The Warren/Reeve/Duchac Family

The Warren/Reeve/Duchac Family of solutions provides a host of options to fit your exact teaching style—all with an integrated technology solution.

Sole Proprietorship Approach

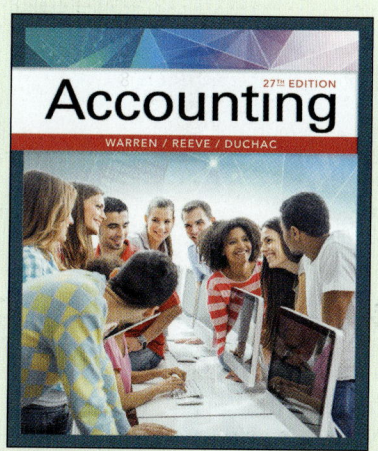

- 26 Chapters
- 65% Financial Accounting/ 35% Managerial Accounting

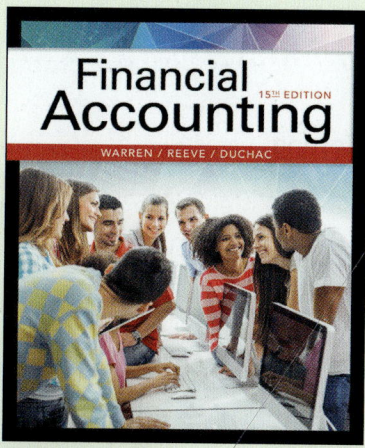

- Financial Chapters 1–17 from *Accounting, 27e*

Corporate Approach

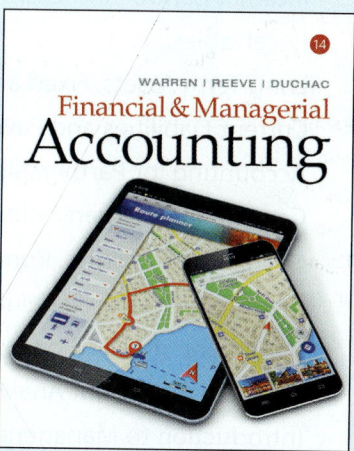

- 26 Chapters
- 50% Financial Accounting/ 50% Managerial Accounting

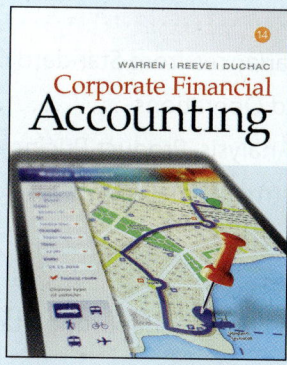 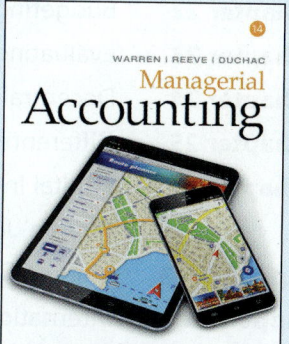

- Chapters 1–14 from *Financial & Managerial Accounting, 14e*
- Chapters 13–26 from *Financial & Managerial Accounting, 14e*

Brief Contents

Chapter 1	Introduction to Accounting and Business	2
Chapter 2	Analyzing Transactions	56
Chapter 3	The Adjusting Process	110
Chapter 4	Completing the Accounting Cycle	160
Chapter 5	Accounting Systems	230
Chapter 6	Accounting for Merchandising Businesses	280
Chapter 7	Inventories	344
Chapter 8	Internal Control and Cash	394
Chapter 9	Receivables	440
Chapter 10	Long-Term Assets: Fixed and Intangible	486
Chapter 11	Current Liabilities and Payroll	536
Chapter 12	Accounting for Partnerships and Limited Liability Companies	584
Chapter 13	Corporations: Organization, Stock Transactions, and Dividends	628
Chapter 14	Long-Term Liabilities: Bonds and Notes	675
Chapter 15	Investments and Fair Value Accounting	719
Chapter 16	Statement of Cash Flows	765
Chapter 17	Financial Statement Analysis	823
Chapter 18	Introduction to Managerial Accounting	883
Chapter 19	Job Order Costing	924
Chapter 20	Process Cost Systems	968
Chapter 21	Cost-Volume-Profit Analysis	1020
Chapter 22	Budgeting	1074
Chapter 23	Evaluating Variances from Standard Costs	1124
Chapter 24	Decentralized Operations	1172
Chapter 25	Differential Analysis, Product Pricing, and Activity-Based Costing	1218
Chapter 26	Capital Investment Analysis	1272
	Mornin' Joe	MJ-1
Appendix A	Interest Tables	A-1
Appendix B	International Financial Reporting Standards (IFRS)	B-1
Appendix C	Revenue Recognition	C-1
Appendix D	Nike Inc., Form 10-K for the Fiscal Year Ended May 31, 2016	D-1
	Glossary	G-1
	Index	I-1

The Warren Vision

Warren/Reeve/Duchac's *Accounting 27e* gives students a solid foundation in accounting to prepare them for future business courses and the real world.

1. Helps students connect concepts to the bigger picture with features such as the new **Chapter-Opening Schema**.

2. **Accounting Cycle Coverage** provides an unmatched foundation so students are prepared to succeed in later chapters.

3. Helps learners appreciate why accounting is important to business and a prosperous society with new tools such as the **Why It Matters Concept Clips**.

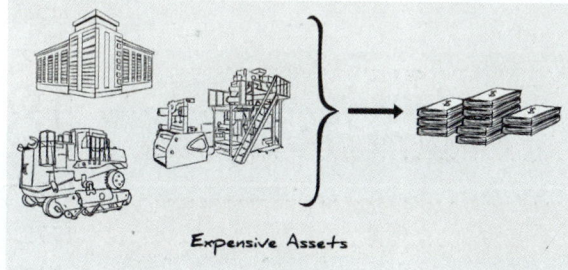

4. A **presentation style** built for the way this generation reads and assimilates information.

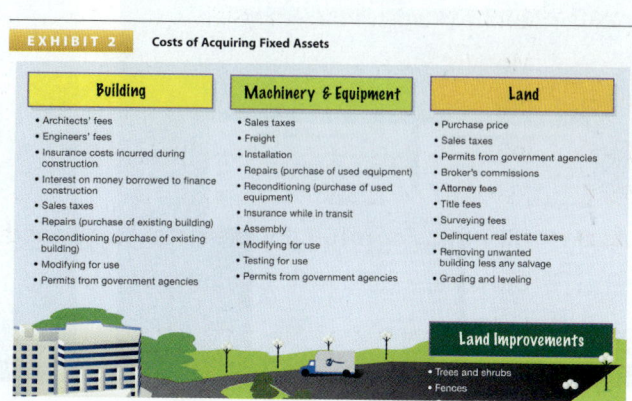

v

Features

Roadmap for Success

Warren/Reeve/Duchac's *Accounting 27e* makes it easy for you to give students a solid foundation in accounting without overwhelming students. Warren covers the fundamentals AND motivates students to learn by showing how accounting is important to a business.

Built for Today's Students

The Warren/Reeve/Duchac presentation style provides content in a way that this generation reads and assimilates information.

- Short, concise paragraphs and bullets
- Stepwise progression
- Meaningful illustrations and graphs

Hallmarks of the Revision

New schemas provide a roadmap of accounting that emphasizes the big picture. Each chapter begins with a new graphic Schema, or Roadmap of Accounting, that shows readers how the chapter material fits within the larger context of the overall book. With this approach, students view chapter concepts as part of a larger whole rather than as mere independent pieces of knowledge, for a truly functional understanding of accounting.

Financial and managerial sections use separate schemas. A four-part schema (Chs. 1–4) demonstrates how chapter content integrates within the accounting cycle. The financial accounting chapters' schema (Chs. 5–17) highlights chapter content within a set of integrated financial statements. A separate managerial accounting schema (Chs. 18–26) shows how chapter content integrates within the managerial accounting functions.

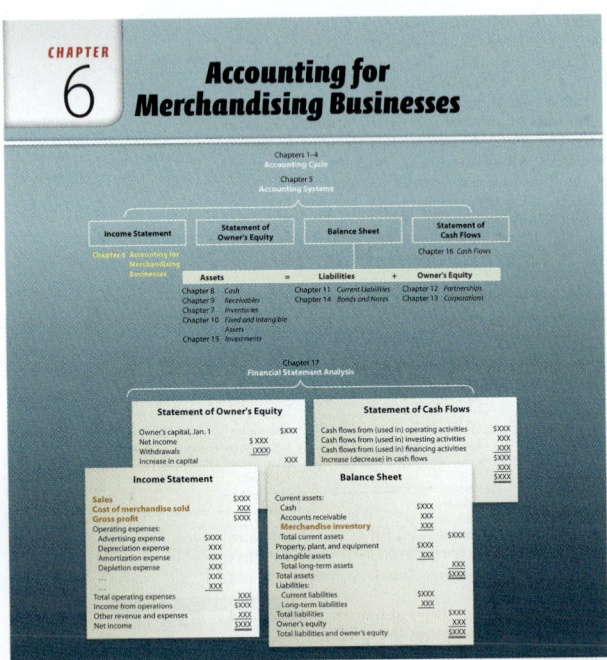

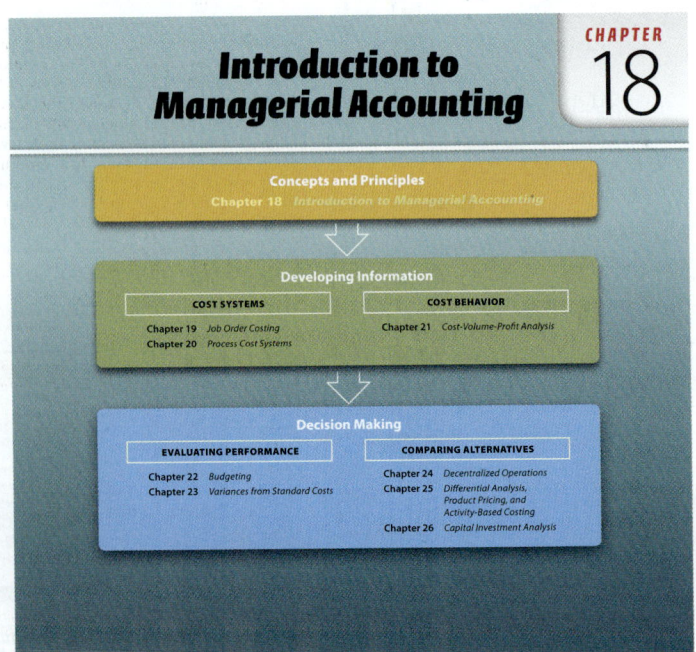

Revised and refreshed real company chapter openers engage readers from the start. New and fresh chapter openers introduce and briefly describe a real company and how its challenges relate to the chapter content. Links to this opening company appear throughout the chapter to reinforce the importance of what readers are learning.

Revised end-of-chapter assignments (homework) provide important hands-on practice. Refined, meaningful review and applications at the end of each chapter include Discussion Questions, Practice Exercises (A and B versions), Exercises, Problems (Series A and B), and Cases & Projects that emphasize ethics, teamwork, and communication skills.

Cases & Projects

Ethics

CP 5-1   Ethics in Action

Netbooks Inc. provides accounting applications for business customers on the Internet for a monthly subscription. Netbooks customers run their accounting system on the Internet; thus, the business data and accounting software reside on the servers of Netbooks Inc. The senior management of Netbooks believes that once a customer begins to use Netbooks, it is very difficult to cancel the service. That is, customers are "locked in" because it is difficult to move the business data from Netbooks to another accounting application even though the customers own their own data. Therefore, Netbooks has decided to entice customers with an initial low monthly price that is half the normal monthly rate for the first year of services. After a year, the price will be increased to the regular monthly rate. Netbooks management believes that customers will have to accept the full price because customers will be "locked in" after one year of use.

a. Discuss whether the half-price offer is an ethical business practice.
b. Discuss whether customer "lock-in" is an ethical business practice.

Team Activity

CP 5-2   Team Activity

The two leading software application providers for supply chain management (SCM) and customer relationship management (CRM) software are JDA and Salesforce.com, respectively. In groups of two or three, go to the website of each company (www.jda.com and www.salesforce.com, respectively) and list the services provided by each company's software.

Communication

CP 5-3   Communication

Internet-based accounting software is a recent trend in business computing. Major software firms such as Oracle, SAP, and NetSuite are running their core products on the Internet using cloud computing. NetSuite is one of the most popular small-business Internet-based accounting systems.

Go to NetSuite Inc.'s website at www.netsuite.com. Read about the product and prepare a memo to management defining cloud-based accounting. Also outline the advantages and disadvantages of using cloud-based accounting compared to running software on a company's internal computer network.

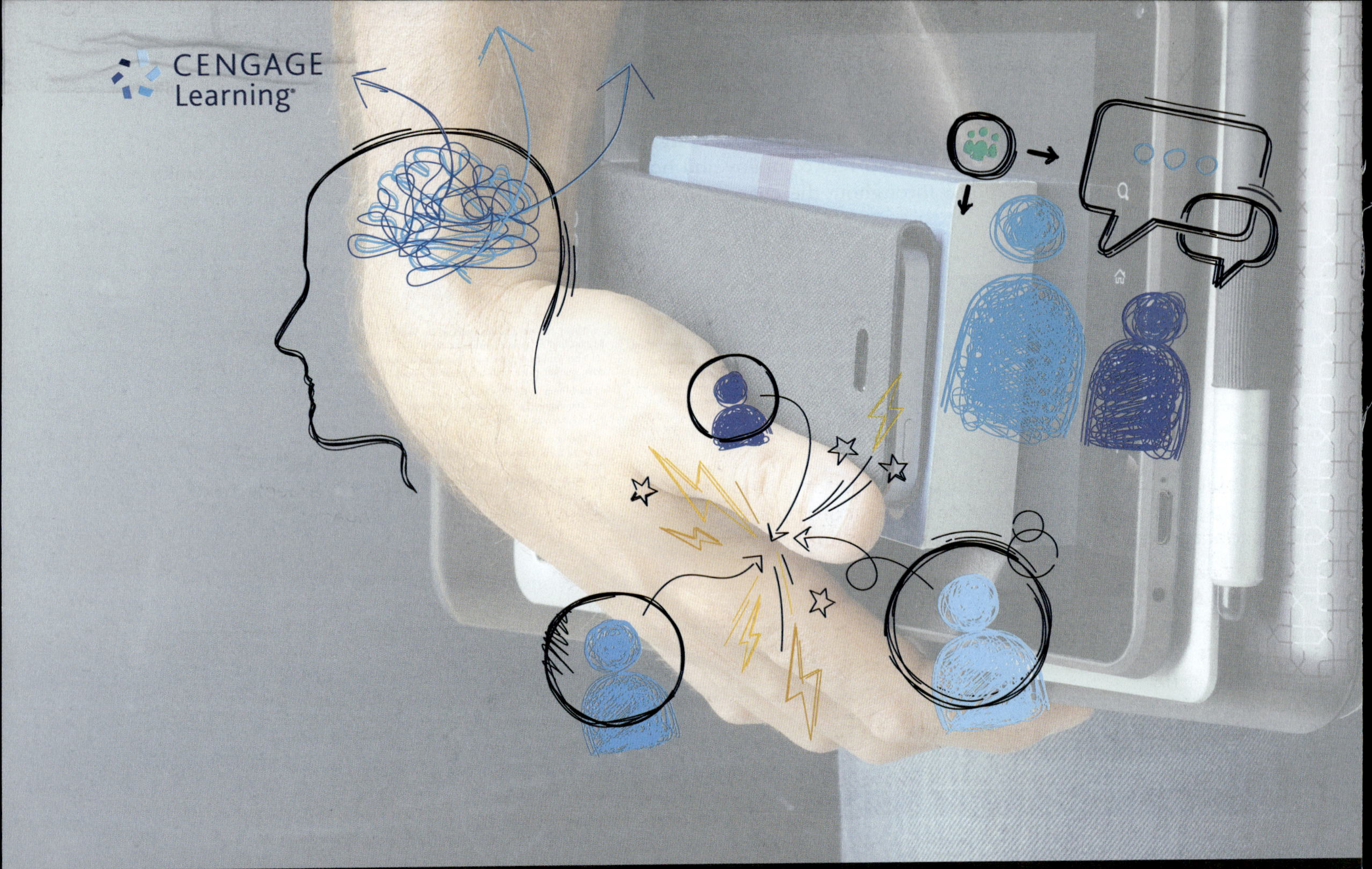

Close the Gap

Between Homework and Exam Performance
with CengageNOWv2.

We've talked with hundreds of accounting instructors across the country, and we are learning that online homework systems have created a new challenge in the accounting course.

We are hearing that students perform well on the homework but poorly on the exam, which leads instructors to believe that students are not truly learning the content, but rather are memorizing their way through the system.

CengageNOWv2 better prepares students for the exam by providing an online homework experience that is similar to what students will experience on the exam and in the real world.

Read on to see how CengageNOWv2 helps close this gap

Closing the gap, one step at a time.

Multi-Panel View

One of the biggest complaints students have about online homework is the scrolling, which prevents students from seeing the big picture and understanding the accounting system. This new Multi-Panel View in CengageNOWv2 enables students to see all the elements of a problem on one screen.

- Students make connections and see the tasks as connected components in the accounting process.
- Dramatically reduced scrolling eliminates student frustration.

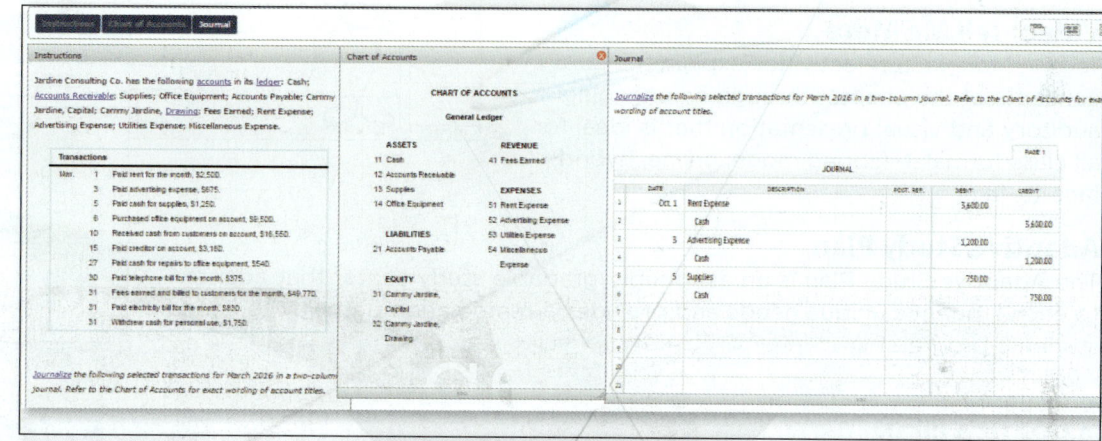

Blank Sheet of Paper Experience

Many students perform well on homework but struggle when it comes to exams. Now, with the new Blank Sheet of Paper Experience, students must problem-solve on their own, just as they would if taking a test on a blank sheet of paper. This discourages overreliance on the system.

- Students must refer to the Chart of Accounts and decide for themselves which account is impacted.
- The number of accounts in each transaction is not given away.
- Whether the account should be debited or credited is not given away.
- Transactions may be entered in any order (as long as the entries are correct).

Adaptive Feedback

Adaptive Feedback responds to students based upon their unique answers and alerts them to the type of error they have made without giving away the answer.

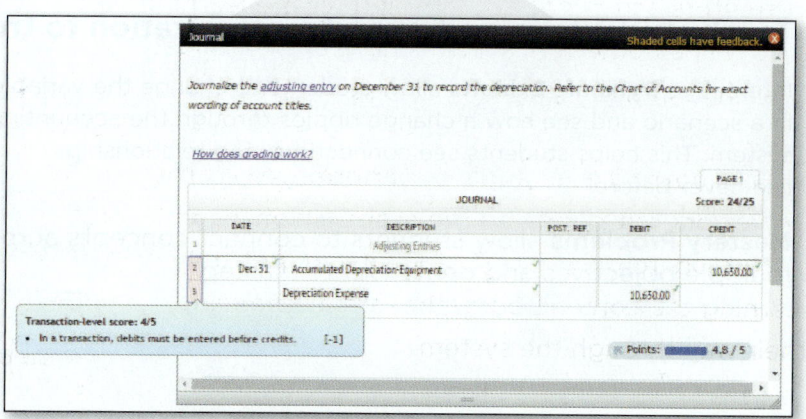

From Motivation to Mastery

MOTIVATION:
Engage students and better prepare them for class.

NEW Video: Animated Concept Clips
Animated Concept Clips are brief captivating video clips that expose students to why a concept is important and how the concept is used in the real world.

Video: Tell Me More
Tell Me More lecture activities explain the core concepts of the chapter through an engaging auditory and visual presentation that is ideal for all class formats—flipped mode, online, hybrid, face-to-face.

Adaptive Study Plan
The Adaptive Study Plan is an assignable/gradable study center that adapts to each student's unique needs and provides a remediation pathway to keep students progressing.

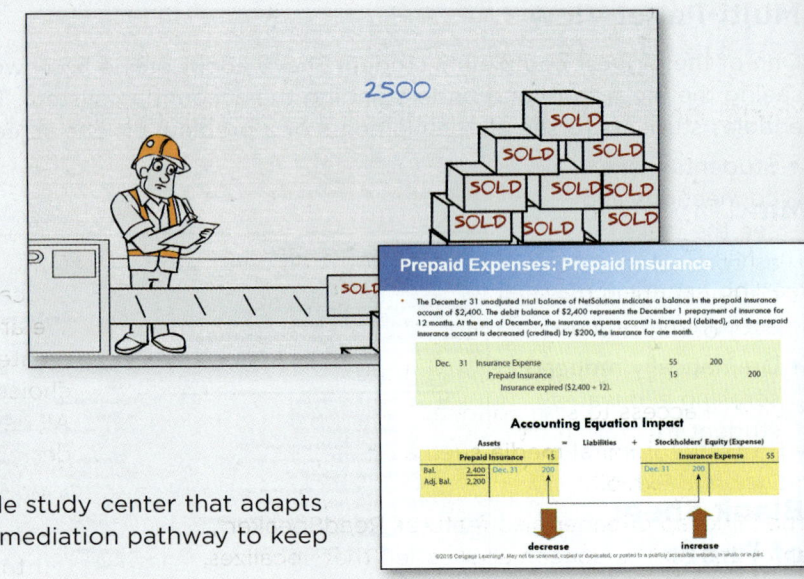

APPLICATION:
Help students apply accounting concepts.

Video: Show Me How
Linked to end-of-chapter problems in CengageNOWv2, Show Me How problem demonstration videos provide a step-by-step model of a similar problem.

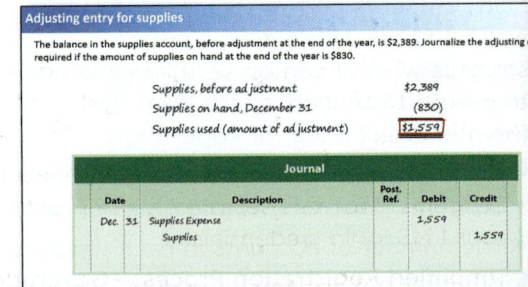

MASTERY:
Teach students to go beyond memorization to true understanding.

Interactive **Dynamic Exhibits** allow students to change the variables in a scenario and see how a change ripples through the accounting system. This helps students see connections and relationships like never before!

Mastery Problems allow students to connect concepts across multiple objectives and demonstrate mastery.

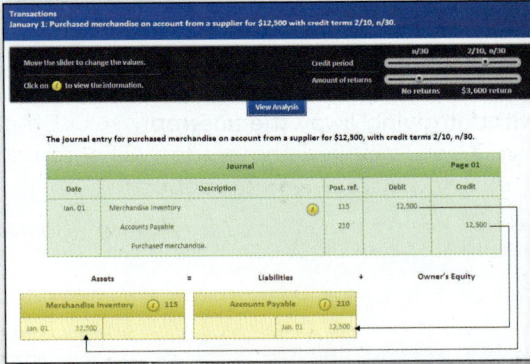

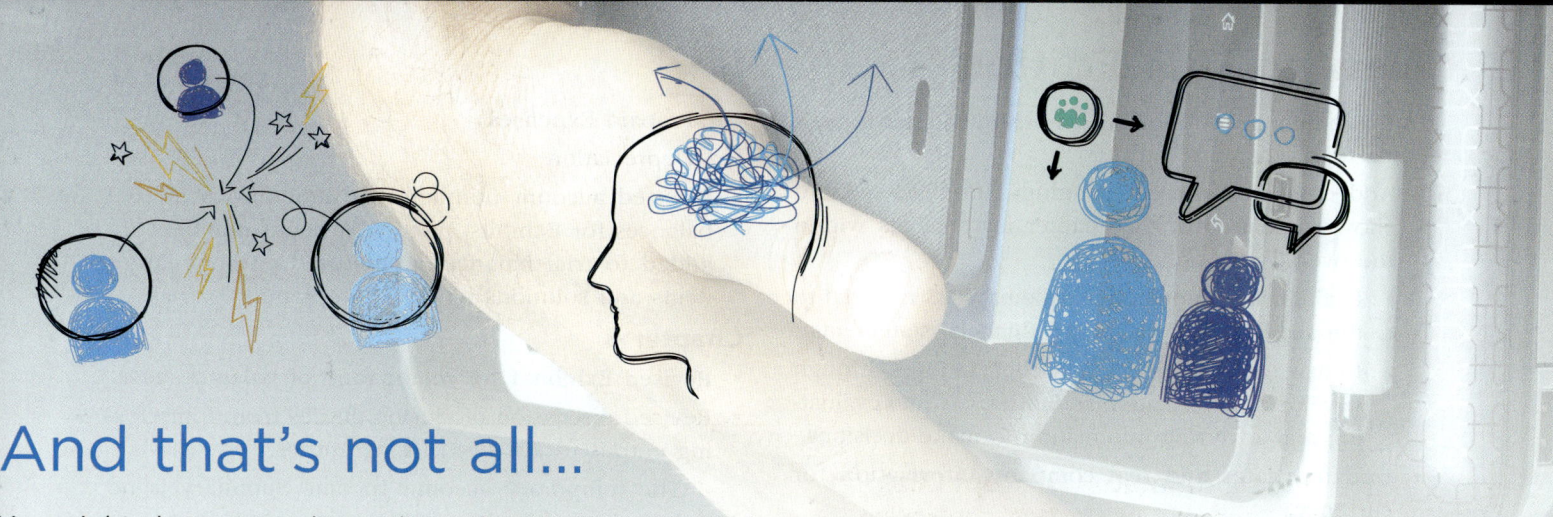

And that's not all...

You might also want to learn about the MindTap eReader, our LMS integration options, and more.

MindTap eReader

The MindTap eReader is the most robust digital reading experience available.

- Fully optimized for the iPad.
- Note-taking, highlighting, and more.
- Offline access to smartphones.
- Embedded digital media such as the Dynamic Exhibits.

The MindTap eReader also features ReadSpeaker®, an online text-to-speech application that vocalizes, or "speechenables," online educational content.

LMS Integration

CengageNOWv2 can be seamlessly integrated with most Learning Management Systems. Adopters will enjoy:

- **A Seamless User Experience**—Access your Cengage resources seamlessly using only your LMS login credentials.
- **Simplified Registration Process**—Get students up and running faster!
- **Content Customization and Deep Linking**—Use our Content Selector to create a unique learning path for students that blends your content with Cengage Learning activities, eText, and more within your LMS course.
- **Automatic Grade Synchronization***—Need to have your course grades recorded in your LMS gradebook? No problem. Simply select the activities you want synched and grades will automatically be recorded in your LMS gradebook.

* Grade synchronization is currently available with Blackboard, Brightspace (powered by D2L), Angel 8, and Canvas.

ADA Accessibility

Cengage Learning is committed to making its educational materials accessible to users of all abilities. We are steadily working to increase accessibility and create a full spectrum of usable tools, features, and choices that are accessible for users of all abilities. All new Cengage Learning products and services are designed with accessibility in mind.

- With the latest release of CengageNOWv2:
  - Images and graphics have been converted to HTML tables so that they can be read by screen readers.
  - The assignment experience now offers proper heading structure to support easy navigation with assistive technology.
- CengageNOWv2 solutions offer high contrast and well-structured HTML, which helps support screen reader interactivity.
- All videos are created with closed captioning and transcripts available for download.
- The MindTap eReader is HTML-based and compatible with most screen reading assistive software. The eReader supports browser settings for high-contrast narrative text, variable font sizes, and multiple foreground and background color options.

For more information on accessibility, please visit www.cengage.com/accessibility.

iPad Tablet Compatibility

CengageNOWv2 is fully compatible with the iPad and other tablet devices, with the exception of General Ledger (CLGL) and Excel Tutorials, which are flash based.

www.cengage.com/cnowv2

New to This Edition

In this edition, the following improvements have been made to all chapters:

- Added schema at the beginning of each chapter to show students how the chapter material fits within the overall textbook.
  - In financial chapters, the schema links material to the accounting cycle or the financial statements.
  - In managerial chapters, the schema moves through developing information and ultimately into evaluating and analyzing information to make decisions.
- Updated dates and real company information for currency.
- Added "Link to" for the opening company to interweave real-world references through each chapter.
- Refreshed end-of-chapter assignments with different numerical values and updated information.
- Revised Cases & Projects to include Ethics in Action, Team Activity, and Communication in every chapter.

Chapter 1

- Added new Exhibit 1 to show a more accurate nature of the flow of information to users.
- Added equality of accounting equation after each transaction A through H.
- Report form of balance sheet shown in Exhibit 9. Report form is used throughout remaining chapter and end of chapter.
- Changed account form presentations to report form presentations.
- Updated ratio of liabilities to owner's equity.

Chapter 2

- Revised Exhibit 3 rules for debits and credits to ease student understanding.
- Inserted account numbers in trial balance of Exhibit 7. Account numbers are added to trial balances in selected end-of-chapter solutions where appropriate.
- Added account numbers to the unadjusted trial balance.
- Updated Microsoft Business Connection box.

Chapter 3

- Revised Nature of the Adjusting Process and updated for new revenue recognition standard.
- New Exhibits 1 and 2.
- Reordered discussion of adjustments from simplest to more complex as follows:
  - Accrued Revenues
  - Accrued Expenses
  - Unearned Revenues
  - Prepaid Expenses
  - Depreciation
- Inserted account numbers of NetSolutions in trial balances for Exhibits 3 and 9. Account numbers are added to trial balances in selected end-of-chapter items and solutions where appropriate.

Chapter 4

- Revised Exhibit 1 for report form of balance sheet.
- Revised discussion of closing entries from four closing entries to just two closing entries.
  - The temporary account Income Summary is no longer used in the closing process.
  - Updated closing process to the one used in modern, computerized accounting systems.
  - Simpler for students to understand.
  - First closing entry closes revenues and expenses yielding net income or net loss, which is transferred to owner's capital, and ties into the income statement.
  - Second closing entry closes owner's drawing account to owner's capital account.
- Revised Exhibits 3 and 4 to reflect new two-entry closing method.
- Added new Exhibit 8 that ties the Chapters 1–4 schema into the accounting cycle and summarizes the accounting cycle.
- Inserted account numbers into trial balances for Exhibits 7 (NetSolutions), 11, 14, and 17 (Kelly Consulting). Account numbers are added to trial balances in selected end-of-chapter items and solutions where appropriate.
- Added new Appendix 2, Reversing Entries, at the end of the chapter. Reversing entries are consistent with most modern, computerized accounting systems.

Chapter 5

- Added a new dedicated schema for Chapter 5, which shows the revenue collection cycle and purchase payment cycle as part of an accounting system.

Chapter 6

- Integrated the new revenue recognition standard (Revenue from Contracts with Customers) throughout the chapter and the NetSolutions illustration.
- Added new Exhibit 2, which shows the chart of accounts for NetSolutions. The chart of accounts includes accounts for Estimated Returns Inventory and Customer Refunds Payable.

- Added journal entry for purchases discounts "not taken."
- Reorganized sales transactions discussion:
  - Journal entry for sales discount "not taken" has been added.
  - Adjusting entries for customer refunds, allowances, and returns have been moved to the end of the chapter with the adjusting entry for inventory shrinkage. This simplifies the initial discussion of customer refunds, allowances, and returns.
  - Discussion of customer refunds, allowances, and returns has been changed so that the discussion flows from simple to complex as follows:
    - Customer cash refunds (no return)
    - Customer allowance against their accounts receivable (no return; credit memorandum)
    - Customer return with refund or allowance
- Revised Exhibit 9 (Recording Merchandise Inventory Transactions) to exclude the effects of adjusting entries for customer refunds, allowances, and returns.
- Revised Exhibit 10 (Illustration of Merchandise Inventory Transactions for Seller and Buyer) to include a customer cash refund and a return with an allowance (credit) memorandum to the customer's accounts receivable.
- Revised discussion of the adjusting process for a merchandise business to include the adjustments for customer refunds, allowances, and returns. The discussion is ordered from simple to complex with the first adjustment (the simplest) for inventory shrinkage followed by the more complex adjustments for customer refunds, allowances, and returns.
- Updated NetSolutions financial statements (Exhibits 11, 12, 13, and 14) include the effects of the new revenue recognition standard. For example, the balance sheet (Exhibit 14) includes Estimated Returns Inventory and Customer Refunds Payable. Note that this is consistent with the chart of accounts presented in Exhibit 2.
- The closing process has been changed to use only two closing entries. This is consistent with the closing entries in Chapter 4. The first closing entry closes the revenue and expense accounts to the owner's capital account. Owner's capital account is credited for net income and debited for a net loss. The second closing entry closes the owner's drawing account to the owner's capital account.
- The chapter appendix (The Periodic Inventory System) using NetSolutions has been revised to include the effects of the new revenue recognition standard.
- The end-of-chapter materials have been revised to include the effects of the chapter reorganization.

Chapter 7
- Added new Business Connection boxes:
  - *Pawn Stars* and Specific Identification
  - Computerized Perpetual Inventory Systems
  - Good Samaritan

Chapter 8
- Revised chapter title to delete reference to Sarbanes-Oxley.
- Exhibit 2 changed from Nike to eBay (consistent with chapter opener).
- Updated example in Ethics box.
- Added new Business Connection boxes:
  - Mobile Payments
  - Managing Apple's Cash

Chapter 9
- New opening company, Keurig Green Mountain, Inc.
- Added new Business Connection boxes:
  - Warning Signs
  - Failure to Collect

Chapter 10
- Changed title to Long-Term Assets: Fixed and Intangible.
- New Business Connection box on Fixed Assets.
- Reorganized chapter as follows:
  - Capital and Revenue Expenditures now appears after discussion of depreciation and before the discussion of disposal of fixed assets. Capital and Revenue Expenditures section is now titled Repair and Improvements.
  - Partial-Year Depreciation is now covered as a separate section after all three depreciation methods have been discussed.
- New Exhibit 3 (Depreciation Expense).
- New Exhibit 4 (Straight-Line Method).
- Added journal entry for recording straight-line depreciation.
- Book value emphasized in discussion of all three depreciation methods.
- New Exhibit 5 (Straight-Line Method: Depreciation Expense and Book Value).
- Added journal entry for recording units-of-activity method.
- New Exhibit 6 (Units-of-Activity Method).
- Added journal entry for recording double-declining-balance method.
- New Exhibit 7 (Double-Declining-Balance Method).

- New Partial-Year Depreciation section.
- Added new Repair and Improvements section.
- Added new Business Connection box on Downsizing.

Chapter 11
- Refreshed Financial Analysis and Interpretation discussion of quick ratio.
- Added Business Connection box on State Pension Obligations.
- Updated federal wage bracket withholding information.

Chapter 12
- Closing entries are changed to reflect a single-stage approach to closing—closing revenues and expenses to partnership capital directly, without using an income summary account.
- New entries are provided to illustrate closing the partner drawing accounts.
- The term "net assets" is more clearly defined.
- Revised Exhibit 7, Statement of Partnership Liquidation: Loss on Realization—Capital Deficiency, to provide a clearer presentation of the transactions steps.

Chapter 13
- Google name changed to Alphabet (Google), Inc.
- Moved Stock Splits earlier in the chapter. It is now Objective 5, which follows dividends (Obj. 4).
- Treasury stock is now Objective 6.
- New Business Connections boxes:
  - Excerpts from Alphabet (Google)'s Bylaws
  - You Have No Vote
  - Treasury Stock or Dividends?

Chapter 14
- Added Business Connection box on Investor Bond Price Risk.
- Refreshed Financial Analysis and Interpretation discussion of times interest earned, focusing on intra-industry comparisons.

Chapter 15
- Refreshed Interest Timeline exhibits to clearly illustrate the timing of interest accruals.

Chapter 16
- Added Business Connection boxes:
  - Cash Crunch!
  - Growing Pains at Twitter
- Updated and expanded Financial Analysis and Interpretation discussion of free cash flow.

Chapter 17
- Revised learning objectives on liquidity analysis and solvency analysis.
- Added learning objective on Analyzing and Interpreting Financial Statements.
- Name changes to several ratios:
  - From "number of times interest charges are earned" to "times interest earned"
  - From "ratio of assets to sales" to "asset turnover"
  - From "rate earned on total assets" to "return on total assets"
  - From "rate earned on stockholders' equity" to "return on stockholders' equity"
  - From "rate earned on common stockholders' equity" to "return on common stockholders' equity"
- Refreshed Exhibit 13, Summary of Analytical Measures.
- Added Business Connection boxes:
  - Flying off the Shelves
  - Liquidity Crunch at Radio Shack
  - Gearing for Profit
- Updated Comprehensive Problem for Nike's recent financial statements.

Chapter 18
- Revised chapter title.
- Added new learning objective on Sustainability and Accounting.
- Added Business Connection box on Line and Staff for Service Companies.

Chapter 19
- Added Business Connection boxes:
  - 3D Printing
  - Advanced Robotics

Chapter 20
- References to "just-in-time processing" are changed to "lean manufacturing" to reflect use of more contemporary terms.
- Added new Business Connection box on Sustainable Papermaking.

Chapter 21
- Added Business Connection boxes:
  - Booking Fees
  - Airline Industry Break-Even

Chapter 22
- Added new Business Connection box on Mad Men; it shows the U.S. companies with the largest advertising budgets.

Chapter 23
- Revised chapter title.

Chapter 24
- Revised chapter title.
- Refreshed Exhibit 3, Responsibility Accounting Reports for Cost Centers.
- Added Business Connection box on Coca-Cola Company: Go West Young Man.

Chapter 25
- Eliminated the step structure at the beginning of the chapter to provide a less complex analysis framework.
- Improved the explanation of the differential analysis table illustration at the beginning of the chapter.
- The differential make vs. buy analysis table has an added revenue line that is set at "zero." Thus, income and loss can now be arithmetically determined.
- Added new Business Connection box on The ABC's of Schwab; it shows how Charles Schwab Corporation uses activity-based costing.

Chapter 26
- Added new section on capital investment analysis for sustainability.
- Added new exercises for capital investment analysis for sustainability.

Instructor Resources

Solutions Manual
Author-written and carefully verified multiple times to ensure accuracy and consistency with the text, the Solutions Manual contains answers to the Discussion Questions, Practice Exercises, Exercises, Problems (Series A and Series B), Continuing Problems, Comprehensive Problems, and Cases & Projects that appear in the text. These solutions help you easily plan, assign, and efficiently grade assignments.

Test Bank
Test Bank content is delivered via Cengage Learning Testing, powered by Cognero®, a flexible, online system that allows you to:
- Author, edit, and manage test bank content
- Create multiple test versions in an instant
- Deliver tests from your LMS, from your classroom, or through CengageNOWv2
- Export tests in Word format

Companion Website
This robust companion website provides immediate access to a rich array of teaching and learning resources—including the Instructor's Manual, PowerPoint slides, and Excel Template Solutions. Easily download the instructor resources you need from the password-protected, instructor-only section of the site.

Instructor's Manual Discover new ways to engage your students by using the Instructor's Manual ideas for class discussion, group learning activities, writing exercises, and Internet activities. Moreover, simplify class preparation by reviewing a brief summary of each chapter, a detailed chapter synopsis, teaching tips regarding a suggested approach to the material, questions students frequently ask in the classroom, lecture aids, and demonstration problems in the Instructor's Manual. Quickly identify the assignments that best align your course with the assignment preparation grid that includes information about learning objective coverage, difficulty level and Bloom's taxonomy categorization, time estimates, and accrediting standard alignment for business programs, AICPA, ACBSP, and IMA.

PowerPoint Slides Bring your lectures to life with slides designed to clarify difficult concepts for your students. The lecture PowerPoints include key terms and definitions, equations, examples, and exhibits from the textbook. Descriptions for all graphics in the PowerPoints are included to enhance PowerPoint usability for students with disabilities.

Excel Template Solutions Excel Templates are provided for selected long or complicated end-of-chapter exercises and problems to assist students as they set up and work the problems. Certain cells are coded to display a red asterisk when an incorrect answer is entered, which helps students stay on track. Selected problems that can be solved using these templates are designated by an icon in the textbook and are listed in the assignment preparation grid in the Instructor's Manual. The Excel Template Solutions provide answers to these templates.

Practice Set Solutions Establish a fundamental understanding of the accounting cycle for your students with Practice Sets, which require students to complete one month of transactions for a fictional company. Brief descriptions of each Practice Set are provided in the Table of Contents. The Practice Set Solutions provide answers to these practice sets.

Student Resources

Study Guide

Now available free in CengageNOWv2, the Study Guide allows students to easily assess what they know with a "Do You Know" checklist covering the key points in each chapter. To further test their comprehension, students can work through Practice Exercises, which include a "strategy" hint and solution so they can continue to practice applying key accounting concepts.

Working Papers

Students will find the tools they need to help work through end-of-chapter assignments with the Working Papers. The preformatted templates provide a starting point by giving students a basic structure for problems and journal entries. Working Papers are available in a printed format as a bundle option.

Practice Sets

For more in-depth application of accounting practices, instructors may choose from among six different Practice Sets for long-term assignments. Each Practice Set requires students to complete one month of transactions for a fictional company. Practice Sets can be solved manually or with the Cengage Learning General Ledger software.

Website

Designed specifically for your students' accounting needs, this website features student PowerPoint slides and Excel Templates, along with the Study Guides.

- **PowerPoint Slides:** Students can easily take notes or review difficult concepts with the student version of this edition's PowerPoint slides.
- **Excel Templates:** These Excel Templates help students stay on track. If students enter an incorrect answer in certain cells, a red asterisk will appear to let them know something is wrong. Problems that can be solved using these templates are designated by an icon.

Acknowledgments

The many enhancements to this edition of *Accounting* are the direct result of one-on-one interviews, surveys, reviews, and focus groups with instructors at institutions across the country. We would like to take this opportunity to thank those who helped us better understand the challenges of the principles of accounting course and provided valuable feedback on our content and digital assets.

Debbie Adkins, Remington College Online
Sharon Agee, Rollins College
Sol. Ahiarah, SUNY Buffalo State
John G. Ahmad, Northern Virginia Community College
Janice Akeo, Butler Community College
Dave Alldredge, Salt Lake Community College
Robert Almon, South Texas College
Lynn Almond, Virginia Tech
Elizabeth Ammann, Lindenwood University
Sheila Ammons, Austin Community College
Anne Marie Anderson, Raritan Valley Community College
Rick Andrews, Sinclair Community College
Leah Arrington, Northwest Mississippi Community College
Christopher Ashley, Everest College
John Babich, Kankakee Community College
Felicia R. Baldwin, Richard J. Daley College
Sara Barritt, Northeast Community College
Geoffrey D. Bartlett, Drake University
Jan Barton, Emory University
Robert E. (Reb) Beatty, Anne Arundel Community College
Eric Blazer, Millersville University
Cindy Bleasdal, Hilbert College
Cynthia Bolt, The Citadel
Anna Boulware, St. Charles Community College
Gary Bower, Community College of Rhode Island
Thomas Branton, Alvin Community College
Gregory Brookins, Santa Monica College

Esther S. Bunn, Stephen F. Austin State University
Jacqueline Burke, Hofstra University
Lisa Busto, William Rainey Harper College
Thane Butt, Champlain College
Marci Butterfield, University of Utah
Magan Calhoun, Austin Peay State University
Julia M. Camp, Providence College
Kirk Canzano, Long Beach City College
Roy Carson, Anne Arundel Community College
Cassandra H. Catlett, Carson Newman University
David Centers, Grand Valley State University
Machiavelli W. Chao, University of California, Irvine
Bea Chiang, The College of New Jersey
Linda Christiansen, Indiana University Southeast
Lawrence Chui, University of St. Thomas
Colleen Chung, Miami Dade College
Tony Cioffi, Lorain County Community College
Sandra Cohen, Columbia College Chicago
Debora Constable, Georgia Perimeter College
Susan Cordes, Johnson County Community College
Leonard Cronin, University Center Rochester
Louann Hofheins Cummings, The University of Findlay
Sue Cunningham, Rowan Cabarrus Community College
Don Curfman, McHenry County College

Robin D'Agati, Palm Beach State College
Dori Danko, Grand Valley State University
Emmanuel Danso, Palm Beach State College
Bruce L. Darling, University of Oregon
Dorothy Davis, University of Louisiana Monroe
Rebecca Grava Davis, East Mississippi Community College
Julie Dawson, Carthage College
Christopher Demaline, Central Arizona College
Carol Dickerson, Chaffey College
Patricia Doherty, Boston University School of Management
Michael P. Dole, Marquette University
Karen C. Elsom, Fayetteville Technical Community College
Nancy Emerson, North Dakota State University
James M. Emig, Villanova University
Bruce England, Massasoit Community College
Lucile Faurel, University of California, Irvine
Robert Foster, Los Angeles Pierce College
Kimberly Franklin, St. Louis Community College
Michael J. Gallagher, DeSales University
Ann Gervais, Springfield Technical Community College
Alex Gialanella, Manhattanville College
Michael Goeken, Northwest Vista College
Nino Gonzalez, El Paso Community College
Saturnino (Nino) Gonzalez, El Paso Community College

Lori A. Grady, Bucks County Community College
Carol Graham, The University of San Francisco
Marina Grau, Houston Community College
Gloria Grayless, Sam Houston State University
Tim Green, North Georgia Technical College
Ann Gregory, South Plains College
Timothy Griffin, Hillsborough Community College
Sheila Guillot, Lamar State College-Port Arthur
Michael Gurevitz, Montgomery College
Keith Hallmark, Calhoun Community College
Rebecca Hancock, El Paso Community College
Martin Hart, Manchester Community College
Len Heritage, Tacoma Community College
Katherine Sue Hewitt, Klamath Community College
Merrily Hoffman, San Jacinto College
Jose Hortensi, Miami Dade College
Jana Hosmer, Blue Ridge Community College
Aileen Huang, Santa Monica College
Marianne James, California State University, Los Angeles
Cynthia Johnson, University of Arkansas at Little Rock
Lori Johnson, Minnesota State University Moorhead
Odessa Jordan, Calhoun Community College
Stani Kantcheva, Cincinnati State Technical and Community College
Chris Kinney, Mount Wachusett Community College
Taylor Klett, Sam Houston State University
Stacy Kline, Drexel University
Pamela Knight, Columbus Technical College
W. Jeff Knight, Flagler College
Lynn Krausse, Bakersfield College
Barbara Kren, Marquette University
Jeffrey T. Kunz, Carroll University
Steven J. LaFave, Augsburg College
Tara Laken, Joliet Junior College
Meg Costello Lambert, Oakland Community College

Richard Lau, California State University, Los Angeles
Suzanne Laudadio, Durham Technical Community College
Greg Lauer, North Iowa Area Community College
David E. Laurel, South Texas College
Michael Lawrence, Mt. Hood Community College
Charles J. F. Leflar, University of Arkansas
Jennifer LeSure, Ivy Tech Community College
Bruce Leung, City College of San Francisco
Charles Lewis, Houston Community College
Erik Lindquist, Lansing Community College
Harold Little, Western Kentucky University
James Lock, Northern Virginia Community College
Katy Long, Hill College
Dawn Lopez, Johnson & Wales University
Ming Lu, Santa Monica College
Angelo Luciano, Columbia College Chicago
Debbie Luna, El Paso Community College
Jennifer Mack, Lindenwood University
Suneel Maheshwari, Marshall University
Ajay Maindiratta, New York University
Richard Mandau, Piedmont Technical College
Michele Martinez, Hillsborough Community College
Michelle A. McFeaters, Grove City College
Noel McKeon, Florida State College at Jacksonville
Chris McNamara, Finger Lakes Community College
Kevin McNelis, New Mexico State University
Glenn (Mel) McQueary, Houston Community College
Brenda McVey, Green River Community College
Pam Meyer, University of Louisiana at Lafayette
Jeanette Milius, Iowa Western Community College
Cynthia J. Miller, University of Kentucky
Linda Miller, Northeast Community College

Julie Miller Millmann, Chippewa Valley Technical College
Rita Mintz, Calhoun Community College
Jill Mitchell, Northern Virginia Community College
Timothy J. Moran, Aurora University
Michelle Moshier, University at Albany
Linda Muren, Cuyahoga Community College
Andrea Murowski, Brookdale Community College
Johnna Murray, University of Missouri-St. Louis
Adam Myers, Texas A&M University
John Nader, Davenport University
Joseph M. Nicassio, Westmoreland County Community College
Lisa Novak, Mott Community College
Jamie O'Brien, South Dakota State University
Ron O'Brien, Fayetteville Technical Community College
Robert A. Pacheco, Masssasoit Community College
Edwin Pagan, Passaic County Community College
Judy Patrick, Minnesota State Community and Technical College
Sy Pearlman, California State University, Long Beach
Aaron Pennington, York College of Pennsylvania
Rachel Pernia, Essex County College
Dawn Peters, Southwestern Illinois College
April Poe, University of the Incarnate Word
Michael P. Prockton, Finger Lakes Community College
Kristen Quinn, Northern Essex Community College
La Vonda Ramey, Schoolcraft College
Marcela Raphael, Chippewa Valley Technical College
Jenny Resnick, Santa Monica College
Rick Rinetti, Los Angeles City College
Cecile Roberti, Community College of Rhode Island
Shani N. Robinson, Sam Houston State University
Patrick Rogan, Cosumnes River College
Lawrence A. Roman, Cuyahoga Community College
Debbie Rose, Northeast Wisconsin Technical College

Acknowledgments

Leah Russell, Holyoke Community College
John H. Sabbagh, Northern Essex Community College
Lynn K. Saubert, Radford University
Marie Saunders, Dakota County Technical College
Michael G. Schaefer, Blinn College
Jennifer Schneider, University of North Georgia
Darlene Schnuck, Waukesha County Technical College
John Seilo, Irvine Valley College
Mon Sellers, Lone Star College-North Harris
Perry Sellers, Lone Star College System
Jim Shelton, Harding University
Ercan Sinmaz, Houston Community College
Lee Smart, Southwest Tennessee Community College
Gerald Smith, University of Northern Iowa
Judy Smith, Parkland College
Ryan Smith, Columbia College
Jennifer Spring Sneed, Arkansas State University-Newport
Nancy L. Snow, University of Toledo
Sharif Soussi, Charter Oak State College
Marilyn Stansbury, Calvin College
Larry G. Stephens, Austin Community College
Dawn W. Stevens, Northwest Mississippi Community College
Joel Strong, St. Cloud State University
Timothy Swenson, Sullivan University
Linda H. Tarrago, Hillsborough Community College
Denise Teixeira, Chemeketa Community College
Teresa Thompson, Chaffey Community College
Judith A. Toland, Bucks County Community College
Lana Tuss, Chemeketa Community College
Robert Urell, Irvine Valley College
Jeff Varblow, College of Lake County
John Verani, White Mountains Community College
Patricia Walczak, Lansing Community College
Terri Walsh, Seminole State College
James Webb, University of the Pacific
Wanda Wong, Chabot College
Patricia Worsham, Norco College
Judith Zander, Grossmont College
Mary Zenner, College of Lake County

About the Authors

Carl S. Warren

Dr. Carl S. Warren is Professor Emeritus of Accounting at the University of Georgia, Athens. Dr. Warren has taught classes at the University of Georgia, University of Iowa, Michigan State University, and University of Chicago. He focused his teaching efforts on principles of accounting and auditing. Dr. Warren received his PhD from Michigan State University and his BBA and MA from the University of Iowa. During his career, Dr. Warren published numerous articles in professional journals, including *The Accounting Review*, *Journal of Accounting Research*, *Journal of Accountancy*, *The CPA Journal*, and *Auditing: A Journal of Practice & Theory*. Dr. Warren has served on numerous committees of the American Accounting Association, the American Institute of Certified Public Accountants, and the Institute of Internal Auditors. He also has consulted with numerous companies and public accounting firms. His outside interests include handball, golf, skiing, backpacking, and fly-fishing.

James M. Reeve

Dr. James M. Reeve is Professor Emeritus of Accounting and Information Management at the University of Tennessee. Dr. Reeve taught full time as part of the accounting faculty for 25 years after graduating with his PhD from Oklahoma State University. He presently teaches part time at UT. His teaching efforts focused on Senior Executive MBA programs. His research interests are varied and include work in managerial accounting, supply chain management, lean manufacturing, and information management. He has published over 40 articles in academic and professional journals, including *Journal of Cost Management*, *Journal of Management Accounting Research*, *Accounting Review*, *Management Accounting Quarterly*, *Supply Chain Management Review*, and *Accounting Horizons*. He has consulted or provided training around the world for a variety of organizations, including Boeing, Procter & Gamble, Norfolk Southern, Hershey Foods, Coca-Cola, and Sony. When not writing books, Dr. Reeve plays golf and is involved in faith-based activities.

Jonathan Duchac

Dr. Jonathan Duchac is the Wayne Calloway Professor of Accounting and Acting Associate Dean of Accounting Programs at Wake Forest University. He earned his PhD in accounting from the University of Georgia and currently teaches introductory and advanced courses in financial accounting. Dr. Duchac has received a number of awards during his career, including the Wake Forest University Outstanding Graduate Professor Award, the T.B. Rose Award for Instructional Innovation, and the University of Georgia Outstanding Teaching Assistant Award. In addition to his teaching responsibilities, Dr. Duchac has served as Accounting Advisor to Merrill Lynch Equity Research, where he worked with research analysts in reviewing and evaluating the financial reporting practices of public companies. He has testified before the U.S. House of Representatives, the Financial Accounting Standards Board, and the Securities and Exchange Commission and has worked with a number of major public companies on financial reporting and accounting policy issues. In addition to his professional interests, Dr. Duchac is an avid mountain biker and snow skier.

xxi

Contents

Chapter 1 Introduction to Accounting and Business 2

Nature of Business and Accounting 5
- Types of Businesses 5
- Role of Accounting in Business 6
- Role of Ethics in Accounting and Business 6

Integrity, Objectivity, and Ethics in Business: Bernie Madoff 9
- Opportunities for Accountants 9

Business Connection: Pathways Commission 10

Generally Accepted Accounting Principles 10
- Business Entity Concept 11

International Connection: International Financial Reporting Standards (IFRS) 11
- Cost Concept 12

The Accounting Equation 13

Business Connection: The Accounting Equation 13

Business Transactions and the Accounting Equation 14
- Summary 18

Financial Statements 19
- Income Statement 20
- Statement of Owner's Equity 21
- Balance Sheet 21
- Statement of Cash Flows 24
- Interrelationships Among Financial Statements 25

Financial Analysis and Interpretation: Ratio of Liabilities to Owner's Equity 26

Chapter 2 Analyzing Transactions 56

Using Accounts to Record Transactions 59
- Chart of Accounts 61

Business Connection: The Hijacking Receivable 61

Double-Entry Accounting System 62
- Balance Sheet Accounts 62
- Income Statement Accounts 63
- Owner Withdrawals 63
- Normal Balances 63
- Journalizing 64

Integrity, Objectivity, and Ethics in Business: Will Journalizing Prevent Fraud? 67

Journalizing and Posting to Accounts 68

Business Connection: Microsoft's Unearned Revenue 70

Business Connection: Computerized Accounting Systems 72

Trial Balance 77
- Errors Affecting the Trial Balance 78
- Errors Not Affecting the Trial Balance 79

Financial Analysis and Interpretation: Horizontal Analysis 80

Chapter 3 The Adjusting Process 110

Nature of the Adjusting Process 113
- Accrual and Cash Basis of Accounting 113
- Revenue and Expense Recognition 114
- The Adjusting Process 114
- Types of Accounts Requiring Adjustment 115

Adjusting Entries for Accruals 116
- Accrued Revenues 117
- Accrued Expenses 118

Business Connection: Earning Revenues from Season Tickets 120

Adjusting Entries for Deferrals 120
- Unearned Revenues 121
- Prepaid Expenses 122

Business Connection: Sports Signing Bonus 122

xxii

Integrity, Objectivity, and Ethics in Business: Free Issue 123

Adjusting Entries for Depreciation 124

Summary of Adjusting Process 126

Business Connection: Microsoft's Deferred Revenues 126

Adjusted Trial Balance 130

Financial Analysis and Interpretation: Vertical Analysis 131

Chapter 4 Completing the Accounting Cycle 160

Flow of Accounting Information 163

Financial Statements 165
- Income Statement 165

Integrity, Objectivity, and Ethics in Business: CEO's Health? 167
- Statement of Owner's Equity 167
- Balance Sheet 168

International Connection: International Differences 169

Closing Entries 169
- Journalizing and Posting Closing Entries 170
- Post-Closing Trial Balance 174

Accounting Cycle 174

Illustration of the Accounting Cycle 177
- Step 1. Analyzing and Recording Transactions in the Journal 177
- Step 2. Posting Transactions to the Ledger 179
- Step 3. Preparing an Unadjusted Trial Balance 179
- Step 4. Assembling and Analyzing Adjustment Data 180
- Step 5. Preparing an Optional End-of-Period Spreadsheet 180
- Step 6. Journalizing and Posting Adjusting Entries 180
- Step 7. Preparing an Adjusted Trial Balance 182
- Step 8. Preparing the Financial Statements 182
- Step 9. Journalizing and Posting Closing Entries 184
- Step 10. Preparing a Post-Closing Trial Balance 184

Fiscal Year 187

Business Connection: Choosing a Fiscal Year 188

Financial Analysis and Interpretation: Working Capital and Current Ratio 188

End-of-Period Spreadsheet 189
- Step 1. Enter the Title 190
- Step 2. Enter the Unadjusted Trial Balance 190
- Step 3. Enter the Adjustments 191
- Step 4. Enter the Adjusted Trial Balance 192
- Step 5. Extend the Accounts to the Income Statement and Balance Sheet Columns 193
- Step 6. Total the Income Statement and Balance Sheet Columns, Compute the Net Income or Net Loss, and Complete the Spreadsheet 193
- Preparing the Financial Statements from the Spreadsheet 194

Reversing Entries 196

Chapter 5 Accounting Systems 230

Basic Accounting Systems 232

Manual Accounting Systems 233
- Subsidiary Ledgers 233
- Special Journals 233
- Revenue Journal 235
- Cash Receipts Journal 238
- Accounts Receivable Control Account and Subsidiary Ledger 240
- Purchases Journal 240
- Cash Payments Journal 243
- Accounts Payable Control Account and Subsidiary Ledger 245

Business Connection: Accounting Systems and Profit Measurement 246

Computerized Accounting Systems 247

Business Connection: TurboTax 249

E-Commerce 249

Integrity, Objectivity, and Ethics in Business: Online Fraud 250

Financial Analysis and Interpretation: Segment Analysis 250

Chapter 6 Accounting for Merchandising Businesses 280

Nature of Merchandising Businesses 282
- Operating Cycle 282
- Financial Statements 283

Business Connection: Comcast Versus Lowe's 284

Merchandising Transactions 284
- Chart of Accounts for a Merchandising Business 284
- Purchases Transactions 285
- Sales Transactions 290

xxiv Contents

Integrity, Objectivity, and Ethics in Business: The Case of the Fraudulent Price Tags 294
    Freight 295
    Summary: Recording Merchandise Inventory Transactions 297
    Dual Nature of Merchandise Transactions 297
    Sales Taxes and Trade Discounts 299

Business Connection: Sales Taxes 300

The Adjusting Process 300
    Adjusting Entry for Inventory Shrinkage 300

Integrity, Objectivity, and Ethics in Business: The Cost of Employee Theft 301
    Adjusting Entries for Customer Refunds, Allowances, and Returns 301

Financial Statements for a Merchandising Business 303
    Multiple-Step Income Statement 303
    Single-Step Income Statement 305
    Statement of Owner's Equity 305
    Balance Sheet 305
    The Closing Process 306

Financial Analysis and Interpretation: Asset Turnover 307

The Periodic Inventory System 309
    Chart of Accounts Under the Periodic Inventory System 309
    Recording Merchandise Transactions Under the Periodic Inventory System 310
    Adjusting Process Under the Periodic Inventory System 310
    Financial Statements Under the Periodic Inventory System 311
    Closing Entries Under the Periodic Inventory System 312

Practice Set: Lawn Ranger Landscaping
This set covers the complete accounting cycle for a service business operated as a sole proprietorship. Students follow a narrative of transactions to make general journal entries. Includes instructions for an optional solution with no debits and credits. This set can be completed manually or with the General Ledger software.

Chapter 7 Inventories 344

Control of Inventory 346
    Safeguarding Inventory 346
    Reporting Inventory 347

Inventory Cost Flow Assumptions 347

Business Connection: Pawn Stars and Specific Identification 349

Inventory Costing Methods Under a Perpetual Inventory System 350
    First-In, First-Out Method 350
    Last-In, First-Out Method 351

International Connection: International Financial Reporting Standards (IFRS) 353
    Weighted Average Cost Method 353

Business Connection: Computerized Perpetual Inventory Systems 355

Inventory Costing Methods Under a Periodic Inventory System 355
    First-In, First-Out Method 355
    Last-In, First-Out Method 356
    Weighted Average Cost Method 357

Comparing Inventory Costing Methods 358

Integrity, Objectivity, and Ethics in Business: Where's the Bonus? 359

Reporting Merchandise Inventory in the Financial Statements 359
    Valuation at Lower of Cost or Market 359

Business Connection: Good Samaritan 361
    Merchandise Inventory on the Balance Sheet 361
    Effect of Inventory Errors on the Financial Statements 362

Financial Analysis and Interpretation: Inventory Turnover and Days' Sales in Inventory 365

Business Connection: Rapid Inventory at Costco 365

Estimating Inventory Cost 368
    Retail Method of Inventory Costing 368
    Gross Profit Method of Inventory Costing 369

Chapter 8 Internal Control and Cash 394

Sarbanes-Oxley Act 396

Internal Control 398
    Objectives of Internal Control 398

Business Connection: Employee Fraud 398
    Elements of Internal Control 398
    Control Environment 399
    Risk Assessment 400
    Control Procedures 400

Integrity, Objectivity, and Ethics in Business: Tips on Preventing Employee Fraud in Small Companies 401
    Monitoring 402
    Information and Communication 402
    Limitations of Internal Control 403

Contents xxv

Cash Controls over Receipts and Payments 403
    Control of Cash Receipts 404
    Control of Cash Payments 406

Business Connection: Mobile Payments 406

Bank Accounts 407
    Bank Statement 407
    Using the Bank Statement as a Control over Cash 409

Bank Reconciliation 410

Integrity, Objectivity, and Ethics in Business: Bank Error in Your Favor (or Maybe Not) 413

Special-Purpose Cash Funds 413

Financial Statement Reporting of Cash 415

Business Connection: Managing Apple's Cash 415

Financial Analysis and Interpretation: Ratio of Cash to Monthly Cash Expenses 415

Business Connection: Microsoft Corporation 417

Chapter 9 Receivables 440

Classification of Receivables 442
    Accounts Receivable 442
    Notes Receivable 442
    Other Receivables 443

Uncollectible Receivables 443

Business Connection: Warning Signs 444

Direct Write-Off Method for Uncollectible Accounts 444

Allowance Method for Uncollectible Accounts 445

Integrity, Objectivity, and Ethics in Business: Collecting Past Due Accounts 446
    Write-Offs to the Allowance Account 446

Business Connection: Failure to Collect 448
    Estimating Uncollectibles 448

Business Connection: Allowance Percentages Across Companies 453

Comparing Direct Write-Off and Allowance Methods 453

Notes Receivable 454
    Characteristics of Notes Receivable 454
    Accounting for Notes Receivable 456

Reporting Receivables on the Balance Sheet 458

Business Connection: Delta Air Lines 458

Financial Analysis and Interpretation: Accounts Receivable Turnover and Days' Sales in Receivables 459

Chapter 10 Long-Term Assets: Fixed and Intangible 486

Nature of Fixed Assets 488
    Classifying Costs 488

Business Connection: Fixed Assets 489
    The Cost of Fixed Assets 490
    Leasing Fixed Assets 491

Accounting for Depreciation 492
    Factors in Computing Depreciation Expense 492
    Straight-Line Method 493
    Units-of-Activity Method 495
    Double-Declining-Balance Method 497
    Comparing Depreciation Methods 499
    Partial-Year Depreciation 499

Business Connection: Depreciating Animals 500
    Revising Depreciation Estimates 501
    Repair and Improvements 502

Integrity, Objectivity, and Ethics in Business: Capital Crime 503

Disposal of Fixed Assets 504
    Discarding Fixed Assets 504
    Selling Fixed Assets 505

Business Connection: Downsizing 506

Natural Resources 507

Intangible Assets 508
    Patents 508
    Copyrights and Trademarks 509
    Goodwill 509

International Connection: International Financial Reporting Standards (IFRS) 511

Financial Reporting for Long-Term Assets: Fixed and Intangible 511

Financial Analysis and Interpretation: Fixed Asset Turnover Ratio 512
    Fixed Asset Turnover Ratio 512

Business Connection: Hub-and-Spoke or Point-to-Point? 513

Exchanging Similar Fixed Assets 514
    Gain on Exchange 514
    Loss on Exchange 515

Chapter 11 Current Liabilities and Payroll 536

Current Liabilities 538
- Accounts Payable 538
- Current Portion of Long-Term Debt 538
- Short-Term Notes Payable 539

Payroll and Payroll Taxes 541
- Liability for Employee Earnings 541
- Deductions from Employee Earnings 541
- Computing Employee Net Pay 544
- Liability for Employer's Payroll Taxes 545

Business Connection: The Most You Will Ever Pay 545

Accounting Systems for Payroll and Payroll Taxes 545
- Payroll Register 546
- Employee's Earnings Record 549
- Payroll Checks 550
- Computerized Payroll System 551
- Internal Controls for Payroll Systems 551

Integrity, Objectivity, and Ethics in Business: Overbilling Clients 552

Employees' Fringe Benefits 552
- Vacation Pay 552
- Pensions 553
- Postretirement Benefits Other Than Pensions 554
- Current Liabilities on the Balance Sheet 554

Business Connection: State Pension Obligations 555

Contingent Liabilities 555
- Probable and Estimable 555
- Probable and Not Estimable 556
- Reasonably Possible 556
- Remote 557

Financial Analysis and Interpretation: Quick Ratio 557

> **Practice Set: Fit & Fashionable**
> This set is a merchandising business operated as a sole proprietorship. It includes a general journal, special journals, and source documents and can be completed manually or with the General Ledger software.
>
> **Practice Set: Chic Events by Jada**
> This set is a merchandising business operated as a proprietorship. It includes payroll transactions and purchases and sales with discounts, along with source documents. It can be completed manually or with the General Ledger software.

Chapter 12 Accounting for Partnerships and Limited Liability Companies 584

Proprietorships, Partnerships, and Limited Liability Companies 586
- Proprietorships 586
- Partnerships 587

Business Connection: Breaking Up Is Hard To Do 587
- Limited Liability Companies 588
- Comparing Proprietorships, Partnerships, and Limited Liability Companies 588

Business Connection: Organizational Forms in the Accounting Industry 588

Forming a Partnership and Dividing Income 589
- Forming a Partnership 589
- Dividing Income 590

Integrity, Objectivity, and Ethics in Business: Tyranny of the Majority 592

Partner Admission and Withdrawal 593
- Admitting a Partner 593
- Withdrawal of a Partner 598
- Death of a Partner 598

Liquidating Partnerships 599
- Gain on Realization 600
- Loss on Realization 601
- Loss on Realization—Capital Deficiency 603

Statement of Partnership Equity 606

Financial Analysis and Interpretation: Revenue per Employee 606

Chapter 13 Corporations: Organization, Stock Transactions, and Dividends 628

Nature of a Corporation 630
- Characteristics of a Corporation 630
- Forming a Corporation 631

Business Connection: Alphabet (Google)'s Bylaws 632

Stockholders' Equity 633

Paid-In Capital from Stock 634
- Characteristics of Stock 634
- Classes of Stock 635

Business Connection: You Have No Vote 635
- Issuing Stock 636
- Premium on Stock 637
- No-Par Stock 638

Integrity, Objectivity, and Ethics in Business: The Professor Who Knew Too Much 639

Accounting for Dividends 639
Cash Dividends 639
Stock Dividends 641

Stock Splits 642

Business Connection: Buffett on Stock Splits 643

Treasury Stock Transactions 644

Business Connection: Treasury Stock or Dividends? 645

Reporting Stockholders' Equity 645
Stockholders' Equity on the Balance Sheet 645
Reporting Retained Earnings 647
Statement of Stockholders' Equity 648

International Connection: IFRS for SMEs 649
Reporting Stockholders' Equity for Mornin' Joe 649

Financial Analysis and Interpretation: Earnings per Share 651

> **Practice Set: My Place, House of Décor**
> This set is a service and merchandising business operated as a corporation. It includes narrative for six months of transactions to be recorded in a general journal. The set can be completed manually or with the General Ledger software.

Chapter 14 Long-Term Liabilities: Bonds and Notes 675

Financing Corporations 677

Nature of Bonds Payable 679
Bond Characteristics and Terminology 680
Proceeds from Issuing Bonds 680

Business Connection: Investor Bond Price Risk 681

Accounting for Bonds Payable 681
Bonds Issued at Face Amount 681
Bonds Issued at a Discount 682
Amortizing a Bond Discount 683

Business Connection: U.S. Government Debt 684
Bonds Issued at a Premium 685
Amortizing a Bond Premium 686

Business Connection: Bond Ratings 687
Bond Redemption 687

Installment Notes 688
Issuing an Installment Note 689
Annual Payments 689

Integrity, Objectivity, and Ethics in Business: The Ratings Game 691

Reporting Long-Term Liabilities 691

Financial Analysis and Interpretation: Times Interest Earned Ratio 691

Present Value Concepts and Pricing Bonds Payable 693
Present Value Concepts 693
Pricing Bonds 696

Interest Rate Method of Amortization 697
Amortization of Discount by the Interest Method 697
Amortization of Premium by the Interest Method 698

Chapter 15 Investments and Fair Value Accounting 719

Why Companies Invest 721
Investing Cash in Current Operations 721
Investing Cash in Temporary Investments 722
Investing Cash in Long-Term Investments 722

Accounting for Debt Investments 722
Purchase of Bonds 723
Interest Revenue 723
Sale of Bonds 724

Accounting for Equity Investments 725
Cost Method: Less Than 20% Ownership 725
Equity Method: Between 20%–50% Ownership 727
Consolidation: More Than 50% Ownership 729

Business Connection: More Cash Means More Investments for Drug Companies 730

Valuing and Reporting Investments 730
Trading Securities 730

Integrity, Objectivity, and Ethics in Business: Socially Responsible Investing 732
Available-for-Sale Securities 732
Held-to-Maturity Securities 734
Summary 734

Business Connection: Warren Buffett: The Sage of Omaha 736

Fair Value Accounting 737
Effect of Fair Value Accounting on the Financial Statements 737

Financial Analysis and Interpretation: Dividend Yield 737

Comprehensive Income 739

Chapter 16 Statement of Cash Flows 765

Reporting Cash Flows 767
Cash Flows from Operating Activities 768

Business Connection: Cash Crunch! 770

Cash Flows from (Used for) Investing Activities 770
Cash Flows from (Used for) Financing Activities 770
Noncash Investing and Financing Activities 770
Format of the Statement of Cash Flows 771
No Cash Flow per Share 771

Preparing the Statement of Cash Flows—The Indirect Method 772
Net Income 773
Adjustments to Net Income 774

Integrity, Objectivity, and Ethics in Business: Credit Policy and Cash Flow 777

Dividends and Dividends Payable 778
Common Stock 779
Bonds Payable 779
Building and Accumulated Depreciation—Building 780
Land 780
Preparing the Statement of Cash Flows 781

Business Connection: Growing Pains 782

Preparing the Statement of Cash Flows—The Direct Method 782
Cash Received from Customers 783
Cash Payments for Merchandise 783
Cash Payments for Operating Expenses 784
Gain on Sale of Land 785
Interest Expense 785
Cash Payments for Income Taxes 785
Reporting Cash Flows from Operating Activities—Direct Method 786

International Connection: IFRS for Statement of Cash Flows 786

Financial Analysis and Interpretation: Free Cash Flow 787

Spreadsheet (Work Sheet) for Statement of Cash Flows—The Indirect Method 789
Analyzing Accounts 789
Retained Earnings 789
Other Accounts 791
Preparing the Statement of Cash Flows 791

Chapter 17 Financial Statement Analysis 823

Analyzing and Interpreting Financial Statements 825
The Value of Financial Statement Information 825
Techniques for Analyzing Financial Statements 826

Basic Analytical Methods 826
Horizontal Analysis 826
Vertical Analysis 829
Common-Sized Statements 830

Analyzing Liquidity 831
Current Position Analysis 832
Accounts Receivable Analysis 834
Inventory Analysis 835

Business Connection: Flying off the Shelves 837

Analyzing Solvency 837
Ratio of Fixed Assets to Long-Term Liabilities 838
Ratio of Liabilities to Stockholders' Equity 838
Times Interest Earned 839

Business Connection: Liquidity Crunch 840

Analyzing Profitability 840
Asset Turnover 840
Return on Total Assets 841
Return on Stockholders' Equity 842

Business Connection: Gearing for Profit 843

Return on Common Stockholders' Equity 843
Earnings per Share on Common Stock 844
Price-Earnings Ratio 845
Dividends per Share 846
Dividend Yield 847

Business Connection: Investing for Yield 847

Summary of Analytical Measures 847

Corporate Annual Reports 849
Management Discussion and Analysis 849
Report on Internal Control 849

Integrity, Objectivity, and Ethics in Business: Characteristics of Financial Statement Fraud 849

Report on Fairness of the Financial Statements 850

Unusual Items on the Income Statement 850
Unusual Items Affecting the Current Period's Income Statement 850
Unusual Items Affecting the Prior Period's Income Statement 852

Chapter 18 Introduction to Managerial Accounting 883

Managerial Accounting 885
Differences Between Managerial and Financial Accounting 885
The Management Accountant in the Organization 886
The Management Process 888

Contents   **xxix**

Business Connection: Line and Staff for Service Companies 888
  Uses of Managerial Accounting Information 889
Manufacturing Operations: Costs and Terminology 890
  Direct and Indirect Costs 891
  Manufacturing Costs 892
Business Connection: Overhead Costs 893
Sustainability and Accounting 896
  Sustainability 897
  Eco-Efficiency Measures in Managerial Accounting 897
Integrity, Objectivity, and Ethics in Business: Environmental Managerial Accounting 898
Financial Statements for a Manufacturing Business 898
  Balance Sheet for a Manufacturing Business 898
  Income Statement for a Manufacturing Business 898
Service Focus: Managerial Accounting in the Service Industry 903

Chapter 19   Job Order Costing   924

Cost Accounting Systems Overview 926
  Job Order Cost Systems 926
  Process Cost Systems 926
Job Order Cost Systems for Manufacturing Businesses 927
  Materials 927
Integrity, Objectivity, and Ethics in Business: Phony Invoice Scams 929
  Factory Labor 930
Business Connection: 3D Printing 931
  Factory Overhead 931
Business Connection: Advanced Robotics 932
  Work in Process 936
  Finished Goods 937
  Sales and Cost of Goods Sold 938
  Period Costs 938
  Summary of Cost Flows for Legend Guitars 938
Job Order Costing for Decision Making 940
Job Order Cost Systems for Service Businesses 941
  Types of Service Businesses 941
  Flow of Costs in a Service Job Order Cost System 942
Service Focus: Job Order Costing in a Law Firm 943

Practice Set: Hydro Paddle Boards
This practice set is a manufacturing business operated as a corporation. This set uses a job order cost system and includes subsidiary ledgers and job cost records. This set can be solved manually or with the General Ledger software.

Chapter 20   Process Cost Systems   968

Process Cost Systems 970
Integrity, Objectivity, and Ethics in Business: On Being Green 970
  Comparing Job Order and Process Cost Systems 971
  Cost Flows for a Process Manufacturer 973
Business Connection: Sustainable Papermaking 975
Cost of Production Report 976
  Step 1: Determine the Units to Be Assigned Costs 976
  Step 2: Compute Equivalent Units of Production 978
  Step 3: Determine the Cost per Equivalent Unit 981
  Step 4: Allocate Costs to Units Transferred Out and Partially Completed Units 982
  Preparing the Cost of Production Report 984
Journal Entries for a Process Cost System 985
Service Focus: Costing the Power Stack 988
Using the Cost of Production Report for Decision Making 989
  Cost per Equivalent Unit Between Periods 989
  Cost Category Analysis 989
  Yield 990
Lean Manufacturing 991
  Traditional Production Process 991
  Lean Production Process 992
Average Cost Method 993
  Determining Costs Using the Average Cost Method 993
  The Cost of Production Report 995

Chapter 21   Cost-Volume-Profit Analysis   1020

Cost Behavior 1022
  Variable Costs 1022
  Fixed Costs 1024
  Mixed Costs 1024
  Summary of Cost Behavior Concepts 1027

Business Connection: Booking Fees 1028

Cost-Volume-Profit Relationships 1028
    Contribution Margin 1029
    Contribution Margin Ratio 1029
    Unit Contribution Margin 1030

Mathematical Approach to Cost-Volume-Profit Analysis 1031
    Break-Even Point 1031
    Target Profit 1035

Business Connection: Airline Industry Break-Even 1036

Integrity, Objectivity, and Ethics in Business: Orphan Drugs 1037

Graphic Approach to Cost-Volume-Profit Analysis 1037
    Cost-Volume-Profit (Break-Even) Chart 1037
    Profit-Volume Chart 1039
    Use of Computers in Cost-Volume-Profit Analysis 1042
    Assumptions of Cost-Volume-Profit Analysis 1042

Service Focus: Profit, Loss, and Break-Even in Major League Baseball 1042

Special Cost-Volume-Profit Relationships 1042
    Sales Mix Considerations 1043
    Operating Leverage 1044
    Margin of Safety 1046

Variable Costing 1047

Chapter 22 Budgeting 1074

Nature and Objectives of Budgeting 1076
    Objectives of Budgeting 1076
    Human Behavior and Budgeting 1077

Integrity, Objectivity, and Ethics in Business: Budget Games 1078

Budgeting Systems 1078
    Static Budget 1079

Service Focus: Film Budgeting 1080
    Flexible Budget 1080
    Computerized Budgeting Systems 1081

Master Budget 1082

Operating Budgets 1082
    Sales Budget 1082
    Production Budget 1084
    Direct Materials Purchases Budget 1084
    Direct Labor Cost Budget 1086
    Factory Overhead Cost Budget 1088
    Cost of Goods Sold Budget 1088
    Selling and Administrative Expenses Budget 1090

Business Connection: Mad Men 1091
    Budgeted Income Statement 1091

Financial Budgets 1092
    Cash Budget 1092
    Capital Expenditures Budget 1095
    Budgeted Balance Sheet 1096

Chapter 23 Evaluating Variances from Standard Costs 1124

Standards 1126
    Setting Standards 1126
    Types of Standards 1127
    Reviewing and Revising Standards 1127

Integrity, Objectivity, and Ethics in Business: Company Reputation: The Best of the Best 1127
    Criticisms of Standard Costs 1127

Business Connection: Standard Costing in Action: Expanding Brewing Operations 1128

Budgetary Performance Evaluation 1128
    Budget Performance Report 1129
    Manufacturing Cost Variances 1129

Direct Materials and Direct Labor Variances 1131
    Direct Materials Variances 1131

Service Focus: Standard Costing in the Restaurant Industry 1133
    Direct Labor Variances 1134

Factory Overhead Variances 1136
    The Factory Overhead Flexible Budget 1136
    Variable Factory Overhead Controllable Variance 1138
    Fixed Factory Overhead Volume Variance 1139
    Reporting Factory Overhead Variances 1141
    Factory Overhead Account 1142

Recording and Reporting Variances from Standards 1143

Nonfinancial Performance Measures 1146

Chapter 24 Decentralized Operations 1172

Centralized and Decentralized Operations 1174
    Advantages of Decentralization 1174
    Disadvantages of Decentralization 1175

Business Connection: Dover Corporation: Many Pieces, One Picture 1175
    Responsibility Accounting 1175

Responsibility Accounting for Cost Centers 1176

Responsibility Accounting for Profit Centers 1178
- Service Department Charges 1178
- Profit Center Reporting 1180

Responsibility Accounting for Investment Centers 1181
- Return on Investment 1182

Business Connection: Coca-Cola Company: Go West Young Man 1184
- Residual Income 1185
- The Balanced Scorecard 1187

Service Focus: Turning Around Charles Schwab 1188

Transfer Pricing 1188
- Market Price Approach 1189
- Negotiated Price Approach 1190
- Cost Price Approach 1192

Integrity, Objectivity, and Ethics in Business: The Ethics of Transfer Prices 1193

Chapter 25 Differential Analysis, Product Pricing, and Activity-Based Costing 1218

Differential Analysis 1220
- Lease or Sell 1222
- Discontinue a Segment or Product 1223
- Make or Buy 1225
- Replace Equipment 1226
- Process or Sell 1228
- Accept Business at a Special Price 1229

Business Connection: 60% Off! 1230

Setting Normal Product Selling Prices 1231

Service Focus: Revenue Management 1232
- Product Cost Concept 1232

Integrity, Objectivity, and Ethics in Business: Price Fixing 1234
- Target Costing 1234

Production Bottlenecks 1235

Activity-Based Costing 1237
- Estimated Activity Costs 1237
- Activity Rates 1238
- Overhead Allocation 1238

Business Connection: The ABC's of Schwab 1239
- Dangers of Product Cost Distortion 1240

Total and Variable Cost Concepts to Setting Normal Price 1241
- Total Cost Concept 1241
- Variable Cost Concept 1244

Chapter 26 Capital Investment Analysis 1272

Nature of Capital Investment Analysis 1274

Business Connection: Business Use of Investment Analysis Methods 1275

Methods Not Using Present Values 1275
- Average Rate of Return Method 1275
- Cash Payback Method 1276

Methods Using Present Values 1278
- Present Value Concepts 1278
- Net Present Value Method and Index 1281
- Internal Rate of Return Method 1283

Business Connection: Panera Bread Rate of Return 1285

Additional Factors in Capital Investment Analysis 1286
- Income Tax 1286
- Unequal Proposal Lives 1286
- Lease Versus Purchase 1288
- Uncertainty 1288

Service Focus: If You Build It, They Will Come 1288
- Changes in Price Levels 1289
- Qualitative Considerations 1289
- Capital Investment for Sustainability 1289

Integrity, Objectivity, and Ethics in Business: Assumption Fudging 1290

Capital Rationing 1290

Mornin' Joe MJ-1

Financial Statements for Mornin' Joe MJ-2
Financial Statements for Mornin' Joe International MJ-5

Appendix A: Interest Tables A-1

Appendix B: International Financial Reporting Standards (IFRS) B-1

Appendix C: Revenue Recognition C-1

Appendix D: Nike Inc., Form 10-K for the Fiscal Year Ended May 31, 2016 D-1

Glossary G-1

Index I-1

CHAPTER 1
Introduction to Accounting and Business

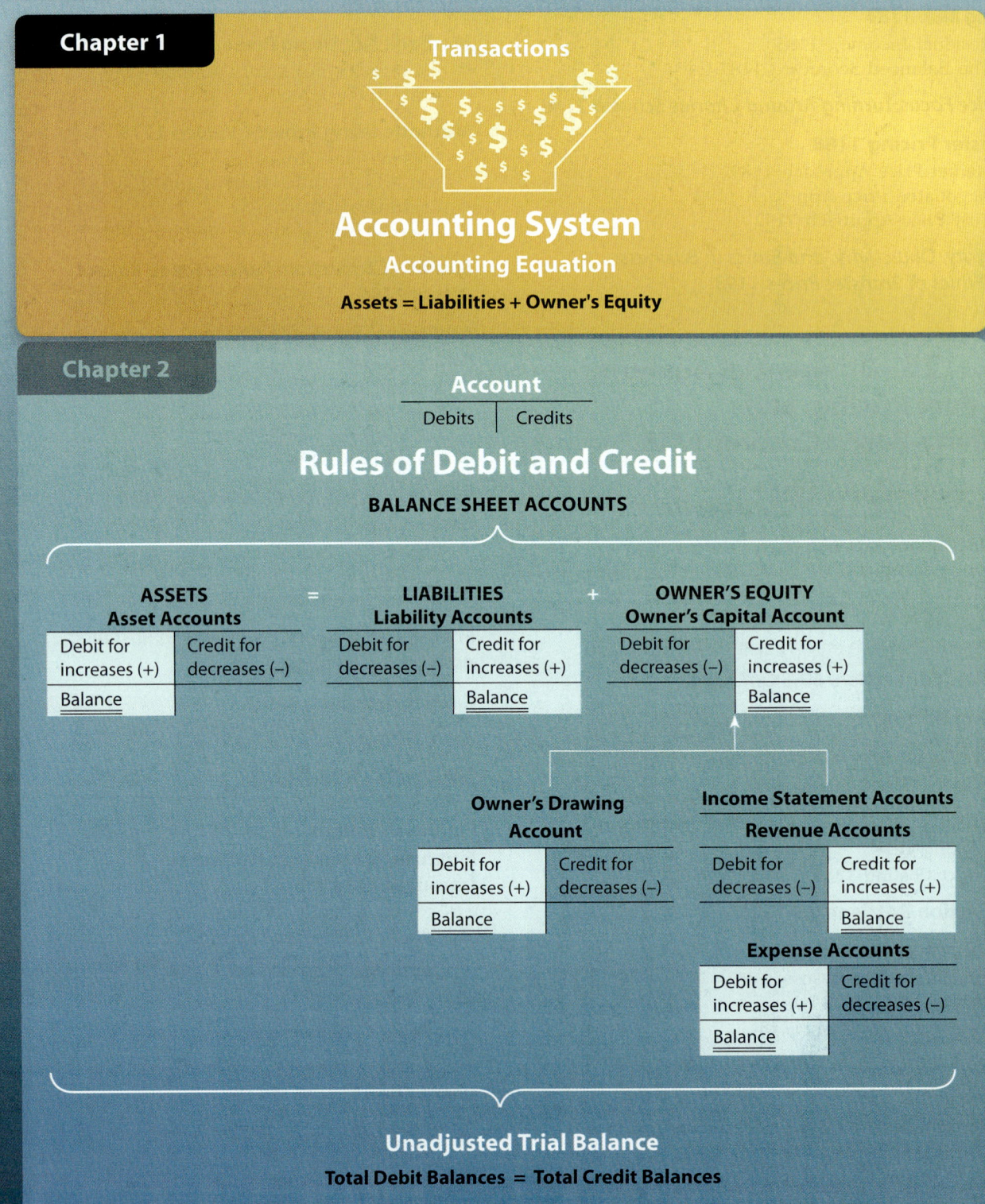

CHAPTER 1

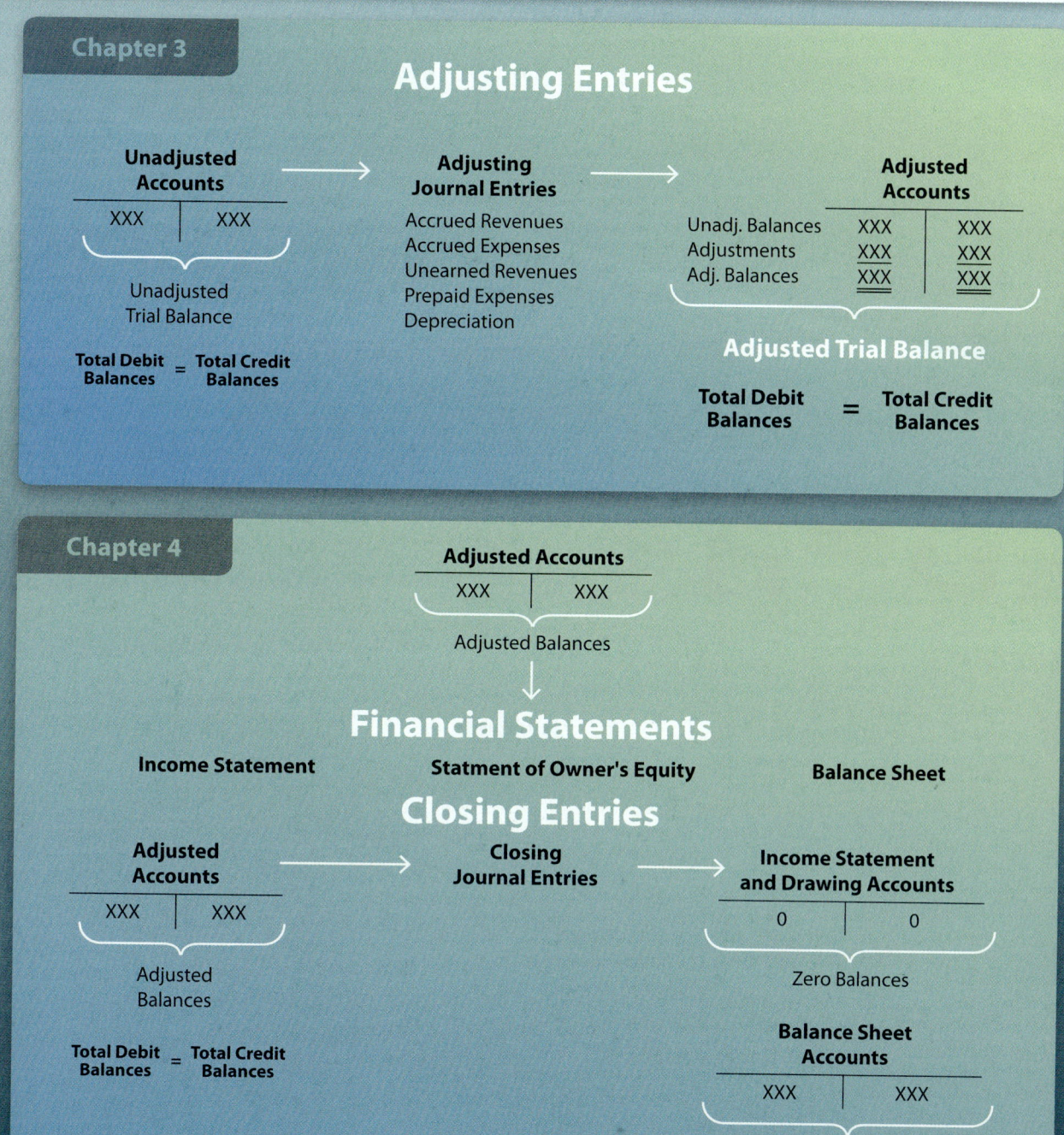

CHAPTER 1

Twitter

When two teams pair up for a game of football, there is often a lot of noise. The band plays, the fans cheer, and fireworks light up the scoreboard. Obviously, the fans are committed and care about the outcome of the game. Just like fans at a football game, the owners of a business want their business to "win" against their competitors in the marketplace. While having your football team win can be a source of pride, winning in the marketplace goes beyond pride and has many tangible benefits. Companies that are winners are better able to serve customers, provide good jobs for employees, and make money for their owners.

Twitter is one of the most visible companies on the Internet. It provides a real-time information network where members can post messages, called tweets, for free. Millions post tweets every day throughout the world.

Do you think Twitter is a successful company? Does it make money? How would you know? Accounting helps to answer these questions.

This textbook introduces you to accounting, the language of business. Chapter 1 begins by discussing what a business is, how it operates, and the role that accounting plays.

Learning Objectives

After studying this chapter, you should be able to:

Example Exercises (EE) are shown in **green**.

Obj. 1 Describe the nature of business and the role of accounting and ethics in business.

Nature of Business and Accounting
Types of Businesses
Role of Accounting in Business
Role of Ethics in Accounting and Business
Opportunities for Accountants

Obj. 2 Summarize the development of accounting principles and relate them to practice.

Generally Accepted Accounting Principles
Business Entity Concept
Cost Concept — EE 1-1

Obj. 3 State the accounting equation and define each element of the equation.

The Accounting Equation
Solving the Accounting Equation — EE 1-2

Obj. 4 Describe and illustrate how business transactions can be recorded in terms of the resulting change in the elements of the accounting equation.

Business Transactions and the Accounting Equation
Recording Transactions — EE 1-3

Obj. 5 Describe the financial statements of a proprietorship and explain how they interrelate.

Financial Statements
Income Statement — EE 1-4
Statement of Owner's Equity — EE 1-5
Balance Sheet — EE 1-6
Statement of Cash Flows — EE 1-7
Interrelationships Among Financial Statements

Obj. 6 Describe and illustrate the use of the ratio of liabilities to owner's equity in evaluating a company's financial condition.

Financial Analysis and Interpretation: Ratio of Liabilities to Owner's Equity
Computing and Interpreting Ratio of Liabilities to Owners' Equity — EE 1-8

At a Glance 1 — Page 28

Nature of Business and Accounting

Obj. 1 Describe the nature of business and the role of accounting and ethics in business.

A **business**[1] is an organization in which basic resources (inputs), such as materials and labor, are assembled and processed to provide goods or services (outputs) to customers. Businesses come in all sizes, from a local coffee house to Starbucks, which sells over $19 billion of coffee and related products each year.

The objective of most businesses is to earn a **profit**. Profit is the difference between the amounts received from customers for goods or services and the amounts paid for the inputs used to provide the goods or services. This text focuses on businesses operating to earn a profit. However, many of the same concepts and principles also apply to not-for-profit organizations such as hospitals, churches, and government agencies.

Types of Businesses

Three types of businesses operating for profit include service, merchandising, and manufacturing businesses. Some examples of each type of business follow:

- **Service businesses** provide services rather than products to customers.
    - Delta Air Lines (transportation services)
    - The Walt Disney Company (entertainment services)

[1] A complete glossary of terms appears at the end of the text.

> **Link to Twitter**
> Twitter is a service company that provides a platform for individuals to send text messages called *tweets*.

- **Merchandising businesses** sell products they purchase from other businesses to customers.
  - Wal-Mart (general merchandise)
  - Amazon.com (Internet books, music, videos)
- **Manufacturing businesses** convert basic inputs into products that are sold to customers.
  - Ford Motor Co. (cars, trucks, vans)
  - Dell Inc. (personal computers)

Role of Accounting in Business

The role of accounting in business is to provide information for managers to use in operating the business. In addition, accounting provides information to other users in assessing the economic performance and condition of the business.

Thus, **accounting** can be defined as an information system that provides reports to users about the economic activities and condition of a business. You could think of accounting as the "language of business." This is because accounting is the means by which businesses' financial information is communicated to users.

> **Note**
> Accounting is an information system that provides reports to users about the economic activities and condition of a business.

The process by which accounting provides information to users is as follows:

1. Identify users.
2. Assess users' information needs.
3. Design the accounting information system to meet users' needs.
4. Record economic data about business activities and events.
5. Prepare accounting reports for users.

As illustrated in Exhibit 1, users of accounting information can be divided into two groups: internal users and external users.

> **Link to Twitter**
> One of the ways Twitter provides information to its investors is by publishing an annual report, which includes general-purpose financial statements.

Managerial Accounting Internal users of accounting information include managers and employees. These users are directly involved in managing and operating the business. The area of accounting that provides internal users with information is called **managerial accounting** or **management accounting**.

The objective of managerial accounting is to provide relevant and timely information for managers' and employees' decision-making needs. Oftentimes, such information is sensitive and is not distributed outside the business. Examples of sensitive information might include information about customers, prices, and plans to expand the business. Managerial accountants employed by a business are employed in **private accounting**.

Financial Accounting External users of accounting information include investors, creditors, customers, and the government. These users are not directly involved in managing and operating the business. The area of accounting that provides external users with information is called **financial accounting**.

The objective of financial accounting is to provide relevant and timely information for the decision-making needs of users outside the business. For example, financial reports on the operations and condition of the business are useful for banks and other creditors in deciding whether to lend money to the business. **General-purpose financial statements** are one type of financial accounting report that is distributed to external users. The term *general-purpose* refers to the wide range of decision-making needs that these reports are designed to serve. Later in this chapter, general-purpose financial statements are described and illustrated.

Role of Ethics in Accounting and Business

The objective of accounting is to provide relevant, timely information for user decision making. Accountants must behave in an ethical manner so that the information they provide users will be trustworthy and, thus, useful for decision making. Managers and employees must also behave in an ethical manner in managing and operating a business. Otherwise, no one will be willing to invest in or loan money to the business.

Accounting as an Information System — EXHIBIT 1

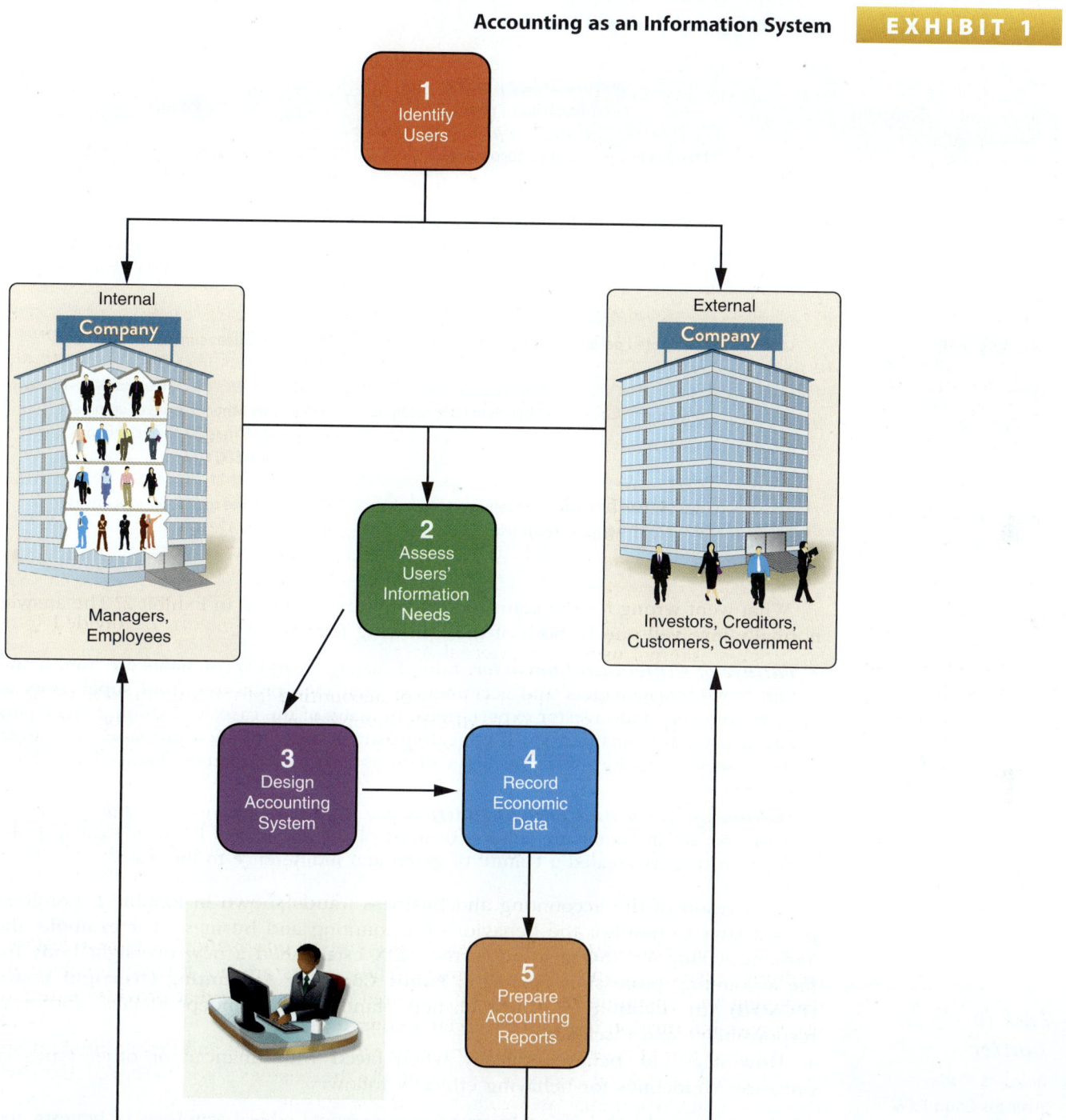

Ethics are moral principles that guide the conduct of individuals. Unfortunately, business managers and accountants sometimes behave in an unethical manner. Many of the managers of the companies listed in Exhibit 2 engaged in accounting or business fraud. These ethical violations led to fines, firings, and lawsuits. In some cases, managers were criminally prosecuted, convicted, and sent to prison.

Chapter 1 Introduction to Accounting and Business

EXHIBIT 2 — Accounting and Business Frauds

Company	Nature of Accounting or Business Fraud	Result
Computer Associates International, Inc.	Fraudulently reported its financial results.	CEO and senior executives indicted. Five executives pled guilty. $225 million fine.
Enron	Fraudulently reported its financial results.	Bankrupcty. Senior executives criminally convicted. More than $60 billion in stock market losses.
HealthSouth	Overstated performance by $4 billion in false entries.	Senior executives criminally convicted.
Qwest Communications International, Inc.	Improperly reported $3 billion in false receipts.	CEO and six other executives criminally convicted of "massive financial fraud." $250 million SEC fine.
Xerox Corporation	Recognized $3 billion in revenue prior to when it should have been recorded.	$10 million fine to SEC. Six executives forced to pay $22 million.

What went wrong for the managers and companies listed in Exhibit 2? The answer normally involved one or both of the following factors:

- **Failure of Individual Character.** Ethical managers and accountants are honest and fair. However, managers and accountants often face pressures from supervisors to meet company and investor expectations. In many of the cases in Exhibit 2, managers and accountants justified small ethical violations to avoid such pressures. However, these small violations became big violations as the company's financial problems became worse.
- **Culture of Greed and Ethical Indifference.** By their behavior and attitude, senior managers set the company culture. In most of the companies listed in Exhibit 2, the senior managers created a culture of greed and indifference to the truth.

As a result of the accounting and business frauds shown in Exhibit 2, Congress passed laws to monitor the behavior of accounting and business. For example, the **Sarbanes-Oxley Act (SOX)** was enacted. SOX established a new oversight body for the accounting profession called the **Public Company Accounting Oversight Board (PCAOB)**. In addition, SOX established standards for independence, corporate responsibility, and disclosure.

How does one behave ethically when faced with financial or other types of pressure? Guidelines for behaving ethically follow:[2]

1. Identify an ethical decision by using your personal ethical standards of honesty and fairness.
2. Identify the consequences of the decision and its effect on others.
3. Consider your obligations and responsibilities to those who will be affected by your decision.
4. Make a decision that is ethical and fair to those affected by it.

> **Link to Twitter**
>
> Twitter's "Code of Business Conduct & Ethics" can be found at https://investor.twitterinc.com/corporate-governance.cfm

---

[2] Many companies have ethical standards of conduct for managers and employees. In addition, the Institute of Management Accountants and the American Institute of Certified Public Accountants have professional codes of conduct, which can be obtained from their websites at www.imanet.org and www.aicpa.org, respectively.

INTEGRITY, OBJECTIVITY, AND ETHICS IN BUSINESS

BERNIE MADOFF

In June 2009, Bernard L. "Bernie" Madoff was sentenced to 150 years in prison for defrauding thousands of investors in one of the biggest frauds in American history. Madoff's fraud started several decades earlier when he began a Ponzi scheme in his investment management firm, Bernard L. Madoff Investment Securities LLC.

In a Ponzi scheme, the investment manager uses funds received from new investors to pay a return to existing investors, rather than basing investment returns on the fund's actual performance. As long as the investment manager is able to attract new investors, he or she will have new funds to pay existing investors and continue the fraud. While most Ponzi schemes collapse quickly when the investment manager runs out of new investors, Madoff's reputation, popularity, and personal contacts provided a steady stream of investors, which allowed the fraud to survive for decades.

Opportunities for Accountants

Numerous career opportunities are available for students majoring in accounting. Currently, the demand for accountants exceeds the number of new graduates entering the job market. This is partly due to the increased regulation of business caused by the accounting and business frauds shown in Exhibit 2. Also, more and more businesses have come to recognize the importance and value of accounting information.

As indicated earlier, accountants employed by a business are employed in private accounting. Private accountants have a variety of possible career options within a company. Some of these career options are shown in Exhibit 3 along with their starting salaries. Accountants who provide audit services, called auditors, attest to the accuracy of financial records, accounts, and systems. As shown in Exhibit 3, several private accounting careers have certification options.

Accounting Career Paths and Salaries — EXHIBIT 3

Accounting Career Track	Description	Career Options	Annual Starting Salaries*	Certification
Private Accounting	Accountants employed by companies, government, and not-for-profit entities.	Bookkeeper	$45,000	
		Payroll clerk	$41,000	Certified Payroll Professional (CPP)
		General accountant	$49,000	
		Budget analyst	$52,000	
		Cost accountant	$53,000	Certified Management Accountant (CMA)
		Internal auditor	$60,000	Certified Internal Auditor (CIA)
		Information technology auditor	$68,000	Certified Information Systems Auditor (CISA)
Public Accounting	Accountants employed individually or within a public accounting firm in audit, tax, or management advisory services.	Large firms (over $250 million in revenue)	$65,000	Certified Public Accountant (CPA)
		Mid-size firms ($25–$250 million in revenue)	$58,000	Certified Public Accountant (CPA)
		Small firms (less than $25 million in revenue)	$54,000	Certified Public Accountant (CPA)

*Average salaries rounded to the nearest thousand. Salaries may vary by size of company and region.
Source: Robert Half *2016 U.S. Salary Guide (Finance and Accounting)*, Robert Half International, Inc. (www.roberthalf.com/workplace-research/salary-guides)

Accountants who provide services on a fee basis are said to be employed in **public accounting**. In public accounting, an accountant may practice as an individual or as a member of a public accounting firm. Public accountants who have met a state's education, experience, and examination requirements may become **Certified Public Accountants (CPAs)**. CPAs typically perform general accounting, audit, or tax services. As can be seen in Exhibit 3, CPAs have slightly better starting salaries than private accountants. Career statistics indicate, however, that these salary differences tend to disappear over time.

Because all functions within a business use accounting information, experience in private or public accounting provides a solid foundation for a career. Many positions in industry and in government agencies are held by individuals with accounting backgrounds.

Business Connection

PATHWAYS COMMISSION

The Pathways Commission issued its study titled *Charting a National Strategy for the Next Generation of Accountants*. The Commission was made up of diverse members and was jointly sponsored by the American Institute of Certified Public Accountants (AICPA) and the American Accounting Association (AAA). The Commission emphasized the importance of accounting for a prosperous society and good decision making. The Commission also emphasized that accountants must be critical thinkers who are comfortable addressing the shades of gray required by accounting judgments.

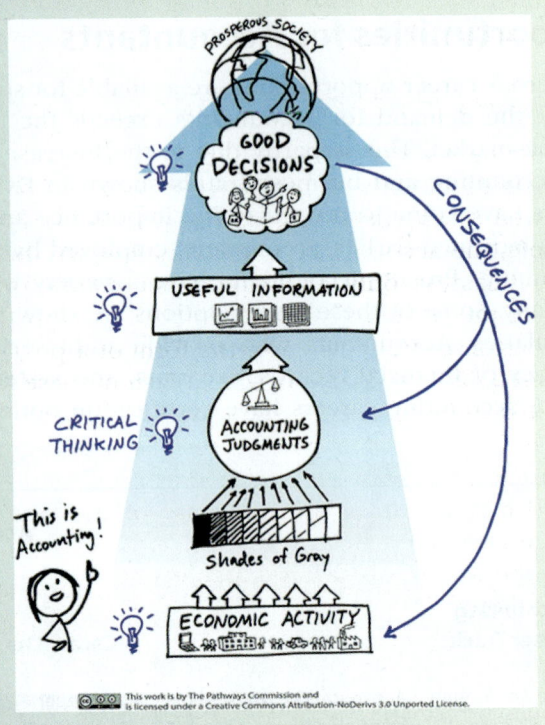

Source: *Charting a National Strategy for the Next Generation of Accountants*, The Pathways Commission, July 2012.

Obj. 2 Summarize the development of accounting principles and relate them to practice.

Generally Accepted Accounting Principles

If companies did not follow the same rules when reporting financial information, comparisons among companies would be difficult, if not impossible. Thus, financial accountants follow **generally accepted accounting principles (GAAP)** in preparing reports. These reports allow investors and other users to compare one company to another.

Accounting principles and concepts develop from research, accepted accounting practices, and pronouncements of regulators. Within the United States, the

Financial Accounting Standards Board (FASB) has the primary responsibility for developing accounting principles. The FASB publishes *Statements of Financial Accounting Standards* as well as *Interpretations* of these Standards. In addition, the **Securities and Exchange Commission (SEC),** an agency of the U.S. government, has authority over the accounting and financial disclosures for companies whose shares of ownership (stock) are traded and sold to the public. The SEC normally accepts the accounting principles set forth by the FASB. However, the SEC may issue *Staff Accounting Bulletins* on accounting matters that may not have been addressed by the FASB.

Many countries outside the United States use accounting principles adopted by the **International Accounting Standards Board (IASB)**. The IASB issues *International Financial Reporting Standards (IFRS)*. Differences currently exist between FASB and IASB accounting principles. Investors and other stakeholders should be alert to these differences in analyzing financial reports of international companies. Throughout this text, International Connection boxes, such as the one at the bottom of this page, highlight many of these differences. In addition, Appendix B at the end of this text summarizes differences between U.S. GAAP and IFRS.

See Appendix B for more information.

In this chapter and text, accounting principles and concepts are emphasized. It is through this emphasis on the "why" as well as the "how" that you will gain an understanding of accounting.

Business Entity Concept

The **business entity concept** limits the economic data in an accounting system to data related directly to the activities of the business. In other words, the business is viewed as an entity separate from its owners, creditors, or other businesses. For example, the accountant for a business with one owner would record the activities of the business only and would not record the personal activities, property, or debts of the owner.

Note

Under the business entity concept, the activities of a business are recorded separately from the activities of its owners, creditors, or other businesses.

A business entity may take the form of a proprietorship, partnership, corporation, or **limited liability company (LLC)**. Each of these forms and their major characteristics are listed in Exhibit 4.

The three types of businesses discussed earlier—service, merchandising, and manufacturing—may be organized as proprietorships, partnerships, corporations, or limited liability companies. Because of the large amount of resources required to operate a manufacturing business, most manufacturers such as Ford Motor Company are corporations. Most large retailers such as Wal-Mart and The Home Depot are also corporations.

International Connection

 INTERNATIONAL FINANCIAL REPORTING STANDARDS (IFRS)

IFRS are considered to be more "principles-based" than U.S. GAAP, which is considered to be more "rules-based." For example, U.S. GAAP consists of approximately 17,000 pages, which include numerous industry-specific accounting rules. In contrast, IFRS allow more judgment in deciding how business transactions are recorded. Many believe that the strong regulatory and litigation environment in the United States is the cause for the more rules-based GAAP approach. Regardless, IFRS and GAAP share many common principles.*

*Differences between U.S. GAAP and IFRS are further discussed and illustrated in Appendix B.

Exhibit 4: Forms of Business Entities

Form of Business Entity	Characteristics	Examples
Proprietorship is owned by one individual.	• 70% of business entities in the United States. • Easy and inexpensive to organize. • Resources are limited to those of the owner. • Used by small businesses.	• A & B Painting
Partnership is owned by two or more individuals.	• 10% of business organizations in the United States (combined with limited liability companies). • Combines the skills and resources of more than one person.	• Jones & Smith, Architects
Corporation is organized under state or federal statutes as a separate legal taxable entity.	• Generates 90% of business revenues. • 20% of the business organizations in the United States. • Ownership is divided into shares called stock. • Can obtain large amounts of resources by issuing stock. • Used by large businesses.	• **Alphabet (Google)** • **Apple** • **Ford Motor Company** • **Twitter**
Limited liability company (LLC) combines the attributes of a partnership and a corporation.	• 10% of business organizations in the United States (combined with partnerships). • Often used as an alternative to a partnership. • Has tax and legal liability advantages for owners.	• Mosel & Farmer, CPAs, LLC

Cost Concept

Under the **cost concept**, amounts are initially recorded in the accounting records at their cost or purchase price. To illustrate, assume that Aaron Publishers purchased a building on February 20, 2017, for $150,000. The following additional information applies to the building:

Price listed by seller on January 1, 2017	$160,000
Aaron Publishers' initial offer to buy on January 31, 2017	140,000
Purchase price on February 20, 2017	150,000
Estimated selling price on December 31, 2019	220,000
Assessed value for property taxes, December 31, 2019	190,000

Under the cost concept, Aaron Publishers records the purchase of the building on February 20, 2017, at the purchase price of $150,000. The other amounts listed have no effect on the accounting records.

The fact that the building has an estimated selling price of $220,000 on December 31, 2019, indicates that the building has increased in value. However, to use the $220,000 in the accounting records would be to record a profit before selling the building. If Aaron Publishers sells the building on January 9, 2021, for $240,000, a profit of $90,000 ($240,000 − $150,000) is then realized and recorded. The new owner would record $240,000 as its cost of the building.

The cost concept also involves the objectivity and unit of measure concepts. The **objectivity concept** requires that the amounts recorded in the accounting records be based on objective evidence. In exchanges between a buyer and a seller, both try to get the best price. Only the final agreed-upon amount is objective enough to be recorded in the accounting records. If amounts in the accounting records were constantly being revised upward or downward based on offers, appraisals, and opinions, accounting reports could become unstable and unreliable.

The **unit of measure concept** requires that economic data be recorded in dollars. Money is a common unit of measurement for reporting financial data and reports.

Example Exercise 1-1 Cost Concept   Obj. 2

On August 25, Gallatin Repair Service extended an offer of $400,000 for land that had been priced for sale at $500,000. On September 3, Gallatin Repair Service accepted the seller's counteroffer of $460,000. On October 20, the land was assessed at a value of $300,000 for property tax purposes. On December 4, a national retail chain offered Gallatin Repair Service $525,000 for the land. At what value should the land be recorded in Gallatin Repair Service's records?

Follow My Example 1-1

$460,000. Under the cost concept, the land should be recorded at the cost to Gallatin Repair Service.

Practice Exercises: PE 1-1A, PE 1-1B

The Accounting Equation

Obj. 3 State the accounting equation and define each element of the equation.

The resources owned by a business are its **assets**. Examples of assets include cash, land, buildings, and equipment. The rights or claims to the assets are divided into two types: (1) the rights of creditors and (2) the rights of owners. The rights of creditors are the debts of the business and are called **liabilities**. The rights of the owners of a proprietorship, partnership, or limited liability company are called **owner's equity**. Since stockholders own a corporation, the rights of owners of a corporation are called **stockholders' equity**.

The following equation shows the relationship among assets, liabilities, and owner's equity:

Assets = Liabilities + Owner's Equity

This equation is called the **accounting equation**. Liabilities usually are shown before owner's equity in the accounting equation because creditors have first rights to the assets.

Given any two amounts, the accounting equation may be solved for the third unknown amount. To illustrate, if the assets owned by a business amount to $100,000 and the liabilities amount to $30,000, the owner's equity is equal to $70,000, computed as follows:

Assets	−	Liabilities	=	Owner's Equity
$100,000	−	$30,000	=	$70,000

Link to Twitter

Twitter's accounting equation for a recent year: Assets ($3,366 million) = Liabilities ($416 million) + Stockholders' Equity ($2,950 million)

Business Connection

THE ACCOUNTING EQUATION

The accounting equation serves as the basic foundation for the accounting systems of all companies. From the smallest business, such as the local convenience store, to the largest business, such as The Coca-Cola Company, companies use the accounting equation. Some examples taken from recent financial reports of well-known corporations follow:

Company	Assets*	=	Liabilities	+	Stockholders' Equity
Alphabet (Google)	$110,920	=	$23,611	+	$87,309
The Coca-Cola Company	$92,023	=	$61,462	+	$30,561
DuPont	$49,876	=	$36,498	+	$13,378
eBay	$45,132	=	$25,226	+	$19,906
McDonald's	$34,281	=	$21,428	+	$12,853
Microsoft Corporation	$172,384	=	$82,600	+	$89,784
Southwest Airlines	$20,200	=	$13,425	+	$6,775
Wal-Mart	$203,706	=	$117,769	+	$85,937

*Amounts are shown in millions of dollars.

Example Exercise 1-2 Accounting Equation   Obj. 3

John Joos is the owner and operator of You're A Star, a motivational consulting business. At the end of its accounting period, December 31, 2018, You're A Star has assets of $800,000 and liabilities of $350,000. Using the accounting equation, determine the following amounts:

a. Owner's equity as of December 31, 2018.

b. Owner's equity as of December 31, 2019, assuming that assets increased by $130,000 and liabilities decreased by $25,000 during 2019.

Follow My Example 1-2

a. Assets = Liabilities + Owner's Equity

$800,000 = $350,000 + Owner's Equity

Owner's Equity = $450,000

b. First, determine the change in owner's equity during 2019 as follows:

Assets = Liabilities + Owner's Equity

$130,000 = −$25,000 + Owner's Equity

Owner's Equity = $155,000

Next, add the change in owner's equity during 2019 to the owner's equity on December 31, 2018, to arrive at owner's equity on December 31, 2019, as follows:

Owner's Equity on December 31, 2019 = $450,000 (Owner's Equity on 12/31/18) + $155,000 (change in Owner's Equity) = $605,000

Practice Exercises: PE 1-2A, PE 1-2B

Obj. 4 Describe and illustrate how business transactions can be recorded in terms of the resulting change in the elements of the accounting equation.

Note

All business transactions can be stated in terms of changes in the elements of the accounting equation.

Business Transactions and the Accounting Equation

Paying a monthly bill, such as a telephone bill of $168, affects a business's financial condition because it now has less cash on hand. Such an economic event or condition that directly changes an entity's financial condition or its results of operations is a **business transaction**. For example, purchasing land for $50,000 is a business transaction. In contrast, a change in a business's credit rating does not directly affect cash or any other asset, liability, or owner's equity amount.

All business transactions can be stated in terms of changes in the elements of the accounting equation. How business transactions affect the accounting equation can be illustrated by using some typical transactions. As a basis for illustration, a business organized by Chris Clark is used.

Assume that on November 1, 2018, Chris Clark begins a business that will be known as NetSolutions. The first phase of Chris's business plan is to operate NetSolutions as a service business assisting individuals and small businesses in developing web pages and installing computer software. Chris expects this initial phase of the business to last one to two years. During this period, Chris plans on gathering information on the software and hardware needs of customers. During the second phase of the business plan, Chris plans to expand NetSolutions into a personalized retailer of software and hardware for individuals and small businesses.

Each transaction during NetSolutions' first month of operations is described in the following paragraphs. The effect of each transaction on the accounting equation is then shown.

Nov. 1, 2018   *Chris Clark deposited $25,000 in a bank account in the name of NetSolutions.*

Transaction A

This transaction increases the asset cash (on the left side of the equation) by $25,000. To balance the equation, the owner's equity (on the right side of the equation) increases by the same amount. The equity of the owner is identified using the owner's name and "Capital," such as "Chris Clark, Capital."

The effect of this transaction on NetSolutions' accounting equation is as follows:

	Assets	=	Owner's Equity
	Cash		Chris Clark, Capital
a.	25,000	=	25,000

Since Chris Clark is the sole owner, NetSolutions is a proprietorship. Also, the preceding accounting equation is only for the business, NetSolutions. Under the business entity concept, Chris's personal assets, such as his home, personal bank account, and personal liabilities are excluded from the equation.

Nov. 5, 2018   *NetSolutions paid $20,000 for the purchase of land as a future building site.*

Transaction B

The land is located in a business park with access to transportation facilities. Chris Clark plans to rent office space and equipment during the first phase of the business plan. During the second phase, Chris plans to build an office and a warehouse on the land.

The purchase of the land changes the makeup of the assets, but it does not change the total assets. The items in the equation prior to this transaction and the effect of the transaction follow. The new amounts are called *balances*.

	Assets		=	Owner's Equity
	Cash	+ Land	=	Chris Clark, Capital
Bal.	25,000			25,000
b.	−20,000	+20,000		
Bal.	5,000	20,000		25,000
	25,000		=	25,000

Nov. 10, 2018   *NetSolutions purchased supplies for $1,350 and agreed to pay the supplier in the near future.*

Transaction C

You have probably used a credit card to buy clothing or other merchandise. In this type of transaction, you received clothing for a promise to pay your credit card bill in the future. That is, you received an asset and incurred a liability to pay a future bill. NetSolutions entered into a similar transaction by purchasing supplies for $1,350 and agreeing to pay the supplier in the near future. This type of transaction is called a purchase *on account* and is often described as follows: *Purchased supplies on account, $1,350.*

The liability created by a purchase on account is called an **account payable**. Items such as supplies that will be used in the business in the future are called **prepaid expenses**, which are assets. Thus, the effect of this transaction is to increase assets (Supplies) and liabilities (Accounts Payable) by $1,350, as follows:

16 Chapter 1 Introduction to Accounting and Business

	Assets			=	Liabilities	+	Owner's Equity
	Cash	+ Supplies +	Land	=	Accounts Payable	+	Chris Clark, Capital
Bal.	5,000		20,000				25,000
c.		+1,350			+1,350		
Bal.	5,000	1,350	20,000		1,350		25,000

$$\underbrace{26{,}350} = \underbrace{26{,}350}$$

Transaction D   Nov. 18, 2018   *NetSolutions received cash of $7,500 for providing services to customers.*

You may have earned money by painting houses or mowing lawns. If so, you received money for rendering services to a customer. Likewise, a business earns money by selling goods or services to its customers. This amount is called **revenue**.

During its first month of operations, NetSolutions received cash of $7,500 for providing services to customers. The receipt of cash increases NetSolutions' assets and also increases Chris Clark's equity in the business. The revenues of $7,500 are recorded in a Fees Earned column to the right of Chris Clark, Capital. The effect of this transaction is to increase Cash and Fees Earned by $7,500, as follows:

	Assets			=	Liabilities	+	Owner's Equity	
	Cash	+ Supplies +	Land	=	Accounts Payable	+	Chris Clark, Capital	+ Fees Earned
Bal.	5,000	1,350	20,000		1,350		25,000	
d.	+7,500							+7,500
Bal.	12,500	1,350	20,000		1,350		25,000	7,500

$$\underbrace{33{,}850} = \underbrace{33{,}850}$$

Different terms are used for the various types of revenues. As illustrated for NetSolutions, revenue from providing services is recorded as **fees earned**. Revenue from the sale of merchandise is recorded as **sales**. Other examples of revenue include rent, which is recorded as **rent revenue**, and interest, which is recorded as **interest revenue**.

Instead of receiving cash at the time services are provided or goods are sold, a business may accept payment at a later date. Such revenues are described as *fees earned on account* or *sales on account*. For example, if NetSolutions had provided services on account instead of for cash, transaction (d) would have been described as follows: *Fees earned on account, $7,500.*

In such cases, the firm has an asset, called an **account receivable**, which is a claim against the customer. Fees earned on account are recorded as increases in Accounts Receivable and Fees Earned. When customers pay their accounts, Cash increases, and Accounts Receivable decreases.

Transaction E   Nov. 30, 2018   *NetSolutions paid the following expenses during the month: wages, $2,125; rent, $800; utilities, $450; and miscellaneous, $275.*

During the month, NetSolutions spent cash or used up other assets in earning revenue. Assets used in this process of earning revenue are called **expenses**. Expenses include supplies used and payments for employee wages, utilities, and other services.

NetSolutions paid the following expenses during the month: wages, $2,125; rent, $800; utilities, $450; and miscellaneous, $275. Miscellaneous expenses include small amounts paid for such items as postage, coffee, and newspapers. The effect of expenses is the opposite of revenues in that expenses reduce assets and owner's equity. Like fees earned, the expenses are recorded in columns to the right of Chris Clark, Capital. However, since expenses reduce owner's equity, the expenses are entered as negative amounts. The effect of this transaction is as follows:

Chapter 1 Introduction to Accounting and Business 17

	Assets			=	Liabilities +		Owner's Equity				
	Cash	+ Supplies +	Land	=	Accounts Payable +	Chris Clark, Capital	Fees + Earned −	Wages Exp. −	Rent Exp. −	Utilities Exp. −	Misc. Exp.
Bal.	12,500	1,350	20,000		1,350	25,000	7,500				
e.	−3,650							−2,125	−800	−450	−275
Bal.	8,850	1,350	20,000		1,350	25,000	7,500	−2,125	−800	−450	−275
	_____						_____				
	30,200			=			30,200				

Businesses usually record each revenue and expense transaction as it occurs. However, to simplify, NetSolutions' revenues and expenses are summarized for the month in transactions (d) and (e).

Nov. 30, 2018   *NetSolutions paid creditors on account, $950.*   **Transaction F**

When you pay your monthly credit card bill, you decrease the cash and decrease the amount you owe to the credit card company. Likewise, when NetSolutions pays $950 to creditors during the month, it reduces assets and liabilities, as follows:

	Assets			=	Liabilities +		Owner's Equity				
	Cash	+ Supplies +	Land	=	Accounts Payable +	Chris Clark, Capital	Fees + Earned −	Wages Exp. −	Rent Exp. −	Utilities Exp. −	Misc. Exp.
Bal.	8,850	1,350	20,000		1,350	25,000	7,500	−2,125	−800	−450	−275
f.	−950				−950						
Bal.	7,900	1,350	20,000		400	25,000	7,500	−2,125	−800	−450	−275
	29,250			=			29,250				

Paying an amount on account is different from paying an expense. The paying of an expense reduces owner's equity, as illustrated in transaction (e). Paying an amount on account reduces the amount owed on a liability.

Nov. 30, 2018   *Chris Clark determined that the cost of supplies on hand at the end of the month was $550.*   **Transaction G**

The cost of the supplies on hand (not yet used) at the end of the month is $550. Thus, $800 ($1,350 − $550) of supplies must have been used during the month. This decrease in supplies is recorded as an expense, as follows:

	Assets			=	Liabilities +		Owner's Equity					
	Cash	+ Supplies +	Land	=	Accounts Payable +	Chris Clark, Capital	Fees + Earned −	Wages Exp. −	Rent Exp. −	Supplies Exp. −	Utilities Exp. −	Misc. Exp.
Bal.	7,900	1,350	20,000		400	25,000	7,500	−2,125	−800		−450	−275
g.		−800								−800		
Bal.	7,900	550	20,000		400	25,000	7,500	−2,125	−800	−800	−450	−275
	28,450			=			28,450					

Nov. 30, 2018   *Chris Clark withdrew $2,000 from NetSolutions for personal use.*   **Transaction H**

At the end of the month, Chris Clark withdrew $2,000 in cash from the business for personal use. This transaction is the opposite of an investment in the business by the owner. Withdrawals by the owner should not be confused with expenses. Withdrawals *do not* represent assets or services used in the process of earning revenues. Instead, withdrawals are a distribution of capital to the owner. Owner withdrawals are identified by the owner's name and *Drawing*. For example, Chris's withdrawal is identified as Chris Clark, Drawing. Like expenses, withdrawals are recorded in a column to the right of Chris Clark, Capital. The effect of the $2,000 withdrawal is as follows:

	Assets			=	Liabilities +		Owner's Equity						
					Accounts	Chris Clark,	Chris Clark,	Fees	Wages	Rent	Supplies	Utilities	Misc.
	Cash	+ Supp. +	Land	=	Payable +	Capital −	Drawing +	Earned −	Exp. −	Exp. −	Exp. −	Exp. −	Exp.
Bal.	7,900	550	20,000		400	25,000		7,500	−2,125	−800	−800	−450	−275
h.	−2,000						−2,000						
Bal.	5,900	550	20,000		400	25,000	−2,000	7,500	−2,125	−800	−800	−450	−275

$$\underbrace{\hspace{3cm}}_{26,450} = \underbrace{\hspace{8cm}}_{26,450}$$

Summary

The transactions of **NetSolutions** are summarized in Exhibit 5. Each transaction is identified by letter, and the balance of each accounting equation element is shown after every transaction.

EXHIBIT 5   Summary of Transaction for NetSolutions

	Assets			=	Liabilities +		Owner's Equity						
					Accounts	Chris Clark,	Chris Clark,	Fees	Wages	Rent	Supplies	Utilities	Misc.
	Cash	+ Supp. +	Land	=	Payable +	Capital −	Drawing +	Earned −	Exp. −	Exp. −	Exp. −	Exp. −	Exp.
a.	+25,000					+25,000							
b.	−20,000		+20,000										
Bal.	5,000		20,000			25,000							
c.		+1,350			+1,350								
Bal.	5,000	+1,350	20,000		+1,350	25,000							
d.	+7,500							+7,500					
Bal.	12,500	1,350	20,000		1,350	25,000		7,500					
e.	−3,650								−2,125	−800		−450	−275
Bal.	8,850	1,350	20,000		1,350	25,000		7,500	−2,125	−800		−450	−275
f.	−950				−950								
Bal.	7,900	1,350	20,000		400	25,000		7,500	−2,125	−800		−450	−275
g.		−800									−800		
Bal.	7,900	550	20,000		400	25,000		7,500	−2,125	−800	−800	−450	−275
h.	−2,000						−2,000						
Bal.	5,900	550	20,000		400	25,000	−2,000	7,500	−2,125	−800	−800	−450	−275

$$\underbrace{\hspace{3cm}}_{26,450} = \underbrace{\hspace{8cm}}_{26,450}$$

Dynamic Exhibit

You should note the following:

- The effect of every transaction *is an increase or a decrease in one or more of the accounting equation elements*.
- The two sides of the accounting equation are *always equal*.
- The owner's equity is *increased by amounts invested by the owner* and is *decreased by withdrawals by the owner*. In addition, the owner's equity is *increased by revenues* and is *decreased by expenses*.

The four types of transactions affecting owner's equity are illustrated in Exhibit 6.

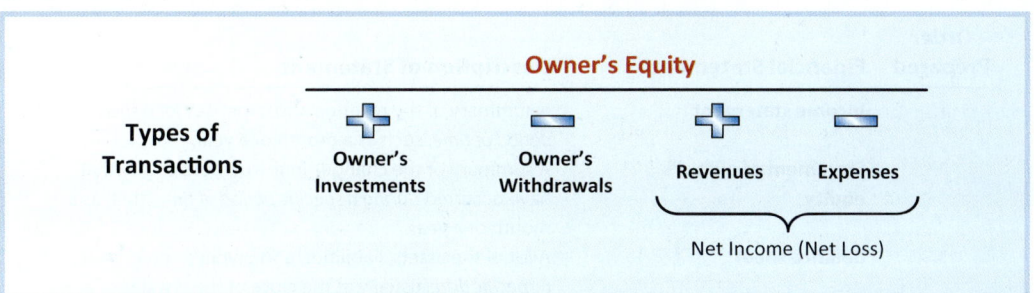

EXHIBIT 6

Types of Transactions Affecting Owner's Equity

Example Exercise 1-3 Transactions — Obj. 4

Salvo Delivery Service is owned and operated by Joel Salvo. The following selected transactions were completed by Salvo Delivery Service during February:

1. Received cash from owner as additional investment, $35,000.
2. Paid creditors on account, $1,800.
3. Billed customers for delivery services on account, $11,250.
4. Received cash from customers on account, $6,740.
5. Paid cash to owner for personal use, $1,000.

Indicate the effect of each transaction on the accounting equation elements (Assets, Liabilities, Owner's Equity, Drawing, Revenue, and Expense). Also indicate the specific item within the accounting equation element that is affected. To illustrate, the answer to (1) follows:

(1) Asset (Cash) increases by $35,000; Owner's Equity (Joel Salvo, Capital) increases by $35,000.

Follow My Example 1-3

(2) Asset (Cash) decreases by $1,800; Liability (Accounts Payable) decreases by $1,800.
(3) Asset (Accounts Receivable) increases by $11,250; Revenue (Delivery Service Fees) increases by $11,250.
(4) Asset (Cash) increases by $6,740; Asset (Accounts Receivable) decreases by $6,740.
(5) Asset (Cash) decreases by $1,000; Drawing (Joel Salvo, Drawing) increases by $1,000.

Practice Exercises: PE 1-3A, PE 1-3B

Financial Statements

Obj. 5 Describe the financial statements of a proprietorship and explain how they interrelate.

After transactions have been recorded and summarized, reports are prepared for users. The accounting reports providing this information are called **financial statements**. The primary financial statements of a proprietorship are the income statement, the statement of owner's equity, the balance sheet, and the statement of cash flows. The order in which the financial statements are prepared and the nature of each statement are described in Exhibit 7.

The four financial statements and their interrelationships are illustrated in Exhibit 8. The data for the statements are taken from the summary of NetSolutions' transactions in Exhibit 5.

All financial statements are identified by the name of the business, the title of the statement, and the *date* or *period of time*. The data presented in the income statement, the statement of owner's equity, and the statement of cash flows are for a period of time. The data presented in the balance sheet are for a specific date.

EXHIBIT 7

Financial Statements

Order Prepared	Financial Statement	Description of Statement
1.	Income statement	A summary of the revenue and expenses *for a specific period of time*, such as a month or a year.
2.	Statement of owner's equity	A summary of the changes in the owner's equity that have occurred *during a specific period of time*, such as a month or a year.
3.	Balance sheet	A list of the assets, liabilities, and owner's equity *as of a specific date*, usually at the close of the last day of a month or a year.
4.	Statement of cash flows	A summary of the cash receipts and cash payments for a *specific period of time*, such as a month or a year.

Income Statement

Note
When revenues exceed expenses, it is referred to as *net income, net profit,* or *earnings*. When expenses exceed revenues, it is referred to as *net loss*.

The income statement reports the revenues and expenses for a *period of time*, based on the **matching concept**. This concept is applied by *matching* the expenses incurred during a period with the revenue that those expenses generated. The excess of the revenue over the expenses is called **net income**, **net profit**, or **earnings**. If the expenses exceed the revenue, the excess is a **net loss**.

The revenue and expenses for **NetSolutions** were shown in the accounting equation as separate increases and decreases. Net income for a period increases the owner's equity (capital) for the period. A net loss decreases the owner's equity (capital) for the period.

The revenue, the expenses, and the net income of $3,050 for NetSolutions are reported in the income statement in Exhibit 8. The order in which the expenses are listed in the income statement varies among businesses. Most businesses list expenses in order of size, beginning with the larger items. Miscellaneous expense is usually shown as the last item, regardless of the amount.

Link to Twitter
For a recent year, **Twitter** reported a net loss of $645 million.

Example Exercise 1-4 Income Statement   Obj. 5

The revenues and expenses of Chickadee Travel Service for the year ended April 30, 2019, follow:

Fees earned	$263,200
Miscellaneous expense	12,950
Office expense	63,000
Wages expense	131,700

Prepare an income statement for the year ended April 30, 2019.

Follow My Example 1-4

Chickadee Travel Service
Income Statement
For the Year Ended April 30, 2019

Fees earned.............................		$263,200
Expenses:		
Wages expense......................	$131,700	
Office expense.......................	63,000	
Miscellaneous expense	12,950	
Total expenses..................		207,650
Net income		$ 55,550

Practice Exercises: PE 1-4A, PE 1-4B

Statement of Owner's Equity

The statement of owner's equity reports the changes in the owner's equity for a period of time. It is prepared *after* the income statement because the net income or net loss for the period must be reported in this statement. Similarly, it is prepared *before* the balance sheet because the amount of owner's equity at the end of the period must be reported on the balance sheet. As a result, the statement of owner's equity is often viewed as the connecting link between the income statement and balance sheet.

Three types of transactions affected owner's equity of **NetSolutions** during November:

- the original investment of $25,000,
- the revenue of $7,500 and expenses of $4,450 that resulted in net income of $3,050 for the month, and
- a withdrawal of $2,000 by the owner.

The preceding information is summarized in the statement of owner's equity in Exhibit 8.

Example Exercise 1-5 Statement of Owner's Equity   Obj. 5

Using the income statement for Chickadee Travel Service shown in Example Exercise 1-4, prepare a statement of owner's equity for the year ended April 30, 2019. Adam Cellini, the owner, invested an additional $50,000 in the business and withdrew cash of $30,000 for personal use during the year. The capital of Adam Cellini was $80,000 on May 1, 2018.

Follow My Example 1-5

Chickadee Travel Service
Statement of Owner's Equity
For the Year Ended April 30, 2019

Adam Cellini, capital, May 1, 2018		$ 80,000
Additional investment by owner during year	$ 50,000	
Net income for the year	55,550	
Withdrawals	(30,000)	
Increase in owner's equity		75,550
Adam Cellini, capital, April 30, 2019		$155,550

Practice Exercises: PE 1-5A, PE 1-5B

Balance Sheet

The balance sheet in Exhibit 8 reports the amounts of **NetSolutions**' assets, liabilities, and owner's equity as of November 30, 2018. The asset and liability amounts are taken from the last line of the summary of transactions in Exhibit 5. Chris Clark, Capital as of November 30, 2018, is taken from the statement of owner's equity. The form of balance sheet shown in Exhibit 8 is called the **account form**. This is because it resembles the basic format of the accounting equation, with assets on the left side and the liabilities and owner's equity sections on the right side.

The assets section of the balance sheet presents assets in the order that they will be converted into cash or used in operations. Cash is presented first, followed by receivables, supplies, prepaid insurance, and other assets. The assets of a more permanent nature are shown next, such as land, buildings, and equipment.

In the liabilities section of the balance sheet in Exhibit 8, accounts payable is the only liability. When there are two or more liabilities, each should be listed and the total amount of liabilities presented as follows:

Bank loan officers use a business's financial statements in deciding whether to grant a loan to the business. Once the loan is granted, the borrower may be required to maintain a certain level of assets in excess of liabilities. The business's financial statements are used to monitor this level.

Liabilities		
Accounts payable	$12,900	
Wages payable	2,570	
Total liabilities		$15,470

EXHIBIT 8

Financial Statements for NetSolutions

NetSolutions
Income Statement
For the Month Ended November 30, 2018

Fees earned..		$7,500
Expenses:		
Wages expense	$2,125	
Rent expense	800	
Supplies expense......................................	800	
Utilities expense	450	
Miscellaneous expense	275	
Total expenses		4,450
Net income		$3,050

NetSolutions
Statement of Owner's Equity
For the Month Ended November 30, 2018

Chris Clark, capital, November 1, 2018...............................		$ 0
Investment on November 1, 2018	$25,000	
Net income for November	3,050	
Withdrawals...	(2,000)	
Increase in owner's equity		26,050
Chris Clark, capital, November 30, 2018............................		$26,050

NetSolutions
Balance Sheet
November 30, 2018

Assets		Liabilities	
Cash	$ 5,900	Accounts payable	$ 400
Supplies...............	550	**Owner's Equity**	
Land	20,000	Chris Clark, capital......................	26,050
Total assets	$26,450	Total liabilities and owner's equity......	$26,450

NetSolutions
Statement of Cash Flows
For the Month Ended November 30, 2018

Cash flows from operating activities:		
Cash receipts from customers.......................	$ 7,500	
Deduct Cash payments for expenses and payments		
to creditors	(4,600)	
Net cash flow from operating activities		$ 2,900
Cash flows used for investing activities:		
Cash payments for purchase of land................		(20,000)
Cash flows from financing activities:		
Cash receipt of owner's investment	$25,000	
Deduct Cash withdrawal by owner	(2,000)	
Net cash flow from financing activities		23,000
Net increase in cash and November 30, 2018, cash balance		$ 5,900

The form of balance sheet shown in Exhibit 9 is called the **report form**. It lists the assets, liabilities, and owner's equity in a downward sequence. The report form is the most common form of reporting the balance sheet and for that reason is used in the remainder of this text.

EXHIBIT 9

Report Form of Balance Sheet

NetSolutions
Balance Sheet
November 30, 2018

Assets

Cash	$ 5,900
Supplies	550
Land	20,000
Total assets	$26,450

Liabilities

Accounts payable	$ 400

Owner's Equity

Chris Clark, Capital	26,050
Total liabilities and owner's equity	$26,450

Example Exercise 1-6 Balance Sheet *Obj. 5*

Using the following data for Chickadee Travel Service as well as the statement of owner's equity shown in Example Exercise 1-5, prepare a balance sheet as of April 30, 2019.

Accounts payable	$12,200
Accounts receivable	31,350
Cash	53,050
Land	80,000
Supplies	3,350

Follow My Example 1-6

Chickadee Travel Service
Balance Sheet
April 30, 2019

Assets

Cash	$ 53,050
Accounts receivable	31,350
Supplies	3,350
Land	80,000
Total assets	$167,750

Liabilities

Accounts payable	$ 12,200

Owner's Equity

Adam Cellini, capital	155,550
Total liabilities and owner's equity	$167,750

Practice Exercises: PE 1-6A, PE 1-6B

Statement of Cash Flows

The statement of cash flows consists of the following three sections, as shown in Exhibit 8:

1. operating activities
2. investing activities
3. financing activities

Each of these sections is briefly described in this section.

Cash Flows from Operating Activities This section reports a summary of cash receipts and cash payments from operations. The net cash flow from operating activities normally differs from the amount of net income for the period. In Exhibit 8, NetSolutions reported net cash flows from operating activities of $2,900 and net income of $3,050. This difference occurs because revenues and expenses may not be recorded at the same time that cash is received from customers or paid to creditors.

Cash Flows from Investing Activities This section reports the cash transactions for the acquisition and sale of relatively permanent assets such as land, buildings, and equipment. Exhibit 8 reports that NetSolutions paid $20,000 for the purchase of land during November.

Cash Flows from Financing Activities This section reports the cash transactions related to cash investments by the owner, borrowings, and withdrawals by the owner. Exhibit 8 shows that Chris Clark invested $25,000 in NetSolutions and withdrew $2,000 during November.

> *Link to Twitter*
>
> For a recent year, **Twitter** reported $1.4 million of cash inflows from operating activities, $1,306.1 million of cash used for investing activities, $1,942.2 million of cash from financing activities, and net increase in cash of $637.5 million.

Preparing NetSolutions' Statement of Cash Flows Preparing the statement of cash flows requires that each of the November cash transactions for NetSolutions be classified as an operating, investing, or financing activity. Using the summary of transactions shown in Exhibit 5, the November cash transactions for NetSolutions are classified as follows:

Transaction	Amount	Cash Flow Activity
a.	$25,000	Financing (Investment by Chris Clark)
b.	−20,000	Investing (Purchase of land)
d.	7,500	Operating (Fees earned)
e.	−3,650	Operating (Payment of expenses)
f.	−950	Operating (Payment of account payable)
h.	−2,000	Financing (Withdrawal by Chris Clark)

Transactions (c) and (g) are not listed since they did not involve a cash receipt or payment. In addition, the payment of accounts payable in transaction (f) is classified as an operating activity because the account payable arose from the purchase of supplies, which are used in operations. Using the preceding classifications of November cash transactions, the statement of cash flows is prepared as shown in Exhibit 8.[3]

The ending cash balance shown on the statement of cash flows is also reported on the balance sheet as of the end of the period. To illustrate, the ending cash of $5,900 reported on the November statement of cash flows in Exhibit 8 is also reported as the amount of cash on hand in the November 30, 2018, balance sheet.

Since November is NetSolutions' first period of operations, the net cash flow for November and the November 30, 2018, cash balance are the same amount, $5,900, as shown in Exhibit 8. In later periods, NetSolutions will report in its statement of cash flows a beginning cash balance, an increase or a decrease in cash for the period, and an ending cash balance. For example, assume that for December NetSolutions

---

[3] This method of preparing the statement of cash flows is called the "direct method." This method and the indirect method are discussed further in Chapter 16.

has a decrease in cash of $3,835. The last three lines of NetSolutions' statement of cash flows for December would be as follows:

Decrease in cash	$(3,835)
Cash as of December 1, 2018	5,900
Cash as of December 31, 2018	$ 2,065

Example Exercise 1-7 Statement of Cash Flows — Obj. 5

A summary of cash flows for Chickadee Travel Service for the year ended April 30, 2019, follows:

Cash receipts:	
Cash received from customers	$251,000
Cash received from additional investment of owner	50,000
Cash payments:	
Cash paid for expenses	210,000
Cash paid for land	80,000
Cash paid to owner for personal use	30,000

The cash balance as of May 1, 2018, was $72,050. Prepare a statement of cash flows for Chickadee Travel Service for the year ended April 30, 2019.

Follow My Example 1-7

Chickadee Travel Service
Statement of Cash Flows
For the Year Ended April 30, 2019

Cash flows from operating activities:		
Cash receipts from customers	$ 251,000	
Cash payments for expenses	(210,000)	
Net cash flow from operating activities		$ 41,000
Cash flows from investing activities:		
Cash payments for purchase of land		(80,000)
Cash flows from financing activities:		
Cash receipt from owner as investment	$ 50,000	
Cash withdrawals by owner	(30,000)	
Net cash flow from financing activities		20,000
Net decrease in cash during year		$(19,000)
Cash as of May 1, 2018		72,050
Cash as of April 30, 2019		$ 53,050

Practice Exercises: PE 1-7A, PE 1-7B

Interrelationships Among Financial Statements

Financial statements are prepared in the order of the income statement, statement of owner's equity, balance sheet, and statement of cash flows. This order is important because the financial statements are interrelated. These interrelationships for **NetSolutions** are shown in Exhibit 8 and are described in Exhibit 10.[4]

The preceding interrelationships are important in analyzing financial statements and the impact of transactions on a business. In addition, these interrelationships serve as a check on whether the financial statements are prepared correctly. For example, if the ending cash on the statement of cash flows does not agree with the balance sheet cash, then an error has occurred.

---

[4] Depending on the method of preparing the cash flows from operating activities section of the statement of cash flows, net income (or net loss) may also appear on the statement of cash flows. This interrelationship or method of preparing the statement of cash flows, called the "indirect method," is described and illustrated in Chapter 16.

EXHIBIT 10 Financial Statement Interrelationships

Financial Statements	Interrelationship	NetSolutions Example (Exhibit 8)
Income Statement *and* Statement of Owner's Equity	Net income or net loss reported on the income statement is also reported on the statement of owner's equity as either an addition (net income) to or deduction (net loss) from the beginning owner's equity and any additional investments by the owner during the period.	NetSolutions' net income of $3,050 for November is added to Chris Clark's investment of $25,000 on the statement of owner's equity.
Statement of Owner's Equity *and* Balance Sheet	Owner's capital at the end of the period reported on the statement of owner's equity is also reported on the balance sheet as owner's capital.	Chris Clark, Capital of $26,050 as of November 30, 2018, on the statement of owner's equity also appears on the November 30, 2018, balance sheet as Chris Clark, Capital.
Balance Sheet *and* Statement of Cash Flows	The cash reported on the balance sheet is also reported as the end-of-period cash on the statement of cash flows.	Cash of $5,900 reported on the balance sheet as of November 30, 2018, is also reported on the November statement of cash flows as the end-of-period cash.

Obj. 6 Describe and illustrate the use of the ratio of liabilities to owner's equity in evaluating a company's financial condition.

Financial Analysis and Interpretation: Ratio of Liabilities to Owner's Equity

The basic financial statements illustrated in this chapter are useful to bankers, creditors, owners, and others in analyzing and interpreting the financial performance and condition of a company. Throughout this text, various tools and techniques that are often used to analyze and interpret a company's financial performance and condition are described and illustrated. The first such tool that is discussed is useful in analyzing the ability of a company to pay its creditors.

The relationship between liabilities and owner's equity, expressed as a **ratio of liabilities to owner's equity**, is computed as follows:

$$\text{Ratio of Liabilities to Owner's Equity} = \frac{\text{Total Liabilities}}{\text{Total Owner's Equity (or Total Stockholders' Equity)}}$$

NetSolutions' ratio of liabilities to owner's equity at the end of November is 0.015, computed as follows:

$$\text{Ratio of Liabilities to Owner's Equity} = \frac{\$400}{\$26,050} = 0.015 \text{ (Rounded)}$$

Corporations refer to total owner's equity as total stockholders' equity. Thus, total stockholders' equity is substituted for total owner's equity when computing this ratio.

To illustrate, recent balance sheet data (in millions) for **Alphabet (Google) Inc.** and **McDonald's Corporation** follow:

	Recent Year	Prior Year
Alphabet Inc.		
Total liabilities	$22,083	$14,429
Total stockholders' equity	71,715	58,145
McDonald's Corporation		
Total liabilities	$18,600	$17,341
Total stockholders' equity	14,390	14,634

The ratio of liabilities to stockholders' equity for Alphabet and McDonald's for a recent year and the prior year is computed as follows:

	Recent Year*	Prior Year*
Alphabet Inc.		
Ratio of liabilities to stockholders' equity	0.31	0.25
	($22,083 ÷ $71,715)	($14,429 ÷ $58,145)
McDonald's Corporation		
Ratio of liabilities to stockholders' equity	1.29	1.18
	($18,600 ÷ $14,390)	($17,341 ÷ $14,634)

*Rounded to two decimal places.

The rights of creditors to a business's assets come before the rights of the owners or stockholders. Thus, the lower the ratio of liabilities to owner's equity, the better able the company is to withstand poor business conditions and to pay its obligations to creditors.

Alphabet is unusual in that it has a very low amount of liabilities. Its ratio of liabilities to stockholders' equity of 0.31 in the recent year and 0.25 in the prior year is low. In contrast, McDonald's has more liabilities; its ratio of liabilities to stockholders' equity is 1.29 in the recent year and 1.18 in the prior year. Because McDonald's ratio of liabilities to stockholders' equity increased slightly, its creditors are slightly more at risk at the end of the recent year. Also, McDonald's creditors are more at risk than are Alphabet's creditors. As well-established companies, however, the creditors of both companies are protected against the risk of nonpayment.

Example Exercise 1-8 Ratio of Liabilities to Owner's Equity   Obj. 6

The following data were taken from Hawthorne Company's balance sheet:

	Dec. 31, 2019	Dec. 31, 2018
Total liabilities	$120,000	$105,000
Total owner's equity	80,000	75,000

a. Compute the ratio of liabilities to owner's equity.
b. Has the creditors' risk increased or decreased from December 31, 2018, to December 31, 2019?

Follow My Example 1-8

a.

	Dec. 31, 2019	Dec. 31, 2018
Total liabilities	$120,000	$105,000
Total owner's equity	80,000	75,000
Ratio of liabilities to owner's equity	1.50	1.40
	($120,000 ÷ $80,000)	($105,000 ÷ $75,000)

b. Increased

Practice Exercises: PE 1-8A, PE 1-8B

At a Glance 1

Obj. 1   Describe the nature of business and the role of accounting and ethics in business.

Key Points   A business provides goods or services (outputs) to customers with the objective of earning a profit. Three types of businesses include service, merchandising, and manufacturing businesses.

Accounting is an information system that provides reports to users about the economic activities and condition of a business.

Ethics are moral principles that guide the conduct of individuals. Good ethical conduct depends on individual character and firm culture.

Accountants are engaged in private accounting or public accounting.

Learning Outcomes	Example Exercises	Practice Exercises
• Distinguish among service, merchandising, and manufacturing businesses.		
• Describe the role of accounting in business and explain why accounting is called the "language of business."		
• Define ethics and list two factors affecting ethical conduct.		
• Differentiate between private and public accounting.		

Obj. 2   Summarize the development of accounting principles and relate them to practice.

Key Points   Generally accepted accounting principles (GAAP) are used in preparing financial statements. Accounting principles and concepts develop from research, practice, and pronouncements of authoritative bodies.

The business entity concept views the business as an entity separate from its owners, creditors, or other businesses. Businesses may be organized as proprietorships, partnerships, corporations, and limited liability companies. The cost concept requires that purchases by a business be recorded in terms of actual cost. The objectivity concept requires that the accounting records and reports be based on objective evidence. The unit of measure concept requires that economic data be recorded in dollars.

Learning Outcomes	Example Exercises	Practice Exercises
• Explain what is meant by generally accepted accounting principles.		
• Describe how generally accepted accounting principles are developed.		
• Describe and give an example of what is meant by the business entity concept.		
• Describe the characteristics of a proprietorship, partnership, corporation, and limited liability company.		
• Describe and give an example of what is meant by the cost concept.	EE1-1	PE1-1A, 1-1B
• Describe and give an example of what is meant by the objectivity concept.		
• Describe and give an example of what is meant by the unit of measure concept.		

Chapter 1 Introduction to Accounting and Business 29

Obj. 3 — State the accounting equation and define each element of the equation.

Key Points The resources owned by a business and the rights or claims to these resources may be stated in the form of an equation, as follows: Assets = Liabilities + Owner's Equity

Learning Outcomes	Example Exercises	Practice Exercises
• State the accounting equation.		
• Define assets, liabilities, and owner's equity.		
• Given two elements of the accounting equation, solve for the third element.	EE1-2	PE1-2A, 1-2B

Obj. 4 — Describe and illustrate how business transactions can be recorded in terms of the resulting change in the elements of the accounting equation.

Key Points All business transactions can be stated in terms of the change in one or more of the three elements of the accounting equation.

Learning Outcomes	Example Exercises	Practice Exercises
• Define a business transaction.		
• Using the accounting equation as a framework, record transactions.	EE1-3	PE1-3A, 1-3B

Obj. 5 — Describe the financial statements of a proprietorship and explain how they interrelate.

Key Points The primary financial statements of a proprietorship are the income statement, the statement of owner's equity, the balance sheet, and the statement of cash flows. The income statement reports a period's net income or net loss, which is also reported on the statement of owner's equity. The ending owner's capital reported on the statement of owner's equity is also reported on the balance sheet. The ending cash balance is reported on the balance sheet and the statement of cash flows.

Learning Outcomes	Example Exercises	Practice Exercises
• List and describe the financial statements of a proprietorship.		
• Prepare an income statement.	EE1-4	PE1-4A, 1-4B
• Prepare a statement of owner's equity.	EE1-5	PE1-5A, 1-5B
• Prepare a balance sheet.	EE1-6	PE1-6A, 1-6B
• Prepare a statement of cash flows.	EE1-7	PE1-7A, 1-7B
• Explain how the financial statements of a proprietorship are interrelated.		

Obj. 6 — Describe and illustrate the use of the ratio of liabilities to owner's equity in evaluating a company's financial condition.

Key Points A ratio useful in analyzing the ability of a business to pay its creditors is the ratio of liabilities to owner's (stockholders') equity. The lower the ratio of liabilities to owner's equity, the better able the company is to withstand poor business conditions and to pay its obligations to creditors.

Learning Outcomes	Example Exercises	Practice Exercises
• Describe the usefulness of the ratio of liabilities to owner's (stockholders') equity.		
• Compute the ratio of liabilities to owner's (stockholders') equity.	EE1-8	PE1-8A, 1-8B

Illustrative Problem

Cecil Jameson, Attorney-at-Law, is a proprietorship owned and operated by Cecil Jameson. On July 1, 2018, the company has the following assets and liabilities: cash, $1,000; accounts receivable, $3,200; supplies, $850; land, $10,000; accounts payable, $1,530. Office space and office equipment are currently being rented, pending the construction of an office complex on land purchased last year. Business transactions during July are summarized as follows:

a. Received cash from clients for services, $3,928.

b. Paid creditors on account, $1,055.

c. Received cash from Cecil Jameson as an additional investment, $3,700.

d. Paid office rent for the month, $1,200.

e. Charged clients for legal services on account, $2,025.

f. Purchased supplies on account, $245.

g. Received cash from clients on account, $3,000.

h. Received invoice for paralegal services from Legal Aid Inc. for July (to be paid on August 10), $1,635.

i. Paid the following: wages expense, $850; utilities expense, $325; answering service expense, $250; and miscellaneous expense, $75.

j. Determined that the cost of supplies on hand was $980; therefore, the cost of supplies used during the month was $115.

k. Jameson withdrew $1,000 in cash from the business for personal use.

Instructions

1. Determine the amount of owner's equity (Cecil Jameson's capital) as of July 1, 2018.

2. State the assets, liabilities, and owner's equity as of July 1 in equation form similar to that shown in this chapter. In tabular form below the equation, indicate the increases and decreases resulting from each transaction and the new balances after each transaction.

3. Prepare an income statement for July, a statement of owner's equity for July, and a balance sheet as of July 31, 2018.

4. (Optional) Prepare a statement of cash flows for July.

Solution

1.

$$\text{Assets} - \text{Liabilities} = \text{Owner's Equity (Cecil Jameson, capital)}$$
$$(\$1{,}000 + \$3{,}200 + \$850 + \$10{,}000) - \$1{,}530 = \text{Owner's Equity (Cecil Jameson, capital)}$$
$$\$15{,}050 - \$1{,}530 = \text{Owner's Equity (Cecil Jameson, capital)}$$
$$\$13{,}520 = \text{Owner's Equity (Cecil Jameson, capital)}$$

2.

	Assets				=	Liabilities +			Owner's Equity						
	Cash +	Accts. Rec. +	Supp. +	Land	=	Accts. Pay. +	Cecil Jameson, Capital −	Cecil Jameson, Drawing +	Fees Earned −	Paralegal Exp. −	Rent Exp. −	Wages Exp. −	Utilities Exp. −	Answering Service Exp. −	Supp. Exp. −	Misc. Exp.
Bal.	1,000	3,200	850	10,000		1,530	13,520									
a.	+3,928								3,928							
Bal.	4,928	3,200	850	10,000		1,530	13,520		3,928							
b.	−1,055					−1,055										
Bal.	3,873	3,200	850	10,000		475	13,520		3,928							
c.	+3,700						+3,700									
Bal.	7,573	3,200	850	10,000		475	17,220		3,928							
d.	−1,200										−1,200					
Bal.	6,373	3,200	850	10,000		475	17,220		3,928		−1,200					
e.		+2,025							+2,025							
Bal.	6,373	5,225	850	10,000		475	17,220		5,953		−1,200					
f.			+245			+245										
Bal.	6,373	5,225	1,095	10,000		720	17,220		5,953		−1,200					
g.	+3,000	−3,000														
Bal.	9,373	2,225	1,095	10,000		720	17,220		5,953		−1,200					
h.						+1,635				−1,635						
Bal.	9,373	2,225	1,095	10,000		2,355	17,220		5,953	−1,635	−1,200					
i.	−1,500											−850	−325	−250		−75
Bal.	7,873	2,225	1,095	10,000		2,355	17,220		5,953	−1,635	−1,200	−850	−325	−250		−75
j.			−115												−115	
Bal.	7,873	2,225	980	10,000		2,355	17,220		5,953	−1,635	−1,200	−850	−325	−250	−115	−75
k.	−1,000							−1,000								
Bal.	6,873	2,225	980	10,000		2,355	17,220	−1,000	5,953	−1,635	−1,200	−850	−325	−250	−115	−75

3.

Cecil Jameson, Attorney-at-Law
Income Statement
For the Month Ended July 31, 2018

Fees earned...		$5,953
Expenses:		
Paralegal expense..	$1,635	
Rent expense..	1,200	
Wages expense...	850	
Utilities expense..	325	
Answering service expense..............................	250	
Supplies expense...	115	
Miscellaneous expense...................................	75	
Total expenses..		4,450
Net income..		$1,503

Cecil Jameson, Attorney-at-Law
Statement of Owner's Equity
For the Month Ended July 31, 2018

Cecil Jameson, capital, July 1, 2018.........................		$13,520
Additional investment by owner.............................	$3,700	
Net income for the month...................................	1,503	
Withdrawals..	(1,000)	
Increase in owner's equity...................................		4,203
Cecil Jameson, capital, July 31, 2018........................		$17,723

(*Continued*)

Cecil Jameson, Attorney-at-Law
Balance Sheet
July 31, 2018

Assets

Cash	$ 6,873
Accounts receivable	2,225
Supplies	980
Land	10,000
Total assets	$20,078

Liabilities

Accounts payable	$ 2,355

Owner's Equity

Cecil Jameson, capital	17,723
Total liabilities and owner's equity	$20,078

4. (Optional)

Cecil Jameson, Attorney-at-Law
Statement of Cash Flows
For the Month Ended July 31, 2018

Cash flows from operating activities:		
Cash receipts from customers	$ 6,928*	
Cash payments for operating expenses	(3,755)**	
Net cash flow from operating activities		$ 3,173
Cash flows from investing activities		—
Cash flows from financing activities:		
Cash receipt from owner as investment	$ 3,700	
Cash withdrawal by owner	(1,000)	
Net cash flow from financing activities		2,700
Net increase in cash during year		$ 5,873
Cash as of July 1, 2018		1,000
Cash as of July 31, 2018		$ 6,873

*$6,928 = $3,928 + $3,000 (from Cash column in Part 2)
**$3,755 = $1,055 + $1,200 + $1,500 (from Cash column in Part 2)

Key Terms

account form (21)
account payable (15)
account receivable (16)
accounting (6)
accounting equation (13)
assets (13)
balance sheet (20)
business (5)
business entity concept (11)
business transaction (14)
Certified Public Accountant (CPA) (10)
corporation (12)

cost concept (12)
earnings (20)
ethics (7)
expenses (16)
fees earned (16)
financial accounting (6)
Financial Accounting Standards Board (FASB) (11)
financial statements (19)
generally accepted accounting principles (GAAP) (10)
general-purpose financial statements (6)

income statement (20)
interest revenue (16)
International Accounting Standards Board (IASB) (11)
liabilities (13)
limited liability company (LLC) (11)
management (or managerial) accounting (6)
manufacturing business (6)
matching concept (20)
merchandising business (6)
net income (or net profit) (20)

net loss (20)
objectivity concept (12)
owner's equity (13)
partnership (12)
prepaid expenses (15)
private accounting (6)
profit (5)
proprietorship (12)

public accounting (10)
Public Company Accounting
 Oversight Board (PCAOB) (8)
ratio of liabilities to owner's
 (stockholders') equity (26)
rent revenue (16)
report form (23)
revenue (16)
sales (16)

Sarbanes-Oxley Act (SOX) (8)
Securities and Exchange
 Commission (SEC) (11)
service business (5)
statement of cash flows (20)
statement of owner's equity (20)
stockholders' equity (13)
unit of measure concept (12)

Discussion Questions

1. Name some users of accounting information.
2. What is the role of accounting in business?
3. Why are most large companies like Microsoft, PepsiCo, Caterpillar, and AutoZone organized as corporations?
4. Josh Reilly is the owner of Dispatch Delivery Service. Recently, Josh paid interest of $4,500 on a personal loan of $75,000 that he used to begin the business. Should Dispatch Delivery Service record the interest payment? Explain.
5. On July 12, Reliable Repair Service extended an offer of $150,000 for land that had been priced for sale at $185,000. On September 3, Reliable Repair Service accepted the seller's counteroffer of $167,500. Describe how Reliable Repair Service should record the land.
6. a. Land with an assessed value of $750,000 for property tax purposes is acquired by a business for $900,000. Ten years later, the plot of land has an assessed value of $1,200,000 and the business receives an offer of $2,000,000 for it. Should the monetary amount assigned to the land in the business records now be increased?
   b. Assuming that the land acquired in (a) was sold for $2,125,000, how would the various elements of the accounting equation be affected?
7. Describe the difference between an account receivable and an account payable.
8. A business had revenues of $679,000 and operating expenses of $588,000. Did the business (a) incur a net loss or (b) realize net income?
9. A business had revenues of $640,000 and operating expenses of $715,000. Did the business (a) incur a net loss or (b) realize net income?
10. The financial statements are interrelated. (a) What item of financial or operating data appears on both the income statement and the statement of owner's equity? (b) What item appears on both the balance sheet and the statement of owner's equity? (c) What item appears on both the balance sheet and the statement of cash flows?

Practice Exercises

Example Exercises

EE 1-1 p. 13 **PE 1-1A Cost concept** OBJ. 2

On February 3, Clairemont Repair Service extended an offer of $360,000 for land that had been priced for sale at $400,000. On February 28, Clairemont Repair Service accepted the seller's counteroffer of $380,000. On October 23, the land was assessed at a value of $390,000 for property tax purposes. On January 15 of the next year, Clairemont Repair Service was offered $450,000 for the land by a national retail chain. At what value should the land be recorded in Clairemont Repair Service's records?

EE 1-1 p. 13 **PE 1-1B Cost concept** OBJ. 2

On March 31, Higgins Repair Service extended an offer of $415,000 for land that had been priced for sale at $460,000. On April 15, Higgins Repair Service accepted the seller's counteroffer of $437,500. On September 9, the land was assessed at a value of $375,000

(Continued)

34 Chapter 1 Introduction to Accounting and Business

for property tax purposes. On December 8, Higgins Repair Service was offered $475,000 for the land by a national retail chain. At what value should the land be recorded in Higgins Repair Service's records?

EE 1-2 *p. 14*

PE 1-2A Accounting equation   OBJ. 3

Terry Fleming is the owner and operator of Go-For-It LLC, a motivational consulting business. At the end of its accounting period, December 31, 2018, Go-For-It has assets of $675,000 and liabilities of $215,000. Using the accounting equation, determine the following amounts:

a. Owner's equity as of December 31, 2018.

b. Owner's equity as of December 31, 2019, assuming that assets increased by $112,300 and liabilities increased by $32,000 during 2019.

EE 1-2 *p. 14*

PE 1-2B Accounting equation   OBJ. 3

Fritz Evans is the owner and operator of Be-The-One, a motivational consulting business. At the end of its accounting period, December 31, 2018, Be-The-One has assets of $395,000 and liabilities of $97,000. Using the accounting equation, determine the following amounts:

a. Owner's equity as of December 31, 2018.

b. Owner's equity as of December 31, 2019, assuming that assets decreased by $65,000 and liabilities increased by $36,000 during 2019.

EE 1-3 *p. 19*

PE 1-3A Transactions   OBJ. 4

Bridgeport Delivery Service is owned and operated by Jerome Foley. The following selected transactions were completed by Bridgeport Delivery Service during February:

1. Received cash from owner as additional investment, $40,000.
2. Billed customers for delivery services on account, $13,750.
3. Paid creditors on account, $2,500.
4. Received cash from customers on account, $9,000.
5. Paid cash to owner for personal use, $1,000.

Indicate the effect of each transaction on the accounting equation elements (Assets, Liabilities, and Owner's Equity). Also indicate the specific item within the accounting equation element that is affected. To illustrate, the answer to (1) follows:

   (1) Asset (Cash) increases by $40,000; Owner's Equity (Jerome Foley, Capital) increases by $40,000.

EE 1-3 *p. 19*

PE 1-3B Transactions   OBJ. 4

Interstate Delivery Service is owned and operated by Katie Wyer. The following selected transactions were completed by Interstate Delivery Service during May:

1. Received cash from owner as additional investment, $18,000.
2. Paid advertising expense, $4,850.
3. Purchased supplies on account, $2,100.
4. Billed customers for delivery services on account, $14,700.
5. Received cash from customers on account, $8,200.

Indicate the effect of each transaction on the accounting equation elements (Assets, Liabilities, and Owner's Equity). Also indicate the specific item within the accounting equation element that is affected. To illustrate, the answer to (1) follows:

   (1) Asset (Cash) increases by $18,000; Owner's Equity (Katie Wyer, Capital) increases by $18,000.

Chapter 1 Introduction to Accounting and Business 35

EE 1-4 *p. 20* **PE 1-4A Income statement** OBJ. 5

The revenues and expenses of Adventure Travel Service for the year ended April 30, 2019, follow:

Fees earned	$2,180,000
Office expense	400,000
Miscellaneous expense	25,000
Wages expense	1,300,000

Prepare an income statement for the year ended April 30, 2019.

EE 1-4 *p. 20* **PE 1-4B Income statement** OBJ. 5

The revenues and expenses of Sentinel Travel Service for the year ended August 31, 2019, follow:

Fees earned	$750,000
Office expense	295,000
Miscellaneous expense	12,000
Wages expense	450,000

Prepare an income statement for the year ended August 31, 2019.

EE 1-5 *p. 21* **PE 1-5A Statement of owner's equity** OBJ. 5

Using the income statement for Adventure Travel Service shown in Practice Exercise 1-4A, prepare a statement of owner's equity for the year ended April 30, 2019. Jerome Foley, the owner, invested an additional $60,000 in the business during the year and withdrew cash of $40,000 for personal use. Jerome Foley, capital as of May 1, 2018, was $1,020,000.

EE 1-5 *p. 21* **PE 1-5B Statement of owner's equity** OBJ. 5

Using the income statement for Sentinel Travel Service shown in Practice Exercise 1-4B, prepare a statement of owner's equity for the year ended August 31, 2019. Barb Schroeder, the owner, invested an additional $36,000 in the business during the year and withdrew cash of $18,000 for personal use. Barb Schroeder, capital as of September 1, 2018, was $380,000.

EE 1-6 *p. 23* **PE 1-6A Balance sheet** OBJ. 5

Using the following data for Adventure Travel Service as well as the statement of owner's equity shown in Practice Exercise 1-5A, prepare a report form balance sheet as of April 30, 2019:

Accounts payable	$105,000
Accounts receivable	485,000
Cash	197,000
Land	900,000
Supplies	18,000

EE 1-6 *p. 23* **PE 1-6B Balance sheet** OBJ. 5

Using the following data for Sentinel Travel Service as well as the statement of owner's equity shown in Practice Exercise 1-5B, prepare a report form balance sheet as of August 31, 2019:

Accounts payable	$ 44,600
Accounts receivable	75,500
Cash	45,400
Land	310,000
Supplies	4,700

36 Chapter 1 Introduction to Accounting and Business

EE 1-7 p. 25   **PE 1-7A Statement of cash flows**   OBJ. 5

A summary of cash flows for Adventure Travel Service for the year ended April 30, 2019, follows:

Cash receipts:	
Cash received from customers	$2,080,000
Cash received from additional investment of owner	60,000
Cash payments:	
Cash paid for operating expenses	1,706,000
Cash paid for land	400,000
Cash paid to owner for personal use	40,000

The cash balance as of May 1, 2018, was $203,000.

Prepare a statement of cash flows for Adventure Travel Service for the year ended April 30, 2019.

EE 1-7 p. 25   **PE 1-7B Statement of cash flows**   OBJ. 5

A summary of cash flows for Sentinel Travel Service for the year ended August 31, 2019, follows:

Cash receipts:	
Cash received from customers	$734,000
Cash received from additional investment of owner	36,000
Cash payments:	
Cash paid for operating expenses	745,600
Cash paid for land	50,000
Cash paid to owner for personal use	18,000

The cash balance as of September 1, 2019, was $89,000.

Prepare a statement of cash flows for Sentinel Travel Service for the year ended August 31, 2019.

EE 1-8 p. 27   **PE 1-8A Ratio of liabilities to owner's equity**   OBJ. 6

The following data were taken from Mesa Company's balance sheet:

	Dec. 31, 2019	Dec. 31, 2018
Total liabilities	$547,800	$518,000
Total owner's equity	415,000	370,000

a. Compute the ratio of liabilities to owner's equity.
b. Has the creditor's risk increased or decreased from December 31, 2018, to December 31, 2019?

EE 1-8 p. 27   **PE 1-8B Ratio of liabilities to owner's equity**   OBJ. 6

The following data were taken from Alvarado Company's balance sheet:

	Dec. 31, 2019	Dec. 31, 2018
Total liabilities	$4,085,000	$2,880,000
Total owner's equity	4,300,000	3,600,000

a. Compute the ratio of liabilities to owner's equity.
b. Has the creditor's risk increased or decreased from December 31, 2018, to December 31, 2019?

Exercises

EX 1-1 Types of businesses
OBJ. 1

The following is a list of well-known companies:

1. Alcoa Inc.
2. Boeing
3. Caterpillar
4. Citigroup Inc.
5. CVS
6. Delta Air Lines
7. eBay Inc.
8. FedEx
9. Ford Motor Company
10. Gap Inc.
11. H&R Block
12. Hilton Hospitality, Inc.
13. Procter & Gamble
14. SunTrust
15. Wal-Mart Stores, Inc.

a. Indicate whether each of these companies is primarily a service, merchandise, or manufacturing business. If you are unfamiliar with the company, use the Internet to locate the company's home page or use the finance website of Yahoo (finance.yahoo.com).

b. For which of the preceding companies is the accounting equation relevant?

EX 1-2 Professional ethics
OBJ. 1

A fertilizer manufacturing company wants to relocate to Lakeside County. A report from a fired researcher at the company indicates the company's product is releasing toxic by-products. The company suppressed that report. A later report commissioned by the company shows there is no problem with the fertilizer.

Should the company's chief executive officer reveal the content of the unfavorable report in discussions with Lakeside County representatives? Discuss.

EX 1-3 Business entity concept
OBJ. 2

Big Sky Sports sells hunting and fishing equipment and provides guided hunting and fishing trips. Big Sky Sports is owned and operated by Joe Flannery, a well-known sports enthusiast and hunter. Joe's wife, Pam, owns and operates Glacier Boutique, a women's clothing store. Joe and Pam have established a trust fund to finance their children's college education. The trust fund is maintained by Kalispell State Bank in the name of the children, Trey and Brooke.

a. For each of the following transactions, identify which of the entities listed should record the transaction in its records:

Entities	
G	Glacier Boutique
K	Kalispell State Bank
B	Big Sky Sports
X	None of the above

1. Pam deposited a $2,000 personal check in the trust fund at Kalispell State Bank.
2. Pam purchased two dozen spring dresses from a Spokane designer for a special spring sale.
3. Joe paid a breeder's fee for an English Springer Spaniel to be used as a hunting guide dog.
4. Pam authorized the trust fund to purchase mutual fund shares.
5. Joe paid a local doctor for his annual physical, which was required by the workmen's compensation insurance policy carried by Big Sky Sports.
6. Received a cash advance from customers for a guided hunting trip.
7. Pam paid her dues to the YWCA.
8. Pam donated several dresses from inventory for a local charity auction for the benefit of a women's abuse shelter.

(Continued)

38 Chapter 1 Introduction to Accounting and Business

9. Joe paid for dinner and a movie to celebrate their thirtieth wedding anniversary.
10. Joe paid for an advertisement in a hunters' magazine.

b. What is a business transaction?

EX 1-4 Accounting equation
OBJ. 3

 Starbucks, $5,818

The total assets and total liabilities (in millions) of **Keurig Green Mountain, Inc.** and **Starbucks Corporation** follow:

	Keurig Green Mountain	Starbucks
Assets	$4,002	$12,446
Liabilities	1,288	6,628

Determine the owners' equity of each company.

EX 1-5 Accounting equation
OBJ. 3

 Dollar Tree, $1,785

The total assets and total liabilities (in millions) of **Dollar Tree Inc.** and **Target Corporation** follow:

	Dollar Tree	Target Corporation
Assets	$3,567	$41,404
Liabilities	1,782	27,407

Determine the owners' equity of each company.

EX 1-6 Accounting equation
OBJ. 3

✓ a. $3,930,000

Determine the missing amount for each of the following:

	Assets	=	Liabilities	+	Owner's Equity
a.	X	=	$556,000	+	$3,374,000
b.	$6,111,200	=	X	+	$5,725,000
c.	$2,150,000	=	$812,500	+	X

EX 1-7 Accounting equation
OBJ. 3, 4

✓ b. $606,500

Annie Rasmussen is the owner and operator of Go44, a motivational consulting business. At the end of its accounting period, December 31, 2018, Go44 has assets of $720,000 and liabilities of $180,000. Using the accounting equation and considering each case independently, determine the following amounts:

a. Annie Rasmussen, capital, as of December 31, 2018.

b. Annie Rasmussen, capital, as of December 31, 2019, assuming that assets increased by $96,500 and liabilities increased by $30,000 during 2019.

c. Annie Rasmussen, capital, as of December 31, 2019, assuming that assets decreased by $168,000 and liabilities increased by $15,000 during 2019.

d. Annie Rasmussen, capital, as of December 31, 2019, assuming that assets increased by $175,000 and liabilities decreased by $18,000 during 2019.

e. Net income (or net loss) during 2019, assuming that as of December 31, 2019, assets were $880,000, liabilities were $220,000, and there were no additional investments or withdrawals.

EX 1-8 Asset, liability, and owner's equity items
OBJ. 3

Indicate whether each of the following is identified with (1) an asset, (2) a liability, or (3) owner's equity:

a. accounts receivable
b. accounts payable
c. cash
d. fees earned
e. land
f. rent expense
g. supplies

EX 1-9 Effect of transactions on accounting equation
OBJ. 4

Describe how the following business transactions affect the three elements of the accounting equation:

a. Invested cash in business.
b. Paid for utilities used in the business.
c. Purchased supplies for cash.
d. Purchased supplies on account.
e. Received cash for services performed.

EX 1-10 Effect of transactions on accounting equation
OBJ. 4

✔ a. (1) increase $183,000

a. A vacant lot acquired for $115,000 is sold for $298,000 in cash. What is the effect of the sale on the total amount of the seller's (1) assets, (2) liabilities, and (3) owner's equity?

b. Assume that the seller owes $80,000 on a loan for the land. After receiving the $298,000 cash in (a), the seller pays the $80,000 owed. What is the effect of the payment on the total amount of the seller's (1) assets, (2) liabilities, and (3) owner's equity?

c. Is it true that a transaction always affects at least two elements (Assets, Liabilities, or Owner's Equity) of the accounting equation? Explain.

EX 1-11 Effect of transactions on owner's equity
OBJ. 4

Indicate whether each of the following types of transactions will either (a) increase owner's equity or (b) decrease owner's equity:

1. expenses
2. owner's investments
3. owner's withdrawals
4. revenues

EX 1-12 Transactions
OBJ. 4

The following selected transactions were completed by Silverado Delivery Service during February:

1. Received cash from owner as additional investment, $25,000.
2. Purchased supplies for cash, $750.
3. Paid rent for February, $3,000.
4. Paid advertising expense, $1,500.
5. Received cash for providing delivery services, $16,800.
6. Billed customers for delivery services on account, $32,500.
7. Paid creditors on account, $1,400.
8. Received cash from customers on account, $23,770.
9. Determined that the cost of supplies on hand was $275 and $475 of supplies had been used during the month.
10. Paid cash to owner for personal use, $5,000.

Indicate the effect of each transaction on the accounting equation by listing the numbers identifying the transactions, (1) through (10), in a column and inserting at the right of each number the appropriate letter from the following list:

a. Increase in an asset, decrease in another asset.
b. Increase in an asset, increase in a liability.
c. Increase in an asset, increase in owner's equity.
d. Decrease in an asset, decrease in a liability.
e. Decrease in an asset, decrease in owner's equity.

Chapter 1 Introduction to Accounting and Business

✓ d. $22,800

EX 1-13 Nature of transactions OBJ. 4

Teri West operates her own catering service. Summary financial data for July are presented in equation form as follows. Each line designated by a number indicates the effect of a transaction on the equation. Each increase and decrease in owner's equity, except transaction (5), affects net income.

	Assets			= Liabilities +		Owner's Equity		
	Cash	+ Supplies +	Land	= Accounts Payable +	Teri West, Capital −	Teri West, Drawing	+ Fees Earned	− Expenses
Bal.	40,000	3,000	82,000	7,500	117,500			
1.	+71,800						+71,800	
2.	−15,000		+15,000					
3.	−47,500							−47,500
4.		+1,100		+1,100				
5.	−5,000					−5,000		
6.	−4,000			−4,000				
7.		−1,500						−1,500
Bal.	40,300	2,600	97,000	4,600	117,500	−5,000	71,800	−49,000

a. Describe each transaction.
b. What is the amount of the net increase in cash during the month?
c. What is the amount of the net increase in owner's equity during the month?
d. What is the amount of the net income for the month?
e. How much of the net income for the month was retained in the business?

EX 1-14 Net income and owner's withdrawals OBJ. 5

The income statement of a proprietorship for the month of February indicates a net income of $17,500. During the same period, the owner withdrew $25,500 in cash from the business for personal use.

Would it be correct to say that the business had incurred a net loss of $8,000 during the month? Discuss.

✓ Mars: Net income, $225,000

EX 1-15 Net income and owner's equity for four businesses OBJ. 5

Four different proprietorships, Jupiter, Mars, Saturn, and Venus, show the same balance sheet data at the beginning and end of a year. These data, exclusive of the amount of owner's equity, are summarized as follows:

	Total Assets	Total Liabilities
Beginning of the year	$550,000	$215,000
End of the year	844,000	320,000

On the basis of the preceding data and the following additional information for the year, determine the net income (or loss) of each company for the year. (*Hint:* First, determine the amount of increase or decrease in owner's equity during the year.)

Jupiter: The owner had made no additional investments in the business and had made no withdrawals from the business.

Mars: The owner had made no additional investments in the business but had withdrawn $36,000.

Saturn: The owner had made an additional investment of $60,000 but had made no withdrawals.

Venus: The owner had made an additional investment of $60,000 and had withdrawn $36,000.

Chapter 1 Introduction to Accounting and Business

EX 1-16 Balance sheet items
OBJ. 5

From the following list of selected items taken from the records of Rosewood Appliance Service as of a specific date, identify those that would appear on the balance sheet:

1. Accounts Payable
2. Accounts Receivable
3. Andrew King, Capital
4. Cash
5. Fees Earned
6. Land
7. Rent Expense
8. Supplies
9. Wages Expense
10. Wages Payable

EX 1-17 Income statement items
OBJ. 5

Based on the data presented in Exercise 1-16, identify those items that would appear on the income statement.

EX 1-18 Statement of owner's equity
OBJ. 5

✔ Mark Kominksy, capital, April 30, 2019: $525,500

Financial information related to Udder Products Company, a proprietorship, for the month ended April 30, 2019, is as follows:

Net income for April	$166,000
Mark Kominksy's withdrawals during April	25,000
Mark Kominksy's capital, April 1, 2019	384,500

a. Prepare a statement of owner's equity for the month ended April 30, 2019.
b. Why is the statement of owner's equity prepared before the April 30, 2019, balance sheet?

EX 1-19 Income statement
OBJ. 5

✔ Net income: $178,100

Dairy Services was organized on August 1, 2019. A summary of the revenue and expense transactions for August follows:

Fees earned	$783,000
Wages expense	550,000
Rent expense	35,000
Supplies expense	8,500
Miscellaneous expense	11,400

Prepare an income statement for the month ended August 31.

EX 1-20 Missing amounts from balance sheet and income statement data
OBJ. 5

✔ (a) $135,000

One item is omitted in each of the following summaries of balance sheet and income statement data for the following four different proprietorships:

	Freeman	Heyward	Jones	Ramirez
Beginning of the year:				
Assets	$ 900,000	$490,000	$115,000	(d)
Liabilities	360,000	260,000	81,000	$120,000
End of the year:				
Assets	1,260,000	675,000	100,000	270,000
Liabilities	330,000	220,000	80,000	136,000
During the year:				
Additional investment in the business	(a)	150,000	10,000	55,000
Withdrawals from the business	75,000	32,000	(c)	39,000
Revenue	570,000	(b)	115,000	115,000
Expenses	240,000	128,000	122,500	128,000

Determine the missing amounts, identifying them by letter. (*Hint:* First, determine the amount of increase or decrease in owner's equity during the year.)

42 Chapter 1 Introduction to Accounting and Business

✔ b. $135,000

EX 1-21 Balance sheets, net income OBJ. 5

Financial information related to the proprietorship of Ebony Interiors for February and March 2019 is as follows:

	February 29, 2019	March 31, 2019
Accounts payable	$310,000	$400,000
Accounts receivable	800,000	960,000
Cash	320,000	380,000
Justin Berk, capital	?	?
Supplies	30,000	35,000

a. Prepare balance sheets for Ebony Interiors as of February 29 and March 31, 2019.
b. Determine the amount of net income for March, assuming that the owner made no additional investments or withdrawals during the month.
c. Determine the amount of net income for March, assuming that the owner made no additional investments but withdrew $50,000 during the month.

EX 1-22 Financial statements OBJ. 5

Each of the following items is shown in the financial statements of **Exxon Mobil Corporation**:

1. Accounts payable
2. Cash equivalents
3. Crude oil inventory
4. Equipment
5. Exploration expenses
6. Income taxes payable
7. Investments
8. Long-term debt
9. Marketable securities
10. Notes and loans payable
11. Notes receivable
12. Operating expenses
13. Prepaid taxes
14. Sales
15. Selling expenses

a. Identify the financial statement (balance sheet or income statement) in which each item would appear.
b. Can an item appear on more than one financial statement?
c. Is the accounting equation relevant for Exxon Mobil Corporation?

EX 1-23 Statement of cash flows OBJ. 5

Indicate whether each of the following activities would be reported on the statement of cash flows as (a) an operating activity, (b) an investing activity, or (c) a financing activity:

1. Cash received from fees earned.
2. Cash paid for expenses.
3. Cash paid for land.
4. Cash paid to owner for personal use.

EX 1-24 Statement of cash flows OBJ. 5

✔ Net increase in cash during year, $117,500

A summary of cash flows for Ethos Consulting Group for the year ended May 31, 2019, follows:

Cash receipts:	
Cash received from customers	$637,500
Cash received from additional investment of owner	62,500
Cash payments:	
Cash paid for operating expenses	475,000
Cash paid for land	90,000
Cash paid to owner for personal use	17,500

The cash balance as of June 1, 2018, was $58,000.
Prepare a statement of cash flows for Ethos Consulting Group for the year ended May 31, 2019.

Chapter 1 Introduction to Accounting and Business

EX 1-25 Financial statements
OBJ. 5

✔ Correct amount of total assets is $51,500.

We-Sell Realty, organized August 1, 2019, is owned and operated by Omar Farah. How many errors can you find in the following statements for We-Sell Realty, prepared after its first month of operations?

We-Sell Realty
Income Statement
August 31, 2019

Sales commissions		$140,000
Expenses:		
Office salaries expense	$87,000	
Rent expense	18,000	
Automobile expense	7,500	
Miscellaneous expense	2,200	
Supplies expense	1,150	
Total expenses		115,850
Net income		$ 25,000

Omar Farah
Statement of Owner's Equity
August 31, 2018

Omar Farah, capital, August 1, 2019		$ 0
Withdrawals during August		(10,000)
		$(10,000)
Investment on August 1, 2019		15,000
		$ 5,000
Net income for August		25,000
Omar Farah, capital, August 31, 2019		$ 30,000

Balance Sheet
For the Month Ended August 31, 2019

Assets

Cash	$ 8,900
Accounts payable	22,350
Total assets	$31,250

Liabilities

Accounts receivable	$38,600
Supplies	4,000

Owner's Equity

Omar Farah, capital	30,000
Total liabilities and owner's equity	$72,600

EX 1-26 Ratio of liabilities to stockholders' equity
OBJ. 6

✔ a. Year 2: $30,624

The Home Depot is the world's largest home improvement retailer and one of the largest retailers in the United States based on net sales volume. The Home Depot operates over 2,200 Home Depot® stores that sell a wide assortment of building materials and home improvement and lawn and garden products.

The Home Depot recently reported the following balance sheet data (in millions):

	Year 2	Year 1
Total assets	$39,946	$40,518
Total stockholders' equity	9,322	12,522

a. Determine the total liabilities at the end of Years 2 and 1.
b. Determine the ratio of liabilities to stockholders' equity for Year 2 and Year 1. Round to two decimal places.
c. What conclusions regarding the margin of protection to the creditors can you draw from (b)?

44 Chapter 1 Introduction to Accounting and Business

EX 1-27 Ratio of liabilities to stockholders' equity OBJ. 6

✔ b. Year 2: 2.19

Lowe's Companies Inc., a major competitor of The Home Depot in the home improvement business, operates over 1,800 stores. Lowe's recently reported the following balance sheet data (in millions):

	Year 2	Year 1
Total assets	$31,827	$32,732
Total liabilities	21,859	20,879

a. Determine the total stockholders' equity at the end of Years 2 and 1.

b. Determine the ratio of liabilities to stockholders' equity for Year 2 and Year 1. Round to two decimal places.

c. What conclusions regarding the risk to the creditors can you draw from (b)?

d. Using the balance sheet data for The Home Depot in Exercise 1-26, how does the ratio of liabilities to stockholders' equity of Lowe's compare to that of The Home Depot?

Problems: Series A

PR 1-1A Transactions OBJ. 4

✔ Cash bal. at end of June: $21,020

On June 1 of the current year, Chad Wilson established a business to manage rental property. He completed the following transactions during June:

a. Opened a business bank account with a deposit of $30,000 from personal funds.

b. Purchased office supplies on account, $1,800.

c. Received cash from fees earned for managing rental property, $10,000.

d. Paid rent on office and equipment for the month, $4,500.

e. Paid creditors on account, $1,250.

f. Billed customers for fees earned for managing rental property, $16,800.

g. Paid automobile expenses (including rental charges) for the month, $750, and miscellaneous expenses, $980.

h. Paid office salaries, $4,000.

i. Determined that the cost of supplies on hand was $680; therefore, the cost of supplies used was $1,120.

j. Withdrew cash for personal use, $7,500.

Instructions

1. Indicate the effect of each transaction and the balances after each transaction, using the following tabular headings:

Assets	= Liabilities +	Owner's Equity
Cash + Accounts Receivable + Supplies =	Accounts Payable +	Chad Wilson, Capital − Chad Wilson, Drawing + Fees Earned − Rent Expense − Salaries Expense − Supplies Expense − Auto Expense − Misc. Expense

2. Briefly explain why the owner's investment and revenues increased owner's equity, while withdrawals and expenses decreased owner's equity.

3. Determine the net income for June.

4. How much did June's transactions increase or decrease Chad Wilson's capital?

PR 1-2A Financial statements OBJ. 5

✔ 1. Net income: $327,500

The amounts of the assets and liabilities of Nordic Travel Agency at December 31, 2019, the end of the year, and its revenue and expenses for the year follow. The capital of Ian Eisele, owner, was $670,000 on January 1, 2019, the beginning of the year. During the year, Ian withdrew $42,000.

Chapter 1 Introduction to Accounting and Business 45

Accounts payable	$ 69,500	Rent expense	$ 36,000
Accounts receivable	285,000	Supplies	5,500
Cash	190,500	Supplies expense	4,100
Fees earned	912,500	Utilities expense	28,500
Land	544,000	Wages expense	510,000
Miscellaneous expense	6,400		

Instructions

1. Prepare an income statement for the year ended December 31, 2019.
2. Prepare a statement of owner's equity for the year ended December 31, 2019.
3. Prepare a balance sheet as of December 31, 2019.
4. What item appears on both the statement of owner's equity and the balance sheet?

PR 1-3A Financial statements OBJ. 5

✓ 1. Net income: $31,200

Seth Feye established Reliance Financial Services on July 1, 2019. Reliance Financial Services offers financial planning advice to its clients. The effect of each transaction and the balances after each transaction for July follow:

	Assets			= Liabilities +		Owner's Equity							
	Cash	+ Accounts Receivable	+ Supplies =	Accounts Payable	+ Seth Feye, Capital	− Seth Feye, Drawing	+ Fees Earned	− Salaries Expense	− Rent Expense	− Auto Expense	− Supplies Expense	− Misc. Expense
a.	+50,000				+50,000							
b.			+7,000	+7,000								
Bal.	50,000		7,000	7,000	50,000							
c.	−3,600			−3,600								
Bal.	46,400		7,000	3,400	50,000							
d.	+110,000						+110,000					
Bal.	156,400		7,000	3,400	50,000		110,000					
e.	−33,000								−33,000			
Bal.	123,400		7,000	3,400	50,000		110,000		−33,000			
f.	−20,800										−16,000	−4,800
Bal.	102,600		7,000	3,400	50,000		110,000		−33,000		−16,000	−4,800
g.	−55,000							−55,000				
Bal.	47,600		7,000	3,400	50,000		110,000	−55,000	−33,000		−16,000	−4,800
h.			−4,500								−4,500	
Bal.	47,600		2,500	3,400	50,000		110,000	−55,000	−33,000		−4,500	−4,800
i.		+34,500					+34,500					
Bal.	47,600	34,500	2,500	3,400	50,000		144,500	−55,000	−33,000	−16,000	−4,500	−4,800
j.	−15,000					−15,000						
Bal.	32,600	34,500	2,500	3,400	50,000	−15,000	144,500	−55,000	−33,000	−16,000	−4,500	−4,800

Instructions

1. Prepare an income statement for the month ended July 31, 2019.
2. Prepare a statement of owner's equity for the month ended July 31, 2019.
3. Prepare a balance sheet as of July 31, 2019.
4. *(Optional)* Prepare a statement of cash flows for the month ending July 31, 2019.

PR 1-4A Transactions; financial statements OBJ. 4, 5

✓ 2. Net income: $27,350

On July 1, 2019, Pat Glenn established Half Moon Realty. Pat completed the following transactions during the month of July:

a. Opened a business bank account with a deposit of $25,000 from personal funds.
b. Purchased office supplies on account, $1,850.

(Continued)

c. Paid creditor on account, $1,200.
d. Earned sales commissions, receiving cash, $41,500.
e. Paid rent on office and equipment for the month, $3,600.
f. Withdrew cash for personal use, $4,000.
g. Paid automobile expenses (including rental charge) for the month, $3,050, and miscellaneous expenses, $1,600.
h. Paid office salaries, $5,000.
i. Determined that the cost of supplies on hand was $950; therefore, the cost of supplies used was $900.

Instructions

1. Indicate the effect of each transaction and the balances after each transaction, using the following tabular headings:

Assets	= Liabilities +	Owner's Equity
Cash + Supplies =	Accounts Payable +	Pat Glenn, Capital − Pat Glenn, Drawing + Sales Commissions − Salaries Expense − Rent Expense − Auto Expense − Supplies Expense − Misc. Expense

2. Prepare an income statement for July, a statement of owner's equity for July, and a balance sheet as of July 31.

PR 1-5A Transactions; financial statements OBJ. 4, 5

✔ 3. Net income: $63,775

Excel

D'Lite Dry Cleaners is owned and operated by Joel Palk. A building and equipment are currently being rented, pending expansion to new facilities. The actual work of dry cleaning is done by another company for a fee. The assets and liabilities of the business on July 1, 2019, are as follows: Cash, $45,000; Accounts Receivable, $93,000; Supplies, $7,000; Land, $75,000; Accounts Payable, $40,000. Business transactions during July are summarized as follows:

a. Joel Palk invested additional cash in the business with a deposit of $35,000 in the business bank account.
b. Paid $50,000 for the purchase of land adjacent to land currently owned by D'Lite Dry Cleaners as a future building site.
c. Received cash from cash customers for dry cleaning revenue, $32,125.
d. Paid rent for the month, $6,000.
e. Purchased supplies on account, $2,500.
f. Paid creditors on account, $22,800.
g. Charged customers for dry cleaning revenue on account, $84,750.
h. Received monthly invoice for dry cleaning expense for July (to be paid on August 10), $29,500.
i. Paid the following: wages expense, $7,500; truck expense, $2,500; utilities expense, $1,300; miscellaneous expense, $2,700.
j. Received cash from customers on account, $88,000.
k. Determined that the cost of supplies on hand was $5,900; therefore, the cost of supplies used during the month was $3,600.
l. Withdrew $12,000 cash for personal use.

Instructions

1. Determine the amount of Joel Palk's capital as of July 1 of the current year.
2. State the assets, liabilities, and owner's equity as of July 1 in equation form similar to that shown in Exhibit 5. In tabular form below the equation, indicate increases and decreases resulting from each transaction and the new balances after each transaction.
3. Prepare an income statement for July, a statement of owner's equity for July, and a balance sheet as of July 31.
4. *(Optional)* Prepare a statement of cash flows for July.

PR 1-6A Missing amounts from financial statements

OBJ. 5

✓ k. $750,000

The financial statements at the end of Wolverine Realty's first month of operations are as follows:

Wolverine Realty
Income Statement
For the Month Ended April 30, 2019

Fees earned		$ (a)
Expenses:		
Wages expense	$300,000	
Rent expense	100,000	
Supplies expense	(b)	
Utilities expense	20,000	
Miscellaneous expense	25,000	
Total expenses		475,000
Net income		$275,000

Wolverine Realty
Statement of Owner's Equity
For the Month Ended April 30, 2019

Dakota Rowe, capital, April 1, 2019		$ (c)
Investment on April 1, 2019	$ 375,000	
Net income for April	(d)	
Withdrawals	(125,000)	
Increase in owner's equity		(e)
Dakota Rowe, capital, April 30, 2019		$ (f)

Wolverine Realty
Balance Sheet
April 30, 2019

Assets

Cash	$462,500
Supplies	12,500
Land	150,000
Total assets	$ (g)

Liabilities

Accounts payable	$ 100,000

Owner's Equity

Dakota Rowe, capital	(h)
Total liabilities and owner's equity	$ (i)

Wolverine Realty
Statement of Cash Flows
For the Month Ended April 30, 2019

Cash flows from operating activities:		
Cash receipts from customers	$ (j)	
Cash payments for expenses and payments to creditors	(387,500)	
Net cash flow from operating activities		$ (k)
Cash flows from investing activities:		
Cash payments for acquisition of land		(l)
Cash flows from financing activities:		
Cash receipt of owner's investment	$ (m)	
Cash withdrawals by owner	(n)	
Net cash flow from financing activities		(o)
Net increase (decrease) in cash and April 30, 2019, cash balance		$ (p)

Instructions

By analyzing the interrelationships among the four financial statements, determine the proper amounts for (a) through (p).

Problems: Series B

PR 1-1B Transactions
OBJ. 4

✔ Cash bal. at end of March: $48,650

Amy Austin established an insurance agency on March 1 of the current year and completed the following transactions during March:

a. Opened a business bank account with a deposit of $50,000 from personal funds.
b. Purchased supplies on account, $4,000.
c. Paid creditors on account, $2,300.
d. Received cash from fees earned on insurance commissions, $13,800.
e. Paid rent on office and equipment for the month, $5,000.
f. Paid automobile expenses for the month, $1,150, and miscellaneous expenses, $300.
g. Paid office salaries, $2,500.
h. Determined that the cost of supplies on hand was $2,700; therefore, the cost of supplies used was $1,300.
i. Billed insurance companies for sales commissions earned, $12,500.
j. Withdrew cash for personal use, $3,900.

Instructions

1. Indicate the effect of each transaction and the balances after each transaction, using the following tabular headings:

Assets	= Liabilities +	Owner's Equity
Cash + Accounts Receivable + Supplies	= Accounts Payable +	Amy Austin, Capital − Amy Austin, Drawing + Fees Earned − Rent Expense − Salaries Expense − Supplies Expense − Auto Expense − Misc. Expense

2. Briefly explain why the owner's investment and revenues increased owner's equity, while withdrawals and expenses decreased owner's equity.
3. Determine the net income for March.
4. How much did March's transactions increase or decrease Amy Austin's capital?

PR 1-2B Financial statements
OBJ. 5

✔ 1. Net income: $200,000

The amounts of the assets and liabilities of Wilderness Travel Service at April 30, 2019, the end of the year, and its revenue and expenses for the year follow. The capital of Harper Borg, owner, was $180,000 at May 1, 2018, the beginning of the year, and the owner withdrew $40,000 during the year.

Accounts payable	$ 25,000	Supplies	$ 9,000
Accounts receivable	210,000	Supplies expense	12,000
Cash	146,000	Taxes expense	10,000
Fees earned	875,000	Utilities expense	38,000
Miscellaneous expense	15,000	Wages expense	525,000
Rent expense	75,000		

Instructions

1. Prepare an income statement for the year ended April 30, 2019.
2. Prepare a statement of owner's equity for the year ended April 30, 2019.
3. Prepare a balance sheet as of April 30, 2019.
4. What item appears on both the income statement and statement of owner's equity?

Chapter 1 Introduction to Accounting and Business   49

PR 1-3B Financial statements   OBJ. 5

✔ 1. Net income: $10,900

Jose Loder established Bronco Consulting on August 1, 2019. The effect of each transaction and the balances after each transaction for August follow:

	Assets			= Liabilities +		Owner's Equity						
	Cash	+ Accounts Receivable	+ Supplies	= Accounts Payable	+ Jose Loder, Capital	− Jose Loder, Drawing	+ Fees Earned	− Salaries Expense	− Rent Expense	− Auto Expense	− Supplies Expense	− Misc. Expense
a.	+75,000				+75,000							
b.			+9,000	+9,000								
Bal.	75,000		9,000	9,000	75,000							
c.	+92,000						+92,000					
Bal.	167,000		9,000	9,000	75,000		92,000					
d.	−27,000								−27,000			
Bal.	140,000		9,000	9,000	75,000		92,000		−27,000			
e.	−6,000			−6,000								
Bal.	134,000		9,000	3,000	75,000		92,000		−27,000			
f.		+33,000					+33,000					
Bal.	134,000	33,000	9,000	3,000	75,000		125,000		−27,000			
g.	−23,000									−15,500		−7,500
Bal.	111,000	33,000	9,000	3,000	75,000		125,000		−27,000	−15,500		−7,500
h.	−58,000							−58,000				
Bal.	53,000	33,000	9,000	3,000	75,000		125,000	−58,000	−27,000	−15,500		−7,500
i.			−6,100								−6,100	
Bal.	53,000	33,000	2,900	3,000	75,000		125,000	−58,000	−27,000	−15,500	−6,100	−7,500
j.	−15,000					−15,000						
Bal.	38,000	33,000	2,900	3,000	75,000	−15,000	125,000	−58,000	−27,000	−15,500	−6,100	−7,500

Instructions

1. Prepare an income statement for the month ended August 31, 2019.
2. Prepare a statement of owner's equity for the month ended August 31, 2019.
3. Prepare a balance sheet as of August 31, 2019.
4. *(Optional)* Prepare a statement of cash flows for the month ending August 31, 2019.

PR 1-4B Transactions; financial statements   OBJ. 4, 5

✔ 2. Net income: $10,850

On April 1, 2019, Maria Adams established Custom Realty. Maria completed the following transactions during the month of April:

a. Opened a business bank account with a deposit of $24,000 from personal funds.
b. Paid rent on office and equipment for the month, $3,600.
c. Paid automobile expenses (including rental charge) for the month, $1,350, and miscellaneous expenses, $600.
d. Purchased office supplies on account, $1,200.
e. Earned sales commissions (revenue) from selling real estate, receiving cash, $19,800.
f. Paid creditor on account, $750.
g. Paid office salaries, $2,500.
h. Withdrew cash for personal use, $3,500.
i. Determined that the cost of supplies on hand was $300; therefore, the cost of supplies used was $900.

(Continued)

Instructions

1. Indicate the effect of each transaction and the balances after each transaction, using the following tabular headings:

Assets	= Liabilities +	Owner's Equity
Cash + Supplies	= Accounts Payable +	Maria Adams, Capital − Maria Adams, Drawing + Sales Commissions − Rent Expense − Salaries Expense − Auto Expense − Supplies Expense − Misc. Expense

2. Prepare an income statement for April, a statement of owner's equity for April, and a balance sheet as of April 30.

PR 1-5B Transactions; financial statements OBJ. 4, 5

✔ 3. Net income: $40,150

Excel

Bev's Dry Cleaners is owned and operated by Beverly Zahn. A building and equipment are currently being rented, pending expansion to new facilities. The actual work of dry cleaning is done by another company for a fee. The assets and the liabilities of the business on November 1, 2019, are as follows: Cash, $39,000; Accounts Receivable, $80,000; Supplies, $11,000; Land, $50,000; Accounts Payable, $31,500. Business transactions during November are summarized as follows:

a. Beverly Zahn invested additional cash in the business with a deposit of $21,000 in the business bank account.
b. Purchased land adjacent to land currently owned by Bev's Dry Cleaners to use in the future as a parking lot, paying cash of $35,000.
c. Paid rent for the month, $4,000.
d. Charged customers for dry cleaning revenue on account, $72,000.
e. Paid creditors on account, $20,000.
f. Purchased supplies on account, $8,000.
g. Received cash from cash customers for dry cleaning revenue, $38,000.
h. Received cash from customers on account, $77,000.
i. Received monthly invoice for dry cleaning expense for November (to be paid on December 10), $29,450.
j. Paid the following: wages expense, $24,000; truck expense, $2,100; utilities expense, $1,800; miscellaneous expense, $1,300.
k. Determined that the cost of supplies on hand was $11,800; therefore, the cost of supplies used during the month was $7,200.
l. Withdrew $5,000 for personal use.

Instructions

1. Determine the amount of Beverly Zahn's capital as of November 1.
2. State the assets, liabilities, and owner's equity as of November 1 in equation form similar to that shown in Exhibit 5. In tabular form below the equation, indicate increases and decreases resulting from each transaction and the new balances after each transaction.
3. Prepare an income statement for November, a statement of owner's equity for November, and a balance sheet as of November 30.
4. (Optional) Prepare a statement of cash flows for November.

PR 1-6B Missing amounts from financial statements

OBJ. 5

✓ i. $208,000

The financial statements at the end of Atlas Realty's first month of operations follow:

Atlas Realty
Income Statement
For the Month Ended May 31, 2019

Fees earned..		$400,000
Expenses:		
Wages expense	$ (a)	
Rent expense	48,000	
Supplies expense	17,600	
Utilities expense	14,400	
Miscellaneous expense	4,800	
Total expenses		288,000
Net income		$ (b)

Atlas Realty
Statement of Owner's Equity
For the Month Ended May 31, 2019

LuAnn Martin, capital, May 1, 2019		$ (c)
Investment on May 1, 2019..	$ (d)	
Net income for May	(e)	
Withdrawals	(f)	
Increase in owner's equity		(g)
LuAnn Martin, capital, May 31, 2019		$ (h)

Atlas Realty
Balance Sheet
May 31, 2019

Assets

Cash	$123,200
Supplies...	12,800
Land	(i)
Total assets	$ (j)

Liabilities

Accounts payable	$ 48,000

Owner's Equity

LuAnn Martin, capital..	(k)
Total liabilities and owner's equity.............................	$ (l)

Atlas Realty
Statement of Cash Flows
For the Month Ended May 31, 2019

Cash flows from operating activities:		
Cash receipts from customers	$ (m)	
Cash payments for expenses and payments to creditors...........	(252,800)	
Net cash flow from operating activities		$ (n)
Cash flows from investing activities:		
Cash payments for acquisition of land		(120,000)
Cash flows from financing activities:		
Cash receipt of owner's investment....................	$ 160,000	
Cash withdrawals by owner	(64,000)	
Net cash flow from financing activities...............		(o)
Net increase (decrease) in cash and May 31, 2019, cash balance.......		$ (p)

Instructions

By analyzing the interrelationships among the four financial statements, determine the proper amounts for (a) through (p).

Continuing Problem

✔ 2. Net income: $1,340

Peyton Smith enjoys listening to all types of music and owns countless CDs. Over the years, Peyton has gained a local reputation for knowledge of music from classical to rap and the ability to put together sets of recordings that appeal to all ages.

During the last several months, Peyton served as a guest disc jockey on a local radio station. In addition, Peyton has entertained at several friends' parties as the host deejay.

On June 1, 2019, Peyton established a proprietorship known as PS Music. Using an extensive collection of music MP3 files, Peyton will serve as a disc jockey on a fee basis for weddings, college parties, and other events. During June, Peyton entered into the following transactions:

June 1. Deposited $4,000 in a checking account in the name of PS Music.

2. Received $3,500 from a local radio station for serving as the guest disc jockey for June.

2. Agreed to share office space with a local real estate agency, Pinnacle Realty. PS Music will pay one-fourth of the rent. In addition, PS Music agreed to pay a portion of the wages of the receptionist and to pay one-fourth of the utilities. Paid $800 for the rent of the office.

4. Purchased supplies from City Office Supply Co. for $350. Agreed to pay $100 within 10 days and the remainder by July 5, 2019.

6. Paid $500 to a local radio station to advertise the services of PS Music twice daily for two weeks.

8. Paid $675 to a local electronics store for renting digital recording equipment.

12. Paid $350 (music expense) to Cool Music for the use of its current music demos to make various music sets.

13. Paid City Office Supply Co. $100 on account.

16. Received $300 from a dentist for providing two music sets for the dentist to play for her patients.

22. Served as disc jockey for a wedding party. The father of the bride agreed to pay $1,000 in July.

25. Received $500 for serving as the disc jockey for a cancer charity ball hosted by the local hospital.

29. Paid $240 (music expense) to Galaxy Music for the use of its library of music demos.

30. Received $900 for serving as PS disc jockey for a local club's monthly dance.

30. Paid Pinnacle Realty $400 for PS Music's share of the receptionist's wages for June.

30. Paid Pinnacle Realty $300 for PS Music's share of the utilities for June.

30. Determined that the cost of supplies on hand is $170. Therefore, the cost of supplies used during the month was $180.

30. Paid for miscellaneous expenses, $415.

30. Paid $1,000 royalties (music expense) to National Music Clearing for use of various artists' music during the month.

30. Withdrew $500 of cash from PS Music for personal use.

Instructions

1. Indicate the effect of each transaction and the balances after each transaction, using the following tabular headings:

Assets	=	Liabilities	+	Owner's Equity
Cash + Accts. Rec. + Supplies	=	Accounts Payable	+	Peyton Smith, Capital − Peyton Smith, Drawing + Fees Earned − Music Exp. − Office Rent Exp. − Equipment Rent Exp. − Advertising Exp. − Wages Exp. − Utilities Exp. − Supplies Exp. − Misc. Exp.

2. Prepare an income statement for PS Music for the month ended June 30, 2019.
3. Prepare a statement of owner's equity for PS Music for the month ended June 30, 2019.
4. Prepare a balance sheet for PS Music as of June 30, 2019.

Cases & Projects

CP 1-1 Ethics in Action

Marco Brolo is one of three partners who own and operate Silkroad Partners, a global import–export business. Marco is the partner in charge of recording partnership transactions in the accounts. On his way to work one day, Marco's car broke down. At the repair shop, Marco learned that his car's engine had significant damage, and it will cost over $2,000 to repair the damage. He does not have enough money in his bank account to cover the cost of the repair, and his credit cards are at their limit. This car is the only form of transportation that Marco has to get to and from work every day. He does not use his car for any business travel.

After considering his options, Marco decides to take $2,000 from the partnership for the repair and record it as an expense of the partnership. He believes that this is appropriate since he needs his car to get to work every day.

1. Is Marco behaving ethically? Why or why not?
2. Who is affected by Marco's decision?
3. What other alternatives might Marco consider?

CP 1-2 Ethics in Action

Colleen Fernandez, president of Rhino Enterprises, applied for a $175,000 loan from First Federal Bank. The bank requested financial statements from Rhino Enterprises as a basis for granting the loan. Colleen has told her accountant to provide the bank with a balance sheet. Colleen has decided to omit the other financial statements because there was a net loss during the past year.

In groups of three or four, discuss the following questions:

1. Is Colleen behaving in a professional manner by omitting some of the financial statements?
2. a. What types of information about their businesses would owners be willing to provide bankers? What types of information would owners not be willing to provide?
   b. What types of information about a business would bankers want before extending a loan?
   c. What common interests are shared by bankers and business owners?

CP 1-3 Team Activity

In teams, select a public company that interests you. Obtain the company's most recent annual report on Form 10-K. The Form 10-K is a company's annually required filing with the Securities and Exchange Commission (SEC). It includes the company's financial statements and accompanying notes. The Form 10-K can be obtained either (A) by referring to the investor relations section of the company's website or (B) by using the company search feature of the SEC's EDGAR database service found at www.sec.gov/edgar/searchedgar/companysearch.html.

Based on the information in the company's most recent annual report, answer the following questions:

1. What is the official name of the company?
2. Where are the company's principal offices located?

(Continued)

3. Who is the company's chief executive officer?
4. Is the company primarily a service, merchandising, or manufacturing business?
5. How does the company describe its business?
6. Which financial statements are included in the annual report?

CP 1-4 Communication

There are two common causes of business and accounting fraud:

- A failure of individual character
- A culture of greed or ethical indifference within an organization

Write a brief memo describing how these two factors could lead to accounting fraud.

CP 1-5 Net income

On January 1, 2018, Dr. Marcie Cousins established Health-Wise Medical, a medical practice organized as a proprietorship. The following conversation occurred the following August between Dr. Cousins and a former medical school classmate, Dr. Avi Abu, at an American Medical Association convention in Seattle:

Dr. Abu: Marcie, good to see you again. Why didn't you call when you were in Miami? We could have had dinner together.

Dr. Cousins: Actually, I never made it to Miami this year. My husband and kids went up to our Vail condo twice, but I got stuck in Jacksonville. I opened a new consulting practice this January and haven't had any time for myself since.

Dr. Abu: I heard about it . . . Health . . . something . . . right?

Dr. Cousins: Yes, Health-Wise Medical. My husband chose the name.

Dr. Abu: I've thought about doing something like that. Are you making any money? I mean, is it worth your time?

Dr. Cousins: You wouldn't believe it. I started by opening a bank account with $25,000, and my July bank statement has a balance of $80,000. Not bad for six months—all pure profit.

Dr. Abu: Maybe I'll try it in Miami! Let's have breakfast together tomorrow, and you can fill me in on the details.

Comment on Dr. Cousins' statement that the difference between the opening bank balance ($25,000) and the July statement balance ($80,000) is pure profit.

CP 1-6 Transactions and financial statements

Lisa Duncan, a junior in college, has been seeking ways to earn extra spending money. As an active sports enthusiast, Lisa plays tennis regularly at the Phoenix Tennis Club, where her family has a membership. The president of the club recently approached Lisa with the proposal that she manage the club's tennis courts. Lisa's primary duty would be to supervise the operation of the club's 4 indoor and 10 outdoor courts, including court reservations.

In return for her services, the club would pay Lisa $325 per week, plus Lisa could keep whatever she earned from lessons. The club and Lisa agreed to a one-month trial, after which both would consider an arrangement for the remaining two years of Lisa's college career. On this basis, Lisa organized Serve-N-Volley. During September 2019, Lisa managed the tennis courts and entered into the following transactions:

a. Opened a business account by depositing $950.
b. Paid $300 for tennis supplies (practice tennis balls, etc.).
c. Paid $275 for the rental of video equipment to be used in offering lessons during September.
d. Arranged for the rental of two ball machines during September for $250. Paid $100 in advance, with the remaining $150 due October 1.
e. Received $1,750 for lessons given during September.

f. Received $600 in fees from the use of the ball machines during September.

g. Paid $800 for salaries of part-time employees who answered the telephone and took reservations while Lisa was giving lessons.

h. Paid $290 for miscellaneous expenses.

i. Received $1,300 from the club for managing the tennis courts during September.

j. Determined that the cost of supplies on hand at the end of the month totaled $180; therefore, the cost of supplies used was $120.

k. Withdrew $400 for personal use on September 30.

As a friend and an accounting student, you have been asked by Lisa to aid her in assessing the venture.

1. Indicate the effect of each transaction and the balances after each transaction, using the following tabular headings:

Assets	=	Liabilities	+	Owner's Equity
Cash + Supplies	=	Accounts Payable	+	Lisa Duncan, Capital − Lisa Duncan, Drawing + Fees Earned − Salaries Expense − Rent Expense − Supplies Expense − Misc. Expense

2. Prepare an income statement for September.

3. Prepare a statement of owner's equity for September.

4. Prepare a balance sheet as of September 30.

5. a. Assume that Lisa Duncan could earn $10 per hour working 30 hours a week as a waitress. Evaluate which of the two alternatives, working as a waitress or operating Serve-N-Volley, would provide Lisa with the most income per month.

   b. Discuss any other factors that you believe Lisa should consider before discussing a long-term arrangement with the Phoenix Tennis Club.

CP 1-7 Certification requirements for accountants

By satisfying certain specific requirements, accountants may become certified as public accountants (CPAs), management accountants (CMAs), or internal auditors (CIAs). Find the certification requirements for one of these accounting groups by accessing one of the following websites:

Site	Description
www.ais-cpa.com	This site lists the address and/or Internet link for each state's board of accountancy. Find your state's requirements.
www.imanet.org	This site lists the requirements for becoming a CMA.
www.theiia.org	This site lists the requirements for becoming a CIA.

CP 1-8 Cash flows

Amazon.com, an Internet retailer, was incorporated and began operation in the mid-nineties. On the statement of cash flows, would you expect Amazon.com's net cash flows from operating, investing, and financing activities to be positive or negative for its first three years of operations? Use the following format for your answers and briefly explain your logic.

	First Year	Second Year	Third Year
Net cash flows from operating activities	negative		
Net cash flows from investing activities			
Net cash flows from financing activities			

CHAPTER 2
Analyzing Transactions

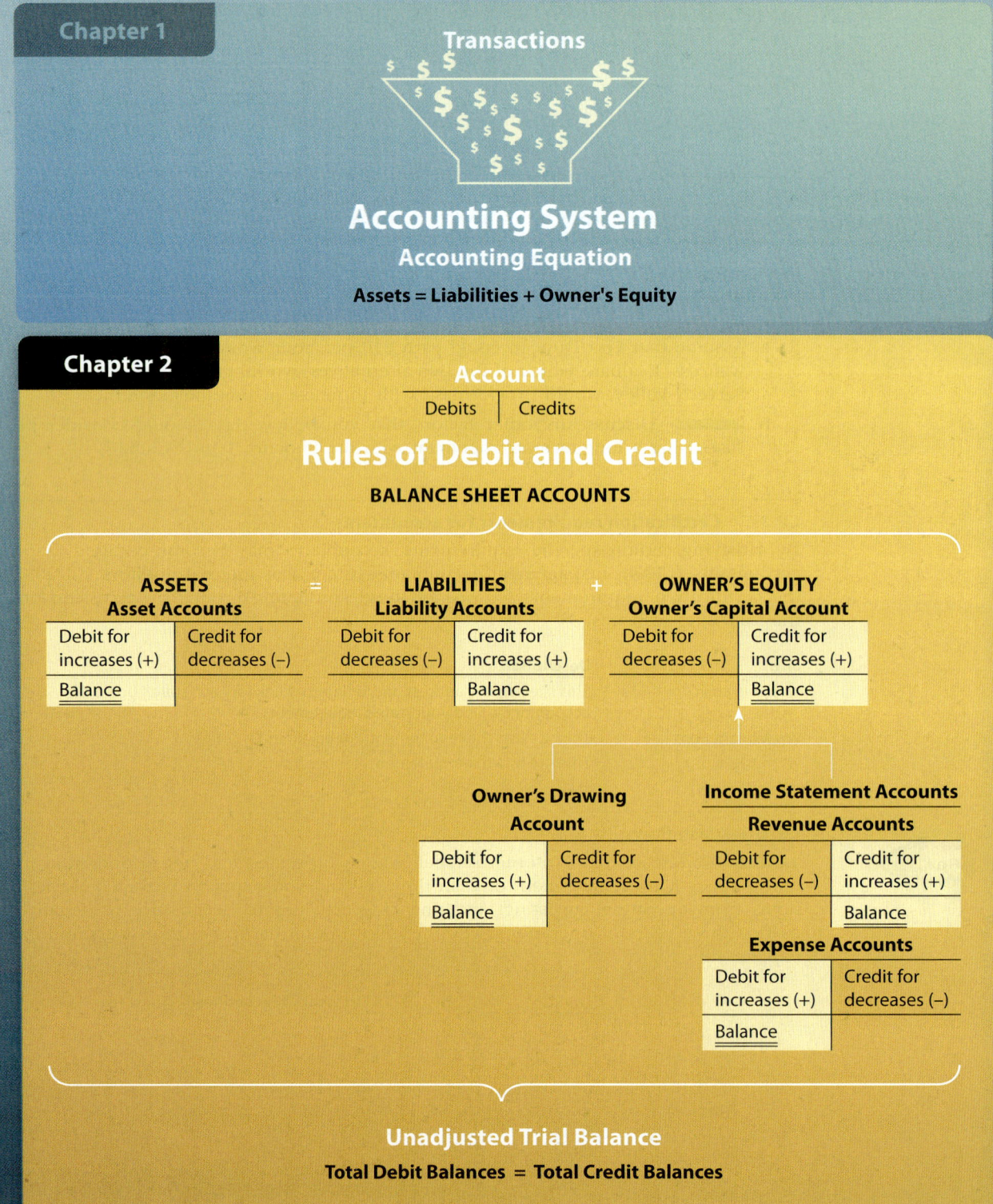

CHAPTER 2

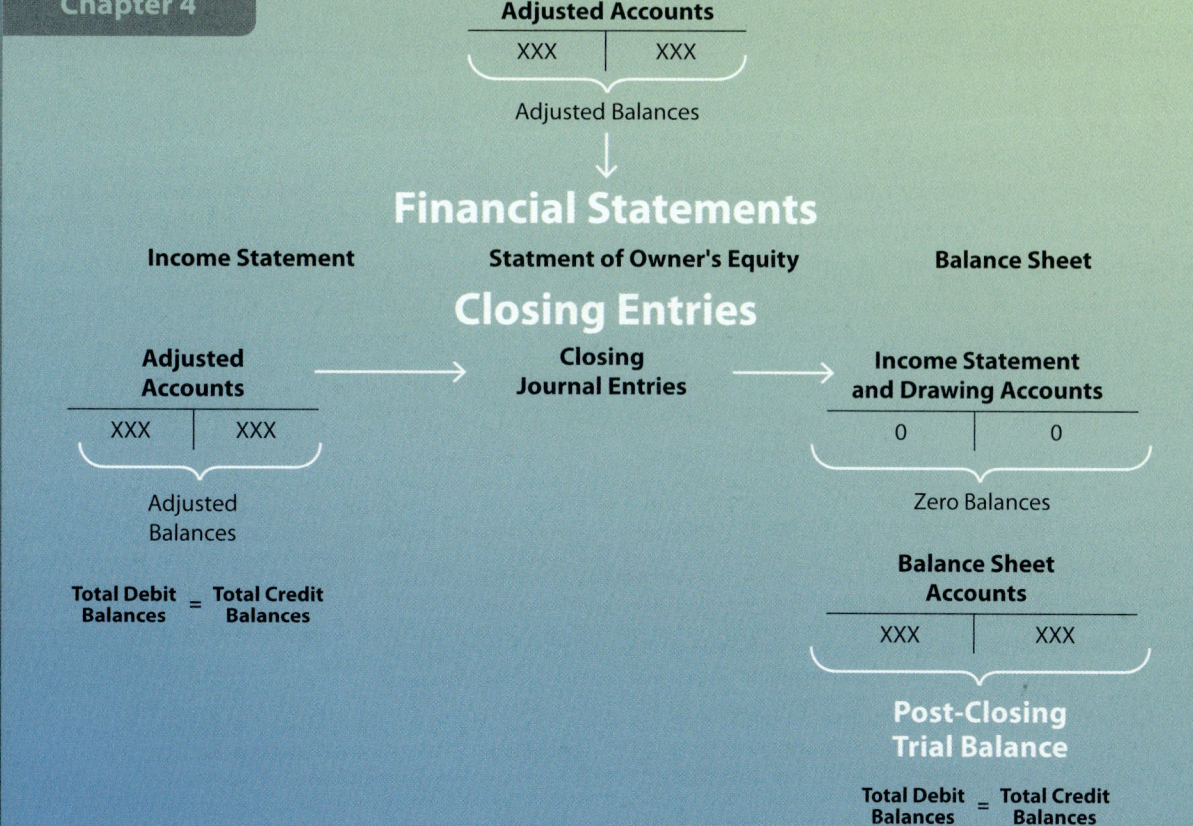

CHAPTER 2

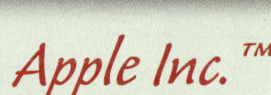

Apple Inc.™

Every day it seems like we get an incredible amount of incoming e-mail messages—from friends, relatives, subscribed e-mail lists, and even spammers! But how do you organize all of these messages? You might create folders to sort messages by sender, topic, or project. Perhaps you use keyword search utilities. You might even use filters or rules to automatically delete spam or send messages from your best friend to a special folder. In any case, you are organizing information so that it is simple to retrieve and allows you to understand, respond, or refer to the messages.

In the same way that you organize your e-mail, companies develop an organized method for processing, recording, and summarizing financial transactions. For example, **Apple Inc.** has a huge volume of financial transactions, resulting from sales of its innovative computers, digital media (iTunes), iPods, iPhones, and iPads. When Apple sells an iPad, a customer has the option of paying with a credit card, a debit or check card, an Apple gift card, a financing arrangement, or cash. In order to analyze only the information related to Apple's cash transactions, the company must record or summarize all these similar sales using a single category or "cash" account. Similarly, Apple will record sales from financing arrangements in different accounts (records).

While Chapter 1 used the accounting equation (Assets = Liabilities + Owner's Equity) to analyze and record financial transactions, this chapter presents more practical and efficient recording methods that most companies use. In addition, this chapter discusses possible accounting errors that may occur, along with methods to detect and correct them.

Learning Objectives

After studying this chapter, you should be able to:

Example Exercises (EE) are shown in **green**.

Obj. 1 Describe the characteristics of an account and a chart of accounts.

Using Accounts to Record Transactions
Chart of Accounts

Obj. 2 Describe and illustrate journalizing transactions using the double-entry accounting system.

Double-Entry Accounting System
Balance Sheet Accounts
Income Statement Accounts
Owner Withdrawals
Normal Balances — EE 2-1
Journalizing: Asset Purchase — EE 2-2

Obj. 3 Describe and illustrate the journalizing and posting of transactions to accounts.

Journalizing and Posting to Accounts
Journalizing: Fees Earned — EE 2-3
Journalizing: Withdrawals — EE 2-4
Missing Amount from Account — EE 2-5

Obj. 4 Prepare an unadjusted trial balance and explain how it can be used to discover errors.

Trial Balance
Errors Affecting the Trial Balance — EE 2-6
Correcting Entries — EE 2-7

Obj. 5 Describe and illustrate the use of horizontal analysis in evaluating a company's performance and financial condition.

Financial Analysis and Interpretation: Horizontal Analysis
Horizontal Analysis Report — EE 2-8

At a Glance 2 Page 82

Using Accounts to Record Transactions

Obj. 1 Describe the characteristics of an account and a chart of accounts.

In Chapter 1, the November transactions for **NetSolutions** were recorded using the accounting equation format shown in Exhibit 1. However, this format is not efficient or practical for companies that have to record thousands or millions of transactions daily. As a result, accounting systems are designed to show the increases and decreases in each accounting equation element as a separate record. This record is called an **account**.

To illustrate, the Cash column of NetSolutions' November transactions in Exhibit 1 records the increases and decreases in cash. Likewise, the other columns in Exhibit 1 record the increases and decreases in the other accounting equation elements. Each of these columns can be organized into a separate account.

An account, in its simplest form, has three parts.

- A title, which is the name of the accounting equation element recorded in the account
- A space for recording increases in the amount of the element
- A space for recording decreases in the amount of the element

The account form that follows is called a **T account** because it resembles the letter T. The left side of the account is called the *debit* side, and the right side is called the *credit* side:[1]

Title	
Left side	Right side
debit	credit

---

[1] The terms *debit* and *credit* are derived from the Latin *debere* and *credere*, respectively.

Chapter 2 Analyzing Transactions

EXHIBIT 1 — NetSolutions' November Transactions

	Assets			=	Liabilities	+			Owner's Equity				
					Accounts		Chris Clark,	Chris Clark,	Fees	Wages	Rent	Supplies	Utilities	Misc.
	Cash	+ Supp.	+ Land	=	Payable	+	Capital	− Drawing	+ Earned	− Exp.	− Exp.	− Exp.	− Exp.	− Exp.
a.	+25,000						+25,000							
b.	−20,000		+20,000											
Bal.	5,000		20,000				25,000							
c.		+1,350			+1,350									
Bal.	5,000	1,350	20,000		1,350		25,000							
d.	+7,500								+7,500					
Bal.	12,500	1,350	20,000		1,350		25,000		7,500					
e.	−3,650									−2,125	−800		−450	−275
Bal.	8,850	1,350	20,000		1,350		25,000		7,500	−2,125	−800		−450	−275
f.	−950				−950									
Bal.	7,900	1,350	20,000		400		25,000		7,500	−2,125	−800		−450	−275
g.		−800										−800		
Bal.	7,900	550	20,000		400		25,000		7,500	−2,125	−800	−800	−450	−275
h.	−2,000							−2,000						
Bal.	5,900	550	20,000		400		25,000	−2,000	7,500	−2,125	−800	−800	−450	−275

> **Note**
> Amounts entered on the left side of an account are debits, and amounts entered on the right side of an account are credits.

The amounts shown in the Cash column of Exhibit 1 would be recorded in a cash account as follows:

Cash

Debit Side of Account			Credit Side of Account
(a) 25,000	(b) 20,000		
(d) 7,500	(e) 3,650		
	(f) 950		
	(h) 2,000		
Balance 5,900			

Balance of Account

Recording transactions in accounts must follow certain rules. For example, increases in assets are recorded on the **debit** (left) side of an account. Likewise, decreases in assets are recorded on the **credit** (right) side of an account. The excess of the debits of an asset account over its credits is the **balance of the account**.

To illustrate, the receipt (increase in Cash) of $25,000 in transaction (a) is entered on the debit (left) side of the cash account. The letter or date of the transaction is also entered into the account. That way, if any questions later arise related to the entry, the entry can be traced back to the underlying transaction data. In contrast, the payment (decrease in Cash) of $20,000 to purchase land in transaction (b) is entered on the credit (right) side of the account.

The balance of the cash account of $5,900 is the excess of the debits over the credits, computed as follows:

Debits ($25,000 + $7,500)	$32,500
Less credits ($20,000 + $3,650 + $950 + $2,000)	26,600
Balance of Cash as of November 30, 2018	$ 5,900

> **Link to Apple**
> In a recent balance sheet, **Apple Inc.** reported $13.8 billion of cash.

The balance of the cash account is inserted in the account in the Debit column. In this way, the balance is identified as a debit balance.[2] This balance represents NetSolutions' cash on hand as of November 30, 2018. This balance of $5,900 is reported on the November 30, 2018, balance sheet for NetSolutions as shown in Exhibit 8 of Chapter 1.

In an actual accounting system, a more formal account form replaces the T account. Later in this chapter, a four-column account is illustrated. The T account, however, is

---
[2] The totals of the Debit and Credit columns may be shown separately in an account. When this is done, these amounts should be identified in some way so that they are not mistaken for entries or the ending balance of the account.

a simple way to illustrate the effects of transactions on accounts and financial statements. For this reason, T accounts are often used in business to explain transactions.

Each of the columns in Exhibit 1 can be converted into an account form in a similar manner as was done for the Cash column of Exhibit 1. However, as mentioned earlier, recording increases and decreases in accounts must follow certain rules. These rules are discussed after the chart of accounts is described.

Chart of Accounts

A group of accounts for a business entity is called a **ledger**. A list of the accounts in the ledger is called a **chart of accounts**. The accounts are normally listed in the order in which they appear in the financial statements. The balance sheet accounts are listed first, in the order of assets, liabilities, and owner's equity. The income statement accounts are then listed in the order of revenues and expenses.

Assets **Assets** are resources owned by the business entity. These resources can be physical items, such as cash and supplies, or intangibles that have value. Examples of intangible assets include patent rights, copyrights, and trademarks. Assets also include accounts receivable, prepaid expenses (such as insurance), buildings, equipment, and land.

Liabilities **Liabilities** are debts owed to outsiders (creditors). Liabilities are often identified on the balance sheet by titles that include *payable*. Examples of liabilities include accounts payable, notes payable, and wages payable. Cash received before services are delivered creates a liability to perform the services. These future service commitments are called *unearned revenues*. Examples of unearned revenues include magazine subscriptions received by a publisher and tuition received at the beginning of a term by a college.

Owner's Equity **Owner's equity** is the owner's right to the assets of the business after all liabilities have been paid. For a proprietorship, the owner's equity is represented by the balance of the owner's **capital account**. A **drawing** account represents the amount of withdrawals made by the owner.

Revenues **Revenues** are increases in assets and owner's equity as a result of selling services or products to customers. Examples of revenues include fees earned, fares earned, commissions revenue, and rent revenue.

Business Connection

THE HIJACKING RECEIVABLE

A company's chart of accounts should reflect the basic nature of its operations. Occasionally, however, transactions take place that give rise to unusual accounts. The following is a story of one such account.

Before strict airport security was implemented across the United States, several airlines experienced hijacking incidents. One such incident occurred when a Southern Airways jet en route from Memphis to Miami was hijacked during a stopover in Birmingham, Alabama. The three hijackers boarded the plane in Birmingham armed with handguns and hand grenades. At gunpoint, the hijackers took the plane, the plane's crew, and the passengers to nine American cities, Toronto, and eventually Havana, Cuba.

During the long flight, the hijackers demanded a ransom of $10 million. Southern Airways, however, was only able to come up with $2 million. Eventually, the pilot talked the hijackers into settling for the $2 million when the plane landed in Chattanooga for refueling.

Upon landing in Havana, the Cuban authorities arrested the hijackers and, after a brief delay, sent the plane, passengers, and crew back to the United States. The hijackers and the $2 million stayed in Cuba.

How did Southern Airways account for and report the hijacking payment in its subsequent financial statements? As you might have analyzed, the initial entry credited Cash for $2 million. The debit was to an account entitled "Hijacking Payment." This account was reported as a type of receivable under "other assets" on Southern Airways' balance sheet. The company maintained that it would be able to collect the cash from the Cuban government and that, therefore, a receivable existed. In fact, Southern Airways was later repaid $2 million by the Cuban government, which was, at that time, attempting to improve relations with the United States.

Expenses Expenses result from using up assets or consuming services in the process of generating revenues. Examples of expenses include wages expense, rent expense, utilities expense, supplies expense, and miscellaneous expense.

Illustration of Chart of Accounts A chart of accounts should meet the needs of a company's managers and other users of its financial statements. The accounts within the chart of accounts are numbered for use as references. A numbering system is normally used so that new accounts can be added without affecting other account numbers.

Exhibit 2 is NetSolutions' chart of accounts that is used in this chapter. Additional accounts will be introduced in later chapters. In Exhibit 2, each account number has two digits. The first digit indicates the major account group of the ledger in which the account is located. Accounts beginning with 1 represent assets; 2, liabilities; 3, owner's equity; 4, revenue; and 5, expenses. The second digit indicates the location of the account within its group.

EXHIBIT 2

Chart of Accounts for NetSolutions

Balance Sheet Accounts	Income Statement Accounts
1. Assets	**4. Revenue**
11 Cash	41 Fees Earned
12 Accounts Receivable	**5. Expenses**
14 Supplies	51 Wages Expense
15 Prepaid Insurance	52 Supplies Expense
17 Land	53 Rent Expense
18 Office Equipment	54 Utilities Expense
2. Liabilities	59 Miscellaneous Expense
21 Accounts Payable	
23 Unearned Rent	
3. Owner's Equity	
31 Chris Clark, Capital	
32 Chris Clark, Drawing	

Each of the columns in Exhibit 1 has been assigned an account number in the chart of accounts shown in Exhibit 2. In addition, Accounts Receivable, Prepaid Insurance, Office Equipment, and Unearned Rent have been added. These accounts will be used in recording NetSolutions' December transactions.

Obj. 2 Describe and illustrate journalizing transactions using the double-entry accounting system.

Double-Entry Accounting System

All businesses use what is called the **double-entry accounting system**. This system is based on the accounting equation and requires:

- Every business transaction to be recorded in at least two accounts.
- The total debits recorded for each transaction to be equal to the total credits recorded.

The double-entry accounting system also has specific **rules of debit and credit** for recording transactions in the accounts.

Balance Sheet Accounts

Link to Apple
Apple records transactions using double-entry accounting.

The debit and credit rules for balance sheet accounts are as follows:

Balance Sheet Accounts

ASSETS Asset Accounts	=	LIABILITIES Liability Accounts	+	OWNER'S EQUITY Owner's Equity Accounts
Debit for increases (+) | Credit for decreases (−)		Debit for decreases (−) | Credit for increases (+)		Debit for decreases (−) | Credit for increases (+)

Income Statement Accounts

The debit and credit rules for income statement accounts are based on their relationship with owner's equity. As shown for balance sheet accounts, owner's equity accounts are increased by credits. Because revenues increase owner's equity, revenue accounts are increased by credits and decreased by debits. Because owner's equity accounts are decreased by debits, expense accounts are increased by debits and decreased by credits. Thus, the rules of debit and credit for revenue and expense accounts are as follows:

Income Statement Accounts			
Revenue Accounts		**Expense Accounts**	
Debit for decreases (−)	Credit for increases (+)	Debit for increases (+)	Credit for decreases (−)

Owner Withdrawals

The debit and credit rules for recording owner withdrawals are based on the effect of owner withdrawals on owner's equity. Because an owner's withdrawals decrease owner's equity, the owner's drawing account is increased by debits. Likewise, the owner's drawing account is decreased by credits. Thus, the rules of debit and credit for the owner's drawing account are as follows:

Drawing Account	
Debit for increases (+)	Credit for decreases (−)

Normal Balances

The sum of the increases in an account is usually equal to or greater than the sum of the decreases in the account. Thus, the **normal balance of an account** is either a debit or credit depending on whether increases in the account are recorded as debits or credits. For example, because asset accounts are increased with debits, asset accounts normally have debit balances. Likewise, liability accounts normally have credit balances.

The rules of debit and credit and the normal balances of the various types of accounts are summarized in Exhibit 3. Debits and credits are sometimes abbreviated as Dr. for debit and Cr. for credit.

Rules of Debit and Credit, Normal Balances of Accounts — **EXHIBIT 3**

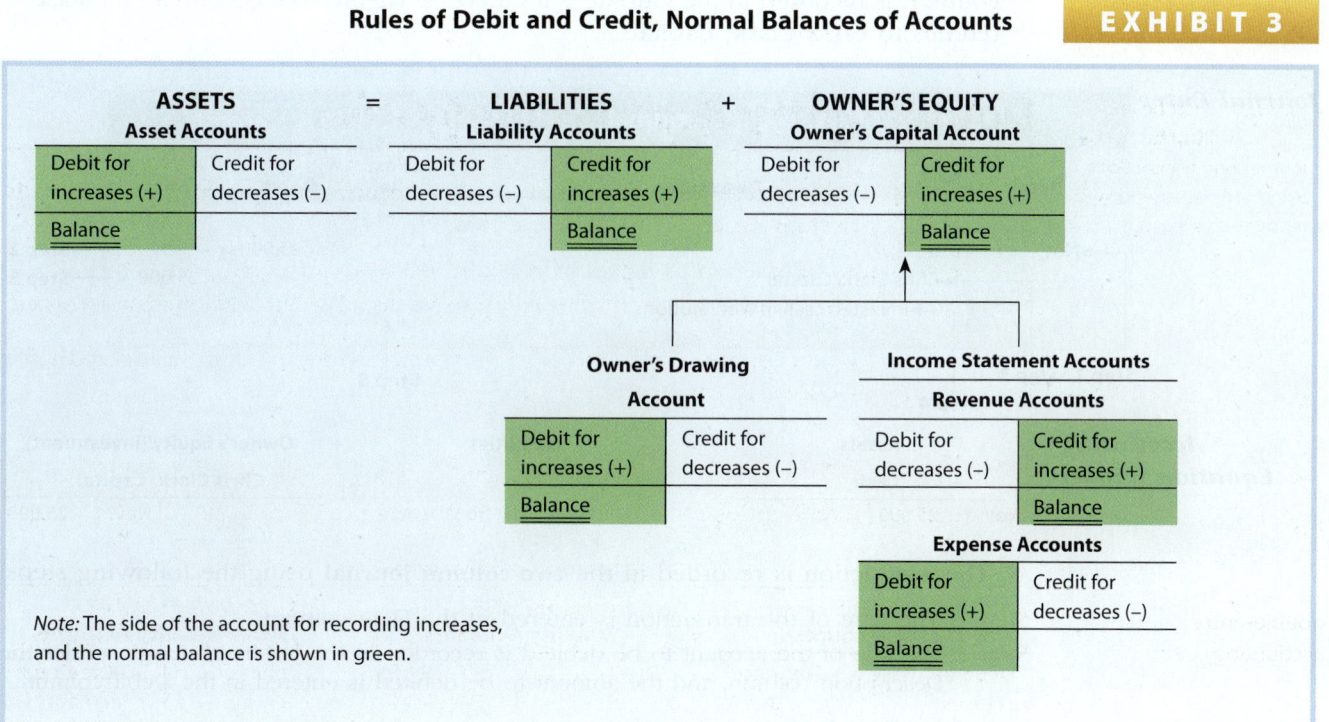

Note: The side of the account for recording increases, and the normal balance is shown in green.

64 Chapter 2 Analyzing Transactions

When an account with a normal debit balance has a credit balance, or vice versa, an error may have occurred or an unusual situation may exist. For example, a credit balance in the office equipment account could result only from an error. This is because a business cannot have more decreases than increases of office equipment. On the other hand, a debit balance in an accounts payable account could result from an overpayment.

Example Exercise 2-1 Rules of Debit and Credit and Normal Balances   Obj. 2

State for each account whether it is likely to have (a) debit entries only, (b) credit entries only, or (c) both debit and credit entries. Also indicate its normal balance.

1. Amber Saunders, Drawing
2. Accounts Payable
3. Cash
4. Fees Earned
5. Supplies
6. Utilities Expense

Follow My Example 2-1

1. Debit entries only; normal debit balance
2. Debit and credit entries; normal credit balance
3. Debit and credit entries; normal debit balance
4. Credit entries only; normal credit balance
5. Debit and credit entries; normal debit balance
6. Debit entries only; normal debit balance

Practice Exercises: PE 2-1A, PE 2-1B

Journalizing

Using the rules of debit and credit, transactions are initially entered in a record called a **journal**. In this way, the journal serves as a record of when transactions occurred and were recorded. To illustrate, the November transactions of **NetSolutions** from Chapter 1 are used.

Transaction A Nov. 1 Chris Clark deposited $25,000 in a bank account in the name of NetSolutions.

Analysis This transaction increases an asset account and increases an owner's equity account. It is recorded in the journal as an increase (debit) to Cash and an increase (credit) to Chris Clark, Capital.

Journal Entry

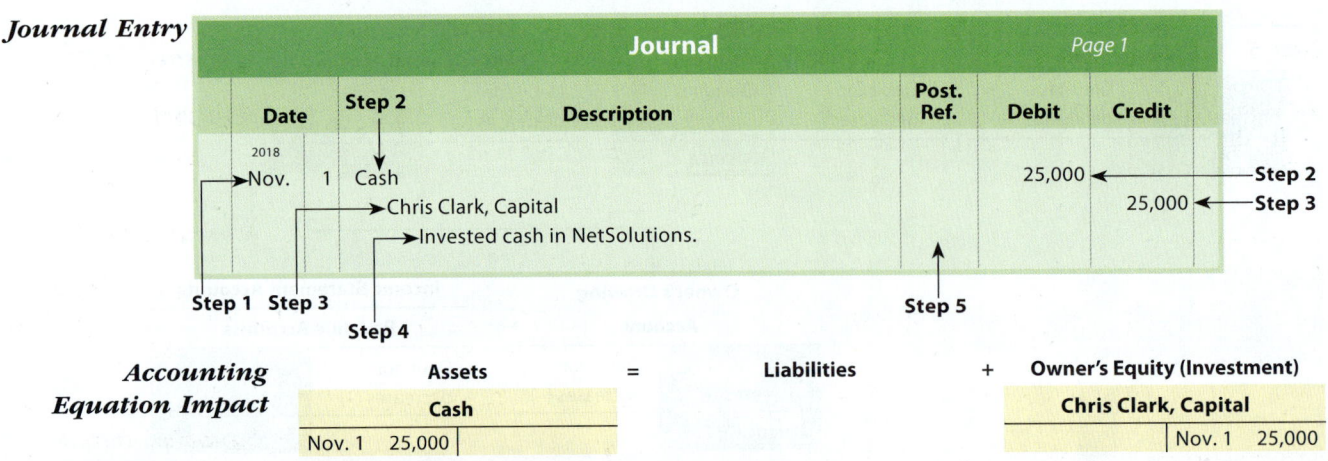

The transaction is recorded in the **two-column journal** using the following steps:

Step 1. The date of the transaction is entered in the Date column.

Step 2. The title of the account to be debited is recorded in the left-hand margin under the Description column, and the amount to be debited is entered in the Debit column.

Step 3. The title of the account to be credited is listed below and to the right of the debited account title, and the amount to be credited is entered in the Credit column.

Step 4. A brief description may be entered below the credited account.

Step 5. The Post. Ref. (Posting Reference) column is left blank when the journal entry is initially recorded. This column is used later in this chapter when the journal entry amounts are transferred to the accounts in the ledger.

The process of recording a transaction in the journal is called **journalizing**. The entry in the journal is called a **journal entry**.

A useful method for analyzing and journalizing transactions is as follows:

Step 1. Carefully read the description of the transaction to determine whether an asset, a liability, an owner's equity, a revenue, an expense, or a drawing account is affected.

Step 2. For each account affected by the transaction, determine whether the account increases or decreases.

Step 3. Determine whether each increase or decrease should be recorded as a debit or a credit to the account, following the rules of debit and credit shown in Exhibit 3.

Step 4. Record the transaction using a journal entry.

Exhibit 4 summarizes terminology that is often used in describing a transaction along with the related accounts that would be debited and credited.

EXHIBIT 4
Transaction Terminology and Related Journal Entry Accounts

Common Transaction Terminology	Journal Entry Account Debit	Credit
Received cash for services provided	Cash	Fees Earned
Services provided on account	Accounts Receivable	Fees Earned
Received cash on account	Cash	Accounts Receivable
Purchased on account	Asset account	Accounts Payable
Paid on account	Accounts Payable	Cash
Paid cash	Asset or expense account	Cash
Owner investments	Cash and/or other assets	(Owner's name), Capital
Owner withdrawals	(Owner's name), Drawing	Cash

The remaining transactions of **NetSolutions** for November are analyzed and journalized next.

Nov. 5 NetSolutions paid $20,000 for the purchase of land as a future building site.

Transaction B

This transaction increases one asset account and decreases another. It is recorded in the journal as a $20,000 increase (debit) to Land and a $20,000 decrease (credit) to Cash.

Analysis

Nov.	5	Land		20,000	
		Cash			20,000
		Purchased land for building site.			

Journal Entry

Assets	=	Liabilities	+	Owner's Equity
Land				
Nov. 5 20,000				

Cash

| Nov. 5 | 20,000 |

Accounting Equation Impact

66 Chapter 2 Analyzing Transactions

Transaction C Nov. 10 *NetSolutions purchased supplies on account for $1,350.*

Analysis

This transaction increases an asset account and increases a liability account. It is recorded in the journal as a $1,350 increase (debit) to Supplies and a $1,350 increase (credit) to Accounts Payable.

Journal Entry

Nov.	10	Supplies		1,350	
		Accounts Payable			1,350
		Purchased supplies on account.			

Accounting Equation Impact

Assets = Liabilities + Owner's Equity

Supplies		Accounts Payable
Nov. 10 1,350		Nov. 10 1,350

Transaction D Nov. 18 *NetSolutions received cash of $7,500 from customers for services provided.*

Analysis

This transaction increases an asset account and increases a revenue account. It is recorded in the journal as a $7,500 increase (debit) to Cash and a $7,500 increase (credit) to Fees Earned.

Journal Entry

Nov.	18	Cash		7,500	
		Fees Earned			7,500
		Received fees from customers.			

Accounting Equation Impact

Assets = Liabilities + Owner's Equity (Revenue)

Cash		Fees Earned
Nov. 18 7,500		Nov. 18 7,500

Transaction E Nov. 30 *NetSolutions incurred the following expenses: wages, $2,125; rent, $800; utilities, $450; and miscellaneous, $275.*

Analysis

This transaction increases various expense accounts and decreases an asset (Cash) account. You should note that regardless of the number of accounts, *the sum of the debits is always equal to the sum of the credits in a journal entry.* It is recorded in the journal with increases (debits) to the expense accounts (Wages Expense, $2,125; Rent Expense, $800; Utilities Expense, $450; and Miscellaneous Expense, $275) and a decrease (credit) to Cash, $3,650.

Journal Entry

Nov.	30	Wages Expense		2,125	
		Rent Expense		800	
		Utilities Expense		450	
		Miscellaneous Expense		275	
		Cash			3,650
		Paid expenses.			

Accounting Equation Impact

Assets = Liabilities + Owner's Equity (Expense)

Cash		Wages Expense
	Nov. 30 3,650	Nov. 30 2,125

Rent Expense
Nov. 30   800

Utilities Expense
Nov. 30   450

Miscellaneous Expense
Nov. 30   275

Nov. 30 NetSolutions paid creditors on account, $950. *Transaction F*

This transaction decreases a liability account and decreases an asset account. It is recorded in the journal as a $950 decrease (debit) to Accounts Payable and a $950 decrease (credit) to Cash. *Analysis*

Nov.	30	Accounts Payable	950	
		Cash		950
		Paid creditors on account.		

Journal Entry

Assets	=	Liabilities	+	Owner's Equity
Cash		Accounts Payable		
Nov. 30 950		Nov. 30 950		

Accounting Equation Impact

Nov. 30 Chris Clark determined that the cost of supplies on hand at November 30 was $550. *Transaction G*

NetSolutions purchased $1,350 of supplies on November 10. Thus, $800 ($1,350 purchased − $550 on hand) of supplies have been used during November. This transaction is recorded in the journal as an $800 increase (debit) to Supplies Expense and an $800 decrease (credit) to Supplies. *Analysis*

Nov.	30	Supplies Expense	800	
		Supplies		800
		Supplies used during November.		

Journal Entry

Assets	=	Liabilities	+	Owner's Equity (Expense)
Supplies				Supplies Expense
Nov. 30 800				Nov. 30 800

Accounting Equation Impact

Nov. 30 Chris Clark withdrew $2,000 from NetSolutions for personal use. *Transaction H*

This transaction decreases assets and owner's equity. It is recorded in the journal as a $2,000 increase (debit) to Chris Clark, Drawing and a $2,000 decrease (credit) to Cash. *Analysis*

Journal Entry

Journal   Page 2

Date	Description	Post. Ref.	Debit	Credit
2018				
Nov. 30	Chris Clark, Drawing		2,000	
	Cash			2,000
	Chris Clark withdrew cash for personal use.			

Assets	=	Liabilities	+	Owner's Equity (Drawing)
Cash				Chris Clark, Drawing
Nov. 30 2,000				Nov. 30 2,000

Accounting Equation Impact

INTEGRITY, OBJECTIVITY, AND ETHICS IN BUSINESS

WILL JOURNALIZING PREVENT FRAUD?

While journalizing transactions reduces the possibility of fraud, it by no means eliminates it. For example, embezzlement can be hidden within the double-entry bookkeeping system by creating fictitious suppliers to whom checks are issued.

68 Chapter 2 Analyzing Transactions

Example Exercise 2-2 Journal Entry for Asset Purchase — Obj. 2

Prepare a journal entry for the purchase of a truck on June 3 for $42,500, paying $8,500 cash and the remainder on account.

Follow My Example 2-2

June 3	Truck...	42,500	
	Cash..		8,500
	Accounts Payable..		34,000

Practice Exercises: PE 2-2A, PE 2-2B

Obj. 3 Describe and illustrate the journalizing and posting of transactions to accounts.

Journalizing and Posting to Accounts

As illustrated, a transaction is first recorded in a journal. Periodically, the journal entries are transferred to the accounts in the ledger. The process of transferring the debits and credits from the journal entries to the accounts is called **posting**.

The December transactions of **NetSolutions** are used to illustrate posting from the journal to the ledger. By using the December transactions, an additional review of analyzing and journalizing transactions is provided.

Transaction Dynamic Exhibit Analysis

Dec. 1 NetSolutions paid a premium of $2,400 for an insurance policy for liability, theft, and fire. The policy covers a one-year period.

Prepayments of expenses, such as for insurance premiums, are called prepaid expenses. Prepaid expenses are assets. For NetSolutions, the asset purchased is insurance protection for 12 months. This transaction is recorded as a $2,400 increase (debit) to Prepaid Insurance and a $2,400 decrease (credit) to Cash.

Journal Entry

Dec.	1	Prepaid Insurance	2,400	
		Cash		2,400
		Paid premium on one-year policy.		

Accounting Equation Impact

Assets = Liabilities + Owner's Equity

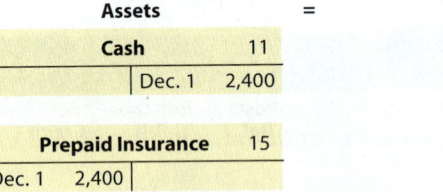

The posting of the preceding December 1 transaction is shown in Exhibit 5. Notice that the T account form is not used in Exhibit 5. In practice, the T account is usually replaced with a standard **four-column account** as shown in Exhibit 5.

The debits and credits for each journal entry are posted to the accounts in the order in which they occur in the journal. To illustrate, the debit portion of the December 1 journal entry is posted to the prepaid insurance account in Exhibit 5 using the following four steps:

Step 1. The date (Dec. 1) of the journal entry is entered in the Date column of Prepaid Insurance.

Step 2. The amount (2,400) is entered into the Debit column of Prepaid Insurance.

Step 3. The journal page number (2) is entered in the Posting Reference (Post. Ref.) column of Prepaid Insurance.

Step 4. The account number (15) is entered in the Posting Reference (Post. Ref.) column in the journal.

As shown in Exhibit 5, the credit portion of the December 1 journal entry is posted to the cash account in a similar manner.

Chapter 2   Analyzing Transactions   69

Diagram of the Recording and Posting of a Debit and a Credit Ledger, NetSolutions   EXHIBIT 5

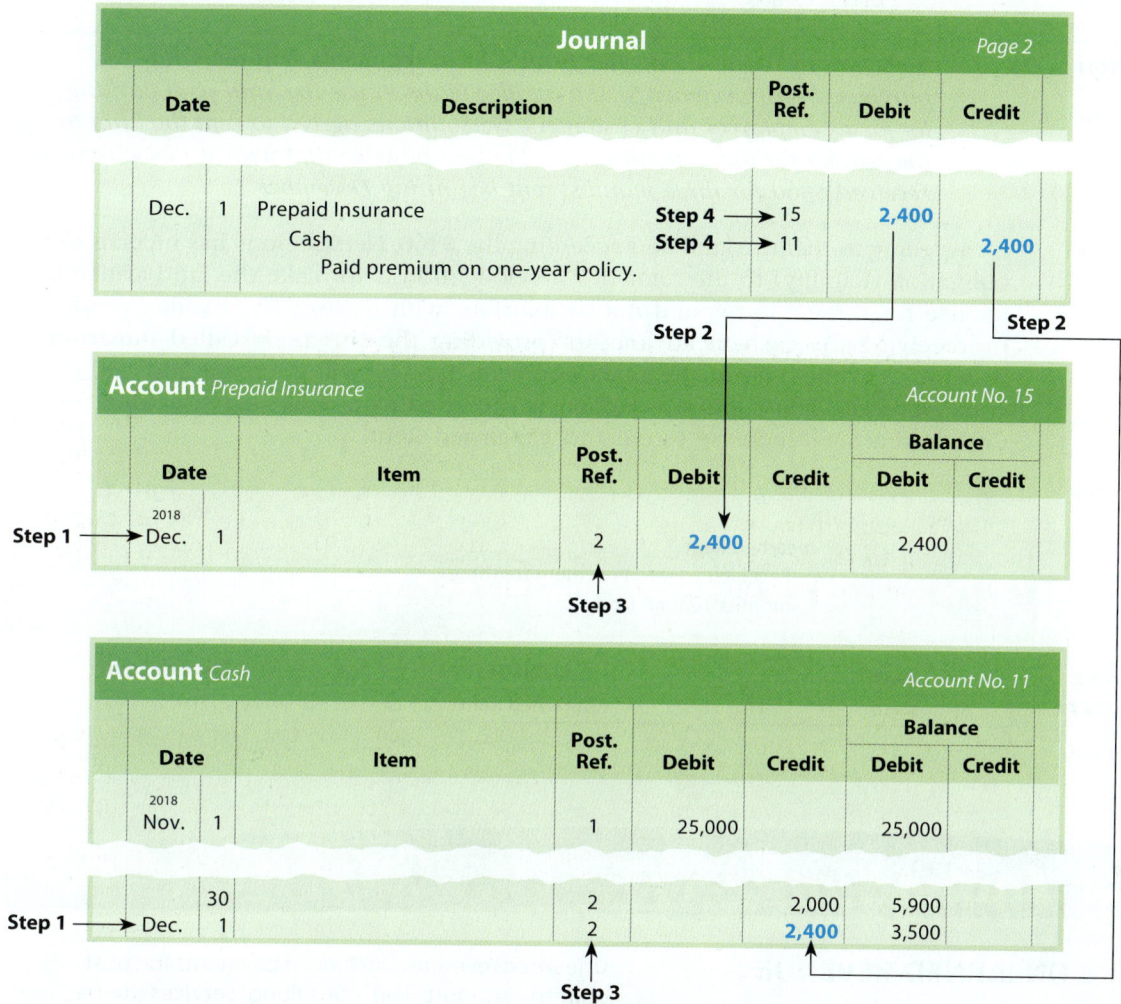

The remaining December transactions for **NetSolutions** are analyzed and journalized in the following paragraphs. These transactions are posted to the ledger later in this chapter (see Exhibit 6). To simplify, some of the December transactions are stated in summary form. For example, cash received for services is normally recorded on a daily basis. However, only summary totals are recorded at the middle and end of the month for NetSolutions.

Dec. 1   NetSolutions paid rent for December, $800. The company from which NetSolutions is renting its office space now requires the payment of rent on the first of each month rather than at the end of the month.   *Transaction*

The prepayment of rent is an asset, much like the advance payment of the insurance premium in the preceding transaction. However, unlike the insurance premium, this prepaid rent will expire in one month. When an asset is purchased with the expectation that it will be used up in a short period of time, such as a month, it is normal to debit an expense account initially. This avoids having to transfer the balance from an asset account (Prepaid Rent) to an expense account (Rent Expense) at the end of the month. Thus, this transaction is recorded as an $800 increase (debit) to Rent Expense and an $800 decrease (credit) to Cash.   *Analysis*

Dec.	1	Rent Expense	53	800	
		Cash	11		800
		Paid rent for December.			

Journal Entry

Chapter 2 Analyzing Transactions

Accounting Equation Impact

Assets	=	Liabilities	+	Owner's Equity (Expense)
Cash 11				Rent Expense 53
Dec. 1 800				Dec. 1 800

Transaction — *Dynamic Exhibit*

Dec. 1 NetSolutions received an offer from a local retailer to rent the land purchased on November 5. The retailer plans to use the land as a parking lot for its employees and customers. NetSolutions agreed to rent the land to the retailer for three months, with the rent payable in advance. NetSolutions received $360 for three months' rent beginning December 1.

Analysis

By agreeing to rent the land and accepting the $360, NetSolutions has incurred an obligation (liability) to the retailer. This obligation is to make the land available for use for three months and not to interfere with its use. The liability created by receiving the cash in advance of providing the service is called **unearned revenue**. As time passes, the unearned rent liability will decrease and will become revenue. Thus, this transaction is recorded as a $360 increase (debit) to Cash and a $360 increase (credit) to Unearned Rent.

Journal Entry

Dec.	1	Cash	11	360	
		Unearned Rent	23		360
		Received advance payment for three months' rent on land.			

Accounting Equation Impact

Assets	=	Liabilities	+	Owner's Equity
Cash 11		Unearned Rent 23		
Dec. 1 360		Dec. 1 360		

Business Connection

MICROSOFT'S UNEARNED REVENUE

Microsoft Corporation develops, manufactures, licenses, and supports a wide range of computer software products, including, Word®, Excel®, and the Xbox® gaming system. When Microsoft sells its products, it also provides technical support and periodic updates on those products for a period of time. Thus, at the time of sale, a portion of the proceeds is unearned (deferred) for these services. As time passes and services are provided to customers, Microsoft records a portion of its unearned (deferred) revenue as revenue.[3]

To illustrate, the following excerpt was taken from a recent financial statement of Microsoft:

Unearned revenue ... include(s) payments for: post-delivery support and consulting services to be performed in the future; Xbox Live subscriptions and prepaid points; Microsoft Dynamics business solutions products; Office 365 subscriptions; Skype prepaid credits and subscriptions; Bundled Offerings; and other offerings for which we have been paid in advance....

During a recent year, Microsoft recognized as revenue $48,498 million of unearned revenue, which is 57% of its total revenues. For a recent year ending June 30, Microsoft also reported on its balance sheet a liability for unearned revenue of $33,909 million. Thus, the recording of unearned revenue is a significant item for Microsoft.

Source: Microsoft Corporation, Form 10-K, For the Year Ended June 30, 2016.

---

[3] Separating unearned revenue from the initial sale of a product or service is consistent with Revenue Recognition (Topic 605), June 24, 2010, paras. 23, 35-36.

Dec. 4 NetSolutions purchased office equipment on account from Executive Supply Co. for $1,800. — *Transaction*

The asset (Office Equipment) and liability accounts (Accounts Payable) increase. This transaction is recorded as an $1,800 increase (debit) to Office Equipment and an $1,800 increase (credit) to Accounts Payable. — *Analysis*

Dec.	4	Office Equipment	18	1,800	
		Accounts Payable	21		1,800
		Purchased office equipment on account.			

Journal Entry

Assets	=	Liabilities	+	Owner's Equity
Office Equipment 18		**Accounts Payable** 21		
Dec. 4 1,800		Dec. 4 1,800		

Accounting Equation Impact

Dec. 6 NetSolutions paid $180 for a newspaper advertisement. — *Transaction*

An expense increases, and an asset (Cash) decreases. Expense items that are expected to be minor in amount are normally included as part of the miscellaneous expense. This transaction is recorded as a $180 increase (debit) to Miscellaneous Expense and a $180 decrease (credit) to Cash. — *Analysis*

Dec.	6	Miscellaneous Expense	59	180	
		Cash	11		180
		Paid for newspaper advertisement.			

Journal Entry

Assets	=	Liabilities	+	Owner's Equity (Expense)
Cash 11				**Miscellaneous Exp.** 59
Dec. 6 180				Dec. 6 180

Accounting Equation Impact

Dec. 11 NetSolutions paid creditors $400. — *Transaction*

A liability (Accounts Payable) and an asset (Cash) decrease. This transaction is recorded as a $400 decrease (debit) to Accounts Payable and a $400 decrease (credit) to Cash. — *Analysis*

Dec.	11	Accounts Payable	21	400	
		Cash	11		400
		Paid creditors on account.			

Journal Entry

Assets	=	Liabilities	+	Owner's Equity
Cash 11		**Accounts Payable** 21		
Dec. 11 400		Dec. 11 400		

Accounting Equation Impact

Dec. 13 NetSolutions paid a receptionist and a part-time assistant $950 for two weeks' wages. — *Transaction*

This transaction is similar to the December 6 transaction, where an expense account is increased and Cash is decreased. This transaction is recorded as a $950 increase (debit) to Wages Expense and a $950 decrease (credit) to Cash. — *Analysis*

Link to Apple

In a recent year, **Apple** incurred advertising expense of $1.2 billion. Apple reports advertising expense as part of Selling, General, and Administrative Expenses.

72 Chapter 2 Analyzing Transactions

Journal Entry

		Journal			Page 3
Date		Description	Post. Ref.	Debit	Credit

2018 Dec.	13	Wages Expense
		    Cash
		        Paid two weeks' wages.
			51
			11
				950	950

Accounting Equation Impact

Assets = Liabilities + Owner's Equity (Expense)

Cash	11			Wages Expense	51
Dec. 13	950			Dec. 13	950

Business Connection

COMPUTERIZED ACCOUNTING SYSTEMS

Computerized accounting systems are widely used by even the smallest companies. These systems simplify the record-keeping process in that transactions are recorded in electronic forms. Forms used to bill customers for services provided are often completed using drop-down menus that list services that are normally provided to customers. An auto-complete entry feature may also be used to fill in customer names. For example, type "ca" to display customers with names beginning with "Ca" (Caban, Cahill, Carey, and Caswell). And to simplify data entry, entries are automatically posted to the ledger accounts when the electronic form is completed.

One popular accounting software package used by small- to medium-sized businesses is QuickBooks®. Some examples of using QuickBooks to record accounting transactions are illustrated and discussed in Chapter 5.

Transaction   Dec. 16   NetSolutions received $3,100 from fees earned for the first half of December.

Dynamic Exhibit

Analysis   An asset account (Cash) and a revenue account (Fees Earned) increase. This transaction is recorded as a $3,100 increase (debit) to Cash and a $3,100 increase (credit) to Fees Earned.

Journal Entry

Dec.	16	Cash
		    Fees Earned
		        Received fees from customers.
			11
			41
				3,100	3,100

Accounting Equation Impact

Assets = Liabilities + Owner's Equity (Revenue)

Cash	11			Fees Earned	41
Dec. 16 3,100				Dec. 16	3,100

Transaction   Dec. 16   Fees earned on account totaled $1,750 for the first half of December.

Analysis   When a business allows a customer to pay for services provided at a later date, an **account receivable** is created. An account receivable is a claim against the customer, and, thus, is an asset for the seller. Revenue is earned even though no cash has been received. Thus, this transaction is recorded as a $1,750 increase (debit) to Accounts Receivable and a $1,750 increase (credit) to Fees Earned.

Journal Entry

Dec.	16	Accounts Receivable
		    Fees Earned
		        Fees earned on account.
			12
			41
				1,750	1,750

Assets	=	Liabilities	+	Owner's Equity (Revenue)	Accounting Equation Impact
Accounts Receivable 12				Fees Earned 41	
Dec. 16 1,750				Dec. 16 1,750	

Example Exercise 2-3 Journal Entry for Fees Earned *Obj. 3*

Prepare a journal entry on August 7 for the fees earned on account, $115,000.

Follow My Example 2-3

| Aug. 7 | Accounts Receivable............................... | 115,000 | |
| | Fees Earned .... | | 115,000 |

Practice Exercises: PE 2-3A, PE 2-3B

Dec. 20 NetSolutions paid $900 to Executive Supply Co. on the $1,800 debt owed from the December 4 transaction. *Transaction*

This is similar to the transaction of December 11. This transaction is recorded as a $900 decrease (debit) to Accounts Payable and a $900 decrease (credit) to Cash. *Analysis*

Journal Entry

Dec.	20	Accounts Payable	21	900	
		Cash	11		900
		Paid creditors on account.			

Assets	=	Liabilities	+	Owner's Equity	Accounting Equation Impact
Cash 11		Accounts Payable 21			
Dec. 20 900		Dec. 20 900			

Dec. 21 NetSolutions received $650 from customers in payment of their accounts. *Transaction*

Dynamic Exhibit

When customers pay amounts owed for services they have previously received, one asset increases and another asset decreases. This transaction is recorded as a $650 increase (debit) to Cash and a $650 decrease (credit) to Accounts Receivable. *Analysis*

Journal Entry

Dec.	21	Cash	11	650	
		Accounts Receivable	12		650
		Received cash from customers on account.			

Assets	=	Liabilities	+	Owner's Equity	Accounting Equation Impact
Cash 11					
Dec. 21 650					
Accounts Receivable 12					
Dec. 21 650					

Dec. 23 NetSolutions paid $1,450 for supplies. *Transaction*

One asset account (Supplies) increases, and another asset account (Cash) decreases. This transaction is recorded as a $1,450 increase (debit) to Supplies and a $1,450 decrease (credit) to Cash. *Analysis*

74 Chapter 2 Analyzing Transactions

Journal Entry

	Dec.	23	Supplies	14	1,450	
			Cash	11		1,450
			Purchased supplies.			

Accounting Equation Impact

Assets = Liabilities + Owner's Equity

Cash	11
Dec. 23	1,450

Supplies	14
Dec. 23 1,450	

Transaction Dec. 27 NetSolutions paid the receptionist and the part-time assistant $1,200 for two weeks' wages.

Analysis This transaction is similar to the transaction of December 13. This transaction is recorded as a $1,200 increase (debit) to Wages Expense and a $1,200 decrease (credit) to Cash.

Journal Entry

	Dec.	27	Wages Expense	51	1,200	
			Cash	11		1,200
			Paid two weeks' wages.			

Accounting Equation Impact

Assets = Liabilities + Owner's Equity (Expense)

Cash	11
Dec. 27 1,200	

Wages Expense	51
Dec. 27 1,200	

Transaction Dec. 31 NetSolutions paid its $310 telephone (utility) bill for the month.

Analysis This is similar to the transaction of December 6. This transaction is recorded as a $310 increase (debit) to Utilities Expense and a $310 decrease (credit) to Cash.

Journal Entry

	Dec.	31	Utilities Expense	54	310	
			Cash	11		310
			Paid telephone bill.			

Accounting Equation Impact

Assets = Liabilities + Owner's Equity (Expense)

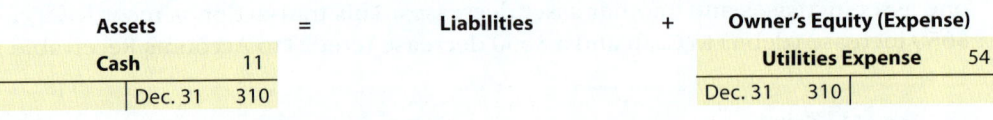

Transaction Dec. 31 NetSolutions paid its $225 electric (utility) bill for the month.

Analysis This is similar to the preceding transaction. This transaction is recorded as a $225 increase (debit) to Utilities Expense and a $225 decrease (credit) to Cash.

Journal Entry

Journal Page 4

Date	Description	Post. Ref.	Debit	Credit
2018 Dec. 31	Utilities Expense	54	225	
	Cash	11		225
	Paid electric bill.			

Assets	=	Liabilities	+	Owner's Equity (Expense)	Accounting Equation Impact
Cash 11				Utilities Expense 54	
Dec. 31 225				Dec. 31 225	

Dec. 31 NetSolutions received $2,870 from fees earned for the second half of December. — *Transaction*

This is similar to the transaction of December 16. This transaction is recorded as a $2,870 increase (debit) to Cash and a $2,870 increase (credit) to Fees Earned. — *Analysis*

Journal Entry

Dec.	31	Cash	11	2,870	
		Fees Earned	41		2,870
		Received fees from customers.			

Assets	=	Liabilities	+	Owner's Equity (Revenue)	Accounting Equation Impact
Cash 11				Fees Earned 41	
Dec. 31 2,870				Dec. 31 2,870	

Dec. 31 Fees earned on account totaled $1,120 for the second half of December. — *Transaction*

This is similar to the transaction of December 16. This transaction is recorded as a $1,120 increase (debit) to Accounts Receivable and a $1,120 increase (credit) to Fees Earned. — *Analysis*

Journal Entry

Dec.	31	Accounts Receivable	12	1,120	
		Fees Earned	41		1,120
		Fees earned on account.			

Assets	=	Liabilities	+	Owner's Equity (Revenue)	Accounting Equation Impact
Accounts Receivable 12				Fees Earned 41	
Dec. 31 1,120				Dec. 31 1,120	

Dec. 31 Chris Clark withdrew $2,000 for personal use. — *Transaction*

This transaction decreases owner's equity and assets. This transaction is recorded as a $2,000 increase (debit) to Chris Clark, Drawing and a $2,000 decrease (credit) to Cash. — *Analysis*

Journal Entry

Dec.	31	Chris Clark, Drawing	32	2,000	
		Cash	11		2,000
		Chris Clark withdrew cash for personal use.			

Assets	=	Liabilities	+	Owner's Equity (Drawing)	Accounting Equation Impact
Cash 11				Chris Clark, Drawing 32	
Dec. 31 2,000				Dec. 31 2,000	

Example Exercise 2-4 Journal Entry for Owner's Withdrawal — Obj. 3

Prepare a journal entry on December 29 for the payment of $12,000 to the owner of Smartstaff Consulting Services, Dominique Walsh, for personal use.

Follow My Example 2-4

Dec. 29	Dominique Walsh, Drawing	12,000	
	Cash		12,000

Practice Exercises: PE 2-4A, PE 2-4B

Chapter 2 Analyzing Transactions

Exhibit 6 shows the December 31, 2018 ledger for **NetSolutions** after the transactions for both November and December have been posted.

EXHIBIT 6 — General Ledger for NetSolutions on December 31, 2018

Ledger

Account Cash — Account No. 11

Date	Item	Post. Ref.	Debit	Credit	Balance Debit	Balance Credit
2018						
Nov. 1		1	25,000		25,000	
5		1		20,000	5,000	
18		1	7,500		12,500	
30		1		3,650	8,850	
30		1		950	7,900	
30		2		2,000	5,900	
Dec. 1		2		2,400	3,500	
1		2		800	2,700	
1		2	360		3,060	
6		2		180	2,880	
11		2		400	2,480	
13		3		950	1,530	
16		3	3,100		4,630	
20		3		900	3,730	
21		3	650		4,380	
23		3		1,450	2,930	
27		3		1,200	1,730	
31		3		310	1,420	
31		4		225	1,195	
31		4	2,870		4,065	
31		4		2,000	2,065	

Account Accounts Receivable — Account No. 12

Date	Item	Post. Ref.	Debit	Credit	Balance Debit	Balance Credit
2018						
Dec. 16		3	1,750		1,750	
21		3		650	1,100	
31		4	1,120		2,220	

Account Supplies — Account No. 14

Date	Item	Post. Ref.	Debit	Credit	Balance Debit	Balance Credit
2018						
Nov. 10		1	1,350		1,350	
30		1		800	550	
Dec. 23		3	1,450		2,000	

Account Prepaid Insurance — Account No. 15

Date	Item	Post. Ref.	Debit	Credit	Balance Debit	Balance Credit
2018						
Dec. 1		2	2,400		2,400	

Account Land — Account No. 17

Date	Item	Post. Ref.	Debit	Credit	Balance Debit	Balance Credit
2018						
Nov. 5		1	20,000		20,000	

Account Office Equipment — Account No. 18

Date	Item	Post. Ref.	Debit	Credit	Balance Debit	Balance Credit
2018						
Dec. 4		2	1,800		1,800	

Account Accounts Payable — Account No. 21

Date	Item	Post. Ref.	Debit	Credit	Balance Debit	Balance Credit
2018						
Nov. 10		1		1,350		1,350
30		1	950			400
Dec. 4		2		1,800		2,200
11		2	400			1,800
20		3	900			900

Account Unearned Rent — Account No. 23

Date	Item	Post. Ref.	Debit	Credit	Balance Debit	Balance Credit
2018						
Dec. 1		2		360		360

Account Chris Clark, Capital — Account No. 31

Date	Item	Post. Ref.	Debit	Credit	Balance Debit	Balance Credit
2018						
Nov. 1		1		25,000		25,000

Account Chris Clark, Drawing — Account No. 32

Date	Item	Post. Ref.	Debit	Credit	Balance Debit	Balance Credit
2018						
Nov. 30		2	2,000		2,000	
Dec. 31		4	2,000		4,000	

General Ledger for NetSolutions on December 31, 2018 (Concluded)

EXHIBIT 6

Account Fees Earned — Account No. 41

Date	Item	Post. Ref.	Debit	Credit	Balance Debit	Balance Credit
2018						
Nov. 18		1		7,500		7,500
Dec. 16		3		3,100		10,600
16		3		1,750		12,350
31		4		2,870		15,220
31		4		1,120		16,340

Account Wages Expense — Account No. 51

Date	Item	Post. Ref.	Debit	Credit	Balance Debit	Balance Credit
2018						
Nov. 30		1	2,125		2,125	
Dec. 13		3	950		3,075	
27		3	1,200		4,275	

Account Supplies Expense — Account No. 52

Date	Item	Post. Ref.	Debit	Credit	Balance Debit	Balance Credit
2018						
Nov. 30		1	800		800	

Account Rent Expense — Account No. 53

Date	Item	Post. Ref.	Debit	Credit	Balance Debit	Balance Credit
2018						
Nov. 30		1	800		800	
Dec. 1		2	800		1,600	

Account Utilities Expense — Account No. 54

Date	Item	Post. Ref.	Debit	Credit	Balance Debit	Balance Credit
2018						
Nov. 30		1	450		450	
Dec. 31		3	310		760	
31		4	225		985	

Account Miscellaneous Expense — Account No. 59

Date	Item	Post. Ref.	Debit	Credit	Balance Debit	Balance Credit
2018						
Nov. 30		1	275		275	
Dec. 6		2	180		455	

Example Exercise 2-5 Missing Amount from an Account *Obj. 3*

On March 1, the cash account balance was $22,350. During March, cash receipts totaled $241,880, and the March 31 balance was $19,125. Determine the cash payments made during March.

Follow My Example 2-5

Using the following T account, solve for the amount of cash payments (indicated by ?):

```
                          Cash
        Mar. 1 Bal.       22,350   |   ?   Cash payments
        Cash receipts    241,880   |
        Mar. 31 Bal.      19,125   |
```

$19,125 = $22,350 + $241,880 − Cash payments
Cash payments = $22,350 + $241,880 − $19,125
Cash payments = $245,105

Practice Exercises: PE 2-5A, PE 2-5B

Trial Balance

Obj. 4 Prepare an unadjusted trial balance and explain how it can be used to discover errors.

Errors may occur in posting debits and credits from the journal to the ledger. One way to detect such errors is by preparing a **trial balance**. Double-entry accounting requires that debits must always equal credits. The trial balance verifies this equality. The steps in preparing a trial balance are as follows:

Step 1. List the name of the company, the title of the trial balance, and the date the trial balance is prepared.
Step 2. List the accounts from the ledger, and enter their debit or credit balance in the Debit or Credit column of the trial balance.
Step 3. Total the Debit and Credit columns of the trial balance.
Step 4. Verify that the total of the Debit column equals the total of the Credit column.

The trial balance for **NetSolutions** as of December 31, 2018, is shown in Exhibit 7. The account balances in Exhibit 7 are taken from the ledger shown in Exhibit 6. Before a trial balance is prepared, each account balance in the ledger must be determined. When the standard account form is used as in Exhibit 6, the balance of each account appears in the balance column on the same line as the last posting to the account.

The trial balance shown in Exhibit 7 is titled an **unadjusted trial balance**. This is to distinguish it from other trial balances that will be prepared in later chapters. These other trial balances include an adjusted trial balance and a post-closing trial balance.[4]

EXHIBIT 7 — Trial Balance

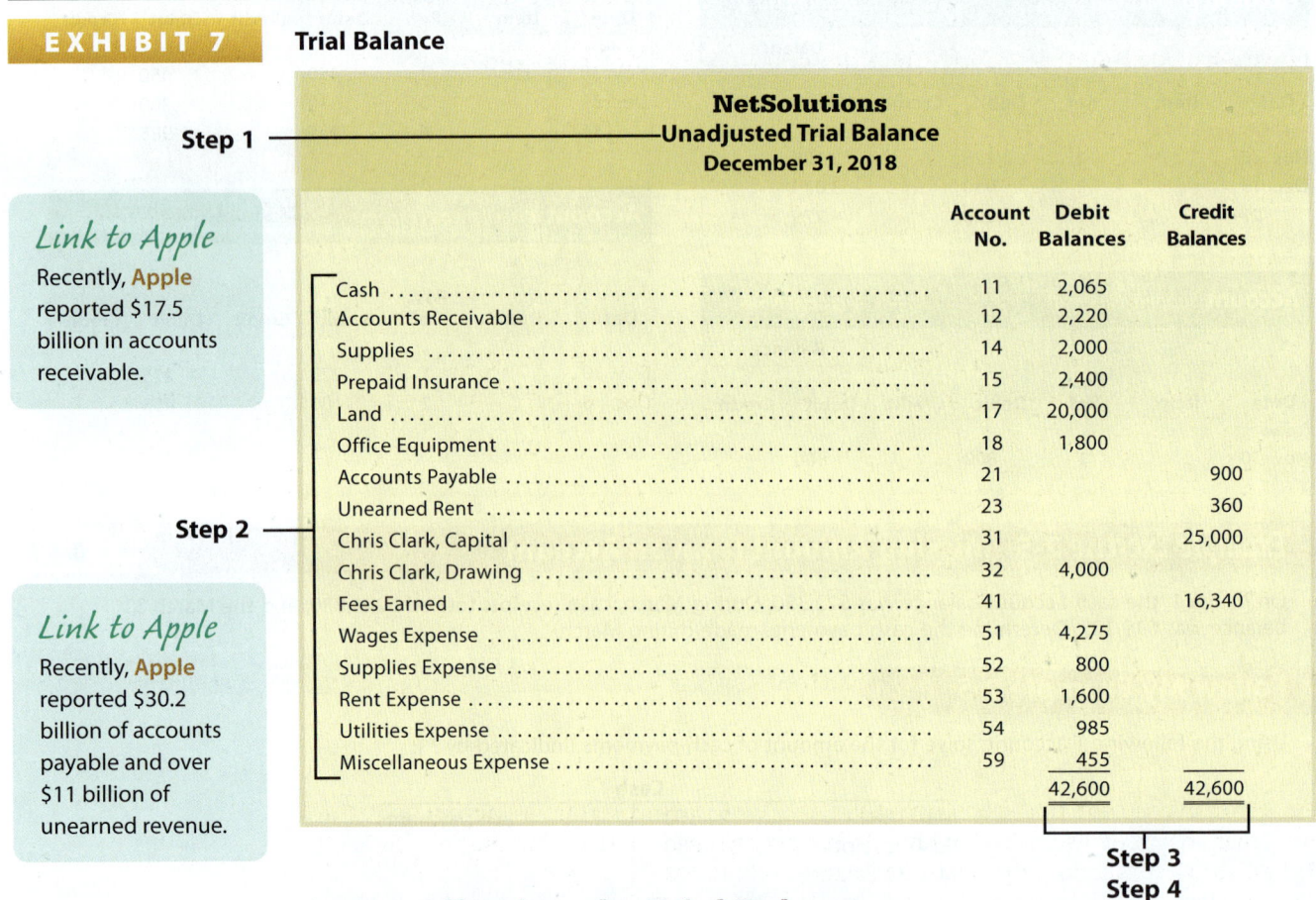

NetSolutions
Unadjusted Trial Balance
December 31, 2018

	Account No.	Debit Balances	Credit Balances
Cash	11	2,065	
Accounts Receivable	12	2,220	
Supplies	14	2,000	
Prepaid Insurance	15	2,400	
Land	17	20,000	
Office Equipment	18	1,800	
Accounts Payable	21		900
Unearned Rent	23		360
Chris Clark, Capital	31		25,000
Chris Clark, Drawing	32	4,000	
Fees Earned	41		16,340
Wages Expense	51	4,275	
Supplies Expense	52	800	
Rent Expense	53	1,600	
Utilities Expense	54	985	
Miscellaneous Expense	59	455	
		42,600	42,600

Link to Apple — Recently, **Apple** reported $17.5 billion in accounts receivable.

Link to Apple — Recently, **Apple** reported $30.2 billion of accounts payable and over $11 billion of unearned revenue.

Errors Affecting the Trial Balance

If the trial balance totals are not equal, an error has occurred. In this case, the error must be found and corrected. A method useful in discovering errors is as follows:

1. If the difference between the Debit and Credit column totals is 10, 100, or 1,000, an error in addition may have occurred. In this case, re-add the trial balance column totals. If the error still exists, recompute the account balances.
2. If the difference between the Debit and Credit column totals can be evenly divisible by 2, the error may be due to the entering of a debit balance as a credit balance, or vice versa. In this case, review the trial balance for account balances of one-half the difference that may have been entered in the wrong column. For example, if the Debit column total is $20,640 and the Credit column total is $20,236, the difference of $404 ($20,640 − $20,236) may be due to a credit account balance of $202 that was entered as a debit account balance.

[4] The adjusted trial balance will be discussed in Chapter 3 and the post-closing trial balance in Chapter 4.

3. If the difference between the Debit and Credit column totals is evenly divisible by 9, trace the account balances back to the ledger to see if an account balance was incorrectly copied from the ledger. Two common types of copying errors are transpositions and slides. A **transposition** occurs when the order of the digits is copied incorrectly, such as writing $542 as $452 or $524. In a **slide**, the entire number is copied incorrectly one or more spaces to the right or the left, such as writing $542.00 as $54.20 or $5,420.00. In both cases, the resulting error will be evenly divisible by 9.
4. If the difference between the Debit and Credit column totals is not evenly divisible by 2 or 9, review the ledger to see if an account balance in the amount of the error has been omitted from the trial balance. If the error is not discovered, review the journal postings to see if a posting of a debit or credit may have been omitted.
5. If an error is not discovered by the preceding steps, the accounting process must be retraced, beginning with the last journal entry.

The trial balance does not provide complete proof of the accuracy of the ledger. It indicates only that the debits and the credits are equal. This proof is of value, however, because errors often affect the equality of debits and credits.

Example Exercise 2-6 Errors Affecting the Trial Balance   Obj. 4

For each of the following errors, considered individually, indicate whether the error would cause the trial balance totals to be unequal. If the error would cause the trial balance totals to be unequal, indicate whether the debit or credit total is higher and by how much.

a. Payment of a cash withdrawal of $5,600 was journalized and posted as a debit of $6,500 to Salary Expense and a credit of $6,500 to Cash.
b. A fee of $2,850 earned from a client was debited to Accounts Receivable for $2,580 and credited to Fees Earned for $2,850.
c. A payment of $3,500 to a creditor was posted as a debit of $3,500 to Accounts Payable and a debit of $3,500 to Cash.

Follow My Example 2-6

a. The trial balance totals are equal since both the debit and credit entries were journalized and posted for $6,500.
b. The trial balance totals are unequal. The credit total is higher by $270 ($2,850 − $2,580).
c. The trial balance totals are unequal. The debit total is higher by $7,000 ($3,500 + $3,500).

Practice Exercises: PE 2-6A, PE 2-6B

Errors Not Affecting the Trial Balance

An error may occur that does not cause the trial balance totals to be unequal. Such an error may be discovered when preparing the trial balance or may be indicated by an unusual account balance. For example, a credit balance in the land account indicates an error has occurred. This is because a business cannot have "negative" land. When such errors are discovered, they should be corrected. If the error has already been journalized and posted to the ledger, a **correcting journal entry** is normally prepared.

To illustrate, assume that on May 5, a $12,500 purchase of office equipment on account was incorrectly journalized and posted as a debit to Supplies and a credit to Accounts Payable for $12,500. This posting of the incorrect entry is shown in the following T accounts:

Posting of Incorrect Journal Entry

Supplies	Accounts Payable
12,500	12,500

Before making a correcting journal entry, it is best to determine the debit(s) and credit(s) that should have been recorded. These are shown in the following T accounts:

Posting of Correct Journal Entry

Office Equipment		Accounts Payable
12,500		12,500

Comparing the two sets of T accounts shows that the incorrect debit to Supplies may be corrected by debiting Office Equipment for $12,500 and crediting Supplies for $12,500. The following correcting entry is then journalized and posted:

Entry to Correct Error:

May	31	Office Equipment	18	12,500	
		Supplies	14		12,500
		To correct erroneous debit to Supplies on May 5.			

Example Exercise 2-7 Correcting Entries *Obj. 4*

The following errors took place in journalizing and posting transactions:

a. A withdrawal of $6,000 by Cheri Ramey, owner of the business, was recorded as a debit to Office Salaries Expense and a credit to Cash.

b. Utilities Expense of $4,500 paid for the current month was recorded as a debit to Miscellaneous Expense and a credit to Accounts Payable.

Journalize the entries to correct the errors. Omit explanations.

Follow My Example 2-7

a.	Cheri Ramey, Drawing...............................	6,000	
	Office Salaries Expense........................		6,000
b.	Accounts Payable	4,500	
	Miscellaneous Expense........................		4,500
	Utilities Expense..................................	4,500	
	Cash		4,500

Note: The first entry in (b) reverses the incorrect entry, and the second entry records the correct entry. These two entries could also be combined into one entry; however, preparing two entries will make it easier for someone later to understand what happened and why the entries were necessary.

Practice Exercises: PE 2-7A, PE 2-7B

Obj. 5 Describe and illustrate the use of horizontal analysis in evaluating a company's performance and financial condition.

Financial Analysis and Interpretation: Horizontal Analysis

A single item in a financial statement, such as net income, is often useful in interpreting the financial performance of a company. However, a comparison with prior periods often makes the financial information even more useful. For example, comparing net income of the current period with the net income of the prior period will indicate whether the company's operating performance has improved.

In **horizontal analysis**, the amount of each item on a current financial statement is compared with the same item on an earlier statement. The increase or decrease in the *amount* of the item is computed together with the *percent* of increase or decrease.

When two statements are being compared, the earlier statement is used as the base for computing the amount and the percent of change.

To illustrate, the horizontal analysis of two income statements for J. Holmes, Attorney-at-Law follows:

J. Holmes, Attorney-at-Law
Income Statements
For the Years Ended December 31

	Year 2	Year 1	Increase (Decrease) Amount	Percent
Fees earned	$187,500	$150,000	$37,500	25.0%*
Operating expenses:				
Wages expense	$ 60,000	$ 45,000	$15,000	33.3
Rent expense	15,000	12,000	3,000	25.0
Utilities expense	12,500	9,000	3,500	38.9
Supplies expense	2,700	3,000	(300)	(10.0)
Miscellaneous expense	2,300	1,800	500	27.8
Total operating expenses	$ 92,500	$ 70,800	$21,700	30.6
Net income	$ 95,000	$ 79,200	$15,800	19.9

*$37,500 ÷ $150,000

The horizontal analysis for J. Holmes, Attorney-at-Law, indicates both favorable and unfavorable changes. The increase in fees earned is a favorable change, as is the decrease in supplies expense. Unfavorable changes include the increase in wages expense, utilities expense, and miscellaneous expense. These expenses increased more than the increase in revenues, with total operating expenses increasing by 30.6%. Overall, net income increased by $15,800, or 19.9%, a favorable change.

The significance of the various increases and decreases in the revenue and expense items should be investigated to see if operations could be further improved. For example, the increase in utilities expense of 38.9% was the result of renting additional office space for use by a part-time law student in performing paralegal services. This explains the increase in rent expense of 25.0% and the increase in wages expense of 33.3%. The increase in revenues of 25.0% reflects the fees generated by the new paralegal.

The preceding example illustrates how horizontal analysis can be useful in interpreting and analyzing the income statement. Horizontal analyses can also be performed for the balance sheet, the statement of owner's equity, and the statement of cash flows.

To illustrate, horizontal analysis for two recent years of **Apple Inc.**'s statements of cash flows (in millions) follows:

Apple Inc.
Statements of Cash Flows

	Year 2	Year 1	Increase (Decrease) Amount	Percent
Cash flows from operating activities	$ 50,856	$ 37,529	$13,327	35.5%
Cash flows used for investing activities	(48,227)	(40,419)	(7,808)	(19.3)
Cash flows from financing activities	(1,698)	1,444	(3,142)	(217.6)
Net increase (decrease) in cash	$ 931	$ (1,446)	$ 2,377	164.4
Beginning of the year balance of cash	9,815	11,261	(1,446)	(12.8)
End of the year balance of cash	$ 10,746	$ 9,815	$ 931	9.5

The horizontal analysis of cash flows for Apple Inc. indicates an increase in cash flows from operating activities of 35.5%, which is a favorable change. At the same time, Apple increased the cash used in its investing activities by 19.3% and decreased the cash it received from financing activities by 217.6%. Overall, Apple had a 164.4% increase in cash for the year, which increased the end-of-the-year cash balance by 9.5%. In contrast, in the prior year, Apple decreased its ending cash balance, which is the beginning cash balance of the current year, by 12.8%.

Example Exercise 2-8 Horizontal Analysis — Obj. 5

Two income statements for McCorkle Company follow:

McCorkle Company
Income Statements
For the Years Ended December 31

	2019	2018
Fees earned	$210,000	$175,000
Operating expenses	172,500	150,000
Net income	$ 37,500	$ 25,000

Prepare a horizontal analysis of McCorkle Company's income statements.

Follow My Example 2-8

McCorkle Company
Income Statements
For the Years Ended December 31

	2019	2018	Increase (Decrease) Amount	Percent
Fees earned	$210,000	$175,000	$35,000	20%
Operating expenses	172,500	150,000	22,500	15
Net income	$ 37,500	$ 25,000	$12,500	50

Practice Exercises: PE 2-8A, PE 2-8B

At a Glance 2

Obj. 1 Describe the characteristics of an account and a chart of accounts.

Key Points The simplest form of an account, a T account, has three parts: (1) a title, which is the name of the item recorded in the account; (2) a left side, called the debit side; and (3) a right side, called the credit side. Periodically, the debits in an account are added, the credits in the account are added, and the balance of the account is determined.

The system of accounts that make up a ledger is called a chart of accounts.

Learning Outcomes	Example Exercises	Practice Exercises
• Record transactions in T accounts.		
• Determine the balance of a T account.		
• Prepare a chart of accounts for a proprietorship.		

Obj. 2 Describe and illustrate journalizing transactions using the double-entry accounting system.

Key Points Transactions are initially entered in a record called a journal. The rules of debit and credit for recording increases or decreases in accounts are shown in Exhibit 3. Each transaction is recorded so that the sum of the debits is always equal to the sum of the credits. The normal balance of an account is indicated by the side of the account (debit or credit) that receives the increases.

Learning Outcomes	Example Exercises	Practice Exercises
• Indicate the normal balance of an account.	EE2-1	PE2-1A, 2-1B
• Journalize transactions using the rules of debit and credit.	EE2-2	PE2-2A, 2-2B

Obj. 3 Describe and illustrate the journalizing and posting of transactions to accounts.

Key Points Transactions are journalized and posted to the ledger using the rules of debit and credit. The debits and credits for each journal entry are posted to the accounts in the order in which they occur in the journal.

Learning Outcomes	Example Exercises	Practice Exercises
• Journalize transactions using the rules of debit and credit.	EE2-3	PE2-3A, 2-3B
• Given other account data, determine the missing amount of an account entry.	EE2-4	PE2-4A, 2-4B
• Post journal entries to a standard account.	EE2-5	PE2-5A, 2-5B
• Post journal entries to a T account.		

Obj. 4 Prepare an unadjusted trial balance and explain how it can be used to discover errors.

Key Points A trial balance is prepared by listing the accounts from the ledger and their balances. The totals of the Debit column and Credit column of the trial balance must be equal. If the two totals are not equal, an error has occurred. Errors may occur even though the trial balance totals are equal. Such errors may require a correcting journal entry.

Learning Outcomes	Example Exercises	Practice Exercises
• Prepare an unadjusted trial balance.	EE2-6	PE2-6A, 2-6B
• Discover errors that cause unequal totals in the trial balance.		
• Prepare correcting journal entries for various errors.	EE2-7	PE2-7A, 2-7B

Obj. 5 Describe and illustrate the use of horizontal analysis in evaluating a company's performance and financial condition.

Key Points In horizontal analysis, the amount of each item on a current financial statement is compared with the same item on an earlier statement. The increase or decrease in the *amount* of the item is computed, together with the *percent* of increase or decrease. When two statements are being compared, the earlier statement is used as the base for computing the amount and the percent of change.

Learning Outcomes	Example Exercises	Practice Exercises
• Describe horizontal analysis.		
• Prepare a horizontal analysis report of a financial statement.	EE2-8	PE2-8A, 2-8B

Illustrative Problem

J. F. Outz, M.D., has been practicing as a cardiologist for three years. During April 2018, Outz completed the following transactions in her practice of cardiology:

Apr. 1. Paid office rent for April, $800.

3. Purchased equipment on account, $2,100.

5. Received cash on account from patients, $3,150.

8. Purchased X-ray film and other supplies on account, $245.

9. One of the items of equipment purchased on April 3 was defective. It was returned with the permission of the supplier, who agreed to reduce the account for the amount charged for the item, $325.

12. Paid cash to creditors on account, $1,250.

17. Paid cash for renewal of a six-month property insurance policy, $370.

20. Discovered that the balances of the cash account and the accounts payable account as of April 1 were overstated by $200. A payment of that amount to a creditor in March had not been recorded. Journalize the $200 payment as of April 20.

24. Paid cash for laboratory analysis, $545.

27. Dr. Outz withdrew $1,250 for personal use.

30. Recorded the cash received in payment of services to patients during April, $1,720.

30. Paid salaries of receptionist and nurses, $1,725.

30. Paid various utility expenses, $360.

30. Recorded fees charged to patients on account for services performed in April, $5,145.

30. Paid miscellaneous expenses, $132.

Outz's account titles, numbers, and balances as of April 1 (all normal balances) are listed as follows: Cash, 11, $4,123; Accounts Receivable, 12, $6,725; Supplies, 13, $290; Prepaid Insurance, 14, $465; Equipment, 18, $19,745; Accounts Payable, 22, $765; J. F. Outz, Capital, 31, $30,583; J. F. Outz, Drawing, 32, $0; Professional Fees, 41, $0; Salary Expense, 51, $0; Rent Expense, 53, $0; Laboratory Expense, 55, $0; Utilities Expense, 56, $0; Miscellaneous Expense, 59, $0.

Instructions

1. Open a ledger of standard four-column accounts for Dr. Outz as of April 1. Enter the balances in the appropriate balance columns and place a check mark (✓) in the Posting Reference column. (*Hint:* Verify the equality of the debit and credit balances in the ledger before proceeding with the next instruction.)

2. Journalize each transaction in a two-column journal.

3. Post the journal to the ledger, extending the balances to the appropriate balance columns after each posting.

4. Prepare an unadjusted trial balance as of April 30.

Chapter 2 Analyzing Transactions

Solution 1., 2., and 3.

Journal — Page 27

Date	Description	Post. Ref.	Debit	Credit
2018				
Apr. 1	Rent Expense	53	800	
	Cash	11		800
	Paid office rent for April.			
3	Equipment	18	2,100	
	Accounts Payable	22		2,100
	Purchased equipment on account.			
5	Cash	11	3,150	
	Accounts Receivable	12		3,150
	Received cash on account.			
8	Supplies	13	245	
	Accounts Payable	22		245
	Purchased supplies.			
9	Accounts Payable	22	325	
	Equipment	18		325
	Returned defective equipment.			
12	Accounts Payable	22	1,250	
	Cash	11		1,250
	Paid creditors on account.			
17	Prepaid Insurance	14	370	
	Cash	11		370
	Renewed six-month property policy.			
20	Accounts Payable	22	200	
	Cash	11		200
	Recorded March payment to creditor.			

Journal — Page 28

Date	Description	Post. Ref.	Debit	Credit
2018				
Apr. 24	Laboratory Expense	55	545	
	Cash	11		545
	Paid for laboratory analysis.			
27	J. F. Outz, Drawing	32	1,250	
	Cash	11		1,250
	J. F. Outz withdrew cash for personal use.			
30	Cash	11	1,720	
	Professional Fees	41		1,720
	Received fees from patients.			
30	Salary Expense	51	1,725	
	Cash	11		1,725
	Paid salaries.			
30	Utilities Expense	56	360	
	Cash	11		360
	Paid utilities.			
30	Accounts Receivable	12	5,145	
	Professional Fees	41		5,145
	Recorded fees earned on account.			
30	Miscellaneous Expense	59	132	
	Cash	11		132
	Paid expenses.			

Account: Cash — Account No. 11

Date	Item	Post. Ref.	Debit	Credit	Balance Debit	Balance Credit
2018						
Apr. 1	Balance	✓			4,123	
1		27		800	3,323	
5		27	3,150		6,473	
12		27		1,250	5,223	
17		27		370	4,853	
20		27		200	4,653	
24		28		545	4,108	
27		28		1,250	2,858	
30		28	1,720		4,578	
30		28		1,725	2,853	
30		28		360	2,493	
30		28		132	2,361	

Account: Accounts Receivable — Account No. 12

Date	Item	Post. Ref.	Debit	Credit	Balance Debit	Balance Credit
2018						
Apr. 1	Balance	✓			6,725	
5		27		3,150	3,575	
30		28	5,145		8,720	

Account: Supplies — Account No. 13

Date	Item	Post. Ref.	Debit	Credit	Balance Debit	Balance Credit
2018						
Apr. 1	Balance	✓			290	
8		27	245		535	

(Continued)

Account Prepaid Insurance — Account No. 14

Date	Item	Post. Ref.	Debit	Credit	Balance Debit	Balance Credit
2018 Apr. 1	Balance	✓			465	
17		27	370		835	

Account Equipment — Account No. 18

Date	Item	Post. Ref.	Debit	Credit	Balance Debit	Balance Credit
2018 Apr. 1	Balance	✓			19,745	
3		27	2,100		21,845	
9		27		325	21,520	

Account Accounts Payable — Account No. 22

Date	Item	Post. Ref.	Debit	Credit	Balance Debit	Balance Credit
2018 Apr. 1	Balance	✓				765
3		27		2,100		2,865
8		27		245		3,110
9		27	325			2,785
12		27	1,250			1,535
20		27	200			1,335

Account J. F. Outz, Capital — Account No. 31

Date	Item	Post. Ref.	Debit	Credit	Balance Debit	Balance Credit
2018 Apr. 1	Balance	✓				30,583

Account J. F. Qutz, Drawing — Account No. 32

Date	Item	Post. Ref.	Debit	Credit	Balance Debit	Balance Credit
2018 Apr. 27		28	1,250		1,250	

Account Professional Fees — Account No. 41

Date	Item	Post. Ref.	Debit	Credit	Balance Debit	Balance Credit
2018 Apr. 30		28		1,720		1,720
30		28		5,145		6,865

Account Salary Expense — Account No. 51

Date	Item	Post. Ref.	Debit	Credit	Balance Debit	Balance Credit
2018 Apr. 30		28	1,725		1,725	

Account Rent Expense — Account No. 53

Date	Item	Post. Ref.	Debit	Credit	Balance Debit	Balance Credit
2018 Apr. 1		27	800		800	

Account Laboratory Expense — Account No. 55

Date	Item	Post. Ref.	Debit	Credit	Balance Debit	Balance Credit
2018 Apr. 24		28	545		545	

Account Utilities Expense — Account No. 56

Date	Item	Post. Ref.	Debit	Credit	Balance Debit	Balance Credit
2018 Apr. 30		28	360		360	

Account Miscellaneous Expense — Account No. 59

Date	Item	Post. Ref.	Debit	Credit	Balance Debit	Balance Credit
2018 Apr. 30		28	132		132	

4.

J. F. Outz, M.D.
Unadjusted Trial Balance
April 30, 2018

	Account No.	Debit Balances	Credit Balances
Cash	11	2,361	
Accounts Receivable	12	8,720	
Supplies	13	535	
Prepaid Insurance	14	835	
Equipment	18	21,520	
Accounts Payable	22		1,335
J. F. Outz, Capital	31		30,583
J. F. Outz, Drawing	32	1,250	
Professional Fees	41		6,865
Salary Expense	51	1,725	
Rent Expense	53	800	
Laboratory Expense	55	545	
Utilities Expense	56	360	
Miscellaneous Expense	59	132	
		38,783	38,783

Key Terms

account (59)
account receivable (72)
assets (61)
balance of the account (60)
capital account (61)
chart of accounts (61)
correcting journal entry (79)
credit (60)
debit (60)
double-entry accounting system (62)
drawing (61)

expenses (62)
four-column account (68)
horizontal analysis (80)
journal (64)
journal entry (65)
journalizing (65)
ledger (61)
liabilities (61)
normal balance of an account (63)
owner's equity (61)
posting (68)

revenues (61)
rules of debit and credit (62)
slide (79)
T account (59)
transposition (79)
trial balance (77)
two-column journal (64)
unadjusted trial balance (78)
unearned revenue (70)

Discussion Questions

1. What is the difference between an account and a ledger?

2. Do the terms *debit* and *credit* signify increase or decrease, or can they signify either? Explain.

3. McIntyre Company adheres to a policy of depositing all cash receipts in a bank account and making all payments by check. The cash account as of December 31 has a credit balance of $1,850, and there is no undeposited cash on hand. (a) Assuming that no errors occurred during journalizing or posting, what caused this unusual balance? (b) Is the $1,850 credit balance in the cash account an asset, a liability, owner's equity, a revenue, or an expense?

4. eCatalog Services Company performed services in October for a specific customer for a fee of $7,890. Payment was received the following November.

(a) Was the revenue earned in October or November? (b) What accounts should be debited and credited in (1) October and (2) November?

5. If the two totals of a trial balance are equal, does it mean that there are no errors in the accounting records? Explain.

6. Assume that a trial balance is prepared with an account balance of $8,900 listed as $9,800 and an account balance of $1,000 listed as $100. Identify the transposition and the slide.

7. Assume that when a purchase of supplies of $2,650 for cash was recorded, both the debit and the credit were journalized and posted as $2,560. (a) Would this error cause the trial balance to be out of balance? (b) Would the trial balance be out of balance if the $2,650 entry had been journalized correctly but the credit to Cash had been posted as $2,560?

8. Assume that Muscular Consulting erroneously recorded the payment of $7,500 of owner withdrawals as a debit to Salary Expense. (a) How would this error affect the equality of the trial balance? (b) How would this error affect the income statement, statement of owner's equity, and balance sheet?

9. Assume that Sunshine Realty Co. borrowed $300,000 from Columbia First Bank and Trust. In recording the transaction, Sunshine erroneously recorded the receipt as a debit to Cash, $300,000, and a credit to Fees Earned, $300,000. (a) How would this error affect the equality of the trial balance? (b) How would this error affect the income statement, statement of owner's equity, and balance sheet?

10. Checking accounts are a common form of deposits for banks. Assume that Surety Storage has a checking account at Ada Savings Bank. What type of account (asset, liability, owner's equity, revenue, expense, drawing) does the account balance of $11,375 represent from the viewpoint of (a) Surety Storage and (b) Ada Savings Bank?

Practice Exercises

Example Exercises

EE 2-1 p. 64

PE 2-1A Rules of debit and credit and normal balances   OBJ. 2

State for each account whether it is likely to have (a) debit entries only, (b) credit entries only, or (c) both debit and credit entries. Also indicate its normal balance.

1. Accounts Receivable
2. Commissions Earned
3. Heidi Schmidt, Capital
4. Rent Expense
5. Rent Revenue
6. Wages Payable

EE 2-1 p. 64

PE 2-1B Rules of debit and credit and normal balances   OBJ. 2

State for each account whether it is likely to have (a) debit entries only, (b) credit entries only, or (c) both debit and credit entries. Also indicate its normal balance.

1. Accounts Payable
2. Cash
3. Del Robinson, Drawing
4. Miscellaneous Expense
5. Insurance Expense
6. Fees Earned

EE 2-2 p. 68

PE 2-2A Journal entry for asset purchase   OBJ. 2

Prepare a journal entry for the purchase of office equipment on February 19 for $18,500 paying $4,500 cash and the remainder on account.

EE 2-2 p. 68

PE 2-2B Journal entry for asset purchase   OBJ. 2

Prepare a journal entry for the purchase of office supplies on September 30 for $2,500, paying $800 cash and the remainder on account.

Chapter 2 Analyzing Transactions 89

EE 2-3 p. 73 **PE 2-3A** **Journal entry for fees earned** OBJ. 3

Prepare a journal entry on April 30 for fees earned on account, $11,250.

EE 2-3 p. 73 **PE 2-3B** **Journal entry for fees earned** OBJ. 3

Prepare a journal entry on August 13 for cash received for services rendered, $9,000.

EE 2-4 p. 75 **PE 2-4A** **Journal entry for owner's withdrawal** OBJ. 3

Prepare a journal entry on December 23 for the withdrawal of $20,000 by Steve Buckley for personal use.

EE 2-4 p. 75 **PE 2-4B** **Journal entry for owner's withdrawal** OBJ. 3

Prepare a journal entry on June 30 for the withdrawal of $11,500 by Dawn Pierce for personal use.

EE 2-5 p. 77 **PE 2-5A** **Missing amount from an account** OBJ. 3

On July 1, the cash account balance was $37,450. During July, cash payments totaled $115,860 and the July 31 balance was $29,600. Determine the cash receipts during July.

EE 2-5 p. 77 **PE 2-5B** **Missing amount from an account** OBJ. 3

On August 1, the supplies account balance was $1,025. During August, supplies of $3,110 were purchased, and $1,324 of supplies were on hand as of August 31. Determine supplies expense for August.

EE 2-6 p. 79 **PE 2-6A** **Trial balance errors** OBJ. 4

For each of the following errors, considered individually, indicate whether the error would cause the trial balance totals to be unequal. If the error would cause the trial balance totals to be unequal, indicate whether the debit or credit total is higher and by how much.

a. The payment of an insurance premium of $5,400 for a three-year policy was debited to Prepaid Insurance for $5,400 and credited to Cash for $4,500.

b. A payment of $270 on account was debited to Accounts Payable for $720 and credited to Cash for $720.

c. A purchase of supplies on account for $1,600 was debited to Supplies for $1,600 and debited to Accounts Payable for $1,600.

EE 2-6 p. 79 **PE 2-6B** **Trial balance errors** OBJ. 4

For each of the following errors, considered individually, indicate whether the error would cause the trial balance totals to be unequal. If the error would cause the trial balance totals to be unequal, indicate whether the debit or credit total is higher and by how much.

a. The payment of cash for the purchase of office equipment of $12,900 was debited to Land for $12,900 and credited to Cash for $12,900.

b. The payment of $1,840 on account was debited to Accounts Payable for $184 and credited to Cash for $1,840.

c. The receipt of cash on account of $3,800 was recorded as a debit to Cash for $8,300 and a credit to Accounts Receivable for $3,800.

90 Chapter 2 Analyzing Transactions

EE 2-7 p. 80

PE 2-7A Correcting entries OBJ. 4

The following errors took place in journalizing and posting transactions:

a. Rent expense of $4,650 paid for the current month was recorded as a debit to Miscellaneous Expense and a credit to Rent Expense.

b. The payment of $3,700 from a customer on account was recorded as a debit to Cash and a credit to Accounts Payable.

Journalize the entries to correct the errors. Omit explanations.

EE 2-7 p. 80

PE 2-7B Correcting entries OBJ. 4

The following errors took place in journalizing and posting transactions:

a. The receipt of $8,400 for services rendered was recorded as a debit to Accounts Receivable and a credit to Fees Earned.

b. The purchase of supplies of $2,500 on account was recorded as a debit to Office Equipment and a credit to Supplies.

Journalize the entries to correct the errors. Omit explanations.

EE 2-8 p. 82

PE 2-8A Horizontal analysis OBJ. 5

Two income statements for Fuller Company follow:

Fuller Company
Income Statements
For Years Ended December 31

	2019	2018
Fees earned	$680,000	$850,000
Operating expenses	541,875	637,500
Net income	$138,125	$212,500

Prepare a horizontal analysis of Fuller Company's income statements.

EE 2-8 p. 82

PE 2-8B Horizontal analysis OBJ. 5

Two income statements for Paragon Company follow:

Paragon Company
Income Statements
For Years Ended December 31

	2019	2018
Fees earned	$1,416,000	$1,200,000
Operating expenses	1,044,000	900,000
Net income	$ 372,000	$ 300,000

Prepare a horizontal analysis of Paragon Company's income statements.

Exercises

EX 2-1 Chart of accounts OBJ. 1

The following accounts appeared in recent financial statements of **Delta Air Lines**:

Accounts Payable	Flight Equipment
Advanced Payments for Equipment	Frequent Flyer (Obligations)
Air Traffic Liability	Fuel Inventory
Aircraft Fuel (Expense)	Landing Fees (Expense)
Aircraft Maintenance (Expense)	Parts and Supplies
Aircraft Rent (Expense)	Passenger Commissions (Expense)
Cargo Revenue	Passenger Revenue
Cash	Prepaid Expenses
Contract Carrier Arrangements (Expense)	Taxes Payable

Identify each account as either a balance sheet account or an income statement account. For each balance sheet account, identify it as an asset, a liability, or owner's equity. For each income statement account, identify it as a revenue or an expense.

EX 2-2 Chart of accounts OBJ. 1

Oak Interiors is owned and operated by Fred Biggs, an interior decorator. In the ledger of Oak Interiors, the first digit of the account number indicates its major account classification (1—assets, 2—liabilities, 3—owner's equity, 4—revenues, 5—expenses). The second digit of the account number indicates the specific account within each of the preceding major account classifications.

Match each account number with its most likely account in the list that follows. The account numbers are 11, 12, 13, 21, 31, 32, 41, 51, 52, and 53.

Accounts Payable	Fred Biggs, Drawing
Accounts Receivable	Land
Cash	Miscellaneous Expense
Fees Earned	Supplies Expense
Fred Biggs, Capital	Wages Expense

EX 2-3 Chart of accounts OBJ. 1

Outdoor Leadership School is a newly organized business that teaches people how to inspire and influence others. The list of accounts to be opened in the general ledger is as follows:

Accounts Payable	Miscellaneous Expense
Accounts Receivable	Prepaid Insurance
Cash	Rent Expense
Equipment	Supplies
Fees Earned	Supplies Expense
Lorri Ross, Capital	Unearned Rent
Lorri Ross, Drawing	Wages Expense

List the accounts in the order in which they should appear in the ledger of Outdoor Leadership School and assign account numbers. Each account number is to have two digits: the first digit is to indicate the major classification (1 for assets, for example), and the second digit is to identify the specific account within each major classification (11 for Cash, for example).

EX 2-4 Rules of debit and credit OBJ. 1, 2

The following table summarizes the rules of debit and credit. For each of the items (a) through (l), indicate whether the proper answer is a debit or a credit.

	Increase	Decrease	Normal Balance
Balance sheet accounts:			
Asset	(a)	(b)	(c)
Liability	(d)	Debit	(e)
Owner's equity:			
Capital	Credit	(f)	Credit
Drawing	(g)	(h)	(i)
Income statement accounts:			
Revenue	(j)	(k)	Credit
Expense	(l)	Credit	Debit

EX 2-5 Normal entries for accounts OBJ. 2

During the month, Midwest Labs Co. has a substantial number of transactions affecting each of the following accounts. State for each account whether it is likely to have (a) debit entries only, (b) credit entries only, or (c) both debit and credit entries.

1. Accounts Payable
2. Accounts Receivable
3. Cash
4. Fees Earned
5. Insurance Expense
6. Jerri Holt, Drawing
7. Utilities Expense

EX 2-6 Normal balances of accounts OBJ. 1, 2

Identify each of the following accounts of Dispatch Services Co. as asset, liability, owner's equity, revenue, or expense and state in each case whether the normal balance is a debit or a credit:

a. Accounts Payable
b. Accounts Receivable
c. Ashley Griffin, Capital
d. Ashley Griffin, Drawing
e. Cash
f. Fees Earned
g. Office Equipment
h. Rent Expense
i. Supplies
j. Wages Expense

EX 2-7 Transactions OBJ. 2

Concrete Consulting Co. has the following accounts in its ledger: Cash; Accounts Receivable; Supplies; Office Equipment; Accounts Payable; Jason Payne, Capital; Jason Payne, Drawing; Fees Earned; Rent Expense; Advertising Expense; Utilities Expense; Miscellaneous Expense.

Journalize the following selected transactions for October 2019 in a two-column journal. Journal entry explanations may be omitted.

Oct. 1. Paid rent for the month, $3,600.
  3. Paid advertising expense, $1,200.
  5. Paid cash for supplies, $750.
  6. Purchased office equipment on account, $8,000.
  10. Received cash from customers on account, $14,800.
  15. Paid creditors on account, $7,110.
  27. Paid cash for miscellaneous expenses, $400.
  30. Paid telephone bill (utility expense) for the month, $250.
  31. Fees earned and billed to customers for the month, $33,100.
  31. Paid electricity bill (utility expense) for the month, $1,050.
  31. Withdrew cash for personal use, $2,500.

EX 2-8 Journalizing and posting OBJ. 2, 3

On September 18, 2019, Afton Company purchased $2,475 of supplies on account. In Afton Company's chart of accounts, the supplies account is No. 15, and the accounts payable account is No. 21.

a. Journalize the September 18, 2019, transaction on page 87 of Afton Company's two-column journal. Include an explanation of the entry.
b. Prepare a four-column account for Supplies. Enter a debit balance of $840 as of September 1, 2019. Place a check mark (✓) in the Posting Reference column.
c. Prepare a four-column account for Accounts Payable. Enter a credit balance of $10,900 as of September 1, 2019. Place a check mark (✓) in the Posting Reference column.
d. Post the September 18, 2019, transaction to the accounts.
e. Do the rules of debit and credit apply to all companies?

EX 2-9 Transactions and T accounts OBJ. 2, 3

The following selected transactions were completed during August of the current year:

1. Billed customers for fees earned, $73,900.
2. Purchased supplies on account, $1,960.
3. Received cash from customers on account, $62,770.
4. Paid creditors on account, $820.

a. Journalize these transactions in a two-column journal, using the appropriate number to identify the transactions. Journal entry explanations may be omitted.

b. Post the entries prepared in (a) to the following T accounts: Cash, Supplies, Accounts Receivable, Accounts Payable, Fees Earned. To the left of each amount posted in the accounts, place the appropriate number to identify the transactions.

c. Assume that the unadjusted trial balance on August 31 shows a credit balance for Accounts Receivable. Does this credit balance mean that an error has occurred?

EX 2-10 Cash account balance   OBJ. 1, 2, 3

During the month, Warwick Co. received $515,000 in cash and paid out $375,000 in cash.

a. Do the data indicate that Warwick Co. had net income of $140,000 during the month? Explain.

b. If the balance of the cash account is $200,000 at the end of the month, what was the cash balance at the beginning of the month?

EX 2-11 Account balances   OBJ. 1, 2, 3

✓ c. $238,050

a. During February, $186,500 was paid to creditors on account, and purchases on account were $201,400. Assuming that the February 28 balance of Accounts Payable was $59,900, determine the account balance on February 1.

b. On October 1, the accounts receivable account balance was $115,800. During October, $449,600 was collected from customers on account. Assuming that the October 31 balance was $130,770, determine the fees billed to customers on account during October.

c. On April 1, the cash account balance was $46,220. During April, cash receipts totaled $248,600 and the April 30 balance was $56,770. Determine the cash payments made during April.

EX 2-12 Capital account balance   OBJ. 1, 2

As of January 1, Terrace Waters, Capital had a credit balance of $500,000. During the year, withdrawals totaled $10,000, and the business incurred a net loss of $320,000.

a. Compute the balance of Terrace Waters, Capital as of the end of the year.

b. Assuming that there have been no recording errors, will the balance sheet prepared at December 31 balance? Explain.

EX 2-13 Identifying transactions   OBJ. 1, 2

National Park Tours Co. is a travel agency. The nine transactions recorded by National Park Tours during May 2019, its first month of operations, are indicated in the following T accounts:

Cash				Equipment		Beth Worley, Drawing	
(1) 75,000	(2) 900		(3) 8,000		(9) 2,500	
(7) 8,150	(3) 1,600					
	(4) 6,280					
	(6) 2,700					
	(9) 2,500					

Accounts Receivable			Accounts Payable			Fees Earned	
(5) 12,300	(7) 8,150	(6) 2,700	(3) 6,400		(5) 12,300

Supplies			Beth Worley, Capital		Operating Expenses	
(2) 900	(8) 660		(1) 75,000	(4) 6,280	
				(8) 660	

(Continued)

Indicate for each debit and each credit (a) whether an asset, liability, owner's equity, drawing, revenue, or expense account was affected and (b) whether the account was increased (+) or decreased (−). Present your answers in the following form, with transaction (1) given as an example:

	Account Debited		Account Credited	
Transaction	Type	Effect	Type	Effect
(1)	asset	+	owner's equity	+

EX 2-14 Journal entries OBJ. 1, 2

Based upon the T accounts in Exercise 2-13, prepare the nine journal entries from which the postings were made. Journal entry explanations may be omitted.

EX 2-15 Trial balance OBJ. 4

Based upon the data presented in Exercise 2-13, (a) prepare an unadjusted trial balance, listing the accounts in their proper order. (b) Based upon the unadjusted trial balance, determine the net income or net loss.

✔ (a) Total of Debit column: $91,000

EX 2-16 Trial balance OBJ. 4

The accounts in the ledger of Hickory Furniture Company as of December 31, 2019, are listed in alphabetical order as follows. All accounts have normal balances. The balance of the cash account has been intentionally omitted.

✔ Total of Credit column: $925,000

Accounts Payable	$ 42,770	Notes Payable	$ 50,000
Accounts Receivable	116,900	Prepaid Insurance	21,600
Cash	?	Rent Expense	48,000
Elaine Wells, Capital	75,000	Supplies	4,275
Elaine Wells, Drawing	24,000	Supplies Expense	6,255
Fees Earned	745,230	Unearned Rent	12,000
Insurance Expense	3,600	Utilities Expense	26,850
Land	50,000	Wages Expense	580,700
Miscellaneous Expense	9,500		

Prepare an unadjusted trial balance, listing the accounts in their normal order and inserting the missing figure for cash.

EX 2-17 Effect of errors on trial balance OBJ. 4

Indicate which of the following errors, each considered individually, would cause the trial balance totals to be unequal:

a. A fee of $21,000 earned and due from a client was not debited to Accounts Receivable or credited to a revenue account, because the cash had not been received.

b. A receipt of $11,300 from an account receivable was journalized and posted as a debit of $11,300 to Cash and a credit of $11,300 to Fees Earned.

c. A payment of $4,950 to a creditor was posted as a debit of $4,950 to Accounts Payable and a debit of $4,950 to Cash.

d. A payment of $5,000 for equipment purchased was posted as a debit of $500 to Equipment and a credit of $500 to Cash.

e. Payment of a cash withdrawal of $19,000 was journalized and posted as a debit of $1,900 to Salary Expense and a credit of $19,000 to Cash.

Indicate which of the preceding errors would require a correcting entry.

EX 2-18 Errors in trial balance OBJ. 4

✔ Total of Credit column: $525,000

The following preliminary unadjusted trial balance of Ranger Co., a sports ticket agency, does not balance:

Ranger Co.
Unadjusted Trial Balance
August 31, 2019

	Debit Balances	Credit Balances
Cash	77,600	
Accounts Receivable	37,750	
Prepaid Insurance		12,000
Equipment	19,000	
Accounts Payable		29,100
Unearned Rent		10,800
Carmen Meeks, Capital	110,000	
Carmen Meeks, Drawing	13,000	
Fees Earned		385,000
Wages Expense		213,000
Advertising Expense	16,350	
Miscellaneous Expense		18,400
	273,700	668,300

When the ledger and other records are reviewed, you discover the following: (1) the debits and credits in the cash account total $77,600 and $62,100, respectively; (2) a billing of $9,000 to a customer on account was not posted to the accounts receivable account; (3) a payment of $4,500 made to a creditor on account was not posted to the accounts payable account; (4) the balance of the unearned rent account is $5,400; (5) the correct balance of the equipment account is $190,000; and (6) each account has a normal balance.

Prepare a corrected unadjusted trial balance.

EX 2-19 Effect of errors on trial balance OBJ. 4

The following errors occurred in posting from a two-column journal:

1. A credit of $6,000 to Accounts Payable was not posted.
2. An entry debiting Accounts Receivable and crediting Fees Earned for $5,300 was not posted.
3. A debit of $2,700 to Accounts Payable was posted as a credit.
4. A debit of $480 to Supplies was posted twice.
5. A debit of $3,600 to Cash was posted to Miscellaneous Expense.
6. A credit of $780 to Cash was posted as $870.
7. A debit of $12,620 to Wages Expense was posted as $12,260.

Considering each case individually (i.e., assuming that no other errors had occurred), indicate (a) by "yes" or "no" whether the trial balance would be out of balance; (b) if answer to (a) is "yes," the amount by which the trial balance totals would differ; and (c) whether the Debit or Credit column of the trial balance would have the larger total. Answers should be presented in the following form, with error (1) given as an example:

Error	(a) Out of Balance	(b) Difference	(c) Larger Total
1.	yes	$6,000	debit

Chapter 2 Analyzing Transactions

✔ Total of Credit column: $1,040,000

EX 2-20 Errors in trial balance   OBJ. 4

Identify the errors in the following trial balance. All accounts have normal balances.

Mascot Co.
Unadjusted Trial Balance
For the Month Ending July 31, 2019

	Account No.	Debit Balances	Credit Balances
Cash	11	36,000	
Accounts Receivable	12		112,600
Prepaid Insurance	13	18,000	
Equipment	14	375,000	
Accounts Payable	21	53,300	
Salaries Payable	22		7,500
Samuel Parson, Capital	31		297,200
Samuel Parson, Drawing	32		17,000
Fees Earned	41		682,000
Salary Expense	51	396,800	
Advertising Expense	52		73,000
Miscellaneous Expense	59	11,600	
		1,189,300	1,189,300

EX 2-21 Entries to correct errors   OBJ. 4

The following errors took place in journalizing and posting transactions:

a. Insurance of $18,000 paid for the current year was recorded as a debit to Insurance Expense and a credit to Prepaid Insurance.

b. A withdrawal of $10,000 by Brian Phillips, owner of the business, was recorded as a debit to Wages Expense and a credit to Cash.

Journalize the entries to correct the errors. Omit explanations.

EX 2-22 Entries to correct errors   OBJ. 4

The following errors took place in journalizing and posting transactions:

a. Cash of $8,800 received on account was recorded as a debit to Fees Earned and a credit to Cash.

b. A $1,760 purchase of supplies for cash was recorded as a debit to Supplies Expense and a credit to Accounts Payable.

Journalize the entries to correct the errors. Omit explanations.

EX 2-23 Horizontal analysis of income statement   OBJ. 5

✔ a. 1. 1.9% increase

The following data (in millions) are taken from the financial statements of **Target Corporation**:

	Recent Year	Prior Year
Revenue	$72,618	$71,279
Operating expenses	68,083	66,109
Operating income	$ 4,535	$ 5,170

a. For Target Corporation, determine the amount of change in millions and the percent of change (round to one decimal place) from the prior year to the recent year for:

1. Revenue
2. Operating expenses
3. Operating income

b. What conclusions can you draw from your analysis of the revenue and the total operating expenses?

EX 2-24 Horizontal analysis of income statement   OBJ. 5

✓ a. 2. 2.9% increase

The following data (in millions) were taken from the financial statements of **Costco Wholesale Corporation**:

	Recent Year	Prior Year
Revenue	$116,199	$112,640
Operating expenses	112,575	109,420
Operating income	$ 3,624	$ 3,220

a. For Costco, determine the amount of change in millions and the percent of change (round to one decimal place) from the prior year to the recent year for:
   1. Revenue
   2. Operating expenses
   3. Operating income

b. ✏️ Comment on the results of your horizontal analysis in part (a).

c. Based upon Exercise 2-23, compare and comment on the operating results of Target and Costco for the recent year.

Problems: Series A

PR 2-1A Entries into T accounts and trial balance   OBJ. 1, 2, 3, 4

✓ 3. Total of Debit column: $93,890

Connie Young, an architect, opened an office on October 1, 2019. During the month, she completed the following transactions connected with her professional practice:

a. Transferred cash from a personal bank account to an account to be used for the business, $36,000.
b. Paid October rent for office and workroom, $2,400.
c. Purchased used automobile for $32,800, paying $7,800 cash and giving a note payable for the remainder.
d. Purchased office and computer equipment on account, $9,000.
e. Paid cash for supplies, $2,150.
f. Paid cash for annual insurance policies, $4,000.
g. Received cash from client for plans delivered, $12,200.
h. Paid cash for miscellaneous expenses, $815.
i. Paid cash to creditors on account, $4,500.
j. Paid $5,000 on note payable.
k. Received invoice for blueprint service, due in November, $2,890.
l. Recorded fees earned on plans delivered, payment to be received in November, $18,300.
m. Paid salary of assistants, $6,450.
n. Paid gas, oil, and repairs on automobile for October, $1,020.

Instructions

1. Record these transactions directly in the following T accounts, without journalizing: Cash; Accounts Receivable; Supplies; Prepaid Insurance; Automobiles; Equipment; Accounts Payable; Notes Payable; Connie Young, Capital; Professional Fees; Salary Expense; Blueprint Expense; Rent Expense; Automobile Expense; Miscellaneous Expense. To the left of the amount entered in the accounts, place the appropriate letter to identify the transaction.
2. Determine account balances of the T accounts. Accounts containing a single entry only (such as Prepaid Insurance) do not need a balance.
3. Prepare an unadjusted trial balance for Connie Young, Architect, as of October 31, 2019.
4. Determine the net income or net loss for October.

Chapter 2 Analyzing Transactions

✔ 4. c. $3,550

PR 2-2A Journal entries and trial balance   OBJ. 1, 2, 3, 4

On January 1, 2019, Sharon Matthews established Tri-City Realty, which completed the following transactions during the month:

a. Sharon Matthews transferred cash from a personal bank account to an account to be used for the business, $40,000.
b. Paid rent on office and equipment for the month, $6,000.
c. Purchased supplies on account, $3,200.
d. Paid creditor on account, $1,750.
e. Earned fees, receiving cash, $18,250.
f. Paid automobile expenses (including rental charge) for month, $1,880, and miscellaneous expenses, $420.
g. Paid office salaries, $5,000.
h. Determined that the cost of supplies used was $1,400.
i. Withdrew cash for personal use, $2,000.

Instructions

1. Journalize entries for transactions (a) through (i), using the following account titles: Cash; Supplies; Accounts Payable; Sharon Matthews, Capital; Sharon Matthews, Drawing; Fees Earned; Rent Expense; Office Salaries Expense; Automobile Expense; Supplies Expense; Miscellaneous Expense. Explanations may be omitted.
2. Prepare T accounts, using the account titles in (1). Post the journal entries to these accounts, placing the appropriate letter to the left of each amount to identify the transactions. Determine the account balances after all posting is complete. Accounts containing only a single entry do not need a balance.
3. Prepare an unadjusted trial balance as of January 31, 2019.
4. Determine the following:
   a. Amount of total revenue recorded in the ledger.
   b. Amount of total expenses recorded in the ledger.
   c. Amount of net income for January.
5. Determine the increase or decrease in owner's equity for January.

✔ 3. Total of Credit column: $91,875

PR 2-3A Journal entries and trial balance   OBJ. 1, 2, 3, 4

On June 1, 2019, Kris Storey established an interior decorating business, Eco-Centric Designs. During the month, Kris completed the following transactions related to the business:

June 1. Kris transferred cash from a personal bank account to an account to be used for the business, $35,000.
     1. Paid rent for period of June 1 to end of month, $4,750.
     6. Purchased office equipment on account, $14,100.
     8. Purchased a van for $28,500 paying $4,500 cash and giving a note payable for the remainder.
     10. Purchased supplies for cash, $2,380.
     12. Received cash for job completed, $12,200.
     15. Paid annual premiums on property and casualty insurance, $3,600.
     23. Recorded jobs completed on account and sent invoices to customers, $11,900.
     24. Received an invoice for van expenses, to be paid in June, $1,500.

Enter the following transactions on Page 2 of the two-column journal:

June 29. Paid utilities expense, $3,100.

     29. Paid miscellaneous expenses, $950.

     30. Received cash from customers on account, $7,330.

     30. Paid wages of employees, $5,070.

     30. Paid creditor a portion of the amount owed for equipment purchased on June 6, $6,825.

     30. Withdrew cash for personal use, $1,600.

Instructions

1. Journalize each transaction in a two-column journal beginning on Page 1, referring to the following chart of accounts in selecting the accounts to be debited and credited. (Do not insert the account numbers in the journal at this time.) Explanations may be omitted.

11 Cash	31 Kris Storey, Capital
12 Accounts Receivable	32 Kris Storey, Drawing
13 Supplies	41 Fees Earned
14 Prepaid Insurance	51 Wages Expense
16 Equipment	53 Rent Expense
18 Van	54 Utilities Expense
21 Notes Payable	55 Van Expense
22 Accounts Payable	59 Miscellaneous Expense

2. Post the journal to a ledger of four-column accounts, inserting appropriate posting references as each item is posted. Extend the balances to the appropriate balance columns after each transaction is posted.

3. Prepare an unadjusted trial balance for Eco-Centric Designs as of June 30, 2019.

4. Determine the excess of revenues over expenses for June.

5. Can you think of any reason why the amount determined in (4) might not be the net income for June?

PR 2-4A   **Journal entries and trial balance**   OBJ. 1, 2, 3, 4

✔ 4. Total of Debit column: $532,525

General Ledger

Elite Realty acts as an agent in buying, selling, renting, and managing real estate. The unadjusted trial balance on March 31, 2019, follows:

Elite Realty
Unadjusted Trial Balance
March 31, 2019

	Account No.	Debit Balances	Credit Balances
Cash	11	26,300	
Accounts Receivable	12	61,500	
Prepaid Insurance	13	3,000	
Office Supplies	14	1,800	
Land	16	—	
Accounts Payable	21		14,000
Unearned Rent	22		—
Notes Payable	23		—
Lester Wagner, Capital	31		46,000
Lester Wagner, Drawing	32	2,000	
Fees Earned	41		240,000
Salary and Commission Expense	51	148,200	
Rent Expense	52	30,000	
Advertising Expense	53	17,800	
Automobile Expense	54	5,500	
Miscellaneous Expense	59	3,900	
		300,000	300,000

(Continued)

The following business transactions were completed by Elite Realty during April 2019:

Apr. 1. Paid rent on office for month, $6,500.
2. Purchased office supplies on account, $2,300.
5. Paid insurance premiums, $6,000.
10. Received cash from clients on account, $52,300.
15. Purchased land for a future building site for $200,000, paying $30,000 in cash and giving a note payable for the remainder.
17. Paid creditors on account, $6,450.
20. Returned a portion of the office supplies purchased on April 2, receiving full credit for their cost, $325.
23. Paid advertising expense, $4,300.

Enter the following transactions on Page 19 of the two-column journal:

27. Discovered an error in computing a commission; received cash from the salesperson for the overpayment, $2,500.
28. Paid automobile expense (including rental charges for an automobile), $1,500.
29. Paid miscellaneous expenses, $1,400.
30. Recorded revenue earned and billed to clients during the month, $57,000.
30. Paid salaries and commissions for the month, $11,900.
30. Withdrew cash for personal use, $4,000.
30. Rented land purchased on April 15 to local merchants association for use as a parking lot in May and June, during a street rebuilding program; received advance payment of $10,000.

Instructions

1. Record the April 1, 2019, balance of each account in the appropriate balance column of a four-column account, write *Balance* in the item section, and place a check mark (✓) in the Posting Reference column.
2. Journalize the transactions for April in a two-column journal beginning on Page 18. Journal entry explanations may be omitted.
3. Post to the ledger, extending the account balance to the appropriate balance column after each posting.
4. Prepare an unadjusted trial balance of the ledger as of April 30, 2019.
5. Assume that the April 30 transaction for salaries and commissions should have been $19,100. (a) Why did the unadjusted trial balance in (4) balance? (b) Journalize the correcting entry. (c) Is this error a transposition or slide?

✓ 1. Total of Debit column: $725,000

PR 2-5A   Corrected trial balance   OBJ. 4

The Colby Group has the following unadjusted trial balance as of August 31, 2019:

The Colby Group
Unadjusted Trial Balance
August 31, 2019

	Debit Balances	Credit Balances
Cash	17,300	
Accounts Receivable	37,000	
Supplies	7,400	
Prepaid Insurance	1,900	
Equipment	196,000	
Notes Payable		97,600
Accounts Payable		26,000
Terry Colby, Capital		129,150
Terry Colby, Drawing	56,000	
Fees Earned		454,450
Wages Expense	270,000	
Rent Expense	51,800	
Advertising Expense	25,200	
Miscellaneous Expense	5,100	
	667,700	707,200

The debit and credit totals are not equal as a result of the following errors:
a. The cash entered on the trial balance was understated by $6,000.
b. A cash receipt of $5,600 was posted as a debit to Cash of $6,500.
c. A debit of $11,000 to Accounts Receivable was not posted.
d. A return of $150 of defective supplies was erroneously posted as a $1,500 credit to Supplies.
e. An insurance policy acquired at a cost of $1,200 was posted as a credit to Prepaid Insurance.
f. The balance of Notes Payable was understated by $20,000.
g. A credit of $4,800 in Accounts Payable was overlooked when determining the balance of the account.
h. A debit of $7,000 for a withdrawal by the owner was posted as a credit to Terry Colby, Capital.
i. The balance of $58,100 in Rent Expense was entered as $51,800 in the trial balance.
j. Gas, Electricity, and Water Expense, with a balance of $24,150, was omitted from the trial balance.

Instructions

1. Prepare a corrected unadjusted trial balance as of August 31, 2019.
2. Does the fact that the unadjusted trial balance in (1) is balanced mean that there are no errors in the accounts? Explain.

Problems: Series B

PR 2-1B Entries into T accounts and trial balance OBJ. 1, 2, 3, 4

✔ 3. Total of Debit column: $69,550

Ken Jones, an architect, opened an office on April 1, 2019. During the month, he completed the following transactions connected with his professional practice:

a. Transferred cash from a personal bank account to an account to be used for the business, $18,000.
b. Purchased used automobile for $19,500, paying $2,500 cash and giving a note payable for the remainder.
c. Paid April rent for office and workroom, $3,150.
d. Paid cash for supplies, $1,450.
e. Purchased office and computer equipment on account, $6,500.
f. Paid cash for annual insurance policies on automobile and equipment, $2,400.
g. Received cash from a client for plans delivered, $12,000.
h. Paid cash to creditors on account, $1,800.
i. Paid cash for miscellaneous expenses, $375.
j. Received invoice for blueprint service, due in May, $2,500.
k. Recorded fees earned on plans delivered, payment to be received in May, $15,650.
l. Paid salary of assistant, $2,800.
m. Paid cash for miscellaneous expenses, $200.
n. Paid $300 on note payable.
o. Paid gas, oil, and repairs on automobile for April, $550.

Instructions

1. Record these transactions directly in the following T accounts without journalizing: Cash; Accounts Receivable; Supplies; Prepaid Insurance; Automobiles; Equipment; Accounts Payable; Notes Payable; Ken Jones, Capital; Professional Fees; Rent Expense; Salary Expense; Blueprint Expense; Automobile Expense; Miscellaneous Expense. To the left of each amount entered in the accounts, place the appropriate letter to identify the transaction.
2. Determine account balances of the T accounts. Accounts containing a single entry only (such as Prepaid Insurance) do not need a balance.

(Continued)

102 Chapter 2 Analyzing Transactions

3. Prepare an unadjusted trial balance for Ken Jones, Architect, as of April 30, 2019.
4. Determine the net income or net loss for April.

PR 2-2B Journal entries and trial balance OBJ. 1, 2, 3, 4

✔ 4. c. $4,550

On August 1, 2019, Rafael Masey established Planet Realty, which completed the following transactions during the month:

a. Rafael Masey transferred cash from a personal bank account to an account to be used for the business, $17,500.
b. Purchased supplies on account, $2,300.
c. Earned fees, receiving cash, $13,300.
d. Paid rent on office and equipment for the month, $3,000.
e. Paid creditor on account, $1,150.
f. Withdrew cash for personal use, $1,800.
g. Paid automobile expenses (including rental charge) for month, $1,500, and miscellaneous expenses, $400.
h. Paid office salaries, $2,800.
i. Determined that the cost of supplies used was $1,050.

Instructions

1. Journalize entries for transactions (a) through (i), using the following account titles: Cash; Supplies; Accounts Payable; Rafael Masey, Capital; Rafael Masey, Drawing; Fees Earned; Rent Expense; Office Salaries Expense; Automobile Expense; Supplies Expense; Miscellaneous Expense. Journal entry explanations may be omitted.
2. Prepare T accounts, using the account titles in (1). Post the journal entries to these accounts, placing the appropriate letter to the left of each amount to identify the transactions. Determine the account balances after all posting is complete. Accounts containing only a single entry do not need a balance.
3. Prepare an unadjusted trial balance as of August 31, 2019.
4. Determine the following:
    a. Amount of total revenue recorded in the ledger.
    b. Amount of total expenses recorded in the ledger.
    c. Amount of net income for August.
5. Determine the increase or decrease in owner's equity for August.

PR 2-3B Journal entries and trial balance OBJ. 1, 2, 3, 4

✔ 3. Total of Credit column: $70,300

On October 1, 2019, Jay Pryor established an interior decorating business, Pioneer Designs. During the month, Jay completed the following transactions related to the business:

Oct. 1. Jay transferred cash from a personal bank account to an account to be used for the business, $18,000.
   4. Paid rent for period of October 4 to end of month, $3,000.
   10. Purchased a used truck for $23,750, paying $3,750 cash and giving a note payable for the remainder.
   13. Purchased equipment on account, $10,500.
   14. Purchased supplies for cash, $2,100.
   15. Paid annual premiums on property and casualty insurance, $3,600.
   15. Received cash for job completed, $8,950.

Enter the following transactions on Page 2 of the two-column journal:

   21. Paid creditor a portion of the amount owed for equipment purchased on October 13, $2,000.
   24. Recorded jobs completed on account and sent invoices to customers, $14,150.
   26. Received an invoice for truck expenses, to be paid in November, $700.
   27. Paid utilities expense, $2,240.
   27. Paid miscellaneous expenses, $1,100.

Oct. 29. Received cash from customers on account, $7,600.
30. Paid wages of employees, $4,800.
31. Withdrew cash for personal use, $3,500.

Instructions

1. Journalize each transaction in a two-column journal beginning on Page 1, referring to the following chart of accounts in selecting the accounts to be debited and credited. (Do not insert the account numbers in the journal at this time.) Journal entry explanations may be omitted.

11 Cash	31 Jay Pryor, Capital
12 Accounts Receivable	32 Jay Pryor, Drawing
13 Supplies	41 Fees Earned
14 Prepaid Insurance	51 Wages Expense
16 Equipment	53 Rent Expense
18 Truck	54 Utilities Expense
21 Notes Payable	55 Truck Expense
22 Accounts Payable	59 Miscellaneous Expense

2. Post the journal to a ledger of four-column accounts, inserting appropriate posting references as each item is posted. Extend the balances to the appropriate balance columns after each transaction is posted.
3. Prepare an unadjusted trial balance for Pioneer Designs as of October 31, 2019.
4. Determine the excess of revenues over expenses for October.
5.  Can you think of any reason why the amount determined in (4) might not be the net income for October?

PR 2-4B Journal entries and trial balance   OBJ. 1, 2, 3, 4

✔ 4. Total of Debit column: $945,000

Valley Realty acts as an agent in buying, selling, renting, and managing real estate. The unadjusted trial balance on July 31, 2019, follows:

Valley Realty
Unadjusted Trial Balance
July 31, 2019

	Account No.	Debit Balances	Credit Balances
Cash	11	52,500	
Accounts Receivable	12	100,100	
Prepaid Insurance	13	12,600	
Office Supplies	14	2,800	
Land	16	—	
Accounts Payable	21		21,000
Unearned Rent	22		—
Notes Payable	23		—
Cindy Getman, Capital	31		87,500
Cindy Getman, Drawing	32	44,800	
Fees Earned	41		591,500
Salary and Commission Expense	51	385,000	
Rent Expense	52	49,000	
Advertising Expense	53	32,200	
Automobile Expense	54	15,750	
Miscellaneous Expense	59	5,250	
		700,000	700,000

The following business transactions were completed by Valley Realty during August 2019:

Aug. 1. Purchased office supplies on account, $3,150.
2. Paid rent on office for month, $7,200.
3. Received cash from clients on account, $83,900.
5. Paid insurance premiums, $12,000.
9. Returned a portion of the office supplies purchased on August 1, receiving full credit for their cost, $400.

(Continued)

Aug. 17. Paid advertising expense, $8,000.
23. Paid creditors on account, $13,750.

Enter the following transactions on Page 19 of the two-column journal:

29. Paid miscellaneous expenses, $1,700.
30. Paid automobile expense (including rental charges for an automobile), $2,500.
31. Discovered an error in computing a commission during July; received cash from the salesperson for the overpayment, $2,000.
31. Paid salaries and commissions for the month, $53,000.
31. Recorded revenue earned and billed to clients during the month, $183,500.
31. Purchased land for a future building site for $75,000, paying $7,500 in cash and giving a note payable for the remainder.
31. Withdrew cash for personal use, $1,000.
31. Rented land purchased on August 31 to a local university for use as a parking lot during football season (September, October, and November); received advance payment of $5,000.

Instructions

1. Record the August 1 balance of each account in the appropriate balance column of a four-column account, write *Balance* in the item section, and place a check mark (✓) in the Posting Reference column.
2. Journalize the transactions for August in a two-column journal beginning on Page 18. Journal entry explanations may be omitted.
3. Post to the ledger, extending the account balance to the appropriate balance column after each posting.
4. Prepare an unadjusted trial balance of the ledger as of August 31, 2019.
5. Assume that the August 31 transaction for Cindy Getman's cash withdrawal should have been $10,000. (a) Why did the unadjusted trial balance in (4) balance? (b) Journalize the correcting entry. (c) Is this error a transposition or slide?

PR 2-5B Corrected trial balance   OBJ. 4

✔ 1. Total of Debit column: $712,500

Tech Support Services has the following unadjusted trial balance as of January 31, 2019:

Tech Support Services
Unadjusted Trial Balance
January 31, 2019

	Debit Balances	Credit Balances
Cash	25,550	
Accounts Receivable	44,050	
Supplies	6,660	
Prepaid Insurance	3,600	
Equipment	162,000	
Notes Payable		75,000
Accounts Payable		13,200
Thad Engelberg, Capital		101,850
Thad Engelberg, Drawing	33,000	
Fees Earned		534,000
Wages Expense	306,000	
Rent Expense	62,550	
Advertising Expense	23,850	
Gas, Electricity, and Water Expense	17,000	
	684,260	724,050

The debit and credit totals are not equal as a result of the following errors:

a. The cash entered on the trial balance was overstated by $8,000.
b. A cash receipt of $4,100 was posted as a debit to Cash of $1,400.

c. A debit of $12,350 to Accounts Receivable was not posted.
d. A return of $235 of defective supplies was erroneously posted as a $325 credit to Supplies.
e. An insurance policy acquired at a cost of $3,000 was posted as a credit to Prepaid Insurance.
f. The balance of Notes Payable was overstated by $21,000.
g. A credit of $3,450 in Accounts Payable was overlooked when the balance of the account was determined.
h. A debit of $6,000 for a withdrawal by the owner was posted as a debit to Thad Engelberg, Capital.
i. The balance of $28,350 in Advertising Expense was entered as $23,850 in the trial balance.
j. Miscellaneous Expense, with a balance of $4,600, was omitted from the trial balance.

Instructions

1. Prepare a corrected unadjusted trial balance as of January 31, 2019.
2. Does the fact that the unadjusted trial balance in (1) is balanced mean that there are no errors in the accounts? Explain.

Continuing Problem

✔ 4. Total of Debit column: $40,750

The transactions completed by PS Music during June 2019 were described at the end of Chapter 1. The following transactions were completed during July, the second month of the business's operations:

July 1. Peyton Smith made an additional investment in PS Music by depositing $5,000 in PS Music's checking account.
1. Instead of continuing to share office space with a local real estate agency, Peyton decided to rent office space near a local music store. Paid rent for July, $1,750.
1. Paid a premium of $2,700 for a comprehensive insurance policy covering liability, theft, and fire. The policy covers a one-year period.
2. Received $1,000 cash from customers on account.
3. On behalf of PS Music, Peyton signed a contract with a local radio station, KXMD, to provide guest spots for the next three months. The contract requires PS Music to provide a guest disc jockey for 80 hours per month for a monthly fee of $3,600. Any additional hours beyond 80 will be billed to KXMD at $40 per hour. In accordance with the contract, Peyton received $7,200 from KXMD as an advance payment for the first two months.
3. Paid $250 to creditors on account.
4. Paid an attorney $900 for reviewing the July 3 contract with KXMD. (Record as Miscellaneous Expense.)
5. Purchased office equipment on account from Office Mart, $7,500.
8. Paid for a newspaper advertisement, $200.
11. Received $1,000 for serving as a disc jockey for a party.
13. Paid $700 to a local audio electronics store for rental of digital recording equipment.
14. Paid wages of $1,200 to receptionist and part-time assistant.

Enter the following transactions on Page 2 of the two-column journal:

16. Received $2,000 for serving as a disc jockey for a wedding reception.
18. Purchased supplies on account, $850.

(Continued)

July 21. Paid $620 to Upload Music for use of its current music demos in making various music sets.
22. Paid $800 to a local radio station to advertise the services of PS Music twice daily for the remainder of July.
23. Served as disc jockey for a party for $2,500. Received $750, with the remainder due August 4, 2019.
27. Paid electric bill, $915.
28. Paid wages of $1,200 to receptionist and part-time assistant.
29. Paid miscellaneous expenses, $540.
30. Served as a disc jockey for a charity ball for $1,500. Received $500, with the remainder due on August 9, 2019.
31. Received $3,000 for serving as a disc jockey for a party.
31. Paid $1,400 royalties (music expense) to National Music Clearing for use of various artists' music during July.
31. Withdrew $1,250 cash from PS Music for personal use.

PS Music's chart of accounts and the balance of accounts as of July 1, 2019 (all normal balances), are as follows:

11	Cash	$3,920	41	Fees Earned	$6,200
12	Accounts Receivable	1,000	50	Wages Expense	400
14	Supplies	170	51	Office Rent Expense	800
15	Prepaid Insurance	—	52	Equipment Rent Expense	675
17	Office Equipment	—	53	Utilities Expense	300
21	Accounts Payable	250	54	Music Expense	1,590
23	Unearned Revenue	—	55	Advertising Expense	500
31	Peyton Smith, Capital	4,000	56	Supplies Expense	180
32	Peyton Smith, Drawing	500	59	Miscellaneous Expense	415

Instructions

1. Enter the July 1, 2019, account balances in the appropriate balance column of a four-column account. Write *Balance* in the Item column and place a check mark (✓) in the Posting Reference column. (*Hint:* Verify the equality of the debit and credit balances in the ledger before proceeding with the next instruction.)
2. Analyze and journalize each transaction in a two-column journal beginning on Page 1, omitting journal entry explanations.
3. Post the journal to the ledger, extending the account balance to the appropriate balance column after each posting.
4. Prepare an unadjusted trial balance as of July 31, 2019.

Cases & Projects

Ethics

CP 2-1 Ethics in Action

Buddy Dupree is the accounting manager for On-Time Geeks, a tech support company for individuals and small businesses. As part of his job, Buddy is responsible for preparing the company's trial balance. His supervisor placed a "hard deadline" of Friday at 5 PM for the completion of the trial balance. Unfortunately, Buddy was unable to get the trial balance to balance by the due date. The credit side of the trial balance exceeded the debit side by $3,000. To make the deadline, Buddy decided to add a $3,000 debit to the vehicles account balance. He selected the vehicles account because it will not be significantly affected by the additional $3,000.

1. Is Buddy behaving ethically? Why or why not?
2. Who is affected by Buddy's decision?
3. How should Buddy have handled this situation?

CP 2-2 Team Activity

In teams, select a public company that interests you. Obtain the company's most recent annual report on Form 10-K. The Form 10-K is a company's annually required filing with the Securities and Exchange Commission (SEC). It includes the company's financial statements and accompanying notes. The Form 10-K can be obtained either (a) by referring to the investor relations section of the company's website or (b) by using the company search feature of the SEC's EDGAR database service found at www.sec.gov/edgar/searchedgar/companysearch.html.

Based on the information in the company's most recent annual report, answer the following questions:

1. What amount of total assets does the company report on its balance sheet?
2. What amount of total liabilities does the company report on its balance sheet?
3. Using the accounting equation, determine the company's stockholders' equity. Compare this amount to the amount of stockholders' equity reported on the company's balance sheet.
4. How many years of information are reported on the company's income statement?
5. How many years of information are reported on the company's balance sheet?
6. What is the difference between the information reported on the income statement and the information reported on the balance sheet?

CP 2-3 Team Activity

The following excerpt is from a conversation between Kate Purvis, the president and chief operating officer of Light House Company, and her neighbor, Dot Evers:

Dot: Kate, I'm taking a course in night school, "Intro to Accounting." I was wondering—could you answer a couple of questions for me?

Kate: Well, I will if I can.

Dot: Okay, our instructor says that it's critical we understand the basic concepts of accounting, or we'll never get beyond the first test. My problem is with those rules of debit and credit . . . you know, assets increase with debits, decrease with credits, etc.

Kate: Yes, pretty basic stuff. You just have to memorize the rules. It shouldn't be too difficult.

Dot: Sure, I can memorize the rules, but my problem is I want to be sure I understand the basic concepts behind the rules. For example, why can't assets be increased with credits and decreased with debits like revenue? As long as everyone did it that way, why not? It would seem easier if we had the same rules for all increases and decreases in accounts. Also, why is the left side of an account called the debit side? Why couldn't it be called something simple . . . like the "LE" for Left Entry? The right side could be called just "RE" for Right Entry. Finally, why are there just two sides to an entry? Why can't there be three or four sides to an entry?

In a group of four or five, select one person to play the role of Kate and one person to play the role of Dot.

1. After listening to the conversation between Kate and Dot, help Kate answer Dot's questions.
2. What information (other than just debit and credit journal entries) could the accounting system gather that might be useful to Kate in managing Light House Company?

CP 2-4 Communication

The complexity of the current business and regulatory environment has increased the demand for individuals in all fields of business who have the ability to analyze business transactions and interpret their effects on the financial statements. Search the Internet or your local newspaper for job opportunities in business. One possible website is www.careerbuilder.com.

Select a job opportunity to explore further. Write a brief memo to your instructor describing how the ability to analyze business transactions and interpret their effects on the financial statements would be needed for the job opportunity you have selected.

CP 2-5 Account for revenue

Bozeman College requires students to pay tuition each term before classes begin. Students who have not paid their tuition are not allowed to enroll or to attend classes.

 What journal entry do you think Bozeman College would use to record the receipt of the students' tuition payments? Describe the nature of each account in the entry.

CP 2-6 Record transactions

The following discussion took place between Tony Cork, the office manager of Hallmark Data Company, and a new accountant, Cassie Miles:

Cassie: I've been thinking about our method of recording entries. It seems inefficient.

Tony: In what way?

Cassie: Well—correct me if I'm wrong—it seems like we have unnecessary steps in the process. We could easily develop a trial balance by posting our transactions directly into the ledger and bypassing the journal altogether. In this way, we could combine the recording and posting process into one step and save ourselves a lot of time. What do you think?

Tony: We need to have a talk.

 What should Tony say to Cassie?

CP 2-7 Transactions and income statement

Cory Neece is planning to manage and operate Eagle Caddy Service at Canyon Lake Golf and Country Club during June through August 2019. Cory will rent a small maintenance building from the country club for $500 per month and will offer caddy services, including cart rentals, to golfers. Cory has had no formal training in record keeping.

Cory keeps notes of all receipts and expenses in a shoe box. An examination of Cory's shoe box records for June revealed the following:

June 1. Transferred $2,000 from personal bank account to be used to operate the caddy service.
- 1. Paid rent expense to Canyon Lake Golf and Country Club, $500.
- 2. Paid for golf supplies (practice balls, for example), $750.
- 3. Arranged for the rental of 40 regular (pulling) golf carts and 20 gasoline-driven carts for $3,000 per month. Paid $600 in advance, with the remaining $2,400 due June 20.
- 7. Purchased supplies, including gasoline, for the golf carts on account, $1,000. Canyon Lake Golf and Country Club has agreed to allow Cory to store the gasoline in one of its fuel tanks at no cost.
- 15. Received cash for services from June 1–15, $5,400.
- 17. Paid cash to creditors on account, $1,000.
- 20. Paid remaining rental on golf carts, $2,400.
- 22. Purchased supplies, including gasoline, on account, $850.
- 25. Earned fees from customers on account, $1,800.
- 28. Paid miscellaneous expenses, $395.
- 30. Received cash for services from June 16–30, $4,200.
- 30. Paid telephone and electricity (utilities) expenses, $340.
- 30. Paid wages of part-time employees, $850.
- 30. Received cash on account, $1,500.
- 30. Determined the amount of supplies on hand at the end of June, $675.

Cory has asked you several questions concerning his financial affairs to date, and he has asked you to assist with his record keeping and reporting of financial data.

a. To assist Cory with his record keeping, prepare a chart of accounts that would be appropriate for Eagle Caddy Service.

b. Prepare an income statement for June in order to help Cory assess the profitability of Eagle Caddy Service. For this purpose, the use of T accounts may be helpful in analyzing the effects of each June transaction.

c. Based on Cory's records of receipts and payments, compute the amount of cash on hand on June 30. For this purpose, a T account for cash may be useful.

d. A count of the cash on hand on June 30 totaled $6,175. Briefly discuss the possible causes of the difference between the amount of cash computed in (c) and the actual amount of cash on hand.

CHAPTER 3

The Adjusting Process

Chapter 1

Transactions

Accounting System

Accounting Equation

Assets = Liabilities + Owner's Equity

Chapter 2

Account

| Debits | Credits |

Rules of Debit and Credit

BALANCE SHEET ACCOUNTS

ASSETS = **LIABILITIES** + **OWNER'S EQUITY**
Asset Accounts | Liability Accounts | Owner's Capital Account

| Debit for increases (+) | Credit for decreases (−) |
| Balance | |

| Debit for decreases (−) | Credit for increases (+) |
| | Balance |

| Debit for decreases (−) | Credit for increases (+) |
| | Balance |

Owner's Drawing Account

| Debit for increases (+) | Credit for decreases (−) |
| Balance | |

Income Statement Accounts

Revenue Accounts

| Debit for decreases (−) | Credit for increases (+) |
| | Balance |

Expense Accounts

| Debit for increases (+) | Credit for decreases (−) |
| Balance | |

Unadjusted Trial Balance

Total Debit Balances = Total Credit Balances

CHAPTER 3

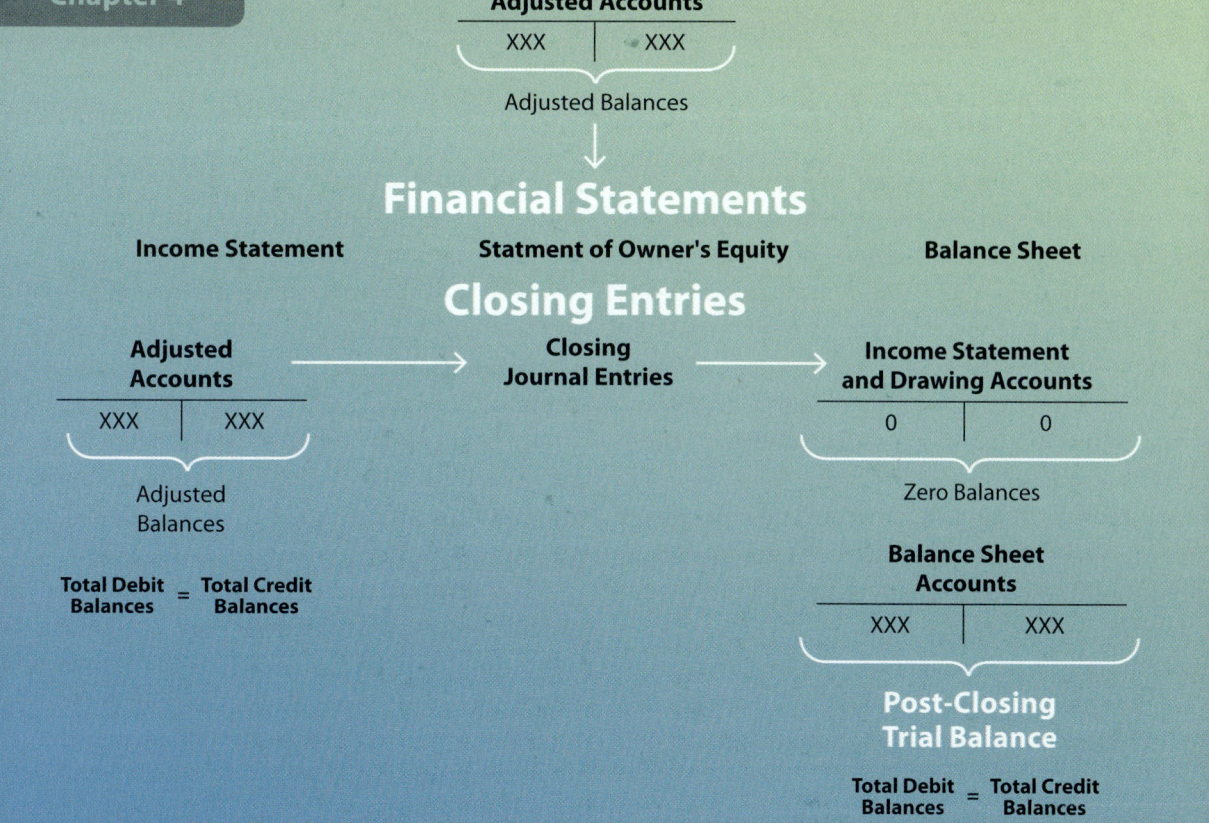

CHAPTER 3

Pandora Media, Inc.

Do you use an Internet-based music service such as Pandora? Using playlist-generating algorithms, **Pandora Media, Inc.** predicts a listener's music preferences based on his or her initial music selections. Pandora selects music it thinks the listener will enjoy, including music of new artists that match the listener's preferences. Pandora also developed similar comedy-generating algorithms that match a listener's preferences for comedy with more than 1,000 comedians.

Most of Pandora's services are offered free to listeners with only 12.5% of its revenues generated from subscription services. So, where do most of Pandora's revenues come from?

Pandora generates more than 85% of its revenues from selling advertising banners that surround the video displays on its tuner. By analyzing its listener interactions, Pandora identifies listener age, gender, zip code, and content preferences. These attributes can then be matched with advertiser needs and desires.

When should Pandora record revenue from its advertisers and subscribers? Revenue should be recorded when earned. Advertising revenue is earned as ads are displayed, while subscriber revenue is earned when the service has been delivered to the listener. As a result, companies like Pandora must update their accounting records for such items as unearned advertising and subscription revenue before preparing financial statements.

This chapter describes and illustrates the process by which companies update their accounting records before preparing financial statements. This discussion includes the adjustments to update revenue and expense accounts at the end of the accounting period.

Learning Objectives

After studying this chapter, you should be able to:

Example Exercises (EE) are shown in **green**.

Obj. 1 Describe the nature of the adjusting process.

Nature of the Adjusting Process
Accrual and Cash Basis of Accounting
Revenue and Expense Recognition
The Adjusting Process — EE 3-1
Types of Accounts Requiring Adjustment — EE 3-2

Obj. 2 Prepare adjusting entries for accruals.

Adjusting Entries for Accruals
Accrued Revenues — EE 3-3
Accrued Expenses — EE 3-4

Obj. 3 Prepare adjusting entries for deferrals.

Adjusting Entries for Deferrals
Unearned Revenues — EE 3-5
Prepaid Expenses — EE 3-6

Obj. 4 Prepare adjusting entries for depreciation.

Adjusting Entries for Depreciation
Journalizing Depreciation — EE 3-7

Obj. 5 Summarize the adjusting process.

Summary of Adjusting Process
Effects of Adjustments — EE 3-8

Obj. 6 Prepare an adjusted trial balance.

Adjusted Trial Balance
Effects of Errors — EE 3-9

Obj. 7 Describe and illustrate the use of vertical analysis in evaluating a company's performance and financial condition.

Financial Analysis and Interpretation: Vertical Analysis
Vertical Analysis of Income Statement — EE 3-10

At a Glance 3 — Page 134

Nature of the Adjusting Process

Obj. 1 Describe the nature of the adjusting process.

In Chapter 2, the November and December transactions for **NetSolutions** were recorded using the double-entry accounting system. After the transactions were recorded, an unadjusted trial balance was prepared on December 31 verifying that the total debit balances equal the total credit balances. Before financial statements can be prepared, however, some accounts in the unadjusted trial balance must be adjusted. These adjustments are necessary because the transactions for NetSolutions were recorded using the accrual basis of accounting.

Accrual and Cash Basis of Accounting

Under the **accrual basis of accounting**, revenues and their related expenses are reported on the income statement in the period in which a service has been performed or a product has been delivered. Cash may or may not be received from customers during this period. For example, a cleaning company will record revenue after it cleans an office building, even if it is not paid for several weeks. The accrual basis of accounting also requires expenses to be recorded when they are incurred, not necessarily when cash is paid.

Although generally accepted accounting principles (GAAP) require the accrual basis of accounting, most individuals and some businesses use the cash basis of accounting. Under the **cash basis of accounting**, revenues and expenses are reported on the income statement in the period in which cash is received or paid. For example, fees are recorded when cash is received from clients; likewise, wages are recorded when cash is paid to employees. The net income (or net loss) is the difference between the cash receipts (revenues) and the cash payments (expenses).

Link to Pandora
Pandora uses the accrual basis of accounting in preparing its financial statements.

Small service businesses may use the cash basis because they have few receivables and payables. For example, attorneys, physicians, and real estate agents may use the cash basis. For them, the cash basis provides financial statements similar to those of the accrual basis. For most large businesses, however, the cash basis will not provide accurate financial statements for user needs. For this reason, the accrual basis is required by GAAP and is used in this text.

Revenue and Expense Recognition

To be useful for decision making, financial statements must be provided on a periodic basis. As a result, the economic life of a business is divided into time periods such as a month, quarter of a year, or full year. Under accrual accounting, the net income of a period is reported using revenue and expense recognition principles.

Under the **revenue recognition principle**, revenues are recorded when services have been performed or products have been delivered to customers. Revenue is measured as the value of the assets received, such as cash or accounts receivable.[1] The process of recognizing revenues is called **revenue recognition**.[2]

Under the **expense recognition principle**, the expenses incurred in generating revenue must be reported in the same period as the related revenue. This is also called the **matching principle**. By matching revenues and expenses, net income or loss for the period is properly reported on the income statement. Adjusting entries are required to properly match revenues and expenses.

The Adjusting Process

At the end of an accounting period, an unadjusted trial balance is prepared to verify that the total debit balances equal the total credit balances. Many of these account balances are reported in the financial statements without change. For example, the balances of the cash and land accounts are normally the amounts reported on the balance sheet.

Some accounts on the unadjusted trial balance, however, require adjustments for the following reasons:

- Some revenues and expenses may be unrecorded at the end of the accounting period. For example, a company may have provided services to customers that it has not billed or recorded at the end of the accounting period. Likewise, a company may not pay its employees until the next accounting period even though the employees have earned their wages in the current period.
- Some expenses are not recorded daily. For example, the daily use of supplies would require many entries with small amounts. Also, information about the amount of supplies on hand on a day-to-day basis is normally not needed.
- Some revenues and expenses are incurred as time passes rather than as separate transactions. For example, rent received in advance (unearned rent) expires and becomes revenue with the passage of time. Likewise, prepaid insurance expires and becomes an expense with the passage of time.

The analysis and updating of accounts at the end of the period before the financial statements are prepared is called the **adjusting process**. The journal entries that bring the accounts up to date at the end of the accounting period are called **adjusting entries**. All adjusting entries affect at least one income statement account and one balance sheet account. Thus, an adjusting entry will always involve a revenue or an expense account *and* an asset or a liability account.

> **Link to Pandora**
> Subscription revenues from **Pandora**'s customers are recorded equally over the subscription periods. For example, a yearly subscription would be recorded equally over 12 months.

> **Link to Pandora**
> **Pandora** computes royalty expense paid to an artist for a song that is streamed to listeners based upon the number of times it is played/streamed.

---

1 As will be illustrated later in this chapter, revenues may also be measured as a decrease in a liability such as unearned revenue.
2 FASB Accounting Standards Update, Revenue from Contracts with Customers (Topic 606), Financial Accounting Standards Board, May 2014, Norwalk, CT.

> **Example Exercise 3-1 Accounts Requiring Adjustment** Obj. 1
>
> Indicate with a Yes or No whether or not each of the following accounts normally requires an adjusting entry:
>
> a. Cash
> b. Utilities Expense
> c. Wages Expense
> d. Land
> e. Accounts Receivable
> f. Unearned Rent
>
> **Follow My Example 3-1**
>
> a. No
> b. Yes
> c. Yes
> d. No
> e. Yes
> f. Yes
>
> Practice Exercises: PE 3-1A, PE 3-1B

Types of Accounts Requiring Adjustment

The two general classifications of accounts requiring adjustment are as follows:

- Accruals
- Deferrals

Accruals An **accrual** occurs when revenue has been earned or an expense has been incurred but has not been recorded. If the accrual is for revenue, the adjusting entry debits an asset (Accounts Receivable) and credits a revenue account. If the accrual is for an expense, the adjusting entry debits an expense account and credits a related liability account such as Accounts Payable or Wages Payable. Exhibit 1 summarizes the accounting for accruals.

EXHIBIT 1 Accruals

ACCRUED REVENUE

Initial Recording		End-of-Period	
Transaction	**Journal Entry**	**Adjustment Data**	**Adjusting Entry**
Revenue has been earned.	No journal entry has been made.	Revenue earned.	Accounts Receivable XXX Revenue XXX

ACCRUED EXPENSE

Initial Recording		End-of-Period	
Transaction	**Journal Entry**	**Adjustment Data**	**Adjusting Entry**
Expense has been incurred.	No journal entry has been made.	Expense incurred.	Expense XXX Accounts Payable XXX

Deferrals A **deferral** occurs when cash related to a future revenue or expense has been initially recorded as a liability or an asset. If the cash received is related to future revenue, it is initially recorded as a liability called **unearned revenue**. The adjusting entry in the period when the revenue is earned debits an unearned revenue account and credits a revenue account. If the cash paid is related to a future expense, it is initially recorded as an asset called **prepaid expense**. The adjusting entry in the period when the expense is incurred debits an expense account and credits a prepaid expense (asset) account. Exhibit 2 summarizes the accounting for deferrals.

EXHIBIT 2 Deferrals

UNEARNED REVENUE

Initial Recording		End-of-Period	
Transaction	**Journal Entry**	**Adjustment Data**	**Adjusting Entry**

Cash has been received for revenue that will be earned in a future period.	Cash XXX
	   Unearned Revenue XXX
		Revenue has been earned.	Unearned Revenue XXX
			   Revenue XXX

PREPAID EXPENSE

Initial Recording		End-of-Period	
Transaction	**Journal Entry**	**Adjustment Data**	**Adjusting Entry**

Cash has been paid for a future expense.	Prepaid Expense XXX
	   Cash XXX
		Prepaid expense has been used to generate revenue.	Expense XXX
			   Prepaid Expense XXX

Example Exercise 3-2 Type of Adjustment *Obj. 1*

Classify the following items as (1) prepaid expense, (2) unearned revenue, (3) accrued expense, or (4) accrued revenue:

a. Wages owed but not yet paid.
b. Supplies on hand.
c. Fees received but not yet earned.
d. Fees earned but not yet received.

Follow My Example 3-2

a. Accrued expense
b. Prepaid expense
c. Unearned revenue
d. Accrued revenue

Practice Exercises: PE 3-2A, PE 3-2B

Adjusting Entries for Accruals

Obj. 2 Prepare adjusting entries for accruals.

To illustrate adjusting entries, the December 31, 2018, unadjusted trial balance of NetSolutions, shown in Exhibit 3, is used. An expanded chart of accounts for NetSolutions is shown in Exhibit 4. The additional accounts used in this chapter are highlighted. The rules of debit and credit shown in Exhibit 3 of Chapter 2 are used to record the adjusting entries.

EXHIBIT 3 Unadjusted Trial Balance for NetSolutions

NetSolutions
Unadjusted Trial Balance
December 31, 2018

	Account No.	Debit Balances	Credit Balances
Cash	11	2,065	
Accounts Receivable	12	2,220	
Supplies	14	2,000	
Prepaid Insurance	15	2,400	
Land	17	20,000	
Office Equipment	18	1,800	
Accounts Payable	21		900
Unearned Rent	23		360
Chris Clark, Capital	31		25,000
Chris Clark, Drawing	32	4,000	
Fees Earned	41		16,340
Wages Expense	51	4,275	
Supplies Expense	52	800	
Rent Expense	53	1,600	
Utilities Expense	54	985	
Miscellaneous Expense	59	455	
		42,600	42,600

EXHIBIT 4
Expanded Chart of Accounts for NetSolutions

Balance Sheet Accounts	Income Statement Accounts
1. Assets	**4. Revenue**
11 Cash	41 Fees Earned
12 Accounts Receivable	42 Rent Revenue
14 Supplies	**5. Expenses**
15 Prepaid Insurance	51 Wages Expense
17 Land	52 Supplies Expense
18 Office Equipment	53 Rent Expense
19 Accumulated Depreciation—Office Equipment	54 Utilities Expense
2. Liabilities	55 Insurance Expense
21 Accounts Payable	56 Depreciation Expense
22 Wages Payable	59 Miscellaneous Expense
23 Unearned Rent	
3. Owner's Equity	
31 Chris Clark, Capital	
32 Chris Clark, Drawing	

Accrued Revenues

During an accounting period, some revenues are recorded only when cash is received. Thus, at the end of an accounting period, there may be revenue that has been earned *but has not been recorded*. In such cases, the revenue is recorded by increasing (debiting) an asset account (Accounts Receivable) and increasing (crediting) a revenue account (Fees Earned).

To illustrate, assume that **NetSolutions** signed an agreement with Dankner Co. on December 15. The agreement provides that NetSolutions will answer computer questions and render assistance to Dankner Co.'s employees. The services will be billed to Dankner Co. on the fifteenth of each month at a rate of $20 per hour. As of December 31, NetSolutions had provided 25 hours of assistance to Dankner Co. The revenue of $500 (25 hours × $20) will be billed on January 15. However, NetSolutions earned the revenue in December.

The claim against the customer for payment of the $500 is an account receivable (*an asset*). Thus, the accounts receivable account is increased (debited) by $500, and the fees earned account is increased (credited) by $500. The adjusting journal entry and T accounts are as follows:

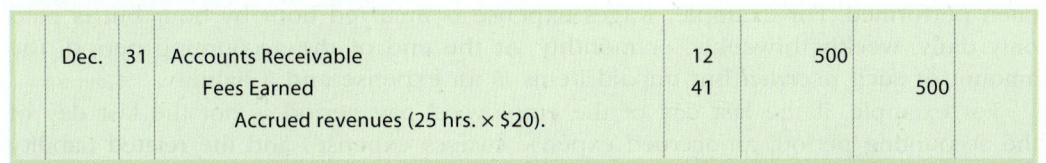

Adjusting Journal Entry

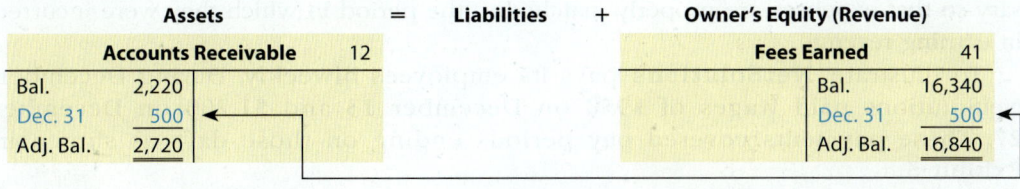

Accounting Equation Impact

If the adjustment for the accrued revenue ($500) is not recorded, Fees Earned and the net income will be understated by $500 on the income statement. On the balance sheet, assets (Accounts Receivable) and owner's equity (Chris Clark, Capital) will be understated by $500. The effects of omitting this adjusting entry are as follows:

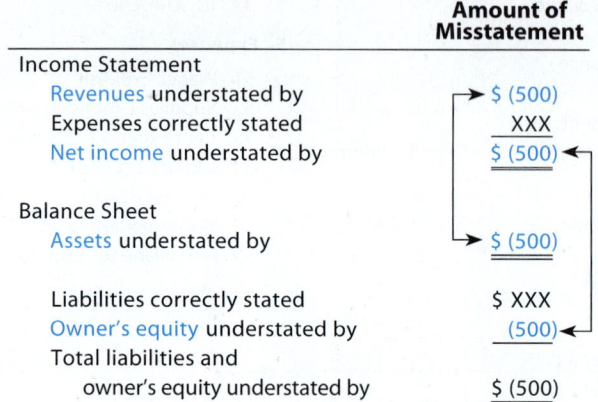

> **Link to Pandora**
>
> **Pandora**'s accrued revenues from advertising are recorded in its accounts receivable at the end of the year.

Example Exercise 3-3 Adjustment for Accrued Revenues   Obj. 2

At the end of the current year, $13,680 of fees have been earned but have not been billed to clients. Journalize the adjusting entry to record the accrued fees.

Follow My Example 3-3

Accounts Receivable	13,680	
Fees Earned		13,680
Accrued fees.		

Practice Exercises: PE 3-3A, PE 3-3B

Accrued Expenses

Some types of services used in earning revenues are paid for *after* the service has been performed. For example, wages expense is incurred hour by hour but is paid only daily, weekly, biweekly, or monthly. At the end of the accounting period, the amount of such *accrued* but unpaid items is an expense and a liability.

For example, if the last day of the employees' pay period is not the last day of the accounting period, an accrued expense (wages expense) and the related liability (wages payable) must be recorded by an adjusting entry. This adjusting entry is necessary so that expenses are properly matched to the period in which they were incurred in earning revenue.

To illustrate, **NetSolutions** pays its employees biweekly. During December, NetSolutions paid wages of $950 on December 13 and $1,200 on December 27. These payments covered pay periods ending on those days as shown in Exhibit 5.

As of December 31, NetSolutions owes $250 of wages to employees for Monday and Tuesday, December 30 and 31. Thus, the wages expense account is increased

EXHIBIT 5
Accrued Wages

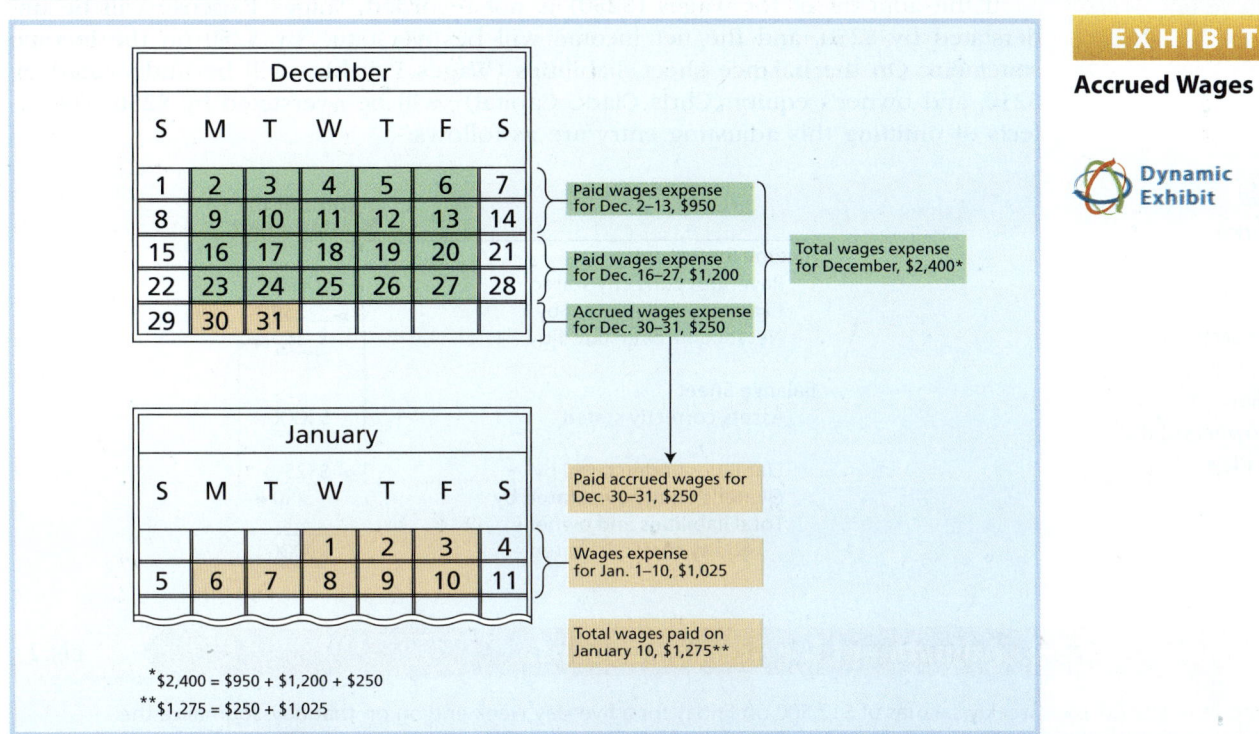

(debited) by $250, and the wages payable account is increased (credited) by $250. The adjusting journal entry and T accounts are as follows:

Dec.	31	Wages Expense	51	250	
		Wages Payable	22		250
		Accrued wages.			

Adjusting Journal Entry

Accounting Equation Impact

After the adjusting entry is recorded and posted, the debit balance of the wages expense account is $4,525. This balance of $4,525 is the wages expense for two months, November and December. The credit balance of $250 in Wages Payable is the liability for wages owed on December 31.

As shown in Exhibit 5, NetSolutions paid wages of $1,275 on January 10. This payment includes the $250 of accrued wages recorded on December 31. Thus, on January 10, the wages payable account is decreased (debited) by $250. Also, the wages expense account is increased (debited) by $1,025 ($1,275 − $250), which is the wages expense for January 1–10. Finally, the cash account is decreased (credited) by $1,275. The journal entry for the payment of wages on January 10 follows:[3]

Jan.	10	Wages Expense	51	1,025	
		Wages Payable	22	250	
		Cash	11		1,275

[3] To simplify the subsequent recording of the following period's transactions, some accountants use what is known as reversing entries for certain types of adjustments. Reversing entries are discussed and illustrated in an appendix to Chapter 4.

If the adjustment for wages ($250) is not recorded, Wages Expense will be understated by $250, and the net income will be overstated by $250 on the income statement. On the balance sheet, liabilities (Wages Payable) will be understated by $250, and owner's equity (Chris Clark, Capital) will be overstated by $250. The effects of omitting this adjusting entry are as follows:

	Amount of Misstatement
Income Statement	
Revenues correctly stated	$ XXX
Expenses understated by	(250)
Net income overstated by	$ 250
Balance Sheet	
Assets correctly stated	$ XXX
Liabilities understated by	$ (250)
Owner's equity overstated by	250
Total liabilities and owner's equity correctly stated	$ XXX

> **Link to Pandora**
> On a recent balance sheet, **Pandora** reported accrued royalties payable of $66 million, which it pays to owners of the music it plays.

Example Exercise 3-4 Adjustment for Accrued Expense Obj. 2

Sanregret Realty Co. pays weekly salaries of $12,500 on Friday for a five-day week ending on that day. Journalize the necessary adjusting entry at the end of the accounting period, assuming that the period ends on Thursday.

Follow My Example 3-4

Salaries Expense 10,000
    Salaries Payable 10,000
        Accrued salaries [($12,500 ÷ 5 days) × 4 days].

Practice Exercises: PE 3-4A, PE 3-4B

Business Connection

EARNING REVENUES FROM SEASON TICKETS

Madison Square Garden Company (MSG) owns the New York Knicks basketball team and the New York Rangers hockey team. The company sells season tickets prior to the season. The amounts received for season tickets are recognized as unearned revenue, a current liability. MSG recognizes revenue and reduces unearned revenue as the games are played through the season.

Obj. 3 Prepare adjusting entries for deferrals.

Adjusting Entries for Deferrals

The unadjusted trial balance for **NetSolutions** in Exhibit 3 indicates Unearned Rent of $360. In addition, Exhibit 3 indicates that NetSolutions has prepaid assets consisting of Supplies of $2,000 and Prepaid Insurance of $2,400. Each of these deferrals requires an adjusting entry.

Unearned Revenues

The December 31 unadjusted trial balance of **NetSolutions** indicates a balance in the unearned rent account of $360. This balance represents the receipt of three months' rent on December 1 for December, January, and February. At the end of December, one month's rent has been earned. Thus, the unearned rent account is decreased (debited) by $120, and the rent revenue account is increased (credited) by $120. The $120 represents the rental revenue for one month ($360 ÷ 3). The adjusting journal entry and T accounts are as follows:

Adjusting Journal Entry

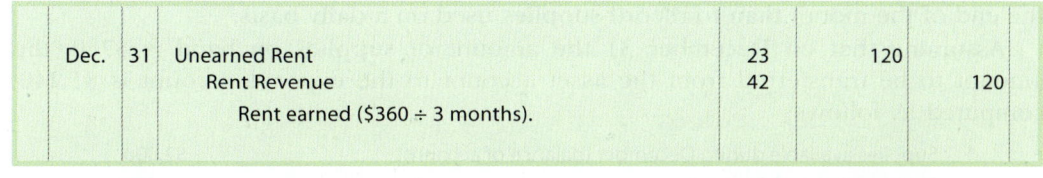

Dec.	31	Unearned Rent	23	120	
		Rent Revenue	42		120
		Rent earned ($360 ÷ 3 months).			

Accounting Equation Impact

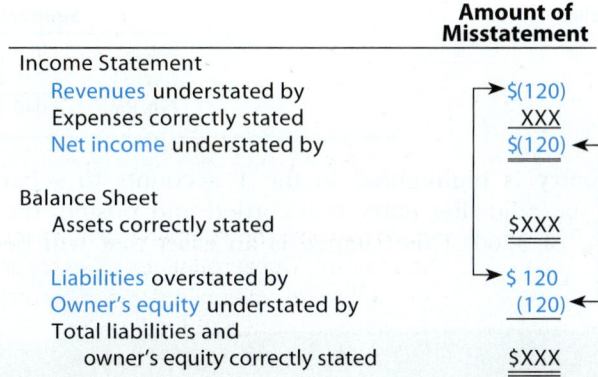

After the adjusting entry is recorded and posted, the unearned rent account has a credit balance of $240. This balance is a liability that will become revenue in a future period. Rent Revenue has a balance of $120, which is revenue earned during the current period.

If the preceding adjustment of unearned rent and rent revenue is not recorded, the financial statements prepared on December 31 will be misstated. On the income statement, Rent Revenue and the net income will be understated by $120. On the balance sheet, liabilities (Unearned Rent) will be overstated by $120, and owner's equity (Chris Clark, Capital) will be understated by $120. The effects of omitting this adjusting entry are as follows:

> **Link to Pandora**
> On a recent balance sheet, **Pandora** reported unearned (deferred) revenue of $43 million.

	Amount of Misstatement
Income Statement	
Revenues understated by	$(120)
Expenses correctly stated	XXX
Net income understated by	$(120)
Balance Sheet	
Assets correctly stated	$XXX
Liabilities overstated by	$ 120
Owner's equity understated by	(120)
Total liabilities and owner's equity correctly stated	$XXX

Example Exercise 3-5 Adjustment for Unearned Revenue *Obj. 3*

The balance in the unearned fees account, before adjustment at the end of the year, is $44,900. Journalize the adjusting entry required if the amount of unearned fees at the end of the year is $12,300.

Follow My Example 3-5

Unearned Fees...	32,600	
Fees Earned..		32,600
Fees earned ($44,900 − $12,300).		

Practice Exercises: PE 3-5A, PE 3-5B

Prepaid Expenses

The December 31, 2018, unadjusted trial balance of **NetSolutions** indicates a balance in the supplies account of $2,000. In addition, the prepaid insurance account has a balance of $2,400. Each of these accounts requires an adjusting entry.

Supplies The balance in NetSolutions' supplies account on December 31 is $2,000. Some of these supplies (paper and envelopes, for example) were used during December, and some are still on hand (not used). If either amount is known, the other can be determined. It is normally easier to determine the cost of the supplies on hand at the end of the month than to record supplies used on a daily basis.

Assuming that on December 31 the amount of supplies on hand is $760, the amount to be transferred from the asset account to the expense account is $1,240, computed as follows:

Supplies available during December (balance of account)	$2,000
Supplies on hand, December 31	760
Supplies used (amount of adjustment)	$1,240

At the end of December, the supplies expense account is increased (debited) for $1,240, and the supplies account is decreased (credited) for $1,240 to record the supplies used during December. The adjusting journal entry and T accounts for Supplies and Supplies Expense are as follows:

Adjusting Journal Entry

Journal *Page 2*

Date	Description	Post. Ref.	Debit	Credit
2018 Dec. 31	Supplies Expense	52	1,240	
	Supplies	14		1,240
	Supplies used ($2,000 − $760).			

Accounting Equation Impact

Assets = Liabilities + Owner's Equity (Expense)

Supplies	14
Bal. 2,000	Dec. 31 1,240
Adj. Bal. 760	

Supplies Expense	52
Bal. 800	
Dec. 31 1,240	
Adj. Bal. 2,040	

The adjusting entry is highlighted in the T accounts to separate it from other transactions. After the adjusting entry is recorded and posted, the supplies account has a debit balance of $760. This balance is an asset that will become an expense in a future period.

Business Connection

SPORTS SIGNING BONUS

The **National Football League** (NFL), **National Basketball Association** (NBA), and **National Hockey League** (NHL) all have team salary caps that are used to create parity in the sport league. The salary cap limits the total salaries that a team can pay each year. Teams use signing bonuses as a way to reduce the impact of salaries on the salary cap. Under cap rules, the bonus is spread over the length of the player's contract. For example, if a player receives a $6 million bonus for a six-year contract, the player will receive the complete $6 million upon signing the contract, but only $1 million will be applied to the salary cap for each year of the contract. This is similar to how GAAP accounts for the bonus. The bonus is treated as a prepaid salary expense that is amortized over the life of the contract. If a player is released prior to the end of the contract, any remaining unamortized balance is expensed immediately.

Prepaid Insurance The debit balance of $2,400 in **NetSolutions**' prepaid insurance account represents a December 1 prepayment of insurance for 12 months. At the end of December, the insurance expense account is increased (debited) and the prepaid insurance account is decreased (credited) by $200, the insurance for one month. The adjusting journal entry and T accounts for Prepaid Insurance and Insurance Expense are as follows:

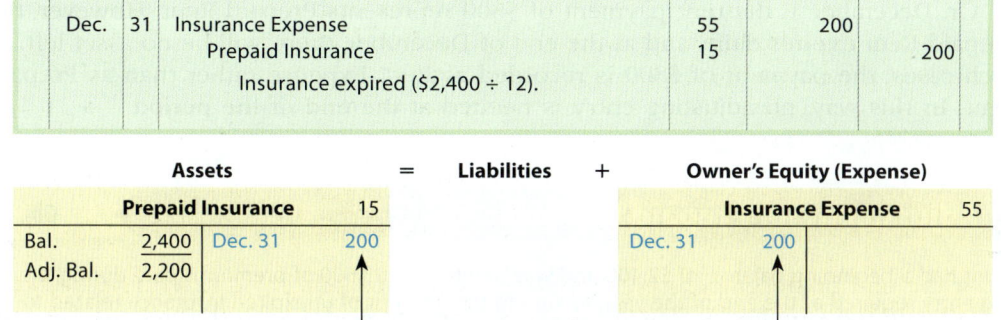

Adjusting Journal Entry

Accounting Equation Impact

After the adjusting entry is recorded and posted, the prepaid insurance account has a debit balance of $2,200. This balance is an asset that will become an expense in future periods. The insurance expense account has a debit balance of $200, which is an expense of the current period.

If the preceding adjustments for supplies ($1,240) and insurance ($200) are not recorded, the financial statements prepared as of December 31 will be misstated. On the income statement, Supplies Expense and Insurance Expense will be understated by a total of $1,440 ($1,240 + $200), and net income will be overstated by $1,440. On the balance sheet, Supplies and Prepaid Insurance will be overstated by a total of $1,440. Because net income increases owner's equity, Chris Clark, Capital will also be overstated by $1,440 on the balance sheet. The effects of omitting these adjusting entries on the income statement and balance sheet are as follows:

> **Link to Pandora**
> On a recent balance sheet, **Pandora** reported prepaid expenses and other current assets of $10 million.

	Amount of Misstatement
Income Statement	
Revenues correctly stated	$ XXX
Expenses understated by	(1,440)
Net income overstated by	$1,440
Balance Sheet	
Assets overstated by	$1,440
Liabilities correctly stated	$ XXX
Owner's equity overstated by	1,440
Total liabilities and	
owner's equity overstated by	$1,440

INTEGRITY, OBJECTIVITY, AND ETHICS IN BUSINESS

FREE ISSUE

Office supplies are often available to employees on a "free issue" basis. This means that employees do not have to "sign" for the release of office supplies but merely obtain the necessary supplies from a local storage area as needed. Just because supplies are easily available, however, doesn't mean they can be taken for personal use. There are many instances where employees have been terminated for taking supplies home for personal use.

Arrow (1) indicates the effect of the understated expenses on assets. Arrow (2) indicates the effect of the overstated net income on owner's equity.

Payments for prepaid expenses are sometimes made at the beginning of the period in which they will be *entirely used or consumed*. To illustrate, the following December 1 transaction of NetSolutions is used:

Dec. 1 *NetSolutions paid rent of $800 for the month.*

On December 1, the rent payment of $800 represents Prepaid Rent. However, the Prepaid Rent expires daily, and at the end of December, there will be no asset left. In such cases, the payment of $800 is recorded as Rent Expense rather than as Prepaid Rent. In this way, no adjusting entry is needed at the end of the period.

Example Exercise 3-6 Adjustment for Prepaid Expense — Obj. 3

The prepaid insurance account had a beginning balance of $2,400 and was debited for $3,600 of premiums paid during the year. Journalize the adjusting entry required at the end of the year, assuming the amount of unexpired insurance related to future periods is $3,250.

Follow My Example 3-6

Insurance Expense..	2,750	
Prepaid Insurance...................................		2,750
Insurance expired ($2,400 + $3,600 − $3,250).		

Practice Exercises: PE 3-6A, PE 3-6B

Obj. 4 Prepare adjusting entries for depreciation.

Adjusting Entries for Depreciation

Fixed assets, or **plant assets**, are physical resources that are owned and used by a business and are permanent or have a long life. Examples of fixed assets include land, buildings, and equipment. In a sense, fixed assets are a type of *long-term* prepaid expense. However, because of their normally high dollar amount and long life, they are discussed separately from other prepaid expenses.

Fixed assets, such as office equipment, are used to generate revenue much like supplies are used to generate revenue. Unlike supplies, however, there is no visible reduction in the quantity of the equipment. Instead, as time passes, the equipment loses its ability to provide useful services. This decrease in usefulness is called **depreciation**.

All fixed assets, except land, lose their usefulness and, thus, are said to **depreciate**. As a fixed asset depreciates, a portion of its cost should be recorded as an expense. This periodic expense is called **depreciation expense**.

The adjusting entry to record depreciation expense is similar to the adjusting entry for supplies used. The depreciation expense account is increased (debited) for the amount of depreciation. However, the fixed asset account is not decreased (credited). This is because both the original cost of a fixed asset and the depreciation recorded since its purchase are reported on the balance sheet. Instead, an account entitled **Accumulated Depreciation** is increased (credited).

Accumulated depreciation accounts are called **contra accounts**, or **contra asset accounts**. This is because accumulated depreciation accounts are deducted from their related fixed asset accounts on the balance sheet. The normal balance of a contra account is opposite the account from which it is deducted. Because the normal balance of a fixed asset account is a debit, the normal balance of an accumulated depreciation account is a credit.

The normal titles for fixed asset accounts and their related contra asset accounts are as follows:

Fixed Asset Account	Contra Asset Account
Land	None—Land is not depreciated.
Buildings	Accumulated Depreciation—Buildings
Store Equipment	Accumulated Depreciation—Store Equipment
Office Equipment	Accumulated Depreciation—Office Equipment

The December 31, 2018, unadjusted trial balance of **NetSolutions** (Exhibit 3) indicates that NetSolutions owns two fixed assets: land and office equipment. Land does not depreciate, and therefore does not have a contra account or an adjusting entry. Office equipment, however, does depreciate and requires an adjusting entry. Assume that the office equipment depreciates $50 during December. The depreciation expense account is increased (debited) by $50, and the contra account Accumulated Depreciation—Office Equipment is increased (credited) by $50.[4] The adjusting journal entry and T accounts are as follows:

Adjusting Journal Entry

Dec.	31	Depreciation Expense	56	50	
		Accumulated Depreciation—Office Equip.	19		50
		Depreciation on office equipment.			

Accounting Equation Impact

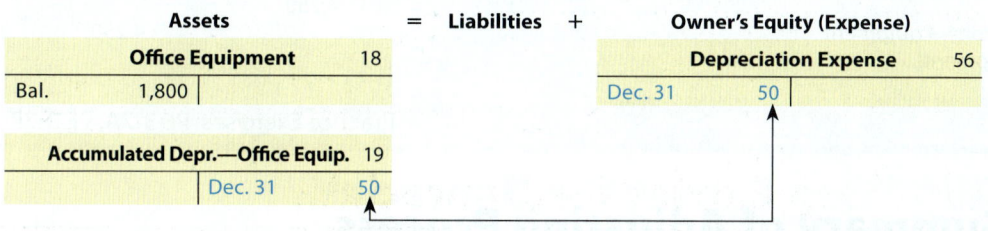

After the adjusting journal entry is recorded and posted, the office equipment account still has a debit balance of $1,800. This is the original cost of the office equipment that was purchased on December 4. The accumulated depreciation—office equipment account has a credit balance of $50. The difference between these two balances is the cost of the office equipment that has not yet been depreciated. This amount, called the **book value of the asset** (or **net book value**), is computed as follows:

Book Value of Asset = Cost of Asset − Accumulated Depreciation of Asset

Thus, the book value of NetSolutions' office equipment at the end of December is $1,750 ($1,800 − $50). The office equipment and its related accumulated depreciation are reported on the December 31, 2018, balance sheet as follows:

Office equipment	$1,800	
Accumulated depreciation	(50)	$1,750

The market value of a fixed asset usually differs from its book value. This is because depreciation is an *allocation* method, not a *valuation* method. That is, depreciation allocates the cost of a fixed asset to expense over its estimated life. Depreciation does not measure changes in market values, which vary from year to year. Thus, on December 31, 2018, the market value of NetSolutions' office equipment could be more or less than $1,750.

If the adjustment for depreciation ($50) is not recorded, Depreciation Expense on the income statement will be understated by $50, and the net income will be overstated by $50. On the balance sheet, assets (the book value of Office Equipment)

Link to Pandora

On a recent balance sheet, **Pandora** reported property, plant, and equipment of $57 million, accumulated depreciation of $22 million, and a net book value of $35 million.

---

[4] Methods of computing depreciation expense are described and illustrated in Chapter 10.

and owner's equity (Chris Clark, Capital) will be overstated by $50. The effects of omitting the adjustment for depreciation are as follows:

	Amount of Misstatement
Income Statement	
Revenues correctly stated	$ XX
Expenses understated by	(50)
Net income overstated by	$ 50
Balance Sheet	
Assets overstated by	$ 50
Liabilities correctly stated	$ XX
Owner's equity overstated by	50
Total liabilities and owner's equity overstated by	$ 50

Example Exercise 3-7 Adjustment for Depreciation — Obj. 4

The estimated amount of depreciation on equipment for the current year is $4,250. Journalize the adjusting entry to record the depreciation.

Follow My Example 3-7

Depreciation Expense... 4,250
   Accumulated Depreciation—Equipment................................. 4,250
   Depreciation on equipment.

Practice Exercises: PE 3-7A, PE 3-7B

Summary of Adjusting Process

Obj. 5 Summarize the adjusting process.

A summary of the basic types of adjusting entries is shown in Exhibit 6. The adjusting entries for **NetSolutions** are shown in Exhibit 7. The adjusting entries are dated as of the last day of the period. However, because collecting the adjustment data requires time, the entries are usually recorded at a later date. An explanation is normally included with each adjusting entry.

NetSolutions' adjusting entries are posted to the ledger shown in Exhibit 8. The adjustments are highlighted in Exhibit 8 to distinguish them from other transactions.

Business Connection

MICROSOFT'S DEFERRED REVENUES

Microsoft Corporation develops, manufactures, licenses, and supports a wide range of computer software products, including Windows® operating systems, Word®, Excel®, and the Xbox® gaming system. When Microsoft sells its products, it incurs an obligation to support its software with technical support and periodic updates. As a result, not all the revenue is earned on the date of sale; some of the revenue on the date of sale is unearned. The portion of revenue related to support services, such as updates and technical support, is earned as time passes and support is provided to customers. Thus, each year Microsoft makes adjusting entries transferring some of its unearned revenue to revenue. The following were taken from recent financial statements of Microsoft:

	Year 2	Year 1
Unearned revenue (in millions)	$25,158	$22,348

During Year 3, Microsoft expects to recognize $23,150 of revenue from the $25,158 of unearned revenue, which will have a significant impact on its operating results. At the same time, Microsoft will record additional unearned revenue from Year 3 sales.

Summary of Adjustments — EXHIBIT 6

ACCRUED REVENUES

Examples	Reason for Adjustment	Adjusting Entry			Examples from NetSolutions			Financial Statement Impact if Adjusting Entry Is Omitted	
Services performed but not billed, interest to be received	Services have been provided to the customer but have not been billed or recorded. Interest has been earned but has not been received or recorded.	Asset Revenue	Dr.	Cr.	Accounts Receivable Fees Earned	500	500	Income Statement: Revenues Expenses Net income Balance Sheet: Assets Liabilities Owner's equity (Owner's Capital)	Understated No effect Understated Understated No effect Understated

ACCRUED EXPENSES

Examples	Reason for Adjustment	Adjusting Entry			Examples from NetSolutions			Financial Statement Impact if Adjusting Entry Is Omitted	
Wages or salaries incurred but not paid, interest incurred but not paid	Expenses have been incurred, but have not been paid or recorded.	Expense Liability	Dr.	Cr.	Wages Expense Wages Payable	250	250	Income Statement: Revenues Expenses Net income Balance Sheet: Assets Liabilities Owner's equity (Owner's Capital)	No effect Understated Overstated No effect Understated Overstated

UNEARNED REVENUES

Examples	Reason for Adjustment	Adjusting Entry			Examples from NetSolutions			Financial Statement Impact if Adjusting Entry Is Omitted	
Unearned rent, magazine subscriptions received in advance, fees received in advance of services	Cash received before the services have been provided is recorded as a liability. Some services have been provided to the customer before the end of the accounting period.	Liability Revenue	Dr.	Cr.	Unearned Rent Rent Revenue	120	120	Income Statement: Revenues Expenses Net income Balance Sheet: Assets Liabilities Owner's equity (Owner's Capital)	Understated No effect Understated No effect Overstated Understated

PREPAID EXPENSES

Examples	Reason for Adjustment	Adjusting Entry			Examples from NetSolutions			Financial Statement Impact if Adjusting Entry Is Omitted	
Supplies, prepaid insurance	Prepaid expenses (assets) have been used or consumed in the business operations.	Expense Asset	Dr.	Cr.	Supplies Expense Supplies Insurance Expense Prepaid Insurance	1,240 200	1,240 200	Income Statement: Revenues Expenses Net income Balance Sheet: Assets Liabilities Owner's equity (Owner's Capital)	No effect Understated Overstated Overstated No effect Overstated

DEPRECIATION

Examples	Reason for Adjustment	Adjusting Entry			Examples from NetSolutions			Financial Statement Impact if Adjusting Entry Is Omitted	
Depreciation of equipment and buildings	Fixed assets depreciate as they are used or consumed in the business operations.	Expense Contra Asset	Dr.	Cr.	Depreciation Expense Accum. Depr.— Office Equipment	50	50	Income Statement: Revenues Expenses Net income Balance Sheet: Assets Liabilities Owner's equity (Owner's Capital)	No effect Understated Overstated Overstated No effect Overstated

EXHIBIT 7
Adjusting Entries—NetSolutions

Journal — Page 5

Date		Description	Post. Ref.	Debit	Credit
		Adjusting Entries			
2018 Dec.	31	Accounts Receivable	12	500	
		Fees Earned	41		500
		Accrued fees (25 hrs. × $20).			
	31	Wages Expense	51	250	
		Wages Payable	22		250
		Accrued wages.			
	31	Unearned Rent	23	120	
		Rent Revenue	42		120
		Rent earned ($360 ÷ 3 months).			
	31	Supplies Expense	52	1,240	
		Supplies	14		1,240
		Supplies used ($2,000 − $760).			
	31	Insurance Expense	55	200	
		Prepaid Insurance	15		200
		Insurance expired ($2,400 ÷ 12 months).			
	31	Depreciation Expense	56	50	
		Accum. Depreciation—Office Equipment	19		50
		Depreciation on office equipment.			

EXHIBIT 8
Ledger with Adjusting Entries—NetSolutions

Account: Cash — Account No. 11

Date	Item	Post. Ref.	Debit	Credit	Balance Debit	Balance Credit
2018 Nov. 1		1	25,000		25,000	
5		1		20,000	5,000	
18		1	7,500		12,500	
30		1		3,650	8,850	
30		1		950	7,900	
30		2		2,000	5,900	
Dec. 1		2		2,400	3,500	
1		2		800	2,700	
1		2	360		3,060	
6		2		180	2,880	
11		2		400	2,480	
13		3		950	1,530	
16		3	3,100		4,630	
20		3		900	3,730	
21		3	650		4,380	
23		3		1,450	2,930	
27		3		1,200	1,730	
31		3		310	1,420	
31		4		225	1,195	
31		4	2,870		4,065	
31		4		2,000	2,065	

Account: Accounts Receivable — Account No. 12

Date	Item	Post. Ref.	Debit	Credit	Balance Debit	Balance Credit
2018 Dec. 16		3	1,750		1,750	
21		3		650	1,100	
31		4	1,120		2,220	
31	Adjusting	5	500		2,720	

Account: Supplies — Account No. 14

Date	Item	Post. Ref.	Debit	Credit	Balance Debit	Balance Credit
2018 Nov. 10		1	1,350		1,350	
30		1		800	550	
Dec. 23		3	1,450		2,000	
31	Adjusting	5		1,240	760	

Ledger with Adjusting Entries—NetSolutions (Continued)   EXHIBIT 8

Account Prepaid Insurance — Account No. 15

Date	Item	Post. Ref.	Debit	Credit	Balance Debit	Balance Credit
2018 Dec. 1		2	2,400		2,400	
31	Adjusting	5		200	2,200	

Account Land — Account No. 17

Date	Item	Post. Ref.	Debit	Credit	Balance Debit	Balance Credit
2018 Nov. 5		1	20,000		20,000	

Account Office Equipment — Account No. 18

Date	Item	Post. Ref.	Debit	Credit	Balance Debit	Balance Credit
2018 Dec. 4		2	1,800		1,800	

Account Accum. Depr.—Office Equip. — Account No. 19

Date	Item	Post. Ref.	Debit	Credit	Balance Debit	Balance Credit
2018 Dec. 31	Adjusting	5		50		50

Account Accounts Payable — Account No. 21

Date	Item	Post. Ref.	Debit	Credit	Balance Debit	Balance Credit
2018 Nov. 10		1		1,350		1,350
30		1	950			400
Dec. 4		2		1,800		2,200
11		2	400			1,800
20		3		900		900

Account Wages Payable — Account No. 22

Date	Item	Post. Ref.	Debit	Credit	Balance Debit	Balance Credit
2018 Dec. 31	Adjusting	5		250		250

Account Unearned Rent — Account No. 23

Date	Item	Post. Ref.	Debit	Credit	Balance Debit	Balance Credit
2018 Dec. 1		2		360		360
31	Adjusting	5	120			240

Account Chris Clark, Capital — Account No. 31

Date	Item	Post. Ref.	Debit	Credit	Balance Debit	Balance Credit
2018 Nov. 1		1		25,000		25,000

Account Chris Clark, Drawing — Account No. 32

Date	Item	Post. Ref.	Debit	Credit	Balance Debit	Balance Credit
2018 Nov. 30		2	2,000		2,000	
Dec. 31		4	2,000		4,000	

Account Fees Earned — Account No. 41

Date	Item	Post. Ref.	Debit	Credit	Balance Debit	Balance Credit
2018 Nov. 18		1		7,500		7,500
Dec. 16		3		3,100		10,600
16		3		1,750		12,350
31		4		2,870		15,220
31		4		1,120		16,340
31	Adjusting	5		500		16,840

Account Rent Revenue — Account No. 42

Date	Item	Post. Ref.	Debit	Credit	Balance Debit	Balance Credit
2018 Dec. 31	Adjusting	5		120		120

Account Wages Expense — Account No. 51

Date	Item	Post. Ref.	Debit	Credit	Balance Debit	Balance Credit
2018 Nov. 30		1	2,125		2,125	
Dec. 13		3	950		3,075	
27		3	1,200		4,275	
31	Adjusting	5	250		4,525	

(Continued)

EXHIBIT 8 — Ledger with Adjusting Entries—NetSolutions (Concluded)

Account Supplies Expense — Account No. 52

Date	Item	Post. Ref.	Debit	Credit	Balance Debit	Balance Credit
2018						
Nov. 30		1	800		800	
Dec. 31	Adjusting	5	1,240		2,040	

Account Rent Expense — Account No. 53

Date	Item	Post. Ref.	Debit	Credit	Balance Debit	Balance Credit
2018						
Nov. 30		1	800		800	
Dec. 1		2	800		1,600	

Account Utilities Expense — Account No. 54

Date	Item	Post. Ref.	Debit	Credit	Balance Debit	Balance Credit
2018						
Nov. 30		1	450		450	
Dec. 31		3	310		760	
31		4	225		985	

Account Insurance Expense — Account No. 55

Date	Item	Post. Ref.	Debit	Credit	Balance Debit	Balance Credit
2018						
Dec. 31	Adjusting	5	200		200	

Account Depreciation Expense — Account No. 56

Date	Item	Post. Ref.	Debit	Credit	Balance Debit	Balance Credit
2018						
Dec. 31	Adjusting	5	50		50	

Account Miscellaneous Expense — Account No. 59

Date	Item	Post. Ref.	Debit	Credit	Balance Debit	Balance Credit
2018						
Nov. 30		1	275		275	
Dec. 6		2	180		455	

Example Exercise 3-8 Effects of Adjustments   Obj. 5

For the year ending December 31, 2019, Mann Medical Co. mistakenly omitted adjusting entries for (1) $8,600 of unearned revenue that was earned, (2) earned revenue of $12,500 that was not billed, and (3) accrued wages of $2,900. Indicate the combined effect of the errors on (a) revenues, (b) expenses, and (c) net income for the year ended December 31, 2019.

Follow My Example 3-8

a. Revenues were understated by $21,100 ($8,600 + $12,500).
b. Expenses were understated by $2,900.
b. Net income was understated by $18,200 ($8,600 + $12,500 − $2,900).

Practice Exercises: PE 3-8A, PE 3-8B

Obj. 6 Prepare an adjusted trial balance.

Adjusted Trial Balance

After the adjusting entries are posted, an **adjusted trial balance** is prepared. The adjusted trial balance verifies the equality of the total debit and credit balances before the financial statements are prepared. If the adjusted trial balance does not balance, an error has occurred. However, as discussed in Chapter 2, errors may occur even though the adjusted trial balance totals agree. For example, if an adjusting entry were omitted, the adjusted trial balance totals would still agree.

Exhibit 9 shows the adjusted trial balance for NetSolutions as of December 31, 2018. Chapter 4 discusses how financial statements, including a classified balance sheet, are prepared from an adjusted trial balance.

EXHIBIT 9
Adjusted Trial Balance

NetSolutions
Adjusted Trial Balance
December 31, 2018

	Account No.	Debit Balances	Credit Balances
Cash	11	2,065	
Accounts Receivable	12	2,720	
Supplies	14	760	
Prepaid Insurance	15	2,200	
Land	17	20,000	
Office Equipment	18	1,800	
Accumulated Depreciation—Office Equipment	19		50
Accounts Payable	21		900
Wages Payable	22		250
Unearned Rent	23		240
Chris Clark, Capital	31		25,000
Chris Clark, Drawing	32	4,000	
Fees Earned	41		16,840
Rent Revenue	42		120
Wages Expense	51	4,525	
Supplies Expense	52	2,040	
Rent Expense	53	1,600	
Utilities Expense	54	985	
Insurance Expense	55	200	
Depreciation Expense	56	50	
Miscellaneous Expense	59	455	
		43,400	43,400

Example Exercise 3-9 Effect of Errors   *Obj. 6*

For each of the following errors, considered individually, indicate whether the error would cause the adjusted trial balance totals to be unequal. If the error would cause the adjusted trial balance totals to be unequal, indicate whether the debit or credit total is higher and by how much.

a. The adjustment for accrued fees of $5,340 was journalized as a debit to Accounts Payable for $5,340 and a credit to Fees Earned of $5,340.

b. The adjustment for depreciation of $3,260 was journalized as a debit to Depreciation Expense for $3,620 and a credit to Accumulated Depreciation for $3,260.

Follow My Example 3-9

a. The totals are equal even though the debit should have been to Accounts Receivable instead of Accounts Payable.
b. The totals are unequal. The debit total is higher by $360 ($3,620 − $3,260).

Practice Exercises: PE 3-9A, PE 3-9B

Financial Analysis and Interpretation: Vertical Analysis

Obj. 7 Describe and illustrate the use of vertical analysis in evaluating a company's performance and financial condition.

Comparing each item on a financial statement with a total amount from the same statement is useful in analyzing relationships within the financial statement. **Vertical analysis** is the term used to describe such comparisons.

In vertical analysis of a balance sheet, each asset item is stated as a percent of the total assets. Each liability and owner's equity item is stated as a percent of total liabilities and owner's equity. In vertical analysis of an income statement, each item is stated as a percent of revenues or fees earned.

Vertical analysis is also useful for analyzing changes in financial statements over time. To illustrate, a vertical analysis of two years of income statements for J. Holmes, Attorney-at-Law, follows:

J. Holmes, Attorney-at-Law
Income Statements
For the Years Ended December 31

	Year 2 Amount	Year 2 Percent*	Year 1 Amount	Year 1 Percent*
Fees earned	$187,500	100.0%	$150,000	100.0%
Operating expenses:				
Wages expense	$ 60,000	32.0%	$ 45,000	30.0%
Rent expense	15,000	8.0%	12,000	8.0%
Utilities expense	12,500	6.7%	9,000	6.0%
Supplies expense	2,700	1.4%	3,000	2.0%
Miscellaneous expense	2,300	1.2%	1,800	1.2%
Total operating expenses	$ 92,500	49.3%	$ 70,800	47.2%
Net income	$ 95,000	50.7%	$ 79,200	52.8%

*Rounded to one decimal place

The preceding vertical analysis indicates both favorable and unfavorable trends affecting the income statement of J. Holmes, Attorney-at-Law. The increase in wages expense of 2% (32.0% − 30.0%) is an unfavorable trend, as is the increase in utilities expense of 0.7% (6.7% − 6.0%). A favorable trend is the decrease in supplies expense of 0.6% (2.0% − 1.4%). Rent expense and miscellaneous expense as a percent of fees earned were constant. The net result of these trends is that net income decreased as a percent of fees earned from 52.8% to 50.7%.

The analysis of the various percentages shown for J. Holmes, Attorney-at-Law, can be enhanced by comparisons with industry averages. Such averages are published by trade associations and financial information services. Any major differences between industry averages should be investigated.

Vertical analysis of operating income taken from two recent years of income statements for **Pandora Media, Inc.** follows:

Pandora Media, Inc.
Operating Income Statements
For the Years Ended January 31
(in thousands)

	Year 2 Amount	Year 2 Percent*	Year 1 Amount	Year 1 Percent*
Revenues:				
Advertising	$732,338	79.5%	$489,340	81.5%
Subscription	188,464	20.5%	110,893	18.5%
Total revenues	$920,802	100.0%	$600,233	100.0%
Expenses:				
Cost of revenues	$508,004	55.2%	$357,083	59.5%
Sales and marketing	277,330	30.1%	169,005	28.2%
General and administrative	112,443	12.2%	69,300	11.5%
Product development	53,153	5.8%	31,294	5.2%
Total expenses	$950,930	103.3%	$626,682	104.4%
Operating income (loss)	$ (30,128)	(3.3)%	$ (26,449)	(4.4)%

*Rounded to one decimal place

The preceding illustration shows the usefulness of vertical analysis. Since Year 2 revenues are significantly larger than those of Year 1, it is difficult to compare operating results using only dollar amounts. Vertical analysis, however, provides a relative comparison. The analysis reveals that the operating loss decreased from 4.4% to 3.3% as a percent of total revenues. This improvement was the result of the net change in expenses as a percent of revenue. The cost of revenues decreased from 59.5% to 55.2% of revenues, while sales and marketing, general and administrative, and product development expenses all increased as a percent of sales. The percentage increase in these latter expenses was less than the percentage decrease in the cost of revenues. Thus, total expenses decreased from 104.4% to 103.3% as a percent of revenues.

Example Exercise 3-10 Vertical Analysis

Obj. 7

Two income statements for Fortson Company follow:

Fortson Company
Income Statements
For the Years Ended December 31, 2019 and 2018

	2019	2018
Fees earned	$425,000	$375,000
Operating expenses	263,500	210,000
Operating income	$161,500	$165,000

a. Prepare a vertical analysis of Fortson Company's income statements.
b. Does the vertical analysis indicate a favorable or an unfavorable trend?

Follow My Example 3-10

a.

Fortson Company
Income Statements
For the Years Ended December 31, 2019 and 2018

	2019 Amount	2019 Percent	2018 Amount	2018 Percent
Fees earned	$425,000	100%	$375,000	100%
Operating expenses	263,500	62	210,000	56
Operating income	$161,500	38%	$165,000	44%

b. An unfavorable trend of increasing operating expenses and decreasing operating income is indicated.

Practice Exercises: PE 3-10A, PE 3-10B

At a Glance 3

Obj. 1 Describe the nature of the adjusting process.

Key Points The accrual basis of accounting requires that revenues be reported in the period in which they are earned and expenses be matched with the revenues they generate. The updating of accounts at the end of the accounting period is called the adjusting process. Each adjusting entry affects an income statement and balance sheet account. The two general classifications for accounts requiring adjustment are accruals and deferrals. Accruals include accrued revenues and accrued expenses. Deferrals include unearned revenues and prepaid expenses.

Learning Outcomes	Example Exercises	Practice Exercises
• Explain why accrual accounting requires adjusting entries.		
• Describe the revenue and expense recognition principles.		
• List accounts that do and do *not* require adjusting entries at the end of the accounting period.	EE3-1	PE3-1A, 3-1B
• Give an example of accrued revenue, accrued expense, deferrred (unearned) revenue, and deferred (prepaid) expense.	EE3-2	PE3-2A, 3-2B

Obj. 2 Prepare adjusting entries for accruals.

Key Points Adjusting entries for accruals include accrued revenues and expenses. The adjusting entry for an accrued revenue debits Accounts Receivable and credits a revenue account such as Fees Earned. The adjusting entry for an accrued expense debits an expense account such as Wages Expense and credits a liability account such as Wages Payable.

Learning Outcomes	Example Exercises	Practice Exercises
• Prepare an adjusting entry for an accrued revenue.	EE3-3	PE3-3A, 3-3B
• Prepare an adjusting entry for an accrued expense.	EE3-4	PE3-4A, 3-4B

Obj. 3 Prepare adjusting entries for deferrals.

Key Points Adjusting entries for deferrals include unearned revenues and prepaid expenses. The adjusting entry for an unearned revenue debits an unearned revenue account such as Unearned Rent and credits a revenue account such as Rent Revenue. The adjusting entry for an accrued expense debits an expense account such as Wages Expense and credits a liability account such as Wages Payable.

Learning Outcomes	Example Exercises	Practice Exercises
• Prepare an adjusting entry for an unearned revenue.	EE3-5	PE3-5A, 3-5B
• Prepare an adjusting entry for a prepaid expense.	EE3-6	PE3-6A, 3-6B

Obj. 4 — Prepare adjusting entries for depreciation.

Key Points The adjusting entry for depreciation of a fixed asset debits Depreciation Expense and credits a contra asset account, Accumulated Depreciation. The book value of a fixed asset equals its cost less its accumulated depreciation. Land is a fixed asset that does not depreciate.

Learning Outcomes	Example Exercises	Practice Exercises
• Describe assets that require the recording of an adjusting entry for depreciation. • Prepare an adjusting entry for depreciation expense.	EE3-7	PE3-7A, 3-7B

Obj. 5 — Summarize the adjusting process.

Key Points A summary of adjustments, including the type of adjustment, reason for the adjustment, the adjusting entry, and the effect of omitting an adjustment on the financial statements, is shown in Exhibit 6.

Learning Outcomes	Example Exercises	Practice Exercises
• Determine the effect on the income statement and balance sheet of omitting an adjusting entry for prepaid expense, unearned revenue, accrued revenue, accrued expense, and depreciation.	EE3-8	PE3-8A, 3-8B

Obj. 6 — Prepare an adjusted trial balance.

Key Points After all of the adjusting entries have been posted, the equality of the total debit balances and the total credit balances is verified using an adjusted trial balance.

Learning Outcomes	Example Exercises	Practice Exercises
• Prepare an adjusted trial balance. • Determine the effect of errors on the equality of the adjusted trial balance.	EE3-9	PE3-9A, 3-9B

Obj. 7 — Describe and illustrate the use of vertical analysis in evaluating a company's performance and financial condition.

Key Points Comparing each item on a financial statement with a total amount from the same statement is called vertical analysis. On the balance sheet, each asset is expressed as a percent of total assets, and each liability and owner's equity is expressed as a percent of total liabilities and owner's equity. On the income statement, each revenue and expense is expressed as a percent of total revenues or fees earned.

Learning Outcomes	Example Exercises	Practice Exercises
• Describe vertical analysis. • Prepare a vertical analysis report of a financial statement.	EE3-10	PE3-10A, 3-10B

Illustrative Problem

Three years ago, T. Roderick organized Harbor Realty. At July 31, 2019, the end of the current year, the unadjusted trial balance of Harbor Realty follows:

Harbor Realty
Unadjusted Trial Balance
July 31, 2019

	Debit Balances	Credit Balances
Cash	3,425	
Accounts Receivable	7,000	
Supplies	1,270	
Prepaid Insurance	620	
Office Equipment	51,650	
Accumulated Depreciation—Office Equipment		9,700
Accounts Payable		925
Wages Payable		0
Unearned Fees		1,250
T. Roderick, Capital		29,000
T. Roderick, Drawing	5,200	
Fees Earned		59,125
Wages Expense	22,415	
Depreciation Expense	0	
Rent Expense	4,200	
Utilities Expense	2,715	
Supplies Expense	0	
Insurance Expense	0	
Miscellaneous Expense	1,505	
	100,000	100,000

The data needed to determine year-end adjustments follow:
- Supplies on hand at July 31, 2019, $380.
- Insurance premiums expired during the year, $315.
- Depreciation of equipment during the year, $4,950.
- Wages accrued but not paid at July 31, 2019, $440.
- Accrued fees earned but not recorded at July 31, 2019, $1,000.
- Unearned fees on July 31, 2019, $750.

Instructions

1. Prepare the necessary adjusting journal entries on July 31. Include journal entry explanations.

2. Determine the balance of the accounts affected by the adjusting entries and prepare an adjusted trial balance.

Solution

1.

Journal

Date		Description	Post. Ref.	Debit	Credit
2019 July	31	Supplies Expense		890	
		Supplies			890
		Supplies used ($1,270 – $380).			
	31	Insurance Expense		315	
		Prepaid Insurance			315
		Insurance expired.			
	31	Depreciation Expense		4,950	
		Accumulated Depreciation—Office Equipment			4,950
		Depreciation expense.			
	31	Wages Expense		440	
		Wages Payable			440
		Accrued wages.			
	31	Accounts Receivable		1,000	
		Fees Earned			1,000
		Accrued fees.			
	31	Unearned Fees		500	
		Fees Earned			500
		Fees earned ($1,250 – $750).			

2.

Harbor Realty
Adjusted Trial Balance
July 31, 2019

	Debit Balances	Credit Balances
Cash	3,425	
Accounts Receivable	8,000	
Supplies	380	
Prepaid Insurance	305	
Office Equipment	51,650	
Accumulated Depreciation—Office Equipment		14,650
Accounts Payable		925
Wages Payable		440
Unearned Fees		750
T. Roderick, Capital		29,000
T. Roderick, Drawing	5,200	
Fees Earned		60,625
Wages Expense	22,855	
Depreciation Expense	4,950	
Rent Expense	4,200	
Utilities Expense	2,715	
Supplies Expense	890	
Insurance Expense	315	
Miscellaneous Expense	1,505	
	106,390	106,390

Key Terms

accrual (115)
accrual basis of accounting (113)
Accumulated Depreciation (124)
adjusted trial balance (130)
adjusting entries (114)
adjusting process (114)
book value of the asset (or net book value) (125)

cash basis of accounting (113)
contra accounts (or contra asset accounts) (124)
deferral (115)
depreciate (124)
depreciation (124)
depreciation expense (124)
expense recognition principle (114)

fixed assets (or plant assets) (124)
matching principle (114)
prepaid expense (115)
revenue recognition (114)
revenue recognition principle (114)
unearned revenue (115)
vertical analysis (131)

Discussion Questions

1. How are revenues and expenses reported on the income statement under (a) the cash basis of accounting and (b) the accrual basis of accounting?

2. Is the matching concept related to (a) the cash basis of accounting or (b) the accrual basis of accounting?

3. Why are adjusting entries needed at the end of an accounting period?

4. What is the difference between adjusting entries and correcting entries?

5. Identify the four different categories of adjusting entries frequently required at the end of an accounting period.

6. If the effect of the debit portion of an adjusting entry is to increase the balance of an asset account, which of the following statements describes the effect of the credit portion of the entry?
   a. Increases the balance of a revenue account.
   b. Increases the balance of an expense account.
   c. Increases the balance of a liability account.

7. If the effect of the credit portion of an adjusting entry is to increase the balance of a liability account, which of the following statements describes the effect of the debit portion of the entry?
   a. Increases the balance of a revenue account.
   b. Increases the balance of an expense account.
   c. Increases the balance of an asset account.

8. Does every adjusting entry affect net income for a period? Explain.

9. On November 1 of the current year, a business paid the November rent on the building that it occupies. (a) Do the rights acquired at November 1 represent an asset or an expense? (b) What is the justification for debiting Rent Expense at the time of payment?

10. (a) Explain the purpose of the two accounts: Depreciation Expense and Accumulated Depreciation. (b) What is the normal balance of each account? (c) Is it customary for the balances of the two accounts to be equal in amount? (d) In what financial statements, if any, will each account appear?

Practice Exercises

Example Exercises

 EE 3-1 p.115

PE 3-1A Accounts requiring adjustment   OBJ. 1, 2, 3

Indicate with a Yes or No whether or not each of the following accounts normally requires an adjusting entry:
a. Building
b. Cash
c. Wages Expense
d. Miscellaneous Expense
e. Nancy Palmer, Capital
f. Prepaid Insurance

Chapter 3 The Adjusting Process 139

EE 3-1 p. 115 **PE 3-1B Accounts requiring adjustment** OBJ. 1
Indicate with a Yes or No whether or not each of the following accounts normally requires an adjusting entry:
a. Accumulated Depreciation
b. Frank Kent, Drawing
c. Land
d. Salaries Payable
e. Supplies
f. Unearned Rent

EE 3-2 p. 116 **PE 3-2A Type of adjustment** OBJ. 1
Classify the following items as (1) prepaid expense, (2) unearned revenue, (3) accrued revenue, or (4) accrued expense:
a. Cash received for use of land next month.
b. Fees earned but not received in cash.
c. Wages owed but not yet paid.
d. Supplies on hand.

EE 3-2 p. 116 **PE 3-2B Type of adjustment** OBJ. 1
Classify the following items as (1) prepaid expense, (2) unearned revenue, (3) accrued revenue, or (4) accrued expense:
a. Cash received for services not yet rendered.
b. Insurance paid for the next year.
c. Interest revenue earned but not received.
d. Salaries owed but not yet paid.

EE 3-3 p. 118 **PE 3-3A Adjustment for accrued revenues** OBJ. 2
At the end of the current year, $17,555 of fees have been earned but have not been billed to clients. Journalize the adjusting entry (include an explanation) to record the accrued fees.

EE 3-3 p. 118 **PE 3-3B Adjustment for accrued revenues** OBJ. 2
At the end of the current year, $23,570 of fees have been earned but have not been billed to clients. Journalize the adjusting entry (include an explanation) to record the accrued fees.

EE 3-4 p. 120 **PE 3-4A Adjustment for accrued expense** OBJ. 2
Prospect Realty Co. pays weekly salaries of $27,600 for a six-day workweek (Monday thru Saturday). Journalize the necessary adjusting entry (include an explanation) assuming that the accounting period ends on Friday.

EE 3-4 p. 120 **PE 3-4B Adjustment for accrued expense** OBJ. 2
We-Sell Realty Co. pays weekly salaries of $11,800 on Friday for a five-day workweek ending on that day. Journalize the necessary adjusting entry (include an explanation) assuming that the accounting period ends on Wednesday.

EE 3-5 p. 121 **PE 3-5A Adjustment for unearned revenue** OBJ. 3
On June 1, 2019, Herbal Co. received $18,900 for the rent of land for 12 months. Journalize the adjusting entry (include an explanation) required for unearned rent on December 31, 2019.

EE 3-5 p. 121 **PE 3-5B Adjustment for unearned revenue** OBJ. 3
The balance in the unearned fees account, before adjustment at the end of the year, is $272,500. Journalize the adjusting entry (include an explanation) required if the amount of unearned fees at the end of the year is $189,750.

140 Chapter 3 The Adjusting Process

EE 3-6 *p. 124* **PE 3-6A Adjustment for prepaid expense** OBJ. 3
The prepaid insurance account had a beginning balance of $4,500 and was debited for $16,600 of premiums paid during the year. Journalize the adjusting entry (include an explanation) required at the end of the year, assuming the amount of unexpired insurance related to future periods is $5,600.

EE 3-6 *p. 124* **PE 3-6B Adjustment for prepaid expense** OBJ. 3
The supplies account had a beginning balance of $3,375 and was debited for $6,450 for supplies purchased during the year. Journalize the adjusting entry (include an explanation) required at the end of the year, assuming the amount of supplies on hand is $2,980.

EE 3-7 *p. 126* **PE 3-7A Adjustment for depreciation** OBJ. 4
The estimated amount of depreciation on equipment for the current year is $7,700. Journalize the adjusting entry (include an explanation) to record the depreciation.

EE 3-7 *p. 126* **PE 3-7B Adjustment for depreciation** OBJ. 4
The estimated amount of depreciation on equipment for the current year is $6,880. Journalize the adjusting entry (include an explanation) to record the depreciation.

EE 3-8 *p. 130* **PE 3-8A Effect of omitting adjustments** OBJ. 5
For the year ending April 30, Urology Medical Services Co. mistakenly omitted adjusting entries for (1) $1,400 of supplies that were used, (2) unearned revenue of $6,600 that was earned, and (3) insurance of $9,000 that expired. Indicate the effect of the errors on (a) revenues, (b) expenses, and (c) net income for the year ended April 30.

EE 3-8 *p. 130* **PE 3-8B Effect of omitting adjustments** OBJ. 5
For the year ending August 31, Mammalia Medical Co. mistakenly omitted adjusting entries for (1) depreciation of $5,800, (2) fees earned that were not billed of $44,500, and (3) accrued wages of $7,300. Indicate the effect of the errors on (a) revenues, (b) expenses, and (c) net income for the year ended August 31.

EE 3-9 *p. 131* **PE 3-9A Effect of errors on adjusted trial balance** OBJ. 6
For each of the following errors, considered individually, indicate whether the error would cause the adjusted trial balance totals to be unequal. If the error would cause the adjusted trial balance totals to be unequal, indicate whether the debit or credit total is higher and by how much.
  a. The adjustment for accrued wages of $5,200 was journalized as a debit to Wages Expense for $5,200 and a credit to Accounts Payable for $5,200.
  b. The entry for $1,125 of supplies used during the period was journalized as a debit to Supplies Expense of $1,125 and a credit to Supplies of $1,152.

EE 3-9 *p. 131* **PE 3-9B Effect of errors on adjusted trial balance** OBJ. 6
For each of the following errors, considered individually, indicate whether the error would cause the adjusted trial balance totals to be unequal. If the error would cause the adjusted trial balance totals to be unequal, indicate whether the debit or credit total is higher and by how much.
  a. The adjustment of $9,800 for accrued fees earned was journalized as a debit to Accounts Receivable for $9,800 and a credit to Fees Earned for $8,900.
  b. The adjustment of depreciation of $3,600 was omitted from the end-of-period adjusting entries.

Chapter 3 The Adjusting Process 141

EE 3-10 *p. 133* **PE 3-10A Vertical analysis**   OBJ. 7

Two income statements for Hemlock Company follow:

Hemlock Company
Income Statements
For Years Ended December 31

	2019	2018
Fees earned	$725,000	$615,000
Operating expenses	435,000	356,700
Operating income	$290,000	$258,300

a. Prepare a vertical analysis of Hemlock Company's income statements.

b.  Does the vertical analysis indicate a favorable or an unfavorable trend?

EE 3-10 *p. 133* **PE 3-10B Vertical analysis**   OBJ. 7

Two income statements for Cornea Company follow:

Cornea Company
Income Statements
For Years Ended December 31

	2019	2018
Fees earned	$1,640,000	$1,300,000
Operating expenses	869,200	715,000
Operating income	$ 770,800	$ 585,000

a. Prepare a vertical analysis of Cornea Company's income statements.

b. 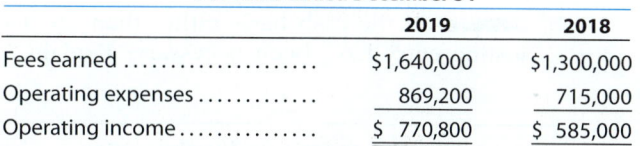 Does the vertical analysis indicate a favorable or an unfavorable trend?

Exercises

EX 3-1 Classifying types of adjustments   OBJ. 1, 2, 3

Classify the following items as (a) accrued revenue, (b) accrued expense, (c) unearned revenue, or (d) prepaid expense:

1. Bill for ads that appeared in prior month's local newspaper.
2. Fees received but not yet earned.
3. Fees earned but not yet received.
4. Premium paid on a one-year insurance policy.
5. Rent received in advance for rental of office space.
6. Supplies on hand.
7. Rent paid in advance.
8. Wages owed but payable in the following period.

EX 3-2 Classifying adjusting entries   OBJ. 1, 2, 3

The following accounts were taken from the unadjusted trial balance of Legislative Results Inc., a congressional lobbying firm. Indicate whether or not each account would normally require an adjusting entry. If the account normally requires an adjusting entry, use the following notation to indicate the type of adjustment:

AR—Accrued Revenue
AE—Accrued Expense
UR—Unearned Revenue
PE—Prepaid Expense

(Continued)

142 Chapter 3 The Adjusting Process

To illustrate, the answer for the first account follows:

Account	Answer
Accounts Receivable	Normally requires adjustment (AR).
Cash	
Harriet Kasun, Capital	
Interest Expense	
Interest Receivable	
Land	
Office Equipment	
Prepaid Rent	
Supplies	
Unearned Fees	
Wages Expense	

EX 3-3 Adjusting entry for accrued fees OBJ. 2

At the end of the current year, $59,500 of fees have been earned but have not been billed to clients.

a. Journalize the adjusting entry to record the accrued fees.

b. If the cash basis rather than the accrual basis had been used, would an adjusting entry have been necessary? Explain.

EX 3-4 Effect of omitting adjusting entry OBJ. 2, 5

The adjusting entry for accrued fees was omitted at the end of the current year. Indicate which items will be in error, because of the omission, on (a) the income statement for the current year and (b) the balance sheet at the end of the year. Also indicate whether the items in error will be overstated or understated.

✔ a. Amount of entry: $10,350

EX 3-5 Adjusting entries for accrued salaries OBJ. 2

Garcia Realty Co. pays weekly salaries of $17,250 on Friday for a five-day workweek ending on that day. Journalize the necessary adjusting entry at the end of the accounting period, assuming that the period ends (a) on Wednesday and (b) on Thursday.

EX 3-6 Determining wages paid OBJ. 2

The wages payable and wages expense accounts at May 31, after adjusting entries have been posted at the end of the first month of operations, are shown in the following T accounts:

Wages Payable		Wages Expense	
	Bal. 7,175	Bal. 73,250	

Determine the amount of wages paid during the month.

EX 3-7 Effect of omitting adjusting entry OBJ. 2, 5

Accrued salaries owed to employees for October 30 and 31 are not considered in preparing the financial statements for the year ended October 31. Indicate which items will be erroneously stated, because of the error, on (a) the income statement for the year and (b) the balance sheet as of October 31. Also indicate whether the items in error will be overstated or understated.

EX 3-8 Effect of omitting adjusting entry
OBJ. 2, 5

When preparing the financial statements for the year ended October 31, accrued salaries owed to employees for October 30 and 31 were omitted. The accrued salaries were included in the first salary payment in November. Indicate which items will be erroneously stated, because of failure to correct the initial error, on (a) the income statement for the month of November and (b) the balance sheet as of November 30.

EX 3-9 Adjusting entries for unearned fees
OBJ. 3

The balance in the unearned fees account, before adjustment at the end of the year, is $18,000. Journalize the adjusting entry required if the amount of unearned fees at the end of the year is $3,600.

EX 3-10 Effect of omitting adjusting entry
OBJ. 3, 5

At the end of January, the first month of the business year, the usual adjusting entry transferring rent earned from the unearned rent account to a revenue account was omitted. Indicate which items will be incorrectly stated, because of the error, on (a) the income statement for January and (b) the balance sheet as of January 31. Also indicate whether the items in error will be overstated or understated.

EX 3-11 Adjusting entry for supplies
OBJ. 3

The balance in the supplies account, before adjustment at the end of the year, is $4,850. Journalize the adjusting entry required if the amount of supplies on hand at the end of the year is $880.

EX 3-12 Determining supplies purchased
OBJ. 3

The supplies and supplies expense accounts at February 28, after adjusting entries have been posted at the end of the first year of operations, are shown in the following T accounts:

Supplies		Supplies Expense	
Bal. 690		Bal. 4,110	

Determine the amount of supplies purchased during the year.

EX 3-13 Effect of omitting adjusting entry
OBJ. 3, 5

At August 31, the end of the first month of operations, the usual adjusting entry transferring prepaid insurance expired to an expense account is omitted. Which items will be incorrectly stated, because of the error, on (a) the income statement for August and (b) the balance sheet as of August 31? Also indicate whether the items in error will be overstated or understated.

EX 3-14 Adjusting entries for prepaid insurance
OBJ. 3

The balance in the prepaid insurance account, before adjustment at the end of the year, is $27,000. Journalize the adjusting entry required under each of the following alternatives for determining the amount of the adjustment: (a) the amount of insurance expired during the year is $20,250; (b) the amount of unexpired insurance applicable to future periods is $6,750.

144 Chapter 3 The Adjusting Process

EX 3-15 Adjusting entries for prepaid insurance OBJ. 3

The prepaid insurance account had a balance of $3,000 at the beginning of the year. The account was debited for $32,500 for premiums on policies purchased during the year. Journalize the adjusting entry required under each of the following alternatives for determining the amount of the adjustment: (a) the amount of unexpired insurance applicable to future periods is $4,800; (b) the amount of insurance expired during the year is $30,700.

EX 3-16 Adjusting entries for unearned and accrued fees OBJ. 2, 3

The balance in the unearned fees account, before adjustment at the end of the year, is $97,770. Of these fees, $39,750 have been earned. In addition, $24,650 of fees have been earned but have not been billed. Journalize the adjusting entries (a) to adjust the unearned fees account and (b) to record the accrued fees.

✔ b. $57,320

EX 3-17 Adjusting entries for prepaid and accrued taxes OBJ. 2, 3

A-Z Construction Company was organized on May 1 of the current year. On May 2, A-Z Construction prepaid $18,480 to the city for taxes (license fees) for the *next* 12 months and debited the prepaid taxes account. A-Z Construction is also required to pay in January an annual tax (on property) for the current calendar year of $45,000.

a. Journalize the two adjusting entries required to bring the accounts affected by the two taxes up to date as of December 31, the end of the current year.

b. What is the amount of tax expense for the current year?

EX 3-18 Adjustment for depreciation OBJ. 4

The estimated amount of depreciation on equipment for the current year is $8,200. Journalize the adjusting entry to record the depreciation.

EX 3-19 Determining fixed asset's book value OBJ. 4

The balance in the equipment account is $3,150,000, and the balance in the accumulated depreciation—equipment account is $2,075,000.

a. What is the book value of the equipment?

b. Does the balance in the accumulated depreciation account mean that the equipment's loss of value is $2,075,000? Explain.

EX 3-20 Book value of fixed assets OBJ. 4

In a recent balance sheet, **Microsoft Corporation** reported *Property, Plant, and Equipment* of $27,804 million and *Accumulated Depreciation* of $14,793 million.

a. What was the book value of the fixed assets?

b. Would the book value of Microsoft's fixed assets normally approximate their market values?

Chapter 3   The Adjusting Process   145

EX 3-21 Effects of errors on financial statements OBJ. 2, 5

For a recent period, the balance sheet for **Costco Wholesale Corporation** reported accrued expenses of $3,446 million. For the same period, Costco reported income before income taxes of $3,197 million. Assume that the adjusting entry for $3,446 million of accrued expenses was not recorded at the end of the current period. What would have been the income (loss) before income taxes?

EX 3-22 Effects of errors on financial statements OBJ. 2, 5

For a recent year, the balance sheet for **The Campbell Soup Company** includes accrued expenses of $553 million. The income before taxes for Campbell for the year was $1,073 million.

a. Assume the adjusting entry for $553 million of accrued expenses was not recorded at the end of the year. By how much would income before taxes have been misstated?

b. What is the percentage of the misstatement in (a) to the reported income of $1,073 million? Round to one decimal place.

EX 3-23 Effects of errors on financial statements OBJ. 2, 3, 5

✔ 1. a. Revenue understated, $34,900

The accountant for Healthy Life Company, a medical services consulting firm, mistakenly omitted adjusting entries for (a) unearned revenue earned during the year ($34,900) and (b) accrued wages ($12,770). Indicate the effect of each error, considered individually, on the income statement for the current year ended July 31. Also indicate the effect of each error on the July 31 balance sheet. Set up a table similar to the following, and record your answers by inserting the dollar amount in the appropriate spaces. Insert a zero if the error does not affect the item.

	Error (a) Over-stated	Error (a) Under-stated	Error (b) Over-stated	Error (b) Under-stated
1. Revenue for the year would be	$___	$___	$___	$___
2. Expenses for the year would be	$___	$___	$___	$___
3. Net income for the year would be	$___	$___	$___	$___
4. Assets at July 31 would be	$___	$___	$___	$___
5. Liabilities at July 31 would be	$___	$___	$___	$___
6. Owner's equity at July 31 would be	$___	$___	$___	$___

EX 3-24 Effects of errors on financial statements OBJ. 2, 3, 5

If the net income for the current year had been $196,400 in Exercise 3-23, what would have been the correct net income if the proper adjusting entries had been made?

EX 3-25 Adjusting entries for depreciation; effect of error OBJ. 4, 5

On December 31, a business estimates depreciation on equipment used during the first year of operations to be $13,900.

a. Journalize the adjusting entry required as of December 31.

b. If the adjusting entry in (a) were omitted, which items would be erroneously stated on (1) the income statement for the year and (2) the balance sheet as of December 31?

EX 3-26 Adjusting entries from trial balances OBJ. 6

The unadjusted and adjusted trial balances for American Leaf Company on October 31, 2019, follow:

(Continued)

American Leaf Company
Trial Balances
October 31, 2019

	Unadjusted Debit Balances	Unadjusted Credit Balances	Adjusted Debit Balances	Adjusted Credit Balances
Cash	16		16	
Accounts Receivable	38		44	
Supplies	12		10	
Prepaid Insurance	20		8	
Land	26		26	
Equipment	40		40	
Accumulated Depreciation—Equipment		8		12
Accounts Payable		26		26
Wages Payable		0		2
Les Huff, Capital		92		92
Les Huff, Drawing	8		8	
Fees Earned		74		80
Wages Expense	24		26	
Rent Expense	8		8	
Insurance Expense	0		12	
Utilities Expense	4		4	
Depreciation Expense	0		4	
Supplies Expense	0		2	
Miscellaneous Expense	4		4	
	200	200	212	212

Journalize the five entries that adjusted the accounts at October 31, 2019. None of the accounts were affected by more than one adjusting entry.

EX 3-27 Adjusting entries from trial balances OBJ. 6

✔ Corrected trial balance totals, $369,000

The accountant for Eva's Laundry prepared the following unadjusted and adjusted trial balances. Assume that all balances in the unadjusted trial balance and the amounts of the adjustments are correct. Identify the errors in the accountant's adjusting entries, assuming that none of the accounts were affected by more than one adjusting entry.

Eva's Laundry
Trial Balances
May 31, 2019

	Unadjusted Debit Balances	Unadjusted Credit Balances	Adjusted Debit Balances	Adjusted Credit Balances
Cash	7,500		7,500	
Accounts Receivable	18,250		23,250	
Laundry Supplies	3,750		6,750	
Prepaid Insurance*	5,200		1,600	
Laundry Equipment	190,000		177,000	
Accumulated Depreciation—Laundry Equipment		48,000		48,000
Accounts Payable		9,600		9,600
Wages Payable				1,000
Eva Baldwin, Capital		110,300		110,300
Eva Baldwin, Drawing	28,775		28,775	
Laundry Revenue		182,100		182,100
Wages Expense	49,200		49,200	
Rent Expense	25,575		25,575	
Utilities Expense	18,500		18,500	
Depreciation Expense			13,000	
Laundry Supplies Expense			3,000	
Insurance Expense			600	
Miscellaneous Expense	3,250		3,250	
	350,000	350,000	358,000	351,000

*$3,600 of insurance expired during the year.

Chapter 3 The Adjusting Process 147

EX 3-28 Vertical analysis OBJ. 7

Amazon.com, Inc. is the largest Internet retailer in the United States. Amazon's income statements through income from operations for two recent years are as follows (in millions):

Amazon.com, Inc.
Operating Income Statements
For the Years Ended December 31
(in millions)

	Year 2	Year 1
Product sales	$70,080	$60,903
Service sales	18,908	13,549
Total sales	$88,988	$74,452
Cost of sales	$62,752	$54,181
Fulfillment	10,766	8,585
Marketing	4,332	3,133
Technology and content	9,275	6,565
General and administrative	1,552	1,129
Other operating expense (income), net	133	114
Total operating expenses	$88,810	$73,707
Income from operations	$ 178	$ 745

a. Prepare a vertical analysis of the two operating income statements. Round percentages to one decimal place.
b. Use the vertical analysis to explain the decrease in income from operations.

EX 3-29 Vertical analysis OBJ. 7

The following data are taken from recent financial statement of Nike, Inc. (in millions):

	Year 2	Year 1
Sales (revenues)	$30,601	$27,799
Net income	3,273	2,693

a. Determine the amount of change (in millions) and percent of change in net income from Year 1 to Year 2. Round to one decimal place.
b. Determine the percentage relationship between net income and sales for Year 2 and Year 1. Round to one decimal place.
c. What conclusions can you draw from your analyses?

EX 3-30 Vertical analysis OBJ. 7

The following income statement data for AT&T Inc. and Verizon Communications Inc. were taken from their recent annual reports (in millions):

	AT&T	Verizon
Revenues	$132,447	$127,079
Cost of services (expense)	60,611	49,931
Selling and marketing expense	39,697	41,016
Depreciation and other expenses	20,393	16,533
Operating income	$ 11,746	$ 19,599

a. Prepare a vertical analysis of the income statement for AT&T. Round to one decimal place.
b. Prepare a vertical analysis of the income statement for Verizon. Round to one decimal place.
c. Based on Requirements (a) and (b), how does AT&T compare to Verizon?

Problems: Series A

PR 3-1A Adjusting entries OBJ. 2, 3, 4

On December 31, the following data were accumulated for preparing the adjusting entries for Bellingham Realty:

- The supplies account balance on December 31 is $1,375. The supplies on hand on December 31 are $280.
- The unearned rent account balance on December 31 is $9,000 representing the receipt of an advance payment on December 1 of four months' rent from tenants.
- Wages accrued but not paid at December 31 are $3,220.
- Fees earned but unbilled at December 31 are $18,750.
- Depreciation of office equipment is $2,900.

Instructions

1. Journalize the adjusting entries required at December 31.
2. Briefly explain the difference between adjusting entries and entries that would be made to correct errors.

PR 3-2A Adjusting entries OBJ. 2, 3, 4, 5

Selected account balances before adjustment for Atlantic Coast Realty at July 31, the end of the current year, are as follows:

	Debits	Credits
Accounts Receivable	$ 75,000	
Equipment	345,700	
Accumulated Depreciation—Equipment		$112,500
Prepaid Rent	9,000	
Supplies	3,350	
Wages Payable		—
Unearned Fees		12,000
Fees Earned		660,000
Wages Expense	325,000	
Rent Expense	—	
Depreciation Expense	—	
Supplies Expense	—	

Data needed for year-end adjustments are as follows:

- Unbilled fees at July 31, $11,150.
- Supplies on hand at July 31, $900.
- Rent expired, $6,000.
- Depreciation of equipment during year, $8,950.
- Unearned fees at July 31, $2,000.
- Wages accrued but not paid at July 31, $4,840.

Instructions

1. Journalize the six adjusting entries required at July 31, based on the data presented.
2. What would be the effect on the income statement if the adjustments for unbilled fees and accrued wages were omitted at the end of the year?
3. What would be the effect on the balance sheet if the adjustments for unbilled fees and accrued wages were omitted at the end of the year?
4. What would be the effect on the "Net increase or decrease in cash" on the statement of cash flows if the adjustments for unbilled fees and accrued wages were omitted at the end of the year?

PR 3-3A Adjusting entries
OBJ. 2, 3, 4, 5

Milbank Repairs & Service, an electronics repair store, prepared the following unadjusted trial balance at the end of its first year of operations:

Milbank Repairs & Service
Unadjusted Trial Balance
June 30, 2019

	Debit Balances	Credit Balances
Cash	10,350	
Accounts Receivable	67,500	
Supplies	16,200	
Equipment	166,100	
Accounts Payable		15,750
Unearned Fees		18,000
Nancy Townes, Capital		171,500
Nancy Townes, Drawing	13,500	
Fees Earned		294,750
Wages Expense	94,500	
Rent Expense	72,000	
Utilities Expense	51,750	
Miscellaneous Expense	8,100	
	500,000	500,000

For preparing the adjusting entries, the following data were assembled:

- Fees earned but unbilled on June 30 were $7,380.
- Supplies on hand on June 30 were $2,775.
- Depreciation of equipment was estimated to be $11,000 for the year.
- The balance in unearned fees represented the June 1 receipt in advance for services to be provided. During June, $16,500 of the services were provided.
- Unpaid wages accrued on June 30 were $3,880.

Instructions

1. Journalize the adjusting entries necessary on June 30, 2019.
2. Determine the revenues, expenses, and net income of Milbank Repairs & Service before the adjusting entries.
3. Determine the revenues, expenses, and net income of Milbank Repairs & Service after the adjusting entries.
4. Determine the effect of the adjusting entries on Nancy Townes, Capital.

150 Chapter 3 The Adjusting Process

PR 3-4A Adjusting entries
OBJ. 2, 3, 4, 5, 6

Good Note Company specializes in the repair of music equipment and is owned and operated by Robin Stahl. On November 30, 2019, the end of the current year, the accountant for Good Note prepared the following trial balances:

Good Note Company
Trial Balances
November 30, 2019

	Unadjusted Debit Balances	Unadjusted Credit Balances	Adjusted Debit Balances	Adjusted Credit Balances
Cash	38,250		38,250	
Accounts Receivable	89,500		89,500	
Supplies	11,250		2,400	
Prepaid Insurance	14,250		3,850	
Equipment	290,450		290,450	
Accumulated Depreciation—Equipment		94,500		106,100
Automobiles	129,500		129,500	
Accumulated Depreciation—Automobiles		54,750		62,050
Accounts Payable		24,930		26,130
Salaries Payable		—		8,100
Unearned Service Fees		18,000		9,000
Robin Stahl, Capital		324,020		324,020
Robin Stahl, Drawing	75,000		75,000	
Service Fees Earned		733,800		742,800
Salary Expense	516,900		525,000	
Rent Expense	54,000		54,000	
Supplies Expense	—		8,850	
Depreciation Expense—Equipment	—		11,600	
Depreciation Expense—Automobiles	—		7,300	
Utilities Expense	12,900		14,100	
Taxes Expense	8,175		8,175	
Insurance Expense	—		10,400	
Miscellaneous Expense	9,825		9,825	
	1,250,000	1,250,000	1,278,200	1,278,200

Instructions
Journalize the seven entries that adjusted the accounts at November 30. None of the accounts were affected by more than one adjusting entry.

PR 3-5A Adjusting entries and adjusted trial balances
OBJ. 2, 3, 4, 5, 6

✔ 2. Total of Debit column: $933,450

Pitman Company is a small editorial services company owned and operated by Jan Pitman. On October 31, 2019 the end of the current year, Pitman Company's accounting clerk prepared the following unadjusted trial balance:

Pitman Company
Unadjusted Trial Balance
October 31, 2019

	Debit Balances	Credit Balances
Cash	7,500	
Accounts Receivable	38,400	
Prepaid Insurance	7,200	
Supplies	1,980	
Land	112,500	
Building	300,250	
Accumulated Depreciation—Building		87,550
Equipment	135,300	
Accumulated Depreciation—Equipment		97,950
Accounts Payable		12,150

Unearned Rent..		6,750
Jan Pitman, Capital		371,000
Jan Pitman, Drawing..	15,000	
Fees Earned...		324,600
Salaries and Wages Expense..	193,370	
Utilities Expense	42,375	
Advertising Expense..	22,800	
Repairs Expense...	17,250	
Miscellaneous Expense	6,075	
	900,000	900,000

The data needed to determine year-end adjustments are as follows:

- Unexpired insurance at October 31, $600.
- Supplies on hand at October 31, $675.
- Depreciation of building for the year, $12,000.
- Depreciation of equipment for the year, $8,600.
- Unearned rent at October 31, $2,250.
- Accrued salaries and wages at October 31, $2,800.
- Fees earned but unbilled on October 31, $10,050.

Instructions

1. Journalize the adjusting entries using the following additional accounts: Salaries and Wages Payable, Rent Revenue, Insurance Expense, Depreciation Expense—Building, Depreciation Expense—Equipment, and Supplies Expense.
2. Determine the balances of the accounts affected by the adjusting entries and prepare an adjusted trial balance.

PR 3-6A Adjusting entries and errors   OBJ. 2, 3, 4, 5

✔ 2. Corrected net income: $137,750

At the end of April, the first month of operations, the following selected data were taken from the financial statements of Shelby Crawford, an attorney:

Net income for April	$120,000
Total assets at April 30	750,000
Total liabilities at April 30	300,000
Total owner's equity at April 30	450,000

In preparing the financial statements, adjustments for the following data were overlooked:

- Supplies used during April, $2,750.
- Unbilled fees earned at April 30, $23,700.
- Depreciation of equipment for April, $1,800.
- Accrued wages at April 30, $1,400.

Instructions

1. Journalize the entries to record the omitted adjustments.
2. Determine the correct amount of net income for April and the total assets, liabilities, and owner's equity at April 30. In addition to indicating the corrected amounts, indicate the effect of each omitted adjustment by setting up and completing a columnar table similar to the following. The adjustment for supplies used is presented as an example.

(*Continued*)

	Net Income	Total Assets	=	Total Liabilities	+	Total Owner's Equity
Reported amounts	$120,000	$750,000		$300,000		$450,000
Corrections:						
Supplies used	−2,750	−2,750		0		−2,750
Unbilled fees earned						
Equipment depreciation						
Accrued wages						
Corrected amounts						

Problems: Series B

PR 3-1B Adjusting entries
OBJ. 2, 3, 4

On May 31, the following data were accumulated to assist the accountant in preparing the adjusting entries for Oceanside Realty:

- Fees accrued but unbilled at May 31 are $19,750.
- The supplies account balance on May 31 is $12,300. The supplies on hand at May 31 are $4,150.
- Wages accrued but not paid at May 31 are $2,700.
- The unearned rent account balance at May 31 is $9,000, representing the receipt of an advance payment on May 1 of three months' rent from tenants.
- Depreciation of office equipment is $3,200.

Instructions
1. Journalize the adjusting entries required at May 31.
2. Briefly explain the difference between adjusting entries and entries that would be made to correct errors.

PR 3-2B Adjusting entries
OBJ. 2, 3, 4, 5

Selected account balances before adjustment for Intuit Realty at November 30, the end of the current year, follow:

	Debits	Credits
Accounts Receivable	$ 75,000	
Equipment	250,000	
Accumulated Depreciation—Equipment		$ 12,000
Prepaid Rent	12,000	
Supplies	3,170	
Wages Payable		—
Unearned Fees		10,000
Fees Earned		400,000
Wages Expense	140,000	
Rent Expense	—	
Depreciation Expense	—	
Supplies Expense	—	

Data needed for year-end adjustments are as follows:

- Supplies on hand at November 30, $550.
- Depreciation of equipment during year, $1,675.
- Rent expired during year, $8,500.
- Wages accrued but not paid at November 30, $2,000.
- Unearned fees at November 30, $4,000.
- Unbilled fees at November 30, $5,380.

Instructions

1. Journalize the six adjusting entries required at November 30, based on the data presented.
2. What would be the effect on the income statement if the adjustments for equipment depreciation and unearned fees were omitted at the end of the year?
3. What would be the effect on the balance sheet if the adjustments for equipment depreciation and unearned fees were omitted at the end of the year?
4. What would be the effect on the "Net increase or decrease in cash" on the statement of cash flows if the adjustments for equipment depreciation and unearned fees were omitted at the end of the year?

PR 3-3B Adjusting entries
OBJ. 2, 3, 4, 5

Crazy Mountain Outfitters Co., an outfitter store for fishing treks, prepared the following unadjusted trial balance at the end of its first year of operations:

Crazy Mountain Outfitters Co.
Unadjusted Trial Balance
April 30, 2019

	Debit Balances	Credit Balances
Cash	11,400	
Accounts Receivable	72,600	
Supplies	7,200	
Equipment	112,000	
Accounts Payable		12,200
Unearned Fees		19,200
John Bridger, Capital		137,800
John Bridger, Drawing	10,000	
Fees Earned		305,800
Wages Expense	157,800	
Rent Expense	55,000	
Utilities Expense	42,000	
Miscellaneous Expense	7,000	
	475,000	475,000

For preparing the adjusting entries, the following data were assembled:

- Supplies on hand on April 30 were $1,380.
- Fees earned but unbilled on April 30 were $3,900.
- Depreciation of equipment was estimated to be $3,000 for the year.
- Unpaid wages accrued on April 30 were $2,475.
- The balance in unearned fees represented the April 1 receipt in advance for services to be provided. Only $14,140 of the services was provided between April 1 and April 30.

Instructions

1. Journalize the adjusting entries necessary on April 30, 2019.
2. Determine the revenues, expenses, and net income of Crazy Mountain Outfitters Co. before the adjusting entries.
3. Determine the revenues, expenses, and net income of Crazy Mountain Outfitters Co. after the adjusting entries.
4. Determine the effect of the adjusting entries on John Bridger, Capital.

PR 3-4B Adjusting entries
OBJ. 2, 3, 4, 5, 6

The Signage Company specializes in the maintenance and repair of signs, such as billboards. On March 31, 2019, the accountant for The Signage Company prepared the trial balances shown at the top of the following page.

(Continued)

154 Chapter 3 The Adjusting Process

The Signage Company
Trial Balances
March 31, 2019

	Unadjusted Debit Balances	Unadjusted Credit Balances	Adjusted Debit Balances	Adjusted Credit Balances
Cash	4,750		4,750	
Accounts Receivable	17,400		17,400	
Supplies	6,200		2,175	
Prepaid Insurance	9,000		1,150	
Land	100,000		100,000	
Buildings	170,000		170,000	
Accumulated Depreciation—Buildings		51,500		61,000
Trucks	75,000		75,000	
Accumulated Depreciation—Trucks		12,000		17,000
Accounts Payable		6,920		8,750
Salaries Payable		—		1,400
Unearned Service Fees		10,500		3,850
Mary Bakken, Capital		256,400		256,400
Mary Bakken, Drawing	7,500		7,500	
Service Fees Earned		162,680		169,330
Salary Expense	80,000		81,400	
Depreciation Expense—Trucks	—		5,000	
Rent Expense	11,900		11,900	
Supplies Expense	—		4,025	
Utilities Expense	6,200		8,030	
Depreciation Expense—Buildings	—		9,500	
Taxes Expense	2,900		2,900	
Insurance Expense	—		7,850	
Miscellaneous Expense	9,150		9,150	
	500,000	500,000	517,730	517,730

Instructions
Journalize the seven entries that adjusted the accounts at March 31. None of the accounts were affected by more than one adjusting entry.

PR 3-5B Adjusting entries and adjusted trial balances OBJ. 2, 3, 4, 5, 6

✓ 2. Total of Debit column: $420,300

Reece Financial Services Co., which specializes in appliance repair services, is owned and operated by Joni Reece. Reece Financial Services' accounting clerk prepared the following unadjusted trial balance at July 31, 2019:

Reece Financial Services Co.
Unadjusted Trial Balance
July 31, 2019

	Debit Balances	Credit Balances
Cash	10,200	
Accounts Receivable	34,750	
Prepaid Insurance	6,000	
Supplies	1,725	
Land	50,000	
Building	155,750	
Accumulated Depreciation—Building		62,850
Equipment	45,000	
Accumulated Depreciation—Equipment		17,650
Accounts Payable		3,750
Unearned Rent		3,600
Joni Reece, Capital		153,550
Joni Reece, Drawing	8,000	
Fees Earned		158,600
Salaries and Wages Expense	56,850	
Utilities Expense	14,100	
Advertising Expense	7,500	
Repairs Expense	6,100	
Miscellaneous Expense	4,025	
	400,000	400,000

The data needed to determine year-end adjustments are as follows:

- Depreciation of building for the year, $6,400.
- Depreciation of equipment for the year, $2,800.
- Accrued salaries and wages at July 31, $900.
- Unexpired insurance at July 31, $1,500.
- Fees earned but unbilled on July 31, $10,200.
- Supplies on hand at July 31, $615.
- Rent unearned at July 31, $300.

Instructions

1. Journalize the adjusting entries using the following additional accounts: Salaries and Wages Payable, Rent Revenue, Insurance Expense, Depreciation Expense—Building, Depreciation Expense—Equipment, and Supplies Expense.
2. Determine the balances of the accounts affected by the adjusting entries and prepare an adjusted trial balance.

PR 3-6B   Adjusting entries and errors   OBJ. 2, 3, 4, 5

✔ 2. Corrected net income: $128,700

Excel

At the end of August, the first month of operations, the following selected data were taken from the financial statements of Tucker Jacobs, an attorney:

Net income for August	$112,500
Total assets at August 31	650,000
Total liabilities at August 31	225,000
Total owner's equity at August 31	425,000

In preparing the financial statements, adjustments for the following data were overlooked:

- Unbilled fees earned at August 31, $31,900.
- Depreciation of equipment for August, $7,500.
- Accrued wages at August 31, $5,200.
- Supplies used during August, $3,000.

Instructions

1. Journalize the entries to record the omitted adjustments.
2. Determine the correct amount of net income for August and the total assets, liabilities, and owner's equity at August 31. In addition to indicating the corrected amounts, indicate the effect of each omitted adjustment by setting up and completing a columnar table similar to the following. The first adjustment is presented as an example.

	Net Income	Total Assets	=	Total Liabilities	+	Total Owner's Equity
Reported amounts	$112,500	$650,000		$225,000		$425,000
Corrections:						
Unbilled fees earned	+31,900	+31,900		0		+31,900
Equipment depreciation	_____	_____		_____		_____
Accrued wages	_____	_____		_____		_____
Supplies used	_____	_____		_____		_____
Corrected amounts						

Chapter 3 The Adjusting Process

Continuing Problem

✓ 3. Total of Debit column: $42,340

The unadjusted trial balance that you prepared for PS Music at the end of Chapter 2 should appear as follows:

PS Music
Unadjusted Trial Balance
July 31, 2019

	Account No.	Debit Balances	Credit Balances
Cash	11	9,945	
Accounts Receivable	12	2,750	
Supplies	14	1,020	
Prepaid Insurance	15	2,700	
Office Equipment	17	7,500	
Accounts Payable	21		8,350
Unearned Revenue	23		7,200
Peyton Smith, Capital	31		9,000
Peyton Smith, Drawing	32	1,750	
Fees Earned	41		16,200
Wages Expense	50	2,800	
Office Rent Expense	51	2,550	
Equipment Rent Expense	52	1,375	
Utilities Expense	53	1,215	
Music Expense	54	3,610	
Advertising Expense	55	1,500	
Supplies Expense	56	180	
Miscellaneous Expense	59	1,855	
		40,750	40,750

The data needed to determine adjustments are as follows:

- During July, PS Music provided guest disc jockeys for KXMD for a total of 115 hours. For information on the amount of the accrued revenue to be billed to KXMD, see the contract described in the July 3 transaction at the end of Chapter 2.
- Supplies on hand at July 31, $275.
- The balance of the prepaid insurance account relates to the July 1 transaction in Chapter 2.
- Depreciation of the office equipment is $50.
- The balance of the unearned revenue account relates to the contract between PS Music and KXMD, described in the July 3 transaction in Chapter 2.
- Accrued wages as of July 31 were $140.

Instructions

1. Prepare adjusting journal entries. You will need the following additional accounts:
    - 18 Accumulated Depreciation—Office Equipment
    - 22 Wages Payable
    - 57 Insurance Expense
    - 58 Depreciation Expense
2. Post the adjusting entries, inserting balances in the accounts affected.
3. Prepare an adjusted trial balance.

Cases & Projects

CP 3-1 Ethics in Action

Chris P. Bacon is the chief accountant for CV Industries, a large manufacturing company. In addition to its normal business activities, the company has excess warehouse space that it rents out to local businesses. Because the typical renter is a small business, CV Industries requires renters to make lease payments for the entire rental period on the day the lease is signed. As a result, CV Industries typically reports a large unearned rent balance on its balance sheet.

After making adjusting entries for the current year, Chris prepares the adjusted trial balance and notices that the company's earnings will decline significantly. He presents the adjusted trial balance to the company's CFO, Antonio Beldin, who is concerned about the earnings decline. Mr. Beldin notices the large unearned rent balance and proposes making an additional end-of-period adjusting entry to recognize the entire unearned rent balance as revenue in the current period. Chris protests, reminding Mr. Beldin that the adjusting entry for unearned rent has already been made. Mr. Beldin assures Chris that his proposal is acceptable, reminding Chris that "because we have already received the cash, we have the right to recognize the revenue in the current period." He instructs Chris to make the additional adjusting journal entry. Chris is hesitant to follow these instructions, but he is sensitive to the company's emphasis on earnings growth and makes the adjusting entry as instructed.

1. Is Chris behaving ethically? Why or why not?
2. Who is affected by Chris's decision?

CP 3-2 Ethics in Action

Daryl Kirby opened Squid Realty Co. on January 1, 2018. At the end of the first year, the business needed additional capital. On behalf of Squid Realty Co., Daryl applied to Ocean National Bank for a loan of $375,000. Based on Squid Realty Co.'s financial statements, which had been prepared on a cash basis, the Ocean National Bank loan officer rejected the loan as too risky.

After receiving the rejection notice, Daryl instructed his accountant to prepare the financial statements on an accrual basis. These statements included $65,000 in accounts receivable and $25,000 in accounts payable. Daryl then instructed his accountant to record an additional $30,000 of accounts receivable for commissions on property for which a contract had been signed on December 28, 2018. The title to the property is to transfer on January 5, 2019, when an attorney formally records the transfer of the property to the buyer.

Daryl then applied for a $375,000 loan from Free Spirit Bank, using the revised financial statements. On this application, Daryl indicated that he had not previously been rejected for credit.

Discuss the ethical and professional conduct of Daryl Kirby in applying for the loan from Free Spirit Bank.

CP 3-3 Team Activity

In teams, select a public company that interests you. Obtain the company's most recent annual report on Form 10-K. The Form 10-K is a company's annually required filing with the Securities and Exchange Commission (SEC). It includes the company's financial statements and accompanying notes. The Form 10-K can be obtained either (a) from the investor relations section of the company's website or (b) by using the company search feature of the SEC's EDGAR database service found at www.sec.gov/edgar/searchedgar/companysearch.html.

(Continued)

158 Chapter 3 The Adjusting Process

Based on the information in the company's most recent annual report, answer the following questions:

1. In what industry does the company operate?
2. How many years of information are reported on the company's income statement?
3. How much net income does the company report on its income statement for each year presented?
4. How much revenue does the company report on its income statement for each year presented?
5. Within the notes to the financial statements, find the note on significant accounting policies. Based on the information in this note, when does the company recognize revenue?
6. ✏️ Based solely on the company's net income, has the company's performance improved, remained constant, or deteriorated over the periods presented? Briefly explain your answer.

Communication

Real World

CP 3-4 Communication

Delta Air Lines is a major passenger airline headquartered in the United States. Most Delta passengers purchase their tickets several weeks prior to taking their trip and use a credit card such as VISA or American Express to pay for their tickets. The credit card company pays the airline at the time the flight is booked, several weeks prior to the flight.

✏️ Write a brief memo to your instructor explaining when Delta should recognize revenue from ticket sales.

CP 3-5 Adjustments and financial statements

Several years ago, your brother opened Magna Appliance Repairs. He made a small initial investment and added money from his personal bank account as needed. He withdrew money for living expenses at irregular intervals. As the business grew, he hired an assistant. He is now considering adding more employees, purchasing additional service trucks, and purchasing the building he now rents. To secure funds for the expansion, your brother submitted a loan application to the bank and included the most recent financial statements (which follow) prepared from accounts maintained by a part-time bookkeeper.

Magna Appliance Repairs
Income Statement
For the Year Ended October 31, 2019

Service revenue		$675,000
Less: Rent paid	$187,200	
Wages paid	148,500	
Supplies paid	42,000	
Utilities paid	39,000	
Insurance paid	21,600	
Miscellaneous payments	54,600	492,900
Net income		$182,100

Magna Appliance Repairs
Balance Sheet
October 31, 2019

Assets

Cash	$ 95,400
Amounts due from customers	112,500
Truck	332,100
Total assets	$540,000

Equities

Owner's capital	$540,000

After reviewing the financial statements, the loan officer at the bank asked your brother if he used the accrual basis of accounting for revenues and expenses. Your brother responded that he did and that is why he included an account for "Amounts Due from Customers." The loan officer then asked whether or not the accounts were adjusted prior to the preparation of the statements. Your brother answered that they had not been adjusted.

a. ✏️ Why do you think the loan officer suspected that the accounts had not been adjusted prior to the preparation of the statements?

b. Indicate possible accounts that might need to be adjusted before an accurate set of financial statements could be prepared.

CHAPTER 4
Completing the Accounting Cycle

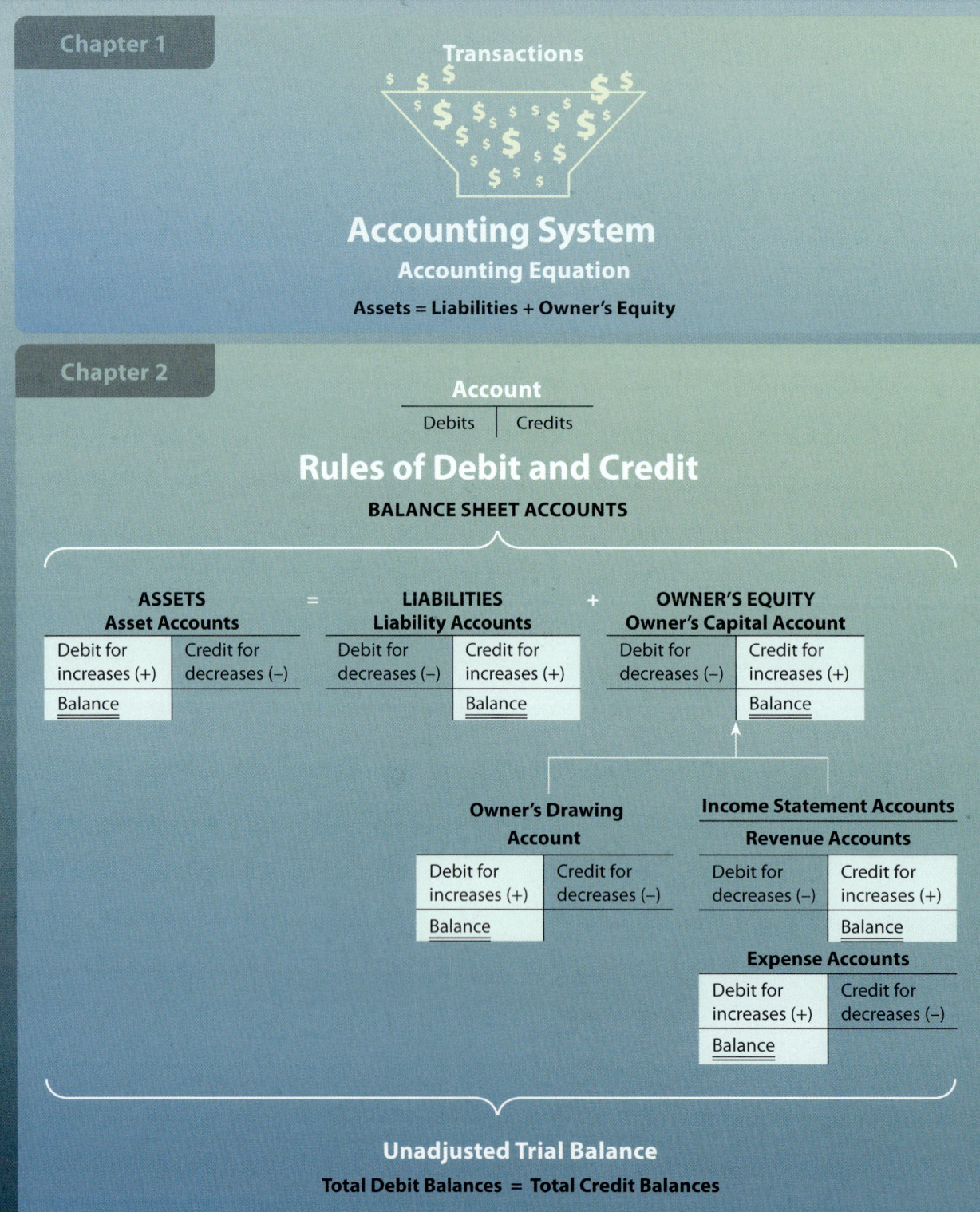

CHAPTER 4

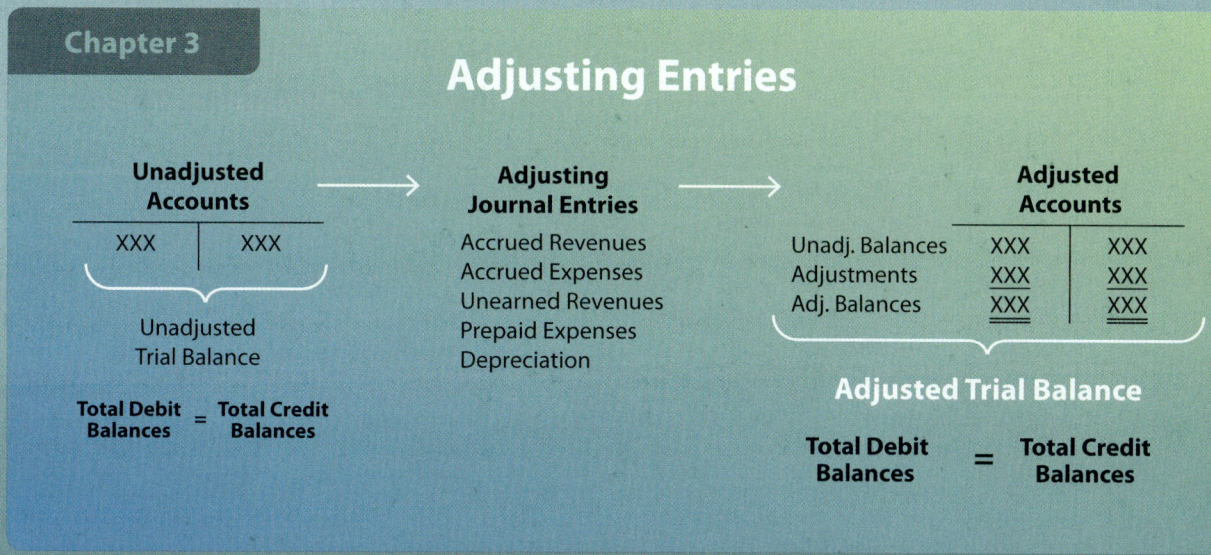

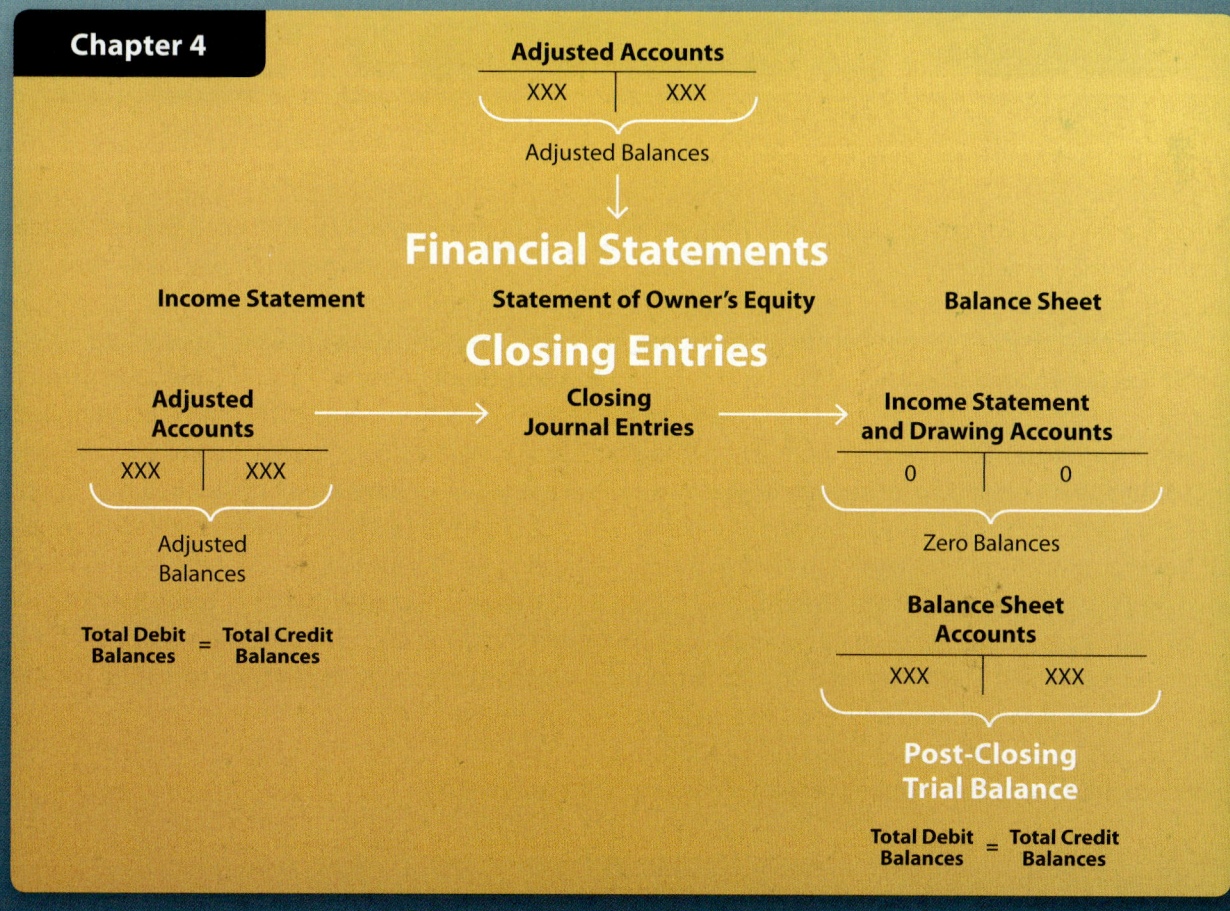

CHAPTER 4

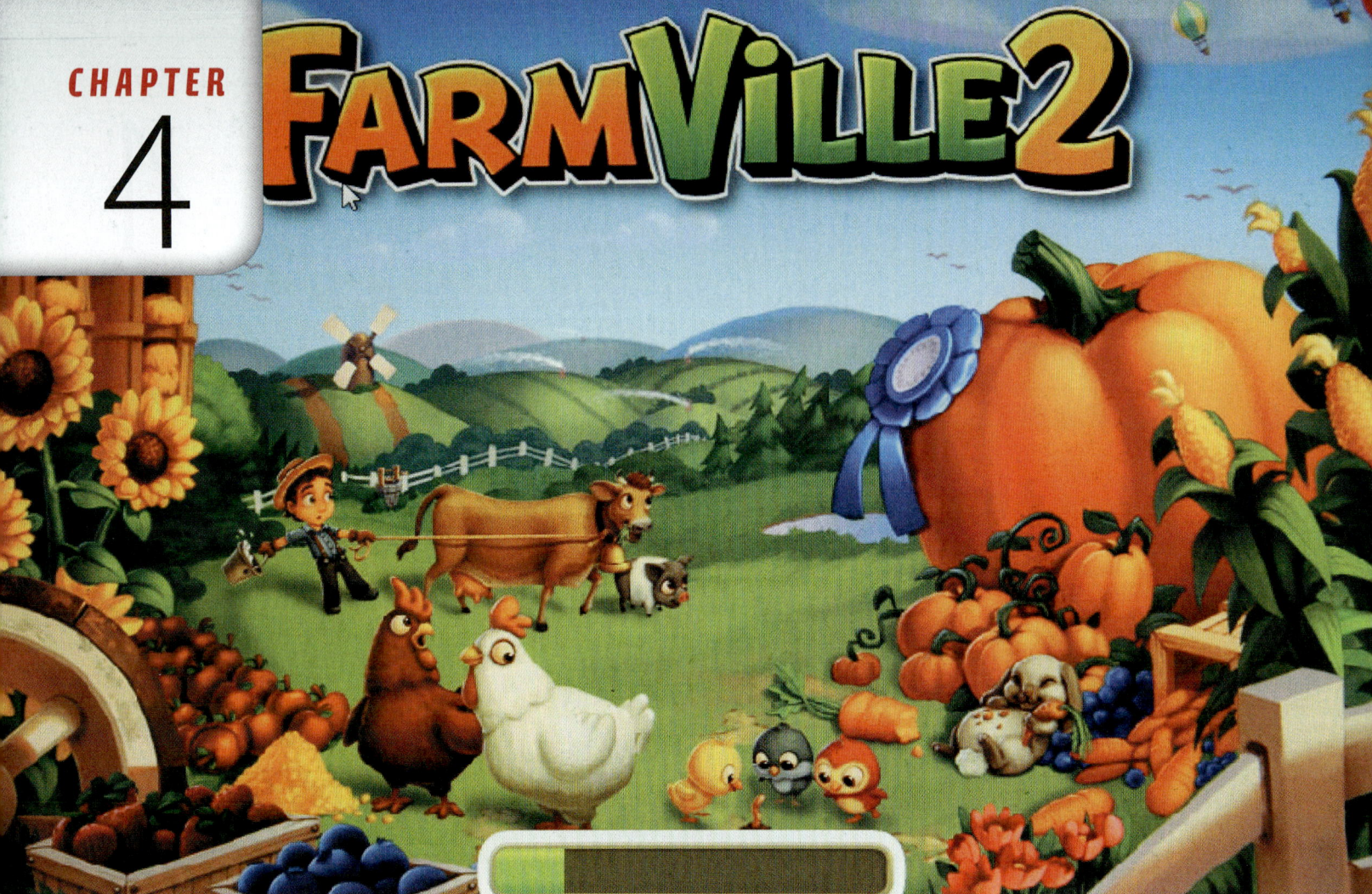

Zynga

Zynga is a leading provider of social games with more than 240 million active players per month. Zynga's games, such as CityVille, FarmVille, CastleVille, and Café World, can be played on a variety of platforms including Facebook, Google Android, and Apple iOS.

Zynga was founded in 2007 and is named after CEO (chief executive officer) Mark Pincus's dog. Zinga is an American Bulldog who is known for her human-like qualities, which include sitting on chairs and eating at the dinner table. Because she is playful, loyal, and lovable, Zinga is considered the guiding spirit of the company.

In developing its games, Zynga goes through a game development cycle that starts with the initial gaming concept, program development, and ends with testing and debugging errors. Businesses also go through a cycle of accounting activities that begins with recording transactions and ends with preparing financial statements and getting the accounting records ready for recording the next period's transactions.

In Chapter 1, the initial accounting cycle for **NetSolutions** began with Chris Clark's investment in the business on November 1, 2018. The cycle continued with recording NetSolutions' transactions for November and December, as we discussed and illustrated in Chapters 1 and 2. In Chapter 3, the cycle continued when the adjusting entries for the two months ending December 31, 2018, were recorded. In this chapter, the cycle is completed for NetSolutions by preparing financial statements and getting the accounts ready for recording transactions of the next period.

Source: Zynga.com

Learning Objectives

After studying this chapter, you should be able to:

Example Exercises (EE) are shown in **green**.

Obj. 1 Describe the flow of accounting information from the unadjusted trial balance into the adjusted trial balance and financial statements.

Flow of Accounting Information
Flow of Accounts into Financial Statements   EE **4-1**

Obj. 2 Prepare financial statements from adjusted account balances.

Financial Statements
Income Statement
Statement of Owner's Equity   EE **4-2**
Balance Sheet   EE **4-3**

Obj. 3 Prepare closing entries.

Closing Entries
Journalizing and Posting Closing Entries   EE **4-4**
Post-Closing Trial Balance

Obj. 4 Describe the accounting cycle.

Accounting Cycle
Steps of the Accounting Cycle   EE **4-5**

Obj. 5 Illustrate the accounting cycle for one period.

Illustration of the Accounting Cycle

Obj. 6 Explain what is meant by the fiscal year and the natural business year.

Fiscal Year

Obj. 7 Describe and illustrate the use of working capital and the current ratio in evaluating a company's financial condition.

Financial Analysis and Interpretation: Working Capital and Current Ratio
Computing Working Capital and Current Ratio   EE **4-6**

At a Glance 4   Page 198

Flow of Accounting Information

Obj. 1 Describe the flow of accounting information from the unadjusted trial balance into the adjusted trial balance and financial statements.

The process of adjusting the accounts and preparing financial statements is one of the most important in accounting. Using the NetSolutions illustration from Chapters 1–3 and an end-of-period spreadsheet, the flow of accounting data in adjusting accounts and the preparation of financial statements are summarized in Exhibit 1.

The end-of-period spreadsheet in Exhibit 1 begins with the unadjusted trial balance. The unadjusted trial balance verifies that the total of the debit balances equals the total of the credit balances. If the trial balance totals are unequal, an error has occurred. Any errors must be found and corrected before the end-of-period process can continue.

The adjustments for NetSolutions from Chapter 3 are shown in the Adjustments columns of the spreadsheet. Cross-referencing (by letters) the debit and credit of each adjustment is useful in reviewing the effect of the adjustments on the unadjusted account balances. The adjustments are normally entered in the order in which the data are assembled. If the titles of the accounts to be adjusted do not appear in the unadjusted trial balance, the accounts are inserted in their proper order in the Account Title column. The total of the Adjustments columns verifies that the total debits equal the total credits for the adjusting entries. The total of the Debit column must equal the total of the Credit column.

Many companies use Microsoft's Excel® software to prepare end-of-period spreadsheets.

The adjustments in the spreadsheet are added to or subtracted from the amounts in the Unadjusted Trial Balance columns to arrive at the amounts inserted in the Adjusted Trial Balance columns. In this way, the Adjusted Trial Balance columns of the spreadsheet illustrate the effect of the adjusting entries on the unadjusted accounts. The totals of the Adjusted Trial Balance columns verify that the totals of the debit and credit balances are equal after adjustment.

164 Chapter 4 Completing the Accounting Cycle

EXHIBIT 1 End-of-Period Spreadsheet and Flow of Accounting Data—NetSolutions

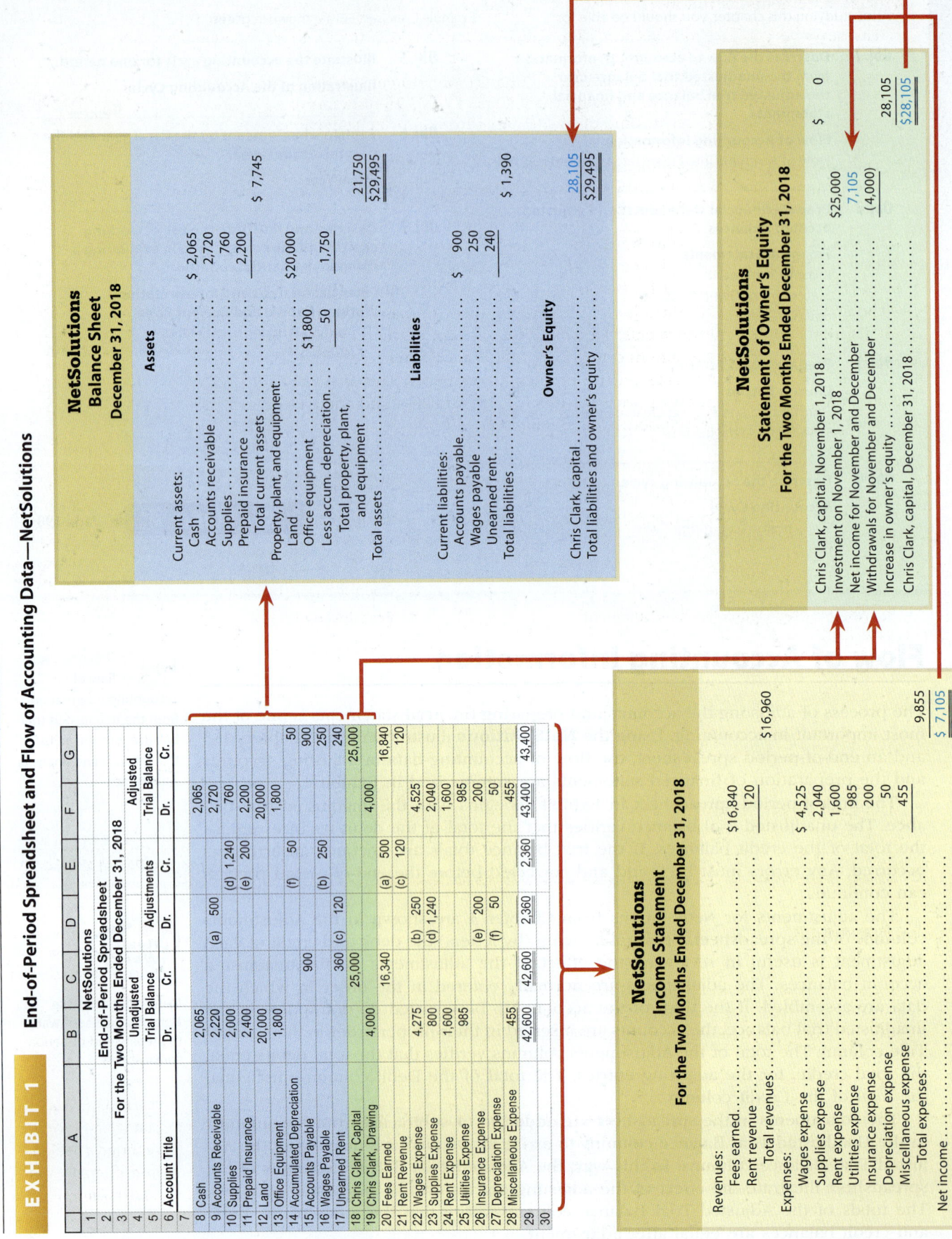

Exhibit 1 illustrates the flow of accounts from the adjusted trial balance into the financial statements as follows:

1. The revenue and expense accounts (spreadsheet lines 20–28) flow into the income statement.
2. The owner's capital account, Chris Clark, Capital (spreadsheet line 18), and owner's drawing account, Chris Clark, Drawing (spreadsheet line 19), flow into the statement of owner's equity. The net income of $7,105 also flows into the statement of owner's equity from the income statement.
3. The asset and liability accounts (spreadsheet lines 8–17) flow into the balance sheet. The end-of-period owner's equity (Chris Clark, Capital of $28,105) also flows into the balance sheet from the statement of owner's equity.

To summarize, Exhibit 1 illustrates the process by which accounts are adjusted. In addition, Exhibit 1 illustrates how the adjusted accounts flow into the financial statements. The financial statements for NetSolutions can be prepared directly from Exhibit 1.

The spreadsheet in Exhibit 1 is not required. However, many accountants prepare such a spreadsheet, sometimes called a *work sheet*, as part of the normal end-of-period process. The primary advantage in doing so is that it allows managers and accountants to see the effect of adjustments on the financial statements. This is especially useful for adjustments that depend upon estimates. Such estimates and their effect on the financial statements are discussed in later chapters.[1]

Example Exercise 4-1 Flow of Accounts into Financial Statements   Obj. 1

The balances for the accounts that follow appear in the Adjusted Trial Balance columns of the end-of-period spreadsheet. Indicate whether each account would flow into the income statement, statement of owner's equity, or balance sheet.

1. Office Equipment
2. Utilities Expense
3. Accumulated Depreciation—Equipment
4. Unearned Rent
5. Fees Earned
6. Doug Johnson, Drawing
7. Rent Revenue
8. Supplies

Follow My Example 4-1

1. Balance sheet
2. Income statement
3. Balance sheet
4. Balance sheet
5. Income statement
6. Statement of owner's equity
7. Income statement
8. Balance sheet

Practice Exercises: PE 4-1A, PE 4-1B

Financial Statements

Obj. 2 Prepare financial statements from adjusted account balances.

Using the adjusted trial balance shown in Exhibit 1, the financial statements for NetSolutions can be prepared. The income statement, the statement of owner's equity, and the balance sheet are shown in Exhibit 2.

Income Statement

The income statement is prepared directly from the Adjusted Trial Balance columns of the Exhibit 1 spreadsheet, beginning with fees earned of $16,840. The expenses in the income statement in Exhibit 2 are listed in order of size, beginning with the larger items. Miscellaneous expense is the last item, regardless of its amount.

Link to Zynga

In a recent income statement, **Zynga** reported a net loss from operations of $226 million.

---

[1] Appendix 1 to this chapter describes and illustrates how to prepare an end-of-period spreadsheet that includes financial statement columns.

EXHIBIT 2

Financial Statements, NetSolutions

NetSolutions
Income Statement
For the Two Months Ended December 31, 2018

Revenues:		
Fees earned	$16,840	
Rent revenue	120	
Total revenues		$16,960
Expenses:		
Wages expense	$ 4,525	
Supplies expense	2,040	
Rent expense	1,600	
Utilities expense	985	
Insurance expense	200	
Depreciation expense	50	
Miscellaneous expense	455	
Total expenses		9,855
Net income		$ 7,105

NetSolutions
Statement of Owner's Equity
For the Two Months Ended December 31, 2018

Chris Clark, capital, November 1, 2018		$ 0
Investment on November 1, 2018	$25,000	
Net income for November and December	7,105	
Withdrawals during November and December	(4,000)	
Increase in owner's equity		28,105
Chris Clark, capital, December 31, 2018		$28,105

NetSolutions
Balance Sheet
December 31, 2018

Assets

Current assets:			
Cash		$ 2,065	
Accounts receivable		2,720	
Supplies		760	
Prepaid insurance		2,200	
Total current assets			$ 7,745
Property, plant, and equipment:			
Land		$20,000	
Office equipment	$1,800		
Less accumulated depreciation	50	1,750	
Total property, plant, and equipment			21,750
Total assets			$29,495

Liabilities

Current liabilities:		
Accounts payable	$ 900	
Wages payable	250	
Unearned rent	240	
Total liabilities		$ 1,390

Owner's Equity

Chris Clark, capital	28,105
Total liabilities and owner's equity	$29,495

INTEGRITY, OBJECTIVITY, AND ETHICS IN BUSINESS

CEO'S HEALTH?

How much and what information to disclose in financial statements and to investors presents a common ethical dilemma for managers and accountants. For example, Steve Jobs, co-founder and CEO of Apple Inc., had been diagnosed and treated for pancreatic cancer. Apple Inc. had insisted that the status of Steve Jobs's health was a "private" matter and did not have to be disclosed to investors. Apple maintained this position even though Jobs was a driving force behind Apple's innovation and financial success.

Steve Jobs's health deteriorated significantly, however, and that disclosure was eventually provided. On October 5, 2011, Steve Jobs died at the age of 56.

Statement of Owner's Equity

The first item presented on the statement of owner's equity is the balance of the owner's capital account at the beginning of the period. The amount listed as owner's capital in the spreadsheet, however, is not always the account balance at the beginning of the period. The owner may have invested additional assets in the business during the period. For the beginning balance and any additional investments, it is necessary to refer to the owner's capital account in the ledger. These amounts, along with the net income (or net loss) and the drawing account balance, are used to determine the ending owner's capital account balance.

The basic form of the statement of owner's equity is shown in Exhibit 2. For NetSolutions, the amount of drawings by the owner was less than the net income. If the owner's withdrawals had exceeded the net income, the difference between the two items would then be deducted from the beginning capital account balance. Other factors, such as additional investments or a net loss, also require some change in the form, as follows:

Allan Johnson, capital, January 1, 2018		$39,000
Investment during year	$ 6,000	
Net loss for year	(5,600)	
Withdrawals	(9,500)	
Decrease in owner's equity		(9,100)
Allan Johnson, capital, December 31, 2018		$29,900

Example Exercise 4-2 Statement of Owner's Equity *Obj. 2*

Zack Gaddis owns and operates Gaddis Employment Services. On January 1, 2018, Zack Gaddis, Capital had a balance of $186,000. During the year, Zack invested an additional $40,000 and withdrew $25,000. For the year ended December 31, 2018, Gaddis Employment Services reported a net income of $18,750. Prepare a statement of owner's equity for the year ended December 31, 2018.

Follow My Example 4-2

Gaddis Employment Services
Statement of Owner's Equity
For the Year Ended December 31, 2018

Zack Gaddis, capital, January 1, 2018		$186,000
Investment during 2018	$ 40,000	
Net income	18,750	
Withdrawals	(25,000)	
Increase in owner's equity		33,750
Zack Gaddis, capital, December 31, 2018		$219,750

Practice Exercises: PE 4-2A, PE 4-2B

Balance Sheet

The balance sheet is prepared directly from the Adjusted Trial Balance columns of the Exhibit 1 spreadsheet, beginning with Cash of $2,065. The asset and liability amounts are taken from the spreadsheet. The owner's equity amount, however, is taken from the statement of owner's equity, as illustrated in Exhibit 2.

The balance sheet in Exhibit 2 shows subsections for assets and liabilities. Such a balance sheet is a *classified balance sheet*. These subsections are described next.

Assets Assets are commonly divided into two sections on the balance sheet: (1) current assets and (2) property, plant, and equipment.

Current Assets Cash and other assets that are expected to be converted to cash or sold or used up usually within one year or less, through the normal operations of the business, are called **current assets**. In addition to cash, the current assets may include notes receivable, accounts receivable, supplies, and other prepaid expenses.

Notes receivable are amounts that customers owe. They are written promises to pay the amount of the note and interest. Accounts receivable are also amounts customers owe, but they are less formal than notes. Accounts receivable normally result from providing services or selling merchandise on account. Notes receivable and accounts receivable are current assets because they are usually converted to cash within one year or less.

Property, Plant, and Equipment The property, plant, and equipment section may also be described as **fixed assets** or **plant assets**. These assets include equipment, machinery, buildings, and land. With the exception of land, as discussed in Chapter 3, fixed assets depreciate over a period of time. The original cost, accumulated depreciation, and book value of each major type of fixed asset are normally reported on the balance sheet or in the notes to the financial statements.

Liabilities Liabilities are the amounts the business owes to creditors. Liabilities are commonly divided into two sections on the balance sheet: (1) current liabilities and (2) long-term liabilities.

Current Liabilities Liabilities that will be due within a short time (usually one year or less) and that are to be paid out of current assets are called **current liabilities**. The most common liabilities in this group are notes payable and accounts payable. Other current liabilities may include Wages Payable, Interest Payable, Taxes Payable, and Unearned Fees.

Long-Term Liabilities Liabilities that will not be due for a long time (usually more than one year) are called **long-term liabilities**. If NetSolutions had long-term liabilities, they would be reported below the current liabilities. As long-term liabilities come due and are to be paid within one year, they are reported as current liabilities. If they are to be renewed rather than paid, they would continue to be reported as long term. When an asset is pledged as security for a liability, the obligation may be called a *mortgage note payable* or a *mortgage payable*.

Owner's Equity The owner's right to the assets of the business is presented on the balance sheet below the liabilities section. The owner's equity is added to the total liabilities, and this total must be equal to the total assets.

> **Note**
> Two common classes of assets are current assets and property, plant, and equipment.

> **Link to Zynga**
> In a recent balance sheet, Zynga reported current assets of $1.1 billion; property, plant, and equipment and other assets of $1.2 billion; and total assets of $2.3 billion.

> **Note**
> Two common classes of liabilities are current liabilities and long-term liabilities.

> **Link to Zynga**
> In a recent balance sheet, Zynga reported current liabilities of $369 million, long-term and other liabilities of $84 million, and total liabilities of $453 million.

Example Exercise 4-3 Classified Balance Sheet Obj. 2

The following accounts appear in an adjusted trial balance of Hindsight Consulting. Indicate whether each account would be reported in the (a) current asset; (b) property, plant, and equipment; (c) current liability; (d) long-term liability; or (e) owner's equity section of the December 31, 2018, balance sheet of Hindsight Consulting.

1. Jason Corbin, Capital
2. Notes Receivable (due in six months)
3. Notes Payable (due in 10 years)
4. Land
5. Cash
6. Unearned Rent (three months)
7. Accumulated Depreciation—Equipment
8. Accounts Payable

Follow My Example 4-3

1. Owner's equity
2. Current asset
3. Long-term liability
4. Property, plant, and equipment
5. Current asset
6. Current liability
7. Property, plant, and equipment
8. Current liability

Practice Exercises: PE 4-3A, PE 4-3B

International Connection

IFRS INTERNATIONAL DIFFERENCES

Financial statements prepared under accounting practices in other countries often differ from those prepared under generally accepted accounting principles in the United States. This is to be expected because cultures and market structures differ from country to country.

To illustrate, **BMW Group** prepares its financial statements under International Financial Reporting Standards as adopted by the European Union. In doing so, BMW's balance sheet reports fixed assets first, followed by current assets. It also reports owner's equity before the liabilities. In contrast, balance sheets prepared under U.S. accounting principles report current assets followed by fixed assets and current liabilities followed by long-term liabilities

and owner's equity. The U.S. form of balance sheet is organized to emphasize creditor interpretation and analysis. For example, current assets and current liabilities are presented first to facilitate their interpretation and analysis by creditors. Likewise, to emphasize their importance, liabilities are reported before owner's equity.*

Regardless of these differences, the basic principles underlying the accounting equation and the double-entry accounting system are the same in Germany and the United States. Even though differences in recording and reporting exist, the accounting equation holds true: The total assets still equal the total liabilities and owner's equity.

*Examples of U.S. and IFRS financial statement reporting differences are further discussed and illustrated in Appendix B.

Closing Entries

Obj. 3 Prepare closing entries.

As discussed in Chapter 3, the adjusting entries are recorded in the journal at the end of the accounting period. For **NetSolutions**, the adjusting entries are shown in Exhibit 7 of Chapter 3. After the adjusting entries are posted to NetSolutions' ledger, shown in Exhibit 6, the ledger agrees with the data reported on the financial statements.

The balances of the accounts reported on the balance sheet are carried forward from period to period. Because these accounts are carried forward from period to period, they are called **permanent accounts** or **real accounts**. For example, Cash, Accounts Receivable, Equipment, Accumulated Depreciation, Accounts Payable, and Owner's Capital are permanent accounts.

The balances of the accounts reported on the income statement are not carried forward from year to year. Also, the balance of the owner's drawing account, which is reported on the statement of owner's equity, is not carried forward. Because these accounts report amounts for only one period, they are called **temporary accounts** or **nominal accounts**. Temporary accounts are not carried forward because they relate only to one period. For example, the Fees Earned of $16,840 and Wages Expense of $4,525 for NetSolutions shown in Exhibit 2 are for the two months ending December 31, 2018, and should not be carried forward to 2019.

170 Chapter 4 Completing the Accounting Cycle

Closing entries transfer the balances of temporary accounts to the owner's capital account.

At the beginning of the next period, temporary accounts should have zero balances. To achieve this, temporary account balances are transferred to permanent accounts at the end of the accounting period. The entries that transfer these balances are called **closing entries**. The transfer process is called the **closing process** and is sometimes referred to as **closing the books**.

The closing process involves the following two closing journal entries.

First Closing Entry:
Revenue and expense account balances are transferred to the owner's capital account.

Second Closing Entry:
The balance of the owner's drawing account is transferred to the owner's capital account.

Exhibit 3 diagrams the closing process.

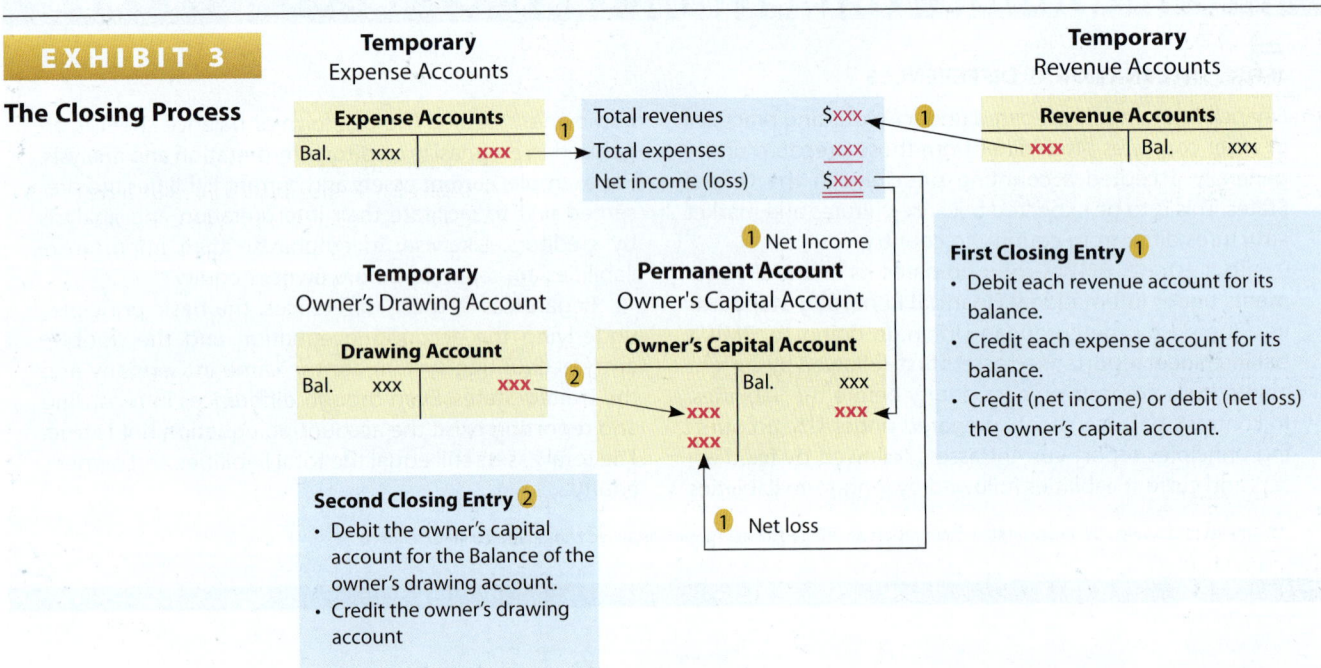

EXHIBIT 3 The Closing Process

The two closing entries required in the closing process are as follows:[2]

1. Debit each revenue account for its balance, credit each expense account for its balance, and credit (net income) or debit (net loss) the owner's capital account.
2. Debit the owner's capital account for the balance of the drawing account and credit the drawing account.

Closing entries are recorded in the journal and are dated as of the last day of the accounting period. In the journal, closing entries are recorded immediately following the adjusting entries. The caption, *Closing Entries*, may be inserted above the closing entries to separate them from the adjusting entries.

Journalizing and Posting Closing Entries

A flowchart of the two closing entries for **NetSolutions** is shown in Exhibit 4. The balances in the accounts are those shown in the Adjusted Trial Balance columns of the end-of-period spreadsheet shown in Exhibit 1.

---

[2] It is possible to close the temporary revenue and expense accounts using a clearing account such as Income Summary, Revenue and Expense Summary, or Profit and Loss Summary. In this case, four closing entries are made. The first entry closes the revenue accounts to Income Summary. The second entry closes the expense accounts to Income Summary. The third entry closes the income summary account to owner's equity. The fourth entry closes the owner's drawing account to owner's equity.

Chapter 4 Completing the Accounting Cycle 171

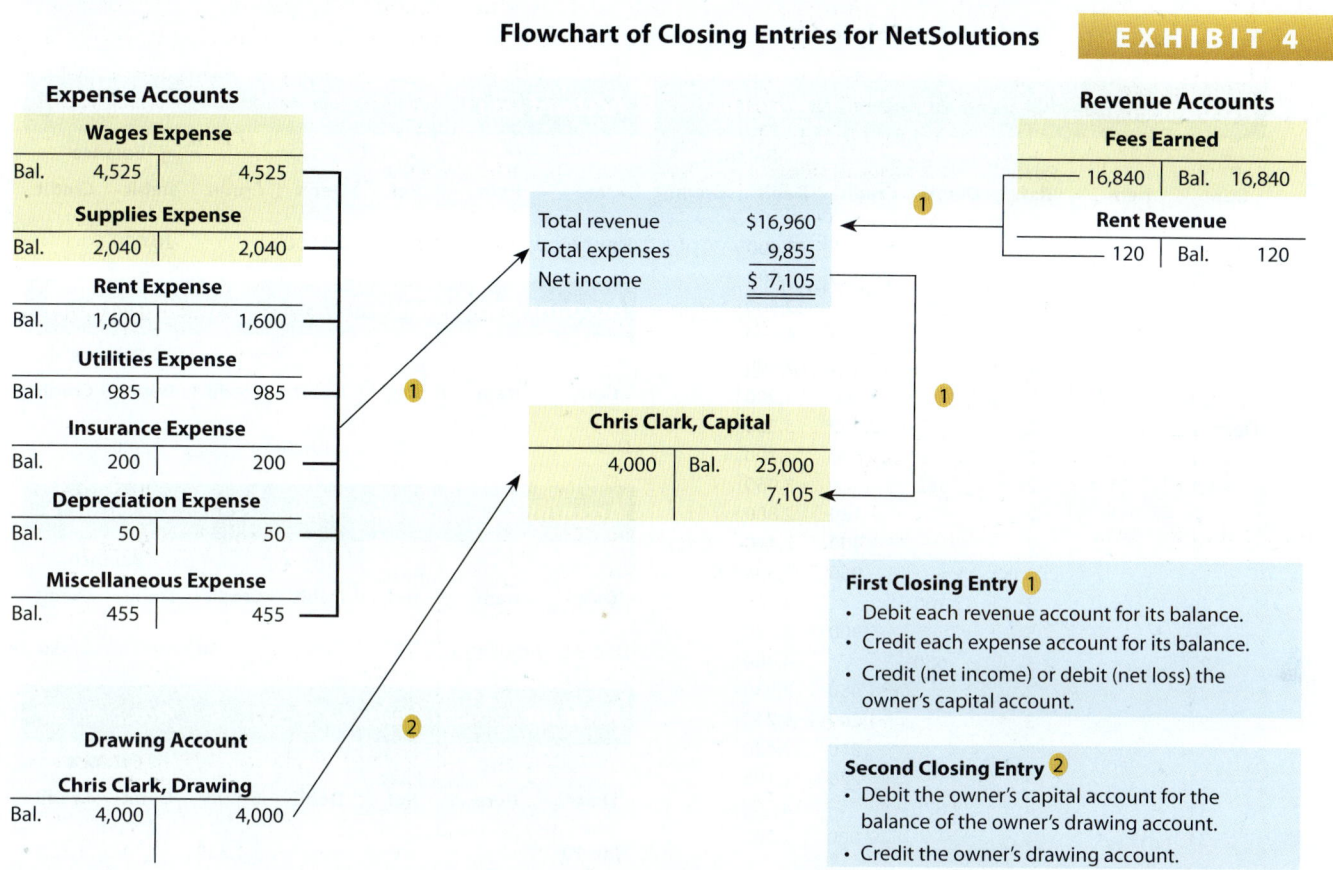

Flowchart of Closing Entries for NetSolutions — EXHIBIT 4

The closing entries for **NetSolutions** are shown in Exhibit 5. The account titles and balances for these entries may be obtained from the end-of-period spreadsheet, the adjusted trial balance, the income statement, the statement of owner's equity, or the ledger.

		Journal			Page 6
Date		Description	Post. Ref.	Debit	Credit
2018		Closing Entries			
Dec.	31	Fees Earned	41	16,840	
		Rent Revenue	42	120	
		Wages Expense	51		4,525
		Supplies Expense	52		2,040
		Rent Expense	53		1,600
		Utilities Expense	54		985
		Insurance Expense	55		200
		Depreciation Expense	56		50
		Miscellaneous Expense	59		455
		Chris Clark, Capital	31		7,105
	31	Chris Clark, Capital	31	4,000	
		Chris Clark, Drawing	32		4,000

EXHIBIT 5

Closing Entries, NetSolutions

The closing entries are posted to NetSolutions' ledger as shown in Exhibit 6. After the closing entries are posted, NetSolutions' ledger has the following characteristics:

- The balance of Chris Clark, Capital of $28,105 agrees with the amount reported on the statement of owner's equity and the balance sheet.
- The revenue, expense, and drawing accounts will have zero balances.

EXHIBIT 6 — Ledger, NetSolutions

Account: Cash — Account No. 11

Date	Item	Post. Ref.	Debit	Credit	Balance Debit	Balance Credit
2018 Nov. 1		1	25,000		25,000	
5		1		20,000	5,000	
18		1	7,500		12,500	
30		1		3,650	8,850	
30		1		950	7,900	
30		2		2,000	5,900	
Dec. 1		2		2,400	3,500	
1		2		800	2,700	
1		2	360		3,060	
6		2		180	2,880	
11		2		400	2,480	
13		3		950	1,530	
16		3	3,100		4,630	
20		3		900	3,730	
21		3	650		4,380	
23		3		1,450	2,930	
27		3		1,200	1,730	
31		3		310	1,420	
31		4		225	1,195	
31		4	2,870		4,065	
31		4		2,000	2,065	

Account: Accounts Receivable — Account No. 12

Date	Item	Post. Ref.	Debit	Credit	Balance Debit	Balance Credit
2018 Dec. 16		3	1,750		1,750	
21		3		650	1,100	
31		4	1,120		2,220	
31	Adjusting	5	500		2,720	

Account: Supplies — Account No. 14

Date	Item	Post. Ref.	Debit	Credit	Balance Debit	Balance Credit
2018 Nov. 10		1	1,350		1,350	
30		1		800	550	
Dec. 23		3	1,450		2,000	
31	Adjusting	5		1,240	760	

Account: Prepaid Insurance — Account No. 15

Date	Item	Post. Ref.	Debit	Credit	Balance Debit	Balance Credit
2018 Dec. 1		2	2,400		2,400	
31	Adjusting	5		200	2,200	

Account: Land — Account No. 17

Date	Item	Post. Ref.	Debit	Credit	Balance Debit	Balance Credit
2018 Nov. 5		1	20,000		20,000	

Account: Office Equipment — Account No. 18

Date	Item	Post. Ref.	Debit	Credit	Balance Debit	Balance Credit
2018 Dec. 4		2	1,800		1,800	

Account: Accumulated Depreciation — Account No. 19

Date	Item	Post. Ref.	Debit	Credit	Balance Debit	Balance Credit
2018 Dec. 31	Adjusting	5		50		50

Account: Accounts Payable — Account No. 21

Date	Item	Post. Ref.	Debit	Credit	Balance Debit	Balance Credit
2018 Nov. 10		1		1,350		1,350
30		1	950			400
Dec. 4		2		1,800		2,200
11		2	400			1,800
20		3	900			900

Account: Wages Payable — Account No. 22

Date	Item	Post. Ref.	Debit	Credit	Balance Debit	Balance Credit
2018 Dec. 31	Adjusting	5		250		250

Account: Unearned Rent — Account No. 23

Date	Item	Post. Ref.	Debit	Credit	Balance Debit	Balance Credit
2018 Dec. 1		2		360		360
31	Adjusting	5	120			240

Account: Chris Clark, Capital — Account No. 31

Date	Item	Post. Ref.	Debit	Credit	Balance Debit	Balance Credit
2018 Nov. 1		1		25,000		25,000
Dec. 31	Closing	6		7,105		32,105
31	Closing	6	4,000			28,105

Ledger, NetSolutions (*Concluded*) — EXHIBIT 6

Account Chris Clark, Drawing — Account No. 32

Date	Item	Post. Ref.	Debit	Credit	Balance Debit	Balance Credit
2018						
Nov. 30		2	2,000		2,000	
Dec. 31		4	2,000		4,000	
31	Closing	6		4,000	—	—

Account Fees Earned — Account No. 41

Date	Item	Post. Ref.	Debit	Credit	Balance Debit	Balance Credit
2018						
Nov. 18		1		7,500		7,500
Dec. 16		3		3,100		10,600
16		3		1,750		12,350
31		4		2,870		15,220
31		4		1,120		16,340
31	Adjusting	5		500		16,840
31	Closing	6	16,840		—	—

Account Rent Revenue — Account No. 42

Date	Item	Post. Ref.	Debit	Credit	Balance Debit	Balance Credit
2018						
Dec. 31	Adjusting	5		120		120
31	Closing	6	120		—	—

Account Wages Expense — Account No. 51

Date	Item	Post. Ref.	Debit	Credit	Balance Debit	Balance Credit
2018							
Nov. 30		1	2,125		2,125	
Dec. 13		3	950		3,075	
27		3	1,200		4,275	
31	Adjusting	5	250		4,525	
31	Closing	6		4,525	—	—

Account Supplies Expense — Account No. 52

Date	Item	Post. Ref.	Debit	Credit	Balance Debit	Balance Credit
2018						
Nov. 30		1	800		800	
Dec. 31	Adjusting	5	1,240		2,040	
31	Closing	6		2,040	—	—

Account Rent Expense — Account No. 53

Date	Item	Post. Ref.	Debit	Credit	Balance Debit	Balance Credit
2018						
Nov. 30		1	800		800	
Dec. 1		2	800		1,600	
31	Closing	6		1,600	—	—

Account Utilities Expense — Account No. 54

Date	Item	Post. Ref.	Debit	Credit	Balance Debit	Balance Credit
2018						
Nov. 30		1	450		450	
Dec. 31		3	310		760	
31		4	225		985	
31	Closing	6		985	—	—

Account Insurance Expense — Account No. 55

Date	Item	Post. Ref.	Debit	Credit	Balance Debit	Balance Credit
2018						
Dec. 31	Adjusting	5	200		200	
31	Closing	6		200	—	—

Account Depreciation Expense — Account No. 56

Date	Item	Post. Ref.	Debit	Credit	Balance Debit	Balance Credit
2018						
Dec. 31	Adjusting	5	50		50	
31	Closing	6		50	—	—

Account Miscellaneous Expense — Account No. 59

Date	Item	Post. Ref.	Debit	Credit	Balance Debit	Balance Credit
2018						
Nov. 30		1	275		275	
Dec. 6		2	180		455	
31	Closing	6		455	—	—

174 Chapter 4 Completing the Accounting Cycle

As shown in Exhibit 6, the closing entries are normally identified in the ledger as "Closing." In addition, a line is often inserted in both balance columns after a closing entry is posted. This separates next period's revenue, expense, and withdrawal transactions from those of the current period. Next period's transactions will be posted directly below the closing entry.

Example Exercise 4-4 Closing Entries — Obj. 3

After the accounts have been adjusted at July 31, the end of the year, the following balances are taken from the ledger of Cabriolet Services Co.:

Terry Lambert, Capital	$615,850
Terry Lambert, Drawing	25,000
Fees Earned	380,450
Wages Expense	250,000
Rent Expense	65,000
Supplies Expense	18,250
Miscellaneous Expense	6,200

Journalize the two entries required to close the accounts.

Follow My Example 4-4

July	31	Fees Earned	380,450	
		Wages Expense		250,000
		Rent Expense		65,000
		Supplies Expense		18,250
		Miscellaneous Expense		6,200
		Terry Lambert, Capital		41,000
	31	Terry Lambert, Capital	25,000	
		Terry Lambert, Drawing		25,000

Practice Exercises: PE 4-4A, PE 4-4B

Post-Closing Trial Balance

A post-closing trial balance is prepared after the closing entries have been posted. The purpose of the post-closing (after closing) trial balance is to verify that the ledger is in balance at the beginning of the next period. The accounts and amounts should agree exactly with the accounts and amounts listed on the balance sheet at the end of the period. The post-closing trial balance for **NetSolutions** is shown in Exhibit 7.

Obj. 4 Describe the accounting cycle.

Accounting Cycle

The accounting process that begins with analyzing and journalizing transactions and ends with the post-closing trial balance is called the **accounting cycle**. The steps in the accounting cycle are as follows:

Step 1. Transactions are analyzed and recorded in the journal.
Step 2. Transactions are posted to the ledger.
Step 3. An unadjusted trial balance is prepared.
Step 4. Adjustment data are assembled and analyzed.
Step 5 (optional). An optional end-of-period spreadsheet is prepared.

Step 6. Adjusting entries are journalized and posted to the ledger.
Step 7. An adjusted trial balance is prepared.
Step 8. Financial statements are prepared.
Step 9. Closing entries are journalized and posted to the ledger.
Step 10. A post-closing trial balance is prepared.[3]

EXHIBIT 7
Post-Closing Trial Balance, NetSolutions

NetSolutions
Post-Closing Trial Balance
December 31, 2018

	Account No.	Debit Balances	Credit Balances
Cash	11	2,065	
Accounts Receivable	12	2,720	
Supplies	14	760	
Prepaid Insurance	15	2,200	
Land	17	20,000	
Office Equipment	18	1,800	
Accumulated Depreciation	19		50
Accounts Payable	21		900
Wages Payable	22		250
Unearned Rent	23		240
Chris Clark, Capital	31		28,105
		29,545	29,545

Exhibit 8 illustrates the accounting cycle in graphic form. It also illustrates how the accounting cycle begins with the source documents for a transaction and flows through the accounting system and into the financial statements.

Example Exercise 4-5 Accounting Cycle   Obj. 4

From the following list of steps in the accounting cycle, identify what two steps are missing:
a. Transactions are analyzed and recorded in the journal:
b. Transactions are posted to the ledger.
c. Adjustment data are assembled and analyzed.
d. An optional end-of-period spreadsheet is prepared.
e. Adjusting entries are journalized and posted to the ledger.
f. Financial statements are prepared.
g. Closing entries are journalized and posted to the ledger.
h. A post-closing trial balance is prepared.

Follow My Example 4-5

The following two steps are missing: (1) the preparation of an unadjusted trial balance and (2) the preparation of the adjusted trial balance. The unadjusted trial balance should be prepared after step (b). The adjusted trial balance should be prepared after step (e).

Practice Exercises: PE 4-5A, PE 4-5B

---

[3] Some accountants include the journalizing and posting of "reversing entries" as the last step in the accounting cycle. Because reversing entries are not required, they are described and illustrated in Appendix 2 to this chapter.

176 Chapter 4 Completing the Accounting Cycle

EXHIBIT 8
Accounting Cycle

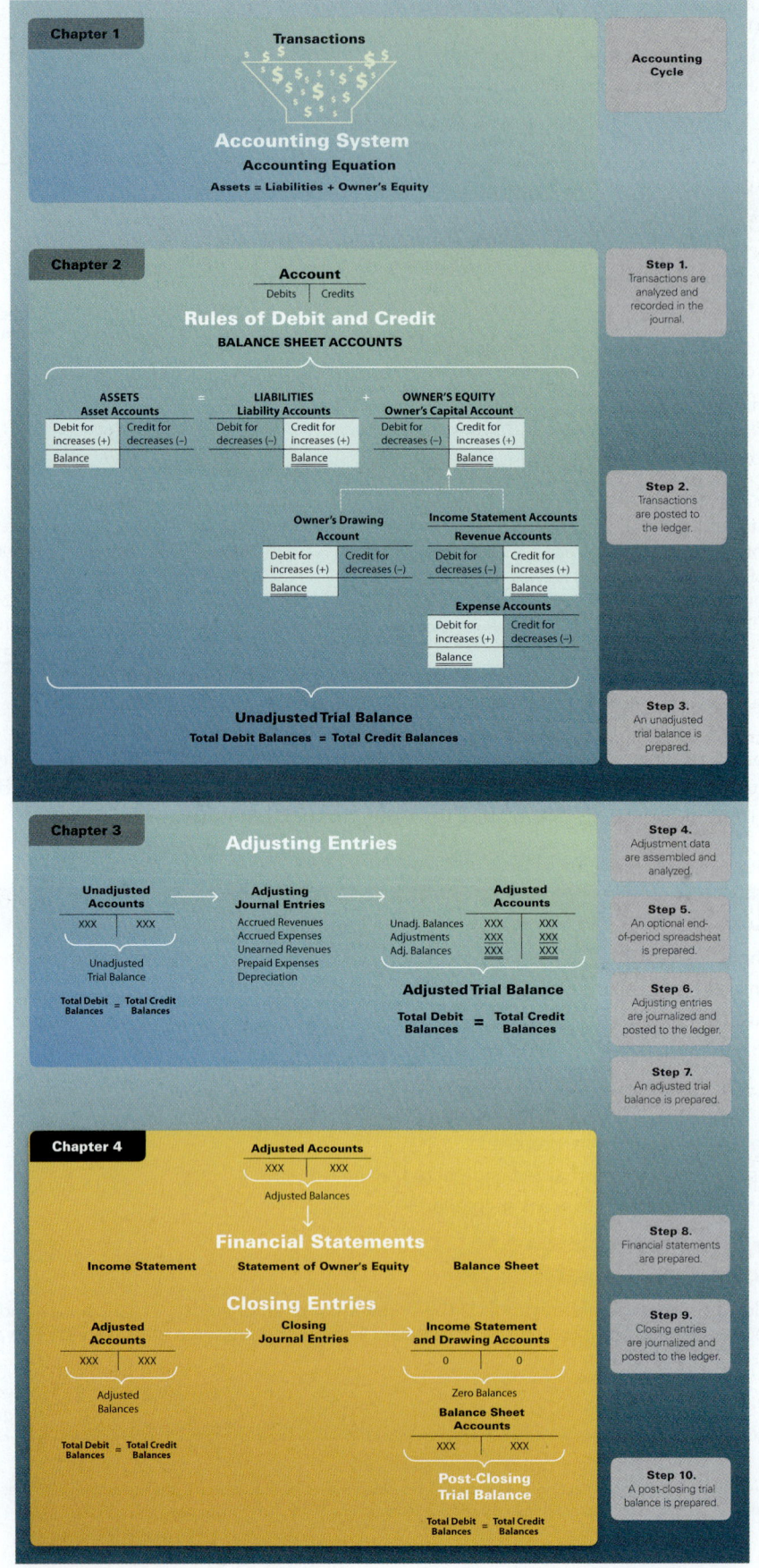

Illustration of the Accounting Cycle

Obj. 5 Illustrate the accounting cycle for one period.

In this section, the complete accounting cycle for one period is illustrated. Assume that for several years Kelly Pitney has operated a part-time consulting business from her home. As of April 1, 2019, Kelly decided to move to rented quarters and to operate the business on a full-time basis. The business will be known as Kelly Consulting. During April, Kelly Consulting entered into the following transactions:

Apr. 1. The following assets were received from Kelly Pitney: cash, $13,100; accounts receivable, $3,000; supplies, $1,400; and office equipment, $12,500. There were no liabilities received.
1. Paid three months' rent on a lease rental contract, $4,800.
2. Paid the premiums on property and casualty insurance policies, $1,800.
4. Received cash from clients as an advance payment for services to be provided and recorded it as unearned fees, $5,000.
5. Purchased additional office equipment on account from Office Station Co., $2,000.
6. Received cash from clients on account, $1,800.
10. Paid cash for a newspaper advertisement, $120.
12. Paid Office Station Co. for part of the debt incurred on April 5, $1,200.
12. Provided services on account for the period April 1–12, $4,200.
14. Paid part-time receptionist for two weeks' salary, $750.
17. Received cash from cash clients for fees earned during the period April 1–16, $6,250.
18. Paid cash for supplies, $800.
20. Provided services on account for the period April 13–20, $2,100.
24. Recorded cash from cash clients for fees earned for the period April 17–24, $3,850.
26. Received cash from clients on account, $5,600.
27. Paid part-time receptionist for two weeks' salary, $750.
29. Paid telephone bill for April, $130.
30. Paid electricity bill for April, $200.
30. Received cash from cash clients for fees earned for the period April 25–30, $3,050.
30. Provided services on account for the remainder of April, $1,500.
30. Kelly withdrew $6,000 for personal use.

Step 1. Analyzing and Recording Transactions in the Journal

The first step in the accounting cycle is to analyze and record transactions in the journal using the double-entry accounting system. As illustrated in Chapter 2, transactions are analyzed and journalized using the following steps:

Step 1. Carefully read the description of the transaction to determine whether an asset, liability, owner's equity, revenue, expense, or drawing account is affected.
Step 2. For each account affected by the transaction, determine whether the account increases or decreases.
Step 3. Determine whether each increase or decrease should be recorded as a debit or a credit, following the rules of debit and credit shown in Exhibit 3 of Chapter 2.
Step 4. Record the transaction using a journal entry.

The company's chart of accounts is useful in determining which accounts are affected by the transaction. The chart of accounts for Kelly Consulting is shown in Exhibit 9.

EXHIBIT 9
Chart of Accounts for Kelly Consulting

11	Cash	31	Kelly Pitney, Capital
12	Accounts Receivable	32	Kelly Pitney, Drawing
14	Supplies	41	Fees Earned
15	Prepaid Rent	51	Salary Expense
16	Prepaid Insurance	52	Rent Expense
18	Office Equipment	53	Supplies Expense
19	Accumulated Depreciation	54	Depreciation Expense
21	Accounts Payable	55	Insurance Expense
22	Salaries Payable	59	Miscellaneous Expense
23	Unearned Fees		

After analyzing each of Kelly Consulting's transactions for April, the journal entries are recorded as shown in Exhibit 10.

EXHIBIT 10
Journal Entries for April, Kelly Consulting

Journal — Page 1

Date		Description	Post. Ref.	Debit	Credit
2019 Apr.	1	Cash	11	13,100	
		Accounts Receivable	12	3,000	
		Supplies	14	1,400	
		Office Equipment	18	12,500	
		Kelly Pitney, Capital	31		30,000
	1	Prepaid Rent	15	4,800	
		Cash	11		4,800
	2	Prepaid Insurance	16	1,800	
		Cash	11		1,800
	4	Cash	11	5,000	
		Unearned Fees	23		5,000
	5	Office Equipment	18	2,000	
		Accounts Payable	21		2,000
	6	Cash	11	1,800	
		Accounts Receivable	12		1,800
	10	Miscellaneous Expense	59	120	
		Cash	11		120
	12	Accounts Payable	21	1,200	
		Cash	11		1,200
	12	Accounts Receivable	12	4,200	
		Fees Earned	41		4,200
	14	Salary Expense	51	750	
		Cash	11		750

Journal — Page 2

Date		Description	Post. Ref.	Debit	Credit
2019 Apr.	17	Cash	11	6,250	
		Fees Earned	41		6,250
	18	Supplies	14	800	
		Cash	11		800

EXHIBIT 10

Journal Entries for April, Kelly Consulting (*Continued*)

Date	Description	Post. Ref.	Debit	Credit
20	Accounts Receivable	12	2,100	
	Fees Earned	41		2,100
24	Cash	11	3,850	
	Fees Earned	41		3,850
26	Cash	11	5,600	
	Accounts Receivable	12		5,600
27	Salary Expense	51	750	
	Cash	11		750
29	Miscellaneous Expense	59	130	
	Cash	11		130
30	Miscellaneous Expense	59	200	
	Cash	11		200
30	Cash	11	3,050	
	Fees Earned	41		3,050
30	Accounts Receivable	12	1,500	
	Fees Earned	41		1,500
30	Kelly Pitney, Drawing	32	6,000	
	Cash	11		6,000

Step 2. Posting Transactions to the Ledger

Periodically, the transactions recorded in the journal are posted to the accounts in the ledger. The debits and credits for each journal entry are posted to the accounts in the order in which they occur in the journal. As illustrated in Chapters 2 and 3, journal entries are posted to the accounts using the following four steps:

Step 1. The date is entered in the Date column of the account.
Step 2. The amount is entered in the Debit or Credit column of the account.
Step 3. The journal page number is entered in the Posting Reference column.
Step 4. The account number is entered in the Posting Reference (Post. Ref.) column in the journal.

The journal entries for Kelly Consulting have been posted to the ledger shown in Exhibit 18.

Step 3. Preparing an Unadjusted Trial Balance

An unadjusted trial balance is prepared to determine whether any errors have been made in posting the debits and credits to the ledger. The unadjusted trial balance shown in Exhibit 11 does not provide complete proof of the accuracy of the ledger. It indicates only that the debits and the credits are equal. This proof is of value, however, because errors often affect the equality of debits and credits. If the two totals of a trial balance are not equal, an error has occurred that must be discovered and corrected.

The unadjusted account balances shown in Exhibit 11 were taken from Kelly Consulting's ledger shown in Exhibit 18, before any adjusting entries were recorded.

EXHIBIT 11

Unadjusted Trial Balance, Kelly Consulting

Kelly Consulting
Unadjusted Trial Balance
April 30, 2019

	Account No.	Debit Balances	Credit Balances
Cash	11	22,100	
Accounts Receivable	12	3,400	
Supplies	14	2,200	
Prepaid Rent	15	4,800	
Prepaid Insurance	16	1,800	
Office Equipment	18	14,500	
Accumulated Depreciation	19		0
Accounts Payable	21		800
Salaries Payable	22		0
Unearned Fees	23		5,000
Kelly Pitney, Capital	31		30,000
Kelly Pitney, Drawing	32	6,000	
Fees Earned	41		20,950
Salary Expense	51	1,500	
Rent Expense	52	0	
Supplies Expense	53	0	
Depreciation Expense	54	0	
Insurance Expense	55	0	
Miscellaneous Expense	59	450	
		56,750	56,750

Step 4. Assembling and Analyzing Adjustment Data

Before the financial statements can be prepared, the accounts must be updated. The four types of accounts that normally require adjustment (updating) include prepaid expenses, unearned revenue, accrued revenue, and accrued expenses. In addition, depreciation expense must be recorded for fixed assets other than land. The following data have been assembled on April 30, 2019, for analysis of possible adjustments for Kelly Consulting:

a. Insurance expired during April is $300.
b. Supplies on hand on April 30 are $1,350.
c. Depreciation of office equipment for April is $330.
d. Accrued receptionist salary on April 30 is $120.
e. Rent expired during April is $1,600.
f. Unearned fees on April 30 are $2,500.

Step 5. Preparing an Optional End-of-Period Spreadsheet

Although an end-of-period spreadsheet is not required, it is useful in showing the flow of accounting information from the unadjusted trial balance to the adjusted trial balance. In addition, an end-of-period spreadsheet is useful in analyzing the impact of proposed adjustments on the financial statements. The end-of-period spreadsheet for Kelly Consulting is shown in Exhibit 12.

Step 6. Journalizing and Posting Adjusting Entries

Based on the adjustment data shown in Step 4, adjusting entries for Kelly Consulting are prepared as shown in Exhibit 13. Each adjusting entry affects at least one income statement account and one balance sheet account. Explanations for each adjustment including any computations are normally included with each adjusting entry.

EXHIBIT 12
End-of-Period Spreadsheet, Kelly Consulting

	A	B	C	D	E	F	G
1		Kelly Consulting					
2		End-of-Period Spreadsheet					
3		For the Month Ended April 30, 2019					
4		Unadjusted				Adjusted	
5		Trial Balance		Adjustments		Trial Balance	
6	Account Title	Dr.	Cr.	Dr.	Cr.	Dr.	Cr.
7							
8	Cash	22,100				22,100	
9	Accounts Receivable	3,400				3,400	
10	Supplies	2,200			(b) 850	1,350	
11	Prepaid Rent	4,800			(e) 1,600	3,200	
12	Prepaid Insurance	1,800			(a) 300	1,500	
13	Office Equipment	14,500				14,500	
14	Accum. Depreciation				(c) 330		330
15	Accounts Payable		800				800
16	Salaries Payable				(d) 120		120
17	Unearned Fees		5,000	(f) 2,500			2,500
18	Kelly Pitney, Capital		30,000				30,000
19	Kelly Pitney, Drawing	6,000				6,000	
20	Fees Earned		20,950		(f) 2,500		23,450
21	Salary Expense	1,500		(d) 120		1,620	
22	Rent Expense			(e) 1,600		1,600	
23	Supplies Expense			(b) 850		850	
24	Depreciation Expense			(c) 330		330	
25	Insurance Expense			(a) 300		300	
26	Miscellaneous Expense	450				450	
27		56,750	56,750	5,700	5,700	57,200	57,200
28							

EXHIBIT 13
Adjusting Entries, Kelly Consulting

Journal — Page 3

Date	Description	Post. Ref.	Debit	Credit
	Adjusting Entries			
2019 Apr. 30	Insurance Expense	55	300	
	Prepaid Insurance	16		300
	Expired insurance.			
30	Supplies Expense	53	850	
	Supplies	14		850
	Supplies used ($2,200 − $1,350).			
30	Depreciation Expense	54	330	
	Accumulated Depreciation	19		330
	Depreciation of office equipment.			
30	Salary Expense	51	120	
	Salaries Payable	22		120
	Accrued salary.			
30	Rent Expense	52	1,600	
	Prepaid Rent	15		1,600
	Rent expired during April.			
30	Unearned Fees	23	2,500	
	Fees Earned	41		2,500
	Fees earned ($5,000 − $2,500).			

Each of the adjusting entries shown in Exhibit 13 is posted to Kelly Consulting's ledger shown in Exhibit 18. The adjusting entries are identified in the ledger as "Adjusting."

Step 7. Preparing an Adjusted Trial Balance

After the adjustments have been journalized and posted, an adjusted trial balance is prepared to verify the equality of the total of the debit and credit balances. This is the last step before preparing the financial statements. If the adjusted trial balance does not balance, an error has occurred and must be found and corrected. The adjusted trial balance for Kelly Consulting as of April 30, 2019, is shown in Exhibit 14.

EXHIBIT 14

Adjusted Trial Balance, Kelly Consulting

Kelly Consulting
Adjusted Trial Balance
April 30, 2019

	Account No.	Debit Balances	Credit Balances
Cash	11	22,100	
Accounts Receivable	12	3,400	
Supplies	14	1,350	
Prepaid Rent	15	3,200	
Prepaid Insurance	16	1,500	
Office Equipment	18	14,500	
Accumulated Depreciation	19		330
Accounts Payable	21		800
Salaries Payable	22		120
Unearned Fees	23		2,500
Kelly Pitney, Capital	31		30,000
Kelly Pitney, Drawing	32	6,000	
Fees Earned	41		23,450
Salary Expense	51	1,620	
Rent Expense	52	1,600	
Supplies Expense	53	850	
Depreciation Expense	54	330	
Insurance Expense	55	300	
Miscellaneous Expense	59	450	
		57,200	57,200

Step 8. Preparing the Financial Statements

The most important outcome of the accounting cycle is the financial statements. The income statement is prepared first, followed by the statement of owner's equity and then the balance sheet. The statements can be prepared directly from the adjusted trial balance, the end-of-period spreadsheet, or the ledger. The net income or net loss shown on the income statement is reported on the statement of owner's equity along with any additional investments by the owner and any withdrawals. The ending owner's capital is reported on the balance sheet and is added with total liabilities to equal total assets.

The financial statements for Kelly Consulting are shown in Exhibit 15. Kelly Consulting earned net income of $18,300 for April. As of April 30, 2019, Kelly Consulting has total assets of $45,720, total liabilities of $3,420, and total owner's equity of $42,300.

EXHIBIT 15

Financial Statements, Kelly Consulting

Kelly Consulting
Income Statement
For the Month Ended April 30, 2019

Fees earned...		$23,450
Expenses:		
Salary expense	$1,620	
Rent expense	1,600	
Supplies expense...	850	
Depreciation expense.......................................	330	
Insurance expense...	300	
Miscellaneous expense	450	
Total expenses		5,150
Net income		$18,300

Kelly Consulting
Statement of Owner's Equity
For the Month Ended April 30, 2019

Kelly Pitney, capital, April 1, 2019.................................		$ 0
Investment during the month	$30,000	
Net income for the month	18,300	
Withdrawals	(6,000)	
Increase in owner's equity		42,300
Kelly Pitney, capital, April 30, 2019...............................		$42,300

Kelly Consulting
Balance Sheet
April 30, 2019

Assets

Current assets:		
Cash	$22,100	
Accounts receivable...	3,400	
Supplies...	1,350	
Prepaid rent	3,200	
Prepaid insurance..	1,500	
Total current assets		$31,550
Property, plant, and equipment:		
Office equipment	$14,500	
Less accumulated depreciation	330	
Total property, plant, and equipment...........		14,170
Total assets..		$45,720

Liabilities

Current liabilities:		
Accounts payable..	$ 800	
Salaries payable	120	
Unearned fees	2,500	
Total liabilities...		$ 3,420

Owner's Equity

Kelly Pitney, capital		42,300
Total liabilities and owner's equity		$45,720

Step 9. Journalizing and Posting Closing Entries

As described earlier in this chapter, two closing entries are required at the end of an accounting period. These two closing entries are as follows:

First Closing Entry:
Debit each revenue account for its balance, credit each expense account for its balance, and credit (net income) or debit (net loss) the owner's capital account.

Second Closing Entry:
Debit the owner's capital account for the balance of the drawing account and credit the drawing account.

The two closing entries for Kelly Consulting are shown in Exhibit 16. The closing entries are posted to Kelly Consulting's ledger as shown in Exhibit 18. After the closing entries are posted, Kelly Consulting's ledger has the following characteristics:

- The balance of Kelly Pitney, Capital of $42,300 agrees with the amount reported on the statement of owner's equity and the balance sheet.
- The revenue, expense, and drawing accounts will have zero balances.

EXHIBIT 16

Closing Entries, Kelly Consulting

Journal
Page 4

Date	Description	Post. Ref.	Debit	Credit
2019	Closing Entries			
Apr. 30	Fees Earned	41	23,450	
	Salary Expense	51		1,620
	Rent Expense	52		1,600
	Supplies Expense	53		850
	Depreciation Expense	54		330
	Insurance Expense	55		300
	Miscellaneous Expense	59		450
	Kelly Pitney, Capital	31		18,300
30	Kelly Pitney, Capital	31	6,000	
	Kelly Pitney, Drawing	32		6,000

The closing entries are normally identified in the ledger as "Closing." In addition, a line is often inserted in both balance columns after a closing entry is posted. This separates next period's revenue, expense, and withdrawal transactions from those of the current period.

Step 10. Preparing a Post-Closing Trial Balance

A post-closing trial balance is prepared after the closing entries have been posted. The purpose of the post-closing trial balance is to verify that the ledger is in balance at the beginning of the next period. The accounts and amounts in the post-closing trial balance should agree exactly with the accounts and amounts listed on the balance sheet at the end of the period.

The post-closing trial balance for Kelly Consulting is shown in Exhibit 17. The balances shown in the post-closing trial balance are taken from the ending balances in the ledger shown in Exhibit 18. These balances agree with the amounts shown on Kelly Consulting's balance sheet in Exhibit 15.

EXHIBIT 17
Post-Closing Trial Balance, Kelly Consulting

Kelly Consulting
Post-Closing Trial Balance
April 30, 2019

	Account No.	Debit Balances	Credit Balances
Cash	11	22,100	
Accounts Receivable	12	3,400	
Supplies	14	1,350	
Prepaid Rent	15	3,200	
Prepaid Insurance	16	1,500	
Office Equipment	18	14,500	
Accumulated Depreciation	19		330
Accounts Payable	21		800
Salaries Payable	22		120
Unearned Fees	23		2,500
Kelly Pitney, Capital	31		42,300
		46,050	46,050

EXHIBIT 18
Ledger, Kelly Consulting

Ledger

Account Cash — Account No. 11

Date	Item	Post. Ref.	Debit	Credit	Balance Debit	Balance Credit
2019						
Apr. 1		1	13,100		13,100	
1		1		4,800	8,300	
2		1		1,800	6,500	
4		1	5,000		11,500	
6		1	1,800		13,300	
10		1		120	13,180	
12		1		1,200	11,980	
14		1		750	11,230	
17		2	6,250		17,480	
18		2		800	16,680	
24		2	3,850		20,530	
26		2	5,600		26,130	
27		2		750	25,380	
29		2		130	25,250	
30		2		200	25,050	
30		2	3,050		28,100	
30		2		6,000	22,100	

Account Accounts Receivable — Account No. 12

Date	Item	Post. Ref.	Debit	Credit	Balance Debit	Balance Credit
2019						
Apr. 1		1	3,000		3,000	
6		1		1,800	1,200	
12		1	4,200		5,400	
20		2	2,100		7,500	
26		2		5,600	1,900	
30		2	1,500		3,400	

Account Supplies — Account No. 14

Date	Item	Post. Ref.	Debit	Credit	Balance Debit	Balance Credit
2019						
Apr. 1		1	1,400		1,400	
18		2	800		2,200	
30	Adjusting	3		850	1,350	

Account Prepaid Rent — Account No. 15

Date	Item	Post. Ref.	Debit	Credit	Balance Debit	Balance Credit
2019						
Apr. 1		1	4,800		4,800	
30	Adjusting	3		1,600	3,200	

Account Prepaid Insurance — Account No. 16

Date	Item	Post. Ref.	Debit	Credit	Balance Debit	Balance Credit
2019						
Apr. 2		1	1,800		1,800	
30	Adjusting	3		300	1,500	

Account Office Equipment — Account No. 18

Date	Item	Post. Ref.	Debit	Credit	Balance Debit	Balance Credit
2019						
Apr. 1		1	12,500		12,500	
5		1	2,000		14,500	

(Continued)

EXHIBIT 18 — Ledger, Kelly Consulting (*Continued*)

Account Accumulated Depreciation — Account No. 19

Date	Item	Post. Ref.	Debit	Credit	Balance Debit	Balance Credit
2019 Apr. 30	Adjusting	3		330		330

Account Accounts Payable — Account No. 21

Date	Item	Post. Ref.	Debit	Credit	Balance Debit	Balance Credit
2019 Apr. 5		1		2,000		2,000
12		1	1,200			800

Account Salaries Payable — Account No. 22

Date	Item	Post. Ref.	Debit	Credit	Balance Debit	Balance Credit
2019 Apr. 30	Adjusting	3		120		120

Account Unearned Fees — Account No. 23

Date	Item	Post. Ref.	Debit	Credit	Balance Debit	Balance Credit
2019 Apr. 4		1		5,000		5,000
30	Adjusting	3	2,500			2,500

Account Kelly Pitney, Capital — Account No. 31

Date	Item	Post. Ref.	Debit	Credit	Balance Debit	Balance Credit
2019 Apr. 1		1		30,000		30,000
30	Closing	4		18,300		48,300
30	Closing	4	6,000			42,300

Account Kelly Pitney, Drawing — Account No. 32

Date	Item	Post. Ref.	Debit	Credit	Balance Debit	Balance Credit
2019 Apr. 30		2	6,000		6,000	
30	Closing	4		6,000	—	—

Account Fees Earned — Account No. 41

Date	Item	Post. Ref.	Debit	Credit	Balance Debit	Balance Credit
2019 Apr. 12		1		4,200		4,200
17		2		6,250		10,450
20		2		2,100		12,550
24		2		3,850		16,400
30		2		3,050		19,450
30		2		1,500		20,950
30	Adjusting	3		2,500		23,450
30	Closing	4	23,450		—	—

Account Salary Expense — Account No. 51

Date	Item	Post. Ref.	Debit	Credit	Balance Debit	Balance Credit
2019 Apr. 14		1	750		750	
27		2	750		1,500	
30	Adjusting	3	120		1,620	
30	Closing	4		1,620	—	—

Account Rent Expense — Account No. 52

Date	Item	Post. Ref.	Debit	Credit	Balance Debit	Balance Credit
2019 Apr. 30	Adjusting	3	1,600		1,600	
30	Closing	4		1,600	—	—

Account Supplies Expense — Account No. 53

Date	Item	Post. Ref.	Debit	Credit	Balance Debit	Balance Credit
2019 Apr. 30	Adjusting	3	850		850	
30	Closing	4		850	—	—

Account Depreciation Expense — Account No. 54

Date	Item	Post. Ref.	Debit	Credit	Balance Debit	Balance Credit
2019 Apr. 30	Adjusting	3	330		330	
30	Closing	4		330	—	—

Ledger, Kelly Consulting (Concluded) — EXHIBIT 18

Account Insurance Expense					Account No. 55	
		Post.			Balance	
Date	Item	Ref.	Debit	Credit	Debit	Credit
2019						
Apr. 30	Adjusting	3	300		300	
30	Closing	4		300	—	—

Account Miscellaneous Expense					Account No. 59	
		Post.			Balance	
Date	Item	Ref.	Debit	Credit	Debit	Credit
2019						
Apr. 10		1	120		120	
29		2	130		250	
30		2	200		450	
30	Closing	4		450	—	—

Fiscal Year

Obj. 6 Explain what is meant by the fiscal year and the natural business year.

The annual accounting period adopted by a business is known as its **fiscal year**. Fiscal years begin with the first day of the month selected and end on the last day of the following twelfth month. The period most commonly used is the calendar year. Other periods are not unusual, especially for businesses organized as corporations. For example, a corporation may adopt a fiscal year that ends when business activities have reached the lowest point in its annual operating cycle. Such a fiscal year is called the **natural business year**. At the low point in its operating cycle, a business has more time to analyze the results of operations and to prepare financial statements.

Because companies with fiscal years often have highly seasonal operations, investors and others should be careful in interpreting partial-year reports for such companies. That is, you should expect the results of operations for these companies to vary significantly throughout the fiscal year.

The financial history of a business may be shown by a series of balance sheets and income statements for several fiscal years. If the life of a business is expressed by a line moving from left to right, the series of balance sheets and income statements may be graphed as shown in Exhibit 19.

Link to Zynga
Zynga uses an accounting period ending December 31.

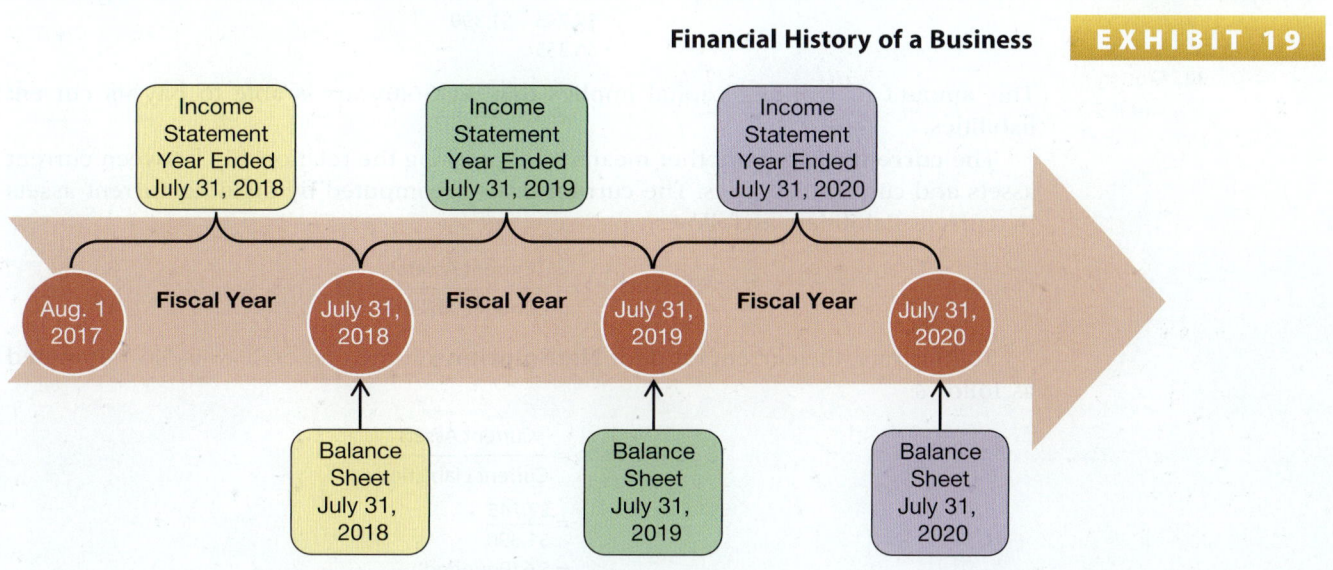

Financial History of a Business — EXHIBIT 19

Business Connection

CHOOSING A FISCAL YEAR

CVS Caremark Corporation (CVS) operates more than 7,000 pharmacies throughout the United States and fills more than one billion prescriptions annually. CVS recently chose December 31 as its fiscal year-end and described its decision as follows:

.... our Board of Directors approved a change in our fiscal year-end ... to December 31 of each year to better reflect our position in the health care ... industry.

In contrast, most large retailers such as **Wal-Mart** and **Target** use fiscal years ending January 31, when their operations are the slowest following the December holidays.

Obj. 7 Describe and illustrate the use of working capital and the current ratio in evaluating a company's financial condition.

Financial Analysis and Interpretation: Working Capital and Current Ratio

The ability to convert assets into cash is called **liquidity**, while the ability of a business to pay its debts is called **solvency**. Two financial measures for evaluating a business's liquidity and solvency are working capital and the current ratio.

Working capital is the excess of the current assets of a business over its current liabilities, computed as follows:

$$\text{Working Capital} = \text{Current Assets} - \text{Current Liabilities}$$

Current assets are more liquid than long-term assets. Thus, an increase in a company's current assets increases or improves its liquidity. An increase in working capital increases or improves liquidity in the sense that current assets are available for uses other than paying current liabilities.

A positive working capital implies that the business is able to pay its current liabilities and is solvent. Thus, an increase in working capital increases or improves a company's short-term solvency.

To illustrate, **NetSolutions**' working capital at the end of 2018 is $6,355 computed as follows:

$$\text{Working Capital} = \text{Current Assets} - \text{Current Liabilities}$$
$$= \$7,745 - \$1,390$$
$$= \$6,355$$

This amount of working capital implies that NetSolutions is able to pay its current liabilities.

The **current ratio** is another means of expressing the relationship between current assets and current liabilities. The current ratio is computed by dividing current assets by current liabilities, as follows:

$$\text{Current Ratio} = \frac{\text{Current Assets}}{\text{Current Liabilities}}$$

To illustrate, the current ratio for **NetSolutions** at the end of 2018 is 5.6, computed as follows:

$$\text{Current Ratio} = \frac{\text{Current Assets}}{\text{Current Liabilities}}$$
$$= \frac{\$7,745}{\$1,390}$$
$$= 5.6 \text{ (Rounded)}$$

The current ratio is more useful than working capital in making comparisons across companies or with industry averages. To illustrate, the following data (in millions) were taken from recent financial statements of Electronic Arts Inc., Take-Two Interactive Software, Inc., and Zynga, Inc.:

	Electronic Arts		Take-Two		Zynga	
	Year 2	Year 1	Year 2	Year 1	Year 2	Year 1
Current assets	$3,720	$3,138	$1,781	$1,399	$1,112	$1,083
Current liabilities	2,747	2,390	966	475	236	369
Working capital	$ 973	$ 748	$ 815	$ 924	$ 876	$ 714
Current ratio*	1.35	1.31	1.84	2.95	4.71	2.93

*Rounded to two decimal places.

Comparing current ratios in Year 2, Zynga has the strongest liquidity position with a current ratio of 4.71. This compares to Electronic Arts' current ratio of 1.35 and Take-Two's current ratio of 1.84. In addition, Zynga's current ratio has increased from 2.93 in Year 1 to 4.71 in Year 2. Electronic Arts' current ratio increased slightly from 1.31 in Year 1 to 1.35 in Year 2. In contrast, Take-Two's current ratio decreased from 2.95 in Year 1 to 1.84 in Year 2. Overall, all three companies have current ratios exceeding 1; thus, there is little risk to short-term creditors that the companies will not meet their current liabilities.

Example Exercise 4-6 Working Capital and Current Ratio Obj. 7

Current assets and current liabilities for Fortson Company follow:

	2019	2018
Current assets	$310,500	$262,500
Current liabilities	172,500	150,000

a. Determine the working capital and current ratio for 2019 and 2018.
b. Does the change in the current ratio from 2018 to 2019 indicate a favorable or an unfavorable change?

Follow My Example 4-6

a.

	2019	2018
Current assets	$310,500	$262,500
Current liabilities	172,500	150,000
Working capital	$138,000	$112,500
Current ratio	1.80	1.75
	($310,500 ÷ $172,500)	($262,500 ÷ $150,000)

b. The change from 1.75 to 1.80 indicates a favorable change.

Practice Exercises: PE 4-6A, PE 4-6B

APPENDIX 1

End-of-Period Spreadsheet

Accountants often use spreadsheets for analyzing and summarizing data. Such spreadsheets are not a formal part of the accounting records. This is in contrast to the chart of accounts, the journal, and the ledger, which are essential parts of an accounting system. Spreadsheets are usually prepared by using a computer program such as Microsoft's Excel.®

Exhibit 1 is an end-of-period spreadsheet used to summarize adjusting entries and their effects on the accounts. As illustrated in the chapter, the financial statements for NetSolutions can be prepared directly from the spreadsheet's Adjusted Trial Balance columns.

Some accountants prefer to expand the end-of-period spreadsheet shown in Exhibit 1 to include financial statement columns. Exhibits 20 through 24 illustrate the step-by-step process of how to prepare this expanded spreadsheet. As a basis for illustration, **NetSolutions** is used.

Step 1. Enter the Title

The spreadsheet is started by entering the following data:

1. Name of the business: *NetSolutions*
2. Type of spreadsheet: *End-of-Period Spreadsheet*
3. The period of time: *For the Two Months Ended December 31, 2018*

Exhibit 20 shows the preceding data entered for NetSolutions.

EXHIBIT 20 — Spreadsheet with Unadjusted Trial Balance Entered

	A	B	C	D	E	F	G	H	I	J	K
1				NetSolutions							
2				End-of-Period Spreadsheet							
3				For the Two Months Ended December 31, 2018							
4		Unadjusted				Adjusted					
5		Trial Balance		Adjustments		Trial Balance		Income Statement		Balance Sheet	
6	Account Title	Dr.	Cr.	Dr.	Cr.	Dr.	Cr.	Dr.	Cr.	Dr.	Cr.
7											
8	Cash	2,065									
9	Accounts Receivable	2,220									
10	Supplies	2,000									
11	Prepaid Insurance	2,400									
12	Land	20,000									
13	Office Equipment	1,800									
14	Accumulated Depreciation										
15	Accounts Payable		900								
16	Wages Payable										
17	Unearned Rent		360								
18	Chris Clark, Capital		25,000								
19	Chris Clark, Drawing	4,000									
20	Fees Earned		16,340								
21	Rent Revenue										
22	Wages Expense	4,275									
23	Supplies Expense	800									
24	Rent Expense	1,600									
25	Utilities Expense	985									
26	Insurance Expense										
27	Depreciation Expense										
28	Miscellaneous Expense	455									
29		42,600	42,600								
30											

The spreadsheet is used for summarizing the effects of adjusting entries. It also aids in preparing financial statements.

Step 2. Enter the Unadjusted Trial Balance

Enter the unadjusted trial balance on the spreadsheet. The spreadsheet in Exhibit 20 shows the unadjusted trial balance for NetSolutions at December 31, 2018.

Step 3. Enter the Adjustments

The adjustments for NetSolutions from Chapter 3 are entered in the Adjustments columns, as shown in Exhibit 21. Cross-referencing (by letters) the debit and credit of each adjustment is useful in reviewing the spreadsheet. It is also helpful for identifying the adjusting entries that need to be recorded in the journal. This cross-referencing process is sometimes referred to as *keying* the adjustments.

Spreadsheet with Unadjusted Trial Balance and Adjustments — **EXHIBIT 21**

	A	B	C	D	E	F	G	H	I	J	K
1				NetSolutions							
2				End-of-Period Spreadsheet							
3				For the Two Months Ended December 31, 2018							
4		Unadjusted				Adjusted					
5		Trial Balance		Adjustments		Trial Balance		Income Statement		Balance Sheet	
6	Account Title	Dr.	Cr.	Dr.	Cr.	Dr.	Cr.	Dr.	Cr.	Dr.	Cr.
7											
8	Cash	2,065									
9	Accounts Receivable	2,220		(a) 500							
10	Supplies	2,000			(d) 1,240						
11	Prepaid Insurance	2,400			(e) 200						
12	Land	20,000									
13	Office Equipment	1,800									
14	Accumulated Depreciation				(f) 50						
15	Accounts Payable		900								
16	Wages Payable				(b) 250						
17	Unearned Rent		360	(c) 120							
18	Chris Clark, Capital		25,000								
19	Chris Clark, Drawing	4,000									
20	Fees Earned		16,340		(a) 500						
21	Rent Revenue				(c) 120						
22	Wages Expense	4,275		(b) 250							
23	Supplies Expense	800		(d) 1,240							
24	Rent Expense	1,600									
25	Utilities Expense	985									
26	Insurance Expense			(e) 200							
27	Depreciation Expense			(f) 50							
28	Miscellaneous Expense	455									
29		42,600	42,600	2,360	2,360						
30											

The adjustments on the spreadsheet are used in preparing the adjusting journal entries.

The adjustments are normally entered in the order in which the data are assembled. If the titles of the accounts to be adjusted do not appear in the unadjusted trial balance, the accounts are inserted in their proper order in the Account Title column.

The adjusting entries for NetSolutions that are entered in the Adjustments columns are as follows:

(a) **Accrued Fees.** Fees accrued at the end of December but not recorded total $500. This amount is an increase in an asset and an increase in revenue. The adjustment is entered as (1) $500 in the Adjustments Debit column on the same line as Accounts Receivable and (2) $500 in the Adjustments Credit column on the same line as Fees Earned.

(b) **Wages.** Wages accrued but not paid at the end of December total $250. This amount is an increase in expenses and an increase in liabilities. The adjustment is entered as (1) $250 in the Adjustments Debit column on the same line as Wages Expense and (2) $250 in the Adjustments Credit column on the same line as Wages Payable.

(c) **Unearned Rent.** The unearned rent account has a credit balance of $360. This balance represents the receipt of three months' rent, beginning with December. Thus, the rent revenue for December is $120 ($360 ÷ 3). The adjustment is entered as (1) $120 in the Adjustments Debit column on the same line as Unearned Rent and (2) $120 in the Adjustments Credit column on the same line as Rent Revenue.

(d) **Supplies.** The supplies account has a debit balance of $2,000. The cost of the supplies on hand at the end of the period is $760. The supplies expense for December is the difference between the two amounts, or $1,240 ($2,000 − $760). The adjustment is entered as (1) $1,240 in the Adjustments Debit column on the same line as Supplies Expense and (2) $1,240 in the Adjustments Credit column on the same line as Supplies.

(e) **Prepaid Insurance.** The prepaid insurance account has a debit balance of $2,400. This balance represents the prepayment of insurance for 12 months beginning December 1. Thus, the insurance expense for December is $200 ($2,400 ÷ 12). The adjustment is entered as (1) $200 in the Adjustments Debit column on the same line as Insurance Expense and (2) $200 in the Adjustments Credit column on the same line as Prepaid Insurance.

(f) **Depreciation.** Depreciation of the office equipment is $50 for December. The adjustment is entered as (1) $50 in the Adjustments Debit column on the same line as Depreciation Expense and (2) $50 in the Adjustments Credit column on the same line as Accumulated Depreciation.

After the adjustments have been entered, the Adjustments columns are totaled to verify the equality of the debits and credits. The total of the Debit column must equal the total of the Credit column.

Step 4. Enter the Adjusted Trial Balance

The adjusted trial balance is entered by combining the adjustments with the unadjusted balances for each account. The adjusted amounts are then extended to the Adjusted Trial Balance columns, as shown in Exhibit 22.

EXHIBIT 22 Spreadsheet with Unadjusted Trial Balance, Adjustments, and Adjusted Trial Balance Entered

	A	B	C	D	E	F	G	H	I	J	K
1					NetSolutions						
2					End-of-Period Spreadsheet						
3					For the Two Months Ended December 31, 2018						
4		Unadjusted				Adjusted					
5		Trial Balance		Adjustments		Trial Balance		Income Statement		Balance Sheet	
6	Account Title	Dr.	Cr.	Dr.	Cr.	Dr.	Cr.	Dr.	Cr.	Dr.	Cr.
7											
8	Cash	2,065				2,065					
9	Accounts Receivable	2,220		(a) 500		2,720					
10	Supplies	2,000			(d) 1,240	760					
11	Prepaid Insurance	2,400			(e) 200	2,200					
12	Land	20,000				20,000					
13	Office Equipment	1,800				1,800					
14	Accumulated Depreciation				(f) 50		50				
15	Accounts Payable		900				900				
16	Wages Payable				(b) 250		250				
17	Unearned Rent		360	(c) 120			240				
18	Chris Clark, Capital		25,000				25,000				
19	Chris Clark, Drawing	4,000				4,000					
20	Fees Earned		16,340		(a) 500		16,840				
21	Rent Revenue				(c) 120		120				
22	Wages Expense	4,275		(b) 250		4,525					
23	Supplies Expense	800		(d) 1,240		2,040					
24	Rent Expense	1,600				1,600					
25	Utilities Expense	985				985					
26	Insurance Expense			(e) 200		200					
27	Depreciation Expense			(f) 50		50					
28	Miscellaneous Expense	455				455					
29		42,600	42,600	2,360	2,360	43,400	43,400				
30											

> The adjusted trial balance amounts are determined by adding the adjustments to or subtracting the adjustments from the trial balance amounts. For example, the Wages Expense debit of $4,525 is the trial balance amount of $4,275 plus the $250 adjustment debit.

To illustrate, the cash amount of $2,065 is extended to the Adjusted Trial Balance Debit column since no adjustments affected Cash. Accounts Receivable has an initial balance of $2,220 and a debit adjustment of $500. Thus, $2,720 ($2,220 + $500) is entered in the Adjusted Trial Balance Debit column for Accounts Receivable. The same process continues until all account balances are extended to the Adjusted Trial Balance columns.

After the accounts and adjustments have been extended, the Adjusted Trial Balance columns are totaled to verify the equality of debits and credits. The total of the Debit column must equal the total of the Credit column.

Step 5. Extend the Accounts to the Income Statement and Balance Sheet Columns

The adjusted trial balance amounts are extended to the Income Statement and Balance Sheet columns. The amounts for revenues and expenses are extended to the Income Statement columns. The amounts for assets, liabilities, owner's capital, and drawing are extended to the Balance Sheet columns.[4]

The first account listed in the Adjusted Trial Balance columns is Cash with a debit balance of $2,065. Cash is an asset, is listed on the balance sheet, and has a debit balance. Therefore, $2,065 is extended to the Balance Sheet Debit column. The Fees Earned balance of $16,840 is extended to the Income Statement Credit column. The same process continues until all account balances have been extended to the proper columns, as shown in Exhibit 23.

Step 6. Total the Income Statement and Balance Sheet Columns, Compute the Net Income or Net Loss, and Complete the Spreadsheet

After the account balances are extended to the Income Statement and Balance Sheet columns, each of the columns is totaled. The difference between the two Income Statement column totals is the amount of the net income or the net loss for the period. This difference (net income or net loss) will also be the difference between the two Balance Sheet column totals.

If the Income Statement Credit column total (total revenue) is greater than the Income Statement Debit column total (total expenses), the difference is the net income. If the Income Statement Debit column total is greater than the Income Statement Credit column total, the difference is a net loss.

As shown in Exhibit 24, the total of the Income Statement Credit column is $16,960, and the total of the Income Statement Debit column is $9,855. Thus, the net income for NetSolutions is $7,105, computed as follows:

Total of Income Statement Credit column (revenues)	$16,960
Total of Income Statement Debit column (expenses)	9,855
Net income (excess of revenues over expenses)	$ 7,105

The amount of the net income, $7,105, is entered in the Income Statement Debit column and the Balance Sheet Credit column. *Net income* is also entered in the Account Title column. Entering the net income of $7,105 in the Balance Sheet Credit column has the effect of transferring the net balance of the revenue and expense accounts to the owner's capital account.

If there was a net loss instead of net income, the amount of the net loss would be entered in the Income Statement Credit column and the Balance Sheet Debit column. *Net loss* would also be entered in the Account Title column.

After the net income or net loss is entered on the spreadsheet, the Income Statement and Balance Sheet columns are totaled. The totals of the two Income Statement columns must now be equal. The totals of the two Balance Sheet columns must also be equal.

---

[4] The balance of the drawing account is extended to the Balance Sheet columns because the spreadsheet does not have separate Statement of Owner's Equity columns.

EXHIBIT 23 — Spreadsheet with Amounts Extended to Income Statement and Balance Sheet Columns

NetSolutions
End-of-Period Spreadsheet
For the Two Months Ended December 31, 2018

	A	B	C	D	E	F	G	H	I	J	K
		Unadjusted Trial Balance		Adjustments		Adjusted Trial Balance		Income Statement		Balance Sheet	
	Account Title	Dr.	Cr.	Dr.	Cr.	Dr.	Cr.	Dr.	Cr.	Dr.	Cr.
8	Cash	2,065				2,065				2,065	
9	Accounts Receivable	2,220		(a) 500		2,720				2,720	
10	Supplies	2,000			(d) 1,240	760				760	
11	Prepaid Insurance	2,400			(e) 200	2,200				2,200	
12	Land	20,000				20,000				20,000	
13	Office Equipment	1,800				1,800				1,800	
14	Accumulated Depreciation				(f) 50		50				50
15	Accounts Payable		900				900				900
16	Wages Payable				(b) 250		250				250
17	Unearned Rent		360	(c) 120			240				240
18	Chris Clark, Capital		25,000				25,000				25,000
19	Chris Clark, Drawing	4,000				4,000				4,000	
20	Fees Earned		16,340		(a) 500		16,840		16,840		
21	Rent Revenue				(c) 120		120		120		
22	Wages Expense	4,275		(b) 250		4,525		4,525			
23	Supplies Expense	800		(d) 1,240		2,040		2,040			
24	Rent Expense	1,600				1,600		1,600			
25	Utilities Expense	985				985		985			
26	Insurance Expense			(e) 200		200		200			
27	Depreciation Expense			(f) 50		50		50			
28	Miscellaneous Expense	455				455		455			
29		42,600	42,600	2,360	2,360	43,400	43,400				

The revenue and expense amounts are extended to (entered in) the Income Statement columns.

The asset, liability, owner's capital, and drawing amounts are extended to (entered in) the Balance Sheet columns.

Preparing the Financial Statements from the Spreadsheet

The spreadsheet can be used to prepare the income statement, the statement of owner's equity, and the balance sheet shown in Exhibit 2. The income statement is normally prepared directly from the spreadsheet. The expenses are listed in the income statement in Exhibit 2 in order of size, beginning with the larger items. Miscellaneous expense is the last item, regardless of its amount.

The first item normally presented on the statement of owner's equity is the balance of the owner's capital account at the beginning of the period. The amount listed as owner's capital in the spreadsheet, however, is not always the account balance at the beginning of the period. The owner may have invested additional assets in the business during the period. Thus, for the beginning balance and any additional investments,

Completed Spreadsheet with Net Income Shown — EXHIBIT 24

NetSolutions
End-of-Period Spreadsheet
For the Two Months Ended December 31, 2018

	A	B	C	D	E	F	G	H	I	J	K
		Unadjusted Trial Balance		Adjustments		Adjusted Trial Balance		Income Statement		Balance Sheet	
	Account Title	Dr.	Cr.	Dr.	Cr.	Dr.	Cr.	Dr.	Cr.	Dr.	Cr.
8	Cash	2,065				2,065				2,065	
9	Accounts Receivable	2,220		(a) 500		2,720				2,720	
10	Supplies	2,000			(d) 1,240	760				760	
11	Prepaid Insurance	2,400			(e) 200	2,200				2,200	
12	Land	20,000				20,000				20,000	
13	Office Equipment	1,800				1,800				1,800	
14	Accumulated Depreciation				(f) 50		50				50
15	Accounts Payable		900				900				900
16	Wages Payable				(b) 250		250				250
17	Unearned Rent		360	(c) 120			240				240
18	Chris Clark, Capital		25,000				25,000				25,000
19	Chris Clark, Drawing	4,000				4,000				4,000	
20	Fees Earned		16,340		(a) 500		16,840		16,840		
21	Rent Revenue				(c) 120		120		120		
22	Wages Expense	4,275		(b) 250		4,525		4,525			
23	Supplies Expense	800		(d) 1,240		2,040		2,040			
24	Rent Expense	1,600				1,600		1,600			
25	Utilities Expense	985				985		985			
26	Insurance Expense			(e) 200		200		200			
27	Depreciation Expense			(f) 50		50		50			
28	Miscellaneous Expense	455				455		455			
29		42,600	42,600	2,360	2,360	43,400	43,400	9,855	16,960	33,545	26,440
30	Net income							7,105			7,105
31								16,960	16,960	33,545	33,545

> The difference between the Income Statement column totals of $7,105 is the net income for the period. The difference between the Balance Sheet column totals is also $7,105 the net income for the period.

it is necessary to refer to the capital account in the ledger. These amounts, along with the net income (or net loss) and the drawing amount shown in the spreadsheet, are used to determine the ending capital account balance.

The balance sheet can be prepared directly from the spreadsheet columns except for the ending balance of owner's capital. The ending balance of owner's capital is taken from the statement of owner's equity.

When a spreadsheet is used, the adjusting and closing entries are normally not journalized or posted until after the spreadsheet and financial statements have been prepared. The data for the adjusting entries are taken from the Adjustments columns of the spreadsheet. The data for the first two closing entries are taken from the Income Statement columns of the spreadsheet. The amount for the third closing entry is the net income or net loss appearing at the bottom of the spreadsheet. The amount for the fourth closing entry is the drawing account balance that appears in the Balance Sheet Debit column of the spreadsheet.

APPENDIX 2

Reversing Entries

Some adjusting entries recorded at the end of an accounting period affect how transactions are recorded in the next period. For this reason, some companies add another step to the accounting cycle. This additional step records journal entries on the first day of the next period that are the exact *opposite* of the related adjusting entry from the last day of the prior period. These journal entries are called **reversing entries**.

To illustrate, the NetSolutions data for accrued wages from Chapter 3 are used. These data are summarized in Exhibit 25.

EXHIBIT 25

Accrued Wages

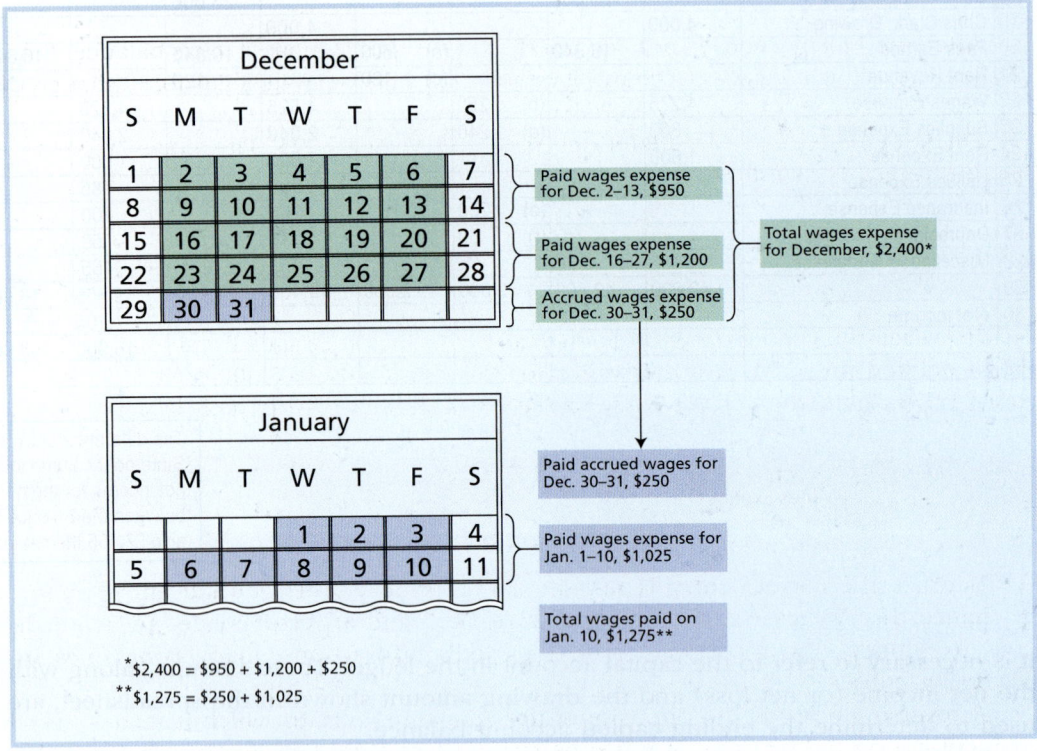

*$2,400 = $950 + $1,200 + $250
**$1,275 = $250 + $1,025

Based upon Exhibit 25, accrued wages for December 30 and 31 of $250 were recorded with the following adjusting entry:

2018					
Dec.	31	Wages Expense	51	250	
		Wages Payable	22		250

Exhibit 26 shows Wages Payable and Wages Expense after the adjusting entry has been recorded and posted. Wages Payable has a credit balance of $250, and Wages Expense has a debit balance of $4,525.

EXHIBIT 26

Wages Expense and Wages Payable

After Adjustment

Account Wages Payable Account No. 22

Date	Item	Post. Ref.	Debit	Credit	Balance Debit	Balance Credit
2018 Dec. 31	Adjusting	5		250		250

Account Wages Expense Account No. 51

Date	Item	Post. Ref.	Debit	Credit	Balance Debit	Balance Credit
2018 Nov. 30		1	2,125		2,125	
Dec. 13		3	950		3,075	
27		3	1,200		4,275	
31	Adjusting	5	250		4,525	

After the closing entries are recorded, Wages Expense has a zero balance. Since Wages Payable is a liability account, it is not closed. Thus, Wages Payable has a credit balance of $250 as of January 1, 2019.

On January 10, 2019, NetSolutions pays wages of $1,275. The *normal* entry for paying wages is as follows:

Jan.	10	Wages Expense	51	1,275	
		Cash	11		1,275

However, the preceding entry is incorrect. Specifically, Wages Payable should have been debited for $250, and the wages for January 1–10 are $1,025 ($1,275 − $250), not $1,275. Thus, the correct entry to record the January 10 payroll is as follows:

Jan.	10	Wages Payable	22	250	
		Wages Expense	51	1,025	
		Cash	11		1,275

Because the correct entry is not the same as the normal journal entry, there is a chance that Wages Payable will be overlooked and an error made. To avoid this and to simplify the recording of next period's transactions, many companies use reversing entries.

A reversing entry is the opposite of the adjusting entry to which it relates, which is recorded on the first day of the subsequent accounting period. Thus, it is an entry that reverses the effects of an adjusting entry in the preceding period. For example, the reversing entry for the accrued payroll for NetSolutions is as follows:

Jan.	1	Wages Payable	22	250	
		Wages Expense	51		250
		Reversing entry.			

Reversing entries are recorded on the first day of the subsequent accounting period. Exhibit 27 shows the wages payable and wages expense accounts after the reversing entry has been recorded and posted.

Exhibit 27 indicates that on January 1, Wages Payable has a zero balance and Wages Expense has a credit balance of $250. The Wages Expense credit balance of $250 is only temporary. Wages Expense will have a debit balance as soon as the first payroll is paid on January 10.

EXHIBIT 27
Wages Expense and Wages Payable

After Reversing Entry

Account Wages Payable — Account No. 22

Date	Item	Post. Ref.	Debit	Credit	Balance Debit	Balance Credit
2018 Dec. 31	Adjusting	5		250		250
2019 Jan. 1	Reversing	7	250		—	—

Account Wages Expense — Account No. 51

Date	Item	Post. Ref.	Debit	Credit	Balance Debit	Balance Credit
2018 Nov. 30		1	2,125		2,125	
Dec. 13		3	950		3,075	
27		3	1,200		4,275	
31	Adjusting	5	250		4,525	
31	Closing	6		4,525	—	—
2019 Jan. 1	Reversing	7		250		250

To illustrate, the January 10 payroll of $1,275 would be recorded in the normal manner as follows:

Jan.	10	Wages Expense			51	1,275
		Cash			11	1,275

After the preceding entry is posted, Wages Expense will have a debit balance of $1,025 ($1,275 − $250), which is the correct wages expense for January 1–10.

The use of reversing entries is optional. However, in computerized accounting systems, routine transactions are processed in a standard manner. In such cases, reversing entries are useful in avoiding errors and simplifying the recording of the subsequent period's transactions.

At a Glance 4

Obj. 1 Describe the flow of accounting information from the unadjusted trial balance into the adjusted trial balance and financial statements.

Key Points Exhibit 1 illustrates the end-of-period process by which accounts are adjusted and how the adjusted accounts flow into the financial statements.

Learning Outcomes	Example Exercises	Practice Exercises
• Using an end-of-period spreadsheet, describe how the unadjusted trial balance accounts are affected by adjustments and how the adjusted trial balance accounts flow into the income statement and balance sheet.	EE4-1	PE4-1A, 4-1B

Chapter 4 Completing the Accounting Cycle 199

Obj. 2 Prepare financial statements from adjusted account balances.

Key Points Using the end-of-period spreadsheet shown in Exhibit 1, the income statement and balance sheet for NetSolutions can be prepared. The statement of owner's equity is prepared by referring to transactions that have been posted to owner's capital accounts in the ledger. A classified balance sheet has sections for current assets; property, plant, and equipment; current liabilities; long-term liabilities; and owner's equity.

Learning Outcomes	Example Exercises	Practice Exercises
• Describe how the net income or net loss from the period can be determined from an end-of-period spreadsheet.		
• Prepare an income statement, a statement of owner's equity, and a balance sheet.	EE4-2	PE4-2A, 4-2B
• Indicate how accounts would be reported on a classified balance sheet.	EE4-3	PE4-3A, 4-3B

Obj. 3 Prepare closing entries.

Key Points Two entries are required in closing the temporary accounts. The first entry debits each revenue account for its balance, credits each expense account for its balance, and credits (net income) or debits (net loss) the owner's capital account. The second entry closes the drawing account to the owner's capital account.

After the closing entries have been posted to the ledger, the balance in the capital account agrees with the amount reported on the statement of owner's equity and balance sheet. In addition, the revenue, expense, and drawing accounts will have zero balances.

Learning Outcomes	Example Exercises	Practice Exercises
• Prepare the closing entry for revenues and expenses.	EE4-4	PE4-4A, 4-4B
• Prepare the closing entry for the owner's drawing account.	EE4-4	PE4-4A, 4-4B

Obj. 4 Describe the accounting cycle.

Key Points The ten basic steps of the accounting cycle are as follows:

1. Transactions are analyzed and recorded in the journal.
2. Transactions are posted to the ledger.
3. An unadjusted trial balance is prepared.
4. Adjustment data are assembled and analyzed.
5. An optional end-of-period spreadsheet is prepared.
6. Adjusting entries are journalized and posted to the ledger.
7. An adjusted trial balance is prepared.
8. Financial statements are prepared.
9. Closing entries are journalized and posted to the ledger.
10. A post-closing trial balance is prepared.

Learning Outcomes	Example Exercises	Practice Exercises
• List the ten steps of the accounting cycle.		
• Determine whether any steps are out of order in a listing of accounting cycle steps.		
• Determine whether there are any missing steps in a listing of accounting cycle steps.	EE4-5	PE4-5A, 4-5B

Obj. 5 — Illustrate the accounting cycle for one period.

Key Points The complete accounting cycle for Kelly Consulting for the month of April is described and illustrated in this chapter.

Learning Outcomes	Example Exercises	Practice Exercises
• Complete the accounting cycle for a period from beginning to end.		

Obj. 6 — Explain what is meant by the fiscal year and the natural business year.

Key Points The annual accounting period adopted by a business is its fiscal year. A company's fiscal year that ends when business activities have reached the lowest point in its annual operating cycle is called the natural business year.

Learning Outcomes	Example Exercises	Practice Exercises
• Explain why companies use a fiscal year that is different from the calendar year.		

Obj. 7 — Describe and illustrate the use of working capital and the current ratio in evaluating a company's financial condition.

Key Points The ability to convert assets into cash is called liquidity, while the ability of a business to pay its debts is called solvency. Two financial measures for evaluating a business's liquidity and solvency are working capital and the current ratio. Working capital is computed by subtracting current liabilities from current assets. An excess of current assets over current liabilities implies that the business is able to pay its current liabilities. The current ratio is computed by dividing current assets by current liabilities. The current ratio is more useful than working capital in making comparisons across companies or with industry averages.

Learning Outcomes	Example Exercises	Practice Exercises
• Define liquidity and solvency.		
• Compute working capital.	EE4-6	PE4-6A, 4-6B
• Compute the current ratio.	EE4-6	PE4-6A, 4-6B

Illustrative Problem

Three years ago, T. Roderick organized Harbor Realty. At July 31, 2019, the end of the fiscal year, the following end-of-period spreadsheet was prepared:

Harbor Realty
End-of-Period Spreadsheet
For the Year Ended July 31, 2019

Account Title	Unadjusted Trial Balance Dr.	Unadjusted Trial Balance Cr.	Adjustments Dr.	Adjustments Cr.	Adjusted Trial Balance Dr.	Adjusted Trial Balance Cr.
Cash	3,425				3,425	
Accounts Receivable	7,000		(e) 1,000		8,000	
Supplies	1,270			(a) 890	380	
Prepaid Insurance	620			(b) 315	305	
Office Equipment	51,650				51,650	
Accum. Depreciation		9,700		(c) 4,950		14,650
Accounts Payable		925				925
Unearned Fees		1,250	(f) 500			750
Wages Payable				(d) 440		440
T. Roderick, Capital		29,000				29,000
T. Roderick, Drawing	5,200				5,200	
Fees Earned		59,125		(e) 1,000		60,625
				(f) 500		
Wages Expense	22,415		(d) 440		22,855	
Depreciation Expense			(c) 4,950		4,950	
Rent Expense	4,200				4,200	
Utilities Expense	2,715				2,715	
Supplies Expense			(a) 890		890	
Insurance Expense			(b) 315		315	
Miscellaneous Expense	1,505				1,505	
	100,000	100,000	8,095	8,095	106,390	106,390

Instructions

1. Prepare an income statement, a statement of owner's equity (no additional investments were made during the year), and a balance sheet.

2. On the basis of the data in the end-of-period spreadsheet, journalize the closing entries.

Solution

1.

Harbor Realty
Income Statement
For the Year Ended July 31, 2019

Fees earned..		$60,625
Expenses:		
Wages expense	$22,855	
Depreciation expense	4,950	
Rent expense	4,200	
Utilities expense..	2,715	
Supplies expense	890	
Insurance expense...	315	
Miscellaneous expense	1,505	
Total expenses		37,430
Net income		$23,195

Harbor Realty
Statement of Owner's Equity
For the Year Ended July 31, 2019

T. Roderick, capital, August 1, 2018		$29,000
Net income for the year..	$23,195	
Withdrawals	(5,200)	
Increase in owner's equity		17,995
T. Roderick, capital, July 31, 2019		$46,995

Harbor Realty
Balance Sheet
July 31, 2019

Assets

Current assets:		
Cash	$ 3,425	
Accounts receivable......................................	8,000	
Supplies..	380	
Prepaid insurance..	305	
Total current assets		$12,110
Property, plant, and equipment:		
Office equipment..	$51,650	
Less accum. depreciation..............................	14,650	
Total property, plant, and equipment.		37,000
Total assets..		$49,110

Liabilities

Current liabilities:		
Accounts payable...	$ 925	
Unearned fees	750	
Wages payable..	440	
Total liabilities		$ 2,115

Owner's Equity

T. Roderick, capital...		46,995
Total liabilities and owner's equity		$49,110

2.

Journal					Page
Date		Description	Post. Ref.	Debit	Credit
		Closing Entries			
2019 July	31	Fees Earned		60,625	
		Wages Expense			22,855
		Depreciation Expense			4,950
		Rent Expense			4,200
		Utilities Expense			2,715
		Supplies Expense			890
		Insurance Expense			315
		Miscellaneous Expense			1,505
		T. Roderick, Capital			23,195
	31	T. Roderick, Capital		5,200	
		T. Roderick, Drawing			5,200

Key Terms

accounting cycle (174)
closing entries (170)
closing process (170)
closing the books (170)
current assets (168)
current liabilities (168)
current ratio (188)

first closing entry (170)
fiscal year (187)
fixed (plant) assets (168)
liquidity (188)
long-term liabilities (168)
natural business year (187)
notes receivable (168)

real (permanent) accounts (169)
reversing entries (196)
second closing entry (170)
solvency (188)
temporary (nominal) accounts (169)
working capital (188)

Discussion Questions

1. Why do some accountants prepare an end-of-period spreadsheet?

2. Describe the nature of the assets that compose the following sections of a balance sheet: (a) current assets and (b) property, plant, and equipment.

3. What is the difference between a current liability and a long-term liability?

4. What types of accounts are referred to as temporary accounts?

5. Why are closing entries required at the end of an accounting period?

6. What is the difference between adjusting entries and closing entries?

7. What is the purpose of the post-closing trial balance?

8. (a) What is the most important output of the accounting cycle? (b) Do all companies have an accounting cycle? Explain.

9. What is the natural business year?

10. Recent fiscal years for several well-known companies are as follows:

Company	Fiscal Year Ending
JCPenney	January 27
Limited Brands, Inc.	January 27
Sears	January 27
Target Corp.	January 27
The Home Depot	January 28
Tiffany & Co.	January 30

What general characteristic shared by these companies explains why they do not have fiscal years ending December 31?

204 Chapter 4 Completing the Accounting Cycle

Practice Exercises

Example Exercises

 EE 4-1 *p. 165*

PE 4-1A Flow of accounts into financial statements OBJ. 1

The balances for the accounts that follow appear in the Adjusted Trial Balance columns of the end-of-period spreadsheet. Indicate whether each account would flow into the income statement, statement of owner's equity, or balance sheet.

1. Accounts Payable
2. Depreciation Expense
3. Nat Hager, Capital (beginning of period)
4. Office Equipment
5. Rent Revenue
6. Supplies Expense
7. Unearned Rent
8. Wages Payable

EE 4-1 *p. 165*

PE 4-1B Flow of accounts into financial statements OBJ. 1

The balances for the accounts that follow appear in the Adjusted Trial Balance columns of the end-of-period spreadsheet. Indicate whether each account would flow into the income statement, statement of owner's equity, or balance sheet.

1. Accumulated Depreciation
2. Cash
3. Fees Earned
4. Insurance Expense
5. Prepaid Rent
6. Supplies
7. Tina Greer, Drawing
8. Wages Expense

 EE 4-2 *p. 167*

PE 4-2A Statement of owner's equity OBJ. 2

Marcie Davies owns and operates Gemini Advertising Services. On January 1, 2018, Marcie Davies, Capital had a balance of $618,500. During the year, Marcie invested an additional $40,000 and withdrew $15,000. For the year ended December 31, 2018, Gemini Advertising Services reported a net income of $92,330. Prepare a statement of owner's equity for the year ended December 31, 2018.

EE 4-2 *p. 167*

PE 4-2B Statement of owner's equity OBJ. 2

Blake Knudson owns and operates Grab Bag Delivery Services. On January 1, 2018, Blake Knudson, Capital had a balance of $918,000. During the year, Blake made no additional investments and withdrew $15,000. For the year ended December 31, 2018, Grab Bag Delivery Services reported a net loss of $43,500. Prepare a statement of owner's equity for the year ended December 31, 2018.

 EE 4-3 *p. 168*

PE 4-3A Classified balance sheet OBJ. 2

The following accounts appear in an adjusted trial balance of Waterloo Consulting. Indicate whether each account would be reported in the (a) current asset; (b) property, plant, and equipment; (c) current liability; (d) long-term liability; or (e) owner's equity section of the December 31, 2018, balance sheet of Waterloo Consulting.

1. Building
2. Cindy Sue Delaney, Capital
3. Notes Payable (due in five years)
4. Prepaid Rent
5. Salaries Payable
6. Supplies
7. Taxes Payable
8. Unearned Service Fees

Chapter 4 Completing the Accounting Cycle 205

EE 4-3 p. 168   **PE 4-3B**   **Classified balance sheet**   OBJ. 2

The following accounts appear in an adjusted trial balance of Kangaroo Consulting. Indicate whether each account would be reported in the (a) current asset; (b) property, plant, and equipment; (c) current liability; (d) long-term liability; or (e) owner's equity section of the December 31, 2018, balance sheet of Kangaroo Consulting.

1. Accounts Payable
2. Accounts Receivable
3. Accumulated Depreciation—Building
4. Cash
5. Lea Gabel, Capital
6. Note Payable (due in ten years)
7. Supplies
8. Wages Payable

EE 4-4 p. 174   **PE 4-4A**   **Closing entries**   OBJ. 3

After the accounts have been adjusted at December 31, the end of the fiscal year, the following balances were taken from the ledger of Pioneer Delivery Services Co.:

Kerry Buckner, Capital	$9,556,300
Kerry Buckner, Drawing	80,000
Fees Earned	1,878,400
Wages Expense	1,415,500
Rent Expense	125,000
Supplies Expense	30,600
Miscellaneous Expense	22,100

Journalize the two entries required to close the accounts.

EE 4-4 p. 174   **PE 4-4B**   **Closing entries**   OBJ. 3

After the accounts have been adjusted at April 30, the end of the fiscal year, the following balances were taken from the ledger of Nuclear Landscaping Co.:

Felix Godwin, Capital	$643,600
Felix Godwin, Drawing	10,500
Fees Earned	356,500
Wages Expense	283,100
Rent Expense	56,000
Supplies Expense	11,500
Miscellaneous Expense	13,000

Journalize the two entries required to close the accounts.

EE 4-5 p. 175   **PE 4-5A**   **Accounting cycle**   OBJ. 4

From the following list of steps in the accounting cycle, identify what two steps are missing:

a. Transactions are analyzed and recorded in the journal.
b. An unadjusted trial balance is prepared.
c. Adjustment data are assembled and analyzed.
d. An optional end-of-period spreadsheet is prepared.
e. Adjusting entries are journalized and posted to the ledger.
f. An adjusted trial balance is prepared.
g. Closing entries are journalized and posted to the ledger.
h. A post-closing trial balance is prepared.

EE 4-5 p. 175   **PE 4-5B**   **Accounting cycle**   OBJ. 4

From the following list of steps in the accounting cycle, identify what two steps are missing:

a. Transactions are analyzed and recorded in the journal.
b. Transactions are posted to the ledger.

(Continued)

206 Chapter 4 Completing the Accounting Cycle

    c. An unadjusted trial balance is prepared.
    d. An optional end-of-period spreadsheet is prepared.
    e. Adjusting entries are journalized and posted to the ledger.
    f. An adjusted trial balance is prepared.
    g. Financial statements are prepared.
    h. A post-closing trial balance is prepared.

EE 4-6 p. 189

PE 4-6A Working capital and current ratio OBJ. 7

Current assets and current liabilities for HQ Properties Company follow:

	2019	2018
Current assets	$2,175,000	$1,900,000
Current liabilities	1,500,000	1,250,000

a. Determine the working capital and current ratio for 2019 and 2018.
b. ✏️ Does the change in the current ratio from 2018 to 2019 indicate a favorable or an unfavorable change?

EE 4-6 p. 189

PE 4-6B Working capital and current ratio OBJ. 7

Current assets and current liabilities for Brimstone Company follow:

	2019	2018
Current assets	$1,586,250	$1,210,000
Current liabilities	705,000	550,000

a. Determine the working capital and current ratio for 2019 and 2018.
b. ✏️ Does the change in the current ratio from 2018 to 2019 indicate a favorable or an unfavorable change?

Exercises

EX 4-1 Flow of accounts into financial statements OBJ. 1, 2

The balances for the accounts that follow appear in the Adjusted Trial Balance columns of the end-of-period spreadsheet. Indicate whether each account would flow into the income statement, statement of owner's equity, or balance sheet.

1. Accounts Payable
2. Accounts Receivable
3. Cash
4. Eddy Rosewood, Drawing
5. Fees Earned
6. Supplies
7. Unearned Rent
8. Utilities Expense
9. Wages Expense
10. Wages Payable

EX 4-2 Classifying accounts OBJ. 1, 2

Balances for each of the following accounts appear in an adjusted trial balance. Identify each as (a) asset, (b) liability, (c) revenue, or (d) expense.

1. Accounts Receivable
2. Equipment
3. Fees Earned
4. Insurance Expense
5. Land
6. Prepaid Rent
7. Rent Revenue
8. Salary Expense
9. Salary Payable
10. Supplies
11. Unearned Rent
12. Wages Payable

Chapter 4 Completing the Accounting Cycle

EX 4-3 Financial statements from the end-of-period spreadsheet   OBJ. 1, 2

Bamboo Consulting is a consulting firm owned and operated by Lisa Gooch. The following end-of-period spreadsheet was prepared for the year ended July 31, 2019:

	A	B	C	D	E	F	G
1		\multicolumn{6}{c|}{Bamboo Consulting}
2		\multicolumn{6}{c|}{End-of-Period Spreadsheet}
3		\multicolumn{6}{c|}{For the Year Ended July 31, 2019}
4		\multicolumn{2}{c|}{Unadjusted}			\multicolumn{2}{c|}{Adjusted}
5		\multicolumn{2}{c|}{Trial Balance}	\multicolumn{2}{c|}{Adjustments}	\multicolumn{2}{c|}{Trial Balance}
6	Account Title	Dr.	Cr.	Dr.	Cr.	Dr.	Cr.
7							
8	Cash	58,000				58,000	
9	Accounts Receivable	106,200				106,200	
10	Supplies	11,900			(a) 7,500	4,400	
11	Office Equipment	515,000				515,000	
12	Accumulated Depreciation		28,000		(b) 5,600		33,600
13	Accounts Payable		20,500				20,500
14	Salaries Payable				(c) 2,500		2,500
15	Lisa Gooch, Capital		516,700				516,700
16	Lisa Gooch, Drawing	25,000				25,000	
17	Fees Earned		348,500				348,500
18	Salary Expense	186,500		(c) 2,500		189,000	
19	Supplies Expense			(a) 7,500		7,500	
20	Depreciation Expense			(b) 5,600		5,600	
21	Miscellaneous Expense	11,100				11,100	
22		913,700	913,700	15,600	15,600	921,800	921,800
23							

Based on the preceding spreadsheet, prepare an income statement, statement of owner's equity, and balance sheet for Bamboo Consulting.

EX 4-4 Financial statements from the end-of-period spreadsheet   OBJ. 1, 2

Elliptical Consulting is a consulting firm owned and operated by Jayson Neese. The following end-of-period spreadsheet was prepared for the year ended June 30, 2019:

	A	B	C	D	E	F	G
1		\multicolumn{6}{c|}{Elliptical Consulting}
2		\multicolumn{6}{c|}{End-of-Period Spreadsheet}
3		\multicolumn{6}{c|}{For the Year Ended June 30, 2019}
4		\multicolumn{2}{c|}{Unadjusted}			\multicolumn{2}{c|}{Adjusted}
5		\multicolumn{2}{c|}{Trial Balance}	\multicolumn{2}{c|}{Adjustments}	\multicolumn{2}{c|}{Trial Balance}
6	Account Title	Dr.	Cr.	Dr.	Cr.	Dr.	Cr.
7							
8	Cash	27,000				27,000	
9	Accounts Receivable	53,500				53,500	
10	Supplies	3,000			(a) 2,100	900	
11	Office Equipment	30,500				30,500	
12	Accumulated Depreciation		4,500		(b) 1,500		6,000
13	Accounts Payable		3,300				3,300
14	Salaries Payable				(c) 375		375
15	Jayson Neese, Capital		82,200				82,200
16	Jayson Neese, Drawing	2,000				2,000	
17	Fees Earned		60,000				60,000
18	Salary Expense	32,000		(c) 375		32,375	
19	Supplies Expense			(a) 2,100		2,100	
20	Depreciation Expense			(b) 1,500		1,500	
21	Miscellaneous Expense	2,000				2,000	
22		150,000	150,000	3,975	3,975	151,875	151,875
23							

Based on the preceding spreadsheet, prepare an income statement, statement of owner's equity, and balance sheet for Elliptical Consulting.

208 Chapter 4 Completing the Accounting Cycle

✔ Net income, $218,000

EX 4-5 Income statement   OBJ. 2

The following account balances were taken from the adjusted trial balance for Laser Messenger Service, a delivery service firm, for the fiscal year ended April 30, 2019:

Depreciation Expense	$ 8,650	Rent Expense	$ 60,000
Fees Earned	674,000	Salaries Expense	336,900
Insurance Expense	1,500	Supplies Expense	4,100
Miscellaneous Expense	3,650	Utilities Expense	41,200

Prepare an income statement.

✔ Net loss, $(20,900)

EX 4-6 Income statement; net loss   OBJ. 2

The following revenue and expense account balances were taken from the ledger of Wholistic Health Services Co. after the accounts had been adjusted on February 28, 2019, the end of the fiscal year:

Depreciation Expense	$ 7,500	Service Revenue	$448,400
Insurance Expense	3,000	Supplies Expense	2,750
Miscellaneous Expense	8,150	Utilities Expense	33,900
Rent Expense	54,000	Wages Expense	360,000

Prepare an income statement.

✔ a. Net income, $1,050

EX 4-7 Income statement   OBJ. 2

FedEx Corporation had the following revenue and expense account balances (in millions) for a recent year ending May 31:

Depreciation Expense	$2,611	Purchased Transportation	$ 8,483
Fuel Expense	3,720	Rentals and Landing Fees	2,682
Maintenance and Repairs Expense	2,099	Revenues	47,453
Other Expense (Revenue) Net	9,121	Salaries and Employee Benefits	17,110
Provision for Income Taxes	577		

Prepare an income statement.

✔ Bart Nesbit, capital, Dec. 31, 2019: $1,640,000

EX 4-8 Statement of owner's equity   OBJ. 2

Apex Systems Co. offers its services to residents in the Seattle area. Selected accounts from the ledger of Apex Systems Co. for the fiscal year ended December 31, 2019, are as follows:

Bart Nesbit, Capital				Bart Nesbit, Drawing			
Dec. 31	90,000	Jan. 1 (2019)	1,375,000	Mar. 31	22,500	Dec. 31	90,000
		Dec. 31	355,000	June 30	22,500		
				Sept. 30	22,500		
				Dec. 31	22,500		

Prepare a statement of owner's equity for the year.

✔ Doug Stone, capital, April 30, 2019: $439,300

EX 4-9 Statement of owner's equity; net loss   OBJ. 2

Selected accounts from the ledger of Restoration Arts for the fiscal year ended April 30, 2019, are as follows:

Doug Stone, Capital				Doug Stone, Drawing			
Apr. 30	31,200	May 1 (2018)	475,500	July 31	1,250	Apr. 30	5,000
30	5,000			Oct. 31	1,250		
				Jan. 31	1,250		
				April 30	1,250		

Prepare a statement of owner's equity for the year.

EX 4-10 Classifying assets   OBJ. 2

Identify each of the following as (a) a current asset or (b) property, plant, and equipment:

1. Accounts Receivable
2. Building
3. Cash
4. Land
5. Prepaid Insurance
6. Supplies

EX 4-11 Balance sheet classification OBJ. 2

At the balance sheet date, a business owes a mortgage note payable of $375,000, the terms of which provide for monthly payments of $1,250.

Explain how the liability should be classified on the balance sheet.

EX 4-12 Balance sheet OBJ. 2

✔ Total assets: $775,000

Optimum Weight Loss Co. offers personal weight reduction consulting services to individuals. After all the accounts have been closed on November 30, 2019, the end of the fiscal year, the balances of selected accounts from the ledger of Optimum Weight Loss Co. are as follows:

Accounts Payable	$ 37,700	Prepaid Insurance	$ 7,200
Accounts Receivable	116,750	Prepaid Rent	21,000
Accumulated Depreciation—Equipment	186,400	Salaries Payable	9,000
Cash	?	Cheryl Viers, Capital	710,300
Equipment	474,150	Supplies	4,800
Land	300,000	Unearned Fees	18,000

Prepare a classified balance sheet that includes the correct balance for Cash.

EX 4-13 Balance sheet OBJ. 2

✔ Corrected balance sheet, total assets: $625,000

List the errors you find in the following balance sheet. Prepare a corrected balance sheet.

Labyrinth Services Co.
Balance Sheet
For the Year Ended August 31, 2019

Assets

Current assets:
Cash	$ 18,500	
Accounts payable	31,300	
Supplies	6,500	
Prepaid insurance	16,600	
Land	225,000	
Total current assets		$297,900

Property, plant, and equipment:
Building	$400,000	
Equipment	97,000	
Total property, plant, and equipment		635,400
Total assets		$933,300

Liabilities

Current liabilities:
Accounts receivable	$ 41,400	
Accumulated depreciation—building	155,000	
Accumulated depreciation—equipment	25,000	
Net income	118,200	
Total liabilities		$339,600

Owner's Equity

Wages payable	$ 6,500	
Ruben Daniel, capital	587,200	
Total owner's equity		593,700
Total liabilities and owner's equity		$933,300

EX 4-14 Identifying accounts to be closed
OBJ. 3

From the list that follows, identify the accounts that should be closed to the owner's capital account at the end of the fiscal year:

a. Accounts Receivable
b. Accumulated Depreciation
c. Building
d. Depreciation Expense
e. Fees Earned
f. Jackie Lindsay, Capital
g. Jackie Lindsay, Drawing
h. Land
i. Supplies
j. Supplies Expense
k. Unearned Rent
l. Wages Expense

EX 4-15 Closing entries
OBJ. 3

Prior to closing, total revenues were $12,840,000 and total expenses were $9,975,000. During the year, the owner made no additional investments and withdrew $630,000. After the closing entries, how much did the owner's capital account change?

EX 4-16 Closing entries with net income
OBJ. 3

Assume that the entry closing total revenues of $3,190,000 and total expenses of $2,350,000 has been made for the year. At the end of the fiscal year, Teresa Schafer, Capital has a credit balance of $1,885,000 and Teresa Schafer, Drawing has a balance of $770,000.
(a) Journalize the entry required to close the Teresa Schafer, Drawing account.
(b) Determine the amount of Teresa Schafer, Capital at the end of the period.

EX 4-17 Closing entries with net loss
OBJ. 3

Stylist Services Co. offers its services to individuals desiring to improve their personal images. After the accounts have been adjusted at July 31, the end of the fiscal year, the following balances were taken from the ledger of Stylist Services Co.:

Marlena Fenton, Capital	$1,060,000	Rent Expense	$60,000
Marlena Fenton, Drawing	75,000	Supplies Expense	19,500
Fees Earned	618,200	Miscellaneous Expense	6,150
Wages Expense	388,400		

Journalize the two entries required to close the accounts.

EX 4-18 Identifying permanent accounts
OBJ. 3

Which of the following accounts will usually appear in the post-closing trial balance?

a. Accounts Receivable
b. Cash
c. Depreciation Expense
d. Fees Earned
e. Doug Woods, Capital
f. Doug Woods, Drawing
g. Equipment
h. Land
i. Salaries Payable
j. Unearned Rent
k. Wages Expense

Chapter 4 Completing the Accounting Cycle   211

EX 4-19 Post-closing trial balance   OBJ. 3

✔ Correct column totals, $300,000

An accountant prepared the following post-closing trial balance:

La Casa Services Co.
Post-Closing Trial Balance
March 31, 2019

	Debit Balances	Credit Balances
Cash	46,540	
Accounts Receivable	122,260	
Supplies		4,000
Equipment		127,200
Accumulated Depreciation—Equipment	33,600	
Accounts Payable	52,100	
Salaries Payable		6,400
Unearned Rent	9,000	
Sonya Flynn, Capital	198,900	
	462,400	137,600

Prepare a corrected post-closing trial balance. Assume that all accounts have normal balances and that the amounts shown are correct.

EX 4-20 Steps in the accounting cycle   OBJ. 4

Rearrange the following steps in the accounting cycle in proper sequence:
a. Transactions are analyzed and recorded in the journal.
b. An unadjusted trial balance is prepared.
c. Transactions are posted to the ledger.
d. Adjustment data are assembled and analyzed.
e. An adjusted trial balance is prepared.
f. Adjusting entries are journalized and posted to the ledger.
g. An optional end-of-period spreadsheet is prepared.
h. A post-closing trial balance is prepared.
i. Financial statements are prepared.
j. Closing entries are journalized and posted to the ledger.

EX 4-21 Working capital and current ratio   OBJ. 7

The following data (in thousands) were taken from recent financial statements of **Under Armour, Inc.**:

	December 31	
	Year 2	Year 1
Current assets	$1,498,763	$1,549,399
Current liabilities	478,810	421,627

a. Compute the working capital and the current ratio as of December 31, Year 2 and Year 1. Round to two decimal places.
b. What conclusions concerning the company's ability to meet its financial obligations can you draw from part (a)?

212 Chapter 4 Completing the Accounting Cycle

EX 4-22 Working capital and current ratio   OBJ. 7

The following data (in thousands) were taken from recent financial statements of Starbucks Corporation:

	Year 2	Year 1
Current assets	$4,352,700	$4,168,700
Current liabilities	3,653,500	3,038,700

a. Compute the working capital and the current ratio for Year 2 and Year 1. Round to two decimal places.

b. ✏️ What conclusions concerning the company's ability to meet its financial obligations can you draw from part (a)?

Appendix 1

EX 4-23 Completing an end-of-period spreadsheet

List (a) through (j) in the order they would be performed in preparing and completing an end-of-period spreadsheet.

a. Add the Debit and Credit columns of the Unadjusted Trial Balance columns of the spreadsheet to verify that the totals are equal.

b. Add the Debit and Credit columns of the Balance Sheet and Income Statement columns of the spreadsheet to verify that the totals are equal.

c. Add or deduct adjusting entry data to trial balance amounts, and extend amounts to the Adjusted Trial Balance columns.

d. Add the Debit and Credit columns of the Adjustments columns of the spreadsheet to verify that the totals are equal.

e. Add the Debit and Credit columns of the Balance Sheet and Income Statement columns of the spreadsheet to determine the amount of net income or net loss for the period.

f. Add the Debit and Credit columns of the Adjusted Trial Balance columns of the spreadsheet to verify that the totals are equal.

g. Enter the adjusting entries into the spreadsheet, based on the adjustment data.

h. Enter the amount of net income or net loss for the period in the proper Income Statement column and Balance Sheet column.

i. Enter the unadjusted account balances from the general ledger into the Unadjusted Trial Balance columns of the spreadsheet.

j. Extend the adjusted trial balance amounts to the Income Statement columns and the Balance Sheet columns.

Appendix 1

EX 4-24 Adjustment data on an end-of-period spreadsheet

✔ Total debits of Adjustments column: $31

Alert Security Services Co. offers security services to business clients. The trial balance for Alert Security Services Co. has been prepared on the following end-of-period spreadsheet for the year ended October 31, 2019:

Alert Security Services Co.
End-of-Period Spreadsheet
For the Year Ended October 31, 2019

Account Title	Unadjusted Trial Balance Dr.	Cr.	Adjustments Dr.	Cr.	Adjusted Trial Balance Dr.	Cr.
Cash	12					
Accounts Receivable	90					
Supplies	8					
Prepaid Insurance	12					
Land	190					
Equipment	50					

Accum. Depr.—Equipment		4
Accounts Payable		36
Wages Payable		0
Brenda Schultz, Capital		260
Brenda Schultz, Drawing	8	
Fees Earned		200
Wages Expense	110	
Rent Expense	12	
Insurance Expense	0	
Utilities Expense	6	
Supplies Expense	0	
Depreciation Expense	0	
Miscellaneous Expense	2	
	500	500

The data for year-end adjustments are as follows:
a. Fees earned but not yet billed, $13.
b. Supplies on hand, $4.
c. Insurance premiums expired, $10.
d. Depreciation expense, $3.
e. Wages accrued but not paid, $1.

Enter the adjustment data and place the balances in the Adjusted Trial Balance columns.

Appendix 1

EX 4-25 Completing an end-of-period spreadsheet

✔ Net income: $65

Excel

Alert Security Services Co. offers security services to business clients. Complete the following end-of-period spreadsheet for Alert Security Services Co.:

Alert Security Services Co.
End-of-Period Spreadsheet
For the Year Ended October 31, 2019

Account Title	Adjusted Trial Balance Dr.	Adjusted Trial Balance Cr.	Income Statement Dr.	Income Statement Cr.	Balance Sheet Dr.	Balance Sheet Cr.
Cash	12					
Accounts Receivable	103					
Supplies	4					
Prepaid Insurance	2					
Land	190					
Equipment	50					
Accum. Depr.—Equipment		7				
Accounts Payable		36				
Wages Payable		1				
Brenda Schultz, Capital		260				
Brenda Schultz, Drawing	8					
Fees Earned		213				
Wages Expense	111					
Rent Expense	12					
Insurance Expense	10					
Utilities Expense	6					
Supplies Expense	4					
Depreciation Expense	3					
Miscellaneous Expense	2					
Net income (loss)	517	517				

✔ Brenda Schultz, capital, October 31, 2019: $317

Appendix 1
EX 4-26 Financial statements from an end-of-period spreadsheet
Based on the data in Exercise 4-25, prepare an income statement, statement of owner's equity, and balance sheet for Alert Security Services Co.

Appendix 1
EX 4-27 Adjusting entries from an end-of-period spreadsheet
Based on the data in Exercise 4-24, prepare the adjusting entries for Alert Security Services Co.

Appendix 1
EX 4-28 Closing entries from an end-of-period spreadsheet
Based on the data in Exercise 4-25, prepare the two closing entries for Alert Security Services Co.

Appendix 2
EX 4-29 Reversing entry
The following adjusting entry for accrued wages was recorded on December 31:

| Dec. 31 | Wages Expense | 5,500 | |
| | Wages Payable | | 5,500 |

a. Journalize the reversing entry that would be made on January 1 of the next period.
b. Assume that the first paid period of the following year ends on January 6 and that wages of $61,375 were paid. Journalize the entry to record the payment of the January 6 wages.
c. Journalize the entry to record the payment of the January 6 wages assuming that a reversing entry was not made on January 1.
d. What is wages expense for the period January 1–6?

Appendix 2
EX 4-30 Adjusting and reversing entries
On the basis of the following data, (a) journalize the adjusting entries at December 31, the end of the current fiscal year, and (b) journalize the reversing entries on January 1, the first day of the following year:

1. Sales salaries are $2,350 per day for a five-day workweek, ending on Friday. The last payday of the year was Friday, December 26.
2. Accrued fees earned but not recorded at December 31, $51,300.

Appendix 2
EX 4-31 Adjusting and reversing entries
On the basis of the following data, (a) journalize the adjusting entries at June 30, the end of the current fiscal year, and (b) journalize the reversing entries on July 1, the first day of the following year:

1. Wages are $13,200 per day for a five-day workweek, ending on Friday. The last payday of the year was Thursday, June 27.
2. Accrued fees earned but not recorded at June 30, $25,000.

Chapter 4 Completing the Accounting Cycle 215

Appendix 2

EX 4-32 Entries posted to wages expense account

Portions of the wages expense account of a business follow:

Account Wages Expense **Account No. 53**

Date	Item	Post. Ref.	Dr.	Cr.	Balance Dr.	Balance Cr.
2018 Dec. 26	(1)	125	15,400		800,000	
31	(2)	126	9,250		809,250	
31	(3)	127		809,250	—	—
2019 Jan. 1	(4)	128		9,250		9,250
2	(5)	129	14,800		5,550	

a. Indicate the nature of the entry (payment, adjusting, closing, reversing) from which each numbered posting was made.

b. Journalize the complete entry from which each numbered posting was made. Close revenues and expenses to D. Bower, Capital.

Appendix 2

EX 4-33 Entries posted to wages expense account

Portions of the salaries expense account of a business follow:

Account Salaries Expense **Account No. 62**

Date	Item	Post. Ref.	Dr.	Cr.	Balance Dr.	Balance Cr.
2018 Dec. 27	(1)	29	22,000		1,200,000	
31	(2)	30	13,200		1,213,200	
31	(3)	31		1,213,200	—	—
2019 Jan. 1	(4)	32		13,200		13,200
2	(5)	33	24,000		10,800	

a. Indicate the nature of the entry (payment, adjusting, closing, reversing) from which each numbered posting was made.

b. Journalize the complete entry from which each numbered posting was made. Close revenues and expenses to J. McHenry, Capital.

Problems: Series A

PR 4-1A Financial statements and closing entries OBJ. 1, 2, 3

✔ 3. Total assets: $418,950

Beacon Signals Company maintains and repairs warning lights, such as those found on radio towers and lighthouses. Beacon Signals Company prepared the following end-of-period spreadsheet at December 31, 2019, the end of the fiscal year:

(Continued)

216 Chapter 4 Completing the Accounting Cycle

	A	B	C	D	E	F	G
1		\multicolumn{6}{c}{Beacon Signals Company}
2		\multicolumn{6}{c}{End-of-Period Spreadsheet}
3		\multicolumn{6}{c}{For the Year Ended December 31, 2019}
4		Unadjusted				Adjusted	
5		Trial Balance		Adjustments		Trial Balance	
6	Account Title	Dr.	Cr.	Dr.	Cr.	Dr.	Cr.
7							
8	Cash	13,000				13,000	
9	Accounts Receivable	40,500		(a) 12,500		53,000	
10	Prepaid Insurance	4,200			(b) 3,000	1,200	
11	Supplies	3,000			(c) 2,250	750	
12	Land	98,000				98,000	
13	Building	500,000				500,000	
14	Accum. Depr.—Building		255,300		(d) 9,000		264,300
15	Equipment	121,900				121,900	
16	Accum. Depr.—Equipment		100,100		(e) 4,500		104,600
17	Accounts Payable		15,700				15,700
18	Salaries and Wages Payable				(f) 4,900		4,900
19	Unearned Rent		2,100	(g) 1,300			800
20	Sarah Colin, Capital		238,100				238,100
21	Sarah Colin, Drawing	10,000				10,000	
22	Fees Earned		388,700		(a)12,500		401,200
23	Rent Revenue				(g) 1,300		1,300
24	Salaries and Wages Expense	163,100		(f) 4,900		168,000	
25	Advertising Expense	21,700				21,700	
26	Utilities Expense	11,400				11,400	
27	Depr. Exp.—Building			(d) 9,000		9,000	
28	Repairs Expense	8,850				8,850	
29	Depr. Exp.—Equipment			(e) 4,500		4,500	
30	Insurance Expense			(b) 3,000		3,000	
31	Supplies Expense			(c) 2,250		2,250	
32	Misc. Expense	4,350				4,350	
33		1,000,000	1,000,000	37,450	37,450	1,030,900	1,030,900
34							

Show Me How

Instructions

1. Prepare an income statement for the year ended December 31.
2. Prepare a statement of owner's equity for the year ended December 31. No additional investments were made during the year.
3. Prepare a balance sheet as of December 31.
4. Based upon the end-of-period spreadsheet, journalize the closing entries.
5. Prepare a post-closing trial balance.

✓ 1. Stacy Tanner, capital, June 30: $483,300

PR 4-2A Financial statements and closing entries   OBJ. 2, 3

Finders Investigative Services is an investigative services firm that is owned and operated by Stacy Tanner. On June 30, 2019, the end of the fiscal year, the accountant for Finders Investigative Services prepared an end-of-period spreadsheet, a part of which follows:

Chapter 4 Completing the Accounting Cycle

	A	F	G
1	Finders Investigative Services		
2	End-of-Period Spreadsheet		
3	For the Year Ended June 30, 2019		
4		Adjusted	
5		Trial Balance	
6	Account Title	Dr.	Cr.
7			
8	Cash	28,000	
9	Accounts Receivable	69,600	
10	Supplies	4,600	
11	Prepaid Insurance	2,500	
12	Building	439,500	
13	Accumulated Depreciation—Building		44,200
14	Accounts Payable		11,700
15	Salaries Payable		3,000
16	Unearned Rent		2,000
17	Stacy Tanner, Capital		373,800
18	Stacy Tanner, Drawing	12,000	
19	Service Fees		718,000
20	Rent Revenue		12,000
21	Salaries Expense	522,100	
22	Rent Expense	48,000	
23	Supplies Expense	10,800	
24	Depreciation Expense—Building	8,750	
25	Utilities Expense	7,150	
26	Repairs Expense	3,000	
27	Insurance Expense	2,500	
28	Miscellaneous Expense	6,200	
29		1,164,700	1,164,700

Instructions

1. Prepare an income statement, a statement of owner's equity (no additional investments were made during the year), and a balance sheet.
2. Journalize the entries that were required to close the accounts at June 30.
3. If Stacy Tanner, Capital has instead decreased $30,000 after the closing entries were posted, and the withdrawals remained the same, what would have been the amount of net income or net loss?

PR 4-3A T accounts, adjusting entries, financial statements, and closing entries; optional end-of-period spreadsheet   OBJ. 2, 3

✔ 5. Net income: $10,700

The unadjusted trial balance of Epicenter Laundry at June 30, 2019, the end of the fiscal year, follows:

Excel

Epicenter Laundry
Unadjusted Trial Balance
June 30, 2019

	Debit Balances	Credit Balances
Cash	11,000	
Laundry Supplies	21,500	
Prepaid Insurance	9,600	
Laundry Equipment	232,600	
Accumulated Depreciation		125,400
Accounts Payable		11,800
Sophie Perez, Capital		105,600
Sophie Perez, Drawing	10,000	
Laundry Revenue		232,200
Wages Expense	125,200	
Rent Expense	40,000	
Utilities Expense	19,700	
Miscellaneous Expense	5,400	
	475,000	475,000

(Continued)

218 Chapter 4 Completing the Accounting Cycle

The data needed to determine year-end adjustments are as follows:
a. Laundry supplies on hand at June 30 are $3,600.
b. Insurance premiums expired during the year are $5,700.
c. Depreciation of laundry equipment during the year is $6,500.
d. Wages accrued but not paid at June 30 are $1,100.

Instructions

1. For each account listed in the unadjusted trial balance, enter the balance in a T account. Identify the balance as "June 30 Bal." In addition, add T accounts for Wages Payable, Depreciation Expense, Laundry Supplies Expense, and Insurance Expense.
2. *(Optional)* Enter the unadjusted trial balance on an end-of-period spreadsheet and complete the spreadsheet. Add the accounts listed in part (1) as needed.
3. Journalize and post the adjusting entries. Identify the adjustments as "Adj." and the new balances as "Adj. Bal."
4. Prepare an adjusted trial balance.
5. Prepare an income statement, a statement of owner's equity (no additional investments were made during the year), and a balance sheet.
6. Journalize and post the closing entries. Identify the closing entries as "Clos."
7. Prepare a post-closing trial balance.

PR 4-4A Ledger accounts, adjusting entries, financial statements, and closing entries; optional spreadsheet   OBJ. 2, 3

✔ 5. Net income: $51,150

Excel

The unadjusted trial balance of Lakota Freight Co. at March 31, 2019, the end of the year, follows:

Lakota Freight Co.
Unadjusted Trial Balance
March 31, 2019

	Account No.	Debit Balances	Credit Balances
Cash	11	12,000	
Supplies	13	30,000	
Prepaid Insurance	14	3,600	
Equipment	16	110,000	
Accumulated Depreciation—Equipment	17		25,000
Trucks	18	60,000	
Accumulated Depreciation—Trucks	19		15,000
Accounts Payable	21		4,000
Kaya Tarango, Capital	31		96,000
Kaya Tarango, Drawing	32	15,000	
Service Revenue	41		160,000
Wages Expense	51	45,000	
Rent Expense	53	10,600	
Truck Expense	54	9,000	
Miscellaneous Expense	59	4,800	
		300,000	300,000

The data needed to determine year-end adjustments are as follows:
a. Supplies on hand at March 31 are $7,500.
b. Insurance premiums expired during the year are $1,800.
c. Depreciation of equipment during the year is $8,350.
d. Depreciation of trucks during the year is $6,200.
e. Wages accrued but not paid at March 31 are $600.

Instructions

1. For each account listed in the trial balance, enter the balance in the appropriate Balance column of a four-column account and place a check mark (✓) in the Posting Reference column.
2. *(Optional)* Enter the unadjusted trial balance on an end-of-period spreadsheet and complete the spreadsheet. Add the accounts listed in part (3) as needed.
3. Journalize and post the adjusting entries, inserting balances in the accounts affected. Record the adjusting entries on Page 26 of the journal. The following additional accounts from Lakota Freight Co.'s chart of accounts should be used: Wages Payable, 22; Supplies Expense, 52; Depreciation Expense—Equipment, 55; Depreciation Expense—Trucks, 56; Insurance Expense, 57.
4. Prepare an adjusted trial balance.
5. Prepare an income statement, a statement of owner's equity (no additional investments were made during the year), and a balance sheet.
6. Journalize and post the closing entries. Record the closing entries on Page 27 of the journal. Indicate closed accounts by inserting a line in both Balance columns opposite the closing entry.
7. Prepare a post-closing trial balance.

PR 4-5A Complete accounting cycle OBJ. 4, 5

✓ 8. Net income: $50,335

For the past several years, Jolene Upton has operated a part-time consulting business from her home. As of July 1, 2019, Jolene decided to move to rented quarters and to operate the business, which was to be known as Gourmet Consulting, on a full-time basis. Gourmet Consulting entered into the following transactions during July:

July 1. The following assets were received from Jolene Upton: cash, $19,000; accounts receivable, $22,300; supplies, $3,800; and office equipment, $8,900. There were no liabilities received.

1. Paid three months' rent on a lease rental contract, $6,000.
2. Paid the premiums on property and casualty insurance policies, $4,500.
4. Received cash from clients as an advance payment for services to be provided and recorded it as unearned fees, $8,000.
5. Purchased additional office equipment on account from Office Necessities Co., $5,100.
6. Received cash from clients on account, $12,750.
10. Paid cash for a newspaper advertisement, $500.
12. Paid Office Necessities Co. for part of the debt incurred on July 5, $3,000.
12. Provided services on account for the period July 1–12, $14,200.
14. Paid receptionist for two weeks' salary, $1,500.

Record the following transactions on Page 2 of the journal:

17. Received cash from cash clients for fees earned during the period July 1–17, $10,400.
18. Paid cash for supplies, $1,000.
20. Provided services on account for the period July 13–20, $9,000.
24. Received cash from cash clients for fees earned for the period July 17–24, $8,500.
26. Received cash from clients on account, $12,000.
27. Paid receptionist for two weeks' salary, $1,500.
29. Paid telephone bill for July, $325.
31. Paid electricity bill for July, $675.
31. Received cash from cash clients for fees earned for the period July 25–31, $7,100.
31. Provided services on account for the remainder of July, $5,500.
31. Jolene withdrew $20,000 for personal use.

(Continued)

220 Chapter 4 Completing the Accounting Cycle

Instructions

1. Journalize each transaction in a two-column journal starting on Page 1, referring to the following chart of accounts in selecting the accounts to be debited and credited. (Do not insert the account numbers in the journal at this time.)

11	Cash	31	Jolene Upton, Capital
12	Accounts Receivable	32	Jolene Upton, Drawing
14	Supplies	41	Fees Earned
15	Prepaid Rent	51	Salary Expense
16	Prepaid Insurance	52	Rent Expense
18	Office Equipment	53	Supplies Expense
19	Accumulated Depreciation—Office Equipment	54	Depreciation Expense
21	Accounts Payable	55	Insurance Expense
22	Salaries Payable	59	Miscellaneous Expense
23	Unearned Fees		

2. Post the journal to a ledger of four-column accounts.
3. Prepare an unadjusted trial balance.
4. At the end of July, the following adjustment data were assembled. Analyze and use these data to complete parts (5) and (6).
    a. Insurance expired during July is $375.
    b. Supplies on hand on July 31 are $2,850.
    c. Depreciation of office equipment for July is $400.
    d. Accrued receptionist salary on July 31 is $140.
    e. Rent expired during July is $2,000.
    f. Unearned fees on July 31 are $3,000.
5. *(Optional)* Enter the unadjusted trial balance on an end-of-period spreadsheet and complete the spreadsheet.
6. Journalize and post the adjusting entries. Record the adjusting entries on Page 3 of the journal.
7. Prepare an adjusted trial balance.
8. Prepare an income statement, a statement of owner's equity, and a balance sheet.
9. Prepare and post the closing entries. Record the closing entries on Page 4 of the journal. Indicate closed accounts by inserting a line in both Balance columns opposite the closing entry.
10. Prepare a post-closing trial balance.

Problems: Series B

PR 4-1B Financial statements and closing entries OBJ. 1, 2, 3

✔ 3. Total assets: $342,425

Last Chance Company offers legal consulting advice to prison inmates. Last Chance Company prepared the end-of-period spreadsheet shown at the top of the following page at June 30, 2019, the end of the fiscal year.

Instructions

1. Prepare an income statement for the year ended June 30.
2. Prepare a statement of owner's equity for the year ended June 30. No additional investments were made during the year.
3. Prepare a balance sheet as of June 30.
4. On the basis of the end-of-period spreadsheet, journalize the closing entries.
5. Prepare a post-closing trial balance.

Chapter 4 Completing the Accounting Cycle

Last Chance Company
End-of-Period Spreadsheet
For the Year Ended June 30, 2019

Account Title	Unadjusted Trial Balance Dr.	Unadjusted Trial Balance Cr.	Adjustments Dr.	Adjustments Cr.	Adjusted Trial Balance Dr.	Adjusted Trial Balance Cr.
Cash	5,100				5,100	
Accounts Receivable	22,750		(a) 3,750		26,500	
Prepaid Insurance	3,600			(b) 1,300	2,300	
Supplies	2,025			(c) 1,500	525	
Land	80,000				80,000	
Building	340,000				340,000	
Accum. Depr.—Building		190,000		(d) 3,000		193,000
Equipment	140,000				140,000	
Accum. Depr.—Equipment		54,450		(e) 4,550		59,000
Accounts Payable		9,750				9,750
Salaries and Wages Payable				(f) 1,900		1,900
Unearned Rent		4,500	(g) 3,000			1,500
Tami Garrigan, Capital		361,300				361,300
Tami Garrigan, Drawing	20,000				20,000	
Fees Earned		280,000		(a) 3,750		283,750
Rent Revenue				(g) 3,000		3,000
Salaries and Wages Expense	145,100		(f) 1,900		147,000	
Advertising Expense	86,800				86,800	
Utilities Expense	30,000				30,000	
Travel Expense	18,750				18,750	
Depr. Exp.—Equipment			(e) 4,550		4,550	
Depr. Exp.—Building			(d) 3,000		3,000	
Supplies Expense			(c) 1,500		1,500	
Insurance Expense			(b) 1,300		1,300	
Misc. Expense	5,875				5,875	
	900,000	900,000	19,000	19,000	913,200	913,200

PR 4-2B Financial statements and closing entries **OBJ. 2, 3**

✓ 1. Nicole Gorman, capital, October 31: $313,000

The Gorman Group is a financial planning services firm owned and operated by Nicole Gorman. As of October 31, 2019, the end of the fiscal year, the accountant for The Gorman Group prepared an end-of-period spreadsheet, part of which follows:

The Gorman Group
End-of-Period Spreadsheet
For the Year Ended October 31, 2019

Account Title	Adjusted Trial Balance Dr.	Adjusted Trial Balance Cr.
Cash	11,000	
Accounts Receivable	28,150	
Supplies	6,350	
Prepaid Insurance	9,500	
Land	75,000	
Buildings	250,000	
Accumulated Depreciation—Buildings		117,200
Equipment	240,000	
Accumulated Depreciation—Equipment		151,700
Accounts Payable		33,300
Salaries Payable		3,300
Unearned Rent		1,500
Nicole Gorman, Capital		220,000
Nicole Gorman, Drawing	20,000	
Service Fees		468,000
Rent Revenue		5,000
Salaries Expense	291,000	
Depreciation Expense—Equipment	17,500	
Rent Expense	15,500	
Supplies Expense	9,000	
Utilities Expense	8,500	
Depreciation Expense—Buildings	6,600	
Repairs Expense	3,450	
Insurance Expense	3,000	
Miscellaneous Expense	5,450	
	1,000,000	1,000,000

(Continued)

222 Chapter 4 Completing the Accounting Cycle

Instructions

1. Prepare an income statement, a statement of owner's equity (no additional investments were made during the year), and a balance sheet.
2. Journalize the entries that were required to close the accounts at October 31.
3. If the balance of Nicole Gorman, Capital had instead increased $115,000 after the closing entries were posted and the withdrawals remained the same, what would have been the amount of net income or net loss?

PR 4-3B T accounts, adjusting entries, financial statements, and closing entries; optional end-of-period spreadsheet   OBJ. 2, 3

✔ 5. Net income: $27,350

The unadjusted trial balance of La Mesa Laundry at August 31, 2019, the end of the fiscal year, follows:

La Mesa Laundry
Unadjusted Trial Balance
August 31, 2019

	Debit Balances	Credit Balances
Cash	3,800	
Laundry Supplies	9,000	
Prepaid Insurance	6,000	
Laundry Equipment	180,800	
Accumulated Depreciation		49,200
Accounts Payable		7,800
Bobbi Downey, Capital		95,000
Bobbi Downey, Drawing	2,400	
Laundry Revenue		248,000
Wages Expense	135,800	
Rent Expense	43,200	
Utilities Expense	16,000	
Miscellaneous Expense	3,000	
	400,000	400,000

The data needed to determine year-end adjustments are as follows:
a. Wages accrued but not paid at August 31 are $2,200.
b. Depreciation of equipment during the year is $8,150.
c. Laundry supplies on hand at August 31 are $2,000.
d. Insurance premiums expired during the year are $5,300.

Instructions

1. For each account listed in the unadjusted trial balance, enter the balance in a T account. Identify the balance as "Aug. 31 Bal." In addition, add T accounts for Wages Payable, Depreciation Expense, Laundry Supplies Expense, and Insurance Expense.
2. *(Optional)* Enter the unadjusted trial balance on an end-of-period spreadsheet and complete the spreadsheet. Add the accounts listed in part (1) as needed.
3. Journalize and post the adjusting entries. Identify the adjustments as "Adj." and the new balances as "Adj. Bal."
4. Prepare an adjusted trial balance.
5. Prepare an income statement, a statement of owner's equity (no additional investments were made during the year), and a balance sheet.
6. Journalize and post the closing entries. Identify the closing entries as "Clos."
7. Prepare a post-closing trial balance.

Chapter 4 Completing the Accounting Cycle 223

PR 4-4B Ledger accounts, adjusting entries, financial statements, and closing entries; optional end-of-period spreadsheet OBJ. 2, 3

✓ 5. Net income: $46,150

The unadjusted trial balance of Recessive Interiors at January 31, 2019, the end of the year, follows:

Recessive Interiors
Unadjusted Trial Balance
January 31, 2019

	Account No.	Debit Balances	Credit Balances
Cash	11	13,100	
Supplies	13	8,000	
Prepaid Insurance	14	7,500	
Equipment	16	113,000	
Accumulated Depreciation—Equipment	17		12,000
Trucks	18	90,000	
Accumulated Depreciation—Trucks	19		27,100
Accounts Payable	21		4,500
Jeanne McQuay, Capital	31		126,400
Jeanne McQuay, Drawing	32	3,000	
Service Revenue	41		155,000
Wages Expense	51	72,000	
Rent Expense	52	7,600	
Truck Expense	53	5,350	
Miscellaneous Expense	59	5,450	
		325,000	325,000

The data needed to determine year-end adjustments are as follows:

a. Supplies on hand at January 31 are $2,850.
b. Insurance premiums expired during the year are $3,150.
c. Depreciation of equipment during the year is $5,250.
d. Depreciation of trucks during the year is $4,000.
e. Wages accrued but not paid at January 31 are $900.

Instructions

1. For each account listed in the unadjusted trial balance, enter the balance in the appropriate Balance column of a four-column account and place a check mark (✓) in the Posting Reference column.
2. *(Optional)* Enter the unadjusted trial balance on an end-of-period spreadsheet and complete the spreadsheet. Add the accounts listed in part (3) as needed.
3. Journalize and post the adjusting entries, inserting balances in the accounts affected. Record the adjusting entries on Page 26 of the journal. The following additional accounts from Recessive Interiors' chart of accounts should be used: Wages Payable, 22; Depreciation Expense—Equipment, 54; Supplies Expense, 55; Depreciation Expense—Trucks, 56; Insurance Expense, 57.
4. Prepare an adjusted trial balance.
5. Prepare an income statement, a statement of owner's equity (no additional investments were made during the year), and a balance sheet.
6. Journalize and post the closing entries. Record the closing entries on Page 27 of the journal. Indicate closed accounts by inserting a line in both Balance columns opposite the closing entry.
7. Prepare a post-closing trial balance.

224　Chapter 4　Completing the Accounting Cycle

✔ 8. Net income: $53,775

Excel

PR 4-5B　Complete accounting cycle　　OBJ. 4, 5

For the past several years, Jeff Horton has operated a part-time consulting business from his home. As of April 1, 2019, Jeff decided to move to rented quarters and to operate the business, which was to be known as Rosebud Consulting, on a full-time basis. Rosebud Consulting entered into the following transactions during April:

Apr. 1. The following assets were received from Jeff Horton: cash, $20,000; accounts receivable, $14,700; supplies, $3,300; and office equipment, $12,000. There were no liabilities received.

　　1. Paid three months' rent on a lease rental contract, $6,000.
　　2. Paid the premiums on property and casualty insurance policies, $4,200.
　　4. Received cash from clients as an advance payment for services to be provided and recorded it as unearned fees, $9,400.
　　5. Purchased additional office equipment on account from Smith Office Supply Co., $8,000.
　　6. Received cash from clients on account, $11,700.
　　10. Paid cash for a newspaper advertisement, $350.
　　12. Paid Smith Office Supply Co. for part of the debt incurred on April 5, $6,400.
　　12. Provided services on account for the period April 1–12, $21,900.
　　14. Paid receptionist for two weeks' salary, $1,650.

Record the following transactions on Page 2 of the journal:

　　17. Received cash from cash clients for fees earned during the period April 1–16, $6,600.
　　18. Paid cash for supplies, $725.
　　20. Provided services on account for the period April 13–20, $16,800.
　　24. Received cash from cash clients for fees earned for the period April 17–24, $4,450.
　　26. Received cash from clients on account, $26,500.
　　27. Paid receptionist for two weeks' salary, $1,650.
　　29. Paid telephone bill for April, $540.
　　30. Paid electricity bill for April, $760.
　　30. Received cash from cash clients for fees earned for the period April 25–30, $5,160.
　　30. Provided services on account for the remainder of April, $2,590.
　　30. Jeff withdrew $18,000 for personal use.

Instructions

1. Journalize each transaction in a two-column journal starting on Page 1, referring to the following chart of accounts in selecting the accounts to be debited and credited. (Do not insert the account numbers in the journal at this time.)

11	Cash		31	Jeff Horton, Capital
12	Accounts Receivable		32	Jeff Horton, Drawing
14	Supplies		41	Fees Earned
15	Prepaid Rent		51	Salary Expense
16	Prepaid Insurance		52	Supplies Expense
18	Office Equipment		53	Rent Expense
19	Accumulated Depreciation—Office Equipment		54	Depreciation Expense
21	Accounts Payable		55	Insurance Expense
22	Salaries Payable		59	Miscellaneous Expense
23	Unearned Fees			

2. Post the journal to a ledger of four-column accounts.
3. Prepare an unadjusted trial balance.

Chapter 4 Completing the Accounting Cycle   225

4. At the end of April, the following adjustment data were assembled. Analyze and use these data to complete parts (5) and (6).

   a. Insurance expired during April is $350.

   b. Supplies on hand on April 30 are $1,225.

   c. Depreciation of office equipment for April is $400.

   d. Accrued receptionist salary on April 30 is $275.

   e. Rent expired during April is $2,000.

   f. Unearned fees on April 30 are $2,350.

5. *(Optional)* Enter the unadjusted trial balance on an end-of-period spreadsheet and complete the spreadsheet.

6. Journalize and post the adjusting entries. Record the adjusting entries on Page 3 of the journal.

7. Prepare an adjusted trial balance.

8. Prepare an income statement, a statement of owner's equity, and a balance sheet.

9. Prepare and post the closing entries. Record the closing entries on Page 4 of the journal. Indicate closed accounts by inserting a line in both Balance columns opposite the closing entry.

10. Prepare a post-closing trial balance.

Continuing Problem

✔ 2. Net income: $4,955

The unadjusted trial balance of PS Music as of July 31, 2019, along with the adjustment data for the two months ended July 31, 2019, are shown in Chapter 3. Based upon the adjustment data, the following adjusted trial balance was prepared:

PS Music
Adjusted Trial Balance
July 31, 2019

	Debit Balances	Credit Balances
Cash	9,945	
Accounts Receivable	4,150	
Supplies	275	
Prepaid Insurance	2,475	
Office Equipment	7,500	
Accumulated Depreciation—Office Equipment		50
Accounts Payable		8,350
Wages Payable		140
Unearned Revenue		3,600
Peyton Smith, Capital		9,000
Peyton Smith, Drawing	1,750	
Fees Earned		21,200
Music Expense	3,610	
Wages Expense	2,940	
Office Rent Expense	2,550	
Advertising Expense	1,500	
Equipment Rent Expense	1,375	
Utilities Expense	1,215	
Supplies Expense	925	
Insurance Expense	225	
Depreciation Expense	50	
Miscellaneous Expense	1,855	
	42,340	42,340

(Continued)

Instructions

1. *(Optional)* Using the data from Chapter 3, prepare an end-of-period spreadsheet.
2. Prepare an income statement, a statement of owner's equity, and a balance sheet. (*Note:* Peyton Smith made investments in PS Music on June 1 and July 1, 2019.)
3. Journalize and post the closing entries. Indicate closed accounts by inserting a line in both Balance columns opposite the closing entry.
4. Prepare a post-closing trial balance.

Comprehensive Problem 1

✔ 8. Net income, $33,425

Kelly Pitney began her consulting business, Kelly Consulting, on April 1, 2019. The accounting cycle for Kelly Consulting for April, including financial statements, was illustrated in this chapter. During May, Kelly Consulting entered into the following transactions:

May 3. Received cash from clients as an advance payment for services to be provided and recorded it as unearned fees, $4,500.
- 5. Received cash from clients on account, $2,450.
- 9. Paid cash for a newspaper advertisement, $225.
- 13. Paid Office Station Co. for part of the debt incurred on April 5, $640.
- 15. Provided services on account for the period May 1–15, $9,180.
- 16. Paid part-time receptionist for two weeks' salary including the amount owed on April 30, $750.
- 17. Received cash from cash clients for fees earned during the period May 1–16, $8,360.

Record the following transactions on Page 6 of the journal:

- 20. Purchased supplies on account, $735.
- 21. Provided services on account for the period May 16–20, $4,820.
- 25. Received cash from cash clients for fees earned for the period May 17–23, $7,900.
- 27. Received cash from clients on account, $9,520.
- 28. Paid part-time receptionist for two weeks' salary, $750.
- 30. Paid telephone bill for May, $260.
- 31. Paid electricity bill for May, $810.
- 31. Received cash from cash clients for fees earned for the period May 26–31, $3,300.
- 31. Provided services on account for the remainder of May, $2,650.
- 31. Kelly withdrew $10,500 for personal use.

Instructions

1. The chart of accounts for Kelly Consulting is shown in Exhibit 9, and the post-closing trial balance as of April 30, 2019, is shown in Exhibit 17. For each account in the post-closing trial balance, enter the balance in the appropriate Balance column of a four-column account. Date the balances May 1, 2019, and place a check mark (✓) in the Posting Reference column. Journalize each of the May transactions in a two-column journal starting on Page 5 of the journal and using Kelly Consulting's chart of accounts. (Do not insert the account numbers in the journal at this time.)
2. Post the journal to a ledger of four-column accounts.
3. Prepare an unadjusted trial balance.
4. At the end of May, the following adjustment data were assembled. Analyze and use these data to complete parts (5) and (6).
   a. Insurance expired during May is $275.
   b. Supplies on hand on May 31 are $715.

c. Depreciation of office equipment for May is $330.

d. Accrued receptionist salary on May 31 is $325.

e. Rent expired during May is $1,600.

f. Unearned fees on May 31 are $3,210.

5. *(Optional)* Enter the unadjusted trial balance on an end-of-period spreadsheet and complete the spreadsheet.

6. Journalize and post the adjusting entries. Record the adjusting entries on Page 7 of the journal.

7. Prepare an adjusted trial balance.

8. Prepare an income statement, a statement of owner's equity, and a balance sheet.

9. Prepare and post the closing entries. Record the closing entries on Page 8 of the journal. Indicate closed accounts by inserting a line in both Balance columns opposite the closing entry.

10. Prepare a post-closing trial balance.

Cases & Projects

CP 4-1 Ethics in Action

New Wave Images is a graphics design firm that prepares its financial statements using a calendar year. Manny Kinn, the company treasurer and vice president of finance, has prepared a classified balance sheet as of December 31. In January, this balance sheet will be submitted along with an application for a loan from First Peoples Community Bank. An excerpt from the balance sheet follows:

Cash	$ 25,000
Accounts receivable	85,000
......	
Total assets	$250,000

The accounts receivable balance includes a $56,000 loan to Tom Morrow, the company president. Tom borrowed the money from New Wave 18 months earlier for a down payment on a new home. Tom has orally assured Manny that he will pay off the loan within the next year. Because Tom is the company president, Manny treats the amount due as part of its normal accounts receivable. In addition, Manny knows that the bank will consider a large balance in accounts receivable more favorably than a large personal loan to a single individual. Manny reported the $56,000 in the same manner on the preceding year's balance sheet.

1. Is Manny behaving ethically by reporting the loan to Tom as a trade account receivable? Why or why not?

2. Who will be affected by Manny's decision?

CP 4-2 Team Activity

In teams, select two public companies of different industries that interest you. Obtain each company's most recent annual report on Form 10-K. The Form 10-K is a company's annually required filing with the Securities and Exchange Commission (SEC). It includes the company's financial statements and accompanying notes. The Form 10-K can be obtained either (a) from the investor relations section of the company's website or (b) by using the company search feature of the SEC's EDGAR database service found at www.sec.gov/edgar/searchedgar/companysearch.html.

Find the balance sheet for each of the two companies you have selected. Compare the balance sheets of the two companies as follows:

1. What is each company's fiscal year?

(Continued)

2. Which balance sheet accounts do the two companies have in common?
3. Which balance sheet accounts stand out as different between the two companies? Why do these differences exist?

Communication

CP 4-3 Communication

Your friend, Daniel Nat, recently began work as the lead accountant for the Asheville Company. Dan prepared the following balance sheet for December 31, 2018:

Asheville Company
Balance Sheet
For the Year Ended December 31, 2018

Assets	
Land...	$100,000
Accounts payable...	10,000
Accounts receivable.......................................	12,500
Cash..	10,000
Daniel Nat, capital..	235,000
Total assets..	$367,500

Liabilities	
Equipment..	$125,000
Wages payable..	2,500
Total liabilities...	$127,500

White a brief memo to Daniel explaining the errors in the Asheville Company balance sheet and the correct presentation for the balance sheet.

CP 4-4 Financial statements

The following is an excerpt from a telephone conversation between Ben Simpson, president of Main Street Co., and Tami Lundgren, owner of Reliable Employment Co.:

Ben: Tami, you're going to have to do a better job of finding me a new computer programmer. That last guy was great at programming, but he didn't have any common sense.

Tami: What do you mean? The guy had a master's degree with straight A's.

Ben: Yes, well, last month he developed a new financial reporting system. He said we could do away with manually preparing an end-of-period spreadsheet and financial statements. The computer would automatically generate our financial statements with "a push of a button."

Tami: So what's the big deal? Sounds to me like it would save you time and effort.

Ben: Right! The balance sheet showed a minus for supplies!

Tami: Minus supplies? How can that be?

Ben: That's what I asked.

Tami: So, what did he say?

Ben: Well, after he checked the program, he said that it must be right. The minuses were greater than the pluses....

Tami: Didn't he know that Supplies can't have a credit balance—it must have a debit balance?

Ben: He asked me what a debit and credit were.

Tami: I see your point.

1. Comment on (a) the desirability of computerizing Main Street Co.'s financial reporting system, (b) the elimination of the end-of-period spreadsheet in a computerized accounting system, and (c) the computer programmer's lack of accounting knowledge.

2. Explain to the programmer why Supplies could not have a credit balance.

CP 4-5 Financial statements

Assume that you recently accepted a position with Five Star National Bank & Trust as an assistant loan officer. As one of your first duties, you have been assigned the responsibility of evaluating a loan request for $300,000 from West Gate Auto Co., a small proprietorship. In support of the loan application, Joan Whalen, owner, submitted a "Statement of Accounts" (trial balance) for the first year of operations ended October 31, 2019.

West Gate Auto Co.
Statement of Accounts
October 31, 2019

Cash	5,000	
Billings Due from Others	40,000	
Supplies (chemicals, etc.)	7,500	
Building	222,300	
Equipment	50,000	
Amounts Owed to Others		31,000
Investment in Business		179,000
Service Revenue		215,000
Wages Expense	75,000	
Utilities Expense	10,000	
Rent Expense	8,000	
Insurance Expense	6,000	
Other Expenses	1,200	
	425,000	425,000

1. Explain to Joan Whalen why a set of financial statements (income statement, statement of owner's equity, and balance sheet) would be useful to you in evaluating the loan request.

2. In discussing the "Statement of Accounts" with Joan Whalen, you discovered that the accounts had not been adjusted at October 31. Analyze the "Statement of Accounts" and indicate possible adjusting entries that might be necessary before an accurate set of financial statements could be prepared.

3. Assuming that an accurate set of financial statements will be submitted by Joan Whalen in a few days, what other considerations or information would you require before making a decision on the loan request?

CHAPTER 5

Accounting Systems

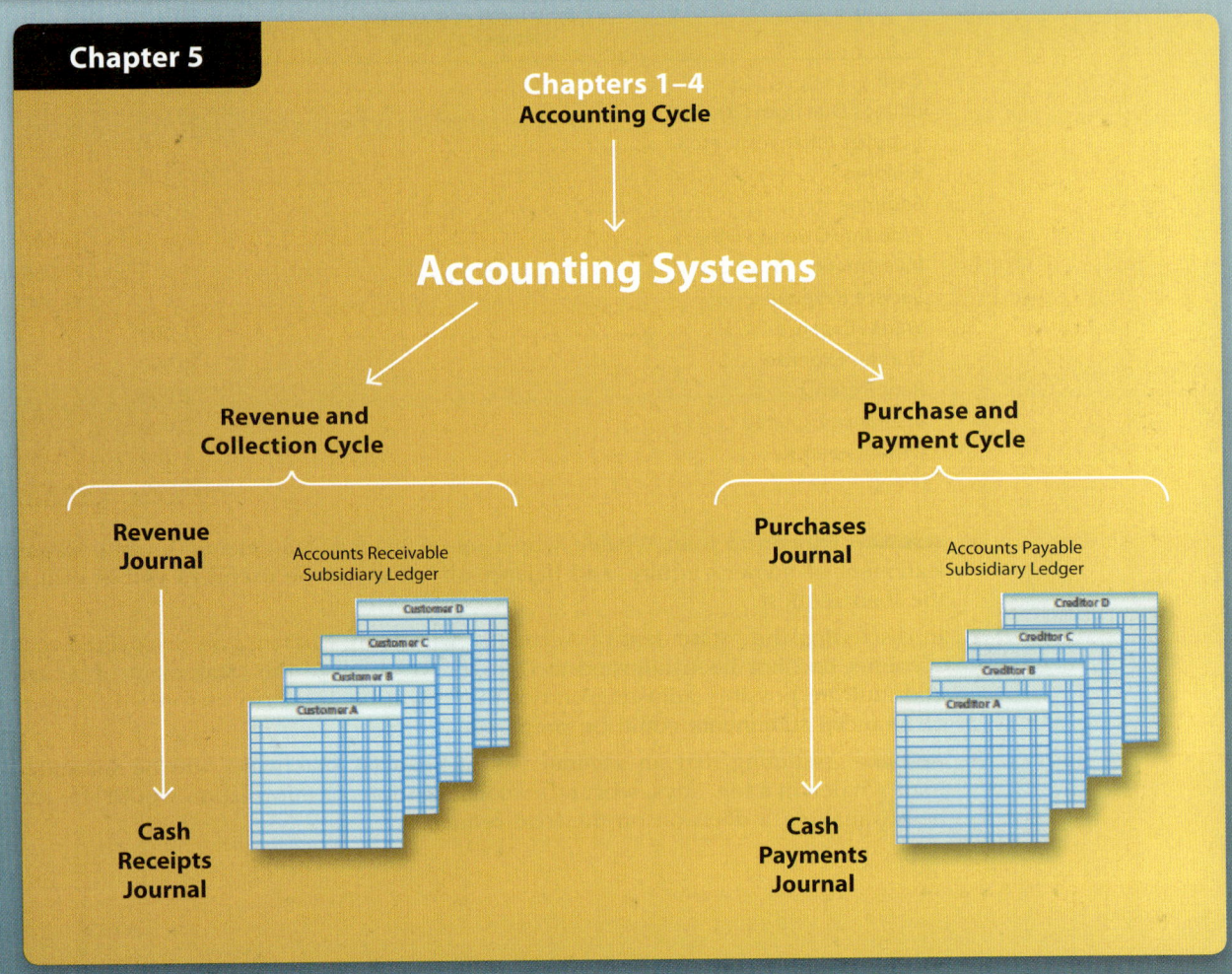

CHAPTER 5

Intuit Inc.

You likely interact with accounting systems as part of your everyday life. For example, your bank statement is a type of accounting system. When you make a deposit, the bank records an addition to your cash; when you withdraw cash, the bank records a reduction in your cash. Such a simple accounting system works well for a person with just a few transactions per month. However, over time, you may find that your financial affairs will become more complex and involve many different types of transactions, including investments and loan payments. At this point, relying on your bank statement may not be sufficient for managing your financial affairs. Personal financial planning software, such as **Intuit**'s Quicken®, can be useful when your financial affairs become more complex.

What happens if you decide to begin a small business? Transactions expand to include customers, vendors, and employees. As a result, the accounting system will need to adjust to this complexity. Thus, many small businesses use small-business accounting software, such as Intuit's QuickBooks®, as their first accounting system. As a business grows, more sophisticated accounting systems will be needed. Companies, such as **SAP**, **Oracle**, **Microsoft**, and **Sage Software, Inc.**, offer accounting system solutions for businesses that become larger with more complex accounting needs.

Accounting systems used by large and small businesses employ the basic principles of the accounting cycle discussed in the previous chapters. However, these accounting systems include features that simplify the recording and summary process. In this chapter, we will discuss these simplifying procedures as they apply to both manual and computerized systems.

Learning Objectives

After studying this chapter, you should be able to:

Example Exercises (EE) are shown in green.

Obj. 1 Define and describe an accounting system.

Basic Accounting Systems

Obj. 2 Journalize and post transactions in a manual accounting system that uses subsidiary ledgers and special journals.

Manual Accounting Systems
Subsidiary Ledgers
Special Journals
Revenue Journal — EE 5-1
Cash Receipts Journal
Accounts Receivable Control Account and Subsidiary Ledger — EE 5-2
Purchases Journal — EE 5-3
Cash Payments Journal
Accounts Payable Control Account and Subsidiary Ledger — EE 5-4

Obj. 3 Describe and illustrate the use of a computerized accounting system.

Computerized Accounting Systems

Obj. 4 Describe the basic features of e-commerce.

E-Commerce

Obj. 5 Use segment analysis in evaluating the operating performance of a company.

Financial Analysis and Interpretation: Segment Analysis
Evaluate Segment Operating Performance — EE 5-5

At a Glance 5 — Page 252

Obj. 1 Define and describe an accounting system.

Basic Accounting Systems

In Chapters 1–4, an accounting system for **NetSolutions** was described and illustrated. An **accounting system** is the methods and procedures for collecting, classifying, summarizing, and reporting a business's financial and operating information. Most accounting systems, however, are more complex than NetSolutions'. For example, **Southwest Airlines**'s accounting system not only records basic transaction data but also records data on such items as ticket reservations, credit card collections, frequent-flier mileage, and aircraft maintenance.

As a business grows and changes, its accounting system also changes in a three-step process. This three-step process is as follows:

Step 1. *Analyze* user information needs.
Step 2. *Design* the system to meet the user needs.
Step 3. *Implement* the system.

For NetSolutions, our analysis determined that Chris Clark needed financial statements for the new business (Step 1). In Chapters 1–4, we designed the system using a basic manual system that included a chart of accounts, a two-column journal, and a general ledger (Step 2). Finally, we implemented the system to record transactions and prepare financial statements (Step 3).

Once a system has been implemented, input from users is used to analyze and improve the system. For example, in later chapters, NetSolutions expands its chart of accounts to record more complex transactions.

The accounting system design consists of:

- internal controls and
- information processing methods.

Internal controls are the policies and procedures that protect assets from misuse, ensure that business information is accurate, and ensure that laws and regulations are being followed. Internal controls are discussed in Chapter 8.

Processing methods are the means by which the accounting system collects, summarizes, and reports accounting information. These methods may be either *manual* or *computerized*. We begin by describing and illustrating a simple manual accounting system that uses special journals and subsidiary ledgers. This is followed by a discussion of more complex computerized accounting systems.

Manual Accounting Systems

Obj. 2 Journalize and post transactions in a manual accounting system that uses subsidiary ledgers and special journals.

Accounting systems are manual or computerized. Understanding a manual accounting system is useful in identifying relationships between accounting data and reports. Also, most computerized systems use principles from manual systems.

In Chapters 1–4, the transactions for NetSolutions were manually recorded in an all-purpose (two-column) journal. The journal entries were then posted individually to the accounts in the ledger. Such a system is simple to use and easy to understand when there are a small number of transactions. However, when a business has a large number of *similar* transactions, using an all-purpose journal is inefficient and impractical. In such cases, subsidiary ledgers and special journals are useful.

Subsidiary Ledgers

A large number of individual accounts with a common characteristic can be grouped together in a separate ledger called a **subsidiary ledger**. The primary ledger, which contains all of the balance sheet and income statement accounts, is then called the **general ledger**. Each subsidiary ledger is represented in the general ledger by a summarizing account, called a **controlling account**. The sum of the balances of the accounts in a subsidiary ledger must equal the balance of the related controlling account. Thus, a subsidiary ledger is a secondary ledger that supports a controlling account in the general ledger.

Two of the most common subsidiary ledgers are as follows:

- Accounts receivable subsidiary ledger
- Accounts payable subsidiary ledger

The **accounts receivable subsidiary ledger**, or *customers ledger*, lists the individual customer accounts in alphabetical order. The controlling account in the general ledger that summarizes the debits and credits to the individual customer accounts is Accounts Receivable.

The **accounts payable subsidiary ledger**, or *creditors ledger*, lists individual creditor accounts in alphabetical order. The related controlling account in the general ledger is Accounts Payable.

The relationship between the general ledger and the accounts receivable and accounts payable subsidiary ledgers is illustrated in Exhibit 1.

Many businesses use subsidiary ledgers for other accounts in addition to Accounts Receivable and Accounts Payable. For example, businesses often use an equipment subsidiary ledger to keep track of each item of equipment purchased, its cost, location, and other data. Moreover, merchandising and manufacturing businesses use additional types of subsidiary ledgers that are unique to them. We simplify by illustrating accounting systems for a service business.

Note: Subsidiary ledgers provide detail of individual accounts that are summarized in a controlling account in the general ledger.

Special Journals

One method of processing transactions more efficiently in a manual system is to use special journals. **Special journals** are designed to record a single kind of transaction that occurs frequently. For example, since most businesses have many transactions in which cash is paid out, they will likely use a special journal for recording cash payments. Likewise, they will use another special journal for recording cash receipts.

Link to Intuit

Intuit has subsidiary ledgers for property and equipment, inventory, and investments.

EXHIBIT 1

General Ledger and Subsidiary Ledgers

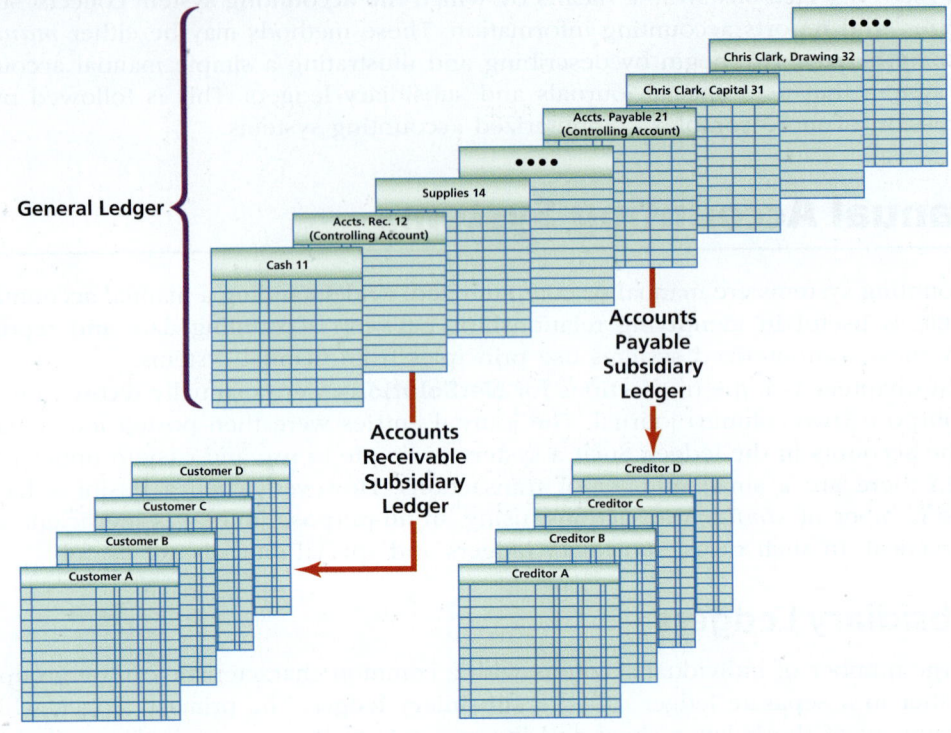

Note

Special journals summarize common transactions that are used frequently.

The format and number of special journals that a business uses depends on the nature of the business. The common transactions and their related special journals used by small service businesses are as follows:

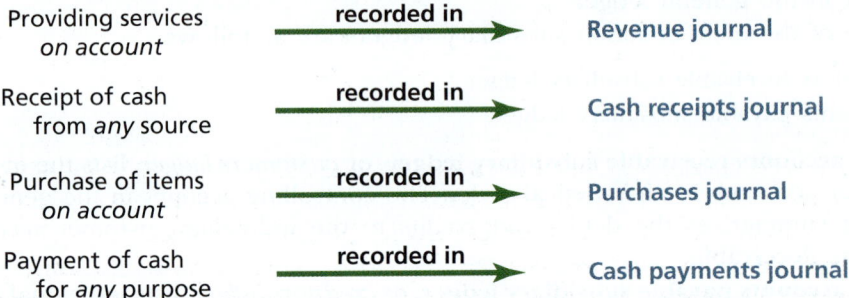

The all-purpose two-column journal, called the **general journal** or simply the *journal*, can be used for entries that do not fit into any of the special journals. For example, adjusting and closing entries are recorded in the general journal.

The following types of transactions, special journals, and subsidiary ledgers are described and illustrated for **NetSolutions**:

Transaction	Special Journal	Subsidiary Ledger
Fees earned on account	Revenue journal	Accounts receivable subsidiary ledger
Cash receipts	Cash receipts journal	Accounts receivable subsidiary ledger
Purchases on account	Purchases journal	Accounts payable subsidiary ledger
Cash payments	Cash payments journal	Accounts payable subsidiary ledger

As shown, transactions that are recorded in the revenue and cash receipts journals will affect the accounts receivable subsidiary ledger as part of the *revenue and collection cycle*. Likewise, transactions that are recorded in the purchases and cash payments journals will affect the accounts payable subsidiary ledger as part of the *purchases and payments cycle*.

We will assume that NetSolutions had the following selected general ledger balances on March 1, 2019:

Account Number	Account	Balance
11	Cash	$6,200
12	Accounts Receivable	3,400
14	Supplies	2,500
18	Office Equipment	2,500
21	Accounts Payable	1,230

Revenue Journal

Fees earned on account would be recorded in the **revenue journal**. *Cash fees earned* would be recorded in the cash receipts journal.

To illustrate the efficiency of using a revenue journal, an example for NetSolutions is used. Specifically, assume that NetSolutions recorded the following four revenue transactions for March in its general journal:

Date	Description	Post. Ref.	Debit	Credit
2019 Mar. 2	Accounts Receivable—Accessories By Claire	12/✓	2,200	
	Fees Earned	41		2,200
6	Accounts Receivable—RapZone	12/✓	1,750	
	Fees Earned	41		1,750
18	Accounts Receivable—Web Cantina	12/✓	2,650	
	Fees Earned	41		2,650
27	Accounts Receivable—Accessories By Claire	12/✓	3,000	
	Fees Earned	41		3,000

For the preceding entries, NetSolutions recorded eight accounts and eight amounts. In addition, NetSolutions made 12 postings to the ledgers—four to Accounts Receivable in the general ledger, four to the accounts receivable subsidiary ledger (indicated by each check mark), and four to Fees Earned in the general ledger.

The preceding revenue transactions could be recorded more efficiently in a revenue journal, as shown in Exhibit 2. In each revenue transaction, the amount of the debit to Accounts Receivable is the same as the amount of the credit to Fees Earned. Thus, only a single amount column is necessary. The date, invoice number, customer name, and amount are entered separately for each transaction.

Revenues are normally recorded in the revenue journal when the company sends an invoice to the customer. An **invoice** is the bill that is sent to the customer by the company. Each invoice is normally numbered in sequence for future reference.

To illustrate, assume that on March 2, NetSolutions issued Invoice No. 615 to Accessories By Claire for fees earned of $2,200. This transaction is entered in the revenue journal, shown in Exhibit 2, by entering the following items:

1. Date column: *Mar. 2*
2. Invoice No. column: *615*
3. Account Debited column: *Accessories By Claire*
4. Accts. Rec. Dr./Fees Earned Cr. column: *2,200*

EXHIBIT 2
Revenue Journal

			Revenue Journal		Page 35
Date		Invoice No.	Account Debited	Post. Ref.	Accts. Rec. Dr. Fees Earned Cr.
2019					
Mar.	2	615	Accessories By Claire		2,200
	6	616	RapZone		1,750
	18	617	Web Cantina		2,650
	27	618	Accessories By Claire		3,000
	31				9,600

The process of posting from a revenue journal, shown in Exhibit 3, is as follows:

Step 1. Each transaction is posted individually to a customer account in the accounts receivable subsidiary ledger. Postings to customer accounts should be made on a regular basis. In this way, the customer's account will show a current balance.

To illustrate, Exhibit 3 shows the posting of the $2,200 debit to Accessories By Claire in the accounts receivable subsidiary ledger. After the posting, Accessories By Claire has a debit balance of $2,200.

Step 2. To provide a trail of the entries posted to the general and subsidiary ledgers, the source of these entries is indicated in the Posting Reference column of each account by inserting the letter R (for revenue journal) and the page number of the revenue journal.

To illustrate, Exhibit 3 shows that after $2,200 is posted to Accessories By Claire's account, R35 is inserted in the Post. Ref. column of the account.

Step 3. To indicate that the transaction has been posted to the accounts receivable subsidiary ledger, a check mark (✓) is inserted in the Post. Ref. column of the revenue journal, as shown in Exhibit 3.

To illustrate, Exhibit 3 shows that a check mark (✓) has been inserted in the Post. Ref. column next to Accessories By Claire in the revenue journal to indicate that the $2,200 has been posted.

Step 4. A single monthly total is posted to Accounts Receivable and Fees Earned in the general ledger. This total is equal to the sum of the month's debits to the individual accounts in the subsidiary ledger. It is posted in the general ledger as a debit to Accounts Receivable and a credit to Fees Earned, as shown in Exhibit 3. The accounts receivable account number (12) and the fees earned account number (41) are then inserted below the total in the revenue journal to indicate that the posting is completed.

To illustrate, Exhibit 3 shows that the monthly total of $9,600 was posted as a debit to Accounts Receivable (12) and as a credit to Fees Earned (41).

Exhibit 3 illustrates the efficiency gained by using the revenue journal rather than the general journal. Specifically, all of the transactions for fees earned during the month are posted to the general ledger only once—at the end of the month.

Chapter 5 Accounting Systems 237

Revenue Journal and Postings — EXHIBIT 3

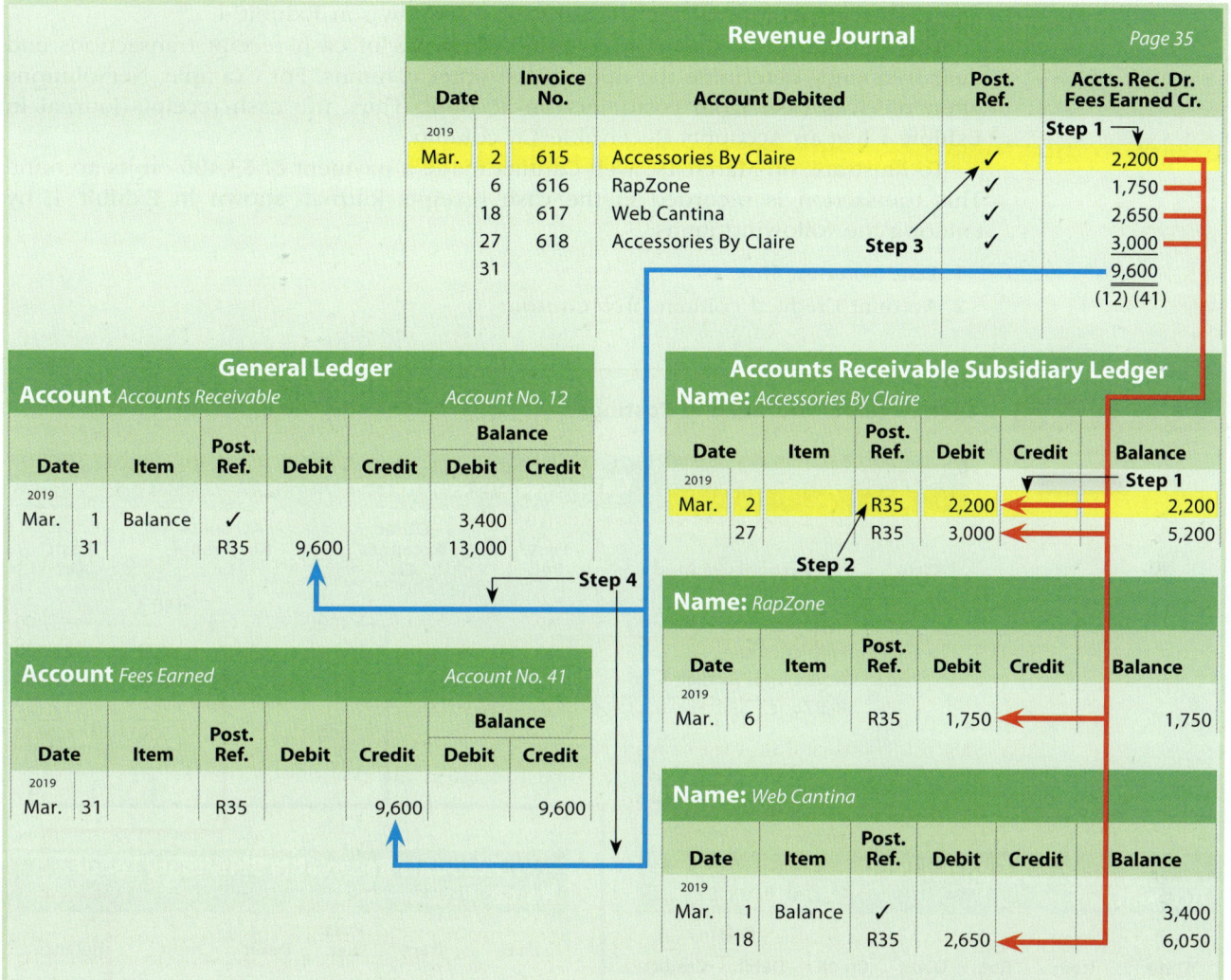

Example Exercise 5-1 Revenue Journal   Obj. 2

The following revenue transactions occurred during December:

Dec. 5. Issued Invoice No. 302 to Butler Company for services provided on account, $5,000.
    9. Issued Invoice No. 303 to JoJo Enterprises for services provided on account, $2,100.
    15. Issued Invoice No. 304 to Salinas Inc. for services provided on account, $3,250.

Record these transactions in a revenue journal as illustrated in Exhibit 2.

Follow My Example 5-1

REVENUE JOURNAL

Date	Invoice No.	Account Debited	Post. Ref.	Accts. Rec. Dr. Fees Earned Cr.
Dec. 5	302	Butler Company		5,000
9	303	JoJo Enterprises		2,100
15	304	Salinas Inc.		3,250

Practice Exercises: PE 5-1A, PE 5-1B

Cash Receipts Journal

All transactions that involve the receipt of cash are recorded in a **cash receipts journal**. The cash receipts journal for NetSolutions is shown in Exhibit 4.

This journal has a Cash Dr. column. The types of cash receipt transactions and their frequency determine the titles of the other columns. For example, NetSolutions often receives cash from customers on account. Thus, the cash receipts journal in Exhibit 4 has an Accounts Receivable Cr. column.

To illustrate, on March 19, Web Cantina made a payment of $3,400 on its account. This transaction is recorded in the cash receipts journal, shown in Exhibit 4, by entering the following items:

1. Date column: *Mar. 19*
2. Account Credited column: *Web Cantina*

EXHIBIT 4   Cash Receipts Journal and Postings

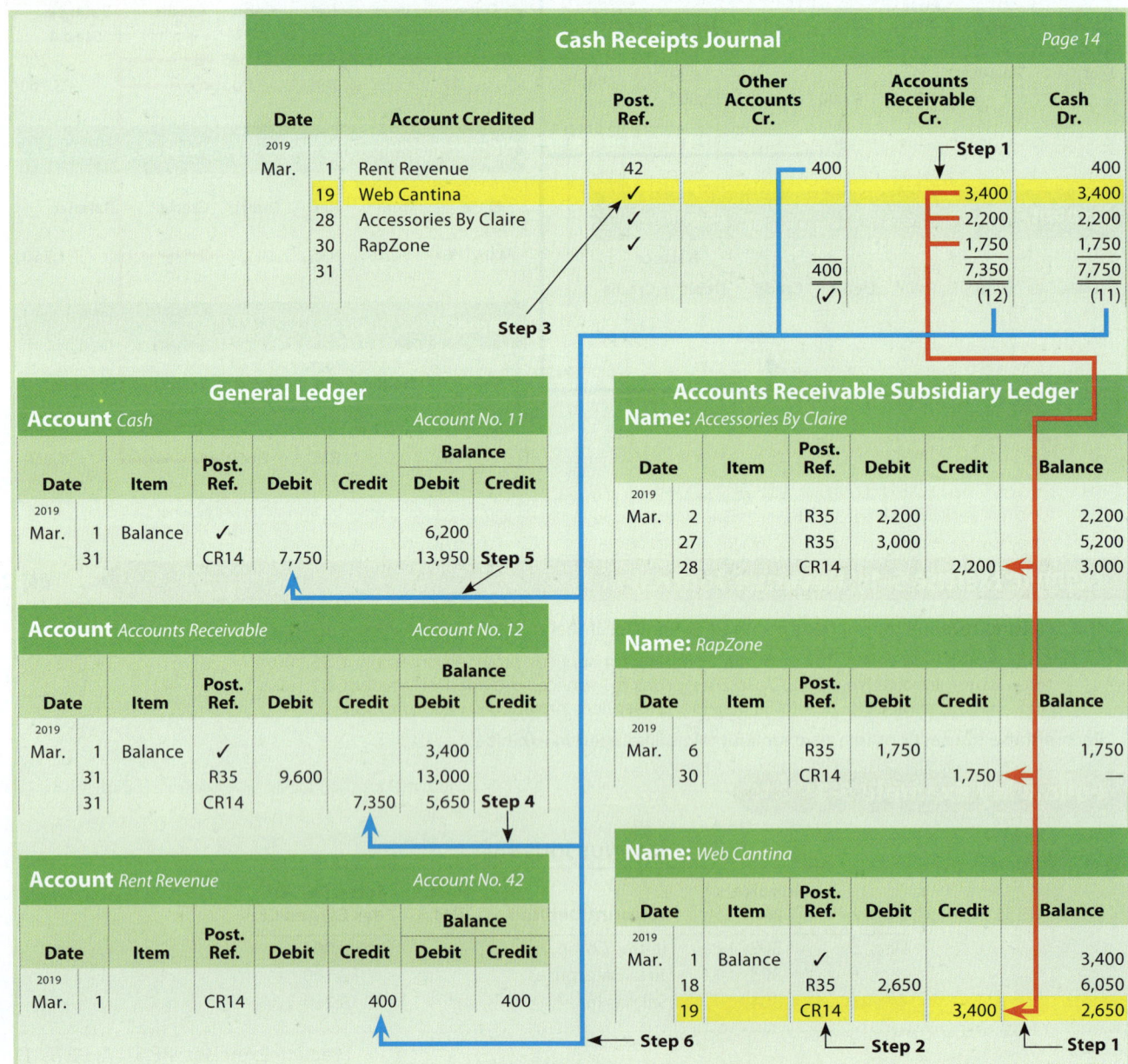

3. Accounts Receivable Cr. column: *3,400*
4. Cash Dr. column: *3,400*

The Other Accounts Cr. column in Exhibit 4 is used for recording credits to any account for which there is no special credit column. For example, NetSolutions received cash on March 1 for rent. Since no special column exists for Rent Revenue, Rent Revenue is entered in the Account Credited column. Thus, this transaction is recorded in the cash receipts journal, shown in Exhibit 4, by entering the following items:

1. Date column: *Mar. 1*
2. Account Credited column: *Rent Revenue*
3. Other Accounts Cr. column: *400*
4. Cash Dr. column: *400*

The process of posting from the cash receipts journal, shown in Exhibit 4, is as follows:

Step 1. Each transaction involving the receipt of cash on account is posted individually to a customer account in the accounts receivable subsidiary ledger. Postings to customer accounts should be made on a regular basis. In this way, the customer's account will show a current balance.

To illustrate, Exhibit 4 shows on March 19 the receipt of $3,400 on account from Web Cantina. The posting of the $3,400 credit to Web Cantina in the accounts receivable subsidiary ledger is also shown in Exhibit 4. After the posting, Web Cantina has a debit balance of $2,650.

Step 2. To provide a trail of the entries posted to the subsidiary ledger, the source of these entries is indicated in the Posting Reference column of each account by inserting the letters CR (for cash receipts journal) and the page number of the cash receipts journal.

To illustrate, Exhibit 4 shows that after $3,400 is posted to Web Cantina's account in the accounts receivable subsidiary ledger, CR14 is inserted in the Post. Ref. column of the account.

Step 3. To indicate that the transaction has been posted to the accounts receivable subsidiary ledger, a check mark (✓) is inserted in the Posting Reference column of the cash receipts journal.

To illustrate, Exhibit 4 shows that a check mark (✓) has been inserted in the Post. Ref. column next to Web Cantina to indicate that the $3,400 has been posted.

Step 4. A single monthly total of the Accounts Receivable Cr. column is posted to the accounts receivable general ledger account. This is the total cash received on account and is posted as a credit to Accounts Receivable. The accounts receivable account number (12) is then inserted below the Accounts Receivable Cr. column to indicate that the posting is complete.

To illustrate, Exhibit 4 shows that the monthly total of $7,350 was posted as a credit to Accounts Receivable (12).

Step 5. A single monthly total of the Cash Dr. column is posted to the cash general ledger account. This is the total cash received during the month and is posted as a debit to Cash. The cash account number (11) is then inserted below the Cash Dr. column to indicate that the posting is complete.

To illustrate, Exhibit 4 shows that the monthly total of $7,750 was posted as a debit to Cash (11).

Step 6. The accounts listed in the Other Accounts Cr. column are posted on a regular basis as a separate credit to each account. The account number is then inserted in the Post. Ref. column to indicate that the posting is complete. Because accounts in the

240 Chapter 5 Accounting Systems

Other Accounts Cr. column are posted individually, a check mark is placed below the column total at the end of the month to show that no further action is needed.

To illustrate, Exhibit 4 shows that $400 was posted as a credit to Rent Revenue in the general ledger and the rent revenue account number (42) was entered in the Post. Ref. column of the cash receipts journal. Also, at the end of the month, a check mark (✓) is entered below the Other Accounts Cr. column to indicate that no further action is needed.

Accounts Receivable Control Account and Subsidiary Ledger

After all posting has been completed for the month, the balances in the accounts receivable subsidiary ledger should be totaled. This total can be summarized in a separate schedule of customer balances. The total should then be compared with the balance of the accounts receivable controlling account in the general ledger. If the controlling account and the subsidiary ledger do not agree, an error has occurred and must be located and corrected.

The total of **NetSolutions**' accounts receivable customer balances is $5,650. This total agrees with the balance of its accounts receivable controlling account on March 31, 2019, as follows:

> **Note**
> The balance of the accounts receivable controlling account equals the sum of the customer account balances.

> **Link to Intuit**
> **Helm Inc.**, an **Intuit** customer, will be represented by a subsidiary customer ledger in Intuit's accounting system.

Accounts Receivable (Controlling)

Balance, March 1, 2019	$ 3,400
Total debits (from revenue journal)	9,600
Total credits (from cash receipts journal)	(7,350)
Balance, March 31, 2019	$ 5,650

NetSolutions
Accounts Receivable Customer Balances
March 31, 2019

Accessories By Claire	$3,000
RapZone	0
Web Cantina	2,650
Total accounts receivable	$5,650

Equal debit balances

Example Exercise 5-2 Accounts Receivable Subsidiary Ledger   Obj. 2

The debits and credits from two transactions are presented in the following customer account:

NAME   Sweet Tooth Confections
ADDRESS 1212 Lombard St.

Date	Item	Post. Ref.	Debit	Credit	Balance
July 1	Balance	✓			625
7	Invoice 35	R12	86		711
31	Invoice 31	CR4		122	589

Describe each transaction and the source of each posting.

Follow My Example 5-2

July 7. Provided $86 of services on account to Sweet Tooth Confections, itemized on Invoice No. 35. Amount posted from Page 12 of the revenue journal.
   31. Collected cash of $122 from Sweet Tooth Confections (Invoice No. 31). Amount posted from Page 4 of the cash receipts journal.

Practice Exercises: PE 5-2A, PE 5-2B

Purchases Journal

All *purchases on account* are recorded in the **purchases journal**. *Cash purchases would be recorded in the cash payments journal.* The purchases journal for **NetSolutions** is shown in Exhibit 5.

Purchases Journal and Postings — EXHIBIT 5

Purchases Journal — Page 11

Date	Account Credited	Post. Ref.	Accounts Payable Cr.	Supplies Dr.	Other Accounts Dr.	Post. Ref.	Amount
2019				Step 1			
Mar. 3	Howard Supplies	✓	600	600			
7	Donnelly Supplies	✓	420	420			
12	Jewett Business Systems	✓	2,800		Office Equipment	18	2,800
19	Donnelly Supplies	✓	1,450	1,450			
27	Howard Supplies	✓	960	960			
31			6,230	3,430			2,800
			(21)	(14)			(✓)

Step 3

General Ledger

Account Supplies — Account No. 14

Date	Item	Post. Ref.	Debit	Credit	Balance Debit	Balance Credit
2019						
Mar. 1	Balance	✓			2,500	
31		P11	3,430		5,930 Step 5	

Account Office Equipment — Account No. 18

Date	Item	Post. Ref.	Debit	Credit	Balance Debit	Balance Credit
2019						
Mar. 1	Balance	✓			2,500	
12		P11	2,800		5,300 Step 6	

Account Accounts Payable — Account No. 21

Date	Item	Post. Ref.	Debit	Credit	Balance Debit	Balance Credit
2019						
Mar. 1	Balance	✓				1,230
31		P11		6,230		7,460 Step 4

Accounts Payable Subsidiary Ledger

Name: Donnelly Supplies

Date	Item	Post. Ref.	Debit	Credit	Balance
2019					
Mar. 7		P11		420	420
19		P11		1,450	1,870

Name: Grayco Supplies

Date	Item	Post. Ref.	Debit	Credit	Balance
2019					
Mar. 1	Balance	✓			1,230

Step 1

Name: Howard Supplies

Date	Item	Post. Ref.	Debit	Credit	Balance
2019					
Mar. 3		P11		600	600
27		P11		960	1,560

Step 2

Name: Jewett Business Systems

Date	Item	Post. Ref.	Debit	Credit	Balance
2019					
Mar. 12		P11		2,800	2,800

The amounts purchased on account are recorded in the purchases journal in an Accounts Payable Cr. column. The items most often purchased on account determine the titles of the other columns. For example, NetSolutions often purchases supplies on account. Thus, the purchases journal in Exhibit 5 has a Supplies Dr. column.

To illustrate, on March 3, NetSolutions purchased $600 of supplies on account from Howard Supplies. This transaction is recorded in the purchases journal, shown in Exhibit 5, by entering the following items:

1. Date column: *Mar. 3*
2. Account Credited column: *Howard Supplies*
3. Accounts Payable Cr. column: *600*
4. Supplies Dr. column: *600*

The Other Accounts Dr. column in Exhibit 5 is used to record purchases on account of any item for which there is no special debit column. The title of the account to be debited is entered in the Other Accounts Dr. column, and the amount is entered in the Amount column.

At the end of the month, all of the amount columns are totaled. The debits must equal the credits. If the debits do not equal the credits, an error has occurred. Before proceeding further, the error must be found and corrected.

The process of posting from the purchases journal shown in Exhibit 5 is as follows:

Step 1. Each transaction involving a purchase on account is posted individually to a creditor's account in the accounts payable subsidiary ledger. Postings to creditor accounts should be made on a regular basis. In this way, the creditor's account will show a current balance.

To illustrate, Exhibit 5 shows on March 3 the purchase of supplies of $600 on account from Howard Supplies. The posting of the $600 credit to Howard Supplies accounts payable subsidiary ledger is also shown in Exhibit 5. After the posting, Howard Supplies has a credit balance of $600.

Step 2. To provide a trail of the entries posted to the subsidiary and general ledgers, the source of these entries is indicated in the Posting Reference column of each account by inserting the letter P (for purchases journal) and the page number of the purchases journal.

To illustrate, Exhibit 5 shows that after $600 is posted to Howard Supplies account, P11 is inserted in the Post. Ref. column of the account.

Step 3. To indicate that the transaction has been posted to the accounts payable subsidiary ledger, a check mark (✓) is inserted in the Posting Reference column of the purchases journal, as shown in Exhibit 5.

To illustrate, Exhibit 5 shows that a check mark (✓) has been inserted in the Post. Ref. column next to Howard Supplies to indicate that the $600 has been posted.

Step 4. A single monthly total of the Accounts Payable Cr. column is posted to the accounts payable general ledger account. This is the total amount purchased on account and is posted as a credit to Accounts Payable. The accounts payable account number (21) is then inserted below the Accounts Payable Cr. column to indicate that the posting is complete.

To illustrate, Exhibit 5 shows that the monthly total of $6,230 was posted as a credit to Accounts Payable (21).

Step 5. A single monthly total of the Supplies Dr. column is posted to the supplies general ledger account. This is the total supplies purchased on account during the month and is posted as a debit to Supplies. The supplies account number (14) is then inserted below the Supplies Dr. column to indicate that the posting is complete.

To illustrate, Exhibit 5 shows that the monthly total of $3,430 was posted as a debit to Supplies (14).

Step 6. The accounts listed in the Other Accounts Dr. column are posted on a regular basis as a separate debit to each account. The account number is then inserted in the Post. Ref. column to indicate that the posting is complete. Because accounts in the Other Accounts Dr. column are posted individually, a check mark is placed below the column total at the end of the month to show that no further action is needed.

To illustrate, Exhibit 5 shows that $2,800 was posted as a debit to Office Equipment in the general ledger and the office equipment account number (18) was entered in the Post. Ref. column of the purchases journal. Also, at the end of the month, a check mark (✓) is entered below the Amount column to indicate that no further action is needed.

Example Exercise 5-3 Purchases Journal *Obj. 2*

The following purchase transactions occurred during October for Helping Hand Cleaners:

Oct. 11. Purchased cleaning supplies for $235, on account, from General Supplies.
    19. Purchased cleaning supplies for $110, on account, from Hubble Supplies.
    24. Purchased office equipment for $850, on account, from Office Warehouse.

Record these transactions in a purchases journal as illustrated at the top of Exhibit 5.

Follow My Example 5-3

PURCHASES JOURNAL

Date	Account Credited	Post. Ref.	Accounts Payable Cr.	Cleaning Supplies Dr.	Other Accounts Dr.	Post. Ref.	Amount
Oct. 11	General Supplies		235	235			
19	Hubble Supplies		110	110			
24	Office Warehouse		850		Office Equipment		850

Practice Exercises: PE 5-3A, PE 5-3B

Cash Payments Journal

All transactions that involve the payment of cash are recorded in a **cash payments journal**. The cash payments journal for NetSolutions is shown in Exhibit 6.

The cash payments journal shown in Exhibit 6 has a Cash Cr. column. The kinds of transactions in which cash is paid and how often they occur determine the titles of the other columns. For example, NetSolutions often pays cash to creditors on account. Thus, the cash payments journal in Exhibit 6 has an Accounts Payable Dr. column. In addition, NetSolutions makes all payments by check. Thus, a check number is entered for each payment in the Ck. No. (Check Number) column to the right of the Date column. The check numbers are helpful in controlling cash payments and provide a useful cross-reference.

To illustrate, on March 15, NetSolutions issued Check No. 151 for $1,230 to Grayco Supplies for payment on its account. This transaction is recorded in the cash payments journal shown in Exhibit 6 by entering the following items:

1. Date column: *Mar. 15*
2. Ck. No. column: *151*
3. Account Debited column: *Grayco Supplies*
4. Accounts Payable Dr. column: *1,230*
5. Cash Cr. column: *1,230*

The Other Accounts Dr. column in Exhibit 6 is used for recording debits to any account for which there is no special debit column. For example, NetSolutions issued Check No. 150 on March 2 for $1,600 in payment of March rent. This transaction is recorded in the cash payments journal, shown in Exhibit 6, by entering these items:

1. Date column: *Mar. 2*
2. Ck. No. column: *150*
3. Account Debited column: *Rent Expense*
4. Other Accounts Dr. column: *1,600*
5. Cash Cr. column: *1,600*

244 Chapter 5 Accounting Systems

EXHIBIT 6 Cash Payments Journal and Postings

Cash Payments Journal — Page 7

Date	Ck. No.	Account Debited	Post. Ref.	Other Accounts Dr.	Accounts Payable Dr.	Cash Cr.
2019 Mar. 2	150	Rent Expense	52	1,600		1,600
15	151	Grayco Supplies	✓		1,230	1,230
21	152	Jewett Business Systems	✓		2,800	2,800
22	153	Donnelly Supplies	✓		420	420
30	154	Utilities Expense	54	1,050		1,050
31	155	Howard Supplies	✓		600	600
31				2,650	5,050	7,700
				(✓)	(21)	(11)

Step 1, Step 3

General Ledger

Account Cash — Account No. 11

Date	Item	Post. Ref.	Debit	Credit	Balance Debit	Balance Credit
2019 Mar. 1	Balance	✓			6,200	
31		CR14	7,750		13,950	
31		CP7		7,700	6,250	

Step 5

Account Accounts Payable — Account No. 21

Date	Item	Post. Ref.	Debit	Credit	Balance Debit	Balance Credit
2019 Mar. 1	Balance	✓				1,230
31		P11		6,230		7,460
31		CP7	5,050			2,410

Step 4

Account Rent Expense — Account No. 52

Date	Item	Post. Ref.	Debit	Credit	Balance Debit	Balance Credit
2019 Mar. 2		CP7	1,600		1,600	

Step 6

Account Utilities Expense — Account No. 54

Date	Item	Post. Ref.	Debit	Credit	Balance Debit	Balance Credit
2019 Mar. 30		CP7	1,050		1,050	

Accounts Payable Subsidiary Ledger

Name: Donnelly Supplies

Date	Item	Post. Ref.	Debit	Credit	Balance
2019 Mar. 7		P11		420	420
19		P11		1,450	1,870
22		CP7	420		1,450

Name: Grayco Supplies

Date	Item	Post. Ref.	Debit	Credit	Balance
2019 Mar. 1	Balance	✓			1,230
15		CP7	1,230		—

Step 1, Step 2

Name: Howard Supplies

Date	Item	Post. Ref.	Debit	Credit	Balance
2019 Mar. 3		P11		600	600
27		P11		960	1,560
31		CP7	600		960

Name: Jewett Business Systems

Date	Item	Post. Ref.	Debit	Credit	Balance
2019 Mar. 12		P11		2,800	2,800
21		CP7	2,800		—

The process of posting from the cash payments journal, Exhibit 6, is as follows:

Step 1. Each transaction involving the payment of cash on account is posted individually to a creditor account in the accounts payable subsidiary ledger. Postings to creditor accounts should be made on a regular basis. In this way, the creditor's account will show a current balance.

To illustrate, Exhibit 6 shows on March 15 the payment of $1,230 on account to Grayco Supplies. The posting of the $1,230 debit to Grayco Supplies in the accounts payable subsidiary ledger is also shown in Exhibit 6. After the posting, Grayco Supplies has a zero balance.

Step 2. To provide a trail of the entries posted to the subsidiary and general ledgers, the source of these entries is indicated in the Posting Reference column of each account by inserting the letters CP (for cash payments journal) and the page number of the cash payments journal.

To illustrate, Exhibit 6 shows that after $1,230 is posted to Grayco Supplies account, CP7 is inserted in the Post. Ref. column of the account.

Step 3. To indicate that the transaction has been posted to the accounts payable subsidiary ledger, a check mark (✓) is inserted in the Posting Reference column of the cash payments journal.

To illustrate, Exhibit 6 shows that a check mark (✓) has been inserted in the Post. Ref. column next to Grayco Supplies to indicate that the $1,230 has been posted.

Step 4. A single monthly total of the Accounts Payable Dr. column is posted to the accounts payable general ledger account. This is the total cash paid on account and is posted as a debit to Accounts Payable. The accounts payable account number (21) is then inserted below the Accounts Payable Dr. column to indicate that the posting is complete.

To illustrate, Exhibit 6 shows that the monthly total of $5,050 was posted as a debit to Accounts Payable (21).

Step 5. A single monthly total of the Cash Cr. column is posted to the cash general ledger account. This is the total cash payments during the month and is posted as a credit to Cash. The cash account number (11) is then inserted below the Cash Cr. column to indicate that the posting is complete.

To illustrate, Exhibit 6 shows that the monthly total of $7,700 was posted as a credit to Cash (11).

Step 6. The accounts listed in the Other Accounts Dr. column are posted on a regular basis as a separate debit to each account. The account number is then inserted in the Post. Ref. column to indicate that the posting is complete. Because accounts in the Other Accounts Dr. column are posted individually, a check mark is placed below the column total at the end of the month to show that no further action is needed.

To illustrate, Exhibit 6 shows that $1,600 was posted as a debit to Rent Expense (52) and $1,050 was posted as a debit to Utilities Expense (54) in the general ledger. The account numbers (52 and 54, respectively) were entered in the Post. Ref. column of the cash payments journal. Also, at the end of the month, a check mark (✓) is entered below the Other Accounts Dr. column to indicate that no further action is needed.

Accounts Payable Control Account and Subsidiary Ledger

After all posting has been completed for the month, the balances in the accounts payable subsidiary ledger should be totaled. This total can be summarized in a separate schedule of creditor balances. The total should then be compared with the balance of the accounts payable controlling account in the general ledger. If the controlling account and the subsidiary ledger do not agree, an error has occurred and must be located and corrected.

Note

The balance of the accounts payable controlling account equals the sum of the creditor account balances.

246 Chapter 5 Accounting Systems

Link to Intuit
Ernst and Young, LLP, is **Intuit**'s financial statement auditor and, as such, will be represented by an accounts payable subsidiary ledger account in Intuit's accounting system.

The total of **NetSolutions**' accounts payable creditor balances is $2,410. This total agrees with the balance of its accounts payable controlling account on March 31, 2019, as follows:

Accounts Payable (Controlling)			NetSolutions Accounts Payable Creditor Balances March 31, 2019	
Balance, March 1, 2019	$1,230		Donnelly Supplies	$1,450
Total credits (from purchases journal)	6,230		Grayco Supplies	0
Total debits			Howard Supplies	960
(from cash payments journal)	(5,050)		Jewett Business Systems	0
Balance, March 31, 2019	$2,410		Total accounts payable	$2,410

Equal credit balances

Example Exercise 5-4 Accounts Payable Subsidiary Ledger *Obj. 2*

The debits and credits from two transactions are presented in the following creditor's (supplier's) account:

NAME   Lassiter Services Inc.
ADDRESS   301 St. Bonaventure Ave.

Date	Item	Post. Ref.	Debit	Credit	Balance
Aug. 1	Balance	✓			320
12	Invoice No. 101	CP36	200		120
22	Invoice No. 106	P16		140	260

Describe each transaction and the source of each posting.

Follow My Example 5-4

Aug. 12. Paid $200 to Lassiter Services Inc. on account (Invoice No. 101). Amount posted from Page 36 of the cash payments journal.

22. Purchased $140 of services on account from Lassiter Services Inc. itemized on Invoice No. 106. Amount posted from Page 16 of the purchases journal.

Practice Exercises: PE 5-4A, PE 5-4B

Business Connection

ACCOUNTING SYSTEMS AND PROFIT MEASUREMENT

A Greek restaurant owner in Canada had his own system of accounting. He kept his accounts payable in a cigar box on the left-hand side of his cash register, his daily cash returns in the cash register, and his receipts for paid bills in another cigar box on the right. A truly "manual" system.

When his youngest son graduated as an accountant, he was appalled by his father's primitive methods. "I don't know how you can run a business that way," he said. "How do you know what your profits are?"

"Well, son," the father replied, "when I got off the boat from Greece, I had nothing but the pants I was wearing. Today, your brother is a doctor. You are an accountant. Your sister is a speech therapist. Your mother and I have a nice car, a city house, and a country home. We have a good business, and everything is paid for...."

"So, you add all that together, subtract the pants, and there's your profit!"

Computerized Accounting Systems

Obj. 3 Describe and illustrate the use of a computerized accounting system.

Computerized accounting systems are widely used by even the smallest of companies. Computerized accounting systems have the following three main advantages over manual systems:

- Computerized systems simplify the record-keeping process by recording transactions in electronic journals or forms and, at the same time, posting them electronically to general and subsidiary ledger accounts.
- Computerized systems are generally more accurate than manual systems.
- Computerized systems provide management with current account balance information to support decision making, since account balances are posted as the transactions occur.

The popular QuickBooks accounting software for small- to medium-sized businesses is used to illustrate a computerized accounting system for **NetSolutions**. To simplify, the illustration is limited to transactions involving revenue earned on account and the subsequent recording of cash collections. Exhibit 7 illustrates the use of QuickBooks for NetSolutions to record transactions as follows:

Large companies have their accounting systems integrated within the company's automated business systems. Such integrated software is termed ERP, or enterprise resource planning.

Step 1. Record fees by completing an electronic invoice form and sending to customer (print and mail, or e-mail).

Sales transactions are entered using an electronic invoice form. The electronic form appears like a paper form with fields to input transaction data. The fields may have drop-down lists to ease data entry. After the form is completed, it is printed out and mailed, or e-mailed, to the customer.

To illustrate, on March 2, NetSolutions earned $2,200 on account from Accessories By Claire. As shown in Exhibit 7, Invoice No. 615 was created using an electronic form. Upon submitting the invoice form, QuickBooks automatically posts a $2,200 debit to the Accessories By Claire customer account and a credit to Fees Earned. An invoice is either e-mailed or printed for mailing to Accessories By Claire.

Step 2. Record collection of payment by completing a "receive payment" form.

Upon collection from the customer, a "receive payment" electronic form is opened and completed. As with the "invoice form," data are input into the various fields directly or by using drop-down lists.

To illustrate, a $2,200 payment was collected from Accessories By Claire on March 28. The $2,200 was applied to Invoice No. 615, as shown by the check mark (✓) next to the March 2 date at the bottom of the form in Exhibit 7. As shown at the bottom of the form, the March 27 invoice of $3,000 remains uncollected. When the screen is completed and submitted, a debit of $2,200 is automatically posted to the cash account and a credit for $2,200 is posted to the Accessories By Claire account. This causes the balance of the Accessories By Claire account to be reduced from $5,200 to $3,000.

Step 3. Prepare reports.

At any time, managers may request reports from the software. Three such reports include the following:

- "Accounts Receivable Customer Balances" lists as of a specific date the accounts receivable balances by customer.

To illustrate, the Accounts Receivable Customer Balances report shown in Exhibit 7 for NetSolutions was generated as of March 31, 2019. The total of the balances of the Accounts Receivable Customer Balances report of $5,650 agrees with the accounts receivable subsidiary ledger balance total we illustrated using a manual system for NetSolutions in Exhibit 4.

- "Fees Earned by Customer" lists revenue by customer for the month. It is created from the electronic invoice form used in step 1.

To illustrate, the Fees Earned by Customer report shown in Exhibit 7 for NetSolutions is for the month of March 2019. The $9,600 of total consulting fees earned agrees with the total of the revenue journal we illustrated using a manual system for NetSolutions in Exhibits 2 and 3.

248 Chapter 5 Accounting Systems

- "Cash Receipts" lists the cash receipts during the month.

To illustrate, the Cash Receipts report shown in Exhibit 7 for NetSolutions is for the month of March 2019. The total cash receipts of $7,750 agree with the total of the Cash Dr. column of the cash receipts journal we illustrated using a manual system for NetSolutions in Exhibit 4.

Quickbooks and other computerized accounting systems use electronic forms. Alternatively, some computerized systems use electronic special journals. Such journals are designed similar to those illustrated in the text. Additionally, electronic general journals are found in all computerized systems.

> **Link to Intuit**
> **Intuit** derives 50% of its revenues from small business accounting software.

EXHIBIT 7   **Revenue and Cash Receipts in QuickBooks**

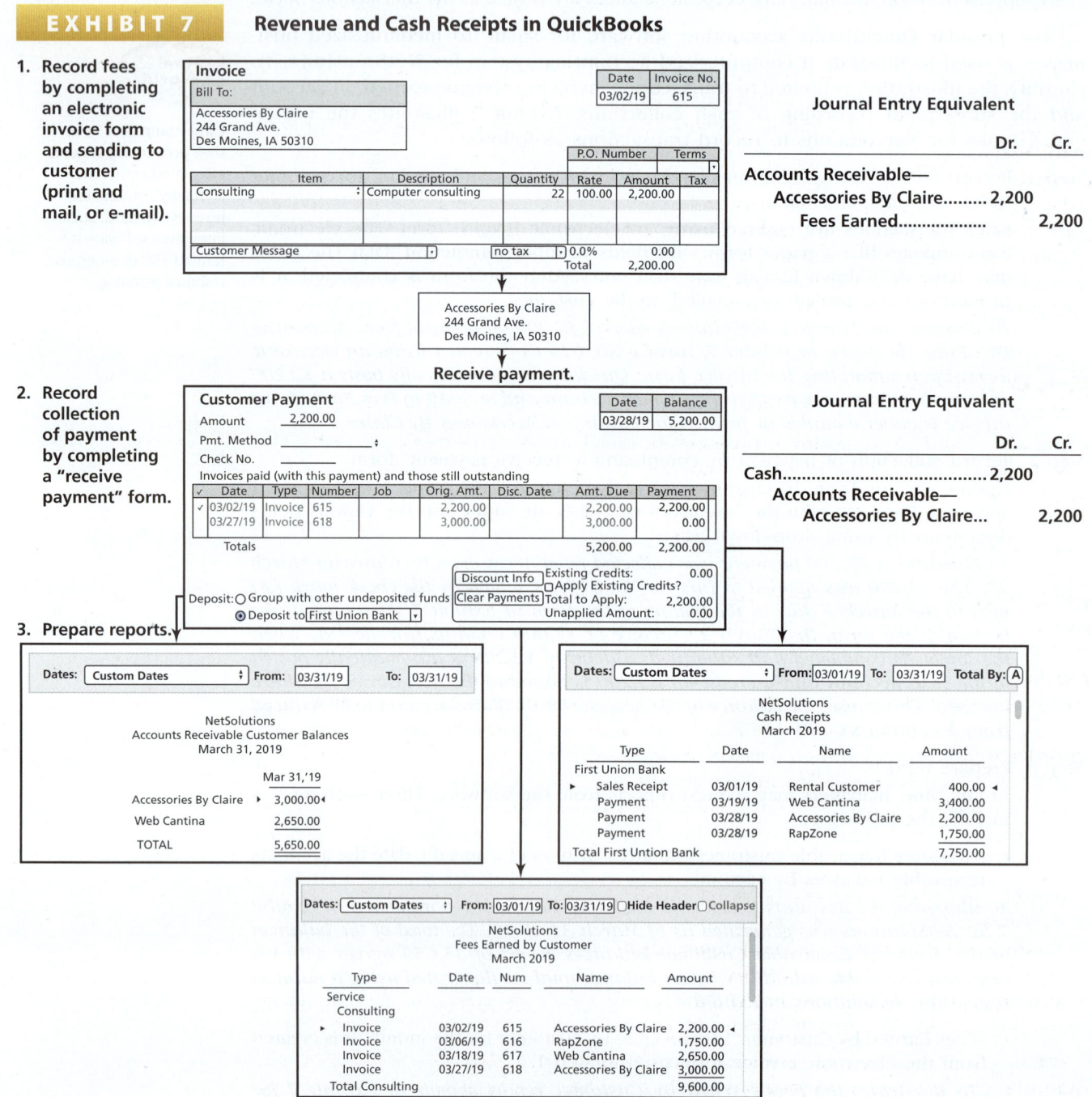

Business Connection

TURBOTAX

Intuit sells TurboTax®, one of the most popular tax preparation software products for individuals. With this product, the tax return is prepared using electronic tax forms. Thus, the familiar Form 1040 is presented as an electronic form with data-entry fields provided for the various line items. The advantage of this approach is that all the arithmetic and linking between forms is done automatically. A change in one field automatically updates all other linked fields.

In using these tools, the computer program prevents transactions in which the total debits do not equal the total credits. In such cases, an error screen will notify the user to correct data inputs. Likewise, the software will not make posting or mathematical errors.

In this section, revenue and cash receipt transactions are illustrated for NetSolutions using QuickBooks accounting software. Similar illustrations could be provided for purchases and cash payment transactions. A complete illustration of a computerized accounting system is beyond the scope of this text. However, this chapter provides a solid foundation for applying accounting system concepts in either a manual or a computerized system.

E-Commerce

Obj. 4 Describe the basic features of e-commerce.

Using the Internet to perform business transactions is termed **e-commerce**. The U.S. Census Bureau indicates that e-commerce represents more than $340 billion in retail sales, or more than 7% of all retail sales.[1] When transactions are between a company and a consumer, it is termed *B2C (business-to-consumer) e-commerce*. Examples of companies engaged in B2C e-commerce include Amazon.com, priceline.com Incorporated, and Apple Inc. The B2C business allows consumers to shop and receive goods at home, rather than going to the store. For example, Apple Inc. allows consumers to use its website to select and purchase Apple products for direct shipment to the home.

When transactions are conducted between two companies, it is termed *B2B (business-to-business) e-commerce*. Examples of companies engaged in B2B e-commerce include Cisco Systems, Inc., an Internet equipment manufacturer, and Union Pacific Corporation, a railroad. Union Pacific, for example, allows its business customers to order freight transportation services from its website.

The Internet creates opportunities for improving the speed and efficiency of transactions. As discussed, many companies are realizing these benefits of using e-commerce. Three additional areas where the Internet is being used for business purposes are as follows:

- **Supply chain management (SCM):** Internet applications to plan supply needs and coordinate them with suppliers.
- **Customer relationship management (CRM):** Internet applications to plan and coordinate marketing and sales effort.
- **Product life-cycle management (PLM):** Internet applications to plan and coordinate the product development and design process.

Many web applications generate accounting transactions as they occur. For example, shopping cart transactions on e-commerce sites generate the accounting revenue transactions for the seller.

---

[1] *Quarterly Retail E-commerce Sales*, U.S. Census Bureau News, U.S. Department of Commerce, February 17, 2016, p. 1.

INTEGRITY, OBJECTIVITY, AND ETHICS IN BUSINESS

ONLINE FRAUD

Online fraud accounted for losses equal to approximately 0.9% of all online revenue. As a result, online retailers are using address verification and credit card security codes as additional security measures. Address verification matches the customer's address to the address on file with the credit card company, while the security code is the additional four-digit code designed to reduce fictitious credit card transactions. In addition, merchants are using Google Maps lookups to verify that order addresses match real locations. Online fraud has been decreasing the last several years as a result of these and other measures.

Source: 15th Annual CyberSource Online Fraud Benchmark Survey, *CyberSource*, January 2015.

As the Internet continues to become the preferred method of conducting business, new applications will be developed. Many of these applications will be linked to the accounting system as transactions flow inside and outside the organization.

Obj. 5 Use segment analysis in evaluating the operating performance of a company.

Financial Analysis and Interpretation: Segment Analysis

Accounting systems often use computers to collect, classify, summarize, and report financial and operating information in a variety of ways. One way is to report revenue earned by different segments of business. Businesses may be segmented by region, by product or service, or by type of customer. Segment revenues are determined from the invoice data that are entered into the accounting system.

For example, **Intuit Inc.** uses invoice data from the accounting system to determine the amount of revenue earned by different products and services. Segment analysis uses horizontal and vertical comparisons to analyze the contributions of various segments to the total operating performance of a company. To illustrate, selected product and service segment revenue information from the notes to Intuit's financial statements for two recent fiscal years follows:

Segment	Recent Year (in millions)	Prior Year (in millions)
Small Business	$2,108	$2,158
Consumer Tax	1,800	1,663
Professional Tax	284	422
Total revenues	$4,192	$4,243

This segment information can be used to perform horizontal analysis using the prior year as the base year as follows:

Segment	Recent Year (in millions)	Prior Year (in millions)	Increase (Decrease) Amount	Percent
Small Business	$2,108	$2,158	$ (50)	(2.3)%
Consumer Tax	1,800	1,663	137	8.2
Professional Tax	284	422	(138)	(32.7)
Total revenues	$4,192	$4,243	$ (51)	(1.2)

Intuit's total revenues declined by over 1% between the two years. This decline was caused by a decline in both the Small Business and Professional Tax segments that were more than the increase in the Consumer Tax segment.

In addition, vertical analysis could be performed on the segment disclosures as follows:

	Recent Year		Prior Year	
Segment	Amount (in millions)	Percent	Amount (in millions)	Percent
Small Business	$2,108	50.3%	$2,158	50.9%
Consumer Tax	1,800	42.9	1,663	39.2
Professional Tax	284	6.8	422	9.9
Total revenues	$4,192	100.0%	$4,243	100.0%

The preceding analysis shows that revenue in the Consumer Tax segment increased as a percent of total revenues between the two years. The Small Business and the Professional Tax segments decreased as a percent of total revenues between the two years.

Both analyses together show that Intuit has declining revenue between the two years, caused mostly by a decline in Professional Tax, its smallest segment. The Consumer Tax segment exhibited revenue growth between the two years and is increasing its share of the total revenue between the two years. However, this growth was not sufficient to offset the declines in Small Business and Professional Tax.

Example Exercise 5-5 Segment Analysis   Obj. 5

Morse Company does business in two regional segments: East and West. The following annual revenue information was determined from the accounting system's invoice information:

Segment	20Y6	20Y5
East	$25,000	$20,000
West	50,000	60,000
Total revenues	$75,000	$80,000

Prepare horizontal and vertical analyses of the segments. Round to one decimal place.

Follow My Example 5-5

Horizontal analysis:

			Increase (Decrease)	
Segment	20Y6	20Y5	Amount	Percent
East	$25,000	$20,000	$ 5,000	25.0%
West	50,000	60,000	(10,000)	(16.7)
Total revenues	$75,000	$80,000	$ (5,000)	(6.3)

Vertical analysis:

	20Y6		20Y5	
Segment	Amount	Percent	Amount	Percent
East	$25,000	33.3%	$20,000	25.0%
West	50,000	66.7	60,000	75.0
Total revenues	$75,000	100.0%	$80,000	100.0%

Practice Exercises: PE 5-5A, PE 5-5B

At a Glance 5

Obj. 1 Define and describe an accounting system.

Key Points An accounting system is the methods and procedures for collecting, classifying, summarizing, and reporting a business's financial information. The three steps through which an accounting system evolves are (1) analysis of information needs, (2) design of the system, and (3) implementation of the system design.

Learning Outcomes	Example Exercises	Practice Exercises
• Define an accounting system.		
• Describe the three steps for designing an accounting system: (1) analysis, (2) design, and (3) implementation.		

Obj. 2 Journalize and post transactions in a manual accounting system that uses subsidiary ledgers and special journals.

Key Points Subsidiary ledgers may be used to maintain separate records for customers and creditors (vendors). A controlling account in the general ledger summarizes the subsidiary ledger accounts. The sum of the subsidiary ledger account balances must agree with the balance in the related controlling account.

Learning Outcomes	Example Exercises	Practice Exercises
• Prepare a revenue journal and post services provided on account to individual customer accounts and the column total to the corresponding general ledger accounts.	EE5-1	PE5-1A, 5-1B
• Prepare a cash receipts journal and post collections on account to individual customer accounts. Post Other Accounts column entries individually and special column totals to the corresponding general ledger accounts.	EE5-2	PE5-2A, 5-2B
• Prepare a purchases journal and post amounts owed to individual creditor accounts. Post Other Accounts column entries individually and special column totals to the corresponding general ledger accounts.	EE5-3	PE5-3A, 5-3B
• Prepare a cash payments journal and post the amounts paid to individual creditor accounts. Post Other Accounts column entries individually and special column totals to the corresponding general ledger accounts.	EE5-4	PE5-4A, 5-4B

Obj. 3 Describe and illustrate the use of a computerized accounting system.

Key Points Computerized accounting systems are similar to manual systems. The main advantages of a computerized accounting system are the simultaneous recording and posting of transactions, high degree of accuracy, and timeliness of reporting.

Learning Outcomes	Example Exercises	Practice Exercises
• Differentiate between a manual and a computerized accounting system.		
• Illustrate revenue and cash receipts transactions using QuickBooks.		

Obj. 4 — Describe the basic features of e-commerce.

Key Points Using the Internet to perform business transactions is termed e-commerce. B2C e-commerce involves Internet transactions between a business and consumer, while B2B e-commerce involves Internet transactions between businesses. More elaborate e-commerce involves planning and coordinating suppliers, customers, and product design.

Learning Outcomes	Example Exercises	Practice Exercises
• Define e-commerce and describe the major trends in e-commerce.		

Obj. 5 — Use segment analysis in evaluating the operating performance of a company.

Key Points Businesses may be segmented by region, by product or service, or by type of customer. Segment revenues can be analyzed using horizontal and vertical analyses. Such analyses are useful to management for evaluating the causes of business performance.

Learning Outcomes	Example Exercises	Practice Exercises
• Prepare horizontal and vertical analyses for business segments.	EE5-5	PE5-5A, 5-5B

Illustrative Problem

Selected transactions of O'Malley Co. for the month of May are as follows:

a. May 1. Issued Check No. 1001 in payment of rent for May, $1,200.
b.   2. Purchased office supplies on account from McMillan Co., $3,600.
c.   4. Issued Check No. 1003 in payment of freight charges on the supplies purchased on May 2, $320.
d.   8. Provided services on account to Waller Co., Invoice No. 51, $4,500.
e.   9. Issued Check No. 1005 for office supplies purchased, $450.
f.   10. Received cash for monthly rental of unused storage space, $120.
g.   11. Purchased office equipment on account from Fender Office Products, $15,000.
h.   12. Issued Check No. 1010 in payment of the supplies purchased from McMillan Co. on May 2, $3,600.
i.   16. Provided services on account to Riese Co., Invoice No. 58, $8,000.
j.   18. Received $4,500 from Waller Co. in payment of May 8 invoice.
k.   20. Invested additional cash in the business, $10,000.
l.   25. Provided services for cash, $15,900.
m.   30. Issued Check No. 1040 for withdrawal of cash for personal use, $1,000.
n.   30. Issued Check No. 1041 in payment of electricity and water invoices, $690.
o.   30. Issued Check No. 1042 in payment of office and sales salaries for May, $15,800.
p.   31. Journalized adjusting entries from the work sheet prepared for the fiscal year ended May 31.

(Continued)

254 Chapter 5 Accounting Systems

O'Malley Co. maintains journals and subsidiary ledgers as follows:

Journals	Subsidiary Ledgers
Revenue	Accounts Receivable
Purchases	Accounts Payable
Cash Receipts	
Cash Payments	
General	

Instructions

1. Indicate the journal in which each of the preceding transactions, (a) through (p), would be recorded.

2. Indicate whether an account in the accounts receivable or accounts payable subsidiary ledgers would be affected for each of the preceding transactions.

3. Journalize transactions (b), (c), (d), (h), and (j) in the appropriate journals.

Solution

	1. Journal	2. Subsidiary Ledger
a.	Cash payments journal	None
b.	Purchases journal	Accounts payable ledger
c.	Cash payments journal	None
d.	Revenue journal	Accounts receivable ledger
e.	Cash payments journal	None
f.	Cash receipts journal	None
g.	Purchases journal	Accounts payable ledger
h.	Cash payments journal	Accounts payable ledger
i.	Revenue journal	Accounts receivable ledger
j.	Cash receipts journal	Accounts receivable ledger
k.	Cash receipts journal	None
l.	Cash receipts journal	None
m.	Cash payments journal	None
n.	Cash payments journal	None
o.	Cash payments journal	None
p.	General journal	None

3.
Transaction (b):

Purchases Journal

Date	Account Credited	Post. Ref.	Accounts Payable Cr.	Office Supplies Dr.	Other Accounts Dr.	Post. Ref.	Amount
May 2	McMillan Co.		3,600	3,600			

Transactions (c) and (h):

Cash Payments Journal

Date	Ck. No.	Account Debited	Post. Ref.	Other Accounts Dr.	Accounts Payable Dr.	Cash Cr.
May 4	1003	Freight Expense		320		320
12	1010	McMillan Co.			3,600	3,600

Transaction (d):

Revenue Journal				
Date	Invoice No.	Account Debited	Post. Ref.	Accts. Rec. Dr. Fees Earned Cr.
May 8	51	Waller Co.		4,500

Transaction (j):

Cash Receipts Journal					
Date	Account Credited	Post. Ref.	Other Accounts Cr.	Accounts Receivable Cr.	Cash Dr.
May 18	Waller Co.			4,500	4,500

Key Terms

accounting system (232)
accounts payable subsidiary ledger (233)
accounts receivable subsidiary ledger (233)
cash payments journal (243)

cash receipts journal (238)
controlling account (233)
e-commerce (249)
general journal (234)
general ledger (233)
internal controls (232)

invoice (235)
purchases journal (240)
revenue journal (235)
special journals (233)
subsidiary ledger (233)

Discussion Questions

1. Why would a company maintain separate accounts receivable ledgers for each customer, as opposed to maintaining a single accounts receivable ledger for all customers?

2. What are the major advantages of the use of special journals?

3. In recording 400 fees earned on account during a single month, how many times will it be necessary to write Fees Earned (a) if each transaction, including fees earned, is recorded individually in a two-column general journal; (b) if each transaction for fees earned is recorded in a revenue journal?

4. How many postings to Fees Earned for the month would be needed in Discussion Question 3 if the procedure described in (a) had been used; if the procedure described in (b) had been used?

5. During the current month, the following errors occurred in recording transactions in the purchases journal or in posting from it:

   a. An invoice for $1,875 of supplies from Kelly Co. was recorded as having been received from Kelley Co., another supplier.
   b. A credit of $420 to Blackstone Company was posted as $240 in the subsidiary ledger.
   c. An invoice for equipment of $4,800 was recorded as $4,000.
   d. The Accounts Payable column of the purchases journal was overstated by $3,600.

   How will each error come to the bookkeeper's attention, other than by chance discovery?

6. Assuming the use of a two-column general journal, a purchases journal, and a cash payments journal as illustrated in this chapter, indicate the journal in which each of the following transactions should be recorded:

   a. Purchase of office supplies on account.
   b. Purchase of supplies for cash.
   c. Purchase of store equipment on account.

256 Chapter 5 Accounting Systems

d. Payment of cash on account to creditor.
e. Payment of cash for office supplies.

7. What is an electronic form, and how is it used in a computerized accounting system?

8. When are transactions posted in a computerized accounting system?

9. What happens to the special journal in a computerized accounting system that uses electronic forms?

10. How would e-commerce improve the revenue/collection cycle?

Practice Exercises

Example Exercises

EE 5-1 p. 237 **PE 5-1A Revenue journal** OBJ. 2

The following revenue transactions occurred during August:

Aug. 4. Issued Invoice No. 162 to Carson Enterprises Co. for services provided on account, $255.

15. Issued Invoice No. 163 to City Electric Inc. for services provided on account, $340.

25. Issued Invoice No. 164 to Juniper Co. for services provided on account, $185.

Record these three transactions in the following revenue journal format:

REVENUE JOURNAL

Date	Invoice No.	Account Debited	Post. Ref.	Accts. Rec. Dr. Fees Earned Cr.

EE 5-1 p. 237 **PE 5-1B Revenue journal** OBJ. 2

The following revenue transactions occurred during April:

Apr. 6. Issued Invoice No. 78 to Lemon Co. for services provided on account, $1,240.

11. Issued Invoice No. 79 to Hitchcock Inc. for services provided on account, $2,570.

19. Issued Invoice No. 80 to Fletcher Inc. for services provided on account, $990.

Record these three transactions in the following revenue journal format:

REVENUE JOURNAL

Date	Invoice No.	Account Debited	Post. Ref.	Accts. Rec. Dr. Fees Earned Cr.

EE 5-2 p. 240 **PE 5-2A Accounts receivable subsidiary ledger** OBJ. 2

The debits and credits from two transactions are presented in the following customer account:

NAME Horizon Entertainment
ADDRESS 125 Wycoff Ave.

Date	Item	Post. Ref.	Debit	Credit	Balance
Feb. 1	Balance	✓			280
22	Invoice No. 422	CR106		120	160
27	Invoice No. 445	R92	170		330

Describe each transaction and the source of each posting.

Chapter 5 Accounting Systems   257

EE 5-2 p. 240   **PE 5-2B   Accounts receivable subsidiary ledger**   OBJ. 2

The debits and credits from two transactions are presented in the following customer account:

NAME   Moravian Products Inc.
ADDRESS 46 W. Main St.

Date	Item	Post. Ref.	Debit	Credit	Balance
Aug. 1	Balance	✓			1,200
10	Invoice No. 119	R24	750		1,950
17	Invoice No. 106	CR46		610	1,340

Describe each transaction and the source of each posting.

EE 5-3 p. 243   **PE 5-3A   Purchases journal**   OBJ. 2

The following purchase transactions occurred during October for K-Town Inc.:

Oct. 6. Purchased office supplies for $190, on account from U-Save Supply Inc.

14. Purchased office equipment for $2,100, on account from Zell Computer Inc.

26. Purchased office supplies for $295, on account from U-Save Supply Inc.

Record these transactions in the following purchases journal format:

PURCHASES JOURNAL

Date	Account Credited	Post. Ref.	Accounts Payable Cr.	Office Supplies Dr.	Other Accounts Dr.	Post. Ref.	Amount

EE 5-3 p. 243   **PE 5-3B   Purchases journal**   OBJ. 2

The following purchase transactions occurred during March for Celebration Catering Service:

Mar. 11. Purchased party supplies for $610, on account from Party Hearty Supplies Inc.

14. Purchased party supplies for $312, on account from Fun 4 All Supplies Inc.

27. Purchased office furniture for $2,480, on account from Office Space Inc.

Record these transactions in the following purchases journal format:

PURCHASES JOURNAL

Date	Account Credited	Post. Ref.	Accounts Payable Cr.	Party Supplies Dr.	Other Accounts Dr.	Post. Ref.	Amount

EE 5-4 p. 246   **PE 5-4A   Accounts payable subsidiary ledger**   OBJ. 2

The debits and credits from two transactions are presented in the following creditor's (supplier's) account:

NAME   Migrant Technology
ADDRESS 2199 Commerce Place

Date	Item	Post. Ref.	Debit	Credit	Balance
Nov. 1	Balance	✓			9,400
11	Invoice No. 85	P8		1,845	11,245
22	Invoice No. 43	CP46	3,270		7,975

Describe each transaction and the source of each posting.

258   Chapter 5   Accounting Systems

EE 5-4 *p. 246* **PE 5-4B** Accounts payable subsidiary ledger   OBJ. 2

The debits and credits from two transactions are presented in the following creditor's (supplier's) account:

NAME   Colonial Inc.
ADDRESS   5000 Grand Ave.

Date	Item	Post. Ref.	Debit	Credit	Balance
Jan. 1	Balance	✓			92
11	Invoice No. 122	CP71	64		28
26	Invoice No. 139	P55		72	100

Describe each transaction and the source of each posting.

EE 5-5 *p. 251* **PE 5-5A** Segment analysis   OBJ. 5

McHale Company does business in two customer segments, Retail and Wholesale. The following annual revenue information was determined from the accounting system's invoice information:

	20Y5	20Y4
Retail	$126,000	$120,000
Wholesale	150,000	164,000
Total revenues	$276,000	$284,000

Prepare horizontal and vertical analyses of the segments. Round to one decimal place.

EE 5-5 *p. 251* **PE 5-5B** Segment analysis   OBJ. 5

Back Country Life, Inc., does business in two product segments, Camping and Fishing. The following annual revenue information was determined from the accounting system's invoice information:

	20Y3	20Y2
Camping	$280,000	$240,000
Fishing	140,000	160,000
Total revenues	$420,000	$400,000

Prepare horizontal and vertical analyses of the segments. Round to one decimal place.

Exercises

EX 5-1 Identify postings from revenue journal   OBJ. 2

Using the following revenue journal for Bowman Cleaners Inc., identify each of the posting references, indicated by a letter, as representing (1) posting to general ledger accounts or (2) posting to subsidiary ledger accounts:

REVENUE JOURNAL

Date	Invoice No.	Account Debited	Post. Ref.	Accounts Rec. Dr. Fees Earned Cr.
20Y3				
May 1	112	Hazmat Safety Co.	(a)	$2,050
10	113	Masco Co.	(b)	980
20	114	Alpha GenCorp	(c)	2,800
27	115	Tillman Inc.	(d)	1,240
31				$7,070
				(e)

EX 5-2 Accounts receivable ledger OBJ. 2

✔ d. Total accounts receivable, $7,660

Based on the data presented in Exercise 5-1, assume that the beginning balances for the customer accounts were zero, except for Tillman Inc., which had a $590 beginning balance. In addition, there were no collections during the period.

a. Set up a T account for Accounts Receivable and T accounts for the four accounts needed in the customer ledger.
b. Post to the T accounts.
c. Determine the balance in the accounts.
d. Prepare a listing of the accounts receivable customer balances as of May 31, 20Y3.

EX 5-3 Identify journals OBJ. 2

Assuming the use of a two-column (all-purpose) general journal, a revenue journal, and a cash receipts journal as illustrated in this chapter, indicate the journal in which each of the following transactions should be recorded:

a. Receipt of cash refund from overpayment of taxes.
b. Adjustment to record accrued salaries at the end of the year.
c. Providing services on account.
d. Investment of additional cash in the business by the owner.
e. Receipt of cash on account from a customer.
f. Receipt of cash for rent.
g. Receipt of cash from sale of office equipment.
h. Sale of used office equipment on account, at cost, to a neighboring business.
i. Closing of drawing account at the end of the year.
j. Providing services for cash.

EX 5-4 Identify journals OBJ. 2

Assuming the use of a two-column (all-purpose) general journal, a purchases journal, and a cash payments journal as illustrated in this chapter, indicate the journal in which each of the following transactions should be recorded:

a. Payment of six months' rent in advance.
b. Purchase of an office computer on account.
c. Purchase of office supplies on account.
d. Adjustment to record depreciation at the end of the month.
e. Adjustment to record accrued salaries at the end of the period.
f. Purchase of services on account.
g. Adjustment to prepaid rent at the end of the month.
h. Purchase of office equipment for cash.
i. Adjustment to prepaid insurance at the end of the month.
j. Purchase of office supplies for cash.
k. Advance payment of a one-year fire insurance policy on the office.

260 Chapter 5 Accounting Systems

EX 5-5 Identify transactions in accounts receivable subsidiary ledger OBJ. 2

The debits and credits from three related transactions are presented in the following customer's account taken from the accounts receivable subsidiary ledger:

NAME Mission Design
ADDRESS 1319 Elm Street

Date	Item	Post. Ref.	Debit	Credit	Balance
20Y7					
Apr. 3		R44	740		740
6		J11		60	680
24		CR81		680	—

Describe each transaction and identify the source of each posting.

EX 5-6 Prepare journal entries in a revenue journal OBJ. 2

Horizon Consulting Company had the following transactions during the month of October:

Oct. 2. Issued Invoice No. 321 to Pryor Corp. for services rendered on account, $595.

3. Issued Invoice No. 322 to Armor Inc. for services rendered on account, $310.

14. Issued Invoice No. 323 to Pryor Corp. for services rendered on account, $205.

24. Issued Invoice No. 324 to Rose Co. for services rendered on account, $850.

29. Collected Invoice No. 321 from Pryor Corp.

a. Record the October revenue transactions for Horizon Consulting Company in the following revenue journal format:

REVENUE JOURNAL

Date	Invoice No.	Account Debited	Post. Ref.	Accts. Rec. Dr. Fees Earned Cr.

b. What is the total amount posted to the accounts receivable and fees earned accounts from the revenue journal for October?

c. What is the October 31 balance of the Pryor Corp. customer account assuming a zero balance on October 1?

EX 5-7 Posting a revenue journal OBJ. 2, 3

The revenue journal for Sapling Consulting Inc. follows. The accounts receivable controlling account has a July 1, 20Y2, balance of $625 consisting of an amount due from Aladdin Co. There were no collections during July.

REVENUE JOURNAL Page 12

Date	Invoice No.	Account Debited	Post. Ref.	Accts. Rec. Dr. Fees Earned Cr.
20Y2				
July 4	355	Clearmark Co.		1,890
9	356	Life Star Inc.		3,410
18	357	Aladdin Co.		950
22	359	Clearmark Co.		3,660
31				9,910

a. Prepare a T account for the accounts receivable customer accounts.

b. Post the transactions from the revenue journal to the customer accounts and determine their ending balances.

c. Prepare T accounts for the accounts receivable and fees earned accounts. Post control totals to the two accounts and determine the ending balances.

d. Prepare a schedule of the customer account balances to verify the equality of the sum of the customer account balances and the accounts receivable controlling account balance.

e. How might a computerized system differ from a revenue journal in recording revenue transactions?

Chapter 5 Accounting Systems 261

✓ Accounts Receivable balance, January 31, $8,280

EX 5-8 Accounts receivable subsidiary ledger OBJ. 2

The revenue and cash receipts journals for Polaris Productions Inc. follow. The accounts receivable control account has a January 1, 20Y4, balance of $3,790 consisting of an amount due from Clear Pointe Studios Inc.

REVENUE JOURNAL — Page 16

Date	Invoice No.	Account Debited	Post. Ref.	Accts. Rec. Dr. Fees Earned Cr.
20Y4				
Jan. 6	1	Echo Broadcasting Co.	✓	2,300
14	2	Gold Coast Media Inc.	✓	5,100
22	3	Echo Broadcasting Co.	✓	2,980
25	4	Clear Pointe Studios Inc.	✓	1,650
29	5	Amber Communications Inc.	✓	3,650
31				15,680
				(12) (41)

CASH RECEIPTS JOURNAL — Page 36

Date	Account Credited	Post. Ref.	Fees Earned Cr.	Accts. Rec. Cr.	Cash Dr.
20Y4					
Jan. 6	Clear Pointe Studios Inc.	✓	—	3,790	3,790
11	Fees Earned		3,200		3,200
18	Echo Broadcasting Co.	✓	—	2,300	2,300
28	Gold Coast Media Inc.	✓	—	5,100	5,100
31			3,200	11,190	14,390
			(41)	(12)	(11)

Prepare a listing of the accounts receivable customer balances and verify that the total agrees with the ending balance of the accounts receivable controlling account.

EX 5-9 Revenue and cash receipts journals OBJ. 2

Transactions related to revenue and cash receipts completed by Sycamore Inc. during the month of March 20Y8 are as follows:

Mar. 2. Issued Invoice No. 512 to Santorini Co., $905.

4. Received cash from CMI Inc., on account, for $205.

8. Issued Invoice No. 513 to Gabriel Co., $220.

12. Issued Invoice No. 514 to Yarnell Inc., $845.

19. Received cash from Yarnell Inc., on account, $555.

20. Issued Invoice No. 515 to Electronic Central Inc., $195.

28. Received cash from Marshall Inc. for services provided, $160.

29. Received cash from Santorini Co. for Invoice No. 512 of March 2.

31. Received cash from McCleary Co. for services provided, $85.

Prepare a single-column revenue journal and a cash receipts journal to record these transactions. Use the following column headings for the cash receipts journal: Fees Earned Cr., Accounts Receivable Cr., and Cash Dr. Place a check mark (✓) in the Post. Ref. column to indicate when the accounts receivable subsidiary ledger should be posted.

262 Chapter 5 Accounting Systems

✔ a. Revenue journal total, $8,700

EX 5-10 Revenue and cash receipts journals   OBJ. 2

Lasting Summer Inc. has $2,510 in the October 1 balance of the accounts receivable account consisting of $1,060 from Champion Co. and $1,450 from Wayfarer Co. Transactions related to revenue and cash receipts completed by Lasting Summer Inc. during the month of October 20Y5 are as follows:

Oct. 3. Issued Invoice No. 622 for services provided to Palace Corp., $2,890.
    5. Received cash from Champion Co., on account, for $1,060.
    8. Issued Invoice No. 623 for services provided to Sunny Style Inc., $1,940.
   12. Received cash from Wayfarer Co., on account, for $1,450.
   18. Issued Invoice No. 624 for services provided to Amex Services Inc., $2,970.
   23. Received cash from Palace Corp. for Invoice No. 622 of October 3.
   28. Issued Invoice No. 625 to Wayfarer Co., on account, for $900.
   30. Received cash from Rogers Co. for services provided, $120.

a. Prepare a single-column revenue journal and a cash receipts journal to record these transactions. Use the following column headings for the cash receipts journal: Fees Earned Cr., Accounts Receivable Cr., and Cash Dr. Place a check mark (✓) in the Post. Ref. column to indicate when the accounts receivable subsidiary ledger should be posted.

b. Prepare a listing of the accounts receivable customer balances and verify that the total of the accounts receivable customer balances equals the balance of the accounts receivable controlling account on October 31, 20Y5.

c. Why does Lasting Summer Inc. use a subsidiary ledger for accounts receivable?

EX 5-11 Identify postings from purchases journal   OBJ. 2

Using the following purchases journal, identify each of the posting references, indicated by a letter, as representing (1) a posting to a general ledger account, (2) a posting to a subsidiary ledger account, or (3) that no posting is required:

PURCHASES JOURNAL   Page 49

Date	Account Credited	Post. Ref.	Accounts Payable Cr.	Store Supplies Dr.	Office Supplies Dr.	Other Accounts Dr.	Post. Ref.	Amount
20Y9								
Jan. 4	Coastal Equipment Co.	(a)	5,325			Warehouse Equipment	(g)	5,325
6	Arrow Supply Co.	(b)	4,000		4,000			
9	Valley Products	(c)	1,875	1,600	275			
14	Office Warehouse	(d)	2,200			Office Equipment	(h)	2,200
20	Office Warehouse	(e)	6,000			Store Equipment	(i)	6,000
25	Metro Supply Co.	(f)	2,740	2,740				
31			22,140	4,340	4,275			13,525
			(j)	(k)	(l)			(m)

EX 5-12 Identify postings from cash payments journal   OBJ. 2

Using the following cash payments journal, identify each of the posting references, indicated by a letter, as representing (1) a posting to a general ledger account, (2) a posting to a subsidiary ledger account, or (3) that no posting is required.

Chapter 5 Accounting Systems 263

CASH PAYMENTS JOURNAL Page 46

Date	Ck. No.	Account Debited	Post. Ref.	Other Accounts Dr.	Accounts Payable Dr.	Cash Cr.
20Y1						
July 3	611	Energy Systems Co.	(a)		4,000	4,000
5	612	Utilities Expense	(b)	310		310
10	613	Prepaid Rent	(c)	3,200		3,200
16	614	Flowers to Go, Inc.	(d)		1,250	1,250
19	615	Advertising Expense	(e)	640		640
22	616	Office Equipment	(f)	3,600		3,600
25	617	Echo Co.	(g)		5,500	5,500
26	618	Office Supplies	(h)	250		250
31	619	Salaries Expense	(i)	1,750		1,750
31				9,750	10,750	20,500
				(j)	(k)	(l)

EX 5-13 Identify transactions in accounts payable subsidiary ledger   OBJ. 2

The debits and credits from three related transactions are presented in the following creditor's account taken from the accounts payable ledger:

NAME Apex Performance Co.
ADDRESS 101 W. Stratford Ave.

Date	Item	Post. Ref.	Debit	Credit	Balance
20Y7					
June 6		P49		12,000	12,000
14		J12	150		11,850
16		CP23	11,850		—

Describe each transaction and identify the source of each posting.

EX 5-14 Prepare journal entries in a purchases journal   OBJ. 2

Guardian Services Inc. had the following transactions during the month of April:

Apr. 4. Purchased office supplies from Officemate Inc. on account, $415.

9. Purchased office equipment on account from Tek Village Inc., $2,460.

16. Purchased office supplies from Officemate Inc. on account, $185.

19. Purchased office supplies from Paper-to-Go Inc. on account, $195.

27. Paid invoice on April 4 purchase from Officemate Inc.

a. Record the June purchase transactions for Guardian Services Inc. in the following purchases journal format:

PURCHASES JOURNAL

Date	Account Credited	Post. Ref.	Accts. Payable Cr.	Office Supplies Dr.	Other Accounts Dr.	Post. Ref.	Amount

b. What is the total amount posted to the accounts payable and office supplies accounts from the purchases journal for April?

c. What is the April 30 balance of the Officemate Inc. creditor account assuming a zero balance on April 1?

EX 5-15 Posting a purchases journal
OBJ. 2, 3

✓ d. Total, $5,840

The purchases journal for Newmark Exterior Cleaners Inc. follows. The accounts payable account has a March 1, 20Y2, balance of $580 for an amount owed to Nicely Co. No payments were made on creditor invoices during March.

PURCHASES JOURNAL   Page 16

Date	Account Credited	Post. Ref.	Accts. Payable Cr.	Cleaning Supplies Dr.	Other Accounts Dr.	Post. Ref.	Amount
20Y2							
Mar. 4	Enviro-Wash Supplies Inc.		690	690			
15	Nicely Co.		325	325			
20	Office Mate Inc.		3,860		Office Equipment		3,860
26	Enviro-Wash Supplies Inc.		385	385			
31			5,260	1,400			3,860

a. Prepare a T account for the accounts payable creditor accounts.
b. Post the transactions from the purchases journal to the creditor accounts and determine their ending balances.
c. Prepare T accounts for the accounts payable control and cleaning supplies accounts. Post control totals to the two accounts, and determine their ending balances. Cleaning Supplies had a zero balance at the beginning of the month.
d. Prepare a schedule of the creditor account balances to verify the equality of the sum of the accounts payable creditor balances and the accounts payable controlling account balance.
e. How might a computerized accounting system differ from the use of a purchases journal in recording purchase transactions?

EX 5-16 Accounts payable subsidiary ledger
OBJ. 2

✓ Accts. Pay., June 30, $21,580

The cash payments and purchases journals for Outdoor Artisan Landscaping follow. The accounts payable control account has a June 1, 20Y1, balance of $2,230, consisting of an amount owed to Augusta Sod Co.

CASH PAYMENTS JOURNAL   Page 31

Date	Ck. No.	Account Debited	Post. Ref.	Other Accounts Dr.	Accounts Payable Dr.	Cash Cr.
20Y1						
June 4	203	Augusta Sod Co.	✓		2,230	2,230
5	204	Utilities Expense	54	440		440
15	205	Home Centers Lumber Co.	✓		5,210	5,210
24	206	Nu Lawn Fertilizer	✓		910	910
30				440	8,350	8,790
				(✓)	(21)	(11)

PURCHASES JOURNAL   Page 22

Date	Account Credited	Post. Ref.	Accounts Payable Cr.	Landscaping Supplies Dr.	Other Accounts Dr.	Post. Ref.	Amount
20Y1							
June 3	Home Centers Lumber Co.	✓	5,210	5,210			
7	Concrete Equipment Co.	✓	6,700		Equipment	18	6,700
14	Nu Lawn Fertilizer	✓	910	910			
24	Augusta Sod Co.	✓	6,450	6,450			
29	Home Centers Lumber Co.	✓	8,430	8,430			
30			27,700	21,000			6,700
			(21)	(14)			(✓)

Prepare a schedule of the accounts payable creditor balances and determine that the total agrees with the ending balance of the accounts payable controlling account.

Chapter 5 Accounting Systems 265

EX 5-17 Purchases and cash payments journals   OBJ. 2

✓ Purchases journal, Accts. Pay., Total, $910

Transactions related to purchases and cash payments completed by Wisk Away Cleaning Services Inc. during the month of May 20Y5 are as follows:

May 1. Issued Check No. 57 to Bio Safe Supplies Inc. in payment of account, $345.
   3. Purchased cleaning supplies on account from Brite N' Shine Products Inc., $200.
   8. Issued Check No. 58 to purchase equipment from Carson Equipment Sales, $2,860.
   12. Purchased cleaning supplies on account from Porter Products Inc., $360.
   15. Issued Check No. 59 to Bowman Electrical Service in payment of account, $145.
   18. Purchased supplies on account from Bio Safe Supplies Inc., $240.
   20. Purchased electrical repair services from Bowman Electrical Service on account, $110.
   26. Issued Check No. 60 to Brite N' Shine Products Inc. in payment of May 3 invoice.
   31. Issued Check No. 61 in payment of salaries, $5,600.

Prepare a purchases journal and a cash payments journal to record these transactions. The forms of the journals are similar to those illustrated in the text. Place a check mark (✓) in the Post. Ref. column to indicate when the accounts payable subsidiary ledger should be posted. Wisk Away Cleaning Services Inc. uses the following accounts:

Cash	11
Cleaning Supplies	14
Equipment	18
Accounts Payable	21
Salary Expense	51
Electrical Service Expense	53

EX 5-18 Purchases and cash payments journals   OBJ. 2

Happy Tails Inc. has a September 1, 20Y4, accounts payable balance of $620, which consists of $320 due Labradore Inc. and $300 due Meow Mart Inc. Transactions related to purchases and cash payments completed by Happy Tails Inc. during the month of September 20Y4 are as follows:

Sept. 4. Purchased pet supplies from Best Friend Supplies Inc. on account, $295.
   6. Issued Check No. 345 to Labradore Inc. in payment of account, $320.
   13. Purchased pet supplies from Poodle Pals Inc. on account, $790.
   18. Issued Check No. 346 to Meow Mart Inc. in payment of account, $300.
   19. Purchased office equipment from Office Helper Inc. on account, $2,510.
   23. Issued Check No. 347 to Best Friend Supplies Inc. in payment of account from purchase made on September 4.
   27. Purchased pet supplies from Meow Mart Inc. on account, $450.
   30. Issued Check No. 348 to Jennings Inc. for cleaning expenses, $80.

a. Prepare a purchases journal and a cash payments journal to record these transactions. The forms of the journals are similar to those used in the text. Place a check mark (✓) in the Post. Ref. column to indicate when the accounts payable subsidiary ledger should be posted. Happy Tails Inc. uses the following accounts:

Cash	11
Pet Supplies	14
Office Equipment	18
Accounts Payable	21
Cleaning Expense	54

b. Prepare a listing of accounts payable creditor balances on September 30, 20Y4. Verify that the total of the accounts payable creditor balances equals the balance of the accounts payable controlling account on September 30, 20Y4.

c. Why does Happy Tails Inc. use a subsidiary ledger for accounts payable?

EX 5-19 Error in accounts payable subsidiary ledger

OBJ. 2

After Bunker Hill Assay Services Inc. had completed all postings for March in the current year (20Y4), the sum of the balances in the following accounts payable ledger did not agree with the $36,600 balance of the controlling account in the general ledger:

NAME C. D. Greer and Son
ADDRESS 972 S. Tenth Street

Date	Item	Post. Ref.	Debit	Credit	Balance
20Y4					
Mar. 17		P30		3,750	3,750
27		P31		12,000	15,750

NAME Carbon Supplies Inc.
ADDRESS 1170 Mattis Avenue

Date	Item	Post. Ref.	Debit	Credit	Balance
20Y4					
Mar. 1	Balance	✓			8,300
9		P30		7,000	14,000
12		J7	300		13,700
20		CP23	5,800		7,900

NAME Cutler and Powell
ADDRESS 717 Elm Street

Date	Item	Post. Ref.	Debit	Credit	Balance
20Y4					
Mar. 1	Balance	✓			6,100
18		CP23	6,100		—
29		P31		7,800	7,800

NAME Hudson Bay Minerals Co.
ADDRESS 1240 W. Main Street

Date	Item	Post. Ref.	Debit	Credit	Balance
20Y4					
Mar. 1	Balance	✓			4,750
10		CP22	4,750		—
17		P30		3,700	3,700
25		J7	3,000		1,700

NAME Valley Power
ADDRESS 915 E. Walnut Street

Date	Item	Post. Ref.	Debit	Credit	Balance
20Y4					
Mar. 5		P30		3,150	3,150

Assuming that the controlling account balance of $36,600 has been verified as correct, (a) determine the error(s) in the preceding accounts and (b) prepare a listing of accounts payable creditor balances (from the corrected accounts payable subsidiary ledger).

EX 5-20 Identify postings from special journals

OBJ. 2

Pinnacle Consulting Company makes most of its sales and purchases on credit. It uses the five journals described in this chapter (revenue, cash receipts, purchases, cash payments, and general). Identify the journal most likely used in recording the postings for selected transactions indicated by letter in the T accounts, as follows:

Chapter 5 Accounting Systems 267

	Cash				Prepaid Rent		
a.	10,940	b.	6,500	e.	1,200		

	Accounts Receivable				Accounts Payable		
c.	11,790	a.	10,940	b.	6,500	d.	7,400

	Office Supplies				Fees Earned		
d.	7,400					c.	11,790

	Rent Expense
e.	1,200

EX 5-21 Cash receipts journal   OBJ. 2

The following cash receipts journal headings have been suggested for a small service firm. List the errors you find in the headings.

CASH RECEIPTS JOURNAL   Page 12

Date	Account Credited	Post. Ref.	Fees Earned Cr.	Accts. Rec. Cr.	Cash Cr.	Other Accounts Dr.

EX 5-22 Computerized accounting systems   OBJ. 3

Most computerized accounting systems use electronic forms to record transaction information, such as the invoice form illustrated at the top of Exhibit 7 in this chapter.

a. Identify the key input fields (spaces) in an electronic invoice form.

b. What accounts are posted from an electronic invoice form?

c. Why aren't special journal totals posted to control accounts at the end of the month in an electronic accounting system?

EX 5-23 Computerized accounting systems and e-commerce   OBJ. 3, 4

Apple Inc.'s iTunes® provides digital products, such as music, video, and software, which can be downloaded to portable devices such as the iPhone® and iPad®. Purchases from iTunes are made with credit cards that are on file with the credit card processing company. Such transactions are considered cash transactions. Once the purchases are made, consumers can download the requested digital products to their portable devices for their enjoyment and the charges will show up on their credit card bills.

a. What kind of e-commerce application is described by Apple iTunes?

b. Assume you purchased 12 songs for $1.25 each on iTunes. Provide the journal entry generated by Apple's e-commerce application.

c. If a special journal were used, what type of special journal would be used to record this sales transaction?

d. If an electronic form were used, what type of electronic form would be used to record this sales transaction?

e. Would it be appropriate for Apple to use either special journals or electronic forms for sales transactions from iTunes? Explain.

EX 5-24 E-commerce   OBJ. 4

For each of the following companies, determine what they primarily sell and whether their e-commerce strategy is primarily business-to-consumer (B2C), business-to-business (B2B), or both. Use the Internet to investigate each company's site in conducting your research.

a. **Amazon.com**

b. **Dell Inc.**

c. **DuPont**

d. **Intuit Inc.**

e. **L.L. Bean, Inc.**

f. **W.W. Grainger, Inc.**

268 Chapter 5 Accounting Systems

EX 5-25 Segment revenue horizontal analysis
OBJ. 5

Starbucks Corporation reported the following geographical segment revenues for a recent and a prior fiscal year:

	Recent Year (in millions, rounded)	Prior Year (in millions, rounded)
Americas	$13,293	$11,980
EMEA*	1,217	1,295
China/Asia Pacific	2,396	1,130
Channel Development**	1,731	1,546
Other	526	497
Total	$19,163	$16,448

*Europe, Middle East, and Africa
**Sells packaged coffee and teas globally

a. Prepare a horizontal analysis of the segment data using the prior year as the base year. Round whole percents to one decimal place.

b. Prepare a vertical analysis of the segment data. Round whole percents to one decimal place.

c. What conclusions can be drawn from your analyses?

EX 5-26 Segment revenue vertical analysis
OBJ. 5

Twenty-First Century Fox, Inc. is one of the world's largest entertainment companies that includes Twentieth Century Fox films, Fox Broadcasting, Fox News, the FX, and various satellite properties. The company provided revenue disclosures by its major product segments in the notes to its financial statements as follows:

Major Product Segments	For a Recent Year (in millions)
Cable Network Programming	$13,773
Television	4,895
Filmed Entertainment	9,525
Direct Broadcast Satellite Television	2,112
Total revenues of major segments	$30,305

a. Provide a vertical analysis of the product segment revenue. Round whole percents to one decimal place.

b. Are the revenues of Twenty-First Century Fox, Inc. diversified or concentrated within a product segment? Explain.

EX 5-27 Segment revenue horizontal and vertical analyses
OBJ. 5

The comparative segment revenues for **Yum! Brands**, a global quick-serve restaurant company, are as follows:

	Recent Year (in millions)	Prior Year (in millions)
China	$ 6,909	$ 6,934
KFC	2,948	3,193
Pizza Hut	1,145	1,148
Taco Bell	1,988	1,863
India	115	141
Total	$13,105	$13,279

a. Provide a horizontal analysis of the segment revenues using the prior year as the base year. Round whole percents to one decimal place.

b. Provide a vertical analysis of the segment revenues for both years. Round whole percents to one decimal place.

c. What conclusions can be drawn from your analyses?

Problems: Series A

✔ 1. Revenue journal, total fees earned, $1,170

PR 5-1A Revenue journal; accounts receivable subsidiary and general ledgers OBJ. 2, 3

Sage Learning Centers was established on July 20 to provide educational services. The services provided during the remainder of the month are as follows:

July 21. Issued Invoice No. 1 to J. Dunlop for $115 on account.
  22. Issued Invoice No. 2 to K. Tisdale for $350 on account.
  24. Issued Invoice No. 3 to T. Quinn for $85 on account.
  25. Provided educational services, $300, to K. Tisdale in exchange for educational supplies.
  27. Issued Invoice No. 4 to F. Mintz for $225 on account.
  30. Issued Invoice No. 5 to D. Chase for $170 on account.
  30. Issued Invoice No. 6 to K. Tisdale for $120 on account.
  31. Issued Invoice No. 7 to T. Quinn for $105 on account.

Instructions

1. Journalize the transactions for July, using a single-column revenue journal and a two-column general journal. Post to the following customer accounts in the accounts receivable ledger and insert the balance immediately after recording each entry: D. Chase; J. Dunlop; F. Mintz; T. Quinn; K. Tisdale.

2. Post the revenue journal and the general journal to the following accounts in the general ledger, inserting the account balances only after the last postings:

    12 Accounts Receivable
    13 Supplies
    41 Fees Earned

3. a. What is the sum of the balances of the customer accounts in the subsidiary ledger at July 31?
   b. What is the balance of the accounts receivable controlling account at July 31?

4. Assume Sage Learning Centers began using a computerized accounting system to record the sales transactions on August 1. What are some of the benefits of the computerized system over the manual system?

PR 5-2A Revenue and cash receipts journals; accounts receivable subsidiary and general ledgers OBJ. 2, 3

✔ 3. Total cash receipts, $34,390

Transactions related to revenue and cash receipts completed by Crowne Business Services Co. during the period April 2–30 are as follows:

Apr. 2. Issued Invoice No. 793 to Ohr Co., $4,680.
  5. Received cash from Mendez Co. for the balance owed on its account.
  6. Issued Invoice No. 794 to Pinecrest Co., $1,990.
  13. Issued Invoice No. 795 to Shilo Co., $3,450.

  Post revenue and collections to the accounts receivable subsidiary ledger.

  15. Received cash from Pinecrest Co. for the balance owed on April 1.
  16. Issued Invoice No. 796 to Pinecrest Co., $5,500.

  Post revenue and collections to the accounts receivable subsidiary ledger.

  19. Received cash from Ohr Co. for the balance due on invoice of April 2.
  20. Received cash from Pinecrest Co. for balance due on invoice of April 6.
  22. Issued Invoice No. 797 to Mendez Co., $7,470.
  25. Received $3,200 note receivable in partial settlement of the balance due on the Shilo Co. account.

(Continued)

270 Chapter 5 Accounting Systems

Apr. 30. Received cash from fees earned, $12,890.

Post revenue and collections to the accounts receivable subsidiary ledger.

Instructions

1. Insert the following balances in the general ledger as of April 1:

11	Cash	$11,350
12	Accounts Receivable	14,830
14	Notes Receivable	6,000
41	Fees Earned	—

2. Insert the following balances in the accounts receivable subsidiary ledger as of April 1:

Mendez Co.	$8,710
Ohr Co.	—
Pinecrest Co.	6,120
Shilo Co.	—

3. Prepare a single-column revenue journal (p. 40) and a cash receipts journal (p. 36). Use the following column headings for the cash receipts journal: Fees Earned Cr., Accounts Receivable Cr., and Cash Dr. The Fees Earned column is used to record cash fees. Insert a check mark (✓) in the Post. Ref. column when recording cash fees.

4. Using the two special journals and the two-column general journal (p. 1), journalize the transactions for April. Post to the accounts receivable subsidiary ledger, and insert the balances at the points indicated in the narrative of transactions. Determine the balance in the customer's account before recording a cash receipt.

5. Total each of the columns of the special journals and post the individual entries and totals to the general ledger. Insert account balances after the last posting.

6. Determine that the sum of the customer balances agrees with the accounts receivable controlling account in the general ledger.

7. Why would an automated system omit postings to a controlling account as performed in step 5 for Accounts Receivable?

PR 5-3A Purchases, accounts payable subsidiary account, and accounts payable ledger OBJ. 2, 4

✓ 5b. $18,110

Sterling Forest Landscaping designs and installs landscaping. The landscape designers and office staff use office supplies, while field supplies (rock, bark, etc.) are used in the actual landscaping. Purchases on account completed by Sterling Forest Landscaping during October are as follows:

Oct. 2. Purchased office supplies on account from Meade Co., $400.

5. Purchased office equipment on account from Peach Computers Co., $3,980.

9. Purchased office supplies on account from Executive Office Supply Co., $320.

13. Purchased field supplies on account from Yamura Co., $1,420.

14. Purchased field supplies on account from Omni Co., $2,940.

17. Purchased field supplies on account from Yamura Co., $1,890.

24. Purchased field supplies on account from Omni Co., $3,880.

29. Purchased office supplies on account from Executive Office Supply Co., $310.

31. Purchased field supplies on account from Omni Co., $1,800.

Instructions

1. Insert the following balances in the general ledger as of October 1:

14	Field Supplies	$ 5,920
15	Office Supplies	750
18	Office Equipment	12,300
21	Accounts Payable	1,170

2. Insert the following balances in the accounts payable subsidiary ledger as of October 1:

Executive Office Supply Co.	$390
Meade Co.	780
Omni Co.	—
Peach Computers Co.	—
Yamura Co.	—

3. Journalize the transactions for October, using a purchases journal (p. 30) similar to the one illustrated in this chapter. Prepare the purchases journal with columns for Accounts Payable, Field Supplies, Office Supplies, and Other Accounts. Post to the creditor accounts in the accounts payable subsidiary ledger immediately after each entry.

4. Post the purchases journal to the accounts in the general ledger.

5. a. What is the sum of the creditor balances in the subsidiary ledger at October 31?
   b. What is the balance of the accounts payable controlling account at October 31?

6. What type of e-commerce application would be used to plan and coordinate transactions with suppliers?

PR 5-4A Purchases and cash payments journals; accounts payable subsidiary and general ledgers OBJ. 2

✔ 1. Total cash payments, $203,940

AquaFresh Water Testing Service was established on April 16. AquaFresh uses field equipment and field supplies (chemicals and other supplies) to analyze water for unsafe contaminants in streams, lakes, and ponds. Transactions related to purchases and cash payments during the remainder of April are as follows:

Apr. 16. Issued Check No. 1 in payment of rent for the remainder of April, $3,500.
16. Purchased field supplies on account from Hydro Supply Co., $5,340.
16. Purchased field equipment on account from Pure Equipment Co., $21,450.
17. Purchased office supplies on account from Best Office Supply Co., $510.
19. Issued Check No. 2 in payment of field supplies, $3,340, and office supplies, $400.

Post the journals to the accounts payable subsidiary ledger.

23. Purchased office supplies on account from Best Office Supply Co., $660.
23. Issued Check No. 3 to purchase land, $140,000.
24. Issued Check No. 4 to Hydro Supply Co. in payment of April 16 invoice, $5,340.
26. Issued Check No. 5 to Pure Equipment Co. in payment of April 16 invoice, $21,450.

Post the journals to the accounts payable subsidiary ledger.

30. Acquired land in exchange for field equipment having a cost of $12,000.
30. Purchased field supplies on account from Hydro Supply Co., $7,650.
30. Issued Check No. 6 to Best Office Supply Co. in payment of April 17 invoice, $510.
30. Purchased the following from Pure Equipment Co. on account: field supplies, $1,340, and field equipment, $4,700.
30. Issued Check No. 7 in payment of salaries, $29,400.

Post the journals to the accounts payable subsidiary ledger.

Instructions

1. Journalize the transactions for April. Use a purchases journal and a cash payments journal, similar to those illustrated in this chapter, and a two-column general journal. Use debit columns for Field Supplies, Office Supplies, and Other Accounts in the purchases journal. Refer to the following partial chart of accounts:

11	Cash	19	Land
14	Field Supplies	21	Accounts Payable
15	Office Supplies	61	Salary Expense
17	Field Equipment	71	Rent Expense

(Continued)

At the points indicated in the narrative of transactions, post to the following accounts in the accounts payable subsidiary ledger:

Best Office Supply Co.
Hydro Supply Co.
Pure Equipment Co.

2. Post the individual entries (Other Accounts columns of the purchases journal and the cash payments journal and both columns of the general journal) to the appropriate general ledger accounts.

3. Total each of the columns of the purchases journal and the cash payments journal and post the appropriate totals to the general ledger. (Because the problem does not include transactions related to cash receipts, the cash account in the ledger will have a credit balance.)

4. Prepare a schedule of the accounts payable creditor balances.

5. Why might AquaFresh consider using a subsidiary ledger for the field equipment?

PR 5-5A All journals and general ledger; trial balance OBJ. 2

✔ 2. Total cash receipts, $53,880

The transactions completed by Revere Courier Company during December, the first month of the fiscal year, were as follows:

Dec. 1. Issued Check No. 610 for December rent, $4,200.
2. Issued Invoice No. 940 to Clifford Co., $1,740.
3. Received check for $4,800 from Ryan Co. in payment of account.
5. Purchased a vehicle on account from Platinum Motors, $37,300.
6. Purchased office equipment on account from Austin Computer Co., $4,500.
6. Issued Invoice No. 941 to Ernesto Co., $3,870.
9. Issued Check No. 611 for fuel expense, $600.
10. Received check from Sing Co. in payment of $4,040 invoice.
10. Issued Check No. 612 for $330 to Office To Go Inc. in payment of invoice.
10. Issued Invoice No. 942 to Joy Co., $1,970.
11. Issued Check No. 613 for $3,090 to Essential Supply Co. in payment of account.
11. Issued Check No. 614 for $500 to Porter Co. in payment of account.
12. Received check from Clifford Co. in payment of $1,740 invoice of December 2.
13. Issued Check No. 615 to Platinum Motors in payment of $37,300 balance of December 5.
16. Issued Check No. 616 for $39,800 for cash purchase of a vehicle.
16. Cash fees earned for December 1–16, $20,300.
17. Issued Check No. 617 for miscellaneous administrative expense, $500.
18. Purchased maintenance supplies on account from Essential Supply Co., $1,750.
19. Purchased the following on account from McClain Co.: maintenance supplies, $1,500; office supplies, $375.
20. Issued Check No. 618 in payment of advertising expense, $1,780.
20. Used $3,200 maintenance supplies to repair delivery vehicles.
23. Purchased office supplies on account from Office To Go Inc., $400.
24. Issued Invoice No. 943 to Sing Co., $6,100.
24. Issued Check No. 619 to S. Holmes as a personal withdrawal, $3,000.
25. Issued Invoice No. 944 to Ernesto Co., $5,530.
25. Received check for $4,100 from Ryan Co. in payment of balance.
26. Issued Check No. 620 to Austin Computer Co. in payment of $4,500 invoice of December 6.
30. Issued Check No. 621 for monthly salaries as follows: driver salaries, $16,900; office salaries, $7,100.

Dec. 31. Cash fees earned for December 17–31, $18,900.

31. Issued Check No. 622 in payment for office supplies, $340.

Instructions

1. Enter the following account balances in the general ledger as of December 1:

11	Cash	$161,680	32	S. Holmes, Drawing	—
12	Accounts Receivable	12,940	41	Fees Earned	—
14	Maintenance Supplies	10,850	51	Driver Salaries Expense	—
15	Office Supplies	4,900	52	Maintenance Supplies Exp.	—
16	Office Equipment	28,500	53	Fuel Expense	—
17	Accum. Depr.—Office Equip.	6,900	61	Office Salaries Expense	—
18	Vehicles	95,900	62	Rent Expense	—
19	Accum. Depr.—Vehicles	14,700	63	Advertising Expense	—
21	Accounts Payable	3,920	64	Miscellaneous Administrative Expense	—
31	S. Holmes, Capital	289,250			

2. Journalize the transactions for December, using the following journals similar to those illustrated in this chapter: cash receipts journal (p. 31), purchases journal (p. 37, with columns for Accounts Payable, Maintenance Supplies, Office Supplies, and Other Accounts), single-column revenue journal (p. 35), cash payments journal (p. 34), and two-column general journal (p. 1). Assume that the daily postings to the individual accounts in the accounts payable subsidiary ledger and the accounts receivable subsidiary ledger have been made.

3. Post the appropriate individual entries to the general ledger.

4. Total each of the columns of the special journals and post the appropriate totals to the general ledger; insert the account balances.

5. Prepare a trial balance.

Problems: Series B

✔ 1. Revenue journal, total fees earned, $2,875

PR 5-1B Revenue journal; accounts receivable subsidiary and general ledgers   OBJ. 2, 3

Guardian Security Services was established on January 15 to provide security services. The services provided during the remainder of the month are as follows:

Jan. 18. Issued Invoice No. 1 to Murphy Co. for $490 on account.

20. Issued Invoice No. 2 to Qwik-Mart Co. for $340 on account.

24. Issued Invoice No. 3 to Hopkins Co. for $750 on account.

27. Issued Invoice No. 4 to Carson Co. for $680 on account.

28. Issued Invoice No. 5 to Amber Waves Co. for $120 on account.

28. Provided security services, $100, to Qwik-Mart Co. in exchange for supplies.

30. Issued Invoice No. 6 to Qwik-Mart Co. for $200 on account.

31. Issued Invoice No. 7 to Hopkins Co. for $295 on account.

Instructions

1. Journalize the transactions for January, using a single-column revenue journal and a two-column general journal. Post to the following customer accounts in the accounts receivable ledger and insert the balance immediately after recording each entry: Amber Waves Co.; Carson Co.; Hopkins Co.; Murphy Co.; Qwik-Mart Co.

2. Post the revenue journal to the following accounts in the general ledger, inserting the account balances only after the last postings:

12	Accounts Receivable
14	Supplies
41	Fees Earned

(*Continued*)

274 Chapter 5 Accounting Systems

3. a. What is the sum of the balances of the customer accounts in the subsidiary ledger at January 31?

   b. What is the balance of the accounts receivable controlling account at January 31?

4. Assume Guardian Security Services began using a computerized accounting system to record the sales transactions on February 1. What are some of the benefits of the computerized system over the manual system?

PR 5-2B Revenue and cash receipts journals; accounts receivable subsidiary and general ledgers **OBJ. 2, 3**

✔ 3. Total cash receipts, $9,270

Show Me How

Transactions related to revenue and cash receipts completed by Sterling Engineering Services during the period June 2–30 are as follows:

June 2. Issued Invoice No. 717 to Yee Co., $1,430.

    3. Received cash from Auto-Flex Co. for the balance owed on its account.

    7. Issued Invoice No. 718 to Cooper Development Co., $670.

    10. Issued Invoice No. 719 to Ridge Communities, $2,840.

        Post revenue and collections to the accounts receivable subsidiary ledger.

    14. Received cash from Cooper Development Co. for the balance owed on June 1.

    16. Issued Invoice No. 720 to Cooper Development Co., $400.

        Post revenue and collections to the accounts receivable subsidiary ledger.

    18. Received cash from Yee Co. for the balance due on invoice of June 2.

    20. Received cash from Cooper Development Co. for invoice of June 7.

    23. Issued Invoice No. 721 to Auto-Flex Co., $860.

    30. Received cash from fees earned, $4,520.

    30. Received office equipment of $1,800 in partial settlement of balance due on the Ridge Communities account.

        Post revenue and collections to the accounts receivable subsidiary ledger.

Instructions

1. Insert the following balances in the general ledger as of June 1:

11	Cash	$18,340
12	Accounts Receivable	2,650
18	Office Equipment	34,700
41	Fees Earned	—

2. Insert the following balances in the accounts receivable subsidiary ledger as of June 1:

Auto-Flex Co.	$1,670
Cooper Development Co.	980
Ridge Communities	—
Yee Co.	—

3. Prepare a single-column revenue journal (p. 40) and a cash receipts journal (p. 36). Use the following column headings for the cash receipts journal: Fees Earned Cr., Accounts Receivable Cr., and Cash Dr. The Fees Earned column is used to record cash fees. Insert a check mark (✓) in the Post. Ref. column when recording cash fees.

4. Using the two special journals and the two-column general journal (p. 1), journalize the transactions for June. Post to the accounts receivable subsidiary ledger and insert the balances at the points indicated in the narrative of transactions. Determine the balance in the customer's account before recording a cash receipt.

5. Total each of the columns of the special journals and post the individual entries and totals to the general ledger. Insert account balances after the last posting.

Chapter 5 Accounting Systems 275

6. Determine that the sum of the customer accounts agrees with the accounts receivable controlling account in the general ledger.

7. Why would an automated system omit postings to a control account as performed in step 5 for Accounts Receivable?

✔ 5a. $31,300

PR 5-3B Purchases, accounts payable account, and accounts payable subsidiary ledger
OBJ. 2, 4

Plumb Line Surveyors provides survey work for construction projects. The office staff use office supplies, while surveying crews use field supplies. Purchases on account completed by Plumb Line Surveyors during May are as follows:

May 1. Purchased field supplies on account from Wendell Co., $3,240.
      3. Purchased office supplies on account from Lassiter Co., $340.
      8. Purchased field supplies on account from Tri Cities Supplies, $4,500.
     12. Purchased field supplies on account from Wendell Co., $3,670.
     15. Purchased office supplies on account from J-Mart Co., $500.
     19. Purchased office equipment on account from Accu-Vision Supply Co., $8,150.
     23. Purchased field supplies on account from Tri Cities Supplies, $2,450.
     26. Purchased office supplies on account from J-Mart Co., $265.
     30. Purchased field supplies on account from Tri Cities Supplies, $3,040.

Instructions

1. Insert the following balances in the general ledger as of May 1:

14	Field Supplies	$ 6,200
15	Office Supplies	1,490
18	Office Equipment	19,400
21	Accounts Payable	5,145

2. Insert the following balances in the accounts payable subsidiary ledger as of May 1:

Accu-Vision Supply Co.	$3,900
J-Mart Co.	730
Lassiter Co.	515
Tri Cities Supplies	—
Wendell Co.	—

3. Journalize the transactions for May, using a purchases journal (p. 30) similar to the one illustrated in this chapter. Prepare the purchases journal with columns for Accounts Payable, Field Supplies, Office Supplies, and Other Accounts. Post to the creditor accounts in the accounts payable subsidiary ledger immediately after each entry.

4. Post the purchases journal to the accounts in the general ledger.

5. a. What is the sum of the creditor balances in the subsidiary ledger at May 31?
   b. What is the balance of the accounts payable controlling account at May 31?

6. What type of e-commerce application would be used to plan and coordinate transactions with suppliers?

✔ 1. Total cash payments, $327,920

PR 5-4B Purchases and cash payments journals; accounts payable subsidiary and general ledgers
OBJ. 2

West Texas Exploration Co. was established on October 15 to provide oil-drilling services. West Texas uses field equipment (rigs and pipe) and field supplies (drill bits and lubricants) in its operations. Transactions related to purchases and cash payments during the remainder of October are as follows:

Oct. 16. Issued Check No. 1 in payment of rent for the remainder of October, $7,000.
     16. Purchased field equipment on account from Petro Services Inc., $32,600.

(*Continued*)

276 Chapter 5 Accounting Systems

Oct. 17. Purchased field supplies on account from Midland Supply Co., $9,780.

18. Issued Check No. 2 in payment of field supplies, $4,570, and office supplies, $650.

20. Purchased office supplies on account from A-One Office Supply Co., $1,320.

Post the journals to the accounts payable subsidiary ledger.

24. Issued Check No. 3 to Petro Services Inc., in payment of October 16 invoice.

26. Issued Check No. 4 to Midland Supply Co. in payment of October 17 invoice.

28. Issued Check No. 5 to purchase land, $240,000.

28. Purchased office supplies on account from A-One Office Supply Co., $3,670.

Post the journals to the accounts payable subsidiary ledger.

30. Purchased the following from Petro Services Inc. on account: field supplies, $25,300 and office equipment, $5,500.

30. Issued Check No. 6 to A-One Office Supply Co. in payment of October 20 invoice.

30. Purchased field supplies on account from Midland Supply Co., $12,450.

31. Issued Check No. 7 in payment of salaries, $32,000.

31. Rented building for one year in exchange for field equipment having a cost of $15,000.

Post the journals to the accounts payable subsidiary ledger.

Instructions

1. Journalize the transactions for October. Use a purchases journal and a cash payments journal similar to those illustrated in this chapter and a two-column general journal. Set debit columns for Field Supplies, Office Supplies, and Other Accounts in the purchases journal. Refer to the following partial chart of accounts:

11	Cash	18	Office Equipment
14	Field Supplies	19	Land
15	Office Supplies	21	Accounts Payable
16	Prepaid Rent	61	Salary Expense
17	Field Equipment	71	Rent Expense

At the points indicated in the narrative of transactions, post to the following subsidiary accounts in the accounts payable ledger:

A-One Office Supply Co.
Midland Supply Co.
Petro Services Inc.

2. Post the individual entries (Other Accounts columns of the purchases journal and the cash payments journal; both columns of the general journal) to the appropriate general ledger accounts.

3. Total each of the columns of the purchases journal and the cash payments journal, and post the appropriate totals to the general ledger. (Because the problem does not include transactions related to cash receipts, the cash account in the ledger will have a credit balance.)

4. Sum the balances of the accounts payable creditor balances.

5. Why might West Texas consider using a subsidiary ledger for the field equipment?

PR 5-5B All journals and general ledger; trial balance **OBJ. 2**

✔ 2. Total cash receipts, $96,050

The transactions completed by AM Express Company during March, the first month of the fiscal year, were as follows:

Mar. 1. Issued Check No. 205 for March rent, $2,450.

2. Purchased a vehicle on account from McIntyre Sales Co., $26,900.

3. Purchased office equipment on account from Office Mate Inc., $1,570.

5. Issued Invoice No. 91 to Ellis Co., $7,000.

6. Received check for $7,950 from Chavez Co. in payment of invoice.

Mar. 7. Issued Invoice No. 92 to Trent Co., $9,840.
  9. Issued Check No. 206 for fuel expense, $820.
  10. Received check for $10,000 from Sajeev Co. in payment of invoice.
  10. Issued Check No. 207 to Office City in payment of $450 invoice.
  10. Issued Check No. 208 to Bastille Co. in payment of $1,890 invoice.
  11. Issued Invoice No. 93 to Jarvis Co., $7,200.
  11. Issued Check No. 209 to Porter Co. in payment of $415 invoice.
  12. Received check for $7,000 from Ellis Co. in payment of March 5 invoice.
  13. Issued Check No. 210 to McIntyre Sales Co. in payment of $26,900 invoice of March 2.
  16. Cash fees earned for March 1–16, $26,800.
  16. Issued Check No. 211 for purchase of a vehicle, $28,500.
  17. Issued Check No. 212 for miscellaneous administrative expense, $4,680.
  18. Purchased maintenance supplies on account from Bastille Co., $2,430.
  18. Received check for rent revenue on office space, $900.
  19. Purchased the following on account from Master Supply Co.: maintenance supplies, $2,640, and office supplies, $1,500.
  20. Issued Check No. 213 in payment of advertising expense, $8,590.
  20. Used maintenance supplies with a cost of $4,400 to repair vehicles.
  21. Purchased office supplies on account from Office City, $990.
  24. Issued Invoice No. 94 to Sajeev Co., $9,200.
  25. Received check for $14,000 from Chavez Co. in payment of invoice.
  25. Issued Invoice No. 95 to Trent Co., $6,300.
  26. Issued Check No. 214 to Office Mate Inc. in payment of $1,570 invoice of March 3.
  27. Issued Check No. 215 to J. Wu as a personal withdrawal, $4,000.
  30. Issued Check No. 216 in payment of driver salaries, $33,300.
  31. Issued Check No. 217 in payment of office salaries, $21,200.
  31. Issued Check No. 218 for office supplies, $600.
  31. Cash fees earned for March 17–31, $29,400.

Instructions

1. Enter the following account balances in the general ledger as of March 1:

11	Cash	$ 65,200	32	J. Wu, Drawing	—
12	Accounts Receivable	31,950	41	Fees Earned	—
14	Maintenance Supplies	7,240	42	Rent Revenue	—
15	Office Supplies	3,690	51	Driver Salaries Expense	—
16	Office Equipment	17,300	52	Maintenance Supplies Expense	—
17	Accum. Depr.—Office Equip.	4,250	53	Fuel Expense	—
18	Vehicles	62,400	61	Office Salaries Expense	—
19	Accum. Depr.—Vehicles	17,800	62	Rent Expense	—
21	Accounts Payable	2,755	63	Advertising Expense	—
31	J. Wu, Capital	162,975	64	Miscellaneous Administrative Exp.	—

2. Journalize the transactions for March, using the following journals similar to those illustrated in this chapter: single-column revenue journal (p. 35), cash receipts journal (p. 31), purchases journal (p. 37, with columns for Accounts Payable, Maintenance Supplies, Office Supplies, and Other Accounts), cash payments journal (p. 34), and two-column general journal (p. 1). Assume that the daily postings to the individual accounts in the accounts payable subsidiary ledger and the accounts receivable subsidiary ledger have been made.

(Continued)

3. Post the appropriate individual entries to the general ledger.
4. Total each of the columns of the special journals and post the appropriate totals to the general ledger; insert the account balances.
5. Prepare a trial balance.

Cases & Projects

CP 5-1 Ethics in Action

Netbooks Inc. provides accounting applications for business customers on the Internet for a monthly subscription. Netbooks customers run their accounting system on the Internet; thus, the business data and accounting software reside on the servers of Netbooks Inc. The senior management of Netbooks believes that once a customer begins to use Netbooks, it is very difficult to cancel the service. That is, customers are "locked in" because it is difficult to move the business data from Netbooks to another accounting application even though the customers own their own data. Therefore, Netbooks has decided to entice customers with an initial low monthly price that is half the normal monthly rate for the first year of services. After a year, the price will be increased to the regular monthly rate. Netbooks management believes that customers will have to accept the full price because customers will be "locked in" after one year of use.

a. Discuss whether the half-price offer is an ethical business practice.
b. Discuss whether customer "lock-in" is an ethical business practice.

CP 5-2 Team Activity

The two leading software application providers for supply chain management (SCM) and customer relationship management (CRM) software are **JDA** and **Salesforce.com**, respectively. In groups of two or three, go to the website of each company (www.jda.com and www.salesforce.com, respectively) and list the services provided by each company's software.

CP 5-3 Communication

Internet-based accounting software is a recent trend in business computing. Major software firms such as **Oracle**, **SAP**, and **NetSuite** are running their core products on the Internet using cloud computing. NetSuite is one of the most popular small-business Internet-based accounting systems.

Go to NetSuite Inc.'s website at www.netsuite.com. Read about the product and prepare a memo to management defining cloud-based accounting. Also outline the advantages and disadvantages of using cloud-based accounting compared to running software on a company's internal computer network.

CP 5-4 Manual vs. computerized accounting systems

The following conversation took place between Durable Construction Co.'s bookkeeper, Kyle Byers, and the accounting supervisor, Sarah Nelson:

Sarah: Kyle, I'm thinking about bringing in a new computerized accounting system to replace our manual system. I guess this means that you will need to learn how to do computerized accounting.

Kyle: What does computerized accounting mean?

Sarah: I'm not sure, but you'll need to prepare for this new way of doing business.

Kyle: I'm not so sure we need a computerized system. I've been looking at some of the sample reports from the software vendor. It looks to me as if the computer will not add much to what we are already doing.

Sarah: What do you mean?

Kyle: Well, look at these reports. This Sales by Customer Report looks like our revenue journal, and the Deposit Detail Report looks like our cash receipts journal. Granted, the computer types them, so they look much neater than my special journals, but I don't see that we're gaining much from this change.

Sarah: Well, surely there's more to it than nice-looking reports. I've got to believe that a computerized system will save us time and effort someplace.

Kyle: I don't see how. We still need to key transactions into the computer. If anything, there may be more work when it's all said and done.

➤ Do you agree with Kyle? Why might a computerized environment be preferred over the manual system?

CP 5-5 Accounts receivable and accounts payable

A subsidiary ledger is used for accounts receivable and accounts payable. Thus, transactions that are made "on account" are posted to the individual customer or creditor accounts.

a. Why do companies use subsidiary ledgers for accounts payable and accounts receivable?

b. Identify another account that could benefit from using a subsidiary ledger.

CP 5-6 Design of accounting systems

For the past few years, your client, Omni Care, has operated a small medical practice. Omni Care's current annual revenues are $945,000. Because the accountant has been spending more time each month recording all transactions in a two-column journal and preparing the financial statements, Omni Care is considering improving the accounting system by adding special journals and subsidiary ledgers. Omni Care has asked you to help with this project and has compiled the following information:

Type of Transaction	Estimated Frequency per Month
Fees earned on account	240
Purchase of medical supplies on account	190
Cash receipts from patients on account	175
Cash payments on account	160
Cash receipts from patients at time services are provided	120
Purchase of office supplies on account	35
Purchase of magazine subscriptions on account	5
Purchase of medical equipment on account	4
Cash payments for office salaries	3
Cash payments for utilities expense	3

1. ➤ Briefly discuss the circumstances under which special journals would be used in place of a two-column (all-purpose) journal. Include in your answer your recommendations for Omni Care's medical practice.

2. Assume that Omni Care has decided to use a revenue journal and a purchases journal. Design the format for each journal, giving special consideration to the needs of the medical practice.

3. Which subsidiary ledgers would you recommend for the medical practice?

CHAPTER 6
Accounting for Merchandising Businesses

Chapters 1–4
Accounting Cycle

Chapter 5
Accounting Systems

| Income Statement | Statement of Owner's Equity | Balance Sheet | Statement of Cash Flows |

Chapter 6 Accounting for Merchandising Businesses

Chapter 16 *Cash Flows*

Assets = Liabilities + Owner's Equity

Chapter 8	*Cash*	Chapter 11	*Current Liabilities*	Chapter 12	*Partnerships*
Chapter 9	*Receivables*	Chapter 14	*Bonds and Notes*	Chapter 13	*Corporations*
Chapter 7	*Inventories*				
Chapter 10	*Fixed and Intangible Assets*				
Chapter 15	*Investments*				

Chapter 17
Financial Statement Analysis

Statement of Owner's Equity

Owner's capital, Jan. 1		$XXX
Net income	$ XXX	
Withdrawals	(XXX)	
Increase in capital		XXX

Statement of Cash Flows

Cash flows from (used in) operating activities	$XXX
Cash flows from (used in) investing activities	XXX
Cash flows from (used in) financing activities	XXX
Increase (decrease) in cash flows	$XXX
	XXX
	$XXX

Income Statement

Sales		$XXX
Cost of merchandise sold		XXX
Gross profit		$XXX
Operating expenses:		
Advertising expense	$XXX	
Depreciation expense	XXX	
Amortization expense	XXX	
Depletion expense	XXX	
…	XXX	
…	XXX	
Total operating expenses		XXX
Income from operations		$XXX
Other revenue and expenses		XXX
Net income		$XXX

Balance Sheet

Current assets:		
Cash	$XXX	
Accounts receivable	XXX	
Merchandise inventory	XXX	
Total current assets		$XXX
Property, plant, and equipment	$XXX	
Intangible assets	XXX	
Total long-term assets		XXX
Total assets		$XXX
Liabilities:		
Current liabilities	$XXX	
Long-term liabilities	XXX	
Total liabilities		$XXX
Owner's equity		XXX
Total liabilities and owner's equity		$XXX

CHAPTER 6

Dollar Tree Stores, Inc.

When you are low on cash but need to pick up party supplies, housewares, or other consumer items, where do you go? Many shoppers are turning to **Dollar Tree Stores, Inc.**, the nation's largest single price point dollar retailer with more than 4,000 stores in 48 states. For the fixed price of $1 on merchandise in its stores, Dollar Tree provides "new treasures" every week for the entire family.

Despite the fact that items cost only $1, the accounting for a merchandiser, like Dollar Tree, is more complex than for a service company. This is because a service company sells only services and has no inventory. Because of Dollar Tree's many locations and wide variety of merchandise, the company must design its accounting system to record the receipt of goods for sale and keep track of where the merchandise is located. The company must also record the sales and cost of merchandise sold for each of its stores. Finally, Dollar Tree must record such data as delivery costs, merchandise discounts, and merchandise returns.

This chapter focuses on the accounting principles and concepts for a merchandising business. In doing so, the basic differences between merchandiser and service company activities are highlighted. The financial statements of a merchandising business and accounting for merchandise transactions are also described and illustrated.

Learning Objectives

After studying this chapter, you should be able to:

Example Exercises (EE) are shown in **green**.

Obj. 1 Distinguish between the activities and financial statements of service and merchandising businesses.

Nature of Merchandising Businesses
Operating Cycle
Gross Profit — EE **6-1**

Obj. 2 Describe and illustrate the accounting for merchandise transactions.

Merchandising Transactions
Chart of Accounts for a Merchandising Business
Purchases Transactions — EE **6-2**
Sales Transactions — EE **6-3**
Freight — EE **6-4**
Summary: Recording Merchandise Inventory Transactions
Dual Nature of Merchandise Transactions — EE **6-5**
Sales Taxes and Trade Discounts

Obj. 3 Describe and illustrate the adjusting process for a merchandising business.

The Adjusting Process
Adjusting Entry for Inventory Shrinkage — EE **6-6**
Adjusting Entries for Customer Allowances and Returns — EE **6-7**

Obj. 4 Describe and illustrate the financial statements of a merchandising business.

Financial Statements for a Merchandising Business
Multiple-Step Income Statement
Single-Step Income Statement
Statement of Owner's Equity
Balance Sheet
The Closing Process

Obj. 5 Describe and illustrate the use of asset turnover in evaluating a company's operating performance.

Financial Analysis and Interpretation: Asset Turnover
Compute Asset Turnover — EE **6-8**

At a Glance 6 — Page 314

Obj. 1 Distinguish between the activities and financial statements of service and merchandising businesses.

Nature of Merchandising Businesses

The activities of a service business differ from those of a merchandising business. These differences are reflected in the operating cycles of a service and merchandising business as well as in their financial statements.

Operating Cycle

The **operating cycle** is the process by which a company spends cash, generates revenues, and receives cash either at the time the revenues are generated or later by collecting an account receivable. The operating cycle of a service and merchandising business differs in that a merchandising business must purchase merchandise for sale to customers. The operating cycle for a merchandise business is shown in Exhibit 1.

EXHIBIT 1
The Operating Cycle for a Merchandising Business

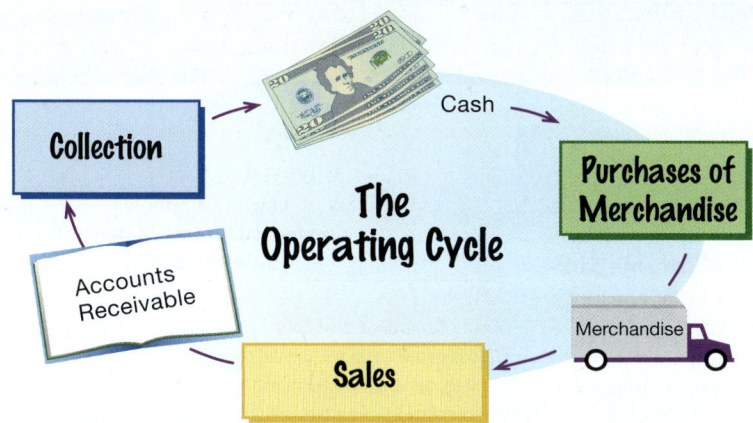

The time in days to complete an operating cycle differs significantly among merchandise businesses. Grocery stores normally have short operating cycles because of the nature of their merchandise. For example, many grocery items, such as milk, must be sold within their expiration dates of a week or two. In contrast, jewelry stores often carry expensive items that are displayed months before being sold to customers.

Financial Statements

The differences between service and merchandising businesses are also reflected in their financial statements. For example, these differences are illustrated in the following condensed income statements:

Service Business		Merchandising Business	
Fees earned	$ XXX	Sales	$ XXX
Operating expenses	(XXX)	Cost of merchandise sold	(XXX)
Operating income	$ XXX	Gross profit	$ XXX
		Operating expenses	(XXX)
		Operating income	$ XXX

The revenue activities of a service business involve providing services to customers. On the income statement for a service business, the revenues from services are reported as *fees earned*. The operating expenses incurred in providing the services are subtracted from the fees earned to arrive at *operating income*.

In contrast, the revenue activities of a merchandising business involve the buying and selling of merchandise. A merchandising business first purchases merchandise to sell to its customers. When this merchandise is sold, the revenue is reported as **sales**, and its cost is recognized as an expense. This expense is called the **cost of merchandise sold**. The cost of merchandise sold is subtracted from sales to arrive at gross profit. This amount is called **gross profit** because it is the profit *before* deducting operating expenses.

Merchandise on hand (not sold) at the end of an accounting period is called **merchandise inventory**. Merchandise inventory is reported as a current asset on the balance sheet.

Link to Dollar Tree

In a recent income statement, **Dollar Tree** reported the following (in billions):
Sales . . . . $ 8.6
Cost of merch. sold . . . . (5.6)
Gross profit . . . . $ 3.0
Operating expenses . . . . . . (2.0)
Operating income . . . . $ 1.0
On its balance sheet, it reported merchandise inventory of $1.0 billion.

Business Connection

COMCAST VERSUS LOWE'S

Comcast Corporation is a service business that offers cable communications, broadcast television (NBC television), filmed entertainment (Universal Pictures), and theme parks (Universal Parks) to its customers. **Lowe's Companies** is a large home improvement retailer. The differences in the operations of a service and merchandising business are illustrated in their recent income statements, as follows:

Comcast Corporation
Condensed Income Statement
(in millions)

Revenue	$ 68,775
Programming and production expenses	(20,912)
Selling and administrative expenses	(24,940)
Depreciation and amortization expenses	(8,019)
Operating income	$ 14,904

Lowe's Companies
Condensed Income Statement
(in millions)

Sales	$ 56,223
Cost of merchandise sold	(36,665)
Gross profit	$ 19,558
Selling, general, and administrative expenses	(13,281)
Depreciation expense	(1,485)
Operating income	$ 4,792

As a merchandising company, Lowe's subtracts cost of merchandise sold from sales to disclose gross profit. As a service company, Comcast shows neither cost of merchandise sold nor a gross profit line. Rather, service expenses are subtracted from revenue straight to operating income.

Example Exercise 6-1 Gross Profit   Obj. 1

During the current year, merchandise is sold for $250,000 cash and for $975,000 on account. The cost of the merchandise sold is $735,000. What is the amount of the gross profit?

Follow My Example 6-1

The gross profit is $490,000 ($250,000 + $975,000 − $735,000).

Practice Exercises: PE 6-1A, PE 6-1B

Obj. 2 Describe and illustrate the accounting for merchandise transactions.

Merchandising Transactions

This section illustrates merchandise transactions for **NetSolutions** after it becomes a retailer of computer hardware and software. During 2018, Chris Clark implemented the second phase of NetSolutions' business plan. In doing so, Chris notified clients that beginning July 1, 2019, NetSolutions would no longer offer consulting services. Instead, it would become a merchandising business.

NetSolutions' business strategy is to offer personalized service to individuals and small businesses that are upgrading or purchasing new computer systems. NetSolutions' personal service includes a no-obligation, on-site assessment of the customer's computer needs. By providing personalized service and follow-up, Chris believes that NetSolutions can compete effectively against such retailers as **Best Buy**, **Office Depot**, and **Dell**.

Chart of Accounts for a Merchandising Business

NetSolutions merchandise transactions are recorded in the accounts, using the rules of debit and credit that are described and illustrated in Chapter 2. However, since

EXHIBIT 2

Chart of Accounts for NetSolutions as a Merchandising Business

Balance Sheet Accounts	Income Statement Accounts
100 Assets	**400 Revenues**
110 Cash	410 Sales
112 Accounts Receivable	**500 Costs and Expenses**
115 Merchandise Inventory	510 Cost of Merchandise Sold
116 Estimated Returns Inventory	520 Sales Salaries Expense
117 Office Supplies	521 Advertising Expense
118 Prepaid Insurance	522 Depreciation Expense— Store Equipment
120 Land	523 Delivery Expense
123 Store Equipment	529 Miscellaneous Selling Expense
124 Accumulated Depreciation— Store Equipment	530 Office Salaries Expense
125 Office Equipment	531 Rent Expense
126 Accumulated Depreciation— Office Equipment	532 Depreciation Expense— Office Equipment
200 Liabilities	533 Insurance Expense
210 Accounts Payable	534 Office Supplies Expense
211 Salaries Payable	539 Misc. Administrative Expense
212 Unearned Rent	**600 Other Revenue**
213 Customer Refunds Payable	610 Rent Revenue
215 Notes Payable	**700 Other Expense**
300 Owner's Equity	710 Interest Expense
310 Chris Clark, Capital	
311 Chris Clark, Drawing	

merchandising transactions differ from those of a service business, NetSolutions adopted the new chart of accounts shown in Exhibit 2.

The accounts related to merchandising transactions are highlighted in pink in Exhibit 2. The nature of these accounts will be described and illustrated as the related merchandising transactions are discussed.

As shown in Exhibit 2, NetSolutions' chart of accounts now consists of three-digit account numbers. The first digit indicates the major financial statement classification (1 for assets, 2 for liabilities, etc.). The second digit indicates the subclassification (e.g., 11 for current assets and 12 for noncurrent assets). The third digit identifies the specific account (e.g., 110 for Cash and 123 for Store Equipment).

Most merchandising companies use accounting systems with computerized reports that are similar to special journals and subsidiary ledgers illustrated in Chapter 5. For example, a merchandise accounting system typically produces sales and inventory reports. However, for the sake of simplicity, the transactions in this chapter will be illustrated using a two-column general journal.

Purchases Transactions

There are two systems for accounting for merchandise transactions: perpetual and periodic. In a **perpetual inventory system**, each purchase and sale of merchandise is recorded in the inventory account and related subsidiary ledger. In this way, the amount of merchandise available for sale and the amount sold are continuously (perpetually) updated in the inventory records. In a **periodic inventory system**, the inventory does not show the amount of merchandise available for sale and the amount sold. Instead, a listing of inventory on hand, called a **physical inventory**, is prepared at the end of the accounting period. This physical inventory is used to determine the cost of merchandise on hand at the end of the period and the cost of merchandise sold during the period.

Link to Dollar Tree

Dollar Tree uses point-of-sale computerized software to plan purchases and track inventory. This system automatically reorders key items based on sales and inventory levels.

Most merchandise companies use computerized perpetual inventory systems. Such systems use bar codes or radio frequency identification codes embedded in a product. An optical scanner or radio frequency identification device is then used to read the product codes and track inventory on hand and sold.

Because computerized perpetual inventory systems are widely used, this chapter illustrates merchandise transactions using a perpetual inventory system. The periodic system is described and illustrated in an appendix at the end of this chapter.

Under the perpetual inventory system, cash purchases of $2,510 of merchandise are recorded as follows:

		Journal			Page 24
Date		Description	Post. Ref.	Debit	Credit
2020 Jan.	3	Merchandise Inventory		2,510	
		Cash			2,510
		Purchased inventory from Bowen Co.			

Purchases of $9,250 of merchandise on account are recorded as follows:

Jan.	4	Merchandise Inventory		9,250	
		Accounts Payable—Thomas Corporation			9,250
		Purchased inventory on account.			

The terms of purchases on account are normally indicated on the **invoice** or bill that the seller sends the buyer. An example of an invoice sent to NetSolutions by Alpha Technologies is shown in Exhibit 3.

EXHIBIT 3

Invoice

Alpha Technologies
1000 Matrix Blvd.
San Jose, CA 95116-1000

Made in U.S.A.

INVOICE 106-8

SOLD TO	CUSTOMER ORDER NO.	ORDER DATE
NetSolutions	412	Jan. 3, 2020
5101 Washington Ave.		
Cincinnati, OH 45227-5101		

DATE SHIPPED	HOW SHIPPED AND ROUTE	TERMS	INVOICE DATE
Jan. 5, 2020	US Express Trucking Co.	2/10, n/30	Jan. 5, 2020

FROM	F.O.B.		
San Jose	Cincinnati		

QUANTITY	DESCRIPTION	UNIT PRICE	AMOUNT
20	HC9 Printer/Fax/Copier	150.00	3,000.00

The terms for when payments for merchandise are to be made are called the **credit terms**. If payment is required on delivery, the terms are cash or net cash. Otherwise, the buyer is allowed an amount of time, known as the **credit period**, in which to pay. The credit period usually begins with the date of the sale as shown on the invoice.

If payment is due within a stated number of days after the invoice date, such as 30 days, the terms are net 30 days. These terms may be written as *n/30*.[1] If payment is due by the end of the month in which the sale was made, the terms are written as *n/eom*.

Purchases Discounts To encourage the buyer to pay before the end of the credit period, the seller may offer a discount. For example, a seller may offer a 2% discount if the buyer pays within 10 days of the invoice date. If the buyer does not take the discount, the total invoice amount is due within 30 days. These terms are expressed as 2/10, n/30 and are read as "2% discount if paid within 10 days, net amount due within 30 days." The credit terms of 2/10, n/30 are summarized in Exhibit 4, using the invoice in Exhibit 3.

EXHIBIT 4 Credit Terms

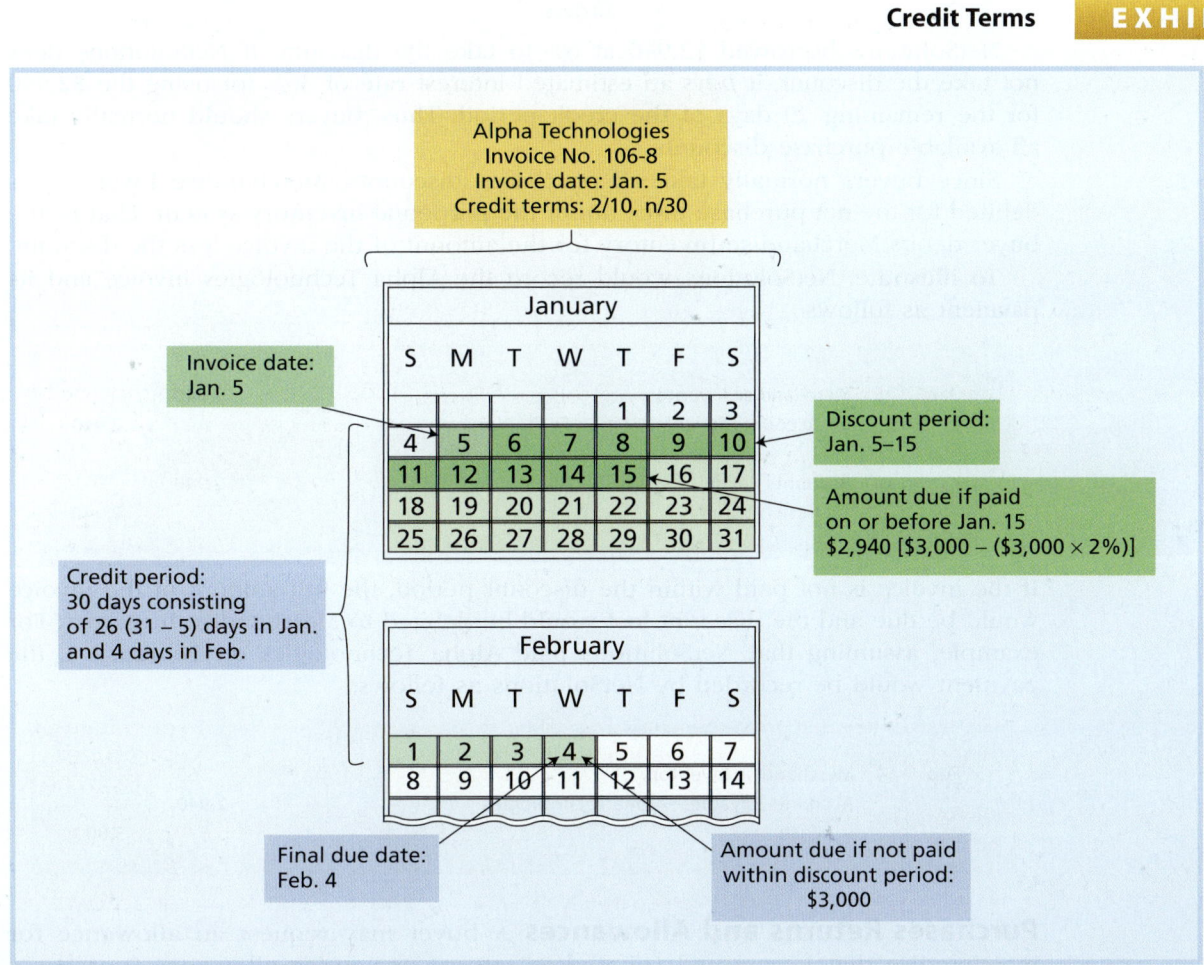

Discounts taken by the buyer for early payment of an invoice are called **purchases discounts**. Purchases discounts taken by a buyer reduce the cost of the merchandise purchased. Even if the buyer has to borrow to pay within a discount period, it is normally to the buyer's advantage to do so. For this reason, accounting systems are normally designed so that all available discounts are taken.

To illustrate, the invoice shown in Exhibit 3 is used. The last day of the discount period is January 15 (invoice date of January 5 plus 10 days). Assume that in order to pay the invoice on January 15, **NetSolutions** borrows $2,940, which is $3,000 less

---

1 The word *net* as used here does not have the usual meaning of a number after deductions have been subtracted, as in *net income*.

the discount of $60 ($3,000 × 2%). If an annual interest rate of 6% and a 360-day year is also assumed, the interest on the loan of $2,940 for the remaining 20 days of the credit period is $9.80 ($2,940 × 6% × 20 ÷ 360).[2]

The net savings to NetSolutions of taking the discount is $50.20, computed as follows:

Discount of 2% on $3,000	$60.00
Interest for 20 days at a rate of 6% on $2,940	9.80
Savings from taking the discount	$50.20

The savings can also be seen by comparing the interest rate on the money *saved* by taking the discount and the interest rate on the money *borrowed* to take the discount. The interest rate on the money saved in the prior example is estimated by converting 2% for 20 days to a yearly rate, as follows:

$$2\% \times \frac{360 \text{ days}}{20 \text{ days}} = 2\% \times 18 = 36\%$$

NetSolutions borrowed $2,940 at 6% to take the discount. If NetSolutions does not take the discount, it *pays* an estimated interest rate of 36% for using the $2,940 for the remaining 20 days of the credit period. Thus, buyers should normally take all available purchase discounts.

Since buyers normally take all purchases discounts, Merchandise Inventory is debited for the net purchase price under the perpetual inventory system. That is, the buyer debits Merchandise Inventory for the amount of the invoice less the discount.

To illustrate, NetSolutions would record the Alpha Technologies invoice and its payment as follows:

Jan.	5	Merchandise Inventory	2,940	
		Accounts Payable—Alpha Technologies		2,940
	15	Accounts Payable—Alpha Technologies	2,940	
		Cash		2,940

If the invoice is not paid within the discount period, the full amount of the invoice would be due and the discount lost would be debited to Merchandise Inventory. For example, assuming that NetSolutions paid Alpha Technologies on February 4, the payment would be recorded by NetSolutions as follows:

Feb.	4	Merchandise Inventory	60	
		Accounts Payable—Alpha Technologies	2,940	
		Cash		3,000

Purchases Returns and Allowances A buyer may request an allowance for merchandise that is returned (purchases return) or a price allowance (purchases allowance) for damaged or defective merchandise. From a buyer's perspective, such returns and allowances are called **purchases returns and allowances**. In both cases, the buyer normally sends the seller a debit memorandum to notify the seller of reasons for the return (purchase return) or to request a price reduction (purchase allowance).

A **debit memorandum**, often called a **debit memo**, is shown in Exhibit 5. A debit memo informs the seller of the amount the buyer proposes to *debit* to the account payable due the seller. It also states the reasons for the return or the request for the price allowance.

---

[2] To simplify computations and rounding, we use a 360-day year rather than a 365-day year.

EXHIBIT 5
Debit Memo

```
                    NetSolutions              No. 18
                 5101 Washington Ave.
                 Cincinnati, OH  45227-5101

DEBIT MEMO

TO                                        DATE
Maxim Systems                             March 7, 2020
7519 East Wilson Ave.
Seattle, WA  98101-7519

WE DEBITED YOUR ACCOUNT AS FOLLOWS
10   Server Network Interface Cards, your invoice No. 7291,
     are being returned via parcel post. Our order specified
     No. 825X, but we received No. 835c.           @ 90.00      900.00
```

The buyer may use the debit memo as the basis for recording the return or allowance or wait for approval from the seller (creditor). In either case, the buyer debits Accounts Payable and credits Merchandise Inventory.

To illustrate, **NetSolutions** records the return of the merchandise indicated in the debit memo in Exhibit 5 as follows:

Mar.	7	Accounts Payable—Maxim Systems	900	
		Merchandise Inventory		900
		Debit Memo No. 18.		

Before paying an invoice, a buyer may return merchandise or be granted a price allowance for an invoice with a purchase discount. In this case, the amount of the return is recorded at its invoice amount less the discount.

To illustrate, assume the following data concerning a purchase of merchandise by NetSolutions on May 2:

May 2. Purchased $5,000 of merchandise on account from Delta Data Link, terms 2/10, n/30.
     4. Returned $1,000 of the merchandise purchased on May 2.
    12. Paid for the purchase of May 2 less the return and discount.

NetSolutions would record these transactions as follows:

May	2	Merchandise Inventory	4,900	
		Accounts Payable—Delta Data Link		4,900
		Purchased merchandise.		
		[$5,000 − ($5,000 × 2%)]		
	4	Accounts Payable—Delta Data Link	980	
		Merchandise Inventory		980
		Returned portion of merch. purchased.		
		[$1,000 − ($1,000 × 2%)]		
	12	Accounts Payable—Delta Data Link	3,920	
		Cash		3,920
		($4,900 − $980)		

Chapter 6 Accounting for Merchandising Businesses

> ### Example Exercise 6-2 Purchases Transactions Obj. 2
>
> Rofles Company purchased merchandise on account from a supplier for $11,500, terms 2/10, n/30. Rofles Company returned $2,500 of the merchandise and received full credit.
>
> a. If Rofles Company pays the invoice within the discount period, what is the amount of cash required for the payment?
>
> b. Under a perpetual inventory system, what account is credited by Rofles Company to record the return?
>
> ### Follow My Example 6-2
>
> a. $8,820. Purchase of $11,270 [$11,500 − ($11,500 × 2%)] less the return of $2,450 [$2,500 − ($2,500 × 2%)].
>
> b. Merchandise Inventory
>
> Practice Exercises: PE 6-2A, PE 6-2B

Sales Transactions

Revenue from merchandise sales is usually recorded as *Sales*. Sometimes a business may use the title *Sales of Merchandise*.

Cash Sales A business may sell merchandise for cash. Cash sales are normally entered on a cash register and recorded in the accounts. To illustrate, assume that on March 3, **NetSolutions** sells merchandise for $1,800. These cash sales are recorded as follows:

	Journal			Page 25
Date	Description	Post. Ref.	Debit	Credit
2020 Mar. 3	Cash		1,800	
	Sales			1,800
	To record cash sales.			

Using the perpetual inventory system, the cost of merchandise sold and the decrease in merchandise inventory are also recorded. In this way, the merchandise inventory account indicates the amount of merchandise on hand (not sold).

To illustrate, assume that the cost of merchandise sold on March 3 is $1,200. The entry to record the cost of merchandise sold and the decrease in the merchandise inventory is as follows:

Mar. 3	Cost of Merchandise Sold		1,200	
	Merchandise Inventory			1,200
	To record the cost of merchandise sold.			

Sales may be made to customers using credit cards such as **MasterCard** or **VISA**. Such sales are recorded as cash sales. This is because these sales are normally processed by a clearinghouse that contacts the bank that issued the card. The issuing bank then electronically transfers cash directly to the retailer's bank account.[3] Thus, the retailer normally receives cash within a few days of making the credit card sale.

---

[3] CyberSource is one of the major credit card clearinghouses. For a more detailed description of how credit card sales are processed, see the following CyberSource web page: www.cybersource.com. Click Products and under Payment Processing, click Payment Cards and then How it Works.

If customers use MasterCards to pay for their purchases, the sales would be recorded exactly as shown in the first March 3 entry illustrated in this section. Any processing fees charged by the clearinghouse or issuing bank are periodically recorded as an expense. This expense is normally reported on the income statement as an administrative expense. To illustrate, assume that NetSolutions paid credit card processing fees of $4,150 on March 31. These fees would be recorded as follows:

Mar.	31	Credit Card Expense		4,150	
		Cash			4,150
		To record service charges on credit card sales for the month.			

> **Link to Dollar Tree**
> **Dollar Tree** normally receives cash from credit card sales within three business days and thus records credit card sales as cash sales.

Sales on Account A business may sell merchandise on account. The seller records such sales as a debit to Accounts Receivable and a credit to Sales. An example of an entry for a **NetSolutions** sale on account of $6,000 to Jones Consulting follows. The cost of merchandise sold was $3,500.

Mar.	10	Accounts Receivable—Jones Consulting		6,000	
		Sales			6,000
		Invoice No. 7172.			
	10	Cost of Merchandise Sold		3,500	
		Merchandise Inventory			3,500
		Cost of merch. sold on Invoice No. 7172.			

> **Link to Dollar Tree**
> **Dollar Tree** only accepts cash, checks, credit cards, and debit cards from its customers.

Customer Discounts A seller may grant customers a variety of discounts, called **customer discounts**, as incentives to encourage customers to act in a way benefiting the seller. For example, a seller may offer customer discounts to encourage customers to purchase in volume or order early.

A common discount, called a **sales discount**, encourages customers to pay their invoice early. For example, a seller may offer credit terms of 2/10, n/30, which provides a 2% sales discount if the invoice is paid within 10 days. If not paid within 10 days, the total invoice amount is due within 30 days.[4]

To illustrate the accounting for sales discounts, assume that **NetSolutions** sold $18,000 of merchandise to Digital Technologies on March 10 with credit terms 2/10, n/30. The cost of merchandise sold was $10,800. The March 10 sale would be recorded as follows:[5]

> **Link to Dollar Tree**
> Because **Dollar Tree** does not sell merchandise to customers on account, but only accepts cash, checks, credit cards, and debit cards, it did not report any accounts receivable on a recent balance sheet.

Mar.	10	Accounts Receivable—Digital Technologies		17,640	
		Sales [$18,000 − ($18,000 × 2%)]			17,640
	10	Cost of Merchandise Sold		10,800	
		Merchandise Inventory			10,800

The sale to Digital Technologies is recorded by **NetSolutions** as $17,640, which is the invoice amount of $18,000 less the sales discount of $360 ($18,000 × 2%).[6]

---

[4] From the buyer's perspective, a sales discount is referred to as a purchases discount, which was discussed earlier in this chapter.
[5] The accounting for customer discounts other than sales discounts is discussed in advanced accounting courses.

The payment by Digital Technologies on March 19 is recorded as follows:

Mar.	19	Cash	17,640	
		Accounts Receivable—Digital Technologies		17,640

If Digital Technologies did not pay within the discount period, NetSolutions would receive $18,000 and Sales would be credited for the amount of the discount. For example, assuming that Digital Technologies paid NetSolutions on April 9, the payment would be recorded by NetSolutions as follows:

Apr.	9	Cash	18,000	
		Accounts Receivable—Digital Technologies		17,640
		Sales		360

Cash Refunds and Allowances A buyer may receive merchandise that is defective, has been damaged during shipment, or does not meet the buyer's expectations. In these cases, the seller may pay the buyer a **cash refund** or grant a **customer allowance** that reduces the account receivable owed on the original selling price.

If the buyer is paid a refund, the seller debits Customer Refunds Payable and credits Cash. For example, assume that on March 4, NetSolutions pays Jones & Hunt a refund of $400 for merchandise that was damaged in shipment. Jones & Hunt has agreed to keep the merchandise and make any necessary repairs. Netsolutions would record the payment of the refund as follows:[7]

Mar.	4	Customer Refunds Payable	400	
		Cash		400

Customer refunds payable is a liability account for estimated refunds and allowances that will be paid or granted customers in the future. It is recorded at the end of the accounting period as part of the adjusting process. The adjusting entry for customer refunds payable is illustrated later in this chapter.

In some cases, a customer who is due a refund has an outstanding account receivable balance. Instead of paying a cash refund, the seller may grant the customer an allowance against the customer's account receivable. When this is done, the seller sends the buyer a **credit memorandum**, or **credit memo**, indicating its intent to credit the customer's account receivable.

To illustrate, assume that NetSolutions granted Blake & Sons a customer allowance of $900 against its outstanding accounts receivable. NetSolutions notifies Blake & Sons of the allowance by issuing the credit memo shown in Exhibit 6.

The credit memo indicates that NetSolutions intends to reduce Blake & Sons' accounts receivable for $900 due to merchandise damaged in shipment. NetSolutions would record the granting of the customer allowance as follows:

> **Link to Dollar Tree**
>
> **Dollar Tree** does not offer refunds, and all sales are final.

Mar.	4	Customer Refunds Payable	900	
		Accounts Receivable—Blake & Sons		900

---

6 This is consistent with *Revenue from Contracts with Customers, Topic 606, FASB Accounting Standards Update,* Financial Accounting Standards Board, Norwalk, CT, May 2014.

7 The accounting illustrated is based upon *Revenue from Contracts with Customers, Topic 606, FASB Accounting Standards Update,* Financial Accounting Standards Board, Norwalk, CT, May 2014.

> **EXHIBIT 6**
>
> **Credit Memo**

NetSolutions
5101 Washington Ave.
Cincinnati, OH 45227-5101

CREDIT MEMO

TO	DATE
Blake & Sons	March 4, 2020
7608 Melton Avenue	
Los Angeles, CA 90025-3942	

WE DEBITED YOUR ACCOUNT AS FOLLOWS	
Allowance for merchandise damaged in shipment	900

Customer Returns In the preceding example, Blake & Sons did not return merchandise. When customers return merchandise for a cash refund or allowance, an additional entry must be made. This additional entry debits Merchandise Inventory and credits Estimated Returns Inventory for the seller's original cost of the returned merchandise.

To illustrate, assume that on January 15 Bormann Enterprises returned merchandise with a selling price of $3,000 for a cash refund. The merchandise originally cost NetSolutions $2,100. NetSolutions would record the cash refund and the return with the following two entries:

Jan.	15	Customer Refunds Payable		3,000	
		Cash			3,000
	15	Merchandise Inventory		2,100	
		Estimated Returns Inventory			2,100

The first entry records the cash refund payment of $3,000. The second entry records the receipt of the $2,100 of returned merchandise by debiting Merchandise Inventory and crediting Estimated Returns Inventory.[8]

Estimated returns inventory is a current asset that is reported on the balance sheet after Merchandise Inventory. It represents an estimate of merchandise that will be returned by customers. It is recorded at the end of the accounting period as part of the adjusting process. The adjusting entry for estimated returns inventory is illustrated later in this chapter.

If Bormann Enterprises had an outstanding accounts receivable balance on January 15, NetSolutions could have issued a $3,000 credit memo to Bormann Enterprises. In this case, NetSolutions would have credited Accounts Receivable—Bormann Enterprises instead of Cash.

The journal entries to record customer refunds, allowances, and returns are summarized in Exhibit 7.

> *Link to Dollar Tree*
>
> Although all sales are final, with the original receipt, **Dollar Tree** will "exchange" any unopened item.

---

[8] Because of wear, tear, and damage, companies may segregate returned items from normal inventory by using a separate returns inventory account.

EXHIBIT 7 — Journal Entries to Record Customer Refunds, Allowances, and Returns

	Cash Refund Paid	Credit Memorandum Issued

Customer does not return merchandise	Customer Refunds Payable XXX
	    Cash XXX
		Customer Refunds Payable XXX
		    Accounts Receivable.......... XXX

Customer returns merchandise	Customer Refunds Payable XXX
	    Cash XXX
	Merchandise Inventory.......... XXX
	    Estimated Returns Inventory ... XXX
		Customer Refunds Payable XXX
		    Accounts Receivable.......... XXX
		Merchandise Inventory.......... XXX
		    Estimated Returns Inventory ... XXX

Example Exercise 6-3 — Sales Transactions   Obj. 2

Journalize the following merchandise transactions:

a. Sold merchandise on account to Smith Inc., $7,500, with terms 2/10, n/30. The cost of the merchandise sold was $5,625.

b. Received payment for the sale in (a) less the discount.

c. Issued a credit memo to Wilson Company for returned merchandise that was sold for $4,000, terms n/30. The cost of the merchandise returned was $2,275.

Follow My Example 6-3

a. Accounts Receivable—Smith Inc. [$7,500 − ($7,500 × 2%)] 7,350
    Sales 7,350
   Cost of Merchandise Sold.. 5,625
    Merchandise Inventory 5,625

b. Cash.. 7,350
    Accounts Receivable—Smith Inc. 7,350

c. Customer Refunds Payable... 4,000
    Accounts Receivable—Wilson Company 4,000
   Merchandise Inventory 2,275
    Estimated Returns Inventory... 2,275

Practice Exercises: PE 6-3A, PE 6-3B

INTEGRITY, OBJECTIVITY, AND ETHICS IN BUSINESS

THE CASE OF THE FRAUDULENT PRICE TAGS

One of the challenges for a retailer is policing its sales return policy. There are many ways in which customers can unethically or illegally abuse such policies. In one case, a couple was accused of attaching Marshalls' store price tags to cheaper merchandise bought or obtained elsewhere. The couple then returned the cheaper goods and received the substantially higher refund amount. Company security officials discovered the fraud and had the couple arrested after they had allegedly bilked the company for more than $1 million.

Freight

Purchases and sales of merchandise often involve freight. The terms of a sale indicate when ownership (title and control) of the merchandise passes from the seller to the buyer. This point determines whether the buyer or the seller pays the freight costs.[9]

The ownership of the merchandise may pass to the buyer when the seller delivers the merchandise to the freight carrier. In this case, the terms are said to be **FOB (free on board) shipping point**. This term means that the buyer pays the freight costs from the shipping point to the final destination. Such costs are part of the buyer's total cost of purchasing inventory and are added to the cost of the inventory by debiting Merchandise Inventory.

> **Note**
> The buyer bears the freight costs if the shipping terms are FOB shipping point.

To illustrate, assume that on June 10, NetSolutions purchased merchandise as follows:

June 10. Purchased merchandise from Magna Data, $900, terms FOB shipping point.
10. Paid freight of $50 on June 10 purchase from Magna Data.

NetSolutions would record these two transactions as follows:

June	10	Merchandise Inventory	900	
		Accounts Payable—Magna Data		900
		Purchased merchandise, terms FOB shipping point.		
	10	Merchandise Inventory	50	
		Cash		50
		Paid shipping cost on merchandise purchased.		

The ownership of the merchandise may pass to the buyer when the buyer receives the merchandise. In this case, the terms are said to be **FOB (free on board) destination**. This term means that the seller pays the freight costs from the shipping point to the buyer's final destination. When the seller pays the delivery charges, the seller debits Delivery Expense or Freight Out. Delivery Expense is reported on the seller's income statement as a selling expense.

> **Note**
> The seller bears the freight costs if the shipping terms are FOB destination.

To illustrate, assume that NetSolutions sells merchandise as follows:

June 15. Sold merchandise to Kranz Company on account, $700, terms FOB destination. The cost of the merchandise sold is $480.
15. NetSolutions pays freight of $40 on the sale of June 15.

NetSolutions records the sale, the cost of the sale, and the freight cost as follows:

June	15	Accounts Receivable—Kranz Company	700	
		Sales		700
		Sold merchandise, terms FOB destination.		
	15	Cost of Merchandise Sold	480	
		Merchandise Inventory		480
		Recorded cost of merchandise sold to Kranz Company.		
	15	Delivery Expense	40	
		Cash		40
		Paid shipping cost on merchandise sold.		

[9] The passage of title also determines whether the buyer or seller must pay other costs, such as the cost of insurance, while the merchandise is in transit.

The seller may prepay the freight even though the terms are FOB shipping point. The seller will then add the freight to the invoice. The buyer debits Merchandise Inventory for the total amount of the invoice, including the freight. Any discount terms would not apply to the prepaid freight.

To illustrate, assume that NetSolutions sells merchandise as follows:

June 20. Sold merchandise to Planter Company on account, $800, terms FOB shipping point. NetSolutions paid freight of $45, which was added to the invoice. The cost of the merchandise sold is $360.

NetSolutions records the sale, the cost of the sale, and the freight as follows:

June	20	Accounts Receivable—Planter Company	800	
		Sales		800
		Sold merchandise, terms FOB shipping point.		
	20	Cost of Merchandise Sold	360	
		Merchandise Inventory		360
		Recorded cost of merchandise sold to Planter Company.		
	20	Accounts Receivable—Planter Company	45	
		Cash		45
		Prepaid shipping cost on merchandise sold.		

Shipping terms, the passage of title (control), and whether the buyer or seller is to pay the freight costs are summarized in Exhibit 8.

EXHIBIT 8 Freight Terms

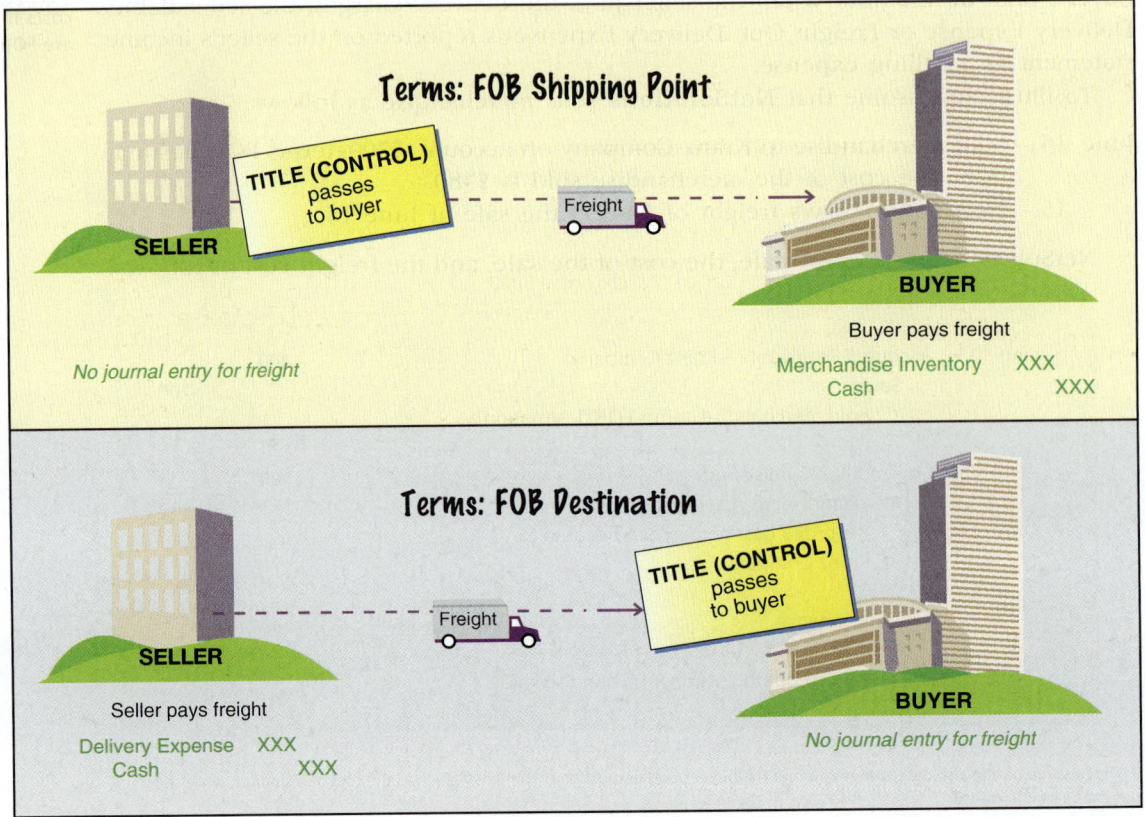

Example Exercise 6-4 Freight Terms   Obj. 2

Determine the amount to be paid in full settlement of each of the two invoices, (a) and (b), assuming that credit for returns and allowances was received prior to payment and that all invoices were paid within the discount period.

	Merchandise	Freight Paid by Seller	Freight Terms	Returns and Allowances
a.	$4,500	$200	FOB shipping point, 1/10, n/30	$ 800
b.	5,000	60	FOB destination, 2/10, n/30	2,500

Follow My Example 6-4

a. $3,863. Purchase of $4,455 [$4,500 − ($4,500 × 1%)] less return of $792 [$800 − ($800 × 1%)] plus $200 of shipping.
b. $2,450. Purchase of $4,900 [$5,000 − ($5,000 × 2%)] less return of $2,450 [$2,500 − ($2,500 × 2%)].

Practice Exercises: PE 6-4A, PE 6-4B

Summary: Recording Merchandise Inventory Transactions

Recording merchandise inventory transactions under the perpetual inventory system has been described and illustrated in the preceding sections. These transactions involved purchases, purchases returns and allowances, freight, cost of merchandise sold (from sales), and customer returns. Exhibit 9 summarizes how these transactions are recorded in T account form.

EXHIBIT 9
Recording Merchandise Inventory Transactions

Merchandise Inventory

Purchases (net of discounts)	XXX	Purchases returns and allowances (net of discounts)	XXX
Freight for merchandise purchased FOB shipping point	XXX	Cost of merchandise sold	XXX
Customer returns	XXX		

Estimated Returns Inventory

		Customer returns	XXX

Cost of Merchandise Sold

Cost of merchandise sold	XXX		

Dual Nature of Merchandise Transactions

Each merchandising transaction affects a buyer and a seller. In Exhibit 10, a series of merchandise transactions are presented. For each transaction, the journal entry that should be recorded by both the seller (Scully Company) and the buyer (Burton Company) is shown.

Chapter 6 Accounting for Merchandising Businesses

EXHIBIT 10 — Illustration of Merchandise Inventory Transactions for Seller and Buyer

Transaction	Scully Company (Seller)	Burton Co. (Buyer)

July 1. Scully Company sold merchandise on account to Burton Co., $7,500, terms FOB shipping point, n/45. The cost of the goods sold was $4,500.	Accounts Receivable—Burton Co. 7,500
	    Sales 7,500
	
	Cost of Merchandise Sold 4,500
	    Merchandise Inventory 4,500
		Merchandise Inventory 7,500
		    Accounts Payable—Scully Co. ... 7,500

July 2. Burton Co. paid freight of $150 on July 1 purchase from Scully Company.	No journal entry.	Merchandise Inventory .... 150 Cash 150

July 5. Scully Company sold merchandise on account to Burton Co., $5,000, terms FOB destination, n/15. The cost of the goods sold was $3,500.	Accounts Receivable—Burton Co. 5,000
	    Sales 5,000
	
	Cost of Merchandise Sold 3,500
	    Merchandise Inventory 3,500
		Merchandise Inventory 5,000
		    Accounts Payable—Scully Co. ... 5,000

July 7. Scully Company paid freight of $250 for delivery of merchandise sold to Burton Co. on July 5.	Delivery Expense .... 250 Cash 250	No journal entry.

July 15. Scully Company received payment from Burton Co. for purchase of July 5.	Cash 5,000
	    Accounts Receivable—Burton Co. 5,000
		Accounts Payable—Scully Co. 5,000
		    Cash 5,000

July 18. Scully Company sold merchandise on account to Burton Co., $12,000, terms FOB shipping point, 2/10, n/eom. Scully Company prepaid freight of $500, which was added to the invoice. The cost of the goods sold was $7,200.	Accounts Receivable—Burton Co. 11,760
	    Sales 11,760
	
	Accounts Receivable—Burton Co. 500
	    Cash 500
	
	Cost of Merchandise Sold 7,200
	    Merchandise Inventory 7,200
		Merchandise Inventory 12,260
		    Accounts Payable—Scully Co. ... 12,260

July 22. Scully Company paid Burton Co. a refund of $750 for merchandise damaged in the July 5 purchase. Burton kept the merchandise.	Customer Refunds Payable 750
	    Cash 750
		Cash 750
		    Merchandise Inventory 750

July 28. Scully Company received payment from Burton Co. for purchase of July 18.	Cash 12,260
	    Accounts Receivable—Burton Co. 12,260
		Accounts Payable—Scully Co. 12,260
		    Cash 12,260

July 31. Scully Company granted a customer allowance (credit memo) to Burton Co. for $2,500 for merchandise returned from July 1 purchase. The cost of the merchandise returned was $1,500.	Customer Refunds Payable 2,500
	    Accounts Receivable—Burton Co. 2,500
	
	Merchandise Inventory 1,500
	    Estimated Returns Inventory 1,500
		Accounts Payable—Scully Co. 2,500
		    Merchandise Inventory 2,500

Chapter 6 Accounting for Merchandising Businesses

> **Example Exercise 6-5 Transactions for Buyer and Seller** Obj. 2
>
> Sievert Co. sold merchandise to Bray Co. on account, $11,500, terms 2/15, n/30. The cost of the merchandise sold is $6,900. Journalize the entries for Sievert Co. and Bray Co. for the sale, purchase, and payment of amount due. Assume that all discounts are taken.
>
> **Follow My Example 6-5**
>
> Sievert Co. journal entries:
>
> | | | |
> |---|---:|---:|
> | Accounts Receivable [$11,500 − ($11,500 × 2%)] | 11,270 | |
> | Sales | | 11,270 |
> | Cost of Merchandise Sold | 6,900 | |
> | Merchandise Inventory | | 6,900 |
> | Cash | 11,270 | |
> | Accounts Receivable—Bray Co. | | 11,270 |
>
> Bray Co. journal entries:
>
> | | | |
> |---|---:|---:|
> | Merchandise Inventory [$11,500 − ($11,500 × 2%)] | 11,270 | |
> | Accounts Payable | | 11,270 |
> | Accounts Payable—Sievert Co. | 11,270 | |
> | Cash | | 11,270 |
>
> Practice Exercises: PE 6-5A, PE 6-5B

Sales Taxes and Trade Discounts

Sales of merchandise often involve sales taxes. Also, the seller may offer buyers trade discounts.

Sales Taxes Almost all states levy a tax on sales of merchandise.[10] The liability for the sales tax is incurred when the sale is made.

At the time of a cash sale, the seller collects the sales tax. When a sale is made on account, the seller charges the tax to the buyer by debiting Accounts Receivable. The seller credits the sales account for the amount of the sale and credits the tax to Sales Tax Payable. For example, the seller would record a sale of $100 on account to Lemon Co., subject to a tax of 6%, as follows:

Aug.	12	Accounts Receivable—Lemon Co.	106	
		Sales		100
		Sales Tax Payable		6
		Invoice No. 339.		

On a regular basis, the seller pays to the taxing authority (state) the amount of the sales tax collected. The seller records such a payment of $2,900 as follows:

Sept.	15	Sales Tax Payable	2,900	
		Cash		2,900
		Payment for sales taxes collected during August.		

---

[10] Businesses that purchase merchandise for resale to others are normally exempt from paying sales taxes on their purchases. Only final buyers of merchandise normally pay sales taxes.

Business Connection

SALES TAXES

While there is no federal sales tax, most states have enacted statewide sales taxes. In addition, many states allow counties and cities to collect a "local option" sales tax. Delaware, Montana, New Hampshire, and Oregon have no state or local sales taxes. Tennessee (9.45%), Washington (8.8%), and Louisiana (8.75%) have the highest average combined rates (including state and local option taxes). Several towns in Tuscaloosa County, Alabama, have the highest combined rates in the United States of 11%, while Chicago, Illinois, has the highest combined city rate of 10.25%.

What about companies that sell merchandise over the Internet? The general rule is that if the company ships merchandise to a customer in a state where the company does not have a physical location, no sales tax is due. For example, a customer in Montana who purchases merchandise online from a New York retailer (which has no physical location in Montana) does not have to pay sales tax to either Montana or New York.

Source: The Sales Tax Clearinghouse at www.thestc.com/FAQ.stm.

Trade Discounts **Wholesalers** are companies that sell merchandise to other businesses rather than to the public. Many wholesalers publish or upload sales catalogs online. However, wholesalers often offer special discounts to government agencies or businesses that order large quantities. Such discounts are called **trade discounts**.

Sellers and buyers do not normally record the list prices of merchandise and trade discounts in their accounts. For example, assume that an item has a list price of $1,000 and a 40% trade discount. The seller records the sale of the item at $600 [$1,000 less the trade discount of $400 ($1,000 × 40%)]. Likewise, the buyer records the purchase at $600.

The Adjusting Process

Obj. 3 Describe and illustrate the adjusting process for a merchandising business.

Thus far, the chart of accounts and the recording of transactions for a merchandising business (NetSolutions) have been described and illustrated. Next, the adjusting process for a merchandising business is described and illustrated. This discussion focuses on the following adjusting entries that differ from those of a service business:

- Inventory Shrinkage
- Customer Returns and Allowances

Adjusting Entry for Inventory Shrinkage

Under the perpetual inventory system, the merchandise inventory account is continually updated for purchase and sales transactions. As a result, the balance of the inventory account is the amount of merchandise available for sale at that point in time. However, retailers normally experience some loss of inventory due to shoplifting, employee theft, or errors. Thus, the physical inventory on hand at the end of the accounting period is usually less than the balance of Merchandise Inventory. This difference is called **inventory shrinkage** or **inventory shortage**.

To illustrate, NetSolutions' inventory is as follows on December 31, 2020:

Account balance of Merchandise Inventory	$63,950
Physical inventory on hand	62,150
Inventory shrinkage	$ 1,800

At the end of the accounting period, inventory shrinkage is recorded by the following adjusting entry:

			Adjusting Entry		
Dec.	31	Cost of Merchandise Sold		1,800	
		Merchandise Inventory			1,800
		Inventory shrinkage ($63,950 – $62,150).			

After the preceding entry is recorded, the balance of Merchandise Inventory agrees with the physical inventory on hand at the end of the period. Since inventory shrinkage cannot be totally eliminated, it is considered a normal cost of operations. If, however, the amount of the shrinkage is unusually large, it may be disclosed separately on the income statement. In such cases, the shrinkage may be recorded in a separate account, such as Loss from Inventory Shrinkage.

Example Exercise 6-6 Inventory Shrinkage *Obj. 3*

Pulmonary Company's perpetual inventory records indicate that $382,800 of merchandise should be on hand on March 31, 2019. The physical inventory indicates that $371,250 of merchandise is actually on hand. Journalize the adjusting entry for the inventory shrinkage for Pulmonary Company for the year ended March 31, 2019. Assume that the inventory shrinkage is a normal amount.

Follow My Example 6-6

Mar. 31   Cost of Merchandise Sold..   11,550
                  Merchandise Inventory......................................   11,550
                  Inventory shrinkage ($382,800 – $371,250).

Practice Exercises: PE 6-6A, PE 6-6B

INTEGRITY, OBJECTIVITY, AND ETHICS IN BUSINESS

THE COST OF EMPLOYEE THEFT

One survey reported that the 24 largest U.S. retail store chains have lost more than $6 billion to shoplifting and employee theft. The stores apprehended over 1 million shoplifters and dishonest employees and recovered more than $161 million from these thieves. Approximately 1 out of every 36 employees was apprehended for theft from his or her employer. Each dishonest employee stole approximately 6 times the amount stolen by shoplifters ($665.77 versus $113.30).

Source: Jack L. Hayes International, 24th Annual Retail Theft Survey, 2012.

Adjusting Entries for Customer Refunds, Allowances, and Returns

Sellers are required to estimate returns and allowances at the end of an accounting period and prepare two adjusting entries:

1. The first adjusting entry reduces the sales account and creates a customer refund liability account for the estimated refunds and allowances that will be granted to customers in the future.
2. The second adjusting entry creates an estimated returns inventory account for the cost of merchandise that is expected to be returned and reduces cost of merchandise sold.

302 Chapter 6 Accounting for Merchandising Businesses

To illustrate, assume the following for **NetSolutions** on December 31, 2020, before any adjustments:

	Unadjusted Balances December 31, 2020	
	Debit	Credit
Sales	$715,409	
Cost of Merchandise Sold		$523,505
Estimated Returns Inventory	300	
Customer Refunds Payable		800
Estimated cost of merchandise returned for 2020 sales	$5,000	
Estimated percent of refunds of 2020 sales	1%	

On December 31, 2020, NetSolutions makes the following two adjusting entries:[11]

Dec.	31	Sales (1% × $715,409)	7,154	
		Customer Refunds Payable		7,154
	31	Estimated Returns Inventory	5,000	
		Cost of Merchandise Sold		5,000

The first adjusting entry reduces 2020 sales by the amount of estimated refunds that may occur in 2021. Since 1% of sales are expected to be refunded, Sales is debited for $7,154 (1% × $715,409). In addition, a liability is recorded for $7,154 by crediting Customer Refunds Payable for the estimated customer refunds in 2021.

The second adjusting entry debits the asset Estimated Returns Inventory and reduces Cost of Merchandise Sold for the cost of merchandise that is expected to be returned in 2021 of $5,000. Estimated Returns Inventory is debited rather than Merchandise Inventory because the type of merchandise returned will not be known until the returns actually occur.

After the adjusting entries are posted to the ledger, Estimated Returns Inventory will have an adjusted balance of $5,300 ($300 + $5,000), and Customer Refunds Payable

---

Example Exercise 6-7 Customer Allowances and Returns Obj. 3

Assume the following data for Bighorn Inc. before its year-end adjustments:

	Unadjusted Balances	
	Debit	Credit
Sales		$18,440,000
Cost of Merchandise Sold	$10,000,000	
Estimated Returns Inventory	9,000	
Customer Refunds Payable		17,200
Estimated cost of merchandise that will be returned in the next year	$128,100	
Estimated percent of refunds for current year sales	1.5%	

Journalize the adjusting entries for the following:

a. Estimated customer refunds and allowances
b. Estimated customer returns

(Continued)

---

[11] The accounting illustrated is based upon *Revenue from Contracts with Customers, Topic 606, FASB Accounting Standards Update*, Financial Accounting Standards Board, Norwalk, CT, May 2014.

> **Follow My Example 6-7**
>
> | | | | |
> |---|---|---:|---:|
> | a. | Sales ($18,440,000 × 1.5%)... | 276,600 | |
> | | Customer Refunds Payable .... | | 276,600 |
> | b. | Estimated Returns Inventory .... | 128,100 | |
> | | Cost of Merchandise Sold...................................... | | 128,100 |
>
> Practice Exercises: PE 6-7A, PE 6-7B

will have a balance of $7,954 ($800 + $7,154). Estimated returns inventory of $5,300 is reported on the balance sheet in Exhibit 14 as a current asset following Merchandise Inventory. Customer refunds payable of $7,954 is reported in Exhibit 14 as a current liability following Accounts Payable. The adjusting entries ensure that the current period sales are matched with the related cost of merchandise sold on the income statement.

Financial Statements for a Merchandising Business

Obj. 4 Describe and illustrate the financial statements of a merchandising business.

Although merchandising transactions affect the balance sheet in reporting inventory, they primarily affect the income statement. An income statement for a merchandising business is normally prepared using either a multiple-step or single-step format.

Multiple-Step Income Statement

The 2020 income statement for **NetSolutions** is shown in Exhibit 11. This form of income statement, called a **multiple-step income statement**, contains several sections, subsections, and subtotals.

Sales The total amount of sales to customers for cash and on account is reported in this section. NetSolutions reported sales of $708,255 for the year ended December 31, 2020.

Cost of Merchandise Sold As shown in Exhibit 11, NetSolutions reported cost of merchandise sold of $520,305 during 2020. This amount is the cost of merchandise sold to customers. Cost of merchandise sold may also be reported as cost of goods sold or cost of sales.

Gross Profit The excess of sales over cost of merchandise sold is gross profit. As shown in Exhibit 11, NetSolutions reported gross profit of $187,950 in 2020.

Income from Operations Income from operations, sometimes called **operating income**, is determined by subtracting operating expenses from gross profit. Operating expenses are normally classified as either selling expenses or administrative expenses.

Selling expenses are incurred directly in the selling of merchandise. Examples of selling expenses include sales salaries, store supplies used, depreciation of store equipment, delivery expense, and advertising.

Administrative expenses, sometimes called **general expenses**, are incurred in the administration or general operations of the business. Examples of administrative expenses include office salaries, depreciation of office equipment, and office supplies used.

> **Link to Dollar Tree**
>
> **Dollar Tree** reports its income using the multiple-step income statement format.

304 Chapter 6 Accounting for Merchandising Businesses

EXHIBIT 11
Multiple-Step Income Statement

NetSolutions
Income Statement
For the Year Ended December 31, 2020

Sales			$708,255
Cost of merchandise sold			520,305
Gross profit			$187,950
Operating expenses:			
Selling expenses:			
Sales salaries expense	$53,430		
Advertising expense	10,860		
Depreciation expense—store equipment	3,100		
Delivery expense	2,800		
Miscellaneous selling expense	630		
Total selling expenses		$70,820	
Administrative expenses:			
Office salaries expense	$21,020		
Rent expense	8,100		
Depreciation expense—office equipment	2,490		
Insurance expense	1,910		
Office supplies expense	610		
Miscellaneous administrative expense	760		
Total administrative expenses		34,890	
Total operating expenses			105,710
Income from operations			$ 82,240
Other revenue and expense:			
Rent revenue		$ 600	
Interest expense		(2,440)	(1,840)
Net income			$ 80,400

Each selling and administrative expense may be reported separately as shown in Exhibit 11. However, many companies report selling, administrative, and operating expenses as single line items, as follows for NetSolutions:

IFRS

See Appendix B for more information.

Gross profit		$187,950
Operating expenses:		
Selling expenses	$70,820	
Administrative expenses	34,890	
Total operating expenses		105,710
Income from operations		$ 82,240

Other Revenue and Expense Other revenue and expense items are not related to the primary operations of the business. **Other revenue** is revenue from sources other than the primary operating activity of a business. Examples of other revenue include revenue from interest, rent, and gains resulting from the sale of fixed assets. **Other expense** is an expense that cannot be traced directly to the normal operations of the business. Examples of other expenses include interest expense and losses from disposing of fixed assets.

Other revenue and other expense are offset against each other on the income statement. If the total of other revenue exceeds the total of other expense, the difference is added to income from operations to determine net income. If the reverse is true, the difference is subtracted from income from operations. The other revenue and expense items of NetSolutions are reported as follows and in Exhibit 11:

Income from operations		$82,240
Other revenue and expense:		
Rent revenue	$ 600	
Interest expense	(2,440)	(1,840)
Net income		$80,400

Single-Step Income Statement

An alternate form of income statement is the **single-step income statement.** As shown in Exhibit 12, the income statement for NetSolutions deducts the total of all expenses *in one step* from the total of all revenues.

The single-step form emphasizes total revenues and total expenses in determining net income. A criticism of the single-step form is that gross profit and income from operations are not reported.

EXHIBIT 12
Single-Step Income Statement

NetSolutions
Income Statement
For the Year Ended December 31, 2020

Revenues:		
Sales		$708,255
Rent revenue		600
Total revenues		$708,855
Expenses:		
Cost of merchandise sold	$520,305	
Selling expenses	70,820	
Administrative expenses	34,890	
Interest expense	2,440	
Total expenses		628,455
Net income		$ 80,400

Statement of Owner's Equity

The statement of owner's equity for NetSolutions is shown in Exhibit 13. This statement is prepared in the same manner as for a service business.

EXHIBIT 13
Statement of Owner's Equity for Merchandising Business

NetSolutions
Statement of Owner's Equity
For the Year Ended December 31, 2020

Chris Clark, capital, January 1, 2020		$153,800
Net income for the year	$ 80,400	
Withdrawals	(18,000)	
Increase in owner's equity		62,400
Chris Clark, capital, December 31, 2020		$216,200

Balance Sheet

The balance sheet for NetSolutions is shown in Exhibit 14. In Exhibit 14, merchandise inventory of $62,150 and estimated returns inventory of $5,300 are reported as current assets and the current portion of the note payable of $5,000 is reported as a current liability.

EXHIBIT 14

Balance Sheet for Merchandising Business

NetSolutions
Balance Sheet
December 31, 2020

Assets

Current assets:		
Cash		$52,650
Accounts receivable		91,080
Merchandise inventory		62,150
Estimated returns inventory		5,300
Office supplies		480
Prepaid insurance		2,650
Total current assets		$214,310
Property, plant, and equipment:		
Land		$20,000
Store equipment	$27,100	
Less accumulated depreciation	5,700	21,400
Office equipment	$15,570	
Less accumulated depreciation	4,720	10,850
Total property, plant, and equipment		52,250
Total assets		$266,560

Liabilities

Current liabilities:		
Accounts payable		$14,466
Customer refunds payable		7,954
Note payable (current portion)		5,000
Salaries payable		1,140
Unearned rent		1,800
Total current liabilities		$ 30,360
Long-term liabilities:		
Note payable (final payment due in ten years)		20,000
Total liabilities		$ 50,360

Owner's Equity

Chris Clark, capital	216,200
Total liabilities and owner's equity	$266,560

The Closing Process

The closing entries for a merchandising business are similar to those for a service business. The two closing entries for a merchandising business are as follows:

1. Debit each revenue account for its balance, credit each expense account for its balance, and credit owner's capital account for net income. Debit the owner's capital account for a net loss. Cost of merchandise sold is a temporary account and is closed like an expense account.
2. Debit the owner's capital account for the balance of the drawing account and credit the drawing account.

The two closing entries for **NetSolutions** are as follows:

		Journal			Page 29
Date		Item	Post. Ref.	Debit	Credit
2020		Closing Entries			
Dec.	31	Sales	410	708,255	
		Rent Revenue	610	600	
		Cost of Merchandise Sold	510		520,305
		Sales Salaries Expense	520		53,430
		Advertising Expense	521		10,860
		Depr. Expense—Store Equipment	522		3,100
		Delivery Expense	523		2,800
		Miscellaneous Selling Expense	529		630
		Office Salaries Expense	530		21,020
		Rent Expense	531		8,100
		Depr. Expense—Office Equipment	532		2,490
		Insurance Expense	533		1,910
		Office Supplies Expense	534		610
		Misc. Administrative Expense	539		760
		Interest Expense	710		2,440
		Chris Clark, Capital	310		80,400
	31	Chris Clark, Capital	310	18,000	
		Chris Clark, Drawing	311		18,000

After the closing entries are posted to the accounts, a post-closing trial balance is prepared. The only accounts that should appear on the post-closing trial balance are the asset, contra asset, liability, and owner's capital accounts with balances. These are the same accounts that appear on the end-of-period balance sheet. If the two totals of the trial balance columns are not equal, an error has occurred that must be found and corrected.

Financial Analysis and Interpretation: Asset Turnover

Obj. 5 Describe and illustrate the use of asset turnover in evaluating a company's operating performance.

Asset turnover, sometimes called the ratio of sales to assets, measures how effectively a business is using its assets to generate sales. A high ratio indicates an effective use of assets.

The asset turnover is computed as follows:

$$\text{Asset Turnover} = \frac{\text{Sales}}{\text{Average Total Assets}}$$

To illustrate, the following data (in millions) were taken from recent annual reports of **Dollar Tree, Inc.**:

	Year 2	Year 1
Total revenues (sales)	$8,602	$7,840
Total assets:		
Beginning of year	2,772	2,752
End of year	3,567	2,772

The asset turnover for each year is as follows:

	Year 2	Year 1
Asset turnover*	2.71	2.84
	$8,602 ÷ [($2,772 + $3,567) ÷ 2]	$7,840 ÷ [($2,752 + $2,772) ÷ 2]

*Rounded to two decimal places.

Dollar Tree's asset turnover declined from 2.84 in Year 1 to 2.71 in Year 2. Thus, Dollar Tree's utilization of its assets to generate sales declined slightly in Year 2.

Using the asset turnover for comparisons to competitors and with industry averages could also be beneficial in interpreting Dollar Tree's use of its assets. For example, the following data (in millions) were taken from recent annual reports of **Dollar General Corporation**:

	Year 2
Total revenues (sales)	$18,910
Total assets:	
Beginning of year	10,868
End of year	11,224

Dollar General's asset turnover for Year 2 is as follows:

	Year 2
Asset turnover*	1.71
	$18,910 ÷ [($10,868 + $11,224) ÷ 2]

*Rounded to two decimal places.

Comparing Dollar General's Year 2 asset turnover of 1.71 to Dollar Tree's Year 2 ratio of 2.71 implies that Dollar Tree is using its assets more efficiently than is Dollar General.

Example Exercise 6-8 Asset Turnover *Obj. 5*

Financial statement data for the years ending December 31, 2019 and 2018, for Gilbert Company follow:

	2019	2018
Sales	$1,305,000	$962,500
Total assets:		
Beginning of year	840,000	700,000
End of year	900,000	840,000

a. Determine the asset turnover for 2019 and 2018.
b. Does the change in the asset turnover from 2018 to 2019 indicate a favorable or an unfavorable trend?

Follow My Example 6-8

a.

	2019	2018
Asset turnover	1.50	1.25
	$1,305,000 ÷ [($840,000 + $900,000) ÷ 2]	$962,500 ÷ [($700,000 + $840,000) ÷ 2]

b. The change from 1.25 to 1.50 indicates a favorable trend in using assets to generate sales.

Practice Exercises: PE 6-8A, PE 6-8B

APPENDIX

The Periodic Inventory System

Throughout this chapter, the perpetual inventory system was used to record purchases and sales of merchandise. Not all merchandise businesses, however, use the perpetual inventory system. For example, small merchandise businesses, such as a local hardware store, may use a manual accounting system. A manual perpetual inventory system is time-consuming and costly to maintain. For these reasons, a business may elect to use the periodic inventory system.

Under the periodic inventory system, purchases are normally recorded at their invoice amount. If the invoice is paid within the discount period, the discount is recorded in a separate account called Purchases Discounts. Likewise, purchases returns are recorded in a separate account called Purchases Returns and Allowances.

Chart of Accounts Under the Periodic Inventory System

The chart of accounts for **NetSolutions** under a periodic inventory system is shown in Exhibit 15. The accounts used to record transactions under the periodic inventory system are highlighted in Exhibit 15.

EXHIBIT 15

Chart of Accounts Under the Periodic Inventory System

Balance Sheet Accounts	Income Statement Accounts
100 Assets	400 Revenues
110 Cash	410 Sales
112 Accounts Receivable	500 Costs and Expenses
115 Merchandise Inventory	510 Purchases
116 Estimated Returns Inventory	511 Purchases Returns and Allowances
117 Office Supplies	512 Purchases Discounts
118 Prepaid Insurance	513 Freight In
120 Land	520 Sales Salaries Expense
123 Store Equipment	521 Advertising Expense
124 Accumulated Depreciation—Store Equipment	522 Depreciation Expense—Store Equipment
125 Office Equipment	523 Delivery Expense
126 Accumulated Depreciation—Office Equipment	529 Miscellaneous Selling Expense
200 Liabilities	530 Office Salaries Expense
210 Accounts Payable	531 Rent Expense
211 Salaries Payable	532 Depreciation Expense—Office Equipment
212 Unearned Rent	533 Insurance Expense
213 Customer Refunds Payable	534 Office Supplies Expense
215 Notes Payable	539 Misc. Administrative Expense
300 Owner's Equity	600 Other Revenue
310 Chris Clark, Capital	610 Rent Revenue
311 Chris Clark, Drawing	700 Other Expense
	710 Interest Expense

Recording Merchandise Transactions Under the Periodic Inventory System

Using the periodic inventory system, purchases of inventory are not recorded in the merchandise inventory account. Instead, purchases, purchases discounts, and purchases returns and allowances accounts are used. In addition, the sales of merchandise are not recorded in the merchandise inventory account. Thus, there is no detailed record of the amount of inventory on hand at any given time. At the end of the period, a physical count of merchandise inventory on hand is taken. This physical count is used to determine the cost of merchandise sold, as will be illustrated later.

The use of purchases, purchases discounts, purchases returns and allowances, and freight in accounts are described in this section.

Purchases Purchases of inventory are recorded in a purchases account rather than in the merchandise inventory account. Purchases is debited for the invoice amount of a purchase.

Purchases Discounts Purchases discounts are normally recorded in a separate purchases discounts account. The balance of the purchases discounts account is reported as a deduction from Purchases for the period. Thus, Purchases Discounts is a contra (or offsetting) account to Purchases.

Purchases Returns and Allowances Purchases returns and allowances are recorded in a similar manner as purchases discounts. A separate purchases returns and allowances account is used to record returns and allowances. Purchases returns and allowances are reported as a deduction from Purchases for the period. Thus, Purchases Returns and Allowances is a contra (or offsetting) account to Purchases.

Freight In When merchandise is purchased FOB shipping point, the buyer pays for the freight. Under the periodic inventory system, freight paid when purchasing merchandise FOB shipping point is debited to Freight In, Transportation In, or a similar account.

The preceding periodic inventory accounts and their effect on the cost of merchandise purchased are summarized as follows:

Account	Entry to Increase	Normal Balance	Effect on Cost of Merchandise Purchased
Purchases	Debit	Debit	Increases
Purchases Discounts	Credit	Credit	Decreases
Purchases Returns and Allowances	Credit	Credit	Decreases
Freight In	Debit	Debit	Increases

Exhibit 16 illustrates the recording of merchandise transactions using the periodic system.

Adjusting Process Under the Periodic Inventory System

The adjusting process is the same under the periodic and perpetual inventory systems except for the inventory shrinkage adjustment and customer refunds and allowances. The ending inventory is determined by a physical count under both systems.

Under the perpetual inventory system, the ending inventory physical count is compared to the balance of Merchandise Inventory. The difference is the amount of inventory shrinkage. The inventory shrinkage is then recorded as a debit to Cost of Merchandise Sold and a credit to Merchandise Inventory.

EXHIBIT 16
Transactions Using the Periodic Inventory System

Transaction	Periodic Inventory System		
June 5. Purchased $30,000 of merchandise on account, terms 2/10, n/30.	Purchases .... Accounts Payable	30,000	30,000
June 8. Returned merchandise purchased on account on June 5, $500.	Accounts Payable............. Purchases Returns and Allowances..............	500	500
June 15. Paid for purchase of June 5, less return of $500 and discount of $590 [($30,000 − $500) × 2%].	Accounts Payable............. Cash....................... Purchases Discounts	29,500	28,910 590
June 18. Sold merchandise on account, $12,500, 1/10, n/30. The cost of the merchandise sold was $9,000.	Accounts Receivable [$12,500 − ($12,500 × 1%)] .... Sales	12,375	12,375
June 22. Purchased merchandise, $15,000, terms FOB shipping point, 2/15, n/30, with prepaid freight of $750 added to the invoice.	Purchases .... Freight In...................... Accounts Payable	15,000 750	15,750
June 28. Received payment on account from June 18 sale.	Cash .... Accounts Receivable	12,375	12,375
June 29. Received $19,600 from cash sales. The cost of the merchandise sold was $13,800.	Cash .... Sales	19,600	19,600

Under the periodic inventory system, the merchandise inventory account is not kept up to date for purchases and sales. As a result, the inventory shrinkage cannot be directly determined. Instead, any inventory shrinkage is included indirectly in the computation of the cost of merchandise sold as shown in Exhibit 17. This is a major disadvantage of the periodic inventory system. That is, inventory shrinkage is not separately determined.

Like the perpetual inventory system, the periodic system records the same adjusting entry debiting Sales and crediting Customer Refunds Payable for estimated customer refunds and allowances of $7,154. No entry, however, is made for estimated returns inventory. Instead, cost of merchandise sold is reduced by the cost of the estimated returns inventory for the current year. The estimated cost of the returns for NetSolutions' 2020 sales is $5,000. This amount is subtracted from the cost of merchandise sold before estimated returns of $525,305 to yield cost of merchandise sold of $520,305 shown in Exhibit 17.

Financial Statements Under the Periodic Inventory System

The financial statements are similar under the perpetual and periodic inventory systems. When the multiple-step format of income statement is used, the cost of merchandise sold may be reported as shown in Exhibit 17.

EXHIBIT 17

Determining Cost of Merchandise Sold Using Periodic Inventory

Merchandise inventory, January 1, 2020		$ 59,700
Cost of merchandise purchased:		
Purchases	$521,980	
Purchases returns and allowances	(9,100)	
Purchases discounts	(2,525)	
Net purchases	$510,355	
Freight in	17,400	
Total cost of merchandise purchased		527,755
Merchandise available for sale		$587,455
Merchandise inventory, December 31, 2020		(62,150)
Cost of merchandise sold before estimated returns		$525,305
Increase in estimated returns inventory		(5,000)
Cost of merchandise sold		$520,305

Closing Entries Under the Periodic Inventory System

In the periodic inventory system, the purchases, purchases discounts, purchases returns and allowances, and freight in accounts are closed to Chris Clark, Capital. In addition, the merchandise inventory account is adjusted to the end-of-period physical inventory count during the closing process. The estimated returns inventory account is also adjusted for the estimated returns from the current period's sales.

The two closing entries under the periodic inventory system are as follows:

1. a. Debit Merchandise Inventory for its end-of-period balance based on the physical inventory.
   b. Debit Estimated Returns Inventory for the cost of the future estimated returns of the current period's sales.
   c. Debit each revenue account and the following temporary periodic inventory accounts for their balances.
      - Purchases Discounts
      - Purchases Returns and Allowances
   d. Credit Merchandise Inventory for its balance as of the beginning of the period.
   e. Credit each expense account and the following temporary periodic inventory accounts for their balances.
      - Purchases
      - Freight In
   f. Credit the owner's capital account (Chris Clark, Capital) for the net income. Debit the owner's capital account for a net loss.
2. Debit the owner's capital account (Chris Clark, Capital) and credit the owner's drawing account (Chris Clark, Drawing) for its balance.

The two closing entries for **NetSolutions** under the periodic inventory system are shown in Exhibit 18.

In the first closing entry, Merchandise Inventory is debited for $62,150. This is the ending physical inventory count on December 31, 2020. In addition, the cost of the estimated merchandise returns from 2020 sales is debited to Estimated Returns Inventory for $5,000. Merchandise Inventory is credited for its January 1, 2020, balance of $59,700. In this way, the closing entries reflect the effects of the beginning and ending inventory in determining the cost of merchandise sold, as shown in Exhibit 17. After the closing entries are posted, Merchandise Inventory

EXHIBIT 18
Closing Entries: Periodic Method

Journal					
Date		Item	Post. Ref.	Debit	Credit
2020 Dec.	31	Closing Entries			
		Merchandise Inventory (December 31, 2020)	115	62,150	
		Estimated Returns Inventory	116	5,000	
		Sales	410	708,255	
		Purchases Returns and Allowances	511	9,100	
		Purchases Discounts	512	2,525	
		Rent Revenue	610	600	
		Merchandise Inventory (January 1, 2020)	115		59,700
		Purchases	510		521,980
		Freight In	513		17,400
		Sales Salaries Expense	520		53,430
		Advertising Expense	521		10,860
		Depreciation Expense—Store Equipment	522		3,100
		Delivery Expense	523		2,800
		Miscellaneous Selling Expense	529		630
		Office Salaries Expense	530		21,020
		Rent Expense	531		8,100
		Depreciation Expense—Office Equipment	532		2,490
		Insurance Expense	533		1,910
		Office Supplies Expense	534		610
		Miscellaneous Administrative Expense	539		760
		Interest Expense	710		2,440
		Chris Clark, Capital	310		80,400
	31	Chris Clark, Capital	310	18,000	
		Chris Clark, Drawing	311		18,000

will have a balance of $62,150 and Estimated Returns Inventory will have a balance of $5,300, which are the amounts reported on the December 31, 2020, balance sheet.

In Exhibit 18, the periodic inventory accounts are highlighted. Under the perpetual inventory system, the highlighted periodic inventory accounts are replaced with the cost of merchandise sold account.

At a Glance 6

Obj. 1 Distinguish between the activities and financial statements of service and merchandising businesses.

Key Points Merchandising businesses purchase merchandise for selling to customers. On a merchandising business's income statement, revenue from selling merchandise is reported as sales. The cost of the merchandise sold is subtracted from sales to arrive at gross profit. The operating expenses are subtracted from gross profit to arrive at net income. Merchandise inventory, which is merchandise not sold at the end of the accounting period, is reported as a current asset on the balance sheet.

Learning Outcomes	Example Exercises	Practice Exercises
• Describe how the activities of a service and a merchandising business differ.		
• Describe the differences between the income statements of a service and a merchandising business.		
• Compute gross profit.	EE6-1	PE6-1A, 6-1B
• Describe how merchandise inventory is reported on the balance sheet.		

Obj. 2 Describe and illustrate the accounting for merchandise transactions.

Key Points A chart of accounts for a merchandising business differs from that of a service business. The chart of accounts for NetSolutions as a merchandising business is shown in Exhibit 2. Under the perpetual inventory system, purchases of merchandise for cash or on account are recorded as Merchandise Inventory. Discounts for early payment of purchases on account are purchases discounts. Purchases of merchandise inventory subject to purchase discounts are recorded net of the discount. Price adjustments for returned merchandise are purchases returns and allowances. Price adjustments for returned merchandise are recorded net of any purchase discount.

Sales of merchandise for cash or on account are recorded as sales. The cost of merchandise sold and the reduction in merchandise inventory are also recorded at the time of sale.

A seller may grant customers a variety of discounts, called customer discounts. A sales discount encourages customers to pay their invoice early. Sales subject to a sales discount are recorded net of the discount.

A seller may pay a customer a refund or grant a price allowance for returned or damaged merchandise, called customer returns and allowances. When merchandise is returned for a refund, Customer Refunds Payable is debited and Cash is credited for the amount of the refund. The returned merchandise is recorded as a debit to Merchandise Inventory and a credit to Estimated Returns Inventory. When a customer doesn't return merchandise but is granted an allowance, Customer Refunds Payable is debited and either Cash (if the customer has already paid for the merchandise) or Accounts Receivable is credited.

When merchandise is shipped FOB shipping point, the buyer pays the freight and debits Merchandise Inventory. When merchandise is shipped FOB destination, the seller pays the freight and debits Delivery Expense or Freight Out. Merchandise transactions can be summarized in T account form as shown in Exhibit 9. Each merchandising transaction affects a buyer and a seller. The liability for sales tax is incurred when the sale is made and is recorded by the seller as a credit to the sales tax payable account. Trade discounts are discounts off the list price of merchandise.

Chapter 6 Accounting for Merchandising Businesses 315

Learning Outcomes	Example Exercises	Practice Exercises
• Prepare a chart of accounts for a merchandising business.		
• Prepare journal entries to record the purchases of merchandise for cash.		
• Prepare journal entries to record the purchases of merchandise on account.	EE6-2	PE6-2A, 6-2B
• Prepare journal entries to record purchases discounts and purchases returns and allowances.	EE6-2	PE6-2A, 6-2B
• Prepare journal entries to record sales of merchandise for cash or using a credit card.		
• Prepare journal entries to record sales of merchandise on account.	EE6-3	PE6-3A, 6-3B
• Prepare journal entries to record sales discounts and customer returns and allowances.	EE6-3	PE6-3A, 6-3B
• Prepare journal entries for freight from the point of view of the buyer and seller.		
• Determine the total cost of the purchase of merchandise under differing freight terms.	EE6-4	PE6-4A, 6-4B
• Record the same merchandise transactions for the buyer and seller.	EE6-5	PE6-5A, 6-5B
• Determine the cost of merchandise purchased when a trade discount is offered by the seller.		
• Record sales transactions involving sales taxes and trade discounts.		

Obj. 3 Describe and illustrate the adjusting process for a merchandising business.

Key Points The normal adjusting entry for inventory shrinkage is to debit Cost of Merchandise Sold and credit Merchandise Inventory. Two adjusting entries are necessary for estimated allowances and returns. The first adjusting entry debits Sales and credits Customer Refunds Payable. The second entry debits Estimated Returns Inventory and credits Cost of Merchandise Sold.

Learning Outcomes	Example Exercises	Practice Exercises
• Prepare the adjusting journal entry for inventory shrinkage.	EE6-6	PE6-6A, 6-6B
• Prepare adjusting entries for customer allowances and returns.	EE6-7	PE6-7A, 6-7B

Obj. 4 Describe and illustrate the financial statements of a merchandising business.

Key Points The multiple-step income statement of a merchandiser reports sales. The cost of the merchandise sold is subtracted from sales to determine the gross profit. Operating income is determined by subtracting selling and administrative expenses from gross profit. Net income is determined by adding or subtracting the net of other revenue and expense. The income statement may also be reported in a single-step form.

The statement of owner's equity is similar to that for a service business.

The balance sheet reports merchandise inventory and estimated returns inventory at the end of the period as current assets. Also, customer refunds payable is reported as a current liability.

The closing entries for a merchandising business are similar to those for a service business except that the cost of merchandise sold is also closed.

Learning Outcomes	Example Exercises	Practice Exercises
• Prepare a multiple-step income statement for a merchandising business.		
• Prepare a single-step income statement.		
• Prepare a statement of owner's equity for a merchandising business.		
• Prepare a balance sheet for a merchandising business.		
• Prepare the closing entries for a merchandising business.		

Obj. 5 Describe and illustrate the use of asset turnover in evaluating a company's operating performance.

Key Points Asset turnover measures how effectively a business is using its assets to generate sales. A high ratio indicates an effective use of assets. Asset turnover is computed as follows:

$$\text{Asset Turnover} = \frac{\text{Sales}}{\text{Average Total Assets}}$$

Learning Outcomes	Example Exercises	Practice Exercises
• Interpret a high asset turnover.		
• Compute the asset turnover.	EE6-8	PE6-8A, 6-8B

Illustrative Problem

The following transactions were completed by Montrose Company during May of the current year. Montrose Company uses a perpetual inventory system.

May 3. Purchased merchandise on account from Floyd Co., $4,000, terms FOB shipping point, 2/10, n/30, with prepaid freight of $120 added to the invoice.

5. Purchased merchandise on account from Kramer Co., $8,500, terms FOB destination, 1/10, n/30.

6. Sold merchandise on account to C. F. Howell Co., list price $4,000, trade discount 30%, terms 2/10, n/30. The cost of the merchandise sold was $1,125.

May 8. Purchased office supplies for cash, $150.
   10. Returned merchandise purchased on May 5 from Kramer Co., $1,300.
   13. Paid Floyd Co. on account for purchase of May 3.
   14. Purchased merchandise for cash, $10,500.
   15. Paid Kramer Co. on account for purchase of May 5, less return of May 10.
   16. Received cash on account from sale of May 6 to C. F. Howell Co.
   19. Sold merchandise on MasterCard credit cards, $2,450. The cost of the merchandise sold was $980.
   22. Sold merchandise for cash to Comer Co., $3,480. The cost of the merchandise sold was $1,400.
   24. Sold merchandise on account to Smith Co., $4,350, terms n/30. The cost of the merchandise sold was $1,750.
   25. Refunded Comer Co. $1,480 for returned merchandise from sale on May 22. The cost of the returned merchandise was $600.
   31. Paid a service processing fee of $140 for MasterCard sales.

Instructions

1. Journalize the preceding transactions.
2. Journalize the adjusting entry for merchandise inventory shrinkage, $3,750.
3. Journalize the adjusting entries for estimated customer refunds and returns. Assume that sales of $3,000 are estimated to be refunded and inventory costing $1,800 is estimated to be returned.

Solution

1.

May	3	Merchandise Inventory [$4,000 − ($4,000 × 2%)] + $120	4,040	
		Accounts Payable—Floyd Co.		4,040
	5	Merchandise Inventory [$8,500 − ($8,500 × 1%)]	8,415	
		Accounts Payable—Kramer Co.		8,415
	6	Accounts Receivable—C. F. Howell Co.	2,744	
		Sales		2,744
		[$4,000 − (30% × $4,000)] = $2,800		
		[$2,800 − ($2,800 × 2%)] = $2,744		
	6	Cost of Merchandise Sold	1,125	
		Merchandise Inventory		1,125
	8	Office Supplies	150	
		Cash		150
	10	Accounts Payable—Kramer Co. [$1,300 − ($1,300 × 1%)]	1,287	
		Merchandise Inventory		1,287
	13	Accounts Payable—Floyd Co.	4,040	
		Cash		4,040
	14	Merchandise Inventory	10,500	
		Cash		10,500
	15	Accounts Payable—Kramer Co. ($8,415 − $1,287)	7,128	
		Cash		7,128
	16	Cash	2,744	
		Accounts Receivable—C. F. Howell Co.		2,744
	19	Cash	2,450	
		Sales		2,450
	19	Cost of Merchandise Sold	980	
		Merchandise Inventory		980
	22	Cash	3,480	
		Sales		3,480

(Continued)

	May 22	Cost of Merchandise Sold	1,400	
		Merchandise Inventory		1,400
	24	Accounts Receivable—Smith Co.	4,350	
		Sales		4,350
	24	Cost of Merchandise Sold	1,750	
		Merchandise Inventory		1,750
	25	Customer Refunds Payable	1,480	
		Cash		1,480
	25	Merchandise Inventory	600	
		Estimated Returns Inventory		600
	31	Credit Card Expense	140	
		Cash		140
2.	May 31	Cost of Merchandise Sold	3,750	
		Merchandise Inventory		3,750
3.	May 31	Sales	3,000	
		Customer Refunds Payable		3,000
	31	Estimated Returns Inventory	1,800	
		Cost of Merchandise Sold		1,800

Key Terms

administrative expenses (general expenses) (303)
asset turnover (307)
cash refund (292)
cost of merchandise sold (283)
credit memorandum (credit memo) (292)
credit period (286)
credit terms (286)
customer allowance (292)
customer discounts (291)
customer refunds payable (292)
debit memorandum (debit memo) (288)

estimated returns inventory (293)
FOB (free on board) destination (295)
FOB (free on board) shipping point (295)
gross profit (283)
income from operations (operating income) (303)
inventory shrinkage (inventory shortage) (300)
invoice (286)
merchandise inventory (283)
multiple-step income statement (303)
operating cycle (282)

other expense (304)
other revenue (304)
periodic inventory system (285)
perpetual inventory system (285)
physical inventory (285)
purchases discounts (287)
purchases returns and allowances (288)
sales (283)
sales discounts (291)
selling expenses (303)
single-step income statement (305)
trade discounts (300)
wholesalers (300)

Discussion Questions

1. What distinguishes a merchandising business from a service business?

2. Can a business earn a gross profit but incur a net loss? Explain.

3. The credit period during which the buyer of merchandise is allowed to pay usually begins with what date?

4. What is the meaning of (a) 1/15, n/60; (b) n/30; (c) n/eom?

5. How are sales to customers using MasterCard and VISA recorded?

6. What is the nature of (a) a credit memo issued by the seller of merchandise, (b) a debit memo issued by the buyer of merchandise?

7. Who bears the freight when the terms of sale are (a) FOB shipping point, (b) FOB destination?

8. Name four accounts that would normally appear in the chart of accounts of a merchandising business but would not appear in the chart of accounts of a service business.

9. Audio Outfitter Inc., which uses a perpetual inventory system, experienced a normal inventory shrinkage of $13,675. What accounts would be debited and credited to record the adjustment for the inventory shrinkage at the end of the accounting period?

10. Assume that Audio Outfitter Inc. in Discussion Question 9 experienced an abnormal inventory shrinkage of $98,600. Audio Outfitter Inc. has decided to record the abnormal inventory shrinkage so that it would be disclosed separately on the income statement. What account would be debited for the abnormal inventory shrinkage?

Practice Exercises

Example Exercises

EE 6-1 p. 284   **PE 6-1A**   **Gross profit**   OBJ. 1

During the current year, merchandise is sold for $315,800 cash and $1,225,000 on account. The cost of the merchandise sold is $875,000. What is the amount of the gross profit?

EE 6-1 p. 284   **PE 6-1B**   **Gross profit**   OBJ. 1

During the current year, merchandise is sold for $18,300 cash and $295,700 on account. The cost of the merchandise sold is $188,000. What is the amount of the gross profit?

EE 6-2 p. 290   **PE 6-2A**   **Purchases transactions**   OBJ. 2

Halibut Company purchased merchandise on account from a supplier for $18,600, terms 2/10, n/30. Halibut Company returned $5,000 of the merchandise and received full credit.

a. If Halibut Company pays the invoice within the discount period, what is the amount of cash required for the payment?

b. What account is credited by Halibut Company to record the return?

EE 6-2 p. 290   **PE 6-2B**   **Purchases transactions**   OBJ. 2

Hoffman Company purchased merchandise on account from a supplier for $65,000, terms 1/10, n/30. Hoffman Company returned $7,500 of the merchandise and received full credit.

a. If Hoffman Company pays the invoice within the discount period, what is the amount of cash required for the payment?

b. What account is debited by Hoffman Company to record the return?

EE 6-3 p. 294   **PE 6-3A**   **Sales transactions**   OBJ. 2

Journalize the following merchandise transactions:

a. Sold merchandise on account, $72,500 with terms 2/10, n/30. The cost of the merchandise sold was $43,500.

b. Received payment less the discount.

c. Issued a credit memo for returned merchandise that was sold for $2,300 terms n/30. The cost of the merchandise returned was $1,600.

320 Chapter 6 Accounting for Merchandising Businesses

EE 6-3 *p. 294* **PE 6-3B Sales transactions** OBJ. 2

Journalize the following merchandise transactions:

a. Sold merchandise on account, $92,500 with terms 1/10, n/30. The cost of the merchandise sold was $55,500.
b. Received payment less the discount.
c. Issued a credit memo for returned merchandise that was sold for $10,400 terms n/30. The cost of the merchandise returned was $6,500.

EE 6-4 *p. 297* **PE 6-4A Freight terms** OBJ. 2

Determine the amount to be paid in full settlement of each of two invoices, (a) and (b), assuming that credit for returns and allowances was received prior to payment and that all invoices were paid within the discount period.

	Merchandise	Freight Paid by Seller	Freight Terms	Returns and Allowances
a.	$ 90,000	$1,000	FOB shipping point, 1/10, n/30	$15,000
b.	110,000	1,575	FOB destination, 2/10, n/30	8,500

EE 6-4 *p. 297* **PE 6-4B Freight terms** OBJ. 2

Determine the amount to be paid in full settlement of each of two invoices, (a) and (b), assuming that credit for returns and allowances was received prior to payment and that all invoices were paid within the discount period.

	Merchandise	Freight Paid by Seller	Freight Terms	Returns and Allowances
a.	$36,000	$800	FOB destination, 1/10, n/30	$4,000
b.	44,900	375	FOB shipping point, 2/10, n/30	2,400

EE 6-5 *p. 299* **PE 6-5A Transactions for buyer and seller** OBJ. 2

Sather Co. sold merchandise to Boone Co. on account, $31,800, terms 2/15, n/30. The cost of the merchandise sold is $19,000. Journalize the entries for Sather Co. and Boone Co. for the sale, purchase, and payment of amount due. Assume all discounts are taken.

EE 6-5 *p. 299* **PE 6-5B Transactions for buyer and seller** OBJ. 2

Shore Co. sold merchandise to Blue Star Co. on account, $112,000, terms FOB shipping point, 2/10, n/30. The cost of the merchandise sold is $67,200. Shore Co. paid freight of $1,800. Journalize the entries for Shore Co. and Blue Star Co. for the sale, purchase, and payment of amount due. Assume all discounts are taken.

EE 6-6 *p. 301* **PE 6-6A Inventory shrinkage** OBJ. 3

Castle Furnishings Company's perpetual inventory records indicate that $675,400 of merchandise should be on hand on November 30, 2019. The physical inventory indicates that $663,800 of merchandise is actually on hand. Journalize the adjusting entry for the inventory shrinkage for Castle Furnishings Company for the year ended November 30, 2019. Assume that the inventory shrinkage is a normal amount.

EE 6-6 *p. 301* **PE 6-6B Inventory shrinkage** OBJ. 3

Hahn Flooring Company's perpetual inventory records indicate that $1,333,150 of merchandise should be on hand on December 31, 2019. The physical inventory indicates that $1,309,900 of merchandise is actually on hand. Journalize the adjusting entry for the inventory shrinkage for Hahn Flooring Company for the year ended December 31, 2019. Assume that the inventory shrinkage is a normal amount.

Chapter 6 Accounting for Merchandising Businesses   321

EE 6-7 *p. 302*   **PE 6-7A   Customer allowances and returns**   OBJ. 3

Assume the following data for Lusk Inc. before its year-end adjustments:

	Unadjusted Balances	
	Debit	Credit
Sales		$3,600,000
Cost of Merchandise Sold	$2,100,000	
Estimated Returns Inventory	1,800	
Customer Refunds Payable		900
Estimated cost of merchandise that will be returned in the next year	$15,000	
Estimated percent of refunds for current year sales	0.8%	

Journalize the adjusting entries for the following:

a. Estimated customer allowances

b. Estimated customer returns

EE 6-7 *p. 302*   **PE 6-7B   Customer allowances and returns**   OBJ. 3

Assume the following data for Casper Company before its year-end adjustments:

	Unadjusted Balances	
	Debit	Credit
Sales		$1,750,000
Cost of Merchandise Sold	$1,000,000	
Estimated Returns Inventory	600	
Customer Refunds Payable		400
Estimated cost of merchandise that will be returned in the next year	$8,000	
Estimated percent of refunds for current year sales	0.6%	

Journalize the adjusting entries for the following:

a. Estimated customer allowances

b. Estimated customer returns

EE 6-8 *p. 308*   **PE 6-8A   Asset turnover**   OBJ. 5

Financial statement data for years ending December 31, 2019 and 2018, for Latchkey Company follow:

	2019	2018
Sales	$1,734,000	$1,645,000
Total assets:		
Beginning of year	480,000	460,000
End of year	540,000	480,000

a. Determine the asset turnover for 2019 and 2018.

b.  Does the change in the asset turnover from 2018 to 2019 indicate a favorable or an unfavorable trend?

322 Chapter 6 Accounting for Merchandising Businesses

EE 6-8 p. 308   **PE 6-8B**   **Asset turnover**   OBJ. 5

Financial statement data for years ending December 31, 2019 and 2018, for Edison Company follow:

	2019	2018
Sales	$1,884,000	$1,562,000
Total assets:		
Beginning of year	770,000	650,000
End of year	800,000	770,000

a. Determine the asset turnover for 2019 and 2018.

b. Does the change in the asset turnover from 2018 to 2019 indicate a favorable or an unfavorable trend?

Exercises

EX 6-1   **Determining gross profit**   OBJ. 1

During the current year, merchandise is sold for $31,850,000. The cost of the merchandise sold is $24,206,000.

a. What is the amount of the gross profit?

b. Compute the gross profit percentage (gross profit divided by sales).

c. Will the income statement necessarily report a net income? Explain.

EX 6-2   **Determining cost of merchandise sold**   OBJ. 1

For a recent year, **Best Buy** reported sales of $40,339 million. Its gross profit was $9,047 million. What was the amount of Best Buy's cost of merchandise sold?

EX 6-3   **Chart of accounts**   OBJ. 2

Monet Paints Co. is a newly organized business with a list of accounts arranged in alphabetical order, as follows:

Accounts Payable	Merchandise Inventory
Accounts Receivable	Miscellaneous Administrative Expense
Accumulated Depreciation—Office Equipment	Miscellaneous Selling Expense
Accumulated Depreciation—Store Equipment	Notes Payable
Advertising Expense	Office Equipment
Cash	Office Salaries Expense
Cost of Merchandise Sold	Office Supplies
Customer Refunds Payable	Office Supplies Expense
Delivery Expense	Prepaid Insurance
Depreciation Expense—Office Equipment	Rent Expense
Depreciation Expense—Store Equipment	Salaries Payable
Estimated Returns Inventory	Sales
Insurance Expense	Sales Salaries Expense
Interest Expense	Store Equipment
Kailey Garner, Capital	Store Supplies
Kailey Garner, Drawing	Store Supplies Expense
Land	

Construct a chart of accounts, assigning account numbers and arranging the accounts in balance sheet and income statement order, as illustrated in Exhibit 2. Each account number is three digits: the first digit is to indicate the major classification (1 for assets,

Chapter 6 Accounting for Merchandising Businesses 323

for example); the second digit is to indicate the subclassification (11 for current assets, for example); and the third digit is to identify the specific account (110 for Cash, 112 for Accounts Receivable, 114 for Merchandise Inventory, etc.).

EX 6-4 Purchase-related transactions   OBJ. 2

The Wheatland Company purchased merchandise on account from a supplier for $30,000, terms 1/10, n/30. The Wheatland Company returned $8,000 of the merchandise and received full credit.

a. What is the amount of cash required for the payment within the discount period?
b. Under a perpetual inventory system, what account is credited by The Wheatland Company to record the return?

EX 6-5 Purchase-related transactions   OBJ. 2

A retailer is considering the purchase of 500 units of a specific item from either of two suppliers. Their offers are as follows:

Supplier One: $40 a unit, total of $20,000, 1/10, n/30, no charge for freight.
Supplier Two: $39 a unit, total of $19,500, 2/10, n/30, plus freight of $500.

Which of the two offers, Supplier One or Supplier Two, yields the lower price?

EX 6-6 Purchase-related transactions   OBJ. 2

The debits and credits for four related entries for a purchase of $40,000, terms 2/10, n/30, are presented in the following T accounts. Describe each transaction.

Cash				Accounts Payable			
		(2)	450	(3)	4,900	(1)	39,200
		(4)	34,300	(4)	34,300		

Merchandise Inventory			
(1)	39,200	(3)	4,900
(2)	450		

EX 6-7 Purchase-related transactions   OBJ. 2

✔ c. Cash, cr. $64,680

Warwick's Co., a women's clothing store, purchased $75,000 of merchandise from a supplier on account, terms FOB destination, 2/10, n/30. Warwick's returned $9,000 of the merchandise, receiving a credit memo, and then paid the amount due within the discount period. Journalize Warwick's entries to record (a) the purchase, (b) the merchandise return, and (c) the payment.

EX 6-8 Purchase-related transactions   OBJ. 2

✔ e. Cash, dr. $7,640

Journalize entries for the following related transactions of Manville Heating & Air Company:

a. Purchased $90,000 of merchandise from Wright Co. on account, terms 2/10, n/30.
b. Paid the amount owed on the invoice within the discount period.
c. Discovered that $18,000 of the merchandise purchased in (a) was defective and returned items, receiving credit for $17,640 [$18,000 − ($18,000 × 2%)].
d. Purchased $10,000 of merchandise from Wright Co. on account, terms n/30.
e. Received a refund from Wright Co. for return in (c) less the purchase in (d).

EX 6-9 Sales-related transactions, including the use of credit cards   OBJ. 2

Journalize the entries for the following transactions:

a. Sold merchandise for cash, $116,300. The cost of the merchandise sold was $72,000.
b. Sold merchandise on account, $755,000. The cost of the merchandise sold was $400,000.
c. Sold merchandise to customers who used MasterCard and VISA, $1,950,000. The cost of the merchandise sold was $1,250,000.

(Continued)

EX 6-10 Sales-related transactions OBJ. 2

After the amount due on a sale of $28,000, terms 2/10, n/eom, is received from a customer within the discount period, the seller consents to the return of the entire shipment for a cash refund. The cost of the merchandise returned was $16,800. (a) What is the amount of the refund owed to the customer? (b) Journalize the entries made by the seller to record the return and the refund.

EX 6-11 Sales-related transactions OBJ. 2

The debits and credits for four related entries for a sale of $15,000, terms 1/10, n/30, are presented in the following T accounts. Describe each transaction.

Cash				Sales			
(5)	13,860					(1)	14,850

Accounts Receivable				Cost of Merchandise Sold			
(1)	14,850	(3)	990	(2)	8,800		
		(5)	13,860				

Merchandise Inventory			
(4)	575	(2)	8,800

Estimated Returns Inventory			
		(4)	575

Customer Refunds Payable			
(3)	990		

EX 6-12 Sales-related transactions OBJ. 2

✓ c. $57,470

Merchandise is sold on account to a customer for $56,500, terms FOB shipping point, 2/10, n/30. The seller paid the freight of $2,100. Determine the following: (a) amount of the sale, (b) amount debited to Accounts Receivable, and (c) amount received within the discount period.

EX 6-13 Determining amounts to be paid on invoices OBJ. 2

✓ a. $10,750

Determine the amount to be paid in full settlement of each of the following invoices, assuming that credit for returns and allowances was received prior to payment and that all invoices were paid within the discount period:

	Merchandise	Freight Paid by Seller		Customer Returns and Allowances
a.	$14,000	—	FOB destination, n/30	$3,250
b.	21,200	$380	FOB shipping point, 2/10, n/30	4,000
c.	16,400	—	FOB shipping point, 1/10, n/30	900
d.	7,500	250	FOB shipping point, 2/10, n/30	1,200
e.	28,800	—	FOB destination, 1/10, n/30	—

EX 6-14 Sales-related transactions OBJ. 2

Showcase Co., a furniture wholesaler, sells merchandise to Balboa Co. on account, $254,500, terms n/30. The cost of the merchandise sold is $152,700. Showcase Co. issues a credit memo for $30,000 for merchandise returned prior to Balboa Co. paying the original invoice. The cost of the merchandise returned is $17,500. Journalize Showcase Co.'s entries for (a) the sale, including the cost of the merchandise sold; (b) the credit memo, including the cost of the returned merchandise; and (c) the receipt of the check for the amount due from Balboa Co.

EX 6-15 Purchase-related transactions OBJ. 2

Based on the data presented in Exercise 6-14, journalize Balboa Co.'s entries for (a) the purchase, (b) the return of the merchandise for credit, and (c) the payment of the invoice.

EX 6-16 Sales tax OBJ. 2

✓ c. $38,880

A sale of merchandise on account for $36,000 is subject to an 8% sales tax. (a) Should the sales tax be recorded at the time of sale or when payment is received? (b) What is the amount recorded as sales? (c) What is the amount debited to Accounts Receivable? (d) What is the title of the account to which the $2,880 ($36,000 × 8%) is credited?

EX 6-17 Sales tax transactions OBJ. 2

Journalize the entries to record the following selected transactions:

a. Sold $62,800 of merchandise on account, subject to a sales tax of 5%. The cost of the merchandise sold was $37,500.

b. Paid $39,650 to the state sales tax department for taxes collected.

EX 6-18 Normal balances of merchandise accounts OBJ. 2

What is the normal balance of the following accounts: (a) Cost of Merchandise Sold, (b) Customer Refunds Payable, (c) Delivery Expense, (d) Estimated Returns Inventory, (e) Merchandise Inventory, (f) Sales, (g) Sales Tax Payable.

EX 6-19 Adjusting entry for merchandise inventory shrinkage OBJ. 3

Paragon Tire Co.'s perpetual inventory records indicate that $2,780,000 of merchandise should be on hand on March 31, 2019. The physical inventory indicates that $2,734,800 of merchandise is actually on hand. Journalize the adjusting entry for the inventory shrinkage for Paragon Tire Co. for the year ended March 31, 2019.

EX 6-20 Adjusting entries for refunds, allowances, and returns OBJ. 3

Assume the following data for Oshkosh Company before its year-end adjustments:

	Unadjusted Balances	
	Debit	Credit
Sales		$51,600000
Cost of Merchandise Sold	$31,750,000	
Estimated Returns Inventory	28,100	
Customer Refunds Payable		115,400
Estimated cost of merchandise that will be returned in the next year	$400,000	
Estimated percent of refunds for current year sales	1.2%	

Journalize the adjusting entries for the following:

a. Estimated customer refunds and allowances

b. Estimated customer returns

EX 6-21 Customer returns and allowances   OBJ. 2, 3

Zell Company had sales of $1,800,000 and related cost of merchandise sold of $1,150,000 for its first year of operations ending December 31, 2019. Zell Company provides customers a refund for any returned or damaged merchandise. At the end of the year, Zell Company estimates that customers will request refunds and allowances for 1.5% of sales and estimates that merchandise costing $16,000 will be returned. Assume that on February 3, 2020, Anderson Co. returned merchandise with a selling price of $5,000 for a cash refund. The returned merchandise originally cost Zell Company $3,100. (a) Journalize the adjusting entries on December 31, 2019, to record the expected customer refunds, allowances, and returns. (b) Journalize the entries to record the returned merchandise and cash refund to Anderson Co.

EX 6-22 Income statement and accounts for merchandiser   OBJ. 4

For the fiscal year, sales were $191,350,000 and the cost of merchandise sold was $114,800,000.

a. What was the amount of gross profit?
b. If total operating expenses were $18,250,000, could you determine net income?
c. Is Customer Refunds Payable an asset, liability, or owner's equity account, and what is its normal balance?
d. Is Estimated Returns Inventory an asset, liability, or owner's equity account, and what is its normal balance?

EX 6-23 Income statement for merchandiser   OBJ. 4

The following expenses were incurred by a merchandising business during the year. In which expense section of the income statement should each be reported: (a) selling, (b) administrative, or (c) other?

1. Advertising expense
2. Depreciation expense on store equipment
3. Insurance expense on office equipment
4. Interest expense on notes payable
5. Rent expense on office building
6. Salaries of office personnel
7. Salary of sales manager
8. Sales supplies used

EX 6-24 Determining amounts for items omitted from income statement   OBJ. 4

One item is omitted in each of the following four lists of income statement data. Determine the amounts of the missing items, identifying them by letter.

Sales	$463,400	(b)	$1,295,000	(d)
Cost of merchandise sold	(a)	$410,000	(c)	$900,000
Gross profit	83,500	277,500	275,000	600,000

EX 6-25 Multiple-step income statement   OBJ. 4

✔ a. Net income: $538,000

On March 31, 2019, the balances of the accounts appearing in the ledger of Racine Furnishings Company, a furniture wholesaler, are as follows:

Accumulated Depreciation—Building	$ 300,000	Merchandise Inventory	$ 392,000
Administrative Expenses	216,000	Notes Payable	100,000
Building	1,000,000	Office Supplies	8,000
Cash	70,000	Salaries Payable	3,200
Cost of Merchandise Sold	1,520,000	Sales	2,564,000
Interest Expense	4,000	Selling Expenses	286,000
Kathy Melman, Capital	634,800	Store Supplies	36,000
Kathy Melman, Drawing	70,000		

a. Prepare a multiple-step income statement for the year ended March 31, 2019.
b. ➤ Compare the major advantages and disadvantages of the multiple-step and single-step forms of income statements.

EX 6-26 Multiple-step income statement
OBJ. 4

Identify the errors in the following income statement:

Curbstone Company
Income Statement
For the Year Ended August 31, 2019

Sales		$8,595,000
Cost of merchandise sold		6,110,000
Income from operations		$2,485,000
Expenses:		
Selling expenses	$800,000	
Administrative expenses	575,000	
Delivery expense	425,000	
Total expenses		1,800,000
		$ 685,000
Other expense:		
Interest revenue		45,000
Gross profit		$ 640,000

EX 6-27 Single-step income statement
OBJ. 4

✔ Net income: $1,277,500

Show Me How

Summary operating data for Custom Wire & Tubing Company during the year ended April 30, 2019, are as follows: cost of merchandise sold, $6,100,000; administrative expenses, $740,000; interest expense, $25,000; rent revenue, $60,000; sales, $9,332,500; and selling expenses, $1,250,000. Prepare a single-step income statement.

EX 6-28 Closing the accounts of a merchandiser
OBJ. 4

From the following list, identify the accounts that should be closed to Tim Button, Capital at the end of the fiscal year under a perpetual inventory system: (a) Accounts Receivable, (b) Cost of Merchandise Sold, (c) Customer Refunds Payable, (d) Estimated Returns Inventory, (e) Merchandise Inventory, (f) Sales, (g) Supplies, (h) Supplies Expense, (i) Tim Button, Drawing, (j) Wages Expense.

EX 6-29 Closing entries; net income
OBJ. 4

Based on the data presented in Exercise 6-25, journalize the closing entries.

EX 6-30 Closing entries
OBJ. 4

On July 31, 2019, the balances of the accounts appearing in the ledger of Serbian Interiors Company, a furniture wholesaler, are as follows:

Accumulated Depr.—Building	$365,000	Peter Bronsky, Capital	$ 530,000
Administrative Expenses	440,000	Peter Bronsky, Drawing	15,000
Building	810,000	Sales	1,437,000
Cash	78,000	Sales Tax Payable	4,500
Cost of Merchandise Sold	775,000	Selling Expenses	160,000
Interest Expense	6,000	Store Supplies	16,000
Merchandise Inventory	115,000	Store Supplies Expense	21,500
Notes Payable	100,000		

Prepare the July 31, 2019, closing entries for Serbian Interiors Company.

EX 6-31 Asset turnover   OBJ. 5

The Home Depot reported the following data (in millions) in its recent financial statements:

	Year 2	Year 1
Sales	$83,176	$78,812
Total assets at the end of the year	39,946	40,518
Total assets at the beginning of the year	40,518	41,084

a. Determine the asset turnover for The Home Depot for Year 2 and Year 1. Round to two decimal places.

b.  What conclusions can be drawn concerning the trend in the ability of The Home Depot to effectively use its assets to generate sales?

EX 6-32 Asset turnover   OBJ. 5

Kroger Co., a national supermarket chain, reported the following data (in millions) in its financial statements for a recent year:

Total revenue	$108,465
Total assets at end of year	30,556
Total assets at beginning of year	29,281

a. Compute the asset turnover. Round to two decimal places.

b. Tiffany & Co. is a large North American retailer of jewelry with an asset turnover of 0.86. Why would Tiffany's asset turnover be lower than that of Kroger?

Appendix
EX 6-33 Rules of debit and credit for periodic inventory accounts

Complete the following table by indicating for (a) through (g) whether the proper answer is debit or credit:

Account	Increase	Decrease	Normal Balance
Purchases	debit	(a)	(b)
Purchases Discounts	credit	(c)	credit
Purchases Returns and Allowances	(d)	(e)	(f)
Freight In	debit	(g)	debit

Appendix
EX 6-34 Journal entries using the periodic inventory system

The following selected transactions were completed by Air Systems Company during January of the current year. Air Systems Company uses the periodic inventory system.

Jan. 2. Purchased $18,200 of merchandise on account, FOB shipping point, terms 2/15, n/30.

  5. Paid freight of $190 on the January 2 purchase.

  6. Returned $2,750 of the merchandise purchased on January 2.

  13. Sold merchandise on account, $37,300, FOB destination, 1/10, n/30. The cost of merchandise sold was $22,400.

  15. Paid freight of $215 for the merchandise sold on January 13.

  17. Paid for the purchase of January 2 less the return and discount.

  23. Received payment on account for the sale of January 13 less the discount.

Journalize the entries to record the transactions of Air Systems Company.

Appendix
EX 6-35 Identify items missing in determining cost of merchandise sold

For (a) through (d), identify the items designated by X and Y.

a. Purchases − (X + Y) = Net purchases.
b. Net purchases + X = Cost of merchandise purchased.
c. Merchandise inventory (beginning) + Cost of merchandise purchased = X.
d. Merchandise available for sale − X = Cost of merchandise sold before estimated returns.
e. Cost of merchandise sold before estimated returns − X = Cost of merchandise sold.

Appendix
EX 6-36 Cost of merchandise sold and related items

✔ a. Cost of merchandise sold, $3,540,000

The following data were extracted from the accounting records of Harkins Company for the year ended April 30, 2019:

Increase in estimated returns inventory	$ 11,600
Merchandise inventory, May 1, 2018	380,000
Merchandise inventory, April 30, 2019	415,000
Purchases	3,800,000
Purchases returns and allowances	150,000
Purchases discounts	80,000
Sales	5,850,000
Freight in	16,600

a. Prepare the cost of merchandise sold section of the income statement for the year ended April 30, 2019, using the periodic inventory system.
b. Determine the gross profit to be reported on the income statement for the year ended April 30, 2019.
c. ✏️ Would gross profit be different if the perpetual inventory system was used instead of the periodic inventory system?

Appendix
EX 6-37 Cost of merchandise sold

Based on the following data, determine the cost of merchandise sold for November:

Increase in estimated returns inventory	$ 14,500
Merchandise inventory, November 1	28,000
Merchandise inventory, November 30	31,500
Purchases	475,000
Purchases returns and allowances	15,000
Purchases discounts	9,000
Freight in	7,000

Appendix
EX 6-38 Cost of merchandise sold

Based on the following data, determine the cost of merchandise sold for July:

Increase in estimated returns inventory	$ 34,900
Merchandise inventory, July 1	190,850
Merchandise inventory, July 31	160,450
Purchases	1,126,000
Purchases returns and allowances	46,000
Purchases discounts	23,000
Freight in	17,500

Chapter 6 Accounting for Merchandising Businesses

✔ Correct cost of merchandise sold, $990,000

Appendix
EX 6-39 Cost of merchandise sold

Identify the errors in the following schedule of the cost of merchandise sold for the year ended May 31, 2018:

Cost of merchandise sold:		
Merchandise inventory, May 31, 2018		$ 105,000
Cost of merchandise purchased:		
Purchases	$1,110,000	
Purchases returns and allowances	55,000	
Purchases discounts	30,000	
Freight in	(22,000)	
Total cost of merchandise purchased		1,173,000
Inventory available for sale		$1,278,000
Merchandise inventory, June 1, 2017		91,300
Cost of merchandise sold before estimated returns		$1,186,700
Increase in estimated returns inventory		43,300
Cost of merchandise sold		$1,230,000

Appendix
Ex 6-40 Closing entries using periodic inventory system

United Rug Company is a small rug retailer owned and operated by Pat Kirwan. After the accounts have been adjusted on December 31, the following selected account balances were taken from the ledger:

Advertising Expense	$ 36,000
Depreciation Expense	13,000
Freight In	17,000
Merchandise Inventory, January 1	375,000
Merchandise Inventory, December 31	460,000
Miscellaneous Expense	9,000
Purchases	1,760,000
Purchases Discounts	35,000
Purchases Returns and Allowances	45,000
Pat Kirwan, Drawing	65,000
Salaries Expense	375,000
Sales	2,220,000

The estimated cost of merchandise returns from December sales is $20,000. Journalize the closing entries on December 31.

Problems: Series A

PR 6-1A Purchase-related transactions using perpetual inventory system   OBJ. 2

The following selected transactions were completed by Capers Company during October of the current year:

Oct. 1. Purchased merchandise from UK Imports Co., $14,448, terms FOB destination, n/30.

3. Purchased merchandise from Hoagie Co., $9,950, terms FOB shipping point, 2/10, n/eom. Prepaid freight of $220 was added to the invoice.

4. Purchased merchandise from Taco Co., $13,650, terms FOB destination, 2/10, n/30.

6. Issued debit memo to Taco Co. for $4,550 of merchandise returned from purchase on October 4.

Oct. 13. Paid Hoagie Co. for invoice of October 3.

14. Paid Taco Co. for invoice of October 4 less debit memo of October 6.

19. Purchased merchandise from Veggie Co., $27,300, terms FOB shipping point, n/eom.

19. Paid freight of $400 on October 19 purchase from Veggie Co.

20. Purchased merchandise from Caesar Salad Co., $22,000, terms FOB destination, 1/10, n/30.

30. Paid Caesar Salad Co. for invoice of October 20.

31. Paid UK Imports Co. for invoice of October 1.

31. Paid Veggie Co. for invoice of October 19.

Instructions

Journalize the entries to record the transactions of Capers Company for October.

PR 6-2A Sales-related transactions using perpetual inventory system OBJ. 2

The following selected transactions were completed by Amsterdam Supply Co., which sells office supplies primarily to wholesalers and occasionally to retail customers:

Mar. 2. Sold merchandise on account to Equinox Co., $18,900, terms FOB destination, 1/10, n/30. The cost of the merchandise sold was $13,300.

3. Sold merchandise for $11,350 plus 6% sales tax to retail cash customers. The cost of merchandise sold was $7,000.

4. Sold merchandise on account to Empire Co., $55,400, terms FOB shipping point, n/eom. The cost of merchandise sold was $33,200.

5. Sold merchandise for $30,000 plus 6% sales tax to retail customers who used MasterCard. The cost of merchandise sold was $19,400.

12. Received check for amount due from Equinox Co. for sale on March 2.

14. Sold merchandise to customers who used American Express cards, $13,700. The cost of merchandise sold was $8,350.

16. Sold merchandise on account to Targhee Co., $27,500, terms FOB shipping point, 1/10, n/30. The cost of merchandise sold was $16,000.

18. Issued credit memo for $4,800 to Targhee Co. for merchandise returned from sale on March 16. The cost of the merchandise returned was $2,900.

19. Sold merchandise on account to Vista Co., $8,250, terms FOB shipping point, 2/10, n/30. Added $75 to the invoice for prepaid freight. The cost of merchandise sold was $5,000.

26. Received check for amount due from Targhee Co. for sale on March 16 less credit memo of March 18.

28. Received check for amount due from Vista Co. for sale of March 19.

31. Received check for amount due from Empire Co. for sale of March 4.

31. Paid Fleetwood Delivery Service $5,600 for delivery of merchandise in March to customers under shipping terms of FOB destination.

Apr. 3. Paid City Bank $940 for service fees for handling MasterCard and American Express sales during March.

15. Paid $6,544 to state sales tax division for taxes owed on sales.

Instructions

Journalize the entries to record the transactions of Amsterdam Supply Co.

PR 6-3A Sales-related and purchase-related transactions using perpetual inventory system   OBJ. 2

The following were selected from among the transactions completed by Babcock Company during November of the current year:

Nov. 3. Purchased merchandise on account from Moonlight Co., list price $85,000, trade discount 25%, terms FOB destination, 2/10, n/30.

    4. Sold merchandise for cash, $37,680. The cost of the merchandise sold was $22,600.

    5. Purchased merchandise on account from Papoose Creek Co., $47,500, terms FOB shipping point, 2/10, n/30, with prepaid freight of $810 added to the invoice.

    6. Returned $13,500 ($18,000 list price less trade discount of 25%) of merchandise purchased on November 3 from Moonlight Co.

    8. Sold merchandise on account to Quinn Co., $15,600 with terms n/15. The cost of the merchandise sold was $9,400.

   13. Paid Moonlight Co. on account for purchase of November 3, less return of November 6.

   14. Sold merchandise on VISA, $236,000. The cost of the merchandise sold was $140,000.

   15. Paid Papoose Creek Co. on account for purchase of November 5.

   23. Received cash on account from sale of November 8 to Quinn Co.

   24. Sold merchandise on account to Rabel Co., $56,900, terms 1/10, n/30. The cost of the merchandise sold was $34,000.

   28. Paid VISA service fee of $3,540.

   30. Paid Quinn Co. a cash refund of $6,000 for returned merchandise from sale of November 8. The cost of the returned merchandise was $3,300.

Instructions
Journalize the transactions.

PR 6-4A Sales-related and purchase-related transactions for seller and buyer using perpetual inventory system   OBJ. 2

The following selected transactions were completed during August between Summit Company and Beartooth Co.:

Aug. 1. Summit Company sold merchandise on account to Beartooth Co., $48,000, terms FOB destination, 2/15, n/eom. The cost of the merchandise sold was $28,800.

    2. Summit Company paid freight of $1,150 for delivery of merchandise sold to Beartooth Co. on August 1.

    5. Summit Company sold merchandise on account to Beartooth Co., $66,000, terms FOB shipping point, n/45. The cost of the merchandise sold was $40,000.

    9. Beartooth Co. paid freight of $2,300 on August 5 purchase from Summit Company.

   15. Summit Company sold merchandise on account to Beartooth Co., $58,700, terms FOB shipping point, 1/10, n/30. Summit Company paid freight of $1,675, which was added to the invoice. The cost of the merchandise sold was $35,000.

   16. Beartooth Co. paid Summit Company for purchase of August 1.

   20. Summit Company paid Beartooth Co. a refund of $1,800 for defective merchandise in the August 1 purchase. Beartooth Co. agreed to keep the merchandise.

   25. Beartooth Co. paid Summit Company on account for purchase of August 15.

   31. Summit Company granted a customer allowance (credit memo) to Beartooth Co. for $6,000 (invoiced amount) for merchandise that was returned from the August 1 purchase. The cost of the merchandise returned was $3,200.

Instructions
Journalize the August transactions for (1) Summit Company and (2) Beartooth Co.

Chapter 6 Accounting for Merchandising Businesses 333

✔ 1. Net income
$943,400

PR 6-5A Multiple-step income statement and balance sheet   OBJ. 3

The following selected accounts and their current balances appear in the ledger of Clairemont Co. for the fiscal year ended May 31, 2019:

Cash	$ 240,000	Kristina Marble, Drawing	$ 100,000
Accounts Receivable	966,000	Sales	11,343,000
Merchandise Inventory	1,690,000	Cost of Merchandise Sold	7,850,000
Estimated Returns Inventory	22,500	Sales Salaries Expense	916,000
Office Supplies	13,500	Advertising Expense	550,000
Prepaid Insurance	8,000	Depreciation Expense—	
Office Equipment	830,000	Store Equipment	140,000
Accumulated Depreciation—		Miscellaneous Selling Expense	38,000
Office Equipment	550,000	Office Salaries Expense	650,000
Store Equipment	3,600,000	Rent Expense	94,000
Accumulated Depreciation—		Depreciation Expense—	
Store Equipment	1,820,000	Office Equipment	50,000
Accounts Payable	326,000	Insurance Expense	48,000
Customer Refunds Payable	40,000	Office Supplies Expense	28,100
Salaries Payable	41,500	Miscellaneous Administrative Exp.	14,500
Note Payable		Interest Expense	21,000
(final payment due 2022)	300,000		
Kristina Marble, Capital	3,449,100		

Instructions

1. Prepare a multiple-step income statement.
2. Prepare a statement of owner's equity.
3. Prepare a balance sheet, assuming that the current portion of the note payable is $50,000.
4. Briefly explain how multiple-step and single-step income statements differ.

PR 6-6A Single-step income statement   OBJ. 3

Selected accounts and related amounts for Clairemont Co. for the fiscal year ended May 31, 2019, are presented in Problem 6-5A.

Instructions

1. Prepare a single-step income statement in the format shown in Exhibit 12.
2. Prepare closing entries as of May 31, 2019.

Appendix
PR 6-7A Purchase-related transactions using periodic inventory system

Selected transactions for Capers Company during October of the current year are listed in Problem 6-1A.

Instructions

Journalize the entries to record the transactions of Capers Company for October using the periodic inventory system.

Appendix
PR 6-8A Sales-related and purchase-related transactions using periodic inventory system

Selected transactions for Babcock Company during November of the current year are listed in Problem 6-3A.

Instructions

Journalize the entries to record the transactions of Babcock Company for November using the periodic inventory system.

334 Chapter 6 Accounting for Merchandising Businesses

✔ 2. Net income, $210,000

Excel

Appendix
PR 6-9A Periodic inventory accounts, multiple-step income statement, closing entries

On December 31, 2019, the balances of the accounts appearing in the ledger of Wyman Company are as follows:

Cash	$ 13,500	Purchases	$2,650,000
Accounts Receivable	72,000	Purchases Returns and Allowances	93,000
Merchandise Inventory,		Purchases Discounts	37,000
January 1, 2019	257,000	Freight In	48,000
Estimated Returns Inventory	35,000	Sales Salaries Expense	300,000
Office Supplies	3,000	Advertising Expense	45,000
Prepaid Insurance	4,500	Delivery Expense	9,000
Land	150,000	Depreciation Expense—	
Store Equipment	270,000	Store Equipment	6,000
Accumulated Depreciation—		Miscellaneous Selling Expense	12,000
Store Equipment	55,900	Office Salaries Expense	175,000
Office Equipment	78,500	Rent Expense	28,000
Accumulated Depreciation—		Insurance Expense	3,000
Office Equipment	16,000	Office Supplies Expense	2,000
Accounts Payable	27,800	Depreciation Expense—	
Customer Refunds Payable	50,000	Office Equipment	1,500
Salaries Payable	3,000	Miscellaneous Administrative Expense	3,500
Unearned Rent	8,300	Rent Revenue	7,000
Notes Payable	50,000	Interest Expense	2,000
Shirley Wyman, Capital	515,600		
Shirley Wyman, Drawing	25,000		
Sales	3,280,000		

Instructions

1. ✏ Does Wyman Company use a periodic or perpetual inventory system? Explain.
2. Prepare a multiple-step income statement for Wyman Company for the year ended December 31, 2019. The merchandise inventory as of December 31, 2019, was $305,000. The adjustment for estimated returns inventory for sales for the year ending December 31, 2019, was $30,000.
3. Prepare the closing entries for Wyman Company as of December 31, 2019.
4. What would the net income have been if the perpetual inventory system had been used?

Problems: Series B

PR 6-1B Purchase-related transactions using perpetual inventory system   OBJ. 2

The following selected transactions were completed by Niles Co. during March of the current year:

Mar. 1. Purchased merchandise from Haas Co., $43,250, terms FOB shipping point, 2/10, n/eom. Prepaid freight of $650 was added to the invoice.

5. Purchased merchandise from Whitman Co., $19,175, terms FOB destination, n/30.

10. Paid Haas Co. for invoice of March 1.

13. Purchased merchandise from Jost Co., $15,550, terms FOB destination, 2/10, n/30.

14. Issued debit memo to Jost Co. for $3,750 of merchandise returned from purchase on March 13.

Mar. 18. Purchased merchandise from Fairhurst Company, $13,560, terms FOB shipping point, n/eom.

18. Paid freight of $140 on March 18 purchase from Fairhurst Company.

19. Purchased merchandise from Bickle Co., $6,500, terms FOB destination, 2/10, n/30.

23. Paid Jost Co. for invoice of March 13 less debit memo of March 14.

29. Paid Bickle Co. for invoice of March 19.

31. Paid Fairhurst Company for invoice of March 18.

31. Paid Whitman Co. for invoice of March 5.

Instructions
Journalize the entries to record the transactions of Niles Co. for March.

PR 6-2B Sales-related transactions using perpetual inventory system OBJ. 2

The following selected transactions were completed by Green Lawn Supplies Co., which sells irrigation supplies primarily to wholesalers and occasionally to retail customers:

July 1. Sold merchandise on account to Landscapes Co., $33,450, terms FOB shipping point, n/eom. The cost of merchandise sold was $20,000.

2. Sold merchandise for $86,000 plus 8% sales tax to retail cash customers. The cost of merchandise sold was $51,600.

5. Sold merchandise on account to Peacock Company, $17,500, terms FOB destination, 1/10, n/30. The cost of merchandise sold was $10,000.

8. Sold merchandise for $112,000 plus 8% sales tax to retail customers who used VISA cards. The cost of merchandise sold was $67,200.

13. Sold merchandise to customers who used MasterCard cards, $96,000. The cost of merchandise sold was $57,600.

14. Sold merchandise on account to Loeb Co., $16,000, terms FOB shipping point, 1/10, n/30. The cost of merchandise sold was $9,000.

15. Received check for amount due from Peacock Company for sale on July 5.

16. Issued credit memo for $3,000 to Loeb Co. for merchandise returned from sale on July 14. The cost of the merchandise returned was $1,800.

18. Sold merchandise on account to Jennings Company, $11,350, terms FOB shipping point, 2/10, n/30. Paid $475 for freight and added it to the invoice. The cost of merchandise sold was $6,800.

24. Received check for amount due from Loeb Co. for sale on July 14 less credit memo of July 16.

28. Received check for amount due from Jennings Company for sale of July 18.

31. Paid Black Lab Delivery Service $8,550 for delivery of merchandise in July to customers under shipping terms of FOB destination.

31. Received check for amount due from Landscapes Co. for sale of July 1.

Aug. 3. Paid Hays Federal Bank $3,770 for service fees for handling MasterCard and VISA sales during July.

10. Paid $41,260 to state sales tax division for taxes owed on sales.

Instructions
Journalize the entries to record the transactions of Green Lawn Supplies Co.

336 Chapter 6 Accounting for Merchandising Businesses

PR 6-3B Sales-related and purchase-related transactions using perpetual inventory system OBJ. 2

The following were selected from among the transactions completed by Essex Company during July of the current year:

July 3. Purchased merchandise on account from Hamling Co., list price $72,000, trade discount 15%, terms FOB shipping point, 2/10, n/30, with prepaid freight of $1,450 added to the invoice.

5. Purchased merchandise on account from Kester Co., $33,450, terms FOB destination, 2/10, n/30.

6. Sold merchandise on account to Parsley Co., $36,000, terms n/15. The cost of the merchandise sold was $25,000.

7. Returned $6,850 of merchandise purchased on July 5 from Kester Co.

13. Paid Hamling Co. on account for purchase of July 3.

15. Paid Kester Co. on account for purchase of July 5, less return of July 7.

21. Received cash on account from sale of July 6 to Parsley Co.

21. Sold merchandise on MasterCard, $108,000. The cost of the merchandise sold was $64,800.

22. Sold merchandise on account to Tabor Co., $16,650, terms 2/10, n/30. The cost of the merchandise sold was $10,000.

23. Sold merchandise for cash, $91,200. The cost of the merchandise sold was $55,000.

28. Paid Parsley Co. a cash refund of $7,150 for returned merchandise from sale of July 6. The cost of the returned merchandise was $4,250.

31. Paid MasterCard service fee of $1,650.

Instructions
Journalize the transactions.

PR 6-4B Sales-related and purchase-related transactions for seller and buyer using perpetual inventory system OBJ. 2

The following selected transactions were completed during April between Swan Company and Bird Company:

Apr. 2. Swan Company sold merchandise on account to Bird Company, $32,000, terms FOB shipping point, 2/10, n/30. Swan Company paid freight of $330, which was added to the invoice. The cost of the merchandise sold was $19,200.

8. Swan Company sold merchandise on account to Bird Company, $49,500, terms FOB destination, 1/15, n/30. The cost of the merchandise sold was $29,700.

8. Swan Company paid freight of $710 for delivery of merchandise sold to Bird Company on April 8.

12. Bird Company paid Swan Company for purchase of April 2.

18. Swan Company paid Bird Company a refund of $2,000 for defective merchandise in the April 2 purchase. Bird Company agreed to keep the merchandise.

23. Bird Company paid Swan Company for purchase of April 8.

24. Swan Company sold merchandise on account to Bird Company, $67,350, terms FOB shipping point, n/45. The cost of the merchandise sold was $40,400.

26. Bird Company paid freight of $875 on April 24 purchase from Swan Company.

30. Swan Company granted a customer allowance (credit memo) to Bird Company for $11,300 for merchandise that was returned from the August 24 purchase. The cost of the merchandise returned was $6,500.

Instructions
Journalize the April transactions for (1) Swan Company and (2) Bird Company.

PR 6-5B Multiple-step income statement and balance sheet OBJ. 3

✔ 1. Net income: $1,340,000

The following selected accounts and their current balances appear in the ledger of Kanpur Co. for the fiscal year ended June 30, 2019:

Cash	$ 92,000	Gerri Faber, Drawing	$ 300,000
Accounts Receivable	450,000	Sales	8,925,000
Merchandise Inventory	370,000	Cost of Merchandise Sold	5,620,000
Estimated Returns Inventory	5,000	Sales Salaries Expense	850,000
Office Supplies	10,000	Advertising Expense	420,000
Prepaid Insurance	12,000	Depreciation Expense—	
Office Equipment	220,000	Store Equipment	33,000
Accumulated Depreciation—		Miscellaneous Selling Expense	18,000
Office Equipment	58,000	Office Salaries Expense	540,000
Store Equipment	650,000	Rent Expense	48,000
Accumulated Depreciation—		Insurance Expense	24,000
Store Equipment	87,500	Depreciation Expense—	
Accounts Payable	38,500	Office Equipment	10,000
Customer Refunds Payable	10,000	Office Supplies Expense	4,000
Salaries Payable	4,000	Miscellaneous Administrative Exp.	6,000
Note Payable		Interest Expense	12,000
(final payment due 2032)	140,000		
Gerri Faber, Capital	431,000		

Instructions

1. Prepare a multiple-step income statement.
2. Prepare a statement of owner's equity.
3. Prepare a balance sheet, assuming that the current portion of the note payable is $7,000.
4. ✏️ Briefly explain how multiple-step and single-step income statements differ.

PR 6-6B Single-step income statement OBJ. 3

Selected accounts and related amounts for Kanpur Co. for the fiscal year ended June 30, 2019, are presented in Problem 6-5B.

Instructions

1. Prepare a single-step income statement in the format shown in Exhibit 12.
2. Prepare closing entries as of June 30, 2019.

Appendix
PR 6-7B Purchase-related transactions using periodic inventory system

Selected transactions for Niles Co. during March of the current year are listed in Problem 6-1B.

Instructions

Journalize the entries to record the transactions of Niles Co. for March using the periodic inventory system.

Appendix
PR 6-8B Sales-related and purchase-related transactions using periodic inventory system

Selected transactions for Essex Company during July of the current year are listed in Problem 6-3B.

Instructions

Journalize the entries to record the transactions of Essex Company for July using the periodic inventory system.

Chapter 6 Accounting for Merchandising Businesses

Appendix
PR 6-9B Periodic inventory accounts, multiple-step income statement, closing entries

✔ 2. Net income, $1,233,000

Excel

On June 30, 2019, the balances of the accounts appearing in the ledger of Simkins Company are as follows:

Cash	$ 125,000	Purchases	$4,100,000
Accounts Receivable	340,000	Purchases Returns and Allowances	32,000
Merchandise Inventory, July 1, 2018	415,000	Purchases Discounts	13,000
Estimated Returns Inventory	25,000	Freight In	45,000
Office Supplies	9,000	Sales Salaries Expense	580,000
Prepaid Insurance	18,000	Advertising Expense	315,000
Land	300,000	Delivery Expense	18,000
Store Equipment	550,000	Depreciation Expense—	
Accumulated Depreciation—		Store Equipment	12,000
Store Equipment	190,000	Miscellaneous Selling Expense	28,000
Office Equipment	250,000	Office Salaries Expense	375,000
Accumulated Depreciation—		Rent Expense	43,000
Office Equipment	110,000	Insurance Expense	17,000
Accounts Payable	85,000	Office Supplies Expense	5,000
Customer Refunds Payable	20,000	Depreciation Expense—	
Salaries Payable	9,000	Office Equipment	4,000
Unearned Rent	6,000	Miscellaneous Administrative Expense	16,000
Notes Payable	50,000	Rent Revenue	32,500
Amy Gant, Capital	820,000	Interest Expense	2,500
Amy Gant, Drawing	275,000		
Sales	6,590,000		

Instructions

1. ✏️ Does Simkins Company use a periodic or perpetual inventory system? Explain.
2. Prepare a multiple-step income statement for Simkins Company for the year ended June 30, 2019. The merchandise inventory as of June 30, 2019, was $508,000. The adjustment for estimated returns inventory for sales for the year ending December 31, 2019, was $33,000.
3. Prepare the closing entries for Simkins Company as of June 30, 2019.
4. What would the net income have been if the perpetual inventory system had been used?

Comprehensive Problem 2

✔ 8. Net income: $741,855

Palisade Creek Co. is a merchandising business that uses the perpetual inventory system. The account balances for Palisade Creek Co. as of May 1, 2019 (unless otherwise indicated), are as follows:

110	Cash	$ 83,600
112	Accounts Receivable	233,900
115	Merchandise Inventory	624,400
116	Estimated Returns Inventory	28,000
117	Prepaid Insurance	16,800
118	Store Supplies	11,400
123	Store Equipment	569,500
124	Accumulated Depreciation—Store Equipment	56,700
210	Accounts Payable	96,600
211	Customer Refunds Payable	50,000
212	Salaries Payable	—
310	Lynn Tolley, Capital, June 1, 2018	685,300
311	Lynn Tolley, Drawing	135,000

410	Sales	$5,069,000
510	Cost of Merchandise Sold	2,823,000
520	Sales Salaries Expense	664,800
521	Advertising Expense	281,000
522	Depreciation Expense	—
523	Store Supplies Expense	—
529	Miscellaneous Selling Expense	12,600
530	Office Salaries Expense	382,100
531	Rent Expense	83,700
532	Insurance Expense	—
539	Miscellaneous Administrative Expense	7,800

During May, the last month of the fiscal year, the following transactions were completed:

May 1. Paid rent for May, $5,000.

3. Purchased merchandise on account from Martin Co., terms 2/10, n/30, FOB shipping point, $36,000.

4. Paid freight on purchase of May 3, $600.

6. Sold merchandise on account to Korman Co., terms 2/10, n/30, FOB shipping point, $68,500. The cost of the merchandise sold was $41,000.

7. Received $22,300 cash from Halstad Co. on account.

10. Sold merchandise for cash, $54,000. The cost of the merchandise sold was $32,000.

13. Paid for merchandise purchased on May 3.

15. Paid advertising expense for last half of May, $11,000.

16. Received cash from sale of May 6.

19. Purchased merchandise for cash, $18,700.

19. Paid $33,450 to Buttons Co. on account.

20. Paid Korman Co. a cash refund of $13,230 for returned merchandise from sale of May 6. The invoice amount of the returned merchandise was $13,500, and the cost of the returned merchandise was $8,000.

Record the following transactions on Page 21 of the journal:

20. Sold merchandise on account to Crescent Co., terms 1/10, n/30, FOB shipping point, $110,000. The cost of the merchandise sold was $70,000.

21. For the convenience of Crescent Co., paid freight on sale of May 20, $2,300.

21. Received $42,900 cash from Gee Co. on account.

21. Purchased merchandise on account from Osterman Co., terms 1/10, n/30, FOB destination, $88,000.

24. Returned damaged merchandise purchased on May 21, receiving a credit memo from the seller for $5,000.

26. Refunded cash on sales made for cash, $7,500. The cost of the merchandise returned was $4,800.

28. Paid sales salaries of $56,000 and office salaries of $29,000.

29. Purchased store supplies for cash, $2,400.

30. Sold merchandise on account to Turner Co., terms 2/10, n/30, FOB shipping point, $78,750. The cost of the merchandise sold was $47,000.

30. Received cash from sale of May 20 plus freight paid on May 21.

31. Paid for purchase of May 21, less return of May 24.

Instructions

1. Enter the balances of each of the accounts in the appropriate balance column of a four-column account. Write *Balance* in the item section and place a check mark (✓) in the Posting Reference column. Journalize the transactions for May, starting on Page 20 of the journal.

(Continued)

2. Post the journal to the general ledger, extending the month-end balances to the appropriate balance columns after all posting is completed. In this problem, you are not required to update or post to the accounts receivable and accounts payable subsidiary ledgers.
3. Prepare an unadjusted trial balance.
4. At the end of May, the following adjustment data were assembled. Analyze and use these data to complete (5) and (6).

a.	Merchandise inventory on May 31	$570,000
b.	Insurance expired during the year	12,000
c.	Store supplies on hand on May 31	4,000
d.	Depreciation for the current year	14,000
e.	Accrued salaries on May 31:	
	Sales salaries $7,000	
	Office salaries 6,600	13,600

f. The adjustment for customer returns and allowances is $60,000 for sales and $35,000 for cost of merchandise sold.

5. *(Optional)* Enter the unadjusted trial balance on a 10-column end-of-period spreadsheet (work sheet), and complete the spreadsheet.
6. Journalize and post the adjusting entries. Record the adjusting entries on Page 22 of the journal.
7. Prepare an adjusted trial balance.
8. Prepare an income statement, a statement of owner's equity, and a balance sheet.
9. Prepare and post the closing entries. Record the closing entries on Page 23 of the journal. Indicate closed accounts by inserting a line in both Balance columns opposite the closing entry. Insert the new balance in the owner's capital account.
10. Prepare a post-closing trial balance.

Cases & Projects

CP 6-1 Ethics in Action
Margie Johnson is a staff accountant at ToolEx Company, a manufacturer of tools and equipment. The company is under pressure from investors to increase earnings, and the president of the company expects the accounting department to "make this happen." Margie's boss, who has been a mentor to her, is concerned that if earnings do not increase, he will be terminated.

Shortly after the end of the fiscal year, the company performs a physical count of the inventory. When Margie compares the physical count to the balance in the inventory account, she finds a significant amount of inventory shrinkage. The amount is so large that it will result in a significant drop in earnings this period. Margie's boss asks her not to make the adjusting entry for shrinkage this period. He assures her that they will get "caught up" on shrinkage in the next period, after the pressure is off to reach this period's earnings goal. Margie's boss asks her to do this as a personal favor to him.

➤ What should Margie do in this situation? Why?

CP 6-2 Ethics in Action
On April 18, 2019, Bontanica Company, a garden retailer, purchased $9,800 of seed, terms 2/10, n/30, from Whitetail Seed Co. Even though the discount period had expired, Shelby Davey subtracted the discount of $196 when he processed the documents for payment on May 1, 2019.

➤ Discuss whether Shelby Davey behaved in a professional manner by subtracting the discount even though the discount period had expired.

Chapter 6 Accounting for Merchandising Businesses

CP 6-3 Team Activity

In teams, select a public company that interests you. Obtain the company's most recent annual report on Form 10-K. The Form 10-K is a company's annually required filing with the Securities and Exchange Commission (SEC). It includes the company's financial statements and accompanying notes. The Form 10-K can be obtained either (a) from the investor relations section of the company's website or (b) by using the company search feature of the SEC's EDGAR database service found at www.sec.gov/edgar/searchedgar/companysearch.html.

1. Based on the information in the company's most recent annual report, determine each of the following for all the years presented:
   a. Gross profit
   b. Gross profit rate (Gross profit ÷ Sales)
   c. Income from operations
   d. Percentage change in income from operations
   e. Net income
   f. Percentage change in net income

2. Based solely on your responses to item 1, has the company's performance improved, remained constant, or deteriorated over the periods presented? Briefly explain your answer.

CP 6-4 Communication

Suzi Nomro operates Watercraft Supply Company, an online boat parts distributorship that is in its third year of operation. The following income statement was prepared for the year ended October 31, 2019.

Watercraft Supply Company
Income Statement
For the Year Ended October 31, 2019

Revenues:		
Sales		$1,350,000
Interest		15,000
Total revenues		$1,365,000
Expenses:		
Cost of merchandise sold	$810,000	
Selling expenses	140,000	
Administrative expenses	90,000	
Interest expense	4,000	
Total expenses		1,044,000
Net income		$ 321,000

Suzi is considering a proposal to increase net income by offering sales discounts of 2/15, n/30 and by shipping all merchandise FOB shipping point. Currently, no sales discounts are allowed and merchandise is shipped FOB destination. It is estimated that the new terms will increase sales by 10%. The ratio of the cost of merchandise sold to sales is expected to be 60%. All selling and administrative expenses are expected to remain unchanged, except for store supplies and miscellaneous selling expenses, which are expected to increase proportionately with increased sales. The amounts of these items for the year ended October 31, 2019, were as follows:

Store supplies expense	$12,000
Miscellaneous selling expenses	6,000

The interest revenue and expense items will remain unchanged. The shipment of all merchandise FOB shipping point will eliminate all delivery expenses, which for the year ended October 31, 2019, were $12,000.

(Continued)

✏️ Write a brief memo to Suzi discussing the potential benefits and limitations of this proposal. Include a determination of the net income that Watercraft Supply could generate next year under the new proposal, assuming that all sales are collected within the discount period.

CP 6-5 Purchases discounts and accounts payable

Rustic Furniture Co. is owned and operated by Cam Pfeifer. The following is an excerpt from a conversation between Cam Pfeifer and Mitzi Wheeler, the chief accountant for Rustic Furniture Co.:

Cam: Mitzi, I've got a question about this recent balance sheet.

Mitzi: Sure, what's your question?

Cam: Well, as you know, I'm applying for a bank loan to finance our new store in Garden Grove, and I noticed that the accounts payable are listed as $320,000.

Mitzi: That's right. Approximately $275,000 of that represents amounts due our suppliers, and the remainder is miscellaneous payables to creditors for utilities, office equipment, supplies, etc.

Cam: That's what I thought. But as you know, we normally receive a 2% discount from our suppliers for earlier payment, and we always try to take the discount.

Mitzi: That's right. I can't remember the last time we missed a discount.

Cam: Well, in that case, it seems to me the accounts payable should be listed minus the 2% discount. Let's list the accounts payable due suppliers as $314,500 rather than $320,000. Every little bit helps. You never know. It might make the difference between getting and not getting the loan.

✏️ How would you respond to Cam Pfeifer's request?

CP 6-6 Determining cost of purchase

The following is an excerpt from a conversation between Mark Loomis and Krista Huff. Mark is debating whether to buy a stereo system from Tru-Sound Systems, a locally owned electronics store, or Wholesale Stereo, an online electronics company.

Mark: Krista, I don't know what to do about buying my new stereo.

Krista: What's the problem?

Mark: Well, I can buy it locally at Tru-Sound Systems for $1,175.00. However, Wholesale Stereo has the same system listed for $1,200.00.

Krista: What's the big deal? Buy it from Tru-Sound Systems.

Mark: It's not quite that simple. Wholesale Stereo charges $49.99 for shipping and handling. If I have Wholesale Stereo send it next-day air, it'll cost $89.99 for shipping and handling.

Krista: So?

Mark: But, that's not all. Tru-Sound Systems will give an additional 2% discount if I pay cash. Otherwise, they will let me use my VISA, or I can pay it off in three monthly installments. In addition, if I buy it from Tru-Sound Systems, I have to pay 9% sales tax. I won't have to pay sales tax if I buy it from Wholesale Stereo, since they are out of state.

Krista: Anything else???

Mark: Well . . . Wholesale Stereo says I have to charge it on my VISA. They don't accept checks.

Krista: I am not surprised. Many online stores don't accept checks.

Mark: I give up. What would you do?

1. Assuming that Wholesale Stereo doesn't charge sales tax on the sale to Mark, which company is offering the best buy?
2. ✏️ What might be some considerations other than price that influence Mark's decision on where to buy the stereo system?

CP 6-7 Shopping for a television

Assume that you are planning to purchase a 55-inch LED, LCD flat-screen television. In groups of three or four, determine the lowest cost for the television, considering the available alternatives and the advantages and disadvantages of each alternative. For example, you could purchase from a local store, through mail order, or through an Internet shopping service. Consider such factors as delivery charges, interest-free financing, discounts, coupons, and availability of warranty services. Prepare a report for presentation to the class.

CHAPTER 7

Inventories

Chapters 1–4
Accounting Cycle

Chapter 5
Accounting Systems

Income Statement	Statement of Owner's Equity	Balance Sheet	Statement of Cash Flows

Chapter 6 *Accounting for Merchandising Businesses*

Chapter 16 *Cash Flows*

Assets	=	Liabilities	+	Owner's Equity
Chapter 8 *Cash*		Chapter 11 *Current Liabilities*		Chapter 12 *Partnerships*
Chapter 9 *Receivables*		Chapter 14 *Bonds and Notes*		Chapter 13 *Corporations*
Chapter 7 Inventories				
Chapter 10 *Fixed and Intangible Assets*				
Chapter 15 *Investments*				

Chapter 17
Financial Statement Analysis

Statement of Owner's Equity

Owner's capital, Jan. 1		$XXX
Net income	$ XXX	
Withdrawals	(XXX)	
Increase in capital		XXX

Statement of Cash Flows

Cash flows from (used in) operating activities	$XXX
Cash flows from (used in) investing activities	XXX
Cash flows from (used in) financing activities	XXX
Increase (decrease) in cash flows	$XXX
	XXX
	$XXX

Income Statement

Sales		$XXX
Cost of merchandise sold		XXX
Gross profit		$XXX
Operating expenses:		
Advertising expense	$XXX	
Depreciation expense	XXX	
Amortization expense	XXX	
Depletion expense	XXX	
…	XXX	
…	XXX	
Total operating expenses		XXX
Income from operations		$XXX
Other revenue and expenses		XXX
Net income		$XXX

Balance Sheet

Current assets:		
Cash	$XXX	
Accounts receivable	XXX	
Merchandise inventory	XXX	
Total current assets		$XXX
Property, plant, and equipment	$XXX	
Intangible assets	XXX	
Total long-term assets		XXX
Total assets		$XXX
Liabilities:		
Current liabilities	$XXX	
Long-term liabilities	XXX	
Total liabilities		$XXX
Owner's equity		XXX
Total liabilities and owner's equity		$XXX

CHAPTER 7

Best Buy

Assume that in September, you purchased a Sony HDTV from **Best Buy**. At the same time, you purchased a Denon surround sound system for $599.99. You liked your surround sound so well that in November, you purchased an identical Denon system on sale for $549.99 for your bedroom TV. Over the holidays, you moved to a new apartment and in the process of unpacking discovered that one of the Denon surround sound systems was missing. Luckily, your renters or homeowners insurance policy will cover the theft, but the insurance company needs to know the cost of the system that was stolen.

The Denon systems were identical. However, to respond to the insurance company, you will need to identify which system was stolen. Was it the first system, which cost $599.99, or was it the second system, which cost $549.99? Whichever system you choose will determine the amount that you receive from the insurance company.

Merchandising businesses such as Best Buy make similar assumptions when identical merchandise is purchased at different costs. For example, Best Buy may have purchased thousands of Denon surround sound systems over the past year at different costs. At the end of a period, some of the Denon systems will still be in inventory, and some will have been sold. But which costs relate to the sold systems, and which costs relate to the systems still in inventory? Best Buy's assumption about inventory costs can involve large dollar amounts and, thus, can have a significant impact on the financial statements. For example, Best Buy reported $5,731 million of inventory and net loss of $1,231 million for a recent year.

This chapter discusses such issues as how to determine the cost of merchandise in inventory and the cost of merchandise sold. However, it begins by discussing the importance of control over inventory.

Learning Objectives

After studying this chapter, you should be able to:

Example Exercises (EE) are shown in **green**.

Obj. 1 Describe the importance of control over inventory.
- Control of Inventory
- Safeguarding Inventory
- Reporting Inventory

Obj. 2 Describe three inventory cost flow assumptions and explain how they impact the income statement and balance sheet.
- Inventory Cost Flow Assumptions
- Cost Flow Methods — EE 7-1

Obj. 3 Determine the cost of inventory under the perpetual inventory system, using the FIFO, LIFO, and weighted average cost methods.
- Inventory Costing Methods Under a Perpetual Inventory System
- First-In, First-Out Method — EE 7-2
- Last-In, First-Out Method — EE 7-3
- Weighted Average Cost Method — EE 7-4

Obj. 4 Determine the cost of inventory under the periodic inventory system, using the FIFO, LIFO, and weighted average cost methods.
- Inventory Costing Methods Under a Periodic Inventory System
- First-In, First-Out Method — EE 7-5
- Last-In, First-Out Method — EE 7-5
- Weighted Average Cost Method — EE 7-5

Obj. 5 Compare and contrast the use of the three inventory costing methods.
- Comparing Inventory Costing Methods

Obj. 6 Describe and illustrate the reporting of merchandise inventory in the financial statements.
- Reporting Merchandise Inventory in the Financial Statements
- Valuation at Lower of Cost or Market — EE 7-6
- Merchandise Inventory on the Balance Sheet
- Effect of Inventory Errors on the Financial Statements — EE 7-7

Obj. 7 Describe and illustrate the inventory turnover and the days' sales in inventory in analyzing the efficiency and effectiveness of inventory management.
- Financial Analysis and Interpretation: Inventory Turnover and Days' Sales in Inventory
- Compute Inventory Turnover and Day's Sales in Inventory — EE 7-8

At a Glance 7 — Page 370

Obj. 1 Describe the importance of control over inventory.

Control of Inventory

Two primary objectives of control over inventory are as follows:[1]

- Safeguarding the inventory from damage or theft.
- Reporting inventory in the financial statements.

Safeguarding Inventory

Controls for safeguarding inventory begin as soon as the inventory is ordered. The following documents are often used for inventory control:

- Purchase order
- Receiving report
- Vendor's invoice

The **purchase order** authorizes the purchase of the inventory from an approved vendor. As soon as the inventory is received, a receiving report is completed. The **receiving report** establishes an initial record of the receipt of the inventory. To make

---

[1] Additional controls used by businesses are described and illustrated in Chapter 8, "Internal Control and Cash."

sure the inventory received is what was ordered, the receiving report is compared with the purchase order. The price, quantity, and description of the item on the purchase order and receiving report are then compared to the vendor's invoice. If the receiving report, purchase order, and vendor's invoice agree, the inventory is recorded in the accounting records. If any differences exist, they should be investigated and reconciled.

Recording inventory using a perpetual inventory system is also an effective means of control. The amount of inventory is always available in the **subsidiary inventory ledger**. This helps keep inventory quantities at proper levels. For example, comparing inventory quantities with maximum and minimum levels allows for the timely reordering of inventory and prevents ordering excess inventory.

Finally, controls for safeguarding inventory should include security measures to prevent damage and customer or employee theft. Some examples of security measures include the following:

- Storing inventory in areas that are restricted to only authorized employees
- Locking high-priced inventory in cabinets
- Using two-way mirrors, cameras, security tags, and guards

Reporting Inventory

A **physical inventory** or *count of inventory* should be taken near year-end to make sure that the quantity of inventory reported in the financial statements is accurate. After the quantity of inventory on hand is determined, the cost of the inventory is assigned for reporting in the financial statements. Most companies assign costs to inventory using one of three inventory cost flow assumptions. If a physical count is not possible or inventory records are not available, the inventory cost may be estimated as described in the appendix at the end of this chapter.

> **Link to Best Buy**
> **Best Buy** uses scanners to screen customers as they leave the store for merchandise that has not been purchased. In addition, Best Buy stations greeters at the store's entrance to keep customers from bringing in bags that can be used to shoplift merchandise.

> **Link to Best Buy**
> **Best Buy** conducts ongoing physical counts of inventory throughout the year as a basis for monitoring and predicting loss adjustments for theft.

Inventory Cost Flow Assumptions

Obj. 2 Describe three inventory cost flow assumptions and explain how they impact the income statement and balance sheet.

An accounting issue arises when identical units of merchandise are acquired at different unit costs during a period. In such cases, when an item is sold, it is necessary to determine its cost using a cost flow assumption and related inventory costing method.

To illustrate, assume that three identical units of merchandise are purchased during May, as follows:

			Units	Cost
May	10	Purchase	1	$ 9
	18	Purchase	1	13
	24	Purchase	1	14
		Total	3	$36

Average cost per unit: $12 ($36 ÷ 3 units)

Assume that one unit is sold on May 30 for $20. Depending upon which unit was sold, the gross profit varies from $11 to $6, computed as follows:

	May 10 Unit Sold	May 18 Unit Sold	May 24 Unit Sold
Sales	$20	$20	$20
Cost of merchandise sold	9	13	14
Gross profit	$11	$ 7	$ 6
Ending inventory	$27	$23	$22
	($13 + $14)	($9 + $14)	($9 + $13)

Under the **specific identification inventory cost flow method**, the unit sold is identified with a specific purchase. The ending inventory is made up of the remaining units

348 **Chapter 7** Inventories

on hand. Thus, the gross profit, cost of merchandise sold, and ending inventory can vary as illustrated. For example, if the May 18 unit was sold, the cost of merchandise sold is $13, the gross profit is $7, and the ending inventory is $23.

The specific identification method is not practical unless each inventory unit can be identified separately. For example, an automobile dealer may use the specific identification method because each automobile has a unique serial number. However, most businesses cannot identify each inventory unit separately. In such cases, one of the following three inventory cost flow methods is used.

Three common cost flow assumptions and related inventory costing methods are shown in Exhibit 1.

EXHIBIT 1 **Cost Flow Assumptions**

Cost Flow Assumption

1. Cost flow is in the order in which the costs were incurred.
2. Cost flow is in the reverse order in which the costs were incurred.
3. Cost flow is an average of the costs.

Inventory Costing Method

First-in, First-out (FIFO)

Last-in, First-out (LIFO)

Weighted Average Cost

Link to Best Buy
Best Buy uses the first-in, first-out method for some of its inventory.

Under the **first-in, first-out (FIFO) inventory cost flow method**, the first units purchased are assumed to be sold and the ending inventory is made up of the most recent purchases. In the preceding example, the May 10 unit would be assumed to have been sold. Thus, the gross profit would be $11 ($20 − $9), and the ending inventory would be $27 ($13 + $14).

Under the **last-in, first-out (LIFO) inventory cost flow method**, the last units purchased are assumed to be sold and the ending inventory is made up of the first purchases. In the preceding example, the May 24 unit would be assumed to have been sold. Thus, the gross profit would be $6 ($20 − $14), and the ending inventory would be $22 ($9 + $13).

Link to Best Buy
Best Buy also uses the weighted average cost method for some of its inventory.

Under the **weighted average inventory cost flow method**, sometimes called the *average cost flow method*, the cost of the units sold and in ending inventory is a weighted average of the purchase costs. The purchase costs are weighted by the quantities purchased at each cost, thus the term *weighted average*. In the preceding example, the cost of the unit sold would be $12 ($36 ÷ 3 units), the gross profit would be $8 ($20 − $12), and the ending inventory would be $24 ($12 × 2 units). In this example, the purchase costs are weighted equally, since the same quantity (one) was purchased at each cost.

The three inventory cost flow methods, FIFO, LIFO, and weighted average, are shown in Exhibit 2. The FIFO method is used most frequently, followed by LIFO and weighted average methods.

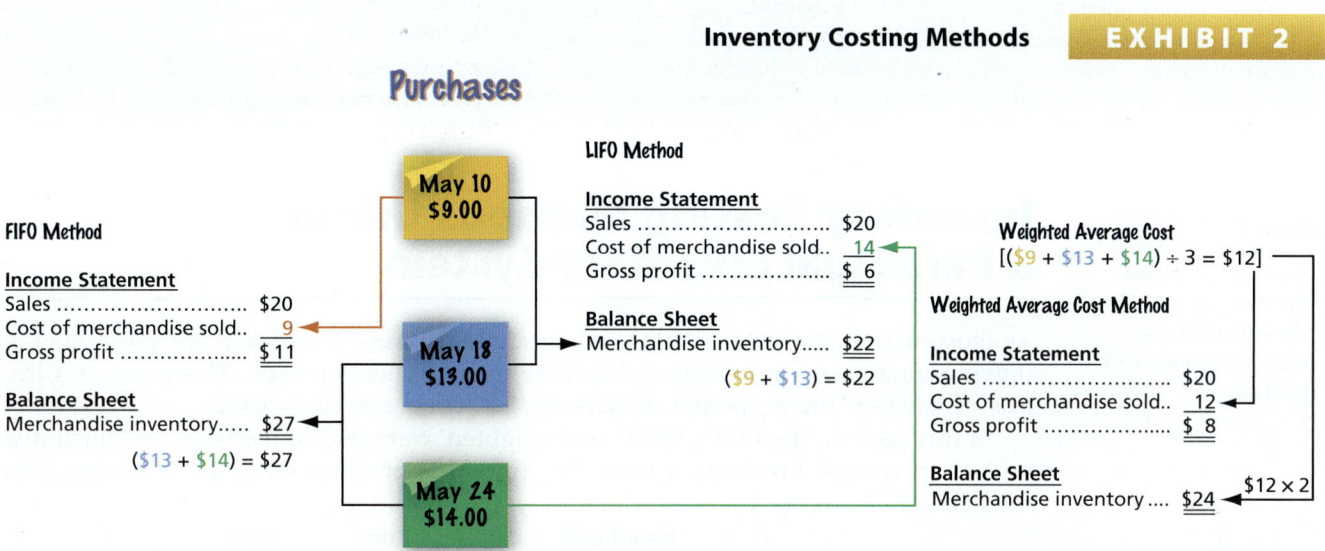

Inventory Costing Methods — EXHIBIT 2

Business Connection

PAWN STARS AND SPECIFIC IDENTIFICATION

Pawn Stars is the History Channel's TV series featuring Rick Harrison's **Gold & Silver Pawn Shop** of Las Vegas, Nevada. As Rick says in the opening of every show, "you never know what is gonna come through that door." The show features the purchase of everything from antique pistols, original movie props, vintage cars and motorcycles, famous autographed memorabilia, and many other types of unusual collectibles. Each item needs to be appraised and a price negotiated with the seller. Once purchased, the pawn shop has an item of inventory to be presented to the public for sale. Gold & Silver Pawn uses the specific identification method for valuing inventory.

Example Exercise 7-1 Cost Flow Methods   Obj. 2

The following three identical units of Item QBM are purchased during February:

	Item QBM	Units	Cost
Feb. 8	Purchase	1	$ 45
15	Purchase	1	48
26	Purchase	1	51
	Total	3	$144
	Average cost per unit		$ 48 ($144 ÷ 3 units)

Assume that one unit is sold on February 27 for $70.
   Determine the gross profit for February and ending inventory on February 28 using the (a) first-in, first-out (FIFO); (b) last-in, first-out (LIFO); and (c) weighted average cost methods.

(Continued)

Follow My Example 7-1

	Gross Profit	Ending Inventory
a. First-in, first-out (FIFO)..............	$25 ($70 − $45)	$99 ($48 + $51)
b. Last-in, first-out (LIFO)..............	$19 ($70 − $51)	$93 ($45 + $48)
c. Weighted average cost..............	$22 ($70 − $48)	$96 ($48 × 2)

Practice Exercises: PE 7-1A, PE 7-1B

Obj. 3 Determine the cost of inventory under the perpetual inventory system, using the FIFO, LIFO, and weighted average cost methods.

Inventory Costing Methods Under a Perpetual Inventory System

As illustrated in the prior section, when identical units of an item are purchased at different unit costs, an inventory cost flow method must be used. This is true regardless of whether the perpetual or periodic inventory system is used.

In this section, the FIFO, LIFO, and weighted average cost methods are illustrated under a perpetual inventory system. For purposes of illustration, the following data for Item 127B are used:

		Item 127B	Units	Cost
Jan.	1	Inventory	1,000	$20.00
	4	Sale at $30 per unit	700	
	10	Purchase	500	22.40
	22	Sale at $30 per unit	360	
	28	Sale at $30 per unit	240	
	30	Purchase	600	23.30

First-In, First-Out Method

When the FIFO method is used, costs are included in the cost of merchandise sold in the order in which they were purchased. This is often the same as the physical flow of the merchandise. Thus, the FIFO method often provides results that are about the same as those that would have been obtained using the specific identification method. For example, grocery stores shelve milk and other perishable products by expiration dates. Products with early expiration dates are stocked in front. In this way, the oldest products (earliest purchases) are sold first.

To illustrate, Exhibit 3 shows the use of FIFO under a perpetual inventory system for Item 127B. The journal entries and the subsidiary inventory ledger for Item 127B are shown in Exhibit 3 as follows:

1. The beginning balance on January 1 is $20,000 (1,000 units at a unit cost of $20).

2. On January 4, 700 units were sold at a price of $30 each for sales of $21,000 (700 units at a selling price of $30 per unit). The cost of merchandise sold is $14,000 (700 units at a unit cost of $20). After the sale, there remains $6,000 of inventory (300 units at a unit cost of $20).

3. On January 10, $11,200 is purchased (500 units at a unit cost of $22.40). After the purchase, the inventory is reported on two lines, $6,000 (300 units at a unit cost of $20.00) from the beginning inventory and $11,200 (500 units at a unit cost of $22.40) from the January 10 purchase.

4. On January 22, 360 units are sold at a price of $30 each for sales of $10,800 (360 units at a selling price of $30 per unit). Using FIFO, the cost of merchandise sold of $7,344 consists of $6,000 (300 units at a unit cost of $20.00) from the beginning inventory plus $1,344 (60 units at a unit cost of $22.40) from the January 10 purchase. After the sale, there remains $9,856 of inventory (440 units at a unit cost of $22.40) from the January 10 purchase.

5. The January 28 sale and January 30 purchase are recorded in a similar manner.

EXHIBIT 3 Entries and Perpetual Inventory Account (FIFO)

Jan. 4	Accounts Receivable	21,000	
	Sales		21,000
4	Cost of Merchandise Sold	14,000	
	Merchandise Inventory		14,000
10	Merchandise Inventory	11,200	
	Accounts Payable		11,200
22	Accounts Receivable	10,800	
	Sales		10,800
22	Cost of Merchandise Sold	7,344	
	Merchandise Inventory		7,344
28	Accounts Receivable	7,200	
	Sales		7,200
28	Cost of Merchandise Sold	5,376	
	Merchandise Inventory		5,376
30	Merchandise Inventory	13,980	
	Accounts Payable		13,980

Item 127B

	Purchases			Cost of Merchandise Sold			Inventory		
Date	Quantity	Unit Cost	Total Cost	Quantity	Unit Cost	Total Cost	Quantity	Unit Cost	Total Cost
Jan. 1							1,000	20.00	20,000
4				700	20.00	14,000	300	20.00	6,000
10	500	22.40	11,200				300	20.00	6,000
							500	22.40	11,200
22				300	20.00	6,000			
				60	22.40	1,344	440	22.40	9,856
28				240	22.40	5,376	200	22.40	4,480
30	600	23.30	13,980				200	22.40	4,480
							600	23.30	13,980
31	Balances					**26,720**			**18,460**

Cost of merchandise sold ← 26,720

January 31 inventory ← 18,460

6. The ending balance on January 31 is $18,460. This balance is made up of two layers of inventory as follows:

	Date of Purchase	Quantity	Unit Cost	Total Cost
Layer 1	Jan. 10	200	$22.40	$ 4,480
Layer 2	Jan. 30	600	23.30	13,980
Total		800		$18,460

Example Exercise 7-2 Perpetual Inventory Using FIFO   Obj. 3

Beginning inventory, purchases, and sales for Item ER27 are as follows:

Dynamic Exhibit

Nov.	1	Inventory	40 units at $5
	5	Sale	30 units
	11	Purchase	70 units at $7
	21	Sale	36 units

Assuming a perpetual inventory system and using the first-in, first-out (FIFO) method, determine (a) the cost of merchandise sold on November 21 and (b) the inventory on November 30.

Follow My Example 7-2

a. Cost of merchandise sold (November 21):
   10 units at $5 $ 50
   26 units at $7   182
   36 units $232

b. Inventory, November 30:
   $308 (44 units × $7)

Practice Exercises: PE 7-2A, PE 7-2B

Last-In, First-Out Method

When the LIFO method is used, the cost of the units sold is the cost of the most recent purchases. The LIFO method was originally used in those rare cases where the units sold were taken from the most recently purchased units. However, for tax

IFRS
See Appendix B for more information.

purposes, LIFO is now widely used even when it does not represent the physical flow of units. The tax impact of LIFO is discussed later in this chapter.

To illustrate, Exhibit 4 shows the use of LIFO under a perpetual inventory system for Item 127B. The journal entries and the subsidiary inventory ledger for Item 127B are shown in Exhibit 4 as follows:

1. The beginning balance on January 1 is $20,000 (1,000 units at a unit of cost of $20.00).
2. On January 4, 700 units were sold at a price of $30 each for sales of $21,000 (700 units at a selling price of $30 per unit). The cost of merchandise sold is $14,000 (700 units at a unit cost of $20). After the sale, there remains $6,000 of inventory (300 units at a unit cost of $20).
3. On January 10, $11,200 is purchased (500 units at a unit cost of $22.40). After the purchase, the inventory is reported on two lines, $6,000 (300 units at a unit cost of $20.00) from the beginning inventory and $11,200 (500 units at $22.40 per unit) from the January 10 purchase.
4. On January 22, 360 units are sold at a price of $30 each for sales of $10,800 (360 units at a selling price of $30 per unit). Using LIFO, the cost of merchandise sold is $8,064 (360 units at unit cost of $22.40) from the January 10 purchase. After the sale, there remains $9,136 of inventory consisting of $6,000 (300 units at a unit cost of $20.00) from the beginning inventory and $3,136 (140 units at a unit cost of $22.40) from the January 10 purchase.
5. The January 28 sale and January 30 purchase are recorded in a similar manner.
6. The ending balance on January 31 is $17,980. This balance is made up of two layers of inventory as follows:

	Date of Purchase	Quantity	Unit Cost	Total Cost
Layer 1	Beg. inv. (Jan. 1)	200	$20.00	$ 4,000
Layer 2	Jan. 30	600	23.30	13,980
	Total	800		$17,980

When the LIFO method is used, the subsidiary inventory ledger is sometimes maintained in units only. The units are converted to dollars when the financial statements are prepared at the end of the period.

EXHIBIT 4 — Entries and Perpetual Inventory Account (LIFO)

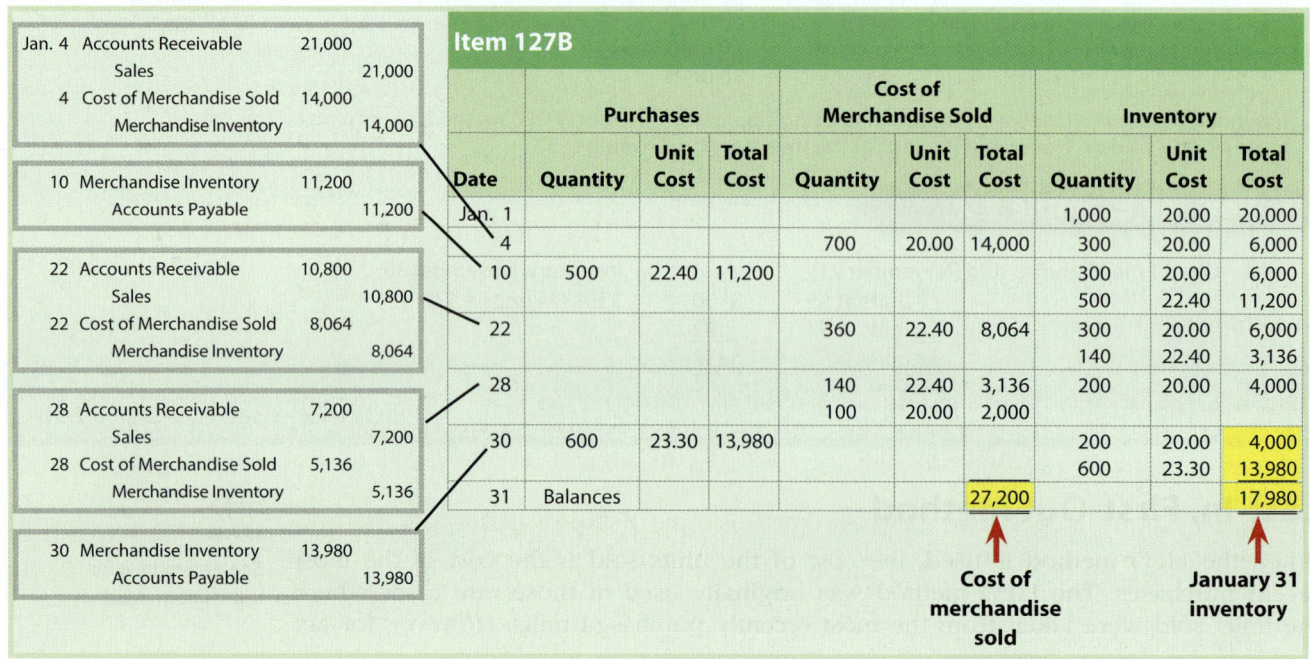

Example Exercise 7-3 Perpetual Inventory Using LIFO   Obj. 3

Beginning inventory, purchases, and sales for Item ER27 are as follows:

Nov.	1	Inventory	40 units at $5
	5	Sale	30 units
	11	Purchase	70 units at $7
	21	Sale	36 units

Assuming a perpetual inventory system and using the last-in, first-out (LIFO) method, determine (a) the cost of the merchandise sold on November 21 and (b) the inventory on November 30.

Follow My Example 7-3

a. Cost of merchandise sold (November 21): $252 (36 units × $7)

b. Inventory, November 30:
  10 units at $5 $ 50
  34 units at $7   238
  44 units $288

Practice Exercises: PE 7-3A, PE 7-3B

International Connection

IFRS   INTERNATIONAL FINANCIAL REPORTING STANDARDS (IFRS)

IFRS permit the first-in, first-out (FIFO) and weighted average cost methods but prohibit the last-in, first-out (LIFO) method for determining inventory costs. Since LIFO is used in the United States, adoption of IFRS could have a significant impact on many U.S. companies. For example, **Caterpillar Inc.** uses LIFO. For a recent year, Caterpillar reported that its inventories would have been $2,750 million higher if FIFO had been used. Since Caterpillar reported profits of $5,681 million for the year, the adoption of IFRS would have significantly affected net income if IFRS and FIFO had been used.*

*Differences between U.S. GAAP and IFRS are further discussed and illustrated in Appendix B.

Weighted Average Cost Method

When the weighted average cost method is used in a perpetual inventory system, a weighted average unit cost for each item is computed each time a purchase is made. This unit cost is used to determine the cost of each sale until another purchase is made and a new average is computed. This technique is called a *moving average*.

To illustrate, Exhibit 5 shows the use of weighted average under a perpetual inventory system for Item 127B.

The journal entries and the subsidiary inventory ledger for Item 127B are shown in Exhibit 5 as follows:

1. The beginning balance on January 1 is $20,000 (1,000 units at a unit cost of $20).
2. On January 4, 700 units were sold at a price of $30 each for sales of $21,000 (700 units at a selling price of $30 per unit). The cost of merchandise sold is $14,000 (700 units at a unit cost of $20.00). After the sale, there remains $6,000 of inventory (300 units at a unit cost of $20.00).
3. On January 10, $11,200 is purchased (500 units at a unit cost of $22.40). After the purchase, the weighted average unit cost of $21.50 is determined by dividing the total cost of the inventory on hand of $17,200 ($6,000 + $11,200) by the total quantity of inventory on hand of 800 (300 + 500) units. Thus, after the purchase, the inventory consists of 800 units at $21.50 per unit for a total cost of $17,200.

EXHIBIT 5 — Entries and Perpetual Inventory Account (Weighted Average)

Date		Jan. 4	Accounts Receivable	21,000	
			Sales		21,000
		4	Cost of Merchandise Sold	14,000	
			Merchandise Inventory		14,000
		10	Merchandise Inventory	11,200	
			Accounts Payable		11,200
		22	Accounts Receivable	10,800	
			Sales		10,800
		22	Cost of Merchandise Sold	7,740	
			Merchandise Inventory		7,740
		28	Accounts Receivable	7,200	
			Sales		7,200
		28	Cost of Merchandise Sold	5,160	
			Merchandise Inventory		5,160
		30	Merchandise Inventory	13,980	
			Accounts Payable		13,980

Item 127B

	Purchases			Cost of Merchandise Sold			Inventory		
Date	Quantity	Unit Cost	Total Cost	Quantity	Unit Cost	Total Cost	Quantity	Unit Cost	Total Cost
Jan. 1							1,000	20.00	20,000
4				700	20.00	14,000	300	20.00	6,000
10	500	22.40	11,200				800	21.50	17,200
22				360	21.50	7,740	440	21.50	9,460
28				240	21.50	5,160	200	21.50	4,300
30	600	23.30	13,980				800	22.85	18,280
31	Balances					26,900	800	22.85	18,280

26,900 → Cost of merchandise sold
18,280 → January 31 inventory

4. On January 22, 360 units are sold at a price of $30 each for sales of $10,800 (360 units at a selling price of $30 per unit). Using weighted average, the cost of merchandise sold is $7,740 (360 units × $21.50 per unit). After the sale, there remains $9,460 of inventory (440 units × $21.50 per unit).
5. The January 28 sale and January 30 purchase are recorded in a similar manner.
6. The ending balance on January 31 is $18,280 (800 units × $22.85 per unit).

Example Exercise 7-4 Perpetual Inventory Using Weighted Average *Obj. 3*

Beginning inventory, purchases, and sales for ER27 are as follows:

Nov. 1	Inventory	40 units at $5
5	Sale	30 units
11	Purchase	70 units at $7
21	Sale	36 units

Assuming a perpetual inventory system using the weighted average method, determine (a) the weighted average unit cost after the November 11 purchase, (b) the cost of the merchandise sold on November 21, and (c) the inventory on November 30.

Follow My Example 7-4

a. Weighted average unit cost: $6.75
   Inventory total cost after purchase on November 21:

	Cost
10 units at $5	$ 50
70 units at $7	490
80 units	$540

Weighted average unit cost = $6.75 ($540 ÷ 80 units)

b. Cost of merchandise sold (November 21):
   $243 (36 units × $6.75)

c. Inventory, November 30:
   $297 (44 units at $6.75)

Practice Exercises: PE 7-4A, PE 7-4B

Business Connection

COMPUTERIZED PERPETUAL INVENTORY SYSTEMS

Your purchases are scanned when you go through the checkout line at **Best Buy**. The scanned data are used to identify the price and adjust the inventory levels. Computerized perpetual inventory systems are used like this when there are many inventory transactions and a manual system is simply not feasible.

Computerized perpetual inventory systems are useful to managers in controlling and managing inventory. For example, if Best Buy has fast-selling items, they can be reordered before the stock runs out. Sales patterns can also be analyzed to determine when to mark down merchandise or when to restock seasonal merchandise. Finally, computerized inventory data can be used to evaluate the effectiveness of advertising campaigns and promotions.

Inventory Costing Methods Under a Periodic Inventory System

Obj. 4 Determine the cost of inventory under the periodic inventory system, using the FIFO, LIFO, and weighted average cost methods.

When the periodic inventory system is used, only revenue is recorded each time a sale is made. No entry is made at the time of the sale to record the cost of the merchandise sold. At the end of the accounting period, a physical inventory is taken to determine the cost of the inventory and the cost of the merchandise sold.[2]

Like the perpetual inventory system, a cost flow assumption must be made when identical units are acquired at different unit costs during a period. In such cases, the FIFO, LIFO, or weighted average cost method is used.

First-In, First-Out Method

To illustrate the use of the FIFO method in a periodic inventory system, we use the same data for Item 127B as in the perpetual inventory example. The beginning inventory and purchases of Item 127B in January are as follows:

Jan. 1	Inventory	1,000 units at	$20.00	$20,000
10	Purchase	500 units at	22.40	11,200
30	Purchase	600 units at	23.30	13,980
Available for sale during month		2,100		$45,180

The physical count on January 31 shows that 800 units are on hand. Using the FIFO method, the cost of the merchandise on hand at the end of the period is made up of the most recent costs. The cost of the 800 units in the ending inventory on January 31 is determined as follows:

Most recent costs, January 30 purchase	600 units at	$23.30	$13,980
Next most recent costs, January 10 purchase	200 units at	$22.40	4,480
Inventory, January 31	800 units		$18,460

Deducting the cost of the January 31 inventory of $18,460 from the cost of merchandise available for sale of $45,180 yields the cost of merchandise sold of $26,720, computed as follows:

Beginning inventory, January 1	$20,000
Purchases ($11,200 + $13,980)	25,180
Cost of merchandise available for sale in January	$45,180
Less ending inventory, January 31	18,460
Cost of merchandise sold	$26,720

---

[2] Determining the cost of merchandise sold using the periodic system was illustrated in the appendix to Chapter 6.

The $18,460 cost of the ending merchandise inventory on January 31 is made up of the most recent costs. The $26,720 cost of merchandise sold is made up of the beginning inventory and the earliest costs. Exhibit 6 shows the relationship of the cost of merchandise sold for January and the ending inventory on January 31.

EXHIBIT 6

First-In, First-Out Flow of Costs

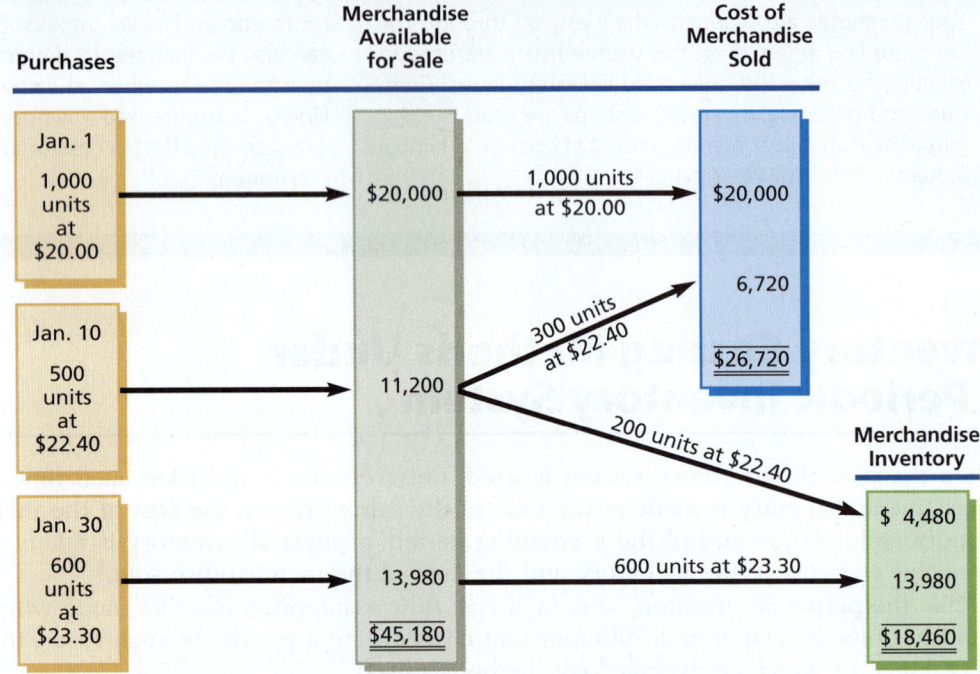

Last-In, First-Out Method

See Appendix B for more information.

When the LIFO method is used, the cost of merchandise on hand at the end of the period is made up of the earliest costs. Based on the same data as in the FIFO example, the cost of the 800 units in ending inventory on January 31 is $16,000, which consists of 800 units from the beginning inventory at a cost of $20.00 per unit.

Deducting the cost of the January 31 inventory of $16,000 from the cost of merchandise available for sale of $45,180 yields the cost of merchandise sold of $29,180, computed as follows:

Beginning inventory, January 1	$20,000
Purchases ($11,200 + $13,980)	25,180
Cost of merchandise available for sale in January	$45,180
Less ending inventory, January 31	16,000
Cost of merchandise sold	$29,180

The $16,000 cost of the ending merchandise inventory on January 31 is made up of the earliest costs. The $29,180 cost of merchandise sold is made up of the most recent costs. Exhibit 7 shows the relationship of the cost of merchandise sold for January and the ending inventory on January 31.

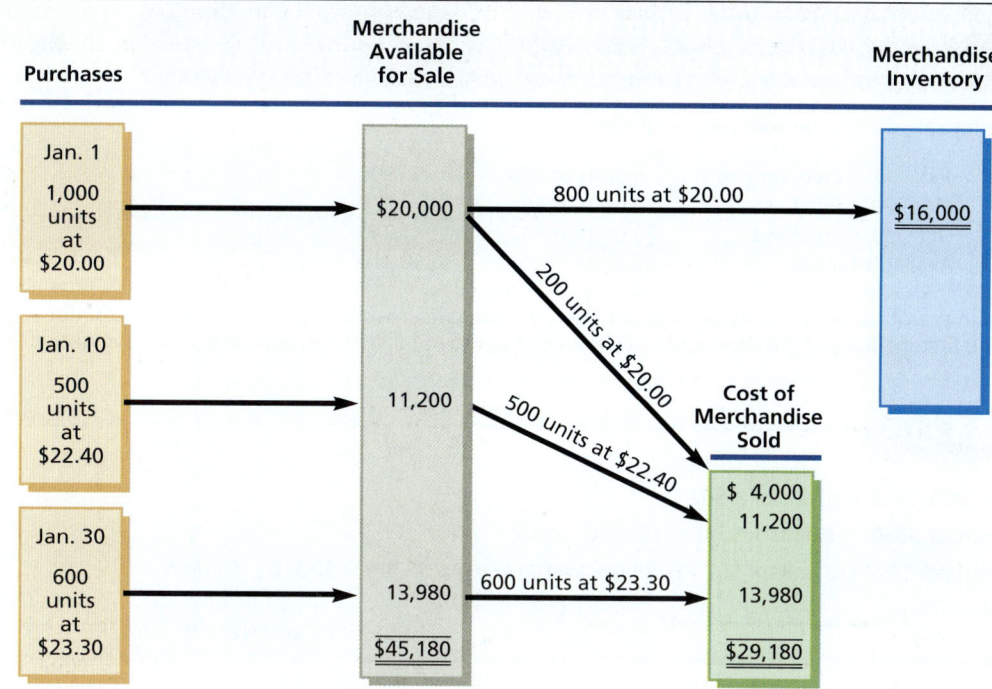

EXHIBIT 7

Last-In, First-Out Flow of Costs

Weighted Average Cost Method

The weighted average cost method uses the weighted average unit cost for determining the cost of merchandise sold and the ending merchandise inventory. If purchases are relatively uniform during a period, the weighted average cost method provides results that are similar to the physical flow of goods.

The weighted average unit cost is determined as follows:

$$\text{Weighted Average Unit Cost} = \frac{\text{Total Cost of Units Available for Sale}}{\text{Units Available for Sale}}$$

To illustrate, the data for Item 127B are used as follows:

$$\text{Weighted Average Unit Cost} = \frac{\text{Total Cost of Units Available for Sale}}{\text{Units Available for Sale}} = \frac{\$45{,}180}{2{,}100 \text{ units}}$$

$$= \$21.51 \text{ per unit (Rounded)}$$

The cost of the January 31 ending inventory is as follows:

Inventory, January 31: $17,208 (800 units × $21.51)

Deducting the cost of the January 31 inventory of $17,208 from the cost of merchandise available for sale of $45,180 yields the cost of merchandise sold of $27,972, computed as follows:

Beginning inventory, January 1	$20,000
Purchases ($11,200 + $13,980)	25,180
Cost of merchandise available for sale in January	$45,180
Less ending inventory, January 31	17,208
Cost of merchandise sold	$27,972

358 Chapter 7 Inventories

Example Exercise 7-5 Periodic Inventory Using FIFO, LIFO, and Weighted Average Cost Methods Obj. 4

The units of an item available for sale during the year were as follows:

Jan. 1	Inventory	6 units at $50	$ 300
Mar. 20	Purchase	14 units at $55	770
Oct. 30	Purchase	20 units at $62	1,240
	Available for sale	40 units	$2,310

There are 16 units of the item in the physical inventory at December 31. The periodic inventory system is used. Determine the inventory cost using (a) the first-in, first-out (FIFO) method; (b) the last-in, first-out (LIFO) method; and (c) the weighted average cost method.

Follow My Example 7-5

a. First-in, first-out (FIFO) method: $992 = (16 units × $62)
b. Last-in, first-out (LIFO) method: $850 = (6 units × $50) + (10 units × $55)
c. Weighted average cost method: $924 (16 units × $57.75), where average cost = $57.75 = $2,310 ÷ 40 units

Practice Exercises: PE 7-5A, PE 7-5B

Comparing Inventory Costing Methods

Obj. 5 Compare and contrast the use of the three inventory costing methods.

A different cost flow is assumed for the FIFO, LIFO, and weighted average inventory cost flow methods. As a result, the three methods normally yield different amounts for the following:

- Cost of merchandise sold
- Gross profit
- Net income
- Ending merchandise inventory

See Appendix B for more information.

Using the perpetual inventory system illustration with sales of $39,000 (1,300 units × $30), the following differences are apparent:[3]

Partial Income Statements

	First-In, First-Out	Weighted Average Cost	Last-In, First-Out
Sales	$39,000	$39,000	$39,000
Cost of merchandise sold	26,720	26,900	27,200
Gross profit	$12,280	$12,100	$11,800
Merchandise Inventory, Jan. 31	$18,460	$18,280	$17,980

The preceding differences show the effect of increasing costs (prices). If costs (prices) remain the same, all three methods would yield the same results. However, costs (prices) normally do change. The effects of changing costs (prices) on the FIFO and LIFO methods are summarized in Exhibit 8. The weighted average cost method will always yield results between those of FIFO and LIFO.

FIFO reports higher gross profit and net income than the LIFO method when costs (prices) are increasing, as shown in Exhibit 8. However, in periods of rapidly rising costs, the inventory that is sold must be replaced at increasingly higher costs. In such cases, the larger FIFO gross profit and net income are sometimes called *inventory profits* or *illusory profits*.

---

[3] Similar results would also occur when comparing inventory costing methods under a periodic inventory system.

EXHIBIT 8

Effects of Changing Costs (Prices): FIFO and LIFO Cost Methods

	↑ Increasing Costs (Prices)		↓ Decreasing Costs (Prices)	
	Highest Amount	Lowest Amount	Highest Amount	Lowest Amount
Cost of merchandise sold	LIFO	FIFO	FIFO	LIFO
Gross profit	FIFO	LIFO	LIFO	FIFO
Net income	FIFO	LIFO	LIFO	FIFO
Ending merchandise inventory	FIFO	LIFO	LIFO	FIFO

During a period of increasing costs, LIFO matches more recent costs against sales on the income statement. Thus, it can be argued that the LIFO method more nearly matches current costs with current revenues. LIFO also offers an income tax savings during periods of increasing costs. This is because LIFO reports the lowest amount of gross profit and, thus, taxable net income. However, under LIFO, the ending inventory on the balance sheet may be quite different from its current replacement cost. In such cases, the financial statements normally include a note that estimates what the inventory would have been if FIFO had been used.

The weighted average cost method is, in a sense, a compromise between FIFO and LIFO. The effect of cost (price) trends is averaged in determining the cost of merchandise sold and the ending inventory.

INTEGRITY, OBJECTIVITY, AND ETHICS IN BUSINESS

WHERE'S THE BONUS?

Managers are often given bonuses based on reported earnings numbers. This can create a conflict. LIFO can improve the value of the company through lower taxes. However, in periods of rising costs (prices), LIFO also produces a lower earnings number and, therefore, lower management bonuses. Ethically, managers should select accounting procedures that will maximize the value of the firm rather than their own compensation. Compensation specialists can help avoid this ethical dilemma by adjusting the bonus plan for the accounting procedure differences.

Reporting Merchandise Inventory in the Financial Statements

Obj. 6 Describe and illustrate the reporting of merchandise inventory in the financial statements.

Cost is the primary basis for valuing and reporting inventories in the financial statements. However, inventory may be valued at other than cost in the following cases:

1. The cost of replacing items in inventory is below the recorded cost.
2. The inventory cannot be sold at normal prices due to imperfections, style changes, spoilage, damage, obsolescence, or other causes.

Valuation at Lower of Cost or Market

If the market is lower than the purchase cost, the **lower-of-cost-or-market (LCM) method** is used to value the inventory. *Market*, as used in *lower of cost or market*, is

See Appendix B for more information.

the **net realizable value** of the merchandise.[4] Net realizable value is determined as follows:

Net Realizable Value = Estimated Selling Price − Direct Costs of Disposal

Direct costs of disposal include selling expenses such as special advertising or sales commissions.

To illustrate, assume the following data about an item of damaged merchandise:

Original cost	$1,000
Estimated selling price	800
Estimated selling expenses	150

In applying LCM, the market value of the merchandise is $650, computed as follows:

Market Value (Net Realizable Value) = $800 − $150 = $650

Thus, the merchandise would be valued at $650, which is the lower of its cost of $1,000 and its market value of $650.

The lower-of-cost-or-market method can be applied in one of three ways. The cost, market price, and any declines could be determined for:

- Each item in the inventory
- Each major class or category of inventory
- Inventory as a whole

The amount of any price decline is included in the cost of merchandise sold. This, in turn, reduces gross profit and net income in the period in which the price declines occur. This matching of price declines to the period in which they occur is the primary advantage of using the lower-of-cost-or-market method.

To illustrate, assume the following data for 400 identical units of Item Echo in inventory on December 31:

Cost per unit	$10.25
Market value (net realizable value) per unit	9.50

Since the market value of Item Echo is $9.50 per unit, $9.50 is used under the lower-of-cost-or-market method.

Exhibit 9 illustrates applying the lower-of-cost-or-market method to each inventory item (Echo, Foxtrot, Sierra, Tango). As applied on an item-by-item basis, the total lower-of-cost-or-market is $15,070, which is a market decline of $450 ($15,520 − $15,070). This market decline of $450 is included in the cost of merchandise sold.

In Exhibit 9, Items Echo, Foxtrot, Sierra, and Tango could be viewed as a class of inventory items. If the lower-of-cost-or-market method is applied to the class, the inventory would be valued at $15,472, which is a market decline of $48 ($15,520 − $15,472). Likewise, if Items Echo, Foxtrot, Sierra, and Tango make up the total inventory, the lower-of-cost-or-market method as applied to the total inventory would be the same amount, $15,472.

> **Link to Best Buy**
> Best Buy values its inventory at lower of cost or market based upon cost and the amount it expects to realize from the sale.

> **Link to Best Buy**
> The excess of cost over the amount Best Buy expects to receive from the sale of an item is called a *markdown*.

EXHIBIT 9
Determining Inventory at Lower of Cost or Market (LCM)

	A	B	C	D	E	F	G
1				Market Value			
2		Inventory	Cost per	per Unit		Total	
3	Item	Quantity	Unit	(Net Realizable Value)	Cost	Market	LCM
4	Echo	400	$10.25	$ 9.50	$ 4,100	$ 3,800	$ 3,800
5	Foxtrot	120	22.50	24.10	2,700	2,892	2,700
6	Sierra	600	8.00	7.75	4,800	4,650	4,650
7	Tango	280	14.00	14.75	3,920	4,130	3,920
8	Total				$15,520	$15,472	$15,070
9							

---

4 Accounting Standards Update, *Inventory* (Topic 330): *Simplifying the Measurement of Inventory*, No. 2015-11, July 2015, FASB (Norwalk, CT).

Example Exercise 7-6 Lower-of-Cost-or-Market Method   Obj. 6

On the basis of the following data, determine the value of the inventory at the lower of cost or market. Apply lower of cost or market to each inventory item as shown in Exhibit 9.

Item	Inventory Quantity	Cost per Unit	Market Value per Unit (Net Realizable Value)
C17Y	10	$ 39	$40
B563	7	110	98

Follow My Example 7-6

	A	B	C	D	E	F	G
1				Market Value			
2		Inventory	Cost per	per Unit		Total	
3	Item	Quantity	Unit	(Net Realizable Value)	Cost	Market	LCM
4	C17Y	10	$ 39	$40	$ 390	$ 400	$ 390
5	B563	7	110	98	770	686	686
6	Total				$1,160	$1,086	$1,076
7							

Practice Exercises: PE 7-6A, PE 7-6B

Business Connection

GOOD SAMARITAN

A corporation may decide that the best way to dispose of unwanted inventory is to give it to charity. Under the Internal Revenue Code, a corporation may take an "enhanced" deduction for charitable contributions of select inventory, such as food, clothing, and medical supplies, used for the ill, the needy, or infants. Thus, for example, disaster relief contributions would be subject to the enhanced deduction. The enhanced deduction is for amounts up to half the planned profit on the item but not greater than twice what the company paid for it. Websites such as www.wastetocharity.org can help corporations donate unwanted items to recyclers and organizations.

Merchandise Inventory on the Balance Sheet

Merchandise inventory is usually reported in the Current assets section of the balance sheet. In addition to this amount, the following are reported:

- The method of determining the cost of the inventory (FIFO, LIFO, or weighted average)
- The method of valuing the inventory (cost or the lower of cost or market)

IFRS

See Appendix B for more information.

The financial statement reporting for the topics covered in Chapters 7–15 is illustrated using excerpts from the financial statements of **Mornin' Joe**. Mornin' Joe is a fictitious company that offers drip and espresso coffee in a coffeehouse setting. The complete financial statements of Mornin' Joe are illustrated at the end of the last chapter.

The balance sheet presentation for merchandise inventory for Mornin' Joe is as follows:

Mornin' Joe
Balance Sheet
December 31, 20Y6

Current assets:	
Cash and cash equivalents	$235,000
...	
Merchandise inventory—at lower of cost (first-in, first-out method) or market	120,000

> **Link to Best Buy**
> **Best Buy** uses the weighted average cost and first-in, first-out methods for recording inventory.

It is not unusual for a large business to use different costing methods for segments of its inventories. Also, a business may change its inventory costing method. In such cases, the effect of the change and the reason for the change are disclosed in the financial statements.

Effect of Inventory Errors on the Financial Statements

Any errors in merchandise inventory will affect the balance sheet and income statement. Some reasons that inventory errors may occur include the following:

- Physical inventory on hand was miscounted.
- Costs were incorrectly assigned to inventory. For example, the FIFO, LIFO, or weighted average cost method was incorrectly applied.
- Inventory in transit was incorrectly included or excluded from inventory.
- Consigned inventory was incorrectly included or excluded from inventory.

Inventory errors often arise from merchandise that is in transit at year-end. As discussed in Chapter 6, shipping terms determine when the title to merchandise passes. When goods are purchased or sold *FOB shipping point*, title passes to the buyer when the goods are shipped. When the terms are *FOB destination*, title passes to the buyer when the goods are received.

To illustrate, assume that SysExpress ordered the following merchandise from American Products:

Date ordered:	December 27, 20Y1
Amount:	$10,000
Terms:	FOB shipping point, 2/10, n/30
Date shipped by seller:	December 30
Date delivered:	January 3, 20Y2

When SysExpress counts its physical inventory on December 31, 20Y1, the merchandise is still in transit. In such cases, it would be easy for SysExpress not to include the $10,000 of merchandise in its December 31 physical inventory. However, since the merchandise was purchased *FOB shipping point*, SysExpress owns the merchandise was not delivered until January 3. Thus, it should be included in the December 31 inventory even though it was not delivered until January 3. Likewise, any merchandise *sold* by SysExpress *FOB destination* is still SysExpress's inventory even if it is in transit to the buyer on December 31.

Inventory errors often arise from **consigned inventory**. Manufacturers sometimes ship merchandise to retailers who act as the manufacturer's selling agent. The manufacturer, called the **consignor**, retains title until the goods are sold. Such merchandise is said to be shipped *on consignment* to the retailer, called the **consignee**.

Any unsold merchandise at year-end is a part of the manufacturer's (consignor's) inventory even though the merchandise is at the retailer (consignee). At year-end, it would be easy for the retailer (consignee) to incorrectly include the consigned merchandise in its physical inventory. Likewise, the manufacturer (consignor) should include consigned inventory in its physical inventory even though the inventory is not on hand.

Income Statement Effects Inventory errors will misstate the income statement amounts for cost of merchandise sold, gross profit, and net income. The effects of inventory errors on the current period's income statement are summarized in Exhibit 10.

	Income Statement Effect		
Inventory Error	**Cost of Merchandise Sold**	**Gross Profit**	**Net Income**
Beginning inventory is:			
Understated ↓	Understated ↓	↑ Overstated	↑ Overstated
↑ Overstated	↑ Overstated	Understated ↓	Understated ↓
Ending inventory is:			
Understated ↓	↑ Overstated	Understated ↓	Understated ↓
↑ Overstated	Understated ↓	↑ Overstated	↑ Overstated

EXHIBIT 10

Effect of Inventory Errors on Current Period's Income Statement

To illustrate, the effects of inventory errors are shown on the income statements of SysExpress in Exhibit 11.[5] On December 31, 20Y1, assume that SysExpress incorrectly records its physical inventory as $50,000 instead of the correct amount of $60,000. Thus, the December 31, 20Y1, inventory is understated by $10,000 ($60,000 – $50,000). As a result, the cost of merchandise sold is overstated by $10,000. The gross profit and the net income for the year will also be understated by $10,000.

The December 31, 20Y1, merchandise inventory becomes the January 1, 20Y2, inventory. Thus, the beginning inventory for 20Y2 is understated by $10,000. As a result, the cost of merchandise sold is understated by $10,000 for 20Y2. The gross profit and net income for 20Y2 will be overstated by $10,000.

As shown in Exhibit 11, because the ending inventory of one period is the beginning inventory of the next period, the effects of inventory errors carry forward to the next period. Specifically, if uncorrected, the effects of inventory errors reverse themselves in the next period. In Exhibit 11, the combined net income for the two years of $525,000 is correct even though the 20Y1 and 20Y2 income statements were incorrect.

Balance Sheet Effects Inventory errors misstate the merchandise inventory, current assets, total assets, and owner's equity on the balance sheet. The effects of inventory errors on the current period's balance sheet are summarized in Exhibit 12.

For the SysExpress illustration shown in Exhibit 11, the December 31, 20Y1, ending inventory was understated by $10,000. As a result, the merchandise inventory, current assets, and total assets would be understated by $10,000 on the December 31, 20Y1, balance sheet. Because the ending physical inventory is understated, the cost of merchandise sold for 20Y1 will be overstated by $10,000. Thus, the gross profit and the net income for 20Y1 are understated by $10,000. Because the net income is closed to owner's equity (capital) at the end of the period, the owner's equity on the December 31, 20Y1, balance sheet is also understated by $10,000.

---

5 The effects of inventory errors will be illustrated using the periodic system. This is because it is easier to see the impacts of inventory errors on the income statement using the periodic system. The effects of inventory errors would be the same under the perpetual inventory system.

EXHIBIT 11 — Effects of Inventory Errors on Two Years' Income Statements

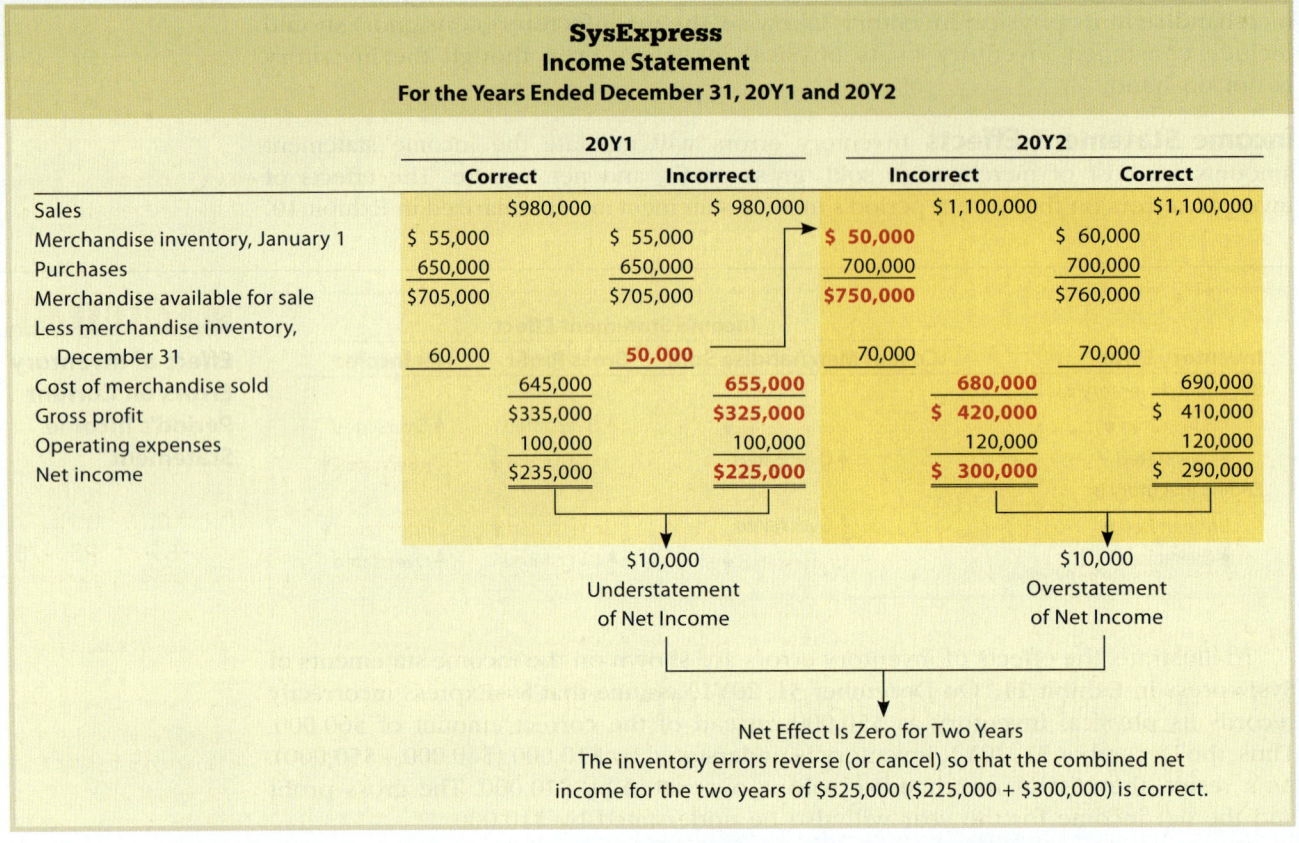

EXHIBIT 12 — Effect of Inventory Errors on Current Period's Balance Sheet

Ending Inventory Error	Balance Sheet Effect				
	Merchandise Inventory	Current Assets	Total Assets	Owner's Equity (Capital)
Understated ↓	Understated ↓	Understated ↓	Understated ↓	Understated ↓
↑ Overstated	↑ Overstated	↑ Overstated	↑ Overstated	↑ Overstated

Inventory errors reverse themselves within two years. As a result, the balance sheet will be correct as of December 31, 20Y2. Using the SysExpress illustration from Exhibit 11, these effects are summarized as follows:

	Amount of Misstatement	
Balance Sheet:	December 31, 20Y1	December 31, 20Y2
Merchandise inventory overstated (understated)	$(10,000)	Correct
Current assets overstated (understated)	(10,000)	Correct
Total assets overstated (understated)	(10,000)	Correct
Owner's equity overstated (understated)	(10,000)	Correct
Income Statement:	20Y1	20Y2
Cost of merchandise sold overstated (understated)	$ 10,000	$(10,000)
Gross profit overstated (understated)	(10,000)	10,000
Net income overstated (understated)	(10,000)	10,000

Example Exercise 7-7 Effect of Inventory Errors Obj. 6

Zula Repair Shop incorrectly counted its December 31, 20Y8, inventory as $250,000 instead of the correct amount of $220,000. Indicate the effect of the misstatement on Zula's December 31, 20Y8, balance sheet and income statement for the year ended December 31, 20Y8.

Follow My Example 7-7

	Amount of Misstatement Overstatement (Understatement)
Balance Sheet:	
Merchandise inventory overstated	$ 30,000
Current assets overstated	30,000
Total assets overstated	30,000
Owner's equity overstated	30,000
Income Statement:	
Cost of merchandise sold understated	$(30,000)
Gross profit overstated	30,000
Net income overstated	30,000

Practice Exercises: PE 7-7A, PE 7-7B

Financial Analysis and Interpretation: Inventory Turnover and Days' Sales in Inventory

Obj. 7 Describe and illustrate the inventory turnover and the days' sales in inventory in analyzing the efficiency and effectiveness of inventory management.

A merchandising business should keep enough inventory on hand to meet its customers' needs. A failure to do so may result in lost sales. However, too much inventory ties up funds that could be used to improve operations. Also, excess inventory increases expenses such as storage and property taxes. Finally, excess inventory increases the risk of losses due to price declines, damage, or changes in customer tastes.

Two measures to analyze the efficiency and effectiveness of inventory management are:

- inventory turnover and
- days' sales in inventory.

Inventory turnover measures the relationship between the cost of merchandise sold and the amount of inventory carried during the period. It is computed as follows:

$$\text{Inventory Turnover} = \frac{\text{Cost of Merchandise Sold}}{\text{Average Inventory}}$$

Business Connection

RAPID INVENTORY AT COSTCO

Costco Wholesale Corporation operates more than 650 membership warehouses that offer members low prices on a limited selection of nationally branded and selected private-label products. Costco emphasizes high sales volumes and rapid inventory turnover. This enables Costco to operate profitably at lower gross margins than traditional wholesalers, discount retailers, and supermarkets. In addition, Costco's rapid inventory turnover allows it to conserve its working capital, described as follows:

We operate membership warehouses . . . [that] . . . will produce high sales volumes and rapid inventory turnover. . . . We generally sell inventory before we are required to pay for it, even while taking advantage of early payment discounts when available. To the extent that sales increase and inventory turnover becomes more rapid, more inventory is financed through payment terms provided by suppliers rather than by our working capital.

Source: Costco Wholesale Corporation, *Form 10-K for the Fiscal Year Ended September 1, 2015.*

To illustrate, inventory turnover for **Best Buy** is computed from the following data (in millions) taken from two recent annual reports:

	For the Year Ended	
	Year 2	Year 1
Cost of merchandise sold	$31,292	$31,212
Inventories:		
Beginning of year	5,376	5,731
End of year	5,174	5,376
Average inventory:*		
($5,376 + $5,174) ÷ 2	5,275.00	
($5,731 + $5,376) ÷ 2		5,553.50
Inventory turnover:*		
$31,292 ÷ $5,275.00	5.93	
$31,212 ÷ $5,553.50		5.62

*Rounded to two decimal places.

Generally, the larger the inventory turnover is, the more efficient and effective the company is in managing inventory. In the preceding example, inventory turnover increased slightly from 5.62 to 5.93 during Year 2, and thus Best Buy's inventory efficiency increased during Year 2.

The **days' sales in inventory** measures the length of time it takes to acquire, sell, and replace the inventory. It is computed as follows:[6]

$$\text{Days' Sales in Inventory} = \frac{\text{Average Inventory}}{\text{Average Daily Cost of Merchandise Sold}}$$

The average daily cost of merchandise sold is determined by dividing the cost of merchandise sold by 365.[7] Based upon the preceding data, the days' sales in inventory for **Best Buy** is computed as follows:

	For the Year Ended	
	Year 2	Year 1
Cost of merchandise sold	$31,292	$31,212
Average daily cost of merchandise sold:*		
$31,292 ÷ 365 days	85.7	
$31,212 ÷ 365 days		85.5
Average inventory:*		
($5,376 + $5,174) ÷ 2	5,275.0	
($5,731 + $5,376) ÷ 2		5,553.5
Days' sales in inventory:*		
$5,275.0 ÷ $85.7	61.6 days	
$5,553.5 ÷ $85.5		65.0 days

*Rounded to one decimal place.

Generally, the lower the days' sales in inventory, the more efficient and effective the company is in managing inventory. As shown previously, the days' sales in inventory decreased from 65.0 to 61.6 during Year 2; thus, Best Buy's inventory management improved. This is consistent with the increase in inventory turnover during the year.

---

[6] Days' sales in inventory may also be computed as 365 days divided by the inventory turnover.
[7] We use 365 days for all computations involving real-world companies and data. We do this to highlight differences among companies and because computations using real-world data normally require rounding.

As with most financial ratios, differences exist among industries. To illustrate, **Tiffany & Co.** is a large retailer of fine jewelry. Because jewelry doesn't sell as rapidly as Best Buy's consumer electronics, Tiffany's inventory turnover and days' sales in inventory should be significantly different from Best Buy's. For a recent year, this is confirmed as follows:

	Best Buy	Tiffany
Inventory turnover	5.93	0.73
Days' sales in inventory	61.6 days	499.6 days

Example Exercise 7-8 Inventory Turnover and Days' Sales in Inventory *Obj. 7*

Financial statement data for years ending December 31 for Beadle Company follow:

	20Y4	20Y3
Cost of merchandise sold	$877,500	$615,000
Inventories:		
Beginning of year	225,000	185,000
End of year	315,000	225,000

a. Determine the inventory turnover for 20Y4 and 20Y3.
b. Determine the days' sales in inventory for 20Y4 and 20Y3, using 365 days.
c. Does the change in the inventory turnover and the days' sales in inventory from 20Y3 to 20Y4 indicate a favorable or an unfavorable trend?

Follow My Example 7-8

a. Inventory turnover:

	20Y4	20Y3
Average inventory:		
($225,000 + $315,000) ÷ 2	$270,000	
($185,000 + $225,000) ÷ 2		$205,000
Inventory turnover:		
$877,500 ÷ $270,000	3.25	
$615,000 ÷ $205,000		3.00

b. Days' sales in inventory:

	20Y4	20Y3
Average daily cost of merchandise sold:		
$877,500 ÷ 365 days	$2,404	
$615,000 ÷ 365 days		$1,685
Average inventory:		
($225,000 + $315,000) ÷ 2	$270,000	
($185,000 + $225,000) ÷ 2		$205,000
Days' sales in inventory:		
$270,000 ÷ $2,404	112.3 days	
$205,000 ÷ $1,685		121.7 days

c. The increase in the inventory turnover from 3.00 to 3.25 and the decrease in the days' sales in inventory from 121.7 days to 112.3 days indicate favorable trends in managing inventory.

Practice Exercises: PE 7-8A, PE 7-8B

Appendix

Estimating Inventory Cost

A business may need to estimate the amount of inventory for the following reasons:

- Perpetual inventory records are not maintained.
- A fire or flood has destroyed inventory.
- A computer security breach has destroyed inventory records.
- Monthly or quarterly financial statements are needed, but a physical inventory is taken only once a year.

This appendix describes and illustrates two widely used methods of estimating inventory cost.

Retail Method of Inventory Costing

The **retail inventory method** of estimating inventory cost requires costs and retail prices to be maintained for the merchandise available for sale. A ratio of cost to retail price is then used to convert ending inventory at retail to estimate the ending inventory cost.

The retail inventory method is applied as follows:

Step 1. Determine the total merchandise available for sale at cost and retail.
Step 2. Determine the ratio of the cost to retail of the merchandise available for sale.
Step 3. Determine the ending inventory at retail by deducting the sales from the merchandise available for sale at retail.
Step 4. Estimate the ending inventory cost by multiplying the ending inventory at retail by the cost to retail ratio.

Exhibit 13 illustrates the retail inventory method.

EXHIBIT 13

Determining Inventory by the Retail Method

	A	B	C
1		Cost	Retail
2	Merchandise inventory, January 1	$19,400	$ 36,000
3	Purchases in January (net)	42,600	64,000
4	Merchandise available for sale (Step 1)	$62,000	$100,000
5	Ratio of cost to retail price (Step 2): $\frac{\$62,000}{\$100,000} = 62\%$		
6	Sales for January		70,000
7	Merchandise inventory, January 31, at retail (Step 3)		$ 30,000
8	Merchandise inventory, January 31, at estimated cost (Step 4)		
9	($30,000 × 62%)		$ 18,600

When estimating the cost to retail ratio, the mix of items in the ending inventory is assumed to be the same as the merchandise available for sale. If the ending inventory is made up of different classes of merchandise, cost to retail ratios may be developed for each class of inventory.

An advantage of the retail method is that it provides inventory figures for preparing monthly statements. Department stores and similar retailers often determine gross profit and operating income each month but may take a physical inventory only once or twice a year. Thus, the retail method allows management to monitor operations more closely.

The retail method may also be used as an aid in taking a physical inventory. In this case, the items are counted and recorded at their retail (selling) prices instead of their costs. The physical inventory at retail is then converted to cost by using the cost to retail ratio.

Gross Profit Method of Inventory Costing

The **gross profit method** uses the estimated gross profit for the period to estimate the inventory at the end of the period. The gross profit is estimated from the preceding year, adjusted for any current period changes in the cost and sales prices.

The gross profit method is applied as follows:

Step 1. Determine the merchandise available for sale at cost.

Step 2. Determine the estimated gross profit by multiplying the sales by the gross profit percentage.

Step 3. Determine the estimated cost of merchandise sold by deducting the estimated gross profit from the sales.

Step 4. Estimate the ending inventory cost by deducting the estimated cost of merchandise sold from the merchandise available for sale.

Exhibit 14 illustrates the gross profit method.

EXHIBIT 14
Estimating Inventory by Gross Profit Method

	A	B	C
1			Cost
2	Merchandise inventory, January 1		$ 57,000
3	Purchases in January (net)		180,000
4	Merchandise available for sale		$237,000
5	Sales for January	$250,000	
6	Less estimated gross profit ($250,000 × 30%)	75,000	
7	Estimated cost of merchandise sold		175,000
8	Estimated merchandise inventory, January 31		$ 62,000
9			

Step 1 → row 4
Step 2 → row 6
Step 3 → row 7
Step 4 → row 8

The gross profit method is useful for estimating inventories for monthly or quarterly financial statements. It is also useful in estimating the cost of merchandise destroyed by fire or other disasters.

At a Glance 7

Obj. 1 Describe the importance of control over inventory.

Key Points Two objectives of inventory control are safeguarding the inventory and properly reporting it in the financial statements. The perpetual inventory system and physical count enhance control over inventory.

Learning Outcomes	Example Exercises	Practice Exercises
• Describe controls for safeguarding inventory.		
• Describe how a perpetual inventory system enhances control over inventory.		
• Describe why taking a physical inventory enhances control over inventory.		

Obj. 2 Describe three inventory cost flow assumptions and explain how they impact the income statement and balance sheet.

Key Points The three common inventory cost flow assumptions used in business are the (1) first-in, first-out method (FIFO); (2) last-in, first-out method (LIFO); and (3) weighted average cost method. The cost flow assumption affects the income statement and balance sheet.

Learning Outcomes	Example Exercises	Practice Exercises
• Describe the FIFO, LIFO, and weighted average cost flow methods.		
• Describe how the choice of a cost flow method affects the income statement and balance sheet.	EE7-1	PE7-1A, 7-1B

Obj. 3 Determine the cost of inventory under the perpetual inventory system, using the FIFO, LIFO, and weighted average cost methods.

Key Points In a perpetual inventory system, the number of units and the cost of each type of merchandise are recorded in a subsidiary inventory ledger, with a separate account for each type of merchandise.

Learning Outcomes	Example Exercises	Practice Exercises
• Determine the cost of inventory and the cost of merchandise sold, using a perpetual inventory system under the FIFO method.	EE7-2	PE7-2A, 7-2B
• Determine the cost of inventory and the cost of merchandise sold, using a perpetual inventory system under the LIFO method.	EE7-3	PE7-3A, 7-3B
• Determine the cost of inventory and the cost of merchandise sold, using a perpetual inventory system under the weighted average cost method.	EE7-4	PE7-4A, 7-4B

Chapter 7 Inventories

Obj. 4 — Determine the cost of inventory under the periodic inventory system, using the FIFO, LIFO, and weighted average cost methods.

Key Points In a periodic inventory system, a physical inventory is taken to determine the cost of the inventory and the cost of merchandise sold.

Learning Outcomes	Example Exercises	Practice Exercises
• Determine the cost of inventory and the cost of merchandise sold, using a periodic inventory system under the FIFO method.	EE7-5	PE7-5A, 7-5B
• Determine the cost of inventory and the cost of merchandise sold, using a periodic inventory system under the LIFO method.	EE7-5	PE7-5A, 7-5B
• Determine the cost of inventory and the cost of merchandise sold, using a periodic inventory system under the weighted average cost method.	EE7-5	PE7-5A, 7-5B

Obj. 5 — Compare and contrast the use of the three inventory costing methods.

Key Points The three inventory costing methods will normally yield different amounts for (1) the ending inventory, (2) the cost of merchandise sold for the period, and (3) the gross profit (and net income) for the period.

Learning Outcomes	Example Exercises	Practice Exercises
• Indicate which inventory cost flow method will yield the highest and lowest ending inventory and net income during periods of increasing prices.		
• Indicate which inventory cost flow method will yield the highest and lowest ending inventory and net income during periods of decreasing prices.		

Obj. 6 — Describe and illustrate the reporting of merchandise inventory in the financial statements.

Key Points The lower of cost or market is used to value inventory. The market value is the net realizable value of the merchandise.

Merchandise inventory is usually presented in the Current assets section of the balance sheet, following receivables. The method of determining the cost and valuing the inventory is reported.

Errors in reporting inventory based on the physical inventory will affect the balance sheet and income statement.

Learning Outcomes	Example Exercises	Practice Exercises
• Determine inventory using lower of cost or market.	EE7-6	PE7-6A, 7-6B
• Prepare the Current assets section of the balance sheet that includes inventory.		
• Determine the effect of inventory errors on the balance sheet and income statement.	EE7-7	PE7-7A, 7-7B

Obj. 7 Describe and illustrate the inventory turnover and the days' sales in inventory in analyzing the efficiency and effectiveness of inventory management.

Key Points Two measures to analyze the efficiency and effectiveness of inventory management are (1) inventory turnover and (2) days' sales in inventory.

Learning Outcomes	Example Exercises	Practice Exercises
• Describe the use of inventory turnover and days' sales in inventory in analyzing how well a company manages inventory.		
• Compute the inventory turnover.	EE7-8	PE7-8A, 7-8B
• Compute the days' sales in inventory.	EE7-8	PE7-8A, 7-8B

Illustrative Problem

Stewart Co.'s beginning inventory and purchases during the year ended December 31, 20Y2, were as follows:

		Unit	Unit Cost	Total Cost
January 1	Inventory	1,000	$50.00	$ 50,000
March 10	Purchase	3,000	52.00	156,000
June 25	Sold 1,600 units			
August 30	Purchase	2,600	55.00	143,000
October 5	Sold 4,000 units			
November 26	Purchase	1,000	57.68	57,680
December 31	Sold 800 units			
Total		7,600		$406,680

Instructions

1. Determine the cost of inventory on December 31, 20Y2, using the perpetual inventory system and each of the following inventory costing methods:
   a. first-in, first-out
   b. last-in, first-out
   c. weighted average

2. Determine the cost of inventory on December 31, 20Y2, using the periodic inventory system and each of the following inventory costing methods:
   a. first-in, first-out
   b. last-in, first-out
   c. weighted average cost

3. (Appendix) Assume that during the fiscal year ended December 31, 20Y2, sales were $530,000 and the estimated gross profit rate was 36%. Estimate the ending inventory at December 31, 20Y2, using the gross profit method.

Solution

1. The perpetual inventory ledgers follow:
   a. First-in, first-out method: $68,680 ($11,000 + $57,680)
   b. Last-in, first-out method: $61,536 ($50,000 + $11,536)
   c. Weighted average cost method: $66,600 (1,200 units × $55.50)

2. a. First-in, first-out method:

1,000 units at $57.68	$57,680
200 units at $55.00	11,000
1,200 units	$68,680

b. Last-in, first-out method:

1,000 units at $50.00	$50,000
200 units at $52.00	10,400
1,200 units	$60,400

c. Weighted average cost method:

Weighted average cost per unit: ($406,680 ÷ 7,600 units = $53.51 (Rounded)
Inventory, December 31, 20Y2: 1,200 units at $53.51 = $64,212

1. a. First-in, first-out method: $68,680 ($11,000 + $57,680)

Date	Purchases Quantity	Purchases Unit Cost	Purchases Total Cost	Cost of Merchandise Sold Quantity	Cost of Merchandise Sold Unit Cost	Cost of Merchandise Sold Total Cost	Inventory Quantity	Inventory Unit Cost	Inventory Total Cost
20Y2									
Jan. 1							1,000	50.00	50,000
Mar. 10	3,000	52.00	156,000				1,000	50.00	50,000
							3,000	52.00	156,000
June 25				1,000	50.00	50,000	2,400	52.00	124,800
				600	52.00	31,200			
Aug. 30	2,600	55.00	143,000				2,400	52.00	124,800
							2,600	55.00	143,000
Oct. 5				2,400	52.00	124,800	1,000	55.00	55,000
				1,600	55.00	88,000			
Nov. 26	1,000	57.68	57,680				1,000	55.00	55,000
							1,000	57.68	57,680
Dec. 31				800	55.00	44,000	200	55.00	11,000
							1,000	57.68	57,680
31 Balances						338,000			68,680

b. Last-in, first-out method: $61,536 ($50,000 + $11,536)

Date	Purchases Quantity	Purchases Unit Cost	Purchases Total Cost	Cost of Merchandise Sold Quantity	Cost of Merchandise Sold Unit Cost	Cost of Merchandise Sold Total Cost	Inventory Quantity	Inventory Unit Cost	Inventory Total Cost
20Y2									
Jan. 1							1,000	50.00	50,000
Mar. 10	3,000	52.00	156,000				1,000	50.00	50,000
							3,000	52.00	156,000
June 25				1,600	52.00	83,200	1,000	50.00	50,000
							1,400	52.00	72,800
Aug. 30	2,600	55.00	143,000				1,000	50.00	50,000
							1,400	52.00	72,800
							2,600	55.00	143,000
Oct. 5				2,600	55.00	143,000	1,000	50.00	50,000
				1,400	52.00	72,800			
Nov. 26	1,000	57.68	57,680				1,000	50.00	50,000
							1,000	57.68	57,680
Dec. 31				800	57.68	46,144	1,000	50.00	50,000
							200	57.68	11,536
31 Balances						345,144			61,536

(Continued)

c. Weighted average cost method: $66,600 (1,200 units × $55.50)

| | Purchases ||| Cost of Merchandise Sold ||| Inventory |||
Date	Quantity	Unit Cost	Total Cost	Quantity	Unit Cost	Total Cost	Quantity	Unit Cost	Total Cost
Jan. 1							1,000	50.00	50,000
Mar. 10	3,000	52.00	156,000				4,000	51.50	206,000
June 25				1,600	51.50	82,400	2,400	51.50	123,600
Aug. 30	2,600	55.00	143,000				5,000	53.32	266,600
Oct. 5				4,000	53.32	213,280	1,000	53.32	53,320
Nov. 26	1,000	57.68	57,680				2,000	55.50	111,000
Dec. 31				800	55.50	44,400	1,200	55.50	66,600
31 Balances						340,080	1,200	55.50	66,600

3. (Appendix)

Merchandise inventory, January 1, 20Y2...............		$ 50,000
Purchases (net)...		356,680
Merchandise available for sale.........................		$406,680
Sales...	$530,000	
Less estimated gross profit ($530,000 × 36%).........	190,800	
Estimated cost of merchandise sold....................		339,200
Estimated merchandise inventory, December 31, 20Y2....		$ 67,480

Key Terms

consigned inventory (362)
consignee (362)
consignor (362)
days' sales in inventory (366)
first-in, first-out (FIFO) inventory cost flow method (348)
gross profit method (369)

inventory turnover (365)
last-in, first-out (LIFO) inventory cost flow method (348)
lower-of-cost-or-market (LCM) method (359)
net realizable value (360)
physical inventory (347)
purchase order (346)

receiving report (346)
retail inventory method (368)
specific identification inventory cost flow method (347)
subsidiary inventory ledger (347)
weighted average inventory cost flow method (348)

Discussion Questions

1. Before inventory purchases are recorded, the receiving report should be reconciled to what documents?

2. Why is it important to take a physical inventory periodically when using a perpetual inventory system?

3. Do the terms *FIFO, LIFO, and weighted average* refer to techniques used in determining quantities of the various classes of merchandise on hand? Explain.

4. If merchandise inventory is being valued at cost and the price level is decreasing, which of the three methods of costing—FIFO, LIFO, or weighted average cost—will yield (a) the highest inventory cost, (b) the lowest inventory cost, (c) the highest gross profit, and (d) the lowest gross profit?

5. Which of the three methods of inventory costing—FIFO, LIFO, or weighted average cost—will in general yield an inventory cost most nearly approximating current replacement cost?

6. If inventory is being valued at cost and the price level is steadily rising, which of the three methods of costing—FIFO, LIFO, or weighted average cost—will yield the lowest annual income tax expense? Explain.

7. Using the following data, how should the merchandise be valued under lower of cost or market?

Original cost	$1,350
Estimated selling price	1,475
Selling expenses	180

8. The inventory at the end of the year was understated by $14,750. (a) Did the error cause an overstatement or an understatement of the gross profit for the year? (b) Which items on the balance sheet at the end of the year were overstated or understated as a result of the error?

9. Hutch Co. sold merchandise to Bibbins Company on May 31, FOB shipping point. If the merchandise is in transit on May 31, the end of the fiscal year, which company would report it in its financial statements? Explain.

10. A manufacturer shipped merchandise to a retailer on a consignment basis. If the merchandise is unsold at the end of the period, in whose inventory should the merchandise be included?

Practice Exercises

Example Exercises

EE 7-1 p. 349   **PE 7-1A**   **Cost flow methods**   OBJ. 2

The following three identical units of Item A are purchased during April:

Item A		Units	Cost
Apr. 2	Purchase	1	$ 68
14	Purchase	1	73
28	Purchase	1	75
Total		3	$216
Average cost per unit			$ 72 ($216 ÷ 3 units)

Assume that one unit is sold on April 30 for $118.

Determine the gross profit for April and ending inventory on April 30 using the (a) first-in, first-out (FIFO); (b) last-in, first-out (LIFO); and (c) weighted average cost methods.

EE 7-1 p. 349   **PE 7-1B**   **Cost flow methods**   OBJ. 2

The following three identical units of Item Beta are purchased during June:

Item Beta		Units	Cost
June 2	Purchase	1	$ 50
12	Purchase	1	60
23	Purchase	1	70
Total		3	$180
Average cost per unit			$ 60 ($180 ÷ 3 units)

Assume that one unit is sold on June 27 for $110.

Determine the gross profit for June and ending inventory on June 30 using the (a) first-in, first-out (FIFO); (b) last-in, first-out (LIFO); and (c) weighted average cost methods.

EE 7-2 p. 351   **PE 7-2A**   **Perpetual inventory using FIFO**   OBJ. 3

Beginning inventory, purchases, and sales for Item Widget are as follows:

Mar. 1	Inventory	200 units at $8
9	Sale	175 units
13	Purchase	160 units at 9
25	Sale	150 units

Assuming a perpetual inventory system and using the first-in, first-out (FIFO) method, determine (a) the cost of merchandise sold on March 25 and (b) the inventory on March 31.

376 Chapter 7 Inventories

EE 7-2 *p. 351* **PE 7-2B Perpetual inventory using FIFO** OBJ. 3

Beginning inventory, purchases, and sales for Item Delta are as follows:

July	1	Inventory	50 units at $15
	7	Sale	44 units
	15	Purchase	90 units at $18
	24	Sale	40 units

Assuming a perpetual inventory system and using the first-in, first-out (FIFO) method, determine (a) the cost of merchandise sold on July 24 and (b) the inventory on July 31.

EE 7-3 *p. 353* **PE 7-3A Perpetual inventory using LIFO** OBJ. 3

Beginning inventory, purchases, and sales for Item Gidget are as follows:

Sept.	1	Inventory	80 units at $175
	10	Sale	65 units
	18	Purchase	75 units at $180
	27	Sale	70 units

Assuming a perpetual inventory system and using the last-in, first-out (LIFO) method, determine (a) the cost of merchandise sold on September 27 and (b) the inventory on September 30.

EE 7-3 *p. 353* **PE 7-3B Perpetual inventory using LIFO** OBJ. 3

Beginning inventory, purchases, and sales for Item Foxtrot are as follows:

Mar.	1	Inventory	270 units at $18
	8	Sale	225 units
	15	Purchase	375 units at $20
	27	Sale	240 units

Assuming a perpetual inventory system and using the last-in, first-out (LIFO) method, determine (a) the cost of merchandise sold on March 27 and (b) the inventory on March 31.

EE 7-4 *p. 354* **PE 7-4A Perpetual inventory using weighted average** OBJ. 3

Beginning inventory, purchases, and sales for Meta-B1 are as follows:

July	1	Inventory	100 units at $400
	12	Sale	70 units
	23	Purchase	120 units at $450
	26	Sale	110 units

Assuming a perpetual inventory system and using the weighted average method, determine (a) the weighted average unit cost after the July 23 purchase, (b) the cost of the merchandise sold on July 26, and (c) the inventory on July 31.

EE 7-4 *p. 354* **PE 7-4B Perpetual inventory using weighted average** OBJ. 3

Beginning inventory, purchases, and sales for WCS12 are as follows:

Oct.	1	Inventory	300 units at $8
	13	Sale	175 units
	22	Purchase	375 units at $10
	29	Sale	280 units

Assuming a perpetual inventory system and using the weighted average method, determine (a) the weighted average unit cost after the October 22 purchase, (b) the cost of the merchandise sold on October 29, and (c) the inventory on October 31.

Chapter 7 Inventories 377

EE 7-5 p. 358   **PE 7-5A Periodic inventory using FIFO, LIFO, and weighted average cost methods** OBJ. 4

The units of an item available for sale during the year were as follows:

Jan. 1	Inventory	12 units at $5,400	$ 64,800
Aug. 7	Purchase	18 units at $6,000	108,000
Dec. 11	Purchase	15 units at $6,480	97,200
Available for sale		45 units	$270,000

There are 14 units of the item in the physical inventory at December 31. The periodic inventory system is used. Determine the inventory cost using (a) the first-in, first-out (FIFO) method; (b) the last-in, first-out (LIFO) method; and (c) the weighted average cost method.

EE 7-5 p. 358   **PE 7-5B Periodic inventory using FIFO, LIFO, and weighted average cost methods** OBJ. 4

The units of an item available for sale during the year were as follows:

Jan. 1	Inventory	20 units at $360	$ 7,200
Aug. 13	Purchase	260 units at $342	88,920
Nov. 30	Purchase	40 units at $357	14,280
Available for sale		320 units	$110,400

There are 57 units of the item in the physical inventory at December 31. The periodic inventory system is used. Determine the inventory cost using (a) the first-in, first-out (FIFO) method; (b) the last-in, first-out (LIFO) method; and (c) the weighted average cost method.

EE 7-6 p. 361   **PE 7-6A Lower-of-cost-or-market method** OBJ. 6

On the basis of the following data, determine the value of the inventory at the lower of cost or market. Apply lower of cost or market to each inventory item, as shown in Exhibit 9.

Item	Inventory Quantity	Cost per Unit	Market Value per Unit (Net Realizable Value)
Raven 10	1,200	$115	$112
Dove 23	6,500	17	22

EE 7-6 p. 361   **PE 7-6B Lower-of-cost-or-market method** OBJ. 6

On the basis of the following data, determine the value of the inventory at the lower of cost or market. Apply lower of cost or market to each inventory item, as shown in Exhibit 9.

Item	Inventory Quantity	Cost per Unit	Market Value per Unit (Net Realizable Value)
JFW1	6,330	$10	$11
SAW9	1,140	36	34

EE 7-7 p. 365   **PE 7-7A Effect of inventory errors** OBJ. 6

During the taking of its physical inventory on August 31, 2019, Kate Interiors Company incorrectly counted its inventory as $366,900 instead of the correct amount of $378,500. Indicate the effect of the misstatement on Kate Interiors' August 31, 2019, balance sheet and income statement for the year ended August 31, 2019.

EE 7-7 p. 365   **PE 7-7B Effect of inventory errors** OBJ. 6

During the taking of its physical inventory on December 31, 2019, Waterjet Bath Company incorrectly counted its inventory as $728,660 instead of the correct amount of $719,880. Indicate the effect of the misstatement on Waterjet Bath's December 31, 2019, balance sheet and income statement for the year ended December 31, 2019.

378 Chapter 7 Inventories

EE 7-8 p. 367   **PE 7-8A Inventory turnover and days' sales in inventory**   OBJ. 7

Financial statement data for years ending December 31 for Holland Company follow:

	20Y4	20Y3
Cost of merchandise sold	$4,504,500	$3,715,200
Inventories:		
Beginning of year	788,000	760,000
End of year	850,000	788,000

a. Determine the inventory turnover for 20Y4 and 20Y3.

b. Determine the days' sales in inventory for 20Y4 and 20Y3. Use 365 days and round to one decimal place.

c. Does the change in inventory turnover and the days' sales in inventory from 20Y3 to 20Y4 indicate a favorable or an unfavorable trend?

EE 7-8 p. 367   **PE 7-8B Inventory turnover and days' sales in inventory**   OBJ. 7

Financial statement data for years ending December 31 for Tango Company follow:

	20Y7	20Y6
Cost of merchandise sold	$3,864,000	$4,001,500
Inventories:		
Beginning of year	770,000	740,000
End of year	840,000	770,000

a. Determine the inventory turnover for 20Y7 and 20Y6.

b. Determine the days' sales in inventory for 20Y7 and 20Y6. Use 365 days and round to one decimal place.

c. Does the change in inventory turnover and the days' sales in inventory from 20Y6 to 20Y7 indicate a favorable or an unfavorable trend?

Exercises

EX 7-1 Control of inventories   OBJ. 1

Triple Creek Hardware Store currently uses a periodic inventory system. Kevin Carlton, the owner, is considering the purchase of a computer system that would make it feasible to switch to a perpetual inventory system.

Kevin is unhappy with the periodic inventory system because it does not provide timely information on inventory levels. Kevin has noticed on several occasions that the store runs out of good-selling items, while too many poor-selling items are on hand.

Kevin is also concerned about lost sales while a physical inventory is being taken. Triple Creek Hardware currently takes a physical inventory twice a year. To minimize distractions, the store is closed on the day inventory is taken. Kevin believes that closing the store is the only way to get an accurate inventory count.

▶ Will switching to a perpetual inventory system strengthen Triple Creek Hardware's control over inventory items? Will switching to a perpetual inventory system eliminate the need for a physical inventory count? Explain.

EX 7-2 Control of inventories   OBJ. 1

Hardcase Luggage Shop is a small retail establishment located in a large shopping mall. This shop has implemented the following procedures regarding inventory items:

a. Because the shop carries mostly high-quality, designer luggage, all inventory items are tagged with a control device that activates an alarm if a tagged item is removed from the store.

Chapter 7 Inventories 379

b. Because the display area of the store is limited, only a sample of each piece of luggage is kept on the selling floor. Whenever a customer selects a piece of luggage, the salesclerk gets the appropriate piece from the store's stockroom. Because all salesclerks need access to the stockroom, it is not locked. The stockroom is adjacent to the break room used by all mall employees.

c. Whenever Hardcase Luggage Shop receives a shipment of new inventory, the items are taken directly to the stockroom. Hardcase's accountant uses the vendor's invoice to record the amount of inventory received.

State whether each of these procedures is appropriate or inappropriate. If it is inappropriate, explain why.

EX 7-3 Perpetual inventory using FIFO OBJ. 2, 3

✔ Inventory balance, April 30, $5,360

Beginning inventory, purchases, and sales data for portable game players are as follows:

Apr.	1	Inventory	120 units at $26
	10	Sale	90 units
	15	Purchase	140 units at $28
	20	Sale	110 units
	24	Sale	40 units
	30	Purchase	160 units at $30

The business maintains a perpetual inventory system, costing by the first-in, first-out method.

a. Determine the cost of the merchandise sold for each sale and the inventory balance after each sale, presenting the data in the form illustrated in Exhibit 3.

b. Based upon the preceding data, would you expect the inventory to be higher or lower using the last-in, first-out method?

EX 7-4 Perpetual inventory using LIFO OBJ. 2, 3

✔ Inventory balance, April 30, $5,320

Assume that the business in Exercise 7-3 maintains a perpetual inventory system, costing by the last-in, first-out method. Determine the cost of merchandise sold for each sale and the inventory balance after each sale, presenting the data in the form illustrated in Exhibit 4.

EX 7-5 Perpetual inventory using LIFO OBJ. 2, 3

✔ Inventory balance, May 31, $20,160

Beginning inventory, purchases, and sales data for prepaid cell phones for May are as follows:

Inventory		Purchases		Sales	
May 1	1,550 units at $44	May 10	720 units at $45	May 12	1,200 units
		20	1,200 units at $48	14	830 units
				31	1,000 units

a. Assuming that the perpetual inventory system is used, costing by the LIFO method, determine the cost of merchandise sold for each sale and the inventory balance after each sale, presenting the data in the form illustrated in Exhibit 4.

b. Based upon the preceding data, would you expect the inventory to be higher or lower using the first-in, first-out method?

EX 7-6 Perpetual inventory using FIFO OBJ. 2, 3

✔ Inventory balance, May 31, $21,120

Assume that the business in Exercise 7-5 maintains a perpetual inventory system, costing by the first-in, first-out method. Determine the cost of merchandise sold for each sale and the inventory balance after each sale, presenting the data in the form illustrated in Exhibit 3.

380 Chapter 7 Inventories

✔ b. $763,200

EX 7-7 FIFO and LIFO costs under perpetual inventory system OBJ. 2, 3

The following units of an item were available for sale during the year:

Beginning inventory	21,600 units at $20.00
Sale	14,400 units at $40.00
First purchase	48,000 units at $25.20
Sale	36,000 units at $40.00
Second purchase	45,000 units at $26.40
Sale	33,000 units at $40.00

The firm uses the perpetual inventory system, and there are 31,200 units of the item on hand at the end of the year. What is the total cost of the ending inventory according to (a) FIFO, (b) LIFO?

✔ Total Cost of Merchandise Sold, $2,110,500

EX 7-8 Weighted average cost flow method under perpetual inventory system OBJ. 3

The following units of a particular item were available for sale during the calendar year:

Jan.	1	Inventory	30,000 units at $30.00
Mar.	18	Sale	24,000 units
May	2	Purchase	54,000 units at $31.00
Aug.	9	Sale	45,000 units
Oct.	20	Purchase	21,000 units at $32.10

The firm uses the weighted average cost method with a perpetual inventory system. Determine the cost of merchandise sold for each sale and the inventory balance after each sale. Present the data in the form illustrated in Exhibit 5.

✔ Total Cost of Merchandise Sold, $154,400

EX 7-9 Weighted average cost flow method under perpetual inventory system OBJ. 3

The following units of a particular item were available for sale during the calendar year:

Jan.	1	Inventory	4,000 units at $20
Apr.	19	Sale	2,500 units
June	30	Purchase	6,000 units at $24
Sept.	2	Sale	4,500 units
Nov.	15	Purchase	1,000 units at $25

The firm uses the weighted average cost method with a perpetual inventory system. Determine the cost of merchandise sold for each sale and the inventory balance after each sale. Present the data in the form illustrated in Exhibit 5.

✔ Total Cost of Merchandise Sold, $152,000

EX 7-10 Perpetual inventory using FIFO OBJ. 3

Assume that the business in Exercise 7-9 maintains a perpetual inventory system. Determine the cost of merchandise sold for each sale and the inventory balance after each sale, assuming the first-in, first-out method. Present the data in the form illustrated in Exhibit 3.

✔ Total Cost of Merchandise Sold, $158,000

EX 7-11 Perpetual inventory using LIFO OBJ. 3

Assume that the business in Exercise 7-9 maintains a perpetual inventory system. Determine the cost of merchandise sold for each sale and the inventory balance after each sale, assuming the last-in, first-out method. Present the data in the form illustrated in Exhibit 4.

Chapter 7 Inventories 381

EX 7-12 Periodic inventory by three methods OBJ. 2, 4

✔ b. $167,700

The units of an item available for sale during the year were as follows:

Jan.	1	Inventory	1,000 units at $120
Feb.	17	Purchase	1,375 units at $128
July	21	Purchase	1,500 units at $136
Nov.	23	Purchase	1,125 units at $140

There are 1,200 units of the item in the physical inventory at December 31. The periodic inventory system is used. Determine the inventory cost by (a) the first-in, first-out method; (b) the last-in, first-out method; and (c) the weighted average cost method.

EX 7-13 Periodic inventory by three methods; cost of merchandise sold OBJ. 2, 4

✔ a. Inventory, $239,840

The units of an item available for sale during the year were as follows:

Jan.	1	Inventory	1,800 units at $108
Mar.	10	Purchase	2,240 units at $110
Aug.	30	Purchase	2,000 units at $116
Dec.	12	Purchase	1,960 units at $120

There are 2,000 units of the item in the physical inventory at December 31. The periodic inventory system is used. Determine the inventory cost and the cost of merchandise sold by three methods, presenting your answers in the following form:

	Cost	
Inventory Method	**Merchandise Inventory**	**Merchandise Sold**
a. First-in, first-out	$	$
b. Last-in, first-out		
c. Weighted average cost		

EX 7-14 Comparing inventory methods OBJ. 5

Assume that a firm separately determined inventory under FIFO and LIFO and then compared the results.

a. In each space that follows, place the correct sign [less than (<), greater than (>), or equal (=)] for each comparison, assuming periods of rising prices.

1. FIFO inventory _____ LIFO inventory
2. FIFO cost of merchandise sold _____ LIFO cost of merchandise sold
3. FIFO net income _____ LIFO net income
4. FIFO income taxes _____ LIFO income taxes

b. Why would management prefer to use LIFO over FIFO in periods of rising prices?

EX 7-15 Lower-of-cost-or-market inventory OBJ. 6

✔ LCM: $41,880

On the basis of the following data, determine the value of the inventory at the lower of cost or market. Assemble the data in the form illustrated in Exhibit 9.

Inventory Item	Inventory Quantity	Cost per Unit	Market Value per Unit (Net Realizable Value)
Birch	100	$125	$120
Cypress	75	100	108
Mountain Ash	80	90	86
Spruce	130	74	80
Willow	60	105	98

382 Chapter 7 Inventories

EX 7-16 Merchandise inventory on the balance sheet   OBJ. 6
Based on the data in Exercise 7-15 and assuming that cost was determined by the FIFO method, show how the merchandise inventory would appear on the balance sheet.

EX 7-17 Effect of errors in physical inventory   OBJ. 6
Missouri River Supply Co. sells canoes, kayaks, whitewater rafts, and other boating supplies. During the taking of its physical inventory on December 31, 20Y2, Missouri River Supply incorrectly counted its inventory as $233,400 instead of the correct amount of $238,600.

a. State the effect of the error on the December 31, 20Y2, balance sheet of Missouri River Supply.
b. State the effect of the error on the income statement of Missouri River Supply for the year ended December 31, 20Y2.
c. If uncorrected, what would be the effect of the error on the 20Y3 income statement?
d. If uncorrected, what would be the effect of the error on the December 31, 20Y3, balance sheet?

EX 7-18 Effect of errors in physical inventory   OBJ. 6
Fonda Motorcycle Shop sells motorcycles, ATVs, and other related supplies and accessories. During the taking of its physical inventory on December 31, 20Y8, Fonda Motorcycle Shop incorrectly counted its inventory as $337,500 instead of the correct amount of $328,850.

a. State the effect of the error on the December 31, 20Y8, balance sheet of Fonda Motorcycle Shop.
b. State the effect of the error on the income statement of Fonda Motorcycle Shop for the year ended December 31, 20Y8.
c. If uncorrected, what would be the effect of the error on the 20Y9 income statement?
d. If uncorrected, what would be the effect of the error on the December 31, 20Y9, balance sheet?

EX 7-19 Error in inventory   OBJ. 6
During 20Y5, the accountant discovered that the physical inventory at the end of 20Y4 had been understated by $42,750. Instead of correcting the error, however, the accountant assumed that the error would balance out (correct itself) in 20Y5.

Are there any flaws in the accountant's assumption? Explain.

EX 7-20 Inventory turnover   OBJ. 7
The following data (in millions) were taken from recent annual reports of Apple Inc., a manufacturer of personal computers and related products, and Mattel Inc., a manufacturer of toys, including Barbie®, Hot Wheels®, and Disney Classics:

	Apple	Mattel
Cost of merchandise sold	$140,089	$2,896
Inventory, end of year	2,349	588
Inventory, beginning of the year	2,111	562

a. Determine the inventory turnover for Apple and Mattel. Round to one decimal place.
b. Would you expect Mattel's inventory turnover to be higher or lower than Apple's? Why?

EX 7-21 Inventory turnover and days' sales in inventory   OBJ. 7
Kroger, Sprouts Farmers Market, Inc., and Whole Foods Markets, Inc. are three grocery chains in the United States. Inventory management is an important aspect of the grocery retail busi-

✔ a. Kroger, inventory turnover, 15.08

Chapter 7 Inventories 383

ness. Recent balance sheets for these three companies indicated the following merchandise inventory (in millions) information:

	Kroger	Sprouts	Whole Foods
Cost of merchandise sold	$85,512	$2,541	$9,973
Inventory, end of year	5,688	165	500
Inventory, beginning of year	5,651	143	441

a. Determine the inventory turnover. Round to two decimal places.
b. Determine the days' sales in inventory. Round to one decimal place.
c. Interpret your results in parts (a) and (b).
d. If Kroger had Whole Foods' days' sales in inventory, how much additional cash flow (rounded to nearest million) would have been generated from the smaller inventory relative to its actual average inventory position?

Appendix

EX 7-22 Retail method

A business using the retail method of inventory costing determines that merchandise inventory at retail is $1,235,000. If the ratio of cost to retail price is 54%, what is the amount of inventory to be reported on the financial statements?

Appendix

EX 7-23 Retail method

A business using the retail method of inventory costing determines that merchandise inventory at retail is $396,400. If the ratio of cost to retail price is 61%, what is the amount of inventory to be reported on the financial statements?

Appendix

EX 7-24 Retail method

A business using the retail method of inventory costing determines that merchandise inventory at retail is $775,000. If the ratio of cost to retail price is 66%, what is the amount of inventory to be reported on the financial statements?

Appendix

EX 7-25 Retail method

On the basis of the following data, estimate the cost of the merchandise inventory at June 30 by the retail method:

		Cost	Retail
June 1	Merchandise inventory	$ 165,000	$ 275,000
June 1–30	Purchases (net)	2,361,500	3,800,000
June 1–30	Sales		3,550,000

Appendix

EX 7-26 Gross profit method

✔ a. Merchandise destroyed: $414,000

The merchandise inventory was destroyed by fire on December 13. The following data were obtained from the accounting records:

Jan. 1	Merchandise inventory	$ 350,000
Jan. 1–Dec. 31	Purchases (net)	2,950,000
	Sales	4,440,000
	Estimated gross profit rate	35%

a. Estimate the cost of the merchandise destroyed.
b. Briefly describe the situations in which the gross profit method is useful.

Appendix
EX 7-27 Gross profit method

Based on the following data, estimate the cost of the ending merchandise inventory:

Sales	$9,250,000
Estimated gross profit rate	36%
Beginning merchandise inventory	$ 180,000
Purchases (net)	5,945,000
Merchandise available for sale	$6,125,000

Appendix
EX 7-28 Gross profit method

Based on the following data, estimate the cost of the ending merchandise inventory:

Sales	$1,450,000
Estimated gross profit rate	42%
Beginning merchandise inventory	$ 100,000
Purchases (net)	860,000
Merchandise available for sale	$ 960,000

Problems: Series A

PR 7-1A FIFO perpetual inventory
OBJ. 2, 3

✓ 3. $8,983,125

The beginning inventory at Midnight Supplies and data on purchases and sales for a three-month period ending March 31, are as follows:

Date	Transaction	Number of Units	Per Unit	Total
Jan. 1	Inventory	7,500	$ 75.00	$ 562,500
10	Purchase	22,500	85.00	1,912,500
28	Sale	11,250	150.00	1,687,500
30	Sale	3,750	150.00	562,500
Feb. 5	Sale	1,500	150.00	225,000
10	Purchase	54,000	87.50	4,725,000
16	Sale	27,000	160.00	4,320,000
28	Sale	25,500	160.00	4,080,000
Mar. 5	Purchase	45,000	89.50	4,027,500
14	Sale	30,000	160.00	4,800,000
25	Purchase	7,500	90.00	675,000
30	Sale	26,250	160.00	4,200,000

Instructions

1. Record the inventory, purchases, and cost of merchandise sold data in a perpetual inventory record similar to the one illustrated in Exhibit 3, using the first-in, first-out method.
2. Determine the total sales and the total cost of merchandise sold for the period. Journalize the entries in the sales and cost of merchandise sold accounts. Assume that all sales were on account.
3. Determine the gross profit from sales for the period.

4. Determine the ending inventory cost as of March 31.
5. Based upon the preceding data, would you expect the inventory using the last-in, first-out method to be higher or lower?

PR 7-2A LIFO perpetual inventory OBJ. 2, 3

✔ 2. Gross profit, $8,853,750

The beginning inventory at Midnight Supplies and data on purchases and sales for a three-month period are shown in Problem 7-1A.

Instructions
1. Record the inventory, purchases, and cost of merchandise sold data in a perpetual inventory record similar to the one illustrated in Exhibit 4, using the last-in, first-out method.
2. Determine the total sales, the total cost of merchandise sold, and the gross profit from sales for the period.
3. Determine the ending inventory cost as of March 31.

PR 7-3A Weighted average cost method with perpetual inventory OBJ. 2, 3

✔ 2. Gross profit, $8,973,750

The beginning inventory for Midnight Supplies and data on purchases and sales for a three-month period are shown in Problem 7-1A.

Instructions
1. Record the inventory, purchases, and cost of merchandise sold data in a perpetual inventory record similar to the one illustrated in Exhibit 5, using the weighted average cost method.
2. Determine the total sales, the total cost of merchandise sold, and the gross profit from sales for the period.
3. Determine the ending inventory cost as of March 31.

PR 7-4A Periodic inventory by three methods OBJ. 2, 3

✔ 2. Inventory, $881,250

The beginning inventory for Midnight Supplies and data on purchases and sales for a three-month period are shown in Problem 7-1A.

Instructions
1. Determine the inventory on March 31 and the cost of merchandise sold for the three-month period, using the first-in, first-out method and the periodic inventory system.
2. Determine the inventory on March 31 and the cost of merchandise sold for the three-month period, using the last-in, first-out method and the periodic inventory system.
3. Determine the inventory on March 31 and the cost of merchandise sold for the three-month period, using the weighted average cost method and the periodic inventory system. Round the weighted average unit cost to the nearest cent.
4. Compare the gross profit and the March 31 inventories, using the following column headings:

	FIFO	LIFO	Weighted Average
Sales			
Cost of merchandise sold			
Gross profit			
Inventory, March 31			

386 Chapter 7 Inventories

✔ 1. $10,700

Excel

PR 7-5A Periodic inventory by three methods OBJ. 2, 4

Dymac Appliances uses the periodic inventory system. Details regarding the inventory of appliances at January 1, purchases invoices during the next 12 months, and the inventory count at December 31 are summarized as follows:

Model	Inventory, November 1	Purchases Invoices 1st	2nd	3rd	Inventory Count, October 31
A10	—	4 at $64	4 at $70	4 at $76	6
B15	8 at $176	4 at 158	3 at 170	6 at 184	8
E60	3 at 75	3 at 65	15 at 68	9 at 70	5
G83	7 at 242	6 at 250	5 at 260	10 at 259	9
J34	12 at 240	10 at 246	16 at 267	16 at 270	15
M90	2 at 108	2 at 110	3 at 128	3 at 130	5
Q70	5 at 160	4 at 170	4 at 175	7 at 180	8

Instructions

1. Determine the cost of the inventory on December 31 by the first-in, first-out method. Present data in columnar form, using the following headings:

Model	Quantity	Unit Cost	Total Cost

    If the inventory of a particular model comprises one entire purchase plus a portion of another purchase acquired at a different unit cost, use a separate line for each purchase.

2. Determine the cost of the inventory on December 31 by the last-in, first-out method, following the procedures indicated in (1).

3. Determine the cost of the inventory on December 31 by the weighted average cost method, using the columnar headings indicated in (1).

4. ✏️ Discuss which method (FIFO or LIFO) would be preferred for income tax purposes in periods of (a) rising prices and (b) declining prices.

PR 7-6A Lower-of-cost-or-market inventory OBJ. 6

✔ Total LCM, $39,873

Data on the physical inventory of Ashwood Products Company as of December 31 follow:

Inventory Item	Inventory Quantity	Market Value per Unit (Net Realizable Value)
B12	38	$57
E41	18	180
G19	33	126
L88	18	550
N94	400	7
P24	90	18
R66	8	250
T33	140	20
Z16	15	752

Quantity and cost data from the last purchases invoice of the year and the next-to-the-last purchases invoice are summarized as follows:

Inventory Item	Last Purchases Invoice Quantity Purchased	Unit Cost	Next-to-the-Last Purchases Invoice Quantity Purchased	Unit Cost
B12	30	$60	30	$59
E41	35	178	20	180
G19	20	128	25	129
L88	10	563	10	560
N94	500	8	500	7
P24	80	22	50	21
R66	5	248	4	260
T33	100	21	100	19
Z16	10	750	9	745

Instructions

Determine the inventory at cost as well as at the lower of cost or market, using the first-in, first-out method. Record the appropriate unit costs on the inventory sheet and complete the pricing of the inventory. When there are two different unit costs applicable to an item, proceed as follows:

1. Draw a line through the quantity and insert the quantity and unit cost of the last purchase.
2. On the following line, insert the quantity and unit cost of the next-to-the-last purchase.
3. Total the cost and market columns and insert the lower of the two totals in the Lower of C or M column. The first item on the inventory sheet has been completed as an example.

Inventory Sheet
December 31

Inventory Item	Inventory Quantity	Cost per Unit	Market Value per Unit (Net Realizable Value)	Total Cost	Total Market	Lower of C or M
B12	~~38~~ 30	$60	$57	$1,800	$1,710	
	8	59	57	472	456	
				$2,272	$2,166	$2,166

Appendix

PR 7-7A Retail method; gross profit method

✔ 1. $483,600

Selected data on merchandise inventory, purchases, and sales for Celebrity Tan Co. and Ranchworks Co. are as follows:

	Cost	Retail
Celebrity Tan		
Merchandise inventory, August 1	$ 300,000	$ 575,000
Transactions during August:		
Purchases (net)	2,149,000	3,375,000
Sales		3,170,000
Ranchworks Co.		
Merchandise inventory, March 1	$ 880,000	
Transactions during March through November:		
Purchases (net)	9,500,000	
Sales	15,800,000	
Estimated gross profit rate	38%	

Instructions

1. Determine the estimated cost of the merchandise inventory of Celebrity Tan Co. on August 31 by the retail method, presenting details of the computations.
2. a. Estimate the cost of the merchandise inventory of Ranchworks Co. on November 30 by the gross profit method, presenting details of the computations.
   b. Assume that Ranchworks Co. took a physical inventory on November 30 and discovered that $369,750 of merchandise was on hand. What was the estimated loss of inventory due to theft or damage during March through November?

Problems: Series B

✔ 3. $214,474

PR 7-1B   FIFO perpetual inventory   OBJ. 2, 3

The beginning inventory of merchandise at Dunne Co. and data on purchases and sales for a three-month period ending June 30 are as follows:

Date		Transaction	Number of Units	Per Unit	Total
Apr.	3	Inventory	25	$1,200	$ 30,000
	8	Purchase	75	1,240	93,000
	11	Sale	40	2,000	80,000
	30	Sale	30	2,000	60,000
May	8	Purchase	60	1,260	75,600
	10	Sale	50	2,000	100,000
	19	Sale	20	2,000	40,000
	28	Purchase	80	1,260	100,800
June	5	Sale	40	2,250	90,000
	16	Sale	25	2,250	56,250
	21	Purchase	35	1,264	44,240
	28	Sale	44	2,250	99,000

Instructions

1. Record the inventory, purchases, and cost of merchandise sold data in a perpetual inventory record similar to the one illustrated in Exhibit 3, using the first-in, first-out method.
2. Determine the total sales and the total cost of merchandise sold for the period. Journalize the entries in the sales and cost of merchandise sold accounts. Assume that all sales were on account.
3. Determine the gross profit from sales for the period.
4. Determine the ending inventory cost on June 30.
5. Based upon the preceding data, would you expect the inventory using the last-in, first-out method to be higher or lower?

✔ 2. Gross profit, $213,170

PR 7-2B   LIFO perpetual inventory   OBJ. 2, 3

The beginning inventory for Dunne Co. and data on purchases and sales for a three-month period are shown in Problem 7-1B.

Instructions

1. Record the inventory, purchases, and cost of merchandise sold data in a perpetual inventory record similar to the one illustrated in Exhibit 4, using the last-in, first-out method.
2. Determine the total sales, the total cost of merchandise sold, and the gross profit from sales for the period.
3. Determine the ending inventory cost on June 30.

✔ 2. Gross profit, $214,396

PR 7-3B   Weighted average cost method with perpetual inventory   OBJ. 2, 3

The beginning inventory for Dunne Co. and data on purchases and sales for a three-month period are shown in Problem 7-1B.

Instructions

1. Record the inventory, purchases, and cost of merchandise sold data in a perpetual inventory record similar to the one illustrated in Exhibit 5, using the weighted average cost method.

2. Determine the total sales, the total cost of merchandise sold, and the gross profit from sales for the period.

3. Determine the ending inventory cost on June 30.

PR 7-4B Periodic inventory by three methods OBJ. 2, 3

✓ 2. Inventory, $31,240

The beginning inventory for Dunne Co. and data on purchases and sales for a three-month period are shown in Problem 7-1B.

Instructions

1. Determine the inventory on June 30 and the cost of merchandise sold for the three-month period, using the first-in, first-out method and the periodic inventory system.
2. Determine the inventory on June 30 and the cost of merchandise sold for the three-month period, using the last-in, first-out method and the periodic inventory system.
3. Determine the inventory on June 30 and the cost of merchandise sold for the three-month period, using the weighted average cost method and the periodic inventory system. Round the weighted average unit cost to the dollar.
4. Compare the gross profit and June 30 inventories using the following column headings:

	FIFO	LIFO	Weighted Average
Sales			
Cost of merchandise sold			
Gross profit			
Inventory, June 30			

PR 7-5B Periodic inventory by three methods OBJ. 2, 4

✓ 1. $18,545

Excel

Pappa's Appliances uses the periodic inventory system. Details regarding the inventory of appliances at January 1, purchases invoices during the year, and the inventory count at December 31 are summarized as follows:

Model	Inventory, January 1	Purchases Invoices 1st	2nd	3rd	Inventory Count, December 31
C55	3 at $1,040	3 at $1,054	3 at $1,060	3 at $1,070	4
D11	9 at 639	7 at 645	6 at 666	6 at 675	11
F32	5 at 240	3 at 260	1 at 260	1 at 280	2
H29	6 at 305	3 at 310	3 at 316	4 at 317	4
K47	6 at 520	8 at 531	4 at 549	6 at 542	8
S33	—	4 at 222	4 at 232	—	2
X74	4 at 35	6 at 36	8 at 37	7 at 39	7

Instructions

1. Determine the cost of the inventory on December 31 by the first-in, first-out method. Present data in columnar form, using the following headings:

Model	Quantity	Unit Cost	Total Cost

If the inventory of a particular model comprises one entire purchase plus a portion of another purchase acquired at a different unit cost, use a separate line for each purchase.

2. Determine the cost of the inventory on December 31 by the last-in, first-out method, following the procedures indicated in (1).
3. Determine the cost of the inventory on December 31 by the weighted average cost method, using the columnar headings indicated in (1).
4. Discuss which method (FIFO or LIFO) would be preferred for income tax purposes in periods of (a) rising prices and (b) declining prices.

PR 7-6B Lower-of-cost-or-market inventory OBJ. 6

✓ Total LCM, $41,873

Data on the physical inventory of Katus Products Co. as of December 31 follow:

Inventory Item	Inventory Quantity	Market Value per Unit (Net Realizable Value)
A54	37	$ 56
C77	24	178
F66	30	132
H83	21	545
K12	375	5
Q58	90	18
S36	8	235
V97	140	20
Y88	17	744

Quantity and cost data from the last purchases invoice of the year and the next-to-the-last purchases invoice are summarized as follows:

	Last Purchases Invoice		Next-to-the-Last Purchases Invoice	
Inventory Item	Quantity Purchased	Unit Cost	Quantity Purchased	Unit Cost
A54	30	$ 60	40	$ 58
C77	25	174	15	180
F66	20	130	15	128
H83	6	547	15	540
K12	500	6	500	7
Q58	75	25	80	26
S36	5	256	4	260
V97	100	17	115	16
Y88	10	750	8	740

Instructions

Determine the inventory at cost as well as at the lower of cost or market, using the first-in, first-out method. Record the appropriate unit costs on the inventory sheet and complete the pricing of the inventory. When there are two different unit costs applicable to an item:

1. Draw a line through the quantity and insert the quantity and unit cost of the last purchase.
2. On the following line, insert the quantity and unit cost of the next-to-the-last purchase.
3. Total the cost and market columns and insert the lower of the two totals in the LCM column. The first item on the inventory sheet has been completed as an example.

Inventory Sheet
December 31

Inventory Item	Inventory Quantity	Cost per Unit	Market Value per Unit (Net Realizable Value)	Total Cost	Total Market	LCM
A54	~~37~~ 30	60	$56	$1,800	$1,680	
	7	58	56	406	392	
				$2,206	$2,072	$2,072

Appendix

PR 7-7B Retail method; gross profit method

✓ 1. $630,000

Selected data on merchandise inventory, purchases, and sales for Jaffe Co. and Coronado Co. are as follows:

	Cost	Retail
Jaffe Co.		
Merchandise inventory, February 1	$ 400,000	$ 615,000
Transactions during February:		
Purchases (net)	4,055,000	5,325,000
Sales		5,100,000

Coronado Co.

Merchandise inventory, May 1	$ 400,000
Transactions during May through October:	
Purchases (net)	3,150,000
Sales	4,750,000
Estimated gross profit rate	35%

Instructions

1. Determine the estimated cost of the merchandise inventory of Jaffe Co. on February 28 by the retail method, presenting details of the computations.

2. a. Estimate the cost of the merchandise inventory of Coronado Co. on October 31 by the gross profit method, presenting details of the computations.

    b. Assume that Coronado Co. took a physical inventory on October 31 and discovered that $366,500 of merchandise was on hand. What was the estimated loss of inventory due to theft or damage during May through October?

Cases & Projects

CP 7-1 Ethics in Action

Sizemo Elektroniks sells semiconductors that are used in games and small toys. The company has been extremely successful in recent years, recording an increase in earnings each of the past six quarters. At the end of the current quarter, Jay Shulz, the company's staff accountant, calculated the ending inventory for the semiconductors and was surprised to find that the quantity of the Hayden 537X model had not changed during the quarter. Jay confirmed his calculation with the inventory control manager, who indicated that sales of the Hayden 537X had stopped when the Hayden 637X semiconductor was released early in the quarter. Jay researched the issue further and found that the Hayden 637X semiconductor has the same applications as the Hayden 537X, but has more computing power and a lower cost than the 537X. Jay e-mailed this information to Tina Vereen, the chief financial officer, and recommended that the company apply the lower-of-cost-or-market method to the Hayden 537X semiconductors in inventory. Later that day, Tina e-mailed Jay back, instructing him not to apply the lower-of-cost-or-market method to the 537X inventory because "the company is under considerable pressure to maintain its track record of earnings growth, and a lower-of-cost-or-market adjustment would result in a significant decline in earnings this quarter." Reluctantly, Jay followed Tina's instructions.

Evaluate the decision not to apply the lower-of-cost-or-market method in the current quarter.

1. Who benefits from this decision?
2. Who is harmed by this decision?
3. Are Jay and Tina acting in an ethical manner? Explain.

CP 7-2 Ethics in Action

Anstead Co. is experiencing a decrease in sales and operating income for the fiscal year ending October 31. Ryan Frazier, controller of Anstead Co., has suggested that all orders received before the end of the fiscal year be shipped by midnight, October 31, even if the shipping department must work overtime. Because Anstead Co. ships all merchandise FOB shipping point, it would record all such shipments as sales for the year ending October 31, thereby offsetting some of the decreases in sales and operating income.

Discuss whether Ryan Frazier is behaving in a professional manner.

CP 7-3 Team Activity

In teams, select a public company in the merchandising industry that interests you. Obtain the company's most recent annual report on Form 10-K. The Form 10-K is a company's annually required filing with the Securities and Exchange Commission (SEC). It includes the company's financial statements and accompanying notes. The Form 10-K can be obtained either (a) by referring to the investor relations section of the company's website or (b) by using the company search feature of the SEC's EDGAR database service found at www.sec.gov/edgar/searchedgar/companysearch.html.

(Continued)

1. Based on the information in the company's most recent annual report, answer the following questions:

    a. What types of items are included in the company's inventory?
    b. What inventory costing method or methods does the company use to determine the inventory amount reported on its balance sheet?
    c. How much inventory does the company have at the end of the most recent year?
    d. What percentage of total current assets is inventory during the three years presented? Has this percentage increased, decreased, or remained the same during this period?
    e. How much cost of merchandise sold does the company report for the most recent year?

2. Using the information presented in the company's annual report, calculate the company's inventory turnover for the current and previous years. Based on this information, has the company's performance improved? Briefly explain your answer.

CP 7-4 Communication

Golden Eagle Company began operations on April 1 by selling a single product. Data on purchases and sales for the year are as follows:

Purchases:

Date	Units Purchased	Unit Cost	Total Cost
April 6	31,000	$36.60	$1,134,600
May 18	33,000	39.00	1,287,000
June 6	40,000	39.60	1,584,000
July 10	40,000	42.00	1,680,000
August 10	27,200	42.75	1,162,800
October 25	12,800	43.50	556,800
November 4	8,000	44.85	358,800
December 10	8,000	48.00	384,000
	200,000		$8,148,000

Sales:

April	16,000 units
May	16,000
June	20,000
July	24,000
August	28,000
September	28,000
October	18,000
November	10,000
December	8,000
Total units	168,000
Total sales	$10,000,000

The president of the company, Connie Kilmer, has asked for your advice on which inventory cost flow method should be used for the 32,000-unit physical inventory that was taken on December 31. The company plans to expand its product line in the future and uses the periodic inventory system.

Write a brief memo to Ms. Kilmer comparing and contrasting the LIFO and FIFO inventory cost flow methods and their potential impacts on the company's financial statements.

CP 7-5 LIFO and inventory flow

The following is an excerpt from a conversation between Paula Marlo, the warehouse manager for Musick Foods Wholesale Co., and its accountant, Mike Hayes. Musick Foods operates a large regional warehouse that supplies produce and other grocery products to grocery stores in smaller communities.

Paula: Mike, can you explain what's going on here with these monthly statements?

Mike: Sure, Paula. How can I help you?

Paula: I don't understand this last-in, first-out inventory procedure. It just doesn't make sense.

Mike: Well, what it means is that we assume that the last goods we receive are the first ones sold. So the inventory consists of the items we purchased first.

Paula: Yes, but that's my problem. It doesn't work that way! We always distribute the oldest produce first. Some of that produce is perishable! We can't keep any of it very long or it'll spoil.

Mike: Paula, you don't understand. We only *assume* that the products we distribute are the last ones received. We don't actually have to distribute the goods in this way.

Paula: I always thought that accounting was supposed to show what really happened. It all sounds like "make believe" to me! Why not report what really happens?

Respond to Paula's concerns.

CP 7-6 Comparing inventory ratios for two companies

Target Corp. sells merchandise primarily through its retail stores. On the other hand, **Amazon.com** uses its e-commerce services, features, and technologies to sell its products through the Internet. Recent balance sheet inventory disclosures for Target and Amazon.com (in millions) are as follows:

	Target	Amazon.com
Cost of merchandise sold	$51,997	$71,651
Inventory, end of year	8,601	10,243
Inventory, beginning of year	8,282	8,299

a. Determine the inventory turnover for Target and Amazon.com. Round to two decimal places.

b. Determine the days' sales in inventory for Target and Amazon.com. Use 365 days and round to one decimal place.

c. Interpret your results.

CP 7-7 Comparing inventory ratios for three companies

The general merchandise retail industry has a number of segments represented by the following companies:

Company Name	Merchandise Concept
Costco Wholesale Corporation	Membership warehouse
Wal-Mart	Discount general merchandise
JCPenney Company	Department store

For a recent year, the following cost of merchandise sold and beginning and ending inventories have been provided from corporate annual reports (in millions) for these three companies:

	Costco	Wal-Mart	JCPenney
Cost of merchandise sold	$101,065	$365,086	$8,074
Merchandise inventory, beginning	8,908	45,141	2,721
Merchandise inventory, ending	8,456	44,858	2,652

a. Determine the inventory turnover ratio for all three companies. Round to two decimal places.

b. Determine the days' sales in inventory for all three companies. Use 365 days and round to one decimal place.

c. Interpret these results based on each company's merchandise concept.

CHAPTER 8

Internal Control and Cash

Chapters 1–4
Accounting Cycle

Chapter 5
Accounting Systems

| Income Statement | Statement of Owner's Equity | Balance Sheet | Statement of Cash Flows |

Chapter 6 *Accounting for Merchandising Businesses*

Chapter 16 *Cash Flows*

| Assets | = | Liabilities | + | Owner's Equity |

Chapter 8 *Cash*
Chapter 9 *Receivables*
Chapter 7 *Inventories*
Chapter 10 *Fixed and Intangible Assets*
Chapter 15 *Investments*

Chapter 11 *Current Liabilities*
Chapter 14 *Bonds and Notes*

Chapter 12 *Partnerships*
Chapter 13 *Corporations*

Chapter 17
Financial Statement Analysis

Statement of Owner's Equity

Owner's capital, Jan. 1		$XXX
Net income	$ XXX	
Withdrawals	(XXX)	
Increase in capital		XXX

Statement of Cash Flows

Cash flows from (used in) operating activities	$XXX
Cash flows from (used in) investing activities	XXX
Cash flows from (used in) financing activities	XXX
Increase (decrease) in cash flows	$XXX
	XXX
	$XXX

Income Statement

Sales		$XXX
Cost of merchandise sold		XXX
Gross profit		$XXX
Operating expenses:		
Advertising expense	$XXX	
Depreciation expense	XXX	
Amortization expense	XXX	
Depletion expense	XXX	
…	XXX	
…	XXX	
Total operating expenses		XXX
Income from operations		$XXX
Other revenue and expenses		XXX
Net income		$XXX

Balance Sheet

Current assets:		
Cash	$XXX	
Accounts receivable	XXX	
Merchandise inventory	XXX	
Total current assets		$XXX
Property, plant, and equipment	$XXX	
Intangible assets	XXX	
Total long-term assets		XXX
Total assets		$XXX
Liabilities:		
Current liabilities	$XXX	
Long-term liabilities	XXX	
Total liabilities		$XXX
Owner's equity		XXX
Total liabilities and owner's equity		$XXX

CHAPTER 8

eBay Inc.

Controls are a part of your everyday life. At one extreme, laws are used to limit your behavior. For example, speed limits are designed to control your driving for traffic safety. In addition, you may use many nonlegal controls. For example, you can keep credit card receipts in order to compare your transactions to the monthly credit card statement. Comparing receipts to the monthly statement is a control designed to catch mistakes made by the credit card company. In addition, banks give you a personal identification number (PIN) as a control against unauthorized access to your cash if you lose your automated teller machine (ATM) card. Dairies (milk producers) use freshness dating on their milk containers as a control to prevent the purchase or sale of soured milk. As you can see, you use and encounter controls every day.

Just as there are many examples of controls throughout society, businesses must also implement controls to help guide the behavior of their managers, employees, and customers. For example, **eBay Inc.** maintains an Internet-based marketplace for the sale of goods and services. Using eBay's online platform, buyers and sellers can browse, buy, and sell a wide variety of items including antiques and used cars. However, in order to maintain the integrity and trust of its buyers and sellers, eBay must have controls to ensure that buyers pay for their items and sellers don't misrepresent their items or fail to deliver sales. One such control eBay uses is a feedback forum that establishes buyers' and sellers' reputations. A prospective buyer or seller can view the member's reputation and feedback comments before completing a transaction. Dishonest or unfair trading can lead to a negative reputation and even suspension or cancellation of the member's ability to trade on eBay.

This chapter discusses controls that can be included in accounting systems to provide reasonable assurance that the financial statements are reliable. Controls to discover and prevent errors to a bank account are also discussed. This chapter begins by discussing the Sarbanes-Oxley Act and its impact on controls and financial reporting.

Learning Objectives

After studying this chapter, you should be able to:

Example Exercises (EE) are shown in **green**.

Obj. 1 Describe the Sarbanes-Oxley Act and its impact on internal controls and financial reporting.
- Sarbanes-Oxley Act

Obj. 2 Describe and illustrate the objectives and elements of internal control.
- Internal Control
- Objectives of Internal Control
- Elements of Internal Control
- Control Environment — EE 8-1
- Risk Assessment — EE 8-1
- Control Procedures — EE 8-1
- Monitoring — EE 8-1
- Information and Communication — EE 8-1
- Limitations of Internal Control

Obj. 3 Describe and illustrate the application of internal controls to cash.
- Cash Controls over Receipts and Payments
- Control of Cash Receipts
- Control of Cash Payments

Obj. 4 Describe the nature of a bank account and its use in controlling cash.
- Bank Accounts
- Bank Statement — EE 8-2
- Using the Bank Statement as a Control over Cash

Obj. 5 Describe and illustrate the use of a bank reconciliation in controlling cash.
- Bank Reconciliation
- Adjusted Balance and Entries — EE 8-3

Obj. 6 Describe the accounting for special-purpose cash funds.
- Special-Purpose Cash Funds
- Petty Cash Fund — EE 8-4

Obj. 7 Describe and illustrate the reporting of cash and cash equivalents in the financial statements.
- Financial Statement Reporting of Cash

Obj. 8 Describe and illustrate the use of the ratio of cash to monthly cash expenses to assess the ability of a company to continue in business.
- Financial Analysis and Interpretation: Ratio of Cash to Monthly Cash Expenses
- Compute Ratio of Cash to Monthly Cash Expenses — EE 8-5

At a Glance 8 — Page 418

Obj. 1 Describe the Sarbanes-Oxley Act and its impact on internal controls and financial reporting.

Sarbanes-Oxley Act

The **Sarbanes-Oxley Act** is one of the most important laws affecting U.S. companies in recent history. The purpose of Sarbanes-Oxley is to foster public confidence and trust in the financial reporting of companies. In addition, Sarbanes-Oxley is designed to prevent fraud, theft, and financial scandals.

Sarbanes-Oxley applies only to companies whose stock is traded on public exchanges, referred to as *publicly held companies*. However, Sarbanes-Oxley highlighted the importance of assessing the financial controls and reporting of all companies. As a result, companies of all sizes have been influenced by Sarbanes-Oxley.

Sarbanes-Oxley emphasizes the importance of effective internal control.[1] **Internal control** is defined as the procedures and processes used by a company to:

- Safeguard its assets.
- Process information accurately.
- Ensure compliance with laws and regulations.

Sarbanes-Oxley requires companies to maintain effective internal controls over the recording of transactions and the preparing of financial statements. Such controls

---

[1] Sarbanes-Oxley also has important implications for corporate governance and the regulation of the public accounting profession. This chapter, however, focuses on the internal control implications of Sarbanes-Oxley.

are important because they deter fraud and prevent misleading financial statements as shown in Exhibit 1.

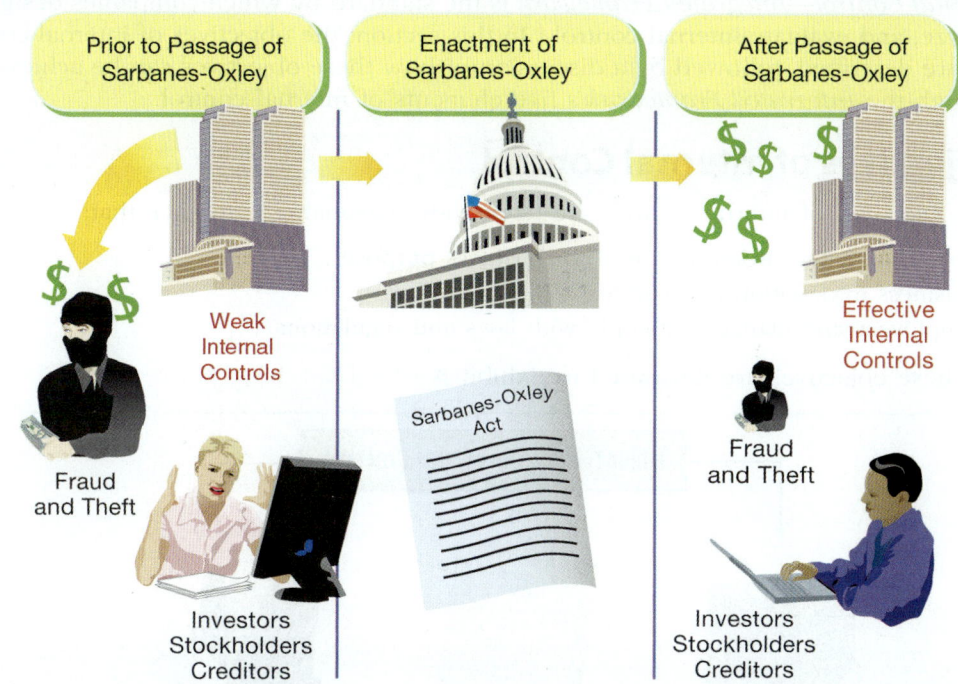

EXHIBIT 1

Effect of Sarbanes-Oxley

Sarbanes-Oxley also requires companies and their independent accountants to report on the effectiveness of the company's internal controls.[2] These reports are required to be filed with the company's annual 10-K report with the Securities and Exchange Commission. Companies are also encouraged to include these reports in their annual reports to stockholders. An example of such a report by the management of eBay is shown in Exhibit 2.

Link to eBay

Exhibit 2 is taken from the annual (10-K) report of **eBay**.

Management's Annual Report on Internal Control Over Financial Reporting

Our management is responsible for establishing and maintaining adequate internal control over financial reporting. Our management, including our principal executive officer and principal financial officer, conducted an evaluation of the effectiveness of our internal control over financial reporting based on the framework in *Internal Control—Integrated Framework (2013)* issued by the Committee of Sponsoring Organizations of the Treadway Commission. Based on its evaluation under the framework in *Internal Control—Integrated Framework*, our management concluded that our internal control over financial reporting was effective as of December 31, . . .

Source: eBay Inc., *Form 10-K for the Fiscal Year Ended December 31, 2015*.

EXHIBIT 2

eBay's Report of Compliance with Sarbanes-Oxley

Exhibit 2 indicates that the evaluation of internal controls is based on *Internal Control—Integrated Framework*, which was issued by the Committee of Sponsoring Organizations (COSO) of the Treadway Commission. This framework is the standard by which companies design, analyze, and evaluate internal controls. For this reason, this framework is used as the basis for discussing internal controls.[3]

---

2 These reporting requirements are required under Section 404 of the act. As a result, these requirements and reports are often referred to as 404 requirements and 404 reports.
3 Information on *Internal Control—Integrated Framework* can be found on COSO's website at www.coso.org/.

Obj. 2 Describe and illustrate the objectives and elements of internal control.

Internal Control

Internal Control—Integrated Framework is the standard by which companies design, analyze, and evaluate internal control.[4] In this section, the objectives of internal control are described, followed by a discussion of how these objectives can be achieved through the *Integrated Framework's* five elements of internal control.

Objectives of Internal Control

The objectives of internal control are to provide reasonable assurance that:

- Assets are safeguarded and used for business purposes.
- Business information is accurate.
- Employees and managers comply with laws and regulations.

These objectives are illustrated in Exhibit 3.

EXHIBIT 3
Objectives of Internal Control

Internal control can safeguard assets by preventing theft, fraud, misuse, or misplacement. A serious concern of internal control is preventing employee fraud. **Employee fraud** is the intentional act of deceiving an employer for personal gain. Such fraud may range from minor overstating of a travel expense report to stealing millions of dollars. Employees stealing from a business often adjust the accounting records in order to hide their fraud. Thus, employee fraud usually affects the accuracy of business information.

Accurate information is necessary to operate a business successfully. Businesses must also comply with laws, regulations, and financial reporting standards. Examples of such standards include environmental regulations, safety regulations, and generally accepted accounting principles (GAAP).

Business Connection

EMPLOYEE FRAUD

The Association of Fraud Examiners estimates that 5% of annual revenues worldwide, or more than $3.5 trillion, is lost to employee fraud. A common cash receipts employee fraud can occur when employees accept cash payments from customers, do not record the sale, and then pocket the cash. A common cash payments employee fraud can occur when employees bill their employer for false services or personal items.

Source: *2014 Report to the Nation on Occupational Fraud and Abuse*, Association of Fraud Examiners.

Elements of Internal Control

The three internal control objectives can be achieved by applying the five **elements of internal control** set forth by the *Integrated Framework*.[5] These elements are as follows:

[4] *Internal Control—Integrated Framework* by the Committee of Sponsoring Organizations of the Treadway Commission, 2013.
[5] Ibid., pp. 12–14.

- Control environment
- Risk assessment
- Control procedures
- Monitoring
- Information and communication

The elements of internal control are illustrated in Exhibit 4.

EXHIBIT 4

Elements of Internal Control

In Exhibit 4, the elements of internal control form an umbrella over the business to protect it from control threats. The control environment is the size of the umbrella. Risk assessment, control procedures, and monitoring are the fabric of the umbrella, which keep it from leaking. Information and communication connect the umbrella to management.

Link to eBay

As technology changes, **eBay** must continually monitor and strengthen its controls over e-commerce transactions.

Control Environment

The **control environment** is the overall attitude of management and employees about the importance of controls. Three factors influencing a company's control environment include the following, as shown in Exhibit 5:

- Management's philosophy and operating style
- The company's organizational structure
- The company's personnel policies

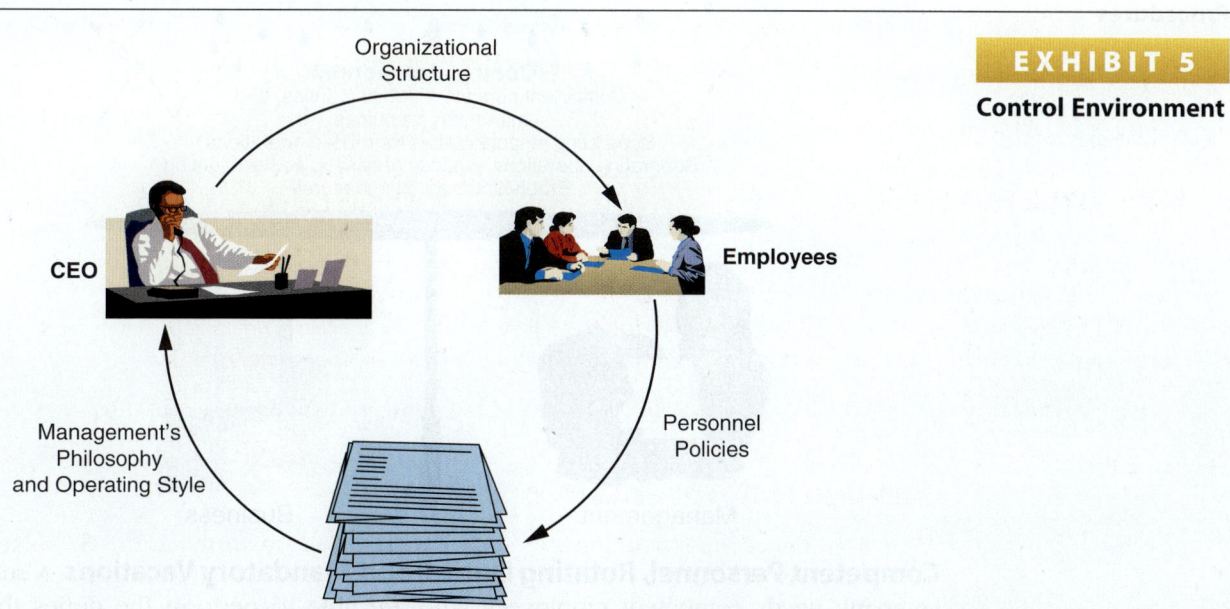

EXHIBIT 5

Control Environment

Management's philosophy and operating style relate to whether management emphasizes the importance of internal controls. An emphasis on controls and adherence to control policies creates an effective control environment. In contrast, overemphasizing operating goals and tolerating deviations from control policies creates an ineffective control environment.

The business's organizational structure is the framework for planning and controlling operations. For example, a retail store chain might organize each of its stores as separate business units. Each store manager has full authority over pricing and other operating activities. In such a structure, each store manager has the responsibility for establishing an effective control environment.

The business's personnel policies involve the hiring, training, evaluation, compensation, and promotion of employees. In addition, job descriptions, employee codes of ethics, and conflict-of-interest policies are part of the personnel policies. Such policies can enhance the internal control environment if they provide reasonable assurance that only competent, honest employees are hired and retained.

Risk Assessment

All businesses face risks such as changes in customer requirements, competitive threats, regulatory changes, and changes in economic factors. Management should identify such risks, analyze their significance, assess their likelihood of occurring, and take any necessary actions to minimize them.

Control Procedures

Control procedures provide reasonable assurance that business goals will be achieved, including the prevention of fraud. Control procedures, which constitute one of the most important elements of internal control, include the following as shown in Exhibit 6:

- Competent personnel, rotating duties, and mandatory vacations
- Separating responsibilities for related operations
- Separating operations, custody of assets, and accounting
- Proofs and security measures

EXHIBIT 6

Internal Control Procedures

Competent Personnel, Rotating Duties, and Mandatory Vacations A successful company needs competent employees who are able to perform the duties that they are assigned. Procedures should be established for properly training and supervising employees. It is also advisable to rotate duties of accounting personnel and mandate vacations for all employees. In this way, employees are encouraged to adhere to procedures. Cases of employee fraud are often discovered when a long-term employee, who never took vacations, missed work because of an illness or another unavoidable reason.

Separating Responsibilities for Related Operations The responsibility for related operations should be divided among two or more people. This decreases the possibility of errors and fraud. For example, if the same person orders supplies, verifies the receipt of the supplies, and pays the supplier, the following abuses may occur:

- Orders may be placed on the basis of friendship with a supplier rather than on price, quality, and other objective factors.
- The quantity and quality of supplies received may not be verified; thus, the company may pay for supplies that are not received or that are of poor quality.
- Supplies may be stolen by the employee.
- The validity and accuracy of invoices may not be verified; hence, the company may pay false or inaccurate invoices.

For the preceding reasons, the responsibilities for purchasing, receiving, and paying for supplies should be divided among three persons or departments.

Separating Operations, Custody of Assets, and Accounting The responsibilities for operations, custody of assets, and accounting should be separated. In this way, the accounting records serve as an independent check on the operating managers and the employees who have custody of assets.

To illustrate, employees who handle cash receipts should not record cash receipts in the accounting records. To do so would allow employees to borrow or steal cash and hide the theft in the accounting records. Likewise, operating managers should not record the results of operations. To do so would allow the managers to distort the accounting reports to show favorable results, which might allow them to receive larger bonuses.

Proofs and Security Measures Proofs and security measures are used to safeguard assets and ensure reliable accounting data. Proofs involve procedures such as authorization, approval, and reconciliation. For example, an employee planning to travel on company business may be required to complete a "travel request" form for a manager's authorization and approval.

INTEGRITY, OBJECTIVITY, AND ETHICS IN BUSINESS

TIPS ON PREVENTING EMPLOYEE FRAUD IN SMALL COMPANIES

- Do not have the same employee write company checks and keep the books. Look for payments to vendors you don't know or payments to vendors whose names appear to be misspelled.
- If your business has a computer system, restrict access to accounting files as much as possible. Also, keep a backup copy of your accounting files and store it at an off-site location.
- Be wary of anybody working in finance who declines to take vacations. They may be afraid that a replacement will uncover fraud.
- Require and monitor supporting documentation (such as vendor invoices) before signing checks.
- Track the number of credit card bills you sign monthly.
- Limit and monitor access to important documents and supplies, such as blank checks and signature stamps.
- Check W-2 forms against your payroll annually to make sure you're not carrying any fictitious employees.
- Rely on yourself, not on your accountant, to spot fraud.

Source: Steve Kaufman, "Embezzlement Common at Small Companies," Knight-Ridder Newspapers, reported in *Athens Daily News/Athens Banner-Herald,* March 10, 1996, p. 4D.

Documents used for authorization and approval should be prenumbered, accounted for, and safeguarded. Prenumbering of documents helps prevent transactions from being recorded more than once or not at all. In addition, accounting for and safeguarding prenumbered documents helps prevent fraudulent transactions from being recorded. For example, blank checks are prenumbered and safeguarded. Once a payment has been properly authorized and approved, the checks are filled out and issued.

Reconciliations are also an important control. Later in this chapter, the use of bank reconciliations as an aid in controlling cash is described and illustrated.

Security measures involve measures to safeguard assets. For example, cash on hand should be kept in a cash register or safe. Inventory not on display should be stored in a locked storeroom or warehouse. Accounting records such as the accounts receivable subsidiary ledger should also be safeguarded to prevent their loss. For example, electronically maintained accounting records should be safeguarded with access codes and backed up so that any lost or damaged files could be recovered if necessary.

Monitoring

Monitoring the internal control system is used to locate weaknesses and improve controls. Monitoring often includes observing employee behavior and the accounting system for indicators of control problems. Some such indicators are shown in Exhibit 7.[6]

EXHIBIT 7

Warning Signs of Internal Control Problems

Warning signs with regard to people

- Abrupt change in lifestyle (without winning the lottery).
- Close social relationships with suppliers.
- Refusing to take a vacation.
- Frequent borrowing from other employees.
- Excessive use of alcohol or drugs.

Warning signs from the accounting system

- Missing documents or gaps in transaction numbers (could mean documents are being used for fraudulent transactions).
- An unusual increase in customer refunds (refunds may be phony).
- Differences between daily cash receipts and bank deposits (could mean receipts are being pocketed before being deposited).
- Sudden increase in slow payments (employee may be pocketing the payments).
- Backlog in recording transactions (possibly an attempt to delay detection of fraud).

Evaluations of controls are often performed when there are major changes in strategy, senior management, business structure, or operations. Internal auditors, who are independent of operations, usually perform such evaluations. Internal auditors are also responsible for day-to-day monitoring of controls. External auditors also evaluate and report on internal control as part of their annual financial statement audit.

Link to eBay
eBay reduces fraudulent activities by restricting or suspending buyers and sellers with questionable transaction histories.

Information and Communication

Information and communication is an essential element of internal control. Information about the control environment, risk assessment, control procedures, and monitoring is used by management for guiding operations and ensuring compliance with reporting, legal, and regulatory requirements. Management also uses external information to assess events and conditions that impact decision making and external reporting. For example, management uses pronouncements of the Financial Accounting Standards Board (FASB) to assess the impact of changes in reporting standards on the financial statements.

---

6 Edwin C. Bliss, "Employee Theft," *Boardroom Reports*, July 15, 1994, pp. 5–6.

> **Example Exercise 8-1 Internal Control Elements**   *Obj. 2*
>
> Identify each of the following as relating to (a) the control environment, (b) risk assessment, or (c) control procedures:
> 1. Mandatory vacations
> 2. Personnel policies
> 3. Report of outside consultants on future market changes
>
> **Follow My Example 8-1**
>
> 1. (c) control procedures
> 2. (a) the control environment
> 3. (b) risk assessment
>
> Practice Exercises: PE 8-1A, PE 8-1B

Limitations of Internal Control

Internal control systems can provide only reasonable assurance for safeguarding assets, processing accurate information, and complying with laws and regulations. In other words, internal controls are not a guarantee. This is due to the following factors:

- The human element of controls
- Cost-benefit considerations

The *human element* recognizes that controls are applied and used by humans. As a result, human errors can occur because of fatigue, carelessness, confusion, or misjudgment. For example, an employee may unintentionally shortchange a customer or miscount the amount of inventory received from a supplier. In addition, two or more employees may collude to defeat or circumvent internal controls. This latter case often involves fraud and the theft of assets. For example, the cashier and the accounts receivable clerk might collude to steal customer payments on account.

Cost-benefit considerations recognize that the cost of internal controls should not exceed their benefits. For example, retail stores could eliminate shoplifting by searching all customers before they leave the store. However, such a control procedure would upset customers and result in lost sales. Instead, retailers use cameras or signs saying, *"We prosecute all shoplifters."*

> **Link to eBay**
> The auditor's report for **eBay** includes this statement: "…internal control over financial reporting is a process designed to provide reasonable assurance regarding the reliability of financial reporting…"

Cash Controls over Receipts and Payments

Obj. 3 Describe and illustrate the application of internal controls to cash.

Cash includes coins, currency (paper money), checks, and money orders. Money on deposit with a bank or another financial institution that is available for withdrawal is also considered cash. Normally, you can think of cash as anything that a bank would accept for deposit in your account. For example, a check made payable to you could normally be deposited in a bank and, thus, is considered cash.

Businesses usually have several bank accounts. For example, a business might have one bank account for general cash payments and another for payroll. A separate ledger account is normally used for each bank account. For example, a bank account at City Bank could be identified in the ledger as *Cash in Bank—City Bank*. To simplify, this chapter assumes that a company has only *one* bank account, which is identified in the ledger as *Cash*.

Cash is the asset most likely to be stolen or used improperly in a business. For this reason, businesses must carefully control cash and cash transactions.

Control of Cash Receipts

To protect cash from theft and misuse, a business must control cash from the time it is received until it is deposited in a bank. Businesses normally receive cash from two main sources.

- Customers purchasing products or services
- Customers making payments on account

Cash Received from Cash Sales
An important control used to protect cash received in over-the-counter sales is a cash register. The use of a cash register to control cash is shown in Exhibit 8.

EXHIBIT 8

Cash Register as a Control

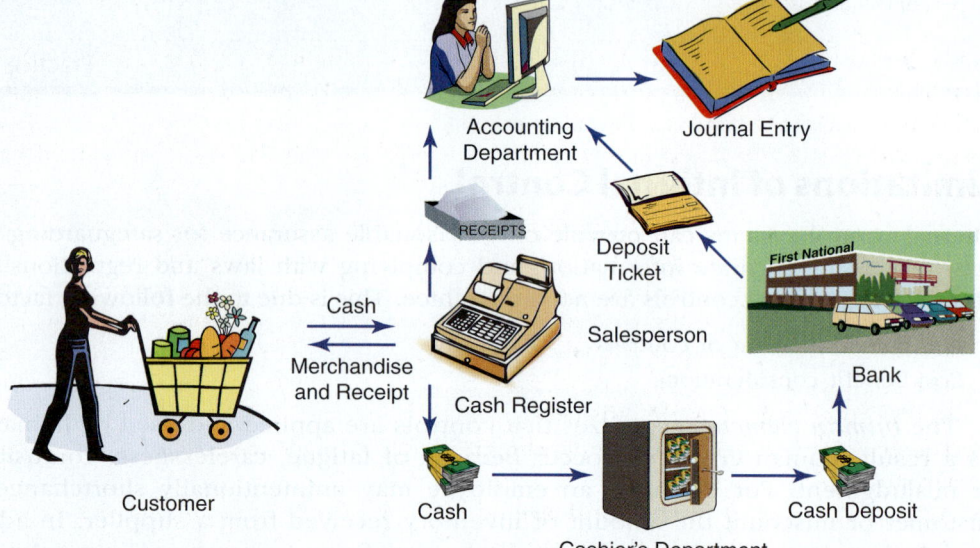

A cash register controls cash as follows:

1. At the beginning of every work shift, each cash register clerk is given a cash drawer containing a predetermined amount of cash. This amount is used for making change for customers and is sometimes called a *change fund*.
2. When a salesperson enters the amount of a sale, the cash register displays the amount to the customer. This allows the customer to verify that the clerk has charged the correct amount. The customer also receives a cash receipt.
3. At the end of the shift, the clerk and the supervisor count the cash in the clerk's cash drawer. The amount of cash in each drawer should equal the beginning amount of cash plus the cash sales for the day.
4. The supervisor takes the cash to the Cashier's Department where it is placed in a safe.
5. The supervisor forwards the clerk's cash register receipts to the Accounting Department.
6. The cashier prepares a bank deposit ticket.
7. The cashier deposits the cash in the bank, or the cash is picked up by an armored car service, such as **Wells Fargo**.
8. The Accounting Department summarizes the cash receipts and records the day's cash sales.
9. When cash is deposited in the bank, the bank normally stamps a duplicate copy of the deposit ticket with the amount received. This bank receipt is returned to the Accounting Department, where it is compared to the total amount that should have been deposited. This control helps ensure that all the cash is deposited and that no cash is lost or stolen on the way to the bank. Any shortages are thus promptly detected.

Salespersons may make errors in making change for customers or in ringing up cash sales. As a result, the amount of cash on hand may differ from the amount of cash sales. Such differences are recorded in a **cash short and over account**.

To illustrate, assume the following cash register data for May 3:

Cash register total for cash sales	$35,690
Cash receipts from cash sales	35,668

The cash sales, receipts, and shortage of $22 ($35,690 − $35,668) would be recorded as follows:

May	3	Cash	35,668	
		Cash Short and Over	22	
		Sales		35,690

If there had been cash over, Cash Short and Over would have been credited for the overage. At the end of the accounting period, a debit balance in Cash Short and Over is included in miscellaneous expense on the income statement. A credit balance is included in the Other revenue section. If a salesperson consistently has large cash short and over amounts, the supervisor may require the clerk to take additional training.

Cash Received in the Mail Cash is received in the mail when customers pay their bills. This cash is usually in the form of checks and money orders. Most companies design their invoices so that customers return a portion of the invoice, called a *remittance advice*, with their payment. Remittance advices may be used to control cash received in the mail as follows:

1. An employee opens the incoming mail and compares the amount of cash received with the amount shown on the remittance advice. If a customer does not return a remittance advice, the employee prepares one. The remittance advice serves as a record of the cash initially received. It also helps ensure that the posting to the customer's account is for the amount of cash received.
2. The employee opening the mail stamps checks and money orders "For Deposit Only" in the bank account of the business.
3. The remittance advices and their summary totals are delivered to the Accounting Department.
4. All cash and money orders are delivered to the Cashier's Department.
5. The cashier prepares a bank deposit ticket.
6. The cashier deposits the cash in the bank, or the cash is picked up by an armored car service, such as **Wells Fargo**.
7. An accounting clerk records the cash received and posts the amounts to the customer accounts.
8. When cash is deposited in the bank, the bank normally stamps a duplicate copy of the deposit ticket with the amount received. This bank receipt is returned to the Accounting Department, where it is compared to the total amount that should have been deposited. This control helps ensure that all cash is deposited and that no cash is lost or stolen on the way to the bank. Any shortages are thus promptly detected.

Separating the duties of the Cashier's Department, which handles cash, and the Accounting Department, which records cash, is a control. If Accounting Department employees both handle and record cash, an employee could steal cash and change the accounting records to hide the theft.

Cash Received by EFT Cash may also be received from customers through **electronic funds transfer (EFT)**. For example, customers may authorize automatic electronic transfers from their checking accounts to pay monthly bills for such items as cell phone, Internet, and electric services. In such cases, the company sends the customer's bank a signed form from the customer authorizing the monthly electronic transfers. Each month, the company notifies the customer's bank of the amount of the transfer and the date the transfer should take place. On the due date, the company records the electronic transfer as a receipt of cash to its bank account and posts the amount paid to the customer's account.

Companies encourage customers to use EFT for the following reasons:

- EFTs cost less than receiving cash payments through the mail.
- EFTs enhance internal controls over cash, since the cash is received directly by the bank without any employees handling cash.
- EFTs reduce late payments from customers and speed up the processing of cash receipts.

Howard Schultz & Associates (HS&A) specializes in reviewing cash payments for its clients. HS&A searches for errors such as duplicate payments, failure to take discounts, and inaccurate computations. Amounts recovered for clients range from thousands to millions of dollars.

Control of Cash Payments

The control of cash payments should provide reasonable assurance that:

- Payments are made only for authorized transactions.
- Cash is used effectively and efficiently. For example, controls should ensure that all available purchase discounts are taken.

In a small business, an owner/manager may authorize payments based on personal knowledge. In a large business, however, purchasing goods, inspecting the goods received, and verifying the invoices are usually performed by different employees. These duties must be coordinated to ensure that proper payments are made to creditors. One system used for this purpose is the voucher system.

Voucher System A **voucher system** is a set of procedures for authorizing and recording liabilities and cash payments. A **voucher** is any document that serves as proof of authority to pay cash or issue an electronic funds transfer. An invoice that has been approved for payment could be considered a voucher. In many businesses, however, a voucher is a special form used to record data about a liability and the details of its payment.

In a manual system, a voucher is normally prepared after all necessary supporting documents have been received. For the purchase of goods, a voucher is supported by the supplier's invoice, a purchase order, and a receiving report. After a voucher is prepared, it is submitted for approval. Once approved, the voucher is recorded in the accounts and filed by due date. Upon payment, the voucher is recorded in the same manner as the payment of an account payable.

In a computerized system, data from the supporting documents (such as purchase orders, receiving reports, and suppliers' invoices) are entered directly into computer files. At the due date, the checks are automatically generated and mailed to creditors. At that time, the voucher is electronically transferred to a paid voucher file.

Cash Paid by EFT Cash can also be paid by electronic funds transfer (EFT) systems. For example, you can withdraw cash from your bank account using an ATM machine. Your withdrawal is a type of EFT transfer.

Companies also use EFT transfers. For example, many companies pay their employees via EFT. Under such a system, employees authorize the deposit of their payroll checks directly into their checking accounts. Each pay period, the company transfers the employees' net pay to their checking accounts through the use of EFT. Many companies also use EFT systems to pay their suppliers and other vendors.

Link to eBay

eBay purchased **PayPal**, which was developed to enable individuals and businesses to send and receive payments safely online. Because of new online payment systems such as Apple Pay™, eBay discontinued its PayPal operations in 2015 and established PayPal as a separate, publicly held company.

Business Connection

MOBILE PAYMENTS

A rapidly emerging method of payments using EFT is mobile payments, such as those made with Apple Pay™. With mobile payments, our phones become our wallets and our cash is transferred digitally from our bank accounts or credit cards.

Security is enhanced with fingerprint log-in to the smartphone. In this way, only the phone's owner can open the "wallet." Many of the internal control features required for managing cash payments are eliminated by this technology, much like EFT transactions. Moreover, even credit card slips are replaced by electronic authorizations and transactions. Internal controls are still required to verify that prices are accurate and goods are properly delivered for authenticated purchases.

Bank Accounts

Obj. 4 Describe the nature of a bank account and its use in controlling cash.

A major reason that companies use bank accounts is for internal control. Some of the control advantages of using bank accounts are as follows:

- Bank accounts reduce the amount of cash on hand.
- Bank accounts provide an independent recording of cash transactions. Reconciling the balance of the cash account in the company's records with the cash balance according to the bank is an important control.
- Use of bank accounts facilitates the transfer of funds using EFT systems.

Bank Statement

Banks usually maintain a record of all checking account transactions. A summary of all transactions, called a **bank statement**, is mailed, usually each month, to the company (depositor) or made available online. The bank statement shows the beginning balance, additions, deductions, and the ending balance. A typical bank statement is shown in Exhibit 9.

EXHIBIT 9 Bank Statement

```
                              MEMBER FDIC                                  PAGE   1
   VALLEY NATIONAL BANK                    ACCOUNT NUMBER   1627042
   OF LOS ANGELES
                                           FROM  6/30/20Y5 TO  7/31/20Y5
   LOS ANGELES, CA 90020-4253  (310)555-5151
                                           BALANCE                    4,218.60

                                        22 DEPOSITS                  13,749.75

                                        52 WITHDRAWALS               14,698.57
        POWER NETWORKING
        1000 Belkin Street               3 OTHER DEBITS
        Los Angeles, CA 90014-1000         AND CREDITS                  90.00CR

                                           NEW BALANCE                3,359.78
```

CHECKS AND OTHER DEBITS				DEPOSITS	DATE	BALANCE
No. 850	819.40	No. 852	122.54	585.75	07/01	3,862.41
No. 854	369.50	No. 853	20.15	421.53	07/02	3,894.29
No. 851	600.00	No. 856	190.70	781.30	07/03	3,884.89
No. 855	25.93	No. 857	52.50		07/04	3,806.46
No. 860	921.20	No. 858	160.00	662.50	07/05	3,387.76
No. 862	91.07	NSF	300.00	503.18	07/07	3,499.87
No. 880	32.26	No. 877	535.09	ACH 932.00	07/29	4,136.66
No. 881	21.10	No. 879	732.26	705.21	07/30	4,088.51
No. 882	126.20	SC	18.00	MS 408.00	07/30	4,352.31
No. 874	26.12	ACH	1,615.13	648.72	07/31	3,359.78

EC — ERROR CORRECTION   ACH — AUTOMATED CLEARING HOUSE
MS — MISCELLANEOUS
NSF — NOT SUFFICIENT FUNDS   SC — SERVICE CHARGE

THE RECONCILEMENT OF THIS STATEMENT WITH YOUR RECORDS IS ESSENTIAL.
ANY ERROR OR EXCEPTION SHOULD BE REPORTED IMMEDIATELY.

Checks or copies of the checks listed in the order they were paid by the bank may accompany the bank statement. If paid checks are returned, they are stamped "Paid," along with the date of payment. Many banks no longer return checks or check copies. Instead, the check payment information is available online.

The company's checking account balance *in the bank records* is a liability. Thus, in the bank's records, the company's account has a credit balance. Because the bank statement is prepared from the bank's point of view, a credit memo entry on the bank statement indicates an increase (a credit) to the company's account. Likewise, a debit memo entry on the bank statement indicates a decrease (a debit) in the company's account. This relationship is shown in Exhibit 10.

EXHIBIT 10

Checking Account: Company and Bank Perspectives

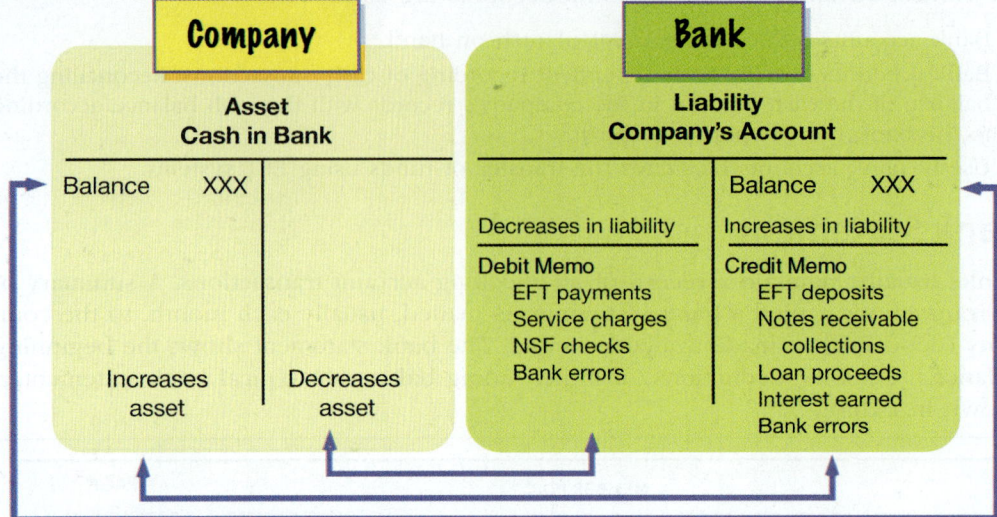

A bank makes credit entries (issues credit memos) for the following:

- Deposits made by electronic funds transfer (EFT)
- Collections of notes receivable for the company
- Proceeds for a loan made to the company by the bank
- Interest earned on the company's account
- Correction (if any) of bank errors

A bank makes debit entries (issues debit memos) for the following:

- Payments made by electronic funds transfer (EFT)
- Service charges
- Customer checks returned for not sufficient funds
- Correction (if any) of bank errors

Customers' checks returned for not sufficient funds, called *NSF checks*, are customer checks that were initially deposited but were not paid by the customer's bank. Because the company's bank credited the customer's check to the company's account when it was deposited, the bank debits the company's account (issues a debit memo) when the check is returned without payment.

The reason for a credit or debit memo entry is indicated on the bank statement. Exhibit 9 identifies the following types of credit and debit memo entries:

- EC: Error correction to correct bank error
- NSF: Not sufficient funds check
- SC: Service charge
- ACH: Automated clearing house entry for electronic funds transfer
- MS: Miscellaneous item such as collection of a note receivable on behalf of the company or receipt of a loan by the company from the bank

The preceding list includes the notation "ACH" for electronic funds transfers. ACH is a network for clearing electronic funds transfers among individuals, companies, and banks.[7] Because electronic funds transfers may be either deposits or payments, ACH entries may indicate either a debit or credit entry to the company's account. Likewise, entries to correct bank errors and miscellaneous items may indicate a debit or credit entry to the company's account.

---

7 For further information on ACH, go to www.nacha.org/. Click on "NACHA and the ACH Network" and then click on "ACH Network: How it Works."

Example Exercise 8-2 — Items on Company's Bank Statement — Obj. 4

The following items may appear on a bank statement:

1. NSF check
2. EFT deposit
3. Service charge
4. Bank correction of an error from recording a $400 check as $40

Using the following format, indicate whether the item would appear as a debit or credit memo on the bank statement and whether the item would increase or decrease the balance of the company's account:

Item No.	Appears on the Bank Statement as a Debit or Credit Memo	Increases or Decreases the Balance of the Company's Bank Account

Follow My Example 8-2

Item No.	Appears on the Bank Statement as a Debit or Credit Memo	Increases or Decreases the Balance of the Company's Bank Account
1	debit memo	decreases
2	credit memo	increases
3	debit memo	decreases
4	debit memo	decreases

Practice Exercises: PE 8-2A, PE 8-2B

Using the Bank Statement as a Control over Cash

The bank statement is a primary control that a company uses over cash. A company uses the bank's statement by comparing the company's recording of cash transactions to those recorded by the bank.

The cash balance shown by a bank statement is usually different from the company's cash balance, as shown in Exhibit 11 for Power Networking.

EXHIBIT 11
Power Networking's Records and Bank Statement

Bank Statement

Beginning balance		$ 4,218.60
Additions:		
Deposits	$13,749.75	
Miscellaneous	408.00	14,157.75
Deductions:		
Checks	$14,698.57	
NSF check	300.00	
Service charge	18.00	(15,016.57)
Ending balance		$ 3,359.78

Power Networking Records

Beginning balance	$ 4,227.60
Deposits	14,565.95
Checks	(16,243.56)
Ending balance	$ 2,549.99

Power Networking should determine the reason for the difference in these two amounts.

Differences between the company and bank balance may arise because of a delay by either the company or bank in recording transactions. For example, there is normally a time lag of one or more days between the date a check is written and the date it is paid by the bank. Likewise, there is normally a time lag between when the company mails a deposit to the bank (or uses the night depository) and when the bank receives and records the deposit.

Differences may also arise because the bank has debited or credited the company's account for transactions that the company will not know about until the bank statement is received. Finally, differences may arise from errors made by either the company or the bank. For example, the company may incorrectly post to Cash a check written for $4,500 as $450. Likewise, a bank may incorrectly record the amount of a check.

Bank Reconciliation

Obj. 5 Describe and illustrate the use of a bank reconciliation in controlling cash.

A **bank reconciliation** is an analysis of the items and amounts that result in the cash balance reported in the bank statement to differ from the balance of the cash account in the ledger. The adjusted cash balance determined in the bank reconciliation is reported on the balance sheet.

A bank reconciliation is usually divided into two sections as follows:

- The *bank section* begins with the cash balance according to the bank statement and ends with the *adjusted balance*.
- The *company section* begins with the cash balance according to the company's records and ends with the *adjusted balance*.

The *adjusted balance* from bank and company sections must be equal. The format of the bank reconciliation is shown in Exhibit 12.

EXHIBIT 12

Bank Reconciliation Format

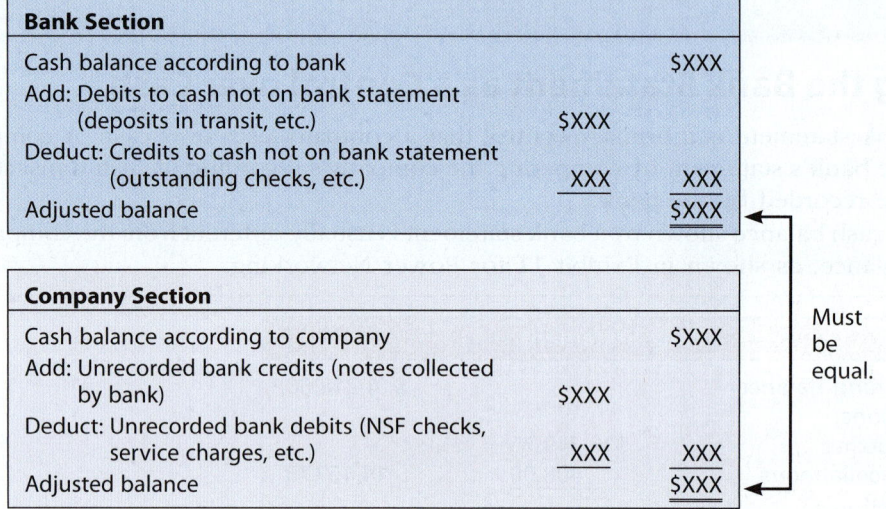

A bank reconciliation is prepared using the steps illustrated in Exhibit 13. The adjusted balances in the bank and company sections of the reconciliation must be equal. If the balances are not equal, an item has been overlooked and must be found.

Sometimes the adjusted balances are not equal because either the company or the bank has made an error. In such cases, the error is often discovered by comparing the amount of each item (deposit and check) on the bank statement with that in the company's records.

Any bank or company errors discovered should be added to or deducted from the bank or company section of the reconciliation, depending on the nature of the error. For example, assume that the bank incorrectly recorded a company check for $50 as $500. This bank error of $450 ($500 – $50) would be added to the bank balance in the bank section of the reconciliation. In addition, the bank would be notified of the error so that it could be corrected. On the other hand, assume that the company recorded a deposit of $1,200 as $2,100. This company error of $900 ($2,100 – $1,200) would be deducted from the cash balance in the company section of the bank reconciliation. The company would later correct the error using a journal entry.

To illustrate, the bank statement for Power Networking in Exhibit 9 is used. This bank statement shows a balance of $3,359.78 as of July 31. The cash balance in Power

Chapter 8 Internal Control and Cash 411

Bank Section

Step 1. Enter the *Cash balance according to bank* from the ending cash balance according to the bank statement.

Step 2. *Add deposits not recorded by the bank.*

Identify deposits not recorded by the bank by comparing each deposit listed on the bank statement with unrecorded deposits appearing in the preceding period's reconciliation and with the current period's deposits.

Examples: Deposits in transit at the end of the period

Step 3. *Deduct outstanding checks that have not been paid by the bank.*

Identify outstanding checks by comparing paid checks with outstanding checks appearing on the preceding period's reconciliation and with recorded checks.

Examples: Outstanding checks at the end of the period

Step 4. Determine the *Adjusted balance* by adding Step 2 and deducting Step 3.

Company Section

Step 5. Enter the *Cash balance according to company* from the ending cash balance in the ledger.

Step 6. *Add credit memos that have not been recorded.*

Identify the bank credit memos that have not been recorded by comparing the bank statement credit memos to entries in the journal.

Examples: A note receivable and interest that the bank has collected for the company

Step 7. *Deduct debit memos that have not been recorded.*

Identify the bank debit memos that have not been recorded by comparing the bank statement debit memos to entries in the journal.

Examples: Customers' not sufficient funds (NSF) checks; bank service charges

Step 8. Determine the *Adjusted balance* by adding Step 6 and deducting Step 7.

Verify that Adjusted Balances Are Equal

Step 9. Verify that the adjusted balances determined in Steps 4 and 8 are equal. If the adjusted balances in Steps 4 and 8 are unequal, search for any bank or company errors. Add or deduct the effects of any errors and verify that the adjusted balances are equal.

EXHIBIT 13

How to Prepare a Bank Reconciliation

Networking's ledger on the same date is $2,549.99. Using the preceding steps, the following reconciling items were identified:

Step 2. Deposit of July 31, not recorded on bank statement: $816.20
Step 3. Outstanding checks:

Check No. 812		$1,061.00
Check No. 878		435.39
Check No. 883		48.60
Total		$1,544.99

Step 6. Note receivable of $400 plus interest of $8 collected by bank not recorded in the journal as indicated by a credit memo of $408.00.

Step 7. Check from customer (Thomas Ivey) for $300 returned by bank because of insufficient funds (NSF) as indicated by a debit memo of $300.00.
Bank service charges of $18, not recorded in the journal as indicated by a debit memo of $18.00.

Step 9. An error of $9 was discovered. This error occurred when Check No. 879 for $732.26 to Taylor Co., on account, was recorded in the company's journal as $723.26.

The bank reconciliation, based on the Exhibit 9 bank statement and the preceding reconciling items, is shown in Exhibit 14. The company's records do not need to be updated for any items in the *bank section* of the reconciliation. This section begins with the cash balance according to the bank statement. However, the bank should be notified of any errors that need to be corrected.

412 Chapter 8 Internal Control and Cash

EXHIBIT 14 Bank Reconciliation for Power Networking

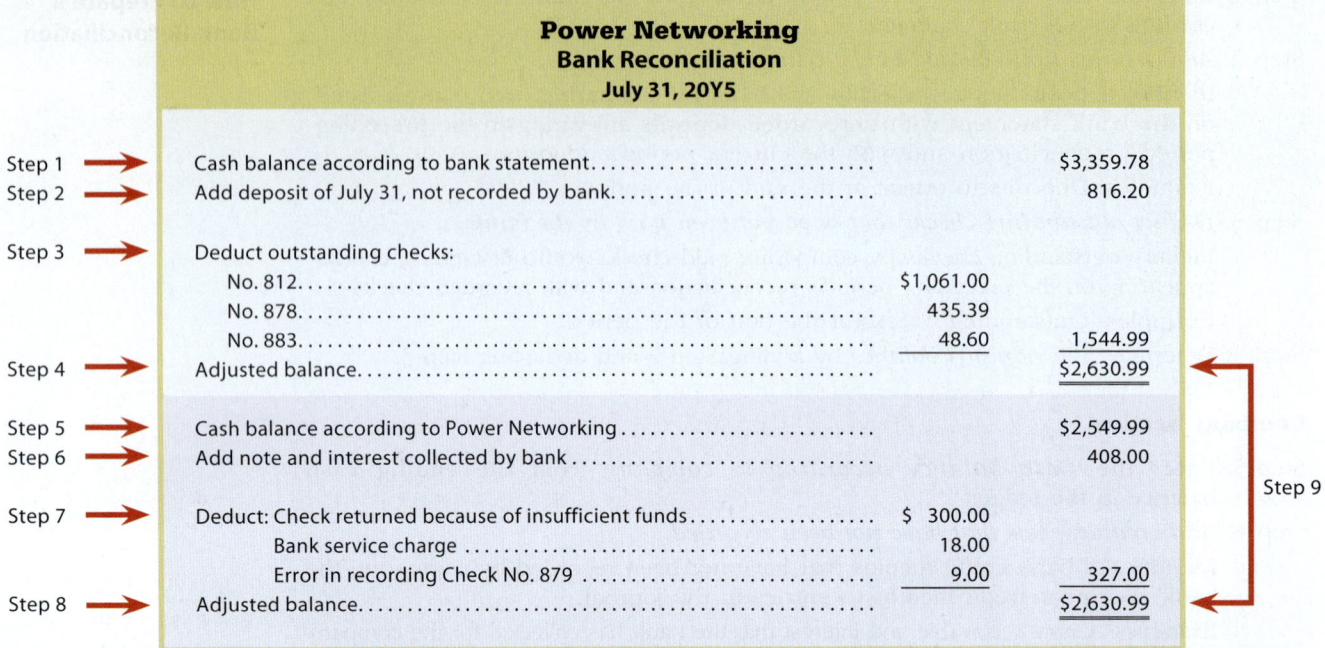

The company's records do need to be updated for any items in the *company section* of the bank reconciliation. The company's records are updated using journal entries. For example, journal entries should be made for any unrecorded bank memos and any company errors.

The journal entries for Power Networking, based on the bank reconciliation shown in Exhibit 14, are as follows:

20Y5					
July	31	Cash		408	
		Notes Receivable			400
		Interest Revenue			8
	31	Accounts Receivable—Thomas Ivey		300	
		Miscellaneous Expense		18	
		Accounts Payable—Taylor Co.		9	
		Cash			327

After the preceding journal entries are recorded and posted, the cash account will have a debit balance of $2,630.99. This cash balance agrees with the adjusted balance shown on the bank reconciliation. This is the amount of cash on July 31 and is the amount that is reported on Power Networking's July 31 balance sheet.

Businesses may reconcile their bank accounts in a slightly different format from that shown in Exhibit 13. Regardless, the objective is to control cash by reconciling the company's records with the bank statement. In doing so, any errors or misuse of cash may be detected.

To enhance internal control, the bank reconciliation should be prepared by an employee who does not take part in or record cash transactions. Otherwise, mistakes may occur, and it is more likely that cash will be stolen or misapplied. For example, an employee who handles cash and also reconciles the bank statement could steal a cash deposit, omit the deposit from the accounts, and omit it from the reconciliation.

Bank reconciliations are also an important part of computerized systems where deposits and checks are stored in electronic files and records. Some systems use computer software to determine the difference between the bank statement and company cash balances. The software then adjusts for deposits in transit and outstanding checks. Any remaining differences are reported for further analysis.

Example Exercise 8-3 Bank Reconciliation   Obj. 5

The following data were gathered to use in reconciling the bank account of Photo Op:

Balance per bank	$14,500
Balance per company records	13,875
Bank service charges	75
Deposit in transit	3,750
NSF check	800
Outstanding checks	5,250

a. What is the adjusted balance on the bank reconciliation?
b. Journalize any necessary entries for Photo Op based on the bank reconciliation.

Follow My Example 8-3

a. $13,000, computed as follows:

Bank section of reconciliation: $14,500 + $3,750 − $5,250 = $13,000
Company section of reconciliation: $13,875 − $75 − $800 = $13,000

b. Accounts Receivable... 800
    Miscellaneous Expense 75
        Cash 875

Practice Exercises: PE 8-3A, PE 8-3B

INTEGRITY, OBJECTIVITY, AND ETHICS IN BUSINESS

BANK ERROR IN YOUR FAVOR (OR MAYBE NOT)

A New Zealand couple expected a $100,000 deposit into their checking account but discovered the bank accidentally deposited $10,000,000. The couple immediately transferred the $10,000,000 to another account and left the country, hoping to cash in on this supposed windfall. Not surprisingly, they were found, arrested, and prosecuted for fraud. So, if you find a bank error in your favor, it really isn't like getting a Monopoly card. You cannot keep the cash, but must return it to the bank. Banks typically have a long time to correct such errors, and if it can be reasonably determined that you knew of the error but failed to report it, you could be prosecuted for bank fraud.

Source: Nickel, "Bank Error in Your Favor?" *Forbes.com*, May 2012 (www.forbes.com/sites/moneybuilder/2012/05/24/bank-error-in-your-favor/).

Special-Purpose Cash Funds

Obj. 6 Describe the accounting for special-purpose cash funds.

A company often has to pay small amounts for such items as postage, office supplies, and minor repairs. Although small, such payments may occur often enough to total a significant amount. Thus, it is desirable to control such payments. However, writing a check for each small payment is not practical. Instead, a special cash fund, called a **petty cash fund**, is used.

A petty cash fund is established by estimating the amount of payments needed from the fund during a period, such as a week or a month. A check is then written and cashed for this amount. The money obtained from cashing the check is then given to an employee, called the *petty cash custodian*. The petty cash custodian disburses monies from the fund as needed. For control purposes, the company may place restrictions on the maximum amount and the types of payments that can be made from the fund. Each time money is paid from petty cash, the custodian records the details on a petty cash receipts form.

The petty cash fund is normally replenished at periodic intervals, when it is depleted, or when it reaches a minimum amount. When a petty cash fund is replenished, the accounts debited are determined by summarizing the petty cash receipts. A check is then written for this amount, payable to Petty Cash.

To illustrate, assume that a petty cash fund of $500 is established on August 1. The entry to record this transaction is as follows:

Aug.	1	Petty Cash	500	
		Cash		500

The only time Petty Cash is debited is when the fund is initially established, as shown in the preceding entry, or when the fund is being increased. The only time Petty Cash is credited is when the fund is being decreased.

At the end of August, the petty cash receipts indicate expenditures for the following items:

Office supplies	$380
Postage (debit Office Supplies)	22
Store supplies	35
Miscellaneous administrative expense	30
Total	$467

The entry to replenish the petty cash fund on August 31 is as follows:

Aug.	31	Office Supplies	402	
		Store Supplies	35	
		Miscellaneous Administrative Expense	30	
		Cash		467

Petty Cash is not debited when the fund is replenished. Instead, the accounts affected by the petty cash disbursements are debited, as shown in the preceding entry. Replenishing the petty cash fund restores the fund to its original amount of $500.

Companies often use other cash funds for special needs, such as payroll or travel expenses. Such funds are called **special-purpose funds**. For example, each salesperson might be given $1,000 for travel-related expenses. Periodically, each salesperson submits an expense report, and the fund is replenished. Special-purpose funds are established and controlled in a manner similar to that of the petty cash fund.

Example Exercise 8-4 Petty Cash Fund — Obj. 6

Prepare journal entries for each of the following:

a. Issued a check to establish a petty cash fund of $500.

b. The amount of cash in the petty cash fund is $120. Issued a check to replenish the fund, based on the following summary of petty cash receipts: office supplies, $300, and miscellaneous administrative expense, $75. Record any missing funds in the cash short and over account.

Follow My Example 8-4

a.	Petty Cash	500	
	Cash		500
b.	Office Supplies	300	
	Miscellaneous Administrative Expense	75	
	Cash Short and Over	5	
	Cash		380

Practice Exercises: PE 8-4A, PE 8-4B

Financial Statement Reporting of Cash

Obj. 7 Describe and illustrate the reporting of cash and cash equivalents in the financial statements.

Cash is normally listed as the first asset in the Current Assets section of the balance sheet. Most companies present only a single cash amount on the balance sheet by combining all their bank and cash fund accounts.

A company may temporarily have excess cash. In such cases, the company usually invests in highly liquid investments in order to earn interest. These investments are called **cash equivalents**.[8] Examples of cash equivalents include U.S. Treasury bills, notes issued by major corporations (referred to as *commercial paper*), and money market funds. In such cases, companies usually report *Cash and cash equivalents* as one amount on the balance sheet.

Link to eBay
On a recent balance sheet, **eBay** reported over $6 billion in cash and cash equivalents.

The balance sheet presentation for cash for **Mornin' Joe** follows:

Mornin' Joe
Balance Sheet
December 31, 20Y6

Assets

Current assets:
  Cash and cash equivalents $235,000

Banks may require that companies maintain minimum cash balances in their bank accounts. Such a balance is called a **compensating balance**. This is often required by the bank as part of a loan agreement or line of credit. A *line of credit* is a preapproved amount the bank is willing to lend to a customer upon request. Compensating balance requirements are normally disclosed in notes to the financial statements.

Business Connection

MANAGING APPLE'S CASH

Apple Inc. has investments and cash that total over $205 billion. This represents over 70% of Apple's total assets and thus requires significant management attention. How does Apple manage these assets? Apple owns **Braeburn Capital**, a Nevada-based asset management company. Braeburn was established for one purpose: to manage Apple's cash and investments. Braeburn operates under a veil of secrecy, and little is known about the firm. It is simply described as follows: "Braeburn Capital Inc. is the asset management arm of Apple Inc. The firm invests in the public equity markets." Apple's financial statement footnotes provide some detail describing its holdings. More than $21 billion is incuded as cash or cash equivalents, such as money market funds. The remainder is divided between short- and long-term investments.

Source: Apple Inc., *Form 10-K for the Year Ended September 26, 2015.*

Financial Analysis and Interpretation: Ratio of Cash to Monthly Cash Expenses

Obj. 8 Describe and illustrate the use of the ratio of cash to monthly cash expenses to assess the ability of a company to continue in business.

For startup companies or companies in financial distress, cash is critical for survival. In their first few years, startup companies often report losses and negative net cash flows from operations. Moreover, companies in financial distress can also report losses and

---

[8] To be classified as a cash equivalent, according to FASB *Accounting Standards Codification*, Section 305.10, the investment is expected to be converted to cash within three months.

negative cash flows from operations. In such cases, the **ratio of cash to monthly cash expenses** is useful for assessing how long a company can continue to operate without:

- Additional financing, or
- Positive cash flows generated from operations

The ratio of cash to monthly cash expenses is computed as follows:

$$\text{Ratio of Cash to Monthly Cash Expenses} = \frac{\text{Cash as of Year-End}}{\text{Monthly Cash Expenses}}$$

The cash, including any cash equivalents, is taken from the balance sheet as of year-end. The monthly cash expenses, sometimes called *cash burn*, are estimated from the operating activities section of the statement of cash flows as follows:

$$\text{Monthly Cash Expenses} = \frac{\text{Negative Cash Flow from Operations}}{12}$$

To illustrate, **Ocean Power Technologies, Inc.**, develops and markets systems that generate electricity from the rising and falling of ocean waves. The following data (in thousands) were taken from financial statements of Ocean Power Technologies:

	For Years Ended April 29			
	Year 4	Year 3	Year 2	Year 1
Cash and cash equivalents at year-end	$ 17,336	$13,859	$ 6,373	$ 9,353
Cash flow from operations	(17,174)	(6,497)	(10,846)	(13,915)

Based on the preceding data, the monthly cash expenses and ratio of cash to monthly cash expenses are computed as follows:

	For Years Ended April 29			
	Year 4	Year 3	Year 2	Year 1
Monthly cash expenses:*				
$17,174 ÷ 12	$1,431			
$6,497 ÷ 12		$541		
$10,846 ÷ 12			$904	
$13,915 ÷ 12				$1,160
Ratio of cash to monthly cash expenses:**				
$17,336 ÷ $1,431	12.1 months			
$13,859 ÷ $541		25.6 months		
$6,373 ÷ $904			7.0 months	
$9,353 ÷ $1,160				8.1 months

*Rounded to nearest dollar.
**Rounded to one decimal place.

The preceding computations indicate that Ocean Power had 8.1 months of cash available at the end of Year 1 to continue its operations. At the end of Year 2, Ocean Power had 7.0 months of cash available to continue its operations. During Year 2, Ocean Power reduced its monthly cash expenses from $1,160 in Year 1 to $904. At the end of Year 3, Ocean Power had 25.6 months of cash available to continue its operations. During Year 3, Ocean Power issued common stock of $20,526, which increased its ratio of cash to monthly cash expenses from 7.0 months at the end of Year 2 to 25.6 months at the end of Year 3. At the end of Year 4, Ocean Power had 12.1 months of cash available to continue its operations.

The preceding analysis indicates that Ocean Power has generated negative cash flows from operations in each of the last four years. Ocean Power was able to fund its operations by issuing common stock. However, in the long term, Ocean Power must generate positive cash flows from its operations to survive and continue operating.

Example Exercise 8-5 Ratio of Cash to Monthly Cash Expenses *Obj. 8*

Financial data for Chapman Company follow:

	For Year Ended December 31
Cash on December 31	$ 102,000
Cash flow from operations	(144,000)

a. Compute the ratio of cash to monthly cash expenses.
b. Interpret the results computed in (a).

Follow My Example 8-5

a. $$\text{Monthly Cash Expenses} = \frac{\text{Negative Cash Flow from Operations}}{12} = \frac{\$144,000}{12} = \$12,000 \text{ per month}$$

$$\frac{\text{Ratio of Cash to}}{\text{Monthly Cash Expenses}} = \frac{\text{Cash as of Year-End}}{\text{Monthly Cash Expenses}} = \frac{\$102,000}{\$12,000 \text{ per month}} = 8.5 \text{ months}$$

b. The preceding computations indicate that Chapman Company has 8.5 months of cash remaining as of December 31. To continue operations beyond 8.5 months, Chapman Company will need to generate positive cash flows from operations or raise additional financing from its owners or by issuing debt.

Practice Exercises: PE 8-5A, PE 8-5B

Business Connection

MICROSOFT CORPORATION

Microsoft Corporation develops, manufactures, licenses, and supports software products for computing devices. Microsoft software products include computer operating systems, such as Windows®, and application software, such as Microsoft Word® and Excel®. Microsoft is actively involved in the video game market through its Xbox® and is also involved in online products and services.

Microsoft is known for its strong cash position. The following recent balance sheet of Microsoft reported more than $96 billion of cash and short-term investments:

Balance Sheet
(In millions)

Assets

Current assets:	
Cash and equivalents	$ 5,595
Short-term investments	90,931
Total cash and short-term investments	$96,526

The cash and cash equivalents of $5,595 million are further described in the notes to the financial statements, as follows:

Cash and equivalents:	
Cash	$3,679
Mutual funds	1,100
Commercial paper	1
U.S. government and agency securities	39
Certificates of deposit	776
Total cash and equivalents	$5,595

Source: Microsoft Corporation, *Form 10-K for the Fiscal Year Ended June 30, 2015*.

At a Glance 8

Obj. 1 Describe the Sarbanes-Oxley Act and its impact on internal controls and financial reporting.

Key Points Sarbanes-Oxley requires companies to maintain strong and effective internal controls and to report on the effectiveness of the internal controls.

Learning Outcomes	Example Exercises	Practice Exercises
• Describe why Congress passed Sarbanes-Oxley.		
• Describe the purpose of Sarbanes-Oxley.		
• Define internal control.		

Obj. 2 Describe and illustrate the objectives and elements of internal control.

Key Points The objectives of internal control are to provide reasonable assurance that (1) assets are safeguarded and used for business purposes, (2) business information is accurate, and (3) the company is complying with laws and regulations. The elements of internal control are the control environment, risk assessment, control procedures, monitoring, and information and communication.

Learning Outcomes	Example Exercises	Practice Exercises
• List the objectives of internal control.		
• List the elements of internal control.		
• Describe each element of internal control and factors influencing each element.	EE8-1	PE8-1A, 8-1B

Obj. 3 Describe and illustrate the application of internal controls to cash.

Key Points A cash register is a control for protecting cash received in over-the-counter sales. A remittance advice is a control for cash received through the mail. Separating the duties of handling cash and recording cash is also a control. A voucher system is a control system for cash payments. Many companies use electronic funds transfers for cash receipts and cash payments.

Learning Outcomes	Example Exercises	Practice Exercises
• Describe and give examples of controls for cash received from cash sales, cash received in the mail, and cash received by EFT.		
• Describe and give examples of controls for cash payments made using a voucher system and cash payments made by EFT.		

Obj. 4 Describe the nature of a bank account and its use in controlling cash.

Key Points Bank accounts control cash by reducing the amount of cash on hand and facilitating the transfer of cash between businesses and locations. In addition, the bank statement allows a business to reconcile the cash transactions recorded in the accounting records to those recorded by the bank.

Learning Outcomes	Example Exercises	Practice Exercises
• Describe how the use of bank accounts helps control cash.	EE8-2	PE8-2A, 8-2B
• Describe a bank statement and provide examples of items that appear on a bank statement as debit and credit memos.		

Obj. 5 Describe and illustrate the use of a bank reconciliation in controlling cash.

Key Points A bank reconciliation is prepared using the nine steps summarized in Exhibit 12. The items in the company section of a bank reconciliation must be journalized on the company's records.

Learning Outcomes	Example Exercises	Practice Exercises
• Describe a bank reconciliation.		
• Prepare a bank reconciliation.	EE8-3	PE8-3A, 8-3B
• Journalize any necessary entries on the company's records, based on the bank reconciliation.	EE8-3	PE8-3A, 8-3B

Obj. 6 Describe the accounting for special-purpose cash funds.

Key Points Special-purpose cash funds, such as a petty cash fund or travel funds, are used by businesses to meet specific needs. Each fund is established by cashing a check for the amount of cash needed. At periodic intervals, the fund is replenished and the disbursements recorded.

Learning Outcomes	Example Exercises	Practice Exercises
• Describe the use of special-purpose cash funds.		
• Journalize the entry to establish a petty cash fund.	EE8-4	PE8-4A, 8-4B
• Journalize the entry to replenish a petty cash fund.	EE8-4	PE8-4A, 8-4B

Obj. 7 Describe and illustrate the reporting of cash and cash equivalents in the financial statements.

Key Points Cash is listed as the first asset in the Current assets section of the balance sheet. Companies that have invested excess cash in highly liquid investments usually report *Cash and cash equivalents* on the balance sheet.

Learning Outcomes	Example Exercises	Practice Exercises
• Describe the reporting of cash and cash equivalents in the financial statements.		
• Illustrate the reporting of cash and cash equivalents in the financial statements.		

Chapter 8 Internal Control and Cash

Obj. 8 Describe and illustrate the use of the ratio of cash to monthly cash expenses to assess the ability of a company to continue in business.

Key Points The ratio of cash to monthly cash expenses is useful for assessing how long a company can continue to operate without (1) additional financing or (2) generating positive cash flows from operations.

Learning Outcomes	Example Exercises	Practice Exercises
• Describe the use of the ratio of cash to monthly cash expenses.		
• Compute the ratio of cash to monthly cash expenses.	EE8-5	PE8-5A, 8-5B

Illustrative Problem

The bank statement for Urethane Company for June 30 indicates a balance of $9,293.11. All cash receipts are deposited in a night depository each evening after banking hours. The accounting records indicate the following summary data for cash receipts and payments for June:

Cash balance as of June 1	$ 3,943.50
Total cash receipts for June	28,971.60
Total amount of checks issued in June	28,388.85

Comparing the bank statement and the accompanying canceled checks and memos with the records reveals the following reconciling items:

a. The bank had collected for Urethane Company $1,030 on a note left for collection. The face amount of the note was $1,000.

b. A deposit of $1,852.21, representing receipts of June 30, had been made too late to appear on the bank statement.

c. Checks outstanding totaled $5,265.27.

d. A check drawn for $139 had been incorrectly charged by the bank as $157.

e. A check for $370 returned with the statement had been recorded in the company's records as $730. The check was for the payment of an obligation to Avery Equipment Company for the purchase of office supplies on account.

f. Bank service charges for June amounted to $18.20.

Instructions

1. Prepare a bank reconciliation for June.
2. Journalize the entries that should be made by Urethane Company.

Solution

1.

Urethane Company
Bank Reconciliation
June 30

Cash balance according to bank statement		$ 9,293.11
Add: Deposit of June 30, not recorded by bank	$1,852.21	
Bank error in charging check as $157 instead of $139	18.00	1,870.21
Deduct outstanding checks		5,265.27
Adjusted balance		$ 5,898.05
Cash balance according to company's records		$ 4,526.25*
Add: Note and interest collected by bank	$1,030.00	
Error in recording check	360.00**	1,390.00
Deduct bank service charges		18.20
Adjusted balance		$ 5,898.05

*$3,943.50 + $28,971.60 − $28,388.85
**$730 − $370 = $360

2.

June	30	Cash	1,390.00	
		Notes Receivable		1,000.00
		Interest Revenue		30.00
		Accounts Payable—Avery Equipment Company		360.00
	30	Miscellaneous Administrative Expense	18.20	
		Cash		18.20

Key Terms

bank reconciliation (410)
bank statement (407)
cash (403)
cash equivalents (415)
cash short and over account (404)
compensating balance (415)

control environment (399)
electronic funds transfer (EFT) (405)
elements of internal control (398)
employee fraud (398)
internal control (396)
petty cash fund (413)

ratio of cash to monthly cash expenses (416)
Sarbanes-Oxley Act (396)
special-purpose funds (414)
voucher (406)
voucher system (406)

Discussion Questions

1. (a) Name and describe the five elements of internal control. (b) Is any one element of internal control more important than another?

2. Why should the employee who handles cash receipts not have the responsibility for maintaining the accounts receivable records? Explain.

3. The ticket seller at a movie theater doubles as a ticket taker for a few minutes each day while the ticket taker is on a break. Which control procedure

of a business's system of internal control is violated in this situation?

4. Why should the responsibility for maintaining the accounting records be separated from the responsibility for operations? Explain.

5. Assume that Brooke Miles, accounts payable clerk for West Coast Design Inc., stole $48,350 by paying fictitious invoices for goods that were never received. The clerk set up accounts in the names of the fictitious companies and cashed the checks at a local bank. Describe a control procedure that would have prevented or detected the fraud.

6. Before a voucher for the purchase of merchandise is approved for payment, supporting documents should be compared to verify the accuracy of the liability. Give an example of supporting documents for the purchase of merchandise.

7. The balance of Cash is likely to differ from the bank statement balance. What two factors are likely to be responsible for the difference?

8. What is the purpose of preparing a bank reconciliation?

9. Knott Inc. has a petty cash fund of $750. (a) Since the petty cash fund is only $750, should Knott Inc. implement controls over petty cash? (b) What controls, if any, could be used for the petty cash fund?

10. (a) How are cash equivalents reported in the financial statements? (b) What are some examples of cash equivalents?

Practice Exercises

Example Exercises

EE 8-1 p. 403

PE 8-1A Internal control elements OBJ. 2

Identify each of the following as relating to (a) the control environment, (b) control procedures, or (c) monitoring:

1. Hiring of external auditors to review the adequacy of controls
2. Personnel policies
3. Safeguarding inventory in a locked warehouse

EE 8-1 p. 403

PE 8-1B Internal control elements OBJ. 2

Identify each of the following as relating to (a) the control environment, (b) control procedures, or (c) information and communication:

1. Organizational structure
2. Report of company's conformity with environmental laws and regulations
3. Proofs and security measures

EE 8-2 p. 409

PE 8-2A Items on company's bank statement OBJ. 4

The following items may appear on a bank statement:

1. Bank correction of an error from posting another customer's check (disbursement) to the company's account
2. EFT deposit
3. Loan proceeds
4. NSF check

Using the following format, indicate whether each item would appear as a debit or credit memo on the bank statement and whether the item would increase or decrease the balance of the company's account:

Item No.	Appears on the Bank Statement as a Debit or Credit Memo	Increases or Decreases the Balance of the Company's Bank Account

EE 8-2 *p. 409* **PE 8-2B Items on company's bank statement** OBJ. 4

The following items may appear on a bank statement:

1. Bank correction of an error from recording a $6,200 deposit as $2,600
2. EFT payment
3. Note collected for company
4. Service charge

Using the following format, indicate whether each item would appear as a debit or credit memo on the bank statement and whether the item would increase or decrease the balance of the company's account:

Item No.	Appears on the Bank Statement as a Debit or Credit Memo	Increases or Decreases the Balance of the Company's Bank Account

EE 8-3 *p. 413* **PE 8-3A Bank reconciliation** OBJ. 5

The following data were gathered to use in reconciling the bank account of Torres Company:

Balance per bank	$12,175
Balance per company records	9,480
Bank service charges	50
Deposit in transit	1,800
NSF check	1,250
Outstanding checks	5,795

a. What is the adjusted balance on the bank reconciliation?
b. Journalize any necessary entries for Torres Company based on the bank reconciliation.

EE 8-3 *p. 413* **PE 8-3B Bank reconciliation** OBJ. 5

The following data were gathered to use in reconciling the bank account of Conway Company:

Balance per bank	$23,900
Balance per company records	8,700
Bank service charges	50
Deposit in transit	5,500
Note collected by bank with $450 interest	9,450
Outstanding checks	11,300

a. What is the adjusted balance on the bank reconciliation?
b. Journalize any necessary entries for Conway Company based on the bank reconciliation.

EE 8-4 *p. 414* **PE 8-4A Petty cash fund** OBJ. 6

Prepare journal entries for each of the following:

a. Issued a check to establish a petty cash fund of $1,000.
b. The amount of cash in the petty cash fund is $315. Issued a check to replenish the fund, based on the following summary of petty cash receipts: repair expense, $600, and miscellaneous selling expense, $56. Record any missing funds in the cash short and over account.

EE 8-4 *p. 414* **PE 8-4B Petty cash fund** OBJ. 6

Prepare journal entries for each of the following:

a. Issued a check to establish a petty cash fund of $900.
b. The amount of cash in the petty cash fund is $115. Issued a check to replenish the fund, based on the following summary of petty cash receipts: store supplies, $550, and miscellaneous selling expense, $200. Record any missing funds in the cash short and over account.

424 Chapter 8 Internal Control and Cash

EE 8-5 p.417   **PE 8-5A**   **Ratio of cash to monthly cash expenses**   OBJ. 8

Financial data for Otto Company follow:

	For Year Ended December 31
Cash on December 31	$ 69,350
Cash flow from operations	(114,000)

a. Compute the ratio of cash to monthly cash expenses.

b. Interpret the results computed in (a).

EE 8-5 p.417   **PE 8-5B**   **Ratio of cash to monthly cash expenses**   OBJ. 8

Financial data for Bonita Company follow:

	For Year Ended December 31
Cash on December 31	$ 187,180
Cash flow from operations	(458,400)

a. Compute the ratio of cash to monthly cash expenses.

b. Interpret the results computed in (a).

Exercises

EX 8-1   **Sarbanes-Oxley internal control report**   OBJ. 1

Using Wikipedia (www.wikipedia.com), look up the entry for Sarbanes-Oxley Act. Look over the table of contents and find the section that describes Section 404.

➤ What does Section 404 require of management's internal control report?

EX 8-2   **Internal controls**   OBJ. 2, 3

Jimmy Pace has recently been hired as the manager of Jittery Jon's Coffee Shop. Jittery Jon's Coffee Shop is a national chain of franchised coffee shops. During his first month as store manager, Jimmy encountered the following internal control situations:

a. Jittery Jon's Coffee Shop has one cash register. Prior to Jimmy's joining the coffee shop, each employee working on a shift would take a customer order, accept payment, and then prepare the order. Jimmy made one employee on each shift responsible for taking orders and accepting the customer's payment. Other employees prepare the orders.

b. Because only one employee uses the cash register, that employee is responsible for counting the cash at the end of the shift and verifying that the cash in the drawer matches the amount of cash sales recorded by the cash register. Jimmy expects each cashier to balance the drawer to the penny *every* time—no exceptions.

c. Jimmy caught an employee putting a case of 1,000 single-serving tea bags in her car. Not wanting to create a scene, Jimmy smiled and said, "I don't think you're putting those tea bags on the right shelf. Don't they belong inside the coffee shop?" The employee returned the tea bags to the stockroom.

➤ State whether you agree or disagree with Jimmy's method of handling each situation and explain your answer.

EX 8-3   **Internal controls**   OBJ. 2, 3

Ramona's Clothing is a retail store specializing in women's clothing. The store has established a liberal return policy for the holiday season in order to encourage gift purchases. Any item purchased during November and December may be returned through January 31, with a receipt, for cash or exchange. If the customer does not have a receipt, cash will still be refunded for any item under $75. If the item is more than $75, a check is mailed to the customer.

Whenever an item is returned, a store clerk completes a return slip, which the customer signs. The return slip is placed in a special box. The store manager visits the return counter approximately once every two hours to authorize the return slips. Clerks are instructed to place the returned merchandise on the proper rack on the selling floor as soon as possible.

This year, returns at Ramona's Clothing have reached an all-time high. There are a large number of returns under $75 without receipts.

a. How can salesclerks employed at Ramona's Clothing use the store's return policy to steal money from the cash register?
b. What internal control weaknesses do you see in the return policy that make cash thefts easier?
c. Would issuing a store credit in place of a cash refund for all merchandise returned without a receipt reduce the possibility of theft? List some advantages and disadvantages of issuing a store credit in place of a cash refund.
d. Assume that Ramona's Clothing is committed to the current policy of issuing cash refunds without a receipt. What changes could be made in the store's procedures regarding customer refunds to improve internal control?

EX 8-4 Internal controls for bank lending   OBJ. 2, 3

Pacific Bank provides loans to businesses in the community through its Commercial Lending Department. Small loans (less than $100,000) may be approved by an individual loan officer, while larger loans (greater than $100,000) must be approved by a board of loan officers. Once a loan is approved, the funds are made available to the loan applicant under agreed-upon terms. Pacific Bank has instituted a policy whereby its president has the individual authority to approve loans up to $5,000,000. The president believes that this policy will allow flexibility to approve loans to valued clients much quicker than under the previous policy.

As an internal auditor of Pacific Bank, how would you respond to this change in policy?

EX 8-5 Internal controls   OBJ. 2, 3

One of the largest losses in history from unauthorized securities trading involved a securities trader for the French bank **Societe Generale**. The trader was able to circumvent internal controls and create more than $7 billion in trading losses in six months. The trader apparently escaped detection by using knowledge of the bank's internal control systems learned from a previous back-office monitoring job. Much of this monitoring involved the use of software to monitor trades. In addition, traders were usually kept to tight trading limits. Apparently, these controls failed in this case.

What general weaknesses in Societe Generale's internal controls contributed to the occurrence and size of the losses?

EX 8-6 Internal controls   OBJ. 2, 3

An employee of **JHT Holdings, Inc.**, a trucking company, was responsible for resolving roadway accident claims under $25,000. The employee created fake accident claims and wrote settlement checks of between $5,000 and $25,000 to friends or acquaintances acting as phony "victims." One friend recruited subordinates at his place of work to cash some of the checks. Beyond this, the JHT employee also recruited lawyers, whom he paid to represent both the trucking company and the fake victims in the bogus accident settlements. When the lawyers cashed the checks, they allegedly split the money with the corrupt JHT employee. This fraud went undetected for two years.

Why would it take so long to discover such a fraud?

EX 8-7 Internal controls   OBJ. 2, 3

All-Around Sound Co. discovered a fraud whereby one of its front office administrative employees used company funds to purchase goods such as computers, digital cameras, and other electronic items for her own use. The fraud was discovered when employees noticed an increase in the frequency of deliveries from vendors and the use of unusual vendors. After some investigation, it was discovered that the employee would alter the description or change the quantity on an invoice in order to explain the cost on the bill.

What general internal control weaknesses contributed to this fraud?

426 Chapter 8 Internal Control and Cash

EX 8-8 Financial statement fraud
OBJ. 2, 3

A former chairman, CFO, and controller of Donnkenny, Inc., an apparel company that makes sportswear for Pierre Cardin and Victoria Jones, pleaded guilty to financial statement fraud. These managers used false journal entries to record fictitious sales, hid inventory in public warehouses so that it could be recorded as "sold," and required sales orders to be backdated so that the sale could be moved to an earlier period. The combined effect of these actions caused $25 million out of $40 million in quarterly sales to be phony.

a. Why might control procedures listed in this chapter be insufficient in stopping this type of fraud?
b. How could this type of fraud be stopped?

EX 8-9 Internal control of cash receipts
OBJ. 2, 3

The procedures used for over-the-counter receipts are as follows: At the close of each day's business, the salesclerks count the cash in their respective cash drawers, after which they determine the amount recorded by the cash register and prepare the memo cash form, noting any discrepancies. An employee from the cashier's office counts the cash, compares the total with the memo, and takes the cash to the cashier's office.

a. Indicate the weak link in internal control.
b. How can the weakness be corrected?

EX 8-10 Internal control of cash receipts
OBJ. 2, 3

Sergio Flores works at the drive-through window of Big & Bad Burgers. Occasionally, when a drive-through customer orders, Sergio fills the order and pockets the customer's money. He does not ring up the order on the cash register.

Identify the internal control weaknesses that exist at Big & Bad Burgers and discuss what can be done to prevent this theft.

EX 8-11 Internal control of cash receipts
OBJ. 2, 3

The mailroom employees send all remittances and remittance advices to the cashier. The cashier deposits the cash in the bank and forwards the remittance advices and duplicate deposit slips to the Accounting Department.

a. Indicate the weak link in internal control in the handling of cash receipts.
b. How can the weakness be corrected?

EX 8-12 Entry for cash sales; cash short
OBJ. 2, 3

The actual cash received from cash sales was $18,371, and the amount indicated by the cash register total was $18,400. Journalize the entry to record the cash receipts and cash sales.

EX 8-13 Entry for cash sales; cash over
OBJ. 2, 3

The actual cash received from cash sales was $71,315, and the amount indicated by the cash register total was $71,220. Journalize the entry to record the cash receipts and cash sales.

EX 8-14 Internal control of cash payments
OBJ. 2, 3

Abbe Co. is a small merchandising company with a manual accounting system. An investigation revealed that in spite of a sufficient bank balance, a significant amount of available cash discounts had been lost because of failure to make timely payments. In addition, it was discovered that the invoices for several purchases had been paid twice.

Outline procedures for the payment of vendors' invoices so that the possibilities of losing available cash discounts and of paying an invoice a second time will be minimized.

EX 8-15 Internal control of cash payments
OBJ. 2, 3

Paragon Tech Company, a communications equipment manufacturer, recently fell victim to a fraud scheme developed by one of its employees. To understand the scheme, it is necessary to review Paragon Tech's procedures for the purchase of services.

The purchasing agent is responsible for ordering services (such as repairs to a photocopy machine or office cleaning) after receiving a service requisition from an authorized manager. However, because no tangible goods are delivered, a receiving report is not prepared. When the Accounting Department receives an invoice billing Paragon Tech for a service call, the accounts payable clerk calls the manager who requested the service in order to verify that it was performed.

The fraud scheme involves Mae Jansma, the manager of plant and facilities. Mae arranged for her uncle's company, Radiate Systems, to be placed on Paragon Tech's approved vendor list. Mae did not disclose the family relationship.

On several occasions, Mae would submit a requisition for services to be provided by Radiate Systems. However, the service requested was really not needed, and it was never performed. Radiate Systems would bill Paragon Tech for the service and then split the cash payment with Mae.

Explain what changes should be made to Paragon Tech's procedures for ordering and paying for services in order to prevent such occurrences in the future.

EX 8-16 Bank reconciliation
OBJ. 5

Identify each of the following reconciling items as: (a) an addition to the cash balance according to the bank statement, (b) a deduction from the cash balance according to the bank statement, (c) an addition to the cash balance according to the company's records, or (d) a deduction from the cash balance according to the company's records. (None of the transactions reported by bank debit and credit memos have been recorded by the company.)

1. Bank service charges, $30.
2. Check of a customer returned by bank to company because of insufficient funds, $400.
3. Check for $320 incorrectly recorded by the company as $230.
4. Check for $1,100 incorrectly charged by bank as $110.
5. Deposit in transit, $3,300.
6. Outstanding checks, $7,950.
7. Note collected by bank, $10,500.

EX 8-17 Entries based on bank reconciliation
OBJ. 5

Which of the reconciling items listed in Exercise 8-16 require an entry in the company's accounts?

EX 8-18 Bank reconciliation
OBJ. 5

✔ Adjusted balance: $32,630

Show Me How

The following data were accumulated for use in reconciling the bank account of Mathers Co. for July:

1. Cash balance according to the company's records at July 31, $32,110.
2. Cash balance according to the bank statement at July 31, $31,350.
3. Checks outstanding, $2,870.
4. Deposit in transit, not recorded by bank, $4,150.
5. A check for $170 in payment of an account was erroneously recorded in the check register as $710.
6. Bank debit memo for service charges, $20.

a. Prepare a bank reconciliation, using the format shown in Exhibit 13.
b. If the balance sheet is prepared for Mathers Co. on July 31, what amount should be reported for cash?
c. Must a bank reconciliation always balance (reconcile)?

428 Chapter 8 Internal Control and Cash

EX 8-19 Entries for bank reconciliation
OBJ. 5

Using the data presented in Exercise 8-18, journalize the entry or entries that should be made by the company.

EX 8-20 Entries for note collected by bank
OBJ. 5

Accompanying a bank statement for Santee Company is a credit memo for $15,120 representing the principal ($14,000) and interest ($1,120) on a note that had been collected by the bank. The company had been notified by the bank at the time of the collection but had made no entries. Journalize the entry that should be made by the company to bring the accounting records up to date.

EX 8-21 Bank reconciliation
OBJ. 5

An accounting clerk for Chesner Co. prepared the following bank reconciliation:

Chesner Co.
Bank Reconciliation
August 31

Cash balance according to company's records		$11,100
Add: Outstanding checks	$ 3,585	
Error by Chesner Co. in recording Check No. 1056 as $950 instead of $590	360	
Note for $12,000 collected by bank, including interest	12,480	16,425
		$27,525
Deduct: Deposit in transit on August 31	$ 7,200	
Bank service charges	25	7,225
Cash balance according to bank statement		$20,300

a. From the data in this bank reconciliation, prepare a new bank reconciliation for Chesner Co., using the format shown in the illustrative problem.

b. If a balance sheet is prepared for Chesner Co. on August 31, what amount should be reported for cash?

EX 8-22 Bank reconciliation
OBJ. 5

✔ Corrected adjusted balance: $19,780

The following June 30 bank reconciliation was prepared for Poway Co.

Poway Co.
Bank Reconciliation
For the Month Ended June 30

Cash balance according to bank statement			$16,185
Add outstanding checks:			
No. 1067		$ 575	
1106		470	
1110		1,050	
1113		910	3,005
			$19,190
Deduct deposit of June 30, not recorded by bank			6,600
Adjusted balance			$12,590
Cash balance according to company's records			$ 8,985
Add: Proceeds of note collected by bank:			
Principal	$6,000		
Interest	300	$6,300	
Service charges		15	6,315
			$15,300
Deduct: Check returned because of insufficient funds		$ 890	
Error in recording June 17 deposit of $7,150 as $1,750		5,400	6,290
Adjusted balance			$ 9,010

a. Identify the errors in the following bank reconciliation:

b. Prepare a new bank reconciliation for Poway Co., using the format shown in the illustrative problem.

EX 8-23 Using bank reconciliation to determine cash receipts stolen   OBJ. 2, 3, 5

Alaska Impressions Co. records all cash receipts on the basis of its cash register tapes. Alaska Impressions Co. discovered during October that one of its salesclerks had stolen an undetermined amount of cash receipts while taking the daily deposits to the bank. The following data have been gathered for October:

Cash in bank according to the general ledger	$11,680
Cash according to the October 31 bank statement	13,275
Outstanding checks as of October 31	3,670
Bank service charge for October	40
Note receivable, including interest collected by bank in October	2,100

No deposits were in transit on October 31.

a. Determine the amount of cash receipts stolen by the salesclerk.

b. What accounting controls would have prevented or detected this theft?

EX 8-24 Petty cash fund entries   OBJ. 6

Journalize the entries to record the following:

a. Check is issued to establish a petty cash fund of $750.

b. The amount of cash in the petty cash fund is now $176. Check is issued to replenish the fund, based on the following summary of petty cash receipts: office supplies, $248; miscellaneous selling expense, $212; miscellaneous administrative expense, $96. (Because the amount of the check to replenish the fund plus the balance in the fund do not equal $750, record the discrepancy in the cash short and over account.)

EX 8-25 Variation in cash flows   OBJ. 7

Mattel, Inc., designs, manufactures, and markets toy products worldwide. Mattel's toys include Barbie® fashion dolls and accessories, Hot Wheels®, and Fisher-Price brands. For a recent year, Mattel reported the following net cash flows from operating activities (in thousands):

First quarter ending March 31	$ (53,110)
Second quarter ending June 30	(187,663)
Third quarter ending September 30	18,435
Fourth quarter ending December 31	956,895

Explain why Mattel reported negative net cash flows from operating activities during the first and second quarters and a large positive cash flow for the fourth quarter, with overall net positive cash flow for the year.

EX 8-26 Cash to monthly cash expenses ratio   OBJ. 8

El Dorado Inc. has monthly cash expenses of $168,500. On December 31, the cash balance is $1,415,400.

a. Compute the ratio of cash to monthly cash expenses.

b. Based on (a), what are the implications for El Dorado Inc.?

EX 8-27 Cash to monthly cash expenses ratio   OBJ. 8

Capstone Turbine Corporation produces and sells turbine generators for such applications as charging electric, hybrid vehicles. Capstone Turbine reported the following financial data for a recent year (in thousands):

Net cash flows from operating activities	$(23,018)
Cash and cash equivalents	32,221

a. Determine the monthly cash expenses. Round to one decimal place.

b. Determine the ratio of cash to monthly cash expenses. Round to one decimal place.

c. Based on your analysis, do you believe that Capstone Turbine will remain in business?

430　Chapter 8　Internal Control and Cash

EX 8-28　Cash to monthly cash expenses ratio　　OBJ. 8

Amicus Therapeutics, Inc., is a biopharmaceutical company that develops drugs for the treatment of various diseases, including Parkinson's disease. Amicus Therapeutics reported the following financial data (in thousands) for three recent years:

	For Years Ended December 31		
	Year 3	Year 2	Year 1
Cash and cash equivalents	$ 69,485	$ 24,074	$ 43,640
Net cash flows from operations	(100,139)	(51,669)	(45,794)

a. Determine the monthly cash expenses for Year 3, Year 2, and Year 1. Round to one decimal place.

b. Determine the ratio of cash to monthly cash expenses for Year 3, Year 2, and Year 1 as of December 31. Round to one decimal place.

c. Based on (a) and (b), comment on Amicus Therapeutics' ratio of cash to monthly operating expenses for Year 3, Year 2, and Year 1.

Problems: Series A

PR 8-1A　Evaluating internal control of cash　　OBJ. 2, 3

The following procedures were recently installed by Raspberry Creek Company:

a. After necessary approvals have been obtained for the payment of a voucher, the treasurer signs and mails the check. The treasurer then stamps the voucher and supporting documentation as paid and returns the voucher and supporting documentation to the accounts payable clerk for filing.

b. The accounts payable clerk prepares a voucher for each disbursement. The voucher along with the supporting documentation is forwarded to the treasurer's office for approval.

c. Along with petty cash expense receipts for postage, office supplies, etc., several postdated employee checks are in the petty cash fund.

d. At the end of the day, cash register clerks are required to use their own funds to make up any cash shortages in their registers.

e. At the end of each day, all cash receipts are placed in the bank's night depository.

f. At the end of each day, an accounting clerk compares the duplicate copy of the daily cash deposit slip with the deposit receipt obtained from the bank.

g. All mail is opened by the mail clerk, who forwards all cash remittances to the cashier. The cashier prepares a listing of the cash receipts and forwards a copy of the list to the accounts receivable clerk for recording in the accounts.

h. The bank reconciliation is prepared by the cashier, who works under the supervision of the treasurer.

Instructions

Indicate whether each of the procedures of internal control over cash represents (1) a strength or (2) a weakness. For each weakness, indicate why it exists.

PR 8-2A　Transactions for petty cash, cash short and over　　OBJ. 3, 6

Jeremiah Restoration Company completed the following selected transactions during January:

Jan.　1.　Established a petty cash fund of $900.

　　12.　The cash sales for the day, according to the cash register records, totaled $6,148. The actual cash received from cash sales was $6,180.

　　31.　Petty cash on hand was $75. Replenished the petty cash fund for the following disbursements, each evidenced by a petty cash receipt:

Jan. 3. Store supplies, $470.

7. Express charges on merchandise sold, $55 (Delivery Expense).

9. Office supplies, $30.

13. Office supplies, $11.

19. Postage stamps, $55 (Office Supplies).

21. Repair to office file cabinet lock, $60 (Miscellaneous Administrative Expense).

22. Postage due on special delivery letter, $30 (Miscellaneous Administrative Expense).

24. Express charges on merchandise sold, $85 (Delivery Expense).

30. Office supplies, $14.

Jan. 31. The cash sales for the day, according to the cash register records, totaled $4,550. The actual cash received from cash sales was $4,536.

31. Decreased the petty cash fund by $200.

Instructions
Journalize the transactions.

PR 8-3A Bank reconciliation and entries OBJ. 5

✔ 1. Adjusted balance: $370,000

The cash account for American Medical Co. at April 30 indicated a balance of $334,985. The bank statement indicated a balance of $388,600 on April 30. Comparing the bank statement and the accompanying canceled checks and memos with the records revealed the following reconciling items:

a. Checks outstanding totaled $61,280.

b. A deposit of $42,500, representing receipts of April 30, had been made too late to appear on the bank statement.

c. The bank collected $42,000 on a $40,000 note, including interest of $2,000.

d. A check for $7,600 returned with the statement had been incorrectly recorded by American Medical Co. as $760. The check was for the payment of an obligation to Targhee Supply Co. for a purchase on account.

e. A check drawn for $240 had been erroneously charged by the bank as $420.

f. Bank service charges for April amounted to $145.

Instructions
1. Prepare a bank reconciliation.
2. Journalize the necessary entries. The accounts have not been closed.
3. If a balance sheet is prepared for American Medical Co. on April 30, what amount should be reported as cash?

PR 8-4A Bank reconciliation and entries OBJ. 5

✔ 1. Adjusted balance: $39,475

The cash account for Brentwood Bike Co. at May 1 indicated a balance of $34,250. During May, the total cash deposited was $140,300, and checks written totaled $138,880. The bank statement indicated a balance of $43,525 on May 31. Comparing the bank statement, the canceled checks, and the accompanying memos with the records revealed the following reconciling items:

a. Checks outstanding totaled $6,440.

b. A deposit of $1,850 representing receipts of May 31 had been made too late to appear on the bank statement.

c. The bank had collected for Brentwood Bike Co. $5,250 on a note left for collection. The face of the note was $5,000.

d. A check for $390 returned with the statement had been incorrectly charged by the bank as $930.

e. A check for $210 returned with the statement had been recorded by Brentwood Bike Co. as $120. The check was for the payment of an obligation to Adkins Co. on account.

(Continued)

432 Chapter 8 Internal Control and Cash

f. Bank service charges for May amounted to $30.

g. A check for $1,325 from Jennings Co. was returned by the bank due to insufficient funds.

Instructions

1. Prepare a bank reconciliation as of May 31.
2. Journalize the necessary entries. The accounts have not been closed.
3. If a balance sheet is prepared for Brentwood Bike Co. on May 31, what amount should be reported as cash?

PR 8-5A Bank reconciliation and entries   OBJ. 5

✔ 1. Adjusted balance: $13,216

Beeler Furniture Company deposits all cash receipts each Wednesday and Friday in a night depository after banking hours. The data required to reconcile the bank statement as of June 30 have been taken from various documents and records and are reproduced as follows. The sources of the data are printed in capital letters. All checks were written for payments on account.

CASH ACCOUNT:
  Balance as of June 1 .... $9,317.40
  CASH RECEIPTS FOR MONTH OF JUNE $9,223.76
DUPLICATE DEPOSIT TICKETS:
  Date and amount of each deposit in June:

Date	Amount	Date	Amount	Date	Amount
June 1	$1,080.50	June 10	$ 996.61	June 22	$ 897.34
3	854.17	15	882.95	24	947.21
8	840.50	17	1,606.74	30	1,117.74

CHECKS WRITTEN:
  Number and amount of each check issued in June:

Check No.	Amount	Check No.	Amount	Check No.	Amount
740	$237.50	747	Void	754	$ 449.75
741	495.15	748	$450.90	755	272.75
742	501.90	749	640.13	756	113.95
743	761.30	750	276.77	757	407.95
744	506.88	751	299.37	758	259.60
745	117.25	752	537.01	759	901.50
746	298.66	753	380.95	760	486.39

Total amount of checks issued in June $8,395.66

BANK RECONCILIATION FOR PRECEDING MONTH:

Beeler Furniture Company
Bank Reconciliation
May 31 20Y2

Cash balance according to bank statement..........................		$ 9,447.20
Add deposit for May 31, not recorded by bank......................		690.25
Deduct outstanding checks:		
No. 731	$162.15	
736	345.95	
738	251.40	
739	60.55	820.05
Adjusted balance...		$ 9,317.40
Cash balance according to company's records		$ 9,352.50
Deduct bank service charges.......................................		35.10
Adjusted balance...		$ 9,317.40

Instructions

1. Prepare a bank reconciliation as of June 30, 20Y2. If errors in recording deposits or checks are discovered, assume that the errors were made by the company. Assume that all deposits are from cash sales. All checks are written to satisfy accounts payable.

2. Journalize the necessary entries. The accounts have not been closed.
3. What is the amount of Cash that should appear on the balance sheet as of June 30?
4. Assume that a canceled check for $390 has been incorrectly recorded by the bank as $930. Briefly explain how the error would be included in a bank reconciliation and how it should be corrected.

JUNE BANK STATEMENT:

AMERICAN NATIONAL BANK OF CHICAGO
CHICAGO, IL 60603   (312) 441-1239
MEMBER FDIC
PAGE 1

ACCOUNT NUMBER
FROM 6/01/20Y2   TO 6/30/20Y2

BALANCE	9,447.20
9 DEPOSITS	8,691.77
20 WITHDRAWALS	7,599.26
4 OTHER DEBITS AND CREDITS	3,085.00CR
NEW BALANCE	13,624.71

BEELER FURNITURE COMPANY

CHECKS AND OTHER DEBITS				DEPOSITS	DATE	BALANCE
No.731	162.15	No.736	345.95	690.25	6/01	9,629.35
No.739	60.55	No.740	237.50	1,080.50	6/02	10,411.80
No.741	495.15	No.742	501.90	854.17	6/04	10,268.92
No.743	671.30	No.744	506.88	840.50	6/09	9,931.24
No.745	117.25	No.746	298.66	MS 3,500.00	6/09	13,015.33
No.748	450.90	No.749	640.13	MS 210.00	6/09	12,134.30
No.750	276.77	No.751	299.37	896.61	6/11	12,454.77
No.752	537.01	No.753	380.95	882.95	6/16	12,419.76
No.754	449.75	No.755	272.75	1,606.74	6/18	13,304.00
No.757	407.95	No.760	486.39	897.34	6/23	13,307.00
				942.71	6/25	14,249.71
		NSF	550.00		6/28	13,699.71
		SC	75.00		6/30	13,624.71

EC — ERROR CORRECTION   OD — OVERDRAFT
MS — MISCELLANEOUS   PS — PAYMENT STOPPED
NSF — NOT SUFFICIENT FUNDS   SC — SERVICE CHARGE

THE RECONCILEMENT OF THIS STATEMENT WITH YOUR RECORDS IS ESSENTIAL.
ANY ERROR OR EXCEPTION SHOULD BE REPORTED IMMEDIATELY.

Problems: Series B

PR 8-1B Evaluating internal control of cash
OBJ. 2, 3

The following procedures were recently installed by The China Shop:

a. All sales are rung up on the cash register, and a receipt is given to the customer. All sales are recorded on a record locked inside the cash register.

b. Each cashier is assigned a separate cash register drawer to which no other cashier has access.

c. At the end of a shift, each cashier counts the cash in his or her cash register, unlocks the cash register record, and compares the amount of cash with the amount on the record to determine cash shortages and overages.

d. Checks received through the mail are given daily to the accounts receivable clerk for recording collections on account and for depositing in the bank.

(Continued)

e. Vouchers and all supporting documents are perforated with a PAID designation after being paid by the treasurer.
f. Disbursements are made from the petty cash fund only after a petty cash receipt has been completed and signed by the payee.
g. The bank reconciliation is prepared by the cashier.

Instructions

Indicate whether each of the procedures of internal control over cash represents (1) a strength or (2) a weakness. For each weakness, indicate why it exists.

PR 8-2B Transactions for petty cash, cash short and over   OBJ. 3, 6

Cedar Springs Company completed the following selected transactions during June:

June 1. Established a petty cash fund of $1,000.
12. The cash sales for the day, according to the cash register records, totaled $9,440. The actual cash received from cash sales was $9,506.
30. Petty cash on hand was $46. Replenished the petty cash fund for the following disbursements, each evidenced by a petty cash receipt:

June 2. Store supplies, $375.
10. Express charges on merchandise purchased, $105 (Merchandise Inventory).
14. Office supplies, $85.
15. Office supplies, $90.
18. Postage stamps, $33 (Office Supplies).
20. Repair to fax, $100 (Miscellaneous Administrative Expense).
21. Repair to office door lock, $25 (Miscellaneous Administrative Expense).
22. Postage due on special delivery letter, $9 (Miscellaneous Administrative Expense).
28. Express charges on merchandise purchased, $110 (Merchandise Inventory).

30. The cash sales for the day, according to the cash register records, totaled $13,390. The actual cash received from cash sales was $13,350.
30. Increased the petty cash fund by $200.

Instructions

Journalize the transactions.

✔ 1. Adjusted balance: $24,305

PR 8-3B Bank reconciliation and entries   OBJ. 5

The cash account for Stone Systems at July 31 indicated a balance of $17,750. The bank statement indicated a balance of $33,650 on July 31. Comparing the bank statement and the accompanying canceled checks and memos with the records reveals the following reconciling items:

a. Checks outstanding totaled $17,865.
b. A deposit of $9,150, representing receipts of July 31, had been made too late to appear on the bank statement.
c. The bank had collected $6,095 on a note left for collection. The face of the note was $5,750.
d. A check for $390 returned with the statement had been incorrectly recorded by Stone Systems as $930. The check was for the payment of an obligation to Holland Co. for the purchase of office supplies on account.
e. A check drawn for $1,810 had been incorrectly charged by the bank as $1,180.
f. Bank service charges for July amounted to $80.

Instructions

1. Prepare a bank reconciliation.
2. Journalize the necessary entries. The accounts have not been closed.
3. If a balance sheet is prepared for Stone Systems on July 31, what amount should be reported as cash?

Chapter 8 Internal Control and Cash

PR 8-4B Bank reconciliation and entries OBJ. 5

✔ 1. Adjusted balance: $78,535

The cash account for Collegiate Sports Co. on November 1 indicated a balance of $81,145. During November, the total cash deposited was $293,150, and checks written totaled $307,360. The bank statement indicated a balance of $112,675 on November 30. Comparing the bank statement, the canceled checks, and the accompanying memos with the records revealed the following reconciling items:

a. Checks outstanding totaled $41,840.
b. A deposit of $12,200, representing receipts of November 30, had been made too late to appear on the bank statement.
c. A check for $7,250 had been incorrectly charged by the bank as $2,750.
d. A check for $760 returned with the statement had been recorded by Collegiate Sports Co. as $7,600. The check was for the payment of an obligation to Ramirez Co. on account.
e. The bank had collected for Collegiate Sports Co. $7,385 on a note left for collection. The face of the note was $7,000.
f. Bank service charges for November amounted to $125.
g. A check for $2,500 from Hallen Academy was returned by the bank because of insufficient funds.

Instructions

1. Prepare a bank reconciliation as of November 30.
2. Journalize the necessary entries. The accounts have not been closed.
3. If a balance sheet is prepared for Collegiate Sports Co. on November 30, what amount should be reported as cash?

PR 8-5B Bank reconciliation and entries OBJ. 5

✔ 1. Adjusted balance: $11,494

Sunshine Interiors deposits all cash receipts each Wednesday and Friday in a night depository after banking hours. The data required to reconcile the bank statement as of July 31 have been taken from various documents and records and are reproduced as follows. The sources of the data are printed in capital letters. All checks were written for payments on account.

BANK RECONCILIATION FOR PRECEDING MONTH (DATED JUNE 30):

Cash balance according to bank statement		$ 9,422.80
Add deposit of June 30, not recorded by bank		780.80
Deduct outstanding checks:		
No. 580	$310.10	
No. 602	85.50	
No. 612	92.50	
No. 613	137.50	625.60
Adjusted balance		$ 9,578.00
Cash balance according to company's records		$ 9,605.70
Deduct bank service charges		27.70
Adjusted balance		$ 9,578.00

CASH ACCOUNT:

Balance as of July 1	$ 9,578.00
CASH RECEIPTS FOR MONTH OF JULY	6,465.42

DUPLICATE DEPOSIT TICKETS:

Date and amount of each deposit in July:

Date	Amount	Date	Amount	Date	Amount
July 2	$569.50	July 12	$580.70	July 23	$ 713.45
5	701.80	16	600.10	26	601.50
9	819.24	19	701.26	31	1,177.87

(*Continued*)

CHECKS WRITTEN:
Number and amount of each check issued in July:

Check No.	Amount	Check No.	Amount	Check No.	Amount
614	$243.50	621	$309.50	628	$ 837.70
615	350.10	622	Void	629	329.90
616	279.90	623	Void	630	882.80
617	395.50	624	707.01	631	1,081.56
618	435.40	625	158.63	632	325.40
619	320.10	626	550.03	633	310.08
620	238.87	627	381.73	634	241.71

Total amount of checks issued in July $8,379.42

JULY BANK STATEMENT:

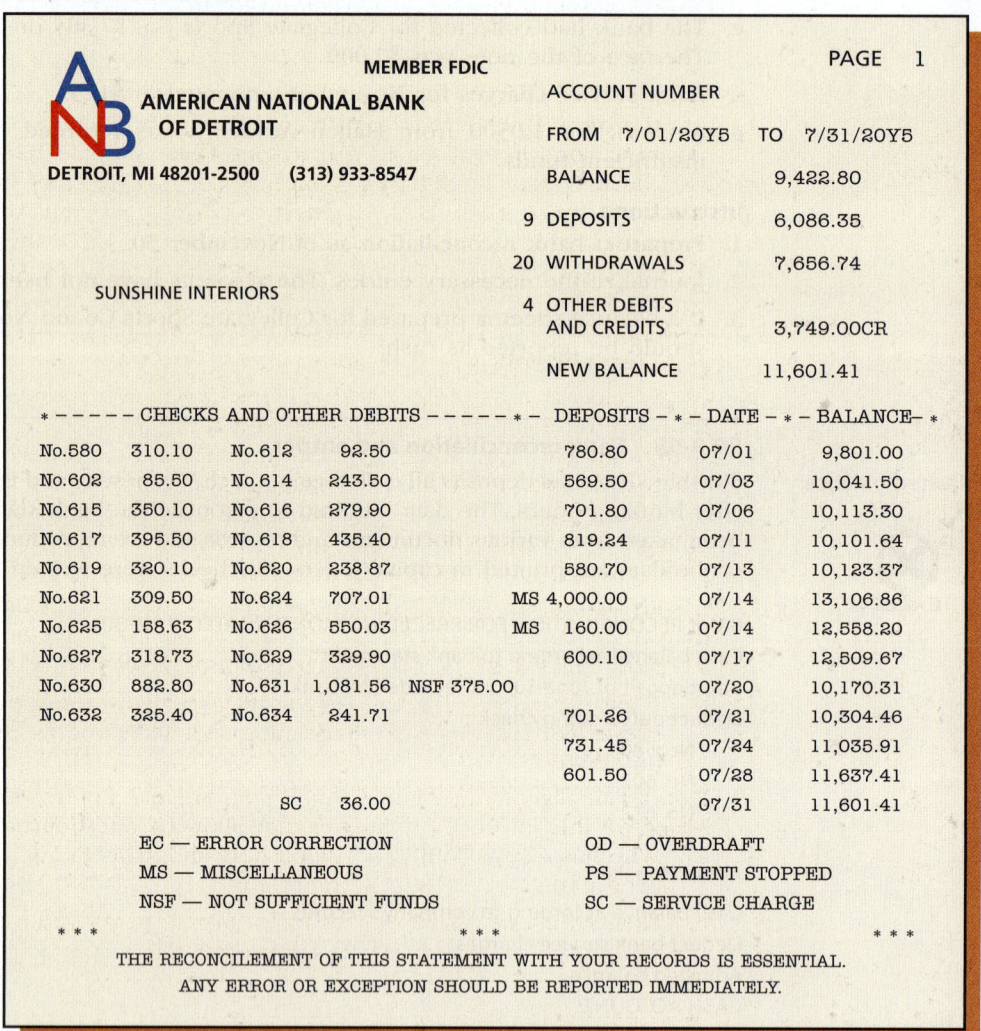

Instructions

1. Prepare a bank reconciliation as of July 31. If errors in recording deposits or checks are discovered, assume that the errors were made by the company. Assume that all deposits are from cash sales. All checks are written to satisfy accounts payable.
2. Journalize the necessary entries. The accounts have not been closed.
3. What is the amount of Cash that should appear on the balance sheet as of July 31?
4. Assume that a canceled check for $180 has been incorrectly recorded by the bank as $1,800. Briefly explain how the error would be included in a bank reconciliation and how it should be corrected.

Cases & Projects

CP 8-1 Ethics in Action

Tehra Dactyl is an accountant for Skeds, Inc., a footwear and apparel company. The company's revenue and net income have increased by more than 100% over the past three years. During the same period, Tehra and her colleagues in the Accounting Department have not received a raise or salary increase. Frustrated by not receiving a raise while the company has thrived, Tehra has begun submitting expense reimbursements for personal purchases. Tehra has a good relationship with her supervisor, and he simply "signs off" on Tehra's expense reimbursements. Tehra suspects that he knows she is submitting personal expenses for reimbursement and is "looking the other way" because Tehra has not received a raise in the past three years.

> Are Tehra and her supervisor acting in an ethical manner? Why or why not?

CP 8-2 Ethics in Action

During the preparation of the bank reconciliation for Building Concepts Co., Joel Knolls, the assistant controller, discovered that Lone Peak National Bank incorrectly recorded a $3,290 check written by Building Concepts Co. as $329. Joel has decided not to notify the bank but wait for the bank to detect the error. Joel plans to record the $2,961 error as Other Income if the bank fails to detect the error within the next three months.

> Discuss whether Joel is behaving in a professional manner.

CP 8-3 Team Activity

In teams, select a public company that interests you and is a business that requires inventory. Obtain the company's most recent annual report on Form 10-K. The Form 10-K is a company's annually required filing with the Securities and Exchange Commission (SEC). It includes the company's financial statements and accompanying notes. The Form 10-K can be obtained either (a) by referring to the investor relations section of the company's website or (b) by using the company search feature of the SEC's EDGAR database service found at www.sec.gov/edgar/searchedgar/companysearch.html.

1. Based on the information in the company's most recent annual report, answer the following questions:
   a. How much cash does the company have at the end of the most recent year?
   b. What percentage of total current assets is cash during the most recent two years presented? Has this percentage increased, decreased, or remained the same during this period?
2. Review Management's Annual Report on Internal Control Over Financial Reporting. Based on this information, answer the following questions:
   a. Who has responsibility for establishing and maintaining adequate internal controls over a company's financial reporting?
   b. How is "internal control over financial reporting" defined in this report?
   c. What level of assurance is provided that fraud will be detected?

CP 8-4 Team Activity

Select a business in your community and observe its internal controls over cash receipts and cash payments. The business could be a bank or a bookstore, a restaurant, a department store, or another retailer. In groups of three or four, identify and discuss the similarities and differences in each business's cash internal controls.

CP 8-5 Communication

Wholesome and Happy Foods is a farm-to-family grocery store located in the Pacific Northwest. The company recently installed four self-checkout lanes that allow customers

(Continued)

to scan their own groceries and pay for their purchases using an automated checkout kiosk. The kiosks are monitored by a single attendant. In recent weeks, management has become concerned that some customers are not scanning all of the items when using the self-checkout lanes.

✏️ Write a brief memo to your instructor suggesting features and capabilities for the kiosks that would serve as control procedures, ensuring that all items brought through the self-checkout lanes are properly scanned and purchased.

CP 8-6   Internal controls

The following is an excerpt from a conversation between two salesclerks, Jean Moen and Sara Cheney. Jean and Sara are employed by Turpin Meadows Electronics, a locally owned and operated electronics retail store.

Jean: Did you hear the news?

Sara: What news?

Jean: Neal and Linda were both arrested this morning.

Sara: What? Arrested? You're putting me on!

Jean: No, really! The police arrested them first thing this morning. Put them in handcuffs, read them their rights—the whole works. It was unreal!

Sara: What did they do?

Jean: Well, apparently they were filling out merchandise refund forms for fictitious customers and then taking the cash.

Sara: I guess I never thought of that. How did they catch them?

Jean: The store manager noticed that returns were twice that of last year and seemed to be increasing. When he confronted Neal, he became flustered and admitted to taking the cash, apparently more than $9,000 in just three months. They're going over the transactions of the last six months to try to determine how much Linda stole. She apparently started stealing first.

✏️ Suggest appropriate control procedures that would have prevented or detected the theft of cash.

CP 8-7   Internal controls

The following is an excerpt from a conversation between the store manager of Wholesome Grocery Stores, Kara Dahl, and Lynn Shutes, president of Wholesome Grocery Stores:

Lynn: Kara, I'm concerned about this new scanning system.

Kara: What's the problem?

Lynn: Well, how do we know the clerks are ringing up all the merchandise?

Kara: That's one of the strong points about the system. The scanner automatically rings up each item based on its bar code. We update the prices daily, so we're sure the sale is rung up for the right price.

Lynn: That's not my concern. What keeps a clerk from pretending to scan items and then simply not charging his friends? If his friends were buying 10–15 items, it would be easy for the clerk to pass several items through putting his finger over the bar code or just pass the merchandise through the scanner with the wrong side showing. It would look normal for anyone observing. In the old days, we at least could hear the cash register ringing up each sale.

Kara: I see your point.

✏️ Suggest ways that Wholesome Grocery Stores could prevent or detect the theft of merchandise as described.

CP 8-8   Bank reconciliation and internal control

The records of Parker Company indicate a July 31 cash balance of $10,400, which includes undeposited receipts for July 30 and 31. The cash balance on the bank statement as of July 31 is $10,575. This balance includes a note of $2,250 plus $150 interest collected by the bank but not recorded in the journal. Checks outstanding on July 31 were as follows: No. 2670, $1,050; No. 3679, $675; No. 3690, $1,650; No. 5148, $225; No. 5149, $750; and No. 5151, $800.

On July 25, the cashier resigned, effective at the end of the month. Before leaving on July 31, the cashier prepared the following bank reconciliation:

Cash balance per books, July 31		$10,400
Add outstanding checks:		
No. 5148	$225	
5149	750	
5151	800	1,675
		$12,075
Less undeposited receipts		1,500
Cash balance per bank, July 31		$10,575
Deduct unrecorded note with interest		2,400
True cash, July 31		$ 8,175

```
Calculator Tape of Outstanding Checks:
             0*
           225+
           750+
           800+
         1,675*
```

Subsequently, the owner of Parker Company discovered that the cashier had stolen an unknown amount of undeposited receipts, leaving only $1,500 to be deposited on July 31. The owner, a close family friend, has asked for your help in determining the amount that the former cashier stole.

1. Determine the amount the cashier stole from Parker Company. Show your computations in good form.

2. How did the cashier attempt to conceal the theft?

3. a. Identify two major weaknesses in internal controls that allowed the cashier to steal the undeposited cash receipts.

   b. Recommend improvements in internal controls so that similar types of thefts of undeposited cash receipts can be prevented.

CP 8-9 Cash to monthly cash expenses ratio

TearLab Corp. is a health care company that specializes in developing diagnostic devices for eye disease. TearLab reported the following data (in thousands) for three recent years:

	For Years Ended December 31		
	Year 3	Year 2	Year 1
Cash and cash equivalents	$ 13,838	$ 16,338	$ 37,778
Net cash flows from operations	(23,703)	(18,172)	(13,234)

1. Determine the monthly cash expenses for Year 3, Year 2, and Year 1. Round to one decimal place.

2. Determine the ratio of cash to monthly cash expenses as of December 31 for Year 3, Year 2, and Year 1. Round to one decimal place.

3. Based on (1) and (2), comment on TearLab's ratio of cash to monthly operating expenses for Year 3, Year 2, and Year 1.

CHAPTER 9
Receivables

Chapters 1–4
Accounting Cycle

Chapter 5
Accounting Systems

Income Statement	Statement of Owner's Equity	Balance Sheet	Statement of Cash Flows

Chapter 6 *Accounting for Merchandising Businesses*

Chapter 16 *Cash Flows*

Assets	=	Liabilities	+	Owner's Equity
Chapter 8 *Cash*		Chapter 11 *Current Liabilities*		Chapter 12 *Partnerships*
Chapter 9 **Receivables**		Chapter 14 *Bonds and Notes*		Chapter 13 *Corporations*
Chapter 7 *Inventories*				
Chapter 10 *Fixed and Intangible Assets*				
Chapter 15 *Investments*				

Chapter 17
Financial Statement Analysis

Statement of Owner's Equity

Owner's capital, Jan. 1		$XXX
Net income	$ XXX	
Withdrawals	(XXX)	
Increase in capital		XXX

Statement of Cash Flows

Cash flows from (used in) operating activities	$XXX
Cash flows from (used in) investing activities	XXX
Cash flows from (used in) financing activities	XXX
Increase (decrease) in cash flows	$XXX
	XXX
	$XXX

Income Statement

Sales		$XXX
Cost of merchandise sold		XXX
Gross profit		$XXX
Operating expenses:		
Advertising expense	$XXX	
Depreciation expense	XXX	
Amortization expense	XXX	
Depletion expense	XXX	
Bad debt expense	XXX	
…	XXX	
…	XXX	
Total operating expenses		XXX
Income from operations		$XXX
Other revenue and expenses		XXX
Interest revenue		XXX
Net income		$XXX

Balance Sheet

Current assets:		
Cash	$XXX	
Accounts receivable	XXX	
Allowance for doubtful accounts	XXX	
…	XXX	
Notes receivable	XXX	
Merchandise inventory	XXX	
Total current assets		$XXX
Property, plant, and equipment:	$XXX	
Intangible assets	XXX	
Total long-term assets		XXX
Total assets		$XXX
Liabilities:		
Current liabilities	$XXX	
Long-term liabilities	XXX	
Total liabilities		$XXX
Owner's equity		XXX
Total liabilities and owner's equity		$XXX

CHAPTER 9

Keurig Green Mountain, Inc.*

A company generates revenues by providing goods or services to customers. For example, **Keurig Green Mountain, Inc.**, sells brewing systems and related beverage packets to supermarkets, department stores, convenience stores, and club stores. Keurig also sells directly to consumers through its website at www.keurig.com.

If you were to buy a brewing system at Keurig.com, you would use a credit card to complete the purchase. In this case, Keurig would record the transaction as a cash sale. However, Keurig allows its business customers to purchase its products "on account." Sales on account create accounts receivable with credit terms requiring payment within the credit period.

Unlike cash sales, not all credit sales will generate cash. That is, some customers will not pay their account receivable and the company will have to record a bad debt expense. Companies like Keurig try to reduce uncollectible accounts by reviewing a customer's credit rating and payment history prior to a sale. Even with such procedures, however, companies will experience bad debts.

This chapter describes common classifications of receivables, including notes receivable. In addition, methods of accounting for and estimating uncollectible accounts are described and illustrated. Finally, the reporting of receivables, the allowance for uncollectible accounts, and bad debt expense in the financial statements is described and illustrated.

*Keurig Green Mountain, Inc., was sold to private equity firm **JAB Holding Co.** in December 2015.

Learning Objectives

After studying this chapter, you should be able to:

Example Exercises (EE) are shown in **green.**

Obj. 1 Describe the common classes of receivables.
- Classification of Receivables
  - Accounts Receivable
  - Notes Receivable
  - Other Receivables

Obj. 2 Describe the accounting for uncollectible receivables.
- Uncollectible Receivables

Obj. 3 Describe the direct write-off method of accounting for uncollectible receivables.
- Direct Write-Off Method for Uncollectible Accounts
  - Write-Offs to Bad Debt Expense — EE 9-1

Obj. 4 Describe the allowance method of accounting for uncollectible receivables.
- Allowance Method for Uncollectible Accounts
  - Write-Offs to the Allowance Account — EE 9-2
  - Percent of Sales Method — EE 9-3
  - Analysis of Receivables Method — EE 9-4

Obj. 5 Compare the direct write-off and allowance methods of accounting for uncollectible accounts.
- Comparing Direct Write-Off and Allowance Methods

Obj. 6 Describe the accounting for notes receivable.
- Notes Receivable
  - Characteristics of Notes Receivable
  - Accounting for Notes Receivable — EE 9-5

Obj. 7 Describe the reporting of receivables on the balance sheet.
- Reporting Receivables on the Balance Sheet

Obj. 8 Describe and illustrate the use of accounts receivable turnover and days' sales in receivables to evaluate a company's efficiency in collecting its receivables.
- Financial Analysis and Interpretation: Accounts Receivable Turnover and Days' Sales in Receivables
  - Compute Accounts Receivable Turnover and Days' Sales in Receivables — EE 9-6

At a Glance 9 — Page 461

Obj. 1 Describe the common classes of receivables.

Classification of Receivables

The receivables that result from sales on account are normally accounts receivable or notes receivable. The term **receivables** includes all money claims against other entities, including people, companies, and other organizations. Receivables are usually a significant portion of the total current assets.

Accounts Receivable

The most common transaction creating a receivable is selling merchandise or services on account (on credit). The receivable is recorded as a debit to Accounts Receivable. Such **accounts receivable** are normally collected within a short period, such as 30 or 60 days. They are classified on the balance sheet as a current asset.

Notes Receivable

Notes receivable are amounts that customers owe for which a formal, written instrument of credit has been issued. If notes receivable are expected to be collected within a year, they are classified on the balance sheet as a current asset.

Notes are often used for credit periods of more than 60 days. For example, a seller may require a down payment at the time of sale and accept a note or a series of notes for the remainder. Such notes usually provide for monthly payments.

Link to Keurig

In a recent annual report, **Keurig** reported an account receivable from **Costco** of over $100 million.

Notes may also be used to settle a customer's account receivable. Notes and accounts receivable that result from sales transactions are sometimes called *trade receivables*. In this chapter, all notes and accounts receivable are from sales transactions.

Other Receivables

Other receivables include interest receivable, taxes receivable, and receivables from officers or employees. Other receivables are normally reported separately on the balance sheet. If they are expected to be collected within one year, they are classified as current assets. If collection is expected beyond one year, they are classified as noncurrent assets and reported under the caption *Investments*.

Uncollectible Receivables

Obj. 2 Describe the accounting for uncollectible receivables.

In prior chapters, the accounting for sales of merchandise or services on account (on credit) was described and illustrated. A major issue that has not yet been discussed is that some customers will not pay their accounts. That is, some accounts receivable will be uncollectible.

Companies may shift the risk of uncollectible receivables to other companies. For example, some retailers do not accept sales on account but will only accept cash or credit cards. Such policies shift the risk to the credit card companies.

Companies may also sell their receivables. This is often the case when a company issues its own credit card. For example, Macy's and JCPenney issue their own credit cards. An advantage of a company selling its receivables is that it immediately receives cash for operating and other needs. Also, depending on the sales agreement, some of the risk of uncollectible accounts is shifted to the buyer.

Regardless of how careful a company is in granting credit, some credit sales will be uncollectible. The operating expense recorded from uncollectible receivables is called **bad debt expense**, *uncollectible accounts expense*, or *doubtful accounts expense*.

There is no general rule for when an account becomes uncollectible. Some indications that an account may be uncollectible include the following:

- The receivable is past due.
- The customer does not respond to the company's attempts to collect.
- The customer files for bankruptcy.
- The customer closes its business.
- The company cannot locate the customer.

If a customer doesn't pay, a company may turn the account over to a collection agency. After the collection agency attempts to collect payment, any remaining balance in the account is considered worthless.

The two methods of accounting for uncollectible receivables are as follows:

- The **direct write-off method** records bad debt expense only when an account is determined to be worthless.
- The **allowance method** records bad debt expense by estimating uncollectible accounts at the end of the accounting period.

The direct write-off method is often used by small companies and companies with few receivables.[1] Generally accepted accounting principles (GAAP), however, require companies with a large amount of receivables to use the allowance method. As a result, most well-known companies such as General Electric, Pepsi, Intel, and FedEx use the allowance method.

Link to Keurig

Keurig uses the allowance method and estimates uncollectible accounts based upon historical experience and specific customer risk, such as a customer who is experiencing financial difficulties.

---

1 The direct write-off method is also required for federal income tax purposes.

Business Connection

WARNING SIGNS

A business must manage the risk of extending credit. The following early warning signs can be used to signal the need to moderate future sales and accelerate collection efforts:

- You're only receiving partial payments.
- The customer's ordering pattern has declined dramatically, or the customer has stopped buying from you.
- The customer requests frequent changes in the payment schedule.
- You are repeatedly told that late payments are in process.
- The customer refuses to make payment, claiming dissatisfaction with the product.
- You can't reach your customer, or the customer refuses to acknowledge you.

Source: BMO Harris Bank website, Small Business Learning Center, Managing Your Trade Credit, 2015, www.bmoharris.com/us/small-business/learning-center/101/trade-credit.

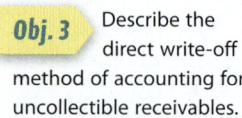

Obj. 3 Describe the direct write-off method of accounting for uncollectible receivables.

Direct Write-Off Method for Uncollectible Accounts

Under the direct write-off method, Bad Debt Expense is not recorded until the customer's account is determined to be worthless. At that time, the customer's account receivable is written off.

To illustrate, assume that on May 10, a $4,200 account receivable from D. L. Ross has been determined to be uncollectible. The entry to write off the account is as follows:

| May | 10 | Bad Debt Expense | 4,200 | |
| | | Accounts Receivable—D. L. Ross | | 4,200 |

An account receivable that has been written off may be collected later. In such cases, the account is reinstated by an entry that reverses the write-off entry. The cash received in payment is then recorded as a receipt on account.

To illustrate, assume that the D. L. Ross account of $4,200 written off on May 10 is later collected on November 21. The reinstatement and receipt of cash is recorded as follows:

Nov.	21	Accounts Receivable—D. L. Ross	4,200	
		Bad Debt Expense		4,200
	21	Cash	4,200	
		Accounts Receivable—D. L. Ross		4,200

The direct write-off method is used by businesses that sell most of their goods or services for cash or through the acceptance of MasterCard or VISA, which are recorded as cash sales. In such cases, receivables are a small part of the current assets and any bad debt expense is small. Examples of such businesses are a restaurant, a convenience store, and a small retail store.

Example Exercise 9-1 — Direct Write-Off Method
Obj. 3

Journalize the following transactions, using the direct write-off method of accounting for uncollectible receivables:

July 9. Received $1,200 from Jay Burke and wrote off the remainder owed of $3,900 as uncollectible.

Oct. 11. Reinstated the account of Jay Burke and received $3,900 cash in full payment.

Follow My Example 9-1

July	9	Cash	1,200	
		Bad Debt Expense	3,900	
		Accounts Receivable—Jay Burke		5,100
Oct.	11	Accounts Receivable—Jay Burke	3,900	
		Bad Debt Expense		3,900
	11	Cash	3,900	
		Accounts Receivable—Jay Burke		3,900

Practice Exercises: PE 9-1A, PE 9-1B

Allowance Method for Uncollectible Accounts

Obj. 4 Describe the allowance method of accounting for uncollectible receivables.

The allowance method estimates the uncollectible accounts receivable at the end of the accounting period. Based on this estimate, Bad Debt Expense is recorded by an adjusting entry.

To illustrate, assume that **ExTone Company** began operations on August 1. As of the end of its accounting period on December 31, 20Y7, ExTone has outstanding accounts receivable of $200,000. This balance includes some past due accounts. Based on industry averages, ExTone estimates that $30,000 of the December 31 accounts receivable will be uncollectible. However, on December 31, ExTone doesn't know which customer accounts will be uncollectible. Thus, specific customer accounts cannot be decreased or credited. Instead, a contra asset account, **Allowance for Doubtful Accounts**, is credited for the estimated bad debts.

Using the $30,000 estimate, the following adjusting entry is made on December 31:

20Y7				
Dec.	31	Bad Debt Expense	30,000	
		Allowance for Doubtful Accounts		30,000
		Uncollectible accounts estimate.		

The preceding adjusting entry affects the income statement and balance sheet. On the income statement, the $30,000 of Bad Debt Expense will be matched against the related revenues of the period. On the balance sheet, the value of the receivables is reduced to the amount that is expected to be collected or realized. This amount, $170,000 ($200,000 − $30,000), is called the **net realizable value** of the receivables.

After the preceding adjusting entry is recorded, Accounts Receivable still has a debit balance of $200,000. This balance is the total amount owed by customers on account on December 31 as supported by the accounts receivable subsidiary ledger. The accounts receivable contra account, Allowance for Doubtful Accounts, has a credit balance of $30,000.

Note

The adjusting entry reduces receivables to their net realizable value and matches the uncollectible expense with revenues.

INTEGRITY, OBJECTIVITY, AND ETHICS IN BUSINESS

COLLECTING PAST DUE ACCOUNTS

Companies should make reasonable attempts (steps) to collect past due accounts. Many companies send a collection reminder as a first step. As a second step, a company may send a collection letter that offers options such as a willingness to negotiate a schedule for future payments. The next step is normally to turn the past due amount over to a collection agency or to file action in court. However, in no case should a company employee harass or misrepresent himself or herself to the customer as an attorney, a collection agent, or an agent of the court.

Write-Offs to the Allowance Account

When a customer's account is identified as uncollectible, it is written off against the allowance account. This requires the company to remove the specific accounts receivable and an equal amount from the allowance account.

To illustrate, on January 21, 20Y8, John Parker's account of $6,000 with **ExTone Company** is written off as follows:

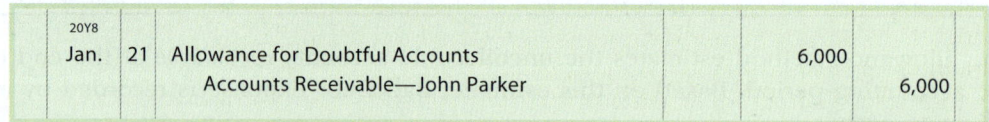

At the end of a period, Allowance for Doubtful Accounts will normally have a balance. This is because Allowance for Doubtful Accounts is based on an estimate. As a result, the total write-offs to the allowance account during the period will rarely equal the balance of the account at the beginning of the period. The allowance account will have a credit balance at the end of the period if the write-offs during the period are less than the beginning balance. It will have a debit balance if the write-offs exceed the beginning balance.

Exhibit 1 illustrates the allowance method where the adjusting entry increases the Allowance for Doubtful Accounts (fills the bucket) while writing off accounts decreases the Allowance for Doubtful Accounts (empties the bucket).

EXHIBIT 1

The Allowance Method

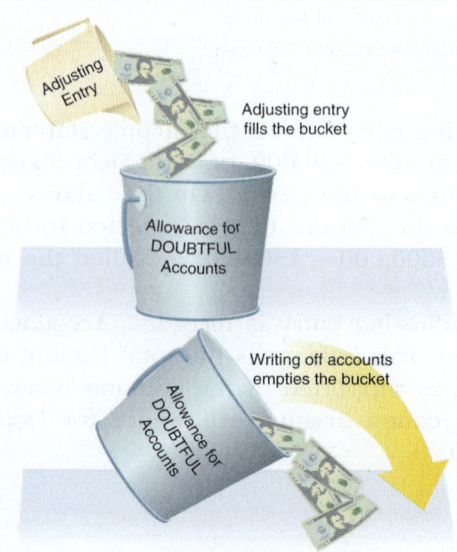

To illustrate, assume that during 20Y8 **ExTone Company** writes off $26,750 of uncollectible accounts, including the $6,000 account of John Parker recorded on January 21. Allowance for Doubtful Accounts will have a credit balance of $3,250 ($30,000 − $26,750), computed as follows:

ALLOWANCE FOR DOUBTFUL ACCOUNTS

				Jan. 1	Balance	30,000
Total accounts written off $26,750	Jan. 21	6,000				
	Feb. 2	3,900				
	⋮	⋮				
				Dec. 31	Unadjusted balance	3,250

If ExTone had written off $32,100 in accounts receivable during 20Y8, Allowance for Doubtful Accounts would have had a debit balance of $2,100, computed as follows:

ALLOWANCE FOR DOUBTFUL ACCOUNTS

				Jan. 1	Balance	30,000
Total accounts written off $32,100	Jan. 21	6,000				
	Feb. 2	3,900				
	⋮	⋮				
Dec. 31	Unadjusted balance	2,100				

The allowance account balances (credit balance of $3,250 and debit balance of $2,100) in the preceding illustrations are *before* the end-of-period adjusting entry. After the end-of-period adjusting entry is recorded, Allowance for Doubtful Accounts should always have a credit balance.

An account receivable that has been written off against the allowance account may be collected later. Like the direct write-off method, the account is reinstated by an entry that reverses the write-off entry. The cash received in payment is then recorded as a receipt on account.

To illustrate, assume that Nancy Smith's account of $5,000, which was written off on April 2, is collected later on June 10. **ExTone Company** records the reinstatement and the collection as follows:

20Y8				
June	10	Accounts Receivable—Nancy Smith	5,000	
		Allowance for Doubtful Accounts		5,000
	10	Cash	5,000	
		Accounts Receivable—Nancy Smith		5,000

Example Exercise 9-2 Allowance Method   Obj. 4

Journalize the following transactions, using the allowance method of accounting for uncollectible receivables:

July 9. Received $1,200 from Jay Burke and wrote off the remainder owed of $3,900 as uncollectible.

Oct. 11. Reinstated the account of Jay Burke and received $3,900 cash in full payment.

Follow My Example 9-2

July	9	Cash	1,200	
		Allowance for Doubtful Accounts	3,900	
		Accounts Receivable—Jay Burke		5,100
Oct.	11	Accounts Receivable—Jay Burke	3,900	
		Allowance for Doubtful Accounts		3,900
	11	Cash	3,900	
		Accounts Receivable—Jay Burke		3,900

Practice Exercises: PE 9-2A, PE 9-2B

Business Connection

FAILURE TO COLLECT

When customers fail to pay their accounts, a business has the option of seeking payment through various means. The easiest recourse is simply to inquire about the cause of non-payment and adjust terms to maximize the potential for collection. For large amounts, the cost and time of legal remedies can be appropriate. However, for smaller amounts, most businesses want to minimize the time, effort, and cost of collecting amounts that are past due. Thus, after exhausting their internal efforts to collect, businesses typically use the services of a collection agency to collect overdue accounts. Such services must abide by a number of consumer protection laws in collecting overdue accounts. The final amount collected will often be less than the full amount due, of which the collection agency will often keep 25–45% as a fee. Thus, the collection agency is often the last resort before a final write-off.

Estimating Uncollectibles

The allowance method requires an estimate of uncollectible accounts at the end of the period. This estimate is normally based on past experience, industry averages, and forecasts of the future.

The two methods used to estimate uncollectible accounts are as follows:

- Percent of sales method
- Analysis of receivables method

Percent of Sales Method

Since accounts receivable are created by credit sales, uncollectible accounts can be estimated as a percent of credit sales. If the portion of credit sales to sales is relatively constant, the percent may be applied to total sales.

To illustrate, assume the following data for **ExTone Company** on December 31, 20Y8, before any adjustments:

Balance of Accounts Receivable	$ 240,000
Balance of Allowance for Doubtful Accounts	3,250 (Cr.)
Total credit sales	3,000,000
Bad debt as a percent of credit sales	¾%

Bad Debt Expense of $22,500 is estimated as follows:

Bad Debt Expense = Credit Sales × Bad Debt as a Percent of Credit Sales
Bad Debt Expense = $3,000,000 × ¾% = $22,500

The adjusting entry for uncollectible accounts on December 31, 20Y8, is as follows:

20Y8					
Dec.	31	Bad Debt Expense		22,500	
		Allowance for Doubtful Accounts			22,500
		Uncollectible accounts estimate			
		($3,000,000 × ¾% = $22,500).			

After the adjusting entry is posted to the ledger, Bad Debt Expense will have an adjusted balance of $22,500. Allowance for Doubtful Accounts will have an adjusted balance of $25,750 ($3,250 + $22,500). Both T accounts follow:

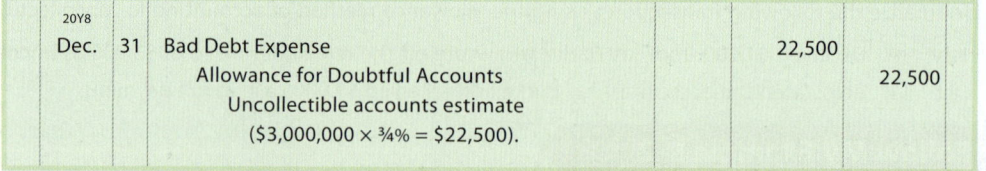

BAD DEBT EXPENSE

| Dec. 31 | Adjusting entry | 22,500 |
| 31 | Adjusted balance | 22,500 |

ALLOWANCE FOR DOUBTFUL ACCOUNTS

			Jan. 1	Balance	30,000
Total accounts written off $26,750	Jan. 21	6,000			
	Feb. 2	3,900			
	⋮	⋮	Dec. 31	Unadjusted balance	3,250
			31	Adjusting entry	22,500
			31	Adjusted balance	25,750

Under the percent of sales method, the amount of the adjusting entry is the amount estimated for Bad Debt Expense. This estimate is credited to whatever the unadjusted balance is for Allowance for Doubtful Accounts. For example, in the preceding illustration, the Allowance for Doubtful Accounts had a beginning credit balance of $3,250. After the adjusting entry, the balance of Allowance for Doubtful Accounts is an adjusted balance of $25,750 ($3,250 + $22,500), and the net realizable value of the receivables is $214,250 ($240,000 − $25,750).

Assume that in the preceding example, Allowance for Doubtful Accounts had a beginning debit balance of $2,100. After the adjusting entry, the balance of Allowance for Doubtful Accounts will have an adjusted balance of $20,400 ($22,500 − $2,100), and the net realizable value of the receivables is $219,600 ($240,000 − $20,400).

Note: The estimate based on sales is added to any balance in Allowance for Doubtful Accounts.

Example Exercise 9-3 Percent of Sales Method   Obj. 4

At the end of the current year, Accounts Receivable has a balance of $800,000; Allowance for Doubtful Accounts has a credit balance of $7,500; and sales for the year total $3,500,000. Bad debt expense is estimated at ½% of sales.

Determine (a) the amount of the adjusting entry for uncollectible accounts; (b) the adjusted balances of Accounts Receivable, Allowance for Doubtful Accounts, and Bad Debt Expense; and (c) the net realizable value of accounts receivable.

Follow My Example 9-3

a. $17,500 ($3,500,000 × 1/2%)

		Adjusted Balance Debt (Credit)
b.	Accounts Receivable	$800,000
	Allowance for Doubtful Accounts ($7,500 + $17,500)	(25,000)
	Bad Debt Expense	17,500

c. $775,000 ($800,000 − $25,000)

Practice Exercises: PE 9-3A, PE 9-3B

Analysis of Receivables Method

The analysis of receivables method is based on the assumption that the longer an account receivable is outstanding, the less likely it will be collected. The analysis of receivables method is applied as follows:

Dynamic Exhibit

Step 1. The due date of each account receivable is determined.
Step 2. The number of days each account is past due is determined. This is the number of days between the due date of the account and the date of the analysis.
Step 3. Each account is placed in an aged class according to its days past due. Typical aged classes include the following:

Not past due
1–30 days past due
31–60 days past due
61–90 days past due
91–180 days past due
181–365 days past due
Over 365 days past due

Step 4. The totals for each aged class are determined.

Step 5. The total for each aged class is multiplied by an estimated percentage of uncollectible accounts for that class.

Step 6. The estimated total of uncollectible accounts is determined as the sum of the estimated uncollectible accounts for each aged class.

The preceding steps are summarized in an aging schedule, and this overall process is called **aging the receivables**.

To illustrate, assume that ExTone Company uses the analysis of receivables method instead of the percent of sales method. ExTone prepared an aging schedule for its accounts receivable of $240,000 as of December 31, 20Y8, as shown in Exhibit 2.

EXHIBIT 2 — Aging of Receivables Schedule, December 31, 20Y8

	A	B	C	D	E	F	G	H	I
1			Not			Days Past Due			
2			Past						Over
3	Customer	Balance	Due	1–30	31–60	61–90	91–180	181–365	365
4	Ashby & Co.	1,500			1,500				
5	B. T. Barr	6,100						3,500	2,600
6	Brock Co.	4,700	4,700						
...	...	...	...	...	...	...	...	...	...
22	Saxon Woods Co.	600						600	
23	Total	240,000	125,000	64,000	13,100	8,900	5,000	10,000	14,000
24	Percent uncollectible			2%	5%	10%	20%	30%	50%	80%
25	Estimate of uncollectible accounts	26,490	2,500	3,200	1,310	1,780	1,500	5,000	11,200

Steps 1–3 correspond to rows 4–22. Step 4 → row 23. Step 5 → row 24. Step 6 → row 25.

Assume that ExTone sold merchandise to Saxon Woods Co. on August 29 with terms 2/10, n/30. Thus, the due date (Step 1) of Saxon Woods' account is September 28, computed as follows:

Credit terms, net	30 days
Less: Aug. 29 to Aug. 31	2 days
Days in September	28 days

As of December 31, Saxon Woods' account is 94 days past due (Step 2), computed as follows:

Number of days past due in September	2 days (30 − 28)
Number of days past due in October	31 days
Number of days past due in November	30 days
Number of days past due in December	31 days
Total number of days past due	94 days

Exhibit 2 shows that the $600 account receivable for Saxon Woods Co. was placed in the 91–180 days past due class (Step 3).

The total for each of the aged classes is determined (Step 4). Exhibit 2 shows that $125,000 of the accounts receivable are not past due, while $64,000 are 1–30 days past due. ExTone applies a different estimated percentage of uncollectible accounts to the totals of each of the aged classes (Step 5). As shown in Exhibit 2, the percent is 2% for accounts not past due, while the percent is 80% for accounts over 365 days past due.

The sum of the estimated uncollectible accounts for each aged class (Step 6) is the estimated uncollectible accounts on December 31, 20Y8. This is the desired adjusted balance for Allowance for Doubtful Accounts. For ExTone, this amount is $26,490, as shown in Exhibit 2.

Comparing the estimate of $26,490 with the unadjusted balance of the allowance account determines the amount of the adjustment for Bad Debt Expense. For ExTone, the unadjusted balance of the allowance account is a credit balance of $3,250. The amount to be added to this balance is therefore $23,240 ($26,490 − $3,250). The adjusting entry is as follows:

20Y8				
Dec.	31	Bad Debt Expense	23,240	
		Allowance for Doubtful Accounts		23,240
		Uncollectible accounts estimate		
		($26,490 − $3,250).		

Note

The estimate based on receivables is compared to the balance in the allowance account to determine the amount of the adjusting entry.

After the preceding adjusting entry is posted to the ledger, Bad Debt Expense will have an adjusted balance of $23,240. Allowance for Doubtful Accounts will have an adjusted balance of $26,490, and the net realizable value of the receivables is $213,510 ($240,000 − $26,490). Both T accounts follow:

BAD DEBT EXPENSE

| Dec. 31 | Adjusting entry | 23,240 | | |
| 31 | Adjusted balance | 23,240 | | |

ALLOWANCE FOR DOUBTFUL ACCOUNTS

			Dec. 31	Unadjusted balance	3,250
			31	Adjusting entry	23,240
			31	Adjusted balance	26,490

Under the analysis of receivables method, the amount of the adjusting entry is the amount that will yield an adjusted balance for Allowance for Doubtful Accounts equal to that estimated by the aging schedule. For example, assume that the unadjusted balance of the allowance account had been a debit of $2,100. The amount of the adjustment is $28,590 ($26,490 + $2,100). The Allowance for Doubtful Accounts will have an adjusted balance is $26,490 ($28,590 − $2,100), and the net realizable value of the receivables is $213,510 ($240,000 − $26,490). Bad Debt Expense will have an adjusted balance of $28,590. The T accounts appear as follows:

BAD DEBT EXPENSE

| Dec. 31 | Adjusting entry | 28,590 | | |
| 31 | Adjusted balance | 28,590 | | |

ALLOWANCE FOR DOUBTFUL ACCOUNTS

| Dec. 31 | Unadjusted balance | 2,100 | Dec. 31 | Adjusting entry | 28,590 |
| | | | 31 | Adjusted balance | 26,490 |

Link to Keurig

In a recent balance sheet, **Keurig** reported an allowance for uncollectible accounts of $66,120,000 and a net realizable value of receivables of $621,451,000.

Example Exercise 9-4 Analysis of Receivables Method   Obj. 4

At the end of the current year, Accounts Receivable has a balance of $800,000, Allowance for Doubtful Accounts has a credit balance of $7,500, and sales for the year total $3,500,000. Using the aging method, the balance of Allowance for Doubtful Accounts is estimated as $30,000.

Determine (a) the amount of the adjusting entry for uncollectible accounts; (b) the adjusted balances of Accounts Receivable, Allowance for Doubtful Accounts, and Bad Debt Expense; and (c) the net realizable value of accounts receivable.

Follow My Example 9-4

a. $22,500 ($30,000 − $7,500)

		Adjusted Balance Debit (Credit)
b.	Accounts Receivable	$800,000
	Allowance for Doubtful Accounts	(30,000)
	Bad Debt Expense	22,500

c. $770,000 ($800,000 − $30,000)

Practice Exercises: PE 9-4A, PE 9-4B

Comparing Estimation Methods Both the percent of sales and analysis of receivables methods estimate uncollectible accounts. However, each method has a slightly different focus and financial statement emphasis.

Under the percent of sales method, Bad Debt Expense is the focus of the estimation process. The percent of sales method places more emphasis on matching revenues and expenses and, thus, emphasizes the income statement. That is, the amount of the adjusting entry is based on the estimate of Bad Debt Expense for the period. Allowance for Doubtful Accounts is then credited for this amount.

Under the analysis of receivables method, Allowance for Doubtful Accounts is the focus of the estimation process. The analysis of receivables method places more emphasis on the net realizable value of the receivables and, thus, emphasizes the balance sheet. That is, the amount of the adjusting entry is the amount that will yield an adjusted balance for Allowance for Doubtful Accounts equal to that estimated by the aging schedule. Bad Debt Expense is then debited for this amount.

Exhibit 3 summarizes these differences between the percent of sales and the analysis of receivables methods. Exhibit 3 also shows the results of the ExTone Company

EXHIBIT 3
Difference Between Estimation Methods

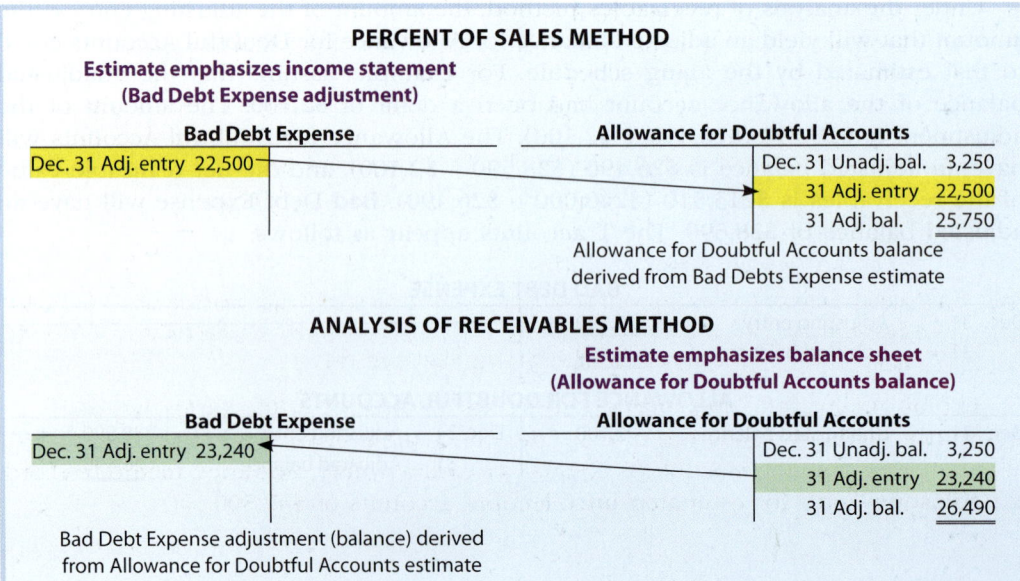

illustration for the percent of sales and analysis of receivables methods. The amounts shown in Exhibit 3 assume an unadjusted credit balance of $3,250 for Allowance for Doubtful Accounts. While the methods normally yield different amounts for any one period, over several periods, the amounts should be similar.

Business Connection

ALLOWANCE PERCENTAGES ACROSS COMPANIES

The percent of the allowance for doubtful accounts to total accounts receivable varies across companies and industries. For example, the following percentages were computed from recent annual reports:

Company	Industry	Percent of Allowance for Doubtful Accounts to Total Accounts Receivable
Coca-Cola	Beverages	7.1%
DuPont	Chemicals	3.8%
HCA	Health services	46.8%
Nike	Apparel	2.2%
Union Pacific	Transportation services	0.3%
Wynn Resorts	Casino gaming	23.9%

HCA's higher percentage is due in part to providing health care to patients without the means to pay. Wynn Resorts' high percentage is typical for casinos, representing the challenges in collecting gambling debts.

Comparing Direct Write-Off and Allowance Methods

Obj. 5 Compare the direct write-off and allowance methods of accounting for uncollectible accounts.

Journal entries for the direct write-off and allowance methods are illustrated and compared in this section. As a basis for illustration, the following transactions, taken from the records of Hobbs Company for the year ending December 31 are used:

Mar. 1. Wrote off account of C. York, $3,650.

Apr. 12. Received $2,250 as partial payment on the $5,500 account of Cary Bradshaw. Wrote off the remaining balance as uncollectible.

June 22. Received the $3,650 from C. York, which had been written off on March 1. Reinstated the account and recorded the cash receipt.

Sept. 7. Wrote off the following accounts as uncollectible (record as one journal entry):

Jason Bigg	$1,100	Stanford Noonan	$1,360
Steve Bradey	2,220	Aiden Wyman	990
Samantha Neeley	775		

Dec. 31. Hobbs Company uses the percent of credit sales method of estimating uncollectible expenses. Based on past history and industry averages, 1.25% of credit sales are expected to be uncollectible. Hobbs recorded $3,400,000 of credit sales during the year.

Exhibit 4 illustrates the journal entries for Hobbs using the direct write-off and allowance methods. Using the direct write-off method, there is no adjusting entry on December 31 for uncollectible accounts. In contrast, the allowance method records an adjusting entry for estimated uncollectible accounts of $42,500.

EXHIBIT 4 — Comparing Direct Write-Off and Allowance Methods

		Direct Write-Off Method			Allowance Method		
Mar.	1	Bad Debt Expense	3,650		Allowance for Doubtful Accounts	3,650	
		Accounts Receivable—C. York		3,650	Accounts Receivable—C. York		3,650
Apr.	12	Cash	2,250		Cash	2,250	
		Bad Debt Expense	3,250		Allowance for Doubtful Accounts	3,250	
		Accounts Receivable—Cary Bradshaw		5,500	Accounts Receivable—Cary Bradshaw		5,500
June	22	Accounts Receivable—C. York	3,650		Accounts Receivable—C. York	3,650	
		Bad Debt Expense		3,650	Allowance for Doubtful Accounts		3,650
	22	Cash	3,650		Cash	3,650	
		Accounts Receivable—C. York		3,650	Accounts Receivable—C. York		3,650
Sept.	7	Bad Debt Expense	6,445		Allowance for Doubtful Accounts	6,445	
		Accounts Receivable—Jason Bigg		1,100	Accounts Receivable—Jason Bigg		1,100
		Accounts Receivable—Steve Bradey		2,220	Accounts Receivable—Steve Bradey		2,220
		Accounts Receivable—Samantha Neeley		775	Accounts Receivable—Samantha Neeley		775
		Accounts Receivable—Stanford Noonan		1,360	Accounts Receivable—Stanford Noonan		1,360
		Accounts Receivable—Aiden Wyman		990	Accounts Receivable—Aiden Wyman		990
Dec.	31	No Entry			Bad Debt Expense	42,500	
					Allowance for Doubtful Accounts		42,500
					Uncollectible accounts estimate ($3,400,000 × 1.25% = $42,500).		

The primary differences between the direct write-off and allowance methods are summarized in Exhibit 5.

EXHIBIT 5 — Direct Write-Off and Allowance Methods

	Direct Write-Off Method	Allowance Method
Bad debt expense is recorded	When a specific customer account is determined to be uncollectible.	Using estimate based on (1) a percent of sales or (2) an analysis of receivables.
Allowance account	No allowance account is used.	The allowance account is used.
Primary users	Small companies and companies with few receivables.	Large companies and those with a large amount of receivables.

Obj. 6 Describe the accounting for notes receivable.

Notes Receivable

A note has some advantages over an account receivable. By signing a note, the debtor recognizes the debt and agrees to pay it according to its terms. Thus, a note is a stronger legal claim.

Characteristics of Notes Receivable

A promissory note is a written promise to pay the face amount, usually with interest, on demand or at a date in the future.[2] Characteristics of a promissory note are as follows:

1. The *maker* is the party making the promise to pay.
2. The *payee* is the party to whom the note is payable.

[2] You may see references to non-interest-bearing notes. Such notes are not widely used and carry an assumed or implicit interest rate.

3. The *face amount* is the amount for which the note is written on its face.
4. The *issuance date* is the date a note is issued.
5. The *due date* or *maturity date* is the date the note is to be paid.
6. The *term* of a note is the amount of time between the issuance and due dates.
7. The *interest rate* is that rate of interest that must be paid on the face amount for the term of the note.

Exhibit 6 illustrates a promissory note.

Promissory Note — **EXHIBIT 6**

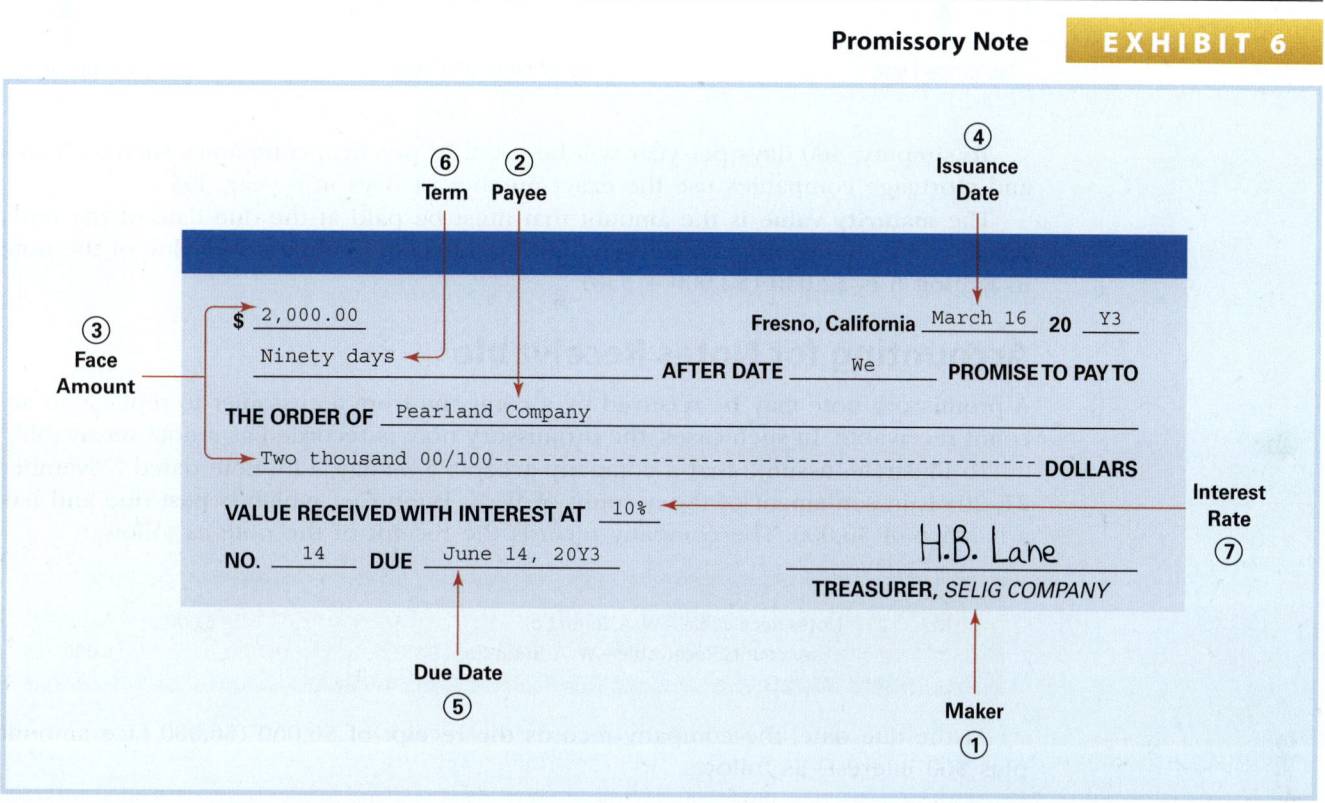

The maker of the note is Selig Company, and the payee is Pearland Company. The face value of the note is $2,000, the interest rate is 10%, and the issuance date is March 16, 20Y3. The term of the note is 90 days, which results in a due date of June 14, 20Y3, computed as follows and shown in Exhibit 7:

Days in March	31 days
Minus issuance date of note	16
Days remaining in March	15 days
Add days in April	30
Add days in May	31
Add days in June (due date of June 14)	14
Term of note	90 days

The interest on a note is computed as follows:

$$\text{Interest} = \text{Face Amount} \times \text{Interest Rate} \times (\text{Term} \div 360 \text{ days})$$

The interest rate is stated on an annual (yearly) basis, while the term is expressed as days. Thus, the interest on the note in Exhibit 6 is computed as follows:

$$\text{Interest} = \$2{,}000 \times 10\% \times (90 \div 360) = \$50$$

EXHIBIT 7

Determining Due Date of Promissory Note

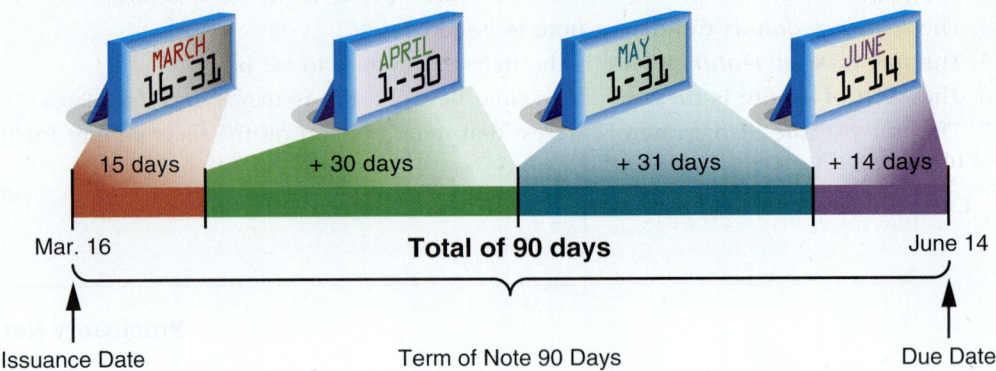

To simplify, 360 days per year will be used. In practice, companies such as banks and mortgage companies use the exact number of days in a year, 365.

The **maturity value** is the amount that must be paid at the due date of the note, which is the sum of the face amount and the interest. The maturity value of the note in Exhibit 6 is $2,050 ($2,000 + $50).

Accounting for Notes Receivable

A promissory note may be received by a company from a customer to replace an account receivable. In such cases, the promissory note is recorded as a note receivable.[3]

To illustrate, assume that a company accepts a 30-day, 12% note dated November 21, 20Y1, in settlement of the account of W. A. Bunn Co., which is past due and has a balance of $6,000. The company records the receipt of the note as follows:

20Y1				
Nov.	21	Notes Receivable—W. A. Bunn Co.	6,000	
		Accounts Receivable—W. A. Bunn Co.		6,000

At the due date, the company records the receipt of $6,060 ($6,000 face amount plus $60 interest) as follows:

20Y1				
Dec.	21	Cash	6,060	
		Notes Receivable—W. A. Bunn Co.		6,000
		Interest Revenue		60
		[$6,060 = $6,000 + ($6,000 × 12% × 30 ÷ 360)].		

If the maker of a note fails to pay the note on the due date, the note is a **dishonored note receivable**. A company that holds a dishonored note transfers the face amount of the note plus any interest due back to an accounts receivable account. For example, assume that the $6,000, 30-day, 12% note received from W. A. Bunn Co. and recorded on November 21 is dishonored. The company holding the note transfers the note and interest back to the customer's account as follows:

20Y1				
Dec.	21	Accounts Receivable—W. A. Bunn Co.	6,060	
		Notes Receivable—W. A. Bunn Co.		6,000
		Interest Revenue		60

---

3 The accounting for notes payable is described and illustrated in Chapter 14.

The company has earned the interest of $60, even though the note is dishonored. If the account receivable is uncollectible, the company will write off $6,060 against Allowance for Doubtful Accounts.

A company receiving a note should record an adjusting entry for any accrued interest at the end of the period. For example, assume that Crawford Company issues a $4,000, 90-day, 12% note dated December 1, 20Y4, to settle its account receivable. If the accounting period ends on December 31, the company receiving the note would record the following entries:

20Y4					
Dec.	1	Notes Receivable—Crawford Company		4,000	
		Accounts Receivable—Crawford Company			4,000
	31	Interest Receivable		40	
		Interest Revenue			40
		Accrued interest			
		($4,000 × 12% × 30 ÷ 360).			
20Y5					
Mar.	1	Cash		4,120	
		Notes Receivable—Crawford Company			4,000
		Interest Receivable			40
		Interest Revenue			80
		Total interest of $120			
		($4,000 × 12% × 90 ÷ 360).			

The interest revenue account is closed at the end of each accounting period. The amount of interest revenue is normally reported in the Other revenue section of the income statement.

Example Exercise 9-5   Note Receivable   Obj. 6

Same Day Surgery Center received a 120-day, 6% note for $40,000, dated March 14, from a patient on account.

a. Determine the due date of the note.
b. Determine the maturity value of the note.
c. Journalize the entry to record the receipt of the payment of the note at maturity.

Follow My Example 9-5

a. The due date of the note is July 12, determined as follows:

March	17 days (31 – 14)	
April	30 days	
May	31 days	
June	30 days	
July	12 days	
Total	120 days	

b. $40,800 [$40,000 + ($40,000 × 6% × 120 ÷ 360)]

c. July 12   Cash 40,800
   Notes Receivable... 40,000
   Interest Revenue.. 800

Practice Exercises: PE 9-5A, PE 9-5B

Reporting Receivables on the Balance Sheet

Obj. 7 Describe the reporting of receivables on the balance sheet.

All receivables that are expected to be realized in cash within a year are reported in the Current assets section of the balance sheet. Current assets are normally reported in the order of their liquidity, beginning with cash and cash equivalents.

The balance sheet presentation for receivables for **Mornin' Joe** follows:

Mornin' Joe
Balance Sheet
December 31, 20Y6

Assets

Current assets:		
Cash and cash equivalents		$235,000
Accounts receivable	$305,000	
Less allowance for doubtful accounts	12,300	292,700

In Mornin' Joe's financial statements, the allowance for doubtful accounts is subtracted from accounts receivable. Some companies report receivables at their net realizable value with a note showing the amount of the allowance.

Other disclosures related to receivables are reported either on the face of the financial statements or in the financial statement notes. Such disclosures include the market (fair) value of the receivables. In addition, if unusual credit risks exist within the receivables, the nature of the risks are disclosed. For example, if the majority of the receivables are due from one customer or are due from customers located in one area of the country or one industry, these facts are disclosed.[4]

Link to Keurig
Keurig uses **M. Block & Sons** to process its sales to department stores, supermarkets, and other retailers in the United States. As a result, Keurig reported a significant credit risk related to its accounts receivable from M. Block.

Business Connection

DELTA AIR LINES

Delta Air Lines is a major air carrier that services cities throughout the United States and the world. In its operations, Delta generates accounts receivable as reported in the following note to its financial statements:

Our accounts receivable are generated largely from the sale of passenger airline tickets and cargo transportation services, the majority of which are processed through major credit card companies. We also have receivables from the sale of mileage credits under our SkyMiles Program to participating airlines and non-airline businesses such as credit card companies, hotels, and car rental agencies. The credit risk associated with our receivables is minimal.

In a recent balance sheet, Delta reported the following accounts receivable (in millions):

	Dec. 31, Year 2	Dec. 31, Year 1
Current Assets:		
Accounts receivable, net of an allowance for uncollectible accounts of $9 at December 31 (Year 2) and $11 at December 31 (Year 1)	$2,020	$2,297

Source: Delta Air Lines, Inc., *Form 10-K for the Fiscal Year Ended December 31, 2015.*

---

[4] *FASB Accounting Standards Codification*, Section 210-10-50.

Financial Analysis and Interpretation: Accounts Receivable Turnover and Days' Sales in Receivables

Obj. 8 Describe and illustrate the use of accounts receivable turnover and days' sales in receivables to evaluate a company's efficiency in collecting its receivables.

Two financial measures that are especially useful in evaluating efficiency in collecting receivables are the following:

- the accounts receivable turnover
- the days' sales in receivables

The **accounts receivable turnover** measures how frequently during the year the accounts receivable are being converted to cash. For example, with credit terms of n/30, the accounts receivable should turn over about 12 (360 days ÷ 30 days) times per year.

The accounts receivable turnover is computed as follows:[5]

$$\text{Accounts Receivable Turnover} = \frac{\text{Sales}}{\text{Average Accounts Receivable}}$$

The average accounts receivable can be determined by using monthly data or by simply adding the beginning and ending accounts receivable balances and dividing by two. For example, using the following financial data (in millions) for **Keurig**, the Year 2 and Year 1 accounts receivable turnover is 7.94 and 8.65, computed as follows:

	Year 2	Year 1
Sales	$4,520	$4,708
Accounts receivable:		
Beginning of year	621	468
End of year	518	621
Average accounts receivable:		
($621 + $518) ÷ 2	569.5	
($468 + $621) ÷ 2		544.5
Accounts receivable turnover:*		
$4,520 ÷ $569.5	7.94	
$4,708 ÷ $544.5		8.65

* Rounded to two decimal places.

The accounts receivable turnover has declined in Year 2. This suggests that Keurig is allowing customers to take longer to pay their accounts.

The **days' sales in receivables** is an estimate of the length of time the accounts receivable have been outstanding. With credit terms of n/30, the days' sales in receivables should be about 30 days. It is computed as follows:[6]

$$\text{Days' Sales in Receivables} = \frac{\text{Average Accounts Receivable}}{\text{Average Daily Sales}}$$

Average daily sales are determined by dividing sales by 365 days.[7] For example, using the preceding data for Keurig, the days' sales in receivables of 45.9 for Year 2 and 42.2 for Year 1 are computed as follows:

---

[5] If known, credit sales can be used in the numerator. However, because credit sales are not normally disclosed to external users, most analysts use sales in the numerator.

[6] Days' sales in receivables may also be computed as 365 days divided by the accounts receivable turnover.

[7] We use 365 days for all computations involving real-world companies and data. We do this because it highlights differences among companies and because computations using real-world data normally require rounding.

	Year 2	Year 1
Average daily sales:*		
$4,520 ÷ 365	12.4	
$4,708 ÷ 365		12.9
Days' sales in receivables:*		
$569.5 ÷ 12.4	45.9	
$544.5 ÷ 12.9		42.2

*Rounded to one decimal place.

The days' sales in receivables confirms that Keurig's efficiency in collecting accounts receivable decreased from Year 1 to Year 2. Generally, the efficiency in collecting accounts receivable has improved when the accounts receivable turnover increases or the days' sales in receivables decreases.[8]

Example Exercise 9-6 Accounts Receivable Turnover and Days' Sales in Receivables

Obj. 8

Financial statement data for years ending December 31 for Osterman Company follow:

	20Y9	20Y8
Sales	$4,284,000	$3,040,000
Accounts receivable:		
Beginning of year	550,000	400,000
End of year	640,000	550,000

Follow My Example 9-6

a. Determine the accounts receivable turnover for 20Y9 and 20Y8.
b. Determine the days' sales in receivables for 20Y9 and 20Y8. Use 365 days and round to one decimal place.
c. Does the change in accounts receivable turnover and the days' sales in receivables from 20Y8 to 20Y9 indicate a favorable or unfavorable change?

a. Accounts receivable turnover:

	20Y9	20Y8
Average accounts receivable:		
($550,000 + $640,000) ÷ 2	$595,000	
($400,000 + $550,000) ÷ 2		$475,000
Accounts receivable turnover:		
$4,284,000 ÷ $595,000	7.2	
$3,040,000 ÷ $475,000		6.4

b. Days' sales in receivables:

	20Y9	20Y8
Average daily sales:		
$4,284,000 ÷ 365 days	$11,737.0	
$3,040,000 ÷ 365 days		$8,328.8
Days' sales in receivables:		
$595,000 ÷ $11,737.0	50.7 days	
$475,000 ÷ $8,328.8		57.0 days

c. The increase in the accounts receivable turnover from 6.4 to 7.2 and the decrease in the days' sales in receivables from 57.0 days to 50.7 days indicate favorable changes in the efficiency of collecting accounts receivable.

Practice Exercises: PE 9-6A, PE 9-6B

---

[8] Days' sales in receivables could also be computed by dividing 365 days by the accounts receivable turnover. For example, Year 1 days' sales in receivables of 42.2 days could be computed as 365 days ÷ 8.65.

At a Glance 9

Obj. 1 Describe the common classes of receivables.

Key Points *Receivables* includes all money claims against other entities. Receivables are normally classified as accounts receivable, notes receivable, or other receivables.

Learning Outcomes	Example Exercises	Practice Exercises
• Define the term *receivables*. • List some common classifications of receivables.		

Obj. 2 Describe the accounting for uncollectible receivables.

Key Points The operating expense recorded from uncollectible receivables is called *bad debt expense*. The two methods of accounting for uncollectible receivables are the direct write-off method and the allowance method.

Learning Outcomes	Example Exercises	Practice Exercises
• Describe how a company may shift the risk of uncollectible receivables to other companies. • List factors that indicate an account receivable is uncollectible. • Describe two methods of accounting for uncollectible accounts receivable.		

Obj. 3 Describe the direct write-off method of accounting for uncollectible receivables.

Key Points Under the direct write-off method, the entry to write off an account debits Bad Debt Expense and credits Accounts Receivable. Neither an allowance account nor an adjusting entry is needed at the end of the period.

Learning Outcomes	Example Exercises	Practice Exercises
• Prepare journal entries to write off an account, using the direct write-off method.	EE9-1	PE9-1A, 9-1B
• Prepare journal entries for the reinstatement and collection of an account previously written off.	EE9-1	PE9-1A, 9-1B

Obj. 4 Describe the allowance method of accounting for uncollectible receivables.

Key Points Under the allowance method, an adjusting entry is made for uncollectible accounts. When an account is determined to be uncollectible, it is written off against the allowance account. The allowance account is a contra asset account that normally has a credit balance after the adjusting entry has been posted.

The estimate of uncollectibles may be based on a percent of sales or an analysis of receivables. Exhibit 3 compares and contrasts these two methods.

462 Chapter 9 Receivables

Learning Outcomes	Example Exercises	Practice Exercises
• Prepare journal entries to write off an account, using the allowance method.	EE9-2	PE9-2A, 9-2B
• Prepare journal entries for the reinstatement and collection of an account previously written off.	EE9-2	PE9-2A, 9-2B
• Determine the adjustment for uncollectible accounts, bad debt expense, and net realizable value of accounts receivable, using the percent of sales method.	EE9-3	PE9-3A, 9-3B
• Determine the adjustment for uncollectible accounts, bad debt expense, and net realizable value of accounts receivable, using the analysis of receivables method.	EE9-4	PE9-4A, 9-4B

Obj. 5 — Compare the direct write-off and allowance methods of accounting for uncollectible accounts.

Key Points Exhibit 4 illustrates the differences between the direct write-off and allowance methods of accounting for uncollectible accounts.

Learning Outcomes	Example Exercises	Practice Exercises
• Describe the differences in accounting for uncollectible accounts under the direct write-off and allowance methods.		
• Record journal entries, using the direct write-off and allowance methods.		

Obj. 6 — Describe the accounting for notes receivable.

Key Points A note received to settle an account receivable is recorded as a debit to Notes Receivable and a credit to Accounts Receivable. When a note is paid at maturity, Cash is debited, Notes Receivable is credited, and Interest Revenue is credited. If the maker of a note fails to pay, the dishonored note is recorded by debiting an account receivable for the amount due from the maker of the note.

Learning Outcomes	Example Exercises	Practice Exercises
• Describe the characteristics of a note receivable.		
• Determine the due date and maturity value of a note receivable.	EE9-5	PE9-5A, 9-5B
• Prepare journal entries for the receipt of the payment of a note receivable.	EE9-5	PE9-5A, 9-5B
• Prepare a journal entry for the dishonored note receivable.		

Obj. 7 — Describe the reporting of receivables on the balance sheet.

Key Points All receivables that are expected to be realized in cash within a year are reported in the Current Assets section of the balance sheet. In addition to the allowance for doubtful accounts, additional receivable disclosures include the market (fair) value and unusual credit risks.

Learning Outcomes	Example Exercises	Practice Exercises
• Describe how receivables are reported in the Current Assets section of the balance sheet.		
• Describe the disclosures related to receivables that should be reported in the financial statements.		

Obj. 8 — Describe and illustrate the use of accounts receivable turnover and days' sales in receivables to evaluate a company's efficiency in collecting its receivables.

Key Points Two financial measures that are especially useful in evaluating efficiency in collecting receivables are (1) the accounts receivable turnover and (2) the days' sales in receivables. Generally, the efficiency in collecting accounts receivable has improved when the accounts receivable turnover increases or there is a decrease in the days' sales in receivables.

Learning Outcomes	Example Exercises	Practice Exercises
• Describe two measures of the efficiency of managing receivables.		
• Compute and interpret the accounts receivable turnover and the days' sales in receivables.	EE9-6	PE9-6A, 9-6B

Illustrative Problem

Ditzler Company, a construction supply company, uses the allowance method of accounting for uncollectible accounts receivable. Selected transactions completed by Ditzler Company are as follows:

Feb. 1. Sold merchandise on account to Ames Co., $8,000. The cost of the merchandise sold was $4,500.

Mar. 15. Accepted a 60-day, 12% note for $8,000 from Ames Co. on account.

Apr. 9. Wrote off a $2,500 account from Dorset Co. as uncollectible.

21. Loaned $7,500 cash to Jill Klein, receiving a 90-day, 14% note.

May 14. Received the interest due from Ames Co. and a new 90-day, 14% note as a renewal of the loan. (Record both the debit and the credit to the notes receivable account.)

June 13. Reinstated the account of Dorset Co., written off on April 9, and received $2,500 in full payment.

July 20. Jill Klein dishonored her note.

Aug. 12. Received from Ames Co. the amount due on its note of May 14.

19. Received from Jill Klein the amount owed on the dishonored note, plus interest for 30 days at 15%, computed on the maturity value of the note.

(Continued)

Dec. 16. Accepted a 60-day, 12% note for $12,000 from Global Company on account.

31. It is estimated that 3% of the credit sales of $1,375,000 for the year ended December 31 will be uncollectible.

Instructions

1. Journalize the transactions.
2. Journalize the adjusting entry to record the accrued interest on December 31 on the Global Company note.

Solution

1.

Date		Description	Debit	Credit
Feb.	1	Accounts Receivable—Ames Co.	8,000.00	
		Sales		8,000.00
	1	Cost of Merchandise Sold	4,500.00	
		Merchandise Inventory		4,500.00
Mar.	15	Notes Receivable—Ames Co.	8,000.00	
		Accounts Receivable—Ames Co.		8,000.00
Apr.	9	Allowance for Doubtful Accounts	2,500.00	
		Accounts Receivable—Dorset Co.		2,500.00
	21	Notes Receivable—Jill Klein	7,500.00	
		Cash		7,500.00
May	14	Notes Receivable—Ames Co.	8,000.00	
		Cash	160.00	
		Notes Receivable—Ames Co.		8,000.00
		Interest Revenue		160.00
		($8,000 × 12% × 60 ÷ 360).		
June	13	Accounts Receivable—Dorset Co.	2,500.00	
		Allowance for Doubtful Accounts		2,500.00
	13	Cash	2,500.00	
		Accounts Receivable—Dorset Co.		2,500.00
July	20	Accounts Receivable—Jill Klein	7,762.50	
		Notes Receivable—Jill Klein		7,500.00
		Interest Revenue		262.50
		($7,500 × 14% × 90 ÷ 360).		
Aug.	12	Cash	8,280.00	
		Notes Receivable—Ames Co.		8,000.00
		Interest Revenue		280.00
		($8,000 × 14% × 90 ÷ 360).		
	19	Cash	7,859.53	
		Accounts Receivable—Jill Klein		7,762.50
		Interest Revenue		97.03
		($7,762.50 × 15% × 30 ÷ 360).		
Dec.	16	Notes Receivable—Global Company	12,000.00	
		Accounts Receivable—Global Company		12,000.00
	31	Bad Debt Expense	41,250.00	
		Allowance for Doubtful Accounts		41,250.00
		Uncollectible accounts estimate ($1,375,000 × 3%).		

2.

Dec.	31	Interest Receivable	60.00	
		Interest Revenue		60.00
		Accrued interest		
		($12,000 × 12% × 15 ÷ 360).		

Key Terms

accounts receivable (442)
accounts receivable turnover (459)
aging the receivables (450)
Allowance for Doubtful Accounts (445)
allowance method (443)
bad debt expense (443)
days' sales in receivables (459)
direct write-off method (443)
dishonored note receivable (456)
maturity value (456)
net realizable value (445)
notes receivable (442)
receivables (442)

Discussion Questions

1. What are the three classifications of receivables?

2. Dan's Hardware is a small hardware store in the rural township of Twin Bridges. It rarely extends credit to its customers in the form of an account receivable. The few customers who are allowed to carry accounts receivable are long-time residents of Twin Bridges with a history of doing business at Dan's Hardware. What method of accounting for uncollectible receivables should Dan's Hardware use? Why?

3. What kind of an account (asset, liability, etc.) is Allowance for Doubtful Accounts, and is its normal balance a debit or a credit?

4. After the accounts are adjusted and closed at the end of the fiscal year, Accounts Receivable has a balance of $673,400 and Allowance for Doubtful Accounts has a balance of $11,900. Describe how the accounts receivable and the allowance for doubtful accounts are reported on the balance sheet.

5. A firm has consistently adjusted its allowance account at the end of the fiscal year by adding a fixed percent of the period's sales on account. After seven years, the balance in Allowance for Doubtful Accounts has become very large in relation to the balance in Accounts Receivable. Give two possible explanations.

6. Which of the two methods of estimating uncollectibles provides for the most accurate estimate of the current net realizable value of the receivables?

7. Neptune Company issued a note receivable to Sailfish Company. (a) Who is the payee? (b) What is the title of the account used by Sailfish Company in recording the note?

8. If a note provides for payment of principal of $85,000 and interest at the rate of 6%, will the interest amount to $5,100? Explain.

9. The maker of a $240,000, 6%, 90-day note receivable failed to pay the note on the due date of November 30. What accounts should be debited and credited by the payee to record the dishonored note receivable?

10. The note receivable dishonored in Discussion Question 9 is paid on December 30 by the maker, plus interest for 30 days at 9%. What entry should be made to record the receipt of the payment?

Practice Exercises

Example Exercises

EE 9-1 *p. 445*

PE 9-1A Direct write-off method — OBJ. 3

Journalize the following transactions, using the direct write-off method of accounting for uncollectible receivables:

Apr. 15. Received $800 from Jean Tooley and wrote off the remainder owed of $1,200 as uncollectible.

Aug. 7. Reinstated the account of Jean Tooley and received $1,200 cash in full payment.

EE 9-1 *p. 445*

PE 9-1B Direct write-off method — OBJ. 3

Journalize the following transactions, using the direct write-off method of accounting for uncollectible receivables:

Oct. 2. Received $600 from Rachel Elpel and wrote off the remainder owed of $1,350 as uncollectible.

Dec. 20. Reinstated the account of Rachel Elpel and received $1,350 cash in full payment.

EE 9-2 *p. 447*

PE 9-2A Allowance method — OBJ. 4

Journalize the following transactions, using the allowance method of accounting for uncollectible receivables:

Apr. 15. Received $800 from Jean Tooley and wrote off the remainder owed of $1,200 as uncollectible.

Aug. 7. Reinstated the account of Jean Tooley and received $1,200 cash in full payment.

EE 9-2 *p. 447*

PE 9-2B Allowance method — OBJ. 4

Journalize the following transactions, using the allowance method of accounting for uncollectible receivables:

Oct. 2. Received $600 from Rachel Elpel and wrote off the remainder owed of $1,350 as uncollectible.

Dec. 20. Reinstated the account of Rachel Elpel and received $1,350 cash in full payment.

EE 9-3 *p. 449*

PE 9-3A Percent of sales method — OBJ. 4

At the end of the current year, Accounts Receivable has a balance of $3,750,000, Allowance for Doubtful Accounts has a credit balance of $22,750, and sales for the year total $48,400,000. Bad debt expense is estimated at ¾ of 1% of sales.

Determine (a) the amount of the adjusting entry for uncollectible accounts; (b) the adjusted balances of Accounts Receivable, Allowance for Doubtful Accounts, and Bad Debt Expense; and (c) the net realizable value of accounts receivable.

EE 9-3 *p. 449*

PE 9-3B Percent of sales method — OBJ. 4

At the end of the current year, Accounts Receivable has a balance of $3,460,000, Allowance for Doubtful Accounts has a debit balance of $12,500, and sales for the year total $46,300,000. Bad debt expense is estimated at ½ of 1% of sales.

Determine (a) the amount of the adjusting entry for uncollectible accounts; (b) the adjusted balances of Accounts Receivable, Allowance for Doubtful Accounts, and Bad Debt Expense; and (c) the net realizable value of accounts receivable.

Chapter 9 Receivables 467

EE 9-4 p. 452

PE 9-4A Analysis of receivables method OBJ. 4

At the end of the current year, Accounts Receivable has a balance of $3,750,000, Allowance for Doubtful Accounts has a credit balance of $22,750, and sales for the year total $48,400,000. Using the aging method, the balance of Allowance for Doubtful Accounts is estimated as $390,000.

Determine (a) the amount of the adjusting entry for uncollectible accounts; (b) the adjusted balances of Accounts Receivable, Allowance for Doubtful Accounts, and Bad Debt Expense; and (c) the net realizable value of accounts receivable.

EE 9-4 p. 452

PE 9-4B Analysis of receivables method OBJ. 4

At the end of the current year, Accounts Receivable has a balance of $3,460,000, Allowance for Doubtful Accounts has a debit balance of $12,500, and sales for the year total $46,300,000. Using the aging method, the balance of Allowance for Doubtful Accounts is estimated as $245,000.

Determine (a) the amount of the adjusting entry for uncollectible accounts; (b) the adjusted balances of Accounts Receivable, Allowance for Doubtful Accounts, and Bad Debt Expense; and (c) the net realizable value of accounts receivable.

EE 9-5 p. 457

PE 9-5A Note receivable OBJ. 6

Lundquist Company received a 60-day, 9% note for $28,000, dated July 23, from a customer on account.

a. Determine the due date of the note.
b. Determine the maturity value of the note.
c. Journalize the entry to record the receipt of the payment of the note at maturity.

EE 9-5 p. 457

PE 9-5B Note receivable OBJ. 6

Prefix Supply Company received a 120-day, 8% note for $450,000, dated April 9, from a customer on account.

a. Determine the due date of the note.
b. Determine the maturity value of the note.
c. Journalize the entry to record the receipt of the payment of the note at maturity.

EE 9-6 p. 460

PE 9-6A Accounts receivable turnover and days' sales in receivables OBJ. 8

Financial statement data for years ending December 31 for Chiro-Solutions Company follow:

	20Y2	20Y1
Sales	$2,912,000	$2,958,000
Accounts receivable:		
Beginning of year	300,000	280,000
End of year	340,000	300,000

a. Determine the accounts receivable turnover for 20Y2 and 20Y1.
b. Determine the days' sales in receivables for 20Y2 and 20Y1. Use 365 days and round to one decimal place.
c. Does the change in accounts receivable turnover and the days' sales in receivables from 20Y1 to 20Y2 indicate a favorable or unfavorable change?

EE 9-6 p. 460

PE 9-6B Accounts receivable turnover and days' sales in receivables OBJ. 8

Financial statement data for years ending December 31 for Robinhood Company follow:

	20Y9	20Y8
Sales	$7,906,000	$6,726,000
Accounts receivable:		
Beginning of year	600,000	540,000
End of year	580,000	600,000

(Continued)

468 Chapter 9 Receivables

a. Determine the accounts receivable turnover for 20Y9 and 20Y8.
b. Determine the days' sales in receivables for 20Y9 and 20Y8. Use 365 days and round to one decimal place.
c. Does the change in accounts receivable turnover and the days' sales in receivables from 20Y8 to 20Y9 indicate a favorable or unfavorable change?

Exercises

EX 9-1 Classifications of receivables   OBJ. 1

Boeing is one of the world's major aerospace firms with operations involving commercial aircraft, military aircraft, missiles, satellite systems, and information and battle management systems. As of a recent year, Boeing had $4,864 million of receivables involving U.S. government contracts and $2,250 million of receivables involving commercial aircraft customers such as Delta Air Lines and United Airlines.

Should Boeing report these receivables separately in the financial statements or combine them into one overall accounts receivable amount? Explain.

EX 9-2 Nature of uncollectible accounts   OBJ. 2

✓ a. 15.7%

MGM Resorts International owns and operates hotels and casinos including the MGM Grand and the Bellagio in Las Vegas, Nevada. As of a recent year, MGM reported accounts receivable of $570,348,000 and allowance for doubtful accounts of $89,789,000. Johnson & Johnson manufactures and sells a wide range of health care products including Band-Aid® bandages and Tylenol®. As of a recent year, Johnson & Johnson reported accounts receivable of $11,002,000,000 and allowance for doubtful accounts of $268,000,000.

a. Compute the percentage of the allowance for doubtful accounts to the accounts receivable for MGM Resorts International. Round to one decimal place.
b. Compute the percentage of the allowance for doubtful accounts to the accounts receivable for Johnson & Johnson. Round to one decimal place.
c. Discuss possible reasons for the difference in the two ratios computed in (a) and (b).

EX 9-3 Entries for uncollectible accounts, using direct write-off method   OBJ. 3

Journalize the following transactions in the accounts of Champion Medical Co., a medical equipment company that uses the direct write-off method of accounting for uncollectible receivables:

Jan. 19. Sold merchandise on account to Dr. Dale Van Dyken, $30,000. The cost of the merchandise sold was $20,500.

July 7. Received $12,000 from Dr. Dale Van Dyken and wrote off the remainder owed on the sale of January 19 as uncollectible.

Nov. 2. Reinstated the account of Dr. Dale Van Dyken that had been written off on July 7 and received $18,000 cash in full payment.

EX 9-4 Entries for uncollectible receivables, using allowance method   OBJ. 4

Journalize the following transactions in the accounts of Sedona Interiors Company, a restaurant supply company that uses the allowance method of accounting for uncollectible receivables:

May 1. Sold merchandise on account to Beijing Palace Co., $18,900. The cost of the merchandise sold was $11,200.

Aug. 30. Received $8,000 from Beijing Palace Co. and wrote off the remainder owed on the sale of May 1 as uncollectible.

Dec. 8. Reinstated the account of Beijing Palace Co. that had been written off on August 30 and received $10,900 cash in full payment.

EX 9-5 Entries to write off accounts receivable OBJ. 3, 4

Quantum Solutions Company, a computer consulting firm, has decided to write off the $33,550 balance of an account owed by a customer, Alliance Inc. Journalize the entry to record the write-off, assuming that (a) the direct write-off method is used and (b) the allowance method is used.

EX 9-6 Providing for doubtful accounts OBJ. 4

✔ a. $611,250
✔ b. $643,250

At the end of the current year, the accounts receivable account has a debit balance of $6,800,000 and sales for the year total $81,500,000. Determine the amount of the adjusting entry to provide for doubtful accounts under each of the following assumptions:

a. The allowance account before adjustment has a debit balance of $68,250. Bad debt expense is estimated at ¾ of 1% of sales.
b. The allowance account before adjustment has a debit balance of $68,250. An aging of the accounts in the customer ledger indicates estimated doubtful accounts of $575,000.
c. The allowance account before adjustment has a credit balance of $45,000. Bad debt expense is estimated at ½ of 1% of sales.
d. The allowance account before adjustment has a credit balance of $45,000. An aging of the accounts in the customer ledger indicates estimated doubtful accounts of $450,000.

EX 9-7 Number of days past due OBJ. 4

✔ Avalanche Auto, 84 days

Toot Auto Supply distributes new and used automobile parts to local dealers throughout the Midwest. Toot's credit terms are n/30. As of the end of business on October 31, the following accounts receivable were past due:

Account	Due Date	Amount
Avalanche Auto	August 8	$12,000
Bales Auto	October 11	2,400
Derby Auto Repair	June 23	3,900
Lucky's Auto Repair	September 2	6,600
Pit Stop Auto	September 19	1,100
Reliable Auto Repair	July 15	9,750
Trident Auto	August 24	1,800
Valley Repair & Tow	May 17	4,000

Determine the number of days each account is past due as of October 31.

EX 9-8 Aging of receivables schedule OBJ. 4

The accounts receivable clerk for Kirchhoff Industries prepared the following partially completed aging of receivables schedule as of the end of business on August 31:

	A	B	C	D	E	F	G
1			Not		Days Past Due		
2			Past				Over
3	Customer	Balance	Due	1–30	31–60	61–90	90
4	Academy Industries Inc.	3,000	3,000				
5	Ascent Company	4,500		4,500			
...							
21	Zoot Company	5,000			5,000		
22	Subtotals	1,050,000	600,000	220,000	115,000	85,000	30,000

(Continued)

The following accounts were unintentionally omitted from the aging schedule and not included in the preceding subtotals:

Customer	Balance	Due Date
Conover Industries	$30,000	March 22
Keystone Company	18,000	July 1
Moxie Creek Inc.	9,000	July 25
Rainbow Company	26,400	September 10
Swanson Company	46,600	August 3

a. Determine the number of days past due for each of the preceding accounts as of August 31.

b. Complete the aging of receivables schedule by adding the omitted accounts to the bottom of the schedule and updating the totals.

EX 9-9 Estimating allowance for doubtful accounts OBJ. 4

✔ Allowance for doubtful accounts, $131,712

Kirchhoff Industries has a past history of uncollectible accounts, as follows. Estimate the allowance for doubtful accounts, based on the aging of receivables schedule you completed in Exercise 9-8.

Age Class	Percent Uncollectible
Not past due	2%
1–30 days past due	4
31–60 days past due	18
61–90 days past due	40
Over 90 days past due	75

EX 9-10 Adjustment for uncollectible accounts OBJ. 4

Using data in Exercise 9-9, assume that the allowance for doubtful accounts for Kirchhoff Industries has a credit balance of $10,112 before adjustment on August 31. Journalize the adjusting entry for uncollectible accounts as of August 31.

EX 9-11 Estimating doubtful accounts OBJ. 4

Performance Bike Co. is a wholesaler of motorcycle supplies. An aging of the company's accounts receivable on December 31 and a historical analysis of the percentage of uncollectible accounts in each age category are as follows:

Age Interval	Balance	Percent Uncollectible
Not past due	$3,250,000	0.8%
1–30 days past due	1,050,000	2.4
31–60 days past due	780,000	7.0
61–90 days past due	320,000	18.0
91–180 days past due	240,000	34.0
Over 180 days past due	150,000	85.0
	$5,790,000	

Estimate the proper balance of the allowance for doubtful accounts as of December 31.

EX 9-12 Entry for uncollectible accounts OBJ. 4

Using the data in Exercise 9-11, assume that the allowance for doubtful accounts for Performance Bike Co. had a debit balance of $28,400 as of December 31.

Journalize the adjusting entry for uncollectible accounts as of December 31.

Chapter 9 Receivables 471

EX 9-13 Entries for bad debt expense under the direct write-off and allowance methods   OBJ. 5

✔ c. $8,225 higher

The following selected transactions were taken from the records of Shipway Company for the first year of its operations ending December 31:

Apr. 13. Wrote off account of Dean Sheppard, $8,450.

May 15. Received $500 as partial payment on the $7,100 account of Dan Pyle. Wrote off the remaining balance as uncollectible.

July 27. Received $8,450 from Dean Sheppard, whose account had been written off on April 13. Reinstated the account and recorded the cash receipt.

Dec. 31. Wrote off the following accounts as uncollectible (record as one journal entry):

Paul Chapman	$2,225
Duane DeRosa	3,550
Teresa Galloway	4,770
Ernie Klatt	1,275
Marty Richey	1,690

31. If necessary, record the year-end adjusting entry for uncollectible accounts.

a. Journalize the transactions under the direct write-off method.

b. Journalize the transactions under the allowance method. Shipway Company uses the percent of credit sales method of estimating uncollectible accounts expense. Based on past history and industry averages, ¾% of credit sales are expected to be uncollectible. Shipway Company recorded $3,778,000 of credit sales during the year.

c. How much higher (lower) would Shipway Company's net income have been under the direct write-off method than under the allowance method?

EX 9-14 Entries for bad debt expense under the direct write-off and allowance methods   OBJ. 5

✔ c. $11,090 higher

The following selected transactions were taken from the records of Rustic Tables Company for the year ending December 31:

June 8. Wrote off account of Kathy Quantel, $8,440.

Aug. 14. Received $3,000 as partial payment on the $12,500 account of Rosalie Oakes. Wrote off the remaining balance as uncollectible.

Oct. 16. Received the $8,440 from Kathy Quantel, whose account had been written off on June 8. Reinstated the account and recorded the cash receipt.

Dec. 31. Wrote off the following accounts as uncollectible (record as one journal entry):

Wade Dolan	$4,600
Greg Gagne	3,600
Amber Kisko	7,150
Shannon Poole	2,975
Niki Spence	6,630

31. If necessary, record the year-end adjusting entry for uncollectible accounts.

a. Journalize the transactions under the direct write-off method.

b. Journalize the transactions under the allowance method, assuming that the allowance account had a beginning credit balance of $36,000 on January 1 and the company uses the analysis of receivables method. Rustic Tables Company prepared the following aging schedule for its accounts receivable:

Aging Class (Number of Days Past Due)	Receivables Balance on December 31	Estimated Percent of Uncollectible Accounts
0–30 days	$320,000	1%
31–60 days	110,000	3
61–90 days	24,000	10
91–120 days	18,000	33
More than 120 days	43,000	75
Total receivables	$515,000	

(*Continued*)

EX 9-15 Effect of doubtful accounts on net income OBJ. 5

During its first year of operations, Mack's Plumbing Supply Co. had sales of $3,250,000, wrote off $27,800 of accounts as uncollectible using the direct write-off method, and reported net income of $487,500. Determine what the net income would have been if the allowance method had been used and the company estimated that 1% of sales would be uncollectible.

EX 9-16 Effect of doubtful accounts on net income OBJ. 5

✓ b. $11,700 credit balance

Using the data in Exercise 9-15, assume that during the second year of operations, Mack's Plumbing Supply Co. had sales of $4,100,000, wrote off $34,000 of accounts as uncollectible using the direct write-off method, and reported net income of $600,000.

a. Determine what net income would have been in the second year if the allowance method (using 1% of sales) had been used in both the first and second years.

b. Determine what the balance of the allowance for doubtful accounts would have been at the end of the second year if the allowance method had been used in both the first and second years. Hint: Use an Allowance for Doubtful Accounts T account.

EX 9-17 Entries for bad debt expense under the direct write-off and allowance methods OBJ. 5

✓ c. $9,375 higher

Show Me How

Casebolt Company wrote off the following accounts receivable as uncollectible for the first year of its operations ending December 31:

Customer	Amount
Shawn Brooke	$ 4,650
Eve Denton	5,180
Art Malloy	11,050
Cassie Yost	9,120
Total	$30,000

a. Journalize the write-offs under the direct write-off method.

b. Journalize the write-offs under the allowance method. Also, journalize the adjusting entry for uncollectible accounts. The company recorded $5,250,000 of credit sales during the year. Based on past history and industry averages, ¾% of credit sales are expected to be uncollectible.

c. How much higher (lower) would Casebolt Company's net income have been under the direct write-off method than under the allowance method?

EX 9-18 Entries for bad debt expense under the direct write-off and allowance methods OBJ. 5

Seaforth International wrote off the following accounts receivable as uncollectible for the year ending December 31:

Customer	Amount
Kim Abel	$ 21,550
Lee Drake	33,925
Jenny Green	27,565
Mike Lamb	19,460
Total	$102,500

The company prepared the following aging schedule for its accounts receivable on December 31:

Aging Class (Number of Days Past Due)	Receivables Balance on December 31	Estimated Percent of Uncollectible Accounts
0–30 days	$ 715,000	1%
31–60 days	310,000	2
61–90 days	102,000	15
91–120 days	76,000	30
More than 120 days	97,000	60
Total receivables	$1,300,000	

a. Journalize the write-offs under the direct write-off method.

b. Journalize the write-offs and the year-end adjusting entry under the allowance method, assuming that the allowance account had a beginning credit balance of $95,000 on January 1 and the company uses the analysis of receivables method.

c. How much higher (lower) would Seaforth International's net income have been under the allowance method than under the direct write-off method?

EX 9-19 Determine due date and interest on notes   OBJ. 6

✔ a. Apr. 10, $500

Determine the due date and the amount of interest due at maturity on the following notes:

	Date of Note	Face Amount	Interest Rate	Term of Note
a.	January 10*	$40,000	5%	90 days
b.	March 19	18,000	8	180 days
c.	June 5	90,000	7	30 days
d.	September 8	36,000	3	90 days
e.	November 20	27,000	4	60 days

*Assume that February has 28 days.

EX 9-20 Entries for notes receivable   OBJ. 6

✔ b. $60,800

Spring Designs & Decorators issued a 120-day, 4% note for $60,000, dated April 13 to Jaffe Furniture Company on account.

a. Determine the due date of the note.

b. Determine the maturity value of the note.

c. Journalize the entries to record the following: (1) receipt of the note by Jaffe Furniture and (2) receipt of payment of the note at maturity.

EX 9-21 Entries for notes receivable   OBJ. 6

The series of five transactions recorded in the following T accounts were related to a sale to a customer on account and the receipt of the amount owed. Briefly describe each transaction.

Cash	
(e) 76,500	

Notes Receivable	
(c) 75,000	(d) 75,000

Accounts Receivable	
(a) 75,000	(c) 75,000
(d) 75,400	(b) 75,400

Cost of Goods Sold	
(b) 45,000	

Inventory	
	(b) 45,000

Interest Revenue	
	(d) 400
	(e) 1,100

Sales	
	(a) 75,000

474　Chapter 9　Receivables

EX 9-22　Entries for notes receivable, including year-end entries　　OBJ. 6

The following selected transactions were completed by Fasteners Inc. Co., a supplier of buttons and zippers for clothing:

20Y3

Nov. 21. Received from McKenna Outer Wear Co., on account, a $96,000, 60-day, 3% note dated November 21 in settlement of a past due account.

Dec. 31. Recorded an adjusting entry for accrued interest on the note of November 21.

20Y4

Jan. 20. Received payment of note and interest from McKenna Outer Wear Co.

Journalize the entries to record the transactions.

EX 9-23　Entries for receipt and dishonor of note receivable　　OBJ. 6

Journalize the following transactions of Trapper Jon's Productions:

June 23. Received a $48,000, 90-day, 8% note dated June 23 from Radon Express Co. on account.

Sept. 21. The note is dishonored by Radon Express Co.

Oct. 21. Received the amount due on the dishonored note plus interest for 30 days at 10% on the total amount charged to Radon Express Co. on September 21.

EX 9-24　Entries for receipt and dishonor of notes receivable　　OBJ. 4, 6

Journalize the following transactions in the accounts of Safari Games Co., which operates a riverboat casino:

Apr. 18. Received a $60,000, 30-day, 7% note dated April 18 from Glenn Cross on account.

　　30. Received a $42,000, 60-day, 8% note dated April 30 from Rhoni Melville on account.

May 18. The note dated April 18 from Glenn Cross is dishonored, and the customer's account is charged for the note, including interest.

June 29. The note dated April 30 from Rhoni Melville is dishonored, and the customer's account is charged for the note, including interest.

Aug. 16. Cash is received for the amount due on the dishonored note dated April 18 plus interest for 90 days at 8% on the total amount debited to Glenn Cross on May 18.

Oct. 22. Wrote off against the allowance account the amount charged to Rhoni Melville on June 29 for the dishonored note dated April 30.

EX 9-25　Receivables on the balance sheet　　OBJ. 7

List any errors you can find in the following partial balance sheet:

Napa Vino Company
Balance Sheet
December 31, 20Y9

Assets

Current assets:		
Cash		$ 78,500
Notes receivable	$ 300,000	
Less interest receivable	4,500	295,500
Accounts receivable	$1,200,000	
Plus allowance for doubtful accounts	11,500	1,211,500

EX 9-26　Accounts receivable turnover and days' sales in receivables　　OBJ. 8

✓ a. Year 2: 9.20

Ralph Lauren Corporation designs, markets, and distributes a variety of apparel, home decor, accessory, and fragrance products. The company's products include such brands as Polo by Ralph Lauren, Ralph Lauren Purple Label, Ralph Lauren, Polo Jeans Co., and Chaps. Polo Ralph Lauren reported the following (in thousands) for two recent years:

	For the Period Ending	
	Year 2	Year 1
Sales	$7,620,000	$7,450,000
Accounts receivable	857,000	800,000

Assume that accounts receivable (in millions) were $607,000 at the beginning of Year 1.

a. Compute the accounts receivable turnover for Year 2 and Year 1. Round to two decimal places.

b. Compute the days' sales in receivables for Year 2 and Year 1. Use 365 days and round to one decimal place.

c.  What conclusions can be drawn from these analyses regarding Ralph Lauren's efficiency in collecting receivables?

EX 9-27 Accounts receivable turnover and days' sales in receivables OBJ. 8

✔ a. Year 2: 12.27

The **Campbell Soup Company** manufactures and markets food products throughout the world. The following sales and receivable data (in millions) were reported by Campbell Soup for two recent years:

	Year 2	Year 1
Sales	$8,082	$8,268
Accounts receivable	647	670

Assume that the accounts receivable (in thousands) were $635 million at the beginning of Year 1.

a. Compute the accounts receivable turnover for Year 2 and Year 1. Round average accounts receivable to one decimal place and accounts receivable turnover to two decimal places.

b. Compute the days' sales in receivables at the end of Year 2 and Year 1. Use 365 days and round to one decimal place.

c. What conclusions can be drawn from these analyses regarding Campbell's efficiency in collecting receivables?

EX 9-28 Accounts receivable turnover and days' sales in receivables OBJ. 8

American Eagle Outfitters, Inc. sells clothing, accessories, and personal care products for men and women through its retail stores. American Eagle reported the following data (in millions) for two recent years:

	Year 2	Year 1
Sales	$3,522	$3,283
Accounts receivable	81	68

Assume that accounts receivable (in millions) were $74 million at the beginning of Year 1.

a. Compute the accounts receivable turnover for Year 2 and Year 1. Round to two decimal places.

b. Compute the day's sales in receivables for Year 2 and Year 1. Use 365 days and round to one decimal place.

c. What conclusions can be drawn from these analyses regarding American Eagle Outfitters' efficiency in collecting receivables?

EX 9-29 Accounts receivable turnover OBJ. 8

Use the data in Exercises 9-27 and 9-28 to analyze the accounts receivable turnover ratios of the **Campbell Soup Company** and **American Eagle Outfitters, Inc.**

a. Compute the average accounts receivable turnover ratio for **Campbell Soup** and **American Eagle** for the years shown in Exercises 9-27 and 9-28.

b. ⬛ Does **Campbelll Soup** or **American Eagle** have the higher average accounts receivable turnover ratio?

c. ⬛ Explain why the average turnover ratios are different in (b).

Problems: Series A

✓ 3. $1,390,000

PR 9-1A Entries related to uncollectible accounts OBJ. 4

The following transactions were completed by Daws Company during the current fiscal year ended December 31:

Jan. 29. Received 35% of the $9,000 balance owed by Kovar Co., a bankrupt business, and wrote off the remainder as uncollectible.

Apr. 18. Reinstated the account of Spencer Clark, which had been written off in the preceding year as uncollectible. Journalized the receipt of $4,000 cash in full payment of Clark's account.

Aug. 9. Wrote off the $11,850 balance owed by Iron Horse Co., which has no assets.

Nov. 7. Reinstated the account of Vinyl Co., which had been written off in the preceding year as uncollectible. Journalized the receipt of $7,000 cash in full payment of the account.

Dec. 31. Wrote off the following accounts as uncollectible (one entry): Beth Connelly Inc., $12,100; DeVine Co., $8,110; Moser Distributors, $21,950; Oceanic Optics, $10,000.

31. Based on an analysis of the $1,450,000 of accounts receivable, it was estimated that $60,000 will be uncollectible. Journalized the adjusting entry.

Instructions

1. Record the January 1 credit balance of $54,200 in a T account for Allowance for Doubtful Accounts.
2. Journalize the transactions. Post each entry that affects the following selected T accounts and determine the new balances:

    Allowance for Doubtful Accounts
    Bad Debt Expense

3. Determine the expected net realizable value of the accounts receivable as of December 31.
4. Assuming that instead of basing the provision for uncollectible accounts on an analysis of receivables the adjusting entry on December 31 had been based on an estimated expense of ½ of 1% of the sales of $13,200,000 for the year, determine the following:

    a. Bad debt expense for the year.
    b. Balance in the allowance account after the adjustment of December 31.
    c. Expected net realizable value of the accounts receivable as of December 31.

✓ 3. $121,000

Excel

PR 9-2A Aging of receivables; estimating allowance for doubtful accounts OBJ. 4

Trophy Fish Company supplies flies and fishing gear to sporting goods stores and outfitters throughout the western United States. The accounts receivable clerk for Trophy Fish prepared the following partially completed aging of receivables schedule as of the end of business on December 31, 20Y6:

	A	B	C	D	E	F	G	H
1			Not		Days Past Due			
2			Past					
3	Customer	Balance	Due	1–30	31–60	61–90	91–120	Over 120
4	AAA Outfitters	20,000	20,000					
5	Brown Trout Fly Shop	7,500			7,500			
30	Zigs Fish Adventures	4,000		4,000				
31	Subtotals	1,300,000	750,000	290,000	120,000	40,000	20,000	80,000

The following accounts were unintentionally omitted from the aging schedule:

Customer	Due Date	Balance
Adams Sports & Flies	May 22, 20Y6	$5,000
Blue Dun Flies	Oct. 10, 20Y6	4,900
Cicada Fish Co.	Sept. 29, 20Y6	8,400
Deschutes Sports	Oct. 20, 20Y6	7,000
Green River Sports	Nov. 7, 20Y6	3,500
Smith River Co.	Nov. 28, 20Y6	2,400
Western Trout Company	Dec. 7, 20Y6	6,800
Wolfe Sports	Jan. 20, 20Y7	4,400

Trophy Fish has a past history of uncollectible accounts by age category, as follows:

Age Class	Percent Uncollectible
Not past due	1%
1–30 days past due	2
31–60 days past due	10
61–90 days past due	30
91–120 days past due	40
Over 120 days past due	80

Instructions

1. Determine the number of days past due for each of the preceding accounts.
2. Complete the aging of receivables schedule by adding the omitted accounts to the bottom of the schedule and updating the totals.
3. Estimate the allowance for doubtful accounts, based on the aging of receivables schedule.
4. Assume that the allowance for doubtful accounts for Trophy Fish Company has a debit balance of $3,600 before adjustment on December 31, 20Y6. Journalize the adjusting entry for uncollectible accounts.
5. Assuming that the adjusting entry in (4) was inadvertently omitted, how would the omission affect the balance sheet and income statement?

PR 9-3A Compare two methods of accounting for uncollectible receivables OBJ. 3, 4, 5

✔ 1. Year 4: Balance of allowance account, end of year, $15,050

Call Systems Company, a telephone service and supply company, has just completed its fourth year of operations. The direct write-off method of recording bad debt expense has been used during the entire period. Because of substantial increases in sales volume and the amount of uncollectible accounts, the company is considering changing to the allowance method. Information is requested as to the effect that an annual provision of 1% of sales would have had on the amount of bad debt expense reported for each of the past four years. It is also considered desirable to know what the balance of Allowance for Doubtful Accounts would have been at the end of each year. The following data have been obtained from the accounts:

Year	Sales	Uncollectible Accounts Written Off	1st	2nd	3rd	4th
1st	$ 900,000	$ 4,500	$4,500			
2nd	1,250,000	9,600	3,000	$6,600		
3rd	1,500,000	12,800	1,000	3,700	$8,100	
4th	2,200,000	16,550		1,500	4,300	$10,750

Year of Origin of Accounts Receivable Written Off as Uncollectible

Instructions

1. Assemble the desired data, using the following column headings:

Year	Expense Actually Reported	Expense Based on Estimate	Increase (Decrease) in Amount of Expense	Balance of Allowance Account, End of Year

Bad Debt Expense

(*Continued*)

2. Experience during the first four years of operations indicated that the receivables either were collected within two years or had to be written off as uncollectible. Does the estimate of 1% of sales appear to be reasonably close to the actual experience with uncollectible accounts originating during the first two years? Explain.

PR 9-4A Details of notes receivable and related entries OBJ. 6

✔ 1. Note 2: Due date, June 22; Interest due at maturity, $360

Flush Mate Co. wholesales bathroom fixtures. During the current fiscal year, Flush Mate Co. received the following notes:

	Date	Face Amount	Interest Rate	Term
1.	Mar. 6	$80,000	5%	45 days
2.	Apr. 23	24,000	9	60 days
3.	July 20	42,000	6	120 days
4.	Sept. 6	54,000	7	90 days
5.	Nov. 29	27,000	6	60 days
6.	Dec. 30	72,000	5	30 days

Instructions

1. Determine for each note (a) the due date and (b) the amount of interest due at maturity, identifying each note by number.
2. Journalize the entry to record the dishonor of Note (3) on its due date.
3. Journalize the adjusting entry to record the accrued interest on Notes (5) and (6) on December 31.
4. Journalize the entries to record the receipt of the amounts due on Notes (5) and (6) in January.

PR 9-5A Notes receivable entries OBJ. 6

The following data relate to notes receivable and interest for CGH Cable Co., a cable manufacturer and supplier. (All notes are dated as of the day they are received.)

Apr. 10. Received a $144,000, 5%, 60-day note on account.
May 15. Received a $270,000, 7%, 120-day note on account.
June 9. Received $145,200 on note of April 10.
Aug. 22. Received a $150,000, 4%, 45-day note on account.
Sept. 12. Received $276,300 on note of May 15.
  30. Received a $210,000, 8%, 60-day note on account.
Oct. 6. Received $150,750 on note of August 22.
  18. Received a 120,000, 5%, 60-day note on account.
Nov. 29. Received $212,800 on note of September 30.
Dec. 17. Received $121,000 on note of October 18.

Instructions
Journalize the entries to record the transactions.

PR 9-6A Sales and notes receivable transactions OBJ. 6

The following were selected from among the transactions completed by Caldemeyer Co. during the current year. Caldemeyer Co. sells and installs home and business security systems.

Jan. 3. Loaned $18,000 cash to Trina Gelhaus, receiving a 90-day, 8% note.
Feb. 10. Sold merchandise on account to Bradford & Co., $24,000. The cost of the merchandise sold was $14,400.
  13. Sold merchandise on account to Dry Creek Co., $60,000. The cost of merchandise sold was $54,000.

Mar. 12. Accepted a 60-day, 7% note for $24,000 from Bradford & Co. on account.

14. Accepted a 60-day, 9% note for $60,000 from Dry Creek Co. on account.

Apr. 3. Received the interest due from Trina Gelhaus and a new 120-day, 9% note as a renewal of the loan of January 3. (Record both the debit and the credit to the notes receivable account.)

May 11. Received from Bradford & Co. the amount due on the note of March 12.

13. Dry Creek Co. dishonored its note dated March 14.

July 12. Received from Dry Creek Co. the amount owed on the dishonored note, plus interest for 60 days at 12% computed on the maturity value of the note.

Aug. 1. Received from Trina Gelhaus the amount due on her note of April 3.

Oct. 5. Sold merchandise on account to Halloran Co., $13,500. The cost of the merchandise sold was $8,100.

15. Received from Halloran Co. the amount of the invoice of October 5.

Instructions

Journalize the entries to record the transactions.

Problems: Series B

PR 9-1B Entries related to uncollectible accounts
OBJ. 4

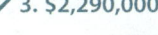
✓ 3. $2,290,000

Show Me How

The following transactions were completed by The Wild Trout Gallery during the current fiscal year ended December 31:

Jan. 19. Reinstated the account of Arlene Gurley, which had been written off in the preceding year as uncollectible. Journalized the receipt of $2,660 cash in full payment of Arlene's account.

Apr. 3. Wrote off the $12,750 balance owed by Premier GS Co., which is bankrupt.

July 16. Received 25% of the $22,000 balance owed by Hayden Co., a bankrupt business, and wrote off the remainder as uncollectible.

Nov. 23. Reinstated the account of Harry Carr, which had been written off two years earlier as uncollectible. Recorded the receipt of $4,000 cash in full payment.

Dec. 31. Wrote off the following accounts as uncollectible (one entry): Cavey Co., $3,300; Fogle Co., $8,100; Lake Furniture, $11,400; Melinda Shryer, $1,200.

31. Based on an analysis of the $2,350,000 of accounts receivable, it was estimated that $60,000 will be uncollectible. Journalized the adjusting entry.

Instructions

1. Record the January 1 credit balance of $50,000 in a T account for Allowance for Doubtful Accounts.

2. Journalize the transactions. Post each entry that affects the following T accounts and determine the new balances:

    Allowance for Doubtful Accounts
    Bad Debt Expense

3. Determine the expected net realizable value of the accounts receivable as of December 31.

4. Assuming that instead of basing the provision for uncollectible accounts on an analysis of receivables the adjusting entry on December 31 had been based on an estimated expense of ½ of 1% of the sales of $15,800,000 for the year, determine the following:

    a. Bad debt expense for the year.

    b. Balance in the allowance account after the adjustment of December 31.

    c. Expected net realizable value of the accounts receivable as of December 31.

480 Chapter 9 Receivables

✓ 3. $123,235

Excel

PR 9-2B Aging of receivables; estimating allowance for doubtful accounts OBJ. 4

Wig Creations Company supplies wigs and hair care products to beauty salons throughout Texas and the Southwest. The accounts receivable clerk for Wig Creations prepared the following partially completed aging of receivables schedule as of the end of business on December 31, 20Y1:

	A	B	C	D	E	F	G	H
1			Not		Days Past Due			
2			Past					
3	Customer	Balance	Due	1–30	31–60	61–90	91–120	Over 120
4	ABC Beauty	15,000	15,000					
5	Angel Wigs	8,000			8,000			
...								
30	Zodiac Beauty	3,000		3,000				
31	Subtotals	875,000	415,000	210,000	112,000	55,000	18,000	65,000

The following accounts were unintentionally omitted from the aging schedule:

Customer	Due Date	Balance
Arcade Beauty	Aug. 17, 20Y1	$10,000
Creative Images	Oct. 30, 20Y1	8,500
Excel Hair Products	July 3, 20Y1	7,500
First Class Hair Care	Sept. 8, 20Y1	6,600
Golden Images	Nov. 23, 20Y1	3,600
Oh That Hair	Nov. 29, 20Y1	1,400
One Stop Hair Designs	Dec. 7, 20Y1	4,000
Visions Hair & Nail	Jan. 11, 20Y2	9,000

Wig Creations has a past history of uncollectible accounts by age category, as follows:

Age Class	Percent Uncollectible
Not past due	1%
1–30 days past due	4
31–60 days past due	16
61–90 days past due	25
91–120 days past due	40
Over 120 days past due	80

Instructions

1. Determine the number of days past due for each of the preceding accounts.
2. Complete the aging of receivables schedule by adding the omitted accounts to the bottom of the schedule and updating the totals.
3. Estimate the allowance for doubtful accounts, based on the aging of receivables schedule.
4. Assume that the allowance for doubtful accounts for Wig Creations has a credit balance of $7,375 before adjustment on December 31, 20Y1. Journalize the adjustment for uncollectible accounts.
5. Assuming that the adjusting entry in (4) was inadvertently omitted, how would the omission affect the balance sheet and income statement?

✓ 1. Year 4: Balance of allowance account, end of year, $32,550

PR 9-3B Compare two methods of accounting for uncollectible receivables OBJ. 3, 4, 5

Digital Depot Company, which operates a chain of 40 electronics supply stores, has just completed its fourth year of operations. The direct write-off method of recording bad debt expense has been used during the entire period. Because of substantial increases in sales volume and the amount of uncollectible accounts, the firm is considering changing to the allowance method. Information is requested as to the effect that an annual provision of ¼% of sales would have had on the amount of bad debt expense reported for each of the past four years. It is also considered desirable to know what the balance of Allowance for Doubtful Accounts would have been at the end of each year. The following data have been obtained from the accounts:

			Year of Origin of Accounts Receivable Written Off as Uncollectible			
Year	Sales	Uncollectible Accounts Written Off	1st	2nd	3rd	4th
1st	$12,500,000	$18,000	$18,000			
2nd	14,800,000	30,200	9,000	$21,200		
3rd	18,000,000	39,900	3,600	9,300	$27,000	
4th	24,000,000	52,600		5,100	12,500	$35,000

Instructions

1. Assemble the desired data, using the following column headings:

	Bad Debt Expense			
Year	Expense Actually Reported	Expense Based on Estimate	Increase (Decrease) in Amount of Expense	Balance of Allowance Account, End of Year

2. Experience during the first four years of operations indicated that the receivables either were collected within two years or had to be written off as uncollectible. Does the estimate of ¼% of sales appear to be reasonably close to the actual experience with uncollectible accounts originating during the first two years? Explain.

PR 9-4B Details of notes receivable and related entries OBJ. 6

✔ 1. Note 1: Due date, Feb. 13; Interest due at maturity, $110

Gen-X Ads Co. produces advertising videos. During the current fiscal year, Gen-X Ads Co. received the following notes:

	Date	Face Amount	Interest Rate	Term
1.	Jan. 14	$33,000	4%	30 days
2.	Mar. 9	60,000	7	45 days
3.	July 12	48,000	5	90 days
4.	Aug. 23	16,000	6	75 days
5.	Nov. 15	36,000	8	60 days
6.	Dec. 10	24,000	6	60 days

Instructions

1. Determine for each note (a) the due date and (b) the amount of interest due at maturity, identifying each note by number.
2. Journalize the entry to record the dishonor of Note (3) on its due date.
3. Journalize the adjusting entry to record the accrued interest on Notes (5) and (6) on December 31.
4. Journalize the entries to record the receipt of the amounts due on Notes (5) and (6) in January and February.

PR 9-5B Notes receivable entries OBJ. 6

The following data relate to notes receivable and interest for Owens Co., a financial services company. (All notes are dated as of the day they are received.)

Mar. 8. Received a $33,000, 5%, 60-day note on account.

   31. Received an $80,000, 7%, 90-day note on account.

May 7. Received $33,275 on note of March 8.

   16. Received a $72,000, 7%, 90-day note on account.

(*Continued*)

June 11. Received a $36,000, 6%, 45-day note on account.

29. Received $81,400 on note of March 31.

July 26. Received $36,270 on note of June 11.

Aug. 4. Received a $48,000, 9%, 120-day note on account.

14. Received $73,260 on note of May 16.

Dec. 2. Received $49,440 on note of August 4.

Instructions

Journalize the entries to record the transactions.

PR 9-6B   Sales and notes receivable transactions   OBJ. 6

The following were selected from among the transactions completed during the current year by Danix Co., an appliance wholesale company:

Jan. 21. Sold merchandise on account to Black Tie Co., $28,000. The cost of merchandise sold was $16,800.

Mar. 18. Accepted a 60-day, 6% note for $28,000 from Black Tie Co. on account.

May 17. Received from Black Tie Co. the amount due on the note of March 18.

June 15. Sold merchandise on account to Pioneer Co. for $17,700. The cost of merchandise sold was $10,600.

21. Loaned $18,000 cash to JR Stutts, receiving a 30-day, 8% note.

25. Received from Pioneer Co. the amount due on the invoice of June 15.

July 21. Received the interest due from JR Stutts and a new 60-day, 9% note as a renewal of the loan of June 21. (Record both the debit and the credit to the notes receivable account.)

Sept. 19. Received from JR Stutts the amount due on her note of July 21.

22. Sold merchandise on account to Wycoff Co., $20,000. The cost of merchandise sold was $12,000.

Oct. 14. Accepted a 30-day, 6% note for $20,000 from Wycoff Co. on account.

Nov. 13. Wycoff Co. dishonored the note dated October 14.

Dec. 28. Received from Wycoff Co. the amount owed on the dishonored note, plus interest for 45 days at 8% computed on the maturity value of the note.

Instructions

Journalize the entries to record the transactions.

Cases & Projects

Ethics

CP 9-1   Ethics in Action

Bud Lighting Co. is a retailer of commercial and residential lighting products. Gowen Geter, the company's chief accountant, is in the process of making year-end adjusting entries for uncollectible accounts receivable. In recent years, the company has experienced an increase in accounts that have become uncollectible. As a result, Gowen believes that the company should increase the percentage used for estimating doubtful accounts from 2% to 4% of credit sales. This change will significantly increase bad debt expense, resulting in a drop in earnings for the first time in company history. The company president, Tim Burr, is under considerable pressure to meet earnings goals. He suggests that this is "not the right time" to change the estimate. He instructs Gowen to keep the estimate at 2%. Gowen is confident that 2% is too low, but he follows Tim's instructions.

➤ Evaluate the decision to use the lower percentage to improve earnings. Are Tim and Gowen acting in an ethical manner?

CP 9-2 Ethics in Action

Bev Wynn, vice president of operations for Dillon County Bank, has instructed the bank's computer programmer to use a 365-day year to compute interest on depository accounts (liabilities). Bev also instructed the programmer to use a 360-day year to compute interest on loans (assets).

Discuss whether Bev is behaving in a professional manner.

CP 9-3 Team Activity

In teams, select a public company that interests you and is a business that has accounts receivable. Obtain the company's most recent annual report on Form 10-K. The Form 10-K is a company's annually required filing with the Securities and Exchange Commission (SEC). It includes the company's financial statements and accompanying notes. The Form 10-K can be obtained either (a) by referring to the investor relations section of the company's website or (b) by using the company search feature of the SEC's EDGAR database service found at www.sec.gov/edgar/searchedgar/companysearch.html.

1. Based on the information in the company's most recent annual report, answer the following questions:
   a. What amount of accounts receivable did the company report at the end of the most recent year?
   b. What is the balance in the company's Allowance for Uncollectible Accounts at the end of the most recent year?
   c. What percentage of total current assets is accounts receivable at the end of each of the two years presented? Has this percentage increased, decreased, or remained the same during this period?
   d. How much bad debt expense did the company report for the most recent year?
2. Using the information presented in the company's annual report, calculate the company's accounts receivable turnover for the current and previous years. Based on this information, has the company's management of accounts receivable improved? Briefly explain your answer.

CP 9-4 Communication

On January 1, Xtreme Co. began offering credit with terms of n/30. Uncollectible accounts are estimated to be 1% of credit sales, which is the average for the industry. The CEO, Todd Hurley, has no background in accounting and is struggling to understand the allowance method.

Write a brief memo to Todd, explaining the allowance method and how this information is reported in the financial statements.

CP 9-5 Estimate uncollectible accounts

For several years, Xtreme Co.'s sales have been on a "cash only" basis. On January 1, 20Y4, however, Xtreme Co. began offering credit on terms of n/30. The amount of the adjusting entry to record the estimated uncollectible receivables at the end of each year has been ½ of 1% of credit sales, which is the rate reported as the average for the industry. Credit sales and the year-end credit balances in Allowance for Doubtful Accounts for the past four years are as follows:

Year	Credit Sales	Allowance for Doubtful Accounts
20Y4	$4,000,000	$ 5,000
20Y5	4,400,000	8,250
20Y6	4,800,000	10,200
20Y7	5,100,000	14,400

(*Continued*)

484 Chapter 9 Receivables

Laurie Jones, president of Xtreme Co., is concerned that the method used to account for and write off uncollectible receivables is unsatisfactory. She has asked for your advice in the analysis of past operations in this area and for recommendations for change.

1. Determine the amount of (a) the addition to Allowance for Doubtful Accounts and (b) the accounts written off for each of the four years.
2. a.  Advise Laurie Jones as to whether the estimate of ½ of 1% of credit sales appears reasonable.
   b.  Assume that after discussing (a) with Laurie Jones, she asked you what action might be taken to determine what the balance of Allowance for Doubtful Accounts should be at December 31, 20Y7, and what possible changes, if any, you might recommend in accounting for uncollectible receivables. How would you respond?

CP 9-6 Accounts receivable turnover and days' sales in receivables

Best Buy is a specialty retailer of consumer electronics, including personal computers, entertainment software, and appliances. Best Buy operates retail stores in addition to the Best Buy, Media Play, On Cue, and Magnolia Hi-Fi websites. For two recent years, Best Buy reported the following (in millions):

	Year 2	Year 1
Sales	$39,528	$40,339
Accounts receivable at end of year	1,162	1,280

Assume that the accounts receivable (in millions) were $1,308 at the beginning of fiscal Year 1.

1. Compute the accounts receivable turnover for Year 2 and Year 1. Round to two decimal places.
2. Compute the days' sales in receivables at the end of Year 2 and Year 1. Use 365 days and round to one decimal place.
3. What conclusions can be drawn from (1) and (2) regarding Best Buy's efficiency in collecting receivables?
4. What assumption did we make about sales for the Best Buy ratio computations that might distort the ratios and therefore cause the ratios not to be comparable for Year 2 and Year 1?

CP 9-7 Accounts receivable turnover and days' sales in receivables

Apple Inc. designs, manufactures, and markets personal computers and related personal computing and communicating solutions for sale primarily to education, creative, consumer, and business customers. Substantially all of the company's sales over the last five years are from sales of its Macs, iPods, iPads, and related software and peripherals. For two recent fiscal years, Apple reported the following (in millions):

	Year 2	Year 1
Sales	$233,715	$182,795
Accounts receivable at end of year	35,889	31,537

Assume that the accounts receivable (in millions) were $24,094 at the beginning of fiscal Year 1.

1. Compute the accounts receivable turnover for Year 2 and Year 1. Round to two decimal places.
2. Compute the days' sales in receivables at the end of Year 2 and Year 1. Use 365 days and round to one decimal place.
3. What conclusions can be drawn from (1) and (2) regarding Apple's efficiency in collecting receivables?

CP 9-8 Accounts receivable turnover and days' sales in receivables

Costco Wholesale Corporation operates membership warehouses that sell a variety of branded and private label products. Headquartered in Issaquah, Washington, it also sells merchandise online in the United States (Costco.com) and in Canada (Costco.ca). For two recent years, Costco reported the following (in millions):

	Year 2	Year 1
Sales	$116,199	$112,640
Accounts receivable at end of year	1,972	1,817

Assume that the accounts receivable (in thousands) were $1,822 at the beginning of Year 1.

1. Compute the accounts receivable turnover for Year 2 and Year 1. Round to two decimal places.
2. Compute the days' sales in receivables at the end of Year 2 and Year 1. Use 365 days and round to one decimal place.
3. ✏️ What conclusions can be drawn from (1) and (2) regarding Costco's efficiency in collecting receivables?
4. ✏️ Given the nature of Costco's operations, do you believe Costco's accounts receivable turnover ratio would be higher or lower than a typical manufacturing company such as the Campbell Soup Company? Explain.

CP 9-9 Accounts receivable turnover

The accounts receivable turnover ratio will vary across companies, depending on the nature of the company's operations. For example, an accounts receivable turnover of 6 for a retailer is unacceptable but might be excellent for a manufacturer of specialty milling equipment. A list of well-known companies follows:

Alcoa Inc.	The Coca-Cola Company	Kroger
AutoZone, Inc.	Delta Air Lines	Procter & Gamble
Barnes & Noble, Inc.	The Home Depot	Wal-Mart
Caterpillar	IBM	Whirlpool Corporation

1. Categorize each of the preceding companies as to whether its turnover ratio is likely to be above or below 15.
2. ✏️ Based on (1), identify a characteristic of companies with accounts receivable turnover ratios above 15.

CHAPTER 10
Long-Term Assets: Fixed and Intangible

Chapters 1–4
Accounting Cycle

Chapter 5
Accounting Systems

| Income Statement | Statement of Owner's Equity | Balance Sheet | Statement of Cash Flows |

Chapter 6 *Accounting for Merchandising Businesses*

Chapter 16 *Cash Flows*

Assets = Liabilities + Owner's Equity

Chapter 7 *Inventories*
Chapter 8 *Internal Control and Cash*
Chapter 9 *Receivables*
Chapter 10 Fixed and Intangible Assets
Chapter 15 *Investments*

Chapter 11 *Current Liabilities*
Chapter 14 *Bonds and Notes*

Chapter 12 *Partnerships*
Chapter 13 *Corporations*

Chapter 17
Financial Statement Analysis

Statement of Owner's Equity

Owner's capital, Jan. 1		$XXX
Net income	$ XXX	
Withdrawals	(XXX)	
Increase in capital		XXX

Statement of Cash Flows

Cash flows from (used in) operating activities	$XXX
Cash flows from (used in) investing activities	XXX
Cash flows from (used in) financing activities	XXX
Increase (decrease) in cash flows	$XXX
	XXX
	$XXX

Income Statement

Sales		$XXX
Cost of merchandise sold		XXX
Gross profit		$XXX
Operating expenses:		
Advertising expense	$XXX	
Depreciation expense	XXX	
Amortization expense	XXX	
Depletion expense	XXX	
…	XXX	
…	XXX	
Total operating expenses		XXX
Income from operations		$XXX
Other revenue and expenses		XXX
Net income		$XXX

Balance Sheet

Current assets:		
Cash	$XXX	
Accounts receivable	XXX	
Merchandise inventory	XXX	
Total current assets		$XXX
Property, plant, and equipment	$XXX	
Intangible assets	XXX	
Total long-term assets		XXX
Total assets		$XXX
Liabilities:		
Current liabilities	$XXX	
Long-term liabilities	XXX	
Total liabilities		$XXX
Owner's equity		XXX
Total liabilities and owner's equity		$XXX

CHAPTER 10

McDonald's

McDonald's began in 1940 in San Bernardino, California, as a Bar-B-Q restaurant operated by two brothers, Dick and Mac McDonald. In 1954, Ray Kroc visited the restaurant and convinced the McDonald brothers to let him franchise its operations nationwide. Ray Kroc opened his first McDonald's in Des Plaines, Illinois, in 1955, with its distinguishing, newly designed Golden Arches. Today, McDonald's operates in more than 100 countries, has more than 30,000 restaurants, employs more than 400,000 people, sells millions of hamburgers each year, and generates yearly revenues in excess of $27 billion.

Would you like to own and operate a McDonald's restaurant? McDonald's grants 20-year franchises to individuals who want to become owner/operators of a restaurant. Individuals may either purchase an existing restaurant or open a new restaurant. When opening a new restaurant, the owner must invest in the store equipment, signs, seating, and décor. McDonald's normally owns the land and the building. McDonald's also provides training for its owner/operators. In return, McDonald's is paid a monthly service charge, which is either a fixed amount or a percent of sales. The total cost of opening a new restaurant may exceed several million dollars.

Obviously, the decision to open a McDonald's restaurant is a major commitment with long-term implications. This chapter discusses the accounting for investments in long-term, fixed assets such as a new restaurant. This accounting addresses such issues as how much of the investment should be recorded as an asset, how much should be written off as an expense each year, and how the disposal of a fixed asset should be recorded. Finally, accounting for natural resources, such as mineral deposits, and for intangible assets, such as patents, copyrights, trademarks, and goodwill, are discussed.

Source: www.aboutmcdonalds.com

Learning Objectives

After studying this chapter, you should be able to: Example Exercises (EE) are shown in **green**.

Obj. 1 Define, classify, and account for the cost of fixed assets.

Nature of Fixed Assets
Classifying Costs
The Cost of Fixed Assets
Leasing Fixed Assets

Obj. 2 Compute depreciation using the following methods: straight-line, units-of-activity, and double-declining-balance.

Accounting for Depreciation
Factors in Computing Depreciation Expense
Straight-Line Method — EE 10-1
Units-of-Activity Method — EE 10-2
Double-Declining-Balance Method — EE 10-3
Comparing Depreciation Methods
Partial-Year Depreciation
Revising Depreciation Estimates — EE 10-4
Repair and Improvements — EE 10-5

Obj. 3 Journalize the disposal of fixed assets.

Disposal of Fixed Assets
Discarding Fixed Assets
Selling Fixed Assets — EE 10-6

Obj. 4 Describe the accounting for natural resources, including the journal entry for depletion.

Natural Resources
Compute and record depletion — EE 10-7

Obj. 5 Describe the accounting for intangible assets, such as patents, copyrights, and goodwill.

Intangible Assets
Patents — EE 10-8
Copyrights and Trademarks
Goodwill — EE 10-8

Obj. 6 Describe how depreciation expense is reported on an income statement and prepare a balance sheet that includes fixed assets and intangible assets.

Financial Reporting for Long-Term Assets: Fixed and Intangible

Obj. 7 Describe and illustrate the fixed asset turnover ratio to assess the efficiency of a company's use of its fixed assets.

Financial Analysis and Interpretation: Fixed Asset Turnover Ratio
Compute Fixed Asset Turnover Ratio — EE 10-9

At a Glance 10 — Page 516

Obj. 1 Define, classify, and account for the cost of fixed assets.

Nature of Fixed Assets

Fixed assets are long-term or relatively permanent assets such as equipment, machinery, buildings, and land. Other descriptive titles for fixed assets are *plant assets* or *property, plant, and equipment*. Fixed assets have the following characteristics:

- They exist physically and, thus, are *tangible* assets.
- They are owned and used by the company in its normal operations.
- They are not offered for sale as part of normal operations.

Fixed assets are critical to the success of many businesses. For example, computers and Internet servers are critical fixed assets for a business that provides online retail or technology services.

See Appendix B for more information.

Classifying Costs

A cost that has been incurred may be classified as a fixed asset, an investment, or an expense. Exhibit 1 shows how to determine the proper classification of a cost and how it should be recorded.

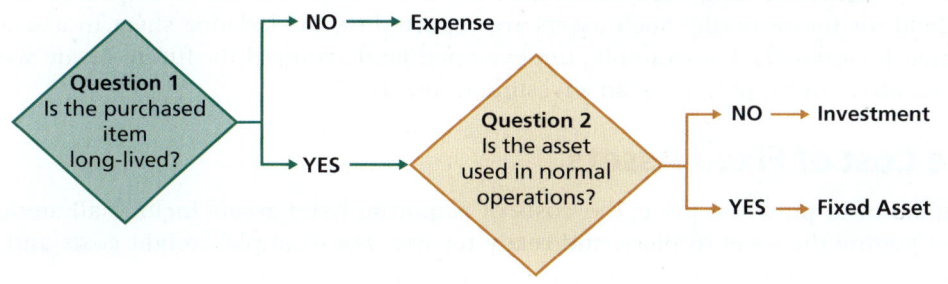

EXHIBIT 1

Classifying Costs

As shown in Exhibit 1, classifying a cost involves the following questions:

Question 1. Is the purchased item long-lived (more than one year)?
  If *yes*, the item is recorded as an asset on the balance sheet, either as a fixed asset or an investment. Proceed to Question 2.
  If *no*, the item is classified and recorded as an *expense*.

Question 2. Is the asset used in normal operations?
  If *yes*, the asset is classified and recorded as a *fixed asset*.
  If *no*, the asset is classified and recorded as an *investment*.

Items that are classified and recorded as fixed assets include equipment, buildings, and land. Such assets normally last more than a year and are used in the normal operations of the business. However, standby equipment for use during peak periods or when other equipment breaks down is still classified as a fixed asset, even though it is not used very often. In contrast, fixed assets that have been abandoned or are no longer used in operations are not classified as fixed assets.

Although fixed assets may be sold, they should not be offered for sale as part of normal operations. For example, cars and trucks offered for sale by an automotive dealership are not fixed assets of the dealership. On the other hand, a tow truck used in the normal operations of the dealership is a fixed asset of the dealership.

Link to McDonald's

In a recent financial statement, **McDonald's** reported total property, plant, and equipment of over $40 billion, which consists of land, buildings, and equipment.

Business Connection

FIXED ASSETS

Fixed assets often represent a significant portion of a company's total assets. The table that follows shows the fixed assets as a percent of total assets for some select companies across a variety of industries. As can be seen, the type of industry will impact the proportion of fixed assets to total assets. Retail has the highest percent of fixed assets to total assets, while social media and software have much lower percentages. High-tech service companies often use fewer fixed assets to deliver their services than companies that use stores, equipment, planes, cell towers, or theme parks.

Company	Industry	Percent of Fixed Assets to Total Assets
McDonald's Corporation	Food Retail	72%
Target Corporation	Merchandise Retail	63%
Alcoa Inc.	Heavy Industry	44%
Delta Air Lines, Inc.	Transportation	41%
Verizon Communications Inc.	Communications	39%
The Walt Disney Company	Entertainment	28%
Facebook, Inc.	Social Media	10%
Microsoft Corporation	Software	8%

Investments are long-lived assets that are not used in the normal operations and are held for future resale. Such assets are reported on the balance sheet in a section entitled *Investments*. For example, undeveloped land acquired for future resale would be classified and reported as an investment, not land.

The Cost of Fixed Assets

In addition to purchase price, the costs of acquiring fixed assets include all amounts spent getting the asset in place and ready for use. For example, freight costs and the costs of installing equipment are part of the asset's total cost.

Exhibit 2 summarizes some of the common costs of acquiring fixed assets. These costs are recorded by debiting the related fixed asset account, such as Land,[1] Building, Land Improvements, or Machinery and Equipment.

EXHIBIT 2 Costs of Acquiring Fixed Assets

Building
- Architects' fees
- Engineers' fees
- Insurance costs incurred during construction
- Interest on money borrowed to finance construction
- Sales taxes
- Repairs (purchase of existing building)
- Reconditioning (purchase of existing building)
- Modifying for use
- Permits from government agencies

Machinery & Equipment
- Sales taxes
- Freight
- Installation
- Repairs (purchase of used equipment)
- Reconditioning (purchase of used equipment)
- Insurance while in transit
- Assembly
- Modifying for use
- Testing for use
- Permits from government agencies

Land
- Purchase price
- Sales taxes
- Permits from government agencies
- Broker's commissions
- Attorney fees
- Title fees
- Surveying fees
- Delinquent real estate taxes
- Removing unwanted building less any salvage
- Grading and leveling

Land Improvements
- Trees and shrubs
- Fences
- Outdoor lighting
- Paved parking areas or walkways

Only costs necessary for preparing the fixed asset for use are included as a cost of the asset. Unnecessary costs that do not increase the asset's usefulness are recorded as an expense. For example, the following costs are recorded as expenses:

- Vandalism
- Mistakes in installation
- Uninsured theft

---

[1] As discussed here, land is assumed to be used only as a location or site and not for its mineral deposits or other natural resources.

- Damage during unpacking and installing
- Fines for not obtaining proper permits from governmental agencies

To illustrate, assume Kimble Inc. purchased equipment for $12,000. Freight costs of $600 were incurred to transport the equipment to the installation site. On site, installation costs of $1,500 were incurred, including $500 due to an error in installation. The journal entry to record the equipment is as follows:

| Equipment ($12,500 + $600 + $1,500 − $500) | 13,600 | |
| Cash | | 13,600 |

The cost of the error in installing the equipment of $500 is not included in the cost of the equipment, but instead is recorded as an expense.

A company may incur costs associated with constructing a fixed asset such as a new building. The direct costs incurred in the construction, such as labor and materials, should be capitalized as a debit to an account entitled *Construction in Progress*. When the construction is complete, the costs are reclassified by crediting Construction in Progress and debiting the proper fixed asset account such as Building.

Leasing Fixed Assets

A *lease* is a contract for the use of an asset for a period of time. Leases are often used in business. For example, automobiles, computers, medical equipment, buildings, and airplanes are often leased.

The two parties to a lease contract are as follows:

- The *lessor* is the party who owns the asset.
- The *lessee* is the party to whom the rights to use the asset are granted by the lessor.

Under a lease contract, the lessee pays rent on a periodic basis for the lease term. An advantage of leasing an asset is that the lessee has access to an asset without having to spend a large amount of funds or borrow to buy the asset. In addition, expenses such as maintenance and repair costs may be the responsibility of the lessor. Finally, the risk of incurring additional cost because the asset becomes obsolete before the end of its useful life can be mitigated by leasing an asset.

The Financial Accounting Standards Board (FASB) and the International Accounting Standards Board (IASB) recently completed a project to merge U.S. and international standards on leasing.[2] The new FASB standard distinguishes between finance leases and operating leases. Under a finance lease, the lessee records an asset and a liability similar to having purchased the asset. Under an operating lease, the lessee records prepaid rent (and, if necessary, a liability for future lease payments) and records rent expense as the asset is used.

For purposes of this text, we assume that all leases are operating leases that do not extend beyond one year. Thus, lease payments are recorded by debiting Rent Expense and crediting Cash. In some cases, like those illustrated in earlier chapters, Prepaid Rent is initially recorded with an adjusting entry at the end of the period to record Rent Expense.

Regardless of the type of lease, lease terms should be disclosed in the notes to the financial statements. These disclosures would include such items as the length of the lease, termination rights, and renewal options.

> **Link to McDonald's**
> McDonald's recently reported that it is the lessee in over 14,000 locations. The leases are normally for 20 years with an option to renew.

IFRS
See Appendix B for more information.

---

2 Accounting Standards Update, *Leases (Topic 842)*, February 2016, FASB (Norwalk, CT).

Obj. 2 Compute depreciation using the following methods: straight-line, units-of-activity, and double-declining-balance.

Accounting for Depreciation

Over time, fixed assets, with the exception of land, lose their ability to provide services. Thus, the costs of fixed assets such as equipment, buildings, and land improvements should be recorded as an expense over their useful lives. Recording the cost of fixed assets as an expense is called **depreciation**. Because land has an unlimited life, it is not depreciated.

Depreciation can be caused by physical or functional factors.

- *Physical depreciation* factors include wear and tear during use or from exposure to weather.
- *Functional depreciation* factors include obsolescence and changes in customer needs that cause the asset to no longer provide services for which it was intended. For example, equipment may become obsolete due to changing technology.

Two common misunderstandings about depreciation as used in accounting include:

- Depreciation does not measure a decline in the market value of a fixed asset. Instead, depreciation is an allocation of a fixed asset's cost to expense over the asset's useful life. Thus, the book value of a fixed asset (cost less accumulated depreciation) usually does not agree with the asset's market value. This is justified in accounting because a fixed asset is for use in a company's operations rather than for resale.
- Depreciation does not provide cash to replace fixed assets as they wear out. This misunderstanding may occur because depreciation, unlike many expenses, does not represent an outlay of cash, but instead is an allocation of the asset's initial cost to expense.

Factors in Computing Depreciation Expense

The three factors that determine the depreciation expense for a fixed asset are as follows:

- The asset's initial cost
- The asset's expected useful life
- The asset's estimated residual value

The **initial cost** of a fixed asset is the purchase price of the asset plus all costs to obtain and ready it for use. This initial cost is determined using the concepts discussed and illustrated earlier in this chapter.

The **expected useful life** of a fixed asset is the estimated length of time the asset will be used in normal operations. It is estimated at the time the asset is placed into service. Estimates of expected useful lives are available from industry trade associations. The Internal Revenue Service also publishes guidelines for useful lives, which may be helpful for financial reporting purposes. However, it is not uncommon for different companies to use a different useful life for similar assets.

The **residual value** of a fixed asset is the estimated value of the asset at the end of its useful life. It is estimated at the time the asset is placed into service. Residual value is sometimes referred to as *scrap value*, *salvage value*, or *trade-in value*.

The difference between a fixed asset's initial cost and its residual value is called the asset's **depreciable cost**. This is the asset's cost that is allocated over its useful life as depreciation expense. If a fixed asset has no residual value, then its entire cost should be allocated to depreciation.

To illustrate depreciation methods, assume that **Exeter Company** purchased a new forklift on January 1 as follows:

Initial cost	$24,000
Expected useful life	5 years
Estimated residual value	$2,000

Link to McDonald's

McDonald's uses a useful life of up to 40 years for its buildings and from 3–5 years for its equipment.

Exhibit 3 shows the relationship between depreciation expense and the forklift's initial cost, expected useful life, and estimated residual value.

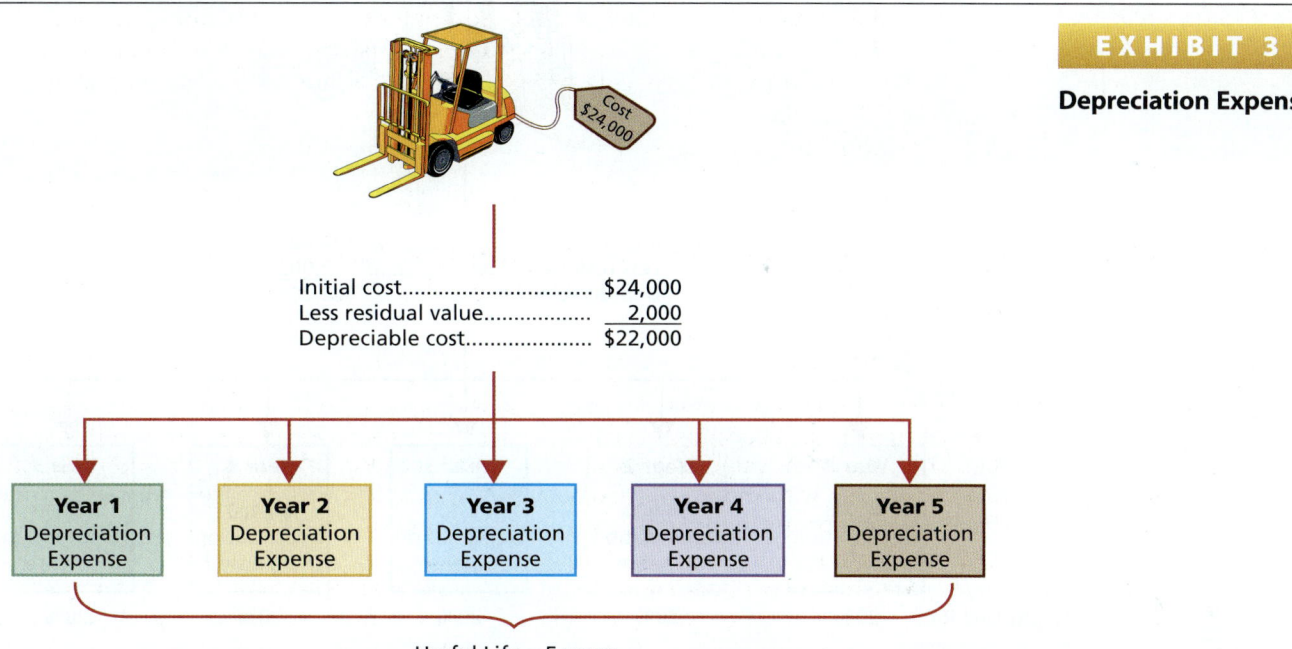

EXHIBIT 3

Depreciation Expense

The three depreciation methods used most often are as follows:[3]

- Straight-line depreciation
- Units-of-activity depreciation
- Double-declining-balance depreciation

It is not necessary for a company to use only one method of computing depreciation for all of its fixed assets. For example, a company may use one method for depreciating equipment and another method for depreciating buildings.

Straight-Line Method

The **straight-line method** provides for the same amount of depreciation expense for each year of the asset's useful life. The annual straight-line depreciation for **Exeter**'s forklift is $4,400, computed as follows:

$$\text{Annual Depreciation} = \frac{\text{Cost} - \text{Residual Value}}{\text{Useful Life}} = \frac{\$24,000 - \$2,000}{5 \text{ Years}} = \$4,400$$

The straight-line method reports the same amount of depreciation expense each year, as illustrated in Exhibit 4.

Computing straight-line depreciation may be simplified by converting the annual depreciation to a percentage of depreciable cost.[4] The straight-line percentage is de-

---

[3] Another method not often used today, called the *sum-of-the-years-digits method*, is described and illustrated in an online appendix located at www.cengagebrain.com.

[4] The depreciation rate may also be expressed as a fraction. For example, the annual straight-line rate for an asset with a three-year useful life is 1/3.

EXHIBIT 4 Straight-Line Method

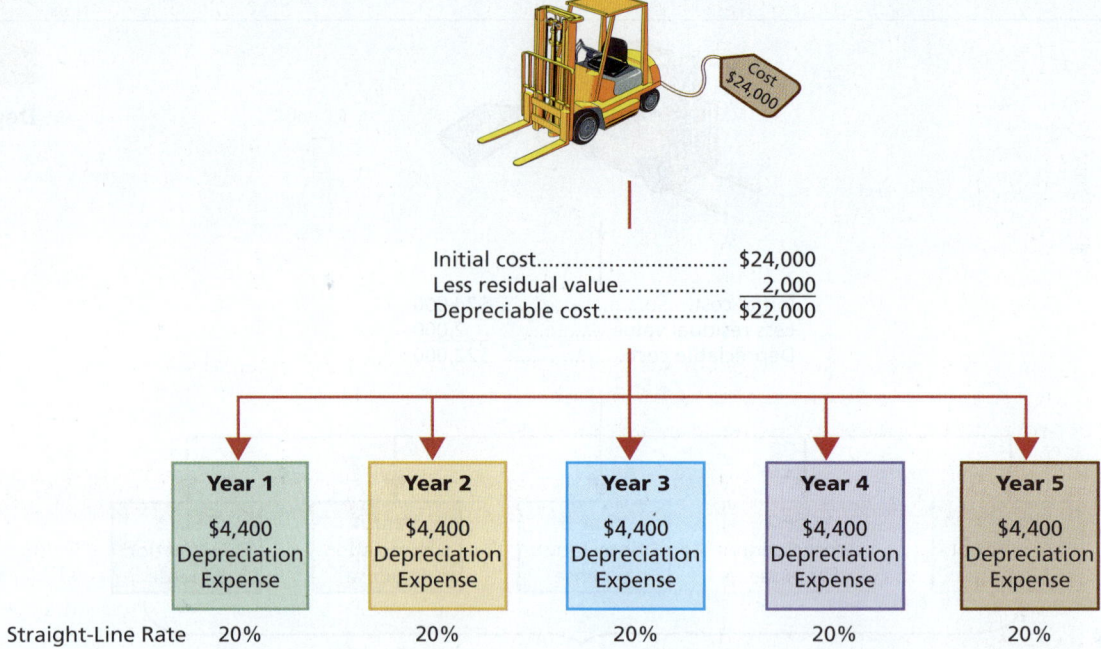

Expected Years of Useful Life	Straight-Line Percentage
5 years	20% (100% ÷ 5)
8 years	12.5% (100% ÷ 8)
10 years	10% (100% ÷ 10)
20 years	5% (100% ÷ 20)
25 years	4% (100% ÷ 25)

For the preceding equipment, the annual depreciation of $4,400 can be computed by multiplying the depreciable cost of $22,000 by 20% (100% ÷ 5).

Depreciation of the forklift for the first year using the straight-line method is recorded as follows:

Dec.	31	Depreciation Expense—Forklift	4,400	
		Accumulated Depreciation—Forklift		4,400

Accumulated depreciation accounts are called *contra accounts* or *contra asset accounts*. This is because accumulated depreciation accounts are deducted from their related fixed asset accounts on the balance sheet. The difference between the fixed asset account and its related accumulated depreciation account is called the asset's **book value** or *net book value of the asset*.

The book value of the forklift at the end of the first year is $19,600. It would be reported on the balance sheet as follows:

Equipment	$24,000
Less accumulated depreciation	4,400
Book value	$19,600

As shown in Exhibit 5, as depreciation expense is recorded each year, Accumulated Depreciation—Forklift will increase and the book value of the forklift will decrease.

Straight-Line Method: Depreciation Expense and Book Value

EXHIBIT 5

The straight-line method is simple to use. When an asset's revenues are about the same from period to period, straight-line depreciation provides a good matching of depreciation expense with the asset's revenues.

Example Exercise 10-1 Straight-Line Depreciation Obj. 2

Equipment acquired at the beginning of the year at a cost of $125,000 has an estimated residual value of $5,000 and an estimated useful life of 10 years. Determine (a) the depreciable cost, (b) the straight-line rate, and (c) the annual straight-line depreciation.

Follow My Example 10-1

a. $120,000 ($125,000 − $5,000)
b. 10% = 100% ÷ 10
c. $12,000 ($120,000 × 10%) or ($120,000 ÷ 10 years)

Practice Exercises: PE 10-1A, PE 10-1B

Units-of-Activity Method

The **units-of-activity method** provides the same amount of depreciation expense for each unit of activity of the asset. Depending on the asset, the units of activity can be expressed in terms of hours, miles driven, or quantity produced. For example, the unit of activity for a truck is normally expressed in miles driven. For manufacturing assets, the units of activity are often expressed as units of product. In this case, the units-of-activity method may be called the *units-of-production method* or *units-of-output method*.

The units-of-activity method is applied in the following two steps:

Step 1. Determine the depreciation per unit as follows:

$$\text{Depreciation per Unit} = \frac{\text{Cost} - \text{Residual Value}}{\text{Total Estimated Units of Activity}}$$

Step 2. Compute the depreciation expense as follows:

$$\text{Depreciation Expense} = \text{Depreciation per Unit} \times \text{Units of Activity for Period}$$

To illustrate, assume that **Exeter**'s forklift is estimated to have a useful life of 10,000 operating hours. During the first year, the forklift was operated 2,100 hours. The units-of-activity depreciation for the year is $4,620, computed as follows:

Step 1. Determine the depreciation per hour as follows:

$$\text{Depreciation per Hour} = \frac{\text{Cost} - \text{Residual Value}}{\text{Total Estimated Units of Activity}} = \frac{\$24,000 - \$2,000}{10,000 \text{ Hours}} = \$2.20 \text{ per Hour}$$

Step 2. Compute the depreciation expense as follows:

Depreciation Expense = Depreciation per Unit × Units of Activity for Period
= $2.20 per Hour × 2,100 Hours = $4,620

Depreciation for the first year using the units-of-activity method is recorded as follows:

| Dec. | 31 | Depreciation Expense—Forklift | 4,620 | |
| | | Accumulated Depreciation—Forklift | | 4,620 |

Assume that during its five-year life, the forklift was used as follows:

Year 1	2,100 hours
Year 2	1,500
Year 3	2,600
Year 4	1,800
Year 5	2,000
Total	10,000 hours

Exhibit 6 illustrates the depreciation expense and book value of the forklift over its five-year life using the units-of-activity method.

EXHIBIT 6 Units-of-Activity Method

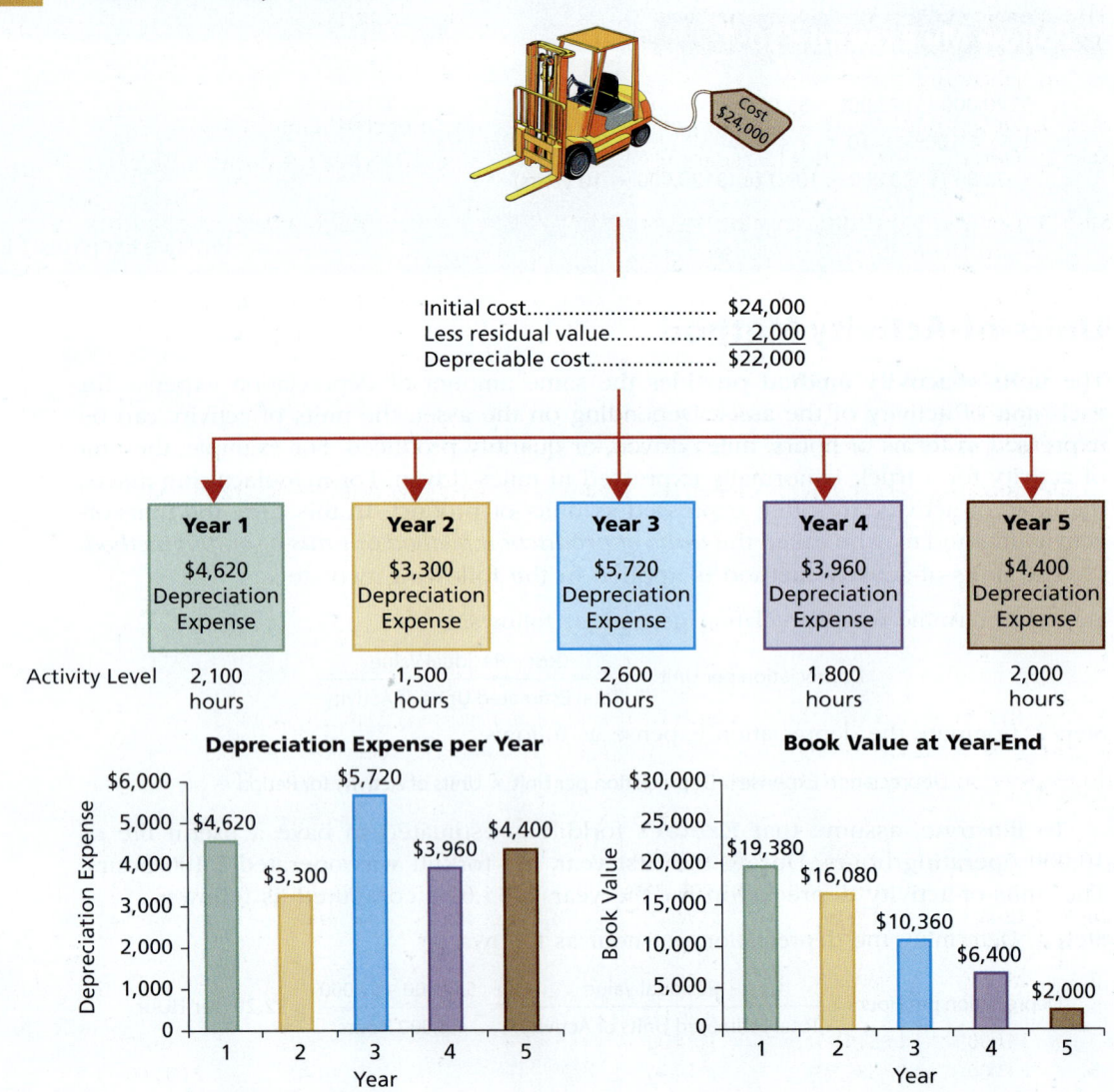

As shown in Exhibit 6, depreciation expense and book value varies each year depending on the hours the forklift is operated.

The units-of-activity method is often used when a fixed asset's use varies from year to year. In such cases, the units-of-activity method matches depreciation expense with the asset's revenues.

Example Exercise 10-2 Units-of-Activity Depreciation Obj. 2

Equipment acquired at the beginning of the year at a cost of $180,000 has an estimated residual value of $10,000, has an estimated useful life of 40,000 hours, and was operated 3,600 hours during the year. Determine (a) the depreciable cost, (b) the depreciation rate, and (c) the units-of-activity depreciation for the year.

Follow My Example 10-2

a. $170,000 ($180,000 − $10,000)
b. $4.25 per hour ($170,000 ÷ 40,000 hours)
c. $15,300 (3,600 hours × $4.25)

Practice Exercises: PE 10-2A, PE 10-2B

Double-Declining-Balance Method

The **double-declining-balance method** provides for a declining periodic expense over the expected useful life of the asset. The double-declining-balance method is applied in the following three steps:

Step 1. Determine the straight-line percentage, using the expected useful life.
Step 2. Determine the double-declining-balance rate by multiplying the straight-line rate (from Step 1) by 2.
Step 3. Compute the depreciation expense by multiplying the double-declining-balance rate (from Step 2) times the book value of the asset.

To illustrate, the purchase of **Exeter**'s forklift is used to compute double-declining-balance depreciation. For the first year, the depreciation is $9,600, computed as follows:

Step 1. Straight-line percentage = 20% (100% ÷ 5)
Step 2. Double-declining-balance rate = 40% (20% × 2)
Step 3. Depreciation expense = $9,600 ($24,000 × 40%)

Depreciation of the forklift for the first year using the double-declining-balance method is recorded as follows:

| Dec. | 31 | Depreciation Expense—Forklift | 9,600 | |
| | | Accumulated Depreciation—Forklift | | 9,600 |

For the first year, the book value of the equipment is its initial cost of $24,000. After the first year, the book value declines, and thus, the depreciation also declines. The double-declining-balance depreciation for the full five-year life of the forklift is as follows:

Year	Cost	Acc. Dep. at Beginning of Year	Book Value at Beginning of Year		Double-Declining-Balance Rate	Depreciation for Year	Book Value at End of Year
1	$24,000		$24,000.00	×	40%	$9,600.00	$14,400.00
2	24,000	$ 9,600.00	14,400.00	×	40%	5,760.00	8,640.00
3	24,000	15,360.00	8,640.00	×	40%	3,456.00	5,184.00
4	24,000	18,816.00	5,184.00	×	40%	2,073.60	3,110.40
5	24,000	20,889.60	3,110.40		—	1,110.40	2,000.00

When the double-declining-balance method is used, the estimated residual value is *not* considered. However, the asset should not be depreciated below its estimated residual value. In the preceding example, the estimated residual value was $2,000. Therefore, the depreciation for the fifth year is $1,110.40 ($3,110.40 − $2,000.00) instead of $1,244.16 (40% × $3,110.40).

Exhibit 7 illustrates the depreciation expense and book value of the forklift over its five-year life using the double-declining-balance method. As shown in Exhibit 7, the double-declining-balance method has higher depreciation in the first year of the asset's life, followed by declining depreciation amounts. For this reason, the double-declining-balance method is called an **accelerated depreciation method**.

EXHIBIT 7   Double-Declining-Balance Method

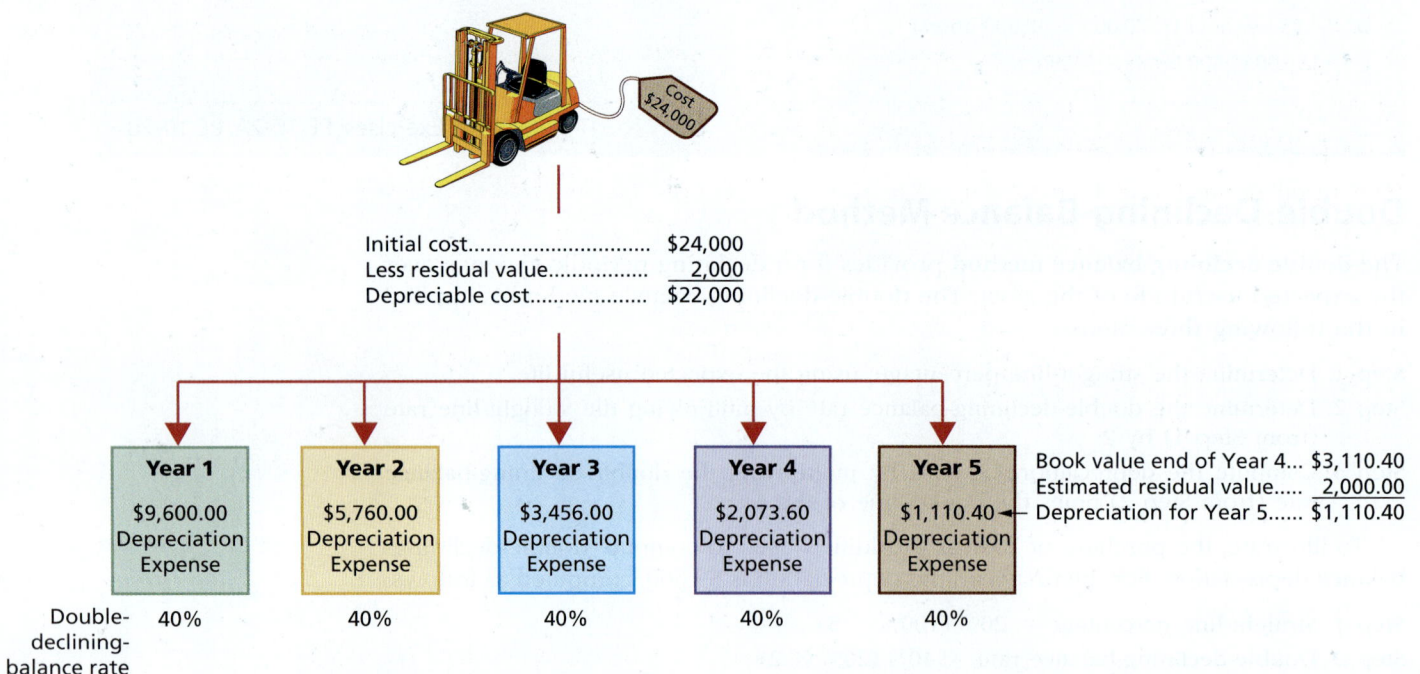

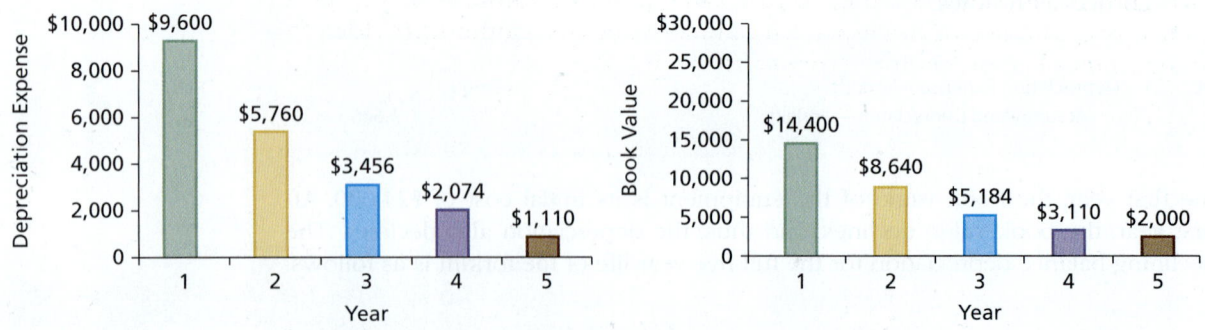

Revenues generated by an asset are often greater in the early years of its use than in later years. In such cases, the double-declining-balance method provides a good matching of depreciation expense with the asset's revenues.

Example Exercise 10-3 Double-Declining-Balance Depreciation — Obj. 2

Equipment acquired at the beginning of the year at a cost of $125,000 has an estimated residual value of $5,000 and an estimated useful life of 10 years. Determine (a) the double-declining-balance rate and (b) the double-declining-balance depreciation for the first year.

Follow My Example 10-3

a. 20% [(100% ÷ 10) × 2]
b. $25,000 ($125,000 × 20%)

Practice Exercises: PE 10-3A, PE 10-3B

Comparing Depreciation Methods

The three depreciation methods are summarized in Exhibit 8. All three methods allocate the total cost of an asset to depreciation expense over the asset's useful life while never depreciating an asset below its residual value.

Method	Useful Life	Depreciable Cost	Depreciation Rate	Depreciation Expense
Straight-line	Years	Cost less residual value	Straight-line rate*	Constant
Units-of-activity	Units of activity	Cost less residual value	(Cost − Residual value) / Total units of activity	Variable
Double-declining-balance	Years	Declining book value, but not below residual value	Straight-line rate* × 2	Declining

*Straight-line rate = (100% ÷ Useful life)

EXHIBIT 8

Summary of Depreciation Methods

The straight-line method provides for the same periodic amounts of depreciation expense over the life of the asset. The units-of-activity method provides for periodic amounts of depreciation expense that vary, depending on the amount the asset is used. The double-declining-balance method provides for a higher depreciation amount in the first year of the asset's use, followed by declining amounts.

Exhibit 9 illustrates depreciation expense for each depreciation method over the five-year life of the forklift.

Partial-Year Depreciation

A fixed asset may be purchased and placed in service other than the first month of an accounting period. In such cases, depreciation is prorated based on the month the asset is placed in service. For example, assume that an asset is placed in service on March 1. For an accounting period ending December 31, depreciation would be computed (prorated) for 10 months (March 1 to December 31).

500 Chapter 10 Long-Term Assets: Fixed and Intangible

EXHIBIT 9

Comparing Depreciation Methods

Dynamic Exhibit

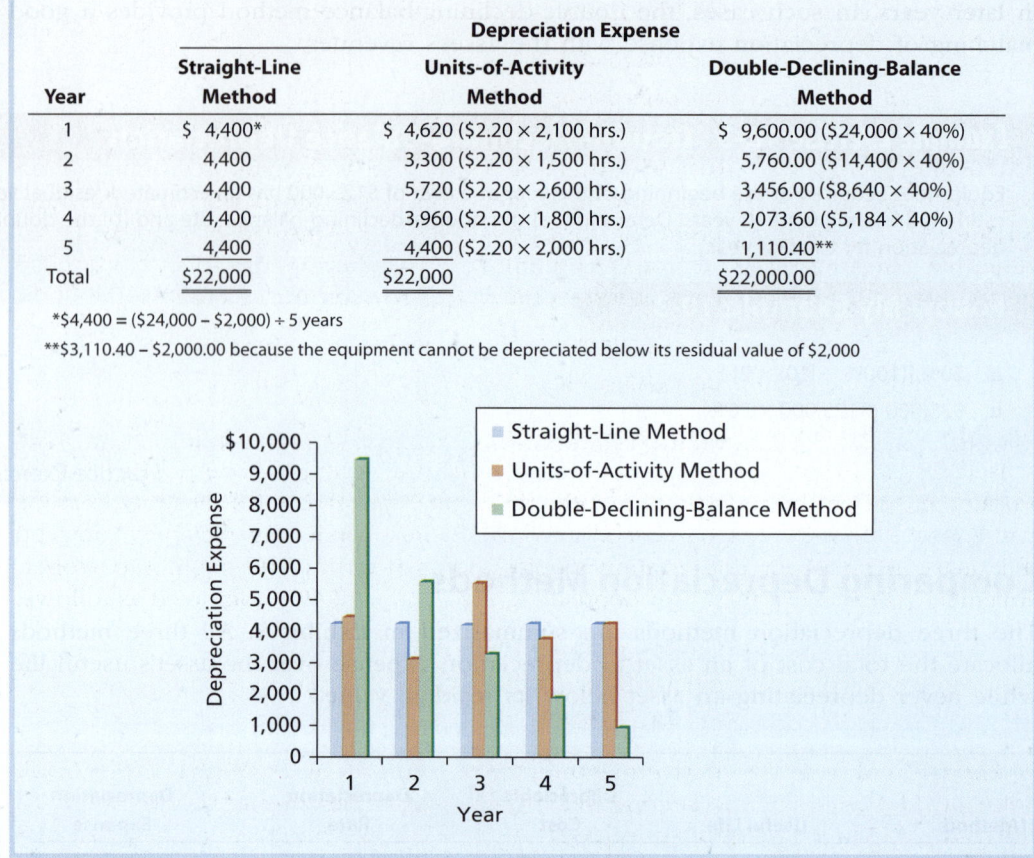

Year	Straight-Line Method	Units-of-Activity Method	Double-Declining-Balance Method
1	$ 4,400*	$ 4,620 ($2.20 × 2,100 hrs.)	$ 9,600.00 ($24,000 × 40%)
2	4,400	3,300 ($2.20 × 1,500 hrs.)	5,760.00 ($14,400 × 40%)
3	4,400	5,720 ($2.20 × 2,600 hrs.)	3,456.00 ($8,640 × 40%)
4	4,400	3,960 ($2.20 × 1,800 hrs.)	2,073.60 ($5,184 × 40%)
5	4,400	4,400 ($2.20 × 2,000 hrs.)	1,110.40**
Total	$22,000	$22,000	$22,000.00

*$4,400 = ($24,000 − $2,000) ÷ 5 years

**$3,110.40 − $2,000.00 because the equipment cannot be depreciated below its residual value of $2,000

Assets may also be placed in service other than the first day of a month. In such cases, assets placed in service during the first half of a month are normally treated as having been purchased on the first day of *that* month. Likewise, asset purchases during the second half of a month are treated as having been placed in service on the first day of the *next* month.

Straight-Line Method Under the straight-line method, depreciation is prorated based on the number of months the asset is in service. To illustrate, assume that Exeter Company purchased the forklift on October 1 instead of January 1. The first-year

Business Connection

DEPRECIATING ANIMALS

The Internal Revenue Code uses the Modified Accelerated Cost Recovery System (MACRS) to compute depreciation for tax purposes. Under MACRS, various farm animals may be depreciated. The period (years) over which some common classes of farm animals may be depreciated are shown in the table that follows.

Depreciation for farm animals begins when the animal reaches the age of maturity, which is normally when it can be worked, milked, or bred. For racehorses, depreciation begins when a horse is put into training.

Class of Animal	Years
Dairy or breeding cattle	7–10
Goats and sheep	5
Hogs	3
Horses	3–12

depreciation would be based upon three months (October, November, December). First-year depreciation would be $1,100, computed as follows:

$$\text{Annual Depreciation} = (\$22{,}000 - \$2{,}000) \div 5 \text{ years} = \$4{,}400$$
$$\text{First-Year Depreciation} = \$4{,}400 \times (3 \div 12) = \$1{,}100$$

Units-of-Activity Method The units-of-activity method computes depreciation expense using an activity rate and the activity level for the period. To illustrate, assume that **Exeter** purchased the forklift on October 1 instead of January 1. Assume that during the period from October 1 to December 31, the forklift was used for 400 hours. First-year depreciation would be $880, computed as follows:

$$\text{Depreciation per Hour} = (\$24{,}000 - \$2{,}000) \div 10{,}000 \text{ Hours} = \$2.20 \text{ per Hour}$$
$$\text{First-Year Depreciation} = \$2.20 \text{ per Hour} \times 400 \text{ Hours} = \$880$$

Double-Declining-Balance Method Like straight-line depreciation, if an asset is used for only part of a year, the annual double-declining-balance depreciation is prorated based on the number of months the asset is in service. To illustrate, assume that **Exeter**'s forklift was purchased and placed into service on October 1 instead of January 1. First-year depreciation would be based upon three months (October, November, December). First-year depreciation would be $2,400, computed as follows:

$$\text{Double-Declining-Balance Rate} = (100\% \div 5) \times 2 = 40\%$$
$$\text{First-Year Annual Depreciation} = \$24{,}000 \times 40\% = \$9{,}600$$
$$\text{First-Year Partial Depreciation} = \$9{,}600 \times (3 \div 12) = \$2{,}400$$

The second-year depreciation would be computed by multiplying the book value on January 1 of the second year by the double-declining-balance rate. To illustrate, assume that Exeter purchased the forklift on October 1 and that $2,400 partial depreciation was recorded on December 31. The book value on January 1 of the second year is $21,600 ($24,000 − $2,400). The second-year depreciation would then be $8,640, computed as follows:

$$\text{Second-Year Annual Depreciation} = \$21{,}600 \times 40\% = \$8{,}640$$

Revising Depreciation Estimates

Estimates of residual values and useful lives of fixed assets may change due to abnormal wear and tear or obsolescence. When new estimates are made by management, they are used to determine the depreciation expense in future periods. The depreciation expense recorded in earlier years is not affected.[5]

To illustrate, assume the following data for a machine that was purchased on January 1:

Initial machine cost	$140,000
Expected useful life	5 years
Estimated residual value	$10,000
Annual depreciation using the straight-line method [($140,000 − $10,000) ÷ 5 years]	$26,000

At the end of the second year, the machine's book value (undepreciated cost) is $88,000, computed as follows:

Initial machine cost	$140,000
Less accumulated depreciation ($26,000 per year × 2 years)	52,000
Book value (undepreciated cost), end of second year	$ 88,000

---

[5] *FASB Accounting Standards Codification*, Section 250-10-05.

502 Chapter 10 Long-Term Assets: Fixed and Intangible

At the beginning of the third year, the company estimates that the machine's remaining useful life is eight years (instead of three) and that its residual value is $8,000 (instead of $10,000). The depreciation expense for each of the remaining eight years is $10,000, computed as follows:

$$\text{Revised Depreciation Expense} = \frac{\text{Book Value} - \text{Revised Residual Value}}{\text{Revised Remaining Useful Life}} = \frac{\$88,000 - \$8,000}{8 \text{ Years}} = \$10,000$$

Exhibit 10 shows the book value of the asset over its original and revised lives. After the depreciation is revised at the end of the second year, book value declines at a slower rate. At the end of the tenth year, the book value reaches the revised residual value of $8,000.

EXHIBIT 10
Book Value of Asset with Change in Estimate

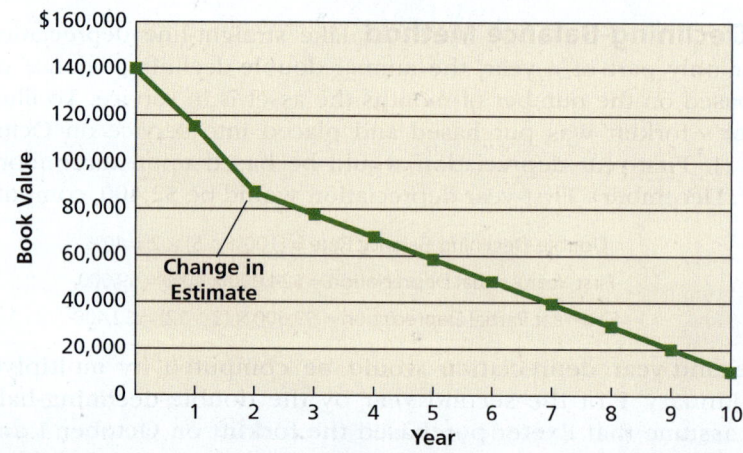

Example Exercise 10-4 Revision of Depreciation *Obj. 2*

A warehouse with a cost of $500,000 has an estimated residual value of $120,000, has an estimated useful life of 40 years, and is depreciated by the straight-line method. (a) Determine the amount of the annual depreciation. (b) Determine the book value at the end of the twentieth year of use. (c) Assuming that at the start of the twenty-first year the remaining life is estimated to be 25 years and the residual value is estimated to be $150,000, determine the depreciation expense for each of the remaining 25 years.

Follow My Example 10-4

a. $9,500 [($500,000 − $120,000) ÷ 40]
b. $310,000 [$500,000 − ($9,500 × 20)]
c. $6,400 [($310,000 − $150,000) ÷ 25]

Practice Exercises: PE 10-4A, PE 10-4B

IFRS

See Appendix B for more information.

Repair and Improvements

Once a fixed asset has been acquired and placed into service, costs may be incurred for ordinary maintenance and repairs. In addition, costs may be incurred for improving an asset or for extraordinary repairs that extend the asset's useful life. Costs that benefit only the current period are called **revenue expenditures**. Costs that improve the asset or extend its useful life are **capital expenditures**.

Ordinary Maintenance and Repairs Costs related to the ordinary maintenance and repairs of a fixed asset are recorded as an expense of the current period. Such expenditures are *revenue expenditures* and are recorded as debits to Repairs and Maintenance Expense. For example, $300 paid for a tune-up of a delivery truck is recorded as follows:

| Repairs and Maintenance Expense | 300 | |
| Cash | | 300 |

Extraordinary Repairs After a fixed asset has been placed into service, costs may be incurred to extend the asset's useful life. For example, the engine of a forklift that is near the end of its useful life may be overhauled at a cost of $4,500, extending its useful life by eight years. Such costs are *capital expenditures* and are recorded as a decrease in an accumulated depreciation account. In the case of the forklift, the expenditure is recorded as follows:

| Accumulated Depreciation—Forklift | 4,500 | |
| Cash | | 4,500 |

Because the forklift's remaining useful life has changed, depreciation for the forklift will also change based on the new book value of the forklift.

Asset Improvements After a fixed asset has been placed into service, costs may be incurred to improve the asset. For example, the service value of a delivery truck might be improved by adding a $5,500 hydraulic lift to allow for easier and quicker loading of cargo. Such costs are *capital expenditures* and are recorded as increases to the fixed asset account. In the case of the hydraulic lift, the expenditure is recorded as follows:

| Delivery Truck | 5,500 | |
| Cash | | 5,500 |

Because the cost of the delivery truck has increased, depreciation for the truck will also change over its remaining useful life.

INTEGRITY, OBJECTIVITY, AND ETHICS IN BUSINESS

CAPITAL CRIME

One of the largest accounting frauds in history involved the improper accounting for maintenance expenditures. WorldCom, the second largest telecommunications company in the United States at the time, improperly treated maintenance expenditures on its telecommunications network as capital expenditures. As a result, the company had to restate its prior years' earnings downward by nearly $4 billion to correct this error. The company declared bankruptcy within months of disclosing the error, and the CEO was sentenced to 25 years in prison.

The accounting for revenue and capital expenditures is summarized in Exhibit 11.

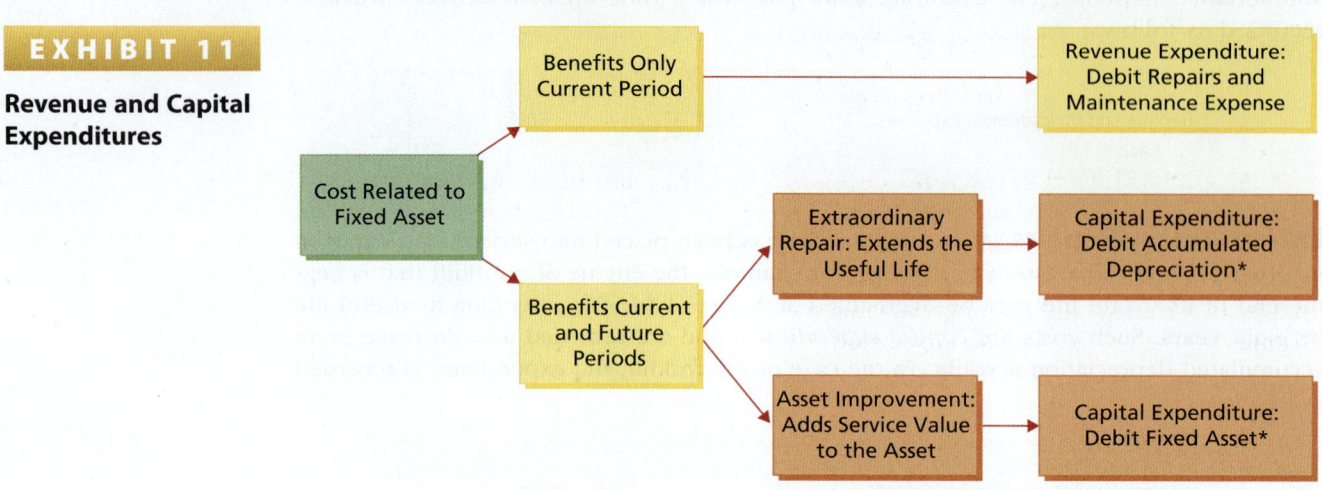

EXHIBIT 11

Revenue and Capital Expenditures

*Revise depreciation.

Example Exercise 10-5 Capital and Revenue Expenditures   Obj. 2

On June 18, GTS Co. paid $1,200 to upgrade a hydraulic lift and $45 for an oil change for one of its delivery trucks. Journalize the entries for the hydraulic lift upgrade and oil change expenditures.

Follow My Example 10-5

June 18	Delivery Truck	1,200	
	Cash		1,200
18	Repairs and Maintenance Expense	45	
	Cash		45

Practice Exercises: PE 10-5A, PE 10-5B

Obj. 3 Journalize the disposal of fixed assets.

Disposal of Fixed Assets

Fixed assets that are no longer useful may be discarded or sold.[6] In such cases, the fixed asset is removed from the accounts. Just because a fixed asset is fully depreciated, however, does not mean that it should be removed from the accounts.

If a fixed asset is still being used, its cost and accumulated depreciation should remain in the ledger even if the asset is fully depreciated. If the asset was removed from the ledger, the accounts would contain no evidence of their continued existence. In addition, cost and accumulated depreciation data on such assets are often needed for property tax and income tax reports.

Discarding Fixed Assets

If a fixed asset is no longer used and has no residual value, it is discarded. For example, assume that a fixed asset is fully depreciated, has no residual value, and is discarded. The discarded asset and its accumulated depreciation are removed from the accounts and ledger.

6 The accounting for the exchange of fixed assets is described and illustrated in the appendix at the end of this chapter.

To illustrate, assume that equipment acquired at a cost of $25,000 with no residual value is fully depreciated. On February 14, the equipment is discarded. The entry to record the discard is as follows:

Feb.	14	Accumulated Depreciation—Equipment	25,000	
		Equipment		25,000
		To write off equipment discarded.		

If an asset has not been fully depreciated, depreciation should be recorded before removing the asset from the accounting records. To illustrate, assume that equipment costing $6,000 with no estimated residual value is depreciated at a straight-line rate of 10%. The accumulated depreciation balance, after adjusting entries, is $4,650 on December 31. On March 24 of the following year, the asset is removed from service and discarded. The entry to record the depreciation for the three months before the asset is discarded is as follows:

Mar.	24	Depreciation Expense—Equipment	150	
		Accumulated Depreciation—Equipment		150
		To record current depreciation on equipment discarded ($600 × 3/12).		

The discarding of the equipment is then recorded as follows:

Mar.	24	Accumulated Depreciation—Equipment	4,800	
		Loss on Disposal of Equipment	1,200	
		Equipment		6,000
		To write off equipment discarded.		

The loss of $1,200 is recorded because the balance of the accumulated depreciation account ($4,800) is less than the balance in the equipment account ($6,000). Losses on the discarding of fixed assets are reported on the income statement.

Selling Fixed Assets

Dynamic Exhibit

The entry to record the sale of a fixed asset is similar to the entry for discarding an asset. The only difference is that the receipt of cash is also recorded. If the selling price is more than the book value of the asset, a gain is recorded. If the selling price is less than the book value, a loss is recorded.

To illustrate, assume that equipment is purchased at a cost of $10,000 with no estimated residual value and is depreciated at a straight-line rate of 10%. The equipment is sold for cash on October 12 of the eighth year of its use. The balance of the accumulated depreciation account as of the preceding December 31 is $7,000. The entry to update the depreciation for the nine months of the current year is as follows:

Oct.	12	Depreciation Expense—Equipment	750	
		Accumulated Depreciation—Equipment		750
		To record current depreciation on equipment sold ($10,000 × 9/12 × 10%).		

After the current depreciation is recorded, the book value of the asset is $2,250 ($10,000 − $7,750). The entries to record the sale, assuming three different selling prices, are as follows:

Sold at book value, for $2,250. No gain or loss.

Oct.	12	Cash	2,250	
		Accumulated Depreciation—Equipment	7,750	
		Equipment		10,000

Sold below book value, for $1,000. Loss of $1,250.

Oct.	12	Cash	1,000	
		Accumulated Depreciation—Equipment	7,750	
		Loss on Sale of Equipment	1,250	
		Equipment		10,000

Sold above book value, for $2,800. Gain of $550.

Oct.	12	Cash	2,800	
		Accumulated Depreciation—Equipment	7,750	
		Equipment		10,000
		Gain on Sale of Equipment		550

Example Exercise 10-6 Sale of Equipment *Obj. 3*

Equipment was acquired at the beginning of the year at a cost of $91,000. The equipment was depreciated using the straight-line method based on an estimated useful life of nine years and an estimated residual value of $10,000.

a. What was the depreciation for the first year?
b. Assuming that the equipment was sold at the end of the second year for $78,000, determine the gain or loss on the sale of the equipment.
c. Journalize the entry to record the sale.

Follow My Example 10-6

a. $9,000 [($91,000 − $10,000) ÷ 9]
b. $5,000 gain {$78,000 − [$91,000 − ($9,000 × 2)]}
c.
Cash	78,000	
Accumulated Depreciation—Equipment	18,000	
Equipment		91,000
Gain on Sale of Equipment		5,000

Practice Exercises: PE 10-6A, PE 10-6B

Business Connection

DOWNSIZING

Management may decide to sell a fixed asset when it is perceived to no longer meet business objectives. This can happen when the strategy of the business changes or the business is downsizing operations. For example, **Ruby Tuesday**, a national restaurant chain, sold stores and equipment at a book value of $14 million for cash of $15.4 million, resulting in a $1.4 million gain. These fixed assets were sold in order to focus on more profitable restaurants.

Natural Resources

Obj. 4 Describe the accounting for natural resources, including the journal entry for depletion.

Some businesses own natural resources such as timber, minerals, or oil. The characteristics of natural resources are as follows:

- **Naturally Occurring:** An asset that is created through natural growth or naturally through the passage of time. For example, timber is a natural resource that naturally grows over time.
- **Removed for Sale:** The asset is consumed by removing it from its land source. For example, timber is removed for use when it is harvested, and minerals are removed when they are mined.
- **Removed and Sold over More Than One Year:** The natural resource is removed and sold over a period of more than one year.

Natural resources are classified as a type of fixed asset. The cost of a natural resource includes the cost of obtaining and preparing it for use. For example, legal fees incurred in purchasing a natural resource are included as part of its cost.

As natural resources are harvested or mined and then sold, a portion of their cost is debited to an expense account called **depletion expense**.

Depletion is determined as follows:[7]

Step 1. Determine the depletion rate as follows:

$$\text{Depletion Rate} = \frac{\text{Cost of Resource}}{\text{Estimated Total Units of Resource}}$$

Step 2. Multiply the depletion rate by the quantity removed from the resource during the period.

$$\text{Depletion Expense} = \text{Depletion Rate} \times \text{Quantity Removed}$$

To illustrate, assume that Karst Company purchased mining rights as follows:

Cost of mineral deposit	$ 400,000
Estimated total units of resource	1,000,000 tons
Tons mined during year	90,000 tons

The depletion expense of $36,000 for the year is computed as follows:

Step 1. $\text{Depletion Rate} = \dfrac{\text{Cost of Resource}}{\text{Estimated Total Units of Resource}} = \dfrac{\$400,000}{1,000,000 \text{ Tons}} = \$0.40 \text{ per Ton}$

Step 2. Depletion Expense = $0.40 per Ton × 90,000 Tons = $36,000

The adjusting entry to record the depletion is as follows:

Dec.	31	Depletion Expense	36,000	
		Accumulated Depletion		36,000
		Depletion of mineral deposit.		

Like the accumulated depreciation account, Accumulated Depletion is a contra asset account. It is reported on the balance sheet as a deduction from the cost of the mineral deposit.

---

[7] We assume that there is no significant residual value after all the natural resource is removed.

Example Exercise 10-7 Depletion Obj. 4

Earth's Treasures Mining Co. acquired mineral rights for $45,000,000. The mineral deposit is estimated at 50,000,000 tons. During the current year, 12,600,000 tons were mined and sold.

a. Determine the depletion rate.
b. Determine the amount of depletion expense for the current year.
c. Journalize the adjusting entry on December 31 to recognize the depletion expense.

Follow My Example 10-7

a. $0.90 per ton ($45,000,000 ÷ 50,000,000 tons)
b. $11,340,000 (12,600,000 tons × $0.90 per ton)
c. Dec. 31 Depletion Expense 11,340,000
             Accumulated Depletion 11,340,000
             Depletion of mineral deposit.

Practice Exercises: PE 10-7A, PE 10-7B

Obj. 5 Describe the accounting for intangible assets, such as patents, copyrights, and goodwill.

Intangible Assets

Long-term assets that are used in the operations of the business but do not exist physically are called intangible assets. **Intangible assets** may be acquired through innovative, creative activities or through the purchase of the rights from another company. Examples of intangible assets include patents, copyrights, trademarks, and goodwill.

The accounting for intangible assets is similar to that for fixed assets. The major issues are:

- Determining the initial cost.
- Determining the **amortization**, which is the amount of cost to transfer to expense.

See Appendix B for more information.

Amortization results from the passage of time or a decline in the usefulness of the intangible asset.

Patents

Manufacturers may acquire exclusive rights to produce and sell goods with one or more unique features. Such rights are granted by **patents**, which the federal government issues to inventors. These rights continue in effect for 20 years. A business may purchase patent rights from others, or it may obtain patents developed by its own research and development.

The initial cost of a purchased patent, including any legal fees, is debited to an asset account. This cost is written off, or amortized, over the years of the patent's expected useful life. The expected useful life of a patent may be less than its legal life. For example, a patent may become worthless due to changing technology or consumer tastes.

Patent amortization is normally computed using the straight-line method. The amortization is recorded by debiting an amortization expense account and crediting the patents account. A separate contra asset account is usually *not* used for intangible assets.

To illustrate, assume that at the beginning of its fiscal year, a company acquires patent rights for $100,000. Although the patent will not expire for 14 years, its remaining useful life is estimated as 5 years. The adjusting entry to amortize the patent at the end of the year is as follows:

Dec.	31	Amortization Expense—Patents	20,000	
		Patents		20,000
		Patent amortization ($100,000 ÷ 5).		

Some companies develop their own patents through research and development. In such cases, any *research and development costs* are usually recorded as current operating expenses in the period in which they are incurred. This accounting for research and development costs is justified on the basis that any future benefits from current research and development are highly uncertain.

Copyrights and Trademarks

The exclusive right to publish and sell a literary, artistic, or musical composition is granted by a **copyright**. Copyrights are issued by the federal government and extend for 70 years beyond the author's death. The costs of a copyright include all costs of creating the work plus any other costs of obtaining the copyright. A copyright that is purchased is recorded at the price paid for it. Copyrights are amortized over their estimated useful lives.

A **trademark** is a name, term, or symbol used to identify a business and its products. Under federal law, businesses can protect their trademarks by registering them for 10 years and renewing the registration for 10-year periods. Like a copyright, the legal costs of registering a trademark are recorded as an asset. Most businesses identify their registered trademarks with ® in their advertisements and on their products.

If a trademark is purchased from another business, its cost is recorded as an asset. In such cases, the cost of the trademark is considered to have an indefinite useful life. Thus, trademarks are not amortized. Instead, trademarks are reviewed periodically for impaired value. When a trademark is impaired, the trademark should be written down and a loss recognized.

Goodwill

Goodwill refers to an intangible asset of a business that is created from such favorable factors as location, product quality, reputation, and managerial skill. Goodwill allows a business to earn a greater rate of return than normal.

Generally accepted accounting principles (GAAP) allow goodwill to be recorded only if it is objectively determined by a transaction. An example of such a transaction is the purchase of a business at a price in excess of the fair value of its net assets (assets less liabilities). The excess is recorded as goodwill and reported as an intangible asset.

Unlike patents and copyrights, goodwill is not amortized. However, a loss should be recorded if the future prospects of the purchased firm become impaired. This loss would normally be disclosed in the Other expense section of the income statement.

To illustrate, assume that on December 31, FaceCard Company has determined that $250,000 of the goodwill created from the purchase of Electronic Systems is impaired. The entry to record the impairment is as follows:

Dec.	31	Loss from Impaired Goodwill		250,000	
		Goodwill			250,000
		Impaired goodwill.			

Exhibit 12 shows common intangible asset disclosures for 500 large firms. Goodwill is the most often reported intangible asset. This is because goodwill arises from merger transactions, which are common.

Link to McDonald's

McDonald's Corporation owns trademarks on "McDonald's" and the Golden Arches logo.

Link to McDonald's

On a recent balance sheet, **McDonald's** reported goodwill of $2.9 billion. Most of McDonald's goodwill arises when it purchases existing restaurants from franchisees.

Link to McDonald's

McDonald's compares fair value to book (carrying) value to determine whether goodwill is impaired. In a recent annual report, McDonald's reported that it did not have any goodwill at risk of impairment.

EXHIBIT 12

Frequency of Intangible Asset Disclosures for 500 Firms

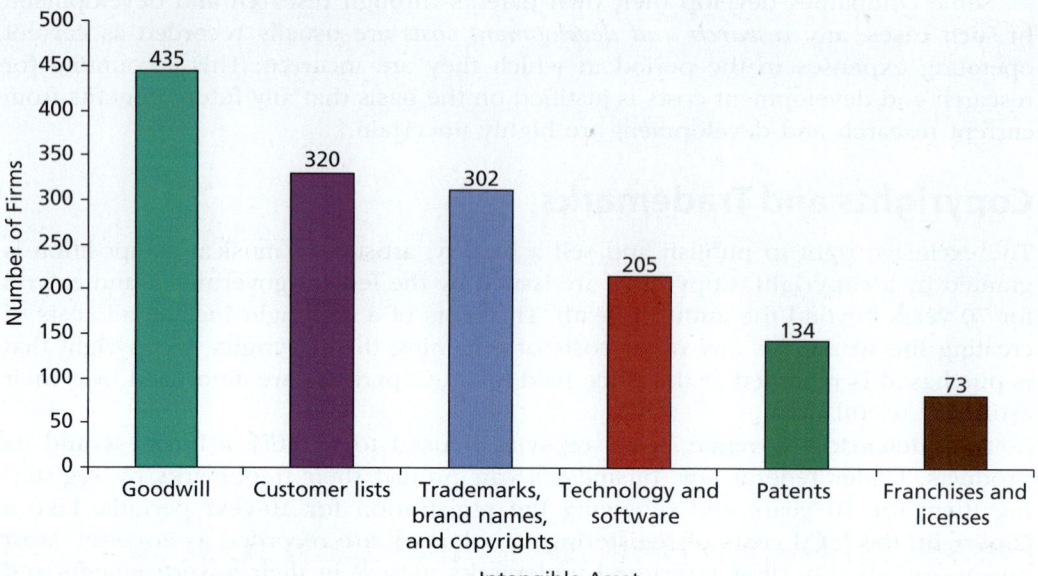

Note: Some firms have multiple disclosures.
Source: *Accounting Trends & Techniques*, 66th ed., American Institute of Certified Public Accountants, New York.

Exhibit 13 summarizes the characteristics of intangible assets.

EXHIBIT 13

Comparison of Intangible Assets

Intangible Asset	Description	Amortization Period	Periodic Expense
Patent	Exclusive right to benefit from an innovation	Estimated useful life not to exceed legal life	Amortization expense
Copyright	Exclusive right to benefit from a literary, artistic, or musical composition	Estimated useful life not to exceed legal life	Amortization expense
Trademark	Exclusive use of a name, term, or symbol	None	Impairment loss if fair value less than carrying value (impaired)
Goodwill	Excess of purchase price of a business over the fair value of its net assets (assets − liabilities)	None	Impairment loss if fair value less than carrying value (impaired)

Example Exercise 10-8 Impaired Goodwill and Amortization of Patent   Obj. 5

On December 31, it was estimated that goodwill of $40,000 was impaired. In addition, a patent with an estimated useful economic life of 12 years was acquired for $84,000 on July 1.

a. Journalize the adjusting entry on December 31 for the impaired goodwill.
b. Journalize the adjusting entry on December 31 for the amortization of the patent rights.

Follow My Example 10-8

a. Dec. 31 Loss from Impaired Goodwill 40,000
              Goodwill 40,000
           Impaired goodwill.
b. Dec. 31 Amortization Expense—Patents 3,500
              Patents 3,500
           Amortized patent rights [($84,000 ÷ 12) × (6 ÷ 12)].

Practice Exercises: PE 10-8A, PE 10-8B

International Connection

INTERNATIONAL FINANCIAL REPORTING STANDARDS (IFRS)

IFRS allow certain research and development (R&D) costs to be recorded as assets when incurred. Typically, R&D costs are classified as either research costs or development costs. If certain criteria are met, research costs can be recorded as an expense, while development costs can be recorded as an asset. This criterion includes such considerations as the company's intent to use or to sell the intangible asset. For example, **Nokia Corporation** (Finland) reported capitalized development costs of €40 million in a recent statement of financial position (balance sheet), where € represents the euro, the common currency of the European Economic Union.*

*Differences between U.S. GAAP and IFRS are further discussed and illustrated in Appendix B.

Financial Reporting for Long-Term Assets: Fixed and Intangible

Obj. 6 Describe how depreciation expense is reported on an income statement and prepare a balance sheet that includes fixed assets and intangible assets.

On the income statement, depreciation and amortization expense should be reported separately or disclosed in a note. A description of the methods used in computing depreciation should also be reported.

On the balance sheet, each class of fixed assets should be disclosed on the face of the statement along with its related accumulated depreciation. Fixed assets may also be reported at their *book value* (net amount) with accumulated depreciation shown in the notes.

If there are many classes of fixed assets, a single amount may be presented on the balance sheet, supported by a note with a separate listing. Fixed assets may be reported under the more descriptive caption of property, plant, and equipment.

Intangible assets are usually reported on the balance sheet in a separate section following fixed assets. The balance of each class of intangible assets should be disclosed net of any amortization.

The balance sheet presentation for **Mornin' Joe**'s fixed and intangible assets follows:

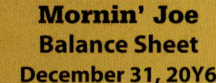

Mornin' Joe
Balance Sheet
December 31, 20Y6

Property, plant, and equipment:			
Land			$1,850,000
Buildings	$2,650,000		
Less accumulated depreciation	420,000	2,230,000	
Office equipment	$ 350,000		
Less accumulated depreciation	102,000	248,000	
Total property, plant, and equipment			4,328,000
Intangible assets:			
Patents			140,000

Chapter 10 Long-Term Assets: Fixed and Intangible

If a company has natural resources, depletion expense is reported on the income statement. In addition, the cost and related accumulated depletion of the natural resources are reported as part of the Property, plant, and equipment section of the balance sheet.

Obj. 7 Describe and illustrate the fixed asset turnover ratio to assess the efficiency of a company's use of its fixed assets.

Financial Analysis and Interpretation: Fixed Asset Turnover Ratio

Fixed Asset Turnover Ratio

The **fixed asset turnover ratio** measures the number of sales dollars earned per dollar of fixed assets. The higher the ratio, the more efficiently a company is using its fixed assets in generating sales. The ratio is computed as follows:

$$\text{Fixed Asset Turnover Ratio} = \frac{\text{Sales}}{\text{Average Book Value of Fixed Assets}}$$

To illustrate, the following data (in millions) were taken from a recent financial statement of **McDonald's Corporation**:

Sales	$25,413
Fixed assets (net):	
Beginning of year	24,558
End of year	23,118

McDonald's fixed asset turnover ratio for the year is computed as follows (rounded to one decimal place):

$$\text{Fixed Asset Turnover Ratio} = \frac{\text{Sales}}{\text{Average Book Value of Fixed Assets}} = \frac{\$25,413}{(\$24,558 + \$23,118) \div 2} = \frac{\$25,413}{\$23,838}$$

$$= 1.1$$

Is 1.1 efficient? To answer this question, McDonald's fixed asset turnover ratio can be compared to other quick-service restaurant companies, as shown in Exhibit 14. **Yum! Brands** operates **KFC**, **Pizza Hut**, and **Taco Bell** quick-service restaurants. The other restaurants are likely familiar by name.

EXHIBIT 14

Fixed Asset Turnover: Selected Quick-Service Restaurants

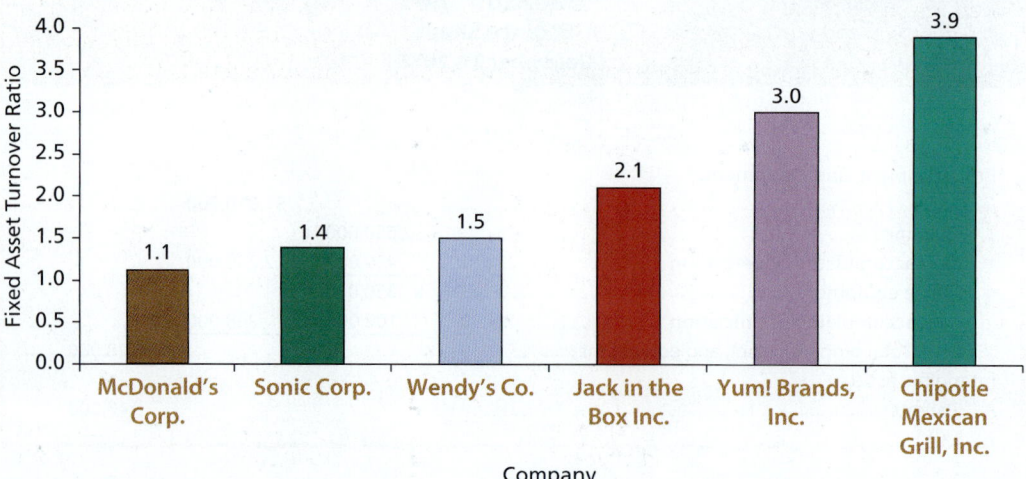

Differences in the fixed asset turnover between these companies can be due to a number of factors, including differences in both the average fixed asset book value and sales per restaurant. Explaining McDonald's low fixed asset turnover ratio relative to the other restaurants would require a deeper analysis into these variables.

Comparing companies within industries is useful because the fixed asset turnover ratio should be comparable within an industry. The fixed asset turnover ratio will vary across industries because of differences in how industries use fixed assets. For example, the fixed asset turnover ratio for selected companies in different industries is shown in Exhibit 15.

EXHIBIT 15

Fixed Asset Turnover Ratio: Various Industries

Company (Industry)	Fixed Asset Turnover Ratio
Disney (entertainment)	2.2
ExxonMobil (petrochemical)	1.0
ManpowerGroup (temporary employment)	130.5
McDonald's (quick-service restaurant)	1.1
Union Pacific (railroad)	0.5

The smaller fixed asset turnover ratios are associated with industries that require large fixed asset investments to generate revenues. The larger fixed asset turnover ratios are associated with industries that require smaller fixed asset investments to generate revenues. Thus, for example, the difference in the fixed asset turnover ratio between Union Pacific and ManpowerGroup is due to the difference in the way fixed assets are used in their respective industries. Railroads require extensive investments in track, engines, and railcars, while temporary employment agencies require few investments in fixed assets.

Business Connection

HUB-AND-SPOKE OR POINT-TO-POINT?

Southwest Airlines Co. uses a simple fare structure featuring low, unrestricted, unlimited, everyday coach fares. These fares are made possible by Southwest's use of a point-to-point rather than a hub-and-spoke business approach.

United Airlines, Inc., Delta Air Lines, and American Airlines employ a hub-and-spoke approach in which an airline establishes major hubs that serve as connecting links to other cities. For example, Delta has major connecting hubs in Atlanta and Salt Lake City.

In contrast, Southwest focuses on nonstop, point-to-point service between selected cities. As a result, Southwest minimizes connections, delays, and total trip time. This operating approach permits Southwest to achieve high utilization of its fixed assets, such as its 737 aircraft.

Example Exercise 10-9 Fixed Asset Turnover Ratio   Obj. 7

Financial statement data for years ending December 31 for Broadwater Company follow:

	Year 2	Year 1
Sales	$2,862,000	$2,025,000
Fixed assets:		
Beginning of year	750,000	600,000
End of year	840,000	750,000

a. Determine the fixed asset turnover ratio for Year 1 and Year 2.
b. Does the change in the fixed asset turnover ratio from Year 1 to Year 2 indicate a favorable or an unfavorable change?

(Continued)

Follow My Example 10-9

a. Fixed asset turnover:

	Year 2	Year 1
Sales	$2,862,000	$2,025,000
Fixed assets:		
Beginning of year	$750,000	$600,000
End of year	$840,000	$750,000
Average fixed assets	$795,000	$675,000
	[($750,000 + $840,000) ÷ 2]	[($600,000 + $750,000) ÷ 2]
Fixed asset turnover	3.6	3.0
	($2,862,000 ÷ $795,000)	($2,025,000 ÷ $675,000)

b. The increase in the fixed asset turnover ratio from 3.0 to 3.6 indicates a favorable change in the efficiency of using fixed assets to generate sales.

Practice Exercises: PE 10-9A, PE 10-9B

APPENDIX

Exchanging Similar Fixed Assets

Old equipment is often traded in for new equipment having a similar use. In such cases, the seller allows the buyer an amount for the old equipment traded in. This amount, called the **trade-in allowance**, may be either greater or less than the book value of the old equipment. The remaining balance—the amount owed—is either paid in cash or recorded as a liability. It is normally called **boot**, which is its tax name.

Accounting for the exchange of similar assets depends on whether the transaction has *commercial substance*.[8] An exchange has commercial substance if future cash flows change as a result of the exchange. If an exchange of similar assets has commercial substance, a gain or loss is recognized. In such cases, the exchange is accounted for similar to that of a sale of a fixed asset. The gain or loss is determined as the difference between the fair market value (trade-in allowance) of the asset given up (exchanged) and its book value. Alternatively, the gain or loss can be determined as the difference between the fair market value of the new asset received and the assets given up in the exchange (cash and book value of the old asset).

Gain on Exchange

To illustrate a gain on an exchange of similar assets, assume the following:

Similar equipment acquired (new):
Price (fair market value) of new equipment	$5,000
Less trade-in allowance on old equipment	1,100
Cash paid at June 19, date of exchange	$3,900

Equipment traded in (old):
Cost of old equipment	$4,000
Less accumulated depreciation at date of exchange	3,200
Book value at June 19, date of exchange	$ 800

---
8 *FASB Accounting Standards Codification*, Section 360-10-30.

The entry to record this exchange and payment of cash is as follows:

June	19	Accumulated Depreciation—Equipment	3,200	
		Equipment (new equipment)	5,000	
		Equipment (old equipment)		4,000
		Cash		3,900
		Gain on Exchange of Equipment		300

The gain on the exchange, $300, is the difference between the fair market value (trade-in allowance) of the asset given up (exchanged) of $1,100 and its book value of $800, computed as follows:

Fair market value (trade-in allowance) of old equipment	$1,100
Less book value of old equipment	800
Gain on exchange of assets	$ 300

The gain on the exchange, $300, can also be determined as the difference between the fair market value of the new asset of $5,000 and the book value of the old asset traded in of $800 plus the cash paid of $3,900, computed as follows:

Price (fair market value) of new equipment		$5,000
Assets given up in exchange:		
Book value of old equipment ($4,000 − $3,200)	$ 800	
Cash paid on the exchange	3,900	4,700
Gain on exchange of assets		$ 300

Loss on Exchange

To illustrate a loss on an exchange of similar assets, assume that instead of a trade-in allowance of $1,100, a trade-in allowance of only $675 was allowed in the preceding example. In this case, the cash paid on the exchange is $4,325, computed as follows:

Price (fair market value) of new equipment	$5,000
Less trade-in allowance of old equipment	675
Cash paid at June 19, date of exchange	$4,325

The entry to record this exchange and payment of cash is as follows:

June	19	Accumulated Depreciation—Equipment	3,200	
		Equipment (new equipment)	5,000	
		Loss on Exchange of Equipment	125	
		Equipment (old equipment)		4,000
		Cash		4,325

The loss on the exchange, $125, is the difference between the fair market value (trade-in allowance) of the asset given up (exchanged) of $675 and its book value of $800, computed as follows:

Fair market value (trade-in allowance) of old equipment	$ 675
Less book value of old equipment	800
Loss on exchange of assets	$(125)

The loss on the exchange, $125, can also be determined as the difference between the fair market value of the new asset of $5,000 and the book value of the old asset traded in of $800 plus the cash paid of $4,325, computed as follows:

Price (fair market value) of new equipment		$5,000
Assets given up in exchange:		
Book value of old equipment ($4,000 − $3,200)	$ 800	
Cash paid on the exchange	4,325	5,125
Loss on exchange of assets		$ (125)

In those cases where an asset exchange *lacks commercial substance*, no gain is recognized on the exchange. Instead, the cost of the new asset is adjusted for any gain. For example, in the first illustration, the gain of $300 would be subtracted from the purchase price of $5,000 and the new asset would be recorded at $4,700. Accounting for the exchange of assets that lack commercial substance is discussed in more advanced accounting texts.[9]

At a Glance 10

Obj. 1 Define, classify, and account for the cost of fixed assets.

Key Points Fixed assets are long-term tangible assets used in the normal operations of the business such as equipment, buildings, and land. The initial cost of a fixed asset includes all amounts spent to get the asset in place and ready for use.

Learning Outcomes	Example Exercises	Practice Exercises
• Define *fixed assets*.		
• List the types of costs that should be included in the cost of a fixed asset.		

---

[9] The exchange of similar assets also involves complex tax issues, which are discussed in advanced accounting courses.

Obj. 2 — Compute depreciation, using the following methods: straight-line, units-of-activity, and double-declining-balance.

Key Points All fixed assets except land should be depreciated over time. Three factors are considered in determining depreciation: (1) the fixed asset's initial cost, (2) the useful life of the asset, and (3) the residual value of the asset.

Depreciation may be determined using the straight-line, units-of-activity, and double-declining-balance methods.

Depreciation may be revised into the future for changes in an asset's useful life or residual value.

Learning Outcomes	Example Exercises	Practice Exercises
• Define and describe *depreciation*.		
• List the factors used in determining depreciation.		
• Compute straight-line depreciation.	EE10-1	PE10-1A, 10-1B
• Compute units-of-activity depreciation.	EE10-2	PE10-2A, 10-2B
• Compute double-declining-balance depreciation.	EE10-3	PE10-3A, 10-3B
• Compute revised depreciation for a change in an asset's useful life and residual value.	EE10-4	PE10-4A, 10-4B
• Provide examples of ordinary repairs, asset improvements, and extraordinary repairs.		
• Prepare journal entries for ordinary repairs, asset improvements, and extraordinary repairs.	EE10-5	PE10-5A, 10-5B

Obj. 3 — Journalize the disposal of fixed assets.

Key Points When discarding a fixed asset, any depreciation for the current period should be recorded, and the book value of the asset is then removed from the accounts.

When a fixed asset is sold, the book value is removed, and the cash or other asset received is recorded. If the selling price is more than the book value of the asset, the transaction results in a gain. If the selling price is less than the book value, there is a loss.

Learning Outcomes	Example Exercises	Practice Exercises
• Prepare the journal entry for discarding a fixed asset.		
• Prepare journal entries for the sale of a fixed asset.	EE10-6	PE10-6A, 10-6B

Obj. 4 — Describe the accounting for natural resources, including the journal entry for depletion.

Key Points The amount of periodic depletion is computed by multiplying the quantity of minerals extracted during the period by a depletion rate. The depletion rate is computed by dividing the cost of the mineral deposit by its estimated total units of resource. The entry to record depletion debits a depletion expense account and credits an accumulated depletion account.

Learning Outcomes	Example Exercises	Practice Exercises
• Define and describe *depletion*.		
• Compute a depletion rate.	EE10-7	PE10-7A, 10-7B
• Prepare the journal entry to record depletion.	EE10-7	PE10-7A, 10-7B

Chapter 10 Long-Term Assets: Fixed and Intangible

Obj. 5   Describe the accounting for intangible assets, such as patents, copyrights, and goodwill.

Key Points   Long-term assets such as patents, copyrights, trademarks, and goodwill are intangible assets. The cost of patents and copyrights should be amortized over the years of the asset's expected usefulness by debiting an expense account and crediting the intangible asset account. Trademarks and goodwill are not amortized but are written down only upon impairment.

Learning Outcomes	Example Exercises	Practice Exercises
• Define, describe, and provide examples of *intangible assets*.		
• Prepare a journal entry for the purchase of an intangible asset.		
• Prepare a journal entry to amortize the costs of patents and copyrights.	EE10-8	PE10-8A, 10-8B
• Prepare the journal entry to record the impairment of goodwill.	EE10-8	PE10-8A, 10-8B

Obj. 6   Describe how depreciation expense is reported on an income statement and prepare a balance sheet that includes fixed assets and intangible assets.

Key Points   The amount of depreciation expense and the depreciation methods used should be disclosed in the financial statements. Each major class of fixed assets should be disclosed, along with the related accumulated depreciation. Intangible assets are usually presented in a separate section following fixed assets. Each major class of intangible assets should be disclosed net of the amortization recorded to date.

Learning Outcomes	Example Exercises	Practice Exercises
• Describe and illustrate how fixed assets are reported on the income statement and balance sheet.		
• Describe and illustrate how intangible assets are reported on the income statement and balance sheet.		
• Describe and illustrate how natural resources are reported on the income statement and balance sheet.		

Obj. 7   Describe and illustrate the fixed asset turnover ratio to assess the efficiency of a company's use of its fixed assets.

Key Points   A measure of a company's efficiency in using its fixed assets to generate sales is the fixed asset turnover ratio. The fixed asset turnover ratio measures the number of dollars of sales earned per dollar of fixed assets and is computed by dividing sales by the average book value of fixed assets.

Learning Outcomes	Example Exercises	Practice Exercises
• Describe a measure of the efficiency of a company's use of fixed assets to generate revenue.		
• Compute and interpret the fixed asset turnover ratio.	EE10-9	PE10-9A, 10-9B

Illustrative Problem

McCollum Company, a furniture wholesaler, acquired new equipment at a cost of $150,000 at the beginning of the fiscal year. The equipment has an estimated life of five years and an estimated residual value of $12,000. Ellen McCollum, the president, has requested information regarding alternative depreciation methods.

Instructions

1. Determine the annual depreciation for each of the five years of estimated useful life of the equipment, the accumulated depreciation at the end of each year, and the book value of the equipment at the end of each year by (a) the straight-line method and (b) the double-declining-balance method.
2. Assume that the equipment was depreciated under the double-declining-balance method. In the first week of the fifth year, the equipment was sold for $10,000. Journalize the entry to record the sale.

Solution

1.

	Year	Depreciation Expense	Accumulated Depreciation, End of Year	Book Value, End of Year
a.	1	$27,600*	$ 27,600	$122,400
	2	27,600	55,200	94,800
	3	27,600	82,800	67,200
	4	27,600	110,400	39,600
	5	27,600	138,000	12,000

*$27,600 = ($150,000 − $12,000) ÷ 5

	1	$60,000**	$ 60,000	$90,000
b.	2	36,000	96,000	54,000
	3	21,600	117,600	32,400
	4	12,960	130,560	19,440
	5	7,440***	138,000	12,000

**$60,000 = $150,000 × 40%

***The asset is not depreciated below the estimated residual value of $12,000.
$7,440 = $150,000 − $130,560 − $12,000

2.

Cash	10,000	
Accumulated Depreciation—Equipment	130,560	
Loss on Sale of Equipment	9,440	
Equipment		150,000

Key Terms

accelerated depreciation method (498)
amortization (508)
book value (494)
boot (514)
capital expenditures (502)
copyright (509)
depletion expense (507)

depreciable cost (492)
depreciation (492)
double-declining-balance method (497)
expected useful life (492)
fixed asset turnover ratio (512)
fixed assets (488)
goodwill (509)
initial cost (492)

intangible assets (508)
patents (508)
residual value (492)
revenue expenditures (502)
straight-line method (493)
trade-in allowance (514)
trademark (509)
units-of-activity method (495)

Discussion Questions

1. O'Neil Office Supplies has a fleet of automobiles and trucks for use by salespersons and for delivery of office supplies and equipment. Collins Auto Sales Co. has automobiles and trucks for sale. Under what caption would the automobiles and trucks be reported in the balance sheet of (a) O'Neil Office Supplies and (b) Collins Auto Sales Co.?

2. Bullwinkle Co. acquired an adjacent vacant lot with the hope of selling it in the future at a gain. The lot is not intended to be used in Bullwinkle business operations. Where should such real estate be listed on the balance sheet?

3. Alpine Company solicited bids from several contractors to construct an addition to its office building. The lowest bid received was for $1,200,000. Alpine decided to construct the addition itself at a cost of $1,100,000. What amount should be recorded in the building account?

4. Keyser Company purchased a machine that has a manufacturer's suggested life of 20 years. The company plans to use the machine on a special project that will last 12 years. At the completion of the project, the machine will be sold. Over how many years should the machine be depreciated?

5. Is it necessary for a business to use the same method of computing depreciation for all classes of its depreciable assets?

6. a. Under what conditions is the use of the straight-line depreciation method most appropriate?
   b. Under what conditions is the use of the units-of-activity depreciation method most appropriate?
   c. Under what conditions is the use of the double-declining-balance depreciation method most appropriate?

7. Distinguish between the accounting for capital expenditures and revenue expenditures.

8. Immediately after a used truck is acquired, a new motor is installed at a total cost of $3,850. Is this a capital expenditure or a revenue expenditure?

9. For some of the fixed assets of a business, the balance in Accumulated Depreciation is equal to the cost of the asset. (a) Is it permissible to record additional depreciation on the assets if they are still useful to the business? Explain. (b) When should an entry be made to remove the cost and the accumulated depreciation from the accounts?

10. a. Over what period of time should the cost of a patent acquired by purchase be amortized?
    b. In general, what is the required accounting treatment for research and development costs?
    c. How should goodwill be amortized?

Practice Exercises

Example Exercises

EE 10-1 *p. 495* **PE 10-1A Straight-line depreciation** OBJ. 2

A building acquired at the beginning of the year at a cost of $1,450,000 has an estimated residual value of $300,000 and an estimated useful life of 10 years. Determine (a) the depreciable cost, (b) the straight-line rate, and (c) the annual straight-line depreciation.

EE 10-1 *p. 495* **PE 10-1B Straight-line depreciation** OBJ. 2

Equipment acquired at the beginning of the year at a cost of $340,000 has an estimated residual value of $45,000 and an estimated useful life of 10 years. Determine (a) the depreciable cost, (b) the straight-line rate, and (c) the annual straight-line depreciation.

EE 10-2 *p. 497* **PE 10-2A Units-of-activity depreciation** OBJ. 2

A truck acquired at a cost of $69,000 has an estimated residual value of $12,000, has an estimated useful life of 300,000 miles, and was driven 77,000 miles during the year. Determine (a) the depreciable cost, (b) the depreciation rate, and (c) the units-of-activity depreciation for the year.

Chapter 10 Long-Term Assets: Fixed and Intangible 521

EE 10-2 *p. 497* **PE 10-2B Units-of-activity depreciation** OBJ. 2

A tractor acquired at a cost of $420,000 has an estimated residual value of $30,000, has an estimated useful life of 25,000 hours, and was operated 1,850 hours during the year. Determine (a) the depreciable cost, (b) the depreciation rate, and (c) the units-of-activity depreciation for the year.

EE 10-3 *p. 499* **PE 10-3A Double-declining-balance depreciation** OBJ. 2

A building acquired at the beginning of the year at a cost of $1,375,000 has an estimated residual value of $250,000 and an estimated useful life of 40 years. Determine (a) the double-declining-balance rate and (b) the double-declining-balance depreciation for the first year.

EE 10-3 *p. 499* **PE 10-3B Double-declining-balance depreciation** OBJ. 2

Equipment acquired at the beginning of the year at a cost of $175,000 has an estimated residual value of $12,000 and an estimated useful life of 10 years. Determine (a) the double-declining-balance rate and (b) the double-declining-balance depreciation for the first year.

EE 10-4 *p. 502* **PE 10-4A Revision of depreciation** OBJ. 2

Equipment with a cost of $180,000 has an estimated residual value of $14,400, has an estimated useful life of 16 years, and is depreciated by the straight-line method. (a) Determine the amount of the annual depreciation. (b) Determine the book value at the end of the tenth year of use. (c) Assuming that at the start of the eleventh year the remaining life is estimated to be eight years and the residual value is estimated to be $10,500, determine the depreciation expense for each of the remaining eight years.

EE 10-4 *p. 502* **PE 10-4B Revision of depreciation** OBJ. 2

A truck with a cost of $82,000 has an estimated residual value of $16,000, has an estimated useful life of 12 years, and is depreciated by the straight-line method. (a) Determine the amount of the annual depreciation. (b) Determine the book value at the end of the seventh year of use. (c) Assuming that at the start of the eighth year the remaining life is estimated to be six years and the residual value is estimated to be $12,000, determine the depreciation expense for each of the remaining six years.

EE 10-5 *p. 504* **PE 10-5A Capital and revenue expenditures** OBJ. 2

On February 14, Garcia Associates Co. paid $2,300 to repair the transmission on one of its delivery vans. In addition, Garcia paid $450 to install a GPS system in its van. Journalize the entries for the transmission and GPS system expenditures.

EE 10-5 *p. 504* **PE 10-5B Capital and revenue expenditures** OBJ. 2

On August 7, Green River Inflatables Co. paid $1,675 to install a hydraulic lift and $40 for an air filter for one of its delivery trucks. Journalize the entries for the new lift and air filter expenditures.

EE 10-6 *p. 506* **PE 10-6A Sale of equipment** OBJ. 3

Equipment was acquired at the beginning of the year at a cost of $600,000. The equipment was depreciated using the double-declining-balance method based on an estimated useful life of 16 years and an estimated residual value of $60,000.

a. What was the depreciation for the first year?
b. Assuming that the equipment was sold at the end of the second year for $480,000, determine the gain or loss on the sale of the equipment.
c. Journalize the entry to record the sale.

522 Chapter 10 Long-Term Assets: Fixed and Intangible

EE 10-6 *p. 506*   **PE 10-6B**   **Sale of equipment**   OBJ. 3

Equipment was acquired at the beginning of the year at a cost of $465,000. The equipment was depreciated using the straight-line method based on an estimated useful life of 15 years and an estimated residual value of $45,000.

a. What was the depreciation for the first year?
b. Assuming the equipment was sold at the end of the eighth year for $235,000, determine the gain or loss on the sale of the equipment.
c. Journalize the entry to record the sale.

EE 10-7 *p. 508*   **PE 10-7A**   **Depletion**   OBJ. 4

Glacier Mining Co. acquired mineral rights for $494,000,000. The mineral deposit is estimated at 475,000,000 tons. During the current year, 31,500,000 tons were mined and sold.

a. Determine the depletion rate.
b. Determine the amount of depletion expense for the current year.
c. Journalize the adjusting entry on December 31 to recognize the depletion expense.

EE 10-7 *p. 508*   **PE 10-7B**   **Depletion**   OBJ. 4

Caldwell Mining Co. acquired mineral rights for $127,500,000. The mineral deposit is estimated at 425,000,000 tons. During the current year, 42,000,000 tons were mined and sold.

a. Determine the depletion rate.
b. Determine the amount of depletion expense for the current year.
c. Journalize the adjusting entry on December 31 to recognize the depletion expense.

EE 10-8 *p. 510*   **PE 10-8A**   **Impaired goodwill and amortization of patent**   OBJ. 5

On December 31, it was estimated that goodwill of $6,000,000 was impaired. In addition, a patent with an estimated useful economic life of 12 years was acquired for $1,500,000 on April 1.

a. Journalize the adjusting entry on December 31 for the impaired goodwill.
b. Journalize the adjusting entry on December 31 for the amortization of the patent rights.

EE 10-8 *p. 510*   **PE 10-8B**   **Impaired goodwill and amortization of patent**   OBJ. 5

On December 31, it was estimated that goodwill of $4,000,000 was impaired. In addition, a patent with an estimated useful economic life of 15 years was acquired for $900,000 on August 1.

a. Journalize the adjusting entry on December 31 for the impaired goodwill.
b. Journalize the adjusting entry on December 31 for the amortization of the patent rights.

EE 10-9 *p. 513*   **PE 10-9A**   **Fixed asset turnover ratio**   OBJ. 7

Financial statement data for years ending December 31 for DePuy Company follow:

	Year 2	Year 1
Sales	$5,510,000	$4,880,000
Fixed assets:		
Beginning of year	1,600,000	1,450,000
End of year	2,200,000	1,600,000

a. Determine the fixed asset turnover ratio for Year 1 and Year 2.
b. Does the change in the fixed asset turnover ratio from Year 1 to Year 2 indicate a favorable or an unfavorable change?

PE 10-9B Fixed asset turnover ratio   OBJ. 7

EE 10-9 p. 513

Financial statement data for years ending December 31 for Davenport Company follow:

	Year 2	Year 1
Sales	$1,668,000	$1,125,000
Fixed assets:		
Beginning of year	670,000	580,000
End of year	720,000	670,000

a. Determine the fixed asset turnover ratio for Year 1 and Year 2.

b. Does the change in the fixed asset turnover ratio from Year 1 to Year 2 indicate a favorable or an unfavorable change?

Exercises

EX 10-1 Costs of acquiring fixed assets   OBJ. 1

Melinda Stoffers owns and operates ABC Print Co. During February, ABC incurred the following costs in acquiring two printing presses. One printing press was new, and the other was purchased from a business that recently filed for bankruptcy.

Costs related to new printing press:

1. Fee paid to factory representative for installation
2. Freight
3. Insurance while in transit
4. New parts to replace those damaged in unloading
5. Sales tax on purchase price
6. Special foundation

Costs related to used printing press:

7. Fees paid to attorney to review purchase agreement
8. Freight
9. Installation
10. Repair of damage incurred in reconditioning the press
11. Replacement of worn-out parts
12. Vandalism repairs during installation

a. Indicate which costs incurred in acquiring the new printing press should be debited to the asset account.

b. Indicate which costs incurred in acquiring the used printing press should be debited to the asset account.

EX 10-2 Determining cost of land   OBJ. 1, 2

Bridger Ski Co. has developed a tract of land into a ski resort. The company has cut the trees, cleared and graded the land and hills, and constructed ski lifts. (a) Should the tree cutting, land clearing, and grading costs of constructing the ski slopes be debited to the land account? (b) If such costs are debited to Land, should they be depreciated? Explain.

EX 10-3 Determining cost of land   OBJ. 1

On-Time Delivery Company acquired an adjacent lot to construct a new warehouse, paying $90,000 and giving a short-term note for $50,000. Legal fees paid were $1,750, delinquent taxes assumed were $25,000, and fees paid to remove an old building from the land were $9,000. Materials salvaged from the demolition of the building were sold for $1,000. A contractor was paid $415,000 to construct a new warehouse. Determine the cost of the land to be reported on the balance sheet.

EX 10-4 Nature of depreciation — OBJ. 2

Tri-City Ironworks Co. reported $44,500,000 for equipment and $29,800,000 for accumulated depreciation—equipment on its balance sheet.

Does this mean (a) that the replacement cost of the equipment is $44,500,000 and (b) that $29,800,000 is set aside in a special fund for the replacement of the equipment? Explain.

EX 10-5 Straight-line depreciation rates — OBJ. 2

✓ c. 4%

Convert each of the following estimates of useful life to a straight-line depreciation rate, stated as a percentage: (a) 10 years, (b) 8 years, (c) 25 years, (d) 40 years, (e) 5 years, (f) 4 years, (g) 20 years.

EX 10-6 Straight-line depreciation — OBJ. 2

A refrigerator used by a wholesale warehouse has a cost of $64,000, an estimated residual value of $5,200, and an estimated useful life of 12 years. What is the amount of the annual depreciation computed by the straight-line method?

EX 10-7 Depreciation by units-of-activity method — OBJ. 2

A diesel-powered tractor with a cost of $90,000 and estimated residual value of $15,000 is expected to have a useful operating life of 30,000 hours. During April, the tractor was operated 120 hours. Determine the depreciation for the month.

EX 10-8 Depreciation by units-of-activity method — OBJ. 2

✓ a. Truck #1, credit to Accumulated Depreciation, $5,460

Prior to adjustment at the end of the year, the balance in Trucks is $296,900 and the balance in Accumulated Depreciation—Trucks is $99,740. Details of the subsidiary ledger are as follows:

Truck No.	Cost	Estimated Residual Value	Estimated Useful Life	Accumulated Depreciation at Beginning of Year	Miles Operated During Year
1	$80,000	$15,000	250,000 miles	—	21,000 miles
2	54,000	6,000	300,000	$14,400	33,500
3	72,900	10,900	200,000	60,140	8,000
4	90,000	22,800	240,000	25,200	22,500

a. Determine for each truck the depreciation rate per mile and the amount to be credited to the accumulated depreciation section of each subsidiary account for the miles operated during the current year.

b. Journalize the entry on December 31 to record depreciation for the year.

EX 10-9 Depreciation by two methods — OBJ. 2

✓ a. $8,500

A Kubota tractor acquired on January 8 at a cost of $85,000 has an estimated useful life of 10 years. Assuming that it will have no residual value, determine the depreciation for each of the first two years (a) by the straight-line method and (b) by the double-declining-balance method.

EX 10-10 Depreciation by two methods — OBJ. 2

✓ a. $3,250

A storage tank acquired at the beginning of the fiscal year at a cost of $75,000 has an estimated residual value of $10,000 and an estimated useful life of 20 years. Determine the following: (a) the amount of annual depreciation by the straight-line method and (b) the amount of depreciation for the first and second years computed by the double-declining-balance method.

Chapter 10 Long-Term Assets: Fixed and Intangible 525

✔ a. First year, $6,200

EX 10-11 Partial-year depreciation OBJ. 2
Equipment acquired at a cost of $105,000 has an estimated residual value of $12,000 and an estimated useful life of 10 years. It was placed into service on May 1 of the current fiscal year, which ends on December 31. Determine the depreciation for the current fiscal year and for the following fiscal year by (a) the straight-line method and (b) the double-declining-balance method.

✔ a. $23,750

EX 10-12 Revision of depreciation OBJ. 2
A building with a cost of $1,200,000 has an estimated residual value of $250,000, has an estimated useful life of 40 years, and is depreciated by the straight-line method. (a) What is the amount of the annual depreciation? (b) What is the book value at the end of the twenty-eighth year of use? (c) If at the start of the twenty-ninth year it is estimated that the remaining life is 10 years and that the residual value is $180,000, what is the depreciation expense for each of the remaining 10 years?

EX 10-13 Capital and revenue expenditures OBJ. 2
US Freight Lines Co. incurred the following costs related to trucks and vans used in operating its delivery service:

1. Installed GPS systems on the trucks.
2. Replaced the transmission fluid on a truck that had been in service for the past four years.
3. Overhauled the engine on one of the trucks purchased three years ago.
4. Performed annual service of installing new spark plugs, changing the oil, and greasing the joints of all trucks and vans.
5. Rebuilt the engine on one of the vans that had been driven 80,000 miles.
6. Repaired a flat tire on one of the vans.
7. Installed a hydraulic lift to a truck.
8. Tinted the back and side windows of the vans and installed a security system to discourage theft of contents.
9. Replaced a truck's suspension system with a new suspension system, allowing for heavier loads.
10. Installed an optional third-row seat on one of the vans.

Classify each of the costs as a capital expenditure or a revenue expenditure.

EX 10-14 Capital and revenue expenditures OBJ. 2
Jackie Fox owns and operates Platinum Transport Co. During the past year, Jackie incurred the following costs related to an 18-wheel truck:

1. Changed engine oil.
2. Installed a television in the sleeping compartment of the truck.
3. Installed a wind deflector on top of the cab to increase fuel mileage.
4. Modified the factory-installed turbo charger with a special-order kit designed to add 50 more horsepower to the engine performance.
5. Replaced a headlight that had burned out.
6. Replaced a shock absorber that had worn out.
7. Replaced fog and cab light bulbs.
8. Replaced the hydraulic brake system that had begun to fail during his latest trip through the Rocky Mountains.
9. Removed the old radio and replaced it with a new communications module.
10. Replaced the old radar detector with a newer model that is fastened to the truck with a locking device that prevents its removal.

Classify each of the costs as a capital expenditure or a revenue expenditure.

526 Chapter 10 Long-Term Assets: Fixed and Intangible

EX 10-15 Capital and revenue expenditures
OBJ. 1, 2

Quality Move Company made the following expenditures on one of its delivery trucks:

Mar. 20. Replaced the transmission at a cost of $1,890.
June 11. Paid $1,350 for installation of a hydraulic lift.
Nov. 30. Paid $55 to change the oil and air filter.

Prepare journal entries for each expenditure.

✔ b. Depreciation Expense, $800

EX 10-16 Capital expenditure and depreciation; parital-year depreciation
OBJ. 1, 2

Willow Creek Company purchased and installed carpet in its new general offices on April 30 for a total cost of $18,000. The carpet is estimated to have a 15-year useful life and no residual value.

a. Prepare the journal entry necessary for recording the purchase of the new carpet.
b. Record the December 31 adjusting entry for the partial-year depreciation expense for the carpet, assuming that Willow Creek uses the straight-line method.

✔ a. $134,000

EX 10-17 Entries for sale of fixed asset
OBJ. 3

Equipment acquired on January 8 at a cost of $168,000 has an estimated useful life of 18 years, has an estimated residual value of $15,000, and is depreciated by the straight-line method.

a. What was the book value of the equipment at December 31 the end of the fourth year?
b. Assuming that the equipment was sold on April 1 of the fifth year for $125,000, journalize the entries to record (1) depreciation for the three months until the sale date and (2) the sale of the equipment.

✔ b. $322,500

EX 10-18 Disposal of fixed asset
OBJ. 3

Equipment acquired on January 6 at a cost of $375,000 has an estimated useful life of 20 years and an estimated residual value of $25,000.

a. What was the annual amount of depreciation for the Years 1–3 using the straight-line method of depreciation?
b. What was the book value of the equipment on January 1 of Year 4?
c. Assuming that the equipment was sold on January 3 of Year 4 for $300,000, journalize the entry to record the sale.
d. Assuming that the equipment had been sold on January 3 of Year 4 for $325,000 instead of $300,000, journalize the entry to record the sale.

✔ a. $9,000,000

EX 10-19 Depletion entries
OBJ. 4

Alaska Mining Co. acquired mineral rights for $67,500,000. The mineral deposit is estimated at 30,000,000 tons. During the current year, 4,000,000 tons were mined and sold.

a. Determine the amount of depletion expense for the current year.
b. Journalize the adjusting entry on December 31 to recognize the depletion expense.

✔ a. $357,600

EX 10-20 Amortization entries
OBJ. 5

Kleen Company acquired patent rights on January 10 of Year 1 for $2,800,000. The patent has a useful life equal to its legal life of eight years. On January 7 of Year 4, Kleen successfully defended the patent in a lawsuit at a cost of $38,000.

a. Determine the patent amortization expense for Year 4 ended December 31.
b. Journalize the adjusting entry on December 31 of Year 4 to recognize the amortization.

Chapter 10 Long-Term Assets: Fixed and Intangible   527

EX 10-21 Book value of fixed assets   OBJ. 6

Apple Inc. designs, manufactures, and markets personal computers and related software. Apple also manufactures and distributes music players (iPod) and mobile phones (iPhone) along with related accessories and services, including online distribution of third-party music, videos, and applications. The following information was taken from a recent annual report of Apple:

Property, Plant, and Equipment (in millions):

	Current Year	Preceding Year
Land and buildings	$ 6,956	$ 4,863
Machinery, equipment, and internal-use software	37,038	29,639
Other fixed assets	5,263	4,513
Accumulated depreciation and amortization	(26,786)	(18,391)

a. Compute the book value of the fixed assets for the current year and the preceding year and explain the differences, if any.

b. Would you normally expect Apple's book value of fixed assets to increase or decrease during the year? Why?

EX 10-22 Balance sheet presentation   OBJ. 6

List the errors you find in the following partial balance sheet:

Burnt Red Company
Balance Sheet
December 31, 20Y2

Assets

Total current assets.. $350,000

	Replacement Cost	Accumulated Depreciation	Book Value
Property, plant, and equipment:			
Land	$ 250,000	$ 50,000	$200,000
Buildings..................................	450,000	160,000	290,000
Factory equipment.........................	375,000	140,000	235,000
Office equipment	125,000	60,000	65,000
Patents....................................	90,000	—	90,000
Goodwill	60,000	10,000	50,000
Total property, plant, and equipment.....	$1,350,000	$420,000	$930,000

EX 10-23 Fixed asset turnover ratio   OBJ. 7

Amazon.com, Inc. is the world's leading Internet retailer of merchandise and media. Amazon also designs and sells electronic products, such as e-readers. **Netflix, Inc.** is the world's leading Internet television network. Both companies compete in the digital media and streaming space. However, Netflix is more narrowly focused in the digital streaming business than is Amazon. Sales and average book value of fixed assets information (in millions) are provided for Amazon and Netflix for a recent year as follows:

	Amazon	Netflix
Sales	$107,006	$6,780
Average book value of fixed assets	19,403	162

a. Compute the fixed asset turnover ratio for each company. Round to one decimal place.
b. Which company is more efficient in generating sales from fixed assets?
c. Interpret your results.

Chapter 10 Long-Term Assets: Fixed and Intangible

EX 10-24 Fixed asset turnover ratio
OBJ. 7

Verizon Communications Inc. is a major telecommunications company in the United States. Two recent balance sheets for Verizon disclosed the following information regarding fixed assets:

	End of Year (in millions)	Beginning of Year (in millions)
Property, plant, and equipment	$220,163	$230,508
Less accumulated depreciation	136,622	140,561
Property, plant, and equipment (net)	$ 83,541	$ 89,947

Verizon's revenue for the year was $131,620 million. Assume that the fixed asset turnover ratio for the telecommunications industry averages approximately 1.1.

a. Determine Verizon's fixed asset turnover ratio. Round to one decimal place.
b. Interpret this ratio with respect to the industry average.

EX 10-25 Fixed asset turnover ratio
OBJ. 7

FedEx Corporation and **United Parcel Service, Inc.** compete in the package delivery business. The major fixed assets for each business include aircraft, sorting and handling facilities, delivery vehicles, and information technology. The sales and average book value of fixed assets reported on recent financial statements for each company were as follows:

	FedEx	UPS
Sales (in millions)	$47,453	$58,363
Average book value of fixed assets (in millions)	20,213	18,317

a. Compute the fixed asset turnover ratio for each company. Round to one decimal place.
b. Which company appears more efficient in using fixed assets?
c. Interpret the meaning of the ratio for the more efficient company.

EX 10-26 Fixed asset turnover ratio
OBJ. 7

The following table shows the sales and average book value of fixed assets for three different companies from three different industries for a recent year:

Company (Industry)	Sales (in millions)	Average Book Value of Fixed Assets (in millions)
Alphabet (Google) Inc. (Internet)	$ 74,989	$ 26,450
Comcast Corporation (communications)	74,510	32,309
Wal-Mart Stores, Inc. (retail)	485,651	117,281

a. For each company, determine the fixed asset turnover ratio. Round to one decimal place.
b. Explain Comcast's fixed asset turnover ratio relative to the other two companies.

Appendix
EX 10-27 Asset traded for similar asset

✔ a. $185,000

A printing press priced at a fair market value of $275,000 is acquired in a transaction that has commercial substance by trading in a similar press and paying cash for the difference between the trade-in allowance and the price of the new press.

a. Assuming that the trade-in allowance is $90,000, what is the amount of cash given?
b. Assuming that the book value of the press traded in is $68,000, what is the gain or loss on the exchange?

Appendix
EX 10-28 Asset traded for similar asset

✔ b. $(18,500) loss

Assume the same facts as in Exercise 9-27, except that the book value of the press traded in is $108,500. (a) What is the amount of cash given? (b) What is the gain or loss on the exchange?

Appendix

EX 10-29 Entries for trade of fixed asset

On July 1, Twin Pines Co., a water distiller, acquired new bottling equipment with a list price (fair market value) of $220,000. Twin Pines received a trade-in allowance (fair market value) of $45,000 on the old equipment of a similar type and paid cash of $175,000. The following information about the old equipment is obtained from the account in the equipment ledger: cost, $180,000; accumulated depreciation on December 31, the end of the preceding fiscal year, $120,000; annual depreciation, $12,000. Assuming that the exchange has commercial substance, journalize the entries to record (a) the current depreciation of the old equipment to the date of trade-in and (b) the exchange transaction on July 1.

Appendix

EX 10-30 Entries for trade of fixed asset

On October 1, Bentley Delivery Services acquired a new truck with a list price (fair market value) of $75,000. Bentley Delivery received a trade-in allowance (fair market value) of $24,000 on an old truck of similar type and paid cash of $51,000. The following information about the old truck is obtained from the account in the equipment ledger: cost, $56,000; accumulated depreciation on December 31, the end of the preceding fiscal year, $35,000; annual depreciation, $7,000. Assuming that the exchange has commercial substance, journalize the entries to record (a) the current depreciation of the old truck to the date of trade-in and (b) the transaction on October 1.

Problems: Series A

PR 10-1A Allocating payments and receipts to fixed asset accounts   OBJ. 1

✔ Land, $400,000

The following payments and receipts are related to land, land improvements, and buildings acquired for use in a wholesale ceramic business. The receipts are identified by an asterisk.

a.	Fee paid to attorney for title search	$ 2,500
b.	Cost of real estate acquired as a plant site: Land	285,000
	Building (to be demolished)	55,000
c.	Delinquent real estate taxes on property, assumed by purchaser	15,500
d.	Cost of tearing down and removing building acquired in (b)	5,000
e.	Proceeds from sale of salvage materials from old building	4,000*
f.	Special assessment paid to city for extension of water main to the property	29,000
g.	Architect's and engineer's fees for plans and supervision	60,000
h.	Premium on one-year insurance policy during construction	6,000
i.	Cost of filling and grading land	12,000
j.	Money borrowed to pay building contractor	900,000*
k.	Cost of repairing windstorm damage during construction	5,500
l.	Cost of paving parking lot to be used by customers	32,000
m.	Cost of trees and shrubbery planted	11,000
n.	Cost of floodlights installed on parking lot	2,000
o.	Cost of repairing vandalism damage during construction	2,500
p.	Proceeds from insurance company for windstorm and vandalism damage	7,500*
q.	Payment to building contractor for new building	800,000
r.	Interest incurred on building loan during construction	34,500
s.	Refund of premium on insurance policy (h) canceled after 11 months	500*

(*Continued*)

530 Chapter 10 Long-Term Assets: Fixed and Intangible

Instructions

1. Assign each payment and receipt to Land (unlimited life), Land Improvements (limited life), Building, or Other Accounts. Indicate receipts by an asterisk. Identify each item by letter and list the amounts in columnar form, as follows:

Item	Land	Land Improvements	Building	Other Accounts

2. Determine the amount debited to Land, Land Improvements, and Building.
3. The costs assigned to the land, which is used as a plant site, will not be depreciated, while the costs assigned to land improvements will be depreciated. Explain this seemingly contradictory application of the concept of depreciation.
4. What would be the effect on the current year's income statement and balance sheet if the cost of filling and grading land of $12,000 [payment (i)] was incorrectly classified as Land Improvements rather than Land? Assume that Land Improvements are depreciated over a 20-year life using the double-declining-balance method.

PR 10-2A Comparing three depreciation methods OBJ. 2

✔ 1. a. Year 1: straight-line depreciation, $22,500

Dexter Industries purchased packaging equipment on January 8 for $72,000. The equipment was expected to have a useful life of three years, or 18,000 operating hours, and a residual value of $4,500. The equipment was used for 7,600 hours during Year 1, 6,000 hours in Year 2, and 4,400 hours in Year 3.

Instructions

1. Determine the amount of depreciation expense for the three years ending December 31 by (a) the straight-line method, (b) the units-of-activity method, and (c) the double-declining-balance method. Also determine the total depreciation expense for the three years by each method. The following columnar headings are suggested for recording the depreciation expense amounts:

	Depreciation Expense		
Year	Straight-Line Method	Units-of-Activity Method	Double-Declining-Balance Method

2. What method yields the highest depreciation expense for Year 1?
3. What method yields the most depreciation over the three-year life of the equipment?

PR 10-3A Depreciation by three methods; partial years OBJ. 2

✔ a. Year 1: $65,250

Perdue Company purchased equipment on April 1 for $270,000. The equipment was expected to have a useful life of three years, or 18,000 operating hours, and a residual value of $9,000. The equipment was used for 7,500 hours during Year 1, 5,500 hours in Year 2, 4,000 hours in Year 3, and 1,000 hours in Year 4.

Instructions

Determine the amount of depreciation expense for the years ended December 31, Year 1, Year 2, Year 3, and Year 4, by (a) the straight-line method, (b) the units-of-activity method, and (c) the double-declining-balance method.

PR 10-4A Depreciation by two methods; sale of fixed asset OBJ. 2, 3

✔ 1. b. Year 1: $320,000 depreciation expense

New lithographic equipment, acquired at a cost of $800,000 on March 1 of Year 1 (beginning of the fiscal year), has an estimated useful life of five years and an estimated residual value of $90,000. The manager requested information regarding the effect of alternative methods on the amount of depreciation expense each year.

On March 4 of Year 5, the equipment was sold for $135,000.

Instructions

1. Determine the annual depreciation expense for each of the estimated five years of use, the accumulated depreciation at the end of each year, and the book value of the equipment at the end of each year by (a) the straight-line method and (b) the double-declining-balance method. The following columnar headings are suggested for each schedule:

Year	Depreciation Expense	Accumulated Depreciation, End of Year	Book Value, End of Year

2. Journalize the entry to record the sale assuming that the manager chose the double-declining-balance method.

3. Journalize the entry to record the sale in (2) assuming that the equipment was sold for $88,750 instead of $135,000.

PR 10-5A Transactions for fixed assets, including sale   OBJ. 1, 2, 3

The following transactions and adjusting entries were completed by Legacy Furniture Co. during a three-year period. All are related to the use of delivery equipment. The double-declining-balance method of depreciation is used.

Year 1

Jan. 4. Purchased a used delivery truck for $28,000, paying cash.
Nov. 2. Paid garage $675 for miscellaneous repairs to the truck.
Dec. 31. Recorded depreciation on the truck for the year. The estimated useful life of the truck is four years, with a residual value of $5,000 for the truck.

Year 2

Jan. 6. Purchased a new truck for $48,000, paying cash.
Apr. 1. Sold the used truck purchased on Jan. 4 of Year 1 for $15,000. (Record depreciation to date in Year 2 for the truck.)
June 11. Paid garage $450 for miscellaneous repairs to the truck.
Dec. 31. Record depreciation for the new truck. It has an estimated residual value of $9,000 and an estimated life of five years.

Year 3

July 1. Purchased a new truck for $54,000, paying cash.
Oct. 2. Sold the truck purchased January 6, Year 2, for $16,750. (Record depreciation to date for Year 3 for the truck.)
Dec. 31. Recorded depreciation on the remaining truck purchased on July 1. It has an estimated residual value of $12,000 and an estimated useful life of eight years.

Instructions

Journalize the transactions and the adjusting entries.

PR 10-6A Amortization and depletion entries   OBJ. 4, 5

✓ 1. a. $352,000

Data related to the acquisition of timber rights and intangible assets during the current year ended December 31 are as follows:

a. Timber rights on a tract of land were purchased for $1,600,000 on February 22. The stand of timber is estimated at 5,000,000 board feet. During the current year, 1,100,000 board feet of timber were cut and sold.
b. On December 31, the company determined that $3,750,000 of goodwill was impaired.
c. Governmental and legal costs of $6,600,000 were incurred on April 3 in obtaining a patent with an estimated economic life of 12 years. Amortization is to be for three-fourths of a year.

Instructions

1. Determine the amount of the amortization, depletion, or impairment for the current year for each of the foregoing items.
2. Journalize the adjusting entries required to record the amortization, depletion, or impairment for each item.

Chapter 10 Long-Term Assets: Fixed and Intangible

Problems: Series B

PR 10-1B Allocating payments and receipts to fixed asset accounts OBJ. 1

✔ Land, $860,000

The following payments and receipts are related to land, land improvements, and buildings acquired for use in a wholesale apparel business. The receipts are identified by an asterisk.

a.	Fee paid to attorney for title search	$ 3,600
b.	Cost of real estate acquired as a plant site: Land	720,000
	Building (to be demolished)	60,000
c.	Finder's fee paid to real estate agency	23,400
d.	Delinquent real estate taxes on property, assumed by purchaser	15,000
e.	Architect's and engineer's fees for plans for new building	75,000
f.	Cost of removing building purchased with land in (b)	10,000
g.	Proceeds from sale of salvage materials from old building	3,400*
h.	Cost of filling and grading land	18,000
i.	Premium on one-year insurance policy during construction	8,400
j.	Money borrowed to pay building contractor	800,000*
k.	Special assessment paid to city for extension of water main to the property	13,400
l.	Cost of repairing windstorm damage during construction	3,000
m.	Cost of repairing vandalism damage during construction	2,000
n.	Cost of trees and shrubbery planted	14,000
o.	Cost of paving parking lot to be used by customers	21,600
p.	Interest incurred on building loan during construction	40,000
q.	Proceeds from insurance company for windstorm and vandalism damage	4,500*
r.	Payment to building contractor for new building	800,000
s.	Refund of premium on insurance policy (i) canceled after 10 months	1,400*

Instructions

1. Assign each payment and receipt to Land (unlimited life), Land Improvements (limited life), Building, or Other Accounts. Indicate receipts by an asterisk. Identify each item by letter and list the amounts in columnar form, as follows:

Item	Land	Land Improvements	Building	Other Accounts

2. Determine the amount debited to Land, Land Improvements, and Building.

3. ✏️ The costs assigned to the land, which is used as a plant site, will not be depreciated, while the costs assigned to land improvements will be depreciated. Explain this seemingly contradictory application of the concept of depreciation.

4. What would be the effect on the current year's income statement and balance sheet if the cost of paving the parking lot of $21,600 [payment (o)] was incorrectly classified as Land rather than Land Improvements? Assume that Land Improvements are depreciated over a 10-year life using the double-declining-balance method.

PR 10-2B Comparing three depreciation methods OBJ. 2

✔ 1. a. Year 1: straight-line depreciation, $71,250

Excel

Show Me How

Waylander Coatings Company purchased waterproofing equipment on January 6 for $320,000. The equipment was expected to have a useful life of four years, or 20,000 operating hours, and a residual value of $35,000. The equipment was used for 7,200 hours during Year 1, 6,400 hours in Year 2, 4,400 hours in Year 3, and 2,000 hours in Year 4.

Instructions

1. Determine the amount of depreciation expense for the years ended December 31, Year 1, Year 2, Year 3, and Year 4, by (a) the straight-line method, (b) the units-of-activity method, and (c) the double-declining-balance method. Also determine the total depreciation expense for the four years by each method. The following columnar headings are suggested for recording the depreciation expense amounts:

	Depreciation Expense		
Year	Straight-Line Method	Units-of-Activity Method	Double-Declining-Balance Method

2. What method yields the highest depreciation expense for Year 1?
3. What method yields the most depreciation over the four-year life of the equipment?

PR 10-3B   Depreciation by three methods; partial years   OBJ. 2

✔ a. Year 1, $8,400

Excel

Layton Company purchased tool sharpening equipment on October 1 for $108,000. The equipment was expected to have a useful life of three years, or 12,000 operating hours, and a residual value of $7,200. The equipment was used for 1,350 hours during Year 1, 4,200 hours in Year 2, 3,650 hours in Year 3, and 2,800 hours in Year 4.

Instructions
Determine the amount of depreciation expense for the years ended December 31, Year 1, Year 2, Year 3, and Year 4, by (a) the straight-line method, (b) the units-of-activity method, and (c) the double-declining-balance method.

PR 10-4B   Depreciation by two methods; sale of fixed asset   OBJ. 2, 3

✔ 1. b. Year 1, $55,000 depreciation expense

New tire retreading equipment, acquired at a cost of $110,000 on September 1 of Year 1 (beginning of the fiscal year), has an estimated useful life of four years and an estimated residual value of $7,500. The manager requested information regarding the effect of alternative methods on the amount of depreciation expense each year. On the basis of the data presented to the manager, the double-declining-balance method was selected.

On September 6 of Year 4, the equipment was sold for $18,000.

Instructions
1. Determine the annual depreciation expense for each of the estimated four years of use, the accumulated depreciation at the end of each year, and the book value of the equipment at the end of each year by (a) the straight-line method and (b) the double-declining-balance method. The following columnar headings are suggested for each schedule:

Year	Depreciation Expense	Accumulated Depreciation, End of Year	Book Value, End of Year

2. Journalize the entry to record the sale.
3. Journalize the entry to record the sale, assuming that the equipment sold for $10,500 instead of $18,000.

PR 10-5B   Transactions for fixed assets, including sale   OBJ. 1, 2, 3

The following transactions and adjusting entries were completed by Robinson Furniture Co. during a three-year period. All are related to the use of delivery equipment. The double-declining-balance method of depreciation is used.

Year 1
Jan. 8. Purchased a used delivery truck for $24,000, paying cash.
Mar. 7. Paid garage $900 for changing the oil, replacing the oil filter, and tuning the engine on the delivery truck.
Dec. 31. Recorded depreciation on the truck for the fiscal year. The estimated useful life of the truck is four years, with a residual value of $4,000 for the truck.

Year 2
Jan. 9. Purchased a new truck for $50,000, paying cash.
Feb. 28. Paid garage $250 to tune the engine and make other minor repairs on the used truck.
Apr. 30. Sold the used truck for $9,500. (Record depreciation to date in Year 2 for the truck.)
Dec. 31. Record depreciation for the new truck. It has an estimated residual value of $12,000 and an estimated life of eight years.

Year 3
Sept. 1. Purchased a new truck for $58,500, paying cash.
4. Sold the truck purchased January 9, Year 2, for $36,000. (Record depreciation to date for Year 3 for the truck.)
Dec. 31. Recorded depreciation on the remaining truck. It has an estimated residual value of $16,000 and an estimated useful life of 10 years.

Instructions
Journalize the transactions and the adjusting entries.

534 Chapter 10 Long-Term Assets: Fixed and Intangible

✔ b. $150,000

PR 10-6B Amortization and depletion entries OBJ. 4, 5

Data related to the acquisition of timber rights and intangible assets during the current year ended December 31 are as follows:

a. On December 31, the company determined that $3,400,000 of goodwill was impaired.
b. Governmental and legal costs of $4,800,000 were incurred on September 30 in obtaining a patent with an estimated economic life of eight years. Amortization is to be for one-fourth of a year.
c. Timber rights on a tract of land were purchased for $2,975,000 on February 4. The stand of timber is estimated at 12,500,000 board feet. During the current year, 4,150,000 board feet of timber were cut and sold.

Instructions

1. Determine the amount of the amortization, depletion, or impairment for the current year for each of the foregoing items.
2. Journalize the adjusting entries to record the amortization, depletion, or impairment for each item.

Cases & Projects

CP 10-1 Ethics in Action

Hard Bodies Co. is a fitness chain that has just completed its second year of operations. At the beginning of its first fiscal year, the company purchased fitness equipment at a cost of $600,000 and estimated that the equipment would have a useful life of five years and no residual value. The company uses the straight-line depreciation method. The company reported net income for the first two years of operations as follows:

Year	Net Income (Loss)
1	$50,000
2	(2,000)

Mike Gambit, the company's chief financial officer (CFO), has recently run financial models to predict future net income, and he expects net losses to continue at $(2,000) per year for the next three years. James Steed, the president of Hard Bodies, is concerned about these predictions, as he is under pressure from the company's owner to return the company to Year 1 net income levels. If the company does not meet these goals, both he and Mike will likely be fired. Mike suggests that the company change the estimated useful life of the fitness equipment to 10 years and increase the equipment's estimated residual value to $50,000. This will reduce depreciation expense and increase net income.

1. ✏ Evaluate the decision to change the equipment's estimated useful life and estimated residual value to improve earnings. How does this change impact the usefulness of the company's net income for external decision makers?
2. ✏ If Mike and James make the change, are they acting in an ethical manner? Explain.

CP 10-2 Ethics in Action

Dave Elliott, CPA, is an assistant to the controller of Lyric Consulting Co. In his spare time, Dave also prepares tax returns and performs general accounting services for clients. Frequently, Dave performs these services after his normal working hours, using Lyric Consulting Co.'s computers and laser printers. Occasionally, Dave's clients will call him at the office during regular working hours.

✏ Discuss whether Dave is performing in a professional manner.

CP 10-3 Team Activity

In teams, select a public company that interests you. Obtain the company's most recent annual report on Form 10-K. The Form 10-K is a company's annually required filing with the Securities and Exchange Commission (SEC). It includes the company's financial statements and accompanying notes. The Form 10-K can be obtained either (a) by referring to the investor relations section of the company's website or (b) by using the company search feature of the SEC's EDGAR database service found at www.sec.gov/edgar/searchedgar/companysearch.html.

1. Based on the information in the company's most recent annual report, answer the following questions:
   a. What depreciation methods does the company use to compute depreciation expense?
   b. How much depreciation expense does the company report on its income statement?
   c. What is the initial cost of the company's fixed assets?
   d. What is the book value of the company's fixed assets?
   e. What types of intangible assets, if any, does the company report on its balance sheet?
2. Does the book value of the company's fixed assets reflect its current market value? Explain your answer.

CP 10-4 Team Activity

Go to the Internet and review the procedures for applying for a patent, a copyright, and a trademark. You may find information available on Wikipedia (Wikipedia.org) useful for this purpose. Prepare a brief written summary of these procedures.

CP 10-5 Communication

Godwin Co. owns three delivery trucks. Details for each truck at the end of the most recent year follow:

	Age	Expected Useful Life	Initial Cost	Accumulated Depreciation
Truck 1	3	6	$22,500	$11,250
Truck 2	5	6	26,250	21,875
Truck 3	2	6	28,500	9,500

- At the beginning of the year, a hydraulic lift is added to Truck 1 at a cost of $4,500. The addition of the hydraulic lift will allow the company to deliver much larger objects than could previously be delivered.
- At the beginning of the year, the engine of Truck 2 is overhauled at a cost of $5,000. The engine overhaul will extend the truck's useful life by three years.

Write a short memo to Godwin's chief financial officer explaining the financial statement effects of the expenditures associated with Trucks 1 and 2.

CP 10-6 Financial versus tax depreciation

The following is an excerpt from a conversation between two employees of WXT Technologies, Nolan Sears and Stacy Mays. Nolan is the accounts payable clerk, and Stacy is the cashier.

Nolan: Stacy, could I get your opinion on something?

Stacy: Sure, Nolan.

Nolan: Do you know Rita, the fixed assets clerk?

Stacy: I know who she is, but I don't know her real well. Why?

Nolan: Well, I was talking to her at lunch last Monday about how she liked her job. You know, the usual; and she mentioned something about having to keep two sets of books—one for taxes and one for the financial statements. That can't be good accounting, can it? What do you think?

Stacy: Two sets of books? It doesn't sound right.

Nolan: It doesn't seem right to me either. I was always taught that you had to use generally accepted accounting principles. How can there be two sets of books? What can be the difference between the two?

How would you respond to Nolan and Stacy if you were Rita?

CHAPTER 11
Current Liabilities and Payroll

Chapters 1–4
Accounting Cycle

Chapter 5
Accounting Systems

Income Statement	Statement of Owner's Equity	Balance Sheet	Statement of Cash Flows

Chapter 6 *Accounting for Merchandising Businesses*

Chapter 16 *Cash Flows*

Assets = Liabilities + Owner's Equity

Chapter 8 *Cash*
Chapter 9 *Receivables*
Chapter 7 *Inventories*
Chapter 10 *Fixed and Intangible Assets*
Chapter 15 *Investments*

Chapter 11 Current Liabilities and Payroll
Chapter 14 *Bonds and Notes*

Chapter 12 *Partnerships*
Chapter 13 *Corporations*

Chapter 17
Financial Statement Analysis

Statement of Owner's Equity

Owner's capital, Jan. 1	$XXX
Net income	$ XXX
Withdrawals	(XXX)
Increase in capital	XXX

Statement of Cash Flows

Cash flows from (used in) operating activities	$XXX
Cash flows from (used in) investing activities	XXX
Cash flows from (used in) financing activities	XXX
Increase (decrease) in cash flows	$XXX
	XXX
	$XXX

Income Statement

Sales		$XXX
Cost of merchandise sold		XXX
Gross profit		$XXX
Operating expenses:		
Wages expense	$XXX	
Advertising expense	XXX	
Depreciation expense	XXX	
Amortization expense	XXX	
Depletion expense	XXX	
...	XXX	
...	XXX	
Total operating expenses		XXX
Income from operations		$XXX
Other revenue and expenses		XXX
Interest expense		XXX
Net income		$XXX

Balance Sheet

Current assets:		
Cash	$XXX	
Accounts receivable	XXX	
Merchandise inventory	XXX	
Total current assets		$XXX
Property, plant, and equipment	$XXX	
Intangible assets	XXX	
Total long-term assets		XXX
Total assets		$XXX
Liabilities:		
Accounts payable	$XXX	
Payroll liabilities	XXX	
Notes payable	XXX	
Total liabilities		$XXX
Owner's equity		XXX
Total liabilities and owner's equity		$XXX

CHAPTER 11

Starbucks

Buying goods on credit is essential for businesses to run efficiently. The use of credit makes transactions more convenient and improves buying power. For *individuals*, the most common form of short-term credit is a credit card. Credit cards allow individuals to purchase items before they are paid for while removing the need for individuals to carry large amounts of cash. They also provide documentation of purchases through a monthly credit card statement.

Short-term credit is also used by *businesses* to make purchasing items for manufacture or resale more convenient. It also gives the business control over the payment for goods and services. When **Starbucks** opened its first coffee shop in 1971, it relied on short-term trade credit, or accounts payable, to purchase ingredients for its coffee shop in Seattle's historic Pike Place Market. Today, Starbucks still relies on accounts payable and short-term trade credit, which also gives the company control over cash payments by separating the purchase function from the payment function. Thus, the employee responsible for purchasing the ingredients is separated from the employee responsible for paying for the purchase. This separation of duties can help prevent unauthorized purchases or payments.

In addition to accounts payable, a business like Starbucks can also have current liabilities related to payroll, payroll taxes, employee benefits, short-term notes, unearned revenue, and contingencies. This chapter discusses each of these types of current liabilities.

Learning Objectives

After studying this chapter, you should be able to:

Example Exercises (EE) are shown in **green**.

Obj. 1 Describe and illustrate current liabilities related to accounts payable, current portion of long-term debt, and notes payable.

Current Liabilities
Accounts Payable
Current Portion of Long-Term Debt
Short-Term Notes Payable   EE 11-1

Obj. 2 Determine employer liabilities for payroll, including liabilities arising from employee earnings and deductions from earnings.

Payroll and Payroll Taxes
Liability for Employee Earnings
Deductions from Employee Earnings   EE 11-2
Computing Employee Net Pay   EE 11-3
Liability for Employer's Payroll Taxes

Obj. 3 Describe payroll accounting systems that use a payroll register, employee earnings records, and a general journal.

Accounting Systems for Payroll and Payroll Taxes
Payroll Register   EE 11-4, 11-5
Employee's Earnings Record
Payroll Checks
Computerized Payroll System
Internal Controls for Payroll Systems

Obj. 4 Journalize entries for employee fringe benefits, including vacation pay and pensions.

Employees' Fringe Benefits
Vacation Pay
Pensions   EE 11-6
Postretirement Benefits Other Than Pensions
Current Liabilities on the Balance Sheet

Obj. 5 Describe the accounting treatment for contingent liabilities and journalize entries for product warranties.

Contingent Liabilities
Probable and Estimable   EE 11-7
Probable and Not Estimable
Reasonably Possible
Remote

Obj. 6 Describe and illustrate the use of the quick ratio in analyzing a company's ability to pay its current liabilities.

Financial Analysis and Interpretation: Quick Ratio
Compute the Quick Ratio   EE 11-8

At a Glance 11 ▶ Page 560

Obj. 1 Describe and illustrate current liabilities related to accounts payable, current portion of long-term debt, and notes payable.

Current Liabilities

When a company or a bank advances *credit,* it is making a loan. The company or bank is called a *creditor* (or *lender*). The individuals or companies receiving the loan are called *debtors* (or *borrowers*).

Debt is recorded as a liability by the debtor. *Long-term liabilities* are debts due beyond one year. Thus, a 30-year mortgage used to purchase property is a long-term liability. *Current liabilities* are debts that will be paid out of current assets and are due within one year.

Three types of current liabilities are discussed in this section—accounts payable, the current portion of long-term debt, and short-term notes payable.

Link to Starbucks
On a recent balance sheet, **Starbucks** reported $684.2 million of accounts payable and $1,760.7 million of accrued liabilities, which made up over two-thirds of its current liabilities.

Accounts Payable

Accounts payable transactions have been described and illustrated in earlier chapters. These transactions involve a variety of purchases on account, including the purchase of merchandise and supplies. For most companies, accounts payable is the largest current liability.

Current Portion of Long-Term Debt

Long-term liabilities are often paid back in periodic payments, called *installments*. Such installments that are due *within* the coming year are classified as a current liability. The installments due *after* the coming year are classified as a long-term liability.

To illustrate, Adichie Company reported the following debt payments schedule in a recent year (in millions):

Fiscal year ending	
20Y2	$ 1,577
20Y3	2,633
20Y4	2,451
20Y5	1,705
20Y6	1,439
Thereafter	6,508
Total principal payments	$16,313

The debt of $1,577 due in 20Y2 would be reported as a current liability on the December 31, 20Y1 balance sheet. The remaining debt of $14,736 ($16,313 − $1,577) would be reported as a long-term liability on the balance sheet.

Short-Term Notes Payable

Notes may be issued to purchase merchandise or other assets. Notes may also be issued to creditors to satisfy an account payable created earlier.[1]

To illustrate, assume that Nature's Sunshine Company issued a 90-day, 12% note for $1,000, dated August 1, 20Y7, to Murray Co. for a $1,000 overdue account. The entry to record the issuance of the note is as follows:

Aug.	1	Accounts Payable—Murray Co.	1,000	
		Notes Payable		1,000
		Issued a 90-day, 12% note on account.		

When the note matures, the entry to record the payment of $1,000 plus $30 interest ($1,000 × 12% × 90 ÷ 360[2]) is as follows:

Oct.	30	Notes Payable	1,000	
		Interest Expense	30	
		Cash		1,030
		Paid principal and interest due on note.		

The interest expense is reported in the Other expense section of the income statement for the year ended December 31, 20Y7. The interest expense account is closed at December 31.

Each note transaction affects a debtor (borrower) and creditor (lender). The following illustration shows how the same transactions are recorded by the debtor and creditor. In this illustration, the debtor (borrower) is Bowden Co., and the creditor (lender) is Coker Co.

	Bowden Co. (Borrower)		Coker Co. (Creditor)	

May 1. Bowden Co. purchased merchandise on account from Coker Co., $10,000, 2/10, n/30. The merchandise cost Coker Co. $7,500.	Merchandise Inventory 10,000
	   Accounts Payable
		10,000	Accounts Receivable 10,000
			   Sales
			
			Cost of Merchandise Sold 7,500
			   Merchandise Inventory
				10,000
				
				7,500

May 31. Bowden Co. issued a 60-day, 12% note for $10,000 to Coker Co. on account.	Accounts Payable 10,000
	   Notes Payable
		10,000	Notes Receivable 10,000
			   Accounts Receivable
				10,000

(Continued)

---

1 The accounting for notes received to satisfy an account receivable was described and illustrated in Chapter 9.
2 To simplify computations and rounding, 360 days per year are used. In practice, companies use 365 days.

540 Chapter 11 Current Liabilities and Payroll

	Bowden Co. (Borrower)		Coker Co. (Creditor)	
July 30. Bowden Co. paid Coker Co. the amount due on the note of May 31. Interest: $10,000 × 12% × 60 ÷ 360.	Notes Payable Interest Expense Cash	10,000 200 10,200	Cash Interest Revenue Notes Receivable	10,200 200 10,000

A company may also borrow from a bank by issuing a note. To illustrate, assume that on September 19, Iceburg Company borrowed cash from First National Bank by issuing a $4,000, 90-day, 15% note to the bank. The entry to record the issuance of the note and the cash proceeds received by Iceburg is as follows:

Sept.	19	Cash	4,000	
		Notes Payable		4,000
		Issued a 90-day, 15% note to First National Bank.		

On the due date of the note (December 18), Iceburg Company owes First National Bank $4,000 plus interest of $150 ($4,000 × 15% × 90 ÷ 360). The entry to record the payment of the note is as follows:

Dec.	18	Notes Payable	4,000	
		Interest Expense	150	
		Cash		4,150
		Paid principal and interest due on note.		

In some cases, a *discounted note* may be issued rather than an interest-bearing note. A discounted note has the following characteristics:

- The interest rate on the note is called the *discount rate*.
- The amount of interest on the note, called the *discount*, is computed by multiplying the discount rate times the face amount of the note.
- The debtor (borrower) receives the face amount of the note less the discount. The amount of cash received at issuance is called the *proceeds*.
- The debtor must repay the face amount of the note on the due date.

Dynamic Exhibit

To illustrate, assume that on August 10, Cary Company issues a $20,000, 90-day discounted note to Western National Bank. The discount rate is 15%, and the amount of the discount is $750 ($20,000 × 15% × 90 ÷ 360). Thus, the proceeds received by Cary Company are $19,250. The entry by Cary Company is as follows:

Aug.	10	Cash	19,250	
		Interest Expense	750	
		Notes Payable		20,000
		Issued a 90-day discounted note to Western National Bank at a 15% discount rate.		

The entry to record the repayment of the discounted note on November 8 is as follows:[3]

Nov.	8	Notes Payable	20,000	
		Cash		20,000
		Paid note due.		

---

[3] If the accounting period ends before a discounted note is paid, an adjusting entry should record the prepaid (deferred) interest that is not yet an expense. This deferred interest would be deducted from Notes Payable in the Current liabilities section of the balance sheet.

Other current liabilities that have been discussed in earlier chapters include accrued expenses, unearned revenue, and interest payable. The accounting for wages and salaries, termed *payroll accounting*, is discussed next.

Example Exercise 11-1 Proceeds from Notes Payable — Obj. 1

On July 1, Bella Salon Company borrowed cash from Best Bank by issuing a 60-day note with a face amount of $60,000.

a. Determine the proceeds of the note, assuming that the note carries an interest rate of 6%.
b. Determine the proceeds of the note, assuming that the note is discounted at 6%.

Follow My Example 11-1

a. $60,000
b. $59,400 [$60,000 − ($60,000 × 6% × 60 ÷ 360)]

Practice Exercises: PE 11-1A, PE 11-1B

Payroll and Payroll Taxes

Obj. 2 Determine employer liabilities for payroll, including liabilities arising from employee earnings and deductions from earnings.

In accounting, **payroll** refers to the amount paid to employees for services they provided during the period. A company's payroll is important for the following reasons:

- Payroll and related payroll taxes significantly affect the net income of most companies.
- Payroll is subject to federal and state regulations.
- Good employee morale requires payroll to be paid timely and accurately.

Liability for Employee Earnings

Salary usually refers to payment for managerial and administrative services. Salary is payment to employees for services that is typically expressed in terms of a month or a year. *Wages* usually refers to payment to employees for services that is stated on an hourly or weekly basis. The salary or wage of an employee may be increased by bonuses, commissions, profit sharing, or other adjustments.

Note
Employee salaries and wages are expenses to an employer.

Companies engaged in interstate commerce must follow the Fair Labor Standards Act. This act, sometimes called the Federal Wage and Hour Law, requires employers to pay a minimum rate of 1½ times the regular rate for all hours worked in excess of 40 hours per week. Exemptions are provided for executive, administrative, and some supervisory positions. Increased rates for working overtime, nights, or holidays are common, even when not required by law. These rates may be as much as twice the regular rate.

To illustrate computing an employee's earnings, assume that John T. McGrath is a salesperson employed by McDermott Supply Co. McGrath's regular rate is $34 per hour, and any hours worked in excess of 40 hours per week are paid at 1½ times the regular rate. McGrath worked 42 hours for the week ended December 27. His earnings of $1,462 for the week are computed as follows:

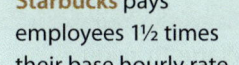

Link to Starbucks
Starbucks pays employees 1½ times their base hourly rate for any hours worked on holidays such as New Year's Day, Thanksgiving Day, and Christmas Day.

Earnings at regular rate (40 hrs. × $34)	$1,360
Earnings at overtime rate [2 hrs. × ($34 × 1½)]	102
Total earnings	$1,462

Deductions from Employee Earnings

The total earnings of an employee for a payroll period, including any overtime pay, are called **gross pay**. From this amount is subtracted one or more *deductions* to arrive at **net pay**. Deductions include items such as federal, state, and local income taxes; medical insurance; and pension contributions. Net pay is the amount the employee receives after deductions are subtracted from gross pay.

Note
Net Pay = Gross Pay − Deductions

542 Chapter 11 Current Liabilities and Payroll

Income Taxes Employers normally withhold a portion of employee earnings for payment of the employees' federal income tax. Each employee authorizes the amount to be withheld by completing an "Employee's Withholding Allowance Certificate," called a W-4. Exhibit 1 is the W-4 form submitted by John T. McGrath.

EXHIBIT 1

Employee's Withholding Allowance Certificate (W-4 Form)

Separate here and give Form W-4 to your employer. Keep the top part for your records.

Form W-4 — Employee's Withholding Allowance Certificate — OMB No. 1545-0074
Department of the Treasury, Internal Revenue Service
▶ Whether you are entitled to claim a certain number of allowances or exemption from withholding is subject to review by the IRS. Your employer may be required to send a copy of this form to the IRS.
20Y6

1. Your first name and middle initial: John T.   Last name: McGrath   2. Your social security number: 381 48 9120
Home address (number and street or rural route): 1830 4th Street
3. ☒ Single   ☐ Married   ☐ Married, but withhold at higher Single rate.
Note. If married, but legally separated, or spouse is a nonresident alien, check the "Single" box.
City or town, state, and ZIP code: Clinton, Iowa 52732-6142
4. If your last name differs from that shown on your social security card, check here. You must call 1-800-772-1213 for a replacement card. ▶ ☐

5. Total number of allowances you are claiming (from line H above or from the applicable worksheet on page 2)   5
6. Additional amount, if any, you want withheld from each paycheck   6 $
7. I claim exemption from withholding for 20Y5, and I certify that I meet **both** of the following conditions for exemption.
   - Last year I had a right to a refund of **all** federal income tax withheld because I had **no** tax liability, **and**
   - This year I expect a refund of **all** federal income tax withheld because I expect to have **no** tax liability.
   If you meet both conditions, write "Exempt" here . . . . ▶ 7

Under penalties of perjury, I declare that I have examined this certificate and, to the best of my knowledge and belief, it is true, correct, and complete.

Employee's signature (This form is not valid unless you sign it.) ▶ *John T. McGrath*   Date ▶ June 2, 20Y6

8. Employer's name and address (Employer: Complete lines 8 and 10 only if sending to the IRS.)   9. Office code (optional)   10. Employer identification number (EIN)

For Privacy Act and Paperwork Reduction Act Notice, see page 2.   Cat. No. 10220Q   Form **W-4** (20Y5)

*The W-4 Form is issued yearly by the U.S. Treasury Department.

On the W-4, an employee indicates marital status and the number of withholding allowances. A single employee may claim one withholding allowance. A married employee may claim an additional allowance for a spouse. An employee may also claim an allowance for each dependent other than a spouse. Each allowance reduces the federal income tax withheld from the employee's pay. Exhibit 1 indicates that McGrath is single and, thus, claimed one withholding allowance.

The federal income tax withheld depends on each employee's gross pay and W-4 allowance. Withholding tables issued by the Internal Revenue Service (IRS) are used to determine amounts to withhold. Exhibit 2 is an example of an IRS wage withholding table for a single person who is paid weekly.[4]

In Exhibit 2, each row is the employee's wages after deducting the employee's withholding allowances. Each year, the amount of the standard withholding allowance is determined by the IRS. For ease of computation and because this amount changes

EXHIBIT 2

Wage Bracket Withholding Table

Table for Percentage Method of Withholding WEEKLY Payroll Period

(a) SINGLE person (including head of household)—

If the amount of wages (after subtracting withholding allowances) is: The amount of income tax to withhold is:
Not over $43 . . . . $0

Over—	But not over—		of excess over—
$43	—$222	$0.00 plus 10%	$43
$222	—$767	$17.90 plus 15%	$222
$767	**—$1,796**	**$99.65 plus 25%**	**$767** ← McGrath wage bracket
$1,796	—$3,700	$356.90 plus 28%	$1,796
$3,700	—$7,992	$890.02 plus 33%	$3,700
$7,992	—$8,025	$2,306.38 plus 35%	$7,992
$8,025	. . . .	$2,317.93 plus 39.6%	$8,025

---

[4] IRS withholding tables are also available for married employees and for pay periods other than weekly.

each year, we assume that the standard withholding allowance to be deducted in Exhibit 2 for a single person paid weekly is $75.[5] Thus, if two withholding allowances are claimed, $150 ($75 × 2) is deducted.

To illustrate, John T. McGrath made $1,462 for the week ended December 27. McGrath's W-4 claims one withholding allowance of $75. Thus, the wages used in determining McGrath's withholding bracket in Exhibit 2 are $1,387 ($1,462 − $75).

After the person's withholding wage bracket has been computed, the federal income tax to be withheld is determined as follows:

Step 1. Locate the proper withholding wage bracket in Exhibit 2.

McGrath's wages after deducting one standard IRS withholding allowance are $1,387 ($1,462 − $75). Therefore, the wage bracket for McGrath is $767–$1,796.

Step 2. Compute the withholding for the proper wage bracket using the directions in the two right-hand columns in Exhibit 2.

For McGrath's wage bracket, the withholding is computed as "$99.65 plus 25% of the excess over $767." Hence, McGrath's withholding is $254.65, computed as follows:

Initial withholding from wage bracket	$ 99.65
Plus [25% × ($1,387 − $767)]	155.00
Total withholding	$254.65

Employers may also be required to withhold state or city income taxes. The amounts to be withheld are determined on state-by-state and city-by-city bases.

Example Exercise 11-2 Federal Income Tax Withholding *Obj. 2*

Karen Dunn's weekly gross earnings for the present week were $2,250. Dunn has two exemptions. Using the wage bracket withholding table in Exhibit 2 with a $75 standard withholding allowance for each exemption, what is Dunn's federal income tax withholding?

Follow My Example 11-2

Total wage payment		$ 2,250
One allowance (provided by IRS)	$75	
Multiplied by allowances claimed on Form W-4	× 2	150
Amount subject to withholding		$ 2,100
Initial withholding from wage bracket in Exhibit 2		$356.90
Plus additional withholding: 28% of excess over $1,796		85.12*
Federal income tax withholding		$442.02

*28% × ($2,100 − $1,796)

Practice Exercises: PE 11-2A, PE 11-2B

FICA Tax Employers are required by the Federal Insurance Contributions Act (FICA) to withhold a portion of the earnings of each employee. The **FICA tax** withheld contributes to the following two federal programs:

- *Social security*, which provides payments for retirees, survivors, and disability insurance.
- *Medicare*, which provides health insurance for senior citizens.

The amount withheld from each employee is based on the employee's earnings *paid* in the *calendar* year. The withholding tax rates and maximum earnings subject

---

[5] The actual IRS standard withholding allowance changes every year and was $77.90 for 2016.

to tax are often revised by Congress.[6] To simplify, this chapter assumes the following rates and earnings subject to tax:

- Social security: 6% on all earnings
- Medicare: 1.5% on all earnings

To illustrate, assume that John T. McGrath's earnings for the week ending December 27 are $1,462 and the total FICA tax to be withheld is $109.65, computed as follows:

Earnings subject to 6% social security tax		$1,462
Social security tax rate		× 6%
Social security tax		$ 87.72
Earnings subject to 1.5% Medicare tax		$1,462
Medicare tax rate		× 1.5%
Medicare tax		21.93
Total FICA tax		$109.65

Other Deductions Employees may choose to have additional amounts deducted from their gross pay. For example, an employee may authorize deductions for retirement savings, charitable contributions, or life insurance. A union contract may also require the deduction of union dues.

Computing Employee Net Pay

Gross earnings less payroll deductions equals *net pay*, sometimes called *take-home pay*. Assuming that John T. McGrath authorized deductions for retirement savings and for a United Fund contribution, McGrath's net pay for the week ended December 27 is $1,072.70, computed as follows:

Gross earnings for the week		$1,462.00
Deductions:		
Federal income tax	$254.65	
Social security tax	87.72	
Medicare tax	21.93	
Retirement savings	20.00	
United Fund	5.00	
Total deductions		389.30
Net pay		$1,072.70

Example Exercise 11-3   Employee Net Pay   Obj. 2

Karen Dunn's weekly gross earnings for the week ending December 3 were $2,250, and her federal income tax withholding was $442.02. Assuming that the social security rate is 6% and Medicare is 1.5%, what is Dunn's net pay?

Follow My Example 11-3

Total wage payment		$2,250.00
Less: Federal income tax withholding	$442.02	
Social security tax ($2,250 × 6%)	135.00	
Medicare tax ($2,250 × 1.5%)	33.75	610.77
Net pay		$1,639.23

Practice Exercises: PE 11-3A, PE 11-3B

---

[6] For 2016, the social security tax rate was 6.2% and the Medicare tax rate was 1.45%. Earnings subject to the social security tax are limited to an annual threshold amount, but for text examples and problems, assume that all accumulated annual earnings are below this threshold and subject to the tax.

Liability for Employer's Payroll Taxes

Employers are subject to the following payroll taxes for amounts paid their employees:

- *FICA Tax*: Employers must match the employee's FICA tax contribution.
- *Federal Unemployment Compensation Tax (FUTA)*: This employer tax provides for temporary payments to those who become unemployed. The tax collected by the federal government is allocated among the states for use in state programs rather than paid directly to employees. Congress often revises the FUTA tax rate and maximum earnings subject to tax.
- *State Unemployment Compensation Tax (SUTA)*: This employer tax also provides temporary payments to those who become unemployed. The FUTA and SUTA programs are closely coordinated, with the states distributing the unemployment checks. SUTA tax rates and earnings subject to tax vary by state.[7]

The preceding employer taxes are an operating expense of the company. Exhibit 3 summarizes the responsibility for employee and employer payroll taxes.

EXHIBIT 3
Responsibility for Tax Payments

Business Connection

THE MOST YOU WILL EVER PAY

In 1936, the Social Security Board described how the tax was expected to affect a worker's pay, as follows:

The taxes called for in this law will be paid both by your employer and by you. For the next 3 years you will pay maybe 15 cents a week, maybe 25 cents a week, maybe 30 cents or more, according to what you earn. That is to say, during the next 3 years, beginning January 1, 1937, you will pay 1 cent for every dollar you earn, and at the same time your employer will pay 1 cent for every dollar you earn, up to $3,000 a year....

...Beginning in 1940 you will pay, and your employer will pay, 1½ cents for each dollar you earn, up to $3,000 a year.

...and then beginning in 1943, you will pay 2 cents, and so will your employer, for every dollar you earn for the next three years. After that, you and your employer will each pay half a cent more for 3 years, and finally, beginning in 1949,... you and your employer will each pay 3 cents on each dollar you earn, up to $3,000 a year. That is the most you will ever pay.

The rate on January 1, 2015, was 7.65 cents per dollar earned (7.65%). The social security portion was 6.20% on the first $118,500 of earnings. The Medicare portion was 1.45% on all earnings. In addition, there is an additional Medicare tax of 0.9% on wages in excess of $200,000 for the calendar year.

Source: Arthur Lodge, "That Is the Most You Will Ever Pay," *Journal of Accountancy*, October 1985, p. 44.

Accounting Systems for Payroll and Payroll Taxes

Obj. 3 Describe payroll accounting systems that use a payroll register, employee earnings records, and a general journal.

Payroll systems should be designed to:

- Pay employees accurately and timely.
- Meet regulatory requirements of federal, state, and local agencies.
- Provide useful data for management decision-making needs.

---

[7] For 2016, the FUTA tax rate is 6.0% of the first $7,000 of each employee's earnings during a calendar year. Employers may get a credit of up to 5.4% for state unemployment taxes, resulting in a net FUTA rate of 0.6% (6.0% FUTA rate − 5.4% credit).

EXHIBIT 4 Payroll Register

	Employee Name	Total Hours	Earnings: Week Ended December 27			
			Regular	Overtime	Total	
1	Abrams, Julie S.	40	500.00		500.00	1
2	Elrod, Fred G.	44	392.00	58.80	450.80	2
3	Gomez, Jose C.	40	840.00		840.00	3
4	**McGrath, John T.**	42	1,360.00	102.00	1,462.00	4
25	Wilkes, Glenn K.	40	480.00		480.00	25
26	Zumpano, Michael W.	40	600.00		600.00	26
27	Total		13,328.00	574.00	13,902.00	27
28						28

Although payroll systems differ among companies, the major elements of most payroll systems are as follows:

- Payroll register
- Employee's earnings record
- Payroll checks

Payroll Register

The **payroll register** is a multicolumn report used for summarizing the data for each payroll period. Although payroll registers vary by company, a payroll register normally includes the following columns:

- Employee name
- Total hours worked
- Regular earnings
- Overtime earnings
- Total gross earnings
- Social security tax withheld
- Medicare tax withheld
- Federal income tax withheld
- Retirement savings withheld
- Miscellaneous items withheld
- Total withholdings
- Net pay
- Check number of payroll check issued
- Accounts debited for payroll expense

Exhibit 4 illustrates a payroll register for **McDermott Supply Co.** The two right-hand columns of the payroll register indicate the accounts debited for the payroll expense. These columns are often referred to as the *payroll distribution*.

Recording Employees' Earnings The column totals of the payroll register provide the basis for recording the journal entry for payroll. The entry based on the payroll register in Exhibit 4 follows:

Dec.	27	Sales Salaries Expense		11,122.00	
		Office Salaries Expense		2,780.00	
		Social Security Tax Payable			834.12
		Medicare Tax Payable			208.53
		Employees Federal Income Tax Payable			3,332.00
		Retirement Savings Deductions Payable			680.00
		United Fund Deductions Payable			520.00
		Salaries Payable			8,327.35
		Payroll for week ended December 27.			

Chapter 11 Current Liabilities and Payroll   547

(Concluded)   **EXHIBIT 4**

	Deductions Withheld					Paid		Accounts Debited	
	Social Security Tax	Medicare Tax	Federal Income Tax	Retirement Savings	Misc.	Total	Net Pay	Check No.	Sales Salaries Expense	Office Salaries Expense
1	30.00	7.50	48.35	20.00	UF 10.00	115.85	384.15	6857	500.00	
2	27.05	6.76	40.85		UF 50.00	124.66	326.14	6858		450.80
3	50.40	12.60	117.90	25.00	UF 10.00	215.90	624.10	6859	840.00	
4	87.72	21.93	254.65	20.00	UF 5.00	389.30	1,072.70	6860	1,462.00	
25	28.80	7.20	45.35	10.00		91.35	388.65	6880	480.00	
26	36.00	9.00	63.35	5.00	UF 2.00	115.35	484.65	6881		600.00
27	834.12	208.53	3,332.00	680.00	UF 520.00	5,574.65	8,327.35		11,122.00	2,780.00

Miscellaneous Deductions: UF—United Fund

Recording and Paying Payroll Taxes Payroll taxes are recorded as liabilities when the payroll is *paid* to employees. In addition, employers compute and report payroll taxes on a *calendar-year* basis, which may differ from the company's fiscal year.

Note
Payroll taxes become a liability to the employer when the payroll is paid.

Example Exercise 11-4 Journalize Period Payroll   Obj. 3

The payroll register of Chen Engineering Services indicates $900 of social security withheld and $225 of Medicare tax withheld on total salaries of $15,000 for the period. Federal withholding for the period totaled $2,925.
  Provide the journal entry for the period's payroll.

Follow My Example 11-4

Salaries Expense	15,000	
Social Security Tax Payable		900
Medicare Tax Payable		225
Employees Federal Income Tax Payable		2,925
Salaries Payable		10,950

Practice Exercises: PE 11-4A, PE 11-4B

On December 27, McDermott Supply has the following payroll data:

Sales salaries	$11,122
Office salaries owed	2,780
Wages owed employees on December 27	$13,902
Wages subject to payroll taxes:	
Social security tax (6%)	$13,902
Medicare tax (1.5%)	13,902
State (5.4%) and federal (0.6%)	
unemployment compensation tax	2,710

Employers must match the employees' social security and Medicare tax contributions. In addition, the employer must pay state unemployment compensation tax (SUTA) of 5.4% and federal unemployment compensation tax (FUTA) of 0.6%. When payroll is paid on December 27, these payroll taxes are computed as follows:

548 Chapter 11 Current Liabilities and Payroll

Social security tax	$ 834.12	($13,902 × 6%, and from Social Security Tax column of Exhibit 4)
Medicare tax	208.53	($13,902 × 1.5%, and from Medicare Tax column of Exhibit 4)
SUTA	146.34	($2,710 × 5.4%)
FUTA	16.26	($2,710 × 0.6%)
Total payroll taxes	$1,205.25	

The entry to journalize the payroll tax expense for Exhibit 4 follows:

Dec.	27	Payroll Tax Expense	1,205.25	
		Social Security Tax Payable		834.12
		Medicare Tax Payable		208.53
		State Unemployment Tax Payable		146.34
		Federal Unemployment Tax Payable		16.26
		Payroll taxes for week ended December 27.		

The preceding entry records a liability for each payroll tax. When the payroll taxes are paid, an entry is recorded debiting the payroll tax liability accounts and crediting Cash.

Example Exercise 11-5 Journalize Payroll Tax Obj. 3

The payroll register of Chen Engineering Services indicates $900 of social security withheld and $225 of Medicare tax withheld on total salaries of $15,000 for the period. Earnings of $5,250 are subject to state and federal unemployment compensation taxes at the federal rate of 0.6% and the state rate of 5.4%.

Provide the journal entry to record the payroll tax expense for the period.

(Continued)

EXHIBIT 5
Employee's Earnings Record

John T. McGrath
1830 4th St.
Clinton, IA 52732-6142   PHONE: 555-3148

SINGLE   **NUMBER OF WITHHOLDING ALLOWANCES: 1**   **PAY RATE:** $1,360.00 Per Week

OCCUPATION: Salesperson   **EQUIVALENT HOURLY RATE: $34**

	Period Ending	Total Hours	Regular Earnings	Overtime Earnings	Total Earnings	Total
42	SEPT. 27	53	1,360.00	663.00	2,023.00	75,565.00
43	THIRD QUARTER		17,680.00	7,605.00	25,285.00	
44	OCT. 4	51	1,360.00	561.00	1,921.00	77,486.00
50	NOV. 15	50	1,360.00	510.00	1,870.00	89,382.00
51	NOV. 22	53	1,360.00	663.00	2,023.00	91,405.00
52	NOV. 29	47	1,360.00	357.00	1,717.00	93,122.00
53	DEC. 6	53	1,360.00	663.00	2,023.00	95,145.00
54	DEC. 13	52	1,360.00	612.00	1,972.00	97,117.00
55	DEC. 20	51	1,360.00	561.00	1,921.00	99,038.00
56	DEC. 27	42	1,360.00	102.00	1,462.00	100,500.00
57	FOURTH QUARTER		17,680.00	7,255.00	24,935.00	
58	YEARLY TOTAL		70,720.00	29,780.00	100,500.00	

Follow My Example 11-5

Payroll Tax Expense...	1,440.00	
Social Security Tax Payable		900.00
Medicare Tax Payable		225.00
State Unemployment Tax Payable		283.50*
Federal Unemployment Tax Payable		31.50**

*$5,250 × 5.4%
**$5,250 × 0.6%

Practice Exercises: PE 11-5A, PE 11-5B

Employee's Earnings Record

Each employee's earnings to date must be determined at the end of each payroll period. This total is necessary for computing the employee's social security tax withholding and the employer's payroll taxes. Thus, detailed payroll records must be kept for each employee. This record is called an **employee's earnings record**.

Exhibit 5 shows a portion of John T. McGrath's employee's earnings record. An employee's earnings record and the payroll register are interrelated. For example, McGrath's earnings record for December 27 can be traced to the fourth line of the payroll register in Exhibit 4.

(Concluded) EXHIBIT 5

SOC. SEC. NO.: 381-48-9120   EMPLOYEE NO.: 814

DATE OF BIRTH: February 15, 1982

DATE EMPLOYMENT TERMINATED:

	Deductions						Paid	
	Social Security Tax	Medicare Tax	Federal Income Tax	Retirement Savings	Other		Total	Net Amount	Check No.
42	121.38	30.35	399.46	20.00			571.19	1,451.81	6175
43	1,517.10	379.28	5,391.71	260.00	UF	40.00	7,588.09	17,696.91	
44	115.26	28.82	370.90	20.00			534.98	1,386.02	6225
50	112.20	28.05	356.65	20.00			516.90	1,353.10	6530
51	121.38	30.35	399.46	20.00			571.19	1,451.81	6582
52	103.02	25.76	318.40	20.00			467.18	1,249.82	6640
53	121.38	30.35	399.46	20.00	UF	5.00	576.19	1,446.81	6688
54	118.32	29.58	385.18	20.00			553.08	1,418.92	6743
55	115.26	28.82	370.90	20.00			534.98	1,386.02	6801
56	87.72	21.93	254.65	20.00	UF	5.00	389.30	1,072.70	6860
57	1,506.90	376.73	5,293.71	260.00	UF	15.00	7,452.34	17,482.66	
58	6,030.00	1,507.50	21,387.65	1,040.00	UF	100.00	30,065.15	70,434.85	

As shown in Exhibit 5, an employee's earnings record has quarterly and yearly totals. These totals are used for tax, insurance, and other reports. For example, one such report is the Wage and Tax Statement, commonly called a *W-2*. This form is provided annually to each employee as well as to the Social Security Administration. The W-2 shown in Exhibit 6 is based on John T. McGrath's employee's earnings record shown in Exhibit 5.

EXHIBIT 6 — Employee's Wage and Tax Statement (W-2 Form)

a Employee's social security number	381-48-9120
22222 Void	
OMB No. 1545-0008	
b Employer identification number (EIN)	61-8436524
c Employer's name, address, and ZIP code	McDermott Supply Co. / 415 5th Ave. So. / Dubuque, IA 52736-0142
1 Wages, tips, other compensation	100,500.00
2 Federal income tax withheld	21,387.65
3 Social security wages	100,500.00
4 Social security tax withheld	6,030.00
5 Medicare wages and tips	100,500.00
6 Medicare tax withheld	1,507.50
7 Social security tips	
8 Allocated tips	
d Control number	
9	
10 Dependent care benefits	
e Employee's first name and initial	John T.
Last name	McGrath
11 Nonqualified plans	
12a See instructions for box 12	
13 Statutory employee / Retirement plan / Third-party sick pay	
14 Other	
f Employee's address and ZIP code	1830 4th St. / Clinton, IA 52732-6142
15 State	IA
16 State wages, tips, etc.	
17 State income tax	
18 Local wages, tips, etc.	
19 Local income tax	
20 Locality name	Dubuque

Form **W-2** Wage and Tax Statement **20Y6**
Copy A For Social Security Administration — Send this entire page with Form W-3 to the Social Security Administration; photocopies are **not** acceptable.
Do Not Cut, Fold, or Staple Forms on This Page
Department of the Treasury—Internal Revenue Service
For Privacy Act and Paperwork Reduction Act Notice, see the separate instructions.
Cat. No. 10134D

Payroll Checks

Companies pay employees either by electronic funds transfer or by *payroll checks*. With electronic funds transfers, the employee's net pay is electronically deposited into their bank account each period. Later, the employees receive a payroll statement summarizing how the net pay was computed. A payroll statement for the electronic funds transfer of John T. McGrath's pay is shown in Exhibit 7. Each payroll check includes a detachable statement showing how the net pay was computed, which is typically identical to the payroll statement accompanying electronic funds transfers (EFTs).

Most companies use a special payroll bank account to disburse payroll. In such cases, payroll is processed as follows:

1. The total net pay for the period is determined from the payroll register.
2. The company authorizes an electronic funds transfer (EFT) from its regular bank account to the special payroll bank account for the total net pay.
3. Individual EFTs or payroll checks are disbursed from the payroll account.
4. The numbers of the individual payroll disbursements are inserted in the payroll register.

> **EXHIBIT 7**
>
> **Payroll Statement**

McDermott Supply Co.
415 5th Ave. So.
Dubuque, IA 52736-0142

John T. McGrath
1830 4th St.
Clinton, IA 52732-6142

Check Number: 6860
Pay Period Ending: 12/27/Y6

HOURS & EARNINGS

DESCRIPTION	AMOUNT
Rate of Pay Reg.	34
Rate of Pay O.T.	51
Hours Worked Reg.	40
Hours Worked O.T.	2
Net Pay	1,072.70
Total Gross Pay	1,462.00
Total Gross Y-T-D	100,500.00

TAXES & DEDUCTIONS

DESCRIPTION	CURRENT AMOUNT	Y-T-D AMOUNT
Social Security Tax	87.72	6,030.00
Medicare Tax	21.93	1,507.50
Fed. Income Tax	254.65	21,387.65
Retirement Savings	20.00	1,040.00
United Fund	5.00	100.00
Total	389.30	30,065.15

An advantage of using a separate payroll bank account is that reconciling the bank statements is simplified. In addition, a payroll bank account establishes control over payroll checks and, thus, prevents their theft or misuse.

Computerized Payroll System

The inputs into a payroll system may be classified as follows:

- *Constants:* Data that remain unchanged from payroll to payroll
  Examples: Employee names, social security numbers, marital status, number of income tax withholding allowances, rates of pay, tax rates, and withholding tables
- *Variables:* Data that change from payroll to payroll
  Examples: Number of hours or days worked for each employee, accrued days of sick leave, vacation credits, total earnings to date, and total taxes withheld

In a computerized accounting system, constants are stored within a payroll file. The variables are input each pay period by a payroll clerk. In some systems, employees swipe their identification (ID) cards when they report for and leave from work. In such cases, the hours worked by each employee are automatically updated.

A computerized payroll system also maintains electronic versions of the payroll register and employee earnings records. Payroll system outputs, such as payroll checks, electronic funds transfers, and tax records, are automatically produced each pay period.

Internal Controls for Payroll Systems

The cash payment controls described in Chapter 8 also apply to payrolls. Some examples of payroll controls include the following:

- If a check-signing machine is used, blank payroll checks and access to the machine should be restricted to prevent their theft or misuse.
- The hiring and firing of employees should be properly authorized and approved in writing.
- All changes in pay rates should be properly authorized and approved in writing.
- Employees should be observed when arriving for work to verify that employees are "checking in" for work only once and only for themselves. Employees may "check in" for work by using a time card or by swiping their employee ID card.
- Payroll checks should be distributed by someone other than employee supervisors.
- A special payroll bank account should be used.

INTEGRITY, OBJECTIVITY, AND ETHICS IN BUSINESS

OVERBILLING CLIENTS

The U.S. government makes payments to hospitals for the medical costs of patients covered under Medicaid. In some cases, computer glitches result in hospitals overbilling the U.S. government, causing overpayments to the hospital. When this happens, hospitals must return the overpayments to the U.S. government within 60 days of identifying the overpayment. If a hospital fails to return the funds within this time frame, it is subject to a penalty of three times the original liability plus additional fines. In one case, **Continuum Health Partners, Inc.**, determined that a computer glitch resulted in over $1,000,000 in claims being incorrectly submitted to and reimbursed by the U.S. government. After identifying the overpayments, it took Continuum over two years to return the funds. In 2014, a U.S. Attorney filed a claim to recover penalties and fines for the late return of these overpayments. The case is still pending.

Source: New York Health Law, July 17, 2014.

Obj. 4 Journalize entries for employee fringe benefits, including vacation pay and pensions.

Employees' Fringe Benefits

Many companies provide their employees with benefits in addition to salary and wages earned. Such **fringe benefits** may include vacation, medical, and retirement benefits.

The cost of employee fringe benefits is recorded as an expense by the employer. To match revenues and expenses, the estimated cost of fringe benefits is recorded as an expense during the period in which employees earn the benefits.

Link to Starbucks
Starbucks offers eligible employees the Starbucks College Achievement Plan, which provides full tuition reimbursement for 50 undergraduate degree programs, delivered online at Arizona State University.

Vacation Pay

Most employers provide employees vacations, sometimes called *compensated absences*. The liability to pay for employee vacations could be accrued as a liability at the end of each pay period. However, many companies wait and record an adjusting entry for accrued vacation at the end of the year.

To illustrate, assume that employees earn one day of vacation for each month worked. The estimated vacation pay for the year ending December 31 is $325,000. The adjusting entry for the accrued vacation is as follows:

Dec.	31	Vacation Pay Expense		325,000	
		Vacation Pay Payable			325,000
		Accrued vacation pay for the year.			

Note: Vacation pay becomes the employer's liability as the employee earns vacation rights.

Employees may be required to take all their vacation time within one year. In such cases, any accrued vacation pay will be paid within one year. Thus, the vacation pay payable is reported as a current liability on the balance sheet. If employees are allowed to accumulate their vacation pay, the estimated vacation pay payable that will *not* be taken within a year is reported as a long-term liability.

When employees take vacations, the liability for vacation pay is decreased by debiting Vacation Pay Payable. Salaries or Wages Payable and the other related payroll accounts for taxes and withholdings are credited.

Pensions

A **pension** is a cash payment to retired employees. Pension benefits are accrued by employees as they work, based on the employer's pension plan. Two basic types of pension plans are defined contribution and defined benefit plans.[8]

Defined Contribution Plans In a **defined contribution plan**, the company invests contributions on behalf of the employee during the employee's working years. Normally, both the employee and employer contribute to the plan. The employee's pension depends on the total contributions and the investment returns earned on those contributions.

One of the more popular defined contribution plans is the 401k plan. Under this plan, employees contribute a portion of their gross pay to investments, such as mutual funds. A 401k plan offers employees two advantages.

- The employee contribution is deducted before taxes.
- The contributions and related earnings are not taxed until withdrawn at retirement.

In most cases, the employer matches some portion of the employee's contribution. The employer's cost is debited to *Pension Expense*. To illustrate, assume that Heaven Scent Perfumes Company contributes 10% of employee monthly salaries to an employee 401k plan. Assuming $500,000 of monthly salaries, the journal entry to record the monthly contribution is as follows:

Dec.	31	Pension Expense	50,000	
		Cash		50,000
		Contributed 10% of monthly salaries to pension plan.		

Defined Benefit Plans In a **defined benefit plan**, the company pays the employee a fixed annual pension based on a formula. The formula is normally based on such factors as the employee's years of service, age, and past salary.

In a defined benefit plan, the employer is obligated to pay for (fund) the employee's future pension benefits. As a result, many companies are replacing their defined benefit plans with defined contribution plans.

The pension cost of a defined benefit plan is debited to *Pension Expense*. Cash is credited for the amount contributed (funded) by the employer. Any unfunded amount is credited to *Unfunded Pension Liability*.

To illustrate, assume that the defined benefit plan of Hinkle Co. requires an annual pension cost of $80,000. This annual contribution is based on estimates of Hinkle's future pension liabilities. On December 31, Hinkle Co. pays $60,000 to the pension fund. The entry to record the payment and the unfunded liability is as follows:

Dec.	31	Pension Expense	80,000	
		Cash		60,000
		Unfunded Pension Liability		20,000
		Annual pension cost and contribution.		

If the unfunded pension liability is to be paid within one year, it is reported as a current liability on the balance sheet. Any portion of the unfunded pension liability that will be paid beyond one year is a long-term liability.

---

[8] The accounting for pensions is complex due to the uncertainties of estimating future pension liabilities. These estimates depend on such factors as employee life expectancies, employee turnover, expected employee compensation levels, and investment income on pension contributions. Additional accounting and disclosures related to pensions are covered in advanced accounting courses.

Example Exercise 11-6 Vacation Pay and Pension Benefits Obj. 4

Manfield Services Company provides its employees with vacation benefits and a defined contribution pension plan. Employees earned vacation pay of $44,000 for the period. The pension plan requires a contribution to the plan administrator equal to 8% of employee salaries. Salaries were $450,000 during the period.

Provide the journal entry for the (a) vacation pay and (b) pension benefit.

Follow My Example 11-6

a. Vacation Pay Expense 44,000
    Vacation Pay Payable... 44,000
      Vacation pay accrued for the period.

b. Pension Expense 36,000
    Cash 36,000
      Pension contribution, 8% of $450,000 salary.

Practice Exercises: PE 11-6A, PE 11-6B

Link to Starbucks

On a recent balance sheet, **Starbucks** reported a $984 million dollar liability for "Stored Value Cards," which are prepaid purchases loaded onto a gift card or a mobile device, that have not yet been redeemed by customers.

Postretirement Benefits Other Than Pensions

Employees may earn rights to other postretirement benefits from their employer. Such benefits may include dental care, eye care, medical care, life insurance, tuition assistance, tax services, and legal services.

The accounting for other postretirement benefits is similar to that of defined benefit pension plans. The estimate of the annual benefits expense is recorded by debiting *Postretirement Benefits Expense*. If the benefits are fully funded, Cash is credited for the same amount. If the benefits are not fully funded, a postretirement benefits plan liability account is also credited.

The financial statements should disclose the nature of the postretirement benefit liabilities. These disclosures are usually included as notes to the financial statements. Additional accounting and disclosures for postretirement benefits are covered in advanced accounting courses.

Current Liabilities on the Balance Sheet

Accounts payable, the current portion of long-term debt, notes payable, and any other debts that are due within one year are reported as current liabilities on the balance sheet. The balance sheet presentation of current liabilities for **Mornin' Joe** follows:

Mornin' Joe
Balance Sheet
December 31, 20Y6

Liabilities

Current liabilities:		
Accounts payable	$133,000	
Notes payable (current portion)	200,000	
Salaries and wages payable	42,000	
Payroll taxes payable	16,400	
Interest payable	40,000	
Total current liabilities		$431,400

Business Connection

STATE PENSION OBLIGATIONS

Each state has a pension plan for its employees. The plan is determined by the state legislature through the normal political process. The funding of each state's plan relative to the outstanding obligation differs across the states, again according to political decisions regarding the funding level. Some states are well funded, while others face significant pension shortfalls. Only 13 out of 50 states have pension assets greater than 80% of their pension obligations, which is considered a healthy funding ratio. The U.S. Census Bureau provides an annual survey on the status of state pension plans. According to a recent survey, the top and bottom five states by the percent of pension obligations funded are as follows:

Rank	State	Percent of Pension Funded	Pension Contributions as a Percent of State Payroll	Pension Liability per State Resident
1	Wisconsin	102%	12.6%	$ 0
2	North Carolina	95	12.7	407
3	New York	93	15.7	877
4	South Dakota	93	13.3	730
5	Tennessee	89	15.1	693
46	New Jersey	55	16.4	6,447
47	Alaska	53	31.6	11,028
48	Kentucky	50	21.6	5,907
49	Connecticut	49	25.7	7,027
50	Illinois	47	31.9	7,636

As can be seen, the states with the most severe underfunding are also the states making the largest contributions to their pension plans as a percent of the state's governmental payroll. This is likely an attempt to "catch up" to their obligations, but it is coming at a high cost to the state's taxpayers.

Contingent Liabilities

Obj. 5 Describe the accounting treatment for contingent liabilities and journalize entries for product warranties.

Some liabilities may arise from past transactions only if certain events occur in the future. These *potential* liabilities are called **contingent liabilities**.

The accounting for contingent liabilities depends on the following two factors:

- *Likelihood of occurring:* Probable, reasonably possible, or remote
- *Measurement:* Estimable or not estimable

The likelihood that the event creating the liability occurring is classified as *probable*, *reasonably possible*, or *remote*. The ability to estimate the potential liability is classified as *estimable* or *not estimable*.

Probable and Estimable

If a contingent liability is *probable* and the amount of the liability can be *reasonably estimated*, it is recorded and disclosed. The liability is recorded by debiting an expense and crediting a liability.

To illustrate, assume that during June, a company sold a product for $60,000 that includes a 36-month warranty for repairs.[9] The average cost of repairs over the warranty period is estimated at 5% of the sales price. The entry to record the estimated product warranty expense for June is as follows:

---

[9] This discussion is limited to assurance type warranties. A more detailed discussion of the types of warranties and their accounting is covered in intermediate and advanced accounting texts.

Link to Starbucks

In 2011, **Starbucks** terminated a contract with **Kraft Foods** that allowed Kraft to sell bagged Starbucks coffee in grocery stores. The early termination resulted in litigation between Kraft and Starbucks. After an arbitrator found in Kraft's favor, Starbucks recorded a liability for $2.8 billion.

June	30	Product Warranty Expense		3,000	
		Product Warranty Payable			3,000
		Warranty expense for June, 5% × $60,000.			

The preceding entry records warranty expense in the same period in which the sale is recorded. In this way, warranty expense is matched with the related revenue (sales).

If the product is repaired under warranty, the repair costs are recorded by debiting *Product Warranty Payable* and crediting *Cash, Supplies, Wages Payable*, or other appropriate accounts. Thus, if a $200 part is replaced under warranty on August 16, the entry is as follows:

Aug.	16	Product Warranty Payable		200	
		Supplies			200
		Replaced defective part under warranty.			

Example Exercise 11-7 Estimated Warranty Liability — Obj. 5

Cook-Rite Co. sold $140,000 of kitchen appliances during August under a six-month warranty. The cost to repair defects under the warranty is estimated at 6% of the sales price. On September 12, a customer required a $200 part replacement plus $90 of labor under the warranty.

Provide the journal entry for (a) the estimated warranty expense on August 31 for August sales and (b) the September 12 warranty work.

Follow My Example 11-7

a. Product Warranty Expense 8,400
       Product Warranty Payable 8,400
          To record warranty expense for August, 6% × $140,000.
b. Product Warranty Payable 290
       Supplies 200
       Wages Payable 90
          Replaced defective part under warranty.

Practice Exercises: PE 11-7A, PE 11-7B

Probable and Not Estimable

A contingent liability may be probable but cannot be estimated. In this case, the contingent liability is disclosed in the notes to the financial statements. For example, a company may have accidentally polluted a local river by dumping waste products. At the end of the period, the cost of the cleanup and any fines may not be able to be estimated.

Reasonably Possible

A contingent liability may be only possible. For example, a company may have lost a lawsuit for infringing on another company's patent rights. However, the verdict is under appeal and the company's lawyers believe that the verdict will be reversed or significantly reduced. In this case, the contingent liability is disclosed in the notes to the financial statements.

Remote

A contingent liability may be remote. For example, a ski resort may be sued for injuries incurred by skiers. In most cases, the courts have found that a skier accepts the risk of injury when participating in the activity. Thus, unless the ski resort is grossly negligent, the resort will not incur a liability for ski injuries. In such cases, no disclosure needs to be made in the notes to the financial statements. The accounting treatment of contingent liabilities is summarized in Exhibit 8.

Common examples of contingent liabilities disclosed in notes to the financial statements are litigation, environmental matters, guarantees, and contingencies from the sale of receivables.

Professional judgment is necessary in distinguishing between classes of contingent liabilities. This is especially the case when distinguishing between probable and reasonably possible contingent liabilities.

> **Link to Starbucks**
> In a recent annual report, **Starbucks** reported that in its normal course of business, it is party to a variety of legal actions. However, the management of Starbucks believes none of these actions will have a material effect on its financial statements.

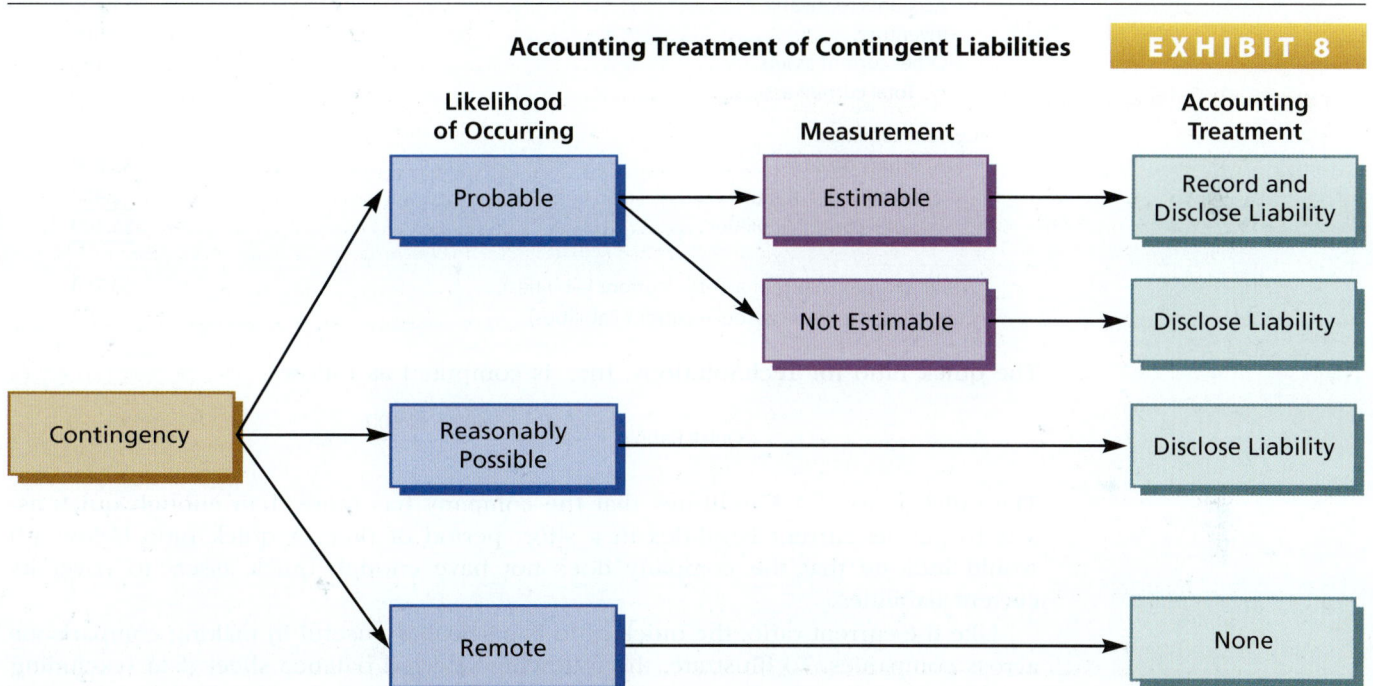

EXHIBIT 8 Accounting Treatment of Contingent Liabilities

Financial Analysis and Interpretation: Quick Ratio

Obj. 6 Describe and illustrate the use of the quick ratio in analyzing a company's ability to pay its current liabilities.

Current position analysis helps creditors evaluate a company's ability to pay its current liabilities. This analysis is based on the following three measures:

- Working capital
- Current ratio
- Quick ratio

Working capital and the current ratio were discussed in Chapter 4 and are computed as follows:

$$\text{Working Capital} = \text{Current Assets} - \text{Current Liabilities}$$

$$\text{Current Ratio} = \frac{\text{Current Assets}}{\text{Current Liabilities}}$$

While these two measures can be used to evaluate a company's ability to pay its current liabilities, they do not provide insight into the company's ability to pay these liabilities within a short period of time. This is because some current assets, such as inventory, cannot be converted into cash as quickly as other current assets, such as cash and accounts receivable.

The **quick ratio** overcomes this limitation by measuring the "instant" debt-paying ability of a company and is computed as follows:

$$\text{Quick Ratio} = \frac{\text{Quick Assets}}{\text{Current Liabilities}}$$

Quick assets are cash and other current assets that can be easily converted to cash. This normally includes cash, temporary investments, and accounts receivable. To illustrate, consider the following data for TechSolutions, Inc., at the end of 20Y7:

Current assets:	
Cash	$2,020
Temporary investments	3,400
Accounts receivable	1,600
Inventory	2,000
Other current assets	160
Total current assets	$9,180
Current liabilities:	
Accounts payable	$3,000
Other current liabilities	2,400
Total current liabilities	$5,400
Working capital (current assets − current liabilities)	$3,780
Current ratio (current assets ÷ current liabilities)	1.7

The quick ratio for TechSolutions, Inc., is computed as follows:

$$\text{Quick Ratio} = \frac{\$2{,}020 + \$3{,}400 + \$1{,}600}{\$5{,}400} = 1.3$$

The quick ratio of 1.3 indicates that the company has more than enough quick assets to pay its current liabilities in a short period of time. A quick ratio below 1.0 would indicate that the company does not have enough quick assets to cover its current liabilities.

Like the current ratio, the quick ratio is particularly useful in making comparisons across companies. To illustrate, the following selected balance sheet data (excluding ratios) were taken from recent financial statements of **Dunkin' Brands Group, Inc.,** and **Starbucks Corporation** (in thousands):

	Dunkin'	Starbucks
Current assets:		
Cash and cash equivalents	$370,901	$1,530,100
Temporary investments	—	81,300
Accounts receivable	128,360	1,100,700
Inventory	—	1,306,400
Other current assets	58,563	334,200
Total current assets	$557,824	$4,352,700

	Dunkin'	Starbucks
Current liabilities:		
Accounts payable	$ 68,852	$2,669,700
Other current liabilities	349,940	983,800
Total current liabilities	$418,792	$3,653,500
Working capital (current assets − current liabilities)	$139,032	$699,200
Current ratio (current assets ÷ current liabilities)	1.3	1.2
Quick ratio (quick assets ÷ current liabilities)*	1.2	0.7

*The quick ratio for each company is computed as follows:
Dunkin': ($370,901 + $128,360) ÷ $418,792 = 1.2
Starbucks: ($1,530,100 + $81,300 + $1,100,700) ÷ $3,653,500 = 0.7

Starbucks is larger than Dunkin' and has more than five times the amount of working capital. Such size differences make working capital comparisons between companies difficult. In contrast, the current and quick ratios provide better comparisons across companies. In this example, Starbucks has a slightly lower current ratio than Dunkin'. However, Starbucks' 0.7 quick ratio reveals that it does not have enough quick assets to cover its current liabilities, while Dunkin's quick ratio of 1.2 indicates that the company has more than enough quick assets to meet its current liabilities.

Example Exercise 11-8 Quick Ratio   Obj. 6

Sayer Company reported the following current assets and current liabilities for the years ended December 31, 20Y9 and 20Y8:

	20Y9	20Y8
Cash	$1,250	$1,000
Temporary investments	1,925	1,650
Accounts receivable	1,775	1,350
Inventory	1,900	1,700
Accounts payable	2,750	2,500

a. Compute the quick ratio for 20Y9 and 20Y8.
b. Interpret the company's quick ratio across the two time periods.

Follow My Example 11-8

a. December 31, 20Y9:
   Quick Ratio = Quick Assets ÷ Current Liabilities
          = ($1,250 + $1,925 + $1,775) ÷ $2,750
          = 1.8

   December 31, 20Y8:
   Quick Ratio = Quick Assets ÷ Current Liabilities
          = ($1,000 + $1,650 + $1,350) ÷ $2,500
          = 1.6

b. The quick ratio of Sayer Company has improved from 1.6 in 20Y8 to 1.8 in 20Y9. This increase is the result of a large increase in the three types of quick assets (cash, temporary investments, and accounts receivable) compared to a relatively smaller increase in the current liability, accounts payable.

Practice Exercises: PE 11-8A, PE 11-8B

At a Glance 11

Obj. 1 Describe and illustrate current liabilities related to accounts payable, current portion of long-term debt, and notes payable.

Key Points Current liabilities are obligations that are to be paid out of current assets and are due within a short time, usually within one year. The three primary types of current liabilities are accounts payable, notes payable, and the current portion of long-term debt.

Learning Outcomes	Example Exercises	Practice Exercises
• Identify and define the most frequently reported current liabilities on the balance sheet.		
• Determine the interest from interest-bearing and discounted notes payable.	EE11-1	PE11-1A, 11-1B

Obj. 2 Determine employer liabilities for payroll, including liabilities arising from employee earnings and deductions from earnings.

Key Points An employer's liability for payroll is determined from employee total earnings, including overtime pay. From this amount, employee deductions are subtracted to arrive at the net pay to be paid to each employee. Most employers also incur liabilities for payroll taxes, such as social security tax, Medicare tax, federal unemployment compensation tax, and state unemployment compensation tax.

Learning Outcomes	Example Exercises	Practice Exercises
• Compute the federal withholding tax from a wage bracket withholding table.	EE11-2	PE11-2A, 11-2B
• Compute employee net pay, including deductions for social security and Medicare tax.	EE11-3	PE11-3A, 11-3B

Obj. 3 Describe payroll accounting systems that use a payroll register, employee earnings records, and a general journal.

Key Points The payroll register is used in assembling and summarizing the data needed for each payroll period. The payroll register is supported by a detailed payroll record for each employee, called an *employee's earnings record*.

Learning Outcomes	Example Exercises	Practice Exercises
• Journalize the employee's earnings, net pay, and payroll liabilities from the payroll register.	EE11-4	PE11-4A, 11-4B
• Journalize the payroll tax expense.		
• Describe elements of a payroll system, including the employee's earnings record, payroll checks, and internal controls.	EE11-5	PE11-5A, 11-5B

Obj. 4 — Journalize entries for employee fringe benefits, including vacation pay and pensions.

Key Points Fringe benefits are expenses of the period in which the employees earn the benefits. Fringe benefits are recorded by debiting an expense account and crediting a liability account.

Learning Outcomes	Example Exercises	Practice Exercises
• Journalize vacation pay.	EE11-6	PE11-6A, 11-6B
• Distinguish and journalize defined contribution and defined benefit pension plans.	EE11-6	PE11-6A, 11-6B

Obj. 5 — Describe the accounting treatment for contingent liabilities and journalize entries for product warranties.

Key Points A contingent liability is a potential obligation that results from a past transaction but depends on a future event. The accounting for contingent liabilities is summarized in Exhibit 8.

Learning Outcomes	Example Exercises	Practice Exercises
• Describe the accounting for contingent liabilities.		
• Journalize estimated warranty obligations and services granted under warranty.	EE11-7	PE11-7A, 11-7B

Obj. 6 — Describe and illustrate the use of the quick ratio in analyzing a company's ability to pay its current liabilities.

Key Points The quick ratio is a measure of a company's ability to pay current liabilities within a short period of time. The quick ratio is computed by dividing quick assets by current liabilities. Quick assets include cash, temporary investments, accounts receivable, and other current assets that can be easily converted into cash. A quick ratio exceeding 1.0 is usually desirable.

Learning Outcomes	Example Exercises	Practice Exercises
• Describe the quick ratio.		
• Compute and evaluate the quick ratio.	EE11-8	PE11-8A, 11-8B

Illustrative Problem

Selected transactions of Taylor Company, completed during the fiscal year ended December 31, are as follows:

Mar. 1. Purchased merchandise on account from Kelvin Co., $20,000.

Apr. 10. Issued a 60-day, 9% note for $20,000 to Kelvin Co. on account.

June 9. Paid Kelvin Co. the amount owed on the note of April 10.

Aug. 1. Issued a $50,000, 90-day note to Harold Co. in exchange for a building. Harold Co. discounted the note at 6%.

Oct. 30. Paid Harold Co. the amount due on the note of August 1.

(Continued)

Dec. 27. Journalized the entry to record the biweekly payroll. A summary of the payroll record follows:

Salary distribution:		
Sales	$63,400	
Officers	36,600	
Office	10,000	$110,000
Deductions:		
Social security tax	$ 6,600	
Medicare tax	1,650	
Federal income tax	17,600	
State income tax	4,950	
Retirement savings	850	
Medical insurance	1,120	32,770
Net amount		$ 77,230

27. Journalized the entry to record payroll taxes for social security and Medicare from the biweekly payroll.

30. Issued a check in payment of liabilities for employees' federal income tax of $17,600, social security tax of $13,200, and Medicare tax of $3,300.

31. Issued a check for $9,500 to the pension fund trustee to fully fund the pension cost for December.

31. Journalized an entry to record the employees' accrued vacation pay, $36,100.

31. Journalized an entry to record the estimated accrued product warranty liability, $37,240.

Instruction

Journalize the preceding transactions.

Solution

Mar.	1	Merchandise Inventory		20,000	
		Accounts Payable—Kelvin Co.			20,000
Apr.	10	Accounts Payable—Kelvin Co.		20,000	
		Notes Payable			20,000
June	9	Notes Payable		20,000	
		Interest Expense		300	
		Cash			20,300
Aug.	1	Building		49,250	
		Interest Expense		750	
		Notes Payable			50,000
Oct.	30	Notes Payable		50,000	
		Cash			50,000

Dec.	27	Sales Salaries Expense		63,400	
		Officers Salaries Expense		36,600	
		Office Salaries Expense		10,000	
		Social Security Tax Payable			6,600
		Medicare Tax Payable			1,650
		Employees Federal Income Tax Payable			17,600
		Employees State Income Tax Payable			4,950
		Retirement Savings Deductions Payable			850
		Medical Insurance Payable			1,120
		Salaries Payable			77,230
	27	Payroll Tax Expense		8,250	
		Social Security Tax Payable			6,600
		Medicare Tax Payable			1,650
	30	Employees Federal Income Tax Payable		17,600	
		Social Security Tax Payable		13,200	
		Medicare Tax Payable		3,300	
		Cash			34,100
	31	Pension Expense		9,500	
		Cash			9,500
		Fund pension cost.			
	31	Vacation Pay Expense		36,100	
		Vacation Pay Payable			36,100
		Accrue vacation pay.			
	31	Product Warranty Expense		37,240	
		Product Warranty Payable			37,240
		Accrue warranty expense.			

Key Terms

contingent liabilities (555)
current position analysis (557)
defined benefit plan (553)
defined contribution plan (553)
employee's earnings record (549)

FICA tax (543)
fringe benefits (552)
gross pay (541)
net pay (541)
payroll (541)

payroll register (546)
pension (553)
quick assets (558)
quick ratio (558)

Discussion Questions

1. Does a discounted note payable provide credit without interest? Discuss.
2. Employees are subject to taxes withheld from their paychecks.
   a. List the federal taxes withheld from most employee paychecks.
   b. Give the title of the accounts credited by amounts withheld.
3. Why are deductions from employees' earnings classified as liabilities for the employer?
4. For each of the following payroll-related taxes, indicate whether they generally apply to (a) employees only, (b) employers only, or (c) both employees and employers:
   1. Federal income tax
   2. Medicare tax

(Continued)

3. Social security tax
4. Federal unemployment compensation tax
5. State unemployment compensation tax

5. What are the principal reasons for using a special payroll bank account?

6. In a payroll system, what types of input data are referred to as (a) constants and (b) variables?

7. To match revenues and expenses properly, should the expense for employee vacation pay be recorded in the period during which the vacation privilege is earned or during the period in which the vacation is taken? Discuss.

8. Explain how a defined contribution pension plan works.

9. When should the liability associated with a product warranty be recorded? Discuss.

10. **General Motors Corporation** reported $2.6 billion of product warranties in the Current Liabilities section of a recent balance sheet. How would costs of repairing a defective product be recorded?

Practice Exercises

Example Exercises

EE 11-1 p. 541 **PE 11-1A Proceeds from notes payable** OBJ. 1

On May 15, Maynard Co. borrowed cash from Texas Bank by issuing a 60-day note with a face amount of $100,000.

a. Determine the proceeds of the note, assuming that the note carries an interest rate of 6%.
b. Determine the proceeds of the note, assuming that the note is discounted at 6%.

EE 11-1 p. 541 **PE 11-1B Proceeds from notes payable** OBJ. 1

On January 26, Nyree Co. borrowed cash from Conrad Bank by issuing a 45-day note with a face amount of $150,000.

a. Determine the proceeds of the note, assuming that the note carries an interest rate of 10%.
b. Determine the proceeds of the note, assuming that the note is discounted at 10%.

EE 11-2 p. 543 **PE 11-2A Federal income tax withholding** OBJ. 2

Tam Worldly's weekly gross earnings for the present week were $2,000. Worldly has two exemptions. Using the wage bracket withholding table in Exhibit 2 with a $75 standard withholding allowance for each exemption, what is Worldly's federal income tax withholding?

EE 11-2 p. 543 **PE 11-2B Federal income tax withholding** OBJ. 2

Marsha Mellow's weekly gross earnings for the present week were $1,250. Mellow has one exemption. Using the wage bracket withholding table in Exhibit 2 with a $75 standard withholding allowance for each exemption, what is Mellow's federal income tax withholding?

EE 11-3 p. 544 **PE 11-3A Employee net pay** OBJ. 2

Tam Worldly's weekly gross earnings for the week ended April 22 were $2,000, and her federal income tax withholding was $372.02. Assuming that the social security rate is 6% and Medicare is 1.5% of all earnings, what is Worldly's net pay?

EE 11-3 p. 544 **PE 11-3B Employee net pay** OBJ. 2

Marsha Mellow's weekly gross earnings for the week ended May 23 were $1,250, and her federal income tax withholding was $201.65. Assuming that the social security rate is 6% and Medicare is 1.5% of all earnings, what is Mellow's net pay?

Chapter 11 Current Liabilities and Payroll 565

PE 11-4A Journalize period payroll OBJ. 3

EE 11-4 p. 547

The payroll register of Ruggerio Co. indicates $10,500 of social security withheld and $2,625 of Medicare tax withheld on total salaries of $175,000 for the period. Federal withholding for the period totaled $34,650.

Provide the journal entry for the period's payroll.

PE 11-4B Journalize period payroll OBJ. 3

EE 11-4 p. 547

The payroll register of Longboat Co. indicates $5,400 of social security withheld and $1,350 of Medicare tax withheld on total salaries of $90,000 for the period. Retirement savings withheld from employee paychecks were $5,400 for the period. Federal withholding for the period totaled $17,820.

Provide the journal entry for the period's payroll.

PE 11-5A Journalize payroll tax OBJ. 3

EE 11-5 p. 548

The payroll register of Ruggerio Co. indicates $10,500 of social security withheld and $2,625 of Medicare tax withheld on total salaries of $175,000 for the period. Earnings of $30,000 are subject to state and federal unemployment compensation taxes at the federal rate of 0.6% and the state rate of 5.4%.

Provide the journal entry to record the payroll tax expense for the period.

PE 11-5B Journalize payroll tax OBJ. 3

EE 11-5 p. 548

The payroll register of Longboat Co. indicates $5,400 of social security withheld and $1,350 of Medicare tax withheld on total salaries of $90,000 for the period. Earnings of $10,000 are subject to state and federal unemployment compensation taxes at the federal rate of 0.6% and the state rate of 5.4%.

Provide the journal entry to record the payroll tax expense for the period.

PE 11-6A Vacation pay and pension benefits OBJ. 4

EE 11-6 p. 554

Fukushima Company provides its employees with vacation benefits and a defined contribution pension plan. Employees earned vacation pay of $19,500 for the period. The pension plan requires a contribution to the plan administrator equal to 6% of employee salaries. Salaries were $260,000 during the period, and the full amount due was contributed to the pension plan administrator.

Provide the journal entry for the (a) vacation pay and (b) pension benefit.

PE 11-6B Vacation pay and pension benefits OBJ. 4

EE 11-6 p. 554

Regling Company provides its employees vacation benefits and a defined benefit pension plan. Employees earned vacation pay of $35,000 for the period. The pension formula calculated a pension cost of $201,250. Only $175,000 was contributed to the pension plan administrator.

Provide the journal entry for the (a) vacation pay and (b) pension benefit.

PE 11-7A Estimated warranty liability OBJ. 5

EE 11-7 p. 556

EarlKeen Co. sold $260,000 of equipment during January under a one-year warranty. The cost to repair defects under the warranty is estimated at 4% of the sales price. On August 15, a customer required a $100 part replacement plus $50 of labor under the warranty.

Provide the journal entry for (a) the estimated warranty expense on January 31 for January sales and (b) the August 15 warranty work.

PE 11-7B Estimated warranty liability OBJ. 5

EE 11-7 p. 556

Quantas Industries sold $325,000 of consumer electronics during July under a nine-month warranty. The cost to repair defects under the warranty is estimated at 4.5% of the sales price. On November 11, a customer was given $220 cash under terms of the warranty.

Provide the journal entry for (a) the estimated warranty expense on July 31 for July sales and (b) the November 11 cash payment.

566 Chapter 11 Current Liabilities and Payroll

EE 11-8 p. 559 **PE 11-8A Quick ratio** OBJ. 6

Nabors Company reported the following current assets and liabilities for December 31 for two recent years:

	Dec. 31, Current Year	Dec. 31, Previous Year
Cash	$ 650	$ 680
Temporary investments	1,500	1,550
Accounts receivable	700	770
Inventory	1,250	1,400
Accounts payable	2,375	2,000

a. Compute the quick ratio on December 31 of both years.

b. Interpret the company's quick ratio. Is the quick ratio improving or declining?

EE 11-8 p. 559 **PE 11-8B Quick ratio** OBJ. 6

Adieu Company reported the following current assets and liabilities for December 31 for two recent years:

	Dec. 31, Current Year	Dec. 31, Previous Year
Cash	$1,000	$1,140
Temporary investments	1,200	1,400
Accounts receivable	800	910
Inventory	2,200	2,300
Accounts payable	1,875	2,300

a. Compute the quick ratio on December 31 of both years.

b. Interpret the company's quick ratio. Is the quick ratio improving or declining?

Exercises

✓ Total current liabilities, $1,929,750

EX 11-1 Current liabilities OBJ. 1

Bon Nebo Co. sold 25,000 annual subscriptions of *Magazine 20XX* for $85 during December 20Y8. These new subscribers will receive monthly issues, beginning in January 20Y9. In addition, the business had taxable income of $840,000 during the first calendar quarter of 20Y9. The federal tax rate is 40%. A quarterly tax payment will be made on April 12, 20Y9.

Prepare the Current liabilities section of the balance sheet for Bon Nebo Co. on March 31, 20Y9.

EX 11-2 Entries for notes payable OBJ. 1

Cosimo Enterprises issues a $260,000, 45-day, 5% note to Dixon Industries for merchandise inventory.

a. Journalize Cosimo Enterprises' entries to record:
   1. the issuance of the note.
   2. the payment of the note at maturity.

b. Journalize Dixon Industries' entries to record:
   1. the receipt of the note.
   2. the receipt of the payment of the note at maturity.

Chapter 11 Current Liabilities and Payroll 567

EX 11-3 Entries for discounting notes payable
OBJ. 1

Ramsey Company issues an $800,000, 45-day note to Buckner Company for merchandise inventory. Buckner discounts the note at 7%.

a. Journalize Ramsey's entries to record:
  1. the issuance of the note.
  2. the payment of the note at maturity.
b. Journalize Buckner's entries to record:
  1. the receipt of the note.
  2. the receipt of the payment of the note at maturity.

EX 11-4 Evaluating alternative notes
OBJ. 1

A borrower has two alternatives for a loan: (1) issue a $360,000, 60-day, 5% note or (2) issue a $360,000, 60-day note that the creditor discounts at 5%.

a. Calculate the amount of the interest expense for each option.
b. Determine the proceeds received by the borrower in each situation.
c. Which alternative is more favorable to the borrower? Explain.

EX 11-5 Entries for notes payable
OBJ. 1

A business issued a 45-day, 6% note for $210,000 to a creditor on account. Journalize the entries to record (a) the issuance of the note and (b) the payment of the note at maturity, including interest.

EX 11-6 Entries for discounted note payable
OBJ. 1

A business issued a 45-day note for $80,000 to a creditor on account. The note was discounted at 5%. Journalize the entries to record (a) the issuance of the note and (b) the payment of the note at maturity.

EX 11-7 Entries for notes payable
OBJ. 1

Bull City Industries is considering issuing a $100,000, 7% note to a creditor on account.
a. If the note is issued with a 45-day term, journalize the entries to record:
  1. the issuance of the note.
  2. the payment of the note at maturity.
b. If the note is issued with a 90-day term, journalize the entries to record:
  1. the issuance of the note.
  2. the payment of the note at maturity.

✔ a. $4,071

EX 11-8 Current portion of long-term debt
OBJ. 1

PepsiCo, Inc., reported the following information about its long-term debt in the notes to a recent financial statement (in millions):

Long-term debt is comprised of the following:

	December 31	
	Current Year	Previous Year
Total long term-debt	$33,284	$28,897
Less current portion	(4,071)	(5,076)
Long-term debt	$29,213	$23,821

a. How much of the long-term debt was disclosed as a current liability on the current year's December 31 balance sheet?
b. How much did the total current liabilities change between the preceding year and the current year as a result of the current portion of long-term debt?
c. If PepsiCo did not issue additional long-term debt next year, what would be the total long-term debt on December 31 of the upcoming year?

568 Chapter 11 Current Liabilities and Payroll

✔ b. Net pay, $1,055.85

EX 11-9 Calculate payroll   OBJ. 2

An employee earns $25 per hour and 2 times that rate for all hours in excess of 40 hours per week. Assume that the employee worked 48 hours during the week. Assume further that the social security tax rate was 6.0%, the Medicare tax rate was 1.5%, and federal income tax to be withheld was $239.15.

a. Determine the gross pay for the week.
b. Determine the net pay for the week.

✔ Consultant net pay, $2,760.48

EX 11-10 Calculate payroll   OBJ. 2

Breakin Away Company has three employees—a consultant, a computer programmer, and an administrator. The following payroll information is available for each employee:

	Consultant	Computer Programmer	Administrator
Regular earnings rate	$4,000 per week	$60 per hour	$50 per hour
Overtime earnings rate*	Not applicable	1.5 times hourly rate	2 times hourly rate
Number of withholding allowances	2	1	2

*For hourly employees, overtime is paid for hours worked in excess of 40 hours per week.

For the current pay period, the computer programmer worked 50 hours and the administrator worked 48 hours. The federal income tax withheld for all three employees, who are single, can be determined from the wage bracket withholding table in Exhibit 2 in the chapter. Assume further that the social security tax rate was 6.0%, the Medicare tax rate was 1.5%, and one withholding allowance is $75.

Determine the gross pay and the net pay for each of the three employees for the current pay period.

✔ a. (3) Total earnings, $540,000

EX 11-11 Summary payroll data   OBJ. 2, 3

In the following summary of data for a payroll period, some amounts have been intentionally omitted:

Earnings:
 1. At regular rate   ?
 2. At overtime rate $ 80,000
 3. Total earnings   ?
Deductions:
 4. Social security tax   32,400
 5. Medicare tax   8,100
 6. Income tax withheld   135,000
 7. Medical insurance   18,900
 8. Union dues   ?
 9. Total deductions   201,150
10. Net amount paid   338,850
Accounts debited:
11. Factory Wages   285,000
12. Sales Salaries   ?
13. Office Salaries   120,000

a. Calculate the amounts omitted in lines (1), (3), (8), and (12).
b. Journalize the entry to record the payroll accrual.
c. Journalize the entry to record the payment of the payroll.

✔ a. $45,600

EX 11-12 Payroll tax entries   OBJ. 3

According to a summary of the payroll of Guthrie Co., $560,000 was subject to the 6.0% social security tax and the 1.5% Medicare tax. Also, $60,000 was subject to state and federal unemployment taxes.

a. Calculate the employer's payroll taxes, using the following rates: state unemployment, 5.4%; federal unemployment, 0.6%.
b. Journalize the entry to record the accrual of payroll taxes.

EX 11-13 Payroll entries   OBJ. 3

The payroll register for Gamble Company for the week ended April 29 indicated the following:

Salaries	$1,250,000
Social security tax withheld	75,000
Medicare tax withheld	18,750
Federal income tax withheld	250,000

In addition, state and federal unemployment taxes were calculated at the rate of 5.4% and 0.6%, respectively, on $225,000 of salaries.

a. Journalize the entry to record the payroll for the week of April 29.
b. Journalize the entry to record the payroll tax expense incurred for the week of April 29.

EX 11-14 Payroll entries   OBJ. 3

Urban Window Company had gross wages of $320,000 during the week ended July 15. The amount of wages subject to social security tax was $320,000, while the amount of wages subject to federal and state unemployment taxes was $40,000. Tax rates are as follows:

Social security	6.0%
Medicare	1.5%
State unemployment	5.4%
Federal unemployment	0.6%

The total amount withheld from employee wages for federal taxes was $75,200.

a. Journalize the entry to record the payroll for the week of July 15.
b. Journalize the entry to record the payroll tax expense incurred for the week of July 15.

EX 11-15 Payroll internal control procedures   OBJ. 3

Big Howie's Hot Dog Stand is a fast-food restaurant specializing in hot dogs and hamburgers. The store employs 8 full-time and 12 part-time workers. The store's weekly payroll averages $5,600 for all 20 workers.

Big Howie's Hot Dog Stand uses a personal computer to assist in preparing paychecks. Each week, the store's accountant collects employee time cards and enters the hours worked into the payroll program. The payroll program calculates each employee's pay and prints a paycheck. The accountant uses a check-signing machine to sign the paychecks. Next, the restaurant's owner authorizes the transfer of funds from the restaurant's regular bank account to the payroll account.

For the week of May 12, the accountant accidentally recorded 100 hours worked instead of 40 hours for one of the full-time employees.

Does Big Howie's Hot Dog Stand have internal controls in place to catch this error? If so, how will this error be detected?

EX 11-16 Internal control procedures   OBJ. 3

Dave's Scooters is a small manufacturer of specialty scooters. The company employs 14 production workers and four administrative persons. The following procedures are used to process the company's weekly payroll:

a. Whenever an employee receives a pay raise, the supervisor must fill out a wage adjustment form, which is signed by the company president. This form is used to change the employee's wage rate in the payroll system.

b. All employees are required to record their hours worked by clocking in and out on a time clock. Employees must clock out for lunch break. Due to congestion around the time clock area at lunch time, management has not objected to having one employee clock in and out for an entire department.

c. Whenever a salaried employee is terminated, Personnel authorizes Payroll to remove the employee from the payroll system. However, this procedure is not required when

(*Continued*)

570 Chapter 11 Current Liabilities and Payroll

an hourly worker is fired. Hourly employees only receive a paycheck if their time cards show hours worked. The computer automatically drops an employee from the payroll system when that employee has six consecutive weeks with no hours worked.

d. Paychecks are signed using a check-signing machine. This machine is located in the main office so that it can be easily accessed by anyone needing a check signed.

e. Dave's Scooters maintains a separate checking account for payroll checks. Each week the total net pay for all employees is transferred from the company's regular bank account to the payroll account.

State whether each of the procedures is appropriate or inappropriate, after considering the principles of internal control. If a procedure is inappropriate, describe the appropriate procedure.

EX 11-17 Accrued vacation pay   OBJ. 4

A business provides its employees with varying amounts of vacation per year, depending on the length of employment. The estimated amount of the current year's vacation pay is $54,000.

a. Journalize the adjusting entry required on January 31, the end of the first month of the current year, to record the accrued vacation pay.

b. How is the vacation pay reported on the company's balance sheet? When is this amount removed from the company's balance sheet?

EX 11-18 Pension plan entries   OBJ. 4

Yuri Co. operates a chain of gift shops. The company maintains a defined contribution pension plan for its employees. The plan requires quarterly installments to be paid to the funding agent, Whims Funds, by the fifteenth of the month following the end of each quarter. Assume that the pension cost is $365,000 for the quarter ended December 31.

a. Journalize the entries to record the accrued pension liability on December 31 and the payment to the funding agent on January 15.

b. How does a defined contribution plan differ from a defined benefit plan?

EX 11-19 Defined benefit pension plan terms   OBJ. 4

In a recent year's financial statements, Procter & Gamble showed an unfunded pension liability of $5,599 million and a periodic pension cost of $434 million.

Explain the meaning of the $5,599 million unfunded pension liability and the $434 million periodic pension cost.

EX 11-20 Accrued product warranty   OBJ. 5

Parker Manufacturing Co. warrants its products for one year. The estimated product warranty is 2.5% of sales. Assume that sales were $600,000 for January. In February, a customer received warranty repairs requiring $200 of parts and $110 of labor.

a. Journalize the adjusting entry required at January 31, the end of the first month of the current fiscal year, to record the accrued product warranty.

b. Journalize the entry to record the warranty work provided in February.

EX 11-21 Accrued product warranty   OBJ. 5

General Motors Corporation (GM) disclosed estimated product warranty payable for comparative years as follows:

	(in millions)	
	Year 2	Year 1
Current estimated product warranty payable	$3,059	$2,884
Noncurrent estimated product warranty payable	4,327	4,147
Total	$7,386	$7,031

Presume that GM's sales were $135,592 million in Year 2 and that the total paid on warranty claims during Year 2 was $3,000 million.

a. ✏ Why are short- and long-term estimated warranty liabilities disclosed separately?
b. Provide the journal entry for the Year 2 product warranty expense.
c. What two conditions must be met in order for a product warranty liability to be reported in the financial statements?

EX 11-22 Contingent liabilities OBJ. 5

Several months ago, Ayers Industries Inc. experienced a hazardous materials spill at one of its plants. As a result, the Environmental Protection Agency (EPA) fined the company $240,000. The company is contesting the fine. In addition, an employee is seeking $220,000 in damages related to the spill. Finally, a homeowner has sued the company for $310,000. The homeowner lives 35 miles from the plant but believes that the incident has reduced the home's resale value by $310,000.

Ayers' legal counsel believes that it is probable that the EPA fine will stand. In addition, counsel indicates that an out-of-court settlement of $125,000 has recently been reached with the employee. The final papers will be signed next week. Counsel believes that the homeowner's case is much weaker and will be decided in favor of Ayers. Other litigation related to the spill is possible, but the damage amounts are uncertain.

a. Journalize the contingent liabilities associated with the hazardous materials spill. Use the account "Damage Awards and Fines" to recognize the expense for the period.
b. ✏ Prepare a note disclosure relating to this incident.

EX 11-23 Quick ratio OBJ. 6

✓ a. Current year: 1.2

Gmeiner Co. had the following current assets and liabilities on December 31 of two recent years:

	Current Year	Previous Year
Current assets:		
Cash	$ 486,000	$ 500,000
Accounts receivable	210,000	200,000
Inventory	375,000	350,000
Total current assets	$1,071,000	$1,050,000
Current liabilities:		
Current portion of long-term debt	$ 145,000	$ 110,000
Accounts payable	175,000	150,000
Accrued and other current liabilities	260,000	240,000
Total current liabilities	$ 580,000	$ 500,000

a. Determine the quick ratio for December 31 of both years.
b. ✏ Interpret the change in the quick ratio between the two balance sheet dates.

EX 11-24 Quick ratio OBJ. 6

✓ a. Apple, 1.0

The current assets and current liabilities for Apple Inc. and HP, Inc., are as follows at the end of a recent fiscal period:

	Apple Inc. (in millions)	HP, Inc. (in millions)
Current assets:		
Cash and cash equivalents	$21,120	$17,433
Short-term investments	20,481	0
Accounts receivable	35,889	16,281
Inventories	2,349	6,485
Other current assets*	9,539	11,588
Total current assets	$89,378	$51,787
Current liabilities:		
Accounts payable	$60,671	$32,418
Accrued and other current liabilities	19,939	9,773
Total current liabilities	$80,610	$42,191

*These represent prepaid expense and other nonquick current assets.

(*Continued*)

572 Chapter 11 Current Liabilities and Payroll

a. Determine the quick ratio for both companies. Round to one decimal place.
b. Interpret the quick ratio difference between the two companies.

Problems: Series A

PR 11-1A Liability transactions
OBJ. 1, 5

The following items were selected from among the transactions completed by O'Donnel Co. during the current year:

Jan. 10. Purchased merchandise on account from Laine Co., $240,000, terms n/30.
Feb. 9. Issued a 30-day, 4% note for $240,000 to Laine Co., on account.
Mar. 11. Paid Laine Co. the amount owed on the note of February 9.
May 1. Borrowed $160,000 from Tabata Bank, issuing a 45-day, 5% note.
June 1. Purchased tools by issuing a $180,000, 60-day note to Gibala Co., which discounted the note at the rate of 5%.
15. Paid Tabata Bank the interest due on the note of May 1 and renewed the loan by issuing a new 45-day, 7% note for $160,000. (Journalize both the debit and credit to the notes payable account.)
July 30. Paid Tabata Bank the amount due on the note of June 15.
30. Paid Gibala Co. the amount due on the note of June 1.
Dec. 1. Purchased office equipment from Warick Co. for $400,000, paying $100,000 and issuing a series of ten 5% notes for $30,000 each, coming due at 30-day intervals.
15. Settled a product liability lawsuit with a customer for $260,000, payable in January. O'Donnel accrued the loss in a litigation claims payable account.
31. Paid the amount due Warick Co. on the first note in the series issued on December 1.

Instructions
1. Journalize the transactions.
2. Journalize the adjusting entry for each of the following accrued expenses at the end of the current year:
   a. Product warranty cost, $23,000.
   b. Interest on the nine remaining notes owed to Warick Co.

PR 11-2A Entries for payroll and payroll taxes
OBJ. 2, 3

✔ 1. (b) Dr. Payroll Tax Expense, $60,675

The following information about the payroll for the week ended December 30 was obtained from the records of Pharrell Co.:

Salaries:		Deductions:	
Sales salaries	$402,000	Income tax withheld	$135,975
Warehouse salaries	210,000	Social security tax withheld	46,620
Office salaries	165,000	Medicare tax withheld	11,655
	$777,000	Retirement savings	17,094
		Group insurance	13,986
			$225,330

Tax rates assumed:
   Social security, 6%
   Medicare, 1.5%
   State unemployment (employer only), 5.4%
   Federal unemployment (employer only), 0.6%

Instructions

1. Assuming that the payroll for the last week of the year is to be paid on December 31, journalize the following entries:

   a. December 30, to record the payroll.

   b. December 30, to record the employer's payroll taxes on the payroll to be paid on December 31. Of the total payroll for the last week of the year, $40,000 is subject to unemployment compensation taxes.

2. Assuming that the payroll for the last week of the year is to be paid on January 5 of the following fiscal year, journalize the following entries:

   a. December 30, to record the payroll.

   b. January 5, to record the employer's payroll taxes on the payroll to be paid on January 5. Because it is a new fiscal year, all salaries are subject to unemployment compensation taxes.

PR 11-3A   Wage and tax statement data on employer FICA tax   OBJ. 2, 3

✓ 2. (e) $28,450.80

Ehrlich Co. began business on January 2, 20Y8. Salaries were paid to employees on the last day of each month, and social security tax, Medicare tax, and federal income tax were withheld in the required amounts. An employee who is hired in the middle of the month receives half the monthly salary for that month. All required payroll tax reports were filed, and the correct amount of payroll taxes was remitted by the company for the calendar year. Early in 20Y9, before the Wage and Tax Statements (Form W-2) could be prepared for distribution to employees and for filing with the Social Security Administration, the employees' earnings records were inadvertently destroyed.

None of the employees resigned or were discharged during the year, and there were no changes in salary rates. The social security tax was withheld at the rate of 6.0% and Medicare tax at the rate of 1.5%. Data on dates of employment, salary rates, and employees' income taxes withheld, which are summarized as follows, were obtained from personnel records and payroll records:

Employee	Date First Employed	Monthly Salary	Monthly Income Tax Withheld
Arnett	Nov. 16	$ 5,500	$ 944
Cruz	Jan. 2	4,800	833
Edwards	Oct. 1	8,000	1,592
Harvin	Dec. 1	6,000	1,070
Nicks	Feb. 1	10,000	2,350
Shiancoe	Mar. 1	11,600	2,600
Ward	Nov. 16	5,220	876

Instructions

1. Calculate the amounts to be reported on each employee's Wage and Tax Statement (Form W-2) for 20Y8, arranging the data in the following form:

Employee	Gross Earnings	Federal Income Tax Withheld	Social Security Tax Withheld	Medicare Tax Withheld

2. Calculate the following employer payroll taxes for the year: (a) social security; (b) Medicare; (c) state unemployment compensation at 5.4% on the first $10,000 of each employee's earnings; (d) federal unemployment compensation at 0.6% on the first $10,000 of each employee's earnings; (e) total.

574 Chapter 11 Current Liabilities and Payroll

PR 11-4A Payroll register
OBJ. 2, 3

✓ 1. Total net pay
$15,424.12

The following data for Throwback Industries Inc. relate to the payroll for the week ended December 9, 20Y8:

Employee	Hours Worked	Hourly Rate	Weekly Salary	Federal Income Tax	Retirement Savings
Aaron	46	$68.00		$750.20	$100
Cobb	41	62.00		537.68	110
Clemente	48	70.00		832.64	120
DiMaggio	35	56.00		366.04	0
Griffey, Jr.	45	62.00		641.84	130
Mantle			$1,800	342.45	120
Robinson	36	54.00		382.56	130
Williams			2,000	398.24	125
Vaughn	42	62.00		584.72	50

Employees Mantle and Williams are office staff, and all of the other employees are sales personnel. All sales personnel are paid 1½ times the regular rate for all hours in excess of 40 hours per week. The social security tax rate is 6.0%, and Medicare tax is 1.5% of each employee's annual earnings. The next payroll check to be used is No. 901.

Instructions

1. Prepare a payroll register for Throwback Industries Inc. for the week ended December 9, 20Y8. Use the following columns for the payroll register: Employee, Total Hours, Regular Earnings, Overtime Earnings, Total Earnings, Social Security Tax, Medicare Tax, Federal Income Tax, Retirement Savings, Total Deductions, Net Pay, Ck. No., Sales Salaries Expense, and Office Salaries Expense.
2. Journalize the entry to record the payroll for the week.

PR 11-5A Payroll accounts and year-end entries
OBJ. 2, 3, 4

The following accounts, with the balances indicated, appear in the ledger of Garcon Co. on December 1 of the current year:

211	Salaries Payable	—	218	Retirement Savings Deductions Payable	$ 3,400
212	Social Security Tax Payable	$ 9,273	219	Medical Insurance Payable	27,000
213	Medicare Tax Payable	2,318	411	Operations Salaries Expense	950,000
214	Employees Federal Income Tax Payable	15,455	511	Officers Salaries Expense	600,000
215	Employees State Income Tax Payable	13,909	512	Office Salaries Expense	150,000
216	State Unemployment Tax Payable	1,400	519	Payroll Tax Expense	137,951
217	Federal Unemployment Tax Payable	500			

The following transactions relating to payroll, payroll deductions, and payroll taxes occurred during December:

Dec. 2. Issued Check No. 410 for $3,400 to Jay Bank to invest in a retirement savings account for employees.

2. Issued Check No. 411 to Jay Bank for $27,046, in payment of $9,273 of social security tax, $2,318 of Medicare tax, and $15,455 of employees' federal income tax due.

13. Journalized the entry to record the biweekly payroll. A summary of the payroll record follows:

Salary distribution:		
Operations	$43,200	
Officers	27,200	
Office	6,800	$77,200
Deductions:		
Social security tax	$ 4,632	
Medicare tax	1,158	
Federal income tax withheld	15,440	
State income tax withheld	3,474	
Retirement savings deductions	1,700	
Medical insurance deductions	4,500	30,904
Net amount		$46,296

Dec. 13. Issued Check No. 420 in payment of the net amount of the biweekly payroll to fund the payroll bank account.

13. Journalized the entry to record payroll taxes on employees' earnings of December 13: social security tax, $4,632; Medicare tax, $1,158; state unemployment tax, $350; federal unemployment tax, $125.

16. Issued Check No. 424 to Jay Bank for $27,020, in payment of $9,264 of social security tax, $2,316 of Medicare tax, and $15,440 of employees' federal income tax due.

19. Issued Check No. 429 to Sims-Walker Insurance Company for $31,500, in payment of the semiannual premium on the group medical insurance policy.

27. Journalized the entry to record the biweekly payroll. A summary of the payroll record follows:

Salary distribution:		
Operations	$42,800	
Officers	28,000	
Office	7,000	$77,800
Deductions:		
Social security tax	$ 4,668	
Medicare tax	1,167	
Federal income tax withheld	15,404	
State income tax withheld	3,501	
Retirement savings deductions	1,700	26,440
Net amount		$51,360

27. Issued Check No. 541 in payment of the net amount of the biweekly payroll to fund the payroll bank account.

27. Journalized the entry to record payroll taxes on employees' earnings of December 27: social security tax, $4,668; Medicare tax, $1,167; state unemployment tax, $225; federal unemployment tax, $75.

27. Issued Check No. 543 for $20,884 to State Department of Revenue in payment of employees' state income tax due on December 31.

31. Issued Check No. 545 to Jay Bank for $3,400 to invest in a retirement savings account for employees.

31. Paid $45,000 to the employee pension plan. The annual pension cost is $60,000. (Record both the payment and unfunded pension liability.)

Instructions

1. Journalize the transactions.
2. Journalize the following adjusting entries on December 31:
   a. Salaries accrued: operations salaries, $8,560; officers salaries, $5,600; office salaries, $1,400. The payroll taxes are immaterial and are not accrued.
   b. Vacation pay, $15,000.

Problems: Series B

PR 11-1B Liability transactions   OBJ. 1, 5

The following items were selected from among the transactions completed by Aston Martin Inc. during the current year:

Apr. 15. Borrowed $225,000 from Audi Company, issuing a 30-day, 6% note for that amount.

May 1. Purchased equipment by issuing a $320,000, 180-day note to Spyder Manufacturing Co., which discounted the note at the rate of 6%.

15. Paid Audi Company the interest due on the note of April 15 and renewed the loan by issuing a new 60-day, 8% note for $225,000. (Record both the debit and credit to the notes payable account.)

July 14. Paid Audi Company the amount due on the note of May 15.

(Continued)

576 Chapter 11 Current Liabilities and Payroll

Aug. 16. Purchased merchandise on account from Exige Co., $90,000, terms, n/30.

Sept. 15. Issued a 45-day, 6% note for $90,000 to Exige Co., on account.

Oct. 28. Paid Spyder Manufacturing Co. the amount due on the note of May 1.

30. Paid Exige Co. the amount owed on the note of September 15.

Nov. 16. Purchased store equipment from Gallardo Co. for $450,000, paying $50,000 and issuing a series of twenty 9% notes for $20,000 each, coming due at 30-day intervals.

Dec. 16. Paid the amount due Gallardo Co. on the first note in the series issued on November 16.

28. Settled a personal injury lawsuit with a customer for $87,500, to be paid in January. Aston Martin Inc. accrued the loss in a litigation claims payable account.

Instructions

1. Journalize the transactions.
2. Journalize the adjusting entry for each of the following accrued expenses at the end of the current year:
   a. Product warranty cost, $26,800.
   b. Interest on the 19 remaining notes owed to Gallardo Co.

PR 11-2B Entries for payroll and payroll taxes   OBJ. 2, 3

✓ 1. (b) Dr. Payroll Tax Expense, $90,675

The following information about the payroll for the week ended December 30 was obtained from the records of Saine Co.:

Salaries:		Deductions:	
Sales salaries	$ 625,000	Income tax withheld	$232,260
Warehouse salaries	240,000	Social security tax withheld	71,100
Office salaries	320,000	Medicare tax withheld	17,775
	$1,185,000	Retirement savings	35,500
		Group insurance	53,325
			$409,960

Tax rates assumed:
  Social security, 6%
  Medicare, 1.5%
  State unemployment (employer only), 5.4%
  Federal unemployment (employer only), 0.6%

Instructions

1. Assuming that the payroll for the last week of the year is to be paid on December 31, journalize the following entries:
   a. December 30, to record the payroll.
   b. December 30, to record the employer's payroll taxes on the payroll to be paid on December 31. Of the total payroll for the last week of the year, $30,000 is subject to unemployment compensation taxes.
2. Assuming that the payroll for the last week of the year is to be paid on January 4 of the following fiscal year, journalize the following entries:
   a. December 30, to record the payroll.
   b. January 4, to record the employer's payroll taxes on the payroll to be paid on January 4. Because it is a new fiscal year, all $1,185,000 in salaries is subject to unemployment compensation taxes.

PR 11-3B Wage and tax statement data and employer FICA tax   OBJ. 2, 3

✓ 2. (e) $25,017.38

Excel

Jocame Inc. began business on January 2, 20Y7. Salaries were paid to employees on the last day of each month, and social security tax, Medicare tax, and federal income tax were withheld in the required amounts. An employee who is hired in the middle of the month receives half the monthly salary for that month. All required payroll tax reports were filed, and the correct amount of payroll taxes was remitted by the company for the calendar year. Early in 20Y8, before the Wage and Tax Statements (Form W-2) could be prepared for distribution to employees and for filing with the Social Security Administration, the employees' earnings records were inadvertently destroyed.

None of the employees resigned or were discharged during the year, and there were no changes in salary rates. The social security tax was withheld at the rate of 6.0% and Medicare tax at the rate of 1.5% on salary. Data on dates of employment, salary rates, and employees' income taxes withheld, which are summarized as follows, were obtained from personnel records and payroll records:

Employee	Date First Employed	Monthly Salary	Monthly Income Tax Withheld
Addai	July 16	$ 8,160	$1,704
Kasay	June 1	3,600	533
McGahee	Feb. 16	6,420	1,238
Moss	Jan. 1	4,600	783
Stewart	Dec. 1	4,500	758
Tolbert	Nov. 16	3,250	446
Wells	May 1	10,500	2,359

Instructions

1. Calculate the amounts to be reported on each employee's Wage and Tax Statement (Form W-2) for 20Y7, arranging the data in the following form:

Employee	Gross Earnings	Federal Income Tax Withheld	Social Security Tax Withheld	Medicare Tax Withheld

2. Calculate the following employer payroll taxes for the year: (a) social security; (b) Medicare; (c) state unemployment compensation at 5.4% on the first $10,000 of each employee's earnings; (d) federal unemployment compensation at 0.6% on the first $10,000 of each employee's earnings; (e) total.

PR 11-4B Payroll register OBJ. 2, 3

✔ 1. Total net pay, $16,592.58

The following data for Flexco Inc. relate to the payroll for the week ended December 9, 20Y8:

Employee	Hours Worked	Hourly Rate	Weekly Salary	Federal Income Tax	Retirement Savings
Carlton	52	$50.00		$667.00	$ 60
Grove			$4,000	860.00	100
Johnson	36	52.00		355.68	0
Koufax	45	58.00		578.55	44
Maddux	37	45.00		349.65	62
Seaver			3,200	768.00	120
Spahn	46	52.00		382.20	0
Winn	48	50.00		572.00	75
Young	43	54.00		480.60	80

Employees Grove and Seaver are office staff, and all of the other employees are sales personnel. All sales personnel are paid 1½ times the regular rate for all hours in excess of 40 hours per week. The social security tax rate is 6.0% of each employee's annual earnings, and Medicare tax is 1.5% of each employee's annual earnings. The next payroll check to be used is No. 328.

Instructions

1. Prepare a payroll register for Flexco Inc. for the week ended December 9, 20Y8. Use the following columns for the payroll register: Employee, Total Hours, Regular Earnings, Overtime Earnings, Total Earnings, Social Security Tax, Medicare Tax, Federal Income Tax, Retirement Savings, Total Deductions, Net Pay, Ck. No., Sales Salaries Expense, and Office Salaries Expense.

2. Journalize the entry to record the payroll for the week.

PR 11-5B Payroll accounts and year-end entries OBJ. 2, 3, 4

The following accounts, with the balances indicated, appear in the ledger of Codigo Co. on December 1 of the current year:

101	Salaries Payable	—	108	Retirement Savings Deductions Payable	$ 2,300
102	Social Security Tax Payable	$2,913	109	Medical Insurance Payable	2,520
103	Medicare Tax Payable	728	201	Sales Salaries Expense	700,000
104	Employees Federal Income Tax Payable	4,490	301	Officers Salaries Expense	340,000
105	Employees State Income Tax Payable	4,078	401	Office Salaries Expense	125,000
106	State Unemployment Tax Payable	1,260	408	Payroll Tax Expense	59,491
107	Federal Unemployment Tax Payable	360			

The following transactions relating to payroll, payroll deductions, and payroll taxes occurred during December:

Dec. 1. Issued Check No. 815 to Aberderas Insurance Company for $2,520, in payment of the semiannual premium on the group medical insurance policy.

1. Issued Check No. 816 to Alvarez Bank for $8,131, in payment for $2,913 of social security tax, $728 of Medicare tax, and $4,490 of employees' federal income tax due.

2. Issued Check No. 817 for $2,300 to Alvarez Bank to invest in a retirement savings account for employees.

12. Journalized the entry to record the biweekly payroll. A summary of the payroll record follows:

Salary distribution:
Sales	$14,500	
Officers	7,100	
Office	2,600	$24,200

Deductions:
Social security tax	$ 1,452	
Medicare tax	363	
Federal income tax withheld	4,308	
State income tax withheld	1,089	
Retirement savings deductions	1,150	
Medical insurance deductions	420	8,782
Net amount		$15,418

12. Issued Check No. 822 in payment of the net amount of the biweekly payroll to fund the payroll bank account.

12. Journalized the entry to record payroll taxes on employees' earnings of December 12: social security tax, $1,452; Medicare tax, $363; state unemployment tax, $315; federal unemployment tax, $90.

15. Issued Check No. 830 to Alvarez Bank for $7,938, in payment of $2,904 of social security tax, $726 of Medicare tax, and $4,308 of employees' federal income tax due.

26. Journalized the entry to record the biweekly payroll. A summary of the payroll record follows:

Salary distribution:
Sales	$14,250	
Officers	7,250	
Office	2,750	$24,250

Deductions:
Social security tax	$ 1,455	
Medicare tax	364	
Federal income tax withheld	4,317	
State income tax withheld	1,091	
Retirement savings deductions	1,150	8,377
Net amount		$15,873

26. Issued Check No. 840 for the net amount of the biweekly payroll to fund the payroll bank account.

Dec. 26. Journalized the entry to record payroll taxes on employees' earnings of December 26: social security tax, $1,455; Medicare tax, $364; state unemployment tax, $150; federal unemployment tax, $40.

30. Issued Check No. 851 for $6,258 to State Department of Revenue, in payment of employees' state income tax due on December 31.

30. Issued Check No. 852 to Alvarez Bank for $2,300 to invest in a retirement savings account for employees.

31. Paid $55,400 to the employee pension plan. The annual pension cost is $65,500. (Record both the payment and the unfunded pension liability.)

Instructions

1. Journalize the transactions.
2. Journalize the following adjusting entries on December 31:
   a. Salaries accrued: sales salaries, $4,275; officers salaries, $2,175; office salaries, $825. The payroll taxes are immaterial and are not accrued.
   b. Vacation pay, $13,350.

Comprehensive Problem 3

✔ 5. Total assets, $3,569,290

Selected transactions completed by Kornett Company during its first fiscal year ended December 31, 20Y8, were as follows:

Jan. 3. Issued a check to establish a petty cash fund of $4,500.

Feb. 26. Replenished the petty cash fund, based on the following summary of petty cash receipts: office supplies, $1,680; miscellaneous selling expense, $570; miscellaneous administrative expense, $880.

Apr. 14. Purchased $31,300 of merchandise on account, terms, n/30. The perpetual inventory system is used to account for inventory.

May 13. Paid the invoice of April 14.

17. Received cash from daily cash sales for $21,200. The amount indicated by the cash register was $21,240.

June 2. Received a 60-day, 8% note for $180,000 on the Ryanair account.

Aug. 1. Received amount owed on June 2 note plus interest at the maturity date.

24. Received $7,600 on the Finley account and wrote off the remainder owed on a $9,000 accounts receivable balance. (The allowance method is used in accounting for uncollectible receivables.)

Sept. 15. Reinstated the Finley account written off on August 24 and received $1,400 cash in full payment.

15. Purchased land by issuing a $670,000, 90-day note to Zahorik Co., which discounted it at 9%.

Oct. 17. Sold office equipment in exchange for $135,000 cash plus receipt of a $100,000, 90-day, 9% note. The equipment had a cost of $320,000 and accumulated depreciation of $64,000 as of October 17.

(Continued)

Nov. 30. Journalized the monthly payroll for November, based on the following data:

Salaries		Deductions	
Sales salaries	$135,000	Income tax withheld	$39,266
Office salaries	77,250	Social security tax withheld	12,735
	$212,250	Medicare tax withheld	3,184

Unemployment tax rates:
- State unemployment 5.4%
- Federal unemployment 0.6%

Amount subject to unemployment taxes:
- State unemployment $5,000
- Federal unemployment 5,000

30. Journalized the employer's payroll taxes on the payroll.

Dec. 14. Journalized the payment of the September 15 note at maturity.

31. The pension cost for the year was $190,400, of which $139,700 was paid to the pension plan trustee.

Instructions

1. Journalize the selected transactions.
2. Based on the following data, prepare a bank reconciliation for December of the current year:
   a. Balance according to the bank statement at December 31, $283,000.
   b. Balance according to the ledger at December 31, $245,410.
   c. Checks outstanding at December 31, $68,540.
   d. Deposit in transit, not recorded by bank, $29,500.
   e. Bank debit memo for service charges, $750.
   f. A check for $12,700 in payment of an invoice was incorrectly recorded in the accounts as $12,000.
3. Based on the bank reconciliation prepared in (2), journalize the entry or entries to be made by Kornett Company.
4. Based on the following selected data, journalize the adjusting entries as of December 31 of the current year:
   a. Estimated uncollectible accounts at December 31, $16,000, based on an aging of accounts receivable. The balance of Allowance for Doubtful Accounts at December 31 was $2,000 (debit).
   b. The physical inventory on December 31 indicated an inventory shrinkage of $3,300.
   c. Prepaid insurance expired during the year, $22,820.
   d. Office supplies used during the year, $3,920.
   e. Depreciation is computed as follows:

Asset	Cost	Residual Value	Acquisition Date	Useful Life in Years	Depreciation Method Used
Buildings	$900,000	$ 0	January 2	50	Double-declining-balance
Office Equip.	246,000	26,000	January 3	5	Straight-line
Store Equip.	112,000	12,000	July 1	10	Straight-line

   f. A patent costing $48,000 when acquired on January 2 has a remaining legal life of 10 years and is expected to have value for eight years.
   g. The cost of mineral rights was $546,000. Of the estimated deposit of 910,000 tons of ore, 50,000 tons were mined and sold during the year.
   h. Vacation pay expense for December, $10,500.
   i. A product warranty was granted beginning December 1 and covering a one-year period. The estimated cost is 4% of sales, which totaled $1,900,000 in December.
   j. Interest was accrued on the note receivable received on October 17.

5. Based on the following information and the post-closing trial balance that follows, prepare a balance sheet in report form at December 31 of the current year:

The merchandise inventory is stated at cost by the LIFO method.
The product warranty payable is a current liability.

Vacation pay payable:
    Current liability $7,140
    Long-term liability   3,360

The unfunded pension liability is a long-term liability.

Notes payable:
    Current liability $ 70,000
    Long-term liability   630,000

Kornett Company
Post-Closing Trial Balance
December 31, 20Y8

	Debit Balances	Credit Balances
Petty Cash	4,500	
Cash	243,960	
Notes Receivable	100,000	
Accounts Receivable	470,000	
Allowance for Doubtful Accounts		16,000
Merchandise Inventory	320,000	
Interest Receivable	1,875	
Prepaid Insurance	45,640	
Office Supplies	13,390	
Land	654,925	
Buildings	900,000	
Accumulated Depreciation—Buildings		36,000
Office Equipment	246,000	
Accumulated Depreciation—Office Equipment		44,000
Store Equipment	112,000	
Accumulated Depreciation—Store Equipment		5,000
Mineral Rights	546,000	
Accumulated Depletion		30,000
Patents	42,000	
Social Security Tax Payable		25,470
Medicare Tax Payable		4,710
Employees Federal Income Tax Payable		40,000
State Unemployment Tax Payable		270
Federal Unemployment Tax Payable		30
Salaries Payable		157,000
Accounts Payable		131,600
Interest Payable		28,000
Product Warranty Payable		76,000
Vacation Pay Payable		10,500
Unfunded Pension Liability		50,700
Notes Payable		700,000
J. Kornett, Capital		2,345,010
	3,700,290	3,700,290

Cases & Projects

CP 11-1 Ethics in Action

Tonya Latirno is a staff accountant for Cannally and Kennedy, a local CPA firm. For the past 10 years, the firm has given employees a year-end bonus equal to two weeks' salary. On November 15, the firm's management team announced that there would be no annual bonus this year. Because of the firm's long history of giving a year-end bonus, Tonya and her coworkers had come to expect the bonus and believed that Cannally and Kennedy had breached an implicit agreement by discontinuing the bonus. As a result, Tonya decided that she would make up for the lost bonus by working an extra six hours of overtime per week for the rest of the year. Cannally and Kennedy's policy is to pay overtime at 150% of straight time.

Tonya's supervisor was surprised to see overtime being reported, because there is generally very little additional or unusual client service demands at the end of the calendar year. However, the overtime was not questioned, because employees are on the "honor system" in reporting their work hours.

1. Is Cannally and Kennedy acting in an ethical manner by eliminating the bonus? Explain your answer.
2. Is Tonya behaving ethically by making up the bonus with unnecessary overtime? Why or why not?

CP 11-2 Ethics in Action

Marvin Turner was discussing summer employment with Tina Song, president of Motown Construction Service:

Tina: I'm glad you're thinking about joining us for the summer. We certainly can use the help.

Marvin: Sounds good. I enjoy outdoor work, and I could use the money to help with next year's school expenses.

Tina: I've got a plan that can help you out on that. As you know, I'll pay you $14 per hour, but in addition, I'd like to pay you with cash. Since you're only working for the summer, it really doesn't make sense for me to go to the trouble of formally putting you on our payroll system. In fact, I do some jobs for my clients on a strictly cash basis, so it would be easy just to pay you that way.

Marvin: Well, that's a bit unusual, but I guess money is money.

Tina: Yeah, not only that, it's tax-free!

Marvin: What do you mean?

Tina: Didn't you know? Any money that you receive in cash is not reported to the IRS on a W-2 form; therefore, the IRS doesn't know about the income—hence, it's the same as tax-free earnings.

a. Why does Tina Song want to conduct business transactions using cash (not check or credit card)?
b. How should Marvin respond to Tina's suggestion?

CP 11-3 Team Activity

In teams, select a public company that interests you. Obtain the company's most recent annual report on Form 10-K. The Form 10-K is a company's annually required filing with the Securities and Exchange Commission (SEC). It includes the company's financial statements and accompanying notes. The Form 10-K can be obtained either (a) by referring to the investor relations section of the company's website or (b) by using the company search feature of the SEC's EDGAR database service found at www.sec.gov/edgar/searchedgar/companysearch.html.

Based on the information in the company's annual report, answer the following questions:

1. What amount of current liabilities does the company report on its balance sheet at the end of the most recent year? What types of current liabilities does the company report?
2. Have current liabilities increased or decreased from the prior year? If so, by what amount?
3. Does the company disclose any contingent liabilities in the notes to the financial statements? If so, briefly describe the nature of these contingent liabilities.
4. How much of the company's long-term debt will come due in the coming year?

CP 11-4 Payroll forms

Payroll accounting involves the use of government-supplied forms to account for payroll taxes. Three common forms are the W-2, Form 940, and Form 941. Form a team with three of your classmates and retrieve copies of each of these forms. They may be obtained from a local IRS office, a library, or the Internet at www.irs.gov (go to forms and publications).

▸ Briefly describe the purpose of each of the three forms.

CP 11-5 Communication

WBM Motorworks is a manufacturer of high-end touring and off-road motorcycles. On November 30, the company was sued by a customer who was injured when the front shock absorber on the WBM Series 3 motorcycle cracked during use. The company conducted a preliminary investigation into the matter during December and found evidence of a manufacturing defect in the shock absorber. While it is uncertain whether the manufacturing defect is the source of the product failure, the company has voluntarily recalled the front shock absorbers on the Series 3 motorcycles. The company is uncertain how the lawsuit will be resolved. Similar lawsuits against other manufacturers have been settled for approximately $2,000,000.

▸ Write a brief memo to the president of WBM Motorworks, U. D. Mach III, discussing how the lawsuit might be reported in the financial statements.

CP 11-6 Recognizing pension expense

The annual examination of Felton Company's financial statements by its external public accounting firm (auditors) is nearing completion. The following conversation took place between the controller of Felton Company (Francie) and the audit manager from the public accounting firm (Sumana):

Sumana: You know, Francie, we are about to wrap up our audit for this fiscal year. Yet, there is one item still to be resolved.

Francie: What's that?

Sumana: Well, as you know, at the beginning of the year, Felton began a defined benefit pension plan. This plan promises your employees an annual payment when they retire, using a formula based on their salaries at retirement and their years of service. I believe that a pension expense should be recognized this year, equal to the amount of pension earned by your employees.

Francie: Wait a minute. I think you have it all wrong. The company doesn't have a pension expense until it actually pays the pension in cash when the employee retires. After all, some of these employees may not reach retirement, and if they don't, the company doesn't owe them anything.

Sumana: You're not really seeing this the right way. The pension is earned by your employees during their working years. You actually make the payment much later—when they retire. It's like one long accrual—much like incurring wages in one period and paying them in the next. Thus, I think you should recognize the expense in the period the pension is earned by the employees.

Francie: Let me see if I've got this straight. I should recognize an expense this period for something that may or may not be paid to the employees in 20 or 30 years, when they finally retire. How am I supposed to determine what the expense is for the current year? The amount of the final retirement depends on many uncertainties: salary levels, employee longevity, mortality rates, and interest earned on investments to fund the pension. I don't think an amount can be determined even if I accepted your arguments.

▸ Evaluate Sumana's position. Is she right, or is Francie correct?

CP 11-7 Contingent liabilities

Reynolds American, Inc., has numerous pages dedicated to describing contingent liabilities in the notes to recent financial statements. These pages include extensive descriptions of multiple contingent liabilities. Use the Internet to research Reynolds American, Inc., at www.reynoldsamerican.com.

a. ▸ What are the major business units of Reynolds American Inc.?

b. ▸ Based on your understanding of this company, why would Reynolds American require so many pages of contingency disclosure?

CHAPTER 12
Accounting for Partnerships and Limited Liability Companies

Chapters 1–4
Accounting Cycle

Chapter 5
Accounting Systems

| Income Statement | Statement of Owner's Equity | Balance Sheet | Statement of Cash Flows |

Chapter 6 *Accounting for Merchandising Businesses*

Chapter 16 *Cash Flows*

Assets = Liabilities + Owner's Equity

Chapter 8 *Cash*
Chapter 9 *Receivables*
Chapter 7 *Inventories*
Chapter 10 *Fixed and Intangible Assets*
Chapter 15 *Investments*

Chapter 11 *Current Liabilities*
Chapter 14 *Bonds and Notes*

Chapter 12 Partnerships
Chapter 13 *Corporations*

Chapter 17
Financial Statement Analysis

Statement of Partnership Equity

	J. Stone, Capital	C. Mills, Capital	Total
Balance, Jan. 1	$ XXX	$ XXX	$ XXX
Capital additions	XXX	XXX	XXX
Net income	XXX	XXX	XXX
Partner withdrawals	(XXX)	(XXX)	(XXX)
Balance, Dec. 31	$ XXX	$ XXX	$ XXX

Statement of Cash Flows

Cash flows from (used in) operating activities	$XXX
Cash flows from (used in) investing activities	XXX
Cash flows from (used in) financing activities	XXX
Increase (decrease) in cash flows	$XXX
Cash as of January 1, 20Y5	XXX
Cash as of December 31, 20Y5	$XXX

Sales		$XXX
Cost of merchandise sold		XXX
Gross profit		$XXX
Operating expenses:		
Advertising expense	$XXX	
Depreciation expense	XXX	
Amortization expense	XXX	
Depletion expense	XXX	
...	XXX	
...	XXX	
Total operating expenses		XXX
Income from operations		$XXX
Other revenue and expenses		XXX
Net income		$XXX

Balance Sheet

Assets:		
Current assets		$XXX
Property, plant, and equipment		XXX
Intangible assets		XXX
Total assets		$XXX
Liabilities:		
Current liabilities	$XXX	
Long-term liabilities	XXX	
Total liabilities		$XXX
Partners' Equity:		
Jennifer Stone, capital	**$XXX**	
Crystal Mills, capital	**XXX**	
Total partners' equity		**XXX**
Total liabilities and partners' equity		$XXX

CHAPTER 12

Boston Basketball Partners LLC

Boston Basketball Partners (BBP) LLC are the owners of the Boston Celtics NBA basketball franchise. The letters "LLC" stand for *limited liability company*. Unlike sole proprietorships illustrated in prior chapters, an LLC is a business form that normally has multiple owners. BBP LLC is led by Wic Grousbeck, a former venture fund manager from Boston, with the assistance of more than 15 other owners. Grousbeck called investing in the Celtics "a chance of a lifetime." Surprisingly, Grousbeck claims "money would not be the first priority." Even so, *Forbes* estimates the team is now worth $1.2 billion, which is more than three times what BBP LLC originally paid, while ranking the Celtics as the fourth most valuable team in the NBA. So, Grousbeck must be doing something right. Grousbeck and his team have turned their venture capital skills toward the Celtics. Some of their innovations off the court include building a cable partnership, using technology to evaluate seat usage, and adding advertising sponsors.

So why would BBP LLC choose the LLC form of organization?

The entity form chosen by a business has an important impact on the owners' legal liability, taxation, and ability to raise money. The four major forms of business entities discussed in this text are the proprietorship, partnership, limited liability company, and corporation. Proprietorships have been discussed in prior chapters. Partnerships and limited liability companies will be discussed in this chapter, and corporations will be introduced in the next chapter.

Learning Objectives

After studying this chapter, you should be able to:

Example Exercises (EE) are shown in **green**.

Obj. 1 Describe the characteristics of proprietorships, partnerships, and limited liability companies.

Proprietorships, Partnerships, and Limited Liability Companies
- Proprietorships
- Partnerships
- Limited Liability Companies
- Comparing Proprietorships, Partnerships, and Limited Liability Companies

Obj. 2 Describe and illustrate the accounting for forming a partnership and for dividing the net income and net loss of a partnership.

Forming a Partnership and Dividing Income
- Forming a Partnership — EE 12-1
- Dividing Income — EE 12-2

Obj. 3 Describe and illustrate the accounting for partner admission and withdrawal.

Partner Admission and Withdrawal
- Admitting a Partner — EE 12-3
- Withdrawal of a Partner — EE 12-4
- Death of a Partner

Obj. 4 Describe and illustrate the accounting for liquidating a partnership.

Liquidating Partnerships
- Gain on Realization
- Loss on Realization — EE 12-5
- Loss on Realization—Capital Deficiency — EE 12-6

Obj. 5 Prepare the statement of partnership equity.

Statement of Partnership Equity

Obj. 6 Analyze and interpret employee efficiency.

Financial Analysis and Interpretation: Revenue per Employee
- Compute and Analyze Revenue per Employee — EE 12-7

At a Glance 12 Page 608

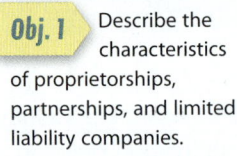

Obj. 1 Describe the characteristics of proprietorships, partnerships, and limited liability companies.

Proprietorships, Partnerships, and Limited Liability Companies

The four most common legal forms for organizing and operating a business are as follows:

- Proprietorship
- Corporation
- Partnership
- Limited liability company

In this section, the characteristics of proprietorships, partnerships, and limited liability companies are described. The characteristics of corporations are described in Chapter 13.

Proprietorships

A *proprietorship* is a company owned by a single individual. The most common proprietorships are professional service providers, such as lawyers, architects, realtors, and physicians.

Characteristics of proprietorships include the following:

- *Simple to form*. There are no legal restrictions or forms to file.
- *No limitation on legal liability*. The owner is personally liable for any debts or legal claims against the business. Thus, creditors can take the personal assets of the owner if the business debts exceed the owner's investment in the company.
- *Not taxable*. For federal income tax purposes, a proprietorship is not taxed. Instead, the proprietorship's income or loss is "passed through" to the owner's individual income tax return.[1]

[1] The proprietor's statement of income is included on Schedule C of the individual 1040 tax return.

- *Limited life.* When the owner dies or retires, the proprietorship ceases to exist.
- *Limited ability to raise capital (funds).* The ability to raise capital (funds) is limited to what the owner can provide from personal resources or through borrowing.

Partnerships

A **partnership** is an association of two or more persons who own and manage a business for profit.[2] Partnerships are less widely used than proprietorships.

Characteristics of a partnership include the following:

> **Note**
>
> A partnership is a nontaxable entity that has a limited life and unlimited liability.

- *Moderately complex to form.* A partnership is often formed with a partnership agreement. A **partnership agreement** includes matters such as amounts to be invested, limits on withdrawals, distributions of income and losses, and admission and withdrawal of partners. Thus, an attorney is often used in forming a partnership.
- *No limitation on legal liability.* The partners are personally liable for any debts or legal claims against the partnership. Therefore, creditors can take the personal assets of the partners if the business debts exceed the partners' investment in the business.
- *Not taxable.* For federal income tax purposes, a partnership is not taxed. Instead, the partnership's income or loss is "passed through" to the partners' individual income tax returns. However, partnerships must still report revenues, expenses, and income or loss annually to the Internal Revenue Service.
- *Limited life.* When a partner dies or retires, the partnership ceases to exist. Likewise, the admission of a new partner dissolves the old partnership, and a new partnership must be formed if operations are to continue.
- *Limited ability to raise capital (funds).* The ability to raise capital (funds) for the partnership is limited to what the partners can provide from personal resources or through borrowing.

In addition to those characteristics, some unique aspects of partnerships are:

- *Co-ownership of partnership property.* The property invested in a partnership by a partner becomes the joint property of all the partners. When a partnership is dissolved, each partner's share of the partnership assets is the balance in his or her capital account.
- *Mutual agency.* Each partner is an agent of the partnership and may act on behalf of the entire partnership. Thus, any liabilities created by one partner become liabilities of all the partners.
- *Participation in income.* Net income and net loss are distributed among the partners according to their partnership agreement. If the partnership agreement does not provide for distribution of income and losses, then income and losses are divided equally among the partners.

Business Connection

BREAKING UP IS HARD TO DO

Former partners of Adam Carolla filed court papers accusing the star of The Adam Carolla Show (adamcarolla.com) of a breach of their partnership agreement. They claimed the partnership agreement gave 30% ownership to Donny Misraje, 10% to Sandy Ganz, and 60% to Carolla. The suit alleges that Carolla began his popular podcast with the help of his partners at a time when future success of the venture was risky and unknown. The former partners claim to have given up jobs, invested money and equipment, and provided expertise to launch the show. Once the show achieved success, the former partners claim Carolla unfairly kicked them out of the partnership. The court will, in part, use the partnership agreement to help settle this dispute. A partnership agreement helps protect the interests of all parties to a business venture.

Source: Radar Staff, "Best Friend Sues Adam Carolla Over Hit Podcast Show," January 18, 2013.

---

[2] The definition of a partnership is included in the Uniform Partnership Act, which has been adopted by most states.

Limited Liability Companies

A **limited liability company (LLC)** is a form of legal entity that provides limited liability to its owners but is treated as a partnership for tax purposes. Thus, the LLC organizational form is popular for small businesses.

Characteristics of an LLC include the following:

- *Moderately complex to form.* An LLC requires an agreement among the owners, who are called members. The *operating agreement* includes matters such as amounts to be invested, limits on withdrawals, distributions of income and losses, and admission and withdrawal of members. An attorney is normally used in forming an LLC.
- *Limited legal liability.* The members have *limited liability* even if they are active in the company. Thus, the members' personal assets are legally protected against creditor claims made against the LLC. That is, only the members' investments in the company are subject to claims of creditors.
- *Not taxable.* An LLC may elect to be treated as a partnership for tax purposes. In this way, income passes through the LLC and is taxed on the individual members' tax returns.[3]
- *Unlimited life.* Most LLC operating agreements specify continuity of life for the LLC, even when a member withdraws or new members join the LLC.
- *Moderate ability to raise capital (funds).* Because of their limited liability, LLCs are attractive to many investors, thus allowing for greater access to capital (funds) than is normally the case in a partnership.

An LLC may elect to operate as a *member-managed* or *manager-managed* company. In a member-managed LLC, individual members may legally bind the LLC, like partners bind a partnership. In a manager-managed LLC, only authorized members may legally bind the LLC. Thus, in a manager-managed LLC, members may share in the income of the LLC without concern for managing the company.

Link to Boston Basketball Partners LLC

BBP LLC is formed as an LLC. The LLC members include individuals and **The Abbey Group**, a real estate development company in Boston.

Comparing Proprietorships, Partnerships, and Limited Liability Companies

Exhibit 1 summarizes the characteristics of proprietorships, partnerships, and limited liability companies.

EXHIBIT 1 — Characteristics of Proprietorships, Partnerships, and Limited Liability Companies

Organizational Form	Complexity of Formation	Legal Liability	Taxation	Limitation on Life of Entity	Access to Capital
Proprietorship	Simple	No limitation	Nontaxable (pass-through) entity	Limited	Limited
Partnership	Moderate	No limitation	Nontaxable (pass-through) entity	Limited	Limited
Limited Liability Company	Moderate	Limited liability	Nontaxable (pass-through) entity by election	Unlimited	Moderate

Business Connection

ORGANIZATIONAL FORMS IN THE ACCOUNTING INDUSTRY

The four major accounting firms, **KPMG LLP**, **Ernst & Young**, **PricewaterhouseCoopers**, and **Deloitte & Touche**, all began as partnerships. This form was legally required due to the theory of mutual agency. That is, the partnership form was thought to create public trust by requiring all partners to be jointly liable and responsible for each other's judgments. In addition, investment in the partnerships was limited to practicing accountants. This prevented any pressures from outside investors affecting professional decisions.

As these firms grew and the risk increased, all of these firms were allowed to change, by law, to limited liability partnerships (LLPs). Thus, while remaining a partnership, the liability of the partners was limited to their investment in the firm. The LLP form is very similar to an LLC, except that investment is restricted to professionals.

---

[3] An LLC may also be taxed as a separate entity. However, doing so would remove these tax benefits, making this a less common election.

Forming a Partnership and Dividing Income

Obj. 2 Describe and illustrate the accounting for forming a partnership and for dividing the net income and net loss of a partnership.

Most of the day-to-day accounting for a partnership or an LLC is similar to that illustrated in earlier chapters. However, the formation, division of net income or net loss, dissolution, and liquidation of partnerships and LLCs give rise to unique transactions.

In the remainder of this chapter, the unique transactions for partnerships and LLCs are described and illustrated. The accounting for an LLC is the same as a partnership, except that the terms *member* and *members' equity* are used rather than *partner* or *owners' capital*. For this reason, the journal entries for an LLC are shown alongside the partnership entries.

Forming a Partnership

In forming a partnership, the investments of each partner are recorded in separate entries. The assets contributed by a partner are debited to the partnership asset accounts. If any liabilities are assumed by the partnership, the partnership liability accounts are credited. The partner's capital account is credited for the net amount.

To illustrate, assume that Joseph Stevens and Earl Foster, owners of competing hardware stores, agree to combine their businesses in a partnership. Stevens agrees to contribute the following:

Cash	$ 7,200	Office equipment	$2,500
Accounts receivable	16,300	Allowance for doubtful accounts	1,500
Merchandise inventory	28,700	Accounts payable	2,600
Store equipment	5,400		

Link to Boston Basketball Partners LLC

BBP LLC announced the completed purchase of the Boston Celtics basketball team on December 31, 2002, for an estimated $360 million.

The entry to record the assets and liabilities contributed by Stevens is as follows:

LLC

Cash	7,200	
Accounts Receivable	16,300	
Merchandise Inventory	28,700	
Store Equipment	5,400	
Office Equipment	2,500	
Allowance for Doubtful Accounts		1,500
Accounts Payable		2,600
Joseph Stevens, Member Equity		56,000

Apr.	1	Cash	7,200	
		Accounts Receivable	16,300	
		Merchandise Inventory	28,700	
		Store Equipment	5,400	
		Office Equipment	2,500	
		Allowance for Doubtful Accounts		1,500
		Accounts Payable		2,600
		Joseph Stevens, Capital		56,000

In the preceding entry, the noncash assets are recorded at values agreed upon by the partners. These values are normally based on current market values. As a result, the previous book value of the assets contributed by the partners normally differs from that recorded by the new partnership.

To illustrate, the store equipment contributed by Stevens may have had a book value of $3,500 in Stevens' ledger (cost of $10,000 less accumulated depreciation of $6,500). However, the store equipment is recorded at its current market value of $5,400 in the preceding entry. The contributions of Foster would be recorded in an entry similar to the entry for Stevens.

Example Exercise 12-1   Journalize Partner's Original Investment   Obj. 2

Reese Howell contributed equipment, inventory, and $34,000 cash to a partnership. The equipment had a book value of $23,000 and a market value of $29,000. The inventory had a book value of $60,000 but only had a market value of $15,000 due to obsolescence. The partnership also assumed a $12,000 note payable owed by Howell that was used originally to purchase the equipment.

Provide the journal entry for Howell's contribution to the partnership.

(Continued)

> **Follow My Example 12-1**
>
> | | | |
> |---|---:|---:|
> | Cash | 34,000 | |
> | Inventory | 15,000 | |
> | Equipment | 29,000 | |
> | Notes Payable | | 12,000 |
> | Reese Howell, Capital | | 66,000 |
>
> Practice Exercises: PE 12-1A, PE 12-1B

Dividing Income

Income or losses of the partnership are divided as specified in the partnership agreement. If there is no specification or agreement, income and losses are divided equally.

Common methods of dividing partnership income are based on the following:

- Services of the partners
- Services and investments of the partners

Services of Partners One method of dividing partnership income is based on the services provided by each partner to the partnership. These services are often recognized by partner salary allowances. Such allowances reflect differences in partners' abilities and time devoted to the partnership. Since partners are not employees, such allowances are recorded as divisions of net income and are credited to the partners' capital accounts.

To illustrate, assume that the partnership agreement of Jennifer Stone and Crystal Mills provides for the following:

	Monthly Salary Allowance
Jennifer Stone	$5,000
Crystal Mills	4,000
Remaining net income:	Divided Equally

The division of income may be reported at the bottom of the partnership income statement. Using this format, the division of $150,000 of net income would be reported on the bottom of the partnership income statement as follows:

Revenues		$650,000
Expenses		500,000
Net income		$150,000

Division of net income:

	J. Stone	C. Mills	Total
Annual salary allowance (mo. × 12)	$60,000	$48,000	$108,000
Remaining income	21,000	21,000	42,000
Net income	$81,000	$69,000	$150,000

As with other business forms, a partnership makes two closing entries at the end of the accounting period. The first closing entry closes all revenues and expenses to the partners' equity accounts. Each partner's equity account is credited for the partner's share of net income (or debited for the partner's share of a net loss). The second closing entry closes each partner's drawing account to the partner's equity account.

Based upon the preceding division of income, the first closing entry for the Stone and Mills partnership is as follows:

LLC		
Revenues	650,000*	
Expenses		500,000
Jennifer Stone, Member Equity		81,000
Crystal Mills, Member Equity		69,000

Dec.	31	Revenues	650,000*	
		Expenses		500,000
		Jennifer Stone, Capital		81,000
		Crystal Mills, Capital		69,000

*We illustrate the closing of revenue and expense totals for simplicity, though in practice, the individual revenue and expense accounts would be closed.

The second closing entry, assuming that Stone and Mills only withdrew their monthly salary allowances is as follows:

LLC		
Jennifer Stone, Member Equity	60,000	
Crystal Mills, Member Equity	48,000	
Jennifer Stone, Drawing		60,000
Crystal Mills, Drawing		48,000

Dec.	31	Jennifer Stone, Capital	60,000	
		Crystal Mills, Capital	48,000	
		Jennifer Stone, Drawing		60,000
		Crystal Mills, Drawing		48,000

Services of Partners and Investments A partnership agreement may divide income based upon salary allowances, as discussed, and also based upon interest on capital balances of each partner. In this way, partners with more invested in the partnership are rewarded by receiving more of the partnership income. One such method of dividing partnership income would be as follows:

1. Partner salary allowances
2. Interest on capital investments
3. Any remaining income equally

To illustrate, assume that the partnership agreement for Stone and Mills provides for the following:

1.

	Monthly Salary Allowance
Jennifer Stone	$5,000
Crystal Mills	4,000

2. Interest of 12% on each partner's capital balance as of January 1.

Capital, Jennifer Stone, January 1	$160,000
Capital, Crystal Mills, January 1	120,000

3. Remaining income: Divided Equally

The $150,000 net income for the year is divided as follows:

Revenues	$650,000
Expenses	500,000
Net income	$150,000

Division of net income:

	J. Stone	C. Mills	Total
Annual salary allowance	$60,000	$48,000	$108,000
Interest allowance	19,200[1]	14,400[2]	33,600
Total	$79,200	$62,400	$141,600
Remaining income	4,200	4,200	8,400
Net income	$83,400	$66,600	$150,000

[1] 12% × $160,000
[2] 12% × $120,000

Link to Boston Basketball Partners LLC

BBP LLC has a seven-member executive committee responsible for running the business.

Link to Boston Basketball Partners LLC

BBP LLC had 14 founding investors.

The entry for closing revenue and expenses and dividing net income is as follows:

LLC		
Revenues	650,000	
Expenses		500,000
Jennifer Stone, Member Equity		83,400
Crystal Mills, Member Equity		66,600

Dec.	31	Revenues		650,000	
		Expenses			500,000
		Jennifer Stone, Capital			83,400
		Crystal Mills, Capital			66,600

INTEGRITY, OBJECTIVITY, AND ETHICS IN BUSINESS

TYRANNY OF THE MAJORITY

Some partnerships involve the contribution of money by one partner and the contribution of effort and expertise by another. This can create a conflict between the two partners, because one works and the other doesn't. Without a properly developed partnership agreement, the working partner could take income in the form of a salary allowance, leaving little for the investor partner. Thus, partnership agreements often require all partners to agree on salary allowances provided to working partners.

Link to Boston Basketball Partners LLC

BBP LLC's estimated operating income for a recent year was $57.4 million.

Allowances Exceed Net Income In the preceding example, the net income is $150,000. The total of the salary ($108,000) and interest ($33,600) allowances is $141,600. Thus, the net income exceeds the salary and interest allowances. In some cases, however, the net income may be less than the total of the allowances. In this case, the remaining net income to divide is a *negative* amount. This negative amount is divided among the partners as though it were a net loss.

To illustrate, assume the same salary and interest allowances as in the preceding example but the net income is $100,000. In this case, the total of the allowances of $141,600 exceeds the net income by $41,600 ($100,000 − $141,600). This amount is divided equally between Stone and Mills. Thus, $20,800 ($41,600 ÷ 2) is deducted from each partner's share of the allowances. The final division of net income between Stone and Mills is as follows:

Revenues	$600,000
Expenses	500,000
Net income	$100,000

Division of net income:

	J. Stone	C. Mills	Total
Annual salary allowance	$60,000	$48,000	$108,000
Interest allowance	19,200	14,400	33,600
Total	$79,200	$62,400	$141,600
Deduct excess of allowances over income	20,800	20,800	41,600
Net income[4]	$58,400	$41,600	$100,000

The entry for closing revenue and expenses and dividing net income is as follows:

LLC		
Revenues	600,000	
Expenses		500,000
Jennifer Stone, Member Equity		58,400
Crystal Mills, Member Equity		41,600

Dec.	31	Revenues		600,000	
		Expenses			500,000
		Jennifer Stone, Capital			58,400
		Crystal Mills, Capital			41,600

[4] In the event of a net loss, the amount deducted from the total allowances would be the "excess of allowances over loss" or the sum of the net loss and the allowances, divided according to the sharing ratio.

Example Exercise 12-2 — Dividing Partnership Net Income — Obj. 2

Steve Prince and Chelsy Bernard formed a partnership, dividing income as follows:

1. Annual salary allowance to Prince of $42,000.
2. Interest of 9% on each partner's capital balance on January 1.
3. Any remaining net income divided equally.

Prince and Bernard had $20,000 and $150,000 in their January 1 capital balances, respectively. Net income for the year was $240,000.
  How much net income should be distributed to Prince and Bernard?

Follow My Example 12-2

	S. Prince	C. Bernard	Total
Annual salary allowance	$ 42,000	$ 0	$ 42,000
Interest allowance	1,800[1]	13,500[2]	15,300
Total	$ 43,800	$ 13,500	$ 57,300
Remaining income	91,350[3]	91,350	182,700
Net income	$135,150	$104,850	$240,000

[1] $20,000 × 9%
[2] $150,000 × 9%
[3] ($240,000 − $42,000 − $15,300) × 50%

Practice Exercises: PE 12-2A, PE 12-2B

Partner Admission and Withdrawal

Obj. 3 Describe and illustrate the accounting for partner admission and withdrawal.

Many partnerships provide for admitting new partners and for partner withdrawals by amending the existing partnership agreement. In this way, the company may continue operating without having to form a new partnership and prepare a new partnership agreement.

Admitting a Partner

As shown in Exhibit 2, a person may be admitted to a partnership by either of the following:

- Purchasing an interest from one or more of the existing partners
- Contributing assets to the partnership

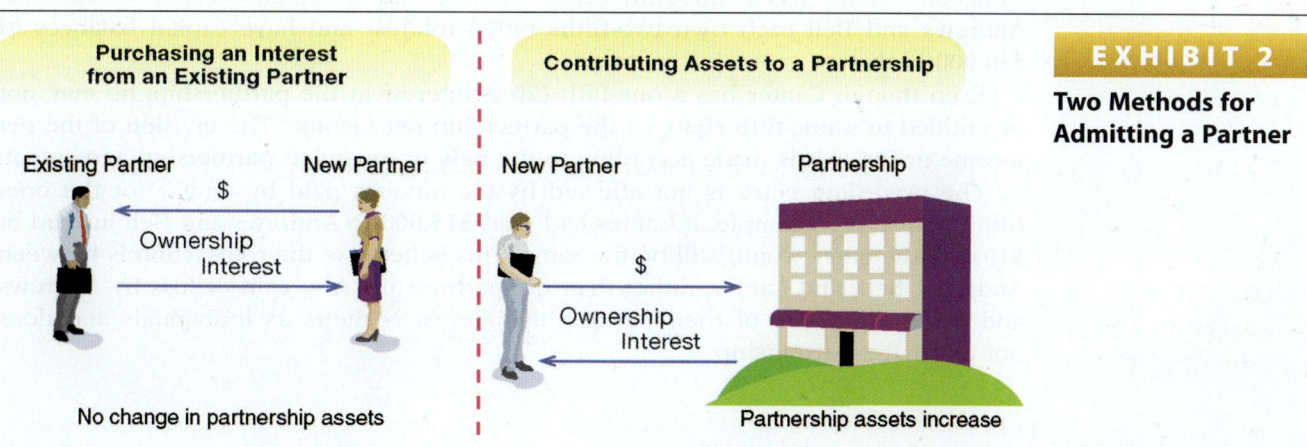

EXHIBIT 2

Two Methods for Admitting a Partner

When a new partner is admitted by *purchasing an interest* from one or more of the existing partners, the total assets and the total owners' equity of the partnership are not affected. The capital (equity) of the new partner is recorded by transferring capital (equity) from the existing partners.

When a new partner is admitted by *contributing assets* to the partnership, the total assets and the total owners' equity of the partnership are increased. The capital (equity) of the new partner is recorded as the amount of assets contributed to the partnership by the new partner.

Purchasing an Interest from Existing Partners

When a new partner is admitted by purchasing an interest from one or more of the existing partners, the transaction is between the new and existing partners acting as individuals. The admission of the new partner is recorded by transferring owners' equity amounts from the capital accounts of the selling partners to the capital account of the new partner.

To illustrate, assume that on June 1, Tom Andrews and Nathan Bell each sell one-fifth of their partnership equity of Bring It Consulting to Joe Canter for $10,000 in cash. On June 1, the partnership has total assets of $120,000 and total liabilities of $20,000, or net assets of $100,000 ($120,000 − $20,000). Both existing partners have capital balances of $50,000 each. This transaction is between Andrews, Bell, and Canter. The only entry required by Bring It Consulting is to record the transfer of capital (equity) from Andrews and Bell to Canter, as follows:

LLC

Tom Andrews, Member Equity	10,000	
Nathan Bell, Member Equity	10,000	
Joe Canter, Member Equity		20,000

June	1	Tom Andrews, Capital	10,000	
		Nathan Bell, Capital	10,000	
		Joe Canter, Capital		20,000

The effect of the transaction on the partnership accounts is as follows:

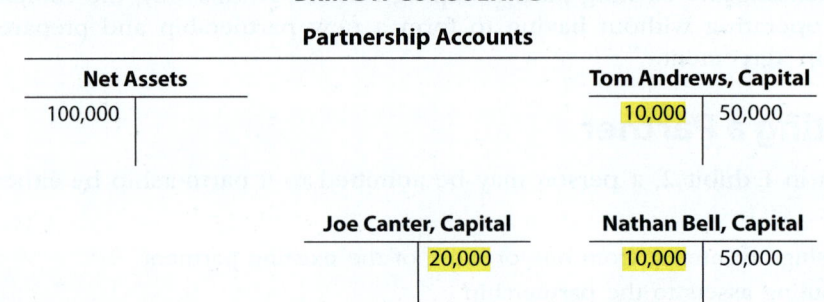

After Canter is admitted to Bring It Consulting, the total owners' equity is still $100,000. Canter has a one-fifth (20%) interest and a capital balance of $20,000. Andrews and Bell each own two-fifths (40%) interest and have capital balances of $40,000 each.

Even though Canter has a one-fifth (20%) interest in the partnership, he may not be entitled to a one-fifth share of the partnership net income. The division of the net income or net loss is made according to the new or amended partnership agreement.

The preceding entry is not affected by the amount paid by Canter for the one-fifth interest. For example, if Canter had paid $15,000 to Andrews and Bell instead of $10,000, the entry would still be the same. This is because the transaction is between Andrews, Bell, and Canter, rather than the partnership. Any gain or loss by Andrews and Bell on the sale of their partnership interest is theirs as individuals and does not affect the partnership.

Contributing Assets to a Partnership When a new partner is admitted by contributing assets to the partnership, the total assets and the total owners' equity of the partnership are increased. This is because the transaction is between the new partner and the partnership.

To illustrate, assume that instead of purchasing a one-fifth ownership in Bring It Consulting directly from Tom Andrews and Nathan Bell, Joe Canter contributes $20,000 cash to Bring It Consulting for ownership equity of $20,000. The entry to record this transaction is as follows:

LLC				June	1	Cash		20,000	
Cash		20,000				Joe Canter, Capital			20,000
Joe Canter, Member Equity			20,000						

The effect of the transaction on the partnership accounts is as follows:

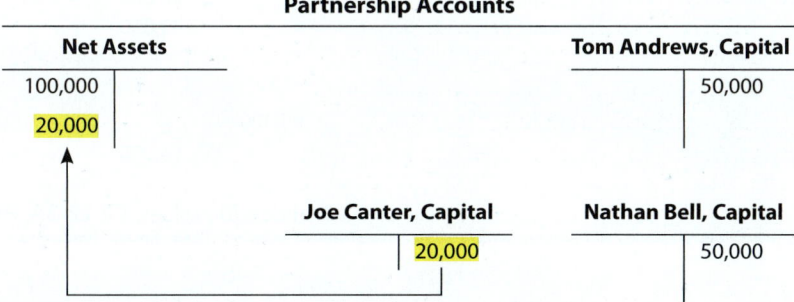

After the admission of Canter, the net assets and total owners' equity of Bring It Consulting increase to $120,000, of which Joe Canter has a $20,000 interest. In contrast, in the prior example, the net assets and total owners' equity of Bring It Consulting did not change from $100,000.

Revaluation of Assets Before a new partner is admitted, the balances of a partnership's asset accounts should be stated at current values. If necessary, the accounts should be adjusted. Any net adjustment (increase or decrease) in asset values is divided among the capital accounts of the existing partners, similar to the division of income.

To illustrate, assume that in the preceding example, the balance of the merchandise inventory account is $14,000 and the current replacement value is $17,000. If Andrews and Bell share net income equally, the revaluation is recorded as follows:

LLC				June	1	Merchandise Inventory		3,000	
Merchandise Inventory		3,000				Tom Andrews, Capital			1,500
Tom Andrews, Member Equity			1,500			Nathan Bell, Capital			1,500
Nathan Bell, Member Equity			1,500						

In the case of fixed assets, the accumulated depreciation is removed and fixed assets are revalued to current value. For example, assume that the partnership of Andrews and Bell in the previous example had equipment of $15,000, with accumulated depreciation of $4,000, that was revalued down to $10,000. The $1,000 ($11,000 − $10,000) revaluation decrease is recorded as follows:

LLC				June	1	Accumulated Depreciation		4,000	
Accumulated Depreciation		4,000				Tom Andrews, Capital		500	
Tom Andrews, Member Equity		500				Nathan Bell, Capital		500	
Nathan Bell, Member Equity		500				Equipment			5,000*
Equipment			5,000						

*$15,000 − $10,000

596 Chapter 12 Accounting for Partnerships and Limited Liability Companies

Failure to adjust the partnership accounts for current values before admitting a new partner may result in the new partner sharing in asset gains or losses that occurred prior to their admission to the partnership.

Example Exercise 12-3 Revaluing and Contributing Assets to a Partnership — Obj. 3

Blake Nelson invested $45,000 in the Lawrence & Kerry partnership for ownership equity of $45,000. Prior to the investment, land was revalued to a market value of $260,000 from a book value of $200,000. Lynne Lawrence and Tim Kerry share net income in a 1:2 ratio.

a. Provide the journal entry for the revaluation of land.
b. Provide the journal entry to admit Nelson.

Follow My Example 12-3

a. Land	60,000	
Lynne Lawrence, Capital		20,000
Tim Kerry, Capital		40,000

[1] $60,000 × 1/3
[2] $60,000 × 2/3

b. Cash	45,000	
Blake Nelson, Capital		45,000

Practice Exercises: PE 12-3A, PE 12-3B

Partner Bonuses A new partner may pay existing partners a bonus to join a partnership. In other cases, existing partners may pay a new partner a bonus to join the partnership.

Bonuses are usually paid because of higher than normal profits the new or existing partners are expected to contribute in the future. For example, a new partner may bring special qualities or skills to the partnership. Celebrities such as actors, musicians, or sports figures often provide name recognition that is expected to increase a partnership's profits.

Partner bonuses are illustrated in Exhibit 3. Existing partners receive a bonus when the ownership interest received by the new partner is less than the amount paid. In contrast, the new partner receives a bonus when the ownership interest received by the new partner is greater than the amount paid.

Bonus to Existing Partners To illustrate, assume that on March 1, the partnership of Marsha Jenkins and Helen Kramer is considering a new partner, Alex Diaz. After the assets of the partnership have been adjusted to current market values, the capital balances of Jenkins and Kramer are as follows:

Marsha Jenkins, Capital	$20,000
Helen Kramer, Capital	24,000
Total owners' equity *before* admitting Diaz	$44,000

EXHIBIT 3
Partner Bonuses

Jenkins and Kramer agree to admit Diaz to the partnership for $31,000. In return, Diaz will receive a one-third equity in the partnership and will share equally with Jenkins and Kramer in partnership income or losses. In this case, Diaz is paying Jenkins and Kramer a $6,000 bonus to join the partnership, computed as follows:

Marsha Jenkins, Capital	$20,000
Helen Kramer, Capital	24,000
Diaz's contribution	31,000
Total owners' equity *after* admitting Diaz	$75,000
Diaz's equity interest after admission	× 1/3
Alex Diaz, Capital	$25,000
Diaz's contribution	$31,000
Alex Diaz, Capital	25,000
Bonus paid to Jenkins and Kramer	$ 6,000

The $6,000 bonus paid by Diaz increases Jenkins' and Kramer's capital accounts. It is distributed to the capital accounts of Jenkins and Kramer according to their income-sharing ratio.[5] Assuming that Jenkins and Kramer share profits and losses equally, the entry to record the admission of Diaz to the partnership is as follows:

LLC

Cash	31,000	
Alex Diaz, Member Equity		25,000
Marsha Jenkins, Member Equity		3,000
Helen Kramer, Member Equity		3,000

Mar.	1	Cash	31,000	
		Alex Diaz, Capital		25,000
		Marsha Jenkins, Capital		3,000
		Helen Kramer, Capital		3,000

Bonus to New Partners Existing partners may agree to pay the new partner a bonus to join a partnership. To illustrate, assume that after adjusting assets to market values, the capital balances of Janice Cowen and Steve Dodd are as follows:

Janice Cowen, Capital	$ 80,000
Steve Dodd, Capital	40,000
Total owners' equity *before* admitting Chou	$120,000

Cowen and Dodd agree to admit Ellen Chou to the partnership on June 1 for an investment of $30,000. In return, Chou will receive a one-fourth equity interest in the partnership and will share in one-fourth of the profits and losses. In this case, Cowen and Dodd are paying Chou a $7,500 bonus to join the partnership, computed as follows:

Janice Cowen, Capital	$ 80,000
Steve Dodd, Capital	40,000
Chou's contribution	30,000
Total owners' equity *after* admitting Chou	$150,000
Chou's equity interest after admission	× 1/4
Ellen Chou, Capital	$ 37,500
Ellen Chou, Capital	$ 37,500
Chou's contribution	30,000
Bonus paid to Chou	$ 7,500

The $7,500 bonus paid to Chou decreases Cowen's and Dodd's capital accounts. It is distributed to the capital accounts of Cowen and Dodd according to their income-sharing ratio. Assuming that the income-sharing ratio of Cowen and Dodd was 2:1 before the admission of Chou, the entry to record the admission of Chou to the partnership is as follows:

---

[5] Another method used to record the admission of partners attributes goodwill rather than a bonus to the partners. This method is discussed in advanced accounting textbooks.

LLC			
Cash	30,000		
Janice Cowen, Member Equity	5,000¹		
Steve Dodd, Member Equity	2,500²		
Ellen Chou, Member Equity		37,500	

June	1	Cash	30,000	
		Janice Cowen, Capital	5,000¹	
		Steve Dodd, Capital	2,500²	
		Ellen Chou, Capital		37,500

¹ $7,500 × 2/3
² $7,500 × 1/3

Example Exercise 12-4 Partner Bonus   *Obj. 3*

Lowman has a capital balance of $51,000 after adjusting assets to fair market value. Conrad contributes $24,000 to receive a 30% interest in a new partnership with Lowman.
   Determine the amount and recipient of the partner bonus.

Follow My Example 12-4

Equity of Lowman	$51,000
Conrad's contribution	24,000
Total equity after admitting Conrad	$75,000
Conrad's equity interest	× 30%
Conrad's equity after admission	$22,500
Conrad's contribution	$24,000
Conrad's equity after admission	22,500
Bonus paid to Lowman	$ 1,500

Practice Exercises: PE 12-4A, PE 12-4B

Withdrawal of a Partner

A partner may retire or withdraw from a partnership. In such cases, the withdrawing partner's interest is normally sold to the:

- Existing partners or
- Partnership

If the *existing partners* purchase the withdrawing partner's interest, the purchase and sale of the partnership interest is between the partners as individuals. The only entry on the partnership's records is to debit the capital account of the partner withdrawing and to credit the capital account of the partner or partners buying the additional interest.

If the *partnership purchases* the withdrawing partner's interest, the assets and the owners' equity of the partnership are reduced by the purchase price. Before the purchase, the asset accounts should be adjusted to current values. The net amount of any adjustment should be divided among the capital accounts of the partners according to their income-sharing ratio.

The entry to record the purchase debits the capital account of the withdrawing partner and credits Cash for the amount of the purchase. If not enough partnership cash is available to pay the withdrawing partner, a liability may be created (credited) for the amount owed the withdrawing partner.

Death of a Partner

When a partner dies, the partnership accounts should be closed as of the date of death. The net income for the current period should then be determined and divided among the partners' capital accounts. The asset accounts should also be adjusted to current values and the amount of any adjustment divided among the capital accounts of the partners.

After the income is divided and any assets are revalued, an entry is recorded to close the deceased partner's capital account. The entry debits the deceased partner's capital account for its balance and credits a liability account, which is payable to the deceased's estate. The remaining partner or partners may then decide to continue the business or liquidate it.

Liquidating Partnerships

Obj. 4 Describe and illustrate the accounting for liquidating a partnership.

When a partnership goes out of business, it sells the assets, pays the creditors, and distributes the remaining cash or other assets to the partners. This winding-up process is called the **liquidation** of the partnership. Although *liquidating* refers to the payment of liabilities, it includes the entire winding-up process.

When the partnership goes out of business and the normal operations are discontinued, the accounts should be adjusted and closed. The only accounts remaining open will be the asset, contra asset, liability, and owners' equity accounts.

The liquidation process is illustrated in Exhibit 4. The steps in the liquidation process are as follows:

Step 1. Sell the partnership assets. This step is called **realization**.
Step 2. Distribute any gains or losses from realization to the partners based on their income-sharing ratio.
Step 3. Pay the claims of creditors, using the cash from the step 1 realization.
Step 4. Distribute the remaining cash to the partners based on the balances in their capital accounts.

Note

In liquidation, cash is distributed to partners according to their capital balances.

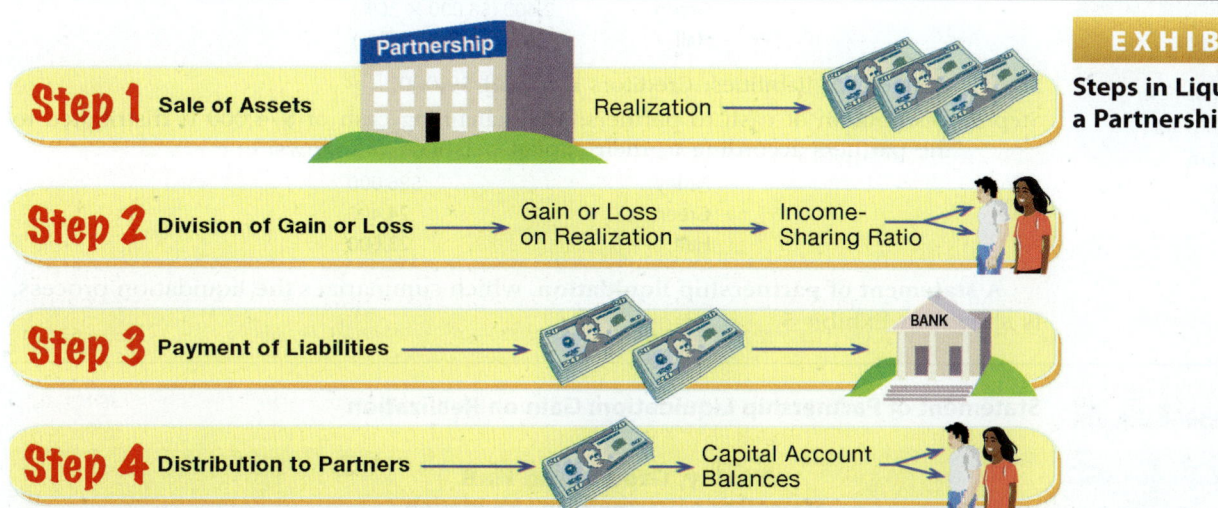

EXHIBIT 4

Steps in Liquidating a Partnership

To illustrate, assume that Farley, Green, and Hall decide to liquidate their partnership. On April 9, after discontinuing business operations of the partnership and closing the accounts, the following trial balance is prepared:

600 CHAPTER 12 Accounting for Partnerships and Limited Liability Companies

Farley, Green, and Hall
Post-Closing Trial Balance
April 9

	Debit Balances	Credit Balances
Cash	11,000	
Noncash Assets	64,000	
Liabilities		9,000
Jean Farley, Capital		22,000
Brad Green, Capital		22,000
Alice Hall, Capital		22,000
	75,000	75,000

Farley, Green, and Hall share income and losses in a ratio of 5:3:2 (50%, 30%, 20%). To simplify, assume that all noncash assets are sold in a single transaction and that all liabilities are paid at one time. In addition, Noncash Assets and Liabilities will be used as account titles in place of the various asset, contra asset, and liability accounts.

Gain on Realization

> **Link to Boston Basketball Partners LLC**
>
> *Forbes Magazine* has estimated the Boston Celtics as the fourth most valuable NBA franchise at $2.1 billion.
> Source: "The Business of Basketball," *Forbes,* January 20, 2016.

Assume that Farley, Green, and Hall sell all noncash assets for $72,000. Thus, a gain of $8,000 ($72,000 – $64,000) is realized. The partnership is liquidated during April as follows:

Step 1. Sale of assets: $72,000 is realized from sale of all the noncash assets.

Step 2. Division of gain: The gain of $8,000 is distributed to Farley, Green, and Hall in the income-sharing ratio of 5:3:2. Thus, the partner capital accounts are credited as follows:

Farley	$4,000 ($8,000 × 50%)
Green	2,400 ($8,000 × 30%)
Hall	1,600 ($8,000 × 20%)

Step 3. Payment of liabilities: Creditors are paid $9,000.

Step 4. Distribution of cash to partners: The remaining cash of $74,000 is distributed to the partners according to their capital balances as follows:

Farley	$26,000
Green	24,400
Hall	23,600

A **statement of partnership liquidation**, which summarizes the liquidation process, is shown in Exhibit 5.

EXHIBIT 5 Statement of Partnership Liquidation: Gain on Realization

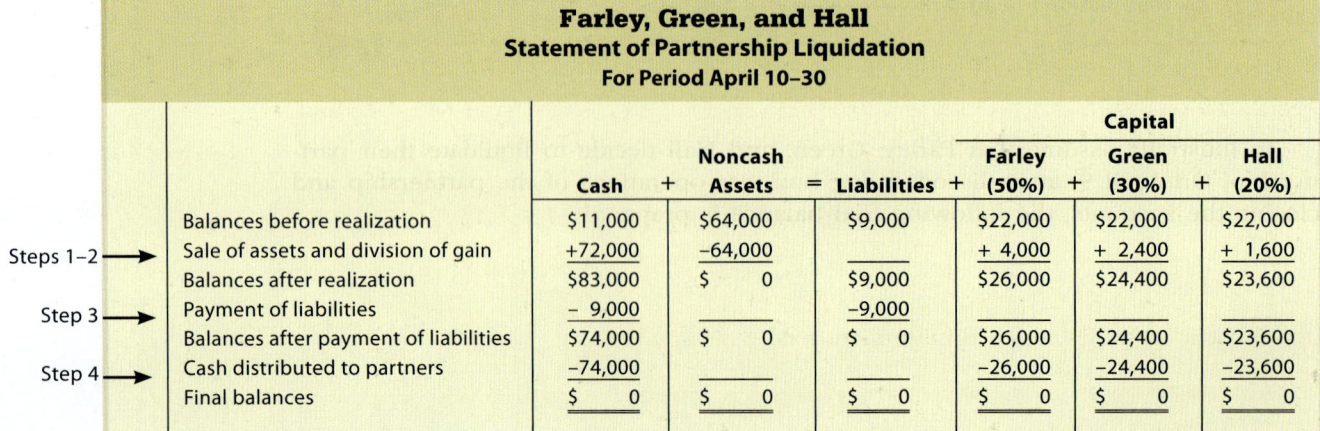

The entries to record the steps in the liquidating process are as follows:

Sale of assets (Step 1):

LLC		
Cash	72,000	
Noncash Assets		64,000
Gain on Realization		8,000

Cash	72,000	
Noncash Assets		64,000
Gain on Realization		8,000

Division of gain (Step 2):

LLC		
Gain on Realization	8,000	
Jean Farley, Member Equity		4,000
Brad Green, Member Equity		2,400
Alice Hall, Member Equity		1,600

Gain on Realization	8,000	
Jean Farley, Capital		4,000
Brad Green, Capital		2,400
Alice Hall, Capital		1,600

Payment of liabilities (Step 3):

LLC		
Liabilities	9,000	
Cash		9,000

Liabilities	9,000	
Cash		9,000

Distribution of cash to partners (Step 4):

LLC		
Jean Farley, Member Equity	26,000	
Brad Green, Member Equity	24,400	
Alice Hall, Member Equity	23,600	
Cash		74,000

Jean Farley, Capital	26,000	
Brad Green, Capital	24,400	
Alice Hall, Capital	23,600	
Cash		74,000

As shown in Exhibit 5, *the cash is distributed to the partners based on the balances of their capital accounts.* These balances are determined after the gain on realization has been divided among the partners and the liabilities are paid. *The income-sharing ratio should not be used as a basis for distributing the cash to partners.*

Loss on Realization

Assume that Farley, Green, and Hall sell all noncash assets for $44,000. Thus, a loss of $20,000 ($64,000 − $44,000) is realized. The liquidation of the partnership is as follows:

Step 1. Sale of assets: $44,000 is realized from the sale of all the noncash assets.

Step 2. Division of loss: The loss of $20,000 is distributed to Farley, Green, and Hall in the income-sharing ratio of 5:3:2. Thus, the partner capital accounts are debited as follows:

Farley	$10,000 ($20,000 × 50%)
Green	6,000 ($20,000 × 30%)
Hall	4,000 ($20,000 × 20%)

Step 3. Payment of liabilities: Creditors are paid $9,000.

602 Chapter 12 Accounting for Partnerships and Limited Liability Companies

Step 4. Distribution of cash to partners: The remaining cash of $46,000 is distributed to the partners according to their capital balances as follows:

Farley	$12,000
Green	16,000
Hall	18,000

The steps in liquidating the partnership are summarized in the statement of partnership liquidation shown in Exhibit 6.

EXHIBIT 6 — **Statement of Partnership Liquidation: Loss on Realization**

Farley, Green, and Hall
Statement of Partnership Liquidation
For Period April 10–30

	Cash	+	Noncash Assets	=	Liabilities	+	Farley (50%)	+	Green (30%)	+	Hall (20%)
Balances before realization	$11,000		$64,000		$9,000		$22,000		$22,000		$22,000
Steps 1–2 → Sale of assets and division of loss	+44,000		−64,000				−10,000		−6,000		−4,000
Balances after realization	$55,000		$ 0		$9,000		$12,000		$16,000		$18,000
Step 3 → Payment of liabilities	−9,000				−9,000						
Balances after payment of liabilities	$46,000		$ 0		$ 0		$12,000		$16,000		$18,000
Step 4 → Cash distributed to partners	−46,000						−12,000		−16,000		−18,000
Final balances	$ 0		$ 0		$ 0		$ 0		$ 0		$ 0

The entries to liquidate the partnership are as follows:

Sale of assets (Step 1):

LLC		
Cash	44,000	
Loss on Realization	20,000	
Noncash Assets		64,000

Cash	44,000	
Loss on Realization	20,000	
Noncash Assets		64,000

Division of loss (Step 2):

LLC		
Jean Farley, Member Equity	10,000	
Brad Green, Member Equity	6,000	
Alice Hall, Member Equity	4,000	
Loss on Realization		20,000

Jean Farley, Capital	10,000	
Brad Green, Capital	6,000	
Alice Hall, Capital	4,000	
Loss on Realization		20,000

Payment of liabilities (Step 3):

LLC		
Liabilities	9,000	
Cash		9,000

Liabilities	9,000	
Cash		9,000

Distribution of cash to partners (Step 4):

LLC		
Jean Farley, Member Equity	12,000	
Brad Green, Member Equity	16,000	
Alice Hall, Member Equity	18,000	
Cash		46,000

Jean Farley, Capital	12,000	
Brad Green, Capital	16,000	
Alice Hall, Capital	18,000	
Cash		46,000

Example Exercise 12-5 Liquidating Partnerships   Obj. 4

Prior to liquidating their partnership, Todd and Gentry had capital accounts of $50,000 and $100,000, respectively. Prior to liquidation, the partnership had no other cash assets than what was realized from the sale of assets. These assets were sold for $220,000. The partnership had $20,000 of liabilities. Todd and Gentry share income and losses equally. Determine the amount received by Gentry as a final distribution from the liquidation of the partnership.

Follow My Example 12-5

Gentry's equity prior to liquidation...		$100,000
Realization of asset sale..	$220,000	
Book value of assets ($50,000 + $100,000 + $20,000).................................	170,000	
Gain on liquidation...	$ 50,000	
Gentry's share of gain (50% × $50,000)..		25,000
Gentry's cash distribution..		$125,000

Practice Exercises: PE 12-5A, PE 12-5B

Loss on Realization—Capital Deficiency

The share of a loss on realization may be greater than the balance in a partner's capital account. The resulting debit balance in the capital account is called a **deficiency**. It represents a claim of the partnership against the partner.

To illustrate, assume that Farley, Green, and Hall sell all noncash assets for $10,000. Thus, a loss of $54,000 ($64,000 − $10,000) is realized. The liquidation of the partnership is as follows:

Step 1. Sale of assets: $10,000 is realized from the sale of all the noncash assets.

Step 2. Division of loss: The loss of $54,000 is distributed to Farley, Green, and Hall in the income-sharing ratio of 5:3:2. The partner capital accounts are debited as follows:

Farley	$27,000 ($54,000 × 50%)
Green	16,200 ($54,000 × 30%)
Hall	10,800 ($54,000 × 20%)

Step 3. Payment of liabilities: Creditors are paid $9,000.

Step 4. Distribution of cash to partners: (a) The share of the loss allocated to Farley, $27,000 (50% × $54,000), exceeds the $22,000 balance in her capital account. This $5,000 deficiency represents an amount that Farley owes the partnership. (b) Assuming that Farley pays the deficiency, the cash of $17,000 is distributed to the partners according to their capital balances as follows:

Farley	$ 0
Green	5,800
Hall	11,200

The steps in liquidating the partnership are summarized in the statement of partnership liquidation shown in Exhibit 7.

EXHIBIT 7 — Statement of Partnership Liquidation: Loss on Realization—Capital Deficiency

Farley, Green, and Hall
Statement of Partnership Liquidation
For Period April 10–30

		Cash	+	Noncash Assets	=	Liabilities	+	Farley Capital (50%)	+	Green Capital (30%)	+	Hall Capital (20%)
	Balances before realization	$11,000		$64,000		$9,000		$22,000		$22,000		$22,000
Steps 1–2 →	Sale of assets and division of loss	+10,000		−64,000				−27,000		−16,200		−10,800
	Balances after realization	$21,000		$ 0		$9,000		$(5,000)		$ 5,800		$11,200
Step 3 →	Payment of liabilities	− 9,000				−9,000						
	Balances after payment of liabilities	$12,000		$ 0		$ 0		$(5,000)		$ 5,800		$11,200
a. →	Receipt of deficiency	+ 5,000						+ 5,000				
Step 4	Balances	$17,000		$ 0		$ 0		$ 0		$ 5,800		$11,200
	Cash distributed to partners	−17,000								− 5,800		−11,200
b. →	Final balances	$ 0		$ 0		$ 0		$ 0		$ 0		$ 0

The entries to liquidate the partnership are as follows:

Sale of assets (Step 1):

LLC
Cash	10,000	
Loss on Realization	54,000	
Noncash Assets		64,000

Cash	10,000	
Loss on Realization	54,000	
Noncash Assets		64,000

Division of loss (Step 2):

LLC
Jean Farley, Member Equity	27,000	
Brad Green, Member Equity	16,200	
Alice Hall, Member Equity	10,800	
Loss on Realization		54,000

Jean Farley, Capital	27,000	
Brad Green, Capital	16,200	
Alice Hall, Capital	10,800	
Loss on Realization		54,000

Payment of liabilities (Step 3):

LLC
Liabilities	9,000	
Cash		9,000

Liabilities	9,000	
Cash		9,000

Receipt of deficiency (Step 4a):

LLC
Cash	5,000	
Jean Farley, Member Equity		5,000

Cash	5,000	
Jean Farley, Capital		5,000

Distribution of cash to partners (Step 4b):

LLC		
Brad Green, Member Equity	5,800	
Alice Hall, Member Equity	11,200	
Cash		17,000

Brad Green, Capital	5,800	
Alice Hall, Capital	11,200	
Cash		17,000

If the deficient partner does not pay the partnership the deficiency, there will not be sufficient partnership cash to pay the remaining partners in full. Any uncollected deficiency becomes a loss to the partnership and is divided among the remaining partners' capital balances based on their income-sharing ratio. The cash balance will then equal the sum of the capital account balances. The cash can then be distributed to the remaining partners, based on the balances of their capital accounts.

To illustrate, assume that in the preceding example, Farley could not pay her deficiency. The deficiency would be allocated to Green and Hall based on their income-sharing ratio of 3:2. The remaining cash of $12,000 would then be distributed to Green ($2,800) and Hall ($9,200), computed as follows:

	Capital Balances *Before* Deficiency	Allocated (Deficiency)	Capital Balances *After* Deficiency
Farley	$ (5,000)	$ 5,000	$ 0
Green	5,800	(3,000)*	2,800
Hall	11,200	(2,000)**	9,200
Total	$12,000		$12,000

*$3,000 = ($5,000 × 3/5) or ($5,000 × 60%)
**$2,000 = ($5,000 × 2/5) or ($5,000 × 40%)

The entries to allocate Farley's deficiency and distribute the cash are as follows:

Allocation of deficiency (Step 4a):

LLC		
Brad Green, Member Equity	3,000	
Alice Hall, Member Equity	2,000	
Jean Farley, Member Equity		5,000

Brad Green, Capital	3,000	
Alice Hall, Capital	2,000	
Jean Farley, Capital		5,000

Distribution of cash to partners (Step 4b):

LLC		
Brad Green, Member Equity	2,800	
Alice Hall, Member Equity	9,200	
Cash		12,000

Brad Green, Capital	2,800	
Alice Hall, Capital	9,200	
Cash		12,000

Example Exercise 12-6 Liquidating Partnerships—Deficiency   Obj. 4

Prior to liquidating their partnership, Short and Bain had capital accounts of $20,000 and $80,000, respectively. The partnership assets were sold for $40,000. The partnership had no liabilities. Short and Bain share income and losses equally.

a. Determine the amount of Short's deficiency.
b. Determine the amount distributed to Bain, assuming that Short is unable to satisfy the deficiency.

(Continued)

Follow My Example 12-6

a.
Short's equity prior to liquidation		$ 20,000
Realization of asset sale	$ 40,000	
Book value of assets ($20,000 + $80,000)	100,000	
Loss on liquidation	$ 60,000	
Short's share of loss (50% × $60,000)		30,000
Short's deficiency		$(10,000)

b. $40,000 ($80,000 − $30,000 share of loss − $10,000 Short deficiency)

Practice Exercises: PE 12-6A, PE 12-6B

Obj. 5 Prepare the statement of partnership equity.

Statement of Partnership Equity

Reporting changes in partnership capital accounts is similar to that for a proprietorship. The primary difference is that there is a capital account for each partner. The changes in partner capital accounts for a period of time are reported in a **statement of partnership equity**.

Exhibit 8 illustrates a statement of partnership equity for Investors Associates, a partnership of Dan Cross and Kelly Baker. Each partner's capital account is shown as a separate column. The partner capital accounts may change due to capital additions, net income, or withdrawals, similar to sole proprietorships.

EXHIBIT 8
Statement of Partnership Equity

Investors Associates
Statement of Partnership Equity
For the Year Ended December 31, 20Y8

	Dan Cross, Capital	Kelly Baker, Capital	Total Partnership Capital
Balance, January 1, 20Y8	$245,000	$365,000	$610,000
Capital additions	50,000		50,000
Net income for the year	40,000	80,000	120,000
Partner withdrawals	(5,000)	(45,000)	(50,000)
Balance, December 31, 20Y8	$330,000	$400,000	$730,000

The equity reporting for an LLC is similar to that of a partnership. Instead of a statement of partnership capital, a statement of members' equity is prepared. The **statement of members' equity** reports the changes in member equity for a period. The statement is similar to Exhibit 8, except that the columns represent member equity rather than partner equity.

Obj. 6 Analyze and interpret employee efficiency.

Financial Analysis and Interpretation: Revenue per Employee

Many partnerships and LLCs operate as service-oriented enterprises. This is the case for many professions, such as medical, advertising, and accounting. The performance of such firms can be measured by the amount of net income per partner, as illustrated in this chapter. Another measure used to assess the performance of a service-oriented business is revenue per employee.

Revenue per employee is a measure of the efficiency of the business in generating revenues. It is computed as follows:

$$\text{Revenue per Employee} = \frac{\text{Revenue}}{\text{Number of Employees}}$$

In a partnership, the number of partners may be included with employees, or partners may be evaluated separately. Generally, the higher the revenue per employee, the more efficient the company is in generating revenue from its employees. In evaluating revenue per employee, changes over time as well as comparisons with industry peers or averages are often used.

To illustrate comparisons over time, assume that Washburn & Lovett, CPAs, has the following information for two years:

	20Y5	20Y4
Revenues	$220,000,000	$180,000,000
Number of employees	1,600	1,500

For Washburn & Lovett, the revenue per employee ratio is computed for 20Y5 and 20Y4 as follows:

$$\text{Revenue per employee, 20Y5: } \frac{\$220,000,000}{1,600 \text{ employees}} = \$137,500 \text{ per employee}$$

$$\text{Revenue per employee, 20Y4: } \frac{\$180,000,000}{1,500 \text{ employees}} = \$120,000 \text{ per employee}$$

Washburn & Lovett increased revenues by $40,000,000 ($220,000,000 − $180,000,000), or 22.2% ($40,000,000 ÷ $180,000,000) from 20Y4 to 20Y5. The number of employees increased by 100, or 6.7% (100 employees ÷ 1,500 employees) between the two years. Thus, the firm increased revenues at a rate faster than the increase in employees. As a result, the revenue per employee improved from $120,000 to $137,500 between the two years, suggesting improved efficiency in generating revenues.

To illustrate comparison within an industry, the revenue per employee for **Starbucks** and **McDonald's** for a recent year is computed as follows:

$$\text{Starbucks: } \frac{\$19,162,700,000}{238,000 \text{ employees}} = \$80,516 \text{ per employee}$$

$$\text{McDonald's: } \frac{\$25,413,000,000}{420,000 \text{ employees}} = \$60,507 \text{ per employee}$$

Starbucks is able to generate more revenues per employee than is McDonald's. Many factors may explain this difference, including relative employee efficiency, extent of part-time workforce, and product pricing.

Example Exercise 12-7 Revenue per Employee Obj. 6

AccuTax, CPAs earned $4,200,000 during 20Y7 using 20 employees. During 20Y8, the firm grew revenues to $4,560,000 and expanded the staff to 24 employees.

a. Determine the revenue per employee for each year.
b. Interpret the results.

Follow My Example 12-7

a. 20Y7: $\dfrac{\$4,200,000}{20 \text{ employees}} = \$210,000 \text{ per employee}$

20Y8: $\dfrac{\$4,560,000}{24 \text{ employees}} = \$190,000 \text{ per employee}$

b. While AccuTax grew revenues by $360,000 ($4,560,000 − $4,200,000), or 8.6% ($360,000 ÷ $4,200,000), the number of employees expanded by 4, or 20% (4/20). The growth in revenue was less than the growth in the number of employees; thus, the revenue per employee declined between the two years. The firm was less efficient in generating revenues from its employees in 20Y8.

Practice Exercises: PE 12-7A, PE 12-7B

At a Glance 12

Obj. 1 Describe the characteristics of proprietorships, partnerships, and limited liability companies.

Key Points The advantages and disadvantages of proprietorships, partnerships, and limited liability companies are summarized in Exhibit 1.

Learning Outcomes	Example Exercises	Practice Exercises
• Identify the advantages and disadvantages of proprietorships, partnerships, and limited liability companies.		

Obj. 2 Describe and illustrate the accounting for forming a partnership and for dividing the net income and net loss of a partnership.

Key Points When a partnership is formed, accounts are debited for contributed assets and credited for assumed liabilities, and the partner's capital account is credited for the net amount. The net income of a partnership may be divided among the partners on the basis of services rendered, interest earned on the capital account balance, and the income-sharing ratio.

Learning Outcomes	Example Exercises	Practice Exercises
• Journalize the initial formation of a partnership and establish partner capital.	EE12-1	PE12-1A, 12-1B
• Determine and journalize the income distributed to each partner.	EE12-2	PE12-2A, 12-2B

Obj. 3 Describe and illustrate the accounting for partner admission and withdrawal.

Key Points Partnership assets should be restated to current values prior to the admission or withdrawal of a partner. A new partner may be admitted into a partnership by either purchasing an interest from an existing partner or by purchasing an interest directly from the partnership.

Learning Outcomes	Example Exercises	Practice Exercises
• Prepare for partner admission by revaluing assets to approximate current values.	EE12-3	PE12-3A, 12-3B
• Distinguish between partner admission through purchase from an existing partner or purchase from the partnership.	EE12-3	PE12-3A, 12-3B
• Determine partner bonuses.	EE12-4	PE12-4A, 12-4B

Obj. 4 Describe and illustrate the accounting for liquidating a partnership.

Key Points A partnership is liquidated by the (1) sale of partnership assets (realization), (2) distribution of gain or loss on realization to the partners, (3) payments to creditors, and (4) distribution of the remaining cash to partners according to their capital account balances. A partner may be deficient when the amount of loss distribution exceeds the capital balance.

Learning Outcomes	Example Exercises	Practice Exercises
• Apply the four steps of liquidating a partnership for either gain or loss on realization.	EE12-5	PE12-5A, 12-5B
• Apply the four steps of partnership liquidation when there is a partner deficiency.	EE12-6	PE12-6A, 12-6B

Obj. 5 Prepare the statement of partnership equity.

Key Points A statement of partnership equity reports the changes in partnership equity from capital additions, net income, and withdrawals.

Learning Outcomes	Example Exercises	Practice Exercises
• Prepare a statement of partnership equity.		

Obj. 6 Analyze and interpret employee efficiency.

Key Points The revenue per employee ratio is calculated as the total annual revenues divided by the total employees. This ratio measures the total revenue earned by each employee and, thus, is a measure of the efficiency of each employee in revenue terms. The ratio is often used to measure efficiency trends over time and across similar firms.

Learning Outcomes	Example Exercises	Practice Exercises
• Analyze and interpret the revenue per employee ratio.	EE12-7	PE12-7A, 12-7B

Illustrative Problem

Radcliffe, Sonders, and Towers, who share in income and losses in the ratio of 2:3:5, decided to discontinue operations as of April 30 and liquidate their partnership. After the accounts were closed on April 30, the following trial balance was prepared:

(Continued)

Radcliffe, Sonders, and Towers
Post-Closing Trial Balance
April 30

	Debit Balances	Credit Balances
Cash	5,900	
Noncash Assets	109,900	
Liabilities		26,800
Radcliffe, Capital		14,600
Sonders, Capital		27,900
Towers, Capital		46,500
	115,800	115,800

Between May 1 and May 18, the noncash assets were sold for $27,400, and the liabilities were paid.

Instructions

1. Assuming that the partner with the capital deficiency pays the entire amount owed to the partnership, prepare a statement of partnership liquidation.

2. Journalize the entries to record (a) the sale of the assets, (b) the division of loss on the sale of the assets, (c) the payment of the liabilities, (d) the receipt of the deficiency, and (e) the distribution of cash to the partners.

Solution

1.

Radcliffe, Sonders, and Towers
Statement of Partnership Liquidation
For Period May 1–18

						Capital		
	Cash	+	Noncash Assets	= Liabilities +	Radcliffe (20%) +	Sonders (30%) +	Towers (50%)
Balances before realization	$ 5,900		$109,900	$26,800	$14,600	$27,900	$46,500
Sale of assets and division of loss	+27,400		–109,900		–16,500	–24,750	–41,250
Balances after realization	$33,300		$ 0	$26,800	$ (1,900)	$ 3,150	$ 5,250
Payment of liabilities	–26,800			–26,800			
Balances after payment of liabilities	$ 6,500		$ 0	$ 0	$ (1,900)	$ 3,150	$ 5,250
Receipt of deficiency	+ 1,900				+ 1,900		
Balances	$ 8,400		$ 0	$ 0	$ 0	$ 3,150	$ 5,250
Cash distributed to partners	– 8,400					– 3,150	– 5,250
Final balances	$ 0		$ 0	$ 0	$ 0	$ 0	$ 0

2. a.

Cash		27,400	
Loss on Realization		82,500	
Noncash Assets			109,900

b.

Radcliffe, Capital	16,500	
Sonders, Capital	24,750	
Towers, Capital	41,250	
Loss on Realization		82,500

c.

Liabilities	26,800	
Cash		26,800

d.

Cash	1,900	
Radcliffe, Capital		1,900

e.

Sonders, Capital	3,150	
Towers, Capital	5,250	
Cash		8,400

Key Terms

deficiency (603)
limited liability company (LLC) (588)
liquidation (599)
partnership (587)
partnership agreement (587)
realization (599)
revenue per employee (606)
statement of members' equity (606)
statement of partnership equity (606)
statement of partnership liquidation (600)

Discussion Questions

1. What are the main advantages of (a) proprietorships, (b) partnerships, and (c) limited liability companies?

2. What are the disadvantages of a partnership over a limited liability company form of organization for a profit-making business?

3. Emilio Alvarez and Graciela Zavala joined together to form a partnership. Is it possible for them to lose a greater amount than the amount of their investment in the partnership? Explain.

4. What are the major features of a partnership agreement for a partnership or an operating agreement for a limited liability company?

5. Josiah Barlow, Patty DuMont, and Owen Maholic are contemplating the formation of a partnership. According to the partnership agreement, Barlow is to invest $60,000 and devote one-half time, DuMont is to invest $40,000 and devote three-fourths time, and Maholic is to make no investment and devote full time. Would Maholic be correct in assuming that since he is not contributing any assets to the firm, he is risking nothing? Explain.

612 Chapter 12 Accounting for Partnerships and Limited Liability Companies

6. During the current year, Marsha Engles withdrew $4,000 monthly from the partnership of Engles and Cox Water Management Consultants. Is it possible that her share of partnership net income for the current year might be more or less than $48,000? Explain.

7. a. What accounts are debited and credited to record a partner's cash withdrawal in lieu of salary?

   b. The articles of partnership provide for a salary allowance of $6,000 per month to partner C. If C withdrew only $4,000 per month, would this affect the division of the partnership net income? Explain.

   c. At the end of the fiscal year, what accounts are debited and credited to record the division of net income among partners?

8. Explain the difference between the admission of a new partner to a partnership (a) by purchase of an interest from another partner and (b) by contribution of assets to the partnership.

9. Why is it important to state all partnership assets in terms of current prices at the time of the admission of a new partner?

10. Why might a partnership pay a bonus to a newly admitted partner?

Practice Exercises

Example Exercises

EE 12-1 *p. 589* **PE 12-1A** Journalizing partner's original investment — **OBJ. 2**

Holly Renfro contributed a patent, accounts receivable, and $20,000 cash to a partnership. The patent had a book value of $8,000. However, the technology covered by the patent appeared to have significant market potential. Thus, the patent was appraised at $92,000. The accounts receivable control account was $45,000, with an allowance for doubtful accounts of $3,000. The partnership also assumed a $14,000 account payable owed to a Renfro supplier.

Provide the journal entry for Renfro's contribution to the partnership.

EE 12-1 *p. 589* **PE 12-1B** Journalizing partner's original investment — **OBJ. 2**

Austin Fisher contributed land, inventory, and $36,000 cash to a partnership. The land had a book value of $120,000 and a market value of $175,000. The inventory had a book value of $50,000 and a market value of $42,000. The partnership also assumed a $35,000 note payable owed by Fisher that was used originally to purchase the land.

Provide the journal entry for Fisher's contribution to the partnership.

EE 12-2 *p. 593* **PE 12-2A** Dividing partnership net income — **OBJ. 2**

Lia Chen and Martin Monroe formed a partnership, dividing income as follows:

1. Annual salary allowance to Chen of $35,000.
2. Interest of 4% on each partner's capital balance on January 1.
3. Any remaining net income divided to Chen and Monroe, 2:1.

Chen and Monroe had $90,000 and $140,000, respectively, in their January 1 capital balances. Net income for the year was $70,000.

How much net income should be distributed to Chen and Monroe?

EE 12-2 *p. 593* **PE 12-2B** Dividing partnership net income — **OBJ. 2**

John Prado and Ayana Nicks formed a partnership, dividing income as follows:

1. Annual salary allowance to Prado, $10,000 and Nicks, $28,000.
2. Interest of 5% on each partner's capital balance on January 1.
3. Any remaining net income divided equally.

Prado and Nicks had $20,000 and $50,000, respectively, in their January 1 capital balances. Net income for the year was $30,000.

How much net income should be distributed to Prado and Nicks?

Chapter 12 Accounting for Partnerships and Limited Liability Companies 613

 EE 12-3 p. 596 **PE 12-3A** **Revaluing and contributing assets to a partnership** OBJ. 3

Craig Roberts purchased one-half of Ennis Leighton's interest in the Vale and Leighton partnership for $34,000. Prior to the investment, land was revalued to a market value of $130,000 from a book value of $80,000. Tony Vale and Ennis Leighton share net income equally. Leighton had a capital balance of $36,000 prior to these transactions.

a. Provide the journal entry for the revaluation of land.

b. Provide the journal entry to admit Roberts.

 EE 12-3 p. 596 **PE 12-3B** **Revaluing and contributing assets to a partnership** OBJ. 3

Demarco Lee invested $60,000 in the Camden and Sayler partnership for ownership equity of $60,000. Prior to the investment, equipment was revalued to a market value of $39,000 from a book value of $30,000. Kevin Camden and Chloe Sayler share net income in a 2:1 ratio.

a. Provide the journal entry for the revaluation of equipment.

b. Provide the journal entry to admit Lee.

 EE 12-4 p. 598 **PE 12-4A** **Partner bonus** OBJ. 3

Gomez has a capital balance of $240,000 after adjusting assets to fair market value. Banks contributes $380,000 to receive a 60% interest in a new partnership with Gomez.
Determine the amount and recipient of the partner bonus.

 EE 12-4 p. 598 **PE 12-4B** **Partner bonus** OBJ. 3

Hiro has a capital balance of $75,000 after adjusting assets to fair market value. Marone contributes $20,000 to receive a 40% interest in a new partnership with Hiro.
Determine the amount and recipient of the partner bonus.

 EE 12-5 p. 603 **PE 12-5A** **Liquidating partnerships** OBJ. 4

Prior to liquidating their partnership, Joyce and Xi had capital accounts of $50,000 and $105,000, respectively. Prior to liquidation, the partnership had no cash assets other than what was realized from the sale of assets. These partnership assets were sold for $190,000. The partnership had $10,000 of liabilities. Joyce and Xi share income and losses equally. Determine the amount received by Joyce as a final distribution from liquidation of the partnership.

 EE 12-5 p. 603 **PE 12-5B** **Liquidating partnerships** OBJ. 4

Prior to liquidating their partnership, Manning and Adamo had capital accounts of $240,000 and $150,000, respectively. Prior to liquidation, the partnership had no cash assets other than what was realized from the sale of assets. These partnership assets were sold for $410,000. The partnership had $80,000 of liabilities. Manning and Adamo share income and losses equally. Determine the amount received by Manning as a final distribution from liquidation of the partnership.

 EE 12-6 p. 605 **PE 12-6A** **Liquidating partnerships—deficiency** OBJ. 4

Prior to liquidating their partnership, Wakefield and Barns had capital accounts of $105,000 and $55,000, respectively. The partnership assets were sold for $40,000. The partnership had no liabilities. Wakefield and Barns share income and losses equally.

a. Determine the amount of Barns's deficiency.

b. Determine the amount distributed to Wakefield, assuming that Barns is unable to satisfy the deficiency.

 EE 12-6 p. 605 **PE 12-6B** **Liquidating partnerships—deficiency** OBJ. 4

Prior to liquidating their partnership, Bonilla and Perez had capital accounts of $185,000 and $245,000, respectively. The partnership assets were sold for $30,000. The partnership had no liabilities. Bonilla and Perez share income and losses equally.

a. Determine the amount of Bonilla's deficiency.

b. Determine the amount distributed to Perez, assuming that Bonilla is unable to satisfy the deficiency.

614 Chapter 12 Accounting for Partnerships and Limited Liability Companies

EE 12-7 p. 607 **PE 12-7A Revenue per employee** OBJ. 6

Niles and Cohen, CPAs earned $12,375,000 during 20Y4 using 75 employees. During 20Y5, the firm grew revenues to $15,400,000 and expanded the staff to 88 employees.

a. Determine the revenue per employee for each year.
b. Interpret the results.

EE 12-7 p. 607 **PE 12-7B Revenue per employee** OBJ. 6

Eclipse Architects earned $1,800,000 during 20Y1 using 12 employees. During 20Y2, the firm reduced revenues to $1,440,000 and reduced the staff to nine employees.

a. Determine the revenue per employee for each year.
b. Interpret the results.

Exercises

EX 12-1 Recording partner's original investment OBJ. 2

Kimberly Payne and Arionna Maples decide to form a partnership by combining the assets of their separate businesses. Payne contributes the following assets to the partnership: cash, $20,000; accounts receivable with a face amount of $145,000 and an allowance for doubtful accounts of $4,200; merchandise inventory with a cost of $92,000; and equipment with a cost of $136,000 and accumulated depreciation of $45,000.

The partners agree that $5,000 of the accounts receivable are completely worthless and are not to be accepted by the partnership, that $4,400 is a reasonable allowance for the uncollectibility of the remaining accounts, that the merchandise inventory is to be recorded at the current market price of $101,700, and that the equipment is to be valued at $81,200.

Journalize the partnership's entry to record Payne's investment.

EX 12-2 Recording partner's original investment OBJ. 2

Hannah Freeman and Hugo Hernandez form a partnership by combining assets of their former businesses. The following balance sheet information is provided by Freeman, sole proprietorship:

Hannah Freeman Proprietorship
Balance Sheet
June 1, 20Y3

Cash		$ 65,000
Accounts receivable	$125,000	
Less: Allowance for doubtful accounts	7,200	117,800
Land		215,000
Equipment	$ 78,000	
Less: Accumulated depreciation—equipment	41,000	37,000
Total assets		$434,800
Accounts payable		$ 24,800
Notes payable		76,000
Hannah Freeman, capital		334,000
Total liabilities and owner's equity		$434,800

Freeman obtained appraised values for the land and equipment as follows:

Land	$320,000
Equipment	34,800

An analysis of the accounts receivable indicated that the allowance for doubtful accounts should be increased to $9,500.

Journalize the partnership's entry for Freeman's investment.

Chapter 12 Accounting for Partnerships and Limited Liability Companies   615

EX 12-3 Dividing partnership income   OBJ. 2

✔ b. Hawes, $217,500

Tyler Hawes and Piper Albright formed a partnership, investing $210,000 and $70,000, respectively. Determine their participation in the year's net income of $290,000 under each of the following independent assumptions: (a) no agreement concerning division of net income; (b) divided in the ratio of original capital investment; (c) interest at the rate of 5% allowed on original investments and the remainder divided in the ratio of 2:3; (d) salary allowances of $36,000 and $45,000, respectively, and the balance divided equally; (e) allowance of interest at the rate of 5% on original investments, salary allowances of $36,000 and $45,000, respectively, and the remainder divided equally.

EX 12-4 Dividing partnership income   OBJ. 2

✔ c. Hawes, $46,500

Using each of the five assumptions as to income division listed in Exercise 12-3, determine the income participation of Hawes and Albright if the year's net income is $104,000.

EX 12-5 Dividing partnership net loss   OBJ. 2

Leigh Meadows and Byron Leef formed a partnership in which the partnership agreement provided for salary allowances of $35,000 and $25,000, respectively. Determine the division of a $20,000 net loss for the current year, assuming that remaining income or losses are shared equally by the two partners.

EX 12-6 Negotiating income-sharing ratio   OBJ. 2

Sixty-year-old Wanda Davis retired from her computer consulting business in Boston and moved to Florida. There she met 27-year-old Ava Jain, who had just graduated from Eldon Community College with an associate degree in computer science. Wanda and Ava formed a partnership called D&J Computer Consultants. Wanda contributed $50,000 for startup costs and devoted one-half time to the business. Ava devoted full time to the business. The monthly drawings were $2,500 for Wanda and $5,000 for Ava.

At the end of the first year of operations, the two partners disagreed on the division of net income. Wanda reasoned that the division should be equal. Although she devoted only one-half time to the business, she contributed all of the startup funds. Ava reasoned that the income-sharing ratio should be 2:1 in her favor because she devoted full time to the business and her monthly drawings were twice those of Wanda.

a. What flaws can you identify in the partners' reasoning regarding the income-sharing ratio?

b. How could an income-sharing agreement resolve this dispute?

EX 12-7 Dividing LLC income   OBJ. 2

✔ a. Farley, $86,800

Martin Farley and Ashley Clark formed a limited liability company with an operating agreement that provided a salary allowance of $40,000 and $30,000 to each member, respectively. In addition, the operating agreement specified an income-sharing ratio of 3:2. The two members withdrew amounts equal to their salary allowances. Revenues were $668,000 and expenses were $520,000, for a net income of $148,000.

a. Determine the division of $148,000 net income for the year.

b. Provide journal entries to close the (1) revenues and expenses and (2) drawing accounts for the two members.

c. If the net income was less than the sum of the salary allowances, how would income be divided between the two members of the LLC?

EX 12-8 LLC net income and statement of members' equity   OBJ. 2, 5

✔ a. Sanders, $138,500

Marvel Media, LLC, has three members: WLKT Partners, Madison Sanders, and Observer Newspaper, LLC. On January 1, 20Y2, the three members had equity of $200,000, $40,000, and $160,000, respectively. WLKT Partners contributed an additional $50,000 to Marvel

(Continued)

Media, LLC, on June 1, 20Y2. Madison Sanders received an annual salary allowance of $55,000 during 20Y2. The members' equity accounts are also credited with 10% interest on each member's January 1 capital balance. Any remaining income is to be shared in the ratio of 4:3:3 among the three members. The revenues, expenses, and net income for Marvel Media, LLC, for 20Y2 were $1,260,000, $900,000, and $360,000, respectively. Amounts equal to the salary and interest allowances were withdrawn by the members.

a. Determine the division of income among the three members.

b. Prepare the journal entry to close the revenues, expenses, and withdrawals to the individual member equity accounts.

c. Prepare a statement of members' equity for 20Y2.

d. What are the advantages of an income-sharing agreement for the members of this LLC?

EX 12-9 Admitting new partners   OBJ. 3

Myles Etter and Crystal Santori are partners who share in the income equally and have capital balances of $210,000 and $62,500, respectively. Etter, with the consent of Santori, sells one-third of his interest to Lonnie Davis. What entry is required by the partnership if the sales price is (a) $60,000? (b) $80,000?

EX 12-10 Admitting new partners who buy an interest and contribute assets   OBJ. 3

✔ b. Henry, $128,000

The capital accounts of Trent Henry and Tim Chou have balances of $160,000 and $100,000, respectively. LeAnne Gilbert and Becky Clarke are to be admitted to the partnership. Gilbert buys one-fifth of Henry's interest for $35,000 and one-fourth of Chou's interest for $29,000. Clarke contributes $90,000 cash to the partnership, for which she is to receive an ownership equity of $90,000.

a. Journalize the entries to record the admission of (1) Gilbert and (2) Clarke.

b. What are the capital balances of each partner after the admission of the new partners?

EX 12-11 Admitting new partner who contributes assets   OBJ. 3

✔ b. Neel, $35,000

After the tangible assets have been adjusted to current market prices, the capital accounts of Brad Paulson and Drew Webster have balances of $45,000 and $60,000, respectively. Austin Neel is to be admitted to the partnership, contributing $30,000 cash to the partnership, for which he is to receive an ownership equity of $35,000. All partners share equally in income.

a. Journalize the entry to record the admission of Neel, who is to receive a bonus of $5,000.

b. What are the capital balances of each partner after the admission of the new partner?

c. Why are tangible assets adjusted to current market prices prior to admitting a new partner?

EX 12-12 Admitting new partner with bonus   OBJ. 3

Cody Jenkins and Lacey Tanner formed a partnership to provide landscaping services. Jenkins and Tanner shared profits and losses equally. After all the tangible assets have been adjusted to current market prices, the capital accounts of Cody Jenkins and Lacey Tanner have balances of $78,000 and $46,000, respectively. Valeria Solano has expertise with using the computer to prepare landscape designs, cost estimates, and renderings. Jenkins and Tanner deem these skills useful; thus, Solano is admitted to the partnership at a 30% interest for a purchase price of $32,000.

a. Determine the recipient and amount of the partner bonus.

b. Provide the journal entry to admit Solano into the partnership.

c. Why would a bonus be paid in this situation?

Chapter 12 Accounting for Partnerships and Limited Liability Companies 617

EX 12-13 Admitting a new LLC member with bonus OBJ. 3

✔ b. (2) Bonus paid to Lin, $7,500

Alert Medical, LLC, consists of two doctors, Abrams and Lipscomb, who share in all income and losses according to a 2:3 income-sharing ratio. Dr. Lin has been asked to join the LLC. Prior to admitting Lin, the assets of Alert Medical were revalued to reflect their current market values. The revaluation resulted in medical equipment being increased by $40,000. Prior to the revaluation, the equity balances for Abrams and Lipscomb were $154,000 and $208,000, respectively.

a. Provide the journal entry for the asset revaluation.
b. Provide the journal entry for the bonus under the following independent situations:
   1. Lin purchased a 30% interest in Alert Medical, LLC, for $228,000.
   2. Lin purchased a 25% interest in Alert Medical, LLC, for $124,000.

EX 12-14 Admitting new partner with bonus OBJ. 3

✔ b. (1) Bonus paid to Ortiz, $9,600

L. Bowers and V. Lipscomb are partners in Elegant Event Consultants. Bowers and Lipscomb share income equally. M. Ortiz will be admitted to the partnership. Prior to the admission, equipment was revalued downward by $8,000. The capital balances of each partner are $96,000 and $40,000, respectively, prior to the revaluation.

a. Provide the journal entry for the asset revaluation.
b. Provide the journal entry for Ortiz's admission under the following independent situations:
   1. Ortiz purchased a 20% interest for $20,000.
   2. Ortiz purchased a 30% interest for $60,000.

EX 12-15 Partner bonuses, statement of partnership equity OBJ. 2, 3, 5

✔ Dennis Overton, Capital, Dec. 31, 20Y5, $226,400

The partnership of Angel Investor Associates began operations on January 1, 20Y5, with contributions from two partners as follows:

Dennis Overton	$180,000
Ben Testerman	120,000

The following additional partner transactions took place during the year:

1. In early January, Randy Campbell is admitted to the partnership by contributing $75,000 cash for a 20% interest.
2. Net income of $150,000 was earned in 20Y5. In addition, Dennis Overton received a salary allowance of $40,000 for the year. The three partners agree to an income-sharing ratio equal to their capital balances after admitting Campbell.
3. The partners' withdrawals are equal to half of the increase in their capital balances from salary allowance and income.

Prepare a statement of partnership equity for the year ended December 31, 20Y5.

EX 12-16 Withdrawal of partner OBJ. 3

Lane Stevens is to retire from the partnership of Stevens and Associates as of March 31, the end of the current fiscal year. After closing the accounts, the capital balances of the partners are as follows: Lane Stevens, $150,000; Cherrie Ford, $70,000; and LaMarcus Rollins, $60,000. They have shared net income and net losses in the ratio of 3:2:2. The partners agree that the merchandise inventory should be increased by $22,300 and the allowance for doubtful accounts should be increased by $1,300. Stevens agrees to accept a note for $100,000 in partial settlement of his ownership equity. The remainder of his claim is to be paid in cash. Ford and Rollins are to share equally in the net income or net loss of the new partnership.

Journalize the entries to record (a) the adjustment of the assets to bring them into agreement with current market prices and (b) the withdrawal of Stevens from the partnership.

EX 12-17 Statement of members' equity, admitting new member   OBJ. 2, 3, 5

✔ a. 3:7

The statement of members' equity for Bonanza, LLC, follows:

Bonanza, LLC
Statement of Members' Equity
For the Years Ended December 31, 20Y3 and 20Y4

	Idaho Properties, LLC, Member Equity	Silver Streams, LLC, Member Equity	Thomas Dunn, Member Equity	Total Members' Equity
Members' equity, January 1, 20Y3	$273,000	$307,000		$ 580,000
Net income	57,000	133,000		190,000
Members' equity, December 31, 20Y3	$330,000	$440,000		$ 770,000
Dunn contribution, January 1, 20Y4	3,000	7,000	$220,000	230,000
Net income	62,500	137,500	50,000	250,000
Member withdrawals	(32,000)	(48,000)	(40,000)	(120,000)
Members' equity, December 31, 20Y4	$363,500	$536,500	$230,000	$1,130,000

a. What was the income-sharing ratio in 20Y3?
b. What was the income-sharing ratio in 20Y4?
c. How much cash did Thomas Dunn contribute to Bonanza, LLC, for his interest?
d. Why do the member equity accounts of Idaho Properties, LLC, and Silver Streams, LLC, have positive entries for Thomas Dunn's contribution?
e. What percentage interest of Bonanza did Thomas Dunn acquire?
f. Why are withdrawals less than net income?

EX 12-18 Distribution of cash upon liquidation   OBJ. 4

✔ a. $11,000 loss

Hewitt and Patel are partners, sharing gains and losses equally. They decide to terminate their partnership. Prior to realization, their capital balances are $28,000 and $18,000, respectively. After all noncash assets are sold and all liabilities are paid, there is a cash balance of $35,000.

a. What is the amount of a gain or loss on realization?
b. How should the gain or loss be divided between Hewitt and Patel?
c. How should the cash be divided between Hewitt and Patel?

EX 12-19 Distribution of cash upon liquidation   OBJ. 4

✔ Oliver, $30,000

David Oliver and Umar Ansari, with capital balances of $28,000 and $35,000, respectively, decide to liquidate their partnership. After selling the noncash assets and paying the liabilities, there is $67,000 of cash remaining. If the partners share income and losses equally, how should the cash be distributed?

EX 12-20 Liquidating partnerships—capital deficiency   OBJ. 4

✔ b. $97,500

Lewis, Zapata, and Fowler share equally in net income and net losses. After the partnership sells all assets for cash, divides the losses on realization, and pays the liabilities, the balances in the capital accounts are as follows: Lewis, $73,500 Cr.; Zapata, $41,000 Cr.; Fowler, $17,000 Dr.

a. What term is applied to the debit balance in Fowler's capital account?
b. What is the amount of cash on hand?
c. Journalize the transaction that must take place for Lewis and Zapata to receive cash in the liquidation process equal to their capital account balances.

Chapter 12 Accounting for Partnerships and Limited Liability Companies

EX 12-21 Distribution of cash upon liquidation
OBJ. 4

✔ a. $975

Bray, Lincoln, and Mapes arranged to import and sell orchid corsages for a university dance. They agreed to share equally the net income or net loss of the venture. Bray and Lincoln advanced $225 and $300 of their own respective funds to pay for advertising and other expenses. After collecting for all sales and paying creditors, the partnership has $1,500 in cash.

a. How much net income was earned from the venture?

b. How should the $1,500 be distributed?

c. Assuming that the partnership has only $300 instead of $1,500, do any of the three partners have a capital deficiency? If so, how much?

EX 12-22 Liquidating partnerships—capital deficiency
OBJ. 4

Nettles, King, and Tanaka are partners sharing income 3:2:1. After the firm's loss from liquidation is distributed, the capital account balances were as follows: Nettles, $15,000 Dr.; King, $46,000 Cr.; and Tanaka, $71,000 Cr. If Nettles is personally bankrupt and unable to pay any of the $15,000, what will be the amount of cash received by King and Tanaka upon liquidation?

EX 12-23 Statement of partnership liquidation
OBJ. 4, 5

After closing the accounts on July 1, prior to liquidating the partnership, the capital account balances of Gold, Porter, and Sims are $55,000, $45,000, and $20,000, respectively. Cash, noncash assets, and liabilities total $56,000, $96,000, and $32,000, respectively. Between July 1 and July 29, the noncash assets are sold for $90,000, the liabilities are paid, and the remaining cash is distributed to the partners. The partners share net income and loss in the ratio of 3:2:1. Prepare a statement of partnership liquidation for the period July 1–29.

EX 12-24 Statement of LLC liquidation
OBJ. 4, 5

Lester, Torres, and Hearst are members of Arcadia Sales, LLC, sharing income and losses in the ratio of 2:2:1, respectively. The members decide to liquidate the limited liability company. The members' equity prior to liquidation and asset realization on August 1 are as follows:

Lester	$ 49,000
Torres	61,000
Hearst	27,000
Total	$137,000

In winding up operations during the month of August, noncash assets with a book value of $146,000 are sold for $158,000, and liabilities of $35,000 are satisfied. Prior to realization, Arcadia Sales has a cash balance of $26,000.

a. Prepare a statement of LLC liquidation.

b. Provide the journal entry for the final cash distribution to members.

c. What is the role of the income- and loss-sharing ratio in liquidating an LLC?

EX 12-25 Partnership entries and statement of partnership equity
OBJ. 2, 5

✔ b. Alvarez, Capital, Dec. 31, $54,000

The capital accounts of Angel Alvarez and Emma Allison have balances of $47,000 and $73,000, respectively, on January 1, 20Y4, the beginning of the fiscal year. On March 10, Alvarez invested an additional $8,000. During the year, Alvarez and Allison withdrew $32,000 and $39,000, respectively, and net income for the year was $62,000. Revenues were $483,000, and expenses were $421,000. The articles of partnership make no reference to the division of net income.

a. Journalize the entries to close (1) the revenues and expenses and (2) the drawing accounts.

b. Prepare a statement of partnership equity for the current year for the partnership of Alvarez and Allison.

620 Chapter 12 Accounting for Partnerships and Limited Liability Companies

EX 12-26 Revenue per professional staff OBJ. 6

The accounting firm of Deloitte & Touche is the largest international accounting firm in the world as ranked by total revenues. For two recent years, Deloitte & Touche reported the following for its U.S. operations:

	Current Year	Previous Year
Revenue (in billions)	$16.1	$14.9
Number of professional staff (including partners)	58,585	53,592

a. For the current and previous years, determine the revenue per professional staff.
b. Interpret the trend between the two years.

EX 12-27 Revenue per employee OBJ. 6

Superior Cleaning Services, LLC, provides cleaning services for office buildings. The firm has 10 members in the LLC, which did not change between 20Y8 and 20Y9. During 20Y9, the business terminated two commercial contracts. The following revenue and employee information is provided:

	20Y9	20Y8
Revenues (in thousands)	$16,200	$18,400
Number of employees (excluding members)	150	200

a. For 20Y9 and 20Y8, determine the revenue per employee (excluding members).
b. Interpret the trend between the two years.

Problems: Series A

✔ 3. Keene net income, $33,800

PR 12-1A Entries and balance sheet for partnership OBJ. 2

On March 1, 20Y8, Eric Keene and Renee Wallace form a partnership. Keene agrees to invest $23,400 in cash and merchandise inventory valued at $62,600. Wallace invests certain business assets at valuations agreed upon, transfers business liabilities, and contributes sufficient cash to bring her total capital to $60,000. Details regarding the book values of the business assets and liabilities, and the agreed valuations, follow:

	Wallace's Ledger Balance	Agreed-Upon Valuation
Accounts Receivable	$19,900	$19,500
Allowance for Doubtful Accounts	1,200	1,400
Equipment	83,500	55,400
Accumulated Depreciation—Equipment	29,800	
Accounts Payable	15,000	15,000
Notes Payable (current)	37,500	37,500

The partnership agreement includes the following provisions regarding the division of net income: interest on original investments at 10%, salary allowances of $19,000 (Keene) and $24,000 (Wallace), and the remainder equally.

Instructions

1. Journalize the entries to record the investments of Keene and Wallace in the partnership accounts.
2. Prepare a balance sheet as of March 1, 20Y8, the date of formation of the partnership of Keene and Wallace.
3. After adjustments at February 28, 20Y9, the end of the first full year of operations, the revenues were $300,000 and expenses were $230,000, for a net income of $70,000. The drawing accounts have debit balances of $19,000 (Keene) and $24,000 (Wallace). Journalize the entries to close the revenues and expenses and the drawing accounts at February 28, 20Y9.

Chapter 12 Accounting for Partnerships and Limited Liability Companies

✔ 1. f. Morrison net income, $45,000

PR 12-2A Dividing partnership income
OBJ. 2

Morrison and Greene have decided to form a partnership. They have agreed that Morrison is to invest $150,000 and that Greene is to invest $50,000. Morrison is to devote one-half time to the business, and Greene is to devote full time. The following plans for the division of income are being considered:

a. Equal division

b. In the ratio of original investments

c. In the ratio of time devoted to the business

d. Interest of 6% on original investments and the remainder equally

e. Interest of 6% on original investments, salary allowances of $40,000 to Morrison and $70,000 to Greene, and the remainder equally

f. Plan (e), except that Greene is also to be allowed a bonus equal to 20% of the amount by which net income exceeds the total salary allowances

Instructions
For each plan, determine the division of the net income under each of the following assumptions: (1) net income of $115,000 and (2) net income of $200,000. Present the data in tabular form, using the following columnar headings:

	$115,000		$200,000	
Plan	Morrison	Greene	Morrison	Greene

✔ 2. Dec. 31 capital—Yost, $125,000

PR 12-3A Financial statements for partnership
OBJ. 2, 5

The ledger of Tyler Lambert and Jayla Yost, attorneys-at-law, contains the following accounts and balances after adjustments have been recorded on December 31, 20Y3:

Lambert and Yost
Trial Balance
December 31, 20Y3

	Debit Balances	Credit Balances
Cash	34,000	
Accounts Receivable	47,800	
Supplies	2,000	
Land	120,000	
Building	157,500	
Accumulated Depreciation—Building		67,200
Office Equipment	63,600	
Accumulated Depreciation—Office Equipment		21,700
Accounts Payable		27,900
Salaries Payable		5,100
Tyler Lambert, Capital		135,000
Tyler Lambert, Drawing	50,000	
Jayla Yost, Capital		88,000
Jayla Yost, Drawing	60,000	
Professional Fees		395,300
Salary Expense	154,500	
Depreciation Expense—Building	15,700	
Property Tax Expense	12,000	
Heating and Lighting Expense	8,500	
Supplies Expense	6,000	
Depreciation Expense—Office Equipment	5,000	
Miscellaneous Expense	3,600	
	740,200	740,200

The balance in Yost's capital account includes an additional investment of $10,000 made on April 10, 20Y3.

(Continued)

Instructions

1. Prepare an income statement for 20Y3, indicating the division of net income. The partnership agreement provides for salary allowances of $45,000 to Lambert and $54,700 to Yost, allowances of 10% on each partner's capital balance at the beginning of the fiscal year, and equal division of the remaining net income or net loss.
2. Prepare a statement of partnership equity for 20Y3.
3. Prepare a balance sheet as of the end of 20Y3.

PR 12-4A Admitting new partner   OBJ. 3

✔ 3. Total assets, $326,300

Musa Moshref and Shaniqua Hollins have operated a successful firm for many years, sharing net income and net losses equally. Taylor Anderson is to be admitted to the partnership on July 1 of the current year, in accordance with the following agreement:

a. Assets and liabilities of the old partnership are to be valued at their book values as of June 30, except for the following:
   - Accounts receivable amounting to $2,500 are to be written off, and the allowance for doubtful accounts is to be increased to 5% of the remaining accounts.
   - Merchandise inventory is to be valued at $76,600.
   - Equipment is to be valued at $155,700.

b. Anderson is to purchase $70,000 of the ownership interest of Hollins for $75,000 cash and to contribute another $45,000 cash to the partnership for a total ownership equity of $115,000.

The post-closing trial balance of Moshref and Hollins as of June 30 is as follows:

Moshref and Hollins
Post-Closing Trial Balance
June 30, 20Y7

	Debit Balances	Credit Balances
Cash	8,000	
Accounts Receivable	42,500	
Allowance for Doubtful Accounts		1,600
Merchandise Inventory	72,000	
Prepaid Insurance	3,000	
Equipment	180,500	
Accumulated Depreciation—Equipment		43,100
Accounts Payable		21,300
Notes Payable (current)		35,000
Musa Moshref, Capital		120,000
Shaniqua Hollins, Capital		85,000
	306,000	306,000

Instructions

1. Journalize the entries as of June 30 to record the revaluations, using a temporary account entitled Asset Revaluations. Debits and credits to the Asset Revaluation account are losses and gains from revaluation, respectively. The balance in the accumulated depreciation account is to be eliminated. After journalizing the revaluations, close the balance of the asset revaluations account to the capital accounts of Musa Moshref and Shaniqua Hollins.
2. Journalize the additional entries to record Anderson's entrance to the partnership on July 1, 20Y7.
3. Present a balance sheet for the new partnership as of July 1, 20Y7.

PR 12-5A Statement of partnership liquidation   OBJ. 4

✔ 1d. Gerloff $8,500

After the accounts are closed on February 3, prior to liquidating the partnership, the capital accounts of William Gerloff, Joshua Chu, and Courtney Jewett are $19,300, $4,500, and $22,300, respectively. Cash and noncash assets total $5,200 and $55,900, respectively. Amounts owed to creditors total $15,000. The partners share income and losses in the ratio of 2:1:1. Between February 3 and February 28, the noncash assets are sold for $34,300, the partner with the capital deficiency pays the deficiency to the partnership, and the liabilities are paid.

Instructions

1. Prepare a statement of partnership liquidation, indicating (a) the sale of assets and division of loss, (b) the payment of liabilities, (c) the receipt of the deficiency (from the appropriate partner), and (d) the distribution of cash.

2. Assume that the partner with the capital deficiency declares bankruptcy and is unable to pay the deficiency. Journalize the entries to (a) allocate the partner's deficiency and (b) distribute the remaining cash.

PR 12-6A Statement of partnership liquidation   OBJ. 4

On November 1, the firm of Sails, Welch, and Greenberg decided to liquidate its partnership. The partners have capital balances of $58,000, $72,000, and $10,000, respectively. The cash balance is $32,000, the book values of noncash assets total $128,000, and liabilities total $20,000. The partners share income and losses in the ratio of 2:2:1.

Instructions

1. Prepare a statement of partnership liquidation, covering the period November 1–30, for each of the following independent assumptions:

   a. All of the noncash assets are sold for $156,000 in cash, the creditors are paid, and the remaining cash is distributed to the partners.

   b. All of the noncash assets are sold for $55,000 in cash, the creditors are paid, the partner with the debit capital balance pays the amount owed to the firm, and the remaining cash is distributed to the partners.

2. Assume that the partner with the capital deficiency in part (b) declares bankruptcy and is unable to pay the deficiency. Journalize the entries to (a) allocate the partner's deficiency and (b) distribute the remaining cash.

Problems: Series B

PR 12-1B Entries and balance sheet for partnership   OBJ. 2

✔ 3. Lang net income, $63,400

On April 1, 20Y1, Whitney Lang and Eli Capri form a partnership. Lang agrees to invest $18,000 cash and merchandise inventory valued at $50,000. Capri invests certain business assets at valuations agreed upon, transfers business liabilities, and contributes sufficient cash to bring his total capital to $120,000. Details regarding the book values of the business assets and liabilities, and the agreed valuations, follow:

	Capri's Ledger Balance	Agreed-Upon Balance
Accounts Receivable	$45,700	$43,400
Allowance for Doubtful Accounts	3,200	3,500
Merchandise Inventory	31,500	28,900
Equipment	89,500	63,400
Accumulated Depreciation—Equipment	19,000	
Accounts Payable	23,400	23,400
Notes Payable (current)	15,000	15,000

The partnership agreement includes the following provisions regarding the division of net income: interest of 10% on original investments, salary allowances of $36,000 (Lang) and $22,000 (Capri), and the remainder equally.

Instructions

1. Journalize the entries to record the investments of Lang and Capri in the partnership accounts.

2. Prepare a balance sheet as of April 1, 20Y1, the date of formation of the partnership of Lang and Capri.

3. After adjustments at March 31, 20Y2, the end of the first full year of operations, the revenues were $598,000 and expenses were $480,000, for a net income of $118,000.

(Continued)

624 Chapter 12 Accounting for Partnerships and Limited Liability Companies

The drawing accounts have debit balances of $40,000 (Lang) and $30,000 (Capri). Journalize the entries to close the revenues and expenses and the drawing accounts at March 31, 20Y2.

PR 12-2B Dividing partnership income OBJ. 2

✔ 1. f. Howell net income, $254,550

Dylan Howell and Demond Nickles have decided to form a partnership. They have agreed that Howell is to invest $50,000 and that Nickles is to invest $75,000. Howell is to devote full time to the business, and Nickles is to devote one-half time. The following plans for the division of income are being considered:

a. Equal division
b. In the ratio of original investments
c. In the ratio of time devoted to the business
d. Interest of 10% on original investments and the remainder in the ratio of 3:2
e. Interest of 10% on original investments, salary allowances of $38,000 to Howell and $19,000 to Nickles, and the remainder equally.
f. Plan (e), except that Howell is also to be allowed a bonus equal to 20% of the amount by which net income exceeds the total salary allowances

Instructions

For each plan, determine the division of the net income under each of the following assumptions: (1) net income of $420,000 and (2) net income of $150,000. Present the data in tabular form, using the following columnar headings:

	$420,000		$150,000	
Plan	Howell	Nickles	Howell	Nickles

PR 12-3B Financial statements for partnerships OBJ. 2, 5

✔ 2. Dec. 31 capital— Xue, $179,100

The ledger of Camila Ramirez and Ping Xue, attorneys-at-law, contains the following accounts and balances after adjustments have been recorded on December 31, 20Y2:

Ramirez and Xue
Trial Balance
December 31, 20Y2

	Debit Balances	Credit Balances
Cash	70,300	
Accounts Receivable	33,600	
Supplies	5,800	
Land	128,000	
Building	175,000	
Accumulated Depreciation—Building		80,000
Office Equipment	42,000	
Accumulated Depreciation—Office Equipment		25,300
Accounts Payable		12,400
Salaries Payable		10,000
Camila Ramirez, Capital		125,000
Camila Ramirez, Drawing	35,000	
Ping Xue, Capital		155,000
Ping Xue, Drawing	50,000	
Professional Fees		555,300
Salary Expense	384,900	
Depreciation Expense—Building	12,900	
Heating and Lighting Expense	10,500	
Depreciation Expense—Office Equipment	6,300	
Property Tax Expense	3,200	
Supplies Expense	3,000	
Miscellaneous Expense	2,500	
	963,000	963,000

Chapter 12 Accounting for Partnerships and Limited Liability Companies 625

The balance in Xue's capital account includes an additional investment of $20,000 made on May 5, 20Y2.

Instructions

1. Prepare an income statement for 20Y2, indicating the division of net income. The partnership agreement provides for salary allowances of $50,000 to Ramirez and $65,000 to Xue, allowances of 12% on each partner's capital balance at the beginning of the fiscal year, and equal division of the remaining net income or net loss.
2. Prepare a statement of partnership equity for 20Y2.
3. Prepare a balance sheet as of the end of 20Y2.

PR 12-4B Admitting new partner OBJ. 3

✔ 3. Total assets, $173,900

Brian Caldwell and Adriana Estrada have operated a successful firm for many years, sharing net income and net losses equally. Kris Mays is to be admitted to the partnership on September 1 of the current year, in accordance with the following agreement:

a. Assets and liabilities of the old partnership are to be valued at their book values as of August 31, except for the following:

- Accounts receivable amounting to $1,500 are to be written off, and the allowance for doubtful accounts is to be increased to 5% of the remaining accounts.
- Merchandise inventory is to be valued at $46,800.
- Equipment is to be valued at $64,500.

b. Mays is to purchase $26,000 of the ownership interest of Estrada for $30,000 cash and to contribute $32,000 cash to the partnership for a total ownership equity of $58,000.

The post-closing trial balance of Caldwell and Estrada as of August 31 follows:

Caldwell and Estrada
Post-Closing Trial Balance
August 31, 20Y9

	Debit Balances	Credit Balances
Cash	12,300	
Accounts Receivable	19,500	
Allowance for Doubtful Accounts		600
Merchandise Inventory	42,500	
Prepaid Insurance	1,200	
Equipment	67,500	
Accumulated Depreciation—Equipment		15,500
Accounts Payable		8,900
Notes Payable (current)		15,000
Brian Caldwell, Capital		55,000
Adriana Estrada, Capital		48,000
	143,000	143,000

Instructions

1. Journalize the entries as of August 31 to record the revaluations, using a temporary account entitled Asset Revaluations. Debits and credits to the Asset Revaluation account are losses and gains from revaluation, respectively. The balance in the accumulated depreciation account is to be eliminated. After journalizing the revaluations, close the balance of the asset revaluations account to the capital accounts of Brian Caldwell and Adriana Estrada.
2. Journalize the additional entries to record Mays' entrance to the partnership on September 1, 20Y9.
3. Present a balance sheet for the new partnership as of September 1, 20Y9.

626 Chapter 12 Accounting for Partnerships and Limited Liability Companies

✓1d. Fairchild, $33,000

PR 12-5B Statement of partnership liquidation OBJ. 4

After the accounts are closed on April 10, prior to liquidating the partnership, the capital accounts of Zach Fairchild, Austin Lowes, and Amber Howard are $42,000, $7,500, and $36,500, respectively. Cash and noncash assets total $23,500 and $84,500, respectively. Amounts owed to creditors total $22,000. The partners share income and losses in the ratio of 1:1:2. Between April 10 and April 30, the noncash assets are sold for $48,500, the partner with the capital deficiency pays the deficiency to the partnership, and the liabilities are paid.

Instructions

1. Prepare a statement of partnership liquidation, indicating (a) the sale of assets and division of loss, (b) the payment of liabilities, (c) the receipt of the deficiency (from the appropriate partner), and (d) the distribution of cash.

2. Assume that the partner with the capital deficiency declares bankruptcy and is unable to pay the deficiency. Journalize the entries to (a) allocate the partner's deficiency and (b) distribute the remaining cash.

PR 12-6B Statement of partnership liquidation OBJ. 4

On August 3, the firm of Chapelle, Rock, and Pryor decided to liquidate its partnership. The partners have capital balances of $14,000, $102,000, and $86,000, respectively. The cash balance is $65,000, the book values of noncash assets total $167,000, and liabilities total $30,000. The partners share income and losses in the ratio of 1:2:2.

Instructions

1. Prepare a statement of partnership liquidation, covering the period August 3–29, for each of the following independent assumptions:
   a. All of the noncash assets are sold for $217,000 in cash, the creditors are paid, and the remaining cash is distributed to the partners.
   b. All of the noncash assets are sold for $72,000 in cash, the creditors are paid, the partner with the debit capital balance pays the amount owed to the firm, and the remaining cash is distributed to the partners.

2. Assume that the partner with the capital deficiency in part (b) declares bankruptcy and is unable to pay the deficiency. Journalize the entries to (a) allocate the partner's deficiency and (b) distribute the remaining cash.

Cases & Projects

CP 12-1 Ethics in Action

Taye Barrow, M.D., and James Robbins, M.D., are sole owners of two medical practices that operate in the same medical building. The two doctors agree to combine assets and liabilities of the two businesses to form a partnership. The partnership agreement calls for dividing income equally between the two doctors. After several months, the following conversation takes place between the two doctors:

Barrow: I've noticed that your patient load has dropped over the last couple of months. When we formed our partnership, we were seeing about the same number of patients per week. However, now our patient records show that you have been seeing about half as many patients as I have. Are there any issues that I should be aware of?

Robbins: There's nothing going on. When I was working on my own, I was really putting in the hours. One of the reasons I formed this partnership was to enjoy life a little more and scale back a little bit.

Barrow: I see. Well, I find that I'm working as hard as I did when I was on my own yet making less than I did previously. Essentially, you're sharing in half of my billings and I'm sharing in half of yours. Since you are working much less than I am, I end up on the short end of the bargain.

Robbins: Well, I don't know what to say. An agreement is an agreement. The partnership is based on a 50/50 split. That's what a partnership is all about.

Barrow: If that's so, then it applies equally well on the effort end of the equation as it does on the income end.

➤ Discuss whether Robbins is acting in an ethical manner. How could Barrow renegotiate the partnership agreement to avoid this dispute?

CP 12-2 Team Activity

In groups of two or three, find the most recent "Accounting Today Top 100 Firms" on the Internet.

a. From this document, create an Excel spreadsheet of the total revenues and total partners for Deloitte & Touche, PwC, Ernst & Young, and KPMG.

b. Determine the revenue per partner for each of these four firms. Round to the nearest dollar.

c. Develop a table of the revenue earned per partner of each of these four firms as a percent of the highest revenue per partner firm.

d. Interpret the differences between the firms in terms of your answer in (c).

CP 12-3 Communication

Lindsey Wilson has agreed to invest $200,000 into an LLC with Lacy Lovett and Justin Lassiter. Lovett and Lassiter will not invest any money but will provide effort and expertise to the LLC. Lovett and Lassiter have agreed that the net income of the LLC should be divided so that Wilson is to receive a 10% preferred return on her capital investment prior to any remaining income being divided equally among the partners. In addition, Lovett and Lassiter have suggested that the operating agreement be written so that all matters are settled by majority vote, with each partner having a one-third voting interest in the LLC.
➤ If you were providing Lindsey Wilson counsel, what might you suggest in forming the final agreement?

CP 12-4 Dividing partnership income

Terry Willard and Jasmine Hill decide to form a partnership. Willard will contribute $300,000 to the partnership, while Hill will contribute only $30,000. However, Hill will be responsible for running the day-to-day operations of the partnership, which are anticipated to require about 45 hours per week. In contrast, Willard will only work five hours per week for the partnership. The two partners are attempting to determine a formula for dividing partnership net income. Willard believes the partners should divide income in the ratio of 7:3, favoring Willard, since Willard provides the majority of the capital. Hill believes the income should be divided 7:3, favoring Hill, since Hill provides the majority of effort in running the partnership business.
➤ How would you advise the partners in developing a method for dividing income?

CHAPTER 13
Corporations: Organization, Stock Transactions, and Dividends

Chapters 1–4
Accounting Cycle

Chapter 5
Accounting Systems

| Income Statement | Statement of Owner's Equity | Balance Sheet | Statement of Cash Flows |

Chapter 6 *Accounting for Merchandising Businesses*

Chapter 16 *Cash Flows*

Assets = Liabilities + Owner's Equity

Chapter 8 *Cash*
Chapter 9 *Receivables*
Chapter 7 *Inventories*
Chapter 10 *Fixed and Intangible Assets*
Chapter 15 *Investments*

Chapter 11 *Current Liabilities and Payroll*
Chapter 14 *Bonds and Notes*

Chapter 12 *Partnerships*
Chapter 13 *Corporations: Organization, Stock Transactions, and Dividends*

Chapter 17
Financial Statement Analysis

Statement of Retained Earnings

Retained earnings, Jan. 1		$XXX
Net income	$ XXX	
Dividends	(XXX)	
Increase in retained earnings		XXX
Retained earnings, Dec. 31		$XXX

Statement of Cash Flows

Cash flows from (used in) operating activities	$XXX
Cash flows from (used in) investing activities	XXX
Cash flows from (used in) financing activities	XXX
Change in cash	$XXX

Sales		$XXX
Cost of merchandise sold		XXX
Gross profit		$XXX
Operating expenses:		
Advertising expense	$XXX	
Depreciation expense	XXX	
Amortization expense	XXX	
Depletion expense	XXX	
…	XXX	
…	XXX	
Total operating expenses		XXX
Income from operations		$XXX
Other revenue and expenses		XXX
Net income		$XXX

Balance Sheet

Assets:		
Current assets		$XXX
Property, plant, and equipment		XXX
Intangible assets		XXX
Total assets		$XXX
Liabilities:		
Current liabilities	$ XXX	
Long-term liabilities	XXX	
Total liabilities		$XXX
Stockholders' equity:		
Retained earnings	$ XXX	
Common stock	XXX	
Preferred stock	XXX	
Paid-in capital in excess of par	XXX	
Paid-in capital from sale of treasury stock	XXX	
Treasury stock	(XXX)	
Total stockholders' equity		XXX
Total liabilities and stockholders' equity		$XXX

CHAPTER 13

Alphabet (Google), Inc.*

If you purchase a share of stock from **Google**, you own a small interest in the company. You may request a Google stock certificate as an indication of your ownership.

Google is one of the most visible companies on the Internet. Many of us cannot visit the Web without using Google to power a search or to retrieve our e-mail using Google's Gmail. Yet Google's Internet tools are free to online browsers. Google generates most of its revenue through online advertising.

Purchasing a share of stock from Google may be a great gift idea for the "hard-to-shop-for person." However, a stock certificate represents more than just a picture that you can frame. In fact, the stock certificate is a document that reflects legal ownership of the future financial prospects of Google. In addition, as a shareholder, it represents your claim against the assets and earnings of the corporation.

If you are purchasing Google stock as an investment, you should analyze Google's financial statements and management's plans for the future. For example, Google first offered its stock to the public on August 19, 2004, for $100 per share. Google's stock has sold for more than $1,000 per share, even though it pays no dividends. In addition, Google recently expanded into developing and offering free software platforms for mobile devices such as cell phones. For example, your cell phone may use Google's Android™ operating system. So, should you purchase Google stock?

This chapter describes and illustrates the nature of corporations, including the accounting for stock and dividends. This discussion will aid you in making decisions such as whether or not to buy stock in a company.

* In August 2015, Google, Inc. announced that it was reorganizing and changing the name of its company from Google to Alphabet. Alphabet will be the parent company for a number of different brands, including Google, Android, and YouTube.

Learning Objectives

After studying this chapter, you should be able to:

Example Exercises (EE) are shown in **green**.

Obj. 1 Describe the nature of the corporate form of organization.

Nature of a Corporation
Characteristics of a Corporation
Forming a Corporation

Obj. 2 Describe the two main sources of stockholders' equity.

Stockholders' Equity

Obj. 3 Describe and illustrate the characteristics of stock, classes of stock, and entries for issuing stock.

Paid-In Capital from Stock
Characteristics of Stock
Classes of Stock   EE 13-1
Issuing Stock   EE 13-2
Premium on Stock   EE 13-2
No-Par Stock   EE 13-2

Obj. 4 Describe and illustrate the accounting for cash dividends and stock dividends.

Accounting for Dividends
Cash Dividends   EE 13-3
Stock Dividends   EE 13-4

Obj. 5 Describe the effect of stock splits on corporate financial statements.

Stock Splits

Obj. 6 Describe and illustrate the accounting for treasury stock transactions.

Treasury Stock Transactions
Entries for Treasury Stock   EE 13-5

Obj. 7 Describe and illustrate the reporting of stockholders' equity.

Reporting Stockholders' Equity
Stockholders' Equity on the Balance Sheet   EE 13-6
Reporting Retained Earnings   EE 13-7
Statement of Stockholders' Equity
Reporting Stockholders' Equity for Mornin' Joe

Obj. 8 Describe and illustrate the use of earnings per share in evaluating a company's profitability.

Financial Analysis and Interpretation: Earnings per Share
Compute Earnings per Share   EE 13-8

At a Glance 13   Page 652

Obj. 1 Describe the nature of the corporate form of organization.

Nature of a Corporation

Most large businesses are organized as corporations. As a result, corporations generate more than 90% of the total business dollars in the United States. In contrast, most small businesses are organized as proprietorships, partnerships, or limited liability companies.

Characteristics of a Corporation

A *corporation* is a legal entity, distinct and separate from the individuals who create and operate it. As a legal entity, a corporation may acquire, own, and dispose of property in its own name. It may also incur liabilities and enter into contracts. Most importantly, it can sell shares of ownership, called **stock**. Issuing (selling) stock gives corporations the ability to raise large amounts of capital.

The **stockholders** or *shareholders* who own the stock own the corporation. They can buy and sell stock without affecting the corporation's operations or continued existence. Corporations whose shares of stock are traded in public markets are called *public corporations*. Corporations whose shares are not traded publicly are usually owned by a small group of investors and are called *nonpublic* or *private corporations*.

The stockholders of a corporation have *limited liability*. This means that creditors usually may not go beyond the assets of the corporation to satisfy their claims. Thus, the financial loss that a stockholder may suffer is limited to the amount invested.

Note

Corporations have a separate legal existence, transferable units of ownership, and limited stockholder liability.

The stockholders control a corporation by electing a *board of directors*. This board meets periodically to establish corporate policies. It also selects the chief executive officer (CEO) and other major officers to manage the corporation's day-to-day affairs. Exhibit 1 shows the organizational structure of a corporation.

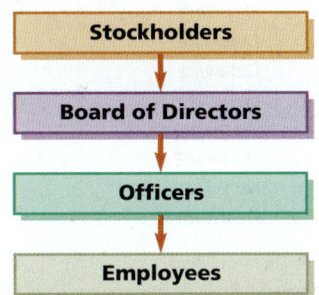

EXHIBIT 1

Organizational Structure of a Corporation

As a separate entity, a corporation is subject to taxes. For example, corporations must pay federal income taxes on their income.[1] Thus, corporate income that is distributed to stockholders in the form of *dividends* has already been taxed. In turn, stockholders must pay income taxes on the dividends they receive. This *double taxation* of corporate earnings is a major disadvantage of the corporate form. The advantages and disadvantages of the corporate form are listed in Exhibit 2.

Advantages and Disadvantages of the Corporate Form **EXHIBIT 2**

Advantages	Explanation
Separate legal existence	A corporation exists separately from its owners.
Continuous life	A corporation's life is separate from its owners; therefore, it exists indefinitely.
Raising large amounts of capital	The corporate form is suited for raising large amounts of money from shareholders.
Ownership rights are easily transferable	A corporation sells shares of ownership, called *stock*. The stockholders of a public company can transfer their shares of stock to other stockholders through stock markets such as the New York Stock Exchange.
Limited liability	A corporation's creditors usually may not go beyond the assets of the corporation to satisfy their claims. Thus, the financial loss that a stockholder may suffer is limited to the amount invested.

Disadvantages	Explanation
Owner is separate from management	Stockholders control management through a board of directors. The board of directors should represent shareholder interests; however, the board is often more closely tied to management than to shareholders. As a result, the board of directors and management may not always behave in the best interests of stockholders.
Double taxation of dividends	As a separate legal entity, a corporation is subject to taxation. Thus, net income distributed as dividends will be taxed once at the corporation level and then again at the individual level.
Regulatory costs	Corporations must satisfy many regulatory requirements, such as those required by the Sarbanes-Oxley Act.

Forming a Corporation

The first step in forming a corporation is to file an *application of incorporation* with the state. State incorporation laws differ, and corporations often organize in those states with the more favorable laws. For this reason, more than half of the largest companies are incorporated in Delaware. Exhibit 3 lists some corporations, their states of incorporation, and the location of their headquarters.

After the application of incorporation has been approved, the state grants a *charter* or *articles of incorporation*. The articles of incorporation formally create the corporation.[2] The corporate management and board of directors then prepare a set of *bylaws*, which are the rules and procedures for conducting the corporation's affairs.

---

[1] A majority of states also require corporations to pay income taxes.
[2] The articles of incorporation may also restrict a corporation's activities in certain areas, such as owning certain types of real estate, conducting certain types of business activities, or purchasing its own stock.

EXHIBIT 3

Examples of Corporations and Their States of Incorporation

Corporation	State of Incorporation	Headquarters
Caterpillar	Delaware	Peoria, Illinois
Deere & Co.	Delaware	Moline, Illinois
Delta Air Lines	Delaware	Atlanta, Georgia
General Electric Company	New York	Fairfield, Connecticut
The Home Depot	Delaware	Atlanta, Georgia
Kellogg Company	Delaware	Battle Creek, Michigan
R.J. Reynolds Tobacco Company	Delaware	Winston-Salem, North Carolina
Starbucks Corporation	Washington	Seattle, Washington
3M Company	Delaware	St. Paul, Minnesota
Walt Disney Company	Delaware	Burbank, California
Whirlpool Corporation	Delaware	Benton Harbor, Michigan

Link to Alphabet (Google)

Alphabet (Google)'s state of incorporation is Delaware, but its headquarters is located in Mountain View, California.

Costs may be incurred in organizing a corporation. These costs include legal fees, taxes, state incorporation fees, license fees, and promotional costs. Such costs are debited to an expense account entitled *Organizational Expenses*.

To illustrate, a corporation's organizing costs of $8,500 on January 5 are recorded as follows:

Jan.	5	Organizational Expenses		8,500	
		Cash			8,500
		Paid costs of organizing the corporation.			

Business Connection

Some excerpts from Alphabet (Google)'s bylaws (amended and restated on October 2, 2015) are as follows:

1.1 REGISTERED OFFICE.
The registered office of Alphabet Inc. shall be fixed in the corporation's certificate of incorporation . . .

ARTICLE II—MEETINGS OF STOCKHOLDERS

2.1 PLACE OF MEETINGS.
. . . stockholders' meetings shall be held at the corporation's principal executive office.

2.2 ANNUAL MEETING.
The annual meeting of stockholders shall be held each year on a date and at a time designated by the Board (of Directors). At the annual meeting, directors shall be elected and any other proper business may be transacted.

2.8 ADMINISTRATION OF THE MEETING.
Meetings of stockholders shall be presided over by the chairman of the Board . . .

ARTICLE V—OFFICERS

5.1 OFFICERS.
The officers of the corporation shall be a chief executive officer and a secretary. The corporation may also have . . . one or more presidents, a chief financial officer, a treasurer, one or more vice presidents, . . .

5.7 CHIEF EXECUTIVE OFFICER.
. . . the chief executive officer shall have general supervision, direction, and control of the business and affairs of the corporation and shall see that all orders and resolutions of the Board are carried into effect. . . .

5.10 SECRETARY.
The secretary shall keep . . . a book of minutes of all meetings and actions of directors, committees of directors, and stockholders.

5.11 CHIEF FINANCIAL OFFICER.
The chief financial officer shall keep and maintain, or cause to be kept and maintained, adequate and correct books and records of accounts of the properties and business transactions of the corporation, including accounts of its assets, liabilities, receipts, disbursements, gains, losses, capital, retained earnings and shares.

5.12 TREASURER.
. . . The treasurer shall deposit all moneys and other valuables in the name and to the credit of the corporation . . . shall disburse the funds of the corporation . . . shall render . . . an account of all his or her transactions as treasurer and of the financial condition of the corporation . . .

Source: https://abc.xyz/investor/other/bylaws.html

Stockholders' Equity

Obj. 2 Describe the two main sources of stockholders' equity.

The owners' equity in a corporation is called **stockholders' equity**, *shareholders' equity, shareholders' investment,* or *capital*. On the balance sheet, stockholders' equity is reported by its following two main sources, as shown in Exhibit 4:

- Capital contributed to the corporation by the stockholders, called **paid-in capital** or *contributed capital*
- Net income retained in the business, called **retained earnings**

EXHIBIT 4
Sources of Stockholders' Equity

Link to Alphabet (Google)
Alphabet (Google) recently reported paid-in capital of $29 billion and retained earnings of $75 billion.

A Stockholders' Equity section of a balance sheet follows:[3]

Stockholders' Equity

Paid-in capital:		
Common stock	$330,000	
Retained earnings	80,000	
Total stockholders' equity		$410,000

The paid-in capital contributed by the stockholders is recorded in separate accounts for each class of stock. If there is only one class of stock, the account is entitled *Common Stock* or *Capital Stock*.

Retained earnings is a corporation's cumulative net income that has not been distributed as dividends. **Dividends** are distributions of a corporation's earnings to stockholders. Sometimes retained earnings that are not distributed as dividends are referred to in the financial statements as *earnings retained for use in the business* and *earnings reinvested in the business*.

Net income increases retained earnings, while a net loss and dividends decrease retained earnings. The net increase or decrease in retained earnings for a period is recorded by the following two closing entries:

1. Debit each revenue account for its balance, credit each expense account for its balance, and credit (net income) or debit (net loss) the retained earnings account.
2. Debit the retained earnings account for the balance of each dividend account and credit each dividend account.

Most companies generate net income. In addition, most companies do not pay out all of their net income in dividends. As a result, Retained Earnings normally has a credit balance. However, in some cases, a debit balance in Retained Earnings may occur. A debit balance in Retained Earnings is called a **deficit**. Such a balance results from accumulated net losses. In the Stockholders' Equity section, a deficit is deducted from paid-in capital in determining total stockholders' equity.

---

[3] The reporting of stockholders' equity is further discussed and illustrated later in this chapter.

634 CHAPTER 13 Corporations: Organization, Stock Transactions, and Dividends

The balance of Retained Earnings represents earnings that have been reinvested back into the company. As cash is reinvested into the company, Cash decreases and Property, Plant, and Equipment or other assets increase. Because Retained Earnings is unaffected by the investments, its balance does not represent cash or cash available for dividends.

Obj. 3 Describe and illustrate the characteristics of stock, classes of stock, and entries for issuing stock.

Paid-In Capital from Stock

The two main sources of stockholders' equity are paid-in capital (or contributed capital) and retained earnings. The main source of paid-in capital is from issuing stock.

Characteristics of Stock

The number of shares of stock that a corporation is *authorized* to issue is stated in its charter. The term *issued* refers to the shares issued to the stockholders. A corporation may reacquire some of the stock it has issued. The stock remaining in the hands of stockholders is then called **outstanding stock**. The relationship between authorized, issued, and outstanding stock is shown in Exhibit 5.

EXHIBIT 5

Authorized, Issued, and Outstanding Stock

Number of shares authorized, issued, and outstanding

Upon request, corporations may issue stock certificates to stockholders to document their ownership. Printed on a stock certificate is the name of the company, the name of the stockholder, and the number of shares owned. The stock certificate may also indicate a dollar amount assigned to each share of stock, called **par value**. Stock may be issued without par, in which case it is called *no-par stock*. In some states, the board of directors of a corporation is required to assign a *stated value* to no-par stock.

Corporations have limited liability; thus, creditors have no claim against stockholders' personal assets. To protect creditors, however, some states require corporations to maintain a minimum amount of paid-in capital. This minimum amount, called *legal capital*, usually includes the par or stated value of the shares issued.

The major rights that accompany ownership of a share of stock are as follows:

- The right to vote in matters concerning the corporation
- The right to share in distributions of earnings
- The right to share in assets upon liquidation

These stock rights normally vary with the class of stock.

Link to Alphabet (Google)
The par value of **Alphabet (Google)**'s stock is $0.001 per share.

Classes of Stock

When only one class of stock is issued, it is called **common stock**. Each share of common stock has equal rights.

A corporation may also issue one or more classes of stock with various preference rights, such as a preference to dividends. Such a stock is called a **preferred stock**. The dividend rights of preferred stock are stated either as dollars per share or as a percent of par. For example, a $50 par value preferred stock with a $4-per-share dividend may be described as either:[4]

preferred $4 stock, $50 par
or
preferred 8% stock, $50 par

As shown in Exhibit 6, preferred stockholders have first rights (preference) to any dividends; thus, they have a greater chance of receiving dividends than common stockholders do. However, since dividends are normally based on earnings, a corporation cannot guarantee dividends even to preferred stockholders.

Link to Alphabet (Google)

Alphabet (Google) has three classes of common stock outstanding: Class A has one vote per share, Class B has 10 votes per share, and Class C has no voting rights. The current executive chairman and the two original founders control over 60% of the voting power through their ownership of Class B stock.

EXHIBIT 6

Dividend Preferences

The payment of dividends is authorized by the corporation's board of directors. When authorized, the directors are said to have *declared* a dividend.

Cumulative preferred stock has a right to receive regular dividends that were not declared (paid) in prior years. Noncumulative preferred stock does not have this right.

Business Connection

YOU HAVE NO VOTE

An emerging trend in technology companies is using multiple classes of stock to concentrate voting control of the company to the founders. For example, Mark Zuckerburg, the founder and CEO of Facebook, owns Class B shares of Facebook. The public owns Class A shares. The Class B shares have 10 votes for every one vote in the Class A shares. As a result, Zuckerburg owns 18% of the stock but 57% of the voting rights of Facebook. Other companies using multiple classes of stock in this way include Groupon, Zynga, and Yelp!. While becoming prevalent among new technology companies, using multiple classes of stock is not a new idea. The Hershey Company has had two classes of stock since becoming a public company in 1927. The Hershey Trust Company, which oversees the Milton Hershey School for orphans, has 80% of the voting control of The Hershey Company by controlling super voting shares. The argument in favor of super voting rights is that the founders can concentrate on the long-term goals of the company without concern for possibly more short-term goals of public shareholders. The argument in opposition is that concentrating control among the founders can eliminate or reduce the public shareholders' ability to hold management accountable.

---

[4] In some cases, preferred stock may receive additional dividends if certain conditions are met. Such stock, called *participating preferred stock*, is not often issued.

636 CHAPTER 13 Corporations: Organization, Stock Transactions, and Dividends

Cumulative preferred stock dividends that have not been paid in prior years are said to be **in arrears**. Any preferred dividends in arrears must be paid before any common stock dividends are paid. In addition, any dividends in arrears are normally disclosed in notes to the financial statements.

To illustrate, assume that a corporation has issued the following preferred and common stock:

1,000 shares of cumulative preferred $4 stock, $50 par
4,000 shares of common stock, $15 par

The corporation was organized on January 1, 20Y7, and paid no dividends in 20Y7 and 20Y8. In 20Y9, the corporation paid $22,000 in dividends, of which $12,000 was paid to preferred stockholders and $10,000 was paid to common stockholders, computed as follows:

Total dividends paid		$22,000
Preferred stockholders:		
20Y7 dividends in arrears (1,000 shares × $4)	$4,000	
20Y8 dividends in arrears (1,000 shares × $4)	4,000	
20Y9 dividend (1,000 shares × $4)	4,000	
Total preferred dividends paid		(12,000)
Dividends available to common stockholders		$10,000

As a result, preferred stockholders received $12.00 per share ($12,000 ÷ 1,000 shares) in dividends, while common stockholders received $2.50 per share ($10,000 ÷ 4,000 shares).

In addition to dividend preference, preferred stock may be given preferences to assets if the corporation goes out of business and is liquidated. However, claims of creditors must be satisfied first. Preferred stockholders are next in line to receive any remaining assets, followed by the common stockholders.

> **Link to Alphabet (Google)**
>
> Alphabet (Google) has 100,000,000 shares of authorized preferred stock with a par of $0.001, which are convertible to common stock. However, there are no shares of preferred stock issued or outstanding.

Note
The two primary classes of paid-in capital are common stock and preferred stock.

Example Exercise 13-1 — Dividends per Share — Obj. 3

Sandpiper Company has 20,000 shares of cumulative preferred 1% stock of $100 par and 100,000 shares of $50 par common stock. The following amounts were distributed as dividends:

Year 1	$10,000
Year 2	45,000
Year 3	80,000

Determine the dividends per share for preferred and common stock for each year.

Follow My Example 13-1

	Year 1	Year 2	Year 3
Amount distributed	$10,000	$45,000	$80,000
Preferred dividend (20,000 shares)	10,000	30,000*	20,000
Common dividend (100,000 shares)	$0	$15,000	$60,000

*Year 1 dividends in arrears of $10,000 plus Year 2 dividends of $20,000

Dividends per share:			
Preferred stock	$0.50	$1.50	$1.00
Common stock	None	$0.15	$0.60

Practice Exercises: PE 13-1A, PE 13-1B

Issuing Stock

A separate account is used for recording the amount of each class of stock issued to investors in a corporation. For example, assume that a corporation is authorized to issue 10,000 shares of $100 par preferred stock and 100,000 shares of $20 par common stock. The corporation issued 5,000 shares of preferred stock and 50,000 shares of common stock at par for cash. The corporation's entry to record the stock issue is as follows:[5]

Cash		1,500,000	
Preferred Stock (5,000 shares x $100)			500,000
Common Stock (50,000 shares x $20)			1,000,000
Issued preferred stock and common			
stock at par for cash.			

Stock is often issued by a corporation at a price other than its par. The price at which stock is sold depends on a variety of factors, such as the following:

- The financial condition, earnings record, and dividend record of the corporation
- Investor expectations of the corporation's potential earning power
- General business and economic conditions and expectations

If stock is issued (sold) for a price that is more than its par, the stock has been sold at a **premium**. For example, if common stock with a par of $50 is sold for $60 per share, the stock has sold at a premium of $10.

If stock is issued (sold) for a price that is less than its par, the stock has been sold at a **discount**. For example, if common stock with a par of $50 is sold for $45 per share, the stock has sold at a discount of $5. Many states do not permit stock to be sold at a discount. In other states, stock may be sold at a discount in only unusual cases. For these reasons, the par value of common stock is often set at a low amount ($1 or less). Because stock is rarely sold at a discount, it is not illustrated.

In order to distribute dividends, financial statements, and other reports, a corporation must keep track of its stockholders. Large public corporations normally use a financial institution, such as a bank, for this purpose.[6] In such cases, the financial institution is referred to as a *transfer agent* or *registrar*.

Premium on Stock

When stock is issued at a premium, Cash is debited for the amount received. Common Stock or Preferred Stock is credited for the par amount. The excess of the amount paid over par is part of the paid-in capital. An account entitled *Paid-In Capital in Excess of Par* is credited for this amount.

To illustrate, assume that Caldwell Company issues 2,000 shares of $50 par preferred stock for cash at $55. The entry to record this transaction is as follows:

Cash (2,000 shares x $55)		110,000	
Preferred Stock (2,000 shares x $50)			100,000
Paid-In Capital in Excess of Par—Preferred Stock			10,000
Issued $50 par preferred stock at $55.			

When stock is issued in exchange for assets other than cash, such as land, buildings, and equipment, the assets acquired are recorded at their fair market value. If this value cannot be determined, the fair market price of the stock issued is used.

---

[5] The accounting for investments in stocks from the point of view of the investor is discussed in Chapter 15.
[6] Small corporations may use a subsidiary ledger, called a *stockholders ledger*. In this case, the stock accounts (Preferred Stock and Common Stock) are controlling accounts for the subsidiary ledger.

To illustrate, assume that a corporation acquired land with a fair market value that cannot be determined. In exchange, the corporation issued 10,000 shares of its $10 par common stock. If the stock has a market price of $12 per share, the transaction is recorded as follows:

Land (10,000 shares × $12)	120,000	
Common Stock (10,000 shares × $10)		100,000
Paid-In Capital in Excess of Par		20,000
Issued $10 par common stock, valued at $12 per share, for land.		

No-Par Stock

In most states, no-par preferred and common stock may be issued. When no-par stock is issued, Cash is debited and Common Stock is credited for the proceeds. As no-par stock is issued over time, this entry is the same even if the issuing price varies.

To illustrate, assume that on January 9, a corporation issues 10,000 shares of no-par common stock at $40 a share. On June 27, the corporation issues an additional 1,000 shares at $36. The entries to record these issuances of the no-par stock are as follows:

Date			Debit	Credit
Jan.	9	Cash	400,000	
		Common Stock		400,000
		Issued 10,000 shares of no-par common stock at $40.		
June	27	Cash	36,000	
		Common Stock		36,000
		Issued 1,000 shares of no-par common stock at $36.		

In some states, no-par stock may be assigned a *stated value per share*. The stated value is recorded like a par value. Any excess of the proceeds over the stated value is credited to *Paid-In Capital in Excess of Stated Value*.

To illustrate, assume that in the preceding example, the no-par common stock is assigned a stated value of $25. The issuance of the stock on January 9 and June 27 is recorded as follows:

Date			Debit	Credit
Jan.	9	Cash (10,000 shares × $40)	400,000	
		Common Stock (10,000 shares × $25)		250,000
		Paid-In Capital in Excess of Stated Value		150,000
		Issued 10,000 shares of no-par common stock at $40; stated value, $25.		
June	27	Cash (1,000 shares × $36)	36,000	
		Common Stock (1,000 shares × $25)		25,000
		Paid-In Capital in Excess of Stated Value		11,000
		Issued 1,000 shares of no-par common stock at $36; stated value, $25.		

INTEGRITY, OBJECTIVITY, AND ETHICS IN BUSINESS

THE PROFESSOR WHO KNEW TOO MUCH

A major Midwestern university released a quarterly "American Customer Satisfaction Index" based on its research of customers of popular U.S. products and services. Before the release of the index to the public, the professor in charge of the research bought and sold stocks of some of the companies in the report. The professor was quoted as saying that he thought it was important to test his theories of customer satisfaction with "real" [his own] money.

Is this proper or ethical? Apparently, the dean of the Business School didn't think so. In a statement to the press, the dean stated: "I have instructed anyone affiliated with the (index) not to make personal use of information gathered in the course of producing the quarterly index, prior to the index's release to the general public, and they [the researchers] have agreed."

Sources: Jon E. Hilsenrath and Dan Morse, "Researcher Uses Index to Buy, Short Stocks," *Wall Street Journal*, February 18, 2003; and Jon E. Hilsenrath, "Satisfaction Theory: Mixed Results," *Wall Street Journal*, February 19, 2003.

Example Exercise 13-2 Entries for Issuing Stock — Obj. 3

On March 6, Limerick Corporation issued for cash 15,000 shares of no-par common stock at $30. On April 13, Limerick issued at par 1,000 shares of preferred 4% stock, $40 par for cash. On May 19, Limerick issued for cash 15,000 shares of 4%, $40 par preferred stock at $42.

Journalize the entries to record the March 6, April 13, and May 19 transactions.

Follow My Example 13-2

Mar. 6	Cash (15,000 shares × $30)	450,000	
	Common Stock		450,000
Apr. 13	Cash (1,000 shares × $40)	40,000	
	Preferred Stock		40,000
May 19	Cash (15,000 shares × $42)	630,000	
	Preferred Stock (15,000 shares × $40)		600,000
	Paid-In Capital in Excess of Par		30,000

Practice Exercises: PE 13-2A, PE 13-2B

Accounting for Dividends

Obj. 4 Describe and illustrate the accounting for cash dividends and stock dividends.

When a board of directors declares a cash dividend, it authorizes the distribution of cash to stockholders. When a board of directors declares a stock dividend, it authorizes the distribution of its stock. In both cases, declaring a dividend reduces the retained earnings of the corporation.[7]

Cash Dividends

A cash distribution of earnings by a corporation to its shareholders is a **cash dividend**. Although dividends may be paid in other assets, cash dividends are the most common.

Three conditions for a cash dividend are as follows:

- Sufficient retained earnings
- Sufficient cash
- Formal action by the board of directors

---

[7] In rare cases, when a corporation is reducing its operations or going out of business, a dividend may be a distribution of paid-in capital. Such a dividend is called a *liquidating dividend*.

Link to Alphabet (Google)

Alphabet (Google) has never paid a cash dividend and has no intention of doing so in the foreseeable future.

There must be a sufficient (large enough) balance in Retained Earnings to declare a cash dividend. That is, the balance of Retained Earnings must be large enough so that the dividend does not create a debit balance in the retained earnings account. However, a large Retained Earnings balance does not mean that there is cash available to pay dividends. This is because the balances, as discussed earlier, of Cash and Retained Earnings are often unrelated.

Even if there are sufficient retained earnings and cash, a corporation's board of directors is not required to pay dividends. Nevertheless, many corporations pay quarterly cash dividends to make their stock more attractive to investors. *Special* or *extra dividends* may also be paid when a corporation experiences higher than normal profits.

Three dates included in a dividend announcement are as follows:

1. Date of declaration
2. Date of record
3. Date of payment

The *date of declaration* is the date the board of directors formally authorizes the payment of the dividend. On this date, the corporation incurs the liability to pay the amount of the dividend.

The *date of record* is the date the corporation uses to determine which stockholders will receive the dividend. During the period of time between the date of declaration and the date of record, the stock price is quoted as selling *with-dividends*. This means that any investors purchasing the stock before the date of record will receive the dividend.

The *date of payment* is the date the corporation will pay the dividend to the stockholders who owned the stock on the date of record. During the period of time between the record date and the payment date, the stock price is quoted as selling *ex-dividends*. This means that since the date of record has passed, any new investors will not receive the dividend.

To illustrate, assume that on October 1, Hiber Corporation declares the following cash dividends with a date of record of November 10 and a date of payment of December 2:

	Dividend per Share	Total Dividends
Preferred stock, $100 par, 5,000 shares outstanding......	$2.50	$12,500
Common stock, $10 par, 100,000 shares outstanding	$0.30	30,000
Total		$42,500

On October 1, the declaration date, Hiber Corporation records the following entry:

Declaration Date

Oct.	1	Cash Dividends	42,500	
		Cash Dividends Payable		42,500
		Declared cash dividends.		

Date of Record

On November 10, the date of record, no entry is necessary. This date merely determines which stockholders will receive the dividends.

On December 2, the date of payment, Hiber Corporation records the payment of the dividends as follows:

Date of Payment

Dec.	2	Cash Dividends Payable	42,500	
		Cash		42,500
		Paid cash dividends.		

At the end of the accounting period, the balance in Cash Dividends will be transferred to Retained Earnings as part of the closing process. This closing entry debits Retained Earnings and credits Cash Dividends for the balance of the cash dividends account. If the cash dividends have not been paid by the end of the period, Cash Dividends Payable will be reported on the balance sheet as a current liability.

Example Exercise 13-3 Entries for Cash Dividends Obj. 4

The important dates in connection with a cash dividend of $75,000 on a corporation's common stock are February 26, March 30, and April 2. Journalize the entries required on each date.

Follow My Example 13-3

Feb. 26	Cash Dividends...	75,000	
	Cash Dividends Payable................................		75,000
Mar. 30	No entry required.		
Apr. 2	Cash Dividends Payable................................	75,000	
	Cash..		75,000

Practice Exercises: PE 13-3A, PE 13-3B

Stock Dividends

A **stock dividend** is a distribution of shares of stock to stockholders. Stock dividends are normally declared only on common stock and issued to common stockholders.

A stock dividend affects only stockholders' equity. Specifically, the amount of the stock dividend is transferred from Retained Earnings to Paid-In Capital. The amount transferred is normally the fair value (market price) of the shares issued in the stock dividend.[8]

To illustrate, assume that the stockholders' equity accounts of Hendrix Corporation as of December 15 are as follows:

Common Stock, $20 par (2,000,000 shares issued)	$40,000,000
Paid-In Capital in Excess of Par—Common Stock	9,000,000
Retained Earnings	26,600,000

On December 15, Hendrix Corporation declares a stock dividend of 5% or 100,000 shares (2,000,000 shares × 5%) to be issued on January 10 to stockholders of record on December 31. The market price of the stock on December 15 (the date of declaration) is $31 per share.

The entry to record the stock dividend is as follows:

Dec.	15	Stock Dividends (100,000 shares × $31)	3,100,000	
		Stock Dividends Distributable (100,000 shares × $20)		2,000,000
		Paid-In Capital in Excess of Par—Common Stock		1,100,000
		Declared 5% (100,000 shares) stock dividend on $20 par common stock with a market price of $31 per share.		

After the preceding entry is recorded, Stock Dividends will have a debit balance of $3,100,000. Like cash dividends, the stock dividends account is closed to Retained Earnings at the end of the accounting period. This closing entry debits Retained Earnings and credits Stock Dividends.

[8] The use of fair market value is justified as long as the number of shares issued for the stock dividend is small (less than 25% of the shares outstanding).

On December 31, the *stock dividends distributable* and *paid-in capital in excess of par—common stock* accounts are reported in the Paid-in capital section of Hendrix Corporation's balance sheet. The effect of the preceding stock dividend is to transfer $3,100,000 of retained earnings to paid-in capital.

On January 10, the stock dividend is distributed to stockholders by issuing 100,000 shares of common stock. The issuance of the stock is recorded by the following entry:

Jan.	10	Stock Dividends Distributable	2,000,000	
		Common Stock		2,000,000
		Issued stock as stock dividend.		

A stock dividend does not change the assets, liabilities, or total stockholders' equity of a corporation. Likewise, a stock dividend does not change an individual stockholder's proportionate interest (equity) in the corporation.

To illustrate, assume that a stockholder owns 1,000 of a corporation's 10,000 shares outstanding. If the corporation declares a 6% stock dividend, the stockholder's proportionate interest will not change, computed as follows:

	Before Stock Dividend	After Stock Dividend
Total shares issued	10,000	10,600 [10,000 + (10,000 × 6%)]
Number of shares owned	1,000	1,060 [1,000 + (1,000 × 6%)]
Proportionate ownership	10% (1,000 ÷ 10,000)	10% (1,060 ÷ 10,600)

Example Exercise 13-4 Entries for Stock Dividends   Obj. 4

Vienna Highlights Corporation has 150,000 shares of $100 par common stock outstanding. On June 14, Vienna Highlights declared a 4% stock dividend to be issued August 15 to stockholders of record on July 1. The market price of the stock was $110 per share on June 14.

Journalize the entries required on June 14, July 1, and August 15.

Follow My Example 13-4

June 14	Stock Dividends (150,000 shares × 4% × $110).............	660,000	
	Stock Dividends Distributable (6,000 shares × $100).........		600,000
	Paid-In Capital in Excess of Par—Common Stock.............		60,000
July 1	No entry required.		
Aug. 15	Stock Dividends Distributable	600,000	
	Common Stock		600,000

Practice Exercises: PE 13-4A, PE 13-4B

Obj. 5 Describe the effect of stock splits on corporate financial statements.

Stock Splits

A **stock split** is a process by which a corporation reduces the par or stated value of its common stock and issues a proportionate number of additional shares. A stock split applies to all common shares including the unissued, issued, and treasury shares.

A major objective of a stock split is to reduce the market price per share of the stock. This attracts more investors and broadens the types and numbers of stockholders.

To illustrate, assume that Rojek Corporation has 10,000 shares of $100 par common stock outstanding with a current market price of $150 per share. The board of directors declares the following stock split:

1. Each common shareholder will receive five shares for each share held. This is called a 5-for-1 stock split. As a result, 50,000 shares (10,000 shares × 5) will be outstanding.
2. The par of each share of common stock will be reduced to $20 ($100 ÷ 5).

The par value of the common stock outstanding is $1,000,000 both before and after the stock split, computed as follows:

	Before Split	After Split
Number of shares	10,000	50,000
Par value per share	× $100	× $20
Total	$1,000,000	$1,000,000

Link to Alphabet (Google)

In 2014, **Alphabet (Google)** implemented a 2-for-1 stock split through the issue of Class C common stock.

In addition, each Rojek Corporation shareholder owns the same total par amount of stock before and after the stock split as shown in Exhibit 7. For example, a stockholder who owned 4 shares of $100 par stock before the split (total par of $400) would own 20 shares of $20 par stock after the split (total par of $400). Only the number of shares and the par value per share have changed.

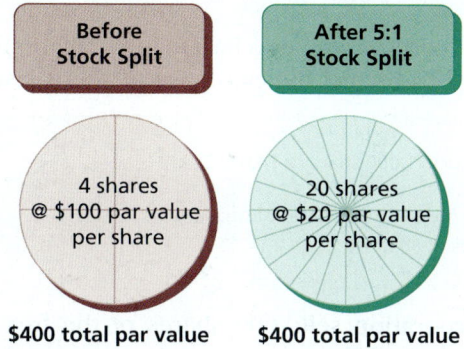

EXHIBIT 7

Stock Split: Before and After

Because there are more shares outstanding after the stock split, the market price of the stock should decrease. For example, in the preceding example, there would be five times as many shares outstanding after the split. Thus, the market price of the stock would be expected to fall from $150 to about $30 ($150 ÷ 5).

Stock splits do not require a journal entry because only the par (or stated) value and number of shares outstanding have changed. However, the details of stock splits are normally disclosed in the notes to the financial statements.

Note

A stock split does not require a journal entry.

Business Connection

BUFFETT ON STOCK SPLITS

Warren E. Buffett, the chairman and chief executive officer of **Berkshire Hathaway Inc.**, opposes stock splits on the basis that they add no value to the company. Since its inception, Berkshire Hathaway has never declared a stock split on its primary (Class A) common stock. As a result, Berkshire Hathaway's Class A common stock sells well above $220,000 per share, which is the most expensive stock on the New York Stock Exchange. Such a high price doesn't bother Buffet because he believes that high stock prices attract more sophisticated and long-term investors and discourage stock speculators and short-term investors.

In contrast, **Microsoft Corporation** has split its stock nine times since it went public in 1986. As a result, one share of Microsoft purchased in 1986 is equivalent to 288 shares today, which would be worth more than $10,000.

Obj. 6 Describe and illustrate the accounting for treasury stock transactions.

Treasury Stock Transactions

Treasury stock is stock that a corporation has issued and then reacquired. A corporation may reacquire (purchase) its own stock for a variety of reasons, including the following:

- To provide shares for resale to employees
- To reissue as bonuses to employees, or
- To support the market price of the stock

The *cost method* is normally used for recording the purchase and resale of treasury stock.[9] Using the cost method, Treasury Stock is debited for the cost (purchase price) of the stock. When the stock is resold, Treasury Stock is credited for its cost. Any difference between the cost and the selling price is debited or credited to *Paid-In Capital from Sale of Treasury Stock*.

To illustrate, assume that a corporation has the following paid-in capital on January 1:

Common stock, $25 par (20,000 shares authorized and issued)	$500,000
Excess of issue price over par	150,000
	$650,000

On February 13, the corporation purchases 1,000 shares of its common stock at $45 per share. The entry to record the purchase of the treasury stock is as follows:

Feb.	13	Treasury Stock (1,000 shares × $45)	45,000	
		Cash		45,000
		Purchased 1,000 shares of treasury stock at $45.		

On April 29, the corporation sells 600 shares of the treasury stock for $60. The entry to record the sale is as follows:

Apr.	29	Cash (600 shares × $60)	36,000	
		Treasury Stock (600 shares × $45)		27,000
		Paid-In Capital from Sale of Treasury Stock		9,000
		Sold 600 shares of treasury stock at $60.		

A sale of treasury stock may result in a decrease in paid-in capital. To the extent that Paid-In Capital from Sale of Treasury Stock has a credit balance, it is debited for any such decrease. Any remaining decrease is then debited to the retained earnings account.

To illustrate, assume that on October 4, the corporation sells the remaining 400 shares of treasury stock for $40 per share. The entry to record the sale is as follows:

Oct.	4	Cash (400 shares × $40)	16,000	
		Paid-In Capital from Sale of Treasury Stock	2,000	
		Treasury Stock (400 shares × $45)		18,000
		Sold 400 shares of treasury stock at $40.		

The preceding October 4 entry decreases paid-in capital by $2,000. Because Paid-in Capital from Sale of Treasury Stock has a credit balance of $9,000, the entire $2,000 was debited to Paid-In Capital from Sale of Treasury Stock.

No dividends (cash or stock) are paid on the shares of treasury stock. To do so would result in the corporation earning dividend revenue from itself.

---

[9] Another method that is used infrequently, called the *par value method*, is discussed in advanced accounting texts.

Example Exercise 13-5 Entries for Treasury Stock Obj. 6

On May 3, Buzz Off Corporation reacquired 3,200 shares of its common stock at $42 per share. On July 22, Buzz Off sold 2,000 of the reacquired shares at $47 per share. On August 30, Buzz Off sold the remaining shares at $40 per share. Journalize the transactions of May 3, July 22, and August 30.

Follow My Example 13-5

May 3	Treasury Stock (3,200 × $42)		134,400	
	Cash			134,400
July 22	Cash (2,000 × $47)		94,000	
	Treasury Stock (2,000 × $42)			84,000
	Paid-In Capital from Sale of Treasury Stock [2,000 × ($47 − $42)]			10,000
Aug. 30	Cash (1,200 × $40)		48,000	
	Paid-In Capital from Sale of Treasury Stock [1,200 × ($42 − $40)]		2,400	
	Treasury Stock (1,200 × $42)			50,400

Practice Exercises: PE 13-5A, PE 13-5B

Business Connection

TREASURY STOCK OR DIVIDENDS?

A company has two major ways to return cash to shareholders: paying cash dividends and repurchasing its stock. A shareholder preferring a current cash income may want to receive a steady cash dividend. A shareholder preferring share price appreciation may want stock repurchases. This is because when a company purchases treasury stock, the amount of shares outstanding will decline and the market value per share should increase. Another consideration is that cash dividends are currently taxed at 15% while the gains on share price increases are tax-deferred until sold. A company may prefer returning cash through stock repurchases because it gives management greater flexibility in managing the company's cash flows. It is considered more difficult to decrease a cash dividend than it is to reduce share repurchases over time. So, overall, the answer to the question depends on circumstances. This is likely why many companies pay dividends and repurchase stock.

Reporting Stockholders' Equity

Obj. 7 Describe and illustrate the reporting of stockholders' equity.

As with other sections of the balance sheet, alternative terms and formats may be used in reporting stockholders' equity. Also, changes in retained earnings and paid-in capital may be reported in separate statements or notes to the financial statements.

Stockholders' Equity on the Balance Sheet

Exhibit 8 shows two methods for reporting stockholders' equity for the December 31, 20Y7, balance sheet for Telex Inc.

Method 1. Each class of stock is reported, followed by its related paid-in capital accounts. Retained earnings is then reported followed by a deduction for treasury stock.

Method 2. The stock accounts are reported, followed by the paid-in capital reported as a single item, Additional paid-in capital. Retained earnings is then reported followed by a deduction for treasury stock.

Link to Alphabet (Google)

Alphabet (Google) has the following shares of common stock outstanding: Class A, 286,560,000; Class B, 53,213,000; and Class C, 340,399,000.

EXHIBIT 8 — Stockholders' Equity Section of a Balance Sheet

Telex Inc.
Balance Sheet
December 31, 20Y7

Method 1

Stockholders' Equity

Paid-in capital:		
Preferred 10% stock, $50 par (2,000 shares authorized and issued)	$100,000	
Excess over par	10,000	
Paid-in capital, preferred stock		$ 110,000
Common stock, $20 par (50,000 shares authorized, 45,000 shares issued)	$900,000	
Excess over par	190,000	
Paid-in capital, common stock		1,090,000
From sale of treasury stock		2,000
Total paid-in capital		$1,202,000
Retained earnings		350,000
Total		$1,552,000
Treasury stock (600 shares at cost)		(27,000)
Total stockholders' equity		$1,525,000

Method 2

Stockholders' Equity

Contributed capital:		
Preferred 10% stock, $50 par (2,000 shares authorized and issued)		$ 100,000
Common stock, $20 par (50,000 shares authorized, 45,000 shares issued)		900,000
Additional paid-in capital		202,000
Total contributed capital		$1,202,000
Retained earnings		350,000
Total		$1,552,000
Treasury stock (600 shares at cost)		(27,000)
Total stockholders' equity		$1,525,000

Significant changes in stockholders' equity during a period may also be presented in a statement of stockholders' equity or in the notes to the financial statements. The statement of stockholders' equity is illustrated later in this section.

Relevant rights and privileges of the various classes of stock outstanding should also be reported.[10] Examples include dividend and liquidation preferences, conversion rights, and redemption rights. Such information may be disclosed on the face of the balance sheet or in the notes to the financial statements.

Example Exercise 13-6 Reporting Stockholders' Equity — Obj. 7

Using the following accounts and balances, prepare the Stockholders' Equity section of the balance sheet using Method 1 of Exhibit 8. Forty thousand shares of common stock are authorized, and 5,000 shares have been reacquired.

Common Stock, $50 par	$1,500,000
Paid-In Capital from Sale of Treasury Stock	44,000
Paid-In Capital in Excess of Par	160,000
Retained Earnings	4,395,000
Treasury Stock	120,000

---

10 *FASB Accounting Standards Codification*, Section 505-10-50.

Follow My Example 13-6

Stockholders' Equity

Paid-in capital:		
Common stock, $50 par (40,000 shares authorized, 30,000 shares issued).....................	$1,500,000	
Excess over par...	160,000	
Paid-in capital, common stock..		$1,660,000
From sale of treasury stock..		44,000
Total paid-in capital...		$1,704,000
Retained earnings..		4,395,000
Total..		$6,099,000
Treasury stock (5,000 shares at cost)..		(120,000)
Total stockholders' equity...		$5,979,000

Practice Exercises: PE 13-6A, PE 13-6B

Reporting Retained Earnings

Changes in retained earnings may be reported using one of the following:

- Separate retained earnings statement
- Combined income and retained earnings statement
- Statement of stockholders' equity

Changes in retained earnings may be reported in a separate retained earnings statement. When a separate **retained earnings statement** is prepared, the beginning balance of retained earnings is reported. The net income is then added (or net loss is subtracted) and any dividends are subtracted to arrive at the ending retained earnings for the period.

To illustrate, a retained earnings statement for Telex Inc. is shown in Exhibit 9.

EXHIBIT 9
Retained Earnings Statement

Telex Inc.
Retained Earnings Statement
For the Year Ended December 31, 20Y7

Retained earnings, January 1, 20Y7.................................		$245,000
Net income..	$180,000	
Dividends:		
Preferred stock dividends...	(10,000)	
Common stock dividends...	(65,000)	
Increase in retained earnings...		105,000
Retained earnings, December 31, 20Y7...............................		$350,000

Changes in retained earnings may also be reported in combination with the income statement. This format emphasizes net income as the connecting link between the income statement and ending retained earnings. Because this format is not often used, it is not illustrated here.

Changes in retained earnings may also be reported in a statement of stockholders' equity. An example of reporting changes in retained earnings in a statement of stockholders' equity for Telex Inc. is shown in Exhibit 10.

> **Link to Alphabet (Google)**
> **Google** does not report a separate retained earnings statement but instead reports changes in retained earnings in its statement of stockholders' equity.

Example Exercise 13-7 Retained Earnings Statement   Obj. 7

Dry Creek Cameras Inc. reported the following results for the year ending March 31, 20Y6:

Retained earnings, April 1, 20Y5	$3,338,500
Net income	461,500
Cash dividends declared	80,000
Stock dividends declared	120,000

Prepare a retained earnings statement for the fiscal year ended March 31, 20Y6.

Follow My Example 13-7

Dry Creek Cameras Inc.
Retained Earnings Statement
For the Year Ended March 31, 20Y6

Retained earnings, April 1, 20Y5		$3,338,500
Net income	$ 461,500	
Dividends declared	(200,000)	
Increase in retained earnings		261,500
Retained earnings, March 31, 20Y6		$3,600,000

Practice Exercises: PE 13-7A, PE 13-7B

Restrictions The use of retained earnings for payment of dividends may be restricted by action of a corporation's board of directors. Such **restrictions**, sometimes called *appropriations*, remain part of the retained earnings.

Restrictions of retained earnings are classified as:

- *Legal*. State laws may require a restriction of retained earnings.

    Example: States may restrict retained earnings by the amount of treasury stock purchased. In this way, legal capital cannot be used for dividends.

- *Contractual*. A corporation may enter into contracts that require restrictions of retained earnings.

    Example: A bank loan may restrict retained earnings so that the amount for repaying the loan cannot be used for dividends.

- *Discretionary*. A corporation's board of directors may restrict retained earnings voluntarily.

    Example: The board may restrict retained earnings and, thus, limit dividend distributions so that earnings are available for expanding the business.

Restrictions of retained earnings must be disclosed in the financial statements. Such disclosures are usually included in the notes to the financial statements.

Prior Period Adjustments An error may arise from a mathematical mistake or from a mistake in applying accounting principles. Such errors may not be discovered within the same period in which they occur. In such cases, the effect of the error should not affect the current period's net income. Instead, the correction of the error, called a **prior period adjustment**, is reported in the retained earnings statement. Such corrections are reported as an adjustment to the beginning balance of retained earnings.[11]

Statement of Stockholders' Equity

When the only change in stockholders' equity is due to net income or net loss and dividends, a retained earnings statement is sufficient. However, when a corporation

---

[11] Prior period adjustments are illustrated in advanced texts.

also has changes in stock and paid-in capital accounts, a **statement of stockholders' equity** is normally prepared.

A statement of stockholders' equity is normally prepared in a columnar format. Each column is a major stockholders' equity classification. Changes in each classification are then described in the left-hand column. Exhibit 10 illustrates a statement of stockholders' equity for Telex Inc.

EXHIBIT 10 — Statement of Stockholders' Equity

Telex Inc.
Statement of Stockholders' Equity
For the Year Ended December 31, 20Y7

	Preferred Stock	Common Stock	Additional Paid-In Capital	Retained Earnings	Treasury Stock	Total
Balance, January 1, 20Y7	$100,000	$850,000	$177,000	$245,000	$(17,000)	$1,355,000
Issuance of additional common stock		50,000	25,000			75,000
Purchase of treasury stock					(10,000)	(10,000)
Net income				180,000		180,000
Dividends on preferred stock				(10,000)		(10,000)
Dividends on common stock				(65,000)		(65,000)
Balance, December 31, 20Y7	$100,000	$900,000	$202,000	$350,000	$(27,000)	$1,525,000

International Connection

IFRS FOR SMEs

In 2010, the International Accounting Standards Board (IASB) issued a set of accounting standards specifically designed for small- and medium-sized enterprises (SMEs) called International Financial Reporting Standards (IFRS) for SMEs. SMEs in the United States are private companies and such small corporations that they do not report to the Securities and Exchange Commission (SEC). IFRS for SMEs consist of only 230 pages, compared to 2,700 pages for full IFRS. These standards are designed to be cost effective for SMEs. Thus, IFRS for SMEs require fewer disclosures and contain no industry-specific standards or exceptions.

The American Institute of CPAs (AICPA) has accepted IFRS for SMEs as part of U.S. generally accepted accounting principles (GAAP) for private companies not reporting to the SEC. If users, such as bankers and investors, accept these financial statements, IFRS for SMEs may become popular in the United States.*

*Differences between U.S. GAAP and IFRS are further discussed and illustrated in Appendix B.

Reporting Stockholders' Equity for Mornin' Joe

Mornin' Joe reports stockholders' equity in its balance sheet. Mornin' Joe also includes a retained earnings statement and statement of stockholders' equity in its financial statements.

The Stockholders' Equity section of Mornin' Joe's balance sheet as of December 31, 20Y6, follows:

Mornin' Joe
Balance Sheet
December 31, 20Y6

Stockholders' Equity

Paid-in capital:		
Preferred 10% stock, $50 par (6,000 shares authorized and issued)	$ 300,000	
Excess of issue price over par	50,000	$ 350,000
Common stock, $20 par (50,000 shares authorized, 45,000 shares issued)	$ 900,000	
Excess of issue price over par	1,450,000	2,350,000
Total paid-in capital		$2,700,000
Retained earnings		1,200,300
Total		$3,900,300
Treasury stock (1,000 shares at cost)		(46,000)
Total stockholders' equity		$3,854,300
Total liabilities and stockholders' equity		$6,169,700

Mornin' Joe's retained earnings statement for the year ended December 31, 20Y6, is as follows:

Mornin' Joe
Retained Earnings Statment
For the Year Ended December 31, 20Y6

Retained earnings, January 1, 20Y6		$ 852,700
Net income	$421,600	
Dividends:		
Preferred stock	(30,000)	
Common stock	(44,000)	
Increase in retained earnings		347,600
Retained earnings, December 31, 20Y6		$1,200,300

The statement of stockholders' equity for Mornin' Joe follows:

Mornin' Joe
Statement of Stockholders' Equity
For the Year Ended December 31, 20Y6

	Preferred Stock	Common Stock	Additional Paid-In Capital	Retained Earnings	Treasury Stock	Total
Balance, January 1, 20Y6	$300,000	$800,000	$1,325,000	$ 852,700	$(36,000)	$3,241,700
Issuance of additional common stock		100,000	175,000			275,000
Purchase of treasury stock					(10,000)	(10,000)
Net income				421,600		421,600
Dividends on preferred stock				(30,000)		(30,000)
Dividends on common stock				(44,000)		(44,000)
Balance, December 31, 20Y6	$300,000	$900,000	$1,500,000	$1,200,300	$(46,000)	$3,854,300

Financial Analysis and Interpretation: Earnings per Share

Obj. 8 Describe and illustrate the use of earnings per share in evaluating a company's profitability.

Net income is often used by investors and creditors in evaluating a company's profitability. However, net income by itself is difficult to use in comparing companies of different sizes. Also, trends in net income may be difficult to evaluate if there have been significant changes in a company's stockholders' equity. Thus, the profitability of companies is often expressed as earnings per share.

Earnings per common share (EPS), sometimes called *basic earnings per share*, is the net income per share of common stock outstanding during a period.[12] Corporations whose stock is traded in a public market must report earnings per common share on their income statements.

Earnings per share is computed as follows:

$$\text{Earnings per Share} = \frac{\text{Net Income} - \text{Preferred Dividends}}{\text{Average Number of Common Shares Outstanding}}$$

If a company has preferred stock outstanding, any preferred dividends are subtracted from net income. This is because the numerator represents only those earnings available to the common shareholders.

To illustrate, the following data (in thousands) were taken from recent financial statements of Google:

	Year 2	Year 1
Net income	$15,826,000	$14,136,000
Average number of common shares outstanding	675,918 shares	675,935 shares
Earnings per share	$23.41	$20.91
	($15,826,000 ÷ 675,918 shares)	($14,136,000 ÷ 675,935 shares)

Google had no preferred stock outstanding; thus, no preferred dividends were subtracted in computing earnings per share. As illustrated, Google's earnings per share increased from $20.91 in Year 1 to $23.41 in Year 2. An increase in earnings per share is generally considered a favorable change.

Earnings per share can be used to compare two companies with different net incomes. For example, the following data (in millions) were taken from a recent year's financial statements for **Bank of America Corporation** and **Wells Fargo & Company**:

	Bank of America	Wells Fargo
Net income	$15,888	$22,894
Preferred dividends	$1,483	$1,424
Average number of common shares outstanding	10,462 shares	5,137 shares

Bank of America:

$$\text{Earnings per Share} = \frac{\text{Net Income} - \text{Preferred Dividends}}{\text{Average Number of Common Shares Outstanding}} = \frac{\$15,888 - \$1,483}{10,462 \text{ shares}} = \frac{\$14,405}{10,462 \text{ shares}} = 1.38$$

Wells Fargo:

$$\text{Earnings per Share} = \frac{\text{Net Income} - \text{Preferred Dividends}}{\text{Average Number of Common Shares Outstanding}} = \frac{\$22,894 - \$1,424}{5,137 \text{ shares}} = \frac{\$21,470}{5,137 \text{ shares}} = 4.18$$

Based on earnings per share, Wells Fargo is more profitable than Bank of America.

---

[12] For complex capital structures, earnings per share assuming dilution may also be reported as described in Chapter 17.

Example Exercise 13-8 Earnings per Share   Obj. 8

Financial statement data for years ending December 31 for Finnegan Company follow:

	20Y2	20Y1
Net income	$350,000	$195,000
Preferred dividends	$20,000	$15,000
Average number of common shares outstanding	75,000 shares	50,000 shares

a. Determine earnings per share for 20Y2 and 20Y1.
b. Does the change in the earnings per share from 20Y1 to 20Y2 indicate a favorable or unfavorable trend?

Follow My Example 13-8

a.
20Y2:

$$\text{Earnings per Share} = \frac{\text{Net Income} - \text{Preferred Dividends}}{\text{Average Number of Common Shares Outstanding}} = \frac{\$350{,}000 - \$20{,}000}{75{,}000 \text{ shares}} = \frac{\$330{,}000}{75{,}000 \text{ shares}} = \$4.40$$

20Y1:

$$\text{Earnings per Share} = \frac{\text{Net Income} - \text{Preferred Dividends}}{\text{Average Number of Common Shares Outstanding}} = \frac{\$195{,}000 - \$15{,}000}{50{,}000 \text{ shares}} = \frac{\$180{,}000}{50{,}000 \text{ shares}} = \$3.60$$

b. The increase in the earnings per share from $3.60 to $4.40 indicates a favorable trend in the company's profitability.

Practice Exercises: PE 13-8A, PE 13-8B

At a Glance 13

Obj. 1 Describe the nature of the corporate form of organization.

Key Points Corporations have a separate legal existence, transferable units of stock, unlimited life, and limited stockholders' liability. The advantages and disadvantages of the corporate form are summarized in Exhibit 2. Costs incurred in organizing a corporation are debited to Organizational Expenses.

Learning Outcomes	Example Exercises	Practice Exercises
• Describe the characteristics of corporations.		
• List the advantages and disadvantages of the corporate form.		
• Prepare a journal entry for the costs of organizing a corporation.		

Obj. 2 — Describe the two main sources of stockholders' equity.

Key Points The two main sources of stockholders' equity are (1) capital contributed by the stockholders and others, called *paid-in capital*, and (2) net income retained in the business, called *retained earnings*. Stockholders' equity is reported in a corporation balance sheet according to these two sources.

Learning Outcomes	Example Exercises	Practice Exercises
• Describe what is meant by paid-in capital.		
• Describe what is meant by net income retained in the business.		
• Prepare a simple Stockholders' Equity section of the balance sheet.		

Obj. 3 — Describe and illustrate the characteristics of stock, classes of stock, and entries for issuing stock.

Key Points The main source of paid-in capital is from issuing common and preferred stock. Stock issued at par is recorded by debiting Cash and crediting the class of stock issued for its par amount. Stock issued for more than par is recorded by debiting Cash, crediting the class of stock for its par, and crediting Paid-In Capital in Excess of Par for the difference. When no-par stock is issued, the entire proceeds are credited to the stock account. No-par stock may be assigned a stated value per share, and the excess of the proceeds over the stated value may be credited to Paid-In Capital in Excess of Stated Value.

Learning Outcomes	Example Exercises	Practice Exercises
• Describe the characteristics of common and preferred stock including rights to dividends.	EE13-1	PE13-1A, 13-1B
• Journalize the entry for common and preferred stock issued at par.	EE13-2	PE13-2A, 13-2B
• Journalize the entry for common and preferred stock issued at more than par.	EE13-2	PE13-2A, 13-2B
• Journalize the entry for issuing no-par stock.	EE13-2	PE13-2A, 13-2B

Obj. 4 — Describe and illustrate the accounting for cash dividends and stock dividends.

Key Points The entry to record a declaration of cash dividends debits Dividends and credits Dividends Payable. When a stock dividend is declared, Stock Dividends is debited for the fair value of the stock to be issued. Stock Dividends Distributable is credited for the par or stated value of the common stock to be issued. The difference between the fair value of the stock and its par or stated value is credited to Paid-In Capital in Excess of Par—Common Stock. When the stock is issued on the date of payment, Stock Dividends Distributable is debited and Common Stock is credited for the par or stated value of the stock issued.

Learning Outcomes	Example Exercises	Practice Exercises
• Journalize the entries for the declaration and payment of cash dividends.	EE13-3	PE13-3A, 13-3B
• Journalize the entries for the declaration and payment of stock dividends.	EE13-4	PE13-4A, 13-4B

Obj. 5 — **Describe the effect of stock splits on corporate financial statements.**

Key Points When a corporation reduces the par or stated value of its common stock and issues a proportionate number of additional shares, a stock split has occurred. There are no changes in the balances of any accounts, and no entry is required for a stock split.

Learning Outcomes	Example Exercises	Practice Exercises
• Define and give an example of a stock split.		
• Describe the accounting for and effects of a stock split on the financial statements.		

Obj. 6 — **Describe and illustrate the accounting for treasury stock transactions.**

Key Points When a corporation buys its own stock, the cost method of accounting is normally used. Treasury Stock is debited for its cost, and Cash is credited. If the stock is resold, Treasury Stock is credited for its cost and any difference between the cost and the selling price is normally debited or credited to Paid-In Capital from Sale of Treasury Stock.

Learning Outcomes	Example Exercises	Practice Exercises
• Define treasury stock.		
• Describe the accounting for treasury stock.		
• Journalize entries for the purchase and sale of treasury stock.	EE13-5	PE13-5A, 13-5B

Obj. 7 — **Describe and illustrate the reporting of stockholders' equity.**

Key Points Two alternatives for reporting stockholders' equity are shown in Exhibit 8. Changes in retained earnings are reported in a retained earnings statement, as shown in Exhibit 9. Restrictions to retained earnings should be disclosed. Any prior period adjustments are reported in the retained earnings statement. Changes in stockholders' equity may be reported on a statement of stockholders' equity, as shown in Exhibit 10.

Learning Outcomes	Example Exercises	Practice Exercises
• Prepare the Stockholders' Equity section of the balance sheet.	EE13-6	PE13-6A, 13-6B
• Prepare a retained earnings statement.	EE13-7	PE13-7A, 13-7B
• Describe retained earnings restrictions and prior period adjustments.		
• Prepare a statement of stockholders' equity.		

Obj. 8 — **Describe and illustrate the use of earnings per share in evaluating a company's profitability.**

Key Points The profitability of companies is often expressed as earnings per share. Earnings per share is computed by subtracting preferred dividends from net income and dividing by the average number of common shares outstanding.

Learning Outcomes	Example Exercises	Practice Exercises
• Describe the use of earnings per share in evaluating a company's profitability.		
• Compute and interpret earnings per share.	EE13-8	PE13-8A, 13-8B

Illustrative Problem

Altenburg Inc. is a lighting fixture wholesaler located in Arizona. During the year ended December 31, Altenburg Inc. completed the following selected transactions:

Feb. 3. Purchased 2,500 shares of its own common stock at $26, recording the stock at cost. (Prior to the purchase, there were 40,000 shares of $20 par common stock outstanding.)

May 1. Declared a semiannual dividend of $1 on the 10,000 shares of preferred stock and a $0.30 dividend on the common stock to stockholders of record on May 31, payable on June 15.

June 15. Paid the cash dividends.

Sept. 23. Sold 1,000 shares of treasury stock at $28, receiving cash.

Nov. 1. Declared semiannual dividends of $1 on the preferred stock and $0.30 on the common stock. In addition, a 5% common stock dividend was declared on the common stock outstanding, to be capitalized at the fair market value of the common stock, which is estimated at $30.

Dec. 1. Paid the cash dividends and issued the certificates for the common stock dividend.

Instructions

Journalize the entries to record the transactions for Altenburg Inc.

Solution

Date		Account	Debit	Credit
Feb.	3	Treasury Stock	65,000	
		Cash		65,000
May	1	Cash Dividends	21,250	
		Cash Dividends Payable		21,250
		(10,000 × $1) + [(40,000 − 2,500) × $0.30].		
June	15	Cash Dividends Payable	21,250	
		Cash		21,250
Sept.	23	Cash	28,000	
		Treasury Stock		26,000
		Paid-In Capital from Sale of Treasury Stock		2,000
Nov.	1	Cash Dividends	21,550	
		Cash Dividends Payable		21,550
		(10,000 × $1) + [(40,000 − 1,500) × $0.30].		
	1	Stock Dividends	57,750*	
		Stock Dividends Distributable		38,500
		Paid-In Capital in Excess of Par—Common Stock		19,250
		*(40,000 − 1,500) × 5% × $30.		
Dec.	1	Cash Dividends Payable	21,550	
		Stock Dividends Distributable	38,500	
		Cash		21,550
		Common Stock		38,500

Key Terms

cash dividend (639)
common stock (635)
cumulative preferred stock (635)
deficit (633)
discount (637)
dividends (633)
earnings per common share (EPS) (651)

in arrears (636)
outstanding stock (634)
paid-in capital (633)
par value (634)
preferred stock (635)
premium (637)
prior period adjustment (648)
restrictions (648)
retained earnings (633)

retained earnings statement (647)
statement of stockholders' equity (649)
stock (630)
stock dividend (641)
stock split (642)
stockholders (630)
stockholders' equity (633)
treasury stock (644)

Discussion Questions

1. Of two corporations organized at approximately the same time and engaged in competing businesses, one issued $80 par common stock and the other issued $1 par common stock. Do the par designations provide any indication as to which stock is preferable as an investment? Explain.

2. A stockbroker advises a client to "buy preferred stock. … With that type of stock, … [you] will never have to worry about losing the dividends." Is the broker correct?

3. A corporation with both preferred stock and common stock outstanding has a substantial credit balance in its retained earnings account at the beginning of the current fiscal year. Although net income for the current year is sufficient to pay the preferred dividend of $150,000 each quarter and a common dividend of $90,000 each quarter, the board of directors declares dividends only on the preferred stock. Suggest possible reasons for passing the dividends on the common stock.

4. An owner of 2,500 shares of Simmons Company common stock receives a stock dividend of 50 shares.
   a. What is the effect of the stock dividend on the stockholder's proportionate interest (equity) in the corporation?
   b. How does the total equity of 2,550 shares compare with the total equity of 2,500 shares before the stock dividend?

5. a. Where should a declared but unpaid cash dividend be reported on the balance sheet?
   b. Where should a declared but unissued stock dividend be reported on the balance sheet?

6. What is the primary purpose of a stock split?

7. A corporation reacquires 60,000 shares of its own $10 par common stock for $3,000,000, recording it at cost.
   a. What effect does this transaction have on revenue or expense of the period?
   b. What effect does it have on stockholders' equity?

8. The treasury stock in Discussion Question 7 is resold for $3,750,000.
   a. What is the effect on the corporation's revenue of the period?
   b. What is the effect on stockholders' equity?

9. What are the three classifications of restrictions of retained earnings, and how are such restrictions normally reported on the financial statements?

10. Indicate how prior period adjustments should be reported on the financial statements presented only for the current period.

Chapter 13 Corporations: Organization, Stock Transactions, and Dividends

Practice Exercises

Example Exercises

EE 13-1 p. 636

PE 13-1A Dividends per share OBJ. 3

Reinhardt Furniture Company has 40,000 shares of cumulative preferred 2% stock, $150 par, and 100,000 shares of $5 par common stock. The following amounts were distributed as dividends:

Year 1	$ 70,000
Year 2	200,000
Year 3	320,000

Determine the dividends per share for preferred and common stock for each year.

EE 13-1 p. 636

PE 13-1B Dividends per share OBJ. 3

Zero Calories Company has 16,000 shares of cumulative preferred 1% stock, $40 par, and 80,000 shares of $150 par common stock. The following amounts were distributed as dividends:

Year 1	$ 21,600
Year 2	4,000
Year 3	100,800

Determine the dividends per share for preferred and common stock for each year.

EE 13-2 p. 639

PE 13-2A Entries for issuing stock OBJ. 3

On May 23, Stoltz Realty Inc. issued for cash 80,000 shares of no-par common stock (with a stated value of $3) at $12. On July 6, Stoltz Realty Inc. issued at par value 18,000 shares of preferred 1% stock, $50 par for cash. On September 15, Stoltz Realty Inc. issued for cash an additional 50,000 shares of no-par common stock (with a stated value of $3) for $15.

Journalize the entries to record the May 23, July 6, and September 15 transactions.

EE 13-2 p. 639

PE 13-2B Entries for issuing stock OBJ. 3

On January 22, Zentric Corporation issued for cash 180,000 shares of no-par common stock at $4. On February 14, Zentric Corporation issued at par value 44,000 shares of preferred 2% stock, $55 par for cash. On August 30, Zentric Corporation issued for cash 9,000 shares of preferred 2% stock, $55 par at $60.

Journalize the entries to record the January 22, February 14, and August 30 transactions.

EE 13-3 p. 641

PE 13-3A Entries for cash dividends OBJ. 4

The declaration, record, and payment dates in connection with a cash dividend of $350,000 on a corporation's common stock are February 28, April 1, and May 15. Journalize the entries required on each date.

EE 13-3 p. 641

PE 13-3B Entries for cash dividends OBJ. 4

The declaration, record, and payment dates in connection with a cash dividend of $480,000 on a corporation's common stock are February 1, March 18, and May 1. Journalize the entries required on each date.

EE 13-4 p. 642

PE 13-4A Entries for stock dividends OBJ. 4

Pro-Builders Corporation has 1,500,000 shares of $5 par common stock outstanding. On September 2, Pro-Builders Corporation declared a 3% stock dividend to be issued November 30 to stockholders of record on October 3. The market price of the stock was $36 per share on September 2.

Journalize the entries required on September 2, October 3, and November 30.

658 Chapter 13 Corporations: Organization, Stock Transactions, and Dividends

EE 13-4 p. 642

PE 13-4B Entries for stock dividends — OBJ. 4

Antique Buggy Corporation has 820,000 shares of $35 par common stock outstanding. On June 8, Antique Buggy Corporation declared a 5% stock dividend to be issued August 12 to stockholders of record on July 13. The market price of the stock was $63 per share on June 8. Journalize the entries required on June 8, July 13, and August 12.

EE 13-5 p. 645

PE 13-5A Entries for treasury stock — OBJ. 6

On January 31, Wilderness Resorts Inc. reacquired 22,500 shares of its common stock at $31 per share. On April 20, Wilderness Resorts sold 12,800 of the reacquired shares at $40 per share. On October 4, Wilderness Resorts sold the remaining shares at $28 per share. Journalize the transactions of January 31, April 20, and October 4.

EE 13-5 p. 645

PE 13-5B Entries for treasury stock — OBJ. 6

On May 27, Hydro Clothing Inc. reacquired 75,000 shares of its common stock at $8 per share. On August 3, Hydro Clothing sold 54,000 of the reacquired shares at $11 per share. On November 14, Hydro Clothing sold the remaining shares at $7 per share. Journalize the transactions of May 27, August 3, and November 14.

EE 13-6 p. 646

PE 13-6A Reporting stockholders' equity — OBJ. 7

Using the following accounts and balances, prepare the Stockholders' Equity section of the balance sheet using Method 1 of Exhibit 8. One hundred thousand shares of common stock are authorized, and 5,000 shares have been reacquired.

Common Stock, $2 par	$ 150,000
Paid-In Capital from Sale of Treasury Stock	60,000
Paid-In Capital in Excess of Par—Common Stock	2,250,000
Retained Earnings	10,880,000
Treasury Stock	140,000

EE 13-6 p. 646

PE 13-6B Reporting stockholders' equity — OBJ. 7

Using the following accounts and balances, prepare the Stockholders' Equity section of the balance sheet using Method 1 of Exhibit 8. Five hundred thousand shares of common stock are authorized, and 40,000 shares have been reacquired.

Common Stock, $120 par	$48,000,000
Paid-In Capital from Sale of Treasury Stock	4,500,000
Paid-In Capital in Excess of Par—Common Stock	6,400,000
Retained Earnings	63,680,000
Treasury Stock	5,200,000

EE 13-7 p. 648

PE 13-7A Retained earnings statement — OBJ. 7

Rockwell Inc. reported the following results for the year ended June 30, 20Y5:

Retained earnings, July 1, 20Y4	$3,900,000
Net income	714,000
Cash dividends declared	100,000
Stock dividends declared	50,000

Prepare a retained earnings statement for the fiscal year ended June 30, 20Y5.

EE 13-7 p. 648

PE 13-7B Retained earnings statement — OBJ. 7

Noric Cruises Inc. reported the following results for the year ended October 31, 20Y9:

Retained earnings, November 1, 20Y8	$12,400,000
Net income	2,350,000
Cash dividends declared	175,000
Stock dividends declared	300,000

Prepare a retained earnings statement for the fiscal year ended October 31, 20Y9.

Chapter 13 Corporations: Organization, Stock Transactions, and Dividends 659

PE 13-8A Earnings per share OBJ. 8

Financial statement data for the years ended December 31 for Dovetail Corporation follow:

	20Y3	20Y2
Net income	$448,750	$376,000
Preferred dividends	$40,000	$40,000
Average number of common shares outstanding	75,000 shares	60,000 shares

a. Determine the earnings per share for 20Y3 and 20Y2.

b. Does the change in the earnings per share from 20Y2 to 20Y3 indicate a favorable or unfavorable trend?

PE 13-8B Earnings per share OBJ. 8

Financial statement data for the years ended December 31 for Black Bull Inc. follow:

	20Y6	20Y5
Net income	$2,485,700	$1,538,000
Preferred dividends	$50,000	$50,000
Average number of common shares outstanding	115,000 shares	80,000 shares

a. Determine the earnings per share for 20Y6 and 20Y5.

b. Does the change in the earnings per share from 20Y5 to 20Y6 indicate a favorable or unfavorable trend?

Exercises

EX 13-1 Dividends per share OBJ. 3

✔ Preferred stock, 1st year: $0.90

Imaging Inc., a developer of radiology equipment, has stock outstanding as follows: 40,000 shares of cumulative preferred 2% stock, $75 par, and 100,000 shares of $50 par common. During its first four years of operations, the following amounts were distributed as dividends: first year, $36,000; second year, $90,000; third year, $115,000; fourth year, $140,000. Compute the dividends per share on each class of stock for each of the four years.

EX 13-2 Dividends per share OBJ. 3

✔ Preferred stock, 1st year: $0.90

Lightfoot Inc., a software development firm, has stock outstanding as follows: 40,000 shares of cumulative preferred 1% stock, $125 par, and 100,000 shares of $150 par common. During its first four years of operations, the following amounts were distributed as dividends: first year, $36,000; second year, $58,000; third year, $75,000; fourth year, $124,000. Compute the dividends per share on each class of stock for each of the four years.

EX 13-3 Entries for issuing par stock OBJ. 3

On October 31, Legacy Rocks Inc., a marble contractor, issued for cash 400,000 shares of $10 par common stock at $18, and on November 19, it issued for cash 50,000 shares of preferred stock, $75 par at $80.

a. Journalize the entries for October 31 and November 19.

b. What is the total amount invested (total paid-in capital) by all stockholders as of November 19?

EX 13-4 Entries for issuing no-par stock OBJ. 3

On February 12, Quality Carpet Inc., a carpet wholesaler, issued for cash 1,000,000 shares of no-par common stock (with a stated value of $0.25) at $1.20, and on August 3, it issued for cash 10,000 shares of preferred stock, $15 par at $21.

a. Journalize the entries for February 12 and August 3, assuming that the common stock is to be credited with the stated value.

b. What is the total amount invested (total paid-in capital) by all stockholders as of August 3?

660 Chapter 13 Corporations: Organization, Stock Transactions, and Dividends

EX 13-5 Issuing stock for assets other than cash   OBJ. 3

On April 5, Fenning Corporation, a wholesaler of hydraulic lifts, acquired land in exchange for 30,000 shares of $80 par common stock valued at $112 per share. Journalize the entry to record the transaction.

EX 13-6 Selected stock transactions   OBJ. 3

Alpha Sounds Corp., an electric guitar retailer, was organized by Michele Kirby, Paul Glenn, and Gretchen Northway. The charter authorized 1,000,000 shares of common stock with a par of $1. The following transactions affecting stockholders' equity were completed during the first year of operations:

a. Issued 100,000 shares of stock at par to Paul Glenn for cash.

b. Issued 3,000 shares of stock at par to Michele Kirby for promotional services provided in connection with the organization of the corporation and issued 45,000 shares of stock at par to Michele Kirby for cash.

c. Purchased land and a building from Gretchen Northway in exchange for stock issued at par. The building is mortgaged for $180,000 for 20 years at 6%, and there is accrued interest of $5,200 on the mortgage note at the time of the purchase. It is agreed that the land is to be priced at $60,000 and the building at $225,000 and that Gretchen Northway's equity will be exchanged for stock at par. The corporation agreed to assume responsibility for paying the mortgage note and the accrued interest.

Journalize the entries to record the transactions.

EX 13-7 Issuing stock   OBJ. 3

Willow Creek Nursery, with an authorization of 75,000 shares of preferred stock and 200,000 shares of common stock, completed several transactions involving its stock on October 1, the first day of operations. The trial balance at the close of the day follows:

Cash	3,780,000	
Land	840,000	
Buildings	2,380,000	
Preferred 1% Stock, $80 par		2,800,000
Paid-In Capital in Excess of Par—Preferred Stock		420,000
Common Stock, $30 par		3,600,000
Paid-In Capital in Excess of Par—Common Stock		180,000
	7,000,000	7,000,000

All shares within each class of stock were sold at the same price. The preferred stock was issued in exchange for the land and buildings.

Journalize the two entries to record the transactions summarized in the trial balance.

EX 13-8 Issuing stock   OBJ. 3

Work Place Products Inc., a wholesaler of office products, was organized on July 1 of the current year, with an authorization of 50,000 shares of preferred 2% stock, $40 par, and 750,000 shares of $7 par common stock. The following selected transactions were completed during the first year of operations:

July 1. Issued 400,000 shares of common stock at par for cash.

1. Issued 1,000 shares of common stock at par to an attorney in payment of legal fees for organizing the corporation.

Aug. 7. Issued 80,000 shares of common stock in exchange for land, buildings, and equipment with fair market prices of $250,000, $400,000, and $70,000, respectively.

Sept. 20. Issued 25,000 shares of preferred stock at $44 for cash.

Journalize the transactions.

Chapter 13 Corporations: Organization, Stock Transactions, and Dividends

EX 13-9 Entries for cash dividends   OBJ. 4
The declaration, record, and payment dates in connection with a cash dividend of $135,000 on a corporation's common stock are January 12, March 13, and April 12. Journalize the entries required on each date.

EX 13-10 Entries for stock dividends   OBJ. 4

✔ b. (1) $3,000,000
(3) $36,500,000

Senior Life Co. is an HMO for businesses in the Portland area. The following account balances appear on the balance sheet of Senior Life Co.: Common stock (800,000 shares authorized; 500,000 shares issued), $4 par, $2,000,000; Paid-in capital in excess of par—common stock, $1,000,000; and Retained earnings, $33,500,000. The board of directors declared a 2% stock dividend when the market price of the stock was $13 a share. Senior Life Co. reported no income or loss for the current year.

a. Journalize the entries to record (1) the declaration of the dividend, capitalizing an amount equal to market value, and (2) the issuance of the stock certificates.
b. Determine the following amounts before the stock dividend was declared: (1) total paid-in capital, (2) total retained earnings, and (3) total stockholders' equity.
c. Determine the following amounts after the stock dividend was declared and closing entries were recorded at the end of the year: (1) total paid-in capital, (2) total retained earnings, and (3) total stockholders' equity.

EX 13-11 Effect of stock split   OBJ. 5

Copper Grill Restaurant Corporation wholesales ovens and ranges to restaurants throughout the Southwest. Copper Grill Restaurant Corporation, which had 50,000 shares of common stock outstanding, declared a 3-for-1 stock split.

a. What will be the number of shares outstanding after the split?
b. If the common stock had a market price of $210 per share before the stock split, what would be an approximate market price per share after the split?

EX 13-12 Effect of cash dividend and stock split   OBJ. 4, 5
Indicate whether the following actions would (+) increase, (–) decrease, or (0) not affect Indigo Inc.'s total assets, liabilities, and stockholders' equity:

	Assets	Liabilities	Stockholders' Equity
(1) Authorizing and issuing stock certificates in a stock split	_____	_____	_____
(2) Declaring a stock dividend	_____	_____	_____
(3) Issuing stock certificates for the stock dividend declared in (2)	_____	_____	_____
(4) Declaring a cash dividend	_____	_____	_____
(5) Paying the cash dividend declared in (4)	_____	_____	_____

EX 13-13 Selected dividend transactions, stock split   OBJ. 4, 5
Selected transactions completed by Canyon Ferry Boating Corporation during the current fiscal year are as follows:

Jan. 8. Split the common stock 2 for 1 and reduced the par from $80 to $40 per share. After the split, there were 150,000 common shares outstanding.

Apr. 30. Declared semiannual dividends of $0.75 on 18,000 shares of preferred stock and $0.28 on the common stock payable on July 1.

July 1. Paid the cash dividends.

Oct. 31. Declared semiannual dividends of $0.75 on the preferred stock and $0.14 on the common stock (before the stock dividend). In addition, a 5% common stock dividend was declared on the common stock outstanding. The fair market value of the common stock is estimated at $52.

Dec. 31. Paid the cash dividends and issued the certificates for the common stock dividend.

Journalize the transactions.

662 Chapter 13 Corporations: Organization, Stock Transactions, and Dividends

EX 13-14 Treasury stock transactions OBJ. 6

✔ b. $210,000 credit

Lava Lake Inc. bottles and distributes spring water. On February 11 of the current year, Lava Lake reacquired 180,000 shares of its common stock at $17 per share. On April 30, Lava Lake Inc. sold 90,000 of the reacquired shares at $20 per share. On August 22, Lava Lake Inc. sold 30,000 shares at $15 per share.

a. Journalize the transactions of February 11, April 30, and August 22.
b. What is the balance in Paid-In Capital from Sale of Treasury Stock on December 31 of the current year?
c. For what reasons might Lava Lake have purchased the treasury stock?

EX 13-15 Treasury stock transactions OBJ. 6, 7

✔ b. $306,000 credit

Lawn Spray Inc. develops and produces spraying equipment for lawn maintenance and industrial uses. On January 31 of the current year, Lawn Spray Inc. reacquired 50,000 shares of its common stock at $51 per share. On June 14, 24,000 of the reacquired shares were sold at $60 per share, and on November 23, 18,000 of the reacquired shares were sold at $56.

a. Journalize the transactions of January 31, June 14, and November 23.
b. What is the balance in Paid-In Capital from Sale of Treasury Stock on December 31 of the current year?
c. What is the balance in Treasury Stock on December 31 of the current year?
d. How will the balance in Treasury Stock be reported on the balance sheet?

EX 13-16 Treasury stock transactions OBJ. 6, 7

✔ b. $55,500 credit

Biscayne Bay Water Inc. bottles and distributes spring water. On May 14 of the current year, Biscayne Bay Water Inc. reacquired 23,500 shares of its common stock at $75 per share. On September 6, Biscayne Bay Water Inc. sold 14,000 of the reacquired shares at $81 per share. The remaining 9,500 shares were sold at $72 per share on November 30.

a. Journalize the transactions of May 14, September 6, and November 30.
b. What is the balance in Paid-In Capital from Sale of Treasury Stock on December 31 of the current year?
c. Where will the balance in Paid-In Capital from Sale of Treasury Stock be reported on the balance sheet?
d. For what reasons might Biscayne Bay Water Inc. have purchased the treasury stock?

EX 13-17 Reporting paid-in capital OBJ. 7

✔ Total paid-in capital, $13,615,000

The following accounts and their balances were selected from the unadjusted trial balance of Point Loma Group Inc., a freight forwarder, at October 31, the end of the current fiscal year:

Common Stock, no par, $14 stated value	$ 4,480,000
Paid-In Capital from Sale of Treasury Stock	45,000
Paid-In Capital in Excess of Par—Preferred Stock	210,000
Paid-In Capital in Excess of Stated Value—Common Stock	480,000
Preferred 2% Stock, $120 par	8,400,000
Retained Earnings	39,500,000

Prepare the Paid-In Capital portion of the stockholders' equity section of the balance sheet using Method 1 of Exhibit 8. There are 375,000 shares of common stock authorized and 85,000 shares of preferred stock authorized.

Chapter 13 Corporations: Organization, Stock Transactions, and Dividends 663

EX 13-18 Stockholders' Equity section of balance sheet OBJ. 7

✔ Total stockholders' equity, $23,676,000

The following accounts and their balances appear in the ledger of Goodale Properties Inc. on June 30 of the current year:

Common Stock, $45 par	$ 3,060,000
Paid-In Capital from Sale of Treasury Stock	115,000
Paid-In Capital in Excess of Par—Common Stock	272,000
Retained Earnings	20,553,000
Treasury Stock	324,000

Prepare the Stockholders' Equity section of the balance sheet as of June 30 using Method 1 of Exhibit 8. Eighty thousand shares of common stock are authorized, and 9,000 shares have been reacquired.

EX 13-19 Stockholders' Equity section of balance sheet OBJ. 7

✔ Total stockholders' equity, $89,100,000

Specialty Auto Racing Inc. retails racing products for BMWs, Porsches, and Ferraris. The following accounts and their balances appear in the ledger of Specialty Auto Racing Inc. on July 31, the end of the current year:

Common Stock, $36 par	$10,080,000
Paid-In Capital from Sale of Treasury Stock—Common	340,000
Paid-In Capital in Excess of Par—Common Stock	420,000
Paid-In Capital in Excess of Par—Preferred Stock	384,000
Preferred 1% Stock, $150 par	7,200,000
Retained Earnings	71,684,000
Treasury Stock—Common	1,008,000

Fifty thousand shares of preferred and 300,000 shares of common stock are authorized. There are 24,000 shares of common stock held as treasury stock.

Prepare the Stockholders' Equity section of the balance sheet as of July 31, the end of the current year using Method 1 of Exhibit 8.

EX 13-20 Retained earnings statement OBJ. 7

✔ Retained earnings, January 31, $64,210,000

Sumter Pumps Corporation, a manufacturer of industrial pumps, reports the following results for the year ended January 31, 20Y2:

Retained earnings, February 1, 20Y1	$59,650,000
Net income	8,160,000
Cash dividends declared	1,000,000
Stock dividends declared	2,600,000

Prepare a retained earnings statement for the fiscal year ended January 31, 20Y2.

EX 13-21 Stockholders' Equity section of balance sheet OBJ. 7

✔ Corrected total stockholders' equity, $122,800,000

List the errors in the following Stockholders' Equity section of the balance sheet prepared as of the end of the current year:

Stockholders' Equity

Paid-in capital:		
Preferred 2% stock, $80 par (125,000 shares authorized and issued)	$10,000,000	
Excess of issue price over par	500,000	$ 10,500,000
Retained earnings		96,700,000
Treasury stock (75,000 shares at cost)		1,755,000
Dividends payable		430,000
Total paid-in capital		$109,385,000
Common stock, $20 par (1,000,000 shares authorized, 825,000 shares issued)		17,655,000
Organizing costs		300,000
Total stockholders' equity		$127,340,000

664 Chapter 13 Corporations: Organization, Stock Transactions, and Dividends

EX 13-22 Statement of stockholders' equity OBJ. 7

✔ Total stockholders' equity, Dec. 31, $21,587,000

The stockholders' equity T accounts of I-Cards Inc. for the fiscal year ended December 31, 20Y9, are as follows. Prepare a statement of stockholders' equity for the year ended December 31, 20Y9.

COMMON STOCK

			Jan. 1	Balance	4,800,000
			Apr. 14	Issued 30,000 shares	1,200,000
			Dec. 31	Balance	6,000,000

PAID-IN CAPITAL IN EXCESS OF PAR

			Jan. 1	Balance	960,000
			Apr. 14	Issued 30,000 shares	300,000
			Dec. 31	Balance	1,260,000

TREASURY STOCK

Aug. 7	Purchased 12,000 shares	552,000			

RETAINED EARNINGS

Mar. 31	Dividend	69,000	Jan. 1	Balance	11,375,000
June 30	Dividend	69,000	Dec. 31	Closing (net income)	3,780,000
Sept. 30	Dividend	69,000			
Dec. 31	Dividend	69,000	Dec. 31	Balance	14,879,000

EX 13-23 EPS OBJ. 8

Junkyard Arts, Inc., had earnings of $316,000 for the year. The company had 40,000 shares of common stock outstanding during the year and issued 15,000 shares of $50 par value preferred stock. The preferred stock has a dividend of $1.60 per share. There were no transactions in either common or preferred stock during the year.

Determine the basic earnings per share for Junkyard Arts for the year.

EX 13-24 EPS OBJ. 8

✔ a. Year 1, $1.83 per share

Pacific Gas and Electric Company is a large gas and electric utility operating in northern and central California. Three recent years of financial data for Pacific Gas and Electric Company are as follows:

	Fiscal Years Ended (in millions)		
	Year 3	Year 2	Year 1
Net income	$888	$1,450	$828
Preferred dividends	$14	$14	$14
Average number of common shares outstanding	484	468	444

a. Determine the earnings per share for fiscal Year 3, Year 2, and Year 1. Round to the nearest cent.

b. Evaluate the growth in earnings per share for the three years in comparison to the growth in net income for the three years.

EX 13-25 EPS OBJ. 8

Caterpillar Inc. and **Deere & Company** are two large companies that manufacture and sell equipment used in the construction, mining, agricultural, and forestry industries. The companies reported the following data (in millions) for two recent years:

Chapter 13 Corporations: Organization, Stock Transactions, and Dividends 665

	Caterpillar		Deere	
	Year 2	Year 1	Year 2	Year 1
Net income	$2,102	$3,695	$1,940	$3,162
Average number of common shares outstanding	594	599	334	363

a. Determine the earnings per share in Year 2 and Year 1 for each company. Round to the nearest cent.

b. Evaluate the relative profitability of the two companies.

Problems: Series A

PR 13-1A Dividends on preferred and common stock   OBJ. 3

✔ 1. Year 3, Preferred Dividends, $130,000

Excel

Show Me How

Pecan Theatre Inc. owns and operates movie theaters throughout Florida and Georgia. Pecan Theatre has declared the following annual dividends over a six-year period: Year 1, $80,000; Year 2, $90,000; Year 3, $150,000; Year 4, $150,000; Year 5, $160,000; and Year 6, $180,000. During the entire period ended December 31 of each year, the outstanding stock of the company was composed of 250,000 shares of cumulative, preferred 2% stock, $20 par, and 500,000 shares of common stock, $15 par.

Instructions

1. Determine the total dividends and the per-share dividends declared on each class of stock for each of the six years. There were no dividends in arrears at the beginning of Year 1. Summarize the data in tabular form, using the following column headings:

Year	Total Dividends	Preferred Dividends Total	Preferred Dividends Per Share	Common Dividends Total	Common Dividends Per Share
Year 1	$ 80,000				
Year 2	90,000				
Year 3	150,000				
Year 4	150,000				
Year 5	160,000				
Year 6	180,000				

2. Determine the average annual dividend per share for each class of stock for the six-year period.

3. Assuming a market price per share of $25.00 for the preferred stock and $17.50 for the common stock, determine the average annual percentage return on initial shareholders' investment, based on the average annual dividend per share (a) for preferred stock and (b) for common stock.

PR 13-2A Stock transactions for corporate expansion   OBJ. 3

On December 1 of the current year, the following accounts and their balances appear in the ledger of Latte Corp., a coffee processor:

Preferred 2% Stock, $50 par (250,000 shares authorized, 80,000 shares issued)	$ 4,000,000
Paid-In Capital in Excess of Par—Preferred Stock	560,000
Common Stock, $35 par (1,000,000 shares authorized, 400,000 shares issued)	14,000,000
Paid-In Capital in Excess of Par—Common Stock	1,200,000
Retained Earnings	180,000,000

At the annual stockholders' meeting on March 31, the board of directors presented a plan for modernizing and expanding plant operations at a cost of approximately $11,000,000.

(Continued)

666 Chapter 13 Corporations: Organization, Stock Transactions, and Dividends

The plan provided (a) that a building, valued at $3,375,000, and the land on which it is located, valued at $1,500,000, be acquired in accordance with preliminary negotiations by the issuance of 125,000 shares of common stock valued at $39 per share, (b) that 40,000 shares of the unissued preferred stock be issued through an underwriter, and (c) that the corporation borrow $4,000,000. The plan was approved by the stockholders and accomplished by the following transactions:

May 11. Issued 125,000 shares of common stock in exchange for land and a building, according to the plan.
  20. Issued 40,000 shares of preferred stock, receiving $52 per share in cash.
  31. Borrowed $4,000,000 from Laurel National, giving a 5% mortgage note.

Instructions
Journalize the entries to record the May transactions.

PR 13-3A Selected stock transactions OBJ. 3, 4, 6

✔ f. Cash dividends, $328,500

The following selected accounts appear in the ledger of Parks Construction Inc. at the beginning of the current year:

Preferred 2% Stock, $75 par (100,000 shares authorized, 80,000 shares issued)	$ 6,000,000
Paid-In Capital in Excess of Par—Preferred Stock	420,000
Common Stock, $8 par (5,000,000 shares authorized, 3,000,000 shares issued)	24,000,000
Paid-In Capital in Excess of Par—Common Stock	1,850,000
Retained Earnings	115,400,000

During the year, the corporation completed a number of transactions affecting the stockholders' equity. They are summarized as follows:

a. Issued 400,000 shares of common stock at $11, receiving cash.
b. Issued 5,000 shares of preferred 2% stock at $90.
c. Purchased 150,000 shares of treasury common for $10 per share.
d. Sold 80,000 shares of treasury common for $13 per share.
e. Sold 20,000 shares of treasury common for $9 per share.
f. Declared cash dividends of $1.50 per share on preferred stock and $0.06 per share on common stock.
g. Paid the cash dividends.

Instructions
Journalize the entries to record the transactions. Identify each entry by letter.

PR 13-4A Entries for selected corporate transactions OBJ. 3, 4, 5, 7

✔ 4. Total stockholders' equity, $44,436,200

Morrow Enterprises Inc. manufactures bathroom fixtures. The stockholders' equity accounts of Morrow Enterprises Inc., with balances on January 1, 20Y5, are as follows:

Common Stock, $20 stated value (500,000 shares authorized, 375,000 shares issued)	$ 7,500,000
Paid-In Capital in Excess of Stated Value—Common Stock	825,000
Retained Earnings	33,600,000
Treasury Stock (25,000 shares, at a cost of $18 per share)	450,000

The following selected transactions occurred during the year:

Jan. 22. Paid cash dividends of $0.08 per share on the common stock. The dividend had been properly recorded when declared on December 1 of the preceding fiscal year for $28,000.
Apr. 10. Issued 75,000 shares of common stock for $24 per share.
June 6. Sold all of the treasury stock for $26 per share.
July 5. Declared a 4% stock dividend on common stock, to be capitalized at the market price of the stock, which is $25 per share.

Aug. 15. Issued the certificates for the dividend declared on July 5.

Nov. 23. Purchased 30,000 shares of treasury stock for $19 per share.

Dec. 28. Declared a $0.10-per-share dividend on common stock.

31. Closed the two dividends accounts to Retained Earnings.

Instructions

1. Enter the January 1 balances in T accounts for the stockholders' equity accounts listed. Also prepare T accounts for the following: Paid-In Capital from Sale of Treasury Stock; Stock Dividends Distributable; Stock Dividends; Cash Dividends.
2. Journalize the entries to record the transactions and post to the eight selected accounts.
3. Prepare a retained earnings statement for the year ended December 31, 20Y5.
4. Prepare the Stockholders' Equity section of the December 31, 20Y5, balance sheet using Method 1 of Exhibit 8.

PR 13-5A Entries for selected corporate transactions OBJ. 3, 4, 5, 6

✔ Oct. 15, Cash dividends, $324,300

Selected transactions completed by ATV Discount Corporation during the current fiscal year are as follows:

Jan. 5. Split the common stock 4 for 1 and reduced the par from $20 to $5 per share. After the split, there were 4,000,000 common shares outstanding.

Mar. 10. Purchased 100,000 shares of the corporation's own common stock at $30, recording the stock at cost.

Apr. 30. Declared semiannual dividends of $0.25 on 30,000 shares of preferred stock and $0.08 on the common stock to stockholders of record on May 15, payable on June 15.

June 15. Paid the cash dividends.

Aug. 20. Sold 60,000 shares of treasury stock at $40, receiving cash.

Oct. 15. Declared semiannual dividends of $0.25 on the preferred stock and $0.08 on the common stock (before the stock dividend). In addition, a 1% common stock dividend was declared on the common stock outstanding. The fair market value of the common stock is estimated at $35. The dividend date of record is November 15 payable on December 19.

Dec. 19. Paid the cash dividends and issued the certificates for the common stock dividend.

Instructions
Journalize the transactions.

Problems: Series B

PR 13-1B Dividends on preferred and common stock OBJ. 3

✔ 1. Common dividends in Year 3: $25,000

Yosemite Bike Corp. manufactures mountain bikes and distributes them through retail outlets in California, Oregon, and Washington. Yosemite Bike Corp. has declared the following annual dividends over a six-year period ended December 31 of each year: Year 1, $24,000; Year 2, $10,000; Year 3, $126,000; Year 4, $100,000; Year 5, $125,000; and Year 6, $125,000. During the entire period, the outstanding stock of the company was composed of 25,000 shares of cumulative preferred 2% stock, $90 par, and 100,000 shares of common stock, $4 par.

Instructions

1. Determine the total dividends and the per-share dividends declared on each class of stock for each of the six years. There were no dividends in arrears on January 1, Year 1. Summarize the data in tabular form, using the following column headings:

(Continued)

668 Chapter 13 Corporations: Organization, Stock Transactions, and Dividends

Year	Total Dividends	Preferred Dividends Total	Preferred Dividends Per Share	Common Dividends Total	Common Dividends Per Share
Year 1	$ 24,000				
Year 2	10,000				
Year 3	126,000				
Year 4	100,000				
Year 5	125,000				
Year 6	125,000				

2. Determine the average annual dividend per share for each class of stock for the six-year period.
3. Assuming a market price of $100 for the preferred stock and $5 for the common stock, calculate the average annual percentage return on initial shareholders' investment, based on the average annual dividend per share (a) for preferred stock and (b) for common stock.

PR 13-2B Stock transaction for corporate expansion OBJ. 3

Pulsar Optics produces medical lasers for use in hospitals. The accounts and their balances appear in the ledger of Pulsar Optics on April 30 of the current year as follows:

Preferred 1% Stock, $120 par (300,000 shares authorized, 36,000 shares issued)	$ 4,320,000
Paid-In Capital in Excess of Par—Preferred Stock	180,000
Common Stock, $15 par (2,000,000 shares authorized, 1,400,000 shares issued)	21,000,000
Paid-In Capital in Excess of Par—Common Stock	3,500,000
Retained Earnings	78,000,000

At the annual stockholders' meeting on August 5, the board of directors presented a plan for modernizing and expanding plant operations at a cost of approximately $9,000,000. The plan provided (a) that the corporation borrow $1,500,000, (b) that 20,000 shares of the unissued preferred stock be issued through an underwriter, and (c) that a building, valued at $4,150,000, and the land on which it is located, valued at $800,000, be acquired in accordance with preliminary negotiations by the issuance of 300,000 shares of common stock valued at $16.50 per share. The plan was approved by the stockholders and accomplished by the following transactions:

Oct. 9. Borrowed $1,500,000 from St. Peter City Bank, giving a 4% mortgage note.

17. Issued 20,000 shares of preferred stock, receiving $126 per share in cash.

28. Issued 300,000 shares of common stock in exchange for land and a building, according to the plan.

Instructions
Journalize the entries to record the October transactions.

PR 13-3B Selected stock transactions OBJ. 3, 4, 6

✔ f. Cash dividends, $234,775

Show Me How

Diamondback Welding & Fabrication Corporation sells and services pipe welding equipment in Illinois. The following selected accounts appear in the ledger of Diamondback Welding & Fabrication Corporation at the beginning of the current fiscal year:

Preferred 2% Stock, $80 par (100,000 shares authorized, 60,000 shares issued)	$ 4,800,000
Paid-In Capital in Excess of Par—Preferred Stock	210,000
Common Stock, $9 par (3,000,000 shares authorized, 1,750,000 shares issued)	15,750,000
Paid-In Capital in Excess of Par—Common Stock	1,400,000
Retained Earnings	52,840,000

Chapter 13 Corporations: Organization, Stock Transactions, and Dividends

During the year, the corporation completed a number of transactions affecting the stockholders' equity. They are summarized as follows:

a. Purchased 87,500 shares of treasury common for $8 per share.
b. Sold 55,000 shares of treasury common for $11 per share.
c. Issued 20,000 shares of preferred 2% stock at $84.
d. Issued 400,000 shares of common stock at $13, receiving cash.
e. Sold 18,000 shares of treasury common for $7.50 per share.
f. Declared cash dividends of $1.60 per share on preferred stock and $0.05 per share on common stock.
g. Paid the cash dividends.

Instructions
Journalize the entries to record the transactions. Identify each entry by letter.

PR 13-4B Entries for selected corporate transactions
OBJ. 3, 4, 5, 7

✔ 4. Total stockholders' equity, $11,262,432

Nav-Go Enterprises Inc. produces aeronautical navigation equipment. The stockholders' equity accounts of Nav-Go Enterprises Inc., with balances on January 1, 20Y3, are as follows:

Common Stock, $5 stated value (900,000 shares authorized, 620,000 shares issued)	$3,100,000
Paid-In Capital in Excess of Stated Value—Common Stock	1,240,000
Retained Earnings	4,875,000
Treasury Stock (48,000 shares, at a cost of $6 per share)	288,000

The following selected transactions occurred during the year:

Jan. 15. Paid cash dividends of $0.06 per share on the common stock. The dividend had been properly recorded when declared on December 1 of the preceding fiscal year for $34,320.

Mar. 15. Sold all of the treasury stock for $6.75 per share.

Apr. 13. Issued 200,000 shares of common stock for $8 per share.

June 14. Declared a 3% stock dividend on common stock, to be capitalized at the market price of the stock, which is $7.50 per share.

July 16. Issued the certificates for the dividend declared on June 14.

Oct. 30. Purchased 50,000 shares of treasury stock for $6 per share.

Dec. 30. Declared a $0.08-per-share dividend on common stock.

31. Closed the two dividends accounts to Retained Earnings.

Instructions
1. Enter the January 1 balances in T accounts for the stockholders' equity accounts listed. Also prepare T accounts for the following: Paid-In Capital from Sale of Treasury Stock; Stock Dividends Distributable; Stock Dividends; Cash Dividends.
2. Journalize the entries to record the transactions and post to the eight selected accounts.
3. Prepare a retained earnings statement for the year ended December 31, 20Y3.
4. Prepare the Stockholders' Equity section of the December 31, 20Y3, balance sheet using Method 1 of Exhibit 8.

PR 13-5B Entries for selected corporate transactions
OBJ. 3, 4, 5, 6

✔ Sept. 1, Cash dividends, $95,200

West Yellowstone Outfitters Corporation manufactures and distributes leisure clothing. Selected transactions completed by West Yellowstone Outfitters during the current fiscal year are as follows:

Jan. 15. Split the common stock 4 for 1 and reduced the par from $120 to $30 per share. After the split, there were 800,000 common shares outstanding.

(Continued)

Mar. 1. Declared semiannual dividends of $0.25 on 100,000 shares of preferred stock and $0.07 on the 800,000 shares of $30 par common stock to stockholders of record on March 31, payable on April 30.

Apr. 30. Paid the cash dividends.

May 31. Purchased 60,000 shares of the corporation's own common stock at $32, recording the stock at cost.

Aug. 17. Sold 40,000 shares of treasury stock at $38, receiving cash.

Sept. 1. Declared semiannual dividends of $0.25 on the preferred stock and $0.09 on the common stock (before the stock dividend). In addition, a 1% common stock dividend was declared on the common stock outstanding, to be capitalized at the fair market value of the common stock, which is estimated at $40. The dividend date of record is September 30, payable on October 31.

Oct. 31. Paid the cash dividends and issued the certificates for the common stock dividend.

Instructions
Journalize the transactions.

Cases & Projects

CP 13-1 Ethics in Action

Tommy Gunn is a division manager for K-Cern Inc., a small pharmaceutical company. Tommy's division has been working on a new drug that has the potential to revolutionize the treatment of skin cancer. Once the drug is proven to be effective in clinical trials, it will be approved for sale by the government and patented by the company. Because of the potential market for this drug, it is highly likely that the company's revenues and net income will increase significantly when it is approved. Tommy recently saw an internal company memo indicating that the drug passed its final clinical trial and that the company has received government approval to sell the drug. The company will issue a press release announcing this news in the next two days, and this announcement is expected to result in a dramatic increase in the company's stock price. Tommy knows that there is "free money" to be made if he invests in the stock before the announcement is made. However, K-Cern has a strict policy against employee purchases of company stock outside of established employee stock purchase plans. To get around this rule, Tommy asks his father to purchase the stock for him. The next morning Tommy's father purchases the stock with the understanding that he will split the profits with Tommy.

▶ Is Tommy behaving ethically? Why or why not?

CP 13-2 Ethics in Action

Lou Hoskins and Shirley Crothers are organizing Red Lodge Metals Unlimited Inc. to undertake a high-risk gold-mining venture in Canada. Lou and Shirley tentatively plan to request authorization for 400,000,000 shares of common stock to be sold to the general public. Lou and Shirley have decided to establish par of $0.03 per share in order to appeal to a wide variety of potential investors. Lou and Shirley believe that investors would be more willing to invest in the company if they received a large quantity of shares for what might appear to be a "bargain" price.

▶ Discuss whether Lou and Shirley are behaving in a professional manner.

CP 13-3 Team Activity

In teams, select a public company that interests you. Obtain the company's most recent annual report on Form 10-K. The Form 10-K is a company's annually required filing with the Securities and Exchange Commission (SEC). It includes the company's financial statements and accompanying notes. The Form 10-K can be obtained either (a) by referring to the investor relations section of the company's website or (b) by using the company search feature of the SEC's EDGAR database service found at www.sec.gov/edgar/searchedgar/companysearch.html.

Based on the information in the company's most recent annual report, determine the following:

1. Name of the corporation
2. State of incorporation
3. Nature of its operations
4. Total assets reported on the most recent balance sheet
5. Total liabilities reported on the most recent balance sheet
6. Total stockholders' equity reported on the most recent balance sheet
7. Total revenues reported on the most recent income statement
8. Net income reported on the most recent income statement
9. The number of shares of common stock authorized, issued, and outstanding
10. The par value per share of each class of stock
11. Market price of the stock outstanding
12. High and low price of the stock for the past year
13. Cash dividends paid for each share of stock during the past year

CP 13-4 Communication

Motion Designs Inc. has paid quarterly cash dividends since 20Y7. These dividends have steadily increased from $0.05 per share to the latest dividend declaration of $0.50 per share. The board of directors would like to continue this trend and is hesitant to suspend or decrease the amount of quarterly dividends. Unfortunately, sales dropped sharply in the fourth quarter of 20Y8 due to worsening economic conditions and increased competition. As a result, the board is uncertain as to whether it should declare a dividend for the last quarter of 20Y8.

On October 1, 20Y8, Motion Designs Inc. borrowed $4,000,000 from Valley National Bank to use in modernizing its retail stores and to expand its product line in response to changes in its industry. The terms of the 10-year, 6% loan require Motion Designs to do the following:

- Pay monthly interest on the last day of the month
- Pay $400,000 of the principal each October 1, beginning in 20Y9
- Maintain a current ratio (current assets ÷ current liabilities) of 2
- Maintain a minimum balance (a compensating balance) of $100,000 in its Valley National Bank account

On December 31, 20Y8, $1,000,000 of the $4,000,000 loan had been disbursed in modernization of the retail stores and in expansion of the product line. Motion Designs Inc.'s balance sheet as of December 31, 20Y8, follows:

(Continued)

Motion Designs Inc.
Balance Sheet
December 31, 20Y8

Assets

Current assets:			
Cash		$ 250,000	
Marketable securities		3,000,000	
Accounts reveivable	$ 800,000		
Allowance for doubtful accounts	(50,000)		
Accounts receivable, net		750,000	
Inventory		2,980,000	
Prepaid expenses		20,000	
Total current assets			$ 7,000,000
Property, plant, and equipment:			
Land		$1,500,000	
Buildings	$ 5,050,000		
Accumulated depreciation—buildings	(1,140,000)		
Buildings, book value		3,910,000	
Equipment	$ 3,320,000		
Accumulated depreciation equipment	(730,000)		
Equipment, book value		2,590,000	
Total property, plant, and equipment			8,000,000
Total assets			$15,000,000

Liabilities

Current liabilities:			
Accounts payable		$ 1,590,000	
Notes payable (Valley National Bank)		400,000	
Salaries payable		10,000	
Total current liabilities			$2,000,000
Long-term liabilities:			
Notes payable (Valley National Bank)			3,600,000
Total liabilities			$ 5,600,000

Stockholders' Equity

Paid-in capital:			
Common stock, $25 par (200,000 shares authorized, 180,000 shares issued)		$ 4,500,000	
Excess of issue price over par		270,000	
Total paid-in capital			$4,770,000
Retained earnings			4,630,000
Total stockholders' equity			9,400,000
Total liabilities and stockholders' equity			$15,000,000

The board of directors is scheduled to meet January 10, 20Y9, to discuss the results of operations for 20Y8 and to consider the declaration of dividends for the fourth quarter of 20Y8. The chairman of the board, Matt Cengage, has asked for your advice on the declaration of dividends.

Write a brief memo to the chairman of the board, outlining the factors that the board should consider in deciding whether to declare a cash dividend.

CP 13-5 Ethics in Action

Bernie Ebbers, the CEO of **WorldCom**, a major telecommunications company, was having personal financial troubles. Ebbers pledged a large stake of his WorldCom stock as security for some personal loans. As the price of WorldCom stock sank, Ebbers's bankers threatened to sell his stock in order to protect their loans. To avoid having his stock sold, Ebbers asked the board of directors of WorldCom to loan him nearly $400 million of corporate assets at 2.5% interest to pay off his bankers. The board agreed to lend him the money.

Comment on the decision of the board of directors in this situation.

CP 13-6 Issuing stock

Epstein Engineering Inc. began operations on January 5, 20Y8, with the issuance of 500,000 shares of $80 par common stock. The sole stockholders of Epstein Engineering Inc. are Barb Abrams and Dr. Amber Epstein, who organized Epstein Engineering Inc. with the objective of developing a new flu vaccine. Dr. Epstein claims that the flu vaccine, which is nearing the final development stage, will protect individuals against 90% of the flu types that have been medically identified. To complete the project, Epstein Engineering Inc. needs $25,000,000 of additional funds. The local banks have been unwilling to loan the funds because of the lack of sufficient collateral and the riskiness of the business.

The following is a conversation between Barb Abrams, the chief executive officer of Epstein Engineering Inc., and Amber Epstein, the leading researcher:

Barb: What are we going to do? The banks won't loan us any more money, and we've got to have $25 million to complete the project. We are so close! It would be a disaster to quit now. The only thing I can think of is to issue additional stock. Do you have any suggestions?

Amber: I guess you're right. But if the banks won't loan us any more money, how can we find any investors to buy stock?

Barb: I've been thinking about that. What if we promise the investors that we will pay them 5% of sales until they receive an amount equal to what they paid for the stock?

Amber: What happens when we pay back the $25 million? Do the investors get to keep the stock? If they do, it'll dilute our ownership.

Barb: How about if after we pay back the $25 million, we make them turn in their stock for $120 per share? That's one and one-half times what they paid for it, and they would have already gotten all their money back. That's a $120 profit per share for the investors.

Amber: It could work. We get our money but don't have to pay any interest, dividends, or the $80 per share until we start generating sales. At the same time, the investors could get their money back plus $120 per share profit.

Barb: We'll need current financial statements for the new investors. I'll get our accountant working on them and contact our attorney to draw up a legally binding contract for the new investors. Yes, this could work.

In late 20Y8, the attorney and the various regulatory authorities approved the new stock offering, and 312,500 shares of common stock were privately sold to new investors at the stock's par of $80.

In preparing financial statements for 20Y8, Barb Abrams and Dan Fisher, the controller for Epstein Engineering Inc., have the following conversation:

Dan: Barb, I've got a problem.

Barb: What's that, Dan?

Dan: Issuing common stock to raise that additional $25 million was a great idea. But . . .

Barb: But what?

Dan: I've got to prepare the 20Y8 annual financial statements, and I am not sure how to classify the common stock.

Barb: What do you mean? It's common stock.

Dan: I'm not so sure. I called the auditor and explained how we are contractually obligated to pay the new stockholders 5% of sales until $80 per share is paid. Then we may be obligated to pay them $120 per share.

Barb: So . . .

Dan: So the auditor thinks that we should classify the additional issuance of $25 million as debt, not stock! And if we put the $25 million on the balance sheet as debt, we will violate our other loan agreements with the banks. And if these agreements are violated, the banks may call in all our debt immediately. If they do that, we are in deep trouble. We'll probably have to file for bankruptcy. We just don't have the cash to pay off the banks.

1. Discuss the arguments for and against classifying the issuance of the $25 million of stock as debt.

2. What might be a practical solution to this classification problem?

CHAPTER 14

Long-Term Liabilities: Bonds and Notes

Chapters 1–4
Accounting Cycle

Chapter 5
Accounting Systems

- **Income Statement**
  - Chapter 6 *Accounting for Merchandising Businesses*
- **Statement of Owner's Equity**
- **Balance Sheet**
- **Statement of Cash Flows**
  - Chapter 16 *Cash Flows*

Assets = Liabilities + Owner's Equity

Assets	Liabilities	Owner's Equity
Chapter 8 *Cash*	Chapter 11 *Current Liabilities*	Chapter 12 *Accounting for Partnerships and Limited Liability Companies*
Chapter 9 *Receivables*	**Chapter 14 Long-Term Liabilities: Bonds and Notes**	
Chapter 7 *Inventories*		
Chapter 10 *Fixed and Intangible Assets*		Chapter 13 *Corporations*
Chapter 15 *Investments*		

Chapter 17
Financial Statement Analysis

Statement of Retained Earnings

Retained earnings, Jan. 1		$XXX
Net income	$ XXX	
Dividends	(XXX)	
Increase in retained earnings		XXX

Statement of Cash Flows

Cash flows from (used in) operating activities	$XXX
Cash flows from (used in) investing activities	XXX
Cash flows from (used in) financing activities	XXX
Increase (decrease) in cash flows	$XXX
	XXX
	$XXX

Income Statement

Sales		$XXX
Cost of merchandise sold		XXX
Gross profit		$XXX
Operating expenses:		
Advertising expense	$XXX	
Depreciation expense	XXX	
Amortization expense	XXX	
Depletion expense	XXX	
…	XXX	
…	XXX	
Total operating expenses		XXX
Income from operations		$XXX
Other revenue and expenses		
Interest expense		XXX
Net income		$XXX

Balance Sheet

Current assets:		
Cash	$XXX	
Accounts receivable	XXX	
Inventory	XXX	
Total current assets		$XXX
Property, plant, and equipment	$XXX	
Intangible assets	XXX	
Total long-term assets		XXX
Total assets		$XXX
Liabilities:		
Current liabilities	$XXX	
Long-term liabilities:	XXX	
Bonds payable	XXX	
Notes payable	XXX	
Total liabilities		$XXX
Stockholders' equity		XXX
Total liabilities and stockholders' equity		$XXX

CHAPTER 14

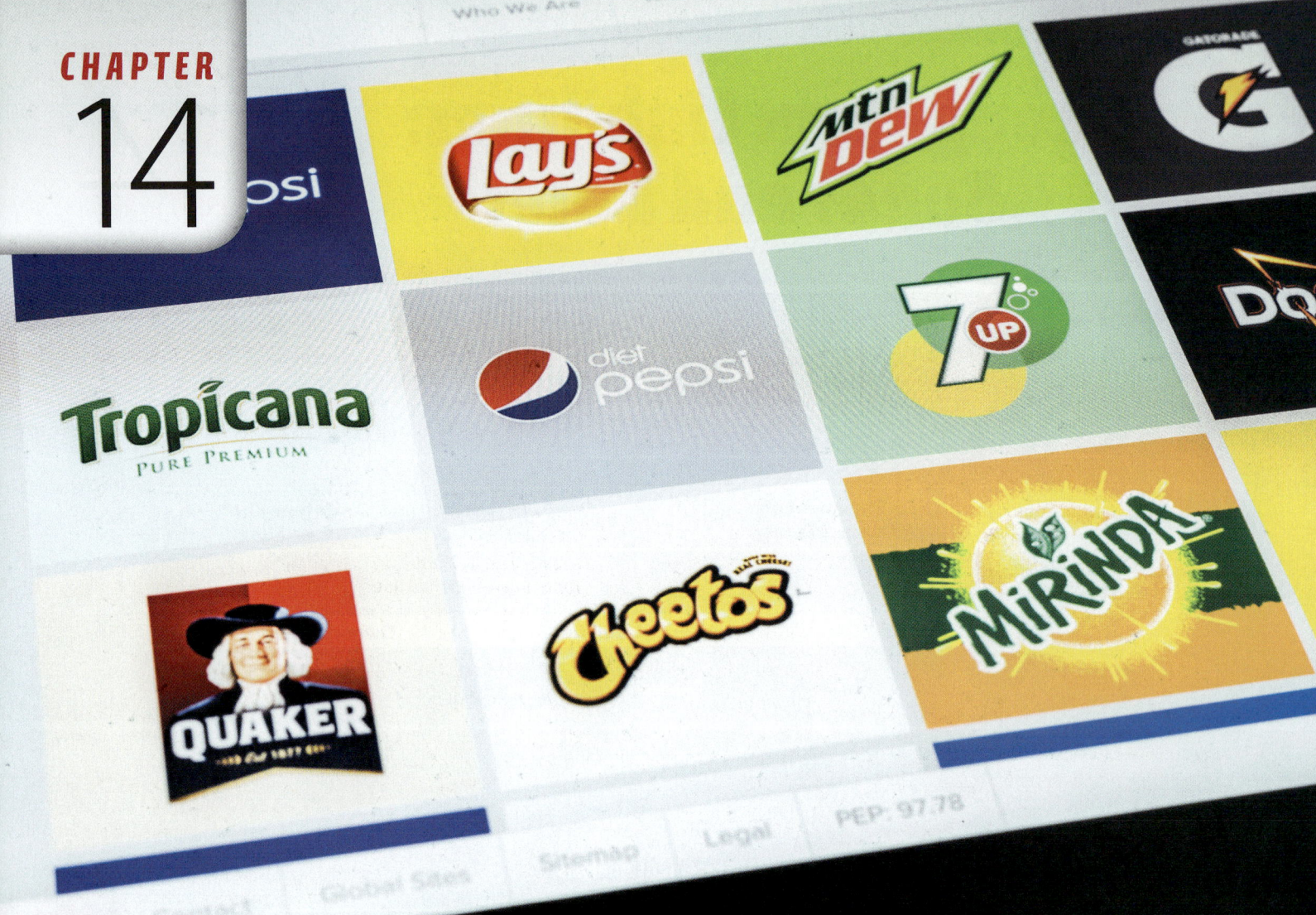

PepsiCo, Inc.

PepsiCo, Inc. is best known for its beverages, which include Pepsi, Diet Pepsi, Gatorade, Mountain Dew, Diet Mountain Dew, Tropicana fruit juices, and Aquafina water.* However, PepsiCo also produces a variety of foods, which include Lay's potato chips, Fritos corn chips, Doritos, Cheetos, Quaker oatmeal, Aunt Jemima mixes and syrups, and Cap'n Crunch cereal. PepsiCo produces, distributes, and sells its products in over 200 countries.

PepsiCo uses a variety of methods to finance its operations, including long-term debt and stock. A recent balance sheet revealed that over 75% of its total assets are financed with liabilities, and 66% of these liabilities are long-term. Included in PepsiCo's long-term liabilities are a variety of notes and bonds. For example, PepsiCo has $13,640 million of bonds maturing throughout 2020–2044 with interest rates of 3.9% and 4.0%. In this chapter, we will discuss the accounting and reporting of bonds payable and installment notes payable.

*The brands listed here are trademarked by PepsiCo.

Learning Objectives

After studying this chapter, you should be able to:

Example Exercises (EE) are shown in **green**.

Obj. 1 Compute the potential impact of long-term borrowing on earnings per share.

Financing Corporations
Determining earnings per share under alternative financing plans — EE 14-1

Obj. 2 Describe the characteristics and terminology of bonds payable.

Nature of Bonds Payable
Bond Characteristics and Terminology
Proceeds from Issuing Bonds

Obj. 3 Describe and illustrate the accounting for bonds payable.

Accounting for Bonds Payable
Bonds Issued at Face Amount — EE 14-2
Bonds Issued at a Discount — EE 14-3
Amortizing a Bond Discount — EE 14-4
Bonds Issued at a Premium — EE 14-5
Amortizing a Bond Premium — EE 14-6
Bond Redemption — EE 14-7

Obj. 4 Describe and illustrate the accounting for installment notes.

Installment Notes
Issuing an Installment Note
Annual Payments — EE 14-8

Obj. 5 Describe and illustrate the reporting of long-term liabilities, including bonds and installment notes payable.

Reporting Long-Term Liabilities

Obj. 6 Describe and illustrate how the times interest earned ratio is used to evaluate a company's financial condition.

Financial Analysis and Interpretation: Times Interest Earned Ratio
Compute Times Interest Earned — EE 14-9

At a Glance 14 ▶ Page 700

Financing Corporations

Obj. 1 Compute the potential impact of long-term borrowing on earnings per share.

Corporations finance their operations using the following sources:

- Short-term debt, such as purchasing goods or services on account
- Long-term debt, such as issuing bonds or notes payable
- Equity, such as issuing common or preferred stock

Short-term debt, including the purchase of goods and services on account and the issuance of short-term notes payable, was discussed in Chapter 11. Issuing equity in the form of common or preferred stock was discussed in Chapter 13. This chapter focuses on the use of long-term debt such as bonds and notes payable to finance a company's operations.

A **bond** is an interest-bearing note that requires periodic interest payments, with the face amount to be repaid at the maturity date. For example, a 12% bond requires the company issuing the bond to pay 12% interest on the face amount of the bonds every year. As creditors of the corporation, bondholder claims on the corporation's assets rank ahead of stockholders.

One of the main factors that influences the decision to issue debt or equity is the effect that various financing alternatives will have on earnings per share. **Earnings per share (EPS)** measures the income earned by each share of common stock. It is computed as follows:[1]

$$\text{Earnings per Share} = \frac{\text{Net Income} - \text{Preferred Dividends}}{\text{Number of Common Shares Outstanding}}$$

---

[1] Earnings per share is also discussed in the *Financial Analysis and Interpretation* section of Chapter 13 and in Chapter 17.

To illustrate the effects that issuing debt can have on earnings per share, consider the following alternative plans for financing Boz Corporation, a $4,000,000 company:

	Plan 1 Amount	Plan 1 Percent	Plan 2 Amount	Plan 2 Percent	Plan 3 Amount	Plan 3 Percent
Issue 12% bonds	—	0%	—	0%	$2,000,000	50%
Issue preferred 9% stock, $50 par value	—	0	$2,000,000	50	1,000,000	25
Issue common stock, $10 par value	$4,000,000	100	2,000,000	50	1,000,000	25
Total amount of financing	$4,000,000	100%	$4,000,000	100%	$4,000,000	100%

The company must choose one of these plans. Each plan finances some of the corporation's operations by issuing common stock. However, the percentage financed by common stock varies from 100% (Plan 1) to 25% (Plan 3).

Assume the following data for Boz Corporation:

- Earnings before interest and income taxes are $800,000.
- The tax rate is 40%.
- All bonds or stocks are issued at their par or face amount.

The effect of the preceding financing plans on Boz's net income and earnings per share is shown in Exhibit 1.

EXHIBIT 1

Effect of Alternative Financing Plans—$800,000 Earnings

Dynamic Exhibit

	Plan 1	Plan 2	Plan 3
12% bonds	—	—	$2,000,000
Preferred 9% stock, $50 par	—	$2,000,000	1,000,000
Common stock, $10 par	$4,000,000	2,000,000	1,000,000
Total	$4,000,000	$4,000,000	$4,000,000
Earnings before interest and income tax	$ 800,000	$ 800,000	$ 800,000
Interest on bonds	—	—	(240,000)[a]
Income before income tax	$ 800,000	$ 800,000	$ 560,000
Income tax	(320,000)[b]	(320,000)[b]	(224,000)[b]
Net income	$ 480,000	$ 480,000	$ 336,000
Dividends on preferred stock	—	(180,000)[c]	(90,000)[c]
Available for dividends on common stock	$ 480,000	$ 300,000	$ 246,000
Shares of common stock outstanding	÷ 400,000[d]	÷ 200,000[d]	÷ 100,000[d]
Earnings per share on common stock	$ 1.20	$ 1.50	$ 2.46

[a] $2,000,000 bonds × 12%
[b] Income before income tax × 40%
[c] Preferred stock × 9%
[d] Common stock ÷ $10 par value per share

Exhibit 1 indicates that when earnings are strong, Plan 3 has the highest earnings per share, making it most attractive for common shareholders. This is because the company is generating more than enough net income to cover the bond interest. If the estimated earnings are more than $800,000, the difference between the earnings per share to common stockholders under Plans 1 and 3 is even greater.[2]

Lower earnings, however, have the opposite effect. If earnings are reduced to $440,000, as illustrated in Exhibit 2, Plans 1 and 2 become more attractive to common stockholders. This is because more of the company's earnings are being used to pay bond interest, leaving less net income attributable to common stockholders.

---

[2] The higher earnings per share under Plan 3 is due to a finance concept known as *leverage*. This concept is discussed further in Chapter 18.

EXHIBIT 2

Effect of Alternative Financing Plans—$440,000 Earnings

	Plan 1	Plan 2	Plan 3
12% bonds	—	—	$2,000,000
Preferred 9% stock, $50 par	—	$2,000,000	1,000,000
Common stock, $10 par	$4,000,000	2,000,000	1,000,000
Total	$4,000,000	$4,000,000	$4,000,000
Earnings before interest and income tax	$ 440,000	$ 440,000	$ 440,000
Interest on bonds	—	—	(240,000)
Income before income tax	$ 440,000	$ 440,000	$ 200,000
Income tax	(176,000)	(176,000)	(80,000)
Net income	$ 264,000	$ 264,000	$ 120,000
Dividends on preferred stock	—	(180,000)	(90,000)
Available for dividends on common stock	$ 264,000	$ 84,000	$ 30,000
Shares of common stock outstanding	÷ 400,000	÷ 200,000	÷ 100,000
Earnings per share on common stock	$ 0.66	$ 0.42	$ 0.30

In addition to earnings per share, the corporation should consider other factors in deciding among the financing plans. For example, if bonds are issued, the interest and the face value of the bonds at maturity must be paid. If these payments are not made, the bondholders could seek court action and force the company into bankruptcy. In contrast, a corporation is not legally obligated to pay dividends on preferred or common stock.

Example Exercise 14-1 Alternative Financing Plans   Obj. 1

Gonzales Co. is considering the following alternative plans for financing its company:

	Plan 1	Plan 2
Issue 10% bonds (at face value)	—	$2,000,000
Issue common stock, $10 par	$3,000,000	1,000,000

Income tax is estimated at 40% of income.
  Determine the earnings per share of common stock under the two alternative financing plans, assuming that income before bond interest and income tax is $750,000.

Follow My Example 14-1

	Plan 1	Plan 2
Earnings before bond interest and income tax	$ 750,000	$ 750,000
Interest on bonds	—	(200,000)[2]
Income before income tax	$ 750,000	$ 550,000
Income tax	(300,000)[1]	(220,000)[3]
Net income	$ 450,000	$ 330,000
Dividends on preferred stock	—	—
Available for dividends on common stock	$ 450,000	$ 330,000
Shares of common stock outstanding	÷300,000	÷100,000
Earnings per share on common stock	$ 1.50	$ 3.30

[1]$750,000 × 40%   [2]$2,000,000 × 10%   [3]$550,000 × 40%

Practice Exercises: PE 14-1A, PE 14-1B

Nature of Bonds Payable

Obj. 2 Describe the characteristics and terminology of bonds payable.

Corporate bonds normally differ in face amount, interest rates, interest payment dates, and maturity dates. Bonds also differ in other ways such as whether corporate assets are pledged in support of the bonds.

Bond Characteristics and Terminology

The face amount of each bond is called the *principal*. This is the amount that must be repaid on the dates the bonds mature. The principal is usually $1,000, or a multiple of $1,000. The interest on bonds may be payable annually, semiannually, or quarterly. Most bonds pay interest semiannually.

The underlying contract between the company issuing bonds and the bondholders is called a **bond indenture**. This contract can be written in different ways, depending on the financing needs of the company. The two most common types of bonds are term bonds and serial bonds. When all bonds of an issue mature at the same time, they are called *term bonds*. If the bonds mature over several dates, they are called *serial bonds*. For example, one-tenth of an issue of $1,000,000 bonds, or $100,000, may mature 16 years from the issue date, another $100,000 in the 17th year, and so on.

There are also a variety of more complicated bond structures. For example, *convertible bonds* may be exchanged for shares of common stock, and *callable bonds* may be redeemed by the corporation prior to maturity. These bonds are discussed in intermediate and advanced accounting texts.

Proceeds from Issuing Bonds

When a corporation issues bonds, the proceeds received for the bonds depend on the following:

- The face amount of the bonds, which is the amount due at the maturity date
- The interest rate on the bonds
- The market rate of interest for similar bonds

The face amount and the interest rate on the bonds are identified in the bond indenture. The interest rate to be paid on the face amount of the bond is called the **contract rate** or *coupon rate*.

The **market rate of interest**, sometimes called the **effective rate of interest**, is the rate determined from sales and purchases of similar bonds. The market rate of interest is affected by a variety of factors, including investors' expectations of current and future economic conditions.

By comparing the market and contract rates of interest, it can be determined whether the bonds will sell for more than, for less than, or at their face amount, as shown in Exhibit 3.

Link to PepsiCo
PepsiCo's 2.75% bonds maturing in 2023 were recently selling for less than their face value.

EXHIBIT 3   Issuing Bonds at a Discount, at Face Amount, and at a Premium

If: Market Rate > Contract Rate	If: Market Rate = Contract Rate	If: Market Rate < Contract Rate
Less than $1,000 < $1,000 Bond	$1,000 = $1,000 Bond	More than $1,000 > $1,000 Bond
Then: Selling Price < Face Amount	Then: Selling Price = Face Amount	Then: Selling Price > Face Amount
Sold at a DISCOUNT	Sold at FACE AMOUNT	Sold at a PREMIUM

If the market rate equals the contract rate, bonds will sell at the **face amount**.

If the market rate is greater than the contract rate, the bonds will sell for less than their face value. The face amount of the bonds less the selling price is called a **discount**. A bond sells at a discount because buyers are not willing to pay the full face amount for bonds with a contract rate that is lower than the market rate.

If the market rate is less than the contract rate, the bonds will sell for more than their face value. The selling price of the bonds less the face amount is called a **premium**. A bond sells at a premium because buyers are willing to pay more than the face amount for bonds with a contract rate that is higher than the market rate.

The price of a bond is quoted as a percentage of the bond's face value. For example, a $1,000 bond quoted at 98 could be purchased or sold for $980 ($1,000 × 0.98). Likewise, bonds quoted at 109 could be purchased or sold for $1,090 ($1,000 × 1.09).

> **Link to PepsiCo**
> PepsiCo's 4.5% bonds maturing in 2023 were recently selling for over 110% of their face value.

Business Connection

INVESTOR BOND PRICE RISK

Corporate bonds are purchased as investments by both individuals and institutions. Bonds issued by financially strong issuers provide a compelling balance of risk and reward, as they provide the investor with both a steady stream of interest payments and the repayment of the principal at maturity. Thus, high-quality bond investments are considered less risky than equity investments. However, this does not mean that bond investors have no price risk. Bond prices move in the opposite direction as changes in market interest rates, as shown below.

Market Rate of Interest	Market Price of Bonds
Increase	Decrease
Decrease	Increase

The magnitude of a bond's price change depends on its maturity. When market interest rates change, the price of short-term bonds fluctuates less than the price of long-term bonds with a comparable interest rate. This is illustrated in the following table:

Bond Term	Contract Rate	Estimated Price of $1,000 Par Value Bond if Market Interest Rate Doubles	Estimated Price of $1,000 Par Value Bond if Market Interest Rate Halves
1 year	0.5%	$995	$1,002
5 years	1.5%	931	1,037
10 years	2.0%	838	1,095
30 years	3.0%	587	1,360

The greater price variability of long-term bonds makes them a riskier investment than short-term bonds. This is one of the reasons longer-term bonds typically have higher coupon rates than shorter-term bonds. As a result, the bond's term must be considered in evaluating both the risk and return of a bond investment.

Accounting for Bonds Payable

Obj. 3 Describe and illustrate the accounting for bonds payable.

Bonds may be issued at their face amount, a discount, or a premium. When bonds are issued at less or more than their face amount, the discount or premium must be amortized over the life of the bonds. At the maturity date, the face amount must be repaid. In some situations, a corporation may redeem bonds before their maturity date by repurchasing them from investors.

Bonds Issued at Face Amount

If the market rate of interest is equal to the contract rate of interest, the bonds will sell for their face amount or at a price of 100. To illustrate, assume that on January 1, 20Y5, Eastern Montana Communications Inc. issued the following bonds:

Face amount	$100,000
Contract rate of interest	12%
Interest paid semiannually on June 30 and December 31.	
Term of bonds	5 years
Market rate of interest	12%

682 **Chapter 14** Long-Term Liabilities: Bonds and Notes

Since the contract rate of interest and the market rate of interest are the same, the bonds will sell at their face amount. The entry to record the issuance of the bonds is as follows:

20Y5					
Jan.	1	Cash		100,000	
		Bonds Payable			100,000
		Issued $100,000 bonds payable at face amount.			

Every six months (on June 30 and December 31) after the bonds are issued, interest of $6,000 ($100,000 × 12% × ½ year) is paid. The first interest payment on June 30, 20Y5, is recorded as follows:

20Y5					
June	30	Interest Expense		6,000	
		Cash			6,000
		Paid six months' interest on bonds.			

At the maturity date, the payment of the principal of $100,000 is recorded as follows:

20Y9					
Dec.	31	Bonds Payable		100,000	
		Cash			100,000
		Paid bond principal at maturity date.			

Example Exercise 14-2 Issuing Bonds at Face Amount   Obj. 3

On January 1, the first day of the fiscal year, a company issues a $1,000,000, 6%, five-year bond that pays semiannual interest of $30,000 ($1,000,000 × 6% × ½ year), receiving cash of $1,000,000. Journalize the entries to record (a) the issuance of the bonds at their face amount, (b) the first interest payment on June 30, and (c) the payment of the principal on the maturity date.

Follow My Example 14-2

a.	Cash		1,000,000	
	Bonds Payable			1,000,000
b.	Interest Expense		30,000	
	Cash			30,000
c.	Bonds Payable		1,000,000	
	Cash			1,000,000

Practice Exercises: PE 14-2A, PE 14-2B

Bonds Issued at a Discount

Note: Bonds will sell at a discount when the market rate of interest is higher than the contract rate.

If the market rate of interest is greater than the contract rate of interest, the bonds will sell for less than their face amount. This is because investors are not willing to pay the full face amount for bonds that pay a lower contract rate of interest than the rate they could earn on similar bonds (market rate). The difference between the face amount and the selling price of the bonds is the bond discount.[3]

---
[3] The price that investors are willing to pay for the bonds depends on present value concepts. Present value concepts, including the computation of bond prices, are described and illustrated in Appendix 1 at the end of this chapter.

To illustrate, assume that on January 1, 20Y5, Western Wyoming Distribution Inc. issued the following bonds:

Face amount	$100,000
Contract rate of interest	12%
Interest paid semiannually on June 30 and December 31.	
Term of bonds	5 years
Market rate of interest	13%

Because the contract rate of interest is less than the market rate of interest, the bonds will sell at less than their face amount. Assuming that the bonds sell for $96,406, the entry to record the issuance of the bonds is as follows:

20Y5					
Jan.	1	Cash		96,406	
		Discount on Bonds Payable		3,594	
		Bonds Payable			100,000
		Issued $100,000 bonds at discount.			

The $96,406 is the amount investors are willing to pay for bonds that have a lower contract rate of interest (12%) than the market rate (13%). The discount is the market's way of adjusting the contract rate of interest to the higher market rate of interest.

The account, Discount on Bonds Payable, is a contra account to Bonds Payable and has a normal debit balance. It is subtracted from Bonds Payable to determine the carrying amount (or book value) of the bonds payable. The **carrying amount** of bonds payable is the face amount of the bonds less any unamortized discount or plus any unamortized premium. Thus, after the preceding entry, the carrying amount of the bonds payable is $96,406 ($100,000 − $3,594).

> **Link to PepsiCo**
> PepsiCo's 3.6% bonds maturing in 2042 were selling for less than 94% of their face value, which implies that the market rate of interest for equivalent bonds is more than the 3.6% contract rate.

Example Exercise 14-3   Issuing Bonds at a Discount   Obj. 3

On the first day of the fiscal year, a company issues a $1,000,000, 6%, five-year bond that pays semiannual interest of $30,000 ($1,000,000 × 6% × ½), receiving cash of $936,420. Journalize the entry to record the issuance of the bonds.

Follow My Example 14-3

Cash	936,420	
Discount on Bonds Payable	63,580	
Bonds Payable		1,000,000

Practice Exercises: PE 14-3A, PE 14-3B

Amortizing a Bond Discount

Every period, a portion of the bond discount must be reduced and added to interest expense to reflect the passage of time. This process, called **amortization**, increases the contract rate of interest on a bond to the market rate of interest that existed on the date the bonds were issued. The entry to amortize a bond discount is as follows:

Interest Expense		XXX	
Discount on Bonds Payable			XXX

684 Chapter 14 Long-Term Liabilities: Bonds and Notes

Business Connection

U.S. GOVERNMENT DEBT

Like many corporations, the U.S. government issues debt to finance its operations. Currently, debt provides approximately 15% of the total annual funding needs of the U.S. government. The remainder comes from taxes. The debt is issued by the U.S. Treasury Department in the form of U.S. Treasury bills, notes, and bonds. An individual investor can purchase these as an investment through the TreasuryDirect® website or through a broker. Treasury securities have the following characteristics:

	Issued at	Interest Paid	Term
U.S. Treasury bills	Discount	None	1 year or less
U.S. Treasury notes	Face value	Semiannual	1 to 10 years
U.S. Treasury bonds	Face value	Semiannual	30 years

Recently, 10-year notes had a contract rate of 2.26%. The contract interest rate for government securities will normally be lowest for Treasury bills and largest for Treasury bonds.

The preceding entry may be made annually as an adjusting entry, or it may be combined with the semiannual interest payment. In the latter case, the entry would be as follows:

Interest Expense		XXX	
Discount on Bonds Payable			XXX
Cash (amount of semiannual interest)			XXX

The straight-line method is used to compute the amortization of a bond discount. This method provides equal amounts of amortization each period[4]. To illustrate, amortization of the Western Wyoming Distribution bond discount of $3,594 is computed as follows:

Discount on bonds payable	$3,594
Term of bonds	5 years
Semiannual amortization	$359.40 ($3,594 ÷ 10 periods)

The combined entry to record the first interest payment and the amortization of the discount is as follows:

20Y5					
June	30	Interest Expense		6,359.40	
		Discount on Bonds Payable			359.40
		Cash			6,000.00
		Paid semiannual interest and			
		amortized 1/10 of bond discount.			

The preceding entry is made on each interest payment date. Thus, the amount of the semiannual interest expense on the bonds ($6,359.40) remains the same over the life of the bonds.

The effect of the discount amortization is to increase the interest expense from $6,000.00 to $6,359.40 on every semiannual interest payment date. In effect, this increases the contract rate of interest from 12% to a rate of interest that approximates the market rate of 13%. In addition, as the discount is amortized, the carrying amount of the bonds increases until it equals the face amount of the bonds on the maturity date.

---

[4] The effective interest rate method is required by generally accepted accounting principles. However, the straight-line method may be used if the results do not differ significantly from the interest method. The straight-line method is used in this chapter. The effective interest rate method is described and illustrated in Appendix 2 at the end of this chapter.

Example Exercise 14-4 Discount Amortization   Obj. 3

Using the bond from Example Exercise 14-3, journalize the first interest payment and the amortization of the related bond discount.

Follow My Example 14-4

Interest Expense	36,358	
Discount on Bonds Payable		6,358
Cash		30,000
Paid interest and amortized the bond discount ($63,580 ÷ 10).		

Practice Exercises: PE 14-4A, PE 14-4B

Bonds Issued at a Premium

If the market rate of interest is less than the contract rate of interest, the bonds will sell for more than their face amount. This is because investors are willing to pay more for bonds that pay a higher contract rate of interest than the rate they could earn on similar bonds (market rate).

To illustrate, assume that on January 1, 20Y5, Northern Idaho Transportation Inc. issued the following bonds:

Face amount	$100,000
Contract rate of interest	12%
Interest paid semiannually on June 30 and December 31.	
Term of bonds	5 years
Market rate of interest	11%

Note: Bonds will sell at a premium when the market rate of interest is less than the contract rate.

Because the contract rate of interest is more than the market rate of interest, the bonds will sell for more than their face amount. Assuming that the bonds sell for $103,769, the entry to record the issuance of the bonds is as follows:

20Y5				
Jan. 1	Cash		103,769	
	Bonds Payable			100,000
	Premium on Bonds Payable			3,769
	Issued $100,000 bonds at a premium.			

The $3,769 premium is the extra amount investors are willing to pay for bonds that have a higher contract rate of interest (12%) than the market rate (11%). The premium is the market's way of adjusting the contract rate of interest to the lower market rate of interest.

The account Premium on Bonds Payable has a normal credit balance. It is added to Bonds Payable to determine the carrying amount (or book value) of the bonds payable. Thus, after the preceding entry, the carrying amount of the bonds payable is $103,769 ($100,000 + $3,769).

Example Exercise 14-5 Issuing Bonds at a Premium   Obj. 3

On the first day of the fiscal year, a company issues a $2,000,000, 12%, five-year bond that pays semiannual interest of $120,000 ($2,000,000 × 12% × ½), receiving cash of $2,154,440. Journalize the bond issuance.

(Continued)

Follow My Example 14-5

Cash	2,154,440
Premium on Bonds Payable	154,440
Bonds Payable	2,000,000

Practice Exercises: PE 14-5A, PE 14-5B

Amortizing a Bond Premium

Like bond discounts, a bond premium must be amortized over the life of the bond. The amortization of a bond premium decreases the contract rate of interest on a bond to the market rate of interest that existed on the date the bonds were issued. The amortization can be computed using either the straight-line or the effective interest rate method. The entry to amortize a bond premium is as follows:

Premium on Bonds Payable	XXX	
Interest Expense		XXX

The preceding entry may be made annually as an adjusting entry, or it may be combined with the semiannual interest payment. In the latter case, it would be:

Interest Expense	XXX	
Premium on Bonds Payable	XXX	
Cash (amount of semiannual interest)		XXX

To illustrate, amortization of the preceding premium of $3,769 is computed as follows using the straight-line method:

Premium on bonds payable	$3,769
Term of bonds	5 years
Semiannual amortization	$376.90 ($3,769 ÷ 10 periods)

The combined entry to record the first interest payment and the amortization of the premium is as follows:

20Y5				
June	30	Interest Expense	5,623.10	
		Premium on Bonds Payable	376.90	
		Cash		6,000.00
		Paid semiannual interest and amortized 1/10 of bond premium.		

The preceding entry is made on each interest payment date. Thus, the amount of the semiannual interest expense ($5,623.10) on the bonds remains the same over the life of the bonds.

The effect of the premium amortization is to decrease the interest expense from $6,000.00 to $5,623.10. In effect, this decreases the rate of interest from 12% to a rate of interest that approximates the market rate of 11%. In addition, as the premium is amortized, the carrying amount of the bonds decreases until it equals the face amount of bonds on the maturity date.

Example Exercise 14-6 Premium Amortization   Obj. 3

Using the bond from Example Exercise 14-5, journalize the first interest payment and the amortization of the related bond premium.

Follow My Example 14-6

Interest Expense	104,556	
Premium on Bonds Payable	15,444	
Cash		120,000
Paid interest and amortized the bond premium ($154,440 ÷ 10).		

Practice Exercises: PE 14-6A, PE 14-6B

Business Connection

BOND RATINGS

When purchasing bonds, investors are very interested in understanding how likely it is that the bond issuer will be able to repay the bond principal and associated interest. To help them assess this likelihood, independent rating agencies review and grade the financial condition of companies that issue bonds. For example, the **Standard & Poor's** rating agency rates bonds on a scale from D (lowest) to AAA (highest). Bonds with a rating of BBB- or higher are called *investment grade* because they are issued by companies in sound financial condition and are considered to be reasonably safe investments. Bonds issued by companies in relatively weak financial condition receive ratings below BBB-, reflecting the higher potential for default or nonpayment. These lesser quality bonds are referred to as *non-investment grade* or *junk* bonds. The market rate of interest on junk bonds is much higher than the market rate on investment grade bonds, which compensates bond investors for junk bonds' higher risk of default.

Bond Redemption

A corporation may redeem or call bonds before they mature. This is often done when the market rate of interest declines below the contract rate of interest. In such cases, the corporation may issue new bonds at a lower interest rate and use the proceeds to redeem the original bond issue.

Callable bonds can be redeemed by the issuing corporation within the period of time and at the price stated in the bond indenture. Normally, the call price is above the face value. A corporation may also redeem its bonds by purchasing them on the open market.[5]

A corporation usually redeems its bonds at a price different from the carrying amount (or book value) of the bonds. A gain or loss may be realized on a bond redemption as follows:

- A *gain* is recorded if the price paid for redemption is below the bond carrying amount.
- A *loss* is recorded if the price paid for the redemption is above the carrying amount.

Gains and losses on the redemption of bonds are reported in the *Other revenue (loss)* section of the income statement.

To illustrate, assume that on June 30, 20Y5, a corporation has the following bond issue:

Face amount of bonds	$100,000
Premium on bonds payable	4,000*

*After the semiannual interest payment and premium amortization have been recorded.

---

[5] Some bond indentures require the corporation issuing the bonds to transfer cash to a special cash fund, called a *sinking fund*, over the life of the bond. Such funds help assure investors that there will be adequate cash to pay the bonds at their maturity date.

688 CHAPTER 14 Long-Term Liabilities: Bonds and Notes

On June 30, 20Y5, the corporation redeemed one-fourth ($25,000) of these bonds in the market for $24,000. The entry to record the redemption is as follows:

20Y5				
June	30	Bonds Payable	25,000	
		Premium on Bonds Payable	1,000	
		Cash		24,000
		Gain on Redemption of Bonds		2,000
		Redeemed $25,000 bonds for $24,000.		

In the preceding entry, only the portion of the premium related to the redeemed bonds ($4,000 × 25% = $1,000) is removed. The difference between the carrying amount of the bonds redeemed, $26,000 ($25,000 + $1,000), and the redemption price, $24,000, is recorded as a gain.

Assume that the corporation calls the remaining $75,000 of outstanding bonds, which are held by a private investor, for $79,500 on July 1, 20Y5. The entry to record the redemption is as follows:

20Y5				
July	1	Bonds Payable	75,000	
		Premium on Bonds Payable	3,000	
		Loss on Redemption of Bonds	1,500	
		Cash		79,500
		Redeemed $75,000 bonds for $79,500.		

Example Exercise 14-7 Redemption of Bonds Payable — Obj. 3

A $500,000 bond issue on which there is an unamortized discount of $40,000 is redeemed for $475,000. Journalize the redemption of the bonds.

Follow My Example 14-7

Bonds Payable	500,000	
Loss on Redemption of Bonds	15,000	
Discount on Bonds Payable		40,000
Cash		475,000

Practice Exercises: PE 14-7A, PE 14-7B

Obj. 4 Describe and illustrate the accounting for installment notes.

Installment Notes

Corporations often finance their operations by issuing bonds payable. As an alternative, corporations may issue a different kind of notes payable called installment notes. An **installment note** is a debt that requires the borrower to make equal periodic payments to the lender for the term of the note. Unlike bonds, each note payment includes the following:

- Payment of a portion of the amount initially borrowed, called the *principal*
- Payment of interest on the outstanding balance

At the end of the note's term, the principal will have been repaid in full.

Installment notes are often used to purchase specific assets such as equipment and are often secured by the purchased asset. When a note is secured by an asset, it is called a **mortgage note**. If the borrower fails to pay a mortgage note, the lender has the right to take possession of the pledged asset and sell it to pay off the debt. Mortgage notes are typically issued by an individual bank.

Individuals typically use mortgage notes when buying a house or car.

Issuing an Installment Note

When an installment note is issued, an entry is recorded debiting Cash and crediting Notes Payable. To illustrate, assume that Lewis Company issues the following installment note to City National Bank on January 1, 20Y4:

Principal amount of note	$24,000
Interest rate	6%
Term of note	5 years
Annual payments	$5,698[6]

The entry to record the issuance of the note is as follows:

20Y4				
Jan.	1	Cash	24,000	
		Notes Payable		24,000
		Issued installment note for cash.		

Annual Payments

The preceding note payable requires Lewis Company to repay the principal and interest in equal payments of $5,698 beginning December 31, 20Y4, for each of the next five years. Unlike bonds, however, each installment note payment includes an interest and principal component.

The interest portion of an installment note payment is computed by multiplying the interest rate by the carrying amount (book value) of the note at the beginning of the period. The principal portion of the payment is then computed as the difference between the total installment note payment (cash paid) and the interest component. These computations are illustrated in Exhibit 4 (rounded to the nearest dollar).

Amortization of Installment Notes — **EXHIBIT 4**

Year Ending December 31	A January 1 Carrying Amount	B Note Payment (Cash Paid)	C Interest Expense (6% of January 1 Note Carrying Amount)	D Decrease in Notes Payable (B – C)	E December 31 Carrying Amount (A – D)
20Y4	$24,000	$ 5,698	$ 1,440 (6% of $24,000)	$ 4,258	$19,742
20Y5	19,742	5,698	1,185 (6% of $19,742)	4,513	15,229
20Y6	15,229	5,698	914 (6% of $15,229)	4,784	10,445
20Y7	10,445	5,698	627 (6% of $10,445)	5,071	5,374
20Y8	5,374	5,698	324* (6% of $5,374)	5,374	—
		$28,490	$4,490	$24,000	

*Rounded ($5,374 – $5,698).

1. The January 1, 20Y4, carrying value (Column A) equals the amount borrowed from the bank. The January 1 balance in the following years equals the December 31 balance from the prior year.
2. The note payment (Column B) remains constant at $5,698, the annual cash payment required by the bank.
3. The interest expense (Column C) is computed at 6% times the installment note carrying amount at the beginning of each year. Since the carrying amount decreases each year, the interest expense decreases each year.
4. Notes payable decreases each year by the amount of the principal repayment (Column D). The principal repayment is computed by subtracting the interest expense (Column C) from the total payment (Column B). The principal repayment (Column D) increases each year as the interest expense decreases (Column C).

[6] The amount of the annual payment is calculated by using the present value concepts discussed in Appendix 1 at the end of this chapter. The annual payment of $5,698 is computed by dividing the $24,000 loan amount by the present value of an annuity of $1 for five periods at 6% (4.21236) from Exhibit 10 (rounded to the nearest dollar).

5. The carrying amount on December 31 (Column E) of the note decreases from $24,000, the initial amount borrowed, to $0 at the end of the five years.

The entry to record the first payment on December 31, 20Y4, is as follows:

20Y4 Dec. 31	Interest Expense	1,440	
	Notes Payable	4,258	
	Cash		5,698
	Paid principal and interest on installment note.		

The entry to record the second payment on December 31, 20Y5, is as follows:

20Y5 Dec. 31	Interest Expense	1,185	
	Notes Payable	4,513	
	Cash		5,698
	Paid principal and interest on installment note.		

As the prior entries show, the cash payment is the same in each year. The interest and principal payments, however, changes each year. This is because the carrying amount (book value) of the note decreases each year as principal is paid, which decreases the interest component the next period.

The entry to record the final payment on December 31, 20Y8, is as follows:

20Y8 Dec. 31	Interest Expense	324	
	Notes Payable	5,374	
	Cash		5,698
	Paid principal and interest on installment note.		

After the final payment, the carrying amount on the note is zero, indicating that the note has been paid in full. Any assets that secure the note would then be released by the bank.

Example Exercise 14-8 Journalizing Installment Notes Obj. 4

On the first day of the fiscal year, a company issues a $30,000, 10%, five-year installment note that has annual payments of $7,914. The first note payment consists of $3,000 of interest and $4,914 of principal repayment.

a. Journalize the entry to record the issuance of the installment note.
b. Journalize the first annual note payment.

Follow My Example 14-8

a. Cash 30,000
        Notes Payable 30,000

b. Interest Expense.. 3,000
    Notes Payable... 4,914
        Cash... 7,914

Practice Exercises: PE 14-8A, PE 14-8B

INTEGRITY, OBJECTIVITY, AND ETHICS IN BUSINESS

THE RATINGS GAME

In February 2013, the United States Justice Department filed a lawsuit against the three main credit rating agencies (Moody's, Standard & Poor's, and Fitch) for inflating their ratings on high risk bond issuances between 2004 and 2007. During this time period, the three ratings agencies gave their highest rating (AAA) to debt securities that were, in fact, highly risky. During the financial crisis of 2008, most of these bonds experienced significant drops in value, leaving investors with huge losses. The Justice Department lawsuit alleges that the ratings agencies were aware of the high risks associated with these bonds but inflated their ratings because of the large fee they received for providing a rating on these bonds. In 2015, Standard & Poor's settled this and related lawsuits for $1.5 billion.

Sources: "U.S. vs. S&P: The Rating Game," *Chicago Tribune*, February 6, 2013; "S&P Reaches $1.5 Billion Deal with U.S., States over Crisis-Era Ratings," Reuters, *Business News*, February 3, 2015.

Reporting Long-Term Liabilities

Obj. 5 Describe and illustrate the reporting of long-term liabilities, including bonds and notes payable.

Bonds payable and notes payable are reported as liabilities on the balance sheet. Any portion of the bonds or notes that is due within one year is reported as a current liability. Any remaining bonds or notes are reported as a long-term liability.

Any unamortized premium is reported as an addition to the face amount of the bonds. Any unamortized discount is reported as a deduction from the face amount of the bonds. A description of the bonds and notes should also be reported either on the face of the financial statements or in the accompanying notes.

The reporting of bonds and notes payable for 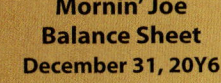 follows:

Mornin' Joe
Balance Sheet
December 31, 20Y6

Current liabilities:		
Accounts payable	$133,000	
Notes payable (current portion)	200,000	
Salaries and wages payable	42,000	
Payroll taxes payable	16,400	
Interest payable	40,000	
Total current liabilities		$ 431,400
Long-term liabilities:		
Bonds payable, 8%, due December 31, 2030	$500,000	
Unamortized discount	(16,000)	$ 484,000
Notes payable		1,400,000
Total long-term liabilities		$1,884,000
Total liabilities		$2,315,400

Financial Analysis and Interpretation: Times Interest Earned Ratio

Obj. 6 Describe and illustrate how the times interest earned ratio is used to evaluate a company's financial condition.

As we have discussed, the assets of a company are subject to (1) the claims of creditors and (2) the rights of owners. As creditors, bondholders are concerned primarily with the company's ability to make its periodic interest payments and repay the face amount of the bonds at maturity.

Analysts assess the risk that bondholders will not receive their interest payments by computing the **times interest earned** ratio during the year as follows:

$$\text{Times Interest Earned} = \frac{\text{Income Before Income Tax} + \text{Interest Expense}}{\text{Interest Expense}}$$

This ratio computes the number of times interest payments could be paid out of current period earnings. Because interest payments reduce income tax expense, the ratio is computed using income before tax. High values of this ratio are considered favorable. In contrast, low values are considered unfavorable. Values of this ratio less than 1.0 suggest that the firm is unable to cover interest payments from current period income before tax. Such a situation could eventually lead to loan defaults.

To illustrate, the following data were taken from recent annual reports of four companies in the soft drink beverage industry—**PepsiCo, Inc.**, **The Coca-Cola Company**, **Dr Pepper Snapple Group, Inc.**, and **Monster Beverage Corporation** (in thousands):

	PepsiCo	Coca-Cola	Dr Pepper Snapple	Monster
Interest expense	$ 909,000	$ 483,000	$ 109,000	$ 1,676
Income before income tax expense	8,757,000	9,325,000	1,073,000	745,788

The times interest earned is computed as follows for all four companies:

	PepsiCo	Coca-Cola	Dr Pepper Snapple	Monster
Interest expense	$ 909,000	$ 483,000	$ 109,000	$ 1,676
Income before income tax expense	8,757,000	9,325,000	1,073,000	745,788
Income before income tax expense + Interest expense	$9,666,000	$9,808,000	$1,182,000	$747,464
Times interest earned	10.6*	20.3**	10.8***	446.0****

*($9,666,000 ÷ $909,000)
**($9,808,000 ÷ $483,000)
***($1,182,000 ÷ $109,000)
****($747,464 ÷ $1,676)

Monster is much smaller than the other three beverage companies. However, it has a times interest earned ratio of 446.0, which is much greater than the other three companies. This is because Monster has no long-term debt and only a small amount of short-term bank loans. Among the other three beverage companies, Coca-Cola has twice the interest coverage of PepsiCo and Dr Pepper Snapple. Since all of the ratios are in excess of 10, all of the companies generate enough income before tax to pay (cover) their interest payments. As a result, bondholders of these companies have extremely good protection in the event of an earnings decline.

Example Exercise 14-9   Times Interest Earned   Obj. 6

Harris Industries reported the following on the company's income statement in 20Y7 and 20Y6:

	20Y7	20Y6
Interest expense	$ 200,000	$180,000
Income before income tax expense	1,000,000	720,000

a. Determine the times interest earned ratio for 20Y7 and 20Y6.
b. Is times interest earned ratio improving or declining?

Follow My Example 14-9

a. 20Y7:

$$\text{Times interest earned:} \quad \frac{\$1{,}000{,}000 + \$200{,}000}{\$200{,}000} = 6.0$$

20Y6:

$$\text{Times interest earned:} \quad \frac{\$720{,}000 + \$180{,}000}{\$180{,}000} = 5.0$$

b. The times interest earned has increased from 5.0 in 20Y6 to 6.0 in 20Y7. Thus, the debtholders have improved confidence in the company's ability to make its interest payments.

Practice Exercises: PE 14-9A, PE 14-9B

APPENDIX 1

Present Value Concepts and Pricing Bonds Payable

When a corporation issues bonds, the price that investors are willing to pay for the bonds depends on the following:

- The face amount of the bonds, which is the amount due at the maturity date
- The periodic interest to be paid on the bonds
- The market rate of interest

An investor determines how much to pay for the bonds by computing the present value of the bond's future cash receipts, using the market rate of interest. A bond's future cash receipts include its face value at maturity and the periodic interest payments.

Present Value Concepts

The concept of present value is based on the time value of money. The *time value of money concept* recognizes that cash received today is worth more than the same amount of cash to be received in the future.

To illustrate, what would you rather have: $1,000 today or $1,000 one year from now? You would rather have the $1,000 today because it could be invested to earn interest. For example, if the $1,000 could be invested to earn 10% interest per year, the $1,000 will accumulate to $1,100 ($1,000 plus $100 interest) in one year. In this sense, you can think of the $1,000 in hand today as the **present value** of $1,100 to be received a year from today. This present value is illustrated in Exhibit 5.

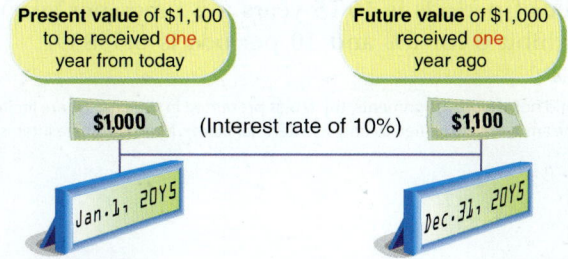

EXHIBIT 5

Present Value and Future Value

694 CHAPTER 14 Long-Term Liabilities: Bonds and Notes

A related concept to present value is **future value**. To illustrate, using the preceding example illustrated in Exhibit 5, the $1,100 to be received on December 31, 20Y5, is the *future value* of $1,000 on January 1, 20Y5, assuming an interest rate of 10%.

Present Value of an Amount

To illustrate the present value of an amount, assume that $1,000 is to be received in one year. If the market rate of interest is 10%, the present value of the $1,000 is $909.09 ($1,000 ÷ 1.10). This present value is illustrated in Exhibit 6.

EXHIBIT 6

Present Value of an Amount to Be Received in One Year

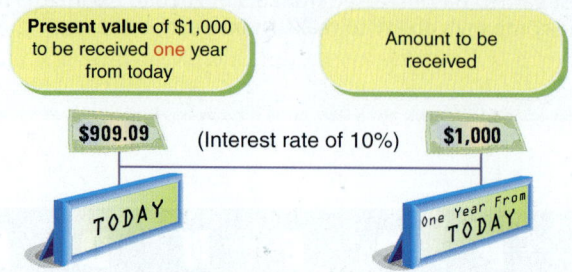

If the $1,000 is to be received in two years, with interest of 10% compounded at the end of the first year, the present value is $826.45 ($909.09 ÷ 1.10). This present value is illustrated in Exhibit 7.

EXHIBIT 7

Present Value of an Amount to Be Received in Two Years

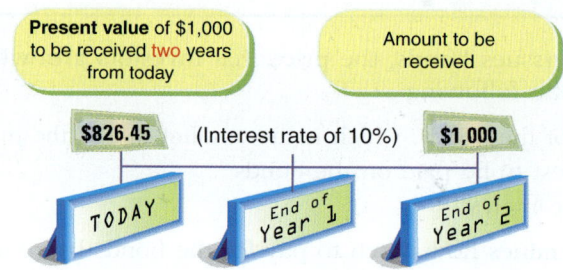

Spreadsheet software and business calculators have built-in present value functions that can also be used to calculate present values.

The present value of an amount to be received in the future can be determined by a series of divisions as illustrated in Exhibits 5, 6, and 7. In practice, however, it is easier to use a table of present values.

The *present value of $1* table is used to find the present value factor for $1 to be received after a number of periods in the future. The amount to be received is then multiplied by this factor to determine its present value.

To illustrate, Exhibit 8 is a partial table of the present value of $1.[7] Exhibit 8 indicates that the present value of $1 to be received in two years with a market rate of interest of 10% a year is 0.82645. Multiplying $1,000 to be received in two years by 0.82645 yields $826.45 ($1,000 × 0.82645). This amount is the same as the amount computed earlier. In Exhibit 8, the Periods column represents the number of compounding periods, and the percentage columns represent the compound interest rate per period. Thus, the present value factor from Exhibit 8 for 12% for five years is 0.56743. If the interest is compounded semiannually, the interest rate is 6% (12% ÷ 2), and the number of periods is 10 (5 years × 2 times per year). Thus, the present value factor from Exhibit 8 for 6% and 10 periods is 0.55839.

---

[7] To simplify the illustrations and homework assignments, the tables presented in this chapter are limited to 10 periods for a small number of interest rates and the amounts are carried to only five decimal places. More complete interest tables are presented in Appendix A of the text.

Present Value of $1 at Compound Interest

EXHIBIT 8

Periods	4%	4½%	5%	5½%	6%	6½%	7%	10%	11%	12%	13%
1	0.96154	0.95694	0.95238	0.94787	0.94340	0.93897	0.93458	0.90909	0.90090	0.89286	0.88496
2	0.92456	0.91573	0.90703	0.89845	0.89000	0.88166	0.87344	0.82645	0.81162	0.79719	0.78315
3	0.88900	0.87630	0.86384	0.85161	0.83962	0.82785	0.81630	0.75131	0.73119	0.71178	0.69305
4	0.85480	0.83856	0.82270	0.80722	0.79209	0.77732	0.76290	0.68301	0.65873	0.63552	0.61332
5	0.82193	0.80245	0.78353	0.76513	0.74726	0.72988	0.71299	0.62092	0.59345	0.56743	0.54276
6	0.79031	0.76790	0.74622	0.72525	0.70496	0.68533	0.66634	0.56447	0.53464	0.50663	0.48032
7	0.75992	0.73483	0.71068	0.68744	0.66506	0.64351	0.62275	0.51316	0.48166	0.45235	0.42506
8	0.73069	0.70319	0.67684	0.65160	0.62741	0.60423	0.58201	0.46651	0.43393	0.40388	0.37616
9	0.70259	0.67290	0.64461	0.61763	0.59190	0.56735	0.54393	0.42410	0.39092	0.36061	0.33288
10	0.67556	0.64393	0.61391	0.58543	0.55839	0.53273	0.50835	0.38554	0.35218	0.32197	0.29459

Some additional examples using Exhibit 8 follow:

	Number of Periods	Interest Rate	Present Value of $1 Factor from Exhibit 8
10% for *two* years compounded *annually*	2	10%	0.82645
10% for *two* years compounded *semiannually*	4	5%	0.82270
10% for *three* years compounded *semiannually*	6	5%	0.74622
12% for *five* years compounded *semiannually*	10	6%	0.55839

Present Value of the Periodic Receipts A series of equal cash receipts spaced equally in time is called an **annuity**. The **present value of an annuity** is the sum of the present values of each cash receipt. To illustrate, assume that $100 is to be received annually for two years and that the market rate of interest is 10%. Using Exhibit 8, the present value of the receipt of the two amounts of $100 is $173.55, as shown in Exhibit 9.

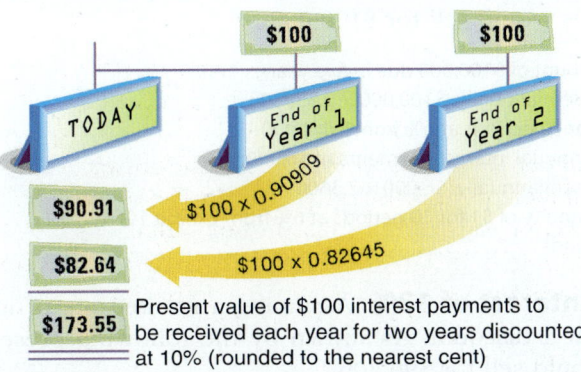

EXHIBIT 9

Present Value of an Annuity

Instead of using present value of $1 tables to determine the present value of each cash flow separately, such as in Exhibit 8, the present value of an annuity can be computed in a single step. Using a value from the *present value of an annuity of $1* table in Exhibit 10, the present value of the entire annuity can be calculated by multiplying the equal cash payment times the appropriate present value of an annuity of $1.

To illustrate, the present value of $100 to be received at the end of each of the next two years at 10% compound interest per period is $173.55 ($100 × 1.73554). This amount is the same amount computed previously using the present value of $1.

EXHIBIT 10 — Present Value of an Annuity of $1 at Compound Interest

Periods	4%	4½%	5%	5½%	6%	6½%	7%	10%	11%	12%	13%
1	0.96154	0.95694	0.95238	0.94787	0.94340	0.93897	0.93458	0.90909	0.90090	0.89286	0.88496
2	1.88609	1.87267	1.85941	1.84632	1.83339	1.82063	1.80802	1.73554	1.71252	1.69005	1.66810
3	2.77509	2.74896	2.72325	2.69793	2.67301	2.64848	2.62432	2.48685	2.44371	2.40183	2.36115
4	3.62990	3.58753	3.54595	3.50515	3.46511	3.42580	3.38721	3.16987	3.10245	3.03735	2.97447
5	4.45182	4.38998	4.32948	4.27028	4.21236	4.15568	4.10020	3.79079	3.69590	3.60478	3.51723
6	5.24214	5.15787	5.07569	4.99553	4.91732	4.84101	4.76654	4.35526	4.23054	4.11141	3.99755
7	6.00205	5.89270	5.78637	5.68297	5.58238	5.48452	5.38929	4.86842	4.71220	4.56376	4.42261
8	6.73274	6.59589	6.46321	6.33457	6.20979	6.08875	5.97130	5.33493	5.14612	4.96764	4.79677
9	7.43533	7.26879	7.10782	6.95220	6.80169	6.65610	6.51523	5.75902	5.53705	5.32825	5.13166
10	8.11090	7.91272	7.72173	7.53763	7.36009	7.18883	7.02358	6.14457	5.88923	5.65022	5.42624

Pricing Bonds

The selling price of a bond is the sum of the present values of:

- The face amount of the bonds due at the maturity date
- The periodic interest to be paid on the bonds

The market rate of interest is used to compute the present value of both the face amount and the periodic interest.

To illustrate the pricing of bonds, assume that Southern Utah Communications Inc. issued the following bond on January 1:

Face amount	$100,000
Contract rate of interest	12%
Interest paid semiannually on June 30 and December 31.	
Term of bonds	5 years

Market Rate of Interest of 12% Assuming a market rate of interest of 12%, the bonds would sell for their face amount. As shown by the following present value computations, the bonds would sell for $100,000:

Present value of face amount of $100,000 due in five years,
   at 12% compounded semiannually: $100,000 × 0.55839
   (present value of $1 for 10 periods at 6% from Exhibit 8) .... $ 55,839
Present value of 10 semiannual interest payments of $6,000,
   at 12% compounded semiannually: $6,000 × 7.36009
   (present value of an annuity of $1 for 10 periods at 6% from Exhibit 10) 44,161
Total present value of bonds $100,000

Market Rate of Interest of 13% Assuming a market rate of interest of 13%, the bonds would sell at a discount. As shown by the following present value computations, the bonds would sell for $96,406:[8]

Present value of face amount of $100,000 due in five years,
   at 13% compounded semiannually: $100,000 × 0.53273
   (present value of $1 for 10 periods at 6½% from Exhibit 8) $53,273
Present value of 10 semiannual interest payments of $6,000,
   at 13% compounded semiannually: $6,000 × 7.18883
   (present value of an annuity of $1 for 10 periods at 6½% from Exhibit 10) 43,133
Total present value of bonds $96,406

---

8 Some corporations issue bonds called *zero-coupon bonds* that provide for only the payment of the face amount at maturity. Such bonds sell for large discounts. In this example, such a bond would sell for $53,273, which is the present value of the face amount.

Market Rate of Interest of 11% Assuming a market rate of interest of 11%, the bonds would sell at a premium. As shown by the following present value computations, the bonds would sell for $103,769:

Present value of face amount of $100,000 due in five years, at 11% compounded semiannually: $100,000 × 0.58543 (present value of $1 for 10 periods at 5½% from Exhibit 8)	$ 58,543
Present value of 10 semiannual interest payments of $6,000, at 11% compounded semiannually: $6,000 × 7.53763 (present value of an annuity of $1 for 10 periods at 5½% from Exhibit 10)	45,226
Total present value of bonds	$103,769

As shown, the selling price of the bond varies with the present value of the bond's face amount at maturity, interest payments, and the market rate of interest.

APPENDIX 2

Interest Rate Method of Amortization

The effective interest rate method of amortization is an alternative method for amortizing the discount or premium on a bond, which provides for a constant *rate* of interest over the life of the bonds. As the discount or premium is amortized, the carrying amount of the bonds changes. As a result, interest expense also changes each period. This is in contrast to the straight-line method, which provides for a constant *amount* of interest expense each period.

The interest rate used in the effective interest rate method of amortization, sometimes called the *interest method*, is the market rate on the date the bonds are issued. The carrying amount of the bonds is multiplied by this interest rate to determine the interest expense for the period. The difference between the interest expense and the interest payment is the amount of discount or premium to be amortized for the period.

Amortization of Discount by the Interest Method

To illustrate, the following data taken from the chapter illustration of issuing bonds at a discount are used:

Face value of 12%, five-year bonds, interest compounded semiannually	$100,000
Present value of bonds at effective (market) rate of interest of 13%	(96,406)
Discount on bonds payable	$ 3,594

Exhibit 11 illustrates the interest method for the preceding bonds. Exhibit 11 begins with six columns. The first column is not lettered. The remaining columns are lettered A through E. The exhibit was then prepared as follows:

Step 1. List the interest payment dates in the first column, which for the preceding bond are 10 interest payment dates (semiannual interest over five years). Also list on the first line (above the first interest payment) the initial amount of discount in Column D and the initial carrying amount (selling price) of the bonds in Column E.

Step 2. List in Column A the semiannual interest payments, which for the preceding bond are $6,000 ($100,000 × 6%).

Step 3. Compute the interest expense in Column B by multiplying the bond carrying amount at the beginning of each period times 6½%, which is the semiannual effective interest (market) rate (13% ÷ 2).

Step 4. In Column C, compute the discount to be amortized each period by subtracting the interest payment in Column A ($6,000) from the interest expense for the period shown in Column B.

EXHIBIT 11 — Amortization of Discount on Bonds Payable

Interest Payment Date	A Interest Paid (6% of Face Amount)	B Interest Expense (6½% of Bond Carrying Amount)	C Discount Amortization (B – A)	D Unamortized Discount (D – C)	E Bond Carrying Amount ($100,000 – D)
				$3,594	$ 96,406
June 30, 20Y5	$6,000	$6,266 (6½% of $96,406)	$266	3,328	96,672
Dec. 31, 20Y5	6,000	6,284 (6½% of $96,672)	284	3,044	96,956
June 30, 20Y6	6,000	6,302 (6½% of $96,956)	302	2,742	97,258
Dec. 31, 20Y6	6,000	6,322 (6½% of $97,258)	322	2,420	97,580
June 30, 20Y7	6,000	6,343 (6½% of $97,580)	343	2,077	97,923
Dec. 31, 20Y7	6,000	6,365 (6½% of $97,923)	365	1,712	98,288
June 30, 20Y8	6,000	6,389 (6½% of $98,288)	389	1,323	98,677
Dec. 31, 20Y8	6,000	6,414 (6½% of $98,677)	414	909	99,091
June 30, 20Y9	6,000	6,441 (6½% of $99,091)	441	468	99,532
Dec. 31, 20Y9	6,000	6,470 (6½% of $99,532)	468*	—	100,000

*Cannot exceed unamortized discount.

Step 5. Compute the remaining unamortized discount by subtracting the amortized discount in Column C for the period from the unamortized discount at the beginning of the period in Column D.

Step 6. Compute the bond carrying amount at the end of the period by subtracting the unamortized discount at the end of the period in Column D from the face amount of the bonds ($100,000).

Steps 3–6 are repeated for each interest payment.

As shown in Exhibit 11, the interest expense increases each period as the carrying amount of the bond increases. Also, the unamortized discount decreases each period to zero at the maturity date. Finally, the carrying amount of the bonds increases from $96,406 to $100,000 (the face amount) at maturity.

The entry to record the first interest payment on June 30, 20Y5, and the related discount amortization is as follows:

20Y5					
June	30	Interest Expense		6,266	
		Discount on Bonds Payable			266
		Cash			6,000
		Paid semiannual interest and amortized bond discount for ½ year.			

If the amortization is recorded only at the end of the year, the amount of the discount amortized on December 31, Year 1, would be $550. This is the sum of the first two semiannual amortization amounts ($266 and $284) from Exhibit 11.

Amortization of Premium by the Interest Method

To illustrate, the following data taken from the chapter illustration of issuing bonds at a premium are used:

Present value of bonds at effective (market) rate of interest of 11%	$103,769
Face value of 12%, five-year bonds, interest compounded semiannually	(100,000)
Premium on bonds payable	$ 3,769

Exhibit 12 illustrates the interest method for the preceding bonds. Exhibit 12 begins with six columns. The first column is not lettered. The remaining columns are lettered A through E. The exhibit was then prepared as follows:

EXHIBIT 12 — Amortization of Premium on Bonds Payable

Interest Payment Date	A Interest Paid (6% of Face Amount)	B Interest Expense (5½% of Bond Carrying Amount)	C Premium Amortization (A – B)	D Unamortized Premium (D – C)	E Bond Carrying Amount ($100,000 + D)
				$3,769	$103,769
June 30, 20Y5	$6,000	$5,707 (5½% of $103,769)	$293	3,476	103,476
Dec. 31, 20Y5	6,000	5,691 (5½% of $103,476)	309	3,167	103,167
June 30, 20Y6	6,000	5,674 (5½% of $103,167)	326	2,841	102,841
Dec. 31, 20Y6	6,000	5,656 (5½% of $102,841)	344	2,497	102,497
June 30, 20Y7	6,000	5,637 (5½% of $102,497)	363	2,134	102,134
Dec. 31, 20Y7	6,000	5,617 (5½% of $102,134)	383	1,751	101,751
June 30, 20Y8	6,000	5,596 (5½% of $101,751)	404	1,347	101,347
Dec. 31, 20Y8	6,000	5,574 (5½% of $101,347)	426	921	100,921
June 30, 20Y9	6,000	5,551 (5½% of $100,921)	449	472	100,472
Dec. 31, 20Y9	6,000	5,526 (5½% of $100,472)	472*	—	100,000

*Cannot exceed unamortized premium.

Step 1. List the number of interest payments in the first column, which for the preceding bond are 10 interest payments (semiannual interest over five years). Also list on the first line the initial amount of premium in Column D and the initial carrying amount of the bonds in Column E.

Step 2. List in Column A the semiannual interest payments, which for the preceding bond are $6,000 ($100,000 × 6%).

Step 3. Compute the interest expense in Column B by multiplying the bond carrying amount at the beginning of each period times 5½%, which is the semiannual effective interest (market) rate (11% ÷ 2).

Step 4. In Column C, compute the premium to be amortized each period by subtracting the interest expense for the period shown in Column B from the interest payment in Column A ($6,000).

Step 5. Compute the remaining unamortized premium by subtracting the amortized premium in Column C for the period from the unamortized premium at the beginning of the period in Column D.

Step 6. Compute the bond carrying amount at the end of the period by adding the unamortized premium at the end of the period in Column D to the face amount of the bonds ($100,000).

Steps 3–6 are repeated for each interest payment.

As shown in Exhibit 12, the interest expense decreases each period as the carrying amount of the bond decreases. Also, the unamortized premium decreases each period to zero at the maturity date. Finally, the carrying amount of the bonds decreases from $103,769 to $100,000 (the face amount) at maturity.

The entry to record the first interest payment on June 30, 20Y5, and the related premium amortization is as follows:

20Y5					
June	30	Interest Expense		5,707	
		Premium on Bonds Payable		293	
		Cash			6,000
		Paid semiannual interest and amortized bond premium for ½ year.			

If the amortization is recorded only at the end of the year, the amount of the premium amortized on December 31, Year 1, would be $602. This is the sum of the first two semiannual amortization amounts ($293 and $309) from Exhibit 12.

At a Glance 14

Obj. 1 Compute the potential impact of long-term borrowing on earnings per share.

Key Points Corporations can finance their operations by issuing short-term debt, long-term debt, or equity. One of the many factors that influence a corporation's decision on whether it should issue long-term debt or equity is the effect each alternative has on earnings per share.

Learning Outcomes	Example Exercises	Practice Exercises
• Define the concept of a bond.		
• Calculate and compare the effect of alternative long-term financing plans on earnings per share.	EE14-1	PE14-1A, 14-1B

Obj. 2 Describe the characteristics and terminology of bonds payable.

Key Points A corporation that issues bonds enters into a contract, or bond indenture.

When a corporation issues bonds, the price that buyers are willing to pay for the bonds depends on (1) the face amount of the bonds, (2) the periodic interest to be paid on the bonds, and (3) the market rate of interest.

Learning Outcomes	Example Exercises	Practice Exercises
• Define the characteristics of a bond.		
• Describe the various types of bonds.		
• Describe the factors that determine the price of a bond.		

Obj. 3 Describe and illustrate the accounting for bonds payable.

Key Points The journal entry for issuing bonds payable debits Cash and credits Bonds Payable. Any difference between the face amount of the bonds and the selling price is debited to Discount on Bonds Payable or credited to Premium on Bonds Payable when the bonds are issued. The discount or premium on bonds payable is amortized to interest expense over the life of the bonds.

At the maturity date, the entry to record the repayment of the face value of a bond is a debit to Bonds Payable and a credit to Cash.

When a corporation redeems bonds before they mature, Bonds Payable is debited for the face amount of the bonds, the premium (discount) on bonds payable account is debited (credited) for its unamortized balance, Cash is credited, and any gain or loss on the redemption is recorded.

Learning Outcomes	Example Exercises	Practice Exercises
• Journalize the issuance of bonds at face value and the payment of periodic interest.	EE14-2	PE14-2A, 14-2B
• Journalize the issuance of bonds at a discount.	EE14-3	PE14-3A, 14-3B
• Journalize the amortization of a bond discount.	EE14-4	PE14-4A, 14-4B
• Journalize the issuance of bonds at a premium.	EE14-5	PE14-5A, 14-5B
• Journalize the amortization of a bond premium.	EE14-6	PE14-6A, 14-6B
• Describe bond redemptions.		
• Journalize the redemption of bonds payable.	EE14-7	PE14-7A, 14-7B

Obj. 4 — Describe and illustrate the accounting for installment notes.

Key Points An installment note requires the borrower to make equal periodic payments to the lender for the term of the note. Unlike bonds, the annual payment in an installment note consists of both principal and interest. The journal entry for the annual payment debits Interest Expense and Notes Payable and credits Cash for the amount of the payment. After the final payment, the carrying amount on the note is zero.

Learning Outcomes	Example Exercises	Practice Exercises
• Define the characteristics of an installment note. • Journalize the issuance of installment notes. • Journalize the annual payment for an installment note.	EE14-8	PE14-8A, 14-8B

Obj. 5 — Describe and illustrate the reporting of long-term liabilities, including bonds and installment notes payable.

Key Points Bonds payable and notes payable are usually reported as long-term liabilities. If the balance sheet date is within one year, they are reported as current liabilities. A discount on bonds should be reported as a deduction from the related bonds payable. A premium on bonds should be reported as an addition to related bonds payable.

Learning Outcomes	Example Exercises	Practice Exercises
• Illustrate the balance sheet presentation of bonds payable and notes payable.		

Obj. 6 — Describe and illustrate how the times interest earned ratio is used to evaluate a company's financial condition.

Key Points The times interest earned ratio measures the risk to bondholders that a company will not be able to make its interest payments. It is computed by dividing income before income tax plus interest expense by interest expense. This ratio computes the number of times interest payments could be paid out of current period earnings.

Learning Outcomes	Example Exercises	Practice Exercises
• Describe and compute the times interest earned ratio. • Interpret the times interest earned ratio.	EE14-9	PE14-9A, 14-9B

Illustrative Problem

The fiscal year of Russell Inc., a manufacturer of acoustical supplies, ends December 31. Selected transactions for the period 20Y1 through 20Y8, involving bonds payable issued by Russell Inc., are as follows:

20Y1

June 30. Issued $2,000,000 of 25-year, 7% callable bonds dated June 30, 20Y1, for cash of $1,920,000. Interest is payable semiannually on June 30 and December 31.

Dec. 31. Paid the semiannual interest on the bonds. The bond discount is amortized annually in a separate journal entry.

(Continued)

702 Chapter 14 Long-Term Liabilities: Bonds and Notes

Dec. 31. Recorded straight-line amortization of $1,600 of discount on the bonds.

20Y2

June 30. Paid the semiannual interest on the bonds. The bond discount is amortized annually in a separate journal entry.

Dec. 31. Paid the semiannual interest on the bonds. The bond discount is amortized annually in a separate journal entry.

31. Recorded straight-line amortization of $3,200 of discount on the bonds.

20Y8

June 30. Recorded the redemption of the bonds, which were called at 101.5. The balance in the bond discount account is $57,600 after the payment of interest and amortization of discount have been recorded. Record the redemption only.

Instructions

1. Journalize entries to record the preceding transactions.
2. Determine the amount of interest expense for 20Y1 and 20Y2.
3. Determine the carrying amount of the bonds as of December 31, 20Y2.

Solution

1.

20Y1					
June	30	Cash		1,920,000	
		Discount on Bonds Payable		80,000	
		Bonds Payable			2,000,000
Dec.	31	Interest Expense*		70,000	
		Cash			70,000
	31	Interest Expense		1,600	
		Discount on Bonds Payable			1,600
		Amortization of discount from July 1			
		to December 31.			
20Y2					
June	30	Interest Expense		70,000	
		Cash			70,000
Dec.	31	Interest Expense		70,000	
		Cash			70,000
	31	Interest Expense		3,200	
		Discount on Bonds Payable			3,200
		Amortization of discount from			
		January 1 to December 31.			
20Y8					
June	30	Bonds Payable		2,000,000	
		Loss on Redemption of Bonds Payable		87,600	
		Discount on Bonds Payable			57,600
		Cash			2,030,000

*$2,000,000 × 7% × 1/2

2. a. 20Y1: $71,600 = $70,000 + $1,600

   b. 20Y2: $143,200 = $70,000 + $70,000 + $3,200

3. Initial carrying amount of bonds $1,920,000
    Discount amortized on December 31, 20Y1   1,600
    Discount amortized on December 31, 20Y2   3,200
    Carrying amount of bonds, December 31, 20Y2 $1,924,800

Key Terms

amortization (683)
annuity (695)
bond (677)
bond indenture (680)
carrying amount (683)
contract rate (680)
discount (680)

earnings per share (EPS) (677)
effective interest rate method (684)
effective rate of interest (680)
face amount (680)
future value (694)
installment note (688)

market rate of interest (680)
mortgage notes (688)
premium (681)
present value (693)
present value of annuity (695)
times interest earned (692)

Discussion Questions

1. Describe the two distinct obligations incurred by a corporation when issuing bonds.

2. Explain the meaning of each of the following terms as they relate to a bond issue: (a) convertible and (b) callable.

3. If you asked your broker to buy you a 12% bond when the market interest rate for such bonds was 11%, would you expect to pay more or less than the face amount for the bond? Explain.

4. A corporation issues $26,000,000 of 9% bonds to yield interest at the rate of 7%. (a) Was the amount of cash received from the sale of the bonds greater or less than $26,000,000? (b) Identify the following amounts as they relate to the bond issue: (1) face amount, (2) market or effective rate of interest, (3) contract rate of interest, and (4) maturity amount.

5. If bonds issued by a corporation are sold at a discount, is the market rate of interest greater or less than the contract rate?

6. The following data relate to a $2,000,000, 8% bond issued for a selected semiannual interest period:

    Bond carrying amount at beginning of period $2,125,000
    Interest paid during period   160,000
    Interest expense allocable to the period   148,750

(a) Were the bonds issued at a discount or at a premium? (b) What is the unamortized amount of the discount or premium account at the beginning of the period? (c) What account was debited to amortize the discount or premium?

7. Bonds Payable has a balance of $5,000,000, and Discount on Bonds Payable has a balance of $150,000. If the issuing corporation redeems the bonds at 98, is there a gain or loss on the bond redemption?

8. What is a mortgage note?

9. Fleeson Company needs additional funds to purchase equipment for a new production facility and is considering either issuing bonds payable or borrowing the money from a local bank in the form of an installment note. How does an installment note differ from a bond payable?

10. In what section of the balance sheet would a bond payable be reported if (a) it is payable within one year and (b) it is payable beyond one year?

Practice Exercises

Example Exercises

EE 14-1 p. 679   **PE 14-1A**   **Alternative financing plans**   OBJ. 1

Frey Co. is considering the following alternative financing plans:

	Plan 1	Plan 2
Issue 5% bonds (at face value)	$6,000,000	$2,000,000
Issue preferred $1 stock, $20 par	—	6,000,000
Issue common stock, $25 par	6,000,000	4,000,000

Income tax is estimated at 40% of income.

Determine the earnings per share of common stock, assuming that income before bond interest and income tax is $800,000.

EE 14-1 p. 679   **PE 14-1B**   **Alternative financing plans**   OBJ. 1

Brower Co. is considering the following alternative financing plans:

	Plan 1	Plan 2
Issue 10% bonds (at face value)	$4,000,000	$2,500,000
Issue preferred $2.50 stock, $25 par	—	3,000,000
Issue common stock, $10 par	4,000,000	2,500,000

Income tax is estimated at 40% of income.

Determine the earnings per share of common stock, assuming that income before bond interest and income tax is $2,000,000.

EE 14-2 p. 682   **PE 14-2A**   **Issuing bonds at face amount**   OBJ. 3

On January 1, the first day of the fiscal year, a company issues a $5,000,000, 6%, 10-year bond that pays semiannual interest of $150,000 ($5,000,000 × 6% × ½ year), receiving cash of $5,000,000. Journalize the entries to record (a) the issuance of the bonds, (b) the first interest payment on June 30, and (c) the payment of the principal on the maturity date.

EE 14-2 p. 682   **PE 14-2B**   **Issuing bonds at face amount**   OBJ. 3

On January 1, the first day of the fiscal year, a company issues an $800,000, 4%, 10-year bond that pays semiannual interest of $16,000 ($800,000 × 4% × ½ year), receiving cash of $800,000. Journalize the entries to record (a) the issuance of the bonds, (b) the first interest payment on June 30, and (c) the payment of the principal on the maturity date.

EE 14-3 p. 683   **PE 14-3A**   **Issuing bonds at a discount**   OBJ. 3

On the first day of the fiscal year, a company issues a $2,500,000, 4%, five-year bond that pays semiannual interest of $50,000 ($2,500,000 × 4% × ½), receiving cash of $2,390,599. Journalize the bond issuance.

EE 14-3 p. 683   **PE 14-3B**   **Issuing bonds at a discount**   OBJ. 3

On the first day of the fiscal year, a company issues a $3,000,000, 11%, five-year bond that pays semiannual interest of $165,000 ($3,000,000 × 11% × ½), receiving cash of $2,889,599. Journalize the bond issuance.

EE 14-4 p. 685   **PE 14-4A**   **Discount amortization**   OBJ. 3

Using the bond from Practice Exercise 14-3A, journalize the first interest payment and the amortization of the related bond discount. Round to the nearest dollar.

Chapter 14 Long-Term Liabilities: Bonds and Notes   705

EE 14-4 *p. 685*   **PE 14-4B** Discount amortization   OBJ. 3

Using the bond from Practice Exercise 14-3B, journalize the first interest payment and the amortization of the related bond discount. Round to the nearest dollar.

EE 14-5 *p. 685*   **PE 14-5A** Issuing bonds at a premium   OBJ. 3

On the first day of the fiscal year, a company issues a $7,500,000, 8%, five-year bond that pays semiannual interest of $300,000 ($7,500,000 × 8% × ½), receiving cash of $7,811,873. Journalize the bond issuance.

EE 14-5 *p. 685*   **PE 14-5B** Issuing bonds at a premium   OBJ. 3

On the first day of the fiscal year, a company issues an $8,000,000, 11%, five-year bond that pays semiannual interest of $440,000 ($8,000,000 × 11% × ½), receiving cash of $8,308,869. Journalize the bond issuance.

EE 14-6 *p. 687*   **PE 14-6A** Premium amortization   OBJ. 3

Using the bond from Practice Exercise 14-5A, journalize the first interest payment and the amortization of the related bond premium. Round to the nearest dollar.

EE 14-6 *p. 687*   **PE 14-6B** Premium amortization   OBJ. 3

Using the bond from Practice Exercise 14-5B, journalize the first interest payment and the amortization of the related bond premium. Round to the nearest dollar.

EE 14-7 *p. 688*   **PE 14-7A** Redemption of bonds payable   OBJ. 3

A $1,500,000 bond issue on which there is an unamortized discount of $70,100 is redeemed for $1,455,000. Journalize the redemption of the bonds.

EE 14-7 *p. 688*   **PE 14-7B** Redemption of bonds payable   OBJ. 3

A $1,200,000 bond issue on which there is an unamortized premium of $63,956 is redeemed for $1,250,000. Journalize the redemption of the bonds.

EE 14-8 *p. 690*   **PE 14-8A** Journalizing installment notes   OBJ. 4

On the first day of the fiscal year, a company issues $65,000, 6%, five-year installment notes that have annual payments of $15,431. The first note payment consists of $3,900 of interest and $11,531 of principal repayment.

a. Journalize the entry to record the issuance of the installment notes.

b. Journalize the first annual note payment.

EE 14-8 *p. 690*   **PE 14-8B** Journalizing installment notes   OBJ. 4

On the first day of the fiscal year, a company issues $45,000, 8%, six-year installment notes that have annual payments of $9,734. The first note payment consists of $3,600 of interest and $6,134 of principal repayment.

a. Journalize the entry to record the issuance of the installment notes.

b. Journalize the first annual note payment.

EE 14-9 *p. 692*   **PE 14-9A** Times interest earned   OBJ. 6

Berry Company reported the following on the company's income statement in two recent years:

	Current Year	Prior Year
Interest expense	$ 320,000	$ 300,000
Income before income tax expense	3,200,000	3,600,000

(Continued)

706 Chapter 14 Long-Term Liabilities: Bonds and Notes

a. Determine the times interest earned ratio for the current year and the prior year. Round to one decimal place.

b. Is the number of times interest charges are earned improving or declining?

EE 14-9 p. 692

PE 14-9B Times interest earned OBJ. 6

Averill Products Inc. reported the following on the company's income statement in two recent years:

	Current Year	Prior Year
Interest expense	$ 440,000	$ 400,000
Income before income tax expense	5,544,000	4,400,000

a. Determine the times interest earned ratio for the current year and the prior year. Round to one decimal place.

b. Is the number of times interest charges are earned improving or declining?

Exercises

EX 14-1 Effect of financing on earnings per share OBJ. 1

✔ b. $1.00

Domanico Co., which produces and sells biking equipment, is financed as follows:

Bonds payable, 6% (issued at face amount)	$5,000,000
Preferred $2.00 stock, $100 par	5,000,000
Common stock, $25 par	5,000,000

Income tax is estimated at 40% of income.

Determine the earnings per share of common stock, assuming that the income before bond interest and income tax is (a) $600,000, (b) $800,000, and (c) $1,200,000.

EX 14-2 Evaluate alternative financing plans OBJ. 1

Based on the data in Exercise 14-1, what factors other than earnings per share should be considered in evaluating these alternative financing plans?

EX 14-3 Corporate financing OBJ. 1

The financial statements for **Nike, Inc.**, are presented in Appendix D at the end of the text. What is the major source of financing for Nike?

EX 14-4 Bond price OBJ. 3

Stone Energy Corporation's 7.5% bonds due in 2022 were reported as selling for 82.95.
Were the bonds selling at a premium or at a discount? Why is Stone Energy Corporation able to sell its bonds at this price?

EX 14-5 Entries for issuing bonds OBJ. 3

Thomson Co. produces and distributes semiconductors for use by computer manufacturers. Thomson Co. issued $900,000 of 10-year, 7% bonds on May 1 of the current year at face value, with interest payable on May 1 and November 1. The fiscal year of the company is the calendar year. Journalize the entries to record the following selected transactions for the current year:

May   1. Issued the bonds for cash at their face amount.

Nov.   1. Paid the interest on the bonds.

Dec. 31. Recorded accrued interest for two months.

Chapter 14 Long-Term Liabilities: Bonds and Notes 707

✔ b. $781,118

EX 14-6 Entries for issuing bonds and amortizing discount by straight-line method OBJ. 2, 3

On the first day of its fiscal year, Chin Company issued $10,000,000 of five-year, 7% bonds to finance its operations of producing and selling home improvement products. Interest is payable semiannually. The bonds were issued at a market (effective) interest rate of 8%, resulting in Chin Company receiving cash of $9,594,415.

a. Journalize the entries to record the following:
  1. Issuance of the bonds.
  2. First semiannual interest payment. The bond discount amortization is combined with the semiannual interest payment. Round your answer to the nearest dollar.
  3. Second semiannual interest payment. The bond discount amortization is combined with the semiannual interest payment. Round your answer to the nearest dollar.
b. Determine the amount of the bond interest expense for the first year.
c. Explain why the company was able to issue the bonds for only $9,594,415 rather than for the face amount of $10,000,000.

EX 14-7 Entries for issuing bonds and amortizing premium by straight-line method OBJ. 2, 3

Smiley Corporation wholesales repair products to equipment manufacturers. On April 1, Year 1, Smiley Corporation issued $20,000,000 of five-year, 9% bonds at a market (effective) interest rate of 8%, receiving cash of $20,811,010. Interest is payable semiannually on April 1 and October 1. Journalize the entries to record the following:

a. Issuance of bonds on April 1.
b. First interest payment on October 1 and amortization of bond premium for six months, using the straight-line method. The bond premium amortization is combined with the semiannual interest payment. Round to the nearest dollar.
c. Explain why the company was able to issue the bonds for $20,811,010 rather than for the face amount of $20,000,000.

EX 14-8 Entries for issuing and calling bonds; loss OBJ. 3

Adele Corp., a wholesaler of music equipment, issued $22,000,000 of 20-year, 7% callable bonds on March 1, 20Y1, at their face amount, with interest payable on March 1 and September 1. The fiscal year of the company is the calendar year. Journalize the entries to record the following selected transactions:

20Y1
Mar. 1. Issued the bonds for cash at their face amount.
Sept. 1. Paid the interest on the bonds.

20Y5
Sept. 1. Called the bond issue at 102, the rate provided in the bond indenture. (Omit entry for payment of interest.)

EX 14-9 Entries for issuing and calling bonds; gain OBJ. 3

Emil Corp. produces and sells wind-energy-driven engines. To finance its operations, Emil Corp. issued $15,000,000 of 20-year, 9% callable bonds on May 1, 20Y1, at their face amount, with interest payable on May 1 and November 1. The fiscal year of the company is the calendar year. Journalize the entries to record the following selected transactions:

20Y1
May 1. Issued the bonds for cash at their face amount.
Nov. 1. Paid the interest on the bonds.

20Y5
Nov. 1. Called the bond issue at 96, the rate provided in the bond indenture. (Omit entry for payment of interest.)

708 Chapter 14 Long-Term Liabilities: Bonds and Notes

EX 14-10 Entries for installment note transactions   OBJ. 4

On the first day of the fiscal year, Shiller Company borrowed $85,000 by giving a seven-year, 7% installment note to Soros Bank. The note requires annual payments of $15,772, with the first payment occurring on the last day of the fiscal year. The first payment consists of interest of $5,950 and principal repayment of $9,822.

a. Journalize the entries to record the following:
   1. Issued the installment note for cash on the first day of the fiscal year.
   2. Paid the first annual payment on the note.
b. Explain how the notes payable would be reported on the balance sheet at the end of the first year.

EX 14-11 Entries for installment note transactions   OBJ. 4

On January 1, Year 1, Luzak Company issued a $120,000, five-year, 6% installment note to McGee Bank. The note requires annual payments of $28,488, beginning on December 31, Year 1. Journalize the entries to record the following:

Year 1

Jan. 1. Issued the note for cash at its face amount.

Dec. 31. Paid the annual payment on the note, which consisted of interest of $7,200 and principal of $21,288.

Year 4

Dec. 31. Paid the annual payment on the note, including $3,134 of interest. The remainder of the payment reduced the principal balance on the note.

EX 14-12 Entries for installment note transactions   OBJ. 4

On January 1, Year 1, Bryson Company obtained a $147,750, four-year, 7% installment note from Campbell Bank. The note requires annual payments of $43,620, beginning on December 31, Year 1.

a. Prepare an amortization table for this installment note, similar to the one presented in Exhibit 4.
b. Journalize the entries for the issuance of the note and the four annual note payments.
c. Describe how the annual note payment would be reported in the Year 1 income statement.

EX 14-13 Reporting bonds   OBJ. 5

At the beginning of the current year, two bond issues (Simmons Industries 7%, 20-year bonds and Hunter Corporation 8%, 10-year bonds) were outstanding. During the year, the Simmons Industries bonds were redeemed and a significant loss on the redemption of bonds was reported as cost of merchandise sold on the income statement. At the end of the year, the Hunter Corporation bonds were reported as a noncurrent liability. The maturity date on the Hunter Corporation bonds was early in the following year.

✏ Identify the flaws in the reporting practices related to the two bond issues.

EX 14-14 Times interest earned   OBJ. 6

The following data were taken from recent annual reports of Southwest Airlines, which operates a low-fare airline service to more than 50 cities in the United States:

	Current Year	Prior Year
Interest expense	$147,000,000	$194,000,000
Income before income tax	685,000,000	323,000,000

a. Determine the times interest earned ratio for the current and preceding years. Round to one decimal place.
b. ✏ What conclusions can you draw?

EX 14-15 Times interest earned
OBJ. 6

Loomis, Inc. reported the following on the company's income statement in two recent years:

	Current Year	Prior Year
Interest expense	$ 13,500,000	$ 16,000,000
Income before income tax expense	310,500,000	432,000,000

a. Determine the times interest earned ratio for the current year and the prior year. Round to one decimal place.

b. ✏️ Is this ratio improving or declining?

EX 14-16 Times interest earned
OBJ. 6

Iacouva Company reported the following on the company's income statement for two recent years:

	Current Year	Prior Year
Interest expense	$5,000,000	$5,000,000
Income before income tax	3,500,000	6,000,000

a. Determine the times interest earned ratio for the current year and the prior year. Round to one decimal place.

b. ✏️ What conclusions can you draw?

Appendix 1
EX 14-17 Present value of amounts due

Tommy John is going to receive $1,000,000 in three years. The current market rate of interest is 10%.

a. Using the present value of $1 table in Exhibit 8, determine the present value of this amount compounded annually.

b. Why is the present value less than the $1,000,000 to be received in the future?

Appendix 1
EX 14-18 Present value of an annuity

Determine the present value of $200,000 to be received at the end of each of four years, using an interest rate of 7%, compounded annually, as follows:

a. By successive computations, using the present value table in Exhibit 8.
b. By using the present value table in Exhibit 10.
c. Why is the present value of the four $200,000 cash receipts less than the $800,000 to be received in the future?

Appendix 1
EX 14-19 Present value of an annuity

✔ $44,160,540

On January 1, you win $60,000,000 in the state lottery. The $60,000,000 prize will be paid in equal installments of $6,000,000 over 10 years. The payments will be made on December 31 of each year, beginning on December 31 of the current year. If the current interest rate is 6%, determine the present value of your winnings. Use the present value tables in Appendix A.

Appendix 1
EX 14-20 Present value of an annuity

Assume the same data as in Exercise 14-19, except that the current interest rate is 10%. ✏️ Will the present value of your winnings using an interest rate of 10% be more than the present value of your winnings using an interest rate of 6%? Why or why not?

Appendix 1
EX 14-21 Present value of bonds payable; discount

Pinder Co. produces and sells high-quality video equipment. To finance its operations, Pinder Co. issued $25,000,000 of five-year, 7% bonds, with interest payable semiannually, at a market (effective) interest rate of 9%. Determine the present value of the bonds payable, using the present value tables in Exhibits 8 and 10. Round to the nearest dollar.

Appendix 1
EX 14-22 Present value of bonds payable; premium

✔ $45,323,443

Moss Co. issued $42,000,000 of five-year, 11% bonds, with interest payable semiannually, at a market (effective) interest rate of 9%. Determine the present value of the bonds payable using the present value tables in Exhibits 8 and 10. Round to the nearest dollar.

Appendix 2
EX 14-23 Amortize discount by interest method

✔ b. $3,923,959

On the first day of its fiscal year, Ebert Company issued $50,000,000 of 10-year, 7% bonds to finance its operations. Interest is payable semiannually. The bonds were issued at a market (effective) interest rate of 9%, resulting in Ebert Company receiving cash of $43,495,895. The company uses the interest method.

a. Journalize the entries to record the following:
   1. Sale of the bonds.
   2. First semiannual interest payment, including amortization of discount. Round to the nearest dollar.
   3. Second semiannual interest payment, including amortization of discount. Round to the nearest dollar.

b. Compute the amount of the bond interest expense for the first year.

c. Explain why the company was able to issue the bonds for only $43,495,895 rather than for the face amount of $50,000,000.

Appendix 2
EX 14-24 Amortize premium by interest method

✔ b. $1,662,619

Shunda Corporation wholesales parts to appliance manufacturers. On January 1, Year 1, Shunda Corporation issued $22,000,000 of five-year, 9% bonds at a market (effective) interest rate of 7%, receiving cash of $23,829,684. Interest is payable semiannually. Shunda Corporation's fiscal year begins on January 1. The company uses the interest method.

a. Journalize the entries to record the following:
   1. Sale of the bonds.
   2. First semiannual interest payment, including amortization of premium. Round to the nearest dollar.
   3. Second semiannual interest payment, including amortization of premium. Round to the nearest dollar.

b. Determine the bond interest expense for the first year.

c. Explain why the company was able to issue the bonds for $23,829,684 rather than for the face amount of $22,000,000.

Appendix 1 and Appendix 2
EX 14-25 Compute bond proceeds, amortizing premium by interest method, and interest expense

✔ a. $37,702,483
✔ c. $225,620

Ware Co. produces and sells motorcycle parts. On the first day of its fiscal year, Ware Co. issued $35,000,000 of five-year, 12% bonds at a market (effective) interest rate of 10%, with interest payable semiannually. Compute the following, presenting figures used in your computations:

a. The amount of cash proceeds from the sale of the bonds. Use the tables of present values in Exhibits 8 and 10. Round to the nearest dollar.

b. The amount of premium to be amortized for the first semiannual interest payment period, using the interest method. Round to the nearest dollar.

c. The amount of premium to be amortized for the second semiannual interest payment period, using the interest method. Round to the nearest dollar.

d. The amount of the bond interest expense for the first year.

Appendix 1 and Appendix 2

EX 14-26 Compute bond proceeds, amortizing discount by interest method, and interest expense

✔ a. $71,167,524
✔ b. $670,051

Boyd Co. produces and sells aviation equipment. On the first day of its fiscal year, Boyd Co. issued $80,000,000 of five-year, 9% bonds at a market (effective) interest rate of 12%, with interest payable semiannually. Compute the following, presenting figures used in your computations:

a. The amount of cash proceeds from the sale of the bonds. Use the tables of present values in Exhibits 8 and 10. Round to the nearest dollar.

b. The amount of discount to be amortized for the first semiannual interest payment period, using the interest method. Round to the nearest dollar.

c. The amount of discount to be amortized for the second semiannual interest payment period, using the interest method. Round to the nearest dollar.

d. The amount of the bond interest expense for the first year.

Problems: Series A

PR 14-1A Effect of financing on earnings per share OBJ. 1

✔ 1. Plan 3: $1.44

Three different plans for financing an $18,000,000 corporation are under consideration by its organizers. Under each of the following plans, the securities will be issued at their par or face amount, and the income tax rate is estimated at 40% of income:

	Plan 1	Plan 2	Plan 3
8% Bonds	—	—	$ 9,000,000
Preferred 4% stock, $20 par	—	$ 9,000,000	4,500,000
Common stock, $10 par	$18,000,000	9,000,000	4,500,000
Total	$18,000,000	$18,000,000	$18,000,000

Instructions

1. Determine the earnings per share of common stock for each plan, assuming that the income before bond interest and income tax is $2,100,000.

2. Determine the earnings per share of common stock for each plan, assuming that the income before bond interest and income tax is $1,050,000.

3. ▶ Discuss the advantages and disadvantages of each plan.

PR 14-2A Bond discount, entries for bonds payable transactions OBJ. 2, 3

✔ 3. $1,535,897

On July 1, Year 1, Danzer Industries Inc. issued $40,000,000 of 10-year, 7% bonds at a market (effective) interest rate of 8%, receiving cash of $37,282,062. Interest on the bonds is payable semiannually on December 31 and June 30. The fiscal year of the company is the calendar year.

Instructions

1. Journalize the entry to record the amount of cash proceeds from the issuance of the bonds on July 1, Year 1.

2. Journalize the entries to record the following:

   a. The first semiannual interest payment on December 31, Year 1, and the amortization of the bond discount, using the straight-line method. Round to the nearest dollar.

(Continued)

712 Chapter 14 Long-Term Liabilities: Bonds and Notes

   b. The interest payment on June 30, Year 2, and the amortization of the bond discount, using the straight-line method. Round to the nearest dollar.
3. Determine the total interest expense for Year 1.
4. Will the bond proceeds always be less than the face amount of the bonds when the contract rate is less than the market rate of interest?
5. (Appendix 1) Compute the price of $37,282,062 received for the bonds by using the present value tables in Appendix A at the end of the text. Round to the nearest dollar.

✓ 3. $1,168,704

PR 14-3A Bond premium, entries for bonds payable transactions   OBJ. 2, 3

Campbell Inc. produces and sells outdoor equipment. On July 1, Year 1, Campbell Inc. issued $25,000,000 of 10-year, 10% bonds at a market (effective) interest rate of 9%, receiving cash of $26,625,925. Interest on the bonds is payable semiannually on December 31 and June 30. The fiscal year of the company is the calendar year.

Instructions
1. Journalize the entry to record the amount of cash proceeds from the issuance of the bonds on July 1, Year 1.
2. Journalize the entries to record the following:
   a. The first semiannual interest payment on December 31, Year 1, and the amortization of the bond premium, using the straight-line method. Round to the nearest dollar.
   b. The interest payment on June 30, Year 2, and the amortization of the bond premium, using the straight-line method. Round to the nearest dollar.
3. Determine the total interest expense for Year 1.
4. Will the bond proceeds always be greater than the face amount of the bonds when the contract rate is greater than the market rate of interest?
5. (Appendix 1) Compute the price of $26,625,925 received for the bonds by using the present value tables in Appendix A at the end of the text. Round to the nearest dollar.

✓ 3. $64,317,346

PR 14-4A Entries for bonds payable and installment note transactions   OBJ. 3, 4

The following transactions were completed by Winklevoss Inc., whose fiscal year is the calendar year:

Year 1

July 1. Issued $74,000,000 of 20-year, 11% callable bonds dated July 1, Year 1, at a market (effective) rate of 13%, receiving cash of $63,532,267. Interest is payable semiannually on December 31 and June 30.

Oct. 1. Borrowed $200,000 by issuing a six-year, 6% installment note to Nicks Bank. The note requires annual payments of $40,673, with the first payment occurring on September 30, Year 2.

Dec. 31. Accrued $3,000 of interest on the installment note. The interest is payable on the date of the next installment note payment.

     31. Paid the semiannual interest on the bonds. The bond discount amortization of $261,693 is combined with the semiannual interest payment.

Year 2

June 30. Paid the semiannual interest on the bonds. The bond discount amortization of $261,693 is combined with the semiannual interest payment.

Sept. 30. Paid the annual payment on the note, which consisted of interest of $12,000 and principal of $28,673.

Dec. 31. Accrued $2,570 of interest on the installment note. The interest is payable on the date of the next installment note payment.

     31. Paid the semiannual interest on the bonds. The bond discount amortization of $261,693 is combined with the semiannual interest payment.

Year 3

June 30. Recorded the redemption of the bonds, which were called at 98. The balance in the bond discount account is $9,420,961 after payment of interest and amortization of discount have been recorded. Record the redemption only.

Sept. 30. Paid the second annual payment on the note, which consisted of interest of $10,280 and principal of $30,393.

Instructions

1. Journalize the entries to record the foregoing transactions. Round all amounts to the nearest dollar.
2. Indicate the amount of the interest expense in (a) Year 1 and (b) Year 2.
3. Determine the carrying amount of the bonds as of December 31, Year 2.

Appendix 1 and Appendix 2
PR 14-5A Bond discount, entries for bonds payable transactions, interest method of amortizing bond discount

✔ 3. $1,491,282

On July 1, Year 1, Danzer Industries Inc. issued $40,000,000 of 10-year, 7% bonds at a market (effective) interest rate of 8%, receiving cash of $37,282,062. Interest on the bonds is payable semiannually on December 31 and June 30. The fiscal year of the company is the calendar year.

Instructions

1. Journalize the entry to record the amount of cash proceeds from the issuance of the bonds.
2. Journalize the entries to record the following:
   a. The first semiannual interest payment on December 31, Year 1, and the amortization of the bond discount, using the interest method. Round to the nearest dollar.
   b. The interest payment on June 30, Year 2, and the amortization of the bond discount, using the interest method. Round to the nearest dollar.
3. Determine the total interest expense for Year 1.

Appendix 1 and Appendix 2
PR 14-6A Bond premium, entries for bonds payable transactions, interest method of amortizing bond premium

✔ 3. $1,198,167

Campbell, Inc. produces and sells outdoor equipment. On July 1, Year 1, Campbell, Inc. issued $25,000,000 of 10-year, 10% bonds at a market (effective) interest rate of 9%, receiving cash of $26,625,925. Interest on the bonds is payable semiannually on December 31 and June 30. The fiscal year of the company is the calendar year.

Instructions

1. Journalize the entry to record the amount of cash proceeds from the issuance of the bonds.
2. Journalize the entries to record the following:
   a. The first semiannual interest payment on December 31, Year 1, and the amortization of the bond premium, using the interest method. Round to the nearest dollar.
   b. The interest payment on June 30, Year 2, and the amortization of the bond premium, using the interest method. Round to the nearest dollar.
3. Determine the total interest expense for Year 1.

Problems: Series B

PR 14-1B Effect of financing on earnings per share
OBJ. 1

✔ 1. Plan 3: $2.84

Three different plans for financing an $80,000,000 corporation are under consideration by its organizers. Under each of the following plans, the securities will be issued at their par or face amount, and the income tax rate is estimated at 40% of income:

(Continued)

714 Chapter 14 Long-Term Liabilities: Bonds and Notes

	Plan 1	Plan 2	Plan 3
9% Bonds	—	—	$40,000,000
Preferred 5% stock, $25 par	—	$40,000,000	20,000,000
Common stock, $20 par	$80,000,000	40,000,000	20,000,000
Total	$80,000,000	$80,000,000	$80,000,000

Instructions

1. Determine for each plan the earnings per share of common stock, assuming that the income before bond interest and income tax is $10,000,000.
2. Determine for each plan the earnings per share of common stock, assuming that the income before bond interest and income tax is $6,000,000.
3. Discuss the advantages and disadvantages of each plan.

PR 14-2B Bond discount, entries for bonds payable transactions OBJ. 2, 3

✔ 3. $2,392,269

Show Me How

On July 1, Year 1, Livingston Corporation, a wholesaler of manufacturing equipment, issued $46,000,000 of 20-year, 10% bonds at a market (effective) interest rate of 11%, receiving cash of $42,309,236. Interest on the bonds is payable semiannually on December 31 and June 30. The fiscal year of the company is the calendar year.

Instructions

1. Journalize the entry to record the amount of cash proceeds from the issuance of the bonds on July 1, Year 1.
2. Journalize the entries to record the following:
   a. The first semiannual interest payment on December 31, Year 1, and the amortization of the bond discount, using the straight-line method. Round to the nearest dollar.
   b. The interest payment on June 30, Year 2, and the amortization of the bond discount, using the straight-line method. Round to the nearest dollar.
3. Determine the total interest expense for Year 1.
4. Will the bond proceeds always be less than the face amount of the bonds when the contract rate is less than the market rate of interest?
5. (Appendix 1) Compute the price of $42,309,236 received for the bonds by using the present value tables in Appendix A at the end of the text. Round to the nearest dollar.

PR 14-3B Bond premium, entries for bonds payable transactions OBJ. 2, 3

✔ 3. $3,494,977

Rodgers Corporation produces and sells football equipment. On July 1, Year 1, Rodgers Corporation issued $65,000,000 of 10-year, 12% bonds at a market (effective) interest rate of 10%, receiving cash of $73,100,469. Interest on the bonds is payable semiannually on December 31 and June 30. The fiscal year of the company is the calendar year.

Instructions

1. Journalize the entry to record the amount of cash proceeds from the issuance of the bonds on July 1, Year 1.
2. Journalize the entries to record the following:
   a. The first semiannual interest payment on December 31, Year 1, and the amortization of the bond premium, using the straight-line method. Round to the nearest dollar.
   b. The interest payment on June 30, Year 2, and the amortization of the bond premium, using the straight-line method. Round to the nearest dollar.
3. Determine the total interest expense for Year 1.
4. Will the bond proceeds always be greater than the face amount of the bonds when the contract rate is greater than the market rate of interest?
5. (Appendix 1) Compute the price of $73,100,469 received for the bonds by using the present value tables in Appendix A at the end of the text. Round to the nearest dollar.

Chapter 14 Long-Term Liabilities: Bonds and Notes   715

PR 14-4B Entries for bonds payable and installment note transactions OBJ. 3, 4

✓ 3. $61,644,484

The following transactions were completed by Montague Inc., whose fiscal year is the calendar year:

Year 1

July 1. Issued $55,000,000 of 10-year, 9% callable bonds dated July 1, Year 1, at a market (effective) rate of 7%, receiving cash of $62,817,040. Interest is payable semiannually on December 31 and June 30.

Oct. 1. Borrowed $450,000 by issuing a six-year, 8% installment note to Intexicon Bank. The note requires annual payments of $97,342, with the first payment occurring on September 30, Year 2.

Dec. 31. Accrued $9,000 of interest on the installment note. The interest is payable on the date of the next installment note payment.

31. Paid the semiannual interest on the bonds. The bond premium amortization of $390,852 is combined with the semiannual interest payment.

Year 2

June 30. Paid the semiannual interest on the bonds. The bond premium amortization of $390,852 is combined with the semiannual interest payment.

Sept. 30. Paid the annual payment on the note, which consisted of interest of $36,000 and principal of $61,342.

Dec. 31. Accrued $7,773 of interest on the installment note. The interest is payable on the date of the next installment note payment.

31. Paid the semiannual interest on the bonds. The bond premium amortization of $390,852 is combined with the semiannual interest payment.

Year 3

June 30. Recorded the redemption of the bonds, which were called at 103. The balance in the bond premium account is $6,253,632 after payment of interest and amortization of premium have been recorded. Record the redemption only.

Sept. 30. Paid the second annual payment on the note, which consisted of interest of $31,093 and principal of $66,249.

Instructions

1. Journalize the entries to record the foregoing transactions.
2. Indicate the amount of the interest expense in (a) Year 1 and (b) Year 2.
3. Determine the carrying amount of the bonds as of December 31, Year 2.

Appendix 1 and Appendix 2
PR 14-5B Bond discount, entries for bonds payable transactions, interest method of amortizing bond discount

✓ 3. $2,327,008

On July 1, Year 1, Livingston Corporation, a wholesaler of manufacturing equipment, issued $46,000,000 of 20-year, 10% bonds at a market (effective) interest rate of 11%, receiving cash of $42,309,236. Interest on the bonds is payable semiannually on December 31 and June 30. The fiscal year of the company is the calendar year.

Instructions

1. Journalize the entry to record the amount of cash proceeds from the issuance of the bonds.
2. Journalize the entries to record the following:
   a. The first semiannual interest payment on December 31, Year 1, and the amortization of the bond discount, using the interest method. Round to the nearest dollar.
   b. The interest payment on June 30, Year 2, and the amortization of the bond discount, using the interest method. Round to the nearest dollar.
3. Determine the total interest expense for Year 1.

Appendix 1 and Appendix 2
PR 14-6B Bond premium, entries for bonds payable transactions, interest method of amortizing bond premium

✓ 3. $3,655,023

Rodgers Corporation produces and sells football equipment. On July 1, Year 1, Rodgers Corporation issued $65,000,000 of 10-year, 12% bonds at a market (effective) interest rate of 10%, receiving cash of $73,100,469. Interest on the bonds is payable semiannually on December 31 and June 30. The fiscal year of the company is the calendar year.

Instructions
1. Journalize the entry to record the amount of cash proceeds from the issuance of the bonds.
2. Journalize the entries to record the following:
   a. The first semiannual interest payment on December 31, Year 1, and the amortization of the bond premium, using the interest method. Round to the nearest dollar.
   b. The interest payment on June 30, Year 2, and the amortization of the bond premium, using the interest method. Round to the nearest dollar.
3. Determine the total interest expense for Year 1.

Cases & Projects

CP 14-1 Ethics in Action
CEG Capital Inc. is a large holding company that uses long-term debt extensively to fund its operations. At December 31, the company reported total assets of $100 million, total debt of $55 million, and total equity of $45 million. In January, the company issued $11 billion in long-term bonds to investors at par value. This was the largest debt issuance in the company's history, and it significantly increased the company's ratio of total debt to total equity. Five days after the debt issuance, CEG filed legal documents to prepare for an additional $50 billion long-term bond issue. As a result of this filing, the price of the $11 billion in bonds that the company issued earlier in the week dropped to 94 because of the increased risk associated with the company's debt. The investors in the original $11 billion bond issuance were not informed of the company's plans to issue additional debt so quickly after the initial bond issue.

▶ Did CEG Capital act unethically by not disclosing to initial bond investors its immediate plans to issue an additional $50 billion debt offering?

CP 14-2 Team Activity
In teams, select a public company that interests you. Obtain the company's most recent annual report on Form 10-K. The Form 10-K is a company's annually required filing with the Securities and Exchange Commission (SEC). It includes the company's financial statements and accompanying notes. The Form 10-K can be obtained either (a) by referring to the investor relations section of the company's website or (b) by using the company search feature of the SEC's EDGAR database service found at www.sec.gov/edgar/searchedgar/companysearch.html.

1. Based on the information in the company's most recent annual report, answer the following questions:
   a. How much long-term debt does the company report at the end of the most recent year presented?
   b. Does the company have any bonds outstanding at the end of the most recent year? If so, read the supporting notes to the financial statements and determine the following:
      (1) The contract rate of interest on the bond issue(s)
      (2) The discount or premium on the bond issue(s)
      (3) The due date of the bond issue(s)
      (4) The total amount of any bonds that will mature within one year of the balance sheet date
2. ▶ Based on your answers to the questions in requirement 1, evaluate the company's debt position.

CP 14-3 Communication

Nordbock Inc. reports the following outstanding bond issue on its December 31, 20Y1, balance sheet:

$1,000,000, 7%, 10-year bonds that pay interest semiannually.

The bonds have been outstanding for five years and were originally issued at face amount. The company is considering redeeming these bonds on January 1, 20Y2, at 103 and issuing new $1,000,000, 5%, five-year bonds at their face amount. These bonds would pay interest semiannually on June 30 and December 31.

✏️ Write a brief memo to Liz Nolan, the chief financial officer, discussing the costs of redeeming the existing bonds, the proceeds from issuing the new bonds, and whether this is a good financial decision.

CP 14-4 Present values

Alex Kelton recently won the jackpot in the Colorado lottery while he was visiting his parents. When he arrived at the lottery office to collect his winnings, he was offered the following three payout options:

a. Receive $100,000,000 in cash today.

b. Receive $25,000,000 today and $9,000,000 per year for eight years, with the first payment being received one year from today.

c. Receive $15,000,000 per year for 10 years, with the first payment being received one year from today.

✏️ Assuming that the effective rate of interest is 7%, which payout option should Alex select? Use the present value tables in Appendix A. Explain your answer and provide any necessary supporting calculations.

CP 14-5 Preferred stock vs. bonds

Xentec Inc. has decided to expand its operations to owning and operating golf courses. The following is an excerpt from a conversation between the chief executive officer, Peter Kilgallon, and the vice president of finance, Dan Baron:

Peter: Dan, have you given any thought to how we're going to manage the acquisition of Sweeping Bluff Golf Course?

Dan: Well, the two basic options, as I see it, are to issue either preferred stock or bonds. The equity market is a little depressed right now. The rumor is that the Federal Reserve Bank's going to increase the interest rates either this month or next.

Peter: Yes. I've heard the rumor. The problem is that we can't wait around to see what's going to happen. We'll have to move on this next week if we want any chance to complete the acquisition of Sweeping Bluff Golf Course.

Dan: Well, the bond market is strong right now. Maybe we should issue debt this time around.

Peter: That's what I would have guessed as well. Sweeping Bluff Golf Course's financial statements look pretty good, except for the volatility of its income and cash flows. But that's characteristic of the industry.

✏️ Discuss the advantages and disadvantages of issuing preferred stock versus bonds.

CP 14-6 Financing business expansion

You hold a 25% common stock interest in YouOwnIt, a family-owned construction equipment company. Your sister, who is the manager, has proposed an expansion of plant facilities at an expected cost of $26,000,000. Two alternative plans have been suggested as methods of financing the expansion. Each plan is briefly described as follows:

Plan 1. Issue $26,000,000 of 20-year, 8% notes at face amount

Plan 2. Issue an additional 550,000 shares of $10 par common stock at $20 per share, and $15,000,000 of 20-year, 8% notes at face amount

(Continued)

The balance sheet as of the end of the previous fiscal year is as follows:

YouOwnIt, Inc.
Balance Sheet
December 31, 20Y7

Assets

Current assets	$15,000,000
Property, plant, and equipment	22,500,000
Total assets	$37,500,000

Liabilities and Stockholders' Equity

Liabilities	$ 11,250,000
Common stock, $10	4,000,000
Paid-in capital in excess of par	500,000
Retained earnings	21,750,000
Total liabilities and stockholders' equity	$ 37,500,000

Net income has remained relatively constant over the past several years. The expansion program is expected to increase yearly income before bond interest and income tax from $2,667,000 in the previous year to $5,000,000 for this year. Your sister has asked you, as the company treasurer, to prepare an analysis of each financing plan.

1. Prepare a table indicating the expected earnings per share on the common stock under each plan. Assume an income tax rate of 40%. Round to the nearest cent.
2. a.  Discuss the factors that should be considered in evaluating the two plans.
   b. Which plan offers greater benefit to the present stockholders? Give reasons for your opinion.

CP 14-7   Times interest earned

The following financial data (in thousands) were taken from recent financial statements of **Staples, Inc.**:

	Year 3	Year 2	Year 1
Interest expense	$ 173,751	$ 214,824	$ 237,025
Earnings before taxes	1,459,141	1,356,595	1,155,894

1. Determine the times interest earned ratio for Staples in Year 3, Year 2, and Year 1? Round your answers to one decimal place.
2. Evaluate this ratio for Staples.

CHAPTER 15
Investments and Fair Value Accounting

Chapters 1–4
Accounting Cycle

Chapter 5
Accounting Systems

Income Statement	Statement of Owner's Equity	Balance Sheet	Statement of Cash Flows
Chapter 6 *Accounting for Merchandising Businesses*			Chapter 16 *Cash Flows*

Assets = Liabilities + Owner's Equity

Assets	Liabilities	Owner's Equity
Chapter 8 *Cash*	Chapter 11 *Current Liabilities*	Chapter 12 *Accounting for Partnerships and Limited Liability Companies*
Chapter 9 *Receivables*	Chapter 14 *Long-Term Liabilities: Bonds and Notes*	
Chapter 7 *Inventories*		
Chapter 10 *Fixed and Intangible Assets*		Chapter 13 *Corporations*
Chapter 15 Investments and Fair Value Accounting		

Chapter 17
Financial Statement Analysis

Statement of Owner's Equity
Owner's capital, Jan. 1 .... $XXX

Statement of Cash Flows
Cash flows from (used in) operating activities .... $XXX
Cash flows from (used in) investing activities XXX
.... XXX
.... $XXX
.... XXX
.... $XXX

Income Statement
Sales	$XXX
Cost of merchandise sold	XXX
Gross profit	$XXX
Total operating expenses	XXX
Income from operations	$XXX
Other revenue and expenses:	
Interest revenue	XXX
Unrealized gain (loss) on available-for-sale investments	XXX
Unrealized gain (loss) on trading investments	XXX
Equity income in investment	XXX
Net income	$XXX

Balance Sheet
Current assets:	
Cash	$XXX
Accounts receivable	XXX
Merchandise inventory	XXX
Available-for-sale investments	XXX
Trading investments	XXX
Total current assets	$XXX
Equity investments	$XXX
Property, plant, and equipment	XXX
Intangible assets	XXX
Total long-term assets	XXX
Total assets	$XXX
Liabilities:	
Current liabilities	$XXX
Long-term liabilities	XXX
Total liabilities	$XXX
Stockholders' equity	XXX
Total liabilities and stockholders' equity	$XXX

CHAPTER 15

Deere & Company

You invest cash to earn more cash. For example, you could deposit cash in a bank account to earn interest. You could also invest in preferred or common stocks; or in corporate or U.S. government notes and bonds.

Preferred and common stock can be purchased through a stock exchange such as the **New York Stock Exchange (NYSE)**. Preferred stock is purchased primarily with the expectation of earning dividends. Common stock is purchased with the expectation of earning dividends and realizing gains from an increase in the price of the stock.

Corporate and U.S. government bonds can also be purchased through a bond exchange. Bonds are purchased with the primary expectation of earning interest revenue.

Companies make investments for many of the same reasons you would as an individual. For example, **Deere & Company**, a manufacturer of agricultural and construction machinery, has invested approximately $437 million of available cash in stocks and bonds. These investments are held by Deere & Company for interest, dividends, and expected price increases.

Unlike most individuals, however, companies also purchase significant amounts of the outstanding common stock of other companies for strategic reasons. For example, Deere & Company has more than $303 million invested in companies where it owns between 20% and 50% of the outstanding shares. The vast majority of these investments are international manufacturing partners.

Investments in debt and equity securities give rise to a number of accounting issues. These issues are described and illustrated in this chapter.

Learning Objectives

After studying this chapter, you should be able to:

Example Exercises (EE) are shown in **green**.

Obj. 1 Describe why companies invest in debt and equity securities.

Why Companies Invest
Investing Cash in Current Operations
Investing Cash in Temporary Investments
Investing Cash in Long-Term Investments

Obj. 2 Describe and illustrate the accounting for debt investments.

Accounting for Debt Investments
Purchase of Bonds
Interest Revenue
Sale of Bonds   EE **15-1**

Obj. 3 Describe and illustrate the accounting for equity investments.

Accounting for Equity Investments
Cost Method: Less Than 20% Ownership   EE **15-2**
Equity Method: Between 20%–50% Ownership   EE **15-3**
Consolidation: More Than 50% Ownership

Obj. 4 Describe and illustrate valuing and reporting investments in the financial statements.

Valuing and Reporting Investments
Trading Securities   EE **15-4**
Available-for-Sale Securities   EE **15-5**
Held-to-Maturity Securities
Summary

Obj. 5 Describe fair value accounting and its effects on the financial statements.

Fair Value Accounting
Effect of Fair Value Accounting on the Financial Statements

Obj. 6 Describe and illustrate the computation of dividend yield.

Financial Analysis and Interpretation:
Dividend Yield   EE **15-6**

At a Glance 15   Page 740

Why Companies Invest

Obj. 1 Describe why companies invest in debt and equity securities.

Most companies generate cash from their operations. This cash can be used for the following investment purposes:

- Investing in current operations
- Investing in temporary investments to earn additional revenue
- Investing in long-term investments in stock of other companies for strategic reasons

Investing Cash in Current Operations

Cash is often used to support the current operating activities of a company. For example, cash may be used to replace worn-out equipment or to purchase new, more efficient and productive equipment. In addition, cash may be reinvested in the company to expand its current operations. For example, a retailer based in the northwest United States might decide to expand by opening stores in the Midwest.

The accounting for the use of cash in current operations has been described and illustrated in earlier chapters. For example, Chapter 10 illustrated the use of cash for purchasing property, plant, and equipment. In this chapter, we describe and illustrate the use of cash for investing in temporary investments and the stock of other companies.

Investing Cash in Temporary Investments

A company may temporarily have excess cash that is not needed for use in its current operations. This is often the case when a company has a seasonal operating cycle. For example, a significant portion of the annual merchandise sales of a retailer occurs during the fall holiday season. As a result, retailers often experience a large increase in cash during this period, which is not needed until the spring buying season.

Instead of letting excess cash remain idle in a checking account, most companies invest their excess cash in temporary investments. In doing so, companies invest in securities such as:

- **Debt securities**, which are notes and bonds that pay interest and have a fixed maturity date.
- **Equity securities**, which are preferred and common stock that represent ownership in a company and do not have a fixed maturity date.

Investments in debt and equity securities, termed **investments** or *temporary investments*, are reported in the Current Assets section of the balance sheet.

The primary objective of investing in temporary investments is as follows:

- Earn interest revenue
- Receive dividends
- Realize gains from increases in the market price of the securities

Investments in certificates of deposit and other securities that do not normally change in value are disclosed on the balance sheet as *cash and cash equivalents*. Such investments are held primarily for their interest revenue.

Investing Cash in Long-Term Investments

A company may invest cash in the debt or equity of another company as a long-term investment. Long-term investments may be held for the same investment objectives as temporary investments. However, long-term investments often involve the purchase of a significant portion of the stock of another company. Such investments usually have a strategic purpose, such as:

- *Reduction of costs:* When one company buys another company, the combined company may be able to reduce administrative expenses. For example, a combined company does not need two chief executive officers (CEOs) or chief financial officers (CFOs).
- *Replacement of management:* If the purchased company has been mismanaged, the acquiring company may replace the company's management and, thus, improve operations and profits.
- *Expansion:* The acquiring company may purchase a company because it has a complementary product line, territory, or customer base. The new combined company may be able to serve customers better than the two companies could separately.
- *Integration:* A company may integrate operations by acquiring a supplier or customer. Acquiring a supplier may provide a more stable or uninterrupted supply of resources. Acquiring a customer may also provide a market for the company's products or services.

Accounting for Debt Investments

Obj. 2 Describe and illustrate the accounting for debt investments.

Debt securities include notes and bonds issued by corporations and governmental organizations. Most companies invest excess cash in bonds as investments to earn interest revenue.

The accounting for bond investments[1] includes recording the following:

- Purchase of bonds
- Interest revenue
- Sale of bonds

---

1 Debt investments may also include installment notes and short-term notes. The accounting for these debt investments is covered in intermediate and advanced accounting courses.

Purchase of Bonds

The purchase of bonds is recorded by debiting an investments account for the purchase price of the bonds, including any brokerage commissions. (A *brokerage commission* is the fee charged by the agent who arranges the transaction between the buyer and seller.) If the bonds are purchased between interest dates, the purchase price includes accrued interest since the last interest payment. This is because the seller has earned the accrued interest, but the buyer will receive the accrued interest when it is paid.

To illustrate, assume that Homer Company purchases $18,000 of U.S. Treasury bonds at their face amount on March 17, 20Y6, plus accrued interest for 45 days. The bonds have an interest rate of 6%, payable on July 31 and January 31.

The entry to record the purchase of the U.S. Treasury bonds is as follows:

20Y6				
Mar.	17	Investments—U.S. Treasury Bonds	18,000	
		Interest Receivable	135	
		Cash		18,135
		Purchased $18,000, 6% U.S. Treasury bonds.		

Because Homer Company purchased the bonds on March 17, it is also purchasing the accrued interest for 45 days (January 31 to March 17), as shown in Exhibit 1. The accrued interest of $135 is computed as follows:[2]

$$\text{Accrued Interest} = \$18,000 \times 6\% \times (45 \div 360) = \$135$$

The accrued interest is recorded by debiting Interest Receivable for $135. Investments is debited for the purchase price of the bonds of $18,000.

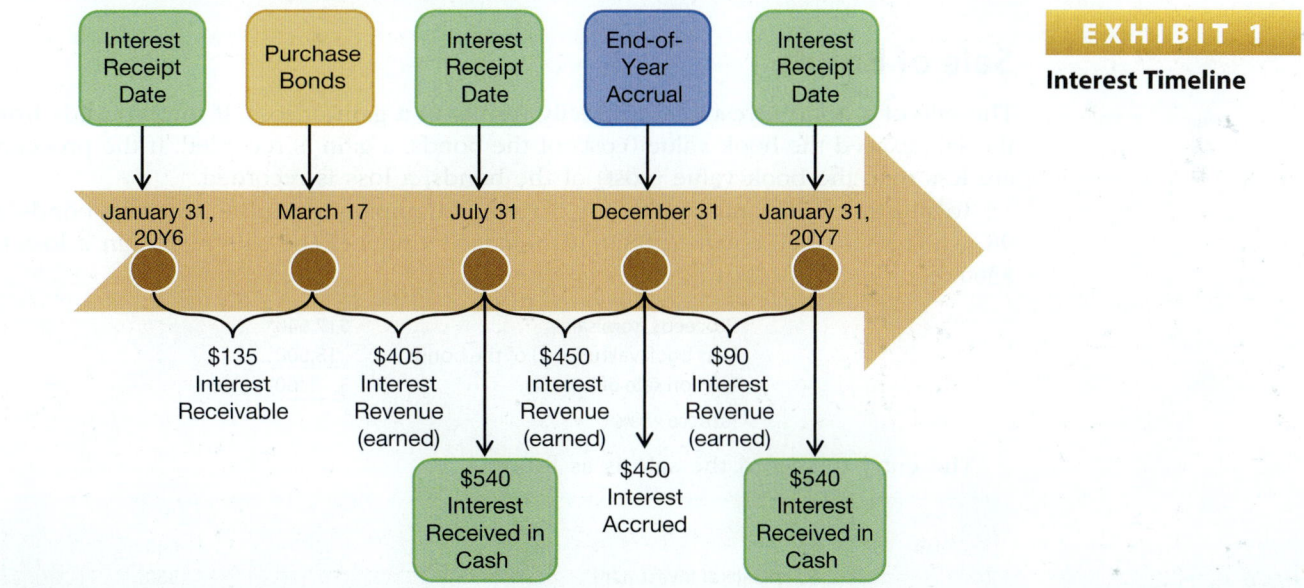

EXHIBIT 1

Interest Timeline

Interest Revenue

On July 31, Homer Company receives a semiannual interest payment of $540 ($18,000 × 6% × ½). The $540 interest includes the $135 accrued interest that Homer Company purchased with the bonds on March 17. Thus, Homer has earned $405 ($540 − $135) of interest revenue since purchasing the bonds, as shown in Exhibit 1.

---

2 To simplify, a 360-day year is used to compute interest.

The receipt of the interest on July 31 is recorded as follows:

20Y6					
July	31	Cash		540	
		Interest Receivable			135
		Interest Revenue			405
		Received semiannual interest.			

Homer Company's accounting period ends on December 31. Thus, an adjusting entry must be made to accrue interest for five months (August 1 to December 31) of $450 ($18,000 × 6% × 5/12), as shown in Exhibit 1. The adjusting entry to record the accrued interest is as follows:

20Y6					
Dec.	31	Interest Receivable		450	
		Interest Revenue			450
		Accrued five months of interest.			

For the year ended December 31, 20Y6, Homer Company would report Interest Revenue of $855 ($405 + $450) as part of Other Income on its income statement.

The receipt of the semiannual interest of $540 on January 31, 20Y7, is recorded as follows:

20Y7					
Jan.	31	Cash		540	
		Interest Revenue			90
		Interest Receivable			450
		Received semiannual interest			

Sale of Bonds

The sale of a bond investment normally results in a gain or loss. If the proceeds from the sale exceed the book value (cost) of the bonds, a gain is recorded. If the proceeds are less than the book value (cost) of the bonds, a loss is recorded.

To illustrate, on January 31, 20Y7, Homer Company sells the Treasury bonds at 98, which is a price equal to 98% of their face amount. The sale results in a loss of $360, computed as follows:

Proceeds from sale	$17,640*
Less book value (cost) of the bonds	18,000
Loss on sale of bonds	$ (360)

*$18,000 × 98%

The entry to record the sale is as follows:

20Y7					
Jan.	31	Cash		17,640	
		Loss on Sale of Investment		360	
		Investments—U.S. Treasury Bonds			18,000
		Sold U.S. Treasury bonds.			

There is no accrued interest upon the sale because the interest payment date is also January 31. If the sale were between interest dates, interest accrued since the last interest payment date would be added to the sale proceeds and credited to Interest Revenue. The loss on the sale of bond investments is reported as part of Other Income (Loss) on Homer Company's income statement.

Link to Deere & Company

Deere & Company recently reported $385 million of investments in government and corporate bonds.

Example Exercise 15-1 Bond Investment Transactions   *Obj. 2*

Journalize the entries to record the following selected bond investment transactions for Fly Company:

1. Purchased for cash $40,000 of Tyler Company 10% bonds at 100 plus accrued interest of $500.
2. Received the first semiannual interest.
3. Sold $30,000 of the bonds at 102 plus accrued interest of $110.

Follow My Example 15-1

1. Investments—Tyler Company Bonds 40,000
    Interest Receivable 500
        Cash 40,500

2. Cash 2,000*
        Interest Receivable.. 500
        Interest Revenue 1,500
    *$40,000 × 10% × ½

3. Cash 30,710*
        Interest Revenue 110
        Gain on Sale of Investments...................................... 600
        Investments—Tyler Company Bonds 30,000

    *Sale proceeds ($30,000 × 102%)................................ $30,600
    Accrued interest 110
    Total proceeds from sale $30,710

Practice Exercises: PE 15-1A, PE 15-1B

Accounting for Equity Investments

Obj. 3 Describe and illustrate the accounting for equity investments.

A company may invest in the preferred or common stock of another company. The company investing in another company's stock is the **investor**. The company whose stock is purchased is the **investee**.

The percent of the investee's outstanding stock purchased by the investor determines the degree of control that the investor has over the investee. This, in turn, determines the accounting method used to record the stock investment, as shown in Exhibit 2.

EXHIBIT 2 Stock Investments

Percent of Outstanding Stock Owned by Investor	Degree of Control of Investor over Investee	Accounting Method
Less than 20%	No control	Cost method
Between 20% and 50%	Significant influence	Equity method
Greater than 50%	Control	Consolidation

Cost Method: Less Than 20% Ownership

If the investor purchases less than 20% of the outstanding stock of the investee, the investor is considered to have no control over the investee. In this case, it is assumed that the investor purchased the stock primarily to earn dividends or to realize gains on price increases of the stock.

Investments of less than 20% of the investee's outstanding stock are accounted for using the **cost method**. Under the cost method, entries are recorded for the following transactions:

- Purchase of stock
- Receipt of dividends
- Sale of stock

Purchase of Stock

The purchase of stock is recorded at its cost. Any brokerage commissions are included as part of the cost.

To illustrate, assume that on May 1, Bart Company purchases 2,000 shares of Lisa Company common stock at $49.90 per share plus a brokerage commission of $200. The entry to record the purchase of the stock is as follows:

May	1	Investments—Lisa Company Stock	100,000	
		Cash		100,000
		Purchased 2,000 shares of Lisa Company common stock [($49.90 × 2,000 shares) + $200].		

Receipt of Dividends

On July 31, Bart Company receives a dividend of $0.40 per share from Lisa Company. The entry to record the receipt of the dividend is as follows:

July	31	Cash	800	
		Dividend Revenue		800
		Received dividend on Lisa Company common stock (2,000 shares × $0.40).		

Dividend Revenue is reported as part of Other Income on Bart Company's income statement.

Sale of Stock

The sale of a stock investment normally results in a gain or loss. A gain is recorded if the proceeds from the sale exceed the book value (cost) of the stock. A loss is recorded if the proceeds from the sale are less than the book value (cost).

To illustrate, on September 1, Bart Company sells 1,500 shares of Lisa Company stock for $54.50 per share less a $160 commission. The sale results in a gain of $6,590, computed as follows:

Proceeds from sale	$81,590*
Book value (cost) of the stock	75,000**
Gain on sale	$ 6,590

*($54.50 × 1,500 shares) − $160
**($100,000 ÷ 2,000 shares) × 1,500 shares

The entry to record the sale is as follows:

Sept.	1	Cash	81,590	
		Gain on Sale of Investments		6,590
		Investments—Lisa Company Stock		75,000
		Sold 1,500 shares of Lisa Company common stock.		

The gain on the sale of investments is reported as part of Other Income on Bart Company's income statement.

> **Example Exercise 15-2 Stock Investment Transactions**   *Obj. 3*
>
> On September 1, 1,500 shares of Monroe Company are acquired at a price of $24 per share plus a $40 brokerage commission. On October 14, a $0.60-per-share dividend was received on the Monroe Company stock. On November 11, 750 shares (half) of Monroe Company stock were sold for $20 per share less a $45 brokerage commission. Prepare the journal entries for the original purchase, dividend, and sale.
>
> **Follow My Example 15-2**
>
> | Sept. 1 | Investments—Monroe Company Stock | 36,040* | |
> | | Cash | | 36,040 |
> | | *(1,500 shares × $24 per share) + $40 | | |
> | Oct. 14 | Cash | 900* | |
> | | Dividend Revenue | | 900 |
> | | *$0.60 per share × 1,500 shares | | |
> | Nov. 11 | Cash | 14,955* | |
> | | Loss on Sale of Investments | 3,065 | |
> | | Investments—Monroe Company Stock | | 18,020** |
> | | *(750 shares × $20) − $45 | | |
> | | **$36,040 × ½ | | |
>
> Practice Exercises: PE 15-2A, PE 15-2B

Equity Method: Between 20%–50% Ownership

If the investor purchases between 20% and 50% of the outstanding stock of the investee, the investor is considered to have a *significant influence* over the investee. In this case, it is assumed that the investor purchased the stock primarily for strategic reasons, such as developing a supplier relationship.

Investments of between 20% and 50% of the investee's outstanding stock are accounted for using the **equity method**. Under the equity method, the stock is recorded initially at its cost, including any brokerage commissions. This is the same as under the cost method.

Under the equity method, the investment account is adjusted for the investor's share of the net income and dividends of the investee. These adjustments are as follows:

- *Net Income:* The investor records its share of the net income of the investee as an increase in the investment account. Its share of any net loss is recorded as a decrease in the investment account.
- *Dividends:* The investor's share of cash dividends received from the investee decreases the investment account.

Purchase of Stock To illustrate, assume that Simpson Inc. purchased a 40% interest in Flanders Corporation's common stock on January 2, 20Y6, for $350,000. The entry to record the purchase is as follows:

20Y6				
Jan. 2	Investment in Flanders Corporation Stock	350,000	
	Cash		350,000
	Purchased 40% of Flanders Corporation stock.		

Recording Investee Net Income For the year ended December 31, 20Y6, Flanders Corporation reported net income of $105,000. Under the equity method, Simpson Inc. (the investor) records its share of Flanders net income, as follows:

	20Y6				
	Dec.	31	Investment in Flanders Corporation Stock	42,000	
			Income of Flanders Corporation		42,000
			Recorded 40% share of Flanders		
			Corporation net income, $105,000 × 40%.		

Income of Flanders Corporation is reported on Simpson Inc.'s income statement. Depending on its significance, it may be reported separately or as part of *Other Income*. If Flanders had a loss during the period, then the journal entry would be a debit to Loss of Flanders Corporation and a credit to the investment account.

Recording Investee Dividends During the year, Flanders Corporation declared and paid cash dividends of $45,000. Under the equity method, Simpson Inc. (the investor) records its share of Flanders dividends as follows:

	20Y6				
	Dec.	31	Cash	18,000	
			Investment in Flanders Corporation Stock		18,000
			Recorded 40% share of Flanders		
			Corporation dividends, $45,000 × 40%.		

The effect of recording 40% of Flanders Corporation's net income and dividends is to increase the investment account by $24,000 ($42,000 − $18,000). Thus, Investment in Flanders Corporation Stock increases from $350,000 to $374,000, as shown in Exhibit 3.

EXHIBIT 3

Investment and Dividends

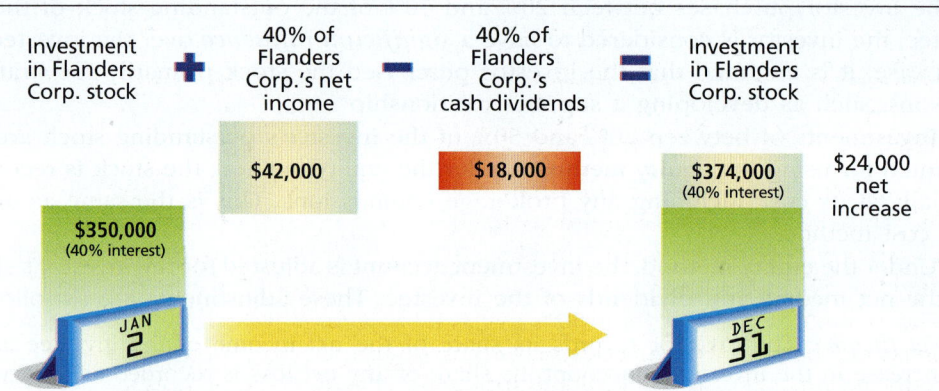

Under the equity method, the investment account reflects the investor's proportional changes in the net book value of the investee. For example, Flanders Corporation's net book value increased by $60,000 (net income of $105,000 less dividends of $45,000) during the year. As a result, Simpson Inc.'s share of Flanders' net book value increased by $24,000 ($60,000 × 40%). Investments accounted for under the equity method are classified on the balance sheet as noncurrent assets.

Sale of Stock Under the equity method, a gain or loss is normally recorded from the sale of an investment. A gain is recorded if the proceeds exceed the *book value* of the investment. A loss is recorded if the proceeds are less than the *book value* of the investment.

To illustrate, if Simpson Inc. sold Flanders Corporation's stock on January 1, 20Y7, for $400,000, a gain of $26,000 would be reported, computed as follows:

Proceeds from sale	$400,000
Book value of stock investment	374,000
Gain on sale	$ 26,000

The entry to record the sale is as follows:

20Y7 Jan.	1	Cash	400,000	
		Investment in Flanders Corporation Stock		374,000
		Gain on Sale of Flanders Corporation Stock		26,000
		Sold Flanders Corporation stock.		

> **Link to Deere & Company**
> In a recent year, **Deere & Company** reported equity method investments of $303.4 million.

Example Exercise 15-3 Equity Method — Obj. 3

On January 2, Olson Company acquired 35% of the outstanding stock of Bryant Company for $140,000. For the year ended December 31, Bryant Company earned income of $44,000 and paid dividends of $20,000. Prepare the entries for Olson Company for the purchase of the stock, the share of Bryant income, and the dividends received from Bryant Company.

Follow My Example 15-3

Jan.	2	Investment in Bryant Company Stock	140,000	
		Cash		140,000
Dec.	31	Investment in Bryant Company Stock	15,400*	
		Income of Bryant Company		15,400

*Recorded 35% of Bryant income, 35% × $44,000

	31	Cash	7,000*	
		Investment in Bryant Company Stock		7,000

*Recorded 35% of Bryant's $20,000 dividend, 35% × $20,000

Practice Exercises: PE 15-3A, PE 15-3B

Consolidation: More Than 50% Ownership

If the investor purchases more than 50% of the outstanding stock of the investee, the investor is considered to have *control* over the investee. In this case, it is assumed that the investor purchased the stock of the investee primarily for strategic reasons.

The purchase of more than 50% ownership of the investee's stock is termed a **business combination**. Companies may combine in order to produce more efficiently, diversify product lines, expand geographically, or acquire know-how.

A corporation owning all or a majority of the voting stock of another corporation is called a **parent company**. The corporation that is controlled is called the **subsidiary company**.

Parent and subsidiary corporations often continue to maintain separate accounting records and prepare their own financial statements. In such cases, at the end of the year, the financial statements of the parent and subsidiary are combined and reported as a single company. These combined financial statements are called **consolidated financial statements**. Such statements are normally identified by adding *and Subsidiary(ies)* to the name of the parent corporation or by adding *Consolidated* to the statement title.

To the external stakeholders of the parent company, consolidated financial statements are more meaningful than separate statements for each corporation. This is because the parent company, in substance, controls the subsidiaries. The accounting for business combinations, including preparing consolidated financial statements, is described and illustrated in advanced accounting courses and textbooks.

> **Link to Deere & Company**
> The financial statements of **Deere & Company** represent the consolidation of all the companies in which Deere & Company owns more than 50%.

Business Connection

MORE CASH MEANS MORE INVESTMENTS FOR DRUG COMPANIES

Patented drugs are the life blood of the pharmaceutical industry. Drug companies with extensive portfolios of patented drugs generate significant cash flows from operating activities. As a result, these companies often have extensive amounts of cash on hand to invest in other companies. Near the end of 2015, the five biggest drug makers had in excess of $45 billion in cash and investments. Many analysts anticipated that these companies would use this excess cash to acquire smaller biotechnology and drug companies for their patented drugs and their ongoing research activities.

Source: "Mergers and Acquisitions on the Rise in 2013 as Big Pharma Companies Hold Record Amounts of Cash on Hand," *Five Star Equities Market Research Report.* February 7, 2013.

Obj. 4 Describe and illustrate valuing and reporting investments in the financial statements.

Valuing and Reporting Investments

Debt and equity securities are *financial assets* that are often traded on public exchanges such as the New York Stock Exchange. As a result, their market value can be observed and, thus, objectively determined. For this reason, generally accepted accounting principles (GAAP) allow some debt securities and require equity securities where there is less than a 20% ownership interest to be valued in the accounting records and financial statements at their fair market values.

These securities are classified as follows:

- Trading securities
- Available-for-sale securities
- Held-to-maturity securities

Trading Securities

Trading securities are debt and equity securities that are purchased to earn short-term profits from changes in their market prices. Trading securities are often held by banks, mutual funds, insurance companies, and other financial institutions.

Because trading securities are held as a short-term investment, they are reported as a current asset on the balance sheet. Trading securities are valued as a portfolio (group) of securities using the securities' fair values. **Fair value** is the market price that the company would receive for a security if it were sold. A change in the fair value of the portfolio (group) of trading securities is recognized as an **unrealized gain or loss** for the period.

To illustrate, assume that Maggie Company purchased a portfolio of trading securities during 20Y6. On December 31, 20Y6, the cost and fair values of the securities were as follows:

Name	Number of Shares	Total Cost	Total Fair Value
Armour Company	400	$ 5,000	$ 7,200
Maven, Inc.	500	11,000	7,500
Polaris Co.	200	8,000	10,600
Total		$24,000	$25,300

The portfolio of trading securities is reported at its fair value of $25,300. An adjusting entry is made to record the increase in the fair value of $1,300 ($25,300 − $24,000). In order to maintain a record of the original cost of the securities, a valuation account, called *Valuation Allowance for Trading Investments*, is debited for $1,300 and Unrealized Gain on Trading Investments is credited for $1,300.[3]

---

[3] We assume that the valuation allowance account has a beginning balance of zero to simplify our illustrations.

The adjusting entry on December 31, 20Y6, to record the fair value of the portfolio of trading securities is as follows:

20Y6				
Dec.	31	Valuation Allowance for Trading Investments	1,300	
		Unrealized Gain on Trading Investments		1,300
		To record increase in fair value of trading securities.		

Unrealized Gain on Trading Investments is reported on the income statement. Depending on its significance, it may be reported separately or as Other Income on the income statement. The valuation allowance is reported on the December 31, 20Y6, balance sheet as follows:

Maggie Company
Balance Sheet (selected items)
December 31, 20Y6

Current assets:		
Cash		$120,000
Trading investments (at cost)	$24,000	
Plus valuation allowance for trading investments	1,300	
Trading investments (at fair value)		25,300

If the fair value of the portfolio of trading securities was less than the cost, then the adjustment would debit Unrealized Loss on Trading Investments and credit Valuation Allowance for Trading Investments for the difference. Unrealized Loss on Trading Investments would be reported on the income statement as Other Expenses. Valuation Allowance for Trading Investments would be shown on the balance sheet as a *deduction* from Trading Investments (at cost).

Over time, the valuation allowance account is adjusted to reflect the difference between the cost and the fair value of the portfolio. Thus, increases in the valuation allowance account from the beginning of the period will result in an adjustment to record an unrealized gain, similar to the preceding journal entry. Likewise, decreases in the valuation allowance account from the beginning of the period will result in an adjustment to record an unrealized loss.

Example Exercise 15-4 Valuing Trading Securities at Fair Value Obj. 4

On January 1, 20Y6, Valuation Allowance for Trading Investments had a zero balance. On December 31, 20Y6, the cost of the trading securities portfolio was $79,200, and the fair value was $76,800. Prepare the December 31, 20Y6, adjusting journal entry to record the unrealized gain or loss on trading investments.

Follow My Example 15-4

20Y6				
Dec. 31		Unrealized Loss on Trading Investments	2,400	
		Valuation Allowance for Trading Investments		2,400*
		To record decrease in fair value of trading investments.		

*Trading investments at fair value, December 31, 20Y6	$ 76,800
Less trading investments at cost, December 31, 20Y6	79,200
Unrealized loss on trading investments	$ (2,400)

Practice Exercises: PE 15-4A, PE 15-4B

INTEGRITY, OBJECTIVITY, AND ETHICS IN BUSINESS

SOCIALLY RESPONSIBLE INVESTING

Socially responsible investing is a growing trend in the United States and Europe that focuses on making investments to improve society. Socially responsible investors attempt to balance investment return with social good by seeking out investments in companies that (1) are environmentally friendly, (2) do not infringe on human rights in the production of a product or provision of a service, and (3) are anti-discriminatory. In some situations, socially responsible investors target emerging markets to both generate a return and help overcome social challenges. In addition, some socially responsible investors refuse to invest in companies that produce alcohol, tobacco, or weapons.

Available-for-Sale Securities

Available-for-sale securities are debt and equity securities that are not held for trading, not held to maturity, and not held for strategic reasons. The accounting for available-for-sale securities is similar to the accounting for trading securities, except for the reporting of changes in fair values. Specifically, changes in the fair values of *trading securities* are reported as an unrealized gain or loss on the income statement. In contrast, changes in the fair values of *available-for-sale securities* are reported as part of stockholders' equity and, thus, excluded from the income statement.

To illustrate, assume that the three securities Maggie Company purchased during 20Y6 are classified as available-for-sale securities instead of as trading securities. On December 31, 20Y6, the cost and fair values of the securities were as follows:

> **Link to Deere & Company**
> Deere & Company has a $14 million valuation allowance for available-for-sale securities.

Name	Number of Shares	Total Cost	Total Fair Value
Armour Company	400	$ 5,000	$ 7,200
Maven, Inc.	500	11,000	7,500
Polaris Co.	200	8,000	10,600
Total		$24,000	$25,300

The portfolio of available-for-sale securities is reported at its fair value of $25,300. An adjusting entry is made to record the increase in fair value of $1,300 ($25,300 − $24,000). In order to maintain a record of the original cost of the securities, a valuation account, called *Valuation Allowance for Available-for-Sale Investments*, is debited for $1,300. This account is similar to the valuation account used for trading securities.

Unlike trading securities, the December 31, 20Y6, adjusting entry credits a stockholders' equity account instead of an income statement account.[4] The $1,300 increase in fair value is credited to Unrealized Gain (Loss) on Available-for-Sale Investments.

The adjusting entry on December 31, 20Y6, to record the fair value of the portfolio of available-for-sale securities is as follows:

20Y6				
Dec. 31	Valuation Allowance for Available-for-Sale Investments		1,300	
	Unrealized Gain (Loss) on Available-for-Sale Investments			1,300
	To record increase in fair value of available-for-sale investments.			

[4] This is a rare exception to the rule that every adjusting entry must affect an income statement and a balance sheet account.

A credit balance in Unrealized Gain (Loss) on Available-for-Sale Investments is added to stockholders' equity, while a debit balance is subtracted from stockholders' equity.

The valuation allowance and the unrealized gain are reported on the December 31, 20Y6, balance sheet as follows:

Maggie Company
Balance Sheet
December 31, 20Y6

Current assets:
Cash		$120,000
Available-for-sale investments (at cost)	$24,000	
Plus valuation allowance for available-for-sale investments	1,300	
Available-for-sale investments (at fair value)		25,300

Stockholders' equity:
Common stock	$ 10,000
Paid-in capital in excess of par	150,000
Retained earnings	250,000
Unrealized gain (loss) on available-for-sale investments	1,300
Total stockholders' equity	$411,300

Equal

As shown, Unrealized Gain (Loss) on Available-for-Sale Investments is reported as an addition to stockholders' equity. In future years, the cumulative effects of unrealized gains and losses are reported in this account. Because 20Y6 was the first year that Maggie Company purchased available-for-sale securities, the unrealized gain is reported as the balance of Unrealized Gain (Loss) on Available-for-Sale Investments. This treatment is supported under the theory that available-for-sale securities will be held longer than trading securities, so changes in fair value over time have a greater opportunity to cancel out. Thus, these changes are not reported on the income statement, as is the case with trading securities.

If the fair value was less than the cost, then the adjustment would debit Unrealized Gain (Loss) on Available-for-Sale Investments and credit Valuation Allowance for Available-for-Sale Investments for the difference. Unrealized Gain (Loss) on Trading Investments would be reported in the Stockholders' Equity section as a negative item. Valuation Allowance for Available-for-Sale Investments would be shown on the balance sheet as a deduction from Available-for-Sale Investments (at cost).

Over time, the valuation allowance account is adjusted to reflect the difference between the cost and the fair value of the portfolio. Thus, increases in the valuation allowance from the beginning of the period will result in an adjustment to record an increase in the valuation and unrealized gain (loss) accounts, similar to the journal entry illustrated earlier. Likewise, decreases in the valuation allowance from the beginning of the period will result in an adjustment to record decreases in the valuation and unrealized gain (loss) accounts.

> **Link to Deere & Company**
> **Deere & Company** classifies all of its investments in debt securities and qualifying equity securities as available-for-sale securities.

> ### Example Exercise 15-5 Valuing Available-for-Sale Securities at Fair Value — Obj. 4
>
> On January 1, 20Y6, Valuation Allowance for Available-for-Sale Investments had a zero balance. On December 31, 20Y6, the cost of the available-for-sale securities was $45,700 and the fair value was $50,000.
>
> Prepare the adjusting entry to record the unrealized gain or loss for available-for-sale investments on December 31, 20Y6.
>
> #### Follow My Example 15-5
>
> | 20Y6 | | | |
> |---|---|---|---|
> | Dec. 31 | Valuation Allowance for Available-for-Sale Investments | 4,300* | |
> | | Unrealized Gain (Loss) on Available-for-Sale Investments | | 4,300 |
> | | To record increase in fair value of available-for-sale securities. | | |
>
> *Available-for-sale investments at fair value, December 31, 20Y6 $50,000
> Less available-for-sale investments at cost, December 31, 20Y6   45,700
> Unrealized gain (loss) on available-for-sale investments $ 4,300
>
> Practice Exercises: PE 15-5A, PE 15-5B

Held-to-Maturity Securities

Held-to-maturity securities are debt investments, such as notes or bonds, that a company intends to hold until their maturity date. Held-to-maturity securities are purchased primarily to earn interest revenue.

If a held-to-maturity security will mature within a year, it is reported as a current asset on the balance sheet. Held-to-maturity securities maturing beyond a year are reported as noncurrent assets.

Only securities with maturity dates, such as corporate notes and bonds, are classified as held-to-maturity securities. Equity securities are not held-to-maturity securities because they have no maturity date.

Held-to-maturity bond investments are recorded at their cost, including any brokerage commissions, as illustrated earlier in this chapter. If the interest rate on the bonds differs from the market rate of interest, the bonds may be purchased at a premium or discount. In such cases, the premium or discount is amortized over the life of the bonds.

Held-to-maturity bond investments are reported on the balance sheet at their amortized cost. The accounting for held-to-maturity investments, including premium and discount amortization, is described in advanced accounting texts.

Summary

Exhibit 4 summarizes the valuation and balance sheet reporting of trading, available-for-sale, and held-to-maturity securities.

EXHIBIT 4
Summary of Valuing and Reporting of Investments

	Trading Securities	Available-for-Sale Securities	Held-to-Maturity Securities
Valued at:	Fair Value	Fair Value	Amortized Cost
Changes in valuation are reported as:	Unrealized gain or loss in the income statement as Other Income (loss).	Accumulated unrealized gain or loss is reported in stockholders' equity on the balance sheet.	Not applicable. Held-to-maturity securities are reported at cost.*
Reported on the balance sheet as:	Cost of investments plus or minus valuation allowance.	Cost of investments plus or minus valuation allowance.	Amortized cost of investment.
Classified on balance sheet as:	A current asset.	Either a current or non-current asset, depending on management's intent.	Either a current or noncurrent asset, depending on remaining term to maturity.

*Premium or discount amortization is reported as part of interest revenue on the income statement.

Common stock investments in trading and available-for-sale securities are typically less than 20% of the outstanding common stock of the investee. The portfolios are reported at fair value using the valuation allowance account, while the individual securities are accounted for using the cost method. Investments between 20% and 50% of the outstanding common stock of the investee are accounted for using the equity method illustrated earlier in this chapter. Equity method investments are classified as noncurrent assets on the balance sheet.

The balance sheet reporting for the investments of **Mornin' Joe** follows:

Mornin' Joe
Balance Sheet
December 31, 20Y6

Assets
Current assets:
Cash and cash equivalents		$235,000
Trading investments (at cost)	$420,000	
Plus valuation allowance for trading investments	45,000	465,000
Accounts receivable	$305,000	
Less allowance for doubtful accounts	12,300	292,700
Merchandise inventory—at lower of cost (first-in, first-out method) or market		120,000
Prepaid insurance		24,000
Total current assets		$1,136,700

Investments:
Investment in AM Coffee (equity method)		565,000

Property, plant, and equipment:

Mornin' Joe invests in trading securities and does not have investments in held-to-maturity or available-for-sale securities. Mornin' Joe also owns 40% of AM Coffee Corporation, which is accounted for using the equity method. Mornin' Joe intends to keep its investment in AM Coffee indefinitely for strategic reasons; thus, its investment in AM Coffee is classified as a noncurrent asset. Such investments are normally reported before property, plant, and equipment.

Mornin' Joe reported an Unrealized Gain on Trading Investments of $5,000 and Equity Income in AM Coffee of $57,000 in the Other Income and Expense section of its income statement, as follows:

Mornin' Joe
Income Statement
For the Year Ended December 31, 20Y6

Sales		$5,402,100
Cost of merchandise sold		2,160,000
Gross profit		$3,242,100
Total operating expenses		2,608,700
Income from operations		$ 633,400
Other revenue and expense:		
Interest revenue	$ 18,000	
Interest expense	(136,000)	
Loss on disposal of fixed asset	(23,000)	
Unrealized gain on trading investments	5,000	
Equity income in AM Coffee	57,000	(79,000)
Income before income taxes		$ 554,400
Income tax expense		132,800
Net income		$ 421,600

Business Connection

WARREN BUFFETT: THE SAGE OF OMAHA

Beginning in 1962, Warren Buffett, one of the world's wealthiest and most successful investors, began buying shares of **Berkshire Hathaway**. He eventually took control of the company and transformed it from a textile manufacturing company into an investment holding company. Today, Berkshire Hathaway holds more than $125 billion in cash and cash equivalents, equity securities, and debt securities. Berkshire's largest holdings include **The Coca-Cola Company**, **American Express**, **Wells Fargo**, and **Procter & Gamble**. Berkshire Class A common stock trades near $212,000 per share, the highest priced share on the **New York Stock Exchange**.

Buffett compares his investment style to hitting a baseball: "Ted Williams, one of the greatest hitters in the game, stated, 'my argument is, to be a good hitter, you've got to get a good ball to hit. It's the first rule of the book. If I have to bite at stuff that is out of my happy zone, I'm not a .344 hitter. I might only be a .250 hitter.'" Buffett states, "Charlie (Buffett's partner) and I agree and will try to wait for (investment) opportunities that are well within our 'happy zone.'" One of Buffet's recent "happy zone" investments was the acquisition of **Burlington Northern Santa Fe Railroad** for $34 billion.

Warren Buffett as the CEO of Berkshire Hathaway earns a salary of only $100,000 per year, which is the lowest CEO salary for a company of its size in the United States. However, he personally owns approximately 38% of the company, making him worth more than $70 billion. What will Buffett do with this wealth? He has decided to give nearly all of it to philanthropic causes through the **Bill and Melinda Gates Foundation**.

Source: Warren E. Buffett, *The Essays of Warren Buffett: Lessons for Corporate America*, edited by Lawrence A. Cunningham, p. 234.

Fair Value Accounting

Obj. 5 Describe fair value accounting and its effects on the financial statements.

Fair value is the price that would be received from selling an asset. Fair value assumes that this transaction occurs under *normal* business conditions.

As illustrated earlier, generally accepted accounting principles require trading and available-for-sale investments to be recorded at their fair value. This differs from the traditional historical cost measurement basis, which records assets such as inventory and property, plant, and equipment at their purchase price. As a result, financial statements include some assets that are reported at their historical cost (inventory, property, plant, and equipment), and other assets that are reported at their fair value (trading and available-for-sale securities).

Over the past several decades, the financial statements of companies in most industries have included more fair value measures. This is partially due to the Financial Accounting Standards Board's increased willingness to apply fair value to certain assets and transactions. As the ability to measure fair value becomes more reliable, a greater number of assets and transactions are likely to be reported at fair value. A more detailed discussion of fair value is provided in intermediate and advanced financial accounting courses.

Effect of Fair Value Accounting on the Financial Statements

The use of fair values for valuing assets and liabilities affects the financial statements. Specifically, the balance sheet and income statement could be affected.

Balance Sheet When an asset is reported at its fair value, any difference between the asset's original cost or prior period's fair value must be recorded. As we illustrated for trading and available-for-sale securities, this difference is reported in a valuation allowance. The account, Valuation Allowance for Trading Investments, was used earlier in this chapter to adjust trading securities to their fair values.

Available-for-sale securities are reported at fair value in the balance sheet. Changes in their fair values are not recognized on the income statement, but are included as part of stockholders' equity through the comprehensive income and accumulated other comprehensive income accounts. These accounts are described in the appendix to this chapter.

Income Statement Trading securities are also reported at fair value in the balance sheet. However, instead of recording the changes in the fair values of trading securities as part of stockholders' equity, the unrealized gains or losses are reported on the income statement.

Financial Analysis and Interpretation: Dividend Yield

Obj. 6 Describe and illustrate the computation of dividend yield.

The **dividend yield** measures the rate of return to stockholders based on cash dividends. Dividend yield is most often computed for common stock because preferred stock has a stated dividend rate. In contrast, the cash dividends paid on common stock normally vary with the profitability of the corporation.

The dividend yield is computed as follows:

$$\text{Dividend Yield} = \frac{\text{Dividends per Share of Common Stock}}{\text{Market Price per Share of Common Stock}}$$

To illustrate, the market price of **Deere & Company** was $76.26 at the end of a recent fiscal year. During the preceding year, Deere & Company had paid dividends of $2.40 per share. Thus, the dividend yield of Deere & Company's common stock is computed as follows:

$$\text{Dividend Yield} = \frac{\text{Dividends per Share of Common Stock}}{\text{Market Price per Share of Common Stock}} = \frac{\$2.40}{\$76.26} = 3.1\%$$

Deere & Company pays a dividend yield of slightly more than 3.1%. The dividend yield is first a function of a company's profitability, or ability to pay a dividend. Deere & Company has sufficient profitability to pay a dividend. Second, a company's dividend yield is a function of management's alternative use of funds. If a company has sufficient growth opportunities, funds may be directed toward internal investment rather than toward paying dividends.

The dividend yield will vary from day to day because the market price of a corporation's stock varies day to day. Current dividend yields are provided with news service quotations of market prices, such as **The Wall Street Journal** or **Yahoo! Finance**.

Recent dividend yields for some selected companies are as follows:

Company	Dividend Yield (%)
Alphabet (Google)	None
Best Buy	3.6
Coca-Cola Company	3.1
Deere & Company	3.1
Duke Energy	4.1
Facebook	None
Microsoft	2.8
Verizon Communications	4.4

As can be seen, the dividend yield varies widely across firms. Growth firms tend to retain their earnings to fund future growth. Thus, **Facebook** and **Alphabet (Google)** pay no dividends. Common stockholders of these companies expect to earn most of their return from stock price appreciation. In contrast, **Duke Energy** and **Verizon Communications** are regulated utilities that provide a return to common stockholders mostly through dividends. **Best Buy**, **Coca-Cola**, **Deere & Company**, and **Microsoft** provide a mix of dividends and expected stock price appreciation to their common stockholders.

Example Exercise 15-6 Dividend Yield — Obj. 6

On March 11, 20Y6, Sheldon Corporation had a market price of $58 per share of common stock. For the previous year, Sheldon paid an annual dividend of $2.90 per share. Compute the dividend yield for Sheldon Corporation.

Follow My Example 15-6

$$\text{Dividend Yield} = \frac{\text{Dividends per Share of Common Stock}}{\text{Market Price per Share of Common Stock}} = \frac{\$2.90}{\$58} = 0.05, \text{ or } 5\%$$

Practice Exercises: PE 15-6A, PE 15-6B

APPENDIX

Comprehensive Income

Comprehensive income is defined as all changes in stockholders' equity during a period, except those resulting from dividends and stockholders' investments. Comprehensive income is computed by adding or subtracting *other comprehensive income* to (from) net income, as follows:

Net income	$XXX
Other comprehensive income	XXX
Comprehensive income	$XXX

Other comprehensive income items include unrealized gains and losses on available-for-sale securities as well as other items such as foreign currency and pension liability adjustments. The *cumulative* effect of other comprehensive income is reported on the balance sheet as **accumulated other comprehensive income**.

Companies are required to report comprehensive income in the financial statements in one of the following two ways:

- On the income statement, or
- In a separate statement of comprehensive income that immediately follows the income statement.

In the earlier illustration, Maggie Company had reported an unrealized gain of $1,300 on available-for-sale investments. This unrealized gain would be reported in the Stockholders' Equity section of Maggie's 20Y6 balance sheet, as follows:

Maggie Company
Balance Sheet
December 31, 20Y6

Stockholders' equity:	
Common stock	$ 10,000
Excess of issue price over par	150,000
Retained earnings	250,000
Unrealized gain (loss) on available-for-sale investments	1,300
Total stockholders' equity	$411,300

Alternatively, Maggie Company could have reported the unrealized gain as part of accumulated other comprehensive income as follows:

Maggie Company
Balance Sheet
December 31, 20Y6

Stockholders' equity:	
Common stock	$ 10,000
Excess of issue price over par	150,000
Retained earnings	250,000
Accumulated other comprehensive income:	
Unrealized gain on available-for-sale investments	1,300
Total stockholders' equity	$411,300

The accounting for comprehensive income is an advanced accounting topic that will be covered in greater detail in advanced accounting courses.

At a Glance 15

Obj. 1 Describe why companies invest in debt and equity securities.

Key Points Cash can be used to (1) invest in current operations, (2) invest to earn additional revenue in marketable securities, or (3) invest in marketable securities for strategic reasons.

Learning Outcomes	Example Exercises	Practice Exercises
• Describe the ways excess cash is used by a business.		
• Describe the purpose of temporary investments.		
• Describe the strategic purpose of long-term investments.		

Obj. 2 Describe and illustrate the accounting for debt investments.

Key Points The accounting for debt investments includes recording the purchase, interest revenue, and sale of the debt. Both the purchase and sale date may include accrued interest.

Learning Outcomes	Example Exercises	Practice Exercises
• Prepare journal entries to record the purchase of a debt investment, including accrued interest.	EE15-1	PE15-1A, 15-1B
• Prepare journal entries for interest revenue from debt investments.	EE15-1	PE15-1A, 15-1B
• Prepare journal entries to record the sale of a debt investment at a gain or loss.	EE15-1	PE15-1A, 15-1B

Obj. 3 Describe and illustrate the accounting for equity investments.

Key Points The accounting for equity investments differs, depending on the degree of control. Accounting for investments of less than 20% of the outstanding stock (no control) of the investee includes recording the purchase of stock, the receipt of dividends, and the sale of stock at a gain or loss. Investments of 20%–50% of the outstanding stock of an investee are considered to have significant influence and are accounted for under the *equity method*. An investment for more than 50% of the outstanding stock of an investee is treated as a *business combination* and is accounted for using *consolidated financial statements*.

Learning Outcomes	Example Exercises	Practice Exercises
• Describe the accounting for less than 20%, 20%–50%, and greater than 50% investments.		
• Prepare journal entries to record the purchase of a stock investment.	EE15-2	PE15-2A, 15-2B
• Prepare journal entries for the receipt of dividends.	EE15-2	PE15-2A, 15-2B
• Prepare journal entries for the sale of a stock investment at a gain or loss.	EE15-2	PE15-2A, 15-2B
• Prepare journal entries for the equity earnings of an equity method investee under the equity method.	EE15-3	PE15-3A, 15-3B
• Prepare journal entries for the dividends received from an equity method investee under the equity method.	EE15-3	PE15-3A, 15-3B
• Describe a business combination, parent company, and subsidiary company.		
• Describe consolidated financial statements.		

Obj. 4 Describe and illustrate valuing and reporting investments in the financial statements.

Key Points Equity security investments of 20%–50% of the outstanding stock (not control) may be classified as either (1) trading securities, or (2) available-for-sale securities Investments in debt securities can be classified as either (1) trading securities, (2) available-for-sale securities, or (3) held-to-maturity securities. *Trading securities* are valued at *fair value*, with unrealized gains and losses reported on the income statement. *Available-for-sale securities* are reported at fair value with unrealized gains or losses reported in the Stockholders' Equity section of the balance sheet. *Held-to-maturity* investments are valued at amortized cost.

Learning Outcomes	Example Exercises	Practice Exercises
• Describe trading securities, held-to-maturity securities, and available-for-sale securities.		
• Prepare journal entries to record the change in the fair value of a trading security portfolio.	EE15-4	PE15-4A, 15-4B
• Describe and illustrate the reporting of trading securities on the balance sheet.		
• Prepare journal entries to record the change in fair value of an available-for-sale security portfolio.	EE15-5	PE15-5A, 15-5B
• Describe and illustrate the reporting of available-for-sale securities on the balance sheet.		
• Describe the accounting for held-to-maturity debt securities.		

Obj. 5 Describe fair value accounting and its effects on the financial statements.

Key Points There is a trend toward fair value accounting in generally accepted accounting principles. Fair value is the price that would be received to sell an asset.

Learning Outcomes	Example Exercises	Practice Exercises
• Describe fair value accounting.		
• Describe how fair value accounting impacts the balance sheet and income statement.		

Obj. 6 Describe and illustrate the computation of dividend yield.

Key Points The dividend yield measures the cash return from common dividends as a percent of the market price of the common stock. The ratio is computed as dividends per share of common stock divided by the market price per share of common stock.

Learning Outcomes	Example Exercises	Practice Exercises
• Compute dividend yield.	EE15-6	PE15-6A, 15-6B
• Describe how dividend yield measures the return to stockholders from dividends.		

Illustrative Problem

The following selected investment transactions were completed by Rosewell Company during Year 1, its first year of operations:

Year 1

Jan. 11. Purchased 800 shares of Bryan Company stock as an available-for-sale security at $23 per share plus an $80 brokerage commission.

Feb. 6. Purchased $40,000 of 8% U.S. Treasury bonds at their face amount plus accrued interest for 36 days. The bonds pay interest on January 1 and July 1. The bonds were classified as held-to-maturity securities.

Mar. 3. Purchased 1,900 shares of Cohen Company stock as a trading security at $48 per share plus a $152 brokerage commission.

Apr. 5. Purchased 2,400 shares of Lyons Inc. stock as an available-for-sale security at $68 per share plus a $120 brokerage commission.

May 12. Purchased 200,000 shares of Myers Company at $37 per share plus an $8,000 brokerage commission. Myers Company has 800,000 common shares issued and outstanding. The equity method was used for this investment.

July 1. Received semiannual interest on bonds purchased on February 6.

Aug. 29. Sold 1,200 shares of Cohen Company stock at $61 per share less a $90 brokerage commission.

Oct. 5. Received an $0.80-per-share dividend on Bryan Company stock.

Nov. 11. Received a $1.10-per-share dividend on Myers Company stock.

16. Purchased 3,000 shares of Morningside Company stock as a trading security for $52 per share plus a $150 brokerage commission.

Chapter 15 Investments and Fair Value Accounting

Year 1

Dec. 31. Accrued interest on U.S. Treasury bonds.

31. Myers Company earned $1,200,000 during the year. Rosewell recorded its share of Myers Company earnings, using the equity method.

31. Prepared adjusting entries for the portfolios of trading and available-for-sale securities based on the following fair values (stock prices):

Bryan Company	$21
Cohen Company	43
Lyons Inc.	88
Myers Company	40
Morningside Company	45

Instructions

1. Journalize the preceding transactions.
2. Prepare the balance sheet disclosure for Rosewell Company's investments on December 31, Year 1. Assume that held-to-maturity investments are classified as noncurrent assets.

Solution

1.

Year 1					
Jan.	11	Investments—Bryan Company		18,480*	
		Cash			18,480
		*(800 shares × $23 per share) + $80			

Feb.	6	Investments—U.S. Treasury Bonds		40,000	
		Interest Receivable		320*	
		Cash			40,320
		*$40,000 × 8% × (36 days ÷ 360 days)			

Mar.	3	Investments—Cohen Company		91,352*	
		Cash			91,352
		*(1,900 shares × $48 per share) + $152			

Apr.	5	Investments—Lyons Inc.		163,320*	
		Cash			163,320
		*(2,400 shares × $68 per share) + $120			

May	12	Investment in Myers Company		7,408,000*	
		Cash			7,408,000
		*(200,000 shares × $37 per share) + $8,000			

July	1	Cash		1,600*	
		Interest Receivable			320
		Interest Revenue			1,280
		*$40,000 × 8% × ½			

(Continued)

Chapter 15 Investments and Fair Value Accounting

Year 1 Aug.	29	Cash		73,110*	
		Investments—Cohen Company			57,696**
		Gain on Sale of Investments			15,414
		*(1,200 shares × $61 per share) − $90			
		**1,200 shares × ($91,352 ÷ 1,900 shares)			

Oct.	5	Cash		640	
		Dividend Revenue			640
		*800 shares × $0.80 per share			

Nov.	11	Cash		220,000	
		Investment in Myers Company Stock			220,000
		*200,000 shares × $1.10 per share			

Nov.	16	Investments—Morningside Company		156,150*	
		Cash			156,150
		*(3,000 shares × $52 per share) + $150			

Dec.	31	Interest Receivable		1,600	
		Interest Revenue			1,600
		Accrued interest, $40,000 × 8% × ½.			

Dec.	31	Investment in Myers Company Stock		300,000	
		Income of Myers Company			300,000
		Recorded equity income,			
		$1,200,000 × (200,000 shares ÷ 800,000 shares).			

Dec.	31	Unrealized Loss on Trading Investments		24,706	
		Valuation Allowance for Trading Investments			24,706
		Recorded decease in fair value of trading			
		investments, $165,100 − $189,806.			

Name	Number of Shares	Total Cost	Total Fair Value
Cohen Company	700	$ 33,656	$ 30,100*
Morningside Company	3,000	156,150	135,000**
Total		$189,806	$165,100

*700 shares × $43 per share
**3,000 shares × $45 per share

Note: Myers Company is valued using the equity method; thus, the fair value is not used.

	Year 1				
	Dec.	31	Valuation Allowance for Available-for-Sale Investments	46,200	
			Unrealized Gain (Loss) on Available-for-Sale Investments		46,200
			Recorded increase in fair value of available-for-sale investments, $228,000 − $181,800.		

Name	Number of Shares	Total Cost	Total Fair Value
Bryan Company	800	$ 18,480	$ 16,800*
Lyons Inc.	2,400	163,320	211,200**
Total		$181,800	$228,000

*800 shares × $21 per share
**2,400 shares × $88 per share

2.

Rosewell Company
Balance Sheet (Selected)
December 31, Year 1

Assets

Current assets:
Cash			$ XXX,XXX
Trading investments (at cost)	$189,806		
Less valuation allowance for trading investments	24,706		
Trading investments at fair value			165,100
Available-for-sale investments (at cost)	$181,800		
Plus valuation allowance for available-for-sale investments	46,200		
Available-for-sale investments at fair value			228,000

Investments:
Held-to-maturity investments	40,000
Investment in Myers Company (equity method)	7,488,000

Stockholders' equity:
Common stock	$ XX,XXX
Paid-in capital in excess of par	XXX,XXX
Retained earnings	XXX,XXX
Unrealized gain on available-for-sale investments	46,200
Total stockholders' equity	$ XXX,XXX

Key Terms

accumulated other comprehensive income (739)
available-for-sale securities (732)
business combination (729)
comprehensive income (739)
consolidated financial statements (729)
cost method (726)

debt securities (722)
dividend yield (737)
equity method (727)
equity securities (722)
fair value (730)
held-to-maturity securities (734)
investee (725)

investments (722)
investor (725)
other comprehensive income (739)
parent company (729)
subsidiary company (729)
trading securities (730)
unrealized gain or loss (730)

Discussion Questions

1. Why might a business invest cash in temporary investments?

2. What causes a gain or loss on the sale of a bond investment?

3. When is the equity method the appropriate accounting for equity investments?

4. How does the accounting for a dividend received differ between the cost method and the equity method?

5. If an investor owns more than 50% of an investee, how is the investment treated on the investor's financial statements?

6. What is the major difference in the accounting for a portfolio of trading securities and a portfolio of available-for-sale securities?

7. If Valuation Allowance for Available-for-Sale Investments has a credit balance, how is it treated on the balance sheet?

8. How would a debit balance in Unrealized Gain (Loss) on Available-for-Sale Investments be reported in the financial statements?

9. What are the factors contributing to the trend toward fair value accounting?

10. How are the balance sheet and income statement affected by fair value accounting?

Practice Exercises

Example Exercises

EE 15-1 p. 725   **PE 15-1A**   Bond investment transactions   OBJ. 2

Journalize the entries to record the following selected bond investment transactions for Hall Trust:

a. Purchased for cash $240,000 of Medina City 6% bonds at 100 plus accrued interest of $3,600.
b. Received first semiannual interest payment.
c. Sold $120,000 of the bonds at 98 plus accrued interest of $600.

EE 15-1 p. 725   **PE 15-1B**   Bond investment transactions   OBJ. 2

Journalize the entries to record the following selected bond investment transactions for Starks Products:

a. Purchased for cash $120,000 of Iceline, Inc. 5% bonds at 100 plus accrued interest of $1,000.
b. Received first semiannual interest payment.
c. Sold $60,000 of the bonds at 101 plus accrued interest of $500.

EE 15-2 p. 727   **PE 15-2A**   Stock investment transactions   OBJ. 3

On January 23, 10,000 shares of Tolle Company are acquired at a price of $30 per share plus a $100 brokerage commission. On April 12, a $0.50-per-share dividend was received on the Tolle Company stock. On June 10, 4,000 shares of the Tolle Company stock were sold for $34 per share less a $100 brokerage commission. Prepare the journal entries for the original purchase, the dividend, and the sale under the cost method.

EE 15-2 p. 727   **PE 15-2B**   Stock investment transactions   OBJ. 3

On September 12, 2,000 shares of Aspen Company are acquired at a price of $50 per share plus a $200 brokerage commission. On October 15, a $0.50-per-share dividend was received on the Aspen Company stock. On November 10, 1,200 shares of the Aspen Company stock were sold for $42 per share less a $150 brokerage commission. Prepare the journal entries for the original purchase, the dividend, and the sale under the cost method.

Chapter 15 Investments and Fair Value Accounting 747

EE 15-3 p. 729 **PE 15-3A Equity method** OBJ. 3

On January 2, Cohan Company acquired 40% of the outstanding stock of Sanger Company for $500,000. For the year ended December 31, Sanger Company earned income of $80,000 and paid dividends of $30,000. Prepare the entries for Cohan Company for the purchase of the stock, the share of Sanger income, and the dividends received from Sanger Company.

EE 15-3 p. 729 **PE 15-3B Equity method** OBJ. 3

On January 2, Yorkshire Company acquired 40% of the outstanding stock of Fain Company for $600,000. For the year ended December 31, Fain Company earned income of $140,000 and paid dividends of $50,000. Prepare the entries for Yorkshire Company for the purchase of the stock, the share of Fain income, and the dividends received from Fain Company.

EE 15-4 p. 731 **PE 15-4A Valuing trading securities at fair value** OBJ. 4

On January 1, Valuation Allowance for Trading Investments had a zero balance. On December 31, the cost of the trading securities portfolio was $260,000, and the fair value was $214,000. Prepare the December 31 adjusting journal entry to record the unrealized gain or loss on trading investments.

EE 15-4 p. 731 **PE 15-4B Valuing trading securities at fair value** OBJ. 4

On January 1, Valuation Allowance for Trading Investments had a zero balance. On December 31, the cost of the trading securities portfolio was $41,500, and the fair value was $46,300. Prepare the December 31 adjusting journal entry to record the unrealized gain or loss on trading investments.

EE 15-5 p. 734 **PE 15-5A Valuing available-for-sale securities at fair value** OBJ. 4

On January 1, Valuation Allowance for Available-for-Sale Investments had a zero balance. On December 31, the cost of the available-for-sale securities was $60,250, and the fair value was $57,500. Prepare the adjusting entry to record the unrealized gain or loss on available-for-sale investments on December 31.

EE 15-5 p. 734 **PE 15-5B Valuing available-for-sale securities at fair value** OBJ. 4

On January 1, Valuation Allowance for Available-for-Sale Investments had a zero balance. On December 31, the cost of the available-for-sale securities was $24,260, and the fair value was $26,350. Prepare the adjusting entry to record the unrealized gain or loss on available-for-sale investments on December 31.

EE 15-6 p. 738 **PE 15-6A Dividend yield** OBJ. 6

On June 30, Setzer Corporation had a market price of $100 per share of common stock. For the previous year, Setzer paid an annual dividend of $4.00. Compute the dividend yield for Setzer Corporation.

EE 15-6 p. 738 **PE 15-6B Dividend yield** OBJ. 6

On October 23, Wilkerson Company had a market price of $40 per share of common stock. For the previous year, Wilkerson paid an annual dividend of $1.20. Compute the dividend yield for Wilkerson Company.

Exercises

EX 15-1 Entries for investment in bonds, interest, and sale of bonds OBJ. 2

Gonzalez Company acquired $200,000 of Walker Co., 6% bonds on May 1 at their face amount. Interest is paid semiannually on May 1 and November 1. On November 1, Gonzalez Company sold $70,000 of the bonds for 97.

Journalize entries to record the following in Year 1:

a. The initial acquisition of the bonds on May 1.
b. The semiannual interest received on November 1.
c. The sale of the bonds on November 1.
d. The accrual of $1,300 interest on December 31.

EX 15-2 Entries for investments in bonds, interest, and sale of bonds OBJ. 2

Torres Investments acquired $160,000 of Murphy Corp., 5% bonds at their face amount on October 1, Year 1. The bonds pay interest on October 1 and April 1. On April 1, Year 2, Torres sold $60,000 of Murphy Corp. bonds at 102.

Journalize the entries to record the following:

a. The initial acquisition of the Murphy Corp. bonds on October 1, Year 1.
b. The adjusting entry for three months of accrued interest earned on the Murphy Corp. bonds on December 31, Year 1.
c. The receipt of semiannual interest on April 1, Year 2.
d. The sale of $60,000 of Murphy Corp. bonds on April 1, Year 2, at 102.

✔ Oct. 31, Loss on sale of investments, $400

EX 15-3 Entries for investment in bonds, interest, and sale of bonds OBJ. 2

Bocelli Co. purchased $120,000 of 6%, 20-year Sanz County bonds on May 11, Year 1, directly from the county, at their face amount plus accrued interest. The bonds pay semiannual interest on April 1 and October 1. On October 31, Year 1, Bocelli Co. sold $30,000 of the Sanz County bonds at 99 plus $150 accrued interest less a $100 brokerage commission.

Provide journal entries for the following:

a. The purchase of the bonds on May 11 plus 40 days of accrued interest.
b. Semiannual interest on October 1.
c. Sale of the bonds on October 31.
d. Adjusting entry for accrued interest of $1,365 on December 31, Year 1.

✔ Aug. 30, Loss on sale of investments, $700

EX 15-4 Entries for investment in bonds, interest, and sale of bonds OBJ. 2

The following bond investment transactions were completed during a recent year by Starks Company:

Year 1

Jan. 31. Purchased 75, $1,000 government bonds at 100 plus accrued interest of $375 (one month). The bonds pay 6% annual interest on July 1 and January 1.

July 1. Received semiannual interest on bond investment.

Aug. 30. Sold 35, $1,000 bonds at 98 plus $350 accrued interest (two months).

a. Journalize the entries for these transactions.
b. Provide the December 31, Year 1, adjusting journal entry for semiannual interest earned on the bonds.

EX 15-5 Interest on bond investments OBJ. 2

On February 1, Hansen Company purchased $120,000 of 5%, 20-year Knight Company bonds at their face amount plus one month's accrued interest. The bonds pay interest on January 1 and July 1. On October 1, Hansen Company sold $40,000 of the Knight Company bonds acquired on February 1, plus three months' accrued interest. On December 31, three months' interest was accrued for the remaining bonds.

Determine the interest earned by Hansen Company on Knight Company bonds for the year.

Chapter 15 Investments and Fair Value Accounting

✔ c. Gain on sale of investments, $47,860

EX 15-6 Entries for investment in stock, receipt of dividends, and sale of shares   OBJ. 3

On February 22, Stewart Corporation acquired 12,000 shares of the 400,000 outstanding shares of Edwards Co. common stock at $50 plus commission charges of $120. On June 1, a cash dividend of $1.40 per share was received. On November 12, 4,000 shares were sold at $62 less commission charges of $100.

Using the cost method, journalize the entries for (a) the purchase of stock, (b) the receipt of dividends, and (c) the sale of 4,000 shares.

✔ Sept. 10, Loss on sale of investments, $6,150

EX 15-7 Entries for investment in stock, receipt of dividends, and sale of shares   OBJ. 3

The following equity investment transactions were completed by Romero Company during a recent year:

Apr. 10. Purchased 5,000 shares of Dixon Company for a price of $25 per share plus a brokerage commission of $75.

July 8. Received a quarterly dividend of $0.60 per share on the Dixon Company investment.

Sept. 10. Sold 2,000 shares for a price of $22 per share less a brokerage commission of $120.

Journalize the entries for these transactions.

✔ Sept. 25, Dividend revenue, $520

EX 15-8 Entries for stock investments, dividends, and sale of stock   OBJ. 3

Yerbury Corp. manufactures construction equipment. Journalize the entries to record the following selected equity investment transactions completed by Yerbury during a recent year:

Feb. 2. Purchased for cash 5,300 shares of Wong Inc. stock for $20 per share plus a $110 brokerage commission.

Mar. 6. Received dividends of $0.30 per share on Wong Inc. stock.

June 7. Purchased 2,000 shares of Wong Inc. stock for $26 per share plus a $120 brokerage commission.

July 26. Sold 6,000 shares of Wong Inc. stock for $35 per share less a $100 brokerage commission. Yerbury assumes that the first investments purchased are the first investments sold.

Sept. 25. Received dividends of $0.40 per share on Wong Inc. stock.

EX 15-9 Entries for stock investments, dividends, and sale of stock   OBJ. 3

Seamus Industries Inc. buys and sells investments as part of its ongoing cash management. The following investment transactions were completed during the year:

Feb. 24. Acquired 1,000 shares of Tett Co. stock for $85 per share plus a $150 brokerage commission.

May 16. Acquired 2,500 shares of Issacson Co. stock for $36 per share plus a $100 commission.

July 14. Sold 400 shares of Tett Co. stock for $100 per share less a $75 brokerage commission.

Aug. 12. Sold 750 shares of Issacson Co. stock for $32.50 per share less an $80 brokerage commission.

Oct. 31. Received dividends of $0.40 per share on Tett Co. stock.

Journalize the entries for these transactions.

EX 15-10 Equity method for stock investment   OBJ. 3

At a total cost of $5,600,000, Herrera Corporation acquired 280,000 shares of Tran Corp. common stock as a long-term investment. Herrera Corporation uses the equity method of accounting for this investment. Tran Corp. has 800,000 shares of common stock outstanding, including the shares acquired by Herrera Corporation.

(*Continued*)

a. Journalize the entries by Herrera Corporation to record the following information:
   1. Tran Corp. reports net income of $600,000 for the current period.
   2. A cash dividend of $0.50 per common share is paid by Tran Corp. during the current period.
b.  Why is the equity method appropriate for the Tran Corp. investment?

EX 15-11 Equity method for stock investment   OBJ. 3

On January 4, Year 1, Ferguson Company purchased 480,000 shares of Silva Company directly from one of the founders for a price of $30 per share. Silva has 1,200,000 shares outstanding, including the Daniels shares. On July 2, Year 1, Silva paid $750,000 in total dividends to its shareholders. On December 31, Year 1, Silva reported a net income of $2,000,000 for the year. Ferguson uses the equity method in accounting for its investment in Silva.

✔ b. $14,900,000

a. Provide the Ferguson Company journal entries for the transactions involving its investment in Silva Company during Year 1.

b. Determine the December 31, Year 1, balance of the investment in Silva Company stock account.

EX 15-12 Equity method for stock investment with loss   OBJ. 3

On January 6, Year 1, Bulldog Co. purchased 34% of the outstanding stock of Gator Co. for $212,000. Gator Co. paid total dividends of $24,000 to all shareholders on June 30. Gator had a net loss of $56,000 for Year 1.

a. Journalize Bulldog's purchase of the stock, receipt of the dividends, and the adjusting entry for the equity loss in Gator Co. stock.

b. Compute the balance of Investment in Gator Co. Stock on December 31, Year 1.

c. How does valuing an investment under the equity method differ from valuing an investment at fair value?

EX 15-13 Equity method for stock investment   OBJ. 3

Hawkeye Company's balance sheet reported, under the equity method, its long-term investment in Raven Company for comparative years as follows:

	Dec. 31, Year 2	Dec. 31, Year 1
Investment in Raven Company stock (in millions)	$281	$264

In addition, the Year 2 Hawkeye Company income statement disclosed equity earnings in the Raven Company investment as $25 million. Hawkeye Company neither purchased nor sold Raven Company stock during Year 2. The fair value of the Raven Company stock investment on December 31, Year 2, was $310 million.

Explain the change in Investment in Raven Company Stock from December 31, Year 1, to December 31, Year 2.

EX 15-14 Missing statement items, trading investments   OBJ. 4

JED Capital Inc. makes investments in trading securities. Selected income statement items for the years ended December 31, Year 2 and Year 3, plus selected items from comparative balance sheets, are as follows:

✔ g. $6,000

JED Capital Inc.
Selected Income Statement Items
For the Years Ended December 31, Year 2 and Year 3

	Year 2	Year 3
Operating income	a.	e.
Unrealized gain (loss)	b.	$(11,000)
Net income	c.	28,000

Chapter 15 Investments and Fair Value Accounting 751

JED Capital Inc.
Selected Balance Sheet Items
December 31, Year 1, Year 2, and Year 3

	Dec. 31, Year 1	Dec. 31, Year 2	Dec. 31, Year 3
Trading investments, at cost	$144,000	$168,000	$205,000
Valuation allowance for trading investments	(12,000)	17,000	g.
Trading investments, at fair value	d.	f.	h.
Retained earnings	$210,000	$245,000	i.

There were no dividends.
Determine the missing lettered items.

EX 15-15 Fair value journal entries, trading investments OBJ. 3, 4

The investments of Charger Inc. include a single investment: 14,500 shares of Raiders Inc. common stock purchased on February 24, Year 1, for $38 per share including brokerage commission. These shares were classified as trading securities. As of the December 31, Year 1, balance sheet date, the share price had increased to $42 per share.

a. Journalize the entries to acquire the investment on February 24 and record the adjustment to fair value on December 31, Year 1.

b. How is the unrealized gain or loss for trading investments reported on the financial statements?

EX 15-16 Fair value journal entries, trading investments OBJ. 3, 4

Gruden Bancorp Inc. purchased a portfolio of trading securities during Year 1. The cost and fair value of this portfolio on December 31, Year 1, was as follows:

Name	Number of Shares	Total Cost	Total Fair Value
Griffin Inc.	1,600	$ 40,000	$ 44,800
Luck Company	1,250	37,500	33,750
Wilson Company	1,000	40,000	37,000
Total		$117,500	$115,550

On May 10, Year 2, Gruden Bancorp Inc. purchased 1,200 shares of Carroll Inc. at $29 per share plus a $100 brokerage commission.
Provide the journal entries to record the following:

a. The adjustment of the trading security portfolio to fair value on December 31, Year 1.
b. The May 10, Year 2, purchase of Carroll Inc. stock.

EX 15-17 Fair value journal entries, trading investments OBJ. 3, 4

Last Unguaranteed Financial Inc. purchased the following trading securities during Year 1, its first year of operations:

✔ a. Dec. 31, Year 1, Unrealized gain on trading investments, $17,500

Name	Number of Shares	Cost
Arden Enterprises Inc.	5,000	$150,000
French Broad Industries Inc.	2,750	66,000
Pisgah Construction Inc.	1,600	104,000
Total		$320,000

The market price per share for the trading security portfolio on December 31, Year 1, was as follows:

	Market Price per Share, Dec. 31, Year 1
Arden Enterprises Inc.	$34
French Broad Industries Inc.	26
Pisgah Construction Inc.	60

a. Provide the journal entry to adjust the trading security portfolio to fair value on December 31, Year 1.

b. Assume that the market prices of the portfolio were the same on December 31, Year 2, as they were on December 31, Year 1. What would be the journal entry to adjust the portfolio to fair value?

EX 15-18 Balance sheet presentation, trading investments — OBJ. 4

The income statement for Delta-tec Inc. for the year ended December 31, Year 2, was as follows:

Delta-tec Inc.
Income Statement (selected items)
For the Year Ended December 31, Year 2

Income from operations	$299,700
Gain on sale of investments	17,800
Unrealized loss on trading investments	(72,500)
Net income	$245,000

The balance sheet dated December 31, Year 1, showed a Retained Earnings balance of $825,000. During Year 2, the company purchased trading investments for the first time at a cost of $346,000. In addition, trading investments with a cost of $66,000 were sold at a gain during Year 2. The company paid $65,000 in dividends during Year 2.

a. Determine the December 31, Year 2, Retained Earnings balance.
b. Provide the December 31, Year 2, balance sheet presentation for Trading Investments.

EX 15-19 Missing statement items, available-for-sale securities — OBJ. 4

✔ f. $(11,000)

Highland Industries Inc. makes investments in available-for-sale securities. Selected income statement items for the years ended December 31, Year 2 and Year 3, plus selected items from comparative balance sheets, are as follows:

Highland Industries Inc.
Selected Income Statement Items
For the Years Ended December 31, Year 2 and Year 3

	Year 2	Year 3
Operating income	a.	g.
Gain (loss) from sale of investments	$7,500	$(12,000)
Net income (loss)	b.	(21,000)

Highland Industries Inc.
Selected Balance Sheet Items
December 31, Year 1, Year 2, and Year 3

	Dec. 31, Year 1	Dec. 31, Year 2	Dec. 31, Year 3
Assets			
Available-for-sale investments, at cost	$ 90,000	$ 86,000	$102,000
Valuation allowance for available-for-sale investments	12,000	(11,000)	h.
Available-for-sale investments, at fair value	c.	e.	i.
Stockholders' Equity			
Unrealized gain (loss) on available-for-sale investments	d.	f.	(16,400)
Retained earnings	$175,400	$220,000	j.

There were no dividends.
Determine the missing lettered items.

EX 15-20 Fair value journal entries, available-for-sale investments — OBJ. 3, 4

The investments of Steelers Inc. include a single investment: 33,100 shares of Bengals Inc. common stock purchased on September 12, Year 1, for $13 per share including brokerage commission. These shares were classified as available-for-sale securities. As of the December 31, Year 1, balance sheet date, the share price declined to $11 per share.

a. Journalize the entries to acquire the investment on September 12 and record the adjustment to fair value on December 31, Year 1.
b. How is the unrealized gain or loss for available-for-sale investments disclosed on the financial statements?

EX 15-21 Fair value journal entries, available-for-sale investments   OBJ. 3, 4

Hurricane Inc. purchased a portfolio of available-for-sale securities in Year 1, its first year of operations. The cost and fair value of this portfolio on December 31, Year 1, was as follows:

Name	Number of Shares	Total Cost	Total Fair Value
Tornado Inc.	800	$14,000	$15,600
Tsunami Corp.	1,250	31,250	35,000
Typhoon Corp.	2,140	43,870	42,800
Total		$89,120	$93,400

On June 12, Year 2, Hurricane purchased 1,450 shares of Rogue Wave Inc. at $45 per share plus a $100 brokerage commission.

a. Provide the journal entries to record the following:

1. The adjustment of the available-for-sale security portfolio to fair value on December 31, Year 1.

2. The June 12, Year 2, purchase of Rogue Wave Inc. stock.

b. How are unrealized gains and losses treated differently for available-for-sale securities than for trading securities?

Excel

EX 15-22 Fair value journal entries, available-for-sale investments   OBJ. 3, 4

Storm, Inc. purchased the following available-for-sale securities during Year 1, its first year of operations:

Name	Number of Shares	Cost
Dust Devil, Inc.	1,900	$ 81,700
Gale Co.	850	68,000
Whirlwind Co.	2,850	114,000
Total		$263,700

The market price per share for the available-for-sale security portfolio on December 31, Year 1, was as follows:

	Market Price per Share, Dec. 31, Year 1
Dust Devil, Inc.	$40
Gale Co.	75
Whirlwind Co.	42

a. Provide the journal entry to adjust the available-for-sale security portfolio to fair value on December 31, Year 1.

b. Describe the income statement impact from the December 31, Year 1, journal entry.

EX 15-23 Balance sheet presentation of available-for-sale investments   OBJ. 4

During Year 1, its first year of operations, Galileo Company purchased two available-for-sale investments as follows:

Security	Shares Purchased	Cost
Hawking Inc.	900	$44,000
Pavlov Co.	1,780	38,000

Assume that as of December 31, Year 1, the Hawking Inc. stock had a market value of $50 per share and the Pavlov Co. stock had a market value of $24 per share. Galileo Company had net income of $300,000 and paid no dividends for the year ended December 31, Year 1. All of the available-for-sale investments are classified as current assets.

(*Continued*)

754 Chapter 15 Investments and Fair Value Accounting

a. Prepare the Current Assets section of the balance sheet presentation for the available-for-sale investments.

b. Prepare the Stockholders' Equity section of the balance sheet to reflect the earnings and unrealized gain (loss) for the available-for-sale investments.

EX 15-24 Balance sheet presentation of available-for-sale investments OBJ. 4

During Year 2, Copernicus Corporation held a portfolio of available-for-sale securities having a cost of $185,000. There were no purchases or sales of investments during the year. The market values at the beginning and end of the year were $225,000 and $160,000, respectively. The net income for Year 2 was $180,000, and no dividends were paid during the year. The Stockholders' Equity section of the balance sheet was as follows on December 31, Year 1:

Copernicus Corporation
Stockholders' Equity
December 31, Year 1

Common stock	$ 50,000
Paid-in capital in excess of par	250,000
Retained earnings	340,000
Unrealized gain on available-for-sale investments	40,000
Total	$680,000

Prepare the Stockholders' Equity section of the balance sheet for December 31, Year 2.

EX 15-25 Dividend yield OBJ. 6

At the market close on May 12 of a recent year, **McDonald's Corporation** had a closing stock price of $129.51. In addition, McDonald's Corporation had a dividend per share of $3.56 during the previous year.

Determine McDonald's Corporation's dividend yield. Round to one decimal place.

EX 15-26 Dividend yield OBJ. 6

✔ a. Dec. 31, current year, 2.24%

The market price for **Microsoft Corporation** closed at $55.48 and $46.45 on December 31, current year, and previous year, respectively. The dividends per share were $1.24 for current year and $1.12 for previous year.

a. Determine the dividend yield for Microsoft on December 31, current year, and previous year. Round percentages to two decimal places.

b. Interpret these measures.

EX 15-27 Dividend yield OBJ. 6

eBay Inc. developed a web-based marketplace at www.ebay.com, in which individuals can buy and sell a variety of items. eBay also acquired **PayPal**, an online payments system that allows businesses and individuals to send and receive online payments securely. In a recent annual report, eBay published the following dividend policy:

We have never paid cash dividends on our stock and currently anticipate that we will continue to retain any future earnings for the foreseeable future.

Given eBay's dividend policy, why would investors be attracted to its stock?

Appendix
EX 15-28 Comprehensive income

On May 12, Year 1, Chewco Co. purchased 2,000 shares of Jedi Inc. for $112 per share, including the brokerage commission. The Jedi investment was classified as an available-for-sale security. On December 31, Year 1, the fair value of Jedi Inc. was $124 per share. The net income of Chewco Co. was $50,000 for Year 1.

Compute the comprehensive income for Chewco Co. for the year ended December 31, Year 1.

Appendix
EX 15-29 Comprehensive income

On December 31, Year 1, Valur Co. had the following available-for-sale investment disclosure within the Current Assets section of the balance sheet:

Available-for-sale investments (at cost)	$145,000
Plus valuation allowance for available-for-sale investments	40,000
Available-for-sale investments (at fair value)	$185,000

There were no purchases or sales of available-for-sale investments during Year 2. On December 31, Year 2, the fair value of the available-for-sale investment portfolio was $200,000. The net income of Valur Co. was $210,000 for Year 2.

Compute the comprehensive income for Valur Co. for the year ended December 31, Year 2.

Problems: Series A

PR 15-1A Debt investment transactions, available-for-sale valuation   OBJ. 2, 4

Soto Industries Inc. is an athletic footware company that began operations on January 1, Year 1. The following transactions relate to debt investments acquired by Soto Industries Inc., which has a fiscal year ending on December 31:

Year 1

Apr. 1. Purchased $100,000 of Welch Co. 6%, 15-year bonds at their face amount plus accrued interest of $500. The bonds pay interest semiannually on March 1 and September 1.

June 1. Purchased $210,000 of Bailey 4%, 10-year bonds at their face amount plus accrued interest of $700. The bonds pay interest semiannually on May 1 and November 1.

Sept. 1. Received semiannual interest on the Welch Co. bonds.

       30. Sold $40,000 of Welch Co. bonds at 97 plus accrued interest of $200.

Nov. 1. Received semiannual interest on the Bailey bonds.

Dec. 31. Accrued $1,200 interest on the Welch Co. bonds.

     31. Accrued $1,400 interest on the Bailey bonds.

Year 2

Mar. 1. Received semiannual interest on the Welch Co. bonds.

May   1. Received semiannual interest on the Bailey bonds.

Instructions

1. Journalize the entries to record these transactions.
2. If the bond portfolio is classified as available for sale, what impact would this have on financial statement disclosure?

PR 15-2A Stock investment transactions, trading securities   OBJ. 3, 4

Rios Financial Co. is a regional insurance company that began operations on January 1, Year 1. The following transactions relate to trading securities acquired by Rios Financial Co., which has a fiscal year ending on December 31:

Year 1

Feb. 1. Purchased 7,500 shares of Caldwell Inc. as a trading security at $50 per share plus a brokerage commission of $75.

May   1. Purchased 3,000 shares of Holland Inc. as a trading security at $42 plus a brokerage commission of $90.

(Continued)

July 1. Sold 4,500 shares of Caldwell Inc. for $46 per share less a $110 brokerage commission.

       31. Received an annual dividend of $0.50 per share on Caldwell Inc. stock.

Dec. 31. The portfolio of trading securities was adjusted to fair values of $47 and $40 per share for Caldwell Inc. and Holland Inc., respectively.

Year 2

Apr. 1. Purchased 5,000 shares of Fuller Inc. as a trading security at $25 per share plus a $100 brokerage commission.

July 31. Received an annual dividend of $0.52 per share on Caldwell Inc. stock.

Oct. 14. Sold 1,000 shares of Fuller Inc. for $28 per share less a $110 brokerage commission.

Dec. 31. The portfolio of trading securities had a cost of $376,200 and a fair value of $420,000, requiring a debit balance in Valuation Allowance for Trading Investments of $43,800 ($420,000 − $376,200). Thus, the credit balance from December 31, Year 1, is to be adjusted to the new balance.

Instructions

1. Journalize the entries to record these transactions.
2. Prepare the investment-related current asset balance sheet presentation for Rios Financial Co. on December 31, Year 2.
3. How are unrealized gains or losses on trading investments presented in the financial statements of Rios Financial Co.?

PR 15-3A Stock investment transactions, equity method and available-for-sale securities OBJ. 3, 4

Forte Inc. produces and sells theater set designs and costumes. The company began operations on January 1, Year 1. The following transactions relate to securities acquired by Forte Inc., which has a fiscal year ending on December 31:

Year 1

Jan. 22. Purchased 22,000 shares of Sankal Inc. as an available-for-sale security at $18 per share, including the brokerage commission.

Mar. 8. Received a cash dividend of $0.22 per share on Sankal Inc. stock.

Sept. 8. A cash dividend of $0.25 per share was received on the Sankal stock.

Oct. 17. Sold 3,000 shares of Sankal Inc. stock at $16 per share less a brokerage commission of $75.

Dec. 31. Sankal Inc. is classified as an available-for-sale investment and is adjusted to a fair value of $25 per share. Use the valuation allowance for available-for-sale investments account in making the adjustment.

Year 2

Jan. 10. Purchased an influential interest in Imboden Inc. for $720,000 by purchasing 96,000 shares directly from the estate of the founder of Imboden Inc. There are 300,000 shares of Imboden Inc. stock outstanding.

Mar. 10. Received a cash dividend of $0.30 per share on Sankal Inc. stock.

Sept. 12. Received a cash dividend of $0.25 per share plus an extra dividend of $0.05 per share on Sankal Inc. stock.

Dec. 31. Received $57,600 of cash dividends on Imboden Inc. stock. Imboden Inc. reported net income of $450,000 in Year 2. Forte Inc. uses the equity method of accounting for its investment in Imboden Inc.

       31. Sankal Inc. is classified as an available-for-sale investment and is adjusted to a fair value of $22 per share. Use the valuation allowance for available-for-sale investments account in making the adjustment for the decrease in fair value from $25 to $22 per share.

Instructions

1. Journalize the entries to record these transactions.
2. Prepare the investment-related asset and stockholders' equity balance sheet presentation for Forte Inc. on December 31, Year 2, assuming that the Retained Earnings balance on December 31, Year 2, is $389,000.

PR 15-4A Investment reporting   OBJ. 2, 3, 4

✓ h. $(5,800)

O'Brien Industries Inc. is a book publisher. The comparative unclassified balance sheets for December 31, Year 2 and Year 1 follow. Selected missing balances are shown by letters.

O'Brien Industries Inc.
Balance Sheet
December 31, Year 2 and Year 1

	Dec. 31, Year 2	Dec. 31, Year 1
Cash	$233,000	$220,000
Accounts receivable (net)	136,530	138,000
Available-for-sale investments (at cost)—Note 1	$ a.	$103,770
Less valuation allowance for available-for-sale investments	b.	2,500
Available-for-sale investments (fair value)	$ c.	$101,270
Interest receivable	$ d.	—
Investment in Jolly Roger Co. stock—Note 2	e.	$ 77,000
Office equipment (net)	115,000	130,000
Total assets	$ f.	$666,270
Accounts payable	$ 69,400	$ 65,000
Common stock	70,000	70,000
Excess of issue price over par	225,000	225,000
Retained earnings	g.	308,770
Unrealized gain (loss) on available-for-sale investments	h.	(2,500)
Total liabilities and stockholders' equity	$ i.	$666,270

Note 1. Investments are classified as available for sale. The investments at cost and fair value on December 31, Year 1, are as follows:

	No. of Shares	Cost per Share	Total Cost	Total Fair Value
Bernard Co. stock	2,250	$17	$ 38,250	$ 37,500
Chadwick Co. stock	1,260	52	65,520	63,770
			$103,770	$101,270

Note 2. The investment in Jolly Roger Co. stock is an equity method investment representing 30% of the outstanding shares of Jolly Roger Co.

The following selected investment transactions occurred during Year 2:

May 5. Purchased 3,080 shares of Gozar Inc. at $30 per share including brokerage commission. Gozar Inc. is classified as an available-for-sale security.

Oct. 1. Purchased $40,000 of Nightline Co. 6%, 10-year bonds at 100. The bonds are classified as available for sale. The bonds pay interest on October 1 and April 1.

  9. Dividends of $12,500 are received on the Jolly Roger Co. investment.

Dec. 31. Jolly Roger Co. reported a total net income of $112,000 for Year 2. O'Brien Industries Inc. recorded equity earnings for its share of Jolly Roger Co. net income.

 31. Accrued three months of interest on the Nightline bonds.

 31. Adjusted the available-for-sale investment portfolio to fair value, using the following fair value per-share amounts:

Available-for-Sale Investments	Fair Value
Bernard Co. stock	$15.40 per share
Chadwick Co. stock	$46.00 per share
Gozar Inc. stock	$32.00 per share
Nightline Co. bonds	$98 per $100 of face amount

(Continued)

Dec. 31. Closed the O'Brien Industries Inc. net income of $146,230. O'Brien Industries Inc. paid no dividends during the year.

Instructions

Determine the missing letters in the unclassified balance sheet. Provide appropriate supporting calculations.

Problems: Series B

PR 15-1B Debt investment transactions, available-for-sale valuation OBJ. 2, 4

Rekya Mart Inc. is a general merchandise retail company that began operations on January 1, Year 1. The following transactions relate to debt investments acquired by Rekya Mart Inc., which has a fiscal year ending on December 31:

Year 1

Apr. 1. Purchased $90,000 of Smoke Bay 6%, 10-year bonds at their face amount plus accrued interest of $900. The bonds pay interest semiannually on February 1 and August 1.

May 16. Purchased $42,000 of Geotherma Co. 4%, 12-year bonds at their face amount plus accrued interest of $70. The bonds pay interest semiannually on May 1 and November 1.

Aug. 1. Received semiannual interest on the Smoke Bay bonds.

Sept. 1. Sold $12,000 of Smoke Bay bonds at 101 plus accrued interest of $60.

Nov. 1. Received semiannual interest on the Geotherma Co. bonds.

Dec. 31. Accrued $1,950 interest on the Smoke Bay bonds.

31. Accrued $280 interest on the Geotherma Co. bonds.

Year 2

Feb. 1. Received semiannual interest on the Smoke Bay bonds.

May 1. Received semiannual interest on the Geotherma Co. bonds.

Instructions

1. Journalize the entries to record these transactions.
2. If the bond portfolio is classified as available for sale, what impact would this have on financial statement disclosure?

PR 15-2B Stock investment transactions, trading securities OBJ. 3, 4

Zeus Investments Inc. is a regional investment company that began operations on January 1, Year 1. The following transactions relate to trading securities acquired by Zeus Investments Inc., which has a fiscal year ending on December 31:

Year 1

Feb. 14. Purchased 4,800 shares of Apollo Inc. as a trading security at $26 per share plus a brokerage commission of $192.

Apr. 1. Purchased 2,300 shares of Ares Inc. as a trading security at $19 per share plus a brokerage commission of $92.

June 1. Sold 600 shares of Apollo Inc. for $32 per share less a $100 brokerage commission.

27. Received an annual dividend of $0.20 per share on Apollo Inc. stock.

Dec. 31. The portfolio of trading securities was adjusted to fair values of $33 and $18.50 per share for Apollo Inc. and Ares Inc., respectively.

Year 2

Mar. 14. Purchased 1,200 shares of Athena Inc. as a trading security at $65 per share plus a $120 brokerage commission.

June 26. Received an annual dividend of $0.21 per share on Apollo Inc. stock.

July 30. Sold 480 shares of Athena Inc. for $60 per share less a $50 brokerage commission.

Dec. 31. The portfolio of trading securities had a cost of $200,032 and a fair value of $188,000, requiring a credit balance in Valuation Allowance for Trading Investments of $12,032 ($188,000 − $200,032). Thus, the debit balance from December 31, Year 1, is to be adjusted to the new balance.

Instructions

1. Journalize the entries to record these transactions.
2. Prepare the investment-related current asset balance sheet presentation for Zeus Investments Inc. on December 31, Year 2.
3. How are unrealized gains or losses on trading investments presented in the financial statements of Zeus Investments Inc.?

PR 15-3B Stock investment transactions, equity method and available-for-sale securities   OBJ. 3, 4

Glacier Products Inc. is a wholesaler of rock climbing gear. The company began operations on January 1, Year 1. The following transactions relate to securities acquired by Glacier Products Inc., which has a fiscal year ending on December 31:

Year 1

Jan. 18. Purchased 9,000 shares of Malmo Inc. as an available-for-sale investment at $40 per share, including the brokerage commission.

July 22. A cash dividend of $3 per share was received on the Malmo stock.

Oct. 5. Sold 500 shares of Malmo Inc. stock at $58 per share less a brokerage commission of $100.

Dec. 18. Received a regular cash dividend of $30 per share on Malmo Inc. stock.

31. Malmo Inc. is classified as an available-for-sale investment and is adjusted to a fair value of $36 per share. Use the valuation allowance for available-for-sale investments account in making the adjustment.

Year 2

Jan. 25. Purchased an influential interest in Helsi Co. for $800,000 by purchasing 75,000 shares directly from the estate of the founder of Helsi. There are 250,000 shares of Helsi Co. stock outstanding.

July 16. Received a cash dividend of $3 per share on Malmo Inc. stock.

Dec. 16. Received a cash dividend of $3 per share plus an extra dividend of $0.20 per share on Malmo Inc. stock.

31. Received $38,000 of cash dividends on Helsi Co. stock. Helsi Co. reported net income of $170,000 in Year 2. Glacier Products Inc. uses the equity method of accounting for its investment in Helsi Co.

31. Malmo Inc. is classified as an available-for-sale investment and is adjusted to a fair value of $44 per share. Use the valuation allowance for available-for-sale investments account in making the adjustment for the increase in fair value from $36 to $44 per share.

Instructions

1. Journalize the entries to record the preceding transactions.
2. Prepare the investment-related asset and stockholders' equity balance sheet presentation for Glacier Products Inc. on December 31, Year 2, assuming that the Retained Earnings balance on December 31, Year 2, is $700,000.

760 Chapter 15 Investments and Fair Value Accounting

PR 15-4B Investment reporting
OBJ. 2, 3, 4

✔ b. $4,680

Teasdale Inc. manufactures and sells commercial and residential security equipment. The comparative unclassified balance sheets for December 31, Year 2 and Year 1 are provided below. Selected missing balances are shown by letters.

Teasdale Inc.
Balance Sheet
December 31, Year 2 and Year 1

	Dec. 31, Year 2	Dec. 31, Year 1
Cash	$160,000	$156,000
Accounts receivable (net)	115,000	108,000
Available-for-sale investments (at cost)—Note 1	$ a.	$ 91,200
Plus valuation allowance for available-for-sale investments	b.	8,776
Available-for-sale investments (fair value)	$ c.	$ 99,976
Interest receivable	$ d.	—
Investment in Wright Co. stock—Note 2	e.	$ 69,200
Office equipment (net)	96,000	105,000
Total assets	$ f.	$538,176
Accounts payable	$ 91,000	$ 72,000
Common stock	80,000	80,000
Excess of issue price over par	250,000	250,000
Retained earnings	g.	127,400
Unrealized gain (loss) on available-for-sale investments	h.	8,776
Total liabilities and stockholders' equity	$ i.	$538,176

Note 1. Investments are classified as available for sale. The investments at cost and fair value on December 31, Year 1, are as follows:

	No. of Shares	Cost per Share	Total Cost	Total Fair Value
Alvarez Inc. stock	960	$38.00	$36,480	$39,936
Hirsch Inc. stock	1,900	28.80	54,720	60,040
			$91,200	$99,976

Note 2. The Investment in Wright Co. stock is an equity method investment representing 30% of the outstanding shares of Wright Co.

The following selected investment transactions occurred during Year 2:

Mar. 18. Purchased 800 shares of Richter Inc. at $40, including brokerage commission. Richter is classified as an available-for-sale security.

July 12. Dividends of $12,000 are received on the Wright Co. investment.

Oct. 1. Purchased $24,000 of Toon Co. 4%, 10-year bonds at 100. The bonds are classified as available for sale. The bonds pay interest on October 1 and April 1.

Dec. 31. Wright Co. reported a total net income of $80,000 for Year 2. Teasdale recorded equity earnings for its share of Wright Co. net income.

31. Accrued interest for three months on the Toon Co. bonds purchased on October 1.

31. Adjusted the available-for-sale investment portfolio to fair value, using the following fair value per-share amounts:

Available-for-Sale Investments	Fair Value
Alvarez Inc. stock	$41.50 per share
Hirsch Inc. stock	$26.00 per share
Richter Inc. stock	$48.00 per share
Toon Co. bonds	101 per $100 of face amount

31. Closed the Teasdale Inc. net income of $51,240. Teasdale Inc. paid no dividends during the year.

Instructions

Determine the missing letters in the unclassified balance sheet. Provide appropriate supporting calculations.

Comprehensive Problem 4

Selected transactions completed by Equinox Products Inc. during the fiscal year ended December 31, Year 1, were as follows:

a. Issued 15,000 shares of $20 par common stock at $30, receiving cash.
b. Issued 4,000 shares of $80 par preferred 5% stock at $100, receiving cash.
c. Issued $500,000 of 10-year, 5% bonds at 104, with interest payable semiannually.
d. Declared a quarterly dividend of $0.50 per share on common stock and $1.00 per share on preferred stock. On the date of record, 100,000 shares of common stock were outstanding, no treasury shares were held and 20,000 shares of preferred stock were outstanding.
e. Paid the cash dividends declared in (d).
f. Purchased 7,500 shares of Solstice Corp. at $40 per share plus a $150 brokerage commission. The investment is classified as an available-for-sale investment.
g. Purchased 8,000 shares of treasury common stock at $33 per share.
h. Purchased 40,000 shares of Pinkberry Co. stock directly from the founders for $24 per share. Pinkberry has 125,000 shares issued and outstanding. Equinox Products Inc. treated the investment as an equity method investment.
i. Declared a $1.00 quarterly cash dividend per share on preferred stock. On the date of record, 20,000 shares of preferred stock had been issued.
j. Paid the cash dividends to the preferred stockholders.
k. Received $27,500 dividend from Pinkberry Co. investment in (h).
l. Purchased $90,000 of Dream Inc. 10-year, 5% bonds, directly from the issuing company, at their face amount plus accrued interest of $375. The bonds are classified as a held-to-maturity long-term investment.
m. Sold, at $38 per share, 2,600 shares of treasury common stock purchased in (g).
n. Received a dividend of $0.60 per share from the Solstice Corp. investment in (f).
o. Sold 1,000 shares of Solstice Corp. at $45, including commission.
p. Recorded the payment of semiannual interest on the bonds issued in (c) and the amortization of the premium for six months. The amortization is determined using the straight-line method.
q. Accrued interest for three months on the Dream Inc. bonds purchased in (l).
r. Pinkberry Co. recorded total earnings of $240,000. Equinox Products recorded equity earnings for its share of Pinkberry Co. net income.
s. The fair value for Solstice Corp. stock was $39.02 per share on December 31, Year 1. The investment is adjusted to fair value, using a valuation allowance account. Assume that Valuation Allowance for Available-for-Sale Investments had a beginning balance of zero.

Instructions

1. Journalize the selected transactions.
2. After all of the transactions for the year ended December 31, Year 1, had been posted [including the transactions recorded in part (1) and all adjusting entries], the data that follows were taken from the records of Equinox Products Inc.

   a. Prepare a multiple-step income statement for the year ended December 31, Year 1, concluding with earnings per share. In computing earnings per share, assume that the average number of common shares outstanding was 100,000 and preferred dividends were $100,000. Round earnings per share to the nearest cent.
   b. Prepare a retained earnings statement for the year ended December 31, Year 1.
   c. Prepare a balance sheet in report form as of December 31, Year 1.

(Continued)

Income statement data:

Advertising expense	$ 150,000
Cost of merchandise sold	3,700,000
Delivery expense	30,000
Depreciation expense—office buildings and equipment	30,000
Depreciation expense—store buildings and equipment	100,000
Dividend revenue	4,500
Gain on sale of investment	4,980
Income from Pinkberry Co. investment	76,800
Income tax expense	140,500
Interest expense	21,000
Interest revenue	2,720
Miscellaneous administrative expense	7,500
Miscellaneous selling expense	14,000
Office rent expense	50,000
Office salaries expense	170,000
Office supplies expense	10,000
Sales	5,254,000
Sales commissions	185,000
Sales salaries expense	385,000
Store supplies expense	21,000

Retained earnings and balance sheet data:

Accounts payable	$ 194,300
Accounts receivable	545,000
Accumulated depreciation—office buildings and equipment	1,580,000
Accumulated depreciation—store buildings and equipment	4,126,000
Allowance for doubtful accounts	8,450
Available-for-sale investments (at cost)	260,130
Bonds payable, 5%, due 20Y2	500,000
Cash	246,000
Common stock, $20 par (400,000 shares authorized; 100,000 shares issued, 94,600 outstanding)	2,000,000
Dividends:	
Cash dividends for common stock	155,120
Cash dividends for preferred stock	100,000
Goodwill	500,000
Income tax payable	44,000
Interest receivable	1,125
Investment in Pinkberry Co. stock (equity method)	1,009,300
Investment in Dream Inc. bonds (long term)	90,000
Merchandise inventory (December 31, Year 1), at lower of cost (FIFO) or market	778,000
Office buildings and equipment	4,320,000
Paid-in capital from sale of treasury stock	13,000
Excess of issue price over par—common stock	886,800
Excess of issue price over par—preferred stock	150,000
Preferred 5% stock, $80 par (30,000 shares authorized; 20,000 shares issued)	1,600,000
Premium on bonds payable	19,000
Prepaid expenses	27,400
Retained earnings, January 1, Year 1	9,319,725
Store buildings and equipment	12,560,000
Treasury stock (5,400 shares of common stock at cost of $33 per share)	178,200
Unrealized gain (loss) on available-for-sale investments	(6,500)
Valuation allowance for available-for-sale investments	(6,500)

Cases & Projects

CP 15-1 Ethics in Action

Financial assets include stocks and bonds. These are fairly simple securities that can often be valued using quoted market prices. However, there are more complex financial instruments that do not have quoted market prices. These complex securities must still be valued on the balance sheet at fair value. Generally accepted accounting principles require that the reporting entity use assumptions in valuing investments when market prices or critical valuation inputs are unobservable.

What are the ethical considerations in making subjective valuations of these complex financial instruments?

CP 15-2 Reporting investments

Group Project

In groups of three or four, find the latest annual report for **Microsoft Corporation**. The annual report can be found on the company's website at www.microsoft.com/msft/default.mspx.

The notes to the financial statements include details of Microsoft's investments. Find the notes that provide details of its investments (Note 4) and the income from its investments (Note 3).

From these disclosures, answer the following questions:

1. What is the total cost of investments?
2. What is the fair value (recorded value) of investments?
3. What is the total unrealized gain from investments?
4. What is the total unrealized loss from investments?
5. What percent of total investments (at fair value) are:
   a. Cash and equivalents?
   b. Short-term investments?
   c. Equity and other investments (long term)?
6. What was the total combined dividend and interest revenue?
7. What was the recognized net gain or loss from sale of investments?

CP 15-3 Warren Buffett and "look-through" earnings

Berkshire Hathaway, the investment holding company of Warren Buffett, reports its "less than 20% ownership" investments according to generally accepted accounting principles. However, it also provides additional disclosures that it terms "look-through" earnings.

Warren Buffett states,

> Many of these companies (in the less than 20%-owned category) pay out relatively small proportions of their earnings in dividends. This means that only a small proportion of their earning power is recorded in our own current operating earnings. But, while our reported operating earnings reflect only the dividends received from such companies, our economic well-being is determined by their earnings, not their dividends.
>
> The value to Berkshire Hathaway of retained earnings (of our investees) is not determined by whether we own 100%, 50%, 20%, or 1% of the businesses in which they reside.... Our perspective on such "forgotten-but-not-gone" earnings is simple: the way they are accounted for is of no importance, but their ownership and subsequent utilization is all-important. We care not whether the auditors hear a tree fall in the forest; we do care who owns the tree and what's next done with it.
>
> I believe the best way to think about our earnings is in terms of "look-through" results, calculated as follows: Take $250 million, which is roughly our share of the operating earnings retained by our investees (<20% ownership holdings); subtract ... incremental taxes we would have owed had that $250 million been paid to us in dividends; then add the remainder, $220 million, to our reported earnings of $371 million. Thus, our "look-through" earnings were about $590 million.
> Source: Warren Buffett, *The Essays of Warren Buffett: Lessons for Corporate America*, edited by Lawrence A. Cunningham, pp. 180–183 (excerpted).

Write a brief memo to your instructor, explaining look through-earnings and why Mr. Buffet favors look-through earnings.

CP 15-4 Benefits of fair value

On July 16, 20Y1, Wyatt Corp. purchased 40 acres of land for $350,000. The land has been held for a future plant site until the current date, December 31, 20Y9. On December 18, 20Y9, TexoPete Inc. purchased 40 acres of land for $2,000,000 to be used for a distribution center. The TexoPete land is located next to the Wyatt Corp. land. Thus, both Wyatt Corp. and TexoPete Inc. own nearly identical pieces of land.

1. What are the valuations of land on the balance sheets of Wyatt Corp. and TexoPete Inc. using generally accepted accounting principles?
2. How might fair value accounting aid comparability when evaluating these two companies?

CP 15-5 International fair value accounting

International Financial Reporting Standard No. 16 provides companies the option of valuing property, plant, and equipment at either historical cost or fair value. If fair value is selected, then the property, plant, and equipment must be revalued periodically to fair value. Under fair value, if there is an increase in the value of the property, plant, and equipment during the reporting period, then the increase is credited to stockholders' equity. However, if there is a decrease in fair value, then the decrease is reported as an expense for the period.

How is the international accounting treatment for changes in fair value for property, plant, and equipment similar to investments?

# CHAPTER 16

Statement of Cash Flows

Chapters 1–4
Accounting Cycle

Chapter 5
Accounting Systems

Income Statement	Retained Earnings Statement	Balance Sheet	Statement of Cash Flows

Chapter 6 *Accounting for Merchandising Businesses*

Chapter 16 Statement of Cash Flows

Assets = Liabilities + Stockholders' Equity

Chapter 8 *Cash*
Chapter 9 *Receivables*
Chapter 7 *Inventories*
Chapter 10 *Fixed and Intangible Assets*
Chapter 15 *Investments*

Chapter 11 *Current Liabilities and Payroll*
Chapter 14 *Bonds and Notes*

Chapter 12 *Partnerships*
Chapter 13 *Corporations*

Chapter 17
Financial Statement Analysis

Retained Earnings Statement

Retained earnings, Jan. 1		$XXX
Net income	$ XXX	
Dividends	(XXX)	

Income Statement

Sales		$XXX
Cost of merchandise sold		XXX
Gross profit		$XXX
Operating expenses:		
Advertising expense	$XXX	
Depreciation expense	XXX	
Wages expense	XXX	
Utilities expense	XXX	
…	XXX	
…	XXX	
Total operating expenses		XXX
Income from operations		$XXX
Other revenue and expenses		XXX
Net income		$XXX

Statement of Cash Flows

Cash flows from operating activities	$XXX
Cash flows from (used for) investing activities	XXX
Cash flows from (used for) financing activities	XXX
Increase (decrease) in cash	$XXX
Cash, January 1	XXX
Cash, December 31	$XXX

Property, plant, and equipment		$XXX
Intangible assets		XXX
Total long-term assets		XXX
Total assets		$XXX
Liabilities:		
Current liabilities	$XXX	
Long-term liabilities	XXX	
Total liabilities		$XXX
Stockholders' equity:		
Retained earnings	$XXX	
Common stock	XXX	
Total stockholders' equity		XXX
Total liabilities and stockholders' equity		$XXX

CHAPTER 16

National Beverage Co.

Suppose you receive $100 from an event. Does it make a difference what the event was? Yes, it does! If you receive $100 for your birthday, then it's a gift. If you receive $100 as a result of working part-time for a week, then it's from earnings. If you receive $100 as a loan, then it's money that you will have to pay back in the future. If you sell your iPod for $100, then it's the result of selling an asset. These examples illustrate that not all cash flows are the same, and the source of the cash has different meanings and implications for your future. You would much rather receive a $100 gift than take out a $100 loan. Likewise, company stakeholders view inflows and outflows of cash differently, depending on their source.

Companies are required to report information about the events causing a change in cash over a period of time. This information is reported in the statement of cash flows. One such company is **National Beverage**, which is known for its innovative soft drinks and alternative beverages. You have probably seen the company's **Shasta** and **Faygo** soft drinks or **LaCroix**, **Everfresh**, and **Crystal Bay** drinks at your local grocery or convenience store. As with any company, cash is important to National Beverage. Without cash, National Beverage would be unable to expand its brands, distribute its product, support extreme sports, or provide a return for its owners. Thus, its managers are concerned about the sources and uses of cash.

In previous chapters, we used the income statement, balance sheet, statement of retained earnings, and other information to analyze the effects of management decisions on a business's financial position and operating performance. In this chapter, we focus on the events causing a change in cash by presenting the preparation and use of the statement of cash flows.

Learning Objectives

After studying this chapter, you should be able to:

Example Exercises (EE) are shown in **green**.

Obj. 1 Describe the cash flow activities reported in the statement of cash flows.

Reporting Cash Flows
Cash Flows from Operating Activities — EE **16-1**
Cash Flows from (used for) Investing Activities — EE **16-1**
Cash Flows from (used for) Financing Activities — EE **16-1**
Noncash Investing and Financing Activities
Format of the Statement of Cash Flows
No Cash Flow per Share

Obj. 2 Prepare a statement of cash flows, using the indirect method.

Preparing the Statement of Cash Flows—The Indirect Method
Net Income
Adjustments to Net Income — EE **16-2, 3, 4**
Dividends and Dividends Payable
Common Stock
Bonds Payable
Building and Accumulated Depreciation—Building
Land — EE **16-5**
Preparing the Statement of Cash Flows

Obj. 3 Prepare a statement of cash flows, using the direct method.

Preparing the Statement of Cash Flows—The Direct Method
Cash Received from Customers — EE **16-6**
Cash Payments for Merchandise — EE **16-7**
Cash Payments for Operating Expenses
Gain on Sale of Land
Interest Expense
Cash Payments for Income Taxes
Reporting Cash Flows from Operating Activities—Direct Method

Obj. 4 Describe and illustrate the use of free cash flow in evaluating a company's cash flow.

Financial Analysis and Interpretation: Free Cash Flow
Compute Free Cash Flow — EE **16-8**

At a Glance 16 Page 792

Reporting Cash Flows

Obj. 1 Describe the cash flow activities reported in the statement of cash flows.

The **statement of cash flows** reports a company's cash inflows and outflows for a period.[1] The statement of cash flows provides useful information about a company's ability to do the following:

- Generate cash from operations
- Maintain and expand its operating capacity
- Meet its financial obligations
- Pay dividends

The statement of cash flows is used by managers in evaluating past operations and in planning future investing and financing activities. It is also used by external users such as investors and creditors to assess a company's profit potential and ability to pay its debt and to pay dividends.

The statement of cash flows reports three types of cash flow activities, as follows:

1. **Cash flows from operating activities** are the cash flows from transactions that affect the net income of the company.
    Example: Purchase and sale of merchandise by a retailer.
2. **Cash flows from (used for) investing activities** are the cash flows received from or used for transactions that affect investments in the noncurrent assets of the company.
    Example: Purchase and sale of fixed assets, such as equipment and buildings.

Note: The statement of cash flows reports cash flows from operating, investing, and financing activities.

---

[1] As used in this chapter, *cash* refers to cash and cash equivalents. Examples of cash equivalents include short-term, highly liquid investments such as money market accounts, bank certificates of deposit, and U.S. Treasury bills.

3. **Cash flows from (used for) financing activities** are the cash flows received from or used for transactions that affect the debt and equity of the company.

Example: Issuing or retiring equity and debt securities.

The cash flows are reported in the statement of cash flows as follows:

Cash flows from operating activities	$XXX
Cash flows from (used for) investing activities	XXX
Cash flows from (used for) financing activities	XXX
Increase (decrease) in cash	$XXX
Cash at the beginning of the period	XXX
Cash at the end of the period	$XXX

The ending cash on the statement of cash flows equals the cash reported on the company's balance sheet at the end of the year.

Exhibit 1 illustrates the sources (increases) and uses (decreases) of cash by each of the three cash flow activities. A *source* of cash causes the cash flow to increase and is called a *cash inflow*. A *use* of cash causes cash flow to decrease and is called *cash outflow*.

EXHIBIT 1 Sources and Uses of Cash

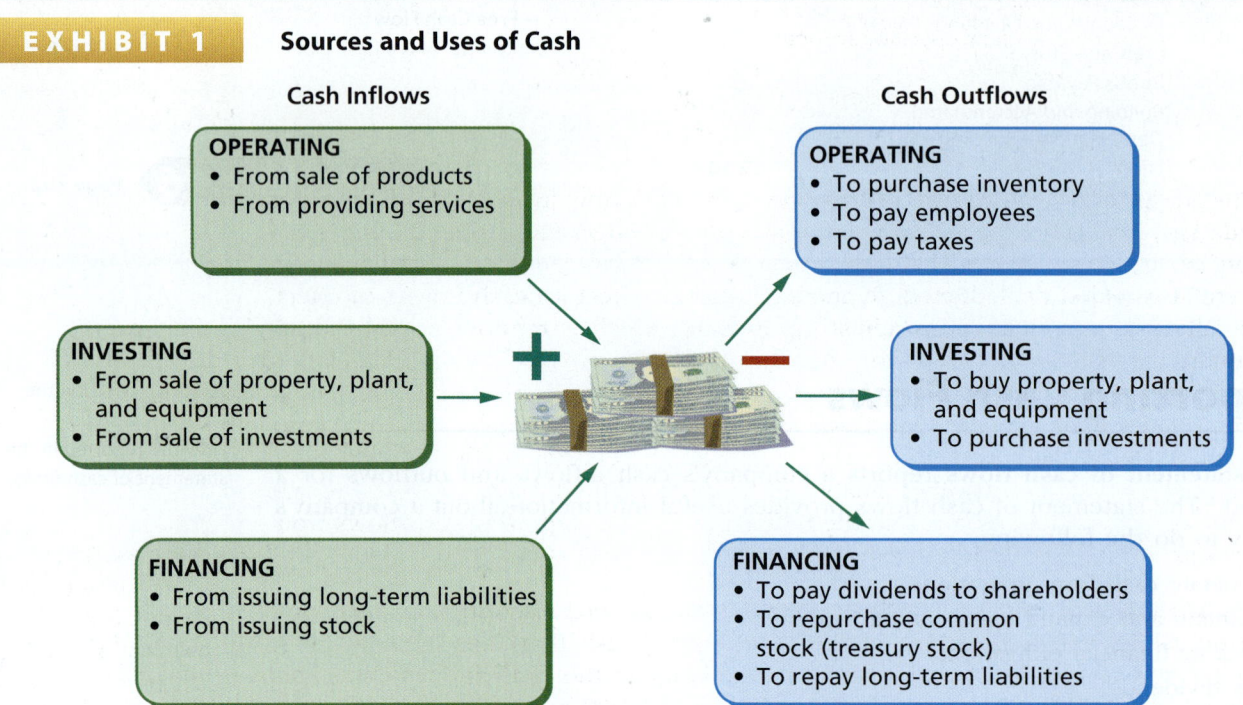

Cash Flows from Operating Activities

Cash flows from operating activities reports the cash inflows and outflows from a company's day-to-day operations. Companies may select one of two alternative methods for reporting cash flows from operating activities in the statement of cash flows:

- The direct method
- The indirect method

Both methods result in the same amount of cash flows from operating activities. They differ in the way they report cash flows from operating activities.

The Direct Method The **direct method** reports operating cash inflows (receipts) and cash outflows (payments) as follows:

```
Cash flows from operating activities:
    Cash received from customers              $ XXX
    Cash payments for merchandise             (XXX)
    Cash payments for operating expenses      (XXX)
    Cash payments for interest                (XXX)
    Cash payments for income taxes            (XXX)
    Net cash flow from operating activities          $XXX
```

The primary operating cash inflow is cash received from customers. The primary operating cash outflows are cash payments for merchandise, operating expenses, interest, and income tax payments. The cash received from operating activities less the cash payments for operating activities is the net cash flow from operating activities.

The primary advantage of the direct method is that it *directly* reports cash receipts and cash payments in the statement of cash flows. Its primary disadvantage is that these data may not be readily available in the accounting records. Thus, the direct method is normally more costly to prepare and, as a result, is used infrequently in practice.

The Indirect Method The **indirect method** reports cash flows from operating activities by beginning with net income and adjusting it for revenues and expenses that do not involve the receipt or payment of cash, as follows:

```
Cash flows from operating activities:
    Net income                                    $XXX
    Adjustments to reconcile net income to net
        cash flow from operating activities        XXX
    Net cash flow from operating activities              $XXX
```

The adjustments to reconcile net income to net cash flow from operating activities include such items as depreciation and gains or losses on fixed assets. Changes in current operating assets and liabilities such as accounts receivable or accounts payable are also added or deducted, depending on their effect on cash flows.[2] In effect, these additions and deductions adjust net income, which is reported on an accrual accounting basis, to cash flows from operating activities, which is a cash basis.

A primary advantage of the indirect method is that it reconciles the differences between net income and net cash flows from operations. In doing so, it shows how net income is related to the ending cash balance that is reported on the balance sheet.

Because the data are readily available, the indirect method is less costly to prepare than the direct method. As a result, the indirect method of reporting cash flows from operations is most commonly used in practice.

Comparing the Direct and Indirect Methods Exhibit 2 illustrates the Cash flows from operating activities section of the statement of cash flows for NetSolutions. Exhibit 2 shows the direct and indirect methods using the NetSolutions data from Chapter 1. As Exhibit 2 illustrates, both methods report the same amount of net cash flow from operating activities, $2,900.

Link to National Beverage

National Beverage uses the indirect method of reporting the cash flows from operating activities in its statement of cash flows.

Cash Flow from Operations: Direct and Indirect Methods—NetSolutions — EXHIBIT 2

Direct Method

Cash flows from operating activities:	
Cash received from customers	$ 7,500
Cash payments for expenses and payments to creditors	(4,600)
Net cash flow from operating activities	$ 2,900

Indirect Method

Cash flows from operating activities:	
Net income	$3,050
Increase in accounts payable	400
Increase in supplies	(550)
Net cash flow from operating activities	$2,900

the same

---

[2] Current operating assets include all current assets other than cash, and all current liabilities other than dividends payable.

Business Connection

CASH CRUNCH!

The Wet Seal, Inc., a young women's clothing retailer, filed for bankruptcy protection. The cash flows from operating activities for the three years prior to bankruptcy (in thousands) follow:

	Year 3	Year 2	Year 1
Cash provided (used in) operating activities	$(17,589)	$(26,191)	$61,900

As can be seen, cash flows from operating activities trended into negative territory during the two years prior to the firm's bankruptcy. Thus, when cash flows from operating activities are negative, it can lead to financial distress.

Cash Flows from (Used for) Investing Activities

Link to National Beverage
For a recent year, **National Beverage** reported net cash used in investing activities of $9,725,000.

Cash flows from (used for) investing activities show the cash inflows and outflows related to changes in a company's long-term assets. Cash flows from (used for) investing activities are reported on the statement of cash flows as follows:

Cash flows from (used for) investing activities:		
Cash from investing activities	$ XXX	
Cash used for investing activities	(XXX)	
Net cash flows from (used for) investing activities		$XXX

Cash inflows from investing activities normally arise when cash is received from selling fixed assets, investments, and intangible assets. Cash outflows normally include payments to purchase fixed assets, investments, and intangible assets.

Cash Flows from (Used for) Financing Activities

Cash flows from (used for) financing activities show the cash inflows and outflows related to changes in a company's long-term liabilities and stockholders' equity. Cash flows from (used for) financing activities are reported on the statement of cash flows as follows:

Cash flows from (used for) financing activities:		
Cash from financing activities	$ XXX	
Cash used for financing activities	(XXX)	
Net cash flow from (used for) financing activities		$XXX

Link to National Beverage
For a recent year, **National Beverage** reported net cash used in financing activities of $25,771,000.

Cash inflows from financing activities normally arise when cash is received from issuing long-term debt or equity securities. For example, issuing bonds, notes payable, preferred stock, and common stock creates cash inflows from financing activities. Cash outflows from financing activities include paying cash dividends, repaying long-term debt, and acquiring treasury stock.

Noncash Investing and Financing Activities

A company may enter into transactions involving investing and financing activities that do not *directly* affect cash. For example, a company may issue common stock to retire long-term debt. Although this transaction does not directly affect cash, it does eliminate future cash payments for interest and for paying the bonds when they mature. Because such transactions *indirectly* affect cash flows, they are reported in a separate section of the statement of cash flows. This section usually appears at the bottom of the statement of cash flows.

Format of the Statement of Cash Flows

The statement of cash flows presents the cash flows generated by, or used for, the three activities previously discussed: operating, investing, and financing. These three activities are always reported in the same order, following the format illustrated in Exhibit 3.

EXHIBIT 3 Format of the Statement of Cash Flows

COMPANY NAME
Statement of Cash Flows
For the Year Ended XXXX

Cash flows from operating activities:		
(List of individual items, as illustrated in Exhibit 1)	$XXX	
Net cash flows from operating activities		$XXX
Cash flows from (used for) investing activities:		
(List of individual items, as illustrated in Exhibit 1)	$XXX	
Net cash flows from (used for) investing activities		XXX
Cash flows from (used for) financing activities:		
(List of individual items, as illustrated in Exhibit 1)	$XXX	
Net cash flows from (used for) financing activities		XXX
Increase (decrease) in cash		$XXX
Cash at the beginning of the period		XXX
Cash at the end of the period		$XXX
Noncash investing and financing activites		$XXX

No Cash Flow per Share

Cash flow per share is sometimes reported in the financial press. As reported, cash flow per share is normally computed as *cash flow from operations divided by the number of common shares outstanding*. However, such reporting may be misleading because of the following:

- Users may misinterpret cash flow per share as the per-share amount available for dividends. This would not be the case if the cash generated by operations is required for repaying loans or for reinvesting in the business.
- Users may misinterpret cash flow per share as equivalent to (or better than) earnings per share.

For these reasons, the financial statements, including the statement of cash flows, should not report cash flow per share.

Example Exercise 16-1 Classifying Cash Flows   Obj. 1

Identify whether each of the following would be reported as an operating, investing, or financing activity in the statement of cash flows:

a. Purchase of patent
b. Payment of cash dividend
c. Disposal of equipment
d. Cash sales
e. Purchase of treasury stock
f. Payment of wages expense

Follow My Example 16-1

a. Investing
b. Financing
c. Investing
d. Operating
e. Financing
f. Operating

Practice Exercises: PE 16-1A, PE 16-1B

772 Chapter 16 Statement of Cash Flows

Obj. 2 Prepare a statement of cash flows, using the indirect method.

Preparing the Statement of Cash Flows— The Indirect Method

The indirect method of reporting cash flows from operating activities uses the logic that a change in any balance sheet account (including cash) can be analyzed in terms of changes in the other balance sheet accounts. Thus, by analyzing changes in noncash balance sheet accounts, any change in the cash account can be *indirectly* determined.

To illustrate, the accounting equation can be solved for cash as follows:

Assets = Liabilities + Stockholders' Equity
Cash + Noncash Assets = Liabilities + Stockholders' Equity
Cash = Liabilities + Stockholders' Equity − Noncash Assets

Therefore, any change in the cash account can be determined by analyzing changes in the liability, stockholders' equity, and noncash asset accounts as follows:

Change in Cash = Change in Liabilities + Change in Stockholders' Equity − Change in Noncash Assets

Under the indirect method, there is no order in which the balance sheet accounts must be analyzed. However, net income (or net loss) is the first amount reported on the statement of cash flows. Because net income (or net loss) is a component of any change in Retained Earnings, the first account normally analyzed is Retained Earnings.

To illustrate the indirect method, the income statement and comparative balance sheets for **Rundell Inc.**, shown in Exhibit 4, are used. Ledger accounts and other data supporting the income statement and balance sheet are presented as needed.[3]

EXHIBIT 4

Income Statement and Comparative Balance Sheet

Rundell Inc.
Income Statement
For the Year Ended December 31, 20Y8

Sales		$1,180,000
Cost of merchandise sold		790,000
Gross profit		$ 390,000
Operating expenses:		
Depreciation expense	$ 7,000	
Other operating expenses	196,000	
Total operating expenses		203,000
Income from operations		$ 187,000
Other revenue and expense:		
Gain on sale of land	$ 12,000	
Interest expense	(8,000)	4,000
Income before income tax		$ 191,000
Income tax expense		83,000
Net income		$ 108,000

---

[3] An appendix that discusses using a spreadsheet (work sheet) as an aid in assembling data for the statement of cash flows is presented at the end of this chapter. This appendix illustrates the use of this spreadsheet in reporting cash flows from operating activities using the indirect method.

EXHIBIT 4

Income Statement and Comparative Balance Sheet (*Continued*)

Rundell Inc.
Comparative Balance Sheet
December 31, 20Y8 and 20Y7

	20Y8	20Y7	Increase (Decrease)
Assets			
Cash	$ 97,500	$ 26,000	$ 71,500
Accounts receivable (net)	74,000	65,000	9,000
Inventories	172,000	180,000	(8,000)
Land	80,000	125,000	(45,000)
Building	260,000	200,000	60,000
Accumulated depreciation—building	(65,300)	(58,300)	(7,000)*
Total assets	$618,200	$537,700	$ 80,500
Liabilities			
Accounts payable (merchandise creditors)	$ 43,500	$ 46,700	$ (3,200)
Accrued expenses payable (operating expenses)	26,500	24,300	2,200
Income taxes payable	7,900	8,400	(500)
Dividends payable	14,000	10,000	4,000
Bonds payable	100,000	150,000	(50,000)
Total liabilities	$191,900	$239,400	$ (47,500)
Stockholders' Equity			
Common stock ($2 par)	$ 24,000	$ 16,000	$ 8,000
Paid-in capital in excess of par	120,000	80,000	40,000
Retained earnings	282,300	202,300	80,000
Total stockholders' equity	$426,300	$298,300	$128,000
Total liabilities and stockholders' equity	$618,200	$537,700	$ 80,500

*There is a $7,000 increase to Accumulated Depreciation—Building, which is a contra asset account. As a result, the $7,000 increase in this account must be subtracted in summing to the increase in Total assets of $80,500.

Net Income

Rundell Inc.'s net income for 20Y8 is $108,000, as shown on the income statement in Exhibit 4. Since net income is closed to Retained Earnings, net income also helps explain the change in retained earnings during the year. The retained earnings account for Rundell is as follows:

Account Retained Earnings   Account No.

					Balance	
Date		Item	Debit	Credit	Debit	Credit
20Y8 Jan.	1	Balance				202,300
June	30	Dividends declared	14,000			188,300
Dec.	31	Net income		108,000		296,300
	31	Dividends declared	14,000			282,300

The retained earnings account indicates that the $80,000 ($108,000 − $28,000) change resulted from net income of $108,000 and cash dividends of $28,000. The net income of $108,000 is the first amount reported in the Cash flows from operating activities section. The impact of the dividends of $28,000 on cash flows will be included as part of financing activities.

Adjustments to Net Income

The net income of $108,000 reported by Rundell Inc. does not equal the cash flows from operating activities for the period. This is because net income is determined using the accrual method of accounting.

Under the accrual method of accounting, revenues and expenses are recorded at different times from when cash is received or paid. For example, merchandise may be sold on account and the cash received at a later date. Likewise, insurance premiums may be paid in the current period but expensed in a following period.

Thus, under the indirect method, adjustments to net income must be made to determine cash flows from operating activities. The typical adjustments to net income are shown in Exhibit 5.[4]

EXHIBIT 5 — Adjustments to Net Income (Loss) Using the Indirect Method

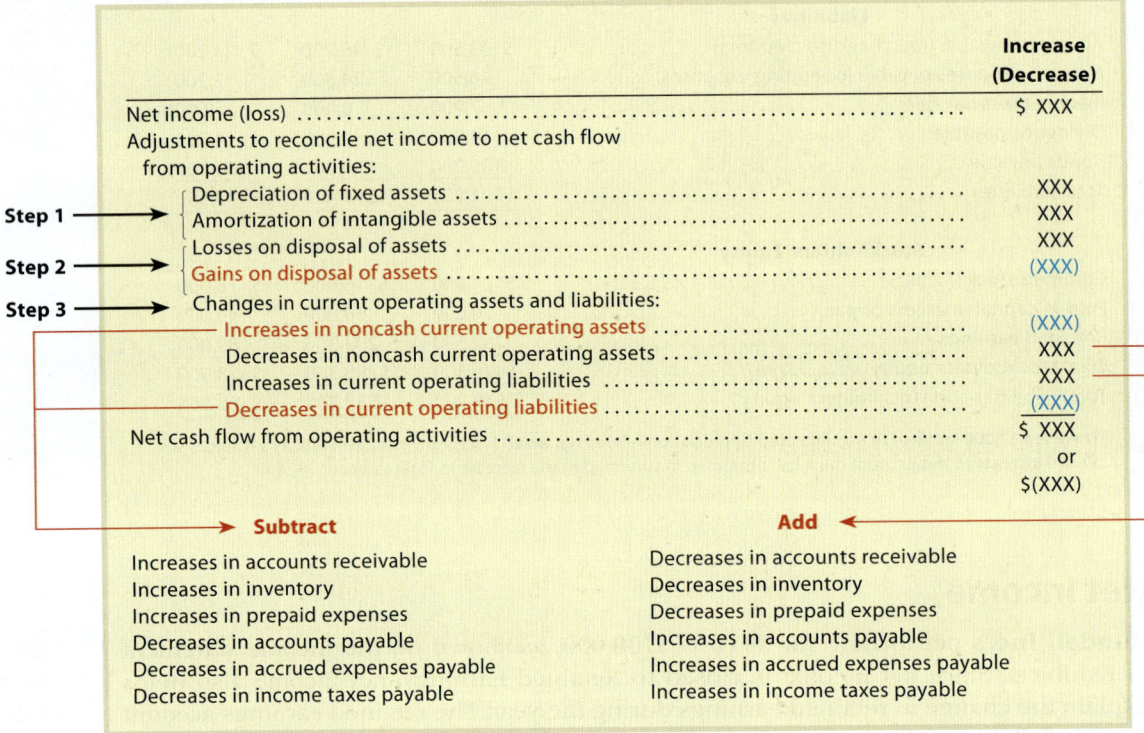

Net income is normally adjusted to cash flows from operating activities, using the following steps:

Step 1. Expenses that do not affect cash are added. Such expenses decrease net income but do not involve cash payments and, thus, are added to net income.

> Example: Depreciation of fixed assets and amortization of intangible assets are non-cash expenses that are added to net income.

Step 2. Losses on the disposal of assets are added and gains on the disposal of assets are deducted. The disposal (sale) of assets is an investing activity rather than an operating activity. However, the losses and gains are reported as part of net income. As a result, any *losses* on disposal of assets are *added* back to net income. Likewise, any *gains* on disposal of assets are *deducted* from net income.

> Example: Land costing $100,000 is sold for $90,000. The loss of $10,000 is added back to net income.

---

[4] Other items that also require adjustments to net income to obtain cash flows from operating activities include amortization of bonds payable discounts (add), losses on debt retirement (add), amortization of bonds payable premiums (deduct), and gains on retirement of debt (deduct). These topics are covered in advanced accounting courses.

Step 3. Changes in current operating assets and liabilities are added or deducted as follows:

- Increases in noncash current operating assets are deducted.
- Decreases in noncash current operating assets are added.
- Increases in current operating liabilities are added.
- Decreases in current operating liabilities are deducted.

Example: A sale of $10,000 on account increases sales, accounts receivable, and net income by $10,000. However, no cash is received or paid. Thus, the $10,000 increase in accounts receivable is deducted from net income. Similar adjustments are required for the changes in the other current asset and liability accounts, such as inventory, prepaid expenses, accounts payable, accrued expenses payable, and income taxes payable, as shown in Exhibit 5.

> **Link to National Beverage**
>
> For a recent year, **National Beverage** reported changes in current asset and liability accounts for accounts receivable, inventory, prepaid assets, accounts payable, and accrued liabilities.

Example Exercise 16-2 Adjustments to Net Income—Indirect Method Obj. 2

Omni Corporation's accumulated depreciation increased by $12,000, while $3,400 of patent amortization was recognized between balance sheet dates. There were no purchases or sales of depreciable or intangible assets during the year. In addition, the income statement showed a gain of $4,100 from the sale of land. Reconcile Omni's net income of $50,000 to net cash flow from operating activities.

Follow My Example 16-2

Net income	$50,000
Adjustments to reconcile net income to net cash flow from operating activities:	
Depreciation	12,000
Amortization of patents	3,400
Gain from sale of land	(4,100)
Net cash flow from operating activities	$61,300

Practice Exercises: PE 16-2A, PE 16-2B

The Cash flows from operating activities section of **Rundell Inc.**'s statement of cash flows is shown in Exhibit 6.

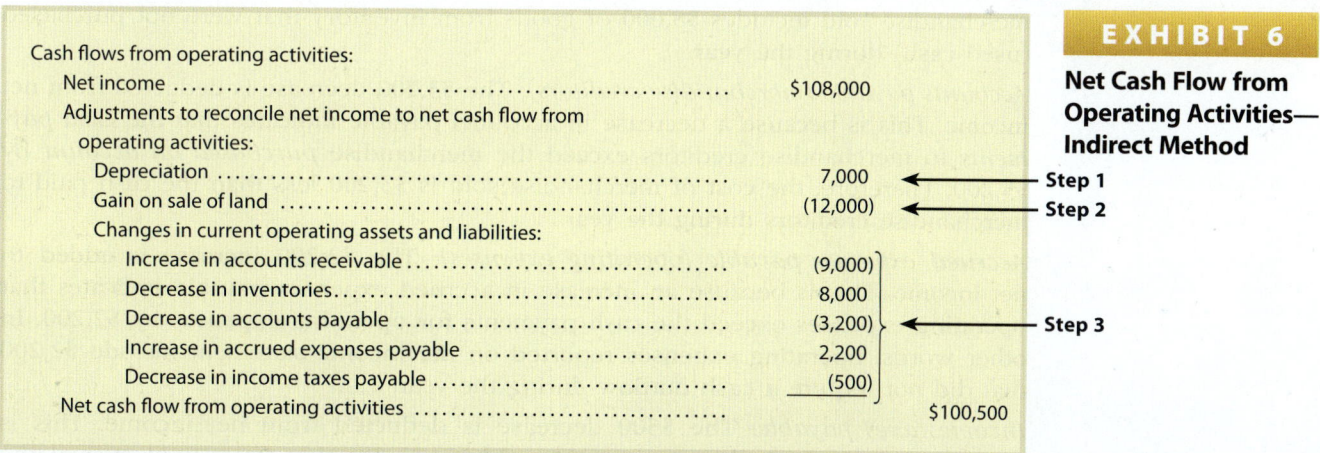

EXHIBIT 6

Net Cash Flow from Operating Activities—Indirect Method

Rundell's net income of $108,000 is converted to cash flows from operating activities of $100,500 as follows:

Step 1. Add depreciation of $7,000.

    Analysis: The comparative balance sheet in Exhibit 4 indicates that Accumulated Depreciation—Building increased by $7,000. Given that there was no other activity in this account, as shown on the following page, depreciation expense for the year was $7,000 on the building:

Account Accumulated Depreciation—Building Account No.

Date		Item	Debit	Credit	Balance Debit	Balance Credit
20Y8 Jan.	1	Balance				58,300
Dec.	31	Depreciation for year		7,000		65,300

Step 2. Deduct the gain on the sale of land of $12,000.

Analysis: The income statement in Exhibit 4 reports a gain of $12,000 from the sale of land. The proceeds, which include the gain, are reported in the Investing section of the statement of cash flows.[5] Thus, the gain of $12,000 is deducted from net income in determining cash flows from operating activities.

Step 3. Add and deduct changes in current operating assets and liabilities excluding cash.

Analysis: The increases and decreases in the current operating asset and current liability accounts excluding cash are as follows:

Accounts	December 31 20Y8	December 31 20Y7	Increase (Decrease)
Accounts Receivable (net)	$ 74,000	$ 65,000	$ 9,000
Inventories	172,000	180,000	(8,000)
Accounts Payable (merchandise creditors)	43,500	46,700	(3,200)
Accrued Expenses Payable (operating expenses)	26,500	24,300	2,200
Income Taxes Payable	7,900	8,400	(500)

Accounts receivable (net): The $9,000 increase is deducted from net income. This is because the $9,000 increase in accounts receivable indicates that sales on account were $9,000 more than the cash received from customers. Thus, sales (and net income) includes $9,000 that was not received in cash during the year.

Inventories: The $8,000 decrease is added to net income. This is because the $8,000 decrease in inventories indicates that the cost of merchandise *sold* exceeds the cost of the merchandise *purchased* during the year by $8,000. In other words, the cost of merchandise sold includes $8,000 of goods from inventory that were not purchased (used cash) during the year.

Accounts payable (merchandise creditors): The $3,200 decrease is deducted from net income. This is because a decrease in accounts payable indicates that the cash *payments* to merchandise creditors exceed the merchandise *purchased on account* by $3,200. Therefore, the cost of merchandise sold is $3,200 less than the cash paid to merchandise creditors during the year.

Accrued expenses payable (operating expenses): The $2,200 increase is added to net income. This is because an increase in accrued expenses payable indicates that operating expenses exceed the cash payments for operating expenses by $2,200. In other words, operating expenses reported on the income statement include $2,200 that did not require a cash outflow during the year.

Income taxes payable: The $500 decrease is deducted from net income. This is because a decrease in income taxes payable indicates that taxes paid exceed the amount of taxes incurred during the year by $500. In other words, the amount reported on the income statement for income tax expense is less than the amount paid by $500.

Using the preceding analyses, Rundell's net income of $108,000 is converted to cash flows from operating activities of $100,500 as shown in Exhibit 6.

---

[5] The reporting of the proceeds (cash flows) from the sale of land as part of investing activities is discussed later in this chapter.

Example Exercise 16-3: Changes in Current Operating Assets and Liabilities—Indirect Method

Obj. 2

Victor Corporation's current operating assets and liabilities from the company's comparative balance sheet were as follows:

	Dec. 31, 20Y8	Dec. 31, 20Y7
Accounts receivable	$ 6,500	$ 4,900
Inventory	12,300	15,000
Accounts payable	4,800	5,200

Adjust Victor's net income of $70,000 for changes in current operating assets and liabilities to arrive at net cash flow from operating activities.

Follow My Example 16-3

Net income	$70,000
Adjustments to reconcile net income to net cash flow from operating activities:	
Changes in current operating assets and liabilities:	
Increase in accounts receivable	(1,600)
Decrease in inventory	2,700
Decrease in accounts payable	(400)
Net cash flow from operating activities	$70,700

Practice Exercises: PE 16-3A, PE 16-3B

INTEGRITY, OBJECTIVITY, AND ETHICS IN BUSINESS

CREDIT POLICY AND CASH FLOW

Investors frequently use net cash flow from operating activities to assess a company's financial health. If a company is financially healthy, net cash flow from operating activities should be roughly consistent with accrual basis net income. Questions arise, however, when a company's net cash flow from operating activities significantly lags net income. Two scenarios can cause this to happen:

- Sales on account are never collected in cash.
- Large cash purchases for inventory are never sold or sell at a very slow pace.

Both of these scenarios increase net income, without a corresponding increase in net cash flow from operating activities. Prudent investors are often skeptical when they observe these scenarios and tend to avoid these types of investments until the cash flows become clear.

Source: M. Argersinger, "How Companies Fake It (With Cash Flow)," *Daily Finance Investor Center*, July 17, 2011.

Example Exercise 16-4: Cash Flows from Operating Activities—Indirect Method

Obj. 2

Omicron Inc. reported the following data:

Net income	$120,000
Depreciation expense	12,000
Loss on disposal of equipment	15,000
Increase in accounts receivable	5,000
Decrease in accounts payable	2,000

Prepare the Cash flows from operating activities section of the statement of cash flows, using the indirect method.

(Continued)

Follow My Example 16-4

Cash flows from operating activities:	
Net income	$120,000
Adjustments to reconcile net income to net cash flow from operating activities:	
Depreciation expense	12,000
Loss on disposal of equipment	15,000
Changes in current operating assets and liabilities:	
Increase in accounts receivable	(5,000)
Decrease in accounts payable	(2,000)
Net cash flow from operating activities	$140,000

Practice Exercises: PE 16-4A, PE 16-4B

Dividends and Dividends Payable

The retained earnings account of **Rundell Inc.** indicates that cash dividends of $28,000 were declared during the year. However, the following dividends payable account indicates that only $24,000 of dividends were paid during the year:

Account Dividends Payable   Account No.

Date		Item	Debit	Credit	Balance Debit	Balance Credit
20Y8						
Jan.	1	Balance				10,000
	10	Cash paid	10,000		—	—
June	30	Dividends declared		14,000		14,000
July	10	Cash paid	14,000		—	—
Dec.	31	Dividends declared		14,000		14,000

Cash dividends paid during the year can also be computed by adjusting the dividends declared during the year for the change in the dividends payable account as follows:

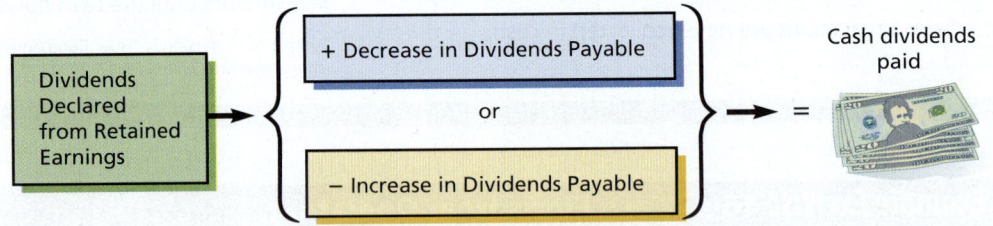

The cash dividends paid by Rundell Inc. during 20Y8 are $24,000, computed as follows:

Dividends declared ($14,000 + $14,000)	$28,000
Increase in Dividends Payable	(4,000)
Cash dividends paid	$24,000

Because dividend payments are a financing activity, the dividend payment of $24,000 is reported in the financing activities section of the statement of cash flows, as follows:

Cash flows from (used for) financing activities:
Cash used for dividends.................................... $(24,000)

Common Stock

The common stock account of **Rundell Inc.** increased by $8,000, and the paid-in capital in excess of par—common stock account increased by $40,000, as follows:

Account Common Stock — Account No.

Date		Item	Debit	Credit	Balance Debit	Balance Credit
20Y8 Jan.	1	Balance				16,000
Nov.	1	4,000 shares issued for cash		8,000		24,000

Account Paid-In Capital in Excess of Par—Common Stock — Account No.

Date		Item	Debit	Credit	Balance Debit	Balance Credit
20Y8 Jan.	1	Balance				80,000
Nov.	1	4,000 shares issued for cash		40,000		120,000

These increases were from issuing 4,000 shares of common stock for $12 per share. This cash inflow is reported in the financing activities section as follows:

Cash flows from (used for) financing activities:
Cash from sale of common stock............................ $48,000

Bonds Payable

The bonds payable account of **Rundell Inc.** decreased by $50,000, as follows:

Account Bonds Payable — Account No.

Date		Item	Debit	Credit	Balance Debit	Balance Credit
20Y8 Jan.	1	Balance				150,000
June	1	Retired by payment of cash at face amount	50,000			100,000

This decrease is from retiring the bonds by a cash payment for their face amount. This cash outflow is reported in the financing activities section as follows:

Cash flows from (used for) financing activities:
Cash used to retire bonds payable........................ $(50,000)

Building and Accumulated Depreciation—Building

The building account of **Rundell Inc.** increased by $60,000, and the accumulated depreciation—building account increased by $7,000, as follows:

Account Building						Account No.
					Balance	
Date		Item	Debit	Credit	Debit	Credit
20Y8 Jan. 1		Balance			200,000	
Dec. 27		Purchased for cash	60,000		260,000	

Account Accumulated Depreciation—Building						Account No.
					Balance	
Date		Item	Debit	Credit	Debit	Credit
20Y8 Jan. 1		Balance				58,300
Dec. 31		Depreciation for the year		7,000		65,300

The purchase of a building for cash of $60,000 is reported as an outflow of cash in the investing activities section as follows:

Cash flows from (used for) investing activities:
Cash used for purchase of building.......................... $(60,000)

The credit in the accumulated depreciation—building account represents depreciation expense for the year. This depreciation expense of $7,000 on the building was added to net income in determining cash flows from operating activities, as reported in Exhibit 6.

Land

The $45,000 decline in the land account of **Rundell Inc.** was from two transactions, as follows:

Account Land						Account No.
					Balance	
Date		Item	Debit	Credit	Debit	Credit
20Y8 Jan. 1		Balance			125,000	
June 8		Sold for $72,000 cash		60,000	65,000	
Oct. 12		Purchased for $15,000 cash	15,000		80,000	

The June 8 transaction is the sale of land with a cost of $60,000 for $72,000 in cash. The $72,000 proceeds from the sale are reported in the investing activities section as follows:

Cash flows from (used for) investing activities:
Cash from sale of land $72,000

The proceeds of $72,000 include the $12,000 gain on the sale of land and the $60,000 cost (book value) of the land. As shown in Exhibit 6, the $12,000 gain is deducted from net income in the Cash flows from operating activities section. This is so that the $12,000 cash inflow related to the gain is not included twice as a cash inflow.

The October 12 transaction is the purchase of land for cash of $15,000. This transaction is reported as an outflow of cash in the investing activities section as follows:

Cash flows from (used for) investing activities:
  Cash used for purchase of land.............................. $(15,000)

Example Exercise 16-5 Land Transactions on the Statement of Cash Flows   Obj. 2

Alpha Corporation purchased land for $125,000. Later in the year, the company sold a different piece of land with a book value of $165,000 for $200,000. How are the effects of these transactions reported on the statement of cash flows?

Follow My Example 16-5

The gain on the sale of the land is deducted from net income, as follows:

Gain on sale of land .... $ (35,000)

The purchase and sale of land are reported as part of cash flows from investing activities, as follows:

Cash received from sale of land .... $ 200,000
Cash used for purchase of land .... (125,000)

Practice Exercises: PE 16-5A, PE 16-5B

Preparing the Statement of Cash Flows

The statement of cash flows for **Rundell Inc.**, using the indirect method, is shown in Exhibit 7. The statement of cash flows indicates that cash increased by $71,500 during the year. The most significant increase in net cash flows ($100,500) was from operating activities. The most significant use of cash ($26,000) was for financing activities. The ending balance of cash on December 31, 20Y8, is $97,500. This ending cash balance is also reported on the December 31, 20Y8, balance sheet shown in Exhibit 4.

Rundell Inc.
Statement of Cash Flows
For the Year Ended December 31, 20Y8

Cash flows from operating activities:		
Net income		$108,000
Adjustments to reconcile net income to net cash flow from operating activities:		
Depreciation	7,000	
Gain on sale of land	(12,000)	
Changes in current operating assets and liabilities:		
Increase in accounts receivable	(9,000)	
Decrease in inventories	8,000	
Decrease in accounts payable	(3,200)	
Increase in accrued expenses payable	2,200	
Decrease in income taxes payable	(500)	
Net cash flow from operating activities		$100,500
Cash flows from (used for) investing activities:		
Cash from sale of land	$ 72,000	
Cash used for purchase of land	(15,000)	
Cash used for purchase of building	(60,000)	
Net cash flow used for investing activities		(3,000)
Cash flows from (used for) financing activities:		
Cash from sale of common stock	$ 48,000	
Cash used to retire bonds payable	(50,000)	
Cash used for dividends	(24,000)	
Net cash flow used for financing activities		(26,000)
Increase (decrease) in cash		$ 71,500
Cash at the beginning of the year		26,000
Cash at the end of the year		$ 97,500

EXHIBIT 7

Statement of Cash Flows—Indirect Method

Link to National Beverage

In a recent statement of cash flows, **National Beverage** reported net cash provided by operating activities of $58,020,000, net cash used for investing activities of $9,725,000, and net cash used for financing activities of $25,771,000 for a net increase in cash of $22,524,000 for the year.

Business Connection

GROWING PAINS

Twitter, Inc. is a global social media platform used for real-time self-expression and conversation within the limits of 140-character tweets. Twitter is a new, fast-growing company. The cash flows from operating, investing, and financing activities are summarized for its first three years as a public company (in thousands):

	Cash provided from (used in)			
	Operating activities	Investing activities	Financing activities	Net change for year
Year 1	$(27,935)	$ 49,443	$ (37,124)	$ (15,616)
Year 2	1,398	(1,306,066)	1,942,176	637,508
Year 3	81,796	(1,097,272)	1,691,722	676,246

One can see the significant improvement in Twitter's cash flows from operations from Year 1 to Year 3. This indicates that Twitter is succeeding as a new company and is able to provide cash from operations after only three years of operating as a public company. However, as a new company, Twitter must make significant investments in order to expand. This is clear in the trend in cash flows used in investing activities. Since the cash flows from operations are insufficient to fund this growth, the company must obtain cash from financing activities. We see significant sources of cash from stockholders in Year 2 and Year 3, which was used to expand and provide future flexibility.

Preparing the Statement of Cash Flows— The Direct Method

Obj. 3 Prepare a statement of cash flows, using the direct method.

The direct method reports cash flows from operating activities as follows:

Cash flows from operating activities:	
Cash received from customers.................................	$ XXX
Cash payments for merchandise.................................	(XXX)
Cash payments for operating expenses	(XXX)
Cash payments for interest....................................	(XXX)
Cash payments for income taxes	(XXX)
Net cash flow from operating activities	$XXX

The investing and financing activities sections of the statement of cash flows are exactly the same under both the direct and indirect methods. The amount of net cash flow from operating activities is also the same, but the manner in which it is reported is different.

Under the direct method, the income statement is adjusted to cash flows from operating activities as shown in Exhibit 8.

EXHIBIT 8
Converting Income Statement to Cash Flows from Operating Activities Using the Direct Method

Income Statement	Adjusted to	Cash Flows from Operating Activities
Sales	→	Cash received from customers
Cost of merchandise sold	→	Cash payments for merchandise
Operating expenses:		
Depreciation expense	N/A	N/A
Other operating expenses	→	Cash payments for operating expenses
Gain on sale of land	N/A	N/A
Interest expense	→	Cash payments for interest
Income tax expense	→	Cash payments for income taxes
Net income	→	Net cash flow from operating activities

N/A—Not applicable

As shown in Exhibit 8, depreciation expense is not adjusted or reported as part of cash flows from operating activities. This is because depreciation expense does not involve a cash outflow. The gain on the sale of the land is also not adjusted and is not reported as part of cash flows from operating activities. This is because the cash flow from operating activities is determined directly, rather than by reconciling net income. The cash proceeds from the sale of the land are reported as an investing activity.

To illustrate the direct method, the income statement and comparative balance sheet for Rundell Inc., shown in Exhibit 4, are used.

Cash Received from Customers

The income statement (shown in Exhibit 4) of **Rundell Inc.** reports sales of $1,180,000. To determine the *cash received from customers*, the $1,180,000 is adjusted for any increase or decrease in accounts receivable. The adjustment is summarized in Exhibit 9.

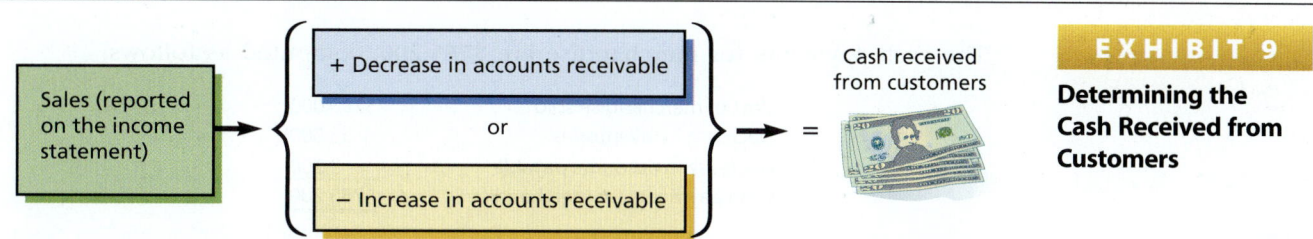

EXHIBIT 9

Determining the Cash Received from Customers

The cash received from customers is $1,171,000, computed as follows:

Sales	$1,180,000
Increase in accounts receivable	(9,000)
Cash received from customers	$1,171,000

The increase of $9,000 in accounts receivable (shown in Exhibit 4) during 20Y8 indicates that sales on account exceeded cash received from customers by $9,000. In other words, sales include $9,000 that did not result in a cash inflow during the year. Thus, $9,000 is deducted from sales to determine the cash received from customers.

Example Exercise 16-6 Cash Received from Customers—Direct Method Obj. 3

Sales reported on the income statement were $350,000. The accounts receivable balance declined $8,000 over the year. Determine the amount of cash received from customers.

Follow My Example 16-6

Sales	$350,000
Decrease in accounts receivable	8,000
Cash received from customers	$358,000

Practice Exercises: PE 16-6A, PE 16-6B

Cash Payments for Merchandise

The income statement (shown in Exhibit 4) for **Rundell Inc.** reports cost of merchandise sold of $790,000. To determine the cash payments for merchandise, the $790,000 is adjusted for any increases or decreases in inventories and accounts payable. Assuming that the accounts payable are owed to merchandise suppliers, the adjustment is summarized in Exhibit 10.

EXHIBIT 10
Determining the Cash Payments for Merchandise

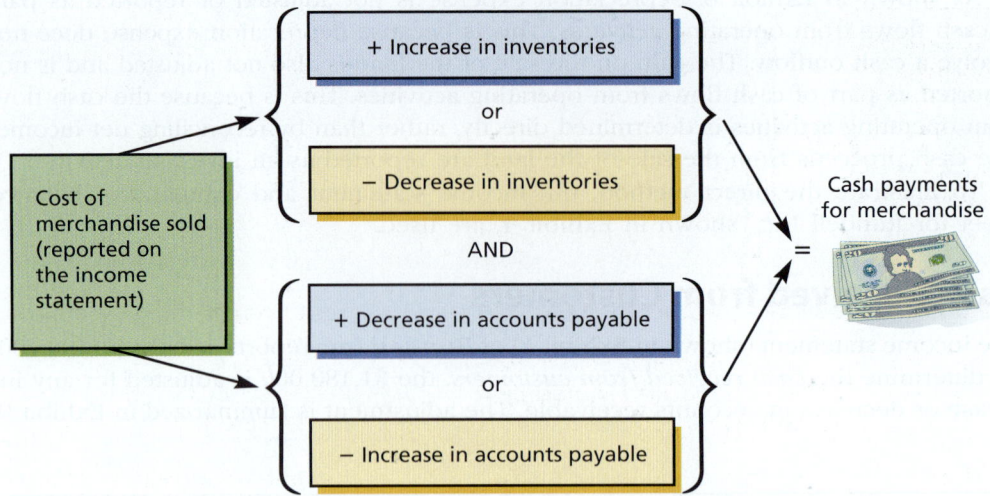

The cash payments for merchandise are $785,200, computed as follows:

Cost of merchandise sold	$790,000
Decrease in inventories	(8,000)
Decrease in accounts payable	3,200
Cash payments for merchandise	$785,200

The $8,000 decrease in inventories (from Exhibit 4) indicates that the merchandise sold exceeded the cost of the merchandise purchased by $8,000. In other words, the cost of merchandise sold includes $8,000 of goods sold from inventory that did not require a cash outflow during the year. Thus, $8,000 is deducted from the cost of merchandise sold in determining the cash payments for merchandise.

The $3,200 decrease in accounts payable (from Exhibit 4) indicates that cash payments for merchandise were $3,200 more than the purchases on account during 20Y8. Therefore, $3,200 is added to the cost of merchandise sold in determining the cash payments for merchandise.

Example Exercise 16-7 Cash Payments for Merchandise—Direct Method   Obj. 3

The cost of merchandise sold reported on the income statement was $145,000. The accounts payable balance increased by $4,000, and the inventory balance increased by $9,000 over the year. Determine the amount of cash paid for merchandise.

Follow My Example 16-7

Cost of merchandise sold	$145,000
Increase in inventories	9,000
Increase in accounts payable	(4,000)
Cash paid for merchandise	$150,000

Practice Exercises: PE 16-7A, PE 16-7B

Cash Payments for Operating Expenses

The income statement for **Rundell Inc.** (from Exhibit 4) reports total operating expenses of $203,000, which includes depreciation expense of $7,000. Because depreciation expense does not require a cash outflow, it is omitted from cash payments for operating expenses.

To determine the cash payments for operating expenses, the other operating expenses (excluding depreciation) of $196,000 ($203,000 − $7,000) are adjusted for any increase or decrease in prepaid and accrued expenses. Assuming that Rundell Inc.'s accrued expenses payable are all operating expenses, this adjustment is summarized in Exhibit 11.

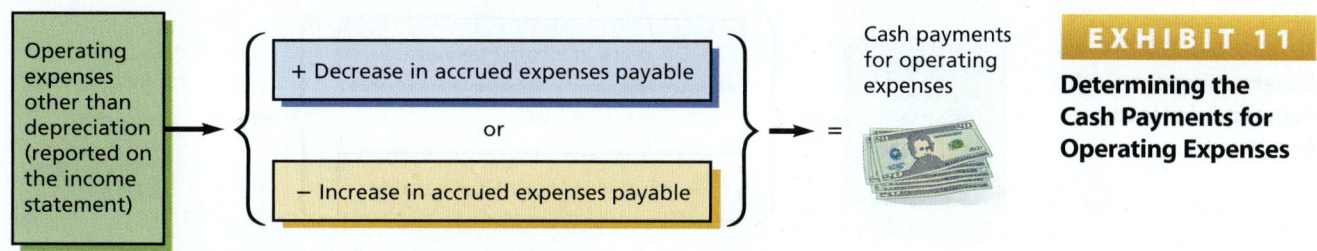

EXHIBIT 11

Determining the Cash Payments for Operating Expenses

The cash payments for operating expenses are $193,800, computed as follows:

Operating expenses other than depreciation	$196,000
Increase in accrued expenses payable	(2,200)
Cash payments for operating expenses	$193,800

The increase in accrued expenses payable (from Exhibit 4) indicates that the cash payments for operating expenses were $2,200 less than the amount reported for operating expenses during the year. Thus, $2,200 is deducted from the operating expenses in determining the cash payments for operating expenses.

Rundell Inc. had no prepaid expenses and thus, there was no operating expense adjustment for prepaid expense. When prepaid expenses exist, operating expenses are also adjusted for any increase or decrease in prepaid expenses. Increases (decreases) in prepaid expenses are added to (subtracted from) other operating expenses to determine the cash payments for operating expenses.

Gain on Sale of Land

The income statement for **Rundell Inc.** (from Exhibit 4) reports a gain of $12,000 on the sale of land. The sale of land is an investing activity. Thus, the proceeds from the sale, which include the gain, are reported as part of the investing activities section.

Interest Expense

The income statement for **Rundell Inc.** (from Exhibit 4) reports interest expense of $8,000. To determine the cash payments for interest, the $8,000 is adjusted for any increases or decreases in interest payable. The adjustment is summarized in Exhibit 12.

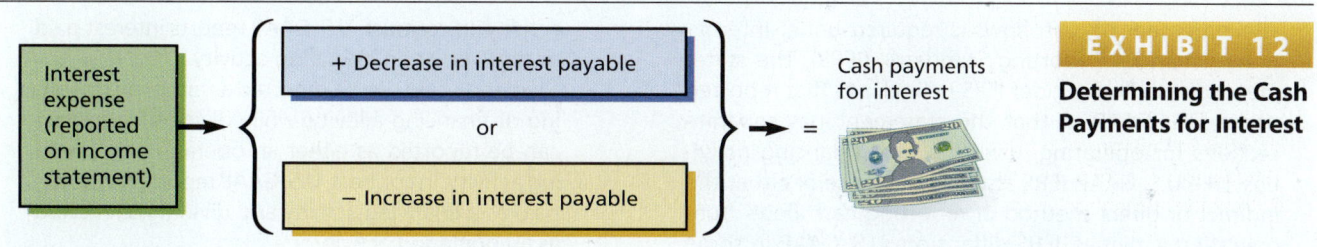

EXHIBIT 12

Determining the Cash Payments for Interest

The comparative balance sheet of Rundell in Exhibit 4 indicates no interest payable. This is because the interest expense on the bonds payable is paid on June 1 and December 31. Because there is no interest payable, no adjustment of the interest expense of $8,000 is necessary.

Cash Payments for Income Taxes

The income statement for **Rundell Inc.** (from Exhibit 4) reports income tax expense of $83,000. To determine the cash payments for income taxes, the $83,000 is adjusted for any increases or decreases in income taxes payable. The adjustment is summarized in Exhibit 13.

EXHIBIT 13
Determining the Cash Payments for Income Taxes

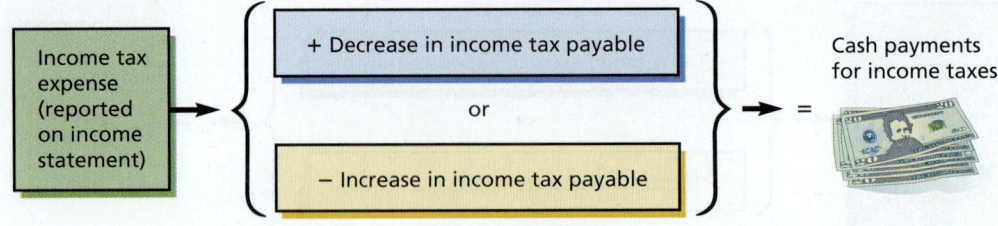

The cash payments for income taxes are $83,500, computed as follows:

Income tax expense	$83,000
Decrease in income taxes payable	500
Cash payments for income taxes	$83,500

The $500 decrease in income taxes payable (from Exhibit 4) indicates that the cash payments for income taxes were $500 more than the amount reported for income tax expense during 20Y8. Thus, $500 is added to the income tax expense in determining the cash payments for income taxes.

Reporting Cash Flows from Operating Activities—Direct Method

The statement of cash flows for **Rundell Inc.**, using the direct method for reporting cash flows from operating activities, is shown in Exhibit 14. The portions of the statement that differ from those prepared under the indirect method are highlighted.

Exhibit 14 also includes the separate schedule reconciling net income and net cash flow from operating activities. This schedule is included in the statement of cash flows when the direct method is used. This schedule is similar to the Cash flows from operating activities section prepared under the indirect method.

International Connection

IFRS FOR STATEMENT OF CASH FLOWS

The statement of cash flows is required under International Financial Reporting Standards (IFRS). The statement of cash flows under IFRS is similar to that reported under U.S. GAAP in that the statement has separate sections for operating, investing, and financing activities. Like U.S. GAAP, IFRS also allow the use of either the indirect or direct method of reporting cash flows from operating activities. IFRS differ from U.S. GAAP in some minor areas, including:

- Interest paid can be reported as either an operating or financing activity, while interest received can be reported as either an operating or investing activity. In contrast, U.S. GAAP reports interest paid or received as an operating activity.
- Dividends paid can be reported as either an operating or financing activity, while dividends received can be reported as either an operating or investing activity. In contrast, U.S. GAAP reports dividends paid as a financing activity and dividends received as an operating activity.
- Cash flows to pay taxes are reported as a separate line in the operating activities, in contrast to U.S. GAAP, which does not require a separate line disclosure.

EXHIBIT 14

Statement of Cash Flows—Direct Method

Rundell Inc.
Statement of Cash Flows
For the Year Ended December 31, 20Y8

Cash flows from operating activities:		
Cash received from customers	$1,171,000	
Cash payments for merchandise	(785,200)	
Cash payments for operating expenses	(193,800)	
Cash payments for interest	(8,000)	
Cash payments for income taxes	(83,500)	
Net cash flow from operating activities		$100,500
Cash flows from (used for) investing activities:		
Cash from sale of land	$ 72,000	
Cash used for purchase of land	(15,000)	
Cash used for purchase of building	(60,000)	
Net cash flow used for investing activities		(3,000)
Cash flows from (used for) financing activities:		
Cash from sale of common stock	$ 48,000	
Cash used to retire bonds payable	(50,000)	
Cash used for dividends	(24,000)	
Net cash flow used for financing activities		(26,000)
Increase (decrease) in cash		$ 71,500
Cash at the beginning of the year		26,000
Cash at the end of the year		$ 97,500
Schedule Reconciling Net Income with Cash		
Flows from Operating Activities:		
Cash flows from operating activities:		
Net income		$108,000
Adjustments to reconcile net income to net cash		
flow from operating activities:		
Depreciation		7,000
Gain on sale of land		(12,000)
Changes in current operating assets and liabilities:		
Increase in accounts receivable		(9,000)
Decrease in inventory		8,000
Decrease in accounts payable		(3,200)
Increase in accrued expenses payable		2,200
Decrease in income taxes payable		(500)
Net cash flow from operating activities		$100,500

Financial Analysis and Interpretation: Free Cash Flow

Obj. 4 Describe and illustrate the use of free cash flow in evaluating a company's cash flow.

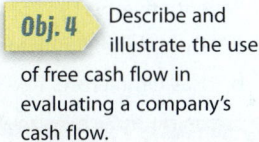

A valuable tool for evaluating the profitability of a business is free cash flow. **Free cash flow** measures the operating cash flow available to a company after it purchases the property, plant, and equipment (PP&E) necessary to maintain its current operations. Since the investments in PP&E necessary to maintain current operations cannot often be determined from financial statements, analysts estimate this amount using the cash used to purchase PP&E, as shown in the statement of cash flows. Thus, free cash flow is computed as follows:

Cash flows from operating activities	$ XXX
Cash used to purchase property, plant, and equipment	(XXX)
Free cash flow	$ XXX

The free cash flow can be expressed as a percentage of sales in order to provide a relative measure that can be compared over time or to other companies. This ratio is computed as follows:

788 Chapter 16 Statement of Cash Flows

$$\text{Ratio of Free Cash Flow to Sales} = \frac{\text{Free Cash Flow}}{\text{Sales}}$$

Positive free cash flow is considered favorable. A company that has free cash flow is able to fund growth and acquisitions, retire debt, purchase treasury stock, and pay dividends. A company with no free cash flow may have limited financial flexibility, potentially leading to liquidity problems.

To illustrate, information from the annual reports of **National Beverage** for three recent years is as follows (in thousands):

	Year 3	Year 2	Year 1
Cash flows from operating activities	$ 58,020	$ 52,383	$ 40,264
Cash used to purchase property, plant, and equipment	11,630	12,124	9,693
Sales	645,825	641,135	662,007

The free cash flow is computed for the three years as follows:

	Year 3	Year 2	Year 1
Cash flows from operating activities	$ 58,020	$ 52,383	$40,264
Cash used to purchase property, plant, and equipment	(11,630)	(12,124)	(9,693)
Free cash flow	$ 46,390	$ 40,259	$30,571

As can be seen, free cash flow has increased across the three years. In Year 3, it is nearly 52% higher than in Year 1 [($46,390 − $30,571) ÷ $30,571]. The ratio of free cash flow to sales is as follows (rounded to one decimal place):

	Year 3	Year 2	Year 1
Ratio of free cash flow to sales	7.2%	6.3%	4.6%
	($46,390 ÷ $645,825)	($40,259 ÷ $641,135)	($30,571 ÷ $662,007)

The ratio of free cash flow to sales has also increased across these three years, from 4.6% in Year 1 to 7.2% in Year 3, which is a 57% increase [(7.2% − 4.6%) ÷ 4.6%].

Example Exercise 16-8 Free Cash Flow *Obj. 4*

Omnicron Inc. reported the following on the company's cash flow statement in 20Y8 and 20Y7:

	20Y8	20Y7
Net cash flow from operating activities	$140,000	$120,000
Net cash flow used for investing activities	(120,000)	(80,000)
Net cash flow used for financing activities	(20,000)	(32,000)

Seventy-five percent of the net cash flow used for investing activities was used to replace existing capacity.

a. Determine Omnicron's free cash flow.
b. Has Omnicron's free cash flow improved or declined from 20Y7 to 20Y8?

Follow My Example 16-8

a.

	20Y8	20Y7
Net cash flow from operating activities	$140,000	$120,000
Investments in fixed assets to maintain current production	(90,000)[1]	(60,000)[2]
Free cash flow	$ 50,000	$ 60,000

[1] $120,000 × 75%
[2] $80,000 × 75%

b. The change from $60,000 to $50,000 indicates an unfavorable trend.

Practice Exercises: PE 16-8A, PE 16-8B

APPENDIX

Spreadsheet (Work Sheet) for Statement of Cash Flows—The Indirect Method

A spreadsheet (work sheet) may be used in preparing the statement of cash flows. However, whether or not a spreadsheet (work sheet) is used, the concepts presented in this chapter are not affected.

The data for **Rundell Inc.**, presented in Exhibit 4, are used as a basis for illustrating the spreadsheet (work sheet) for the indirect method. The steps in preparing this spreadsheet (work sheet), shown in Exhibit 15, are as follows:

Step 1. List the title of each balance sheet account in the Accounts column.

Step 2. For each balance sheet account, enter its balance as of December 31, 20Y7, in the first column and its balance as of December 31, 20Y8, in the last column. Place the credit balances in parentheses.

Step 3. Add the December 31, 20Y7 and 20Y8 column totals, which should total to zero.

Step 4. Analyze the change during the year in each noncash account to determine its net increase (decrease) and classify the change as affecting cash flows from operating activities, investing activities, financing activities, or noncash investing and financing activities.

Step 5. Indicate the effect of the change on cash flows by making entries in the Transactions columns.

Step 6. After all noncash accounts have been analyzed, enter the net increase (decrease) in cash during the period.

Step 7. Add the Debit and Credit Transactions columns. The totals should be equal.

Analyzing Accounts

In analyzing the noncash accounts (Step 4), try to determine the type of cash flow activity (operating, investing, or financing) that led to the change in the account. As each noncash account is analyzed, an entry (Step 5) is made on the spreadsheet (work sheet) for the type of cash flow activity that caused the change. After all noncash accounts have been analyzed, an entry (Step 6) is made for the increase (decrease) in cash during the period.

The entries made on the spreadsheet are not posted to the ledger. They are only used in preparing and summarizing the data on the spreadsheet.

The order in which the accounts are analyzed is not important. However, it is more efficient to begin with Retained Earnings and proceed upward in the account listing.

Retained Earnings

The spreadsheet (work sheet) shows a Retained Earnings balance of $202,300 at December 31, 20Y7, and $282,300 at December 31, 20Y8. Thus, Retained Earnings increased $80,000 during the year. This increase is from the following:

- Net income of $108,000
- Declaring cash dividends of $28,000

To identify the cash flows from these activities, two entries are made on the spreadsheet.

790 Chapter 16 Statement of Cash Flows

EXHIBIT 15 End-of-Period Spreadsheet (Work Sheet) for Statement of Cash Flows—Indirect Method

Rundell Inc.
End-of-Period Spreadsheet (Work Sheet) for Statement of Cash Flows
For the Year Ended December 31, 20Y8

	Accounts	Balance, Dec. 31, 20Y7		Debit		Credit	Balance, Dec. 31, 20Y8
6	Cash	26,000	(o)	71,500			97,500
7	Accounts receivable (net)	65,000	(n)	9,000			74,000
8	Inventories	180,000			(m)	8,000	172,000
9	Land	125,000	(k)	15,000	(l)	60,000	80,000
10	Building	200,000	(j)	60,000			260,000
11	Accumulated depreciation—building	(58,300)			(i)	7,000	(65,300)
12	Accounts payable (merchandise creditors)	(46,700)	(h)	3,200			(43,500)
13	Accrued expenses payable (operating expenses)	(24,300)			(g)	2,200	(26,500)
14	Income taxes payable	(8,400)	(f)	500			(7,900)
15	Dividends payable	(10,000)			(e)	4,000	(14,000)
16	Bonds payable	(150,000)	(d)	50,000			(100,000)
17	Common stock	(16,000)			(c)	8,000	(24,000)
18	Paid-in capital in excess of par	(80,000)			(c)	40,000	(120,000)
19	Retained earnings	(202,300)	(b)	28,000	(a)	108,000	(282,300)
20	Totals	0		237,200		237,200	0
21	Operating activities:						
22	Net income		(a)	108,000			
23	Depreciation of building		(i)	7,000			
24	Gain on sale of land				(l)	12,000	
25	Increase in accounts receivable				(n)	9,000	
26	Decrease in inventories		(m)	8,000			
27	Decrease in accounts payable				(h)	3,200	
28	Increase in accrued expenses payable		(g)	2,200			
29	Decrease in income taxes payable				(f)	500	
30	Investing activities:						
31	Sale of land		(l)	72,000			
32	Purchase of land				(k)	15,000	
33	Purchase of building				(j)	60,000	
34	Financing activities:						
35	Issued common stock		(c)	48,000			
36	Retired bonds payable				(d)	50,000	
37	Declared cash dividends				(b)	28,000	
38	Increase in dividends payable		(e)	4,000			
39	Increase (decrease) in cash				(o)	71,500	
40	Totals			249,200		249,200	

The $108,000 is reported on the statement of cash flows as part of cash flows from operating activities. Thus, an entry is made in the Transactions columns on the spreadsheet, as follows:

(a) Operating Activities—Net Income.................................. 108,000
   Retained Earnings.. 108,000

The preceding entry accounts for the net income portion of the change to Retained Earnings. It also identifies the cash flow in the bottom portion of the spreadsheet as related to operating activities.

The $28,000 of dividends is reported as a financing activity on the statement of cash flows. Thus, an entry is made in the Transactions columns on the spreadsheet, as follows:

(b)	Retained Earnings...	28,000	
	Financing Activities—Declared Cash Dividends		28,000

The preceding entry accounts for the dividends portion of the change to Retained Earnings. It also identifies the cash flow in the bottom portion of the spreadsheet as related to financing activities. The $28,000 of declared dividends will be adjusted later for the actual amount of cash dividends paid during the year.

Other Accounts

The entries for the other noncash accounts are made in the spreadsheet in a manner similar to entries (a) and (b). A summary of these entries follows:

(c)	Financing Activities—Issued Common Stock.......................	48,000	
	Common Stock		8,000
	Paid-In Capital in Excess of Par—Common Stock		40,000
(d)	Bonds Payable	50,000	
	Financing Activities—Retired Bonds Payable....................		50,000
(e)	Financing Activities—Increase in Dividends Payable...............	4,000	
	Dividends Payable		4,000
(f)	Income Taxes Payable	500	
	Operating Activities—Decrease in Income Taxes Payable		500
(g)	Operating Activities—Increase in Accrued Expenses Payable	2,200	
	Accrued Expenses Payable		2,200
(h)	Accounts Payable	3,200	
	Operating Activities—Decrease in Accounts Payable		3,200
(i)	Operating Activities—Depreciation of Building	7,000	
	Accumulated Depreciation—Building		7,000
(j)	Building	60,000	
	Investing Activities—Purchase of Building		60,000
(k)	Land..	15,000	
	Investing Activities—Purchase of Land.........................		15,000
(l)	Investing Activities—Sale of Land.................................	72,000	
	Operating Activities—Gain on Sale of Land		12,000
	Land...		60,000
(m)	Operating Activities—Decrease in Inventories......................	8,000	
	Inventories...		8,000
(n)	Accounts Receivable	9,000	
	Operating Activities—Increase in Accounts Receivable		9,000
(o)	Cash..	71,500	
	Net Increase in Cash..		71,500

After all the balance sheet accounts are analyzed and the entries made on the spreadsheet (work sheet), all the operating, investing, and financing activities are identified in the bottom portion of the spreadsheet. The accuracy of the entries is verified by totaling the Debit and Credit Transactions columns. The totals of the columns should be equal.

Preparing the Statement of Cash Flows

The statement of cash flows prepared from the spreadsheet is identical to the statement in Exhibit 7. The data for the three sections of the statement are obtained from the bottom portion of the spreadsheet.

At a Glance 16

Obj. 1 Describe the cash flow activities reported in the statement of cash flows.

Key Points The statement of cash flows reports cash receipts and cash payments by three types of activities: operating activities, investing activities, and financing activities. Cash flows from operating activities reports the cash inflows and outflows from a company's day-to-day operations. Cash flows from (used for) investing activities reports the cash inflows and outflows related to changes in a company's long-term assets. Cash flows from (used for) financing activities reports the cash inflows and outflows related to changes in a company's long-term liabilities and stockholders' equity. Investing and financing for a business may be affected by transactions that do not involve cash. The effect of such transactions should be reported in a separate schedule accompanying the statement of cash flows.

Learning Outcome	Example Exercises	Practice Exercises
• Classify transactions that either provide or use cash into operating, investing, or financing activities.	EE16-1	PE16-1A, 16-1B

Obj. 2 Prepare a statement of cash flows, using the indirect method.

Key Points The indirect method reports cash flows from operating activities by adjusting net income for revenues and expenses that do not involve the receipt or payment of cash. Noncash expenses such as depreciation are added back to net income. Gains and losses on the disposal of assets are added to or deducted from net income. Changes in current operating assets and liabilities are added to or subtracted from net income, depending on their effect on cash. Cash flows from (used for) investing activities and cash flows from (used for) financing activities are reported below cash flows from operating activities in the statement of cash flows.

Learning Outcomes	Example Exercises	Practice Exercises
• Determine cash flows from operating activities under the indirect method by adjusting net income for noncash expenses and gains and losses from asset disposals.	EE16-2	PE16-2A, 16-2B
• Determine cash flows from operating activities under the indirect method by adjusting net income for changes in current operating assets and liabilities.	EE16-3	PE16-3A, 16-3B
• Prepare the Cash flows from operating activities section of the statement of cash flows, using the indirect method.	EE16-4	PE16-4A, 16-4B
• Prepare the Cash flows from (used for) investing activities and Cash flows from (used for) financing activities sections of the statement of cash flows.	EE16-5	PE16-5A, 16-5B

Obj. 3 Prepare a statement of cash flows, using the direct method.

Key Points The amount of cash flows from operating activities is the same under both the direct and indirect methods, but the manner in which cash flows operating activities is reported is different. The direct method reports cash flows from operating activities by major classes of operating cash receipts and cash payments. The difference between the major classes of total operating cash receipts and total operating cash payments is the net cash flow from operating activities. The Cash flows from (used for) investing and financing activities sections of the statement are the same under both the direct and indirect methods.

Learning Outcome	Example Exercises	Practice Exercises
• Prepare the Cash flows from operating activities section of the statement of cash flows under the direct method.	EE16-6 EE16-7	PE16-6A, 16-6B PE16-7A, 16-7B

Obj. 4 Describe and illustrate the use of free cash flow in evaluating a company's cash flow.

Key Points Free cash flow measures the operating cash flow available for company use after purchasing the fixed assets that are necessary to maintain current productive capacity. It is calculated by subtracting these fixed asset purchases from net cash flow from operating activities. A company with strong free cash flow is able to fund internal growth, retire debt, pay dividends, and enjoy financial flexibility. A company with weak free cash flow has much less financial flexibility.

Learning Outcomes	Example Exercises	Practice Exercises
• Describe free cash flow.		
• Calculate and evaluate free cash flow.	EE16-8	PE16-8A, 16-8B

Illustrative Problem

The comparative balance sheet of Dowling Company for December 31, 20Y6 and 20Y5, is as follows:

Dowling Company
Comparative Balance Sheet
December 31, 20Y6 and 20Y5

	20Y6	20Y5
Assets		
Cash	$ 140,350	$ 95,900
Accounts receivable (net)	95,300	102,300
Inventories	165,200	157,900
Prepaid expenses	6,240	5,860
Investments (long-term)	35,700	84,700
Land	75,000	90,000
Buildings	375,000	260,000
Accumulated depreciation—buildings	(71,300)	(58,300)
Machinery and equipment	428,300	428,300
Accumulated depreciation—machinery and equipment	(148,500)	(138,000)
Patents	58,000	65,000
Total assets	$1,159,290	$1,093,660
Liabilities and Stockholders' Equity		
Accounts payable (merchandise creditors)	$ 43,500	$ 46,700
Accrued expenses payable (operating expenses)	14,000	12,500
Income taxes payable	7,900	8,400
Dividends payable	14,000	10,000
Mortgage note payable, due in 10 years	40,000	0
Bonds payable	150,000	250,000
Common stock, $30 par	450,000	375,000
Excess of issue price over par—common stock	66,250	41,250
Retained earnings	373,640	349,810
Total liabilities and stockholders' equity	$1,159,290	$1,093,660

(Continued)

The income statement for Dowling Company follows:

Dowling Company
Income Statement
For the Year Ended December 31, 20Y6

Sales		$1,100,000
Cost of merchandise sold		710,000
Gross profit		$ 390,000
Operating expenses:		
Depreciation expense	$ 23,500	
Patent amortization	7,000	
Other operating expenses	196,000	
Total operating expenses		226,500
Income from operations		$ 163,500
Other revenue and expense:		
Gain on sale of investments	$ 11,000	
Interest expense	(26,000)	(15,000)
Income before income tax		$ 148,500
Income tax expense		50,000
Net income		$ 98,500

An examination of the accounting records revealed the following additional information applicable to 20Y6:

a. Land costing $15,000 was sold for $15,000.

b. A mortgage note was issued for $40,000.

c. A building costing $115,000 was constructed.

d. 2,500 shares of common stock were issued at $40 in exchange for the bonds payable.

e. Cash dividends declared were $74,670.

Instructions

1. Prepare a statement of cash flows, using the indirect method of reporting cash flows from operating activities.

2. Prepare a statement of cash flows, using the direct method of reporting cash flows from operating activities. For purposes of the direct method, the adjustment to arrive at cash payments for operating expenses includes changes in prepaid expenses.

Solution

1.

Dowling Company
Statement of Cash Flows—Indirect Method
For the Year Ended December 31, 20Y6

Cash flows from operating activities:		
Net income		$ 98,500
Adjustments to reconcile net income to net		
cash flow from operating activities:		
Depreciation	23,500	
Amortization of patents	7,000	
Gain on sale of investments	(11,000)	
Changes in current operating assets and liabilities:		
Decrease in accounts receivable	7,000	
Increase in inventories	(7,300)	
Increase in prepaid expenses	(380)	
Decrease in accounts payable	(3,200)	
Increase in accrued expenses payable	1,500	
Decrease in income taxes payable	(500)	
Net cash flow from operating activities		$115,120
Cash flows from (used for) investing activities:		
Cash from sale of investments	$ 60,000[1]	
Cash from sale of land	15,000	
Cash used for construction of building	(115,000)	
Net cash flow used for investing activities		(40,000)
Cash flows from (used for) financing activities:		
Cash from issuing mortgage note payable	$ 40,000	
Cash used for dividends	(70,670)[2]	
Net cash flow used for financing activities		(30,670)
Increase (decrease) in cash		$ 44,450
Cash at the beginning of the year		95,900
Cash at the end of the year		$140,350
Schedule of Noncash Investing and Financing Activities:		
Issued common stock to retire bonds payable		$100,000

[1] $60,000 = $11,000 gain + $49,000 (decrease in investments)
[2] $70,670 = $74,670 − $4,000 (increase in dividends)

(Continued)

2.

Dowling Company
Statement of Cash Flows—Direct Method
For the Year Ended December 31, 20Y6

Cash flows from operating activities:		
Cash received from customers[1]	$1,107,000	
Cash paid for merchandise[2]	(720,500)	
Cash paid for operating expenses[3]	(194,880)	
Cash paid for interest expense	(26,000)	
Cash paid for income tax[4]	(50,500)	
Net cash flow from operating activities		$115,120
Cash flows from (used for) investing activities:		
Cash from sale of investments	$ 60,000[5]	
Cash from sale of land	15,000	
Cash used for construction of building	(115,000)	
Net cash flow used for investing activities		(40,000)
Cash flows from (used for) financing activities:		
Cash from issuing mortgage note payable	$ 40,000	
Cash used for dividends[6]	(70,670)	
Net cash flow used for financing activities		(30,670)
Increase (decrease) in cash		$ 44,450
Cash at the beginning of the year		95,900
Cash at the end of the year		$140,350
Schedule of Noncash Investing and Financing Activities:		
Issued common stock to retire bonds payable		$100,000
Schedule Reconciling Net Income with Cash Flows		
from Operating Activities[7]		

Computations:

[1] $1,100,000 + $7,000 = $1,107,000
[2] $710,000 + $3,200 + $7,300 = $720,500
[3] $196,000 + $380 − $1,500 = $194,880
[4] $50,000 + $500 = $50,500
[5] $60,000 = $11,000 gain + $49,000 (decrease in investments)
[6] $74,670 + $10,000 − $14,000 = $70,670
[7] The content of this schedule is the same as the operating activities section of part (1) of this solution and is not reproduced here for the sake of brevity.

Key Terms

cash flow per share (771)
cash flows from (used for) financing activities (768)
cash flows from (used for) investing activities (767)
cash flows from operating activities (767)
direct method (768)
free cash flow (787)
indirect method (769)
statement of cash flows (767)

Discussion Questions

1. What is the principal advantage and the principal disadvantage of the direct method of reporting cash flows from operating activities?

2. What are the major advantages of the indirect method of reporting cash flows from operating activities?

3. A corporation issued $2,000,000 of common stock in exchange for $2,000,000 of fixed assets. Where would this transaction be reported on the statement of cash flows?

4. A retail business, using the accrual method of accounting, owed merchandise creditors (accounts payable) $320,000 at the beginning of the year and $350,000 at the end of the year. How would the $30,000 increase be used to adjust net income in determining the amount of cash flows from operating activities by the indirect method?

5. If salaries payable was $100,000 at the beginning of the year and $75,000 at the end of the year, should the $25,000 decrease be added to or deducted from income to determine the amount of cash flows from operating activities by the indirect method? Explain.

6. A long-term investment in bonds with a cost of $500,000 was sold for $600,000 cash. (a) What was the gain or loss on the sale? (b) What was the effect of the transaction on cash flows? (c) How would the transaction be reported on the statement of cash flows if cash flows from operating activities are reported by the indirect method?

7. A corporation issued $2,000,000 of 20-year bonds for cash at 98. How would the transaction be reported on the statement of cash flows?

8. Fully depreciated equipment costing $50,000 is discarded. What is the effect of the transaction on cash flows if (a) $15,000 cash is received for the equipment, (b) no cash is received for the equipment?

9. For the current year, Packers Company decided to switch from the indirect method to the direct method for reporting cash flows from operating activities on the statement of cash flows. Will the change cause the amount of net cash flow from operating activities to be larger, smaller, or the same compared to the indirect method being used? Explain.

10. Name five common major classes of operating cash receipts or operating cash payments presented on the statement of cash flows when the cash flows from operating activities are reported by the direct method.

Practice Exercises

Example Exercises

EE 16-1 p. 771   **PE 16-1A**   Classifying cash flows   OBJ. 1

Identify whether each of the following would be reported as an operating, investing, or financing activity on the statement of cash flows:

a. Retirement of bonds payable
b. Purchase of inventory for cash
c. Cash sales
d. Repurchase of common stock
e. Payment of accounts payable
f. Disposal of equipment

EE 16-1 p. 771   **PE 16-1B**   Classifying cash flows   OBJ. 1

Identify whether each of the following would be reported as an operating, investing, or financing activity on the statement of cash flows:

a. Purchase of investments
b. Purchase of equipment
c. Payment for selling expenses
d. Collection of accounts receivable
e. Cash received from customers
f. Issuance of bonds payable

798 Chapter 16 Statement of Cash Flows

EE 16-2 p. 775

PE 16-2A Adjustments to net income—indirect method OBJ. 2

Ripley Corporation's accumulated depreciation—furniture account increased by $11,575, while $2,500 of patent amortization was recognized between balance sheet dates. There were no purchases or sales of depreciable or intangible assets during the year. In addition, the income statement showed a loss of $3,400 from the sale of land. Reconcile a net income of $224,500 to net cash flow from operating activities.

EE 16-2 p. 775

PE 16-2B Adjustments to net income—indirect method OBJ. 2

Ya Wen Corporation's accumulated depreciation—equipment account increased by $8,750, while $3,250 of patent amortization was recognized between balance sheet dates. There were no purchases or sales of depreciable or intangible assets during the year. In addition, the income statement showed a gain of $18,750 from the sale of investments. Reconcile a net income of $175,000 to net cash flow from operating activities.

EE 16-3 p. 777

PE 16-3A Changes in current operating assets and liabilities—indirect method OBJ. 2

Zwilling Corporation's comparative balance sheet for current assets and liabilities was as follows:

	Dec. 31, Year 2	Dec. 31, Year 1
Accounts receivable	$35,000	$39,500
Inventory	22,500	18,450
Accounts payable	18,500	16,300
Dividends payable	43,200	53,100

Adjust net income of $320,000 for changes in operating assets and liabilities to arrive at net cash flow from operating activities.

EE 16-3 p. 777

PE 16-3B Changes in current operating assets and liabilities—indirect method OBJ. 2

Huluduey Corporation's comparative balance sheet for current assets and liabilities was as follows:

	Dec. 31, Year 2	Dec. 31, Year 1
Accounts receivable	$18,000	$14,400
Inventory	34,800	29,700
Accounts payable	27,600	20,700
Dividends payable	8,400	10,800

Adjust net income of $160,000 for changes in operating assets and liabilities to arrive at net cash flow from operating activities.

EE 16-4 p. 777

PE 16-4A Cash flows from operating activities—indirect method OBJ. 2

Demers Inc. reported the following data:

Net income	$490,000
Depreciation expense	52,000
Gain on disposal of equipment	26,500
Decrease in accounts receivable	32,400
Decrease in accounts payable	12,350

Prepare the Cash flows from operating activities section of the statement of cash flows, using the indirect method.

EE 16-4 p. 777   **PE 16-4B**   **Cash flows from operating activities—indirect method**   OBJ. 2

Staley Inc. reported the following data:

Net income	$280,000
Depreciation expense	48,000
Loss on disposal of equipment	19,520
Increase in accounts receivable	17,280
Increase in accounts payable	8,960

Prepare the Cash flows from operating activities section of the statement of cash flows, using the indirect method.

EE 16-5 p. 781   **PE 16-5A**   **Land transactions on the statement of cash flows**   OBJ. 2

Simkin Corporation purchased land for $420,000. Later in the year, the company sold a different piece of land with a book value of $155,000 for $110,000. How are the effects of these transactions reported on the statement of cash flows?

EE 16-5 p. 781   **PE 16-5B**   **Land transactions on the statement of cash flows**   OBJ. 2

IZ Corporation purchased land for $400,000. Later in the year, the company sold a different piece of land with a book value of $200,000 for $240,000. How are the effects of these transactions reported on the statement of cash flows?

EE 16-6 p. 783   **PE 16-6A**   **Cash received from customers—direct method**   OBJ. 3

Sales reported on the income statement were $480,000. The accounts receivable balance increased $54,000 over the year. Determine the amount of cash received from customers.

EE 16-6 p. 783   **PE 16-6B**   **Cash received from customers—direct method**   OBJ. 3

Sales reported on the income statement were $112,000. The accounts receivable balance decreased $10,500 over the year. Determine the amount of cash received from customers.

EE 16-7 p. 784   **PE 16-7A**   **Cash payments for merchandise—direct method**   OBJ. 3

The cost of merchandise sold reported on the income statement was $770,000. The accounts payable balance decreased $44,000, and the inventory balance decreased by $66,000 over the year. Determine the amount of cash paid for merchandise.

EE 16-7 p. 784   **PE 16-7B**   **Cash payments for merchandise—direct method**   OBJ. 3

The cost of merchandise sold reported on the income statement was $240,000. The accounts payable balance increased $12,000, and the inventory balance increased by $19,200 over the year. Determine the amount of cash paid for merchandise.

EE 16-8 p. 788   **PE 16-8A**   **Free cash flow**   OBJ. 4

McMahon Inc. reported the following on the company's statement of cash flows in Year 2 and Year 1:

	Year 2	Year 1
Net cash flow from operating activities	$ 294,000	$ 280,000
Net cash flow used for investing activities	(224,000)	(252,000)
Net cash flow used for financing activities	(63,000)	(42,000)

Seventy percent of the net cash flow used for investing activities was used to replace existing capacity.

(Continued)

a. Determine McMahon's free cash flow for both years.

b. Has McMahon's free cash flow improved or declined from Year 1 to Year 2?

 EE 16-8 *p. 788* **PE 16-8B Free cash flow** OBJ. 4

Dillin Inc. reported the following on the company's statement of cash flows in Year 2 and Year 1:

	Year 2	Year 1
Net cash flow from operating activities	$476,000	$455,000
Net cash flow used for investing activities	(427,000)	(378,000)
Net cash flow used for financing activities	(42,000)	(58,800)

Eighty percent of the net cash flow used for investing activities was used to replace existing capacity.

a. Determine Dillin's free cash flow for both years.

b. Has Dillin's free cash flow improved or declined from Year 1 to Year 2?

Exercises

EX 16-1 Cash flows from operating activities—net loss OBJ. 1

On its income statement for a recent year, **American Airlines Group, Inc.**, the parent company of American Airlines, reported a net *loss* of $1,834 million from operations. On its statement of cash flows, it reported $675 million of cash flows from operating activities. Explain this apparent contradiction between the loss and the positive cash flows.

EX 16-2 Effect of transactions on cash flows OBJ. 1

✔ a. Cash payment, $411,000

State the effect (cash receipt or payment and amount) of each of the following transactions, considered individually, on cash flows:

a. Retired $400,000 of bonds, on which there was $3,000 of unamortized discount, for $411,000.

b. Sold 20,000 shares of $5 par common stock for $22 per share.

c. Sold equipment with a book value of $55,800 for $60,000.

d. Purchased land for $650,000 cash.

e. Purchased a building by paying $50,000 cash and issuing a $450,000 mortgage note payable.

f. Sold a new issue of $500,000 of bonds at 98.

g. Purchased 10,000 shares of $40 par common stock as treasury stock at $50 per share.

h. Paid dividends of $1.50 per share. There were 1,000,000 shares issued and 120,000 shares of treasury stock.

EX 16-3 Classifying cash flows OBJ. 1

Identify the type of cash flow activity for each of the following events (operating, investing, or financing):

a. Redeemed bonds
b. Issued preferred stock
c. Paid cash dividends
d. Net income
e. Sold equipment
f. Purchased treasury stock
g. Purchased patents
h. Purchased buildings
i. Sold long-term investments
j. Issued bonds
k. Issued common stock

Chapter 16 Statement of Cash Flows   801

EX 16-4 Cash flows from operating activities—indirect method   OBJ. 2

Indicate whether each of the following would be added to or deducted from net income in determining net cash flow from operating activities by the indirect method:

a. Increase in merchandise inventory
b. Increase in prepaid expenses
c. Depreciation of fixed assets
d. Gain on disposal of fixed assets
e. Amortization of patent
f. Increase in notes payable due in 120 days to vendors
g. Increase in accounts payable
h. Decrease in wages payable
i. Decrease in notes receivable due in 60 days from customers
j. Decrease in accounts receivable
k. Loss on retirement of long-term debt

EX 16-5 Cash flows from operating activities—indirect method   OBJ. 1, 2

✔ Net cash flow from operating activities, $103,850

The net income reported on the income statement for the current year was $73,600. Depreciation recorded on store equipment for the year amounted to $27,400. Balances of the current asset and current liability accounts at the beginning and end of the year are as follows:

	End of Year	Beginning of Year
Cash	$23,500	$18,700
Accounts receivable (net)	56,000	48,000
Merchandise inventory	35,500	40,000
Prepaid expenses	4,750	7,000
Accounts payable (merchandise creditors)	21,800	16,800
Wages payable	4,900	5,800

a. Prepare the Cash flows from operating activities section of the statement of cash flows, using the indirect method.
b. Briefly explain why net cash flow from operating activities is different from net income.

EX 16-6 Cash flows from operating activities—indirect method   OBJ. 1, 2

✔ Net cash flow from operating activities, $260,850

The net income reported on the income statement for the current year was $185,000. Depreciation recorded on equipment and a building amounted to $96,000 for the year. Balances of the current asset and current liability accounts at the beginning and end of the year are as follows:

	End of Year	Beginning of Year
Cash	$ 75,000	$ 86,150
Accounts receivable (net)	84,550	90,000
Inventories	186,200	175,000
Prepaid expenses	3,600	4,500
Accounts payable (merchandise creditors)	91,500	110,000
Salaries payable	7,200	4,000

a. Prepare the Cash flows from operating activities section of the statement of cash flows, using the indirect method.
b. If the direct method had been used, would the net cash flow from operating activities have been the same? Explain.

EX 16-7 Cash flows from operating activities—indirect method   OBJ. 1, 2

✔ Net cash flow from operating activities, $651,300

The income statement disclosed the following items for the year:

Depreciation expense	$ 65,000
Gain on disposal of equipment	27,500
Net income	620,000

(Continued)

The changes in the current asset and liability accounts for the year are as follows:

	Increase (Decrease)
Accounts receivable	$11,200
Inventory	(6,350)
Prepaid insurance	(1,200)
Accounts payable	(4,200)
Income taxes payable	1,650
Dividends payable	2,500

a. Prepare the Cash flows from operating activities section of the statement of cash flows, using the indirect method.

b. Briefly explain why net cash flows from operating activities is different from net income.

EX 16-8 Determining cash payments to stockholders   OBJ. 2

The board of directors declared cash dividends totaling $585,000 during the current year. The comparative balance sheet indicates dividends payable of $167,625 at the beginning of the year and $146,250 at the end of the year. What was the amount of cash payments to stockholders during the year?

EX 16-9 Reporting changes in equipment on statement of cash flows   OBJ. 2

An analysis of the general ledger accounts indicates that office equipment, which cost $202,500 and on which accumulated depreciation totaled $84,375 on the date of sale, was sold for $101,250 during the year. Using this information, indicate the items to be reported on the statement of cash flows.

EX 16-10 Reporting changes in equipment on statement of cash flows   OBJ. 2

An analysis of the general ledger accounts indicates that delivery equipment, which cost $200,000 and on which accumulated depreciation totaled $60,000 on the date of sale, was sold for $132,500 during the year. Using this information, indicate the items to be reported on the statement of cash flows.

EX 16-11 Reporting land transactions on statement of cash flows   OBJ. 2

On the basis of the details of the following fixed asset account, indicate the items to be reported on the statement of cash flows:

ACCOUNT Land   **ACCOUNT NO.**

					Balance	
Date		Item	Debit	Credit	Debit	Credit
Jan.	1	Balance			868,000	
Mar.	12	Purchased for cash	104,300		972,300	
Oct.	4	Sold for $95,550		63,840	908,460	

EX 16-12 Reporting stockholders' equity items on statement of cash flows   OBJ. 2

On the basis of the following stockholders' equity accounts, indicate the items, exclusive of net income, to be reported on the statement of cash flows. There were no unpaid dividends at either the beginning or the end of the year.

ACCOUNT Common Stock, $40 par   **ACCOUNT NO.**

					Balance	
Date		Item	Debit	Credit	Debit	Credit
Jan.	1	Balance, 120,000 shares				4,800,000
Apr.	2	30,000 shares issued for cash		1,200,000		6,000,000
June	30	4,400-share stock dividend		176,000		6,176,000

ACCOUNT Paid-In Capital in Excess of Par—Common Stock   **ACCOUNT NO.**

Date		Item	Debit	Credit	Balance Debit	Balance Credit
Jan.	1	Balance				360,000
Apr.	2	30,000 shares issued for cash		720,000		1,080,000
June	30	Stock dividend		114,400		1,194,400

ACCOUNT Retained Earnings   **ACCOUNT NO.**

Date		Item	Debit	Credit	Balance Debit	Balance Credit
Jan.	1	Balance				2,000,000
June	30	Stock dividend	290,440			1,709,560
Dec.	30	Cash dividend	463,200			1,246,360
	31	Net income		1,440,000		2,686,360

EX 16-13   **Reporting land acquisition for cash and mortgage note on statement of cash flows**   **OBJ. 2**

On the basis of the details of the following fixed asset account, indicate the items to be reported on the statement of cash flows:

ACCOUNT Land   **ACCOUNT NO.**

Date		Item	Debit	Credit	Balance Debit	Balance Credit
Jan.	1	Balance			156,000	
Feb.	10	Purchased for cash	246,000		402,000	
Nov.	20	Purchased with long-term mortgage note	324,000		726,000	

EX 16-14   **Reporting issuance and retirement of long-term debt**   **OBJ. 2**

On the basis of the details of the following bonds payable and related discount accounts, indicate the items to be reported in the financing activities section of the statement of cash flows, assuming no gain or loss on retiring the bonds:

ACCOUNT Bonds Payable   **ACCOUNT NO.**

Date		Item	Debit	Credit	Balance Debit	Balance Credit
Jan.	1	Balance				750,000
	2	Retire bonds	150,000			600,000
June	30	Issue bonds		450,000		1,050,000

ACCOUNT Discount on Bonds Payable   **ACCOUNT NO.**

Date		Item	Debit	Credit	Balance Debit	Balance Credit
Jan.	1	Balance			33,750	
	2	Retire bonds		12,000	21,750	
June	30	Issue bonds	30,000		51,750	
Dec.	31	Amortize discount		2,625	49,125	

804 Chapter 16 Statement of Cash Flows

✔ Net income, $341,770

EX 16-15 Determining net income from net cash flow from operating activities OBJ. 2

Curwen Inc. reported net cash flow from operating activities of $357,500 on its statement of cash flows for a recent year ended December 31. The following information was reported in the Cash flows from operating activities section of the statement of cash flows, using the indirect method:

Decrease in income taxes payable	$ 7,700
Decrease in inventories	19,140
Depreciation	29,480
Gain on sale of investments	13,200
Increase in accounts payable	5,280
Increase in prepaid expenses	2,970
Increase in accounts receivable	14,300

a. Determine the net income reported by Curwen Inc. for the year ended December 31.
b. ✏️ Briefly explain why Curwen's net income is different from net cash flow from operating activities.

✔ Net cash flow from operating activities, $58,020

EX 16-16 Cash flows from operating activities—indirect method OBJ. 2

Selected data derived from the income statement and balance sheet of **National Beverage Co.** for a recent year are as follows:

Income statement data (in thousands):

Net income	$49,311
Gain on disposal of property	1,188
Depreciation expense	11,580
Other items involving noncash expense	1,383

Balance sheet data (in thousands):

Increase in accounts receivable	1,746
Decrease in inventory	990
Increase in prepaid expenses	605
Decrease in accounts payable and other current liabilities	1,705

a. Prepare the Cash flows from operating activities section of the statement of cash flows, using the indirect method for National Beverage Co.
b. ✏️ Interpret your results in part (a).

✔ Net cash flow from operating activities, $38

EX 16-17 Statement of cash flows—indirect method OBJ. 2

The comparative balance sheet of Olson-Jones Industries Inc. for December 31, 20Y2 and 20Y1, is as follows:

	Dec. 31, 20Y2	Dec. 31, 20Y1
Assets		
Cash	$183	$ 14
Accounts receivable (net)	55	49
Inventories	117	99
Land	250	330
Equipment	205	175
Accumulated depreciation—equipment	(68)	(42)
Total assets	$742	$625
Liabilities and Stockholders' Equity		
Accounts payable (merchandise creditors)	$ 51	$ 37
Dividends payable	5	—
Common stock, $1 par	125	80
Paid-in capital: Excess of issue price over par—common stock	85	70
Retained earnings	476	438
Total liabilities and stockholders' equity	$742	$625

The following additional information is taken from the records:
1. Land was sold for $120.
2. Equipment was acquired for cash.
3. There were no disposals of equipment during the year.
4. The common stock was issued for cash.
5. There was a $62 credit to Retained Earnings for net income.
6. There was a $24 debit to Retained Earnings for cash dividends declared.

a. Prepare a statement of cash flows, using the indirect method of presenting cash flows from operating activities.

b. ✏️ Was Olson-Jones Industries Inc.'s net cash flow from operations more or less than net income? What is the source of this difference?

EX 16-18 Statement of cash flows—indirect method OBJ. 2

The following statement of cash flows for Shasta Inc. was not correctly prepared:

Shasta Inc.
Statement of Cash Flows
For the Year Ended December 31, 20Y9

Cash flows from operating activities:		
Net income	$ 360,000	
Adjustments to reconcile net income to net cash flow from operating activities:		
Depreciation.	100,800	
Gain on sale of investments	17,280	
Changes in current operating assets and liabilities:		
Increase in accounts receivable	27,360	
Increase in inventories	(36,000)	
Increase in accounts payable	(3,600)	
Decrease in accrued expenses payable	(2,400)	
Net cash flow from operating activities		$ 463,440
Cash flows from (used for) investing activities:		
Cash from sale of investments	$ 240,000	
Cash used for purchase of land	(259,200)	
Cash used for purchase of equipment	(432,000)	
Net cash flow used for investing activities		(415,200)
Cash flows from (used for) financing activities:		
Cash from sale of common stock	$ 312,000	
Cash used for dividends	(132,000)	
Net cash flow from financing activities		180,000
Increase (decrease) in cash		$ 47,760
Cash at the end of the year		192,240
Cash at the beginning of the year		$240,000

a. List the errors you find in the statement of cash flows. The cash balance at the beginning of the year was $240,000. All other amounts are correct, except the cash balance at the end of the year.

b. Prepare a corrected statement of cash flows.

EX 16-19 Cash flows from operating activities—direct method OBJ. 3

✓ a. $801,900

The cash flows from operating activities are reported by the direct method on the statement of cash flows. Determine the following:

a. If sales for the current year were $753,500 and accounts receivable decreased by $48,400 during the year, what was the amount of cash received from customers?

b. If income tax expense for the current year was $50,600 and income tax payable decreased by $5,500 during the year, what was the amount of cash payments for income taxes?

c. ✏️ Briefly explain why the cash received from customers in (a) is different from sales.

806 Chapter 16 Statement of Cash Flows

EX 16-20 Cash paid for merchandise purchases   OBJ. 3

The cost of merchandise sold for **Kohl's Corporation** for a recent year was $12,265 million. The balance sheet showed the following current account balances (in millions):

	Balance, End of Year	Balance, Beginning of Year
Merchandise inventories	$4,038	$3,814
Accounts payable	1,251	1,511

Determine the amount of cash payments for merchandise.

EX 16-21 Determining selected amounts for cash flows from operating activities—direct method   OBJ. 3

✔ a. $1,025,800

Selected data taken from the accounting records of Ginis Inc. for the current year ended December 31 are as follows:

	Balance, December 31	Balance, January 1
Accrued expenses payable (operating expenses)	$ 12,650	$ 14,030
Accounts payable (merchandise creditors)	96,140	105,800
Inventories	178,020	193,430

During the current year, the cost of merchandise sold was $1,031,550 and the operating expenses other than depreciation were $179,400. The direct method is used for presenting the cash flows from operating activities on the statement of cash flows.

Determine the amount reported on the statement of cash flows for (a) cash payments for merchandise and (b) cash payments for operating expenses.

EX 16-22 Cash flows from operating activities—direct method   OBJ. 3

✔ Net cash flow from operating activities, $96,040

The income statement of Booker T Industries Inc. for the current year ended June 30 is as follows:

Sales		$511,000
Cost of merchandise sold		290,500
Gross profit		$220,500
Operating expenses:		
Depreciation expense	$ 39,200	
Other operating expenses	105,000	
Total operating expenses		144,200
Income before income tax		$ 76,300
Income tax expense		21,700
Net income		$ 54,600

Changes in the balances of selected accounts from the beginning to the end of the current year are as follows:

	Increase (Decrease)
Accounts receivable (net)	$(11,760)
Inventories	3,920
Prepaid expenses	(3,780)
Accounts payable (merchandise creditors)	(7,980)
Accrued expenses payable (operating expenses)	1,260
Income tax payable	(2,660)

a. Prepare the Cash flows from operating activities section of the statement of cash flows, using the direct method.

b. ✏ What does the direct method show about a company's cash flows from operating activities that is not shown using the indirect method?

Chapter 16 Statement of Cash Flows 807

EX 16-23 Cash flows from operating activities—direct method
OBJ. 3

✔ Net cash flow from operating activities, $123,860

The income statement for Rhino Company for the current year ended June 30 and balances of selected accounts at the beginning and the end of the year are as follows:

Sales	$445,500
Cost of merchandise sold	154,000
Gross profit	$291,500
Operating expenses:	
Depreciation expense	$ 38,500
Other operating expenses	115,280
Total operating expenses	153,780
Income before income tax	$137,720
Income tax expense	39,600
Net income	$ 98,120

	End of Year	Beginning of Year
Accounts receivable (net)	$36,300	$31,240
Inventories	92,400	80,300
Prepaid expenses	14,520	15,840
Accounts payable (merchandise creditors)	67,540	62,700
Accrued expenses payable (operating expenses)	19,140	20,900
Income tax payable	4,400	4,400

Prepare the Cash flows from operating activities section of the statement of cash flows, using the direct method.

EX 16-24 Free cash flow
OBJ. 4

Sweeter Enterprises Inc. has cash flows from operating activities of $539,000. Cash flows used for investments in property, plant, and equipment totaled $210,000, of which 75% of this investment was used to replace existing capacity.

a. Determine the free cash flow for Sweeter Enterprises Inc.

b. How might a lender use free cash flow to determine whether or not to give Sweeter Enterprises Inc. a loan?

EX 16-25 Free cash flow
OBJ. 4

The financial statements for **Nike, Inc.**, are provided in Appendix C at the end of the text.

a. Determine the free cash flow for the most recent fiscal year. Assume that 90% of the additions to property, plant, and equipment were used to maintain productive capacity. Round to the nearest thousand dollars.

b. How might a lender use free cash flow to determine whether or not to give Nike, Inc., a loan?

c. Would you feel comfortable giving Nike a loan, based on the free cash flow calculated in (a)?

EX 16-26 Free cash flow
OBJ. 4

Lovato Motors Inc. has cash flows from operating activities of $720,000. Cash flows used for investments in property, plant, and equipment totaled $440,000, of which 85% of this investment was used to replace existing capacity.

Determine the free cash flow for Lovato Motors Inc.

Problems: Series A

✔ Net cash flow from operating activities, $490,000

PR 16-1A Statement of cash flows—indirect method   OBJ. 2

The comparative balance sheet of Navaria Inc. for December 31, 20Y3 and 20Y2, is shown as follows:

	Dec. 31, 20Y3	Dec. 31, 20Y2
Assets		
Cash	$ 155,000	$ 150,000
Accounts receivable (net)	450,000	400,000
Inventories	770,000	750,000
Investments	0	100,000
Land	500,000	0
Equipment	1,400,000	1,200,000
Accumulated depreciation—equipment	(600,000)	(500,000)
Total assets	$2,675,000	$2,100,000
Liabilities and Stockholders' Equity		
Accounts payable	$ 340,000	$ 300,000
Accrued expenses payable	45,000	50,000
Dividends payable	30,000	25,000
Common stock, $4 par	700,000	600,000
Paid-in capital: Excess of issue price over par—common stock	200,000	175,000
Retained earnings	1,360,000	950,000
Total liabilities and stockholders' equity	$2,675,000	$2,100,000

Additional data obtained from an examination of the accounts in the ledger for 20Y3 are as follows:

a. The investments were sold for $175,000 cash.
b. Equipment and land were acquired for cash.
c. There were no disposals of equipment during the year.
d. The common stock was issued for cash.
e. There was a $500,000 credit to Retained Earnings for net income.
f. There was a $90,000 debit to Retained Earnings for cash dividends declared.

Instructions
Prepare a statement of cash flows, using the indirect method of presenting cash flows from operating activities.

✔ Net cash flow from operating activities, $225,000

PR 16-2A Statement of cash flows—indirect method   OBJ. 2

The comparative balance sheet of Yellow Dog Enterprises Inc. at December 31, 20Y8 and 20Y7, is as follows:

	Dec. 31, 20Y8	Dec. 31, 20Y7
Assets		
Cash	$ 80,000	$ 100,000
Accounts receivable (net)	275,000	300,000
Merchandise inventory	510,000	400,000
Prepaid expenses	15,000	10,000
Equipment	1,070,000	750,000
Accumulated depreciation—equipment	(200,000)	(160,000)
Total assets	$1,750,000	$1,400,000

	Dec. 31, 20Y8	Dec. 31, 20Y7
Liabilities and Stockholders' Equity		
Accounts payable (merchandise creditors)	$ 100,000	$ 90,000
Mortgage note payable	0	400,000
Common stock, $10 par	600,000	200,000
Paid-in capital: Excess of issue price over par—common stock	300,000	100,000
Retained earnings	750,000	610,000
Total liabilities and stockholders' equity	$1,750,000	$1,400,000

Additional data obtained from the income statement and from an examination of the accounts in the ledger for 20Y8 are as follows:

a. Net income, $190,000.

b. Depreciation reported on the income statement, $115,000.

c. Equipment was purchased at a cost of $395,000, and fully depreciated equipment costing $75,000 was discarded, with no salvage realized.

d. The mortgage note payable was not due for six years, but the terms permitted earlier payment without penalty.

e. 40,000 shares of common stock were issued at $15 for cash.

f. Cash dividends declared and paid, $50,000.

Instructions
Prepare a statement of cash flows, using the indirect method.

PR 16-3A Statement of cash flows—indirect method OBJ. 2

✔ Net cash flow from operating activities, $(169,600)

Excel

The comparative balance sheet of Whitman Co. at December 31, 20Y2 and 20Y1, is as follows:

	Dec. 31, 20Y2	Dec. 31, 20Y1
Assets		
Cash	$ 918,000	$ 964,800
Accounts receivable (net)	828,900	761,940
Inventories	1,268,460	1,162,980
Prepaid expenses	29,340	35,100
Land	315,900	479,700
Buildings	1,462,500	900,900
Accumulated depreciation—buildings	(408,600)	(382,320)
Equipment	512,280	454,680
Accumulated depreciation—equipment	(141,300)	(158,760)
Total assets	$4,785,480	$4,219,020
Liabilities and Stockholders' Equity		
Accounts payable (merchandise creditors)	$ 922,500	$ 958,320
Bonds payable	270,000	0
Common stock, $25 par	317,000	117,000
Paid-in capital: Excess of issue price over par—common stock	758,000	558,000
Retained earnings	2,517,980	2,585,700
Total liabilities and stockholders' equity	$4,785,480	$4,219,020

The noncurrent asset, noncurrent liability, and stockholders' equity accounts for 20Y2 are as follows:

ACCOUNT Land   ACCOUNT NO.

Date		Item	Debit	Credit	Balance Debit	Balance Credit
20Y2						
Jan.	1	Balance			479,700	
Apr.	20	Realized $151,200 cash from sale		163,800	315,900	

(Continued)

ACCOUNT Buildings
ACCOUNT NO.

Date		Item	Debit	Credit	Balance Debit	Balance Credit
20Y2						
Jan.	1	Balance			900,900	
Apr.	20	Acquired for cash	561,600		1,462,500	

ACCOUNT Accumulated Depreciation—Buildings
ACCOUNT NO.

Date		Item	Debit	Credit	Balance Debit	Balance Credit
20Y2						
Jan.	1	Balance				382,320
Dec.	31	Depreciation for year		26,280		408,600

ACCOUNT Equipment
ACCOUNT NO.

Date		Item	Debit	Credit	Balance Debit	Balance Credit
20Y2						
Jan.	1	Balance			454,680	
	26	Discarded, no salvage		46,800	407,880	
Aug.	11	Purchased for cash	104,400		512,280	

ACCOUNT Accumulated Depreciation—Equipment
ACCOUNT NO.

Date		Item	Debit	Credit	Balance Debit	Balance Credit
20Y2						
Jan.	1	Balance				158,760
	26	Equipment discarded	46,800			111,960
Dec.	31	Depreciation for year		29,340		141,300

ACCOUNT Bonds Payable
ACCOUNT NO.

Date		Item	Debit	Credit	Balance Debit	Balance Credit
20Y2						
May	1	Issued 20-year bonds		270,000		270,000

ACCOUNT Common Stock, $25 par
ACCOUNT NO.

Date		Item	Debit	Credit	Balance Debit	Balance Credit
20Y2						
Jan.	1	Balance				117,000
Dec.	7	Issued 8,000 shares of common stock for $50 per share		200,000		317,000

Chapter 16 Statement of Cash Flows 811

ACCOUNT Paid-In Capital in Excess of Par—Common Stock   ACCOUNT NO.

Date		Item	Debit	Credit	Balance Debit	Balance Credit
20Y2						
Jan.	1	Balance				558,000
Dec.	7	Issued 8,000 shares of common stock for $50 per share		200,000		758,000

ACCOUNT Retained Earnings   ACCOUNT NO.

Date		Item	Debit	Credit	Balance Debit	Balance Credit
20Y2						
Jan.	1	Balance				2,585,700
Dec.	31	Net loss	35,320			2,550,380
Dec.	31	Cash dividends	32,400			2,517,980

Instructions

Prepare a statement of cash flows, using the indirect method of presenting cash flows from operating activities.

PR 16-4A   **Statement of cash flows—direct method**   OBJ. 3

✔ Net cash flow from operating activities, $293,600

The comparative balance sheet of Canace Products Inc. for December 31, 20Y6 and 20Y5, is as follows:

	Dec. 31, 20Y6	Dec. 31, 20Y5
Assets		
Cash	$ 643,400	$ 679,400
Accounts receivable (net)	566,800	547,400
Inventories	1,011,000	982,800
Investments	0	240,000
Land	520,000	0
Equipment	880,000	680,000
Accumulated depreciation	(244,400)	(200,400)
Total assets	$3,376,800	$2,929,200
Liabilities and Stockholders' Equity		
Accounts payable	$ 771,800	$ 748,400
Accrued expenses payable	63,400	70,800
Dividends payable	8,800	6,400
Common stock, $2 par	56,000	32,000
Paid-in capital: Excess of issue price over par—common stock	408,000	192,000
Retained earnings	2,068,800	1,879,600
Total liabilities and stockholders' equity	$3,376,800	$2,929,200

The income statement for the year ended December 31, 20Y6, is as follows:

Sales		$5,980,000
Cost of merchandise sold		2,452,000
Gross profit		$3,528,000
Operating expenses:		
Depreciation expense	$ 44,000	
Other operating expenses	3,100,000	
Total operating expenses		3,144,000

(Continued)

Operating income	$384,000
Other expense:	
Loss on sale of investments	(64,000)
Income before income tax	$320,000
Income tax expense	102,800
Net income	$217,200

Additional data obtained from an examination of the accounts in the ledger for 20Y6 are as follows:

a. Equipment and land were acquired for cash.
b. There were no disposals of equipment during the year.
c. The investments were sold for $176,000 cash.
d. The common stock was issued for cash.
e. There was a $28,000 debit to Retained Earnings for cash dividends declared.

Instructions

Prepare a statement of cash flows, using the direct method of presenting cash flows from operating activities.

PR 16-5A Statement of cash flows—direct method applied to PR 16-1A OBJ. 3

✔ Net cash flow from operating activities, $490,000

The comparative balance sheet of Navaria Inc. for December 31, 20Y3 and 20Y2, is as follows:

	Dec. 31, 20Y3	Dec. 31, 20Y2
Assets		
Cash	$155,000	$150,000
Accounts receivable (net)	450,000	400,000
Inventories	770,000	750,000
Investments	0	100,000
Land	500,000	0
Equipment	1,400,000	1,200,000
Accumulated depreciation—equipment	(600,000)	(500,000)
Total assets	$2,675,000	$2,100,000
Liabilities and Stockholders' Equity		
Accounts payable	$340,000	$300,000
Accrued expenses payable	45,000	50,000
Dividends payable	30,000	25,000
Common stock, $4 par	700,000	600,000
Paid-in capital: Excess of issue price over par—common stock	200,000	175,000
Retained earnings	1,360,000	950,000
Total liabilities and stockholders' equity	$2,675,000	$2,100,000

The income statement for the year ended December 31, 20Y3, is as follows:

Sales		$3,000,000
Cost of merchandise sold		1,400,000
Gross profit		$1,600,000
Operating expenses:		
Depreciation expense	$100,000	
Other operating expenses	950,000	
Total operating expenses		1,050,000
Operating income		$550,000
Other income:		
Gain on sale of investments		75,000
Income before income tax		$625,000
Income tax expense		125,000
Net income		$500,000

Additional data obtained from an examination of the accounts in the ledger for 20Y3 are as follows:

a. The investments were sold for $175,000 cash.
b. Equipment and land were acquired for cash.
c. There were no disposals of equipment during the year.
d. The common stock was issued for cash.
e. There was a $90,000 debit to Retained Earnings for cash dividends declared.

Instructions
Prepare a statement of cash flows, using the direct method of presenting cash flows from operating activities.

Problems: Series B

PR 16-1B Statement of cash flows—indirect method   OBJ. 2

✔ Net cash flow from operating activities, $154,260

The comparative balance sheet of Merrick Equipment Co. for December 31, 20Y9 and 20Y8, is as follows:

	Dec. 31, 20Y9	Dec. 31, 20Y8
Assets		
Cash	$ 70,720	$ 47,940
Accounts receivable (net)	207,230	188,190
Inventories	298,520	289,850
Investments	0	102,000
Land	295,800	0
Equipment	438,600	358,020
Accumulated depreciation—equipment	(99,110)	(84,320)
Total assets	$1,211,760	$901,680
Liabilities and Stockholders' Equity		
Accounts payable	$ 205,700	$194,140
Accrued expenses payable	30,600	26,860
Dividends payable	25,500	20,400
Common stock, $1 par	202,000	102,000
Paid-in capital: Excess of issue price over par—common stock	354,000	204,000
Retained earnings	393,960	354,280
Total liabilities and stockholders' equity	$1,211,760	$901,680

Additional data obtained from an examination of the accounts in the ledger for 20Y9 are as follows:

a. Equipment and land were acquired for cash.
b. There were no disposals of equipment during the year.
c. The investments were sold for $91,800 cash.
d. The common stock was issued for cash.
e. There was a $141,680 credit to Retained Earnings for net income.
f. There was a $102,000 debit to Retained Earnings for cash dividends declared.

Instructions
Prepare a statement of cash flows, using the indirect method of presenting cash flows from operating activities.

814 Chapter 16 Statement of Cash Flows

✔ Net cash flow from operating activities, $561,400

PR 16-2B Statement of cash flows—indirect method OBJ. 2

The comparative balance sheet of Harris Industries Inc. at December 31, 20Y4 and 20Y3, is as follows:

	Dec. 31, 20Y4	Dec. 31, 20Y3
Assets		
Cash	$ 443,240	$ 360,920
Accounts receivable (net)	665,280	592,200
Inventories	887,880	1,022,560
Prepaid expenses	31,640	25,200
Land	302,400	302,400
Buildings	1,713,600	1,134,000
Accumulated depreciation—buildings	(466,200)	(414,540)
Machinery and equipment	781,200	781,200
Accumulated depreciation—machinery and equipment	(214,200)	(191,520)
Patents	106,960	112,000
Total assets	$4,251,800	$3,724,420
Liabilities and Stockholders' Equity		
Accounts payable	$ 837,480	$ 927,080
Dividends payable	32,760	25,200
Salaries payable	78,960	87,080
Mortgage note payable, due in 10 years	224,000	0
Bonds payable	0	390,000
Common stock, $5 par	200,400	50,400
Paid-in capital: Excess of issue price over par—common stock	366,000	126,000
Retained earnings	2,512,200	2,118,660
Total liabilities and stockholders' equity	$4,251,800	$3,724,420

An examination of the income statement and the accounting records revealed the following additional information applicable to 20Y4:

a. Net income, $524,580.

b. Depreciation expense reported on the income statement: buildings, $51,660; machinery and equipment, $22,680.

c. Patent amortization reported on the income statement, $5,040.

d. A building was constructed for $579,600.

e. A mortgage note for $224,000 was issued for cash.

f. 30,000 shares of common stock were issued at $13 in exchange for the bonds payable.

g. Cash dividends declared, $131,040.

Instructions
Prepare a statement of cash flows, using the indirect method.

✔ Net cash flow from operating activities, $162,800

PR 16-3B Statement of cash flows—indirect method OBJ. 2

The comparative balance sheet of Coulson, Inc. at December 31, 20Y2 and 20Y1, is as follows:

	Dec. 31, 20Y2	Dec. 31, 20Y1
Assets		
Cash	$ 300,600	$ 337,800
Accounts receivable (net)	704,400	609,600
Inventories	918,600	865,800
Prepaid expenses	18,600	26,400
Land	990,000	1,386,000

Buildings	$1,980,000	$ 990,000
Accumulated depreciation—buildings	(397,200)	(366,000)
Equipment	660,600	529,800
Accumulated depreciation—equipment	(133,200)	(162,000)
Total assets	$5,042,400	$4,217,400

Liabilities and Stockholders' Equity

Accounts payable	$ 594,000	$ 631,200
Income taxes payable	26,400	21,600
Bonds payable	330,000	0
Common stock, $20 par	320,000	180,000
Paid-in capital: Excess of issue price over par—common stock	950,000	810,000
Retained earnings	2,822,000	2,574,600
Total liabilities and stockholders' equity	$5,042,400	$4,217,400

The noncurrent asset, noncurrent liability, and stockholders' equity accounts for 20Y2 are as follows:

ACCOUNT *Land*   ACCOUNT NO.

Date		Item	Debit	Credit	Balance Debit	Balance Credit
20Y2						
Jan.	1	Balance			1,386,000	
Apr.	20	Realized $456,000 cash from sale		396,000	990,000	

ACCOUNT *Buildings*   ACCOUNT NO.

Date		Item	Debit	Credit	Balance Debit	Balance Credit
20Y2						
Jan.	1	Balance			990,000	
Apr.	20	Acquired for cash	990,000		1,980,000	

ACCOUNT *Accumulated Depreciation—Buildings*   ACCOUNT NO.

Date		Item	Debit	Credit	Balance Debit	Balance Credit
20Y2						
Jan.	1	Balance				366,000
Dec.	31	Depreciation for year		31,200		397,200

ACCOUNT *Equipment*   ACCOUNT NO.

Date		Item	Debit	Credit	Balance Debit	Balance Credit
20Y2						
Jan.	1	Balance			529,800	
	26	Discarded, no salvage		66,000	463,800	
Aug.	11	Purchased for cash	196,800		660,600	

(*Continued*)

ACCOUNT Accumulated Depreciation—Equipment   **ACCOUNT NO.**

Date		Item	Debit	Credit	Balance Debit	Balance Credit
20Y2						
Jan.	1	Balance				162,000
	26	Equipment discarded	66,000			96,000
Dec.	31	Depreciation for year		37,200		133,200

ACCOUNT Bonds Payable   **ACCOUNT NO.**

Date		Item	Debit	Credit	Balance Debit	Balance Credit
20Y2						
May	1	Issued 20-year bonds		330,000		330,000

ACCOUNT Common Stock, $20 par   **ACCOUNT NO.**

Date		Item	Debit	Credit	Balance Debit	Balance Credit
20Y2						
Jan.	1	Balance				180,000
Dec.	7	Issued 7,000 shares of common stock for $40 per share		140,000		320,000

ACCOUNT Paid-In Capital in Excess of Par—Common Stock   **ACCOUNT NO.**

Date		Item	Debit	Credit	Balance Debit	Balance Credit
20Y2						
Jan.	1	Balance				810,000
Dec.	7	Issued 7,000 shares of common stock for $40 per share		140,000		950,000

ACCOUNT Retained Earnings   **ACCOUNT NO.**

Date		Item	Debit	Credit	Balance Debit	Balance Credit
20Y2						
Jan.	1	Balance				2,574,600
Dec.	31	Net income		326,600		2,901,200
	31	Cash dividends	79,200			2,822,000

Instructions

Prepare a statement of cash flows, using the indirect method of presenting cash flows from operating activities.

PR 16-4B Statement of cash flows—direct method   OBJ. 3

✔ Net cash flow from operating activities, $509,220

The comparative balance sheet of Martinez Inc. for December 31, 20Y4 and 20Y3, is as follows:

	Dec. 31, 20Y4	Dec. 31, 20Y3
Assets		
Cash	$ 661,920	$ 683,100
Accounts receivable (net)	992,640	914,400
Inventories	1,394,400	1,363,800
Investments	0	432,000
Land	960,000	0
Equipment	1,224,000	984,000
Accumulated depreciation—equipment	(481,500)	(368,400)
Total assets	$4,751,460	$4,008,900
Liabilities and Stockholders' Equity		
Accounts payable	$1,080,000	$ 966,600
Accrued expenses payable	67,800	79,200
Dividends payable	100,800	91,200
Common stock, $5 par	130,000	30,000
Paid-in capital: Excess of issue price over par—common stock	950,000	450,000
Retained earnings	2,422,860	2,391,900
Total liabilities and stockholders' equity	$4,751,460	$4,008,900

The income statement for the year ended December 31, 20Y4, is as follows:

Sales		$4,512,000
Cost of merchandise sold		2,352,000
Gross profit		$2,160,000
Operating expenses:		
Depreciation expense	$ 113,100	
Other operating expenses	1,344,840	
Total operating expenses		1,457,940
Operating income		$ 702,060
Other income:		
Gain on sale of investments		156,000
Income before income tax		$ 858,060
Income tax expense		299,100
Net income		$ 558,960

Additional data obtained from an examination of the accounts in the ledger for 20Y4 are as follows:

a. Equipment and land were acquired for cash.
b. There were no disposals of equipment during the year.
c. The investments were sold for $588,000 cash.
d. The common stock was issued for cash.
e. There was a $528,000 debit to Retained Earnings for cash dividends declared.

Instructions
Prepare a statement of cash flows, using the direct method of presenting cash flows from operating activities.

PR 16-5B Statement of cash flows—direct method applied to PR 16-1B   OBJ. 3

✔ Net cash flow from operating activities, $154,260

The comparative balance sheet of Merrick Equipment Co. for Dec. 31, 20Y9 and 20Y8, is as follows:

	Dec. 31, 20Y9	Dec. 31, 20Y8
Assets		
Cash	$ 70,720	$ 47,940
Accounts receivable (net)	207,230	188,190
Inventories	298,520	289,850
Investments	0	102,000
Land	295,800	0
Equipment	438,600	358,020
Accumulated depreciation—equipment	(99,110)	(84,320)
Total assets	$1,211,760	$901,680
Liabilities and Stockholders' Equity		
Accounts payable	$ 205,700	$194,140
Accrued expenses payable	30,600	26,860
Dividends payable	25,500	20,400
Common stock, $1 par	202,000	102,000
Paid-in capital: Excess of issue price over par—common stock	354,000	204,000
Retained earnings	393,960	354,280
Total liabilities and stockholders' equity	$1,211,760	$901,680

The income statement for the year ended December 31, 20Y9, is as follows:

Sales		$2,023,898
Cost of merchandise sold		1,245,476
Gross profit		$ 778,422
Operating expenses:		
Depreciation expense	$ 14,790	
Other operating expenses	517,299	
Total operating expenses		532,089
Operating income		$ 246,333
Other expenses:		
Loss on sale of investments		(10,200)
Income before income tax		$ 236,133
Income tax expense		94,453
Net income		$ 141,680

Additional data obtained from an examination of the accounts in the ledger for 20Y9 are as follows:

a. Equipment and land were acquired for cash.
b. There were no disposals of equipment during the year.
c. The investments were sold for $91,800 cash.
d. The common stock was issued for cash.
e. There was a $102,000 debit to Retained Earnings for cash dividends declared.

Instructions
Prepare a statement of cash flows, using the direct method of presenting cash flows from operating activities.

Cases & Projects

CP 16-1 Ethics in Action

Lucas Hunter, president of Simmons Industries Inc., believes that reporting operating cash flow per share on the income statement would be a useful addition to the company's just completed financial statements. The following discussion took place between Lucas Hunter and Simmons' controller, John Jameson, in January, after the close of the fiscal year:

Lucas: I've been reviewing our financial statements for the last year. I am disappointed that our net income per share has dropped by 10% from last year. This won't look good to our shareholders. Is there anything we can do about this?

John: What do you mean? The past is the past, and the numbers are in. There isn't much that can be done about it. Our financial statements were prepared according to generally accepted accounting principles, and I don't see much leeway for significant change at this point.

Lucas: No, no. I'm not suggesting that we "cook the books." But look at the cash flow from operating activities on the statement of cash flows. The cash flow from operating activities has increased by 20%. This is very good news—and, I might add, useful information. The higher cash flow from operating activities will give our creditors comfort.

John: Well, the cash flow from operating activities is on the statement of cash flows, so I guess users will be able to see the improved cash flow figures there.

Lucas: This is true, but somehow I think this information should be given a much higher profile. I don't like this information being "buried" in the statement of cash flows. You know as well as I do that many users will focus on the income statement. Therefore, I think we ought to include an operating cash flow per share number on the face of the income statement—someplace under the earnings per share number. In this way, users will get the complete picture of our operating performance. Yes, our earnings per share dropped this year, but our cash flow from operating activities improved! And all the information is in one place where users can see and compare the figures. What do you think?

John: I've never really thought about it like that before. I guess we could put the operating cash flow per share on the income statement, underneath the earnings per share amount. Users would really benefit from this disclosure. Thanks for the idea—I'll start working on it.

Lucas: Glad to be of service.

How would you interpret this situation? Is John behaving in an ethical and professional manner?

CP 16-2 Team Activity

In teams, select a public company that interests you. Obtain the company's most recent annual report on Form 10-K. The Form 10-K is a company's annually required filing with the Securities and Exchange Commission (SEC). It includes the company's financial statements and accompanying notes. The Form 10-K can be obtained either (a) by referring to the investor relations section of the company's website or (b) by using the company search feature of the SEC's EDGAR database service found at www.sec.gov/edgar/searchedgar/companysearch.html.

1. Based on the information in the company's most recent annual report, answer the following questions:
    a. What is the net cash flows from operating activities reported by the company at the end of the most recent year?
    b. What is the net cash flows from (used for) investing activities reported by the company at the end of the most recent year?
    c. What is the net cash flows from (used for) financing activities reported by the company at the end of the most recent year?
    d. What was the net increase (or decrease) in cash during the year?
2. Evaluate the company's cash inflows and outflows.

Communication

CP 16-3 Communication

Tidewater Inc., a retailer, provided the following financial information for its most recent fiscal year:

Net income	$945,000
Return on invested capital	8%
Cash flows from operating activities	$(1,428,000)
Cash flows from investing activities	$600,000
Cash flows from financing activities	$900,000

The company's Cash flows from operating activities section is as follows:

Net income	$ 945,000
Depreciation	210,000
Increase in accounts receivable	(1,134,000)
Increase in inventory	(1,260,000)
Decrease in accounts payable	(189,000)
Net cash flow from operating activities	$(1,428,000)

An examination of the financial statements revealed the following additional information:

- Revenues increased during the year as a result of an aggressive marketing campaign aimed at increasing the number of new "Tidewater Card" credit card customers. This is the company's branded credit card, which can only be used at Tidewater stores. The credit card balances are accounts receivable on Tidewater's balance sheet.
- Some suppliers have made their merchandise available at a deep discount. As a result, the company purchased large quantities of these goods in an attempt to improve the company's profitability.
- In recent years, the company has struggled to pay its accounts payable on time. The company has improved on this during the past year and is nearly caught up on overdue payables balances.
- The company reported net losses in each of the two prior years.

Write a brief memo to your instructor evaluating the financial condition of Tidewater Inc.

CP 16-4 Using the statement of cash flows

You are considering an investment in a new start-up company, Giraffe Inc., an Internet service provider. A review of the company's financial statements reveals a negative retained earnings. In addition, it appears as though the company has been running a negative cash flow from operating activities since the company's inception.

How is the company staying in business under these circumstances? Could this be a good investment?

CP 16-5 Analysis of statement of cash flows

Dillip Lachgar is the president and majority shareholder of Argon Inc., a small retail chain store. Recently, Dillip submitted a loan application for Argon Inc. to Compound Bank. It called for a $600,000, 9%, 10-year loan to help finance the construction of a building and the purchase of store equipment, costing a total of $750,000. This will enable Argon Inc. to open a store in the town of Compound. Land for this purpose was acquired last year. The bank's loan officer requested a statement of cash flows in addition to the most recent income statement, balance sheet, and retained earnings statement that Dillip had submitted with the loan application.

   As a close family friend, Dillip asked you to prepare a statement of cash flows. From the records provided, you prepared the following statement:

Argon Inc.
Statement of Cash Flows
For the Year Ended December 31, 20Y7

Cash flows from operating activities:		
Net income		$ 300,000
Adjustments to reconcile net income to net cash flow from operating activities:		
Depreciation	84,000	
Gain on sale of investments	(30,000)	
Changes in current operating assets and liabilities:		
Decrease in accounts receivable	21,000	
Increase in inventories	(42,000)	
Increase in accounts payable	30,000	
Decrease in accrued expenses payable	(6,000)	
Net cash flow from operating activities		$ 357,000
Cash flows from (used for) investing activities:		
Cash from investments sold	$ 180,000	
Cash used for purchase of store equipment	(120,000)	
Net cash flow from investing activities		60,000
Cash flows from (used for) financing activities:		
Cash used for dividends	$(126,000)	
Net cash flow used for financing activities		(126,000)
Increase (decrease) in cash		$ 291,000
Cash at the beginning of the year		108,000
Cash at the end of the year		$ 399,000

Schedule of Noncash Financing and Investing Activities:

Issued common stock for land	$ 240,000

After reviewing the statement, Dillip telephoned you and commented, "Are you sure this statement is right?" Dillip then raised the following questions:

1. "How can depreciation be a cash flow?"
2. "Issuing common stock for the land is listed in a separate schedule. This transaction has nothing to do with cash! Shouldn't this transaction be eliminated from the statement?"
3. "How can the gain on the sale of investments be a deduction from net income in determining the cash flow from operating activities?"
4. "Why does the bank need this statement anyway? They can compute the increase in cash from the balance sheets for the last two years."

After jotting down Dillip's questions, you assured him that this statement was "right." But to alleviate Dillip's concern, you arranged a meeting for the following day.

a. How would you respond to each of Dillip's questions?
b. Do you think that the statement of cash flows enhances the chances of Argon Inc. receiving the loan? Discuss.

CP 16-6 Team Activity

This activity will require two teams to retrieve cash flow statement information from the Internet. One team is to obtain the most recent year's statement of cash flows for Johnson & Johnson; the other team, the most recent year's statement of cash flows for JetBlue Airways Corp.

The statement of cash flows is included as part of the annual report information that is a required disclosure to the Securities and Exchange Commission (SEC). SEC documents can be retrieved using the EdgarScan™ service at www.sec.gov/edgar/searchedgar/companysearch.html.

(Continued)

To obtain annual report information, key a company name in the appropriate space. EdgarScan will list the reports available to you for the company you've selected. Select the most recent annual report filing, identified as a 10-K or 10-K405. EdgarScan provides an outline of the report, including the separate financial statements.

As a group, compare the two statements of cash flows.

a. How are Johnson & Johnson and JetBlue Airways Corp. similar or different regarding cash flows?

b. Compute and compare the free cash flow for each company, assuming that additions to property, plant, and equipment replace current capacity.

CHAPTER 17

Financial Statement Analysis

Chapters 1–4 Accounting Cycle

Chapter 5 Accounting Systems

| Income Statement | Retained Earnings Statement | Balance Sheet | Statement of Cash Flows |

Chapter 6 *Accounting for Merchandising Businesses*

Chapter 16 *Statement of Cash Flows*

Assets = Liabilities + Stockholders' Equity

Chapter 8 *Cash*
Chapter 9 *Receivables*
Chapter 7 *Inventories*
Chapter 10 *Fixed and Intangible Assets*
Chapter 15 *Investments*

Chapter 11 *Current Liabilities and Payroll*
Chapter 14 *Bonds and Notes*

Chapter 12 *Partnerships*
Chapter 13 *Corporations*

Chapter 17 Financial Statement Analysis

Retained Earnings Statement

Retained earnings, Jan. 1		$XXX
Net income	$ XXX	
Dividends	(XXX)	

Statement of Cash Flows

Cash flows from operating activities	$XXX
Cash flows from investing activities	XXX
Cash flows from financing activities	XXX
	$XXX
	XXX
	$XXX

Income Statement

Sales		$XXX
Cost of goods sold		XXX
Gross profit		$XXX
Operating expenses:		
Advertising expense	$XXX	
Depreciation expense	XXX	
Amortization expense	XXX	
Depletion expense	XXX	
…	XXX	
…	XXX	
Total operating expenses		XXX
Income from operations		$XXX
Other revenue and expenses		XXX
Net income		$XXX

Balance Sheet

Current assets:		
Cash	$XXX	
Accounts receivable	XXX	
Inventory	XXX	
Total current assets		$XXX
Long-term assets:		
Fixed assets	$XXX	
Intangible assets	XXX	
Total long-term assets		XXX
Total assets		$XXX
Liabilities:		
Current liabilities	$XXX	
Long-term liabilities	XXX	
Total liabilities		$XXX
Stockholders' equity		XXX
Total liabilities and stockholders' equity		$XXX

CHAPTER 17

Nike, Inc.

"Just do it." These three words identify one of the most recognizable brands in the world, **Nike**. While this phrase inspires athletes to "compete and achieve their potential," it also defines the company.

Nike began in 1964 as a partnership between University of Oregon track coach Bill Bowerman and one of his former student-athletes, Phil Knight. The two began by selling shoes imported from Japan out of the back of Knight's car to athletes at track-and-field events. As sales grew, the company opened retail outlets, calling itself **Blue Ribbon Sports**. The company also began to develop its own shoes. In 1971, the company commissioned a graphic design student at Portland State University to develop the swoosh logo for a fee of $35. In 1978, the company changed its name to Nike, and in 1980, it sold its first shares of stock to the public.

Nike would have been a great company to invest in at the time. If you had invested in Nike's common stock back in 1990, you would have paid $5 per share. As of September 2016, Nike's stock was worth over $55 per share. Unfortunately, you can't invest using hindsight.

How can you select companies in which to invest? Like any significant purchase, you should do some research to guide your investment decision. If you were buying a car, for example, you might go to **Edmunds.com** to obtain reviews, ratings, prices, specifications, options, and fuel economies to evaluate different vehicles. In selecting companies in which to invest, you can use financial analysis to gain insight into a company's past performance and future prospects. This chapter describes and illustrates common financial data that can be analyzed to assist you in making investment decisions such as whether or not to invest in Nike's stock.

Source: http://news.nike.com

Learning Objectives

After studying this chapter, you should be able to:

Example Exercises (EE) are shown in **green**.

Obj. 1 Describe the techniques and tools used to analyze financial statement information.

Analyzing and Interpreting Financial Statements
The Value of Financial Statement Information
Techniques for Analyzing Financial Statements

Obj. 2 Describe and illustrate basic financial statement analytical methods.

Basic Analytical Methods
Horizontal Analysis — EE 17-1
Vertical Analysis — EE 17-2
Common-Sized Statements

Obj. 3 Describe and illustrate how to use financial statement analysis to assess liquidity.

Analyzing Liquidity
Current Position Analysis — EE 17-3
Accounts Receivable Analysis — EE 17-4
Inventory Analysis — EE 17-5

Obj. 4 Describe and illustrate how to use financial statement analysis to assess solvency.

Analyzing Solvency
Ratio of Fixed Assets to Long-Term Liabilities
Ratio of Liabilities to Stockholders' Equity — EE 17-6
Times Interest Earned — EE 17-7

Obj. 5 Describe and illustrate how to use financial statement analysis to assess profitability.

Analyzing Profitability
Asset Turnover — EE 17-8
Return on Total Assets — EE 17-9
Return on Stockholders' Equity
Return on Common Stockholders' Equity — EE 17-10
Earnings per Share on Common Stock
Price-Earnings Ratio — EE 17-11
Dividends per Share
Dividend Yield
Summary of Analytical Measures

Obj. 6 Describe the contents of corporate annual reports.

Corporate Annual Reports
Management Discussion and Analysis
Report on Internal Control
Report on Fairness of the Financial Statements

At a Glance 17 — Page 852

Analyzing and Interpreting Financial Statements

Obj. 1 Describe the techniques and tools used to analyze financial statement information.

The objective of accounting is to provide relevant and timely information to support the decision-making needs of financial statement users. Bankers, creditors, and investors all rely on financial statements to provide insight into a company's financial condition and performance. This chapter discusses the value of financial statement information, techniques used to evaluate financial statements, and how this information can be used in decision making.

The Value of Financial Statement Information

General-purpose financial statements are distributed to a wide range of potential users, providing each group with valuable information about a company's economic performance and financial condition. Users typically evaluate this information along three dimensions: liquidity, solvency, and profitability.

Liquidity Short-term creditors such as banks and financial institutions are concerned primarily with whether a company will be able to repay short-term borrowings such as loans and notes. As such, they are most interested in evaluating a company's ability to convert assets into cash, which is called **liquidity**.

Solvency Long-term creditors such as bondholders loan money for long periods of time. Thus, they are interested in evaluating a company's ability to make its periodic interest payments and repay the face amount of debt at maturity, which is called **solvency**.

Profitability Investors such as stockholders are the owners of the company. They benefit from increases in the price of a company's shares and are interested in evaluating the potential for the price of the company's stock to increase. The price of a company's stock depends on a variety of factors, including the company's current and potential future earnings. As such, investors focus on evaluating a company's ability to generate earnings, which is called **profitability**.

Techniques for Analyzing Financial Statements

Financial statement users rely on the following techniques to analyze and interpret a company's financial performance and condition:

- **Analytical methods** examine changes in the amount and percentage of financial statement items within and across periods.
- **Ratios** express a financial statement item or set of financial statement items as a percentage of another financial statement item in order to measure an important economic relationship as a single number.

Both analytical methods and ratios can be used to compare a company's financial performance over time or to another company.

- *Comparisons over Time:* The comparison of a financial statement item or ratio with the same item or ratio from a prior period often helps the user identify trends in a company's economic performance, financial condition, liquidity, solvency, and profitability.
- *Comparisons Between Companies:* The comparison of a financial statement item or ratio to another company in the same industry can provide insight into a company's economic performance and financial condition relative to its competitors.

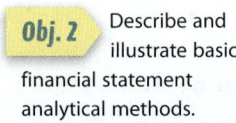

Obj. 2 Describe and illustrate basic financial statement analytical methods.

Basic Analytical Methods

Users analyze a company's financial statements using a variety of analytical methods. Three such methods are:

- Horizontal analysis
- Vertical analysis
- Common-sized statements

Horizontal Analysis

The analysis of increases and decreases in the amount and percentage of comparative financial statement items is called **horizontal analysis**. Each item on the most recent statement is compared with the same item on one or more earlier statements in terms of the following:

- *Amount* of increase or decrease
- *Percent* of increase or decrease

When comparing statements, the earlier statement is normally used as the base year for computing increases and decreases.

Exhibit 1 illustrates horizontal analysis for the December 31, 20Y6 and 20Y5 balance sheets of Lincoln Company. In Exhibit 1, the December 31, 20Y5, balance sheet (the earliest year presented) is used as the base year.

EXHIBIT 1

Comparative Balance Sheet—Horizontal Analysis

Lincoln Company
Comparative Balance Sheet
December 31, 20Y6 and 20Y5

	Dec. 31, 20Y6	Dec. 31, 20Y5	Increase (Decrease) Amount	Percent
Assets				
Current assets	$ 550,000	$ 533,000	$ 17,000	3.2%
Long-term investments	95,000	177,500	(82,500)	(46.5%)
Property, plant, and equipment (net)	444,500	470,000	(25,500)	(5.4%)
Intangible assets	50,000	50,000	—	—
Total assets	$1,139,500	$1,230,500	$ (91,000)	(7.4%)
Liabilities				
Current liabilities	$ 210,000	$ 243,000	$ (33,000)	(13.6%)
Long-term liabilities	100,000	200,000	(100,000)	(50.0%)
Total liabilities	$ 310,000	$ 443,000	$(133,000)	(30.0%)
Stockholders' Equity				
Preferred 6% stock, $100 par	$ 150,000	$ 150,000	$ —	—
Common stock, $10 par	500,000	500,000	—	—
Retained earnings	179,500	137,500	42,000	30.5%
Total stockholders' equity	$ 829,500	$ 787,500	$ 42,000	5.3%
Total liabilities and stockholders' equity	$1,139,500	$1,230,500	$ (91,000)	(7.4%)

Exhibit 1 indicates that total assets decreased by $91,000 (7.4%), liabilities decreased by $133,000 (30.0%), and stockholders' equity increased by $42,000 (5.3%). Since the long-term investments account decreased by $82,500, it appears that most of the decrease in long-term liabilities of $100,000 was achieved through the sale of long-term investments.

The balance sheets in Exhibit 1 may be expanded or supported by a separate schedule that includes the individual asset and liability accounts. For example, Exhibit 2 is a supporting schedule of Lincoln Company's current asset accounts.

EXHIBIT 2

Comparative Schedule of Current Assets—Horizontal Analysis

Lincoln Company
Comparative Schedule of Current Assets
December 31, 20Y6 and 20Y5

	Dec. 31, 20Y6	Dec. 31, 20Y5	Increase (Decrease) Amount	Percent
Cash	$ 90,500	$ 64,700	$ 25,800	39.9%
Temporary investments	75,000	60,000	15,000	25.0%
Accounts receivable, net	115,000	120,000	(5,000)	(4.2%)
Inventories	264,000	283,000	(19,000)	(6.7%)
Prepaid expenses	5,500	5,300	200	3.8%
Total current assets	$550,000	$533,000	$ 17,000	3.2%

Exhibit 2 indicates that while cash and temporary investments increased, accounts receivable and inventories decreased. The decrease in accounts receivable could be caused by improved collection policies, which would increase cash. The decrease in inventories could be caused by increased sales.

Exhibit 3 illustrates horizontal analysis for the 20Y6 and 20Y5 income statements of Lincoln Company. Exhibit 3 indicates an increase in sales of $298,000, or 24.8%.

EXHIBIT 3
Comparative Income Statement—Horizontal Analysis

Lincoln Company
Comparative Income Statement
For the Years Ended December 31, 20Y6 and 20Y5

	20Y6	20Y5	Increase (Decrease) Amount	Percent
Sales	$1,498,000	$1,200,000	$298,000	24.8%
Cost of goods sold	1,043,000	820,000	223,000	27.2%
Gross profit	$ 455,000	$ 380,000	$ 75,000	19.7%
Selling expenses	$ 191,000	$ 147,000	$ 44,000	29.9%
Administrative expenses	104,000	97,400	6,600	6.8%
Total operating expenses	$ 295,000	$ 244,400	$ 50,600	20.7%
Income from operations	$ 160,000	$ 135,600	$ 24,400	18.0%
Other revenue	8,500	11,000	(2,500)	(22.7%)
	$ 168,500	$ 146,600	$ 21,900	14.9%
Other expense (interest)	6,000	12,000	(6,000)	(50.0%)
Income before income tax	$ 162,500	$ 134,600	$ 27,900	20.7%
Income tax expense	71,500	58,100	13,400	23.1%
Net income	$ 91,000	$ 76,500	$ 14,500	19.0%

However, the percentage increase in sales of 24.8% was accompanied by an even greater percentage increase in the cost of goods sold of 27.2%. Thus, gross profit increased by only 19.7% compared to the 24.8% increase in sales.

Exhibit 3 also indicates that selling expenses increased by 29.9%. Thus, the 24.8% increases in sales could have been caused by an advertising campaign, which increased selling expenses. Administrative expenses increased by only 6.8%, total operating expenses increased by 20.7%, and income from operations increased by 18.0%. Interest expense decreased by 50.0%. This decrease was probably caused by the 50.0% decrease in long-term liabilities (Exhibit 1). Overall, net income increased by 19.0%, a favorable result.

Exhibit 4 illustrates horizontal analysis for the 20Y6 and 20Y5 retained earnings statements of **Lincoln Company**. Exhibit 4 indicates that retained earnings increased by 30.5% for the year. The increase is due to net income of $91,000 for the year, less dividends of $49,000.

Link to Nike
For a recent year, **Nike**'s net income increased by 21.5%.

EXHIBIT 4
Comparative Retained Earnings Statement—Horizontal Analysis

Lincoln Company
Comparative Retained Earnings Statement
For the Years Ended December 31, 20Y6 and 20Y5

	20Y6	20Y5	Increase (Decrease) Amount	Percent
Retained earnings, January 1	$137,500	$100,000	$37,500	37.5%
Net income	91,000	76,500	14,500	19.0%
Total	$228,500	$176,500	$52,000	29.5%
Dividends:				
Preferred stock dividends	$ 9,000	$ 9,000	—	—
Common stock dividends	40,000	30,000	$10,000	33.3%
Total dividends	$ 49,000	$ 39,000	$10,000	25.6%
Retained earnings, December 31	$179,500	$137,500	$42,000	30.5%

Example Exercise 17-1   Horizontal Analysis   Obj. 2

The comparative cash and accounts receivable balances for a company follow:

	Dec. 31, Current Year	Dec. 31, Previous Year
Cash	$62,500	$50,000
Accounts receivable (net)	74,400	80,000

Based on this information, what is the amount and percentage of increase or decrease that would be shown on a balance sheet with horizontal analysis?

Follow My Example 17-1

Cash $12,500 increase ($62,500 − $50,000), or 25%
Accounts receivable $5,600 decrease ($74,400 − $80,000), or (7%)

Practice Exercises: PE 17-1A, PE 17-1B

Vertical Analysis

The percentage analysis of the relationship of each component in a financial statement to a total within the statement is called **vertical analysis**. Although vertical analysis is applied to a single statement, it may be applied on the same statement over time. This enhances the analysis by showing how the percentages of each item have changed over time.

In vertical analysis of the balance sheet, the percentages are computed as follows:

- Each asset item is stated as a percent of the total assets.
- Each liability and stockholders' equity item is stated as a percent of the total liabilities and stockholders' equity.

Exhibit 5 illustrates the vertical analysis of the December 31, 20Y6 and 20Y5 balance sheets of **Lincoln Company**. Exhibit 5 indicates that current assets have increased from 43.3% to 48.3% of total assets. Long-term investments decreased from 14.4% to 8.3% of total assets. Stockholders' equity increased from 64.0% to 72.8%, with a comparable decrease in liabilities.

Link to Nike

For a recent year, Nike's current assets were 73.6% of total assets.

EXHIBIT 5

Comparative Balance Sheet—Vertical Analysis

Lincoln Company
Comparative Balance Sheet
December 31, 20Y6 and 20Y5

	Dec. 31, 20Y6 Amount	Percent	Dec. 31, 20Y5 Amount	Percent
Assets				
Current assets	$ 550,000	48.3%	$ 533,000	43.3%
Long-term investments	95,000	8.3	177,500	14.4
Property, plant, and equipment (net)	444,500	39.0	470,000	38.2
Intangible assets	50,000	4.4	50,000	4.1
Total assets	$1,139,500	100.0%	$1,230,500	100.0%
Liabilities				
Current liabilities	$ 210,000	18.4%	$ 243,000	19.7%
Long-term liabilities	100,000	8.8	200,000	16.3
Total liabilities	$ 310,000	27.2%	$ 443,000	36.0%
Stockholders' Equity				
Preferred 6% stock, $100 par	$ 150,000	13.2%	$ 150,000	12.2%
Common stock, $10 par	500,000	43.9	500,000	40.6
Retained earnings	179,500	15.7	137,500	11.2
Total stockholders' equity	$ 829,500	72.8%	$ 787,500	64.0%
Total liabilities and stockholders' equity	$1,139,500	100.0%	$1,230,500	100.0%

In a vertical analysis of the income statement, each item is stated as a percent of sales. Exhibit 6 illustrates the vertical analysis of the 20Y6 and 20Y5 income statements of **Lincoln Company**.

EXHIBIT 6

Comparative Income Statement—Vertical Analysis

Lincoln Company
Comparative Income Statement
For the Years Ended December 31, 20Y6 and 20Y5

	20Y6 Amount	20Y6 Percent	20Y5 Amount	20Y5 Percent
Sales	$1,498,000	100.0%	$1,200,000	100.0%
Cost of goods sold	1,043,000	69.6	820,000	68.3
Gross profit	$ 455,000	30.4%	$ 380,000	31.7%
Selling expenses	$ 191,000	12.8%	$ 147,000	12.3%
Administrative expenses	104,000	6.9	97,400	8.1
Total operating expenses	$ 295,000	19.7%	$ 244,400	20.4%
Income from operations	$ 160,000	10.7%	$ 135,600	11.3%
Other revenue	8,500	0.6	11,000	0.9
	$ 168,500	11.3%	$ 146,600	12.2%
Other expense (interest)	6,000	0.4	12,000	1.0
Income before income tax	$ 162,500	10.9%	$ 134,600	11.2%
Income tax expense	71,500	4.8	58,100	4.8
Net income	$ 91,000	6.1%	$ 76,500	6.4%

Exhibit 6 indicates a decrease in the gross profit rate from 31.7% in 20Y5 to 30.4% in 20Y6. Although this is only a 1.3 percentage point (31.7% − 30.4%) decrease, in dollars of potential gross profit, it represents a decrease of $19,474 (1.3% × $1,498,000) based on 20Y6 sales. Thus, a small percentage decrease can have a large dollar effect.

Example Exercise 17-2 Vertical Analysis   Obj. 2

Income statement information for Lee Corporation follows:

Sales	$100,000
Cost of goods sold	65,000
Gross profit	$ 35,000

Prepare a vertical analysis of the income statement for Lee Corporation.

Follow My Example 17-2

	Amount	Percentage	
Sales	$100,000	100%	($100,000 ÷ $100,000)
Cost of goods sold	65,000	65	($65,000 ÷ $100,000)
Gross profit	$ 35,000	35%	($35,000 ÷ $100,000)

Practice Exercises: PE 17-2A, PE 17-2B

Common-Sized Statements

In a **common-sized statement**, all items are expressed as percentages, with no dollar amounts shown. Common-sized statements are often useful for comparing one company with another or for comparing a company with industry averages.

Exhibit 7 illustrates common-sized income statements for **Lincoln Company** and Madison Corporation. Exhibit 7 indicates that Lincoln has a slightly higher gross profit percentage (30.4%) than Madison (30.0%). However, Lincoln has a higher percentage of selling expenses (12.8%) and administrative expenses (6.9%) than does Madison (11.5% and 4.1%). As a result, the income from operations as a percentage of sales of Lincoln (10.7%) is less than that of Madison (14.4%).

EXHIBIT 7
Common-Sized Income Statements

	Lincoln Company	Madison Corporation
Sales	100.0%	100.0%
Cost of goods sold	69.6	70.0
Gross profit	30.4%	30.0%
Selling expenses	12.8%	11.5%
Administrative expenses	6.9	4.1
Total operating expenses	19.7%	15.6%
Income from operations	10.7%	14.4%
Other revenue	0.6	0.6
	11.3%	15.0%
Other expense (interest)	0.4	0.5
Income before income tax	10.9%	14.5%
Income tax expense	4.8	5.5
Net income	6.1%	9.0%

The unfavorable difference of 3.7 (14.4% − 10.7%) percentage points in income from operations would concern the managers and other stakeholders of Lincoln. The underlying causes of the difference should be investigated and possibly corrected. For example, Lincoln may decide to outsource some of its administrative duties so that its administrative expenses are more comparative to that of Madison.

> **Link to Nike**
> For a recent year, **Nike**'s net income was 9.7% of sales.

Analyzing Liquidity

Obj. 3 Describe and illustrate how to use financial statement analysis to assess liquidity.

Liquidity analysis evaluates the ability of a company to convert current assets into cash. Banks and other short-term creditors rely heavily on liquidity analysis, because they are interested in evaluating a company's ability to repay loans and short-term notes. Exhibit 8 shows three categories of measures used to evaluate a company's liquidity. These ratios and measures focus upon a company's current position (current assets and liabilities), accounts receivable, and inventory.

EXHIBIT 8
Liquidity Ratios and Measures

Current Position Analysis	Accounts Receivable Analysis	Inventory Analysis
Working Capital	Accounts Receivable Turnover	Inventory Turnover
Current Ratio	Number of Days' Sales in Receivables	Number of Days' Sales in Inventory
Quick Ratio		

Current Position Analysis

Current position analysis evaluates a company's ability to pay its current liabilities. This information helps short-term creditors determine how quickly they will be repaid. This analysis includes:

- Working capital
- Current ratio
- Quick ratio

Working Capital

A company's **working capital** is computed as follows:

$$\text{Working Capital} = \text{Current Assets} - \text{Current Liabilities}$$

To illustrate, the working capital for **Lincoln Company** for 20Y6 and 20Y5 is computed as follows:

	20Y6	20Y5
Current assets	$ 550,000	$ 533,000
Current liabilities	(210,000)	(243,000)
Working capital	$ 340,000	$ 290,000

The working capital is used to evaluate a company's ability to pay current liabilities. A company's working capital is often monitored monthly, quarterly, or yearly by creditors and other debtors. However, it is difficult to use working capital to compare companies of different sizes. For example, working capital of $250,000 may be adequate for a local sporting goods store, but it would be inadequate for **Nike**.

Current Ratio

The **current ratio**, sometimes called the *working capital ratio*, is computed as follows:

$$\text{Current Ratio} = \frac{\text{Current Assets}}{\text{Current Liabilities}}$$

To illustrate, the current ratio for **Lincoln Company** is computed as follows:

	20Y6	20Y5
Current assets	$550,000	$533,000
Current liabilities	$210,000	$243,000
Current ratio	2.6 ($550,000 ÷ $210,000)	2.2 ($533,000 ÷ $243,000)

> **Link to Nike**
> For a recent five-year period, Nike's average current ratio was 2.9.

The current ratio is a more reliable indicator of a company's ability to pay its current liabilities than is working capital, and it is much easier to compare across companies. To illustrate, assume that as of December 31, 20Y6, the working capital of a competitor is much greater than Lincoln's $340,000, but its current ratio is only 1.3. Considering these facts alone, Lincoln is in a more favorable position to obtain short-term credit than the competitor because it has a higher current ratio.

Quick Ratio

One limitation of working capital and the current ratio is that they do not consider the types of current assets a company has and how easily they can be turned into cash. Because of this, two companies may have the same working capital and current ratios but differ significantly in their ability to pay their current liabilities.

To illustrate, the current assets and liabilities for **Lincoln Company** and Jefferson Company as of December 31, 20Y6, are as follows:

	Lincoln Company	Jefferson Company
Current assets:		
Cash	$ 90,500	$ 45,500
Temporary investments	75,000	25,000
Accounts receivable (net)	115,000	90,000
Inventories	264,000	380,000
Prepaid expenses	5,500	9,500
Total current assets	$550,000	$550,000
Current assets	$550,000	$550,000
Current liabilities	(210,000)	(210,000)
Working capital	$340,000	$340,000
Current ratio (Current assets ÷ Current liabilities)	2.6	2.6

Lincoln and Jefferson both have a working capital of $340,000 and current ratios of 2.6. Jefferson, however, has more of its current assets in inventories. These inventories must be sold and the receivables collected before all the current liabilities can be paid. This takes time. In addition, if the market for its product declines, Jefferson may have difficulty selling its inventory. This, in turn, could impair its ability to pay its current liabilities.

In contrast, Lincoln's current assets contain more cash, temporary investments, and accounts receivable, which can easily be converted to cash. Thus, Lincoln is in a stronger current position than Jefferson to pay its current liabilities.

A ratio that captures this difference and measures the "instant" debt-paying ability of a company is the **quick ratio**, sometimes called the *acid-test ratio*. The quick ratio is computed as follows:

$$\text{Quick Ratio} = \frac{\text{Quick Assets}}{\text{Current Liabilities}}$$

Quick assets are cash and other current assets that can be easily converted to cash. Quick assets normally include cash, temporary investments, and receivables but exclude inventories and prepaid assets.

To illustrate, the quick ratios for **Lincoln Company** and Jefferson Company are computed as follows:

	Lincoln Company	Jefferson Company
Quick assets:		
Cash	$ 90,500	$ 45,500
Temporary investments	75,000	25,000
Accounts receivable (net)	115,000	90,000
Total quick assets	$280,500	$160,500
Current liabilities	$210,000	$210,000
Quick ratio	1.3 ($280,500 ÷ $210,000)	0.8 ($160,500 ÷ $210,000)

Example Exercise 17-3 Current Position Analysis   Obj. 3

The following items are reported on a company's balance sheet:

Cash	$300,000
Temporary investments	100,000
Accounts receivable (net)	200,000
Inventory	200,000
Accounts payable	400,000

Determine (a) the current ratio and (b) the quick ratio. Round to one decimal place.

(Continued)

Follow My Example 17-3

a. Current Ratio = Current Assets ÷ Current Liabilities
   = ($300,000 + $100,000 + $200,000 + $200,000) ÷ $400,000
   = 2.0

b. Quick Ratio = Quick Assets ÷ Current Liabilities
   = ($300,000 + $100,000 + $200,000) ÷ $400,000
   = 1.5

Practice Exercises: PE 17-3A, PE 17-3B

Accounts Receivable Analysis

A company's ability to collect its accounts receivable is called **accounts receivable analysis**. It includes the computation and analysis of the following:

- Accounts receivable turnover
- Number of days' sales in receivables

Collecting accounts receivable as quickly as possible improves a company's liquidity. In addition, the cash collected from receivables may be used to improve or expand operations. Quick collection of receivables also reduces the risk of uncollectible accounts.

Accounts Receivable Turnover The **accounts receivable turnover** is computed as follows:

$$\text{Accounts Receivable Turnover} = \frac{\text{Sales}[1]}{\text{Average Accounts Receivable}}$$

To illustrate, the accounts receivable turnover for **Lincoln Company** for 20Y6 and 20Y5 is computed as follows. Lincoln's accounts receivable balance at the beginning of 20Y5 is $140,000.

	20Y6	20Y5
Sales	$1,498,000	$1,200,000
Accounts receivable (net):		
Beginning of year	$ 120,000	$ 140,000
End of year	115,000	120,000
Total	$ 235,000	$ 260,000
Average accounts receivable	$117,500 ($235,000 ÷ 2)	$130,000 ($260,000 ÷ 2)
Accounts receivable turnover	12.7 ($1,498,000 ÷ $117,500)	9.2 ($1,200,000 ÷ $130,000)

The increase in Lincoln's accounts receivable turnover from 9.2 to 12.7 indicates that the collection of receivables has improved during 20Y6. This may be due to a change in how credit is granted, collection practices, or both.

For Lincoln, the average accounts receivable was computed using the accounts receivable balance at the beginning and the end of the year. When sales are seasonal and, thus, vary throughout the year, monthly balances of receivables are often used. Also, if sales on account include notes receivable as well as accounts receivable, notes and accounts receivable are normally combined for analysis.

---

[1] If known, *credit* sales should be used in the numerator. Because credit sales are not normally known by external users, we use sales in the numerator.

Number of Days' Sales in Receivables The **number of days' sales in receivables** is computed as follows:

$$\text{Number of Days' Sales in Receivables} = \frac{\text{Average Accounts Receivable}}{\text{Average Daily Sales}}$$

where

$$\text{Average Daily Sales} = \frac{\text{Sales}}{365 \text{ days}}$$

To illustrate, the number of days' sales in receivables for **Lincoln Company** is computed as follows:

	20Y6	20Y5
Average accounts receivable	$117,500 ($235,000 ÷ 2)	$130,000 ($260,000 ÷ 2)
Average daily sales	$4,104 ($1,498,000 ÷ 365)	$3,288 ($1,200,000 ÷ 365)
Number of days' sales in receivables	28.6 ($117,500 ÷ $4,104)	39.5 ($130,000 ÷ $3,288)

The number of days' sales in receivables is an estimate of the time (in days) that the accounts receivable have been outstanding. The number of days' sales in receivables is often compared with a company's credit terms to evaluate the efficiency of the collection of receivables.

To illustrate, if Lincoln's credit terms are 2/10, n/30, then Lincoln was very *inefficient* in collecting receivables in 20Y5. In other words, receivables should have been collected in 30 days or less but were being collected in 39.5 days. Although collections improved during 20Y6 to 28.6 days, there is probably still room for improvement. On the other hand, if Lincoln's credit terms are n/45, then there is probably little room for improving collections.

Example Exercise 17-4 Accounts Receivable Analysis   Obj. 3

A company reports the following:

Sales	$960,000
Average accounts receivable (net)	48,000

Determine (a) the accounts receivable turnover and (b) the number of days' sales in receivables. Round to one decimal place.

Follow My Example 17-4

a. Accounts Receivable Turnover = Sales ÷ Average Accounts Receivable
   = $960,000 ÷ $48,000
   = 20.0

b. Number of Days' Sales in Receivables = Average Accounts Receivable ÷ Average Daily Sales
   = $48,000 ÷ ($960,000 ÷ 365) = $48,000 ÷ $2,630
   = 18.3 days

Practice Exercises: PE 17-4A, PE 17-4B

Inventory Analysis

A company's ability to manage its inventory effectively is evaluated using **inventory analysis**. It includes the computation and analysis of the following:

- Inventory turnover
- Number of days' sales in inventory

Excess inventory decreases liquidity by tying up funds (cash) in inventory. In addition, excess inventory increases insurance expense, property taxes, storage costs, and other related expenses. These expenses further reduce funds that could be used elsewhere to improve or expand operations.

Excess inventory also increases the risk of losses because of price declines or obsolescence of the inventory. On the other hand, a company should keep enough inventory in stock so that it doesn't lose sales because of lack of inventory.

Inventory Turnover The **inventory turnover** is computed as follows:

$$\text{Inventory Turnover} = \frac{\text{Cost of Goods Sold}}{\text{Average Inventory}}$$

To illustrate, the inventory turnover for **Lincoln Company** for 20Y6 and 20Y5 is computed as follows. Lincoln's inventory balance at the beginning of 20Y5 is $311,000.

	20Y6	20Y5
Cost of goods sold	$1,043,000	$820,000
Inventories:		
Beginning of year	$ 283,000	$311,000
End of year	264,000	283,000
Total	$ 547,000	$594,000
Average inventory	$273,500 ($547,000 ÷ 2)	$297,000 ($594,000 ÷ 2)
Inventory turnover	3.8 ($1,043,000 ÷ $273,500)	2.8 ($820,000 ÷ $297,000)

The increase in Lincoln's inventory turnover from 2.8 to 3.8 indicates that the management of inventory has improved in 20Y6. The inventory turnover improved because of an increase in the cost of goods sold, which indicates more sales and a decrease in the average inventories.

What is considered a good inventory turnover varies by type of inventory, company, and industry. For example, grocery stores have a higher inventory turnover than jewelers or furniture stores. Likewise, within a grocery store, perishable foods have a higher turnover than the soaps and cleansers.

> **Link to Nike**
> For a recent five-year period, **Nike**'s average inventory turnover was 4.3.

Number of Days' Sales in Inventory The **number of days' sales in inventory** is computed as follows:

$$\text{Number of Days' Sales in Inventory} = \frac{\text{Average Inventory}}{\text{Average Daily Cost of Goods Sold}}$$

where

$$\text{Average Daily Cost of Goods Sold} = \frac{\text{Cost of Goods Sold}}{365 \text{ days}}$$

To illustrate, the number of days' sales in inventory for **Lincoln Company** is computed as follows:

	20Y6	20Y5
Average inventory	$273,500 ($547,000 ÷ 2)	$297,000 ($594,000 ÷ 2)
Average daily cost of goods sold	$2,858 ($1,043,000 ÷ 365)	$2,247 ($820,000 ÷ 365)
Number of days' sales in inventory	95.7 ($273,500 ÷ $2,858)	132.2 ($297,000 ÷ $2,247)

The number of days' sales in inventory is a rough measure of the length of time it takes to purchase, sell, and replace the inventory. Lincoln's number of days' sales in inventory improved from 132.2 days to 95.7 days during 20Y6. This is a major improvement in managing inventory.

Example Exercise 17-5 Inventory Analysis Obj. 3

A company reports the following:

Cost of goods sold $560,000
Average inventory 112,000

Determine (a) the inventory turnover and (b) the number of days' sales in inventory. Round to one decimal place.

Follow My Example 17-5

a. Inventory Turnover = Cost of Goods Sold ÷ Average Inventory
   = $560,000 ÷ $112,000
   = 5.0

b. Number of Days' Sales in Inventory = Average Inventory ÷ Average Daily Cost of Goods Sold
   = $112,000 ÷ ($560,000 ÷ 365) = $112,000 ÷ $1,534
   = 73.0 days

Practice Exercises: PE 17-5A, PE 17-5B

Business Connection

FLYING OFF THE SHELVES

Two companies with a fast inventory turnover relative to their industries are **Apple Inc.** and **Costco Wholesale Corporation**:

	Inventory Turnover	Industry	Industry Average
Apple	53.2	Technology	15.6
Costco	11.5	Retail	7.7

Apple turns over its inventory approximately every week. There are two primary reasons for this performance. First, Apple does not manufacture its products, but contracts their manufacture by others. Thus, Apple has no inventory related to manufacturing. Second, the Apple Store inventory moves very quickly due to the popularity of its products. Costco is ranked number one in the retail industry for inventory turns. This is because Costco employs a club warehouse model that stocks a minimum variety of highly popular products. Products that don't sell quickly are removed from its offerings.

Analyzing Solvency

Obj. 4 Describe and illustrate how to use financial statement analysis to assess solvency.

Solvency analysis evaluates a company's ability to pay its long-term debts. Bondholders and other long-term creditors use solvency analysis to evaluate a company's ability to (1) repay the face amount of debt at maturity and (2) make periodic interest payments. Three common solvency ratios are shown in Exhibit 9.

Solvency Ratios

| Ratio of Fixed Assets to Long-Term Liabilities | Ratio of Liabilities to Stockholders' Equity | Times Interest Earned |

EXHIBIT 9
Solvency Ratios

Ratio of Fixed Assets to Long-Term Liabilities

Fixed assets are often pledged as security for long-term notes and bonds. The **ratio of fixed assets to long-term liabilities** provides a measure of how much fixed assets a company has to support its long-term debt. This measures a company's ability to repay the face amount of debt at maturity and is computed as follows:

$$\text{Ratio of Fixed Assets to Long-Term Liabilities} = \frac{\text{Fixed Assets (net)}}{\text{Long-Term Liabilities}}$$

To illustrate, the ratio of fixed assets to long-term liabilities for **Lincoln Company** is computed as follows:

	20Y6	20Y5
Fixed assets (net)	$444,500	$470,000
Long-term liabilities	$100,000	$200,000
Ratio of fixed assets to long-term liabilities	4.4 ($444,500 ÷ $100,000)	2.4 ($470,000 ÷ $200,000)

During 20Y6, Lincoln's ratio of fixed assets to long-term liabilities increased from 2.4 to 4.4. This increase was due primarily to Lincoln paying off one-half of its long-term liabilities in 20Y6.

> **Link to Nike**
>
> For a recent year, **Nike**'s ratio of fixed assets to long-term liabilities was 1.0.

Ratio of Liabilities to Stockholders' Equity

The **ratio of liabilities to stockholders' equity** measures how much of the company is financed by debt and equity. It is computed as follows:

$$\text{Ratio of Liabilities to Stockholders' Equity} = \frac{\text{Total Liabilities}}{\text{Total Stockholders' Equity}}$$

To illustrate, the ratio of liabilities to stockholders' equity for **Lincoln Company** is computed as follows:

	20Y6	20Y5
Total liabilities	$310,000	$443,000
Total stockholders' equity	$829,500	$787,500
Ratio of liabilities to stockholders' equity	0.4 ($310,000 ÷ $829,500)	0.6 ($443,000 ÷ $787,500)

Lincoln's ratio of liabilities to stockholders' equity decreased from 0.6 to 0.4 during 20Y6. The lower ratio indicates that Lincoln's liabilities as a proportion of equity is decreasing. This is an improvement and indicates that the margin of safety for Lincoln's creditors is improving.

> **Link to Nike**
>
> For a recent five-year period, **Nike**'s average ratio of liabilities to stockholders' equity was 0.6.

Example Exercise 17-6 Solvency Analysis *Obj. 4*

The following information was taken from Acme Company's balance sheet:

Fixed assets (net)	$1,400,000
Long-term liabilities	400,000
Total liabilities	560,000
Total stockholders' equity	1,400,000

Determine the company's (a) ratio of fixed assets to long-term liabilities and (b) ratio of liabilities to total stockholders' equity. Round to one decimal place.

Follow My Example 17-6

a. Ratio of Fixed Assets to Long-Term Liabilities = Fixed Assets ÷ Long-Term Liabilities
= $1,400,000 ÷ $400,000
= 3.5

b. Ratio of Liabilities to Total Stockholders' Equity = Total Liabilities ÷ Total Stockholders' Equity
= $560,000 ÷ $1,400,000
= 0.4

Practice Exercises: PE 17-6A, PE 17-6B

Times Interest Earned

The **times interest earned**, sometimes called the *coverage ratio*, measures the risk that interest payments will not be made if earnings decrease. It is computed as follows:

$$\text{Times Interest Earned} = \frac{\text{Income Before Income Tax} + \text{Interest Expense}}{\text{Interest Expense}}$$

Interest expense is paid before income taxes. In other words, interest expense is deducted in determining taxable income and, thus, income tax. For this reason, income *before taxes* is used in computing the times interest earned.

The *higher* the ratio, the more likely interest payments will be paid if earnings decrease. To illustrate, the times interest earned for **Lincoln Company** is computed as follows:

	20Y6	20Y5
Income before income tax	$162,500	$134,600
Interest expense	6,000	12,000
Amount available to pay interest	$168,500	$146,600
Times interest earned	28.1 ($168,500 ÷ $6,000)	12.2 ($146,600 ÷ $12,000)

The times interest earned improved from 12.2 to 28.1 during 20Y6. The higher ratio indicates that the relationship between the amount of income available to pay interest and the amount of interest expense has improved. Lincoln has more than enough earnings (28 times) to make its interest payments.

Link to Nike

For a recent year, **Nike**'s times interest earned ratio was nine times higher than the industry average.

Example Exercise 17-7 Times Interest Earned Obj. 4

Acme Company reports the following:

Income before income tax	$250,000
Interest expense	100,000

Determine the times interest earned ratio. Round to one decimal place.

Follow My Example 17-7

Times Interest Earned = (Income Before Income Tax + Interest Expense) ÷ Interest Expense
= ($250,000 + $100,000) ÷ $100,000
= 3.5

Practice Exercises: PE 17-7A, PE 17-7B

Business Connection

LIQUIDITY CRUNCH

RadioShack Corporation, an electronics retailer, filed for bankruptcy protection. Information on the company's liquidity and solvency for the three years prior to bankruptcy follow:

	20Y3	20Y2	20Y1
Liquidity measures:			
Working capital (in thousands)	$748,400	$1,003,700	$1,176,700
Current ratio	2.3	2.0	2.9
Quick ratio	0.7	1.0	1.5
Solvency measures:			
Ratio of liabilities to stockholders' equity	6.7	2.8	1.9
Ratio of fixed assets to long-term liabilities	0.2	0.3	0.3

The data show that the company's liquidity and solvency measures deteriorated in the years prior to the firm's bankruptcy. All three of the company's liquidity measures declined significantly during the three-year period, indicating a growing risk that the company would not be able to repay its current liabilities. The ratio of liabilities to stockholder's equity also increased significantly during this period, indicating that the company might not be able to repay its long-term debts. Finally, the ratio of fixed assets to long-term liabilities began to deteriorate in 20Y3, indicating that fewer assets would be available to secure the company's long-term liabilities.

Obj. 5 Describe and illustrate how to use financial statement analysis to assess profitability.

Analyzing Profitability

Profitability analysis evaluates the ability of a company to generate future earnings. This ability depends on the relationship between the company's operating results and the assets the company has available for use in its operations. Thus, the relationship between income statement and balance sheet items are used to evaluate profitability.

Common profitability ratios are shown in Exhibit 10.

EXHIBIT 10
Profitability Ratios

Profitability Ratios		
Asset Turnover	Return on Stockholders' Equity	Price-Earnings Ratio
Return on Total Assets	Return on Common Stockholders' Equity	Dividends per Share
	Earnings per Share on Common Stock	Dividend Yield

Asset Turnover

The **asset turnover** ratio measures how effectively a company uses its assets. It is computed as follows:

$$\text{Asset Turnover} = \frac{\text{Sales}}{\text{Average Total Assets}}$$

To illustrate, the asset turnover for **Lincoln Company** is computed as follows. Total assets are $1,187,500 at the beginning of 20Y5.

	20Y6	20Y5
Sales	$1,498,000	$1,200,000
Total assets:		
Beginning of year	$1,230,500	$1,187,500
End of year	1,139,500	1,230,500
Total	$2,370,000	$2,418,000
Average total assets	$1,185,000 ($2,370,000 ÷ 2)	$1,209,000 ($2,418,000 ÷ 2)
Asset turnover	1.3 ($1,498,000 ÷ $1,185,000)	1.0 ($1,200,000 ÷ $1,209,000)

For Lincoln, the average total assets was computed using total assets at the beginning and end of the year. The average total assets could also be based on monthly or quarterly averages.

The asset turnover ratio indicates that Lincoln's use of its assets has improved in 20Y6. This was due primarily to the increase in sales in 20Y6.

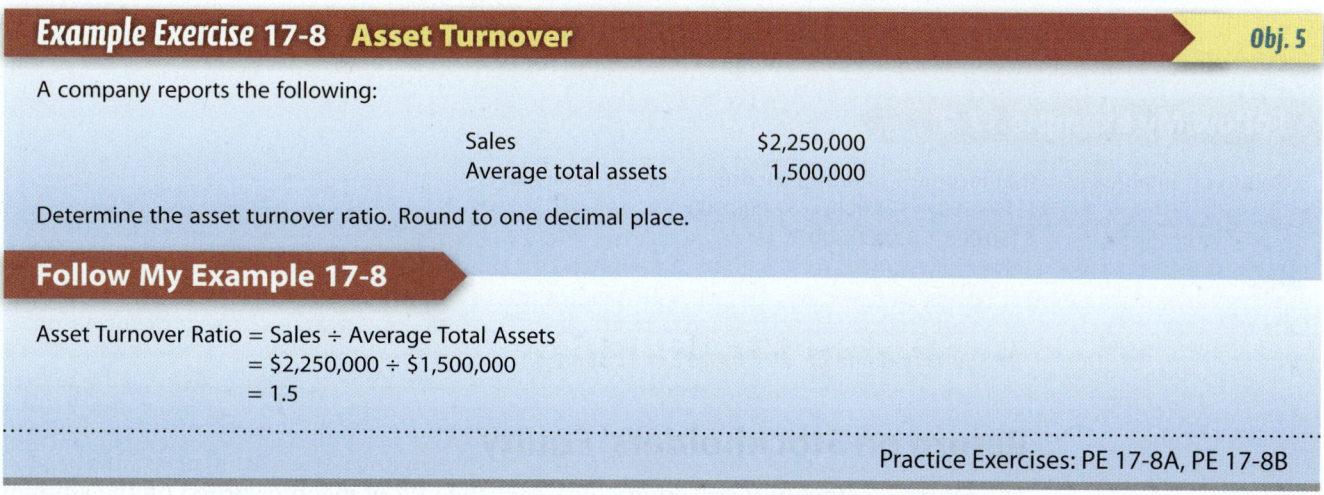

Return on Total Assets

The **return on total assets** measures the profitability of total assets, without considering how the assets are financed. In other words, this rate is not affected by the portion of assets financed by creditors or stockholders. It is computed as follows:

$$\text{Return on Total Assets} = \frac{\text{Income} + \text{Interest Expense}}{\text{Average Total Assets}}$$

The return on total assets is computed by adding interest expense to net income. By adding interest expense to net income, the effect of whether the assets are financed by creditors (debt) or stockholders (equity) is eliminated. Because net income includes any income earned from long-term investments, the average total assets includes long-term investments as well as the net operating assets.

To illustrate, the return on total assets by **Lincoln Company** is computed as follows. Total assets are $1,187,500 at the beginning of 20Y5.

	20Y6	20Y5
Net income	$ 91,000	$ 76,500
Interest expense	6,000	12,000
	$ 97,000	$ 88,500
Total assets:		
Beginning of year	$1,230,500	$1,187,500
End of year	1,139,500	1,230,500
Total	$2,370,000	$2,418,000
Average total assets	$1,185,000 ($2,370,000 ÷ 2)	$1,209,000 ($2,418,000 ÷ 2)
Return on total assets	8.2% ($97,000 ÷ $1,185,000)	7.3% ($88,500 ÷ $1,209,000)

The return on total assets improved from 7.3% to 8.2% during 20Y6.

The *return on operating assets* is sometimes computed when there are large amounts of nonoperating income and expense. It is computed as follows:

$$\text{Return on Operating Assets} = \frac{\text{Income from Operations}}{\text{Average Operating Assets}}$$

Because Lincoln does not have a significant amount of nonoperating income and expense, the return on operating assets is not illustrated.

Example Exercise 17-9 Return on Total Assets   Obj. 5

A company reports the following income statement and balance sheet information for the current year:

Net income	$ 125,000
Interest expense	25,000
Average total assets	2,000,000

Determine the return on total assets. Round percentage to one decimal place.

Follow My Example 17-9

Return on Total Assets = (Net Income + Interest Expense) ÷ Average Total Assets
= ($125,000 + $25,000) ÷ $2,000,000
= $150,000 ÷ $2,000,000
= 7.5%

Practice Exercises: PE 17-9A, PE 17-9B

Return on Stockholders' Equity

The **return on stockholders' equity** measures the rate of income earned on the amount invested by the stockholders. It is computed as follows:

$$\text{Return on Stockholders' Equity} = \frac{\text{Net Income}}{\text{Average Total Stockholders' Equity}}$$

To illustrate, the return on stockholders' equity for **Lincoln Company** is computed as follows. Total stockholders' equity is $750,000 at the beginning of 20Y5.

	20Y6	20Y5
Net income	$ 91,000	$ 76,500
Total stockholders' equity:		
Beginning of year	$ 787,500	$ 750,000
End of year	829,500	787,500
Total	$1,617,000	$1,537,500
Average total stockholders' equity	$808,500 ($1,617,000 ÷ 2)	$768,750 ($1,537,500 ÷ 2)
Return on stockholders' equity	11.3% ($91,000 ÷ $808,500)	10.0% ($76,500 ÷ $768,750)

The return on stockholders' equity improved from 10.0% to 11.3% during 20Y6.

Leverage involves using debt to increase the return on an investment. The return on stockholders' equity is normally higher than the return on total assets. This is because of the effect of leverage.

For **Lincoln Company**, the effect of leverage for 20Y6 is 3.1% and for 20Y5 is 2.7% computed as follows:

	20Y6	20Y5
Return on stockholders' equity	11.3%	10.0%
Return on total assets	(8.2)	(7.3)
Effect of leverage	3.1%	2.7%

Link to Nike
For a recent five-year period, **Nike**'s average return on stockholders' equity was 23.9%.

Exhibit 11 shows the 20Y6 and 20Y5 effects of leverage for Lincoln.

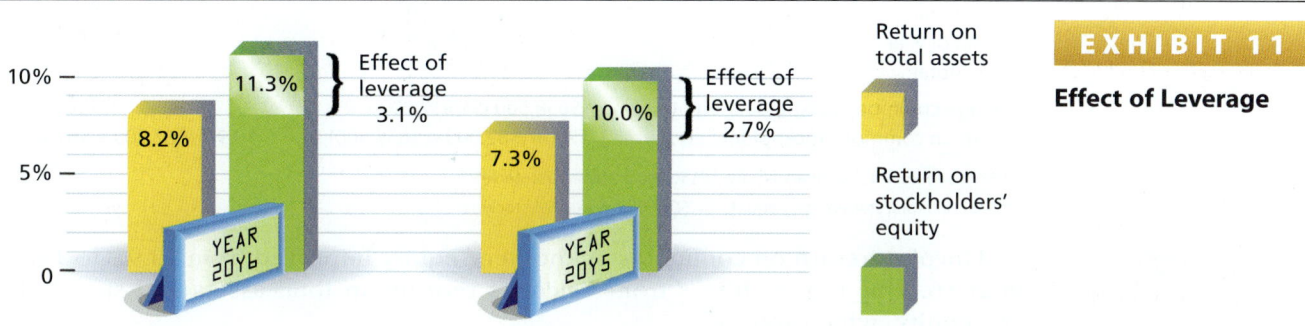

EXHIBIT 11

Effect of Leverage

Business Connection

GEARING FOR PROFIT

Another term for leverage is "financial gearing." **Exxon Mobil Corporation**, a worldwide-integrated energy company, is an example of a company that uses leverage for financial advantage. Exxon had a return on total assets of 9.35% for a recent year, while its return on stockholders' equity was 18.7%. Thus, Exxon is "geared" 2:1 by using debt on its balance sheet. Exxon is very profitable; thus, leverage is beneficial. In contrast, **Chesapeake Energy**, an oil and gas exploration company, had return on assets of −7.5% for a recent 12-month period and return on stockholders' equity of −25%. In this case, the over 3:1 leverage (25% ÷ 7.5%) creates a financial disadvantage because the company is experiencing losses.

Return on Common Stockholders' Equity

The **return on common stockholders' equity** measures the rate of profits earned on the amount invested by the common stockholders. It is computed as follows:

$$\text{Return on Common Stockholders' Equity} = \frac{\text{Net Income} - \text{Preferred Dividends}}{\text{Average Common Stockholders' Equity}}$$

Because preferred stockholders rank ahead of the common stockholders in their claim on earnings, any preferred dividends are subtracted from net income in computing the return on common stockholders' equity.

Lincoln Company had $150,000 par value of 6% preferred stock outstanding on December 31, 20Y6 and 20Y5. Thus, preferred dividends of $9,000 ($150,000 × 6%) are deducted from net income. Lincoln's common stockholders' equity is determined as follows:

	December 31		
	20Y6	20Y5	20Y4
Common stock, $10 par	$500,000	$500,000	$500,000
Retained earnings	179,500	137,500	100,000
Common stockholders' equity	$679,500	$637,500	$600,000

The retained earnings on December 31, 20Y4, of $100,000 is the same as the retained earnings on January 1, 20Y5, as shown in Lincoln's retained earnings statement in Exhibit 4.

Using this information, the return on common stockholders' equity for Lincoln is computed as follows:

	20Y6	20Y5
Net income	$ 91,000	$ 76,500
Preferred dividends	(9,000)	(9,000)
Total	$ 82,000	$ 67,500
Common stockholders' equity:		
Beginning of year	$ 637,500	$ 600,000
End of year	679,500*	637,500**
Total	$1,317,000	$1,237,500
Average common stockholders' equity	$658,500 ($1,317,000 ÷ 2)	$618,750 ($1,237,500 ÷ 2)
Return on common stockholders' equity	12.5% ($82,000 ÷ $658,500)	10.9% ($67,500 ÷ $618,750)

*($829,500 total stockholders' equity − $150,000 preferred 6% stock)
**($787,500 total stockholders' equity − $150,000 preferred 6% stock)

Lincoln's return on common stockholders' equity improved from 10.9% to 12.5% in 20Y6. This return differs from Lincoln's returns on total assets and stockholders' equity, which follow:

	20Y6	20Y5
Return on total assets	8.2%	7.3%
Return on stockholders' equity	11.3%	10.0%
Return on common stockholders' equity	12.5%	10.9%

These returns differ because of leverage, as discussed in the preceding section.

Example Exercise 17-10   Return on Stockholders' Equity   *Obj. 5*

A company reports the following:

Net income	$ 125,000
Preferred dividends	5,000
Average stockholders' equity	1,000,000
Average common stockholders' equity	800,000

Determine (a) the return on stockholders' equity and (b) the return on common stockholders' equity. Round percentages to one decimal place.

Follow My Example 17-10

a.   Return on Stockholders' Equity = Net Income ÷ Average Stockholders' Equity
         = $125,000 ÷ $1,000,000
         = 12.5%

b.   Return on Common Stockholders' Equity = (Net Income − Preferred Dividends) ÷ Average Common Stockholders' Equity
         = ($125,000 − $5,000) ÷ $800,000
         = 15.0%

Practice Exercises: PE 17-10A, PE 17-10B

Earnings per Share on Common Stock

Earnings per share (EPS) on common stock measures the share of profits that are earned by a share of common stock. Earnings per share must be reported on the income statement. As a result, earnings per share (EPS) is often reported in the financial press. It is computed as follows:

$$\text{Earnings per Share (EPS) on Common Stock} = \frac{\text{Net Income} - \text{Preferred Dividends}}{\text{Shares of Common Stock Outstanding}}$$

When preferred and common stock are outstanding, preferred dividends are subtracted from net income to determine the income related to the common shares.

To illustrate, the earnings per share (EPS) of common stock for **Lincoln Company** is computed as follows:

	20Y6	20Y5
Net income	$91,000	$76,500
Preferred dividends	(9,000)	(9,000)
Total	$82,000	$67,500
Shares of common stock outstanding	50,000	50,000
Earnings per share on common stock	$1.64 ($82,000 ÷ 50,000)	$1.35 ($67,500 ÷ 50,000)

Lincoln had $500,000 par value of $10 common stock, and $150,000 par value of 6% preferred stock outstanding on December 31, 20Y6 and 20Y5. The preferred dividends of $9,000 ($150,000 × 6%) are deducted from net income in computing earnings per share on common stock. This amount is divided by the 50,000 common shares outstanding, which is computed by dividing the $500,000 par value of the common stock by the $10 par value per share.

Lincoln did not issue any additional shares of common stock in 20Y6. If Lincoln had issued additional shares in 20Y6, a weighted average of common shares outstanding during the year would have been used.

Lincoln's earnings per share (EPS) on common stock improved from $1.35 to $1.64 during 20Y6.

Lincoln has a simple capital structure with only common stock and preferred stock outstanding. Many corporations, however, have complex capital structures with various types of equity securities outstanding, such as convertible preferred stock, stock options, and stock warrants. In such cases, the possible effects of such securities on the shares of common stock outstanding are considered in reporting earnings per share. These possible effects are reported separately as *earnings per common share assuming dilution* or *diluted earnings per share*. This topic is described and illustrated in advanced accounting courses and textbooks.

> **Link to Nike**
> On a recent income statement, **Nike** reported net income of $2,693 million.

Price-Earnings Ratio

The **price-earnings (P/E) ratio** on common stock measures a company's future earnings prospects. It is often quoted in the financial press and is computed as follows:

$$\text{Price-Earnings (P/E) Ratio} = \frac{\text{Market Price per Share of Common Stock}}{\text{Earnings per Share on Common Stock}}$$

To illustrate, the price-earnings (P/E) ratio for **Lincoln Company** is computed as follows:

	20Y6	20Y5
Market price per share of common stock	$41.00	$27.00
Earnings per share on common stock	$1.64	$1.35
Price-earnings ratio on common stock	25 ($41 ÷ $1.64)	20 ($27 ÷ $1.35)

The price-earnings ratio improved from 20 to 25 during 20Y6. In other words, a share of common stock of Lincoln was selling for 20 times earnings per share at the end of 20Y5. At the end of 20Y6, the common stock was selling for 25 times earnings per share. This indicates that the market expects Lincoln to experience favorable earnings in the future.

Example Exercise 17-11 — Earnings per Share and Price-Earnings Ratio — Obj. 5

A company reports the following:

Net income	$250,000
Preferred dividends	$15,000
Shares of common stock outstanding	20,000
Market price per share of common stock	$35.25

a. Determine the company's earnings per share on common stock.
b. Determine the company's price-earnings ratio. Round to one decimal place.

Follow My Example 17-11

a. Earnings per Share on Common Stock = (Net Income − Preferred Dividends) ÷ Shares of Common Stock Outstanding
   = ($250,000 − $15,000) ÷ 20,000
   = $11.75

b. Price-Earnings Ratio = Market Price per Share of Common Stock ÷ Earnings per Share on Common Stock
   = $35.25 ÷ $11.75
   = 3.0

Practice Exercises: PE 17-11A, PE 17-11B

Dividends per Share

Dividends per share measures the extent to which earnings are being distributed to common shareholders. It is computed as follows:

$$\text{Dividends per Share} = \frac{\text{Dividends on Common Stock}}{\text{Shares of Common Stock Outstanding}}$$

To illustrate, the dividends per share for **Lincoln Company** are computed as follows:

	20Y6	20Y5
Dividends on common stock	$40,000	$30,000
Shares of common stock outstanding	50,000	50,000
Dividends per share of common stock	$0.80 ($40,000 ÷ 50,000)	$0.60 ($30,000 ÷ 50,000)

The dividends per share of common stock increased from $0.60 to $0.80 during 20Y6.

Dividends per share are often reported with earnings per share. Comparing the two per-share amounts indicates the extent to which earnings are being retained for use in operations. To illustrate, the dividends and earnings per share for **Lincoln Company** are shown in Exhibit 12.

EXHIBIT 12

Dividends and Earnings per Share of Common Stock

Dividend Yield

The **dividend yield** on common stock measures the rate of return to common stockholders from cash dividends. It is of special interest to investors whose objective is to earn revenue (dividends) from their investment. It is computed as follows:

$$\text{Dividend Yield} = \frac{\text{Dividends per Share of Common Stock}}{\text{Market Price per Share of Common Stock}}$$

To illustrate, the dividend yield for Lincoln Company is computed as follows:

	20Y6	20Y5
Dividends per share of common stock	$0.80	$0.60
Market price per share of common stock	$41.00	$27.00
Dividend yield on common stock	2.0% ($0.80 ÷ $41)	2.2% ($0.60 ÷ $27)

The dividend yield declined slightly from 2.2% to 2.0% in 20Y6. This decline was due primarily to the increase in the market price of Lincoln's common stock.

Link to Nike

For a recent five-year period, Nike's average dividend yield was 1.24%.

Business Connection

INVESTING FOR YIELD

Companies that provide attractive dividend yields are often mature companies found in stable industries. Examples of such industries are public utilities and food. Coca-Cola, Procter & Gamble, Kellogg's, Consolidated Edison, Southern Company, and General Mills all have attractive dividend yields in excess of 3%. Procter & Gamble has had 58 consecutive years of dividend payouts, and Kellogg's has not reduced its dividend for 56 years. The stability of the food industry has allowed these companies to maintain dividends for many years. Growth companies such as Google and Facebook do not pay dividends, because they use their cash to grow the business. Investors in such growth companies expect to make their return from stock price appreciation rather than dividends. Mark Cuban, billionaire, Shark Tank® investor, and owner of the Dallas Mavericks, stated, "I believe non-dividend stocks aren't much more than baseball cards. They are worth what you can convince someone to pay for it."

Quote source: Tim Parker, "The Top Ten Dividend Quotes," *Dividend.com*, August 29, 2012.

Summary of Analytical Measures

Exhibit 13 shows a summary of the liquidity, solvency and profitability measures discussed in this chapter. The type of industry and the company's operations usually affect which measures are used. In many cases, additional measures are used for a specific industry. For example, airlines use *revenue per passenger mile* and *cost per available seat* as profitability measures. Likewise, hotels use *occupancy rates* as a profitability measure.

EXHIBIT 13 — Summary of Analytical Measures

Liquidity Measures

	Method of Computation	Use
Working Capital	Current Assets − Current Liabilities	Measures the company's ability to pay current liabilities.
Current Ratio	$\dfrac{\text{Current Assets}}{\text{Current Liabilities}}$	
Quick Ratio	$\dfrac{\text{Quick Assets}}{\text{Current Liabilities}}$	Measures the company's instant debt-paying ability.
Accounts Receivable Turnover	$\dfrac{\text{Sales}}{\text{Average Accounts Receivable}}$	Measures the company's efficiency in collecting receivables and in the management of credit.
Numbers of Days' Sales in Receivables	$\dfrac{\text{Average Accounts Receivable}}{\text{Average Daily Sales}}$	
Inventory Turnover	$\dfrac{\text{Cost of Goods Sold}}{\text{Average Inventory}}$	Measures the company's efficiency in managing inventory.
Number of Days' Sales in Inventory	$\dfrac{\text{Average Inventory}}{\text{Average Daily Cost of Goods Sold}}$	

Solvency Measures

	Method of Computation	Use
Ratio of Fixed Assets to Long-Term Liabilities	$\dfrac{\text{Fixed Assets (net)}}{\text{Long-Term Liabilities}}$	Measures the margin of safety available to long-term creditors.
Ratio of Liabilities to Stockholders' Equity	$\dfrac{\text{Total Liabilities}}{\text{Total Stockholders' Equity}}$	Measures how much of the company is financed by debt and equity.
Times Interest Earned	$\dfrac{\text{Income Before Income Tax + Interest Expense}}{\text{Interest Expense}}$	Measures the risk that interest payments will not be made if earnings decrease.

Profitability Measures

	Method of Computation	Use
Asset Turnover	$\dfrac{\text{Sales}}{\text{Average Total Assets}}$	Measures how effectively a company uses its assets.
Return on Total Assets	$\dfrac{\text{Net Income + Interest Expense}}{\text{Average Total Assets}}$	Measures the profitability of a company's assets.
Return on Stockholders' Equity	$\dfrac{\text{Net Income}}{\text{Average Total Stockholders' Equity}}$	Measures the profitability of the investment by stockholders.
Return on Common Stockholders' Equity	$\dfrac{\text{Net Income − Preferred Dividends}}{\text{Average Common Stockholders' Equity}}$	Measures the profitability of the investment by common stockholders.
Earnings per Share (EPS) on Common Stock	$\dfrac{\text{Net Income − Preferred Dividends}}{\text{Shares of Common Stock Outstanding}}$	
Price-Earnings (P/E) Ratio	$\dfrac{\text{Market Price per Share of Common Stock}}{\text{Earnings per Share on Common Stock}}$	Measures future earnings prospects, based on the relationship between market value of common stock and earnings.
Dividends per Share	$\dfrac{\text{Dividends on Common Stock}}{\text{Shares of Common Stock Outstanding}}$	Measures the extent to which earnings are being distributed to common stockholders.
Dividend Yield	$\dfrac{\text{Dividends per Share of Common Stock}}{\text{Market Price per Share of Common Stock}}$	Measures the rate of return to common stockholders in terms of dividends.

The analytical measures shown in Exhibit 13 are a useful starting point for analyzing a company's liquidity, solvency, and profitability. However, they are not a substitute for sound judgment. The general economic and business environment should always be considered in analyzing a company's future prospects. In addition, any trends and interrelationships among the measures should be studied carefully.

Corporate Annual Reports

Obj. 6 Describe the contents of corporate annual reports.

See Appendix B for more information.

Public corporations issue annual reports summarizing their operating activities for the past year and plans for the future. Such annual reports include the financial statements and the accompanying notes. In addition, annual reports normally include the following sections:

- Management discussion and analysis
- Report on internal control
- Report on fairness of the financial statements

Management Discussion and Analysis

Management's Discussion and Analysis (MD&A) is required in annual reports filed with the Securities and Exchange Commission. It includes management's analysis of current operations and its plans for the future. Typical items included in the MD&A are as follows:

- Management's analysis and explanations of any significant changes between the current and prior years' financial statements.
- Important accounting principles or policies that could affect interpretation of the financial statements, including the effect of changes in accounting principles or the adoption of new accounting principles.
- Management's assessment of the company's liquidity and the availability of capital to the company.
- Significant risk exposures that might affect the company.
- Any "off-balance-sheet" arrangements such as leases not included in the financial statements. Such arrangements are discussed in advanced accounting courses and textbooks.

Report on Internal Control

The Sarbanes-Oxley Act of 2002 requires a report on internal control by management. The report states management's responsibility for establishing and maintaining internal control. In addition, management's assessment of the effectiveness of internal controls over financial reporting is included in the report.

INTEGRITY, OBJECTIVITY, AND ETHICS IN BUSINESS

CHARACTERISTICS OF FINANCIAL STATEMENT FRAUD

Each year, the Association of Certified Fraud Examiners conducts a worldwide survey examining the characteristics of corporate fraud. The most recent study found the following:

- 43.3% of frauds were detected by a tip from an employee or someone close to the company.
- Frauds committed by owners and executives tended to be much larger than those caused by employees.
- Most people who are caught committing fraud are first-time offenders with clean employment histories.
- In 81% of the cases, the person committing the fraud displayed one or more behavioral red flags, such as living beyond his or her means, having financial difficulties, and having excessive control issues.

Fraud examiners can use these trends to help them narrow their focus when searching for fraud.

Source: *2012 Report to the Nations*, Association of Certified Fraud Examiners, 2012.

Chapter 17 Financial Statement Analysis

Sarbanes-Oxley also requires a public accounting firm to verify management's conclusions on internal control. Thus, two reports on internal control, one by management and one by a public accounting firm, are included in the annual report. In some situations, these may be combined into a single report on internal control.

Report on Fairness of the Financial Statements

All publicly held corporations are required to have an independent audit (examination) of their financial statements. The Certified Public Accounting (CPA) firm that conducts the audit renders an opinion, called the *Report of Independent Registered Public Accounting Firm*, on the fairness of the statements.

An opinion stating that the financial statements present fairly the financial position, results of operations, and cash flows of the company is said to be an *unmodified opinion*, sometimes called a *clean opinion*. Any report other than an unmodified opinion raises a red flag for financial statement users and requires further investigation as to its cause. The types and nature of audit opinions are covered in more detail in advanced courses on auditing.

The annual report of Nike Inc. is shown in Appendix D. The Nike report includes the financial statements as well as Management's Discussion and Analysis, Report on Internal Control, and the Report on Fairness of the Financial Statements.

APPENDIX

Unusual Items on the Income Statement

Generally accepted accounting principles require that unusual items be reported separately on the income statement. This is because such items do not occur frequently and are typically unrelated to current operations. Without separate reporting of these items, users of the financial statements might be misled about current and future operations.

Unusual items on the income statement are classified as one of the following:

- Affecting the *current period* income statement
- Affecting a *prior period* income statement

Unusual Items Affecting the Current Period's Income Statement

Discontinued operations are an unusual item that affects the current period's:

- Income statement presentation
- Earnings per share presentation

Discontinued operations are reported separately on the income statement for any period in which they occur.

Income Statement Presentation A company may discontinue a component of its operations by selling or abandoning the component's operations. For example, a retailer might decide to sell its product only online and, thus, discontinue selling its merchandise at its retail outlets (stores).

If the discontinued component is (1) the result of a strategic shift and (2) has a major effect on the entity's operations and financial results, any gain or loss on discontinued operations is reported on the income statement as a *Gain (or loss) from discontinued operations*. It is reported immediately following *Income from continuing operations*.

To illustrate, assume that Jones Corporation produces and sells electrical products, hardware supplies, and lawn equipment. Because of a lack of profits, Jones discontinues its electrical products operation and sells the remaining inventory and other assets at a loss of $100,000. Exhibit 14 illustrates the reporting of the loss on discontinued operations.[2]

EXHIBIT 14

Unusual Items in the Income Statement

Jones Corporation
Income Statement
For the Year Ended December 31, 20Y2

Sales	$12,350,000
Cost of goods sold	5,800,000
Gross profit	$ 6,550,000
Selling and administrative expenses	5,240,000
Income from continuing operations before income tax	$ 1,310,000
Income tax expense	620,000
Income from continuing operations	$ 690,000
Loss on discontinued operations	(100,000)
Net income	$ 590,000

In addition, a note to the financial statements should describe the operations sold, including the date operations were discontinued, and details about the assets, liabilities, income, and expenses of the discontinued component.

Earnings per Share Earnings per common share should be reported separately for discontinued operations. To illustrate, a partial income statement for Jones Corporation is shown in Exhibit 15. The company has 200,000 shares of common stock outstanding.

EXHIBIT 15

Income Statement with Earnings per Share

Jones Corporation
Income Statement
For the Year Ended December 31, 20Y2

Earnings per common share:	
Income from continuing operations	$ 3.45
Loss on discontinued operations	(0.50)
Net income	$ 2.95

Exhibit 15 reports earnings per common share for income from continuing operations, discontinued operations. However, only earnings per share for income from continuing operations and net income are required by generally accepted accounting principles. The other per-share amounts may be presented in the notes to the financial statements.

---

[2] The gain or loss on discontinued operations is reported net of any tax effects. To simplify, the tax effects are not specifically identified in Exhibit 14.

Unusual Items Affecting the Prior Period's Income Statement

An unusual item may occur that affects a prior period's income statement. Two such items are as follows:

- Errors in applying generally accepted accounting principles
- Changes from one generally accepted accounting principle to another

If an error is discovered in a prior period's financial statement, the prior-period statement and all following statements are restated and thus corrected.

A company may change from one generally accepted accounting principle to another. In this case, the prior-period financial statements are restated as if the new accounting principle had always been used as discussed in Chapter 11.

For both of the preceding items, the current period earnings are not affected. That is, only the earnings reported in prior periods are restated. However, because the prior earnings are restated, the beginning balance of Retained Earnings may also have to be restated. This, in turn, may cause the restatement of other balance sheet accounts. Illustrations of these types of adjustments and restatements are provided in advanced accounting courses.

At a Glance 17

Obj. 1 Describe the techniques and tools used to analyze financial statement information.

Key Points Financial statements provide important information that users rely on to make economic decisions. This information is evaluated along three dimensions: liquidity, solvency, and profitability. Two common techniques are used to analyze a company's financial performance and condition: analytical methods and ratios. Both analytical methods and ratios can be used to compare a company's financial performance over time or to another company.

Learning Outcome	Example Exercises	Practice Exercises
• Describe the techniques used to analyze a company's financial performance.		

Obj. 2 Describe and illustrate basic financial statement analytical methods.

Key Points Financial statements provide much of the information users need to make economic decisions. Analytical procedures are used to compare items on a current financial statement with related items on earlier financial statements or to examine relationships within a financial statement.

Learning Outcomes	Example Exercises	Practice Exercises
• Prepare a horizontal analysis from a company's financial statements.	EE17-1	PE17-1A, 17-1B
• Prepare a vertical analysis from a company's financial statements.	EE17-2	PE17-2A, 17-2B
• Prepare a common-sized financial statement.		

Obj. 3 Describe and illustrate how to use financial statement analysis to assess liquidity.

Key Points Liquidity analysis evaluates a company's ability to convert current assets into cash. Short-term creditors use liquidity analysis to evaluate a company's ability to repay short-term debts by focusing on a company's current position, accounts receivable, and inventory. The measures and ratios used to evaluate a company's liquidity include (1) working capital, (2) current ratio, (3) quick ratio, (4) accounts receivable turnover, (5) number of days' sales in receivables, (6) inventory turnover, and (7) number of days' sales in inventory.

Learning Outcomes	Example Exercises	Practice Exercises
• Determine working capital.		
• Compute and interpret the current ratio.		
• Compute and interpret the quick ratio.	EE17-3	PE17-3A, 17-3B
• Compute and interpret accounts receivable turnover.	EE17-4	PE17-4A, 17-4B
• Compute and interpret the number of days' sales in receivables.		
• Compute and interpret inventory turnover.		
• Compute and interpret the number of days' sales in inventory.	EE17-5	PE17-5A, 17-5B

Obj. 4 Describe and illustrate how to use financial statement analysis to assess solvency.

Key Points Solvency analysis evaluates the ability of a company to pay its long-term debts. Long-term creditors use solvency analysis to evaluate a company's ability to make its periodic interest payments and repay the face amount of bonds at maturity. Solvency is normally assessed by examining (1) the ratio of fixed assets to long-term liabilities, (2) the ratio of liabilities to stockholders' equity, and (3) the times interest earned ratio.

Learning Outcomes	Example Exercises	Practice Exercises
• Compute and interpret the ratio of fixed assets to long-term liabilities.		
• Compute and interpret the ratio of liabilities to stockholders' equity.	EE17-6	PE17-6A, 17-6B
• Compute and interpret the times interest earned ratio.	EE17-7	PE17-7A, 17-7B

Obj. 5 Describe and illustrate to to use financial statement analysis to assess profitability.

Key Points Profitability analysis focuses on the relationship between operating results (income statement) and assets (balance sheet). Profitability analyses include (1) the asset turnover ratio, (2) the return on total assets, (3) the return on stockholders' equity, (4) the return on common stockholders' equity, (5) earnings per share on common stock, (6) the price-earnings ratio, (7) dividends per share, and (8) dividend yield.

Learning Outcomes	Example Exercises	Practice Exercises
• Compute and interpret the asset turnover ratio.	EE17-8	PE17-8A, 17-8B
• Compute and interpret the return on total assets.	EE17-9	PE17-9A, 17-9B
• Compute and interpret the return on stockholders' equity.		
• Compute and interpret the return on common stockholders' equity.	EE17-10	PE17-10A, 17-10B
• Compute and interpret the price-earnings ratio.	EE17-11	PE17-11A, 17-11B
• Compute and interpret dividends per share and dividend yield.		
• Describe the uses and limitations of analytical measures.		

Obj. 6 Describe the contents of corporate annual reports.

Key Points Public corporations issue annual reports summarizing their operating activities for the past year and plans for the future. In addition to the financial statements and accompanying notes, annual reports include Management's Discussion and Analysis (MD&A), a report on internal control, and a report on fairness of the financial statements.

Learning Outcome	Example Exercises	Practice Exercises
• Describe the elements of a corporate annual report.		

Illustrative Problem

Rainbow Paint Co.'s comparative financial statements for the years ending December 31, 20Y9 and 20Y8, are as follows. The market price of Rainbow Paint's common stock was $25 on December 31, 20Y9, and $30 on December 31, 20Y8.

Rainbow Paint Co.
Comparative Income Statement
For the Years Ended December 31, 20Y9 and 20Y8

	20Y9	20Y8
Sales	$5,000,000	$3,200,000
Cost of goods sold	3,400,000	2,080,000
Gross profit	$1,600,000	$1,120,000
Selling expenses	$ 650,000	$ 464,000
Administrative expenses	325,000	224,000
Total operating expenses	$ 975,000	$ 688,000
Income from operations	$ 625,000	$ 432,000
Other revenue	25,000	19,200
	$ 650,000	$ 451,200
Other expense (interest)	105,000	64,000
Income before income tax	$ 545,000	$ 387,200
Income tax expense	300,000	176,000
Net income	$ 245,000	$ 211,200

Rainbow Paint Co.
Comparative Retained Earnings Statement
For the Years Ended December 31, 20Y9 and 20Y8

	20Y9	20Y8
Retained earnings, January 1	$723,000	$581,800
Net income	245,000	211,200
Total	$968,000	$793,000
Dividends:		
Preferred stock dividends	$ 40,000	$ 40,000
Common stock dividends	45,000	30,000
Total dividends	$ 85,000	$ 70,000
Retained earnings, December 31	$883,000	$723,000

(*Continued*)

Rainbow Paint Co.
Comparative Balance Sheet
December 31, 20Y9 and 20Y8

	20Y9	20Y8
Assets		
Current assets:		
Cash	$ 175,000	$ 125,000
Temporary investments	150,000	50,000
Accounts receivable (net)	425,000	325,000
Inventories	720,000	480,000
Prepaid expenses	30,000	20,000
Total current assets	$1,500,000	$1,000,000
Long-term investments	250,000	225,000
Property, plant, and equipment (net)	2,093,000	1,948,000
Total assets	$3,843,000	$3,173,000
Liabilities		
Current liabilities	$ 750,000	$ 650,000
Long-term liabilities:		
Mortgage note payable, 10%, due in five years	$ 410,000	$ —
Bonds payable, 8%, due in 15 years	800,000	800,000
Total long-term liabilities	$1,210,000	$ 800,000
Total liabilities	$1,960,000	$1,450,000
Stockholders' Equity		
Preferred 8% stock, $100 par	$ 500,000	$ 500,000
Common stock, $10 par	500,000	500,000
Retained earnings	883,000	723,000
Total stockholders' equity	$1,883,000	$1,723,000
Total liabilities and stockholders' equity	$3,843,000	$3,173,000

Instructions

Determine the following measures for 20Y9, rounding percentages and ratios other than per-share amounts to one decimal place:

1. Working capital
2. Current ratio
3. Quick ratio
4. Accounts receivable turnover
5. Number of days' sales in receivables
6. Inventory turnover
7. Number of days' sales in inventory
8. Ratio of fixed assets to long-term liabilities
9. Ratio of liabilities to stockholders' equity
10. Times interest earned
11. Asset turnover
12. Return on total assets
13. Return on stockholders' equity
14. Return on common stockholders' equity
15. Earnings per share on common stock
16. Price-earnings ratio
17. Dividends per share
18. Dividend yield

Solution

(Ratios are rounded to one decimal place.)

1. Working capital: $750,000

    $1,500,000 − $750,000

2. Current ratio: 2.0

    $1,500,000 ÷ $750,000

3. Quick ratio: 1.0

    $750,000 ÷ $750,000

4. Accounts receivable turnover: 13.3

    $5,000,000 ÷ [($425,000 + $325,000) ÷ 2]

5. Number of days' sales in receivables: 27.4 days

    $5,000,000 ÷ 365 days = $13,699 average daily sales

    $375,000 ÷ $13,699

6. Inventory turnover: 5.7

    $3,400,000 ÷ [($720,000 + $480,000) ÷ 2]

7. Number of days' sales in inventory: 64.4 days

    $3,400,000 ÷ 365 days = $9,315 average daily cost of goods sold

    $600,000 ÷ $9,315

8. Ratio of fixed assets to long-term liabilities: 1.7

    $2,093,000 ÷ $1,210,000

9. Ratio of liabilities to stockholders' equity: 1.0

    $1,960,000 ÷ $1,883,000

10. Times interest earned: 6.2

    ($545,000 + $105,000) ÷ $105,000

11. Asset turnover: 1.4

    $5,000,000 ÷ [($3,843,000 + $3,173,000) ÷ 2]

12. Return on total assets: 10.0%

    ($245,000 + $105,000) ÷ [($3,843,000 + $3,173,000) ÷ 2]

13. Return on stockholders' equity: 13.6%

    $245,000 ÷ [($1,883,000 + $1,723,000) ÷ 2]

14. Return on common stockholders' equity: 15.7%

    ($245,000 − $40,000) ÷ [($1,383,000 + $1,223,000) ÷ 2]

15. Earnings per share on common stock: $4.10

    ($245,000 − $40,000) ÷ 50,000 shares

16. Price-earnings ratio: 6.1

    $25 ÷ $4.10

17. Dividends per share: $0.90

    $45,000 ÷ 50,000 shares

18. Dividend yield: 3.6%

    $0.90 ÷ $25

Key Terms

- accounts receivable analysis (834)
- accounts receivable turnover (834)
- analytical methods (826)
- asset turnover (840)
- common-sized statement (830)
- current position analysis (832)
- current ratio (832)
- dividend yield (847)
- dividends per share (846)
- earnings per share (EPS) on common stock (844)
- horizontal analysis (826)
- inventory analysis (835)
- inventory turnover (836)
- leverage (842)
- liquidity (825)
- Management's Discussion and Analysis (MD&A) (849)
- number of days' sales in inventory (836)
- number of days' sales in receivables (835)
- price-earnings (P/E) ratio (845)
- profitability (826)
- quick assets (833)
- quick ratio (833)
- ratio of fixed assets to long-term liabilities (838)
- ratio of liabilities to stockholders' equity (838)
- ratios (826)
- return on common stockholders' equity (843)
- return on stockholders' equity (842)
- return on total assets (841)
- solvency (826)
- times interest earned (839)
- vertical analysis (829)
- working capital (832)

Discussion Questions

1. Briefly explain the difference between liquidity, solvency, and profitability analysis.

2. What is the advantage of using comparative statements for financial analysis rather than statements for a single date or period?

3. A company's current year net income (after income tax) is 25% larger than that of the preceding year. Does this indicate improved operating performance? Why or why not?

4. How would the current and quick ratios of a service business compare?

5. a. Why is a high inventory turnover considered to be a positive indicator?

   b. Is it possible to have a high inventory turnover and a high number of days' sales in inventory? Why?

6. What do the following data, taken from a comparative balance sheet, indicate about the company's ability to borrow additional long-term debt in the current year as compared to the preceding year?

	Current Year	Preceding Year
Fixed assets (net)	$1,260,000	$1,360,000
Total long-term liabilities	300,000	400,000

7. a. How does the return on total assets differ from the return on stockholders' equity?

   b. Which ratio is normally higher? Why?

8. Kroger, a grocery store, recently had a price-earnings ratio of 17.5, while the average price-earnings ratio in the grocery store industry was 21.4. What might explain this difference?

9. The dividend yield of Suburban Propane was 10.2% in a recent year, and the dividend yield of Google was 0% in the same year. What might explain the difference between these ratios?

10. Describe two reports provided by independent auditors in the annual report to shareholders.

Practice Exercises

Example Exercises

EE 17-1 p. 829

PE 17-1A Horizontal analysis OBJ. 2

The comparative temporary investments and inventory balances of a company follow.

	Current Year	Previous Year
Temporary investments	$44,000	$40,000
Inventory	57,000	60,000

Based on this information, what is the amount and percentage of increase or decrease that would be shown on a balance sheet with horizontal analysis?

EE 17-1 p. 829

PE 17-1B Horizontal analysis OBJ. 2

The comparative accounts payable and long-term debt balances for a company follow.

	Current Year	Previous Year
Accounts payable	$111,000	$100,000
Long-term debt	132,680	124,000

Based on this information, what is the amount and percentage of increase or decrease that would be shown on a balance sheet with horizontal analysis?

EE 17-2 p. 830

PE 17-2A Vertical analysis OBJ. 2

Income statement information for Omega Corporation follows:

Sales	$500,000
Cost of goods sold	300,000
Gross profit	200,000

Prepare a vertical analysis of the income statement for Omega Corporation.

EE 17-2 p. 830

PE 17-2B Vertical analysis OBJ. 2

Income statement information for Einsworth Corporation follows:

Sales	$1,200,000
Cost of goods sold	780,000
Gross profit	420,000

Prepare a vertical analysis of the income statement for Einsworth Corporation.

EE 17-3 p. 833

PE 17-3A Current position analysis OBJ. 3

The following items are reported on a company's balance sheet:

Cash	$100,000
Marketable securities	50,000
Accounts receivable (net)	60,000
Inventory	70,000
Accounts payable	140,000

Determine (a) the current ratio and (b) the quick ratio. Round to one decimal place.

860 Chapter 17 Financial Statement Analysis

EE 17-3 *p. 833*

PE 17-3B Current position analysis OBJ. 3

The following items are reported on a company's balance sheet:

Cash	$210,000
Marketable securities	120,000
Accounts receivable (net)	110,000
Inventory	160,000
Accounts payable	200,000

Determine (a) the current ratio and (b) the quick ratio. Round to one decimal place.

EE 17-4 *p. 835*

PE 17-4A Accounts receivable analysis OBJ. 3

A company reports the following:

Sales	$1,500,000
Average accounts receivable (net)	100,000

Determine (a) the accounts receivable turnover and (b) the number of days' sales in receivables. Round to one decimal place.

EE 17-4 *p. 835*

PE 17-4B Accounts receivable analysis OBJ. 3

A company reports the following:

Sales	$4,000,000
Average accounts receivable (net)	200,000

Determine (a) the accounts receivable turnover and (b) the number of days' sales in receivables. Round to one decimal place.

EE 17-5 *p. 837*

PE 17-5A Inventory analysis OBJ. 3

A company reports the following:

Cost of goods sold	$660,000
Average inventory	60,000

Determine (a) the inventory turnover and (b) the number of days' sales in inventory. Round to one decimal place.

EE 17-5 *p. 837*

PE 17-5B Inventory analysis OBJ. 3

A company reports the following:

Cost of goods sold	$435,000
Average inventory	72,500

Determine (a) the inventory turnover and (b) the number of days' sales in inventory. Round to one decimal place.

EE 17-6 *p. 838*

PE 17-6A Long-term solvency analysis OBJ. 4

The following information was taken from Sigmund Company's balance sheet:

Fixed assets (net)	$1,050,000
Long-term liabilities	750,000
Total liabilities	850,000
Total stockholders' equity	500,000

Determine the company's (a) ratio of fixed assets to long-term liabilities and (b) ratio of liabilities to stockholders' equity. Round to one decimal place.

EE 17-6 *p. 838* **PE 17-6B Long-term solvency analysis** OBJ. 4

The following information was taken from Charu Company's balance sheet:

Fixed assets (net)	$860,000
Long-term liabilities	200,000
Total liabilities	600,000
Total stockholders' equity	250,000

Determine the company's (a) ratio of fixed assets to long-term liabilities and (b) ratio of liabilities to stockholders' equity. Round to one decimal place.

EE 17-7 *p. 839* **PE 17-7A Times interest earned** OBJ. 4

A company reports the following:

Income before income tax	$4,000,000
Interest expense	400,000

Determine the times interest earned ratio. Round to one decimal place.

EE 17-7 *p. 839* **PE 17-7B Times interest earned** OBJ. 4

A company reports the following:

Income before income tax	$8,000,000
Interest expense	500,000

Determine the times interest earned ratio. Round to one decimal place.

EE 17-8 *p. 841* **PE 17-8A Asset turnover** OBJ. 5

A company reports the following:

Sales	$1,800,000
Average total assets	1,125,000

Determine the asset turnover ratio. Round to one decimal place.

EE 17-8 *p. 841* **PE 17-8B Asset turnover** OBJ. 5

A company reports the following:

Sales	$4,400,000
Average total assets	2,000,000

Determine the asset turnover ratio. Round to one decimal place.

EE 17-9 *p. 842* **PE 17-9A Return on total assets** OBJ. 5

A company reports the following income statement and balance sheet information for the current year:

Net income	$ 250,000
Interest expense	100,000
Average total assets	2,500,000

Determine the return on total assets. Round percentage to one decimal place.

PE 17-9B Return on total assets OBJ. 5

A company reports the following income statement and balance sheet information for the current year:

Net income	$ 410,000
Interest expense	90,000
Average total assets	5,000,000

Determine the return on total assets. Round percentage to one decimal place.

PE 17-10A Common stockholders' profitability analysis OBJ. 5

A company reports the following:

Net income	$ 375,000
Preferred dividends	75,000
Average stockholders' equity	2,500,000
Average common stockholders' equity	1,875,000

Determine (a) the return on stockholders' equity and (b) the return on common stockholders' equity. Round percentages to one decimal place.

PE 17-10B Common stockholders' profitability analysis OBJ. 5

A company reports the following:

Net income	$1,000,000
Preferred dividends	50,000
Average stockholders' equity	6,250,000
Average common stockholders' equity	3,800,000

Determine (a) the return on stockholders' equity and (b) the return on common stockholders' equity. Round percentages to one decimal place.

PE 17-11A Earnings per share and price-earnings ratio OBJ. 5

A company reports the following:

Net income	$185,000
Preferred dividends	$25,000
Shares of common stock outstanding	100,000
Market price per share of common stock	$20

a. Determine the company's earnings per share on common stock.
b. Determine the company's price-earnings ratio. Round to one decimal place.

PE 17-11B Earnings per share and price-earnings ratio OBJ. 5

A company reports the following:

Net income	$410,000
Preferred dividends	$60,000
Shares of common stock outstanding	50,000
Market price per share of common stock	$84

a. Determine the company's earnings per share on common stock.
b. Determine the company's price-earnings ratio. Round to one decimal place.

Exercises

EX 17-1 Vertical analysis of income statement OBJ. 2

✔ a. Current year net income: $360,000; 9% of sales

Revenue and expense data for Innovation Quarter Inc. for two recent years are as follows:

	Current Year	Previous Year
Sales	$4,000,000	$3,600,000
Cost of goods sold	2,280,000	1,872,000
Selling expenses	600,000	648,000
Administrative expenses	520,000	360,000
Income tax expense	240,000	216,000

a. Prepare an income statement in comparative form, stating each item for both years as a percent of sales. Round to the nearest whole percentage.

b. Comment on the significant changes disclosed by the comparative income statement.

EX 17-2 Vertical analysis of income statement OBJ. 2

✔ a. Current fiscal year income from continuing operations, 12.3% of revenues

The following comparative income statement (in thousands of dollars) for two recent fiscal years was adapted from the annual report of **Speedway Motorsports, Inc.**, owner and operator of several major motor speedways, such as the Atlanta, Texas, and Las Vegas Motor Speedways.

	Current Year	Previous Year
Revenues:		
Admissions	$100,694	$100,798
Event-related revenue	146,980	146,849
NASCAR broadcasting revenue	217,469	207,369
Other operating revenue	31,320	29,293
Total revenues	$496,463	$484,309
Expenses and other:		
Direct expense of events	$104,303	$102,196
NASCAR event management fees	133,682	128,254
Other direct operating expenses	19,541	18,513
General and administrative	177,926	194,120
Total expenses and other	$435,452	$443,083
Income from continuing operations	$ 61,011	$ 41,226

a. Prepare a comparative income statement for these two years in vertical form, stating each item as a percent of revenues. Round percentages to one decimal place.

b. Comment on the significant changes.

EX 17-3 Common-sized income statement OBJ. 2

✔ A. Tannenhill net income: $120,000; 3.0% of sales

Revenue and expense data for the current calendar year for Tannenhill Company and for the electronics industry are as follows. Tannenhill's data are expressed in dollars. The electronics industry averages are expressed in percentages.

(*Continued*)

864 Chapter 17 Financial Statement Analysis

	Tannenhill Company	Electronics Industry Average
Sales	$4,000,000	100%
Cost of goods sold	2,120,000	60
Gross profit	$1,880,000	40%
Selling expenses	$1,080,000	24%
Administrative expenses	640,000	14
Total operating expenses	$1,720,000	38%
Operating income	$ 160,000	2%
Other revenue	120,000	3
	$ 280,000	5%
Other expense	80,000	2
Income before income tax	$ 200,000	3%
Income tax expense	80,000	2
Net income	$ 120,000	1%

a. Prepare a common-sized income statement comparing the results of operations for Tannenhill Company with the industry average. Round to the nearest whole percentage.

b. As far as the data permit, comment on significant relationships revealed by the comparisons.

EX 17-4 Vertical analysis of balance sheet OBJ. 2

✔ Retained earnings, Current year, 36.8%

Balance sheet data for Alvarez Company on December 31, the end of two recent fiscal years, follow:

	Current Year	Previous Year
Current assets	$2,500,000	$1,840,000
Property, plant, and equipment	5,600,000	6,072,000
Intangible assets	1,900,000	1,288,000
Current liabilities	2,000,000	1,380,000
Long-term liabilities	3,400,000	3,680,000
Common stock	920,000	920,000
Retained earnings	3,680,000	3,220,000

Prepare a comparative balance sheet for both years, stating each asset as a percent of total assets and each liability and stockholders' equity item as a percent of the total liabilities and stockholders' equity. Round percentages to one decimal place.

EX 17-5 Horizontal analysis of the income statement OBJ. 2

✔ a. Net income increase, 66.0%

Income statement data for Winthrop Company for two recent years ended December 31 are as follows:

	Current Year	Previous Year
Sales	$2,280,000	$2,000,000
Cost of goods sold	1,960,000	1,750,000
Gross profit	$ 320,000	$ 250,000
Selling expenses	$ 156,500	$ 125,000
Administrative expenses	122,000	100,000
Total operating expenses	$ 278,500	$ 225,000
Income before income tax	$ 41,500	$ 25,000
Income tax expense	16,600	10,000
Net income	$ 24,900	$ 15,000

a. Prepare a comparative income statement with horizontal analysis, indicating the increase (decrease) for the current year when compared with the previous year. Round percentages to one decimal place.

b. What conclusions can be drawn from the horizontal analysis?

Chapter 17 Financial Statement Analysis

EX 17-6 Current position analysis OBJ. 3

✓ a. Current year working capital, $1,170,000

The following data were taken from the balance sheet of Nilo Company at the end of two recent fiscal years:

	Current Year	Previous Year
Current assets:		
Cash	$ 414,000	$ 320,000
Marketable securities	496,800	336,000
Accounts and notes receivable (net)	619,200	464,000
Inventories	351,900	272,000
Prepaid expenses	188,100	208,000
Total current assets	$2,070,000	$1,600,000
Current liabilities:		
Accounts and notes payable (short-term)	$ 675,000	$ 600,000
Accrued liabilities	225,000	200,000
Total current liabilities	$ 900,000	$ 800,000

a. Determine for each year (1) the working capital, (2) the current ratio, and (3) the quick ratio. Round ratios to one decimal place.

b. What conclusions can be drawn from these data as to the company's ability to meet its currently maturing debts?

EX 17-7 Current position analysis OBJ. 3

✓ a. (1) Current year's current ratio, 1.1

PepsiCo, Inc., the parent company of Frito-Lay snack foods and Pepsi beverages, had the following current assets and current liabilities at the end of two recent years:

	Current Year (in millions)	Previous Year (in millions)
Cash and cash equivalents	$ 6,297	$ 4,067
Short-term investments, at cost	322	358
Accounts and notes receivable, net	7,041	6,912
Inventories	3,581	3,827
Prepaid expenses and other current assets	1,479	2,277
Short-term obligations	4,815	6,205
Accounts payable	12,274	11,949

a. Determine the (1) current ratio and (2) quick ratio for both years. Round to one decimal place.

b. What conclusions can you draw from these data about PepsiCo's liquidity?

EX 17-8 Current position analysis OBJ. 3

The bond indenture for the 10-year, 9% debenture bonds issued January 2, 20Y5, required working capital of $100,000, a current ratio of 1.5, and a quick ratio of 1.0 at the end of each calendar year until the bonds mature. At December 31, 20Y6, the three measures were computed as follows:

1. Current assets:
    Cash $102,000
    Temporary investments 48,000
    Accounts and notes receivable (net) 120,000
    Inventories 36,000
    Prepaid expenses 24,000
    Intangible assets 124,800
    Property, plant, and equipment 55,200
       Total current assets (net) $510,000
    Current liabilities:
    Accounts and short-term notes payable .... $ 96,000
    Accrued liabilities 204,000
       Total current liabilities 300,000
    Working capital $210,000

(Continued)

2. Current ratio .... 1.7 $510,000 ÷ $300,000
3. Quick ratio .... 1.2 $115,200 ÷ $ 96,000

a. List the errors in the determination of the three measures of current position analysis.
b. Is the company satisfying the terms of the bond indenture? Explain.

EX 17-9 Accounts receivable analysis   OBJ. 3

✓ a. Accounts receivable turnover, 20Y3, 8.2

The following data are taken from the financial statements of Sigmon Inc. Terms of all sales are 2/10, n/45.

	20Y3	20Y2	20Y1
Accounts receivable, end of year	$ 725,000	$ 650,000	$600,000
Sales on account	5,637,500	4,687,500	

a. For 20Y2 and 20Y3, determine (1) the accounts receivable turnover and (2) the number of days' sales in receivables. Round to the nearest dollar and one decimal place.
b. What conclusions can be drawn from these data concerning accounts receivable and credit policies?

EX 17-10 Accounts receivable analysis   OBJ. 3

✓ a. 1. Lestrade, 7.0

Xavier Stores Company and Lestrade Stores Inc. are large retail department stores. Both companies offer credit to their customers through their own credit card operations. Information from the financial statements for both companies for two recent years is as follows (in millions):

	Xavier	Lestrade
Sales	$8,500,000	$4,585,000
Credit card receivables—beginning	820,000	600,000
Credit card receviables—ending	880,000	710,000

a. Determine the (1) accounts receivable turnover and (2) the number of days' sales in receivables for both companies. Round to one decimal place.
b. Compare the two companies with regard to their credit card policies.

EX 17-11 Inventory analysis   OBJ. 3

✓ a. Inventory turnover, current year, 9.0

The following data were extracted from the income statement of Keever Inc.:

	Current Year	Previous Year
Sales	$18,500,000	$20,000,000
Beginning inventories	940,000	860,000
Cost of goods sold	9,270,000	10,800,000
Ending inventories	1,120,000	940,000

a. Determine for each year (1) the inventory turnover and (2) the number of days' sales in inventory. Round to the nearest dollar and one decimal place.
b. What conclusions can be drawn from these data concerning the inventories?

EX 17-12 Inventory analysis   OBJ. 3

✓ a. QT inventory turnover, 32.1

QT, Inc. and Elppa Computers, Inc. compete with each other in the personal computer market. QT assembles computers to customer orders, building and delivering a computer within four days of a customer entering an order online. Elppa, on the other hand, builds computers for inventory prior to receiving an order. These computers are sold from inventory once an order is received. Selected financial information for both companies from recent financial statements follows (in millions):

	QT	Elppa
Sales	$56,940	$120,357
Cost of goods sold	44,754	92,385
Inventory, beginning of period	1,382	6,317
Inventory, end of period	1,404	7,490

a. Determine for both companies (1) the inventory turnover and (2) the number of days' sales in inventory. Round to one decimal place.

b. ✎ Interpret the inventory ratios in the context of both companies' operating strategies.

EX 17-13 Ratio of liabilities to stockholders' equity and times interest earned   OBJ. 4

✓ a. Ratio of liabilities to stockholders' equity, current year, 0.9

The following data were taken from the financial statements of Hunter Inc. for December 31 of two recent years:

	Current Year	Previous Year
Accounts payable	$ 924,000	$ 800,000
Current maturities of serial bonds payable	200,000	200,000
Serial bonds payable, 10%	1,000,000	1,200,000
Common stock, $10 par value	250,000	250,000
Paid-in capital in excess of par	1,250,000	1,250,000
Retained earnings	860,000	500,000

The income before income tax was $480,000 and $420,000 for the current and previous years, respectively.

a. Determine the ratio of liabilities to stockholders' equity at the end of each year. Round to one decimal place.

b. Determine the times interest earned ratio for both years. Round to one decimal place.

c. ✎ What conclusions can be drawn from these data as to the company's ability to meet its currently maturing debts?

EX 17-14 Ratio of liabilities to stockholders' equity and times interest earned   OBJ. 4

✓ a. Hasbro, 1.8

Real World

Hasbro, Inc. and Mattel, Inc. are the two largest toy companies in North America. Condensed liabilities and stockholders' equity from a recent balance sheet are shown for each company as follows (in thousands):

	Hasbro	Mattel
Liabilities:		
Current liabilities	$ 1,064,647	$ 1,645,572
Long-term debt	1,547,115	1,800,000
Other liabilities	404,883	473,863
Total liabilities	$ 3,016,645	$ 3,919,435
Stockholders' equity:		
Common stock	$ 104,847	$ 441,369
Additional paid in capital	893,630	1,789,870
Retained earnings	3,852,321	3,745,815
Accumulated other comprehensive loss and other equity items	(146,001)	(848,899)
Treasury stock, at cost	(3,040,895)	(2,494,901)
Total stockholders' equity	$ 1,663,902	$ 2,633,254
Total liabilities and stockholders' equity	$ 4,680,547	$ 6,522,689

The income from operations and interest expense from the income statement for each company were as follows (in thousands):

(Continued)

	Hasbro	Mattel
Income from operations (before income tax)	$603,915	$463,915
Interest expense	97,122	85,270

a. Determine the ratio of liabilities to stockholders' equity for both companies. Round to one decimal place.

b. Determine the times interest earned ratio for both companies. Round to one decimal place.

c. Interpret the ratio differences between the two companies.

EX 17-15 Ratio of liabilities to stockholders' equity and ratio of fixed assets to long-term liabilities
OBJ. 4

✔ a. Mondelez International, Inc., 1.3

Recent balance sheet information for two companies in the food industry, Mondelez International, Inc. and The Hershey Company, is as follows (in thousands):

	Mondelez	Hershey
Net property, plant, and equipment	$10,010,000	$1,674,071
Current liabilities	14,873,000	1,471,110
Long-term debt	15,574,000	1,530,967
Other long-term liabilities	12,816,000	716,013
Stockholders' equity	32,215,000	1,036,749

a. Determine the ratio of liabilities to stockholders' equity for both companies. Round to one decimal place.

b. Determine the ratio of fixed assets to long-term liabilities for both companies. Round to one decimal place.

c. Interpret the ratio differences between the two companies.

EX 17-16 Asset turnover
OBJ. 5

✔ a. YRC, 2.5

Three major segments of the transportation industry are motor carriers such as YRC Worldwide, railroads such as Union Pacific, and transportation logistics services such as C.H. Robinson Worldwide, Inc. Recent financial statement information for these three companies follows (in thousands):

	YRC	Union Pacific	C.H. Robinson
Sales	$4,832,400	$21,813,000	$13,476,084
Average total assets	1,939,800	53,486,000	3,199,348

a. Determine the asset turnover for all three companies. Round to one decimal place.

b. Assume that the asset turnover for each company represents its respective industry segment. Interpret the differences in the asset turnover in terms of the operating characteristics of each of the respective segments.

EX 17-17 Profitability ratios
OBJ. 5

✔ a. Return on total assets, 20Y7, 11.0%

The following selected data were taken from the financial statements of Vidahill Inc. for December 31, 20Y7, 20Y6, and 20Y5:

	20Y7	20Y6	20Y5
Total assets	$5,200,000	$5,000,000	$4,800,000
Notes payable (6% interest)	2,500,000	2,500,000	2,500,000
Common stock	250,000	250,000	250,000
Preferred 2.5% stock, $100 par (no change during year)	500,000	500,000	500,000
Retained earnings	1,574,000	1,222,000	750,000

The 20Y7 net income was $411,000, and the 20Y6 net income was $462,500. No dividends on common stock were declared between 20Y5 and 20Y7. Preferred dividends were declared and paid in full in 20Y6 and 20Y7.

a. Determine the return on total assets, the return on stockholders' equity, and the return on common stockholders' equity for the years 20Y6 and 20Y7. Round percentages to one decimal place.

b. What conclusions can be drawn from these data as to the company's profitability?

EX 17-18 Profitability ratios   OBJ. 5

✓a. Year 3 return on total assets, 12.2%

Ralph Lauren Corporation sells apparel through company-owned retail stores. Recent financial information for Ralph Lauren follows (in thousands):

	Fiscal Year 3	Fiscal Year 2	
Net income	$567,600	$479,500	
Interest expense	18,300	22,200	

	Fiscal Year 3	Fiscal Year 2	Fiscal Year 1
Total assets (at end of fiscal year)	$4,981,100	$4,648,900	$4,356,500
Total stockholders' equity (at end of fiscal year)	3,304,700	3,116,600	2,735,100

Assume that the apparel industry average return on total assets is 8.0% and the average return on stockholders' equity is 10.0% for the year ended April 2, Year 3.

a. Determine the return on total assets for Ralph Lauren for fiscal Years 2 and 3. Round percentages to one decimal place.

b. Determine the return on stockholders' equity for Ralph Lauren for fiscal Years 2 and 3. Round percentages to one decimal place.

c. Evaluate the two-year trend for the profitability ratios determined in (a) and (b).

d. Evaluate Ralph Lauren's profit performance relative to the industry.

EX 17-19 Six measures of solvency or profitability   OBJ. 4, 5

✓ c. Asset turnover, 2.5

The following data were taken from the financial statements of Gates Inc. for the current fiscal year.

Property, plant, and equipment (net)		$ 3,200,000
Liabilities:		
Current liabilities	$1,000,000	
Note payable, 6%, due in 15 years	2,000,000	
Total liabilities		$ 3,000,000
Stockholders' equity:		
Preferred $10 stock, $100 par (no change during year)		$ 1,000,000
Common stock, $10 par (no change during year)		2,000,000
Retained earnings:		
Balance, beginning of year	$1,570,000	
Net income	930,000 $2,500,000	
Preferred dividends	$ 100,000	
Common dividends	400,000 500,000	
Balance, end of year		2,000,000
Total stockholders' equity		$ 5,000,000
Sales		$18,750,000
Interest expense		$ 120,000

Assuming that total assets were $7,000,000 at the beginning of the current fiscal year, determine the following: (a) ratio of fixed assets to long-term liabilities, (b) ratio of liabilities to stockholders' equity, (c) asset turnover, (d) return on total assets, (e) return on stockholders' equity, and (f) return on common stockholders' equity. Round ratios and percentages to one decimal place as appropriate.

870 Chapter 17 Financial Statement Analysis

✔ c. Price-earnings ratio, 10.0

EX 17-20 Five measures of solvency or profitability   OBJ. 4, 5

The balance sheet for Garcon Inc. at the end of the current fiscal year indicated the following:

Bonds payable, 8%	$5,000,000
Preferred $4 stock, $50 par	2,500,000
Common stock, $10 par	5,000,000

Income before income tax was $3,000,000, and income taxes were $1,200,000 for the current year. Cash dividends paid on common stock during the current year totaled $1,200,000. The common stock was selling for $32 per share at the end of the year. Determine each of the following: (a) times interest earned ratio, (b) earnings per share on common stock, (c) price-earnings ratio, (d) dividends per share of common stock, and (e) dividend yield. Round ratios and percentages to one decimal place, except for per-share amounts.

✔ b. Price-earnings ratio, 15.0

Show Me How

EX 17-21 Earnings per share, price-earnings ratio, dividend yield   OBJ. 5

The following information was taken from the financial statements of Tolbert Inc. for December 31 of the current fiscal year:

Common stock, $20 par (no change during the year)	$10,000,000
Preferred $4 stock, $40 par (no change during the year)	2,500,000

The net income was $1,750,000, and the declared dividends on the common stock were $1,125,000 for the current year. The market price of the common stock is $45 per share.

For the common stock, determine (a) the earnings per share, (b) the price-earnings ratio, (c) the dividends per share, and (d) the dividend yield. Round ratios and percentages to one decimal place, except for per-share amounts.

✔ a. Alphabet (Google), 29.9

Real World

EX 17-22 Price-earnings ratio; dividend yield   OBJ. 5

The table that follows shows the stock price, earnings per share, and dividends per share for three companies for a recent year:

	Price	Earnings per Share	Dividends per Share
Deere & Company	$ 82.29	$ 4.98	$2.40
Alphabet (Google)	735.72	24.58	0.00
The Coca-Cola Company	44.60	1.66	1.40

a. Determine the price-earnings ratio and dividend yield for the three companies. Round ratios and percentages to one decimal place as appropriate.

b. ✏️ Explain the differences in these ratios across the three companies.

Appendix

EX 17-23 Earnings per share, discontinued operations

✔ b. Earnings per share on common stock, $7.60

The net income reported on the income statement of Cutler Co. was $4,000,000. There were 500,000 shares of $10 par common stock and 100,000 shares of $2 preferred stock outstanding throughout the current year. The income statement included a gain on discontinued operations of $400,000 after applicable income tax. Determine the per-share figures for common stock for (a) income before discontinued operations and (b) net income.

Appendix

EX 17-24 Income statement and earnings per share for discontinued operations

Apex Inc. reports the following for a recent year:

Income from continuing operations before income tax	$1,000,000
Loss from discontinued operations	$240,000*
Weighted average number of shares outstanding	20,000
Applicable tax rate	40%

*Net of any tax effect.

Chapter 17 Financial Statement Analysis 871

a. Prepare a partial income statement for Apex Inc., beginning with income from continuing operations before income tax.

b. Determine the earnings per common share for Apex Inc., including per-share amounts for unusual items.

Appendix

EX 17-25 Unusual items

 Explain whether Colston Company correctly reported the following items in the financial statements:

a. In a recent year, the company discovered a clerical error in the prior year's accounting records. As a result, the reported net income for the previous year was overstated by $45,000. The company corrected this error by restating the prior-year financial statements.

b. In a recent year, the company voluntarily changed its method of accounting for long-term construction contracts from the percentage of completion method to the completed contract method. Both methods are acceptable under generally acceptable accounting principles. The cumulative effect of this change was reported as a separate component of income in the current period income statement.

Problems: Series A

PR 17-1A Horizontal analysis of income statement OBJ. 2

✔ 1. Sales, 12.0% increase

For 20Y2, McDade Company reported a decline in net income. At the end of the year, T. Burrows, the president, is presented with the following condensed comparative income statement:

McDade Company
Comparative Income Statement
For the Years Ended December 31, 20Y2 and 20Y1

	20Y2	20Y1
Sales	$16,800,000	$15,000,000
Cost of goods sold	11,500,000	10,000,000
Gross profit	$ 5,300,000	$ 5,000,000
Selling expenses	$ 1,770,000	$ 1,500,000
Administrative expenses	1,220,000	1,000,000
Total operating expenses	$ 2,990,000	$ 2,500,000
Income from operations	$ 2,310,000	$ 2,500,000
Other revenue	256,950	225,000
Income before income tax	$ 2,566,950	$ 2,725,000
Income tax expense	1,413,000	1,500,000
Net income	$ 1,153,950	$ 1,225,000

Instructions

1. Prepare a comparative income statement with horizontal analysis for the two-year period, using 20Y1 as the base year. Round percentages to one decimal place.

2. To the extent the data permit, comment on the significant relationships revealed by the horizontal analysis prepared in (1).

PR 17-2A Vertical analysis of income statement OBJ. 2

✔ 1. Net income, 20Y2, 10.0%

For 20Y2, Tri-Comic Company initiated a sales promotion campaign that included the expenditure of an additional $50,000 for advertising. At the end of the year, Lumi Neer, the president, is presented with the following condensed comparative income statement:

(Continued)

Tri-Comic Company
Comparative Income Statement
For the Years Ended December 31, 20Y2 and 20Y1

	20Y2	20Y1
Sales	$1,500,000	$1,250,000
Cost of goods sold	510,000	475,000
Gross profit	$ 990,000	$ 775,000
Selling expenses	$ 270,000	$ 200,000
Administrative expenses	180,000	156,250
Total operating expenses	$ 450,000	$ 356,250
Income from operations	$ 540,000	$ 418,750
Other revenue	60,000	50,000
Income before income tax	$ 600,000	$ 468,750
Income tax expense	450,000	375,000
Net income	$ 150,000	$ 93,750

Instructions

1. Prepare a comparative income statement for the two-year period, presenting an analysis of each item in relationship to sales for each of the years. Round percentages to one decimal place.

2. To the extent the data permit, comment on the significant relationships revealed by the vertical analysis prepared in (1).

PR 17-3A Effect of transactions on current position analysis   **OBJ. 3**

 2. c. Current ratio, 2.0

Data pertaining to the current position of Forte Company follow:

Cash	$412,500
Marketable securities	187,500
Accounts and notes receivable (net)	300,000
Inventories	700,000
Prepaid expenses	50,000
Accounts payable	200,000
Notes payable (short-term)	250,000
Accrued expenses	300,000

Instructions

1. Compute (a) the working capital, (b) the current ratio, and (c) the quick ratio. Round ratios in parts b through j to one decimal place.

2. List the following captions on a sheet of paper:

Transaction	Working Capital	Current Ratio	Quick Ratio

Compute the working capital, the current ratio, and the quick ratio after each of the following transactions and record the results in the appropriate columns. *Consider each transaction separately* and assume that only that transaction affects the data given. Round to one decimal place.

a. Sold marketable securities at no gain or loss, $70,000.
b. Paid accounts payable, $125,000.
c. Purchased goods on account, $110,000.
d. Paid notes payable, $100,000.
e. Declared a cash dividend, $150,000.
f. Declared a common stock dividend on common stock, $50,000.
g. Borrowed cash from bank on a long-term note, $225,000.
h. Received cash on account, $125,000.
i. Issued additional shares of stock for cash, $600,000.
j. Paid cash for prepaid expenses, $10,000.

PR 17-4A Measures of liquidity, solvency, and profitability   OBJ. 3, 4, 5

✔ 5. Number of days' sales in receivables, 18.3

The comparative financial statements of Marshall Inc. are as follows. The market price of Marshall common stock was $82.60 on December 31, 20Y2.

Marshall Inc.
Comparative Retained Earnings Statement
For the Years Ended December 31, 20Y2 and 20Y1

	20Y2	20Y1
Retained earnings, January 1	$3,704,000	$3,264,000
Net income	600,000	550,000
Total	$4,304,000	$3,814,000
Dividends:		
On preferred stock	$ 10,000	$ 10,000
On common stock	100,000	100,000
Total dividends	$ 110,000	$ 110,000
Retained earnings, December 31	$4,194,000	$3,704,000

Marshall Inc.
Comparative Income Statement
For the Years Ended December 31, 20Y2 and 20Y1

	20Y2	20Y1
Sales	$10,850,000	$10,000,000
Cost of goods sold	6,000,000	5,450,000
Gross profit	$ 4,850,000	$ 4,550,000
Selling expenses	$ 2,170,000	$ 2,000,000
Administrative expenses	1,627,500	1,500,000
Total operating expenses	$ 3,797,500	$ 3,500,000
Income from operations	$ 1,052,500	$ 1,050,000
Other revenue	99,500	20,000
	$ 1,152,000	$ 1,070,000
Other expense (interest)	132,000	120,000
Income before income tax	$ 1,020,000	$ 950,000
Income tax expense	420,000	400,000
Net income	$ 600,000	$ 550,000

Marshall Inc.
Comparative Balance Sheet
December 31, 20Y2 and 20Y1

	20Y2	20Y1
Assets		
Current assets:		
Cash	$1,050,000	$ 950,000
Marketable securities	301,000	420,000
Accounts receivable (net)	585,000	500,000
Inventories	420,000	380,000
Prepaid expenses	108,000	20,000
Total current assets	$ 2,464,000	$2,270,000
Long-term investments	800,000	800,000
Property, plant, and equipment (net)	5,760,000	5,184,000
Total assets	$ 9,024,000	$8,254,000
Liabilities		
Current liabilities	$ 880,000	$ 800,000
Long-term liabilities:		
Mortgage note payable, 6%	$ 200,000	$ 0
Bonds payable, 4%	3,000,000	3,000,000
Total long-term liabilities	$ 3,200,000	$3,000,000
Total liabilities	$ 4,080,000	$3,800,000
Stockholders' Equity		
Preferred 4% stock, $5 par	$ 250,000	$ 250,000
Common stock, $5 par	500,000	500,000
Retained earnings	4,194,000	3,704,000
Total stockholders' equity	$ 4,944,000	$4,454,000
Total liabilities and stockholders' equity	$ 9,024,000	$8,254,000

(Continued)

Instructions

Determine the following measures for 20Y2, rounding to one decimal place, including percentages, except for per-share amounts:

1. Working capital
2. Current ratio
3. Quick ratio
4. Accounts receivable turnover
5. Number of days' sales in receivables
6. Inventory turnover
7. Number of days' sales in inventory
8. Ratio of fixed assets to long-term liabilities
9. Ratio of liabilities to stockholders' equity
10. Times interest earned
11. Asset turnover
12. Return on total assets
13. Return on stockholders' equity
14. Return on common stockholders' equity
15. Earnings per share on common stock
16. Price-earnings ratio
17. Dividends per share of common stock
18. Dividend yield

PR 17-5A **Solvency and profitability trend analysis** OBJ. 4, 5

✓ 1. c. 20Y8, 1.5

Addai Company has provided the following comparative information:

	20Y8	20Y7	20Y6	20Y5	20Y4
Net income	$ 273,406	$ 367,976	$ 631,176	$ 884,000	$ 800,000
Interest expense	616,047	572,003	528,165	495,000	440,000
Income tax expense	31,749	53,560	106,720	160,000	200,000
Total assets (ending balance)	4,417,178	4,124,350	3,732,443	3,338,500	2,750,000
Total stockholders' equity (ending balance)	3,706,557	3,433,152	3,065,176	2,434,000	1,550,000
Average total assets	4,270,764	3,928,396	3,535,472	3,044,250	2,475,000
Average total stockholders' equity	3,569,855	3,249,164	2,749,588	1,992,000	1,150,000

You have been asked to evaluate the historical performance of the company over the last five years.

Selected industry ratios have remained relatively steady at the following levels for the last five years:

	20Y4–20Y8
Return on total assets	28%
Return on stockholders' equity	18%
Times interest earned	2.7
Ratio of liabilities to stockholders' equity	0.4

Instructions

1. Prepare four line graphs with the ratio on the vertical axis and the years on the horizontal axis for the following four ratios, rounding to one decimal place:
   a. Return on total assets
   b. Return on stockholders' equity
   c. Times interest earned
   d. Ratio of liabilities to stockholders' equity

   Display both the company ratio and the industry benchmark on each graph. That is, each graph should have two lines.

2. ➤ Prepare an analysis of the graphs in (1).

Chapter 17 Financial Statement Analysis 875

Problems: Series B

✔ 1. Sales, 30.0% increase

PR 17-1B Horizontal analysis of income statement   OBJ. 2

For 20Y2, Macklin Inc. reported a significant increase in net income. At the end of the year, John Mayer, the president, is presented with the following condensed comparative income statement:

Macklin Inc.
Comparative Income Statement
For the Years Ended December 31, 20Y2 and 20Y1

	20Y2	20Y1
Sales	$910,000	$700,000
Cost of goods sold	441,000	350,000
Gross profit	$469,000	$350,000
Selling expenses	$139,150	$115,000
Administrative expenses	99,450	85,000
Total operating expenses	$238,600	$200,000
Income from operations	$230,400	$150,000
Other revenue	65,000	50,000
Income before income tax	$295,400	$200,000
Income tax expense	65,000	50,000
Net income	$230,400	$150,000

Instructions

1. Prepare a comparative income statement with horizontal analysis for the two-year period, using 20Y1 as the base year. Round percentages to one decimal place.

2. To the extent the data permit, comment on the significant relationships revealed by the horizontal analysis prepared in (1).

✔ 1. Net income, 20Y1, 14.0%

PR 17-2B Vertical analysis of income statement   OBJ. 2

For 20Y2, Fielder Industries Inc. initiated a sales promotion campaign that included the expenditure of an additional $40,000 for advertising. At the end of the year, Leif Grando, the president, is presented with the following condensed comparative income statement:

Fielder Industries Inc.
Comparative Income Statement
For the Years Ended December 31, 20Y2 and 20Y1

	20Y2	20Y1
Sales	$1,300,000	$1,180,000
Cost of goods sold	682,500	613,600
Gross profit	$ 617,500	$ 566,400
Selling expenses	$ 260,000	$ 188,800
Administrative expenses	169,000	177,000
Total operating expenses	$ 429,000	$ 365,800
Income from operations	$ 188,500	$ 200,600
Other revenue	78,000	70,800
Income before income tax	$ 266,500	$ 271,400
Income tax expense	117,000	106,200
Net income	$ 149,500	$ 165,200

Instructions

1. Prepare a comparative income statement for the two-year period, presenting an analysis of each item in relationship to sales for each of the years. Round percentages to one decimal place.

2. To the extent the data permit, comment on the significant relationships revealed by the vertical analysis prepared in (1).

876 Chapter 17 Financial Statement Analysis

✔ 2. g. Quick ratio, 1.6

PR 17-3B Effect of transactions on current position analysis OBJ. 3

Data pertaining to the current position of Lucroy Industries Inc. follow:

Cash	$ 800,000
Marketable securities	550,000
Accounts and notes receivable (net)	850,000
Inventories	700,000
Prepaid expenses	300,000
Accounts payable	1,200,000
Notes payable (short-term)	700,000
Accrued expenses	100,000

Instructions

1. Compute (a) the working capital, (b) the current ratio, and (c) the quick ratio. Round ratios in parts b through j to one decimal place.
2. List the following captions on a sheet of paper:

Transaction	Working Capital	Current Ratio	Quick Ratio

Compute the working capital, the current ratio, and the quick ratio after each of the following transactions and record the results in the appropriate columns. *Consider each transaction separately* and assume that only that transaction affects the data given. Round to one decimal place.

a. Sold marketable securities at no gain or loss, $500,000.
b. Paid accounts payable, $287,500.
c. Purchased goods on account, $400,000.
d. Paid notes payable, $125,000.
e. Declared a cash dividend, $325,000.
f. Declared a common stock dividend on common stock, $150,000.
g. Borrowed cash from bank on a long-term note, $1,000,000.
h. Received cash on account, $75,000.
i. Issued additional shares of stock for cash, $2,000,000.
j. Paid cash for prepaid expenses, $200,000.

✔ 9. Ratio of liabilities to stockholders' equity, 0.4

PR 17-4B Measures of liquidity, solvency and profitability OBJ. 3, 4, 5

The comparative financial statements of Stargel Inc. are as follows. The market price of Stargel common stock was $119.70 on December 31, 20Y2.

Stargel Inc.
Comparative Retained Earnings Statement
For the Years Ended December 31, 20Y2 and 20Y1

	20Y2	20Y1
Retained earnings, January 1	$5,375,000	$4,545,000
Net income	900,000	925,000
Total	$6,275,000	$5,470,000
Dividends:		
Preferred stock dividends	$ 45,000	$ 45,000
Common stock dividends	50,000	50,000
Total dividends	$ 95,000	$ 95,000
Retained earnings, December 31	$6,180,000	$5,375,000

Stargel Inc.
Comparative Income Statement
For the Years Ended December 31, 20Y2 and 20Y1

	20Y2	20Y1
Sales	$10,000,000	$9,400,000
Cost of goods sold	5,350,000	4,950,000
Gross profit	$ 4,650,000	$4,450,000
Selling expenses	$ 2,000,000	$1,880,000
Administrative expenses	1,500,000	1,410,000
Total operating expenses	$ 3,500,000	$3,290,000
Income from operations	$ 1,150,000	$1,160,000
Other revenue	150,000	140,000
	$ 1,300,000	$1,300,000
Other expense (interest)	170,000	150,000
Income before income tax	$ 1,130,000	$1,150,000
Income tax expense	230,000	225,000
Net income	$ 900,000	$ 925,000

Stargel Inc.
Comparative Balance Sheet
December 31, 20Y2 and 20Y1

	20Y2	20Y1
Assets		
Current assets:		
Cash	$ 500,000	$ 400,000
Marketable securities	1,010,000	1,000,000
Accounts receivable (net)	740,000	510,000
Inventories	1,190,000	950,000
Prepaid expenses	250,000	229,000
Total current assets	$3,690,000	$3,089,000
Long-term investments	2,350,000	2,300,000
Property, plant, and equipment (net)	3,740,000	3,366,000
Total assets	$9,780,000	$8,755,000
Liabilities		
Current liabilities	$ 900,000	$ 880,000
Long-term liabilities:		
Mortgage note payable, 10%	$ 200,000	$ 0
Bonds payable, 10%	1,500,000	1,500,000
Total long-term liabilities	$1,700,000	$1,500,000
Total liabilities	$2,600,000	$2,380,000
Stockholders' Equity		
Preferred $0.90 stock, $10 par	$ 500,000	$ 500,000
Common stock, $5 par	500,000	500,000
Retained earnings	6,180,000	5,375,000
Total stockholders' equity	$7,180,000	$6,375,000
Total liabilities and stockholders' equity	$9,780,000	$8,755,000

Instructions
Determine the following measures for 20Y2, rounding to one decimal place including percentages, except for per-share amounts:
1. Working capital
2. Current ratio
3. Quick ratio
4. Accounts receivable turnover
5. Number of days' sales in receivables

(Continued)

6. Inventory turnover
7. Number of days' sales in inventory
8. Ratio of fixed assets to long-term liabilities
9. Ratio of liabilities to stockholders' equity
10. Times interest earned
11. Asset turnover
12. Return on total assets
13. Return on stockholders' equity
14. Return on common stockholders' equity
15. Earnings per share on common stock
16. Price-earnings ratio
17. Dividends per share of common stock
18. Dividend yield

PR 17-5B Solvency and profitability trend analysis
OBJ. 4, 5

✓ 1. b. 20Y7, 32.9%

Crosby Company has provided the following comparative information:

	20Y8	20Y7	20Y6	20Y5	20Y4
Net income	$ 5,571,720	$ 3,714,480	$ 2,772,000	$ 1,848,000	$ 1,400,000
Interest expense	1,052,060	891,576	768,600	610,000	500,000
Income tax expense	1,225,572	845,222	640,320	441,600	320,000
Total assets (ending balance)	29,378,491	22,598,839	17,120,333	12,588,480	10,152,000
Total stockholders' equity (ending balance)	18,706,200	13,134,480	9,420,000	6,648,000	4,800,000
Average total assets	25,988,665	19,859,586	14,854,406	11,370,240	8,676,000
Average total stockholders' equity	15,920,340	11,277,240	8,034,000	5,724,000	4,100,000

You have been asked to evaluate the historical performance of the company over the last five years.

Selected industry ratios have remained relatively steady at the following levels for the last five years:

	20Y4–20Y8
Return on total assets	19%
Return on stockholders' equity	26%
Times interest earned	3.4
Ratio of liabilities to stockholders' equity	1.4

Instructions

1. Prepare four line graphs with the ratio on the vertical axis and the years on the horizontal axis for the following four ratios, rounding ratios and percentages to one decimal place:

    a. Return on total assets
    b. Return on stockholders' equity
    c. Times interest earned
    d. Ratio of liabilities to stockholders' equity

    Display both the company ratio and the industry benchmark on each graph. That is, each graph should have two lines.

2. Prepare an analysis of the graphs in (1).

Nike, Inc., Problem

Financial statement analysis

The financial statements for **Nike, Inc.**, are presented in Appendix D at the end of the text. Use the following additional information (in thousands):

Accounts receivable at May 31, 2014	$ 3,117
Inventories at May 31, 2014	4,142
Total assets at May 31, 2014	18,594
Stockholders' equity at May 31, 2014	12,000

Instructions

1. Determine the following measures for the fiscal years ended May 31, 2016, and May 31, 2015. Round ratios and percentages to one decimal place.

    a. Working capital
    b. Current ratio
    c. Quick ratio
    d. Accounts receivable turnover
    e. Number of days' sales in receivables
    f. Inventory turnover
    g. Number of days' sales in inventory
    h. Ratio of liabilities to stockholders' equity
    i. Asset turnover
    j. Return on total assets.
    k. Return on common stockholders' equity
    l. Price-earnings ratio, assuming that the market price was $54.90 per share on May 29, 2016, and $52.81 per share on May 30, 2015
    m. Percentage relationship of net income to sales

2. What conclusions can be drawn from these analyses?

Cases & Projects

Ethics

CP 17-1 Ethics in Action

Rodgers Industries Inc. completed its fiscal year on December 31. Near the end of the fiscal year, the company's Internal Audit Department determined that an important internal control procedure had not been functioning properly. The head of Internal Audit, Dash Riprock, reported the internal control failure to the company's chief accountant, Todd Barleywine. Todd reported the failure to the company's chief financial officer, Josh McCoy. After discussing the issue, Josh instructed Todd not to inform the external auditors of the internal control failure and to fix the problem quietly after the end of the fiscal year. The external auditors did not discover the internal control failure during their audit. In March, after the audit was complete, the company released its annual report, including associated reports by management. As chief financial officer, Josh authorized the release of Management's Report on Internal Control, which stated that the management team believed that the company's internal controls were effective during the period covered by the annual report.

Did Josh behave ethically in this situation? Explain your answer.

CP 17-2 Team Activity

In teams, select a public company that interests you. Obtain the company's most recent annual report on Form 10-K. The Form 10-K is a company's annually required filing with the Securities and Exchange Commission (SEC). It includes the company's financial statements and accompanying notes. The Form 10-K can be obtained either (a) by referring to the investor relations section of the company's website or (b) by using the company search feature of the SEC's EDGAR database service found at www.sec.gov/edgar/searchedgar/companysearch.html.

1. Based on the information in the company's annual report, compute the following for the most recent year, rounding ratios and percentages to one decimal place, except for per-share amounts:
   a. Liquidity analysis:
      (1) Working capital
      (2) Current ratio
      (3) Quick ratio
      (4) Accounts receivable turnover
      (5) Number of days' sales in receivables
      (6) Inventory turnover
      (7) Number of days' sales in inventory
   b. Solvency analysis:
      (1) Ratio of liabilities to stockholders' equity
      (2) Times interest earned
   c. Profitability analysis:
      (1) Asset turnover
      (2) Return on total assets
      (3) Return on stockholders' equity
      (4) Earnings per share
      (5) Price-earnings ratio

CP 17-3 Communication

The president of Freeman Industries Inc. made the following statement in the annual report to shareholders: "The founding family and majority shareholders of the company do not believe in using debt to finance future growth. The founding family learned from hard experience during the Great Depression that debt can cause loss of flexibility and eventual loss of corporate control. The company will not place itself at such risk again. As such, all future growth will be financed either by stock sales to the public or by internally generated resources."

➤ Write a brief memo to the company's president, Boss Freeman, outlining the errors in his logic.

CP 17-4 Common-sized income statements

The condensed income statements through income from operations for **Amazon.com, Inc.**, **Best Buy, Inc.**, and **Wal-Mart Stores, Inc.** for a recent fiscal year follow (in millions):

	Amazon	Best Buy	Wal-Mart
Sales	$88,988	$40,339	$485,651
Cost of sales	62,752	31,292	365,086
Gross profit	$26,236	$ 9,047	$120,565
Selling, general, and administrative expenses	26,058	7,592	93,418
Operating expenses	0	5	0
Income from operations	$ 178	$ 1,450	$ 27,147

1. Prepare comparative common-sized income statements for each company. Round percentages to one decimal place.
2. Use the common-sized analysis to compare the financial performance of the three companies.

CP 17-5 Profitability analysis

Deere & Company manufactures and distributes farm and construction machinery that it sells around the world. In addition to its manufacturing operations, Deere's credit division loans money to customers to finance the purchase of their farm and construction equipment.

The following information is available for three recent years (in millions except per-share amounts):

	Year 3	Year 2	Year 1
Net income (loss)	$3,064.7	$2,799.9	$1,865.0
Preferred dividends	$0.00	$0.00	$0.00
Interest expense	$782.8	$759.4	$811.4
Shares outstanding for computing earnings per share	397	417	424
Cash dividend per share	$1.79	$1.52	$1.16
Average total assets	$52,237	$45,737	$42,200
Average stockholders' equity	$6,821	$6,545	$5,555
Average stock price per share	$79.27	$80.48	$61.18

1. Calculate the following ratios for each year, rounding ratios and percentages to one decimal place, except for per-share amounts:
   a. Return on total assets
   b. Return on stockholders' equity
   c. Earnings per share
   d. Dividend yield
   e. Price-earnings ratio
2. Based on these data, evaluate Deere's profitability.

CP 17-6 Comprehensive profitability and solvency analysis

Marriott International, Inc., and **Hyatt Hotels Corporation** are two major owners and managers of lodging and resort properties in the United States. Abstracted income statement information for the two companies is as follows for a recent year (in millions):

	Marriott	Hyatt
Operating profit before other expenses and interest	$ 677	$ 39
Other revenue (expenses)	54	118
Interest expense	(180)	(54)
Income before income taxes	$ 551	$103
Income tax expense	93	37
Net income	$ 458	$ 66

Balance sheet information is as follows:

	Marriott	Hyatt
Total liabilities	$7,398	$2,125
Total stockholders' equity	1,585	5,118
Total liabilities and stockholders' equity	$8,983	$7,243

(Continued)

882 Chapter 17 Financial Statement Analysis

The average liabilities, average stockholders' equity, and average total assets are as follows:

	Marriott	Hyatt
Average total liabilities	$7,095	$2,132
Average total stockholders' equity	1,364	5,067
Average total assets	8,458	7,199

1. Determine the following ratios for both companies, rounding ratios and percentages to one decimal place:
   a. Return on total assets
   b. Return on stockholders' equity
   c. Times interest earned
   d. Ratio of total liabilities to stockholders' equity
2. ✏ Based on the information in (1), analyze and compare the two companies' solvency and profitability.

Introduction to Managerial Accounting

CHAPTER 18

Concepts and Principles
Chapter 18 *Introduction to Managerial Accounting*

Developing Information

COST SYSTEMS
Chapter 19 *Job Order Costing*
Chapter 20 *Process Cost Systems*

COST BEHAVIOR
Chapter 21 *Cost-Volume-Profit Analysis*

Decision Making

EVALUATING PERFORMANCE
Chapter 22 *Budgeting*
Chapter 23 *Variances from Standard Costs*

COMPARING ALTERNATIVES
Chapter 24 *Decentralized Operations*
Chapter 25 *Differential Analysis, Product Pricing, and Activity-Based Costing*
Chapter 26 *Capital Investment Analysis*

CHAPTER 18

Gibson Guitars

Gibson guitars have been used by musical legends over the years, including B.B. King, Chet Atkins, Brian Wilson (Beach Boys), Jimmy Page (Led Zeppelin), Jackson Browne, John Fogerty, Jose Feliciano, Miranda Lambert, and Wynonna Judd. Known for its quality, **Gibson Guitars** celebrated its 120th anniversary in 2014.

Staying in business for 120 years requires a thorough understanding of how to manufacture high-quality guitars. In addition, it requires knowledge of how to account for the costs of making guitars. For example, Gibson needs cost information to answer the following questions:

- What should be the selling price of its guitars?
- How many guitars does it have to sell in a year to cover its costs and earn a profit?
- How many employees should the company have working on each stage of the manufacturing process?
- How would purchasing automated equipment affect the costs of its guitars?

This chapter introduces managerial accounting concepts that are useful in addressing these questions. This chapter begins by describing managerial accounting and its relationship to financial accounting. Following this overview, the management process is described along with the role of managerial accounting. Finally, characteristics of managerial accounting reports, managerial accounting terms, and uses of managerial accounting information are described and illustrated.

Source: www.gibson.com/Gibson/History.aspx

Learning Objectives

After studying this chapter, you should be able to:

Example Exercises (EE) are shown in **green.**

Obj. 1 Describe managerial accounting and the role of managerial accounting in a business.

Managerial Accounting
Differences Between Managerial and Financial Accounting
The Management Accountant in the Organization
The Management Process   EE 18-1
Uses of Managerial Accounting Information

Obj. 2 Describe and illustrate the following costs: direct and indirect costs; direct materials, direct labor, and factory overhead costs; and product and period costs.

Manufacturing Operations: Costs and Terminology
Direct and Indirect Costs
Manufacturing Costs   EE 18-2, 3, 4

Obj. 3 Describe sustainable business activities and eco-efficiency measures.

Sustainability and Accounting
Sustainability
Eco-Efficiency Measures in Managerial Accounting

Obj. 4 Describe and illustrate the following statements for a manufacturing business: balance sheet, statement of cost of goods manufactured, and income statement.

Financial Statements for a Manufacturing Business
Balance Sheet for a Manufacturing Business
Income Statement for a Manufacturing Business   EE 18-5

At a Glance 18 Page 904

Managerial Accounting

Obj. 1 Describe managerial accounting and the role of managerial accounting in a business.

Managers make numerous decisions during the day-to-day operations of a business and in planning for the future. Managerial accounting provides much of the information used for these decisions.

Some examples of managerial accounting information along with the chapter in which it is described and illustrated follow:

- Classifying manufacturing and other costs and reporting them in the financial statements (Chapter 18)
- Determining the cost of manufacturing a product or providing a service (Chapters 19 and 20)
- Estimating the behavior of costs for various levels of activity and assessing cost-volume-profit relationships (Chapter 21)
- Planning for the future by preparing budgets (Chapter 22)
- Evaluating manufacturing costs by comparing actual with expected results (Chapter 23)
- Evaluating decentralized operations by comparing actual and budgeted costs as well as computing various measures of profitability (Chapter 24)
- Evaluating special decision-making situations by comparing differential revenues and costs and allocating product costs using activity-based costing (Chapter 25)
- Evaluating alternative proposals for long-term investments in fixed assets (Chapter 26)

Link to Gibson Guitars

Orville Gibson, founder of **Gibson Guitars**, started producing guitars in 1894 in Kalamazoo, Michigan. He produced guitars and mandolins based on the archtop design of violins.

Differences Between Managerial and Financial Accounting

Accounting information is often divided into two types: financial and managerial. Exhibit 1 shows the relationship between financial accounting and managerial accounting.

Financial accounting information is reported at fixed intervals (monthly, quarterly, yearly) in general-purpose financial statements. These financial statements—the income statement, retained earnings statement, balance sheet, and statement of cash flows—present timely information about the results of operations and the financial

EXHIBIT 1 Financial Accounting and Managerial Accounting

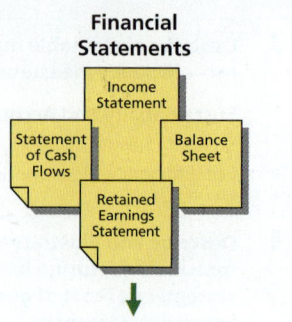
Financial Statements

Management Reports

	Financial Statements	Management Reports
Users of Information	External users and company management	Management
Nature of Information	Objective	Objective and subjective
Guidelines for Preparation	Prepared according to GAAP	Prepared according to management needs
Timeliness of Reporting	Prepared at fixed intervals	Prepared at fixed intervals and on an as-needed basis
Focus of Reporting	Company as a whole	Company as a whole or segment

condition of a business. These statements are based on objective historical data and are prepared according to generally accepted accounting principles (GAAP) in order to meet the decision-making needs of external users such as:

- Investors
- Creditors
- Government agencies
- The general public

Managers of a company also use general-purpose financial statements. For example, in planning future operations, managers often begin by evaluating the current income statement and statement of cash flows.

Managerial accounting information is designed to meet the specific needs of a company's management. This information includes the following:

- Historical data, which provide *objective measures* of past operations
- Estimated data, which provide *subjective estimates* about future decisions

Management uses both types of information in directing daily operations, planning future operations, and developing business strategies.

Unlike the financial statements prepared in financial accounting, managerial accounting reports are not required to be:

- Prepared according to generally accepted accounting principles (GAAP). This is because *only* the company's management uses the information. Also, in many cases, GAAP is not relevant to the specific decision-making needs of management.
- Prepared at fixed intervals (monthly, quarterly, yearly). Although some management reports are prepared at fixed intervals, most reports are prepared as management needs the information.
- Prepared for the business as a whole. Most management reports are prepared for products, projects, sales territories, or other segments of the company.

The Management Accountant in the Organization

In most companies, departments or similar organizational units are assigned responsibilities for specific functions or activities. The operating structure of a company can be shown in an *organization chart*.

Link to Gibson Guitars
Gibson Mandolin-Guitar Mfg. Co., Ltd. was formed in 1902 in Kalamazoo, Michigan, with the support of five investors.

Link to Gibson Guitars
Chicago Musical Instrument Company purchased **Gibson** in 1944.

Exhibit 2 is a partial organization chart for **Callaway Golf Company**, the manufacturer and distributor of golf clubs, clothing, and other products.

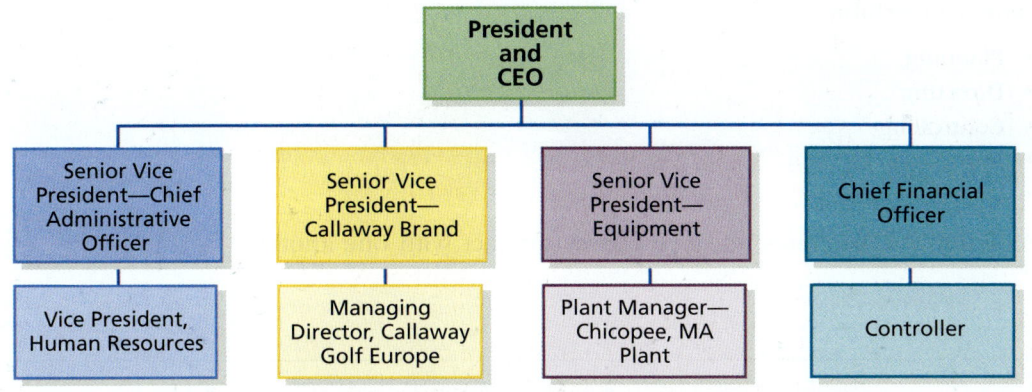

EXHIBIT 2

Partial Organization Chart for Callaway Golf Company

The departments in a company can be viewed as having either of the following:

- Line responsibilities
- Staff responsibilities

A **line department** is directly involved in providing goods or services to the customers of the company. For Callaway Golf (shown in Exhibit 2), the following occupy line positions:

- Senior Vice President—Equipment
- Plant Manager—Chicopee, MA Plant
- Senior Vice President—Callaway Brand
- Managing Director, Callaway Golf Europe

Individuals in these positions are responsible for manufacturing and selling Callaway's products.

A **staff department** provides services, assistance, and advice to the departments with line or other staff responsibilities. A staff department has no direct authority over a line department. For Callaway Golf (Exhibit 2), the following are staff positions:

- Senior Vice President—Chief Administrative Officer
- Vice President, Human Resources
- Chief Financial Officer
- Controller

In most companies, the **controller** is the chief management accountant. The controller's staff consists of a variety of other accountants who are responsible for specialized accounting functions such as the following:

- Systems and procedures
- General accounting
- Budgets and budget analysis
- Special reports and analysis
- Taxes
- Cost accounting

Experience in managerial accounting is often an excellent training ground for senior management positions. This is not surprising because accounting touches all phases of a company's operations.

Link to Gibson Guitars

One of **Gibson**'s most influential managers was Ted McCarty, who was the company president from 1950–1966. During this period, Gibson was known for its innovations. For example, in 1954, McCarty invented the tune-o-matic bridge with adjustable saddles.

The Management Process

As a staff department, managerial accounting supports management and the management process. The **management process** has the following five basic phases, as shown in Exhibit 3:

- Planning
- Directing
- Controlling
- Improving
- Decision making

As Exhibit 3 illustrates, the five phases interact with one another.

EXHIBIT 3
The Management Process

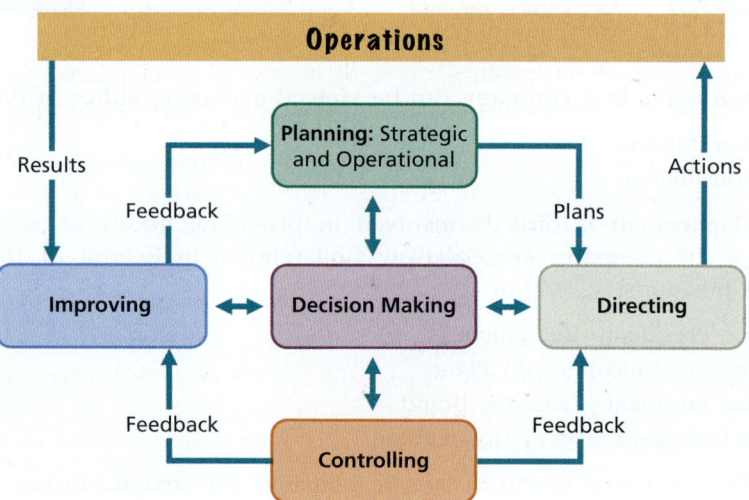

Business Connection

LINE AND STAFF FOR SERVICE COMPANIES

The terms *line* and *staff* may also be applied to service organizations. Some examples follow:

Service Industry	Line	Staff
Airline	Crew, baggage handling, and gate staff	Information systems, accounting, and human resources
Hotel	Housekeeping and reception staff	Maintenance, hotel manager, and grounds
Hospital	Doctors, nurses, and other caregivers	Admissions, records, and billing
Banking	Tellers, loan officers, trust officers, and brokers	Branch manager, information systems
Telecommunications	Sales, customer service, and customer installation staff	Information systems, regional management, and network maintenance

Planning Management uses **planning** in developing the company's **objectives (goals)** and translating these objectives into courses of action. For example, a company may set an objective to increase market share by 15% by introducing three new products. The actions to achieve this objective might be as follows:

- Increase the advertising budget
- Open a new sales territory
- Increase the research and development budget

Planning may be classified as follows:

- **Strategic planning**, which is developing long-term actions to achieve the company's objectives. These long-term actions are called **strategies**, which often involve periods of 5 to 10 years.
- **Operational planning**, which develops short-term actions for managing the day-to-day operations of the company.

Directing The process by which managers run day-to-day operations is called **directing**. An example of directing is a production supervisor's efforts to keep the production line moving without interruption (downtime). A credit manager's development of guidelines for assessing the ability of potential customers to pay their bills is also an example of directing.

Controlling Monitoring operating results and comparing actual results with the expected results is **controlling**. This **feedback** allows management to isolate areas for further investigation and possible remedial action. It may also lead to revising future plans. This philosophy of controlling by comparing actual and expected results is called **management by exception**.

Improving Feedback is also used by managers to support continuous process improvement. **Continuous process improvement** is the philosophy of continually improving employees, business processes, and products. The objective of continuous improvement is to eliminate the *source* of problems in a process. In this way, the right products (services) are delivered in the right quantities at the right time.

Decision Making Inherent in each of the preceding management processes is **decision making**. In managing a company, management must continually decide among alternative actions. For example, in directing operations, managers must decide on an operating structure, training procedures, and staffing of day-to-day operations.

Managerial accounting supports managers in all phases of the management process. For example, accounting reports comparing actual and expected operating results help managers plan and improve current operations. Such a report might compare the actual and expected costs of defective materials. If the cost of defective materials is unusually high, management might decide to change suppliers.

Uses of Managerial Accounting Information

As mentioned earlier, managerial accounting provides information and reports for managers to use in operating a business. Some examples of how managerial accounting could be used by **Gibson Guitars** include the following:

- The cost of manufacturing each guitar could be used to determine its selling price.
- Comparing the costs of guitars over time can be used to monitor and control the cost of direct materials, direct labor, and factory overhead.
- Performance reports could be used to identify any large amounts of scrap or employee downtime. For example, large amounts of unusable wood (scrap) after the cutting process should be investigated to determine the underlying cause. Such scrap may be caused by saws that have not been properly maintained.
- A report could analyze the potential efficiencies and dollar savings of purchasing a new computerized saw to speed up the production process.

Link to Gibson Guitars

Gibson struggled financially from 1966–1986. The company was purchased and sold several times and experienced declining sales.

- A report could analyze how many guitars need to be sold to cover operating costs and expenses. Such information could be used to set monthly selling targets and bonuses for sales personnel.

As the prior examples illustrate, managerial accounting information can be used for a variety of purposes. In the remaining chapters of this text, we examine these and other areas of managerial accounting.

Example Exercise 18-1 The Management Process — Obj. 1

Three phases of the management process are planning, controlling, and improving. Match the following descriptions to the proper phase:

Phase of management process	Description
Planning	a. Monitoring the operating results of implemented plans and comparing the actual results with expected results.
Controlling	b. Rejects solving individual problems with temporary solutions that fail to address the root cause of the problem.
Improving	c. Used by management to develop the company's objectives.

Follow My Example 18-1

Planning (c), Controlling (a), and Improving (b)

Practice Exercises: PE 18-1A, PE 18-1B

Obj. 2 Describe and illustrate the following costs: direct and indirect costs; direct materials, direct labor, and factory overhead costs; and product and period costs.

Manufacturing Operations: Costs and Terminology

The operations of a business can be classified as service, merchandising, or manufacturing. The accounting for service and merchandising businesses has been described and illustrated in earlier chapters. For this reason, the remaining chapters of this text focus primarily on manufacturing businesses. Most of the managerial accounting concepts discussed, however, also apply to service and merchandising businesses.

As a basis for illustration of manufacturing operations, a guitar manufacturer, Legend Guitars, is used. Exhibit 4 is an overview of Legend's guitar manufacturing operations.

EXHIBIT 4 Guitar-Making Operations of Legend Guitars

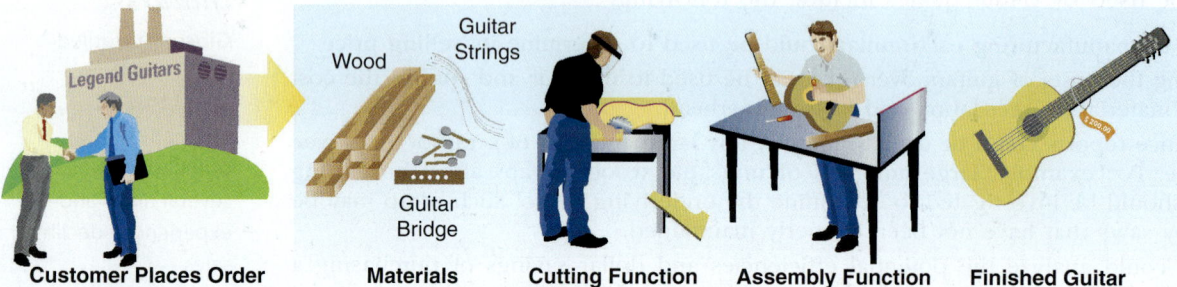

Customer Places Order | Materials | Cutting Function | Assembly Function | Finished Guitar

Legend's guitar-making process begins when a customer places an order for a guitar. Once the order is accepted, the manufacturing process begins by obtaining the necessary materials. An employee then cuts the body and neck of the guitar out of raw lumber. Once the wood is cut, the body and neck of the guitar are assembled. When the assembly is complete, the guitar is painted and finished.

Direct and Indirect Costs

A **cost** is a payment of cash or the commitment to pay cash in the future for the purpose of generating revenues. For example, cash (or credit) used to purchase equipment is the cost of the equipment. If equipment is purchased by exchanging assets other than cash, the current market value of the assets given up is the cost of the equipment purchased.

In managerial accounting, costs are classified according to the decision-making needs of management. For example, costs are often classified by their relationship to a segment of operations, called a **cost object**. A cost object may be a product, a sales territory, a department, or an activity such as research and development. Costs identified with cost objects are either direct costs or indirect costs.

Direct costs are identified with and can be traced to a cost object. For example, as shown in Exhibit 5, the cost of wood (materials) used by Legend Guitars in manufacturing a guitar is a direct cost of the guitar.

> **Link to Gibson Guitars**
>
> **Gibson** provides tours of its Memphis guitar factory located at 145 Lt. George W. Lee Avenue.

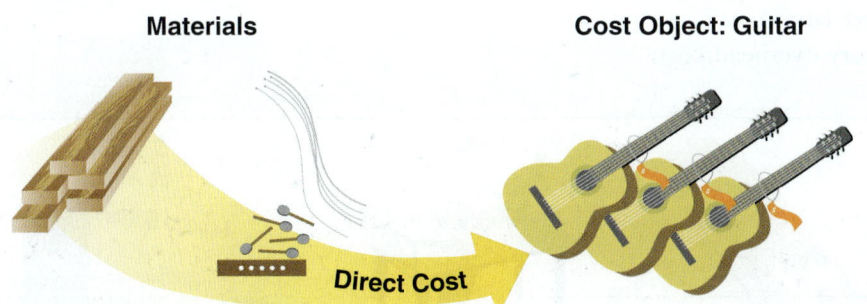

EXHIBIT 5

Direct Costs of Legend Guitars

Indirect costs cannot be identified with or traced to a cost object. For example, as shown in Exhibit 6, the salaries of the Legend Guitars production supervisors are indirect costs of producing a guitar. Although the production supervisors contribute to the production of a guitar, their salaries cannot be identified with or traced to any individual guitar.

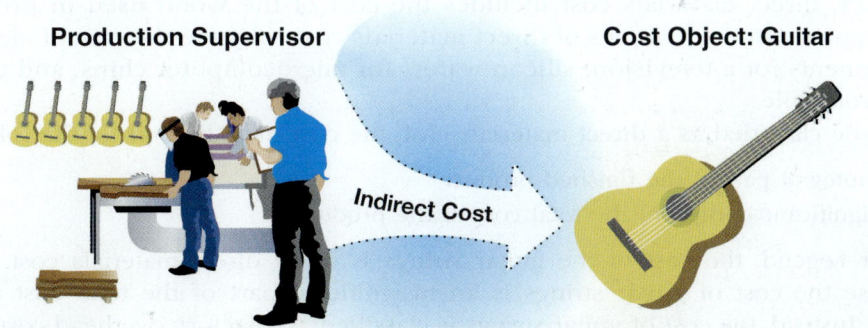

EXHIBIT 6

Indirect Costs of Legend Guitars

Depending on the cost object, a cost may be either a direct or indirect cost. For example, the salaries of production supervisors are indirect costs when the cost object is an individual guitar. If, however, the cost object is Legend Guitars' overall production process, then the salaries of production supervisors are direct costs.

This process of classifying a cost as direct or indirect is illustrated in Exhibit 7.

EXHIBIT 7

Classifying Direct and Indirect Costs

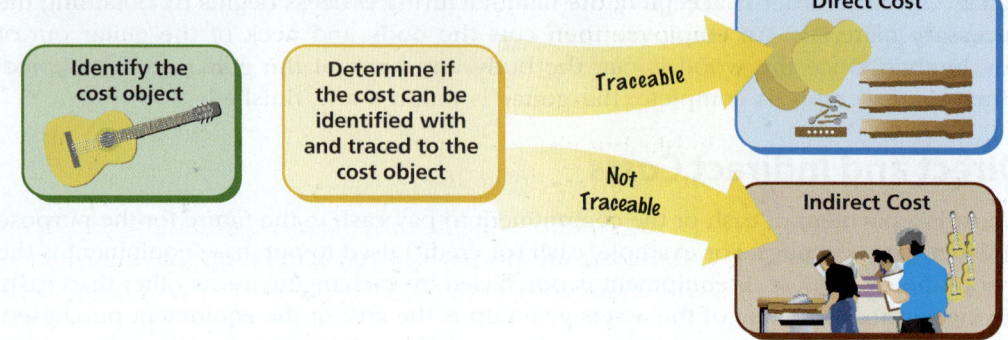

Manufacturing Costs

The cost of a manufactured product includes the cost of materials used in making the product. In addition, the cost of a manufactured product includes the cost of converting the materials into a finished product. For example, Legend Guitars uses employees and machines to convert wood (and other supplies) into finished guitars. Thus, as shown in Exhibit 8, the cost of a finished guitar (the cost object) includes the following:

- Direct materials cost
- Direct labor cost
- Factory overhead cost

EXHIBIT 8

Manufacturing Costs of Legend Guitars

Direct Materials Cost Manufactured products begin with raw materials that are converted into finished products. The cost of any material that is an integral part of the finished product is classified as a **direct materials cost**. For Legend Guitars, direct materials cost includes the cost of the wood used in producing each guitar. Other examples of direct materials costs include the cost of electronic components for a television, silicon wafers for microcomputer chips, and tires for an automobile.

To be classified as a direct materials cost, the cost must be *both* of the following:

- An integral part of the finished product
- A significant portion of the total cost of the product

For Legend, the cost of the guitar strings is not a direct materials cost. This is because the cost of guitar strings is an insignificant part of the total cost of each guitar. Instead, the cost of guitar strings is classified as a factory overhead cost, which is discussed later.

Direct Labor Cost Most manufacturing processes use employees to convert materials into finished products. The cost of employee wages that is an integral part of the finished product is classified as **direct labor cost**. For Legend Guitars, direct labor cost includes the wages of the employees who cut each guitar out of raw lumber and assemble it. Other examples of direct labor costs include mechanics' wages for repairing an automobile, machine operators' wages for manufacturing tools, and assemblers' wages for assembling a laptop computer.

Like a direct materials cost, a direct labor cost must meet *both* of the following criteria:

- An integral part of the finished product
- A significant portion of the total cost of the product

For Legend, the wages of the janitors who clean the factory are not a direct labor cost. This is because janitorial costs are not an integral part or a significant cost of each guitar. Instead, janitorial costs are classified as a factory overhead cost, which is discussed next.

Factory Overhead Cost Costs other than direct materials and direct labor that are incurred in the manufacturing process are combined and classified as **factory overhead cost**. Factory overhead is sometimes called **manufacturing overhead** or **factory burden**.

All factory overhead costs are indirect costs of the product. Some factory overhead costs include the following:

- Cost of heating and lighting the factory
- Cost of repairing and maintaining factory equipment
- Property taxes on factory buildings and land
- Insurance on factory buildings
- Depreciation on factory plant and equipment

Factory overhead cost also includes materials and labor costs that do not enter directly into the finished product. Examples include the cost of oil used to lubricate machinery and the wages of janitorial and supervisory employees. Also, if the costs of direct materials or direct labor are not a significant portion of the total product cost, these costs may be classified as factory overhead costs.

For **Legend Guitars**, the costs of guitar strings and janitorial wages are factory overhead costs. Additional factory overhead costs of making guitars are as follows:

- Sandpaper
- Buffing compound
- Glue
- Power (electricity) to run the machines
- Depreciation of the machines and building
- Salaries of production supervisors

Business Connection

OVERHEAD COSTS

Defense contractors such as **General Dynamics**, **Boeing**, and **Lockheed Martin** sell products such as airplanes, ships, and military equipment to the U.S. Department of Defense. Building large products such as these requires a significant investment in facilities and tools, all of which are classified as factory overhead costs. As a result, factory overhead costs are a much larger portion of the cost of goods sold for defense contractors than they are in other industries. For example, a U.S. General Accounting Office study of six defense contractors found that overhead costs were almost one-third the price of the final product. This is more than three times greater than the factory overhead costs for a laptop computer, which are typically about 10% of the price of the final product.

894 CHAPTER 18 Introduction to Managerial Accounting

Example Exercise 18-2 Direct Materials, Direct Labor, and Factory Overhead Obj. 2

Identify the following costs as direct materials (DM), direct labor (DL), or factory overhead (FO) for a baseball glove manufacturer:

a. Leather used to make a baseball glove
b. Coolants for machines that sew baseball gloves
c. Wages of assembly line employees
d. Ink used to print a player's autograph on a baseball glove

Follow My Example 18-2

a. DM
b. FO
c. DL
d. FO

Practice Exercises: PE 18-2A, PE 18-2B

Prime Costs and Conversion Costs Direct materials, direct labor, and factory overhead costs may be grouped together for analysis and reporting. Two such common groupings are as follows:

- **Prime costs**, which consist of direct materials and direct labor costs
- **Conversion costs**, which consist of direct labor and factory overhead costs

Conversion costs are the costs of converting the materials into a finished product. Direct labor is both a prime cost and a conversion cost, as shown in Exhibit 9.

EXHIBIT 9
Prime Costs and Conversion Costs

Direct Materials

Direct Labor

Factory Overhead

Example Exercise 18-3 Prime and Conversion Costs Obj. 2

Identify the following costs as a prime cost (P), conversion cost (C), or both (B) for a baseball glove manufacturer:

a. Leather used to make a baseball glove
b. Coolants for machines that sew baseball gloves
c. Wages of assembly line employees
d. Ink used to print a player's autograph on a baseball glove

Follow My Example 18-3

a. P
b. C
c. B
d. C

Practice Exercises: PE 18-3A, PE 18-3B

Product Costs and Period Costs For financial reporting purposes, costs are classified as product costs or period costs.

Note: Product costs consist of direct materials, direct labor, and factory overhead costs.

- **Product costs** consist of manufacturing costs: direct materials, direct labor, and factory overhead.
- **Period costs** consist of selling and administrative expenses. *Selling expenses* are incurred in marketing the product and delivering the product to customers. *Administrative expenses* are incurred in managing the company and are not directly related to the manufacturing or selling functions.

Examples of product costs and period costs for Legend Guitars are presented in Exhibit 10.

EXHIBIT 10 — Examples of Product Costs and Period Costs—Legend Guitars

Product (Manufacturing) Costs

Direct Materials Cost
- Wood used in neck and body

Direct Labor Cost
- Wages of saw operator
- Wages of employees who assemble the guitar

Factory Overhead
- Guitar strings
- Wages of janitor
- Power to run the machines
- Depreciation expense—factory building
- Sandpaper and buffing materials
- Glue used in assembly of the guitar
- Salary of production supervisors

Period (Nonmanufacturing) Costs

Selling Expenses
- Advertising expenses
- Sales salaries expenses
- Commissions expenses

Administrative Expenses
- Office salaries expense
- Office supplies expense
- Depreciation expense—office building and equipment

896 CHAPTER 18 Introduction to Managerial Accounting

To facilitate control, selling and administrative expenses may be reported by level of responsibility. For example, selling expenses may be reported by products, salespersons, departments, divisions, or territories. Likewise, administrative expenses may be reported by areas such as human resources, computer services, legal, accounting, or finance.

The impact on the financial statements of product and period costs is summarized in Exhibit 11. As product costs are incurred, they are recorded and reported on the balance sheet as *inventory*. When the inventory is sold, the cost of the manufactured product sold is reported as *cost of goods sold* on the income statement. Period costs are reported as *expenses* on the income statement in the period in which they are incurred and, thus, never appear on the balance sheet.

EXHIBIT 11

Product Costs, Period Costs, and the Financial Statements

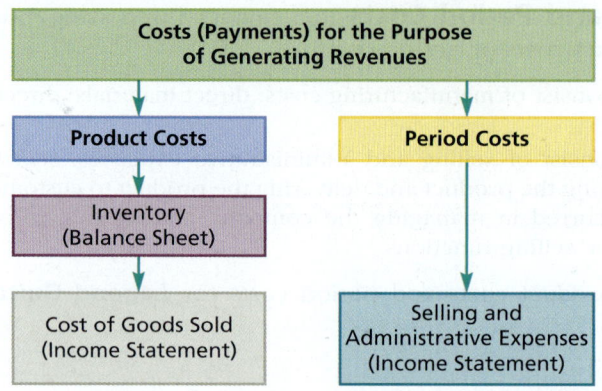

Example Exercise 18-4 Product and Period Costs — Obj. 2

Identify the following costs as a product cost or a period cost for a baseball glove manufacturer:

a. Leather used to make a baseball glove
b. Cost of endorsement from a professional baseball player
c. Office supplies used at the company headquarters
d. Ink used to print a player's autograph on the baseball glove

Follow My Example 18-4

a. Product cost
b. Period cost
c. Period cost
d. Product cost

Practice Exercises: PE 18-4A, PE 18-4B

Obj. 3 Describe sustainable business activities and eco-efficiency measures.

Sustainability and Accounting

Managers must consider the social and environmental settings in which a business operates, in order to make sound strategic and operational decisions. Issues such as population growth, resource scarcity, declining ecosystems, increasing urbanization, and climate change all have a direct impact on a company's potential for success. As a result, managers are using new management techniques and tools that consider these issues.

Sustainability

Sustainability is the practice of operating a business to maximize profits while attempting to preserve the environment, economy, and needs of future generations. Sustainability practices acknowledge that a company's long-term success requires the continued availability of natural resources and a productive social environment. Examples of sustainable business activities are provided in Exhibit 12.

EXHIBIT 12 Sustainable Business Activities

Category	Description	Example
Agriculture	Using farming and ranching techniques that do not damage or disrupt the environment	Mixed farming, crop rotation, multiple cropping
Energy	Generating energy with little or no pollution	Wind turbines, solar power
Engineering and Construction	Designing and constructing buildings that are highly efficient in using natural resources, while minimizing pollution	Recycled building materials, high-efficiency heating and cooling systems, renewable energy generation
Transportation	Using transportation methods that result in little pollution and have a minimal impact on the environment	Expanded public transportation systems, green vehicles, biofuel-powered vehicles
Waste Minimization	Using recycling and reuse practices that reduce the amount of waste disposed in landfills	Curbside recycling collection, composting, reusable products (e.g., water bottles)

Eco-Efficiency Measures in Managerial Accounting

Sustainability information can provide important feedback to guide a company's strategic and operational decision making. Managers can use this information to increase revenue, control costs, and allocate resources efficiently. **Eco-efficiency measures** are a form of managerial accounting information that helps managers evaluate the savings generated by using fewer natural resources in a company's operations. Examples of eco-efficiency measures are provided in Exhibit 13.

EXHIBIT 13 Eco-Efficiency Measures

Energy Efficiency	Energy cost savings from replacing lighting fixtures in a production facility with energy-efficient lighting
Material Use Efficiency	Materials cost savings from reducing the amount of product packaging materials
Fuel Efficiency	Fuel cost savings from replacing gas-powered vehicles with hybrid or alternative energy-source vehicles
Waste Efficiency	Waste removal cost savings from recycling and reusing waste and by-product materials

Sustainability information can also benefit external financial statement users in their decision making. The risks and opportunities that a company faces are tied to the environment in which it operates and provide important insights into the potential for success. As such, external financial statement users may require sustainability information to evaluate investment and credit decisions. The **Sustainability Accounting Standards Board (SASB)** was organized in 2011 to develop accounting standards that help companies report decision-useful sustainability information to external financial statement users. While the SASB's standards are not required, they are designed to provide sustainability information that complements required financial statement information.

INTEGRITY, OBJECTIVITY, AND ETHICS IN BUSINESS

ENVIRONMENTAL MANAGERIAL ACCOUNTING

Throughout the last decade, environmental issues have become an increasingly important part of the business environment for most companies. Companies and managers must now consider the environmental impact of their business decisions in the same way they would consider other operational issues. To help managers make sound business decisions, the emerging field of environmental management accounting focuses on calculating the environmental-related costs of business decisions. Environmental managerial accountants evaluate a variety of issues such as the volume and level of emissions, the estimated costs of different levels of emissions, and the impact that environmental costs have on product cost. Managers use these results to assess the environmental effects of their business decisions.

Obj. 4 Describe and illustrate the following statements for a manufacturing business: balance sheet, statement of cost of goods manufactured, and income statement.

Financial Statements for a Manufacturing Business

The retained earnings and cash flow statements for a manufacturing business are similar to those illustrated in earlier chapters for service and merchandising businesses. However, the balance sheet and income statement for a manufacturing business are more complex. This is because a manufacturer makes the products that it sells and, thus, must record and report product costs. The reporting of product costs affects primarily the balance sheet and the income statement.

Balance Sheet for a Manufacturing Business

A manufacturing business reports three types of inventory on its balance sheet as follows:

- **Materials inventory** (sometimes called raw materials inventory). This inventory consists of the costs of the direct and indirect materials that have not entered the manufacturing process.

    Examples for Legend Guitars: Wood, guitar strings, glue, sandpaper

- **Work in process inventory.** This inventory consists of the direct materials, direct labor, and factory overhead costs for products that have entered the manufacturing process but are not yet completed (in process).

    Example for Legend: Unfinished (partially assembled) guitars

- **Finished goods inventory.** This inventory consists of completed (or finished) products that have not been sold.

    Example for Legend: Unsold guitars

Exhibit 14 illustrates the reporting of inventory on the balance sheet for a merchandising and a manufacturing business. MusicLand Stores, Inc., a retailer of musical instruments, reports only Merchandise Inventory. In contrast, Legend Guitars, a manufacturer of guitars, reports Finished Goods, Work in Process, and Materials inventories. In both balance sheets, inventory is reported in the Current assets section.

Income Statement for a Manufacturing Business

The income statements for merchandising and manufacturing businesses differ primarily in the reporting of the cost of merchandise (goods) *available for sale* and *sold* during the period. These differences are shown in Exhibit 15.

Link to Gibson Guitars

In January 1986, guitar enthusiasts Henry Juszkiewicz and David Berryman purchased Gibson. Together they restored Gibson's reputation for innovation and quality. Under their leadership, Gibson began generating profits.

EXHIBIT 14

Balance Sheet Presentation of Inventory in Manufacturing and Merchandising Companies

MusicLand Stores, Inc.
Balance Sheet
December 31, 20Y8

Current assets:	
Cash	$ 25,000
Accounts receivable (net)	85,000
Merchandise inventory	142,000
Supplies	10,000
Total current assets	$262,000

Legend Guitars
Balance Sheet
December 31, 20Y8

Current assets:		
Cash		$ 21,000
Accounts receivable (net)		120,000
Inventories:		
Finished goods	$62,500	
Work in process	24,000	
Materials	35,000	121,500
Supplies		2,000
Total current assets		$264,500

EXHIBIT 15

Income Statements for Merchandising and Manufacturing Businesses

Merchandising Business

Income Statement

Sales		$XXX
Beginning merchandise inventory	$XXX	
Plus net purchases	XXX	
Merchandise available for sale	$XXX	
Less ending merchandise inventory	XXX	
Cost of merchandise sold		XXX
Gross profit		$XXX

Manufacturing Business

Income Statement

Sales		$XXX
Beginning finished goods inventory	$XXX	
Plus cost of goods manufactured	XXX	
Cost of finished goods available for sale	$XXX	
Less ending finished goods inventory	XXX	
Cost of goods sold		XXX
Gross profit		$XXX

A merchandising business purchases merchandise ready for resale to customers. The total cost of the **merchandise available for sale** during the period is determined as follows:

Beginning Merchandise Inventory + Net Purchases = Merchandise Available for Sale

The **cost of merchandise sold** is determined as follows:

Cost of Merchandise Available for Sale − Ending Merchandise Inventory = Cost of Merchandise Sold

A manufacturer makes the products it sells, using direct materials, direct labor, and factory overhead. The total cost of making products that are available for sale during the period is called the **cost of goods manufactured**.

The **cost of finished goods available for sale** is determined as follows:

Beginning Finished Goods Inventory + Cost of Goods Manufactured = Cost of Finished Goods Available for Sale

The **cost of goods sold** is determined as follows:

Cost of Finished Goods Available for Sale − Ending Finished Goods Inventory = Cost of Goods Sold

Cost of goods manufactured is required to determine the *cost of goods sold* and, thus, to prepare the income statement. The cost of goods manufactured is often determined by preparing a **statement of cost of goods manufactured**.[1] This statement summarizes the cost of goods manufactured during the period, as follows:

Statement of Cost of Goods Manufactured

Beginning work in process inventory............		$XXX
Direct materials:		
Beginning materials inventory..............	$XXX	
Purchases.................................	XXX	
Cost of materials available for use...........	$XXX	
Less ending materials inventory	XXX	
Cost of direct materials used	$XXX	
Direct labor	XXX	
Factory overhead..............................	XXX	
Total manufacturing costs incurred		XXX
Total manufacturing costs		$XXX
Less ending work in process inventory		XXX
Cost of goods manufactured...................		$XXX

To illustrate, the following data for **Legend Guitars** are used:

	Jan. 1, 20Y8	Dec. 31, 20Y8
Inventories:		
Materials.................................	$ 65,000	$ 35,000
Work in process	30,000	24,000
Finished goods...........................	60,000	62,500
Total inventories...........................	$155,000	$121,500
Manufacturing costs incurred during 20Y8:		
Materials purchased.......................		$100,000
Direct labor...............................		110,000
Factory overhead:		
Indirect labor...........................	$ 24,000	
Depreciation on factory equipment.....	10,000	
Factory supplies and utility costs........	10,000	44,000
Total		$254,000
Sales..		$366,000
Selling expenses...............................		20,000
Administrative expenses.......................		15,000

The statement of cost of goods manufactured is prepared using the following three steps:

Step 1. Determine the *cost of materials used*.
Step 2. Determine the *total manufacturing costs incurred*.
Step 3. Determine the *cost of goods manufactured*.

---

[1] Chapters 19 and 20 describe and illustrate the use of job order and process cost systems. As will be discussed, these systems do not require a statement of cost of goods manufactured.

Exhibit 16 summarizes how manufacturing costs flow to the income statement and balance sheet of a manufacturing business.

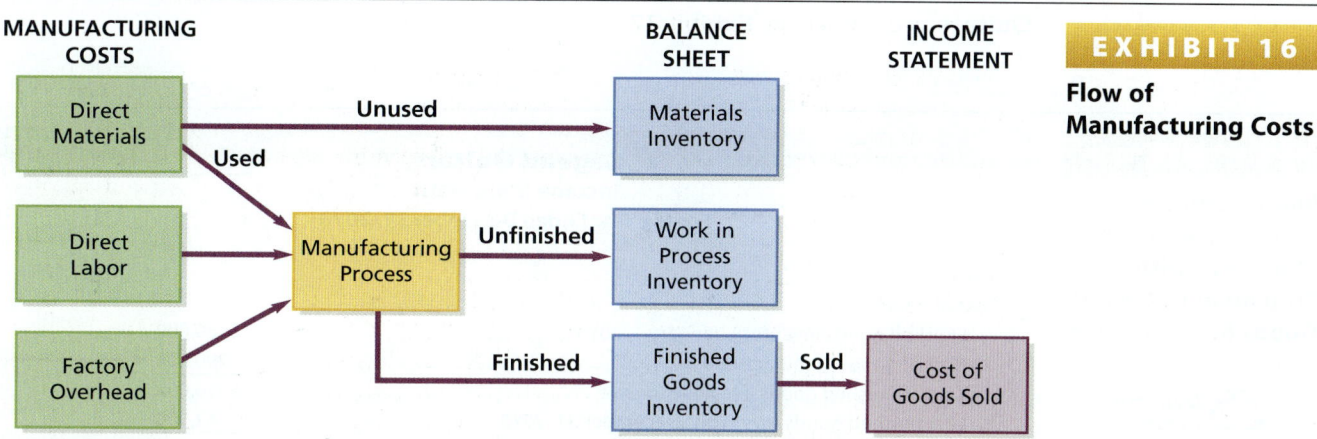

EXHIBIT 16

Flow of Manufacturing Costs

Using the data for **Legend Guitars**, the steps for determining the cost of materials used, total manufacturing costs incurred, and cost of goods manufactured are computed as follows:

Step 1. The *cost of materials used* in production is determined as follows:

Materials inventory, January 1, 20Y8	$ 65,000
Add materials purchased	100,000
Cost of materials available for use	$ 165,000
Less materials inventory, December 31, 20Y8	35,000
Cost of direct materials used	$ 130,000

The January 1, 20Y8 (beginning), materials inventory of $65,000 is added to the cost of materials purchased of $100,000 to yield the $165,000 total cost of materials that are available for use during 20Y8. Deducting the December 31, 20Y8 (ending), materials inventory of $35,000 yields the $130,000 cost of direct materials used in production.

Step 2. The *total manufacturing costs incurred* is determined as follows:

Direct materials used in production (Step 1)	$ 130,000
Direct labor	110,000
Factory overhead	44,000
Total manufacturing costs incurred	$284,000

The total manufacturing costs incurred in 20Y8 of $284,000 are determined by adding the direct materials used in production (Step 1), the direct labor cost, and the factory overhead costs.

Step 3. The *cost of goods manufactured* is determined as follows:

Work in process inventory, January 1, 20Y8	$ 30,000
Total manufacturing costs incurred (Step 2)	284,000
Total manufacturing costs	$ 314,000
Less work in process inventory, December 31, 20Y8	24,000
Cost of goods manufactured	$290,000

The cost of goods manufactured of $290,000 is determined by adding the total manufacturing costs incurred (Step 2) to the January 1, 20Y8 (beginning), work in process inventory of $30,000. This yields total manufacturing costs of $314,000. The December 31, 20Y8 (ending), work in process inventory of $24,000 is then deducted to determine the cost of goods manufactured of $290,000.

The income statement and statement of cost of goods manufactured for **Legend Guitars** are shown in Exhibit 17.

EXHIBIT 17

Manufacturing Company—Income Statement with Statement of Cost of Goods Manufactured

Dynamic Exhibit

Legend Guitars
Income Statement
For the Year Ended December 31, 20Y8

Sales		$366,000
Cost of goods sold:		
Finished goods inventory, January 1, 20Y8	$ 60,000	
Cost of goods manufactured	290,000	
Cost of finished goods available for sale	$350,000	
Less finished goods inventory, December 31, 20Y8	62,500	
Cost of goods sold		287,500
Gross profit		$ 78,500
Operating expenses:		
Selling expenses	$ 20,000	
Administrative expenses	15,000	
Total operating expenses		35,000
Net income		$ 43,500

Legend Guitars
Statement of Cost of Goods Manufactured
For the Year Ended December 31, 20Y8

Work in process inventory, January 1, 20Y8			$ 30,000
Direct materials:			
Materials inventory, January 1, 20Y8	$ 65,000		
Purchases	100,000		
Cost of materials available for use	$165,000		
Less materials inventory, December 31, 20Y8	35,000		
Cost of direct materials used		$130,000	
Direct labor		110,000	
Factory overhead:			
Indirect labor	$ 24,000		
Depreciation on factory equipment	10,000		
Factory supplies and utility costs	10,000		
Total factory overhead		44,000	
Total manufacturing costs incurred			284,000
Total manufacturing costs			$314,000
Less work in process inventory, December 31, 20Y8			24,000
Cost of goods manufactured			$290,000

Example Exercise 18-5 Cost of Goods Sold, Cost of Goods Manufactured   *Obj. 4*

Gauntlet Company has the following information for January:

Cost of direct materials used in production	$25,000
Direct labor	35,000
Factory overhead	20,000
Work in process inventory, January 1	30,000
Work in process inventory, January 31	25,000
Finished goods inventory, January 1	15,000
Finished goods inventory, January 31	12,000

For January, determine (a) the cost of goods manufactured and (b) the cost of goods sold.

Follow My Example 18-5

a.
Work in process inventory, January 1		$ 30,000
Cost of direct materials used	$ 25,000	
Direct labor	35,000	
Factory overhead	20,000	
Total manufacturing costs incurred during January		80,000
Total manufacturing costs		$110,000
Less work in process inventory, January 31		25,000
Cost of goods manufactured		$ 85,000

b.
Finished goods inventory, January 1	$ 15,000	
Cost of goods manufactured	85,000	
Cost of finished goods available for sale	$100,000	
Less finished goods inventory, January 31	12,000	
Cost of goods sold	$ 88,000	

Practice Exercises: PE 18-5A, PE 18-5B

SERVICE FOCUS

MANAGERIAL ACCOUNTING IN THE SERVICE INDUSTRY

All businesses can benefit from managerial accounting whether they manufacture a product or provide a service. Service businesses such as professional service firms, restaurants, maintenance companies, and airlines need managerial accounting information to direct daily operations, plan future operations, and develop business strategies.

For example, The Walt Disney Company relies heavily on managerial accounting to manage its operations. Disney uses budgets and financial forecasts to plan costs and allocate resources between its various business units. Based on these budgets and financial forecasts, Disney directs its operations by determining how to staff its theme parks and off-cycle its theme park rides for maintenance. Operations are controlled by a variety of qualitative and quantitative metrics that provide feedback on the efficiency and quality of the customer experience. To ensure the best guest experience, Disney Theme Parks manages operations in small business units to maximize management ownership and responsibility. The results of Disney's deployment and use of managerial accounting have been impressive. The Walt Disney Company is typically ranked number 1 in *Fortune*'s listing of the 10 most admired companies for quality.

At a Glance 18

Obj. 1 Describe managerial accounting and the role of managerial accounting in a business.

Key Points Managerial accounting is a staff function that supports the management process by providing reports to aid management in planning, directing, controlling, improving, and decision making. This differs from financial accounting, which provides information to users outside the organization. Managerial accounting reports are designed to meet the specific needs of management and aid management in planning long-term strategies and running the day-to-day operations.

Learning Outcomes	Example Exercises	Practice Exercises
• Describe the differences between financial accounting and managerial accounting.		
• Describe the role of the management accountant in the organization.		
• Describe the role of managerial accounting in the management process.	EE18-1	PE18-1A, 18-1B

Obj. 2 Describe and illustrate the following costs: direct and indirect costs; direct materials, direct labor, and factory overhead costs; and product and period costs.

Key Points Manufacturing companies use machinery and labor to convert materials into a finished product. A direct cost can be directly traced to a finished product, while an indirect cost cannot. The cost of a finished product is made up of three components: direct materials, direct labor, and factory overhead.

These three manufacturing costs can be categorized into prime costs (direct materials and direct labor) or conversion costs (direct labor and factory overhead). Product costs consist of the elements of manufacturing cost—direct materials, direct labor, and factory overhead—while period costs consist of selling and administrative expenses.

Learning Outcomes	Example Exercises	Practice Exercises
• Describe a cost object.		
• Classify a cost as a direct or indirect cost for a cost object.		
• Describe direct materials cost.	EE18-2	PE18-2A, 18-2B
• Describe direct labor cost.	EE18-2	PE18-2A, 18-2B
• Describe factory overhead cost.	EE18-2	PE18-2A, 18-2B
• Describe prime costs and conversion costs.	EE18-3	PE18-3A, 18-3B
• Describe product costs and period costs.	EE18-4	PE18-4A, 18-4B

Chapter 18 Introduction to Managerial Accounting

Obj. 3 — Describe sustainable business activities and eco-efficiency measures.

Key Points To make sound strategic and operational decisions, managers must consider the social and environmental conditions in which their company operates. Sustainability is the practice of operating a business to maximize profits while attempting to preserve the environment, economy, and needs of future generations. Sustainability information provides important internal feedback that helps guide a company's strategic and operational decision making. This information also helps users of external financial statements evaluate the risks and opportunities a company faces that are tied to the environment in which it operates.

Learning Outcomes	Example Exercises	Practice Exercises
• Describe sustainability.		
• Describe eco-efficiency measures.		

Obj. 4 — Describe and illustrate the following statements for a manufacturing business: balance sheet, statement of cost of goods manufactured, and income statement.

Key Points The financial statements of manufacturing companies differ from those of merchandising companies. Manufacturing company balance sheets report three types of inventory: materials, work in process, and finished goods. The income statement of manufacturing companies reports the cost of goods sold, which is the total manufacturing cost of the goods sold. The income statement is supported by the statement of cost of goods manufactured, which provides the details of the cost of goods manufactured during the period.

Learning Outcomes	Example Exercises	Practice Exercises
• Describe materials inventory.		
• Describe work in process inventory.		
• Describe finished goods inventory.		
• Describe the differences between merchandising and manufacturing company balance sheets.		
• Prepare a statement of cost of goods manufactured.	EE18-5	PE18-5A, 18-5B
• Prepare an income statement for a manufacturing company.	EE18-5	PE18-5A, 18-5B

Illustrative Problem

The following is a list of costs that were incurred in producing this textbook:

a. Insurance on the factory building and equipment
b. Salary of the vice president of finance
c. Hourly wages of printing press operators during production
d. Straight-line depreciation on the printing presses used to manufacture the text
e. Electricity used to run the presses during the printing of the text
f. Sales commissions paid to textbook representatives for each text sold
g. Paper on which the text is printed
h. Book covers used to bind the pages

(Continued)

Chapter 18 Introduction to Managerial Accounting

i. Straight-line depreciation on an office building
j. Salaries of staff used to develop artwork for the text
k. Glue used to bind pages to cover

Instructions

With respect to the manufacture and sale of this text, classify each cost as either a product cost or a period cost. Indicate whether each product cost is a direct materials cost, a direct labor cost, or a factory overhead cost. Indicate whether each period cost is a selling expense or an administrative expense.

Solution

Cost	Product Cost — Direct Materials Cost	Product Cost — Direct Labor Cost	Product Cost — Factory Overhead Cost	Period Cost — Selling Expense	Period Cost — Administrative Expense
a.			X		
b.					X
c.		X			
d.			X		
e.			X		
f.				X	
g.	X				
h.	X				
i.					X
j.			X		
k.			X		

Key Terms

continuous process improvement (889)
controller (887)
controlling (889)
conversion costs (894)
cost (891)
cost object (891)
cost of finished goods available for sale (900)
cost of goods manufactured (899)
cost of goods sold (900)
cost of merchandise sold (899)
decision making (889)
direct costs (891)
direct labor cost (892)
direct materials cost (892)

directing (889)
eco-efficiency measures (897)
factory burden (893)
factory overhead cost (893)
feedback (889)
financial accounting (885)
finished goods inventory (898)
indirect costs (891)
line department (887)
management by exception (889)
management process (888)
managerial accounting (886)
manufacturing overhead (893)
materials inventory (898)
merchandise available for sale (899)

objectives (goals) (889)
operational planning (889)
period costs (895)
planning (889)
prime costs (894)
product costs (895)
staff department (887)
statement of cost of goods manufactured (900)
strategic planning (889)
strategies (889)
sustainability (897)
Sustainability Accounting Standards Board (SASB) (897)
work in process inventory (898)

Discussion Questions

1. What are the major differences between financial accounting and managerial accounting?
2. a. Differentiate between a department with line responsibility and a department with staff responsibility.
   b. In an organization that has a Sales Department and a Personnel Department, among others, which of the two departments has (1) line responsibility and (2) staff responsibility?
3. What manufacturing cost term is used to describe the cost of materials that are an integral part of the manufactured end product?
4. Distinguish between prime costs and conversion costs.
5. What is the difference between a product cost and a period cost?
6. Name the three inventory accounts for a manufacturing business and describe what each balance represents at the end of an accounting period.
7. In what order should the three inventories of a manufacturing business be presented on the balance sheet?
8. What three categories of manufacturing costs are included in the cost of finished goods and the cost of work in process?
9. Describe sustainability and sustainable business practices.
10. How does the Cost of goods sold section of the income statement differ between merchandising and manufacturing companies?

Practice Exercises

Example Exercises

EE 18-1 p. 890

PE 18-1A Management process OBJ. 1

Three phases of the management process are controlling, planning, and decision making. Match the following descriptions to the proper phase:

Phase of management process	Description
Controlling	a. Monitoring the operating results of implemented plans and comparing the actual results with expected results.
Planning	b. Inherent in planning, directing, controlling, and improving.
Decision making	c. Long-range courses of action.

EE 18-1 p. 890

PE 18-1B Management process OBJ. 1

Three phases of the management process are planning, directing, and controlling. Match the following descriptions to the proper phase:

Phase of management process	Description
Planning	a. Developing long-range courses of action to achieve goals.
Directing	b. Isolating significant departures from plans for further investigation and possible remedial action. It may lead to a revision of future plans.
Controlling	c. Process by which managers, given their assigned levels of responsibilities, run day-to-day operations.

908 Chapter 18 Introduction to Managerial Accounting

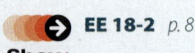 EE 18-2 *p. 894*

PE 18-2A Direct materials, direct labor, and factory overhead OBJ. 2

Identify the following costs as direct materials (DM), direct labor (DL), or factory overhead (FO) for an automobile manufacturer:

a. Wages of employees that operate painting equipment
b. Wages of the plant supervisor
c. Steel
d. Oil used for assembly line machinery

 EE 18-2 *p. 894*

PE 18-2B Direct materials, direct labor, and factory overhead OBJ. 2

Identify the following costs as direct materials (DM), direct labor (DL), or factory overhead (FO) for a magazine publisher:

a. Staples used to bind magazines
b. Wages of printing machine employees
c. Maintenance on printing machines
d. Paper used in the magazine

 EE 18-3 *p. 894*

PE 18-3A Prime and conversion costs OBJ. 2

Identify the following costs as a prime cost (P), conversion cost (C), or both (B) for an automobile manufacturer:

a. Wages of employees that operate painting equipment
b. Wages of the plant manager
c. Steel
d. Oil used for assembly line machinery

 EE 18-3 *p. 894*

PE 18-3B Prime and conversion costs OBJ. 2

Identify the following costs as a prime cost (P), conversion cost (C), or both (B) for a magazine publisher:

a. Paper used for the magazine
b. Wages of printing machine employees
c. Glue used to bind magazine
d. Maintenance on printing machines

 EE 18-4 *p. 896*

PE 18-4A Product and period costs OBJ. 2

Identify the following costs as a product cost or a period cost for an automobile manufacturer:

a. Steel
b. Wages of employees that operate painting equipment
c. Rent on office building
d. Sales staff salaries

 EE 18-4 *p. 896*

PE 18-4B Product and period costs OBJ. 2

Identify the following costs as a product cost or a period cost for a magazine publisher:

a. Sales salaries
b. Paper used for the magazine
c. Maintenance on printing machines
d. Depreciation expense—corporate headquarters

EE 18-5 *p. 903* **PE 18-5A Cost of goods sold, cost of goods manufactured** OBJ. 4

Timbuk 3 Company has the following information for March:

Cost of direct materials used in production	$21,000
Direct labor	54,250
Factory overhead	35,000
Work in process inventory, March 1	87,500
Work in process inventory, March 31	92,750
Finished goods inventory, March 1	36,750
Finished goods inventory, March 31	42,000

For March, determine (a) the cost of goods manufactured and (b) the cost of goods sold.

EE 18-5 *p. 903* **PE 18-5B Cost of goods sold, cost of goods manufactured** OBJ. 4

Glenville Company has the following information for April:

Cost of direct materials used in production	$280,000
Direct labor	324,000
Factory overhead	188,900
Work in process inventory, April 1	72,300
Work in process inventory, April 30	76,800
Finished goods inventory, April 1	39,600
Finished goods inventory, April 30	41,200

For April, determine (a) the cost of goods manufactured and (b) the cost of goods sold.

Exercises

EX 18-1 Classifying costs as materials, labor, or factory overhead OBJ. 2

Indicate whether each of the following costs of an automobile manufacturer would be classified as direct materials cost, direct labor cost, or factory overhead cost:

a. Wheels
b. Glass used in the vehicle's windshield
c. Wages of assembly line worker
d. V8 automobile engine
e. Depreciation of robotic assembly line equipment
f. Steering wheel
g. Painting safety masks for employees working in the paint room
h. Salary of test driver

EX 18-2 Classifying costs as materials, labor, or factory overhead OBJ. 2

Indicate whether the following costs of Procter & Gamble, a maker of consumer products, would be classified as direct materials cost, direct labor cost, or factory overhead cost:

a. Resins for body wash products
b. Scents and fragrances used in making soaps and detergents
c. Plant manager salary for the Iowa City, Iowa, plant
d. Depreciation on the Auburn, Maine, manufacturing plant

(Continued)

e. Depreciation on assembly line in the Mehoopany, Pennsylvania, paper products plant
f. Maintenance supplies
g. Packaging materials, which are a significant portion of the total product cost
h. Wages of production line employees at the Pineville, Louisiana, soap and detergent plant
i. Wages paid to Packaging Department employees in the Bear River City, Utah, paper products plant
j. Salary of process engineers

EX 18-3 Classifying costs as factory overhead OBJ. 2

Which of the following items are properly classified as part of factory overhead for **Ford Motor Company**, a maker of heavy automobiles and trucks?

a. Plant manager's salary at Buffalo, New York, stamping plant, which manufactures auto and truck subassemblies
b. Depreciation on Flat Rock, Michigan, assembly plant
c. Dividends paid to shareholders
d. Machine lubricant used to maintain the assembly line at the Louisville, Kentucky, assembly plant
e. Leather to be used on vehicles that have leather interiors
f. Depreciation on mechanical robots used on the assembly line
g. Consultant fees for a study of production line efficiency
h. Dealership sales incentives
i. Vice president of human resources' salary
j. Property taxes on the Detroit, Michigan, headquarters building

EX 18-4 Classifying costs as product or period costs OBJ. 2

For apparel manufacturer **Abercrombie & Fitch, Inc.**, classify each of the following costs as either a product cost or a period cost:

a. Cost of information technology support for the corporate headquarters
b. Depreciation on sewing machines
c. Fabric used during production
d. Depreciation on office equipment
e. Advertising expenses
f. Repairs and maintenance costs for sewing machines
g. Salary of production quality control supervisor
h. Utility costs for office building
i. Sales commissions
j. Salaries of distribution center personnel
k. Wages of sewing machine operators
l. Factory janitorial supplies
m. Chief financial officer's salary
n. Travel costs of media relations employees
o. Factory supervisors' salaries
p. Oil used to lubricate sewing machines
q. Property taxes on factory building and equipment

EX 18-5 Concepts and terminology OBJ. 1, 2

From the choices presented in parentheses, choose the appropriate term for completing each of the following sentences:

a. Advertising costs are usually viewed as (period, product) costs.
b. Feedback is often used to (improve, direct) operations.
c. Payments of cash or the commitment to pay cash in the future for the purpose of generating revenues are (costs, expenses).

d. A product, a sales territory, a department, or an activity to which costs are traced is called a (direct cost, cost object).

e. The balance sheet of a manufacturer would include an account for (cost of goods sold, work in process inventory).

f. Factory overhead costs combined with direct labor costs are called (prime, conversion) costs.

g. The implementation of automatic, robotic factory equipment normally (increases, decreases) the direct labor component of product costs.

EX 18-6 Concepts and terminology
OBJ. 1, 2

From the choices presented in parentheses, choose the appropriate term for completing each of the following sentences:

a. The phase of the management process that uses process information to eliminate the source of problems in a process so that the process delivers the correct product in the correct quantities is called (directing, improving).

b. Direct labor costs combined with factory overhead costs are called (prime, conversion) costs.

c. The salaries of salespeople are normally considered a (period, product) cost.

d. The plant manager's salary would be considered (direct, indirect) to the product.

e. Long-term plans are called (strategic, operational) plans.

f. Materials for use in production are called (supplies, materials inventory).

g. An example of factory overhead is (electricity used to run assembly line, CEO salary).

EX 18-7 Classifying costs in a service company
OBJ. 2

A partial list of the costs for Wisconsin and Minnesota Railroad, a short hauler of freight, follows. Classify each cost as either indirect or direct. For purposes of classifying each cost, use the train as the cost object.

a. Cost to lease (rent) railroad cars
b. Cost of track and bed (ballast) replacement
c. Diesel fuel costs
d. Cost to lease (rent) train locomotives
e. Depreciation of terminal facilities
f. Maintenance costs of right-of-way, bridges, and buildings
g. Salaries of dispatching and communications personnel
h. Headquarters information technology support staff salaries
i. Safety training costs
j. Wages of train engineers
k. Wages of switch and classification yard personnel
l. Costs of accident cleanup

EX 18-8 Sustainability and eco-efficiency measures
OBJ. 3

Four types of eco-efficiency measures are identified below. Match the following descriptions to the proper eco-efficiency measures:

1. Energy efficiency
2. Fuel efficiency
3. Material use efficiency
4. Waste efficiency

a. Cost savings from recycling and reusing waste and by-product materials
b. Cost savings from reducing the amount of product packaging materials
c. Cost savings from replacing lighting fixtures in a production facility with energy-efficient lighting
d. Cost savings from replacing gas-powered vehicles with hybrid or alternative energy-source vehicles

EX 18-9 Classifying costs
OBJ. 2, 4

The following report was prepared for evaluating the performance of the plant manager of Marching Ants Inc. Evaluate and correct this report.

Marching Ants Inc.
Manufacturing Costs
For the Quarter Ended June 30

Materials used in production (including $56,200 of indirect materials)	$ 607,500
Direct labor (including $84,400 maintenance salaries)	562,500
Factory overhead:	
Supervisor salaries	517,500
Heat, light, and power	140,650
Sales salaries	348,750
Promotional expenses	315,000
Insurance and property taxes—plant	151,900
Insurance and property taxes—corporate offices	219,400
Depreciation—plant and equipment	123,750
Depreciation—corporate offices	90,000
Total	$3,076,950

EX 18-10 Financial statements of a manufacturing firm
OBJ. 4

✔ a. Net income, $145,000

The following events took place for Digital Vibe Manufacturing Company during January, the first month of its operations as a producer of digital video monitors:

a. Purchased $168,500 of materials.
b. Used $149,250 of direct materials in production.
c. Incurred $360,000 of direct labor wages.
d. Incurred $120,000 of factory overhead.
e. Transferred $600,000 of work in process to finished goods.
f. Sold goods for $875,000.
g. Sold goods with a cost of $525,000.
h. Incurred $125,000 of selling expense.
i. Incurred $80,000 of administrative expense.

Using the information given, complete the following:

a. Prepare the January income statement for Digital Vibe Manufacturing Company.
b. Determine the Materials Inventory, Work in Process Inventory, and Finished Goods Inventory balances at the end of the first month of operations.

EX 18-11 Manufacturing company balance sheet
OBJ. 4

Partial balance sheet data for Diesel Additives Company at August 31 are as follows:

Finished goods inventory	$ 89,400	Supplies	$ 13,800
Prepaid insurance	9,000	Materials inventory	26,800
Accounts receivable	348,200	Cash	167,500
Work in process inventory	61,100		

Prepare the Current assets section of Diesel Additives Company's balance sheet at August 31.

EX 18-12 Cost of direct materials used in production for a manufacturing company OBJ. 4

Okaboji Manufacturing Company reported the following materials data for the month ending November 30:

Materials purchased	$490,900
Materials inventory, November 1	64,900
Materials inventory, November 30	81,300

Determine the cost of direct materials used in production by Okaboji during the month ended November 30.

EX 18-13 Cost of goods manufactured for a manufacturing company OBJ. 4

✔ e. $165,000

Two items are omitted from each of the following three lists of cost of goods manufactured statement data. Determine the amounts of the missing items, identifying them by letter.

Work in process inventory, August 1	$ 19,660	$ 41,650	(e)
Total manufacturing costs incurred during August	332,750	(c)	1,075,000
Total manufacturing costs	(a)	$515,770	$1,240,000
Work in process inventory, August 31	23,500	54,000	(f)
Cost of goods manufactured	(b)	(d)	$1,068,000

EX 18-14 Cost of goods manufactured for a manufacturing company OBJ. 4

The following information is available for Ethtridge Manufacturing Company for the month ending July 31:

Cost of direct materials used in production	$1,150,000
Direct labor	966,000
Work in process inventory, July 1	316,400
Work in process inventory, July 31	355,500
Total factory overhead	490,500

Determine Ethtridge's cost of goods manufactured for the month ended July 31.

EX 18-15 Income statement for a manufacturing company OBJ. 4

✔ d. $470,000

Two items are omitted from each of the following three lists of cost of goods sold data from a manufacturing company income statement. Determine the amounts of the missing items, identifying them by letter.

Finished goods inventory, June 1	$ 116,600	$ 38,880	(e)
Cost of goods manufactured	825,900	(c)	180,000
Cost of finished goods available for sale	(a)	$540,000	$1,100,000
Finished goods inventory, June 30	130,000	70,000	(f)
Cost of goods sold	(b)	(d)	$ 945,000

EX 18-16 Statement of cost of goods manufactured for a manufacturing company OBJ. 4

✔ a. Total manufacturing costs, $4,325,700

Cost data for Disksan Manufacturing Company for the month ended January 31 are as follows:

Inventories	January 1	January 31
Materials	$180,000	$145,500
Work in process	334,600	290,700
Finished goods	675,000	715,000

(Continued)

Direct labor	$2,260,000
Materials purchased during January	1,375,000
Factory overhead incurred during January:	
Indirect labor	115,000
Machinery depreciation	90,000
Heat, light, and power	55,000
Supplies	18,500
Property taxes	10,000
Miscellaneous costs	33,100

a. Prepare a cost of goods manufactured statement for January.
b. Determine the cost of goods sold for January.

EX 18-17 Cost of goods sold, profit margin, and net income for a manufacturing company OBJ. 4

✔ a. Cost of goods sold, $4,595,000

The following information is available for Bandera Manufacturing Company for the month ending January 31:

Cost of goods manufactured	$4,490,000
Selling expenses	530,000
Administrative expenses	340,000
Sales	6,600,000
Finished goods inventory, January 1	880,000
Finished goods inventory, January 31	775,000

For the month ended January 31, determine Bandera's (a) cost of goods sold, (b) gross profit, and (c) net income.

EX 18-18 Cost flow relationships OBJ. 4

✔ a. $330,000

The following information is available for the first month of operations of Bahadir Company, a manufacturer of mechanical pencils:

Sales	$792,000
Gross profit	462,000
Cost of goods manufactured	396,000
Indirect labor	171,600
Factory depreciation	26,400
Materials purchased	244,200
Total manufacturing costs for the period	455,400
Materials inventory, ending	33,000

Using the information given, determine the following missing amounts:
a. Cost of goods sold
b. Finished goods inventory at the end of the month
c. Direct materials cost
d. Direct labor cost
e. Work in process inventory at the end of the month

EX 18-19 Uses of managerial accounting in a service company LO 1, 4

Priceline.com allows customers to bid on hotel rooms by "naming their price." This "name your price" process allows customers to obtain a better rate on a hotel room than they might be able to obtain by reserving their room directly from the hotel. The hotel can also benefit from this transaction by filling empty hotel rooms during periods of low occupancy.

Natalie Mooney bids $85 for a night's stay at the Hotel Monaco in Seattle on Saturday August 10. The Hotel Monaco is not fully booked that evening and would likely accept any reasonable bids. How might the Hotel Monaco use managerial accounting information to decide whether or not to accept Natalie's bid?

Problems: Series A

PR 18-1A Classifying costs OBJ. 2

The following is a list of costs that were incurred in the production and sale of large commercial airplanes:

a. Cost of electronic guidance system installed in the airplane cockpit
b. Special advertising campaign in *Aviation World* magazine
c. Salary of chief compliance officer of company
d. Salary of chief financial officer
e. Decals for cockpit door, the cost of which is immaterial to the cost of the final product
f. Cost of electrical wiring throughout the airplane
g. Cost of normal scrap from production of airplane body
h. Instrument panel installed in the airplane cockpit
i. Depreciation on factory equipment
j. Masks for use by painters in painting the airplane body
k. Cost of paving the headquarters employee parking lot
l. Turbo-charged airplane engine
m. Prebuilt leather seats installed in the first-class cabin
n. Human Resources Department costs for the year
o. Hourly wages of employees that assemble the airplane
p. Salary of the Marketing Department personnel
q. Oil to lubricate factory equipment
r. Yearly cost of the maintenance contract for robotic equipment
s. Hydraulic pumps used in the airplane's flight control system
t. Cost of miniature replicas of the airplane used to promote and market the airplane
u. Metal used for producing the airplane body
v. Power used by painting equipment
w. Annual bonus paid to the chief operating officer of the company
x. Interior trim material used throughout the airplane cabin
y. Salary of plant manager
z. Annual fee to a celebrity to promote the aircraft

Instructions

Classify each cost as either a product cost or a period cost. Indicate whether each product cost is a direct materials cost, a direct labor cost, or a factory overhead cost. Indicate whether each period cost is a selling expense or an administrative expense. Use the following tabular headings for your answer, placing an "X" in the appropriate column:

	Product Costs			Period Costs	
Cost	Direct Materials Cost	Direct Labor Cost	Factory Overhead Cost	Selling Expense	Administrative Expense

PR 18-2A Classifying costs OBJ. 2

The following is a list of costs incurred by several businesses:

a. Cost of fabric used by clothing manufacturer
b. Maintenance and repair costs for factory equipment
c. Rent for a warehouse used to store raw materials and work in process
d. Wages of production quality control personnel
e. Oil lubricants for factory plant and equipment

(Continued)

f. Depreciation of robot used to assemble a product
g. Travel costs of marketing executives to annual sales meeting
h. Depreciation of copying machines used by the Marketing Department
i. Fees charged by collection agency on past-due customer accounts
j. Electricity used to operate factory machinery
k. Maintenance costs for factory equipment
l. Pens, paper, and other supplies used by the Accounting Department in preparing various managerial reports
m. Charitable contribution to United Fund
n. Depreciation of microcomputers used in the factory to coordinate and monitor the production schedules
o. Fees paid to lawn service for office grounds upkeep
p. Cost of sewing machine needles used by a shirt manufacturer
q. Cost of plastic for a telephone being manufactured
r. Telephone charges by president's office
s. Cost of 30-second television commercial
t. Surgeon's fee for heart bypass surgery
u. Depreciation of tools used in production
v. Wages of a machine operator on the production line
w. Salary of the vice president of manufacturing operations
x. Factory janitorial supplies

Instructions

Classify each of the preceding costs as a product cost or period cost. Indicate whether each product cost is a direct materials cost, a direct labor cost, or a factory overhead cost. Indicate whether each period cost is a selling expense or an administrative expense. Use the following tabular headings for preparing your answer, placing an "X" in the appropriate column:

Cost	Product Costs			Period Costs	
	Direct Materials Cost	Direct Labor Cost	Factory Overhead Cost	Selling Expense	Administrative Expense

---

PR 18-3A Cost classifications for a service company OBJ. 2

A partial list of Foothills Medical Center's costs follows:

a. Cost of laundry services for operating room personnel
b. Salary of intensive care personnel
c. Depreciation on patient rooms
d. Cost of blood tests
e. Nurses' salaries
f. Cost of patient meals
g. Overtime incurred in the Patient Records Department due to a computer failure
h. Operating room supplies used on patients (catheters, sutures, etc.)
i. Doctor's fee
j. Cost of X-ray test
k. Cost of maintaining the staff and visitors' cafeteria
l. Cost of drugs used for patients
m. Cost of intravenous solutions used for patients
n. Cost of improvements on the employee parking lot
o. Salary of the nutritionist
p. General maintenance of the hospital
q. Cost of advertising hospital services on television
r. Cost of new heart wing
s. Training costs for nurses
t. Depreciation of X-ray equipment
u. Utility costs of the hospital

Instructions

1. What would be Foothills Medical Center's most logical definition for the final cost object? Explain.
2. Identify whether each of the costs is to be classified as direct or indirect. For purposes of classifying each cost as direct or indirect, use the patient as the cost object.

PR 18-4A Manufacturing income statement, statement of cost of goods manufactured   **OBJ. 2, 4**

✔ 1. b. Yakima, $1,330,000

Several items are omitted from the income statement and cost of goods manufactured statement data for two different companies for the month of May.

	Rainier Company	Yakima Company
Materials inventory, May 1	$ 100,000	$ 48,200
Materials inventory, May 31	(a)	50,000
Materials purchased	950,000	710,000
Cost of direct materials used in production	938,500	(a)
Direct labor	2,860,000	(b)
Factory overhead	1,800,000	446,000
Total manufacturing costs incurred during May	(b)	2,484,200
Total manufacturing costs	5,998,500	2,660,600
Work in process inventory, May 1	400,000	176,400
Work in process inventory, May 31	382,000	(c)
Cost of goods manufactured	(c)	2,491,500
Finished goods inventory, May 1	615,000	190,000
Finished goods inventory, May 31	596,500	(d)
Sales	9,220,000	4,550,000
Cost of goods sold	(d)	2,470,000
Gross profit	(e)	(e)
Operating expenses	1,000,000	(f)
Net income	(f)	1,500,000

Instructions

1. Determine the amounts of the missing items, identifying them by letter.
2. Prepare Yakima Company's statement of cost of goods manufactured for May.
3. Prepare Yakima Company's income statement for May.

PR 18-5A Statement of cost of goods manufactured and income statement for a manufacturing company   **OBJ. 2, 4**

✔ 1. Cost of goods manufactured, $1,989,250

The following information is available for Robstown Corporation for 20Y8:

Inventories	January 1	December 31
Materials	$ 44,250	$31,700
Work in process	63,900	80,000
Finished goods	101,200	99,800

(Continued)

Advertising expense	$ 400,000
Depreciation expense—office equipment	30,000
Depreciation expense—factory equipment	80,000
Direct labor	1,100,000
Heat, light, and power—factory	53,300
Indirect labor	115,000
Materials purchased	556,600
Office salaries expense	$ 318,000
Property taxes—factory	40,000
Property taxes—office building	25,000
Rent expense—factory	27,000
Sales	3,850,000
Sales salaries expense	200,000
Supplies—factory	9,500
Miscellaneous costs—factory	11,400

Instructions

1. Prepare the statement of cost of goods manufactured.
2. Prepare the income statement.

Problems: Series B

PR 18-1B Classifying costs   OBJ. 2

The following is a list of costs that were incurred in the production and sale of lawn mowers:

a. Premiums on insurance policy for factory buildings
b. Tires for lawn mowers
c. Filter for spray gun used to paint the lawn mowers
d. Paint used to coat the lawn mowers, the cost of which is immaterial to the cost of the final product
e. Plastic for outside housing of lawn mowers
f. Salary of factory supervisor
g. Hourly wages of operators of robotic machinery used in production
h. Engine oil used in mower engines prior to shipment
i. Salary of vice president of marketing
j. Property taxes on the factory building and equipment
k. Cost of advertising in a national magazine
l. Gasoline engines installed in the lawn mowers
m. Electricity used to run the robotic machinery
n. Straight-line depreciation on the robotic machinery used to manufacture the lawn mowers
o. Salary of quality control supervisor who inspects each lawn mower before it is shipped
p. Attorney fees for drafting a new lease for headquarters offices
q. Payroll taxes on hourly assembly line employees
r. Telephone charges for company controller's office
s. Steering wheels for lawn mowers
t. Factory cafeteria cashier's wages
u. Cash paid to outside firm for janitorial services for factory
v. Maintenance costs for new robotic factory equipment, based on hours of usage
w. Cost of boxes used in packaging lawn mowers, which are a significant portion of the total product cost

x. License fees for use of patent for lawn mower blade, based on the number of lawn mowers produced
y. Steel used in producing the lawn mowers
z. Commissions paid to sales representatives, based on the number of lawn mowers sold

Instructions

Classify each cost as either a product cost or a period cost. Indicate whether each product cost is a direct materials cost, a direct labor cost, or a factory overhead cost. Indicate whether each period cost is a selling expense or an administrative expense. Use the following tabular headings for your answer, placing an "X" in the appropriate column:

	Product Costs			Period Costs	
Cost	Direct Materials Cost	Direct Labor Cost	Factory Overhead Cost	Selling Expense	Administrative Expense

PR 18-2B Classifying costs
OBJ. 2

The following is a list of costs incurred by several businesses:

a. Salary of quality control supervisor
b. Packing supplies for products sold. These supplies are a very small portion of the total cost of the product.
c. Factory operating supplies
d. Depreciation of factory equipment
e. Hourly wages of warehouse laborers
f. Wages of company controller's secretary
g. Maintenance and repair costs for factory equipment
h. Paper used by commercial printer
i. Entertainment expenses for sales representatives
j. Protective glasses for factory machine operators
k. Sales commissions
l. Cost of hogs for meat processor
m. Cost of telephone operators for a toll-free hotline to help customers operate products
n. Hard drives for a microcomputer manufacturer
o. Lumber used by furniture manufacturer
p. Wages of a machine operator on the production line
q. First-aid supplies for factory workers
r. Tires for an automobile manufacturer
s. Paper used by Computer Department in processing various managerial reports
t. Seed for grain farmer
u. Health insurance premiums paid for factory workers
v. Costs of information technology support for the corporate headquarters
w. Costs for television advertisement
x. Executive bonus for vice president of marketing

Instructions

Classify each of the preceding costs as a product cost or period cost. Indicate whether each product cost is a direct materials cost, a direct labor cost, or a factory overhead cost. Indicate whether each period cost is a selling expense or an administrative expense. Use the following tabular headings for preparing your answer. Place an "X" in the appropriate column.

	Product Costs			Period Costs	
Cost	Direct Materials Cost	Direct Labor Cost	Factory Overhead Cost	Selling Expense	Administrative Expense

Chapter 18 Introduction to Managerial Accounting

PR 18-3B Cost classifications for a service company
OBJ. 2

A partial list of The Grand Hotel's costs follows:

a. Cost to mail a customer survey
b. Wages of convention setup employees
c. Pay-per-view movie rental costs (in rooms)
d. Cost of food
e. Cost of room mini-bar supplies
f. Training for hotel restaurant servers
g. Cost to paint lobby
h. Cost of laundering towels and bedding
i. Champagne for guests
j. Salary of the hotel manager
k. Depreciation of the hotel
l. Cost of valet parking
m. Wages of bellhops
n. Cost to replace lobby furniture
o. Cost of advertising in local newspaper
p. Wages of desk clerks
q. Wages of maids
r. Cost of new carpeting
s. Guest room telephone costs for long-distance calls
t. Cost of soaps and shampoos for rooms
u. Utility cost
v. Wages of kitchen employees
w. General maintenance supplies

Instructions

1. What would be The Grand Hotel's most logical definition for the final cost object? Explain.
2. Identify whether each of the costs is to be classified as direct or indirect. For purposes of classifying each cost as direct or indirect, use the hotel guest as the cost object.

PR 18-4B Manufacturing income statement, statement of cost of goods manufactured
OBJ. 2, 4

✓ 1. c. On Company, $800,800

Excel

Several items are omitted from the income statement and cost of goods manufactured statement data for two different companies for the month of December.

	On Company	Off Company
Materials inventory, December 1	$ 65,800	$ 195,300
Materials inventory, December 31	(a)	91,140
Materials purchased	282,800	(a)
Cost of direct materials used in production	317,800	(b)
Direct labor	387,800	577,220
Factory overhead	148,400	256,060
Total manufacturing costs incurred in December	(b)	1,519,000
Total manufacturing costs	973,000	1,727,320
Work in process inventory, December 1	119,000	208,320
Work in process inventory, December 31	172,200	(c)
Cost of goods manufactured	(c)	1,532,020
Finished goods inventory, December 1	$ 224,000	$ 269,080
Finished goods inventory, December 31	197,400	(d)
Sales	1,127,000	1,944,320
Cost of goods sold	(d)	1,545,040
Gross profit	(e)	(e)
Operating expenses	117,600	(f)
Net income	(f)	164,920

Instructions

1. Determine the amounts of the missing items, identifying them by letter.
2. Prepare On Company's statement of cost of goods manufactured for December.
3. Prepare On Company's income statement for December.

PR 18-5B Statement of cost of goods manufactured and income statement for a manufacturing company

OBJ. 2, 4

✔ 1. Cost of goods manufactured, $367,510

The following information is available for Shanika Company for 20Y6:

Inventories	January 1	December 31
Materials	$ 77,350	$ 95,550
Work in process	109,200	96,200
Finished goods	113,750	100,100

Advertising expense	$ 68,250
Depreciation expense—office equipment	22,750
Depreciation expense—factory equipment	14,560
Direct labor	186,550
Heat, light, and power—factory	5,850
Indirect labor	23,660
Materials purchased	123,500
Office salaries expense	77,350
Property taxes—factory	4,095
Property taxes—headquarters building	13,650
Rent expense—factory	6,825
Sales	864,500
Sales salaries expense	136,500
Supplies—factory	3,250
Miscellaneous costs—factory	4,420

Instructions
1. Prepare the statement of cost of goods manufactured.
2. Prepare the income statement.

Cases & Projects

CP 18-1 Ethics in Action

Avett Manufacturing Company allows employees to purchase materials, such as metal and lumber, for personal use at a price equal to the company's cost. To purchase materials, an employee must complete a materials requisition form, which must then be approved by the employee's immediate supervisor. Brian Dadian, an assistant cost accountant, then charges the employee an amount based on Avett's net purchase cost.

Brian is in the process of replacing a deck on his home and has requisitioned lumber for personal use, which has been approved in accordance with company policy. In computing the cost of the lumber, Brian reviewed all the purchase invoices for the past year. He then used the lowest price to compute the amount due the company for the lumber.

The Institute of Management Accountants (IMA) is the professional organization for managerial accountants. The IMA has established four principles of ethical conduct for its members: honesty, fairness, objectivity, and responsibility. These principles are available at the IMA Web site: www.imanet.org.

▶ Using the IMA's four principles of ethical conduct, evaluate Brian's behavior. Has he acted in an ethical manner? Why?

CP 18-2 Team Activity

In teams, visit a local restaurant. As you observe the operation, consider the costs associated with running the business. As a team, identify as many costs as you can and classify them according to the following table headings:

Cost	Direct Materials	Direct Labor	Overhead	Selling Expenses

CP 18-3 Communication

Todd Johnson is the vice president of Finance for Boz Zeppelin Industries, Inc. At a recent finance meeting, Todd made the following statement: "The managers of a company should use the same information as the shareholders of the firm. When managers use the same information to guide their internal operations as shareholders use in evaluating their investments, the managers will be aligned with the stockholders' profit objectives." Prepare a one-half page memo to Todd discussing any concerns you might have with his statement.

CP 18-4 Managerial accounting in the management process

For each of the following managers, describe how managerial accounting could be used to satisfy strategic or operational objectives:

1. The vice president of the Information Systems Division of a bank.
2. A hospital administrator.
3. The chief executive officer of a food company. The food company is divided into three divisions: Nonalcoholic Beverages, Snack Foods, and Fast-Food Restaurants.
4. The manager of the local campus copy shop.

CP 18-5 Classifying costs

Geek Chic Company provides computer repair services for the community. Obie Won's computer was not working, and he called Geek Chic for a home repair visit. Geek Chic Company's technician arrived at 2:00 PM to begin work. By 4:00 PM, the problem was diagnosed as a failed circuit board. Unfortunately, the technician did not have a new circuit board in the truck because the technician's previous customer had the same problem and a board was used on that visit. Replacement boards were available back at Geek Chic Company's shop. Therefore, the technician drove back to the shop to retrieve a replacement board. From 4:00 to 5:00 PM, Geek Chic Company's technician drove the round trip to retrieve the replacement board from the shop.

At 5:00 PM, the technician was back on the job at Obie's home. The replacement procedure is somewhat complex because a variety of tests must be performed once the board is installed. The job was completed at 6:00 PM.

Obie's repair bill showed the following:

Circuit board	$100
Labor charges	300
Total	$400

Obie was surprised at the size of the bill and asked for more detail supporting the calculations. Geek Chic Company responded with the following explanations:

Cost of materials:	
Purchase price of circuit board	$ 80
Markup on purchase price to cover storage and handling	20
Total materials charge	$100

The labor charge per hour is detailed as follows:

2:00–3:00 PM	$ 70
3:00–4:00 PM	60
4:00–5:00 PM	80
5:00–6:00 PM	90
Total labor charge	$300

Further explanations in the differences in the hourly rates are as follows:

First hour:
Base labor rate	$42
Fringe benefits	10
Overhead (other than storage and handling)	8
Total base labor rate	$60
Additional charge for first hour of any job to cover the cost of vehicle depreciation, fuel, and employee time in transit. A 30-minute transit time is assumed.	10
	$70

Third hour:
Base labor rate	$60
The trip back to the shop includes vehicle depreciation and fuel; therefore, a charge was added to the hourly rate to cover these costs. The round trip took an hour.	20
	$80

Fourth hour:
Base labor rate	$60
Overtime premium for time worked in excess of an eight-hour day (starting at 5:00 PM) is equal to 1.5 times the base rate.	30
	$90

1. If you were in Obie's position, how would you respond to the bill? Are there parts of the bill that appear incorrect to you? If so, what argument would you employ to convince Geek Chic Company that the bill is too high?

2. Use the headings that follow to construct a table. Fill in the table by listing the costs identified in the activity in the left-hand column. For each cost, place a check mark in the appropriate column identifying the correct cost classification. Assume that each service call is a job.

Cost	Direct Materials	Direct Labor	Overhead

CP 18-6 Using managerial accounting information

The following situations describe decision scenarios that could use managerial accounting information:

1. The manager of High Times Restaurant wants to determine the price to charge for various lunch plates.
2. By evaluating the cost of leftover materials, the plant manager of a precision tool facility wants to determine how effectively the plant is being run.
3. The division controller of West Coast Supplies needs to determine the cost of products left in inventory.
4. The manager of the Maintenance Department of a large manufacturing company wants to plan next year's anticipated expenditures.

For each situation, discuss how managerial accounting information could be used.

CHAPTER 19

Job Order Costing

Concepts and Principles
Chapter 18 *Introduction to Managerial Accounting*

Developing Information

COST SYSTEMS
Chapter 19 *Job Order Costing*
Chapter 20 *Process Cost Systems*

COST BEHAVIOR
Chapter 21 *Cost-Volume-Profit Analysis*

Decision Making

EVALUATING PERFORMANCE
Chapter 22 *Budgeting*
Chapter 23 *Variances from Standard Costs*

COMPARING ALTERNATIVES
Chapter 24 *Decentralized Operations*
Chapter 25 *Differential Analysis, Product Pricing, and Activity-Based Costing*
Chapter 26 *Capital Investment Analysis*

CHAPTER 19

Gibson Guitar

The selling price of a Gibson guitar ranges from less than $500 to over $11,000 for a Gibson 2015 Wes Montgomery electric guitar. These differences in selling prices reflect the quality of the materials and the craftsmanship required in making a guitar. In all cases, however, the selling price of a guitar must be greater than the cost of producing it. So how does **Gibson** determine the cost of producing a guitar?

Costs associated with creating a guitar include materials such as wood and strings, the wages of employees who build the guitar, and factory overhead. To determine the purchase price of a guitar, Gibson identifies and records the costs that go into the guitar during each step of the manufacturing process. As the guitar moves through the production process, the costs of direct materials, direct labor, and factory overhead are recorded. When the guitar is complete, the costs that have been recorded are added up to determine the cost of the guitar. The company then prices the guitar to achieve a level of profit.

This chapter describes a job order cost accounting system that illustrates how costs could be recorded and accumulated in manufacturing a guitar. The chapter also describes how a job order cost system could be used by service businesses.

Source: www.gibson.com/Gibson/History.aspx

Learning Objectives

After studying this chapter, you should be able to:

Example Exercises (EE) are shown in **green**.

Obj. 1 Describe cost accounting systems used by manufacturing businesses.

Cost Accounting Systems Overview
Job Order Cost Systems
Process Cost Systems

Obj. 2 Describe and illustrate a job order cost accounting system.

Job Order Cost Systems for Manufacturing Businesses
- Materials — EE 19-1
- Factory Labor — EE 19-2
- Factory Overhead — EE 19-3, 19-4
- Work in Process — EE 19-5
- Finished Goods
- Sales and Cost of Goods Sold
- Period Costs
- Summary of Cost Flows for Legend Guitars

Obj. 3 Describe the use of job order cost information for decision making.

Job Order Costing for Decision Making

Obj. 4 Describe job order cost accounting systems for service businesses.

Job Order Cost Systems for Service Businesses
- Types of Service Businesses
- Flow of Costs in a Service Job Order Cost System

At a Glance 19 — Page 943

Obj. 1 Describe cost accounting systems used by manufacturing businesses.

Cost Accounting Systems Overview

Cost accounting systems measure, record, and report product costs. Managers use product costs for setting product prices, controlling operations, and developing financial statements.

The two main types of cost accounting systems for manufacturing operations are job order cost and process cost systems. Each system differs in how it accumulates and records costs.

Job Order Cost Systems

A **job order cost system** provides product costs for each quantity of product that is manufactured. Each quantity of product that is manufactured is called a *job*. Job order cost systems are often used by companies that manufacture custom products for customers or batches of similar products. For example, an apparel manufacturer such as **Levi Strauss & Co.** or a guitar manufacturer such as **Gibson Guitars** would use a job order cost system.

This chapter illustrates the job order cost system. As a basis for illustration, **Legend Guitars**, a manufacturer of guitars, is used.[1]

Process Cost Systems

A **process cost system** provides product costs for each manufacturing department or process. Process cost systems are often used by companies that manufacture units of a product that are indistinguishable from each other and are manufactured using a continuous production process. Examples are oil refineries, paper producers, chemical processors, and food processors. The process cost system is illustrated in Chapter 20.

---

1 Legend Guitars' manufacturing operation is described in more detail in Chapter 18.

Job Order Cost Systems for Manufacturing Businesses

Obj. 2 Describe and illustrate a job order cost accounting system.

A job order cost system records and summarizes manufacturing costs by jobs. The flow of manufacturing costs in a job order system is illustrated in Exhibit 1.

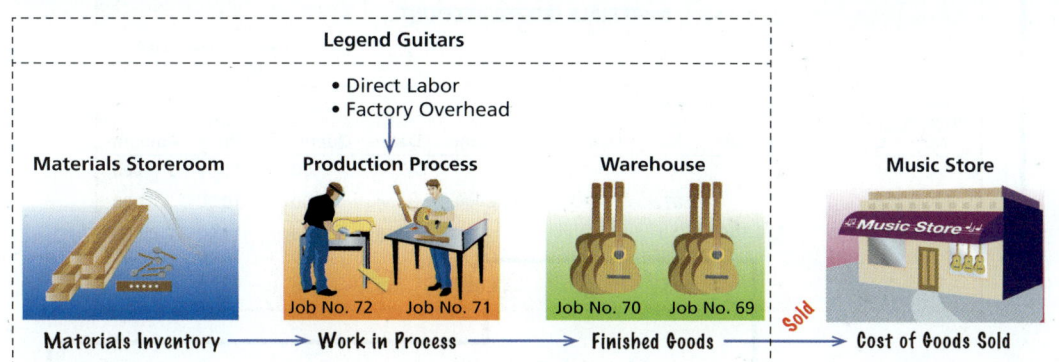

EXHIBIT 1

Flow of Manufacturing Costs

Exhibit 1 indicates that although the materials for Jobs 71 and 72 have been added, both jobs are still in the production process. Thus, Jobs 71 and 72 are part of *Work in Process Inventory*. In contrast, Exhibit 1 indicates that Jobs 69 and 70 have been completed. Thus, Jobs 69 and 70 are part of *Finished Goods Inventory*. Exhibit 1 also indicates that when finished guitars are sold to music stores, their costs become part of *Cost of Goods Sold*.

In a job order cost accounting system, perpetual inventory controlling accounts and subsidiary ledgers are maintained for materials, work in process, and finished goods inventories as shown in Exhibit 2.

Link to Gibson Guitars
At any one point in time, **Gibson** will have materials, work in process, and finished goods inventories.

Inventory Ledger Accounts

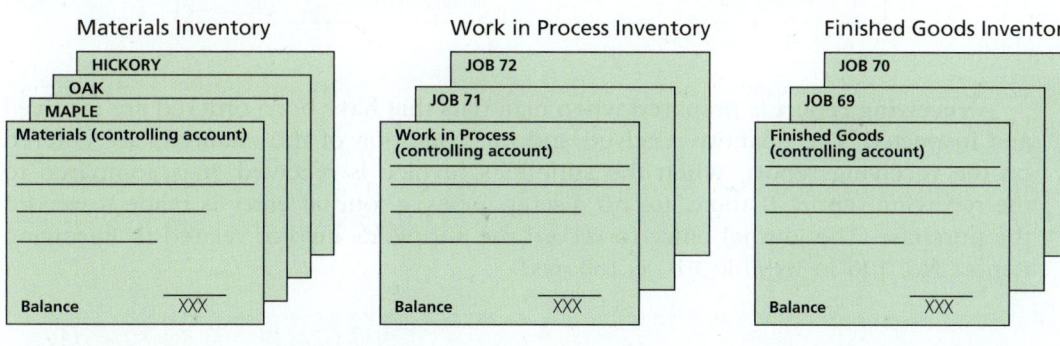

EXHIBIT 2

Materials

The materials account in the general ledger is a controlling account. A separate account for each type of material is maintained in a subsidiary **materials ledger**.

Exhibit 3 shows **Legend Guitars**' materials ledger account for maple. Increases (debits) and decreases (credits) to the materials account are as follows:

- Increases (debits) are based on *receiving reports* such as Receiving Report No. 196 for $10,500, which is supported by the supplier's invoice.

928 Chapter 19 Job Order Costing

- Decreases (credits) are based on *materials requisitions* such as Requisition No. 672 for $2,000 for Job 71 and Requisition No. 704 for $11,000 for Job 72.

EXHIBIT 3
Materials Information and Cost Flows

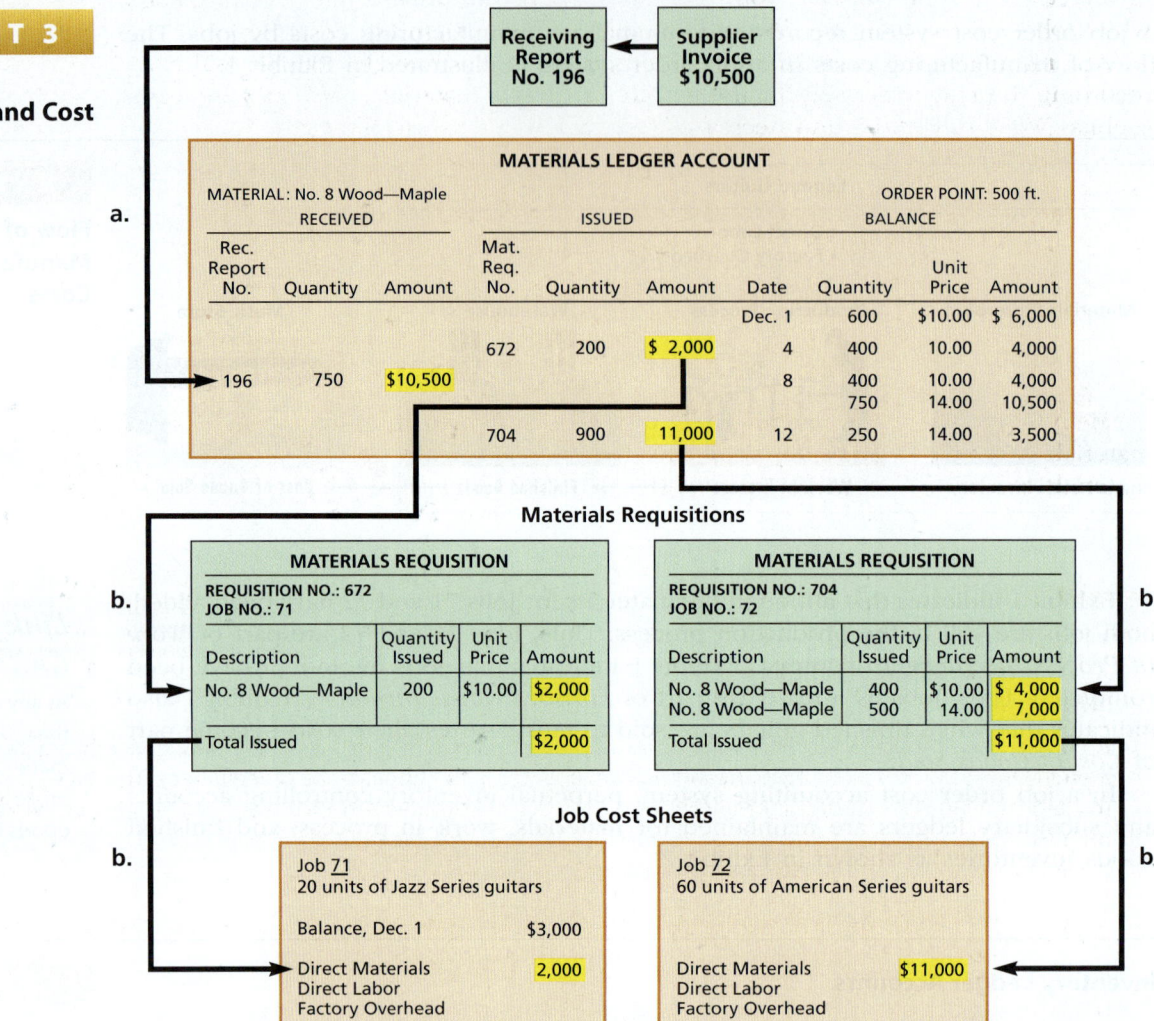

Link to Gibson Guitars

Gibson Guitars uses a variety of woods (direct materials) in making guitars, including cedar.

A **receiving report** is prepared when materials that have been ordered are received and inspected. The quantity received and the condition of the materials are entered on the receiving report. When the supplier's invoice is received, it is compared to the receiving report. If there are no discrepancies, a journal entry is made to record the purchase. The journal entry to record the supplier's invoice related to Receiving Report No. 196 in Exhibit 3 is as follows:

a.	Materials	10,500	
	Accounts Payable		10,500
	Materials purchased during December.		

The storeroom releases materials for use in manufacturing when a **materials requisition** is received. Examples of materials requisitions are shown in Exhibit 3.

The materials requisitions for each job serve as the basis for recording materials used. For direct materials, the quantities and amounts from the materials requisitions are posted to job cost sheets. **Job cost sheets**, which are also illustrated in Exhibit 3, make up the work in process subsidiary ledger.

Exhibit 3 shows the posting of $2,000 of direct materials to Job 71 and $11,000 of direct materials to Job 72.[2] Job 71 is an order for 20 units of Jazz Series guitars, while Job 72 is an order for 60 units of American Series guitars.

A summary of the materials requisitions is used as a basis for the journal entry recording the materials used for the month. For direct materials, this entry increases (debits) Work in Process and decreases (credits) Materials as follows:

b.	Work in Process		13,000	
	Materials			13,000
	Materials requisitioned to jobs ($2,000 + $11,000).			

Many companies use computerized information processes to record the use of materials. In such cases, storeroom employees electronically record the release of materials, which automatically updates the materials ledger and job cost sheets.

INTEGRITY, OBJECTIVITY, AND ETHICS IN BUSINESS

PHONY INVOICE SCAMS

A popular method for defrauding a company is to issue a phony invoice. The scam begins by initially contacting the target firm to discover details of key business contacts, business operations, and products. The swindler then uses this information to create a fictitious invoice. The invoice will include names, figures, and other details to give it the appearance of legitimacy. This type of scam can be avoided if invoices are matched with receiving documents prior to issuing a check.

Example Exercise 19-1 Issuance of Materials   Obj. 2

On March 5, Hatch Company purchased 400 units of raw materials at $14 per unit. During March, raw materials were requisitioned for production as follows: 200 units for Job 101 at $12 per unit and 300 units for Job 102 at $14 per unit. Journalize the entry on March 5 to record the purchase and on March 31 to record the requisition from the materials storeroom.

Follow My Example 19-1

Mar. 5	Materials	5,600*	
	Accounts Payable		5,600
31	Work in Process	6,600**	
	Materials		6,600

*$5,600 = 400 × $14

**Job 101	$2,400 = 200 × $12
Job 102	4,200 = 300 × $14
Total	$6,600

Practice Exercises: PE 19-1A, PE 19-1B

---

[2] To simplify, Exhibit 4 and this chapter use the first-in, first-out cost flow method.

Factory Labor

When employees report for work, they may use *electronic badges, clock cards,* or *in-and-out cards* to clock in. When employees work on an individual job, they use **time tickets** to record the amount of time they have worked on a specific job. Exhibit 4 illustrates time tickets for Jobs 71 and 72 at Legend Guitars.

EXHIBIT 4
Labor Information and Cost Flows

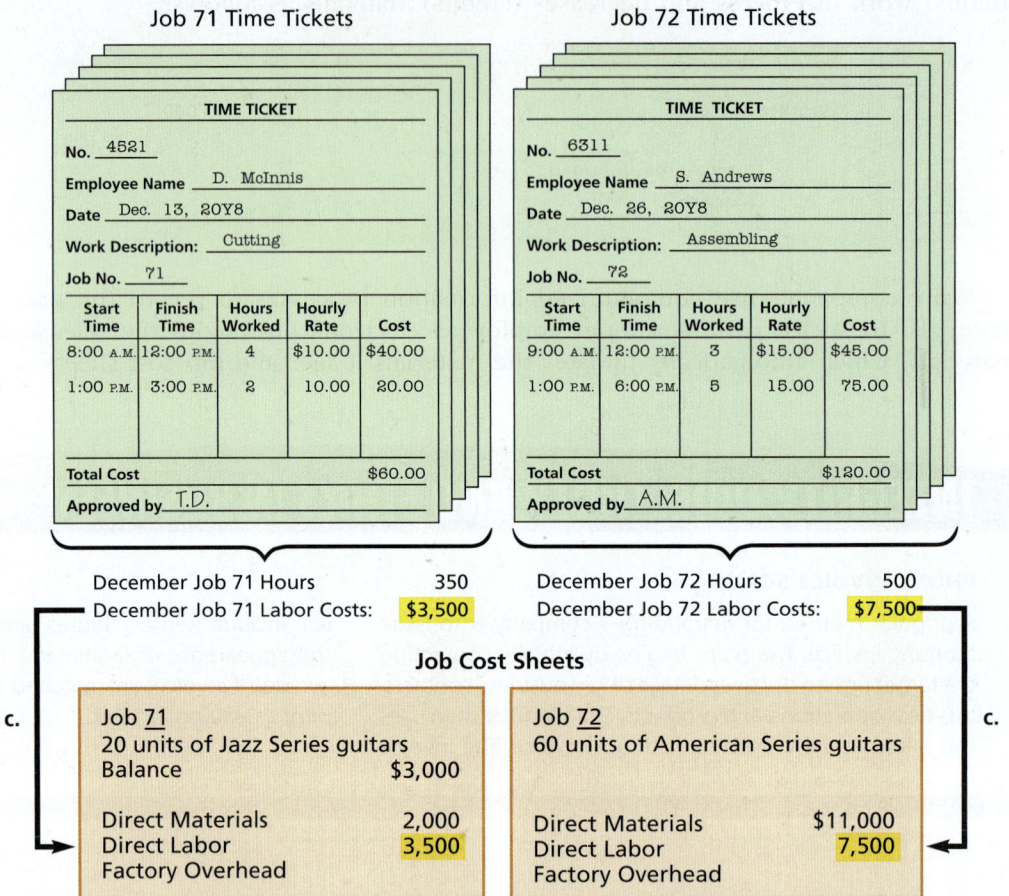

Link to Gibson Guitars

Gibson uses workers (factory labor) to perform a variety of tasks in making guitars, including cutting, matching wood grains, fitting braces, shaping and fitting necks, coloring, polishing, tuning, and inspecting.

Exhibit 4 shows that on December 13, 20Y8, D. McInnis spent six hours working on Job 71 at an hourly rate of $10 for a cost of $60 (6 hrs. × $10). Exhibit 4 also indicates that a total of 350 hours was spent by employees on Job 71 during December for a total cost of $3,500. This total direct labor cost of $3,500 is posted to the job cost sheet for Job 71, as shown in Exhibit 4.

Likewise, Exhibit 4 shows that on December 26, 20Y8, S. Andrews spent eight hours on Job 72 at an hourly rate of $15 for a cost of $120 (8 hrs. × $15). A total of 500 hours was spent by employees on Job 72 during December for a total cost of $7,500. This total direct labor cost of $7,500 is posted to the job cost sheet for Job 72, as shown in Exhibit 4.

A summary of the time tickets is used as the basis for the journal entry recording direct labor for the month. This entry increases (debits) Work in Process and increases (credits) Wages Payable, as follows:

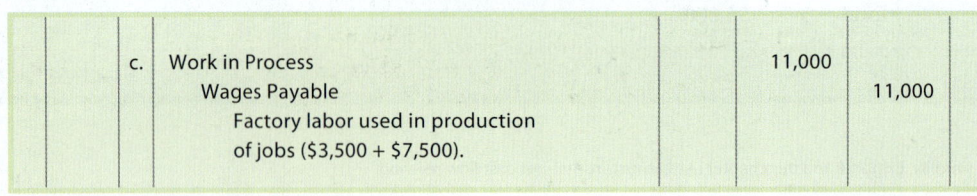

As with direct materials, many businesses use computerized information processing to record direct labor. In such cases, employees may log their time directly into computer terminals at their workstations. In other cases, employees may be issued magnetic cards, much like credit cards, to log in and out of work assignments.

Example Exercise 19-2 Direct Labor Costs   Obj. 2

During March, Hatch Company accumulated 800 hours of direct labor costs on Job 101 and 600 hours on Job 102. The total direct labor was incurred at a rate of $16 per direct labor hour for Job 101 and $12 per direct labor hour for Job 102. Journalize the entry to record the flow of labor costs into production during March.

Follow My Example 19-2

Work in Process	20,000*	
Wages Payable		20,000

*Job 101 $12,800 = 800 hrs. × $16
 Job 102   7,200 = 600 hrs. × $12
 Total $20,000

Practice Exercises: PE 19-2A, PE 19-2B

Business Connection

3D PRINTING

3D printing is a technology that creates a three-dimensional product from an "additive" process. "Additive" means the product is built from plastic, metal, or other material that is built layer by successive layer until the final object is complete. The layers are very thin, allowing for extremely precise final specifications. The process is like printing on a piece of paper (which adds a layer of ink), but in three dimensions, hence the term 3D printing. The machines that add the thin material layers are computer controlled, so that the layers are added in exactly the right way to create the final product. 3D printers can manufacture very complex final products. 3D printing fits well within a job shop environment because the technology provides an economical way to create custom products.

Factory Overhead

Factory overhead includes all manufacturing costs except direct materials and direct labor. Factory overhead costs come from a variety of sources, including the following:

- *Indirect materials* comes from a summary of materials requisitions.
- *Indirect labor* comes from the salaries of production supervisors and the wages of other employees such as janitors.
- *Factory power* comes from utility bills.
- *Factory depreciation* comes from Accounting Department computations of depreciation.

To illustrate the recording of factory overhead, assume that Legend Guitars incurred $4,600 of overhead during December, which included $500 of indirect materials, $2,000 of indirect labor, $900 of utilities, and $1,200 of factory depreciation.

The $500 of indirect materials consisted of $200 of glue and $300 of sandpaper. The entry to record the factory overhead is as follows:

d.	Factory Overhead		4,600	
	Materials			500
	Wages Payable			2,000
	Utilities Payable			900
	Accumulated Depreciation			1,200
	Factory overhead incurred in production.			

Business Connection

ADVANCED ROBOTICS

Boston Consulting Group (BCG) believes that the use of advanced robotics in manufacturing is about to take off. It estimates that by 2025, 25% of all tasks will be automated through robotics, driving a 10–30% increase in productivity. China, the United States, Japan, Germany, and South Korea will be the primary drivers of this trend. BCG anticipates that significant use of advanced robotics will have a number of important impacts on manufacturing:

- Robotics will reduce the need to move factories to low-labor cost countries to save costs.
- Robotics will reduce the size of manufacturing facilities, allowing for greater flexibility and a more regional focus.
- The economic costs of robotics will decline, opening up their broad use.
- The workforce will require new skills, such as programming and technical maintenance, to support robotic manufacturing. For example, **Shenzhen Everwin Precision Technology** recently announced plans to replace 90% of its 1,800 employees with advanced robotics in the near future. The remaining employees will be retrained to work with the robots.

Increasing use of robots will cause direct labor to go down while factory overhead will increase. As a result, accurate factory overhead allocation will become increasingly important in these advanced manufacturing environments.

Source: Boston Consulting Group, *The Shifting Economics of Global Manufacturing: How a Takeoff in Advanced Robotics Will Power the Next Productivity Surge*, February 2015.

Example Exercise 19-3 Factory Overhead Costs Obj. 2

During March, Hatch Company incurred factory overhead costs as follows: indirect materials, $800; indirect labor, $3,400; utilities cost, $1,600; and factory depreciation, $2,500. Journalize the entry to record the factory overhead incurred during March.

Follow My Example 19-3

Factory Overhead	8,300	
Materials		800
Wages Payable		3,400
Utilities Payable		1,600
Accumulated Depreciation—Factory		2,500

Practice Exercises: PE 19-3A, PE 19-3B

Allocating Factory Overhead Unlike direct labor and direct materials, factory overhead is *indirectly* related to the jobs. That is, factory overhead costs cannot be identified with or traced to specific jobs. For this reason, factory overhead costs are allocated to jobs. The process by which factory overhead or other costs are assigned to a cost object, such as a job, is called **cost allocation**.

The factory overhead costs are *allocated* to jobs using a common measure related to each job. This measure is called an **activity base**, *allocation base*, or *activity driver*. The activity base used to allocate overhead should reflect the consumption or use of factory overhead costs. Three common activity bases used to allocate factory overhead costs are direct labor hours, direct labor cost, and machine hours.

Predetermined Factory Overhead Rate Factory overhead costs are normally allocated or *applied* to jobs using a **predetermined factory overhead rate**. The predetermined factory overhead rate is computed as follows:

$$\text{Predetermined Factory Overhead Rate} = \frac{\text{Estimated Total Factory Overhead Costs}}{\text{Estimated Activity Base}}$$

To illustrate, assume that **Legend Guitars** estimates the total factory overhead cost as $50,000 for the year and the activity base as 10,000 direct labor hours. The predetermined factory overhead rate of $5 per direct labor hour is computed as follows:

$$\text{Predetermined Factory Overhead Rate} = \frac{\$50,000}{10,000 \text{ direct labor hours}} = \$5 \text{ per direct labor hour}$$

As illustrated, the predetermined overhead rate is computed using *estimated* amounts at the beginning of the period. This is because managers need timely information on the product costs of each job. If a company waited until all overhead costs were known at the end of the period, the allocated factory overhead would be accurate but not timely. Only through timely reporting can managers adjust manufacturing methods or product pricing.

Many companies use a more precise method for accumulating and allocating factory overhead costs called **activity-based costing**. This method uses a different overhead rate for each type of factory overhead activity, such as inspecting, moving, and machining. Activity-based costing is discussed and illustrated in Chapter 25.

Applying Factory Overhead to Work in Process **Legend Guitars** applies factory overhead using a rate of $5 per direct labor hour. The factory overhead applied to each job is recorded in the job cost sheets, as shown in Exhibit 5.

Exhibit 5 shows that 850 direct labor hours were used in Legend Guitars' December operations. Based on the time tickets, 350 hours can be traced to Job 71 and 500 hours can be traced to Job 72.

Using a factory overhead rate of $5 per direct labor hour, $4,250 of factory overhead is applied as follows:

	Direct Labor Hours	Factory Overhead Rate	Factory Overhead Applied
Job 71	350	$5	$1,750 (350 hrs. × $5)
Job 72	500	5	2,500 (500 hrs. × $5)
Total	850		$4,250

As shown in Exhibit 5, the applied overhead is posted to each job cost sheet. Factory overhead of $1,750 is posted to Job 71, which results in a total product cost on December 31, 20Y8, of $10,250. Factory overhead of $2,500 is posted to Job 72, which results in a total product cost on December 31, 20Y8, of $21,000.

The journal entry to apply factory overhead increases (debits) Work in Process and credits Factory Overhead. This journal entry to apply overhead to Jobs 71 and 72 is as follows:

e.	Work in Process		4,250	
	Factory Overhead			4,250
	Factory overhead applied to jobs according to the predetermined overhead rate (850 hrs. × $5).			

934 Chapter 19 Job Order Costing

EXHIBIT 5

Applying Factory Overhead to Jobs

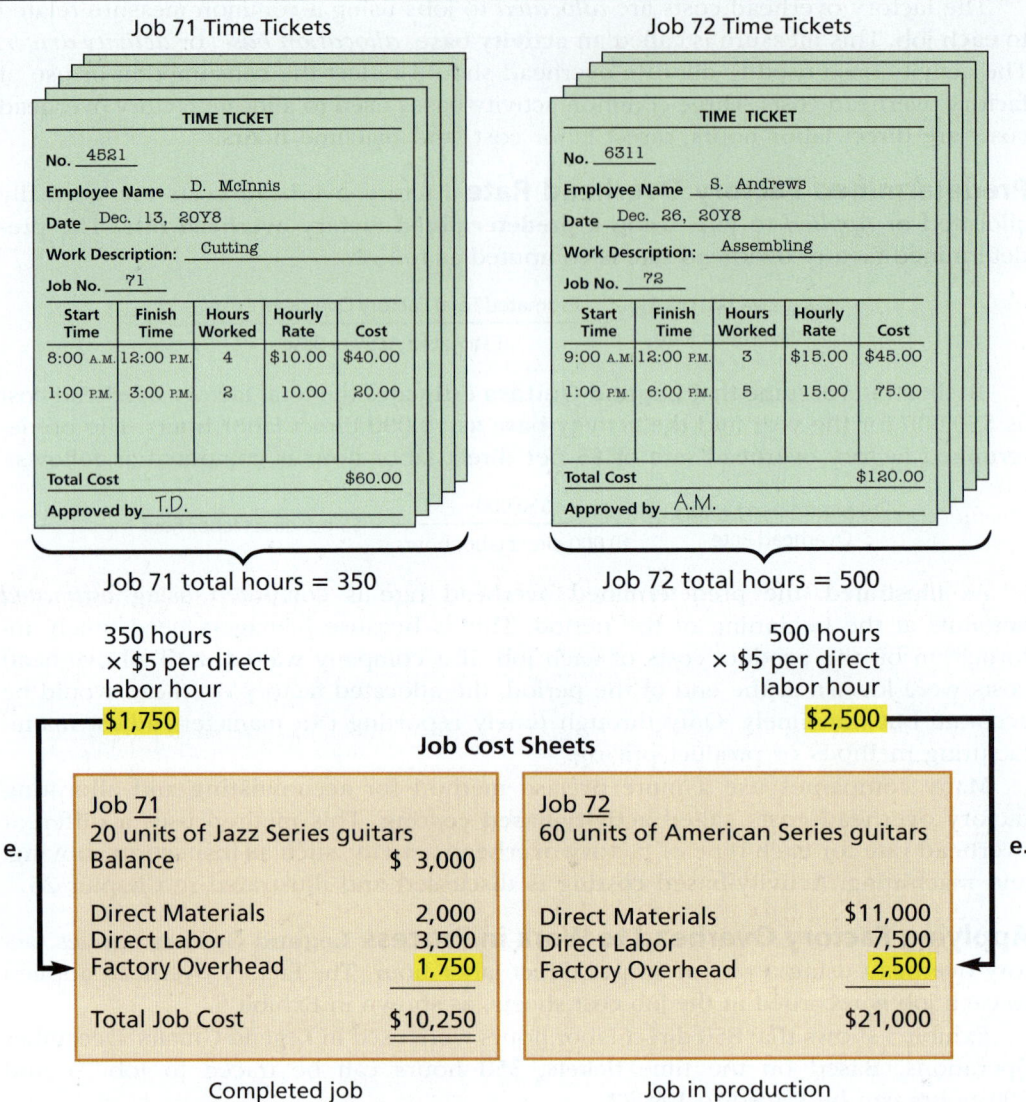

To summarize, the factory overhead account is:

- Increased (debited) for the *actual overhead* costs incurred, as shown for transaction (d).
- Decreased (credited) for the *applied overhead*, as shown for transaction (e).

The actual and applied overhead usually differ because the actual overhead costs are normally different from the estimated overhead costs. Depending on whether actual overhead is greater or less than applied overhead, the factory overhead account will have either a debit or credit ending balance as follows:

- If the applied overhead is *less than* the actual overhead incurred, the factory overhead account will have a debit balance. This debit balance is called **underapplied factory overhead** or *underabsorbed factory overhead*.
- If the applied overhead is *more than* the actual overhead incurred, the factory overhead account will have a credit balance. This credit balance is called **overapplied factory overhead** or *overabsorbed factory overhead*.

The factory overhead account for Legend Guitars, which follows, illustrates both underapplied and overapplied factory overhead. Specifically, the December 1, 20Y8, credit balance of $200 represents overapplied factory overhead. In contrast, the December 31, 20Y8, debit balance of $150 represents underapplied factory overhead.

Account Factory Overhead					Account No.		
						Balance	
Date	Item	Post. Ref.	Debit	Credit	Debit	Credit
20Y8 Dec. 1	Balance					200
31	Factory overhead cost incurred		4,600		4,400	
31	Factory overhead cost applied			4,250	150	

Underapplied balance ⟶ (150)
Overapplied balance ⟶ (200)

If the balance of factory overhead (either underapplied or overapplied) becomes large, the balance and related overhead rate should be investigated. For example, a large balance could be caused by changes in manufacturing methods. In this case, the factory overhead rate should be revised.

Example Exercise 19-4   Applying Factory Overhead   Obj. 2

Hatch Company estimates that total factory overhead costs will be $100,000 for the year. Direct labor hours are estimated to be 25,000. For Hatch Company, (a) determine the predetermined factory overhead rate using direct labor hours as the activity base, (b) determine the amount of factory overhead applied to Jobs 101 and 102 in March using the data on direct labor hours from Example Exercise 19-2, and (c) prepare the journal entry to apply factory overhead to both jobs in March according to the predetermined overhead rate.

Follow My Example 19-4

a. $4.00 per direct labor hour = $100,000 ÷ 25,000 direct labor hours

b. Job 101 $3,200 = 800 hours × $4.00 per hour
    Job 102   2,400 = 600 hours × $4.00 per hour
    Total $5,600

c. Work in Process 5,600
        Factory Overhead   5,600

Practice Exercises: PE 19-4A, PE 19-4B

Disposal of Factory Overhead Balance During the year, the balance in the factory overhead account is carried forward and reported as a deferred debit or credit on the monthly (interim) balance sheets. However, any balance in the factory overhead account should not be carried over to the next year. This is because any such balance applies only to operations of the current year.

If the estimates for computing the predetermined overhead rate are reasonably accurate, the ending balance of Factory Overhead should be relatively small. For this reason, the balance of Factory Overhead at the end of the year is disposed of by transferring it to the cost of goods sold account as follows:[3]

- If there is an ending debit balance (underapplied overhead) in the factory overhead account, it is disposed of by the entry that follows:

		Cost of Goods Sold		XXX	
		Factory Overhead			XXX
		Transfer of underapplied overhead to cost of goods sold.			

Link to Gibson Guitars

Gibson incurs a variety of overhead costs in making guitars, including depreciation on buildings and equipment.

[3] An ending balance in the factory overhead account may also be allocated among the work in process, finished goods, and cost of goods sold accounts. This brings these accounts into agreement with the actual costs incurred. This approach is rarely used and is only required for large ending balances in the factory overhead account. For this reason, it will not be used in this text.

936 Chapter 19 Job Order Costing

- If there is an ending credit balance (overapplied overhead) in the factory overhead account, it is disposed of by the entry that follows:

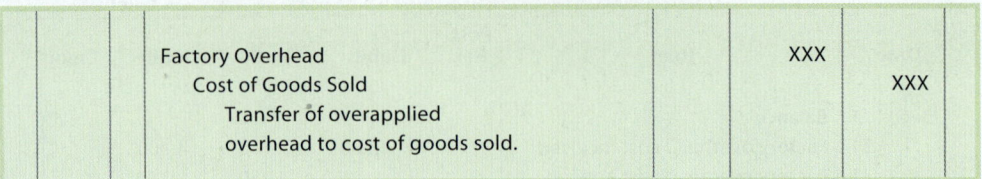

To illustrate, the journal entry to dispose of Legend Guitars' December 31, 20Y8, underapplied overhead balance of $150 is as follows:

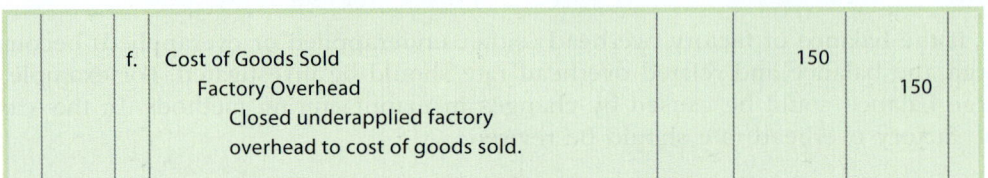

Work in Process

During the period, Work in Process is increased (debited) for the following:

- Direct materials cost
- Direct labor cost
- Applied factory overhead cost

To illustrate, the work in process account for Legend Guitars is shown in Exhibit 6. The balance of Work in Process on December 1, 20Y8 (beginning balance), was $3,000.

EXHIBIT 6

Job Cost Sheets and the Work in Process Controlling Account

Job Cost Sheets

Job 71
20 units of Jazz Series guitars

Balance	$ 3,000
Direct Materials	2,000
Direct Labor	3,500
Factory Overhead	1,750
Total Job Cost	$10,250
Unit Cost	$512.50

Job 72
60 units of American Series guitars

Direct Materials	$11,000
Direct Labor	7,500
Factory Overhead	2,500
Total Job Cost	$21,000

Account Work in Process   Account No.

Date		Item	Post. Ref.	Debit	Credit	Balance Debit	Balance Credit
20Y8 Dec.	1	Balance				3,000	
	31	Direct materials		13,000		16,000	
	31	Direct labor		11,000		27,000	
	31	Factory overhead		4,250		31,250	
	31	Jobs completed—Job 71			10,250	21,000	

g.

As shown in Exhibit 6, this balance relates to Job 71, which was the only job in process on this date. During December, Work in Process was debited for the following:

- Direct materials cost of $13,000 [transaction (b)] based on materials requisitions
- Direct labor cost of $11,000 [transaction (c)] based on time tickets
- Applied factory overhead of $4,250 [transaction (e)] based on the predetermined overhead rate of $5 per direct labor hour

The preceding Work in Process debits are supported by the detail postings to job cost sheets for Jobs 71 and 72, as shown in Exhibit 6.

During December, Job 71 was completed. Upon completion, the product costs (direct materials, direct labor, factory overhead) are totaled. This total is divided by the number of units produced to determine the cost per unit. Thus, the 20 Jazz Series guitars produced as Job 71 cost $512.50 ($10,250 ÷ 20) per guitar.

After completion, Job 71 is transferred from Work in Process to Finished Goods by the following entry:

g.	Finished Goods		10,250	
	Work in Process			10,250
	Job 71 completed in December.			

Job 72 was started in December but was not completed by December 31, 20Y8. Thus, Job 72 is still part of work in process on December 31, 20Y8. As shown in Exhibit 6, the balance of the job cost sheet for Job 72 ($21,000) is also the December 31, 20Y8, balance of Work in Process.

Example Exercise 19-5 Job Costs   Obj. 2

At the end of March, Hatch Company had completed Jobs 101 and 102. Job 101 is for 500 units, and Job 102 is for 1,000 units. Using the data from Example Exercises 19-1, 19-2, and 19-4, determine (a) the balance on the job cost sheets for Jobs 101 and 102 at the end of March and (b) the cost per unit for Jobs 101 and 102 at the end of March.

Follow My Example 19-5

a.
	Job 101	Job 102
Direct materials	$ 2,400	$ 4,200
Direct labor	12,800	7,200
Factory overhead	3,200	2,400
Total costs	$18,400	$13,800

b. Job 101 $36.80 = $18,400 ÷ 500 units
   Job 102 $13.80 = $13,800 ÷ 1,000 units

Practice Exercises: PE 19-5A, PE 19-5B

Finished Goods

The finished goods account is a controlling account for the subsidiary **finished goods ledger** or *stock ledger*. Each account in the finished goods ledger contains cost data for the units manufactured, units sold, and units on hand.

Exhibit 7 illustrates the finished goods ledger account for Legend Guitars' Jazz Series guitars.

Exhibit 7 indicates that 40 Jazz Series guitars were on hand on December 1, 20Y8. During the month, 20 additional Jazz guitars were completed and transferred to Finished Goods from the completion of Job 71. In addition, the beginning inventory of 40 Jazz guitars was sold during the month.

EXHIBIT 7

Finished Goods Ledger Account

ITEM: *Jazz Series guitars*

Manufactured			Shipped			Balance			
Job Order No.	Quantity	Amount	Ship Order No.	Quantity	Amount	Date	Quantity	Amount	Unit Cost
			643	40	$20,000	Dec. 1	40	$20,000	$500.00
						9	—	—	—
71	20	$10,250				31	20	10,250	512.50

Sales and Cost of Goods Sold

During December, **Legend Guitars** sold 40 Jazz Series guitars for $850 each, generating total sales of $34,000 ($850 × 40 guitars). Exhibit 7 indicates that the cost of these guitars was $500 per guitar, or a total cost of $20,000 ($500 × 40 guitars). The entries to record the sale and related cost of goods sold are as follows:

h.	Accounts Receivable		34,000	
	Sales			34,000
	Revenue received from guitars sold on account.			

i.	Cost of Goods Sold		20,000	
	Finished Goods			20,000
	Cost of 40 Jazz Series guitars sold.			

In a job order cost accounting system, the preparation of a statement of cost of goods manufactured, which was discussed in Chapter 18, is not necessary. This is because job order costing uses the perpetual inventory system; thus, the cost of goods sold can be determined directly from the finished goods ledger as illustrated in Exhibit 7.

Period Costs

Period costs are used in generating revenue during the current period but are not involved in the manufacturing process. As discussed in Chapter 18, *period costs* are recorded as expenses of the current period as either selling or administrative expenses.

Selling expenses are incurred in marketing the product and delivering sold products to customers. Administrative expenses are incurred in managing the company but are not related to the manufacturing or selling functions. During December, **Legend Guitars** recorded the following selling and administrative expenses:

j.	Sales Salaries Expense		2,000	
	Office Salaries Expense		1,500	
	Salaries Payable			3,500
	Recorded December period costs.			

Summary of Cost Flows for Legend Guitars

Exhibit 8 shows the cost flows through the manufacturing accounts of **Legend Guitars** for December. In addition, summary details of the following subsidiary ledgers are shown:

- *Materials Ledger*—the subsidiary ledger for Materials

Link to Gibson Guitars

A virtual tour of **Gibson**'s Bozeman, Montana, manufacturing plant can be found at www2.gibson.com. The Bozeman plant makes acoustical guitars similar to those illustrated in this chapter. Acoustical guitars that do not require power or amps to produce sound are often used for folk and country music. Electric guitars are most often used for heavy metal and rock music.

Chapter 19 Job Order Costing 939

EXHIBIT 8 Flow of Manufacturing Costs for Legend Guitars

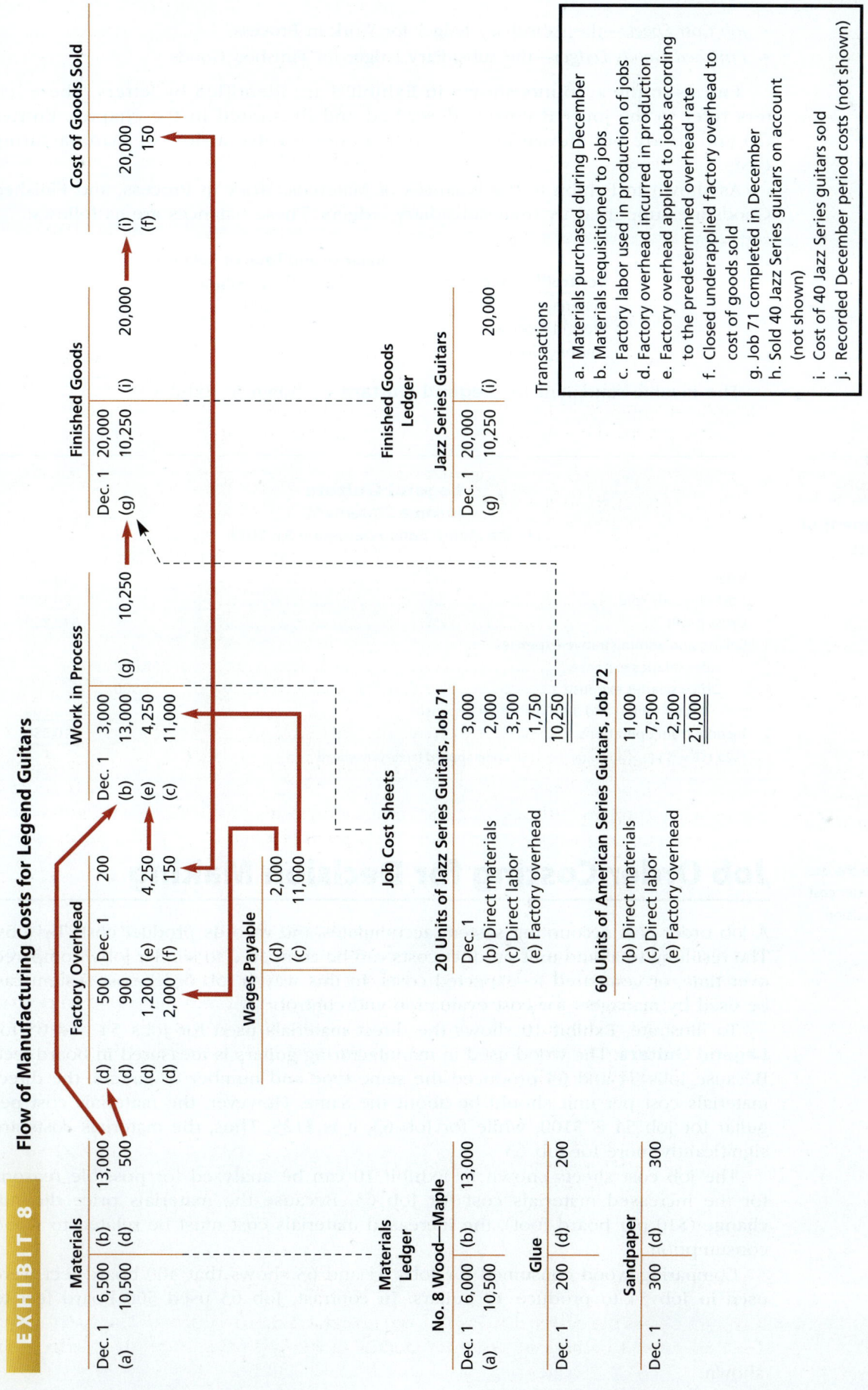

- *Job Cost Sheets*—the subsidiary ledger for Work in Process
- *Finished Goods Ledger*—the subsidiary ledger for Finished Goods

Entries in the accounts shown in Exhibit 8 are identified by letters. These letters refer to the journal entries described and illustrated in the chapter. Entries (h) and (j) are not shown because they do not involve a flow of manufacturing costs.

As shown in Exhibit 8, the balances of Materials, Work in Process, and Finished Goods are supported by their subsidiary ledgers. These balances are as follows:

Controlling Account	Balance and Total of Related Subsidiary Ledger
Materials	$ 3,500
Work in Process	21,000
Finished Goods	10,250

The income statement for **Legend Guitars** is shown in Exhibit 9.

EXHIBIT 9
Income Statement of Legend Guitars

Legend Guitars
Income Statement
For the Month Ended December 31, 20Y8

Sales		$34,000
Cost of goods sold		20,150*
Gross profit		$13,850
Selling and administrative expenses:		
Sales salaries expense	$2,000	
Office salaries expense	1,500	
Total selling and administrative expenses		3,500
Income from operations		$10,350

*$20,150 = ($500 × 40 guitars) + $150 underapplied factory overhead

Job Order Costing for Decision Making

Obj. 3 Describe the use of job order cost information for decision making.

A job order cost accounting system accumulates and records product costs by jobs. The resulting total and unit product costs can be compared to similar jobs, compared over time, or compared to expected costs. In this way, a job order cost system can be used by managers for cost evaluation and control.

To illustrate, Exhibit 10 shows the direct materials used for Jobs 54 and 63 for **Legend Guitars**. The wood used in manufacturing guitars is measured in board feet. Because Jobs 54 and 63 produced the same type and number of guitars, the direct materials cost per unit should be about the same. However, the materials cost per guitar for Job 54 is $100, while for Job 63, it is $125. Thus, the materials costs are significantly more for Job 63.

The job cost sheets shown in Exhibit 10 can be analyzed for possible reasons for the increased materials cost for Job 63. Because the materials price did not change ($10 per board foot), the increased materials cost must be related to wood consumption.

Comparing wood consumed for Jobs 54 and 63 shows that 400 board feet were used in Job 54 to produce 40 guitars. In contrast, Job 63 used 500 board feet to

> **EXHIBIT 10**
>
> Comparing Data from Job Cost Sheets

Job 54
Item: 40 Jazz Series guitars

	Materials Quantity (board feet)	Materials Price	Materials Amount
Direct materials:			
No. 8 Wood—Maple	400	$10.00	$4,000
Direct materials per guitar			$ 100*

*$4,000 ÷ 40

Job 63
Item: 40 Jazz Series guitars

	Materials Quantity (board feet)	Materials Price	Materials Amount
Direct materials:			
No. 8 Wood—Maple	500	$10.00	$5,000
Direct materials per guitar			$ 125*

*$5,000 ÷ 40

produce the same number of guitars. Thus, an investigation should be undertaken to determine the cause of the extra 100 board feet used for Job 63. Possible explanations could include the following:

- A new employee who was not properly trained cut the wood for Job 63. As a result, there was excess waste and scrap.
- The wood used for Job 63 was purchased from a new supplier. The wood was of poor quality, which created excessive waste and scrap.
- The cutting tools needed repair and were not properly maintained. As a result, the wood was miscut, which created excessive waste and scrap.
- The instructions attached to the job were incorrect. The wood was cut according to the instructions. The incorrect instructions were discovered later in assembly. As a result, the wood had to be recut and the initial cuttings scrapped.

Job Order Cost Systems for Service Businesses

Obj. 4 Describe job order cost accounting systems for service businesses.

A job order cost accounting system may be used by a service business. However, whether a service business uses a job order cost system depends upon the nature of the service provided to customers.

Types of Service Businesses

Hotels, taxis, newspapers, attorneys, accountants, and hospitals provide services to customers. Some of these businesses, such as law firms, accounting firms, and hospitals, rely on job order costing to manage and control costs. However, not all service businesses are able to practically apply job order costing. These include businesses such as hotels, taxi services, and newspapers.

A service business using job order costing normally renders a service that is unique to each customer with related costs that vary significantly with each customer. For example, while hotels provide a service, the service is the same for each guest on any given night.

In contrast, an attorney or a hospital provides a unique service for each client or patient. In addition, each client or patient incurs costs that are unique to him or her. For this reason, law firms and hospitals normally use job order cost systems.[4] Other examples of service businesses using job order cost systems include advertising agencies, event planners, and car repair shops.

Flow of Costs in a Service Job Order Cost System

A service business using a job order cost system views each customer, client, or patient as a separate job for which costs are accumulated and reported.

Since a service is being provided, the primary product costs are normally direct labor and overhead. Any materials or supplies used in rendering services are usually insignificant. As a result, materials and supply costs may be included as part of the overhead cost.

Like a manufacturing business, the direct labor and overhead costs of rendering services to clients are accumulated in a work in process account. Work in Process is supported by a cost ledger with a job cost sheet for each client.

When a job is completed and the client is billed, the costs are transferred to a cost of services account. Cost of Services is similar to the cost of goods sold account for a merchandising or manufacturing business. A finished goods account and related finished goods ledger are not necessary. This is because services cannot be inventoried and the revenues for the services are recorded upon completion.

In practice, other considerations unique to service businesses may need to be considered. For example, a service business may bill clients on a weekly or monthly basis rather than upon completion of a job. In such cases, a portion of the costs related to each billing is transferred from the work in process account to the cost of services account. A service business may also bill clients for services in advance, which would be accounted for as deferred revenue until the services are completed.

The flow of costs through a service business using a job order cost accounting system is shown in Exhibit 11.

EXHIBIT 11 — Flow of Costs Through a Service Business

Wages Payable		Work in Process		Cost of Services
Paid XXX	Direct labor XXX →	XXX	Completed jobs XXX →	XXX
	Indirect labor XXX	XXX		

Supplies		Overhead	
Purchased XXX	Used XXX	XXX	Applied XXX
		XXX	
		Other costs XXX	

[4] Service businesses using job order cost systems normally require each customer, client, or patient to sign a contract that describes the nature of the service being rendered.

SERVICE FOCUS

JOB ORDER COSTING IN A LAW FIRM

Law firms typically use job order costing to track the costs of individual legal cases or client engagements. The costs of each job are accumulated in a job cost sheet, just as in a manufacturing firm. However, because a law firm is a service firm, there are no direct materials costs. The primary cost comes from the direct labor of the professional staff.

Law firms like **Constangy, Brooks, Smith & Prophete**, a national law firm specializing in employment law and labor relations, uses a job order costing system to track the cost of individual cases. The direct labor costs of the professional staff are determined by multiplying the time that each attorney spends on an individual case by the attorney's hourly billing rate. Billing rates vary depending on the rank of the attorney doing the work. In addition, any costs that can be attributed directly to a specific engagement are added to the engagement's job cost sheet. For example, if a case requires the legal team to travel to another city to interview witnesses, the cost of that travel is added to the job cost sheet for that specific client. Indirect costs such as support staff, office supplies, and office rent are accumulated as overhead costs and allocated to individual jobs using an activity base such as professional service hours.

At a Glance 19

Obj. 1 Describe cost accounting systems used by manufacturing businesses.

Key Points A cost accounting system accumulates product costs. The two primary cost accounting systems are the job order and the process cost systems. Job order cost systems accumulate costs for each quantity of product that passes through the factory. Process cost systems accumulate costs for each department or process within the factory.

Learning Outcomes	Example Exercises	Practice Exercises
• Describe a cost accounting system.		
• Describe a job order cost system.		
• Describe a process cost system.		

Chapter 19 Job Order Costing

Obj. 2 Describe and illustrate a job order cost accounting system.

Key Points A job order cost system accumulates costs for each quantity of product, or "job," that passes through the factory. Direct materials, direct labor, and factory overhead are accumulated on the job cost sheet, which is the subsidiary cost ledger for each job. Direct materials and direct labor are assigned to individual jobs based on the quantity used. Factory overhead costs are assigned to each job based on an activity base that reflects the use of factory overhead costs.

Learning Outcomes	Example Exercises	Practice Exercises
• Describe the flow of materials and how materials costs are assigned.		
• Prepare the journal entry to record materials used in production.	EE19-1	PE19-1A, 19-1B
• Describe how factory labor hours are recorded and how labor costs are assigned.		
• Prepare the journal entry to record factory labor used in production.	EE19-2	PE19-2A, 19-2B
• Describe and illustrate how factory overhead costs are accumulated and assigned.	EE19-3 EE19-4	PE19-3A, 19-3B PE19-4A, 19-4B
• Compute the predetermined overhead rate.	EE19-4	PE19-4A, 19-4B
• Describe and illustrate how to dispose of the balance in the factory overhead account.		
• Describe and illustrate how costs are accumulated for work in process and finished goods inventories.	EE19-5	PE19-5A, 19-5B
• Describe how costs are assigned to the cost of goods sold.	EE19-6	PE19-6A, 19-6B
• Describe and illustrate the flow of costs.		

Obj. 3 Describe the use of job order cost information for decision making.

Key Points Job order cost systems can be used to evaluate cost performance. Unit costs can be compared over time to determine whether product costs are staying within expected ranges.

Learning Outcome	Example Exercises	Practice Exercises
• Describe and illustrate how job cost sheets can be used to investigate possible reasons for increased product costs.		

Obj. 4 Describe job order cost accounting systems for service businesses.

Key Points Job order cost accounting systems can be used by service businesses to plan and control operations. Because the product is a service, the focus is on direct labor and overhead costs. The costs of providing a service are accumulated in a work in process account and transferred to a cost of services account upon completion.

Learning Outcome	Example Exercises	Practice Exercises
• Describe how service businesses use a job order cost system.		

Illustrative Problem

Wildwing Entertainment Inc. is a manufacturer that uses a job order cost system. The following data summarize the operations related to production for March, the first month of operations:

a. Materials purchased on account, $15,500.

b. Materials requisitioned and labor used:

	Materials	Factory Labor
Job No. 100	$2,650	$1,770
Job No. 101	1,240	650
Job No. 102	980	420
Job No. 103	3,420	1,900
Job No. 104	1,000	500
Job No. 105	2,100	1,760
For general factory use	450	650

c. Factory overhead costs incurred on account, $2,700.

d. Depreciation of machinery, $1,750.

e. Factory overhead is applied at a rate of 70% of direct labor cost.

f. Jobs completed: Nos. 100, 101, 102, 104.

g. Jobs 100, 101, and 102 were shipped, and customers were billed for $8,100, $3,800, and $3,500, respectively.

Instructions

1. Journalize the entries to record these transactions.
2. Determine the account balances for Work in Process and Finished Goods.
3. Prepare a schedule of unfinished jobs to support the balance in the work in process account.
4. Prepare a schedule of completed jobs on hand to support the balance in the finished goods account.

Solution

1.
a. Materials 15,500
　　Accounts Payable 15,500
b. Work in Process 11,390
　　Materials 11,390
　Work in Process 7,000
　　Wages Payable 7,000
　Factory Overhead 1,100
　　Materials 450
　　Wages Payable 650
c. Factory Overhead 2,700
　　Accounts Payable 2,700
d. Factory Overhead 1,750
　　Accumulated Depreciation—Machinery ... 1,750
e. Work in Process 4,900
　　Factory Overhead (70% of $7,000) ... 4,900
f. Finished Goods 11,548
　　Work in Process 11,548

(Continued)

Computation of the cost of jobs finished:

Job	Direct Materials	Direct Labor	Factory Overhead	Total
Job No. 100	$2,650	$1,770	$1,239	$ 5,659
Job No. 101	1,240	650	455	2,345
Job No. 102	980	420	294	1,694
Job No. 104	1,000	500	350	1,850
				$11,548

g. Accounts Receivable   15,400
    Sales   15,400
    Cost of Goods Sold   9,698
        Finished Goods   9,698

Cost of jobs sold computation:

Job No. 100	$5,659
Job No. 101	2,345
Job No. 102	1,694
	$9,698

2. Work in Process: $11,742 ($11,390 + $7,000 + $4,900 − $11,548)

   Finished Goods: $1,850 ($11,548 − $9,698)

3. **Schedule of Unfinished Jobs**

Job	Direct Materials	Direct Labor	Factory Overhead	Total
Job No. 103	$3,420	$1,900	$1,330	$ 6,650
Job No. 105	2,100	1,760	1,232	5,092
Balance of Work in Process, March 31				$11,742

4. **Schedule of Completed Jobs**

   Job No. 104:
Direct materials	$1,000
Direct labor	500
Factory overhead	350
Balance of Finished Goods, March 31	$1,850

Key Terms

activity base (933)
activity-based costing (933)
cost accounting systems (926)
cost allocation (932)
finished goods ledger (937)
job cost sheets (929)

job order cost system (926)
materials ledger (927)
materials requisition (928)
overapplied factory overhead (934)
predetermined factory overhead rate (933)

process cost system (926)
receiving report (928)
time tickets (930)
underapplied factory overhead (934)

Discussion Questions

1. a. Name two principal types of cost accounting systems.
   b. Which system provides for a separate record of each particular quantity of product that passes through the factory?
   c. Which system accumulates the costs for each department or process within the factory?
2. What kind of firm would use a job order cost system?
3. Which account is used in the job order cost system to accumulate direct materials, direct labor, and factory overhead applied to production costs for individual jobs?
4. What document is the source for (a) debiting the accounts in the materials ledger and (b) crediting the accounts in the materials ledger?
5. What is a job cost sheet?
6. What is the difference between a clock card and time ticket?
7. Discuss how the predetermined factory overhead rate can be used in job order cost accounting to assist management in pricing jobs.
8. a. How is a predetermined factory overhead rate calculated?
   b. Name three common bases used in calculating the rate.
9. a. What is (1) overapplied factory overhead and (2) underapplied factory overhead?
   b. If the factory overhead account has a debit balance, was factory overhead underapplied or overapplied?
10. Describe how a job order cost system can be used for professional service businesses.

Practice Exercises

Example Exercises

EE 19-1 *p. 929*   **PE 19-1A**   **Issuance of materials**   OBJ. 2

On May 7, Bergan Company purchased on account 10,000 units of raw materials at $8 per unit. During May, raw materials were requisitioned for production as follows: 7,500 units for Job 200 at $8 per unit and 1,480 units for Job 305 at $5 per unit. Journalize the entry on May 7 to record the purchase and on May 31 to record the requisition from the materials storeroom.

EE 19-1 *p. 929*   **PE 19-1B**   **Issuance of materials**   OBJ. 2

On August 4, Rothchild Company purchased on account 12,000 units of raw materials at $14 per unit. During August, raw materials were requisitioned for production as follows: 5,000 units for Job 40 at $8 per unit and 6,200 units for Job 42 at $14 per unit. Journalize the entry on August 4 to record the purchase and on August 31 to record the requisition from the materials storeroom.

EE 19-2 *p. 931*   **PE 19-2A**   **Direct labor costs**   OBJ. 2

During May, Bergan Company accumulated 2,500 hours of direct labor costs on Job 200 and 3,000 hours on Job 305. The total direct labor was incurred at a rate of $28 per direct labor hour for Job 200 and $24 per direct labor hour for Job 305. Journalize the entry to record the flow of labor costs into production during May.

948 Chapter 19 Job Order Costing

PE 19-2B Direct labor costs OBJ. 2

During August, Rothchild Company accumulated 3,500 hours of direct labor costs on Job 40 and 4,200 hours on Job 42. The total direct labor was incurred at a rate of $25.00 per direct labor hour for Job 40 and $23.50 per direct labor hour for Job 42. Journalize the entry to record the flow of labor costs into production during August.

EE 19-2 *p. 931*

PE 19-3A Factory overhead costs OBJ. 2

During May, Bergan Company incurred factory overhead costs as follows: indirect materials, $8,800; indirect labor, $6,600; utilities cost, $4,800; and factory depreciation, $9,000. Journalize the entry to record the factory overhead incurred during May.

EE 19-3 *p. 932*

PE 19-3B Factory overhead costs OBJ. 2

During August, Rothchild Company incurred factory overhead costs as follows: indirect materials, $17,500; indirect labor, $22,000; utilities cost, $9,600; and factory depreciation, $17,500. Journalize the entry to record the factory overhead incurred during August.

EE 19-3 *p. 932*

PE 19-4A Applying factory overhead OBJ. 2

Bergan Company estimates that total factory overhead costs will be $620,000 for the year. Direct labor hours are estimated to be 80,000. For Bergan Company, (a) determine the predetermined factory overhead rate using direct labor hours as the activity base, (b) determine the amount of factory overhead applied to Jobs 200 and 305 in May using the data on direct labor hours from Practice Exercise 19-2A, and (c) prepare the journal entry to apply factory overhead to both jobs in May according to the predetermined overhead rate.

EE 19-4 *p. 935*

PE 19-4B Applying factory overhead OBJ. 2

Rothchild Company estimates that total factory overhead costs will be $810,000 for the year. Direct labor hours are estimated to be 90,000. For Rothchild Company, (a) determine the predetermined factory overhead rate using direct labor hours as the activity base, (b) determine the amount of factory overhead applied to Jobs 40 and 42 in August using the data on direct labor hours from Practice Exercise 19-2B, and (c) prepare the journal entry to apply factory overhead to both jobs in August according to the predetermined overhead rate.

EE 19-4 *p. 935*

PE 19-5A Job costs OBJ. 2

At the end of May, Bergan Company had completed Jobs 200 and 305. Job 200 is for 2,390 units, and Job 305 is for 2,053 units. Using the data from Practice Exercises 19-1A, 19-2A, and 19-4A, determine (a) the balance on the job cost sheets for Jobs 200 and 305 at the end of May and (b) the cost per unit for Jobs 200 and 305 at the end of May.

EE 19-5 *p. 937*

PE 19-5B Job costs OBJ. 2

At the end of August, Rothchild Company had completed Jobs 40 and 42. Job 40 is for 10,000 units, and Job 42 is for 11,000 units. Using the data from Practice Exercises 19-1B, 19-2B, and 19-4B, determine (a) the balance on the job cost sheets for Jobs 40 and 42 at the end of August and (b) the cost per unit for Jobs 40 and 42 at the end of August.

EE 19-5 *p. 937*

Exercises

EX 19-1 Transactions in a job order cost system   OBJ. 2

Five selected transactions for the current month are indicated by letters in the following T accounts in a job order cost accounting system:

Materials		Work in Process	
(a)		(a)	(d)
		(b)	
		(c)	

Wages Payable		Finished Goods	
	(b)	(d)	(e)

Factory Overhead		Cost of Goods Sold	
(a)	(c)	(e)	
(b)			

Describe each of the five transactions.

EX 19-2 Cost of materials issuances under the FIFO method   OBJ. 2

✔ b. $2,280

An incomplete subsidiary ledger of materials inventory for May is as follows:

RECEIVED			ISSUED			BALANCE		
Receiving Report Number	Quantity	Unit Price	Materials Requisition Number	Quantity	Amount	Date	Quantity	Unit Price	Amount
						May 1	285	$30.00	$8,550
40	130	$32.00				May 4	___	___	___
			91	365		May 10	___	___	___
44	110	38.00				May 21	___	___	___
			97	100		May 27	___	___	___

a. Complete the materials issuances and balances for the materials subsidiary ledger under FIFO.
b. Determine the materials inventory balance at the end of May.
c. Journalize the summary entry to transfer materials to work in process.
d. Explain how the materials ledger might be used as an aid in maintaining inventory quantities on hand.

EX 19-3 Entry for issuing materials   OBJ. 2

Materials issued for the current month are as follows:

Requisition No.	Material	Job No.	Amount
103	Plastic	400	$ 2,800
104	Steel	402	24,000
105	Glue	Indirect	1,620
106	Rubber	403	3,200
107	Titanium	404	31,600

Journalize the entry to record the issuance of materials.

950 Chapter 19 Job Order Costing

✓ c. Fabric, $35,500

EX 19-4 Entries for materials
OBJ. 2

GenX Furnishings manufactures designer furniture. GenX Furnishings uses a job order cost system. Balances on June 1 from the materials ledger are as follows:

Fabric	$40,500
Polyester filling	28,600
Lumber	62,400
Glue	6,550

The materials purchased during June are summarized from the receiving reports as follows:

Fabric	$440,000
Polyester filling	180,000
Lumber	360,000
Glue	40,000

Materials were requisitioned to individual jobs as follows:

	Fabric	Polyester Filling	Lumber	Glue	Total
Job 601	$205,000	$ 75,000	$120,000		$400,000
Job 602	110,000	36,000	88,000		234,000
Job 603	130,000	55,000	125,000		310,000
Factory overhead—indirect materials				$34,800	34,800
Total	$445,000	$166,000	$333,000	$34,800	$978,800

The glue is not a significant cost, so it is treated as indirect materials (factory overhead).

a. Journalize the entry to record the purchase of materials in June.
b. Journalize the entry to record the requisition of materials in June.
c. Determine the June 30 balances that would be shown in the materials ledger accounts.

EX 19-5 Entry for factory labor costs
OBJ. 2

A summary of the time tickets for the current month follows:

Job No.	Amount	Job No.	Amount
100	$ 3,500	Indirect	$ 9,100
101	6,650	111	8,620
104	21,900	115	2,760
108	14,440	117	18,550

Journalize the entry to record the factory labor costs.

EX 19-6 Entry for factory labor costs
OBJ. 2

The weekly time tickets indicate the following distribution of labor hours for three direct labor employees:

	Hours			
	Job 301	Job 302	Job 303	Process Improvement
Tom Couro	10	15	13	2
David Clancy	12	12	14	2
Jose Cano	11	13	15	1

The direct labor rate earned per hour by the three employees is as follows:

Tom Couro	$32
David Clancy	36
Jose Cano	28

The process improvement category includes training, quality improvement, and other indirect tasks.

a. Journalize the entry to record the factory labor costs for the week.
b. Assume that Jobs 301 and 302 were completed but not sold during the week and that Job 303 remained incomplete at the end of the week. How would the direct labor costs for all three jobs be reflected on the financial statements at the end of the week?

EX 19-7 Entries for direct labor and factory overhead OBJ. 2

Townsend Industries Inc. manufactures recreational vehicles. Townsend uses a job order cost system. The time tickets from November jobs are summarized as follows:

Job 201	$6,240
Job 202	7,000
Job 203	5,210
Job 204	6,750
Factory supervision	4,000

Factory overhead is applied to jobs on the basis of a predetermined overhead rate of $18 per direct labor hour. The direct labor rate is $40 per hour.

a. Journalize the entry to record the factory labor costs.
b. Journalize the entry to apply factory overhead to production for November.

EX 19-8 Factory overhead rates, entries, and account balance OBJ. 2

✔ b. $40.80 per direct labor hour

Sundance Solar Company operates two factories. The company applies factory overhead to jobs on the basis of machine hours in Factory 1 and on the basis of direct labor hours in Factory 2. Estimated factory overhead costs, direct labor hours, and machine hours are as follows:

	Factory 1	Factory 2
Estimated factory overhead cost for fiscal year beginning March 1	$12,900,000	$10,200,000
Estimated direct labor hours for year		250,000
Estimated machine hours for year	600,000	
Actual factory overhead costs for March	$12,990,000	$10,090,000
Actual direct labor hours for March		245,000
Actual machine hours for March	610,000	

a. Determine the factory overhead rate for Factory 1.
b. Determine the factory overhead rate for Factory 2.
c. Journalize the entries to apply factory overhead to production in each factory for March.
d. Determine the balances of the factory overhead accounts for each factory as of March 31 and indicate whether the amounts represent over- or underapplied factory overhead.

952 Chapter 19 Job Order Costing

EX 19-9 Predetermined factory overhead rate   OBJ. 2

Street Runner Engine Shop uses a job order cost system to determine the cost of performing engine repair work. Estimated costs and expenses for the coming period are as follows:

Engine parts	$ 740,000
Shop direct labor	500,000
Shop and repair equipment depreciation	40,000
Shop supervisor salaries	133,000
Shop property taxes	22,000
Shop supplies	10,000
Advertising expense	20,000
Administrative office salaries	71,400
Administrative office depreciation expense	6,000
Total costs and expenses	$1,542,400

The average shop direct labor rate is $20 per hour.

Determine the predetermined shop overhead rate per direct labor hour.

EX 19-10 Predetermined factory overhead rate   OBJ. 2

✓ a. $290 per hour

Poehling Medical Center has a single operating room that is used by local physicians to perform surgical procedures. The cost of using the operating room is accumulated by each patient procedure and includes the direct materials costs (drugs and medical devices), physician surgical time, and operating room overhead. On January 1 of the current year, the annual operating room overhead is estimated to be:

Disposable supplies	$299,600
Depreciation expense	75,000
Utilities	32,000
Nurse salaries	278,500
Technician wages	126,900
Total operating room overhead	$812,000

The overhead costs will be assigned to procedures based on the number of surgical room hours. Poehling Medical Center expects to use the operating room an average of eight hours per day, seven days per week. In addition, the operating room will be shut down two weeks per year for general repairs.

a. Calculate the estimated number of operating room hours for the year.
b. Determine the predetermined operating room overhead rate for the year.
c. Bill Harris had a five-hour procedure on January 22. How much operating room overhead would be charged to his procedure, using the rate determined in part (b)?
d. During January, the operating room was used 240 hours. The actual overhead costs incurred for January were $67,250. Determine the overhead under- or overapplied for the period.

EX 19-11 Entry for jobs completed; cost of unfinished jobs   OBJ. 2

✓ b. $62,200

The following account appears in the ledger prior to recognizing the jobs completed in January:

Work in Process

Balance, January 1	$ 72,000
Direct materials	390,000
Direct labor	500,000
Factory overhead	250,000

Jobs finished during January are summarized as follows:

| Job 210 | $200,000 | Job 224 | $225,000 |
| Job 216 | 288,000 | Job 230 | 436,800 |

a. Journalize the entry to record the jobs completed.
b. Determine the cost of the unfinished jobs at January 31.

EX 19-12 Entries for factory costs and jobs completed   OBJ. 2

✓ d. $73,750

Old School Publishing Inc. began printing operations on January 1. Jobs 301 and 302 were completed during the month, and all costs applicable to them were recorded on the related cost sheets. Jobs 303 and 304 are still in process at the end of the month, and all applicable costs except factory overhead have been recorded on the related cost sheets. In addition to the materials and labor charged directly to the jobs, $8,000 of indirect materials and $12,400 of indirect labor were used during the month. The cost sheets for the four jobs entering production during the month are as follows, in summary form:

Job 301		Job 302	
Direct materials	$10,000	Direct materials	$20,000
Direct labor	8,000	Direct labor	17,000
Factory overhead	6,000	Factory overhead	12,750
Total	$24,000	Total	$49,750

Job 303		Job 304	
Direct materials	$24,000	Direct materials	$14,000
Direct labor	18,000	Direct labor	12,000
Factory overhead	—	Factory overhead	—

Journalize the summary entry to record each of the following operations for January (one entry for each operation):

a. Direct and indirect materials used
b. Direct and indirect labor used
c. Factory overhead applied to all four jobs (a single overhead rate is used based on direct labor cost)
d. Completion of Jobs 301 and 302

EX 19-13 Financial statements of a manufacturing firm   OBJ. 2

✓ a. Income from operations, $137,200

Excel

The following events took place for Focault Inc. during July 20Y2, the first month of operations as a producer of road bikes:

- Purchased $320,000 of materials
- Used $275,000 of direct materials in production
- Incurred $236,000 of direct labor wages
- Applied factory overhead at a rate of 75% of direct labor cost
- Transferred $652,000 of work in process to finished goods
- Sold goods with a cost of $630,000
- Sold goods for $1,120,000
- Incurred $252,800 of selling expenses
- Incurred $100,000 of administrative expenses

a. Prepare the July income statement for Focault. Assume that Focault uses the perpetual inventory method.
b. Determine the inventory balances at the end of the first month of operations.

EX 19-14 Decision making with job order costs   OBJ. 3

Alvarez Manufacturing Inc. is a job shop. The management of Alvarez Manufacturing Inc. uses the cost information from the job sheets to assess cost performance. Information on the total cost, product type, and quantity of items produced is as follows:

Date	Job No.	Product	Quantity	Amount
Jan. 2	1	TT	520	$16,120
Jan. 15	22	SS	1,610	20,125
Feb. 3	30	SS	1,420	25,560
Mar. 7	41	TT	670	15,075
Mar. 24	49	SLK	2,210	22,100
May 19	58	SLK	2,550	31,875
June 12	65	TT	620	10,540
Aug. 18	78	SLK	3,110	48,205
Sept. 2	82	SS	1,210	16,940
Nov. 14	92	TT	750	8,250
Dec. 12	98	SLK	2,700	52,650

a. Develop a graph for *each* product (three graphs) with Job Number (in date order) on the horizontal axis and Unit Cost on the vertical axis. Use this information to determine Alvarez Manufacturing Inc.'s cost performance over time for the three products.

b. ➤ What additional information would you require in order to investigate Alvarez Manufacturing Inc.'s cost performance more precisely?

EX 19-15 Decision making with job order costs   OBJ. 3

Raneri Trophies Inc. uses a job order cost system for determining the cost to manufacture award products (plaques and trophies). Among the company's products is an engraved plaque that is awarded to participants who complete a training program at a local business. The company sells the plaques to the local business for $80 each.

Each plaque has a brass plate engraved with the name of the participant. Engraving requires approximately 30 minutes per name. Improperly engraved names must be redone. The plate is screwed to a walnut backboard. This assembly takes approximately 15 minutes per unit. Improper assembly must be redone using a new walnut backboard.

During the first half of the year, Raneri had two separate plaque orders. The job cost sheets for the two separate jobs indicated the following information:

Job 101   May 4

	Cost per Unit	Units	Job Cost
Direct materials:			
Wood	$20/unit	40 units	$ 800
Brass	15/unit	40 units	600
Engraving labor	20/hr.	20 hrs.	400
Assembly labor	30/hr.	10 hrs.	300
Factory overhead	10/hr.	30 hrs.	300
			$2,400
Plaques shipped			÷ 40
Cost per plaque			$ 60

Job 105	June 10		
	Cost per Unit	Units	Job Cost
Direct materials:			
Wood	$20/unit	34 units	$ 680
Brass	15/unit	34 units	510
Engraving labor	20/hr.	17 hrs.	340
Assembly labor	30/hr.	8.5 hrs.	255
Factory overhead	10/hr.	25.5 hrs.	255
			$2,040
Plaques shipped			÷ 30
Cost per plaque			$ 68

a. Why did the cost per plaque increase from $60 to $68?

b. What improvements would you recommend for Raneri Trophies Inc.?

EX 19-16 Job order cost accounting for a service company OBJ. 4

✔ b. Underapplied, $5,530

The law firm of Furlan and Benson accumulates costs associated with individual cases, using a job order cost system. The following transactions occurred during July:

July 3. Charged 175 hours of professional (lawyer) time at a rate of $150 per hour to the Obsidian Co. breech of contract suit to prepare for the trial

10. Reimbursed travel costs to employees for depositions related to the Obsidian case, $12,500

14. Charged 260 hours of professional time for the Obsidian trial at a rate of $185 per hour

18. Received invoice from consultants Wadsley and Harden for $30,000 for expert testimony related to the Obsidian trial

27. Applied office overhead at a rate of $62 per professional hour charged to the Obsidian case

31. Paid administrative and support salaries of $28,500 for the month

31. Used office supplies for the month, $4,000

31. Paid professional salaries of $74,350 for the month

31. Billed Obsidian $172,500 for successful defense of the case

a. Provide the journal entries for each of these transactions.

b. How much office overhead is over- or underapplied?

c. Determine the gross profit on the Obsidian case, assuming that over- or underapplied office overhead is closed monthly to cost of services.

EX 19-17 Job order cost accounting for a service company OBJ. 4

✔ d. Dr. Cost of Services, $2,827,750

The Fly Company provides advertising services for clients across the nation. The Fly Company is presently working on four projects, each for a different client. The Fly Company accumulates costs for each account (client) on the basis of both direct costs and allocated indirect costs. The direct costs include the charged time of professional personnel and media purchases (air time and ad space). Overhead is allocated to each project as a percentage of media purchases. The predetermined overhead rate is 65% of media purchases.

On August 1, the four advertising projects had the following accumulated costs:

	August 1 Balances
Vault Bank	$270,000
Take Off Airlines	80,000
Sleepy Tired Hotels	210,000
Tastee Beverages	115,000
Total	$675,000

(Continued)

During August, The Fly Company incurred the following direct labor and media purchase costs related to preparing advertising for each of the four accounts:

	Direct Labor	Media Purchases
Vault Bank	$ 190,000	$ 710,000
Take Off Airlines	85,000	625,000
Sleepy Tired Hotels	372,000	455,000
Tastee Beverages	421,000	340,000
Total	$1,068,000	$2,130,000

At the end of August, both the Vault Bank and Take Off Airlines campaigns were completed. The costs of completed campaigns are debited to the cost of services account. Journalize the summary entry to record each of the following for the month:

a. Direct labor costs
b. Media purchases
c. Overhead applied
d. Completion of Vault Bank and Take Off Airlines campaigns

Problems: Series A

PR 19-1A Entries for costs in a job order cost system OBJ. 2

Munson Co. uses a job order cost system. The following data summarize the operations related to production for July:

a. Materials purchased on account, $225,750
b. Materials requisitioned, $217,600, of which $17,600 was for general factory use
c. Factory labor used, $680,000, of which $72,300 was indirect
d. Other costs incurred on account for factory overhead, $330,000; selling expenses, $180,000; and administrative expenses, $126,000
e. Prepaid expenses expired for factory overhead, $27,500; for selling expenses, $8,100; and for administrative expenses, $5,250
f. Depreciation of office building was $44,500; of office equipment, $16,800; and of factory equipment, $55,100
g. Factory overhead costs applied to jobs, $548,000
h. Jobs completed, $1,140,000
i. Cost of goods sold, $1,128,000

Instructions
Journalize the entries to record the summarized operations.

PR 19-2A Entries and schedules for unfinished jobs and completed jobs OBJ. 2

✔ 3. Work in Process balance, $27,288

Tybee Industries Inc. uses a job order cost system. The following data summarize the operations related to production for January, the first month of operations:

a. Materials purchased on account, $29,800.

b. Materials requisitioned and factory labor used:

Job	Materials	Factory Labor
301	$2,960	$2,775
302	3,620	3,750
303	2,400	1,875
304	8,100	6,860
305	5,100	5,250
306	3,750	3,340
For general factory use	1,080	4,100

c. Factory overhead costs incurred on account, $5,500.
d. Depreciation of machinery and equipment, $1,980.
e. The factory overhead rate is $54 per machine hour. Machine hours used:

Job	Machine Hours
301	25
302	36
303	30
304	72
305	40
306	25
Total	228

f. Jobs completed: 301, 302, 303, and 305.
g. Jobs were shipped and customers were billed as follows: Job 301, $8,250; Job 302, $11,200; Job 303, $15,000.

Instructions

1. Journalize the entries to record the summarized operations.
2. Post the appropriate entries to T accounts for Work in Process and Finished Goods, using the identifying letters as transaction codes. Insert memo account balances as of the end of the month.
3. Prepare a schedule of unfinished jobs to support the balance in the work in process account.
4. Prepare a schedule of completed jobs on hand to support the balance in the finished goods account.

Excel

PR 19-3A Job order cost sheet OBJ. 2, 3

Remnant Carpet Company sells and installs commercial carpeting for office buildings. Remnant Carpet Company uses a job order cost system. When a prospective customer asks for a price quote on a job, the estimated cost data are inserted on an unnumbered job cost sheet. If the offer is accepted, a number is assigned to the job and the costs incurred are recorded in the usual manner on the job cost sheet. After the job is completed, reasons for the variances between the estimated and actual costs are noted on the sheet. The data are then available to management in evaluating the efficiency of operations and in preparing quotes on future jobs. On October 1, Remnant Carpet Company gave Jackson

(Continued)

Consulting an estimate of $9,450 to carpet the consulting firm's newly leased office. The estimate was based on the following data:

Estimated direct materials:	
200 sq. ft. at $35 per sq. ft.	$7,000
Estimated direct labor:	
16 hours at $20 per hour	320
Estimated factory overhead (75% of direct labor cost)	240
Total estimated costs	$7,560
Markup (25% of production costs)	1,890
Total estimate	$9,450

On October 3, Jackson Consulting signed a purchase contract, and the delivery and installation was completed on October 10.

The related materials requisitions and time tickets are summarized as follows:

Materials Requisition No.	Description	Amount
112	140 sq. ft. at $35	$4,900
114	68 sq. ft. at $35	2,380

Time Ticket No.	Description	Amount
H10	10 hours at $20	$200
H11	10 hours at $20	200

Instructions

1. Complete that portion of the job order cost sheet that is prepared when the estimate is given to the customer.
2. ➤ Record the costs incurred and prepare a job order cost sheet. Comment on the reasons for the variances between actual costs and estimated costs. For this purpose, assume that the additional square feet of material used in the job were spoiled, the factory overhead rate has proven to be satisfactory, and an inexperienced employee performed the work.

PR 19-4A **Analyzing manufacturing cost accounts**   OBJ. 2

✓ g. $751,870

Fire Rock Company manufactures designer paddle boards in a wide variety of sizes and styles. The following incomplete ledger accounts refer to transactions that are summarized for June:

Materials

June 1	Balance	82,500	June 30	Requisitions	(a)
30	Purchases	330,000			

Work in Process

June 1	Balance	(b)	June 30	Completed jobs	(f)
30	Materials	(c)			
30	Direct labor	(d)			
30	Factory overhead applied	(e)			

Finished Goods

June 1	Balance	0	June 30	Cost of goods sold	(g)
30	Completed jobs	(f)			

Wages Payable

		June 30 Wages incurred	330,000

Factory Overhead

June 1	Balance	33,000	June 30	Factory overhead applied	(e)
30	Indirect labor	(h)			
30	Indirect materials	44,000			
30	Other overhead	237,500			

In addition, the following information is available:

a. Materials and direct labor were applied to the following jobs in June:

Job No.	Style	Quantity	Direct Materials	Direct Labor
201	T100	550	$ 55,000	$ 41,250
202	T200	1,100	93,500	71,500
203	T400	550	38,500	22,000
204	S200	660	82,500	69,300
205	T300	480	60,000	48,000
206	S100	380	22,000	12,400
Total		3,720	$351,500	$264,450

b. Factory overhead is applied to each job at a rate of 140% of direct labor cost.

c. The June 1 Work in Process balance consisted of two jobs, as follows:

Job No.	Style	Work in Process, June 1
201	T100	$16,500
202	T200	44,000
Total		$60,500

d. Customer jobs completed and units sold in June were as follows:

Job No.	Style	Completed in June	Units Sold in June
201	T100	X	440
202	T200	X	880
203	T400		0
204	S200	X	570
205	T300	X	420
206	S100		0

Instructions

1. Determine the missing amounts associated with each letter. Provide supporting calculations by completing a table with the following headings:

Job No.	Quantity	June 1 Work in Process	Direct Materials	Direct Labor	Factory Overhead	Total Cost	Unit Cost	Units Sold	Cost of Goods Sold

2. Determine the June 30 balances for each of the inventory accounts and factory overhead.

PR 19-5A Flow of costs and income statement OBJ. 2

✔ 1. Income from operations, $432,000

Excel

Ginocera Inc. is a designer, manufacturer, and distributor of low-cost, high-quality stainless steel kitchen knives. A new kitchen knife series called the Kitchen Ninja was released for production in early 20Y8. In January, the company spent $600,000 to develop a late-night advertising infomercial for the new product. During 20Y8, the company spent $1,400,000 advertising the product through these infomercials. In addition, the company incurred $800,000 in legal costs. The knives were ready for manufacture on January 1, 20Y8.

Ginocera uses a job order cost system to accumulate costs associated with the kitchen knife. The unit direct materials cost for the knife is as follows:

Hardened steel blanks (used for knife shaft and blade)	$4.00
Wood (for handle)	1.50
Packaging	0.50

(Continued)

960 Chapter 19 Job Order Costing

The production process is straightforward. First, the hardened steel blanks, which are purchased directly from a raw material supplier, are stamped into a single piece of metal that includes both the blade and the shaft. The stamping machine requires one hour per 250 knives.

After the knife shafts are stamped, they are brought to an assembly area where an employee attaches the handle to the shaft and packs the knife in a decorative box. The direct labor cost is $0.50 per unit.

The knives are sold to stores. Each store is given promotional materials such as posters and aisle displays. Promotional materials cost $60.00 per store. In addition, shipping costs average $0.20 per knife.

Total completed production was 1,200,000 units during the year. Other information is as follows:

Number of customers (stores)	60,000
Number of knives sold	1,120,000
Wholesale price (to store) per knife	$16

Factory overhead cost is applied to jobs at the rate of $800 per stamping machine hour after the knife blanks are stamped. There were an additional 25,000 stamped knives, handles, and cases waiting to be assembled on December 31, 20Y8.

Instructions

1. Prepare an annual income statement for the Kitchen Ninja knife series, including supporting calculations, from the information provided.
2. Determine the balances in the work in process and finished goods inventories for the Kitchen Ninja knife series on December 31, 20Y8.

Problems: Series B

PR 19-1B Entries for costs in a job order cost system   OBJ. 2

Royal Technology Company uses a job order cost system. The following data summarize the operations related to production for March:

a. Materials purchased on account, $770,000
b. Materials requisitioned, $680,000, of which $75,800 was for general factory use
c. Factory labor used, $756,000, of which $182,000 was indirect
d. Other costs incurred on account for factory overhead, $245,000; selling expenses, $171,500; and administrative expenses, $110,600
e. Prepaid expenses expired for factory overhead, $24,500; for selling expenses, $28,420; and for administrative expenses, $16,660
f. Depreciation of factory equipment was $49,500; of office equipment, $61,800; and of office building, $14,900
g. Factory overhead costs applied to jobs, $568,500
h. Jobs completed, $1,500,000
i. Cost of goods sold, $1,375,000

Instruction
Journalize the entries to record the summarized operations.

✔ 3. Work in Process balance, $127,880

PR 19-2B Entries and schedules for unfinished jobs and completed jobs   OBJ. 2

Hildreth Company uses a job order cost system. The following data summarize the operations related to production for April, the first month of operations:

a. Materials purchased on account, $147,000.

b. Materials requisitioned and factory labor used:

Job No.	Materials	Factory Labor
101	$19,320	$19,500
102	23,100	28,140
103	13,440	14,000
104	38,200	36,500
105	18,050	15,540
106	18,000	18,700
For general factory use	9,000	20,160

c. Factory overhead costs incurred on account, $6,000.
d. Depreciation of machinery and equipment, $4,100.
e. The factory overhead rate is $40 per machine hour. Machine hours used:

Job	Machine Hours
101	154
102	160
103	126
104	238
105	160
106	174
Total	1,012

f. Jobs completed: 101, 102, 103, and 105.
g. Jobs were shipped and customers were billed as follows: Job 101, $62,900; Job 102, $80,700; Job 105, $45,500.

Instructions

1. Journalize the entries to record the summarized operations.
2. Post the appropriate entries to T accounts for Work in Process and Finished Goods, using the identifying letters as transaction codes. Insert memo account balances as of the end of the month.
3. Prepare a schedule of unfinished jobs to support the balance in the work in process account.
4. Prepare a schedule of completed jobs on hand to support the balance in the finished goods account.

PR 19-3B Job order cost sheet   OBJ. 2, 3

Stretch and Trim Carpet Company sells and installs commercial carpeting for office buildings. Stretch and Trim Carpet Company uses a job order cost system. When a prospective customer asks for a price quote on a job, the estimated cost data are inserted on an unnumbered job cost sheet. If the offer is accepted, a number is assigned to the job, and the costs incurred are recorded in the usual manner on the job cost sheet. After the job is completed, reasons for the variances between the estimated and actual costs are noted on the sheet. The data are then available for management to use in evaluating the efficiency of operations and in preparing quotes on future jobs. On May 9, Stretch and Trim gave Lunden Consulting an estimate of $18,044 to carpet the consulting firm's newly leased office. The estimate was based on the following data:

Estimated direct materials:	
400 sq. ft. at $32 per sq. ft.	$12,800
Estimated direct labor:	
30 hours at $20 per hour	600
Estimated factory overhead (80% of direct labor cost)	480
Total estimated costs	$13,880
Markup (30% of production costs)	4,164
Total estimate	$18,044

(*Continued*)

962 Chapter 19 Job Order Costing

On May 10, Lunden Consulting signed a purchase contract, and the carpet was delivered and installed on May 15.

The related materials requisitions and time tickets are summarized as follows:

Materials Requisition No.	Description	Amount
132	360 sq. ft. at $32	$11,520
134	50 sq. ft. at $32	1,600

Time Ticket No.	Description	Amount
H9	18 hours at $19	$342
H12	18 hours at $19	342

Instructions

1. Complete that portion of the job order cost sheet that would be prepared when the estimate is given to the customer. Round factory overhead applied to the nearest dollar.
2. Record the costs incurred and prepare a job order cost sheet. Comment on the reasons for the variances between actual costs and estimated costs. For this purpose, assume that the additional square feet of material used in the job were spoiled, the factory overhead rate has proven to be satisfactory, and an inexperienced employee performed the work.

PR 19-4B Analyzing manufacturing cost accounts   OBJ. 2

✓ g. $700,284

Clapton Company manufactures custom guitars in a wide variety of styles. The following incomplete ledger accounts refer to transactions that are summarized for May:

Materials

May 1	Balance	105,600	May 31	Requisitions		(a)
31	Purchases	500,000				

Work in Process

May 1	Balance	(b)	May 31	Completed jobs		(f)
31	Materials	(c)				
31	Direct labor	(d)				
31	Factory overhead applied	(e)				

Finished Goods

May 1	Balance	0	May 31	Cost of goods sold		(g)
31	Completed jobs	(f)				

Wages Payable

		May 31	Wages incurred	396,000

Factory Overhead

May 1	Balance	26,400	May 31	Factory overhead applied		(e)
31	Indirect labor	(h)				
31	Indirect materials	15,400				
31	Other overhead	122,500				

In addition, the following information is available:

a. Materials and direct labor were applied to the following jobs in May:

Job No.	Style	Quantity	Direct Materials	Direct Labor
101	AF1	330	$ 82,500	$ 59,400
102	AF3	380	105,400	72,600
103	AF2	500	132,000	110,000
104	VY1	400	66,000	39,600
105	VY2	660	118,800	66,000
106	AF4	330	66,000	30,800
Total		2,600	$570,700	$378,400

b. Factory overhead is applied to each job at a rate of 50% of direct labor cost.
c. The May 1 Work in Process balance consisted of two jobs, as follows:

Job No.	Style	Work in Process, May 1
101	AF1	$26,400
102	AF3	46,000
Total		$72,400

d. Customer jobs completed and units sold in May were as follows:

Job No.	Style	Completed in May	Units Sold in May
101	AF1	X	264
102	AF3	X	360
103	AF2		0
104	VY1	X	384
105	VY2	X	530
106	AF4		0

Instructions

1. Determine the missing amounts associated with each letter. Provide supporting calculations by completing a table with the following headings:

Job No.	Quantity	May 1 Work in Process	Direct Materials	Direct Labor	Factory Overhead	Total Cost	Unit Cost	Units Sold	Cost of Goods Sold

2. Determine the May 31 balances for each of the inventory accounts and factory overhead.

PR 19-5B Flow of costs and income statement OBJ. 2

✔ 1. Income from operations, $656,000

Excel

Technology Accessories Inc. is a designer, manufacturer, and distributor of accessories for consumer electronic products. Early in 20Y3, the company began production of a leather cover for tablet computers, called the iLeather. The cover is made of stitched leather with a velvet interior and fits around most tablet computers. In January, $750,000 was spent on developing marketing and advertising materials. For the first six months of 20Y2, the company spent $1,400,000 promoting the iLeather. The product was ready for manufacture on January 21, 20Y3.

Technology Accessories Inc. uses a job order cost system to accumulate costs for the iLeather. Direct materials unit costs for the iLeather are as follows:

Leather	$10.00
Velvet	5.00
Packaging	0.40
Total	$15.40

The actual production process for the iLeather is fairly straightforward. First, leather is brought to a cutting and stitching machine. The machine cuts the leather and stitches an exterior edge into the product. The machine requires one hour per 125 iLeathers.

After the iLeather is cut and stitched, it is brought to assembly, where assembly personnel affix the velvet interior and pack the iLeather for shipping. The direct labor cost for this work is $0.50 per unit.

The completed packages are then sold to retail outlets through a sales force. The sales force is compensated by a 20% commission on the wholesale price for all sales.

Total completed production was 500,000 units during the year. Other information is as follows:

Number of iLeather units sold in 20Y3	460,000
Wholesale price per unit	$40

(Continued)

Factory overhead cost is applied to jobs at the rate of $1,250 per machine hour. An additional 22,000 cut and stitched iLeathers were waiting to be assembled on December 31, 20Y3.

Instructions

1. Prepare an annual income statement for the iLeather product, including supporting calculations, from the information provided.
2. Determine the balances in the finished goods and work in process inventories for the iLeather product on December 31, 20Y3.

Cases & Projects

CP 19-1 Communication

TAC Industries sells heavy equipment to large corporations and to federal, state, and local governments. Corporate sales are the result of a competitive bidding process, where TAC competes against other companies based on selling price. Sales to the government, however, are determined on a cost plus basis, where the selling price is determined by adding a fixed markup percentage to the total job cost.

Tandy Lane is the cost accountant for the Equipment Division of TAC Industries Inc. The division is under pressure from senior management to improve income from operations. As Tandy reviewed the division's job cost sheets, she realized that she could increase the division's income from operations by moving a portion of the direct labor hours that had been assigned to the job order cost sheets of corporate customers onto the job order costs sheets of government customers. She believed that this would create a win–win for the division by (1) reducing the cost of corporate jobs and (2) increasing the cost of government jobs whose profit is based on a percentage of job cost. Tandy submitted this idea to her division manager, who was impressed by her creative solution for improving the division's profitability.

• Is Tandy's plan ethical? Explain.

CP 19-2 Predetermined overhead rates

As an assistant cost accountant for Mississippi Industries, you have been assigned to review the activity base for the predetermined factory overhead rate. The president, Tony Favre, has expressed concern that the over- or underapplied overhead has fluctuated excessively over the years.

An analysis of the company's operations and use of the current overhead rate (direct labor cost) has narrowed the possible alternative overhead bases to direct labor cost and machine hours. For the past five years, the following data have been gathered:

	Year 5	Year 4	Year 3	Year 2	Year 1
Actual overhead	$ 790,000	$ 870,000	$ 935,000	$ 845,000	$ 760,000
Applied overhead	777,000	882,000	924,000	840,000	777,000
(Over-) underapplied overhead	$ 13,000	$ (12,000)	$ 11,000	$ 5,000	$ (17,000)
Direct labor cost	$3,885,000	$4,410,000	$4,620,000	$4,200,000	$3,885,000
Machine hours	93,000	104,000	111,000	100,400	91,600

In teams:

1. Calculate a predetermined factory overhead rate for each alternative base, assuming that rates would have been determined by relating the total amount of factory overhead for the past five years to the base.
2. For each of the past five years, determine the over- or underapplied overhead based on the two predetermined overhead rates developed in part (1).
3. • Which predetermined overhead rate would you recommend? Discuss the basis for your recommendation.

Communication

CP 19-3 Communication

Carol Creedence, the plant manager of the Clearwater Company's Revival plant, has prepared the following graph of the unit costs from the job cost reports for the plant's highest volume product, Product CCR:

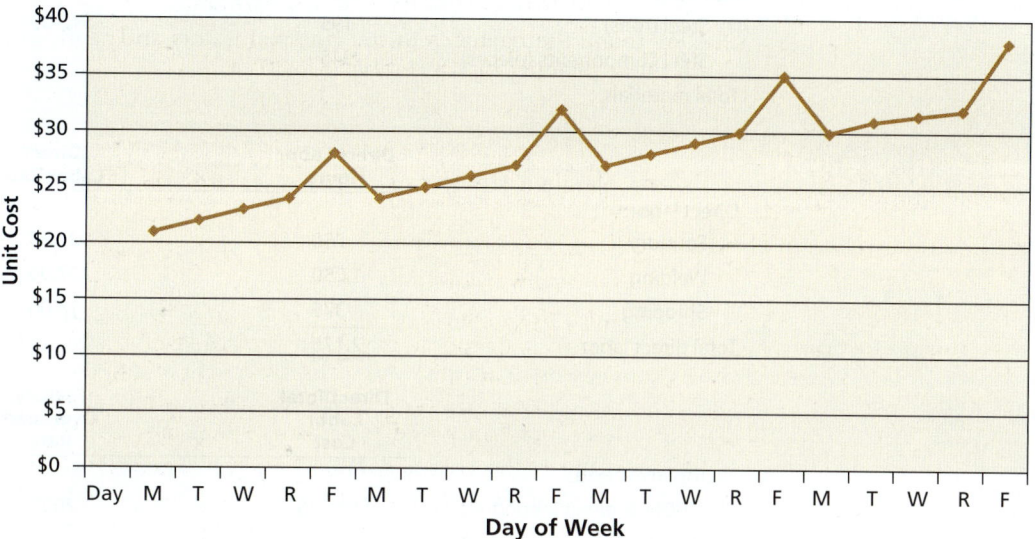

Carol is concerned about the erratic and increasing cost of Product CCR and has asked for your help. Prepare a half-page memo to Carol, interpreting this graph and requesting any additional information that might be needed to explain this situation.

CP 19-4 Job order decision making and rate deficiencies

RIRA Company makes attachments such as backhoes and grader and bulldozer blades for construction equipment. The company uses a job order cost system. Management is concerned about cost performance and evaluates the job cost sheets to learn more about the cost effectiveness of the operations. To facilitate a comparison, the cost sheet for Job 206 (50 backhoe buckets completed in October) was compared with Job 228, which was for 75 backhoe buckets completed in December. The two job cost sheets follow:

Job 206

Item: 50 backhoe buckets

Materials:	Direct Materials Quantity	×	Direct Materials Price	=	Amount
Steel (tons)	105		$1,200		$126,000
Steel components (pieces)	630		7		4,410
Total materials					$130,410

Direct labor:	Direct Labor Hours	×	Direct Labor Rate	=	Amount
Foundry	400		$22.50		$ 9,000
Welding	550		27.00		14,850
Shipping	180		18.00		3,240
Total direct labor	1,130				$ 27,090

	Direct Total Labor Cost	×	Factory Overhead Rate	=	Amount
Factory overhead (200% of direct labor dollars)	$27,090		200%		$ 54,180
Total cost					$ 211,680
Total units					÷ 50
Unit cost (rounded)					$4,233.60

(Continued)

Job 228

Item: 75 backhoe buckets

	Direct Materials Quantity	×	Direct Materials Price	=	Amount
Materials:					
Steel (tons)	195		$1,100		$214,500
Steel components (pieces)	945		7		6,615
Total materials					$221,115

	Direct Labor Hours	×	Direct Labor Rate	=	Amount
Direct labor:					
Foundry	750		$22.50		$ 16,875
Welding	1,050		27.00		28,350
Shipping	375		18.00		6,750
Total direct labor	2,175				$ 51,975

	Direct Total Labor Cost	×	Factory Overhead Rate	=	Amount
Factory overhead					
(200% of direct labor dollars)	$51,975		200%		$ 103,950
Total cost					$ 377,040
Total units					÷ 75
Unit cost					$5,027.20

Management is concerned with the increase in unit costs over the months from October to December. To understand what has occurred, management interviewed the purchasing manager and quality manager.

Purchasing Manager: Prices have been holding steady for our raw materials during the first half of the year. I found a new supplier for our bulk steel that was willing to offer a better price than we received in the past. I saw these lower steel prices and jumped at them, knowing that a reduction in steel prices would have a very favorable impact on our costs.

Quality Manager: Something happened around mid-year. All of a sudden, we were experiencing problems with respect to the quality of our steel. As a result, we've been having all sorts of problems on the shop floor in our foundry and welding operation.

1. Analyze the two job cost sheets and identify why the unit costs have changed for the backhoe buckets. Complete the following schedule to help in your analysis:

Item	Input Quantity per Unit—Job 206	Input Quantity per Unit—Job 228
Steel		
Foundry labor		
Welding labor		

2. How would you interpret what has happened in light of your analysis and the interviews?

CP 19-5 Recording manufacturing costs

Todd Lay just began working as a cost accountant for Enteron Industries Inc., which manufactures gift items. Todd is preparing to record summary journal entries for the month. Todd begins by recording the factory wages as follows:

| Wages Expense | 60,000 | |
| Wages Payable | | 60,000 |

Then the factory depreciation:

Depreciation Expense—Factory Machinery	20,000	
Accumulated Depreciation—Factory Machinery		20,000

Todd's supervisor, Jeff Fastow, walks by and notices the entries. The following conversation takes place:

Jeff: That's a very unusual way to record our factory wages and depreciation for the month.

Todd: What do you mean? This is the way I was taught in school to record wages and depreciation. You know, debit an expense and credit Cash or payables or, in the case of depreciation, credit Accumulated Depreciation.

Jeff: Well, it's not the credits I'm concerned about. It's the debits—I don't think you've recorded the debits correctly. I wouldn't mind if you were recording the administrative wages or office equipment depreciation this way, but I've got real questions about recording factory wages and factory machinery depreciation this way.

Todd: Now I'm really confused. You mean this is correct for administrative costs but not for factory costs? Well, what am I supposed to do—and why?

1. Play the role of Jeff and answer Todd's questions.
2. Why would Jeff accept the journal entries if they were for administrative costs?

CHAPTER 20
Process Cost Systems

Concepts and Principles
Chapter 18 *Introduction to Managerial Accounting*

Developing Information

COST SYSTEMS
Chapter 19 *Job Order Costing*
Chapter 20 *Process Cost Systems*

COST BEHAVIOR
Chapter 21 *Cost-Volume-Profit Analysis*

Decision Making

EVALUATING PERFORMANCE
Chapter 22 *Budgeting*
Chapter 23 *Variances from Standard Costs*

COMPARING ALTERNATIVES
Chapter 24 *Decentralized Operations*
Chapter 25 *Differential Analysis, Product Pricing, and Activity-Based Costing*
Chapter 26 *Capital Investment Analysis*

Dreyer's Ice Cream

In making ice cream, an electric ice cream maker is used to mix ingredients, which include milk, cream, sugar, and flavoring. After the ingredients are added, the mixer is packed with ice and salt to cool the ingredients and then turned on.

After mixing for half of the required time, would you have ice cream? Of course not, because the ice cream needs to mix longer to freeze. Now assume that you ask the question:

What costs have I incurred so far in making ice cream?

The answer to this question requires knowing the cost of the ingredients and electricity. The ingredients are added at the beginning; thus, all the ingredient costs have been incurred. Because the mixing is only half complete, only 50% of the electricity cost has been incurred. Therefore, the answer to the preceding question is:

All the materials costs and half the electricity costs have been incurred.

These same cost concepts apply to larger ice cream processes like those of **Dreyer's Ice Cream** (a subsidiary of **Nestlé**), manufacturer of Dreyer's® and Edy's® ice cream. Dreyer's mixes ingredients in 3,000-gallon vats in much the same way you would using an electric ice cream maker. Dreyer's also records the costs of the ingredients, labor, and factory overhead used in making ice cream. These costs are used by managers for decisions such as setting prices and improving operations.

This chapter describes and illustrates process cost systems that are used by manufacturers such as Dreyer's. In addition, the use of cost of production reports in decision making is described. Finally, the principles of lean manufacturing are discussed.

Learning Objectives

After studying this chapter, you should be able to:

Example Exercises (EE) are shown in **green**.

Obj. 1 Describe process cost systems.

Process Cost Systems
Comparing Job Order and Process Cost Systems — EE **20-1**
Cost Flows for a Process Manufacturer

Obj. 2 Prepare a cost of production report.

Cost of Production Report
Step 1: Determine the Units to Be Assigned Costs — EE **20-2**
Step 2: Compute Equivalent Units of Production — EE **20-3, 20-4**
Step 3: Determine the Cost per Equivalent Unit — EE **20-5**
Step 4: Allocate Costs to Units Transferred Out and Partially Completed Units — EE **20-6**
Preparing the Cost of Production Report

Obj. 3 Journalize entries for transactions using a process cost system.

Journal Entries for a Process Cost System — EE **20-7**

Obj. 4 Describe and illustrate the use of cost of production reports for decision making.

Using the Cost of Production Report for Decision Making
Cost per Equivalent Unit Between Periods
Cost Category Analysis — EE **20-8**
Yield

Obj. 5 Compare lean manufacturing with traditional manufacturing processing.

Lean Manufacturing
Traditional Production Process
Lean Production Process

At a Glance 20 — Page 996

Obj. 1 Describe process cost systems.

Process Cost Systems

A **process manufacturer** produces products that are indistinguishable from each other using a continuous production process. For example, an oil refinery processes crude oil through a series of steps to produce a barrel of gasoline. One barrel of gasoline, the product, cannot be distinguished from another barrel. Other examples of process manufacturers include paper producers, chemical processors, aluminum smelters, and food processors.

INTEGRITY, OBJECTIVITY, AND ETHICS IN BUSINESS

ON BEING GREEN

Process manufacturing often involves significant energy and material resources, which can be harmful to the environment. Thus, many process manufacturing companies, such as chemical, electronic, and metal processors, must address environmental issues. Companies such as **DuPont**, **Intel**, **Apple**, and **Alcoa** are at the forefront of providing environmental solutions for their products and processes.

For example, Apple provides free recycling programs for Macs®, iPhones®, and iPads®. Apple recovers more than 90% by weight of the original product in reusable components, glass, and plastic. You can even receive a free gift card for voluntarily recycling an older Apple product.

Source: Apple website.

The cost accounting system used by process manufacturers is called the **process cost system.** A process cost system records product costs for each manufacturing department or process.

In contrast, a job order manufacturer produces custom products for customers or batches of similar products. For example, a custom printer produces wedding invitations, graduation announcements, or other special print items that are tailored to the specifications of each customer. Each item manufactured is unique to itself. Other examples of job order manufacturers include furniture manufacturers, shipbuilders, and home builders.

As described and illustrated in Chapter 19, the cost accounting system used by job order manufacturers is called the *job order cost system*. A job order cost system records product cost for each job, using job cost sheets.

Some examples of process and job order companies and their products are shown in Exhibit 1.

EXHIBIT 1
Examples of Process Cost and Job Order Companies

Process Manufacturing Companies		Job Order Companies	
Company	Product	Company	Product
Pepsi	soft drinks	Walt Disney	movies
Alcoa	aluminum	Nike, Inc.	athletic shoes
Intel	computer chip	Nicklaus Design	golf courses
ExxonMobil	Gasoline	Tennessee Heritage	log homes
Hershey	chocolate bars	DDB Advertising Agency	advertising

Comparing Job Order and Process Cost Systems

Process and job order cost systems are similar in that each system:

- Records and summarizes product costs.
- Classifies product costs as direct materials, direct labor, and factory overhead.
- Allocates factory overhead costs to products.
- Uses perpetual inventory system for materials, work in process, and finished goods.
- Provides useful product cost information for decision making.

Process and job costing systems are different in several ways. As a basis for illustrating these differences, the cost systems for Frozen Delight and Legend Guitars are used.

Exhibit 2 illustrates the process cost system for Frozen Delight, an ice cream manufacturer. As a basis for comparison, Exhibit 2 also illustrates the job order cost system for Legend Guitars, a custom guitar manufacturer. Legend Guitars was described and illustrated in Chapters 18 and 19.

Exhibit 2 indicates that Frozen Delight manufactures ice cream, using two departments:

- The Mixing Department mixes the ingredients, using large vats.
- The Packaging Department puts the ice cream into cartons for shipping to customers.

Because each gallon of ice cream is similar, product costs are recorded in each department's work in process account. As shown in Exhibit 2, Frozen Delight accumulates (records) the cost of making ice cream in *work in process accounts* for the Mixing and Packaging departments.

The product costs of making a gallon of ice cream include:

- *Direct materials costs*, which include milk, cream, sugar, and packing cartons. All materials costs are added at the beginning of the process for both the Mixing Department and the Packaging Department.

Link to Dreyer's Ice Cream

William Dreyer, an ice cream maker, and Joseph Edy, a candy maker, founded **Dreyer's** and **Edy's Grand Ice Cream** in 1928. The ice cream was sold out of their ice cream parlor on Grand Avenue in Oakland, California.

EXHIBIT 2 — Process Cost and Job Order Cost Systems

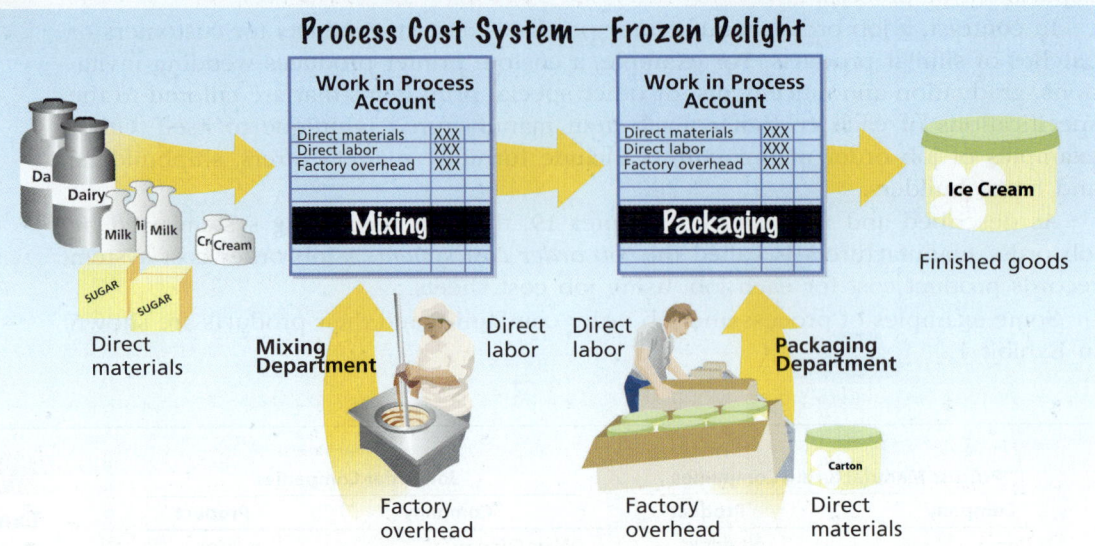

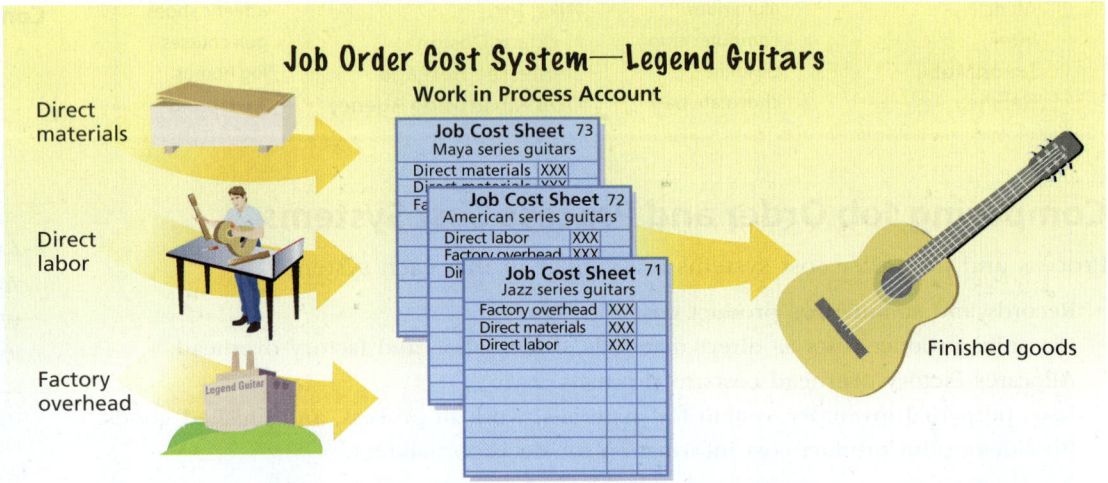

- *Direct labor costs,* which are incurred by employees in each department who run the equipment and load and unload product.
- *Factory overhead costs,* which include the utility costs (power) and depreciation on the equipment.

When the Mixing Department completes the mixing process, its product costs are transferred to the Packaging Department. When the Packaging Department completes its process, the product costs are transferred to Finished Goods. In this way, the cost of the product (a gallon of ice cream) accumulates across the entire production process.

In contrast, Exhibit 2 shows that Legend Guitars accumulates (records) product costs by jobs, using a job cost sheet for each type of guitar. Thus, Legend Guitars uses just one work in process account. As each job is completed, its product costs are transferred to Finished Goods.

In a job order cost system, the work in process at the end of the period is the sum of the job cost sheets for partially completed jobs. In a process cost system, the work in process at the end of the period is the sum of the costs remaining in each department account at the end of the period.

Chapter 20 Process Cost Systems

Example Exercise 20-1 Job Order versus Process Costing *Obj. 1*

Which of the following industries would normally use job order costing systems, and which would normally use process costing systems?

Home construction	Computer chips
Beverages	Cookies
Military aircraft	Video game design and production

Follow My Example 20-1

Home construction	Job order costing
Beverages	Process costing
Military aircraft	Job order costing
Computer chips	Process costing
Cookies	Process costing
Video game design and production	Job order costing

Practice Exercises: PE 20-1A, PE 20-1B

Cost Flows for a Process Manufacturer

Exhibit 3 illustrates the *physical flow* of materials for **Frozen Delight**. Ice cream is made in a manufacturing plant in much the same way you would make it at home, except on a larger scale.

Physical Flows for a Process Manufacturer — **EXHIBIT 3**

In the Mixing Department, direct materials in the form of milk, cream, and sugar are placed into a vat. An employee fills each vat, sets the cooling temperature, and sets the mix speed. The vat is cooled as the direct materials are being mixed by agitators (paddles). Factory overhead includes equipment depreciation and indirect materials.

In the Packaging Department, the ice cream is received from the Mixing Department in a form ready for packaging. The Packaging Department uses direct labor and factory overhead to package the ice cream into one-gallon containers. The ice cream is then transferred to finished goods, where it is frozen and stored in refrigerators prior to shipment to customers.

The *cost flows* in a process cost accounting system are similar to the *physical flow* of materials illustrated in Exhibit 3. The cost flows for **Frozen Delight** are illustrated in Exhibit 4 as follows:

a. The cost of materials purchased is recorded in the materials account.
b. The cost of direct materials used by the Mixing and Packaging departments is recorded in the work in process accounts for each department.

Link to Dreyer's Ice Cream

Dreyer's slow-churned ice cream uses a proprietary process that mixes nonfat milk slowly. This process, called low-temperature extrusion, allows ice cream to be made with one-third fewer calories and half the fat while tasting like normal ice cream.

Materials costs can be as high as 70% of the total product costs for many process manufacturers.

974 Chapter 20 Process Cost Systems

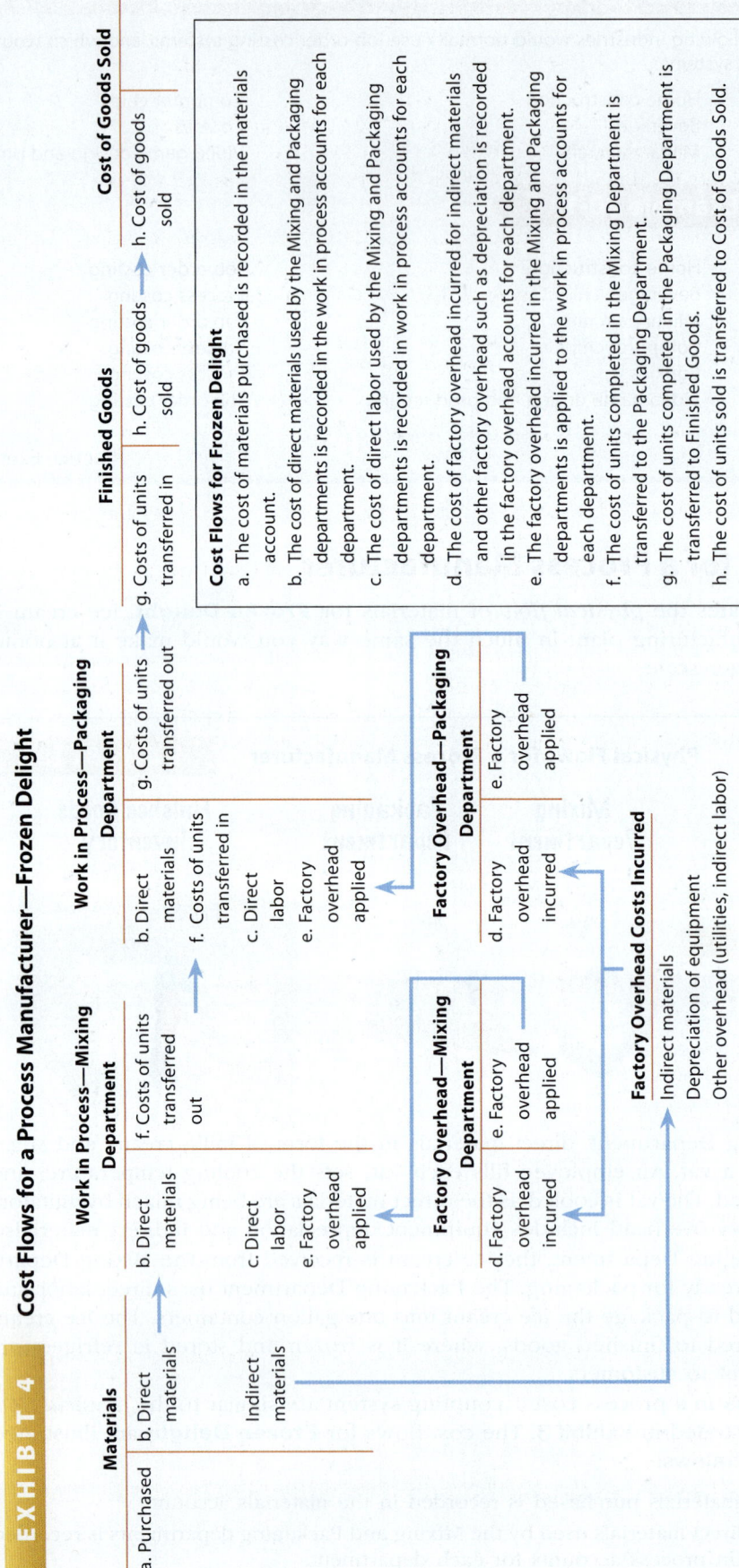

EXHIBIT 4 Cost Flows for a Process Manufacturer—Frozen Delight

c. The cost of direct labor used by the Mixing and Packaging departments is recorded in work in process accounts for each department.
d. The cost of factory overhead incurred for indirect materials and other factory overhead such as depreciation is recorded in the factory overhead accounts for each department.
e. The factory overhead incurred in the Mixing and Packaging departments is applied to the work in process accounts for each department.
f. The cost of units completed in the Mixing Department is transferred to the Packaging Department.
g. The cost of units completed in the Packaging Department is transferred to Finished Goods.
h. The cost of units sold is transferred to Cost of Goods Sold.

As shown in Exhibit 4, the Mixing and Packaging departments have separate factory overhead accounts. The factory overhead costs incurred for indirect materials, depreciation, and other overhead are debited to each department's factory overhead account. The overhead is applied to work in process by debiting each department's work in process account and crediting the department's factory overhead account.

Exhibit 4 illustrates how the Mixing and Packaging departments have separate work in process accounts. Each work in process account is debited for direct materials, direct labor, and applied factory overhead. In addition, the work in process account for the Packaging Department is debited for the cost of the units transferred in from the Mixing Department. Each work in process account is credited for the cost of the units transferred to the next department.

Finally, Exhibit 4 shows that the finished goods account is debited for the cost of the units transferred from the Packaging Department. The finished goods account is credited for the cost of the units sold, which is debited to the cost of goods sold account.

> *Link to Dreyer's Ice Cream*
>
> **Dreyer's** is currently a subsidiary of **Nestlé**, which produces Dreyer's ice cream at its Bakersfield, California, plant.

Business Connection

SUSTAINABLE PAPERMAKING

We discussed social and environmental sustainability in the introductory managerial chapter. Processing companies involved with papermaking, refining, and chemical processing focus on sustainability because of their impact on the environment. For example, papermaking requires the use of large amounts of wood fiber (cellulous), energy, and water. Thus, papermakers are actively involved in sustainability efforts to reduce the negative environmental impacts from the use of these resources. To illustrate, **International Paper Company** provides an annual report to external stakeholders identifying its progress toward several sustainability objectives. A recent report identified six sustainability areas:

1. **Safety:** Improve worker health and safety, resulting in a 68% reduction in life-impacting injuries.
2. **Water use:** Identify and implement water conservation opportunities at each paper mill.
3. **Greenhouse gas emissions:** Reduce greenhouse gases by using renewable carbon-neutral biomass to meet over 70% of energy needs.
4. **Forest stewardship:** Implement sustainable forest management practices that provide a low-cost wood supply while simultaneously conserving primary forests.
5. **Ethics and compliance:** Train suppliers in the company's Supplier Code of Conduct.
6. **Stakeholder engagement:** Engage with communities, customers, and governments by participating in conferences, providing donations, and volunteering.

Source: *In Our Nature: Sustainability Year in Review 2014*, International Paper Company.

Cost of Production Report

Obj. 2 Prepare a cost of production report.

In a process cost system, the cost of units transferred out of each processing department must be determined along with the cost of any partially completed units remaining in the department. The report that summarizes these costs is a cost of production report.

The **cost of production report** summarizes the production and cost data for a department as follows:

- The units the department is accountable for and the disposition of those units
- The product costs incurred by the department and the allocation of those costs between completed (transferred out) and partially completed units

A cost of production report is prepared using the following four steps:

Step 1. Determine the units to be assigned costs.
Step 2. Compute equivalent units of production.
Step 3. Determine the cost per equivalent unit.
Step 4. Allocate costs to units transferred out and partially completed units.

Preparing a cost of production report requires making a cost flow assumption. Like merchandise inventory, costs can be assumed to flow through the manufacturing process, using the first-in, first-out (FIFO), last in, first-out (LIFO), or average cost methods. Because the **first-in, first-out (FIFO) method** is often the same as the physical flow of units, the FIFO method is used in this chapter.[1]

To illustrate, a cost of production report for the Mixing Department of **Frozen Delight** for July is prepared. The July data for the Mixing Department are as follows:

Inventory in process, July 1, 5,000 gallons:	
Direct materials cost, for 5,000 gallons	$5,000
Conversion costs, for 5,000 gallons, 70% completed	1,225
Total inventory in process, July 1	$ 6,225
Direct materials cost for July, 60,000 gallons	66,000
Direct labor cost for July	10,500
Factory overhead applied for July	7,275
Total production costs to account for	$90,000
Gallons transferred to Packaging in July (includes units in process on July 1), 62,000 gallons	?
Inventory in process, July 31, 3,000 gallons, 25% completed as to conversion costs	?

By preparing a cost of production report, the cost of the gallons transferred to the Packaging Department in July and the ending work in process inventory in the Mixing Department are determined. These amounts are indicated by question marks (?).

Step 1: Determine the Units to Be Assigned Costs

The first step is to determine the units to be assigned costs. A unit can be any measure of completed production, such as tons, gallons, pounds, barrels, or cases. For **Frozen Delight**, a unit is a gallon of ice cream.

The Mixing Department is accountable for 65,000 gallons of direct materials during July, computed as follows:

---

[1] The average cost method is illustrated in an appendix to this chapter.

Total units (gallons) charged to production:
  In process, July 1 .... 5,000 gallons
  Received from materials storage 60,000
    Total units (gallons) accounted for .... 65,000 gallons

For July, the following three groups of units (gallons) are assigned costs:

Group 1. Units (gallons) in beginning work in process inventory on July 1.
Group 2. Units (gallons) started and completed during July.
Group 3. Units (gallons) in ending work in process inventory on July 31.

Exhibit 5 illustrates these groups of units (gallons) in the Mixing Department for July. The 5,000 gallons of beginning inventory were completed and transferred to the Packaging Department. During July, 60,000 gallons of material were started (entered into mixing). Of the 60,000 gallons started in July, 3,000 gallons were incomplete on July 31. Thus, 57,000 gallons (60,000 − 3,000) were started and completed in July.

The total units (gallons) to be assigned costs for July are summarized as follows:

Group 1	Inventory in process, July 1, completed in July	5,000 gallons
Group 2	Started and completed in July	57,000
	Transferred out to the Packaging Department in July	62,000 gallons
Group 3	Inventory in process, July 31	3,000
	Total units (gallons) to be assigned costs	65,000 gallons

The total gallons to be assigned costs (65,000) equal the total gallons accounted for (65,000) by the Mixing Department.

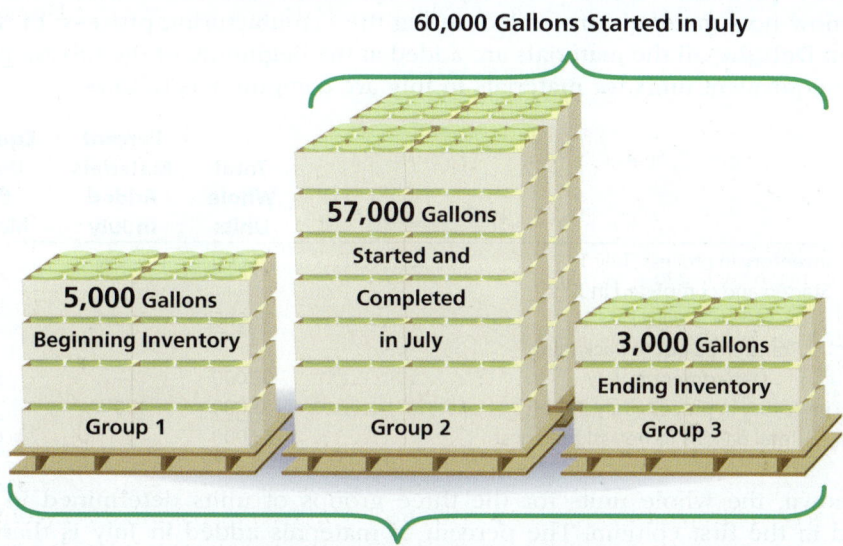

EXHIBIT 5

July Units to Be Costed—Mixing Department

Example Exercise 20-2   Units to Be Assigned Costs   Obj. 2

Rocky Springs Beverage Company has two departments, Blending and Bottling. The Bottling Department received 57,000 liters from the Blending Department. During the period, the Bottling Department completed 58,000 liters, including 4,000 liters of work in process at the beginning of the period. The ending work in process was 3,000 liters. How many liters were started and completed during the period?

Follow My Example 20-2

54,000 liters started and completed (58,000 completed − 4,000 beginning work in process), or (57,000 started − 3,000 ending work in process)

Practice Exercises: PE 20-2A, PE 20-2B

Step 2: Compute Equivalent Units of Production

Whole units are the number of units in production during a period, whether completed or not. **Equivalent units of production** are the portion of whole units that are complete with respect to materials or conversion (direct labor and factory overhead) costs.

To illustrate, assume that a 1,000-gallon batch (vat) of ice cream at **Frozen Delight** is only 40% complete in the mixing process on May 31. Thus, the batch is only 40% complete as to conversion costs such as power. In this case, the whole units and equivalent units of production are as follows:

	Whole Units	Equivalent Units
Materials costs	1,000 gallons	1,000 gallons
Conversion costs	1,000 gallons	400 gallons (1,000 × 40%)

Because the materials costs are all added at the beginning of the process, the materials costs are 100% complete for the 1,000-gallon batch of ice cream. Thus, the whole units and equivalent units for materials costs are 1,000 gallons. However, because the batch is only 40% complete as to conversion costs, the equivalent units for conversion costs are 400 gallons.

Equivalent units for materials and conversion costs are usually determined separately as shown earlier. This is because materials and conversion costs normally enter production at different times and rates. In contrast, direct labor and factory overhead normally enter production at the same time and rate. For this reason, direct labor and factory overhead are combined as conversion costs in computing equivalent units.

Materials Equivalent Units To compute equivalent units for materials, it is necessary to know how materials are added during the manufacturing process. In the case of **Frozen Delight**, all the materials are added at the beginning of the mixing process. Thus, the equivalent units for materials in July are computed as follows:

		Total Whole Units	Percent Materials Added in July	Equivalent Units for Direct Materials
Group 1	Inventory in process, July 1	5,000	0%	0
Group 2	Started and completed in July (62,000 − 5,000)	57,000	100%	57,000
	Transferred out to Packaging Department in July	62,000	—	57,000
Group 3	Inventory in process, July 31	3,000	100%	3,000
	Total gallons to be assigned cost	65,000		60,000

As shown, the whole units for the three groups of units determined in Step 1 are listed in the first column. The percent of materials added in July is then listed. The equivalent units are determined by multiplying the whole units by the percent of materials added.

To illustrate, the July 1 inventory (Group 1) has 5,000 gallons of whole units, which are complete as to materials. That is, all the direct materials for the 5,000 gallons in process on July 1 were added in June. Thus, the percent of materials added in July is zero, and the equivalent units added in July are zero.

The 57,000 gallons started and completed in July (Group 2) are 100% complete as to materials. Thus, the equivalent units for the gallons started and completed in July are 57,000 (57,000 × 100%) gallons. The 3,000 gallons in process on July 31 (Group 3) are also 100% complete as to materials because all materials are added at the beginning of the process. Therefore, the equivalent units for the inventory in process on July 31 are 3,000 (3,000 × 100%) gallons.

The equivalent units for direct materials for **Frozen Delight** are summarized in Exhibit 6.

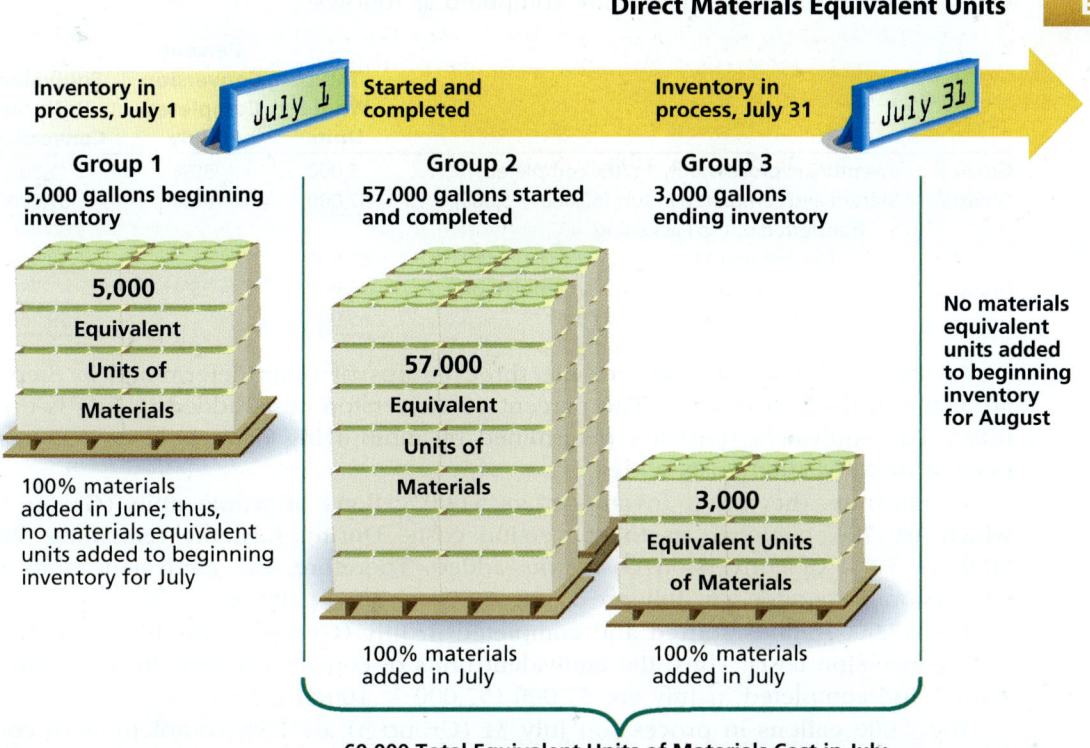

EXHIBIT 6 Direct Materials Equivalent Units

Example Exercise 20-3 Equivalent Units of Materials Cost
Obj. 2

The Bottling Department of Rocky Springs Beverage Company had 4,000 liters in the beginning work in process inventory (30% complete). During the period, 58,000 liters were completed. The ending work in process inventory was 3,000 liters (60% complete). What are the total equivalent units for direct materials if materials are added at the beginning of the process?

Follow My Example 20-3

Total equivalent units for direct materials are 57,000, computed as follows:

	Total Whole Units	Percent Materials Added in Period	Equivalent Units for Direct Materials
Inventory in process, beginning of period	4,000	0%	0
Started and completed during the period	54,000*	100%	54,000
Transferred out of Bottling (completed)	58,000	—	54,000
Inventory in process, end of period	3,000	100%	3,000
Total units to be assigned costs	61,000		57,000

*58,000 − 4,000

Practice Exercises: PE 20-3A, PE 20-3B

Conversion Equivalent Units To compute equivalent units for conversion costs, it is necessary to know how direct labor and factory overhead enter the manufacturing process. Direct labor, utilities, and equipment depreciation are often incurred uniformly during processing. For this reason, it is assumed that **Frozen Delight** incurs conversion costs evenly throughout its manufacturing process. Thus, the equivalent units for conversion costs in July are computed as follows:

		Total Whole Units	Percent Conversion Completed in July	Equivalent Units for Conversion
Group 1	Inventory in process, July 1 (70% completed)	5,000	30%	1,500
Group 2	Started and completed in July (62,000 − 5,000)	57,000	100%	57,000
	Transferred out to Packaging Department in July	62,000	—	58,500
Group 3	Inventory in process, July 31 (25% completed)	3,000	25%	750
	Total gallons to be assigned cost	65,000		59,250

As shown, the whole units for the three groups of units determined in Step 1 are listed in the first column. The percent of conversion costs added in July is then listed. The equivalent units are determined by multiplying the whole units by the percent of conversion costs added.

To illustrate, the July 1 inventory has 5,000 gallons of whole units (Group 1), which are 70% complete as to conversion costs. During July, the remaining 30% (100% − 70%) of conversion costs was added. Therefore, the equivalent units of conversion costs added in July are 1,500 (5,000 × 30%) gallons.

The 57,000 gallons started and completed in July (Group 2) are 100% complete as to conversion costs. Thus, the equivalent units of conversion costs for the gallons started and completed in July are 57,000 (57,000 × 100%) gallons.

The 3,000 gallons in process on July 31 (Group 3) are 25% complete as to conversion costs. Hence, the equivalent units for the inventory in process on July 31 are 750 (3,000 × 25%) gallons.

The equivalent units for conversion costs for **Frozen Delight** are summarized in Exhibit 7.

EXHIBIT 7 Conversion Equivalent Units

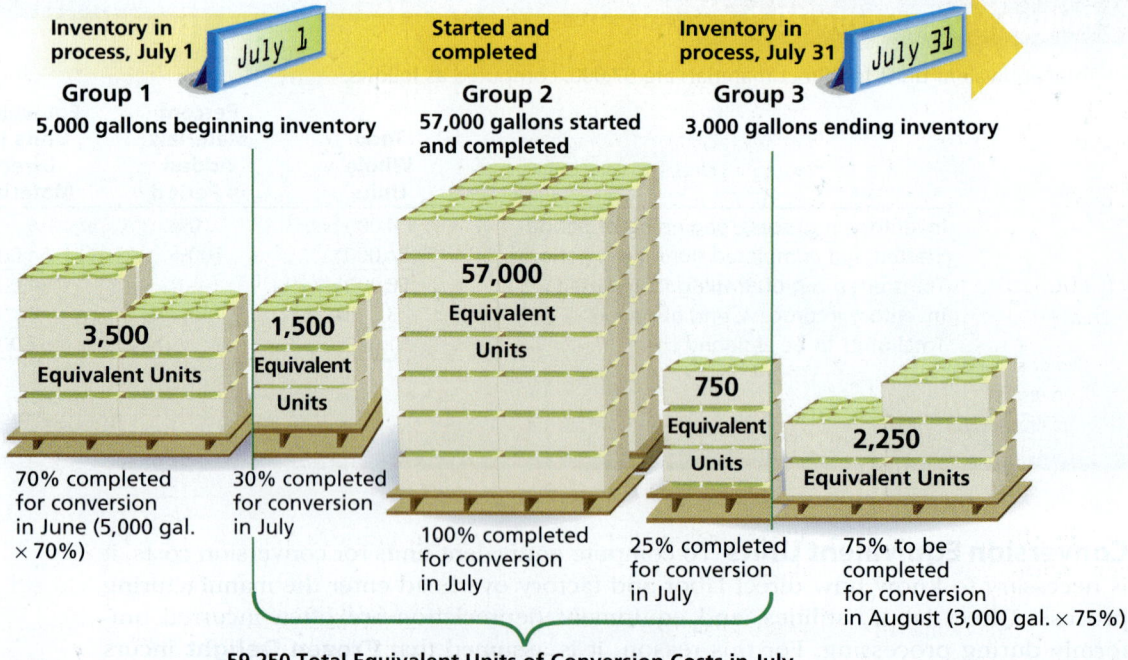

Example Exercise 20-4 Equivalent Units of Conversion Costs Obj. 2

The Bottling Department of Rocky Springs Beverage Company had 4,000 liters in the beginning work in process inventory (30% complete). During the period, 58,000 liters were completed. The ending work in process inventory was 3,000 liters (60% complete). What are the total equivalent units for conversion costs?

Follow My Example 20-4

	Total Whole Units	Percent Conversion Completed in Period	Equivalent Units for Conversion
Inventory in process, beginning of period	4,000	70%	2,800
Started and completed during the period	54,000*	100%	54,000
Transferred out of Bottling (completed)	58,000	—	56,800
Inventory in process, end of period	3,000	60%	1,800
Total units to be assigned costs	61,000		58,600

*58,000 − 4,000

Practice Exercises: PE 20-4A, PE 20-4B

Step 3: Determine the Cost per Equivalent Unit

The next step in preparing the cost of production report is to compute the cost per equivalent unit for direct materials and conversion costs. The **cost per equivalent unit** for direct materials and conversion costs is computed as follows:

$$\text{Direct Materials Cost per Equivalent Unit} = \frac{\text{Total Direct Materials Cost for the Period}}{\text{Total Equivalent Units of Direct Materials}}$$

$$\text{Conversion Cost per Equivalent Unit} = \frac{\text{Total Conversion Costs for the Period}}{\text{Total Equivalent Units of Conversion Costs}}$$

The July direct materials and conversion cost equivalent units for **Frozen Delight**'s Mixing Department from Step 2 are as follows:

		Equivalent Units	
		Direct Materials	Conversion
Group 1	Inventory in process, July 1	0	1,500
Group 2	Started and completed in July (62,000 − 5,000)	57,000	57,000
	Transferred out to Packaging Department in July	57,000	58,500
Group 3	Inventory in process, July 31	3,000	750
	Total gallons to be assigned cost	60,000	59,250

The direct materials and conversion costs incurred by Frozen Delight in July are repeated as follows:

Direct materials		$66,000
Conversion costs:		
Direct labor	$10,500	
Factory overhead	7,275	17,775
Total product costs		$83,775

The direct materials and conversion costs per equivalent unit are $1.10 and $0.30 per gallon, computed as follows:

$$\text{Direct Materials Cost per Equivalent Unit} = \frac{\text{Total Direct Materials Cost for the Period}}{\text{Total Equivalent Units of Direct Materials}}$$

982 Chapter 20 Process Cost Systems

$$\text{Direct Materials Cost per Equivalent Unit} = \frac{\$66,000}{60,000 \text{ gallons}} = \$1.10 \text{ per gallon}$$

$$\text{Conversion Cost per Equivalent Unit} = \frac{\text{Total Conversion Costs for the Period}}{\text{Total Equivalent Units of Conversion Costs}}$$

$$\text{Conversion Cost per Equivalent Unit} = \frac{\$17,775}{59,250 \text{ gallons}} = \$0.30 \text{ per gallon}$$

The preceding costs per equivalent unit are used in Step 4 to allocate the direct materials and conversion costs to the completed and partially completed units.

Example Exercise 20-5 Cost per Equivalent Unit — Obj. 2

The cost of direct materials transferred into the Bottling Department of Rocky Springs Beverage Company is $22,800. The conversion cost for the period in the Bottling Department is $8,790. The total equivalent units for direct materials and conversion are 57,000 liters and 58,600 liters, respectively. Determine the direct materials and conversion costs per equivalent unit.

Follow My Example 20-5

$$\text{Direct Materials Cost per Equivalent Unit} = \frac{\$22,800}{57,000 \text{ liters}} = \$0.40 \text{ per liter}$$

$$\text{Conversion Cost per Equivalent Unit} = \frac{\$8,790}{58,600 \text{ liters}} = \$0.15 \text{ per liter}$$

Practice Exercises: PE 20-5A, PE 20-5B

Step 4: Allocate Costs to Units Transferred Out and Partially Completed Units

Product costs must be allocated to the units transferred out and the partially completed units on hand at the end of the period. The product costs are allocated using the costs per equivalent unit for materials and conversion costs that were computed in Step 3.

The total production costs to be assigned for **Frozen Delight** in July are $90,000, computed as follows:

Inventory in process, July 1, 5,000 gallons:	
Direct materials cost, for 5,000 gallons	$ 5,000
Conversion costs, for 5,000 gallons, 70% completed	1,225
Total inventory in process, July 1	$ 6,225
Direct materials cost for July, 60,000 gallons	66,000
Direct labor cost for July	10,500
Factory overhead applied for July	7,275
Total production costs to account for	$90,000

The units to be assigned these costs follow. The costs to be assigned these units are indicated by question marks (?).

			Units	Total Cost
Group 1	Inventory in process, July 1, completed in July		5,000 gallons	?
Group 2	Started and completed in July		57,000	?
	Transferred out to the Packaging Department in July		62,000 gallons	?
Group 3	Inventory in process, July 31		3,000	?
	Total		65,000 gallons	$90,000

Group 1: Inventory in Process on July 1

The 5,000 gallons of inventory in process on July 1 (Group 1) were completed and transferred out to the Packaging Department in July. The cost of these units of $6,675 is determined as follows:

	Direct Materials Costs	Conversion Costs	Total Costs
Inventory in process, July 1 balance..................			$6,225
Equivalent units for completing the July 1 in-process inventory.......................	0	1,500	
Cost per equivalent unit............................	× $1.10	× $0.30	
Cost to complete July 1 in-process inventory.........	0	$450	450
Cost of July 1 in-process inventory transferred to Packaging Department............			$6,675

As shown, $6,225 of the cost of the July 1 in-process inventory of 5,000 gallons was carried over from June. This cost plus the cost of completing the 5,000 gallons in July was transferred to the Packaging Department during July. The cost of completing the 5,000 gallons during July is $450. The $450 represents the conversion costs necessary to complete the remaining 30% of the processing. No direct materials costs were added in July because all the materials costs had been added in June. Thus, the cost of the 5,000 gallons in process on July 1 (Group 1) transferred to the Packaging Department is $6,675.

Group 2: Started and Completed

The 57,000 units started and completed in July (Group 2) incurred all (100%) of their direct materials and conversion costs in July. Thus, the cost of the 57,000 gallons started and completed is $79,800, computed by multiplying 57,000 gallons by the costs per equivalent unit for materials and conversion costs as follows:

	Direct Materials Costs	Conversion Costs	Total Costs
Units started and completed in July.................	57,000 gallons	57,000 gallons	
Cost per equivalent unit............................	× $1.10	× $0.30	
Cost of the units started and completed in July............................	$62,700	$17,100	$79,800

The total cost of $86,475 transferred to the Packaging Department in July is the sum of the beginning inventory cost and the costs of the units started and completed in July, computed as follows:

Group 1	Cost of July 1 in-process inventory	$ 6,675
Group 2	Cost of the units started and completed in July	79,800
	Total costs transferred to Packaging Department in July	$86,475

Group 3: Inventory in Process on July 31

The 3,000 gallons in process on July 31 (Group 3) incurred all their direct materials costs and 25% of their conversion costs in July. The cost of these partially completed units of $3,525 is computed as follows:

	Direct Materials Costs	Conversion Costs	Total Costs
Equivalent units in ending inventory.................	3,000 gallons	750 gallons	
Cost per equivalent unit............................	× $1.10	× $0.30	
Cost of July 31 in-process inventory.................	$3,300	$225	$3,525

The 3,000 gallons in process on July 31 received all (100%) of their materials in July. Therefore, the direct materials cost incurred in July is $3,300 (3,000 × $1.10). The conversion costs of $225 represent the cost of the 750 (3,000 × 25%) equivalent gallons multiplied by the cost of $0.30 per equivalent unit for conversion costs. The sum of the direct materials cost ($3,300) and the conversion costs ($225) equals the total cost of the July 31 work in process inventory of $3,525 ($3,300 + $225).

To summarize, the total manufacturing costs for Frozen Delight in July were assigned as follows. In doing so, the question marks (?) for the costs to be assigned to units in Groups 1, 2, and 3 have been answered.

		Units	Total Cost
Group 1	Inventory in process, July 1, completed in July	5,000 gallons	$ 6,675
Group 2	Started and completed in July	57,000	79,800
	Transferred out to the Packaging Department in July	62,000 gallons	$86,475
Group 3	Inventory in process, July 31	3,000	3,525
	Total	65,000 gallons	$90,000

Example Exercise 20-6 Cost of Units Transferred Out and Ending Work in Process

Obj. 2

The costs per equivalent unit of direct materials and conversion in the Bottling Department of Rocky Springs Beverage Company are $0.40 and $0.15, respectively. The equivalent units to be assigned costs are as follows:

	Equivalent Units	
	Direct Materials	Conversion
Inventory in process, beginning of period	0	2,800
Started and completed during the period	54,000	54,000
Transferred out of Bottling (completed)	54,000	56,800
Inventory in process, end of period	3,000	1,800
Total units to be assigned costs	57,000	58,600

The beginning work in process inventory had a cost of $1,860. Determine the cost of units transferred out and the ending work in process inventory.

Follow My Example 20-6

	Direct Materials Costs	Conversion Costs	Total Costs
Inventory in process, beginning balance			$ 1,860
Inventory in process, to complete	0 +	2,800 × $0.15	420
Started and completed during the period	54,000 × $0.40 +	54,000 × $0.15	29,700
Transferred out of Bottling (completed)			$31,980
Inventory in process, end of period	3,000 × $0.40 +	1,800 × $0.15	1,470
Total costs assigned by the Bottling Department			$33,450
Completed and transferred out of production	$31,980		
Inventory in process, ending	$ 1,470		

Practice Exercises: PE 20-6A, PE 20-6B

Preparing the Cost of Production Report

A cost of production report is prepared for each processing department at periodic intervals. The report summarizes the following production quantity and cost data:

- The units for which the department is accountable and the disposition of those units
- The production costs incurred by the department and the allocation of those costs between completed (transferred out) and partially completed units

Using Steps 1–4, the July cost of production report for **Frozen Delight**'s Mixing Department is shown in Exhibit 8. During July, the Mixing Department was accountable for 65,000 units (gallons). Of these units, 62,000 units were completed and transferred to the Packaging Department. The remaining 3,000 units are partially completed and are part of the in-process inventory as of July 31.

The Mixing Department was responsible for $90,000 of production costs during July. The cost of goods transferred to the Packaging Department in July was $86,475. The remaining cost of $3,525 is part of the in-process inventory as of July 31.

EXHIBIT 8 Cost of Production Report for Frozen Delight's Mixing Department—FIFO

	A	B	C	D	E
1		Frozen Delight			
2		Cost of Production Report—Mixing Department			
3		For the Month Ended July 31			
4					
5		Whole Units	Equivalent Units		
6	**UNITS**		Direct Materials	Conversion	
7	Units charged to production:				
8	Inventory in process, July 1	5,000			
9	Received from materials storeroom	60,000			
10	Total units accounted for by the Mixing Department	65,000			
11					
12	Units to be assigned costs:				
13	Inventory in process, July 1 (70% completed)	5,000	0	1,500	
14	Started and completed in July	57,000	57,000	57,000	
15	Transferred to Packaging Department in July	62,000	57,000	58,500	
16	Inventory in process, July 31 (25% completed)	3,000	3,000	750	
17	Total units to be assigned costs	65,000	60,000	59,250	
18					
19				Costs	
20	**COSTS**		Direct Materials	Conversion	Total
21					
22	Cost per equivalent unit:				
23	Total costs for July in Mixing Department		$ 66,000	$ 17,775	
24	Total equivalent units (from Step 2)		÷ 60,000	÷ 59,250	
25	Cost per equivalent unit		$ 1.10	$ 0.30	
26					
27	Costs assigned to production:				
28	Inventory in process, July 1				$ 6,225
29	Costs incurred in July				83,775[a]
30	Total costs accounted for by the Mixing Department				$90,000
31					
32					
33	Cost allocated to completed and partially				
34	completed units:				
35	Inventory in process, July 1 balance				$ 6,225
36	To complete inventory in process, July 1		$ 0 +	$ 450[b] =	450
37	Cost of completed July 1 work in process				$ 6,675
38	Started and completed in July		62,700[c] +	17,100[d] =	79,800
39	Transferred to Packaging Department in July				$86,475
40	Inventory in process, July 31		$ 3,300[e] +	$ 225[f] =	3,525
41	Total costs assigned by the Mixing Department				$90,000

Step 1, Step 2, Step 3, Step 4

[a] $66,000 + $10,500 + $7,275 = $83,775 [b] 1,500 units × $0.30 = $450 [c] 57,000 units × $1.10 = $62,700 [d] 57,000 units × $0.30 = $17,100
[e] 3,000 units × $1.10 = $3,300 [f] 750 units × $0.30 = $225

Journal Entries for a Process Cost System

Obj. 3 Journalize entries for transactions using a process cost system.

The journal entries to record the cost flows and transactions for a process cost system are illustrated in this section. As a basis for illustration, the July transactions for Frozen Delight are used. To simplify, the entries are shown in summary form, even though many of the transactions would be recorded daily.

a. Purchased materials, including milk, cream, sugar, packaging, and indirect materials on account, $88,000.

a.	Materials		88,000	
	Accounts Payable			88,000

b. The Mixing Department requisitioned milk, cream, and sugar, $66,000. This is the total amount from the original July data. Packaging materials of $8,000 were requisitioned by the Packaging Department. Indirect materials for the Mixing and Packaging departments were $4,125 and $3,000, respectively.

b.	Work in Process—Mixing		66,000	
	Work in Process—Packaging		8,000	
	Factory Overhead—Mixing		4,125	
	Factory Overhead—Packaging		3,000	
	Materials			81,125

c. Incurred direct labor in the Mixing and Packaging departments of $10,500 and $12,000, respectively.

c.	Work in Process—Mixing		10,500	
	Work in Process—Packaging		12,000	
	Wages Payable			22,500

d. Recognized equipment depreciation for the Mixing and Packaging departments of $3,350 and $1,000, respectively.

d.	Factory Overhead—Mixing		3,350	
	Factory Overhead—Packaging		1,000	
	Accumulated Depreciation—Equipment			4,350

e. Applied factory overhead to Mixing and Packaging departments of $7,275 and $3,500, respectively.

e.	Work in Process—Mixing		7,275	
	Work in Process—Packaging		3,500	
	Factory Overhead—Mixing			7,275
	Factory Overhead—Packaging			3,500

f. Transferred costs of $86,475 from the Mixing Department to the Packaging Department per the cost of production report in Exhibit 8.

f.	Work in Process—Packaging		86,475	
	Work in Process—Mixing			86,475

g. Transferred goods of $106,000 out of the Packaging Department to Finished Goods according to the Packaging Department cost of production report (not illustrated).

g.	Finished Goods—Ice Cream		106,000	
	Work in Process—Packaging			106,000

h. Recorded the cost of goods sold out of the finished goods inventory of $107,000.

	h.	Cost of Goods Sold		107,000	
		Finished Goods—Ice Cream			107,000

Exhibit 9 shows the flow of costs for each transaction. The highlighted amounts in Exhibit 9 were determined from assigning the costs in the Mixing Department. These amounts were computed and are shown at the bottom of the cost of production report for the Mixing Department in Exhibit 8. Likewise, the amount transferred out of the Packaging Department to Finished Goods would have also been determined from a cost of production report for the Packaging Department.

Frozen Delight's Cost Flows **EXHIBIT 9**

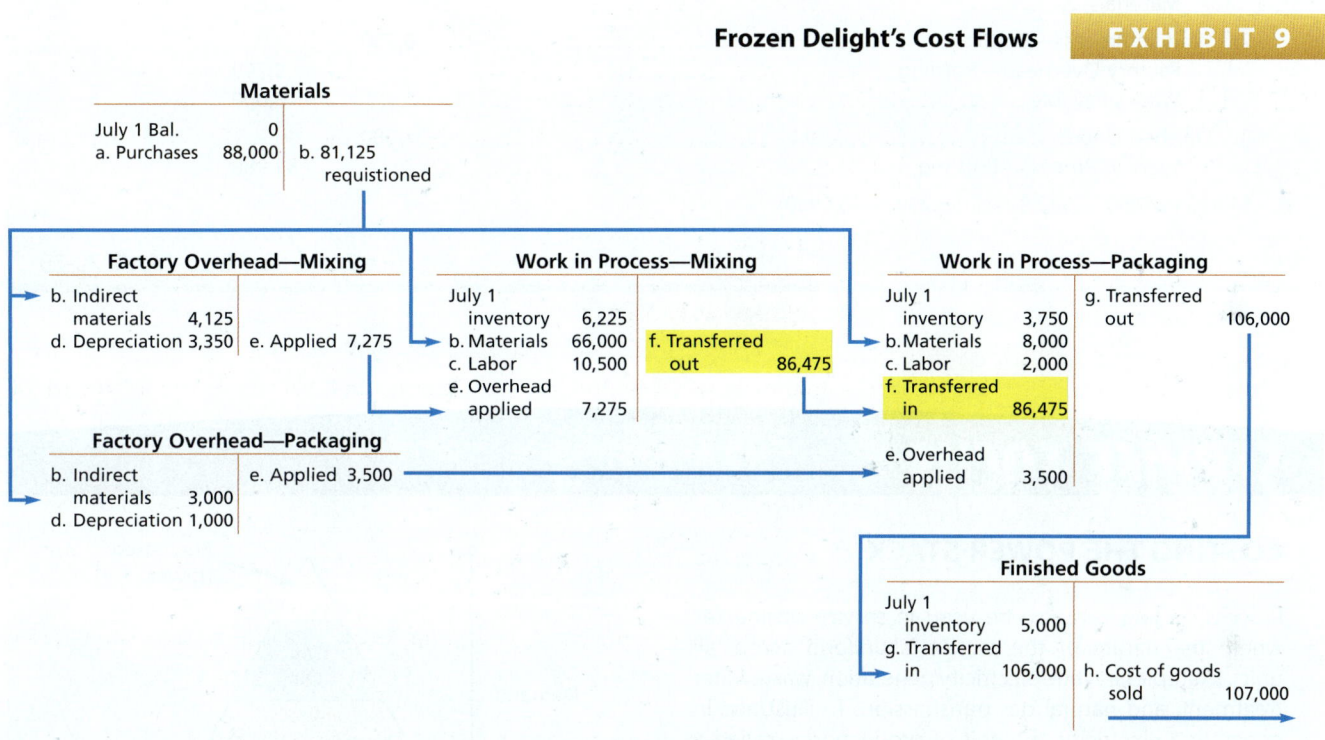

The ending inventories for Frozen Delight are reported on the July 31 balance sheet as follows:

Materials	$ 6,875
Work in Process—Mixing Department	3,525
Work in Process—Packaging Department	7,725
Finished Goods	4,000
Total inventories	$22,125

The $3,525 balance of Work in Process—Mixing Department is the amount determined from the bottom of the cost of production report in Exhibit 8.

Example Exercise 20-7 Process Cost Journal Entries   Obj. 3

The cost of materials transferred into the Bottling Department of Rocky Springs Beverage Company is $22,800, including $20,000 from the Blending Department and $2,800 from the materials storeroom. The conversion cost for the period in the Bottling Department is $8,790 ($3,790 factory overhead applied and $5,000 direct labor). The total cost transferred to Finished Goods for the period was $31,980. The Bottling Department had a beginning inventory of $1,860.

a. Journalize (1) the cost of transferred-in materials, (2) conversion costs, and (3) the costs transferred out to Finished Goods.
b. Determine the balance of Work in Process—Bottling at the end of the period.

Follow My Example 20-7

a. 1. Work in Process—Bottling 22,800
          Work in Process—Blending   20,000
          Materials   2,800
   2. Work in Process—Bottling 8,790
          Factory Overhead—Bottling   3,790
          Wages Payable   5,000
   3. Finished Goods 31,980
          Work in Process—Bottling   31,980

b. $1,470 ($1,860 + $22,800 + $8,790 − $31,980)

Practice Exercises: PE 20-7A, PE 20-7B

SERVICE FOCUS

COSTING THE POWER STACK

Process costing can also be used in service businesses where the nature of the service is uniform across all units. Examples include electricity generation, wastewater treatment, and natural gas transmission. To illustrate, in generating electricity, the unit of production is called a *megawatt hour*, where each megawatt hour is the same across all sources of generation.

Unlike product manufacturing, service companies often do not have inventory. For example, in generating electricity, the electricity cannot be stored. Thus, electric companies such as Duke Energy Corporation match the production of electricity to the demand in real time. Electric companies use what is termed the *power stack* to match power supply to demand by arranging generating facilities in order of cost per megawatt hour. The least cost per megawatt hour facilities satisfy initial demand at the bottom of the stack, while the highest cost per megawatt hour power sources are placed at top of the stack to satisfy peak loads, as illustrated in the following graph:

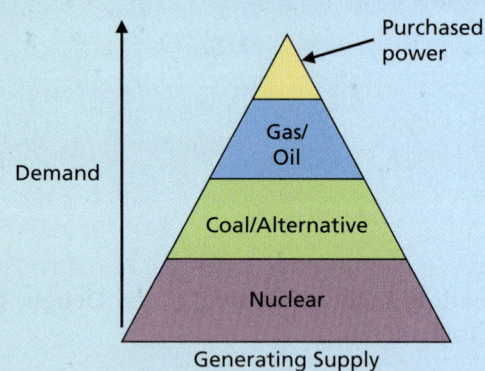

The cost per megawatt hour is determined using process costing by accumulating the conversion costs such as equipment depreciation, labor, and maintenance plus the cost of fuel for each facility. These costs are divided by the megawatt hours generated. Because there are no inventories, the additional complexity of equivalent units is avoided. The resulting cost per megawatt hour by facility is used to develop the power stack.

Using the Cost of Production Report for Decision Making

Obj. 4 Describe and illustrate the use of cost of production reports for decision making.

The cost of production report is often used by managers for decisions involving the control and improvement of operations. To illustrate, cost of production reports for **Frozen Delight** and **Holland Beverage Company** are used. Finally, the computation and use of yield are discussed.

Cost per Equivalent Unit Between Periods

The cost of production report for the Mixing Department is shown in Exhibit 8. The cost per equivalent unit for June can be determined from the beginning inventory. The original Frozen Delight data indicate that the July 1 inventory in process of $6,225 consists of the following costs:

Direct materials cost, 5,000 gallons	$5,000
Conversion costs, 5,000 gallons, 70% completed	1,225
Total inventory in process, July 1	$6,225

Using the preceding data, the June costs per equivalent unit of materials and conversion costs can be determined as follows:

$$\text{Direct Materials Cost per Equivalent Unit} = \frac{\text{Total Direct Materials Cost for the Period}}{\text{Total Equivalent Units of Direct Materials}}$$

$$\text{Direct Materials Cost per Equivalent Unit} = \frac{\$5,000}{5,000 \text{ gallons}} = \$1.00 \text{ per gallon}$$

$$\text{Conversion Cost per Equivalent Unit} = \frac{\text{Total Conversion Costs for the Period}}{\text{Total Equivalent Units of Conversion Costs}}$$

$$\text{Conversion Cost per Equivalent Unit} = \frac{\$1,225}{(5,000 \times 70\%) \text{ gallons}} = \$0.35 \text{ per gallon}$$

In July, the cost per equivalent unit of materials increased by $0.10 per gallon, while the cost per equivalent unit for conversion costs decreased by $0.05 per gallon, computed as follows:

	July*	June	Increase (Decrease)
Cost per equivalent unit for direct materials	$1.10	$1.00	$ 0.10
Cost per equivalent unit for conversion costs	0.30	0.35	(0.05)

*From Exhibit 8

Frozen Delight's management could use the preceding analysis as a basis for investigating the increase in the direct materials cost per equivalent unit and the decrease in the conversion cost per equivalent unit.

Cost Category Analysis

A cost of production report may be prepared showing more cost categories beyond just direct materials and conversion costs. This greater detail can help managers isolate problems and seek opportunities for improvement.

To illustrate, the Blending Department of Holland Beverage Company prepared cost of production reports for April and May. To simplify, assume that the Blending Department had no beginning or ending work in process inventory in either month. That is, all units started were completed in each month. The cost of production reports showing multiple cost categories for April and May in the Blending Department are as follows:

	A	B	C
1	Cost of Production Reports		
2	Holland Beverage Company—Blending Department		
3	For the Months Ended April 30 and May 31		
4		April	May
5	Direct materials	$ 20,000	$ 40,600
6	Direct labor	15,000	29,400
7	Energy	8,000	20,000
8	Repairs	4,000	8,000
9	Tank cleaning	3,000	8,000
10	Total	$ 50,000	$106,000
11	Units completed	÷100,000	÷200,000
12	Cost per unit	$ 0.50	$ 0.53

The May results indicate that total unit costs have increased from $0.50 to $0.53, or 6% in May. To determine the possible causes for this increase, the cost of production report is restated in per-unit terms by dividing the costs by the number of units completed, as follows:

	A	B	C	D
1	Blending Department			
2	Per-Unit Expense Comparisons			
3		April	May	% Change
4	Direct materials	$0.200	$0.203	1.50%
5	Direct labor	0.150	0.147	−2.00%
6	Energy	0.080	0.100	25.00%
7	Repairs	0.040	0.040	0.00%
8	Tank cleaning	0.030	0.040	33.33%
9	Total	$0.500	$0.530	6.00%

Both energy and tank cleaning per-unit costs have increased significantly in May. These increases should be further investigated. For example, the increase in energy may be due to the machines losing fuel efficiency. This could lead management to repair the machines. The tank cleaning costs could be investigated in a similar fashion.

Yield

In addition to unit costs, managers of process manufacturers are also concerned about yield. The **yield** is computed as follows:

$$\text{Yield} = \frac{\text{Quantity of Material Output}}{\text{Quantity of Material Input}}$$

To illustrate, assume that 1,000 pounds of sugar enter the Packaging Department and 980 pounds of sugar were packed. The yield is 98%, computed as follows:

$$\text{Yield} = \frac{\text{Quantity of Material Output}}{\text{Quantity of Material Input}} = \frac{980 \text{ pounds}}{1{,}000 \text{ pounds}} = 98\%$$

Thus, two percent (100% − 98%) or 20 pounds of sugar were lost or spilled during the packing process. Managers can investigate significant changes in yield over time or significant differences in yield from industry standards.

Example Exercise 20-8 — Using Process Costs for Decision Making — Obj. 4

The cost of energy consumed in producing good units in the Bottling Department of Rocky Springs Beverage Company was $4,200 and $3,700 for March and April, respectively. The number of equivalent units produced in March and April was 70,000 liters and 74,000 liters, respectively. Evaluate the change in the cost of energy between the two months.

Follow My Example 20-8

$$\text{Energy cost per liter, March} = \frac{\$4,200}{70,000 \text{ liters}} = \$0.06$$

$$\text{Energy cost per liter, April} = \frac{\$3,700}{74,000 \text{ liters}} = \$0.05$$

The cost of energy has improved by 1 cent per liter between March and April.

Practice Exercises: PE 20-8A, PE 20-8B

Lean Manufacturing

Obj. 5 Compare lean manufacturing with traditional manufacturing processing.

The objective of most manufacturers is to produce products with high quality, low cost, and instant availability. In attempting to achieve this objective, many manufacturers have implemented lean manufacturing. **Lean manufacturing** is a management approach that produces products with high quality, low cost, fast response, and immediate availability. Lean manufacturing obtains efficiencies and flexibility by reorganizing the traditional production process.

Traditional Production Process

A traditional manufacturing process for a furniture manufacturer is shown in Exhibit 10. The product (chair) moves through seven processes. In each process, workers are assigned a specific job, which is performed repeatedly as unfinished products are received from the preceding department. The product moves from process to process as each function or step is completed.

EXHIBIT 10

Traditional Production Line

For the furniture maker in Exhibit 10, the product (chair) moves through the following processes:

1. In the Cutting Department, the wood is cut to design specifications.
2. In the Drilling Department, the wood is drilled to design specifications.
3. In the Sanding Department, the wood is sanded.
4. In the Staining Department, the wood is stained.
5. In the Varnishing Department, varnish and other protective coatings are applied.
6. In the Upholstery Department, fabric and other materials are added.
7. In the Assembly Department, the product (chair) is assembled.

In the traditional production process, supervisors enter materials into manufacturing to keep all the manufacturing departments (processes) operating. Some departments, however, may process materials more rapidly than others. In addition, if one department stops because of machine breakdowns, for example, the preceding departments usually continue production in order to avoid idle time. In such cases, a buildup of work in process inventories results in some departments.

Lean Production Process

In lean manufacturing, processing functions are combined into work centers, sometimes called **manufacturing cells**. For example, the seven departments illustrated in Exhibit 10 might be reorganized into the following three work centers:

1. Work Center 1 performs the cutting, drilling, and sanding functions.
2. Work Center 2 performs the staining and varnishing functions.
3. Work Center 3 performs the upholstery and assembly functions.

The preceding lean manufacturing process is illustrated in Exhibit 11.

Lean Production Line

In traditional manufacturing, a worker typically performs only one function. However, in lean manufacturing, work centers complete several functions. Thus, workers are often cross-trained to perform more than one function. Research has indicated that workers who perform several functions identify better with the end product. This creates pride in the product and improves quality and productivity.

The activities supporting the manufacturing process are called *service activities*. For example, repair and maintenance of manufacturing equipment are service activities. In lean manufacturing, service activities may be assigned to individual work centers rather than to centralized service departments. For example, each work center may be assigned responsibility for the repair and maintenance of its machinery and equipment. This creates an environment in which workers gain a better understanding of the production process and their machinery. In turn, workers tend to take better care of the machinery, which decreases repairs and maintenance costs, reduces machine downtime, and improves product quality.

In lean manufacturing, the product is often placed on a movable carrier that is centrally located in the work center. After the workers in a work center have completed their activities with the product, the entire carrier and any additional materials are moved just in time to satisfy the demand or need of the next work center. In this sense, the product is said to be "pulled through." Each work center is connected to other work centers through information contained on a Kanban, which is a Japanese term for cards.

In summary, the primary objective of lean manufacturing is to increase the efficiency of operations. This is achieved by eliminating waste and simplifying the production process. At the same time, lean manufacturing continually improves the manufacturing process and product quality.

Before **Caterpillar** implemented JIT, a transmission traveled 10 miles through the factory and required 1,000 pieces of paper to support the manufacturing process. After implementing lean manufacturing, a transmission travels only 200 feet and requires only 10 pieces of paper.

APPENDIX

Average Cost Method

A cost flow assumption must be used as product costs flow through manufacturing processes. In this chapter, the first-in, first-out cost flow method was used for the Mixing Department of Frozen Delight. In this appendix, the average cost flow method is illustrated for **S&W Ice Cream Company (S&W)**.

Determining Costs Using the Average Cost Method

S&W's operations are similar to those of Frozen Delight. Like Frozen Delight, S&W mixes direct materials (milk, cream, sugar) in refrigerated vats and has two manufacturing departments, Mixing and Packaging.

The manufacturing data for the Mixing Department for July are as follows:

Inventory in process, July 1, 5,000 gallons (70% completed)	$ 6,200
Direct materials cost incurred in July, 60,000 gallons	66,000
Direct labor cost incurred in July	10,500
Factory overhead applied in July	6,405
Total production costs to account for	$89,105
Cost of goods transferred to Packaging in July (includes units in process on July 1), 62,000 gallons	?
Cost of work in process inventory, July 31, 3,000 gallons, 25% completed as to conversion costs	?

Using the average cost method, the objective is to allocate the total costs of production of $89,105 to the following:

- The 62,000 gallons completed and transferred to the Packaging Department
- The 3,000 gallons in the July 31 (ending) work in process inventory

The preceding costs show two question marks. These amounts are determined by preparing a cost of production report, using the following four steps:

Step 1. Determine the units to be assigned costs.
Step 2. Compute equivalent units of production.
Step 3. Determine the cost per equivalent unit.
Step 4. Allocate costs to transferred out and partially completed units.

Under the average cost method, all production costs (materials and conversion costs) are combined for determining equivalent units and cost per equivalent unit.

Step 1: Determine the Units to Be Assigned Costs

The first step is to determine the units to be assigned costs. A unit can be any measure of completed production, such as tons, gallons, pounds, barrels, or cases. For **S&W**, a unit is a gallon of ice cream.

S&W's Mixing Department had 65,000 gallons of direct materials to account for during July, as shown here.

Total gallons to account for:
Inventory in process, July 1 .... 5,000 gallons
Received from materials storeroom 60,000
    Total units to account for by the Packaging Department .... 65,000 gallons

There are two groups of units to be assigned costs for the period.

Group 1   Units completed and transferred out
Group 2   Units in the July 31 (ending) work in process inventory

During July, the Mixing Department completed and transferred 62,000 gallons to the Packaging Department. Of the 60,000 gallons started in July, 57,000 (60,000 − 3,000) gallons were completed and transferred to the Packaging Department. Thus, the ending work in process inventory consists of 3,000 gallons.

The total units (gallons) to be assigned costs for S&W can be summarized as follows:

Group 1   Units transferred out to the Packaging Department in July   62,000 gallons
Group 2   Inventory in process, July 31   3,000
           Total gallons to be assigned costs....................................   65,000 gallons

The total units (gallons) to be assigned costs (65,000 gallons) equal the total units to account for (65,000 gallons).

Step 2: Compute Equivalent Units of Production

S&W has 3,000 gallons of whole units in the work in process inventory for the Mixing Department on July 31. Because these units are 25% complete, the number of equivalent units in process in the Mixing Department on July 31 is 750 gallons (3,000 gallons × 25%). Because the units transferred to the Packaging Department have been completed, the whole units (62,000 gallons) transferred are the same as the equivalent units transferred.

The total equivalent units of production for the Mixing Department are determined by adding the equivalent units in the ending work in process inventory to the units transferred and completed during the period, computed as follows:

Equivalent units completed and transferred to the
    Packaging Department during July .... 62,000 gallons
Equivalent units in ending work in process, July 31   750
    Total equivalent units .... 62,750 gallons

Step 3: Determine the Cost per Equivalent Unit

Because materials and conversion costs are combined under the average cost method, the cost per equivalent unit is determined by dividing the total production costs by the total equivalent units of production as follows:

$$\text{Cost per Equivalent Unit} = \frac{\text{Total Production Costs}}{\text{Total Equivalent Units}}$$

$$\text{Cost per Equivalent Unit} = \frac{\text{Total Production Costs}}{\text{Total Equivalent Units}} = \frac{\$89,105}{62,750 \text{ gallons}} = \$1.42$$

The cost per equivalent unit is used in Step 4 to allocate the production costs to the completed and partially completed units.

Step 4: Allocate Costs to Transferred Out and Partially Completed Units

The cost of transferred and partially completed units is determined by multiplying the cost per equivalent unit times the equivalent units of production. For **S&W**'s Mixing Department, these costs are determined as follows:

Group 1	Transferred out to the Packaging Department (62,000 gallons × $1.42)		$88,040
Group 2	Inventory in process, July 31 (3,000 gallons × 25% × $1.42).................		1,065
	Total production costs assigned		$89,105

The Cost of Production Report

The July cost of production report for **S&W**'s Mixing Department is shown in Exhibit 12.

This cost of production report summarizes the following:

- The units for which the department is accountable and the disposition of those units
- The production costs incurred by the department and the allocation of those costs between completed and partially completed units

Cost of Production Report for S&W's Mixing Department—Average Cost

EXHIBIT 12

	A	B	C
1	S&W Ice Cream Company		
2	Cost of Production Report—Mixing Department		
3	For the Month Ended July 31		
4	**UNITS**		
5		Whole Units	Equivalent Units
6			of Production
7	Units to account for during production:		
8	Inventory in process, July 1	5,000	
9	Received from materials storeroom	60,000	
10	Total units accounted for by the Mixing Department	65,000	
11			
12	Units to be assigned costs:		
13	Transferred to Packaging Department in July	62,000	62,000
14	Inventory in process, July 31 (25% completed)	3,000	750
15	Total units to be assigned costs	65,000	62,750
16			
17	**COSTS**		Costs
18			
19	Cost per equivalent unit:		
20	Total production costs for July in Mixing Department		$89,105
21	Total equivalent units (from Step 2)		÷62,750
22	Cost per equivalent unit		$ 1.42
23			
24	Costs assigned to production:		
25	Inventory in process, July 1		$ 6,200
26	Direct materials, direct labor, and factory overhead incurred in July		82,905
27	Total costs accounted for by the Mixing Department		$89,105
28			
29			
30	Costs allocated to completed and partially completed units:		
31	Transferred to Packaging Department in July (62,000 gallons × $1.42)		$88,040
32	Inventory in process, July 31 (3,000 gallons × 25% × $1.42)		1,065
33	Total costs assigned by the Mixing Department		$89,105
34			

Step 1 — rows 4–10
Step 2 — rows 12–15
Step 3 — rows 19–27
Step 4 — rows 30–33

At a Glance 20

Obj. 1 Describe process cost systems.

Key Points The process cost system is best suited for industries that mass produce identical units of a product. Costs are charged to processing departments rather than to jobs as with the job order cost system. These costs are transferred from one department to the next until production is completed.

Learning Outcomes	Example Exercises	Practice Exercises
• Identify the characteristics of a process manufacturer.		
• Compare and contrast the job order cost system with the process cost system.	EE20-1	PE20-1A, 20-1B
• Describe the physical and cost flows of a process manufacturer.		

Obj. 2 Prepare a cost of production report.

Key Points Manufacturing costs must be allocated between the units that have been completed and those that remain within the department. This allocation is accomplished by allocating costs using equivalent units of production.

Learning Outcomes	Example Exercises	Practice Exercises
• Determine the whole units charged to production and to be assigned costs.	EE20-2	PE20-2A, 20-2B
• Compute the equivalent units with respect to materials.	EE20-3	PE20-3A, 20-3B
• Compute the equivalent units with respect to conversion.	EE20-4	PE20-4A, 20-4B
• Compute the costs per equivalent unit.	EE20-5	PE20-5A, 20-5B
• Allocate the costs to beginning inventory, units started and completed, and ending inventory.	EE20-6	PE20-6A, 20-6B
• Prepare a cost of production report.		

Obj. 3 Journalize entries for transactions using a process cost system.

Key Points Prepare the summary journal entries for materials, labor, applied factory overhead, and transferred costs incurred in production.

Learning Outcomes	Example Exercises	Practice Exercises
• Prepare journal entries for process costing transactions.	EE20-7	PE20-7A, 20-7B
• Summarize cost flows in T account form.		
• Compute the ending inventory balances.		

Obj. 4 Describe and illustrate the use of cost of production reports for decision making.

Key Points The cost of production report provides information for controlling and improving operations. The report(s) can provide details of a department for a single period or over a period of time.
Yield measures the quantity of output of production relative to the inputs.

Learning Outcomes	Example Exercises	Practice Exercises
• Evaluate the change in the cost per equivalent unit between two periods.		
• Prepare and evaluate a report showing the change in costs per unit by multiple cost categories for comparative periods.	EE20-8	PE20-8A, 20-8B
• Compute and interpret yield.		

Obj. 5 Compare lean manufacturing with traditional manufacturing processing.

Key Points The lean manufacturing philosophy focuses on reducing time, cost, and poor quality within the process.

Learning Outcome	Example Exercises	Practice Exercises
• Identify the characteristics of lean manufacturing.		

Illustrative Problem

Southern Aggregate Company manufactures concrete by a series of four processes. All materials are introduced in Crushing. From Crushing, the materials pass through Sifting, Baking, and Mixing, emerging as finished concrete. All inventories are costed by the first-in, first-out method.

The balances in the accounts Work in Process—Mixing and Finished Goods were as follows on May 1:

Inventory in Process—Mixing (2,000 units, 1/4 completed with regard to conversion)	$ 13,700
Finished Goods (1,800 units at $8.00 a unit)	14,400

The following costs were charged to Work in Process—Mixing during May:

Direct materials transferred from Baking: 15,200 units at $6.50 a unit	$ 98,800
Direct labor	17,200
Factory overhead	11,780
Total	$127,780

During May, 16,000 units of concrete were completed and 15,800 units were sold. Inventories on May 31 were as follows:

Inventory in Process—Mixing: 1,200 units, 1/2 completed with regard to conversion
Finished Goods: 2,000 units

(Continued)

Instructions

1. Prepare a cost of production report for the Mixing Department.
2. Determine the cost of goods sold (indicate number of units and unit costs).
3. Determine the finished goods inventory, May 31.

Solution

1.

Southern Aggregate Company
Cost of Production Report—Mixing Department
For the Month Ended May 31

	Whole Units	Equivalent Units Direct Materials	Equivalent Units Conversion
UNITS			
Units charged to production:			
Inventory in process, May 1	2,000		
Received from Baking	15,200		
Total units accounted for by the Mixing Department	17,200		
Units to be assigned costs:			
Inventory in process, May 1 (25% completed with regards to conversion)	2,000	0	1,500
Started and completed in May	14,000	14,000	14,000
Transferred to finished goods in May	16,000	14,000	15,500
Inventory in process, May 31 (50% completed with regards to conversion)	1,200	1,200	600
Total units to be assigned costs	17,200	15,200	16,100

	Costs Direct Materials	Costs Conversion	Total
COSTS			
Cost per equivalent unit:			
Total costs for May in Mixing Department	$98,800	$28,980*	
Total equivalent units (row 16)	÷15,200	÷16,100	
Cost per equivalent unit	$6.50	$1.80	
*$17,200 + $11,780			
Costs assigned to production:			
Inventory in process, May 1			$13,700
Costs incurred in May			127,780
Total costs accounted for by the Mixing Department			$141,480
Cost allocated to completed and partially completed units:			
Inventory in process, May 1 balance			$13,700
To complete inventory in process, May 1	$ 0	$2,700[a]	2,700
Cost of completed May 1 work in process			$16,400
Started and completed in May	91,000[b]	25,200[c]	116,200
Transferred to finished goods in May			$132,600
Inventory in process, May 31	7,800[d]	1,080[e]	8,880
Total costs assigned by the Mixing Department			$141,480

[a]1,500 × $1.80 = $2,700 [b]14,000 × $6.50 = $91,000 [c]14,000 × $1.80 = $25,200 [d]1,200 × $6.50 = $7,800 [e]600 × $1.80 = $1,080

2. Cost of goods sold:

1,800 units at $8.00	$ 14,400	(from finished goods beginning inventory)
2,000 units at $8.20*	16,400	(from inventory in process beginning inventory)
12,000 units at $8.30**	99,600	(from May production started and completed)
15,800 units	$130,400	

*($13,700 + $2,700) ÷ 2,000
**$116,200 ÷ 14,000

3. Finished goods inventory, May 31:

2,000 units at $8.30 $16,600

Key Terms

cost of production report (976)
cost per equivalent unit (981)
equivalent units of production (978)
first-in, first-out (FIFO) method (976)
lean manufacturing (991)
manufacturing cells (992)
process cost system (971)
process manufacturer (970)
whole units (978)
yield (990)

Discussion Questions

1. Which type of cost system, process or job order, would be best suited for each of the following: (a) TV assembler, (b) building contractor, (c) automobile repair shop, (d) paper manufacturer, and (e) custom jewelry manufacturer? Give reasons for your answers.
2. In job order cost accounting, the three elements of manufacturing cost are charged directly to job orders. Why is it not necessary to charge manufacturing costs in process cost accounting to job orders?
3. In a job order cost system, direct labor and factory overhead applied are debited to individual jobs. How are these items treated in a process cost system and why?
4. Why is the cost per equivalent unit often determined separately for direct materials and conversion costs?
5. What is the purpose for determining the cost per equivalent unit?
6. Rameriz Company is a process manufacturer with two production departments, Blending and Filling. All direct materials are introduced in Blending from the materials store area. What is included in the cost transferred to Filling?
7. What is the most important purpose of the cost of production report?
8. How are cost of production reports used for controlling and improving operations?
9. How is "yield" determined for a process manufacturer?
10. How does lean manufacturing differ from the conventional manufacturing process?

Practice Exercises

Example Exercises

EE 20-1 p. 973 **PE 20-1A Job order versus process costing** OBJ. 1

Which of the following industries would typically use job order costing, and which would typically use process costing?

Steel manufactuirng	Computer chip manufacturing
Business consulting	Candy making
Web designer	Designer clothes manufacturing

EE 20-1 p. 973 **PE 20-1B Job order versus process costing** OBJ. 1

Which of the following industries would typically use job order costing, and which would typically use process costing?

Dentist	Movie studio
Gasoline refining	Paper manufacturing
Flour mill	Custom printing

1000 Chapter 20 Process Cost Systems

EE 20-2 p. 977 **PE 20-2A** Units to be assigned costs OBJ. 2

Eve Cosmetics Company consists of two departments, Blending and Filling. The Filling Department received 50,000 ounces from the Blending Department. During the period, the Filling Department completed 46,000 ounces, including 4,000 ounces of work in process at the beginning of the period. The ending work in process inventory was 8,000 ounces. How many ounces were started and completed during the period?

EE 20-2 p. 977 **PE 20-2B** Units to be assigned costs OBJ. 2

Keystone Steel Company has two departments, Casting and Rolling. In the Rolling Department, ingots from the Casting Department are rolled into steel sheet. The Rolling Department received 8,500 tons from the Casting Department. During the period, the Rolling Department completed 7,900 tons, including 400 tons of work in process at the beginning of the period. The ending work in process inventory was 1,000 tons. How many tons were started and completed during the period?

EE 20-3 p. 979 **PE 20-3A** Equivalent units of materials cost OBJ. 2

The Filling Department of Eve Cosmetics Company had 4,000 ounces in beginning work in process inventory (60% complete). During the period, 46,000 ounces were completed. The ending work in process inventory was 8,000 ounces (25% complete). What are the total equivalent units for direct materials if materials are added at the beginning of the process?

EE 20-3 p. 979 **PE 20-3B** Equivalent units of materials cost OBJ. 2

The Rolling Department of Keystone Steel Company had 400 tons in beginning work in process inventory (20% complete). During the period, 7,900 tons were completed. The ending work in process inventory was 1,000 tons (30% complete). What are the total equivalent units for direct materials if materials are added at the beginning of the process?

EE 20-4 p. 981 **PE 20-4A** Equivalent units of conversion costs OBJ. 2

The Filling Department of Eve Cosmetics Company had 4,000 ounces in beginning work in process inventory (60% complete). During the period, 46,000 ounces were completed. The ending work in process inventory was 8,000 ounces (25% complete). What are the total equivalent units for conversion costs?

EE 20-4 p. 981 **PE 20-4B** Equivalent units of conversion costs OBJ. 2

The Rolling Department of Keystone Steel Company had 400 tons in beginning work in process inventory (20% complete). During the period, 7,900 tons were completed. The ending work in process inventory was 1,000 tons (30% complete). What are the total equivalent units for conversion costs?

EE 20-5 p. 982 **PE 20-5A** Cost per equivalent unit OBJ. 2

The cost of direct materials transferred into the Filling Department of Eve Cosmetics Company is $20,000. The conversion cost for the period in the Filling Department is $4,560. The total equivalent units for direct materials and conversion are 50,000 ounces and 45,600 ounces, respectively. Determine the direct materials and conversion costs per equivalent unit.

EE 20-5 p. 982 **PE 20-5B** Cost per equivalent unit OBJ. 2

The cost of direct materials transferred into the Rolling Department of Keystone Steel Company is $510,000. The conversion cost for the period in the Rolling Department is $81,200. The total equivalent units for direct materials and conversion are 8,500 tons and 8,120 tons, respectively. Determine the direct materials and conversion costs per equivalent unit.

EE 20-6 p. 984

PE 20-6A Cost of units transferred out and ending work in process OBJ. 2

The costs per equivalent unit of direct materials and conversion in the Filling Department of Eve Cosmetics Company are $0.40 and $0.10, respectively. The equivalent units to be assigned costs are as follows:

	Equivalent Units	
	Direct Materials	Conversion
Inventory in process, beginning of period	0	1,600
Started and completed during the period	42,000	42,000
Transferred out of Filling (completed)	42,000	43,600
Inventory in process, end of period	8,000	2,000
Total units to be assigned costs	50,000	45,600

The beginning work in process inventory had a cost of $1,800. Determine the cost of completed and transferred-out production and the ending work in process inventory.

EE 20-6 p. 984

PE 20-6B Cost of units transferred out and ending work in process OBJ. 2

The costs per equivalent unit of direct materials and conversion in the Rolling Department of Keystone Steel Company are $60 and $10, respectively. The equivalent units to be assigned costs are as follows:

	Equivalent Units	
	Direct Materials	Conversion
Inventory in process, beginning of period	0	320
Started and completed during the period	7,500	7,500
Transferred out of Rolling (completed)	7,500	7,820
Inventory in process, end of period	1,000	300
Total units to be assigned costs	8,500	8,120

The beginning work in process inventory had a cost of $25,000. Determine the cost of completed and transferred-out production and the ending work in process inventory.

EE 20-7 p. 988

PE 20-7A Process cost journal entries OBJ. 3

The cost of materials transferred into the Filling Department of Eve Cosmetics Company is $20,000, including $14,000 from the Blending Department and $6,000 from the materials storeroom. The conversion cost for the period in the Filling Department is $4,560 ($1,600 factory overhead applied and $2,960 direct labor). The total cost transferred to Finished Goods for the period was $22,960. The Filling Department had a beginning inventory of $1,800.

a. Journalize (1) the cost of transferred-in materials, (2) conversion costs, and (3) the costs transferred out to Finished Goods.

b. Determine the balance of Work in Process—Filling at the end of the period.

EE 20-7 p. 988

PE 20-7B Process cost journal entries OBJ. 3

The cost of materials transferred into the Rolling Department of Keystone Steel Company is $510,000 from the Casting Department. The conversion cost for the period in the Rolling Department is $81,200 ($54,700 factory overhead applied and $26,500 direct labor). The total cost transferred to Finished Goods for the period was $553,200. The Rolling Department had a beginning inventory of $25,000.

a. Journalize (1) the cost of transferred-in materials, (2) conversion costs, and (3) the costs transferred out to Finished Goods.

b. Determine the balance of Work in Process—Rolling at the end of the period.

1002 Chapter 20 Process Cost Systems

EE 20-8 *p. 991*   **PE 20-8A**   **Using process costs for decision making**   OBJ. 4

The costs of energy consumed in producing good units in the Baking Department of Pan Company were $14,875 and $14,615 for June and July, respectively. The number of equivalent units produced in June and July was 42,500 pounds and 39,500 pounds, respectively. Evaluate the change in the cost of energy between the two months.

EE 20-8 *p. 991*   **PE 20-8B**   **Using process costs for decision making**   OBJ. 4

The costs of materials consumed in producing good units in the Forming Department of Thomas Company were $76,000 and $77,350 for September and October, respectively. The number of equivalent units produced in September and October was 800 tons and 850 tons, respectively. Evaluate the change in the cost of materials between the two months.

Exercises

EX 20-1   **Entries for materials cost flows in a process cost system**   OBJ. 1, 3

The Hershey Company manufactures chocolate confectionery products. The three largest raw materials are cocoa, sugar, and dehydrated milk. These raw materials first go into the Blending Department. The blended product is then sent to the Molding Department, where the bars of candy are formed. The candy is then sent to the Packing Department, where the bars are wrapped and boxed. The boxed candy is then sent to the distribution center, where it is eventually sold to food brokers and retailers.

Show the accounts debited and credited for each of the following business events:

a. Materials used by the Blending Department
b. Transfer of blended product to the Molding Department
c. Transfer of chocolate to the Packing Department
d. Transfer of boxed chocolate to the distribution center
e. Sale of boxed chocolate

EX 20-2   **Flowchart of accounts related to service and processing departments**   OBJ. 1

Alcoa Inc. is the world's largest producer of aluminum products. One product that Alcoa manufactures is aluminum sheet products for the aerospace industry. The entire output of the Smelting Department is transferred to the Rolling Department. Part of the fully processed goods from the Rolling Department are sold as rolled sheet, and the remainder of the goods are transferred to the Converting Department for further processing into sheared sheet.

Prepare a diagram using T accounts showing the flow of costs from the processing department accounts into the finished goods accounts and then into the cost of goods sold account. The relevant accounts are as follows:

Cost of Goods Sold	Finished Goods—Rolled Sheet
Materials	Finished Goods—Sheared Sheet
Factory Overhead—Smelting Department	Work in Process—Smelting Department
Factory Overhead—Rolling Department	Work in Process—Rolling Department
Factory Overhead—Converting Department	Work in Process—Converting Department

EX 20-3   **Entries for flow of factory costs for process cost system**   OBJ. 1, 3

Domino Foods, Inc., manufactures a sugar product by a continuous process involving three production departments—Refining, Sifting, and Packing. Assume that records indicate that direct materials, direct labor, and applied factory overhead for the first department, Refining, were $400,000, $150,000, and $100,000, respectively. Also, work in process in the Refining Department at the beginning of the period totaled $40,000, and work in process at the end of the period totaled $35,000.

Journalize the entries to record (a) the flow of costs into the Refining Department during the period for (1) direct materials, (2) direct labor, and (3) factory overhead and to record (b) the transfer of production costs to the second department, Sifting.

EX 20-4 Factory overhead rate, entry for applying factory overhead, and factory overhead account balance
OBJ. 1, 3

✔ a. 125%

The chief cost accountant for Kenner Beverage Co. estimated that total factory overhead cost for the Blending Department for the coming fiscal year beginning May 1 would be $3,000,000 and total direct labor costs would be $2,400,000. During May, the actual direct labor cost totaled $198,400 and factory overhead cost incurred totaled $253,200.

a. What is the predetermined factory overhead rate based on direct labor cost?
b. Journalize the entry to apply factory overhead to production for May.
c. What is the May 31 balance of the account Factory Overhead—Blending Department?
d. Does the balance in part (c) represent over- or underapplied factory overhead?

EX 20-5 Equivalent units of production
OBJ. 2

✔ Direct materials, 16,800 units

The Converting Department of Soft Touch Towel and Tissue Company had 1,200 units in work in process at the beginning of the period, which were 25% complete. During the period, 16,000 units were completed and transferred to the Packing Department. There were 2,000 units in process at the end of the period, which were 40% complete. Direct materials are placed into the process at the beginning of production. Determine the number of equivalent units of production with respect to direct materials and conversion costs.

EX 20-6 Equivalent units of production
OBJ. 2

✔ a. Conversion, 96,720 units

Units of production data for the two departments of Pacific Cable and Wire Company for November of the current fiscal year are as follows:

	Drawing Department	Winding Department
Work in process, November 1	5,000 units, 40% completed	3,200 units, 80% completed
Completed and transferred to next processing department during November	95,000 units	95,100 units
Work in process, November 30	6,200 units, 60% completed	3,100 units, 15% completed

If all direct materials are placed in process at the beginning of production, determine the direct materials and conversion equivalent units of production for November for (a) the Drawing Department and (b) the Winding Department.

EX 20-7 Equivalent units of production
OBJ. 2

✔ b. Conversion, 335,100

The following information concerns production in the Baking Department for March. All direct materials are placed in process at the beginning of production.

ACCOUNT Work in Process—Baking Department   ACCOUNT NO.

Date		Item	Debit	Credit	Balance Debit	Balance Credit
Mar.	1	Bal., 18,000 units, ¼ completed			14,760	
	31	Direct materials, 336,000 units	252,000		266,760	
	31	Direct labor	40,000		306,760	
	31	Factory overhead	60,530		367,290	
	31	Goods finished, 330,000 units		346,410	20,880	
	31	Bal. ? units, ⅖ completed			20,880	

a. Determine the number of units in work in process inventory at March 31.
b. Determine the equivalent units of production for direct materials and conversion costs in March.

1004 Chapter 20 Process Cost Systems

EX 20-8 Costs per equivalent unit OBJ. 2, 4

✔ a. 2. Conversion cost per equivalent unit, $0.30

a. Based on the data in Exercise 20-7, determine the following for March:
 1. Direct materials cost per equivalent unit
 2. Conversion cost per equivalent unit
 3. Cost of the beginning work in process completed during March
 4. Cost of units started and completed during March
 5. Cost of the ending work in process

b. Assuming that the direct materials cost is the same for February and March, did the conversion cost per equivalent unit increase, decrease, or remain the same in March?

EX 20-9 Equivalent units of production OBJ. 2

Kellogg Company manufactures cold cereal products, such as *Frosted Flakes*. Assume that the inventory in process on March 1 for the Packing Department included 1,200 pounds of cereal in the packing machine hopper (enough for 800 24-oz. boxes) and 800 empty 24-oz. boxes held in the package carousel of the packing machine. During March, 65,400 boxes of 24-oz. cereal were packaged. Conversion costs are incurred when a box is filled with cereal. On March 31, the packing machine hopper held 900 pounds of cereal and the package carousel held 600 empty 24-oz. (1½-lb.) boxes. Assume that once a box is filled with cereal, it is immediately transferred to the finished goods warehouse.

Determine the equivalent units of production for cereal, boxes, and conversion costs for March. An equivalent unit is defined as "pounds" for cereal and "24-oz. boxes" for boxes and conversion costs.

EX 20-10 Costs per equivalent unit OBJ. 2

✔ c. $2.40

Georgia Products Inc. completed and transferred 89,000 particle board units of production from the Pressing Department. There was no beginning inventory in process in the department. The ending in-process inventory was 2,400 units, which were ⅗ complete as to conversion cost. All materials are added at the beginning of the process. Direct materials cost incurred was $219,360, direct labor cost incurred was $28,100, and factory overhead applied was $12,598.

Determine the following for the Pressing Department:

a. Total conversion cost
b. Conversion cost per equivalent unit
c. Direct materials cost per equivalent unit

EX 20-11 Equivalent units of production and related costs OBJ. 2

✔ a. 1,000 units

The charges to Work in Process—Assembly Department for a period, together with information concerning production, are as follows. All direct materials are placed in process at the beginning of production.

Work in Process—Assembly Department			
Bal., 1,600 units, 35% completed	17,440	To Finished Goods, 29,600 units	?
Direct materials, 29,000 units @ $9.50	275,500		
Direct labor	84,600		
Factory overhead	39,258		
Bal. ? units, 45% completed	?		

Determine the following:

a. The number of units in work in process inventory at the end of the period
b. Equivalent units of production for direct materials and conversion
c. Costs per equivalent unit for direct materials and conversion
d. Cost of the units started and completed during the period

EX 20-12 Cost of units completed and in process   OBJ. 2, 4

✓ a. 1. $21,808

a. Based on the data in Exercise 20-11, determine the following:
   1. Cost of beginning work in process inventory completed this period
   2. Cost of units transferred to finished goods during the period
   3. Cost of ending work in process inventory
   4. Cost per unit of the completed beginning work in process inventory, rounded to the nearest cent
b. Did the production costs change from the preceding period? Explain.
c. Assuming that the direct materials cost per unit did not change from the preceding period, did the conversion costs per equivalent unit increase, decrease, or remain the same for the current period?

EX 20-13 Errors in equivalent unit computation   OBJ. 2

Napco Refining Company processes gasoline. On June 1 of the current year, 6,400 units were $3/5$ completed in the Blending Department. During June, 55,000 units entered the Blending Department from the Refining Department. During June, the units in process at the beginning of the month were completed. Of the 55,000 units entering the department, all were completed except 5,200 units that were $1/5$ completed. The equivalent units for conversion costs for June for the Blending Department were computed as follows:

Equivalent units of production in June:	
To process units in inventory on June 1: 6,400 × $3/5$	3,840
To process units started and completed in June: 55,000 – 6,400	48,600
To process units in inventory on June 30: 5,200 × $1/5$	1,040
Equivalent units of production	53,480

List the errors in the computation of equivalent units for conversion costs for the Blending Department for June.

EX 20-14 Cost per equivalent unit   OBJ. 2

✓ a. 12,400 units

The following information concerns production in the Forging Department for November. All direct materials are placed into the process at the beginning of production, and conversion costs are incurred evenly throughout the process. The beginning inventory consists of $9,000 of direct materials.

ACCOUNT Work in Process—Forging Department   **ACCOUNT NO.**

				Balance	
Date	Item	Debit	Credit	Debit	Credit
Nov. 1	Bal., 900 units, 60% completed			10,566	
30	Direct materials, 12,900 units	123,840		134,406	
30	Direct labor	21,650		156,056	
30	Factory overhead	16,870		172,926	
30	Goods transferred, ? units		?	?	
30	Bal., 1,400 units, 70% completed			?	

a. Determine the number of units transferred to the next department.
b. Determine the costs per equivalent unit of direct materials and conversion.
c. Determine the cost of units started and completed in November.

1006 Chapter 20 Process Cost Systems

EX 20-15 Costs per equivalent unit and production costs — OBJ. 2, 4

✓ a. $11,646

Based on the data in Exercise 20-14, determine the following:

a. Cost of beginning work in process inventory completed in November
b. Cost of units transferred to the next department during November
c. Cost of ending work in process inventory on November 30
d. Costs per equivalent unit of direct materials and conversion included in the November 1 beginning work in process
e. The November increase or decrease in costs per equivalent unit for direct materials and conversion from the previous month

---

EX 20-16 Cost of production report — OBJ. 2, 4

✓ a. 4. $2,092

Excel

The debits to Work in Process—Roasting Department for Morning Brew Coffee Company for August, together with information concerning production, are as follows:

Work in process, August 1, 700 pounds, 20% completed		$ 3,479*
*Direct materials (700 × $4.70)	$3,290	
Conversion (700 × 20% × $1.35)	189	
	$3,479	
Coffee beans added during August, 14,300 pounds		65,780
Conversion costs during August		21,942
Work in process, August 31, 400 pounds, 42% completed		?
Goods finished during August, 14,600 pounds		?

All direct materials are placed in process at the beginning of production.

a. Prepare a cost of production report, presenting the following computations:
  1. Direct materials and conversion equivalent units of production for August
  2. Direct materials and conversion costs per equivalent unit for August
  3. Cost of goods finished during August
  4. Cost of work in process at August 31
b. Compute and evaluate the change in cost per equivalent unit for direct materials and conversion from the previous month (July).

EX 20-17 Cost of production report — OBJ. 2, 4

✓ Conversion cost per equivalent unit, $5.10

The Cutting Department of Karachi Carpet Company provides the following data for January. Assume that all materials are added at the beginning of the process.

Work in process, January 1, 1,400 units, 75% completed		$ 22,960*
*Direct materials (1,400 × $12.65)	$17,710	
Conversion (1,400 × 75% × $5.00)	5,250	
	$22,960	
Materials added during January from Weaving Department, 58,000 units		$742,400
Direct labor for January		134,550
Factory overhead for January		151,611
Goods finished during January (includes goods in process, January 1), 56,200 units		—
Work in process, January 31, 3,200 units, 30% completed		—

a. Prepare a cost of production report for the Cutting Department.
b. Compute and evaluate the change in the costs per equivalent unit for direct materials and conversion from the previous month (December).

Chapter 20   Process Cost Systems   1007

EX 20-18   Cost of production and journal entries   OBJ. 1, 2, 3, 4

✔ b. $29,760

AccuBlade Castings Inc. casts blades for turbine engines. Within the Casting Department, alloy is first melted in a crucible, then poured into molds to produce the castings. On May 1, there were 230 pounds of alloy in process, which were 60% complete as to conversion. The Work in Process balance for these 230 pounds was $32,844, determined as follows:

Direct materials (230 × $132)	$30,360
Conversion (230 × 60% × $18)	2,484
	$32,844

During May, the Casting Department was charged $350,000 for 2,500 pounds of alloy and $19,840 for direct labor. Factory overhead is applied to the department at a rate of 150% of direct labor. The department transferred out 2,530 pounds of finished castings to the Machining Department. The May 31 inventory in process was 44% complete as to conversion.

a. Prepare the following May journal entries for the Casting Department:
   1. The materials charged to production
   2. The conversion costs charged to production
   3. The completed production transferred to the Machining Department
b. Determine the Work in Process—Casting Department May 31 balance.
c. Compute and evaluate the change in the costs per equivalent unit for direct materials and conversion from the previous month (April).

EX 20-19   Cost of production and journal entries   OBJ. 1, 2, 3

✔ b. $14,319

Lighthouse Paper Company manufactures newsprint. The product is manufactured in two departments, Papermaking and Converting. Pulp is first placed into a vessel at the beginning of papermaking production. The following information concerns production in the Papermaking Department for March:

ACCOUNT Work in Process—Papermaking Department   **ACCOUNT NO.**

Date	Item	Debit	Credit	Balance Debit	Balance Credit
Mar. 1	Bal., 2,600 units, 35% completed			9,139	
31	Direct materials, 105,000 units	330,750		339,889	
31	Direct labor	40,560		380,449	
31	Factory overhead	54,795		435,244	
31	Goods transferred, 103,900 units		?	?	
31	Bal., 3,700 units, 80% completed			?	

a. Prepare the following March journal entries for the Papermaking Department:
   1. The materials charged to production
   2. The conversion costs charged to production
   3. The completed production transferred to the Converting Department
b. Determine the Work in Process—Papermaking Department March 31 balance.

EX 20-20   Process costing for a service company   OBJ. 4

Madison Electric Company uses a fossil fuel (coal) plant for generating electricity. The facility can generate 900 megawatts (million watts) per hour. The plant operates 600 hours during March. Electricity is used as it is generated; thus, there are no inventories at the beginning or end of the period. The March conversion and fuel costs are as follows:

Conversion costs	$40,500,000
Fuel	10,800,000
Total	$51,300,000

(Continued)

Madison also has a wind farm that can generate 100 megawatts per hour. The wind farm receives sufficient wind to run 300 hours for March. The March conversion costs for the wind farm (mostly depreciation) are as follows:

Conversion costs $2,700,000

a. Determine the cost per megawatt hour (MWh) for the fossil fuel plant and the wind farm to identify the lowest cost facility in March.
b. Why are equivalent units of production not needed in determining the cost per megawatt hour (MWh) for generating electricity?
c. What advantage does the fossil fuel plant have over the wind farm?

EX 20-21 Decision making   OBJ. 4

Mystic Bottling Company bottles popular beverages in the Bottling Department. The beverages are produced by blending concentrate with water and sugar. The concentrate is purchased from a concentrate producer. The concentrate producer sets higher prices for the more popular concentrate flavors. A simplified Bottling Department cost of production report separating the cost of bottling the four flavors follows:

	A	B	C	D	E
1		Orange	Cola	Lemon-Lime	Root Beer
2	Concentrate	$ 4,625	$129,000	$105,000	$ 7,600
3	Water	1,250	30,000	25,000	2,000
4	Sugar	3,000	72,000	60,000	4,800
5	Bottles	5,500	132,000	110,000	8,800
6	Flavor changeover	3,000	4,800	4,000	10,000
7	Conversion cost	1,750	24,000	20,000	2,800
8	Total cost transferred to finished goods	$19,125	$391,800	$324,000	$36,000
9	Number of cases	2,500	60,000	50,000	4,000
10					

Beginning and ending work in process inventories are negligible, so they are omitted from the cost of production report. The flavor changeover cost represents the cost of cleaning the bottling machines between production runs of different flavors.

Prepare a memo to the production manager, analyzing this comparative cost information. In your memo, provide recommendations for further action, along with supporting schedules showing the total cost per case and cost per case by cost element. Round all supporting calculations to the nearest cent.

EX 20-22 Decision making   OBJ. 4

Pix Paper Inc. produces photographic paper for printing digital images. One of the processes for this operation is a coating (solvent spreading) operation, where chemicals are coated onto paper stock. There has been some concern about the cost performance of this operation. As a result, you have begun an investigation. You first discover that all materials and conversion prices have been stable for the last six months. Thus, increases in prices for inputs are not an explanation for increasing costs. However, you have discovered three possible problems from some of the operating personnel whose quotes follow:

Operator 1: "I've been keeping an eye on my operating room instruments. I feel as though our energy consumption is becoming less efficient."

Operator 2: "Every time the coating machine goes down, we produce waste on shutdown and subsequent startup. It seems as though during the last half year, we have had more unscheduled machine shutdowns than in the past. Thus, I think our yields must be dropping."

Operator 3: "My sense is that our coating costs are going up. It seems as though we are spreading a thicker coating than we should. Perhaps the coating machine needs to be recalibrated."

The Coating Department had no beginning or ending inventories for any month during the study period. The following data from the cost of production report are made available:

	A	B	C	D	E	F	G
1		January	February	March	April	May	June
2	Paper stock	$67,200	$63,840	$60,480	$64,512	$57,120	$53,760
3	Coating	$11,520	$11,856	$12,960	$15,667	$16,320	$18,432
4	Conversion cost (incl. energy)	$38,400	$36,480	$34,560	$36,864	$32,640	$30,720
5	Pounds input to the process	100,000	95,000	90,000	96,000	85,000	80,000
6	Pounds transferred out	96,000	91,200	86,400	92,160	81,600	76,800
7							

a. Prepare a table showing the paper cost per output pound, coating cost per output pound, conversion cost per output pound, and yield (pounds transferred out/pounds input) for each month. Round costs to the nearest cent and yield to the nearest whole percent.

b. ✏️ Interpret your table results.

EX 20-23 Lean manufacturing
OBJ. 5

The following are some quotes provided by a number of managers at Hawkeye Machining Company regarding the company's planned move toward a lean manufacturing system:

Director of Sales: I'm afraid we'll miss some sales if we don't keep a large stock of items on hand just in case demand increases. It only makes sense to me to keep large inventories in order to ensure product availability for our customers.

Director of Purchasing: I'm very concerned about moving to a lean system for materials. What would happen if one of our suppliers were unable to make a shipment? A supplier could fall behind in production or have a quality problem. Without some safety stock in our materials, our whole plant would shut down.

Director of Manufacturing: If we go to lean manufacturing, I think our factory output will drop. We need in-process inventory in order to "smooth out" the inevitable problems that occur during manufacturing. For example, if a machine that is used to process a product breaks down, it will starve the next machine if I don't have in-process inventory between the two machines. If I have in-process inventory, then I can keep the next operation busy while I fix the broken machine. Thus, the in-process inventories give me a safety valve that I can use to keep things running when things go wrong.

✏️ How would you respond to these managers?

Appendix
EX 20-24 Equivalent units of production: average cost method

✔ a. 17,000

The Converting Department of Tender Soft Tissue Company uses the average cost method and had 1,900 units in work in process that were 60% complete at the beginning of the period. During the period, 15,800 units were completed and transferred to the Packing Department. There were 1,200 units in process that were 30% complete at the end of the period.

a. Determine the number of whole units to be accounted for and to be assigned costs for the period.

b. Determine the number of equivalent units of production for the period.

Appendix
EX 20-25 Equivalent units of production: average cost method

✔ a. 12,100 units to be accounted for

Units of production data for the two departments of Atlantic Cable and Wire Company for July of the current fiscal year are as follows:

	Drawing Department	Winding Department
Work in process, July 1	500 units, 50% completed	350 units, 30% completed
Completed and transferred to next processing department during July	11,400 units	10,950 units
Work in process, July 31	700 units, 55% completed	800 units, 25% completed

Each department uses the average cost method.

a. Determine the number of whole units to be accounted for and to be assigned costs and the equivalent units of production for the Drawing Department.

b. Determine the number of whole units to be accounted for and to be assigned costs and the equivalent units of production for the Winding Department.

1010 Chapter 20 Process Cost Systems

Appendix
EX 20-26 Equivalent units of production: average cost method

✔ a. 3,100

The following information concerns production in the Finishing Department for May. The Finishing Department uses the average cost method.

ACCOUNT Work in Process—Finishing Department   ACCOUNT NO.

Date		Item	Debit	Credit	Balance Debit	Balance Credit
May	1	Bal., 4,200 units, 70% completed			36,500	
	31	Direct materials, 23,600 units	125,800		162,300	
	31	Direct labor	75,400		237,700	
	31	Factory overhead	82,675		320,375	
	31	Goods transferred, 24,700 units		308,750	11,625	
	31	Bal., ? units, 30% completed			11,625	

a. Determine the number of units in work in process inventory at the end of the month.
b. Determine the number of whole units to be accounted for and to be assigned costs and the equivalent units of production for May.

Appendix
EX 20-27 Equivalent units of production and related costs

✔ b. 8,820 units

Excel

The charges to Work in Process—Baking Department for a period as well as information concerning production are as follows. The Baking Department uses the average cost method, and all direct materials are placed in process during production.

Work in Process—Baking Department

Bal., 900 units, 40% completed	2,466	To Finished Goods, 8,100 units	?
Direct materials, 8,400 units	34,500		
Direct labor	16,200		
Factory overhead	8,574		
Bal., 1,200 units, 60% completed	?		

Determine the following:
a. The number of whole units to be accounted for and to be assigned costs
b. The number of equivalent units of production
c. The cost per equivalent unit
d. The cost of units transferred to Finished Goods
e. The cost of units in ending Work in Process

Appendix
EX 20-28 Cost per equivalent unit: average cost method

✔ a. $26.00

The following information concerns production in the Forging Department for June. The Forging Department uses the average cost method.

ACCOUNT Work in Process—Forging Department   ACCOUNT NO.

Date		Item	Debit	Credit	Balance Debit	Balance Credit
June	1	Bal., 500 units, 40% completed			5,000	
	30	Direct materials, 3,700 units	49,200		54,200	
	30	Direct labor	25,200		79,400	
	30	Factory overhead	25,120		104,520	
	30	Goods transferred, 3,600 units		?	?	
	30	Bal., 600 units, 70% completed			?	

a. Determine the cost per equivalent unit.
b. Determine cost of units transferred to Finished Goods.
c. Determine the cost of units in ending Work in Process.

Appendix
EX 20-29 Cost of production report: average cost method

✔ Cost per equivalent unit, $3.60

The increases to Work in Process—Roasting Department for Highlands Coffee Company for May as well as information concerning production are as follows:

Work in process, May 1, 1,150 pounds, 40% completed	$ 1,700
Coffee beans added during May, 10,900 pounds	28,600
Conversion costs during May	12,504
Work in process, May 31, 800 pounds, 80% completed	—
Goods finished during May, 11,250 pounds	—

Prepare a cost of production report, using the average cost method.

Appendix
EX 20-30 Cost of production report: average cost method

✔ Cost per equivalent unit, $9.00

Prepare a cost of production report for the Cutting Department of Dalton Carpet Company for January. Use the average cost method with the following data:

Work in process, January 1, 3,400 units, 75% completed	$ 23,000
Materials added during January from Weaving Department, 64,000 units	366,200
Direct labor for January	105,100
Factory overhead for January	80,710
Goods finished during January (includes goods in process, January 1), 63,500 units	—
Work in process, January 31, 3,900 units, 10% completed	—

Problems: Series A

PR 20-1A Entries for process cost system
OBJ. 1, 3

✔ 2. Materials January 31 balance, $46,500

Port Ormond Carpet Company manufactures carpets. Fiber is placed in process in the Spinning Department, where it is spun into yarn. The output of the Spinning Department is transferred to the Tufting Department, where carpet backing is added at the beginning of the process and the process is completed. On January 1, Port Ormond Carpet Company had the following inventories:

Finished Goods	$62,000
Work in Process—Spinning Department	35,000
Work in Process—Tufting Department	28,500
Materials	17,000

Departmental accounts are maintained for factory overhead, and both have zero balances on January 1.

Manufacturing operations for January are summarized as follows:

a. Materials purchased on account $500,000

b. Materials requisitioned for use:

Fiber—Spinning Department	$275,000
Carpet backing—Tufting Department	110,000
Indirect materials—Spinning Department	46,000
Indirect materials—Tufting Department	39,500

(Continued)

1012 Chapter 20 Process Cost Systems

c. Labor used:
Direct labor—Spinning Department	$185,000
Direct labor—Tufting Department	98,000
Indirect labor—Spinning Department	18,500
Indirect labor—Tufting Department	9,000

d. Depreciation charged on fixed assets:
Spinning Department	$ 12,500
Tufting Department	8,500

e. Expired prepaid factory insurance:
Spinning Department	$ 2,000
Tufting Department	1,000

f. Applied factory overhead:
Spinning Department	$ 80,000
Tufting Department	55,000

g. Production costs transferred from Spinning Department to Tufting Department $547,000
h. Production costs transferred from Tufting Department to Finished Goods $807,200
i. Cost of goods sold during the period $795,200

Instructions

1. Journalize the entries to record the operations, identifying each entry by letter.
2. Compute the January 31 balances of the inventory accounts.
3. Compute the January 31 balances of the factory overhead accounts.

PR 20-2A Cost of production report OBJ. 2, 4

✔ 1. Conversion cost per equivalent unit, $0.76

Arabica Highland Coffee Company roasts and packs coffee beans. The process begins by placing coffee beans into the Roasting Department. From the Roasting Department, coffee beans are then transferred to the Packing Department. The following is a partial work in process account of the Roasting Department at July 31:

ACCOUNT Work in Process—Roasting Department ACCOUNT NO.

Date		Item	Debit	Credit	Balance Debit	Balance Credit
July	1	Bal., 30,000 units, 10% completed			121,800	
	31	Direct materials, 155,000 units	620,000		741,800	
	31	Direct labor	90,000		831,800	
	31	Factory overhead	33,272		865,072	
	31	Goods transferred, 149,000 units		?		
	31	Bal., ? units, 45% completed			?	

Instructions

1. Prepare a cost of production report and identify the missing amounts for Work in Process—Roasting Department.
2. Assuming that the July 1 work in process inventory includes $119,400 of direct materials, determine the increase or decrease in the cost per equivalent unit for direct materials and conversion between June and July.

PR 20-3A Equivalent units and related costs; cost of production report; entries OBJ. 2, 3, 4

✔ 2. Transferred to Packaging Dept., $40,183

White Diamond Flour Company manufactures flour by a series of three processes, beginning with wheat grain being introduced in the Milling Department. From the Milling Department, the materials pass through the Sifting and Packaging departments, emerging as packaged refined flour.

The balance in the account Work in Process—Sifting Department was as follows on July 1:

Work in Process—Sifting Department (900 units, ⅗ completed):
Direct materials (900 × $2.05) $1,845
Conversion (900 × ⅗ × $0.40) 216
$2,061

The following costs were charged to Work in Process—Sifting Department during July:

Direct materials transferred from Milling Department:
15,700 units at $2.15 a unit $33,755
Direct labor 4,420
Factory overhead 2,708

During July, 15,500 units of flour were completed. Work in Process—Sifting Department on July 31 was 1,100 units, ⅘ completed.

Instructions

1. Prepare a cost of production report for the Sifting Department for July.
2. Journalize the entries for costs transferred from Milling to Sifting and the costs transferred from Sifting to Packaging.
3. Determine the increase or decrease in the cost per equivalent unit from June to July for direct materials and conversion costs.
4. Discuss the uses of the cost of production report and the results of part (3).

PR 20-4A Work in process account data for two months; cost of production reports OBJ. 1, 2, 3, 4

✔ 1. c. Transferred to finished goods in April, $49,818

Hearty Soup Co. uses a process cost system to record the costs of processing soup, which requires the cooking and filling processes. Materials are entered from the cooking process at the beginning of the filling process. The inventory of Work in Process—Filling on April 1 and debits to the account during April were as follows:

Bal., 800 units, 30% completed:
Direct materials (800 × $4.30) .... $ 3,440
Conversion (800 × 30% × $1.75) 420
$ 3,860

From Cooking Department, 7,800 units $34,320
Direct labor 8,562
Factory overhead 6,387

During April, 800 units in process on April 1 were completed, and of the 7,800 units entering the department, all were completed except 550 units that were 90% completed. Charges to Work in Process—Filling for May were as follows:

From Cooking Department, 9,600 units $44,160
Direct labor 12,042
Factory overhead 6,878

During May, the units in process at the beginning of the month were completed, and of the 9,600 units entering the department, all were completed except 300 units that were 35% completed.

Instructions

1. Enter the balance as of April 1 in a four-column account for Work in Process—Filling. Record the debits and credits in the account for April. Construct a cost of production report and present computations for determining (a) equivalent units of production for materials and conversion; (b) cost per equivalent unit; (c) cost of goods finished, differentiating between units started in the prior period and units started and finished in April; and (d) work in process inventory.

2. Provide the same information for May by recording the May transactions in the four-column work in process account. Construct a cost of production report and present the May computations (a through d) listed in part (1).

(*Continued*)

1014 Chapter 20 Process Cost Systems

3. ✏️ Comment on the change in costs per equivalent unit for March through May for direct materials and conversion costs.

Appendix
PR 20-5A Cost of production report: average cost method

✔ Cost per equivalent unit, $2.70

Sunrise Coffee Company roasts and packs coffee beans. The process begins in the Roasting Department. From the Roasting Department, the coffee beans are transferred to the Packing Department. The following is a partial work in process account of the Roasting Department at December 31:

ACCOUNT Work in Process—Roasting Department   **ACCOUNT NO.**

Date		Item	Debit	Credit	Balance Debit	Balance Credit
Dec.	1	Bal., 10,500 units, 75% completed			21,000	
	31	Direct materials, 210,400 units	246,800		267,800	
	31	Direct labor	135,700		403,500	
	31	Factory overhead	168,630		572,130	
	31	Goods transferred, 208,900 units		?	?	
	31	Bal., ? units, 25% completed			?	

Instructions

Prepare a cost of production report, using the average cost method, and identify the missing amounts for Work in Process—Roasting Department.

Problems: Series B

PR 20-1B Entries for process cost system   **OBJ. 1, 3**

✔ 2. Materials July 31 balance, $11,390

Preston & Grover Soap Company manufactures powdered detergent. Phosphate is placed in process in the Making Department, where it is turned into granulars. The output of Making is transferred to the Packing Department, where packaging is added at the beginning of the process. On July 1, Preston & Grover Soap Company had the following inventories:

Finished Goods	$13,500
Work in Process—Making	6,790
Work in Process—Packing	7,350
Materials	5,100

Departmental accounts are maintained for factory overhead, which both have zero balances on July 1.

Manufacturing operations for July are summarized as follows:

a. Materials purchased on account	$149,800
b. Materials requisitioned for use:	
Phosphate—Making Department	$105,700
Packaging—Packing Department	31,300
Indirect materials—Making Department	4,980
Indirect materials—Packing Department	1,530
c. Labor used:	
Direct labor—Making Department	$ 32,400
Direct labor—Packing Department	40,900
Indirect labor—Making Department	15,400
Indirect labor—Packing Department	18,300

d. Depreciation charged on fixed assets:
   Making Department.. $ 10,700
   Packing Department 7,900

e. Expired prepaid factory insurance:
   Making Department.. $ 2,000
   Packing Department 1,500

f. Applied factory overhead:
   Making Department.. $ 32,570
   Packing Department 30,050

g. Production costs transferred from Making Department to Packing Department $166,790

h. Production costs transferred from Packing Department to Finished Goods.......... $263,400

i. Cost of goods sold during the period $265,200

Instructions

1. Journalize the entries to record the operations, identifying each entry by letter.
2. Compute the July 31 balances of the inventory accounts.
3. Compute the July 31 balances of the factory overhead accounts.

PR 20-2B Cost of production report OBJ. 2, 4

✔ 1. Conversion cost per equivalent unit, $6.00

Bavarian Chocolate Company processes chocolate into candy bars. The process begins by placing direct materials (raw chocolate, milk, and sugar) into the Blending Department. All materials are placed into production at the beginning of the blending process. After blending, the milk chocolate is then transferred to the Molding Department, where the milk chocolate is formed into candy bars. The following is a partial work in process account of the Blending Department at October 31:

ACCOUNT Work in Process—Blending Department   ACCOUNT NO.

Date		Item	Debit	Credit	Balance Debit	Balance Credit
Oct.	1	Bal., 2,300 units, ⅗ completed			46,368	
	31	Direct materials, 26,000 units	429,000		475,368	
	31	Direct labor	100,560		575,928	
	31	Factory overhead	48,480		624,408	
	31	Goods transferred, 25,700 units		?		
	31	Bal., ? units, ⅕ completed			?	

Instructions

1. Prepare a cost of production report and identify the missing amounts for Work in Process—Blending Department.
2. Assuming that the October 1 work in process inventory includes direct materials of $38,295, determine the increase or decrease in the cost per equivalent unit for direct materials and conversion between September and October.

PR 20-3B Equivalent units and related costs; cost of production report; entries OBJ. 2, 3, 4

✔ 2. Transferred to finished goods, $705,376

Dover Chemical Company manufactures specialty chemicals by a series of three processes, all materials being introduced in the Distilling Department. From the Distilling Department, the materials pass through the Reaction and Filling departments, emerging as finished chemicals.

The balance in the account Work in Process—Filling was as follows on January 1:

(Continued)

1016 Chapter 20 Process Cost Systems

Work in Process—Filling Department
(3,400 units, 60% completed):
Direct materials (3,400 × $9.58)	$32,572
Conversion (3,400 × 60% × $3.90)	7,956
	$40,528

The following costs were charged to Work in Process—Filling during January:

Direct materials transferred from Reaction Department: 52,300 units at $9.50 a unit	$496,850
Direct labor	101,560
Factory overhead	95,166

During January, 53,000 units of specialty chemicals were completed. Work in Process—Filling Department on January 31 was 2,700 units, 30% completed.

Instructions

1. Prepare a cost of production report for the Filling Department for January.
2. Journalize the entries for costs transferred from Reaction to Filling and the costs transferred from Filling to Finished Goods.
3. Determine the increase or decrease in the cost per equivalent unit from December to January for direct materials and conversion costs.
4. Discuss the uses of the cost of production report and the results of part (3).

PR 20-4B Work in process account data for two months; cost of production reports OBJ. 1, 2, 3, 4

✔ 1. c. Transferred to finished goods in September, $702,195

Pittsburgh Aluminum Company uses a process cost system to record the costs of manufacturing rolled aluminum, which consists of the smelting and rolling processes. Materials are entered from smelting at the beginning of the rolling process. The inventory of Work in Process—Rolling on September 1 and debits to the account during September were as follows:

Bal., 2,600 units, ¼ completed:	
Direct materials (2,600 × $15.50)	$40,300
Conversion (2,600 × ¼ × $8.50)	5,525
	$45,825
From Smelting Department, 28,900 units	462,400
Direct labor	158,920
Factory overhead	101,402

During September, 2,600 units in process on September 1 were completed, and of the 28,900 units entering the department, all were completed except 2,900 units that were ⅘ completed.

Charges to Work in Process—Rolling for October were as follows:

From Smelting Department, 31,000 units	$511,500
Direct labor	162,850
Factory overhead	104,494

During October, the units in process at the beginning of the month were completed, and of the 31,000 units entering the department, all were completed except 2,000 units that were ⅖ completed.

Instructions

1. Enter the balance as of September 1 in a four-column account for Work in Process—Rolling. Record the debits and credits in the account for September. Construct a cost of production report and present computations for determining (a) equivalent units of production for materials and conversion; (b) cost per equivalent unit; (c) cost of goods finished, differentiating between units started in the prior period and units started and finished in September; and (d) work in process inventory.

2. Provide the same information for October by recording the October transactions in the four-column work in process account. Construct a cost of production report and present the October computations (a through d) listed in part (1).

3. Comment on the change in costs per equivalent unit for August through October for direct materials and conversion cost.

✔ Transferred to Packaging Dept., $54,000

Appendix
PR 20-5B Cost of production report: average cost method

Blue Ribbon Flour Company manufactures flour by a series of three processes, beginning in the Milling Department. From the Milling Department, the materials pass through the Sifting and Packaging departments, emerging as packaged refined flour.

The balance in the account Work in Process—Sifting Department was as follows on May 1:

Work in Process—Sifting Department (1,500 units, 75% completed)	$3,400

The following costs were charged to Work in Process—Sifting Department during May:

Direct materials transferred from Milling Department: 18,300 units	$32,600
Direct labor	14,560
Factory overhead	7,490

During May, 18,000 units of flour were completed and transferred to finished goods. Work in Process—Sifting Department on May 31 was 1,800 units, 75% completed.

Instructions
Prepare a cost of production report for the Sifting Department for May, using the average cost method.

Cases & Projects

CP 20-1 Ethics in Action
Assume that you are the division controller for Auntie M's Cookie Company. Auntie M has introduced a new chocolate chip cookie called Full of Chips, and it is a success. As a result, the product manager responsible for the launch of this new cookie was promoted to division vice president and became your boss. A new product manager, Bishop, has been brought in to replace the promoted manager. Bishop notices that the Full of Chips cookie uses a great deal of chips, which increases the cost of the cookie. As a result, Bishop has ordered that the amount of chips used in the cookies be reduced by 10%. The manager believes that a 10% reduction in chips will not adversely affect sales but will reduce costs and, hence, improve margins. The increased margins would help Bishop meet profit targets for the period.

You are looking over some cost of production reports segmented by cookie line. You notice that there is a drop in the materials costs for Full of Chips. On further investigation, you discover why the chip costs have declined (fewer chips). Both you and Bishop report to the division vice president, who was the original product manager for Full of Chips. You are trying to decide what to do, if anything.

Discuss the options you might consider.

CP 20-2 Team Activity
The following categories represent typical process manufacturing industries:

Beverages	Metals
Chemicals	Petroleum refining
Food	Pharmaceuticals
Forest and paper products	Soap and cosmetics

In groups of two or three, for each category, identify one company (following your instructor's specific instructions) and determine the following:

(Continued)

1. Typical products manufactured by the selected company, including brand names
2. Typical raw materials used by the selected company
3. Types of processes used by the selected company

Use annual reports, the Internet, or library resources in doing this activity.

Communication

CP 20-3 Communication

Jamarcus Bradshaw, plant manager of Georgia Paper Company's papermaking mill, was looking over the cost of production reports for July and August for the Papermaking Department. The reports revealed the following:

	July	August
Pulp and chemicals	$295,600	$304,100
Conversion cost	146,000	149,600
Total cost	$441,600	$453,700
Number of tons	÷ 1,200	÷ 1,130
Cost per ton	$ 368	$ 401.50

Jamarcus was concerned about the increased cost per ton from the output of the department. As a result, he asked the plant controller to perform a study to help explain these results. The controller, Leann Brunswick, began the analysis by performing some interviews of key plant personnel in order to understand what the problem might be. Excerpts from an interview with Len Tyson, a paper machine operator, follow:

Len: We have two papermaking machines in the department. I have no data, but I think paper machine No. 1 is applying too much pulp and, thus, is wasting both conversion and materials resources. We haven't had repairs on paper machine No. 1 in a while. Maybe this is the problem.

Leann: How does too much pulp result in wasted resources?

Len: Well, you see, if too much pulp is applied, then we will waste pulp material. The customer will not pay for the extra product; we just use more material to make the product. Also, when there is too much pulp, the machine must be slowed down in order to complete the drying process. This results in additional conversion costs.

Leann: Do you have any other suspicions?

Len: Well, as you know, we have two products—green paper and yellow paper. They are identical except for the color. The color is added to the papermaking process in the paper machine. I think that during August these two color papers have been behaving differently. I don't have any data, but it seems as though the amount of waste associated with the green paper has increased.

Leann: Why is this?

Len: I understand that there has been a change in specifications for the green paper, starting near the beginning of August. This change could be causing the machines to run poorly when making green paper. If that is the case, the cost per ton would increase for green paper.

Leann also asked for a database printout providing greater detail on August's operating results.

September 9   Requested by: Leann Brunswick

Papermaking Department—August detail

	A	B	C	D	E	F
1	Production					
2	Run	Paper		Material	Conversion	
3	Number	Machine	Color	Costs	Costs	Tons
4	1	1	Green	40,300	18,300	150
5	2	1	Yellow	41,700	21,200	140
6	3	1	Green	44,600	22,500	150
7	4	1	Yellow	36,100	18,100	120
8	5	2	Green	38,300	18,900	160
9	6	2	Yellow	33,900	15,200	140
10	7	2	Green	35,600	18,400	130
11	8	2	Yellow	33,600	17,000	140
12			Total	304,100	149,600	1,130
13						

Prior to preparing a report, Leann resigned from Georgia Paper Company to start her own business. You have been asked to take the data that Leann collected and write a memo to Jamarcus Bradshaw with a recommendation to management. Your memo should include analysis of the August data to determine whether the paper machine or the paper color explains the increase in the unit cost from July. Include any supporting schedules that are appropriate. Round all calculations to the nearest cent.

CP 20-4 Accounting for materials costs

In papermaking operations for companies such as **International Paper Company**, wet pulp is fed into paper machines, which press and dry pulp into a continuous sheet of paper. The paper is formed at very high speeds (60 mph). Once the paper is formed, the paper is rolled onto a reel at the back end of the paper machine. One of the characteristics of papermaking is the creation of "broke" paper. Broke is paper that fails to satisfy quality standards and is therefore rejected for final shipment to customers. Broke is recycled back to the beginning of the process by combining the recycled paper with virgin (new) pulp material. The combination of virgin pulp and recycled broke is sent to the paper machine for papermaking. Broke is fed into this recycle process continuously from all over the facility.

In this industry, it is typical to charge the papermaking operation with the cost of direct materials, which is a mixture of virgin materials and broke. Broke has a much lower cost than does virgin pulp. Therefore, the more broke in the mixture, the lower the average cost of direct materials to the department. Papermaking managers frequently comment on the importance of broke for keeping their direct materials costs down.

a. How do you react to this accounting procedure?

b. What "hidden costs" are not considered when accounting for broke as described?

CP 20-5 Analyzing unit costs

Midstate Containers Inc. manufactures cans for the canned food industry. The operations manager of a can manufacturing operation wants to conduct a cost study investigating the relationship of tin content in the material (can stock) to the energy cost for enameling the cans. The enameling was necessary to prepare the cans for labeling. A higher percentage of tin content in the can stock increases the cost of material. The operations manager believed that a higher tin content in the can stock would reduce the amount of energy used in enameling. During the analysis period, the amount of tin content in the steel can stock was increased every month from April to September. The following operating reports were available from the controller:

	A	B	C	D	E	F	G
1		April	May	June	July	August	September
2	Materials	$ 14,000	$ 34,800	$ 33,000	$ 21,700	$ 28,800	$ 33,000
3	Energy	13,000	28,800	24,200	14,000	17,100	16,000
4	Total cost	$ 27,000	$ 63,600	$ 57,200	$ 35,700	$ 45,900	$ 49,000
5	Units produced	÷50,000	÷120,000	÷110,000	÷70,000	÷90,000	÷100,000
6	Cost per unit	$ 0.54	$ 0.53	$ 0.52	$ 0.51	$ 0.51	$ 0.49
7							

Differences in materials unit costs were entirely related to the amount of tin content.

Interpret this information and report to the operations manager your recommendations with respect to tin content.

CHAPTER 21
Cost-Volume-Profit Analysis

Concepts and Principles
Chapter 18 *Introduction to Managerial Accounting*

Developing Information

COST SYSTEMS
Chapter 19 *Job Order Costing*
Chapter 20 *Process Costing*

COST BEHAVIOR
Chapter 21 *Cost-Volume-Profit Analysis*

Decision Making

EVALUATING PERFORMANCE
Chapter 22 *Budgeting*
Chapter 23 *Variances from Standard Costs*

COMPARING ALTERNATIVES
Chapter 24 *Decentralized Operations*
Chapter 25 *Differential Analysis, Product Pricing, and Activity-Based Costing*
Chapter 26 *Capital Investment Analysis*

CHAPTER 21

Ford Motor Company

Making a profit isn't easy for U.S. auto manufacturers like the **Ford Motor Company**. The cost of materials, labor, equipment, and advertising means it is very expensive to produce cars and trucks.

How many cars does Ford need to produce and sell to break even? The answer depends on the relationship between Ford's sales revenue and costs. Some of Ford's costs, like direct labor and materials, change in direct proportion to the number of vehicles that are built. Other costs, such as the costs of manufacturing equipment, are fixed and do not change with the number of vehicles that are produced. Ford breaks even when it generates enough sales revenue to cover both its fixed and variable costs.

During the depths of the 2009 recession, Ford renegotiated labor contracts with its employees. These renegotiations reduced the direct labor cost incurred to build each car, which lowered the number of cars the company needed to sell to break even by 45%.

As with Ford, understanding how costs behave and the relationship between costs, profits, and volume is important for all businesses. This chapter discusses commonly used methods for classifying costs according to how they change, and illustrates how to determine the number of units that must be sold for a company to break even. Techniques that management can use to evaluate costs in order to make sound business decisions are also discussed.

Source: J. Booton, "Moody's Upgrades Ford's Credit Rating, Returns Blue Oval Trademark," *Fox Business*, May 22, 2012.

Learning Objectives

After studying this chapter, you should be able to:

Example Exercises (EE) are shown in **green**.

Obj. 1 Classify costs as variable costs, fixed costs, or mixed costs.

Cost Behavior
Variable Costs
Fixed Costs
Mixed Costs   EE 21-1
Summary of Cost Behavior Concepts

Obj. 2 Compute the contribution margin, the contribution margin ratio, and the unit contribution margin.

Cost-Volume-Profit Relationships
Contribution Margin
Contribution Margin Ratio
Unit Contribution Margin   EE 21-2

Obj. 3 Determine the break-even point and sales necessary to achieve a target profit.

Mathematical Approach to Cost-Volume-Profit Analysis
Break-Even Point   EE 21-3
Target Profit   EE 21-4

Obj. 4 Using a cost-volume-profit chart and a profit-volume chart, determine the break-even point and sales necessary to achieve a target profit.

Graphic Approach to Cost-Volume-Profit Analysis
Cost-Volume-Profit (Break-Even) Chart
Profit-Volume Chart
Use of Computers in Cost-Volume-Profit Analysis
Assumptions of Cost-Volume-Profit Analysis

Obj. 5 Compute the break-even point for a company selling more than one product, the operating leverage, and the margin of safety.

Special Cost-Volume-Profit Relationships
Sales Mix Considerations   EE 21-5
Operating Leverage   EE 21-6
Margin of Safety   EE 21-7

At a Glance 21 Page 1050

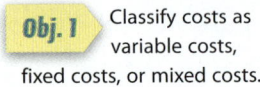

Obj. 1 Classify costs as variable costs, fixed costs, or mixed costs.

Cost Behavior

Cost behavior is the manner in which a cost changes as a related activity changes. The behavior of costs is useful to managers for a variety of reasons. For example, knowing how costs behave allows managers to predict profits as sales and production volumes change. Knowing how costs behave is also useful for estimating costs, which affects a variety of decisions such as whether to replace a machine.

Understanding the behavior of a cost depends on the following:

- Identifying the activities that cause the cost to change. These activities are called **activity bases** (or *activity drivers*).
- Specifying the range of activity over which the changes in the cost are of interest. This range of activity is called the **relevant range**.

To illustrate, assume that a hospital is concerned about planning and controlling patient food costs. A good activity base is the number of patients who *stay* overnight in the hospital. The number of patients who are *treated* is not as good an activity base because some patients are outpatients and, thus, do not consume food. Once an activity base is identified, food costs can then be analyzed over the range of the number of patients who normally stay in the hospital (the relevant range).

Costs are normally classified as variable costs, fixed costs, or mixed costs.

Variable Costs

Variable costs are costs that vary in proportion to changes in the activity base. When the activity base is units produced, direct materials and direct labor costs are normally classified as variable costs.

Link to Ford Motor Company

The first vehicle built by Henry Ford in 1896 was a Quadracycle that consisted of four bicycle wheels powered by a four-horsepower engine. The first Ford Model A was sold by **Ford Motor Company** in 1903. In 1908, the Ford Model T was introduced, which had sales of 15 million before its production was halted in 1927.

Source: www.corporate.ford.com

To illustrate, assume that Jason Sound Inc. produces stereo systems. The parts for the stereo systems are purchased from suppliers for $10 per unit and are assembled by Jason Sound. For Model JS-12, the direct materials costs for the relevant range of 5,000 to 30,000 units of production are as follows:

Number of Units of Model JS-12 Produced	Direct Materials Cost per Unit	Total Direct Materials Cost
5,000 units	$10	$ 50,000
10,000	10	100,000
15,000	10	150,000
20,000	10	200,000
25,000	10	250,000
30,000	10	300,000

Link to Ford Motor Company
Changing emission, fuel economy, and safety standards increase the variable cost of each vehicle manufactured by **Ford Motor Company**.

As shown, variable costs have the following characteristics:

- *Cost per unit* remains the same regardless of changes in the activity base. For Jason Sound, units produced is the activity base. For Model JS-12, the cost per unit is $10.
- *Total cost* changes in proportion to changes in the activity base. For Model JS-12, the direct materials cost for 10,000 units ($100,000) is twice the direct materials cost for 5,000 units ($50,000).

Exhibit 1 illustrates how the variable costs for direct materials for Model JS-12 behave in total and on a per-unit basis as production changes.

EXHIBIT 1 Variable Cost Graphs

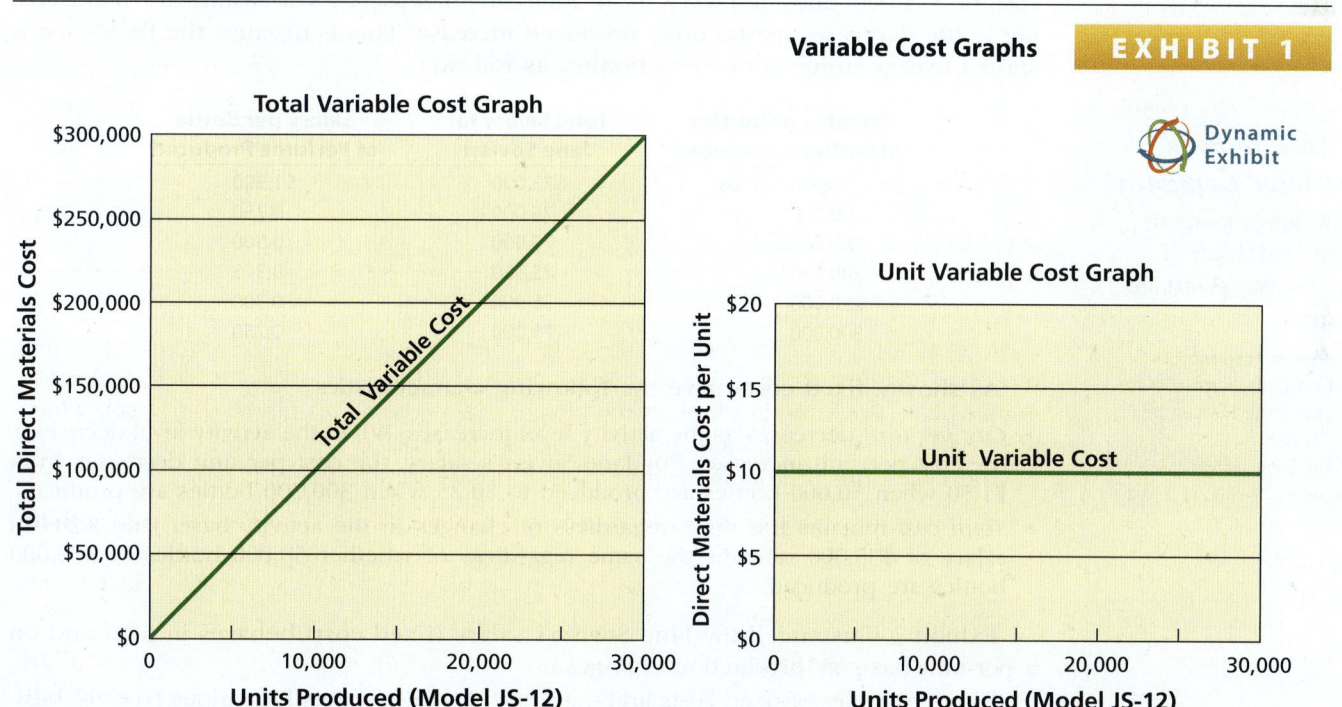

Some examples of variable costs and their related activity bases for various types of businesses are shown in Exhibit 2.

EXHIBIT 2
Variable Costs and Their Activity Bases

Type of Business	Cost	Activity Base
University	Instructor salaries	Number of classes
Passenger airline	Fuel	Number of miles flown
Manufacturing	Direct materials	Number of units produced
Hospital	Nurse wages	Number of patients
Hotel	Maid wages	Number of guests
Bank	Teller wages	Number of banking transactions

Fixed Costs

Fixed costs are costs that remain the same in total dollar amount as the activity base changes. When the activity base is units produced, many factory overhead costs such as straight-line depreciation are classified as fixed costs.

To illustrate, assume that Minton Inc. manufactures, bottles, and distributes perfume. The production supervisor is Jane Sovissi, who is paid a salary of $75,000 per year. For the relevant range of 50,000 to 300,000 bottles of perfume, the total fixed cost of $75,000 does not vary as production increases. As a result, the fixed cost per bottle decreases as the units produced increase. This is because the fixed cost is spread over a larger number of bottles, as follows:

Number of Bottles of Perfume Produced	Total Salary for Jane Sovissi	Salary per Bottle of Perfume Produced
50,000 bottles	$75,000	$1.500
100,000	75,000	0.750
150,000	75,000	0.500
200,000	75,000	0.375
250,000	75,000	0.300
300,000	75,000	0.250

> **Link to Ford Motor Company**
>
> A high proportion of **Ford Motor Company**'s costs are fixed.
>
> Source: Ford Motor Company, Form 10-K for Year Ended December 31, 2015.

As shown, fixed costs have the following characteristics:

- *Cost per unit* decreases as the activity level increases. When the activity level decreases, the cost per unit increases. For Jane Sovissi's salary, the cost per unit decreases from $1.50 when 50,000 bottles are produced to $0.25 when 300,000 bottles are produced.
- *Total cost* remains the same regardless of changes in the activity base. Jane Sovissi's salary of $75,000 remains the same regardless of whether 50,000 bottles or 300,000 bottles are produced.

Exhibit 3 illustrates how Jane Sovissi's salary (fixed cost) behaves in total and on a per-unit basis as production changes.

Some examples of fixed costs and their related activity bases for various types of businesses are shown in Exhibit 4. In each of these cases, the cost is fixed to the level of activity.

Mixed Costs

Mixed costs are costs that have characteristics of both a variable and a fixed cost. Mixed costs are sometimes called *semivariable* or *semifixed costs*.

To illustrate, assume that Simpson Inc. manufactures sails, using rented machinery. The rental charges are as follows:

Rental Charge = $15,000 per year + $1 for each hour used in excess of 10,000 hours

Fixed Cost Graphs

EXHIBIT 3

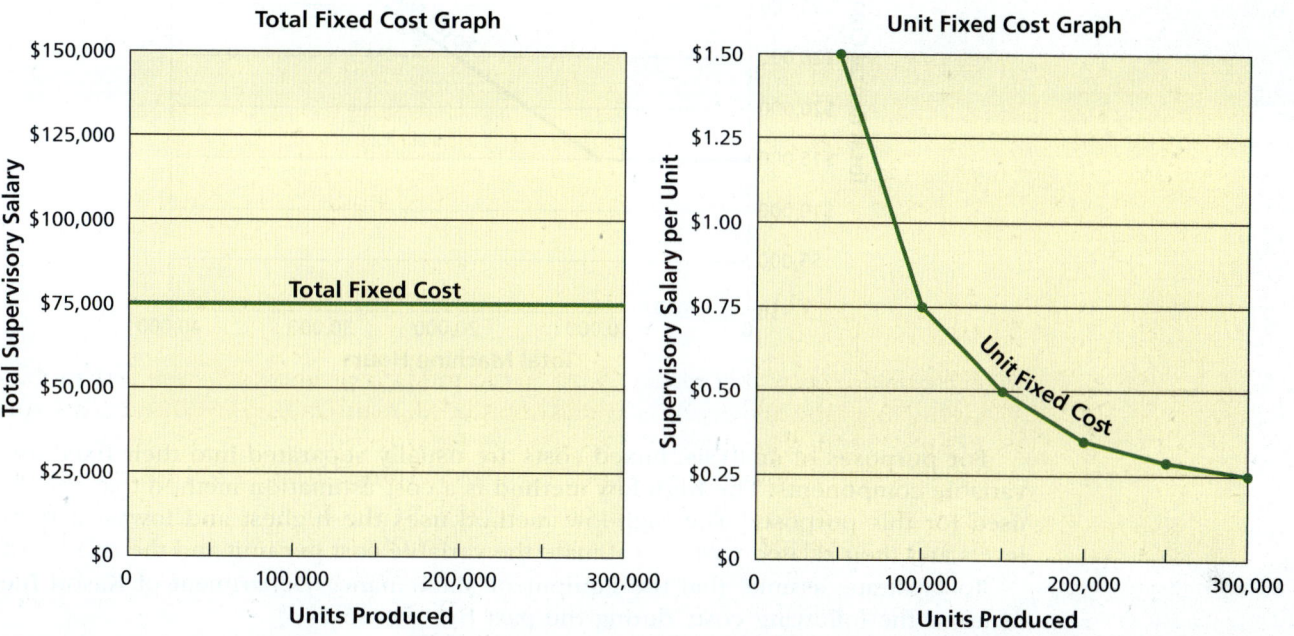

EXHIBIT 4

Fixed Costs and Their Activity Bases

Type of Business	Fixed Cost	Activity Base
University	Building (straight-line) depreciation	Number of students
Passenger airline	Airplane (straight-line) depreciation	Number of miles flown
Manufacturing	Plant manager salary	Number of units produced
Hospital	Property insurance	Number of patients
Hotel	Property taxes	Number of guests
Bank	Branch manager salary	Number of customer accounts

The rental charges for various hours used within the relevant range of 8,000 hours to 40,000 hours are as follows:

Hours Used	Rental Charge
8,000 hours	$15,000
12,000	$17,000 {$15,000 + [(12,000 hrs. − 10,000 hrs.) × $1]}
20,000	$25,000 {$15,000 + [(20,000 hrs. − 10,000 hrs.) × $1]}
40,000	$45,000 {$15,000 + [(40,000 hrs. − 10,000 hrs.) × $1]}

Exhibit 5 illustrates the preceding mixed cost behavior.

EXHIBIT 5
Mixed Costs

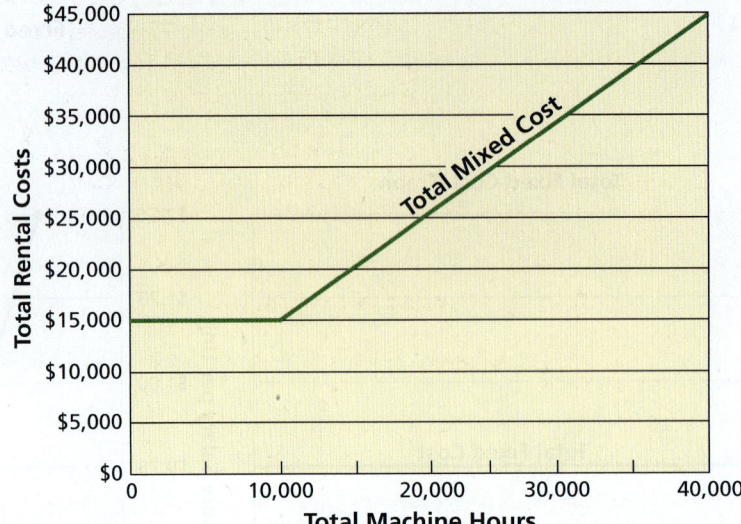

For purposes of analysis, mixed costs are usually separated into their fixed and variable components. The **high-low method** is a cost estimation method that may be used for this purpose.[1] The high-low method uses the highest and lowest activity levels and their related costs to estimate the variable cost per unit and the fixed cost.

To illustrate, assume that the Equipment Maintenance Department of Kason Inc. incurred the following costs during the past five months:

	Units Produced	Total Cost
June	1,000 units	$45,550
July	1,500	52,000
August	2,100	61,500
September	1,800	57,500
October	750	41,250

The number of units produced is the activity base, and the relevant range is the units produced between June and October. For Kason, the difference between the units produced and the total costs at the highest and lowest levels of production are as follows:

	Units Produced	Total Cost
Highest level	2,100 units	$61,500
Lowest level	750	41,250
Difference	1,350 units	$20,250

The total fixed cost does not change with changes in production. Thus, the $20,250 difference in the total cost is the change in the total variable cost. Dividing this difference of $20,250 by the difference in production is an estimate of the variable cost per unit. For Kason, this estimate is $15, computed as follows:

$$\text{Variable Cost per Unit} = \frac{\text{Difference in Total Cost}}{\text{Difference in Units Produced}}$$

$$= \frac{\$20,250}{1,350 \text{ units}} = \$15 \text{ per unit}$$

The fixed cost is estimated by subtracting the total variable costs from the total costs for the units produced, as follows:

$$\text{Fixed Cost} = \text{Total Costs} - (\text{Variable Cost per Unit} \times \text{Units Produced})$$

---

[1] Other methods of estimating costs, such as the scattergraph method and the least squares method, are discussed in cost accounting textbooks.

The fixed cost is the same at the highest and lowest levels of production, as follows for Kason:

Highest level (2,100 units)

Fixed Cost = Total Costs − (Variable Cost per Unit × Units Produced)
= $61,500 − ($15 × 2,100 units)
= $61,500 − $31,500
= $30,000

Lowest level (750 units)

Fixed Cost = Total Costs − (Variable Cost per Unit × Units Produced)
= $41,250 − ($15 × 750 units)
= $41,250 − $11,250
= $30,000

Using the variable cost per unit and the fixed cost, the total equipment maintenance cost for Kason can be computed for various levels of production as follows:

Total Cost = (Variable Cost per Unit × Units Produced) + Fixed Costs
= ($15 × Units Produced) + $30,000

To illustrate, the estimated total cost of 2,000 units of production is $60,000, computed as follows:

Total Cost = ($15 × Units Produced) + $30,000
= ($15 × 2,000 units) + $30,000 = $30,000 + $30,000
= $60,000

Link to Ford

In 2011, **Ford Motor Company** entered into a collective bargaining agreement with the United Auto Workers union that provides for lump-sum payments in lieu of general wage increases. This has the effect of making wages more like a mixed cost.

Source: Ford Motor Company, Form 10-K for Year Ended December 31, 2011.

Example Exercise 21-1 High-Low Method *Obj. 1*

The manufacturing costs of Alex Industries for the first three months of the year follow:

	Total Cost	Units Produced
January	$ 80,000	1,000 units
February	125,000	2,500
March	100,000	1,800

Using the high-low method, determine (a) the variable cost per unit and (b) the total fixed cost.

Follow My Example 21-1

a. $30 per unit = ($125,000 − $80,000) ÷ (2,500 − 1,000)
b. $50,000 = $125,000 − ($30 × 2,500), or $80,000 − ($30 × 1,000)

Practice Exercises: PE 21-1A, PE 21-1B

Summary of Cost Behavior Concepts

The cost behavior of variable costs and fixed costs is summarized in Exhibit 6.

EXHIBIT 6 — Variable and Fixed Cost Behavior

Cost	Effect of Changing Activity Level	
	Total Amount	Per-Unit Amount
Variable	Increases and decreases proportionately with activity level.	Remains the same regardless of activity level.
Fixed	Remains the same regardless of activity level.	Increases and decreases inversely with activity level.

Mixed costs contain a fixed cost component that is incurred even if nothing is produced. For analysis, the fixed and variable cost components of mixed costs are separated using the high-low method.

Exhibit 7 provides some examples of variable, fixed, and mixed costs for the activity base of *units produced*.

EXHIBIT 7
Variable, Fixed, and Mixed Costs

Variable Costs	Fixed Costs	Mixed Costs
• Direct materials	• Straight-line depreciation	• Quality Control Department salaries
• Direct labor	• Property taxes	• Purchasing Department salaries
• Electricity expense	• Production supervisor salaries	• Maintenance expenses
• Supplies	• Insurance expense	• Warehouse expenses

One method of reporting variable and fixed costs is called **variable costing** or *direct costing*. Under variable costing, only the variable manufacturing costs (direct materials, direct labor, and variable factory overhead) are included in the product cost. The fixed factory overhead is treated as an expense of the period in which it is incurred. Variable costing is described and illustrated in the appendix to this chapter.

Business Connection

BOOKING FEES

A major fixed cost for a concert promoter is the booking fee for the act. The booking fee is the amount to be paid to the act for a single show at a venue. **Degy Entertainment**, a booking agency, provided a list of asking prices for several popular acts. The following is a sampling from the list.

Taylor Swift	$1,000,000+
Justin Timberlake	$1,000,000+
Rihanna	$500K–$750K
Katy Perry	$500K
Keith Urban	$400K–$600K
Maroon 5	$400K–$600K
Kanye West	$400K–$600K
Carrie Underwood	$400K–$500K
Alicia Keys	$350k–$500K
Bruno Mars	$200K–$400K
Pitbull	$200K–$300K
Ke$ha	$150K–$200K
The Script	$125K–$175K

The promoter must cover these fixed costs with ticket revenues; thus, the size of the booking fee is necessarily related to the popularity of the act represented by the number of potential tickets sold and the ticket price.

Source: Zachery Crockett, "How Much Does It Cost to Book Your Favorite Band?" *Priceconomics.com*, May 16, 2014.

Obj. 2 Compute the contribution margin, the contribution margin ratio, and the unit contribution margin.

Cost-Volume-Profit Relationships

Cost-volume-profit analysis is the examination of the relationships among selling prices, sales and production volume, costs, expenses, and profits. Cost-volume-profit analysis is useful for managerial decision making. Some of the ways cost-volume-profit analysis may be used include the following:

- Analyzing the effects of changes in selling prices on profits
- Analyzing the effects of changes in costs on profits
- Analyzing the effects of changes in volume on profits
- Setting selling prices
- Selecting the mix of products to sell
- Choosing among marketing strategies

Contribution Margin

Contribution margin is especially useful because it provides insight into the profit potential of a company. **Contribution margin** is the excess of sales over variable costs, computed as follows:

$$\text{Contribution Margin} = \text{Sales} - \text{Variable Costs}$$

To illustrate, assume the following data for Lambert Inc.:

Sales	50,000 units
Sales price per unit	$20 per unit
Variable cost per unit	$12 per unit
Fixed costs	$300,000

Exhibit 8 illustrates an income statement for Lambert prepared in a contribution margin format.

EXHIBIT 8 — Contribution Margin Income Statement Format

Sales (50,000 units × $20)	$1,000,000
Variable costs (50,000 units × $12)	600,000
Contribution margin (50,000 units × $8)	$ 400,000
Fixed costs	300,000
Income from operations	$ 100,000

Lambert's contribution margin of $400,000 is available to cover the fixed costs of $300,000. Once the fixed costs are covered, any additional contribution margin increases income from operations.

Contribution Margin Ratio

Contribution margin can also be expressed as a percentage. The **contribution margin ratio**, sometimes called the *profit-volume ratio*, indicates the percentage of each sales dollar available to cover fixed costs and to provide income from operations. The contribution margin ratio is computed as follows:

$$\text{Contribution Margin Ratio} = \frac{\text{Contribution Margin}}{\text{Sales}}$$

The contribution margin ratio is 40% for Lambert Inc., computed as follows:

$$\text{Contribution Margin Ratio} = \frac{\$400{,}000}{\$1{,}000{,}000} = 40\%$$

The contribution margin ratio is most useful when the increase or decrease in sales volume is measured in sales *dollars*. In this case, the change in sales dollars multiplied by the contribution margin ratio equals the change in income from operations, computed as follows:

$$\text{Change in Income from Operations} = \text{Change in Sales Dollars} \times \text{Contribution Margin Ratio}$$

To illustrate, if Lambert adds $80,000 in sales from the sale of an additional 4,000 units, its income from operations will increase by $32,000, computed as follows:

$$\begin{aligned}\text{Change in Income from Operations} &= \text{Change in Sales Dollars} \times \text{Contribution Margin Ratio} \\ &= \$80{,}000 \times 40\% \\ &= \$32{,}000\end{aligned}$$

The preceding analysis is confirmed by the contribution margin income statement of Lambert that follows:

Sales (54,000 units × $20)	$1,080,000
Variable costs (54,000 units × $12)	648,000*
Contribution margin (54,000 units × $8)	$ 432,000**
Fixed costs	300,000
Income from operations	$ 132,000

*$1,080,000 × 60%
**$1,080,000 × 40%

Income from operations increased from $100,000 to $132,000 when sales increased from $1,000,000 to $1,080,000. Variable costs as a percentage of sales are equal to 100% minus the contribution margin ratio. Thus, in the preceding income statement, the variable costs are 60% (100% – 40%) of sales, or $648,000 ($1,080,000 × 60%). The total contribution margin, $432,000, can also be computed directly by multiplying the total sales by the contribution margin ratio ($1,080,000 × 40%).

In the preceding analysis, factors other than sales volume, such as variable cost per unit and sales price, are assumed to remain constant. If such factors change, their effect must also be considered.

The contribution margin ratio is also useful in developing business strategies. For example, assume that a company has a high contribution margin ratio and is producing below 100% of capacity. In this case, a large increase in income from operations can be expected from an increase in sales volume. Therefore, the company might consider implementing a special sales campaign to increase sales. In contrast, a company with a small contribution margin ratio will probably want to give more attention to reducing costs before attempting to promote sales.

Unit Contribution Margin

The unit contribution margin is also useful for analyzing the profit potential of proposed decisions. The **unit contribution margin** is computed as follows:

Unit Contribution Margin = Sales Price per Unit – Variable Cost per Unit

To illustrate, if Lambert Inc.'s unit selling price is $20 and its variable cost per unit is $12, the unit contribution margin is $8, computed as follows:

Unit Contribution Margin = Sales Price per Unit – Variable Cost per Unit
= $20 – $12
= $8

The unit contribution margin is most useful when the increase or decrease in sales volume is measured in sales *units* (quantities). In this case, the change in sales volume (units) multiplied by the unit contribution margin equals the change in income from operations, computed as follows:

Change in Income from Operations = Change in Sales Units × Unit Contribution Margin

To illustrate, assume that Lambert's sales could be increased by 15,000 units, from 50,000 units to 65,000 units. Lambert's income from operations would increase by $120,000 (15,000 units × $8), computed as follows:

Change in Income from Operations = Change in Sales Units × Unit Contribution Margin
= 15,000 units × $8
= $120,000

The preceding analysis is confirmed by the contribution margin income statement of Lambert that follows, which shows that income increased to $220,000 when 65,000 units are sold. The income statement in Exhibit 8 indicates income of $100,000 when 50,000 units are sold. Thus, selling an additional 15,000 units increases income by $120,000 ($220,000 – $100,000).

Sales (65,000 units × $20)	$1,300,000
Variable costs (65,000 units × $12)	780,000
Contribution margin (65,000 units × $8)	$ 520,000
Fixed costs	300,000
Income from operations	$ 220,000

Unit contribution margin analysis is useful information for managers. For example, in the preceding illustration, Lambert could spend up to $120,000 for special advertising or other product promotions to increase sales by 15,000 units and still increase income.

Example Exercise 21-2 Contribution Margin Obj. 2

Molly Company sells 20,000 units at $12 per unit. Variable costs are $9 per unit, and fixed costs are $25,000. Determine the (a) contribution margin ratio, (b) unit contribution margin, and (c) income from operations.

Follow My Example 21-2

a. 25% = ($12 − $9) ÷ $12, or ($240,000 − $180,000) ÷ $240,000
b. $3 per unit = $12 − $9
c.
Sales	$240,000	(20,000 units × $12 per unit)
Variable costs	180,000	(20,000 units × $9 per unit)
Contribution margin	$ 60,000	[20,000 units × ($12 − $9)]
Fixed costs	25,000	
Income from operations	$ 35,000	

Practice Exercises: PE 21-2A, PE 21-2B

Mathematical Approach to Cost-Volume-Profit Analysis

Obj. 3 Determine the break-even point and sales necessary to achieve a target profit.

The mathematical approach to cost-volume-profit analysis uses equations to determine the following:

- Sales necessary to break even
- Sales necessary to make a target or desired profit

Break-Even Point

The **break-even point** is the level of operations at which a company's revenues and expenses are equal, as shown in Exhibit 9. At break-even, a company reports neither income nor a loss from operations.

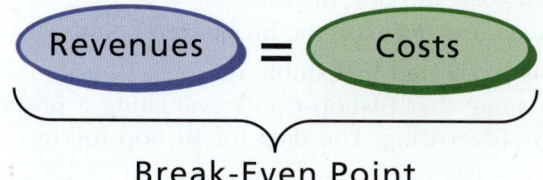

EXHIBIT 9
Break-Even Point

The break-even point in *sales units* is computed as follows:

$$\text{Break-Even Sales (units)} = \frac{\text{Fixed Costs}}{\text{Unit Contribution Margin}}$$

To illustrate, assume the following data for Baker Corporation:

Fixed costs	$90,000
Unit selling price	$25
Unit variable cost	15
Unit contribution margin	$10

The break-even point for Baker is 9,000 units, computed as follows:

$$\text{Break-Even Sales (units)} = \frac{\text{Fixed Costs}}{\text{Unit Contribution Margin}} = \frac{\$90,000}{\$10} = 9,000 \text{ units}$$

The following income statement for Baker verifies the break-even point of 9,000 units:

Sales (9,000 units × $25)	$225,000
Variable costs (9,000 units × $15)	135,000
Contribution margin	$ 90,000
Fixed costs	90,000
Income from operations	$ 0

As shown in Baker's income statement, the break-even point is $225,000 (9,000 units × $25) of sales. The break-even point in *sales dollars* can be determined directly as follows:

$$\text{Break-Even Sales (dollars)} = \frac{\text{Fixed Costs}}{\text{Contribution Margin Ratio}}$$

The contribution margin ratio can be computed using the unit contribution margin and unit selling price as follows:

$$\text{Contribution Margin Ratio} = \frac{\text{Unit Contribution Margin}}{\text{Unit Selling Price}}$$

The contribution margin ratio for Baker is 40%, computed as follows:

$$\text{Contribution Margin Ratio} = \frac{\text{Unit Contribution Margin}}{\text{Unit Selling Price}} = \frac{\$10}{\$25} = 40\%$$

Thus, the break-even sales dollars for Baker of $225,000 can be computed directly as follows:

$$\text{Break-Even Sales (dollars)} = \frac{\text{Fixed Costs}}{\text{Contribution Margin Ratio}} = \frac{\$90,000}{40\%} = \$225,000$$

> **Link to Ford Motor Company**
>
> **Ford Motor** reported that its 2014 operations in the Middle East and Africa were at break-even.
>
> Source: Ford Motor Company, Form 10-K for Year Ended December 31, 2014.

The break-even point is affected by changes in the fixed costs, unit variable costs, and unit selling price.

Effect of Changes in Fixed Costs

Fixed costs do not change in total with changes in the level of activity. However, fixed costs may change because of other factors such as advertising campaigns, changes in property tax rates, or changes in factory supervisors' salaries.

Changes in fixed costs affect the break-even point as follows:

- Increases in fixed costs increase the break-even point.
- Decreases in fixed costs decrease the break-even point.

This relationship is illustrated in Exhibit 10.

To illustrate, assume that Bishop Co. is evaluating a proposal to budget an additional $100,000 for advertising. The data for Bishop follow:

	Current	Proposed
Unit selling price	$90	$90
Unit variable cost	70	70
Unit contribution margin	$20	$20
Fixed costs	$600,000	$700,000

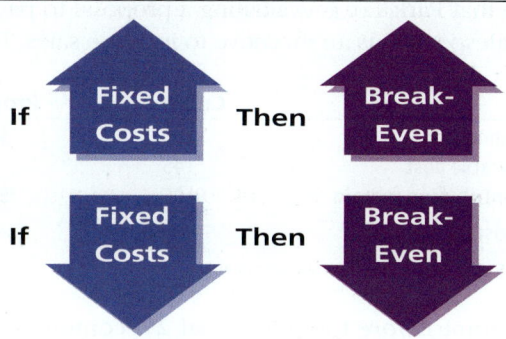

EXHIBIT 10

Effect of Change in Fixed Costs on Break-Even Point

Bishop's break-even point *before* the additional advertising expense of $100,000 is 30,000 units, computed as follows:

$$\text{Break-Even Sales (units)} = \frac{\text{Fixed Costs}}{\text{Unit Contribution Margin}} = \frac{\$600,000}{\$20} = 30,000 \text{ units}$$

Bishop's break-even point *after* the additional advertising expense of $100,000 is 35,000 units, computed as follows:

$$\text{Break-Even Sales (units)} = \frac{\text{Fixed Costs}}{\text{Unit Contribution Margin}} = \frac{\$700,000}{\$20} = 35,000 \text{ units}$$

As shown for Bishop, the $100,000 increase in advertising (fixed costs) requires an additional 5,000 units (35,000 − 30,000) of sales to break even.[2] In other words, an increase in sales of 5,000 units is required in order to generate an additional $100,000 of total contribution margin (5,000 units × $20) to cover the increased fixed costs.

Effect of Changes in Unit Variable Costs Unit variable costs do not change with changes in the level of activity. However, unit variable costs may be affected by other factors such as changes in the cost per unit of direct materials, changes in the wage rate for direct labor, or changes in the sales commission paid to salespeople.

Changes in unit variable costs affect the break-even point as follows:

- Increases in unit variable costs increase the break-even point.
- Decreases in unit variable costs decrease the break-even point.

This relationship is illustrated in Exhibit 11.

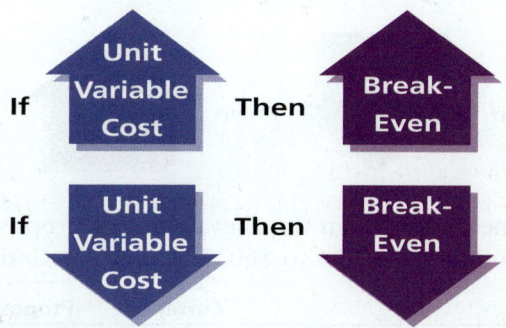

EXHIBIT 11

Effect of Change in Unit Variable Cost on Break-Even Point

---

2 The increase of 5,000 units can also be computed by dividing the increase in fixed costs of $100,000 by the unit contribution margin, $20, as follows: 5,000 units = $100,000 ÷ $20.

To illustrate, assume that Park Co. is evaluating a proposal to pay an additional 2% commission on sales to its salespeople as an incentive to increase sales. The data for Park follow:

	Current	Proposed
Unit selling price	$250	$250
Unit variable cost	145	150*
Unit contribution margin	$105	$100
Fixed costs	$840,000	$840,000

*$150 = $145 + (2% × $250 unit selling price)

Park's break-even point *before* the additional 2% commission is 8,000 units, computed as follows:

$$\text{Break-Even Sales (units)} = \frac{\text{Fixed Costs}}{\text{Unit Contribution Margin}} = \frac{\$840{,}000}{\$105} = 8{,}000 \text{ units}$$

If the 2% sales commission proposal is adopted, unit variable costs will increase by $5 ($250 × 2%), from $145 to $150 per unit. This increase in unit variable costs will decrease the unit contribution margin from $105 to $100 ($250 − $150). Thus, Park's break-even point *after* the additional 2% commission is 8,400 units, computed as follows:

$$\text{Break-Even Sales (units)} = \frac{\text{Fixed Costs}}{\text{Unit Contribution Margin}} = \frac{\$840{,}000}{\$100} = 8{,}400 \text{ units}$$

As shown for Park, an additional 400 units of sales will be required in order to break even. This is because if 8,000 units are sold, the new unit contribution margin of $100 provides only $800,000 (8,000 units × $100) of contribution margin. Thus, $40,000 more contribution margin is necessary to cover the total fixed costs of $840,000. This additional $40,000 of contribution margin is provided by selling 400 more units (400 units × $100).

Effect of Changes in Unit Selling Price Changes in the unit selling price affect the unit contribution margin and, thus, the break-even point. Specifically, changes in the unit selling price affect the break-even point as follows:

- Increases in the unit selling price decrease the break-even point.
- Decreases in the unit selling price increase the break-even point.

This relationship is illustrated in Exhibit 12.

EXHIBIT 12

Effect of Change in Unit Selling Price on Break-Even Point

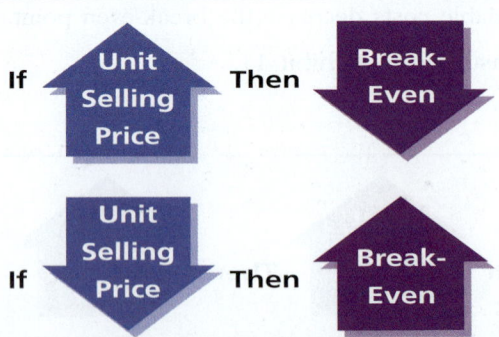

To illustrate, assume that Graham Co. is evaluating a proposal to increase the unit selling price of its product from $50 to $60. The data for Graham follow:

	Current	Proposed
Unit selling price	$50	$60
Unit variable cost	30	30
Unit contribution margin	$20	$30
Fixed costs	$600,000	$600,000

Graham's break-even point *before* the price increase is 30,000 units, computed as follows:

$$\text{Break-Even Sales (units)} = \frac{\text{Fixed Costs}}{\text{Unit Contribution Margin}} = \frac{\$600,000}{\$20} = 30,000 \text{ units}$$

The increase of $10 per unit in the selling price increases the unit contribution margin by $10. Thus, Graham's break-even point *after* the price increase is 20,000 units, computed as follows:

$$\text{Break-Even Sales (units)} = \frac{\text{Fixed Costs}}{\text{Unit Contribution Margin}} = \frac{\$600,000}{\$30} = 20,000 \text{ units}$$

As shown for Graham, the price increase of $10 increased the unit contribution margin by $10, which decreased the break-even point by 10,000 units (30,000 units − 20,000 units).

Summary of Effects of Changes on Break-Even Point The break-even point in sales changes in the same direction as changes in the variable cost per unit and fixed costs. In contrast, the break-even point in sales changes in the opposite direction as changes in the unit selling price. These changes on the break-even point in sales are summarized in Exhibit 13.

EXHIBIT 13
Effects of Changes in Selling Price and Costs on Break-Even Point

Type of Change	Direction of Change	Effect of Change on Break-Even Sales
Fixed cost	↑ ↓	↑ ↓
Unit variable cost	↑ ↓	↑ ↓
Unit selling price	↑ ↓	↓ ↑

Example Exercise 21-3 Break-Even Point Obj. 3

Nicolas Enterprises sells a product for $60 per unit. The variable cost is $35 per unit, while fixed costs are $80,000. Determine the (a) break-even point in sales units and (b) break-even point in sales units assuming that the selling price is increased to $67 per unit.

Follow My Example 21-3

a. 3,200 units = $80,000 ÷ ($60 − $35)
b. 2,500 units = $80,000 ÷ ($67 − $35)

Practice Exercises: PE 21-3A, PE 21-3B

Target Profit

At the break-even point, sales and costs are exactly equal. However, the goal of most companies is to make a profit.

Business Connection

AIRLINE INDUSTRY BREAK-EVEN

Airlines measure revenues and costs by available seat miles. An available seat mile is one seat (empty or filled) flying one mile. Thus, the average revenue earned per available seat mile is termed the RASM, and the average cost per available seat mile is termed the CASM. The operating break-even occurs when the RASM equals the CASM. Since airlines have high aircraft fixed costs, filling passenger seats is an important contributor to exceeding break-even. This is measured by the average proportion of seats filled across all flights, which is termed the load factor. In addition, important variable costs such as labor and fuel impact the break-even performance. Thus, airlines monitor employee productivity and fuel costs to maintain profitability. The RASM, CASM, and load factor for a recent year for major airlines are as follows:

	American Airlines	United Airlines	Delta Air Lines	Southwest Airlines	US Airways
RASM	$0.129	$0.124	$0.132	$0.135	$0.125
CASM	0.082	0.079	0.089	0.075	0.077
RASM – CASM	$0.047	$0.045	$0.043	$0.060	$0.048
Load factor	82%	84%	85%	82%	83%

As can be seen, all the major airlines are operating above their break-even points, with Southwest Airlines demonstrating the best profit performance by these metrics. All the load factors are more than 80%, indicating that the airlines are using their aircraft efficiently.

Source: MIT Airline Data Project.

By modifying the break-even equation, the sales required to earn a target or desired amount of profit may be computed. For this purpose, target profit is added to the break-even equation, as follows:

$$\text{Sales (units)} = \frac{\text{Fixed Costs} + \text{Target Profit}}{\text{Unit Contribution Margin}}$$

To illustrate, assume the following data for Waltham Co.:

Fixed costs	$200,000
Target profit	100,000
Unit selling price	$75
Unit variable cost	45
Unit contribution margin	$30

The sales necessary for Waltham to earn the target profit of $100,000 would be 10,000 units, computed as follows:

$$\text{Sales (units)} = \frac{\text{Fixed Costs} + \text{Target Profit}}{\text{Unit Contribution Margin}} = \frac{\$200{,}000 + \$100{,}000}{\$30} = 10{,}000 \text{ units}$$

The following income statement for Waltham verifies this computation:

Sales (10,000 units × $75)	$750,000
Variable costs (10,000 units × $45)	450,000
Contribution margin (10,000 units × $30)	$300,000
Fixed costs	200,000
Income from operations	$100,000 ←Target profit

As shown in the income statement for Waltham, sales of $750,000 (10,000 units × $75) are necessary to earn the target profit of $100,000. The sales of $750,000 needed to earn the target profit of $100,000 can be computed directly using the contribution margin ratio, computed as follows:

$$\text{Contribution Margin Ratio} = \frac{\text{Unit Contribution Margin}}{\text{Unit Selling Price}} = \frac{\$30}{\$75} = 40\%$$

$$\text{Sales (dollars)} = \frac{\text{Fixed Costs + Target Profit}}{\text{Contribution Margin Ratio}}$$

$$= \frac{\$200{,}000 + \$100{,}000}{40\%} = \frac{\$300{,}000}{40\%} = \$750{,}000$$

Example Exercise 21-4 Target Profit Obj. 3

Forest Company sells a product for $140 per unit. The variable cost is $60 per unit, and fixed costs are $240,000. Determine the (a) break-even point in sales units and (b) the sales units required to achieve a target profit of $50,000.

Follow My Example 21-4

a. 3,000 units = $240,000 ÷ ($140 − $60)

b. 3,625 units = ($240,000 + $50,000) ÷ ($140 − $60)

Practice Exercises: PE 21-4A, PE 21-4B

INTEGRITY, OBJECTIVITY, AND ETHICS IN BUSINESS

ORPHAN DRUGS

Each year, pharmaceutical companies develop new drugs that cure a variety of physical conditions. In order to be profitable, drug companies must sell enough of a product for a reasonable price to exceed break-even. Break-even points, however, create a problem for drugs, called "orphan drugs," targeted at rare diseases. These drugs are typically expensive to develop and have low sales volumes, making it impossible to achieve break-even.

To ensure that orphan drugs are not overlooked, Congress passed the Orphan Drug Act, which provides incentives for pharmaceutical companies to develop drugs for rare diseases that might not generate enough sales to reach break-even. The program has been a great success. Since 1982, more than 200 orphan drugs have come to market, such as **Novartis AG**'s drug for the treatment of Paget's disease.

Graphic Approach to Cost-Volume-Profit Analysis

Obj. 4 Using a cost-volume-profit chart and a profit-volume chart, determine the break-even point and sales necessary to achieve a target profit.

Cost-volume-profit analysis can be presented as a graph as well as an equation. Many managers prefer the graphic form because the operating profit or loss for different levels can be easily seen.

Cost-Volume-Profit (Break-Even) Chart

A **cost-volume-profit chart**, sometimes called a *break-even chart*, graphically shows sales, costs, and the related profit or loss for various levels of units sold. It assists in understanding the relationship among sales, costs, and operating profit or loss.

1038 Chapter 21 Cost-Volume-Profit Analysis

To illustrate, the cost-volume-profit chart in Exhibit 14 is based on the following data for Munoz Co.:

Total fixed costs	$100,000
Unit selling price	$50
Unit variable cost	30
Unit contribution margin	$20

The cost-volume-profit chart in Exhibit 14 is constructed using the following steps:

Step 1. Volume in units of sales is indicated along the horizontal axis. The range of volume shown is the relevant range in which the company expects to operate. Dollar amounts of total sales and total costs are indicated along the vertical axis.

Step 2. A total sales line is plotted by connecting the point at zero on the left corner of the graph to a second point on the chart. The second point is determined by multiplying the maximum number of units in the relevant range, which is found on the far right of the horizontal axis, by the unit sales price. A line is then drawn through both of these points. This is the total sales line. For Munoz, the maximum number of units in the relevant range is 10,000. The second point on the line is determined by multiplying the 10,000 units by the $50 unit selling price to get the second point for the total sales line of $500,000 (10,000 units × $50). The sales line is drawn upward to the right from zero through the $500,000 point at the end of the relevant range.

Step 3. A total cost line is plotted by beginning with total fixed costs on the vertical axis. A second point is determined by multiplying the maximum number of units in the relevant range, which is found on the far right of the horizontal axis by the unit variable costs, and adding the total fixed costs. A line is then drawn through both of these points. This is the total cost line. For Munoz, the maximum number of units in the relevant range is 10,000. The second point on the line is determined by multiplying the 10,000 units by the $30 unit variable cost and then adding the $100,000 total fixed costs to get the second point for the total estimated costs of $400,000 [(10,000 units × $30) + $100,000]. The cost line is drawn upward to the right from $100,000 on the vertical axis through the $400,000 point at the end of the relevant range.

Step 4. The break-even point is the intersection point of the total sales and total cost lines. A vertical dotted line drawn downward at the intersection point indicates the units of sales at the break-even point. A horizontal dotted line drawn to the left at the intersection point indicates the sales dollars and costs at the break-even point.

EXHIBIT 14

Cost-Volume-Profit Chart

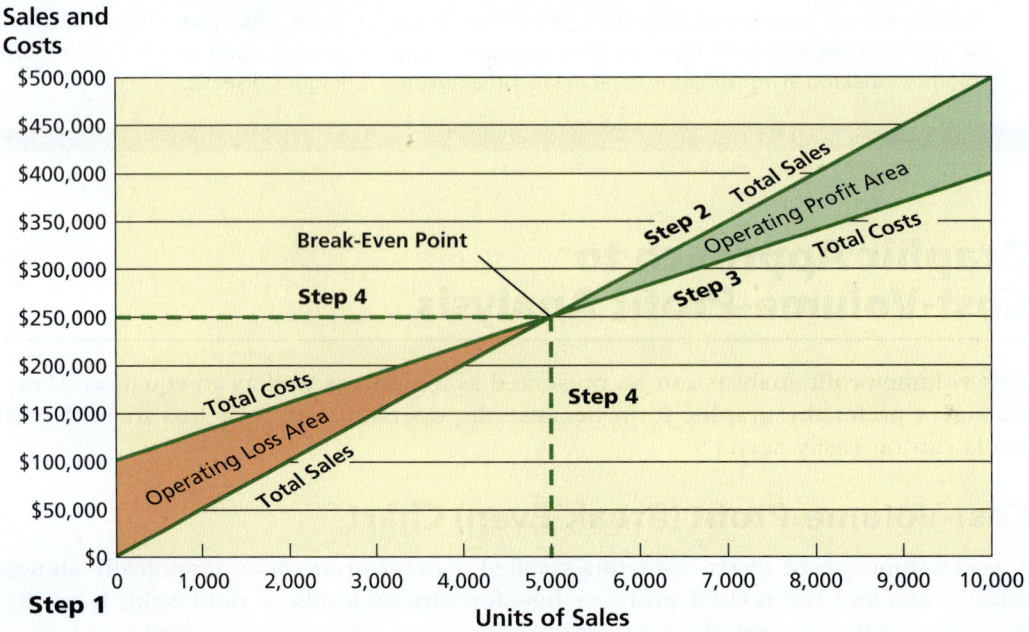

In Exhibit 14, the break-even point for Munoz is $250,000 of sales, which represents sales of 5,000 units. Operating profits will be earned when sales levels are to the right of the break-even point (*operating profit area*). Operating losses will be incurred when sales levels are to the left of the break-even point (*operating loss area*).

Changes in the unit selling price, total fixed costs, and unit variable costs can be analyzed by using a cost-volume-profit chart. Using the data in Exhibit 14, assume that Munoz is evaluating a proposal to reduce fixed costs by $20,000. In this case, the total fixed costs would be $80,000 ($100,000 – $20,000).

Under this scenario, the total sales line is not changed, but the total cost line will change. As shown in Exhibit 15, the total cost line is redrawn, starting at the $80,000 point (total fixed costs) on the vertical axis. The second point is determined by multiplying the maximum number of units in the relevant range, which is found on the far right of the horizontal axis, by the unit variable costs and adding the fixed costs. For Munoz, this is the total estimated cost for 10,000 units, which is $380,000 [(10,000 units × $30) + $80,000]. The cost line is drawn upward to the right from $80,000 on the vertical axis through the $380,000 point. The revised cost-volume-profit chart in Exhibit 15 indicates that the break-even point for Munoz decreases to $200,000 and 4,000 units of sales.

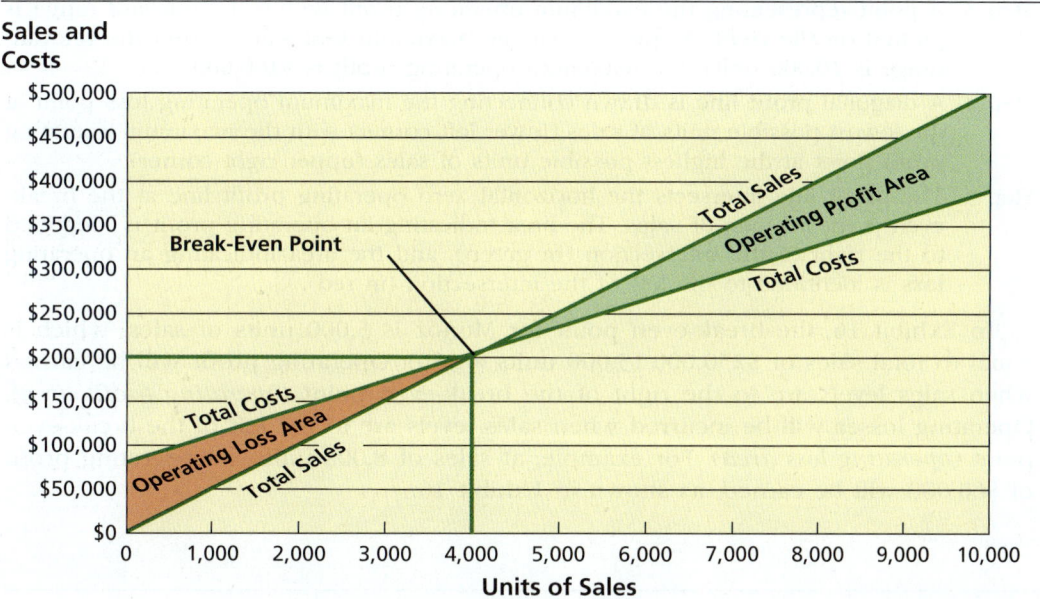

EXHIBIT 15

Revised Cost-Volume-Profit Chart

Profit-Volume Chart

Another graphic approach to cost-volume-profit analysis is the profit-volume chart. The **profit-volume chart** plots only the difference between total sales and total costs (or profits). In this way, the profit-volume chart allows managers to determine the operating profit (or loss) for various levels of units sold.

To illustrate, the profit-volume chart for Munoz Co. in Exhibit 16 is based on the same data used in Exhibit 14. These data are as follows:

Total fixed costs	$100,000
Unit selling price	$50
Unit variable cost	30
Unit contribution margin	$20

The maximum operating loss is equal to the fixed costs of $100,000. Assuming that the maximum units that can be sold within the relevant range is 10,000 units, the maximum operating profit is $100,000, computed as follows:

Sales (10,000 units × $50)	$500,000
Variable costs (10,000 units × $30)	300,000
Contribution margin (10,000 units × $20)	$200,000
Fixed costs	100,000
Operating profit	$100,000 ← Maximum profit

The profit-volume chart in Exhibit 16 is constructed using the following steps:

Step 1. Volume in units of sales is indicated along the horizontal axis. The range of volume shown is the relevant range in which the company expects to operate. In Exhibit 16, the maximum units of sales is 10,000 units. Dollar amounts indicating operating profits and losses are shown along the vertical axis.

Step 2. A point representing the maximum operating loss is plotted on the vertical axis at the left. This loss is equal to the total fixed costs at the zero level of sales. Thus, the maximum operating loss is equal to the fixed costs of $100,000.

Step 3. A point representing the maximum operating profit within the relevant range is plotted on the right. Assuming that the maximum unit sales within the relevant range is 10,000 units, the maximum operating profit is $100,000.

Step 4. A diagonal profit line is drawn connecting the maximum operating loss point at the lowest possible units of sales (lower left corner) with the maximum operating profit point at the highest possible units of sales (upper right corner).

Step 5. The profit line intersects the horizontal zero operating profit line at the break-even point in units of sales. The area indicating an operating profit is identified to the right of the intersection (in green), and the area indicating an operating loss is identified to the left of the intersection (in red).

In Exhibit 16, the break-even point for Munoz is 5,000 units of sales, which is equal to total sales of $250,000 (5,000 units × $50). Operating profit will be earned when sales levels are to the right of the break-even point (*operating profit area*). Operating losses will be incurred when sales levels are to the left of the break-even point (*operating loss area*). For example, at sales of 8,000 units, an operating profit of $60,000 will be earned, as shown in Exhibit 16.

EXHIBIT 16

Profit-Volume Chart

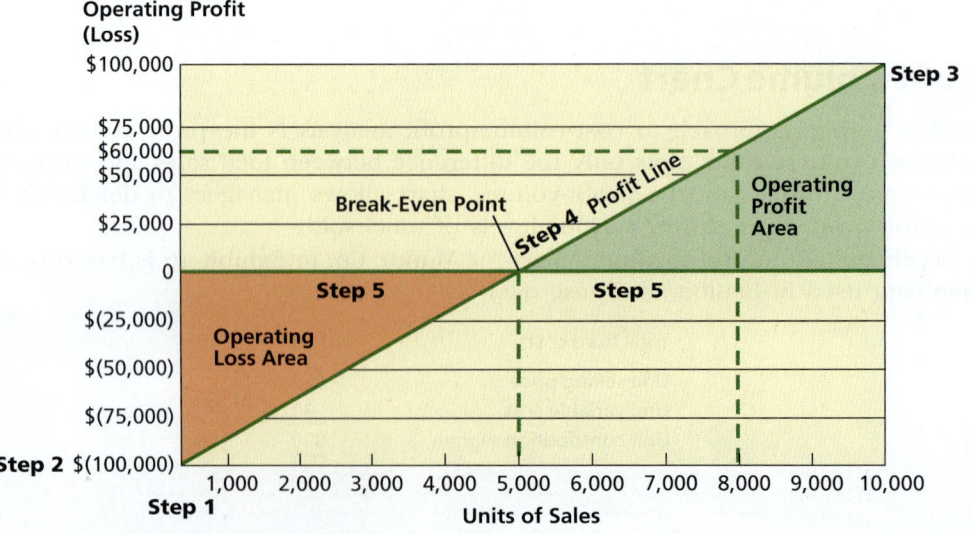

The effect of changes in the unit selling price, total fixed costs, and unit variable costs on profit can be analyzed using a profit-volume chart. Using the data in Exhibit 16, consider the effect that a $20,000 increase in fixed costs will have on profit. In this case, the total fixed costs will increase to $120,000 ($100,000 + $20,000), and the maximum operating loss will also increase to $120,000. At the maximum sales of 10,000 units, the maximum operating profit would be $80,000, computed as follows:

Sales (10,000 units × $50)	$500,000
Variable costs (10,000 units × $30)	300,000
Contribution margin (10,000 units × $20)	$200,000
Fixed costs	120,000
Operating profit	$ 80,000 ← Revised maximum profit

A revised profit-volume chart is constructed by plotting the maximum operating loss and maximum operating profit points and drawing the revised profit line. The original and revised profit-volume charts for Munoz are shown in Exhibit 17.

EXHIBIT 17 Original Profit-Volume Chart and Revised Profit-Volume Chart

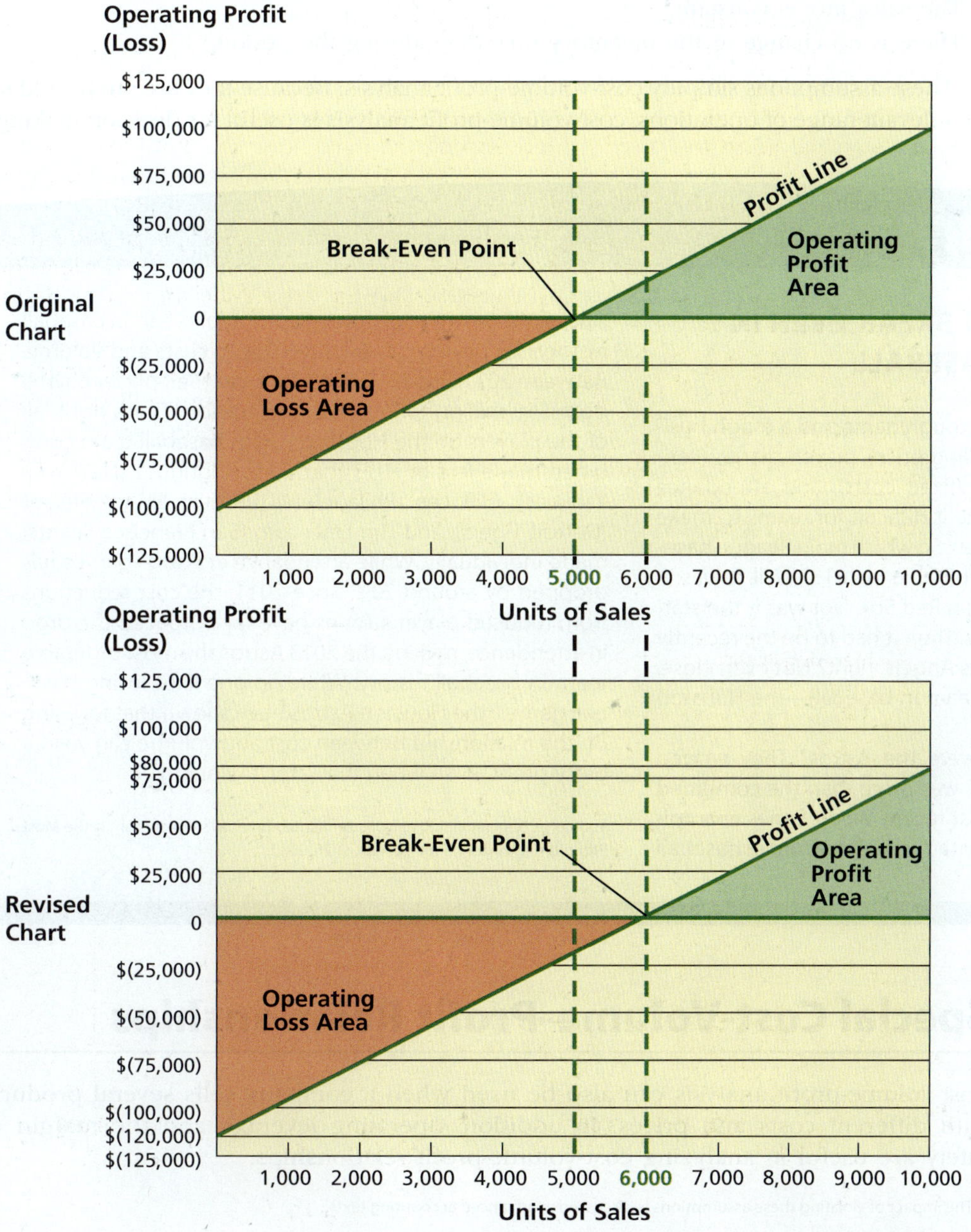

The revised profit-volume chart indicates that the break-even point for Munoz is 6,000 units of sales. This is equal to total sales of $300,000 (6,000 units × $50). The operating loss area of the chart has increased, while the operating profit area has decreased.

Use of Computers in Cost-Volume-Profit Analysis

With computers, the graphic approach and the mathematical approach to cost-volume-profit analysis are easy to use. Managers can vary assumptions regarding selling prices, costs, and volume and can observe the effects of each change on the break-even point and profit. Such an analysis is called a *"what if"* analysis or *sensitivity* analysis.

Assumptions of Cost-Volume-Profit Analysis

Cost-volume-profit analysis depends on several assumptions. The primary assumptions are as follows:

- Total sales and total costs can be represented by straight lines.
- Within the relevant range of operating activity, the efficiency of operations does not change.
- Costs can be divided into fixed and variable components.
- The sales mix is constant.
- There is no change in the inventory quantities during the period.

These assumptions simplify cost-volume-profit analysis. Because they are often valid for the relevant range of operations, cost-volume-profit analysis is useful for decision making.[3]

SERVICE FOCUS

PROFIT, LOSS, AND BREAK-EVEN IN MAJOR LEAGUE BASEBALL

Major League Baseball is a tough game and a tough business. Ticket prices (unit selling price), player salaries (variable costs), stadium fees (fixed costs), and attendance (volume) converge to make it difficult for teams to make a profit or at least break even. So which major league baseball team was the most profitable in 2013? Well, it wasn't the World Champion Boston Red Sox. Nor was it the star-studded New York Yankees. Then it had to be the recently turned around Los Angeles Angels, right? Not even close. It was actually the worst team in baseball—the Houston Astros.

Just how profitable were the Astros? They earned $99 million in 2013, which was more than the combined 2013 profits of the six most recent World Series champions. How could the team with the worst record in baseball since 2005 have one of the most profitable years in baseball history? By paying careful attention to costs and volume. Between 2011 and 2013, the Astros cut their player payroll from $56 million to less than $13 million. That's right; all of the players on the Houston Astros baseball team combined made less in 2013 than Alex Rodriguez (New York Yankees), Cliff Lee (Philadelphia Phillies), Prince Fielder (Detroit Tigers), and Tim Lincecum (San Francisco Giants) made individually. While attendance at Astros games has dropped by around 20% since 2011, the cost reductions from reduced player salaries have far outpaced the drop in attendance, making the 2013 Astros the most profitable team in baseball history. While no one likes losing baseball games, the Houston Astros have shown that focusing on the relationship between cost and volume can yield a hefty profit, even when they aren't winning.

Source: D. Alexander, "2013 Houston Astros: Baseball's Worst Team Is the Most Profitable In History," *Forbes*, August 26, 2013.

Obj. 5 Compute the break-even point for a company selling more than one product, the operating leverage, and the margin of safety.

Special Cost-Volume-Profit Relationships

Cost-volume-profit analysis can also be used when a company sells several products with different costs and prices. In addition, operating leverage and the margin of safety are useful in analyzing cost-volume-profit relationships.

---

3 The impact of violating these assumptions is discussed in advanced accounting texts.

Sales Mix Considerations

Many companies sell more than one product at different selling prices. In addition, the products normally have different unit variable costs and, thus, different unit contribution margins. In such cases, break-even analysis can still be performed by considering the sales mix. The **sales mix** is the relative distribution of sales among the products sold by a company.

To illustrate, assume that Cascade Company sold Products A and B during the past year, as follows:

		Product A	Product B
Total fixed costs	$200,000		
Unit selling price		$90	$140
Unit variable cost		70	95
Unit contribution margin		$20	$ 45
Units sold		8,000	2,000
Sales mix		80%	20%

The sales mix for Products A and B is expressed as a percentage of total units sold. For Cascade, a total of 10,000 (8,000 + 2,000) units were sold during the year. Therefore, the sales mix is 80% (8,000 ÷ 10,000) for Product A and 20% for Product B (2,000 ÷ 10,000), as shown in Exhibit 18. The sales mix could also be expressed as the ratio 80:20.

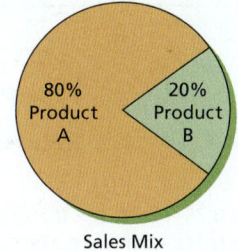

Sales Mix

EXHIBIT 18

Multiple Product Sales Mix

For break-even analysis, it is useful to think of Products A and B as components of one overall enterprise product called E. The unit selling price of E equals the sum of the unit selling prices of each product multiplied by its sales mix percentage. Likewise, the unit variable cost and unit contribution margin of E equal the sum of the unit variable costs and unit contribution margins of each product multiplied by its sales mix percentage.

For Cascade, the unit selling price, unit variable cost, and unit contribution margin for E are computed as follows:

Product E		Product A	Product B
Unit selling price of E	$100 =	($90 × 0.8) +	($140 × 0.2)
Unit variable cost of E	75 =	($70 × 0.8) +	($95 × 0.2)
Unit contribution margin of E	$ 25 =	($20 × 0.8) +	($45 × 0.2)

Link to Ford Motor Company
The sales mix of cars and trucks has a major impact on profitability. **Ford Motor Company**'s overall profitability.

Cascade has total fixed costs of $200,000. The break-even point of 8,000 units of E can be determined as follows using the unit selling price, unit variable cost, and unit contribution margin of E:

$$\text{Break-Even Sales (units) for E} = \frac{\text{Fixed Costs}}{\text{Unit Contribution Margin}} = \frac{\$200,000}{\$25} = 8,000 \text{ units}$$

Because the sales mix for Products A and B is 80% and 20%, respectively, the break-even quantity of A is 6,400 units (8,000 units × 80%) and B is 1,600 units (8,000 units × 20%). The preceding break-even analysis is verified in Exhibit 19.

EXHIBIT 19

Break-Even Sales: Multiple Products

	Product A	Product B	Total
Sales:			
6,400 units × $90	$576,000		$576,000
1,600 units × $140		$224,000	224,000
Total sales	$576,000	$224,000	$800,000
Variable costs:			
6,400 units × $70	$448,000		$448,000
1,600 units × $95		$152,000	152,000
Total variable costs	$448,000	$152,000	$600,000
Contribution margin	$128,000	$ 72,000	$200,000
Fixed costs			200,000
Income from operations		Break-even point →	$ 0

The effects of changes in the sales mix on the break-even point can be determined by assuming a different sales mix. The break-even point of E can then be recomputed.

Example Exercise 21-5 Sales Mix and Break-Even Analysis   Obj. 5

Megan Company has fixed costs of $180,000. The unit selling price, variable cost per unit, and contribution margin per unit for the company's two products are as follows:

Product	Selling Price	Variable Cost per Unit	Contribution Margin per Unit
Q	$160	$100	$60
Z	100	80	20

The sales mix for products Q and Z is 75% and 25%, respectively. Determine the break-even point in units of Q and Z.

Follow My Example 21-5

Unit selling price of E: [($160 × 0.75) + ($100 × 0.25)] = $145
Unit variable cost of E: [($100 × 0.75) + ($80 × 0.25)] =   95
Unit contribution margin of E $ 50

Break-Even Sales (units) for E = $180,000 ÷ $50 = 3,600 units
Break-Even Sales (units) for Q = 3,600 units of E × 75% = 2,700 units of Product Q
Break-Even Sales (units) for Z = 3,600 units of E × 25% = 900 units of Product Z

Practice Exercises: PE 21-5A, PE 21-5B

Operating Leverage

The relationship between a company's contribution margin and income from operations is measured by **operating leverage**. A company's operating leverage is computed as follows:

$$\text{Operating Leverage} = \frac{\text{Contribution Margin}}{\text{Income from Operations}}$$

The difference between contribution margin and income from operations is fixed costs. Thus, companies with high fixed costs will normally have high operating leverage. Examples of such companies include airline and automotive companies, like **Ford Motor Company**. Low operating leverage is normal for companies that are labor-intensive, such as professional service companies, which have low fixed costs.

To illustrate operating leverage, assume the following data for Jones Inc. and Wilson Inc.:

	Jones Inc.	Wilson Inc.
Sales	$400,000	$400,000
Variable costs	300,000	300,000
Contribution margin	$100,000	$100,000
Fixed costs	80,000	50,000
Income from operations	$ 20,000	$ 50,000

As shown, Jones and Wilson have the same sales, the same variable costs, and the same contribution margin. However, Jones has larger fixed costs than Wilson and, thus, a higher operating leverage. The operating leverage for each company is computed as follows:

Jones Inc.

$$\text{Operating Leverage} = \frac{\text{Contribution Margin}}{\text{Income from Operations}} = \frac{\$100,000}{\$20,000} = 5$$

Wilson Inc.

$$\text{Operating Leverage} = \frac{\text{Contribution Margin}}{\text{Income from Operations}} = \frac{\$100,000}{\$50,000} = 2$$

Operating leverage can be used to measure the impact of changes in sales on income from operations. Using operating leverage, the effect of changes in sales on income from operations is computed as follows:

$$\frac{\text{Percent Change in}}{\text{Income from Operations}} = \frac{\text{Percent Change in}}{\text{Sales}} \times \frac{\text{Operating}}{\text{Leverage}}$$

To illustrate, assume that sales increased by 10%, or $40,000 ($400,000 × 10%), for Jones and Wilson. The percent increase in income from operations for Jones and Wilson is computed as follows:

Jones Inc.

$$\frac{\text{Percent Change in}}{\text{Income from Operations}} = \frac{\text{Percent Change in}}{\text{Sales}} \times \frac{\text{Operating}}{\text{Leverage}}$$

$$= 10\% \times 5 = 50\%$$

Wilson Inc.

$$\frac{\text{Percent Change in}}{\text{Income from Operations}} = \frac{\text{Percent Change in}}{\text{Sales}} \times \frac{\text{Operating}}{\text{Leverage}}$$

$$= 10\% \times 2 = 20\%$$

As shown, Jones's income from operations increases by 50%, while Wilson's income from operations increases by only 20%. The validity of this analysis is shown in the following income statements for Jones and Wilson based on the 10% increase in sales:

	Jones Inc.	Wilson Inc.
Sales	$440,000	$440,000
Variable costs	330,000	330,000
Contribution margin	$110,000	$110,000
Fixed costs	80,000	50,000
Income from operations	$ 30,000	$ 60,000

The preceding income statements indicate that Jones's income from operations increased from $20,000 to $30,000, a 50% increase ($10,000 ÷ $20,000). In contrast, Wilson's income from operations increased from $50,000 to $60,000, a 20% increase ($10,000 ÷ $50,000).

Because even a small increase in sales will generate a large percentage increase in income from operations, Jones might consider ways to increase sales. Such actions

> **Link to Ford Motor Company**
>
> **Ford Motor Company** has a high proportion of fixed costs with the result that small changes in units sold can significantly affect its overall profitability.
>
> Source: Ford Motor Company, Form 10-K for Year Ended December 31, 2014.

could include special advertising or sales promotions. In contrast, Wilson might consider ways to increase operating leverage by reducing variable costs.

The impact of a change in sales on income from operations for companies with high and low operating leverage is summarized in Exhibit 20.

EXHIBIT 20

Effect of Operating Leverage on Income from Operations

Operating Leverage	Percentage Impact on Income from Operations from a Change in Sales
High	Large
Low	Small

Example Exercise 21-6 Operating Leverage — Obj. 5

Tucker Company reports the following data:

Sales	$750,000
Variable costs	500,000
Contribution margin	$250,000
Fixed costs	187,500
Income from operations	$ 62,500

Determine Tucker Company's operating leverage.

Follow My Example 21-6

$$\text{Operating Leverage} = \frac{\text{Contribution Margin}}{\text{Income from Operations}} = \frac{\$250,000}{\$62,500} = 4.0$$

Practice Exercises: PE 21-6A, PE 21-6B

Margin of Safety

The **margin of safety** indicates the possible decrease in sales that may occur before an operating loss results. Thus, if the margin of safety is low, even a small decline in sales revenue may result in an operating loss.

The margin of safety may be expressed in the following ways:

- Dollars of sales
- Units of sales
- Percent of current sales

To illustrate, assume the following data:

Sales	$250,000
Sales at the break-even point	200,000
Unit selling price	25

The margin of safety in dollars of sales is $50,000 ($250,000 − $200,000). The margin of safety in units is 2,000 units ($50,000 ÷ $25). The margin of safety expressed as a percent of current sales is 20%, computed as follows:

$$\text{Margin of Safety} = \frac{\text{Sales} - \text{Sales at Break-Even Point}}{\text{Sales}}$$

$$= \frac{\$250,000 - \$200,000}{\$250,000} = \frac{\$50,000}{\$250,000} = 20\%$$

Therefore, the current sales may decline $50,000, 2,000 units, or 20% before an operating loss occurs.

Chapter 21 Cost-Volume-Profit Analysis

Example Exercise 21-7 Margin of Safety Obj. 5

Rachel Company has sales of $400,000, and the break-even point in sales dollars is $300,000. Determine the company's margin of safety as a percent of current sales.

Follow My Example 21-7

$$\text{Margin of Safety} = \frac{\text{Sales} - \text{Sales at Break-Even Point}}{\text{Sales}} = \frac{\$400,000 - \$300,000}{\$400,000} = \frac{\$100,000}{\$400,000} = 25\%$$

Practice Exercises: PE 21-7A, PE 21-7B

APPENDIX

Variable Costing

The cost of manufactured products consists of direct materials, direct labor, and factory overhead. The reporting of all these costs in financial statements is called **absorption costing**. Absorption costing is required under generally accepted accounting principles for financial statements distributed to external users. However, alternative reports may be prepared for decision-making purposes by managers and other internal users. One such alternative reporting is *variable costing* or *direct costing*.

In *variable costing*, the cost of goods manufactured is composed only of variable costs. Thus, the cost of goods manufactured consists of direct materials, direct labor, and *variable* factory overhead.

In a variable costing income statement, *fixed* factory overhead costs do not become a part of the cost of goods manufactured. Instead, fixed factory overhead costs are treated as a period expense. The differences between absorption and variable cost of goods manufactured is summarized in Exhibit 21.

EXHIBIT 21
Absorption Versus Variable Cost of Goods Manufactured

Cost of Goods Manufactured	
Absorption Costing	**Variable Costing**
Direct materials	Direct materials
Direct labor	Direct labor
Variable factory overhead	Variable factory overhead
Fixed factory overhead	

The form of a variable costing income statement is as follows:

Sales		$XXX
Variable cost of goods sold		XXX
Manufacturing margin		$XXX
Variable selling and administrative expenses		XXX
Contribution margin		$XXX
Fixed costs:		
Fixed manufacturing costs	$XXX	
Fixed selling and administrative expenses	XXX	XXX
Income from operations		$XXX

1048 Chapter 21 Cost-Volume-Profit Analysis

Manufacturing margin is the excess of sales over variable cost of goods sold.

Manufacturing Margin = Sales − Variable Cost of Goods Sold

Variable cost of goods sold consists of direct materials, direct labor, and variable factory overhead for the units sold. *Contribution margin* is the excess of manufacturing margin over variable selling and administrative expenses.

Contribution Margin = Manufacturing Margin − Variable Selling and Administrative Expenses

Subtracting fixed costs from contribution margin yields *income from operations*.

Income from Operations = Contribution Margin − Fixed Costs

The variable costing income statement facilitates managerial decision making because manufacturing margin and contribution margin are reported directly. As illustrated in this chapter, contribution margin is used in break-even analysis and other analyses.

To illustrate the variable costing income statement, assume that Martinez Co. manufactures 15,000 units, which are sold at a price of $50. The related costs and expenses for Martinez are as follows:

	Total Cost	Number of Units	Unit Cost
Manufacturing costs:			
Variable	$375,000	15,000	$25
Fixed	150,000	15,000	10
Total	$525,000		$35
Selling and administrative expenses:			
Variable ($5 per unit sold)	$ 75,000		
Fixed	50,000		
Total	$125,000		

Exhibit 22 shows the variable costing income statement prepared for Martinez. The computations are shown in parentheses.

EXHIBIT 22
Variable Costing Income Statement

Sales (15,000 × $50)		$750,000
Variable cost of goods sold (15,000 × $25)		375,000
Manufacturing margin		$375,000
Variable selling and administrative expenses (15,000 × $5)		75,000
Contribution margin		$300,000
Fixed costs:		
Fixed manufacturing costs	$150,000	
Fixed selling and administrative expenses	50,000	200,000
Income from operations		$100,000

Exhibit 23 illustrates the absorption costing income statement prepared for Martinez. The absorption costing income statement does not distinguish between variable and fixed costs. All manufacturing costs are included in the cost of goods sold. Deducting the cost of goods sold from sales yields the *gross profit*. Deducting the selling and administrative expenses from gross profit yields the *income from operations*.

The relationship between variable and absorption costing *income from operations* is summarized in Exhibit 24.

EXHIBIT 23
Absorption Costing Income Statement

Sales (15,000 × $50)	$750,000
Cost of goods sold (15,000 × $35)	525,000
Gross profit	$225,000
Selling and administrative expenses ($75,000 + $50,000)	125,000
Income from operations	$100,000

EXHIBIT 24 — Relationship Between Variable and Absorption Costing Income

If Units Sold < Units Manufactured
Then Variable Costing Income < Absorption Costing Income

If Units Sold > Units Manufactured
Then Variable Costing Income > Absorption Costing Income

In Exhibits 22 and 23, Martinez manufactured and sold 15,000 units. Thus, the variable and absorption costing income statements reported the same income from operations of $100,000. However, assume that only 12,000 units of the 15,000 units Martinez manufactured were sold. Exhibit 25 shows the related variable and absorption costing income statements.

Exhibit 25 shows a $30,000 ($70,000 − $40,000) difference in income from operations. This difference is due to the fixed manufacturing costs. All of the $150,000 of fixed manufacturing costs is included as a period expense in the variable costing statement. However, the 3,000 units of ending inventory in the absorption costing statement include $30,000 (3,000 units × $10) of fixed manufacturing costs. By being included in inventory, this $30,000 is excluded from the current cost of goods sold. Thus, the absorption costing income from operations is $30,000 higher than the income from operations for variable costing.

A similar analysis could be used to illustrate that income from operations under variable costing is greater than income from operations under absorption costing when the units manufactured are less than the units sold.

Under absorption costing, increases or decreases in income from operations can result from changes in inventory levels. For example, for Martinez, a 3,000 increase in ending inventory created a $30,000 increase in income from operations under absorption costing. Such increases (decreases) could be misinterpreted by managers using absorption costing as operating efficiencies (inefficiencies). This is one of the reasons that variable costing is often used by managers for cost control, product pricing, and production planning. Such uses of variable costing are discussed in advanced accounting texts.

EXHIBIT 25 — Units Manufactured Exceed Units Sold

Variable Costing Income Statement

Sales (12,000 × $50)		$600,000
Variable cost of goods sold:		
Variable cost of goods manufactured (15,000 × $25)	$375,000	
Less ending inventory (3,000 × $25)	75,000	
Variable cost of goods sold		300,000
Manufacturing margin		$300,000
Variable selling and administrative expenses (12,000 × $5)		60,000
Contribution margin		$240,000
Fixed costs:		
Fixed manufacturing costs	$150,000	
Fixed selling and administrative expenses	50,000	200,000
Income from operations		$ 40,000

Absorption Costing Income Statement

Sales (12,000 × $50)		$600,000
Cost of goods sold:		
Cost of goods manufactured (15,000 × $35)	$525,000	
Less ending inventory (3,000 × $35)	105,000	
Cost of goods sold		420,000
Gross profit		$180,000
Selling and administrative expenses [(12,000 × $5) + $50,000]		110,000
Income from operations		$ 70,000

At a Glance 21

Obj. 1 Classify costs as variable costs, fixed costs, or mixed costs.

Key Points   Variable costs vary in proportion to changes in the level of activity. Fixed costs remain the same in total dollar amount as the level of activity changes. Mixed costs are comprised of both fixed and variable costs.

Learning Outcomes	Example Exercises	Practice Exercises
• Describe variable costs.		
• Describe fixed costs.		
• Describe mixed costs.		
• Separate mixed costs, using the high-low method.	EE21-1	PE21-1A, 21-1B

Obj. 2 Compute the contribution margin, the contribution margin ratio, and the unit contribution margin.

Key Points   Contribution margin is the excess of sales revenue over variable costs and can be expressed as a ratio (contribution margin ratio) or a dollar amount (unit contribution margin).

Learning Outcomes	Example Exercises	Practice Exercises
• Describe the contribution margin.		
• Compute the contribution margin ratio.	EE21-2	PE21-2A, 21-2B
• Compute the unit contribution margin.	EE21-2	PE21-2A, 21-2B

Obj. 3 Determine the break-even point and sales necessary to achieve a target profit.

Key Points   The break-even point is the point at which a business's revenues exactly equal costs. The mathematical approach to cost-volume-profit analysis uses the unit contribution margin concept and mathematical equations to determine the break-even point and the volume necessary to achieve a target profit.

Learning Outcomes	Example Exercises	Practice Exercises
• Compute the break-even point in units.	EE21-3	PE21-3A, 21-3B
• Describe how changes in fixed costs affect the break-even point.		
• Describe how changes in variable costs affect the break-even point.		
• Describe how a change in the unit selling price affects the break-even point.	EE21-3	PE21-3A, 21-3B
• Modify the break-even equation to compute the unit sales required to earn a target profit.	EE21-4	PE21-4A, 21-4B

Obj. 4 — Using a cost-volume-profit chart and a profit-volume chart, determine the break-even point and sales necessary to achieve a target profit.

Key Points Graphical methods can be used to determine the break-even point and the volume necessary to achieve a target profit. A cost-volume-profit chart focuses on the relationship among costs, sales, and operating profit or loss. The profit-volume chart focuses on profits rather than revenues and costs.

Learning Outcomes	Example Exercises	Practice Exercises
• Describe how to construct a cost-volume-profit chart.		
• Determine the break-even point, using a cost-volume-profit chart.		
• Describe how to construct a profit-volume chart.		
• Determine the break-even point, using a profit-volume chart.		
• Describe factors affecting the reliability of cost-volume-profit analysis.		

Obj. 5 — Compute the break-even point for a company selling more than one product, the operating leverage, and the margin of safety.

Key Points Cost-volume-profit relationships can be used for analyzing (1) sales mix, (2) operating leverage, and (3) margin of safety.

Learning Outcomes	Example Exercises	Practice Exercises
• Compute the break-even point for a mix of products.	EE21-5	PE21-5A, 21-5B
• Compute operating leverage.	EE21-6	PE21-6A, 21-6B
• Compute the margin of safety.	EE21-7	PE21-7A, 21-7B

Illustrative Problem

Wyatt Inc. expects to maintain the same inventories at the end of the year as at the beginning of the year. The estimated fixed costs for the year are $288,000, and the estimated variable costs per unit are $14. It is expected that 60,000 units will be sold at a price of $20 per unit. Maximum sales within the relevant range are 70,000 units.

Instructions

1. What is (a) the contribution margin ratio and (b) the unit contribution margin?
2. Determine the break-even point in units.
3. Construct a cost-volume-profit chart, indicating the break-even point.
4. Construct a profit-volume chart, indicating the break-even point.
5. What is the margin of safety?

(Continued)

Solution

1. a. Contribution Margin Ratio = $\dfrac{\text{Sales} - \text{Variable Costs}}{\text{Sales}}$

   $= \dfrac{(60{,}000 \text{ units} \times \$20) - (60{,}000 \text{ units} \times \$14)}{(60{,}000 \text{ units} \times \$20)}$

   $= \dfrac{\$1{,}200{,}000 - \$840{,}000}{\$1{,}200{,}000} = \dfrac{\$360{,}000}{\$1{,}200{,}000}$

   $= 30\%$

   b. Unit Contribution Margin = Unit Selling Price − Unit Variable Costs
      = $20 − $14 = $6

2. Break-Even Sales (units) = $\dfrac{\text{Fixed Costs}}{\text{Unit Contribution Margin}}$

   $= \dfrac{\$288{,}000}{\$6} = 48{,}000 \text{ units}$

3. Sales and Costs

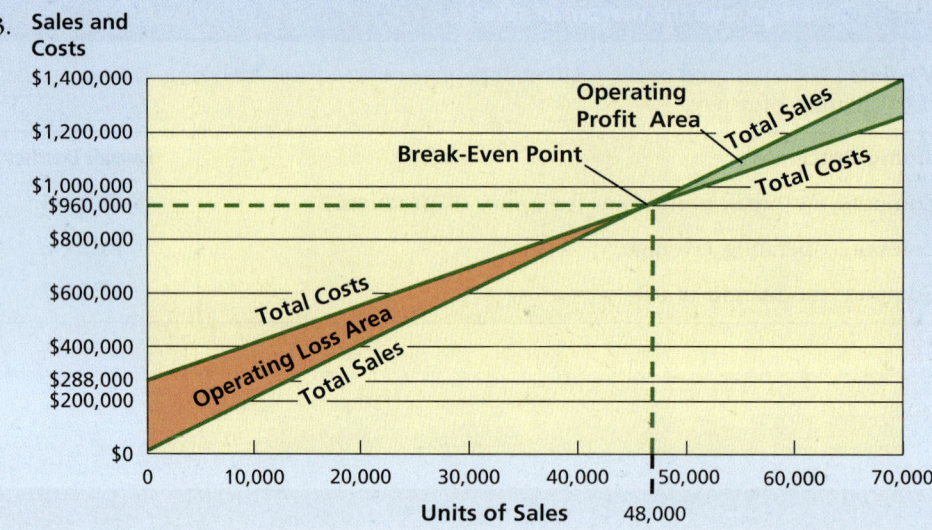

4. Operating Profit (Loss)

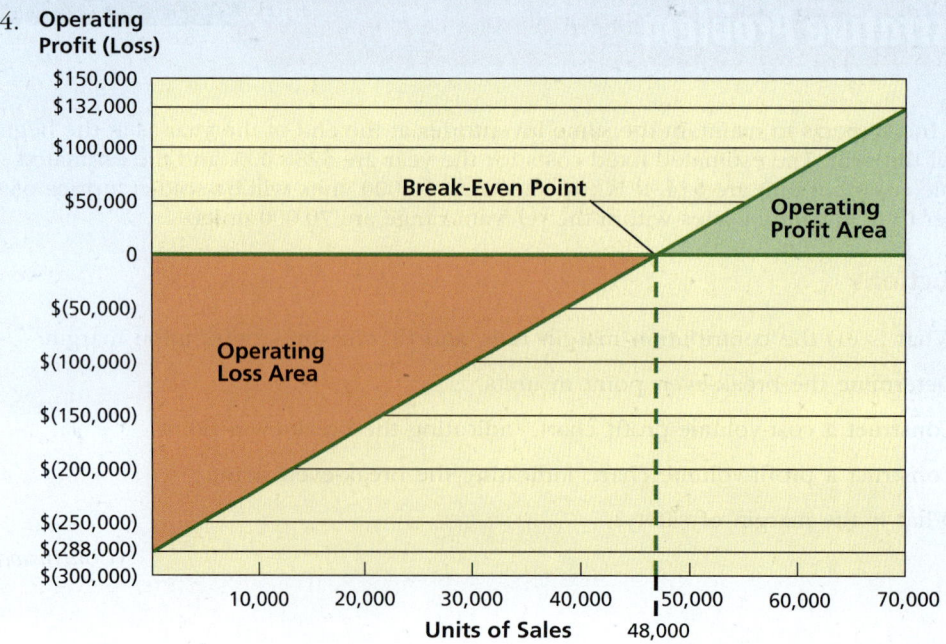

5. Margin of safety:

Expected sales (60,000 units × $20)	$1,200,000
Break-even point (48,000 units × $20)	960,000
Margin of safety	$ 240,000

or

$$\text{Margin of Safety} = \frac{\text{Sales} - \text{Sales at Break-Even Point}}{\text{Sales}}$$

$$= \frac{\$240,000}{\$1,200,000} = 20\%$$

Key Terms

absorption costing (1047)
activity bases (drivers) (1022)
break-even point (1031)
contribution margin (1029)
contribution margin ratio (1029)
cost behavior (1022)
cost-volume-profit analysis (1028)
cost-volume-profit chart (1037)
fixed costs (1024)
high-low method (1026)
margin of safety (1046)
mixed costs (1024)
operating leverage (1044)
profit-volume chart (1039)
relevant range (1022)
sales mix (1043)
unit contribution margin (1030)
variable costing (1028)
variable costs (1022)

Discussion Questions

1. Describe how total variable costs and unit variable costs behave with changes in the level of activity.

2. How would the following costs be classified (variable or fixed) if units produced was the activity base?
   a. Direct materials costs
   b. Electricity costs of $0.35 per kilowatt-hour

3. Describe how total fixed costs and unit fixed costs behave with changes in the level of activity.

4. In applying the high-low method of cost estimation to mixed costs, how is the total fixed cost estimated?

5. If fixed costs increase, what would be the impact on the (a) contribution margin? (b) income from operations?

6. An examination of the accounting records of Clowney Company disclosed a high contribution margin ratio and production at a level below maximum capacity. Based on this information, suggest a likely means of improving income from operations. Explain.

7. If the unit cost of direct materials is decreased, what effect will this change have on the break-even point?

8. Both Austin Company and Hill Company had the same unit sales, total costs, and income from operations for the current fiscal year; yet, Austin Company had a lower break-even point than Hill Company. Explain the reason for this difference in break-even points.

9. How does the sales mix affect the calculation of the break-even point?

10. What does operating leverage measure, and how is it computed?

Practice Exercises

Example Exercises

PE 21-1A High-low method OBJ. 1

The manufacturing costs of Ackerman Industries for the first three months of the year follow:

	Total Cost	Units Produced
January	$1,900,000	20,000 units
February	2,250,000	27,000
March	2,400,000	30,000

Using the high-low method, determine (a) the variable cost per unit and (b) the total fixed cost.

PE 21-1B High-low method OBJ. 1

The manufacturing costs of Carrefour Enterprises for three months of the year follow:

	Total Cost	Units Produced
July	$300,000	2,700 units
August	440,000	5,500
September	325,000	3,500

Using the high-low method, determine (a) the variable cost per unit and (b) the total fixed cost.

PE 21-2A Contribution margin OBJ. 2

Lanning Company sells 160,000 units at $45 per unit. Variable costs are $27 per unit, and fixed costs are $975,000. Determine (a) the contribution margin ratio, (b) the unit contribution margin, and (c) income from operations.

PE 21-2B Contribution margin OBJ. 2

Weidner Company sells 22,000 units at $30 per unit. Variable costs are $24 per unit, and fixed costs are $40,000. Determine (a) the contribution margin ratio, (b) the unit contribution margin, and (c) income from operations.

PE 21-3A Break-even point OBJ. 3

Bigelow Inc. sells a product for $800 per unit. The variable cost is $600 per unit, while fixed costs are $1,200,000. Determine (a) the break-even point in sales units and (b) the break-even point if the selling price were increased to $850 per unit.

PE 21-3B Break-even point OBJ. 3

Elrod Inc. sells a product for $75 per unit. The variable cost is $45 per unit, while fixed costs are $48,000. Determine (a) the break-even point in sales units and (b) the break-even point if the selling price were increased to $95 per unit.

PE 21-4A Target profit OBJ. 3

Ramirez Inc. sells a product for $80 per unit. The variable cost is $60 per unit, and fixed costs are $2,000,000. Determine (a) the break-even point in sales units and (b) the break-even point in sales units if the company desires a target profit of $250,000.

Chapter 21 Cost-Volume-Profit Analysis 1055

EE 21-4 p. 1037 **PE 21-4B Target profit** OBJ. 3

Scrushy Company sells a product for $150 per unit. The variable cost is $110 per unit, and fixed costs are $200,000. Determine (a) the break-even point in sales units and (b) the break-even point in sales units if the company desires a target profit of $50,000.

EE 21-5 p. 1044 **PE 21-5A Sales mix and break-even analysis** OBJ. 5

Wide Open Industries Inc. has fixed costs of $475,000. The unit selling price, variable cost per unit, and contribution margin per unit for the company's two products follow:

Product	Selling Price	Variable Cost per Unit	Contribution Margin per Unit
AA	$145	$105	$40
BB	110	75	35

The sales mix for Products AA and BB is 60% and 40%, respectively. Determine the break-even point in units of AA and BB.

EE 21-5 p. 1044 **PE 21-5B Sales mix and break-even analysis** OBJ. 5

Einhorn Company has fixed costs of $105,000. The unit selling price, variable cost per unit, and contribution margin per unit for the company's two products follow:

Product	Selling Price	Variable Cost per Unit	Contribution Margin per Unit
QQ	$50	$35	$15
ZZ	60	30	30

The sales mix for Products QQ and ZZ is 40% and 60%, respectively. Determine the break-even point in units of QQ and ZZ.

EE 21-6 p. 1046 **PE 21-6A Operating leverage** OBJ. 5

SungSam Enterprises reports the following data:

Sales	$340,000
Variable costs	180,000
Contribution margin	$160,000
Fixed costs	80,000
Income from operations	$ 80,000

Determine SungSam Enterprises's operating leverage.

EE 21-6 p. 1046 **PE 21-6B Operating leverage** OBJ. 5

Westminster Co. reports the following data:

Sales	$875,000
Variable costs	425,000
Contribution margin	$450,000
Fixed costs	150,000
Income from operations	$300,000

Determine Westminster Co.'s operating leverage.

EE 21-7 p. 1047 **PE 21-7A Margin of safety** OBJ. 5

Liu Inc. has sales of $48,500,000, and the break-even point in sales dollars is $31,040,000. Determine the company's margin of safety as a percent of current sales.

EE 21-7 p. 1047 **PE 21-7B Margin of safety** OBJ. 5

Junck Company has sales of $550,000, and the break-even point in sales dollars is $385,000. Determine the company's margin of safety as a percent of current sales.

Exercises

EX 21-1 Classify costs
OBJ. 1

Following is a list of various costs incurred in producing replacement automobile parts. With respect to the production and sale of these auto parts, classify each cost as variable, fixed, or mixed.

1. Cost of labor for hourly workers
2. Factory cleaning costs, $6,000 per month
3. Hourly wages of machine operators
4. Computer chip (purchased from a vendor)
5. Electricity costs, $0.20 per kilowatt-hour
6. Metal
7. Salary of plant manager
8. Property taxes, $165,000 per year on factory building and equipment
9. Plastic
10. Oil used in manufacturing equipment
11. Rent on warehouse, $10,000 per month plus $25 per square foot of storage used
12. Property insurance premiums, $3,600 per month plus $0.01 for each dollar of property over $1,200,000
13. Straight-line depreciation on the production equipment
14. Pension cost, $1.00 per employee hour on the job
15. Packaging

EX 21-2 Identify cost graphs
OBJ. 1

The following cost graphs illustrate various types of cost behavior:

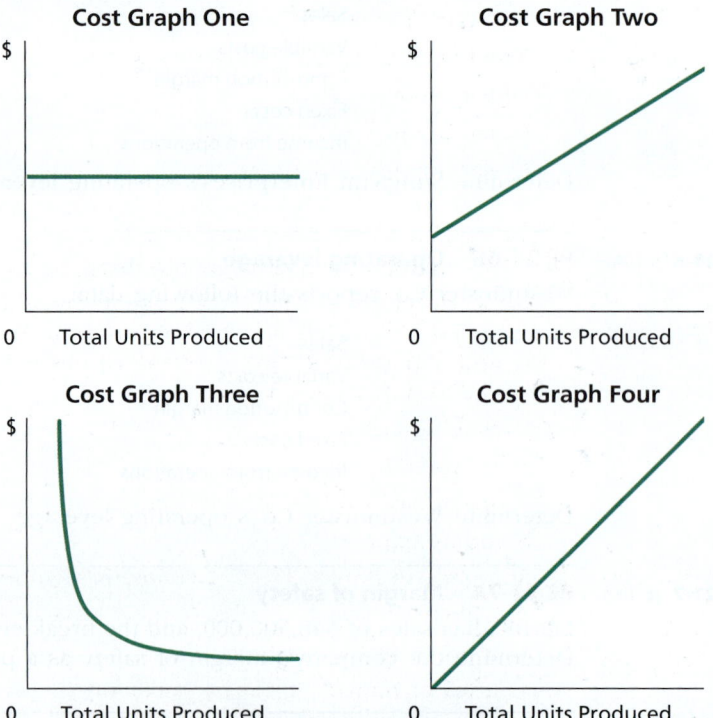

For each of the following costs, identify the cost graph that best illustrates its cost behavior as the number of units produced increases:

a. Total direct materials cost
b. Electricity costs of $1,000 per month plus $0.10 per kilowatt-hour
c. Per-unit cost of straight-line depreciation on factory equipment
d. Salary of quality control supervisor, $20,000 per month
e. Per-unit direct labor cost

EX 21-3 Identify activity bases OBJ. 1

For a major university, match each cost in the following table with the activity base most appropriate to it. An activity base may be used more than once or not used at all.

Cost:
1. Instructor salaries
2. Admissions office salaries
3. Student records office salaries
4. Financial aid office salaries
5. Housing personnel wages
6. Office supplies

Activity Base:
a. Student credit hours
b. Number of students living on campus
c. Number of enrollment applications
d. Number of students
e. Number of enrolled students and alumni
f. Number of financial aid applications

EX 21-4 Identify activity bases OBJ. 1

From the following list of activity bases for an automobile dealership, select the base that would be most appropriate for each of these costs: (1) preparation costs (cleaning, oil, and gasoline costs) for each car received, (2) salespersons' commission of 5% of the sales price for each car sold, and (3) administrative costs for ordering cars.

a. Number of cars sold
b. Dollar amount of cars ordered
c. Number of cars ordered
d. Number of cars on hand
e. Number of cars received
f. Dollar amount of cars sold
g. Dollar amount of cars received
h. Dollar amount of cars on hand

EX 21-5 Identify fixed and variable costs OBJ. 1

Intuit Inc. develops and sells software products for the personal finance market, including popular titles such as Quickbooks® and TurboTax®. Classify each of the following costs and expenses for this company as either variable or fixed to the number of units produced and sold:

a. Packaging costs
b. Sales commissions
c. Property taxes on general offices
d. Shipping expenses
e. Straight-line depreciation of computer equipment
f. President's salary
g. Salaries of software developers
h. Salaries of human resources personnel
i. Wages of telephone order assistants
j. Users' guides

1058 Chapter 21 Cost-Volume-Profit Analysis

EX 21-6 Relevant range and fixed and variable costs   OBJ. 1

✔ a. $30.00

Vogel Inc. manufactures memory chips for electronic toys within a relevant range of 45,000 to 75,000 memory chips per year. Within this range, the following partially completed manufacturing cost schedule has been prepared:

Components produced	45,000	60,000	75,000
Total costs:			
Total variable costs	$1,350,000	(d)	(j)
Total fixed costs	810,000	(e)	(k)
Total costs	$2,160,000	(f)	(l)
Cost per unit:			
Variable cost per unit	(a)	(g)	(m)
Fixed cost per unit	(b)	(h)	(n)
Total cost per unit	(c)	(i)	(o)

Complete the cost schedule, identifying each cost by the appropriate letter (a) through (o).

EX 21-7 High-low method   OBJ. 1

✔ a. $175.50 per unit

Ziegler Inc. has decided to use the high-low method to estimate the total cost and the fixed and variable cost components of the total cost. The data for various levels of production are as follows:

Units Produced	Total Costs
80,000	$25,100,000
92,000	27,206,000
120,000	32,120,000

a. Determine the variable cost per unit and the total fixed cost.
b. Based on part (a), estimate the total cost for 115,000 units of production.

EX 21-8 High-low method for a service company   OBJ. 1

✔ Fixed cost, $600,000

Boston Railroad decided to use the high-low method and operating data from the past six months to estimate the fixed and variable components of transportation costs. The activity base used by Boston Railroad is a measure of railroad operating activity, termed "gross-ton miles," which is the total number of tons multiplied by the miles moved.

	Transportation Costs	Gross-Ton Miles
January	$1,776,000	560,000
February	2,700,000	1,000,000
March	1,650,000	500,000
April	1,860,000	600,000
May	1,440,000	400,000
June	1,566,000	460,000

Determine the variable cost per gross-ton mile and the total fixed cost.

EX 21-9 Contribution margin ratio   OBJ. 2

✔ a. 35%

a. Yountz Company budgets sales of $2,400,000, fixed costs of $525,000, and variable costs of $1,560,000. What is the contribution margin ratio for Yountz Company?
b. If the contribution margin ratio for Vera Company is 40%, sales were $3,400,000, and fixed costs were $800,000, what was the income from operations?

EX 21-10 Contribution margin and contribution margin ratio
OBJ. 2

✓ b. 34.6%

For a recent year, McDonald's company-owned restaurants had the following sales and expenses (in millions):

Sales	$18,169.3
Food and packaging	$ 6,129.7
Payroll	4,756.0
Occupancy (rent, depreciation, etc.)	4,402.6
General, selling, and administrative expenses	2,487.9
	$17,776.2
Income from operations	$ 393.1

Assume that the variable costs consist of food and packaging; payroll; and 40% of the general, selling, and administrative expenses.

a. What is McDonald's contribution margin? Round to the nearest tenth of a million (one decimal place).

b. What is McDonald's contribution margin ratio? Round to one decimal place.

c. How much would income from operations increase if same-store sales increased by $500 million for the coming year, with no change in the contribution margin ratio or fixed costs? Round your answer to the nearest tenth of a million (one decimal place).

EX 21-11 Break-even sales and sales to realize income from operations
OBJ. 3

✓ b. 154,000 units

For the current year ended October 31, Yentling Company expects fixed costs of $14,000,000, a unit variable cost of $200, and a unit selling price of $300.

a. Compute the anticipated break-even sales (units).

b. Compute the sales (units) required to realize income from operations of $1,400,000.

EX 21-12 Break-even sales
OBJ. 3

✓ a. 168.9 million barrels

Anheuser-Busch InBev Companies, Inc., reported the following operating information for a recent year (in millions):

Net sales	$47,063
Cost of goods sold	$18,756
Selling, general and administration	12,999
	$31,755
Income from operations	$15,308*
*Before special items	

In addition, assume that Anheuser-Busch InBev sold 400 million barrels of beer during the year. Assume that variable costs were 75% of the cost of goods sold and 50% of selling, general and administration expenses. Assume that the remaining costs are fixed. For the following year, assume that Anheuser-Busch InBev expects pricing, variable costs per barrel, and fixed costs to remain constant, except that new distribution and general office facilities are expected to increase fixed costs by $300 million.

a. Compute the break-even number of barrels for the current year. *Note:* For the selling price per barrel and variable costs per barrel, round to the nearest cent. Also present the break-even units in millions of barrels.

b. Compute the anticipated break-even number of barrels for the following year.

EX 21-13 Break-even sales
OBJ. 3

✓ a. 15,000 units

Currently, the unit selling price of a product is $1,500, the unit variable cost is $1,200, and the total fixed costs are $4,500,000. A proposal is being evaluated to increase the unit selling price to $1,600.

a. Compute the current break-even sales (units).

b. Compute the anticipated break-even sales (units), assuming that the unit selling price is increased to the proposed $1,600, and all costs remain constant.

EX 21-14 Break-even analysis
OBJ. 3

The Junior League of Yadkinville, California, collected recipes from members and published a cookbook entitled *Food for Everyone*. The book will sell for $18 per copy. The chairwoman of the cookbook development committee estimated that the club needed to sell 2,000 books to break even on its $4,000 investment. What is the variable cost per unit assumed in the Junior League's analysis?

EX 21-15 Break-even analysis
OBJ. 3

Media outlets such as **ESPN** and **Fox Sports** often have websites that provide in-depth coverage of news and events. Portions of these websites are restricted to members who pay a monthly subscription to gain access to exclusive news and commentary. These websites typically offer a free trial period to introduce viewers to the site. Assume that during a recent fiscal year, ESPN.com spent $4,200,000 on a promotional campaign for the ESPN.com website that offered two free months of service for new subscribers. In addition, assume the following information:

Number of months an average new customer stays with the service (including the two free months)	14 months
Revenue per month per customer subscription	$10.00
Variable cost per month per customer subscription	$5.00

Determine the number of new customer accounts needed to break even on the cost of the promotional campaign. In forming your answer, (1) treat the cost of the promotional campaign as a fixed cost and (2) treat the revenue less variable cost per account for the subscription period as the unit contribution margin.

EX 21-16 Break-even analysis for a service company
OBJ. 3

Sprint Nextel is one of the largest digital wireless service providers in the United States. In a recent year, it had approximately 32.5 million direct subscribers (accounts) that generated revenue of $35,345 million. Costs and expenses for the year were as follows (in millions):

Cost of revenue	$20,841
Selling, general, and administrative expenses	9,765
Depreciation	2,239

Assume that 70% of the cost of revenue and 30% of the selling, general, and administrative expenses are variable to the number of direct subscribers (accounts).

a. What is Sprint Nextel's break-even number of accounts, using the data and assumptions given? Round units (accounts) and per-account amounts to one decimal place.

b. How much revenue per account would be sufficient for Sprint Nextel to break even if the number of accounts remained constant?

EX 21-17 Cost-volume-profit chart
OBJ. 4

✔ b. $1,500,000

For the coming year, Loudermilk Inc. anticipates fixed costs of $600,000, a unit variable cost of $75, and a unit selling price of $125. The maximum sales within the relevant range are $2,500,000.

a. Construct a cost-volume-profit chart.

b. Estimate the break-even sales (dollars) by using the cost-volume-profit chart constructed in part (a).

c. What is the main advantage of presenting the cost-volume-profit analysis in graphic form rather than equation form?

EX 21-18 Profit-volume chart   OBJ. 4

✔ b. $400,000

Using the data for Loudermilk Inc. in Exercise 21-17, (a) determine the maximum possible operating loss, (b) compute the maximum possible operating profit, (c) construct a profit-volume chart, and (d) estimate the break-even sales (units) by using the profit-volume chart constructed in part (c).

EX 21-19 Break-even chart   OBJ. 4

Name the following chart and identify the items represented by the letters (a) through (f):

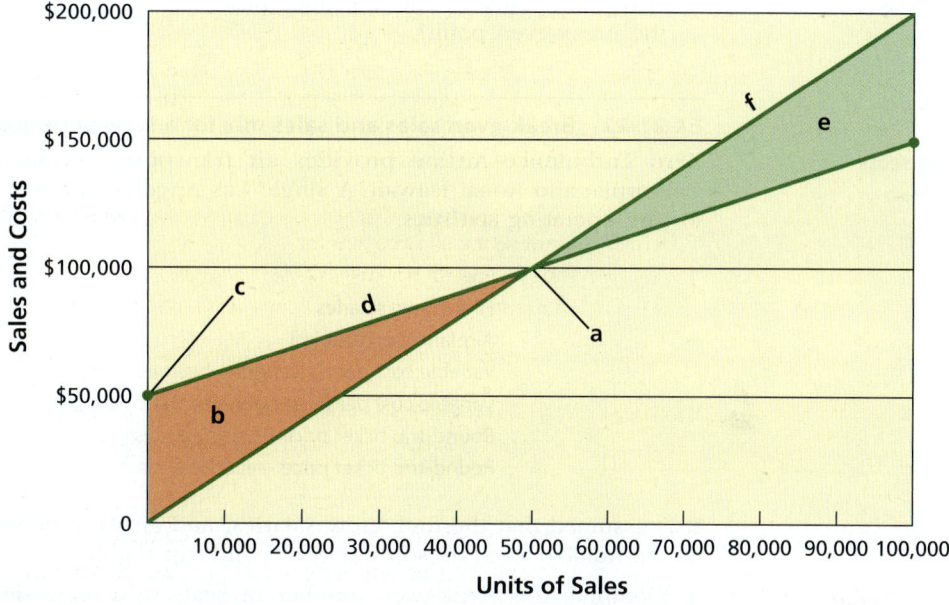

EX 21-20 Break-even chart   OBJ. 4

Name the following chart and identify the items represented by the letters (a) through (f):

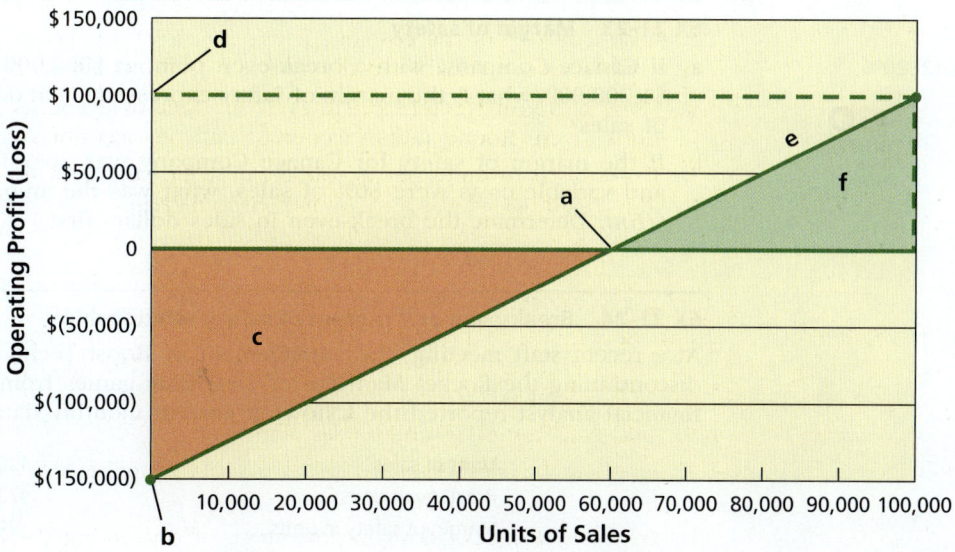

1062 Chapter 21 Cost-Volume-Profit Analysis

✔ a. 15,500 units

EX 21-21 Sales mix and break-even sales
OBJ. 5

Dragon Sports Inc. manufactures and sells two products, baseball bats and baseball gloves. The fixed costs are $620,000, and the sales mix is 40% bats and 60% gloves. The unit selling price and the unit variable cost for each product are as follows:

Products	Unit Selling Price	Unit Variable Cost
Bats	$ 90	$50
Gloves	105	65

a. Compute the break-even sales (units) for the overall product, E.

b. How many units of each product, baseball bats and baseball gloves, would be sold at the break-even point?

✔ a. 60 seats

EX 21-22 Break-even sales and sales mix for a service company
OBJ. 5

Zero Turbulence Airline provides air transportation services between Los Angeles, California; and Kona, Hawaii. A single Los Angeles to Kona round-trip flight has the following operating statistics:

Fuel	$7,000
Flight crew salaries	3,200
Airplane depreciation	3,480
Variable cost per passenger—business class	140
Variable cost per passenger—economy class	120
Round-trip ticket price—business class	800
Round-trip ticket price—economy class	300

It is assumed that the fuel, crew salaries, and airplane depreciation are fixed, regardless of the number of seats sold for the round-trip flight.

a. Compute the break-even number of seats sold on a single round-trip flight for the overall product, E. Assume that the overall product mix is 10% business class and 90% economy class tickets.

b. How many business class and economy class seats would be sold at the break-even point?

✔ a. (2) 20%

EX 21-23 Margin of safety
OBJ. 5

a. If Canace Company, with a break-even point at $960,000 of sales, has actual sales of $1,200,000, what is the margin of safety expressed (1) in dollars and (2) as a percentage of sales?

b. If the margin of safety for Canace Company was 20%, fixed costs were $1,875,000, and variable costs were 80% of sales, what was the amount of actual sales (dollars)? (*Hint:* Determine the break-even in sales dollars first.)

EX 21-24 Break-even and margin of safety relationships
OBJ. 5

At a recent staff meeting, the management of Boost Technologies Inc. was considering discontinuing the Rocket Man line of electronic games from the product line. The chief financial analyst reported the following current monthly data for the Rocket Man:

Units of sales	420,000
Break-even units	472,500
Margin of safety in units	29,400

➤ For what reason would you question the validity of these data?

Chapter 21 Cost-Volume-Profit Analysis

EX 21-25 Operating leverage
OBJ. 5

✔ a. Beck, 5.0

Beck Inc. and Bryant Inc. have the following operating data:

	Beck Inc.	Bryant Inc.
Sales	$1,250,000	$2,000,000
Variable costs	750,000	1,250,000
Contribution margin	$ 500,000	$ 750,000
Fixed costs	400,000	450,000
Income from operations	$ 100,000	$ 300,000

a. Compute the operating leverage for Beck Inc. and Bryant Inc.

b. How much would income from operations increase for each company if the sales of each increased by 20%?

c. Why is there a difference in the increase in income from operations for the two companies? Explain.

Appendix
EX 21-26 Items on variable costing income statement

In the following equations, based on the variable costing income statement, identify the items designated by X:

a. Net Sales − X = Manufacturing Margin

b. Manufacturing Margin − X = Contribution Margin

c. Contribution Margin − X = Income from Operations

Appendix
EX 21-27 Variable costing income statement

✔ a. Contribution margin, $1,934,400

On July 31, the end of the first month of operations, Rhys Company prepared the following income statement, based on the absorption costing concept:

Sales (96,000 units)...........................		$4,440,000
Cost of goods sold:		
Cost of goods manufactured...............	$3,120,000	
Less ending inventory (24,000 units)	624,000	
Cost of goods sold........................		2,496,000
Gross profit...................................		$1,944,000
Selling and administrative expenses............		288,000
Income from operations.......................		$1,656,000

a. Prepare a variable costing income statement, assuming that the fixed manufacturing costs were $132,000 and the variable selling and administrative expenses were $115,200.

b. Reconcile the absorption costing income from operations of $1,656,000 with the variable costing income from operations determined in (a).

Appendix
EX 21-28 Absorption costing income statement

✔ a. Gross profit, $1,435,600

On June 30, the end of the first month of operations, Tudor Manufacturing Co. prepared the following income statement, based on the variable costing concept:

(Continued)

Sales (420,000 units)			$7,450,000
Variable cost of goods sold:			
Variable cost of goods manufactured (500,000 units × $14 per unit)		$7,000,000	
Less ending inventory (80,000 units × $14 per unit)		1,120,000	
Variable cost of goods sold			5,880,000
Manufacturing margin			$1,570,000
Variable selling and administrative expenses			80,000
Contribution margin			$1,490,000
Fixed costs:			
Fixed manufacturing costs		$ 160,000	
Fixed selling and administrative expenses		75,000	235,000
Income from operations			$1,255,000

a. Prepare an absorption costing income statement.

b. Reconcile the variable costing income from operations of $1,255,000 with the absorption costing income from operations determined in (a).

Problems: Series A

PR 21-1A Classify costs   OBJ. 1

Seymour Clothing Co. manufactures a variety of clothing types for distribution to several major retail chains. The following costs are incurred in the production and sale of blue jeans:

a. Shipping boxes used to ship orders
b. Consulting fee of $200,000 paid to industry specialist for marketing advice
c. Straight-line depreciation on sewing machines
d. Salesperson's salary, $10,000 plus 2% of the total sales
e. Fabric
f. Dye
g. Thread
h. Salary of designers
i. Brass buttons
j. Legal fees paid to attorneys in defense of the company in a patent infringement suit, $50,000 plus $87 per hour
k. Insurance premiums on property, plant, and equipment, $70,000 per year plus $5 per $30,000 of insured value over $8,000,000
l. Rental costs of warehouse, $5,000 per month plus $4 per square foot of storage used
m. Supplies
n. Leather for patches identifying the brand on individual pieces of apparel
o. Rent on plant equipment, $50,000 per year
p. Salary of production vice president
q. Janitorial services, $2,200 per month
r. Wages of machine operators
s. Electricity costs of $0.10 per kilowatt-hour
t. Property taxes on property, plant, and equipment

Instructions

Classify the preceding costs as fixed, variable, or mixed. Use the following tabular headings and place an X in the appropriate column. Identify each cost by letter in the cost column.

Cost	Fixed Cost	Variable Cost	Mixed Cost

PR 21-2A Break-even sales under present and proposed conditions OBJ. 2, 3

✔ 2. (b) $50

Darby Company, operating at full capacity, sold 500,000 units at a price of $94 per unit during the current year. Its income statement is as follows:

Sales		$47,000,000
Cost of goods sold		25,000,000
Gross profit		$22,000,000
Expenses:		
Selling expenses	$4,000,000	
Administrative expenses	3,000,000	
Total expenses		7,000,000
Income from operations		$15,000,000

The division of costs between variable and fixed is as follows:

	Variable	Fixed
Cost of goods sold	70%	30%
Selling expenses	75%	25%
Administrative expenses	50%	50%

Management is considering a plant expansion program for the following year that will permit an increase of $3,760,000 in yearly sales. The expansion will increase fixed costs by $1,800,000 but will not affect the relationship between sales and variable costs.

Instructions
1. Determine the total variable costs and the total fixed costs for the current year.
2. Determine (a) the unit variable cost and (b) the unit contribution margin for the current year.
3. Compute the break-even sales (units) for the current year.
4. Compute the break-even sales (units) under the proposed program for the following year.
5. Determine the amount of sales (units) that would be necessary under the proposed program to realize the $15,000,000 of income from operations that was earned in the current year.
6. Determine the maximum income from operations possible with the expanded plant.
7. If the proposal is accepted and sales remain at the current level, what will the income or loss from operations be for the following year?
8. ✏ Based on the data given, would you recommend accepting the proposal? Explain.

PR 21-3A Break-even sales and cost-volume-profit chart OBJ. 3, 4

✔ 1. 12,000 units

For the coming year, Cleves Company anticipates a unit selling price of $100, a unit variable cost of $60, and fixed costs of $480,000.

Instructions
1. Compute the anticipated break-even sales (units).
2. Compute the sales (units) required to realize a target profit of $240,000.
3. Construct a cost-volume-profit chart, assuming maximum sales of 20,000 units within the relevant range.
4. Determine the probable income (loss) from operations if sales total 16,000 units.

PR 21-4A Break-even sales and cost-volume-profit chart OBJ. 3, 4

✔ 1. 1,000 units

Last year Hever Inc. had sales of $500,000, based on a unit selling price of $250. The variable cost per unit was $175, and fixed costs were $75,000. The maximum sales within Hever Inc.'s relevant range are 2,500 units. Hever Inc. is considering a proposal to spend an additional $33,750 on billboard advertising during the current year in an attempt to increase sales and utilize unused capacity.

(Continued)

Instructions

1. Construct a cost-volume-profit chart indicating the break-even sales for last year. Verify your answer, using the break-even equation.
2. Using the cost-volume-profit chart prepared in part (1), determine (a) the income from operations for last year and (b) the maximum income from operations that could have been realized during the year. Verify your answers using the mathematical approach to cost-volume-profit analysis.
3. Construct a cost-volume-profit chart indicating the break-even sales for the current year, assuming that a noncancellable contract is signed for the additional billboard advertising. No changes are expected in the unit selling price or other costs. Verify your answer, using the break-even equation.
4. Using the cost-volume-profit chart prepared in part (3), determine (a) the income from operations if sales total 2,000 units and (b) the maximum income from operations that could be realized during the year. Verify your answers using the mathematical approach to cost-volume-profit analysis.

PR 21-5A Sales mix and break-even sales OBJ. 5

✓ 1. 4,030 units

Data related to the expected sales of laptops and tablets for Tech Products Inc. for the current year, which is typical of recent years, are as follows:

Products	Unit Selling Price	Unit Variable Cost	Sales Mix
Laptops	$1,600	$800	40%
Tablets	850	350	60%

The estimated fixed costs for the current year are $2,498,600.

Instructions

1. Determine the estimated units of sales of the overall (total) product, E, necessary to reach the break-even point for the current year.
2. Based on the break-even sales (units) in part (1), determine the unit sales of both laptops and tablets for the current year.
3. Assume that the sales mix was 50% laptops and 50% tablets. Compare the break-even point with that in part (1). Why is it so different?

PR 21-6A Contribution margin, break-even sales, cost-volume-profit chart, margin of safety, and operating leverage OBJ. 2, 3, 4, 5

✓ 2. 25%

Wolsey Industries Inc. expects to maintain the same inventories at the end of 20Y8 as at the beginning of the year. The total of all production costs for the year is therefore assumed to be equal to the cost of goods sold. With this in mind, the various department heads were asked to submit estimates of the costs for their departments during the year. A summary report of these estimates is as follows:

	Estimated Fixed Cost	Estimated Variable Cost (per unit sold)
Production costs:		
Direct materials	—	$ 46
Direct labor	—	40
Factory overhead	$200,000	20
Selling expenses:		
Sales salaries and commissions	110,000	8
Advertising	40,000	—
Travel	12,000	—
Miscellaneous selling expense	7,600	1
Administrative expenses:		
Office and officers' salaries	132,000	—
Supplies	10,000	4
Miscellaneous administrative expense	13,400	1
Total	$525,000	$120

It is expected that 21,875 units will be sold at a price of $160 a unit. Maximum sales within the relevant range are 27,000 units.

Instructions
1. Prepare an estimated income statement for 20Y8.
2. What is the expected contribution margin ratio?
3. Determine the break-even sales in units and dollars.
4. Construct a cost-volume-profit chart indicating the break-even sales.
5. What is the expected margin of safety in dollars and as a percentage of sales?
6. Determine the operating leverage.

Problems: Series B

PR 21-1B Classify costs   OBJ. 1
Cromwell Furniture Company manufactures sofas for distribution to several major retail chains. The following costs are incurred in the production and sale of sofas:

a. Fabric for sofa coverings
b. Wood for framing the sofas
c. Legal fees paid to attorneys in defense of the company in a patent infringement suit, $25,000 plus $160 per hour
d. Salary of production supervisor
e. Cartons used to ship sofas
f. Rent on experimental equipment, $50 for every sofa produced
g. Straight-line depreciation on factory equipment
h. Rental costs of warehouse, $30,000 per month
i. Property taxes on property, plant, and equipment
j. Insurance premiums on property, plant, and equipment, $25,000 per year plus $25 per $25,000 of insured value over $16,000,000
k. Springs
l. Consulting fee of $120,000 paid to efficiency specialists
m. Electricity costs of $0.13 per kilowatt-hour
n. Salesperson's salary, $80,000 plus 4% of the selling price of each sofa sold
o. Foam rubber for cushion fillings
p. Janitorial supplies, $2,500 per month
q. Employer's FICA taxes on controller's salary of $180,000
r. Salary of designers
s. Wages of sewing machine operators
t. Sewing supplies

Instructions
Classify the preceding costs as fixed, variable, or mixed. Use the following tabular headings and place an X in the appropriate column. Identify each cost by letter in the cost column.

Cost	Fixed Cost	Variable Cost	Mixed Cost

PR 21-2B Break-even sales under present and proposed conditions OBJ. 2, 3

✓ 3. 29,375 units

Howard Industries Inc., operating at full capacity, sold 64,000 units at a price of $45 per unit during the current year. Its income statement is as follows:

Sales	$2,880,000
Cost of goods sold	1,400,000
Gross profit	$1,480,000
Expenses:	
Selling expenses ... $400,000	
Administrative expenses ... 387,500	
Total expenses	787,500
Income from operations	$ 692,500

The division of costs between variable and fixed is as follows:

	Variable	Fixed
Cost of goods sold	75%	25%
Selling expenses	60%	40%
Administrative expenses	80%	20%

Management is considering a plant expansion program for the following year that will permit an increase of $900,000 in yearly sales. The expansion will increase fixed costs by $212,500 but will not affect the relationship between sales and variable costs.

Instructions
1. Determine the total fixed costs and the total variable costs for the current year.
2. Determine (a) the unit variable cost and (b) the unit contribution margin for the current year.
3. Compute the break-even sales (units) for the current year.
4. Compute the break-even sales (units) under the proposed program for the following year.
5. Determine the amount of sales (units) that would be necessary under the proposed program to realize the $692,500 of income from operations that was earned in the current year.
6. Determine the maximum income from operations possible with the expanded plant.
7. If the proposal is accepted and sales remain at the current level, what will the income or loss from operations be for the following year?
8. Based on the data given, would you recommend accepting the proposal? Explain.

PR 21-3B Break-even sales and cost-volume-profit chart OBJ. 3, 4

✓ 1. 20,000 units

For the coming year, Culpeper Products Inc. anticipates a unit selling price of $150, a unit variable cost of $110, and fixed costs of $800,000.

Instructions
1. Compute the anticipated break-even sales (units).
2. Compute the sales (units) required to realize income from operations of $300,000.
3. Construct a cost-volume-profit chart, assuming maximum sales of 40,000 units within the relevant range.
4. Determine the probable income (loss) from operations if sales total 32,000 units.

PR 21-4B Break-even sales and cost-volume-profit chart OBJ. 3, 4

✓ 1. 3,000 units

Last year Parr Co. had sales of $900,000, based on a unit selling price of $200. The variable cost per unit was $125, and fixed costs were $225,000. The maximum sales within Parr Co.'s relevant range are 7,500 units. Parr Co. is considering a proposal to spend an additional $112,500 on billboard advertising during the current year in an attempt to increase sales and utilize unused capacity.

Instructions

1. Construct a cost-volume-profit chart indicating the break-even sales for last year. Verify your answer, using the break-even equation.
2. Using the cost-volume-profit chart prepared in part (1), determine (a) the income from operations for last year and (b) the maximum income from operations that could have been realized during the year. Verify your answers.
3. Construct a cost-volume-profit chart indicating the break-even sales for the current year, assuming that a noncancellable contract is signed for the additional billboard advertising. No changes are expected in the selling price or other costs. Verify your answer, using the break-even equation.
4. Using the cost-volume-profit chart prepared in part (3), determine (a) the income from operations if sales total 6,000 units and (b) the maximum income from operations that could be realized during the year. Verify your answers.

PR 21-5B Sales mix and break-even sales   OBJ. 5

✔ 1. 4,500 units

Data related to the expected sales of two types of frozen pizzas for Norfolk Frozen Foods Inc. for the current year, which is typical of recent years, are as follows:

Products	Unit Selling Price	Unit Variable Cost	Sales Mix
12" Pizza	$12	$3	30%
16" Pizza	15	4	70%

The estimated fixed costs for the current year are $46,800.

Instructions

1. Determine the estimated units of sales of the overall (total) product, E, necessary to reach the break-even point for the current year.
2. Based on the break-even sales (units) in part (1), determine the unit sales of both the 12" pizza and 16" pizza for the current year.
3. Assume that the sales mix was 50% 12" pizza and 50% 16" pizza. Compare the break-even point with that in part (1). Why is it so different?

PR 21-6B Contribution margin, break-even sales, cost-volume-profit chart, margin of safety, and operating leverage   OBJ. 2, 3, 4, 5

✔ 3. 8,000 units

Belmain Co. expects to maintain the same inventories at the end of 20Y7 as at the beginning of the year. The total of all production costs for the year is therefore assumed to be equal to the cost of goods sold. With this in mind, the various department heads were asked to submit estimates of the costs for their departments during the year. A summary report of these estimates is as follows:

	Estimated Fixed Cost	Estimated Variable Cost (per unit sold)
Production costs:		
Direct materials	—	$50.00
Direct labor	—	30.00
Factory overhead	$ 350,000	6.00
Selling expenses:		
Sales salaries and commissions	340,000	4.00
Advertising	116,000	—
Travel	4,000	—
Miscellaneous selling expense	2,300	1.00
Administrative expenses:		
Office and officers' salaries	325,000	—
Supplies	6,000	4.00
Miscellaneous administrative expense	8,700	1.00
Total	$1,152,000	$96.00

(*Continued*)

It is expected that 12,000 units will be sold at a price of $240 a unit. Maximum sales within the relevant range are 18,000 units.

Instructions

1. Prepare an estimated income statement for 20Y7.
2. What is the expected contribution margin ratio?
3. Determine the break-even sales in units and dollars.
4. Construct a cost-volume-profit chart indicating the break-even sales.
5. What is the expected margin of safety in dollars and as a percentage of sales?
6. Determine the operating leverage.

Cases & Projects

CP 21-1 Ethics in Action

Edward Seymour is a financial consultant to Cornish Inc., a real estate syndicate. Cornish finances and develops commercial real estate (office buildings) projects. The completed projects are then sold as limited partnership interests to individual investors. The syndicate makes a profit on the sale of these partnership interests. Edward provides financial information for prospective investors in a document called the offering "prospectus." This document discusses the financial and legal details of the limited partnership investment.

One of the company's current projects, called JEDI 2, has the partnership borrowing money from a local bank to build a commercial office building. The interest rate on the loan is 6.5% for the first four years. After four years, the interest rate jumps to 15% for the remaining 20 years of the loan. The interest expense is one of the major costs of this project and significantly affects the number of renters needed for the project to break even. In the prospectus, Edward has prominently reported that the break-even occupancy for the first four years is 65%. This is the amount of office space that must be leased to cover the interest and general upkeep costs during the first four years. The 65% break-even point is very low compared to similar projects and thus communicates a low risk to potential investors. Edward uses the 65% break-even rate as a major marketing tool in selling the limited partnership interests. Buried in the fine print of the prospectus is additional information that would allow an astute investor to determine that the break-even occupancy jumps to 95% after the fourth year when the interest rate on the loan increases to 15%. Edward believes prospective investors are adequately informed of the investment's risk.

> Is Edward behaving ethically? Explain your answer.

CP 21-2 Team Activity

Break-even analysis is an important tool for managing any business, including colleges and universities. In a group, identify three areas where break-even analysis might be used at your college or university. For each area, identify the revenues, fixed costs, and variable costs.

CP 21-3 Communication

Sun Airlines is a commercial airline that targets business and nonbusiness travelers. In recent months, the airline has been unprofitable. The company has break-even sales volume of 75% of capacity, which is significantly higher than the industry average of 65%. Sun's CEO, Neil Armstrong, is concerned about the recent string of losses and is considering a strategic plan that could reduce the break-even sales volume by increasing ticket prices. He has asked for your help in evaluating this plan.

> Write a brief memo to Neil Armstrong evaluating this strategy.

CP 21-4 Break-even analysis

Somerset Inc. has finished a new video game, *Snowboard Challenge*. Management is now considering its marketing strategies. The following information is available:

Anticipated sales price per unit	$80
Variable cost per unit*	$35
Anticipated volume	1,000,000 units
Production costs	$20,000,000
Anticipated advertising	$15,000,000

*The cost of the video game, packaging, and copying costs.

Two managers, James Hamilton and Thomas Seymour, had the following discussion of ways to increase the profitability of this new offering:

James: I think we need to think of some way to increase our profitability. Do you have any ideas?

Thomas: Well, I think the best strategy would be to become aggressive on price.

James: How aggressive?

Thomas: If we drop the price to $60 per unit and maintain our advertising budget at $15,000,000, I think we will generate total sales of 2,000,000 units.

James: I think that's the wrong way to go. You're giving up too much on price. Instead, I think we need to follow an aggressive advertising strategy.

Thomas: How aggressive?

James: If we increase our advertising to a total of $25,000,000, we should be able to increase sales volume to 1,400,000 units without any change in price.

Thomas: I don't think that's reasonable. We'll never cover the increased advertising costs.

▶ Which strategy is best: Do nothing, follow the advice of Thomas Seymour, or follow James Hamilton's strategy?

CP 21-5 Variable costs and activity bases in decision making

The owner of Warwick Printing, a printing company, is planning direct labor needs for the upcoming year. The owner has provided you with the following information for next year's plans:

	One Color	Two Color	Three Color	Four Color	Total
Number of banners	212	274	616	698	1,800

Each color on the banner must be printed one at a time. Thus, for example, a four-color banner will need to be run through the printing operation four separate times. The total production volume last year was 800 banners, as follows:

	One Color	Two Color	Three Color	Total
Number of banners	180	240	380	800

▶ As you can see, the four-color banner is a new product offering for the upcoming year. The owner believes that the expected 1,000-unit increase in volume from last year means that direct labor expenses should increase by 125% (1,000 ÷ 800). What do you think?

CP 21-6 Variable costs and activity bases in decision making

Sales volume has been dropping at Mumford Industries. During this time, however, the Shipping Department manager has been under severe financial constraints. The manager knows that most of the Shipping Department's effort is related to pulling inventory from the warehouse for each order and performing the paperwork. The paperwork involves preparing shipping documents for each order. Thus, the pulling and paperwork effort associated with each sales order is essentially the same, regardless of the size of the

(Continued)

order. The Shipping Department manager has discussed the financial situation with senior management. Senior management has responded by pointing out that because sales volume has been dropping, the amount of work in the Shipping Department also should be dropping. Thus, senior management told the Shipping Department manager that costs should be decreasing in the department.

The Shipping Department manager prepared the following information:

Month	Sales Volume	Number of Customer Orders	Sales Volume per Order
January	$472,000	1,180	400
February	475,800	1,220	390
March	456,950	1,235	370
April	425,000	1,250	340
May	464,750	1,430	325
June	421,200	1,350	312
July	414,000	1,380	300
August	430,700	1,475	292

Given this information, how would you respond to senior management?

CHAPTER 22

Budgeting

Concepts and Principles

Chapter 18 *Introduction to Managerial Accounting*

Developing Information

COST SYSTEMS
Chapter 19 *Job Order Costing*
Chapter 20 *Process Costing*

COST BEHAVIOR
Chapter 21 *Cost-Volume-Profit Analysis*

Decision Making

EVALUATING PERFORMANCE
Chapter 22 *Budgeting*
Chapter 23 *Variances from Standard Costs*

COMPARING ALTERNATIVES
Chapter 24 *Decentralized Operations*
Chapter 25 *Differential Analysis, Product Pricing, and Activity-Based Costing*
Chapter 26 *Capital Investment Analysis*

CHAPTER 22

Hendrick Motorsports

You may have financial goals for your life. To achieve these goals, it is necessary to plan for future expenses. For example, you may consider taking a part-time job to save money for school expenses for the coming school year. How much money would you need to earn and save in order to pay these expenses? One way to find an answer to this question would be to prepare a budget. A budget would show an estimate of your expenses associated with school, such as tuition, fees, and books. In addition, you would have expenses for day-to-day living, such as rent, food, and clothing. You might also have expenses for travel and entertainment. Once the school year begins, you can use the budget as a tool for guiding your spending priorities during the year.

The budget is used in businesses in much the same way it can be used in personal life. For example, **Hendrick Motorsports**, featuring drivers Dale Earnhardt, Jr., Jeff Gordon, and Jimmie Johnson, uses budget information to remain one of the most valuable racing teams in NASCAR. Hendrick uses budgets to keep revenues greater than expenses. For example, Hendrick plans revenues from car sponsorships and winnings. Primary and secondary sponsorships (car decals) can provide as much as 70% of the revenues for a typical race team. Costs include salaries, engines, tires, cars, travel, and research and development. In addition, star drivers such as Dale Earnhardt, Jr. can earn as much as $28 million in salary, winnings, and endorsements. Overall, Hendrick is estimated to earn $179 million in revenues and $16.6 million in operating income from its four race teams. The budget provides the company with a "game plan" for the year. In this chapter, you will see how budgets can be used for financial planning and control.

Sources: Kurt Badenhausen, "Hendrick Motorsports Tops List of Nascar's Most Valuable Teams," *Forbes*, March 13, 2013; Bob Pockrass, "NASCAR's Highest Paid Drivers Make Their Money from a Variety of Sources," *Sporting News*, December 4, 2012; and Ed Hilton, "Under the Hood at Hendrick Motorsports", *Chicago Tribune*, July 13, 2007.

Learning Objectives

After studying this chapter, you should be able to:

Example Exercises (EE) are shown in **green**.

Obj. 1 Describe budgeting, its objectives, and its impact on human behavior.

Nature and Objectives of Budgeting
Objectives of Budgeting
Human Behavior and Budgeting

Obj. 2 Describe the basic elements of the budget process, the two major types of budgeting, and the use of computers in budgeting.

Budgeting Systems
Static Budget
Flexible Budget — EE 22-1
Computerized Budgeting Systems

Obj. 3 Describe the master budget for a manufacturing company.

Master Budget

Obj. 4 Prepare the basic operating budgets for a manufacturing company.

Operating Budgets
Sales Budget
Production Budget — EE 22-2
Direct Materials Purchases Budget — EE 22-3
Direct Labor Cost Budget — EE 22-4
Factory Overhead Cost Budget
Cost of Goods Sold Budget — EE 22-5
Selling and Administrative Expenses Budget
Budgeted Income Statement

Obj. 5 Prepare financial budgets for a manufacturing company.

Financial Budgets
Cash Budget — EE 22-6
Capital Expenditures Budget
Budgeted Balance Sheet

At a Glance 22 — Page 1096

Obj. 1 Describe budgeting, its objectives, and its impact on human behavior.

Nature and Objectives of Budgeting

Budgets play an important role for organizations of all sizes and forms. For example, budgets are used in managing the operations of government agencies, churches, hospitals, and other nonprofit organizations. Individuals and families also use budgeting in managing their financial affairs. This chapter describes and illustrates budgeting for a manufacturing company.

Link to Hendrick Motorsports
Hendrick Motorsports holds a record of 11 NASCAR Sprint Cup Series Championships won by the following drivers: 6 by Jimmie Johnson, 4 by Jeff Gordon, and 1 by Terry Labonte.

Objectives of Budgeting

Budgeting involves (1) establishing specific goals, (2) executing plans to achieve the goals, and (3) periodically comparing actual results with the goals. In doing so, budgeting affects the following managerial functions:

- Planning
- Directing
- Controlling

The relationships of these activities are illustrated in Exhibit 1.

EXHIBIT 1   Planning, Directing, and Controlling

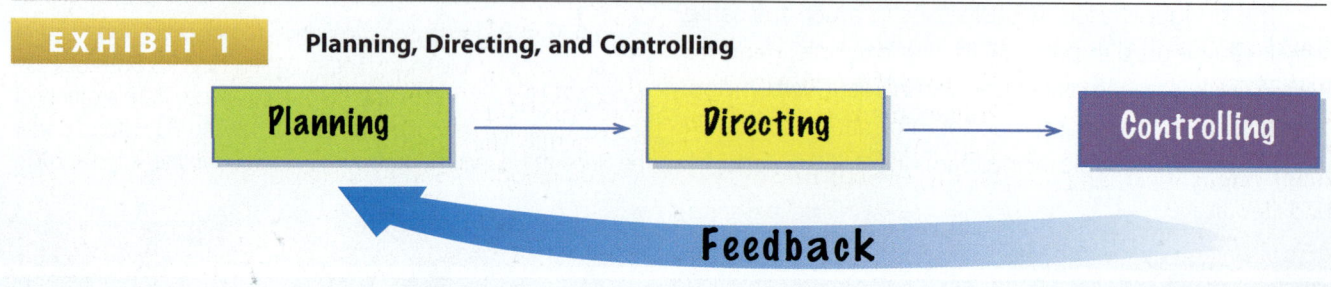

Planning involves setting goals to guide decisions and help motivate employees. The planning process often identifies where operations can be improved.

Directing involves decisions and actions to achieve budgeted goals. A budgetary unit of a company is called a **responsibility center**. Each responsibility center is led by a manager who has the authority and responsibility for achieving the center's budgeted goals.

Controlling involves comparing actual performance against the budgeted goals. Such comparisons provide feedback to managers and employees about their performance. If necessary, responsibility centers can use such feedback to adjust their activities in the future.

Human Behavior and Budgeting

Human behavior problems can arise in the budgeting process in the following situations:

- Budgeted goals are set too tight, which are very hard or impossible to achieve.
- Budgeted goals are set too loose, which are very easy to achieve.
- Budgeted goals conflict with the objectives of the company and employees.

These behavior problems are illustrated in Exhibit 2.

EXHIBIT 2

Human Behavior Problems in Budgeting

Setting Budget Goals Too Tightly Employees and managers may become discouraged if budgeted goals are set too high. That is, if budgeted goals are viewed as unrealistic or unachievable, the budget may have a negative effect on the ability of the company to achieve its goals.

Reasonable, attainable goals are more likely to motivate employees and managers. For this reason, it is important for employees and managers to be involved in the budgeting process. Involving employees in the budgeting process provides them with a sense of control and, thus, more of a commitment in meeting budgeted goals.

Setting Budget Goals Too Loosely Although it is desirable to establish attainable goals, it is undesirable to plan budget goals that are too easy. Such budget "padding" is termed **budgetary slack**. Managers may plan slack in their budgets to provide a "cushion" for unexpected events. However, slack budgets may create inefficiency by reducing the budgetary incentive to trim spending.

Setting Conflicting Budget Goals **Goal conflict** occurs when the employees' or managers' self-interest differs from the company's objectives or goals. To illustrate, assume that the sales department manager is given an increased sales goal and as a result accepts customers who are poor credit risks. Thus, while the sales department might meet sales goals, the overall firm may suffer reduced profitability from bad debts.

INTEGRITY, OBJECTIVITY, AND ETHICS IN BUSINESS

BUDGET GAMES

The budgeting system is designed to plan and control a business. However, it is common for the budget to be "gamed" by its participants. For example, managers may pad their budgets with excess resources. In this way, the managers have additional resources for unexpected events during the period. If the budget is being used to establish the incentive plan, then sales managers have incentives to understate the sales potential of a territory to ensure hitting their quotas. Other times, managers engage in "land grabbing," which occurs when they overstate the sales potential of a territory to guarantee access to resources. If managers believe that unspent resources will not roll over to future periods, then they may be encouraged to "spend it or lose it," causing wasteful expenditures. These types of problems can be partially overcome by separating the budget into planning and incentive components. This is why many organizations have two budget processes, one for planning resources and another more challenging budget for motivating managers.

Obj. 2 Describe the basic elements of the budget process, the two major types of budgeting, and the use of computers in budgeting.

Budgeting Systems

Budgeting systems vary among companies and industries. For example, the budget system used by **Ford Motor Company** differs from that used by **Delta Air Lines**. However, the basic budgeting concepts discussed in this section apply to all types of businesses and organizations.

The budgetary period for operating activities normally includes the fiscal year of a company. A year is short enough that future operations can be estimated fairly accurately, yet long enough that the future can be viewed in a broad context. However, for control purposes, annual budgets are usually subdivided into shorter time periods, such as quarters of the year, months, or weeks.

A variation of fiscal-year budgeting, called **continuous budgeting**, maintains a 12-month projection into the future. The 12-month budget is continually revised by replacing the data for the month just ended with the budget data for the same month in the next year. A continuous budget is illustrated in Exhibit 3.

EXHIBIT 3   **Continuous Budgeting**

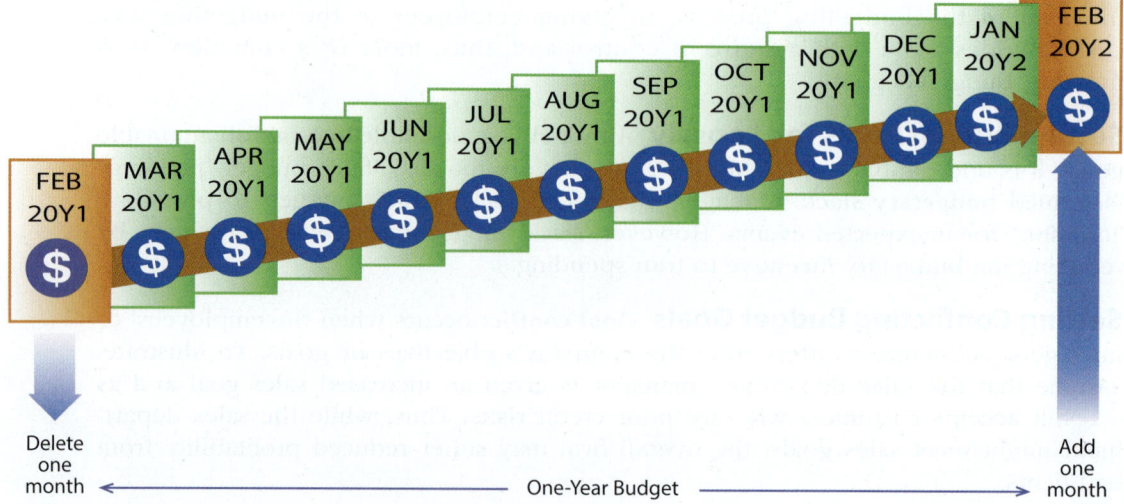

Developing an annual budget usually begins several months prior to the end of the current year. This responsibility is normally assigned to a budget committee. Such a committee often consists of the budget director, the controller, the treasurer, the production manager, and the sales manager. The budget process is monitored and summarized by the Accounting Department, which reports to the committee.

There are several methods of developing budget estimates. One method, called **zero-based budgeting**, requires managers to estimate sales, production, and other operating data as though operations are being started for the first time. This approach has the benefit of taking a fresh view of operations each year. A more common approach is to start with last year's budget and revise it for actual results and expected changes for the coming year. Two major budgets using this approach are the static budget and the flexible budget.

Static Budget

A **static budget** shows the expected results of a responsibility center for only one activity level. Once the budget has been determined, it is not changed, even if the activity changes. Static budgeting is used by many service companies; by governmental entities; and for some functions of manufacturing companies, such as purchasing, engineering, and accounting.

To illustrate, the static budget for the Assembly Department of Colter Manufacturing Company is shown in Exhibit 4.

> **Link to Hendrick Motorsports**
> Rick Hendrick uses budgeting in **Hendrick Motorsports** as well as the **Hendrick Automotive Group**. The Hendrick Automotive Group is the largest privately held dealership group in the United States with 120 retail franchises.

	A	B
1	Colter Manufacturing Company	
2	Assembly Department Budget	
3	For the Year Ending July 31, 20Y8	
4	Direct labor	$40,000
5	Electric power	5,000
6	Supervisor salaries	15,000
7	Total department costs	$60,000
8		

EXHIBIT 4

Static Budget

A disadvantage of static budgets is that they do not adjust for changes in activity levels. For example, assume that the Assembly Department of Colter Manufacturing spent $70,800 for the year ended July 31, 20Y8. Thus, the Assembly Department spent $10,800 ($70,800 − $60,000), or 18% ($10,800 ÷ $60,000) more than budgeted. Is this good news or bad news?

The first reaction is that this is bad news and the Assembly Department was inefficient in spending more than budgeted. However, assume that the Assembly Department's budget was based on plans to assemble 8,000 units during the year. If 10,000 units were actually assembled, the additional $10,800 spent in excess of budget might be good news. That is, the Assembly Department assembled 25% (2,000 units ÷ 8,000 units) more than planned for only 18% more cost. In this case, a static budget may not be useful for controlling costs.

SERVICE FOCUS

FILM BUDGETING

Service businesses, like film and entertainment, use budgets as a road map to control expenses. In film production, the budget is a valuable tool to manage the tension between creative expression and cost.

The film budget is a static budget that can be divided into three major categories:

- above the line
- below the line
- post-production costs

The *above the line* costs include costs attributed to creative talent, such as the lead cast's and director's salaries and script fees. The *below the line* costs include the remaining costs to create the film, including location, costume, and prop rentals; permits; and other production costs. The *post-production costs* include the costs to complete the film, including editing, sound, and special effects. Marketing has a separate budget.

The total cost of the film is influenced by many decisions, including the cost of story rights, location, star quality of creative talent, union representation in the production crew, music, and special effects. Even a low-budget indie (independent) documentary could easily have a budget of more than $1 million. In contrast, a special effect-laden Hollywood film could have a budget in excess of $200 million.

Flexible Budget

Note: Flexible budgets show expected results for several activity levels.

Unlike static budgets, **flexible budgets** show the expected results of a responsibility center for several activity levels. A flexible budget is, in effect, a series of static budgets for different levels of activity.

To illustrate, a flexible budget for the Assembly Department of Colter Manufacturing Company is shown in Exhibit 5.

EXHIBIT 5
Flexible Budget

Link to Hendrick Motorsports
Rick Hendrick started by selling used cars. At age 26, he invested all of his assets in a struggling Chevrolet dealership, becoming the youngest Chevrolet dealer in the United States. This dealership was the predecessor of the **Hendrick Automotive Group**.

	A	B	C	D
1	Colter Manufacturing Company				
2	Assembly Department Budget			
3	For the Year Ending July 31, 20Y8			
4		Level 1	Level 2	Level 3
5	Units of production	8,000	9,000	10,000
6	Variable cost:			
7	Direct labor ($5 per unit)	$40,000	$45,000	$50,000
8	Electric power ($0.50 per unit)	4,000	4,500	5,000
9	Total variable cost	$44,000	$49,500	$55,000
10	Fixed cost:			
11	Electric power	$ 1,000	$ 1,000	$ 1,000
12	Supervisor salaries	15,000	15,000	15,000
13	Total fixed cost	$16,000	$16,000	$16,000
14	Total department costs	$60,000	$65,500	$71,000
15				

Step 1 ← Units of production row
Step 2 ← Variable and Fixed cost sections
Step 3 ← Total columns

A flexible budget is constructed as follows:

Step 1. Identify the relevant activity levels. The relevant levels of activity could be expressed in units, machine hours, direct labor hours, or some other activity base. In Exhibit 5, the levels of activity are 8,000, 9,000, and 10,000 units of production.

Step 2. Identify the fixed and variable cost components of the costs being budgeted. In Exhibit 5, the electric power cost is separated into its fixed cost ($1,000 per year) and variable cost ($0.50 per unit). The direct labor is a variable cost, and the supervisor salaries are all fixed costs.

Step 3. Prepare the budget for each activity level by multiplying the variable cost per unit by the activity level and then adding the monthly fixed cost.

With a flexible budget, actual costs can be compared to the budgeted costs for actual activity. To illustrate, assume that the Assembly Department spent $70,800 to produce 10,000 units. Exhibit 5 indicates that the Assembly Department was *under* budget by $200 ($71,000 − $70,800).

Under the static budget in Exhibit 4, the Assembly Department was $10,800 *over* budget. This comparison is illustrated in Exhibit 6.

The flexible budget for the Assembly Department is more accurate and useful than the static budget. This is because the flexible budget adjusts for changes in the level of activity. Flexible budgets can be used in service businesses when the variable costs can be associated to an activity. For example, hospital room expenses are related to number of patients, or transportation fuel costs are related to number of miles.

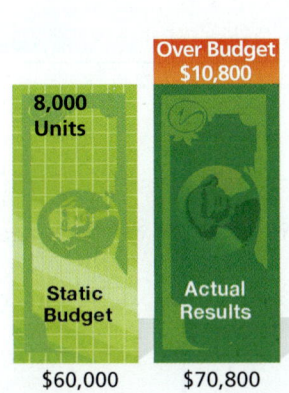
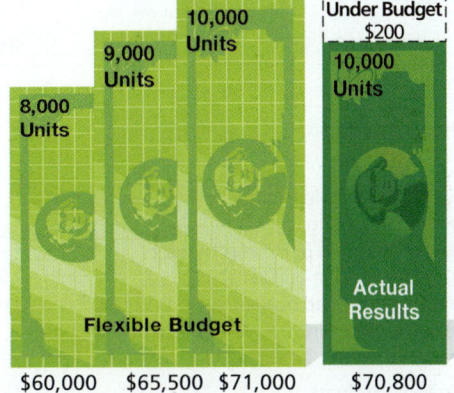

EXHIBIT 6

Static and Flexible Budgets

Example Exercise 22-1 Flexible Budgeting *Obj. 2*

At the beginning of the period, the Assembly Department budgeted direct labor of $45,000 and supervisor salaries of $30,000 for 5,000 hours of production. The department actually completed 6,000 hours of production. Determine the budget for the department, assuming that it uses flexible budgeting.

Follow My Example 22-1

Variable cost:	
Direct labor (6,000 hours × $9* per hour)	$54,000
Fixed cost:	
Supervisor salaries	30,000
Total department costs	$84,000

*$45,000 ÷ 5,000 hours

Practice Exercises: PE 22-1A, PE 22-1B

Computerized Budgeting Systems

In developing budgets, companies use a variety of computerized approaches. Two of the most popular computerized approaches use:

- Spreadsheet software such as Microsoft® Excel®
- Integrated budget and planning (B&P) software systems

Spreadsheets ease budget preparation by summarizing budget information in linked spreadsheets across the organization. In addition, the impact of proposed changes in various assumptions or operating alternatives can be analyzed on a spreadsheet.

B&P software systems use the web (intranet) to link thousands of employees during the budget process. Employees can input budget data onto web pages that are integrated and summarized throughout the company. In this way, a company can quickly and consistently integrate top-level strategies and goals to lower-level operational goals.

Master Budget

Obj. 3 Describe the master budget for a manufacturing company.

The **master budget** is an integrated set of operating and financial budgets for a period of time. Most companies prepare a master budget on a yearly basis. Exhibit 7 shows that the operating budgets can be used to prepare a budgeted income statement, while the financial budgets provide information for a budgeted balance sheet.

EXHIBIT 7

Master Budget for a Manufacturing Company

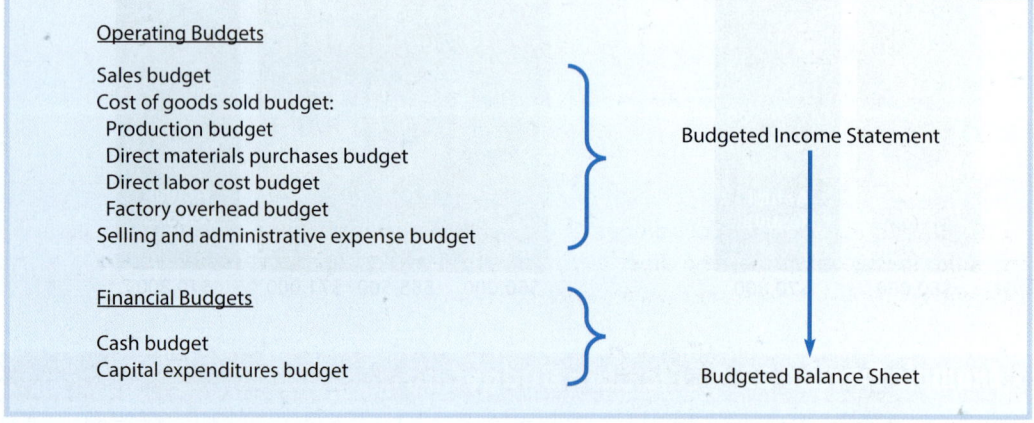

The master budget begins with preparing the operating budgets, which form the budgeted income statement. Exhibit 8 shows the relationships among the operating budgets leading to an income statement budget.

Operating Budgets

Obj. 4 Prepare the basic operating budgets for a manufacturing company.

The integrated operating budgets that support the income statement budget are illustrated for **Elite Accessories Inc.**, a small manufacturing company of personal accessories.

Sales Budget

The **sales budget** begins by estimating the quantity of sales. The prior year's sales are often used as a starting point. These sales quantities are then revised for factors such as planned advertising and promotion, projected pricing changes, and expected industry and general economic conditions.

Once sales quantities are estimated, the budgeted sales revenue can be determined as follows:

$$\text{Budgeted Revenue} = \text{Expected Sales Volume} \times \text{Expected Unit Sales Price}$$

EXHIBIT 8

Operating Budgets

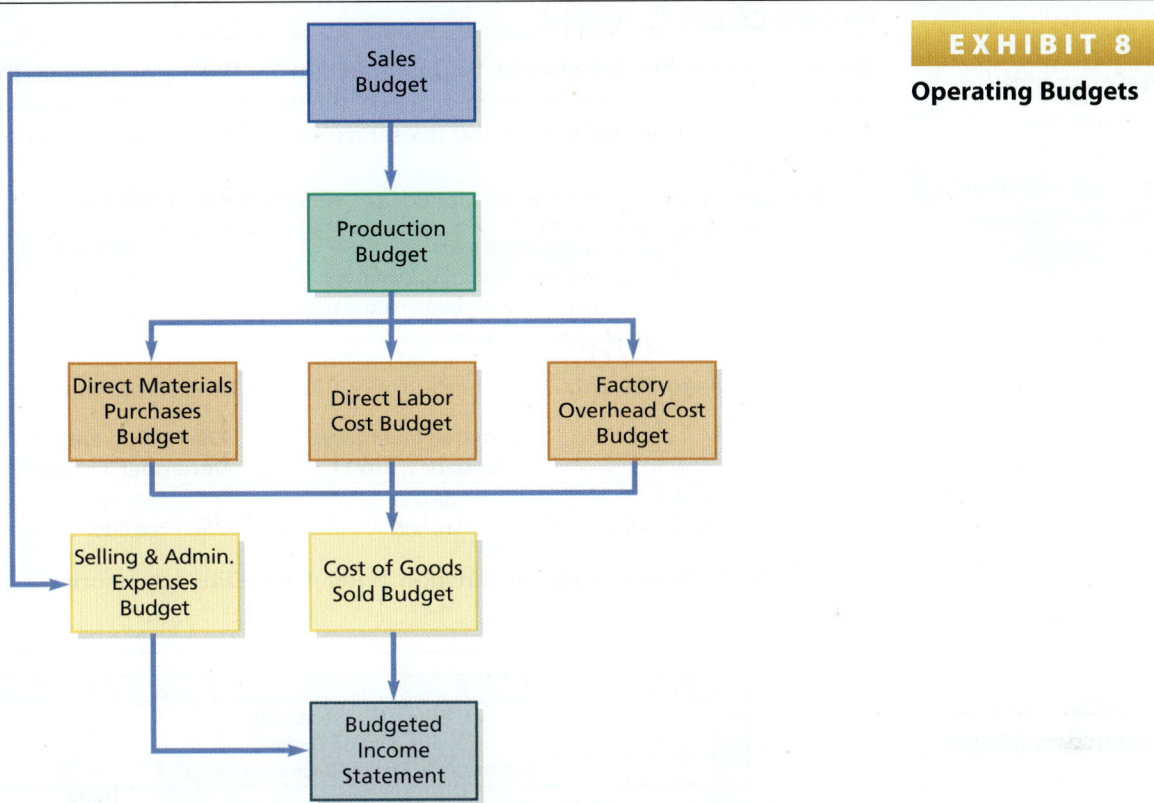

To illustrate, **Elite Accessories Inc.** manufactures wallets and handbags that are sold in two regions, the East and West regions. Elite Accessories estimates the following sales volumes and prices for 20Y1:

	East Region Sales Volume	West Region Sales Volume	Unit Selling Price
Wallets	287,000	241,000	$12
Handbags	156,400	123,600	25

Exhibit 9 illustrates the sales budget for Elite Accessories based on the preceding data.

EXHIBIT 9

Sales Budget

	A	B	C	D
1	\multicolumn{4}{c}{Elite Accessories Inc.}
2	\multicolumn{4}{c}{Sales Budget}
3	\multicolumn{4}{c}{For the Year Ending December 31, 20Y1}
4		Unit Sales	Unit Selling	
5	Product and Region	Volume	Price	Total Sales
6	Wallet:			
7	East	287,000	$12.00	$ 3,444,000
8	West	241,000	12.00	2,892,000
9	Total	528,000		$ 6,336,000
10				
11	Handbag:			
12	East	156,400	$25.00	$ 3,910,000
13	West	123,600	25.00	3,090,000
14	Total	280,000		$ 7,000,000
15				
16	Total revenue from sales			$13,336,000
17				

Production Budget

Link to Hendrick Motorsports

In a recent year, **Hendrick Automotive Group** generated over $7 billion of revenue across 13 states.

The production budget should be integrated with the sales budget to ensure that production and sales are kept in balance during the year. The **production budget** estimates the number of units to be manufactured to meet budgeted sales and desired inventory levels.

The budgeted units to be produced are determined as follows:

Expected units to be sold	XXX units
Plus desired units in ending inventory	+ XXX
Less estimated units in beginning inventory	– XXX
Total units to be produced	XXX units

Elite Accessories Inc. expects the following inventories of wallets and handbags:

	Estimated Inventory, January 1, 20Y1	Desired Inventory, December 31, 20Y1
Wallets	88,000	80,000
Handbags	48,000	60,000

Exhibit 10 illustrates the production budget for Elite Accessories.

EXHIBIT 10
Production Budget

	A	B	C
1	Elite Accessories Inc.		
2	Production Budget		
3	For the Year Ending December 31, 20Y1		
4		Units	
5		Wallet	Handbag
6	Expected units to be sold (from Exhibit 9)	528,000	280,000
7	Plus desired ending inventory, December 31, 20Y1	80,000	60,000
8	Total units required	608,000	340,000
9	Less estimated beginning inventory, January 1, 20Y1	88,000	48,000
10	Total units to be produced	520,000	292,000

Example Exercise 22-2 Production Budget *Obj. 4*

Landon Awards Co. projected sales of 45,000 brass plaques for 20Y5. The estimated January 1, 20Y5, inventory is 3,000 units, and the desired December 31, 20Y5, inventory is 5,000 units. What is the budgeted production (in units) for 20Y5?

Follow My Example 22-2

Expected units to be sold	45,000
Plus desired ending inventory, December 31, 20Y5	5,000
Total units required	50,000
Less estimated beginning inventory, January 1, 20Y5	3,000
Total units to be produced	47,000

Practice Exercises: PE 22-2A, PE 22-2B

Direct Materials Purchases Budget

The direct materials purchases budget should be integrated with the production budget to ensure that production is not interrupted during the year. The **direct materials purchases budget** estimates the quantities of direct materials to be purchased to support budgeted production and desired inventory levels and can be developed in three steps.

Step 1 Determine the budgeted direct material required for production, which is computed as follows:

$$\text{Budgeted Direct Material Required for Production} = \text{Budgeted Production Volume (from Exhibit 10)} \times \text{Direct Material Quantity Expected per Unit}$$

To illustrate, **Elite Accessories Inc.** uses leather and lining in producing wallets and handbags. The quantity of direct materials expected to be used for each unit of product is as follows:

Wallet	Handbag
Leather: 0.30 sq. yd. per unit	Leather: 1.25 sq. yds. per unit
Lining: 0.10 sq. yd. per unit	Lining: 0.50 sq. yd. per unit

For the wallet, the direct material required for production is computed as follows:

Leather: 520,000 units × 0.30 sq. yd. per unit = 156,000 sq. yds.
Lining: 520,000 units × 0.10 sq. yd. per unit = 52,000 sq. yds.

For the handbag, the direct material required for production is computed as follows:

Leather: 292,000 units × 1.25 sq. yd. per unit = 365,000 sq. yds.
Lining: 292,000 units × 0.50 sq. yd. per unit = 146,000 sq. yds.

Step 2 The budgeted material required for production is adjusted for beginning and ending inventories to determine the direct materials to be purchased for each material, as follows:

Materials required for production (Step 1)	XXX
Plus desired ending materials inventory	+XXX
Less estimated beginning materials inventory	−XXX
Direct material quantity to be purchased	XXX

Step 3 The budgeted direct materials to be purchased is computed as follows:

$$\text{Budgeted Direct Material to be Purchased} = \text{Direct Material Quantity to be Purchased (Step 2)} \times \text{Unit Price}$$

Complete Direct Materials Purchases Budget The following inventory and unit price information for **Elite Accessories Inc.** is expected:

	Estimated Direct Materials Inventory, January 1, 20Y1	Desired Direct Materials Inventory, December 31, 20Y1
Leather	18,000 sq. yds.	20,000 sq. yds.
Lining	15,000 sq. yds.	12,000 sq. yds.

The estimated price per square yard of leather and lining during 20Y1 follows:

	Price per Square Yard
Leather	$4.50
Lining	1.20

Exhibit 11 illustrates the complete direct materials purchases budget for Elite Accessories by combining all three steps into a single schedule.

The timing of the direct materials purchases should be coordinated between the Purchasing and Production departments so that production is not interrupted.

EXHIBIT 11
Direct Materials Purchases Budget

	A	B	C	D
1		Elite Accessories Inc.		
2		Direct Materials Purchases Budget		
3		For the Year Ending December 31, 20Y1		
4		Direct Materials		
5		Leather	Lining	Total
6	Square yards required for production:			
7	Wallet (Note A)	156,000	52,000	
8	Handbag (Note B)	365,000	146,000	
9	Plus desired ending inventory, December 31, 20Y1	20,000	12,000	
10	Total square yards required	541,000	210,000	
11	Less estimated beginning inventory, January 1, 20Y1	18,000	15,000	
12	Total square yards to be purchased	523,000	195,000	
13	Unit price (per square yard)	× $4.50	× $1.20	
14	Total direct materials to be purchased	$2,353,500	$234,000	$2,587,500
15				
16	Note A: Leather: 520,000 units × 0.30 sq. yd. per unit = 156,000 sq. yds.			
17	Lining: 520,000 units × 0.10 sq. yd. per unit = 52,000 sq. yds.			
18				
19	Note B: Leather: 292,000 units × 1.25 sq. yds. per unit = 365,000 sq. yds.			
20	Lining: 292,000 units × 0.50 sq. yd. per unit = 146,000 sq. yds.			
21				

Step 1: rows 7–8
Step 2: rows 9–12
Step 3: rows 13–14

Example Exercise 22-3 Direct Materials Purchases Budget Obj. 4

Landon Awards Co. budgeted production of 47,000 brass plaques in 20Y5. Brass sheet is required to produce a brass plaque. Assume that 96 square inches of brass sheet are required for each brass plaque. The estimated January 1, 20Y5, brass sheet inventory is 240,000 square inches. The desired December 31, 20Y5, brass sheet inventory is 200,000 square inches. If brass sheet costs $0.12 per square inch, determine the direct materials purchases budget for 20Y5.

Follow My Example 22-3

Square inches required for production: Brass sheet (47,000 × 96 sq. in.)	4,512,000
Plus desired ending inventory, December 31, 20Y5	200,000
Total square inches required	4,712,000
Less estimated beginning inventory, January 1, 20Y5	240,000
Total square inches to be purchased	4,472,000
Unit price (per square inch)	× $0.12
Total direct materials to be purchased	$ 536,640

Practice Exercises: PE 22-3A, PE 22-3B

Link to Hendrick Motorsports

Hendrick Motorsports uses sheet metal in building its race cars. "Used" sections of sheet metal (from crashed cars) can be purchased from its online store.

Direct Labor Cost Budget

The **direct labor cost budget** estimates the direct labor hours and related cost needed to support budgeted production. Production managers study work methods to provide estimates used in preparing the direct labor cost budget.

The direct labor cost budget for each department is determined in two steps, as follows:

Step 1 Determine the budgeted direct labor hours required for production, which is computed as follows:

$$\text{Budgeted Direct Labor Hours Required for Production} = \text{Budgeted Production Volume (from Exhibit 10)} \times \text{Direct Labor Hours Expected per Unit}$$

To illustrate, **Elite Accessories Inc.**'s production managers estimate that the following direct labor hours are needed to produce a wallet and handbag:

Wallet	Handbag
Cutting Department: 0.10 hr. per unit	Cutting Department: 0.15 hr. per unit
Sewing Department: 0.25 hr. per unit	Sewing Department: 0.40 hr. per unit

Thus, for the wallet, the budgeted direct labor hours required for production is computed as follows:

Cutting: 520,000 units × 0.10 hr. per unit = 52,000 direct labor hours
Sewing: 520,000 units × 0.25 hr. per unit = 130,000 direct labor hours

For the handbag, the budgeted direct labor hours required for production is computed as follows:

Cutting: 292,000 units × 0.15 hr. per unit = 43,800 direct labor hours
Sewing: 292,000 units × 0.40 hr. per unit = 116,800 direct labor hours

Step 2 Determine the total direct labor cost as follows:

Direct Labor Cost = Direct Labor Required for Production (Step 1) × Hourly Rate

The estimated direct labor hourly rates for the Cutting and Sewing departments for **Elite Accessories Inc.** during 20Y1 follow:

	Hourly Rate
Cutting Department	$12
Sewing Department	15

Complete Direct Labor Cost Budget Exhibit 12 illustrates the direct labor cost budget by combining both steps for **Elite Accessories Inc.**

EXHIBIT 12
Direct Labor Cost Budget

Dynamic Exhibit

	A	B	C	D
1		Elite Accessories Inc.		
2		Direct Labor Cost Budget		
3		For the Year Ending December 31, 20Y1		
4		Cutting	Sewing	Total
5	Hours required for production:			
6	Wallet (Note A)	52,000	130,000	
7	Handbag (Note B)	43,800	116,800	
8	Total hours required	95,800	246,800	
9	Hourly rate	× $12.00	× $15.00	
10	Total direct labor cost	$1,149,600	$3,702,000	$4,851,600
11				
12	Note A: Cutting Department: 520,000 units × 0.10 hr. per unit = 52,000 hrs.			
13	Sewing Department: 520,000 units × 0.25 hr. per unit = 130,000 hrs.			
14				
15	Note B: Cutting Department: 292,000 units × 0.15 hr. per unit = 43,800 hrs.			
16	Sewing Department: 292,000 units × 0.40 hr. per unit = 116,800 hrs.			
17				

Rows 6–8 are bracketed as Step 1; rows 9–10 are bracketed as Step 2.

The direct labor needs should be coordinated between the production and personnel departments so that there will be enough labor available for production.

> **Link to Hendrick Motorsports**
>
> **Hendrick Motorsports** offers an internship program for college students who want to experience and learn the operations of a NASCAR team.

Example Exercise 22-4 — Direct Labor Cost Budget — Obj. 4

Landon Awards Co. budgeted production of 47,000 brass plaques in 20Y5. Each plaque requires engraving. Assume that 12 minutes are required to engrave each plaque. If engraving labor costs $11.00 per hour, determine the direct labor cost budget for 20Y5.

Follow My Example 22-4

Hours required for engraving:	
Brass plaque (47,000 × 12 min.)	564,000 min.
Convert minutes to hours	÷ 60 min.
Engraving hours	9,400 hrs.
Hourly rate	× $11.00
Total direct labor cost	$103,400

Practice Exercises: PE 22-4A, PE 22-4B

Factory Overhead Cost Budget

The **factory overhead cost budget** estimates the cost for each item of factory overhead needed to support budgeted production.

Exhibit 13 illustrates the factory overhead cost budget for **Elite Accessories Inc.**

EXHIBIT 13

Factory Overhead Cost Budget

	A	B
1	Elite Accessories Inc.	
2	Factory Overhead Cost Budget	
3	For the Year Ending December 31, 20Y1	
4	Indirect factory wages	$ 732,800
5	Supervisor salaries	360,000
6	Power and light	306,000
7	Depreciation of plant and equipment	288,000
8	Indirect materials	182,800
9	Maintenance	140,280
10	Insurance and property taxes	79,200
11	Total factory overhead cost	$2,089,080
12		

The factory overhead cost budget shown in Exhibit 13 may be supported by departmental schedules. Such schedules normally separate factory overhead costs into fixed and variable costs to better enable department managers to monitor and evaluate costs during the year.

The factory overhead cost budget should be integrated with the production budget to ensure that production is not interrupted during the year.

Cost of Goods Sold Budget

The **cost of goods sold budget** is prepared by integrating the following budgets:

- Direct materials purchases budget (Exhibit 11)
- Direct labor cost budget (Exhibit 12)
- Factory overhead cost budget (Exhibit 13)

In addition, the estimated and desired inventories for direct materials, work in process, and finished goods must be integrated into the cost of goods sold budget.

Elite Accessories Inc. expects the following direct materials, work in process, and finished goods inventories:

	Estimated Inventory, January 1, 20Y1	Desired Inventory, December 31, 20Y1
Direct materials:		
Leather	$ 81,000 (18,000 sq. yds. × $4.50)	$ 90,000 (20,000 sq. yds. × $4.50)
Lining	18,000 (15,000 sq. yds. × $1.20)	14,400 (12,000 sq. yds. × $1.20)
Total direct materials	$ 99,000	$ 104,400
Work in process	$ 214,400	$ 220,000
Finished goods	$1,095,600	$1,565,000

The cost of goods sold budget for Elite Accessories in Exhibit 14 indicates that total manufacturing costs of $9,522,780 are budgeted to be incurred in 20Y1. Of this total, $2,582,100 is budgeted for direct materials, $4,851,600 is budgeted for direct labor, and $2,089,080 is budgeted for factory overhead. After considering work in process inventories, the total budgeted cost of goods manufactured and transferred to finished goods during 20Y1 is $9,517,180. Based on expected sales, the budgeted cost of goods sold is $9,047,780.

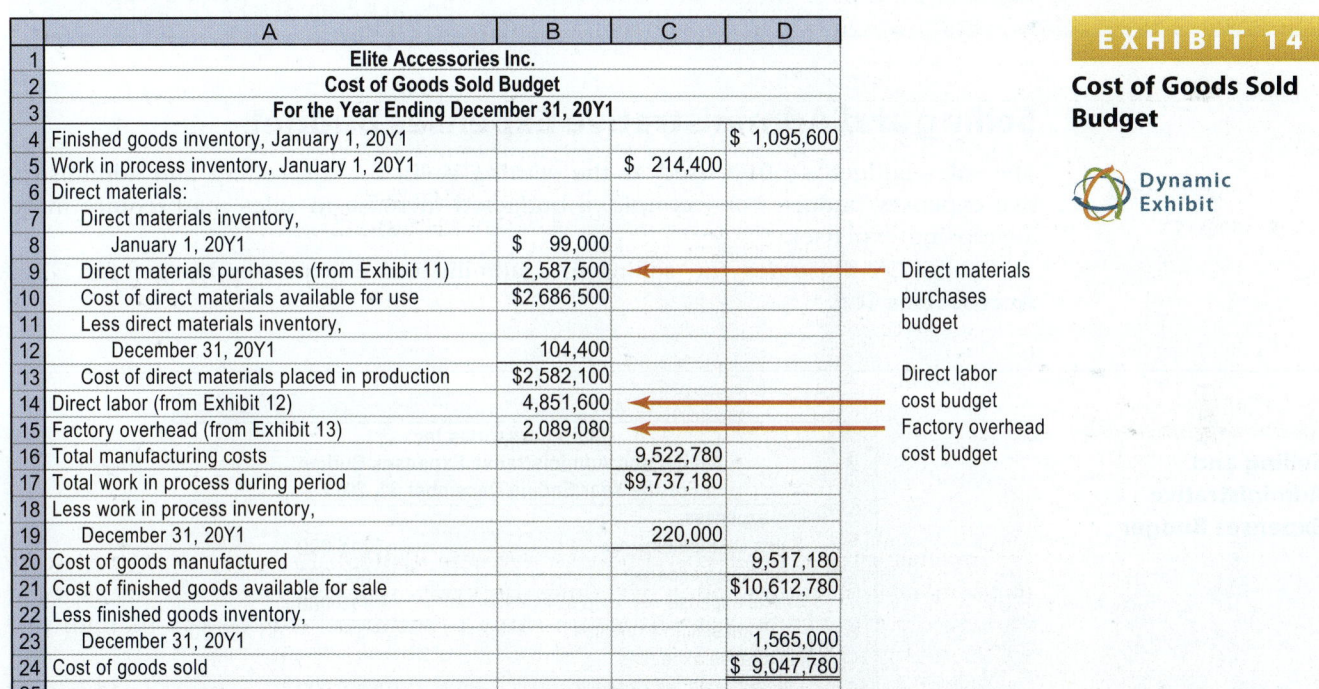

EXHIBIT 14

Cost of Goods Sold Budget

Dynamic Exhibit

Example Exercise 22-5 Cost of Goods Sold Budget — Obj. 4

Prepare a cost of goods sold budget for Landon Awards Co. using the information in Example Exercises 22-3 and 22-4. Assume that the estimated inventories on January 1, 20Y5, for finished goods and work in process were $54,000 and $47,000, respectively. Also assume that the desired inventories on December 31, 20Y5, for finished goods and work in process were $50,000 and $49,000, respectively. Factory overhead was budgeted for $126,000.

(Continued)

Follow My Example 22-5

Finished goods inventory, January 1, 20Y5		$54,000
Work in process inventory, January 1, 20Y5...........................	$47,000	
Direct materials:		
Direct materials inventory, January 1, 20Y5		
(240,000 × $0.12, from EE 22-3).................................	$28,800	
Direct materials purchases (from EE 22-3)	536,640	
Cost of direct materials available for use	$565,440	
Less direct materials inventory, December 31, 20Y5		
(200,000 × $0.12, from EE 22-3).................................	24,000	
Cost of direct materials placed in production.....................	$541,440	
Direct labor (from EE 22-4)...	103,400	
Factory overhead	126,000	
Total manufacturing costs...	770,840	
Total work in process during period....................................	$817,840	
Less work in process inventory, December 31, 20Y5	49,000	
Cost of goods manufactured...		768,840
Cost of finished goods available for sale............................		$822,840
Less finished goods inventory, December 31, 20Y5		50,000
Cost of goods sold..		$772,840

Practice Exercises: PE 22-5A, PE 22-5B

Selling and Administrative Expenses Budget

The sales budget is often used as the starting point for the selling and administrative expenses budget. For example, a budgeted increase in sales may require more advertising expenses.

Exhibit 15 illustrates the selling and administrative expenses budget for **Elite Accessories Inc.**

EXHIBIT 15

Selling and Administrative Expenses Budget

	A	B	C
1	Elite Accessories Inc.		
2	Selling and Administrative Expenses Budget		
3	For the Year Ending December 31, 20Y1		
4	Selling expenses:		
5	Sales salaries expense	$715,000	
6	Advertising expense	360,000	
7	Travel expense	115,000	
8	Total selling expenses		$1,190,000
9	Administrative expenses:		
10	Officers' salaries expense	$360,000	
11	Office salaries expense	258,000	
12	Office rent expense	34,500	
13	Office supplies expense	17,500	
14	Miscellaneous administrative expenses	25,000	
15	Total administrative expenses		695,000
16	Total selling and administrative expenses		$1,885,000
17			

The selling and administrative expenses budget shown in Exhibit 15 is normally supported by departmental schedules. For example, an advertising expense schedule for the Marketing Department could include the advertising media to be used (newspaper, direct mail, television), quantities (column inches, number of pieces, minutes), and related costs per unit.

Business Connection

MAD MEN

The advertising budget can be one of the largest selling and administrative expenses for a business. The top 200 leading national advertisers accounted for 51% of all advertising dollars for all businesses combined. Of this amount, 68.5% went toward video broadcast advertising, 7.2% for Internet display ads, and 24.3% for print and radio. The top five spenders according to *Advertising Age* were:

Company	U.S. Advertising Spending
Procter & Gamble	$4.6 billion
AT&T	3.3 billion
General Motors	3.1 billion
Comcast	3.0 billion
Verizon	2.5 billion

The advertising budget is segmented between "measured" and "unmeasured" media. Measured media are tracked to determine the number of impressions an ad is receiving due to audience, viewership, or readership counts. Unmeasured media are not counted for impressions and include promotions, direct marketing, and coupons.

A major trend is allocating ad budget dollars toward digital strategies, such as search, social, video, and mobile. These strategies are believed to be more efficient and effective than TV or print. For Colgate-Palmolive, digital went from 2% of the advertising budget in 2006 to 13% in 2014, with expectations of growing to 25%.

Source: Bradley Johnson, "Big Spenders on a Budget: What the Top 200 U.S. Advertisers Are Doing to Spend Smarter," *Advertising Age*, July 5, 2015.

Budgeted Income Statement

The budgeted income statement for Elite Accessories Inc. in Exhibit 16 is prepared by integrating the following budgets:

- Sales budget (Exhibit 9)
- Cost of goods sold budget (Exhibit 14)
- Selling and administrative expenses budget (Exhibit 15)

EXHIBIT 16 Budgeted Income Statement

	A	B	C
1	Elite Accessories Inc.		
2	Budgeted Income Statement		
3	For the Year Ending December 31, 20Y1		
4	Revenue from sales (from Exhibit 9)		$13,336,000
5	Cost of goods sold (from Exhibit 14)		9,047,780
6	Gross profit		$ 4,288,220
7	Selling and administrative expenses:		
8	Selling expenses (from Exhibit 15)	$1,190,000	
9	Administrative expenses (from Exhibit 15)	695,000	
10	Total selling and administrative expenses		1,885,000
11	Income from operations		$ 2,403,220
12	Other revenue and expense:		
13	Interest revenue	$ 98,000	
14	Interest expense	(90,000)	8,000
15	Income before income tax		$ 2,411,220
16	Income tax		600,000
17	Net income		$ 1,811,220
18			

Revenue from sales ← Sales budget
Cost of goods sold ← Cost of goods sold budget
Selling expenses, Administrative expenses ← Selling and administrative expenses budget

In addition, estimates of other income, other expense, and income tax are also integrated into the budgeted income statement.

This budget summarizes the budgeted operating activities of the company. In doing so, the budgeted income statement allows management to assess the effects of estimated sales, costs, and expenses on profits for the year.

Financial Budgets

Obj. 5 Prepare financial budgets for a manufacturing company.

While the operating budgets reflect the operating activities of the company, the financial budgets reflect the financing and investing activities. In this section, the following financial budgets are described and illustrated:

- Cash budget
- Capital expenditures budget

Cash Budget

Note: The cash budget presents the expected receipts and payments of cash for a period of time.

The **cash budget** estimates the expected receipts (inflows) and payments (outflows) of cash for a period of time. The cash budget is integrated with the various operating budgets. In addition, the capital expenditures budget, dividends, and equity or long-term debt financing plans of the company affect the cash budget.

To illustrate, a monthly cash budget for January, February, and March 20Y1 for **Elite Accessories Inc.** is prepared. The preparation of the cash budget begins by estimating cash receipts.

Estimated Cash Receipts The primary source of estimated cash receipts is from cash sales and collections on account. In addition, cash receipts may be obtained from plans to issue equity or debt financing as well as other sources such as interest revenue.

To estimate cash receipts from cash sales and collections on account, a *schedule of collections from sales* is prepared. To illustrate, the following data for **Elite Accessories Inc.** are used:

	January	February	March
Sales:			
Budgeted sales	$1,080,000	$1,240,000	$970,000
Accounts receivable:			
Accounts receivable January 1, 20Y1	$480,000		
Receipts from sales on account:			
From prior month's sales on account	40%		
From current month's sales on account	60		
	100%		

The budgeted cash collected for any month is the sum of the cash collected from previous month's sales and the cash collected from current month's sales. To illustrate, the cash collected in February is 40% of cash collected on sales in January ($1,080,000 × 40%) added to 60% of cash collected on sales in February ($1,240,000 × 60%), shown as follows:

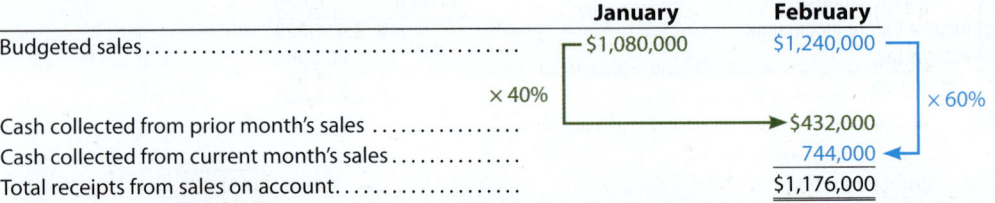

Using the preceding data, Exhibit 17 shows the schedule of collections from sales for Elite Accessories for all three months. To simplify, it is assumed that all accounts receivable are collected and there are no cash sales.

EXHIBIT 17
Schedule of Collections from Sales

	A	B	C	D
1	Elite Accessories Inc.			
2	Schedule of Collections from Sales			
3	For the Three Months Ending March 31, 20Y1			
4		January	February	March
5	Cash collected from prior month's sales—Note A	$ 480,000	$ 432,000	$ 496,000
6	Cash collected from current month's sales—Note B	648,000	744,000	582,000
7	Total receipts from sales on account	$1,128,000	$1,176,000	$1,078,000
8				
9	Note A: $480,000, given as January 1, 20Y1, Accounts Receivable balance			
10	$432,000 = $1,080,000 × 40%			
11	$496,000 = $1,240,000 × 40%			
12				
13	Note B: $648,000 = $1,080,000 × 60%			
14	$744,000 = $1,240,000 × 60%			
15	$582,000 = $970,000 × 60%			
16				

Estimated Cash Payments Estimated cash payments must be budgeted for operating costs and expenses such as manufacturing costs, selling expenses, and administrative expenses. In addition, estimated cash payments may be planned for capital expenditures, dividends, interest payments, or long-term debt payments.

To estimate cash payments for manufacturing costs, a *schedule of payments for manufacturing costs* is prepared. To illustrate, the following data for **Elite Accessories Inc.** are used:

	January	February	March
Manufacturing Costs:			
Budgeted manufacturing costs	$840,000	$780,000	$812,000
Depreciation on machines included in manufacturing costs	24,000	24,000	24,000
Accounts Payable:			
Accounts payable, January 1, 20Y1	$190,000		
Payments of manufacturing costs on account:			
From prior month's manufacturing costs	25%		
From current month's manufacturing costs	75		
	100%		

The budgeted cash payments for any month are the sum of the cash paid from previous month's manufacturing costs (less depreciation) and the cash paid from current month's manufacturing costs (less depreciation). To illustrate, the cash paid in February is 25% of manufacturing costs (less depreciation) in January [($840,000 − $24,000) × 25%] added to 75% of cash paid on manufacturing costs (less depreciation) in February [($780,000 − $24,000) × 75%], computed as follows:

	January	February
Budgeted manufacturing costs	$840,000	$780,000
Less depreciation on machines	24,000	24,000
Manufacturing costs (less depreciation)	$816,000	$756,000
	× 25%	
Payments of prior month's manufacturing costs (less depreciation)		$204,000 × 75%
Payments of current month's manufacturing costs (less depreciation)		567,000
Total payments		$771,000

Using the preceding data, Exhibit 18 shows the schedule of payments for manufacturing costs for Elite Accessories for all three months.

EXHIBIT 18
Schedule of Payments for Manufacturing Costs

	A	B	C	D
1	Elite Accessories Inc.			
2	Schedule of Payments for Manufacturing Costs			
3	For the Three Months Ending March 31, 20Y1			
4		January	February	March
5	Payments of prior month's manufacturing costs			
6	{[25% × previous month's manufacturing costs			
7	(less depreciation)]—Note A}	$190,000	$204,000	$189,000
8	Payments of current month's manufacturing costs			
9	{[75% × current month's manufacturing costs			
10	(less depreciation)]—Note B}	612,000	567,000	591,000
11	Total payments	$802,000	$771,000	$780,000
12				
13	Note A: $190,000, given as January 1, 20Y1, Accounts Payable balance			
14	$204,000 = ($840,000 − $24,000) × 25%			
15	$189,000 = ($780,000 − $24,000) × 25%			
16				
17	Note B: $612,000 = ($840,000 − $24,000) × 75%			
18	$567,000 = ($780,000 − $24,000) × 75%			
19	$591,000 = ($812,000 − $24,000) × 75%			
20				

Completing the Cash Budget The cash budget is structured for a budget period as follows:

Budget Period:

Estimated cash receipts
− Estimated cash payments
Cash increase (decrease)
+ Cash balance at the beginning of the month
Cash balance at the end of the month ⟶ Becomes the beginning balance for the next period
− Minimum cash balance
Excess (deficiency)

The budgeted balance at the end of the period is determined by adding the net increase (decrease) for the period to the beginning cash balance. The ending balance is compared to a minimum cash balance to support operations as determined by management. Any difference between the ending balance and the minimum cash balance represents an excess or a deficiency that may require management action.

To illustrate, assume the following additional data for **Elite Accessories Inc.**:

Cash balance on January 1, 20Y1	$225,000
Quarterly taxes paid on March 31, 20Y1	150,000
Quarterly interest expense paid on January 10, 20Y1	22,500
Quarterly interest revenue received on March 21, 20Y1	24,500
Sewing equipment purchased in February 20Y1	274,000

Selling and administrative expenses (paid in month incurred):

January	February	March
$160,000	$165,000	$145,000

The cash budget for Elite Accessories is shown in Exhibit 19.

The estimated cash receipts include the total receipts from sales on account (Exhibit 17) and interest revenue. The estimated cash payments include the cash payments from manufacturing costs (Exhibit 18), selling and administrative expenses, capital additions, interest expense, and income taxes. In addition, assume that the minimum cash balance is $340,000.

Exhibit 19 indicates that Elite Accessories expects a cash excess at the end of January of $28,500. This excess could be invested in temporary income-producing securities such as U.S. Treasury bills or notes. In contrast, the estimated cash deficiency at the end of February of $5,500 might require Elite Accessories to borrow cash from its bank.

EXHIBIT 19
Cash Budget

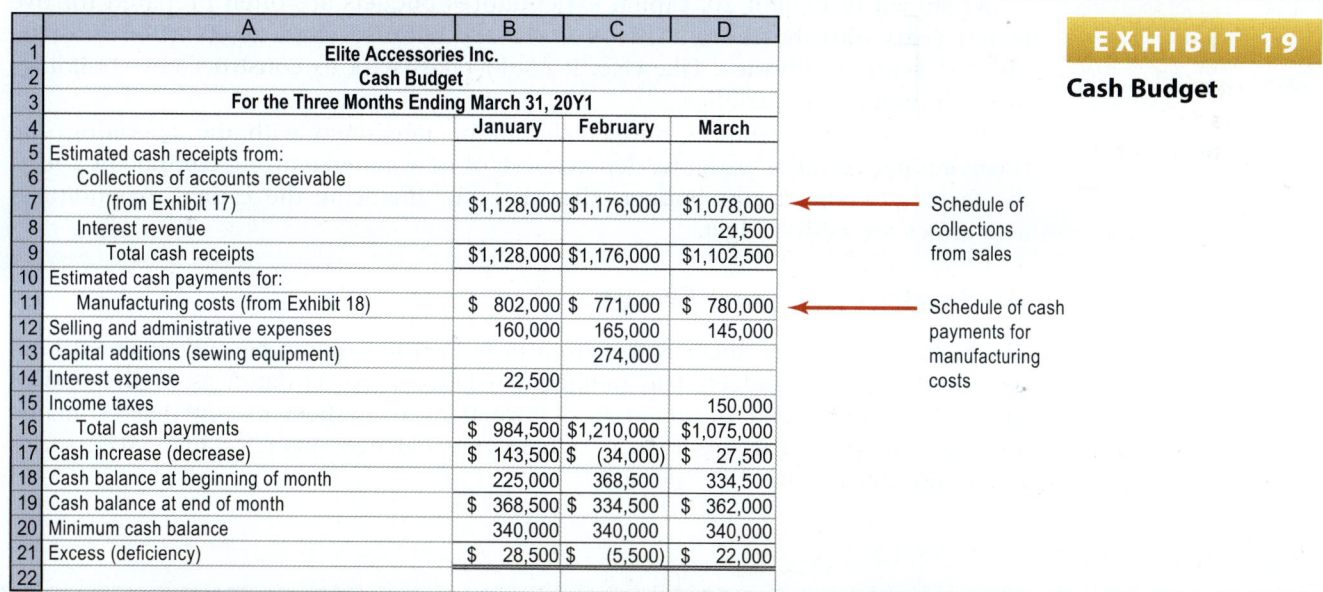

	A	B	C	D
1		Elite Accessories Inc.		
2		Cash Budget		
3		For the Three Months Ending March 31, 20Y1		
4		January	February	March
5	Estimated cash receipts from:			
6	Collections of accounts receivable			
7	(from Exhibit 17)	$1,128,000	$1,176,000	$1,078,000
8	Interest revenue			24,500
9	Total cash receipts	$1,128,000	$1,176,000	$1,102,500
10	Estimated cash payments for:			
11	Manufacturing costs (from Exhibit 18)	$ 802,000	$ 771,000	$ 780,000
12	Selling and administrative expenses	160,000	165,000	145,000
13	Capital additions (sewing equipment)		274,000	
14	Interest expense	22,500		
15	Income taxes			150,000
16	Total cash payments	$ 984,500	$1,210,000	$1,075,000
17	Cash increase (decrease)	$ 143,500	$ (34,000)	$ 27,500
18	Cash balance at beginning of month	225,000	368,500	334,500
19	Cash balance at end of month	$ 368,500	$ 334,500	$ 362,000
20	Minimum cash balance	340,000	340,000	340,000
21	Excess (deficiency)	$ 28,500	$ (5,500)	$ 22,000

Schedule of collections from sales

Schedule of cash payments for manufacturing costs

Example Exercise 22-6 Cash Budget Obj. 5

Landon Awards Co. collects 25% of its sales on account in the month of the sale and 75% in the month following the sale. If sales on account are budgeted to be $100,000 for March and $126,000 for April, what are the budgeted cash receipts from sales on account for April?

Follow My Example 22-6

	April
Collections from March sales (75% × $100,000)	$ 75,000
Collections from April sales (25% × $126,000)	31,500
Total receipts from sales on account	$106,500

Practice Exercises: PE 22-6A, PE 22-6B

Capital Expenditures Budget

The **capital expenditures budget** summarizes plans for acquiring fixed assets. Such expenditures are necessary as machinery and other fixed assets wear out or become obsolete. In addition, purchasing additional fixed assets may be necessary to meet increasing demand for the company's product.

To illustrate, a five-year capital expenditures budget for **Elite Accessories Inc.** is shown in Exhibit 20.

EXHIBIT 20
Capital Expenditures Budget

	A	B	C	D	E	F
1		Elite Accessories Inc.				
2		Capital Expenditures Budget				
3		For the Five Years Ending December 31, 20Y5				
4	Item	20Y1	20Y2	20Y3	20Y4	20Y5
5	Machinery—Cutting Department	$400,000			$280,000	$360,000
6	Machinery—Sewing Department	274,000	$260,000	$560,000	200,000	
7	Office equipment		90,000			60,000
8	Total	$674,000	$350,000	$560,000	$480,000	$420,000

As shown in Exhibit 20, capital expenditures budgets are often prepared for five to ten years into the future. This is necessary because fixed assets often must be ordered years in advance. Likewise, it could take years to construct new buildings or other production facilities.

The capital expenditures budget should be integrated with the operating and financing budgets. For example, depreciation of new manufacturing equipment affects the factory overhead cost budget. The plans for financing the capital expenditures also affect the cash budget.

Budgeted Balance Sheet

The budgeted balance sheet is prepared based on the operating and financial budgets of the master budget. The budgeted balance sheet is dated as of the end of the budget period and is similar to a normal balance sheet except that estimated amounts are used. For this reason, a budgeted balance sheet for Elite Accessories Inc. is not illustrated.

At a Glance 22

Obj. 1 Describe budgeting, its objectives, and its impact on human behavior.

Key Points Budgeting involves (1) establishing plans (planning), (2) directing operations (directing), and (3) evaluating performance (controlling). In addition, budgets should be established to avoid human behavior problems.

Learning Outcomes	Example Exercises	Practice Exercises
• Describe the planning, directing, controlling, and feedback elements of the budget process.		
• Describe the behavioral issues associated with tight goals, loose goals, and goal conflict.		

Obj. 2 Describe the basic elements of the budget process, the two major types of budgeting, and the use of computers in budgeting.

Key Points The budget estimates received by the budget committee should be carefully studied, analyzed, revised, and integrated. The static and flexible budgets are two major budgeting approaches. Computers can be used to make the budget process more efficient and organizationally integrated.

Learning Outcomes	Example Exercises	Practice Exercises
• Describe a static budget and explain when it might be used.		
• Describe and prepare a flexible budget and explain when it might be used.	EE22-1	PE22-1A, 22-1B
• Describe the role of computers in the budget process.		

Obj. 3 Describe the master budget for a manufacturing company.

Key Points The master budget consists of operating and financial budgets.

Learning Outcome	Example Exercises	Practice Exercises
• Illustrate the connection between the major operating and financial budgets.		

Obj. 4 Prepare the basic operating budgets for a manufacturing company.

Key Points The basic operating budgets are the sales budget, production budget, direct materials purchases budget, direct labor cost budget, factory overhead cost budget, cost of goods sold budget, and selling and administrative expenses budget. These can then be combined to prepare an income statement budget.

Learning Outcomes	Example Exercises	Practice Exercises
• Prepare a sales budget.		
• Prepare a production budget.	EE22-2	PE22-2A, 22-2B
• Prepare a direct materials purchases budget.	EE22-3	PE22-3A, 22-3B
• Prepare a direct labor cost budget.	EE22-4	PE22-4A, 22-4B
• Prepare a factory overhead cost budget.		
• Prepare a cost of goods sold budget.	EE22-5	PE22-5A, 22-5B
• Prepare a selling and administrative expenses budget.		
• Prepare an income statement budget.		

Obj. 5 Prepare financial budgets for a manufacturing company.

Key Points The cash budget and capital expenditures budget are financial budgets showing the investing and financing activities of the firm.

Learning Outcomes	Example Exercises	Practice Exercises
• Prepare cash receipts and cash payments schedules.	EE22-6	PE22-6A, 22-6B
• Prepare a cash budget.		
• Prepare a capital expenditures budget.		

Illustrative Problem

Selected information concerning sales and production for Cabot Co. for July are summarized as follows:

a. Estimated sales:

   Product K: 40,000 units at $30 per unit
   Product L: 20,000 units at $65 per unit

b. Estimated inventories, July 1:

Material A:	4,000 lb.	Product K:	3,000 units at $17 per unit	$ 51,000
Material B:	3,500 lb.	Product L:	2,700 units at $35 per unit	94,500
		Total		$145,500

   There were no work in process inventories estimated for July 1.

c. Desired inventories at July 31:

Material A:	3,000 lb.	Product K:	2,500 units at $17 per unit	$ 42,500
Material B:	2,500 lb.	Product L:	2,000 units at $35 per unit	70,000
		Total		$112,500

   There were no work in process inventories desired for July 31.

d. Direct materials used in production:

	Product K	Product L
Material A	0.7 lb. per unit	3.5 lb. per unit
Material B	1.2 lb. per unit	1.8 lb. per unit

e. Unit costs for direct materials:

   Material A: $4.00 per lb.
   Material B: $2.00 per lb.

f. Direct labor requirements:

	Department 1	Department 2
Product K	0.4 hr. per unit	0.15 hr. per unit
Product L	0.6 hr. per unit	0.25 hr. per unit

g.
	Department 1	Department 2
Direct labor rate	$12.00 per hr.	$16.00 per hr.

h. Estimated factory overhead costs for July:

Indirect factory wages	$200,000
Depreciation of plant and equipment	40,000
Power and light	25,000
Indirect materials	34,000
Total	$299,000

Instructions

1. Prepare a sales budget for July.
2. Prepare a production budget for July.
3. Prepare a direct materials purchases budget for July.
4. Prepare a direct labor cost budget for July.
5. Prepare a cost of goods sold budget for July.

Solution

1.

	A	B	C	D
1		Cabot Co.		
2		Sales Budget		
3		For the Month Ending July 31		
4	Product	Unit Sales Volume	Unit Selling Price	Total Sales
5	Product K	40,000	$30.00	$1,200,000
6	Product L	20,000	65.00	1,300,000
7	Total revenue from sales			$2,500,000
8				

2.

	A	B	C
1		Cabot Co.	
2		Production Budget	
3		For the Month Ending July 31	
4		Units	
5		Product K	Product L
6	Expected units to be sold	40,000	20,000
7	Plus desired ending inventory, July 31	2,500	2,000
8	Total units required	42,500	22,000
9	Less estimated beginning inventory, July 1	3,000	2,700
10	Total units to be produced	39,500	19,300
11			

3.

	A	B	C	D
1		Cabot Co.		
2		Direct Materials Purchases Budget		
3		For the Month Ending July 31		
4		Direct Materials		
5		Material A	Material B	Total
6	Pounds required for production:			
7	Product K (39,500 × lb. per unit)	27,650 lb.*	47,400 lb.*	
8	Product L (19,300 × lb. per unit)	67,550 **	34,740 **	
9	Plus desired ending inventory,			
10	July 31	3,000	2,500	
11	Total pounds required	98,200 lb.	84,640 lb.	
12	Less estimated beginning inventory,			
13	July 1	4,000	3,500	
14	Total pounds to be purchased	94,200 lb.	81,140 lb.	
15	Unit price (per pound)	× $4.00	× $2.00	
16	Total direct materials to be purchased	$376,800	$162,280	$539,080
17				
18	*27,650 = 39,500 × 0.7 47,400 = 39,500 × 1.2			
19	**67,550 = 19,300 × 3.5 34,740 = 19,300 × 1.8			
20				

(Continued)

4.

	A	B	C	D
1		Cabot Co.		
2		Direct Labor Cost Budget		
3		For the Month Ending July 31		
4		Department 1	Department 2	Total
5	Hours required for production:			
6	Product K (39,500 × hrs. per unit)	15,800 *	5,925 *	
7	Product L (19,300 × hrs. per unit)	11,580 **	4,825 **	
8	Total hours required	27,380	10,750	
9	Hourly rate	×$12.00	×$16.00	
10	Total direct labor cost	$328,560	$172,000	$500,560
11				
12	*15,800 = 39,500 × 0.4 5,925 = 39,500 × 0.15			
13	**11,580 = 19,300 × 0.6 4,825 = 19,300 × 0.25			
14				

5.

	A	B	C	D
1		Cabot Co.		
2		Cost of Goods Sold Budget		
3		For the Month Ending July 31		
4	Finished goods inventory, July 1			$ 145,500
5	Direct materials:			
6	Direct materials inventory, July 1 (Note A)		$ 23,000	
7	Direct materials purchases		539,080	
8	Cost of direct materials available for use		$562,080	
9	Less direct materials inventory, July 31 (Note B)		17,000	
10	Cost of direct materials placed in production		$545,080	
11	Direct labor		500,560	
12	Factory overhead		299,000	
13	Cost of goods manufactured			1,344,640
14	Cost of finished goods available for sale			$1,490,140
15	Less finished goods inventory, July 31			112,500
16	Cost of goods sold			$1,377,640
17				
18	Note A:			
19	Material A 4,000 lb. at $4.00 per lb.		$16,000	
20	Material B 3,500 lb. at $2.00 per lb.		7,000	
21	Direct materials inventory, July 1		$23,000	
22				
23	Note B:			
24	Material A 3,000 lb. at $4.00 per lb.		$12,000	
25	Material B 2,500 lb. at $2.00 per lb.		5,000	
26	Direct materials inventory, July 31		$17,000	
27				

Key Terms

budget (1076)
budgetary slack (1077)
capital expenditures budget (1095)
cash budget (1092)
continuous budgeting (1078)
cost of goods sold budget (1088)

direct labor cost budget (1086)
direct materials purchases budget (1084)
factory overhead cost budget (1088)
flexible budget (1080)
goal conflict (1077)

master budget (1082)
production budget (1084)
responsibility center (1077)
sales budget (1082)
static budget (1079)
zero-based budgeting (1079)

Discussion Questions

1. What are the three major objectives of budgeting?
2. Briefly describe the type of human behavior problems that might arise if budget goals are set too tightly.
3. What behavioral problems are associated with setting a budget too loosely?
4. What behavioral problems are associated with establishing conflicting goals within the budget?
5. Under what circumstances is a static budget appropriate?
6. How do computerized budgeting systems aid firms in the budgeting process?
7. Why should the production requirements set forth in the production budget be carefully coordinated with the sales budget?
8. Why should the timing of direct materials purchases be closely coordinated with the production budget?
9. a. Discuss the purpose of the cash budget.
   b. If the cash for the first quarter of the fiscal year indicates excess cash at the end of each of the first two months, how might the excess cash be used?
10. Give an example of how the capital expenditures budget affects other operating budgets.

Practice Exercises

Example Exercises

EE 22-1 p. 1081   **PE 22-1A**   **Flexible budgeting**   OBJ. 2

At the beginning of the period, the Assembly Department budgeted direct labor of $120,000 and property tax of $16,000 for 5,000 hours of production. The department actually completed 5,600 hours of production. Determine the budget for the department, assuming that it uses flexible budgeting.

EE 22-1 p. 1081   **PE 22-1B**   **Flexible budgeting**   OBJ. 2

At the beginning of the period, the Fabricating Department budgeted direct labor of $9,280 and equipment depreciation of $2,300 for 640 hours of production. The department actually completed 600 hours of production. Determine the budget for the department, assuming that it uses flexible budgeting.

EE 22-2 p. 1084   **PE 22-2A**   **Production budget**   OBJ. 4

Daybook Inc. projected sales of 400,000 personal journals for 20Y6. The estimated January 1, 20Y6, inventory is 20,000 units, and the desired December 31, 20Y6, inventory is 23,500 units. What is the budgeted production (in units) for 20Y6?

EE 22-2 p. 1084   **PE 22-2B**   **Production budget**   OBJ. 4

Magnolia Candle Inc. projected sales of 75,000 candles for 20Y4. The estimated January 1, 20Y4, inventory is 3,500 units, and the desired December 31, 20Y4, inventory is 2,700 units. What is the budgeted production (in units) for 20Y4?

EE 22-3 p. 1086   **PE 22-3A**   **Direct materials purchases budget**   OBJ. 4

Daybook Inc. budgeted production of 403,500 personal journals in 20Y6. Paper is required to produce a journal. Assume six square yards of paper are required for each journal. The estimated January 1, 20Y6, paper inventory is 40,400 square yards. The desired December 31, 20Y6, paper inventory is 38,900 square yards. If paper costs $0.40 per square yard, determine the direct materials purchases budget for 20Y6.

1102   Chapter 22   Budgeting

EE 22-3 *p. 1086*

PE 22-3B   Direct materials purchases budget   OBJ. 4

Magnolia Candle Inc. budgeted production of 74,200 candles in 20Y4. Wax is required to produce a candle. Assume that eight ounces (one-half of a pound) of wax is required for each candle. The estimated January 1, 20Y4, wax inventory is 2,500 pounds. The desired December 31, 20Y4, wax inventory is 2,100 pounds. If candle wax costs $4.10 per pound, determine the direct materials purchases budget for 20Y4.

EE 22-4 *p. 1088*

PE 22-4A   Direct labor cost budget   OBJ. 4

Daybook Inc. budgeted production of 403,500 personal journals in 20Y6. Each journal requires assembly. Assume that eight minutes are required to assemble each journal. If assembly labor costs $13.00 per hour, determine the direct labor cost budget for 20Y6.

EE 22-4 *p. 1088*

PE 22-4B   Direct labor cost budget   OBJ. 4

Magnolia Candle Inc. budgeted production of 74,200 candles in 20Y4. Each candle requires molding. Assume that 12 minutes are required to mold each candle. If molding labor costs $14.00 per hour, determine the direct labor cost budget for 20Y4.

EE 22-5 *p. 1089*

PE 22-5A   Cost of goods sold budget   OBJ. 4

Prepare a cost of goods sold budget for Daybook Inc. using the information in Practice Exercises 22-3A and 22-4A. Assume the estimated inventories on January 1, 20Y6, for finished goods and work in process were $28,000 and $16,500, respectively. Also assume the desired inventories on December 31, 20Y6, for finished goods and work in process were $30,000 and $14,300, respectively. Factory overhead was budgeted at $214,600.

EE 22-5 *p. 1089*

PE 22-5B   Cost of goods sold budget   OBJ. 4

Prepare a cost of goods sold budget for Magnolia Candle Inc. using the information in Practice Exercises 22-3B and 22-4B. Assume that the estimated inventories on January 1, 20Y4, for finished goods and work in process were $9,800 and $3,600, respectively. Also assume that the desired inventories on December 31, 20Y4, for finished goods and work in process were $12,900 and $3,500, respectively. Factory overhead was budgeted at $109,600.

EE 22-6 *p. 1095*

PE 22-6A   Cash budget   OBJ. 5

Daybook Inc. collects 30% of its sales on account in the month of the sale and 70% in the month following the sale. If sales on account are budgeted to be $105,000 for September and $116,000 for October, what are the budgeted cash receipts from sales on account for October?

EE 22-6 *p. 1095*

PE 22-6B   Cash budget   OBJ. 5

Magnolia Candle Inc. pays 10% of its purchases on account in the month of the purchase and 90% in the month following the purchase. If purchases are budgeted to be $11,900 for March and $12,700 for April, what are the budgeted cash payments for purchases on account for April?

Exercises

EX 22-1 Personal budget
OBJ. 2, 5

✔ a. December 31 cash balance, $3,000

At the beginning of the school year, Katherine Malloy decided to prepare a cash budget for the months of September, October, November, and December. The budget must plan for enough cash on December 31 to pay the spring semester tuition, which is the same as the fall tuition. The following information relates to the budget:

Cash balance, September 1 (from a summer job)...............	$5,750
Purchase season football tickets in September.................	210
Additional entertainment for each month.....................	275
Pay fall semester tuition in September.......................	3,700
Pay rent at the beginning of each month.....................	600
Pay for food each month...................................	235
Pay apartment deposit on September 2 (to be returned December 15)	500
Part-time job earnings each month (net of taxes)	1,400

a. Prepare a cash budget for September, October, November, and December.
b. Are the four monthly budgets that are presented prepared as static budgets or flexible budgets?
c. What are the budget implications for Katherine Malloy?

EX 22-2 Flexible budget for selling and administrative expenses for a service company
OBJ. 2, 4

✔ Total selling and administrative expenses at $400,000 sales, $309,000

Morningside Technologies Inc. uses flexible budgets that are based on the following data:

Sales commissions	15% of sales
Advertising expense.........................	12% of sales
Miscellaneous administrative expense	$8,000 per month plus 10% of sales
Office salaries expense	$32,000 per month
Customer support expenses...................	$14,000 per month plus 18% of sales
Research and development expense...........	$35,000 per month

Prepare a flexible selling and administrative expenses budget for April for sales volumes of $400,000, $500,000, and $600,000.

EX 22-3 Static budget versus flexible budget
OBJ. 2, 4

✔ b. Excess of actual cost over budget for March, $45,750

The production supervisor of the Machining Department for Niland Company agreed to the following monthly static budget for the upcoming year:

Niland Company
Machining Department
Monthly Production Budget

Wages...	$1,125,000
Utilities..	90,000
Depreciation...	50,000
Total	$1,265,000

The actual amount spent and the actual units produced in the first three months in the Machining Department were as follows:

	Amount Spent	Units Produced
January	$1,100,000	80,000
February	1,200,000	90,000
March	1,250,000	95,000

(Continued)

1104 Chapter 22 Budgeting

The Machining Department supervisor has been very pleased with this performance because actual expenditures for January–March have been less than the monthly static budget of $1,265,000. However, the plant manager believes that the budget should not remain fixed for every month but should "flex" or adjust to the volume of work that is produced in the Machining Department. Additional budget information for the Machining Department is as follows:

Wages per hour	$15.00
Utility cost per direct labor hour	$1.20
Direct labor hours per unit	0.75
Planned monthly unit production	100,000

a. Prepare a flexible budget for the actual units produced for January, February, and March in the Machining Department. Assume that depreciation is a fixed cost.

b. Compare the flexible budget with the actual expenditures for the first three months. What does this comparison suggest?

EX 22-4 Flexible budget for Assembly Department OBJ. 2

✔ Total department cost at 18,000 units, $253,700

Steelcase Inc. is one of the largest manufacturers of office furniture in the United States. In Grand Rapids, Michigan, it assembles filing cabinets in an Assembly Department. Assume the following information for the Assembly Department:

Direct labor per filing cabinet	12 minutes
Supervisor salaries	$150,000 per month
Depreciation	$24,500 per month
Direct labor rate	$22 per hour

Prepare a flexible budget for 18,000, 20,000, and 22,000 filing cabinets for the month of August in the Assembly Department, similar to Exhibit 5.

EX 22-5 Production budget OBJ. 4

✔ Bath scale budgeted production, 144,500 units

Weightless Inc. produces a small and large version of its popular electronic scale. The anticipated unit sales for the scales by sales region are as follows:

	Bath Scale	Gym Scale
East Region unit sales	55,000	30,000
West Region unit sales	95,000	60,000
Total	150,000	90,000

The finished goods inventory estimated for October 1 for the Bath and Gym scale models is 18,000 and 10,000 units, respectively. The desired finished goods inventory for October 31 for the Bath and Gym scale models is 12,500 and 8,000 units, respectively.

Prepare a production budget for the Bath and Gym scales for the month ended October 31.

EX 22-6 Sales and production budgets OBJ. 4

✔ b. Model Rumble total production, 25,750 units

Sonic Inc. manufactures two models of speakers, Rumble and Thunder. Based on the following production and sales data for June, prepare (a) a sales budget and (b) a production budget:

	Rumble	Thunder
Estimated inventory (units), June 1	750	300
Desired inventory (units), June 30	500	250
Expected sales volume (units):		
East Region	12,000	3,500
West Region	14,000	4,000
Unit sales price	$160	$200

Chapter 22 Budgeting

✔ Total professional fees earned, $10,270,000

EX 22-7 Professional fees earned budget for a service company OBJ. 4

Rollins and Cohen, CPAs, offer three types of services to clients: auditing, tax, and small business accounting. Based on experience and projected growth, the following billable hours have been estimated for the year ending December 31, 20Y7:

	Billable Hours
Audit Department:	
Staff	22,400
Partners	7,900
Tax Department:	
Staff	13,200
Partners	5,500
Small Business Accounting Department:	
Staff	3,000
Partners	600

The average billing rate for staff is $150 per hour, and the average billing rate for partners is $320 per hour. Prepare a professional fees earned budget for Rollins and Cohen, CPAs, for the year ending December 31, 20Y7, using the following column headings and showing the estimated professional fees by type of service rendered:

Billable Hours	Hourly Rate	Total Revenue

EX 22-8 Professional labor cost budget for a service company OBJ. 4

✔ Staff total labor cost, $1,737,000

Based on the data in Exercise 22-7 and assuming that the average compensation per hour for staff is $45 and for partners is $140, prepare a professional labor cost budget for each department for Rollins and Cohen, CPAs, for the year ending December 31, 20Y7. Use the following column headings:

Staff	Partners

EX 22-9 Direct materials purchases budget OBJ. 4

✔ Total cheese purchases, $96,603

Lorenzo's Frozen Pizza Inc. has determined from its production budget the following estimated production volumes for 12" and 16" frozen pizzas for September:

	Units	
	12" Pizza	16" Pizza
Budgeted production volume	12,500	21,800

Three direct materials are used in producing the two types of pizza. The quantities of direct materials expected to be used for each pizza are as follows:

	12" Pizza	16" Pizza
Direct materials:		
Dough	0.80 lb. per unit	1.50 lb. per unit
Tomato	0.50	0.70
Cheese	0.70	1.30

In addition, Lorenzo's has determined the following information about each material:

	Dough	Tomato	Cheese
Estimated inventory, September 1	490 lb.	230 lb.	275 lb.
Desired inventory, September 30	580 lb.	185 lb.	340 lb.
Price per pound	$0.50	$2.20	$2.60

Prepare September's direct materials purchases budget for Lorenzo's Frozen Pizza Inc.

1106 Chapter 22 Budgeting

✔ Concentrate budgeted purchases, $47,400

EX 22-10 Direct materials purchases budget   OBJ. 4

Coca-Cola Enterprises is the largest bottler of Coca-Cola® in Western Europe. The company purchases Coke® and Sprite® concentrate from **The Coca-Cola Company**, dilutes and mixes the concentrate with carbonated water, and then fills the blended beverage into cans or plastic two-liter bottles. Assume that the estimated production for Coke and Sprite two-liter bottles at the Wakefield, UK, bottling plant is as follows for the month of May:

Coke	153,000 two-liter bottles
Sprite	86,500 two-liter bottles

In addition, assume that the concentrate costs $75 per pound for both Coke and Sprite and is used at a rate of 0.15 pound per 100 liters of carbonated water in blending Coke and 0.10 pound per 100 liters of carbonated water in blending Sprite. Assume that two liters of carbonated water are used for each two-liter bottle of finished product. Assume further that two-liter bottles cost $0.08 per bottle and carbonated water costs $0.06 per liter.

Prepare a direct materials purchases budget for May, assuming that inventories are ignored, because there are no changes between beginning and ending inventories for concentrate, bottles, and carbonated water.

✔ Total steel belt purchases, $291,200

EX 22-11 Direct materials purchases budget   OBJ. 4

Anticipated sales for Safety Grip Company were 42,000 passenger car tires and 19,000 truck tires. Rubber and steel belts are used in producing passenger car and truck tires as follows:

	Passenger Car	Truck
Rubber	35 lb. per unit	78 lb. per unit
Steel belts	5 lb. per unit	8 lb. per unit

The purchase prices of rubber and steel are $1.20 and $0.80 per pound, respectively. The desired ending inventories of rubber and steel belts are 40,000 and 10,000 pounds, respectively. The estimated beginning inventories for rubber and steel belts are 46,000 and 8,000 pounds, respectively.

Prepare a direct materials purchases budget for Safety Grip Company for the year ended December 31, 20Y8.

✔ Total direct labor cost, Assembly, $30,660

EX 22-12 Direct labor cost budget   OBJ. 4

MatchPoint Racket Company manufactures two types of tennis rackets, the Junior and Pro Striker models. The production budget for March for the two rackets is as follows:

	Junior	Pro Striker
Production budget	2,200 units	7,000 units

Both rackets are produced in two departments, Forming and Assembly. The direct labor hours required for each racket are estimated as follows:

	Forming Department	Assembly Department
Junior	0.10 hour per unit	0.20 hour per unit
Pro Striker	0.15 hour per unit	0.25 hour per unit

The direct labor rate for each department is as follows:

Forming Department	$15.00 per hour
Assembly Department	$14.00 per hour

Prepare the direct labor cost budget for March.

Chapter 22 Budgeting 1107

✔ Average weekday total, $2,640

EX 22-13 Direct labor budget for a service business OBJ. 4

Ambassador Suites Inc. operates a downtown hotel property that has 300 rooms. On average, 80% of Ambassador Suites' rooms are occupied on weekdays and 40% are occupied during the weekend. The manager has asked you to develop a direct labor budget for the housekeeping and restaurant staff for weekdays and weekends. You have determined that the housekeeping staff requires 30 minutes to clean each occupied room. The housekeeping staff is paid $14 per hour. The housekeeping labor cost is fully variable to the number of occupied rooms. The restaurant has six full-time staff (eight-hour day) on duty, regardless of occupancy. However, for every 60 occupied rooms, an additional person is brought in to work in the restaurant for the eight-hour day. The restaurant staff is paid $12 per hour.

Determine the estimated housekeeping, restaurant, and total direct labor cost for an average weekday and average weekend day. Format the budget in two columns, labeled as weekday and weekend day.

EX 22-14 Production and direct labor cost budgets OBJ. 4

✔ a. Total production of 501 Jeans, 53,300

Levi Strauss & Co. manufactures slacks and jeans under a variety of brand names, such as Dockers® and 501® Jeans. Slacks and jeans are assembled by a variety of different sewing operations. Assume that the sales budget for Dockers and 501 Jeans shows estimated sales of 23,600 and 53,100 pairs, respectively, for May. The finished goods inventory is assumed as follows:

	Dockers	501 Jeans
May 1 estimated inventory	670	1,660
May 31 desired inventory	420	1,860

Assume the following direct labor data per 10 pairs of Dockers and 501 Jeans for four different sewing operations:

	Direct Labor per 10 Pairs	
	Dockers	501 Jeans
Inseam	18 minutes	9 minutes
Outerseam	20	14
Pockets	6	9
Zipper	12	6
Total	56 minutes	38 minutes

a. Prepare a production budget for May. Prepare the budget in two columns: Dockers® and 501 Jeans®.

b. Prepare the May direct labor cost budget for the four sewing operations, assuming a $13 wage per hour for the inseam and outerseam sewing operations and a $15 wage per hour for the pocket and zipper sewing operations. Prepare the direct labor cost budget in four columns: inseam, outerseam, pockets, and zipper.

EX 22-15 Factory overhead cost budget OBJ. 4

✔ Total variable factory overhead costs, $268,000

Sweet Tooth Candy Company budgeted the following costs for anticipated production for August:

Advertising expenses	$232,000	Production supervisor wages	$135,000
Manufacturing supplies	14,000	Production control wages	32,000
Power and light	48,000	Executive officer salaries	310,000
Sales commissions	298,000	Materials management wages	39,000
Factory insurance	30,000	Factory depreciation	22,000

Prepare a factory overhead cost budget, separating variable and fixed costs. Assume that factory insurance and depreciation are the only fixed factory costs.

1108   Chapter 22   Budgeting

✔ Cost of goods sold, $3,293,600

EX 22-16 Cost of goods sold budget   OBJ. 4

Wilmington Chemical Company uses oil to produce two types of plastic products, P1 and P2. Wilmington budgeted 50,000 barrels of oil for purchase in June for $50 per barrel. Direct labor budgeted in the chemical process was $300,000 for June. Factory overhead was budgeted $500,000 during June. The inventories on June 1 were estimated to be:

Oil	$15,500
P1	25,400
P2	22,900
Work in process	3,400

The desired inventories on June 30 were:

Oil	$16,100
P1	28,500
P2	25,000
Work in process	4,000

Use the preceding information to prepare a cost of goods sold budget for June.

EX 22-17 Cost of goods sold budget   OBJ. 4

✔ Cost of goods sold, $488,360

The controller of MingWare Ceramics Inc. wants to prepare a cost of goods sold budget for September. The controller assembled the following information for constructing the cost of goods sold budget:

Direct materials:	Enamel	Paint	Porcelain	Total
Total direct materials purchases budgeted for September	$36,780	$6,130	$145,500	$188,410
Estimated inventory, September 1	1,240	950	4,250	6,440
Desired inventory, September 30	1,890	1,070	5,870	8,830

Direct labor cost:	Kiln Department	Decorating Department	Total
Total direct labor cost budgeted for September	$47,900	$145,700	$193,600

Finished goods inventories:	Dish	Bowl	Figurine	Total
Estimated inventory, September 1	$5,780	$3,080	$2,640	$11,500
Desired inventory, September 30	3,710	2,670	3,290	9,670

Work in process inventories:	
Estimated inventory, September 1	$3,400
Desired inventory, September 30	1,990

Budgeted factory overhead costs for September:	
Indirect factory wages	$ 81,900
Depreciation of plant and equipment	14,300
Power and light	5,200
Indirect materials	4,100
Total	$105,500

Use the preceding information to prepare a cost of goods sold budget for September.

EX 22-18 Schedule of cash collections of accounts receivable   OBJ. 5

✔ Total cash collected in July, $177,550

Furry Friends Supplies Inc., a pet wholesale supplier, was organized on May 1. Projected sales for each of the first three months of operations are as follows:

May	$156,000
June	175,000
July	180,000

All sales are on account. Seventy percent of sales are expected to be collected in the month of the sale, 25% in the month following the sale, and the remainder in the second month following the sale.

Prepare a schedule indicating cash collections from sales for May, June, and July.

EX 22-19 Schedule of cash collections of accounts receivable OBJ. 5

✔ Total cash collected in October, $675,000

Office World Inc. has "cash and carry" customers and credit customers. Office World estimates that 25% of monthly sales are to cash customers, while the remaining sales are to credit customers. Of the credit customers, 40% pay their accounts in the month of sale, while the remaining 60% pay their accounts in the month following the month of sale. Projected sales for the next three months are as follows:

October	$700,000
November	650,000
December	500,000

The Accounts Receivable balance on September 30 was $290,000.

Prepare a schedule of cash collections from sales for October, November, and December.

EX 22-20 Schedule of cash payments for a service company OBJ. 5

✔ Total cash payments in May, $82,880

SafeMark Financial Inc. was organized on February 28. Projected selling and administrative expenses for each of the first three months of operations are as follows:

March	$78,400
April	83,500
May	96,900

Depreciation, insurance, and property taxes represent $10,000 of the estimated monthly expenses. The annual insurance premium was paid on February 28, and property taxes for the year will be paid in June. Seventy percent of the remainder of the expenses are expected to be paid in the month in which they are incurred, with the balance to be paid in the following month.

Prepare a schedule indicating cash payments for selling and administrative expenses for March, April, and May.

EX 22-21 Schedule of cash payments for a service company OBJ. 5

✔ Total cash payments in March, $113,740

EastGate Physical Therapy Inc. is planning its cash payments for operations for the first quarter (January–March). The Accrued Expenses Payable balance on January 1 is $15,000. The budgeted expenses for the next three months are as follows:

Excel

	January	February	March
Salaries	$56,900	$ 68,100	$ 72,200
Utilities	2,400	2,600	2,500
Other operating expenses	32,300	41,500	44,700
Total	$91,600	$112,200	$119,400

Other operating expenses include $3,000 of monthly depreciation expense and $500 of monthly insurance expense that was prepaid for the year on May 1 of the previous year. Of the remaining expenses, 70% are paid in the month in which they are incurred, with the remainder paid in the following month. The Accrued Expenses Payable balance on January 1 relates to the expenses incurred in December.

Prepare a schedule of cash payments for operations for January, February, and March.

1110 Chapter 22 Budgeting

✔ Total capital expenditures in 20Y2, $4,000,000

EX 22-22 Capital expenditures budget
OBJ. 5

On January 1, 20Y2, the controller of Omicron Inc. is planning capital expenditures for the years 20Y2–20Y5. The following interviews helped the controller collect the necessary information for the capital expenditures budget:

Director of Facilities: A construction contract was signed in late 20Y1 for the construction of a new factory building at a contract cost of $10,000,000. The construction is scheduled to begin in 20Y2 and be completed in 20Y3.

Vice President of Manufacturing: Once the new factory building is finished, we plan to purchase $1.5 million in equipment in late 20Y3. I expect that an additional $200,000 will be needed early in the following year (20Y4) to test and install the equipment before we can begin production. If sales continue to grow, I expect we'll need to invest another $1,000,000 in equipment in 20Y5.

Chief Operating Officer: We have really been growing lately. I wouldn't be surprised if we need to expand the size of our new factory building in 20Y5 by at least 35%. Fortunately, we expect inflation to have minimal impact on construction costs over the next four years. In addition, I would expect the cost of the expansion to be proportional to the size of the expansion.

Director of Information Systems: We need to upgrade our information systems to wireless network technology. It doesn't make sense to do this until after the new factory building is completed and producing product. During 20Y4, once the factory is up and running, we should equip the whole facility with wireless technology. I think it would cost us $800,000 today to install the technology. However, prices have been dropping by 25% per year, so it should be less expensive at a later date.

Chief Financial Officer: I am excited about our long-term prospects. My only short-term concern is managing our cash flow while we expend the $4,000,000 of construction costs on the portion of the new factory building scheduled to be completed in 20Y2.

Use this interview information to prepare a capital expenditures budget for Omicron Inc. for the years 20Y2–20Y5.

Problems: Series A

✔ 3. Total revenue from sales, $878,403

PR 22-1A Forecast sales volume and sales budget
OBJ. 4

For 20Y6, Raphael Frame Company prepared the sales budget that follows.

At the end of December 20Y6, the following unit sales data were reported for the year:

	Unit Sales	
	8" × 10" Frame	12" × 16" Frame
East	8,755	3,686
Central	6,510	3,090
West	12,348	5,616

Raphael Frame Company
Sales Budget
For the Year Ending December 31, 20Y6

Product and Area	Unit Sales Volume	Unit Selling Price	Total Sales
8" × 10" Frame:			
East	8,500	$16	$136,000
Central	6,200	16	99,200
West	12,600	16	201,600
Total	27,300		$436,800
12" × 16" Frame:			
East	3,800	$30	$114,000
Central	3,000	30	90,000
West	5,400	30	162,000
Total	12,200		$366,000
Total revenue from sales			$802,800

For the year ending December 31, 20Y7, unit sales are expected to follow the patterns established during the year ending December 31, 20Y6. The unit selling price for the 8" × 10" frame is expected to increase to $17, and the unit selling price for the 12" × 16" frame is expected to increase to $32, effective January 1, 20Y7.

Instructions

1. Compute the increase or decrease of actual unit sales for the year ended December 31, 20Y6, over budget. Place your answers in a columnar table with the following format:

	Unit Sales, Year Ended 20Y6		Increase (Decrease) Actual Over Budget	
	Budget	Actual Sales	Amount	Percent
8" × 10" Frame:				
East				
Central				
West				
12" × 16" Frame:				
East				
Central				
West				

2. Assuming that the increase or decrease in actual sales to budget indicated in part (1) is to continue in 20Y7, compute the unit sales volume to be used for preparing the sales budget for the year ending December 31, 20Y7. Place your answers in a columnar table similar to that in part (1) but with the following column heads. Round budgeted units to the nearest unit.

20Y6 Actual Units	Percentage Increase (Decrease)	20Y7 Budgeted Units (rounded)

3. Prepare a sales budget for the year ending December 31, 20Y7.

PR 22-2A Sales, production, direct materials purchases, and direct labor cost budgets   **OBJ. 4**

✔ 3. Total direct materials purchases, $1,183,680

Excel

The budget director of Gourmet Grill Company requests estimates of sales, production, and other operating data from the various administrative units every month. Selected information concerning sales and production for March is summarized as follows:

a. Estimated sales for March by sales territory:

   Maine:
      Backyard Chef .... 350 units at $800 per unit
      Master Chef... 200 units at $1,400 per unit
   Vermont:
      Backyard Chef .... 400 units at $825 per unit
      Master Chef... 240 units at $1,500 per unit
   New Hampshire:
      Backyard Chef .... 320 units at $850 per unit
      Master Chef... 200 units at $1,600 per unit

b. Estimated inventories at March 1:

Direct materials:		Finished products:	
Grates	320 units	Backyard Chef	30 units
Stainless steel	1,700 lb.	Master Chef	36 units
Burner subassemblies	190 units		
Shelves	350 units		

(*Continued*)

c. Desired inventories at March 31:

Direct materials:		Finished products:	
Grates	300 units	Backyard Chef	40 units
Stainless steel	1,500 lb.	Master Chef	26 units
Burner subassemblies	210 units		
Shelves	400 units		

d. Direct materials used in production:

In manufacture of Backyard Chef:
Grates	3 units per unit of product
Stainless steel	24 lb. per unit of product
Burner subassemblies	2 units per unit of product
Shelves	4 units per unit of product

In manufacture of Master Chef:
Grates	6 units per unit of product
Stainless steel	42 lb. per unit of product
Burner subassemblies	4 units per unit of product
Shelves	5 units per unit of product

e. Anticipated purchase price for direct materials:

Grates	$16 per unit	Burner subassemblies	$120 per unit
Stainless steel	$8 per lb.	Shelves	$12 per unit

f. Direct labor requirements:

Backyard Chef:
Stamping Department	0.50 hr. at $18 per hr.
Forming Department	0.60 hr. at $16 per hr.
Assembly Department	1.00 hr. at $15 per hr.

Master Chef:
Stamping Department	0.60 hr. at $18 per hr.
Forming Department	0.80 hr. at $16 per hr.
Assembly Department	1.50 hrs. at $15 per hr.

Instructions

1. Prepare a sales budget for March.
2. Prepare a production budget for March.
3. Prepare a direct materials purchases budget for March.
4. Prepare a direct labor cost budget for March.

PR 22-3A Budgeted income statement and supporting budgets OBJ. 4

✔ 4. Total direct labor cost in Fabrication Dept., $44,880

The budget director of Birds of a Feather Inc., with the assistance of the controller, treasurer, production manager, and sales manager, has gathered the following data for use in developing the budgeted income statement for January:

a. Estimated sales for January:

Birdhouse	6,000 units at $55 per unit
Bird feeder	4,500 units at $75 per unit

b. Estimated inventories at January 1:

Direct materials:		Finished products:	
Wood	220 ft.	Birdhouse	300 units at $23 per unit
Plastic	250 lb.	Bird feeder	240 units at $34 per unit

c. Desired inventories at January 31:

Direct materials:		Finished products:	
Wood	180 ft.	Birdhouse	340 units at $23 per unit
Plastic........	210 lb.	Bird feeder.......	200 units at $34 per unit

d. Direct materials used in production:

In manufacture of Birdhouse:		In manufacture of Bird Feeder:	
Wood	0.80 ft. per unit of product	Wood	1.20 ft. per unit of product
Plastic........	0.50 lb. per unit of product	Plastic...........	0.75 lb. per unit of product

e. Anticipated cost of purchases and beginning and ending inventory of direct materials:

Wood	$8.00 per ft.	Plastic.................	$1.20 per lb.

f. Direct labor requirements:

Birdhouse:
Fabrication Department .... 0.20 hr. at $15 per hr.
Assembly Department... 0.30 hr. at $12 per hr.
Bird Feeder:
Fabrication Department .... 0.40 hr. at $15 per hr.
Assembly Department... 0.35 hr. at $12 per hr.

g. Estimated factory overhead costs for January:

Indirect factory wages	$80,000	Power and light	$8,000
Depreciation of plant and equipment	25,000	Insurance and property tax	2,000

h. Estimated operating expenses for January:

Sales salaries expense	$90,000
Advertising expense	20,000
Office salaries expense	18,000
Depreciation expense—office equipment	800
Telephone expense—selling	500
Telephone expense—administrative	200
Travel expense—selling	5,000
Office supplies expense	250
Miscellaneous administrative expense	450

i. Estimated other income and expense for January:

Interest revenue	$300
Interest expense	224

j. Estimated tax rate: 30%

Instructions

1. Prepare a sales budget for January.
2. Prepare a production budget for January.
3. Prepare a direct materials purchases budget for January.
4. Prepare a direct labor cost budget for January.
5. Prepare a factory overhead cost budget for January.
6. Prepare a cost of goods sold budget for January. Work in process at the beginning of January is estimated to be $29,000, and work in process at the end of January is estimated to be $35,400.
7. Prepare a selling and administrative expenses budget for January.
8. Prepare a budgeted income statement for January.

1114 Chapter 22 Budgeting

✔ 1. July deficiency, $2,200

PR 22-4A Cash budget   OBJ. 5

The controller of Sonoma Housewares Inc. instructs you to prepare a monthly cash budget for the next three months. You are presented with the following budget information:

	May	June	July
Sales	$86,000	$90,000	$95,000
Manufacturing costs	34,000	39,000	44,000
Selling and administrative expenses	15,000	16,000	22,000
Capital expenditures	—	—	80,000

The company expects to sell about 10% of its merchandise for cash. Of sales on account, 70% are expected to be collected in the month following the sale and the remainder the following month (second month following sale). Depreciation, insurance, and property tax expense represent $3,500 of the estimated monthly manufacturing costs. The annual insurance premium is paid in September, and the annual property taxes are paid in November. Of the remainder of the manufacturing costs, 80% are expected to be paid in the month in which they are incurred and the balance in the following month.

Current assets as of May 1 include cash of $33,000, marketable securities of $40,000, and accounts receivable of $90,000 ($72,000 from April sales and $18,000 from March sales). Sales on account for March and April were $60,000 and $72,000, respectively. Current liabilities as of May 1 include $6,000 of accounts payable incurred in April for manufacturing costs. All selling and administrative expenses are paid in cash in the period they are incurred. An estimated income tax payment of $14,000 will be made in June. Sonoma's regular quarterly dividend of $5,000 is expected to be declared in June and paid in July. Management wants to maintain a minimum cash balance of $30,000.

Instructions

1. Prepare a monthly cash budget and supporting schedules for May, June, and July.
2. On the basis of the cash budget prepared in part (1), what recommendation should be made to the controller?

✔ 1. Budgeted net income, $96,600

PR 22-5A Budgeted income statement and balance sheet   OBJ. 4, 5

As a preliminary to requesting budget estimates of sales, costs, and expenses for the fiscal year beginning January 1, 20Y4, the following tentative trial balance as of December 31, 20Y3, is prepared by the Accounting Department of Regina Soap Co.:

Cash	$ 85,000	
Accounts Receivable	125,600	
Finished Goods	69,300	
Work in Process	32,500	
Materials	48,900	
Prepaid Expenses	2,600	
Plant and Equipment	325,000	
Accumulated Depreciation—Plant and Equipment		$156,200
Accounts Payable		62,000
Common Stock, $10 par		180,000
Retained Earnings		290,700
	$688,900	$688,900

Factory output and sales for 20Y4 are expected to total 200,000 units of product, which are to be sold at $5.00 per unit. The quantities and costs of the inventories at December 31, 20Y4, are expected to remain unchanged from the balances at the beginning of the year.

Budget estimates of manufacturing costs and operating expenses for the year are summarized as follows:

	Estimated Costs and Expenses	
	Fixed (Total for Year)	Variable (Per Unit Sold)
Cost of goods manufactured and sold:		
Direct materials	—	$1.10
Direct labor	—	0.65
Factory overhead:		
Depreciation of plant and equipment	$40,000	—
Other factory overhead	12,000	0.40
Selling expenses:		
Sales salaries and commissions	46,000	0.45
Advertising	64,000	—
Miscellaneous selling expense	6,000	0.25
Administrative expenses:		
Office and officers salaries	72,400	0.12
Supplies	5,000	0.10
Miscellaneous administrative expense	4,000	0.05

Balances of accounts receivable, prepaid expenses, and accounts payable at the end of the year are not expected to differ significantly from the beginning balances. Federal income tax of $30,000 on 20Y4 taxable income will be paid during 20Y4. Regular quarterly cash dividends of $0.15 per share are expected to be declared and paid in March, June, September, and December on 18,000 shares of common stock outstanding. It is anticipated that fixed assets will be purchased for $75,000 cash in May.

Instructions
1. Prepare a budgeted income statement for 20Y4.
2. Prepare a budgeted balance sheet as of December 31, 20Y4, with supporting calculations.

Problems: Series B

PR 22-1B Forecast sales volume and sales budget OBJ. 4

✔ 3. Total revenue from sales, $2,148,950

Sentinel Systems Inc. prepared the following sales budget for 20Y8:

Sentinel Systems Inc.
Sales Budget
For the Year Ending December 31, 20Y8

Product and Area	Unit Sales Volume	Unit Selling Price	Total Sales
Home Alert System:			
United States	1,700	$200	$ 340,000
Europe	580	200	116,000
Asia	450	200	90,000
Total	2,730		$ 546,000
Business Alert System:			
United States	980	$750	$ 735,000
Europe	350	750	262,500
Asia	240	750	180,000
Total	1,570		$1,177,500
Total revenue from sales			$1,723,500

(Continued)

1116 Chapter 22 Budgeting

At the end of December 20Y8, the following unit sales data were reported for the year:

	Unit Sales	
	Home Alert System	Business Alert System
United States	1,734	1,078
Europe	609	329
Asia	432	252

For the year ending December 31, 20Y9, unit sales are expected to follow the patterns established during the year ending December 31, 20Y8. The unit selling price for the Home Alert System is expected to increase to $250, and the unit selling price for the Business Alert System is expected to be decreased to $820, effective January 1, 20Y9.

Instructions

1. Compute the increase or decrease of actual unit sales for the year ended December 31, 20Y8, over budget. Place your answers in a columnar table with the following format:

	Unit Sales, Year Ended 20Y8		Increase (Decrease) Actual Over Budget	
	Budget	Actual Sales	Amount	Percent
Home Alert System:				
United States				
Europe				
Asia				
Business Alert System:				
United States				
Europe				
Asia				

2. Assuming that the increase or decrease in actual sales to budget indicated in part (1) is to continue in 20Y9, compute the unit sales volume to be used for preparing the sales budget for the year ending December 31, 20Y9. Place your answers in a columnar table similar to that in part (1) but with the following column heads. Round budgeted units to the nearest unit.

20Y8 Actual Units	Percentage Increase (Decrease)	20Y9 Budgeted Units (rounded)

3. Prepare a sales budget for the year ending December 31, 20Y9.

PR 22-2B Sales, production, direct materials purchases, and direct labor cost budgets   **OBJ. 4**

✔ 3. Total direct materials purchases, $987,478

The budget director of Royal Furniture Company requests estimates of sales, production, and other operating data from the various administrative units every month. Selected information concerning sales and production for February is summarized as follows:

a. Estimated sales of King and Prince chairs for February by sales territory:

  Northern Domestic:
    King .... 610 units at $780 per unit
    Prince .... 750 units at $550 per unit
  Southern Domestic:
    King .... 340 units at $780 per unit
    Prince .... 440 units at $550 per unit
  International:
    King .... 360 units at $850 per unit
    Prince .... 290 units at $600 per unit

b. Estimated inventories at February 1:

Direct materials:
Fabric	420 sq. yds.
Wood	580 linear ft.
Filler	250 cu. ft.
Springs	660 units

Finished products:
| King | 90 units |
| Prince | 25 units |

c. Desired inventories at February 28:

Direct materials:
Fabric	390 sq. yds.
Wood	650 linear ft.
Filler	300 cu. ft.
Springs	540 units

Finished products:
| King | 80 units |
| Prince | 35 units |

d. Direct materials used in production:

In manufacture of King:
Fabric	6.0 sq. yds. per unit of product
Wood	38 linear ft. per unit of product
Filler	4.2 cu. ft. per unit of product
Springs	16 units per unit of product

In manufacture of Prince:
Fabric	4.0 sq. yds. per unit of product
Wood	26 linear ft. per unit of product
Filler	3.4 cu. ft. per unit of product
Springs	12 units per unit of product

e. Anticipated purchase price for direct materials:

| Fabric | $12.00 per sq. yd. | Filler | $3.00 per cu. ft. |
| Wood | $7.00 per linear ft. | Springs | $4.50 per unit |

f. Direct labor requirements:

King:
Framing Department	1.2 hrs. at $12 per hr.
Cutting Department	0.5 hr. at $14 per hr.
Upholstery Department	0.8 hr. at $15 per hr.

Prince:
Framing Department	1.0 hr. at $12 per hr.
Cutting Department	0.4 hr. at $14 per hr.
Upholstery Department	0.6 hr. at $15 per hr.

Instructions

1. Prepare a sales budget for February.
2. Prepare a production budget for February.
3. Prepare a direct materials purchases budget for February.
4. Prepare a direct labor cost budget for February.

✔ 4. Total direct labor cost in Assembly Dept., $171,766

Excel

PR 22-3B Budgeted income statement and supporting budgets   **OBJ. 4**

The budget director of Gold Medal Athletic Co., with the assistance of the controller, treasurer, production manager, and sales manager, has gathered the following data for use in developing the budgeted income statement for March:

a. Estimated sales for March:

| Batting helmet | 1,200 units at $40 per unit |
| Football helmet | 6,500 units at $160 per unit |

(Continued)

b. Estimated inventories at March 1:

Direct materials:		Finished products:	
Plastic	90 lb.	Batting helmet	40 units at $25 per unit
Foam lining	80 lb.	Football helmet	240 units at $77 per unit

c. Desired inventories at March 31:

Direct materials:		Finished products:	
Plastic	50 lb.	Batting helmet	50 units at $25 per unit
Foam lining	65 lb.	Football helmet	220 units at $78 per unit

d. Direct materials used in production:

In manufacture of batting helmet:
Plastic	1.20 lb. per unit of product
Foam lining	0.50 lb. per unit of product

In manufacture of football helmet:
Plastic	3.50 lb. per unit of product
Foam lining	1.50 lb. per unit of product

e. Anticipated cost of purchases and beginning and ending inventory of direct materials:

Plastic	$6.00 per lb.
Foam lining	$4.00 per lb.

f. Direct labor requirements:

Batting helmet:
Molding Department	0.20 hr. at $20 per hr.
Assembly Department	0.50 hr. at $14 per hr.

Football helmet:
Molding Department	0.50 hr. at $20 per hr.
Assembly Department	1.80 hrs. at $14 per hr.

g. Estimated factory overhead costs for March:

Indirect factory wages	$86,000	Power and light	$4,000
Depreciation of plant and equipment	12,000	Insurance and property tax	2,300

h. Estimated operating expenses for March:

Sales salaries expense	$184,300
Advertising expense	87,200
Office salaries expense	32,400
Depreciation expense—office equipment	3,800
Telephone expense—selling	5,800
Telephone expense—administrative	1,200
Travel expense—selling	9,000
Office supplies expense	1,100
Miscellaneous administrative expense	1,000

i. Estimated other income and expense for March:

Interest revenue	$940
Interest expense	872

j. Estimated tax rate: 30%

Instructions

1. Prepare a sales budget for March.
2. Prepare a production budget for March.
3. Prepare a direct materials purchases budget for March.
4. Prepare a direct labor cost budget for March.

5. Prepare a factory overhead cost budget for March.
6. Prepare a cost of goods sold budget for March. Work in process at the beginning of March is estimated to be $15,300, and work in process at the end of March is desired to be $14,800.
7. Prepare a selling and administrative expenses budget for March.
8. Prepare a budgeted income statement for March.

PR 22-4B Cash budget   OBJ. 5

✔ 1. August deficiency, $9,000

The controller of Mercury Shoes Inc. instructs you to prepare a monthly cash budget for the next three months. You are presented with the following budget information:

	June	July	August
Sales	$160,000	$185,000	$200,000
Manufacturing costs	66,000	82,000	105,000
Selling and administrative expenses	40,000	46,000	51,000
Capital expenditures	—	—	120,000

The company expects to sell about 10% of its merchandise for cash. Of sales on account, 60% are expected to be collected in the month following the sale and the remainder the following month (second month after sale). Depreciation, insurance, and property tax expense represent $12,000 of the estimated monthly manufacturing costs. The annual insurance premium is paid in February, and the annual property taxes are paid in November. Of the remainder of the manufacturing costs, 80% are expected to be paid in the month in which they are incurred and the balance in the following month.

Current assets as of June 1 include cash of $42,000, marketable securities of $25,000, and accounts receivable of $198,000 ($150,000 from May sales and $48,000 from April sales). Sales on account in April and May were $120,000 and $150,000, respectively. Current liabilities as of June 1 include $13,000 of accounts payable incurred in May for manufacturing costs. All selling and administrative expenses are paid in cash in the period they are incurred. An estimated income tax payment of $24,000 will be made in July. Mercury Shoes' regular quarterly dividend of $15,000 is expected to be declared in July and paid in August. Management wants to maintain a minimum cash balance of $40,000.

Instructions
1. Prepare a monthly cash budget and supporting schedules for June, July, and August.
2. On the basis of the cash budget prepared in part (1), what recommendation should be made to the controller?

PR 22-5B Budgeted income statement and balance sheet   OBJ. 4, 5

✔ 1. Budgeted net income, $114,660

As a preliminary to requesting budget estimates of sales, costs, and expenses for the fiscal year beginning January 1, 20Y8, the following tentative trial balance as of December 31, 20Y7, is prepared by the Accounting Department of Mesa Publishing Co.:

Cash	$ 26,000	
Accounts Receivable	23,800	
Finished Goods	16,900	
Work in Process	4,200	
Materials	6,400	
Prepaid Expenses	600	
Plant and Equipment	82,000	
Accumulated Depreciation—Plant and Equipment		$ 32,000
Accounts Payable		14,800
Common Stock, $1.50 par		30,000
Retained Earnings		83,100
	$159,900	$159,900

(*Continued*)

Factory output and sales for 20Y8 are expected to total 3,800 units of product, which are to be sold at $120 per unit. The quantities and costs of the inventories at December 31, 20Y8, are expected to remain unchanged from the balances at the beginning of the year.

Budget estimates of manufacturing costs and operating expenses for the year are summarized as follows:

	Estimated Costs and Expenses	
	Fixed (Total for Year)	Variable (Per Unit Sold)
Cost of goods manufactured and sold:		
Direct materials	—	$30.00
Direct labor	—	8.40
Factory overhead:		
Depreciation of plant and equipment	$ 4,000	—
Other factory overhead	1,400	4.80
Selling expenses:		
Sales salaries and commissions	12,800	13.50
Advertising	13,200	—
Miscellaneous selling expense	1,000	2.50
Administrative expenses:		
Office and officers salaries	7,800	7.00
Supplies	500	1.20
Miscellaneous administrative expense	400	2.40

Balances of accounts receivable, prepaid expenses, and accounts payable at the end of the year are not expected to differ significantly from the beginning balances. Federal income tax of $35,000 on 20Y8 taxable income will be paid during 20Y8. Regular quarterly cash dividends of $0.20 per share are expected to be declared and paid in March, June, September, and December on 20,000 shares of common stock outstanding. It is anticipated that fixed assets will be purchased for $22,000 cash in May.

Instructions

1. Prepare a budgeted income statement for 20Y8.
2. Prepare a budgeted balance sheet as of December 31, 20Y8, with supporting calculations.

Cases & Projects

Ethics

CP 22-1   Ethics in Action

The director of marketing for Starr Computer Co., Megan Hewitt, had the following discussion with the company controller, Cam Morley, on July 26 of the current year:

Megan: Cam, it looks like I'm going to spend much less than indicated on my July budget.

Cam: I'm glad to hear it.

Megan: Well, I'm not so sure it's good news. I'm concerned that the president will see that I'm under budget and reduce my budget in the future. The only reason I look good is because we delayed an advertising campaign. Once the campaign hits in September, I'm sure my actual expenditures will go up. You see, we are also having our sales convention in September. Having the advertising campaign and the convention at the same time is going to kill my September numbers.

Cam: I don't think that's anything to worry about. We all expect some variation in actual spending month to month. What's really important is staying within the budgeted targets for the year. Does that look as if it's going to be a problem?

Megan: I don't think so, but just the same, I'd like to be on the safe side.

Cam: What do you mean?

Megan: Well, this is what I'd like to do. I want to pay the convention-related costs in advance this month. I'll pay the hotel for room and convention space and purchase the airline tickets in advance. In this way, I can charge all these expenditures to July's budget. This would cause my actual expenses to come close to budget for July. Moreover, when the big advertising campaign hits in September, I won't have to worry about expenditures for the convention on my September budget. The convention costs will already be paid. Thus, my September expenses should be pretty close to budget.

Cam: I can't tell you when to make your convention purchases, but I'm not too sure it should be expensed on July's budget.

Megan: What's the problem? It looks like "no harm, no foul" to me. I can't see that there's anything wrong with this—it's just smart management.

How should Cam Morley respond to Megan Hewitt's request to expense the advanced payments for convention-related costs against July's budget?

CP 22-2 Team Activity

In a group, find the home page of a state that interests you. The home page will be of the form *www.statename.gov*. For example, the state of Tennessee would be found at www.tennessee.gov. At the home page site, search for annual budget information.

1. What are the budgeted sources of revenue and their percentage breakdown?
2. What are the major categories of budgeted expenditures (or appropriations) and their percentage breakdown?
3. Is the projected budget in balance?

CP 22-3 Communication

The city of Milton has an annual budget cycle that begins on July 1 and ends on June 30. At the beginning of each budget year, an annual budget is established for each department. The annual budget is divided by 12 months to provide a constant monthly static budget. On June 30, all unspent budgeted monies for the budget year from the various city departments must be "returned" to the General Fund. Thus, if department heads fail to use their budget by year-end, they will lose it. A budget analyst prepared a chart of the difference between the monthly actual and budgeted amounts for the recent fiscal year. The chart was as follows:

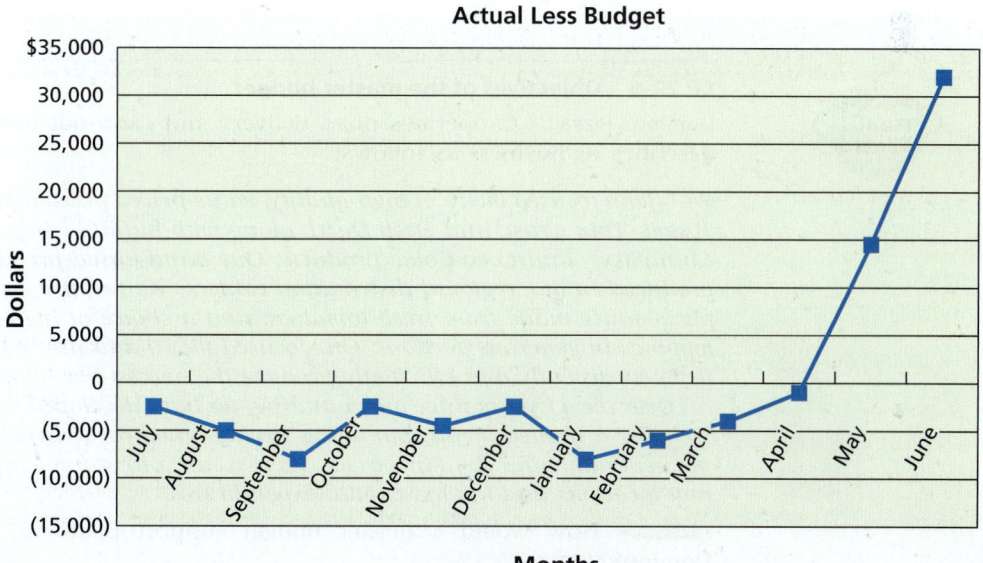

Write a memo to Stacy Collins, the city manager, interpreting the chart and suggesting improvements to the budgeting system.

CP 22-4 Evaluating budgeting systems in a service company

Children's Hospital of the King's Daughters Health System in Norfolk, Virginia, introduced a new budgeting method that allowed the hospital's annual plan to be updated for changes in operating plans. For example, if the budget was based on 400 patient-days (number of patients × number of days in the hospital) and the actual count rose to 450 patient-days, the variable costs of staffing, lab work, and medication costs could be adjusted to reflect this change. The budget manager stated, "I work with hospital directors to turn data into meaningful information and effect change before the month ends."

a. What budgeting methods are being used under the new approach?
b. Why are these methods superior to the former approaches?

CP 22-5 Static budget for a service company

A bank manager of City Savings Bank Inc. uses the managerial accounting system to track the costs of operating the various departments within the bank. The departments include Cash Management, Trust, Commercial Loans, Mortgage Loans, Operations, Credit Card, and Branch Services. The static budget and actual results for the Operations Department are as follows:

Resources	Budget	Actual
Salaries	$200,000	$200,000
Benefits	30,000	30,000
Supplies	45,000	42,000
Travel	20,000	30,000
Training	25,000	35,000
Overtime	25,000	20,000
Total	$345,000	$357,000
Excess of actual over budget		$ 12,000

a. What information is provided by the budget? Specifically, what questions can the bank manager ask of the Operations Department manager?
b. What information does the static budget fail to provide? Specifically, could the budget information be presented differently to provide even more insight for the bank manager?

CP 22-6 Objectives of the master budget

Domino's Pizza L.L.C. operates pizza delivery and carry-out restaurants. The annual report describes its business as follows:

We offer a focused menu of high-quality, value-priced pizza with three types of crust (Hand-Tossed, Thin Crust, and Deep Dish), along with buffalo wings, bread sticks, cheesy bread, CinnaStix®, and Coca-Cola® products. Our hand-tossed pizza is made from fresh dough produced in our regional distribution centers. We prepare every pizza using real cheese, pizza sauce made from fresh tomatoes, and a choice of high-quality meat and vegetable toppings in generous portions. Our focused menu and use of premium ingredients enable us to consistently and efficiently produce the highest-quality pizza.

Over the 41 years since our founding, we have developed a simple, cost-efficient model. We offer a limited menu, our stores are designed for delivery and carry-out, and we do not generally offer dine-in service. As a result, our stores require relatively small, lower-rent locations and limited capital expenditures.

How would a master budget support planning, directing, and control for Domino's?

CHAPTER 23
Evaluating Variances from Standard Costs

Concepts and Principles
Chapter 18 *Introduction to Managerial Accounting*

Developing Information

COST SYSTEMS
Chapter 19 *Job Order Costing*
Chapter 20 *Process Costing*

COST BEHAVIOR
Chapter 21 *Cost-Volume-Profit Analysis*

Decision Making

EVALUATING PERFORMANCE
Chapter 22 *Budgeting*
Chapter 23 *Variances from Standard Costs*

COMPARING ALTERNATIVES
Chapter 24 *Decentralized Operations*
Chapter 25 *Differential Analysis, Product Pricing, and Activity-Based Costing*
Chapter 26 *Capital Investment Analysis*

CHAPTER 23

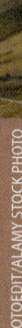

BMW Group—Mini Cooper

When you play a sport, you are evaluated with respect to how well you perform compared to a standard or to a competitor. In bowling, for example, your score is compared to a perfect score of 300 or to the scores of your competitors. In this class, you are compared to performance standards. These standards are often described in terms of letter grades, which provide a measure of how well you achieved the class objectives. In your job, you are also evaluated according to performance standards.

Just as your class performance is evaluated, managers are evaluated according to goals and plans. For example, the **BMW Group** uses manufacturing standards at its automobile assembly plants to guide performance. The Mini Cooper, a BMW Group car, is manufactured in a modern facility in Oxford, England. A number of performance targets are used in this plant. For example, the bodyshell is welded by more than 250 robots so as to be two to three times stiffer than rival cars. In addition, the bodyshell dimensions are tested to the accuracy of the width of a human hair. Such performance standards are not surprising given the automotive racing background of John W. Cooper, the designer of the original Mini Cooper.

If you want to get a view of the BMW manufacturing process, go to the BMW website and search the phrase "How an automobile is born."

Performance is often measured as the difference between actual results and planned results. In this chapter, we will discuss and illustrate the ways in which business performance is evaluated.

Learning Objectives

After studying this chapter, you should be able to:

Example Exercises (EE) are shown in **green**.

Obj. 1 Describe the types of standards and how they are established.

Standards
Setting Standards
Types of Standards
Reviewing and Revising Standards
Criticisms of Standard Costs

Obj. 2 Describe and illustrate how standards are used in budgeting.

Budgetary Performance Evaluation
Budget Performance Report
Manufacturing Cost Variances

Obj. 3 Compute and interpret direct materials and direct labor variances.

Direct Materials and Direct Labor Variances
Direct Materials Variances — EE **23-1**
Direct Labor Variances — EE **23-2**

Obj. 4 Compute and interpret factory overhead controllable and volume variances.

Factory Overhead Variances
The Factory Overhead Flexible Budget
Variable Factory Overhead Controllable Variance — EE **23-3**
Fixed Factory Overhead Volume Variance — EE **23-4**
Reporting Factory Overhead Variances
Factory Overhead Account

Obj. 5 Journalize the entries for recording standards in the accounts and prepare an income statement that includes variances from standard.

Recording and Reporting Variances from Standards
Prepare Standard Cost Journal Entries — EE **23-5**
Prepare Income Statement with Variances — EE **23-6**

Obj. 6 Describe and provide examples of nonfinancial performance measures.

Nonfinancial Performance Measures
Identify Activity Inputs and Outputs — EE **23-7**

At a Glance 23 — Page 1148

Obj. 1 Describe the types of standards and how they are established.

Standards

Standards are performance goals. Manufacturing companies normally use **standard cost** for each of the three following product costs:

- Direct materials
- Direct labor
- Factory overhead

Accounting systems that use standards for product costs are called **standard cost systems**. Standard cost systems enable management to determine the following:

- How much a product *should* cost (standard cost)
- How much it *does* cost (actual cost)

When actual costs are compared with standard costs, the exceptions or cost variances are reported. This reporting by the *principle of exceptions* allows management to focus on correcting the cost variances.

Setting Standards

The standard-setting process normally requires the joint efforts of accountants, engineers, and other management personnel. The accountant converts the results of judgments and process studies into dollars and cents. Engineers with the aid of operation managers identify the materials, labor, and machine requirements needed to

---

Link to BMW Group

BMW began in Germany in the early 1900s as a manufacturer of airplane engines. The BMW emblem, which was first used in 1917, represents a rotating airplane propeller with the white and blue state colors of Bavaria.

produce the product. For example, engineers estimate direct materials by studying the product specifications and estimating normal spoilage. Time and motion studies may be used to determine the direct labor required for each manufacturing operation. Engineering studies may also be used to determine standards for factory overhead, such as the amount of power needed to operate machinery.

Types of Standards

Standards imply an acceptable level of production efficiency. One of the major objectives in setting standards is to motivate employees to achieve efficient operations.

Ideal standards, or *theoretical standards*, are standards that can be achieved only under perfect operating conditions, such as no idle time, no machine breakdowns, and no materials spoilage. Such standards may have a negative impact on performance because they may be viewed by employees as unrealistic.

Currently attainable standards, sometimes called *normal standards*, are standards that can be attained with reasonable effort. Such standards, which are used by most companies, allow for normal production difficulties and mistakes. When reasonable standards are used, employees focus more on cost and are more likely to put forth their best efforts.

An example from the game of golf illustrates the distinction between ideal and normal standards. In golf, *par* is an ideal standard for most players. Each player's USGA (United States Golf Association) handicap is the player's normal standard. The motivation of average players is to beat their handicaps because beating par is unrealistic for most players.

Reviewing and Revising Standards

Standard costs should be reviewed periodically to ensure that they reflect current operating conditions. Standards should not be revised, however, just because they differ from actual costs. For example, the direct labor standard would not be revised just because employees are unable to meet properly set standards. On the other hand, standards should be revised when prices, product designs, labor rates, or manufacturing methods change.

INTEGRITY, OBJECTIVITY, AND ETHICS IN BUSINESS

COMPANY REPUTATION: THE BEST OF THE BEST

Harris Interactive annually ranks American corporations in terms of reputation. The ranking is based on how respondents rate corporations on 20 attributes in six major areas. The six areas are emotional appeal, products and services, financial performance, workplace environment, social responsibility, and vision and leadership. What are the five highest ranked companies in a recent survey? The five highest (best) ranked companies were Amazon.com, Apple Inc., Alphabet (Google), USAA, and The Walt Disney Company.

Source: Harris Interactive, February 2016.

Criticisms of Standard Costs

Some criticisms of using standard costs for performance evaluation include the following:

- Standards limit operating improvements by discouraging improvement beyond the standard.
- Standards are too difficult to maintain in a dynamic manufacturing environment, resulting in "stale standards."

Link to BMW Group

In addition to BMW, Mini Cooper, and Rolls-Royce automobiles, the **BMW Group** manufactures motorcycles.

- Standards can cause employees to lose sight of the larger objectives of the organization by focusing only on efficiency improvement.
- Standards can cause employees to focus unduly on their own operations to the possible harm of other operations that rely on them.

Regardless of these criticisms, standards are used widely. In addition, standard costs are only one part of the performance evaluation system used by most companies. As discussed in this chapter, other nonfinancial performance measures are often used to supplement standard costs, with the result that many of the preceding criticisms are overcome.

Business Connection

STANDARD COSTING IN ACTION: EXPANDING BREWING OPERATIONS

In 2011, U.S. West Coast craft brewers **Sierra Nevada** (CA) and **New Belgium** (CO) announced plans to expand their brewing operations to the Asheville, North Carolina, area. Both companies considered the standard cost of their product when making the decision to expand and in selecting Asheville as their East Coast location. The standard price of direct materials includes the cost of shipping direct materials to the manufacturers' place of business. The Asheville location was desirable when considering these costs.

In addition, New Belgium projected that its Fort Collins, Colorado, brewery would reach maximum capacity in three to five years. While consistently operating at 100% capacity creates a favorable overhead volume variance, it also can make it difficult to meet customer demand. Thus, New Belgium thought that adding a new brewery prior to reaching 100% capacity at Fort Collins was supported. In both cases, standard costing was used to support the expansion and location decisions.

Sources: H. Dornbusch, "The Case for Low Mileage Beer," www.brewersassociation.org; J. McCurry, "Hops City: Beer Culture Comes to a Head in the Asheville Region," *Site Selection*, July 2012; and J. Shikes, "New Belgium, Maker of Fat Tire, Plans a Second Brewery on the East Coast," *Denver Westword*, May 19, 2011.

Obj. 2 Describe and illustrate how standards are used in budgeting.

Budgetary Performance Evaluation

As discussed in Chapter 22, the master budget assists a company in planning, directing, and controlling performance. The control function, or budgetary performance evaluation, compares the actual performance against the budget.

To illustrate, **Western Rider Inc.**, a manufacturer of blue jeans, uses standard costs in its budgets. The standards for direct materials, direct labor, and factory overhead are separated into the following two components:

- Standard price
- Standard quantity

The standard cost per unit for direct materials, direct labor, and factory overhead is computed as follows:

$$\text{Standard Cost per Unit} = \text{Standard Price} \times \text{Standard Quantity}$$

Western Rider's standard costs per unit for its XL jeans are shown in Exhibit 1.

As shown in Exhibit 1, the standard cost per unit (pair) of XL jeans is $19.50, which consists of $7.50 for direct materials, $7.20 for direct labor, and $4.80 for factory overhead.

The standard price and standard quantity are separated for each product cost. For example, Exhibit 1 indicates that for each unit (pair) of XL jeans, the standard price for direct materials is $5.00 per square yard and the standard quantity is 1.5 square yards.

EXHIBIT 1
Standard Cost for XL Jeans

Manufacturing Costs	Standard Price	×	Standard Quantity per Unit	=	Standard Cost per Unit of XL Jeans
Direct materials	$5.00 per sq. yd.	×	1.5 sq. yds.	=	$ 7.50
Direct labor	$9.00 per hr.	×	0.80 hr. per unit	=	7.20
Factory overhead	$6.00 per hr.	×	0.80 hr. per unit	=	4.80
Total standard cost per unit					$19.50

The standard price and quantity are separated because the department responsible for their control is normally different. For example, the direct materials price per square yard is controlled by the Purchasing Department, and the direct materials quantity per unit is controlled by the Production Department.

As illustrated in Chapter 22, the master budget is prepared based on planned sales and production. The budgeted costs for materials purchases, direct labor, and factory overhead are determined by multiplying their standard costs per unit by the planned level of production. Budgeted (standard) costs are then compared to actual costs during the year for control purposes.

Budget Performance Report

The differences between actual and standard costs are called **cost variances**. A **favorable cost variance** occurs when the actual cost is less than the standard cost. An **unfavorable cost variance** occurs when the actual cost exceeds the standard cost. These cost variances are illustrated in Exhibit 2.

EXHIBIT 2
Cost Variances

Favorable Cost Variance	Unfavorable Cost Variance
Actual cost < Standard cost at actual volumes	Actual cost > Standard cost at actual volumes

The report that summarizes actual costs, standard costs, and the differences for the units produced is called a **budget performance report**. To illustrate, assume that Western Rider Inc. reported the following actual production data during June:

XL jeans produced and sold	5,000 units
Actual costs incurred in June:	
Direct materials	$ 40,150
Direct labor	38,500
Factory overhead	22,400
Total costs incurred	$101,050

Exhibit 3 illustrates the budget performance report for June for Western Rider.

The budget performance report shown in Exhibit 3 is based on the actual units produced in June of 5,000 XL jeans. Even though 6,000 XL jeans might have been *planned* for production, the budget performance report is based on *actual* production.

Manufacturing Cost Variances

The **total manufacturing cost variance** is the difference between total standard costs and total actual cost for the units produced. As shown in Exhibit 3, the total manufacturing cost unfavorable variance is $3,550, which consists of an unfavorable direct

1130 Chapter 23 Evaluating Variances from Standard Costs

EXHIBIT 3

Budget Performance Report

Western Rider Inc.
Budget Performance Report
For the Month Ended June 30

Manufacturing Costs	Actual Costs	Standard Cost at Actual Volume (5,000 units of XL Jeans)*	Cost Variance— (Favorable) Unfavorable
Direct materials..........................	$ 40,150	$37,500	$ 2,650
Direct labor	38,500	36,000	2,500
Factory overhead	22,400	24,000	(1,600)
Total manufacturing costs............	$101,050	$97,500	$ 3,550

*5,000 units × $7.50 per unit = $37,500
5,000 units × $7.20 per unit = $36,000
5,000 units × $4.80 per unit = $24,000

materials cost variance of $2,650, an unfavorable direct labor cost variance of $2,500, and a favorable factory overhead cost variance of $1,600.

For control purposes, each product cost variance is separated into two additional variances as shown in Exhibit 4.

EXHIBIT 4 **Manufacturing Cost Variances**

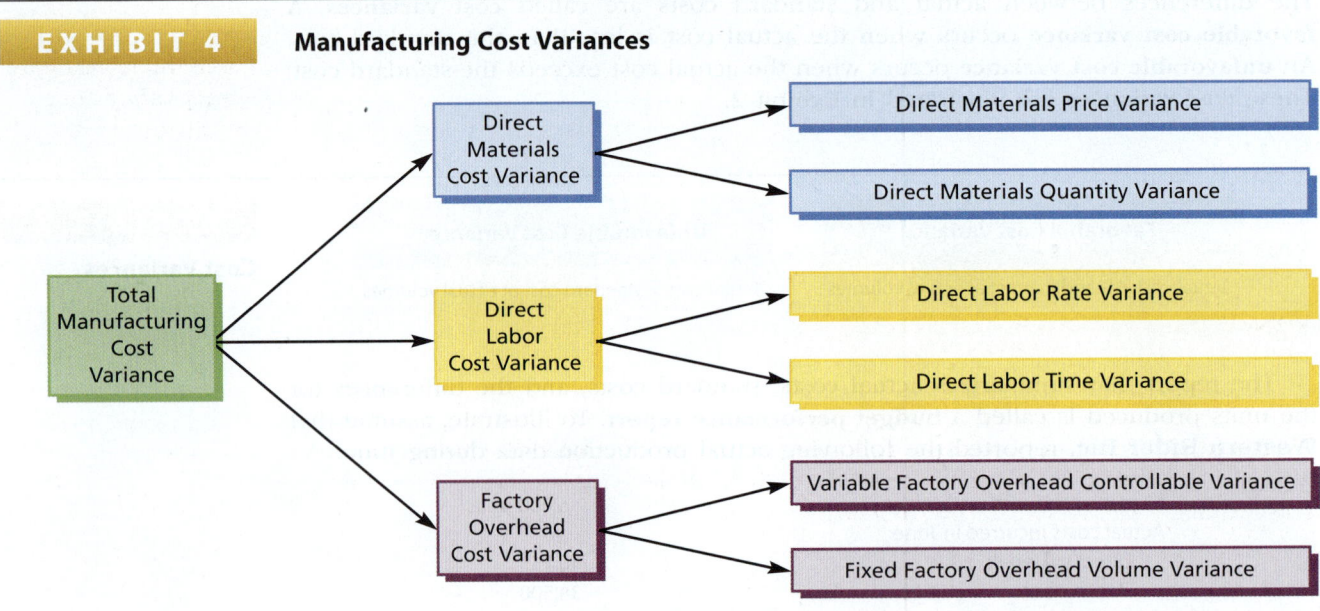

The total direct materials variance is separated into a *price* variance and a *quantity* variance. This is because standard and actual direct materials costs are computed as follows:

Actual Direct Materials Cost = Actual Price × Actual Quantity
Standard Direct Materials Cost = Standard Price × Standard Quantity

Thus, the actual and standard direct materials costs may differ because of a price difference (Actual Price − Standard Price), a quantity difference (Actual Quantity − Standard Quantity), or both.

Likewise, the total direct labor variance is separated into a *rate* variance and a *time* variance. This is because standard and actual direct labor costs are computed as follows:

Actual Direct Labor Cost = Actual Rate × Actual Time
Standard Direct Labor Cost = Standard Rate × Standard Time

Therefore, the actual and standard direct labor costs may differ because of a rate difference (Actual Rate − Standard Rate), a time difference (Actual Time − Standard Time), or both.

The total factory overhead variance is separated into a *controllable* variance and a *volume* variance. Because factory overhead has fixed and variable cost elements, it uses different variances than direct materials and direct labor, which are variable costs.

In the next sections, the price and quantity variances for direct materials, the rate and time variances for direct labor, and the controllable and volume variances for factory overhead are further described and illustrated.

> **Link to BMW Group**
>
> **BMW**'s Spartanburg, South Carolina, plant employs 8,000 workers in its 6 million-square-foot facility where it manufactures X3 and X5 SUVs. Visitors may tour the manufacturing plant and company museum.

Direct Materials and Direct Labor Variances

Obj. 3 Compute and interpret direct materials and direct labor variances.

As indicated in the prior section, the total direct materials and direct labor variances are separated into the direct materials cost and direct labor cost variances for analysis and control purposes. These variances are illustrated in Exhibit 5.

Total Direct Materials Cost Variance ⟶ { Direct Materials Price Variance
                                          Direct Materials Quantity Variance

Total Direct Labor Cost Variance ⟶ { Direct Labor Rate Variance
                                      Direct Labor Time Variance

EXHIBIT 5

Direct Materials and Direct Labor Cost Variances

As a basis for illustration, the variances for Western Rider's June operations shown in Exhibit 3 are used.

Direct Materials Variances

During June, **Western Rider Inc.** reported an unfavorable total direct materials cost variance of $2,650 for the production of 5,000 XL style jeans, as shown in Exhibit 3. This variance was based on the following actual and standard costs:

Actual costs	$40,150
Standard costs	37,500
Total direct materials cost variance	$ 2,650

The actual costs incurred of $40,150 consist of the following:

Actual Direct Materials Cost = Actual Price × Actual Quantity
= ($5.50 per sq. yd.) × (7,300 sq. yds.)
= $40,150

The standard costs of $37,500 consist of the following:

Standard Direct Materials Cost = Standard Price × Standard Quantity
= $5.00 per sq. yd. × 7,500 sq. yds.
= $37,500

The standard price of $5.00 per square yard is established by management as shown in Exhibit 1. In addition, Exhibit 1 indicates that 1.5 square yards is the standard quantity of materials for one unit (pair) of XL jeans. Thus, 7,500 (5,000 units × 1.5 yards per unit) square yards is the standard quantity of materials for producing 5,000 units (pairs) of XL jeans.

Comparing the actual and standard cost computations indicates that the total direct materials unfavorable cost variance of $2,650 is caused by the following:

- A price per square yard of $0.50 ($5.50 − $5.00) more than standard
- A quantity usage of 200 square yards (7,300 sq. yds. − 7,500 sq. yds.) less than standard

The impact of these differences from standard is reported and analyzed as a direct materials *price* variance and direct materials *quantity* variance.

Direct Materials Price Variance

The **direct materials price variance** is computed as follows:

$$\text{Direct Materials Price Variance} = (\text{Actual Price} - \text{Standard Price}) \times \text{Actual Quantity}$$

If the actual price per unit exceeds the standard price per unit, the variance is unfavorable. This positive amount (unfavorable variance) can be thought of as increasing costs (a debit). If the actual price per unit is less than the standard price per unit, the variance is favorable. This negative amount (favorable variance) can be thought of as decreasing costs (a credit).

To illustrate, the direct materials price variance for **Western Rider Inc.** for June is $3,650 (unfavorable), computed as follows:[1]

$$\text{Direct Materials Price Variance} = (\text{Actual Price} - \text{Standard Price}) \times \text{Actual Quantity}$$
$$= (\$5.50 - \$5.00) \times 7{,}300 \text{ sq. yds.}$$
$$= \$3{,}650 \text{ Unfavorable Variance}$$

Direct Materials Quantity Variance

The **direct materials quantity variance** is computed as follows:

$$\text{Direct Materials Quantity Variance} = (\text{Actual Quantity} - \text{Standard Quantity}) \times \text{Standard Price}$$

If the actual quantity for the units produced exceeds the standard quantity, the variance is unfavorable. This positive amount (unfavorable variance) can be thought of as increasing costs (a debit). If the actual quantity for the units produced is less than the standard quantity, the variance is favorable. This negative amount (favorable variance) can be thought of as decreasing costs (a credit).

To illustrate, the direct materials quantity variance for **Western Rider Inc.** for June is $1,000 (favorable), computed as follows:

$$\text{Direct Materials Quantity Variance} = (\text{Actual Quantity} - \text{Standard Quantity}) \times \text{Standard Price}$$
$$= (7{,}300 \text{ sq. yds.} - 7{,}500 \text{ sq. yds.}) \times \$5.00$$
$$= \$(1{,}000) \text{ Favorable Variance}$$

Direct Materials Variance Relationships

The relationship among the *total* direct materials cost variance, the direct materials *price* variance, and the direct materials *quantity* variance is shown in Exhibit 6.

Reporting Direct Materials Variances

The direct materials quantity variances should be reported to the manager responsible for the variance. For example, an unfavorable quantity variance might be caused by either of the following:

- Equipment that has not been properly maintained
- Low-quality (inferior) direct materials

In the first case, the Operating Department responsible for maintaining the equipment should be held responsible for the variance. In the second case, the Purchasing Department should be held responsible.

> **Link to BMW Group**
> Steel and aluminum are pressed into doors and side panels in **BMW**'s stamping facility.

[1] To simplify, it is assumed that there is no change in the beginning and ending materials inventories. Thus, the amount of materials budgeted for production equals the amount purchased.

Direct Materials Variance Relationships

EXHIBIT 6

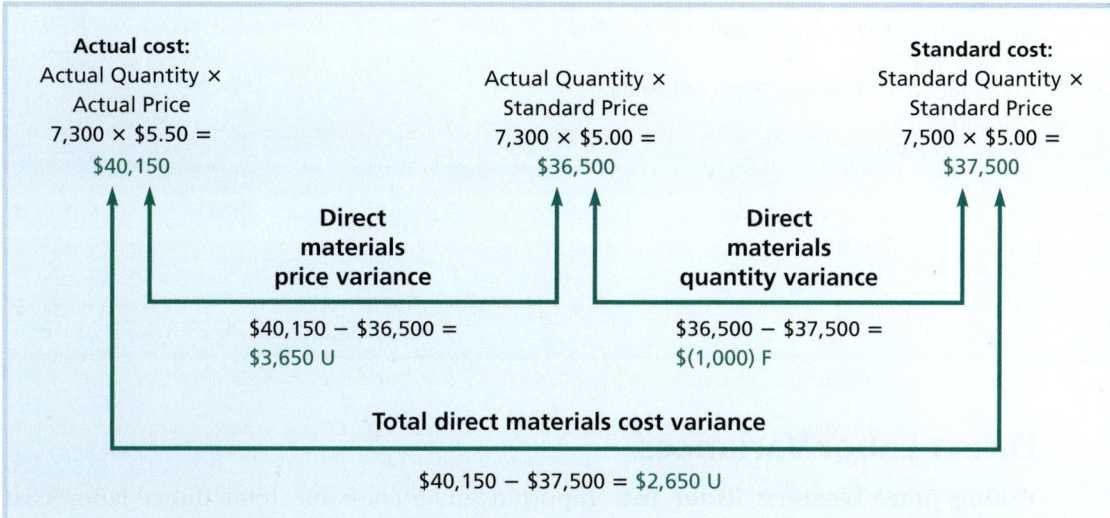

Not all variances are controllable. For example, an unfavorable materials price variance might be due to market-wide price increases. In this case, there is nothing the Purchasing Department might have done to avoid the unfavorable variance. On the other hand, if materials of the same quality could have been purchased from another supplier at the standard price, the variance was controllable.

SERVICE FOCUS

STANDARD COSTING IN THE RESTAURANT INDUSTRY

Many restaurants use standard costs to manage their business. Food costs are typically the largest expense for a restaurant. As a result, many restaurants use food quantity standards to control food costs by establishing the amount of food that is served to a customer. For example, Red Lobster restaurants, a division of **Darden Restuarants, Inc.**, establishes food quantity standards for the number of shrimp, scallops, or clams on a seafood plate.

The second largest cost to most restaurants is labor cost. Many restaurants base their labor cost standards on the labor cost percentage, which is the ratio of total labor cost to total sales. This ratio helps the restaurants of Darden Restaurants, Inc., including Olive Garden and Red Lobster, control and monitor labor costs.

Source: N. Irwin, "What Olive Garden and Red Lobster Tell Us About the Economy," *The Washington Post*, September 21, 2012.

Example Exercise 23-1 Direct Materials Variances   Obj. 3

Tip Top Corp. produces a product that requires six standard pounds per unit. The standard price is $4.50 per pound. If 3,000 units required 18,500 pounds, which were purchased at $4.35 per pound, what is the direct materials (a) price variance, (b) quantity variance, and (c) total direct materials cost variance?

(Continued)

Follow My Example 23-1

a. Direct materials price variance:
 ($4.35 − $4.50) × 18,500 pounds = $(2,775) (favorable)
b. Direct materials quantity variance:
 (18,500 pounds − 18,000 pounds*) × $4.50 = $2,250 (unfavorable)
c. Total direct materials cost variance:**
 $(2,775) + $2,250 = $(525) (favorable)

*3,000 units × 6 pounds
**Also computed as follows:
 ($4.35 × 18,500 pounds) − ($4.50 × 18,000 pounds)
 $80,475 − $81,000 = $(525) (favorable)

Practice Exercises: PE 23-1A, PE 23-1B

Direct Labor Variances

During June, **Western Rider Inc.** reported an unfavorable total direct labor cost variance of $2,500 for the production of 5,000 XL style jeans, as shown in Exhibit 3. This variance was based on the following actual and standard costs:

Actual costs	$38,500
Standard costs	36,000
Total direct labor cost variance	$ 2,500

The actual costs incurred of $38,500 consist of the following:

Actual Direct Labor Cost = Actual Rate per Hour × Actual Time
= $10.00 per hr. × 3,850 hrs.
= $38,500

The standard costs of $36,000 consist of the following:

Standard Direct Labor Cost = Standard Rate per Hour × Standard Time
= $9.00 per hr. × 4,000 hrs.
= $36,000

The standard rate of $9.00 per direct labor hour is set by management and provided in Exhibit 1. In addition, Exhibit 1 indicates that 0.80 hour is the standard time required for producing one unit of XL jeans. Thus, 4,000 (5,000 units × 0.80 hr.) direct labor hours is the standard for producing 5,000 units (pairs) of XL jeans.

Comparing the actual and standard cost computations indicates that the total direct labor unfavorable cost variance of $2,500 is caused by the following:

- A rate of $1.00 per hour ($10.00 − $9.00) more than standard
- A quantity of 150 hours (4,000 hrs. − 3,850 hrs.) less than standard

The impact of these differences from standard is reported and analyzed as a direct labor *rate* variance and a direct labor *time* variance.

Direct Labor Rate Variance

The **direct labor rate variance** is computed as follows:

Direct Labor Rate Variance = (Actual Rate per Hour − Standard Rate per Hour) × Actual Hours

If the actual rate per hour exceeds the standard rate per hour, the variance is unfavorable. This positive amount (unfavorable variance) can be thought of as increasing costs (a debit). If the actual rate per hour is less than the standard rate per hour, the variance is favorable. This negative amount (favorable variance) can be thought of as decreasing costs (a credit).

Link to BMW Group

The camshafts of **BMW**'s engines are manufactured using computer-controlled machine tools to a precision of one-hundredth of a human hair. Workers are used primarily to adjust the machine tools.

To illustrate, the direct labor rate variance for **Western Rider Inc.** in June is $3,850 (unfavorable), computed as follows:

Direct Labor Rate Variance = (Actual Rate per Hour − Standard Rate per Hour) × Actual Hours
= ($10.00 − $9.00) × 3,850 hours
= $3,850 Unfavorable Variance

Direct Labor Time Variance

The **direct labor time variance** is computed as follows:

Direct Labor Time Variance = (Actual Direct Labor Hours − Standard Direct Labor Hours)
× Standard Rate per Hour

If the actual direct labor hours for the units produced exceeds the standard direct labor hours, the variance is unfavorable. This positive amount (unfavorable variance) can be thought of as increasing costs (a debit). If the actual direct labor hours for the units produced is less than the standard direct labor hours, the variance is favorable. This negative amount (favorable variance) can be thought of as decreasing costs (a credit).

To illustrate, the direct labor time variance for **Western Rider Inc.** for June is $1,350 (favorable) computed as follows:

Direct Labor Time Variance = (Actual Direct Labor Hours − Standard Direct Labor Hours)
× Standard Rate per Hour
= (3,850 hours − 4,000 direct labor hours) × $9.00
= $(1,350) Favorable Variance

Direct Labor Variance Relationships

The relationship among the *total* direct labor cost variance, the direct labor *rate* variance, and the direct labor *time* variance is shown in Exhibit 7.

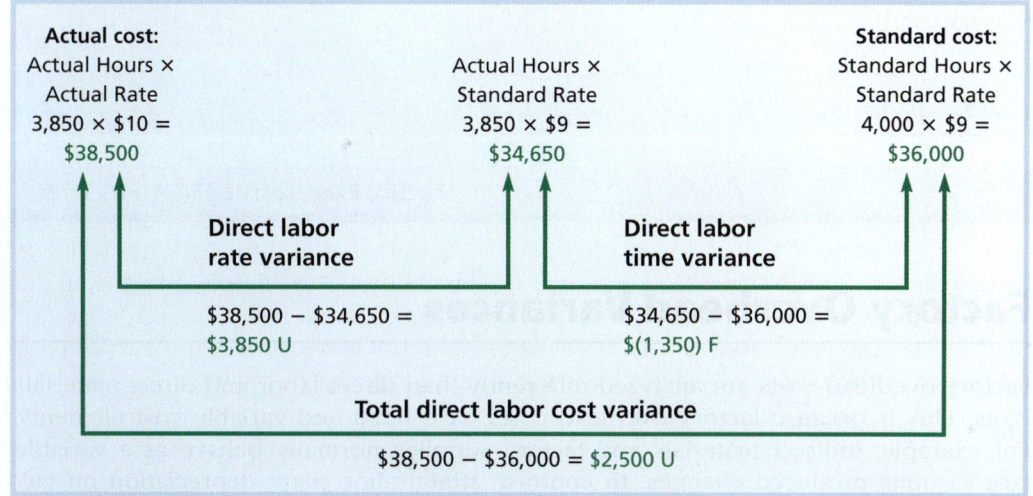

EXHIBIT 7
Direct Labor Variance Relationships

Reporting Direct Labor Variances

Production supervisors are normally responsible for controlling direct labor cost. For example, an investigation could reveal the following causes for unfavorable rate and time variances:

- An unfavorable rate variance may be caused by the improper scheduling and use of employees. In such cases, skilled, highly paid employees may be used in jobs that are normally performed by unskilled, lower-paid employees. In this case, the unfavorable rate variance should be reported to the managers who schedule work assignments.
- An unfavorable time variance may be caused by a shortage of skilled employees. In such cases, there may be an abnormally high turnover rate among skilled employees. In this case, production supervisors with high turnover rates should be questioned as to why their employees are quitting.

Direct Labor Standards for Nonmanufacturing Activities Direct labor time standards can also be developed for use in administrative, selling, and service activities. This is most appropriate when the activity involves a repetitive task that produces a common output. In these cases, the use of standards is similar to that for a manufactured product.

To illustrate, standards could be developed for customer service personnel who process sales orders. A standard time for processing a sales order (the output) could be developed and used to control sales order processing costs. Similar standards could be developed for computer help desk operators, nurses, and insurance application processors.

When labor-related activities are not repetitive, direct labor time standards are less commonly used. For example, the time spent by a senior executive or the work of a research and development scientist would not normally be controlled using time standards.

Example Exercise 23-2 Direct Labor Variances — Obj. 3

Tip Top Corp. produces a product that requires 2.5 standard hours per unit at a standard hourly rate of $12 per hour. If 3,000 units required 7,420 hours at an hourly rate of $12.30 per hour, what is the (a) direct labor rate variance, (b) direct labor time variance, and (c) total direct labor cost variance?

Follow My Example 23-2

a. Direct labor rate variance:
   ($12.30 − $12.00) × 7,420 hours = $2,226 (unfavorable)

b. Direct labor time variance:
   (7,420 hours − 7,500 hours*) × $12.00 = $(960) (favorable)

c. Total direct labor cost variance:**
   $2,226 − $960 = $1,266 (unfavorable)

*3,000 units × 2.5 hours
**Also computed as follows:
   ($12.30 × 7,420 hours) − ($12.00 × 7,500 hours)
   $91,266 − $90,000 = $1,266 (unfavorable)

Practice Exercises: PE 23-2A, PE 23-2B

Factory Overhead Variances

Obj. 4 Compute and interpret factory overhead controllable and volume variances.

Factory overhead costs are analyzed differently than direct labor and direct materials costs. This is because factory overhead costs have fixed and variable cost elements. For example, indirect materials and factory supplies normally behave as a variable cost as units produced changes. In contrast, straight-line plant depreciation on factory machinery is a fixed cost.

Factory overhead costs are budgeted and controlled by separating factory overhead into fixed and variable components. Doing so allows the preparation of flexible budgets and the analysis of factory overhead controllable and volume variances.

The Factory Overhead Flexible Budget

The preparation of a flexible budget was described and illustrated in Chapter 22. Exhibit 8 illustrates a flexible factory overhead budget for **Western Rider Inc.** for June.

Link to BMW Group

The **BMW Group** has significant overhead costs due to its investment in robotic and other state-of-the art technology, machinery, and facilities.

EXHIBIT 8

Factory Overhead Cost Budget Indicating Standard Factory Overhead Rate

	A	B	C	D	E
1	Western Rider Inc.				
2	Factory Overhead Cost Budget				
3	For the Month Ending June 30				
4	Percent of normal capacity	80%	90%	100%	110%
5	Units produced	5,000	5,625	6,250	6,875
6	Direct labor hours (0.80 hr. per unit)	4,000	4,500	5,000	5,500
7	Budgeted factory overhead:				
8	Variable costs:				
9	Indirect factory wages	$ 8,000	$ 9,000	$10,000	$11,000
10	Power and light	4,000	4,500	5,000	5,500
11	Indirect materials	2,400	2,700	3,000	3,300
12	Total variable cost	$14,400	$16,200	$18,000	$19,800
13	Fixed costs:				
14	Supervisory salaries	$ 5,500	$ 5,500	$ 5,500	$ 5,500
15	Depreciation of plant				
16	and equipment	4,500	4,500	4,500	4,500
17	Insurance and property taxes	2,000	2,000	2,000	2,000
18	Total fixed cost	$12,000	$12,000	$12,000	$12,000
19	Total factory overhead cost	$26,400	$28,200	$30,000	$31,800
20					
21	Factory overhead rate per direct labor hour, $30,000 ÷ 5,000 hours = $6.00				
22					

Exhibit 8 indicates that the budgeted factory overhead rate for Western Rider is $6.00, computed as follows:

$$\text{Factory Overhead Rate} = \frac{\text{Budgeted Factory Overhead at Normal Productive Capacity}}{\text{Normal Productive Capacity}}$$

$$= \frac{\$30,000}{5,000 \text{ direct labor hrs.}} = \$6.00 \text{ per direct labor hr.}$$

The normal productive capacity is expressed in terms of an activity base such as direct labor hours, direct labor cost, or machine hours. For Western Rider, 100% of normal capacity is 5,000 direct labor hours. The budgeted factory overhead cost at 100% of normal capacity is $30,000, which consists of variable overhead of $18,000 and fixed overhead of $12,000.

For analysis purposes, the budgeted factory overhead rate is subdivided into a variable factory overhead rate and a fixed factory overhead rate. For Western Rider, the variable overhead rate is $3.60 per direct labor hour and the fixed overhead rate is $2.40 per direct labor hour, computed as follows:

$$\text{Variable Factory Overhead Rate} = \frac{\text{Budgeted Variable Overhead at Normal Productive Capacity}}{\text{Normal Productive Capacity}}$$

$$= \frac{\$18,000}{5,000 \text{ direct labor hrs.}} = \$3.60 \text{ per direct labor hr.}$$

$$\text{Fixed Factory Overhead Rate} = \frac{\text{Budgeted Fixed Overhead at Normal Productive Capacity}}{\text{Normal Productive Capacity}}$$

$$= \frac{\$12,000}{5,000 \text{ direct labor hrs.}} = \$2.40 \text{ per direct labor hr.}$$

To summarize, the budgeted factory overhead rates for Western Rider Inc. are as follows:

Variable factory overhead rate	$3.60
Fixed factory overhead rate	2.40
Total factory overhead rate	$6.00

As mentioned previously, factory overhead variances can be separated into a controllable variance and a volume variance as discussed in the next sections.

Variable Factory Overhead Controllable Variance

The variable factory overhead **controllable variance** is the difference between the actual variable overhead costs and the budgeted variable overhead for actual production. It is computed as follows:

$$\text{Variable Factory Overhead Controllable Variance} = \text{Actual Variable Factory Overhead} - \text{Budgeted Variable Factory Overhead}$$

If the actual variable overhead is less than the budgeted variable overhead, the variance is favorable. If the actual variable overhead exceeds the budgeted variable overhead, the variance is unfavorable.

The **budgeted variable factory overhead** is the standard variable overhead for the *actual* units produced. It is computed as follows:

$$\text{Budgeted Variable Factory Overhead} = \text{Standard Hours for Actual Units Produced} \times \text{Variable Factory Overhead Rate}$$

To illustrate, the budgeted variable overhead for **Western Rider Inc.** for June, when 5,000 units of XL jeans were produced, is $14,400, computed as follows:

$$\begin{aligned}\text{Budgeted Variable Factory Overhead} &= \text{Standard Hours for Actual Units Produced} \\ &\quad \times \text{Variable Factory Overhead Rate} \\ &= 4{,}000 \text{ direct labor hrs.} \times \$3.60 \\ &= \$14{,}400\end{aligned}$$

The preceding computation is based on the fact that Western Rider produced 5,000 XL jeans, which requires a standard of 4,000 (5,000 units × 0.8 hr.) direct labor hours. The variable factory overhead rate of $3.60 was computed earlier. Thus, the budgeted variable factory overhead is $14,400 (4,000 direct labor hrs. × $3.60).

During June, assume that Western Rider incurred the following actual factory overhead costs:

	Actual Costs in June
Variable factory overhead	$10,400
Fixed factory overhead	12,000
Total actual factory overhead	$22,400

Based on the actual variable factory overhead incurred in June, the variable factory overhead controllable variance is a $4,000 favorable variance, computed as follows:

$$\begin{aligned}\text{Variable Factory Overhead Controllable Variance} &= \text{Actual Variable Factory Overhead} - \text{Budgeted Variable Factory Overhead} \\ &= \$10{,}400 - \$14{,}400 \\ &= \$(4{,}000) \text{ Favorable Variance}\end{aligned}$$

The variable factory overhead controllable variance indicates the ability to keep the factory overhead costs within the budget limits. Because variable factory overhead costs are normally controllable at the department level, responsibility for controlling this variance usually rests with department supervisors.

> **Example Exercise 23-3** **Factory Overhead Controllable Variance** **Obj. 4**
>
> Tip Top Corp. produced 3,000 units of product that required 2.5 standard hours per unit. The standard variable overhead cost per unit is $2.20 per hour. The actual variable factory overhead was $16,850. Determine the variable factory overhead controllable variance.
>
> **Follow My Example 23-3**
>
> Variable Factory Overhead Controllable Variance = Actual Variable Factory Overhead − Budgeted Variable Factory Overhead
>
> = $16,850 − [(3,000 units × 2.5 hrs.) × $2.20]
> = $16,850 − $16,500
> = $350 (unfavorable)
>
> Practice Exercises: PE 23-3A, PE 23-3B

Fixed Factory Overhead Volume Variance

Western Rider's budgeted factory overhead is based on a 100% normal capacity of 5,000 direct labor hours, as shown in Exhibit 8. This is the expected capacity that management believes will be used under normal business conditions. Exhibit 8 indicates that the 5,000 direct labor hours is less than the total available capacity of 110%, which is 5,500 direct labor hours.

The fixed factory overhead **volume variance** is the difference between the budgeted fixed overhead at 100% of normal capacity and the standard fixed overhead for the actual units produced. It is computed as follows:

$$\text{Fixed Factory Overhead Volume Variance} = \left(\text{Standard Hours for 100\% of Normal Capacity} - \text{Standard Hours for Actual Units Produced}\right) \times \text{Fixed Factory Overhead Rate}$$

The volume variance measures the use of fixed overhead resources (plant and equipment). The interpretation of an unfavorable and a favorable fixed factory overhead volume variance is as follows:

- *Unfavorable*. The actual units produced is *less than* 100% of normal capacity; thus, the company used its fixed overhead resources (plant and equipment) less than would be expected under normal operating conditions.
- *Favorable*. The actual units produced is *more than* 100% of normal capacity; thus, the company used its fixed overhead resources (plant and equipment) more than would be expected under normal operating conditions.

To illustrate, the fixed factory overhead volume variance for **Western Rider Inc.** is a $2,400 unfavorable variance, computed as follows:

$$\text{Fixed Factory Overhead Volume Variance} = \left(\text{Standard Hours for 100\% of Normal Capacity} - \text{Standard Hours for Actual Units Produced}\right) \times \text{Fixed Factory Overhead Rate}$$

$$= (5{,}000 \text{ direct labor hrs.} - 4{,}000 \text{ direct labor hrs.}) \times \$2.40$$

$$= \$2{,}400 \text{ Unfavorable Variance}$$

Because Western Rider produced 5,000 units of XL jeans during June, the standard for the actual units produced is 4,000 (5,000 units × 0.80) direct labor hours. This is 1,000 hours less than the 5,000 standard hours of normal capacity. The fixed overhead rate of $2.40 was computed earlier. Thus, the unfavorable fixed factory overhead volume variance is $2,400 (1,000 direct labor hrs. × $2.40).

Exhibit 9 illustrates graphically the fixed factory overhead volume variance for **Western Rider Inc.** The budgeted fixed overhead does not change and is $12,000 at all levels of production. At 100% of normal capacity (5,000 direct labor hours), the standard fixed overhead line intersects the budgeted fixed costs line. For production levels *more than* 100% of normal capacity (5,000 direct labor hours), the volume variance is *favorable*. For production levels *less than* 100% of normal capacity (5,000 direct labor hours), the volume variance is *unfavorable*.

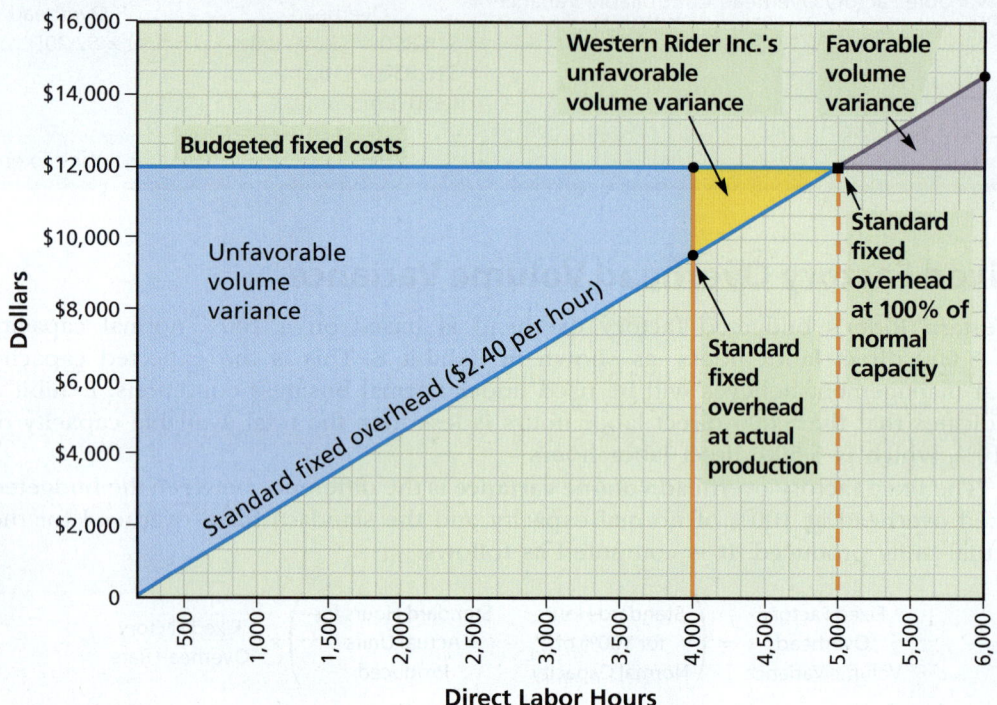

EXHIBIT 9

Graph of Fixed Overhead Volume Variance

Exhibit 9 indicates that Western Rider's fixed factory overhead volume variance is unfavorable in June because the actual production is 4,000 direct labor hours, or 80% of normal volume. The unfavorable volume variance of $2,400 can be viewed as the cost of the unused capacity (1,000 direct labor hours).

An unfavorable volume variance may be due to factors such as the following:

- Failure to maintain an even flow of work
- Machine breakdowns
- Work stoppages caused by lack of materials or skilled labor
- Lack of enough sales orders to keep the factory operating at normal capacity

Management should determine the causes of the unfavorable variance and consider taking corrective action. For example, a volume variance caused by an uneven flow of work could be remedied by changing operating procedures. Lack of sales orders may be corrected through increased advertising.

Favorable volume variances may not always be desirable. For example, in an attempt to create a favorable volume variance, manufacturing managers might run the factory above the normal capacity. However, if the additional production cannot be sold, it must be stored as inventory, which would incur storage costs.

Example Exercise 23-4 Factory Overhead Volume Variance   Obj. 4

Tip Top Corp. produced 3,000 units of product that required 2.5 standard hours per unit. The standard fixed overhead cost per unit is $0.90 per hour at 8,000 hours, which is 100% of normal capacity. Determine the fixed factory overhead volume variance.

> **Follow My Example 23-4**
>
> Fixed Factory Overhead Volume Variance = (Standard Hours for 100% of Normal Capacity − Standard Hours for Actual Units Produced) × Fixed Factory Overhead Rate
> = [8,000 hrs. − (3,000 units × 2.5 hrs.)] × $0.90
> = (8,000 hrs. − 7,500 hrs.) × $0.90
> = $450 (unfavorable)
>
> Practice Exercises: PE 23-4A, PE 23-4B

Reporting Factory Overhead Variances

The total factory overhead cost variance can also be determined as the sum of the variable factory overhead controllable and fixed factory overhead volume variances, computed as follows for **Western Rider Inc.**:

Variable factory overhead controllable variance	$(4,000) Favorable Variance
Fixed factory overhead volume variance	2,400 Unfavorable Variance
Total factory overhead cost variance	$(1,600) Favorable Variance

A **factory overhead cost variance report** is useful to management in controlling factory overhead costs. Budgeted and actual costs for variable and fixed factory overhead along with the related controllable and volume variances are reported by each cost element.

Exhibit 10 illustrates a factory overhead cost variance report for Western Rider Inc. for June.

EXHIBIT 10

Factory Overhead Cost Variance Report

	A	B	C	D	E
1		Western Rider Inc.			
2		Factory Overhead Cost Variance Report			
3		For the Month Ending June 30			
4	Productive capacity for the month (100% of normal)		5,000 hours		
5	Actual production for the month		4,000 hours		
6					
7			Budget		
8			(at Actual	Variances	
9		Actual	Production)	Unfavorable	Favorable
10	Variable factory overhead costs:				
11	Indirect factory wages	$ 5,100	$ 8,000		$(2,900)
12	Power and light	4,200	4,000	$ 200	
13	Indirect materials	1,100	2,400		(1,300)
14	Total variable factory				
15	overhead cost	$10,400	$14,400		
16	Fixed factory overhead costs:				
17	Supervisory salaries	$ 5,500	$ 5,500		
18	Depreciation of plant and				
19	equipment	4,500	4,500		
20	Insurance and property taxes	2,000	2,000		
21	Total fixed factory				
22	overhead cost	$12,000	$12,000		
23	Total factory overhead cost	$22,400	$26,400		
24	Total controllable variances			$ 200	$(4,200)
25					
26					
27	Net controllable variance—favorable [$(4,200) favorable + $200 unfavorable]			$(4,000)	
28	Volume variance—unfavorable:				
29	Capacity not used at the standard rate for fixed				
30	factory overhead—1,000 × $2.40			2,400	
31	Total factory overhead cost variance—favorable			$(1,600)	
32					

Factory Overhead Account

To illustrate, the applied factory overhead for **Western Rider Inc.** for the 5,000 units of XL jeans produced in June is $24,000, computed as follows:

$$\text{Applied Factory Overhead} = \text{Standard Hours for Actual Units Produced} \times \text{Total Factory Overhead Rate}$$

$$= (5,000 \text{ jeans} \times 0.80 \text{ direct labor hr. per unit}) \times \$6.00$$

$$= 4,000 \text{ direct labor hrs.} \times \$6.00 = \$24,000$$

The total actual factory overhead for Western Rider, as shown in Exhibit 10, was $22,400. Thus, the total factory overhead cost variance for Western Rider for June is a $1,600 favorable variance, computed as follows:

$$\text{Total Factory Overhead Cost Variance} = \text{Actual Factory Overhead} - \text{Applied Factory Overhead}$$

$$= \$22,400 - \$24,000 = \$(1,600) \text{ Favorable Variance}$$

At the end of the period, the factory overhead account typically has a debit or credit balance. A debit balance in Factory Overhead represents underapplied overhead. Underapplied overhead occurs when actual factory overhead costs exceed the applied factory overhead. A credit balance in Factory Overhead represents overapplied overhead. Overapplied overhead occurs when actual factory overhead costs are less than the applied factory overhead.

The difference between the actual factory overhead and the applied factory overhead is the total factory overhead cost variance. Thus, underapplied and overapplied factory overhead account balances represent the following total factory overhead cost variances:

- *Underapplied* Factory Overhead = *Unfavorable* Total Factory Overhead Cost Variance
- *Overapplied* Factory Overhead = *Favorable* Total Factory Overhead Cost Variance

The factory overhead account for **Western Rider Inc.** for the month ending June 30 is as follows:

	Factory Overhead	
Actual factory overhead ($10,400 + $12,000)	22,400	24,000 Applied factory overhead (4,000 hrs. × $6.00 per hr.)
	Bal., June 30	1,600 Overapplied factory overhead

The $1,600 overapplied factory overhead account balance and the favorable total factory overhead cost variance shown in Exhibit 10 are the same.

The variable factory overhead controllable variance and the volume variance can be computed by comparing the factory overhead account with the budgeted total overhead for the actual level produced, as shown in Exhibit 11.

The controllable and volume variances are determined as follows:

- The difference between the actual overhead incurred and the budgeted overhead is the *controllable* variance.
- The difference between the applied overhead and the budgeted overhead is the *volume* variance.

If the actual factory overhead exceeds (is less than) the budgeted factory overhead, the controllable variance is unfavorable (favorable). In contrast, if the applied factory overhead is less than (exceeds) the budgeted factory overhead, the volume variance is unfavorable (favorable).

Factory Overhead Variances

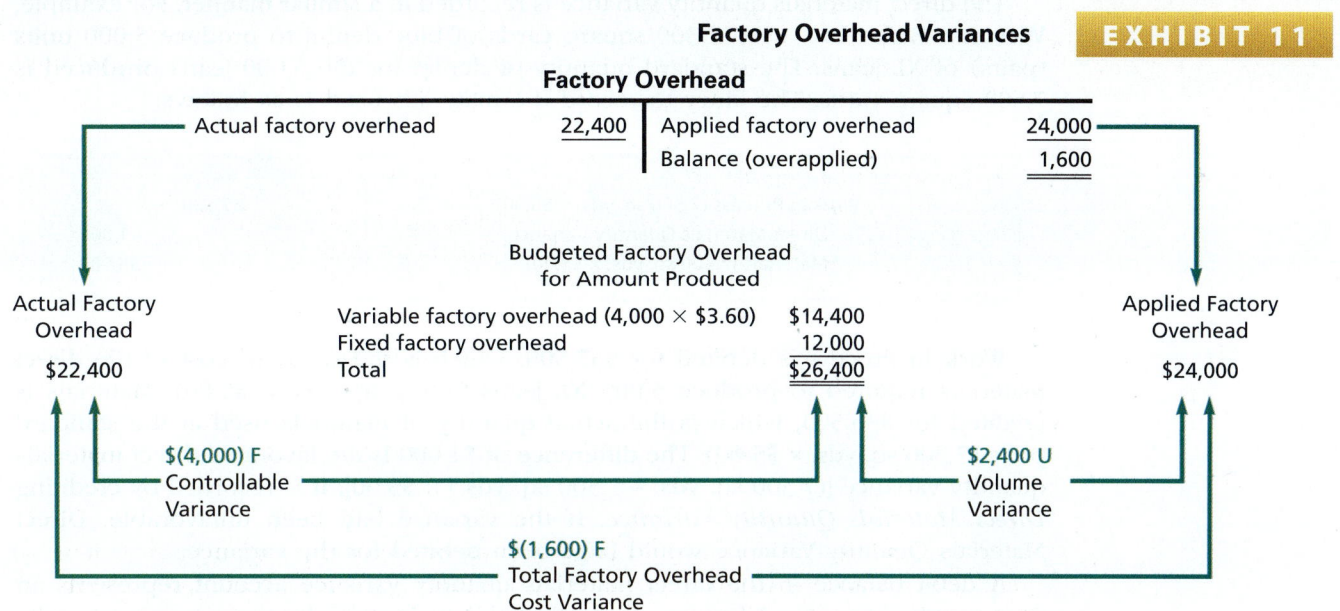

EXHIBIT 11

Recording and Reporting Variances from Standards

Obj. 5 Journalize the entries for recording standards in the accounts and prepare an income statement that includes variances from standard.

Standard costs may be used as a management tool to control costs separately from the accounts in the general ledger. However, many companies include standard costs in their accounts. One method for doing so records standard costs and variances at the same time the actual product costs are recorded.

To illustrate, assume that **Western Rider Inc.** purchased, on account, the 7,300 square yards of blue denim used at $5.50 per square yard. The standard price for direct materials is $5.00 per square yard. The entry to record the purchase and the unfavorable direct materials price variance is as follows:

Materials (7,300 sq. yds. × $5.00)	36,500	
Direct Materials Price Variance	3,650	
Accounts Payable (7,300 sq. yds. × $5.50)		40,150

The materials account is debited for the *actual quantity* purchased at the *standard price*, $36,500 (7,300 square yards × $5.00). Accounts Payable is credited for the $40,150 actual cost and the amount due the supplier. The difference of $3,650 is the unfavorable direct materials price variance [($5.50 − $5.00) × 7,300 sq. yds.]. It is recorded by debiting Direct Materials Price Variance. If the variance had been favorable, Direct Materials Price Variance would have been credited for the variance.

A debit balance in the direct materials price variance account represents an unfavorable variance. Likewise, a credit balance in the direct materials price variance account represents a favorable variance.

The direct materials quantity variance is recorded in a similar manner. For example, Western Rider Inc. used 7,300 square yards of blue denim to produce 5,000 units (pairs) of XL jeans. The standard quantity of denim for the 5,000 jeans produced is 7,500 square yards. The entry to record the materials used is as follows:

Work in Process (7,500 sq. yds. × $5.00)	37,500	
Direct Materials Quantity Variance		1,000
Materials (7,300 sq. yds. × $5.00)		36,500

Work in Process is debited for $37,500, which is the standard cost of the direct materials required to produce 5,000 XL jeans (7,500 sq. yds. × $5.00). Materials is credited for $36,500, which is the actual quantity of materials used at the standard price (7,300 sq. yds. × $5.00). The difference of $1,000 is the favorable direct materials quantity variance [(7,300 sq. yds. – 7,500 sq. yds.) × $5.00]. It is recorded by crediting *Direct Materials Quantity Variance*. If the variance had been unfavorable, Direct Materials Quantity Variance would have been debited for the variance.

A debit balance in the direct materials quantity variance account represents an unfavorable variance. Likewise, a credit balance in the direct materials quantity variance account represents a favorable variance.

Example Exercise 23-5 Standard Cost Journal Entries   Obj. 5

Tip Top Corp. produced 3,000 units that require six standard pounds per unit at the $4.50 standard price per pound. The company actually used 18,500 pounds in production. Journalize the entry to record the standard direct materials used in production.

Follow My Example 23-5

Work in Process (18,000* pounds × $4.50)	81,000	
Direct Materials Quantity Variance [(18,500 pounds – 18,000 pounds) × $4.50]	2,250	
Materials (18,500 pounds × $4.50)		83,250

*3,000 units × 6 pounds per unit = 18,000 standard pounds for units produced

Practice Exercises: PE 23-5A, PE 23-5B

The journal entries to record the standard costs and variances for *direct labor* are similar to those for direct materials. These entries are summarized as follows:

- Work in Process is debited for the standard cost of direct labor.
- Wages Payable is credited for the actual direct labor cost incurred.
- Direct Labor Rate Variance is debited for an unfavorable variance and credited for a favorable variance.
- Direct Labor Time Variance is debited for an unfavorable variance and credited for a favorable variance.

As illustrated in the prior section, the factory overhead account already incorporates standard costs and variances into its journal entries. That is, Factory Overhead is debited for actual factory overhead and credited for applied (standard) factory overhead. The ending balance of factory overhead (overapplied or underapplied) is the total factory overhead cost variance. By comparing the actual factory overhead with the budgeted factory overhead, the controllable variance can be determined. By comparing the budgeted factory overhead with the applied factory overhead, the volume variance can be determined.

When goods are completed, Finished Goods is debited and Work in Process is credited for the standard cost of the product transferred.

At the end of the period, the balances of each of the variance accounts indicate the net favorable or unfavorable variance for the period. These variances may be reported in an income statement prepared for management's use.

Exhibit 12 is an example of an income statement for **Western Rider Inc.** that includes variances. In Exhibit 12, a sales price of $28 per unit (pair) of jeans, selling expenses of $14,500, and administrative expenses of $11,225 are assumed.

EXHIBIT 12
Variance from Standards in Income Statement

Western Rider Inc.
Income Statement
For the Month Ended June 30

	Unfavorable	Favorable	
Sales			$140,000[1]
Cost of goods sold—at standard			97,500[2]
Gross profit—at standard			$ 42,500
Less variance adjustments to gross profit—at standard:			
Direct materials price	$3,650		
Direct materials quantity		$ (1,000)	
Direct labor rate	3,850		
Direct labor time		(1,350)	
Factory overhead controllable		(4,000)	
Factory overhead volume	2,400		
Net variance from standard cost—unfavorable			3,550
Gross profit			$ 38,950
Operating expenses:			
Selling expenses		$14,500	
Administrative expenses		11,225	25,725
Income before income tax			$ 13,225

[1] 5,000 × $28
[2] $37,500 + $36,000 + $24,000 (from Exhibit 3), or 5,000 × $19.50 (from Exhibit 1)

The income statement shown in Exhibit 12 is for internal use by management. That is, variances are not reported to external users. Thus, the variances shown in Exhibit 12 must be transferred to other accounts in preparing an income statement for external users.

In preparing an income statement for external users, the balances of the variance accounts are normally transferred to Cost of Goods Sold. However, if the variances are significant or if many of the products manufactured are still in inventory, the variances should be allocated to Work in Process, Finished Goods, and Cost of Goods Sold. Such an allocation, in effect, converts these account balances from standard cost to actual cost.

Example Exercise 23-6 Income Statement with Variances   Obj. 5

Prepare an income statement for the year ended December 31 through gross profit for Tip Top Corp. using the variance data in Example Exercises 23-1 through 23-4. Assume that Tip Top sold 3,000 units at $100 per unit.

(Continued)

Follow My Example 23-6

Tip Top Corp.
Income Statement Through Gross Profit
For the Year Ended December 31

	Unfavorable	Favorable	
Sales (3,000 units × $100)			$300,000
Cost of goods sold—at standard			194,250*
Gross profit—at standard			$105,750
Less variance adjustments to gross profit—at standard:			
Direct materials price (EE23-1)		$(2,775)	
Direct materials quantity (EE23-1)	$2,250		
Direct labor rate (EE23-2)	2,226		
Direct labor time (EE23-2)		(960)	
Factory overhead controllable (EE23-3)	350		
Factory overhead volume (EE23-4)	450		
Net variance from standard cost—unfavorable			1,541
Gross profit—actual			$104,209

*Direct materials (3,000 units × 6 lb. × $4.50)	$ 81,000	
Direct labor (3,000 units × 2.5 hrs. × $12.00)	90,000	
Factory overhead [3,000 units × 2.5 hrs. × ($2.20 + $0.90)]	23,250	
Cost of goods sold at standard	$194,250	

Practice Exercises: PE 23-6A, PE 23-6B

Obj. 6 Describe and provide examples of nonfinancial performance measures.

Nonfinancial Performance Measures

Many companies supplement standard costs and variances from standards with nonfinancial performance measures. A **nonfinancial performance measure** expresses performance in a measure other than dollars. For example, airlines use on-time performance, percent of bags lost, and number of customer complaints as nonfinancial performance measures. Such measures are often used to evaluate the time, quality, or quantity of a business activity.

Using financial and nonfinancial performance measures aids managers and employees in considering multiple performance objectives. Such measures often bring additional perspectives, such as quality of work, to evaluating performance. Some examples of nonfinancial performance measures are shown in Exhibit 13.

Link to BMW Group

The **BMW Group** uses a variety of nonfinancial performance measures for its vehicles and manufacturing operations, including energy consumption, water consumption, carbon dioxide emissions, percent of women in its workforce, average days of training per employee, and accident frequency.

EXHIBIT 13   Nonfinancial Performance Measures

- Inventory turnover
- Percent of on-time delivery
- Elapsed time between a customer order and product delivery
- Customer preference rankings compared to competitors
- Response time to a service call
- Time to develop new products
- Employee satisfaction
- Number of customer complaints

Nonfinancial measures are often linked to either the inputs or outputs of an activity or process. A **process** is a sequence of activities for performing a task. The relationship between an activity or a process and its inputs and outputs is shown in Exhibit 14.

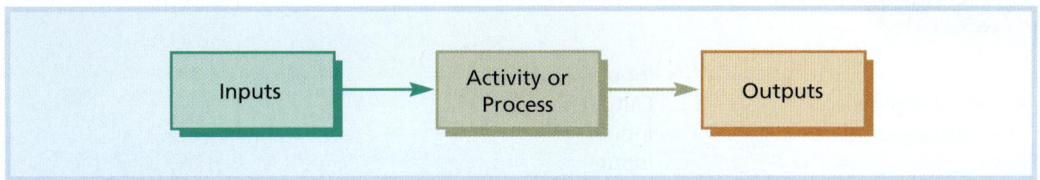

EXHIBIT 14

Relationship Between a Process and Its Inputs and Outputs

To illustrate, the counter service activity of a fast-food restaurant is used. The inputs/outputs for providing counter service at a fast-food restaurant are shown in Exhibit 15.

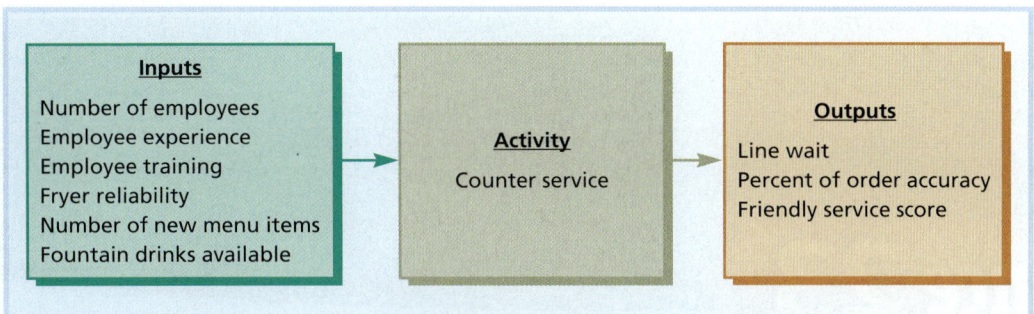

EXHIBIT 15

Inputs/Outputs for a Fast-Food Restaurant

The customer service outputs of the counter service activity include the following:

- Line wait for the customer
- Percent of order accuracy in serving the customer
- Friendly service experience for the customer

Some of the inputs that impact the customer service outputs include the following:

- Number of employees
- Employee experience
- Employee training
- Fryer (and other cooking equipment) reliability
- Number of new menu items
- Fountain drinks available

A fast-food restaurant can develop a set of linked nonfinancial performance measures across inputs and outputs. The output measures tell management how the activity is performing, such as keeping the line wait to a minimum. The input measures are used to improve the output measures. For example, if the customer line wait is too long, then improving employee training or hiring more employees could improve the output (decrease customer line wait).

Link to BMW Group

The **BMW Group** assesses its suppliers using a BMW sustainability standard that measures compliance with human rights, labor, and social issues.

Example Exercise 23-7 Activity Inputs and Outputs   Obj. 6

The following are inputs and outputs to the baggage claim process of an airline:

Baggage handler training
Time customers wait for returned baggage
Maintenance of baggage handling equipment
Number of baggage handlers
Number of damaged bags
On-time flight performance

Identify whether each is an input or output to the baggage claim process.

(Continued)

Follow My Example 23-7

Baggage handler training	Input
Time customers wait for returned baggage	Output
Maintenance of baggage handling equipment	Input
Number of baggage handlers	Input
Number of damaged bags	Output
On-time flight performance	Input

Practice Exercises: PE 23-7A, PE 23-7B

At a Glance 23

Obj. 1 Describe the types of standards and how they are established.

Key Points Standards represent performance goals that can be compared to actual results in evaluating performance. Standards are established so that they are neither too high nor too low but are attainable.

Learning Outcomes	Example Exercises	Practice Exercises
• Define *ideal* and *currently attainable standards* and explain how they are used in setting standards.		
• Describe some of the criticisms of the use of standards.		

Obj. 2 Describe and illustrate how standards are used in budgeting.

Key Points Budgets are prepared by multiplying the standard cost per unit by the planned production. To measure performance, the standard cost per unit is multiplied by the actual number of units produced, and the actual results are compared with the standard cost at actual volumes (cost variance).

Learning Outcomes	Example Exercises	Practice Exercises
• Compute the standard cost per unit of production for materials, labor, and factory overhead.		
• Compute the direct materials, direct labor, and factory overhead cost variances.		
• Prepare a budget performance report.		

Obj. 3 Compute and interpret direct materials and direct labor variances.

Key Points The direct materials cost variance can be separated into direct materials price and quantity variances. The direct labor cost variance can be separated into direct labor rate and time variances.

Learning Outcomes	Example Exercises	Practice Exercises
• Compute and interpret direct materials price and quantity variances.	EE23-1	PE23-1A, 23-1B
• Compute and interpret direct labor rate and time variances.	EE23-2	PE23-2A, 23-2B
• Describe and illustrate how time standards are used in nonmanufacturing settings.		

Obj. 4 Compute and interpret factory overhead controllable and volume variances.

Key Points The factory overhead cost variance can be separated into a variable factory overhead controllable variance and a fixed factory overhead volume variance.

Learning Outcomes	Example Exercises	Practice Exercises
• Prepare a factory overhead flexible budget.		
• Compute and interpret the variable factory overhead controllable variance.	EE23-3	PE23-3A, 23-3B
• Compute and interpret the fixed factory overhead volume variance.	EE23-4	PE23-4A, 23-4B
• Prepare a factory overhead cost variance report.		
• Evaluate factory overhead variances using a T account.		

Obj. 5 Journalize the entries for recording standards in the accounts and prepare an income statement that includes variances from standard.

Key Points Standard costs and variances can be recorded in the accounts at the same time the manufacturing costs are recorded in the accounts. Work in Process is debited at standard. Under a standard cost system, the cost of goods sold will be reported at standard cost. Manufacturing variances can be disclosed on the income statement to adjust the gross profit at standard to the actual gross profit.

Learning Outcomes	Example Exercises	Practice Exercises
• Journalize the entries to record the purchase and use of direct materials at standard, recording favorable or unfavorable variances.	EE23-5	PE23-5A, 23-5B
• Prepare an income statement, disclosing favorable and unfavorable direct materials, direct labor, and factory overhead variances.	EE23-6	PE23-6A, 23-6B

Obj. 6 Describe and provide examples of nonfinancial performance measures.

Key Points Many companies use a combination of financial and nonfinancial measures in order for multiple perspectives to be incorporated in evaluating performance. Nonfinancial measures are often used in conjunction with the inputs or outputs of a process or an activity.

Learning Outcomes	Example Exercises	Practice Exercises
• Define, provide the rationale for, and provide examples of nonfinancial performance measures.		
• Identify nonfinancial inputs and outputs of an activity.	EE23-7	PE23-7A, 23-7B

Illustrative Problem

Hawley Inc. manufactures designer iPod cases for national distribution. The standard costs for the manufacture of Folk Art style baskets were as follows:

	Standard Costs	Actual Costs
Direct materials	1,500 lb. at $35	1,600 lb. at $32
Direct labor	4,800 hrs. at $11	4,500 hrs. at $11.80
Factory overhead	Rates per labor hour, based on 100% of normal capacity of 5,500 labor hrs.:	
	Variable cost, $2.40	$12,300 variable cost
	Fixed cost, $3.50	$19,250 fixed cost

Instructions

1. Determine the direct materials price variance, direct materials quantity variance, and total direct materials cost variance for the designer iPod cases.

2. Determine the direct labor rate variance, direct labor time variance, and total direct labor cost variance for the designer iPod cases.

3. Determine the variable factory overhead controllable variance, fixed factory overhead volume variance, and total factory overhead cost variance for the designer iPod cases.

Solution

1. **Direct Materials Cost Variance**

   Price variance:
   Direct Materials Price Variance = (Actual Price − Standard Price) × Actual Quantity
   = ($32 per lb. − $35 per lb.) × 1,600 lb.
   = $(4,800) Favorable Variance

   Quantity variance:
   Direct Materials Quantity Variance = (Actual Quantity − Standard Quantity) × Standard Price
   = (1,600 lb. − 1,500 lb.) × $35 per lb.
   = $3,500 Unfavorable Variance

   Total direct materials cost variance:
   Direct Materials Cost Variance = Direct Materials Quantity Variance + Direct Materials Price Variance
   = $3,500 Unfavorable + $(4,800) Favorable
   = $(1,300) Favorable Variance

2.
Direct Labor Cost Variance

Rate variance:

Direct Labor Rate Variance = (Actual Rate per Hour − Standard Rate per Hour) × Actual Hours
= ($11.80 − $11.00) × 4,500 hrs.
= $3,600 Unfavorable Variance

Time variance:

Direct Labor Time Variance = (Actual Direct Labor Hours − Standard Direct Labor Hours) × Standard Rate per Hour
= (4,500 hrs. − 4,800 hrs.) × $11.00 per hour
= $(3,300) Favorable Variance

Total direct labor cost variance:

Direct Labor Cost Variance = Direct Labor Time Variance + Direct Labor Rate Variance
= $(3,300) Favorable + $3,600 Unfavorable
= $300 Unfavorable Variance

3.
Factory Overhead Cost Variance

Variable factory overhead controllable variance:

Variable Factory Overhead Controllable Variance = Actual Variable Factory Overhead − Budgeted Variable Factory Overhead
= $12,300 − (4,800 hours × $2.40 per hour)
= $780 Unfavorable Variance

Fixed factory overhead volume variance:

Fixed Factory Overhead Volume Variance = (Standard Hours for 100% of Normal Capacity − Standard Hours for Actual Units Produced) × Fixed Factory Overhead Rate
= (5,500 hrs. − 4,800 hrs.) × $3.50 per hr.
= $2,450 Unfavorable Variance

Total factory overhead cost variance:

Factory Overhead Cost Variance = Variable Factory Overhead Controllable Variance + Fixed Factory Overhead Volume Variance
= $780 Unfavorable + $2,450 Unfavorable
= $3,230 Unfavorable Variance

Factory Overhead

Actual costs	31,550	Applied costs	28,320*
Balance (underapplied)	3,230		

Actual Factory Overhead
$31,550

Budgeted Factory Overhead for Amount Produced
Variable cost ($2.40 per hour × 4,800 hours) $11,520
Fixed cost   19,250
Total $30,770

Applied Factory Overhead
$28,320*

$780 U Controllable Variance

$2,450 U Volume Variance

$3,230 U Total Factory Overhead Cost Variance

*($2.40 + $3.50) × 4,800

Chapter 23 Evaluating Variances from Standard Costs

Key Terms

- budget performance report (1129)
- budgeted variable factory overhead (1138)
- controllable variance (1138)
- cost variance (1129)
- currently attainable standards (1127)
- direct labor rate variance (1134)
- direct labor time variance (1135)
- direct materials price variance (1132)
- direct materials quantity variance (1132)
- factory overhead cost variance report (1141)
- favorable cost variance (1129)
- ideal standards (1127)
- nonfinancial performance measure (1146)
- process (1146)
- standard cost (1126)
- standard cost systems (1126)
- standards (1126)
- total manufacturing cost variance (1129)
- unfavorable cost variance (1129)
- volume variance (1139)

Discussion Questions

1. What are the basic objectives in the use of standard costs?
2. What is meant by reporting by the "principle of exceptions" as the term is used in reference to cost control?
3. What are the two variances between the actual cost and the standard cost for direct materials?
4. The materials cost variance report for Nickols Inc. indicates a large favorable materials price variance and a significant unfavorable materials quantity variance. What might have caused these offsetting variances?
5. a. What are the two variances between the actual cost and the standard cost for direct labor?
   b. Who generally has control over the direct labor cost variances?
6. A new assistant controller recently was heard to remark: "All the assembly workers in this plant are covered by union contracts, so there should be no labor variances." Was the controller's remark correct? Discuss.
7. Would the use of standards be appropriate in a nonmanufacturing setting such as a fast-food restaurant?
8. a. Describe the two variances between the actual costs and the standard costs for factory overhead.
   b. What is a factory overhead cost variance report?
9. If variances are recorded in the accounts at the time the manufacturing costs are incurred, what does a debit balance in Direct Materials Price Variance represent?
10. Briefly explain why firms might use nonfinancial performance measures.

Practice Exercises

Example Exercises

EE 23-1 p. 1133   **PE 23-1A**   Direct materials variances   OBJ. 3

Bellingham Company produces a product that requires 2.5 standard pounds per unit. The standard price is $3.75 per pound. If 15,000 units required 36,000 pounds, which were purchased at $4.00 per pound, what is the direct materials (a) price variance, (b) quantity variance, and (c) total direct materials cost variance?

Chapter 23 Evaluating Variances from Standard Costs 1153

EE 23-1 *p. 1133*   **PE 23-1B**   **Direct materials variances**   OBJ. 3

Dvorak Company produces a product that requires 5 standard pounds per unit. The standard price is $2.50 per pound. If 1,000 units required 4,500 pounds, which were purchased at $3.00 per pound, what is the direct materials (a) price variance, (b) quantity variance, and (c) total direct materials cost variance?

EE 23-2 *p. 1136*   **PE 23-2A**   **Direct labor variances**   OBJ. 3

Bellingham Company produces a product that requires 4 standard hours per unit at a standard hourly rate of $20 per hour. If 15,000 units required 61,800 hours at an hourly rate of $19.85 per hour, what is the direct labor (a) rate variance, (b) time variance, and (c) total direct labor cost variance?

EE 23-2 *p. 1136*   **PE 23-2B**   **Direct labor variances**   OBJ. 3

Dvorak Company produces a product that requires 3 standard hours per unit at a standard hourly rate of $17 per hour. If 1,000 units required 2,800 hours at an hourly rate of $16.50 per hour, what is the direct labor (a) rate variance, (b) time variance, and (c) total direct labor cost variance?

EE 23-3 *p. 1139*   **PE 23-3A**   **Factory overhead controllable variance**   OBJ. 4

Bellingham Company produced 15,000 units of product that required 4 standard hours per unit. The standard variable overhead cost per unit is $0.90 per hour. The actual variable factory overhead was $52,770. Determine the variable factory overhead controllable variance.

EE 23-3 *p. 1139*   **PE 23-3B**   **Factory overhead controllable variance**   OBJ. 4

Dvorak Company produced 1,000 units of product that required 3 standard hours per unit. The standard variable overhead cost per unit is $1.40 per hour. The actual variable factory overhead was $4,000. Determine the variable factory overhead controllable variance.

EE 23-4 *p. 1140*   **PE 23-4A**   **Factory overhead volume variance**   OBJ. 4

Bellingham Company produced 15,000 units of product that required 4 standard hours per unit. The standard fixed overhead cost per unit is $1.15 per hour at 58,000 hours, which is 100% of normal capacity. Determine the fixed factory overhead volume variance.

EE 23-4 *p. 1140*   **PE 23-4B**   **Factory overhead volume variance**   OBJ. 4

Dvorak Company produced 1,000 units of product that required 3 standard hours per unit. The standard fixed overhead cost per unit is $0.60 per hour at 3,500 hours, which is 100% of normal capacity. Determine the fixed factory overhead volume variance.

EE 23-5 *p. 1144*   **PE 23-5A**   **Standard cost journal entries**   OBJ. 5

Bellingham Company produced 15,000 units that require 2.5 standard pounds per unit at $3.75 standard price per pound. The company actually used 36,000 pounds in production. Journalize the entry to record the standard direct materials used in production.

EE 23-5 *p. 1144*   **PE 23-5B**   **Standard cost journal entries**   OBJ. 5

Dvorak Company produced 1,000 units that require 5 standard pounds per unit at $2.50 standard price per pound. The company actually used 4,500 pounds in production. Journalize the entry to record the standard direct materials used in production.

EE 23-6 *p. 1145*   **PE 23-6A**   **Income statement with variances**   OBJ. 5

Prepare an income statement through gross profit for Bellingham Company for the month ended March 31 using the variance data in Practice Exercises 23-1A through 23-4A. Assume that Bellingham sold 15,000 units at $172 per unit.

1154 Chapter 23 Evaluating Variances from Standard Costs

EE 23-6 p. 1145

PE 23-6B Income statement with variances OBJ. 5

Prepare an income statement through gross profit for Dvorak Company for the month ended July 31 using the variance data in Practice Exercises 23-1B through 23-4B. Assume that Dvorak sold 1,000 units at $90 per unit.

EE 23-7 p. 1147

PE 23-7A Activity inputs and outputs OBJ. 6

The following are inputs and outputs to the copying process of a copy shop:

Number of employee errors
Number of times paper supply runs out
Copy machine downtime (broken)
Number of pages copied per hour
Number of customer complaints
Percent of jobs done on time

Identify whether each is an input or output to the copying process.

EE 23-7 p. 1147

PE 23-7B Activity inputs and outputs OBJ. 6

The following are inputs and outputs to the cooking process of a restaurant:

Number of times ingredients are missing
Number of customer complaints
Number of hours kitchen equipment is down for repairs
Number of server order mistakes
Percent of meals prepared on time
Number of unexpected cook absences

Identify whether each is an input or output to the cooking process.

Exercises

EX 23-1 Standard direct materials cost per unit OBJ. 2

Roanoke Company produces chocolate bars. The primary materials used in producing chocolate bars are cocoa, sugar, and milk. The standard costs for a batch of chocolate (5,200 bars) are as follows:

Ingredient	Quantity	Price
Cocoa	400 lb.	$1.25 per lb.
Sugar	80 lb.	$0.40 per lb.
Milk	120 gal.	$2.50 per gal.

Determine the standard direct materials cost per bar of chocolate.

EX 23-2 Standard product cost OBJ. 2

Sana Rosa Furniture Company manufactures designer home furniture. Sana Rosa uses a standard cost system. The direct labor, direct materials, and factory overhead standards for an unfinished dining room table are as follows:

Direct labor:	standard rate	$18.00 per hr.
	standard time per unit	3.5 hrs.
Direct materials (oak):	standard price	$15.00 per bd. ft.
	standard quantity	26 bd. ft.
Variable factory overhead:	standard rate	$4.20 per direct labor hr.
Fixed factory overhead:	standard rate	$1.80 per direct labor hr.

a. Determine the standard cost per dining room table.
b. Why would Sana Rosa Furniture Company use a standard cost system?

EX 23-3 Budget performance report — OBJ. 2

✔ b. Direct labor cost variance, $(580) F

Genie in a Bottle Company (GBC) manufactures plastic two-liter bottles for the beverage industry. The cost standards per 100 two-liter bottles are as follows:

Cost Category	Standard Cost per 100 Two-Liter Bottles
Direct labor	$ 2.00
Direct materials	9.10
Factory overhead	0.55
Total	$11.65

At the beginning of July, GBC management planned to produce 400,000 bottles. The actual number of bottles produced for July was 406,000 bottles. The actual costs for July of the current year were as follows:

Cost Category	Actual Cost for the Month Ended July 31
Direct labor	$ 7,540
Direct materials	35,750
Factory overhead	2,680
Total	$45,970

a. Prepare the July manufacturing standard cost budget (direct labor, direct materials, and factory overhead) for GBC, assuming planned production.

b. Prepare a budget performance report for manufacturing costs, showing the total cost variances for direct materials, direct labor, and factory overhead for July.

c. Interpret the budget performance report.

EX 23-4 Direct materials variances — OBJ. 3

✔ a. Price variance, $7,250 U

The following data relate to the direct materials cost for the production of 10,000 automobile tires:

Actual:	145,000 lb. at $2.80	
Standard:	150,000 lb. at $2.75	

a. Determine the direct materials price variance, direct materials quantity variance, and total direct materials cost variance.

b. To whom should the variances be reported for analysis and control?

EX 23-5 Direct materials variances — OBJ. 3

✔ Quantity variance, $300 U

Silicone Engine Inc. produces wrist-worn tablet computers. The company uses Thin Film Crystal (TFC) LCD displays for its products. Each tablet uses one display. The company produced 580 tablets during December. However, due to LCD defects, the company actually used 600 LCD displays during December. Each display has a standard cost of $15.00. Six hundred LCD displays were purchased for December production at a cost of $8,550.

Determine the price variance, quantity variance, and total direct materials cost variance for December.

EX 23-6 Standard direct materials cost per unit from variance data — OBJ. 2, 3

The following data relating to direct materials cost for October of the current year are taken from the records of Good Clean Fun Inc., a manufacturer of organic toys:

Quantity of direct materials used	3,000 lb.
Actual unit price of direct materials	$5.50 per lb.
Units of finished product manufactured	1,400 units
Standard direct materials per unit of finished product	2 lb.
Direct materials quantity variance—unfavorable	$1,000
Direct materials price variance—unfavorable	$1,500

(*Continued*)

Determine the standard direct materials cost per unit of finished product, assuming that there was no inventory of work in process at either the beginning or end of the month.

EX 23-7 Standard product cost, direct materials variance
OBJ. 2, 3

H.J. Heinz Company uses standards to control its materials costs. Assume that a batch of ketchup (3,128 pounds) has the following standards:

	Standard Quantity	Standard Price
Whole tomatoes	4,000 lb.	$ 0.60 per lb.
Vinegar	260 gal.	2.25 per gal.
Corn syrup	25 gal.	28.00 per gal.
Salt	100 lb.	2.25 per lb.

The actual materials in a batch may vary from the standard due to tomato characteristics. Assume that the actual quantities of materials for batch K-111 were as follows:

4,250 lb. of tomatoes
275 gal. of vinegar
22 gal. of corn syrup
90 lb. of salt

a. Determine the standard unit materials cost per pound for a standard batch.

b. Determine the direct materials quantity variance for batch K-111. Round your answer to the nearest cent.

EX 23-8 Direct labor variances
OBJ. 3

✔ a. Rate variance, $(6,330) F

The following data relate to labor cost for production of 22,000 cellular telephones:

Actual:	4,220 hrs. at $44.50
Standard:	4,160 hrs. at $46.00

a. Determine the direct labor rate variance, direct labor time variance, and total direct labor cost variance.

b. ✎ Discuss what might have caused these variances.

EX 23-9 Direct labor variances
OBJ. 3, 5

✔ a. Time variance, $(5,600) F

La Barte Company manufactures commuter bicycles from recycled materials. The following data for July of the current year are available:

Quantity of direct labor used	5,050 hrs.
Actual rate for direct labor	$16.80 per hr.
Bicycles completed in July	1,000 bicycles
Standard direct labor per bicycle	5.4 hrs.
Standard rate for direct labor	$16.00 per hr.

a. Determine the direct labor rate variance, time variance, and total direct labor cost variance.

b. How much direct labor should be debited to Work in Process?

EX 23-10 Direct labor variances
OBJ. 3

✔ a. Cutting Department rate variance, $(638) F

Greeson Clothes Company produced 25,000 units during June of the current year. The Cutting Department used 6,380 direct labor hours at an actual rate of $10.90 per hour. The Sewing Department used 9,875 direct labor hours at an actual rate of $11.12 per hour. Assume that there were no work in process inventories in either department at the beginning or end of the month. The standard labor rate is $11.00. The standard labor time for the Cutting and Sewing departments is 0.25 hour and 0.40 hour per unit, respectively.

a. Determine the direct labor rate, direct labor time, and total direct labor cost variance for the (1) Cutting Department and (2) Sewing Department.

b. ✎ Interpret your results.

Chapter 23 Evaluating Variances from Standard Costs

✔ a. $2,400

EX 23-11 Direct labor standards for nonmanufacturing expenses OBJ. 3

Englert Hospital began using standards to evaluate its Admissions Department. The standard was broken into two types of admissions as follows:

Type of Admission	Standard Time to Complete Admission Record
Unscheduled admission	30 min.
Scheduled admission	15 min.

The unscheduled admission took longer because name, address, and insurance information needed to be determined and verified at the time of admission. Information was collected on scheduled admissions prior to the admissions, which was less time-consuming.

The Admissions Department employs four full-time people (40 productive hours per week, with no overtime) at $15 per hour. For the most recent week, the department handled 140 unscheduled and 350 scheduled admissions.

a. How much was actually spent on labor for the week?

b. What are the standard hours for the actual volume for the week?

c. Calculate a time variance and report how well the department performed for the week.

✔ a. 28

EX 23-12 Direct labor standards for a service company OBJ. 2, 3

One of the operations in the United States Postal Service is a mechanical mail sorting operation. In this operation, letter mail is sorted at a rate of 1.5 letters per second. The letter is mechanically sorted from a three-digit code input by an operator sitting at a keyboard. The manager of the mechanical sorting operation wants to determine the number of temporary employees to hire for December. The manager estimates that there will be an additional 24,192,000 pieces of mail in December, due to the upcoming holiday season.

Assume that the sorting operators are temporary employees. The union contract requires that temporary employees be hired for one month at a time. Each temporary employee is hired to work 160 hours in the month.

a. How many temporary employees should the manager hire for December?

b. If each temporary employee earns a standard $16.40 per hour, what would be the labor time variance if the actual number of additional letters sorted in December was 23,895,000?

✔ a. Direct labor rate variance, $(12) F

EX 23-13 Direct labor variances for a service company OBJ. 2, 3

Hit-n-Run Food Trucks, Inc. owns and operates food trucks (mobile kitchens) throughout the West Coast. The company's employees have varying wage levels depending on their experience and length of time with the company. Employees work eight-hour shifts and are assigned to a truck each day based on labor needs to support the daily menu. One of the trucks, Jose O'Brien's Mobile Fiesta, specializes in Irish-Mexican fusion cuisine. The truck offers a single menu item that changes daily. On November 11, the truck prepared 200 of its most popular item, the Irish Breakfast Enchilada. The following data are available for that day:

Quantity of direct labor used (3 employees, working 8-hour shifts)	24 hrs.
Actual rate for direct labor	$15.00 per hr.
Standard direct labor per meal	0.1 hr.
Standard rate for direct labor	$15.50 per hr.

a. Determine the direct labor rate variance, the direct labor time variance, and the total direct labor cost variance.

b. Discuss what might have caused these variances.

1158 Chapter 23 Evaluating Variances from Standard Costs

✔ Direct materials quantity variance, $(1,300) F

EX 23-14 Direct materials and direct labor variances OBJ. 3

At the beginning of June, Kimber Toy Company budgeted 4,800 toy action figures to be manufactured in June at standard direct materials and direct labor costs as follows:

Direct materials	$ 60,000
Direct labor	48,000
Total	$108,000

The standard materials price is $5.00 per pound. The standard direct labor rate is $20.00 per hour. At the end of June, the actual direct materials and direct labor costs were as follows:

Actual direct materials	$ 61,200
Actual direct labor	48,000
Total	$109,200

There were no direct materials price or direct labor rate variances for June. In addition, assume no changes in the direct materials inventory balances in June. Kimber Toy Company actually produced 5,000 units during June.

Determine the direct materials quantity and direct labor time variances.

✔ Total factory overhead, 22,000 hrs., $443,600

EX 23-15 Flexible overhead budget OBJ. 4

Leno Manufacturing Company prepared the following factory overhead cost budget for the Press Department for October of the current year, during which it expected to require 20,000 hours of productive capacity in the department:

Variable overhead cost:		
Indirect factory labor	$180,000	
Power and light	12,000	
Indirect materials	64,000	
Total variable overhead cost		$256,000
Fixed overhead cost:		
Supervisory salaries	$ 80,000	
Depreciation of plant and equipment	50,000	
Insurance and property taxes	32,000	
Total fixed overhead cost		162,000
Total factory overhead cost		$418,000

Assuming that the estimated costs for November are the same as for October, prepare a flexible factory overhead cost budget for the Press Department for November for 18,000, 20,000, and 22,000 hours of production.

EX 23-16 Flexible overhead budget OBJ. 4

Wiki Wiki Company has determined that the variable overhead rate is $4.50 per direct labor hour in the Fabrication Department. The normal production capacity for the Fabrication Department is 10,000 hours for the month. Fixed costs are budgeted at $60,000 for the month.

a. Prepare a monthly factory overhead flexible budget for 9,000, 10,000, and 11,000 hours of production.

b. How much overhead would be applied to production if 9,000 hours were used in the department during the month?

✔ Volume variance, $4,000 U

EX 23-17 Factory overhead cost variances OBJ. 4

The following data relate to factory overhead cost for the production of 15,000 computers:

Actual:	Variable factory overhead		$240,000
	Fixed factory overhead		160,000
Standard:	19,500 hrs. at $20		390,000

If productive capacity of 100% was 20,000 hours and the total factory overhead cost budgeted at the level of 19,500 standard hours was $394,000, determine the variable factory overhead controllable variance, fixed factory overhead volume variance, and total factory overhead cost variance. The fixed factory overhead rate was $8.00 per hour.

EX 23-18 Factory overhead cost variances OBJ. 4

✔ a. $(13,000) F

Blumen Textiles Corporation began April with a budget for 90,000 hours of production in the Weaving Department. The department has a full capacity of 100,000 hours under normal business conditions. The budgeted overhead at the planned volumes at the beginning of April was as follows:

Variable overhead	$540,000
Fixed overhead	240,000
Total	$780,000

The actual factory overhead was $782,000 for April. The actual fixed factory overhead was as budgeted. During April, the Weaving Department had standard hours at actual production volume of 92,500 hours.

a. Determine the variable factory overhead controllable variance.
b. Determine the fixed factory overhead volume variance.

EX 23-19 Factory overhead variance corrections OBJ. 4

The data related to Shunda Enterprises Inc.'s factory overhead cost for the production of 100,000 units of product are as follows:

Actual:	Variable factory overhead		$458,000
	Fixed factory overhead		494,000
Standard:	132,000 hrs. at $7.30 ($3.50 for variable factory overhead)		963,600

Productive capacity at 100% of normal was 130,000 hours, and the factory overhead cost budgeted at the level of 132,000 standard hours was $956,000. Based on these data, the chief cost accountant prepared the following variance analysis:

Variable factory overhead controllable variance:		
Actual variable factory overhead cost incurred	$458,000	
Budgeted variable factory overhead for 132,000 hours	462,000	
Variance—favorable		$ (4,000)
Fixed factory overhead volume variance:		
Normal productive capacity at 100%	130,000 hrs.	
Standard for amount produced	132,000	
Productive capacity not used	2,000 hrs.	
Standard variable factory overhead rate	× $7.30	
Variance—unfavorable		14,600
Total factory overhead cost variance—unfavorable		$10,600

Identify the errors in the factory overhead cost variance analysis.

EX 23-20 Factory overhead cost variance report OBJ. 4

✔ Net controllable variance, $900 U

Tannin Products Inc. prepared the following factory overhead cost budget for the Trim Department for July of the current year, during which it expected to use 20,000 hours for production:

Variable overhead cost:		
Indirect factory labor	$46,000	
Power and light	12,000	
Indirect materials	20,000	
Total variable overhead cost		$ 78,000

(*Continued*)

1160 Chapter 23 Evaluating Variances from Standard Costs

Fixed overhead cost:
Supervisory salaries	$54,500
Depreciation of plant and equipment	40,000
Insurance and property taxes	35,500
Total fixed overhead cost	130,000
Total factory overhead cost	$208,000

Tannin has available 25,000 hours of monthly productive capacity in the Trim Department under normal business conditions. During July, the Trim Department actually used 22,000 hours for production. The actual fixed costs were as budgeted. The actual variable overhead for July was as follows:

Actual variable factory overhead cost:
Indirect factory labor	$49,700
Power and light	13,000
Indirect materials	24,000
Total variable cost	$86,700

Construct a factory overhead cost variance report for the Trim Department for July.

EX 23-21 Recording standards in accounts OBJ. 5

Cioffi Manufacturing Company incorporates standards in its accounts and identifies variances at the time the manufacturing costs are incurred. Journalize the entries to record the following transactions:

a. Purchased 2,450 units of copper tubing on account at $52.00 per unit. The standard price is $48.50 per unit.

b. Used 1,900 units of copper tubing in the process of manufacturing 200 air conditioners. Ten units of copper tubing are required, at standard, to produce one air conditioner.

EX 23-22 Recording standards in accounts OBJ. 5

The Assembly Department produced 5,000 units of product during March. Each unit required 2.20 standard direct labor hours. There were 11,500 actual hours used in the Assembly Department during March at an actual rate of $17.60 per hour. The standard direct labor rate is $18.00 per hour. Assuming that direct labor for a month is paid on the fifth day of the following month, journalize the direct labor in the Assembly Department on March 31.

EX 23-23 Income statement indicating standard cost variances OBJ. 5

✔ Income before income tax, $85,900

The following data were taken from the records of Griggs Company for December:

Administrative expenses	$100,800
Cost of goods sold (at standard)	550,000
Direct materials price variance—unfavorable	1,680
Direct materials quantity variance—favorable	(560)
Direct labor rate variance—favorable	(1,120)
Direct labor time variance—unfavorable	490
Variable factory overhead controllable variance—favorable	(210)
Fixed factory overhead volume variance—unfavorable	3,080
Interest expense	2,940
Sales	868,000
Selling expenses	125,000

Prepare an income statement for presentation to management.

EX 23-24 Nonfinancial performance measures OBJ. 6

Diamond Inc. is an Internet retailer of woodworking equipment. Customers order woodworking equipment from the company, using an online catalog. The company processes these orders and delivers the requested product from its warehouse. The company wants to provide customers with an excellent purchase experience in order to expand the

Chapter 23 Evaluating Variances from Standard Costs   1161

business through favorable word-of-mouth advertising and to drive repeat business. To help monitor performance, the company developed a set of performance measures for its order placement and delivery process:

Average computer response time to customer "clicks"
Dollar amount of returned goods
Elapsed time between customer order and product delivery
Maintenance dollars divided by hardware investment
Number of customer complaints divided by the number of orders
Number of misfilled orders divided by the number of orders
Number of orders per warehouse employee
Number of page faults or errors due to software programming errors
Number of software fixes per week
Server (computer) downtime
Training dollars per programmer

a. For each performance measure, identify it as either an input or output measure related to the "order placement and delivery" process.
b. Provide an explanation for each performance measure.

EX 23-25 Nonfinancial performance measures   OBJ. 6

Alpha University wants to monitor the efficiency and quality of its course registration process.

a. Identify three input and three output measures for this process.
b. Why would Alpha University use nonfinancial measures for monitoring this process?

Problems: Series A

PR 23-1A   Direct materials and direct labor variance analysis   OBJ. 2, 3

✔ c. Direct labor time variance, $600 U

Abbeville Company manufactures faucets in a small manufacturing facility. The faucets are made from brass. Manufacturing has 90 employees. Each employee presently provides 36 hours of labor per week. Information about a production week is as follows:

Standard wage per hr.	$15.00
Standard labor time per faucet	40 min.
Standard number of lb. of brass	3 lb.
Standard price per lb. of brass	$2.40
Actual price per lb. of brass	$2.50
Actual lb. of brass used during the week	14,350 lb.
Number of faucets produced during the week	4,800
Actual wage per hr.	$14.40
Actual hrs. for the week	3,240 hrs.

Instructions
Determine (a) the standard cost per unit for direct materials and direct labor; (b) the direct materials price variance, direct materials quantity variance, and total direct materials cost variance; and (c) the direct labor rate variance, direct labor time variance, and total direct labor cost variance.

PR 23-2A   Flexible budgeting and variance analysis   OBJ. 1, 2, 3

✔ 1. a. Direct materials quantity variance, $(625) F

I Love My Chocolate Company makes dark chocolate and light chocolate. Both products require cocoa and sugar. The following planning information has been made available:

	Standard Amount per Case		
	Dark Chocolate	Light Chocolate	Standard Price per Pound
Cocoa	12 lb.	8 lb.	$7.25
Sugar	10 lb.	14 lb.	1.40
Standard labor time	0.50 hr.	0.60 hr.	

(Continued)

1162 Chapter 23 Evaluating Variances from Standard Costs

	Dark Chocolate	Light Chocolate
Planned production	4,700 cases	11,000 cases
Standard labor rate	$15.50 per hr.	$15.50 per hr.

I Love My Chocolate Company does not expect there to be any beginning or ending inventories of cocoa or sugar. At the end of the budget year, I Love My Chocolate Company had the following actual results:

	Dark Chocolate	Light Chocolate
Actual production (cases)	5,000	10,000

	Actual Price per Pound	Actual Pounds Purchased and Used
Cocoa	$7.33	140,300
Sugar	1.35	188,000

	Actual Labor Rate	Actual Labor Hours Used
Dark chocolate	$15.25 per hr.	2,360
Light chocolate	15.80 per hr.	6,120

Instructions

1. Prepare the following variance analyses for both chocolates and the total, based on the actual results and production levels at the end of the budget year:

    a. Direct materials price, quantity, and total variance

    b. Direct labor rate, time, and total variance

2. Why are the standard amounts in part (1) based on the actual production for the year instead of the planned production for the year?

PR 23-3A Direct materials, direct labor, and factory overhead cost variance analysis   OBJ. 3, 4

✔ c. Controllable variance, $(4,800) F

Excel

Mackinaw Inc. processes a base chemical into plastic. Standard costs and actual costs for direct materials, direct labor, and factory overhead incurred for the manufacture of 40,000 units of product were as follows:

	Standard Costs	Actual Costs
Direct materials	120,000 lb. at $3.20	118,500 lb. at $3.25
Direct labor	12,000 hrs. at $24.40	11,700 hrs. at $25.00
Factory overhead	Rates per direct labor hr., based on 100% of normal capacity of 15,000 direct labor hrs.:	
	Variable cost, $8.00	$91,200 variable cost
	Fixed cost, $10.00	$150,000 fixed cost

Each unit requires 0.3 hour of direct labor.

Instructions

Determine (a) the direct materials price variance, direct materials quantity variance, and total direct materials cost variance; (b) the direct labor rate variance, direct labor time variance, and total direct labor cost variance; and (c) the variable factory overhead controllable variance, fixed factory overhead volume variance, and total factory overhead cost variance.

Chapter 23 Evaluating Variances from Standard Costs 1163

✔ Controllable variance, $770 U

PR 23-4A Factory overhead cost variance report
OBJ. 4

Tiger Equipment Inc., a manufacturer of construction equipment, prepared the following factory overhead cost budget for the Welding Department for May of the current year. The company expected to operate the department at 100% of normal capacity of 8,400 hours.

Variable costs:		
Indirect factory wages	$30,240	
Power and light	20,160	
Indirect materials	16,800	
Total variable cost		$ 67,200
Fixed costs:		
Supervisory salaries	$20,000	
Depreciation of plant and equipment	36,200	
Insurance and property taxes	15,200	
Total fixed cost		71,400
Total factory overhead cost		$138,600

During May, the department operated at 8,860 standard hours. The factory overhead costs incurred were indirect factory wages, $32,400; power and light, $21,000; indirect materials, $18,250; supervisory salaries, $20,000; depreciation of plant and equipment, $36,200; and insurance and property taxes, $15,200.

Instructions
Prepare a factory overhead cost variance report for May. To be useful for cost control, the budgeted amounts should be based on 8,860 hours.

✔ 3. $1,600 U

PR 23-5A Standards for nonmanufacturing expenses
OBJ. 3, 6

CodeHead Software Inc. is a software development company. One important activity in software development is writing software code. The manager of the WordPro Development Team determined that the average software programmer could write 25 lines of code in an hour. The plan for the first week in May called for 4,650 lines of code to be written on the WordPro product. The WordPro Team has five programmers. Each programmer is hired from an employment firm that requires temporary employees to be hired for a minimum of a 40-hour week. Programmers are paid $32.00 per hour. The manager offered a bonus if the team could generate more lines for the week, without overtime. Due to a project emergency, the programmers wrote more code in the first week of May than planned. The actual amount of code written in the first week of May was 5,650 lines, without overtime. As a result, the bonus caused the average programmer's hourly rate to increase to $40.00 per hour during the first week in May.

Instructions
1. If the team had generated 4,650 lines of code according to the original plan, what would have been the labor time variance?
2. What was the actual labor time variance as a result of generating 5,650 lines of code?
3. What was the labor rate variance as a result of the bonus?
4. ✏ Are there any performance-related issues that the labor time and rate variances fail to consider? Explain.
5. The manager is trying to determine if a better decision would have been to hire a temporary programmer to meet the higher programming demand in the first week of May, rather than paying out the bonus. If another employee had been hired from the employment firm, what would have been the labor time variance in the first week?
6. ✏ Which decision is better, paying the bonus or hiring another programmer?

Problems: Series B

✔ c. Rate variance, $(200) F

PR 23-1B Direct materials and direct labor variance analysis   OBJ. 2, 3

Lenni Clothing Co. manufactures clothing in a small manufacturing facility. Manufacturing has 25 employees. Each employee presently provides 40 hours of productive labor per week. Information about a production week is as follows:

Standard wage per hr.	$12.00
Standard labor time per unit	12 min.
Standard number of yds. of fabric per unit	5.0 yds.
Standard price per yd. of fabric	$5.00
Actual price per yd. of fabric	$5.10
Actual yds. of fabric used during the week	26,200 yds.
Number of units produced during the week	5,220
Actual wage per hr.	$11.80
Actual hrs. for the week	1,000 hrs.

Instructions

Determine (a) the standard cost per unit for direct materials and direct labor; (b) the price variance, quantity variance, and total direct materials cost variance; and (c) the rate variance, time variance, and total direct labor cost variance.

✔ 1. a. Direct materials price variance, $12,220 U

PR 23-2B Flexible budgeting and variance analysis   OBJ. 1, 2, 3

I'm Really Cold Coat Company makes women's and men's coats. Both products require filler and lining material. The following planning information has been made available:

	Standard Amount per Unit		
	Women's Coats	Men's Coats	Standard Price per Unit
Filler	4.0 lb.	5.2 lb.	$2.00 per lb.
Liner	7.0 yds.	9.4 yds.	8.00 per yd.
Standard labor time	0.40 hr.	0.50 hr.	

	Women's Coats	Men's Coats
Planned production	5,000 units	6,200 units
Standard labor rate	$14.00 per hr.	$13.00 per hr.

I'm Really Cold Coat Company does not expect there to be any beginning or ending inventories of filler and lining material. At the end of the budget year, I'm Really Cold Coat Company experienced the following actual results:

	Women's Coats	Men's Coats
Actual production	4,400	5,800

	Actual Price per Unit	Actual Quantity Purchased and Used
Filler	$1.90 per lb.	48,000
Liner	8.20 per yd.	85,100

	Actual Labor Rate	Actual Labor Hours Used
Women's coats	$14.10 per hr.	1,825
Men's coats	13.30 per hr.	2,800

The expected beginning inventory and desired ending inventory were realized.

Instructions

1. Prepare the following variance analyses for both coats and the total, based on the actual results and production levels at the end of the budget year:

   a. Direct materials price, quantity, and total variance

   b. Direct labor rate, time, and total variance

2. Why are the standard amounts in part (1) based on the actual production at the end of the year instead of the planned production at the beginning of the year?

Chapter 23 Evaluating Variances from Standard Costs 1165

PR 23-3B Direct materials, direct labor, and factory overhead cost variance analysis OBJ. 3, 4

✔ a. Direct materials price variance, $10,100 U

Road Gripper Tire Co. manufactures automobile tires. Standard costs and actual costs for direct materials, direct labor, and factory overhead incurred for the manufacture of 4,160 tires were as follows:

	Standard Costs	Actual Costs
Direct materials	100,000 lb. at $6.40	101,000 lb. at $6.50
Direct labor	2,080 hrs. at $15.75	2,000 hrs. at $15.40
Factory overhead	Rates per direct labor hr., based on 100% of normal capacity of 2,000 direct labor hrs.:	
	Variable cost, $4.00	$8,200 variable cost
	Fixed cost, $6.00	$12,000 fixed cost

Each tire requires 0.5 hour of direct labor.

Instructions

Determine (a) the direct materials price variance, direct materials quantity variance, and total direct materials cost variance; (b) the direct labor rate variance, direct labor time variance, and total direct labor cost variance; and (c) the variable factory overhead controllable variance, fixed factory overhead volume variance, and total factory overhead cost variance.

PR 23-4B Factory overhead cost variance report OBJ. 4

✔ Controllable variance, $(1,450) F

Feeling Better Medical Inc., a manufacturer of disposable medical supplies, prepared the following factory overhead cost budget for the Assembly Department for October of the current year. The company expected to operate the department at 100% of normal capacity of 30,000 hours.

Variable costs:		
Indirect factory wages	$247,500	
Power and light	189,000	
Indirect materials	52,500	
Total variable cost		$489,000
Fixed costs:		
Supervisory salaries	$126,000	
Depreciation of plant and equipment	70,000	
Insurance and property taxes	44,000	
Total fixed cost		240,000
Total factory overhead cost		$729,000

During October, the department operated at 28,500 hours. The factory overhead costs incurred were indirect factory wages, $234,000; power and light, $178,500; indirect materials, $50,600; supervisory salaries, $126,000; depreciation of plant and equipment, $70,000; and insurance and property taxes, $44,000.

Instructions

Prepare a factory overhead cost variance report for October. To be useful for cost control, the budgeted amounts should be based on 28,500 hours.

PR 23-5B Standards for nonmanufacturing expenses for a service company OBJ. 3, 6

✔ 2. $(161) F

The Radiology Department provides imaging services for Emergency Medical Center. One important activity in the Radiology Department is transcribing digitally recorded analyses of images into a written report. The manager of the Radiology Department determined that the average transcriptionist could type 700 lines of a report in an hour. The plan for the first week in May called for 81,900 typed lines to be written. The Radiology Department

(*Continued*)

has three transcriptionists. Each transcriptionist is hired from an employment firm that requires temporary employees to be hired for a minimum of a 40-hour week. Transcriptionists are paid $23.00 per hour. The manager offered a bonus if the department could type more lines for the week, without overtime. Due to high service demands, the transcriptionists typed more lines in the first week of May than planned. The actual amount of lines typed in the first week of May was 88,900 lines, without overtime. As a result, the bonus caused the average transcriptionist hourly rate to increase to $30.00 per hour during the first week in May.

Instructions

1. If the department had typed 81,900 lines according to the original plan, what would have been the labor time variance?
2. What was the labor time variance as a result of typing 88,900 lines?
3. What was the labor rate variance as a result of the bonus?
4. The manager is trying to determine if a better decision would have been to hire a temporary transcriptionist to meet the higher typing demands in the first week of May, rather than paying out the bonus. If another employee had been hired from the employment firm, what would have been the labor time variance in the first week?
5. ✏️ Which decision is better, paying the bonus or hiring another transcriptionist?
6. ✏️ Are there any performance-related issues that the labor time and rate variances fail to consider? Explain.

Comprehensive Problem 5

Genuine Spice Inc. began operations on January 1 of the current year. The company produces eight-ounce bottles of hand and body lotion called *Eternal Beauty*. The lotion is sold wholesale in 12-bottle cases for $100 per case. There is a selling commission of $20 per case. The January direct materials, direct labor, and factory overhead costs are as follows:

DIRECT MATERIALS

	Cost Behavior	Units per Case	Cost per Unit	Direct Materials Cost per Case
Cream base	Variable	100 oz.	$0.02	$ 2.00
Natural oils	Variable	30 oz.	0.30	9.00
Bottle (8-oz.)	Variable	12 bottles	0.50	6.00
				$17.00

DIRECT LABOR

Department	Cost Behavior	Time per Case	Labor Rate per Hour	Direct Labor Cost per Case
Mixing	Variable	20 min.	$18.00	$6.00
Filling	Variable	5	14.40	1.20
		25 min.		$7.20

FACTORY OVERHEAD

	Cost Behavior	Total Cost
Utilities	Mixed	$ 600
Facility lease	Fixed	14,000
Equipment depreciation	Fixed	4,300
Supplies	Fixed	660
		$19,560

Part A—Break-Even Analysis

The management of Genuine Spice Inc. wants to determine the number of cases required to break even per month. The utilities cost, which is part of factory overhead, is a mixed cost. The following information was gathered from the first six months of operation regarding this cost:

	Case Production	Utility Total Cost
January	500	$600
February	800	660
March	1,200	740
April	1,100	720
May	950	690
June	1,025	705

Instructions

✔ 2. $55.60

1. Determine the fixed and variable portion of the utility cost using the high-low method.
2. Determine the contribution margin per case.
3. Determine the fixed costs per month, including the utility fixed cost from part (1).
4. Determine the break-even number of cases per month.

Part B—August Budgets

During July of the current year, the management of Genuine Spice Inc. asked the controller to prepare August manufacturing and income statement budgets. Demand was expected to be 1,500 cases at $100 per case for August. Inventory planning information is provided as follows:

Finished Goods Inventory:

	Cases	Cost
Estimated finished goods inventory, August 1	300	$12,000
Desired finished goods inventory, August 31	175	7,000

Materials Inventory:

	Cream Base (oz.)	Oils (oz.)	Bottles (bottles)
Estimated materials inventory, August 1	250	290	600
Desired materials inventory, August 31	1,000	360	240

There was negligible work in process inventory assumed for either the beginning or end of the month; thus, none was assumed. In addition, there was no change in the cost per unit or estimated units per case operating data from January.

Instructions

✔ 6. Bottles purchased, $8,070

5. Prepare the August production budget.
6. Prepare the August direct materials purchases budget.
7. Prepare the August direct labor cost budget. Round the hours required for production to the nearest hour.
8. Prepare the August factory overhead cost budget.
9. Prepare the August budgeted income statement, including selling expenses.

Part C—August Variance Analysis

During September of the current year, the controller was asked to perform variance analyses for August. The January operating data provided the standard prices, rates, times, and quantities per case. There were 1,500 actual cases produced during August, which was 250 more cases than planned at the beginning of the month. Actual data for August were as follows:

	Actual Direct Materials Price per Unit	Actual Direct Materials Quantity per Case
Cream base	$0.016 per oz.	102 oz.
Natural oils	$0.32 per oz.	31 oz.
Bottle (8-oz.)	$0.42 per bottle	12.5 bottles

(Continued)

	Actual Direct Labor Rate	Actual Direct Labor Time per Case
Mixing	$18.20	19.50 min.
Filling	14.00	5.60 min.
Actual variable overhead	$305.00	
Normal volume	1,600 cases	

The prices of the materials were different from standard due to fluctuations in market prices. The standard quantity of materials used per case was an ideal standard. The Mixing Department used a higher grade labor classification during the month, thus causing the actual labor rate to exceed standard. The Filling Department used a lower grade labor classification during the month, thus causing the actual labor rate to be less than standard.

Instructions

10. Determine and interpret the direct materials price and quantity variances for the three materials.

✔ 11. Mixing time variance, $(225) F

11. Determine and interpret the direct labor rate and time variances for the two departments. Round hours to the nearest hour.

✔ 12. $5 U

12. Determine and interpret the factory overhead controllable variance.

13. Determine and interpret the factory overhead volume variance.

14. Why are the standard direct labor and direct materials costs in the calculations for parts (10) and (11) based on the actual 1,500-case production volume rather than the planned 1,375 cases of production used in the budgets for parts (6) and (7)?

Cases & Projects

Ethics

CP 23-1 Ethics in Action

Dash Riprock is a cost analyst with Safe Insurance Company. Safe is applying standards to its claims payment operation. Claims payment is a repetitive operation that could be evaluated with standards. Dash used time and motion studies to identify an ideal standard of 36 claims processed per hour. The Claims Processing Department manager, Henry Tudor, has rejected this standard and has argued that the standard should be 30 claims processed per hour. Henry and Dash were unable to agree, so they decided to discuss this matter openly at a joint meeting with the vice president of operations, who would arbitrate a final decision. Prior to the meeting, Dash wrote the following memo to the VP:

To: Anne Boleyn, Vice President of Operations
From: Dash Riprock
Re: Standards in the Claims Processing Department

As you know, Henry and I are scheduled to meet with you to discuss our disagreement with respect to the appropriate standards for the Claims Processing Department. I have conducted time and motion studies and have determined that the ideal standard is 36 claims processed per hour. Henry argues that 30 claims processed per hour would be more appropriate. I believe he is trying to "pad" the budget with some slack. I'm not sure what he is trying to get away with, but I believe a tight standard will drive up efficiency in his area. I hope you will agree when we meet with you next week.

▶ Discuss the ethical and professional issues in this situation.

Team Activity

CP 23-2 Team Activity

Many city and county governments are discovering that you can control only what you measure. As a result, many municipal governments are introducing nonfinancial performance measures to help improve municipal services. As a team, use the Google search engine to perform a search for "municipal government performance measurement." Google will provide a list of Internet sites that outline various city efforts in using nonfinancial performance measures. As a team, report on the types of measures used by one of the cities from the search.

Communication

CP 23-3 Communication

The senior management of Tungston Company has proposed the following three performance measures for the company:

1. Net income as a percent of stockholders' equity
2. Revenue growth
3. Employee satisfaction

Management believes that these three measures combine both financial and nonfinancial measures and are thus superior to using just financial measures.

Write a brief memo to David Tungston, the company president, providing suggestions on how to improve the company's performance measurement system.

CP 23-4 Variance interpretation

You have been asked to investigate some cost problems in the Assembly Department of Ruthenium Electronics Co., a consumer electronics company. To begin your investigation, you have obtained the following budget performance report for the department for the last quarter:

Ruthenium Electronics Co.—Assembly Department
Quarterly Budget Performance Report

	Standard Quantity at Standard Rates	Actual Quantity at Standard Rates	Quantity Variances
Direct labor	$157,500	$227,500	$ 70,000 U
Direct materials	297,500	385,000	87,500 U
Total	$455,000	$612,500	$157,500 U

You also obtained the following reports:

Ruthenium Electronics Co.—Purchasing Department
Quarterly Budget Performance Report

	Actual Quantity at Standard Rates	Actual Quantity at Actual Rates	Price Variance
Direct materials	$437,500	$385,000	$(52,500) F

Ruthenium Electronics Co.—Fabrication Department
Quarterly Budget Performance Report

	Standard Quantity at Standard Rates	Actual Quantity at Standard Rates	Quantity Variances
Direct labor	$245,000	$203,000	$(42,000) F
Direct materials	140,000	140,000	0
Total	$385,000	$343,000	$(42,000) F

You also interviewed the Assembly Department supervisor. Excerpts from the interview follow:

Q: What explains the poor performance in your department?

A: Listen, you've got to understand what it's been like in this department recently. Lately, it seems no matter how hard we try, we can't seem to make the standards. I'm not sure what is going on, but we've been having a lot of problems lately.

Q: What kind of problems?

A: Well, for instance, all this quarter we've been requisitioning purchased parts from the material storeroom, and the parts just didn't fit together very well. I'm not sure what is going on, but during most of this quarter, we've had to scrap and sort purchased parts—just to get our assemblies put together. Naturally, all this takes time and material. And that's not all.

(Continued)

Q: Go on.

A: All this quarter the work we've been receiving from the Fabrication Department has been shoddy. I mean, maybe around 20% of the stuff that comes in from Fabrication just can't be assembled. The fabrication is all wrong. As a result, we've had to scrap and rework a lot of the stuff. Naturally, this has just shot our quantity variances.

✏️ Interpret the variance reports in light of the comments by the Assembly Department supervisor.

CP 23-5 Variance interpretation

Vanadium Audio Inc. is a small manufacturer of electronic musical instruments. The plant manager received the following variable factory overhead report for the period:

	Actual	Budgeted Variable Factory Overhead at Actual Production	Controllable Variance
Supplies	$ 42,000	$ 39,780	$ 2,220 U
Power and light	52,500	50,900	1,600 U
Indirect factory wages	39,100	30,600	8,500 U
Total	$133,600	$121,280	$12,320 U

Actual units produced: 15,000 (90% of practical capacity)

The plant manager is not pleased with the $12,320 unfavorable variable factory overhead controllable variance and has come to discuss the matter with the controller. The following discussion occurred:

Plant Manager: I just received this factory report for the latest month of operation. I'm not very pleased with these figures. Before these numbers go to headquarters, you and I need to reach an understanding.

Controller: Go ahead. What's the problem?

Plant Manager: What's the problem? Well, everything. Look at the variance. It's too large. If I understand the accounting approach being used here, you are assuming that my costs are variable to the units produced. Thus, as the production volume declines, so should these costs. Well, I don't believe these costs are variable at all. I think they are fixed costs. As a result, when we operate below capacity, the costs really don't go down. I'm being penalized for costs I have no control over. I need this report to be redone to reflect this fact. If anything, the difference between actual and budget is essentially a volume variance. Listen, I know that you're a team player. You really need to reconsider your assumptions on this one.

✏️ If you were in the controller's position, how would you respond to the plant manager?

CHAPTER 24
Decentralized Operations

Concepts and Principles
Chapter 18 Introduction to Managerial Accounting

Developing Information

COST SYSTEMS
Chapter 19 Job Order Costing
Chapter 20 Process Costing

COST BEHAVIOR
Chapter 21 Cost-Volume-Profit Analysis

Decision Making

EVALUATING PERFORMANCE
Chapter 22 Budgeting
Chapter 23 Variances from Standard Costs

COMPARING ALTERNATIVES
Chapter 24 *Decentralized Operations*
Chapter 25 Differential Analysis, Product Pricing, and Activity-Based Costing
Chapter 26 Capital Investment Analysis

CHAPTER 24

Caterpillar, Inc.

Have you ever wondered why large retail stores like **Macy's**, **JC Penney**, and **Sears** are divided into departments? Organizing into departments allows retailers to provide products and expertise in specialized areas while offering a wide range of products. Departments also allow companies to assign responsibility for financial performance. This information can be used to make product decisions, evaluate operations, and guide company strategy. Strong departmental performance might be attributable to a good department manager, while weak departmental performance may be the result of a product mix that has low customer appeal. By tracking departmental performance, companies can identify and reward excellent performance and take corrective action in departments that are performing poorly.

Like retailers, most businesses organize into operational units such as divisions and departments. For example, **Caterpillar, Inc.**, manufactures a variety of equipment and machinery and is organized into a number of different segments, including Construction Industries, Resource Industries, Energy & Transportation, and Financial Products. The Construction Industries segment manufactures construction equipment such as tractors, dump trucks, and loaders. The Resource Industries segment makes equipment for the mining industry, such as off-highway and mining trucks. The Energy & Transportation segment manufactures equipment that is used to generate power, such as engines and turbines for power plants. The Financial Products segment provides financing for Caterpillar products to customers and dealers.

Managers at Caterpillar, Inc., are responsible for running their business segment. Each segment is evaluated on segment profit, which excludes certain expense items from the calculation of profit that are not within the control of the business segment. The company uses segment profit to determine how to allocate resources between business segments and to plan and control the company's operations.

In this chapter, the role of accounting in assisting managers in planning and controlling organizational units such as departments, divisions, and stores is described and illustrated.

Learning Objectives

After studying this chapter, you should be able to:

Example Exercises (EE) are shown in **green**.

Obj. 1 Describe the advantages and disadvantages of decentralized operations.

Centralized and Decentralized Operations
Advantages of Decentralization
Disadvantages of Decentralization
Responsibility Accounting

Obj. 2 Prepare a responsibility accounting report for a cost center.

Responsibility Accounting for Cost Centers
Budgetary Performance for Cost Centers   EE **24-1**

Obj. 3 Prepare responsibility accounting reports for a profit center.

Responsibility Accounting for Profit Centers
Service Department Charges   EE **24-2**
Profit Center Reporting   EE **24-3**

Obj. 4 Compute and interpret the return on investment, the residual income, and the balanced scorecard for an investment center.

Responsibility Accounting for Investment Centers
Return on Investment   EE **24-4**
Residual Income   EE **24-5**
The Balanced Scorecard

Obj. 5 Describe and illustrate how the market price, negotiated price, and cost price approaches to transfer pricing may be used by decentralized segments of a business.

Transfer Pricing
Market Price Approach
Negotiated Price Approach   EE **24-6**
Cost Price Approach

At a Glance 24   Page 1194

Obj. 1 Describe the advantages and disadvantages of decentralized operations.

Centralized and Decentralized Operations

In a *centralized* company, all major planning and operating decisions are made by top management. For example, a one-person, owner–manager operated company is centralized because all plans and decisions are made by one person. In a small owner–manager operated business, centralization may be desirable. This is because the owner–manager's close supervision ensures that the business will be operated the way the owner-manager chooses.

In a *decentralized* company, managers of separate divisions or units are delegated operating responsibility. The division (unit) managers are responsible for planning and controlling the operations of their divisions. Divisions are often structured around products, customers, or regions.

The proper amount of decentralization for a company depends on the company's size, organizational culture, and business strategy. For example, in some companies, division managers have authority over all operations, including fixed asset purchases. In other companies, division managers have authority over profits but not fixed asset purchases.

Advantages of Decentralization

For large companies, it is difficult for top management to:

- Maintain daily contact with all operations, and
- Maintain operating expertise in all product lines and services

In such cases, delegating authority to managers closest to the operations usually results in better decisions. These managers can typically anticipate and react to operating data more quickly than top management. Decentralization also allows managers to focus their attention on becoming "experts" in their area of operation.

Decentralized operations provide excellent training for managers. Delegating responsibility allows managers to develop managerial experience early in their careers.

This helps a company retain managers, some of whom may be later promoted to top management positions.

Managers of decentralized operations often work closely with customers. As a result, they tend to identify with customers and, thus, are often more creative in suggesting operating and product improvements. This helps create good customer relations.

Disadvantages of Decentralization

A primary disadvantage of decentralized operations is that decisions made by one manager may negatively affect the profits of the company. For example, managers of divisions whose products compete with one another might start a price war that decreases the profits of both divisions and, thus, the overall company.

Another disadvantage of decentralized operations is that assets and expenses may be duplicated across divisions. For example, each manager of a product line might have a separate sales force and office support staff.

The advantages and disadvantages of decentralization are summarized in Exhibit 1.

> **Link to Caterpillar**
> **Caterpillar** uses a decentralized network of over a thousand dealers to sell its products.

EXHIBIT 1

Advantages and Disadvantages of Decentralized Operations

Advantages of Decentralization
- Allows managers closest to the operations to make decisions
- Provides excellent training for managers
- Allows managers to become experts in their area of operation
- Helps retain managers
- Improves creativity and customer relations

Disadvantages of Decentralization
- Decisions made by managers may negatively affect the profits of the company
- Duplicates assets and expenses

Business Connection

DOVER CORPORATION: MANY PIECES, ONE PICTURE

Dover Corporation has grown over 45 years by acquiring more than 100 different manufacturing companies within a variety of industries. Dover uses a highly decentralized operating strategy. For example, of Dover's 30,000 employees, only about 50 employees staff the headquarters. Thus, almost all of the employees work within the 100 operating companies. The primary benefit of this approach is giving the operating companies room to respond to threats and opportunities without the bureaucratic hindrance of a centralized structure. As a result, the operating company presidents have unusual levels of autonomy. As stated by the company, "Dover company presidents set the direction of their own companies, make their own decisions, and nurture and grow their own organizations." The presidents are evaluated using metrics similar to those discussed in this chapter to keep the businesses aligned to the performance objectives of the overall organization.

Source: Dover Corporation website, Dover's Culture and Operating Philosophy.

Responsibility Accounting

In a decentralized business, accounting assists managers in evaluating and controlling their areas of responsibility, called *responsibility centers*. **Responsibility accounting** is the process of measuring and reporting operating data by responsibility center.

Link to Caterpillar
Caterpillar's corporate headquarters are located in Peoria, Illinois.

Obj. 2 Prepare a responsibility accounting report for a cost center.

Three types of responsibility centers are as follows:
- *Cost centers*, which have responsibility over costs
- *Profit centers*, which have responsibility over revenues and costs
- *Investment centers*, which have responsibility over revenues, costs, and investment in assets

Responsibility Accounting for Cost Centers

A **cost center** manager has responsibility for controlling costs. For example, the supervisor of the Power Department has responsibility for the costs of providing power. A cost center manager does not make decisions concerning sales or the amount of fixed assets invested in the center.

Cost centers may vary in size from a small department to an entire manufacturing plant. In addition, cost centers may exist within other cost centers. For example, an entire university or college could be viewed as a cost center, and each college and department within the university could also be a cost center, as shown in Exhibit 2.

EXHIBIT 2
Cost Centers in a University

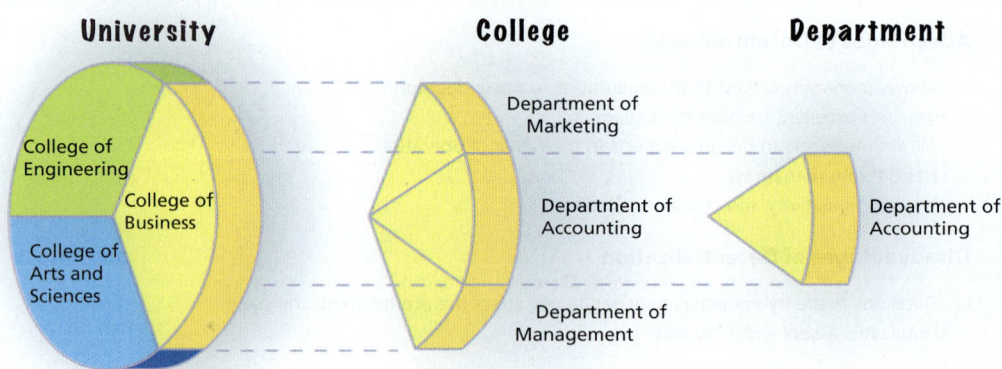

Link to Caterpillar
Caterpillar's "Corporate Services" group performs support services for its operating segments and is organized as a cost center.

Responsibility accounting for cost centers focuses on the controlling and reporting of costs. Budget performance reports that report budgeted and actual costs are normally prepared for each cost center.

Exhibit 3 illustrates budget performance reports for the following cost centers:
- Vice President, Production
- Manager, Plant A
- Supervisor, Department 1—Plant A

Exhibit 3 shows how cost centers are often linked within a company. For example, the budget performance report for Department 1—Plant A supports the report for Plant A, which supports the report for the vice president of production.

The reports in Exhibit 3 show the budgeted costs and actual costs along with the differences. Each difference is classified as either *over* budget or *under* budget. Such reports allow cost center managers to focus on areas of significant differences.

For example, the supervisor for Department 1 of Plant A can focus on why the materials cost was over budget. The supervisor might discover that excess materials were scrapped. This could be due to such factors as machine malfunctions, improperly trained employees, or low-quality materials.

As shown in Exhibit 3, responsibility accounting reports are usually more summarized for higher levels of management. For example, the budget performance report for the manager of Plant A shows only administration and departmental data. This report enables the plant manager to identify the departments responsible for major differences. Likewise, the report for the vice president of production summarizes the cost data for each plant.

EXHIBIT 3

Responsibility Accounting Reports for Cost Centers

Budget Performance Report
Vice President, Production
For the Month Ended October 31

	Actual	Budget	Over Budget	Under Budget
Administration	$ 19,700	$ 19,500	$ 200	
Plant A	470,330	467,475	2,855	
Plant B	394,300	395,225		$ (925)
	$884,330	$882,200	$3,055	$ (925)

Budget Performance Report
Manager, Plant A
For the Month Ended October 31

	Actual	Budget	Over Budget	Under Budget
Administration	$ 17,350	$ 17,500		$(150)
Department 1	111,280	109,725	$1,555	
Department 2	192,600	190,500	2,100	
Department 3	149,100	149,750		(650)
	$470,330	$467,475	$3,655	$(800)

Budget Performance Report
Supervisor, Department 1—Plant A
For the Month Ended October 31

	Actual	Budget	Over Budget	Under Budget
Factory wages	$ 58,000	$ 58,100		$(100)
Materials	34,225	32,500	$1,725	
Supervisory salaries	6,400	6,400		
Power and light	5,690	5,750		(60)
Depreciation of plant and equipment	4,000	4,000		
Maintenance	1,990	2,000		(10)
Insurance and property taxes	975	975		
	$111,280	$109,725	$1,725	$(170)

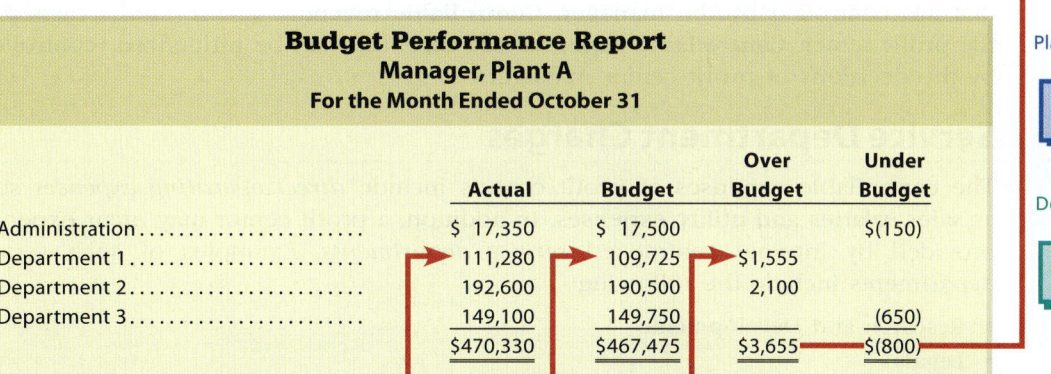

Example Exercise 24-1 Budgetary Performance for Cost Center   Obj. 2

Nuclear Power Company's costs were over budget by $24,000. The company is divided into North and South regions. The North Region's costs were under budget by $2,000. Determine the amount the South Region's costs were over or under budget.

Follow My Example 24-1

$26,000 over budget [$24,000 over budget + $(2,000) under budget]

Practice Exercises: PE 24-1A, PE 24-1B

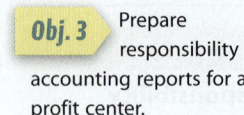

Obj. 3 Prepare responsibility accounting reports for a profit center.

Responsibility Accounting for Profit Centers

A **profit center** manager has the responsibility and authority for making decisions that affect revenues and costs and, thus, profits. Profit centers may be divisions, departments, or products.

The manager of a profit center does not make decisions concerning the fixed assets invested in the center. However, profit centers are an excellent training assignment for new managers.

Responsibility accounting for profit centers focuses on reporting revenues, expenses, and income from operations. Thus, responsibility accounting reports for profit centers take the form of income statements.

The profit center income statement should include only revenues and expenses that are controlled by the manager. **Controllable revenues** are revenues earned by the profit center. **Controllable expenses** are costs that can be influenced (controlled) by the decisions of profit center managers.

Service Department Charges

The controllable expenses of profit centers include *direct operating expenses* such as sales salaries and utility expenses. In addition, a profit center may incur expenses provided by internal centralized *service departments*. Examples of such service departments include the following:

- Research and Development
- Legal
- Telecommunications
- Information and Computer Systems
- Facilities Management
- Purchasing
- Advertising
- Payroll Accounting
- Transportation
- Human Resources

Link to Caterpillar
Caterpillar's research and development is conducted at its Tech Center in Mossville, Illinois.

Service department charges are *indirect* expenses to a profit center. They are similar to the expenses that would be incurred if the profit center purchased the services from outside the company. A profit center manager has control over service department expenses if the manager is free to choose how much service is used. In such cases, **service department charges** are allocated to profit centers based on the usage of the service by each profit center.

To illustrate, Nova Entertainment Group (NEG), a diversified entertainment company, is used. NEG has the following two operating divisions organized as profit centers:

- Theme Park Division
- Movie Production Division

The revenues and direct operating expenses for the two divisions follow. The operating expenses consist of direct expenses such as the wages and salaries of a division's employees.

	Theme Park Division	Movie Production Division
Revenues	$6,000,000	$2,500,000
Operating expenses	2,495,000	405,000

NEG's service departments and the expenses they incurred for the year ended December 31 are as follows:

Purchasing	$400,000
Payroll Accounting	255,000
Legal	250,000
Total	$905,000

An activity base for each service department is used to charge service department expenses to the Theme Park and Movie Production divisions. The activity base for each service department is a measure of the services performed. For NEG, the service department activity bases are as follows:

Department	Activity Base
Purchasing	Number of purchase requisitions
Payroll Accounting	Number of payroll checks
Legal	Number of billed hours

The use of services by the Theme Park and Movie Production divisions is as follows:

	Service Usage		
Division	Purchasing	Payroll Accounting	Legal
Theme Park	25,000 purchase requisitions	12,000 payroll checks	100 billed hrs.
Movie Production	15,000	3,000	900
Total	40,000 purchase requisitions	15,000 payroll checks	1,000 billed hrs.

The rates at which services are charged to each division are called *service department charge rates*. These rates are computed as follows:

$$\text{Service Department Charge Rate} = \frac{\text{Service Department Expense}}{\text{Total Service Department Usage}}$$

NEG's service department charge rates are computed as follows:

$$\text{Purchasing Charge Rate} = \frac{\$400,000}{40,000 \text{ purchase requisitions}} = \$10 \text{ per purchase requisition}$$

$$\text{Payroll Charge Rate} = \frac{\$255,000}{15,000 \text{ payroll checks}} = \$17 \text{ per payroll check}$$

$$\text{Legal Charge Rate} = \frac{\$250,000}{1,000 \text{ billed hrs.}} = \$250 \text{ per hr.}$$

The services used by each division are multiplied by the service department charge rates to determine the service charges for each division, computed as follows:

$$\text{Service Department Charge} = \text{Service Usage} \times \text{Service Department Charge Rate}$$

Exhibit 4 illustrates the service department charges and related computations for NEG's Theme Park and Movie Production divisions.

EXHIBIT 4
Service Department Charges to NEG Divisions

Nova Entertainment Group
Service Department Charges to NEG Divisions
For the Year Ended December 31, 20Y8

Service Department	Theme Park Division	Movie Production Division
Purchasing (Note A)	$250,000	$150,000
Payroll Accounting (Note B)	204,000	51,000
Legal (Note C)	25,000	225,000
Total service department charges	$479,000	$426,000

Note A:
25,000 purchase requisitions × $10 per purchase requisition = $250,000
15,000 purchase requisitions × $10 per purchase requisition = $150,000
Note B:
12,000 payroll checks × $17 per check = $204,000
 3,000 payroll checks × $17 per check = $51,000
Note C:
100 hours × $250 per hour = $25,000
900 hours × $250 per hour = $225,000

The differences in the service department charges between the two divisions can be explained by the nature of their operations and, thus, usage of services. For example, the Theme Park Division employs many part-time employees who are paid weekly. As a result, the Theme Park Division requires 12,000 payroll checks and incurs a $204,000 payroll service department charge (12,000 × $17). In contrast, the Movie Production Division has more permanent employees who are paid monthly. Thus, the Movie Production Division requires only 3,000 payroll checks and incurs a payroll service department charge of $51,000 (3,000 × $17).

Example Exercise 24-2 Service Department Charges   Obj. 3

The centralized legal department of Johnson Company has expenses of $600,000. The department has provided a total of 2,000 hours of service for the period. The East Division has used 500 hours of legal service during the period, and the West Division has used 1,500 hours. How much should each division be charged for legal services?

Follow My Example 24-2

East Division Service Charge for Legal Department:
$150,000 = 500 billed hours × ($600,000 ÷ 2,000 hours)

West Division Service Charge for Legal Department:
$450,000 = 1,500 billed hours × ($600,000 ÷ 2,000 hours)

Practice Exercises: PE 24-2A, PE 24-2B

Profit Center Reporting

The divisional income statements for NEG are shown in Exhibit 5.

EXHIBIT 5

Divisional Income Statements—NEG

Nova Entertainment Group
Divisional Income Statements
For the Year Ended December 31, 20Y8

	Theme Park Division	Movie Production Division
Revenues*	$6,000,000	$2,500,000
Operating expenses	2,495,000	405,000
Income from operations before service department charges	$3,505,000	$2,095,000
Less service department charges:		
Purchasing	$ 250,000	$ 150,000
Payroll Accounting	204,000	51,000
Legal	25,000	225,000
Total service department charges	$ 479,000	$ 426,000
Income from operations	$3,026,000	$1,669,000

*For a profit center that sells products, the income statement would show: Sales − Cost of goods sold = Gross profit. The operating expenses would be deducted from the gross profit to get the income from operations before service department charges.

In evaluating the profit center manager, the income from operations should be compared over time to a budget. However, it should not be compared across profit centers because the profit centers are usually different in terms of size, products, and customers.

Example Exercise 24-3 Income from Operations for Profit Center *Obj. 3*

Using the data for Johnson Company from Example Exercise 24-2 along with the following data, determine the divisional income from operations for the East and West divisions:

	East Division	West Division
Sales	$3,000,000	$8,000,000
Cost of goods sold	1,650,000	4,200,000
Selling expenses	850,000	1,850,000

Follow My Example 24-3

	East Division	West Division
Sales	$3,000,000	$8,000,000
Cost of goods sold	1,650,000	4,200,000
Gross profit	$1,350,000	$3,800,000
Selling expenses	850,000	1,850,000
Income from operations before service department charges	$ 500,000	$1,950,000
Service department charges	150,000	450,000
Income from operations	$ 350,000	$1,500,000

Practice Exercises: PE 24-3A, PE 24-3B

Responsibility Accounting for Investment Centers

Obj. 4 — Compute and interpret the return on investment, the residual income, and the balanced scorecard for an investment center.

An **investment center** manager has the responsibility and the authority to make decisions that affect not only costs and revenues but also the assets invested in the center. Investment centers are often used in diversified companies organized by divisions. In such cases, the divisional manager has authority similar to that of a chief operating officer or president of a company.

Because investment center managers have responsibility for revenues and expenses, *income from operations* is part of investment center reporting. In addition, because the manager has responsibility for the assets invested in the center, the following two additional measures of performance are used:

- Return on investment
- Residual income

To illustrate, DataLink Inc., a cellular phone company with three regional divisions, is used. Condensed divisional income statements for the Northern, Central, and Southern divisions of DataLink are shown in Exhibit 6.

Link to Caterpillar

Caterpillar has four group presidents who are responsible for the operations of each of its four segments: Construction Industries, Resource Industries, Energy & Transportation, and Financial Products. A fifth group president is responsible for three smaller operating segments.

Divisional Income Statements—DataLink Inc. EXHIBIT 6

DataLink Inc.
Divisional Income Statements
For the Year Ended December 31, 20Y8

	Northern Division	Central Division	Southern Division
Revenues	$560,000	$672,000	$750,000
Operating expenses	336,000	470,400	562,500
Income from operations before service department charges	$224,000	$201,600	$187,500
Service department charges	154,000	117,600	112,500
Income from operations	$ 70,000	$ 84,000	$ 75,000

Using only income from operations, the Central Division is the most profitable division. However, income from operations does not reflect the amount of assets invested in each center. For example, the Central Division could have twice as many assets as the Northern Division. For this reason, performance measures that consider the amount of invested assets, such as the return on investment and residual income, are used.

Return on Investment

Because investment center managers control the amount of assets invested in their centers, they should be evaluated based on the use of these assets. One measure that considers the amount of assets invested is the **return on investment (ROI)** or *return on assets*. It is computed as follows:

$$\text{Return on Investment (ROI)} = \frac{\text{Income from Operations}}{\text{Invested Assets}}$$

The return on investment is useful because the three factors subject to control by divisional managers (revenues, expenses, and invested assets) are considered. The higher the return on investment, the better the division is using its assets to generate income. In effect, the return on investment measures the income (return) on each dollar invested. As a result, the return on investment can be used as a common basis for comparing divisions with each other.

To illustrate, the invested assets of DataLink's three divisions are as follows:

	Invested Assets
Northern Division	$350,000
Central Division	700,000
Southern Division	500,000

Using the income from operations for each division shown in Exhibit 6, the return on investment for each division is computed as follows:

Northern Division:

$$\text{Return on Investment} = \frac{\text{Income from Operations}}{\text{Invested Assets}} = \frac{\$70,000}{\$350,000} = 20\%$$

Central Division:

$$\text{Return on Investment} = \frac{\text{Income from Operations}}{\text{Invested Assets}} = \frac{\$84,000}{\$700,000} = 12\%$$

Southern Division:

$$\text{Return on Investment} = \frac{\text{Income from Operations}}{\text{Invested Assets}} = \frac{\$75,000}{\$500,000} = 15\%$$

Although the Central Division generated the largest income from operations, its return on investment (12%) is the lowest. Hence, relative to the assets invested, the Central Division is the least profitable division. In comparison, the return on investment of the Northern Division is 20%, and the Southern Division is 15%.

To analyze differences in the return on investment across divisions, the **DuPont formula** for the return on investment is often used.[1] The DuPont formula views the return on investment as the product of the following two factors:

- **Profit margin**, which is the ratio of income from operations to sales.
- **Investment turnover**, which is the ratio of sales to invested assets.

> **Link to Caterpillar**
>
> Based upon recent financial statements, the return on investment for each of Caterpillar's four segments was as follows: Construction Industries 33.8%; Resource Industries 5.2%; Energy & Transportation 48.1%; Financial Products 2.7%

---

[1] The DuPont formula was created by a financial executive of E. I. du Pont de Nemours and Company in 1919.

Using the DuPont formula, the return on investment is expressed as follows:

$$\text{Return on Investment} = \text{Profit Margin} \times \text{Investment Turnover}$$

$$\text{Return on Investment} = \frac{\text{Income from Operations}}{\text{Sales}} \times \frac{\text{Sales}}{\text{Invested Assets}}$$

The DuPont formula is useful in evaluating divisions. This is because the profit margin and the investment turnover reflect the following underlying operating relationships of each division:

- Profit margin indicates *operating profitability* by computing the rate of profit earned on each sales dollar.
- Investment turnover indicates *operating efficiency* by computing the number of sales dollars generated by each dollar of invested assets.

If a division's profit margin increases and all other factors remain the same, the division's return on investment will increase. For example, a division might add more profitable products to its sales mix and, thus, increase its operating profit, profit margin, and return on investment.

If a division's investment turnover increases and all other factors remain the same, the division's return on investment will increase. For example, a division might attempt to increase sales through special sales promotions and thus increase operating efficiency, investment turnover, and return on investment.

The return on investment, profit margin, and investment turnover operate in relationship to one another. Specifically, more income can be earned by increasing the investment turnover, increasing the profit margin, or both.

Using the DuPont formula yields the same return on investment for each of DataLink's divisions, computed as follows:

$$\text{Return on Investment} = \frac{\text{Income from Operations}}{\text{Sales}} \times \frac{\text{Sales}}{\text{Invested Assets}}$$

Northern Division:

$$\text{Return on Investment} = \frac{\$70{,}000}{\$560{,}000} \times \frac{\$560{,}000}{\$350{,}000} = 12.5\% \times 1.6 = 20\%$$

Central Division:

$$\text{Return on Investment} = \frac{\$84{,}000}{\$672{,}000} \times \frac{\$672{,}000}{\$700{,}000} = 12.5\% \times 0.96 = 12\%$$

Southern Division:

$$\text{Return on Investment} = \frac{\$75{,}000}{\$750{,}000} \times \frac{\$750{,}000}{\$500{,}000} = 10\% \times 1.5 = 15\%$$

The Northern and Central divisions have the same profit margins of 12.5%. However, the Northern Division's investment turnover of 1.6 is larger than that of the Central Division's turnover of 0.96. By using its invested assets more efficiently, the Northern Division's return on investment of 20% is 8 percentage points higher than the Central Division's return of 12%.

The Southern Division's profit margin of 10% and investment turnover of 1.5 are lower than those of the Northern Division. The product of these factors results in a return on investment of 15% for the Southern Division, compared to 20% for the Northern Division.

Even though the Southern Division's profit margin is lower than the Central Division's, its higher turnover of 1.5 results in a return of 15%, which is greater than the Central Division's return of 12%.

To increase the return on investment, the profit margin and investment turnover for a division may be analyzed. For example, assume that the Northern Division is in

> **Link to Caterpillar**
> Based upon recent financial statements, **Caterpillar**'s Construction Industries segment had a Profit Margin of 11.3%, Investment Turnover of 3.0, resulting in a Return on Investment (ROI) of 33.9% (11.3% × 3.0).

a highly competitive industry in which the profit margin cannot be easily increased. As a result, the division manager might focus on increasing the investment turnover.

To illustrate, assume that the revenues of the Northern Division could be increased by $56,000 through increasing operating expenses, such as advertising, to $385,000. The Northern Division's income from operations will increase from $70,000 to $77,000, computed as follows:

Revenues ($560,000 + $56,000)	$616,000
Operating expenses	385,000
Income from operations before service department charges	$231,000
Service department charges	154,000
Income from operations	$ 77,000

The return on investment for the Northern Division, using the DuPont formula, is recomputed as follows:

$$\text{Return on Investment} = \frac{\$77,000}{\$616,000} \times \frac{\$616,000}{\$350,000} = 12.5\% \times 1.76 = 22\%$$

Although the Northern Division's profit margin remains the same (12.5%), the investment turnover has increased from 1.6 to 1.76, an increase of 10% (0.16 ÷ 1.6). The 10% increase in investment turnover increases the return on investment by 10% (from 20% to 22%).

The return on investment is also useful in deciding where to invest additional assets or expand operations. For example, DataLink should give priority to expanding operations in the Northern Division because it earns the highest return on investment. In other words, an investment in the Northern Division will return 20 cents (20%) on each dollar invested. In contrast, investments in the Central and Southern divisions will earn only 12 cents and 15 cents, respectively, per dollar invested.

A disadvantage of the return on investment as a performance measure is that it may lead divisional managers to reject new investments that could be profitable for the company as a whole. To illustrate, assume the following returns for the Northern Division of DataLink:

Current return on investment	20%
Minimum acceptable return on investment set by top management	10%
Expected return on investment for new project	14%

If the manager of the Northern Division invests in the new project, the Northern Division's overall return will decrease from 20% due to averaging. Thus, the division manager might decide to reject the project, even though the new project's expected return of 14% exceeds DataLink's minimum acceptable return of 10%.

Business Connection

COCA-COLA COMPANY: GO WEST YOUNG MAN

A major decision early in the history of Coca-Cola was to expand outside the United States to the rest of the world. As a result, Coca-Cola is known today the world over. What is revealing is how this decision has impacted the revenues and profitability of Coca-Cola across its international and North American segments. The following table shows the percent of revenues and percent of income from operations from the international and North American geographic segments.

	Revenues	Income from Operations
International segments	35.4%	94.3%
North American segment	49.2	28.5
Other (bottling companies, headquarters)	15.4	(22.8)
Total	100%	100%

The first column shows that the international segments provide over 35% of the revenues, while North America provides over 49% of the revenues, as the United States is a large market for Coca-Cola products. However, the income from operations tells a different story. More than 94% of Coca-Cola's profitability comes from international segments. Given the revenue segmentation, this suggests that the international profit margins must be much higher than the North American profit margin. Indeed this is the case, as can be seen in the following table:

	Profit Margin
International average	52.5%
North America	11.4%
Overall average	19.7%

The average profit margin for all the international segments is over four times as large as the North American segment. These results speak to the heart of the Coca-Cola marketing strategy. In the United States, Coca-Cola faces competition from many other beverage alternatives. However, outside the United States, Coca-Cola is able to earn higher profit margins because international consumers want to associate with the Coca-Cola brand identity.

Source: The Coca-Cola Company, Form 10-K for the Fiscal Year Ended December 31, 2015.

Example Exercise 24-4 Profit Margin, Investment Turnover, and ROI Obj. 4

Campbell Company has income from operations of $35,000, invested assets of $140,000, and sales of $437,500. Use the DuPont formula to compute the return on investment and show (a) the profit margin, (b) the investment turnover, and (c) the return on investment.

Follow My Example 24-4

a. Profit Margin = $35,000 ÷ $437,500 = 8%
b. Investment Turnover = $437,500 ÷ $140,000 = 3.125
c. Return on Investment = 8% × 3.125 = 25%

Practice Exercises: PE 24-4A, PE 24-4B

Residual Income

Residual income is useful in overcoming some of the disadvantages of the return on investment. **Residual income** is the excess of income from operations over a minimum acceptable income from operations, as shown in Exhibit 7.

Income from operations	$XXX
Less minimum acceptable income from operations as a percent of invested assets	XXX
Residual income	$XXX

EXHIBIT 7
Residual Income

The minimum acceptable income from operations is computed by multiplying the company minimum return by the invested assets. The minimum return is set by top management, based on such factors as the cost of financing.

To illustrate, assume that DataLink Inc. has established 10% as the minimum acceptable return on divisional assets. The residual incomes for the three divisions are shown in Exhibit 8.

EXHIBIT 8

Residual Income—DataLink, Inc.

	Northern Division	Central Division	Southern Division
Income from operations	$70,000	$84,000	$75,000
Less minimum acceptable income from operations as a percent of invested assets:			
$350,000 × 10%	35,000		
$700,000 × 10%		70,000	
$500,000 × 10%			50,000
Residual income	$35,000	$14,000	$25,000

As shown in Exhibit 8, the Northern Division has more residual income ($35,000) than the other divisions, even though it has the least amount of income from operations ($70,000). This is because the invested assets are less for the Northern Division than for the other divisions.

The major advantage of residual income as a performance measure is that it considers the minimum acceptable return, invested assets, and the income from operations for each division. In doing so, residual income encourages division managers to maximize income from operations in excess of the minimum. This provides an incentive to accept any project that is expected to have a return in excess of the minimum.

To illustrate, assume the following return for the Northern Division of DataLink:

Current return on investment	20%
Minimum acceptable return on investment set by top management	10%
Expected return on investment for new project	14%

If the manager of the Northern Division is evaluated on new projects using only return on investment, the division manager might decide to reject the new project. This is because investing in the new project will decrease Northern's current return of 20%. While this helps the division maintain its high ROI, it hurts the company as a whole because the expected return of 14% exceeds DataLink's minimum acceptable return of 10%.

In contrast, if the manager of the Northern Division is evaluated using residual income, the new project would probably be accepted because it will increase the Northern Division's residual income. In this way, residual income supports both divisional and overall company objectives.

Example Exercise 24-5 Residual Income   Obj. 4

The Wholesale Division of PeanutCo has income from operations of $87,000 and assets of $240,000. The minimum acceptable return on assets is 12%. What is the residual income for the division?

Follow My Example 24-5

Income from operations	$87,000
Less: minimum acceptable income from operations as a percent of assets ($240,000 × 12%)	28,800
Residual income	$58,200

Practice Exercises: PE 24-5A, PE 24-5B

The Balanced Scorecard[2]

The **balanced scorecard** is a set of multiple performance measures for a company. In addition to financial performance, a balanced scorecard normally includes performance measures for customer service, innovation and learning, and internal processes, as shown in Exhibit 9.

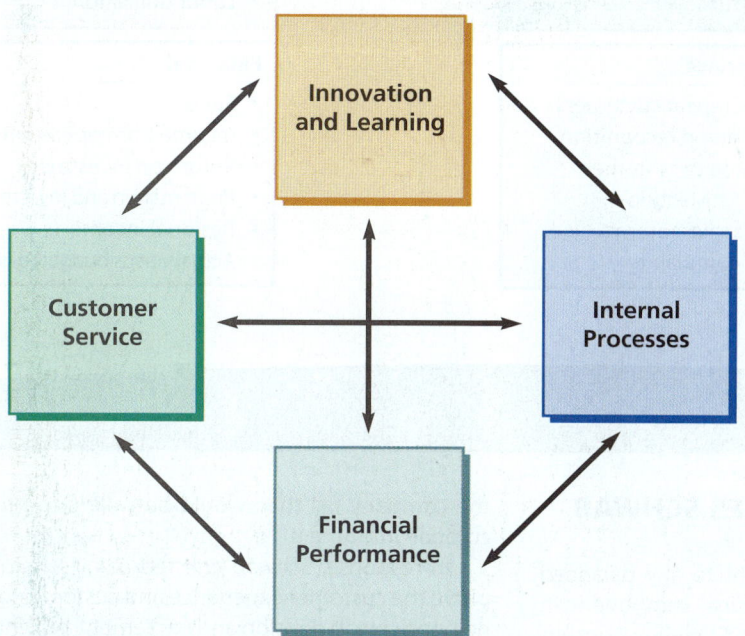

EXHIBIT 9

The Balanced Scorecard

Performance measures for learning and innovation often revolve around a company's research and development efforts. For example, the number of new products developed during a year and the time it takes to bring new products to the market are performance measures for innovation. Performance measures for learning could include the number of employee training sessions and the number of employees who are cross-trained in several skills.

Performance measures for customer service include the number of customer complaints and the number of repeat customers. Customer surveys can also be used to gather measures of customer satisfaction with the company as compared to competitors.

Performance measures for internal processes include the length of time it takes to manufacture a product. The amount of scrap and waste is a measure of the efficiency of a company's manufacturing processes. The number of customer returns is a performance measure of both the manufacturing and sales ordering processes.

All companies will use financial performance measures. Some financial performance measures discussed earlier in this chapter include income from operations, return on investment, and residual income.

The balanced scorecard attempts to identify the underlying nonfinancial drivers, or causes, of financial performance related to innovation and learning, customer service, and internal processes. In this way, the financial performance may be improved. For example, customer satisfaction is often measured by the number of repeat customers. By increasing the number of repeat customers, sales and income from operations can be increased.

Some common performance measures used in the balanced scorecard approach are shown in Exhibit 10.

> **Link to Caterpillar**
> The performance of **Caterpillar**'s Financial Products segment is measured by interest coverage and leverage ratios as well as its credit rating and timeliness of financial reporting.

---

[2] The balanced scorecard was developed by R. S. Kaplan and D. P. Norton and explained in *The Balanced Scorecard: Translating Strategy into Action* (Cambridge: Harvard Business School Press, 1996).

EXHIBIT 10
Balanced Scorecard Performance Measures

Innovation and Learning
- Number of new products
- Number of new patents
- Number of cross-trained employees
- Number of training hours
- Number of ethics violations
- Employee turnover

Internal Processes
- Waste and scrap
- Time to manufacture products
- Number of defects
- Number of rejected sales orders
- Number of stockouts
- Labor utilization

Customer Service
- Number of repeat customers
- Customer brand recognition
- Delivery time to customer
- Customer satisfaction
- Number of sales returns
- Customer complaints

Financial
- Sales
- Income from operations
- Return on investment
- Profit margin and investment turnover
- Residual income
- Actual versus budgeted (standard) costs

SERVICE FOCUS

TURNING AROUND CHARLES SCHWAB

Customer service is a key component to any balanced scorecard, and it is a particularly critical component in service industries. Since 2003, **Bain & Company** consulting has helped companies improve customer service by focusing on a customer loyalty metric called the *Net Promoter Score*. This metric, when used as part of a balanced scorecard, evaluates customer service by assessing how likely a customer is to recommend the company to others.

The Charles Schwab Corporation is a full-service financial advisory firm that was founded in 1973. In 2004, the company was struggling. Although Schwab had been built on delivering exceptional customer service, the company had lost its way. When customers were surveyed, they gave Schwab a negative 35% Net Promoter Score, indicating that more customers wanted to see the company fail than would be willing to promote the company to others.

In response, Schwab enlisted Bain to help them improve the customer experience and customer loyalty. Bain helped Schwab develop and implement a Client Promoter System that focused on embedding the Client Promoter Score deep within the company's values and core strategy. As Schwab CEO Walt Bettinger describes, "If you serve clients in the way that you would like to be served, they are going to want to do more business with you." The results were significant. By 2008, the company's stock price had more than doubled, and in 2010, Schwab received a Net Promoter Score of 46%, the highest in its sector.

Sources: "Schwab Earns Highest Customer Loyalty Ranking Among Brokerage & Investment Firms in Satmetrix Net Promoter's 2010 Industry Report," *BusinessWire*, March 25, 2010 and "Seeing the World through the Client's Eyes," Bain & Co., www.netpromotersystem.com/videos/trailblazer-video/charles-schwab.aspx.

Obj. 5 Describe and illustrate how the market price, negotiated price, and cost price approaches to transfer pricing may be used by decentralized segments of a business.

Transfer Pricing

When divisions transfer products or render services to each other, a **transfer price** is used to charge for the products or services.[3] Because transfer prices will affect a division's financial performance, setting a transfer price is a sensitive matter for the managers of both the selling and buying divisions.

Three common approaches to setting transfer prices are as follows:

- Market price approach
- Negotiated price approach
- Cost approach

---

[3] The discussion in this chapter highlights the essential concepts of transfer pricing. In-depth discussion of transfer pricing can be found in advanced texts.

Transfer prices may be used for cost, profit, or investment centers. The objective of setting a transfer price is to motivate managers to behave in a manner that will increase the overall company income. As will be illustrated, however, transfer prices may be misused in such a way that overall company income suffers.

Transfer prices can be set as low as the variable cost per unit or as high as the market price. Often, transfer prices are negotiated at some point between variable cost per unit and market price. Exhibit 11 shows the possible range of transfer prices.

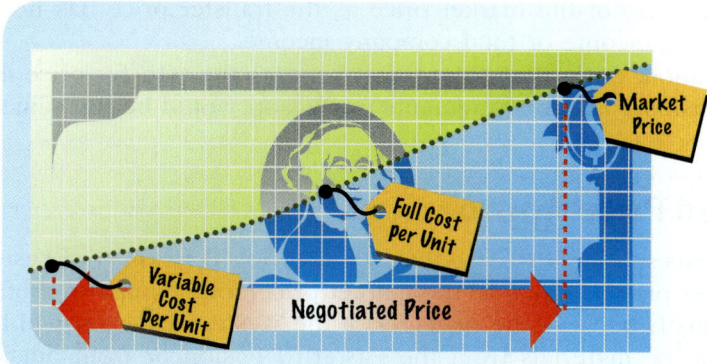

EXHIBIT 11

Commonly Used Transfer Prices

To illustrate, Wilson Company, a packaged snack food company with no service departments, is used. Wilson has two operating divisions (Eastern and Western) that are organized as investment centers. Condensed income statements for Wilson, assuming no transfers between divisions, are shown in Exhibit 12.

EXHIBIT 12

Income Statements—No Transfers Between Divisions

Wilson Company
Income Statements
For the Year Ended December 31, 20Y1

	Eastern Division	Western Division	Total Company
Sales:			
50,000 units × $20 per unit	$1,000,000		$1,000,000
20,000 units × $40 per unit		$800,000	800,000
			$1,800,000
Expenses:			
Variable:			
50,000 units × $10 per unit	$ 500,000		$ 500,000
20,000 units × $30* per unit		$600,000	600,000
Fixed	300,000	100,000	400,000
Total expenses	$ 800,000	$700,000	$1,500,000
Income from operations	$ 200,000	$100,000	$ 300,000

*$20 of the $30 per unit represents materials costs, and the remaining $10 per unit represents other variable conversion expenses incurred within the Western Division.

Market Price Approach

Using the **market price approach**, the transfer price is the price at which the product or service transferred could be sold to outside buyers. If an outside market exists for the product or service transferred, the current market price may be a proper transfer price.

Transfer Price = Market Price

To illustrate, assume that materials used by Wilson in producing snack food in the Western Division are currently purchased from an outside supplier at $20 per unit. The same materials are produced by the Eastern Division. The Eastern Division is operating at full capacity of 50,000 units and can sell all it produces to the Western Division or to outside buyers.

A transfer price of $20 per unit (the market price) has no effect on the Eastern Division's income or total company income. The Eastern Division will earn revenues of $20 per unit on all its production and sales, regardless of who buys its product.

Likewise, the Western Division will pay $20 per unit for materials (the market price). Thus, the use of the market price as the transfer price has no effect on the Eastern Division's income or total company income.

In this situation, the use of the market price as the transfer price is proper. The condensed divisional income statements for Wilson would be the same as shown in Exhibit 12.

Negotiated Price Approach

If unused or excess capacity exists in the supplying division (the Eastern Division) and the transfer price is equal to the market price, total company profit may not be maximized. This is because the manager of the Western Division will be indifferent toward purchasing materials from the Eastern Division or from outside suppliers. That is, in both cases the Western Division manager pays $20 per unit (the market price). As a result, the Western Division may purchase the materials from outside suppliers.

If, however, the Western Division purchases the materials from the Eastern Division, the difference between the market price of $20 and the variable costs of the Eastern Division of $10 per unit (from Exhibit 12) can cover fixed costs and contribute to overall company profits. Thus, the Western Division manager should be encouraged to purchase the materials from the Eastern Division.

The **negotiated price approach** allows the managers to agree (negotiate) among themselves on a transfer price. The only constraint is that the transfer price be less than the market price but greater than the supplying division's variable costs per unit, as follows:

Variable Costs per Unit < Transfer Price < Market Price

To illustrate, assume that instead of a capacity of 50,000 units, the Eastern Division's capacity is 70,000 units. In addition, assume that the Eastern Division can continue to sell only 50,000 units to outside buyers.

A transfer price less than $20 would encourage the manager of the Western Division to purchase from the Eastern Division. This is because the Western Division is currently purchasing its materials from outside suppliers at a cost of $20 per unit. Thus, its materials cost would decrease, and its income from operations would increase.

At the same time, a transfer price above the Eastern Division's variable costs per unit of $10 would encourage the manager of the Eastern Division to supply materials to the Western Division. In doing so, the Eastern Division's income from operations would also increase.

Exhibit 13 illustrates the divisional and company income statements, assuming that the Eastern and Western division managers agree to a transfer price of $15.

The Eastern Division increases its sales by $300,000 (20,000 units × $15 per unit) to $1,300,000. As a result, the Eastern Division's income from operations increases by $100,000 ($300,000 sales − $200,000 variable costs) to $300,000, as shown in Exhibit 13.

> **EXHIBIT 13**
>
> **Income Statements—Negotiated Transfer Price**
>
>
> Dynamic Exhibit

Wilson Company
Income Statements
For the Year Ended December 31, 20Y1

	Eastern Division	Western Division	Total Company
Sales:			
50,000 units × $20 per unit	$1,000,000		$1,000,000
20,000 units × $15 per unit	300,000		300,000
20,000 units × $40 per unit		$800,000	800,000
	$1,300,000	$800,000	$2,100,000
Expenses:			
Variable:			
70,000 units × $10 per unit	$ 700,000		$ 700,000
20,000 units × $25* per unit		$500,000	500,000
Fixed	300,000	100,000	400,000
Total expenses	$1,000,000	$600,000	$1,600,000
Income from operations	$ 300,000	$200,000	$ 500,000

*$10 of the $25 represents variable conversion expenses incurred solely within the Western Division, and $15 per unit represents the transfer price per unit from the Eastern Division.

The increase of $100,000 in the Eastern Division's income can also be computed as follows:

$$\text{Increase in Eastern (Supplying) Division's Income from Operations} = (\text{Transfer Price} - \text{Variable Cost per Unit}) \times \text{Units Transferred}$$

$$= (\$15 - \$10) \times 20{,}000 \text{ units} = \$100{,}000$$

The Western Division's materials cost decreases by $5 per unit ($20 – $15) for a total of $100,000 (20,000 units × $5 per unit). Thus, the Western Division's income from operations increases by $100,000 to $200,000, as shown in Exhibit 13.

The increase of $100,000 in the Western Division's income can also be computed as follows:

$$\text{Increase in Western (Purchasing) Division's Income from Operations} = (\text{Market Price} - \text{Transfer Price}) \times \text{Units Transferred}$$

$$= (\$20 - \$15) \times 20{,}000 \text{ units} = \$100{,}000$$

Comparing Exhibits 12 and 13 shows that Wilson's income from operations increased by $200,000, computed as follows:

	Income from Operations		
	No Units Transferred (Exhibit 12)	20,000 Units Transferred at $15 per Unit (Exhibit 13)	Increase (Decrease)
Eastern Division	$200,000	$300,000	$100,000
Western Division	100,000	200,000	100,000
Wilson Company	$300,000	$500,000	$200,000

In the preceding illustration, any negotiated transfer price between $10 and $20 is acceptable, as shown below:

Variable Costs per Unit < Transfer Price < Market Price
$10 < Transfer Price < $20

Any transfer price within this range will increase the overall income from operations for Wilson by $200,000. However, the increases in the Eastern and Western divisions' income from operations will vary depending on the transfer price.

To illustrate, a transfer price of $16 would increase the Eastern Division's income from operations by $120,000, computed as follows:

Increase in Eastern (Supplying) Division's Income from Operations = (Transfer Price − Variable Cost per Unit) × Units Transferred

= ($16 − $10) × 20,000 units = $120,000

A transfer price of $16 would increase the Western Division's income from operations by $80,000, computed as follows:

Increase in Western (Purchasing) Division's Income from Operations = (Market Price − Transfer Price) × Units Transferred

= ($20 − $16) × 20,000 units = $80,000

With a transfer price of $16, Wilson Company's income from operations still increases by $200,000, which consists of the Eastern Division's increase of $120,000 plus the Western Division's increase of $80,000.

As shown, a negotiated price provides each division manager with an incentive to negotiate the transfer of materials. At the same time, the overall company's income from operations will also increase. However, the negotiated approach only applies when the supplying division has excess capacity. In other words, the supplying division cannot sell all its production to outside buyers at the market price.

Example Exercise 24-6 Transfer Pricing — Obj. 5

The materials used by the Winston-Salem Division of Fox Company are currently purchased from outside suppliers at $30 per unit. These same materials are produced by Fox's Flagstaff Division. The Flagstaff Division can produce the materials needed by the Winston-Salem Division at a variable cost of $15 per unit. The division is currently producing 70,000 units and has capacity of 100,000 units. The two divisions have recently negotiated a transfer price of $22 per unit for 30,000 units. By how much will each division's income increase as a result of this transfer?

Follow My Example 24-6

Increase in Flagstaff (Supplying) Division's Income from Operations = (Transfer Price − Variable Cost per Unit) × Units Transferred

= ($22 − $15) × 30,000 units = $210,000

Increase in Winston-Salem (Purchasing) Division's Income from Operations = (Market Price − Transfer Price) × Units Transferred

= ($30 − $22) × 30,000 units = $240,000

Practice Exercises: PE 24-6A, PE 24-6B

Cost Price Approach

Under the **cost price approach**, cost is used to set transfer prices. A variety of costs may be used in this approach, including the following:

- Total product cost per unit
- Variable product cost per unit

If total product cost per unit is used, direct materials, direct labor, and factory overhead are included in the transfer price. If variable product cost per unit is used, the fixed factory overhead cost is excluded from the transfer price.

Actual costs or standard (budgeted) costs may be used in applying the cost price approach. If actual costs are used, inefficiencies of the producing (supplying) division are transferred to the purchasing division. Thus, there is little incentive for the producing (supplying) division to control costs. For this reason, most companies use standard costs in the cost price approach. In this way, differences between actual and standard costs remain with the producing (supplying) division for cost control purposes.

The cost price approach is most often used when the responsibility centers are organized as cost centers. When the responsibility centers are organized as profit or investment centers, the cost price approach is normally not used.

For example, using the cost price approach when the supplying division is organized as a profit center ignores the supplying division manager's responsibility for earning profits. In this case, using the cost price approach prevents the supplying division from reporting any profit (revenues – costs) on the units transferred. As a result, the division manager has little incentive to transfer units to another division, even though it may be in the best interests of the company.

INTEGRITY, OBJECTIVITY, AND ETHICS IN BUSINESS

THE ETHICS OF TRANSFER PRICES

Transfer prices allow large multinational companies to minimize taxes by shifting taxable income from countries with high tax rates to countries with low taxes. For example, a British company will pay U.S. taxes on income from its U.S. division and British taxes on income from its British division. Because this company can set its own transfer price, it can minimize its overall tax bill by setting a high transfer price when transferring goods to the United States This increases cost of goods sold for the highly taxed U.S division and increases sales for the lesser taxed British division. The overall result is a lower tax bill for the multinational company as a whole. In recent years, government tax authorities like the Internal Revenue Service (IRS) have become concerned with tax avoidance through transfer price manipulation. In response, many countries now have guidelines for setting transfer prices that ensure that transfer prices are not subject to manipulation for tax purposes.

Source: L. Eden and L. M. Smith, "The Ethics of Transfer Pricing," unpublished working paper, Texas A&M University, 2011.

At a Glance 24

Obj. 1 Describe the advantages and disadvantages of decentralized operations.

Key Points In a centralized business, all major planning and operating decisions are made by top management. In a decentralized business, these responsibilities are delegated to unit managers. Decentralization may be more effective because operational decisions are made by the managers closest to the operations.

Learning Outcomes	Example Exercises	Practice Exercises
• Describe the advantages of decentralization.		
• Describe the disadvantages of decentralization.		
• Describe the common types of responsibility centers and the role of responsibility accounting.		

Obj. 2 Prepare a responsibility accounting report for a cost center.

Key Points Cost centers limit the responsibility and authority of managers to decisions related to the costs of their unit. The primary tools for planning and controlling are budgets and budget performance reports.

Learning Outcomes	Example Exercises	Practice Exercises
• Describe cost centers.		
• Describe the responsibility reporting for a cost center.		
• Compute the costs over (under) budget for a cost center.	EE24-1	PE24-1A, 24-1B

Obj. 3 Prepare responsibility accounting reports for a profit center.

Key Points In a profit center, managers have the responsibility and authority to make decisions that affect both revenues and costs. Responsibility reports for a profit center usually show income from operations for the unit.

Learning Outcomes	Example Exercises	Practice Exercises
• Describe profit centers.		
• Determine how service department charges are allocated to profit centers.	EE24-2	PE24-2A, 24-2B
• Describe the responsibility reporting for a profit center.		
• Compute income from operations for a profit center.	EE24-3	PE24-3A, 24-3B

Obj. 4 Compute and interpret the return on investment, the residual income, and the balanced scorecard for an investment center.

Key Points In an investment center, the unit manager has the responsibility and authority to make decisions that affect the unit's revenues, expenses, and assets invested in the center. Three measures are commonly used to assess investment center performance: return on investment (ROI), residual income, and the balanced scorecard. These measures are often used to compare investment center performance.

Learning Outcomes	Example Exercises	Practice Exercises
• Describe investment centers.		
• Describe the responsibility reporting for an investment center.		
• Compute the profit margin, investment turnover, and return on investment (ROI).	EE24-4	PE24-4A, 24-4B
• Compute residual income.	EE24-5	PE24-5A, 24-5B
• Describe the balanced scorecard approach.		

Obj. 5 Describe and illustrate how the market price, negotiated price, and cost price approaches to transfer pricing may be used by decentralized segments of a business.

Key Points When divisions within a company transfer products or provide services to each other, a transfer price is used to charge for the products or services. Transfer prices should be set so that the overall company income is increased when goods are transferred between divisions. One of three approaches is typically used to establish transfer prices: market price, negotiated price, or cost price.

Learning Outcomes	Example Exercises	Practice Exercises
• Describe how companies determine the price used to transfer products or services between divisions.		
• Determine transfer prices using the market price approach.		
• Determine transfer prices using the negotiated price approach.	EE24-6	PE24-6A, 24-6B
• Describe the cost price approach to determining transfer price.		

Illustrative Problem

Quinn Company has two divisions, Domestic and International. Invested assets and condensed income statement data for each division for the year ended December 31, 20Y8, are as follows:

	Domestic Division	International Division
Revenues	$675,000	$480,000
Operating expenses	450,000	372,400
Service department charges	90,000	50,000
Invested assets	600,000	384,000

(Continued)

Instructions

1. Prepare condensed income statements for the past year for each division.
2. Using the DuPont formula, determine the profit margin, investment turnover, and return on investment for each division.
3. If management's minimum acceptable return is 10%, determine the residual income for each division.

Solution

1.

Quinn Company
Divisional Income Statements
For the Year Ended December 31, 20Y8

	Domestic Division	International Division
Revenues	$675,000	$480,000
Operating expenses	450,000	372,400
Income from operations before service department charges	$225,000	$107,600
Service department charges	90,000	50,000
Income from operations	$135,000	$ 57,600

2. Return on Investment = Profit Margin × Investment Turnover

$$\text{Return on Investment} = \frac{\text{Income from Operations}}{\text{Sales}} \times \frac{\text{Sales}}{\text{Invested Assets}}$$

$$\text{Domestic Division: ROI} = \frac{\$135{,}000}{\$675{,}000} \times \frac{\$675{,}000}{\$600{,}000}$$

$$= 20\% \times 1.125$$

$$= 22.5\%$$

$$\text{International Division: ROI} = \frac{\$57{,}600}{\$480{,}000} \times \frac{\$480{,}000}{\$384{,}000}$$

$$= 12\% \times 1.25$$

$$= 15\%$$

3. Domestic Division: $75,000 [$135,000 − (10% × $600,000)]
   International Division: $19,200 [$57,600 − (10% × $384,000)]

Key Terms

balanced scorecard (1187)
controllable expenses (1178)
controllable revenues (1178)
cost center (1176)
cost price approach (1192)
DuPont formula (1182)

investment center (1181)
investment turnover (1182)
market price approach (1189)
negotiated price approach (1190)
profit center (1178)
profit margin (1182)

residual income (1185)
responsibility accounting (1175)
return on investment (ROI) (1182)
service department charges (1178)
transfer price (1188)

Discussion Questions

1. Differentiate between centralized and decentralized operations.
2. Differentiate between a profit center and an investment center.
3. **Weyerhaeuser** developed a system that assigns service department expenses to user divisions on the basis of actual services consumed by the division. Here are a number of Weyerhaeuser's activities in its central Financial Services Department:
   - Payroll
   - Accounts payable
   - Accounts receivable
   - Database administration—report preparation

   For each activity, identify an activity base that could be used to charge user divisions for service.
4. What is the major shortcoming of using income from operations as a performance measure for investment centers?
5. In a decentralized company in which the divisions are organized as investment centers, how could a division be considered the least profitable even though it earned the largest amount of income from operations?
6. How does using the return on investment facilitate comparability between divisions of decentralized companies?
7. Why would a firm use a balanced scorecard in evaluating divisional performance?
8. What is the objective of transfer pricing?
9. When is the negotiated price approach preferred over the market price approach in setting transfer prices?
10. When using the negotiated price approach to transfer pricing, within what range should the transfer price be established?

Practice Exercises

Example Exercises

EE 24-1 p. 1177

PE 24-1A Budgetary performance for cost center   OBJ. 2

Caroline Company's costs were over budget by $319,000. The company is divided into West and East regions. The East Region's costs were under budget by $47,500. Determine the amount that the West Region's costs were over or under budget.

EE 24-1 p. 1177

PE 24-1B Budgetary performance for cost center   OBJ. 2

Conley Company's costs were under budget by $198,000. The company is divided into North and South regions. The North Region's costs were over budget by $52,000. Determine the amount that the South Region's costs were over or under budget.

EE 24-2 p. 1180

PE 24-2A Service department charges   OBJ. 3

The centralized employee travel department of Croce Company has expenses of $724,000. The department has serviced a total of 5,000 travel reservations for the period. The South Division has made 2,850 reservations during the period, and the West Division has made 2,150 reservations. How much should each division be charged for travel services?

EE 24-2 p. 1180

PE 24-2B Service department charges   OBJ. 3

The centralized computer technology department of Hardy Company has expenses of $320,000. The department has provided a total of 4,000 hours of service for the period. The Retail Division has used 2,750 hours of computer technology service during the period, and the Commercial Division has used 1,250 hours of computer technology service. How much should each division be charged for computer technology department services?

1198 Chapter 24 Decentralized Operations

EE 24-3 p. 1181   **PE 24-3A Income from operations for profit center**   OBJ. 3

Using the data for Croce Company from Practice Exercise 24-2A along with the following data, determine the divisional income from operations for the South and West divisions:

	South Division	West Division
Sales	$2,600,000	$2,420,000
Cost of goods sold	1,352,000	1,379,400
Selling expenses	520,000	484,000

EE 24-3 p. 1181   **PE 24-3B Income from operations for profit center**   OBJ. 3

Using the data for Hardy Company from Practice Exercise 24-2B along with the following data, determine the divisional income from operations for the Retail Division and the Commercial Division:

	Retail Division	Commercial Division
Sales	$2,150,000	$1,200,000
Cost of goods sold	1,300,000	800,000
Selling expenses	150,000	175,000

EE 24-4 p. 1185   **PE 24-4A Profit margin, investment turnover, and ROI**   OBJ. 4

Cash Company has income from operations of $112,500, invested assets of $750,000, and sales of $1,875,000. Use the DuPont formula to compute the return on investment and show (a) the profit margin, (b) the investment turnover, and (c) the return on investment.

EE 24-4 p. 1185   **PE 24-4B Profit margin, investment turnover, and ROI**   OBJ. 4

Briggs Company has income from operations of $36,000, invested assets of $180,000, and sales of $720,000. Use the DuPont formula to compute the return on investment and show (a) the profit margin, (b) the investment turnover, and (c) the return on investment.

EE 24-5 p. 1186   **PE 24-5A Residual income**   OBJ. 4

The Consumer Division of Galena Company has income from operations of $12,680,000 and assets of $74,500,000. The minimum acceptable return on assets is 12%. What is the residual income for the division?

EE 24-5 p. 1186   **PE 24-5B Residual income**   OBJ. 4

The Commercial Division of Herring Company has income from operations of $420,000 and assets of $910,000. The minimum acceptable return on assets is 8%. What is the residual income for the division?

EE 24-6 p. 1192   **PE 24-6A Transfer pricing**   OBJ. 5

The materials used by the North Division of Horton Company are currently purchased from outside suppliers at $60 per unit. These same materials are produced by Horton's South Division. The South Division can produce the materials needed by the North Division at a variable cost of $42 per unit. The division is currently producing 200,000 units and has capacity of 250,000 units. The two divisions have recently negotiated a transfer price of $52 per unit for 30,000 units. By how much will each division's income increase as a result of this transfer?

EE 24-6 p. 1192   **PE 24-6B   Transfer pricing**   OBJ. 5

The materials used by the Multnomah Division of Isbister Company are currently purchased from outside suppliers at $90 per unit. These same materials are produced by the Pembroke Division. The Pembroke Division can produce the materials needed by the Multnomah Division at a variable cost of $75 per unit. The division is currently producing 120,000 units and has capacity of 150,000 units. The two divisions have recently negotiated a transfer price of $82 per unit for 15,000 units. By how much will each division's income increase as a result of this transfer?

Exercises

✔ a. (c) $22,950

EX 24-1   Budget performance reports for cost centers   OBJ. 2

Partially completed budget performance reports for Garland Company, a manufacturer of light duty motors, follow:

Garland Company
Budget Performance Report—Vice President, Production
For the Month Ended November 30

Plant	Actual	Budget	Over Budget	Under Budget
Eastern Region	$2,409,400	$2,420,000		$(10,600)
Central Region	2,998,400	3,000,000		(1,600)
Western Region	(g)	(h)	(i)	
	(j)	(k)	$ (l)	$(12,200)

Garland Company
Budget Performance Report—Manager, Western Region Plant
For the Month Ended November 30

Department	Actual	Budget	Over Budget	Under Budget
Chip Fabrication	(a)	(b)	(c)	
Electronic Assembly	$703,200	$700,000	$ 3,200	
Final Assembly	516,600	525,000		$(8,400)
	(d)	(e)	$ (f)	$(8,400)

Garland Company
Budget Performance Report—Supervisor, Chip Fabrication
For the Month Ended November 30

Cost	Actual	Budget	Over Budget	Under Budget
Factory wages	$ 95,500	$ 82,000	$13,500	
Materials	115,300	120,000		$(4,700)
Power and light	49,950	45,000	4,950	
Maintenance	37,200	28,000	9,200	
	$297,950	$275,000	$27,650	$(4,700)

a. Complete the budget performance reports by determining the correct amounts for the lettered spaces.

b. ✏️ Compose a memo to Cassandra Reid, vice president of production for Garland Company, explaining the performance of the production division for November.

1200 Chapter 24 Decentralized Operations

✓ Commercial Division income from operations, $179,890

EX 24-2 Divisional income statements OBJ. 3

The following data were summarized from the accounting records for Jersey Coast Construction Company for the year ended June 30, 20Y8:

Cost of goods sold:		Service department charges:	
Commercial Division	$912,250	Commercial Division	$112,560
Residential Division	423,675	Residential Division	67,830
Administrative expenses:		Sales:	
Commercial Division	$149,800	Commercial Division	$1,354,500
Residential Division	128,625	Residential Division	743,780

Prepare divisional income statements for Jersey Coast Construction Company.

EX 24-3 Service department charges and activity bases OBJ. 3

For each of the following service departments, identify an activity base that could be used for charging the expense to the profit center:

a. Legal
b. Duplication services
c. Information Technology Help Desk
d. Central purchasing
e. Networking
f. Accounts receivable

EX 24-4 Activity bases for service department charges OBJ. 3

✓ c. 4

For each of the following service departments, select the activity base listed that is most appropriate for charging service expenses to responsible units:

Service Department	Activity Base
a. Accounts Receivable	1. Number of employees trained
b. Central Purchasing	2. Number of payroll checks
c. Computer Support	3. Number of sales invoices
d. Conferences	4. Number of computers
e. Employee Travel	5. Number of conference attendees
f. Payroll Accounting	6. Number of travel claims
g. Telecommunications	7. Number of purchase requisitions
h. Training	8. Number of cell phone minutes used

EX 24-5 Service department charges OBJ. 3

✓ b. Residential payroll, $33,000

Show Me How

In divisional income statements prepared for LeFevre Company, the Payroll Department costs are charged back to user divisions on the basis of the number of payroll distributions, and the Purchasing Department costs are charged back on the basis of the number of purchase requisitions. The Payroll Department had expenses of $75,400 and the Purchasing Department had expenses of $42,000 for the year. The following annual data for Residential, Commercial, and Government Contract divisions were obtained from corporate records:

	Residential	Commercial	Government Contract
Sales	$1,000,000	$1,600,000	$3,200,000
Number of employees:			
Weekly payroll (52 weeks per year)	300	150	200
Monthly payroll	75	160	90
Number of purchase requisitions per year	4,000	3,500	3,000

a. Determine the total amount of payroll checks and purchase requisitions processed per year by the company and each division.

b. Using the activity base information in (a), determine the annual amount of payroll and purchasing costs charged back to the Residential, Commercial, and Government Contract divisions from payroll and purchasing services.

c. ➤ Why does the Residential Division have a larger service department charge than the other two divisions even though its sales are lower?

EX 24-6 Service department charges and activity bases OBJ. 3

✔ b. Help desk, $77,200

Middler Corporation, a manufacturer of electronics and communications systems, uses a service department charge system to charge profit centers with Computing and Communications Services (CCS) service department costs. The following table identifies an abbreviated list of service categories and activity bases used by the CCS department. The table also includes some assumed cost and activity base quantity information for each service for October.

CCS Service Category	Activity Base	Budgeted Cost	Budgeted Activity Base Quantity
Help desk	Number of calls	$160,000	3,200
Network center	Number of devices monitored	735,000	9,800
Electronic mail	Number of user accounts	100,000	10,000
Handheld Technology support	Number of handheld devices issued	124,600	8,900

One of the profit centers for Middler Corporation is the Communication Systems (COMM) sector. Assume the following information for the COMM sector:

- The sector has 5,200 employees, of whom 25% are office employees.
- Almost all office employees (99%) have a computer on the network.
- One hundred percent of the employees with a computer also have an e-mail account.
- The average number of help desk calls for October was 1.2 calls per individual with a computer.
- There are 600 additional printers, servers, and peripherals on the network beyond the personal computers.
- All the nonoffice employees have been issued a handheld device.

a. Determine the service charge rate for the four CCS service categories for October.
b. Determine the charges to the COMM sector for the four CCS service categories for October.

EX 24-7 Divisional income statements with service department charges OBJ. 3

✔ Commercial income from operations, $1,071,000

Grael Technology has two divisions, Consumer and Commercial, and two corporate service departments, Tech Support and Purchasing. The corporate expenses for the year ended December 31, 20Y7, are as follows:

Tech Support Department	$336,000
Purchasing Department	67,500
Other corporate administrative expenses	448,000
Total corporate expense	$851,500

The other corporate administrative expenses include officers' salaries and other expenses required by the corporation. The Tech Support Department charges the divisions for services rendered, based on the number of computers in the department, and the Purchasing Department charges divisions for services, based on the number of purchase orders for each department. The usage of service by the two divisions is as follows:

	Tech Support	Purchasing
Consumer Division	300 computers	1,800 purchase orders
Commercial Division	180	2,700
Total	480 computers	4,500 purchase orders

(Continued)

1202　Chapter 24　Decentralized Operations

The service department charges of the Tech Support Department and the Purchasing Department are considered controllable by the divisions. Corporate administrative expenses are not considered controllable by the divisions. The revenues, cost of goods sold, and operating expenses for the two divisions are as follows:

	Consumer	Commercial
Revenues	$5,900,000	$4,950,000
Cost of goods sold	3,304,000	2,475,000
Operating expenses	1,180,000	1,237,500

Prepare the divisional income statements for the two divisions.

EX 24-8 Corrections to service department charges for a service company   OBJ. 3

✔ b. Income from operations, Cargo Division, $84,400

Wild Sun Airlines Inc. has two divisions organized as profit centers, the Passenger Division and the Cargo Division. The following divisional income statements were prepared:

Wild Sun Airlines Inc.
Divisional Income Statements
For the Year Ended December 31, 20Y9

	Passenger Division		Cargo Division	
Revenues		$3,025,000		$3,025,000
Operating expenses		2,450,000		2,736,000
Income from operations before service department charges		$ 575,000		$ 289,000
Less service department charges:				
Training	$125,000		$125,000	
Flight scheduling	108,000		108,000	
Reservations	151,200	384,200	151,200	384,200
Income from operations		$ 190,800		$ (95,200)

The service department charge rate for the service department costs was based on revenues. Because the revenues of the two divisions were the same, the service department charges to each division were also the same.

The following additional information is available:

	Passenger Division	Cargo Division	Total
Number of personnel trained	350	150	500
Number of flights	800	1,200	2,000
Number of reservations requested	20,000	0	20,000

a. Does the income from operations for the two divisions accurately measure performance? Explain.

b. Correct the divisional income statements, using the activity bases provided in revising the service department charges.

EX 24-9 Profit center responsibility reporting   OBJ. 3

✔ Income from operations, Summer Sports Division, $1,717,920

Glades Sporting Goods Co. operates two divisions—the Winter Sports Division and the Summer Sports Division. The following income and expense accounts were provided from the trial balance as of December 31, 20Y8, the end of the fiscal year, after all adjustments, including those for inventories, were recorded and posted:

Sales—Winter Sports Division	$12,600,000
Sales—Summer Sports Division	16,300,000
Cost of Goods Sold—Winter Sports Division	7,560,000
Cost of Goods Sold—Summer Sports Division	9,454,000
Sales Expense—Winter Sports Division	2,016,000
Sales Expense—Summer Sports Division	2,282,000
Administrative Expense—Winter Sports Division	1,260,000
Administrative Expense—Summer Sports Division	1,450,700
Advertising Expense	578,000
Transportation Expense	265,660
Accounts Receivable Collection Expense	174,000
Warehouse Expense	1,540,000

The bases to be used in allocating expenses, together with other essential information, are as follows:

a. Advertising expense—incurred at headquarters, charged back to divisions on the basis of usage: Winter Sports Division, $252,000; Summer Sports Division, $326,000.

b. Transportation expense—charged back to divisions at a charge rate of $7.40 per bill of lading: Winter Sports Division, 17,200 bills of lading; Summer Sports Division, 18,700 bills of lading.

c. Accounts receivable collection expense—incurred at headquarters, charged back to divisions at a charge rate of $6.00 per invoice: Winter Sports Division, 11,500 sales invoices; Summer Sports Division, 17,500 sales invoices.

d. Warehouse expense—charged back to divisions on the basis of floor space used in storing division products: Winter Sports Division, 102,000 square feet; Summer Sports Division, 118,000 square feet.

Prepare a divisional income statement with two column headings: Winter Sports Division and Summer Sports Division. Provide supporting calculations for service department charges.

EX 24-10 Return on investment OBJ. 4

✔ a. Retail, 18%

Show Me How

The income from operations and the amount of invested assets in each division of Beck Industries are as follows:

	Income from Operations	Invested Assets
Retail Division	$5,400,000	$30,000,000
Commercial Division	6,250,000	25,000,000
Internet Division	1,800,000	12,000,000

a. Compute the return on investment for each division.
b. Which division is the most profitable per dollar invested?

EX 24-11 Residual income OBJ. 4

✔ a. Retail Division, $2,700,000

Show Me How

Based on the data in Exercise 24-10, assume that management has established a 9% minimum acceptable return for invested assets.

a. Determine the residual income for each division.
b. Which division has the most residual income?

1204 Chapter 24 Decentralized Operations

✔ d. 3.00

EX 24-12 Determining missing items in return computation OBJ. 4

One item is omitted from each of the following computations of the return on investment:

Return on Investment	=	Profit Margin	×	Investment Turnover
13.2%	=	6%	×	(a)
(b)	=	10%	×	1.80
10.5%	=	(c)	×	1.50
15.0%	=	5%	×	(d)
(e)	=	12%	×	1.10

Determine the missing items, identifying each by the appropriate letter.

EX 24-13 Profit margin, investment turnover, and return on investment OBJ. 4

✔ a. ROI, 24%

The condensed income statement for the Consumer Products Division of Fargo Industries Inc. is as follows (assuming no service department charges):

Sales	$82,500,000
Cost of goods sold	53,625,000
Gross profit	$28,875,000
Administrative expenses	15,675,000
Income from operations	$13,200,000

The manager of the Consumer Products Division is considering ways to increase the return on investment.

a. Using the DuPont formula for return on investment, determine the profit margin, investment turnover, and return on investment of the Consumer Products Division, assuming that $55,000,000 of assets have been invested in the Consumer Products Division.

b. If expenses could be reduced by $1,650,000 without decreasing sales, what would be the impact on the profit margin, investment turnover, and return on investment for the Consumer Products Division?

EX 24-14 Return on investment OBJ. 4

✔ a. Media Networks ROI, 24.5%

The Walt Disney Company has four profitable business segments, described as follows:

- **Media Networks:** The ABC television and radio network, Disney channel, ESPN, A&E, E!, and Disney.com
- **Parks and Resorts:** Walt Disney World Resort, Disneyland, Disney Cruise Line, and other resort properties
- **Studio Entertainment:** Walt Disney Studios, which releases films by Pixar Animation Studios, Marvel Studios, Disney/Lucasfilm, and Touchstone Pictures
- **Consumer Products:** Character merchandising, Disney stores, books, and magazines

Disney recently reported sector income from operations, revenue, and invested assets (in millions) as follows:

	Income from Operations	Revenue	Invested Assets
Media Networks	$7,321	$21,152	$29,887
Parks and Resorts	2,663	15,099	23,335
Studio Entertainment	1,549	6,988	15,155
Consumer Products	1,356	4,274	7,526

a. Use the DuPont formula to determine the return on investment for the four Disney sectors. Round whole percents to one decimal place and investment turnover to two decimal places.

b. How do the four sectors differ in their profit margin, investment turnover, and return on investment?

Chapter 24 Decentralized Operations 1205

EX 24-15 Determining missing items in return and residual income computations
OBJ. 4

✓ c. $46,250

Data for Uberto Company are presented in the following table of returns on investment and residual incomes:

Invested Assets	Income from Operations	Return on Investment	Minimum Return	Minimum Acceptable Income from Operations	Residual Income
$925,000	$185,000	(a)	15%	(b)	(c)
$775,000	(d)	(e)	(f)	$93,000	$23,250
$450,000	(g)	18%	(h)	$58,500	(i)
$610,000	$97,600	(j)	12%	(k)	(l)

Determine the missing items, identifying each item by the appropriate letter.

EX 24-16 Determining missing items from computations
OBJ. 4

✓ a. (e) $300,000

Data for the North, South, East, and West divisions of Free Bird Company are as follows:

	Sales	Income from Operations	Invested Assets	Return on Investment	Profit Margin	Investment Turnover
North	$860,000	(a)	(b)	17.5%	7.0%	(c)
South	(d)	$51,300	(e)	(f)	4.5%	3.8
East	$1,020,000	(g)	$680,000	15.0%	(h)	(i)
West	$1,120,000	$89,600	$560,000	(j)	(k)	(l)

a. Determine the missing items, identifying each by the letters (a) through (l). Round percents and investment turnover to one decimal place.

b. Determine the residual income for each division, assuming that the minimum acceptable return established by management is 12%.

c. Which division is the most profitable in terms of (1) return on investment and (2) residual income?

EX 24-17 Return on investment, residual income for a service company
OBJ. 4

H&R Block Inc. provides tax preparation services throughout the United States and other parts of the world. These services are provided through two segments: company-owned offices and franchised operations.

Recent financial information provided by H&R Block for its company-owned and franchised operations is as follows (in millions):

	Company-Owned	Franchised Operations
Revenues	$2,651	$335
Income from operations	617	86
Total assets	3,930	586

a. Use the DuPont formula to determine the return on investment for each business divisions. Round whole percents to one decimal place and investment turnover to two decimal places.

b. Determine the residual income for each division, assuming a minimum acceptable income of 15% of total assets. Round minimal acceptable return to the nearest million dollars.

c. ✏️ Interpret your results.

EX 24-18 Balanced scorecard for a service company
OBJ. 4

American Express Company is a major financial services company, noted for its American Express® card. Some of the performance measures used by the company in its balanced scorecard follow:

Average card member spending	Number of Internet features
Cards in force	Number of merchant signings
Earnings growth	Number of new card launches
Hours of credit consultant training	Return on equity
Investment in information technology	Revenue growth
Number of card choices	

For each measure, identify whether the measure best fits the innovation, customer, internal process, or financial dimension of the balanced scorecard.

EX 24-19 Building a balanced scorecard
OBJ. 4

Hit-n-Run Inc. owns and operates 10 food trucks (mobile kitchens) throughout metropolitan Los Angeles. Each food truck has a different food theme, such as Irish-Mexican fusion, traditional Mexican street food, Ethiopian cuisine, and Lebanese-Italian fusion. The company was founded three years ago by Juanita O'Brien when she opened a single food truck with a unique menu. As her business has grown, she has become concerned about her ability to manage and control the business. O'Brien describes how the company was built, its key success factors, and its recent growth.

"I built the company from the ground up. In the beginning it was just me. I drove the truck, set the menu, bought the ingredients, prepared the meals, served the meals, cleaned the kitchen, and maintained the equipment. I made unique meals from quality ingredients and didn't serve anything that wasn't perfect. I changed my location daily and notified customers of my location via Twitter.

As my customer base grew, I hired employees to help me in the truck. Then one day I realized that I had a formula that could be expanded to multiple trucks. Before I knew it, I had 10 trucks and was hiring people to do everything that I used to do by myself. Now I work with my team to build the menu, set daily locations for the trucks, and manage the operations of the business.

My business model is based on providing the highest quality street food and charging more for it than other trucks do. You won't get the cheapest meal at one of my trucks, but you will get the best. The superior quality allows me to price my meals a little bit higher than the other trucks do. My employees are critical to my success. I pay them a better wage than they could make on other food trucks, and I expect more from them. I rely on them to maintain the quality that I established when I opened my first truck.

Things are going great, but I'm feeling overwhelmed. So far, the growth in sales has led to a growth in profitability—but I'm getting nervous. If quality starts to fall off, my brand value erodes, and that could affect the prices that I charge for my meals and the success of my business."

Create balanced scorecard measures for Hit-n-Run Food Trucks. Identify whether these measures best fit the innovation, customer, internal process, or financial dimension of the balanced scorecard.

EX 24-20 Decision on transfer pricing
OBJ. 5

✔ a. $2,650,000

Materials used by the Instrument Division of T_Kong Industries are currently purchased from outside suppliers at a cost of $175 per unit. However, the same materials are available from the Components Division. The Components Division has unused capacity and can produce the materials needed by the Instrument Division at a variable cost of $122 per unit.

a. If a transfer price of $148 per unit is established and 50,000 units of materials are transferred, with no reduction in the Components Division's current sales, how much would T_Kong Industries' total income from operations increase?

b. How much would the Instrument Division's income from operations increase?

c. How much would the Components Division's income from operations increase?

EX 24-21 Decision on transfer pricing
OBJ. 5

✔ b. $750,000

Based on T_Kong Industries' data in Exercise 24-20, assume that a transfer price of $160 has been established and that 50,000 units of materials are transferred, with no reduction in the Components Division's current sales.

a. How much would T_Kong Industries' total income from operations increase?
b. How much would the Instrument Division's income from operations increase?
c. How much would the Components Division's income from operations increase?
d. If the negotiated price approach is used, what would be the range of acceptable transfer prices and why?

Problems: Series A

PR 24-1A Budget performance report for a cost center   OBJ. 2

Valotic Tech Inc. sells electronics over the Internet. The Consumer Products Division is organized as a cost center. The budget for the Consumer Products Division for the month ended January 31 is as follows (in thousands):

Customer service salaries	$ 546,840
Insurance and property taxes	114,660
Distribution salaries	872,340
Marketing salaries	1,028,370
Engineer salaries	836,850
Warehouse wages	586,110
Equipment depreciation	183,792
Total	$4,168,962

During January, the costs incurred in the Consumer Products Division were as follows:

Customer service salaries	$ 602,350
Insurance and property taxes	110,240
Distribution salaries	861,200
Marketing salaries	1,085,230
Engineer salaries	820,008
Warehouse wages	562,632
Equipment depreciation	183,610
Total	$4,225,270

Instructions

1. Prepare a budget performance report for the director of the Consumer Products Division for the month of January.
2. For which costs might the director be expected to request supplemental reports?

✔ 1. Income from operations, Central Division, $930,100

PR 24-2A Profit center responsibility reporting for a service company   OBJ. 3

Red Line Railroad Inc. has three regional divisions organized as profit centers. The chief executive officer (CEO) evaluates divisional performance, using income from operations as a percent of revenues. The following quarterly income and expense accounts were provided from the trial balance as of December 31:

Revenues—East	$1,400,000
Revenues—West	2,000,000
Revenues—Central	3,200,000
Operating Expenses—East	800,000
Operating Expenses—West	1,350,000
Operating Expenses—Central	1,900,000
Corporate Expenses—Shareholder Relations	300,000
Corporate Expenses—Customer Support	320,000
Corporate Expenses—Legal	500,000
General Corporate Officers' Salaries	1,200,000

(Continued)

The company operates three service departments: Shareholder Relations, Customer Support, and Legal. The Shareholder Relations Department conducts a variety of services for shareholders of the company. The shareholder Relations Department and general corporate officers' salaries are not controllable by division management. The Customer Support Department is the company's point of contact for new service, complaints, and requests for repair. The department believes that the number of customer contacts is an activity base for this work. The Legal Department provides legal services for division management. The department believes that the number of hours billed is an activity base for this work. The following additional information has been gathered:

	East	West	Central
Number of customer contacts	1,500	2,800	5,700
Number of hours billed	750	1,750	1,500

Instructions

1. Prepare quarterly income statements showing income from operations for the three divisions. Use three column headings: East, West, and Central.
2. Identify the most successful division according to the profit margin.
3. ▬▬▬▶ Provide a recommendation to the CEO for a better method for evaluating the performance of the divisions. In your recommendation, identify the major weakness of the present method.

PR 24-3A Divisional income statements and return on investment analysis OBJ. 4

✓ 2. Cereal Division ROI, 11.0%

Excel

The Whole Life Baked Goods Company is a diversified food company that specializes in all natural foods. The company has three operating divisions organized as investment centers. Condensed data taken from the records of the three divisions for the year ended June 30, 20Y7, are as follows:

	Cereal Division	Snack Cake Division	Retail Bakeries Division
Sales	$17,600,000	$18,000,000	$9,520,000
Cost of goods sold	10,600,000	12,550,000	6,630,000
Operating expenses	6,120,000	4,730,000	2,318,800
Invested assets	8,000,000	6,000,000	6,800,000

The management of The Whole Life Baked Goods Company is evaluating each division as a basis for planning a future expansion of operations.

Instructions

1. Prepare condensed divisional income statements for the three divisions, assuming that there were no service department charges.
2. Using the DuPont formula for return on investment, compute the profit margin, investment turnover, and return on investment for each division. Round percentages and the investment turnover to one decimal place.
3. ▬▬▬▶ If available funds permit the expansion of operations of only one division, which of the divisions would you recommend for expansion, based on parts (1) and (2)? Explain.

PR 24-4A Effect of proposals on divisional performance OBJ. 4

✓ 1. ROI, 16.8%

Excel

A condensed income statement for the Commercial Division of Maxell Manufacturing Inc. for the year ended December 31 is as follows:

Sales	$3,500,000
Cost of goods sold	2,480,000
Gross profit	$1,020,000
Operating expenses	600,000
Income from operations	$ 420,000
Invested assets	$2,500,000

Assume that the Commercial Division received no charges from service departments. The president of Maxell Manufacturing has indicated that the division's return on a $2,500,000 investment must be increased to at least 21% by the end of the next year if operations are to continue. The division manager is considering the following three proposals:

Proposal 1: Transfer equipment with a book value of $312,500 to other divisions at no gain or loss and lease similar equipment. The annual lease payments would exceed the amount of depreciation expense on the old equipment by $105,000. This increase in expense would be included as part of the cost of goods sold. Sales would remain unchanged.

Proposal 2: Purchase new and more efficient machining equipment and thereby reduce the cost of goods sold by $560,000 after considering the effects of depreciation expense on the new equipment. Sales would remain unchanged, and the old equipment, which has no remaining book value, would be scrapped at no gain or loss. The new equipment would increase invested assets by an additional $1,875,000 for the year.

Proposal 3: Reduce invested assets by discontinuing a product line. This action would eliminate sales of $595,000, reduce cost of goods sold by $406,700, and reduce operating expenses by $175,000. Assets of $1,338,000 would be transferred to other divisions at no gain or loss.

Instructions

1. Using the DuPont formula for return on investment, determine the profit margin, investment turnover, and return on investment for the Commercial Division for the past year.
2. Prepare condensed estimated income statements and compute the invested assets for each proposal.
3. Using the DuPont formula for return on investment, determine the profit margin, investment turnover, and return on investment for each proposal. Round percentages and the investment turnover to one decimal place.
4. Which of the three proposals would meet the required 21% return on investment?
5. If the Commercial Division were in an industry where the profit margin could not be increased, how much would the investment turnover have to increase to meet the president's required 21% return on investment? Round to one decimal place.

PR 24-5A   **Divisional performance analysis and evaluation**   **OBJ. 4**

✔ 2. Business Division ROI, 20.0%

Excel

Show Me How

The vice president of operations of Pavone Company is evaluating the performance of two divisions organized as investment centers. Invested assets and condensed income statement data for the past year for each division are as follows:

	Business Division	Consumer Division
Sales	$2,500,000	$2,550,000
Cost of goods sold	1,320,000	1,350,000
Operating expenses	930,000	843,000
Invested assets	1,250,000	2,125,000

Instructions

1. Prepare condensed divisional income statements for the year ended December 31, assuming that there were no service department charges.
2. Using the DuPont formula for return on investment, determine the profit margin, investment turnover, and return on investment for each division. Round percentages and the investment turnover to one decimal place.
3. If management wants a minimum acceptable return of 17%, determine the residual income for each division.
4. Discuss the evaluation of the two divisions, using the performance measures determined in parts (1), (2), and (3).

Chapter 24 Decentralized Operations

✔ 3. Total income from operations, $1,759,680

PR 24-6A Transfer pricing
OBJ. 5

Garcon Inc. manufactures electronic products, with two operating divisions, the Consumer and Commercial divisions. Condensed divisional income statements, which involve no intracompany transfers and include a breakdown of expenses into variable and fixed components, are as follows:

Garcon Inc.
Divisional Income Statements
For the Year Ended December 31, 20Y8

	Consumer Division	Commercial Division	Total
Sales:			
14,400 units @ $144 per unit	$2,073,600		$2,073,600
21,600 units @ $275 per unit		$5,940,000	5,940,000
	$2,073,600	$5,940,000	$8,013,600
Expenses:			
Variable:			
14,400 units @ $104 per unit	$1,497,600		$1,497,600
21,600 units @ $193* per unit		$4,168,800	4,168,800
Fixed	200,000	520,000	720,000
Total expenses	$1,697,600	$4,688,800	$6,386,400
Income from operations	$ 376,000	$1,251,200	$1,627,200

*$150 of the $193 per unit represents materials costs, and the remaining $43 per unit represents other variable conversion expenses incurred within the Commercial Division.

The Consumer Division is presently producing 14,400 units out of a total capacity of 17,280 units. Materials used in producing the Commercial Division's product are currently purchased from outside suppliers at a price of $150 per unit. The Consumer Division is able to produce the materials used by the Commercial Division. Except for the possible transfer of materials between divisions, no changes are expected in sales and expenses.

Instructions

1. Would the market price of $150 per unit be an appropriate transfer price for Garcon Inc.? Explain.

2. If the Commercial Division purchased 2,880 units from the Consumer Division, rather than externally, at a negotiated transfer price of $115 per unit, how much would the income from operations of each division and the total company income from operations increase?

3. Prepare condensed divisional income statements for Garcon Inc. based on the data in part (2).

4. If a transfer price of $126 per unit was negotiated, how much would the income from operations of each division and the total company income from operations increase?

5. a. What is the range of possible negotiated transfer prices that would be acceptable for Garcon Inc.?

   b. Assuming that the managers of the two divisions cannot agree on a transfer price, what price would you suggest as the transfer price?

Problems: Series B

PR 24-1B Budget performance report for a cost center
OBJ. 2

The Eastern District of Adelson Inc. is organized as a cost center. The budget for the Eastern District of Adelson Inc. for the month ended December 31 is as follows (in thousands):

Sales salaries	$ 819,840
System administration salaries	448,152
Customer service salaries	152,600
Billing salaries	98,760
Maintenance	271,104
Depreciation of plant and equipment	92,232
Insurance and property taxes	41,280
Total	$1,923,968

During December, the costs incurred in the Eastern District were as follows:

Sales salaries	$ 818,880
System administration salaries	447,720
Customer service salaries	183,120
Billing salaries	98,100
Maintenance	273,000
Depreciation of plant and equipment	92,232
Insurance and property taxes	41,400
Total	$1,954,452

Instructions

1. Prepare a budget performance report for the manager of the Eastern District of Adelson for the month of December.
2. For which costs might the supervisor be expected to request supplemental reports?

PR 24-2B **Profit center responsibility reporting for a service company**   OBJ. 3

✔ 1. Income from operations, West Region, $820,800

Thomas Railroad Company organizes its three divisions, the North (N), South (S), and West (W) regions, as profit centers. The chief executive officer (CEO) evaluates divisional performance using income from operations as a percent of revenues. The following quarterly income and expense accounts were provided from the trial balance as of December 31:

Revenues—N Region	$3,780,000
Revenues—S Region	5,673,000
Revenues—W Region	5,130,000
Operating Expenses—N Region	2,678,500
Operating Expenses—S Region	4,494,890
Operating Expenses—W Region	3,770,050
Corporate Expenses—Dispatching	182,000
Corporate Expenses—Equipment Management	1,200,000
Corporate Expenses—Treasurer's	734,000
General Corporate Officers' Salaries	1,380,000

The company operates three service departments: the Dispatching Department, the Equipment Management Department, and the Treasurer's Department. The Treasurer's Department and general corporate officers' salaries are not controllable by division management. The Dispatching Department manages the scheduling and releasing of completed trains. The Equipment Management Department manages the inventories of railroad cars. It makes sure the right freight cars are at the right place at the right time. The Treasurer's Department conducts a variety of services for the company as a whole. The following additional information has been gathered:

	North	South	West
Number of scheduled trains	650	1,105	845
Number of railroad cars in inventory	6,000	8,400	9,600

(Continued)

1212 Chapter 24 Decentralized Operations

Instructions

1. Prepare quarterly income statements showing income from operations for the three regions. Use three column headings: North, South, and West.
2. Identify the most successful region according to the profit margin.
3. ✏️ Provide a recommendation to the CEO for a better method for evaluating the performance of the regions. In your recommendation, identify the major weakness of the present method.

PR 24-3B Divisional income statements and return on investment analysis   OBJ. 4

✔ 2. Mutual Fund Division, ROI, 22.4%

Excel

E.F. Lynch Company is a diversified investment company with three operating divisions organized as investment centers. Condensed data taken from the records of the three divisions for the year ended June 30, 20Y8, are as follows:

	Mutual Fund Division	Electronic Brokerage Division	Investment Banking Division
Fee revenue	$4,140,000	$3,360,000	$4,560,000
Operating expenses	2,980,800	3,091,200	3,739,200
Invested assets	5,175,000	1,120,000	3,800,000

The management of E.F. Lynch Company is evaluating each division as a basis for planning a future expansion of operations.

Instructions

1. Prepare condensed divisional income statements for the three divisions, assuming that there were no service department charges.
2. Using the DuPont formula for return on investment, compute the profit margin, investment turnover, and return on investment for each division. Round percentages and the investment turnover to one decimal place.
3. ✏️ If available funds permit the expansion of operations of only one division, which of the divisions would you recommend for expansion, based on parts (1) and (2)? Explain.

PR 24-4B Effect of proposals on divisional performance   OBJ. 4

✔ 3. Proposal 3 ROI, 16.0%

Excel

A condensed income statement for the Electronics Division of Gihbli Industries Inc. for the year ended December 31 is as follows:

Sales	$1,575,000
Cost of goods sold	891,000
Gross profit	$ 684,000
Operating expenses	558,000
Income from operations	$ 126,000
Invested assets	$1,050,000

Assume that the Electronics Division received no charges from service departments.

The president of Gihbli Industries Inc. has indicated that the division's return on a $1,050,000 investment must be increased to at least 20% by the end of the next year if operations are to continue. The division manager is considering the following three proposals:

Proposal 1: Transfer equipment with a book value of $300,000 to other divisions at no gain or loss and lease similar equipment. The annual lease payments would be less than the amount of depreciation expense on the old equipment by $31,400. This decrease in expense would be included as part of the cost of goods sold. Sales would remain unchanged.

Proposal 2: Reduce invested assets by discontinuing a product line. This action would eliminate sales of $180,000, reduce cost of goods sold by $119,550, and reduce operating expenses by $60,000. Assets of $112,500 would be transferred to other divisions at no gain or loss.

Proposal 3: Purchase new and more efficient machinery and thereby reduce the cost of goods sold by $189,000 after considering the effects of depreciation expense on the new equipment. Sales would remain unchanged, and the old machinery, which has no remaining book value, would be scrapped at no gain or loss. The new machinery would increase invested assets by $918,750 for the year.

Instructions

1. Using the DuPont formula for return on investment, determine the profit margin, investment turnover, and return on investment for the Electronics Division for the past year. Round percentages and the investment turnover to one decimal place.
2. Prepare condensed estimated income statements and compute the invested assets for each proposal.
3. Using the DuPont formula for return on investment, determine the profit margin, investment turnover, and return on investment for each proposal. Round percentages and the investment turnover to one decimal place.
4. Which of the three proposals would meet the required 20% return on investment?
5. If the Electronics Division were in an industry where the profit margin could not be increased, how much would the investment turnover have to increase to meet the president's required 20% return on investment? Round to one decimal place.

PR 24-5B   **Divisional performance analysis and evaluation**   OBJ. 4

✔ 2. Road Bike Division ROI, 12.0%

The vice president of operations of Free Ride Bike Company is evaluating the performance of two divisions organized as investment centers. Invested assets and condensed income statement data for the past year for each division are as follows:

	Road Bike Division	Mountain Bike Division
Sales	$1,728,000	$1,760,000
Cost of goods sold	1,380,000	1,400,000
Operating expenses	175,200	236,800
Invested assets	1,440,000	800,000

Instructions

1. Prepare condensed divisional income statements for the year ended December 31, 20Y7, assuming that there were no service department charges.
2. Using the DuPont formula for return on investment, determine the profit margin, investment turnover, and return on investment for each division. Round percentages and the investment turnover to one decimal place.
3. If management's minimum acceptable return is 10%, determine the residual income for each division.
4. Discuss the evaluation of the two divisions, using the performance measures determined in parts (1), (2), and (3).

PR 24-6B Transfer pricing

OBJ. 5

✓ 3. Navigational Systems Division, $179,410

Exoplex Industries Inc. is a diversified aerospace company, including two operating divisions, Semiconductors and Navigational Systems divisions. Condensed divisional income statements, which involve no intracompany transfers and include a breakdown of expenses into variable and fixed components, are as follows:

Exoplex Industries Inc.
Divisional Income Statements
For the Year Ended December 31, 20Y8

	Semiconductors Division	Navigational Systems Division	Total
Sales:			
2,240 units @ $396 per unit	$887,040		$ 887,040
3,675 units @ $590 per unit		$2,168,250	2,168,250
	$887,040	$2,168,250	$3,055,290
Expenses:			
Variable:			
2,240 units @ $232 per unit	$519,680		$ 519,680
3,675 units @ $472* per unit		$1,734,600	1,734,600
Fixed	220,000	325,000	545,000
Total expenses	$739,680	$2,059,600	$2,799,280
Income from operations	$147,360	$ 108,650	$ 256,010

*$432 of the $472 per unit represents materials costs, and the remaining $40 per unit represents other variable conversion expenses incurred within the Navigational Systems Division.

The Semiconductors Division is presently producing 2,240 units out of a total capacity of 2,820 units. Materials used in producing the Navigational Systems Division's product are currently purchased from outside suppliers at a price of $432 per unit. The Semiconductors Division is able to produce the components used by the Navigational Systems Division. Except for the possible transfer of materials between divisions, no changes are expected in sales and expenses.

Instructions

1. Would the market price of $432 per unit be an appropriate transfer price for Exoplex Industries Inc.? Explain.

2. If the Navigational Systems Division purchased 580 units from the Semiconductors Division, rather than externally, at a negotiated transfer price of $310 per unit, how much would the income from operations of each division and total company income from operations increase?

3. Prepare condensed divisional income statements for Exoplex Industries Inc. based on the data in part (2).

4. If a transfer price of $340 per unit was negotiated, how much would the income from operations of each division and total company income from operations increase?

5. a. What is the range of possible negotiated transfer prices that would be acceptable for Exoplex Industries Inc.?

   b. Assuming that the managers of the two divisions cannot agree on a transfer price, what price would you suggest as the transfer price?

Cases & Projects

CP 24-1 Ethics in Action

Sembotix Company has several divisions including a Semiconductor Division that sells semiconductors to both internal and external customers. The company's X-ray Division uses semiconductors as a component in its final product and is evaluating whether to purchase them from the Semiconductor Division or from an external supplier. The market price for semiconductors is $100 per 100 semiconductors. Dave Bryant is the controller of the X-ray Division, and Howard Hillman is the controller of the Semiconductor Division. The following conversation took place between Dave and Howard:

Dave: I hear you are having problems selling semiconductors out of your division. Maybe I can help.

Howard: You've got that right. We're producing and selling at about 90% of our capacity to outsiders. Last year we were selling 100% of capacity. Would it be possible for your division to pick up some of our excess capacity? After all, we are part of the same company.

Dave: What kind of price could you give me?

Howard: Well, you know as well as I that we are under strict profit responsibility in our divisions, so I would expect to get market price, $100 for 100 semiconductors.

Dave: I'm not so sure we can swing that. I was expecting a price break from a "sister" division.

Howard: Hey, I can only take this "sister" stuff so far. If I give you a price break, our profits will fall from last year's levels. I don't think I could explain that. I'm sorry, but I must remain firm—market price. After all, it's only fair—that's what you would have to pay from an external supplier.

Dave: Fair or not, I think we'll pass. Sorry we couldn't have helped.

Is Dave behaving ethically by trying to force the Semiconductor Division into a price break? Comment on Howard's reactions.

CP 24-2 Team Activity

In teams, visit the website of a company that uses the balanced scorecard to evaluate its performance. Identify the performance measures used by the company on its balanced scorecard. For each measure, identify whether the measure best fits the innovation, customer, internal process, or financial dimension of the balanced scorecard.

CP 24-3 Communication

The Norsk Division of Gridiron Concepts Inc. has been experiencing revenue and profit growth during the years 20Y6–20Y8. The divisional income statements follow:

Gridiron Concepts Inc.
Divisional Income Statements, Norsk Division
For the Years Ended December 31, 20Y6–20Y8

	20Y6	20Y7	20Y8
Sales	$1,470,000	$2,100,000	$2,450,000
Cost of goods sold	1,064,000	1,498,000	1,680,000
Gross profit	$ 406,000	$ 602,000	$ 770,000
Operating expenses	185,500	224,000	231,000
Income from operations	$ 220,500	$ 378,000	$ 539,000
Invested assets	$ 735,000	$1,500,000	$3,500,000

There are no service department charges, and the division operates as an investment center that must maintain a 15% return on invested assets.

Determine the profit margins, investment turnover, and return on investment for the Norse Division for 20Y6–20Y8. Based on your calculations, write a brief memo to the president of Gridiron Concepts Inc., Tom Yang, evaluating the division's performance.

CP 24-4 Service department charges

The Customer Service Department of Door Industries Inc. asked the Publications Department to prepare a brochure for its training program. The Publications Department delivered the brochures and charged the Customer Service Department a rate that was 25% higher than could be obtained from an outside printing company. The policy of the company required the Customer Service Department to use the internal publications group for brochures. The Publications Department claimed that it had a drop in demand for its services during the fiscal year, so it had to charge higher prices in order to recover its payroll and fixed costs.

(Continued)

CP 24-5 Evaluating divisional performance

The three divisions of Yummy Foods are Snack Goods, Cereal, and Frozen Foods. The divisions are structured as investment centers. The following responsibility reports were prepared for the three divisions for the prior year:

	Snack Goods	Cereal	Frozen Foods
Revenues	$2,200,000	$2,520,000	$2,100,000
Operating expenses	1,366,600	1,122,000	976,800
Income from operations before service department charges	$ 833,400	$1,398,000	$1,123,200
Service department charges:			
Promotion	$ 300,000	$ 600,000	$ 468,000
Legal	137,400	243,600	235,200
Total service department charges	$ 437,400	$ 843,600	$ 703,200
Income from operations	$ 396,000	$ 554,400	$ 420,000
Invested assets	$2,000,000	$1,680,000	$1,750,000

1. Which division is making the best use of invested assets and should be given priority for future capital investments?
2. Assuming that the minimum acceptable return on new projects is 19%, would all investments that produce a return in excess of 19% be accepted by the divisions? Explain.
3. Identify opportunities for improving the company's financial performance.

CP 24-6 Evaluating division performance

Last Resort Industries Inc. is a privately held diversified company with five separate divisions organized as investment centers. A condensed income statement for the Specialty Products Division for the past year, assuming no service department charges, is as follows:

Last Resort Industries Inc.—Specialty Products Division
Income Statement
For the Year Ended December 31, 20Y5

Sales	$32,400,000
Cost of goods sold	24,300,000
Gross profit	$ 8,100,000
Operating expenses	3,240,000
Income from operations	$ 4,860,000
Invested assets	$27,000,000

The manager of the Specialty Products Division was recently presented with the opportunity to add an additional product line, which would require invested assets of $14,400,000. A projected income statement for the new product line is as follows:

New Product Line
Projected Income Statement
For the Year Ended December 31, 20Y6

Sales	$12,960,000
Cost of goods sold	7,500,000
Gross profit	$ 5,460,000
Operating expenses	3,127,200
Income from operations	$ 2,332,800

The Specialty Products Division currently has $27,000,000 in invested assets, and Last Resort Industries Inc.'s overall return on investment, including all divisions, is 10%. Each division manager is evaluated on the basis of divisional return on investment. A bonus is paid, in $8,000 increments, for each whole percentage point that the division's return on investment exceeds the company average.

The president is concerned that the manager of the Specialty Products Division rejected the addition of the new product line, even though all estimates indicated that the product line would be profitable and would increase overall company income. You have been asked to analyze the possible reasons the Specialty Products Division manager rejected the new product line.

1. Determine the return on investment for the Specialty Products Division for the past year.

2. Determine the Specialty Products Division manager's bonus for the past year.

3. Determine the estimated return on investment for the new product line. Round whole percents to one decimal place and investment turnover to two decimal places.

4. ▸ Why might the manager of the Specialty Products Division decide to reject the new product line? Support your answer by determining the projected return on investment for 20Y6, assuming that the new product line was launched in the Specialty Products Division, and 20Y6 actual operating results were similar to those of 20Y5.

5. ▸ Suggest an alternative performance measure for motivating division managers to accept new investment opportunities that would increase the overall company income and return on investment.

CHAPTER 25: Differential Analysis, Product Pricing, and Activity-Based Costing

Concepts and Principles
Chapter 18 *Introduction to Managerial Accounting*

Developing Information

COST SYSTEMS
Chapter 19 *Job Order Costing*
Chapter 20 *Process Costing*

COST BEHAVIOR
Chapter 21 *Cost-Volume-Profit Analysis*

Decision Making

EVALUATING PERFORMANCE
Chapter 22 *Budgeting*
Chapter 23 *Variances from Standard Costs*

COMPARING ALTERNATIVES
Chapter 24 *Decentralized Operations*
Chapter 25 *Differential Analysis, Product Pricing, and Activity-Based Costing*
Chapter 26 *Capital Investment Analysis*

CHAPTER 25

Facebook

Managers must evaluate the costs and benefits of alternative actions. **Facebook**, the largest social networking site in the world, was cofounded by Mark Zuckerberg in 2004. Since then, it has grown to nearly 1 billion users and made Zuckerberg a multibillionaire.

Facebook has plans to grow to well over 1 billion users worldwide. Such growth involves decisions about where to expand. For example, expanding the site to new languages and countries involves software programming, marketing, and computer hardware costs. The benefits include adding new users to Facebook.

Analysis of the benefits and costs might lead Facebook to expand in some languages before others. For example, such an analysis might lead Facebook to expand in Swedish before it expands in Tok Pisin (the language of Papua New Guinea).

In this chapter, differential analysis, which reports the effects of decisions on total revenues and costs, is discussed. Practical approaches to setting product prices are also described and illustrated. Finally, how production bottlenecks and activity-based costing influence pricing and other decisions is also discussed.

Learning Objectives

After studying this chapter, you should be able to:

Example Exercises (EE) are shown in **green**.

Obj. 1 Prepare differential analysis reports for a variety of managerial decisions.

Differential Analysis
Lease or Sell — EE **25-1**
Discontinue a Segment or Product — EE **25-2**
Make or Buy — EE **25-3**
Replace Equipment — EE **25-4**
Process or Sell — EE **25-5**
Accept Business at a Special Price — EE **25-6**

Obj. 2 Determine the selling price of a product, using the product cost concept.

Setting Normal Product Selling Prices
Product Cost Concept — EE **25-7**
Target Costing

Obj. 3 Compute the relative profitability of products in bottleneck production processes.

Production Bottlenecks
Bottleneck profit — EE **25-8**

Obj. 4 Allocate product costs using activity-based costing.

Activity-Based Costing
Estimated Activity Costs
Activity Rates — EE **25-9**
Overhead Allocation — EE **25-9**
Dangers of Product Cost Distortion

At a Glance 25 ▶ Page 1246

Obj. 1 Prepare differential analysis reports for a variety of managerial decisions.

Link to Facebook
Facebook's purchase of **WhatsApp** in 2014 was estimated to yield differential income.

Differential Analysis

Managerial decision making involves choosing between alternative courses of action. **Differential analysis**, sometimes called *incremental analysis*, analyzes differential revenues and costs in order to determine the differential impact on income of two alternative courses of action.

Differential revenue is the amount of increase or decrease in revenue that is expected from a course of action compared to an alternative. **Differential cost** is the amount of increase or decrease in cost that is expected from a course of action as compared to an alternative. **Differential income (loss)** is the difference between the differential revenue and differential costs. Differential income indicates that a decision is expected to increase income, while a differential loss indicates that the decision is expected to decrease income.

To illustrate, assume Bryant Restaurants is deciding between using selected floor space for existing tables (Alternative 1) or replacing the tables with a salad bar (Alternative 2). Each alternative will produce revenues, costs, and income as shown below:

	Tables (Alternative 1)	Salad Bar (Alternative 2)
Revenues	$100,000	$120,000
Costs	60,000	65,000
Income (loss)	$ 40,000	$ 55,000

The differential analysis as of July 11 for Bryant Restaurants is shown in Exhibit 1. The differential analysis is prepared in three columns, where positive amounts indicate that the effect is to increase income and negative amounts indicate that the effect is to decrease income. The first column is the revenues, costs, and income for maintaining floor space for tables (Alternative 1). The second column is the revenues, costs, and income for using that floor space for a salad bar (Alternative 2).

Exhibit 1 compares the income from keeping the existing tables (Alternative 1 in column 1) to the income from a salad bar (Alternative 2 in column 2). The difference (column 3), is the differential income from selecting Alternative 2 over Alternative 1.

EXHIBIT 1

Differential Analysis—Bryant Restaurants

Differential Analysis
Tables (Alternative 1) or Salad Bar (Alternative 2)
July 11

	Tables (Alternative 1)	Salad Bar (Alternative 2)	Differential Effect on Income (Alternative 2)
Revenues	$100,000	$120,000	$20,000
Costs	–60,000	–65,000	–5,000
Income (loss)	$ 40,000	$ 55,000	$15,000

In Exhibit 1, the differential revenue of a salad bar over tables is $20,000 ($120,000 – $100,000). Because the increased revenue would increase income, it is entered as a positive $20,000 in the Differential Effect on Income column. The differential cost of a salad bar over tables is $5,000 ($65,000 – $60,000). Because the increased costs will decrease income, it is entered as a negative $5,000 in the Differential Effect on Income column.

The differential income (loss) of a salad bar over tables of $15,000 is determined by subtracting the differential costs from the differential revenues in the Differential Effect on Income column. Thus, installing a salad bar increases income by $15,000.

The preceding differential revenue, costs, and income can also be determined using the following formulas:

$$\text{Differential Revenue} = \text{Revenue (Alt. 2)} - \text{Revenue (Alt. 1)}$$
$$= \$120,000 - \$100,000 = \$20,000$$

$$\text{Differential Costs} = \text{Costs (Alt. 2)} - \text{Costs (Alt. 1)}$$
$$= -\$65,000 - (-\$60,000) = -\$5,000$$

$$\text{Differential Income (Loss)} = \text{Income (Alt. 2)} - \text{Income (Alt. 1)}$$
$$= \$55,000 - \$40,000 = \$15,000$$

Based upon the differential analysis report shown in Exhibit 1, Bryant Restaurants should replace some of its tables with a salad bar. Doing so will increase its income by $15,000. Over time, this decision should be reviewed based upon actual revenues and costs. If the actual revenues and costs differ significantly from those gathered in the analysis, another differential analysis may be needed to verify the decision.

In this chapter, differential analysis is illustrated for the following common decisions:

- Leasing or selling equipment
- Discontinuing an unprofitable segment
- Manufacturing or purchasing a needed part
- Replacing fixed assets
- Selling a product or processing further
- Accepting additional business at a special price

> **Link to Facebook**
>
> **Facebook** used differential analyses in deciding to own data centers in Iowa, North Carolina, Oregon, and Luleå, Sweden, but to lease (rent) data centers in California and Virginia.

Lease or Sell

Management may lease or sell a piece of equipment that is no longer needed. This may occur when a company changes its manufacturing process and can no longer use the equipment in the manufacturing process. In making a decision, differential analysis can be used.

To illustrate, assume that on June 22 of the current year, Marcus Company is considering leasing or disposing of the following equipment:

Cost of equipment	$200,000
Less accumulated depreciation	120,000
Book value	$ 80,000
Lease (Alternative 1):	
Total revenue for five-year lease	$160,000
Total estimated repair, insurance, and	
property tax expenses during life of lease	35,000
Residual value at end of fifth year of lease	0
Sell (Alternative 2):	
Sales price	$100,000
Commission on sales	6%

Exhibit 2 shows the differential analysis of whether to lease (Alternative 1) or sell (Alternative 2) the equipment.

EXHIBIT 2
Differential Analysis—Lease or Sell Equipment

Differential Analysis
Lease Equipment (Alternative 1) or Sell Equipment (Alternative 2)
June 22

	Lease Equipment (Alternative 1)	Sell Equipment (Alternative 2)	Differential Effect on Income (Alternative 2)
Revenues.............	$160,000	$100,000	–$60,000
Costs................	–35,000	–6,000*	29,000
Income (loss)..........	$125,000	$ 94,000	–$31,000

*$100,000 × 6%

If the equipment is sold, differential revenues will decrease by $60,000, differential costs will decrease by $29,000, and the differential effect on income is a decrease of $31,000. Thus, the decision should be to lease the equipment.

Exhibit 2 includes only the differential revenues and differential costs associated with the lease-or-sell decision. The $80,000 book value ($200,000 − $120,000) of the equipment is a *sunk* cost and is not considered in the differential analysis. **Sunk costs** are costs that have been incurred in the past, cannot be recouped, and are not relevant to future decisions. That is, the $80,000 is not affected regardless of which decision is made. For example, if the $80,000 were included in Exhibit 2, the costs for each alternative would both increase by $80,000, but the differential effect on income of −$31,000 would remain unchanged.

To simplify, the following factors were not considered in Exhibit 2:

- Differential revenue from investing funds
- Differential income tax

Differential revenue, such as interest revenue, could arise from investing the cash created by the two alternatives. Differential income tax could also arise from differences in income. These factors are discussed in Chapter 26.

Example Exercise 25-1 Lease or Sell *Obj. 1*

Casper Company owns office space with a cost of $100,000 and accumulated depreciation of $30,000 that can be sold for $150,000, less a 6% broker commission. Alternatively, the office space can be leased by Casper Company for 10 years for a total of $170,000, at the end of which there is no residual value. In addition, repair, insurance, and property tax that would be incurred by Casper Company on the rented office space would total $24,000 over the 10 years. Prepare a differential analysis on May 30 as to whether Casper Company should lease (Alternative 1) or sell (Alternative 2) the office space.

Follow My Example 25-1

Differential Analysis
Lease Office Space (Alternative 1) or Sell Office Space (Alternative 2)
May 30

	Lease Office Space (Alternative 1)	Sell Office Space (Alternative 2)	Differential Effect on Income (Alternative 2)
Revenues	$170,000	$150,000	–$20,000
Costs	–24,000	–9,000*	15,000
Income (loss)	$146,000	$141,000	–$ 5,000

*$150,000 × 6%

Casper Company should lease the office space.

Practice Exercises: PE 25-1A, PE 25-1B

Discontinue a Segment or Product

A product, department, branch, territory, or other segment of a business may be generating losses. As a result, management may consider discontinuing (eliminating) the product or segment. In such cases, it may be erroneously assumed that the total company income will increase by eliminating the operating loss.

Discontinuing the product or segment usually eliminates all of the product's or segment's variable costs. Such costs include direct materials, direct labor, variable factory overhead, and sales commissions. However, fixed costs such as depreciation, insurance, and property taxes may not be eliminated. Thus, it is possible for total company income to decrease rather than increase if the unprofitable product or segment is discontinued.

To illustrate, the income statement for Battle Creek Cereal Co. is shown in Exhibit 3. As shown in Exhibit 3, Bran Flakes incurred an operating loss of $11,000. Because Bran Flakes has incurred annual losses for several years, management is considering discontinuing it.

EXHIBIT 3
Income (Loss) by Product

Battle Creek Cereal Co.
Condensed Income Statement
For the Year Ended August 31, 20Y7

	Corn Flakes	Toasted Oats	Bran Flakes	Total Company
Sales	$500,000	$400,000	$100,000	$1,000,000
Cost of goods sold:				
Variable costs	$220,000	$200,000	$ 60,000	$ 480,000
Fixed costs	120,000	80,000	20,000	220,000
Total cost of goods sold	$340,000	$280,000	$ 80,000	$ 700,000
Gross profit	$160,000	$120,000	$ 20,000	$ 300,000
Operating expenses:				
Variable expenses	$ 95,000	$ 60,000	$ 25,000	$ 180,000
Fixed expenses	25,000	20,000	6,000	51,000
Total operating expenses	$120,000	$ 80,000	$ 31,000	$ 231,000
Income (loss) from operations	$ 40,000	$ 40,000	$ (11,000)	$ 69,000

However, the differential analysis dated September 29, 20Y7, in Exhibit 4 indicates that discontinuing Bran Flakes (Alternative 2) actually decreases operating income by $15,000, even though it incurs a net loss of $11,000. This is because discontinuing Bran Flakes has no effect on fixed costs and expenses.

Exhibit 4 only considers the short-term (one-year) effects of discontinuing Bran Flakes. When discontinuing a product or segment, long-term effects should also be considered. For example, employee morale and productivity might suffer if employees are laid off or relocated.

EXHIBIT 4
Differential Analysis—Continue or Discontinue Bran Flakes

Differential Analysis
Continue Bran Flakes (Alternative 1) or Discontinue Bran Flakes (Alternative 2)
September 29, 20Y7

	Continue Bran Flakes (Alternative 1)	Discontinue Bran Flakes (Alternative 2)	Differential Effect on Income (Alternative 2)
Revenues	$100,000	$ 0	–$100,000
Costs:			
Variable	–$ 85,000	$ 0	$ 85,000
Fixed	–26,000	–26,000	0
Total costs	–$111,000	–$26,000	$ 85,000
Income (loss)	–$ 11,000	–$26,000	–$ 15,000

Example Exercise 25-2   Discontinue a Segment   Obj. 1

Product K has revenue of $65,000, variable cost of goods sold of $50,000, variable selling expenses of $12,000, and fixed costs of $25,000, creating a loss from operations of $22,000. Prepare a differential analysis dated February 22 to determine whether Product K should be continued (Alternative 1) or discontinued (Alternative 2), assuming that fixed costs are unaffected by the decision.

Follow My Example 25-2

Differential Analysis
Continue K (Alternative 1) or Discontinue K (Alternative 2)
February 22

	Continue Product K (Alternative 1)	Discontinue Product K (Alternative 2)	Differential Effect on Income (Alternative 2)
Revenues	$65,000	$ 0	–$65,000
Costs:			
Variable	–$62,000*	$ 0	$62,000
Fixed	–25,000	–25,000	0
Total costs	–$87,000	–$25,000	$62,000
Income (loss)	–$22,000	–$25,000	–$ 3,000

*$50,000 + $12,000

Product K should be continued.

Practice Exercises: PE 25-2A, PE 25-2B

Make or Buy

Companies often manufacture products made up of components that are assembled into a final product. For example, an automobile manufacturer assembles tires, radios, motors, interior seats, transmissions, and other parts into a finished automobile. In such cases, the manufacturer must decide whether to make a part or purchase it from a supplier.

Differential analysis can be used to decide whether to make or buy a part. The analysis is similar whether management is considering making a part that is currently being purchased or purchasing a part that is currently being made.

To illustrate, assume that an automobile manufacturer has been purchasing instrument panels for $240 a unit. The factory is currently operating at 80% of capacity, and no major increase in production is expected in the near future. The cost per unit of manufacturing an instrument panel internally is estimated on February 15 as follows:

Direct materials	$ 80
Direct labor	80
Variable factory overhead	52
Fixed factory overhead	68
Total cost per unit	$280

If the make price of $280 is simply compared with the buy price of $240, the decision is to buy the instrument panel. However, if unused capacity could be used in manufacturing the part, only the variable factory overhead costs would increase.

The differential analysis for this make (Alternative 1) or buy (Alternative 2) decision is shown in Exhibit 5. The first line shows that no revenue is earned in this decision, since the component is not sold, but is used in production. The remaining lines show the cost per unit under each alternative. The fixed factory overhead cannot be eliminated by purchasing the panels. Thus, both alternatives include the fixed factory overhead. The differential analysis indicates that there is a loss of $28 per unit from buying the instrument panels. Thus, the instrument panels should be manufactured.

EXHIBIT 5

Differential Analysis—Make or Buy Instrument Panels

Differential Analysis
Make Panels (Alternative 1) or Buy Panels (Alternative 2)
February 15

	Make Panels (Alternative 1)	Buy Panels (Alternative 2)	Differential Effect on Income (Alternative 2)
Sales price	$ 0	$ 0	$ 0
Unit costs:			
Purchase price	$ 0	−$240	−$240
Direct materials	−80	0	80
Direct labor	−80	0	80
Variable factory overhead	−52	0	52
Fixed factory overhead	−68	−68	0
Income (loss)	−$280	−$308	−$ 28

Link to Facebook

Rather than develop its own virtual reality technology, **Facebook** purchased **Oculus VR, LLC**, a privately held company, in 2014.

Other factors should also be considered in the analysis. For example, productive capacity used to make the instrument panel would not be available for other production. The decision may also affect the future business relationship with the instrument panel supplier. For example, if the supplier provides other parts, the company's decision to make instrument panels might jeopardize the timely delivery of other parts.

Example Exercise 25-3 Make or Buy — Obj. 1

A company manufactures a subcomponent of an assembly for $80 per unit, including fixed costs of $25 per unit. A proposal is offered to purchase the subcomponent from an outside source for $60 per unit plus $5 per unit freight. Prepare a differential analysis dated November 2 to determine whether the company should make (Alternative 1) or buy (Alternative 2) the subcomponent, assuming that fixed costs are unaffected by the decision.

Follow My Example 25-3

Differential Analysis
Make Subcomponent (Alternative 1) or Buy Subcomponent (Alternative 2)
November 2

	Make Subcomponent (Alternative 1)	Buy Subcomponent (Alternative 2)	Differential Effect on Income (Alternative 2)
Sales price	$ 0	$ 0	$ 0
Unit costs:			
Purchase price	$ 0	−$60	−$60
Freight	0	−5	−5
Variable costs ($80 − $25)	−55	0	55
Fixed factory overhead	−25	−25	0
Income (loss)	−$80	−$90	−$10

The company should make the subcomponent.

Practice Exercises: PE 25-3A, PE 25-3B

Replace Equipment

The usefulness of a fixed asset may decrease before it is worn out. For example, old equipment may no longer be as efficient as new equipment.

Differential analysis can be used for decisions to replace fixed assets such as equipment and machinery. The analysis normally focuses on the costs of continuing to use the old equipment versus replacing the equipment. The book value of the old equipment is a sunk cost and, thus, is irrelevant.

To illustrate, assume that on November 28 of the current year, a business is considering replacing an old machine with a new machine:

Old Machine	
Book value	$100,000
Estimated annual variable manufacturing costs	225,000
Estimated selling price	25,000
Estimated remaining useful life	5 years
New Machine	
Purchase price of new machine	$250,000
Estimated annual variable manufacturing costs	150,000
Estimated residual value	0
Estimated useful life	5 years

The differential analysis for whether to continue with the old machine (Alternative 1) or replace the old machine with a new machine (Alternative 2) is shown in Exhibit 6.

EXHIBIT 6

Differential Analysis—Continue with or Replace Old Equipment

Differential Analysis
Continue with Old Machine (Alternative 1) or Replace Old Machine (Alternative 2)
November 28

	Continue with Old Machine (Alternative 1)	Replace Old Machine (Alternative 2)	Differential Effect on Income (Alternative 2)
Revenues:			
Proceeds from sale of old machine	$ 0	$ 25,000	$ 25,000
Costs:			
Purchase price	$ 0	–$ 250,000	–$250,000
Variable manufacturing costs (5 years)	–1,125,000*	–750,000**	375,000
Total costs	–$1,125,000	–$1,000,000	$125,000
Income (loss)	–$1,125,000	–$ 975,000	$150,000

*$225,000 × 5 years
**$150,000 × 5 years

As shown in Exhibit 6, there is five-year differential effect on income of $150,000 (or $30,000 per year) from replacing the machine. Thus, the decision should be to purchase the new machine and sell the old machine.

Other factors are often important in equipment replacement decisions. For example, differences between the remaining useful life of the old equipment and the estimated life of the new equipment could exist. In addition, the new equipment might improve the overall quality of the product and, thus, increase sales.

The time value of money and other uses for the cash needed to purchase the new equipment could also affect the decision to replace equipment.[1] The revenue that is forgone from an alternative use of an asset, such as cash, is called an **opportunity cost**. Although the opportunity cost is not recorded in the accounting records, it is useful in analyzing alternative courses of action.

Link to Facebook

Facebook used cash to purchase $1,812 million of property and equipment in 2014.

---

1 The time value of money in purchasing equipment (capital assets) is discussed in Chapter 26.

Example Exercise 25-4 Replace Equipment *Obj. 1*

A machine with a book value of $32,000 has an estimated four-year life. A proposal is offered to sell the old machine for $10,000 and replace it with a new machine at a cost of $45,000. The new machine has a four-year life with no residual value. The new machine would reduce annual direct labor costs from $33,000 to $22,000. Prepare a differential analysis dated October 7 on whether to continue with the old machine (Alternative 1) or replace the old machine (Alternative 2).

Follow My Example 25-4

Differential Analysis
Continue with Old Machine (Alternative 1) or Replace Old Machine (Alternative 2)
October 7

	Continue with Old Machine (Alternative 1)	Replace Old Machine (Alternative 2)	Differential Effect on Income (Alternative 2)
Revenues:			
Proceeds from sale of old machine	$ 0	$ 10,000	$10,000
Costs:			
Purchase price	$ 0	–$ 45,000	–$45,000
Direct labor (4 years)	–132,000*	–88,000**	44,000
Total costs	–$132,000	–$133,000	–$ 1,000
Total income (loss)	–$132,000	–$123,000	$ 9,000

*$33,000 × 4 years
**$22,000 × 4 years

The old machine should be sold and replaced with the new machine.

Practice Exercises: PE 25-4A, PE 25-4B

Process or Sell

During manufacturing, a product normally progresses through various stages or processes. In some cases, a product can be sold at an intermediate stage of production, or it can be processed further and then sold.

Differential analysis can be used to decide whether to sell a product at an intermediate stage or to process it further. In doing so, the differential revenues and costs from further processing are compared. The costs of producing the intermediate product do not change, regardless of whether the intermediate product is sold or processed further.

To illustrate, assume that a business produces kerosene as an intermediate product as follows:

Kerosene:	
Batch size	4,000 gallons
Cost of producing kerosene	$2,400 per batch
Selling price	$2.50 per gallon

The kerosene can be processed further to yield gasoline. When processing kerosene into gasoline, the process will incur additional costs and some evaporation, shown as follows:

Gasoline:	
Input batch size	4,000 gallons
Less evaporation (20%)	800 (4,000 × 20%)
Output batch size	3,200 gallons
Cost of producing gasoline	$3,050 per batch
Selling price	$3.50 per gallon

Exhibit 7 shows the differential analysis dated October 1 for whether to sell kerosene (Alternative 1) or process it further into gasoline (Alternative 2).

As shown in Exhibit 7, there is additional income of $550 per batch from further processing the kerosene into gasoline. Therefore, the decision should be to process the kerosene further into gasoline.

EXHIBIT 7
Differential Analysis—Sell Kerosene or Process Further into Gasoline

Differential Analysis
Sell Kerosene (Alternative 1) or Process Further into Gasoline (Alternative 2)
October 1

	Sell Kerosene (Alternative 1)	Process Further into Gasoline (Alternative 2)	Differential Effect on Income (Alternative 2)
Revenues	$10,000*	$11,200**	$1,200
Costs	−2,400	−3,050	−650
Income (loss)	$ 7,600	$ 8,150	$ 550

*4,000 gallons × $2.50
**(4,000 gallons − 800 gallons) × $3.50

Example Exercise 25-5 Process or Sell *Obj. 1*

Product T is produced for $2.50 per gallon. Product T can be sold without additional processing for $3.50 per gallon or processed further into Product V at an additional total cost of $0.70 per gallon. Product V can be sold for $4.00 per gallon. Prepare a differential analysis dated April 8 on whether to sell Product T (Alternative 1) or process it further into Product V (Alternative 2).

Follow My Example 25-5

Differential Analysis
Sell Product T (Alternative 1) or Process Further into Product V (Alternative 2)
April 8

	Sell Product T (Alternative 1)	Process Further into Product V (Alternative 2)	Differential Effect on Income (Alternative 2)
Revenues, per unit	$3.50	$4.00	$0.50
Costs, per unit	−2.50	−3.20*	−0.70
Income (loss), per unit	$1.00	$0.80	−$0.20

*$2.50 + $0.70

This analysis is conducted on a per-unit basis, as opposed to a per-batch basis as illustrated in the text. Without evaporation, the per-unit approach is acceptable; thus the decision should be to sell Product T.

Practice Exercises: PE 25-5A, PE 25-5B

Accept Business at a Special Price

A company may be offered the opportunity to sell its products at prices other than normal prices. For example, an exporter may offer to sell a company's products overseas at special discount prices.

Differential analysis can be used to decide whether to accept additional business at a special price. The differential revenue from accepting the additional business is compared to the differential costs of producing and delivering the product to the customer.

The differential costs of accepting additional business depend on whether the company is operating at less than capacity. If the company is operating at less than full capacity, then the additional production does not increase fixed manufacturing costs. However, selling and administrative expenses may change because of the additional business.

To illustrate, assume that B-Ball Inc. manufactures basketballs as follows:

Monthly productive capacity	12,500 basketballs
Current monthly sales	10,000 basketballs
Normal (domestic) selling price	$30.00 per basketball
Manufacturing costs:	
Variable costs	$12.50 per basketball
Fixed costs	7.50
Total	$20.00 per basketball

On March 10 of the current year, B-Ball Inc. received an offer from an exporter for 5,000 basketballs at $18 each. Production can be spread over three months without interfering with normal production or incurring overtime costs. Pricing policies in the domestic market will not be affected.

As shown in Exhibit 8, a differential analysis on whether to reject the order (Alternative 1) or accept the order (Alternative 2) shows that the special order should be accepted. The special business is accepted even though the sales price of $18 per unit is less than the manufacturing cost of $20 per unit because the fixed costs are not affected by the decision and are, thus, omitted from the analysis.

EXHIBIT 8

Differential Analysis—Accept Business at a Special Price

Differential Analysis
Reject Order (Alternative 1) or Accept Order (Alternative 2)
March 10

	Reject Order (Alternative 1)	Accept Order (Alternative 2)	Differential Effect on Income (Alternative 2)
Revenues	$0	$90,000*	$90,000
Costs:			
Variable manufacturing costs	0	–62,500**	–62,500
Income (loss)	$0	$27,500	$27,500

*5,000 units × $18
**5,000 units × $12.50 variable cost per unit

Proposals to sell products at special prices often require additional considerations. For example, special prices in one geographic area may result in price reductions in other areas, with the result that total company sales revenues decrease. Manufacturers must also conform to the Robinson-Patman Act, which prohibits price discrimination within the United States unless price differences can be justified by different costs.

Business Connection

60% OFF!

Priceline.com Inc. was founded in the late 1990s and has become a successful online retailer. Priceline offers deep discounts of up to 60% for travel services, such as hotels and travel. How does it work? For hotel services, Priceline has arrangements with hotels to provide deeply discounted rooms. These rooms are resold to customers on Priceline's website. Why do hotels provide rooms at such a large discount? If the hotel has unused rooms, the variable cost of an incremental guest is low relative to the fixed cost of the room. Thus, during low occupancy times, any price greater than the variable cost of providing the room can add to the profitability of the hotel. Thus, hotels view Priceline as an additional source of profit from filling unused rooms during low demand periods.

Example Exercise 25-6 Accept Business at Special Price — Obj. 1

Product D is normally sold for $4.40 per unit. A special price of $3.60 is offered for the export market. The variable production cost is $3.00 per unit. An additional export tariff of 10% of revenue must be paid for all export products. Assume that there is sufficient capacity for the special order. Prepare a differential analysis dated January 14 on whether to reject (Alternative 1) or accept (Alternative 2) the special order.

Follow My Example 25-6

Differential Analysis
Reject Order (Alternative 1) or Accept Order (Alternative 2)
January 14

	Reject Order (Alternative 1)	Accept Order (Alternative 2)	Differential Effect on Income (Alternative 2)
Per unit:			
Revenues	$0	$3.60	$3.60
Costs:			
Variable manufacturing costs	$0	−$3.00	−$3.00
Export tariff	0	−0.36*	−0.36
Total costs	$0	−$3.36	−$3.36
Income (loss)	$0	$0.24	$0.24

*$3.60 × 10%

The special order should be accepted.

Practice Exercises: PE 25-6A, PE 25-6B

Setting Normal Product Selling Prices

Obj. 2 Determine the selling price of a product, using the product cost concept.

The *normal* selling price is the target selling price to be achieved in the long term. The normal selling price must be set high enough to cover all costs and expenses (fixed and variable) and provide a reasonable profit. Otherwise, the business will not survive.

In contrast, in deciding whether to accept additional business at a special price, only differential costs are considered. Any price greater than the differential costs will increase profits in the short term. However, in the long term, products are sold at normal prices rather than special prices.

Managers can use one of two market methods to determine selling price:

- Demand-based concept
- Competition-based concept

The demand-based concept sets the price according to the demand for the product. If there is high demand for the product, then the price is set high. Likewise, if there is a low demand for the product, then the price is set low.

The competition-based concept sets the price according to the price offered by competitors. For example, if a competitor reduces the price, then management adjusts the price to meet the competition. The market-based pricing approaches are discussed in greater detail in marketing courses.

Managers can also use one of three cost-plus methods to determine the selling price:

- Product cost concept
- Total cost concept
- Variable cost concept

The product cost concept is illustrated in this section. The total cost and variable cost concepts are illustrated in the appendix to this chapter.

Link to Facebook

Facebook's prices are affected by its competitors, such as **Google**.

SERVICE FOCUS

REVENUE MANAGEMENT

Did you know that it is common to sit next to a person on a flight who paid much more for that seat than you did for yours (or vice versa)? While this may not seem fair, this practice is consistent with a type of differential analysis called revenue management. Revenue management strives to yield the maximum amount of profit from a perishable good. Examples of perishable goods in service include a seat on a flight, a hotel room for a given night, a ticket for a given event, or a cruise ship berth for a given voyage. The service is perishable because once the date passes, the "product" expires.

Consider **Delta Air Lines**. Delta maximizes the profitability on a given flight by taking into account different customer behaviors and preferences. For example, a businessperson may pay a very high price for an airline ticket booked one day in advance to attend an emergency meeting. Next to her may be a college student on the same flight who booked two months in advance at a very low price. The difference in behavior yields a different price. The airline sells early bookings at very favorable prices to fill out the flight. However, late emergency business bookings are priced high because the inventory of seats has diminished and, thus, seats have become valuable. However, if too many seats remain unoccupied very close to the flight time, the airline may release them at deep discounts to standby passengers to fill the flight. Thus, the flight is filled with different priced seats for different customers, all in attempt to fill the flight as profitably as possible.

Product Cost Concept

Cost-plus methods determine the normal selling price by estimating a cost amount per unit and adding a markup, computed as follows:

Normal Selling Price = Cost Amount per Unit + Markup

Management determines the markup based on the desired profit for the product. The markup should be sufficient to earn the desired profit and cover any costs and expenses that are not included in the cost amount.

As shown in Exhibit 9, under the **product cost concept**, only the costs of manufacturing the product, termed the *product costs,* are included in the cost amount per unit to which the markup is added. Estimated selling expenses, administrative expenses, and desired profit are included in the markup. The markup per unit is then computed and added to the product cost per unit to determine the normal selling price.

EXHIBIT 9

Product Cost Concept

The product cost concept is applied using the following steps:

Step 1. Estimate the total product costs as follows:

> Product costs:
> Direct materials $XXX
> Direct labor XXX
> Factory overhead XXX
> Total product cost $XXX

Step 2. Estimate the total selling and administrative expenses.

Step 3. Divide the total product cost by the number of units expected to be produced and sold to determine the total product cost per unit, computed as follows:

$$\text{Product Cost per Unit} = \frac{\text{Total Product Cost}}{\text{Estimated Units Produced and Sold}}$$

Step 4. Compute the markup percentage as follows:

$$\text{Markup Percentage} = \frac{\text{Desired Profit} + \text{Total Selling and Administrative Expenses}}{\text{Total Product Cost}}$$

The numerator of the markup percentage is the desired profit plus the total selling and administrative expenses. These expenses must be included in the markup percentage because they are not included in the cost amount to which the markup is added.

The desired profit is normally computed based on a rate of return on assets as follows:

$$\text{Desired Profit} = \text{Desired Rate of Return} \times \text{Total Assets}$$

Step 5. Determine the markup per unit by multiplying the markup percentage times the product cost per unit as follows:

$$\text{Markup per Unit} = \text{Markup Percentage} \times \text{Product Cost per Unit}$$

Step 6. Determine the normal selling price by adding the markup per unit to the product cost per unit as follows:

> Product cost per unit $XXX
> Markup per unit XXX
> Normal selling price per unit $XXX

To illustrate, assume the following data for 100,000 calculators that Digital Solutions Inc. expects to produce and sell during the current year:

Manufacturing costs:	
Direct materials ($3.00 × 100,000)	$ 300,000
Direct labor ($10.00 × 100,000)	1,000,000
Factory overhead	200,000
Total manufacturing costs	$1,500,000
Selling and administrative expenses	170,000
Total cost	$1,670,000
Total assets	$ 800,000
Desired rate of return	20%

The normal selling price of $18.30 is determined under the product cost concept as follows:

Step 1. Total product cost: $1,500,000
Step 2. Total selling and administrative expenses: $170,000
Step 3. Total product cost per unit: $15.00

$$\text{Total Cost per Unit} = \frac{\text{Total Product Cost}}{\text{Estimated Units Produced and Sold}} = \frac{\$1,500,000}{100,000 \text{ units}} = \$15.00 \text{ per unit}$$

Step 4. Markup percentage: 22%

Desired Profit = Desired Rate of Return × Total Assets = 20% × $800,000 = $160,000

$$\text{Markup Percentage} = \frac{\text{Desired Profit} + \text{Total Selling and Administrative Expenses}}{\text{Total Product Cost}}$$

$$= \frac{\$160,000 + \$170,000}{\$1,500,000} = \frac{\$330,000}{\$1,500,000} = 22\%$$

Step 5. Markup per unit: $3.30

Markup per Unit = Markup Percentage × Product Cost per Unit
= 22% × $15.00 = $3.30 per unit

Step 6. Normal selling price: $18.30

Total product cost per unit	$15.00
Markup per unit	3.30
Normal selling price per unit	$18.30

Product cost estimates, rather than actual costs, may be used in computing the markup. Management should be careful, however, when using estimated or standard costs in applying the cost-plus approach. Specifically, estimates should be based on normal (attainable) operating levels and not theoretical (ideal) levels of performance. In product pricing, the use of estimates based on ideal operating performance could lead to setting product prices too low.

Example Exercise 25-7 Product Cost Markup Percentage — Obj. 2

Apex Corporation produces and sells Product Z at a total cost of $30 per unit, of which $20 is product cost and $10 is selling and administrative expenses. In addition, the total cost of $30 is made up of $18 variable cost and $12 fixed cost. The desired profit is $3 per unit. Determine the markup percentage on product cost.

Follow My Example 25-7

Markup percentage on product cost: $\dfrac{\$3 + \$10}{\$20} = 65\%$

Practice Exercises: PE 25-7A, PE 25-7B

INTEGRITY, OBJECTIVITY, AND ETHICS IN BUSINESS

PRICE FIXING

Federal law prevents companies competing in similar markets from sharing cost and price information, or what is commonly termed "price fixing." For example, the Federal Trade Commission (FTC) brought a suit against U-Haul for releasing company-wide memorandums to its managers telling them to encourage competitors to match U-Haul price increases. Commenting on the case, the chairman of the FTC stated, "It's a bedrock principle that you can't conspire with your competitors to fix prices, and shouldn't even try."

Source: Edward Wyatt, "U-Haul to Settle with Trade Agency in Case on Truck Rental Price-Fixing," *New York Times*, June 10, 2010, p. B3.

Target Costing

Target costing is a method of setting prices that combines market-based pricing with a cost-reduction emphasis. Under target costing, a future selling price is anticipated, using the demand or competition-based concepts. The target cost is then determined by subtracting a desired profit from the expected selling price, computed as follows:

$$\text{Target Cost} = \text{Expected Selling Price} - \text{Desired Profit}$$

Target costing tries to reduce costs as shown in Exhibit 10. The bar at the left in Exhibit 10 shows the actual cost and profit that can be earned during the current period. The bar at the right shows that the market price is expected to decline in the future. The target cost is estimated as the difference between the expected market price and the desired profit.

The target cost is normally less than the current cost. Thus, managers must try to reduce costs from the design and manufacture of the product. The planned cost reduction is sometimes referred to as the cost drift. Costs can be reduced in a variety of ways such as the following:

- Simplifying the design
- Reducing the cost of direct materials
- Reducing the direct labor costs
- Eliminating waste

Target costing is especially useful in highly competitive markets such as the market for personal computers. Such markets require continual product cost reductions to remain competitive.

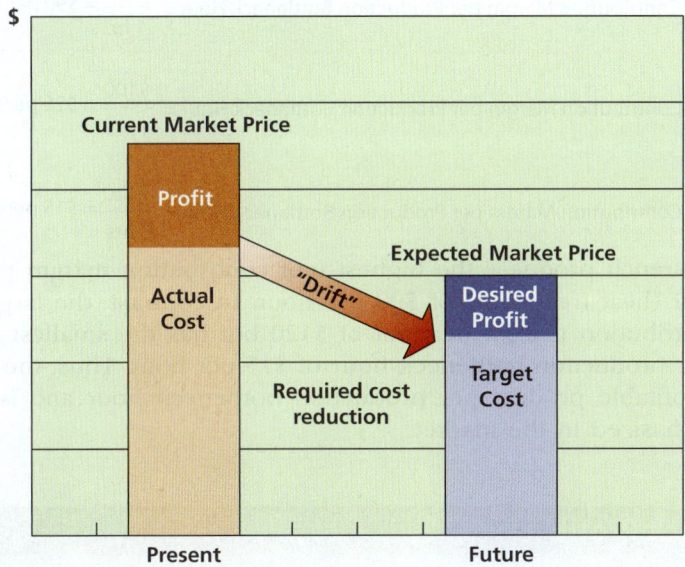

EXHIBIT 10

Target Cost Concept

Production Bottlenecks

Obj. 3 Compute the relative profitability of products in bottleneck production processes.

A **production bottleneck** (or *constraint*) is a point in the manufacturing process where the demand for the company's product exceeds the ability to produce the product. The **theory of constraints (TOC)** is a manufacturing strategy that focuses on reducing the influence of bottlenecks on production processes.

When a company has a production bottleneck in its production process, it should attempt to maximize its profits, subject to the production bottleneck. In doing so, the unit contribution margin of each product per production bottleneck constraint is used.

To illustrate, assume that PrideCraft Tool Company makes three types of wrenches: small, medium, and large. All three products are processed through a heat treatment operation, which hardens the steel tools. PrideCraft Tool's heat treatment process is operating at full capacity and is a production bottleneck. The product unit contribution margin and the number of hours of heat treatment used by each type of wrench are as follows:

	Small Wrench	Medium Wrench	Large Wrench
Unit selling price	$130	$140	$160
Unit variable cost	40	40	40
Unit contribution margin	$ 90	$100	$120
Heat treatment hours per unit	1 hr.	4 hrs.	8 hrs.

The large wrench appears to be the most profitable product because its unit contribution margin of $120 is the greatest. However, the unit contribution margin can be misleading in a production bottleneck operation.

In a production bottleneck operation, the best measure of profitability is the unit contribution margin per production bottleneck constraint. For PrideCraft Tool, the production bottleneck constraint is heat treatment process hours. Therefore, the unit contribution margin per bottleneck constraint is expressed as follows:

$$\text{Unit Contribution Margin per Production Bottleneck Hour} = \frac{\text{Unit Contribution Margin}}{\text{Heat Treatment Hours per Unit}}$$

The unit contribution per production bottleneck hour for each of the wrenches produced by PrideCraft Tool is computed as follows:

Small Wrenches

$$\text{Unit Contribution Margin per Production Bottleneck Hour} = \frac{\$90}{1 \text{ hr.}} = \$90 \text{ per hr.}$$

Medium Wrenches

$$\text{Unit Contribution Margin per Production Bottleneck Hour} = \frac{\$100}{4 \text{ hrs.}} = \$25 \text{ per hr.}$$

Large Wrenches

$$\text{Unit Contribution Margin per Production Bottleneck Hour} = \frac{\$120}{8 \text{ hrs.}} = \$15 \text{ per hr.}$$

The small wrench produces the highest unit contribution margin per production bottleneck hour (heat treatment) of $90 per hour. In contrast, the large wrench has the largest contribution margin per unit of $120 but has the smallest unit contribution margin per production bottleneck hour of $15 per hour. Thus, the small wrench is the most profitable product per production bottleneck hour and is the one that should be emphasized in the market.

Example Exercise 25-8 Bottleneck Profit Obj. 3

Product A has a unit contribution margin of $15. Product B has a unit contribution margin of $20. Product A requires three furnace hours, while Product B requires five furnace hours. Determine the most profitable product, assuming that the furnace is a production bottleneck.

Follow My Example 25-8

	Product A	Product B
Unit contribution margin	$15	$20
Furnace hours per unit	÷ 3	÷ 5
Unit contribution margin per production bottleneck hour	$ 5	$ 4

Product A is the most profitable in using bottleneck resources.

Practice Exercises: PE 25-8A, PE 25-8B

Activity-Based Costing

Obj. 4 Allocate product costs using activity-based costing.

Normal product prices can be computed from a markup on product cost, as illustrated earlier in this chapter. Product cost is the sum of direct material, direct labor, and factory overhead. In Chapter 19, factory overhead was allocated to products (jobs) using a predetermined factory overhead rate. This rate was computed as follows:

$$\text{Predetermined Factory Overhead Rate} = \frac{\text{Estimated Total Factory Overhead Costs}}{\text{Estimated Activity Base}}$$

> **Link to Facebook**
>
> One of **Facebook**'s significant activities is research and development, with a cost of $4.8 billion in a recent year.

The use of a single, predetermined factory overhead rate may, however, allocate factory overhead inaccurately. In such cases, normal product prices based on product cost markup may also be inaccurate. This may occur in manufacturing operations involving more than one product. In such cases, each product may use different types of factory overhead in different ways. Under such conditions, a single factory overhead rate will distort factory overhead allocation.

Activity-based costing (ABC) identifies and traces costs and expenses to activities and then to specific products. The ABC method is an alternative approach for allocating factory overhead when there are diverse products and processes. ABC uses multiple factory overhead rates based on activities. **Activities** are the types of work, or actions, involved in a manufacturing process or service activity. For example, assembly, inspection, and engineering design are activities.

Estimated Activity Costs

ABC initially assigns estimated factory overhead costs to activities, resulting in estimated activity costs. To illustrate, assume that Ruiz Company produces snowmobiles and riding mowers. The overhead activities used in producing each product are as follows:

- *Fabrication*, which consists of cutting metal to shape the product. This activity is machine-intensive.
- *Assembly*, which consists of manually assembling machined pieces into a final product. This activity is labor-intensive.
- *Setup*, which consists of changing the characteristics of a machine to produce a different product. Each production run requires a **setup**.
- *Quality-control inspections*, which consist of inspecting the product for conformance to specifications. Inspection requires product teardown and reassembly.
- *Engineering changes*, which consist of processing changes in design or process specifications for a product. The document that initiates changing a product or process is called an **engineering change order (ECO)**.

Ruiz Company's total estimated factory overhead of $1,600,000 is assigned to each activity as shown in Exhibit 11.

Activity	Estimated Activity Cost
Fabrication	$ 530,000
Assembly	70,000
Setup	480,000
Quality-control inspection	312,000
Engineering changes	208,000
Total estimated activity costs	$1,600,000

EXHIBIT 11

Estimated Activity Costs

Activity Rates

The estimated activity costs are allocated to products using an **activity rate**. Activity rates are determined as follows:

$$\text{Activity Rate} = \frac{\text{Estimated Activity Cost}}{\text{Estimated Activity-Base Usage}}$$

The **activity base** is a measure of physical activity for each activity. For example, the activity base for the setup activity is the number of setups. The activity-base *usage* is the number of setups estimated to be used by the operations.

As shown in Exhibit 11, the estimated activity cost for setups is $480,000. Assume that the activity-base usage for the setup activity is estimated to be 120 setups. The setup activity rate is $4,000 per setup, computed as follows:

$$\text{Setup Activity Rate} = \frac{\$480,000}{120 \text{ setups}} = \$4,000 \text{ per setup}$$

The estimated activity-base usage for each activity is shown in Exhibit 12.

EXHIBIT 12
Ruiz Company Activity-Base Usage

Activity Base	Estimated Activity-Base Usage by Product — Snowmobile	Estimated Activity-Base Usage by Product — Riding Mower	Total Estimated Activity-Base Usage
Number of fabrication direct labor hours	8,000 dlh	2,000 dlh	10,000 dlh
Number of assembly direct labor hours	2,000 dlh	8,000 dlh	10,000 dlh
Number of setups	100 setups	20 setups	120 setups
Number of quality-control inspections	100 insp.	4 insp.	104 insp.
Number of engineering change orders	12 ECOs	4 ECOs	16 ECOs

The activity rates for each activity are determined by dividing the estimated activity cost in Exhibit 11 by the total estimated activity-base usage for each activity in Exhibit 12. The activity rates for Ruiz Company are computed in Exhibit 13.

EXHIBIT 13
Activity Rates—Ruiz Company

Activity	Estimated Activity Cost	÷	Estimated Activity-Base Usage	=	Activity Rate
Fabrication	$530,000	÷	10,000 direct labor hours	=	$53 per direct labor hour
Assembly	$ 70,000	÷	10,000 direct labor hours	=	$7 per direct labor hour
Setup	$480,000	÷	120 setups	=	$4,000 per setup
Quality-control inspection	$312,000	÷	104 inspections	=	$3,000 per inspection
Engineering changes	$208,000	÷	16 engineering changes	=	$13,000 per engineering change order

Overhead Allocation

The estimated activity costs are allocated to the snowmobiles and riding mowers by using the following equation for each product:

$$\text{Activity-Base Usage} \times \text{Activity Rate} = \text{Activity Cost}$$

The sum of these activity costs for each product is the total factory overhead cost for the product. This amount is divided by the total number of units produced to determine the factory overhead cost per unit. These computations are shown in Exhibit 14 for Ruiz Company.

Activity-Based Product Cost Calculations — EXHIBIT 14

	A	B	C	D	E	F	G	H	I	J	K	L
1				Snowmobile						Riding Mower		
2		Activity-		Activity		Activity		Activity-		Activity		Activity
3	Activity	Base Usage	×	Rate	=	Cost		Base Usage	×	Rate	=	Cost
4												
5	Fabrication	8,000 dlh		$53/dlh		$ 424,000		2,000 dlh		$53/dlh		$106,000
6	Assembly	2,000 dlh		$7/dlh		14,000		8,000 dlh		$7/dlh		56,000
7	Setup	100 setups		$4,000/setup		400,000		20 setups		$4,000/setup		80,000
8	Quality-control											
9	inspections	100 insp.		$3,000/insp.		300,000		4 insp.		$3,000/insp.		12,000
10	Engineering											
11	changes	12 ECOs		$13,000/ECO		156,000		4 ECOs		$13,000/ECO		52,000
12	Total factory											
13	overhead cost					$1,294,000						$306,000
14	Budgeted units											
15	of production				÷	1,000					÷	1,000
16	Factory overhead											
17	cost per unit					$ 1,294						$ 306
18												

The allocation of factory overhead using the ABC method for Ruiz Company is illustrated in Exhibit 15.

Activity-Based Costing Method—Ruiz Company — EXHIBIT 15

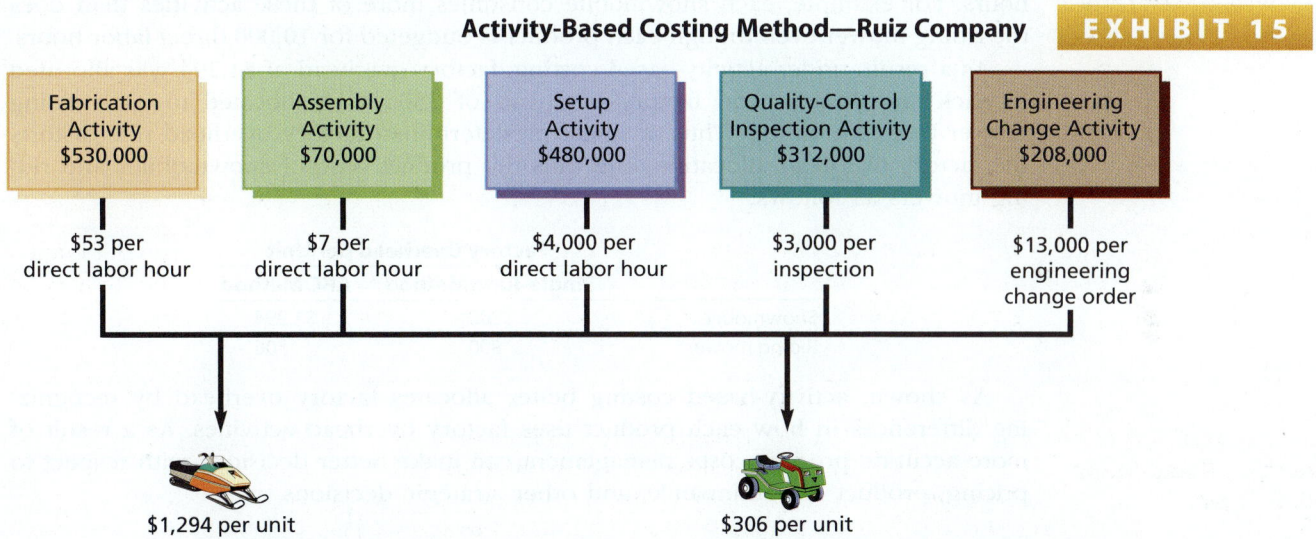

Dangers of Product Cost Distortion

The allocation of factory overhead affects the accuracy of product costs. In turn, product costs are used for decisions such as establishing product price and determining whether to discontinue a product line.

Using an inappropriate factory overhead allocation method can lead to distorted product costs. To illustrate, assume that Ruiz Company used a single predetermined factory overhead rate to allocate factory overhead to the riding mower and snowmobile. Assume that total estimated factory overhead was allocated using direct labor hours. The single predetermined factory overhead rate for Ruiz is computed as follows:

$$\text{Predetermined Factory Overhead Rate} = \frac{\text{Estimated Total Factory Overhead Costs}}{\text{Estimated Activity Base}}$$

$$= \frac{\$1,600,000}{20,000 \text{ direct labor hours}}$$

$$= \$80 \text{ per direct labor hour}$$

Using this rate, riding mowers and snowmobiles are each allocated $800,000 of factory overhead ($80 per direct labor hour × 10,000 direct labor hours), or $800 per unit ($800,000 ÷ 1,000 units). Under the single predetermined factory overhead rate method, each product is allocated the same factory overhead. This is because riding mowers and snowmobiles consume the same amount of direct labor hours.

However, the snowmobiles and riding mowers do not consume setup, quality-control inspection, and engineering change activities in proportion to direct labor hours. For example, each snowmobile consumes more of these activities than does the riding mower even though each product is budgeted for 10,000 direct labor hours.

As a result, under activity-based costing, factory overhead of $1,294 was allocated to each snowmobile and factory overhead of $306 was allocated to each riding mower (see Exhibit 14). Thus, a single predetermined factory overhead rate distorts the factory overhead allocation, and thus the product cost, of snowmobiles and riding mowers as follows:

	Factory Overhead per Unit	
	Single-Rate Method	ABC Method
Snowmobile	$800	$1,294
Riding mower	800	306

As shown, activity-based costing better allocates factory overhead by recognizing differences in how each product uses factory overhead activities. As a result of more accurate product costs, management can make better decisions with respect to pricing, product discontinuance, and other strategic decisions.

Example Exercise 25-9 Activity-Based Costing — Obj. 4

Thor Company has total estimated factory overhead for the year of $600,000, divided into four activities: fabrication, $300,000; assembly, $120,000; setup, $100,000; and materials handling, $80,000. Thor manufactures two products: snowboards and skis. The activity-base usage quantities for each product by each activity are as follows:

	Fabrication	Assembly	Setup	Materials Handling
Snowboards	5,000 dlh	15,000 dlh	30 setups	50 moves
Skis	15,000	5,000	220	350
	20,000 dlh	20,000 dlh	250 setups	400 moves

Each product is budgeted for 5,000 units of production for the year. Determine (a) the activity rates for each activity and (b) the factory overhead cost per unit for each product, using activity-based costing.

Follow My Example 25-9

a. Fabrication: $300,000 ÷ 20,000 direct labor hours = $15 per dlh
   Assembly: $120,000 ÷ 20,000 direct labor hours = $6 per dlh
   Setup: $100,000 ÷ 250 setups = $400 per setup
   Materials handling: $80,000 ÷ 400 moves = $200 per move

b.

Activity	Snowboards Activity-Base Usage	×	Activity Rate	=	Activity Cost	Skis Activity-Base Usage	×	Activity Rate	=	Activity Cost
Fabrication	5,000 dlh		$15/dlh		$ 75,000	15,000 dlh		$15/dlh		$225,000
Assembly	15,000 dlh		$6/dlh		90,000	5,000 dlh		$6/dlh		30,000
Setup	30 setups		$400/setup		12,000	220 setups		$400/setup		88,000
Materials handling	50 moves		$200/move		10,000	350 moves		$200/move		70,000
Total					$187,000					$413,000
Budgeted units					÷ 5,000					÷ 5,000
Factory overhead per unit					$ 37.40					$ 82.60

Practice Exercises: PE 25-9A, PE 25-9B

APPENDIX

Total and Variable Cost Concepts to Setting Normal Price

Recall from the chapter that cost-plus methods determine the normal selling price by estimating a cost amount per unit and adding a markup, as follows:

Normal Selling Price = Cost Amount per Unit + Markup

Management determines the markup based on the desired profit for the product. The markup should be sufficient to earn the desired profit and cover any cost and expenses that are not included in the cost amount. The product cost concept was discussed in the chapter, and the total and variable cost concepts are discussed in this appendix.

Total Cost Concept

As shown in Exhibit 16, under the **total cost concept**, manufacturing cost plus the selling and administrative expenses are included in the total cost per unit. The markup per unit is then computed and added to the total cost per unit to determine the normal selling price.

The total cost concept is applied using the following steps:

Step 1. Estimate the total manufacturing cost as follows:

Manufacturing costs:	
Direct materials	$XXX
Direct labor	XXX
Factory overhead	XXX
Total manufacturing cost	$XXX

> **EXHIBIT 16**
> Total Cost Concept

Step 2. Estimate the total selling and administrative expenses.

Step 3. Estimate the total cost as follows:

Total manufacturing costs	$XXX
Selling and administrative expenses	XXX
Total cost	$XXX

Step 4. Divide the total cost by the number of units expected to be produced and sold to determine the total cost per unit, as follows:

$$\text{Total Cost per Unit} = \frac{\text{Total Cost}}{\text{Estimated Units Produced and Sold}}$$

Step 5. Compute the markup percentage as follows:

$$\text{Markup Percentage} = \frac{\text{Desired Profit}}{\text{Total Cost}}$$

The desired profit is normally computed based on a rate of return on assets as follows:

$$\text{Desired Profit} = \text{Desired Rate of Return} \times \text{Total Assets}$$

Step 6. Determine the markup per unit by multiplying the markup percentage times the total cost per unit as follows:

$$\text{Markup per Unit} = \text{Markup Percentage} \times \text{Total Cost per Unit}$$

Step 7. Determine the normal selling price by adding the markup per unit to the total cost per unit as follows:

Total cost per unit	$XXX
Markup per unit	XXX
Normal selling price per unit	$XXX

To illustrate, assume the following data for 100,000 calculators that Digital Solutions Inc. expects to produce and sell during 20Y4:

Manufacturing costs:		
Direct materials ($3.00 × 100,000)		$ 300,000
Direct labor ($10.00 × 100,000)		1,000,000
Factory overhead:		
Variable costs ($1.50 × 100,000)	$150,000	
Fixed costs	50,000	200,000
Total manufacturing cost		$1,500,000
Selling and administrative expenses:		
Variable expenses ($1.50 × 100,000)	$150,000	
Fixed costs	20,000	
Total selling and administrative expenses		170,000
Total cost		$1,670,000
Desired rate of return		20%
Total assets		$ 800,000

Using the total cost concept, the normal selling price of $18.30 is determined as follows:

Step 1. Total manufacturing cost: $1,500,000
Step 2. Total selling and administrative expenses: $170,000
Step 3. Total cost: $1,670,000
Step 4. Total cost per unit: $16.70

$$\text{Total Cost per Unit} = \frac{\text{Total Cost}}{\text{Estimated Units Produced and Sold}} = \frac{\$1,670,000}{100,000 \text{ units}} = \$16.70 \text{ per unit}$$

Step 5. Markup percentage: 9.6% (rounded)

Desired Profit = Desired Rate of Return × Total Assets = 20% × $800,000 = $160,000

$$\text{Markup Percentage} = \frac{\text{Desired Profit}}{\text{Total Cost}} = \frac{\$160,000}{\$1,670,000} = 9.6\% \text{ (rounded)}$$

Step 6. Markup per unit: $1.60

Markup per Unit = Markup Percentage × Total Cost per Unit
= 9.6% × $16.70 = $1.60 per unit

Step 7. Normal selling price: $18.30

Total cost per unit	$16.70
Markup per unit	1.60
Normal selling price per unit	$18.30

The ability of the selling price of $18.30 to generate the desired profit of $160,000 is illustrated by the income statement that follows:

Digital Solutions Inc.
Income Statement
For the Year Ended December 31, 20Y4

Sales (100,000 units × $18.30)		$1,830,000
Expenses:		
Variable (100,000 units × $16.00)	$1,600,000	
Fixed ($50,000 + $20,000)	70,000	1,670,000
Income from operations		$ 160,000

The total cost concept is often used by contractors who sell products to government agencies. This is because in many cases, government contractors are required by law to be reimbursed for their products on a total-cost-plus-profit basis.

Variable Cost Concept

As shown in Exhibit 17, under the **variable cost concept**, only variable costs are included in the cost amount per unit to which the markup is added. All variable manufacturing costs, as well as variable selling and administrative expenses, are included in the cost amount. Fixed manufacturing costs, fixed selling and administrative expenses, and desired profit are included in the markup. The markup per unit is then added to the variable cost per unit to determine the normal selling price.

EXHIBIT 17

Variable Cost Concept

The variable cost concept is applied using the following steps:

Step 1. Estimate the total variable product cost as follows:

Variable product costs:	
Direct materials	$XXX
Direct labor	XXX
Variable factory overhead	XXX
Total variable product cost	$XXX

Step 2. Estimate the total variable selling and administrative expenses.

Step 3. Determine the total variable cost as follows:

Total variable product cost	$XXX
Total variable selling and administrative expenses	XXX
Total variable cost	$XXX

Step 4. Compute the variable cost per unit as follows:

$$\text{Variable Cost per Unit} = \frac{\text{Total Variable Cost}}{\text{Estimated Units Produced and Sold}}$$

Step 5. Compute the markup percentage as follows:

$$\text{Markup Percentage} = \frac{\text{Desired Profit} + \text{Total Fixed Costs and Expenses}}{\text{Total Variable Cost}}$$

The numerator of the markup percentage is the desired profit plus the total fixed costs (fixed factory overhead) and expenses (selling and administrative). These fixed costs and expenses must be included in the markup percentage because they are not included in the cost amount to which the markup is added.

As illustrated for the total and product cost concepts, the desired profit is normally computed based on a rate of return on assets as follows:

$$\text{Desired Profit} = \text{Desired Rate of Return} \times \text{Total Assets}$$

Step 6. Determine the markup per unit by multiplying the markup percentage times the variable cost per unit as follows:

$$\text{Markup per Unit} = \text{Markup Percentage} \times \text{Variable Cost per Unit}$$

Step 7. Determine the normal selling price by adding the markup per unit to the variable cost per unit as follows:

Variable cost per unit	$XXX
Markup per unit	XXX
Normal selling price per unit	$XXX

To illustrate, assume the same data for the production and sale of 100,000 calculators by Digital Solutions Inc. as in the preceding example. The normal selling price of $18.30 is determined under the variable cost concept as follows:

Step 1. Total variable product cost: $1,450,000

Variable product costs:	
Direct materials ($3 × 100,000)	$ 300,000
Direct labor ($10 × 100,000)	1,000,000
Variable factory overhead ($1.50 × 100,000)	150,000
Total variable product cost	$1,450,000

Step 2. Total variable selling and administrative expenses: $150,000 ($1.50 × 100,000)
Step 3. Total variable cost: $1,600,000 ($1,450,000 + $150,000)
Step 4. Variable cost per unit: $16.00

$$\text{Variable Cost per Unit} = \frac{\text{Total Variable Cost}}{\text{Estimated Units Produced and Sold}} = \frac{\$1,600,000}{100,000 \text{ units}} = \$16 \text{ per unit}$$

Step 5. Markup percentage: 14.4% (rounded)

$$\text{Desired Profit} = \text{Desired Rate of Return} \times \text{Total Assets} = 20\% \times \$800,000 = \$160,000$$

$$\text{Markup Percentage} = \frac{\text{Desired Profit} + \text{Total Fixed Costs and Expenses}}{\text{Total Variable Cost}}$$

$$= \frac{\$160,000 + \$50,000 + \$20,000}{\$1,600,000} = \frac{\$230,000}{\$1,600,000}$$

$$= 14.4\% \text{ (rounded)}$$

Step 6. Markup per unit: $2.30

$$\text{Markup per Unit} = \text{Markup Percentage} \times \text{Variable Cost per Unit}$$
$$= 14.4\% \times \$16.00 = \$2.30 \text{ per unit}$$

Step 7. Normal selling price: $18.30

Total variable cost per unit	$16.00
Markup per unit	2.30
Normal selling price per unit	$18.30

At a Glance 25

Obj. 1 Prepare differential analysis reports for a variety of managerial decisions.

Key Points Differential analysis reports for various decisions are illustrated in the text. Each analysis focuses on the differential effects on income (loss) for alternative courses of action.

Learning Outcomes	Example Exercises	Practice Exercises
• Prepare a lease-or-sell differential analysis.	EE25-1	PE25-1A, 25-1B
• Prepare a discontinued segment differential analysis.	EE25-2	PE25-2A, 25-2B
• Prepare a make-or-buy differential analysis.	EE25-3	PE25-3A, 25-3B
• Prepare an equipment replacement differential analysis.	EE25-4	PE25-4A, 25-4B
• Prepare a process-or-sell differential analysis.	EE25-5	PE25-5A, 25-5B
• Prepare an accept business at a special price differential analysis.	EE25-6	PE25-6A, 25-6B

Obj. 2 Determine the selling price of a product, using the product cost concept.

Key Points The three cost concepts commonly used in applying the cost-plus approach to product pricing are the product cost, total cost (appendix), and variable cost (appendix) concepts.
Target costing combines market-based methods with a cost-reduction emphasis.

Learning Outcomes	Example Exercises	Practice Exercises
• Compute the markup percentage, using the product cost concept.	EE25-7	PE25-7A, 25-7B
• Define and describe target costing.		

Obj. 3 Compute the relative profitability of products in bottleneck production processes.

Key Points The relative profitability of a product in a bottleneck production environment is determined by dividing the unit contribution margin by the bottleneck hours per unit.

Learning Outcome	Example Exercises	Practice Exercises
• Compute the unit contribution margin per bottleneck hour.	EE25-8	PE25-8A, 25-8B

Obj. 4 Allocate product costs using activity-based costing.

Key Points Activity-based costing requires factory overhead to be assigned to activities. The estimated activity costs are allocated to products by multiplying activity rates by the activity-base usage quantity consumed for each product. Activity-based costing may provide more accurate allocation of factory overhead in complex product and manufacturing environments.

Learning Outcomes	Example Exercises	Practice Exercises
• Compute activity rates.		
• Allocate factory overhead costs to products using ABC.	EE25-9	PE25-9A, 25-9B

Illustrative Problem

Inez Company recently began production of a new product, a digital clock, which required the investment of $1,600,000 in assets. The costs of producing and selling 80,000 units of the digital clock are estimated as follows:

Variable costs:	
Direct materials	$10.00 per unit
Direct labor	6.00
Factory overhead	4.00
Selling and administrative expenses	5.00
Total	$25.00 per unit
Fixed costs:	
Factory overhead	$800,000
Selling and administrative expenses	400,000

Inez Company is currently considering establishing a selling price for the digital clock. The president of Inez Company has decided to use the cost-plus approach to product pricing and has indicated that the digital clock must earn a 10% rate of return on invested assets.

Instructions

1. Determine the amount of desired profit from the production and sale of the digital clock.
2. Assuming that the product cost concept is used, determine (a) the cost amount per unit, (b) the markup percentage, and (c) the selling price of the digital clock.
3. Under what conditions should Inez Company consider using activity-based costing rather than a single factory overhead allocation rate in allocating factory overhead to the digital clock?
4. Assume that the market price for similar digital clocks was estimated at $38. Compute the reduction in manufacturing cost per unit needed to maintain the desired profit and existing selling and administrative expenses under target costing.
5. Assume that for the current year, the selling price of the digital clock was $42 per unit. To date, 60,000 units have been produced and sold, and analysis of the domestic market indicates that 15,000 additional units are expected to be sold during the remainder of the year. On August 7, Inez Company received an offer from Wong Inc. for 4,000 units of the digital clock at $28 each. Wong Inc. will market the units in Korea under its own brand name, and no selling and administrative expenses associated with the sale will be incurred by Inez Company. The additional business is not expected to affect the domestic sales of the digital clock, and the additional units could be produced during the current year, using existing capacity. Prepare a differential analysis dated August 7 to determine whether to reject (Alternative 1) or accept (Alternative 2) the special order from Wong.

Solution

1. $160,000 ($1,600,000 × 10%)
2. a. Total manufacturing costs:

Variable ($20 × 80,000 units)	$1,600,000
Fixed factory overhead	800,000
Total	$2,400,000

Cost amount per unit: $2,400,000 ÷ 80,000 units = $30.00

(Continued)

1248 Chapter 25 Differential Analysis, Product Pricing, and Activity-Based Costing

b. Markup Percentage = $\dfrac{\text{Desired Profit + Total Selling and Administrative Expenses}}{\text{Total Product Cost}}$

$= \dfrac{\$160{,}000 + \$400{,}000 + (\$5 \times 80{,}000 \text{ units})}{\$2{,}400{,}000}$

$= \dfrac{\$160{,}000 + \$400{,}000 + \$400{,}000}{\$2{,}400{,}000}$

$= \dfrac{\$960{,}000}{\$2{,}400{,}000} = 40\%$

c.
Cost amount per unit	$30.00
Markup ($30 × 40%)	12.00
Selling price	$42.00

3. Inez should consider using activity-based costing for factory overhead allocation when the product and manufacturing operations are complex. For example, if the digital clock was introduced as one among many different consumer digital products, these products will likely consume factory activities in different ways. If this is combined with complex manufacturing and manufacturing support processes, a single overhead allocation rate will likely lead to distorted factory overhead allocation. Specifically, the digital clock is a new product. Thus, it will likely consume more factory overhead than existing stable and mature products. In this case, a single rate would result in the digital clock being undercosted compared to results using activity-based rates for factory overhead allocation.

4.
Current selling price	$42
Expected selling price	−38
Required reduction in manufacturing cost to maintain same profit	$ 4

Revised revenue and cost figures:

	Current	Desired
Selling price	$42	$38
Costs:		
Variable selling and administrative expenses per unit	$ 5	$ 5
Fixed selling and administrative expenses per unit ($400,000 ÷ 80,000 units)	5	5
Existing manufacturing cost per unit [part (2)]	30	
Target manufacturing cost per unit ($30 − $4)		26
Total costs	$40	$36
Profit	$ 2	$ 2

5.
Differential Analysis—Wong Inc. Special Order
Reject Order (Alternative 1) or Accept Order (Alternative 2)
August 7

	Reject Order (Alternative 1)	Accept Order (Alternative 2)	Differential Effect on Income (Alternative 2)
Revenues	$0	$112,000*	$112,000
Costs:			
Variable manufacturing costs	0	−80,000**	−80,000
Income (loss)	$0	$ 32,000	$ 32,000

*4,000 units × $28 per unit
**4,000 units × $20 per unit

The proposal should be accepted.

Chapter 25 Differential Analysis, Product Pricing, and Activity-Based Costing

Key Terms

activities (1237)
activity base (1238)
activity-based costing (ABC) (1237)
activity rate (1238)
differential analysis (1220)
differential cost (1220)
differential income (loss) (1220)

differential revenue (1220)
engineering change order (ECO) (1237)
opportunity cost (1227)
product cost concept (1232)
production bottleneck (1235)
setup (1237)

sunk cost (1222)
target costing (1234)
theory of constraints (TOC) (1235)
total cost concept (1241)
variable cost concept (1244)

Discussion Questions

1. Explain the meaning of (a) differential revenue, (b) differential cost, and (c) differential income.

2. A company could sell a building for $250,000 or lease it for $2,500 per month. What would need to be considered in determining if the lease option would be preferred?

3. A chemical company has commodity-grade and premium-grade products. Why might the company elect to process the commodity-grade product further to the premium-grade product?

4. A company accepts incremental business at a special price that exceeds the variable cost. What other issues must the company consider in deciding whether to accept the business?

5. A company fabricates a component at a cost of $6.00. A supplier offers to supply the same component for $5.50. Under what circumstances is it reasonable to purchase from the supplier?

6. **Real World** Many fast-food restaurant chains such as McDonald's occasionally discontinue restaurants in their system. What are some financial considerations in deciding to eliminate a store?

7. In the long run, the normal selling price must be set high enough to cover what factors?

8. Although the cost-plus approach to product pricing may be used by management as a general guideline, what are examples of other factors that managers should consider in setting product prices?

9. How does the target cost concept differ from cost-plus approaches?

10. What is the appropriate measure of a product's value when a firm is operating under production bottlenecks?

11. Under what conditions might a company use activity-based costing to allocate factory overhead to products?

Practice Exercises

Example Exercises

 EE 25-1 p. 1223
Show Me How

PE 25-1A Lease or sell OBJ. 1

Duncan Company owns a machine with a cost of $75,000 and accumulated depreciation of $15,000 that can be sold for $54,000 less a 5% sales commission. Alternatively, Duncan Company can lease the machine to another company for three years for a total of $60,000, at the end of which there is no residual value. In addition, the repair, insurance, and property tax expense that would be incurred by Duncan Company on the machine would total $8,500 over the three years. Prepare a differential analysis on February 21 as to whether Duncan Company should lease (Alternative 1) or sell (Alternative 2) the machine.

1250 Chapter 25 Differential Analysis, Product Pricing, and Activity-Based Costing

EE 25-1 *p. 1223* **PE 25-1B Lease or sell** OBJ. 1

Timberlake Company owns equipment with a cost of $165,000 and accumulated depreciation of $60,000 that can be sold for $82,000 less a 6% sales commission. Alternatively, Timberlake Company can lease the equipment to another company for five years for a total of $84,600, at the end of which there is no residual value. In addition, the repair, insurance, and property tax expense that would be incurred by Timberlake Company on the equipment would total $7,950 over the five years. Prepare a differential analysis on March 23 as to whether Timberlake Company should lease (Alternative 1) or sell (Alternative 2) the equipment.

EE 25-2 *p. 1224* **PE 25-2A Discontinue a segment** OBJ. 1

Product Alpha has revenue of $545,000, variable cost of goods sold of $400,000, variable selling expenses of $65,000, and fixed costs of $90,000, creating a loss from operations of $10,000. Prepare a differential analysis as of December 10 to determine whether Product Alpha should be continued (Alternative 1) or discontinued (Alternative 2), assuming that fixed costs are unaffected by the decision.

EE 25-2 *p. 1224* **PE 25-2B Discontinue a segment** OBJ. 1

Product B has revenue of $39,500, variable cost of goods sold of $25,500, variable selling expenses of $16,500, and fixed costs of $15,000, creating a loss from operations of $17,500. Prepare a differential analysis as of May 9 to determine whether Product B should be continued (Alternative 1) or discontinued (Alternative 2), assuming fixed costs are unaffected by the decision.

EE 25-3 *p. 1226* **PE 25-3A Make or buy** OBJ. 1

A restaurant bakes its own bread for a cost of $230 per unit (100 loaves), including fixed costs of $47 per unit. A proposal is offered to purchase bread from an outside source for $180 per unit, plus $18 per unit for delivery. Prepare a differential analysis dated July 7 to determine whether the company should make (Alternative 1) or buy (Alternative 2) the bread, assuming that fixed costs are unaffected by the decision.

EE 25-3 *p. 1226* **PE 25-3B Make or buy** OBJ. 1

A company manufactures various sized plastic bottles for its medicinal product. The manufacturing cost for small bottles is $67 per unit (100 bottles), including fixed costs of $22 per unit. A proposal is offered to purchase small bottles from an outside source for $35 per unit, plus $5 per unit for freight. Prepare a differential analysis dated March 30 to determine whether the company should make (Alternative 1) or buy (Alternative 2) the bottles, assuming that fixed costs are unaffected by the decision.

EE 25-4 *p. 1228* **PE 25-4A Replace equipment** OBJ. 1

A machine with a book value of $250,000 has an estimated six-year life. A proposal is offered to sell the old machine for $320,000 and replace it with a new machine at a cost of $390,000. The new machine has a six-year life with no residual value. The new machine would reduce annual direct labor costs from $75,000 to $61,000. Prepare a differential analysis dated October 3 on whether to continue with the old machine (Alternative 1) or replace the old machine (Alternative 2).

EE 25-4 *p. 1228* **PE 25-4B Replace equipment** OBJ. 1

A machine with a book value of $80,000 has an estimated five-year life. A proposal is offered to sell the old machine for $50,500 and replace it with a new machine at a cost of $75,000. The new machine has a five-year life with no residual value. The new machine would reduce annual direct labor costs from $11,200 to $7,400. Prepare a differential analysis dated April 11 on whether to continue with the old machine (Alternative 1) or replace the old machine (Alternative 2).

PE 25-5A Process or sell
OBJ. 1

Product K is produced for $155 per pound. Product K can be sold without additional processing for $220 per pound or processed further into Product L at an additional cost of $28 per pound. Product L can be sold for $250 per pound. Prepare a differential analysis dated November 15 on whether to sell Product K (Alternative 1) or process further into Product L (Alternative 2).

PE 25-5B Process or sell
OBJ. 1

Product D is produced for $24 per gallon. Product D can be sold without additional processing for $36 per gallon or processed further into Product E at an additional cost of $9 per gallon. Product E can be sold for $43 per gallon. Prepare a differential analysis dated February 26 on whether to sell Product D (Alternative 1) or process further into Product E (Alternative 2).

PE 25-6A Accept business at special price
OBJ. 1

Product AA is normally sold for $120 per unit. A special price of $112 is offered for the export market. The variable production cost is $80 per unit. An additional export tariff of 30% of revenue must be paid for all export products. Assume that there is sufficient capacity for the special order. Prepare a differential analysis dated March 5 on whether to reject (Alternative 1) or accept (Alternative 2) the special order.

PE 25-6B Accept business at special price
OBJ. 1

Product A is normally sold for $9.60 per unit. A special price of $7.20 is offered for the export market. The variable production cost is $5.00 per unit. An additional export tariff of 15% of revenue must be paid for all export products. Assume that there is sufficient capacity for the special order. Prepare a differential analysis dated March 16 on whether to reject (Alternative 1) or accept (Alternative 2) the special order.

PE 25-7A Product cost markup percentage
OBJ. 2

Light Force Inc. produces and sells lighting fixtures. An entry light has a total cost of $180 per unit, of which $100 is product cost and $80 is selling and administrative expenses. In addition, the total cost of $180 is made up of $110 variable cost and $70 fixed cost. The desired profit is $45 per unit. Determine the markup percentage on product cost.

PE 25-7B Product cost markup percentage
OBJ. 2

Green Thumb Garden Tools Inc. produces and sells home and garden tools and equipment. A lawn mower has a total cost of $230 per unit, of which $160 is product cost and $70 is selling and administrative expenses. In addition, the total cost of $230 is made up of $120 variable cost and $110 fixed cost. The desired profit is $58 per unit. Determine the markup percentage on product cost.

PE 25-8A Bottleneck profit
OBJ. 3

Product A has a unit contribution margin of $24. Product B has a unit contribution margin of $30. Product A requires four testing hours, while Product B requires six testing hours. Determine the most profitable product, assuming that the testing is a production bottleneck.

1252 Chapter 25 Differential Analysis, Product Pricing, and Activity-Based Costing

EE 25-8 *p. 1236*

PE 25-8B Bottleneck profit
OBJ. 3

Product K has a unit contribution margin of $120. Product L has a unit contribution margin of $100. Product K requires five furnace hours, while Product L requires four furnace hours. Determine the most profitable product, assuming that the furnace is a production bottleneck.

EE 25-9 *p. 1240*

PE 25-9A Activity-based costing
OBJ. 4

Mainline Marine Company has total estimated factory overhead for the year of $2,090,000, divided into four activities: fabrication, $750,000; assembly, $240,000; setup, $600,000; and inspection, $500,000. Mainline manufactures two types of boats: a speedboat and a bass boat. The activity-base usage quantities for each product by each activity are as follows:

	Fabrication	Assembly	Setup	Inspection
Speedboat	1,200 dlh	1,800 dlh	60 setups	600 inspections
Bass boat	1,800	1,200	100	200
	3,000 dlh	3,000 dlh	160 setups	800 inspections

Each product is budgeted for 200 units of production for the year. Determine (a) the activity rates for each activity and (b) the factory overhead cost per unit for each product, using activity-based costing.

EE 25-9 *p. 1240*

PE 25-9B Activity-based costing
OBJ. 4

Casual Cuts Inc. has total estimated factory overhead for the year of $225,000, divided into four activities: cutting, $90,000; sewing, $22,500; setup, $80,000; and inspection, $32,500. Casual Cuts manufactures two types of men's pants: jeans and khakis. The activity-base usage quantities for each product by each activity are as follows:

	Cutting	Sewing	Setup	Inspection
Jeans	500 dlh	1,000 dlh	250 setups	100 inspections
Khakis	1,000	500	750	400
	1,500 dlh	1,500 dlh	1,000 setups	500 inspections

Each product is budgeted for 10,000 units of production for the year. Determine (a) the activity rates for each activity and (b) the factory overhead cost per unit for each product, using activity-based costing.

Exercises

✔ a. Differential revenue from selling, $3,500

EX 25-1 Differential analysis for a lease-or-sell decision
OBJ. 1

Matrix Construction Company is considering selling excess machinery with a book value of $75,000 (original cost of $200,000 less accumulated depreciation of $125,000) for $60,000 less a 5% brokerage commission. Alternatively, the machinery can be leased to another company for a total of $75,000 for five years, after which it is expected to have no residual value. During the period of the lease, Matrix Construction Company's costs of repairs, insurance, and property tax expenses are expected to be $21,500.

a. Prepare a differential analysis dated May 25 to determine whether Matrix should lease (Alternative 1) or sell (Alternative 2) the machinery.

b. ✏️ On the basis of the data presented, would it be advisable to lease or sell the machinery? Explain.

✔ Loss from buying equipment, −$378,000

EX 25-2 Differential analysis for a lease-or-buy decision
OBJ. 1

D'Amato Corporation is considering new equipment. The equipment can be purchased from an overseas supplier for $315,000. The freight and installation costs for the equip-

Chapter 25   Differential Analysis, Product Pricing, and Activity-Based Costing   1253

ment are $15,000. If purchased, annual repairs and maintenance are estimated to be $12,000 per year over the four-year useful life of the equipment. Alternatively, D'Amato can lease the equipment from a domestic supplier for $95,000 per year for four years, with no additional costs. Prepare a differential analysis dated December 11 to determine whether D'Amato should lease (Alternative 1) or purchase (Alternative 2) the equipment. *Hint:* This is a lease-or-buy decision, which must be analyzed from the perspective of the equipment user, as opposed to the equipment owner.

EX 25-3   Differential analysis for a discontinued product   OBJ. 1

✔ a. Loss to discontinue Star Cola, –$113,300

A condensed income statement by product line for Celestial Beverage Inc. indicated the following for Star Cola for the past year:

Sales	$390,000
Cost of goods sold	184,000
Gross profit	$206,000
Operating expenses	255,000
Loss from operations	$ (49,000)

It is estimated that 20% of the cost of goods sold represents fixed factory overhead costs and that 30% of the operating expenses are fixed. Because Star Cola is only one of many products, the fixed costs will not be materially affected if the product is discontinued.

a. Prepare a differential analysis dated January 21 to determine whether Star Cola should be continued (Alternative 1) or discontinued (Alternative 2).

b. Should Star Cola be retained? Explain.

EX 25-4   Differential analysis for a discontinued product   OBJ. 1

✔ a. Alternative 1 loss, $4,300

The condensed product-line income statement for Dish N' Dat Company for the month of May is as follows:

Dish N' Dat Company
Product-Line Income Statement
For the Month Ended May 31

	Bowls	Plates	Cups
Sales	$71,000	$105,700	$33,500
Cost of goods sold	32,600	42,300	20,600
Gross profit	$38,400	$ 63,400	$12,900
Selling and administrative expenses	27,400	42,800	17,200
Income from operations	$11,000	$ 20,600	$ (4,300)

Fixed costs are 15% of the cost of goods sold and 30% of the selling and administrative expenses. Dish N' Dat assumes that fixed costs would not be materially affected if the Cups line were discontinued.

a. Prepare a differential analysis dated May 31 to determine if Cups should be continued (Alternative 1) or discontinued (Alternative 2).

b. Should the Cups line be retained? Explain.

EX 25-5   Segment analysis for a service company   OBJ. 1

Charles Schwab Corporation is one of the more innovative brokerage and financial service companies in the United States. The company recently provided information about its major business segments as follows (in millions):

	Investor Services	Advisor Services
Revenues	$4,771	$4,597
Income from operations	1,681	1,660
Depreciation	171	154

(Continued)

a. How does a brokerage company like Schwab define the Investor Services and Advisor Services segments? Use the Internet and the Business Connection box in this chapter to develop your answer.

b. Provide a specific example of a variable and fixed cost in the Investor Services segment.

c. Estimate the contribution margin for each segment, assuming that depreciation represents the majority of fixed costs.

d. If Schwab decided to sell its Advisor Services business to another company, estimate how much operating income would decline.

EX 25-6 Decision to discontinue a product   OBJ. 1

 On the basis of the following data, the general manager of Foremost Footwear Inc. decided to discontinue Children's Shoes because it reduced income from operations by $10,000. What is the flaw in this decision if it is assumed that fixed costs would not be materially affected by the discontinuance?

Foremost Footwear Inc.
Product-Line Income Statement
For the Year Ended April 30, 20Y7

	Children's Shoes	Men's Shoes	Women's Shoes	Total
Sales	$165,000	$300,000	$500,000	$965,000
Costs of goods sold:				
Variable costs	$105,000	$150,000	$220,000	$475,000
Fixed costs	32,000	60,000	120,000	212,000
Total cost of goods sold	$137,000	$210,000	$340,000	$687,000
Gross profit	$ 28,000	$ 90,000	$160,000	$278,000
Selling and adminstrative expenses:				
Variable selling and admin. expenses	$ 21,000	$ 45,000	$ 95,000	$161,000
Fixed selling and admin. expenses	17,000	20,000	25,000	62,000
Total selling and admin. expenses	$ 38,000	$ 65,000	$120,000	$223,000
Income (loss) from operations	$ (10,000)	$ 25,000	$ 40,000	$ 55,000

EX 25-7 Make-or-buy decision   OBJ. 1

✔ a. Differential loss from buying, $3.30 per case

Diamond Computer Company has been purchasing carrying cases for its portable computers at a purchase price of $59 per unit. The company, which is currently operating below full capacity, charges factory overhead to production at the rate of 40% of direct labor cost. The fully absorbed unit costs to produce comparable carrying cases are expected to be as follows:

Direct materials	$35.00
Direct labor	18.00
Factory overhead (40% of direct labor)	7.20
Total cost per unit	$60.20

If Diamond Computer Company manufactures the carrying cases, fixed factory overhead costs will not increase and variable factory overhead costs associated with the cases are expected to be 15% of the direct labor costs.

a. Prepare a differential analysis dated February 24 to determine whether the company should make (Alternative 1) or buy (Alternative 2) the carrying case.

b. On the basis of the data presented, would it be advisable to make the carrying cases or to continue buying them? Explain.

Chapter 25 Differential Analysis, Product Pricing, and Activity-Based Costing   1255

EX 25-8 Make-or-buy decision for a service company   OBJ. 1

✓ a. Loss from purchasing layout services, –$364,000

The Theater Arts Guild of Dallas (TAG-D) employs five people in its Publication Department. These people lay out pages for pamphlets, brochures, magazines, and other publications for the TAG-D productions. The pages are delivered to an outside company for printing. The company is considering an outside publication service for the layout work. The outside service is quoting a price of $13 per layout page. The budget for the Publication Department for the current year is as follows:

Salaries	$224,000
Benefits	36,000
Supplies	21,000
Office expenses	39,000
Office depreciation	28,000
Computer depreciation	24,000
Total	$372,000

The department expects to lay out 24,000 pages for the current year. The Publication Department office space and equipment would be used for future administrative needs if the department's function were purchased from the outside.

a. Prepare a differential analysis dated February 22 to determine whether TAG-D should lay out pages internally (Alternative 1) or purchase layout services from the outside (Alternative 2).

b. On the basis of your analysis in part (a), should the page layout work be purchased from an outside company? Explain.

c. What additional considerations might factor into the decision making?

EX 25-9 Machine replacement decision   OBJ. 1

✓ a. Loss from replacing old machine, –$66,700

A company is considering replacing an old piece of machinery, which cost $105,000 and has $55,000 of accumulated depreciation to date, with a new machine that has a purchase price of $83,000. The old machine could be sold for $56,300. The annual variable production costs associated with the old machine are estimated to be $8,500 per year for eight years. The annual variable production costs for the new machine are estimated to be $5,000 per year for eight years.

a. Prepare a differential analysis dated April 29 to determine whether to continue with (Alternative 1) or replace (Alternative 2) the old machine.

b. What is the sunk cost in this situation?

EX 25-10 Differential analysis for machine replacement   OBJ. 1

✓ a. Differential loss, $2,500

Kim Kwon Digital Components Company assembles circuit boards by using a manually operated machine to insert electronic components. The original cost of the machine is $60,000, the accumulated depreciation is $24,000, its remaining useful life is five years, and its residual value is negligible. On May 4 of the current year, a proposal was made to replace the present manufacturing procedure with a fully automatic machine that has a purchase price of $180,000. The automatic machine has an estimated useful life of five years and no significant residual value. For use in evaluating the proposal, the accountant accumulated the following annual data on present and proposed operations:

	Present Operations	Proposed Operations
Sales	$205,000	$205,000
Direct materials	$ 72,000	$ 72,000
Direct labor	51,000	—
Power and maintenance	5,000	18,000
Taxes, insurance, etc.	1,500	4,000
Selling and administrative expenses	45,000	45,000
Total expenses	$174,500	$139,000

(*Continued*)

1256 Chapter 25 Differential Analysis, Product Pricing, and Activity-Based Costing

a. Prepare a differential analysis dated May 4 to determine whether to continue with the old machine (Alternative 1) or replace the old machine (Alternative 2). Prepare the analysis over the useful life of the new machine.
b. Based only on the data presented, should the proposal be accepted?
c. ✏️ What other factors should be considered before a final decision is made?

EX 25-11 Sell or process further OBJ. 1

✔ Income from processing further, $145

Big Fork Lumber Company incurs a cost of $402 per hundred board feet (hbf) in processing certain "rough-cut" lumber, which it sells for $540 per hbf. An alternative is to produce a "finished cut" at a total processing cost of $523 per hbf, which can be sold for $668 per hbf. Prepare a differential analysis dated August 9 on whether to sell rough-cut lumber (Alternative 1) or process further into finished-cut lumber (Alternative 2).

EX 25-12 Sell or process further OBJ. 1

✔ a. Income from processing further, $24,486

Rise N' Shine Coffee Company produces Columbian coffee in batches of 6,000 pounds. The standard quantity of materials required in the process is 6,000 pounds, which cost $5.50 per pound. Columbian coffee can be sold without further processing for $9.22 per pound. Columbian coffee can also be processed further to yield Decaf Columbian, which can be sold for $11.88 per pound. The processing into Decaf Columbian requires additional processing costs of $10,230 per batch. The additional processing also causes a 5% loss of product due to evaporation.

a. Prepare a differential analysis dated October 6 on whether to sell regular Columbian (Alternative 1) or process further into Decaf Columbian (Alternative 2).
b. ✏️ Should Rise N' Shine sell Columbian coffee or process further and sell Decaf Columbian?
c. Determine the price of Decaf Columbian that would cause neither an advantage nor a disadvantage for processing further and selling Decaf Columbian.

EX 25-13 Decision on accepting additional business OBJ. 1

✔ a. Differential income, $54,000

Homestead Jeans Co. has an annual plant capacity of 65,000 units, and current production is 45,000 units. Monthly fixed costs are $54,000, and variable costs are $29 per unit. The present selling price is $42 per unit. On November 12 of the current year, the company received an offer from Dawkins Company for 18,000 units of the product at $32 each. Dawkins Company will market the units in a foreign country under its own brand name. The additional business is not expected to affect the domestic selling price or quantity of sales of Homestead Jeans Co.

a. Prepare a differential analysis dated November 12 on whether to reject (Alternative 1) or accept (Alternative 2) the Dawkins order.
b. ✏️ Briefly explain why accepting this additional business will increase operating income.
c. What is the minimum price per unit that would produce a positive contribution margin?

EX 25-14 Accepting business at a special price OBJ. 1

Portable Power Company expects to operate at 80% of productive capacity during July. The total manufacturing costs for July for the production of 25,000 batteries are budgeted as follows:

Direct materials	$162,500
Direct labor	70,000
Variable factory overhead	30,000
Fixed factory overhead	112,500
Total manufacturing costs	$375,000

Chapter 25 Differential Analysis, Product Pricing, and Activity-Based Costing 1257

The company has an opportunity to submit a bid for 2,500 batteries to be delivered by July 31 to a government agency. If the contract is obtained, it is anticipated that the additional activity will not interfere with normal production during July or increase the selling or administrative expenses. What is the unit cost below which Portable Power Company should not go in bidding on the government contract?

EX 25-15 Decision on accepting additional business   OBJ. 1

✔ a. Differential revenue, $2,320,000

Brightstone Tire and Rubber Company has capacity to produce 170,000 tires. Brightstone presently produces and sells 130,000 tires for the North American market at a price of $175 per tire. Brightstone is evaluating a special order from a European automobile company, Euro Motors. Euro is offering to buy 20,000 tires for $116 per tire. Brightstone's accounting system indicates that the total cost per tire is as follows:

Direct materials	$ 56
Direct labor	22
Factory overhead (60% variable)	25
Selling and administrative expenses (45% variable)	26
Total	$129

Brightstone pays a selling commission equal to 5% of the selling price on North American orders, which is included in the variable portion of the selling and administrative expenses. However, this special order would not have a sales commission. If the order was accepted, the tires would be shipped overseas for an additional shipping cost of $7.50 per tire. In addition, Euro has made the order conditional on receiving European safety certification. Brightstone estimates that this certification would cost $165,000.

a. Prepare a differential analysis dated January 21 on whether to reject (Alternative 1) or accept (Alternative 2) the special order from Euro Motors.

b. What is the minimum price per unit that would be financially acceptable to Brightstone?

EX 25-16 Accepting business at a special price for a service company

Cityscape Hotels has 200 rooms available in a major metropolitan city. The hotel is able to attract business customers during the weekdays and leisure customers during the weekend. However, the leisure customers on weekends occupy fewer rooms than do business customers on weekdays. Thus, Cityscape plans to provide special weekend pricing to attract additional leisure customers. A hotel room is priced at $180 per room night. The cost of a hotel room night includes the following:

	Cost per Room Night (at normal occupancy)
Housekeeping service	$ 23
Utilities	7
Amenities	3
Hotel depreciation	55
Hotel staff (excluding housekeeping)	42
Total	$130

a. What is the contribution margin for a room night if only the hotel depreciation and hotel staff are assumed fixed for all occupancy levels?

b. What should be considered in setting a discount price for the weekends?

EX 25-17 Product cost concept of product pricing   OBJ. 2

✔ b. $40

La Femme Accessories Inc. produces women's handbags. The cost of producing 800 handbags is as follows:

Direct materials	$18,000
Direct labor	8,500
Factory overhead	5,500
Total manufacturing cost	$32,000

(Continued)

1258 Chapter 25 Differential Analysis, Product Pricing, and Activity-Based Costing

The selling and administrative expenses are $17,000. The management wants a profit equal to 22% of invested assets of $250,000.

a. Determine the amount of desired profit from the production and sale of 800 handbags.
b. Determine the product cost per unit for the production of 800 handbags.
c. Determine the product cost markup percentage for handbags.
d. Determine the selling price of handbags.

EX 25-18 Product cost concept of product costing
OBJ. 2

✓ d. $325

Smart Stream Inc. uses the product cost concept of applying the cost-plus approach to product pricing. The costs of producing and selling 10,000 cellular phones are as follows:

Variable costs per unit:		Fixed costs:	
Direct materials	$150	Factory overhead	$350,000
Direct labor	25	Selling and administrative expenses	140,000
Factory overhead	40		
Selling and administrative expenses	25		
Total	$240		

Smart Stream wants a profit equal to a 30% rate of return on invested assets of $1,200,000.

a. Determine the amount of desired profit from the production and sale of 10,000 cellular phones.
b. Determine the product cost and the cost amount per unit for the production of 10,000 cellular phones.
c. Determine the product cost markup percentage for cellular phones.
d. Determine the selling price of cellular phones.

EX 25-19 Target costing
OBJ. 2

Toyota Motor Corporation uses target costing. Assume that Toyota marketing personnel estimate that the competitive selling price for the Camry in the upcoming model year will need to be $27,000. Assume further that the Camry's total unit cost for the upcoming model year is estimated to be $22,500 and that Toyota requires a 20% profit margin on selling price (which is equivalent to a 25% markup on total cost).

a. What price will Toyota establish for the Camry for the upcoming model year?
b. What impact will target costing have on Toyota, given the assumed information?

EX 25-20 Target costing
OBJ. 2

✓ b. $30

Instant Image Inc. manufactures color laser printers. Model J20 presently sells for $460 and has a product cost of $230, as follows:

Direct materials	$175
Direct labor	40
Factory overhead	15
Total	$230

It is estimated that the competitive selling price for color laser printers of this type will drop to $400 next year. Instant Image has established a target cost to maintain its historical markup percentage on product cost. Engineers have provided the following cost-reduction ideas:

1. Purchase a plastic printer cover with snap-on assembly rather than with screws. This will reduce the amount of direct labor by 15 minutes per unit.
2. Add an inspection step that will add six minutes per unit of direct labor but reduce the materials cost by $20 per unit.

3. Decrease the cycle time of the injection molding machine from four minutes to three minutes per part. Forty percent of the direct labor and 48% of the factory overhead are related to running injection molding machines.

The direct labor rate is $30 per hour.

a. Determine the target cost for Model J20, assuming that the historical markup on product cost and selling price is maintained.
b. Determine the required cost reduction.
c. Evaluate the three engineering improvements together to determine whether the required cost reduction (drift) can be achieved.

EX 25-21 Product decisions under bottlenecked operations OBJ. 3

✔ Unit contribution per furnace hour Type 5, $0.30

Mill Metals Inc. has three grades of metal product, Type 5, Type 10, and Type 20. Financial data for the three grades are as follows:

	Type 5	Type 10	Type 20
Revenues	$43,000	$49,000	$56,500
Variable cost	$34,000	$28,000	$26,500
Fixed cost	8,000	8,000	8,000
Total cost	$42,000	$36,000	$34,500
Income from operations	$ 1,000	$13,000	$22,000
Number of units	÷ 5,000	÷ 5,000	÷ 5,000
Income from operations per unit	$ 0.20	$ 2.60	$ 4.40

Mill's operations require all three grades to be melted in a furnace before being formed. The furnace runs 24 hours a day, 7 days a week, and is a production bottleneck. The furnace hours required per unit of each product are as follows:

Type 5:	6 hours
Type 10:	6 hours
Type 20:	12 hours

The Marketing Department is considering a new marketing and sales campaign.
  Which product should be emphasized in the marketing and sales campaign in order to maximize profitability?

EX 25-22 Product decisions under bottlenecked operations OBJ. 3

✔ a. Total income from operations, $269,000

Youngstown Glass Company manufactures three types of safety plate glass: large, medium, and small. All three products have high demand. Thus, Youngstown Glass is able to sell all the safety glass it can make. The production process includes an autoclave operation, which is a pressurized heat treatment. The autoclave is a production bottleneck. Total fixed costs are $85,000 for the company as a whole. In addition, the following information is available about the three products:

	Large	Medium	Small
Unit selling price	$184	$160	$100
Unit variable cost	130	120	76
Unit contribution margin	$ 54	$ 40	$ 24
Autoclave hours per unit	3	2	1
Total process hours per unit	5	4	2
Budgeted units of production	3,000	3,000	3,000

a. Determine the contribution margin by glass type and the total company income from operations for the budgeted units of production.
b. Prepare an analysis showing which product is the most profitable per bottleneck hour.

EX 25-23 Activity-based costing OBJ. 4

✔ Activity cost per stationary bicycle, $92.40

CardioTrainer Equipment Company manufactures stationary bicycles and treadmills. The products are produced in the Fabrication and Assembly production departments. In addition to production activities, several other activities are required to produce the two products. These activities and their associated activity rates are as follows:

Activity	Activity Rate
Fabrication	$22 per machine hour (mh)
Assembly	$12 per direct labor hour (dlh)
Setup	$40 per setup
Inspecting	$18 per inspection
Production scheduling	$8 per production order
Purchasing	$5 per purchase order

The activity-base usage quantities and units produced for each product were as follows:

	Stationary Bicycle	Treadmill
Machine hours	1,680	1,070
Direct labor hours	243	131
Setups	45	20
Inspections	158	94
Production orders	60	32
Purchase orders	240	98
Units produced	500	350

Use the activity rate and usage information to compute the total activity costs and the activity costs per unit for each product.

EX 25-24 Activity-based costing OBJ. 4

✔ b. Custom, $90.65 per unit

Zeus Industries manufactures two types of electrical power units, custom and standard, which involve four factory overhead activities—production setup, procurement, quality control, and materials management. An activity analysis of the overhead revealed the following estimated activity costs and activity bases for these activities:

Activity	Activity Cost	Activity Base
Production setup	$ 44,000	Number of setups
Procurement	13,500	Number of purchase orders (PO)
Quality control	97,500	Number of inspections
Materials management	84,000	Number of components
Total	$239,000	

The activity-base usage quantities for each product are as follows:

	Setups	Purchase Orders	Inspections	Components	Unit Volume
Custom	290	760	1,200	500	2,000
Standard	110	140	300	200	2,000
Total	400	900	1,500	700	4,000

a. Determine an activity rate for each activity.
b. Assign activity costs to each product and determine the unit activity cost, using the activity rates from part (a).
c. Assume that each product required one direct labor hour per unit. Determine the per-unit cost if factory overhead is allocated on the basis of direct labor hours.
d. Explain why the answers in parts (b) and (c) are different.

EX 25-25 Activity rates and product costs using activity-based costing OBJ. 4

✔ b. Dining room lighting fixtures, $71.60 per unit

BriteLite Inc. manufactures entry and dining room lighting fixtures. Five activities are used in manufacturing the fixtures. These activities and their associated activity costs and activity bases are as follows:

Activity	Activity Costs (Budgeted)	Activity Base
Casting	$42,000	Machine hours
Assembly	13,500	Direct labor hours
Inspecting	5,800	Number of inspections
Setup	16,800	Number of setups
Materials handling	3,600	Number of loads

Corporate records were obtained to estimate the amount of activity to be used by the two products. The estimated activity-base usage quantities and units produced for each product and in total are provided in the following table:

Activity Base	Entry	Dining	Total
Machine hours	800	600	1,400
Direct labor hours	500	400	900
Number of inspections	140	150	290
Number of setups	80	60	140
Number of loads	50	40	90
Units produced	1,200	500	1,700

a. Determine the activity rate for each activity.
b. Use the activity rates in (a) to determine the total and per-unit activity costs associated with each product.

Appendix
EX 25-26 Total cost concept of product pricing

✔ b. 12.46%

Based on the data presented in Exercise 25-18, assume that Smart Stream Inc. uses the total cost concept of applying the cost-plus approach to product pricing.

a. Determine the total costs and the total cost amount per unit for the production and sale of 10,000 cellular phones.
b. Determine the total cost markup percentage (rounded to two decimal places) for cellular phones.
c. Determine the selling price of cellular phones. Round to the nearest dollar.

Appendix
EX 25-27 Variable cost concept of product pricing

✔ b. 35.42%

Based on the data presented in Exercise 25-18, assume that Smart Stream Inc. uses the variable cost concept of applying the cost-plus approach to product pricing.

a. Determine the variable costs and the variable cost amount per unit for the production and sale of 10,000 cellular phones.
b. Determine the variable cost markup percentage (rounded to two decimal places) for cellular phones.
c. Determine the selling price of cellular phones. Round to the nearest dollar.

Problems: Series A

✔ 1. Income from investing in bonds, $172,800

PR 25-1A Differential analysis involving opportunity costs OBJ. 1

On October 1, White Way Stores Inc. is considering leasing a building and purchasing the necessary equipment to operate a retail store. Alternatively, the company could use the funds to invest in $180,000 of 6% U.S. Treasury bonds that mature in 16 years. The bonds could be purchased at face value. The following data have been assembled:

Cost of store equipment	$180,000
Life of store equipment	16 years
Estimated residual value of store equipment	$15,000
Yearly costs to operate the store, excluding depreciation of store equipment	$58,000
Yearly expected revenues—years 1–8	$85,000
Yearly expected revenues—years 9–16	$73,000

Instructions

1. Prepare a differential analysis as of October 1 presenting the proposed operation of the store for the 16 years (Alternative 1) as compared with investing in U.S. Treasury bonds (Alternative 2).
2. Based on the results disclosed by the differential analysis, should the proposal be accepted?
3. If the proposal is accepted, what would be the total estimated income from operations of the store for the 16 years?

✔ 1. Loss to replace the old machine, −$131,400

PR 25-2A Differential analysis for machine replacement proposal OBJ. 1

Lexigraphic Printing Company is considering replacing a machine that has been used in its factory for four years. Relevant data associated with the operations of the old machine and the new machine, neither of which has any estimated residual value, are as follows:

Old Machine

Cost of machine, 10-year life	$89,000
Annual depreciation (straight-line)	8,900
Annual manufacturing costs, excluding depreciation	23,600
Annual nonmanufacturing operating expenses	6,100
Annual revenue	74,200
Current estimated selling price of machine	29,700

New Machine

Purchase price of machine, six-year life	$119,700
Annual depreciation (straight-line)	19,950
Estimated annual manufacturing costs, excluding depreciation	6,900

Annual nonmanufacturing operating expenses and revenue are not expected to be affected by purchase of the new machine.

Instructions

1. Prepare a differential analysis as of April 30 comparing operations using the present machine (Alternative 1) with operations using the new machine (Alternative 2). The analysis should indicate the total differential income that would result over the six-year period if the new machine is acquired.
2. List other factors that should be considered before a final decision is reached.

PR 25-3A Differential analysis for sales promotion proposal OBJ. 1

✔ 1. Differential revenue, −$10,000

Parisian Cosmetics Company is planning a one-month campaign for September to promote sales of one of its two cosmetics products. A total of $140,000 has been budgeted for advertising, contests, redeemable coupons, and other promotional activities. The following data have been assembled for their possible usefulness in deciding which of the products to select for the campaign:

	Moisturizer	Perfume
Unit selling price	$55	$60
Unit production costs:		
Direct materials	$ 9	$14
Direct labor	3	5
Variable factory overhead	3	5
Fixed factory overhead	6	4
Total unit production costs	$21	$28
Unit variable selling expenses	16	15
Unit fixed selling expenses	12	6
Total unit costs	$49	$49
Operating income per unit	$ 6	$11

No increase in facilities would be necessary to produce and sell the increased output. It is anticipated that 22,000 additional units of moisturizer or 20,000 additional units of perfume could be sold from the campaign without changing the unit selling price of either product.

Instructions

1. Prepare a differential analysis as of August 21 to determine whether to promote moisturizer (Alternative 1) or perfume (Alternative 2).

2. ━━━━▶ The sales manager had tentatively decided to promote perfume, estimating that operating income would be increased by $80,000 ($11 operating income per unit for 20,000 units less promotion expenses of $140,000). The manager also believed that the selection of moisturizer would reduce operating income by $8,000 ($6 operating income per unit for 22,000 units less promotion expenses of $140,000). State briefly your reasons for supporting or opposing the tentative decision.

PR 25-4A Differential analysis for further processing OBJ. 1

✔ 1. Raw sugar income, $23,800

The management of Dominican Sugar Company is considering whether to process further raw sugar into refined sugar. Refined sugar can be sold for $2.20 per pound, and raw sugar can be sold without further processing for $1.40 per pound. Raw sugar is produced in batches of 42,000 pounds by processing 100,000 pounds of sugar cane, which costs $0.35 per pound of cane. Refined sugar will require additional processing costs of $0.50 per pound of raw sugar, and 1.25 pounds of raw sugar will produce 1 pound of refined sugar.

Instructions

1. Prepare a differential analysis as of March 24 to determine whether to sell raw sugar (Alternative 1) or process further into refined sugar (Alternative 2).

2. ━━━━▶ Briefly report your recommendations.

1264 Chapter 25 Differential Analysis, Product Pricing, and Activity-Based Costing

---

PR 25-5A Product pricing using the cost-plus approach concepts; differential analysis for accepting additional business
OBJ. 1, 2

✓ 2. b. Markup percentage, 44%

Crystal Displays Inc. recently began production of a new product, flat panel displays, which required the investment of $1,500,000 in assets. The costs of producing and selling 5,000 units of flat panel displays are estimated as follows:

Variable costs per unit:		Fixed costs:	
Direct materials	$120	Factory overhead	$250,000
Direct labor	30	Selling and administrative expenses	150,000
Factory overhead	50		
Selling and administrative expenses	35		
Total	$235		

Crystal Displays Inc. is currently considering establishing a selling price for flat panel displays. The president of Crystal Displays has decided to use the cost-plus approach to product pricing and has indicated that the displays must earn a 15% rate of return on invested assets.

Instructions

1. Determine the amount of desired profit from the production and sale of flat panel displays.
2. Assuming that the product cost concept is used, determine (a) the cost amount per unit, (b) the markup percentage, and (c) the selling price of flat panel displays.
3. (*Appendix*) Assuming that the total cost concept is used, determine (a) the cost amount per unit, (b) the markup percentage (rounded to two decimal places), and (c) the selling price of flat panel displays (rounded to nearest whole dollar).
4. (*Appendix*) Assuming that the variable cost concept is used, determine (a) the cost amount per unit, (b) the markup percentage (rounded to two decimal places), and (c) the selling price of flat panel displays (rounded to nearest whole dollar).
5. ━━▶ Comment on any additional considerations that could influence establishing the selling price for flat panel displays.
6. Assume that as of August 1, 3,000 units of flat panel displays have been produced and sold during the current year. Analysis of the domestic market indicates that 2,000 additional units are expected to be sold during the remainder of the year at the normal product price determined under the product cost concept. On August 3, Crystal Displays Inc. received an offer from Maple Leaf Visual Inc. for 800 units of flat panel displays at $225 each. Maple Leaf Visual Inc. will market the units in Canada under its own brand name, and no variable selling and administrative expenses associated with the sale will be incurred by Crystal Displays Inc. The additional business is not expected to affect the domestic sales of flat panel displays, and the additional units could be produced using existing factory, selling, and administrative capacity.
    a. Prepare a differential analysis of the proposed sale to Maple Leaf Visual Inc.
    b. Based on the differential analysis in part (a), should the proposal be accepted?

PR 25-6A Product pricing and profit analysis with bottleneck operations
OBJ. 3

✓ 1. High Grade, $10

Excel

Hercules Steel Company produces three grades of steel: high, good, and regular grade. Each of these products (grades) has high demand in the market, and Hercules is able to sell as much as it can produce of all three. The furnace operation is a bottleneck in the process and is running at 100% of capacity. Hercules wants to improve steel operation profitability. The variable conversion cost is $15 per process hour. The fixed cost is $200,000. In addition, the cost analyst was able to determine the following information about the three products:

	High Grade	Good Grade	Regular Grade
Budgeted units produced	5,000	5,000	5,000
Total process hours per unit	12	11	10
Furnace hours per unit	4	3	2.5
Unit selling price	$280	$270	$250
Direct materials cost per unit	$90	$84	$80

The furnace operation is part of the total process for each of these three products. Thus, for example, 4.0 of the 12.0 hours required to process High Grade steel are associated with the furnace.

Instructions

1. Determine the unit contribution margin for each product.
2. Provide an analysis to determine the relative product profitability, assuming that the furnace is a bottleneck.

PR 25-7A Activity-based costing   OBJ. 4

✔ 2. Brown sugar total activity cost, $138,550

Excel

Pure Cane Sugar Company manufactures three products (white sugar, brown sugar, and powdered sugar) in a continuous production process. Senior management has asked the controller to conduct an activity-based costing study. The controller identified the amount of factory overhead required by the critical activities of the organization as follows:

Activity	Activity Costs
Production	$247,500
Setup	48,000
Inspection	12,500
Shipping	69,300
Customer service	27,600
Total	$404,900

The activity bases identified for each activity are as follows:

Activity	Activity Base
Production	Machine hours
Setup	Number of setups
Inspection	Number of inspections
Shipping	Number of customer orders
Customer service	Number of customer service requests

The activity-base usage quantities and units produced for the three products were determined from corporate records as follows:

	Machine Hours	Number of Setups	Number of Inspections	Number of Customer Orders	Number of Customer Service Requests	Units
White sugar	2,000	50	100	410	25	8,000
Brown sugar	1,250	70	160	1,100	200	5,000
Powdered sugar	1,250	80	240	800	120	5,000
Total	4,500	200	500	2,310	345	18,000

Each product requires 0.25 machine hour per unit.

Instructions

1. Determine the activity rate for each activity.
2. Determine the total and per-unit activity costs for all three products.
3. Why aren't the activity unit costs equal across all three products since they require the same machine time per unit?

Problems: Series B

PR 25-1B Differential analysis involving opportunity costs **OBJ. 1**

✓ 1. Income from investing in bonds, $518,000

On July 1, Coastal Distribution Company is considering leasing a building and buying the necessary equipment to operate a public warehouse. Alternatively, the company could use the funds to invest in $740,000 of 5% U.S. Treasury bonds that mature in 14 years. The bonds could be purchased at face value. The following data have been assembled:

Cost of equipment	$740,000
Life of equipment	14 years
Estimated residual value of equipment	$75,000
Yearly costs to operate the warehouse, excluding depreciation of equipment	$175,000
Yearly expected revenues—years 1–7	$280,000
Yearly expected revenues—years 8–14	$240,000

Instructions

1. Prepare a differential analysis as of July 1 presenting the proposed operation of the warehouse for the 14 years (Alternative 1) as compared with investing in U.S. Treasury bonds (Alternative 2).
2. Based on the results disclosed by the differential analysis, should the proposal be accepted?
3. If the proposal is accepted, what is the total estimated income from operations of the warehouse for the 14 years?

PR 25-2B Differential analysis for machine replacement proposal **OBJ. 1**

✓ 1. Loss to replace the old machine, –$64,500

Flint Tooling Company is considering replacing a machine that has been used in its factory for two years. Relevant data associated with the operations of the old machine and the new machine, neither of which has any estimated residual value, are as follows:

Old Machine

Cost of machine, eight-year life	$38,000
Annual depreciation (straight-line)	4,750
Annual manufacturing costs, excluding depreciation	12,400
Annual nonmanufacturing operating expenses	2,700
Annual revenue	32,400
Current estimated selling price of the machine	12,900

New Machine

Cost of machine, six-year life	$57,000
Annual depreciation (straight-line)	9,500
Estimated annual manufacturing costs, exclusive of depreciation	3,400

Annual nonmanufacturing operating expenses and revenue are not expected to be affected by purchase of the new machine.

Instructions

1. Prepare a differential analysis as of November 8 comparing operations using the present machine (Alternative 1) with operations using the new machine (Alternative 2). The analysis should indicate the differential income that would result over the six-year period if the new machine is acquired.
2. ✏ List other factors that should be considered before a final decision is reached.

Chapter 25 Differential Analysis, Product Pricing, and Activity-Based Costing   **1267**

✔ 1. Differential revenue, $105,000

PR 25-3B   **Differential analysis for sales promotion proposal**   OBJ. 1

Sole Mates Inc. is planning a one-month campaign for July to promote sales of one of its two shoe products. A total of $100,000 has been budgeted for advertising, contests, redeemable coupons, and other promotional activities. The following data have been assembled for their possible usefulness in deciding which of the products to select for the campaign:

	Tennis Shoe	Walking Shoe
Unit selling price	$85	$100
Unit production costs:		
Direct materials	$19	$ 32
Direct labor	8	12
Variable factory overhead	7	5
Fixed factory overhead	16	11
Total unit production costs	$50	$ 60
Unit variable selling expenses	6	10
Unit fixed selling expenses	20	15
Total unit costs	$76	$ 85
Operating income per unit	$ 9	$ 15

No increase in facilities would be necessary to produce and sell the increased output. It is anticipated that 7,000 additional units of tennis shoes or 7,000 additional units of walking shoes could be sold without changing the unit selling price of either product.

Instructions

1. Prepare a differential analysis as of June 19 to determine whether to promote tennis shoes (Alternative 1) or walking shoes (Alternative 2).

2. The sales manager had tentatively decided to promote walking shoes, estimating that operating income would be increased by $5,000 ($15 operating income per unit for 7,000 units less promotion expenses of $100,000). The manager also believed that the selection of tennis shoes would reduce operating income by $37,000 ($9 operating income per unit for 7,000 units less promotion expenses of $100,000). State briefly your reasons for supporting or opposing the tentative decision.

PR 25-4B   **Differential analysis for further processing**   OBJ. 1

✔ 1. Ingot income, $35,500

The management of International Aluminum Co. is considering whether to process aluminum ingot further into rolled aluminum. Rolled aluminum can be sold for $2,200 per ton, and ingot can be sold without further processing for $1,100 per ton. Ingot is produced in batches of 80 tons by smelting 500 tons of bauxite, which costs $105 per ton of bauxite. Rolled aluminum will require additional processing costs of $620 per ton of ingot, and 1.25 tons of ingot will produce 1 ton of rolled aluminum (due to trim losses).

Instructions

1. Prepare a differential analysis as of February 5 to determine whether to sell aluminum ingot (Alternative 1) or process further into rolled aluminum (Alternative 2).

2. Briefly report your recommendations.

1268 Chapter 25 Differential Analysis, Product Pricing, and Activity-Based Costing

PR 25-5B Product pricing using the cost-plus approach concepts; differential analysis for accepting additional business
OBJ. 1, 2

✔ 2. b. Markup percentage, 30%

Night Glow Inc. recently began production of a new product, the halogen light, which required the investment of $600,000 in assets. The costs of producing and selling 10,000 halogen lights are estimated as follows:

Variable costs per unit:		Fixed costs:	
Direct materials	$32	Factory overhead	$180,000
Direct labor	12	Selling and administrative expenses	80,000
Factory overhead	8		
Selling and administrative expenses	7		
Total	$59		

Night Glow Inc. is currently considering establishing a selling price for the halogen light. The president of Night Glow Inc. has decided to use the cost-plus approach to product pricing and has indicated that the halogen light must earn a 10% rate of return on invested assets.

Instructions

1. Determine the amount of desired profit from the production and sale of the halogen light.
2. Assuming that the product cost concept is used, determine (a) the cost amount per unit, (b) the markup percentage, and (c) the selling price of the halogen light.
3. (*Appendix*) Assuming that the total cost concept is used, determine (a) the cost amount per unit, (b) the markup percentage (rounded to two decimal places), and (c) the selling price of the halogen light (rounded to the nearest whole dollar).
4. (*Appendix*) Assuming that the variable cost concept is used, determine (a) the cost amount per unit, (b) the markup percentage (rounded to two decimal places), and (c) the selling price of the halogen light (rounded to nearest whole dollar).
5. ➤ Comment on any additional considerations that could influence establishing the selling price for the halogen light.
6. Assume that as of September 1, 7,000 units of halogen light have been produced and sold during the current year. Analysis of the domestic market indicates that 3,000 additional units of the halogen light are expected to be sold during the remainder of the year at the normal product price determined under the product cost concept. On September 5, Night Glow Inc. received an offer from Tokyo Lighting Inc. for 1,600 units of the halogen light at $57 each. Tokyo Lighting Inc. will market the units in Japan under its own brand name, and no variable selling and administrative expenses associated with the sale will be incurred by Night Glow Inc. The additional business is not expected to affect the domestic sales of the halogen light, and the additional units could be produced using existing productive, selling, and administrative capacity.
   a. Prepare a differential analysis of the proposed sale to Tokyo Lighting Inc.
   b. Based on the differential analysis in part (a), should the proposal be accepted?

PR 25-6B Product pricing and profit analysis with bottleneck operations
OBJ. 3

✔ 1. Ethylene, $15

Wilmington Chemical Company produces three products: ethylene, butane, and ester. Each of these products has high demand in the market, and Wilmington Chemical is able to sell as much as it can produce of all three. The reaction operation is a bottleneck in the process and is running at 100% of capacity. Wilmington wants to improve chemical operation profitability. The variable conversion cost is $10 per process hour. The fixed cost is $400,000. In addition, the cost analyst was able to determine the following information about the three products:

	Ethylene	Butane	Ester
Budgeted units produced	9,000	9,000	9,000
Total process hours per unit	4.0	4.0	3.0
Reactor hours per unit	1.5	1.0	0.5
Unit selling price	$170	$155	$130
Direct materials cost per unit	$115	$88	$85

The reaction operation is part of the total process for each of these three products. Thus, for example, 1.5 of the 4.0 hours required to process ethylene is associated with the reactor.

Instructions

1. Determine the unit contribution margin for each product.
2. Provide an analysis to determine the relative product profitabilities, assuming that the reactor is a bottleneck.

PR 25-7B Activity-based costing OBJ. 4

✔ 2. Newsprint total activity cost, $139,650

Southeastern Paper Company manufactures three products (computer paper, newsprint, and specialty paper) in a continuous production process. Senior management has asked the controller to conduct an activity-based costing study. The controller identified the amount of factory overhead required by the critical activities of the organization as follows:

Activity	Activity Costs
Production	$220,000
Setup	117,000
Moving	21,000
Shipping	105,000
Product engineering	102,000
Total	$565,000

The activity bases identified for each activity are as follows:

Activity	Activity Base
Production	Machine hours
Setup	Number of setups
Moving	Number of moves
Shipping	Number of customer orders
Product engineering	Number of test runs

The activity-base usage quantities and units produced for the three products were determined from corporate records and are as follows:

	Machine Hours	Number of Setups	Number of Moves	Number of Customer Orders	Number of Test Runs	Units
Computer paper	400	80	230	310	50	1,000
Newsprint	500	30	70	140	15	1,250
Specialty paper	200	150	300	550	105	500
Total	1,100	260	600	1,000	170	2,750

Each product requires 0.4 machine hour per unit.

Instructions

1. Determine the activity rate for each activity.
2. Determine the total and per-unit activity cost for all three products.
3. Why aren't the activity unit costs equal across all three products, since they require the same machine time per unit?

Cases & Projects

CP 25-1   Ethics in Action

Aaron McKinney is a cost accountant for Majik Systems Inc. Martin Dodd, vice president of marketing, has asked Aaron to meet with representatives of Majik Systems' major competitor to discuss product cost data. Martin indicates that the sharing of these data will enable Majik Systems to determine a fair and equitable price for its products.

✏ Would it be ethical for Aaron to attend the meeting and share the relevant cost data? Why or why not?

CP 25-2   Team Activity

Many businesses are offering their products and services over the Internet. Some of these companies and their Internet addresses follow:

Company Name	Internet Address (URL)	Product
Delta Air Lines	www.delta.com	Airline tickets
Amazon.com	www.amazon.com	Merchandise
Dell Inc.	www.dell.com	Personal computers

In groups of three, assign each person in your group to one of the Internet sites listed. For each site, determine the following:

1. A product (or service) description
2. A product price
3. Based on your responses to parts (1) and (2), along with the description of the company's business, identify the potential costs that are required to provide the product selected in part (1) and categorize them as fixed or variable.
4. Which product do you believe has the largest contribution margin per incremental unit sold?

CP 25-3   Communication

The following conversation took place between Juanita Jackson, vice president of marketing, and Les Miles, controller of Diamond Computer Company:

Juanita: I am really excited about our new computer coming out. I think it will be a real market success.

Les: I'm really glad you think so. I know that our success will be determined by our price. If our price is too high, our competitors will be the ones with the market success.

Juanita: Don't worry about it. We'll just mark our product cost up by 25%, and it will all work out. I know we'll make money at those markups. By the way, what does the estimated product cost look like?

Les: Well, there's the rub. The product cost looks as if it's going to come in at around $1,200. With a 25% markup, that will give us a selling price of $1,500.

Juanita: I see your concern. That's a little high. Our research indicates that computer prices are dropping and that this type of computer should be selling for around $1,250 when we release it to the market.

Les: I'm not sure what to do.

Juanita: Let me see if I can help. How much of the $1,200 is fixed cost?

Les: About $200.

Juanita: There you go. The fixed cost is sunk. We don't need to consider it in our pricing decision. If we reduce the product cost by $200, the new price with a 25% markup would be right at $1,250. Boy, I was really worried for a minute there. I knew something wasn't right.

✏ Write a brief memo from Les Miles to Juanita Jackson (1) responding to her solution to the pricing problem and (2) explaining how target costing could be used to solve the problem.

CP 25-4 Decision on accepting additional business

A manager of Varden Sporting Goods Company is considering accepting an order from an overseas customer. This customer has requested an order for 20,000 dozen golf balls at a price of $22 per dozen. The variable cost to manufacture a dozen golf balls is $18 per dozen. The full cost is $25 per dozen. Varden has a normal selling price of $35 per dozen. Varden's plant has just enough excess capacity on the second shift to make the overseas order.

➤ What are some considerations in accepting or rejecting this order?

CP 25-5 Accept business at a special price for a service company

If you are not familiar with **Priceline.com Inc.**, go to its website. Assume that an individual "names a price" of $85 on Priceline.com for a room in Nashville, Tennessee, on August 22. Assume that August 22 is a Saturday, with low expected room demand in Nashville at a **Marriott International, Inc.**, hotel, so there is excess room capacity. The fully allocated cost per room per day is assumed from hotel records as follows:

Housekeeping labor cost*	$ 38
Hotel depreciation expense	43
Cost of room supplies (soap, paper, etc.)	8
Laundry labor and material cost*	10
Cost of desk staff	6
Utility cost (mostly air conditioning)	5
Total cost per room per day	$110

*Both housekeeping and laundry staff include many part-time workers so that the workload is variable to demand.

➤ Should Marriott accept the customer bid for a night in Nashville on August 22 at a price of $85? Why or why not?

CP 25-6 Identifying product cost distortion

Peachtree Beverage Company manufactures soft drinks. Information about two products is as follows:

	Volume	Sales Price per Case	Gross Profit per Case
Jamaican Punch	10,000 cases	$30	$12
King Kola	800,000 cases	30	12

It is known that both products have the same direct materials and direct labor costs per case. Peachtree Beverage allocates factory overhead to products by using a single plant-wide factory overhead rate, based on direct labor cost. Additional information about the two products is as follows:

Jamaican Punch: Requires extensive process preparation and sterilization prior to processing. The ingredients are from Jamaica, requiring complex import controls. The formulation is complex, and it is thus difficult to maintain quality. Finally, the product is produced in small production run sizes.

King Kola: Requires minor process preparation and sterilization prior to processing. The ingredients are acquired locally. The formulation is simple, and it is easy to maintain quality. Finally, the product is produced in large production run sizes.

Explain the weakness in the per-case product profitability report in light of the additional data.

CHAPTER 26
Capital Investment Analysis

Concepts and Principles
Chapter 18 *Introduction to Managerial Accounting*

Developing Information

COST SYSTEMS	COST BEHAVIOR
Chapter 19 *Job Order Costing* **Chapter 20** *Process Costing*	**Chapter 21** *Cost-Volume-Profit Analysis*

Decision Making

EVALUATING PERFORMANCE	COMPARING ALTERNATIVES
Chapter 22 *Budgeting* **Chapter 23** *Variances from Standard Costs*	**Chapter 24** *Decentralized Operations* **Chapter 25** *Differential Analysis, Product Pricing, and Activity-Based Costing* **Chapter 26** *Capital Investment Analysis*

CHAPTER 26

Vail Resorts, Inc.

Why are you paying tuition, studying this text, and spending time and money on a higher education? Most people believe that the money and time spent now will return them more earnings in the future. That is, the cost of higher education is an investment in your future earning ability. How would you know if this investment is worth it?

One method would be for you to compare the cost of a higher education with the estimated increase in your future earning power. The bigger the difference between your expected future earnings and the cost of your education, the better the investment. A business also evaluates its investments in fixed assets by comparing the initial cost of the investment to its future earnings and cash flows.

For example, **Vail Resorts, Inc.**, is one of the largest ski resort owner-operators in the world. It is known for its Vail, Breckenridge, and Keystone ski resorts, among others. A ski resort requires significant investments in property and equipment. Thus, Vail routinely makes major investments in new or improved amenities, lodging, retail, lifts, snowmaking and grooming equipment, and technology infrastructure. These investments are evaluated by their ability to enhance cash flows.

In this chapter, the methods used to make investment decisions, which may involve thousands, millions, or even billions of dollars, are described and illustrated. The similarities and differences among the most commonly used methods of evaluating investment proposals, as well as the benefits of each method, are emphasized. Factors that can complicate the analysis are also discussed.

Learning Objectives

After studying this chapter, you should be able to:

Example Exercises (EE) are shown in green.

Obj. 1 Explain the nature and importance of capital investment analysis.

Nature of Capital Investment Analysis

Obj. 2 Evaluate capital investment proposals, using the average rate of return and cash payback methods.

Methods Not Using Present Values
Average Rate of Return Method — EE 26-1
Cash Payback Method — EE 26-2

Obj. 3 Evaluate capital investment proposals, using the net present value and internal rate of return methods.

Methods Using Present Values
Present Value Concepts
Net Present Value Method and Index — EE 26-3
Internal Rate of Return Method — EE 26-4

Obj. 4 List and describe additional factors in capital investment analysis.

Additional Factors in Capital Investment Analysis
Income Tax
Unequal Proposal Lives — EE 26-5
Lease Versus Capital Investment
Uncertainty
Changes in Price Levels
Qualitative Considerations
Capital Investment for Sustainability

Obj. 5 Diagram the capital rationing process.

Capital Rationing

At a Glance 26 — Page 1292

Obj. 1 Explain the nature and importance of capital investment analysis.

Nature of Capital Investment Analysis

Companies use capital investment analysis to evaluate long-term investments. **Capital investment analysis** (or *capital budgeting*) is the process by which management plans, evaluates, and controls investments in fixed assets. Capital investments use funds and affect operations for many years and must earn a reasonable rate of return. Thus, capital investment decisions are some of the most important decisions that management makes.

Capital investment evaluation methods can be grouped into the following categories:

Methods That Do Not Use Present Values

- Average rate of return method
- Cash payback method

Methods That Use Present Values

- Net present value method
- Internal rate of return method

The two methods that use present values consider the time value of money. The **time value of money concept** recognizes that a dollar today is worth more than a dollar tomorrow because today's dollar can earn interest.

Link to Vail Resorts, Inc.
In 2014, **Vail Resorts, Inc.**, purchased the Park City Mountain Resort and ski area in Park City, Utah, for $182.5 million.

Business Connection

BUSINESS USE OF INVESTMENT ANALYSIS METHODS

A survey of chief financial officers of large U.S. companies reported their use of the four investment methods as follows:

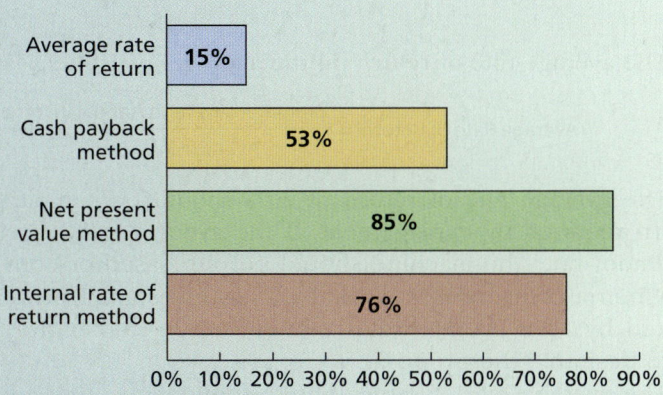

Percentage of Respondents Reporting the Use of the Method as "Always" or "Often"

- Average rate of return: 15%
- Cash payback method: 53%
- Net present value method: 85%
- Internal rate of return method: 76%

Source: Patricia A. Ryan and Glenn P. Ryan, "Capital Budgeting Practice of the Fortune 1000: How Have Things Changed?" *Journal of Business and Management* (Winter 2002).

Methods Not Using Present Values

Obj. 2 Evaluate capital investment proposals, using the average rate of return and cash payback methods.

The methods not using present values are often useful in evaluating capital investment proposals that have relatively short useful lives. In such cases, the timing of the cash flows (the time value of money) is less important.

Because the methods not using present values are easy to use, they are often used to screen proposals. Minimum standards for accepting proposals are set, and proposals not meeting these standards are dropped. If a proposal meets the minimum standards, it may be subject to further analysis using the present value methods.

Average Rate of Return Method

The **average rate of return**, sometimes called the *accounting rate of return*, measures the average income as a percent of the average investment. The average rate of return is computed as follows:

$$\text{Average Rate of Return} = \frac{\text{Estimated Average Annual Income}}{\text{Average Investment}}$$

In the preceding equation, the numerator is the average of the annual income expected to be earned from the investment over its life, after deducting depreciation. The denominator is the average investment (book value) over the life of the investment. Assuming straight-line depreciation, the average investment is computed as follows:

$$\text{Average Investment} = \frac{\text{Initial Cost} + \text{Residual Value}}{2}$$

To illustrate, assume that management is evaluating the purchase of a new machine as follows:

Cost of new machine	$500,000
Residual value	$0
Estimated total income from machine	$200,000
Expected useful life	4 years

The average estimated annual income from the machine is $50,000 ($200,000 ÷ 4 years). The average investment is $250,000, computed as follows:

$$\text{Average Investment} = \frac{\text{Initial Cost} + \text{Residual Value}}{2} = \frac{\$500,000 + \$0}{2} = \$250,000$$

The average rate of return on the average investment is 20%, computed as follows:

$$\text{Average Rate of Return} = \frac{\text{Estimated Average Annual Income}}{\text{Average Investment}} = \frac{\$50,000}{\$250,000} = 20\%$$

The average rate of return of 20% should be compared to the minimum rate of return required by management. If the average rate of return equals or exceeds the minimum rate, the machine should be purchased or considered for further analysis.

When a company has several capital investment proposals, the proposals can be ranked by their average rates of return. The higher the average rate of return, the more desirable the proposal.

The average rate of return has the following three advantages:

- It is easy to compute.
- It includes the entire amount of income earned over the life of the proposal.
- It emphasizes accounting income, which is often used by investors and creditors in evaluating management performance.

The average rate of return has the following two disadvantages:

- It does not directly consider the expected cash flows from the proposal.
- It does not directly consider the timing of the expected cash flows.

Note: The average rate of return method considers the amount of income earned over the life of a proposal.

Example Exercise 26-1 Average Rate of Return — Obj. 2

Determine the average rate of return for a project that is estimated to yield total income of $273,600 over three years, has a cost of $690,000, and has a $70,000 residual value.

Follow My Example 26-1

Estimated average annual income	$91,200 ($273,600 ÷ 3 years)
Average investment	$380,000 ($690,000 + $70,000) ÷ 2
Average rate of return	24% ($91,200 ÷ $380,000)

Practice Exercises: PE 26-1A, PE 26-1B

Link to Vail Resorts, Inc.

Vail Resorts' average rate of return on its property, plant, and equipment is slightly more than 10%.

Cash Payback Method

A capital investment uses cash and must return cash in the future to be successful. The expected period of time between the date of an investment and the recovery in cash of the amount invested is the **cash payback period**.

When annual net cash inflows are equal, the cash payback period is computed as follows:

$$\text{Cash Payback Period} = \frac{\text{Initial Cost}}{\text{Annual Net Cash Inflow}}$$

To illustrate, assume that management is evaluating the purchase of the following new machine:

Cost of new machine	$200,000
Cash revenues from machine per year	50,000
Expenses of machine per year (incl. depreciation)	30,000
Depreciation per year	20,000

To simplify, the revenues and expenses other than depreciation are assumed to be in cash. Hence, the expected net cash inflow per year from use of the machine is as follows:

Net cash inflow per year:		
Cash revenues from machine		$50,000
Less cash expenses of machine:		
Expenses of machine (incl. depreciation)	$30,000	
Less depreciation	20,000	10,000
Net cash inflow per year		$40,000

The time required for the net cash flow to equal the cost of the new machine is the payback period. Thus, the estimated cash payback period for the investment is five years, computed as follows:

$$\text{Cash Payback Period} = \frac{\text{Initial Cost}}{\text{Annual Net Cash Inflow}} = \frac{\$200,000}{\$40,000} = 5 \text{ years}$$

In the preceding illustration, the annual net cash inflows are equal ($40,000 per year). When the annual net cash inflows are not equal, the cash payback period is determined by adding the annual net cash inflows until the cumulative total equals the initial cost of the proposed investment.

To illustrate, assume that a proposed investment has an initial cost of $400,000. The annual and cumulative net cash inflows over the proposal's six-year life are as follows:

Year	Net Cash Flow	Cumulative Net Cash Flow
1	$ 60,000	$ 60,000
2	80,000	140,000
3	105,000	245,000
4	155,000	400,000
5	100,000	500,000
6	90,000	590,000

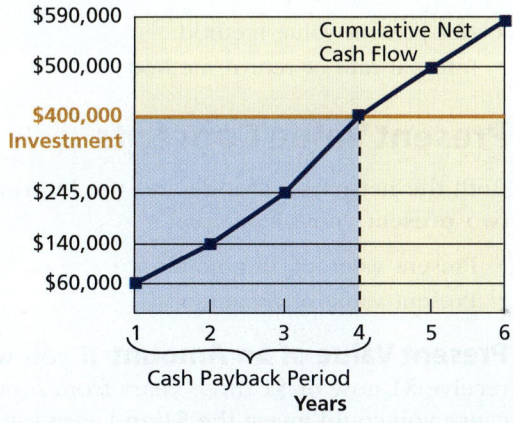

The cumulative net cash flow at the end of Year 4 equals the initial cost of the investment, $400,000. Thus, the payback period is four years.

If the initial cost of the proposed investment had been $450,000, the cash payback period would occur during Year 5. Because $100,000 of net cash flow is expected during Year 5, the additional $50,000 to increase the cumulative total to $450,000 occurs halfway through the year ($50,000 ÷ $100,000). Thus, the cash payback period would be 4½ years.[1]

A short cash payback period is desirable. This is because the sooner cash is recovered, the sooner it can be reinvested in other projects. In addition, there is less chance of losses from changing economic or business conditions. A short cash payback period is also desirable for quickly repaying any debt used to purchase the investment.

Link to Vail Resorts, Inc.
The ski operations are seasonal in nature and typically run from mid-November to mid-April. To increase cash flows, **Vail Resorts** promotes nonski activities in the summer months, including sightseeing, mountain biking, and zip tours.

[1] Unless otherwise stated, net cash inflows are received uniformly throughout the year.

The cash payback method has the following two advantages:

- It is simple to use and understand.
- It analyzes cash flows, which provides insight into how long it takes to return cash equal to the original investment.

The cash payback method has the following two disadvantages:

- It ignores cash flows occurring after the payback period.
- It does not use present value concepts in valuing cash flows occurring in different periods.

Example Exercise 26-2 Cash Payback Period *Obj. 2*

A project has estimated annual net cash flows of $30,000. It is estimated to cost $105,000. Determine the cash payback period.

Follow My Example 26-2

3.5 years ($105,000 ÷ $30,000)

Practice Exercises: PE 26-2A, PE 26-2B

Obj. 3 Evaluate capital investment proposals, using the net present value and internal rate of return methods.

Methods Using Present Values

An investment in fixed assets may be viewed as purchasing a series of net cash flows over a period of time. The timing of when the net cash flows will be received is important in determining the value of a proposed investment.

Present value methods use the amount and timing of the net cash flows in evaluating an investment. The two methods of evaluating capital investments using present values are as follows:

- Net present value method
- Internal rate of return method

Present Value Concepts

Both the net present value and the internal rate of return methods use the following two **present value concepts**:

- Present value of an amount
- Present value of an annuity

Present Value of an Amount If you were given the choice, would you prefer to receive $1 now or $1 three years from now? You should prefer to receive $1 now, because you could invest the $1 and earn interest for three years. As a result, the amount you would have after three years would be greater than $1.

To illustrate, assume that you have $1 to invest as follows:

Amount to be invested	$1
Period to be invested	3 years
Interest rate	12%

After one year, the $1 earns interest of $0.12 ($1 × 12%) and, thus, will grow to $1.12 ($1 × 1.12). In the second year, the $1.12 earns 12% interest of $0.134 ($1.12 × 12%) and, thus, will grow to $1.254 ($1.12 × 1.12) by the end of the second year. This process of interest earning interest is called *compounding*. By the end of the third year, your $1 investment will grow to $1.404 as shown in Exhibit 1.

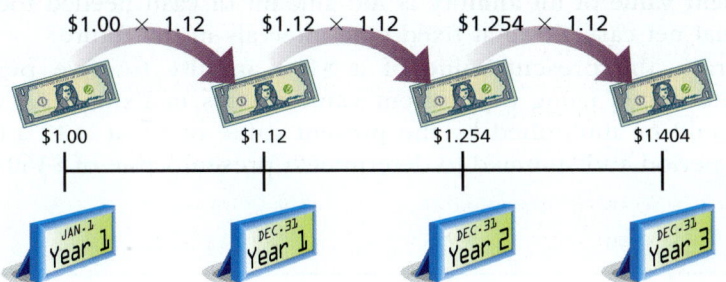

EXHIBIT 1

Compound Amount of $1 for Three Periods at 12%

On January 1, Year 1, what is the present value of $1.404 to be received on December 31, Year 3? This is a present value question. The answer can be determined with the aid of a present value of $1 table. For example, the partial table in Exhibit 2 indicates that the present value of $1 to be received in three years with earnings compounded at the rate of 12% per year is 0.712.[2]

Present Value of $1 at Compound Interest

Year	6%	10%	12%	15%	20%
1	0.943	0.909	0.893	0.870	0.833
2	0.890	0.826	0.797	0.756	0.694
3	0.840	0.751	0.712	0.658	0.579
4	0.792	0.683	0.636	0.572	0.482
5	0.747	0.621	0.567	0.497	0.402
6	0.705	0.564	0.507	0.432	0.335
7	0.665	0.513	0.452	0.376	0.279
8	0.627	0.467	0.404	0.327	0.233
9	0.592	0.424	0.361	0.284	0.194
10	0.558	0.386	0.322	0.247	0.162

EXHIBIT 2

Partial Present Value of $1 Table

Multiplying 0.712 by $1.404 yields $1 as follows:

Present Value		Amount to Be Received in 3 Years		Present Value of $1 to Be Received in 3 Years (from Exhibit 2)
$1	=	$1.404	×	0.712

That is, the present value of $1.404 to be received in three years using a compound interest rate of 12% is $1, as shown in Exhibit 3.

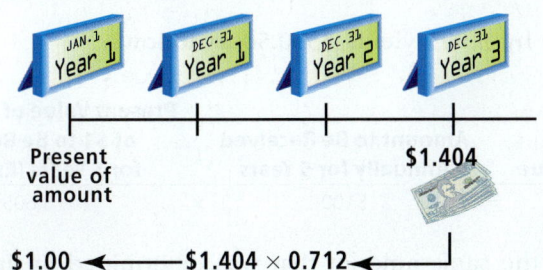

EXHIBIT 3

Present Value of an Amount of $1.404

Present Value of an Annuity An **annuity** is a series of equal net cash flows at fixed time intervals. Annuities are very common in business. Cash payments for monthly rent, salaries, and bond interest are all examples of annuities.

[2] The present value factors in the table are rounded to three decimal places. More complete tables of present values are in Appendix A.

The **present value of an annuity** is the amount of cash needed today to yield a series of equal net cash flows at fixed time intervals in the future.

To illustrate, the present value of a $100 annuity for five periods at 12% could be determined using the present value factors in Exhibit 2. Each $100 net cash flow could be multiplied by the present value of $1 at a 12% factor for the appropriate period and summed to determine a present value of $360.50, as shown in Exhibit 4.

EXHIBIT 4

Present Value of a $100 Amount for Five Consecutive Periods

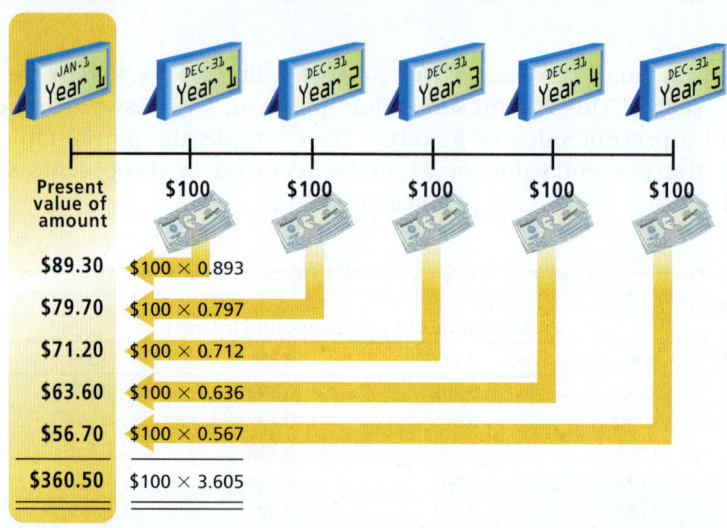

Using a present value of an annuity table is a simpler approach. Exhibit 5 is a partial table of present value annuity factors.[3]

The present value factors in the table shown in Exhibit 5 are the sum of the present value of $1 factors in Exhibit 2 for the number of annuity periods. Thus, 3.605 in the annuity table (Exhibit 5) is the sum of the five present value of $1 factors at 12% from Exhibit 2, computed as follows:

	Present Value of $1 (Exhibit 2)
Present value of $1 for 1 year @12%	0.893
Present value of $1 for 2 years @12%	0.797
Present value of $1 for 3 years @12%	0.712
Present value of $1 for 4 years @12%	0.636
Present value of $1 for 5 years @12%	0.567
Present value of an annuity of $1 for 5 years (from Exhibit 5)	3.605

Multiplying $100 by 3.605 yields $360.50 as follows:

Present Value		Amount to Be Received Annually for 5 Years		Present Value of an Annuity of $1 to Be Received for 5 Years (Exhibit 5)
$360.50	=	$100	×	3.605

Thus, $360.50 is the same amount that was determined in the preceding illustration by five successive multiplications.

---

[3] The present value factors in the table are rounded to three decimal places. More complete tables of present values are in Appendix A.

EXHIBIT 5
Partial Present Value of an Annuity Table

| Year | \multicolumn{5}{c}{Present Value of an Annuity of $1 at Compound Interest} |
	6%	10%	12%	15%	20%
1	0.943	0.909	0.893	0.870	0.833
2	1.833	1.736	1.690	1.626	1.528
3	2.673	2.487	2.402	2.283	2.106
4	3.465	3.170	3.037	2.855	2.589
5	4.212	3.791	**3.605**	3.353	2.991
6	4.917	4.355	4.111	3.785	3.326
7	5.582	4.868	4.564	4.160	3.605
8	6.210	5.335	4.968	4.487	3.837
9	6.802	5.759	5.328	4.772	4.031
10	7.360	6.145	5.650	5.019	4.192

Net Present Value Method and Index

The net present value method and present value index are often used in combination, as illustrated in this section.

Net Present Value Method

The **net present value method** compares the amount to be invested with the present value of the net cash inflows. It is sometimes called the *discounted cash flow method*.

The interest rate (return) used in net present value analysis is the company's minimum desired rate of return. This rate, sometimes termed the *hurdle rate*, is based on such factors as the purpose of the investment and the cost of obtaining funds for the investment. If the present value of the cash inflows equals or exceeds the amount to be invested, the proposal is desirable.

To illustrate, assume the following data for a proposed investment in new equipment:

Cost of new equipment	$200,000
Expected useful life	5 years
Minimum desired rate of return	10%
Expected cash flows to be received each year:	
Year 1	$ 70,000
Year 2	60,000
Year 3	50,000
Year 4	40,000
Year 5	40,000
Total expected cash flows	$260,000

Note

The net present value method compares an investment's initial cash outflow with the present value of its cash inflows.

The present value of the net cash flow for each year is computed by multiplying the net cash flow for the year by the present value factor of $1 for that year, as follows:

Year	Present Value of $1 at 10%	×	Net Cash Flow	=	Present Value of Net Cash Flow
1	0.909		$ 70,000		$ 63,630
2	0.826		60,000		49,560
3	0.751		50,000		37,550
4	0.683		40,000		27,320
5	0.621		40,000		24,840
Total			$260,000		$202,900
Less amount to be invested					200,000
Net present value					$ 2,900

The preceding computations are also graphically illustrated in Exhibit 6.

EXHIBIT 6

Present Value of Equipment Cash Flows

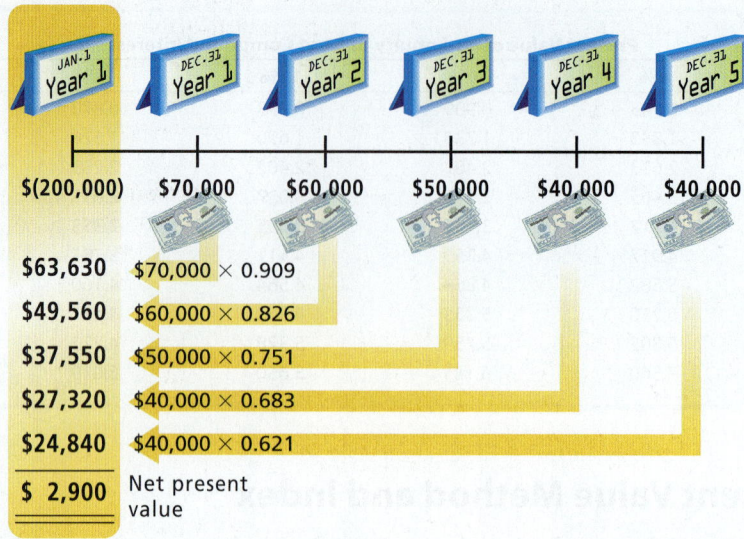

The net present value of $2,900 indicates that the purchase of the new equipment is expected to recover the investment and provide more than the minimum rate of return of 10%. Thus, the purchase of the new equipment is desirable.

The net present value method has the following three advantages:

- It considers the cash flows of the investment.
- It considers the time value of money.
- It can rank projects with equal lives using the present value index, as shown in the next section.

The net present value method has the following two disadvantages:

- It has more complex computations than methods that don't use present value.
- It assumes that the cash flows can be reinvested at the minimum desired rate of return, which may not be valid.

Present Value Index

When capital investment funds are limited and the proposals involve different investments, a ranking of the proposals can be prepared using a present value index. The **present value index** is computed as follows:

$$\text{Present Value Index} = \frac{\text{Total Present Value of Net Cash Flow}}{\text{Amount to Be Invested}}$$

The present value index for the investment in the preceding illustration is 1.0145, computed as follows:

$$\text{Present Value Index} = \frac{\$202,900}{\$200,000} = 1.0145$$

Assume that a company is considering three proposals. The net present value and the present value index for each proposal are as follows:

	Proposal A	Proposal B	Proposal C
Total present value of net cash flow	$107,000	$86,400	$86,400
Less amount to be invested	100,000	80,000	90,000
Net present value	$ 7,000	$ 6,400	$ (3,600)
Present value index:			
Proposal A ($107,000 ÷ $100,000)	1.07		
Proposal B ($86,400 ÷ $80,000)		1.08	
Proposal C ($86,400 ÷ $90,000)			0.96

Link to Vail Resorts, Inc.

Vail Resorts uses present values in determining the value of assets and liabilities acquired in business acquisitions.

Source: Vail Resorts, Inc., Form 10-K for the Fiscal Year Ended July 31, 2015.

A project will have a present value index greater than 1 when the net present value is positive. This is the case for Proposals A and B. When the net present value is negative, the present value index will be less than 1, as is the case for Proposal C.

Although Proposal A has the largest net present value, the present value indices indicate that it is not as desirable as Proposal B. That is, Proposal B returns $1.08 present value per dollar invested, whereas Proposal A returns only $1.07. Proposal B requires an investment of $80,000, compared to an investment of $100,000 for Proposal A. The possible use of the $20,000 difference between Proposals A and B investments should also be considered before making a final decision.

Example Exercise 26-3 Net Present Value   Obj. 3

A project has estimated annual net cash flows of $50,000 for seven years and is estimated to cost $240,000. Assume a minimum acceptable rate of return of 12%. Using Exhibit 5, determine (a) the net present value of the project and (b) the present value index, rounded to two decimal places.

Follow My Example 26-3

a. ($11,800)   [($50,000 × 4.564) − $240,000]
b. 0.95   ($228,200 ÷ $240,000)

Practice Exercises: PE 26-3A, PE 26-3B

Internal Rate of Return Method

The **internal rate of return (IRR) method** determines the rate of return wherein the net present value of a project is zero. This method, sometimes called the *time-adjusted rate of return method*, starts with the proposal's net cash flows and works backward to estimate the proposal's expected rate of return.

To illustrate, assume that management is evaluating the following proposal to purchase new equipment:

Cost of new equipment	$33,530
Yearly expected cash flows to be received	$10,000
Expected life	5 years
Minimum desired rate of return	12%

The present value of the net cash flows, using the present value of an annuity table in Exhibit 5, is $2,520, as shown in Exhibit 7.

Annual net cash flow (at the end of each of five years)	$10,000
Present value of an annuity of $1 at 12% for five years (Exhibit 5)	× 3.605
Present value of annual net cash flows	$36,050
Less amount to be invested	33,530
Net present value	$ 2,520

EXHIBIT 7

Net Present Value Analysis at 12%

Dynamic Exhibit

In Exhibit 7, the $36,050 present value of the cash inflows, based on a 12% rate of return, is greater than the $33,530 to be invested. Thus, the internal rate of return must be greater than 12%. Through trial and error, the rate of return equating the $33,530 cost of the investment with the present value of the net cash flows can be determined to be 15%, as shown in Exhibit 8.

EXHIBIT 8

Present Value of an Annuity at the Internal Rate of Return

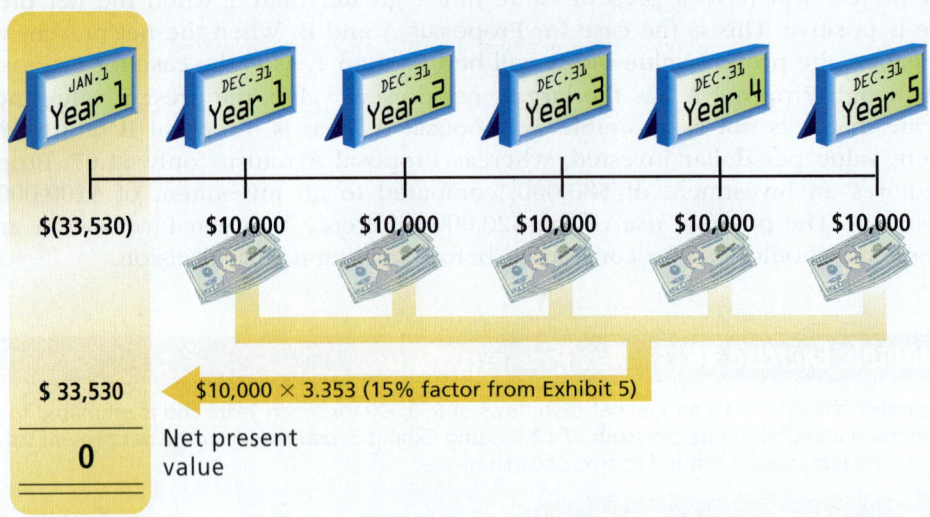

When equal annual net cash flows are expected from a proposal, as in the preceding example, the internal rate of return can be determined as follows:[4]

Step 1. Determine a present value factor for an annuity of $1 as follows:

$$\text{Present Value Factor for an Annuity of \$1} = \frac{\text{Amount to Be Invested}}{\text{Equal Annual Net Cash Flows}}$$

Step 2. Locate the present value factor determined in Step 1 in the present value of an annuity of $1 table (Exhibit 5) as follows:
  a. Locate the number of years of expected useful life of the investment in the Year column.
  b. Proceed horizontally across the table until you find the present value factor computed in Step 1.

Step 3. Identify the internal rate of return by the heading of the column in which the present value factor in Step 2 is located.

To illustrate, assume that management is evaluating the following proposal to purchase new equipment:

Cost of new equipment	$97,360
Yearly expected cash flows to be received	$20,000
Expected useful life	7 years

The present value factor for an annuity of $1 is 4.868, computed as follows:

$$\text{Present Value Factor for an Annuity of \$1} = \frac{\text{Amount to Be Invested}}{\text{Equal Annual Net Cash Flows}}$$

$$= \frac{\$97,360}{\$20,000} = 4.868$$

Using the partial present value of an annuity of $1 table shown in Exhibit 9 and a period of seven years, the factor 4.868 is related to 10%. Thus, the internal rate of return for this proposal is 10%.

---

4 To simplify, equal annual net cash flows are assumed. If the net cash flows are not equal, spreadsheet software can be used to determine the rate of return.

EXHIBIT 9

Steps to Determine the Internal Rate of Return

Present Value of an Annuity of $1 at Compound Interest

	Year	6%	Step 3 10%	12%
	1	0.943	0.909	0.893
	2	1.833	1.736	1.690
	3	2.673	2.487	2.402
	4	3.465	3.170	3.037
	5	4.212	3.791	3.605
	6	4.917	Step 2(b) 4.355	4.111
Step 2(a)	7	5.582	4.868	4.564
	8	6.210	5.335	4.968
	9	6.802	5.759	5.328
	10	7.360	6.145	5.650

Step 1: Determine present value factor for an annuity of $1 $= \dfrac{\$97{,}360}{\$20{,}000} = 4.868$

If the minimum acceptable rate of return is 10%, then the proposal is considered acceptable. Several proposals can be ranked by their internal rates of return. The proposal with the highest rate is the most desirable.

The internal rate of return method has the following three advantages:

- It considers the cash flows of the investment.
- It considers the time value of money.
- It ranks proposals based upon the cash flows over their complete useful life, even if the project lives are not the same.

The internal rate of return method has the following two disadvantages:

- It has complex computations, requiring a computer if the periodic cash flows are not equal.
- It assumes that the cash received from a proposal can be reinvested at the internal rate of return, which may not be valid.

Example Exercise 26-4 Internal Rate of Return   Obj. 3

A project is estimated to cost $208,175 and provide annual net cash flows of $55,000 for six years. Determine the internal rate of return for this project, using Exhibit 5.

Follow My Example 26-4

15% [($208,175 ÷ $55,000) = 3.785, the present value of an annuity factor for six periods at 15%, from Exhibit 5]

Practice Exercises: PE 26-4A, PE 26-4B

Business Connection

PANERA BREAD RATE OF RETURN

Panera Bread owns, operates, and franchises bakery-cafés throughout the United States. A recent annual report to the Securities and Exchange Commission (SEC Form 10-K) allowed the following information to be determined about an average company-owned store:

Operating profit	$ 405,000
Depreciation	115,000
Investment book value	1,500,000

Assume that the operating profit and depreciation will remain unchanged for the next 15 years. Assume that operating profit plus depreciation approximates annual net cash

(Continued)

flows and that the investment residual value will be zero. The average rate of return on a company-owned store is:

$$\frac{\$405{,}000}{\$1{,}500{,}000 \div 2} = 54\%$$

The internal rate of return is calculated by first determining the present value of an annuity of $1:

$$\text{Present Value of an Annuity of } \$1 = \frac{\$1{,}500{,}000}{\$405{,}000 + \$115{,}000} = 2.88$$

For a period of five years, this factor implies an internal rate of return of more than 20% (from Exhibit 5). However, if we more realistically assumed these cash flows for 15 years, Panera's company-owned stores generate an estimated internal rate of return of approximately 34% (from a spreadsheet calculation). Clearly, both investment evaluation methods indicate a highly successful business.

Source: Panera Bread, *Form 10-K for the Fiscal Year Ended December 25, 2015.*

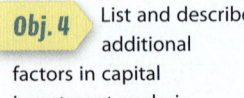

Obj. 4 List and describe additional factors in capital investment analysis.

Additional Factors in Capital Investment Analysis

Four widely used methods of evaluating capital investment proposals have been described and illustrated in this chapter. In practice, additional factors such as the following may impact capital investment decisions:

- Income tax
- Proposals with unequal lives
- Lease versus purchase
- Uncertainty
- Changes in price levels
- Qualitative factors
- Capital investment for sustainability

Income Tax

The impact of income taxes on capital investment decisions can be material. For example, in determining depreciation for federal income tax purposes, useful lives that are much shorter than the actual useful lives are often used. Also, depreciation for tax purposes often differs from depreciation for financial statement purposes. As a result, the timing of the cash flows for income taxes can have a significant impact on capital investment analysis.[5]

Unequal Proposal Lives

The prior capital investment illustrations assumed that the alternative proposals had the same useful lives. In practice, however, proposals often have different lives.

To illustrate, assume that a company is considering purchasing a new truck or a new computer network. The data for each proposal follow:

	Truck	Computer Network
Cost	$100,000	$100,000
Minimum desired rate of return	10%	10%
Expected useful life	8 years	5 years
Yearly expected cash flows to be received:		
Year 1	$ 30,000	$ 30,000
Year 2	30,000	30,000
Year 3	25,000	30,000
Year 4	20,000	30,000
Year 5	15,000	35,000
Year 6	15,000	0
Year 7	10,000	0
Year 8	10,000	0
Total	$155,000	$155,000

[5] The impact of taxes on capital investment analysis is covered in advanced accounting textbooks.

The expected cash flows and net present value for each proposal are shown in Exhibit 10. Because of the unequal useful lives, however, the net present values in Exhibit 10 are not comparable.

EXHIBIT 10 Net Present Value Analysis—Unequal Lives of Proposals

	A	B	C	D
1		Truck		
2		Present	Net	Present
3		Value of	Cash	Value of
4	Year	$1 at 10%	Flow	Net Cash Flow
5	1	0.909	$ 30,000	$ 27,270
6	2	0.826	30,000	24,780
7	3	0.751	25,000	18,775
8	4	0.683	20,000	13,660
9	5	0.621	15,000	9,315
10	6	0.564	15,000	8,460
11	7	0.513	10,000	5,130
12	8	0.467	10,000	4,670
13	Total		$155,000	$112,060
14				
15	Less amount to be invested			100,000
16	Net present value			$ 12,060
17				

	A	B	C	D
1		Computer Network		
2		Present	Net	Present
3		Value of	Cash	Value of
4	Year	$1 at 10%	Flow	Net Cash Flow
5	1	0.909	$ 30,000	$ 27,270
6	2	0.826	30,000	24,780
7	3	0.751	30,000	22,530
8	4	0.683	30,000	20,490
9	5	0.621	35,000	21,735
10	Total		$155,000	$116,805
11				
12	Less amount to be invested			100,000
13	Net present value			$ 16,805
14				

Cannot be compared (unequal lives)

EXHIBIT 11 Net Present Value Analysis—Equalized Lives of Proposals

	A	B	C	D
1		Truck—Revised to 5-Year Life		
2		Present	Net	Present
3		Value of	Cash	Value of
4	Year	$1 at 10%	Flow	Net Cash Flow
5	1	0.909	$ 30,000	$ 27,270
6	2	0.826	30,000	24,780
7	3	0.751	25,000	18,775
8	4	0.683	20,000	13,660
9	5	0.621	15,000	9,315
10	5 (Residual			
11	value)	0.621	40,000	24,840
12	Total		$160,000	$118,640
13				
14	Less amount to be invested			100,000
15	Net present value			$ 18,640
16				

Truck Net Present Value Greater Than Computer Network Net Present Value by $1,835

Compared (equal lives)

To make the proposals comparable, the useful lives are adjusted to end at the same time. In this illustration, this is done by assuming that the truck will be sold at the end of five years. The selling price (residual value) of the truck at the end of five years is estimated and included in the cash inflows. Both proposals will then cover five years; thus, the net present value analyses will be comparable.

To illustrate, assume that the truck's estimated selling price (residual value) at the end of Year 5 is $40,000. Exhibit 11 shows the truck's revised present value analysis assuming a five-year life.

As shown in Exhibit 11, the net present value for the truck exceeds the net present value for the computer network by $1,835 ($18,640 − $16,805). Thus, the truck is the more attractive of the two proposals.

Example Exercise 26-5 Net Present Value—Unequal Lives Obj. 4

Project 1 requires an original investment of $50,000. The project will yield cash flows of $12,000 per year for seven years. Project 2 has a calculated net present value of $8,900 over a five-year life. Project 1 could be sold at the end of five years for a price of $30,000. (a) Determine the net present value of Project 1 over a five-year life, with residual value, assuming a minimum rate of return of 12%. (b) Which project provides the greatest net present value?

Follow My Example 26-5

a.
Present value of $12,000 per year at 12% for 5 years	$43,260	[$12,000 × 3.605 (Exhibit 5, 12%, 5 years)]
Present value of $30,000 at 12% at the end of 5 years	17,010	[$30,000 × 0.567 (Exhibit 2, 12%, 5 years)]
Total present value of Project 1	$60,270	
Total cost of Project 1	50,000	
Net present value of Project 1	$10,270	

b. Project 1—$10,270 is greater than the net present value of Project 2, $8,900.

Practice Exercises: PE 26-5A, PE 26-5B

Lease Versus Purchase

Leasing fixed assets is common in many industries. For example, hospitals often lease medical equipment. Some advantages of leasing a fixed asset include the following:

- The company has use of the fixed asset without spending large amounts of cash to purchase the asset.
- The company eliminates the risk of owning an obsolete asset.
- The company may deduct the annual lease payments for income tax purposes.

A disadvantage of leasing a fixed asset is that it is normally more costly than purchasing the asset. This is because the lessor (owner of the asset) includes in the rental price not only the costs of owning the asset but also a profit.

The methods of evaluating capital investment proposals illustrated in this chapter can also be used to decide whether to lease or purchase a fixed asset.

Uncertainty

All capital investment analyses rely on factors that are uncertain. For example, estimates of revenues, expenses, and cash flows are uncertain. This is especially true for long-term capital investments. Errors in one or more of the estimates could lead to incorrect decisions. Methods that consider the impact of uncertainty on capital investment analysis are discussed in advanced accounting and finance textbooks.

SERVICE FOCUS

IF YOU BUILD IT, THEY WILL COME

A business model describes how an organization delivers products or services to make a profit. Many service companies use what is termed a *network business model*. A network business model connects people and businesses with each other or to a centralized service. Examples of network service businesses include telecommunication, transportation, power and natural gas distribution, cable, satellite, and Internet companies. Network businesses often require significant investment in physical assets in order to create the network. Often, this is described as a *Field of Dreams strategy* (from the movie of that name) because the network can only generate revenue once it is largely built. For example, a cell phone company draws value from having many cell towers linking many callers. A critical mass of cell towers must be pre-built in order to establish the business. This is risky. As a result, network businesses carefully evaluate capital investments prior to building networks.

Changes in Price Levels

Price levels normally change as the economy improves or deteriorates. General price levels often increase in a rapidly growing economy, which is called **inflation**. During such periods, the rate of return on an investment should exceed the rising price level. If this is not the case, the cash returned on the investment will be less than expected.

Price levels may also change for foreign investments. This occurs as currency exchange rates change. **Currency exchange rates** are the rates at which currency in another country can be exchanged for U.S. dollars.

If the amount of local dollars that can be exchanged for one U.S. dollar increases, then the local currency is said to be weakening to the dollar. When a company has an investment in another country where the local currency is weakening, the return on the investment, as expressed in U.S. dollars, is adversely impacted. This is because the expected amount of local currency returned on the investment would purchase fewer U.S. dollars.

Link to Vail Resorts, Inc.
Some of **Vail Resorts**' rental (lease) agreements include increases for inflation that are linked to the Consumer Price Index (CPI).

Qualitative Considerations

Some benefits of capital investments are qualitative in nature and cannot be estimated in dollar terms. However, if a company does not consider qualitative considerations, an acceptable investment proposal could be rejected.

Some examples of qualitative considerations that may influence capital investment analysis include the investment proposal's impact on the following:

- Product quality
- Manufacturing flexibility
- Employee morale
- Manufacturing productivity
- Market (strategic) opportunities

Many qualitative factors may be as important as, if not more important than, quantitative factors.

Capital Investment for Sustainability

Chapter 18 defined sustainability as "the practice of operating a business to maximize profits while attempting to preserve the environment, economy, and needs of future generations." Sustainability practices often require capital investments in order to establish these priorities. Some examples are listed in Exhibit 12.

Link to Vail Resorts, Inc.
Vail recycles 300 tons of material from the resort mountain each year. An example includes vegetable oil from the mountain restaurants being recycled into biodiesel.

Source: www.vail.com sustainability page

EXHIBIT 12

Examples of Capital Investments in Sustainability

Sustainability Objective	Capital Investment Example
Minimize resource waste and environmental degradation	Invest in land, soil, and water reclamation projects for a mining company.
Develop new sustainable markets	Invest in equipment to produce an environmentally safe cleaning product for a consumer product company.
Reduce litigation risks	Invest in wastewater recycling to avoid river contamination and potential legal liability for a papermaking company.
Maintain an attractive and safe working environment	Invest in an employee wellness and fitness center to attract and retain high-performance employees for a software company.

Often, sustainability investments can be analyzed using methods described in this chapter. An example is manufacturing equipment for the new environmentally safe cleaning product listed in Exhibit 12. In contrast, the benefits of some sustainability investments may be difficult to measure and, thus, must be evaluated qualitatively.

An example is the wellness and fitness center for employees listed in Exhibit 12. In addition, sustainability investments may be legally mandated and, thus, are justified more by the requirements of law than by their immediate economic benefits. Examples are the land, soil, and water reclamation project and wastewater recycling projects listed in Exhibit 12.

To illustrate a capital investment analysis, Carpenter Company proposes to install solar panels to satisfy a portion of the power requirements for its manufacturing plant. The cost of the solar panel investment is $150,000. The solar panel operating and maintenance cost is expected to be $20,000 per year. The plant uses an average of 3,000 kilowatt-hours (kwh) per day for 250 sunny days per year. A kilowatt-hour is the use of 1,000 watts per hour and is a standard measure of electricity consumption. The solar panels replace metered electricity from the power company that costs Carpenter $0.12 per kwh. The solar panels are expected to last 10 years with no salvage value.

The annual cost savings can be computed as follows:

Kilowatt-hours per day	3,000	kwh
× Number of sunny operating days	250	days
Kilowatt-hours per year	750,000	kwh
× Metered electricity cost per kwh	$0.12	per kwh
Total metered cost savings	$ 90,000	
Less annual solar panel maintenance cost	20,000	
Net annual savings	$ 70,000	

The net present value of the project assuming a minimum rate of return of 10% is as follows:

Annual net cash flow savings from installing solar panels	$ 70,000
× Present value of a $1 annuity at 10% for 10 periods (Exhibit 5)	× 6.145
Present value of annual savings	$ 430,150
Less amount to be invested	150,000
Net present value	$ 280,150

The net present value is positive; thus, the solar panel proposal is supported by the analysis.

INTEGRITY, OBJECTIVITY, AND ETHICS IN BUSINESS

ASSUMPTION FUDGING

The results of any capital budgeting analysis depend on many subjective estimates, such as the cash flows, discount rate, time period, and total investment amount. The results of the analysis should be used to either support or reject a project. Capital budgeting should not be used to justify an assumed net present value. That is, the analyst should not work backwards, filling in assumed numbers that will produce the desired net present value. Such a reverse approach reduces the credibility of the entire process.

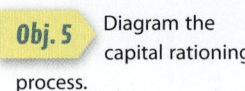

Obj. 5 Diagram the capital rationing process.

Capital Rationing

Capital rationing is the process by which management allocates funds among competing capital investment proposals. In this process, management often uses a combination of the methods described in this chapter.

Exhibit 13 illustrates the capital rationing decision process. Alternative proposals are initially screened by establishing minimum standards, using the cash payback and the average rate of return methods. The proposals that survive this screening are further analyzed, using the net present value and internal rate of return methods.

Capital Rationing Decision Process

EXHIBIT 13

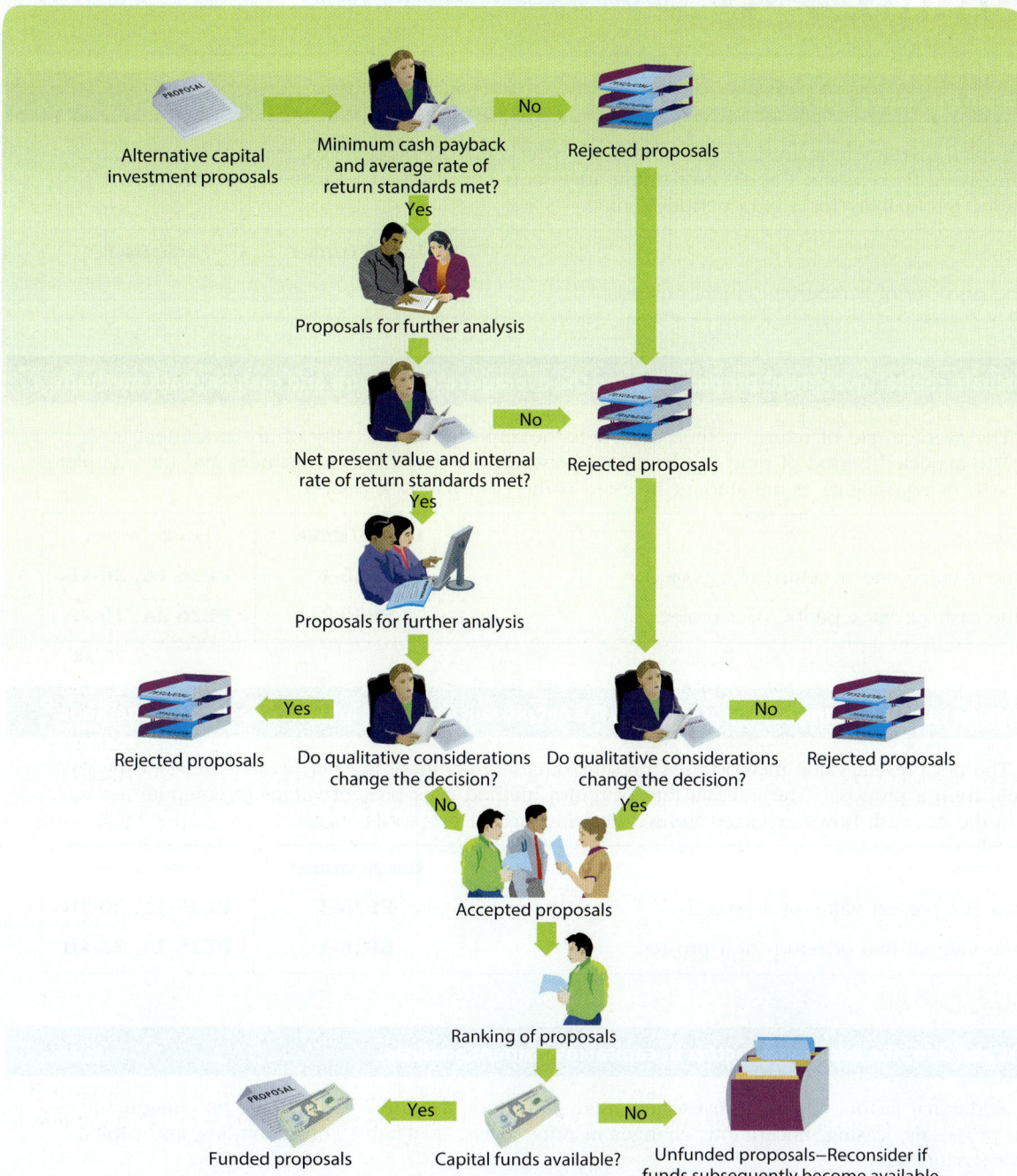

Qualitative factors related to each proposal should also be considered throughout the capital rationing process. For example, new equipment might improve the quality of the product and, thus, increase consumer satisfaction and sales.

At the end of the capital rationing process, accepted proposals are ranked and compared with the funds available. Proposals that are selected for funding are included in the capital expenditures budget. Unfunded proposals may be reconsidered if funds later become available.

At a Glance 26

Obj. 1 Explain the nature and importance of capital investment analysis.

Key Points Capital investment analysis is the process by which management plans, evaluates, and controls investments involving fixed assets. Capital investment analysis is important to a business because such investments affect profitability for a long period of time.

Learning Outcome	Example Exercises	Practice Exercises
• Describe the purpose of capital investment analysis.		

Obj. 2 Evaluate capital investment proposals, using the average rate of return and cash payback methods.

Key Points The average rate of return method measures the expected profitability of an investment in fixed assets. The expected period of time that will pass between the date of an investment and the complete recovery in cash (or equivalent) of the amount invested is the cash payback period.

Learning Outcomes	Example Exercises	Practice Exercises
• Compute the average rate of return of a project.	EE26-1	PE26-1A, 26-1B
• Compute the cash payback period of a project.	EE26-2	PE26-2A, 26-2B

Obj. 3 Evaluate capital investment proposals, using the net present value and internal rate of return methods.

Key Points The net present value method uses present values to compute the net present value of the cash flows expected from a proposal. The internal rate of return method uses present values to compute the rate of return from the net cash flows expected from capital investment proposals.

Learning Outcomes	Example Exercises	Practice Exercises
• Compute the net present value of a project.	EE26-3	PE26-3A, 26-3B
• Compute the internal rate of return of a project.	EE26-4	PE26-4A, 26-4B

Obj. 4 List and describe additional factors in capital investment analysis.

Key Points Additional factors in capital investment analysis include the impact of income tax, unequal lives of alternative proposals, leasing, uncertainty, changes in price levels, qualitative considerations, and capital investment for sustainability.

Learning Outcomes	Example Exercises	Practice Exercises
• Describe the impact of income taxes in capital investment analysis.		
• Evaluate projects with unequal lives.	EE26-5	PE26-5A, 26-5B
• Describe leasing versus capital investment.		
• Describe uncertainty, changes in price levels, and qualitative considerations in capital investment analysis.		
• Describe and illustrate capital investment analysis for sustainability.		

Chapter 26 Capital Investment Analysis

Obj. 5 Diagram the capital rationing process.

Key Points Capital rationing refers to the process by which management allocates available investment funds among competing capital investment proposals. A diagram of the capital rationing process appears in Exhibit 13.

Learning Outcomes	Example Exercises	Practice Exercises
• Define *capital rationing*.		
• Diagram the capital rationing process.		

Illustrative Problem

The capital investment committee of Hopewell Company is currently considering two investments. The estimated income from operations and net cash flows expected from each investment are as follows:

	Truck		Equipment	
Year	Income from Operations	Net Cash Flow	Income from Operations	Net Cash Flow
1	$ 6,000	$ 22,000	$13,000	$ 29,000
2	9,000	25,000	10,000	26,000
3	10,000	26,000	8,000	24,000
4	8,000	24,000	8,000	24,000
5	11,000	27,000	3,000	19,000
	$44,000	$124,000	$42,000	$122,000

Each investment requires $80,000. Straight-line depreciation will be used, and no residual value is expected. The committee has selected a rate of 15% for purposes of the net present value analysis.

Instructions

1. Compute the following:

    a. The average rate of return for each investment.

    b. The net present value for each investment. Use the present value of $1 table appearing in this chapter (Exhibit 2).

2. Why is the net present value of the equipment greater than the truck even though its average rate of return is less?

3. Prepare a summary for the capital investment committee, advising it on the relative merits of the two investments.

Solution

1. a. Average rate of return for the truck:

    $$\frac{\$44,000 \div 5}{(\$80,000 + \$0) \div 2} = 22\%$$

    Average rate of return for the equipment:

    $$\frac{\$42,000 \div 5}{(\$80,000 + \$0) \div 2} = 21\%$$

(Continued)

b. Net present value analysis:

Year	Present Value of $1 at 15%	Net Cash Flow Truck	Net Cash Flow Equipment	Present Value of Net Cash Flow Truck	Present Value of Net Cash Flow Equipment
1	0.870	$ 22,000	$ 29,000	$19,140	$25,230
2	0.756	25,000	26,000	18,900	19,656
3	0.658	26,000	24,000	17,108	15,792
4	0.572	24,000	24,000	13,728	13,728
5	0.497	27,000	19,000	13,419	9,443
Total		$124,000	$122,000	$82,295	$83,849
Less amount to be invested				80,000	80,000
Net present value				$ 2,295	$ 3,849

2. The equipment has a lower average rate of return than the truck because the equipment's total income from operations for the five years is $42,000, which is $2,000 less than the truck's. Even so, the net present value of the equipment is greater than that of the truck because the equipment has higher cash flows in the early years.

3. Both investments exceed the selected rate established for the net present value analysis. The truck has a higher average rate of return, but the equipment offers a larger net present value. Thus, if only one of the two investments can be accepted, the equipment would be the more attractive.

Key Terms

annuity (1279)
average rate of return (1275)
capital investment analysis (1274)
capital rationing (1290)
cash payback period (1276)

currency exchange rate (1289)
inflation (1289)
internal rate of return (IRR) method (1283)
net present value method (1281)

present value concept (1278)
present value index (1282)
present value of an annuity (1280)
time value of money concept (1274)

Discussion Questions

1. What are the principal objections to the use of the average rate of return method in evaluating capital investment proposals?

2. Discuss the principal limitations of the cash payback method for evaluating capital investment proposals.

3. Why would the average rate of return differ from the internal rate of return on the same project?

4. Your boss has suggested that a one-year payback period is the same as a 100% average rate of return. Do you agree? Explain.

5. Why would the cash payback method understate the attractiveness of a project with a large residual value?

6. Why would the use of the cash payback period for analyzing the financial performance of theatrical releases from a motion picture production studio be supported over the net present value method?

7. A net present value analysis used to evaluate a proposed equipment acquisition indicated a $7,900 net present value. What is the meaning of the $7,900 as it relates to the desirability of the proposal?

8. Two projects have an identical net present value of $9,000. Are both projects equal in desirability? Explain.

9. What are the major disadvantages of the use of the net present value method of analyzing capital investment proposals?

10. What are the major disadvantages of the use of the internal rate of return method of analyzing capital investment proposals?

11. What are the major advantages of leasing a fixed asset rather than purchasing it?

12. Give an example of a qualitative factor that should be considered in a capital investment analysis related to acquiring automated factory equipment.

13. How are investments in sustainability justified?

Practice Exercises

Example Exercises

EE 26-1 p. 1276 **PE 26-1A Average rate of return** — OBJ. 2
Determine the average rate of return for a project that is estimated to yield total income of $180,000 over five years, has a cost of $400,000, and has a $50,000 residual value.

EE 26-1 p. 1276 **PE 26-1B Average rate of return** — OBJ. 2
Determine the average rate of return for a project that is estimated to yield total income of $36,000 over three years, has a cost of $70,000, and has a $10,000 residual value.

EE 26-2 p. 1278 **PE 26-2A Cash payback period** — OBJ. 2
A project has estimated annual net cash flows of $95,200. It is estimated to cost $580,720. Determine the cash payback period. Round to one decimal place.

EE 26-2 p. 1278 **PE 26-2B Cash payback period** — OBJ. 2
A project has estimated annual net cash flows of $9,300. It is estimated to cost $41,850. Determine the cash payback period. Round to one decimal place.

EE 26-3 p. 1283 **PE 26-3A Net present value** — OBJ. 3
A project has estimated annual net cash flows of $8,000 for five years and is estimated to cost $28,000. Assume a minimum acceptable rate of return of 12%. Using Exhibit 5, determine (1) the net present value of the project and (2) the present value index, rounded to two decimal places.

EE 26-3 p. 1283 **PE 26-3B Net present value** — OBJ. 3
A project has estimated annual net cash flows of $96,200 for four years and is estimated to cost $315,500. Assume a minimum acceptable rate of return of 10%. Using Exhibit 5, determine (1) the net present value of the project and (2) the present value index, rounded to two decimal places.

EE 26-4 p. 1285 **PE 26-4A Internal rate of return** — OBJ. 3
A project is estimated to cost $90,045 and provide annual net cash flows of $14,500 for eight years. Determine the internal rate of return for this project, using Exhibit 5.

EE 26-4 p. 1285 **PE 26-4B Internal rate of return** — OBJ. 3
A project is estimated to cost $362,672 and provide annual net cash flows of $76,000 for nine years. Determine the internal rate of return for this project, using Exhibit 5.

1296 Chapter 26 Capital Investment Analysis

EE 26-5 *p. 1288* **PE 26-5A Net present value—unequal lives** OBJ. 4

Project A requires an original investment of $32,600. The project will yield cash flows of $7,000 per year for nine years. Project B has a calculated net present value of $3,500 over a six-year life. Project A could be sold at the end of six years for a price of $15,000. (a) Determine the net present value of Project A over a six-year life, with residual value, assuming a minimum rate of return of 12%. (b) Which project provides the greatest net present value?

EE 26-5 *p. 1288* **PE 26-5B Net present value—unequal lives** OBJ. 4

Project 1 requires an original investment of $55,000. The project will yield cash flows of $15,000 per year for seven years. Project 2 has a calculated net present value of $5,000 over a four-year life. Project 1 could be sold at the end of four years for a price of $38,000. (a) Determine the net present value of Project 1 over a four-year life, with residual value, assuming a minimum rate of return of 20%. (b) Which project provides the greatest net present value?

Exercises

EX 26-1 Average rate of return OBJ. 2

✔ 3D Printer, 16%

Show Me How

The following data are accumulated by Lone Peak Inc. in evaluating two competing capital investment proposals:

	3D Printer	Truck
Amount of investment	$40,000	$50,000
Useful life	7 years	10 years
Estimated residual value	$3,000	$6,000
Estimated total income over the useful life	$24,080	$36,400

Determine the expected average rate of return for each proposal.

EX 26-2 Average rate of return—cost savings OBJ. 2

Midwest Fabricators Inc. is considering an investment in equipment that will replace direct labor. The equipment has a cost of $132,000 with a $16,000 residual value and a 10-year life. The equipment will replace one employee who has an average wage of $34,000 per year. In addition, the equipment will have operating and energy costs of $5,380 per year.
  Determine the average rate of return on the equipment, giving effect to straight-line depreciation on the investment.

EX 26-3 Average rate of return—new product OBJ. 2

✔ Average annual income, $744,000

Show Me How

Micro Tek Inc. is considering an investment in new equipment that will be used to manufacture a smartphone. The phone is expected to generate additional annual sales of 4,000 units at $450 per unit. The equipment has a cost of $940,000, residual value of $20,000, and an eight-year life. The equipment can only be used to manufacture the phone. The cost to manufacture the phone follows:

Cost per unit:	
Direct labor	$ 20
Direct materials	205
Factory overhead (including depreciation)	39
Total cost per unit	$264

Determine the average rate of return on the equipment.

Chapter 26 Capital Investment Analysis 1297

Year 1: $(217,400)

EX 26-4 Calculate cash flows
OBJ. 2

Nature's Way Inc. is planning to invest in new manufacturing equipment to make a new garden tool. The garden tool is expected to generate additional annual sales of 1,600 units at $75 each. The new manufacturing equipment will cost $257,000 and is expected to have a 10-year life and $17,000 residual value. Selling expenses related to the new product are expected to be 5% of sales revenue. The cost to manufacture the product includes the following on a per-unit basis:

Direct labor	$12.00
Direct materials	30.00
Fixed factory overhead—depreciation	15.00
Variable factory overhead	4.50
Total	$61.50

Determine the net cash flows for the first year of the project, Years 2–9, and for the last year of the project.

✔ Location 1: 5 years

EX 26-5 Cash payback period for a service company
OBJ. 2

Prime Financial Inc. is evaluating two capital investment proposals for a drive-up ATM kiosk, each requiring an investment of $200,000 and each with an eight-year life and expected total net cash flows of $320,000. Location 1 is expected to provide equal annual net cash flows of $40,000, and Location 2 is expected to have the following unequal annual net cash flows:

Year 1	$60,000		Year 5	$30,000
Year 2	50,000		Year 6	30,000
Year 3	50,000		Year 7	30,000
Year 4	40,000		Year 8	30,000

Determine the cash payback period for both location proposals.

EX 26-6 Cash payback method
OBJ. 2

Lily Products Company is considering an investment in one of two new product lines. The investment required for either product line is $540,000. The net cash flows associated with each product are as follows:

Year	Liquid Soap	Body Lotion
1	$170,000	$ 90,000
2	150,000	90,000
3	120,000	90,000
4	100,000	90,000
5	70,000	90,000
6	40,000	90,000
7	40,000	90,000
8	30,000	90,000
Total	$720,000	$720,000

a. Recommend a product offering to Lily Products Company, based on the cash payback period for each product line.

b. Why is one product line preferred over the other even though they both have the same total net cash flows through eight periods?

EX 26-7 Net present value method   OBJ. 3

✓ a. NPV, $24,520

The following data are accumulated by Paxton Company in evaluating the purchase of $150,000 of equipment having a four-year useful life:

	Net Income	Net Cash Flow
Year 1	$42,500	$80,000
Year 2	27,500	65,000
Year 3	12,500	50,000
Year 4	2,500	40,000

a. Assuming that the desired rate of return is 15%, determine the net present value for the proposal. Use the table of the present value of $1 appearing in Exhibit 2 of this chapter.

b. Would management be likely to look with favor on the proposal? Explain.

EX 26-8 Net present value method for a service company   OBJ. 3

✓ a. 20Y1, $13,000

AM Express Inc. is considering the purchase of an additional delivery vehicle for $55,000 on January 1, 20Y1. The truck is expected to have a five-year life with an expected residual value of $15,000 at the end of five years. The expected additional revenues from the added delivery capacity are anticipated to be $58,000 per year for each of the next five years. A driver will cost $42,000 in 20Y1, with an expected annual salary increase of $1,000 for each year thereafter. The annual operating costs for the truck are estimated to be $3,000 per year.

a. Determine the expected annual net cash flows from the delivery truck investment for 20Y1–20Y5.

b. Calculate the net present value of the investment, assuming that the minimum desired rate of return is 12%. Use the present value of $1 table appearing in Exhibit 2 of this chapter.

c. Is the additional truck a good investment based on your analysis? Explain.

EX 26-9 Net present value method—annuity for a service company   OBJ. 3

✓ a. $14 million

Welcome Inn Hotels is considering the construction of a new hotel for $90 million. The expected life of the hotel is 30 years, with no residual value. The hotel is expected to earn revenues of $26 million per year. Total expenses, including depreciation, are expected to be $15 million per year. Welcome Inn management has set a minimum acceptable rate of return of 14%.

a. Determine the equal annual net cash flows from operating the hotel.

b. Calculate the net present value of the new hotel, using the present value of an annuity of $1 table found in Appendix A. Round to the nearest million dollars.

c. Does your analysis support construction of the new hotel? Explain.

EX 26-10 Net present value method—annuity   OBJ. 3

✓ a. $46,000

Briggs Excavation Company is planning an investment of $132,000 for a bulldozer. The bulldozer is expected to operate for 1,500 hours per year for five years. Customers will be charged $110 per hour for bulldozer work. The bulldozer operator costs $28 per hour in wages and benefits. The bulldozer is expected to require annual maintenance costing $8,000. The bulldozer uses fuel that is expected to cost $46 per hour of bulldozer operation.

a. Determine the equal annual net cash flows from operating the bulldozer.

b. Determine the net present value of the investment, assuming that the desired rate of return is 10%. Use the present value of an annuity of $1 table in the chapter (Exhibit 5). Round to the nearest dollar.

c. Should Briggs invest in the bulldozer, based on this analysis? Explain.

d. Determine the number of operating hours such that the present value of cash flows equals the amount to be invested.

Chapter 26 Capital Investment Analysis 1299

✔ a. $146,320,000

EX 26-11 Net present value method for a service company OBJ. 3

Carnival Corporation has recently placed into service some of the largest cruise ships in the world. One of these ships, the *Carnival Breeze*, can hold up to 3,600 passengers, and it can cost $800 million to build. Assume the following additional information:

- There will be 330 cruise days per year operated at a full capacity of 3,600 passengers.
- The variable expenses per passenger are estimated to be $110 per cruise day.
- The revenue per passenger is expected to be $250 per cruise day.
- The fixed expenses for running the ship, other than depreciation, are estimated to be $20,000,000 per year.
- The ship has a service life of 10 years, with a residual value of $200,000,000 at the end of 10 years.

a. Determine the annual net cash flow from operating the cruise ship.

b. Determine the net present value of this investment, assuming a 12% minimum rate of return. Use the present value tables (Exhibits 2 and 5) provided in the chapter in determining your answer.

EX 26-12 Present value index OBJ. 3

✔ Fort Collins, 0.98

Dip N' Dunk Doughnuts has computed the net present value for capital expenditure at two locations. Relevant data related to the computation are as follows:

	Fort Collins	Boulder
Total present value of net cash flow	$607,600	$624,000
Less amount to be invested	620,000	600,000
Net present value	$(12,400)	$ 24,000

a. Determine the present value index for each proposal.

b. ✏ Which location does your analysis support? Explain.

EX 26-13 Net present value method and present value index OBJ. 3

✔ b. Packing machine, 1.55

Diamond & Turf Inc. is considering an investment in one of two machines. The sewing machine will increase productivity from sewing 150 baseballs per hour to sewing 290 per hour. The contribution margin per unit is $0.32 per baseball. Assume that any increased production of baseballs can be sold. The second machine is an automatic packing machine for the golf ball line. The packing machine will reduce packing labor cost. The labor cost saved is equivalent to $21 per hour. The sewing machine will cost $260,000, will have an eight-year life, and will operate for 1,800 hours per year. The packing machine will cost $85,000, will have an eight-year life, and will operate for 1,400 hours per year. Diamond & Turf seeks a minimum rate of return of 15% on its investments.

a. Determine the net present value for the two machines. Use the present value of an annuity of $1 table in the chapter (Exhibit 5). Round to the nearest dollar.

b. Determine the present value index for the two machines. Round to two decimal places.

c. ✏ If Diamond & Turf has sufficient funds for only one of the machines and qualitative factors are equal between the two machines, in which machine should it invest? Explain.

EX 26-14 Average rate of return, cash payback period, net present value method for a service company OBJ. 2, 3

✔ b. 5 years

Bi-Coastal Railroad Inc. is considering acquiring equipment at a cost of $520,000. The equipment has an estimated life of eight years and no residual value. It is expected to provide yearly net cash flows of $104,000. The company's minimum desired rate of return for net present value analysis is 10%.

(*Continued*)

1300 Chapter 26 Capital Investment Analysis

Compute the following:

a. The average rate of return, assuming the annual earnings are equal to the net cash flows less the annual depreciation expense on the equipment.

b. The cash payback period.

c. The net present value. Use the present value of an annuity of $1 table appearing in this chapter (Exhibit 5). Round to the nearest dollar.

EX 26-15 Cash payback period, net present value analysis, and qualitative considerations
OBJ. 2, 3, 4

✔ a. 4 years

The plant manager of Shenzhen Electronics Company is considering the purchase of new automated assembly equipment. The new equipment will cost $1,400,000. The manager believes that the new investment will result in direct labor savings of $350,000 per year for 10 years.

a. What is the payback period on this project?

b. What is the net present value, assuming a 10% rate of return? Use the present value of an annuity of $1 table in Exhibit 5.

c. ✏ What else should the manager consider in the analysis?

EX 26-16 Internal rate of return method
OBJ. 3

✔ a. 4.111

Show Me How

The internal rate of return method is used by King Bros. Construction Co. in analyzing a capital expenditure proposal that involves an investment of $156,218 and annual net cash flows of $38,000 for each of the six years of its useful life.

a. Determine a present value factor for an annuity of $1, which can be used in determining the internal rate of return. Round to three decimal places.

b. Using the factor determined in part (a) and the present value of an annuity of $1 table appearing in this chapter (Exhibit 5), determine the internal rate of return for the proposal.

EX 26-17 Internal rate of return method for a service company
OBJ. 3, 4

Real World

Park City Mountain Resort, a Utah ski resort, recently announced a $415 million expansion of lodging properties, lifts, and terrain. Assume that this investment is estimated to produce $99 million in equal annual cash flows for each of the first 10 years of the project life.

a. Determine the expected internal rate of return of this project for 10 years, using the present value of an annuity of $1 table found in Exhibit 5.

b. ✏ What are some uncertainties that could reduce the internal rate of return of this project?

EX 26-18 Internal rate of return method—two projects
OBJ. 3

✔ a. Delivery truck, 15%

Munch N' Crunch Snack Company is considering two possible investments: a delivery truck or a bagging machine. The delivery truck would cost $43,056 and could be used to deliver an additional 95,000 bags of pretzels per year. Each bag of pretzels can be sold for a contribution margin of $0.45. The delivery truck operating expenses, excluding depreciation, are $1.35 per mile for 24,000 miles per year. The bagging machine would replace an old bagging machine, and its net investment cost would be $61,614. The new machine would require three fewer hours of direct labor per day. Direct labor is $18 per hour. There are 250 operating days in the year. Both the truck and the bagging machine are estimated to have seven-year lives. The minimum rate of return is 13%. However, Munch N' Crunch has funds to invest in only one of the projects.

a. Compute the internal rate of return for each investment. Use the present value of an annuity of $1 table appearing in this chapter (Exhibit 5).

b. ✏ Provide a recommendation to management in a memo.

Chapter 26 Capital Investment Analysis 1301

EX 26-19 Net present value method and internal rate of return method for a service company   OBJ. 3

✔ a. $(36,750)

Keystone Healthcare Corp. is proposing to spend $260,820 on an eight-year project that has estimated net cash flows of $42,000 for each of the eight years.

a. Compute the net present value, using a rate of return of 10%. Use the present value of an annuity of $1 table in the chapter (Exhibit 5).

b. Based on the analysis prepared in part (a), is the rate of return (1) more than 10%, (2) 10%, or (3) less than 10%? Explain.

c. Determine the internal rate of return by computing a present value factor for an annuity of $1 and using the present value of an annuity of $1 table presented in the text (Exhibit 5).

EX 26-20 Identify error in capital investment analysis calculations   OBJ. 3

Artscape Inc. is considering the purchase of automated machinery that is expected to have a useful life of five years and no residual value. The average rate of return on the average investment has been computed to be 20%, and the cash payback period was computed to be 5.5 years.

Do you see any reason to question the validity of the data presented? Explain.

EX 26-21 Net present value—unequal lives   OBJ. 3, 4

✔ Net present value, Processing mill, $196,220

Bunker Hill Mining Company has two competing proposals: a processing mill and an electric shovel. Both pieces of equipment have an initial investment of $750,000. The net cash flows estimated for the two proposals are as follows:

	Net Cash Flow	
Year	Processing Mill	Electric Shovel
1	$310,000	$330,000
2	260,000	325,000
3	260,000	325,000
4	260,000	320,000
5	180,000	
6	130,000	
7	120,000	
8	120,000	

The estimated residual value of the processing mill at the end of Year 4 is $280,000.

Determine which equipment should be favored, comparing the net present values of the two proposals and assuming a minimum rate of return of 15%. Use the present value table presented in this chapter (Exhibit 2).

EX 26-22 Net present value—unequal lives   OBJ. 3, 4

Daisy's Creamery Inc. is considering one of two investment options. Option 1 is a $75,000 investment in new blending equipment that is expected to produce equal annual cash flows of $19,000 for each of seven years. Option 2 is a $90,000 investment in a new computer system that is expected to produce equal annual cash flows of $27,000 for each of five years. The residual value of the blending equipment at the end of the fifth year is estimated to be $15,000. The computer system has no expected residual value at the end of the fifth year.

Assume that there is sufficient capital to fund only one of the projects. Determine which project should be selected, comparing the (a) net present values and (b) present value indices of the two projects. Assume a minimum rate of return of 10%. Round the present value index to two decimal places. Use the present value tables presented in this chapter (Exhibits 2 and 5).

EX 26-23 Sustainable energy capital investment analysis OBJ. 3, 4

Central Plains Power Company is considering an investment in wind farm technology to replace natural gas-generating capacity. Initial installation cost of a wind turbine is expected to be $1,200 per kilowatt-hour of capacity. The wind turbine has a capacity of generating 2 megawatts per hour. A kilowatt-hour is 1,000 watts generated per hour, and a megawatt hour is 1,000 kilowatts generated per hour.

Annual operating information related to the wind turbine project was developed as follows:

Operating cost per wind turbine megawatt hour	$10
Variable operating, fuel, and maintenance costs of natural gas per megawatt hour	$95
Wind turbine operating days per year	90

a. Determine the initial investment cost of the wind turbine.
b. Determine the annual cost savings from the wind turbine in replacing natural gas generation. Round to the nearest dollar.
c. Determine the net present value of the project assuming a 15-year life and 12% minimum rate of return (use the present value tables in Appendix A). Round to the nearest dollar.

EX 26-24 Sustainable product capital investment analysis OBJ. 3, 4

AutoSource Inc. designs and manufactures tires for automobiles. The company's strategy is to design products that incorporate the full environmental impact of the product over its life cycle. This includes designing tires for fuel efficiency.

The technical team has determined that the tires manufactured with a silica blend will reduce road resistance. Thus, silica-blended tires will be significantly more fuel-efficient for the consumer, without compromising tire life. To produce the silica-blended tires, AutoSource will need to invest $5,000,000 in new equipment. It is expected that the new tire will be attractive to consumers and will result in increased tire sales. However, sales of conventional tires will be reduced as a result of the new silica-based tires. To evaluate the project, the cost and prices of silica and conventional tires are estimated as follows:

	Silica Tires	Conventional Tires
Sales price per tire	$160	$140
Material cost per tire	80	70
Variable manufacturing cost per tire	15	12

It is anticipated that 80,000 silica tires will be sold annually, while the sales of conventional tires will be reduced by 70,000 tires annually.

a. Determine the annual contribution margin for manufacturing and selling the silica-blended tires.
b. Determine the annual cash flows of manufacturing and selling silica-blended tires, incorporating the impact of lost sales from conventional tires.
c. Prepare a net present value analysis of the silica equipment investment, assuming an eight-year life and 12% minimum rate of return (use the Present Value tables in Appendix A). Round to the nearest dollar.

Problems: Series A

PR 26-1A Average rate of return method, net present value method, and analysis   OBJ. 2, 3

✓ 1. a. 30.0%

The capital investment committee of Nature's Portrait Landscaping Company is considering two capital investments. The estimated income from operations and net cash flows from each investment are as follows:

	Front-End Loader		Greenhouse Fixtures	
Year	Income from Operations	Net Cash Flow	Income from Operations	Net Cash Flow
1	$25,000	$ 40,000	$11,250	$ 26,250
2	20,000	35,000	11,250	26,250
3	7,000	22,000	11,250	26,250
4	3,000	18,000	11,250	26,250
5	1,250	16,250	11,250	26,250
Total	$56,250	$131,250	$56,250	$131,250

Each project requires an investment of $75,000. Straight-line depreciation will be used, and no residual value is expected. The committee has selected a rate of 12% for purposes of the net present value analysis.

Instructions

1. Compute the following:

    a. The average rate of return for each investment. Round to one decimal place.

    b. The net present value for each investment. Use the present value of $1 table appearing in this chapter (Exhibit 2). Round present values to the nearest dollar.

2. ✏️ Prepare a brief report for the capital investment committee, advising it on the relative merits of the two investments.

PR 26-2A Cash payback period, net present value method, and analysis   OBJ. 2, 3

✓ 1. b. Plant expansion, $305,040

Elite Apparel Inc. is considering two investment projects. The estimated net cash flows from each project are as follows:

Year	Plant Expansion	Retail Store Expansion
1	$ 450,000	$ 500,000
2	450,000	400,000
3	340,000	350,000
4	280,000	250,000
5	180,000	200,000
Total	$1,700,000	$1,700,000

Each project requires an investment of $900,000. A rate of 15% has been selected for the net present value analysis.

Instructions

1. Compute the following for each product:

    a. Cash payback period.

    b. The net present value. Use the present value of $1 table appearing in this chapter (Exhibit 2).

2. ✏️ Prepare a brief report advising management on the relative merits of each project.

1304 Chapter 26 Capital Investment Analysis

✔ 2. Computer network, 1.20

PR 26-3A Net present value method, present value index, and analysis OBJ. 3

Continental Railroad Company is evaluating three capital investment proposals using the net present value method. Relevant data related to the proposals are summarized as follows:

	Maintenance Equipment	Ramp Facilities	Computer Network
Amount to be invested	$8,000,000	$20,000,000	$9,000,000
Annual net cash flows:			
Year 1	4,000,000	12,000,000	6,000,000
Year 2	3,500,000	10,000,000	5,000,000
Year 3	2,500,000	9,000,000	4,000,000

Instructions

1. Assuming that the desired rate of return is 20%, prepare a net present value analysis for each proposal. Use the present value of $1 table appearing in this chapter (Exhibit 2).
2. Determine a present value index for each proposal. Round to two decimal places.
3. ▶ Which proposal offers the largest amount of present value per dollar of investment? Explain.

✔ 1. a. Wind turbines, $82,600

PR 26-4A Net present value method, internal rate of return method, and analysis OBJ. 3, 4

The management of Advanced Alternative Power Inc. is considering two capital investment projects. The estimated net cash flows from each project are as follows:

Year	Wind Turbines	Biofuel Equipment
1	$280,000	$300,000
2	280,000	300,000
3	280,000	300,000
4	280,000	300,000

The wind turbines require an investment of $887,600, while the biofuel equipment requires an investment of $911,100. No residual value is expected from either project.

Instructions

1. Compute the following for each project:
   a. The net present value. Use a rate of 6% and the present value of an annuity of $1 table appearing in this chapter (Exhibit 5).
   b. A present value index. Round to two decimal places.
2. Determine the internal rate of return for each project by (a) computing a present value factor for an annuity of $1 and (b) using the present value of an annuity of $1 table appearing in this chapter (Exhibit 5).
3. ▶ What advantage does the internal rate of return method have over the net present value method in comparing projects?

✔ 1. Server upgrade, $11,105

PR 26-5A Alternative capital investments OBJ. 3, 4

The investment committee of Sentry Insurance Co. is evaluating two projects, office expansion and upgrade to computer servers. The projects have different useful lives, but each requires an investment of $490,000. The estimated net cash flows from each project are as follows:

	Net Cash Flows	
Year	Office Expansion	Servers
1	$125,000	$165,000
2	125,000	165,000
3	125,000	165,000
4	125,000	165,000
5	125,000	
6	125,000	

The committee has selected a rate of 12% for purposes of net present value analysis. It also estimates that the residual value at the end of each project's useful life is $0, but at the end of the fourth year, the office expansion's residual value would be $180,000.

Instructions

1. For each project, compute the net present value. Use the present value of an annuity of $1 table appearing in this chapter (Exhibit 5). (Ignore the unequal lives of the projects.)

2. For each project, compute the net present value, assuming that the office expansion is adjusted to a four-year life for purposes of analysis. Use the present value of $1 table appearing in this chapter (Exhibit 2).

3. Prepare a report to the investment committee, giving your advice on the relative merits of the two projects.

PR 26-6A   Capital rationing decision for a service company involving four proposals   OBJ. 2, 3, 5

✔ 5. Proposal B, 1.13

Clearcast Communications Inc. is considering allocating a limited amount of capital investment funds among four proposals. The amount of proposed investment, estimated income from operations, and net cash flow for each proposal are as follows:

	Investment	Year	Income from Operations	Net Cash Flow
Proposal A:	$450,000	1	$ 30,000	$120,000
		2	30,000	120,000
		3	20,000	110,000
		4	10,000	100,000
		5	(30,000)	60,000
			$ 60,000	$510,000
Proposal B:	$200,000	1	$ 60,000	$100,000
		2	40,000	80,000
		3	20,000	60,000
		4	(10,000)	30,000
		5	(20,000)	20,000
			$ 90,000	$290,000
Proposal C:	$320,000	1	$ 36,000	$100,000
		2	26,000	90,000
		3	26,000	90,000
		4	16,000	80,000
		5	16,000	80,000
			$120,000	$440,000
Proposal D:	$540,000	1	$ 92,000	$200,000
		2	72,000	180,000
		3	52,000	160,000
		4	12,000	120,000
		5	(8,000)	100,000
			$220,000	$760,000

(Continued)

The company's capital rationing policy requires a maximum cash payback period of three years. In addition, a minimum average rate of return of 12% is required on all projects. If the preceding standards are met, the net present value method and present value indexes are used to rank the remaining proposals.

Instructions

1. Compute the cash payback period for each of the four proposals.
2. Giving effect to straight-line depreciation on the investments and assuming no estimated residual value, compute the average rate of return for each of the four proposals. Round to one decimal place.
3. Using the following format, summarize the results of your computations in parts (1) and (2). By placing the calculated amounts in the first two columns on the left and by placing a check mark in the appropriate column to the right, indicate which proposals should be accepted for further analysis and which should be rejected.

Proposal	Cash Payback Period	Average Rate of Return	Accept for Further Analysis	Reject
A				
B				
C				
D				

4. For the proposals accepted for further analysis in part (3), compute the net present value. Use a rate of 12% and the present value of $1 table appearing in this chapter (Exhibit 2).
5. Compute the present value index for each of the proposals in part (4). Round to two decimal places.
6. Rank the proposals from most attractive to least attractive, based on the present values of net cash flows computed in part (4).
7. Rank the proposals from most attractive to least attractive, based on the present value indexes computed in part (5).
8. Based on the analyses, comment on the relative attractiveness of the proposals ranked in parts (6) and (7).

Problems: Series B

PR 26-1B Average rate of return method, net present value method, and analysis OBJ. 2, 3

✔ 1. a. 18.7%

Show Me How

The capital investment committee of Ellis Transport and Storage Inc. is considering two investment projects. The estimated income from operations and net cash flows from each investment are as follows:

	Warehouse		Tracking Technology	
Year	Income from Operations	Net Cash Flow	Income from Operations	Net Cash Flow
1	$ 61,400	$135,000	$ 34,400	$108,000
2	51,400	125,000	34,400	108,000
3	36,400	110,000	34,400	108,000
4	26,400	100,000	34,400	108,000
5	(3,600)	70,000	34,400	108,000
Total	$172,000	$540,000	$172,000	$540,000

Each project requires an investment of $368,000. Straight-line depreciation will be used, and no residual value is expected. The committee has selected a rate of 15% for purposes of the net present value analysis.

Instructions

1. Compute the following:
   a. The average rate of return for each investment. Round to one decimal place.
   b. The net present value for each investment. Use the present value of $1 table appearing in this chapter (Exhibit 2). Round present values to the nearest dollar.
2. ✏️ Prepare a brief report for the capital investment committee, advising it on the relative merits of the two projects.

✔ 1. b. *Pro Gamer,* $49,465

PR 26-2B Cash payback period, net present value method, and analysis OBJ. 2, 3

Social Circle Publications Inc. is considering two new magazine products. The estimated net cash flows from each product are as follows:

Year	Sound Cellar	Pro Gamer
1	$ 65,000	$ 70,000
2	60,000	55,000
3	25,000	35,000
4	25,000	30,000
5	45,000	30,000
Total	$220,000	$220,000

Each product requires an investment of $125,000. A rate of 10% has been selected for the net present value analysis.

Instructions

1. Compute the following for each product:
   a. Cash payback period.
   b. The net present value. Use the present value of $1 table appearing in this chapter (Exhibit 2).
2. ✏️ Prepare a brief report advising management on the relative merits of each of the two products.

✔ 2. Branch office expansion, 0.95

PR 26-3B Net present value method, present value index, and analysis OBJ. 3

First United Bank Inc. is evaluating three capital investment projects using the net present value method. Relevant data related to the projects are summarized as follows:

	Branch Office Expansion	Computer System Upgrade	ATM Kiosk Expansion
Amount to be invested	$420,000	$350,000	$520,000
Annual net cash flows:			
Year 1	200,000	190,000	275,000
Year 2	160,000	180,000	250,000
Year 3	160,000	170,000	250,000

Instructions

1. Assuming that the desired rate of return is 15%, prepare a net present value analysis for each project. Use the present value of $1 table appearing in this chapter (Exhibit 2).
2. Determine a present value index for each project. Round to two decimal places.
3. ✏️ Which project offers the largest amount of present value per dollar of investment? Explain.

1308 Chapter 26 Capital Investment Analysis

✔ 1. a. *After Hours*, $100,800

PR 26-4B **Net present value method, internal rate of return method, and analysis** OBJ. 3

The management of Style Networks Inc. is considering two TV show projects. The estimated net cash flows from each project are as follows:

Year	After Hours	Sun Fun
1	$320,000	$290,000
2	320,000	290,000
3	320,000	290,000
4	320,000	290,000

After Hours requires an investment of $913,600, while *Sun Fun* requires an investment of $880,730. No residual value is expected from either project.

Instructions

1. Compute the following for each project:

   a. The net present value. Use a rate of 10% and the present value of an annuity of $1 table appearing in this chapter (Exhibit 5).

   b. A present value index. Round to two decimal places.

2. Determine the internal rate of return for each project by (a) computing a present value factor for an annuity of $1 and (b) using the present value of an annuity of $1 table appearing in this chapter (Exhibit 5).

3. What advantage does the internal rate of return method have over the net present value method in comparing projects?

✔ 1. Topeka, $135,600

PR 26-5B **Alternative capital investments** OBJ. 3, 4

The investment committee of Auntie M's Restaurants Inc. is evaluating two restaurant sites. The sites have different useful lives, but each requires an investment of $900,000. The estimated net cash flows from each site are as follows:

	Net Cash Flows	
Year	Wichita	Topeka
1	$310,000	$400,000
2	310,000	400,000
3	310,000	400,000
4	310,000	400,000
5	310,000	
6	310,000	

The committee has selected a rate of 20% for purposes of net present value analysis. It also estimates that the residual value at the end of each restaurant's useful life is $0, but at the end of the fourth year, Wichita's residual value would be $500,000.

Instructions

1. For each site, compute the net present value. Use the present value of an annuity of $1 table appearing in this chapter (Exhibit 5). (Ignore the unequal lives of the projects.)

2. For each site, compute the net present value, assuming that Wichita is adjusted to a four-year life for purposes of analysis. Use the present value of $1 table appearing in this chapter (Exhibit 2).

3. Prepare a report to the investment committee, giving your advice on the relative merits of the two sites.

Chapter 26 Capital Investment Analysis

PR 26-6B Capital rationing decision for a service company involving four proposals   OBJ. 2, 3, 5

✓ 5. Proposal C, 1.57

Excel

Renaissance Capital Group is considering allocating a limited amount of capital investment funds among four proposals. The amount of proposed investment, estimated income from operations, and net cash flow for each proposal are as follows:

	Investment	Year	Income from Operations	Net Cash Flow
Proposal A:	$680,000	1	$ 64,000	$ 200,000
		2	64,000	200,000
		3	64,000	200,000
		4	24,000	160,000
		5	24,000	160,000
			$240,000	$ 920,000
Proposal B:	$320,000	1	$ 26,000	$ 90,000
		2	26,000	90,000
		3	6,000	70,000
		4	6,000	70,000
		5	(44,000)	20,000
			$ 20,000	$ 340,000
Proposal C:	$108,000	1	$ 33,400	$ 55,000
		2	31,400	53,000
		3	28,400	50,000
		4	25,400	47,000
		5	23,400	45,000
			$142,000	$ 250,000
Proposal D:	$400,000	1	$100,000	$ 180,000
		2	100,000	180,000
		3	80,000	160,000
		4	20,000	100,000
		5	0	80,000
			$300,000	$700,000

The company's capital rationing policy requires a maximum cash payback period of three years. In addition, a minimum average rate of return of 12% is required on all projects. If the preceding standards are met, the net present value method and present value indexes are used to rank the remaining proposals.

Instructions

1. Compute the cash payback period for each of the four proposals.
2. Giving effect to straight-line depreciation on the investments and assuming no estimated residual value, compute the average rate of return for each of the four proposals. Round to one decimal place.
3. Using the following format, summarize the results of your computations in parts (1) and (2). By placing the calculated amounts in the first two columns on the left and by placing a check mark in the appropriate column to the right, indicate which proposals should be accepted for further analysis and which should be rejected.

Proposal	Cash Payback Period	Average Rate of Return	Accept for Further Analysis	Reject
A				
B				
C				
D				

4. For the proposals accepted for further analysis in part (3), compute the net present value. Use a rate of 15% and the present value of $1 table appearing in this chapter (Exhibit 2).

(Continued)

5. Compute the present value index for each of the proposals in part (4). Round to two decimal places.
6. Rank the proposals from most attractive to least attractive, based on the present values of net cash flows computed in part (4).
7. Rank the proposals from most attractive to least attractive, based on the present value indexes computed in part (5).
8.  Based on the analyses, comment on the relative attractiveness of the proposals ranked in parts (6) and (7).

Cases & Projects

Ethics

CP 26-1 Ethics in Action

Danielle Hastings was recently hired as a cost analyst by CareNet Medical Supplies Inc. One of Danielle's first assignments was to perform a net present value analysis for a new warehouse. Danielle performed the analysis and calculated a present value index of 0.75. The plant manager, Jerrod Moore, is intent on purchasing the warehouse because he believes that more storage space is needed. Jerrod asks Danielle to come to his office, where the following conversation takes place:

Jerrod: Danielle, you're new here, aren't you?

Danielle: Yes, I am.

Jerrod: Well, Danielle, I'm not at all pleased with the capital investment analysis that you performed on this new warehouse. I need that warehouse for my production. If I don't get it, where am I going to place our output?

Danielle: Well, we need to get product into our customers' hands.

Jerrod: I agree, and we need a warehouse to do that.

Danielle: My analysis does not support constructing a new warehouse. The numbers don't lie; the warehouse does not meet our investment return targets. In fact, it seems to me that purchasing a warehouse does not add much value to the business. We need to be producing product to satisfy customer orders, not to fill a warehouse.

Jerrod: The headquarters people will not allow me to build the warehouse if the numbers don't add up. You know as well as I that many assumptions go into your net present value analysis. Why don't you relax some of your assumptions so that the financial savings will offset the cost?

Danielle: I'm willing to discuss my assumptions with you. Maybe I overlooked something.

Jerrod: Good. Here's what I want you to do. I see in your analysis that you don't project greater sales as a result of the warehouse. It seems to me that if we can store more goods, we will have more to sell. Thus, logically, a larger warehouse translates into more sales. If you incorporate this into your analysis, I think you'll see that the numbers will work out. Why don't you work it through and come back with a new analysis. I'm really counting on you on this one. Let's get off to a good start together and see if we can get this project accepted.

What is your advice to Danielle?

Team Activity

CP 26-2 Team Activity

Divide your team into two groups. In one group, find a local business, such as a copy shop, that rents time on desktop computers for an hourly rate. Determine the hourly rate. In the other group, determine the price of a mid-range desktop computer at www.dell.com. Combine this information from the two groups and perform a capital investment analysis. Assume that one student will use the computer for 40 hours per semester for the next three years. Also assume that the minimum rate of return is 10%. Use the interest tables in Appendix A in performing your analysis. [*Hint:* Use the appropriate present value of an annuity of $1 factor for 5% compounded for six semiannual periods (periods = 6).]

Does your analysis support the student purchasing the computer? Why or why not?

CP 26-3 Communication

Global Electronics Inc. invested $1,000,000 to build a plant in a foreign country. The labor and materials used in production are purchased locally. The plant expansion was estimated to produce an internal rate of return of 20% in U.S. dollar terms. Due to a currency crisis, the currency exchange rate between the local currency and the U.S. dollar doubled from two local units per U.S. dollar to four local units per U.S. dollar.

➤ Write a brief memo to the chief financial officer, Tom Greene, explaining the impact the currency exchange rate change would have on the project's internal rate of return if (1) the plant produced and sold all product in the local economy only and (2) the plant produced all product locally and exported all product to the United States for sale.

CP 26-4 Personal investment analysis for a service company

A Masters of Accountancy degree at Central University costs $12,000 for an additional fifth year of education beyond the bachelor's degree. Assume that all tuition is paid at the beginning of the year. A student considering this investment must evaluate the present value of cash flows from possessing a graduate degree versus holding only the undergraduate degree. Assume that the average student with an undergraduate degree is expected to earn an annual salary of $50,000 per year (assumed to be paid at the end of the year) for 10 years. Assume that the average student with a graduate Masters of Accountancy degree is expected to earn an annual salary of $66,000 per year (assumed to be paid at the end of the year) for nine years after graduation. Assume a minimum rate of return of 10%.

1. Determine the net present value of cash flows from an undergraduate degree. Use the present value table provided in this chapter in Exhibit 5.

2. Determine the net present value of cash flows from a Masters of Accountancy degree, assuming that no salary is earned during the graduate year of schooling.

3. ➤ What is the net advantage or disadvantage of pursuing a graduate degree under these assumptions?

CP 26-5 Qualitative issues in investment analysis

The following are some selected quotes from senior executives:

CEO, **Worthington Industries** (a high-technology steel company): "We try to find the best technology, stay ahead of the competition, and serve the customer.... We'll make any investment that will pay back quickly ... but if it is something that we really see as a must down the road, payback is not going to be that important."

Chairman of **Amgen Inc.** (a biotech company): "You cannot really run the numbers, do net present value calculations, because the uncertainties are really gigantic.... You decide on a project you want to run, and then you run the numbers [as a reality check on your assumptions]. Success in a business like this is much more dependent on tracking rather than on predicting, much more dependent on seeing results over time, tracking and adjusting and readjusting, much more dynamic, much more flexible."

Chief financial officer of **Merck & Co., Inc.** (a pharmaceutical company): "... at the individual product level—the development of a successful new product requires on the order of $230 million in R&D, spread over more than a decade—discounted cash flow style analysis does not become a factor until development is near the point of manufacturing scale-up effort. Prior to that point, given the uncertainties associated with new product development, it would be lunacy in our business to decide that we know exactly what's going to happen to a product once it gets out."

➤ Explain the role of capital investment analysis for these companies.

CP 26-6 Net present value method for a service company

Metro-Goldwyn-Mayer Studios Inc. (MGM) is a major producer and distributor of theatrical and television filmed entertainment. Regarding theatrical films, MGM states, "Our feature films are exploited through a series of sequential domestic and international distribution channels, typically beginning with theatrical exhibition. Thereafter, feature films are first made available for home video (online downloads) generally six months after theatrical release; for pay television, one year after theatrical release; and for syndication, approximately three to five years after theatrical release."

(Continued)

Assume that MGM produces a film during early 2018 at a cost of $340 million and releases it halfway through the year. During the last half of 2018, the film earns revenues of $420 million at the box office. The film requires $90 million of advertising during the release. One year later, by the end of 2019, the film is expected to earn MGM net cash flows from online downloads of $60 million. By the end of 2020, the film is expected to earn MGM $20 million from pay TV, and by the end of 2021, the film is expected to earn $10 million from syndication.

a. Determine the net present value of the film as of the beginning of 2018 if the desired rate of return is 20%. To simplify present value calculations, assume that all annual net cash flows occur at the end of each year. Use the table of the present value of $1 appearing in Exhibit 2 of this chapter. Round to the nearest whole million dollars.

b. Under the assumptions provided here, is the film expected to be financially successful? Explain.

Mornin' Joe

Financial Statements for Mornin' Joe

Financial Statements for Mornin' Joe International

Financial Statements for Mornin' Joe

The financial statements for **Mornin' Joe** follow. Mornin' Joe is a fictitious coffeehouse chain featuring drip and espresso coffee in cafés. The financial statements for Mornin' Joe are provided to illustrate the complete financial statements of a corporation, using the terms, formats, and reporting illustrated throughout this text. In addition, excerpts of the Mornin' Joe financial statements are used to illustrate the financial reporting for the topics discussed in Chapters 7–15. The complete financial statements are shown in Exhibits 1, 2, 3, and 4.

EXHIBIT 1
Income Statement for Mornin' Joe

Mornin' Joe
Income Statement
For the Year Ended December 31, 20Y6

Sales			$5,402,100
Cost of merchandise sold			2,160,000
Gross profit			$3,242,100
Operating expenses			
Selling expenses:			
Wages expense	$825,000		
Advertising expense	678,900		
Depreciation expense—buildings	124,300		
Miscellaneous selling expense	26,500		
Total selling expenses		$1,654,700	
Administrative expenses:			
Office salaries expense	$325,000		
Rent expense	425,600		
Payroll tax expense	110,000		
Depreciation expense—office equipment	68,900		
Bad debt expense	14,000		
Amortization expense	10,500		
Total administrative expenses		954,000	
Total operating expenses			2,608,700
Income from operations			$ 633,400
Other income and expense:			
Interest revenue		$ 18,000	
Interest expense		(136,000)	
Loss on disposal of fixed asset		(23,000)	
Unrealized gain on trading investments		5,000	
Equity income in AM Coffee		57,000	(79,000)
Income before income taxes			$ 554,400
Income tax expense			132,800
Net income			$ 421,600
Basic earnings per share [($421,600 − $30,000) ÷ 44,000 shares issued and outstanding]			$ 8.90

MJ-2

EXHIBIT 2
Balance Sheet for Mornin' Joe

Mornin' Joe
Balance Sheet
December 31, 20Y6

Assets

Current assets:			
Cash and cash equivalents			$ 235,000
Trading investments (at cost)		$ 420,000	
Plus valuation allowance for trading investments		45,000	465,000
Accounts receivable		$ 305,000	
Less allowance for doubtful accounts		12,300	292,700
Merchandise inventory—at lower of cost (first-in, first-out method) or market			120,000
Prepaid insurance			24,000
Total current assets			$1,136,700
Investments:			
Investment in AM Coffee (equity method)			565,000
Property, plant, and equipment:			
Land			$1,850,000
Buildings		$2,650,000	
Less accumulated depreciation		420,000	2,230,000
Office equipment		$ 350,000	
Less accumulated depreciation		102,000	248,000
Total property, plant, and equipment			4,328,000
Intangible assets:			
Patents			140,000
Total assets			$6,169,700

Liabilities

Current liabilities:			
Accounts payable			$ 133,000
Notes payable (current portion)			200,000
Salaries and wages payable			42,000
Payroll taxes payable			16,400
Interest payable			40,000
Total current liabilities			$ 431,400
Long-term liabilities:			
Bonds payable, 8%, due in 25 years		$ 500,000	
Unamortized discount		(16,000)	$ 484,000
Notes payable			1,400,000
Total long-term liabilities			$1,884,000
Total liabilities			$2,315,400

Stockholders' Equity

Paid-in capital:			
Preferred 10% stock, $50 par (6,000 shares authorized and issued)		$ 300,000	
Excess of issue price over par		50,000	$ 350,000
Common stock, $20 par (50,000 shares authorized, 45,000 shares issued)		$ 900,000	
Excess of issue price over par		1,450,000	2,350,000
Total paid-in capital			$2,700,000
Retained earnings			1,200,300
Total			$3,900,300
Treasury stock (1,000 shares at cost)			(46,000)
Total stockholders' equity			$3,854,300
Total liabilities and stockholders' equity			$6,169,700

EXHIBIT 3
Retained Earnings Statement for Mornin' Joe

Mornin' Joe
Retained Earnings Statement
For the Year Ended December 31, 20Y6

Retained earnings, January 1, 20Y6		$ 852,700
Net income	$421,600	
Dividends:		
Preferred stock	(30,000)	
Common stock	(44,000)	
Increase in retained earnings		347,600
Retained earnings, December 31, 20Y6		$1,200,300

EXHIBIT 4
Statement of Stockholders' Equity for Mornin' Joe

Mornin' Joe
Statement of Stockholders' Equity
For the Year Ended December 31, 20Y6

	Preferred Stock	Common Stock	Additional Paid-In Capital	Retained Earnings	Treasury Stock	Total
Balance, January 1, 20Y6	$300,000	$800,000	$1,325,000	$ 852,700	$(36,000)	$3,241,700
Issuance of additional common stock		100,000	175,000			275,000
Purchase of treasury stock					(10,000)	(10,000)
Net income				421,600		421,600
Dividends on preferred stock				(30,000)		(30,000)
Dividends on common stock				(44,000)		(44,000)
Balance, December 31, 20Y6	$300,000	$900,000	$1,500,000	$1,200,300	$(46,000)	$3,854,300

Financial Statements for Mornin' Joe International

Mornin' Joe is planning to expand operations to various places around the world. Financing for this expansion will come from foreign banks. While financial statements prepared under U.S. GAAP may be appropriate for U.S. operations, financial statements prepared for foreign bankers should be prepared using international accounting standards.

The European Union (EU) has developed accounting standards similar in structure to U.S. standards. Its accounting standards board is called the International Accounting Standards Board (IASB). The IASB issues accounting standards that are termed *International Financial Reporting Standards (IFRS)*. The intent of the IASB is to create a set of financial standards that can be used by public companies worldwide, not just in the EU.

Currently, the EU countries and more than 100 other countries around the world have adopted or are planning to adopt IFRS.

Key Reporting Differences Between IFRS and U.S. GAAP

The financial statements of **Mornin' Joe International** using IFRS are presented in Exhibits 1, 2, and 3. This illustration highlights reporting and terminology differences between IFRS and U.S. GAAP. Differences in recording transactions under IFRS and U.S. GAAP are discussed in Appendix B and in various International Connection boxes throughout the text.

The Mornin' Joe International financial statements in Exhibits 5, 6, and 7 are simplified and illustrate only portions of IFRS that are appropriate for introductory accounting. The financial statements are presented in euros (€), which is the standard currency of the European Union. The euro is translated at a 1:1 ratio from the dollar to simplify comparisons. Throughout the illustration, call-outs and end notes to each statement are used to highlight the differences between financial statements prepared under IFRS and under U.S. GAAP.

Statements of Comprehensive Income Versus Income Statements

Exhibit 5 illustrates the statement of comprehensive income for **Mornin' Joe International** and shows key differences from the income statements prepared under U.S. GAAP.

EXHIBIT 5 Statement of Comprehensive Income for Mornin' Joe International

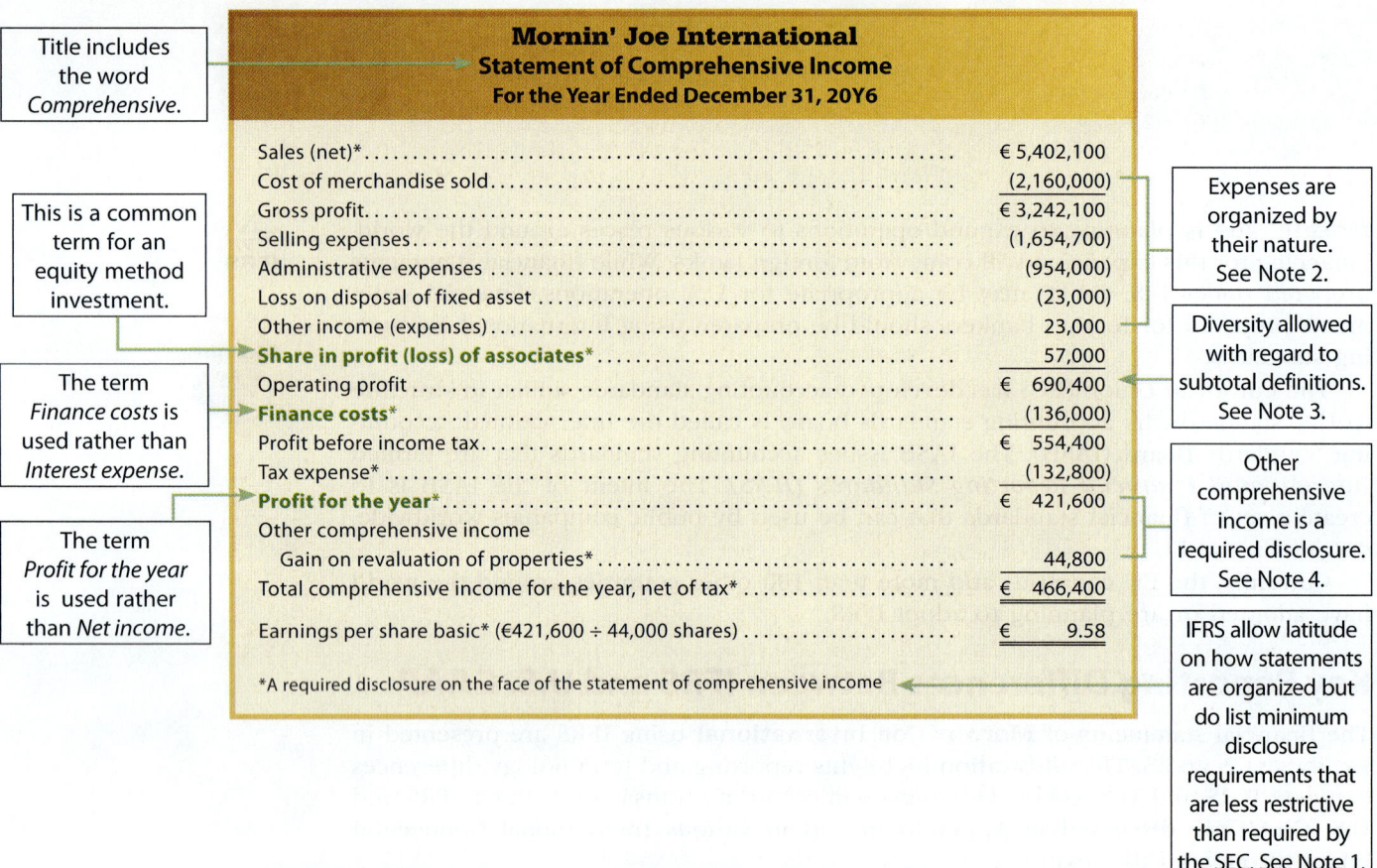

1. IFRS statements are often more summarized than U.S. GAAP statements. To compensate, IFRS require specific disclosures on the face of the financial statements (denoted*) and additional disclosures in the footnotes to the financial statements. Because additions and subtractions are grouped together in sections of IFRS statements, parentheses are used to indicate subtractions.

2. Expenses in an IFRS income statement are classified by either their nature or function. The nature of an expense is how the expense would naturally be recorded in a journal entry reflecting the economic benefit received for that expense. Examples include salaries, depreciation, advertising, and utilities. The function of an expense identifies the purpose of the expense, such as a selling expense or an administrative expense.

   IFRS do not permit the natural and functional classifications to be mixed together on the same statement. That is, all expenses must be classified by either nature or function. However, if a functional classification of expenses is used, a footnote to the income statement must show the natural classification of expenses. To illustrate, because **Mornin' Joe International** uses the functional classification of expenses in its income statement, it must also show the following natural classification of expenses in a footnote:

Cost of product	€2,100,000	The cost of product purchased for resale
Employee benefits expense	1,260,000	Required natural disclosure
Depreciation and amortization expense	203,700	Required natural disclosure
Rent expense	425,600	
Advertising expense	678,900	
Other expenses	58,500	
Total natural expenses	€4,726,700	

3. IFRS provide flexibility with regard to line items, headings, and subtotals on the income statement. There is less flexibility under U.S. GAAP for public companies.
4. IFRS require the reporting of other comprehensive income (see appendix to Chapter 15) either on the income statement (see Exhibit 5) or in a separate statement. U.S. GAAP has a similar disclosure treatment. For **Mornin' Joe International**, other comprehensive income consists of the restatement of café locations to fair value (see Note 6 for more details).
5. Under IFRS, there is no standard format for the balance sheet (statement of financial position, see Exhibit 6). A typical format for European Union companies is to begin the Asset section of the balance sheet with noncurrent assets. This is followed by current assets listed in reverse order of liquidity. That is, the asset side of the balance sheet is reported in reverse order of liquidity from least liquid to most liquid. Listing noncurrent assets first emphasizes the going concern nature of the entity.

    The liability and owners' equity side of the balance sheet is also reported differently than under U.S. GAAP. Specifically, owners' equity is reported first followed by noncurrent liabilities and current liabilities. Listing equity first emphasizes the going concern nature of the entity and the long-term financial interest of the owners in the business.
6. Under IFRS, property, plant, and equipment (PP&E) may be measured at historical cost or fair value. If fair value is used, the revaluation must be for similar classifications of PP&E but need not be for all PP&E. This departs from U.S. GAAP, which requires PP&E to be measured at historical cost. **Mornin' Joe International** restated its Land and Buildings to fair value because the café sites have readily available real estate market prices. Land and buildings are included together because their fair values are not separable. The office equipment remains at historical cost because it does not have a readily available market price. The increase in fair value is recorded by reducing accumulated depreciation and recognizing the gain as other comprehensive income. This element of other comprehensive income is accumulated in stockholders' equity under the heading Property revaluation reserve.* This treatment is similar (with different titles) to the U.S. GAAP treatment of unrealized gains (losses) from available-for-sale securities. For Mornin' Joe International, there is an increase in the property revaluation reserve of €44,800. This amount is the only difference between Mornin' Joe's U.S. GAAP net income, total assets, and total stockholders' equity and Mornin' Joe International's IFRS total comprehensive income, total assets, and total stockholders' equity.
7. **Mornin' Joe International** recently acquired a coffee plantation. This is an example of a biological asset. IFRS require separate reporting of biological assets (principally agricultural assets) at fair value.
8. Inventories are valued at lower of cost or market; however, "market" is defined as net realizable value under IFRS. U.S. GAAP defines "market" as replacement cost under most conditions. In addition, IFRS prohibit LIFO cost valuation.
9. Under IFRS, some elements of other comprehensive income and owner's equity are often aggregated under the term *reserves*. In contrast, under U.S. GAAP, *reserve* is used to identify a liability. IFRS also do not require separate disclosure of treasury stock as does U.S. GAAP. Specifically, treasury stock may be reported as a reduction of a reserve, as a reduction of a stock premium, or as a separate item.
10. The term *provision* is used to denote a liability under IFRS, whereas this term often indicates an expense under U.S. GAAP. For example, *Provision for income taxes* means "Income tax expense" under U.S. GAAP, whereas it would mean "Income taxes payable" under IFRS.
11. Under U.S. GAAP, other comprehensive income items must be included as changes in accumulated other comprehensive income in the statement of changes in stockholders' equity (see Exhibit 7). IFRS allow for similar treatment, with wider latitude for terminology, such as *Property Revaluation Reserve* illustrated by the column title here. In this illustration, treasury stock is included as part of a reserve (Reserve for Own Shares). As discussed in Note 9, under U.S. GAAP, the term *reserve* denotes a liability.

Statements of Financial Position Versus Balance Sheets

Exhibit 6 illustrates the statement of financial position for **Mornin' Joe International** and shows key differences from the balance sheets prepared under U.S. GAAP.

EXHIBIT 6 — Statement of Financial Position for Mornin' Joe International

Mornin' Joe International
Statement of Financial Position
December 31, 20Y6

Preferred title for the balance sheet.

Assets

Noncurrent assets
Property, plant, and equipment*
Land and buildings at fair value	€4,180,000	
Less: Accumulated depreciation	375,200	€3,804,800
Office equipment at cost	€ 350,000	
Less: Accumulated depreciation	102,000	248,000
Biological assets at fair value*		320,000
Patents at amortized cost*		140,000
Investment in AM Coffee (equity method)*		565,000
Total noncurrent assets		€5,077,800

Sub-classifications of PP&E may be valued at fair value. See Note 6.

Biological assets are a required disclosure at fair value. See Note 7.

Current assets
Prepaid insurance	€ 24,000	
Merchandise inventory—at lower of cost (first-in, first-out) or realizable value*	120,000	
Accounts receivable (net of allowance for doubtful accounts)*	292,700	
Financial assets at fair value through profit or loss*	465,000	
Cash and cash equivalents*	235,000	
Total current assets		1,136,700
Total assets*		**€6,214,500**

Inventory valuation. See Note 8.

International terminology for "Trading investments." Same accounting treatment.

Reverse liquidity account order. See Note 5.

Equity attributable to owners
Preferred 10% stock, €50 par (6,000 shares authorized and issued)*	€ 300,000	
Common stock, €20 par (50,000 shares authorized, 45,000 shares issued)*	900,000	
Share premium*	1,500,000	
Reserves*	(1,200)	
Retained earnings*	1,200,300	
Total equity attributable to owners*		€3,899,100

International terminology for "Excess of issue price over par."

Other comprehensive items and treasury stock. See Note 9.

Equities listed first, then liabilities. See Note 5.

Liabilities

Noncurrent liabilities*
Bonds payable, 8%, due December 31, 2036 (net of discount)	€ 484,000	
Notes payable	1,400,000	
Total noncurrent liabilities		€1,884,000

Noncurrent liabilities listed prior to current liabilities.

Current liabilities
Accounts payable*	€ 133,000	
Loans*	200,000	
Employee provisions*	58,400	
Interest payable	40,000	
Total current liabilities		431,400
Total liabilities*		€2,315,400
Total equity and liabilities*		**€6,214,500**

Employee provisions are wages, salaries, and payroll taxes payable. See Note 10.

*Required disclosures. Footnotes provide additional subclassification detail.

Statements of Changes in Equity Versus Statements of Stockholders' Equity

Exhibit 7 illustrates the statement of changes in equity for **Mornin' Joe International** and shows key differences from the statements of stockholders' equity prepared under U.S. GAAP.

EXHIBIT 7 — Statement of Changes in Equity for Mornin' Joe International

Mornin' Joe International
Statement of Changes in Equity
For the Year Ended December 31, 20Y6

	Preferred Stock	Common Stock	Share Premium	Property Revaluation Reserve	Reserve for Own Shares	Retained Earnings	Total Equity Attributable to Owners
Balance, January 1, 20Y6	€300,000	€800,000	€1,325,000	€ 0	€(36,000)	€ 852,700	€3,241,700
Profit for the year						421,600	421,600
Other comprehensive income							
Property revaluation (gain)				44,800			44,800
Total comprehensive income				€44,800		€ 421,600	€ 466,400
Contributions by and distributions to owners							
Dividends on preferred stock						(30,000)	(30,000)
Dividends on common stock						(44,000)	(44,000)
Issuance of additional common stock		100,000	175,000				275,000
Purchase of own shares					(10,000)		(10,000)
Total contributions and distributions to owners	€ 0	€100,000	€ 175,000	€ 0	€(10,000)	€ (74,000)	€ 191,000
Balance, December 31, 20Y6	€300,000	€900,000	€1,500,000	€44,800	€(46,000)	€1,200,300	€3,899,100

"Reserves," see Notes 9 and 11.

Discussion Questions

1. Contrast U.S. GAAP financial statement terms with their different IFRS terms.
2. What is the difference between classifying an expense by nature or function?
3. If a functional expense classification is used for the statement of comprehensive income, what must also be disclosed?
4. How is the term *provision* used differently under IFRS than under U.S. GAAP?
5. What are two main differences in inventory valuation under IFRS compared to U.S. GAAP?
6. What is a "biological asset"?
7. What is the most significant IFRS departure from U.S. GAAP for valuing property, plant, and equipment?
8. What is a "share premium"?
9. How is the term *reserve* used under IFRS, and how does it differ from its meaning under U.S. GAAP?

IFRS Activity 1

Unilever Group is a global company that markets a wide variety of products, including Lever® soap, Breyer's® ice cream, and Hellman's® mayonnaise. A recent income statement and statement of comprehensive income for the Dutch company, Unilever Group, follow:

Unilever Group
Consolidated Income Statement
For the Year Ended December 31
(in millions of euros)

Turnover	€51,324
Operating profit	6,989
After (charging)/crediting:	
Non-core items	(73)
Net finance costs	(397)
Finance income	136
Finance costs	(526)
Pensions and similar obligations	(7)
Share of net profit/(loss) of joint ventures and associations	105
Other income from non-current investments	(14)
Profit before taxation	€ 6,683
Taxation	(1,735)
Net profit	€ 4,948
Earnings per share—basic	€ 1.58
Earnings per share—diluted	€ 1.54

Consolidated Statement of Comprehensive Income
For the Year Ended December 31

Fair value gains (losses), net of tax	€ (125)
Actuarial gains (losses) on pensions, net of tax	(644)
Currency retranslation gains (losses), net of tax	(316)
Net income (expense) recognized directly into equity	€(1,085)
Net profit	4,948
Total comprehensive income	€3,863

a. What do you think is meant by "turnover"?

b. How does Unilever's income statement presentation differ significantly from that of Mornin' Joe?

c. How is the total for net finance costs presented differently from what typically would be found under U.S. GAAP?

IFRS Activity 2

The following is a recent consolidated statement of financial position on December 31 of a recent year for **LVMH**, a French company that markets the Louis Vuitton® and Moët Hennessy® brands:

LVMH
Statement of Financial Position
December 31
(in millions of euros)

Assets	
Brands and other intangible assets—net	€11,510
Goodwill—net	7,806
Property, plant, and equipment—net	8,769
Investment in associates	163
Non-current available for sale financial assets	6,004
Other non-current assets	524
Deferred tax	881
Non-current assets	**€35,657**
Inventories	€ 8,080
Trade accounts receivable	1,985
Income taxes	201
Other current assets	1,811
Cash and cash equivalents	2,196
Current assets	**€14,273**
TOTAL ASSETS	**€49,930**
Liabilities and Equity	
Share capital	€ 152
Share premium	3,848
Treasury shares	(414)
Revaluation reserves	2,819
Other reserves	14,393
Cumulative translation adjustment	342
Net profit, group share	3,424
Equity, group share	€24,564
Minority interests	1,102
Total equity	**€25,666**
Long-term borrowings	€ 3,836
Provisions	1,530
Deferred tax	3,960
Other non-current liabilities	5,456
Total non-current liabilities	**€14,782**
Short-term borrowings	€ 2,976
Trade accounts payable	3,134
Income taxes payable	442
Provisions	335
Other current liabilities	2,595
Total current liabilities	**€ 9,482**
TOTAL LIABILITIES AND EQUITY	**€49,930**

a. Identify presentation differences between the balance sheet of LVMH and a balance sheet prepared under U.S. GAAP. Use the Mornin' Joe balance sheet (Exhibit 2) as an example of a U.S. GAAP balance sheet. (Ignore minority interests and cumulative translation adjustment.)

b. Compare the terms used in this balance sheet with the terms used by Mornin' Joe (Exhibit 2), using the table that follows:

LVMH Term	Mornin' Joe U.S. GAAP Term
Statement of financial position	
Share capital	
Share premium	
Other reserves	
Provisions	

c. What does the "Revaluation reserves" in the Equity section of the balance sheet represent?

IFRS Activity 3

Under U.S. GAAP, LIFO is an acceptable inventory method. Financial statement information for three companies that use LIFO follows. All table numbers are in millions of dollars.

	LIFO Inventory	FIFO Inventory (from notes)	Impact on Net Income from Using LIFO Rather Than FIFO (from notes)	Total Current Assets	Net Income as Reported
ExxonMobil	$9,852	$31,200	$317	$58,984	$30,460
Kroger	4,966	5,793	(57)	7,621	1,116
Ford Motor*	5,917	6,782	4	34,368	4,690

*Autos and trucks only

Assume that these companies adopted IFRS and thus were required to use FIFO rather than LIFO.

a. Prepare a table with the following columns:

(1)	(2)	(3)	(4)
FIFO less LIFO	IFRS Net Income	(FIFO less LIFO) / Total Current Assets	IFRS Net Income (Col. 2) / Reported Net Income

(1) Difference between FIFO and LIFO inventory valuation

(2) Revised IFRS net income using FIFO

(3) Difference between FIFO and LIFO inventory valuation as a percent of total current assets (rounded to the nearest whole percent)

(4) Revised IFRS net income as a percent of the reported net income (rounded to the nearest whole percent)

b. Complete the table for the three companies.

c. For which company would a change to IFRS for inventory valuation have the largest percentage impact on total current assets (Col. 3)?

d. For which company would a change to IFRS for inventory valuation have the largest percentage impact on net income (Col. 4)?

e. Why might Kroger have a negative impact on net income from using LIFO, while the other two companies have a positive impact on net income from using LIFO?

Appendices

A Interest Tables

B International Financial Reporting Standards (IFRS)

C Revenue Recognition

D Nike Inc., Form 10-K for the Fiscal Year Ended May 31, 2016

Appendix A

Interest Tables

Present Value of $1 at Compound Interest Due in n Periods

Periods	4.0%	4.5%	5%	5.5%	6%	6.5%	7%
1	0.96154	0.95694	0.95238	0.94787	0.94340	0.93897	0.93458
2	0.92456	0.91573	0.90703	0.89845	0.89000	0.88166	0.87344
3	0.88900	0.87630	0.86384	0.85161	0.83962	0.82785	0.81630
4	0.85480	0.83856	0.82270	0.80722	0.79209	0.77732	0.76290
5	0.82193	0.80245	0.78353	0.76513	0.74726	0.72988	0.71299
6	0.79031	0.76790	0.74622	0.72525	0.70496	0.68533	0.66634
7	0.75992	0.73483	0.71068	0.68744	0.66506	0.64351	0.62275
8	0.73069	0.70319	0.67684	0.65160	0.62741	0.60423	0.58201
9	0.70259	0.67290	0.64461	0.61763	0.59190	0.56735	0.54393
10	0.67556	0.64393	0.61391	0.58543	0.55839	0.53273	0.50835
11	0.64958	0.61620	0.58468	0.55491	0.52679	0.50021	0.47509
12	0.62460	0.58966	0.55684	0.52598	0.49697	0.46968	0.44401
13	0.60057	0.56427	0.53032	0.49856	0.46884	0.44102	0.41496
14	0.57748	0.53997	0.50507	0.47257	0.44230	0.41410	0.38782
15	0.55526	0.51672	0.48102	0.44793	0.41727	0.38883	0.36245
16	0.53391	0.49447	0.45811	0.42458	0.39365	0.36510	0.33873
17	0.51337	0.47318	0.43630	0.40245	0.37136	0.34281	0.31657
18	0.49363	0.45280	0.41552	0.38147	0.35034	0.32189	0.29586
19	0.47464	0.43330	0.39573	0.36158	0.33051	0.30224	0.27651
20	0.45639	0.41464	0.37689	0.34273	0.31180	0.28380	0.25842
21	0.43883	0.39679	0.35894	0.32486	0.29416	0.26648	0.24151
22	0.42196	0.37970	0.34185	0.30793	0.27751	0.25021	0.22571
23	0.40573	0.36335	0.32557	0.29187	0.26180	0.23494	0.21095
24	0.39012	0.34770	0.31007	0.27666	0.24698	0.22060	0.19715
25	0.37512	0.33273	0.29530	0.26223	0.23300	0.20714	0.18425
26	0.36069	0.31840	0.28124	0.24856	0.21981	0.19450	0.17220
27	0.34682	0.30469	0.26785	0.23560	0.20737	0.18263	0.16093
28	0.33348	0.29157	0.25509	0.22332	0.19563	0.17148	0.15040
29	0.32065	0.27902	0.24295	0.21168	0.18456	0.16101	0.14056
30	0.30832	0.26700	0.23138	0.20064	0.17411	0.15119	0.13137
31	0.29646	0.25550	0.22036	0.19018	0.16425	0.14196	0.12277
32	0.28506	0.24450	0.20987	0.18027	0.15496	0.13329	0.11474
33	0.27409	0.23397	0.19987	0.17087	0.14619	0.12516	0.10723
34	0.26355	0.22390	0.19035	0.16196	0.13791	0.11752	0.10022
35	0.25342	0.21425	0.18129	0.15352	0.13011	0.11035	0.09366
40	0.20829	0.17193	0.14205	0.11746	0.09722	0.08054	0.06678
45	0.17120	0.13796	0.11130	0.08988	0.07265	0.05879	0.04761
50	0.14071	0.11071	0.08720	0.06877	0.05429	0.04291	0.03395

Present Value of $1 at Compound Interest Due in _n_ Periods

Periods	8%	9%	10%	11%	12%	13%	14%
1	0.92593	0.91743	0.90909	0.90090	0.89286	0.88496	0.87719
2	0.85734	0.84168	0.82645	0.81162	0.79719	0.78315	0.76947
3	0.79383	0.77218	0.75131	0.73119	0.71178	0.69305	0.67497
4	0.73503	0.70843	0.68301	0.65873	0.63552	0.61332	0.59208
5	0.68058	0.64993	0.62092	0.59345	0.56743	0.54276	0.51937
6	0.63017	0.59627	0.56447	0.53464	0.50663	0.48032	0.45559
7	0.58349	0.54703	0.51316	0.48166	0.45235	0.42506	0.39964
8	0.54027	0.50187	0.46651	0.43393	0.40388	0.37616	0.35056
9	0.50025	0.46043	0.42410	0.39092	0.36061	0.33288	0.30751
10	0.46319	0.42241	0.38554	0.35218	0.32197	0.29459	0.26974
11	0.42888	0.38753	0.35049	0.31728	0.28748	0.26070	0.23662
12	0.39711	0.35553	0.31863	0.28584	0.25668	0.23071	0.20756
13	0.36770	0.32618	0.28966	0.25751	0.22917	0.20416	0.18207
14	0.34046	0.29925	0.26333	0.23199	0.20462	0.18068	0.15971
15	0.31524	0.27454	0.23939	0.20900	0.18270	0.15989	0.14010
16	0.29189	0.25187	0.21763	0.18829	0.16312	0.14150	0.12289
17	0.27027	0.23107	0.19784	0.16963	0.14564	0.12522	0.10780
18	0.25025	0.21199	0.17986	0.15282	0.13004	0.11081	0.09456
19	0.23171	0.19449	0.16351	0.13768	0.11611	0.09806	0.08295
20	0.21455	0.17843	0.14864	0.12403	0.10367	0.08678	0.07276
21	0.19866	0.16370	0.13513	0.11174	0.09256	0.07680	0.06383
22	0.18394	0.15018	0.12285	0.10067	0.08264	0.06796	0.05599
23	0.17032	0.13778	0.11168	0.09069	0.07379	0.06014	0.04911
24	0.15770	0.12640	0.10153	0.08170	0.06588	0.05323	0.04308
25	0.14602	0.11597	0.09230	0.07361	0.05882	0.04710	0.03779
26	0.13520	0.10639	0.08391	0.06631	0.05252	0.04168	0.03315
27	0.12519	0.09761	0.07628	0.05974	0.04689	0.03689	0.02908
28	0.11591	0.08955	0.06934	0.05382	0.04187	0.03264	0.02551
29	0.10733	0.08215	0.06304	0.04849	0.03738	0.02889	0.02237
30	0.09938	0.07537	0.05731	0.04368	0.03338	0.02557	0.01963
31	0.09202	0.06915	0.05210	0.03935	0.02980	0.02262	0.01722
32	0.08520	0.06344	0.04736	0.03545	0.02661	0.02002	0.01510
33	0.07889	0.05820	0.04306	0.03194	0.02376	0.01772	0.01325
34	0.07305	0.05339	0.03914	0.02878	0.02121	0.01568	0.01162
35	0.06763	0.04899	0.03558	0.02592	0.01894	0.01388	0.01019
40	0.04603	0.03184	0.02209	0.01538	0.01075	0.00753	0.00529
45	0.03133	0.02069	0.01372	0.00913	0.00610	0.00409	0.00275
50	0.02132	0.01345	0.00852	0.00542	0.00346	0.00222	0.00143

Present Value of Ordinary Annuity of $1 per Period

Periods	4.0%	4.5%	5%	5.5%	6%	6.5%	7%
1	0.96154	0.95694	0.95238	0.94787	0.94340	0.93897	0.93458
2	1.88609	1.87267	1.85941	1.84632	1.83339	1.82063	1.80802
3	2.77509	2.74896	2.72325	2.69793	2.67301	2.64848	2.62432
4	3.62990	3.58753	3.54595	3.50515	3.46511	3.42580	3.38721
5	4.45182	4.38998	4.32948	4.27028	4.21236	4.15568	4.10020
6	5.24214	5.15787	5.07569	4.99553	4.91732	4.84101	4.76654
7	6.00205	5.89270	5.78637	5.68297	5.58238	5.48452	5.38929
8	6.73274	6.59589	6.46321	6.33457	6.20979	6.08875	5.97130
9	7.43533	7.26879	7.10782	6.95220	6.80169	6.65610	6.51523
10	8.11090	7.91272	7.72173	7.53763	7.36009	7.18883	7.02358
11	8.76048	8.52892	8.30641	8.09254	7.88687	7.68904	7.49867
12	9.38507	9.11858	8.86325	8.61852	8.38384	8.15873	7.94269
13	9.98565	9.68285	9.39357	9.11708	8.85268	8.59974	8.35765
14	10.56312	10.22283	9.89864	9.58965	9.29498	9.01384	8.74547
15	11.11839	10.73955	10.37966	10.03758	9.71225	9.40267	9.10791
16	11.65230	11.23402	10.83777	10.46216	10.10590	9.76776	9.44665
17	12.16567	11.70719	11.27407	10.86461	10.47726	10.11058	9.76322
18	12.65930	12.15999	11.68959	11.24607	10.82760	10.43247	10.05909
19	13.13394	12.59329	12.08532	11.60765	11.15812	10.73471	10.33560
20	13.59033	13.00794	12.46221	11.95038	11.46992	11.01851	10.59401
21	14.02916	13.40472	12.82115	12.27524	11.76408	11.28498	10.83553
22	14.45112	13.78442	13.16300	12.58317	12.04158	11.53520	11.06124
23	14.85684	14.14777	13.48857	12.87504	12.30338	11.77014	11.27219
24	15.24696	14.49548	13.79864	13.15170	12.55036	11.99074	11.46933
25	15.62208	14.82821	14.09394	13.41393	12.78336	12.19788	11.65358
26	15.98277	15.14661	14.37519	13.66250	13.00317	12.39237	11.82578
27	16.32959	15.45130	14.64303	13.89810	13.21053	12.57500	11.98671
28	16.66306	15.74287	14.89813	14.12142	13.40616	12.74648	12.13711
29	16.98371	16.02189	15.14107	14.33310	13.59072	12.90749	12.27767
30	17.29203	16.28889	15.37245	14.53375	13.76483	13.05868	12.40904
31	17.58849	16.54439	15.59281	14.72393	13.92909	13.20063	12.53181
32	17.87355	16.78889	15.80268	14.90420	14.08404	13.33393	12.64656
33	18.14765	17.02286	16.00255	15.07507	14.23023	13.45909	12.75379
34	18.41120	17.24676	16.19290	15.23703	14.36814	13.57661	12.85401
35	18.66461	17.46101	16.37419	15.39055	14.49825	13.68696	12.94767
40	19.79277	18.40158	17.15909	16.04612	15.04630	14.14553	13.33171
45	20.72004	19.15635	17.77407	16.54773	15.45583	14.48023	13.60552
50	21.48218	19.76201	18.25593	16.93152	15.76186	14.72452	13.80075

Present Value of Ordinary Annuity of $1 per Period

Periods	8%	9%	10%	11%	12%	13%	14%
1	0.92593	0.91743	0.90909	0.90090	0.89286	0.88496	0.87719
2	1.78326	1.75911	1.73554	1.71252	1.69005	1.66810	1.64666
3	2.57710	2.53129	2.48685	2.44371	2.40183	2.36115	2.32163
4	3.31213	3.23972	3.16987	3.10245	3.03735	2.97447	2.91371
5	3.99271	3.88965	3.79079	3.69590	3.60478	3.51723	3.43308
6	4.62288	4.48592	4.35526	4.23054	4.11141	3.99755	3.88867
7	5.20637	5.03295	4.86842	4.71220	4.56376	4.42261	4.28830
8	5.74664	5.53482	5.33493	5.14612	4.96764	4.79677	4.63886
9	6.24689	5.99525	5.75902	5.53705	5.32825	5.13166	4.94637
10	6.71008	6.41766	6.14457	5.88923	5.65022	5.42624	5.21612
11	7.13896	6.80519	6.49506	6.20652	5.93770	5.68694	5.45273
12	7.53608	7.16073	6.81369	6.49236	6.19437	5.91765	5.66029
13	7.90378	7.48690	7.10336	6.74987	6.42355	6.12181	5.84236
14	8.22424	7.78615	7.36669	6.96187	6.62817	6.30249	6.00207
15	8.55948	8.06069	7.60608	7.19087	6.81086	6.46238	6.14217
16	8.85137	8.31256	7.82371	7.37916	6.97399	6.60388	6.26506
17	9.12164	8.54363	8.02155	7.54879	7.11963	6.72909	6.37286
18	9.37189	8.75563	8.20141	7.70162	7.24967	6.83991	6.46742
19	9.60360	8.95011	8.36492	7.83929	7.36578	6.93797	6.55037
20	9.81815	9.12855	8.51356	7.96333	7.46944	7.02475	6.62313
21	10.01680	9.29224	8.64869	8.07507	7.56200	7.10155	6.68696
22	10.20074	9.44243	8.77154	8.17574	7.64465	7.16951	6.74294
23	10.37106	9.58021	8.88322	8.26643	7.71843	7.22966	6.79206
24	10.52876	9.70661	8.98474	8.34814	7.78432	7.28288	6.83514
25	10.67478	9.82258	9.07704	8.42174	7.84314	7.32998	6.87293
26	10.80998	9.92897	9.16095	8.48806	7.89566	7.37167	6.90608
27	10.93516	10.02658	9.23722	8.54780	7.94255	7.40856	6.93515
28	11.05108	10.11613	9.30657	8.60162	7.98442	7.44120	6.96066
29	11.15841	10.19828	9.36961	8.65011	8.02181	7.47009	6.98304
30	11.25778	10.27365	9.42691	8.69379	8.05518	7.49565	7.00266
31	11.34980	10.34280	9.47901	8.73315	8.08499	7.51828	7.01988
32	11.43500	10.40624	9.52638	8.76860	8.11159	7.53830	7.03498
33	11.51389	10.46444	9.56943	8.80054	8.13535	7.55602	7.04823
34	11.58693	10.51784	9.60857	8.82932	8.15656	7.57170	7.05985
35	11.65457	10.56682	9.64416	8.85524	8.17550	7.58557	7.07005
40	11.92461	10.75736	9.77905	8.95105	8.24378	7.63438	7.10504
45	12.10840	10.88120	9.86281	9.00791	8.28252	7.66086	7.12322
50	12.23348	10.96168	9.91481	9.04165	8.30450	7.67524	7.13266

Appendix B

International Financial Reporting Standards (IFRS)

The Need for Global Accounting Standards

As discussed in Chapter 1, the Financial Accounting Standards Board (FASB) establishes generally accepted accounting principles (GAAP) for public companies in the United States. Of course, there is a world beyond the borders of the United States. In recent years, the removal of trade barriers and the growth in cross-border equity and debt issuances have led to a dramatic increase in international commerce. As a result, often companies are reporting financial results to users outside of the United States.

Historically, accounting standards have varied considerably across countries. These variances have been driven by cultural, legal, and political differences and resulted in financial statements that were not easily comparable and difficult to interpret. These differences caused problems for companies in Europe and Asia, where local economies have become increasingly tied to international commerce.

A common set of International Financial Reporting Standards (IFRS) has begun to emerge to reduce cross-country differences in accounting standards. While much of the world has migrated to IFRS, the United States has not. Because of the size of the United States and its significant role in world commerce, U.S. GAAP still has a global impact. As a result, there are currently two major accounting standard-setting efforts in the world, U.S. GAAP and IFRS. These two sets of accounting standards add cost and complexity for companies operating internationally.

Overview of IFRS

International Financial Reporting Standards are designed to meet the financial reporting needs of an increasingly global business environment.

What Is IFRS? International Financial Reporting Standards are a set of global accounting standards developed by an international standard-setting body called the International Accounting Standards Board (IASB). Like the Financial Accounting Standards Board, the IASB is an independent entity that establishes accounting rules. Unlike the FASB, the IASB does not establish accounting rules for any specific country. Rather, it develops accounting rules that can be used by a variety of countries, with the goal of developing a single set of global accounting standards.

Who Uses IFRS? IFRS applies to companies that issue publicly traded debt or equity securities, called **public companies**, in countries that have adopted IFRS as their accounting standards. For example, public companies in the European Union (EU) are required to prepare financial statements using IFRS. The 140 countries and jurisdictions that have adopted or permit the use of IFRS for financial reporting are shown in Exhibit 1.

B-1

EXHIBIT 1 IFRS Adopters

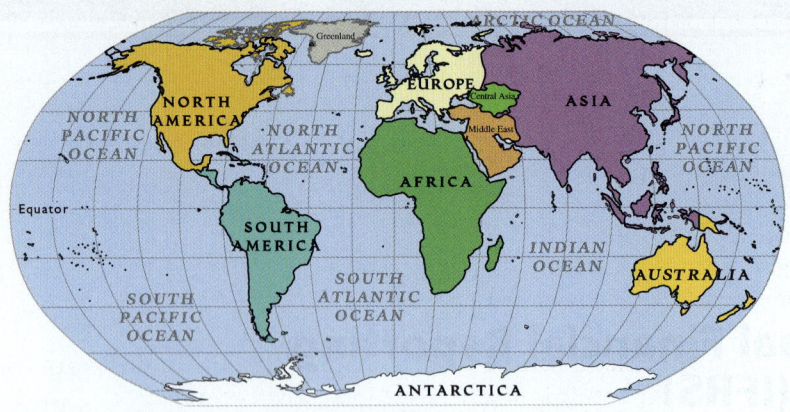

Afghanistan	Bulgaria	Ghana	Liechtenstein	Palestine	Sweden
Albania	Cambodia	Greece	Lithuania	Panama	Switzerland
Angola	Canada	Grenada	Luxembourg	Paraguay	Syria
Anguilla	Cayman Islands	Guatemala	Macao	Peru	Taiwan
Antigua and Barbuda	Chile	Guinea-Bissau	Macedonia	Philippines	Tanzania
Argentina	China	Guyana	Madagascar	Poland	Thailand
Armenia	Colombia	Honduras	Malaysia	Portugal	Trinidad and Tobago
Australia	Costa Rica	Hong Kong	Maldives	Romania	Turkey
Austria	Croatia	Hungary	Malta	Russia	Uganda
Azerbaijan	Cyprus	Iceland	Mauritius	Rwanda	Ukraine
Bahamas	Czech Republic	India	Mexico	Saint Lucia	United Arab Emirates
Bahrain	Denmark	Indonesia	Moldova	Saudi Arabia	United Kingdom
Bangladesh	Dominica	Iraq	Mongolia	Serbia	United States
Barbados	Dominican Republic	Ireland	Montserrat	Sierra Leone	Uruguay
Belarus	Ecuador	Israel	Myanmar	Singapore	Uzbekistan
Belgium	Egypt	Italy	Nepal	Slovakia	Venezuela
Belize	El Salvador	Jamaica	Netherlands	Slovenia	Vietnam
Bermuda	Estonia	Japan	New Zealand	South Africa	Yemen
Bhutan	European Union	Jordan	Nicaragua	Spain	Zambia
Bolivia	Fiji	Kenya	Niger	Sri Lanka	Zimbabwe
Bosnia and Herzegovina	Finland	Korea (South)	Nigeria	St Kitts and Nevis	
Botswana	France	Kosovo	Norway	St Vincent and the Grenadines	
Brazil	Georgia	Latvia	Oman	Suriname	
Brunei	Germany	Lesotho	Pakistan	Swaziland	

Source: *Financial Reporting Standards for the World Economy*, IFRS, June 2015.

U.S. GAAP and IFRS: The Road Forward

The United States has not formally adopted IFRS for U.S. companies. The wide acceptance being gained by IFRS around the world, however, has placed considerable pressure on the United States to align U.S. GAAP with IFRS. There are two possible paths that the United States could take to achieve this: (1) adoption of IFRS by the U.S. Securities and Exchange Commission or (2) convergence of U.S. GAAP and IFRS. These two options are briefly discussed in this section.

Adoption of IFRS by the SEC The U.S. Securities and Exchange Commission (SEC) is the U.S. governmental agency that has authority over the accounting and financial disclosures for U.S. public companies. Only the SEC has the authority to adopt IFRS for U.S. public companies. After considerable deliberation over a period of nearly five years, the SEC published a Final

Report on the issues surrounding IFRS adoption.[1] Notably, this report did not include a final policy decision or recommendation in favor of U.S. public companies adopting IFRS. Indeed, since this report, the SEC has distanced itself from the adoption position, and it is now acknowledged as unsupported. This leaves what remains of the convergence pathway.

Convergence of U.S. GAAP and IFRS Convergence involves aligning IFRS and U.S. GAAP one topic at a time, by slowly merging IFRS and U.S. GAAP into two broadly uniform sets of accounting standards. To this end, the FASB and IASB have agreed to work together on a select number of difficult and high-profile accounting issues. These issues frame a large portion of the disagreement between the two sets of standards and, if accomplished, will significantly reduce the differences between U.S. GAAP and IFRS. The projects selected for the convergence effort represent some of the more technical topics in accounting and are covered in intermediate and advanced accounting courses.

One of the major limitations of convergence is that both the FASB and IASB continue to operate as the accounting standard-setting bodies for their respective jurisdictions. As such, convergence would not result in a single set of global accounting standards. Only those standards that go through the joint FASB–IASB standard-setting process would be released as uniform. Standards that do not go through a joint standard-setting process may create inconsistencies between U.S. GAAP and IFRS.

Differences Between U.S. GAAP and IFRS

U.S. GAAP and IFRS differ both in their approach to standard setting, as well as their financial statement presentation and recording of transactions.

Rules-Based Versus Principles Approach to Standard Setting U.S. GAAP is considered to be a "rules-based" approach to accounting standard setting. The accounting standards provide detailed and specific rules on the accounting for business transactions. There are few exceptions or varying interpretations of the accounting for a business event. This structure is consistent with the U.S. legal and regulatory system, reflecting the social and economic values of the United States.

In contrast, IFRS is designed to meet the needs of many countries. Differences in legal, political, and economic systems create different needs for and uses of financial information in different countries. For example, Germany needs a financial reporting system that reflects the central role of banks in its financial system, while the Netherlands needs a financial reporting system that reflects the significant role of outside equity in its financial system.

To accommodate economic, legal, and social diversity, IFRS must be broad enough to capture these differences while still presenting comparable financial statements. Under IFRS, there is greater opportunity for different interpretations of the accounting treatment of a business event across different business entities. To support this, IFRS often has more extensive disclosures that support alternative assumptions. Thus, IFRS provides more latitude for professional judgment than typically found in comparable U.S. GAAP. Many countries find this feature attractive in reducing regulatory costs associated with using and auditing financial reports. This "principles-based" approach presents one of the most significant challenges to adopting IFRS in the United States.

Technical Differences Between IFRS and U.S. GAAP Although U.S. GAAP is similar to IFRS, differences arise in the presentation format, balance sheet valuations, and technical accounting procedures. The Mornin' Joe International financial statements presented at the end of the last chapter highlight the financial statement format, presentation, and recording differences between U.S. GAAP and IFRS. A more comprehensive summary of the key differences between U.S. GAAP and IFRS that are relevant to an introductory accounting course is provided in Exhibit 2.

---

[1] Work Plan for the Consideration of Incorporating International Financial Accounting Standards into the Financial Reporting System for U.S. Issuers: Final Staff Report, U.S. Securities Exchange Commission, July 13, 2012.

Appendix B International Financial Reporting Standards (IFRS)

EXHIBIT 2 Comparison of Accounting for Selected Items Under U.S. GAAP and IFRS

	U.S. GAAP	IFRS	Text Reference
General:			
Financial statement titles	Balance Sheet Statement of Stockholders' Equity Statement of Cash Flows	Statement of Financial Position Statement of Changes in Equity Statement of Cash Flows	General
Financial periods presented	Public companies must present two years of comparative information for income statement, statement of stockholders' equity, and statement of cash flows	One year of comparative information must be presented	General
Conceptual basis for standard setting	"Rules-based" approach	"Principles-based" approach	General
Internal control requirements	Sarbanes-Oxley Act (SOX) Section 404		Ch 7
Balance Sheet:	**Balance Sheet**	**Statement of Financial Position**	
Terminology differences	"Payable" "Stockholders' Equity" "Net Income (Loss)"	"Provision" "Capital and Reserves" "Profit or (Loss)"	Ch 10 Ch 12 General
Inventory—LIFO	LIFO allowed	LIFO prohibited	Ch 6
Inventory—valuation	Reversal of lower-of-cost-or-market write-downs not allowed	Reversal of write-downs allowed	Ch 6
Long-lived assets	May NOT be revalued to fair value	May be revalued to fair value on a regular basis	Ch 9

(Continued)

EXHIBIT 2 Comparison of Accounting for Selected Items Under U.S. GAAP and IFRS (Continued)

	U.S. GAAP	IFRS	Text Reference
Land held for investment	Treated as held for use or sale, and recorded at historical cost	May be accounted for on a historical cost basis or on a fair value basis with changes in fair value recognized through profit and loss	Ch 9
Property, plant, and equipment—valuation	Historical cost	May select between historical cost or revalued amount (a form of fair value)	Ch 9
	If impaired, impairment loss may NOT be reversed in future periods	If impaired, impairment loss may be reversed in future periods	Ch 9
Cost of major overhaul (Capital and revenue expenditures)	Different treatment for ordinary repairs and maintenance, asset improvement, extraordinary repairs	Typically included as part of the cost of the asset or asset component if future economic benefit is probable and can be reliably measured	Ch 9
Intangible assets—valuation	Acquisition cost, unless impaired	Fair value permitted if the intangible asset trades in an active market	Ch 9
Intangible assets—impairment loss reversal	Prohibited	Prohibited for goodwill but allowed for other intangible assets	Ch 9
Income Statement:	**Income Statement**	**Statement of Comprehensive Income**	
Classification of expenses on income statement	Public companies must present expenses on the income statement by function (e.g., cost of goods sold, selling, administrative)	Expenses may be presented based either by function (e.g., cost of goods sold, selling) or by the nature of expense (e.g., wages expense, interest expense)	Chs 3, 4, 5
Statement of Cash Flows:	**Statement of Cash Flows**	**Statement of Cash Flows**	
Classification of interest paid or received	Treated as an operating activity	Interest paid may be treated as either an operating or a financing activity; interest received may be treated as an operating or investing activity	Ch. 13
Classification of dividend paid or received	Dividend paid treated as a financing activity, dividend received treated as an operating activity	Dividend paid may be treated as either an operating or a financing activity; dividend received may be treated as an operating or investing activity	Ch. 13

Discussion Questions

1. Briefly discuss why global accounting standards are needed in today's business environment.

2. What are International Financial Reporting Standards? Who uses these accounting standards?

3. What body is responsible for setting International Financial Reporting Standards?

4. Briefly discuss the differences between (A) adoption of IFRS by the U.S. Securities and Exchange Commission and (B) convergence of U.S. GAAP with IFRS.

5. Briefly discuss the difference between (A) a "rules-based" approach to accounting standard setting and (B) a "principles-based" approach to accounting standard setting.

6. How is property, plant, and equipment measured on the balance sheet under IFRS? How does this differ from the way property, plant, and equipment is measured on the balance sheet under U.S. GAAP?

7. What inventory costing methods are allowed under IFRS? How does this differ from the treatment under U.S. GAAP?

Appendix C

Revenue Recognition

Companies recognize revenue when services have been performed or products have been delivered to customers. For example, when **McDonald's** sells a hamburger, the revenue is earned when the hamburger is delivered to the customer. In this example, revenue recognition is simple because the hamburger is delivered and cash is received at a single point in time.

Revenue recognition is more complex, however, when a transaction includes several items that are sold together, items that are delivered over time, or items whose prices depend upon future events. To address these more complex transactions, the Financial Accounting Standards Board (FASB) issued a new accounting standard in May 2014.[1] The new Standard uses a five-step method for determining when revenue should be recognized. The five steps are as follows:

Step 1. *Identify the contract with the customer.* The new Standard treats every revenue transaction as a contract. A contract is an agreement by the seller to provide a good or service in exchange for payment from the buyer. A contract may be verbal and implicit, such as the purchase of a **McDonald's** hamburger, or written and explicit, such as a cell phone contract.

Step 2. *Identify the separate performance obligations in the contract.* Every contract requires the seller and buyer to perform. For example, when you purchase a **McDonald's** hamburger, you (the buyer) perform by paying and McDonald's (the seller) performs by delivering a hamburger. When you purchase a cell phone from **Verizon**, the transaction is more complex. You perform by paying cash or charging your credit card and signing a written contract. Verizon performs by delivering you the phone and promising to provide you cellular service in the future. In this case, Verizon has two performance obligations: (1) to provide the phone and (2) to provide cellular service in the future.

Step 3. *Determine the transaction price.* The transaction price is the amount the seller is entitled to receive in exchange for the goods and services they have provided. In the case of the **McDonald's** hamburger, the transaction price is the amount paid for the hamburger. In the case of **Verizon**, the transaction price must be estimated for the phone (the first performance obligation) and cellular service (the second performance obligation).

Step 4. *Allocate the transaction price to the separate performance obligations.* Since the sale of a **McDonald's** hamburger involves the sale of a single item that is immediately delivered, the entire transaction price is allocated to the hamburger. In more complex transactions, such as a **Verizon** cellular service contract, the revenue received from the customer must be allocated among the performance obligations. This allocation is often based on the stand-alone (separate) price of each good or service. For example, Verizon should allocate the revenue from the

---

1 Accounting Standards Update, *Revenue from Contracts with Customers (Topic 606),* Financial Accounting Standards Board, May 2014, Norwalk, CT.

customer between the phone (first performance obligation) and the commitment to provide cellular service (second performance obligation).

Step 5. *Recognize revenue when each separate performance obligation is satisfied.* The seller should recognize (record) revenue as each performance obligation is satisfied. In the case of **McDonald's**, the performance obligation is satisfied when the clerk delivers the hamburger to the customer. At this point, the control of the hamburger has passed to the customer. In the case of **Verizon**, it satisfies its first performance obligation when it delivers you the phone. Verizon satisfies its second performance obligation over time by providing you cellular service. Thus, Verizon should record a portion of the total revenue at the time you sign the contract and receive your phone and the remaining revenue over the period cellular service is provided.

To illustrate, assume that on March 1, Chandler Evans upgrades (replaces) his cell phone with Star Cellular at no cost by signing a two-year agreement. The new agreement cannot be cancelled and requires a payment of $90 per month. The cell phone selected by Evans cost Star Cellular $250.

The five-step method for recognizing revenue from this transaction would be applied as follows:

Step 1. *Identify the contract with the customer.* The contract with Chandler Evans is the two-year cellular service agreement that includes delivery of a new cell phone.

Step 2. *Identify the separate performance obligations in the contract.* Star Cellular has two separate performance obligations under this contract. First, Star Cellular must deliver a new cell phone at the time that Evans signs the service agreement. Second, Star Cellular must provide Evans with cell service for two years.

Step 3. *Determine the transaction price.* The transaction price is the total amount Star Cellular will receive over the contract period. In this case, Star Cellular will receive $2,160 ($90 × 24 months) over the contract period.[2]

Step 4. *Allocate the transaction price to the separate performance obligations.* If Star Cellular sold the cell phone and cell service separately, the individual prices would be as follows:

Cell phone (sold separately)	$ 600
Cell service for two years	3,000
Total price if sold separately	$3,600

The transaction price is allocated to each performance obligation based upon what each obligation would sell for separately as a stand-alone product. To illustrate, the cell phone is allocated $360 of the transaction price of $2,160, computed as follows:

$$\text{Cell Phone} = \text{Transaction Price} \times \frac{\text{Price of Cell Phone Sold Separately}}{\text{Total Price of Cell Phone and Cell Service Sold Separately}}$$

$$= \$2{,}160 \times \frac{\$600}{\$3{,}600} = \$360$$

The cell service is allocated $1,800 of the transaction price of $2,160, computed as follows:

$$\text{Cell Service} = \text{Transaction Price} \times \frac{\text{Price of Cell Service Sold Separately}}{\text{Total Price of Cell Phone and Cell Service Sold Separately}}$$

$$= \$2{,}160 \times \frac{\$3{,}000}{\$3{,}600} = \$1{,}800$$

Step 5. *Recognize revenue when each separate performance obligation is satisfied.* The $360 of revenue assigned to the cell phone is recognized when the customer signs the service agreement and receives the phone. At this point, the first performance obligation has been satisfied by Star Cellular and the control of the phone has passed to the customer. The journal entry to record revenue on March 1 is as follows:

---

2 An interest component may need to be considered in long-term contracts. To simplify, we ignore interest.

Mar.	1	Accounts Receivable—Chandler Evans	360	
		Sales		360
	1	Cost of Goods Sold	250	
		Inventory		250

The $1,800 of cell service revenue is recognized as the performance obligation is satisfied over the two-year term of the contract. For example, $75 ($1,800 ÷ 24 months) of service revenue would be recorded each month. The journal entry to record the service revenue for March is as follows:

Mar.	31	Cash	90	
		Accounts Receivable ($360 ÷ 24 months)		15
		Cell Service Revenue ($1,800 ÷ 24 months)		75

The preceding journal entries illustrate how over the life of the two-year contract the total revenue from the contract of $2,160 is divided between the sale of the cell phone ($360 of revenue) and providing of cell service ($1,800 of revenue). In addition, the journal entries illustrate when revenue from the phone and service is recorded.

Exhibit 1 summarizes the division of revenue and its recording over the two-year contract.

Recording Revenue over Two-Year Contract — **EXHIBIT 1**

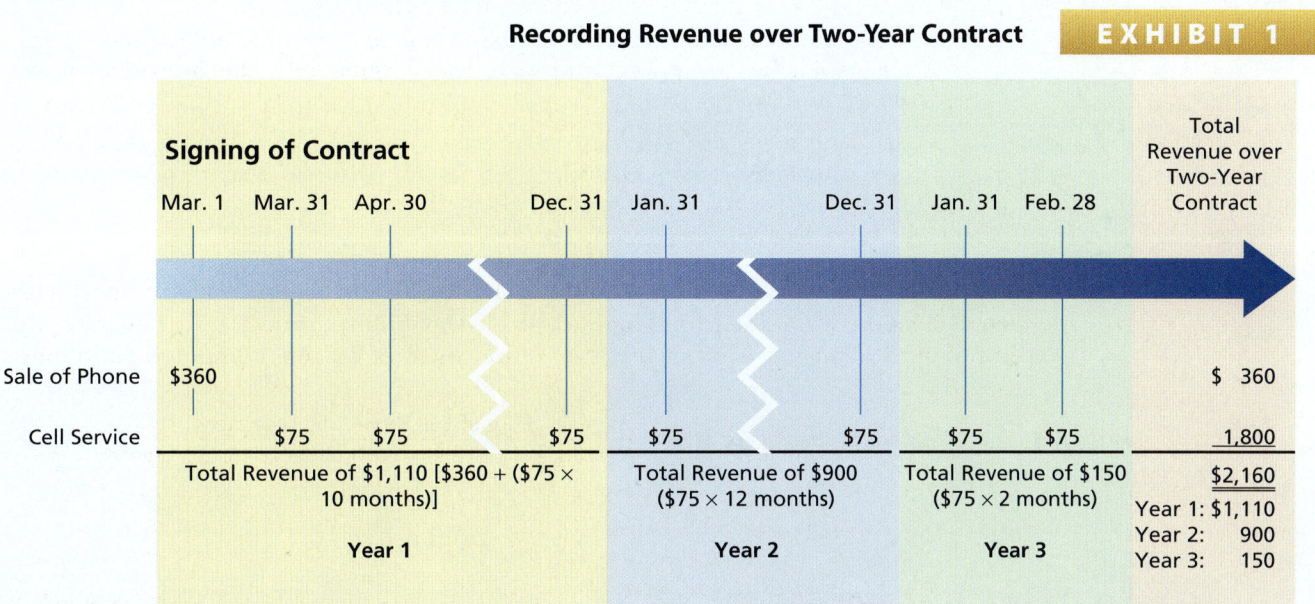

Appendix D

Selected Excerpts from Nike Inc., Form 10-K for the Fiscal Year Ended May 31, 2016

NIKE, Inc .
(Exact name of Registrant as specified in its charter)

Management's Annual Report on Internal Control Over Financial Reporting

Management is responsible for establishing and maintaining adequate internal control over financial reporting, as such term is defined in Rule 13(a) - 15(f) and Rule 15(d) - 15(f) of the Securities Exchange Act of 1934, as amended. Internal control over financial reporting is a process designed to provide reasonable assurance regarding the reliability of financial reporting and the preparation of the financial statements for external purposes in accordance with generally accepted accounting principles in the United States of America. Internal control over financial reporting includes those policies and procedures that: (i) pertain to the maintenance of records that, in reasonable detail, accurately and fairly reflect the transactions and dispositions of assets of the Company; (ii) provide reasonable assurance that transactions are recorded as necessary to permit preparation of financial statements in accordance with generally accepted accounting principles, and that receipts and expenditures of the Company are being made only in accordance with authorizations of our management and directors; and (iii) provide reasonable assurance regarding prevention or timely detection of unauthorized acquisition, use or disposition of assets of the Company that could have a material effect on the financial statements.

While "reasonable assurance" is a high level of assurance, it does not mean absolute assurance. Because of its inherent limitations, internal control over financial reporting may not prevent or detect every misstatement and instance of fraud. Controls are susceptible to manipulation, especially in instances of fraud caused by the collusion of two or more people, including our senior management. Also, projections of any evaluation of effectiveness to future periods are subject to the risk that controls may become inadequate because of changes in conditions, or that the degree of compliance with the policies or procedures may deteriorate.

Under the supervision and with the participation of our Chief Executive Officer and Chief Financial Officer, our management conducted an evaluation of the effectiveness of our internal control over financial reporting based upon the framework in *Internal Control — Integrated Framework (2013)* issued by the Committee of Sponsoring Organizations of the Treadway Commission (COSO). Based on the results of our evaluation, our management concluded that our internal control over financial reporting was effective as of May 31, 2016.

PricewaterhouseCoopers LLP, an independent registered public accounting firm, has audited (1) the Consolidated Financial Statements and (2) the effectiveness of our internal control over financial reporting as of May 31, 2016, as stated in their report herein.

Mark G. Parker
Chairman, President and Chief Executive Officer

Andrew Campion
Chief Financial Officer

Report of Independent Registered Public Accounting Firm

To the Board of Directors and Shareholders of NIKE, Inc.:

In our opinion, the consolidated financial statements listed in the index appearing under Item 15(a)(1) present fairly, in all material respects, the financial position of NIKE, Inc. and its subsidiaries at May 31, 2016 and 2015 , and the results of their operations and their cash flows for each of the three years in the period ended May 31, 2016 in conformity with accounting principles generally accepted in the United States of America. In addition, in our opinion, the financial statement schedule listed in the index appearing under Item 15(a)(2) presents fairly, in all material respects, the information set forth therein when read in conjunction with the related consolidated financial statements. Also in our opinion, the Company maintained, in all material respects, effective internal control over financial reporting as of May 31, 2016 , based on criteria established in *Internal Control — Integrated Framework (2013)* issued by the Committee of Sponsoring Organizations of the Treadway Commission (COSO). The Company's management is responsible for these financial statements and financial statement schedule, for maintaining effective internal control over financial reporting and for its assessment of the effectiveness of internal control over financial reporting, included in Management's Annual Report on Internal Control over Financial Reporting appearing under Item 8. Our responsibility is to express opinions on these financial statements, on the financial statement schedule and on the Company's internal control over financial reporting based on our integrated audits. We conducted our audits in accordance with the standards of the Public Company Accounting Oversight Board (United States). Those standards require that we plan and perform the audits to obtain reasonable assurance about whether the financial statements are free of material misstatement and whether effective internal control over financial reporting was maintained in all material respects. Our audits of the financial statements included examining, on a test basis, evidence supporting the amounts and disclosures in the financial statements, assessing the accounting principles used and significant estimates made by management and evaluating the overall financial statement presentation. Our audit of internal control over financial reporting included obtaining an understanding of internal control over financial reporting, assessing the risk that a material weakness exists and testing and evaluating the design and operating effectiveness of internal control based on the assessed risk. Our audits also included performing such other procedures as we considered necessary in the circumstances. We believe that our audits provide a reasonable basis for our opinions.

A company's internal control over financial reporting is a process designed to provide reasonable assurance regarding the reliability of financial reporting and the preparation of financial statements for external purposes in accordance with generally accepted accounting principles. A company's internal control over financial reporting includes those policies and procedures that (i) pertain to the maintenance of records that, in reasonable detail, accurately and fairly reflect the transactions and dispositions of the assets of the company; (ii) provide reasonable assurance that transactions are recorded as necessary to permit preparation of financial statements in accordance with generally accepted accounting principles, and that receipts and expenditures of the company are being made only in accordance with authorizations of management and directors of the company; and (iii) provide reasonable assurance regarding prevention or timely detection of unauthorized acquisition, use, or disposition of the company's assets that could have a material effect on the financial statements.

Because of its inherent limitations, internal control over financial reporting may not prevent or detect misstatements. Also, projections of any evaluation of effectiveness to future periods are subject to the risk that controls may become inadequate because of changes in conditions, or that the degree of compliance with the policies or procedures may deteriorate.

/S/ PRICEWATERHOUSECOOPERS LLP

Portland, Oregon

July 21, 2016

NIKE, Inc. Consolidated Statements of Income

	Year Ended May 31,		
(In millions, except per share data)	2016	2015	2014
Revenues	$ 32,376	$ 30,601	$ 27,799
Cost of sales	17,405	16,534	15,353
Gross profit	14,971	14,067	12,446
Demand creation expense	3,278	3,213	3,031
Operating overhead expense	7,191	6,679	5,735
Total selling and administrative expense	10,469	9,892	8,766
Interest expense (income), net	19	28	33
Other (income) expense, net	(140)	(58)	103
Income before income taxes	4,623	4,205	3,544
Income tax expense	863	932	851
NET INCOME	**$ 3,760**	**$ 3,273**	**$ 2,693**
Earnings per common share:			
Basic	$ 2.21	$ 1.90	$ 1.52
Diluted	$ 2.16	$ 1.85	$ 1.49
Dividends declared per common share	$ 0.62	$ 0.54	$ 0.47

The accompanying Notes to the Consolidated Financial Statements are an integral part of this statement.

The Notes may be found on the companion website at CengageBrain.com

NIKE, Inc. Consolidated Statements of Comprehensive Income

	Year Ended May 31,		
(In millions)	2016	2015	2014
Net income	$ 3,760	$ 3,273	$ 2,693
Other comprehensive income (loss), net of tax:			
Change in net foreign currency translation adjustment[1]	(176)	(20)	(32)
Change in net gains (losses) on cash flow hedges[2]	(757)	1,188	(161)
Change in net gains (losses) on other[3]	5	(7)	4
Total other comprehensive income (loss), net of tax	(928)	1,161	(189)
TOTAL COMPREHENSIVE INCOME	$ 2,832	$ 4,434	$ 2,504

(1) Net of tax benefit (expense) of $0 million, $0 million and $0 million, respectively.
(2) Net of tax benefit (expense) of $35 million, $(31) million and $18 million, respectively.
(3) Net of tax benefit (expense) of $0 million, $0 million and $0 million, respectively.

The accompanying Notes to the Consolidated Financial Statements are an integral part of this statement.

The Notes may be found on the companion website at CengageBrain.com

NIKE, Inc. Consolidated Balance Sheets

	May 31, 2016	May 31, 2015
(In millions)		
ASSETS		
Current assets:		
Cash and equivalents	$ 3,138	$ 3,852
Short-term investments	2,319	2,072
Accounts receivable, net	3,241	3,358
Inventories	4,838	4,337
Prepaid expenses and other current assets	1,489	1,968
Total current assets	15,025	15,587
Property, plant and equipment, net	3,520	3,011
Identifiable intangible assets, net	281	281
Goodwill	131	131
Deferred income taxes and other assets	2,439	2,587
TOTAL ASSETS	**$ 21,396**	**$ 21,597**
LIABILITIES AND SHAREHOLDERS' EQUITY		
Current liabilities:		
Current portion of long-term debt	$ 44	$ 107
Notes payable	1	74
Accounts payable	2,191	2,131
Accrued liabilities	3,037	3,949
Income taxes payable	85	71
Total current liabilities	5,358	6,332
Long-term debt	2,010	1,079
Deferred income taxes and other liabilities	1,770	1,479
Commitments and contingencies		
Redeemable preferred stock	—	—
Shareholders' equity:		
Common stock at stated value:		
Class A convertible — 353 and 355 shares outstanding	—	—
Class B — 1,329 and 1,357 shares outstanding	3	3
Capital in excess of stated value	7,786	6,773
Accumulated other comprehensive income	318	1,246
Retained earnings	4,151	4,685
Total shareholders' equity	12,258	12,707
TOTAL LIABILITIES AND SHAREHOLDERS' EQUITY	**$ 21,396**	**$ 21,597**

The accompanying Notes to the Consolidated Financial Statements are an integral part of this statement.

The Notes may be found on the companion website at CengageBrain.com

NIKE, Inc. Consolidated Statements of Cash Flows

	Year Ended May 31,		
(In millions)	2016	2015	2014
Cash provided by operations:			
Net income	$ 3,760	$ 3,273	$ 2,693
Income charges (credits) not affecting cash:			
Depreciation	649	606	518
Deferred income taxes	(80)	(113)	(11)
Stock-based compensation	236	191	177
Amortization and other	13	43	68
Net foreign currency adjustments	98	424	56
Changes in certain working capital components and other assets and liabilities:			
Decrease (increase) in accounts receivable	60	(216)	(298)
(Increase) in inventories	(590)	(621)	(505)
(Increase) in prepaid expenses and other current assets	(161)	(144)	(210)
(Decrease) increase in accounts payable, accrued liabilities and income taxes payable	(889)	1,237	525
Cash provided by operations	3,096	4,680	3,013
Cash used by investing activities:			
Purchases of short-term investments	(5,367)	(4,936)	(5,386)
Maturities of short-term investments	2,924	3,655	3,932
Sales of short-term investments	2,386	2,216	1,126
Investments in reverse repurchase agreements	150	(150)	—
Additions to property, plant and equipment	(1,143)	(963)	(880)
Disposals of property, plant and equipment	10	3	3
Decrease (increase) in other assets, net of other liabilities	6	—	(2)
Cash used by investing activities	(1,034)	(175)	(1,207)
Cash used by financing activities:			
Net proceeds from long-term debt issuance	981	—	—
Long-term debt payments, including current portion	(106)	(7)	(60)
(Decrease) increase in notes payable	(67)	(63)	75
Payments on capital lease obligations	(7)	(19)	(17)
Proceeds from exercise of stock options and other stock issuances	507	514	383
Excess tax benefits from share-based payment arrangements	281	218	132
Repurchase of common stock	(3,238)	(2,534)	(2,628)
Dividends — common and preferred	(1,022)	(899)	(799)
Cash used by financing activities	(2,671)	(2,790)	(2,914)
Effect of exchange rate changes on cash and equivalents	(105)	(83)	(9)
Net (decrease) increase in cash and equivalents	(714)	1,632	(1,117)
Cash and equivalents, beginning of year	3,852	2,220	3,337
CASH AND EQUIVALENTS, END OF YEAR	$ 3,138	$ 3,852	$ 2,220
Supplemental disclosure of cash flow information:			
Cash paid during the year for:			
Interest, net of capitalized interest	$ 70	$ 53	$ 53
Income taxes	748	1,262	856
Non-cash additions to property, plant and equipment	252	206	167
Dividends declared and not paid	271	240	209

The accompanying Notes to the Consolidated Financial Statements are an integral part of this statement.

The Notes may be found on the companion website at CengageBrain.com

NIKE, Inc. Consolidated Statements of Shareholders' Equity

(In millions, except per share data)	Common Stock Class A Shares	Amount	Common Stock Class B Shares	Amount	Capital in Excess of Stated Value	Accumulated Other Comprehensive Income	Retained Earnings	Total
Balance at May 31, 2013	356	$—	1,433	$3	$5,184	$274	$5,620	$11,081
Stock options exercised	(1)		22		445			445
Conversion to Class B Common Stock			1					—
Repurchase of Class B Common Stock			(73)		(11)		(2,617)	(2,628)
Dividends on common stock ($0.47 per share)							(821)	(821)
Issuance of shares to employees			3		78			78
Stock-based compensation					177			177
Forfeiture of shares from employees			(1)		(8)		(4)	(12)
Net income							2,693	2,693
Other comprehensive income (loss)						(189)		(189)
Balance at May 31, 2014	355	$—	1,385	$3	$5,865	$85	$4,871	$10,824
Stock options exercised			27		639			639
Repurchase of Class B Common Stock			(58)		(9)		(2,525)	(2,534)
Dividends on common stock ($0.54 per share)							(931)	(931)
Issuance of shares to employees			3		92			92
Stock-based compensation					191			191
Forfeiture of shares from employees			—		(5)		(3)	(8)
Net income							3,273	3,273
Other comprehensive income (loss)						1,161		1,161
Balance at May 31, 2015	355	$—	1,357	$3	$6,773	$1,246	$4,685	$12,707
Stock options exercised			22		680			680
Conversion to Class B Common Stock	(2)		2		—			—
Repurchase of Class B Common Stock			(55)		(8)		(3,230)	(3,238)
Dividends on common stock ($0.62 per share)							(1,053)	(1,053)
Issuance of shares to employees			3		115			115
Stock-based compensation					236			236
Forfeiture of shares from employees			—		(10)		(11)	(21)
Net income							3,760	3,760
Other comprehensive income (loss)						(928)		(928)
Balance at May 31, 2016	353	$—	1,329	3	$7,786	$318	$4,151	$12,258

The accompanying Notes to the Consolidated Financial Statements are an integral part of this statement.

The Notes may be found on the companion website at CengageBrain.com

Glossary

A

absorption costing The reporting of the costs of manufactured products, normally direct materials, direct labor, and factory overhead, as product costs. (Ch. 21)

accelerated depreciation method A depreciation method that provides for a higher depreciation amount in the first year of the asset's use, followed by a gradually declining amount of depreciation. (Ch. 10)

account An accounting form that is used to record the increases and decreases in each financial statement item. (Ch. 2)

account form The form of balance sheet that resembles the basic format of the accounting equation, with assets on the left side and Liabilities and Owner's Equity sections on the right side. (Ch. 1)

account payable The liability created by a purchase on account. (Ch. 1)

account receivable A claim against the customer created by selling merchandise or services on credit. (Chs. 1, 2, 9)

accounting An information system that provides reports to stakeholders about the economic activities and condition of a business. (Ch. 1)

accounting cycle The process that begins with analyzing and journalizing transactions and ends with the post-closing trial balance. (Ch. 4)

accounting equation Assets = Liabilities + Owner's Equity. (Ch. 1)

accounting system The methods and procedures used by a business to collect, classify, summarize, and report financial data for use by management and external users. (Ch. 5)

accounts payable subsidiary ledger The subsidiary ledger containing the individual accounts with creditors (suppliers). (Ch. 5)

accounts receivable analysis A company's ability to collect its accounts receivable. (Ch. 17)

accounts receivable subsidiary ledger The subsidiary ledger containing the individual accounts with customers. (Ch. 5)

accounts receivable turnover The relationship between net sales and accounts receivable, computed by dividing the net sales by the average net accounts receivable; measures how frequently during the year the accounts receivable are being converted to cash. (Chs. 9, 17)

accrual An accrual occurs when revenue has been earned or an expense has been incurred but has not been recorded. (Ch. 3)

accrual basis of accounting Under this basis of accounting, revenues and expenses are reported in the income statement in the period in which they are earned or incurred. (Ch. 3)

Accumulated Depreciation The contra asset account credited when recording the depreciation of a fixed asset. (Ch. 3)

accumulated other comprehensive income The cumulative effects of other comprehensive income items reported separately in the Stockholders' Equity section of the balance sheet. (Ch. 15)

activities The types of work, or actions, involved in a manufacturing process or service activity. (Ch. 25)

activity base (driver) A measure of activity that is related to changes in cost. Used in analyzing and classifying cost behavior. Activity bases are also used in the denominator in calculating the predetermined factory overhead rate to assign overhead costs to cost objects. (Chs. 19, 21, 25)

activity rate The estimated activity cost divided by estimated activity-base usage. (Ch. 25)

activity-based costing (ABC) A cost allocation method that identifies activities causing the incurrence of costs and allocates these costs to products (or other cost objects), based on activity drivers (bases). (Chs. 19, 25)

adjusted trial balance The trial balance prepared after all the adjusting entries have been posted. (Ch. 3)

adjusting entries The journal entries that bring the accounts up to date at the end of the accounting period. (Ch. 3)

adjusting process An analysis and updating of the accounts when financial statements are prepared. (Ch. 3)

administrative expenses (general expenses) Expenses incurred in the administration or general operations of the business. (Ch. 6)

aging the receivables The process of analyzing the accounts receivable and classifying them according to various age groupings, with the due date being the base point for determining age. (Ch. 9)

G-1

Allowance for Doubtful Accounts The contra asset account for accounts receivable. (Ch. 9)

allowance method The method of accounting for uncollectible accounts that provides an expense for uncollectible receivables in advance of their write-off. (Ch. 9)

amortization The periodic transfer of the cost of an intangible asset to expense. (Chs. 10, 14)

analytical methods Methods that examine changes in the amount and percentage of financial statement items within and across periods. (Ch. 17)

annuity A series of equal cash flows at fixed intervals. (Chs. 14, 26)

asset turnover A measure of how effectively a business is using its assets to generate sales. (Chs. 6, 17)

assets The resources owned by a business. (Chs. 1, 2)

available-for-sale securities Securities that management expects to sell in the future but which are not actively traded for profit. (Ch. 15)

average rate of return A method of evaluating capital investment proposals that focuses on the expected profitability of the investment. (Ch. 26)

B

bad debt expense The operating expense incurred because of the failure to collect receivables. (Ch. 9)

balance of the account The amount of the difference between the debits and the credits that have been entered into an account. (Ch. 2)

balance sheet A list of the assets, liabilities, and owner's equity as of a specific date, usually at the close of the last day of a month or a year. (Ch. 1)

balanced scorecard A performance evaluation approach that incorporates multiple performance dimensions by combining financial and nonfinancial measures. (Ch. 24)

bank reconciliation The analysis that details the items responsible for the difference between the cash balance reported in the bank statement and the balance of the cash account in the ledger. (Ch. 8)

bank statement A summary of all transactions mailed to the depositor or made available online by the bank each month. (Ch. 8)

bond A form of an interest-bearing note used by corporations to borrow on a long-term basis. (Ch. 14)

bond indenture The contract between a corporation issuing bonds and the bondholders. (Ch. 14)

book value The cost of a fixed asset minus accumulated depreciation on the asset. (Ch. 10)

book value of the asset (or net book value) The difference between the cost of a fixed asset and its accumulated depreciation. (Ch. 3)

boot The amount a buyer owes a seller when a fixed asset is traded in on a similar asset. (Ch. 10)

break-even point The level of business operations at which revenues and expired costs are equal. (Ch. 21)

budget An accounting device used to plan and control resources of operational departments and divisions. (Ch. 22)

budget performance report A report comparing actual results with budget figures. (Ch. 23)

budgetary slack Excess resources set within a budget to provide for uncertain events. (Ch. 22)

budgeted variable factory overhead The standard variable overhead for the actual units produced. (Ch. 23)

business An organization in which basic resources (inputs), such as materials and labor, are assembled and processed to provide goods or services (outputs) to customers. (Ch. 1)

business combination A business making an investment in another business by acquiring a controlling share, often greater than 50%, of the outstanding voting stock of another corporation by paying cash or exchanging stock. (Ch. 15)

business entity concept A concept of accounting that limits the economic data in the accounting system to data related directly to the activities of the business. (Ch. 1)

business transaction An economic event or condition that directly changes an entity's financial condition or directly affects its results of operations. (Ch. 1)

C

capital account An account used for a proprietorship that represents the owner's equity. (Ch. 2)

capital expenditures The costs of acquiring fixed assets, adding to a fixed asset, improving a fixed asset, or extending a fixed asset's useful life. (Ch. 10)

capital expenditures budget The budget summarizing future plans for acquiring plant facilities and equipment. (Ch. 22)

capital investment analysis The process by which management plans, evaluates, and controls long-term capital investments involving property, plant, and equipment. (Ch. 26)

capital rationing The process by which management plans, evaluates, and controls long-term capital investments involving fixed assets. (Ch. 26)

carrying amount The balance of the bonds payable account (face amount of the bonds) less any unamortized discount or plus any unamortized premium. (Ch. 14)

cash Coins, currency (paper money), checks, money orders, and money on deposit that is available for unrestricted withdrawal from banks and other financial institutions. (Ch. 8)

cash basis of accounting Under this basis of accounting, revenues and expenses are reported in the income statement in the period in which cash is received or paid. (Ch. 3)

cash budget A budget of estimated cash receipts and payments. (Ch. 22)

cash dividend A cash distribution of earnings by a corporation to its shareholders. (Ch. 13)

cash equivalents Highly liquid investments that are usually reported with cash on the balance sheet. (Ch. 8)

cash flow per share Normally computed as cash flow from operations per share. (Ch. 16)

cash flows from (used for) financing activities The section of the statement of cash flows that reports cash flows from transactions affecting the equity and debt of the business. (Ch. 16)

cash flows from (used for) investing activities The section of the statement of cash flows that reports cash flows from transactions affecting investments in noncurrent assets. (Ch. 16)

cash flows from operating activities The section of the statement of cash flows that reports the cash transactions affecting the determination of net income. (Ch. 16)

cash payback period The expected period of time that will elapse between the date of a capital expenditure and the complete recovery in cash (or equivalent) of the amount invested. (Ch. 26)

cash payments journal The special journal in which all cash payments are recorded. (Ch. 5)

cash receipts journal The special journal in which all cash receipts are recorded. (Ch. 5)

cash refund An amount paid by the seller to the buyer for merchandise that is defective, is damaged during shipment, or does not meet the buyer's expectations. (Ch. 6)

cash short and over account An account which has recorded errors in cash sales or errors in making change causing the amount of actual cash on hand to differ from the beginning amount of cash plus the cash sales for the day. (Ch. 8)

Certified Public Accountant (CPA) Public accountants who have met a state's education, experience, and examination requirements. (Ch. 1)

chart of accounts A list of the accounts in the ledger. (Ch. 2)

closing entries The entries that transfer the balances of the revenue, expense, and drawing accounts to the owner's capital account. (Ch. 4)

closing process The transfer process of converting temporary account balances to zero by transferring the revenue and expense account balances to the owner's capital account, and transferring the owner's drawing account balance to the owner's capital account. (Ch. 4)

closing the books The process of transferring temporary accounts balances to permanent accounts at the end of the accounting period. (Ch. 4)

common stock The stock outstanding when a corporation has issued only one class of stock. (Ch. 13)

common-sized statement A financial statement in which all items are expressed only in relative terms. (Ch. 17)

compensating balance A requirement by some banks requiring depositors to maintain minimum cash balances in their bank accounts. (Ch. 8)

comprehensive income All changes in stockholders' equity during a period, except those resulting from dividends and stockholders' investments. (Ch. 15)

consigned inventory Merchandise that is shipped by manufacturers to retailers who act as the manufacturer's selling agent. (Ch. 7)

consignee The name for the retailer in a consigned inventory arrangement. (Ch. 7)

consignor The name for the manufacturer in a consigned inventory arrangement. (Ch. 7)

consolidated financial statements Financial statements resulting from combining parent and subsidiary statements. (Ch. 15)

contingent liabilities Liabilities that may arise from past transactions if certain events occur in the future. (Ch. 11)

continuous budgeting A method of budgeting that provides for maintaining a 12-month projection into the future. (Ch. 22)

continuous process improvement A management approach that is part of the overall total quality management philosophy. The approach requires all employees to constantly improve processes of which they are a part or for which they have managerial responsibility. (Ch. 18)

contra accounts (or contra asset accounts) An account offset against another account. (Ch. 3)

contract rate The periodic interest to be paid on the bonds that is identified in the bond indenture; expressed as a percentage of the face amount of the bond. (Ch. 14)

contribution margin The excess of sales over variable costs. (Ch. 21)

contribution margin ratio The percentage of each sales dollar that is available to cover the fixed costs and provide an operating income. (Ch. 21)

control environment The overall attitude of management and employees about the importance of controls. (Ch. 8)

controllable expenses Costs that can be influenced by the decisions of a manager. (Ch. 24)

controllable revenues Revenues earned by the profit center. (Ch. 24)

controllable variance The difference between the actual amount of variable factory overhead cost incurred and the amount of variable factory overhead budgeted for the standard product. (Ch. 23)

controller The chief management accountant of a division or other segment of a business. (Ch. 18)

controlling A phase in the management process that consists of monitoring the operating results of implemented plans and comparing the actual results with the expected results. (Ch. 18)

controlling account The account in the general ledger that summarizes the balances of the accounts in a subsidiary ledger. (Ch. 5)

conversion costs The combination of direct labor and factory overhead costs. (Ch. 18)

copyright An exclusive right to publish and sell a literary, artistic, or musical composition. (Ch. 10)

corporation A business organized under state or federal statutes as a separate legal entity. (Ch. 1)

Glossary

correcting journal entry An entry that is prepared when an error has already been journalized and posted. (Ch. 2)

cost A payment of cash (or a commitment to pay cash in the future) for the purpose of generating revenues. (Ch. 18)

cost accounting systems Systems that measure, record, and report product costs. (Ch. 19)

cost allocation The process of assigning indirect cost to a cost object, such as a job. (Ch. 19)

cost behavior The manner in which a cost changes in relation to its activity base (driver). (Ch. 21)

cost center A decentralized unit in which the department or division manager has responsibility for the control of costs incurred and the authority to make decisions that affect these costs. (Ch. 24)

cost concept A concept of accounting that determines the amount initially entered into the accounting records for purchases. (Ch. 1)

cost method A method of accounting for equity investments representing less than 20% of the outstanding shares of the investee. The purchase is at original cost, and any gains or losses upon sale are recognized by the difference between the sale proceeds and the original cost. (Ch. 15)

cost object The object or segment of operations to which costs are related for management's use, such as a product or department. (Ch. 18)

cost of finished goods available for sale The beginning finished goods inventory added to the cost of goods manufactured during the period. (Ch. 18)

cost of goods manufactured The total cost of making and finishing a product. (Ch. 18)

cost of goods sold The cost of finished goods available for sale minus the ending finished goods inventory. (Ch. 18)

cost of goods sold budget A budget of the estimated direct materials, direct labor, and factory overhead consumed by sold products. (Ch. 22)

cost of merchandise sold The cost that is reported as an expense when merchandise is sold. (Chs. 6, 18)

cost of production report A report prepared periodically by a processing department, summarizing (1) the units for which the department is accountable and the disposition of those units and (2) the costs incurred by the department and the allocation of those costs between completed and incomplete production. (Ch. 20)

cost per equivalent unit The rate used to allocate costs between completed and partially completed production. (Ch. 20)

cost price approach An approach to transfer pricing that uses cost as the basis for setting the transfer price. (Ch. 24)

cost variance The difference between actual cost and the flexible budget at actual volumes. (Ch. 23)

cost-volume-profit analysis The systematic examination of the relationships among selling prices, volume of sales and production, costs, expenses, and profits. (Ch. 21)

cost-volume-profit chart A chart that graphically shows sales, costs, and the related profit or loss for various levels of units sold. (Ch. 21)

credit Amount entered on the right side of an account. (Ch. 2)

credit memorandum (credit memo) A form used by a seller to inform the buyer of the amount the seller proposes to credit to the account receivable due from the buyer. (Ch. 6)

credit period The amount of time the buyer is allowed in which to pay the seller. (Ch. 6)

credit terms Terms for payment on account by the buyer to the seller. (Ch. 6)

cumulative preferred stock Stock that has a right to receive regular dividends that were not declared (paid) in prior years. (Ch. 13)

currency exchange rate The rate at which currency in another country can be exchanged for local currency. (Ch. 26)

current assets Cash and other assets that are expected to be converted to cash or sold or used up, usually within one year or less, through the normal operations of the business. (Ch. 4)

current liabilities Liabilities that will be due within a short time (usually one year or less) and that are to be paid out of current assets. (Ch. 4)

current position analysis A company's ability to pay its current liabilities. (Chs. 11, 17)

current ratio A financial ratio that is computed by dividing current assets by current liabilities. (Chs. 4, 17)

currently attainable standards Standards that represent levels of operation that can be attained with reasonable effort. (Ch. 23)

customer allowance Returns to the seller by the customer or reductions from the initial selling price due to defective or damaged merchandise or goods that did not meet the customer's expectations. (Ch. 6)

customer discounts A variety of discounts offered by the seller as incentive for the customer to act in a way benefiting the seller. (Ch. 6)

customer refunds payable A liability account for estimated refunds and allowances that will be paid or granted customers in the future. (Ch. 6)

D

debit Amount entered on the left side of an account. (Ch. 2)

debit memorandum (debit memo) A form used by a buyer to inform the seller of the amount the buyer proposes to debit to the account payable due the seller. (Ch. 6)

debt securities Notes and bond investments that provide interest revenue over a fixed maturity. (Ch. 15)

decision making A component inherent in the other management processes of planning, directing, controlling, and improving. (Ch. 18)

deferral A deferral occurs when cash related to a future revenue or expense has been initially recorded as a liability or an asset. (Ch. 3)

deficiency The debit balance in the owner's equity account of a partner. (Ch. 12)

deficit A debit balance in the retained earnings account. (Ch. 13)

defined benefit plan A pension plan that promises employees a fixed annual pension benefit at retirement, based on years of service and compensation levels. (Ch. 11)

defined contribution plan A pension plan that requires a fixed amount of money to be invested on the employee's behalf during the employee's working years. (Ch. 11)

depletion expense A deferral occurs when cash related to a future revenue or expense has been initially recorded as a liability or an asset. (Ch. 10)

depreciable cost The difference between a fixed asset's initial cost and its residual value. (Ch. 10)

depreciate To lose usefulness as all fixed assets except land do. (Ch. 3)

depreciation The systematic periodic transfer of the cost of a fixed asset to an expense account during its expected useful life. (Chs. 3, 10)

depreciation expense The portion of the cost of a fixed asset that is recorded as an expense each year of its useful life. (Ch. 3)

differential analysis The area of accounting concerned with the effect of alternative courses of action on revenues and costs. (Ch. 25)

differential cost The amount of increase or decrease in cost expected from a particular course of action compared with an alternative. (Ch. 25)

differential income (loss) The difference between the differential revenue and the differential costs. (Ch. 25)

differential revenue The amount of increase or decrease in revenue expected from a particular course of action as compared with an alternative. (Ch. 25)

direct costs Costs that can be traced directly to a cost object. (Ch. 18)

direct labor cost The wages of factory workers who are directly involved in converting materials into a finished product. (Ch. 18)

direct labor cost budget Budget that estimates direct labor hours and related costs needed to support budgeted production. (Ch. 22)

direct labor rate variance The cost associated with the difference between the actual rate and the standard rate paid for direct labor multiplied by the actual direct labor hours used in producing a commodity. (Ch. 23)

direct labor time variance The cost associated with the difference between the actual hours and the standard hours of direct labor spent producing a commodity multiplied by the standard direct labor rate per hour. (Ch. 23)

direct materials cost The cost of materials that are an integral part of the finished product. (Ch. 18)

direct materials price variance The cost associated with the difference between the actual price and the standard price of direct materials multiplied by the actual quantity of direct materials used in producing a commodity. (Ch. 23)

direct materials purchases budget A budget that uses the production budget as a starting point to budget materials purchases. (Ch. 22)

direct materials quantity variance The cost associated with the difference between the actual quantity and the standard quantity of direct materials used in producing a commodity multiplied by the standard direct materials price. (Ch. 23)

direct method A method of reporting the cash flows from operating activities as the difference between the operating cash receipts and the operating cash payments. (Ch. 16)

direct write-off method The method of accounting for uncollectible accounts that recognizes the expense only when accounts are judged to be worthless. (Ch. 9)

directing The process by which managers, given their assigned level of responsibilities, run day-to-day operations. (Ch. 18)

discount The interest deducted from the maturity value of a note or the excess of the face amount of bonds over their issue price. (Chs. 13, 14)

dishonored note receivable A note that the maker fails to pay on the due date. (Ch. 9)

dividend yield A ratio, computed by dividing the annual dividends paid per share of common stock by the market price per share at a specific date, that indicates the rate of return to stockholders in terms of cash dividend distributions. (Chs. 15, 17)

dividends Distribution of a corporation's earnings to stockholders. (Ch. 13)

dividends per share Measures the extent to which earnings are being distributed to common shareholders. (Ch. 17)

double-declining-balance method A method of depreciation that provides periodic depreciation expense based on the declining book value of a fixed asset over its estimated life. (Ch. 10)

double-entry accounting system A system of accounting for recording transactions, based on recording increases and decreases in accounts so that debits equal credits. (Ch. 2)

drawing The account used to record amounts withdrawn by an owner of a proprietorship. (Ch. 2)

DuPont formula An expanded expression of return on investment determined by multiplying the profit margin by the investment turnover. (Ch. 24)

E

earnings The amount by which revenues exceed expenses. (Ch. 1)

earnings per common share (EPS) Net income per share of common stock outstanding during a period. (Chs. 13, 14)

earnings per share (EPS) on common stock The profitability ratio of net income available to common shareholders to the number of common shares outstanding. (Ch. 17)

e-commerce The use of the Internet for performing business transactions. (Ch. 5)

eco-efficiency measures Measures that help managers evaluate the savings generated by using fewer natural resources in a company's operations. (Ch. 18)

effective interest rate method The method of amortizing discounts and premiums that provides for a constant rate of interest on the carrying amount of the bonds at the beginning of each period; often called simply the "interest method." (Ch. 14)

effective rate of interest The market rate of interest at the time bonds are issued. (Ch. 14)

electronic funds transfer (EFT) A system in which computers rather than paper (money, checks, etc.) are used to effect cash transactions. (Ch. 8)

elements of internal control The control environment, risk assessment, control activities, information and communication, and monitoring. (Ch. 8)

employee fraud The intentional act of deceiving an employer for personal gain. (Ch. 8)

employee's earnings record A detailed record of each employee's earnings. (Ch. 11)

engineering change order (ECO) The document that initiates changing a product or process. (Ch. 25)

equity method A method of accounting for an investment in common stock by which the investment account is adjusted for the investor's share of periodic net income and cash dividends of the investee. (Ch. 15)

equity securities The common and preferred stock of a firm. (Ch. 15)

equivalent units of production The number of production units that could have been completed within a given accounting period, given the resources consumed. (Ch. 20)

estimated returns inventory A current asset that is reported on the balance sheet after inventory. (Ch. 6)

ethics Moral principles that guide the conduct of individuals. (Ch. 1)

expected useful life The estimated length of time a fixed asset will be used in normal operations. (Ch. 10)

expense recognition principle A principle, sometimes called the matching principle, that requires expenses to be recorded in the same period as the related revenue. (Ch. 3)

expenses Assets used up or services consumed in the process of generating revenues. (Chs. 1, 2)

F

face amount An amount at which bonds sell if the market rate equals the contract rate. (Ch. 14)

factory burden Another term for manufacturing overhead or factory overhead. (Ch. 18)

factory overhead cost All of the costs of producing a product except for direct materials and direct labor. (Ch. 18)

factory overhead cost budget Budget that estimates the cost for each item of factory overhead needed to support budgeted production. (Ch. 22)

factory overhead cost variance report Reports budgeted and actual costs for variable and fixed factory overhead along with the related controllable and volume variances. (Ch. 23)

fair value The price that would be received for selling an asset or paying off a liability, often the market price for an equity or debt security. (Ch. 15)

favorable cost variance A variance that occurs when the actual cost is less than standard cost. (Ch. 23)

feedback Measures provided to operational employees or managers on the performance of subunits of the organization. These measures are used by employees to adjust a process or a behavior to achieve goals. See management by exception. (Ch. 18)

fees earned Revenue from providing services. (Ch. 1)

FICA tax Federal Insurance Contributions Act tax used to finance federal programs for old-age and disability benefits (social security) and health insurance for the aged (Medicare). (Ch. 11)

financial accounting The branch of accounting that is concerned with recording transactions using generally accepted accounting principles (GAAP) for a business or other economic unit and with a periodic preparation of various statements from such records. (Chs. 1, 18)

Financial Accounting Standards Board (FASB) The authoritative body that has the primary responsibility for developing accounting principles. (Ch. 1)

financial statements Financial reports that summarize the effects of events on a business. (Ch. 1)

finished goods inventory The direct materials costs, direct labor costs, and factory overhead costs of finished products that have not been sold. (Ch. 18)

finished goods ledger The subsidiary ledger that contains the individual accounts for each kind of commodity or product produced. (Ch. 19)

first closing entry The first journal entry in the closing process that transfers revenue and the expense account balances to the owner's capital account as either a net income or a net loss. (Ch. 4)

first-in, first-out (FIFO) inventory cost flow method The method of inventory costing based on the assumption that the costs of merchandise sold should be charged against revenue in the order in which the costs were incurred. (Chs. 7, 20)

fiscal year The annual accounting period adopted by a business. (Ch. 4)

fixed asset turnover ratio The number of dollars of sales that are generated from each dollar of average fixed assets during the year, computed by dividing the net sales by the average net fixed assets. (Ch. 10)

fixed assets (or plant assets) Long-term or relatively permanent tangible assets such as equipment, machinery, and buildings that are used in the normal business operations and that depreciate over time. (Chs. 3, 4, 10)

fixed costs Costs that tend to remain the same in amount, regardless of variations in the level of activity. (Ch. 21)

flexible budget A budget that adjusts for varying rates of activity. (Ch. 22)

FOB (free on board) destination Freight terms in which the seller pays the transportation costs from the shipping point to the final destination. (Ch. 6)

FOB (free on board) shipping point Freight terms in which the buyer pays the transportation costs from the shipping point to the final destination. (Ch. 6)

four-column account An account format used for posting journal entries with columns for debits, credits, and a debit or credit balance. (Ch. 2)

free cash flow The amount of operating cash flow remaining after replacing current productive capacity. (Ch. 16)

fringe benefits Benefits provided to employees in addition to wages and salaries. (Ch. 11)

future value The value of an asset or cash at a specified date in the future that is equivalent in value to a specified sum today. (Ch. 14)

G

general journal The two-column form used for entries that do not "fit" in any of the special journals. (Ch. 5)

general ledger The primary ledger, when used in conjunction with subsidiary ledgers, that contains all of the balance sheet and income statement accounts. (Ch. 5)

general-purpose financial statements A type of financial accounting report that is distributed to external users. The term "general purpose" refers to the wide range of decision-making needs that the reports are designed to serve. (Ch. 1)

generally accepted accounting principles (GAAP) Generally accepted guidelines for the preparation of financial statements. (Ch. 1)

goal conflict A condition that occurs when individual objectives conflict with organizational objectives. (Ch. 22)

goodwill An intangible asset that is created from such favorable factors as location, product quality, reputation, and managerial skill. (Ch. 10)

gross pay The total earnings of an employee for a payroll period. (Ch. 11)

gross profit Sales minus the cost of merchandise sold. (Ch. 6)

gross profit method A method of estimating inventory cost that is based on the relationship of gross profit to sales. (Ch. 7)

H

held-to-maturity securities Investments in bonds or other debt securities that management intends to hold to their maturity. (Ch. 15)

high-low method A technique that uses the highest and lowest total costs as a basis for estimating the variable cost per unit and the fixed cost component of a mixed cost. (Ch. 21)

horizontal analysis Financial analysis that compares an item in a current statement with the same item in prior statements. (Chs. 2, 17)

I

ideal standards Standards that can be achieved only under perfect operating conditions, such as no idle time, no machine breakdowns, and no materials spoilage; also called theoretical standards. (Ch. 23)

in arrears Cumulative preferred stock dividends that have not been paid in prior years are said to be in arrears. (Ch. 13)

income from operations (operating income) Revenues less operating expenses and service department charges for a profit or an investment center. (Ch. 6)

income statement A summary of the revenue and expenses for a specific period of time, such as a month or a year. (Ch. 1)

indirect costs Costs that cannot be traced directly to a cost object. (Ch. 18)

indirect method A method of reporting the cash flows from operating activities as the net income from operations adjusted for all deferrals of past cash receipts and payments and all accruals of expected future cash receipts and payments. (Ch. 16)

inflation A period when prices in general are rising and the purchasing power of money is declining. (Ch. 26)

initial cost The purchase price of a fixed asset plus all costs to obtain and ready it for use. (Ch. 10)

installment note A debt that requires the borrower to make equal periodic payments to the lender for the term of the note. (Ch. 14)

intangible assets Long-term assets that are useful in the operations of a business, are not held for sale, and are without physical qualities. (Ch. 10)

interest revenue Money received for interest. (Ch. 1)

internal controls The policies and procedures used to safeguard assets, ensure accurate business information, and ensure compliance with laws and regulations. (Chs. 5, 8)

internal rate of return (IRR) method A method that determines the rate of return wherein the net present value of a project is zero. (Ch. 26)

International Accounting Standards Board (IASB) An organization that issues International Financial Reporting Standards for many countries outside the United States. (Ch. 1)

inventory analysis A company's ability to manage its inventory effectively. (Ch. 17)

inventory shrinkage (inventory shortage) The amount by which the merchandise for sale, as indicated by the balance of the merchandise inventory account, is larger than the total amount of merchandise counted during the physical inventory. (Ch. 6)

inventory turnover The relationship between the volume of goods sold and inventory, computed by dividing the cost of goods sold by the average inventory. (Chs. 7, 17)

investee The company whose stock is purchased by the investor. (Ch. 15)

investment center A decentralized unit in which the manager has the responsibility and authority to make decisions that affect not only costs and revenues but also the fixed assets available to the center. (Ch. 24)

investment turnover A component of the rate of return on investment, computed as the ratio of sales to invested assets. (Ch. 24)

investments The balance sheet caption used to report long-term investments in stocks not intended as a source of cash in the normal operations of the business. (Ch. 15)

investor The company investing in another company's stock. (Ch. 15)

invoice The bill that the seller sends to the buyer. (Chs. 5, 6)

J

job cost sheet An account in the work in process subsidiary ledger in which the costs charged to a particular job order are recorded. (Ch. 19)

job order cost system A type of cost accounting system that provides for a separate record of the cost of each particular quantity of product that passes through the factory. (Ch. 19)

journal The initial record in which the effects of a transaction are recorded. (Ch. 2)

journal entry The form of recording a transaction in a journal. (Ch. 2)

journalizing The process of recording a transaction in the journal. (Ch. 2)

L

last-in, first-out (LIFO) inventory cost flow method A method of inventory costing based on the assumption that the most recent merchandise inventory costs should be charged against revenue. (Ch. 7)

lean manufacturing A manufacturing enterprise that uses lean principles. (Ch. 20)

ledger A group of accounts for a business. (Ch. 2)

leverage Using debt to increase the return on an investment. (Ch. 17)

liabilities The rights of creditors that represent debts of the business. (Chs. 1, 2)

limited liability company (LLC) A business form consisting of one or more persons or entities filing an operating agreement with a state to conduct business with limited liability to the owners, yet treated as a partnership for tax purposes. (Chs. 1, 12)

line department A unit that is directly involved in the basic objectives of an organization. (Ch. 18)

liquidation The winding-up process when a partnership goes out of business. (Ch. 12)

liquidity The ability to convert assets into cash. (Chs. 4, 17)

long-term liabilities Liabilities that usually will not be due for more than one year. (Ch. 4)

lower-of-cost-or-market (LCM) method A method of valuing inventory that reports the inventory at the lower of its cost or current market value (replacement cost). (Ch. 7)

M

management (or managerial) accounting The branch of accounting that uses both historical and estimated data in providing information that management uses in conducting daily operations, in planning future operations, and in developing overall business strategies. (Chs. 1, 18)

management by exception The philosophy of managing that involves monitoring the operating results of implemented plans and comparing the expected results with the actual results. This feedback allows management to isolate significant variations for further investigation and possible remedial action. (Ch. 18)

management process The five basic management functions of (1) planning, (2) directing, (3) controlling, (4) improving, and (5) decision making. (Ch. 18)

Management's Discussion and Analysis (MD&A) An annual report disclosure that provides management's analysis of the results of operations and financial condition. (Ch. 17)

manufacturing business A type of business that changes basic inputs into products that are sold to individual customers. (Ch. 1)

manufacturing cells A grouping of processes where employees are cross-trained to perform more than one function. (Ch. 20)

manufacturing overhead Costs, other than direct materials and direct labor costs, that are incurred in the manufacturing process. (Ch. 18)

margin of safety Indicates the possible decrease in sales that may occur before an operating loss results. (Ch. 21)

market price approach An approach to transfer pricing that uses the price at which the product or service transferred could be sold to outside buyers as the transfer price. (Ch. 24)

market rate of interest The rate determined from sales and purchases of similar bonds. (Ch. 14)

master budget The comprehensive budget plan linking all the individual budgets related to sales, cost of goods sold, operating expenses, projects, capital expenditures, and cash. (Ch. 22)

matching concept (or matching principle) A concept of accounting in which expenses are matched with the revenue generated during a period by those expenses. (Chs. 1, 3)

materials inventory The cost of materials that have not yet entered into the manufacturing process. (Ch. 18)

materials ledger The subsidiary ledger containing the individual accounts for each type of material. (Ch. 19)

materials requisition The form or electronic transmission used by a manufacturing department to authorize materials issuances from the storeroom. (Ch. 19)

maturity value The amount that is due at the maturity or due date of a note. (Ch. 9)

merchandise available for sale The cost of merchandise available for sale to customers calculated by adding the beginning merchandise inventory to net purchases. (Ch. 18)

merchandise inventory Merchandise on hand (not sold) at the end of an accounting period. (Ch. 6)

merchandising business A type of business that purchases products from other businesses and sells them to customers. (Ch. 1)

mixed costs Costs with both variable and fixed characteristics, sometimes called semivariable or semifixed costs. (Ch. 21)

mortgage notes An installment note that may be secured by a pledge of the borrower's assets. (Ch. 14)

multiple-step income statement A form of income statement that contains several sections, subsections, and subtotals. (Ch. 6)

N

natural business year A fiscal year that ends when business activities have reached the lowest point in an annual operating cycle. (Ch. 4)

negotiated price approach An approach to transfer pricing that allows managers of decentralized units to agree (negotiate) among themselves as to the transfer price. (Ch. 24)

net income (or net profit) The amount by which revenues exceed expenses. (Ch. 1)

net loss The amount by which expenses exceed revenues. (Ch. 1)

net pay Gross pay less payroll deductions; the amount the employer is obligated to pay the employee. (Ch. 11)

net present value method A method of analysis of proposed capital investments that subtracts the amount to be invested from the present value of the cash flows expected from the investments. (Ch. 26)

net realizable value The estimated selling price of an item of inventory less any direct costs of disposal, such as sales commissions. (Chs. 7, 9)

nonfinancial performance measure A performance measure expressed in units rather than dollars. (Ch. 23)

normal balance of an account The normal balance of an account can be either a debit or a credit depending on whether increases in the account are recorded as debits or credits. (Ch. 2)

notes receivable A customer's written promise to pay an amount and possibly interest at an agreed-upon rate. (Chs. 4, 9)

number of days' sales in inventory The relationship between the volume of sales and inventory, computed by dividing the inventory at the end of the year by the average daily cost of goods sold. (Chs. 7, 17)

number of days' sales in receivables The relationship between sales and accounts receivable, computed by dividing the net accounts receivable at the end of the year by the average daily sales. (Chs. 9, 17)

O

objectives (goals) Developed in the planning stage, these reflect the direction and desired outcomes of certain courses of action. (Ch. 18)

objectivity concept A concept of accounting that requires accounting records and the data reported in financial statements to be based on objective evidence. (Ch. 1)

operating cycle The process by which a company spends cash, generates revenues, and receives cash either at the time the revenues are generated or later by collecting an accounts receivable. (Ch. 6)

operating leverage A measure of the relative mix of a business's variable costs and fixed costs, computed as contribution margin divided by operating income. (Ch. 21)

operational planning The development of short-term plans to achieve goals identified in a business's strategic plan. Sometimes called tactical planning. (Ch. 18)

opportunity cost The amount of income forgone from an alternative to a proposed use of cash or its equivalent. (Ch. 25)

other comprehensive income Specified items that are reported separately from net income, including foreign currency items, pension liability adjustments, and unrealized gains and losses on investments. (Ch. 15)

other expense Expenses that cannot be traced directly to operations. (Ch. 6)

other revenue Revenue from sources other than the primary operating activity of a business. (Ch. 6)

outstanding stock The stock in the hands of stockholders. (Ch. 13)

overapplied factory overhead The amount of factory overhead applied in excess of the actual factory overhead costs incurred for production during a period. (Ch. 19)

owner's equity The owner's right to the assets of the business. (Chs. 1, 2)

P

paid-in capital Capital contributed to a corporation by the stockholders and others. (Ch. 13)

par value A dollar amount assigned to each share of stock. (Ch. 13)

parent company The corporation owning all or a majority of the voting stock of the other corporation. (Ch. 15)

partnership An unincorporated business form consisting of two or more persons conducting business as co-owners for profit. (Chs. 1, 12)

partnership agreement The formal written contract creating a partnership. (Ch. 12)

patents Exclusive rights to produce and sell goods with one or more unique features. (Ch. 10)

payroll The total amount paid to employees for a certain period. (Ch. 11)

payroll register A multicolumn report used to assemble and summarize payroll data at the end of each payroll period. (Ch. 11)

pension A cash payment to retired employees. (Ch. 11)

period costs Those costs that are used up in generating revenue during the current period and that are not involved in manufacturing a product, such as selling, general, and administrative expenses. (Ch. 18)

periodic inventory system The inventory system in which the inventory records do not show the amount available for sale or sold during the period. (Ch. 6)

perpetual inventory system The inventory system in which each purchase and sale of merchandise is recorded in an inventory account. (Ch. 6)

petty cash fund A special cash fund to pay relatively small amounts. (Ch. 8)

physical inventory A detailed listing of merchandise on hand. (Chs. 6, 7)

planning A phase of the management process whereby objectives are outlined and courses of action determined. (Ch. 18)

posting The process of transferring the debits and credits from the journal entries to the accounts. (Ch. 2)

predetermined factory overhead rate The rate used to apply factory overhead costs to the goods manufactured. The rate is determined by dividing the budgeted overhead cost by the estimated activity usage at the beginning of the fiscal period. (Ch. 19)

preferred stock A class of stock with preferential rights over common stock. (Ch. 13)

premium The excess of the issue price of a stock over its par value or the excess of the issue price of bonds over their face amount. (Chs. 13, 14)

prepaid expenses Items such as supplies that will be used in the business in the future. (Chs. 1, 3)

present value concept Cash to be received (or paid) in the future is not the equivalent of the same amount of money received at an earlier date. (Chs. 14, 26)

present value index An index computed by dividing the total present value of the net cash flow to be received from a proposed capital investment by the amount to be invested. (Ch. 26)

present value of an annuity The sum of the present values of a series of equal cash flows to be received at fixed intervals. (Chs. 14, 26)

price-earnings (P/E) ratio The ratio of the market price per share of common stock, at a specific date, to the annual earnings per share. (Ch. 17)

prime costs The combination of direct materials and direct labor costs. (Ch. 18)

prior period adjustments Corrections of material errors related to a prior period or periods, excluded from the determination of net income. (Ch. 13)

private accounting The field of accounting whereby accountants are employed by a business firm or a not-for-profit organization. (Ch. 1)

process A sequence of activities linked together for performing a particular task. (Ch. 23)

process cost system A type of cost system that accumulates costs for each of the various departments within a manufacturing facility. (Chs. 19, 20)

process manufacturer A manufacturer that uses large machines to process a continuous flow of raw materials through various stages of completion into a finished state. (Ch. 20)

product cost concept A concept used in applying the cost-plus approach to product pricing in which only the costs of manufacturing the product, termed the product cost, are included in the cost amount to which the markup is added. (Ch. 25)

product costs The three components of manufacturing cost: direct materials, direct labor, and factory overhead costs. (Ch. 18)

production bottleneck A condition that occurs when product demand exceeds production capacity. (Ch. 25)

production budget A budget of estimated unit production. (Ch. 22)

profit The difference between the amounts received from customers for goods or services provided and the amounts paid for the inputs used to provide the goods or services. (Ch. 1)

profit center A decentralized unit in which the manager has the responsibility and the authority to make decisions that affect both costs and revenues (and thus profits). (Ch. 24)

profit margin A component of the rate of return on investment, computed as the ratio of income from operations to sales. (Ch. 24)

profit-volume chart A chart used to assist management in understanding the relationship between profit and volume. (Ch. 21)

profitability The ability of a firm to earn income. (Ch. 17)

proprietorship A business owned by one individual. (Ch. 1)

public accounting The field of accounting where accountants and their staff provide services on a fee basis. (Ch. 1)

public companies Companies that issue publicly traded debt or equity securities. (App. B)

Public Company Accounting Oversight Board (PCAOB) A new oversight body for the accounting profession that was established by the Sarbanes-Oxley Act. (Ch. 1)

purchase order The purchase order authorizes the purchase of the inventory from an approved vendor. (Ch. 7)

purchases discounts Discounts taken by the buyer for early payment of an invoice. (Ch. 6)

purchases journal The journal in which all items purchased on account are recorded. (Ch. 5)

purchases returns and allowances From the buyer's perspective, returned merchandise or an adjustment for defective merchandise. (Ch. 6)

Q

quick assets Cash and other current assets that can be quickly converted to cash, such as marketable securities and receivables. (Chs. 11, 17)

quick ratio A financial ratio that measures the ability to pay current liabilities with quick assets (cash, marketable securities, accounts receivable). (Chs. 11, 17)

R

ratio of cash to monthly cash expenses Ratio that helps assess how long a company can continue to operate without additional financing or generating positive cash flows from operations. (Ch. 8)

ratio of fixed assets to long-term liabilities A leverage ratio that measures the margin of safety of long-term creditors, calculated as the net fixed assets divided by the long-term liabilities. (Ch. 17)

ratio of liabilities to owner's (stockholders') equity A comprehensive leverage ratio that measures the relationship of the claims of creditors to stockholders' equity. (Chs. 1, 17)

ratios A number that expresses a financial statement item or set of financial statement items as a percentage of another financial item, in order to measure an important economic relationship as a single number. (Ch. 17)

real (permanent) accounts Term for balance sheet accounts because they are relatively permanent and carried forward from year to year. (Ch. 4)

realization The sale of assets when a partnership is being liquidated. (Ch. 12)

receivables All money claims against other entities, including people, business firms, and other organizations. (Ch. 9)

receiving report The form or electronic transmission used by the receiving personnel to indicate that materials have been received and inspected. (Chs. 7, 19)

relevant range The range of activity over which changes in cost are of interest to management. (Ch. 21)

rent revenue Money received for rent. (Ch. 1)

report form The form of balance sheet with the Liabilities and Owner's Equity sections presented below the Assets section. (Ch. 1)

residual income The excess of divisional income from operations over a "minimum" acceptable income from operations. (Ch. 24)

residual value The estimated value of a fixed asset at the end of its useful life. (Ch. 10)

responsibility accounting The process of measuring and reporting operating data by areas of responsibility. (Ch. 24)

responsibility center An organizational unit for which a manager is assigned responsibility over costs, revenues, or assets. (Ch. 22)

restrictions Amounts of retained earnings that have been limited for use as dividends. (Ch. 13)

retail inventory method A method of estimating inventory cost that is based on the relationship of gross profit to sales. (Ch. 7)

retained earnings Net income retained in a corporation. (Ch. 13)

retained earnings statement A summary of the changes in the retained earnings in a corporation for a specific period of time, such as a month or a year. (Ch. 13)

return on common stockholders' equity A measure of profitability computed by dividing net income, reduced by preferred dividend requirements, by common stockholders' equity. (Ch. 17)

return on investment (ROI) A measure of managerial efficiency in the use of investments in assets, computed as income from operations divided by invested assets. (Ch. 24)

return on stockholders' equity A measure of profitability computed by dividing net income by total stockholders' equity. (Ch. 17)

return on total assets A measure of the profitability of assets, without regard to the equity of creditors and stockholders in the assets. (Ch. 17)

revenue expenditures Costs that benefit only the current period or costs incurred for normal maintenance and repairs of fixed assets. (Ch. 10)

revenue journal The journal in which all sales and services on account are recorded. (Ch. 5)

revenue per employee A measure of the efficiency of the business in generating revenues, which is computed as revenue divided by number of employees. (Ch. 12)

revenue recognition The process of recognizing revenue. (Ch. 3)

revenue recognition principle The concept that supports recording revenues when services have been performed or products delivered to customers. (Ch. 3)

revenues Increases in assets from performing services or delivering products to customers. (Chs. 1, 2)

reversing entries Journal entries made the first day of the period that are the exact opposite of the related adjusting entries of the prior period. (Ch. 4)

rules of debit and credit In the double-entry accounting system, specific rules for recording debits and credits based on the type of account. (Ch. 2)

S

sales The total amount charged customers for merchandise sold, including cash sales and sales on account. (Chs. 1, 6)

sales budget One of the major elements of the income statement budget that indicates the quantity of estimated sales and the expected unit selling price. (Ch. 22)

sales discounts From the seller's perspective, discounts that a seller may offer the buyer for early payment. (Ch. 6)

sales mix The relative distribution of sales among the various products available for sale. (Ch. 21)

Sarbanes-Oxley Act (SOX) An act passed by Congress to restore public confidence and trust in the financial statements of companies. (Chs. 1, 8)

second closing entry The second journal entry of the closing process that transfers the owner's drawing account balance to the owner's capital account. (Ch. 4)

Securities and Exchange Commission (SEC) An agency of the U.S. government that has authority over the accounting and financial disclosures for companies whose shares of ownership (stock) are traded and sold to the public. (Ch. 1)

selling expenses Expenses that are incurred directly in the selling of merchandise. (Ch. 6)

service business A business providing services rather than products to customers. (Ch. 1)

service department charges The costs of services provided by an internal service department and transferred to a responsibility center. (Ch. 24)

setup An overhead activity that consists of changing tooling in machines in preparation for making a new product. (Ch. 25)

single-step income statement A form of income statement in which the total of all expenses is deducted from the total of all revenues. (Ch. 6)

slide An error in which the entire number is moved one or more spaces to the right or the left, such as writing $542.00 as $54.20 or $5,420.00. (Ch. 2)

solvency The ability of a firm to pay its debts as they come due. (Chs. 4, 17)

special journals Journals designed to be used for recording a single type of transaction. (Ch. 5)

special-purpose funds Cash funds used for a special business need. (Ch. 8)

specific identification inventory cost flow method Inventory method in which the unit sold is identified with a specific purchase. (Ch. 7)

staff department A unit that provides services, assistance, and advice to the departments with line or other staff responsibilities. (Ch. 18)

standard cost A detailed estimate of what a product should cost. (Ch. 23)

standard cost systems Accounting systems that use standards for each element of manufacturing cost entering into the finished product. (Ch. 23)

standards Performance goals, often relating to how much a product should cost. (Ch. 23)

statement of cash flows A summary of the cash receipts and cash payments for a specific period of time, such as a month or a year. (Chs. 1, 16)

statement of cost of goods manufactured The income statement of manufacturing companies. (Ch. 18)

statement of members' equity A summary of the changes in each member's equity in a limited liability corporation that have occurred during a specific period of time. (Ch. 12)

statement of owner's equity A summary of the changes in owner's equity that have occurred during a specific period of time, such as a month or a year. (Ch. 1)

statement of partnership equity A summary of the changes in each partner's capital in a partnership that have occurred during a specific period of time. (Ch. 12)

statement of partnership liquidation A summary of the liquidation process whereby cash is distributed to the partners based on the balances in their capital accounts. (Ch. 12)

statement of stockholders' equity A summary of the changes in the stockholders' equity in a corporation that have occurred during a specific period of time. (Ch. 13)

static budget A budget that does not adjust to changes in activity levels. (Ch. 22)

stock Shares of ownership of a corporation. (Ch. 13)

stock dividend A distribution of shares of stock to its stockholders. (Ch. 13)

stock split A reduction in the par or stated value of a common stock and the issuance of a proportionate number of additional shares. (Ch. 13)

stockholders The owners of a corporation. (Ch. 13)

stockholders' equity The owners' equity in a corporation. (Chs. 1, 13)

straight-line method A method of depreciation that provides for equal periodic depreciation expense over the estimated life of a fixed asset. (Ch. 10)

strategic planning The development of a long-range course of action to achieve business goals. (Ch. 18)

strategies The means by which business goals and objectives will be achieved. (Ch. 18)

subsidiary company The corporation that is controlled by a parent company. (Ch. 15)

subsidiary inventory ledger The subsidiary ledger containing individual accounts for items of inventory. (Ch. 7)

subsidiary ledger A ledger containing individual accounts with a common characteristic. (Ch. 5)

sunk cost A cost that is not affected by subsequent decisions. (Ch. 25)

sustainability The practice of operating a business to maximize profits while attempting to preserve the environment, economy, and needs of future generations. (Ch. 18)

Sustainability Accounting Standards Board (SASB) A board that was organized in 2011 to develop accounting standards that help companies report decision-useful sustainability information to external financial statement users. (Ch. 18)

T

T account The simplest form of an account. (Ch. 2)

target costing The target cost is determined by subtracting a desired profit from a market method determined price. The resulting target cost is used to motivate cost improvements in design and manufacture. (Ch. 25)

temporary (nominal) accounts Accounts that report amounts for only one period. (Ch. 4)

theory of constraints (TOC) A manufacturing strategy that attempts to remove the influence of bottlenecks (constraints) on a process. (Ch. 25)

time tickets The form on which the amount of time spent by each employee and the labor cost incurred for each individual job, or for factory overhead, are recorded. (Ch. 19)

time value of money concept The concept that an amount of money invested today will earn income. (Ch. 26)

times interest earned A ratio that measures creditor margin of safety for interest payments, calculated as income before interest and taxes divided by interest expense. (Chs. 14, 17)

total cost concept A concept used in applying the cost-plus approach to product pricing in which all the costs of manufacturing the product plus the selling and administrative expenses are included in the cost amount to which the markup is added. (Ch. 25)

total manufacturing cost variance The difference between total standard costs and total actual costs for units produced. (Ch. 23)

trade discounts Discounts from the list prices in published catalogs or special discounts offered to certain classes of buyers. (Ch. 6)

trade-in allowance The amount a seller allows a buyer for a fixed asset that is traded in for a similar asset. (Ch. 10)

trademark A name, term, or symbol used to identify a business and its products. (Ch. 10)

trading securities Securities that management intends to actively trade for profit. (Ch. 15)

transfer price The price charged one decentralized unit by another for the goods or services provided. (Ch. 24)

transposition An error in which the order of the digits is changed, such as writing $542 as $452 or $524. (Ch. 2)

treasury stock Stock that a corporation has once issued and then reacquires. (Ch. 13)

trial balance A summary listing of the titles and balances of accounts in the ledger. (Ch. 2)

two-column journal A journal format with a debit column and a credit column. (Ch. 2)

U

unadjusted trial balance A summary listing of the titles and balances of accounts in the ledger prior to the posting of adjusting entries. (Ch. 2)

underapplied factory overhead The amount of actual factory overhead in excess of the factory overhead applied to production during a period. (Ch. 19)

unearned revenue The liability created by receiving revenue in advance. (Chs. 2, 3)

unfavorable cost variance A variance that occurs when the actual cost exceeds the standard cost. (Ch. 23)

unit contribution margin The dollars available from each unit of sales to cover fixed costs and provide operating profits. (Ch. 21)

unit of measure concept A concept of accounting requiring that economic data be recorded in dollars. (Ch. 1)

units-of-activity method A method of depreciation that provides for depreciation expense based on each unit of activity of a fixed asset. (Ch. 10)

unrealized gain or loss Changes in the fair value of equity or debt securities for a period. (Ch. 15)

V

variable cost concept A concept used in applying the cost-plus approach to product pricing in which only the variable costs are included in the cost amount to which the markup is added. (Ch. 25)

variable costing The concept that considers the cost of products manufactured to be composed only of those manufacturing costs that increase or decrease as the volume of production rises or falls (direct materials, direct labor, and variable factory overhead). (Ch. 21)

variable costs Costs that vary in total dollar amount as the level of activity changes. (Ch. 21)

vertical analysis An analysis that compares each item in a current statement with a total amount within the same statement. (Chs. 3, 17)

volume variance The difference between the budgeted fixed overhead at 100% of normal capacity and the standard fixed overhead for the actual production achieved during the period. (Ch. 23)

voucher A special form for recording relevant data about a liability and the details of its payment. (Ch. 8)

voucher system A set of procedures for authorizing and recording liabilities and cash payments. (Ch. 8)

W

weighted average inventory cost flow method A method of inventory costing in which the cost of the units sold and in ending inventory is a weighted average of the purchase costs. (Ch. 7)

whole units The number of units in production during a period, whether completed or not. (Ch. 20)

wholesalers Companies that sell merchandise to other businesses rather than to the public. (Ch. 6)

work in process inventory The direct materials costs, the direct labor costs, and the applied factory overhead costs that have entered into the manufacturing process but are associated with products that have not been finished. (Ch. 18)

working capital The excess of the current assets of a business over its current liabilities. (Chs. 4, 17)

Y

yield A measure of materials usage efficiency. (Ch. 20)

Z

zero-based budgeting A concept of budgeting that requires all levels of management to start from zero and estimate budget data as if there had been no previous activities in their units. (Ch. 22)

Index

A

Abbey Group, The, 588
ABC's of **Schwab**, 1239
Abercrombie & Fitch, Inc., 910
Above-the-line costs, 1080
Absences, compensated, 552
Absorption costing
   and variable costing income, relationship between, *illus.*, 1049
   def., 1047
   income statement, *illus.*, 1048
Absorption vs. variable cost of goods manufactured, *illus.*, 1047
Accelerated depreciation method, *def.*, 498
Account form, *def.*, 21
Account payable, *def.*, 15
   See also Accounts payable
Account receivable, *def.*, 16, 72
   See also Accounts receivable
Accountants
   Certified Public Accountants (CPAs), 10
   management, 886–887
   opportunities for, 9–10
Accounting, 401
   accrual and cash basis of, 113–114
   and business frauds, *illus.*, 8
   as information system, *illus.*, 7
   career paths and salaries, *illus.*, 9
   def., 6
   environmental managerial, 898
   financial, 6, 885–886, *illus.*, 886
   for depreciation, 492–504
   for dividends, 639–642
   for notes receivable, 456–457
   management, 6
   managerial, 6, 885–890, 903, *illus.*, 886
   nature of, 5–10
   payroll, 541
   private, 6
   public, 10
   responsibility, 1175–1176
   role of ethics in, 6–9
   role of, in business, 6
   sustainability and, 896–897
   under U.S. GAAP and IFRS, comparison of, *illus.*, B-4–B-5

Accounting cycle, 174–176
   def., 174
   illustration of, 176, 177–187
Accounting data, flow of, and end-of-period spreadsheet, *illus.*, 164
Accounting equation, 13–14
   business transactions and, 14–19
   def., 13
Accounting industry, organizational forms in, 588
Accounting information, flow of, 163–165
Accounting principles. See Generally accepted accounting principles
Accounting rate of return, 1275
Accounting standards, need for global, B-1
Accounting system
   and profit measurement, 246
   basic, 232–233
   computerized, 247–249
   def., 232
   double-entry, 62–68
   for payroll and payroll taxes, 545–551
   manual, 233–246
Accounting treatment of contingent liabilities, *illus.*, 557
Account(s)
   allowance for doubtful, 445
   analyzing, 789
   balance of the, 60
   balance sheet, 62
   bank, 407–410
   cash short and over, 404
   chart of, 61–62, *illus.*, 62
   collecting past due, 446
   contra, 124, 494
   contra asset, 124, 494
   controlling, 233
   def., 59
   factory overhead, 1142
   income statement, 63
   inventory ledger, *illus.*, 927
   journalizing and posting to, 68–77
   nominal, 169
   normal balance of, 63, *illus.*, 63
   other, 791
   permanent, 169
   real, 169
   sales on, 291

   temporary, 169
   types of requiring adjustment, 115–116
   using to record transactions, 59–62
Accounts payable, 538
   control account and subsidiary ledger, 245–246
   subsidiary ledger, *def.*, 233
   See also Account payable
Accounts receivable
   control account and subsidiary ledger, 240
   def., 442
   subsidiary ledger, *def.*, 233
   See also Account receivable
Accounts receivable analysis, 834–835
   def., 834
Accounts receivable turnover, 459–460, 848
   def., 459, 834
Accrual basis of accounting, 113–114
   def., 113
Accrual(s)
   adjusting entries for, 116–120
   def., 115
   illus., 115
Accrued expenses, 118–120
Accrued revenues, 117–118
Accrued wages, *illus.*, 119, 196
Accumulated depreciation, *def.*, 124
Accumulated other comprehensive income, *def.*, 739
ACH, Automated Clearing House, 408
Acid-test ratio, 833
Activities, *def.*, 1237
Activity base(s), *def.*, 933, 1022, 1238
Activity costs, estimated, 1237, *illus.*, 1237
Activity driver, 933, 1022
Activity rate, *def.*, *illus.*, 1238
Activity-base product cost calculations, *illus.*, 1239
Activity-base usage, *illus.*, 1238
Activity-based costing (ABC), 1237–1241
   def., 933, 1237
   method, *illus.*, 1239
Actual overhead, 934
Adjusted trial balance, 130–131
   def., 130
   enter on the spreadsheet, 192–193
   illus., 131, 182

I-1

I-2 Index

preparing, 182
spreadsheet with unadjusted trial balance, adjustments and, *illus.*, 192
Adjusting entries
  def., 114
  for accruals, 116–120
  for customer refunds, allowances, and returns, 301–303
  for deferrals, 120–124
  for depreciation, 124–126
  for inventory shrinkage, 300–301
  illus., 128, 181
  journalizing and posting, 180–182
  ledger with, *illus.*, 128–130
Adjusting process, 114–115, 300–303
  def., 114
  nature of, 113–116
  under periodic inventory system, 310–311
Adjustment data, assembling and analyzing, 180
Adjustment process, summary of, 126–130
Adjustments
  and adjusted trial balance, spreadsheet with unadjusted trial balance, *illus.*, 192
  enter on the spreadsheet, 191–192
  prior period, 648
  spreadsheet with unadjusted trial balance and, *illus.*, 191
  summary of, *illus.*, 127
  types of accounts requiring, 115–116
Administrative expenses, 895
  def., 303
Advanced robotics, 832
Aging of receivables schedule, *illus.*, 450
Aging the receivables, *def.*, 450
Agreement, operating, 588
Alcoa Inc., 37, 485, 489, 970, 971, 1002
Allocation base, 933
Allocation method, 125
Allowance
  for doubtful accounts, *def.*, 445
  percentages across companies, 453
  trade-in, 514
Allowance account, write-offs to, 446–447
Allowance method
  and direct write-off methods, comparing, 453–454, *illus.*, 454
  def., 443
  for uncollectible accounts, 445–453
  illus., 446
Alphabet (Google) Inc., 12, 13, 27, 528, 629, 632, 633, 634, 635, 636, 640, 643, 645, 647, 738, 870, 1127
  See also **Google**
Alternative financing plans, effect of, *illus.*, 678, 679
Amazon.com, Inc., 6, 55, 147, 249, 267, 393, 527, 880–881, 1127, 1270
American Accounting Association (AAA), 10
American Airlines, 513, 1036
American Airlines Group, Inc., 800

American Customer Satisfaction Index, 639
American Eagle Outfitters Inc., 475
American Express Company, 736, 1206
American Institute of Certified Public Accountants (AICPA), 8*fn*, 10, 649
Amgen Inc., 1311
Amicus Therapeutics, Inc., 430
Amortization
  def., 508, 683
  interest rate method of, 697–699
  of installment notes, *illus.*, 689
Amortization of discount
  by interest method, 697–698
  on bonds payable, *illus.*, 698
Amortization of premium
  by interest method, 698–699
  on bonds payable, *illus.*, 699
Amount, present value of, 1278–1279
Analysis
  accounts receivable, 834–835
  assumptions of cost-volume-profit, 1042
  cost-volume-profit, 1028
  current position, 832–834
  differential, 1220–1231, *illus.*, 1221
  horizontal, 826–829
  incremental, 1220
  inventory, 836–837
  of receivables method, 449–452
  vertical, 829–830
  "what if" or sensitivity, 1042
Analytical measures, summary of, 847–849, *illus.*, 848
Analytical methods
  basic, 826–831
  def., 826
Anheuser-Busch InBev Companies, Inc., 1059
Annual payments, 689–690
Annual reports, corporate, 849–850
Annuity
  def., 695, 1279
  of $1 at compound interest, present value of, *illus.*, 696
  present value of, 695, 1279–1281, *illus.*, 1284
Annuity table, partial present value of, *illus.*, 1281
Apple Inc., 12, 58, 60, 62, 71, 78, 81, 167, 249, 267, 382, 415, 484, 527, 571, 837, 970, 1127
Application of incorporation, 631
Applied overhead, 934
Appropriations, 648
Articles of incorporation, 631
Asset disclosures, frequency of intangible, *illus.*, 510
Asset improvements, 503–504
Asset turnover, 307–308, 840–841, 848
  def., 307, 840
Asset with change in estimate, book value of, *illus.*, 502
Assets, 168
  book value of, 125
  contributing to a partnership, 594, 595

current, 168
custody of, 401
def., 13, 61
financial, 730
fixed, 124, 168, 488–491, 504–506, 511–512, 514–516, *illus.*, 490
intangible, 508–510, 511–512, *illus.*, 510
net book value of, 494
plant, 124, 168, 488
quick, 558, 833
ratio of fixed to long-term liabilities, 838
return on, 1182
return on operating, 842
return on total, 841–842, 848
revaluation of in partnership, 595–596
tangible, 488
Association of Certified Fraud Examiners, 398, 849
Assumption fudging, 1290
AT&T, 147, 1091
Auditors, 9
Authorized stock, *illus.*, 634
AutoZone, Inc., 33, 485
Available-for-sale securities, 732–734
  def., 732
Average cost flow method, 348
Average cost method, 976*fn*, 993–995
  determining costs under, 993–995
Average cost per available seat mile (CASM), 1036
Average rate of return
  def., 1275
  method, 1275–1276
Average revenue earned per available seat mile (RASM,) 1036

B

B2B (business-to-business) e-commerce, 249
B2C (business-to-consumer) e-commerce, 249
Bad debt expense, *def.*, 443
Bain & Company, 1188
Balance of the account
  def., 60
  normal, 63, *illus.*, 63
Balance sheet, 21–23, 168–169, 305–306
  budgeted, 1096
  classified, 168
  comparative, *illus.*, 827, 829
  current liabilities on, 554
  def., 20
  effect of fair value accounting on, 737
  effect of inventory errors on current period's, *illus.*, 364
  for manufacturing business, 898
  for merchandising business, *illus.*, 306
  for Mornin' Joe, *illus.*, MJ-3
  income statement and comparative, *illus.*, 772–773
  merchandise inventory on, 361–362

presentation of inventory in manufacturing and merchandising companies, *illus.*, 899
report form of, *illus.*, 23
reporting receivables on, 458
stockholders' equity in, 645–647, *illus.*, 646
vs. statements of financial position, MJ-8
Balance sheet accounts, 62
Balance sheet columns
extend the accounts to, 193
spreadsheet with amounts extended to, *illus.*, 194
total, 193–194
Balance sheet effects, 363–364
Balanced scorecard, 1187–1188
def., illus., 1187
performance measures, *illus.*, 1188
Bank accounts, 407–410
Bank error, in your favor, 413
Bank of America Corporation, 651
Bank reconciliation, 410–413
def., 410
format, *illus.*, 410
how to prepare, *illus.*, 411
illus., 412
Bank statement, 407–409
and records, *illus.*, 409
def., 407
illus., 407
using as control over cash, 409–410
Barnes & Noble, Inc., 485
Basic analytical methods, 826–831
Basic earnings per share, 651
Below-the-line costs, 1080
Benefits other than pensions, postretirement, 554
Berkshire Hathaway Inc., 643, 736, 763
Bernard L. Madoff Investment Securities LLC, 9
Best Buy, Inc., 284, 322, 345, 346, 347, 348, 353, 360, 362, 366, 484, 738, 880–881
Bill and Melinda Gates Foundation, 736
Blue Ribbon Sports, 824
BMW Group, 169, 1125, 1126, 1128, 1131, 1132, 1134, 1136, 1146, 1147
Board of directors, 631
Boeing, 37, 468, 893
Bond discount, amortizing, 683–685
Bond indenture, *def.*, 680
Bond premium, amortizing, 686–687
Bond ratings, 687
Bond redemption, 687–688
Bond(s)
callable, 680, 687
characteristics and terminology of, 680
convertible, 680
def., 677
investment grade, 687
issued at a discount, 682–683, *illus.*, 680
issued at a premium, 685–686, *illus.*, 680

issued at face amount, 681–682, *illus.*, 680
junk, 687
non-investment grade, 687
pricing of, 696–697
proceeds from issuing, , 680–681
purchase of, 723
sale of, 724–725
serial, 680
term, 680
zero-coupon, 696*fn*
Bonds payable, 779
accounting for, 681–688
amortization of discount on, *illus.*, 698
amortization of premium on, *illus.*, 699
nature of, 679–681
pricing, 693–697
Bonuses, 359
partner, 596, *illus.*, 596
to existing partners, 596–597
to new partner, 597–598
Book value, 511, 728
def., 494
Book value of the asset
def., 125
with change in estimate, *illus.*, 502
Booking fees, 1028
Boot, *def.*, 514
Borrowers, 538
Boston Basketball Partners (BBP) LLC, 585, 588, 589, 591, 592, 600
Boston Consulting Group (BCG), 932
Braeburn Capital, 415
Break-even
airline industry, 1036
chart, 1037
profit, and loss in **Major League Baseball**, 1042
sales, multiple products, *illus.*, 1044
Break-even point, 1031–1035
def., 1031
illus., 1031
summary of effects of changes on, 1035, *illus.*, 1033, 1034, 1035
Brokerage commission, 723
Budget games, 1078
Budget performance report
def., 1129
illus., 1130
Budgetary performance evaluation, 1128–1131
Budgetary slack, *def.*, 1077
Budgeted balance sheet, 1096
Budgeted income statement, 1091–1092 *illus.*, 1091
Budgeted variable factory overhead, *def.*, 1138
Budgeting
continuous, 1078, *illus.*, 1078
human behavior and, 1077, *illus.*, 1077
nature and objectives of, 1076–1077
zero-based, 1079
Budgeting systems, 1078–1082
computerized, 1081–1082

Budget(s)
capital expenditures, 1095–1096, *illus.*, 1095
cash, 1092–1095, *illus.*, 1095
cost of goods sold, 1088–1090, *illus.*, 1089
def., 1076
direct labor cost, 1086–1088, *illus.*, 1087
direct materials purchases, 1084–1086, *illus.*, 1086
factory overhead cost, 1088, *illus.*, 1088
factory overhead flexible, 1136–1138
financial, 1092–1096
flexible, 1080–1081, *illus.*, 1080, 1081
master, 1082
operating, 1082–1092, *illus.*, 1083
production, 1084, *illus.*, 1084
sales, 1082–1083, *illus.*, 1083
selling and administrative expenses, 1090, *illus.*, 1090
setting conflicting goals, 1077
setting goals too loosely, 1077
setting goals too tightly, 1077
static, 1079, *illus.*, 1079, 1081
Buffett, Warren E., 643, 736
Building and accumulated depreciation, 780
Burlington Northern Santa Fe Railroad, 736
Business
accept at a special price, 1229–1231, *illus.*, 1230
and accounting frauds, *illus.*, 8
def., 5
financial history of, *illus.*, 187
nature of, 5–10
role of accounting in, 6
role of ethics in, 6–9
types of, 5–6
See also Manufacturing businesses; Merchandising businesses; Service businesses
Business combination, *def.*, 729
Business connection
ABC's of **Schwab**,1239
accounting equation, 13
accounting systems and profit measurement, 246
advanced robotics, 932
airline industry break-even, 1036
allowance percentages across companies, 453
bond ratings, 687
booking fees, 1028
breaking up is hard to do, 587
Buffett on stock splits, 643
business use of investment analysis methods, 1275
cash crunch, 770
choosing a fiscal year, 188
Coca-Cola Company, 1184–1185
Comcast vs. **Lowe's**, 284
computerized accounting systems, 72

Index   I-3

computerized perpetual inventory systems, 355
deferred revenues, 128
Delta Air Lines, 458
depreciating animals, 500
downsizing, 506
earning revenues from season tickets, 120
employee fraud, 398
excerpts from **Alphabet (Google)**'s bylaws, 632
failure to collect, 448
fixed assets, 489
flying off the shelves, 837
gearing for profit, 843
Good Samaritan, 361
growing pains, 782
hijacking receivable, 61
hub-and-spoke or point-to-point, 513
investing for yield, 847
investor bond price risk, 681
line and staff for service companies, 888
liquidity crunch, 840
Mad Men, 1091
managing **Apple**'s cash, 415
many pieces, one picture, 1175
Microsoft Corporation, 417
mobile payments, 406
more cash means more investments for drug companies, 730
organizational forms in the accounting industry, 588
overhead costs, 893
Panera Bread store rate of return, 1285–1286
Pathways Commission, 10
pawn stars and specific identification, 349
rapid inventory at **Costco**, 365
sales taxes, 300
60% off, 1230
sports signing bonus, 122
standard costing in action, 1128
state pension obligations, 555
sustainable papermaking, 975
the most you will ever pay, 545
3D printing, 931
treasury stock or dividends, 645
TurboTax, 249
U.S. government debt, 684
unearned revenue, 70
warning signs, 444
Warren Buffett: The Sage of Omaha, 736
you have no vote, 635
Business entities, forms of, *illus.*, 12
Business entity concept, 11–12
def., 11
Business, integrity, objectivity, and ethics in
assumption fudging, 1290
bank error, 413
Bernie Madoff, 9
bonuses, 359
budget games, 1078
capital crime, 503
case of fraudulent price tags, 294
CEO's health, 167
characteristics of financial statement fraud, 849
collecting past due accounts, 446
company reputation, 1127
cost of employee theft, 301
credit policy and cash flow, 777
environmental managerial accounting, 898
free issue, 123
journalizing and fraud, 67
on being green, 970
online fraud, 250
orphan drugs, 1037
overbilling clients, 552
phony invoice scams, 929
price fixing, 1234
ratings game, 691
socially responsible investing, 732
the professor who know too much, 639
tips on preventing employee fraud, 401
transfer prices, 1193
tyranny of the majority of partnerships, 592
Business transaction
and the accounting equation, 14–19
def., 14
Business use of investment analysis methods, 1275
Buy or make, 1225–1226
differential analysis, *illus.*, 1226
Bylaws, 631
excerpts from **Alphabet (Google)**, 632

C

C.H. Robinson Worldwide Inc., 868
Calendar year, 543, 547
Callable bonds, 680, 687
Callaway Golf Company, 887
Campbell Soup Company, The, 145, 475, 485
Capital, 633
contributed, 633
legal, 634
paid-in, 633
working, 832, 848
Capital account, *def.*, 61
Capital budgeting, 1274
Capital crime, 503
Capital deficiency, loss on realization, 603–606
Capital expenditures, 503
def., 502
illus., 504
Capital expenditures budget, 1095–1096
def., *illus.*, 1095
Capital investment analysis
additional factors in, 1286–1290
def., 1274
nature of, 1274

Capital investment for sustainability, 1289–1290
examples of, *illus.*, 1289
Capital rationing, 1290–1291
decision process, *illus.*, 1291
def., 1290
Capstone Turbine Corporation, 429
Carnival Corporation, 1299
Carrying amount, *def.*, 683
Cash
def., 403
financial statement reporting of, 415
investing in current operations, 721
investing in long-term investments, 722
investing in temporary investments, 722
paid by EFT, 406
sources and uses of, *illus.*, 768
using bank statement as control over, 409–410
Cash basis of accounting, 113–114
def., 113
Cash budget, 1092–1095
completing, 1094–1095
def., 1092
illus., 1095
Cash burn, 416
Cash controls over receipts and payments, 403–406
Cash dividend, 639–641
def., 639
Cash equivalents, *def.*, 415
Cash fees earned, 235
Cash flow from operations: direct and indirect methods, *illus.*, 769
Cash flow per share
def., 771
no, 771
Cash flows
credit policy and, 777
free, 787–788
reporting, 767–771
Cash flows from (used for) financing activities, 24, 770
def., 768
Cash flows from (used for) investing activities, 24, 770
def., 767
Cash flows from operating activities, 24, 768–769
converting income statement to, using direct method, *illus.*, 782
def., 767
direct method, reporting, 786–787
indirect method, *illus.*, 775
Cash flows, statement of, 20, 24–25, 767
direct method, 782–787, *illus.*, 787
indirect method, 772–781, *illus.*, 781
preparing, 24–25, 781, 791
spreadsheet for, indirect method, 789–791, *illus.*, 790
Cash funds, special-purpose, 413–414
Cash inflow, 768
Cash outflow, 768
Cash payback method, 1276–1278
Cash payback period, *def.*, 1276

Index I-5

Cash payments
　control of, 406
　estimated, 1093–1094
　for income taxes, 785–786, *illus.*, 786
　for interest, determining, *illus.*, 785
　for merchandise, 783–784, *illus.*, 784
　for operating expenses, 784–785, *illus.*, 785
Cash payments journal, 243–245
　and postings, *illus.*, 244
　def., 243
Cash purchases, 240
Cash receipts
　and revenue in QuickBooks, *illus.*, 248
　control of, 404–405
　estimated, 1092–1093
Cash receipts journal, 238–240
　and postings, *illus.*, 238
　def., 238
Cash received
　by EFT, 405
　from cash sales, 404–405
　from customers, 783, *illus.*, 783
　in the mail, 405
Cash refund
　and allowances, 292–293
　def., 292
Cash sales, 290–291
Cash short and over account, *def.*, 404
Caterpillar, Inc., 33, 37, 353, 485, 632, 664–665, 992, 1173, 1175, 1176, 1178, 1182, 1183, 1187
Centralized operations, 1174–1176
Certified Public Accountants (CPAs), *def.*, 10
Certified Public Accounting (CPA), 850
Change fund, 404
Character, failure of individual, 8
Charles Schwab Corporation, The, 1188, 1239, 1253–1254
Chart of accounts, 61–62
　def., 61
　expanded, *illus.*, 117
　for a merchandising business, 284–285, *illus.*, 285
　illus., 62, 178
　under periodic inventory system, 309, *illus.*, 309
Charter, 631
Checking account, *illus.*, 408
Chesapeake Energy, 843
Children's Hospital of the King's Daughters Health System, 1122
Chipotle Mexican Grill, Inc., 512
Cisco Systems, Inc., 249
Citigroup Inc., 37
Classified balance sheet, 168
Clean opinion, 850
Clock cards, 930
Closing entries, 169–174
　def., 170
　flowchart of, *illus.*, 171
　illus., 171, 184

journalizing and posting, 170–174, 184
　under periodic inventory system, 312–313, *illus.*, 313
Closing process, 306–307
　def., *illus.*, 170
Closing the books, *def.*, 170
Coca-Cola Company, The, 13, 453, 485, 692, 736, 738, 847, 870, 1106, 1184–1185
Coca-Cola Enterprises, 1106
Colgate-Palmolive, 1091
Collecting past due accounts, 446
Collections from sales, schedule of, 1092 *illus.*, 1093
Comcast Corporation, 284, 528, 1091
Commercial paper, 415
Commercial substance, 514
Committee of Sponsoring Organizations (COSO) of the Treadway Commission, 397
Common stock, 779
　def., 635
　dividends and earnings per share of, *illus.*, 847
　earnings per share on, 844–845, 848
Common-sized income statement, *illus.*, 831
Common-sized statements, 830–831
　def., 830
Communication, information and, 402
Companies, why they invest, 721–722
Company reputation, best of the best, 1127
Comparative balance sheet
　horizontal analysis, *illus.*, 827
　income statement and, *illus.*, 772–773
　vertical analysis, *illus.*, 829
Comparative income statement
　horizontal analysis, *illus.*, 828
　vertical analysis, *illus.*, 830
Comparative retained earnings statement, horizontal analysis, *illus.*, 828
Comparative schedule of current assets, horizontal analysis, *illus.*, 827
Compensated absences, 552
Compensating balance, *def.*, 415
Compound amount of $1 for three periods at 12%, *illus.*, 1279
Compounding, 1278
Comprehensive income, 739–740
　def., 739
Computer Associates International, Inc., 8
Computerized accounting systems, 72, 247–249
Computerized budgeting systems, 1081–1082
Computerized payroll system, 551
Computerized perpetual inventory systems, 355
Computers, use of in cost-volume-profit analysis, 1042
Concept
　business entity, 11–12
　cost, 12–13
　matching, 20

objectivity, 12
　unit of measure, 12
Consigned inventory, *def.*, 362
Consignee, *def.*, 362
Consignor, *def.*, 362
Consolidated balance sheets, Nike Inc., D-6
Consolidated Edison, 847
Consolidated financial statements
　def., 729
　consolidated income statement for Unilever Group, *illus.*, MJ-10
　consolidated statement of comprehensive income for Unilever Group, *illus.*, MJ-10
　consolidated statements of cash flows, Nike Inc., D-7
　consolidated statements of comprehensive income, Nike Inc., D-5
　consolidated statements of income, Nike Inc., D-4
　consolidated statements of shareholders' equity, Nike Inc., D-8–D-10
Consolidation, more than 50% ownership, 729
Constangy, Brooks, Smith & Prophete, 943
Constants, 551
Constraint, 1235
Contingent liabilities, 555–557
　accounting treatment of, *illus.*, 557
　def., 555
Continue or discontinue, differential analysis, *illus.*, 1224
Continue with or replace old equipment, differential analysis, *illus.*, 1227
Continuous budgeting, *def.*, *illus.*, 1078
Continuous process improvement, *def.*, 889
Continuum Health Partners, Inc., 552
Contra accounts, 494
　def., 124
Contra asset accounts, 494
　def., 124
Contract rate, *def.*, 680
Contractual restrictions, 648
Contributed capital, 633
Contribution margin, 1048
　def., 1029
　income statement format, *illus.*, 1029
Contribution margin ratio, 1029–1030
　def., 1029
Control
　cash register as a, *illus.*, 404
　human element of, 403
　internal, 396, 398–403
　of cash payments, 406
　of cash receipts, 404–405
　of inventory, 346–347
　over cash, using bank statement as, 409–410
　procedures, 400–402
Control environment, 399–400
　def., *illus.*, 399
Controllable expenses, *def.*, 1178

Controllable revenues, *def.*, 1178
Controllable variance, 1131
   def., 1138
Controller, *def.*, 887
Controlling, 1077
   def., 889
   account, *def.*, 233
Conversion costs, 894–895
   def., *illus.*, 894
Conversion equivalent units, 979–981
   illus., 980
Convertible bonds, 680
Copyright, *def.*, 509
Corporate annual reports, 849–850
Corporate form, advantages and disadvantages of, *illus.*, 631
Corporation, 11, 586, 630
   and their states of incorporation, examples of, *illus.*, 632
   characteristics of, 630–631
   def., 12
   financing, 677–679
   forming of, 631–932
   nature of, 630–632
   nonpublic, 630
   organizational structure, *illus.*, 631
   private, 630
   public, 630
Correcting journal entry, *def.*, 79
Cost accounting system
   def., 926
   overview, 926
Cost allocation, *def.*, 932
Cost behavior, 1022–1028
   concepts, summary of, 1027–1028
   def., 1022
Cost category analysis, 989–990
Cost center, 1176
   def., *illus.*, 1176
   responsibility accounting for, 1176–1177, *illus.*, 1177
Cost concept, 12–13
   def., 12
   product, 1232–1234
   target, *illus.*, 1235
   total, 1241–1243
   variable, 1244–1245
Cost flow assumptions, *illus.*, 348
Cost flows
   for a process manufacturer, 973–975, *illus.*, 974
   illus., 987
   labor information and, *illus.*, 930
   materials information and, *illus.*, 928
   summary of, 938–940
Cost graphs
   fixed, *illus.*, 1025
   variable, *illus.*, 1023
Cost method, 644
   def., 726
   less than 20% ownership, 725–727
Cost object, *def.*, 891
Cost of finished goods available for sale, *def.*, 900
Cost of goods manufactured
   def., 899
   statement of, 900

Cost of goods sold, *def.*, 900
   sales and, 938
Cost of goods sold budget, 1088–1090
   def., 1088
   illus., 1089
Cost of merchandise sold, 303
   def., 283, 899
   using periodic system, determining, *illus.*, 312
Cost of production report, 976–985, 995
   def., 976
   illus., 985, 995
   preparing, 984–985
   using for decision making, 989–991
Cost per equivalent units
   between periods, 989
   def., 981
   determine, 981–982, 994
Cost per unit, 1023, 1024
Cost price approach, 1192–1193
   def., 1192
Cost variances
   def., 1129
   direct materials and direct labor, *illus.*, 1131
   favorable, 1129
   illus., 1129
   manufacturing, 1129–1131, *illus.*, 1130
   total manufacturing, 1129
   unfavorable, 1129
Cost-benefit considerations, 403
Costco Wholesale Corporation, 97, 145, 365, 393, 442, 485, 837
Costing
   absorption, 1047
   power stack, 988
   variable or direct, 1028, 1047–1049
Cost(s)
   above-the-line, 1080
   allocate to transferred and partially completed units, 982–984, 995
   below-the-line, 1080
   classifying, 488–490, *illus.*, 489
   def., 891
   determine units to be assigned, 976–977, 993–994
   determining under average cost method, 993–995
   differential, 1220
   direct and indirect, 891–892, *illus.*, 892
   effect of changes in unit variable, 1033–1034, *illus.*, 1033
   estimated activity, 1237, *illus.*, 1237
   estimating inventory, 368–369
   fixed, 1024, 1032–1033, *illus.*, 1028, 1033
   flow of in service job order cost system, 942
   flow of through service business, *illus.*, 942
   manufacturing, 892, *illus.*, 892, 901., 927., 939
   manufacturing operations, 890–896
   mixed, 1024–1027, *illus.*, 1026, 1028
   of employee theft, 301

   of fixed assets, 490–491, *illus.*, 490
   opportunity, 1227
   overhead, 893
   period, 895–896, 938, *illus.*, 895, 896
   post-production, 1080
   prime and conversion, 894–895, *illus.*, 894
   product, 895–896, *illus.*, 895, 896
   research and development, 509
   semivariable or semifixed, 1024
   standard, 1126, 1127–1128, *illus.*, 1129
   sunk, 1222
   variable, 1022–1024, *illus.*, 1028
Costs and selling price, effects of changes in on break-even point, *illus.*, 1035
Costs per available seat, 847
Cost-volume-profit analysis
   assumptions of, 1042
   def., 1028
   graphic approach to, 1037–1042
   mathematical approach to, 1031–1037
   use of computers in, 1042
Cost-volume-profit chart, 1037–1039
   def., 1037
   illus., 1038
   revised, *illus.*, 1039
Cost-volume-profit relationships, 1028–1031
Cost-volume-profit, special relationships, 1042–1047
Count of inventory, 347
Coupon rate, 680
Coverage ratio, 839
Credit, 59*fn*, 538
   def., 60
   diagram of the recording and posting of, *illus.*, 69
   line of, 415
   rules of, 62, *illus.*, 63
Credit memo
   def., 292
   illus., 293
Credit memorandum, *def.*, 292
Credit period, *def.*, 286
Credit policy and cash flow, 777
Credit sales, 834*fn*
Credit terms
   def., 286
   illus., 287
Creditor, 538
Creditors ledger, 233
Crime, capital, 503
Crystal Bay, 766
Cumulative preferred stock, *def.*, 635
Currency exchange rates, *def.*, 1289
Current assets
   comparative schedule of, horizontal analysis, *illus.*, 827
   def., 168
Current liabilities, 538–541
   def., 168
   on the balance sheet, 554
Current operations, investing cash in, 721

Current portion of long-term debt, 538–539
Current position analysis, 832–834
　def., 557, 832
Current ratio, 557, 848
　def., 188, 832
Currently attainable standards, def., 1127
Customer allowance
　adjusting entries for, 301–303
　def., 292
　journal entries to record, illus., 294
Customer discounts, 291–292
　def., 291
Customer refunds
　adjusting entries for, 301–303
　journal entries to record, illus., 294
Customer refunds payable, def., 292
Customer relationship management (CRM), 249
Customer returns, 293–294
　adjusting entries for, 301–303
　journal entries to record, illus., 294
Customer service, 1188
Customers
　cash received from, 783, illus., 783
　ledger, 233
CVS Caremark Corporation (CVS), 37, 187
CyberSource, 290fn

D

Dallas Mavericks, 847
Darden Restaurants, Inc., 1133
Data
　assembling and analyzing adjustment, 180
　estimated, 886
　historical, 886
Date of declaration, 640
Date of payment, 640
Date of record, 640
Days' sales in inventory, def., 366
Days' sales in receivables, 459–460
　def., 459
DDB Advertising Agency, 971
Debit, 59fn
　def., 60
　diagram of the recording and posting of, illus., 69
　rules of, 62, illus., 63
Debit memo
　def., 288
　illus., 289
Debit memorandum, def., 288
Debt
　current portion of long-term, 538–539
　U.S. government, 684
Debt investments, accounting for, 722–725
Debt securities, def., 722
Debtors, 538
Decentralization
　advantages of, 1174–1175
　disadvantages of, 1175

Decentralized operations, 1174–1176
　advantages and disadvantages of, illus., 1175
Decision making
　def., 889
　job order costing for, 940–941
　using cost of production report for, 989–991
Deductions
　from employee earnings, 541–544
　other, 544
Deere & Company, 632, 664–665, 720, 724, 729, 732, 733, 738, 870, 881
Deferral(s), 115–116
　adjusting entries for, 120–124
　def., 115
　illus., 116
Deferred revenues, 128
Deficiency, def., 603
Deficit, def., 633
Defined benefit plan, def., 553
Defined contribution plan, def., 553
Degy Entertainment, 1028
Dell Inc., 267, 284, 1270
Deloitte & Touche, 588, 620, 627
Delta Air Lines, Inc., 5, 37, 90, 158, 458, 468, 485, 489, 513, 632, 1036, 1078, 1232, 1270
Depletion expense, def., 507
Depreciable cost, def., 492
Depreciate, def., 124
Depreciating animals, 500
Depreciation
　accounting for, 492–504
　accumulated, 124
　adjusting entries for, 124–126
　def., 124, 492
　functional, 492
　partial-year, 499–501
　physical, 492
　revising estimates, 501–502
Depreciation expense
　and book value, straight-line method, illus., 495
　def., 124
　factors in computing, 492–493
　illus., 493
Depreciation methods
　comparing, 499, illus., 500
　summary of, illus., 499
Differential analysis, 1220–1231
　accept business at a special price, illus., 1230
　continue or discontinue, illus., 1224
　continue with or replace old equipment, illus., 1227
　def., 1220
　illus., 1221
　lease or sell, illus., 1222
　make or buy, illus., 1226
　sell or process further, illus., 1229
Differential cost, def., 1220
Differential income (loss), def., 1220
Differential revenue, def., 1220
Diluted earnings per share, 845
Direct costing, 1028, 1047
Direct costs

and indirect costs, classifying, illus., 892
　def., illus., 891
Direct labor cost, 892–893, 972
　def., 892
Direct labor cost budget, 1086–1088
　def., 1086
　illus., 1087
Direct labor rate variance, 1134–1135
　def., 1134
Direct labor standards for nonmanufacturing activities, 1136
Direct labor time variance, def., 1135
Direct labor variances, 1134–1136
　and direct materials variances, 1131–1136
　relationships, 1135, illus., 1135
　reporting, 1135
Direct materials costs, 971
　def., 892
Direct materials equivalent units, illus., 979
Direct materials price variance, def., 1132
Direct materials purchases budget, 1084–1086
　def., 1084
　illus., 1086
Direct materials quantity variance, def., 1132
Direct materials variances, 1131–1134
　and direct labor variances, 1131–1136, illus., 1131
　relationships, 1132, illus., 1133
　reporting, 1132–1134
Direct method, 24fn, 768–769
　and indirect method, comparing, 769
　cash flow from operations, illus., 769
　converting income statement to cash flows from operating activities using, illus., 782
　def., 768
　reporting cash flows from operating activities, 786–787
　statement of cash flows, 782–787, illus., 787
Direct operating expenses, 1178
Direct write-off method
　and allowance method, comparing, 453–454, illus., 454
　def., 443
　for uncollectible accounts, 444–445
Directing, 1077
　def., 889
Directors, board of, 631
Discontinue a segment or product, 1223–1225
Discontinue or continue, differential analysis, illus., 1224
Discount, 540
　amortization of by interest method, 697–698
　bonds issued at, 682–683, illus., 680
　customer, 291–292
　def., 637, 680

on bonds payable, amortization of, *illus.*, 698
purchases, 287–288
rate, 540
sales, 291
trade, 299, 300
Discounted cash flow method, 1281
Discounted note, 540
Discretionary restrictions, 648
Dishonored note receivable, *def.*, 456
Disney. See **Walt Disney Company**
Disposal of fixed assets, 504–506
Dividend preferences, *illus.*, 635
Dividend yield, , 737–738, 848
def., 737, 847
Dividends, 631, 727
accounting for, 639–642
and dividends payable, 778–779
and earnings per share of common stock, *illus.*, 847
and investment, *illus.*, 728
cash, 639–641
def., 633
liquidating, 639*fn*
receipt of, 726
recording investee, 728
stock, 641–642
treasury stock or, 645
Dividends payable, dividends and, 778–779
Dividends per share, 846–847, 848
def., 846
Divisional income statements, *illus.*, 1180, 1181
Dollar General Corporation, 308
Dollar Tree Stores, Inc., 38, 281, 283, 285, 291, 292, 293, 303, 307
Domino Foods, Inc., 1002–1003
Domino's Pizza L.L.C., 1122
Donnkenny, Inc., 426
Double taxation, 631
Double-declining-balance method, 497–499, 501
def., 497
illus., 498
Double-entry accounting system, 62–68
def., 62
Doubtful accounts, allowance for, 445
Doubtful accounts expense, 443
Dover Corporation, 1175
Downsizing, 506
Dr Pepper Snapple Group, Inc., 692
Drawing, *def.*, 61
Dreyer's and Edy's Grand Ice Cream, 971
Dreyer's Ice Cream, Inc., 969, 973, 975
Due date, 455
Duke Energy Corporation, 738, 988
Dunkin' Brands Group, Inc., 558
DuPont formula, *def.*, 1182
DuPont, 13, 267, 453t, 970
Duties, rotating, 400–401

E

E.I. du Pont de Nemours and Company, 1182*fn*
Earning revenues from season tickets, 120

Earnings
deductions from employee, 541–544
def., 20
recording employees', 546–548
retained, 633, 789–791
Earnings per common share (EPS) assuming dilution, 845
def., 651
Earnings per share (EPS), 851
def., 677
income statement with, *illus.*, 851
Earnings per share (EPS) on common stock, 844–845, 848
def., 844
Earnings record, employee's, 549–550
illus., 548–549
eBay Inc., 13, 37, 395, 397, 399, 402, 403, 406, 415, 754
EC, error correction, 408
Eco-efficiency measures
def., illus., 897
in managerial accounting, 897
E-commerce, 249–250
def., 249
Edmunds.com, 824
Effective interest rate method, 684*fn*
Effective rate of interest, *def.*, 680
Electronic Arts Inc., 189
Electronic badges, 930
Electronic funds transfers (EFT)
cash paid by, 406
cash received by, 405
def., 405
Elements of internal control, 398–399
def., 398
illus., 399
Employee
fringe benefits, 552–554
net pay, computing, 544
revenue per, 606
theft, cost of, 301
wage and tax statement (W-2 form), *illus.*, 550
Withholding Allowance Certificate (W-4), 542, *illus.*, 542
Employee earnings
deductions from, 541–544
liability for, 541
recording, 546–548
Employee fraud, 398
def., 398
tips on preventing, 401
Employee's earnings record, 549–550
def., 549
illus., 548–549
Employer's payroll taxes, liability for, 545
End-of-period spreadsheet, 189–195
and flow of accounting data, *illus.*, 164
for statement of cash flows, indirect method, *illus.*, 790
illus., 181
preparing, 180
Engineering change order (ECO), *def.*, 1237
Enron, 8

Environmental managerial accounting, 898
Equity
owner's, 61, 168
ratio of liabilities to stockholders', 838–839, 848
return on common stockholders', 843–844, 848
return on stockholders', 842–843, 848
shareholders, 633
statement of members', 606
statement of owner's, 305
statement of partnership, 606, *illus.*, 606
statement of stockholders', 648–649, *illus.*, 649
stockholders', 633–634, 645–650
Equity investments, accounting for, 725–729
Equity method
between 20%–50% ownership, 727–729
def., 727
Equity securities, *def.*, 722
Equivalent units
conversion, 979–981, *illus.*, 980
cost per, 981–982, 994
direct materials, *illus.*, 979
materials, 978
Equivalent units of production
compute, 978, 994
def., 978
Ernst & Young, 246, 588, 627
Errors
affecting the trial balance, 78–79
not affecting the trial balance, 79–80
inventory, 362
ESPN, 1060
Estimated data, 886
Estimated returns inventory, *def.*, 293
Estimating uncollectibles, 448–453
Estimation methods, comparing, 452–453
illus., 452
Ethical indifference, culture of, 8
Ethics
def., 7
role of in accounting, 6–9
role of in business, 6–9
European Union (EU), B-1, MJ-5
Everfresh, 766
Exchange
gain on, 514–515
loss on, 515–516
Ex-dividends, 640
Expected useful life, *def.*, 492
Expenditures, revenue and capital, 502
illus., 504
Expense recognition principle, *def.*, 114
Expense(s)
accrued, 118–120
administrative, 303, 895
bad debt, 443
cash payments for operating, 784–785, *illus.*, 785

classifying costs as, 489
def., 16, 62
depletion, 507
depreciation, 124
direct operating, 1178
doubtful accounts, 443
factors in computing depreciation, 492–493
general, 303
interest, 785
other, 304
prepaid, 15, 115, 122–124
selling, 303, 895
uncollectible accounts, 443
Extraordinary repairs, 503
Exxon Mobil Corporation, 42, 513, 843, 971, MJ-12

F

Face amount, 455
bonds issued at, 681–682, *illus.*, 680
def., 680
Facebook Inc., 489, 635, 738, 847, 1219, 1220, 1222, 1227, 1231, 1237
Factory burden, *def.*, 893
Factory depreciation, 931
Factory labor, 930–931
Factory overhead, 931–936
allocating, 932–933
applying to jobs, *illus.*, 934
applying to work in process, 933–935
overapplied or overabsorbed, 934
underapplied or underabsorbed, 934
Factory overhead account, 1142
Factory overhead balance, disposal of, 935–936
Factory overhead cost, 972
def., 893
Factory overhead cost budget
def., illus., 1088
indicating standard factory overhead rate, *illus.*, 1137
Factory overhead cost variance report, *def., illus.*, 1141
Factory overhead flexible budget, 1136–1138
Factory overhead variances, 1136–1143
illus., 1143
reporting, 1141
Factory power, 931
Failure to collect, 448
Fair Labor Standards Act, 541
Fair market value, 641*fn*
Fair value
accounting, 737
def., 730
Favorable cost variance, *def.*, 1129
Favorable fixed factory overhead volume variance, 1139
Favorable total factory overhead cost variance, 1142
Faygo, 766
Federal Insurance Contributions Act. See FICA

Federal unemployment compensation tax. See FUTA tax
Federal Wage and Hour Law, 541
FedEx Corporation, 37, 208, 443, 528
Feedback, *def.*, 889
Fees earned, 283
def., 16
on account, 235
FICA, 543
FICA tax, 543–544, 545
def., 543
FIFO. See First-in, first-out method
Film budgeting, 1080
Financial accounting
and managerial accounting, differences between, 885–886, *illus.*, 886
def., 6, 885
Financial Accounting Standards Board (FASB), 402, 491, 737, B-1, C-1
def., 11
Financial analysis and interpretation
accounts receivable turnover and number of days' sales in receivables, 459–460
asset turnover, 307–308
dividend yield, 737–738
earnings per share, 651–652
fixed asset turnover ratio, 512–514
free cash flow, 787–788
horizontal analysis, 80–82
inventory turnover and number of days' sales in inventory, 365–367
quick ratio, 557–559
ratio of cash to monthly cash expenses, 415–417
ratio of liabilities to owner's equity, 26–27
revenue per employee, 606–607
segment analysis, 250–251
times interest earned ratio, 691–693
vertical analysis, 131–133
working capital and current ratio, 188–189
Financial assets, 730
Financial budgets, 1092–1096
Financial reporting for long-term assets, 511–512
Financial statement fraud, characteristics of, 849
Financial statement information, value of, 825–826
Financial statements, 19–26, 165–169, 283–284
analyzing and interpreting, 825–826
consolidated, 729
def., 19
effect of fair value accounting on, 737
effect of inventory errors on, 362–365
for manufacturing business, 898–903
for merchandising business, 303–307
for Mornin' Joe, MJ-2–MJ-4
for Mornin' Joe International, MJ-5–MJ-9
general-purpose, 6

illus., 20, 22, 166, 183
international differences in, 169
interrelationships among, 25–26
preparing, 182–183
preparing from the spreadsheet, 194–195
product costs, period costs, and, *illus.*, 896
report on fairness of, 850
reporting merchandise inventory in, 359–365
reporting of cash, 415
techniques for analyzing, 826
under periodic inventory system, 311–312
Financing activities
cash flows from (used for), 24, 768, 770
noncash, 770
Finished goods, 937–938
Finished goods inventory, *def.*, 898
Finished goods ledger, 940
account, *illus.*, 938
def., 937
First-in, first-out (FIFO) inventory cost flow method, *def.*, 348
First-in, first-out flow of costs, *illus.*, 356
First-in, first-out method, 350–351, 355–356
and LIFO cost methods, effect of changing costs, *illus.*, 359
def., 976
Fiscal year, 187–188
def., 187
Fitch, 691
Fixed asset turnover, *illus.*, 512
Fixed asset turnover ratio, 512–514
def., 512
illus., 513
Fixed assets, 489
classifying costs as, 489
cost of, 490–491, *illus.*, 490
def., 124, 168, 488
disposal of, 504–506
exchanging similar, 514–516
financial reporting for, 511–512
leasing, 491
nature of, 488–491
selling, 505–506
Fixed assets to long-term liabilities, ratio of, 838, 848
Fixed cost graphs, *illus.*, 1025
Fixed costs
and their activity bases, *illus.*, 1025
and variable cost behavior, *illus.*, 1027
def., 1024
effect of changes in, 1032–1033, *illus.*, 1033
illus., 1028
Fixed factory overhead volume variance, 1139–1141
favorable, 1139
unfavorable, 1139
Fixed overhead volume variance, graph of, *illus.*, 1140

Index

Fixing, price, 1234
Flexible budgets, 1080–1081
   def., illus., 1080, 1081
Flow of manufacturing costs, *illus.*, 939
Flowchart of closing entries, *illus.*, 171
FOB (free on board) destination, 362
   def., 295
FOB (free on board) shipping point, 362
   def., 295
Ford Motor Company, 11, 12, 37, 910, 1021, 1022, 1023, 1024, 1027, 1032, 1043, 1044, 1045, 1078, MJ-12
Form 10-K for the fiscal year ended May 31, 2016, Nike Inc., D-1–D-31
Form W-2, Employee's Wage and Tax Statement, *illus.*, 550
Four-column account, *def.*, 68
Fox Sports, 1060
Fraud
   accounting and business, *illus.*, 8
   Association of Fraud Examiners, 398
   case of fraudulent price tags, 294
   characteristics of financial statement, 849
   employee, 398
   journalizing and, 67
   online, 250
   tips on preventing employee, 401
Free cash flow, 787–788
   def., 787
Free issue basis, office supplies, 123
Freight, 295–297
Freight in, 310
Freight terms, *illus.*, 296
Fringe benefits
   def., 552
   employees', 552–554
Functional depreciation, 492
Fund(s)
   petty cash, 413
   sinking, 687*fn*
   special-purpose, 414
FUTA tax, 545
Future value
   def., 694
   illus., 693

G

GAAP. *See* Generally accepted accounting principles; U.S. GAAP
Gain, 687
   on exchange, 514–515
   on realization, 600–601
   on sale of land, 785
   unrealized, 730
Gap Inc., 37
General accounting principles. *See* Generally accepted accounting principles (GAAP)
General Dynamics, 893
General Electric Company, 443, 632
General expenses, *def.*, 303
General journal, *def.*, 234
General ledger
   and subsidiary ledgers, *illus.*, 234
   def., 233
   illus., 76–77
General Mills, 847
General Motors Corporation (GM), 564, 570, 1091
Generally accepted accounting principles (GAAP), 10–13, 113, 398, 443, 509, 649, 730, 886, B-1
   def., 10
General-purpose financial statements, *def.*, 6
Gibson Guitars, 884, 885, 886, 887, 889, 891, 898, 925, 926, 927, 928, 930, 935, 938
Gibson Mandolin Guitar Mfg. Co., Ltd., 885
Global accounting standards, need for, B-1
Goal conflict, *def.*, 1077
Gold & Silver Pawn Shop, 349
Good Samaritan, 361
Goods manufactured, cost of, 899
   statement of, 900
Goodwill, 509–510
   admission of partners by, 597*fn*
   def., 509
Google, 629, 651, 847, 858, 1231
   See also Alphabet (Google), Inc.
Graph of fixed overhead volume variance, *illus.*, 1140
Graphic approach to cost-volume-profit analysis, 1037–1042
Greed, culture of, 8
Gross pay, *def.*, 541
Gross profit, 303, 1048
   def., 283
Gross profit method
   def., 369
   estimating inventory by, *illus.*, 369
   of inventory costing, 369
Groupon, 635

H

H&R Block Inc., 37, 1205
H.J. Heinz Company, 1156
Harris Interactive, 1127
Hasbro, 867–868
HCA, 453
HealthSouth, 8
Held-to-maturity securities, *def.*, 734
Helm Inc., 240
Hendrick Automotive Group, 1079, 1080, 1084
Hendrick Motorsports, 1075, 1076, 1079, 1086, 1087
Hershey Company, The, 635, 868, 971
Hershey Foods Company, The, 1002
Hershey Trust Company, The, 635
High-low method, *def.*, 1026
Hijacking receivable, 61
Hilton Hospitality, Inc., 37
Historical data, 886
Home Depot, Inc., The, 11, 43, 44, 203, 328, 485, 632
Horizontal analysis, 80–82, 826–829
   comparative balance sheet, *illus.*, 827
   comparative income statement, *illus.*, 828
   comparative retained earnings statement, *illus.*, 828
   comparative schedule of current assets, *illus.*, 827
   def., 80, 826
Howard Schultz & Associates (HS&A), 406
HP, Inc., 571
Hub-and-spoke or point-to-point, 513
Human behavior and budgeting, 1077, *illus.*, 1077
Human element of controls, 403
Hurdle rate, 1281
Hyatt Hotels Corporation, 881–882

I

IBM, 485
Ideal standards, *def.*, 1127
IFRS. *See* International Financial Reporting Standards
Illusory profits, 358
Improvements, repair and, 502–504
In arrears, *def.*, 636
In-and-out cards, 930
Income
   by product, *illus.*, 1224
   comprehensive, 739–740
   differential, 1220
   net, 20, 774–778, *illus.*, 774
   operating, 303
Income from operations, 303–304, 1048, 1181
   def., 303
   effect of operating leverage on, *illus.*, 1046
Income of partnership, dividing, 590–593
Income statement accounts, 63
Income statement columns
   extend the accounts to, 193
   spreadsheet with amounts extended to, *illus.*, 194
   total, 193–194
Income statement effects, 363
Income statement format, contribution margin, *illus.*, 1029
Income statement presentation, 850–851
Income statement(s), 20, 165–166
   absorption costing, *illus.*, 1048
   and comparative balance sheet, *illus.*, 772–773
   budgeted, 1091–1092, *illus.*, 1091
   common-sized, *illus.*, 831
   comparative, *illus.*, 828, 830
   converting to cash flows from operating activities using direct method, *illus.*, 782
   def., 20
   effect of fair value accounting on, 737
   effect of inventory errors on, *illus.*, 363, 364

Index I-11

for a manufacturing company, 898–903, *illus.*, 899
for merchandising businesses, *illus.*, 899
for Mornin' Joe, *illus.*, MJ-2
illus., 940
multiple-step, 303–304, *illus.*, 304
negotiated transfer price, *illus.*, 1191
no transfers between divisions, *illus.*, 1189
single-step, 305, *illus.*, 305
unusual items on, 850–852, *illus.*, 851
variable costing, *illus.*, 1048
variance from standards in, *illus.*, 1145
vs. statements of comprehensive income, MJ-6–MJ-7
with earnings per share, *illus.*, 851
with statement of costs of goods manufactured, (manufacturing company), *illus.*, 902
Income taxes, 542, 1286
cash payments for, 785–786, *illus.*, 786
Incorporation, application of, 631
Incremental analysis, 1220
Independent registered public accounting firm report, **Nike Inc.**, D-3
Indirect costs
and direct costs, classifying, *illus.*, 892
def., illus., 891
Indirect labor, 931
Indirect materials, 931
Indirect method, 25*fn*
adjustments to net income (loss), *illus.*, 774
and direct method, comparing, 769
cash flow from operations, *illus.*, 769, 775
def., 769
spreadsheet for statement of cash flows, 789–791, *illus.*, 790
statement of cash flows, 772–781, *illus.*, 781
Inflation, *def.*, 1289
Information
and communication, 402
flow of accounting, 163–165
Initial cost, *def.*, 492
Inputs and outputs, *illus.*, 1147
Installment note, 688–690
amortization of, *illus.*, 689
def., 688
issuing, 689
Installments, 538
Institute of Management Accountants, 8*fn*
Intangible asset disclosures, frequency of, *illus.*, 510
Intangible assets, 508–510
comparison of, *illus.*, 510
def., 508
financial reporting for, 511–512
Intel, 443, 970, 971

Interest
determining cash payments for, *illus.*, 785
market or effective rate of, 680
Interest expense, 785
Interest in a partnership, purchasing, 594
Interest method
amortization of discount by, 697–698
amortization of premium by, 698–699
Interest rate, 455
method of amortization, 697–699
Interest revenue, 723–724
def., 16
Interest tables, A-2–A-5
Interest timeline, *illus.*, 723
Internal control(s), 398–403
def., 232, 396
elements of, 398–399, *illus.*, 399
for payroll systems, 551
Integrated Framework, 397, 398
limitations of, 403
objectives of, 398, *illus.*, 398
problems, warning signs of, *illus.*, 402
procedures, *illus.*, 400
report on, 849–850
Internal rate of return (IRR) method, 1283–1286
def., 1283
Internal rate of return, steps to determine, *illus.*, 1285
International Accounting Standards Board (IASB), 491, 649, B-1, MJ-5
def., 11
International connection
IFRS for SMEs, 649
IFRS for statement of cash flows, 786
international differences, 169
International Financial Reporting Standards (IFRS), 11, 353, 511
International differences in financial statements, 169
International Financial Reporting Standards (IFRS), 11, 353, 511, 649, B-1–B-6, MJ-5
adopters, *illus.*, B-2
adoption of by SEC, B-2–B-3
for statement of cash flows, 786
overview of, B-1–B-2
International Financial Reporting Standards (IFRS) and U.S. GAAP, B-2–B-3
comparison of accounting under, *illus.*, B-4–B-5
convergence of, B-3
differences between, B-3–B-5
key reporting differences between, MJ-5–MJ-9
technical differences between, B-3
International Paper Company, 975, 1019
Interpretations, 11

Intuit, 231, 233, 240, 246, 248, 249, 250., 267., 1057
Inventory
consigned, 362
control of, 346–347
days' sales in, 366
determining by retail method, *illus.*, 368
estimating by gross profit method, *illus.*, 369
finished goods, 898
in manufacturing and merchandising companies, balance sheet presentation of, *illus.*, 899
in process, 983–984
materials, 898
merchandise, 283
number of days' sales in, 836–837in, 848
physical, 347
raw materials, 898
reporting of, 347
safeguarding of, 346–347
work in process, 898
Inventory analysis, 836–837
def., 835
Inventory at lower of cost or market, determining, *illus.*, 360
Inventory cost, estimating, 368–369
Inventory cost flow assumptions, 347–350
Inventory costing
gross profit method of, 369
retail method of, 368–369
Inventory costing methods
comparing, 358–359
illus., 349
under periodic inventory system, 355–358
under perpetual inventory system, 350–354
Inventory errors
effect of on current period's balance sheet, *illus.*, 364
effect of on current period's income statement, *illus.*, 363
effect of on two year's income statements, *illus.*, 364
on financial statements, effect of, 362–365
Inventory ledger accounts, *illus.*, 927
Inventory ledger, subsidiary, 347
Inventory profits, 358
Inventory shortage, *def.*, 300
Inventory shrinkage
adjusting entry for, 300–301
def., 300
Inventory transactions, recording merchandise, 297, *illus.*, 297
Inventory turnover, 848
and number of days' sales in inventory, 365–367
def., 365, 836
Investee
def., 725
dividends, recording, 728
net income, recording, 727–728

Investing activities
　　cash flows from (used for), 24, 767, 770
　　noncash, 770
Investing for yield, 847
Investing, socially responsible, 732
Investment analysis methods, business use of, 1275
Investment centers, 1176
　　def., 1181
　　responsibility accounting for, 1181–1188
Investment grade bonds, 687
Investment turnover, def., 1182
Investment(s)
　　accounting for debt, 722–725
　　accounting for equity, 725–729
　　and dividends, illus., 728
　　classifying costs as, 489
　　def., 722
　　dividing of partnership income, 591–592
　　investing cash in long-term, 722
　　investing cash in temporary, 722
　　more cash means more, 730
　　return on, 1182
　　shareholders', 633
　　stock, illus., 725
　　valuing and reporting, 730–736, illus., 735
Investor bond price risk, 681
Investor, def., 725
Invoice
　　def., 235, 286
　　illus., 286
　　phony scams, 929
　　vendor's, 346
Issuance date, 455
Issuing stock, 636–637, illus., 634

J

Jack in the Box Inc., 512
JCPenney, 203, 393, 443, 1173
JDA, 278
JetBlue Airways Corp., 821–822
JHT Holdings, Inc., 425
Job, 926
　　applying factory overhead to, illus., 934
Job cost sheets, 940
　　and work in process controlling account, illus., 936
　　comparing data from, illus., 941
　　def., 929
Job order and process cost companies, examples of, illus., 971
Job order cost system, 971
　　and process cost systems, , comparing, 971–973, illus., 972
　　def., 926
　　for manufacturing businesses, 927–940
　　for service businesses, 941–943
Job order costing
　　for decision making, 940–941
　　in a law firm, 943
Jobs, Steve, 167

Johnson & Johnson, 468, 821–822
Journal, 234
　　analyzing and recording transactions in, 177–179
　　cash payments, 243–245
　　def., 64
　　general, 234
　　purchases, 240–243
　　revenue, 235–237, illus., 236
　　special, 233–235
　　two-column, 64
Journal entries
　　for process cost system, 985–988
　　illus., 178–179
　　to record customer refunds, allowances, and returns, illus., 294
Journal entry, def., 65
Journalizing, 64–68
　　adjusting entries, 180–182
　　and fraud, 67
　　and posting to accounts, 68–77
　　closing entries, 170–174, 184
　　def., 65
Junk bonds, 687

K

Kellogg Company, 632, 847, 1004
Keurig Green Mountain, Inc., 38, 441, 442, 443, 451, 458, 459
Keying, 191
KFC, 512
Kohl's Corporation, 806
KPMG LLP, 588, 627
Kraft Foods, 556
Kroger Co., 328r, 382–383, 485, 858, MJ-12

L

L.L. Bean, Inc., 267
Labor information and cost flows, illus., 930
LaCroix, 766
Land, 780–781
　　gain on sale of, 785
Last-in, first-out (LIFO) inventory cost flow method, def., 348
Last-in, first-out flow of costs, illus., 357
Last-in, first-out method, 351–353, 356–357
　　and FIFO cost methods, effect of changing costs, illus., 359
Lean manufacturing, 991–992
　　def., 991
Lean production line, illus., 992
Lean production process, 992
Lease, 491
　　vs. purchase, 1288
Lease or sell, 1222–1223
　　differential analysis, illus., 1222
Leasing fixed assets, 491
Least squares method, 1026fn
Ledger
　　accounts payable subsidiary, 233
　　accounts receivable subsidiary, 233
　　creditors, 233

customers, 233
　　def., 61
　　diagram of the recording and posting of a debit and a credit, illus., 69
　　finished goods, 940
　　general, 233, illus., 234
　　illus., 172–173, 185–187
　　materials, 938
　　posting transactions to, 179
　　stockholders, 637fn
　　subsidiary, 233, illus., 234
　　subsidiary inventory, 347
　　with adjusting entries, illus., 128–130
Legal capital, 634
Legal liability
　　LLCs, 588
　　partnerships, 587
　　proprietorships, 586
Legal restrictions, 648
Lender, 538
Lessee, 491
Lessor, 491
Leverage, 678fn
　　def., 842
　　effect of, illus., 843
Levi Strauss & Co., 926, 1107
Liabilities, 168
　　contingent, 555–557
　　current, 168, 538–541
　　def., 13, 61
　　long-term, 168, 538, 691
　　ratio of fixed assets to long-term, 838, 848
　　to stockholders' equity, ratio of, 838–839, 848
Liability for employee earnings, 541
Liability for employer's payroll taxes, 545
Liability, limited, 630
LIFO. See Last-in, first-out method
Limitations of internal control, 403
Limited Brands, Inc., 203
Limited liability, 630
Limited liability company (LLC), 12, 586
　　characteristics of, illus., 588
　　def., 11, 588
　　proprietorships, and partnerships, comparing, 588
Limited life
　　partnerships, 587
　　proprietorships, 587
Line, 888
Line department, def., 887
Line of credit, 415
Liquidating dividend, 639fn
Liquidating partnerships, 599–606
　　steps in, illus., 599
Liquidation
　　def., 599
　　statement of partnership, 600
Liquidity
　　analyzing, 831–837
　　crunch, 840
　　def., 188, 825
　　measures, 848
　　ratios and measures, illus., 831

Lockheed Martin, 893
Long-term debt, current portion of, 538–539
Long-term investments, investing cash in, 722
Long-term liabilities, 538
   def., 168
   ratio of fixed assets to, 838, 848
   reporting, 691
Loss, 687
   differential, 1220
   net, 20
   profit, and break-even in **Major League Baseball**, 1042
   unrealized, 730
Loss on exchange, 515–516
Loss on realization, 601–603
   capital deficiency, 603–606
   statement of partnership liquidation, *illus.*, 602
Lowe's Companies Inc., 44, 284
Lower of cost or market
   determining inventory at, *illus.*, 360
   valuation at, 359–361
Lower-of-cost-or-market (LCM) method, *def.*, 359
LVMH, MJ-11–MJ-12

M

M. Block & Sons, 458
Macy's, 443, 1173
Madison Square Garden Company (MSG), 120
Madoff, Bernie, 9
Maintenance, ordinary, 503
Major League Baseball, 1042
Make or buy, 1225–1226
   differential analysis, *illus.*, 1226
Maker, 454
Management accountant in the organization, 886–887
Management accounting, *def.*, 6
Management by exception, *def.*, 889
Management process, 888–889
   def., illus., 888
Management's annual report on internal control over financial reporting, **Nike Inc.**, D-2
Management's Discussion and Analysis (MD&A), *def.*, 849
Managerial accounting, 885–890
   and financial accounting, differences between, 885–886, *illus.*, 886
   def., 6, 886
   eco-efficiency measures in, 897
   environmental, 898
   in service industry, 903
   information, uses of, 889–890
Manager-managed company, 588
Mandatory vacations, 400–401
ManpowerGroup, 513
Manual accounting systems, 233–246
Manufacturing businesses
   balance sheet for, 898
   def., 6
   financial statements for, 898–903

   income statements for, *illus.*, 899
   job order cost systems for, 927–940
Manufacturing cells, *def.*, 992
Manufacturing company
   balance sheet presentation of inventory of, *illus.*, 899
   income statement for, 898–903, *illus.*, 902
   master budget for, *illus.*, 1082
Manufacturing cost variances, 1129–1131
   illus., 1130
Manufacturing costs, 892
   flow of, *illus.*, 901, 927, 939
   illus., 892
   schedule of payments for, 1093, *illus.*, 1094
Manufacturing margin, 1048
Manufacturing operations, 890–896
   illus., 890
Manufacturing overhead, *def.*, 893
Margin of safety, 1046–1047
   def., 1046
Market price approach, 1189–1190
   def., 1189
Market rate of interest
   def., 680
   of 11%, 697
   of 12%, 696
   of 13%, 696
Marriott International, Inc., 881–882., 1271
Marshalls, 294
Master budget
   def., 1082
   for manufacturing company, *illus.*, 1082
MasterCard, 290, 444
Matching concept, *def.*, 20
Matching principle, *def.*, 114
Materials, 927–929
Materials equivalent units, 978
Materials information and cost flows, *illus.*, 928
Materials inventory, *def.*, 898
Materials ledger, 938
   def., 927
Materials requisitions, 928
   def., 928
Mathematical approach to cost-volume-profit analysis, 1031–1037
Mattel Inc., 382, 429, 867–868
Maturity date, 455
Maturity value, *def.*, 456
McDonald's Corporation, 13, 27, 487, 489, 491, 492, 509, 512, 513, 607, 754, 1059, 1249, C-1–C-2
Medicare, 543
Megawatt hour, 988
Member-managed company, 588
Members' equity, statement of, 606
Merchandise available for sale, *def.*, 899
Merchandise, cash payments for, 783–784
   illus., 784
Merchandise inventory
   def., 283
   in financial statements, reporting of, 359–365
   on balance sheet, 361–362

Merchandise inventory transactions
   illustration of for seller and buyer, *illus.*, 298
   recording of, 297, *illus.*, 297
Merchandise sold, cost of, 283, 899
Merchandise transactions, 284–300
   dual nature of, 297–299
   recording under periodic inventory system, 310
Merchandising businesses
   balance sheet for, *illus.*, 306
   balance sheet presentation of inventory of, *illus.*, 899
   chart of accounts for, 284–285
   def., 6
   financial statements for, 303–307
   income statements for, *illus.*, 899
   nature of, 282–284
   operating cycle for, *illus.*, 283
   statement of owner's equity for, *illus.*, 305
Merck & Co., Inc., 1311
Metro-Goldwyn-Mayer Studios Inc. (MGM), 1311–1312
MGM Resorts International, 468
Microsoft Corporation, 13, 33, 70, 128, 144, 163, 231, 417, 489, 643, 738, 754, 763
Mixed costs, 1024–1027
   def., 1024
   illus., 1026, 1028
Modified Accelerated Cost Recovery System, (MACRS), 500
Mondelez International, Inc., 868
Monitoring, 402
Monster Beverage Corporation, 692
Moody's, 691
Mortgage note, *def.*, 688
Mortgage note payable, 168
Mortgage payable, 168
Moving average, 353
MS, miscellaneous item, 408
Multiple-step income statement, 303–304
   def., 303
   illus., 304
Mutual agency, partnerships, 587

N

n/30, 287
n/eom, 287
National Basketball Association (NBA), 122
National Beverage Co., 766, 769, 770, 775, 781, 788, 804
National Football League (NFL), 122
National Hockey League (NHL), 122
Natural business year, *def.*, 187
Natural resources, 507–508
Negotiated price approach, 1190–1192
   def., 1190
Nestlé, 969, 975
Net book value
   def., 125
   of the asset, 494

Net income, 727, 773
　　adjustments to, 774–778, *illus.*, 774
　　completed spreadsheet with, *illus.*, 195
　　def., 20
　　dividing of partnership income when allowances exceed, 592
　　or net loss, compute, 193–194
　　recording investee, 727–728
Net loss, *def.*, 20
Net pay
　　computing employee, 544
　　def., 541
Net present value analysis
　　at 12%, *illus.*, 1283
　　equalized lives of proposals, *illus.*, 1287
　　unequal lives of proposals, *illus.*, 1287
Net present value method
　　and index, 1281–1283
　　def., 1281
Net profit, *def.*, 20
Net realizable value, *def.*, 360, 445
Netflix, Inc., 527
NetSuite, 278
Network business model, 1288
New Belgium, 1128
New York Stock Exchange (NYSE), 720, 736
Nicklaus Design, 971
Nike Inc., 147, 453, 706, 807, 824, 828, 829, 831, 832, 836, 838, 839, 843, 845, 847, 850, 879, 971
　　Form 10-K for the fiscal year ended May 31, 2016, D-1–D-31
Nokia Corporation, 511
Nominal accounts, *def.*, 169
Noncash investing and financing activities, 770
Nonfinancial performance measures, 1146–1148
　　def., illus., 1146
Non-investment grade bonds, 687
Nonmanufacturing activities, direct labor standards for, 1136
Nonpublic corporations, 630
No-par stock, 634, 638
Normal balance of an account, *def.*, 63
Normal balances, 63–64
Normal price, total and variable cost concepts to setting, 1241–1245
Normal standards, 1127
Notes
　　amortization of installment, *illus.*, 689
　　installment, 688–690
　　mortgage, 688
Notes payable, short-term, 539–541
Notes receivable, 454–457
　　accounting for, 456–457
　　characteristics of, 454–456
　　def., 168, 442–443
　　dishonored, 456
Novartis AG, 1037
NSF, not sufficient funds check, 408

Number of days' sales in inventory, 836–837, 848
　　def., 836
　　inventory turnover and, 365–367
Number of days' sales in receivables, 848
　　def., 835

O

Objectives (goals), *def.*, 889
Objectivity concept, *def.*, 12
Occupancy rates, 847
Ocean Power Technologies, Inc., 416
Oculus VR, LLC, 1222
Office Depot, 284
Office supplies, free issue basis of, 123
On consignment, 362
Online fraud, 250
Operating activities, cash flows from, 24, 767, 768–769
　　direct method, 786–787
　　indirect method, *illus.*, 775
Operating agreement, 588
Operating assets, return on, 842
Operating budgets, 1082–1092
　　illus., 1083
Operating cycle, 282–283
　　def., 282
　　for merchandising business, *illus.*, 283
Operating efficiency, 1183
Operating expenses, cash payments for, 784–785
　　illus., 785
Operating income, 283
　　def., 303
Operating leverage, 1044–1046
　　def., 1044
　　effect of on income from operations, *illus.*, 1046
Operating loss area, 1039, 1040
Operating profit area, 1039, 1040
Operating profitability, 1183
Operational planning, *def.*, 889
Operations
　　cash flow from, direct and indirect methods, *illus.*, 769
　　centralized and decentralized, 1174–1176
　　income from, 303–304
　　separating responsibilities for related, 401
Opportunity cost, *def.*, 1227
Oracle, 231, 278
Ordinary maintenance and repairs, 503
Organization, management accountant in, 886–887
Organizational chart, 886
　　illus., 887
Organizational forms in the accounting industry, 588
Organizational structure of corporation, *illus.*, 631
Orphan Drug Act, 1037
Orphan drugs, 1037
Other comprehensive income, *def.*, 739

Other expense, *def.*, 304
Other receivables, 443
Other revenue, *def.*, 304
Outstanding stock, *def., illus.*, 634
Overabsorbed factory overhead, 934
Overapplied factory overhead, 1142
　　def., 934
Overbilling clients, 552
Overhead
　　actual, 934
　　applied, 934
Overhead allocation, 1238–1239
Overhead costs, 893
Owner withdrawals, 63
Owner's equity, 168
　　def., 13, 61
　　statement of, 20, 21, 167, 305
　　types of transactions affecting, *illus.*, 19
Ownership
　　between 20%–50%, 727–729
　　less than 20%, 725–727
　　more than 50%, 729

P

Pacific Gas and Electric Company, 664
Paid-in capital
　　def., 633
　　from issuing stock, 634–638
Pandora, 113, 114, 118, 120, 121, 123, 125
Pandora Media, Inc., 112, 132
Panera Bread, 1285–1286
Par value
　　def., 634
　　method, 644*fn*
Parent company, *def.*, 729
Park City Mountain Resort, 1300
Partial-year depreciation, 499–501
Participating preferred stock, 635*fn*
Partner bonuses, 596
Partnership, 11, 586, 587
　　admitting a partner, 593–598, *illus.*, 593
　　characteristics of, *illus.*, 588
　　contributing assets to, 594, 595
　　death of a partner, 598–599
　　def., 12, 587
　　forming of, 589–590
　　liquidating, 599–606, *illus.*, 599
　　partner admission and withdrawal, 593–599
　　partner bonuses, *illus.*, 596
　　proprietorships, and limited liability companies, comparing, 588
　　purchasing an interest in, 594
　　revaluation of assets, 595–596
　　tyranny of the majority, 592
　　withdrawal of a partner, 598
Partnership agreement, *def.*, 587
Partnership equity, statement of, 606, *illus.*, 606
Partnership income, dividing of, 590–593
　　by services and investments of partners, 591–592

by services of partners, 590–591
when allowances exceed net income, 592
Partnership liquidation, statement of, 600
Patents, 508–509
def., 508
Pay
computing employee net, 544
gross, 541
net, 541
take-home, 544
vacation, 552
Payee, 454
Payments and receipts, cash controls over, 403–406
Payments, mobile, 406
Payments for manufacturing costs, schedule of, 1093
illus., 1094
PayPal, 406, 754
Payroll, 541–545
accounting, 541
accounting systems for, 545–551
checks, 550–551
def., 541
distribution, 546
statement, *illus.*, 551
Payroll register
def., 546
illus., 546–547
Payroll system
computerized, 551
internal controls for, 551
Payroll taxes, 541–545
recording and paying, 547–549
Pension, *def.*, 553
PepsiCo, Inc., 33, 443, 567, 676, 680, 681, 683, 692, 865, 971
Percent of sales method, 448–449
Performance measures
balanced scorecard, *illus.*, 1188
nonfinancial, 1146–1148
Period costs, 895–896, 938
def., 895
examples of, *illus.*, 895
product costs, and financial statements, *illus.*, 896
Periodic inventory system, 309–313
adjusting process under, 310–311
chart of accounts under, 309, *illus.*, 309
closing entries under, 312–313
def., 285
determining cost of merchandise sold using, *illus.*, 312
financial statements under, 311–312
inventory costing methods under, 355–358
transactions using, *illus.*, 311
Periodic method, closing entries, *illus.*, 313
Permanent accounts, *def.*, 169
Perpetual inventory account
(FIFO), entries and, *illus.*, 351
(LIFO), entries and, *illus.*, 352
(weighted average), entries and, *illus.*, 354

Perpetual inventory system
computerized, 355
def., 285
inventory costing methods under, 350–354
Personnel, competent, 400–401
Petty cash custodian, 413
Petty cash fund, *def.*, 413
Physical depreciation, 492
Physical flows for a process manufacturers, *illus.*, 973
Physical inventory, *def.*, 285, 347
Pizza Hut, 512
Planning, 1077
def., 889
directing, and controlling, *illus.*, 1076
Plant assets, 488
def., 124, 168
Point-to-point or hub-and-spoke, 513
Polo Ralph Lauren Corporation, 474–475
Ponzi scheme, 9
Post-closing trial balance, 174
illus., 175, 185
preparing, 184–187
Posting
adjusting entries, 180–182
and journalizing to accounts, 68–77
cash payments journal and, *illus.*, 244
cash receipts journal and, *illus.*, 238
closing entries, 170–174, 184
def., 68
purchases journal and, *illus.*, 241
revenue journal and, *illus.*, 237
transactions to ledger, 179
Post-production costs, 1080
Postretirement benefits other than pensions, 554
Power stack, costing, 988
Predetermined factory overhead rate, *def.*, 933
Preferred stock
cumulative, 635
def., 635
participating, 635*fn*
Premium
amortization of by interest method, 698–699
bonds issued at, 685–686, *illus.*, 680
def., 637, 681
on bonds payable, amortization of, *illus.*, 699
on stock, 637–638
Prepaid expenses, 122–124
def., 15, 115
Prepaid insurance, 123–124
Present value
def., *illus.*, 693
methods using, 1278–1285
methods not using, 1275–1278
of equipment cash flows, *illus.*, 1282
of $100 amount for five consecutive periods, *illus.*, 1280
of ordinary annuity of $1 per period (table), A-4–A-5
of the periodic receipts, 695

Present value concepts, 693–697, 1278–1281
def., 1278
Present value index, 1282–1283
def., 1282
Present value of $1 at compound interest (table), A-2–A-3
illus., 695
Present value of $1 table, 694
partial, *illus.*, 1279
Present value of an amount, 694, 1278–1279
illus., 1279
to be received, *illus.*, 694
Present value of an annuity, 1279–1281
at the internal rate of return, *illus.*, 1284
def., 695, 1280
illus., 695
of $1 at compound interest, *illus.*, 69
of $1 table, 695
table, partial, *illus.*, 1281
Price
effect of change in unit selling, on break-even point, *illus.*, 1034
ethics of transfer, 1193
Price fixing, 1234
Price levels, changes in, 1289
Price variance, 1130
Price-earnings (P/E) ratio, 845–846, 848
def., 845
Priceline.com Incorporated, 249, 914, 1230, 1271
PricewaterhouseCoopers, 588
Prime costs, 894–895
and conversion costs, 894–895
def., *illus.*, 894
Principal, 680, 688
Principle of exceptions, 1126
Principles vs. rules-based approach to standard setting, B-3
Prior period adjustments, *def.*, 648
Private accounting, *def.*, 6
Private corporations, 630
Probable and estimable, contingent liabilities, 555–556
Probable and not estimable, contingent liabilities, 556
Proceeds, 540
from issuing bonds, 680–681
Process
and job order cost companies, examples of, *illus.*, 971
def., 1146
or sell, 1228–1229
relationship between inputs and outputs in, *illus.*, 1147
Process cost system, 970–975
and job order cost system, comparing, 971–973, *illus.*, 972
def., 926, 971
journal entries for, 985–988
Process further or sell, differential analysis, *illus.*, 1229

Process manufacturer
  cost flows for, 973–975, *illus.*, 974
  def., 970
  physical flows for, *illus.*, 973
Process manufacturing, on being green, 970
Processing methods, 233
Procter & Gamble, 37, 485, 570, 736, 847, 909–910, 1091
Product cost concept, 1232–1234
  def., illus., 1232
Product cost distortion, dangers of, 1240–1241
Product costs, 895–896, 1232
  def., 895
  examples of, *illus.*, 895
  period costs, and financial statements, *illus.*, 896
Product life-cycle management (PLM), 249
Product selling prices, setting normal, 1231–1235
Product, discontinue a, 1223–1225
Production bottlenecks, 1235–1236
  def., 1235
Production budget, *def., illus.*, 1084
Production, compute equivalent units of, 994
Production report
  cost of, 995, *illus.*, 985, 995
  for decision making, using cost of, 989–991
  preparing cost of, 984–985
Profit
  def., 5
  gearing for, 843
  gross, 283, 303
  illusory, 358
  inventory, 358
  loss, and break-even in **Major League Baseball**, 1042
  net, 20
  target, 1035–1037
Profit center, 1176
  def., 1178
  reporting, 1180–1181
  responsibility accounting for, 1178–1181
Profit margin, *def.*, 1182
Profit measurement, accounting systems and, 246
Profitability
  analyzing, 840–849
  def., 826
  measures, 848
  ratios, *illus.*, 840
Profit-volume chart, 1039–1042
  def., 1039
  illus., 1040
  original and revised, *illus.*, 1041
Profit-volume ratio, 1029
Promissory note
  determining due date of, *illus.*, 456
  illus., 455
Proofs and security measures, 401–402
Property, plant, and equipment, 168, 488

Proprietorship, 11, 586–587
  characteristics of, *illus.*, 588
  def., 12
  partnerships, and limited liability companies, comparing, 588
Public accounting, *def.*, 10
Public companies, *def.*, B-1
Public Company Accounting Oversight Board (PCAOB), *def.*, 8
Public corporations, 630
Publicly held companies, 396
Purchase order, *def.*, 346
Purchase vs. lease, 1288
Purchases, 310
  and payments cycle, 234
  on account, 240
  transactions, 285–290
Purchases discounts, 287–288, 310
  def., 287
Purchases journal, 240–243
  and postings, *illus.*, 241
  def., 240
Purchases returns and allowances, 288–290, 310
  def., 288
PwC, 627

Q

Qualitative considerations, 1289
Quantity variance, 1130
Quick assets, *def.*, 558, 833
Quick ratio, 557–559, 832–834, 848
  def., 558, 833
Qwest Communications International, Inc., 8

R

R.J. Reynolds Tobacco Company, 632
RadioShack Corporation, 840
Ralph Lauren Corp., 869
Rate of return, **Panera Bread** store, 1285–1286
Rate variance, 1131
Ratings game, 691
Ratio of cash to monthly cash expenses, 415–417
  def., 416
Ratio of fixed assets to long-term liabilities, 848
  def., 838
Ratio of liabilities to owner's equity, *def.*, 26
Ratio of liabilities to stockholders' equity, 838–839, 848
  def., 838
Ratios
  acid-test, 833
  contribution margin, 1029–1030
  coverage, 839
  current, 557, 832, 848
  def., 826
  fixed asset turnover, 512
  price-earnings, 845–846, 848
  profit-volume, 1029

  quick, 557–559, 832–834, 848
  working capital, 832
Raw materials inventory, 898
Real accounts, *def.*, 169
Realization
  capital deficiency—loss on, 603–606
  def., 599
  gain on, 600–601
  loss on, 601–603
Reasonably possible, contingent liabilities, 556
Receipts and payments, cash controls over, 403–406
Receivable(s)
  accounts, 442
  aging the, 450
  classification of, 442–443
  days' sales in, 459–460
  def., 442
  notes, 442–443, 454–457
  number of days' sales in, 835, 848
  other, 443
  reporting on the balance sheet, 458
  trade, 443
  uncollectible, 443
Receivables method, analysis of, 449–452
Receivables schedule, aging of, *illus.*, 450
Receiving report, 927
  def., 346, 928
Records and bank statement, *illus.*, 409
Registrar, 637
Related operations, separating responsibilities for, 401
Relevant range, *def.*, 1022
Remittance advice, 405
Remote, contingent liabilities, 557
Rent revenue, *def.*, 16
Repairs
  and improvements, 502–504
  extraordinary, 503
  ordinary, 503
Replace equipment, 1226–1228
Replace or continue with old equipment, differential analysis, *illus.*, 1227
Report form
  def., 23
  of balance sheet, *illus.*, 23
Report of compliance with Sarbanes-Oxley, *illus.*, 397
Report of Independent Registered Public Accounting Firm, 850
Research and development costs, 509
Residual income, 1185–1186
  def., 1185
  illus., 1185, 1186
Residual value, *def.*, 492
Responsibility accounting, 1175–1176
  def., 1175
  for cost centers, 1176–1177
  for investment centers, 1181–1188
  for profit centers, 1178–1181
  reports for cost centers, *illus.*, 1177

Index I-17

Responsibility center, 1175
   def., 1077
Restaurant industry, standard costing in, 1133
Restrictions, *def.*, 648
Retail inventory method, 368–369
   def., illus., 368
Retained earnings, 789–791
   def., 633
   reporting, 647–648
Retained earnings statement
   comparative, horizontal analysis, *illus.*, 828
   def., illus., 647
   for Mornin' Joe, *illus.*, MJ-4
Return on assets, 1182
Return on common stockholders' equity, 843–844, 848
   def., 843
Return on investment (ROI), 1182–1185
   def., 1182
Return on operating assets, 842
Return on stockholders' equity, 842–843, 848
   def., 842
Return on total assets, 841–842, 848
   def., 841
Revenue expenditures, 503
   def., 502
   illus., 504
Revenue journal, 235–237
   and postings, *illus.*, 237
   def., 235
   illus., 236
Revenue management, 1232
Revenue per employee, *def.*, 606
Revenue per passenger mile, 847
Revenue recognition, C-1–C-3
   def., 114
   principle, *def.*, 114
Revenue(s)
   accrued, 117–118
   and cash receipts in QuickBooks, *illus.*, 248
   collection cycle and, 234
   def., 16, 61
   deferred, 128
   differential, 1220
   expense recognition and, 114
   interest, 16
   other, 304
   recording over two-year contract, C-3
   rent, 16
   unearned, 70, 115, 121
Reversing entries, 119*fn*, 196–198, 175*fn*
   def., 196
Reynolds American, Inc., 583
Risk assessment, 400
Risk, investor bond price, 681
Ruby Tuesday, 506
Rules of debit and credit
   def., 62
   illus., 63
Rules-based vs. principles approach to standard setting, B-3

S

Safety, margin of, 1046–1047
Sage Software, Inc., 231
Salary, 541
Sale of bonds, 724–725
Sale of land, gain on, 785
Sale of stock, 726, 728–729
Sales, 303
   cash, 290–291
   def., 16, 283
   on account, 291
   schedule of collections from, 1092, *illus.*, 1093
   taxes, 299, 300
   transactions, 290–294
Sales budget, 1082–1083
   def., 1082
   illus., 1083
Sales discounts, *def.*, 291
Sales method, percent of, 448–449
Sales mix
   considerations, 1043
   def., 1043
   multiple product, *illus.*, 1043
Salesforce.com, 278
Salvage value, 492
SAP, 231, 278
Sarbanes-Oxley Act (SOX), 396–397, 849
   def., 8, 396
   effect of, *illus.*, 397
SC, service charge, 408
Scattergraph method, 1026*fn*
Schedule of collections from sales, 1092
   illus., 1093
Schedule of payments for manufacturing costs, 1093
   illus., 1094
Scrap value, 492
Sears, 203, 1173
Securities
   available-for-sale, 732–734
   debt, 722
   equity, 722
   held-to-maturity, 734
   trading, 730–731, 732
Securities and Exchange Commission (SEC), 397, 649, 1285, B-2
   def., 11
Security measures and proofs, 401–402
Segment analysis, 250–251
Segment, discontinue a, 1223–1225
Sell or lease, 1222–1223
   differential analysis, *illus.*, 1222
Sell or process, 1228–1229
Sell or process further, differential analysis, *illus.*, 1229
Selling and administrative expenses budget, 1090, *illus.*, 1090
Selling expenses, 895
   def., 303
Selling price and costs, effects of changes in on break-even point, *illus.*, 1035
Semifixed costs, 1024
Semivariable costs, 1024

Sensitivity analysis, 1042
Serial bonds, 680
Service activities, 992
Service businesses
   def., 5
   flow of costs through, *illus.*, 942
   job order cost systems for, 941–943
   types of, 941–942
Service companies, line and staff for, 888
Service department charge rates, 1179
Service department charges, 1178–1180
   def., 1178
   illus., 1179
Service departments, 1178
Service industry, managerial accounting in, 903
Service job order cost system, flow of costs in, 942
Services of partners, dividing income, 590–591
Setup, *def.*, 1237
Shareholders, 630
   equity, 633
   investment, 633
Shasta, 766
Shenzhen Everwin Precision Technology, 932
Short-term notes payable, 539–541
Sierra Nevada, 1128
Single-step income statement, *def., illus.*, 305
Sinking fund, 687*fn*
Slide, *def.*, 79
Small- and medium-sized enterprises (SMEs), 649
Social security, 543
Social Security Board, 545
Societe Generale, 425
Solvency
   analyzing, 837–839
   def., 188, 826
   measures, 848
   ratios, *illus.*, 837
Sonic Corp., 512
Sources and uses of cash, *illus.*, 768
Southern Airways, 61
Southern Company, 847
Southwest Airlines Co., 13, 232, 513, 708, 1036
Special journals, 233–235
   def., 233
Special-purpose funds
   cash funds, 413–414
   def., 414
Specific identification
   inventory cost flow method, *def.*, 347
   pawn stars and, 349
Speedway Motorsports, Inc., 863
Sports signing bonus, 122
Spreadsheet
   complete, 193–194, *illus.*, 195
   end-of-period, 180, 189–195, *illus.*, 181
   enter the adjusted trial balance, 192–193
   enter the adjustments, 191–192

enter the title, 190
enter the unadjusted trial balance, 190, *illus.*, 190, 191, 192
extend the accounts to the income statement columns and the balance sheet columns, 193
for statement of cash flows, end-of-period, indirect method, 789–791, *illus.*, 790
preparing financial statements from, 194–195
total income statement and balance sheet columns, 193–194
with amounts extended to income statement and balance sheet columns, *illus.*, 194

Sprint Nextel, 1060
Sprouts Farmers Market, Inc., 382–383
Staff, 888
Staff Accounting Bulletins, 11
Staff department, *def.*, 887
Standard & Poor's, 687, 691
Standard cost
criticisms of, 1127–1128
def., 1126
illus., 1129
Standard cost systems, *def.*, 1126
Standard costing
in action, 1128
restaurant industry, 1133
Standard factory overhead rate, factory overhead cost budget indicating, *illus.*, 1137
Standard setting, rules-based vs. principles approach to, B-3
Standards, 1126–1128
currently attainable, 1127
def., 1126
for nonmanufacturing activities, direct labor, 1136
ideal, 1127
in income statement, variance from, *illus.*, 1145
normal, 1127
recording and reporting variances from, 1143–1146
reviewing and revising, 1127
setting of, 1126–1127
theoretical, 1127
types of, 1127
Staples, Inc., 718
Starbucks Corporation, 5, 38, 212, 268, 537, 538, 541, 552, 554, 556, 557, 558, 607, 632
State pension obligations, 555
State unemployment compensation tax, *See also* SUTA tax
Stated value, 634
per share, 638
Statement of cash flows, 24–25
def., 20, 767
direct method, 782–787, *illus.*, 787
format of, 771, *illus.*, 771
indirect method, 772–781, *illus.*, 781
preparing, 24–25, 781, 791
spreadsheet for, indirect method, 789–791, *illus.*, 790

Statement of changes in equity
for Mornin' Joe International, *illus.*, MJ-9
vs. statements of stockholders' equity, MJ-9
Statement of comprehensive income
for Mornin' Joe International, *illus.*, MJ-6
vs. income statements, MJ-6–MJ-7
Statement of cost of goods manufactured
def., 900
income statement with, (manufacturing company), *illus.*, 902
Statement of financial position
for **LVMH**, *illus.*, MJ-11
for Mornin' Joe International, *illus.*, MJ-8
vs. balance sheets, MJ-8
Statement of members' equity, *def.*, 606
Statement of owner's equity, 21, 167, 305
def., 20
for merchandising business, *illus.*, 305
Statement of partnership equity, *def.*, *illus.*, 606
Statement of partnership liquidation
capital deficiency, *illus.*, 604
def., 600
gain on realization, *illus.*, 600
loss on realization, *illus.*, 602
Statement of stockholders' equity, 648–649
def., 649
for Mornin' Joe, *illus.*, MJ-4
illus., 649
vs. statements of changes in equity, MJ-9
Statements of Financial Accounting Standards, 11
Static budget
def., 1079
illus., 1079, 1081
Steelcase Inc., 1104
Stock
characteristics of, 634
classes of, 635–636
common, 635, 779
cumulative preferred, 635
def., 630
issuing, 636–637
no-par, 634, 638
outstanding, 634
paid-in capital from issuing, 634–638
participating preferred, 635*fn*
preferred, 635
premium on, 637–638
purchase of, 726, 727
sale of, 726, 728–729
treasury, 644
Stock dividend, 641–642
def., 641
Stock investments, *illus.*, 725
Stock ledger, 937

Stock splits, 642–643
before and after, *illus.*, 643
def., 642
Stockholders
def., 630
ledger, 637*fn*
Stockholders' equity, 633–634
def., 13, 633
in balance sheet, 645–647
ratio of liabilities to, 838–839, 848
reporting, 645–650
return on, 842–843, 848
return on common, 843–844, 848
section of balance sheet, *illus.*, 646
sources of, *illus.*, 633
statement of, 648–649, *illus.*, 649
Stone Energy Corporation, 706
Straight-line method, 493–495, 500–501, 684
def., 493
depreciation expense and book value, *illus.*, 495
illus., 494
Strategic planning, *def.*, 889
Strategies, *def.*, 889
Subsidiary company, *def.*, 729
Subsidiary inventory ledger, *def.*, 347
Subsidiary ledger
accounts payable, 233
accounts payable control account and, 245–246
accounts receivable, 233
accounts receivable control account and, 240
and general ledger, *illus.*, 34
def., 233
Suburban Propane, 858
Sum-of-the-years-digits method, 493*fn*
Sunk costs, *def.*, 1222
SunTrust, 37
Supplies, 122
Supply chain management (SCM), 249
Sustainability
and accounting, 896–897
business activities, *illus.*, 897
capital investment for, 1289–1290, *illus.*, 1289
def., 897
Sustainability Accounting Standards Board (SASB), *def.*, 897
Sustainable papermaking, 975
SUTA tax, 545

T

T account, *def.*, 59
Taco Bell, 512
Take-home pay, 544
Take-Two Interactive Software, Inc., 189
Tangible assets, 488
Target Corporation, 38, 96, 187, 203, 393, 489
Target cost concept, *illus.*, 1235
Target costing, 1234–1235
def., 1234
Target profit, 1035–1037

Tax payments, responsibility for, *illus.*, 545
Taxation, double, 631
Taxes
   FICA, 543–544, 545
   FUTA, 545
   income, 542, 785–786, *illus.*, 786
   payroll, 541–545, 545–551, 547–549
   sales, 299
   SUTA, 545
TearLab Corp., 439
Technical differences between IRFS and U.S. GAAP, B-3
Temporary accounts, *def.*, 169
Temporary investments, 722
   investing cash in, 722
Tennessee Heritage, 971
Term, 455
Term bonds, 680
Terminology, manufacturing operations, 890–896
Terms, freight, *illus.*, 296
The Wall Street Journal, 738
The Wet Seal, Inc., 770
Theft, cost of employee, 301
Theoretical standards, 1127
Theory of constraints (TOC), *def.*, 1235
3D printing, 931
3M Company, 632
Tiffany & Co., 203, 328, 367
Time tickets, *def.*, 930
Time value of money concept, 693
   def., 1274
Time variance, 1131
Time-adjusted rate of return method, 1283
Times interest earned, 848
   def., 692, 839
   ratio, 691–693
Title, enter on the spreadsheet, 190
Total assets, return on, 841–842, 848
Total cost, 1023, 1024
Total cost concept, 1241–1243
   def., 1241
   illus., 1242
   to setting normal price, 1241–1245
Total manufacturing cost variance, *def.*, 1129
Toyota Motor Corporation, 1258
Trade discounts, 299
   def., 300
Trade receivables, 443
Trade-in allowance, *def.*, 514
Trade-in value, 492
Trademark, *def.*, 509
Trading securities, 730–731, 732
   def., 730
Traditional production line, *illus.*, 991
Traditional production process, 991–992
Transaction terminology and related journal entry accounts, *illus.*, 65
Transactions
   analyzing and recording in the journal, 177–179
   dual nature of merchandise, 297–299
   illus., 60

   merchandising, 284–300
   posting to ledger, 179
   recording merchandise under the periodic inventory system, 310
   sales, 290–294
   summary of, *illus.*, 18
   treasury stock, 644–645
   types of affecting owner's equity, *illus.*, 19
   using accounts to record, 59–62
   using periodic inventory systems, *illus.*, 311
Transfer agent, 637
Transfer price
   def., 1188
   ethics of, 1193
   illus., 1189
Transfer pricing, 1188–1193
Transposition, *def.*, 79
Treasury stock
   def., 644
   or dividends, 645
   transactions, 644–645
Trial balance, 77–80
   adjusted, 130–131, 182, *illus.*, 131, 182
   def., 77
   errors effecting, 78–79
   errors not affecting, 79–80
   illus., 78
   post-closing, 174, 184–187, *illus.*, 175, 185
   spreadsheet with unadjusted, *illus.*, 190, 191, 192
   unadjusted, 78, 179–180, *illus.*, 180
TurboTax, 249
Turnover
   accounts receivable, 459–460, 834, 848
   inventory, 365, 836, 848
Twenty-First Century Fox, Inc., 268
Twitter, Inc., 4, 6, 8, 12, 13, 20, 24, 782
Two-column journal, *def.*, 64
Tyranny of the majority in partnerships, 592

U

U.S. GAAP, MJ-5
U.S. GAAP and IFRS, B-2–B-3
   comparison of accounting under, *illus.*, B-4–B-5
   convergence of, B-3
   differences between, B-3–B-5
   key reporting differences between, MJ-5–MJ-9
   technical differences between, B-3
U.S. government debt, 684
U-Haul, 1234
Unadjusted trial balance
   def., 78
   enter on the spreadsheet, 190
   illus., 116, 180
   preparing, 179–180
   spreadsheet with, *illus.*, 190, 191, 192
Uncertainty, 1288

Uncollectible accounts
   allowance method for, 445–453
   direct write-off method for, 444–445
   expense, 443
Uncollectible receivables, 443
Uncollectibles, estimating, 448–453
Under Armour, Inc., 211
Underabsorbed factory overhead, 934
Underapplied factory overhead, 1142
   def., 934
Unearned revenue, 61, 121
   def., 70, 115
Unequal proposal lives, 1286–1288
Unfavorable cost variance, *def.*, 1129
Unfavorable fixed factory overhead volume variance, 1139
Unfavorable total factory overhead cost variance, 1142
Uniform Partnership Act, 587*fn*
Unilever Group, MJ-10
Union Pacific Corporation, 249, 453, 513, 868
Unit contribution margin, 1030–1031
   def., 1030
Unit of measure concept, *def.*, 12
Unit selling price, effect of changes in, 1034–1035
   on break-even point, *illus.*, 1033, 1034
Unit variable costs, effect of changes in, 1033–1034
United Airlines, Inc., 468, 513, 1036
United Parcel Service, Inc., 528
United States Postal Service, 1157
Units
   allocate costs to units transferred out and partially completed, 982–984, 995
   manufactured exceed units sold, *illus.*, 1049
   started and completed, 983
   to be assigned costs, determine, 976–977, 993–994
   to be costed—mixing department, *illus.*, 977
   whole, 978
Units-of-activity method, 495–497, 501
   def., illus., 495
Units-of-output method, 495
Units-of-production method, 495
Unlimited life, LLCs, 588
Unqualified opinion, 850
Unrealized gain or loss, *def.*, 730
Unusual items
   affecting the current period's income statement, 850–851
   affecting the prior period's income statement, 852
   on income statement, 850–852, *illus.*, 851
US Airways, 1036
USAA, 1127
Uses and sources of cash, *illus.*, 768

V

Vacation pay, 552
Vacations, mandatory, 400–401

Index

Vail Resorts, Inc., 1273, 1274, 1276, 1277, 1282, 1289
Valuation at lower of cost or market, 359–361
Valuation method, 125
Value
    book, 494, 728
    fair, 730
    fair market, 641*fn*
    future, 694, *illus.*, 693
    maturity, 456
    net book, 125
    net realizable, 360, 445
    present, 693, *illus.*, 693
    residual, scrap, salvage, or trade-in, 492
    stated, 634
Variable cost concept, 1244–1245
    def., illus., 1244
    to setting normal price, 1241–1245
Variable cost graphs, *illus.*, 1023
Variable cost of goods sold, 1048
Variable costing, 1047–1049
    and absorption costing income, relationship between, *illus.*, 1049
    def., 1028
    income statement, *illus.*, 1048
Variable costs, 1022–1024
    and fixed cost behavior, *illus.*, 1027
    and their activity bases, *illus.*, 1024
    def., 1022
    illus., 1028
Variable factory overhead controllable variance, 1138–1139
Variable vs. absorption cost of goods manufactured, *illus.*, 1047
Variables, 551
Variance from standards in income statement, *illus.*, 1145
Variance relationships
    direct labor, 1135, *illus.*, 1135
    direct materials, 1132, *illus.*, 1133
Variance(s)
    controllable, 1131, 1138
    cost, 1129, *illus.*, 1129
    direct labor, 1134–1136
    direct labor rate, 1134–1135
    direct labor time, 1135
    direct materials, 1131–1134
    direct materials price, 1132
    direct materials quantity, 1132
    factory overhead, 1136–1143
    favorable cost, 1129
    favorable fixed factory overhead volume, 1139
    fixed factory overhead volume, 1139–1141
    from standards, recording and reporting, 1143–1146
    graph of fixed overhead volume, *illus.*, 1140
    manufacturing cost, 1129–1131, *illus.*, 1130
    price, 1130
    quantity, 1130
    rate, 1131
    time, 1131
    total manufacturing cost, 1129
    unfavorable cost, 1129
    unfavorable fixed factory overhead volume, 1139
    variable factory overhead controllable, 1138–1139
    volume, 1131, 1139
Vendor's invoice, 346
Verizon Communications Inc., 147, 489, 528, 738, 1091, C-1-C-2
Vertical analysis, 131–133, 829–830
    comparative balance sheet, *illus.*, 829
    comparative income statement, *illus.*, 830
    def., 131, *def.*, 829
VISA, 290, 444
Volume variance, 1131
    def., 1139
Voting control, using multiple classes of stock, 635
Voucher, *def.*, 406
Voucher system, *def.*, 406

W

W.W. Grainger, Inc., 267
W-4 (Employee's Withholding Allowance Certificate), 542
    illus., 542
Wage bracket withholding table, *illus.*, 542
Wages, 541
    accrued, *illus.*, 119
    expense, *illus.*, 197, 198
    payable, *illus.*, 197, 198
Wal-Mart Stores, Inc., 6, 11, 13, 37, 187, 393, 485, 528, 880–881
Walt Disney Company, The, 5, 489, 513, 632, 903, 971, 1127, 1204
Warning signs of internal control problems, *illus.*, 402
Weighted average cost method, 353–354, 357–358
Weighted average inventory cost flow method, *def.*, 348
Wells Fargo & Company, 404, 405, 651, 736
Wendy's Co., 512
Weyerhaeuser, 1197
"What if" analysis, 1042
WhatsApp, 1220
Whirlpool Corporation, 485, 632
Whole Foods Markets, Inc., 382–383
Whole units, *def.*, 978
Wholesalers, *def.*, 300
With-dividends, 640
Withdrawals, owner, 63
Work in process, 936–937
    applying factory overhead to, 933–935
    controlling account and job cost sheets, *illus.*, 936
Work in process inventory, *def.*, 898
Working capital, 557, 848
    def., 188, 832
    ratio, 832
WorldCom, 503, 672
Worthington Industries, 1311
Write-offs to the allowance account, 446–447
Wynn Resorts, 453

X

Xerox Corporation, 8

Y

Yahoo, 37
Yahoo! Finance, 738
Yelp!, 635
Yield
    def., 990
    investing for, 847
YRC Worldwide, 868
Yum! Brands, Inc., 268, 512

Z

Zero-based budgeting, *def.*, 1079
Zero-coupon bonds, 696*fn*
Zynga, Inc., 162, 165, 168, 187, 189, 635

The Basics

Accounting Equation:

Assets = Liabilities + Owner's Equity

T Account:

Account Title	
Left side	Right side
debit	credit

Rules of Debit and Credit:

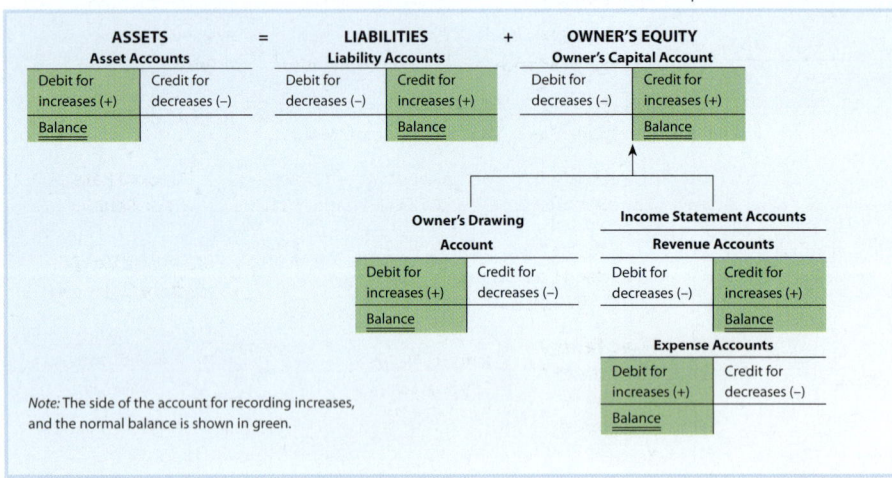

Note: The side of the account for recording increases, and the normal balance is shown in green.

Analyzing and Journalizing Transactions

1. Carefully read the description of the transaction to determine whether an asset, a liability, an owner's equity, a revenue, an expense, or a drawing account is affected.
2. For each account affected by the transaction, determine whether the account increases or decreases.
3. Determine whether each increase or decrease should be recorded as a debit or a credit, following the rules of debit and credit.
4. Record the transaction using a journal entry.
5. Periodically post journal entries to the accounts in the ledger.
6. Prepare an unadjusted trial balance at the end of the period.

Financial Statements:

- **Income statement:** A summary of the revenue and expenses of a business entity for a specific period of time, such as a month or a year.
- **Statement of owner's equity:** A summary of the changes in the owner's equity of a business entity that have occurred during a specific period of time, such as a month or a year.
- **Balance sheet:** A list of the assets, liabilities, and owner's equity of a business entity as of a specific date, usually at the close of the last day of a month or a year.
- **Statement of Cash Flows:** A summary of the cash receipts and cash payments of a business entity for a specific period of time, such as a month or a year.

Accounting Cycle:

1. Transactions are analyzed and recorded in the journal.
2. Transactions are posted to the ledger.
3. An unadjusted trial balance is prepared.
4. Adjustment data are assembled and analyzed.
5. An optional end-of-period spreadsheet is prepared.
6. Adjusting entries are journalized and posted to the ledger.
7. An adjusted trial balance is prepared.
8. Financial statements are prepared.
9. Closing entries are journalized and posted to the ledger.
10. A post-closing trial balance is prepared.

Types of Adjusting Entries:

- Accrued revenue (accrued asset)
- Accrued expense (accrued liability)
- Unearned revenue (deferred revenue)
- Prepaid expense (deferred expense)
- Depreciation expense

Each entry will always affect both a balance sheet account and an income statement account.

Closing Entries:

1. Debit each revenue account for its balance, credit each expense account for its balance, and credit (net income) or debit (net loss) the owner's capital account.
2. Debit the owner's capital account for the balance of the drawing account and credit the drawing account.

Special Journals:

Providing services on account → recorded in → Revenue journal
Receipt of cash from any source → recorded in → Cash receipts journal
Purchase of items on account → recorded in → Purchases journal
Payments of cash for any purpose → recorded in → Cash payments journal

Shipping Terms:

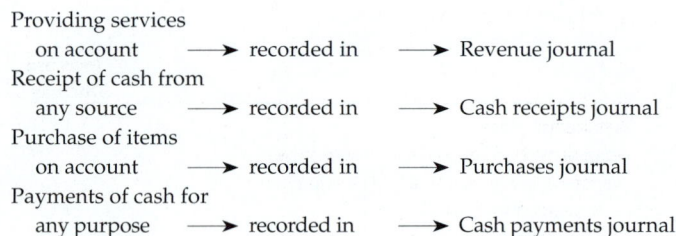

Format for Bank Reconciliation:

Cash balance according to bank statement		$XXX
Add: Additions by company not on bank statement	$XXX	
Bank errors	XXX	XXX
		$XXX
Deduct: Deductions by company not on bank statement	$XXX	
Bank errors	XXX	XXX
Adjusted balance		$XXX
Cash balance according to company's records		$XXX
Add: Additions by bank not recorded by company	$XXX	
Company errors	XXX	XXX
		$XXX
Deduct: Deductions by bank not recorded by company	$XXX	
Company errors	XXX	XXX
Adjusted balance		$XXX

Inventory Costing Methods:

- First-in, First-out (FIFO)
- Last-in, First-out (LIFO)
- Weighted-Average

Interest Computations:

$$\text{Interest} = \text{Face Amount (or Principal)} \times \text{Rate} \times \text{Time}$$

Methods of Determining Annual Depreciation:

Straight-Line: $\dfrac{\text{Cost} - \text{Estimated Residual Value}}{\text{Estimated Life}}$

Double-Declining-Balance: Rate* × Book Value at Beginning of Period

*Rate is commonly twice the straight-line rate (1 ÷ Estimated Life).

Adjustments to Net Income (Loss) Using the Indirect Method:

	Increase (Decrease)
Net income (loss)	$ XXX
Adjustments to reconcile net income to net cash flow from operating activities:	
Depreciation of fixed assets	XXX
Amortization of intangible assets	XXX
Losses on disposal of assets	XXX
Gains on disposal of assets	(XXX)
Changes in current operating assets and liabilities:	
Increases in noncash current operating assets	(XXX)
Decreases in noncash current operating assets	XXX
Increases in current operating liabilities	XXX
Decreases in current operating liabilities	(XXX)
Net cash flow from operating activities	$ XXX
	or
	$(XXX)

Contribution Margin Ratio = $\dfrac{\text{Sales} - \text{Variable Costs}}{\text{Sales}}$

Break-Even Sales (Units) = $\dfrac{\text{Fixed Costs}}{\text{Unit Contribution Margin}}$

Sales (Units) = $\dfrac{\text{Fixed Costs} + \text{Target Profit}}{\text{Unit Contribution Margin}}$

Margin of Safety = $\dfrac{\text{Sales} - \text{Sales at Break-Even Point}}{\text{Sales}}$

Operating Leverage = $\dfrac{\text{Contribution Margin}}{\text{Income from Operations}}$

Variances:

$$\text{Direct Materials Price Variance} = \left(\text{Actual Price} - \text{Standard Price}\right) \times \text{Actual Quantity}$$

$$\text{Direct Materials Quantity Variance} = \left(\text{Actual Quantity} - \text{Standard Quantity}\right) \times \text{Standard Price}$$

$$\text{Direct Labor Rate Variance} = \left(\text{Actual Rate per Hour} - \text{Standard Rate per Hour}\right) \times \text{Actual Hours}$$

$$\text{Direct Labor Time Variance} = \left(\text{Actual Direct Labor Hours} - \text{Standard Direct Labor Hours}\right) \times \text{Standard Rate per Hour}$$

$$\text{Variable Factory Overhead Controllable Variance} = \text{Actual Variable Factory Overhead} - \text{Budgeted Variable Factory Overhead}$$

$$\text{Fixed Factory Overhead Volume Variance} = \left(\text{Standard Hours for 100\% of Normal Capacity} - \text{Standard Hours for Actual Units Produced}\right) \times \text{Fixed Factory Overhead Rate}$$

Rate of Return on Investment (ROI) = $\dfrac{\text{Income from Operations}}{\text{Invested Assets}}$

Alternative ROI Computation:

$$\text{ROI} = \dfrac{\text{Income from Operations}}{\text{Sales}} \times \dfrac{\text{Sales}}{\text{Invested Assets}}$$

Capital Investment Analysis Methods:

Methods That Ignore Present Values:

- Average Rate of Return Method
- Cash Payback Method

Methods That Use Present Values:

- Net Present Value Method
- Internal Rate of Return Method

Average Rate of Return = $\dfrac{\text{Estimated Average Annual Income}}{\text{Average Investment}}$

Present Value Index = $\dfrac{\text{Total Present Value of Net Cash Flow}}{\text{Amount to Be Invested}}$

Present Value Factor for an Annuity of $1 = $\dfrac{\text{Amount to Be Invested}}{\text{Equal Annual Net Cash Flows}}$

Abbreviations and Acronyms Commonly Used in Business and Accounting

AAA	American Accounting Association
ABC	Activity-based costing
AICPA	American Institute of Certified Public Accountants
B2B	Business-to-business
B2C	Business-to-consumer
CFO	Chief Financial Officer
CMA	Certified Management Accountant
COGM	Cost of goods manufactured
COGS	Cost of goods sold
CPA	Certified Public Accountant
Cr.	Credit
CVP	Cost-volume-profit
Dr.	Debit
EFT	Electronic funds transfer
EPS	Earnings per share
ERP	Enterprise resource planning
FASB	Financial Accounting Standards Board
FICA tax	Federal Insurance Contributions Act tax
FIFO	First-in, first-out
FOB	Free on board
FUTA	Federal unemployment compensation tax
GAAP	Generally accepted accounting principles
IASB	International Accounting Standards Board
IFRS	International Financial Reporting Standards
IMA	Institute of Management Accountants
IRC	Internal Revenue Code
IRR	Internal rate of return
IRS	Internal Revenue Service
JIT	Just-in-time
LIFO	Last-in, first-out
LCM	Lower of cost or market
MACRS	Modified Accelerated Cost Recovery System
MD&A	Management's Discussion and Analysis
n/30	Net 30
n/eom	Net, end-of-month
NPV	Net present value
NSF	Not sufficient funds
P/E Ratio	Price-earnings ratio
POS	Point of sale
ROI	Return on investment
R&D	Research and development
SCM	Supply chain management
SEC	Securities and Exchange Commission
SOX	Sarbanes-Oxley Act
TQC	Total quality control
W-4	Employee's Withholding Allowance Certificate
WIP	Work in process

Classification of Accounts

Account Title	Account Classification	Normal Balance	Financial Statement
Accounts Payable	Current liability	Credit	Balance sheet
Accounts Receivable	Current asset	Debit	Balance sheet
Accumulated Depletion	Contra fixed asset	Credit	Balance sheet
Accumulated Depreciation	Contra fixed asset	Credit	Balance sheet
Advertising Expense	Operating expense	Debit	Income statement
Allowance for Doubtful Accounts	Contra current asset	Credit	Balance sheet
Amortization Expense	Operating expense	Debit	Income statement
Bonds Payable	Long-term liability	Credit	Balance sheet
Building	Fixed asset	Debit	Balance sheet
_____ Capital	Owner's equity	Credit	Statement of owner's equity/ Balance sheet
Cash	Current asset	Debit	Balance sheet
Cash Dividends	Stockholders' equity	Debit	Retained earnings statement
Cash Dividends Payable	Current liability	Credit	Balance sheet
Common Stock	Stockholders' equity	Credit	Balance sheet
Cost of Merchandise (Goods) Sold	Cost of merchandise (goods) sold	Debit	Income statement
Customer Refunds Payable	Current liability	Credit	Balance sheet
Delivery Expense	Operating expense	Debit	Income statement
Depletion Expense	Operating expense	Debit	Income statement
Discount on Bonds Payable	Long-term liability	Debit	Balance sheet
Dividend Revenue	Other income	Credit	Income statement
Dividends	Stockholders' equity	Debit	Retained earnings statement
_____ Drawing	Owner's equity	Debit	Statement of owner's equity
Employees Federal Income Tax Payable	Current liability	Credit	Balance sheet
Equipment	Fixed asset	Debit	Balance sheet
Estimated Returns Inventory	Current asset	Debit	Balance sheet
Factory Overhead (Overapplied)	Deferred credit	Credit	Balance sheet (interim)
Factory Overhead (Underapplied)	Deferred debit	Debit	Balance sheet (interim)
Federal Income Tax Payable	Current liability	Credit	Balance sheet
Federal Unemployment Tax Payable	Current liability	Credit	Balance sheet
Finished Goods	Current asset	Debit	Balance sheet
Freight In	Cost of merchandise sold	Debit	Income statement
Freight Out	Operating expense	Debit	Income statement
Gain on Disposal of Fixed Assets	Other income	Credit	Income statement
Gain on Redemption of Bonds	Other income	Credit	Income statement
Gain on Sale of Investments	Other income	Credit	Income statement
Goodwill	Intangible asset	Debit	Balance sheet
Income Tax Expense	Income tax	Debit	Income statement
Income Tax Payable	Current liability	Credit	Balance sheet
Insurance Expense	Operating expense	Debit	Income statement
Interest Expense	Other expense	Debit	Income statement
Interest Receivable	Current asset	Debit	Balance sheet
Interest Revenue	Other income	Credit	Income statement
Investment in Bonds	Investment	Debit	Balance sheet
Investment in Stocks	Investment	Debit	Balance sheet
Investment in Subsidiary	Investment	Debit	Balance sheet
Land	Fixed asset	Debit	Balance sheet
Loss on Disposal of Fixed Assets	Other expense	Debit	Income statement
Loss on Redemption of Bonds	Other expense	Debit	Income statement

Account Title	Account Classification	Normal Balance	Financial Statement
Loss on Sale of Investments	Other expense	Debit	Income statement
Marketable Securities	Current asset	Debit	Balance sheet
Materials	Current asset	Debit	Balance sheet
Medicare Tax Payable	Current liability	Credit	Balance sheet
Merchandise Inventory	Current asset/Cost of merchandise sold	Debit	Balance sheet/Income statement
Net Sales	Revenue from sales	Credit	Income statement
Notes Payable	Current liability/Long-term liability	Credit	Balance sheet
Notes Receivable	Current asset/Investment	Debit	Balance sheet
Patents	Intangible asset	Debit	Balance sheet
Paid-In Capital from Sale of Treasury Stock	Stockholders' equity	Credit	Balance sheet
Paid-In Capital in Excess of Par (Stated Value)	Stockholders' equity	Credit	Balance sheet
Payroll Tax Expense	Operating expense	Debit	Income statement
Pension Expense	Operating expense	Debit	Income statement
Petty Cash	Current asset	Debit	Balance sheet
Preferred Stock	Stockholders' equity	Credit	Balance sheet
Premium on Bonds Payable	Long-term liability	Credit	Balance sheet
Prepaid Insurance	Current asset	Debit	Balance sheet
Prepaid Rent	Current asset	Debit	Balance sheet
Purchases	Cost of merchandise sold	Debit	Income statement
Purchases Discounts	Cost of merchandise sold	Credit	Income statement
Purchases Returns and Allowances	Cost of merchandise sold	Credit	Income statement
Rent Expense	Operating expense	Debit	Income statement
Rent Revenue	Other income	Credit	Income statement
Retained Earnings	Stockholders' equity	Credit	Balance sheet/Retained earnings statement
Salaries Expense	Operating expense	Debit	Income statement
Salaries Payable	Current liability	Credit	Balance sheet
Sales Tax Payable	Current liability	Credit	Balance sheet
Social Security Tax Payable	Current liability	Credit	Balance sheet
State Unemployment Tax Payable	Current liability	Credit	Balance sheet
Stock Dividends	Stockholders' equity	Debit	Retained earnings statement
Stock Dividends Distributable	Stockholders' equity	Credit	Balance sheet
Supplies	Current asset	Debit	Balance sheet
Supplies Expense	Operating expense	Debit	Income statement
Treasury Stock	Stockholders' equity	Debit	Balance sheet
Uncollectible Accounts Expense	Operating expense	Debit	Income statement
Unearned Rent	Current liability	Credit	Balance sheet
Utilities Expense	Operating expense	Debit	Income statement
Vacation Pay Expense	Operating expense	Debit	Income statement
Vacation Pay Payable	Current liability/Long-term liability	Credit	Balance sheet
Work in Process	Current asset	Debit	Balance sheet